Bookman's Price Index

ISSN 0068-0141

Bookman's Price Index

VOLUME 95

A Guide to the Values of
Rare and Other Out of Print Books

Edited by
Anne F. McGrath

Detroit • New York • San Francisco • New Haven, Conn • Waterville, Maine • London

Bookman's Price Index, Vol. 95

Anne F. McGrath

Product Management: Jenai Drouillard

Project Editor: Jeffrey Wilson

Manufacturing: Rita Wimberley

© 2012 Gale, Cengage Learning

ALL RIGHTS RESERVED. No part of this work covered by the copyright herein may be reproduced, transmitted, stored, or used in any form or by any means graphic, electronic, or mechanical, including but not limited to photocopying, recording, scanning, digitizing, taping, Web distribution, information networks, or information storage and retrieval systems, except as permitted under Section 107 or 108 of the 1976 United States Copyright Act, without the prior written permission of the publisher.

This publication is a creative work fully protected by all applicable copyright laws, as well as by misappropriation, trade secret, unfair competition, and other applicable laws. The authors and editors of this work have added value to the underlying factual material herein through one or more of the following: unique and original selection, coordination, expression, arrangement, and classification of the information.

> For product information and technology assistance, contact us at
> Gale Customer Support, 1-800-877-4253.
> For permission to use material from this text or product,
> submit all requests online at www.cengage.com/permissions.
> Further permissions questions can be emailed to
> permissionrequest@cengage.com

While every effort has been made to ensure the reliability of the information presented in this publication, Gale, a part of Cengage Learning, does not guarantee the accuracy of the data contained herein. Gale accepts no payment for listing; and inclusion in the publication of any organization, agency, institution, publication, service, or individual does not imply endorsement of the editors or publisher. Errors brought to the attention of the publisher and verified to the satisfaction of the publisher will be corrected in future editions.

EDITORIAL DATA PRIVACY POLICY
Does this product contain information about you as an individual? If so, for more information about how to access or correct that information or about our data privacy policies please see our Privacy Statement at www.gale.cengage.com

Gale
27500 Drake Rd.
Farmington Hills, MI 48331-3535

LIBRARY OF CONGRESS CATALOG CARD NUMBER 64-008723

ISBN-13: 978-1-4144-0661-9
ISBN-10: 1-4144-0661-4
ISSN 0068-0141

Printed in the United States of America
1 2 3 4 5 6 7 15 14 13 12 11

Contents

Introduction vii
Dealers Represented in This Volume 1
Bookman's Price Index 9
Association Copies 891
Fine Bindings 1177
Fore-edge Paintings 1239

Introduction

Bookman's Price Index, established in 1964, is published two to four times each year as an index to both the prices and availability of antiquarian books in the United States, Canada, and the British Isles. Each issue of *BPI* reports the prices and availability of over 12,000 different antiquarian books. Thus, in the course of an average calendar year, *BPI* reports the prices and availability of about 25,000 antiquarian books that are important to readers in the North Atlantic portion of the English-speaking community.

Definition of Antiquarian Books

An antiquarian book is one that is, or has been, traded on the antiquarian book market. It is, or was, traded there because it is important (or in demand) and scarce.

Importance, in the case of antiquarian books, is national. American, Canadian, and British readers buy and sell the artifacts of their own literature and history, science and art as well as a select number of books that document the Continental and Classical origins of certain aspects of their cultures. There are special enthusiasms, too, such as children's books, sporting books, and books that are important principally for their physical beauty; but even the books of these special enthusiasms reflect the national preoccupations of English-speaking readers.

Scarcity means that the number of copies of any book that might come onto the market is measured, at most, in scores, and that only a dozen or a half-dozen, at most, come onto the market during any calendar year.

Lots of important books are not scarce, and lots of scarce books are not important. And, despite the word *antiquarian*, age is no guarantee of either scarcity or importance. Conversely, many books that are less than a generation old bring a handsome price on the market.

The antiquarian books that do appear on the North Atlantic market are a small percentage of the world's entire antiquarian book market, and, necessarily, they are the tiniest fraction of the total number of books published over the centuries.

Despite their thin ranks and scant number, antiquarian books are usually not outrageously expensive. They often range in price from $50 to $500, with most clustering between $100 and $200, and precious few enjoying four-figure prominence.

Prices Reported in *BPI*

The prices reported in *Bookman's Price Index* each year are established by some 100-200 antiquarian booksellers in the United States, Canada, and the British Isles. Usually, about 50 of these booksellers are represented in any one volume of *BPI*. By drawing information from a large number of antiquarian booksellers across English-speaking North America, as well as the British Isles, *BPI* is able to report broad, consistent, and reliable market patterns in the whole North Atlantic English-speaking community.

Within the ranks of the antiquarian booksellers whose prices are reported in *BPI*, the group most interesting is the specialist dealers, whose stock is limited to books in a single subject such as law, or psychiatry, or maritime studies, or horticulture. Such specialists provide readers of *BPI* with information that is not easily available elsewhere.

The prices that all of these antiquarian booksellers report are retail prices that they have established on the basis of their working experience and familiarity with current market conditions, including supply and demand and the effect upon price of the general physical condition of a book, as well as such extraordinary factors as the presence of important autographs.

The willingness of the various antiquarian booksellers to publish their prices in direct comparison with the prices of all other antiquarian booksellers serves as a general indication of the reliability of the prices reported in *BPI* as well as the probity of the antiquarian booksellers. These prices are public market prices, not private deals.

Availability of Books in *BPI*

Every one of the books in *Bookman's Price Index* was recently available in one of the shops of the antiquarian booksellers whose catalogs are included in this volume of *BPI*. It was upon the basis of a hands-on appraisal of each book that an antiquarian bookseller established its price. Thus, the prices reported in *BPI* are actual prices for specific books rather than approximate prices for probable or possible books.

While a particular book may no longer be in the shop of the antiquarian bookseller who established its price, the fact that the book stood on the shelf there recently means that the book is still to be found on the market and that the antiquarian bookseller who established its price may have access to another copy of the same book, or that a different antiquarian bookseller may price another copy of the book in the following issue of *BPI*. Thus, by reporting prices of actual books and their real availability, *Bookman's Price Index* serves as an index to the general market availability of a particular antiquarian book.

Conversely, *BPI* is an index to the absence of certain antiquarian books from the market: books not priced in *BPI* may be presumed to be generally unavailable on the antiquarian book market. *BPI* makes no effort to predict what such unavailable books might be worth if they were perhaps to someday come on the market; *BPI* reports only what is going on in the market, not what might go on.

For example, if a reader were to search the six most recent issues of *BPI* for the price of the first edition of Edgar Allan Poe's *Tamerlane,* he might not find it and could safely conclude that a first edition of *Tamerlane* was not generally available during the past two years or so. If, on the other hand, the same reader were to make a similar search for a first edition of *The Stand* by Poe's spiritual son Stephen King, he might discover that *The Stand* has been found in the shops from time to time and that it is worth about $1600 for a signed first edition, or between $200 and $400 for an unsigned first, depending on condition.

The Importance of Condition

Condition is critical in antiquarian books as in any other antiquarian artifact. The condition of all of the books priced in *Bookman's Price Index* is stated in elaborate detail because it is impossible to understand or justify the price of any antiquarian book without full knowledge of its condition.

Arrangement of *BPI*

The books priced in *Bookman's Price Index* are arranged in a single main alphabet according to the name of the author: in cases of personal authorship, the author's last name; in cases of books produced by corporate bodies such as governments of countries or states, the name of that corporation; in cases of anonymous books, the title; and in cases of anonymous classics such as the *Arabian Nights,* by customary title.

All names of authors, or titles, are standardized according to the usage of American libraries, thus gathering all works by an author.

The works of an author are arranged under his or her name in alphabetical sequence according to the first word of the title, excepting initial articles. However, editions of an author's collected works are listed, out of alphabetical sequence, at the end of the list of his or her individual works.

Different editions of a single work are arranged according to date of publication, with the earlier preceding the later even though this sequence sometimes disrupts alphabetical regularity. In such cases, the editor has sought to consult the reader's convenience rather than any rigid consistency.

The reasons for the occasional disruption of alphabetical regularity are two: the first is that in reporting prices, antiquarian booksellers sometimes refer to a book elliptically, leaving unknown the complete title. The second reason is that certain books change title without changing substance. The most obvious example of this particular editorial problem is the Bible. Title pages of Bibles can begin with such words as Complete, Holy, Sacred, New, Authorized, and so on: it is still the same book. Therefore all English Bibles appear, under the heading BIBLES – ENGLISH, in chronological order. Following the title of each book is its imprint: the place and date of publication and the name of the publisher (or the name of the printer in cases of certain books produced prior to the late eighteenth century).

Description of the Condition of Books

Following the author, title, and imprint of each book is a thorough description of the physical condition of the book, insofar as the bookseller has provided this information. While antiquarian booksellers do not always apply a standard formula in describing the condition of a book, they generally include, as appropriate, most of the following details:

Edition. *BPI* reports which edition of a book is being priced when this information is critical, as in cases when several editions were published in one year. If an edition was published in more than one issue, or state, *BPI* distinguishes among them and identifies them either by the order in which they appeared, or by the physical peculiarities that characterize them. When necessary, *BPI* even describes those obscure details, called "points," that are used to distinguish among issues or states. The points are often minute and consist of such details as one misspelled word buried in the text. Finally, *BPI* identifies limited editions, stating the number of copies in the press run and, if necessary, the types of paper used and the specific number assigned to the book being priced.

Physical Size. *BPI* describes the height and the bulk of each book when this information is available. Height is usually described in the traditional language of the antiquarian book trade: folio, for a tall book; quarto (4to) for a medium-size book; and octavo (8vo) or duodecimo (12mo) for a smaller book. Miniature books are usually described in inches top to bottom and left to right. The bulk of a book is described by stating its pagination, a custom that operates to assure the reader that the book in question is complete.

Illustrations. Since many antiquarian books are more valuable for their illustrations than for their text, *BPI* describes such illustrations carefully, sometimes in considerable detail, as in the case of a book with hand-colored plates.

Binding. All bindings are described fully as to the material used, be it paper, cloth or leather, and even as to the type and color of the material and the time at which it was applied. ("Contemporary tan calf" means that a binding of cattle hide was made for the book contemporaneously with its printing.) Decorations of the binding are also described, and in the cases of twentieth century books, the presence or absence of the dust jacket is always noted.

Authors' Signatures. These are always cited, as they have a significant effect on the price of a book.

General Physical Condition, Specific Flaws, and Relative Scarcity. Usually, *BPI* provides some advice on the general condition of a book by stating that its condition is good, very good, or fine. Additionally, specific flaws are usually listed; some of them are significant, as in the case of a missing leaf or a worn binding, while others are very minor, as in the case of a worm hole in an ancient tome.

Availability. Frequently *BPI* will point out that certain books are of unusual scarcity or rarity. As all antiquarian books are by definition scarce, a special remark that a book is uncommonly scarce should be noted carefully.

Prices. Following the description, *BPI* gives the price of the book along with the name of the antiquarian bookseller who established the price and provided the physical description. Accompanying the antiquarian bookseller's name is the number of the catalog in which he published the price and description of the book, plus the item number of the book in the catalog. The addresses of the antiquarian booksellers whose prices are reported in *BPI* are listed following this Introduction, in the section entitled Dealers Represented in This Volume.

Association Copies, Fine Bindings, and Fore-edge Paintings

Following the main section of *Bookman's Price Index* are three small sections of association copies of books, books in fine bindings, and books decorated with fore-edge paintings. The books in these three sections take on additional interest and value because of features peculiar to them that are not found in other copies of the same books. Their value, or some portion of it, derives from factors not inherent in the text and not identifiable through the name of the author, thereby requiring that they be isolated so that readers can search them out according to the factors that create, or influence, their worth: association, binding or fore-edge painting.

All books priced and described in one of the special sections are also priced and described in the main section of *BPI*, thus permitting the reader to compare an ordinary copy of a book with one that enjoys added attraction because of a unique feature.

Association Copies. Certain antiquarian books acquire added value because of their association with a prominent owner. For instance, an ordinary eighteenth century book would take on enormous extra worth if it had once belonged to George Washington. Association copies of books priced in the special section of *BPI* are arranged according to the name of the person with whom the book was associated rather than according to the name of the author. (The same book is listed in the main body of *BPI* under the name of the author.)

Fine Bindings. Some books are valuable because custom bindings were applied to them alone, and not to other copies of the same book. In the Fine Bindings section of *BPI*, books are gathered under the name of the binder, when known, and then listed according to author. (Each of the books so listed is also listed under the name of the author in the main section of *BPI*.)

Fore-edge Paintings. Fore-edge paintings are original watercolor drawings upon the vertical edges of the leaves of a book. The book is laid flat with the front cover open so that the vertical edges of the leaves slant a little when the painting is applied; when the book is closed, the painting is not visible. These unusual examples of book decoration are gathered in the Fore-edge section under the year of publication of the book, and then arranged according to the name of the author. Generally, fore-edge paintings are not signed and dated, and it is often difficult, if not impossible, to be sure a fore-edge painting was executed in the year of publication of the book. When there is conclusive evidence as to the name of the artist and the date of a fore-edge painting, the book is listed under the year in which the painting was executed. (All books listed in the Fore-edge section are also listed in the main section of *BPI* under the name of the author.)

Errors in *BPI*

The multiple volumes of *BPI* that appear each year combine to include millions of letters and numerals. The editor makes every effort to get them all right, and she asks the reader to be understanding about an occasional typo.

Suggestions Are Welcome

Comments on the *Bookman's Price Index* series and suggestions for corrections and improvements are always welcome. Please contact:

Editor, *Bookman's Price Index*
Gale
27500 Drake Rd.
Farmington Hills, MI 48331-3535
Phone: 248-699-GALE
Toll-free: 800-877-GALE

Antiquarian Book Dealers
in Volume 95

Charles Agvent
291 Linden Road
Mertztown PA   19539
USA

Telephone: (610) 682-4750
e-mail: info@charlesagvent.com
http://www.charlesagvent.com
Contact: Charles Agvent

Aleph-Bet Books, Inc.
85 Old Mill River Road
Pound Ridge   NY   10576
USA

Telephone: (914) 764-7410
Fax: (914) 764-1356
e-mail: helen@alephbet.com
http://www.alephbet.com
Contact: Helen & Marc Younger
Specialties: Children's & illustrated books for the collector, first editions, pop-ups, picture books, fairy tales and more.

Andrew Isles Natural History Books
Rear 115 Greville Street
PO Box 2305
Pahran 3181
Australia

Telephone: 61 (0) 2 9510 5750
Fax: 61 (0) 3 9529 1256
e-mail: books@AmdrewIsles.com
http://www.AndrewIsles.com
Specialties: Natural history

Any Amount of Books
56 Charing Cross Road
London   WC2H 0QA
England

Telephone: 0207 836 3697
Fax: 0207 240 1769
e-mail: charingx@anyamountofbooks.com
http://www.anyamountofbooks.com

Argonaut Book Shop
786 Sutter Street
San Francisco   CA   94109
USA

Telephone: (415) 474-9067
Fax: (415) 474-2537
e-mail: argonautSF@PacBell.net
http://www.argonautbookshop.com

Athena Rare Books
424 Riverside Drive
Fairfield   CT   06824
USA

Telephone: (203) 254-2727
Fax: (203) 254-3518
e-mail: bill@athenararebooks.com
http://www.athenararebooks.com
Contact: Willliam H. Schaberg
Specialties: Philosophy, Psychology, Science, Literature, History, Alcoholism

Barnaby Rudge Booksellers
1445 Glenneyre Street
Laguna Beach   CA   92651
USA

Telephone: (866) 840-5900; (949) 497-4079
Fax: (949) 376-3111
e-mail: info@barnabyrudge.com
http://www.barnabyrudge.com
Contact: Edward S. Postal
Specialties: Antiquarian, Children's & Illustrated Books, Early Printed Books, Bibles

Bella Luna Books
4697 Stone Canyon Ranch Road
Castle Rock   CO   80104
USA

Telephone: 800-497-4717; (303) 663-2202
Fax: (303) 663-2113
e-mail: info@bellalunabooks.com
http://www.bellalunabooks.com

Between the Covers Rare Books, Inc.
112 Nicholson Road
Gloucester City NJ   08030
USA

Telephone: (856) 456-8008
Fax: (856) 456-7675
e-mail: mail@betweenthecovers.com
http://www.betweenthecovers.com
Contact: Tom Congalton, Heidi Congalton, Gwen Waring, Jessica Luminoso, Dan Gregory, Jennifer Gregory

Blackwell's Rare Books
48-51 Broad Street
Oxford OX1 3BQ
England

Telephone: 01865 333555
Fax: 01865 794143
e-mail: rarebooks@blackwell.co.uk
http://www.rarebooks.blackwell.co.uk

J & S L Bonham
Flat 14
84 Westbourne Terrace
London W2 6QE
England

Telephone: 20 7402 7064
Fax: 20 7402 0955
e-mail: bonbooks@dial.pipex.com
http://www.bonbooks.dial.pipex.com

Bookworm & Silverfish
P.O. Box 639
Wytheville VA   24382
USA

Telephone: (276) 686-5813
Fax: (276) 686-6636
e-mail: bookworm@naxs.com
http://www.bookwormandsilverfish.com
Contact: Jim Presgraves, ABAA
Specialties: General antiquarian, appraisals, 19th & 20th century technology, trade catalogs.

David Brass Rare Books, Inc.
23901 Calabasas Road
Suite 2060
Calabasas CA   91302
USA

Telephone: (818) 222-4103
e-mail: info@davidbrassrareabooks.com
http://www.davidbrassrarebooks.com
Specialties: Children's Books, Color-Plate Books, Early Printed Books, Fine Bindings, Illustrated Books, Literature, Original Artwork, Private Press Books

The Brick Row Book Shop
49 Geary Street #230
San Francisco CA   94108
USA

Telephone: (415) 398-0414
Fax: (415) 398-0435
e-mail: book@brickrow.com
http://www.brickrow.com
Specialties: First Editions, Rare Books and Manuscripts of 17th, 18th & 19th Century English and American Literature

Buckingham Books
8058 Stone Bridge Road
Greencastle PA   17225-9786
USA

Telephone: (717) 597-5657
Fax: (717) 597-1003
e-mail: sales@buckinghambooks.com
http://www.buckinghambooks.com
Specialties: Western Americana, mystery, detective, and espionage fiction.

By the Book, LC ABAA-ILAB
1045 East Camelback Road
Phoenix AZ   85014
USA

Telephone: (602) 222-8806
Fax: (480) 596-1672
e-mail: bythebooklc@qwestoffice.net
http://bythebooklc.com
Specialties: Art, Children's China/Japan/Korea, History of Ideas, Literature, Medicine, Science &Technology, Signed Books

L. W. Currey, Inc.
203 Water Street
Elizabethtown NY   12932
USA

Telephone: (518) 873-6477
http://www.lwcurrey.com
Contact: Lloyd Currey
Specialties: Popular fiction, with emphasis on science fiction and fantasy literature from the earliest times to end of the twentieth century.

Dramatis Personae, Bookseller
P.O. Box 1070
Sheffield MA   01257-1070
USA

Telephone: (413) 229-7735
Fax: (413) 229-7735
e-mail: books@dramatispersonae.com
http://www.dramatispersonae.com
Contact: Jonathan and Lisa Reynolds
Specialties: Theatre, drama, conjuring, circus, puppetry, other amusements, all performing arts pre-1930.

John Drury Rare Books
Strandlands, Wrabness
Manningtree
Essex CO11 2TX
England

Telephone: 01255 886260
Fax: 01255 880303
e-mail: mail@johndruryrarebooks.com
http://www.johndruryrarebooks.com
Contact: David Edmunds, Jennifer Edmunds
Specialties: Economics, education. law, philosophy, social history.

Dumont Maps & Books of the West
314 McKenzie Street
P.O. Box 10250
Santa Fe NM   87504
USA

Telephone: (505) 988-1076
Fax: (505) 986-6114
e-mail: info@dumontbooks.com
http://www.dumontbooks.com

I. D. Edrich
17 Selsdon Road
Wanstead
London E11 2QF
England

Telephone: 020 8989 9541
Fax: 020 8989 9541
e-mail: idedrich@idedrich.co.uk
http://www.idedrich.co.uk

Peter Ellis, Bookseller
18 Cecil Court
London WC2N 4HE
England

Telephone: 20 7836 8880
Fax: 20 8318 4748
e-mail: ellisbooks@lineone.net
http://www.peter-ellis.co.uk

Joseph J. Felcone Inc.
P.O. Box 366
Princeton NJ   08542
USA

Telephone: (609) 924-0539
Fax: (609) 924-9078
e-mail: info@felcone.com
http://www.felcone.com

Simon Finch Rare Books Limited
26 Brook Street
London W1K 5DQ
England

Telephone: 20 7499 0974
Fax: 20 7499 0799
e-mail: Rarebooks@simonfinch.com
http://www.simonfinch.com

Gemini Fine Books & Arts, Ltd.
917 Oakwood Terrace
Hinsdale IL   60521
USA

Telephone: (630) 986-1478
Fax: (630) 986-8992
e-mail: art@geminibooks.com
http://www.geminibooks.com
Specialties: Art Reference Books, French Symbolism, Art Nouveau and Art Deco, German Expressionism, Modern Illustrated Books (Livres D'artistes)

Heritage Book Shop, LLC
8687 Melrose Ave
Suite M46
West Hollywood CA   90069
USA

Telephone: (310) 659-3674
Fax: (310) 659-4872
e-mail: books@heritagebookshop.com
http://www.heritagebookshop.com
Contact: Ben Weinstein
Specialties: Illustrated Books, Bindings, Literature, Manuscripts, Early Printed Books, First Editions

Jeff Hirsch Books
2531 Ashland Avenue
Evanston IL   60201
USA

Telephone: (847) 570-9115
e-mail: mail@jhbooks.com
http://www.jhbooks.com
Contact: Jeff or Susan Hirsch
Specialties: 20th Century Photography, Art Monographs, Drama, Modern Literary Firsts, Poetry, Signed Books, Broadsides

Hobbyhorse Books Inc.
P.O. Box 591
Ho Ho Kus NJ   07423
USA

Telephone: (201) 327-4717
Fax: (201) 327-4717
e-mail: aroldi@hobbyhorsebooks.com
http://www.hobbyhorsebooks.com
Contact: Alberto C. Aroldi
Specialties: Antiquarian Children's Books, 17th-19th Century, Fables and Related Materials

R. F. G. Hollett and Son
6 Finkle Street
Sedbergh
Cumbria LA10 5BZ
England

Telephone: 44 0 15396 20298
Fax: 44 0 15396 21396
e-mail: hollett@sedburgh.demon.co.uk
http://www.holletts-rarebooks.co.uk
Contact: C. G. Hollett
Specialties: Fine, rare and collectable books of all kinds.

C P Hyland
Rosscarbery
Co. Cork
Ireland

Telephone: 023 8848063
e-mail: calbux@gmail.com
http://www.rossbarbery.ie/cphyland
Contact: Cal and Joan Hyland

James S. Jaffe Rare Books Llc
790 Madison Ave
Suite 605
New York NY   10065
USA

Telephone: (212) 988-8042
Fax: (212) 988-8044
e-mail: jamesjaffe@earthlink.net
http://www.jamessjafferarebooks.com
Contact: James Jaffe, Ingrid Lin, Mark Lowe
Specialties: Rare books, literary first editions, poetry, livres d'artistes, association copies, letters and manuscripts, archives.

Jarndyce
Antiquarian Booksellers
46, Great Russell Street
Bloomsbury
London WC1B 3PA
England

Telephone: 020 7631 4220
Fax: 020 7631 1882
e-mail: books@jarndyce.co.uk
http://www.jarndyce.co.uk
Contact: Brian Lake, Janet Nassau
Specialties: Specialty: 18th and particularly 19th century English literature and history; Dickens.

Priscilla Juvelis, Inc.
11 Goose Fair
Kennebunkport ME   04046
USA

Telephone: (207) 967-0909
e-mail: pf@juvelisbooks.com
http://www.juvelisbooks.com
Contact: Priscilla Juvelis
Specialties: Book Arts, Literary First Editions

Kaaterskill Books
PO Box 122
East Jewett NY   12424
USA

Telephone: (518) 589-0555
Fax: (518) 589-0555
e-mail: books@katerskillbooks.com
http://www.kaaterskillbooks.com
Contact: Joan Kutcher, Charles Kutcher
Specialties: Americana, Latin Americana, Asia, Art, Books on Books, History, Literature, Religion

Anthony W. Laywood
Antiquarian Bookseller
Kercheval House
79 Main Street
Balderton
Newark NG24 3NN
England

Telephone: 01636 659031
Fax: 01636 659219
e-mail: books@anthonylaywood.co.uk

Ken Lopez, Bookseller
51 Huntington Rd.
Hadley MA 01035
USA

Telephone: (413) 584-4827
Fax: (413) 584-2045
e-mail: klopez@well.com
http://www.lopezbooks.com
Specialties: Modern literary first editions, literature of the 1960's, Vietnam War, native American literature, nature writing.

Lupack Rare Books
449 New Hanover Ave.
Meriden CT 06451
USA

Telephone: (203) 237-9198
e-mail: slupack@cox.net
Contact: Kathleen & Stephen Lupack
Specialties: Literary first editions; 19th & 20th century English & American literature, Joseph Conrad, Charles Dickens, Ernest Hemingway, John Steinbeck, Mark Twain.

M & S Rare Books. Inc.
P.O. Box 2594
East Side Station
Providence RI   02906
USA

Telephone: (401) 421-1050
Fax: (401) 272-0831
e-mail: dsiegel@msrarebooks.com
http://www.msrarebooks.com
Contact: Daniel G. Siegel
Specialties: Office hours by appointment

Maggs Bros Ltd.
50 Berkeley Square
London W1J 5BA
England

Telephone: 20 7493 7160
Fax: 20 7499 2007
e-mail: enquiries@maggs.com
http://www.maggs.com

Howard S. Mott, Inc.
P. O. Box 309
170 South Main Street
Sheffield MA 01257
USA

Telephone: (413) 229-2019
Fax: (413) 229-8553
e-mail: mottinc@vgernet.net
Contact: Donald N. Mott
Specialties: Americana, English & American literature, unusual imprints, West Indies, historical manuscripts.

Phillip J. Pirages
Fine Books And Manuscripts
P.O. Box 504
2205 Nut Tree Lane
McMinnville OR   97128
USA

Telephone: (503) 472-0476; (800) 962-6666
Fax: (503) 472-5029
e-mail: pirages@onlinemac.com
http://www.pirages.com
Contact: Phil Pirages
Specialties: Early printing, bindings, illuminated manuscripts, illustrated books, private press books.

Jo Ann Reisler, Ltd.
360 Glyndon St., N.E.
Vienna VA 22180
USA

Telephone: (703) 938-2967
Fax: (703) 938-9057
e-mail: email@joannreisler.com
http://www.joannreisler.com
Specialties: Children's books, illustrated books, original illustrative art, paper dolls, paper toys.

Paulette Rose
Fine and Rare Books
10 East 70th Street
New York NY 10021
USA

Telephone: (212) 861-5607
Fax: (212) 861-5619
e-mail: prose326@aol.com
Specialties: By appointment only

Schooner Books Ltd.
5378 Inglis Street
Halifax NS
 B3H 1J5
Canada

Telephone: (902) 423-8419
Fax: (902) 423-8503
e-mail: SchoonerBooks@schoonerbooks.com
http://www.SchoonerBooks.com
Specialties: Second hand and rare books, antique maps & prints.

Second Life Books, Inc.
P.O. Box 242
55 Quarry Road
Lanesborough MA 01237
USA

Telephone: (413) 447-8010
Fax: (413) 499-1540
e-mail: info@secondlifebooks.com
http://www.secondlifebooks.com

Ken Spelman Rare Books
70 Micklegate
York YO1 6LF
England

Telephone: 01904 624414
Fax: 01904 626276
e-mail: ask@kenspelman.com
http://www.kenspelman.com

Raymond M. Sutton, Jr.
430 Main Street
Williamsburg KY 40769
USA

Telephone: (606) 549-3464
Fax: (606) 549-3469
e-mail: suttonbks@2geton.net
http://www.suttonbooks.com
Contact: Raymond M. Sutton, Jr., Chip Sutton
Specialties: Natural history books.

Unsworths Booksellers Ltd.
36, St. Martin's Court
London WC2N 4AL
England

Telephone: 020 7836-6622
e-mail: books@unsworths.com
http://www.unsworths.com
Contact: Charlie Unsworth, Leo Cadogan
Specialties: Scholarly and Antiquarian books on the humanities, especially Classics and History.

Jeff Weber Rare Books
P.O. Box 3368
Glendale CA 91221-0368
USA

Telephone: (323) 344-9332
Fax: (323) 344-9267
e-mail: weberbks@pacbell.net
Contact: Jeff Weber, Linda Weber

Bookman's Price Index

A

Aaronovitch, S. *The Ruling Class.* London: Lawrence & Wishart, 1961, First edition; small 8vo., original cloth gilt, dust jacket, pages 192, edges rather spotted. R. F. G. Hollett & Son Antiquarian Booksellers 175 - 1 2011 £35

Aarons, Slim *A Wonderful Time: an Intimate Portrait of the Good Life.* New York: Harper and Row, 1974, First edition; 4to., copiously illustrated in color and black and white, pages 216, very good+ in bright, clean dust jacket, slightly rubbed at corners and head of spine and with minimal wear, decent condition. Any Amount of Books May 29 2011 - A68306 2011 $383

Abarbanel, Isaac *Don Vitzhaq Abravaniel & R. Mosis Alschechi Comment in Essiae Propbetian 30 (Actually Isaiah 52 v. 13 to 53 v. 12)...* Leiden: B. & A. Elzevier, 1631, 8vo., (16) 291, (13) pages, title printed in red and black, Square & Rabbinic letter, some Arabic type, contemporary English calf, from the library of the Earls of Macclesfield at Shirburn Castle. Maggs Bros. Ltd. 1440 - 1 2011 £550

Abbey, Edward *Abbey's Road.* New York: Dutton, 1979, First edition; near fine, spine pushed in, ghost of small sticker on front free endpapers, dust jacket near fine, two very small closed tears. Bella Luna Books May 26 2011 - t4059 2011 $440

Abbey, Edward *Appalachian Wilderness.* New York: Dutton, 1970, First edition; near fine, photos by Eliot Porter, near fine dust jacket, price clipped. Bella Luna Books May 29 2011 - t9631 2011 $137

Abbey, Edward *Desert Solitaire.* New York: McGraw Hill, 1968, First edition; 8vo., pages 269, drawings by Peter Parnell, nice in little nicked dust jacket, scarce. Second Life Books Inc. 174 - 1 2011 $1500

Abbey, Edward *Desert Solitaire.* New York: McGraw Hill, 1968, First edition; near fine, very minor wear at base of spine, dust jacket very good, 1 inch closed tear on front panel, half inch closed tear on rear panel, light creasing and rubbing to extremities, despite flaws dust jackets colors are true, very good with 1 inch closed tear on front panel, half inch closed tear on rear panel, light creasing and rubbing to extremities. Bella Luna Books May 26 2011 - t4259 2011 $605

Abbey, Edward *Desert Solitaire.* Tucson: University of Arizona Press, 1988, First edition thus; illustrations by Lawrence Ormsby, near fine, few minor spots on page edges, dust jacket fine. Bella Luna Books May 29 2011 - t2013 2011 $137

Abbey, Edward *Fire on the Mountain.* New York: Dial Press, 1962, First edition; book very good, light shelfwear, rear hinge starting, previous owner's name under front flap of dust jacket, dust jacket very good, moderate chipping to spine and corners, light soiling. Bella Luna Books May 26 2011 - t7947 2011 $654

Abbey, Edward *The Fool's Progress.* New York: Henry Holt, 1988, First edition; near fine, previous owner's name and gift inscription, dust jacket fine, first state of dust jacket with uncorrected errors on both front and rear flaps, 'msit' for 'myth' and 'Mickey' for 'Becky', signed by author. Bella Luna Books May 26 2011 - 3668 2011 $330

Abbey, Edward *The Hidden Canyon.* New York: Viking, 1977, First edition; book condition near fine, previous owner's inscription erased from front free endpapers, leaving two small holes and rubbing, dust jacket fine, signed by photographer. Bella Luna Books May 26 2011 - t760 2011 $357

Abbey, Edward *The Journey Home.* New York: Dutton, 1977, First edition; book fine, dust jacket near fine, with 1 inch closed tear at heel of spine and light creasing to spine ends. Bella Luna Books May 26 2011 - t6330 2011 $330

Abbey, Edward *The Monkey Wrench Gang.* Philadelphia: New York: J. B. Lippincott, 1975, First edition; near fine, light wear to extremities, dust jacket very good with chipping to edges and corners, very good, chipping to edges and corners. Bella Luna Books May 26 2011 - 2101 2011 $275

Abbey, Edward *One Life at a Time, Please.* New York: Henry Holt, 1988, First edition; fine, dust jacket fine. Bella Luna Books May 29 2011 - 3672 2011 $82

Abbey, Edward *Slickrock.* San Francisco: Sierra Club Books, 1971, First edition; illustrations by Philip Hyde, near fine very light use, dust jacket is near fine, light scratching and creasing. Bella Luna Books May 26 2011 - t8767 2011 $357

Abbey, Edward *Sunset Canyon.* London: Talmy Franklin, 1972, First UK edition; fine, fine dust jacket. Bella Luna Books May 26 2011 - t2419 2011 $192

Abbey, Edward *Vox Clamantis in Desierto.* Santa Fe: Rydal Press, 1989, Publisher's overrun, this was number 130 but number has been crossed out and "withdrawn" written next to it; fine brown paper covered slipcase, book fine. Bella Luna Books   May 26 2011 - t5813   2011 $247

Abbiatico, Mario *Modern Firearm Engravings.* Italy: Artiche Italiane, 1980, First edition; tall 4to., original cloth, gilt, dust jacket, pages 284, with 67 colored plates and 422 illustrations.   R. F. G. Hollett & Son Antiquarian Booksellers General Catalogue Summer 2010 - 27   2011   £120

Abbot, Abiel *Genealogical Register of the Descendants of George Abbot of Andover...* Boston: 1847, 197 pages, very good, early cloth, fore edge untrimmed, 6 page typed summary laid in.   Bookworm & Silverfish   669 - 1   2011 $150

Abbot, Abiel *Self Preservation. A Sermon Preached Before the Ancient and Honorable Artillery Company in Boston June 7 1802...* First edition; 8vo., 23, (1) pages, illustrated half title, sewn and uncut, original plain front wrapper, presented by militia commander General John Winslow to Judge (Robert Treate) Paine.   M & S Rare Books, Inc.   90 - 1   2011 $125

Abbot, W. Robert *Write Me a Verbal contract.* Charlottesville: 1961, First edition; fine in very good dust jacket with age soil.   Bookworm & Silverfish   676 - 208   2011 $75

Abbott, Berenice *Changing New York.* New York: E. P. Dutton & Co. Inc., 1939, First edition; 4to., pages xiv, 15-208, frontispiece and 96 black and white photos, original blue cloth, spine lettered in gilt, upper side lettered and with device in gilt, top edge dyed blue, light soiling to pastedowns, ink mark and short close tear to page 17, original black and white photo illustrated dust jacket, lightly worn at extremities and around spine, crease, chip and closed tear to head of spine, near fine in very good dust jacket.   Simon Finch Rare Books   Zero - 501   2011   £2500

Abbott, Jacob *Caleb in Town.* London: T. J. Allman, circa, 1865, 32mo., half title, few spots, original dark blue pebble grained cloth, blocked in blind, spine lettered and decorated in gilt, slight rubbing, inner hinge slightly cracked, all edges gilt, very good.   Jarndyce Antiquarian Booksellers CXCI - 32   2011   £35

ABC. New York: Metropolitan Life Ins. Co. circa, 1920, 8vo., pictorial wrappers, light soil, very good, black and white illustrations.   Aleph-Bet Books, Inc.   95 - 3   2011 $125

ABC Alphabet Book. no publication information circa, 1935, Folio, pictorial wrappers, slight fading, else fine, printed on linen like paper.   Aleph-Bet Books, Inc.   95 - 1   2011 $150

ABC Book. Kansas City: Faultless Starch, n.d. circa, 1910, 3 1/8 x 5 inches, pictorial wrappers, near fine, illustrations in blue.   Aleph-Bet Books, Inc.   95 - 2   2011 $125

ABC for Children. no publication information, circa, 1910, 9 x 7 1/2 inches, some soil, but very good, illustrations in full color.   Aleph-Bet Books, Inc.   95 - 10   2011 $150

ABC for Little Ones. London: Nister, n.d. circa, 1890, 4to., cloth backed pictorial boards, some soil and wear to covers else very good, beautiful ABC, printed on thick card pages, illustrations in color on every page.   Aleph-Bet Books, Inc.   95 - 30   2011 $225

ABC of Games and Toys. London: T. Nelson & Sons, n.d., circa, 1910, 4to., flexible pictorial card covers, spine slightly rough, very good+, color illustrations by Rosa Petherick.   Aleph-Bet Books, Inc.   95 - 37   2011 $275

ABC Van Het Naziregiem. Brussels: Leven, 1944, 12mo., pictorial wrappers, slight soil, else near fine, very page illustrated in full color by Herman A. Voss.   Aleph-Bet Books, Inc.   95 - 29   2011 $850

Abeling, James *The History of Roche Abbey, Yorkshire.* Worksop: Robert White, 1870, First edition; tall 8vo., original cloth, gilt over bevelled boards, neatly recased, pages, xiv, 201, frontispiece, title in red and black, 15 lithographed plates, very scarce.   R. F. G. Hollett & Son Antiquarian Booksellers   General Catalogue Summer 2010 - 1314   2011   £180

Abraham, George D. *Motor Ways in Lakeland.* London: Methuen & Co., 1913, First edition; original cloth, gilt, spine trifle faded, few slight marks, pages xi, 307 30, with 24 illustrations and map on front endpapers.   R. F. G. Hollett & Son Antiquarian Booksellers   173 - 3   2011   £45

Abraham, George D. *On Alpine Heights and British Crags.* London: Methuen, 1919, First edition; original cloth, gilt, rather rubbed and bumped, pages x, 307, 24 plates, flyleaves lightly browned.   R. F. G. Hollett & Son Antiquarian Booksellers   General Catalogue Summer 2010 - 936   2011   £65

An Account of Money Raised and Expended for the Relief of the Poor of that Part of the Parish of Whitchurch which Lies within the County of Salop from March 27th 1840 to March 27th 1841.   Whitchurch: printed by J. Davies, 1841,   First edition; 8vo., 21 (1) pages, contemporary related press cutting tipped on to titlepage just affecting few letters of the word "account" but still absolutely legible, signatures of two members of the Corser family also on titlepage, preserved in modern wrappers with printed title label on upper cover, good copy, very rare.   John Drury Rare Books   153 - 171   2011   £125

Accurate Account of the Loss of His Majesty's Ship Litchfield, Captain Barton, of Fifty Guns on the Coast of Barbary, Nov. 30 1758...   London: printed for Thomas Tegg, 1758,   12mo., large folding frontispiece, (2), 7-28 pages, title rather browned.   Anthony W. Laywood   May 26 2011 - 21475   2011 $184

Achilles, Tatius   *De Clitophontis et Leucippes Amoribus Libri VIII.*   Leipzig: Sumtibus Io. Friderici Iunii, 1776,   Facing pages of Greek and Latin text, pages xvi, 731, (13), 8vo., contemporary red morocco, boards bordered with triple gilt fillet, spine divided by gilt square chain rolls between gilt fillets, second compartment gilt lettered direct, rest with central gilt tools, marbled endpapers, all edges gilt, small ink spot to lower board, note on endpaper above binding, near fine, binding unsigned, but 20th century pencil note on verso of front flyleaf attributes it to Derome le Jeune.   Blackwell Rare Books   B166 - 16   2011   £800

Acker, Kathy   *I Dreamt I Was a Nymphomaniac!: Imagining.*   N.P.: Black Tarantula, 1974,   First edition; Chapter 4 ("Imagining") in her self-published sequence - this being pages 72-106, stapled wrappers, several small spots to covers, near fine, scarce.   Ken Lopez Bookseller   154 - 2   2011 $250

Ackermann, Rudolph   1764-1834   *The Microcosm of London.*   London: R. Ackermann's Repository of Arts, 1808-1810,   First edition, early issue with 9 (possibly 10) of Abbey's twelve key plates in their first state; text watermarked 1806-1807 and plates watermarked 1805-1808 and with errata uncorrected, except for that reading 'coustom' for 'custom' on page 218 of volume I, 3 volumes, large quarto, 104 hand colored aquatint plates, contemporary full tree calf, gilt tooled borders, spines neatly rebacked to period style, five compartments with crimson and green morocco labels and gilt ornaments, four gilt tooled raised bands, some offsetting to opposing leaves, extraordinary copy, scarcely seen with all half titles and 9 (possibly 10) of the 12 key plate in first state).   David Brass Rare Books, Inc.   May 26 2011 - 01585   2011 $14,500

Acton, Harold   *The Last of the Medici.*   Florence: privately printed for subscribers by G. Orioli, Lungarno Corsini, 1930,   One of 365 numbered copies; 159 pages, printed on Binda handmade paper, signed by introducer, Norman Douglas, paper boards with gilt medallion on upper cover and gilt title label on spine, fine in fine dust jacket, just slightly faded at spine and in original card mailing box, brilliant copy.   Peter Ellis   May 26 2011 - ACTONHARO11702   2011 $450

Acton, Harold   *The Villas of Tuscany.*   London: Thames and Hudson, 1984,   4to., pages 288, 24 color plates, 126 black and white illustrations, original cloth, gilt, dust jacket.   R. F. G. Hollett & Son Antiquarian Booksellers   177 - 1   2011   £85

Acton, John   *An Essay on Shooting.*   London: printed for T. Cadell, 1789,   First edition in English; 192 x 133mm., xiii, (i), 303 pages (missing A1, blank), original publisher's boards, blue paper sides, plain paper spine with ink titling, untrimmed edges, very nice folding cloth box with leather label on spine, armorial bookplate of Oliver Collett over early ink signature; paper on covers and spine and bit soiled and chafed, as expected, small portion of backstrip perished at bottom, isolated minor foxing internally, extremely desirable copy, binding entirely sound, text clean and fresh and bright.   Phillip J. Pirages   59 - 54   2011 $1250

The Actor; or, a Peep Behind the Curtain.   New York: William H. Graham, 1846,   First edition; 12mo., ex-library, modern blue buckram, library stamps in ink to front flyleaf and titlepage, tear to foot of one leaf, repaired with archival tape, mild foxing (primarily marginal) to a few leaves, scarce.   Dramatis Personae Booksellers   106 - 4   2011 $100

Adam, Alexander   *A Summary of Geography & History, Both Ancient & Modern.*   London: 1824,   xi, 727 pages, with all 13 maps (folding), very free of foxing, this copy without covers.   Bookworm & Silverfish   667 - 19   2011 $250

Adam, John   1721-1792   *Lewis Grant, Trustee for the Creditors of Adam and Thomas Fairholme, Merchants in Edinburgh... Appellant John Adam Architect in Edinburgh,... Respondent.*   London: 1767,   First (only) edition; 2 parts in one volume, large folio, 14, (2) and 9 + (1) pages, drophead and docket titles, recent marbled boards, lettered on spine, very good, large copies, apparently extremely rare.   John Drury Rare Books   153 - 1   2011   £750

Adam, William *A Treatise and Observations on Trial by Jury in Civil Causes, as Now Incorporated with Jurisdiction of the Court of Session.* Edinburgh: Thomas Clark, 1836, First edition; 8vo., recently rebound in half leather, marbled boards lettered gilt on spine with 5 raised bands, all edges gilt, pages xxv, xii, 13-418, with 156 page appendix and 21 page article at rear titled "A Short View of the Difficulties which Surround the Introduction of Trial by Jury in Civil Causes into Scotland and of the Ultimate Success of the Experiment", from the library of the Dukes of Bedford with 2 page signed letter dated 1836 to then Duke from William Adam (Lord Chief Commissioner) dated 1836 tipped in after titlepage, slight foxing to prelims, otherwise sound, clean, near fine condition. Any Amount of Books May 26 2011 - A71748 2011 $671

Adams, C. L. *Castles of Ireland: Some Fortress Histories and Legends.* 1904, Ex-library in library cloth, very good, illustrations. C. P. Hyland May 26 2011 - 255/002 2011 $275

Adams, Charlotte *Boys at Home.* London: Routledge, 1857, New edition; original red blindstamped cloth gilt extra, pages 414, with 8 full page tissue guarded woodcuts by John Gilbert, nice, bright copy, contemporary school prize inscription (Wesleyan School, Ulverston: presented to John Briggs, Christmas 1857). R. F. G. Hollett & Sons Antiquarian Booksellers 170 - 1 2011 £45

Adams, Douglas *The Hitch Hiker's Guide to the Galaxy.* London: Arthur Barker, 1979, First British edition; near fine with light bumping to spine ends, fine dust jacket. Bella Luna Books May 26 2011 - t8480 2011 $1650

Adams, Eleanor B. *The Missions of New Mexico, 1776...* Albuquerque: 1975, Reprint edition, signed limited printing of 150 specially bound, numbered copies signed by editors; xxi, 387 pages, illustrations, half leather in slipcase, issued without dust jacket, but with jacket from trade edition laid in. Dumont Maps & Books of the West 111 - 42 2011 $350

Adams, Francis *Star Castle & Its Garrison.* Liskeard: Belvedere Press, 1984, First edition; pages (iv), 120, 30 illustrations, original faux leather boards, dust jacket. R. F. G. Hollett & Son Antiquarian Booksellers 177 - 2 2011 £40

Adams, Franklin P. *Something Else Again.* Garden City: Doubleday, Page, 1920, First edition; bookplate and ownership signature of Lewis Gensler, boards little soiled, very good in very good dust jacket with some shallow chipping around crown, inscribed by author to Gensler, scarce in jacket. Between the Covers 169 - BTC347699 2011 $225

Adams, H. G. *The Life and Adventures of Dr. Livingstone: in the Interior of South Africa.* London: James Blackwood, 1868, First edition; 8vo., pages xxvi, 322, portrait, map, engravings, original full black decorative morocco, all edges gilt, gilt decoration on cover, corners rubbed, very good. J. & S. L. Bonham Antiquarian Booksellers Africa 4/20/2011 - 9172 2011 £150

Adams, Henry 1838-1918 *Democracy.* New York: Henry Holt and Co., 1880, First edition, first issue with all points; 12mo., 374 pages plus ads, original black stamped white cloth, some soiling, ink scratches on front free endpaper, trifle weary. M & S Rare Books, Inc. 90 - 2 2011 $750

Adams, John 1735-1826 *Defence of the Constitutions of Government of the United States of America.* London: printed for John Stockdale, 1794, New edition; 3 volumes, octavo, 8, xxxii, (3)-392 (2, blank); (2) (1)-451, (1, directions to binder); (2), (1)-528 (36, index) pages, frontispiece in volume I, full contemporary tree calf, rebacked, two red morocco spine labels on each volume, lettered in gilt, boards decoratively ruled in gilt, top edges brown, others speckled brown, marbled endpapers, 2 1/2 inch closed tear to leaf C2 volume I, front board volume III with some slight scuffing, previous owner's bookplate on pastedown of each volume, some light scattered foxing, overall very good, clean set. Heritage Book Shop Holiday 2010 - 2 2011 $4500

Adams, John Quincy 1767-1848 *Lectures on Freemasonry.* Hartford: Joseph Hurlbut, 1833, First edition; 8vo., 32 pages, sewn & uncut. M & S Rare Books, Inc. 90 - 232 2011 $225

Adams, Leonie *Those Not Elect.* New York: Robert M. McBride, 1925, First edition, one of just 10 copies on Ingres paper which are not for sale; signed by author, 8vo., 50 pages, paper over boards (little soiled), near fine. Second Life Books Inc. 174 - 2 2011 $700

Adams, Maurice B. *Examples of Old English Houses and Furniture...* London: B. T. Batsford, 9 + (1) pages, 27 plates, titlepage foxed, old dampstain to rear board which affects edge of final plates, original gilt stamped red cloth, rather rubbed and worn. Ken Spelman Rare Books 68 - 89 2011 £45

Adams, Maurice B. *Examples of Old English Houses and Furniture Drawn by...* London: B. T. Batsford, 1888, First edition; folio, original publisher's red buckram lettered gilt on spine and on front cover, 36 full page drawings, printed verso only, slight fox spotting at sides of prelim pages, otherwise about fine in used and chipped original plain dust jacket, exceptional condition. Any Amount of Books May 26 2011 - A49582 2011 $587

Adams, Ramon F. *Burrs Under the Saddle: A Second Look at Books and Histories of the West.* (with) *More Burrs Under the Saddle; Books & Histories of the West.* Norman: 1964-1979, First editions; x, 61 pages, xiii, 182 pages, first work dust jacket with some edge wear, else clean and very good, second work near fine in like dust jacket. Dumont Maps & Books of the West 111 - 92 2011 $175

Adams, Ramon F. *Western Words: a Dictionary of the Range, Cow Camp and Trail.* Norman: 1944, First edition; xiv, 182 pages, prospectus laid in, light soil and spine fading to dust jacket, book near fine. Dumont Maps & Books of the West 111 - 43 2011 $65

Adams, Richard *The Plague Dogs.* London: Allen Lane, 1977, First edition; original cloth, gilt, dust jacket, pages 462 with illustrations and diagrams. R. F. G. Hollett & Son Antiquarian Booksellers 173 - 8 2011 £50

Adams, Robert *The Narrative of Robert Adams a Sailor.* London: John Murray, 1816, Fiirst edition; quarto, pages xxxix, 231, folding map, some occasional light foxing, small tear repaired page 109, original grey boards with later reback. J. & S. L. Bonham Antiquarian Booksellers Africa 4/20/2011 - 8244 2011 £450

Adams, Robert *West from the Columbia.* New York: Aperture, 1995, Stated first edition; signed by author, fine in fine dust jacket, 4to., 79 pages. By the Book, L. C. 26 - 21 2011 $175

Adams, William *Practical Observations on Ectropium or Eversion of the Eyelids with the Descriptions of a New Operation for the Cure of that Disease and the Description of a Series of New and Improved Operations for the Cure of the Different Species of Cataract.* (bound with) *Official Papers Relating to Operations Performed by Order of the Directors of the Royal Hospital for Seamen at Greenwich on Several of the Pensioners Belonging Thereto for the Purpose of Ascertaining the General Efficacy of the New Modes of Treatment of Dr. Adams...* (and with) *Report Made by Order of the Philomathic Society of Paris, by Drs. Magendie and Blainville on the Subject of the New Operations and Instruments Invented by Sir William Adams for the Cure of Various Diseases of the Eye...* London: J. Callow, 1814, London: W. Winchester, 1814. London: Richard and Arthur Taylor, 1814; 3 works in one volume, 8vo., pages xvi 252 (131-136 misbound after 126), (i) errata, (i) (blank); (iv), 21, (5) blank, 8. 3 stipple engraved plates, included 2 printed in color, all edges gilt, some light sporadic spotting, elaborate contemporary straight grain red morocco, raised bands, decorated in gilt, gilt ruled and decorated border to sides, with blind rolls inside border, gilt inner dentelles, author's presentation inscription to verso of initial blank, his autograph note on inserted leaf bound after the second work, excellent copy, presentation copy inscribed by author to Baron de Stift, Counsellor of the State in the Service of His Majesty the Emperor of Austria. Simon Finch Rare Books Zero - 123 2011 £1800

Adams, William Henry Davenport 1828-1891 *Celebrated Women Travellers of the Nineteenth Century.* London: W. Swan Sonnenschein & Co., 1884, Second edition; original green cloth gilt extra, pages 459, all edges gilt, 8 plates. R. F. G. Hollett & Son Antiquarian Booksellers 175 - 11 2011 £140

Adams, William Henry Davenport 1828-1891 *Celebrated Women Travellers of the Nineteenth Century.* London: Swan Sonnenschein & Co., 1903, Half title, frontispiece, plates, original green pictorial cloth, blocked and lettered in black and orange, little dulled and rubbed, prize inscription dated 1907, good, sound copy. Jarndyce Antiquarian Booksellers CXCI - 536 2011 £40

Adams, William Henry Davenport 1828-1891 *Temples, Tombs and Monuments of Ancient Greece and Rome.* London: T. Nelson and Sons, 1871, Original blue cloth gilt over bevelled boards, pages 307, (xii), 100 woodcut illustrations. R. F. G. Hollett & Son Antiquarian Booksellers 177 - 3 2011 £40

Adams, William Y. *Nubia: Corridor to Africa.* London: Allen Lane, 1977, First edition; fat 8vo., tables, figures, plates, pages 812, ex-British Foreign Office library with few library markings, else very good. Any Amount of Books May 29 2011 - A72739 2011 $238

Adas, Michael 1805-1882 *Technology and European Overseas Enterprise: Diffusion, Adaption and Adoption.* Aldershot & Brookfield: Variorum & Ashgate, 1996, 8vo., xxvi, 433 pages, illustrations, tables, navy cloth, gilt stamped cover and spine titles, fine, from the Bern Dibner reference library, with Burndy bookplate. Jeff Weber Rare Books 161 - 1 2011 $100

Addison, Joseph 1672-1719 *Dialogues Upon the Usefulness of Ancient Medals Especially in Relation to the Latin and Greek Poets.* Glasgow: printed by R. Urie, 1751, 8vo., pages 267 (i) 4, contemporary polished tan calf, spine single rule gilt, red lettering piece gilt, board edges decorative roll in blind, all edges lightly red sprinkled, red and white sewn endbands, marginal browning to first few leaves, joints cracking, extremities bit rubbed, few small marks, ink inscription "Alex Fraser Tytler", from the collection of Christopher Ernest Weston 1947-2010. Unsworths Booksellers 24 - 65 2011 £250

Addison, Joseph 1672-1719 *The Evidences of the Christian Religion.* Oxford: Clarendon Press, 1809, 165 x 100 mm., 354 pages, very attractive dark green straight grain morocco, handsomely gilt, covers with border of multiple blind rules as well as intricate scrolling gilt cornerpieces, wide raised bands, spine compartments densely gilt cornerpieces, wide raised bands, spine compartments densely gilt with many floral and foliate tools emanating from central flower, all edges gilt, excellent fore-edge painting showing Eton College, front flyleaf with signature of Jefry Goddard dated 1819; joints just slightly rubbed, covers bit marked, isolated very minor foxing, generally in quite attractive condition, binding bright and scarcely worn, text fresh and clean. Phillip J. Pirages 59 - 194 2011 $1100

Addison, Joseph 1672-1719 *The Works of the Right Honorable Joseph Addison...* New York: William Duell & Co., 1811, 6 volumes, 12mo., gilt stamping on spine and covers, with two leather labels on spines, very fine, matching contemporary full morocco bindings, printed paper label of Cummings & Hilliard, Boston with date 18/8 and "Sold By", small bookplates neatly removed from inside front covers. M & S Rare Books, Inc. 90 - 4 2011 $750

Addison, Joseph 1672-1719 *The Works.* London: George Bell and Sons, 1893-1898, 7 volumes, 185 x 115 mm., attractive contemporary prize binding of light polished calf done for H. Sotheran & Co. (stamp signed on front turn-in of each volume), covers with double gilt fillet border, upper board of each volume with central gilt crest of St. Peter's College, Westminster, raised bands, spines ornately gilt in compartments with elegant central floral spray, surrounded by a lozenge of small tools and elaborate side and cornerpieces composed of fleurons, curls, volutes and circulets, two pale green morocco labels, filigree gilt turn-ins, marbled endpapers, all edges gilt, volume I with portrait frontispiece and 8 plates of medal and coin designs, pastedown with affixed presentation certificate to B. H. Willet, signed by William ("Gulielmus") Rutherford and dated 1899, leather with bit of dryness, extremities little rubbed, labels slightly faded, one minor neatly repaired tear (into text, but no loss), otherwise fine, elaborately gilt bindings lustrous and with other minor wear and text virtually pristine, pretty set. Phillip J. Pirages 59 - 62 2011 $275

Addison, Paul *Churchill on the Home Front 1900-1955.* London: Cape, 1902, First edition; original cloth, gilt, dust jacket, pages 493, with 12 pages of plates. R. F. G. Hollett & Son Antiquarian Booksellers 175 - 15 2011 £35

An Address to the Supporters of Lord Grey and the Friends of reform. London: Roake & Varty, 1831, First edition; 12mo., 12 pages, preserved in modern wrappers, printed title label on upper cover, very good, uncut. John Drury Rare Books 154 - 1 2011 £50

Addresses, Petitions, etc. from the Kings and Chiefs of Sudan (Africa) and the Inhabitants of Sierra Leone to His Late Majesty, King William the Fourth and His Excellency. London: privately printed, 1838, First edition; 8vo., pages ii 59, original green textured cloth boards, paper label to upper board showing a few marks and light fading, little dust soiling (heavier to front endpapers), and faint age browning, tiny tear to margin of title, binding loosening just slightly, sides rubbed, upper hinge cracking, gilt stamps of BMS Library to upper board, sellotaped shelf label to spine, inscription presented by Lt. Colonel H. D. Campbell, presented to Lord Bishop of London. J. & S. L. Bonham Antiquarian Booksellers Africa 4/20/2011 - 8065 2011 £250

Adelmann, Howard B. *The Correspondenve of Marcello Malpighi.* Ithaca and London: Cornell University Press, 1975, 5 volumes, 4to., maroon cloth, gilt stamped spine title, inner hinge cracked (volume V only), very good, from the Bern Dibner reference library with Burndy bookplate. Jeff Weber Rare Books 161 - 2 2011 $100

Adolphus, John *The Royal Exile; or Memoirs of the Public and Private Life of Her Majesty, Caroline, Queen Consort of Great Britain...* Jones and Co., 1821, Eighteenth edition; 8vo., 2 volumes, most handsome copy, full contemporary calf, gilt decorated spines with red and green morocco labels, extra illustrated with numerous contemporary portrait plates, engravings, cuttings, etc. Ken Spelman Rare Books 68 - 201 2011 £395

Adra *Legends of Lakeland.* Scarborough: S. W. Theakston, 1881, Small 4to., original red cloth gilt over bevelled boards, few slight marks, pages (vi), 166, all edges gilt, single line border to each page in red, edges of first and last leaves little spotted, uncommon. R. F. G. Hollett & Son Antiquarian Booksellers 173 - 9 2011 £85

Adronicus Rhodius *Ethicorum Nichomacheorum Paraphrasis.* Cambridge: Excudebat Johannes Hayes, 1679, Titlepage in red and black, one or two small spots, embossment of Earls of Macclesfield to first two printed leaves, pages (xviii), 530, (30), 8vo., contemporary plain biscuit calf, backstrip with five raised bands, old paper labels in top and bottom compartments, edges speckled red, merest touch of rubbing to edges, South Library bookplate, very good. Blackwell Rare Books B166 - 4 2011 £400

The Adventures of Teasing Tom and Naughty Ned with a Spool of Clarks. New York: F. B. Patterson, 1879, 24mo., pictorial buff paper wrappers, clean copy, 6 leaves (counting covers) with set of amusing illustrations. Jo Ann Reisler, Ltd. 86 - 138 2011 $150

Advice and Select Hymns for the Instruction of Little Children. Seventh Series No. 10. Concord: Atwood & Brown, 1837, 16 pages, original paper wrapper, small engraved vignette on titlepage, full page engraved frontispiece and 4 small engravings in text, upper cover dated 1839, with engraved figure of a crab, lower wrapper with two vignettes and title representing the Moon and a King, both enclosed in decorative printer device, minor foxing, small repair at foot of spine, rare imprint in very good state. Hobbyhorse Books   56 - 20   2011 $125

Aelianus, Claudius   *Claudii Aeliani Praenestini ontificis Opera Quae Extant...* Tiguri: Apud Gesneros Fratres, 1556, Folio, engraved printer's device on title and last page and engraved historiated letters, pages (48), 655, (56), text in double columns of Greek and Latin, double plate included in paging, 19th century red morocco (old stains to covers, flecking near lower edge of covers, some damage to lower margins of endpapers resulting from dampness, piece missing from margin of title, 3 leaves professionally restored, dampstaining, mostly to lower margins of text, throughout; tear near lower margin of a leaf), 5 raised bands, gilt ruling to all panels, gilt decorations near ends of spine, covers triple ruled in gilt, with triple ruled gilt dentelles, all edges gilt, fine.   Raymond M. Sutton, Jr.   May 26 2011 - 41641   2011 $3000

Aesopus   *Fabulae Aesopicae.*   Lvgdvni: Apud Ioan. Tornaesium Typogr. Regium, 1571, 16mo., 637, 18 pages, straight grain morocco with gilt decorative frame and gilt dentelles at edge of covers, professionally rebacked, black label with gilt title on spine, marbled endpapers, text in Latin and Greek, large medallion portrait, 92 superb 1/3 page woodcuts, gilt royal armorial shield laid down inside covers, lacking 18 pages, as bound, inner hinges of covers reinforced, light wear to edges, tiny lower marginal small wormhole on six leaves, not interfering with text, excellent and very rare.   Hobbyhorse Books   56 - 51   2011 $420

Aesopus   *Fables d'Esope.*   Paris: Chez Davidtz, 1763, 2 volumes, 8vo., cxxxv, 287 (3)-426 (4), full leather on boards, marbled endpapers, gilt dentelles at edges of covers, 6 elaborate decorative gilt panels on spine and two gilt red labels with title and numeral, red silk page marker, full page copper engraved frontispiece, wood engraved vignette on titlepage, front margin of three leaves restored, not interfering with text or plates, front edge of one leaf restored, light rubbing along fold of covers, beautiful and rare set with exquisite copper engravings.   Hobbyhorse Books   56 - 47 2011 $900

Aesopus   *Les Fables et la Vie d'Esope.*   Caen: T. Chalopin, n.d circa, 1795, 12mo., 79 pages, original drab blue wrappers, full page woodcut, woodcuts, printed on provincial handmade paper, shelfwear at edges, minor nick at foot of spine, cased on handmade folder with title label, rare in very good state.   Hobbyhorse Books   56 - 49   2011 $800

Aesopus   *Fabulae Aesopi Selectae or Selected Fables.* Lancaster: Burnside and Smith, 1804, 8vo., 155, 1 pages, full leather on boards, red roan spine, rebacked maintaining original covers, scuffing along edges of covers, repaired corner of titlepage and lower edge of a leaf, scattered foxing and browning along fore edges, very good.   Hobbyhorse Books   56 - 50   2011 $270

Aesopus   *Nouveau Choix des Fables d'Esope.*   Paris: Chez Nyon jeune Linraire place de la Monnoise No. 13..., 1808, Small 8vo., viii, 131, (1), 34, (2), original vellum on boards, small engraved vignette on titlepage, wood engraved headpiece, cover rubbed and frayed at corners, rebacked with antique paper, good, rare.   Hobbyhorse Books   56 - 53   2011 $200

Aesopus   *Fables d'Esope.*   Epinal: Chez Pellerin, n.d. circa, 1825, 12mo., 69 pages, pictorial green paper wrappers, thread stitched as published, printed on provincial paper, rebacked with colored matching paper, restored tear lower wrapper not interfering with text, faded stamp at corner of cover, rare.   Hobbyhorse Books   56 - 48   2011 $370

Aesopus   *Familiar Fables in Verse.*   Edinburgh: Oliver and Boyd, 1829, 16mo., 36 pages, pictorial stiff paper covers, full page octagonal wood engraved frontispiece, small vignette on titlepage, 15 superb beautifully printed wood engravings, rounded corners as published, small nick at top section of page 11 and lower edge (restored) of page 21, light soiling of covers, rare, very good.   Hobbyhorse Books 56 - 52   2011 $450

Aesopus   *Some of Aesops Fables...*   London: Macmillan, 1883, First edition; small 4to., original pictorial cloth, rather soiled and edges worn, pages 80, illustrations, few finger marks.   R. F. G. Hollett & Son Antiquarian Booksellers 175 - 216   2011   £45

Aesopus   *Aesop's Fables.*   London: Paris & Melbourne: Cassell & Co., 1896, Small 4to., viii, 422, (13) list of publications, pictorial stamped and gilt brown cloth on boards, gilt title repeated on spine, full page engraved frontispiece, full page engravings, frontispiece lightly creased, new front free endpaper, minor rubbing at edges and corners of covers, very good.   Hobbyhorse Books   56 - 46   2011 $150

Aesopus   *Fables of Aesop.*   New York & Boston: H. M. Caldwell, n.d. circa, 1905, 8vo., green cloth with beautiful gold and black classic art nouveau design on cover and spine, top edge gilt, 255 pages, corner of rear cover darkened, else fine, 7 black and white plate, lovely edition. Aleph-Bet Books, Inc.   95 - 222   2011 $225

Aesopus *Aesop's Fables.* London: William Heinemann; New York: Doubleday, Page & Co., 1912, One of 1450 copies signed by artist (this #417); 290 x 232mm., xxix, (i), 223, (1) pages, very attractive red three quarter morocco (stamp signed "Putnams"), raised bands, spine handsomely gilt compartments, formed by plain and decorative rules, quatrefoil centerpiece surrounded by densely scrolling cornerpieces, sides and endleaves of rose colored linen, top edge gilt, with 20 full page black and white illustrations, numerous illustrations in text, 13 color plates by Arthur Rackham, mounted on heavy brown stock and protected by lettered tissue guard; extremities little rubbed (spine with barely perceptible loss of leather across the top), one plate with corner crease, isolated trivial faint smudges, but excellent copy, fresh, clean and bright internally smudges, but excellent copy, fresh, clean and bright internally, quite pleasing lustrous decorative binding with only minor wear. Phillip J. Pirages   59 - 283   2011 $2400

Affo, Ireneo *Antichita a Pregj della Chiesa Guastallese Ragionamento Storico-Critico del Padre Ireo Affo.* Parma: dalla Reale Stameria, 1774, Small 4to., vii, 199 pages, title within fine ornamental border, original plain wrappers, very good.   Jeff Weber Rare Books   163 - 39   2011 $950

Afternoon Tea. Boston: Joseph Knight Co., 1891, Oblong large 4to., silver decorated salmon colored cloth backed decorated paper covered boards, slight rubbing at corners, rather fresh copy, cloth decorated with lovely silver design and lettering, boards covered with attractive color and golden floral motif, 8 mounted black and white photos by W. G. Mitchell.   Jo Ann Reisler, Ltd.   86 - 190   2011 $400

Agassiz, Louis   1807-1873   *Contributions to the Natural History of the United States of America.* Boston: Little Brown and Co., 1857-1862, 4 volumes, 77 plates, foxing, sometimes heavy to many, dampstaining, mostly marginal to plates in volumes 3 and 4, colored plates of turtles are virtually clean, large 4to., pages li, 452; (4), (451-) 643; xi, 306, 26; viii, 380, 12, original brown cloth (rebacked with later brown cloth, wear to corners and several edges to covers, head of spine perished, staining to front cover, some foxing to front and back pages, dampstaining to gutters and or margins of front and back pages, paper on some inner hinges cracked), from the library of Henry Wadsworth Longfellow, with his signature included twice, tipped into volume 1 is brief ALS, 1 page, from Agassiz to unknown recipient.   Raymond M. Sutton, Jr.   May 26 2011 - 55815   2011 $1200

Agee, James   1909-1955   *On Film. Volume One: Reviews and Comments (and) Volume Two: Five Film scripts by James Agee.* London: Peter Owen, 1963-1965, First UK edition; 2 volumes, photos, illustrations, fine set in near fine, slightly marked dust jackets.   Peter Ellis   May 26 2011 - AGEEJAME007416   2011 $85

Agee, James   1909-1955   *Permit Me Voyage.* New Haven: Yale University Press, 1935, Second edition; near fine in very good dust jacket.   Lupack Rare Books   May 26 2011 - ABE1290099497   2011 $150

Agnes, Sister   *The Story of Kendal: An Outline of the History of the Town of Kendal and Its People from Ancient Times to the Present Day.* Kendal: Westmorland Gazette, 1947, First edition; original cloth, dust jacket little chipped and worn, price clipped, pages 64, with 10 plates, scarce.   R. F. G. Hollett & Son Antiquarian Booksellers   173 - 10   2011   £45

Agnew, Georgette   *Let's Pretend.* London: J. Saville, 1927, Limited to only 156 numbered copies signed by author and artist; 4to., vellum backed cloth, vellum slight soiled, else near fine, illustrations by E. H. Shepard, printed on handmade paper.   Aleph-Bet Books, Inc.   95 - 533   2011 $1250

Agopian, Yovhannes   *l'Argmanout 'iwn Italakansrbazani Xorhdatetern. La Laichiaratione Della Liturgia Armena.* Venice: M. A. Barboni, 1690, 4to., 51, (1) pages, title and text printed in red and black, some leaves cropped close at head, with loss of page numbers, modern half calf, from the library of the Earls of Macclesfield at Shirburn Castle.   Maggs Bros. Ltd.   1440 - 2   2011   £2000

Agrippa Von Nettesheim, Henrich Cornelius   *The Vanity of the Arts and Sciences.* London: printed by J. C. for Samuel Speed and sold by booksellers of London and Westminster, 1676, First edition thus; contemporary leather with raised bands, leather spine label with gilt rear endpapers torn out, interior clean, tight, free of foxing, frontispiece, (20), 368 pages.   G. H. Mott Bookseller   May 26 2011 - 42935   2011 $1600

Ahearn, Allen   *Collected Books. The Guide to Values.* New York: G. P. Putnam's Sons, 2002, Large 8vo., original cloth backed boards, gilt, dust jacket, xii, 788, fine, signed by Patricia and Allen Ahearn.   R. F. G. Hollett & Son Antiquarian Booksellers   General Catalogue Summer 2010 - 360   2011   £35

Ai, Pseud.   *Cruelty Poems.* Boston: Houghton Mifflin, 1973, First edition; 8vo., pages 46, wrinkle in cloth on cover, otherwise nice, somewhat scuffed and soiled dust jacket.   Second Life Books Inc.   174 - 5   2011 $85

Aickman, Robert   *Sub Rosa: Strange Tales.* London: Victor Gollancz Ltd., 1968, First edition; octavo, boards.   L. W. Currey, Inc.   124 - 126   2011 $500

Aiken, Conrad   *Cats and Bats and Things with Wings.* New York: Atheneum, 1965, Stated first edition; 4to., pictorial cloth, fine in dust jacket, wonderfully illustrated by Milton Glaser, this copy inscribed by author.   Aleph-Bet Books, Inc.   95 - 44   2011 $125

Aiken, Conrad *Earth Triumphant.* New York: 1914, First edition; very nearly fine.   Lupack Rare Books   May 26 2011 - ABE750228993   2011 $150

Aiken, Joan *The Butterfly Picnic.* London: Victor Gollancz, 1972,   First edition; head of spine very slightly bumped, fine in fine dust jacket, uncommon.   Peter Ellis   May 26 2011 - AIKENJOA012838   2011 $65

Aiken, Peter Freeland *The People's Charter; and Old England For Ever.* London: L. & G. Seeley, 1839,   First edition (16th thousand); 8vo., woodcut on titlepage, 12 pages, plain wrappers, very good, very scarce.   John Drury Rare Books   153 - 2   2011   £125

Aikin, John *Evenings at Home...* Darton & Co., n.d. circa, 1850,   Small 8vo., original cloth gilt, little rubbed, pages 355, all edges gilt, engraved frontispiece and title (edges rather damp spotted), joints cracked.   R. F. G. Hollett & Sons Antiquarian Booksellers   170 - 5   2011   £35

Ainslie, Peter *Life and Writings of George W. Abell.* Richmond: 1875,   First edition; 272 pages, 12mo., laid down photo frontispiece, excellent copy with a few age defects (one or two opaque spots etc.), scarce.   Bookworm & Silverfish   679 - 171   2011 $85

Ainslie, R. St. J. *Sedbergh School Songs.* Leeds: Richard Jackson, 1896,   First edition; original pictorial blue cloth gilt, 104 pages, all edges gilt, illustrations by author, scarce.   R. F. G. Hollett & Son Antiquarian Booksellers   173 - 11   2011   £65

Ainslie, R. St. J. *Sedbergh School Songs.* Leeds: Richard Jackson, 1896,   Deluxe edition; tall 8vo., original vellum gilt, boards little warped and slight spotted as usual, pages 104, all edges gilt, illustrations by author, scarce.   R. F. G. Hollett & Son Antiquarian Booksellers   173 - 12   2011   £85

Ainslie, R. St. J. *Sedbergh School Songs.* Sedbergh: Jackson & Sons, n.d. circa, 1910,   Large 8vo., original brown cloth gilt, school arms and motto in gilt on upper board, unpaginated, scarce.   R. F. G. Hollett & Son Antiquarian Booksellers   173 - 13   2011   £75

Ainsworth, Cyrus *The Disappearance of Nicholson. A Story.* London: John Ouseley, 1908,   First edition; 107 pages, frontispiece, orange cloth lettered and decoratively lined in black, cheap paper browned, hinges cracked, spine faded, covers lightly soiled, good.   Peter Ellis   May 26 2011 - AINSWORTH011597   2011 $85

Ainsworth, Robert *Thesaurus... or a Compendius Dictionary of the Latin Tongue: Designed for the Use of the British Nations...* London: for various booksellers, 1746,   Second edition; 4to., 2 volumes, contemporary Russia gilt, extremely handsome copy, from the library of the Earls of Macclesfield at Shirburn Castle.   Maggs Bros. Ltd.   1440 - 3   2011   £450

Ainsworth, William Harrison   1805-1882 *Hilary St. Ives.* London: Chapman & Hall, 1870,   First edition; volumes, handsomely bound in later half maroon crushed morocco, raised gilt bands, gilt compartments, small nick to head of volume 1 following hinge of volume III, little rubbed, otherwise handsome.   Jarndyce Antiquarian Booksellers   CXCI - 517   2011   £480

Ainsworth, William Harrison   1805-1882 *Mervyn Clitheroe.* London: George Routledge, 1858,   First edition in book form; 8vo., pages 372, publisher's blue cloth, stamped in gilt, frontispiece, engraved titlepage, 22 plates by Phiz, very rare, fine.   Second Life Books Inc.   174 - 7   2011 $713

Ainsworth, William Harrison   1805-1882 *Le Gentilhomme Des Grandes-Routes (Rockwood).* Paris: Imprimerie de Dubisson et cie, n.d.,   First French edition; 4to., pages 156, bound in original plain wrappers, very good, rare.   Second Life Books Inc.   174 - 6   2011 $1125

Ainsworth, William Harrison   1805-1882 *Saint James's or the Court of Queen Anne. an Historical Romance.* London: John Mortimer, 1844,   First (Magazine) issue; 8vo., unbound and housed in half calf slipcase, not issued with the engraved frontispiece but with 14 engraved plates by Cruikshank, first appearance in print as extracted from "Ainsworth's Magazine" volume 4 and bound with titlepage apparently issued by Mortimer who was publisher of both magazine and three volume first book edition of this, nice, clean, unfoxed, scarce.   Second Life Books Inc.   174 - 9   2011 $563

Ainsworth, William Harrison   1805-1882 *Saint James's or the Court of Queen Anne. an Historical Romance.* London: John Mortimer, 1844,   First (Magazine) issue; 8vo., full red levant, elaborate gilt dentelles, all edges gilt, gilt lettered by Riviere, frontispiece after Maclise and 14 engraved plates by Cruikshank, first appearance in print as extracted from "Ainsworth's Magazine" volume 4 and bound with titlepage apparently issued by Mortimer who was publisher of both Magazine and three volume first book edition of this, nice, clean, unfoxed, scarce.   Second Life Books Inc.   174 - 8   2011 $638

Ainsworth, William Harrison   1805-1882   *The Works of Cheviot Tichburn.*   Manchester: with the type of John Leigh, 1825, Half title, small tear to upper margin of half title and contents leaf, 20th century half calf by Bayntun, very good.   Jarndyce Antiquarian Booksellers   CXCI - 33   2011   £1850

Airay, Christopher   *Fasciculus Praeceptorum Logicorum: In Gratiam Juventutis Academiae (sic)...*   Oxford: Henry Hall, 1660, Title within arched woodcut border, woodcut Porphyrian Tree on verso of *4, lacking initial leaf, probably blank, fore-edge of title brittle, pages (vi), 224, 12mo. in 8s, contemporary sheep, worn, loss to surface leather, rebacked, some contemporary underlinings and few emendations to text, author's name added in MS. on title and date altered to 1679, this being date of an ownership inscription at inside front cover but name indecipherable thanks to wormhole, below this name of L. Burd dated 1890 with his large armorial bookplate below stamp of Repton School.   Blackwell Rare Books   B166 - 1   2011   £750

Aislabie, John   *The Speech of the Right Honourable John Aislabie, Esq. Upon His Defence Made in the House of Lords Against the Bill for Raising Money Upon the Estates of the South Sea Directors on Wednesday 19th of July 1721.*   London: Printed for J. Roberts in Warwick Lane, 1721, Second edition; 4to., (2), 22 pages, titlepage rather soiled and creased and with some marginal fraying, text unaffected, large copy with generous margins, sewn as issued but now preserved loose in marbled wrappers, titlepage apart, fine.   John Drury Rare Books   154 - 4   2011   £275

Akerman, John Yonge   *Remains of Pagan Saxondom.*   John Russell Smith, 1855, First edition; 4to., original quarter polished roan gilt extra, odd scratch to boards, corners trifle softened, pages xxviii, 84, (ii), top edge gilt, 40 tissue guarded chromolithographed plates, many with additional hand coloring, little scattered foxing, but excellent copy, signature of James Farrer, 19th century Yorkshire archaeologist.   R. F. G. Hollett & Son Antiquarian Booksellers   177 - 5   2011   £275

Akers, Floyd   *Boy Fortune Hunters in Panama.*   Chicago: Reilly & Britton, 1908, First edition, first printing; 8vo., brown cloth stamped in black, cream and white, 310 pages, very good-fine (3rd color plate is opposite page 248, cover picture slightly rubbed, small rough area front hinge), 4 color plates by Howard Heath.   Aleph-Bet Books, Inc.   95 - 84   2011 $1200

Albee, Edward   *Malcolm.*   New York: Atheneum, 1966, First edition; Albee's play adaptation of James Purdy's first novel, fine in near fine dust jacket with light rubbing and edge wear, signed by Purdy and Albee, uncommon signed by both.   Ken Lopez Bookseller   154 - 3   2011 $250

Albemarle County Historical Society   *The Magazine of Albemarle County History.*   Charlottesville: 1979+, Volumes 37-38, 40, 41, 43, 46 48 and 53, first rubbed, rest much better.   Bookworm & Silverfish   670 - 187   2011 $100

Albemarle, William Coutts Keppel, 7th Earl of   1832-1894   *Cycling.*   London: Longmans Green and Co., 1889, Second edition; original brown cloth, spine trifle dulled, pages xiii, 452, with 19 plates and numerous woodcuts, joints tender.   R. F. G. Hollett & Son Antiquarian Booksellers   General Catalogue Summer 2010 - 1223   2011   £150

Alden, John Doughty   *The American Steel Navy: a Photographical History of the U.S. Navy from the Introduction of the Steel Hull in 1883 to the Cruise of the Great White Fleet 1907-1909.*   Annapolis & New York: Naval Inst. Press & American Heritage Press, 1972, Square 4to., ix, 396 pages, heavily illustrated with photos, creme cloth, gray stamped spine title, dust jacket, very good, from the Bern Dibner reference library, with Burndy bookplate.   Jeff Weber Rare Books   161 - 3   2011 $75

Alderson, Brian   *Cakes and Custard.*   London: Heinemann, 1974, First edition; large 8vo., original cloth, gilt, dust jacket little worn, price clipped, pages 156, (v), illustrations in color.   R. F. G. Hollett & Sons Antiquarian Booksellers   170 - 494   2011   £40

Aldin, Cecil   *Bunny Borough.*   London: Eyre & Spottiswoode, 1946, Large 8vo., original yellow cloth, dust jacket, few creases, closed tears and small chips, unpaginated, 14 fine color plates and numerous line drawings by Aldin.   R. F. G. Hollett & Sons Antiquarian Booksellers   170 - 6   2011   £75

Aldin, Cecil   *Cathedrals and Abbey Churches of England.*   London: Eyre & Spottiswoode, 1929, Small 4to., original cloth gilt, trifle used, pages vii, 111, with 16 color plates, 15 text illustrations by Aldin, half title rather spotted.   R. F. G. Hollett & Son Antiquarian Booksellers   177 - 7   2011   £60

Aldin, Cecil   *Cecil Aldin's Happy Family.*   London: Henry Frowde/Hodder & Stoughton, 1912, First edition; thick 4to., top edge gilt, elaborate presentation, cloth backed boards with pictorial spine gold lettering on cover and spine and color paste label on front cover with vignette on rear cover, some light overall soiling of quite uncommon book, this copy is ex-libris with stamp on and discreet stamping on cover and spine, lastly there is a bookplate on blank front pastedown.   Jo Ann Reisler, Ltd.   86 - 2   2011 $1500

The Aldine Poets. The Complete Series. London: printed by Charles Whittingham for William Pickering, 1830-1845, 160 x 103mm., 53 volumes, especially pretty polished light brown calf, attractively gilt by Zaehnsdorf (stamp signed), covers with gilt double fillet border and gilt Aldine/Pickering anchor centerpiece, raised bands, spines in gilt compartments with scrolling foliate cornerpieces and looping stem centerpiece surrounded by a diamond frame of circlets and tiny stars, each spine with red and green titling label and at bottom, a red date label elaborately gilt turn-ins, marbled endpapers, all edges gilt, 24 frontispiece portraits, spines uniformly faded to a darker brown, a number of small nicks or tiny scuffs to backstrips, slight offsetting from engraved frontispieces, but fine and in many ways an amazing set, joints and remarkably bright covers almost entirely without wear and text pristine. Phillip J. Pirages 59 - 279 2011 $7800

Aldington, Richard *All Men Are Enemies.* London: Chatto & Windus, 1933, First edition; number 103 of 110 copies signed by Aldington, 8vo., yellow cloth backed boards, top edge gilt, tips of corners very slightly worn, no foxing, binding tight, bright, gilt not faded, overall fine. Gemini Fine Books & Arts, Ltd. Art Reference & Illustrated Books: First Editions 2011 $150

Aldington, Richard *Women Must Work.* London: Chatto & Windus, 1934, First edition; tail of spine slightly bumped, very good in like dust jacket, rubbed, marked and slightly dusty, with few chips and tears. Peter Ellis May 26 2011 - ALDIGNTON012756 2011 $65

Aldini, Tobia *Exactissima Descriptio Rariorum Quarundam Plantarum Que Continetur Rome in Horto Farnesiano.* Rome: Mascardi, 1625, First edition; engraved titlepage, 22 finely engraved plates (print from versos visible in background of plates), few small woodcuts in text, folio, pages (10), 101, (5), late 19th century plain boards, soiled and darkened, corners bumped, head of spine chipped, heel of spine perished, 2 splits to front hinge, scattered foxing some offsetting to text, marginal dampstaining near fore-edge of many pages and plates, occasional soiling to text, small black stain near lower edge of 2 pages, last leaf of text and first leaf of index are heavily browned. Raymond M. Sutton, Jr. May 26 2011 - 28936 2011 $2500

Aldrovandi, Ulyssis *De Piscibus Libri V et de Cetis Lib. Unus.* Bononiae: Apud Nicolaum Thebaldinum, Engraved allegorical title (some light foxing), about 389 woodcuts, engraved headpieces, folio, pages (6), 732, (26), contemporary full vellum, old soiling, vellum missing from a panel on spine, upper rear corner showing, endpapers and last leaf foxed, few tears to lower margin of title and 2 leaves professionally reinforced, some stains to lower margin of first 13 leaves, small dampspot to upper margin of few leaves, browning or tanning to several leaves, 6 raised bands with panel lettered in gilt, later edition, the copy of Robert Rofen. Raymond M. Sutton, Jr. May 26 2011 - 42653 2011 $4500

Aldrovandi, Ulyssis *Quadrupedum Omniu Bisulcoru Historia Joannes Corenlius Uterverius Belga Colliqere Incaepit Thomas Dempsterus Baro a Muresk Scots...* Bonon: Apud Io. Baptistae Ferronii, 1642, colophon lists 1641. Second edition; engraved frontispiece, large woodcut printer's device on colophon, 89 woodcut illustrations, folio, (6), 1040, (12), contemporary half vellum (soiled, some wormholes around margins of pastedowns and margin to front and back pages, few pages with marginal brown spots, lower blank corner to a leaf professionally replaced), overall text remarkably clean. Raymond M. Sutton, Jr. May 26 2011 - 55970 2011 $5250

Alexander, Amir R. *Geometrical Landscapes: The Voyages of Discovery and the Transformation of Mathematical Practice.* Stanford: Stanford University Press, 2002, First printing; 8vo., xv, 293 pages, illustrations, index, blue cloth, white stamped spine title, dust jacket, fine, rare in jacket, from the Bern Dibner reference library, with Burndy bookplate. Jeff Weber Rare Books 161 - 4 2011 $100

Alexander, J. A. *The Life of George Chaffey; a Story of Irrigation Beginnings in California and Australia.* Melbourne & London: Macmillan, 1928, 8vo., xv, 381 page, frontispiece, large folding map, 35 illustrations, pale green cloth, gilt stamped spine title, spine ends frayed, very good, from the Bern Dibner reference library, with Burndy bookplate. Jeff Weber Rare Books 161 - 5 2011 $90

Alexander, James Edward *An Expedition of Discovery into the Interior of Africa through the Hitherto Undescribed Countries of the Great Namaguas...* Philadelphia: E. L. Carey, 1838, First US edition; 2 volumes, small 8vo., pages 216, 215, ink library stamp on titlepages, original purple cloth, small loss of cloth at base volume II, joints cracked, scarce. J. & S. L. Bonham Antiquarian Booksellers Africa 4/20/2011 - 6900 2011 £290

Alexander, Patrick Proctor *Spiritualism: a Narrative with a Discussion.* Edinburgh: William P. Nimmo, 1871, First edition; 2 pages ads, original yellow printed boards, neatly rebacked, dulled, slightly rubbed, slight creasing to boards, contemporary signature of G. S. Thomson on leading pastedown, good, sound copy. Jarndyce Antiquarian Booksellers CXCI - 34 2011 £65

Alexander, Sam *Photographic Scenery of South Africa.* Syracuse: Alexander, n.d., 1880, First edition; quarto, pages 56, 100 photos, occasional foxing of text, original brown decorative morocco, rebacked using damaged backstrip, free endpaper torn and repaired. J. & S. L. Bonham Antiquarian Booksellers Africa 4/20/2011 - 9213 2011 £750

Alexie, Sherman *The Absolutely True Diary of a Part-Time Indian.* New York: Little Brown, 2007, First edition; fine in fine dust jacket. Bella Luna Books May 29 2011 - p34932 2011 $82

Alexie, Sherman *First Indian on the Moon.* New York: Hanging Loose Press, 1993, First edition; fine, signed by author. Bella Luna Books May 26 2011 - 1021 2011 $220

Alexie, Sherman *The Journal of Ethnic Studies.* Bellingham: JES, 1988, First printing, paperback original; printed wrappers, fine, very scarce. Bella Luna Books May 26 2011 - t9517 2011 $825

Alexie, Sherman *Old Shirts and New Skins.* Los Angeles: UCLA, 1993, First edition; illustrations by Elizabeth Woody, fine, paperback original, pictorial wrappers, signed by author. Bella Luna Books May 29 2011 - 1050 2011 $104

Alexie, Sherman *One Stick Song.* Brooklyn: Hanging Loose Press, 2000, First edition; fine in fine dust jacket, signed by author 6/27/2000. Bella Luna Books May 29 2011 - t1172 2011 $82

Alford, Violet *Dances of Austria, Finland, Greece, Norway, Portugal.* Max Parrish, 1948-1951, 5 volumes, small 8vo., original cloth dust jackets, each 40 pages with 4 color plates and map, fine set. R. F. G. Hollett & Son Antiquarian Booksellers 175 - 18 2011 £35

Alfred *My Early Years, for those in Early Life.* London: B. J. Holdsworth, 1828, First edition; 12mo., frontispiece, 2 pages ads, errata slip, slightly foxed, uncut in original drab boards, striped green cloth, spine little wormed at head of following hinge, paper label rubbed, contemporary inscription. Jarndyce Antiquarian Booksellers CXCI - 35 2011 £40

Alger, Horatio *The Western Boy.* New York: 1878, First edition, first printing with G. W. Carleton ad at front and with "American News Co.", in gilt at spine bottom; very good, light shelfwear, bit of spotting, Xmas 1880 presentation to grandson, contemporary seller stamp and owner number, scarce. Lupack Rare Books May 26 2011 - ABE1222942243 2011 $1400

Ali, Monica *Brick Lane.* London: Doubleday, 2003, First edition; signed by author, fine in fine dust jacket. Bella Luna Books May 29 2011 - t7188 2011 $82

Alishan, Ghevond M. *Armenian Popular Songs.* Venice: S. Lazarus, 1867, Second edition; few small tears and slight creasing to margins, unopened, disbound, (86) pages. Jarndyce Antiquarian Booksellers CXCI - 36 2011 £75

Alison, Archibald *Lives of Lord Castlereagh and Sir Charles Stewart the Second and Third Marquesses of Londonderry with Annals of Contemporary Events in which they Bore a Part.* London: William Blackwood and Sons, 1861, Volume 1 and 2 (of 3), cloth chipped at heads and heels, stained, corners bumped, edges soiled, bookplates, foxing to prelims, hinges firm, pages uncut, 693, 642 pages. G. H. Mott Bookseller May 26 2011 - 22432 2011 $200

Alken, Henry *Qualified Horses and Unqualified Riders.* London: S. & J. Fuller, 1815, First edition; watermarked J. Whatman 1815, oblong folio, engraved title and 7 hand colored engraved plates, uncut, late 19th century crushed crimson morocco over marbled board, ruled in gilt, spine with four raised bands, decoratively tooled and lettered in gilt, original printed gray wrappers bound in, occasional light smudges to margins, dampstain to lower right corner of last plate, not affecting image, otherwise excellent copy. David Brass Rare Books, Inc. May 26 2011 - 01691 2011 $6000

Alken, Henry *Specimens of Riding Near London.* London: published by Thomas M'Lean, 1823, Second edition; oblong folio, printed title and 18 hand colored engraved plates, late 19th century half red roan over red cloth boards, ruled in gilt, rectangular red roan gilt lettering label, bordered in gilt on front board, spine with two raised bands, paneled and lettered in gilt, clean tear in inside margin of the seventeenth plate (just touching image), expertly and almost invisible repaired, few other small margins but till near fine, plates watermarked 1821 and 1823. David Brass Rare Books, Inc. May 26 2011 - 01689 2011 $7500

The All About Story Book. New York: Cupples & Leon, 1929, 4to., orange cloth, fine in worn dust jacket, 12 stories, illustrations in full color by Gruelle, Thelma Gooch and others, rare in dust jacket. Aleph-Bet Books, Inc. 95 - 69 2011 $600

Allan, Brian *Wild Orchids of Scotland.* Edinburgh: HMSO, 1993, 4to., original cloth, dust jacket, pages (iv), 135, illustrations in full color, numerous line drawings, maps, field key. R. F. G. Hollett & Son Antiquarian Booksellers General Catalogue Summer 2010 - 942 2011 £35

Allan, Oswald *Worthy a Crown?* Head & Meek, 1876, 4to., illustrations, ads + 4 pages ads, original color printed wrappers, spine slightly chipped, 60 pages. Jarndyce Antiquarian Booksellers CXCI - 692 2011 £150

Allen, Don C. *The Owles Almanacke.* Baltimore: 1943, First edition; vii, 103 pages, reddish brown cloth, pages uncut, has underlining and margin notes, gilt on spine bright, notes on f.e.p. Bookworm & Silverfish 667 - 64 2011 $275

Allen, Frank J. *The Great Church Towers of England.* Cambridge: Cambridge University Press, 1932, First edition; 4to., xi, 305 pages, 52 monochrome plates, original publisher's brown cloth lettered gilt at spine, handsome very good+ copy wit minor rubbing, ownership signature of Professor G. H. Bushnell (1903-1978), with his bookplate and 2 substantial signed handwritten letters from Allen to him loosely inserted.   Any Amount of Books   May 29 2011 - A675761 2011 $213

Allen, George Loscomb, Mrs. *The Views and Flowers from Guzerat and Rajpootana.* Paul Jerrard & Son, circa, 1860, 4to., 12 color plates with text on verso, 1 page ads, apparently lacking frontispiece, some leaves neatly strengthened at hinge, original cream wavy grained cloth, blocked elaborately in gilt on front board and blind on back board, heavily spotted, small nick to upper margin with slight loss of cloth, little rubbed, inner hinges with some slight repair, armorial bookplate of Fenton, internally nice and bright. Jarndyce Antiquarian Booksellers   CXCI - 38 2011   £220

Allen, John   *The Humiliation and Exaltation of Our Redeemer.* London: George Routledge & Co., 1856, First edition; 32 prints, square 8vo. original printed pictorial cloth, faded, pages 64, complete with 22 plates, etched bookplate of M. Snape.   R. F. G. Hollett & Son Antiquarian Booksellers   175 - 20 2011   £85

Allen, Philip Shuyler   *Three Roly-Poly Piglets.*   Collins, n.d., First edition; oblong 4to., original pictorial boards, dust jacket (few closed edge tears), unpaginated, 12 fine full page color plates and numerous drawings, lovely, clean copy, very scarce.   R. F. G. Hollett & Sons Antiquarian Booksellers   170 - 8 2011   £175

Allen, R. E.   *The Concise Oxford Dictionary and the Oxford Thesaurus.* Oxford University Press, 1992, 2 volumes, large 8vo., original cloth, gilt, dust jackets (price clipped), glazed slipcase, pages xxxix, 1454; xi, 1042, all edges sprinkled, fine set.   R. F. G. Hollett & Son Antiquarian Booksellers   General Catalogue Summer 2010 - 362 2011   £35

Allen, Thomas   *A New and Complete History of The County of York.* London: published by I. T. Hinton, 1828, 6 volumes, 8vo., pages (iii)-viii, ii, 359 + engraved title and frontispiece, ii, 431 + engraved title, frontispiece and 12 other plates; ii, 443 + engraved title frontispiece and 7 other plates; ii, 532 + engraved title, frontispiece and 22 other plates; ii, 488 + engraved title, frontispiece and 28 other plates; ii, 404 + engraved title, frontispiece and 67 other plates, contemporary tan half calf, four flat banded spines gilt with blind double rule open centered compartments, green lettering and numbering pieces gilt boards double ruled in blind with green 'swirl' marbled paper sides, matching 'made' endpapers, all edges gilt "French Shell marbled, pink and white sewn flat endbands, light age toning, little offsetting from plates, extremities little rubbed, volume 6 joints just cracking at ends, boards scuffed, bindings blindstamped "I.L" within a 3/8 inch diameter circle at head of front board of all volumes, from the collection of Christopher Ernest Weston 1947-2010.   Unsworths Booksellers   24 - 66 2011   £360

Allen, William   *A Narrative of the Expedition Sent by Her Majesty's Government to the River Niger in 1841...* London: Richard Bentley, 1848, First edition; 2 volumes, 8vo., pages xviii, 509, (1) imprint; viii, 511, (1) imprint, frontispiece volume 1, 3 maps, folding panorama, 17 plates, 25 text illustrations, recent brown half calf, red morocco labels, slight foxing to prelims, good, partially unopened set.   J. & S. L. Bonham Antiquarian Booksellers   Africa 4/20/2011 - 8060 2011   £320

Allen, William   *A Narrative of the Expedition Sent by Her Majesty's Government to the River Niger in 1841...* London: Richard Bentley, 1848, First edition; 2 volumes, 8vo., pages xviii, 509, (1) imprint; viii, 511, (1) imprint, frontispiece volume I, 3 maps, folding panorama, 17 plates (some marginal foxing to some of the plates), 25 textual illustrations, late 19th century red half morocco.   J. & S. L. Bonham Antiquarian Booksellers   Africa 4/20/2011 - 7573 2011   £490

Allerton, Mark   *The Girl on the Green.* London: Methuen, 1914, First edition; 8vo., original publisher's green cloth lettered gilt on spine and cover (gilt golf clubs on spine), pages 295, with 31 page publishers' catalogue at rear, review copy with small circular "Presentation Copy" stamp at bottom of titlepage and printed review slip noting publication date as 26 March 1914, faint handling wear, covers very slightly bumped, otherwise very good+.   Any Amount of Books   May 29 2011 - A75623 2011 $408

Allestree, Richard   *The Whole Duty of Man, laid Down in a Plain and Familiar Way for the Use of All...*   London: printed for N. Norton for George Pawles, 1689, Contemporary calf, rather worn, spine cracked and defective, pages xxii, 472, (vi) (ii ad), engraved frontispiece and title, (both little chipped), little loose, good, complete edition, inscription "Ann Martyn her book....1690".   R. F. G. Hollett & Son Antiquarian Booksellers   175 - 22 2011   £350

Allibone, S. Austin *A Critical Dictionary of English Literature and British and American Authors, Living and Deceased...* Philadelphia: J. B. Lippincott, 1886-1898, 5 volumes, large 8vo., green cloth, gilt stamped spine title, extremities rubbed, some volumes waterstained, some hinges cracked, still strong, very good, from the Bern Dibner reference library, with Burndy bookplate. Jeff Weber Rare Books   161 - 7   2011 $275

Allingham, Helen *Happy England.* London: Adam and Charles Black, 1904, Reprint; 8vo., original publisher's floral illustrated blue cloth lettered gilt on spine and on front cover, pages xi, 204, uncut, unopened, 81 illustrations, endpapers slightly browned, else fne in near fine complete unchipped dust jacket that is faintly browned, exceptional condition, original mailing box which is somewhat worn and used but has printed list of books in same series on inside card.   Any Amount of Books   May 29 2011 - A47324   2011 $306

Allingham, William *Flower Pieces and Other Poems.* London: Longmans, Green and Co., 1893, First edition; 8vo., original publisher's white parchment backed green cloth lettered gilt on spine, frontispiece and one other illustration by Dante Gabriel Rossetti, pages x, 194, pages uncut, sound, decent copy with slight mottling and slight soiling at spine, else very good or better.   Any Amount of Books   May 29 2011 - A76083   2011 $272

Allingham, William *Nightingale Valley: A Collection Including a Great Number of the Choicest Lyrics and Short Poems in the English Language.* London: Bell & Daldy, 1860, First edition; half title, date in ink on titlepage, 11th Feb. 1860, ink inscription, original maroon cloth, slightly rubbed, spine slightly faded to brown, very good.   Jarndyce Antiquarian Booksellers   CXCI - 39   2011   £180

Allinson, Robert *Lectures and Addresses.* London: Arthur L. Humphreys, 1913, First edition; large 8vo., original green cloth, gilt, pages 250, top edge gilt, scarce.   R. F. G. Hollett & Son Antiquarian Booksellers   173 - 16   2011   £45

Allinson, T. *Offical Guide to Keswick on Derwentwater.* Keswick: Urban District Council and Town Publicity Association, n.d. circa, 1925, Oblong 8vo., original pictorial limp cloth, little creased, pages 48, plus numerous ad leaves, illustrations, some lower corners, little worn, scarce.   R. F. G. Hollett & Son Antiquarian Booksellers   173 - 15   2011   £75

Allison, Dorothy *Bastard Out of Carolina.* New York: Dutton, 1992, First edition; fine, fine dust jacket.   Bella Luna Books   May 29 2011 - 42   2011 $88

Allison, Dorothy *Lesbian Poetry.* Watertown: Persephone Press, 1981, First edition; fine, pictorial wrappers.   Bella Luna Books   May 29 2011 - t5833   2011 $82

Allison, Robert *Lectures and Addresses.* London: Arthur L. Humphreys, 1913, First edition; large 8vo., original green cloth gilt, pages 250, top edge gilt, scarce.   R. F. G. Hollett & Son Antiquarian Booksellers   175 - 23   2011   £45

Allix, Susan *Rosas: Roses Real and Imaginary with Poems.* London: Susan Allix, 2009, One of 10 copies, signed by artist (this copy #8); 369 x 277mm., 14 unnumbered leaves, in an exuberant binding of multi-colored morocco and embroidery by Susan Allix, covers inlaid with irregular morocco pieces in various shades of yellow, pink, blue, green, orange and burgundy to achieve a quilt like effects; upper cover with large octagonal centerpiece of hand embroidered roses in reds, yellows and pinks on dark green background, flat spine with vertical titling in blind, handmade endpapers in bright pink and black with pink polka dots, edges untrimmed, original red felt lined folding cloth box with morocco labels and accents in two colors, 9 illustrations, one an original watercolor unique to this volume, as new.   Phillip J. Pirages   59 - 83   2011 $4800

Allix, Susan *Rosas: Roses Real and Imaginary with Poems.* London: Susan Allix, 2009, One of 10 copies of this work, each in a variant binding, signed by artist, this copy #10; 369 x 277mm., 14 unnumbered leaves, wonderful mixed media binding by Susan Allix, upper cover of beige morocco inlaid and onlaid with red and black morocco in a geometrically minimalist design, one horizontal rectangular inlay of silver metal painted with streaks of red, one vertical rectangular inlay of a glass mirror, red design scratched into the silvering, a most unusual protruding black metal sculpture of a rose attached to the horizontal inlay, lower cover with inlays of black and red morocco lines continuing the Mondrian like style, flat black morocco spine with red vertical titling, red and off-white handmade endpapers, edges untrimmed, original cleverly designed red cloth dropback box lined with black felt and with recessed area inside its lid to protect the three dimensional rose, leather title labels on front and spine, 9 illustrations of various sorts and in various media showing roses by Allix, one double page and one an original watercolor.   Phillip J. Pirages   59 - 82   2011 $4800

Allom, Thomas 1804-1872 *Picturesque Rambles in Westmorland, Cumberland, Durham and Northumberland From Drawings Taken on the Spot.* Peter Jackson late Fisher Son & Co., The Caxton Press, n.d. circa, 1832, 3 volumes, 4to., original half calf gilt by D. Batten of Clapham Common, spines with broad raised bands, and lettering pieces, evenly mellowed, pages (ii), 96; (ii), 80; (i), 72, complete with 3 engraved titles and 215 fine full page steel engraved plates, glazed endpapers, occasional spot or mark but clean handsome set of best form of this work, engraved plates, printed on superior paper.   R. F. G. Hollett & Son Antiquarian Booksellers   173 - 18   2011   £850

Allom, Thomas 1804-1872 *Westmorland, Cumberland, Durham and Northumberland Illustrated from Original Drawings.* F. F. Fisher etc., n.d., 1832, 4to., old panelled calf gilt, little scraped, handsomely rebacked in matching calf gilt with raised bands, pages 220, vignette on title and 215 steel engraved plates, little occasional browning and spotting, but very good, sound. R. F. G. Hollett & Son Antiquarian Booksellers 173 - 17 2011 £475

Allsopp, Bruce *Historic Architecture of Northumberland.* Newcastle-upon-Tyne: Oriel Press, 1969, First edition; large 8vo., original cloth, gilt, dust jacket price clipped, pages 96, illustrations. R. F. G. Hollett & Son Antiquarian Booksellers 177 - 9 2011 £30

Allston, Washington *Exhibition of Pictures Painted by Washington Allston at Harding's Gallery School Street.* Boston: John H. Eastburn, 1839, First edition; 8vo., 8 pages, original printed wrappers (some soiling), foxed. M & S Rare Books, Inc. 90 - 12 2011 $400

The Alphabet Annotated for Youth and Adults. London: Ackermann & Co., 1853, First edition; large 4to., engraved titlepage, illustrations, some spotting, few leaves slightly torn without loss, original blue cloth, large paper label on front board, good plus. Jarndyce Antiquarian Booksellers CXCI - 42 2011 £110

Alphabet Book of Coca Cola. Atlanta: Coca Cola Co., 1928, Oblong 12mo., pictorial wrapper, fine, illustrations, rare. Aleph-Bet Books, Inc. 95 - 12 2011 $875

Alphabet of Country Scenes. New York: McLoughlin Bros. n.d. circa, 1880, Large 4to., pictorial wrappers with pages mounted on linen, spine rubbed, else very good-fine, stunning ABC book printed on one side of page with each page of text facing rich full page chromolithograph divided into 4 panels. Aleph-Bet Books, Inc. 95 - 25 2011 $400

Alphabet Story of Famous Cities. N.P.: n.p., copyright, by Horace Fry, 1900, Large 4to., gilt pictorial cloth with flags on cover, some cover soil, else very good+, full page color illustrations. Aleph-Bet Books, Inc. 95 - 9 2011 $600

Althuysen, Jan *Langaene oer dy Fortziesing fin zyn Trogloftigste Haegheyt byrymme Trog Jan Althuysen.* Harlingen: F. van der Plaats, 1747, 4to., 18 pages, imprint and catchwords trimmed, modern half calf over marbled boards, from the library of the Earls of Macclesfield at Shirburn Castle. Maggs Bros. Ltd. 1440 - 4 2011 £500

Alton, Robert *Violin and Cello Building and Repairing.* William Reeves, 1969, Small 8vo., original cloth, dust jacket, pages (ii), 182, 16, 82 text illustrations, near fine. R. F. G. Hollett & Son Antiquarian Booksellers General Catalogue Summer 2010 - 32 2011 £45

Aluminum Company of America *Design Forecast.* Pittsburgh: 1859-1960, 2 volumes, 4to., very good, cloth, ex-library, photos illustrations, each volume has 64 pages. Bookworm & Silverfish 669 - 12 2011 $125

Alywin, David Cooper *A Pamphlet on the Salt Trade of India.* London: Printed by Madden and Malcolm, 1846, Only edition; 4to., large folidng map, colored in outline, (4), 40 pages + 15 leaves of appendix (tables), of which 6 leaves are folded, recent neat repairs to few closed tears, original printed wrappers, respined and repaired, good copy, sometime in the library of Worcester Chamber of Commerce (inked not on upper wrapper), with late 19th century book-plate of Worcester Public Library on both pastedowns (no other marks of ownership), apparently very rare. John Drury Rare Books 154 - 12 2011 £275

Ambler, Louis *The Old Halls & Manor Houses of Yorkshire.* London: Batsford, 1913, First edition; large 8vo., original blindstamped cloth, gilt, spine faded as usual, boards also little faded and marked, pages viii, xv, 97, with 91 plates from photos, 20 plates of measured drawings and numerous text illustrations, labels removed from pastedown, half title rather spotted. R. F. G. Hollett & Son Antiquarian Booksellers 177 - 10 2011 £180

Amend, Ottlile *Jolly Jungle Jingles.* Joliet: Volland, 1929, Large oblong 4to., cloth backed pictorial boards, fine in original box, color unevenly faded, full color drawings on every page by Eleanore Barte, rare in box. Aleph-Bet Books, Inc. 95 - 571 2011 $475

The American and Anglican Pulpit Library Advent to Christmastide. New York: James Pott and Co., 1895, Cloth soiled, chipped at top and bottom of spine, small label on spine, netting exposed at hinge, owner's name, toning, else clean, tight, 561 pages. G. H. Mott Bookseller May 26 2011 - 31555 2011 $400

The American and Anglican Pulpit Library Sexagesima to Good Friday. New York: James Pott and Co., 1895, 573 pages, cloth soiled, chipped a top and bottom of spine, small label on spine, owner's name, toning, else clean, tight, very good. G. H. Mott Bookseller May 26 2011 - 31554 2011 $350

The American and Anglican Pulpit Library Whitsunday to the ninth Sunday Father Trinity. New York: James Pott and Co., 1896, 577 pages, cloth soiled, chipped at top and bottom of spine, small label on spine, owner's name, toning, else clean, tight, 577 pages, illustrations, very good. G. H. Mott Bookseller May 26 2011 - 31553 2011 $350

American Art Association of Paris *The Quartier Latin.* Paris and London: Illiffe and Son, Jul. 1896-, Feb.March 1899. First edition; 8 volumes bound in 4, 8vo., handsome set in half black leather lettered gilt on spine, bound without original wrappers and without ads, nos. 1-30 (all published), copiously illustrated in black and white, pages 1226, boards slightly mottled on third volume, otherwise very good+. Any Amount of Books   May 26 2011 - A68670 2011 $1006

American Book Prices Current 1998-2004. Washington: Bancroft Parkman, 1999-2005, 7 volumes, 8vo., red cloth, gilt stamped cover and spine title, very good.   Jeff Weber Rare Books   163 - 105 2011 $325

American Book-Prices Current, Index 1940-1945 and 1945-1950. New York: 1946+, 2 volumes, very good. Bookworm & Silverfish   670 - 29 2011 $75

American Domestic Cookery, Formed on Principles of Economy for the Use of Private Families. New York: Evert Duyckinck, 1823, 357 pages, frontispiece, engraved fore title and 7 plates, contemporary marbled leather, very skillfully rebacked with original gilt spine laid down, scattered dampstaining on first and last few leaves, plates foxed, very nice.   Joseph J. Felcone Inc.   Fall Miscellany 2010 - 27   2011 $650

American Institute of Mining Engineers *Transactions.* Philadelphia: 1880, First edition; 611 pages, half leather, one inch chip to top of backstrip, library # on backstrip, 2 stamps on titlepage and elsewhere, 2 maps, folding chart, folding map with 1 tear, 8 plates.   Bookworm & Silverfish   671 - 100 2011 $68

American Jewish Publication Society *Constitution and By-Laws (Founded on the 9th of Heshvan 5806) Adopted at Philadelphia on Sunday Nvo. 30 1845.* Philadelphia: C. Sherman, 1845?, First edition; 12mo., 11 pages, contemporary plain wrappers, old oval stamp of the Leeser Library Hebrew Education Society on title and one of Dropsie College on front wrapper, otherwise fine.   M & S Rare Books, Inc.   90 - 198 2011 $2000

American Orchid Society *Awards Quarterly.* 1970-2005, 4to., volumes 1-24, binder's buckram (original covers included), volumes 25-63 in ring binders, included is American Orchid Society Awards 1932-2001, a combined index. Raymond M. Sutton, Jr.   May 26 2011 - 45806 2011 $1250

American Philosophical Society *Transactions of the American Philosophical Society Held at Philadelphia, for Promoting Useful Knowledge.* Philadelphia: Robert Aitken, 1786, First edition; 4 (of 5) folding copperplates (2 are loose, offsetting to 1, a corner missing), 4to., pages xxxii, 297 (8 pages donors), contemporary boards, spine defective, page gathering loose, uncut, boards worn, dampstaining to rear board, last leaf of donations missing, modern cloth covered box.   Raymond M. Sutton, Jr.   May 26 2011 - 55921 2011 $1200

American Tract Society *The Publications of the American Tract Society. Volume I-VIII # 1-253 (First series complete).* New York: American Tract Society, 1825-1831, 12mo., 404; 400; 408; 404; 400; 404; 400; 408, 12, (1) pages, illustrations, contemporary calf, leather labels, most of general titlepage of volume 2 torn away, otherwise very good, text somewhat foxed, bindings rubbed.   M & S Rare Books, Inc.   90 - 15 2011 $1000

Amis, Kingsley *Bright November. Poems.* London: Fortune Press, 1974, First edition; pages 32, foolscap 8vo., original grey boards, backstrip gilt lettered, untrimmed, very good.   Blackwell Rare Books   B166 - 120 2011 £400

Amis, Kingsley *The Green Man.* London: Jonathan Cape, 1969, First edition; very good, light spots of foxing to endpapers and bumping to spine ends, near fine dust jacket, light use.   Bella Luna Books   May 29 2011 - 57095A 2011 $82

Amis, Martin *Heavy Water and Other Stories.* London: Jonathan Cape, 1998, First British edition, true first; signed by author, fine in fine dust jacket.   Bella Luna Books   May 29 2011 - t7220 2011 $82

Ammianus Marcellinus *Rerum Gestarum Libri Decem et Octo.* Lyons: S. Gryphius, 1552, 12mo., 736 (8) pages, aa2 mis-signed, aa3, last 2 leaves blank, contemporary French binding of smooth calf, gilt arabesque in centre of covers, spine in 5 compartments each with small gilt ornament, gilt edges, binding little rubbed, deleted contemporary inscription on titlepage Jacobus Rubeus, from the library of the Earls of Macclesfield at Shirburn Castle.   Maggs Bros. Ltd.   1440 - 6 2011   £450

Amperex Elecronic Corporation *Amperex Eleceronic Tubes.* Hicksville: circa, 1955, 2 volumes, 8 1/4 x 7 1/4 inches, two three ring binders.   Bookworm & Silverfish 679 - 58 2011 $150

Anacreon *Odae et Fragmenta, Graece et Latine.* Utrecht: Apud Guilielmum Kroon, 1732, Light toning and few spots pages (xxxvi), 315, (1), 4to., contemporary Dutch calf, boards panelled in blind with central blind lozenge, backstrip with five raised bands, second compartment dyed dark and gilt lettered, rest plain, front joint rubbed, corners lightly worn, pastedowns lifted and boards bowed slightly, shelf-mark inked to front board, good.   Blackwell Rare Books   B166 - 2   2011   £250

Anacreon *(Title in Greek, then) Anacreontis Teii Odaria (i.e. The Odes).* Parmae: ex Regio Typographeio, 1785, One of 250 copies on "Blue" paper (of a total of 310 copies); 305 x 223mm., 2 p.l., xciv, 100 (1) pages, splendid contemporary crimson morocco, handsomely gilt by Derome Le Jeune (with his ticket), covers framed with double gilt rules, inner rule with scalloped corners, raised bands, compartments with very appealing all over diaper pattern, chain pattern (asterisk and four petal flower) on board edges, endleaves of lavender watered silk, very wide and intricate inner dentelles extending in unusual way from turn-ins onto silk pastedowns, all edges gilt, small author portrait in style of ancient coin to titlepage, large and elaborate armorial vignette on dedication page; tiny bit of wear to spine ends, few leaves with very minor wear or paper flaw at fore edge, especially fine, beautiful book with elegant original binding scarcely worn, text very clean, bright and fresh, margins nothing short of immense.   Phillip J. Pirages   59 - 9   2011 $8500

Anacreon *Anacreontis Odaria. (The Odes).* Londini: Ex Officina B. R. Howlett, Veneunt apud J. Murray, 1813, 188 x 112mm., 2 p.l., 130 pages, very pleasing contemporary crimson straight grain morocco, covers bordered by single gilt fillet upper cover with gilt arms of the Duke of Sutherland, raised bands flanked by gilt rules, spine panels with central gilt wheel ornament, gilt turn-ins, marbled endpaper, all edges gilt, 20 charming hand colored engraved head and tailpieces vignettes, text in Greek, spine slightly and uniformly faded, text with occasional minor foxing and slight yellowing, one opening with offsetting from a pressed flower, otherwise quite excellent contemporary copy, high quality binding with only most minor wear, beautifully set text quite fresh and hand coloring subtly done and very pleasing.   Phillip J. Pirages   59 - 63   2011 $600

Anacreon *Opera.* London: W. Bowyer, 1725, 4to., (8), xlii, xlii, xliii-lxxiv, 75, (3) pages, list of subscribers, contemporary sprinkled calf gilt, rubbed, subscriber's copy, from the library of the Earls of Macclesfield at Shirburn Castle.   Maggs Bros. Ltd.   1440 - 7   2011   £450

Anatomical Dialogues or A Breviary of Anatomy. London: printed for G. Robinson No. 25 Paternoster Row, 1778, First edition; vii, (1), 371, (1), (26) pages, table, 10 engraved plates, 12mo., old repair to clean tear without loss to K3, final leaf of table with old and rather obvious paper repairs, light browning, little dusty and little repairs, little old waterstaining to final pages, contemporary tree calf, spine, gilt ruled, black label.   Jarndyce Antiquarian Booksellers   CXCI - 43   2011   £380

Anaya, Rudolfo *Bless Me. Ultima.* Berkeley: Quinto Sol, 1972, First edition; near fine, light bumping to corners, dust jacket very good-, moderate rubbing, several repaired closed tears, but complete, inscribed by author for Mr. & Mrs. Yeager.   Bella Luna Books   May 26 2011 - t9349   2011 $1650

Andersen, Hans Christian   1805-1875   *Fairy Tales and Sketches.* George Bell and Sons, 1875, New edition; xi, (i) 542 pages, illustrations, very good in bright original dark green decorative cloth, all edges gilt, some slight foxing.   Ken Spelman Rare Books   68 - 202   2011   £95

Andersen, Hans Christian   1805-1875   *Hans Andersen's Fairy Tales.* Philadelphia: J. B. Lippincott, 1899, First US edition; Thick 4to., blue-grey pictorial cloth elaborately decorated, 320 pages, near fine, illustrations by Helen Stratton with more than 400 black and white illustrations.   Aleph-Bet Books, Inc.   95 - 47   2011 $400

Andersen, Hans Christian   1805-1875   *Hans Andersen's Fairy Tales.* London: Hodder & Stoughton for Boots the Chemist, n.d., 1913, 4to., original plum cloth gilt pages 320, 16 tipped in color plates and illustrated with line drawings by W. Heath Robinson.   R. F. G. Hollett & Son Antiquarian Booksellers   General Catalogue Summer 2010 - 892   2011   £175

Andersen, Hans Christian   1805-1875   *Hans Andersen's Fairy Tales.* London: Hodder & Stoughton for Boots the Chemist, n.d., 1913, First edition; pages 320, 16 tipped in color plates and illustrated throughout with line drawings by W. Heath Robinson, 4to., original plum cloth gilt, upper board very slightly differentially faded, few spots to fore edge, otherwise fine.   R. F. G. Hollett & Sons Antiquarian Booksellers   170 - 593   2011   £175

Andersen, Hans Christian   1805-1875   *Andersen's Fairy Stories.* London: Collins, n.d. circa, 1915, 4to., 160 pages, blue cloth stamped in gold, pictorial paste-on, some foxing, very good+, illustrations by Anne Anderson with 8 beautiful color plates plus full and partial page line illustrations and pictorial endpapers.   Aleph-Bet Books, Inc.   95 - 48   2011 $300

Andersen, Hans Christian   1805-1875   *Fairy Tales.* New York: George H. Doran Co., 1924, First American edition; 4to., black cloth with elaborate silver lettering and decoration on spine, silver and orange paste label on front cover with elaborate decorations and embellishments, very clean, fresh copy, housed in original publisher's cardboard box, box top repeats front cover of book and there is little wear to edges of box and some tape strengthening, 280 numbered pages with 12 full color mounted plates, full page black and white drawings, plus decorations and vignettes by Kay Nielsen.   Jo Ann Reisler, Ltd.   86 - 180   2011 $1500

Andersen, Hans Christian 1805-1875 *Fairy Tales by Hans Andersen.* London: Hodder and Stoughton, 1924, Edition deluxe, limited to 500 copies signed by artist, this number 420; quarto, (x), 11-197 (3, blank) pages, 12 mounted color plates, each with descriptive tissue guard and numerous black and white illustrations by Kay Nielsen, beautifully bound in modern full dark blue levant morocco, boards decoratively ruled in blind, spine stamped and lettered in gilt, top edge gilt, others uncut, some very light foxing to prelim pages, housed in custom cloth slipcase, pictorial gilt stamped cloth preserved from original binding and used on front, rear and spine of slipcase, near fine. Heritage Book Shop   Holiday 2010 - 92 2011 $3000

Andersen, Hans Christian 1805-1875 *Fairy Tales by Hans Andersen.* London: Hodder & Stoughton, n.d., 1924, First edition; large 4to., elaborate gilt pictorial green moire silk, fine in pictorial dust jacket slightly frayed, fine in pictorial dust jacket, slightly frayed, illustrations by Kay Nielsen and 12 beautiful tipped in color plates plus many full page black and whites, beautiful copy, scarce in dust jacket. Aleph-Bet Books, Inc.   95 - 392   2011 $2500

Andersen, Hans Christian 1805-1875 *Fairy Tales by Hans Andersen.* London: Harrap (McKay on spine), 1932, 4to., 288 pages, red cloth gilt, top edge gilt, lettering dulled, else fine in dust jacket and pictorial box (box neatly strengthened), illustrations by Rackham with pictorial endpapers, 12 color plates and a profusion of black and whites in text, mounted color plate on jacket and repeated on box, extraordinary copy.   Aleph-Bet Books, Inc.   95 - 471 2011 $1500

Andersen, Hans Christian 1805-1875 *Hans Andersen's Fairy Tales.* London: Strand Publications, n.d., 1938, Large 8vo., original pictorial boards, spine little creased, unpaginated, tinted endpapers, color frontispiece and title, 4 fine colored pop-ups and black and white drawings, inscription dated 1949, otherwise good, crisp, unused condition.   R. F. G. Hollett & Sons Antiquarian Booksellers   170 - 262   2011   £120

Andersen, Hans Christian 1805-1875 *Michael Hague's Favourite Hans Christian Andersen Fairy Tales.* New York: Holt, Rinehart and Winston, 1981, Limited to 350 copies, signed; issued with original drawing on free prelim page, blue cloth with full color paste label, housed in cloth covered slipcase with fading to back of slipcase, otherwise as new, book in original mailing box which is numbered to match the copy, 162 numbered pages with 24 full page color plates by Michael Hague.   Jo Ann Reisler, Ltd.   86 - 124   2011 $350

Andersen, Hans Christian 1805-1875 *Hans Andersen's Fairy Tales.* London: Hodder & Stoughton, 1981, Facsimile edition; large 8vo., original cloth gilt, extra, glassine wrapper, pages 300, 16 color plates, line drawings by W. Heath Robinson.   R. F. G. Hollett & Sons Antiquarian Booksellers   170 - 594   2011   £45

Andersen, Hans Christian 1805-1875 *Fourteen Classic Tales.* London: Andre Deutsch, 1978, First edition thus; original cloth, gilt, dust jacket price clipped, pages 191, 16 color illustrations, numerous drawings.   R. F. G. Hollett & Sons Antiquarian Booksellers   170 - 40   2011   £35

Andersen, Hans Christian 1805-1875 *The Garden of Paradise and other Stories.* London: Heinemann, 1923, First edition; large 8vo., original cloth cloth gilt with pictorial onlay, trifle rubbed and scratched, unpaginated, 10 plates and head and tailpieces, top corners slightly bumped, uncommon.   R. F. G. Hollett & Sons Antiquarian Booksellers   170 - 706   2011   £45

Andersen, Hans Christian 1805-1875 *The Ice Maiden.* London: Richard Bentley, 1863, First English edition; 4to., illustrations, 2 pages ads, original purple cloth, bevelled boards, blocked in gilt and blind, neatly recased repairs to head and tail of spine, endpapers replaced, front board faded to brown, all edges gilt, attractive copy.   Jarndyce Antiquarian Booksellers   CXCI - 41   2011   £180

Andersen, Hans Christian 1805-1875 *The Little Mermaid.* New York: Holiday House, 1935, 56 pages, illustrations by Pamela Bianco, very good in fair dust jacket (soiled and torn with loss), cloth soiled, otherwise book is very clean and tight.   G. H. Mott Bookseller   May 26 2011 - 44550   2011 $375

Andersen, Hans Christian 1805-1875 *The Little Mermaid.* New York: Macmillan, Oct., 1939, First edition; 4to., blue gilt cloth, dedication page slightly rubbed, else fine in dust jacket (few small edge chips, else very good+), 14 full page illustrations by Dorothy Lathrop.   Aleph-Bet Books, Inc.   95 - 320   2011 $400

Andersen, Hans Christian 1805-1875 *Stories from Hans Andersen.* London: Hodder and Stoughton, n.d. 1920's, Original cloth gilt, pictorial dust jacket, pages 195 with 14 tipped in color plates by Edmund Dulac, light spotting to edges and few leaves, otherwise fine in lovely dust jacket.   R. F. G. Hollett & Sons Antiquarian Booksellers   170 - 211   2011   £250

Andersen, Hans Christian 1805-1875 *Stories from Hans Andersen.* London: Hodder & Stoughton, 1911, Edition de luxe, limited to 750 numbered copies, signed by Dulac, this number 308; large quarto, illustrations by Edmund Dulac, publisher's full brown morocco gilt. Heritage Book Shop   Booth A12 51st NY International Antiquarian Book Fair April 8-10 2011 - 49   2011 $3750

Andersen, Hans Christian 1805-1875 *Tales from Denmark.* London: Grant and Griffith, 1848, Early impression of this first edition; engraved illustrations by Count Franz Pocci, including 7 full page plates and original pictorial card covers bound in at front, dark green half leather over marbled paper backed boards, spine has burgundy leather spine label lettered gilt and gilt rules, edges somewhat rubbed and faded with slight chipping at spine top, one 10 page gathering slightly proud of binding but not loose, neat 19th century ink inscription of titlepage, otherwise text very clean and overall condition very decent.   Any Amount of Books   May 26 2011 - A76604   2011 $587

Andersen, Hans Christian 1805-1875 *Wonderful Stories for Children.* New York: Wiley and Putnam, 1847, Early US edition; 12mo., pages 144, frontispiece and one other illustration, with author's name spelled Anderson on spine and titlepage, original publisher's green cloth lettered and decorated gilt on spine and on front cover, small bookplate of Janet and C. R. Ashbee and pictorial bookplate of Janet Ashbee designed by C. R. Ashbee, sound, clean, very good with slight wear at head of spine, slight foxing, very slight shelf wear, some family notes, press cutting on blank prelims.   Any Amount of Books   May 29 2011 - A46337   2011 $340

Anderson, C. W. *Bobcat.* New York: Macmillan, 1949, Stated first edition; 8vo., 97 pages, signed, fine in near fine dust jacket.   By the Book, L. C.   26 - 52   2011 $600

Anderson, Isabel *The Great Sea Horse.* Boston: Little Brown and Co., 1909, Limited, numbered edition of 300 copies; 4to., top edge gilt, white cloth with elaborate gold lettering and wonderful illustration of a little child riding a fish beneath the sea, spine slightly marked, printed dust jacket with some darkening and light edge wear, this copy has appealing signed in full presentation by Anderson, 24 full page color plates from pastel drawings by John Elliott, chapter decorations by Frank Downey.   Jo Ann Reisler, Ltd.   86 - 11   2011 $1000

Anderson, J. Corbet *The Roman City of Uriconium at Wroxeter, Salop...* J. Russell Smith, 1867, First edition; original cloth, gilt, over bevelled boards, extremities trifle rubbed, few marks, pages x, 150, with 12 plates and 57 woodcuts.   R. F. G. Hollett & Son Antiquarian Booksellers   177 - 11   2011   £120

Anderson, James *The New Practical Gardener and Modern Horticulturalist.* London: William Mackenzie, n.c. circa, 1875, Thick 4to., contemporary half calf gilt with raised bands, light crease to head of spine, some bubbling to cloth on upper board, pages (ii), 988, all edges and endpapers marbled, complete, 27 fine hand colored lithograph plates, 12 woodcut plates and numerous text illustrations, excellent copy.   R. F. G. Hollett & Son Antiquarian Booksellers   General Catalogue Summer 2010 - 943   2011   £275

Anderson, James S. M. *The History of the Church of England in the Colonies and Foreign Dependencies of the British Empire.* London: Rivingtons, 1856, Second edition; original brown cloth, blindstamp design to boards and gilt titles to spine, pages xl, 512, (8 pages ads); xix, 582, (2 ads); xx, 654, (2 ads), index, large folding table and folding color map to volume i and folding geological table to volume III, small 8vo., each volume has one outer hinge crack, otherwise very good, very good interiors with small signature "Augustus Jessopp February 1858".   Schooner Books Ltd.   96 - 274   2011 $175

Anderson, Joseph *Scotland in early Christian Times: Rhind Lectures, 1879 & 1880 and Scotland in Pagan Times: Rhind Lectures 1881-1882.* 1881-1886,   4 volumes, xiv, 262; xvii, 263; xx, 314; xxii, 397 pages, illustrations, ex-library, else very good.   C. P. Hyland   May 26 2011 - 255/016   2011 $333

Anderson, Kent *Sympathy for the Devil.* Garden City: Doubleday & Co., 1987, First edition; 8vo., pages (x), 350, original red endpapers, original black cloth backstrip over black paper covered boards, spine lettered in gold, original color pictorial dust jacket designed by Kirschner-Caroff, cover illustration by Alberto Barrerea, lower panel lightly and evenly soiled, light crease to corner, author's inscription, fine in near fine dust jacket.   Simon Finch Rare Books   Zero - 201   2011   £175

Anderson, Laurie *United States.* New York: Harper & Row, 1984, First edition; inscribed by author with an additional hand and lightning-bolt sketch, issue in wrappers, oblong quarto, fine.   Ken Lopez Bookseller   154 - 4   2011 $175

Anderson, Lorin *Charles Bonnet and the Order of the Known.* Dordrecht, Boston, London: D. Reidel, 1982, 8vo., x, 159 pages, frontispiece, brown cloth, gilt stamped spine title, dust jacket, fine, from the Bern Dibner reference library, with Burndy bookplate.   Jeff Weber Rare Books   161 - 9   2011 $75

Anderson, Maxwell *Both Your Houses.* New York: Samuel French, 1933, First edition; 8vo., pages 180, cloth little faded, but very good, tight copy in better than very good pictorial dust jacket with very rare wrap around band.   Second Life Books Inc.   174 - 12   2011 $675

Anderson, Peter John *Fasti Academiae Mariscallanae Aberdonenss.* Aberdeen: The New Spalding Club, 1889, Limited edition, no. 239 of 525 copies; small thick 4to., original cloth gilt, rather soiled, pages xxxi, 577, uncut and large unopened, 5 plates, 2 leaves of index little soiled.   R. F. G. Hollett & Son Antiquarian Booksellers   175 - 24   2011   £75

Anderson, Poul *Brain Wave.* Melbourne: London: Toronto: William Heinemann Ltd., 1955, First British and first hardcover edition; octavo, boards.   L. W. Currey, Inc.   124 - 65   2011 $1250

Anderson, Poul *The Enemy Stars.* Philadelphia and New York: J. B. Lippincott Co., 1959, First edition; octavo, boards.   L. W. Currey, Inc.   124 - 133   2011 $450

Anderson, Poul *Three Hearts and Three Lions.* Garden City: Doubleday and Co., 1961, First edition; octavo, cloth.   L. W. Currey, Inc.   124 - 171   2011 $300

Anderson, Robert *Ballads in the Cumberland Dialect.* Wigton: E. Rook, 1815, Second edition; pages vi, 258, modern half levant morocco gilt.   R. F. G. Hollett & Son Antiquarian Booksellers   173 - 20   2011   £85

Anderson, Robert M. *American Law of Zoning.* Rochester: 1977, Second edition; 5 volumes, fine maroon cloth.   Bookworm & Silverfish   667 - 107   2011 $250

Anderson, Sherwood 1876-1941 *6 Mid-American Chants.* Highlands: Nantahala Foundation, 1964, First edition; oblong spiral bound book, photos by Art Sinsabaugh, clean, very near fine copy with only some minute and incidental wear, superior copy.   Jeff Hirsch Books   ny 2010   2011 $850

Anderson, William *Glimpses of Natural Science and Art for the Young.* Gall & Inglis, n.d., 1853, Small 8vo., original green decorated cloth gilt, pages vi, 250, all edges gilt, 3 woodcut plates, one leaf refixed, upper joint cracked, prize label on flyleaf.   R. F. G. Hollett & Sons Antiquarian Booksellers   170 - 11   2011   £35

Andersson, Charles John 1827-1867 *Lake Ngami; or Explorations and Discoveries During Four Years Wanderings in the Wilds of South Western Africa.* London: Hurst & Blackett, 1856, First edition; royal 8vo., pages xviii, 546, (24), large folding map (repaired), 16 tinted lithographs (including frontispiece), textual illustrations, pages 159 and 434 repaired with sellotape, light foxing to margin of frontispiece, original red decorative cloth, rebacked in later blue morocco.   J. & S. L. Bonham Antiquarian Booksellers   Africa 4/20/2011 - 9184   2011   £90

Andersson, Charles John 1827-1867 *Lake Ngami or Explorations and Discoveries.* New York: Dix, Edwards, London: Hurst & Blackett, 1857, Octavo, xxiii, 433, 4 ads, frontispiece, plates, illustrations, some internal soiling, original green blindstamped cloth, gilt spine, spine ends bit worn, very good plus.   Jeff Weber Rare Books   163 - 122   2011 $200

Andersson, Charles John 1827-1867 *The Okavango River: a Narrative of Travel, Exploration and Adventure.* London: Hurst & Blackett, London: Osgood, 1861, First edition; 8vo., pages xxiii, 364, ads, frontispiece, engraved portrait on titlepage, 15 engraved plates (clean and crisp), contemporary brown calf, rebacked with original gilt spine, library label on front endpaper but no stamps in text, very good.   J. & S. L. Bonham Antiquarian Booksellers   Africa 4/20/2011 - 9162   2011   £980

Andre, R. *Colonel Bogey's Sketch Book.* London: Longmans Green and Co., 1897, Oblong 4to., cloth backed pictorial boards, 44 pages, covers little scratched, hinges neatly strengthened, very good+, illustrations.   Aleph-Bet Books, Inc.   95 - 259   2011 $2750

Andrea De Nerciat, Andre Robert *Le Diable Au Corps, Oeuvre Posthume du Tres-Recommandable Docteur Cazzone, Membre Extraordinaire de la Joyeuse Faculte Phallo...* Mezieres: Fremont, 1803, First edition, large paper copy; 3 volumes, 8vo., pages (iv), x-253; (iv), 252; (iv), 234; 20 erotic engravings, all with decorated frame, old repair to margin of one plate but generally in excellent condition throughout, crisp and bright, all edges marbled, original grey cloth, gilt lettering and "Romantique" decoration to spines, yellow endpapers bumped, lightly rubbed, spines lightly sunned upper hinge of volume i weak, narrow slit to lower joint of volume i but holding firmly, consecutively numbered label to front free endpaper of each volume (373-374), from the collection of Michel Simon.   Simon Finch Rare Books   Zero - 422   2011   £9500

Andrea De Nerciat, Andre Robert *Le Doctorat In-Promptu. (bound with) Les Religieuses au Serail. (with) Les Progres du Libertinage Historiette Trouvee das le Porte-Feuille d'un Carme Reforme.* Paris: Cazin, 1788, Paris: Au ouvent des Filles du Sauveur,1790. Paris: L'Imprimerie de l'Abbesse du Mont-Martre...1794; First editions of first two titles, second edition of third; 3 works in one volume, 12mo., pages (iv), iv, 120, 2 erotic engravings; xii, 13-58, engraved frontispiece, 108 engraved frontispiece (lacking the 3 plates called for by Gay-Lemmonyer), all edges gilt, sporadic light spotting, frontispiece third text expertly remargined, otherwise very crisp and fresh copy, full glazed tan calf, early 19th century, gilt decorated and lettered on spine, endpapers browned in margin, bookplate of F. de Rolland de Lastous.   Simon Finch Rare Books   Zero - 415   2011   £4500

Andrea De Nerciat, Andre Robert *Felicia ou Mes Fredaines, Orne de Figures en taille Douce.* Londres: Paris: Cazin, 1782, First edition; 4 parts bound in 2, 18mo., pages (iv), 160, (iv), 161-352; (iv), 204, (iv), 205-396, with 24 plates by Elluin after Borel, one supplied from another, slightly later copy, apres la lettre, the others all avant la lettre, initial blanks to parts 1 and 3, short tear to margin of volume II A1, otherwise internally fine, all edges gilt, mid 19th century full morocco, gilt filleting to boards, gilt decoration and lettering to spines, marbled endpapers by Hardy, firm, bright with very light negligible shelfwear, bookplates of Leigh D. Brownlee to each volume. Simon Finch Rare Books Zero - 409 2011 £5000

Andrea De Nerciat, Andre Robert *Monrose, ou Suite de Felicia.* Paris: An Cinq, 1797, 4 volumes, pages (ii), x, 179, (1) blank, (2), contents; leaf (ii), 202, (2) contents, (ii), 190, (2) contents; (ii), 194, (2) contents, 20 erotic engraved plates, attributed to Francis Queverdo, completely unsophisticated original pink marbled paper boards, black morocco spines, gilt titled and volume numbering on red morocco spine labels, very pretty copy in remarkably original state. Simon Finch Rare Books Zero - 418 2011 £4500

Andreev, Mikhail *Maslyanitsa. (The Oldest Russian Folk Holiday Which marks the End of Winter, also known as Pancake Week).* Moscow: Raduga, 1926, First edition; 8vo., full color pictorial paper covers loose in stapled binding but clean and fresh, 9 pages within, counting inside rear over), each with fresh, bright colored illustrations. Jo Ann Reisler, Ltd. 86 - 214 2011 $550

Andrewes, Lancelot *The Morall Law Expounded 1. Largely. 2. Learnedly. 3. Orthodoxly.* For Michael Sparke, Robert Milbourne, Richard Cotes and Andrew Crooke, 1642, (8) 132 165-188 181-440 1f. blank, 728-855, (1) 136 (4) 59 (1) pages, frontispiece, good, clean copy in contemporary calf, rebacked with new red morocco label, corners and board edges worn. Ken Spelman Rare Books 68 - 203 2011 £380

Andrews, Elisha *A Candid Reply to the Arguments of the Late Rev. Ethan Winchester Contained in a Work Entitled "The Universal Restoration, Exhibited in Four Dialogues".* Boston: Manning & Loring, 1800, 91 pages, fair, boards detached, soiled, edge worn, interior clean and tight, with foxing. G. H. Mott Bookseller May 26 2011 - 42941 2011 $200

Andrews, James *Flora's Gems; or the Treasure of the Parterre.* London: Charles Tilt, circa, 1830-1837, First edition; 12 finely hand colored plates, including additional title (occasional medium foxing, heavier to one), signed "JA", tissue guards, folio, original brown ribbed moire cloth with ornate gilt stamping of a large flower urn and bouquet on both cover and with leaf scrolls to corners, few faint stains to cover, sympathetically rebacked, corners strengthened, edgewear repaired, excellent restoration, gilt stamped label on spine, all edges gilt, very good. Raymond M. Sutton, Jr. May 26 2011 - 48961 2011 $2000

Andrews, James P. *Cases Argued and Determined in the Supreme Court of Errors of the State of Connecticut.* New York: Banks Law Publishing Co., 1922-1924, First edition; 5 volumes, volumes 96, 97, 98, 99, 100 from February 1921 - June 1924, tan cloth with raised bands, red and black leather labels, near fine set, attractive. Lupack Rare Books May 26 2011 - ABE1401536323 2011 $100

Andrews, Richard *Literary Fables, from the Spanish...* London: Smith, Elder and Co., 1835, First edition thus; modern half morocco gilt, pages xvi, 128, (xvi ads), little fingering in places. R. F. G. Hollett & Son Antiquarian Booksellers 175 - 25 2011 £95

Andrews, Wayne *Architecture in America.* London: Thames and Hudson, 1960, First edition; 4to., original cloth, gilt, dust jacket, pages 179, (iv), with 257 photos, fine. R. F. G. Hollett & Son Antiquarian Booksellers 177 - 12 2011 £60

Andrews, William *Antiquities and Curiosities of the Church.* London: William Andrews & Co., 1897, First edition; original cloth, gilt, pages 285, (x), half title and final leaf lightly browned. R. F. G. Hollett & Son Antiquarian Booksellers 175 - 27 2011 £35

Andrews, William *The Book of Oddities.* London: Simpkin, Marshall and Co., 1882, First edition; pages (ii), 86, title lightly browned in red and black, bound for Eli Simpson of Autwick by Edmondson & Wilson of Settle, with note to that effect by Simpson with his faint stamp on title, very scarce. R. F. G. Hollett & Son Antiquarian Booksellers General Catalogue Summer 2010 - 623 2011 £120

Andrews, William *The Church Treasury of History, Custom, Folk-lore, etc.* London: William Andrews, 1898, First edition; pages (iv), 301, (x), , illustrations, half title and lower flyleaves browned. R. F. G. Hollett & Son Antiquarian Booksellers 175 - 28 2011 £35

Andrews, William *Ecclesiastical Curiosities.* London: William Andrews, 1899, First edition; original cloth, gilt, top of upper hinge frayed, pages (iv), 250, (v), top edge gilt, illustrations, flyleaves lightly browned. R. F. G. Hollett & Son Antiquarian Booksellers 175 - 29 2011 £35

Andrews, William *North Country Poets.* London: Simpkin, Marshall & Co., 1888, First edition; original cloth, gilt, pages 298, (6). R. F. G. Hollett & Son Antiquarian Booksellers 173 - 22 2011 £45

Andrews, William *Old Church Lore.* Hull: William Andrews & Co., 1891, First edition; pages (iv) 255, (vi), illustrations, original quarter roan gilt, spine trifle rubbed and faded. R. F. G. Hollett & Son Antiquarian Booksellers 175 - 26 2011 £40

Andrews, William Eusebius *A Word of Advice to the Inhabitants of Ashton and Adjacent Towns, Catholics and Protestants on the Letters of Parson Sibson.* London: printed by the author, 1822, Unbound tract, as issued, pages 24, uncut, title and last leaf rather dusty. R. F. G. Hollett & Son Antiquarian Booksellers 175 - 30 2011 £45

Andry De Boisregard, Nicolas *L'Orthopedie ou l'Art de Corriger dans les Enfans, les Difformities du Corps.* Paris: La Veuve Alix and Lambert & Durand, 1741, First edition; 2 volumes, 12mo., pages (iv), cxvii (actually xcviii), 345, (3) with engraved frontispiece (bound after title), (ii), vi, 47, (i) blank, 365, (5), 14 engraved plates bound at end, both titlepages with tiny puncture holes close to imprint, contemporary French polished tree sheep, spine gilt and with apricot and black leather labels, marbled endpapers, small wormhole and chip to foot of spine of volume ii, excellent copy in contemporary binding. Simon Finch Rare Books Zero - 114 2011 £3750

Andecdotes of the Chinese Illustrative of Their Character and of Their Conduct Towards Foreigners. London: T. Allman, 1847, First edition; 12mo., original publisher's red cloth lettered and decorated gilt on spine and cover, pages 219, all edges gilt, very good+, neat inscription from father to his daughter on her 13th birthday. Any Amount of Books May 29 2011 - A76508 2011 $255

Angeli, Pietro *Syrias hoc est Expeditio illa Celeberrima Christianorum Principium Qua Hierosolyma Ductu Goffredi Blionis Lotharinguiae...* Florence: F. Giunto, 1591, First edition; 4to., (24), 406 pages, italic type, woodcut initials, 18th century English calf, triple gilt fillet on covers, little rubbed, 17th century French inscription of Vallognes on titlepage, from the library of the Earls of Macclesfield at Shirburn Castle. Maggs Bros. Ltd. 1440 - 8 2011 £950

Angelo, Domenico *The School of Fencing with General Explanation of the Principal Attitudes and Positions Peculiar to the Art.* London: no publisher noted, 1787, First edition thus; small oblong 4to., bound in recent half dark brown leather with part of original leather spine laid down, new endpapers, marbled boards, lettered gilt on spine, pages viii, 105, (1) index 8 pages, 47 engraved plates on 44 sheets, occasional very slight browning to pages, plates clean with some staining to index not affecting plates, handsome copy in very good good with plates dated 1783 in exemplary condition. Any Amount of Books May 26 2011 - A8706 2011 $1593

Angelo, Michael *A Curious and Exact Account of a Voyage to Congo in the Years 1666 and 1667.* London: Churchill, 1704, First UK edition; folio, recent brown speckled quarter calf. J. & S. L. Bonham Antiquarian Booksellers Africa 4/20/2011 - 9062 2011 £100

Angelou, Maya *Gather Together in My Name.* New York: Random House, 1974, First edition; near fine, previous owner's name neatly inked on front free endpapers, dust jacket near fine, very light creasing to top of spine, very bright. Bella Luna Books May 29 2011 - 58 2011 $82

Angelou, Maya *Singin' and Swingin' and Gettin' Merry Like Christ.* New York: Random House, 1976, First edition; fine in fine dust jacket. Bella Luna Books May 29 2011 - 2998 2011 $82

Anger, Kenneth *Hollywood Babylon.* London: Arrow Books Ltd., 1986, First Arrow Books edition; wrappers, small 4to., illustrations in black and white, signed presentation from author for Nick Culpepper, 305 pages, slight rubbing, else sound, very good+. Any Amount of Books May 29 2011 - A73504 2011 $306

Ancient Songs from the Time of King Henry the Third to the Revolution. London: J. Johnson, 1790, 8vo., recently bound in half brown leather with speckled effect and gilt title label in antiquarian lettering, marbled boards, pages (iv), lxx, 322, engraved vignette on titlepage, 5 vignettes in text, wood engraved tailpieces, music illustrations in text, very attractive near fine with very slight browning to edges of prelims and slight fraying to edges of 3 pages not affecting text. Any Amount of Books May 29 2011 - A44868 2011 $306

Animated ABC. Garden City: Garden City Publishing Co., 1945, First edition; 4to., full color pictorial boards with spira binding, very slight shelfwear, clean copy, color illustrations by William Wiesner. Jo Ann Reisler, Ltd. 86 - 9 2011 $350

Annee Galante ou Etrenne AL'Amour. Paris: 1773, First edition; large 8vo., ff. 41 printed on rectos only, hand colored engraved titlepage and 12 half page hand colored engraved illustrations, nicely bound in half morocco, marbled boards, gilt lettered on spine, near fine. Simon Finch Rare Books Zero - 405 2011 £2800

Annual Bibliography of English Language. 1940-1978, First edition; volume 21, 34-47, 50-53, together 19 volumes, some ex-library but all in very good condition. I. D. Edrich May 26 2011 - 84597 2011 $637

Annual Circular and Catalogue of Bryant & Stratton's National Chain of Business Colleges Located in New York City: Philadelphia: Albany; Buffalo; New York: Cleveland: Detroit: Chicago and St. Louis. New York: Office of the American Merchant, 1861, 8vo., (19); 20-80 pages, illustrations, original printed wrappers, light wear and soiling, few corners, creased, very good. M & S Rare Books, Inc. 90 - 118 2011 $225

Ansell, Robert *The Bookplate Designs of Austin Osman Spare.* N.P.: London: The Bookplate Society/Keridwen Press, 1988, No. x of xxx copies with an original bookplate (Denis Bardens) tipped in, book signed by Ansell; 8vo., original quarter leather lettered gilt on spine, pages 35, 23 plates, fine in plain stiff card slipcase.   Any Amount of Books   May 26 2011 - A64758   2011 $419

Anson, George *A Voyage Round the World, in the Years MDCCXL, I, II, III, IV.* London: printed by John and Paul Knapton, 1749, Fifth edition; 10.5 x 8 inches, 43 large folding engraved plates, including maps, plans and charts with extra folding frontispiece map, bound in full recent brown calf, lettered gilt at spine, 5 raised bands, handsome clean, bright copy with plates in fresh state (one plate has short closed tear with no loss), additional fine portrait engraving on blank page opposite titlepage, presumably bound in by former owner, very good.   Any Amount of Books   May 26 2011 - A75274   2011 $2432

Anson, W. S. W. *Asgard and the Gods: the Tales and Traditions and Of Our Northern Ancestors.* London: W. Swan Sonnenschein, 1884, Third edition; original quarter parchment, spine little rubbed and cracked pages xvi, 326, text illustrations.   R. F. G. Hollett & Son Antiquarian Booksellers   175 - 41 2011   £45

Ansted, David Thomas *The Channel Islands.* London: William H. Allen & Co., 1862, First edition; 8vo., dark blue buckram lettered gilt at spine, pages xxix, 604, 59, illustrations in text, 16 maps, plans and diagrams, folding map at rear, ex-Foreign and Commonwealth Office library with their label and stamps (lightly applied) with light marking, very good, bookplate and 2 small stamps on titlepage and one on back.   Any Amount of Books   May 29 2011 - A49556   2011 $238

Anstie, John *A Letter Addressed to Edward Phelips,, Esq. Member for the County of Somerset...* London: printed by Stafford and Davenport for J. Debrett, opposite Old Bond Street, Piccadilly, 1788, Second edition; 4to., half title, final leaf with resolution, signed on page 27: John Anstie, (4), 30, (2) pages, disbound, nice.   Anthony W. Laywood   May 26 2011 - 21695 2011 $587

Antaeus. Tangier/London/New York: Ecco Press, 1970-1991, First edition; Nos. 1-44, 1970-1982, together with No. 55, 58 & 67, Aug. 1985-Autumn 1991, all very good in original wrappers, a run of 44 numbers in 39 plus extra 3 issues,.   I. D. Edrich   May 26 2011 - 82912 2011 $671

Anthony, Gordon *Ballet. Camera Studies.* London: Geoffrey Bles, 1937, First edition; pages 241, untrimmed with 96 tipped in plates, scattered foxing, very nice, attractive label of Gladstone Memorial Prize.   R. F. G. Hollett & Son Antiquarian Booksellers   175 - 42 2011   £45

Anthony, Gordon *John Geilgud. Camera Studies.* London: Bles, 1938, First edition; large 8vo., original black cloth, silvered, dust jacket trifle dusty, odd closed edge tear, pages (viii) plus 24 plates.   R. F. G. Hollett & Son Antiquarian Booksellers   175 - 43 2011   £30

Anthony, Gordon *Russian Ballet. Camera Studies.* London: Geoffrey Bles, 1939, First edition; folio, original two tone cloth, gilt over bevelled boards, pages (28), frontispiece and 96 tipped in plates, endpapers rather foxed but very nice, attractive label of Gladstone Memorial Prize for political science on flyleaf.   R. F. G. Hollett & Son Antiquarian Booksellers   175 - 44 2011   £95

Anthony, Susan B. *The History of Woman Suffrage.* Rochester: Susan B. Anthony, 1902, First edition; Volume IV (only) 1883-1900, 8vo., pages 1144, frontispiece, publisher's cloth, hinge little tender, small paint smudge on rear board, very good much better than most, inscribed by Anthony to temperance worker and suffragist Jessie Ackerman.   Second Life Books Inc.   174 - 14 2011 $4000

Anti-Slavery Monthly Reporter. Volume I. London: Printed for the London Society for the Mitigation and Abolition of Slavery in the British Dominions1827, 1827, First edition of the first volume; first volume with the first 24 numbers, 8vo., pages 392, each issue 12 pages long, bound in recent black half morocco (by Phillip Dusel), marbled sides, red morocco label, gilt rules, decorations and lettering.   Second Life Books Inc.   174 - 15 2011 $1200

An Antidote to Revolution; or a Practical Comment on the Creation of Privilege for Quadrating the Principles of Consumption and Thereby Creating Stimulus for the Unlimited Production of National Wealth Neutralizing the Motives for Political Discontent and Establishing a Solid Base for the Promotion of Morality. Dublin: printed for the author by M. Goodwin, 1830, First edition; 8vo., 16 pages, modern rather oversized green cloth boards, spine lettered in gilt, good, rare.   John Drury Rare Books   153 - 39 2011   £125

Antipas: a Solemn Appeal to the Right Reverend, the Archbishops and Bishops of the United Churches of England and Ireland with Reference to Several Bills Passed or Passing through the Imperial Parliament... London: William Stockdale, 1821, First edtition; 4to., 43, (1) pages, well bound in later 19th century cloth backed marbled boards, very good, large copy, scarce.   John Drury Rare Books   154 - 6 2011   £175

Apican Morsels; or Tales of the Table, Kitchen and Larder.... New York: J. & J. Harper, 1829, First American edition; 8vo, 167, 198-212 plus ads, 2 plates, original cloth backed boards, printed paper label, uncut, some soiling of binding, light foxing, illustration in ink on cover.   M & S Rare Books, Inc.   90 - 99 2011 $450

Apollinaire, Guillaume *Les Onze Mille Verges ou les Amours d'un Hospodar.* Monte Carlo: Les Ygrees; Paris: Rene Bonnet and Pascal Pia, 1930, First bibliophile edition, no. 3 of 3 copies on Imperial Japan; large square 8vo., pages (vi), xii, 168 + limitation leaf, bound in are 14 highly erotic original watercolor drawings , attributed by a penciled note on the flyleaf to Jean Auscher, contemporary full crimson, marbled endpapers, top edge gilt others rough trimmed, in matching (lined) slipcase, original grey printed wrappers bound in, by Bianchi of Nice, fine in immaculate binding. Simon Finch Rare Books Zero - 441 2011 £6000

Apology Addressed to the Travellers Club or Anecdotes of Moneys. London: John Murray, 1825, First edition; 8vo., half light brown leather and marbled boards lettered gilt at spine with 5 raised bands, pages iv (including half title), vi, 184, uncut, sound, clean, very good+ copy, first blank, slightly foxed, inscription in French. Any Amount of Books May 29 2011 - A49300 2011 $221

An Appeal to the Electors of England. London: Roake and Varty, 1831, First edition; 12mo., 12 pages, preserved in mdoern wrappers, printed title label on upper cover, uncut, very good. John Drury Rare Books 154 - 7 2011 £35

Appel, Toby A. *The Cuvier-Geoffroy Debate: French Biology in the Decade before Darwin.* New York and Oxford: Oxford University Press, 1987, First edition; 8vo., 305 pages, plates, navy cloth, gilt stamped cover and spine titles, dust jacket, fine, from the Bern Dibner reference library, with Burndy bookplate. Jeff Weber Rare Books 161 - 11 2011 $150

Appendix to the Comment on the Petition of the British Inhabitants of Bengal, Bahar and Orissa to Parliament. London: 1780, First edition; 4to., first two parts have divisional titlepages, 24, 8, 8, 8, 8, (2), 48 pages, disbound. Anthony W. Laywood May 26 2011 - 21770 2011 $126

Apperley, Charles James 1777-1843 *Memoirs of the Life of the Late John Mytton, Esqre. of Halston, Shropshire...* London: Rudolph Ackermann, 1837, Second edition; additional engraved title with vignette, 18 hand colored aquatint plates by H. Alken, some tissue guards present and foxed, one plate with adjacent text with faint dampstaining, pages ix, (i), (ii), 206, 8vo., slightly later polished calf, backstrip panelled in gilt, hunting emblems and morocco labels with gilt lettering, upper covers with crest and motto "Audactr et Sincere", ochre endpapers, good. Blackwell Rare Books B166 - 74 2011 £400

Apperley, Charles James 1777-1843 *Memoirs of the Life of the Late John Mytton Esq. of Halston Shropshire.* London: Edward Arnold, 1925, New edition; 4to., original red cloth, gilt, spine rather faded, pages ix, 157, 18 color plates. R. F. G. Hollett & Son Antiquarian Booksellers General Catalogue Summer 2010 - 1212 2011 £35

Appert, Fancois *The Art of Preserving all Kinds of Animal and Vegetable Substances for Several Years.* London: printed for Black, Parry and Kingsbury, booksellers to the Hon. East India Co., 1812, Second edition; 12mo., folding, engraved plate (this little soiled and faded), xxv, (1) 164 (2) pages, including half title and final ad leaf, old, perhaps original boards, little stained, recently rebacked and labelled, entirely uncut, good, crisp copy. John Drury Rare Books 154 - 8 2011 £375

Appianus, Alexandrinus *Romanorum Historiarum Libri.* Basel: Hieronymus Froben and Nicolaus Episcopius, 1554, 318 x 216mm., 8 p.l., 506 pages (duplicate leaves pages 437-440), 22 leaves, early 20th century dark brown morocco over pasteboard, covers panelled in gilt and blind with three sets of blind rules, gilt double ruled frame interlaced at lobes on ends and sides, decorated with broad foliate curls, cornerpieces and small bird tools, inner panel with titling in lobed compartment at head, small foliate curl endpiece and sidepieces, flanking upright oval Apollo and Pegasus centerpiece embossed and with traces of gilt and silvering on black background, showing Pegasus with raised foreleg on cliff before a charging Apollo, who races his chariot across steep terrain with reins and whip held aloft and cape fluttering behind, gilt collar with motto in Greek in upper half and chain roll in lower, raised single and double bands, spine panelled gilt and blind with double rules, gilt cinquefoil centerpiece, all edges gilt, fleece lined brown buckram clamshell case, brown morocco labels on spine; woodcut historiated initials, printer's device on titlepage and verso of last leaf; morocco bookplate of Michel Wittock; slightly soiled and with several tiny wormholes, much of text with light overall browning, sprinkled foxing and very occasional faint spotting, little soiling (done on purpose?) to covers, still an obviously appealing volume, wonderful (according to Hobson fraudulent) binding virtually unworn and text perfectly satisfactory with no serious problems, superb example of a replica binding with remarkably persausive tooling and just enough purposefully applied "wear" and discoloration to be deceiving, according to Hobson ths example would not be genuine because Apollo does not lean far enough forward in his chariot and his steeds' front hooves incorrectly touch the cliff. Phillip J. Pirages 59 - 3 2011 $8500

A Apple Pie. Akron: Saalfield, 1907, 12mo., bottom edge cropped unevenly else very good+, muslin book printed on cloth and illustrated on every page in color by Kate Greenaway. Aleph-Bet Books, Inc. 95 - 264 2011 $250

Appleton's Journal Volume V. 1871. Jan.-June number 93-117. New York: 1871, 4to., illustrations. Bookworm & Silverfish 671 - 14 2011 $125

Apuleius *The Golden Ass.* New York: Limited Editions Club, 1932, First edition, one of 1500 copies; signed by artist, tall 8vo., 392 pages, illustrations by Percival Goodman, cream calf (rubbed on spine), housed in publisher's box, very good, included are 4 original pen and ink drawings by Goodman, nicely framed under glass of illustrations from the book, each image approximately 9 1/2 x 8 inches, little browned but in excellent condition.   Second Life Books Inc.   174 - 16 2011 $750

Aquaculture Nutrition. Oxford: Blackwell Science, 1995-2003, 4to., pictorial paperbound, very good plus. Raymond M. Sutton, Jr.   May 26 2011 - 54371 2011 $1250

Aquatic Life. 1915-1942, 1951-1968; 8vo., original wrappers on volume 1 (wrappers on part 1 rough and separated; wrappers on part 9 missing; worn, fair to good), cloth to volumes 2-14 (some wear, good to very good), original printed wrappers on remaining parts (occasional soiling, wrapper detached, and stamp to few front wrappers), good to fine, includes 5 separate booklets written by August M. Roth. Raymond M. Sutton, Jr.   May 26 2011 - 54368 2011 $2500

Arabian Nights *Aladdin or the Wonderful Lamp and Ali-Baba and the Forty Thieves.* Chicago: Albert Whitman, 1929, 4to., cloth, pictorial paste-on, 128 pages, near fine, illustrations by Thomas Mackenzie with 8 stunning color plates and 1 full page and 6 smaller black and whites by Thomas MacKenzie, quite scarce.   Aleph-Bet Books, Inc. 95 - 340 2011 $225

Arabian Nights *Arabian Nights.* New York: Dodd Mead, 1925, Thick 4to., blue gilt cloth, pictorial paste-on, 297 pages, near fine, 12 beautiful mounted color plates with tissue guards plus pictorial titlepage and black and whites in text by E. J. Detmold.   Aleph-Bet Books, Inc. 95 - 187 2011 $1250

Arabian Nights *The Book of the Thousand Nights and a Night. (and) Supplemental Nights.* Benares: printed by the Kamashastra Society for private subscribers only, 1885-1888, First printing of this edition; 250 x 1600, 16 volumes, very pleasing rose colored crushed half morocco over buckram boards by Brian Frost & Co. (signed on verso of front endpaper of each volume), raised bands, spine panels with gilt floral centerpiece or titling, marbled endpapers, top edge gilt, titlepages printed in red and black, first and last leaves of each volume generally with light foxing (few of these leaves bit more foxed), text a shade less than bright because of paper stock chose, still very fine, especially lustrous binding without fault, no signs of use internally. Phillip J. Pirages   59 - 64 2011 $12,500

Arabian Nights *Prince Ahmed and the Fairy Perie Banou from the Arabian Nights.* London: Gay & Hancock, n.d circa, 1916, 8vo., 118 pages, slight spotting, very good+, illustrations by Charles Robinson with 5 lovely color plates, few line illustrations in red and black, uncommon.   Aleph-Bet Books, Inc. 95 - 490 2011 $200

Arabian Nights *Sinbad the Sailor and Other Stories from the Arabian Nights.* London: Hodder and Stoughton, n.d., 1914, Limited to 500 numbered copies signed by artist, not numbered; thick large 4to., full vellum with elaborate gilt decorations on cover and spine, top edge gilt, other edges untrimmed, small area of front and rear lower corners discolored, else very good-fine with original silk ties, sumptuous book, illustrated by Edmund Dulac with 26 tipped in color plates on gilt decorated mounts with lettered guards and with gilt decorations and borders on text pages.   Aleph-Bet Books, Inc. 95 - 210 2011 $6500

Arabian Nights *The Thousand and One Nights Commonly Called in England the Arabian Nights' Entertainments.* London: John Murray, 1849, 222 x 150mm., 3 volumes, 222 x 150mm., elegant contemporary green pebble grain morocco, elaborately gilt by M. Paterson of Edinburgh (his ticket on front pastedown), cover with alcove design, frames with ornate floral decoration, top and bottom panels with semi-circular central portion formed by multiple gilt rules, whole enclosing large central urn filled with flowers, spines gilt in double ruled compartments, with intricate fan style cornerpieces and large complex central fleuron, densely gilt turn-ins, marbled endpapers, all edges gilt, extra engraved titlepage and about 700 wood engravings from designs by William Harvey; spines just slightly and uniformly sunned toward a pleasing olive green, inner half inch of front free endpaper of volume on glued to pastedown and slightly torn, small additional defect, otherwise fine, extremely pretty set, decorative original binding with bright gilt and only trivial wear, text with virtually no signs of use.   Phillip J. Pirages 59 - 65 2011 $1250

Aragon, Louis *Le Con d'Irene.* Paris: Rene Bonnell, 1928, First edition, number 129 of an edition of 135 and of 125 on verge d'Arches; 4to., pages 85, (1) blank, (i) limitation), (i) blank, five original etchings by Andre Masson, each with its own tissue guard, original red wrappers, printed with titlepage design, contemporary red limp suede with titlepage design in gilt, marbled endpapers, near fine in beautiful appropriate contemporary binding.   Simon Finch Rare Books   Zero - 440 2011   £7000

Aragon, Louis *Paris Peasant.* London: Jonathan Cape, 1971, First UK edition; slight bruise at head of spine, near fine in very good dust jacket faded at spine top edge. Peter Ellis   May 26 2011 - ARAGONLO015691 2011 $65

Arblay, Frances Burney D' 1752-1840 *Evelina or a Young Lady's Entrance into the World.* Worcester: Thomas, Son & Thomas, for Thomas, Andrews & Penniman, Booksellers, State Street, Albany, 1796, Second American edition; Small 8vo., 222, 276 pages, original calf on boards, red label with title on spine, dedication page in volume 1, charming wood engraved tailpiece, volume one with repaired portion of lower endpaper, spine rubbed and lightly chipped, water spots on front endleaves of first volume, internally with small chipping and foxing, all uniformly tanned leaves, volume two lacking free endpaper, spines rubbed, scuffed corner of covers, shelfwear at edges.   Hobbyhorse Books   56 - 17 2011 $250

Arbousset, T. *Narrative of an Exploratory Tour to the North East of the Colony of the Cape of Good Hope.* London: John C. Bishop, 1852, First London edition; small 8vo., pages 455, folding map, original blue cloth, little wear to head and tail of spine, rubbing to joints, some light foxing to prelims, inscribed by author to Miss Eardley.   J. & S. L. Bonham Antiquarian Booksellers   Africa 4/20/2011 - 5355 2011   £350

Arbus, Diane *Diane Arbus.* Millerton: Aperture, 1972, First edition; 4to., pages (182), 80 black and white photos, original paper covered boards, spine lettered in black, black and white photo reproduced to upper side, page edges lightly toned, original black and white photo illustrated dust jacket, short closed tear and nick to lower panel, loss of laminate to head of spine, rear flap creased, near fine.   Simon Finch Rare Books   Zero - 502 2011   £2000

Archaeological Institute of Great Britain and Ireland *The Archaeological Journal... Volume II.* London: Longman Brown, 1846, Original cloth, leather spine label, pages 424, (ix), 2 lithographed plates, numerous text woodcuts, some browning or foxing in places, but good, sound copy.   R. F. G. Hollett & Son Antiquarian Booksellers   177 - 16 2011   £40

Archaeological Institute of Great Britain and Ireland *The Archaeological Journal...Volume 126 to volume 149.* Royal Archaeological Institute, 1969-1992, 4to., original wrappers, plates and diagrams, fine run.   R. F. G. Hollett & Son Antiquarian Booksellers   177 - 18 2011   £120

Archaeological Institute of Great Britain and Ireland *The Ecclesiastical and Architectural Topography of England.* John Henry Parker, 1849, First edition; unpaginated, modern half levant morocco gilt.   R. F. G. Hollett & Son Antiquarian Booksellers   177 - 15 2011   £65

Archer, Annie *Family Omnibus.* Kendal: privately printed by titus Wilson for the author, n.d. circa, 1960, Original blue cloth, gilt, pages (iv), 76, illustrations.   R. F. G. Hollett & Son Antiquarian Booksellers   173 - 24 2011   £35

Archer, Francis Bisset *The Gambia Colony and Protectorate: an Official Handbook.* London: St. Brides n.d., 1905, First edition; 8vo., pages xviii, 364, frontispiece, folding map, illustrations, original brown cloth, inner hinges cracked, very good.   J. & S. L. Bonham Antiquarian Booksellers   Africa 4/20/2011 - 8292 2011   £120

Archer, Gleason Leonard *Big Business and Radio.* New York: American Historical Co., 1939, Thick 8vo., vi, 503 pages, photos, plates, silver cloth, blue stamped cover title, silver stamped blue spine label, dust jacket worn, very good, scarce in jacket, from the Bern Dibner reference library, with Burndy bookplate.   Jeff Weber Rare Books   161 - 13 2011 $95

Archer, Jeffrey *Cat O' Nine Tales and other Stories.* London: Macmillan, 2006, First edition; large 8vo., original cloth, dust jacket, pages ix 262, illustrations in color. R. F. G. Hollett & Son Antiquarian Booksellers   General Catalogue Summer 2010 - 899 2011   £35

Archer, Jeffrey *A Prison Diary.* London: Macmillan, 2003-2004, First editions; Volume two and three only, corners little bumped, thus near fine in near fine or better dust jackets, both volumes inscribed to basketball player and former US Senator Bill Bradley and his wife Ernestine. Between the Covers   169 - BTC 343394 2011 $400

Archer, Thomas *Pictures and Royal Portraits Illustrative of English and Scottish History...* London: Blackie & Son Old Bailey, 1880, First edition; 4to., pages 184, 171, 2 frontispieces and 67 full page engravings, 2 volumes, original publisher's full red morocco, Blackie presentation luxury binding with bevelled edges, extensive and elaborate gilt tooling and blindstamping with various English and Scottish heraldic gilt crests on front and back boards, spines with 6 raised bands and elaborate gilt decoration, inner gilt dentelles, all edges gilt, marbled endpapers, some slight rubbing at hinges, cover and edges otherwise very good+ with small label on rear pastedown "bound by Blackie".   Any Amount of Books May 26 2011 - !68988 2011 $1006

Archimedes *De iis Quae Vehuntur in Aqua Libri Duo. A Federico Commandino... in Pristinum Nitorem Restituti et Commentariis Illustrati.* Bologna: Ex Officina Alexandri Benacii, 1565, First edition; 4to., (4), 43, (i.e. 45) leaves + final blank L6, woodcut diagrams in text, later 18th century Italian? limp vellum, lower margin of C1 neatly repaired, not affecting text.   Joseph J. Felcone Inc.   Fall Miscellany 2010 - 4 2011 $3800

Architectural and Arcaheological Society of Durham and Northumberland *Transactions. Volume II 1869-1870.* Durham: Andrews and Co., 1883, Old half morocco gilt with raised bands by Andrews of Durham, pages xciii, 272, iv, with 15 photo plates and 4 folding plans and plates, some little stained.   R. F. G. Hollett & Son Antiquarian Booksellers   177 - 19 2011   £75

The Architectural Review. Architectural Review, 1949-1981, 4to., monthly magazine bound here in 2 volumes per year, this run includes volume 105 to volume 170 (Jan. 1949 to Dec. 1989) inclusive, lacking only volume 157 (Jan-June 1975).   R. F. G. Hollett & Son Antiquarian Booksellers   177 - 743   2011   £1250

Architectural Review. Professional Publications, 1973, 125th Anniversary Special Commemorative Publication; Pages 284, 4to., original wrappers, illustrations.   R. F. G. Hollett & Son Antiquarian Booksellers   177 - 20   2011   £30

Architecture. A Monthly Magazine of Architectural Art. Architecture, 1896,   Volume I, no. 1, tall 4to., original wrappers, foot of spine little worn, slight scratch to lower panel, pages 64, xx (ads), photos, plans and drawings by Herbert Railton an others.   R. F. G. Hollett & Son Antiquarian Booksellers   177 - 584   2011   £45

Ardizzone, Edward   *Tom and Lucy go to Sea.*   London: Oxford University Press, 1938,   First edition; small folio, color illustrated boards, bright copy, some bumps at ends of spine, color pictorial dust jacket, partial wrapper in pieces, illustrations.   Jo Ann Reisler, Ltd.   86 - 13   2011 $500

Ardizzone, Edward   *Tim All Alone.*   Oxford University Press, 1956,   First edition; every page carrying an illustration by Ardizzone, pages (48), imperial 8vo., original boards illustrated overall, edges rubbed, free endpapers foxed, dust jacket rubbed, very good.   Blackwell Rare Books   B166 - 121   2011   £85

Ardley, Patricia B.   *The Adventures of Mr. Horace Hedgehog.*   London: Collins, 1935,   First edition; oblong 4to., original cloth backed pictorial pink boards, trifle dusty, pages 56, 6 full page color plates, numerous line drawings by E. C. Ardley, occasional spot and mark, very nice.   R. F. G. Hollett & Sons Antiquarian Booksellers   170 - 41   2011   £45

Ardley, Patricia B.   *Mr. and Mrs. Hedgehog.*   Collins, 1936,   First edition; oblong 4to., original cloth backed pictorial pink boards, dust jacket (few short closed edge tears), pages 55, 6 full page color plates, numerous line drawings by E. C. Ardley, lovely, clean copy.   R. F. G. Hollett & Sons Antiquarian Booksellers   170 - 42   2011   £85

Aretino, Pietro   *Quatro Comedie...coe Il Marescoalco la Talanta. La Cortegiana L'Hipocrito.*   London: J. Wolfe, 1588,   8vo., ff. (8), 485, (3 errata), early 18th century English calf, spine gilt in compartments, very nice, from the library of the Earls of Macclesfield at Shirburn Castle.   Maggs Bros. Ltd.   1440 - 5   2011   £900

Argens, Jean Baptiste De Boyer, Marquis De   1704-1771
Therese Philosophe ou Memoires Pour servir a l'Histoire du P. Dirrag & De Mademoiselle Eradice.   A La Hay: circa, 1748,   First edition; 2 'parties', 8vo., pages viii (misbound iii-vi, blank leaf, engraved title, titlepage, vii-viii), 140, 72, engraved title, folding frontispiece and 16 explicit engraved plates, marbled endpapers, original calf, red morocco spine label, titled in gilt, spine gilt decorated, triple gilt rule on boards, all edges gilt, all printed pages framed within printed borders, joints beginning to show signs of wear, with slight fraying to top edges, top right upper panel bumped, withal, binding in sound state, with pages still firm in binding.   Simon Finch Rare Books   Zero - 402   2011   £7500

Argens, Jean Baptiste De Boyer, Marquis De   1704-1771
Therese Philosophe ou Memoires Pour servir a l'Histoire du P. Dirrag & De Mademoiselle Eradice...Premiere Partie. Therese Philosophe &c Seconde & Derniere Partie.   A La Haye: circa, 1748,   2 'parties' bound in one, 8vo., pages viii (titlepage) 'explication' of the 17 plates, 'Table des Matieres de la Premiere Partie', page 72 misnumbered 24), 69, 70-72 (Table des matieres de la seconde partie' Page 72 misnumbered 70), (1) (Fautes a Coriger'), final leaf was probably printed as leaf I8 (pages 143-144) of the first partie and subsequently bound in at end of joint volume, frontispiece, 16 erotic plates, all edges gilt, slight scattered age darkening and soiling of paper, original 18th century maroon morocco (slight restoration), marbled endpapers, spine decorated and title label reading "T. PH" in gilt, all within raised bands, bookplate of G. Nordmann.   Simon Finch Rare Books   Zero - 403   2011   £25,000

Argosy. Fleetway Publications, 1926,   First edition; June 1926 - Feb. 1974 (last issue), a monthly magazine of novels, short stories and verse, 510 out of 573 issues, bound volumes from 1926 - June 1939 in excellent condition, wrappers of earlier issues tend to be little frayed at staples rusted, otherwise contents very good and the majority in very good condition.   I. D. Edrich   May 26 2011 - 84732   2011 $4445

Aries, Philippe   *A History of Private Life.*   Cambridge: 1987,   5 volumes, 8vo., approximately 3000 pages, abundantly illustrated, hard back, near fine.   Bookworm & Silverfish   666 - 156   2011 $125

Ariosto, L.   *The Orlando of Ariosto Reduced to XXIV Books.*   London: Printed for J. Dodsley, 1791,   First edition thus; 2 volumes, pages vii, 495 and 473, frontispiece in volume one, 3 illustrations to each volume, full leather tree calf, gilt decoration on spine, red leather spine labels, spine label slightly chipped, slight rubbing and scuffing, otherwise sound and about very good, two former owners neat signatures on front endpaper dated 1798 and 1944.   Any Amount of Books   May 29 2011 - A55095   2011 $204

Aristophanes *The Lysistrata of Aristophanes.* London: 1896, First edition; 4to., pages (x) 61, (1) blank, very good and 7 plates by Aubrey Beardsley, original pale blue gray paper boards, white title label on front cover, top edge rough trimmed, partially unopened, others untrimmed, printed on Van Gelder handmade paper, plates on glossy art paper, rare variant binding.   Simon Finch Rare Books   Zero - 433   2011   £6500

Aristoteles *Commentarii Colelgii Conimbricensis Societatis Iesu in Tres Libros de Anima Aristotelis Stagiritae.* Cologne: Impensis Lazari Zetzneri, 1609, Some light browning and spotting, few marginal paper flaws and touch of marginal worming near end (never affecting text) pages (viii), columns 694, pages (19), 4to., contemporary Oxford blind tooled dark calf boards, outer border of triple blind fillet, frame of triple blind fillet with cornerpieces and central decorative blind lozenge, spine with four raised bands between blind fillets, hatched at top and bottom, little rubbed in places, bit of wear to corners and head of spine, pastedowns lifted and early printed binder's waste exposed to front, ownership inscription of "Chesterton", good. Blackwell Rare Books   B166 - 17   2011   £950

Aristoteles *I tre Libri della Retorica...* Venice: Francesco de' Franceschi, 1571, First edition of this translation by Piccolomini; 4to., (12), 292 pages, device on titlepage, English calf c. 1720, gilt fillet on covers, spine gilt, colored silk marker, from the library of the Earls of Macclesfield at Shirburn Castle.   Maggs Bros. Ltd.   1440 - 12 2011   £550

Aristoteles *The Basic Works of Aristotle.* New York: Random House, 1941, Thick 8vo., xxxix, 1487 pages, frontispiece, beige cloth, gilt stamped black spine label, dust jacket worn along top edge, else very good, scarce in jacket, from the Bern Dibner reference library, with Burndy bookplate.   Jeff Weber Rare Books   161 - 14   2011 $95

Aristotelian Society *Aristotelian Society Proceedings.* London: Methuen/Compton Press/Aristotelian Society, 1969-1987, First edition; 13 volumes, 8vo., most books about 300 pages, from the library of philosophy professor J. N. Findlay, but with no sign of his ownership apart from train times written in his hand on endpaper of 1938 volume, all about very good and complete.   Any Amount of Books   May 29 2011 - B26238 2011 $298

Aristotle, Pseud. *The Works of Aristotle the Famous Philosopher in Four Parts.* New England: printed for the Proprietor, 1813, 12mo., 264 pages, 4 illustrations on pages 54-5, contemporary calf, leather label, text quite browned, bottom of title frayed, one leaf loose. M & S Rare Books, Inc.   90 - 18   2011 $225

Arkell, Reginald *Old Herbaceous.* London: Michael Joseph, 1950, First edition; original pictorial cloth, dust jacket extremities little rubbed, pages 155, green tinted illustrations by Minton.   R. F. G. Hollett & Son Antiquarian Booksellers   General Catalogue Summer 2010 - 852 2011   £30

Arlington, Thomas Bebington, Earl of *The Right Honourable the Earl of Arlington's Letter to Sir W. Temple.* London: Tho. Bener, 1701, First edition; 2 volumes, small 8vo., full leather with blindstamped designs on covers, pages 480 & 454, ex-British Foreign Office library with few library markings, slight splitting at spines, slight shelfwear, else very good.   Any Amount of Books   May 29 2011 - A66990   2011 $255

Armistead, William *Tales and Legends of the English Lakes.* London: Simpkin Marshall & Co., 1891, First edition; original blue cloth gilt, pages xii, 289, uncut, front endpapers little spotted.   R. F. G. Hollett & Son Antiquarian Booksellers   173 - 26   2011   £45

Armistead, Wilson *Tribute for the Negro: Being a Vindication of the Moral, Intellectual and Religious Capabilities of the Coloured Portion of Mankind.* Manchester: William Irwin, 1848, First edition; octavo, (i)-xxxv, (1, blank), (1)- 564, (4, publisher's ads), (2, blank) pages, frontispiece and 11 additional engraved plates, half title and engraved titlepage, text within decorative border, publisher's deluxe gilt binding, full plum morocco, boards ruled in blind, front board and spine decoratively stamped gilt with vignettes of shackled slaves, all edges gilt, yellow endpapers, bookplate of John Ralph Willis, prominent collector of Rare Africana, previous owner's ink inscription dated '48, inner front hinge cracked but firm, hardly noticeable, some light foxing, overall better condition than usually found in publisher's rare deluxe binding.   Heritage Book Shop   Holiday 2010 - 3   2011 $2750

Armitage, Harold *Early Man in Hallamshire.* London: Sampson Low and Co., 1939, First edition; original cloth, gilt, spine rather faded, pages xii, 307, 26 plates.   R. F. G. Hollett & Son Antiquarian Booksellers   177 - 49   2011   £45

Armitage, Merle *Brett Weston: Photographs.* New York: E. Weyhe, Publisher, 1956, First edition; clean, very near fine copy, very small stain to bottom of first two pages in bright near fine dust jacket with small chip and couple of tears to top of spine, as well as some other very minor wear, signed and inscribed by Weston, additionally, a vintage silver gelatin self portrait of Weston is affixed to front endpaper, image signed by Weston in negative, unique copy. Jeff Hirsch Books   ny 2010 2011 $5000

Armstrong, A. M. *The Place Names of Cumberland. English Place Name Society Volumes XX-XXII.* Cambridge: University Press, 1950-1952, First edition; 3 volumes, original cloth, gilt, pages 565, map in rear pocket of final volume, very good. R. F. G. Hollett & Son Antiquarian Booksellers 173 - 30 2011 £150

Armstrong, M. D. *Exodus and Other Poems.* London: Lynwood and Co., 1912, First edition; 8vo., original publisher's brown paper covered boards, white linen spine, pages viii, 77, spine slightly browned, slight split at top hinge, rubbed at edges with slight browning, very good-. Any Amount of Books May 29 2011 - A76082 2011 $230

Arnatt, Keith *Walking the Dog.* London: Omedga Books, 1979, First edition; small 4to., wrappers, unnumbered (56 pages), full page black and white photos, rare, slight sunning at spine, corners faintly rubbed, very slight edgewear, neat small American address label on fe.p., else sound, very good. Any Amount of Books May 29 2011 - A40957 2011 $298

Arnold; or a Trait and It's (sic) Consequences of Civil War. London: for G. Robinson, 1809, First and only edition; 2 volumes, x, 206, (1) pages; (2), 280, (1) pages, including half titles, untrimmed, bound in contemporary sheep backed marbled paper covered boards, hinges tender, spine ends chipped. Joseph J. Felcone Inc. Fall Miscellany 2010 - 6 2011 $2000

Arnold, Fred S. *Garenganze; or Seven Years Pioneer Mission Work in Central Africa.* London: James E. Hawkins, 1889, Pages viii, (iii), 276, 19 illustrations, 2 text maps and large folding map, original pictorial cloth gilt, extremities trifle worn, light crease across upper board, endpapers lightly foxed, crack on front pastedown repaired. R. F. G. Hollett & Son Antiquarian Booksellers 175 - 49 2011 £50

Arnold, Julian *Palms and Temples Being Notes of a Four Months Voyage Upon the Nile.* London: Tinsley Bros., 1882, First edition; 8vo., original publisher's blind patterned maroon cloth lettered gilt on spine and on front cover, gilt decoration on cover of setting sun and tork, page xii, 371, frontispiece, attractive very good+, Victorian prize label on pastedown, some slight foxing to prelims. Any Amount of Books May 29 2011 - A47215 2011 $238

Arnold, Matthew 1822-1888 *Alaric at Rome.* 1893, Limited to a few copies printed for private circulation, type facsimile reprint of original edition; half title, uncut in 20th century quarter calf, brown paper boards, "RBA" in red ink on leading f.e.p., printed by Thomas J. Wise. Jarndyce Antiquarian Booksellers CXCI - 49 2011 £125

Arnold, Matthew 1822-1888 *Essays in Criticism. Second Series.* London: Macmillan, 1888, First edition; half title, 2 pages ads + 32 page catalog (April 1888), original blue cloth, slightly rubbed. Jarndyce Antiquarian Booksellers CXCI - 50 2011 £50

Arnold, Matthew 1822-1888 *New Poems.* London: Macmillan & Co., 1867, First edition; half title, original green cloth by Burn, booksellers ticket of G. G. Walmsley. Jarndyce Antiquarian Booksellers CXCI - 51 2011 £150

Arnold, Matthew 1822-1888 *Poems.* London: Macmillan, 1888-1890, Volume 1 Popular edition, volumes II & III New edition; 3 volumes, half titles, full dark brown morocco by Wells of Winchester, gilt, gilt dentelles, decorated endpapers, slightly rubbed, contemporary inscription, all edges gilt, very good, handsome set. Jarndyce Antiquarian Booksellers CXCI - 52 2011 £150

Arnold, Matthew 1822-1888 *Reports on Elementary Schools 1852-1882.* London: Macmillan, 1889, First collected edition; original cloth, gilt, neatly recased, pages xv, 306, (ii), half title, library stamp on back of title, few blind marginal stamps. R. F. G. Hollett & Son Antiquarian Booksellers 175 - 47 2011 £95

Arnold, Matthew 1822-1888 *The Strayed Reveller and Other Poems.* London: B. Fellowes, 1849, First edition; 8vo., pages vii, 128, full brown grained morocco with green and gilt Celtic device on cover spine tooled and lettered in gilt, 5 raised bands, gilt inner dentelles, top edge gilt, joints slightly rubbed and slightly tender, bookplate, binding elaborate and dated 1904 with monogram that might be CD. Any Amount of Books May 26 2011 - A65769 2011 $419

Arnold, Samuel James *A Letter to All the Proprietors of Drury-Lane Theatre (Excepting Peter Moore, Esq. and others who are, or have been concerned in the management thereof).* London: William Fearman, 1818, First edition; 8vo., (2), 86 pages, recently well bound in watered cloth, spine lettered gilt, good copy. John Drury Rare Books 154 - 9 2011 £250

Arnold, Thomas James *Reynard the Fox.* London: Nattali and Bond, 1855, First edition thus; pages xvi, 320, engraved titlepage and 12 steel engraved plates after Wolf, modern levant morocco backed paper covered gilt, scattered foxing, small neat repairs to frontispiece and engraved title, scarce. R. F. G. Hollett & Son Antiquarian Booksellers 175 - 48 2011 £150

Arnoux, Guy *Histoire De La Ramee Soldat Francais.* Paris: Devambez, 1918, Limited to 325 numbered copies; folio, pictorial wrappers, light cover soil, very good+, 15 hand colored pochoir illustrations by Arnoux. Aleph-Bet Books, Inc. 95 - 435 2011 $600

Arnow, Harriette *The Dollmaker.* London: Heinemann, 1955, First British edition; warmly inscribed by author for Virginia Patterson, laid into book are two autograph Christmas cards signed by Arnow 1968 and 1972 with lengthy notes, uncommon thus, book has tear at upper edge of front endpaper, and lower corner bump, otherwise near fine in fair dust jacket, corner chipped dust jacket fully split at front flap fold, pictorial dust jacket differs markedly from that of US edition, cards are fine.   Ken Lopez Bookseller   154 - 8   2011 $650

Arrowsmith, James *The Paper Hanger's and Upholsterer's Guide; a Treatise on Paper-Hanging and Upholstery...* London: Thomas Dean and Son, n.d., circa, 1850-1854, First and apparently only edition; 8vo., 2 diagrammatic plates 70 (10) pages, original cloth, gilt title on upper cover, spine neatly restored, very good, inscribed "with publisher's compliments".   John Drury Rare Books   153 - 4   2011   £350

The Art Annual. London: Art Journal Office, 1888, Folio, good, salmon gilt, cover soiled.   Barnaby Rudge Booksellers   Art & Architecture & Photography 2011 $75

L'Art de Voyager dans les Airs, ou Les Balloons: Contenant les Moyens de Faire des Globes Aerostatiques Suivant la methode de MM. de Montgolfier & Suivant les Procedes de MM. Charles & Robert. Paris: Chez les Libraires, 1784, First edition; (4), 142, (2) pages, 3 engraved plates, uncut, contemporary marbled paper wrappers as issued, tiny burn mark in center of last few leaves affecting a letter on each of two or three pages, wrappers worn from upper and lower spine, very good, uncut, clean and as issued.   Joseph J. Felcone Inc.   Fall Miscellany 2010 - 9   2011 $2000

The Art Journal. New York: 1876, 380 pages, folio, 24 numbers, each in wrappers as issued, some expected fraying to wrappers, print margins intact, one issue damped at top margin not affecting images, 32 full page steel engravings with modest foxing, , woodcut illustrations.   Bookworm & Silverfish   676 - 79   2011   £225

The Art Journal for 1910. London: Virtue & Co., 1910, 4 etchings, many tipped in color and black and white plates, folio, gray cloth, good, bookplate of Gertrude M. Lawrence.   Barnaby Rudge Booksellers   Art & Architecture & Photography - 017188   2011 $75

The Art of Painting in Miniature. London: G. Smith, 1730, First edition; small 8vo., full leather boards, pages (xvi) 121, titlepage printed in red and black, one illustration on page 7, vignette at beginning and end, boards loose, repair to one page with no loss of text, note on one page in 18th century hand, some wear and rubbing, text block clean and sound overall, very good.   Any Amount of Books   May 29 2011 - A45531   2011 $221

L'Art Revue Hebdomadaire Illustre. Cinquieme Annee Tome III. Paris: Librairie de l'Art, 1879, 440 x 310mm., 2 p.l., 322, (1) pages, in very elaborately inlaid morocco binding by Marius Michel (stamp signed on front turn-in), covers with all over design of entwined floral and foliate sprays incorporating many morocco inlays in 8 different colors (predominately browns, but with some red and two shades of green), front cover with journal title (L'Art) inlaid on a scroll that straps around a foliated branch and budding stem, rear cover similarly decorated but without titling, raised bands, spine compartments with onlaid frame and foliate centerpiece in two shades of brown morocco, wide turn-ins with six gilt rules, especially pleasing brocaded endleaves in very animated floral pattern, marbled flyleaves, all edges gilt, elaborate historiated and decorative initials, headpieces and tailpieces, nearly 200 illustrations in text, 24 full page illustrations, four illustrated borders and 67 engraved plates, including 14 plates, each appearing four times, 28 of these plates done on special paper and mounted, little cockling to some of the mounted plates, otherwise only trivial imperfections, in very fine condition, binding bright and virtually unworn.   Phillip J. Pirages   59 - 117   2011 $5500

Artemidorus *Artemidori Daldiani & Achmetis Sereimi f. Oneirocritica. Astrampsychi & Nicephori Versus Etiam Oneirocritici.* Paris: M. Orry, 1603, 4to. (12), 269, L14 blank, (23) P2 blank, 20, 65; 275, (17) pages, title printed in red and black, 2 columns, later 17th century Cambridge binding of panelled calf, spine gilt, red edges, extremely handsome, inscription Stephanus Joann(is) Stephanius, from the library of the Earls of Macclesfield at Shirburn Castle.   Maggs Bros. Ltd.   1440 - 14   2011   £900

Arts & Crafts Exhibition Society *Art and Life and the Building and Decoration of Cities...* Rivington, Percival & Co., 1897, Half title, recent ownership inscription, uncut, original red brown publisher's gilt monogram on front board, worn paper label on spine, little sunned, presentation inscription for Elie Reclus, from T. J. and Annie Cobden-Sanderson, 5 volumes.   Jarndyce Antiquarian Booksellers   CXCI - 53   2011   £250

Arunachalam, P. *Light from the East: Being Letters of Gnanam. The Divine Knowledge.* London: George Allen & Unwin, 1927, First edition; 8vo. pages 157, original publisher's blue cloth lettered gilt on spine, frontispiece and plate, faint wear at head of spine, corners slightly bumped, otherwise very good, in chipped, nicked and browned dust jacket (very good).   Any Amount of Books   May 29 2011 - A69810   2011 $204

Asbjornsen, P. C. *The Pancake.* London: Sampson Low, Marston, Searle & Rivington, circa, 1880, 4to., full color pictorial paper covers with some minor rippling, book has been rebacked professionally, 6 full page color plates signed with initial monogram.   Jo Ann Reisler, Ltd.   86 - 97   2011 $200

Ascham, Roger *The English Works.* London: printed for R. and J. Dodsley, 1761, First edition, first issue with leaf of additional subscribers; 4to., (10), xvi, 395 pages, engraved armorial headpiece (Earl of Shaftesbury), contemporary calf, spine gilt, red morocco lettering piece (short split at head of upper joint), from the library of the Earls of Macclesfield at Shirburn Castle.   Maggs Bros. Ltd.   1440 - 15   2011   £400

Ashbee, Felicity *The W.A.A.F. Magazine.* Printed in Watford: H.Q.F.C. Unit, 1939-1940, First edition; wrappers, 8vo., first 3 issues, possibly all published, pages 16, 20 and 32, some illustrations, slight wear, otherwise very good.   Any Amount of Books   May 29 2011 - A63895   2011 $255

Ashbee, Paul *The Bronze Age Round Barrow In Britain.* Phoenix House, 1960, First edition; small 4to., original cloth, gilt, dust jacket, pages 222, with 32 pages of plates and 61 text figures.   R. F. G. Hollett & Son Antiquarian Booksellers   177 - 51   2011   £60

Ashbery, John *Turnadot and Other Poems.* New York: Tibor De Nagy Gallery, 1953, first edition, one of 300 copies, Printed under supervision of the artist, Nell Blaine; 8vo., original decorated stitched wrappers with printed paper label on front cover, fine copy with few nicks and tiny closed edge tears in wrappers.   James S. Jaffe Rare Books   May 26 2011 - 20711   2011 $6500

Ashdown, Charles H. *British Castles.* London: A. & C. Black, 1911, First edition; large 8vo., original pictorial green cloth, gilt, pages xx, 208, 32 colored plates and a number of plans and diagrams in text, joints cracking, otherwise very nice.   R. F. G. Hollett & Son Antiquarian Booksellers   177 - 52   2011   £85

Ashe, Robert P. *Chronicles of Uganda.* London: Hodder & Stoughton, 1894, First edition; 8vo., pages xiv, 480, ads, photogravure portrait frontispiece, 26 illustrations, many text illustrations, original blue decorative cloth gilt vignette on upper cover, spine little faded.   J. & S. L. Bonham Antiquarian Booksellers   Africa 4/20/2011 - 6230   2011   £80

Ashe, Robert P. *Two Kings of Uganda; or Life by the Shores of Victoria Nyanza.* London: Sampson Low, 1889, First edition; 8vo., pages ix (iv), 342, appendices, ads, folding map, 4 illustrations, original green decorative cloth, recased, spine faded, new endpapers.   J. & S. L. Bonham Antiquarian Booksellers   Africa 4/20/2011 - 6234   2011   £150

Ashe, Thomas *History of the Azores: or, Western Islands.* London: Sherwood Neely & Jones, 1813, First edition; quarto, 306 pages, frontispiece, 4 plates, 3 maps, some light occasional foxing, 19th century half calf, very good.   J. & S. L. Bonham Antiquarian Booksellers   Africa 4/20/2011 - 8936   2011   £800

Ashley, Evelyn *The Life of Henry John Temple, Viscount Palmerston 1846-1865.* London: Richard Bentley & Son, 1876, 2 volumes, original cloth gilt, spines faded, pages viii, 380; viii, 341, with 2 frontispiece portraits, some joints tender, armorial bookplate of Sir Francis Montefiore.   R. F. G. Hollett & Son Antiquarian Booksellers   175 - 52   2011   £75

Ashley, William H. *The West of William H. Ashley.* Denver: Old West Publishing Co., 1964, First trade edition; folio, liv, 341 pages, numerous plates, facsimiles, maps, pictorial gray cloth stamped in red and gilt, spine ends lightly rubbed, fine.   Argonaut Book Shop   Recent Acquisitions Summer 2010 - 137   2011 $225

Ashmolean Museum *Eric Ravilious 1903-1942.* Oxford: Ashmolean Museum, 1972, Large 8vo., original wrappers, pages (24), patterned endpapers, 7 plates and decorations all by Ravilious, scarce.   R. F. G. Hollett & Son Antiquarian Booksellers   General Catalogue Summer 2010 - 133   2011   £45

Ashmun, Jehudi *History of the American Colony in Liberia from December 1821 to 1825.* Washington City: Way & Gideon, 1826, First edition; 42 pages, large folding map, uncut in contemporary printed wrappers, map moderately foxed, faint dampstaining to last several leaves, else lovely copy, stitched and untrimmed as issued.   Joseph J. Felcone Inc.   Fall Miscellany 2010 - 7   2011 $1000

Ashton, John *Humour, Wit and Satire of the Seventeenth Century.* London: Chatto & Windus, 1883, Original decorated green cloth, gilt, pages viii, 455, illustrations.   R. F. G. Hollett & Son Antiquarian Booksellers   175 - 53   2011   £65

Ashton, John *A Right Merrie Christmasse!!!* London: Leadenhall Press, 1894, 4to., original half calf, gilt, rubbed and scraped, backstrip rather defective at head and fox, pages xii, 250, top edge gilt, uncut, copper etched frontispiece, red ruled borders, scarce.   R. F. G. Hollett & Son Antiquarian Booksellers   175 - 54   2011   £140

Ashton, Thomas *A Sermon Preached in the Parish Church of Christ Church, London on Wednesday May the 14th 1760...* London: J. & W. Oliver and B. Dod, 1760, First edition; 4to., old drab wrappers, pages 30, 3-90, (ii), engraved head and tailpieces and initial letters, rare.   R. F. G. Hollett & Son Antiquarian Booksellers   175 - 55   2011   £180

Asimov, Isaac 1920-1992 *Asimov's Chronology of Science and Discovery.* New York: Harper Collins, 1994, First edition; thick 8vo., 790 pages, illustrations, quarter gray cloth with black paper boards, silver stamped spine title, dust jacket, from the Bern Dibner reference library, with Burndy bookplate.   Jeff Weber Rare Books   161 - 17   2011 $80

Asimov, Isaac 1920-1992   *The Caves of Steel.*   Garden City: Doubleday & Co., 1954,   First edition; octavo, cloth.   L. W. Currey, Inc.   124 - 7   2011 $4500

Asimov, Isaac 1920-1992   *Earth is Room Enough: Science Fiction Tales of Our Own Planet.* Garden City: Doubleday and Co., 1957,   First edition; octavo, cloth.   L. W. Currey, Inc.   124 - 114   2011 $650

Asimov, Isaac 1920-1992   *The End of Eternity.*   Garden City: Doubleday and Co., 1955,   First edition; octavo, cloth.   L. W. Currey, Inc.   124 - 31   2011 $1750

Asimov, Isaac 1920-1992   *Foundation. (with) Foundation and Empire. (with) Second Foundation.*   New York: Gnome Press Pub., Later Gnome Press, Inc., 1951-1953,   First editions; octavo, 3 volumes, first volume bound in cloth, others in boards, dust jackets where required.   L. W. Currey, Inc.   124 - 3   2011 $6500

Asimov, Isaac 1920-1992   *I, Robot.*   New York: Gnome Press Inc., 1950,   First edition; octavo, cloth.   L. W. Currey, Inc.   124 - 32   2011 $1750

Asimov, Isaac 1920-1992   *Isaac Asimov, First Visit to Britain 1974.*   London: Aardvaark House/Steve Odell,   First edition; wrappers, 8vo., pages 18, photos, illustrated wrappers, fine, signed presentation from author for Margery and John Brunner.   Any Amount of Books   May 29 2011 - A66921   2011 $408

Asimov, Isaac 1920-1992   *Lucky Starr and the Big Sun of Mercury.*   Garden City: Doubleday & Co., 1956,   First edition; octavo, boards.   L. W. Currey, Inc.   124 - 134   2011 $450

Asimov, Isaac 1920-1992   *Lucky Starr and the Oceans of Venus.*   Garden City: Doubleday & Co., 1954,   First edition; octavo, cloth.   L. W. Currey, Inc.   124 - 113   2011 $650

Asimov, Isaac 1920-1992   *The Martian Way and Other Stories.*   Garden City: Doubleday & Co., 1955,   First edition; octavo, boards.   L. W. Currey, Inc.   124 - 44   2011 $1500

Asimov, Isaac 1920-1992   *Pebble in the Sky.*   Garden City: Doubleday & Co. Inc., 1950,   First edition; octavo, cloth.   L. W. Currey, Inc.   124 - 115   2011 $650

Asimov, Isaac 1920-1992   *Robots and Empire.*   West Bloomfield: Phantasia Press, 1985,   First edition; octavo, leather.   L. W. Currey, Inc.   124 - 45   2011 $1500

Asimov, Isaac 1920-1992   *The Robots of Dawn.*   Huntington Woods: Phantasia Press, 1983,   First edition; octavo, leather,.   L. W. Currey, Inc.   124 - 46   2011 $1500

Aspin, J.   *Cosmorama: the Manners, Customs and Costumes of all the Nations of the World, Described.*   John Harris, 1834,   New edition; 16mo., color frontispiece and plates, original patterned boards, paper label on front board, slightly rubbed, spine dulled, leading inner hinge slightly cracked with some repair to inner hinge, contemporary inscription.   Jarndyce Antiquarian Booksellers   CXCI - 54   2011   £150

Asquith, Cynthia   *The Flying Carpet.*   Partridge & Co., n.d., 1926,   First edition; pages 200, 4to., 4 tippe in color plates, and monochrome illustrations, original cloth, lower board little soiled, flyleaves rather browned, few spots to fore edge, 2 early Attwell postcards loosely inserted.   R. F. G. Hollett & Sons Antiquarian Booksellers   170 - 45   2011   £40

Asquith, Cynthia   *This Mortal Coil.*   Sauk City: Arkham House, 1947,   First edition; octavo, cloth.   L. W. Currey, Inc.   124 - 47   2011 $1500

Astell, Mary   *Some Reflections Upon Marriage.*   Printed for William Parker, 1730,   Fourth edition; Complete with prelim and terminal ad leaves, pages (viii), 180, (4), 8vo., contemporary sheep, gilt roll tooled borders on sides, unlettered spine with gilt rules on either side of raised bands, joints cracked, bookplate inside front cover of Sir John Cope, good.   Blackwell Rare Books   B166 - 5   2011   £350

Aster, Jane, Pseud.   *The Habits of Good Society: a Handbook of Etiquette for Ladies and Gentlemen.*   London: James Hogg & Sons, n.d., 1859,   First edition; original decorated and stamped cloth gilt, trifle damped and neatly recased, pages 378, 6, woodcut frontispiece, few leaves trifle stained.   R. F. G. Hollett & Son Antiquarian Booksellers   175 - 58   2011   £45

Asterius, Saint   *Homiliae Graece & Latine Nunc Primum Editae Philppo Rubernio Interprete...*   Antwerp: in off. Plantiniana, widoe & sons of J. Moretus, 1615,   4to., (12), 284, (4) pages, engraved device on titlepage, last leaf with woodcut device on recto, engraved portrait by Galle after Rubens, contemporary limp vellum, lower cover slightly damaged, very fine, from the library of the Earls of Macclesfield at Shirburn Castle.   Maggs Bros. Ltd.   1440 - 10   2011   £1200

Aston, Mick   *Landscape Archaeology.*   London: David & Charles, 1974,   First edition; original cloth, gilt, dust jacket, pages 217 with 19 plates and 51 maps and plans top edges little dusty.   R. F. G. Hollett & Son Antiquarian Booksellers   177 - 54   2011   £35

The Astrologer's Magazine and Philosophical Miscellany. London: W. Ocke, 1794, Volume 3, contemporary half sprinkled calf with marbled boards, edges and corners worn, boards rather rubbed, remains of paper label on spine, pages 250, (ii), etched general title and numerous diagrams of bands.   R. F. G. Hollett & Son Antiquarian Booksellers General Catalogue Summer 2010 - 1154   2011   £850

Athanasius, Alexandrini Archiepiscopi   *Omnia Quae Extant Opera.*   Parisiis: Apud Michaelem Sonnium, 1581, Folio, pages (xii), 699 (lxxxvii), contemporary blind tooled pigskin, spine simply ruled, boards panelled with a stylised wheatsheaf roll and two sizes of medallion rolls, paper title label in MS ink at head of spine, inner chamber of boards blind ruled, pink and white sewn endbands, original brass staples but modern clasps, toned bit of spotting, boards marked and bit rubbed at edges, spine darkened, ink inscription "Collegii Caroli iv Paerum No. 17" and lower down "Collegii Soctii Jesu Pragae and S. Clementen Bibliothecae Minoris", from the collection of Christopher Ernest Weston 1947-2010.   Unsworths Booksellers   24 - 1   2011   £750

Athenaeus   *The Deipnosophists or Banquet of the Learned of Athenaeus.*   London: Henry G. Bohn, 1854, First edition translated by Yonge; 3 volumes, 8vo., pages 1252, very good in original publisher's dark blue cloth, inner front hinge of first volume, slightly cracked, else very good+, slightly bumped at corners.   Any Amount of Books   May 29 2011 - A47124   2011 $221

Atherstone, Edwin   *A Midsummer Day's Dream.*   London: printed for Baldwin, Cradock and Joy, 1824, Engraved frontispiece, 2 other plates, edges untrimmed, pages lightly toned and spotted, title washed and bound before frontispiece and half title, tape mark at gutter and some dust soiling, errata slip torn away, pages (ii), 173, (1), 8vo., modern quarter mid brown calf, marbled (old) paper board with long edges, covered in vellum, backstrip with five raised bands, between single gilt rules, red morocco label in second compartment, rest with small central gilt clover stamp, label an tail of spine just bit chipped, good.   Blackwell Rare Books B166 - 6   2011   £100

Atkin, George Duckworth   *House Scraps.*   London: published by the author at the Stock Exchange, 1887, Only edition, printed "for private circulation only", apparently limited to 200 copies; 8vo., vi, 183, (1) pages, 5 plates, numerous text illustrations, original maroon cloth lettered in gilt, very good.   John Drury Rare Books   153 - 5   2011   £50

Atkinson, Dwight   *Scientific Discourse in Sociohistorical Context: The Philosophical Transactions of the Royal Society of London 1675-1975.*   Mahwah and London: Lawrence Erlbaum, 1999, First printing; 8vo., xxxi, 208 pages, figures, pictorial boards, fine, from the Bern Dibner reference library, with Burndy bookplate.   Jeff Weber Rare Books   161 - 18   2011 $75

Atkinson, George   *The Worthies of Westmorland; or Notable Persons Born in the County Since the Reformation.*   London: J. Robinson, 1849, First edition; 2 volumes, original blindstamped red cloth, gilt, few marks to boards, pages 320; 360, steel engraved frontispiece (little spotted), joints tender, very good set, volume 2 inscribed By William Fell to Bernard Gilpin, Belle Vue House Ulverstone.   R. F. G. Hollett & Son Antiquarian Booksellers   173 - 36   2011   £140

Atkinson, H.   *Exercises in the Yokohama Dialect.*   Yokohama: printed at the Japan Gazette Office No. 10 Water Street, 1915, 22 thousandth; (16), 33, (1) pages, original printed wrappers loose and rather chipped, text clean.   Anthony W. Laywood   May 26 2011 - 21738   2011 $252

Atkinson, J. C.   *British Birds' Eggs & Nests.*   London: George Routledge & Sons, n.., 1861, First edition; original decorated blue cloth gilt over bevelled boards, pages viii, 182, (ii), 12 color plates.   R. F. G. Hollett & Son Antiquarian Booksellers   General Catalogue Summer 2010 - 945   2011   £45

Atkinson, J. C.   *Forty Years in Moorland Parish.*   Macmillan and Co., 1892, Original green cloth, gilt, few slight string marks to edges, pages xv, (i), 472, (ii), with 3 illustrations and 2 maps.   R. F. G. Hollett & Son Antiquarian Booksellers   General Catalogue Summer 2010 - 1317   2011   £35

Atkinson, J. C.   *Memorials of Old Whitby or Historical Gleanigns from Ancient Whitby Records.*   London: Macmillan & Co., 1894, First edition; original green cloth, gilt, pages xix, 332, 22 illustrations, very nice, clean and bright.   R. F. G. Hollett & Son Antiquarian Booksellers General Catalogue Summer 2010 - 1318   2011   £85

Atkinson, M. E.   *Challenge to Adventure.*   London: John Lane The Bodley Head, 1943, First reprint; original cloth, dust jacket, edges little worn, few closed tears, pages 288, illustrations by Stuart Tresilian.   R. F. G. Hollett & Son Antiquarian Booksellers   General Catalogue Summer 2010 - 487   2011   £30

Atkinson, Thomas Dunham   *Local Style in English Architecture.*   London: Batsford, 1947, First edition; pages viii, 183, color frontispiece and 126 illustrations, fore-edge lightly spotted, original cloth, dust jacket little rubbed and spotted on reverse.   R. F. G. Hollett & Son Antiquarian Booksellers   177 - 57   2011   £30

Atlantic Monthly 1872.   Jan. to Dec., 1872, Complete, lovely set in nearly fine condition.   Lupack Rare Books May 26 2011 - ABE273695516   2011 $250

Attali, Marc *Les Erotiques du Regard.* Paris: Andre Balland, 1968, First edition; folio, pages (112), 64 black and white photos, original black and white photo illustrated paper covered boards, tinted pink, text and spine printed in black, rubbing to tips and to head and foot of spine, short closed tear to lower panel at foot of spine, horizontal crease towards foot of spine, near fine, from the library of Alessandro Bertolotti.   Simon Finch Rare Books   Zero - 503   2011   £900

Attenborough, David *Zoo Quest in Paraguay.* Lutterworth Press, 1959, First edition; original cloth, gilt, dust jacket, pages 168, with 42 plates.   R. F. G. Hollett & Son Antiquarian Booksellers   General Catalogue Summer 2010 - 946   2011   £30

Atterbury, Francis *The Epistolary Correspondence, Visitation Charges, Speeches and Miscellanies of the Right Reverend Francis Atterbury, D.D., Lord Bishop of Rochester, with Historical Notes.* London: printed by J. Nichols, 1783, First edition; 3 volumes, full light brown leather with darker brown leather spine labels lettered gilt with 5 raised bands, pages xvi, 384; v, 456; xxii, 552, 3 volumes, slight rubbing and scuffing but sound, very good, sound set.   Any Amount of Books   May 29 2011 - A48875   2011 $272

Atterbury, Francis *The Rights, Powers and Priviledges, of an English Convocation, Stated and Vindicated in Answer to a Late Book of Dr. Wake's entitled The Authority of Christian Princes Over Their Ecclesiastical Synods Asserted...* London: printed for Th. Bennet, 1700, First edition; modern quarter morocco, gilt, pages (xxx), 516, folding plate, title within double ruled border, pagination of pages 273-294 in brackets, rare.   R. F. G. Hollett & Son Antiquarian Booksellers   175 - 60   2011   £450

Attersoll, E. *The Curate of Mersden; or Pastoral Conversations Between a Minister and His Parishioners.* London: SPCK, 1839, Large 12mo., bound in 6's, original cloth gilt, pages 83, engraved frontispiece and head and tail-pieces.   R. F. G. Hollett & Son Antiquarian Booksellers   175 - 61   2011   £45

Atton, Henry *The King's Customs. An Account of Maritime Revenue & Contraband Traffic in England, Scotland and Ireland from the Earliest Times to the year 1800.* London: John Murray, 1908, First edition; original red cloth, spine trifle faded and frayed at head, pages xii, 489, 4 plates, some foxing.   R. F. G. Hollett & Son Antiquarian Booksellers   175 - 62   2011   £35

Attwell, Sydney G. *Drifting to Destruction.* London: Henry Walker, 1927, First edition; 280 pages, 6 pages publisher's ads at rear, fine in very good dust jacket slightly darkened at spine and nicked and creased at edges, tail of spine of dust jacket the publisher is given as "Ouseley" which suggests that Walker sold the book, scarce.   Peter Ellis   May 26 2011 - ATTWELL2011213   2011 $125

Atwood, Margaret *Alias Grace.* Toronto: McClelland & Stewart, 1996, First Canadian edition; fine in fine dust jacket, signed by author.   Bella Luna Books   May 29 2011 - t9551   2011 $82

Atwood, Margaret *The Blind Assassin.* London: Bloomsbury, 2000, First British edition; fine in fine dust jacket, signed by author.   Bella Luna Books   May 29 2011 - t1567s   2011 $110

Atwood, Margaret *Dancing Girls & Other Stories.* Toronto: McClelland & Stewart, 1977, First Canadian edition; fine in near fine dust jacket, creasing to spine,.   Bella Luna Books   May 29 2011 - 4043s   2011 $82

Atwood, Margaret *The Journals of Susanna Moodie.* Boston: Houghton Mifflin, 1997, First American edition; small 4to., pages xxiii, remainder of pages, consisting of Pachter's serigraphs in color and Atwoods poetry, not numbered, white paper over boards, blue cloth spine, stamped in copper and black, fine copy, little worn paper slipcase.   Second Life Books Inc.   174 - 19   2011 $75

Atwood, Margaret *Oryx and Crake.* Bloomsbury: 2003, First edition; 381 pages, original patterned boards, dust jacket.   R. F. G. Hollett & Son Antiquarian Booksellers   General Catalogue Summer 2010 - 697   2011   £30

Aubrey, Antoine *L'Histoire du Cardinal Du de Richeliev par le Sievr Avbery advocat av parlement...* Paris: Antoine Bertier, 1660, First edition; large 4to., (20), 628, (26) pages, engraved frontispiece, red and black titlepage with large printer's device, contemporary full brown mottled calf, raised bands, gilt stamped spine panels and title, front hinge beginning to split, cords holding firm, extremities scratched, corners showing, contemporary ink ownership marks on titlepage, very good.   Jeff Weber Rare Books   163 - 18   2011 $800

Aubrey, John *Miscellanies, Viz. i. Day-Fatality. ii. Local Fatality. iii. Ostenta. iv. Omens. v. Dreams. vi. Apparitions. vii. Voices. viii. Impulses. ix. Knockings. x. Blows Invisible. xi, Prophecies. xii. Marvels. xiii. Magick. xiv. Transportation in the Air.* London: Edward Castle, 1696, First edition; 8vo., pages (vi), 179, (1) blank, 4 illustrations in text, exceedingly crisp and clean with only very few spots of soiling confined to outer margin, contemporary calf, repaired, filleted with blind tooled devices to corners of upper and lower boards, spine with raised bands, outlined in gilt, red morocco lettering piece with gilt lettering, bookplate and small ownership label to front pastedown.   Simon Finch Rare Books   Zero - 111   2011   £1750

Aucassin et Nicolete *The Son Story of Aucassin and Nicolete.* New Rochelle: Elston Press, 1902, One of 240 copies; 165 x 125mm., 2 p.l., 66, (3) pages, original publisher's quarter linen, gray paper boards, paper spine abel with vertical titling, fore and tail edges untrimmed, introductory facing pages filled with decoration in white vine style by Helen Marguerite O'Kane, text in red and black, penned signature date 1934, 2 very small dark ink(?) spots on rear board, otherwise virtually pristine, text in mint condition. Phillip J. Pirages   59 - 188 2011 $250

Auch, Lord *Historie De L'Oeil. Nouvelle Version avec six Gravures Originales a l'Eua Forte et au Burin.* Seville: 1940, Paris: Gheerbrant, 1947. Second edition, no. EC 16, one of 10 on velin per fil Johannot, from a total edition of 199; large 8 vo., pages (ii) blank,134, (1) limitation, (7) blank, 6 erotic etchings signed in pencil by the artist, Hans Bellmer, half deep green morocco, marbled boards, top and bottom edges gilt, fore edge untrimmed, original white wrappers bound in, spine and upper side with title printed in red, fine.   Simon Finch Rare Books   Zero - 443 2011   £5750

Auckland, William Eden, 1st Baron 1744-1814 *The Substance of a Speech Made in the House of Peers on Tuesday 8th Jan. 1799...* London: printed for J. Wright, 1799, New (probably second) edition; modern half calf gilt, pages 36, (iv appendix), half title and final page rather soiled and little repaired in margins, library stamp to verso of title, scarce.   R. F. G. Hollett & Son Antiquarian Booksellers 175 - 63 2011   £250

Auden, Wystan Hugh 1907-1973 *Mountains.* London: Faber, 1954, First edition; original wrappers, printed envelope (two edges little faded), pages (4), with colored lithograph and 2 drawings by Bawden.   R. F. G. Hollett & Son Antiquarian Booksellers   General Catalogue Summer 2010 - 707 2011   £45

Audubon, John James 1785-1851 *The Birds of America.* New York: 1937, First edition; small folio, (i-iv) v-x (xi, xii, 500, (2) xiii-xxvi pages, title faded from backstrip, discolored backstrip, cover gilt rubbed, very mild cover wear, endpapers foxed, color onplates brilliant.   Bookworm & Silverfish   671 - 15 2011 $75

Audubon, John James 1785-1851 *Ornithological Biography or an Account of the Habits of the Birds of the United States of America...* Edinburgh: Neill & Co. for Adam Black, 1831-1849, (i.e. 1831-1839). First edition; approximately 140 wood engravings, tall octavo, pages iii-xxiv, 512; iii-xxxii, 588; iii-xvi,638; iii-xxviii, 618; iii-xxxix, 664, contemporary three quarter morocco over marbled boards, 5 raised bands, gilt decorated panels to spines, 3 volumes professionally rebacked, while retaining original spines, piece missing from head of 2 spines skillfully replaced with leather, closed tear to heel of spine, rubbing to edges of 2 spines of 2 volumes, spines have changed color to oxblood brown, half titles missing, tape residue from removal of a letter to gutter of first title, overall nice set, endpapers marbled, top edge gilt.   Raymond M. Sutton, Jr.   May 26 2011 - 54276 2011 $8500

Audubon, John Woodhouse *The Drawings of John Woodhouse Audubon Illustrating His Adventures through Mexico and California 1849-1850.* San Francisco: 1957, (14 pages plus 34 plates with facing text), prospectus laid in, small folio, half cloth and paper covered boards, slight shelfwear nick from corner of spine title label, else near fine. Dumont Maps & Books of the West   113 - 25 2011 $250

Augustinius, Aurelius, Saint, Bp. of Hippo *De Civitate Dei.* Venice: Nicolaus Jenson, 1475, Chancery folio, 302 (of 306) leaves (lacks four blanks), 19th century full calf, rebacked with spine laid down.   Heritage Book Shop Booth A12 51st NY International Antiquarian Book Fair April 8-10 2011 - 4 2011 $25,000

Aulnoy, Marie Catherine Lejmel De Barneville, Comtesse D' *Histoire d'Hypolite, Comte de Douglas.* A La Haie: Chez Jean Swart, R. Christ, Alberts, 1726, Reprint, first issued in 1690; small 8vo., 2 parts in one, pages (6), 138; (139)-318, 22 copperplates, one a frontispiece (signed "D. Coster), other plates unsigned, titlepage of part one printed in red and black, contemporary calf with morocco label, some minor external rubbing, very good, scarce.   Second Life Books Inc.   174 - 20 2011 $600

Aunt Louisa's Birthday Gift Book. London: Frederick Warne and co. n.d. circa, 1869, Large square 8vo., original pictorial and decorated brown cloth gilt, little stained and faded, extremities slightly worn, neatly recased, unpaginated, 23 (ex 24) full page colored plates, almost certainly by Kronheim, with accompanying text.   R. F. G. Hollett & Sons Antiquarian Booksellers   170 - 715 2011   £180

Aunt Louisa's Fairy Legends. New York: McLoughlin Bros. n.d., inscribed, 1875, 4to., brown cloth stamped in black and gold, pictorial paste on, slight fading on rear cover, else near fine, 24 very fine full page chromolithographs.   Aleph-Bet Books, Inc.   95 - 229 2011 $500

Aunt Louisa's National Album Comprising Jack and Jill, Punch and Judy, My Children and The Faithful Friend. London: Frederick Warne and Co., circa, 1880, 4to., green cloth, black and gold lettering and illustration on embossed covers, edges with some light rubbing, 24 pages of color illustrations printed in colors by Kronheim.   Jo Ann Reisler, Ltd.   86 - 244   2011 $400

Aunt Lousia's Nursery Favourite.   London: Warne, n.d., owner inscribed, 1877, 4to., green gilt pictorial cloth, light shelf wear, else fine and clean, near fine, 24 full page chromolithographs, beautiful illustrations printed by Kronheim on one side of the paper, scarce in such nice condition.   Aleph-Bet Books, Inc.   95 - 56   2011 $450

Aurelius Victor, Sextus   *Historiae Romanae Breviarium... (bound with) De Vita et Moribus Imperatorum Romanorum Excerpta ex Libris Sexti Aurelii Victoris.*   Utrecht: Apud Franciscum Halmam, Guilielmum van de Water, 1696, Variorum edition; additional engraved title, printed title in red and black, engravings of coins in text, some browning and spotting, upper inside corner dampmarked, pages (xliv), 434, (74), 8vo; second work lacking one leaf (F7), numerous engraved coin portraits in text, some spotting, pages 96, 99-168, (28), 8vo., old vellum, backstrip with red morocco label (little worn at edges), somewhat soiled, good.   Blackwell Rare Books   B166 - 7   2011   £125

Australian Poetry.   Australia: 1942-1970, First edition; 1942-1948, 1951-1952, 1954, 1955, 1956, 1958, 1961-1963, 1965-1968, 1970, 20 volumes, all save one with dust jackets, all very good, 1955 presentation copy inscribed by V. Vallis, one of the contributors.   I. D. Edrich   May 26 2011 - 84608   2011 $419

Austen, Jane   1775-1817   *Emma: a Novel.*   London: printed for John Murray, 1816, First edition; 3 volumes, 12mo., bound without half titles, contemporary half black polished calf over marbled boards.   Heritage Book Shop Booth A12 51st NY International Antiquarian Book Fair April 8-10 2011 - 5   2011 $25,000

Austen, Jane   1775-1817   *Northanger Abbey.*   London: J. M. Dent, 1907, First edition thus; pages x, 207, original green cloth gilt, spine and upper board decorated in gilt overall, top edges gilt, untrimmed, with 24 color plates by C. E. Brock, flyleaves lightly browned.   R. F. G. Hollett & Son Antiquarian Booksellers   General Catalogue Summer 2010 - 734   2011   £35

Austen, Jane   1775-1817   *The Novels of Jane Austen.*   Edinburgh: John Grant, 1911, Winhester edition; Half titles, frontispiece volume I, untrimmed in original blue cloth, spines blocked and lettered in gilt, top edge gilt, very good, bright.   Jarndyce Antiquarian Booksellers   CXCI - 1   2011   £1200

Austen, Jane   1775-1817   *Persuasion & Northanger Abbey.*   London: Richard Bentley, 1833, First One volume edition and first illustrated edition; 12mo., 2 works bound in one volume, continuous pagination, engraved frontispiece, separate titlepage for each novel, engraved titlepage, 19th century half calf, marbled boards, (gilt) raised bands, little scattered foxing and slight wear, however handsome copy with essentially clean, tight text.   Lupack Rare Books   May 26 2011 - ABE488908796   2011 $1750

Austen, Jane   1775-1817   *Pride and Prejudice.*   London: printed for T. Egerton, Military Library, Whitehall, 1813, First edition, following all points in Gilson and Keynes and complete with all half titles present; 12mo., 3 volumes, (iv), 307, (1, blank); (iv), 239, (1, blank); (v), (323), (1, blank) pages, contemporary speckled calf, blind tooled board edges, edges sprinkled red, original light brown endpapers, expertly rebacked with original spines laid down, later green morocco gilt lettering labels on spines, gilt stamped "Charleton" to upper boards of each volume (possibly that of Charleton House, Montrose), from the library of German artist and music historian Frida Best (1876-1964) with her bookplate in each volume, edges to few leaves professionally and near invisibly repaired, occasional light foxing, excellent and complete copy in original and contemporary binding, housed in modern half red morocco clamshell case with 3 individual spines decoratively lettered and tooled in gilt, Regency binders typically removed half titles, those with half titles rare.   David Brass Rare Books, Inc.   May 26 2011 - 01651   2011 $75,000

Auster, Paul   *Living Hand 1-8.*   V.P.: Living Hand, 1973-1976, First edition; 8 chapbooks in printed color wrappers, from the library of poet Ray di Palma with two books inscribed to him, uncommon to fine complete set, occasional sunning to spines, about fine.   Charles Agvent 2010 Summer Miscellany - 2   2011 $1500

Austin, Alfred   *The Season: a Satire.*   London: Robert Hardwicke, 1861, Half title, color frontispiece by Thomas George Cooper, text slightly spotted, few pages little roughly opened, original purple cloth lettered gilt on front board, spine faded, little rubbed.   Jarndyce Antiquarian Booksellers   CXCI - 55   2011   £55

Austin, Alfred   *The Season: a Satire.*   London: John Camden Hotten, 1869, New edition, being the third; half title, final ad leaf + 4 pages ads, original brown cloth bevelled boards, lettered gilt, slightly dulled, all edges gilt.   Jarndyce Antiquarian Booksellers   CXCI - 56   2011   £35

Austin, William *A Specimen of Sketching Landscapes in a Free and Masterly Manner with a Pen or Pencil; Exemplified in thirty Etchings done from original drawings of Lucatelli after the Life in and about Rome.* by the author in George Street, Hanover Square..., 1781, 4 pages, 30 etchings, some signed Austin F (or Fecit) Lucatelli, inscribed by Frederick Finden for Catherine Ward, very good, contemporary half calf with red morocco label, dark blue glazed paper boards which are rubbed and marked, marginal stain to one plate but clear of image and little old and faint waterstaining the inner lower corner, again not affecting images. Ken Spelman Rare Books   68 - 13 2011   £2200

An Australian Colony The Government Handbook of Victoria. Melbourne: Government printer, 1898, 8vo., 202 pages plus 2 large foldout maps, blue cloth, ex-library binding from Lambeth Library stamps on most photo pages and one map, good.   Barnaby Rudge Booksellers Travel and Exploration - 017240 2011 $90

An Authentic Candid and Circumstantial Narrative, of the Astonishing Transactions at Stockwell, in the County of Surry on Monday and Tuesday the 6th, 7th Days of January 1772... London: W. Bailey, 1772, First edition, variant issue; 8vo., (3)-23, (1) pages, wanting half title, recently well bound in linen backed marbled board lettered, very good, rare.   John Drury Rare Books   154 - 10 2011   £600

An Authentic Narrative of the Events of the Westminster Election Which Commenced on Saturday, February 13th and Closed on Wednesday March 3rd 1819... London: R. Stodart, 1819, First edition; 8vo., engraved portrait frontispiece (torn and repaired - no loss), vii, (1), 412 pages, early to mid 19th century half cloth over marbled boards, spine simply lettered in gilt, slightly worn at head and foot, good copy from the library of Michael Foot, the British labour Party politician with his ownership signature.   John Drury Rare Books 154 - 11 2011   £250

The Automobile Handbook. London: Automobile Club, 1904, First edition; 8vo., original publisher's burgundy cloth lettered gilt on spine and on front cover, pages viii, 2888, xciv, good contemporary ads at prelims and rear, sound near very good with some rubbing, scuffing and slight marks to covers.   Any Amount of Books   May 29 2011 - A43854 2011 $230

Avedon, Richard *An Autobiography.* New York: Random House, 1993, First edition; 284 photos, fine in very near fine printed acetate dust jacket, signed and dated by Avedon on front free endpaper in year of publication.   Jeff Hirsch Books   ny 2010 2011 $500

Adventures of Little Man Chester or Recollections of the Royal Jubilee Exhibition. Manchester: Abel Heywood, 1887, Square 4to., pictorial wrappers, fine, 8 fabulous full page color illustrations and brown line, scarce.   Aleph-Bet Books, Inc. 95 - 430   2011 $600

Averill, Esther *The Cat Club or the Life and Times of Jenny Linksy.* New York: Harper & Bros., 1944, First edition; 12mo., red cloth with yellow lettering and vignette on front cover, color pictorial dust jacket, clean copy with maybe minor dusting to the wrapper, 32 numbered pages which have two color illustrations and drawings.   Jo Ann Reisler, Ltd. 86 - 36 2011 $400

Avery, Gillian *Nineteenth Century Children.* London: Hodder and Stoughton, 1965, First edition; original cloth, gilt, dust jacket, pages 260, 16 pages of plates, uncommon.   R. F. G. Hollett & Sons Antiquarian Booksellers   170 - 52 2011   £35

Avery, Harold *Play the Game!* London: Thomas Nelson & Sons, 1906, First edition; frontispiece and plates, final ad leaf, original brown pictorial cloth, bright and attractive. Jarndyce Antiquarian Booksellers   CXCI - 57 2011   £50

Avery, Harold *Through the Wood.* Thomas Nelson and Sons, n.d., 1907, Pages 50, title in green and black, 24 full page color plates printed throughout on coated paper, very good, clean, sound copy.   R. F. G. Hollett & Sons Antiquarian Booksellers   170 - 315 2011   £45

Awdry, W. *Four Little Engines.* London: Edmund Ward, 1955, First edition; Oblong 16mo., black cloth, 62 numbered pages, fine in slightly edge frayed dust jacket, charming full page color illustration.   Aleph-Bet Books, Inc. 95 - 59 2011 $150

Axelson, G. W. *Commy. The Life Story of Charles A. Comiskey.* Chicago: Reilly, 1919, First edition; mild soil edges and endpapers, very good++ in very good dust jacket with chips, 8vo., 320 pages.   By the Book, L. C. 26 - 72 2011 $425

Axtius, Johann Conrad *Tractatus de Arboribus Coniferis et Pice Conficienda.* Jena: Samuel Krebs for Joann Bielcken, 1679, 16mo., engraved titlepage and 5 plates, 16mo., pages (2), 131, contemporary full mottled calf, corners worn, covers scuffed, some losses to spine, institutional handstamp on a blank, old notations on blanks, occasional foxing, ownership signature of Jean Estienne Guettard, geologist.   Raymond M. Sutton, Jr. May 26 2011 - 28947 2011 $2000

Ayer, A. J. *Part of My Life.* London: Collins, 1977, First edition; 8vo., pages 318, illustrations, signed presentation by author to Lady Caroline Gilmour, very good+, price clipped, very good dust jacket with slight edgewear.   Any Amount of Books   May 29 2011 - A74370 2011 $298

Aylmer, G. E. *A History of York Minster.* Oxford: Clarendon Press, 1977, First edition; small 4to., original cloth, gilt, dust jacket, pages xv, 586, color frontispiece, 182 illustrations and 6 plans.   R. F. G. Hollett & Son Antiquarian Booksellers   177 - 59 2011   £50

Ayre, L. R. *The North Lonsdale Magazine and Furness Miscellany.* Ulverston: W. Holmes, 1894-1902, 4 volumes, 4to., original crimson cloth gilt extra over bevelled boards, spines faded, extremities little worn, illustrations, 3 color frontispieces, very good, sound and clean set, scarce. R. F. G. Hollett & Son Antiquarian Booksellers 173 - 39 2011 £450

Ayton, Emily *Words by the Way-Side; or The Children and the Flowers.* London: Grant and Griffith, Successors to Newbery and Harris, 1855, First edition; 8vo., ii, 159, 16 page publisher's catalog, red blindstamped board, large pictorial gilt title vignette on upper cover signed JL (John Leighton), repeated gilt title along spine, gilt edges, yellow endpapers, two inked and dated inscriptions, 4 very fine full page hand colored engravings, all printed on heavier handmade paper and on one side of the leaf only, small personal engraved label inside upper cover, chipping along spine with missing portion of crown of spine, else fine. Hobbyhorse Books 56 - 3 2011 $170

Aytoun, William Edmonstoun *The Book of Ballads.* William Blackwood Sons, 1903, New edition; illustrations, original blue cloth, gilt, bevelled boards, all edges gilt, fine, presentation inscription to W. G. (Wilhelm) Max Muller Xmas 1903, signed G.M.M. (Georgina Max Muller, 1853-1911, wife of Freidrich Max Muller 1832-1907, to her son). Jarndyce Antiquarian Booksellers CXCI - 318 2011 £50

Azara, Felix De *Essais sur l'Histoire Naturelle des Quadrupedes de la Province du Paraguay...* Paris: Charles Pougens, 1801, First French edition; 8vo., pages lxxx, 366; 2 (5-) 499, contemporary calf backed boards (missing half titles, corners worn, 1 bumped, spines scuffed, a 1 1/2 inch split to front edge of spine, calf on ends of spine perished, small, old sticker on heel of spines, ink number on front flyleaf and blank, small handstamp on titles, scattered tanning and light foxing to text, sometimes heavier in volume 2, short marginal tear to 2 leaves, with gilt lettering and gilt decorations on spines, marbled page edge, rare, the copy of Raul Vaz-Ferreira with his handstamp. Raymond M. Sutton, Jr. May 26 2011 - 45608 2011 $2000

B

Babbage, Charles 1792-1871 *The Works of Charles Babbage.* New York: New York University Press, 1989, 11 volumes, 8vo., 456, 223, 253, 217, 192, 129, 133, 280, 118, 173, 425 pages, blue cloth, gilt stamped spine titles, fine, from the Bern Dibner reference library, with Burndy bookplate.   Jeff Weber Rare Books   161 - 20 2011 $700

Babbage, Charles 1792-1871 *Science and Reform: Selected Works of Charles Babbage Chosen with Introduction and Discussion by Anthony Hyman.* Cambridge et al: Cambridge University Press, 1989, First edition; tall 8vo., vii 336 pages, 18 plates, figures, index, dark blue cloth, gilt stamped spine title, dust jacket, fine, scarce, from the Bern Dibner reference library, with Burndy bookplate.   Jeff Weber Rare Books   161 - 21 2011 $100

Babbington, Charles *Tuning and Repairing Pianofortes.* London: L. Upcott Gill, 1896, Original pictorial wrappers printed in black, back cover ad, very good, 16 page catalog (coded 6-69).   Jarndyce Antiquarian Booksellers   CXCI - 359 2011   £60

The Baby Bears-Little Boy Blue and Little Bo-Peep Fairy Story no. 4. Chicago: John Puhl Products, circa, 1905, 6 x 3 1/2 inches, full color pictorial covers with light dusting to rear cover, four panel panorama that offers full color illustrated story.   Jo Ann Reisler, Ltd.   86 - 21 2011 $150

Babington, Churchill *An Introductory Lecture on Archaeology Delivered Before the University of Cambridge.* Cambridge: Deighton Bell and Co., 1865, First edition; original cloth, gilt, spine chipped at head and tail, pages (iv), 80, 8, presentation copy inscribed to W. A. Wright.   R. F. G. Hollett & Son Antiquarian Booksellers   177 - 60 2011   £65

Babington, Gervase *The Workes.* London: printed by G. Eld and F. Flesher, 1622, reissue of 1615 first edition; folio, contemporary full panelled calf with spine label, little worn, pages (xii), 428, 311, lacks half title, portrait and table, titlepage defective and laid down, some one third of text replaced in mss., few leaves at beginning and end creased and little soiled and edge worn, small piece torn from one fore-edge without loss of text.   R. F. G. Hollett & Son Antiquarian Booksellers   175 - 66 2011   £250

Babson, Roger W. *The Future of the Nations: How Prosperity Must Come: Economic Facts for Workers and Preachers.* Boston: Babson's Statistical Organization, 1914, Second edition; very good, boards lightly edge worn, owner's name and stamp, otherwise very clean and tight, 120 pages, foldout graph, inscribed and signed by author.   G. H. Mott Bookseller   May 26 2011 - 43068 2011 $450

Bacheldor, John *A. D. 2050. Electrical Development of Atlantis.* San Francisco: Bancroft Co., 1890, First edition; 8vo., vi (3)-83 (1) pages, including half title, errata slip pasted on to (blank) fooft of page vi, some general paper browning, original maroon cloth boards, lettered gilt on spine and upepr cover, good.   John Drury Rare Books   154 - 13 2011   £275

The Bachelors & Spinsters. Washington: 1956, 1957. 1958. 1961; Wrappers.   Bookworm & Silverfish   667 - 152 2011 $150

Backhouse, James *Upper Teesdale, Past and Present.* London: Simpkin, Marshall etc. and Barnard Castle; w. R. Atkinson, 1896, First edition; original pictorial boards, little soiled and worn, hinges cracked, pages (iv), 87, (ii), 8 plates and map, flyleaves browned or spotted, upper joint cracked, signature of E. Russell Walton of Cotherstone on half title.   R. F. G. Hollett & Son Antiquarian Booksellers   General Catalogue Summer 2010 - 1320 2011   £35

Bacon, Francis, Viscount St. Albans 1561-1626 *Apophthegmes New and Old...* London: printed for Hanna Barret and Richard Whittaker, 1625, First edition; 16mo., pages (ii), 307, 19th century straight grained morocco, stamped in blind and gilt, all edges gilt, custom clamshell box (little rubbed), later MSS. poem on front blank, nice, clean copy.   Second Life Books Inc.   174 - 21 2011 $3500

Bacon, Francis, Viscount St. Albans 1561-1626 *Essayes or Counsels, Civill and Morall.* London: printed by John Haviland for Hanna Barret and Richard Whitaker, 1625, First complete edition, first issue with titlepage bearing imprint of Barret and Whitaker and the qualifier "Newly enlarged"; small quarto, (xii), 340, (2, blank) pages, complete with both first and final blank, text within printed borders, woodcut initials, full light brown morocco by Riviere, covers with triple gilt fillet borders, densely gilt spine compartments, gilt spine lettering, gilt board edges and dentelles, all edges gilt, leaves O-O3 with light dampstain on lower outer corner, very small wormhole through outer upper corners of leaves Nn-Tt, in slipcase, overall, excellent copy, very clean and complete.   Heritage Book Shop   Holiday 2010 - 6 2011 $5500

Bacon, Francis, Viscount St. Albans   1561-1626   *The Historie of Life and Death.*   printed for I. Okes, for Humphrey Mosley at the Princes Armes in Pauls Church Yard, 1638, (1637). First (Unauthorized) translation into English; engraved additional titlepage with faint ink library stamps (small penned note at head), letterpress title within ornamental border, ink ownership inscription verso of engraved title, ink name verso of title, woodcut headpieces and initials, text printed within single line border, sporadic contemporary ink marginalia, pages (14), 323, (1), 12mo., original brown speckled calf, rebacked in paler calf backstrip divided into five compartments by low raised bands between blind rules, gilt lettered morocco label in second, rest with blindstamped device at centres, gilt dated at foot, sides with triple fillet in blind (lightly worn at corner tips) and single gilt fillet on board edges, ink trials on prelim and final leaves, red speckled edges, good, imprimatur leaf dated 30th Sept. 1637.   Blackwell Rare Books   B166 - 8 2011   £650

Bacon, Francis, Viscount St. Albans   1561-1626   *The New Organon.*   Cambridge: Cambridge University Press, 2000, First edition; 8vo., xxxv, 252, (2) pages, pictorial boards, fine, from the Bern Dibner reference library, with Burndy bookplate.   Jeff Weber Rare Books   161 - 22   2011 $85

Bacon, Francis, Viscount St. Albans   1561-1626   *The Twoo Bookes of Francis Bacon.*   London: printed for Henrie Tomes, 1605, First edition; 2 parts in one quarto volume, mid 19th century speckled calf, rebacked to style. Heritage Book Shop   Booth A12 51st NY International Antiquarian Book Fair April 8-10 2011 - 7   2011 $6500

Bacon, Francis, Viscount St. Albans   1561-1626   *The Two Bookes of Francis Bacon. Of the Proficience and Advancement of learning, Divine and Humane.*   London: for Henrie Tomes, 1605, First edition; 4to., (1), 45, 118 (i.e. 121), leaves, lacks final blank 3H2 an, as always, the rare two leaves of errata at end, late 18th century half calf and marbled boards, extremities of boards worn, very skillfully and imperceptively rebacked retaining entire original spine, small worm trail in bottom margin of quires 2D-2F, occasional minor marginalia in an early hand, else lovely, early signature of Row'd Wetherald on title, signature of Horatio Carlyon 1861, Sachs bookplate and modern leather booklabel, calf backed clamshell box.   Joseph J. Felcone Inc.   Fall Miscellany 2010 - 8   2011 $7500

Bacon, Francis, Viscount St. Albans   1561-1626   *Two Essays of Francis Lord Bacon; of Bvildings & Gardens.*   Ashendene Press, 1897, One of 16 copies printed for private circulation (this copy #6); 225 x 170mm., viii, 36 pages, original gray printed paper wrappers, fore-edge and tail edge untrimmed, green linen clamshell case (slightly soiled) with gilt titling on spine, printer's device on final page, pencilled initials on front free endpaper, apparently those of printer Hornby, professional repairs to bottom edges and one fore edge of overlapping wrapper and to two places on covers, front cover with long faint diagonal crease, very fragile original wrapper entirely intact and mostly quite clean, very fine internally with clean, fresh, bright text.   Phillip J. Pirages   59 - 73   2011 $14,000

Bacon, Francis, Viscount St. Albans   1561-1626   *Works of Francis Bacon.*   London: William Pickering, 1825, New edition; 16 volumes, bound in 17, octavo, several volumes with inserted frontispieces and plates, uniformly bound by Brentanos in half brown morocco over brown cloth, spines lettered and stamped in gilt, some scattered foxing, headcaps of few volumes slightly chipped, previous owner's bookplate on front pastedown of each volume, previous owner's old ink inscription on prelim blank of each volume dated 1928, overall very good, handsome copy. Heritage Book Shop   Holiday 2010 - 7   2011 $1500

Bacon, Francis, Viscount St. Albans   1561-1626   *Opera Omnia Quae Extant: Philosophica Moralia, Politica, Historia.*   Francofvrti: ad Moenvm Impensis Joannis Baptistae Schonwetteri, 1664-165, Folio in sixes, (10 pages), 1324 double columns (29) pages, titlepage in red and black with large engraved printers device, 9 additional titlepage, lacks half title with frontispiece, modern full brown calf, raised bands, contemporary gilt stamped red spine label, fine.   Jeff Weber Rare Books   163 - 19   2011 $775

Bacon, Frederick T.   *Bibliography of the Writings of William Somerset Maugham.*   Unicorn Press, 1931, First edition, 628/950 copies (of an edition of 1000); pages (ii), 82, 8vo., , original red cloth, backstrip gilt lettered on faded backstrip, front cover stamped in blind and with press device in gilt, untrimmed, good, inscribed by bibliographer on dedication page to fellow Maugham enthusiast Cecil Field and note to fellow admirer.   Blackwell Rare Books   B166 - 181   2011   £50

Bacon, Roger   *Roger Bacon's Philosophy of Nature.* Oxford: Clarendon Press, 1983, First edition; 8vo., lxxxi, 420 pages, figures, navy cloth, gilt stamped cover and spine titles, fine, from the Bern Dibner reference library, with Burndy bookplate.   Jeff Weber Rare Books   161 - 24   2011 $120

Bacon, Roger *Specula Mathematica in Qua de Specierum Muiltiplicatione Agitur. Liber... editus Opera.* Frankfurt: W. Richter for A. Hummius, 1614, 4to., (8), 83 pages, woodcut figures in text, rebound in half calf, old style, from the library of the Earls of Macclesfield at Shirburn Castle. Maggs Bros. Ltd.   1440 - 18 2011   £1200

Badge, Peter *Nobel Laureates.* Nobelpreistrager: Herausgeber, 2001, Limited to 1000 copies, this #605; folio, 155 pages, fine in fine dust jacket.   By the Book, L. C. 26 - 23 2011 $165

The Badminton Library. London: Longmans, Green and Co., 1891-1898, Early editions; 29 volumes, octavo, standard trade edition, bound in illustrated brown cloth with gilt titles and decoration to spines, patterned endpapers, slight rubbing and occasional tiny splits to heads of spines, overall clean, very good, internally very good, occasional light foxing to some pages, partly unopened, each volume with armorial Woburn Abbey bookplate of Duke of Bedford.   Any Amount of Books May 26 2011 - A76291 2011 $2348

Baedeker, Karl *Palestine and Syria With Routes through Mesopotamia and Babbylonia and the Island of Cyprus.* Leipzig: Karl Baedeker, 1912, Fifth edition; small 8vo., original publisher's limp red cloth, pages clv, 462, all maps, plans and panorama present, clean, sound, very good+ with slight rubbing and faint tanning at head of spine, otherwise hardly used, excellent.   Any Amount of Books   May 29 2011 - A74025 2011 $306

Baer, Karl Ernst Von *Autobiography of Dr. Karl Ernst von Baer.* Canton: Science History Publications, 1986, 8vo., xiv, 389 pages, frontispiece, gray paper boards, black stamped spine title, dust jacket, very good, from the Bern Dibner reference library, with Burndy bookplate.   Jeff Weber Rare Books 161 - 25 2011 $100

Bagehot, Walter *Lombard Street: a Description of the Money Market.* London: Henry S. King & Co., 1873, First edition; 8vo. viii, 359, (1) pages, complete with half title, with occasional unobtrusive emphasis marks in pencil, small old red inkstamp at foot of three leaves of text, well bound recently in blue quarter calf over cloth boards, gilt lines, raised bands and gilt spine label, very good.   John Drury Rare Books 154 - 14 2011   £750

Bagot, Josceline *Colonel James Grahme of Levens.* Kendal: T. Wilson, 1886, First edition; original parchment, few marks, pages 48, with 4 plates, scarce, gift inscriptions. R. F. G. Hollett & Son Antiquarian Booksellers 173 - 42 2011   £95

Baif, Lazare De *Annotationes in L. II. De Captivis, et Postiliminio Reversis in Qvibvs Tractatvr de Re Navali (and three other works).* Paris: Robert Estienne, 1536, First edition of "De re Navali", first printing of this collection; 215 x 150mm., 4 p.l., (1)-168, (8), (1)-203, (13) pages (with pagination anomalies), striking 16th century calf, heavily and beautifully gilt, covers gilt with border formed by two plain rules flanking a floral roll, this frame enclosing a central file of very many tiny star tools, intricate strapwork, cornerpieces and large central arabesque composed of strapwork interspersed with lilies and volutes; flat spine divided into latticed gilt panels by double plain rules and floral bands, newer (17th or 18th century?) black morocco label, binding almost certainly with some restoration (joints probably worked on, though repairs executed with such skill as to make difficult identifying exactly what has been done), old stock used for replacement endpapers, 32 fine woodcuts in text, 11 of them full page or nearly so, woodcut printer's device on title, decorative initials 4 woodcut diagrams, text in Latin and Greek, covers with minor discoloration, little crackling and minor scratching, gilt bit dulled and eroded, one corner somewhat bumped, half dozen leaves with faint dampstains to lower outer corner, hint of soil in isolated places, extremely pleasing copy, binding solid, serious wear, still very attractive, text clean, fresh and bright, margins generous.   Phillip J. Pirages 59 - 5 2011 $7500

Baif, Lazare De *De Re Vestiaria Libellus ex Bayfi Excerptus...* Paris: Ambroise Girault, 1535, 8vo., 68, (10) pages, later vellum, from the library of the Earls of Macclesfield at Shirburn Castle.   Maggs Bros. Ltd. 1440 - 20 2011   £650

Baikie, William Balfour *Narrative of an Exploring Voyage Up the Rivers Kwo Ra and Bi Nue...* London: John Murray, 1856, First edition; 8vo., pages xvi, 456, frontispiece, folding plan, folding map, vignette on titlepage, original purple blindstamped cloth, inner hinge cracked, spine faded, wear to head, corners rubbed, small hole in cloth on upper board (half cm.), internally good.   J. & S. L. Bonham Antiquarian Booksellers Africa 4/20/2011 - 8527 2011   £280

Baikie, William Balfour *Narrative of an Exploring Voyage Up the Rivers Kwo'ra and Bi'nue (Commonly Known as the Niger and Tsadda) in 1854.* London: John Murray, 1856, First edition; octavo, xvi, 456 pages, frontispiece, title vignette, folding plan, folding map, original mauve blindstamped cloth, gilt spine, spine ends chipped, spine faded, inner hinge broken (needs repair), good.   Jeff Weber Rare Books 163 - 126 2011 $400

Bailes, G. M. *Modern Mining Practice.* Sheffield: The Bennett College, n.d., 1907-1908, 5 volumes, small 4to., original cloth, gilt, little worn in places, 872 illustrations, good, sound set.   R. F. G. Hollett & Son Antiquarian Booksellers General Catalogue Summer 2010 - 1079 2011   £75

Bailey, Alice A. *A Treatise on Cosmic Fire.* New York: 1973, Tenth printing; 1367 pages, very good, blue cloth, gold lettering on backstrip and cover. Bookworm & Silverfish 671 - 182 2011 $60

Bailey, Carolyn Sherwin *Lil' Hannibal.* New York: Platt and Munk, 1938, Small 4to., pictorial cloth, fine in repaired dust jacket, illustrations in color and black and white by George Carlson. Aleph-Bet Books, Inc. 95 - 102 2011 $150

Bailey, H. C. *The Red Castle Mystery.* New York: Doubleday, Doran and Co., 1932, First US edition; fine in sharp, bright dust jacket, exceptional copy. Buckingham Books May 26 2011 - 28277 2011 $2000

Bailey, Henry *Travel and Adventures in the Congo Free State and Its Big Game Shooting.* London: Chapman & Hall, 1894, First edition; 8vo., pages xv, 335, map, illustrations, original green cloth, very good. J. & S. L. Bonham Antiquarian Booksellers Africa 4/20/2011 - 9109 2011 £850

Bailey, Nathaniel *An Universal Etymological English Dictionary.* London: Printed for R. Ware, J. & P. Knapton &c., 1749, Thirteenth edition; rebound in half brown reverse calf, red morocco label, signature of Walter Oakeley on titlepage, very good. Jarndyce Antiquarian Booksellers CXCI - 155 2011 £280

Bailey, Nathaniel *An Universal Etymological English Dictionary.* Edinburgh: William Creech, 1776, Twenty-fourth edition; unpaginated, some dampstaining, mainly at beginning and end, few stains and spots, title neatly repaired at top edge, but very good. R. F. G. Hollett & Son Antiquarian Booksellers General Catalogue Summer 2010 - 363 2011 £175

Bailey, Paul *At the Jerusalem.* London: Cape, 1967, First edition; pages 192, foolscap 8vo., original light blue boards, backstrip lettered, owner's name on front pastedown, dust jacket with design by Charles Raymond, very good. Blackwell Rare Books B166 - 123 2011 £30

Bailey, Richard N. *Viking Age Sculpture in Northern England.* London: Collins, 1980, First edition; original cloth, gilt, dust jacket, pages 288, with 78 plates and 5 maps, fine. R. F. G. Hollett & Son Antiquarian Booksellers 173 - 44 2011 £40

Bailey, Samuel *Essays on the Formation and Publication of Opinions, and on other Subjects.* London: R. Hunter, 1826, Second edition; 8vo., xv, (i), 320 pages, contemporary plum calf gilt, sides panelled in gilt and blind, central unidentified armorial impresses, spine faded and bit worn, label renewed, marbled edges, very good. John Drury Rare Books 153 - 7 2011 £200

Bailey, Stephen A. *L. L. Nunn: a Memoir.* Ithaca: Telluride Association, 1933, First edition; 8vo. 180 pages, frontispiece, plates, navy cloth, gilt stamped cover and spine titles, fine, scarce, from the Bern Dibner reference library, with Burndy bookplate. Jeff Weber Rare Books 161 - 26 2011 $100

Bain, William *An Essay on the Variation of the Compass, Showing How far It Is Influence by a Change in the Direction of the Ship's Head, with an Exposition of the Dangers Arising to Navigators from Not Allowing for This Change of Variation. (bound with) Magnetism. (and) A Popular View of Mr. Barlow's Magnetical Experiments and Discoveries... (article from Edinburgh Philosophical Journal Volume XI No. 21 July 1824, pages 65-86).* Edinburgh: printed for William Blackwood and John Murray, 1817, 3 works in 1 volume, 8vo., pages (vi), 140, tables, throughout, folding chart; pages 96, numerous small illustrations; half calf and marbled boards, spine with lettering and decoration in gilt, slightly rubbed, bookplate of Sir Alexander Milne to front pastedown, his signature, occasional pencil annotations throughout, bookplate of Turner Collection, University of Keele. Simon Finch Rare Books Zero - 124 2011 £475

Bainbridge, John *An Astronomicall Description of the Late Comet from the 18 of Novemb. 1618 to 16 of December following.* London: by Edward Griffin for Iohn Parker, 1619, First edition (2nd state of imprint); 4to., (8), 24 "17" (i.e. 25) (26 (blank), 27-42 pages, folding engraved plate, lacking last blank leaf, errata leaf lightly stained, some light browning, few headlines slightly shaved, from the library of the Earls of Macclesfield at Shirburn Castle. Maggs Bros. Ltd. 1440 - 21 2011 £2500

Baines, Edward *A Companion to the Lakes of Cumberland and Westmoreland and Lancashire...* London: Simpkin and Marshall, 1834, Third edition; original pebble grain green cloth, backstrip rather faded and upper hinge trifle frayed, paper spine label (little chipped and darkened), pages 2, viii, 352, steel engraved frontispiece and folding hand colored map, nice, unsophisticated copy. R. F. G. Hollett & Son Antiquarian Booksellers 173 - 45 2011 £180

Baines, Edward *The History of the County Palatine and Duchy of Lancaster.* London: Routledge and Manchester: L. C. Gent, 1868-1870, Large paper deluxe issue; 2 volumes, large 4to., original publisher's deluxe binding of half morocco gilt over heavy bevelled boards, large roundel comprised of multiple shields surrounding a central coat of arms of the Duchy of Lancaster on each upper board, pages xvi, (vi, subscribers), 690, (ii); xii, 729, large folding colored map (lightly foxed to repair to one fold), few text woodcuts, marbled endpapers, magnificent version, scarce. R. F. G. Hollett & Son Antiquarian Booksellers General Catalogue Summer 2010 - 1323 2011 £450

Baines, Thomas 1806-1881 *The Northern Goldfields - Diaries of Thomas Baines 1869-1872.* London: 1946, 3 volumes, tall 8vo., 3 maps, very good in crimson cloth, top edge gilt. Bookworm & Silverfish 669 - 6 2011 $150

Baird, Spencer Fullerton 1823-1887 *The Birds of North America...* New York: D. Appleton, 1860, 2 volumes, 100 hand colored lithographed plates (some soiling to first plate, toning to 3 plates, tan wash to upper margin of a plate, overall quite nice), 4to., pages (4), lvi, 1005, (2), xl, Modern brown cloth, numbers partially erased near lower corner of title to text volume, ink number on title, light foxing to few leaves, many text pages tanned, few browned, perforated institutional handstamp and ink number to title of atlas volume, very good. Raymond M. Sutton, Jr. May 26 2011 - 43265 2011 $1900

Baird, Spencer Fullerton 1823-1887 *General Report Upon the Zoology of the Several Pacific Railroad Routes.* Washington: 1857, xlviii, 735 pages, with 43 plates as printed, original binding, new backstrip, endpaper foxed, very good. Bookworm & Silverfish 679 - 9 2011 $150

Baker, J. H. *A Flora of the Lake District.* London: George Bell & Sons, 1885, First (only) edition; original green cloth gilt, pages 262, (ii ad leaf), joints cracked. R. F. G. Hollett & Son Antiquarian Booksellers 173 - 46 2011 £120

Baker, James *The Imperial Guide with Picturesque Plans for the Great Post Roads, Containing Miniature Likenesses, Engraved from Real Sketches of the Cities...* London: printed by C. Whittingham sold by H. D. Symonds, 1802, 8vo., additional engraved titlepage incorporating the Prince of Wales feathers and a large allegorical vignette, 18 hand colored plans, 10 uncolored views, iv, 66 pages printed on thick paper, very small stain in extreme upper corner of five of the uncolored views (but not touching printed surface), contemporary tree calf gilt, generally rather worn, sometime rebacked, spine gilt and labelled, very good, crisp. John Drury Rare Books 154 - 15 2011 £1150

Baker, Josephine *La Tribu Arc-En-Ciel.* Netherlands: Mulder & Zoon, Opera Mundi Paris, 1957, 4to., pictorial cloth, fine, illustrations in color by Piet Worm. Aleph-Bet Books, Inc. 95 - 103 2011 $850

Baker, Richard St. Barbe *Among the Trees.* privately Printed by the Men of the Trees, 1935-1941, Limited, signed edition, no. 182 and 792 of 500 copies each; 2 volumes, 4to., original quarter vellum gilt, few slight marks, pages 98, 101, with 98 plates, inscriptions on flyleaves, otherwise excellent set. R. F. G. Hollett & Son Antiquarian Booksellers General Catalogue Summer 2010 - 947 2011 £150

Baker, Samuel White 1821-1893 *The Albert Nyanza, Great Britain of the Nile and Explorations of the Nile Sources.* London: Macmillan, Philadelphia: J. B. Lippincott, 1866, Octavo, xxvi, 516 pages, frontispiece, lithograph, plates, illustrations, color maps, erratum slip at rear, large map is torn and needs repair, some waterstains, foxing, original full mauve blindstamped cloth, gilt spine, spine end bit worn, rubbed, very good. Jeff Weber Rare Books 163 - 127 2011 $70

Baker, Samuel White 1821-1893 *The Albert Nyanza: Great Basin of the Nile and Explorations of the Nile Sources.* London: Macmillan, 1866, First edition; 2 volumes, pages xxx, 395; xi, 384, frontispieces, 2 maps, illustrations, contemporary purple full calf, all edges gilt, small area of scuffing to rear board volume I, internally fine, handsome set. J. & S. L. Bonham Antiquarian Booksellers Africa 4/20/2011 - 8355 2011 £400

Baker, Samuel White 1821-1893 *The Albert N'Yanza Great Basin of the Nile.* London: Macmillan, 1887, 8vo., lacking front free endpaper, library stamp on titlepage, good. Barnaby Rudge Booksellers Travel and Exploration - 019688 2011 $75

Baker, Samuel White 1821-1893 *Exploration of the Nile Tributaries of Abyssinia, The Sources, Supply and Overflow of the Nile, the Country, People, Customs etc....* Hartford: O. D. Case & Co., 1868, First American edition; 9 x 6.75 inches, about 620 pages, 21 illustrations and 2 partly colored maps, including one foldout, bound in burgundy cloth, edgeworn, internal hinges crudely repaired, otherwise clean copy. Gemini Fine Books & Arts, Ltd. Art Reference & Illustrated Books: First Editions 2011 $75

Baker, Samuel White 1821-1893 *Exploration of the Nile Tributaries of Abyssina.* San Francisco: Francis Dewing, 1869, Octavo, xx, (2), 23-624 pages, frontispiece, engraved plates, color folding map, original maroon blindstamped cloth, gilt spine, spine and head partly faded, spine end worn, corners showing some, very good. Jeff Weber Rare Books 163 - 128 2011 $150

Baker, Samuel White 1821-1893 *Ismailia: a Narrative of the Expedition to Central Africa for the Suppression of the Slave Trade Organized by Ismail Khedive of Egypt.* London: Macmillan, 1874, First edition; 2 volumes, 8vo., pages viii, 447, 55 publisher's list, viii, 588, 2 maps colored in outline, frontispieces, 50 plates, original green cloth, gilt vignettes on spines and upper covers, inner hinges cracked, slight rubbing to head and tail of spine. J. & S. L. Bonham Antiquarian Booksellers Africa 4/20/2011 - 7897 2011 £295

Baker, Samuel White   1821-1893   *Ismailia: a Narrative of the Expedition to Central Africa for the Suppression of the Slave Trade.*   New York: Harper and Brothers, 1875, First American edition;   542 pages, octavo, steel plate portrait (tissue guard), frontispiece, map, numerous other plates, couple of signatures sprung a bit, original brick red cloth, gilt stamped upper cover and spine, rear cover blindstamped, signature of Israel Pierce, 1882, very good.   Jeff Weber Rare Books   163 - 129   2011 $125

Baker, Samuel White   1821-1893   *The Nile Tributaries.*   London: Macmillan, 1867, First edition; 8vo., xxii, 596 pages, engraved frontispiece, 23 plates, 2 colored maps, modern quarter calf, marbled boards, gilt spine, bookplate of William Thomlinson, fine.   Jeff Weber Rare Books   163 - 130   2011 $225

Baker, Samuel White   1821-1893   *The Nile Tributaries of Abyssinia and the Sword Hunters of the Hamran Arabs.*   London: Macmillan, 1867, First edition; 8vo., pages xxii, (i) list of illustrations, (i) blank, 596, 2 maps, frontispiece, 23 engraved plates, 1 map repaired, recent blue half morocco, light foxing to prelims.   J. & S. L. Bonham Antiquarian Booksellers   Africa 4/20/2011 - 8543   2011   £350

Baker, Samuel White   1821-1893   *The Nile Tributaries of Abyssinia and the Sword Hunters of the Hamran Arabs.*   London: Macmillan, 1868, Second edition; large 8vo., pages xxiii, 596, 2 maps, 1 folding repaired on fold, illustrations, recent half calf, titlepage and frontispiece foxed and with marginal waterstaining.   J. & S. L. Bonham Antiquarian Booksellers   Africa 4/20/2011 - 8933   2011   £190

Baker, W. S.   *Bibliotheca Washingtoniana.*   Philadelphia: Robert M. Lindsay, 1889,   One of 400 copies; quarto, 179 pages, very good+, inner hinges with tape repair, otherwise near fine.   Lupack Rare Books   May 26 2011 - ABE803414043   2011 $125

Baker, William   *Peregrinations of the Mind through the Most General and Interesting Subjects...*   London: G. Pearch, 1770, First edition; 12mo., (20), 264 pages, sympathetically bound recently in 18th century style quarter calf over marbled boards, raised bands, gilt lines, original label replaced, very good, scarce.   John Drury Rare Books   154 - 16   2011   £300

Balcarres, Colin Lindsay, 3rd Earl of   *An Account of the Affairs of Scotland, Relating to the Revolution in 1688.*   London: printed for J. Baker, 1714, First edition; 8vo., (2) vi, (5)-150, (2) pages, including final ad leaf, short closed tear in upper margin of one leaf (no loss), contemporary panelled calf, neatly rebacked and labelled, very good, crisp copy, uncommon.   John Drury Rare Books   153 - 83   2011   £375

Balch, H. E.   *Wookey Hole.*   Oxford University Press, 1914, First edition; large 4to., original cloth backed pictorial boards very slight wear to corners, pages xiv, 268, untrimmed, 36 plates and 55 text figures, contemporary inscription.   R. F. G. Hollett & Son Antiquarian Booksellers   General Catalogue Summer 2010 - 1324   2011   £120

Baldwin, George   *Political Recollections Relative to Egypt...*   London: T. Cadell and W. Davies, 1801, First edition; 8vo., recent blue cloth lettered gilt with ex-Foreign and Commonwealth Office library copy, blindstamped on cover, bound with half title, handwritten presentation from author "With author's compliments", although not noted in text, the book can show up with 2 plates, not present in this volume and no signs of their removal, pages faintly browned, overall decent copy, very good.   Any Amount of Books   May 26 2011 - A49989   2011 $419

Baldwin, Henry   *The Orchids of New England.*   New York: John Wiley and Sons, 1884, First edition; 8vo., 158, (2) pages, 40 illustrations, very good slightly rubbed original green cloth, gilt lettered.   Ken Spelman Rare Books   68 - 139   2011   £35

Baldwin, James   *No Name in the Street.*   London: Michael Joseph, 1972, First British edition, true first; fine in near fine dust jacket, price clipped, very light edge wear.   Bella Luna Books   May 29 2011 - k181   2011 $110

Baldwin, James   *No Name in the Street.*   London: Michael Joseph, 1972, First British edition, true first; fine in near fine dust jacket, very light foxing to light areas.   Bella Luna Books   May 29 2011 - t8496   2011 $82

Baldwin, James   *Tell Me How Long the Train's Been Gone.*   London: Michael Joseph, 1968, First British edition; dust jacket is very good, offsetting to top 1 inch, wear to top of spine, very good, offsetting to top 1 inch, wear to top of spine.   Bella Luna Books   May 29 2011 - t5505   2011 $82

Balfour, Alice Blanche   *Twelve Hundred Miles in a Wagon.*   London: Ed Arnold, 1895, First edition; 8vo., pages xix, 265, ads, folding map, frontispiece, illustrations, original red decorative cloth, gilt vignette (bullock cart), lacks front free endpaper, otherwise good, clean copy.   J. & S. L. Bonham Antiquarian Booksellers   Africa 4/20/2011 - 8854   2011   £150

Ball Games.   London: George Routledge & Sons, 1867, Ink library marks and ownership inscription, illustrations, ads on endpapers, original blue pictorial boards, neatly rebacked, little rubbed and marked, library label of St. Paul's Brugh, on contents page.   Jarndyce Antiquarian Booksellers   CXCI - 44   2011   £150

Ball, John *Peaks, Passes and Glaciers.* London: Longman, Brown, Green (etc.), 1859, First edition; First Series with title vignette, 8 colored plates and 9 maps, second Series with title vignette, 11 plates, 14 maps, half titles, 3 volumes, pages xvi, 516, 2, 24; xiv, 415; viii, 541, 8vo., original brown diaper grain cloth with backstrip lettered gilt, front covers with mountaineering scenes in gilt, minor wear, extremities bumped, one or two nicks, First Series neatly repaired at head, foot and joints, Second Series with hinges cracked but still strong, good.   Blackwell Rare Books   B166 - 70 2011   £550

Ballard, James Graham *Crash.* London: Jonathan Cape, 1973, First edition; octavo, boards.   L. W. Currey, Inc.   124 - 48 2011 $1500

Ballard, James Graham *The Crystal World.* London: Jonathan Cape, 1966, First edition; boards.   L. W. Currey, Inc.   124 - 50 2011 $1500

Ballou, Adin *Lecture on the Inspiration of the Bible. Delivered in the Town Hall, Milford, Mass. Sunday Evening January 16 1859.* Milford: Hopedale Community, 1859, First edition; 4to., 8 pages, sewn as issued, leaves torn horizontally, nearly across at center fold, first page soiled, scarce.   M & S Rare Books, Inc.   90 - 25 2011 $175

Balmforth, Owen *Handbook of the Twenty-Seventh Annual Co-Operative Congress, to be Held at Huddersfield June 3rd, 4th and 5th 1895.* Manchester: Co-operative Printing Society, 1895, Original brown cloth gilt with shaped pictorial onlay, pages 216 with 2 folding street plans, numerous plates, few scattered spots, but excellent clean and sound copy, scarce.   R. F. G. Hollett & Son Antiquarian Booksellers   General Catalogue Summer 2010 - 1325 2011   £85

Balon, Eugene K. *Environmental Biology of Fishes.* August, 1976-, December 2001; Numerous text figures and photos, tall 8vo., paperbound, overall very good, light edgewear to wrappers on older issues, occasional bump, crease to covers, edges of about 20 issues lightly bumped.   Raymond M. Sutton, Jr.   May 26 2011 - 47083 2011 $2250

Balston, Edward *Interesting Particulars of the Loss of the Hon. East India Company's Ship the Hindostan of 1248 Tons Which Struck on Wedge Sand off Margate Jan. 11 1803.* London: printed for Thomas Tegg, 111 Cheapside, 1803, 12mo., large folding frontispiece, (3), 8-28 pages, good copy, disbound.   Anthony W. Laywood   May 26 2011 - 21476 2011 $101

Baltz, Lewis *The New Industrial Parks Near Irvine, California.* New York: Castelli Graphics, 1974, First edition, one of 960 copies; 4to., pages (10&0, (5) blank, 51 black and white photos, edges lightly toned, original grey boards, spine and upper side lettered in black, corners lightly rubbed, bottom corner of lower side bumped, original black and white photo illustrated dust jacket, text printed in black, lightly tone, creasing to flaps, rubbing to tips and to head and foot of spine, 3 short closed tears internally, strengthened, spotting to verso, dampstain to verso of lower panel, Ralph Gibson's ex-libris stamp in black, ink to front free endpaper, laid in are two postcards from Baltz to Gibson, one signed, the other initialled, near fine in very good dust jacket.   Simon Finch Rare Books   Zero - 506 2011   £2250

Balwhidder, Micah *Annals of the Parish; or the Chronicle of Dalmailling; During the Minstry of the Rev. Micah Balwhidder.* Edinburgh: William Blackwood, 1821, First edition; 8vo., recent half brown leather lettered gilt on spine, 5 raised bands, marbled boards, pages 400, with half title, text clean, very good.   Any Amount of Books   May 26 2011 - A75416 2011 $419

Balzac, Honore De *Les Cent Contes Drolatiques.* Paris: Charles Gosseli and Ed Werdet, 1832, First edition; 3 volumes, octavo, titlepages printed in red and black, later quarter tan calf over marbled boards, spines with four raised bands ruled in gilt and decoratively tooled in blind in compartments with two black morocco gilt lettering labels, marbled endpapers, edges sprinkled red, excellent copy, from the library of the Duc D'Orleans, Louis Philippe (King of the French), with armorial stamp on half title volume two, extremely scarce.   David Brass Rare Books, Inc.   May 26 2011 - 00914 2011 $5500

Balzac, Honore De *Works (Comedie Humaine).* New York: University Society published around, 1900, Limited edition, Edition royale, no. 288 of 1000; 32 volumes, each volume with frontispiece and several other photogravures, half leather with marbled boards, gilt decorations and titles, leather gone from 2 of the volumes, half gone, 2 others, lesser loss on 4 others, interiors tight, clean , top edge gilt.   G. H. Mott Bookseller   May 26 2011 - 34039 2011 $1800

Bamberger, Louis *Memoirs of Sixty Years in the Timber and Pianoforte Trades.* London: Sampson Low, Marston and Co., n.d. early 1930's, First edition; original cloth, gilt, dust jacket head and foot of spine defective, pages xviii, 270, portraits, presentation copy inscribed by author.   R. F. G. Hollett & Son Antiquarian Booksellers   175 - 73 2011   £65

Bancroft, George *Address at Hartford, Below the Delegates of the Democratic Convention of the Young Men of Connecticut, on the Evening of February 18, 1840.* Hartford: 1840, First edition; 8vo., 16 pages, sewn as issued.   M & S Rare Books, Inc.   90 - 26 2011 $175

Bancroft, Joseph *A Persuasvie to Unity, Setting Forth the Ground of that Source of Comfort, in Which Ground of a Clean Heart an Right Spirit...* Philadelphia: Thomas William Stucket, 1877, Pages xi, 336, original pebble grain cloth, gilt. R. F. G. Hollett & Son Antiquarian Booksellers 175 - 74 2011 £30

Bancroft, Laura *Policeman Bluejay.* Chicago: Reilly & Britton, 1907, First edition; 4to., cloth backed pictorial boards, (116) pages (3) pages ads, tips slightly rubbed, else fine, illustrations by Maginel Wright Enright, with 8 color plates and many black and whites, incredible copy, rare. Aleph-Bet Books, Inc. 95 - 88 2011 $1850

Bancroft, Laura *Twinkle and Chubbins...* Chicago: Reilly & Britton, 1911, First and only edition; 8vo., yellow cloth pictorially stamped in green, red and black, 384 pages, mint in dust jacket (with piece off top edge of spine, with loss of lettering and other normal wear, but very good), illustrations by Maginel Wright Enright, with 94 color illustrations plus several black and whites, very scarce, extremely rare in pictorial dust jacket. Aleph-Bet Books, Inc. 95 - 86 2011 $4000

Bandelier, Adolph Francis Alphonse 1840-1914 *The Southwestern Journals of Adolph F. Bandelier 1880-1882/1883-1884/1885-1888/1889-1892.* Albuquerque: 1966, 1970. 1975. 1984. First editions; 4 volumes, xvi, 462; xviii, 582; xviii, 702; xxi, 785 pages, maps and illustrations, hardcovers, dust jackets on volumes I, II and III, edgewear and some paper loss, internally clean volume IV near fine, overall very good. Dumont Maps & Books of the West 112 - 51 2011 $275

Bangs, John Kendrick *Mr. Bonaparte of Corsica.* New York: Harper & Brothers, 1895, First edition; frontispiece, title in red and black, illustrations, 6 pages ads, contemporary pencil inscription on leading f.e.p., original mustard decorated cloth, blocked in red, black and gilt, slightly dulled, very good, illustrations by H. W. McVickar. Jarndyce Antiquarian Booksellers CXCI - 58 2011 £35

Banham, Reyner *The Aspen Papers.* London: Pall Mall Press, 1974, First edition; 8vo., pages 224, illustrations in black and white, fine in fine dust jacket. Any Amount of Books May 29 2011 - A42089 2011 $255

Banim, John *The Smuggler.* London: Richard Bentley, 1837, Series title, frontispiece and additional engraved title dated 1813, waterstain to frontispiece and engraved title, original red cloth, little rubbed & dulled. Jarndyce Antiquarian Booksellers CXCI - 59 2011 £75

Bank of Bombay *Is Government Responsible for Its Failure?* London: Waterlow & Sons, n.d., 1867?, Apparently first (only) edition?; 8vo., 20 pages, recently well bound in blue boards, lettered on upper cover, paper label on spine, very good. John Drury Rare Books 154 - 18 2011 £125

Bank of Bombay *Report of the Committee of English Shareholders.* London: Waterlow & Sons, 1868, Apparently first (only?) edition; very rare, 8vo., 70 pages, recently well bound in blue boards, lettered on upper cover, paper label on spine, very good. John Drury Rare Books 154 - 19 2011 £175

Bank, David *British Biographical Index.* London: Melbourne: Munich and New York: K. G. Saur, 1990, First edition; 4 volumes, 4to., pages 2045, ex-British Foreign Office library with few library markings, else clean, very good+. Any Amount of Books May 26 2011 - A70132 2011 $419

Banks, A. G. *H. W. Schneider of Barrow and Bowness.* Kendal: Titus Wilson, 1984, First edition; original cloth, gilt, dust jacket, pages xvi, 121, 45 illustrations, 5 maps. R. F. G. Hollett & Son Antiquarian Booksellers 173 - 48 2011 £35

Banks, Eualie *Bobby in Bubbleland.* London: Gale & Polden, n.d., 1913, First edition; 4to., original cloth backed pictorial boards, edges rather worn and cloth bubbled, unpaginated, 10 superb color plates tipped in to grey captioned card with broad border and text drawings, one or two short tears to very soft paper, few slight marks here and there, small prize label on pastedown, excellent copy, rare. R. F. G. Hollett & Son Antiquarian Booksellers General Catalogue Summer 2010 - 490 2011 £450

Banks, Ian *The Wasp Factory.* London: Macmillan, 1984, First edition; 8vo., pages 184, publisher's cloth, brown gilt lettering to spine, slightly rubbed with minor bump, original color pictorial dust jacket, spine very lightly second, author's signature to titlepage, near fine. Simon Finch Rare Books Zero - 203 2011 £150

Banks, Joseph *Banks' Florilgieum, a Publication in Thirty-Four Parts of Seven Hundred and Thirty-Eight Copperplate Engravings of Plants Collected on Captain James Cook's First Voyage Round the World in H.M.S. Endeavour 1768-1771.* London: Alecto Historical Editions and the British Museum, 1980-1990, First complete edition; 738 copper engraved plates in titled window mounts, color printed a la Poupee in up to 17 colors with additional watercolor touches from the original plates, the supplement with 5 copper engraved plates in titled window mounts, color printed a la poupee in up to 17 colors with additional watercolor touches from the plates made by the Master Engravers of the Bank of England, after 18th century proofs pulled from 5 stolen plates, the Catalogue with 8 copper engraved uncolored and duplicate plates, 35 solander boxes (including supplement), broadsheet folio and one volume catalog, folio, The Florilegium and supplement in 101 original cloth backed portfolios contained within 35 dark green cloth covered boards (boards slightly warped), top edge gilt. Raymond M. Sutton, Jr. May 26 2011 - 46984 2011 $79,000

Banks, Joseph *Captain Cook's Florilegium.* London: Lion and Uniorn Press, Royal College of Art, 1973, One of 100 copies on handmade paper; folio, black half Nigerian goatskin and Japanese silk by Zaehnsdorf (fine), matching buckram solander case (very good plus), text printed in various colors, list of subscribers, 30 engraved plates. Raymond M. Sutton, Jr. May 26 2011 - 55737 2011 $15,000

Banks, W., & Son *Views of the English lakes.* Windermere: J. Garnett, n.d., Deluxe edition with plates printed on heavy paper; Oblong 8vo., original brown cloth gilt over bevelled boards, extremities trifle frayed, all edges gilt, wood engraved title, 26 tissue guarded vignettes, nice, clean set. R. F. G. Hollett & Son Antiquarian Booksellers 173 - 49 2011 £175

Bannerman, David Armitage *The Birds of West and Equatorial Africa.* Edinburgh: Oliver and Boyd, 1953, First edition; 2 volumes, 8vo. pages xiii, 796; 797-1526; 54 plates, numerous text illustrations, original red cloth, fine set. J. & S. L. Bonham Antiquarian Booksellers Africa 4/20/2011 - 4406 2011 £60

Bannerman, Helen *Der Kleine Schwarze Sambo. (Little Black Sambo).* Oldenburg: Gerhard Stallings, 1928, First edition thus; 4to., cloth backed full color pictorial boards with edge rubbing and weakness to front hinge, every page illustrated with full color pictures to accompany text (in German). Jo Ann Reisler, Ltd. 86 - 14 2011 $575

Bannerman, Helen *Little Black Sambo.* Cleveland: Harter, 1931, Stated first edition; 4to., red patterned cloth, circular pictorial paste-on, near fine, illustrations in color by Fern Bisel Peat with 8 color plates plus 12 full page and 1 smaller black and whites, extremely rare in this first edition. Aleph-Bet Books, Inc. 95 - 60 2011 $875

Bannerman, Helen *El Negrito Sambo.* N.P.: Barcelona: Libro Escenario Juventud, circa, 1940, 4to., cloth backed boards, slightest of cover soil, else very good+, panorama book which opens in center, 7 full page color scenes in center, color illustrations to both side panels, illustrations by J. Vinals, rare version. Aleph-Bet Books, Inc. 95 - 61 2011 $1200

Bannerman, Helen *Little Black Sambo.* New York: Grossett & Dunlap, 1942, Square 4to., pictorial boards, very good+ in worn dust jacket, illustrations in color by Robert Moore, very scarce. Aleph-Bet Books, Inc. 95 - 67 2011 $300

Bannerman, Helen *Little Black Sambo.* New York: Duenewald, 1943, 8vo., spiral backed pictorial boards, slight wear, else near fine in chipped and slightly worn dust jacket, moveable, illustrated in color by Julian Wehr with 6 really terrific moveable plates done in color. Aleph-Bet Books, Inc. 95 - 66 2011 $600

Bannerman, Helen *Little Black Sambo.* no publication information, printed in USA circa, 1945, 8vo., pictorial wrappers, fine, illustrations in color by unknown hand. Aleph-Bet Books, Inc. 95 - 65 2011 $150

Bannerman, Helen *Little Black Sambo.* Racine: Whitman, 1959, Square 12mo., pictorial board, fine, illustrations in color by Violet Lamont. Aleph-Bet Books, Inc. 95 - 68 2011 $150

Banting, John *The Blue Book of Conversation.* London: Editions Poetry/Nicholson and Watson, 1946, First edition; small quarto, pages 57 with 25 plates, one of which is double page, all of which are printed in blue, some slight foxing to endpapers, else near fine in about very good dust jacket that is slightly browned and slightly foxed at rear and has one inch chip at head of spine, loosely inserted is good longish 2 page letter to Raymond Mortimer from Banting. Any Amount of Books May 26 2011 - A39855 2011 $629

Baraga, Frederic *A Dictionary of the Otchipwe Language.* Cincinnati: printed for Jos. A. Hermann, 1853, First edition; 12mo., 7, 662 pages, old calf backed marbled boards, spine repaired, inner margins of first few leaves reinforced, very good. M & S Rare Books, Inc. 90 - 180 2011 $2250

Barba, Alvaro Alonso *A Collection of Scarce and Valuable Treatises Upon Metals, Mines and Minerals.* London: C. Jephson for Olive Payne, 1738, 12mo., (12), 170 (10) 173-275 (5), 66, (2) pages, engraved plate, woodcut illustrations, contemporary morocco, gilt triple fillet and roll tooled border, gilt corner fleurons, spine gilt in compartments, gilt edges, spine chipped at head, joints rubbed and cracking, lacking lettering piece, fine, with publisher's ads (2 pages) at end, glossary (6 pages); from the library of the Earls of Macclesfield at Shirburn Castle. Maggs Bros. Ltd. 1440 - 22 2011 £550

Barbara Peek-a-Boos Holiday. London: Humphrey Milford/ Oxford University Press, n.d. circa, 1915, Square 4to., pictorial boards, color paste-on, slight wear to paper and slight soil, very good+, 8 fine color plates plus numerous black and whites. Aleph-Bet Books, Inc. 95 - 463 2011 $500

Barbara's Song Book. London: George Allen, 1900, Oblong small 4to., original cloth backed boards with pictorial onlay, edges rubbed, pages 55, 17 full and half page color illustrations, joints strengthened. R. F. G. Hollett & Sons Antiquarian Booksellers 170 - 319 2011 £95

Barbauld, Anna Laetitia Aikin 1743-1825 *Lecons pour des Enfans.* Londre: Darton et Harvey, 1834, 12mo., iv, 140 + 36 page dictionary, original green roan spine with gilt title and fillets, marbled paper on boards, light soiling throughout, pencilled and dated signature inside upper cover, bumped corners of cover, minor chipping at edges, good copy, scarce. Hobbyhorse Books 56 - 4 2011 $150

Barbauld, Anna Laetitia Aikin 1743-1825 *Lessons for Children.* London: Longman and Co. et al, 1867, 12mo., iv, 176 pages, green tooled cloth on boards, gilt title on spine, speckled edges, charming full page copper engraved frontispiece, large engraved vignette on titlepage plus four headpieces by Jackson, library inked stamp inside upper board, numbers and dry seal at lower margin on 3 leaves, repaired lower endpaper, near fine.   Hobbyhorse Books   56 - 5   2011 $125

Barber, Lynn *The Heyday of Natural History 1820-1870.* London: Cape, 1980, First edition; large 8vo., original cloth, gilt, dust jacket price clipped, pages 320, illustrations, partly in color.   R. F. G. Hollett & Son Antiquarian Booksellers   General Catalogue Summer 2010 - 9948   2011   £65

Barber, Miss *The True Narrative of the Five Years' Suffering & Perilous Adventures by Miss Barber...* Philadelphia: Barclay & Co., 1873, First edition; octavo, (17)-94, 97-107, (1) pages, complete as issued, 9 full page woodcuts with captions in English and German, lightly foxed, original yellow pictorial wrappers, extremities worn, corners curled, good plus.   Jeff Weber Rare Books   163 - 52   2011 $100

Barber, Richard *Arthurian Literature.* Woodbridge: D. S. Brewer, 1987, First edition, volume 1 reprint of 1987; 11 volumes, 8vo., pages 2200+, very slight edgewear, some pencil underlinings throughout, very slight bumping, otherwise near very good in browned, slightly soiled dust jackets (very good with some closed tears), volumes 10 and 11 lacking dust jackets.   Any Amount of Books   May 29 2011 - A65019   2011 $204

Barber, Samuel *Beneath Helvellyn's Shade.* London: Elliot Stock, 1892, First edition; original pictorial red cloth gilt, spine and edges rather faded, pages viii, 166, scarce, color litho folding plan loosely inserted.   R. F. G. Hollett & Son Antiquarian Booksellers   173 - 52   2011   £85

Barbier, Carl Paul *William Gilpin. His Drawings, Teaching and Theory of the Picturesque.* Oxford: Clarendon Press, 1963, First edition; 196 pages, 16 plates, fine in dust jacket.   Ken Spelman Rare Books   68 - 131   2011   £95

Barclay, Edgar *Stonehenge and Its Earth-Works.* London: D. Nutt, 1895, First edition; 4to. original cloth, gilt, pages xi, 152, top edge gilt, plates and illustrations and 3 plans, bookplate removed from pastedown, otherwise fine.   R. F. G. Hollett & Son Antiquarian Booksellers   177 - 62   2011   £160

Barclay, G. Lippard *The Life and Remarkable Career of Adah Isaacs Menken, the Celebrated Actress.* Philadelphia: Barclay and Co., 1868, First edition; original green pictorial wrappers, extremities dust soiled, chipping to head of backstrip, plates.   Dramatis Personae Booksellers   106 - 10   2011 $250

Barclay, Robert *Theologiae Vere Christianae Apologia.* Amsterdam: Jacob Claus for Benjamin Clark (London), Isaac Van Neer (Rotterdam) and Heinrich Betke (Frankfurt), 1676, First edition; 4to., (24), 374, (25) pages, contemporary sprinkled calf, blind fillet around covers and run twice along spine, gilt sawtooth roll on board edges, spine with gilt fillet above and below each cord, paper ms. title label, hinges split but securely by cords, corners bumped, tips worn through, spine with very faint white-ish cast, internally slight dampstain at top margin, some slight, sporadic foxing and browning, edges of endpapers discolored from leather turn-ins, very good, rare.   Joseph J. Felcone Inc.   Fall Miscellany 2010 - 10   2011 $8000

Bardet De Villeneuve, P. P. A. *Cours De La Science Militaire, A L'Usage De L'Infanterie, De La Cavalerie, De L'Artillerie, Du Genie & De La Marine.* The Hague: Jean Van Duren, 1740-1742, First edition; 202 x 118mm., 10 volumes bound in nine, first and fifth volumes bound without half titles, extremely pleasing late 18th century sprinkled calf, spines very elaborately gilt in diapered compartments (two of the compartments featuring unusual checkerboard and floral pattern), each (flat spine with red and green titling label; engraved vignette devices on all 10 volume titlepages, 8 engraved frontispieces (as called for) and a total of 142 folding plates, titlepages printed in red and black, front pastedown of each volume with armorial bookplate of Lt. Gen. G. L. Parker (4th Earl of Macclesfield), first endpaper with similar armorial bookplate of Macclesfield library, first two leaves of each volume with small embossed Macclesfield stamp, front jont of first volume (only) with just hint of wear, one cover with few small blemishes (superficial worm burrows?), light offsetting from frontispiece, about half the plates in three volumes with headlines and or/plate number partly cropped), no cropping elsewhere), two or three gatherings with minor foxing, but beautifully bound set in remarkably fine condition, bindings showing only most negligible wear, entire series clean and fresh internally.   Phillip J. Pirages   59 - 1   2011 $4800

Barham, Richard Harris 1788-1845 *Ingoldsby Legends or Mirth & Marvels.* London: J. M. Dent & Co., 1898, First Rackham edition; 200 x 135mm., 2 p.l., including frontispiece, xxiii, (i), 638, (1) pages, very attractive contemporary Arts and Crafts style binding of russet Niger Goatskin lavishly gilt, covers with central panel of gilt ruled squares within wide frame of flowers and foliage, raised bands, spine compartments densely gilt with tooling repeating cover frame design, gilt turn-ins, top edge gilt, other edges gilded on the rough, titlepage with green ornamental border, numerous black and white illustrations and 13 color plates, including frontispiece by Arthur Rackham; slight and even darkening to spine, covers with minor soiling, title and frontispiece rather foxed, text with hint of browning at edges, but very attractive copy, nevertheles animated gilt of binding still bright, leather with only insignificant wear and text almost entirely bright, clean and fresh.   Phillip J. Pirages   59 - 84   2011 $1500

Barham, Richard Harris 1788-1845 *Ingoldsby Legends.* London: Dent, 1907, Limited to only 560 copies signed by artist (500 for sale); 24 tipped in color plates mounted on dark paper, 12 full page tinted illustrations and 66 black and white drawings plus pictorial endpapers by Arthur Rackham, large thick 4to., full gilt pictorial vellum, fine with new ties, this copy features a fine half page watercolor drawing signed by artist.   Aleph-Bet Books, Inc.   95 - 473   2011 $13,500

Barham, Richard Harris 1788-1845 *The Ingoldsby Legends, or Mirth & Marvels.* London: J. M. Dent & Co., 1907, First quarto edition; one of 560 copies signed by artist, thi #143, quarto, (550) pages, original signed watercolor on half title, with 24 color plates mounted on dark green paper, 12 full page illustrations tinted but not mounted, 66 drawings in black and white, olive green and black pictorial endpapers by Arthur Rackham, original signed watercolor by Rackham, full original white vellum, front board and spine decorated and lettered in gilt, top edge gilt, others uncut, with renewed yellow silk ties, some very faint soiling to vellum, titlepage with 3 inch closed tear, professionally restored, overall near fine.   Heritage Book Shop Holiday 2010 - 102   2011 $13,500

Barham, Richard Harris 1788-1845 *The Lay of St. Aloys, a Legend of Blois.* London: Eyre & Spottiswoode, n.d. circa, 1885, Folio, original cloth backed pictorial bevelled boards, neatly recased, 34 leaves of stiff paper, printed on one side only in red, black and sepia, illustrations by Ernest Jessop.   R. F. G. Hollett & Son Antiquarian Booksellers   175 - 79   2011   £120

Baring-Gould, Sabine *Yorkshire Oddities.* London: John Hodges, 1880, Fourth edition; 2 volumes in 1, original decorated plum cloth gilt, neatly recased, pages viii, 279, (i), 271, very good, clean and sound, scarce.   R. F. G. Hollett & Son Antiquarian Booksellers   General Catalogue Summer 2010 - 1326   2011   £75

Baring, Maurice *Forget-Me-Not and Lilly of the Valley.* Dublin: Campion Press, 1960, First edition thus; large 8vo., original green cloth, pictorial onlay, dust jacket little stained, long vertical closed tear repaired on reverse, pages v, 40, text printed in blue, color text illustrations.   R. F. G. Hollett & Sons Antiquarian Booksellers   170 - 59   2011   £65

Baring, Maurice *Orpheus in Mayfair and Other Stories and Sketches.* London: Mills and Boon, 1909, First edition; 8vo., pages x, 306, Blanche Warne Cornish's copy with her name and return adress (c/o David Balfour) in blue crayon on halt title, original publisher's green cloth lettered gilt on spine and on front cover, slight rubbing, few minor marks, otherwise decent sound, very good.   Any Amount of Books   May 29 2011 - A36012   2011 $255

Barker, Cicely Mary *Summer Songs.* London: Blackie & Son, n.d., 1927, Large 8vo., original cloth backed boards with pictorial onlay, corners little bruised, unpaginated, 12 tipped in 'flower fairy" plates, flyleaves lightly spotted, pencilled list of flowers on front flyleaf, otherwise very good.   R. F. G. Hollett & Son Antiquarian Booksellers   175 - 80   2011   £80

Barker, Clive *Books of Blood. Volumes I and II.* London: Sphere, 1984, First edition thus; near fine, light shelf wear, dust jacket near fine with creasing to top and bottom of spine.   Bella Luna Books   May 29 2011 - t2444   2011 $82

Barker, Clive *Books of Blood.* London: Sphere, 1984, First edition; near fine, dust jacket fine.   Bella Luna Books   May 26 2011 - t2410   2011 $192

Barker, Clive *Cabal.* New York: Poseidon, 1988, First edition; fine, signed by author.   Bella Luna Books   May 29 2011 - t4089   2011 $82

Barker, George *The Dead Seagull.* London: John Lehman, 1950, First edition; 8vo., pages 142, (2) blank, original bright orange cloth, blocked in black and lettered in gilt to spine, original pictorial dust jacket designed by Humphrey Spender, extremities lightly rubbed, lower panel lightly soiled, couple of nicks to lower edge, inscribed in blue by Stephen And Natasha Spender for Marcelle (Sibon).   Simon Finch Rare Books   Zero - 204   2011   £75

Barker, Joseph *The Abominations of Socialism Exposed in Reply to the Gateshead Observer.* Newcastle: printed by J. Blackwell and Co., 1839-1840, First edition; 12mo., drophead title, 12 pages, recently well bound in linen backed marbled boards lettered, very good, rare.   John Drury Rare Books   153 - 9   2011   £300

Barker, Nugent *Written with My Left Hand.* London: Percival Marshall & Co. Ltd., 1951, First edition; octavo, boards.   L. W. Currey, Inc.   124 - 116   2011 $650

Barker, Pat *The Man Who Wasn't There.* London: Virago, 1989, First British edition; true first edition, fine in like dust jacket.   Bella Luna Books   May 29 2011 - t1620   2011 $93

Barker, William Higgs *The Hebrew and English Lexicon Improved: with Great Additions and Amendments.* Carmarthen: printed for the author by John Ross, 1776, First edition; 8vo., (2), viii, 241, (1), ix, (1) pages, titlepage soiled, 4 leaves of prelims with short closed tears, contemporary blindstamped calf (almost certainly provincial - Welsh?) with little general wear at extremities, rare.   John Drury Rare Books   154 - 20   2011   £450

Barkly, Fanny *Among Boers and Basutos.* Westminster: Roxburghe Press, n.d., 1896, First edition; small 8vo., pages 275, ads, original green decorative cloth, some minor fading.   J. & S. L. Bonham Antiquarian Booksellers   Africa 4/20/2011 - 4682   2011   £95

Barley, M. W. *The English Farmhouse and Cottage.* London: Routledge and Kegan Paul, 1961, First edition; original cloth, gilt, dust jacket (little worn), pages xxi, 297, with 24 pages on plates, 38 text figures and 8 tables, Dr. Arthur Raistrick's copy with his bookplate and stamps, inscribed on flyleaf by his wife.   R. F. G. Hollett & Son Antiquarian Booksellers   177 - 63   2011   £45

Barlow, Alfred *The History and Principles of Weaving by Hand & Power.* London &: 1878, First edition; xii, 443 (23 publisher's catalog) pages, 4to., several hundred illustrations, later cloth, new label, modestly ex-library.   Bookworm & Silverfish   676 - 185   2011 $125

Barlow, William *Magneticall Advertisements or Divers Pertinent Observations and Approved Experiments Concerning the Nature and Properties of the Load-stone...* London: Edward Griffin for Timothy Barlow, 1616, First edition; 4to., (16), 86, (2) pages, woodcut illustrations in text, without final leaf of "Faults escaped" but with penultimate leaf, short tear at head of A4, title and final page dust soiled, small dampstain in upper fore corner and fore margin at beginning and end, disbound, from the library of the Earls of Macclesfield at Shirburn Castle.   Maggs Bros. Ltd. 1440 - 25   2011   £4500

Barman, C. *The Bridge.* London: John Lane The Bodley Head, 1926, First edition; small 4to., original buckram gilt, trifle rubbed and lower board scratched, pages xvii, 249, uncut, 24 colored plates and 22 line drawings by Frank Brangwyn, front flyleaf removed.   R. F. G. Hollett & Son Antiquarian Booksellers   177 - 111   2011   £85

Barnard, J. E. *Practical Photo-Micrography.* London: Edward Arnold, 1936, Third edition; original cloth, gilt, pages xii, 352, with 23 plates and 121 text illustrations.   R. F. G. Hollett & Son Antiquarian Booksellers   General Catalogue Summer 2010 - 1081   2011   £30

Barnes, Jim *The Fish on Poteau Mountain.* De Kalb: Cedar Creek Press, 1980, Wrappered edition; signed by Barnes, fine, uncommon title.   Ken Lopez Bookseller   154 - 132   2011 $200

Barnes, Julian *England, England.* London: Cape, 1998, First edition; fine in fine, first issue dust jacket, signed and dated by author 3/8/98.   Bella Luna Books   May 29 2011 - t7206   2011 $110

Barnes, Julian *Nothing to Be Frightened of.* London: Jonathan Cape, 2008, First edition, number 95 of 100 copies; quarter red leather, lettered gilt at spine, blue and white patterned boards, as new, signed limited edition, fine light brown cloth slipcase.   Any Amount of Books   May 29 2011 - A69881   2011 $272

Barnes, William H. *The Story of Laulii, a Daughter of Samoa.* San Francisco: Jos. Winterburn & Co., 1889, First edition; octavo, 255 pages, frontispiece, engravings, portraits, original full green blind and black stamped cloth, gilt spine, rubbed, very good, scarce.   Jeff Weber Rare Books   163 - 227   2011 $125

Barnum, Phineas Taylor   1810-1891   *Life of P. T. Barnum Written by Himself. Brought up to 1886.* Buffao: Courier Co., 1886, First edition; original brick cloth, 361 pages, engravings, this copy inscribed and signed by author to F. J. Bonnelle, near fine, minor fraying to spine tips.   Charles Agvent   2010 Summer Miscellany - 4   2011 $1000

Baron-Wilson, Cornwel, Mrs. *Memoirs of Harriot, Duchess of St. Albans.* London: Henry Colburn, 1839, First edition; 2 volumes, 8vo., half navy blue leather with marbled boards, gilt border, pages xvi, 362; vii, 354, frontispiece to volume 1, hinges slightly rubbed and very slightly tender, otherwise and clean very good.   Any Amount of Books   May 29 2011 - A69107   2011 $255

Barr, J. S. *A Brief History of the Mahratta Light Infantry.* Bombay: Privately Printed, 1945, First edition; 4to., green leather styled covers lettered yellow on cover, which is mostly faded into black, pages 65, one color plate, stain to near corner of front endpaper, covers slightly dull and faintly marked, otherwise decent, very good.   Any Amount of Books   May 29 2011 - A69336   2011 $213

Barr, Nevada *Bittersweet.* New York: St. Martin's Press, 1984, First edition; near fine, light shelfwear, dust jacket fine, signed by author.   Bella Luna Books   May 26 2011 - t7162   2011 $550

Barr, Nevada *A Superior Death.* New York: Putnam, 1994, Advance reading copy; fine, signed by author, pictorial wrappers.   Bella Luna Books   May 29 2011 - 2715   2011 $82

Barr, Nevada *Track of the Cat.* New York: Putnam, 1993, First edition; fine in like dust jacket, signed by author.   Bella Luna Books   May 26 2011 - t1427   2011 $275

Barr, Nevada *The Track of the Cat.* New York: Putnam, 1993, First edition; near fine, bottom of spine bumped, dust jacket fine, signed by author.   Bella Luna Books   May 26 2011 - 3697   2011 $192

Barrie, James Matthew 1860-1937 *Peter Pan and Wendy.* London: Hodder & Stoughton, n.d., Original green pictorial cloth, spine little faded, pages 144, 7 tinted gravure plates and 13 text drawings by Mabel Lucie Attwell, neat inscription on flyleaf. R. F. G. Hollett & Son Antiquarian Booksellers General Catalogue Summer 2010 - 488 2011 £30

Barrie, James Matthew 1860-1937 *Peter and Wendy.* New York: Scribner's, 1911, First American edition; 8vo., pages 266, illustrations by F. D. Bedford with 12 black and white plates, partially unopened, owner's bookplate, green cloth stamped in gilt, cover somewhat dust scuffed, otherwise very good, tight copy. Second Life Books Inc. 174 - 22 2011 $600

Barrie, James Matthew 1860-1937 *Peter Pan in Kensington Gardens.* London: Hodder & Stoughton. n.d., 1912, Large 4to., green gilt pictorial cloth, 125 numbered pages, slightest of rubbing to spine extremities, else fine in dust jacket with mounted color plate, dust jacket chipped and repaired on verso, illustrations by Arthur Rackham with 50 mounted color plates with tissue guards and with 7 full page black and whites, magnificent copy. Aleph-Bet Books, Inc. 95 - 475 2011 $2750

Barrie, James Matthew 1860-1937 *Peter Pan and Wendy.* London: Hodder & Stoughton, n.d. circa, 1921, Thick 4to., blue cloth, slight fade spots on covers, else very good+, 12 beautiful tipped in color plate and many black and whites in text by Mabel Lucy Attwell, this copy inscribed by Attwell with lovely full page watercolor of baby mermaid playing with bubbles, exceedingly scarce. Aleph-Bet Books, Inc. 95 - 71 2011 $2750

Barrie, James Matthew 1860-1937 *Peter Pan or the Boy Who Would Not Grow Up.* London: Folio Society, 1992, First edition thus, 1 of 100 numbered copies; large tall 8vo., pages xx, 106, (2), 27.5 x 18 cm., frontispiece and 14 color illustrations by Paula Rego, specially bound in quarter Nigerian goatskin with hand marbled sides by Ann Muir, signed by artist, lettered gilt at spine with, fine in fine slipcase, this copy no. "staff 2", superb example of sumptuous special edition. Any Amount of Books May 26 2011 - A48124 2011 $805

Barrie, James Matthew 1860-1937 *Quality Street.* London: Hodder & Stoughton, 1913, First edition; 4to., pages 198, with 22 plates and signed by Hugh Thomson, the artist, one of 1000 numbered copies, full vellum boards, stamped in gilt, boards little warped, otherwise fine, includes announcement card for an exhibition of original drawings by Thomson. Second Life Books Inc. 174 - 23 2011 $563

Barrie, James Matthew 1860-1937 *Rosalind.* New York: Charles Scribner's Sons, 1914, 190 x 130mm., 1 p.l., 89-151 pages, very pleasing dark green pebble grain morocco, attractively gilt by J. S. H. Bates of Leicester (stamp signed on rear turn-in), covers with border of plain and broken gilt fillets around a central rectangular panel formed by the same broken rule (four flap-like panels surrounding the central rectangle in an arrangement resembling fold-over closures) large and very attractive cornerpieces of five grouped tulips on leaves stems, spine with two raised bands, large gilt tulips at either end, vertical titling in middle, gilt turn-ins, top edge gilt, gilt stamped presentation "To Lady Kathleen Curzon-Herrick/ A Memento of June 1918/ from Mr. and Mrs. A. Laxton-Hames", spine faded (as always with green morocco) to a pleasing olive green, hint of wear to extremities, still quite fine, especially attractive, very bright and clean inside and out. Phillip J. Pirages 59 - 87 2011 $850

Barrie, James Matthew 1860-1937 *When a Man's Single.* London: Hodder & Stoughton, 1888, Half title, final ad leaf, partially uncut, original navy blue buckram, bevelled boards, slight string mark to leading edge of spine, signature of Florence A. Baines 1890 on half title, top edge gilt, very good in custom made half dark blue morocco slipcase. Jarndyce Antiquarian Booksellers CXCI - 61 2011 £180

Barrow Naturalists' Field Club *Annual Report and Proceedings.* Barrow: Barrow Times, 1879, Third year, volume 3; original pink wrappers, stained and spotted, pages 144, first few leaves spotted. R. F. G. Hollett & Son Antiquarian Booksellers 173 - 57 2011 £45

Barrow, Isaac *A Brief Exposition of the Lord's Prayer and the Decalogue.* London: M. Flesher for Brabazon Aylmer, 1681, 8vo., pages (vi), 269, (iii) + engraved portrait frontispiece; later dark blue polished turkey, spine decorative roll gilt in compartments with small corner and centre pieces, lettered in gilt direct, boards gilt rule bordered with small stylised floweret in corners, board edges and turn-ins 'zig-zag' decorative roll gilt, crimson turkey doublures with 'dentelle' gilt border, blue 'made' end flyleaves, all edges gilt, pale blue and white sewn endbands (suggestions here of James Brindley binding), faint dampmark to fore-edge, joints rubbed, splitting, endcaps and corners worn, "Shelburne" armorial bookplate, and "Holland House" heraldic bookplate on doublure, from the collection of Christopher Ernest Weston 1947-2010. Unsworths Booksellers 24 - 4 2011 £175

Barrow, Isaac *Several Sermons Against Evil Speaking.* London: printed for Brabazon Aylmer, 1678, 8vo., pages (viii), 243, (i), 140, (iv), contemporary speckled calf, boards blind ruled, board edges 'broken rule', gilt, text block edges densely red sprinkled, blue and white sewn endbands, alte 20th century blind ruled and unlettered calf reback, touch of minor spotting, leather rubbed at extremities, corners just worn, contemporary ink inscription "Rd Scott", ink inscription "Jonathan Scott 1746 Betton", also "J. A. Milner/ Shrewsbury/1889", from the collection of Christopher Ernest Weston 1947-2010. Unsworths Booksellers 24 - 2 2011 £275

Barrow, Isaac *A Treatise of the Pope's Supremacy.* London: Miles Flesher for Barbazon Aylmer, 1680, Small 4to., pages (viii), 428, (ii), 49, (i), engraved portrait frontispiece, contemporary mottled calf, boards blind double rule bordered, board edges "morse code" rule gilt, early 21st century rebacked and restoration by CEW, little faint spotting, old leather crackled, from the collection of Christopher Ernest Weston 1947-2010. Unsworths Booksellers 24 - 3 2011 £275

Barrow, Isaac *The Works of the Learned Isaac Barrow...* London: James Round, Jacob Tonson, and William Taylor, 1716, Third/fourth editions; 3 volumes bound in two, large 4to., (20), 783, (5); (4), 381, (7), (8), 390, (6) pages, frontispiece, full paneled Cambridge style speckled calf, raised bands, gilt stamped spine titles, expertly rebacked, retaining covers and spines, ownership signatures of David Jenks and John A. James, fine. Jeff Weber Rare Books 163 - 31 2011 $1000

Barrow, John 1764-1848 *Mountain Ascents in Cumberland and Westmoreland.* London: Sampson Low etc., 1886, First edition; modern cloth, gilt, pages viii, 208, 32, woodcut frontispiece (little soiled, stained on reverse), 15 woodcut text illustrations and folding map, some foxing and fingering, few annotations and one deletion, but sound, scarce. R. F. G. Hollett & Son Antiquarian Booksellers 173 - 56 2011 £150

Barrow, S. *A Popular Dictionary of Fact and Knowledge, for the Use of Schools and Students..* Poole and Edwards, 1827, Pages iv, 232, (iv), text woodcuts, one or two illustrations with added hand coloring, original green roan gilt, rubbed and scraped, upper hinge cracked, scattered foxing or browning. R. F. G. Hollett & Sons Antiquarian Booksellers 170 - 61 2011 £45

Barruel, Augustin *Memoirs, Illustrating the History of Jacobinism....* London: printed for the translator by T. Burton, 1798, Second edition in English; 4 volumes, 8vo., (4), xvi, 401, (1), and (4), 479, (1); and xviii, 414; xviii, 601, (1), 50 pages, engraved plate of alphabets in volume III, large folding chart in volume IV (slightly cropped at foot affecting letters), one or two very minor marks here and there, contemporary uniform half calf gilt with contrasting red and black labels, vellum tips, little wear to joints but very good in first bindings, 19th century armorial bookplate in each volume of John S. Pakington. John Drury Rare Books 153 - 10 2011 £400

Barry, George *The History of the Orkney Islands...* Edinburgh: printed for the author by D. Willison, 1805, 4to., pages (ii) viii, 509 + engraved frontispiece, 1 folding map, 19 other engraved plates, later tan calf, spine panelled in gilt with 'crowned dolphin" center pieces, dark brown lettering piece gilt, boards double rule gilt bordered with decorative roll gilt within, board edges and turn-ins decorative roll gilt, 'Dutch-curl' 'made' endpapers and all edges matching, brown and white sewn flat endbands, some minor spotting, little foxing to plates, spine bit rubbed, front joint cracking at foot, subscriber's copy of John Spottiswoode of Spottiswoode with his armorial gilt stamped on both boards, from the collection of Christopher Ernest Weston 1947-2010. Unsworths Booksellers 24 - 67 2011 £400

Barry, Philip *Hotel Universe.* New York: Samuel French, 1930, First edition; slight sunning at extremities, top corners tad bumped, very good or better without dust jacket, inscribed by author for Adele and Bob. Between the Covers 169 - BTC347387 2011 $350

Barry, Sebastian *The Secret Scripture.* London: Faber & Faber, 2008, First British hardcover edition; fine in fine dust jacket. Bella Luna Books May 29 2011 - t9436 2011 $110

Bart, Harriet *The Poetry of Chance Encounters.* Minneapolis: Mnemonic Press, 2003, One of 35 numbered copies, all on Rives BFK, from a total edition of 40 (35 + 5 artist proof copies); page size 9 x 6 1/8 inches, 42 pages, bound by Jill Jevne, full brown box calf, matching calf edged and gold paste paper by Claire Maziarcyzk, matching calf over boards slipcase, book contains 16 visual poems on multi-color fields, each imprinted with an icon in 22 karat gold, each printed page has total of five press runs, including a varnish over icon and field with the impression of the gold leaf imparting an embossed effect to the icon, basic typeface is Lydian, a stressed sans serif chose to complement the treatment of image and type throughout the page. Priscilla Juvelis - Rare Books 48 - 1 2011 $2400

Barth, Henry *Travels and Discoveries in North and Central Africa from the Journal of an Expedition Undertaken under the Auspcies of H. B. M.'s Government in the Year 1849-1855.* Philadelphia: J. W. Bradley, 1860, Early one volume issue; octavo, xxiv, 25-538, 9-14 (ads) pages, folding color maps, original full publisher's brown blindstamped cloth, gilt spine title, ownership gift inscription, unusually fine, bit of wear to corners very good plus. Jeff Weber Rare Books   163 - 131   2011 $85

Barth, John *The Friday Book.* New York: 1984, First edition; several lines underscored on pages 1 and 2, otherwise as new in like dust jacket, laid in is 8 x 10 photo of Barth, signed by author. Gemini Fine Books & Arts, Ltd. Art Reference & Illustrated Books: First Editions 2011 $60

Barthelme, Donald *Amateurs.* New York: FSG, 1976, First edition; inscribed by author in year of publication, foxing to fore edge, near fine in near fine dust jacket with two tiny tears at crown. Ken Lopez Bookseller   154 - 10   2011 $125

Barthelme, Donald *The Dead Father.* New York: FSG, 1975, First edition; inscribed by author, slight foxing to top stain, else fine in near fine dust jacket. Ken Lopez Bookseller   154 - 9   2011 $100

Barthelme, Donald *Sixty Stories.* New York: Putnam, 1981, First edition; number 83 of 350 copies signed by author, cloth in slipcase, fine. Gemini Fine Books & Arts, Ltd. Art Reference & Illustrated Books: First Editions 2011 $85

Barthelme, Donald *Snow White.* New York: Atheneum, 1967, First edition; near fine, very light soiling to top edge of cloth, dust jacket fine. Bella Luna Books   May 29 2011 - t5744   2011 $82

Barthes, Roland *Essais Critiques. (Critical Essays).* Paris: Editions du Seuil, 1964, First edition; half title, titlepage, 1 leaf + 9-(276) + 1 leaf - table, octavo, inscribed by author, original paper wrappers, usual review copy perforations "SP" to last few leaves and rear wrapper, very good. Athena Rare Books   10 2011 $950

Barthes, Roland *Sur Racine. (On Racine).* Paris: Editions du Seuil, 1963, First edition; half title + titlepage + 1 leaf + 9-167 2 leafs - table + 1 leaf - imprime, octavo, 3 line inscription and Barthes' signature on half titlepage, original printed wrappers, usual review copy perforations "SP" to last few leaves and rear wrapper, original printer's band loosely laid in. Athena Rare Books   10 2011 $950

Barthes, Roland *S/Z.* Paris: Editions du Seuil, 1970, First edition; frontispiece, 1 blank leaf, half title + titlepage, 1 leaf, 9-(278) + 1 leaf - ads, octavo, inscribed, lovely signed copy, original printed wrappers, very good. Athena Rare Books   10 2011 $950

Barthes, Roland *Sade Fourier, Loyola.* Paris: Editions du Seuil, 1971, First edition; half title, titlepage 7-187 + 2 leaves - table, octavo, 2 line inscription and signature by author, original printed wrappers, usual review copy perforations "SP" to last few leaves and rear wrapper, very good. Athena Rare Books   10 2011 $950

Barthes, Roland *Le Degre Zero de l'Ecriture. (Writing Degree Zero).* Paris: Editions Du Seuil, 1953, First edition; half title, frontispiece+ 7-(126) (1) = table, small octavo, original printed wrappers, some chipping along spine, light creasing to covers, former owner's name in ink to top of half titlepage, internally clean, very good. Athena Rare Books   10 2011   £450

Bartholomew, George *Prof. George Bartholomew's Equine Paradox!* N.P.: 1884, 16 pages, illustrations, 16mo., original blue printed wrappers, light soil, pages browned, couple of pages creased, else very good. Dumont Maps & Books of the West   113 - 15   2011 $125

Bartlett, Benjamin *Manduessedum Romanorum; Being the History and Antiquities of the Parish of Manceter...* printed by and for J. Nichols, Printer to the Society of Antiquaries, 1791, First edition; 24 engraved plates (as called for), chronological charts (some folding, pages viii, 136, 137*-167- (1), 137-142, 143*-146*, 143-168, 4to., modern half tan calf by Ipsley bindery (their ink stamp at foot of rear pastedown), backstrip divided into six compartments by raised bands between blindstamped rules, gilt lettered direct in second compartment, remainder empty, gilt dated at foot, marbled sides, buff endpapers, marbled edges, very good. Blackwell Rare Books   B166 - 9   2011   £150

Bartlett, William Henry 1809-1854 *The Pilgrim Fathers or the Founders of New England in the Reign of James the First.* London: Arthur Hall, Virtue & Co., 1853, 4to., old half crimson calf, gilt with attractively gilt decorated spine, pages 240, top edge gilt, 28 steel engraved plates and many text woodcuts, little light spotting here and there as usual, generally a fine, clean copy. R. F. G. Hollett & Son Antiquarian Booksellers   General Catalogue Summer 2010 - 1626   2011   £195

Bartoli, Pietro Santi 1635-1700 *Le Antiche Lucerne Sepolcrali Figuarate Raccolte dalle Caue Sotteranee, e Grotte di Roma.* In Roma: Nella Stamparia di Gio: Francesco Buagni, 1691, 4to., (8), 16, 15, 12 pages, engraved section titlepages for each of the 3 parts, 116 full page engraved plates, full modern antique style speckled calf, blindstamped covers, raised bands, gilt stamped black calf spine label, fine, rare. Jeff Weber Rare Books   163 - 24   2011 $2750

Barton, O. S. *Three Years with Quantrell: A True Story by His Scout John McCorkle.* Armstrong: Armstrong Herald Print n.d. circa, 1914, First edition; 8vo., variant black cloth (unprinted), 157 pages, frontispiece, illustrations, moderate wear to spine ends with small chips at spine ends and moderate chipping to all fore-edges, else very good, tight copy, housed in cloth slipcase with leather label on spine with gold stamping. Buckingham Books May 26 2011 - 23459 2011 $1750

Barton, William P. C. *Vegetable Materia Medica of the United States; or Medical Botany.* Philadelphia: M. Carey & Son, 1817-1818, First edition; 50 hand colored engraved plates (1 folding, occasional foxing, offsetting from text to many plates in volume I, less so in volume II, 4to., pages vi, (17-) 76, (ad - 4 pages); 273; xvi, (9-) 243, list of subscribers at end volume II, contemporary full sheep (wear to extremities, some splitting to 2 outer hinges but solid, old abrasion to rear cover of volume II, foxing, mostly to volume I, small dark stain to a leaf, ex-libris Dr. James Norris with his signature on titles, a bookplate). Raymond M. Sutton, Jr. May 26 2011 - 55847 2011 $6000

Bartram, Alfred, Mrs. *Recollections of Seven Years Residence at the Mauritius or Isle of France.* London: James Cawthorn, 1830, First edition; 8vo., xi, 208, ads, small mark on 4 pages, rebound in black half calf. J. & S. L. Bonham Antiquarian Booksellers Africa 4/20/2011 - 7884 2011 £375

Bartram, William *Travels through North & South Carolina, Georgia, East and West Florida, the Cherokee Country, The Extensive Territories of the Muscogulges or Creek Confederacy...* Philadelphia: James & Johnson, 1791, First edition; contemporary calf, early rebacking and gilt lettered black morocco spine label, (2), (iii)-xxxiv, 522 pages, engraved folding map and 7 engraved plates, this copy lacks engraved frontispiece portrait of "Mico Chulcco the Long Warrior", moderate foxing throughout, occasionally heavy, map with some wrinkles and wear along top edge with slight loss as with folding plate of Hydrangea Quercifolia; very good example, scarce. Charles Agvent 2010 Summer Miscellany - 6 2011 $6000

Bartram, William *Voyage dans les Parties Sud de L'Amerique Septentrionale...* Paris: Carteret et Brosson; Dugour et Durand An vii, 1799, First Paris edition; engraved frontispiece, 3 folding engraved plates, third plate has dampstaining in gutter and only touching a tip of an image, tear near gutter and third plate, large folding map, with some light dampstaining, 8vo., pages 457, errata; 94), 436, errata, original pink wrappers (chipped; some soiling; paper of spines, especially volume 2, partly perished, front cover to volume 1 detached, marginal tear to 2 pages, small red stain to upper edge of pages, more so volume 2, last gathering of pages in volume 2 nearly loose, light dampstaining to few pages in volume 2). Raymond M. Sutton, Jr. May 26 2011 - 55965 2011 $1250

Bartram, William *William Bartram's Reisen Durch Nord- und Sud-Karolina, Georgien, Ost- und West-Florida, das Gebiet der Tscherokesen...* Berlin: Vossische Buchhandlung, 1793, First German edition; 8 engraved plates, light foxing to 2, 8vo., pages (2), xxvi, 469, contemporary boards, rubbed, edges of covers and corners worn, head of spine perished, remains of old sticker on spine, small abrasions to spine, owner's name on front flyleaf, occasional foxing, mostly to prelim pages, otherwise, text and plates clean and fresh. Raymond M. Sutton, Jr. May 26 2011 - 39652 2011 $1200

Bartruse, Grace *The Children in Japan.* New York: McBride Nast, 1915, 4to., boards, slight cover soil, very good, 16 fine color plates by Willy Pogany and 16 black and whites, quite scarce. Aleph-Bet Books, Inc. 95 - 439 2011 $350

Baruch, Dorothy *Christmas Stocking.* New York: William Scott, 1946, First edition; oblong 12mo., spiral backed pictorial wrappers, slight shelfwear, else very good+, full page color illustrations by Lucienne Bloch. Aleph-Bet Books, Inc. 95 - 146 2011 $300

Barwell, Louisa Bacon *The Novel Adventures of Tom Thumb the Great: Showing How He Visited the Insect World and Learned Much Wisdom.* London: Chapman and Hall, n.d. circa, 1850, 16mo., (ii), 151 pages, blind embossed green cloth on boards with gilt title on upper cover repeated on spine, half title, full page wood engraved frontispiece, fine wood engravings, all printed on heavier paper, dry dealer seal and dated ink inscription on front free endpaper, cover sunned at spine, dampstain lower section of some plates, very good copy. Hobbyhorse Books 56 - 6 2011 $175

Barwick, Peter *Vita Johannis Barwick.* London: Typis Gulielmi Bowyer, 1721, Large paper copy; from the collection of Christopher Ernest Weston 1947-2010, 8vo., pages (lxvi), 464 (44) + 2 engraved portrait plates, contemporary sprinkled calf, gilt panelled spine, boards "Harleian style" gilt bordered board edges, decorative roll gilt, 'Dutch-comb' 'made' endpapers, all edges gilt, mid 1990's conservation/restoration by Weston, little surface wear to leather. Unsworths Booksellers 24 - 5 2011 £250

Barwick, Peter *The Life of the Reverend Dr. John Barwick, D.D.* London: printed by J. Bettenham, 1724, Large paper copy, 8vo., pages (xxiv), 552, (xl) + 2 engraved portrait frontispieces, contemporary calf, gilt panelled spine, orange lettering piece gilt, boards panelled in blind (Cambridge style), board edges decorative roll gilt, 'Dutch-comb' 'made' endpapers, all edges red and grey sprinkled green and white sewn endbands, rubbed at extremities, spine darkened, joints cracked but strong, endcaps worn "James Affleck" book label, contemporary ink inscription "Eliz. Dolben" and above "James Affleck", mid 20th century provenance note by Peter B. G. Binnall, from the collection of Christopher Ernest Weston 1947-2010. Unsworths Booksellers 24 - 6 2011 £200

Basbanes, Nicholas *A Gentle Madness.* New York: Holt, 1995, First edition; book fine, dust jacket near fine, very light rubbing.   Bella Luna Books   May 29 2011 - t9320 2011 $137

Basch, Peter *The Nude as Form and Figure.* New York: 1966, First edition; (112) pages, large 4to., original binding, fine in near fine dust jacket.   Bookworm & Silverfish 679 - 152 2011 $65

Basile, Giovanni Battista *Il Pentamerone or the Tale of Tales.* London: Henry and Co., 1893, First trade edition; 8vo., xvi, vi, 562 pages, continuous pagination, black cloth on boards, gilt title on upper covers repeated along spines, black endpaper, armorial plates inside upper cover of both volumes, trace of pasted down news clipping, very good.   Hobbyhorse Books   56 - 7 2011 $270

Basile, Giovanni Battista *Stories from the Pentamerone.* London: Macmillan, 1911, One of only 150 copies of the edition deluxe; large 4to., (304) pages, original full vellum stamped in gold, top edge gilt, slight toning to covers, some occasional foxing (worse on non pictorial endpapers), near fine in original dust jacket with silk ties renewed, rare.   Aleph-Bet Books, Inc. 95 - 258 2011 $2250

Baskin, Leonard *Birds and Animals.* Gehenna Press, 1972-1974, First edition; square 4to., 65 original wood engravings, full red pigskin with gilt cat profile on front cover by Arno Werner, very fine copy in beautiful Werner binding, half morocco folding box, unique copy, specially bound by Werner, with his pencil annotation on prelim leaf, binder's own copy with his bookplate.   James S. Jaffe Rare Books   May 26 2011 - 20923 2011 $9500

Bass, Rick *The Deer Pasture.* College Station: Texas A. & M, 1985, First edition; fine, dust jacket near fine, price clipped, inscribed by author.   Bella Luna Books   May 26 2011 - 4481 2011 $192

Bass, Rick *The Ninemile Wolves.* Livingston: Clark City Press, 1992, Limited to 125 copies; fine, signed by author, cloth slipcase.   Bella Luna Books   May 26 2011 - 4141 2011 $192

Bass, Rick *Wild to the Heart.* New York: Stackpole, 1987, First edition; illustrations by Elizabeth Hughes (Bass), fine in fine dust jacket, signed by author and artist.   Bella Luna Books   May 26 2011 - p2030 2011 $192

Bass, Rick *Wild to the Heart.* New York: Stackpole, 1987, First edition; illustrations by Elizabeth Hughes (Bass), fine in near fine dust jacket, light sunning to edges, signed by author.   Bella Luna Books   May 29 2011 - 3754 2011 $137

Basta, Giorgio *Counti d'Huszt.* Rouen: Jean Berthelin, 1627, Folio, (12), 76 pages, title within engraved border, woodcut initials and headpieces, 12 double page engraved plates, water damaged at foot throughout with some fraying, including foot of titlepage and on some plates, binding scraped; from the library of the Earls of Macclesfield at Shirburn Castle.   Maggs Bros. Ltd.   1440 - 26 2011   £450

Basterfield, George *Mountain Lure.* Kendal: Titus Wilson, 1947, First edition; original cloth, dust jacket, edges very worn and chipped, pages (12), 166 with 6 plates, loosely inserted are 2 leaflets of climbing poems by Basterfield, one with mss. correction and 8 line song, probably in author's hand, also inserted small card printed with poem "To Garth. The spider" by AW.   R. F. G. Hollett & Son Antiquarian Booksellers   173 - 58 2011   £65

Bataille, Georges *L'Experience Interieure. (Inner Experience).* Paris: Gallimard, 1943, First edition; octavo, 1 blank leaf, half title, titlepage, quote page, half title (9)-247 + 1 blank leaf + 1 leaf - 2 pages (table des Matieres) + 1 blank leaf, octavo, with titlepage marked "S.P." or Service de Presse", review copy, uncut copy, original publisher's printed wrappers, excellent copy, scarce.   Athena Rare Books   10 2011 $500

Bataille, Georges *Le Mort.* Paris: Au vent d'Arles, 1964, No. 5 of 10 copies (tirage de tete, from a total edition of 145) with extra suite of etchings, signed and numbered by artist, with a 'refused' plate, an original drawing and one of the original copper plates; oblong folio, pages (4) blank, lvii (including engravings), (3) blank, (4) limitation, imprints, 2 blanks, (4) blank; plus an original drawing and original rejected copper plate, laid into publisher's full vellum binding, title blindstamped to upper panel, with black lettering to spine, with additional suite of hand colored engravings, plus one refused, all signed by Mason, laid into publisher's oatmeal buckram cloth, vellum spine, publisher's leather edged oatmeal buckram slipcase, slight rubbing to edges of slipcase, overall near fine.   Simon Finch Rare Books   Zero - 444 2011   £10,000

Bateman, H. M. *Burlesques.* London: Duckworth, 1916, First edition; large 8vo., original cloth backed pictorial boards, slightly rubbed and dusty, lower corners worn, pages viii, 72, illustrations.   R. F. G. Hollett & Son Antiquarian Booksellers   General Catalogue Summer 2010 - 698 2011   £45

Bateman, H. M. *H. M. Bateman by Himself.* Collins, 1937, First edition; small 4to., original pictorial cloth, gilt, dust jacket, slightly frayed at head and foot of spine, pages 136, illustrated with cartoons and drawings.   R. F. G. Hollett & Son Antiquarian Booksellers   General Catalogue Summer 2010 - 699 2011   £50

Bateman, James *A Second Century of Orchidaceous Plants.* London: L. Reeve & Co., 1867, 100 hand colored lithographed plates (light foxing to a few, mostly marginal), slight tanning to 3, 2 small marginal stains to a plate, most plates clean and fresh, each with one or two pages of descriptive letterpress, 4to., pages viii, plates and letterpress, original green gilt lettered cloth (flecking to lower margin & lower edge of covers, also slightly to head of spine, few small scuffs & minor stains to covers, corners worn, light rubbing to edges of spine, light foxing to 2 edges of pages, pages and plates restitched, half title and last page tanned, correction slip pasted over imprint on title, scattered light foxing to letterpress pages, heavy to 1, few inner joints open, the copy of Mary Noble McQuerry. Raymond M. Sutton, Jr. May 26 2011 - 13000 2011 $6000

Bateman, Thomas *Ten Years Diggings in Celtic and Saxon Grave Hills, in the Counties of Derby, Stafford and York from 1848 to 1858...* London: J. R. Smith and Dergy: W. Bemrose & sons, 1861, First edition; original blind ruled cloth gilt, spine rather faded and little frayed at head and foot, pages 39, (iii), 59 illustrations, plans, patterned endpapers, labels removed from front endpapers, small library stamps to pastedown and back of title, title rather browned and front joint tender, scarce. R. F. G. Hollett & Son Antiquarian Booksellers 177 - 67 2011 £140

Bateman, William *The Colonist; a Work on the Past and Present Position of the Colony of New Zealand.* Christchurch: J. T. Smith and Co., 1881, First edition; half title, presentation inscription by author to Thomas Ingram, (12), tables in text, 9-486 pages, original cloth, appendix (pages 255-486). Anthony W. Laywood May 26 2011 - 19080 2011 $84

Bates, Elisha *The Doctrines of Friends or Principles of the Christian Religion as Held by the Society of Friends...* Dublin: reprinted by Thomas I. White, 1828, Original cloth backed boards, recased, pages viii, 383, uncut. R. F. G. Hollett & Son Antiquarian Booksellers 175 - 85 2011 £75

Bates, Ely *A Cursory View of Civil Government, Chiefly in Relation to Virtue and Happiness.* London: F. and C. Rivington, 1797, First (and only?) edition; very scarce, 8vo., vi, (ii), 245, (1) pages, contemporary, perhaps original, marbled boards, old paper spine lettered in ink, slightly worn and soiled, entirely uncut, very good, very scarce. John Drury Rare Books 153 - 11 2011 £600

Bates, Herbert Ernest 1905-1974 *In the Heart of the Country.* London: Country Life, 1942, First edition; small 4to., original green cloth, gilt, dust jacket, lower edges and head of spine little frayed, pages 150, 14 fine woodcut illustrations, scattered foxing, mainly to first few leaves, scarce in dust jacket. R. F. G. Hollett & Son Antiquarian Booksellers General Catalogue Summer 2010 - 918 2011 £65

Bates, Herbert Ernest 1905-1974 *Now Sleeps the Crimson Petal and Other Stories.* London: Joseph, 1961, First edition; light partial browning to initial and final letterpress pages, pages 208, crown 8vo., original pink cloth, backstrip gilt lettered, tiny chip to fold to tail of dust jacket, very good. Blackwell Rare Books B166 - 124 2011 £40

Bates, Herbert Ernest 1905-1974 *The Seasons and The Gardener.* Cambridge: University Press, 1945, Large 8vo., original cloth backed pictorial boards, matching dust jacket (trifling wear to extremities), pages 69, drawings throughout. R. F. G. Hollett & Sons Antiquarian Booksellers 170 - 692 2011 £35

Bates, Herbert Ernest 1905-1974 *Through the Woods.* London: Gollancz, 1936, First edition; small 4to., original cloth, gilt, dust jacket, little trifling wer and marking, pages 142, with 73 superb wood engravings, one or two light spots to endpapers, but very good. R. F. G. Hollett & Son Antiquarian Booksellers General Catalogue Summer 2010 - 861 2011 £140

Bateson, F. W. *Essays in Criticism.* 1951-1984, Complete run from volume 1/1-volume 32/4 Jan. 51-Oct. 82, with volume 33/4 & volume 34/2.3. 1984, over 130 issues in original wrappers, very good. I. D. Edrich May 26 2011 - 82788 2011 $1090

Bath, Isabella Elizabeth Thynne, Marchioness of *Cottage Domestic Economy.* Frome: Crockers printers, 1829, 12mo., original grey boards, sheep spine, spine rubbed, nice, scarce. Jarndyce Antiquarian Booksellers CXCI - 120 2011 £500

Batkin, Jonathan *Pottery of the Pueblos of New Mexico 1700-1940.* Colorado Springs: 1987, 215 pages, illustrations, dust jacket edges rubbed, else near fine, scarce. Dumont Maps & Books of the West 111 - 44 2011 $250

The Battle for Native Industry. The Debate Upon the Corn Laws, The Corn Importation and Customs Duties Bills, and Other Financial Measures of the Government in Session 1846. London: Office of the Society for the Protection of Agriculture and British Industry, n.d., 1846, First edition; 2 volumes, large 8vo., xii, 728; xii, 790 pages, original green cloth, printed spine labels, fine copies, untrimmed in virtually original condition. John Drury Rare Books 153 - 55 2011 £275

Baudelaire, Charles *Les Fleurs du Mal.* Paris: Poulet Malassis et De Broisse, 1857, First edition; first printing with six suppressed poems, in second state wrappers, original light yellow printed wrappers, uncut. Heritage Book Shop Booth A12 51st NY International Antiquarian Book Fair April 8-10 2011 - 8 2011 $40,000

Baudelaire, Charles *Les Fleurs Du Mal.* Paris: Poulet Malassis et de Broise, 1857, First edition, first issue cotnaining the six 'notorious' poems for which Baudeliare was fined and which were suppressed in second issue; with following points with "Fleurs" in headline on page 31 and 108, with p. 45 misnumbered 44 and the last word of first line on page 201 'captieux' instead of 'capiteux', 12mo., (4), 248, (4, table of contents) pages, title printed in red and black, original contemporary French binding of brown morocco grain cloth over boards, covers ruled in blind, smooth spine ruled in gilt and blind and lettered in gilt, marbled endpapers, edges sprinkled brown, merest of rubbing to corners and spine extremities, paper very slightly browned at edges, as to be expected, occasional very minor soiling or faint staining (heaviest on pages 52 an 53, 154 and 155 and 184 and 185), contemporary pencil inscription "Sancta Simplicita" at head of half title, spectacular copy in publisher's original binding, housed in three quarter black morocco clamshell cae,.   David Brass Rare Books, Inc.   May 26 2011 - 00219   2011 $19,500

Baughan, Peter E. *North of Leeds.* Roundhouse Books, 1966, First edition; thick 8vo, original cloth, gilt, dust jacket extremities little chipped, pages 500, 58 illustrations and 4 maps, excellent copy.   R. F. G. Hollett & Son Antiquarian Booksellers   173 - 62   2011   £50

Baum, Lyman Frank *The Enchanted Island of Yew.* Indianapolis: Bobbs Merrill, 1903, 4to., first edition, first state with titlepage printed only in orange and black, illustrations, page 238 printed upside down and pictorial endpapers, illustrations by Fanny Corry and 8 lovely color plates plus black and whites in text, beautiful copy.   Aleph-Bet Books, Inc.   95 - 90   2011 $900

Baum, Lyman Frank *The Marvelous Land of Oz.* Chicago: Reilly & Britton Co., 1904, First edition, mixed state unknown to Hanff and Greene (first state of binding - casting A, second state of text, publication date on verso of titlepage, smaller box on page 4, later state illustrations with transposed pictures to correct locations); 4to., light green cloth (casing A) with dark blue lettering and outlines of vignettes (themselves with green silver coloration), lettering and color vignette on spine (some rubbing), rear cover has dark blue outline of Jack Pumpkin-head, book has been resewn but is clean within, 16 full page color plates plus numerous black and white plates and drawings by John Neill, fine set of images.   Jo Ann Reisler, Ltd.   86 - 15   2011 $1200

Baum, Lyman Frank *The Marvelous Land of Oz.* Chicago: Reilly & Britton, 1904, First edition, second state, "A" binding in green with full title on cover and all points; illustrations by J. R. Neill, 16 full color plates plus black and whites in text, photo pictorial endpapers, beautiful copy, rarely found in this condition.   Aleph-Bet Books, Inc.   95 - 76   2011 $3500

Baum, Lyman Frank *The Master Key.* Indianapolis: Bowen Merrill, 1901, First edition, 3rd state with copyright notice 1-25/32 and all 16 page signatures except first; 8vo., 245 page, green gilt cloth, pictorial paste-on, some cover soil and signatures sprung but binding tight and overall very good, illustrations by Fanny Corry with 12 wonderful color plates plus black and white chapter heads and tails.   Aleph-Bet Books, Inc.   95 - 89   2011 $375

Baum, Lyman Frank *Mother Goose in Prose.* Chicago: Way & Williams, 1897, First edition, 2nd issue (all 16 page signatures terminal leaf concluding on page (272); 4to. 265 pages, grey pictorial cloth stamped in color on both covers, name erased from endpaper and slighest soil on covers, else tight, near fine, illustrations by Maxfield Parrish, first book with Parish illustrations.   Aleph-Bet Books, Inc.   95 - 75   2011 $7500

Baum, Lyman Frank *Mother Goose in Prose.* Chicago: Way & Williams, 1897, First edition, first issue; quarto, original grey cloth pictorially stamped in color, illustrations by Maxfield Parrish.   Heritage Book Shop   Booth A12 51st NY International Antiquarian Book Fair April 8-10 2011 - 9   2011 $6500

Baum, Lyman Frank *The Navy Alphabet.* Chicago: George Hill, 1900, First and only edition; folio, cloth backed pictorial boards, slight cover soil, edges rubbed bit as usual, corner of blank endpaper repaired, else very good+, nice, clean copy, very scarce, full color illustrations by Harry Kennedy.   Aleph-Bet Books, Inc.   95 - 85   2011 $2750

Baum, Lyman Frank *Patchwork Girl of Oz.* Chicago: Reilly & Britton, 1913, First edition (H/G VII) (but 'c' in chop, 3 on page 35 does not overlap text); 4to., green pictorial cloth, 341 pages + 5 pages ads, tiny snag at base of spine and name erased from tile, else very fine and bright, rare in this condition, illustrations by J. R. Neill.   Aleph-Bet Books, Inc.   95 - 80   2011 $1800

Baum, Lyman Frank *The Wonderful Wizard of Oz.* Chicago: George M. Hill, 1900, First edition, 2nd state with no box around ads on page 2, first line on page 14 reads 'low wail of', page 81 fourth line from bottom spells 'pieces' correctly, page (227) 1st line reads "While the Woodman", colophon is 13 lines with no box, verso of titlepage has copyright, mperfect type on pages 100, 186, color plates perfect on page 34 and 92, binding sate 'c' with publisher's imprint in red serifed type with the 'o' of "Co." inside the "C"; Large 8vo., pale green cloth stamped in red and green, 261 pages, fine and bright, clean and tight, housed in custom cloth box, wonderful color illustrations by W. W. Denslow, clean copy.   Aleph-Bet Books, Inc.   95 - 73   2011 $32,500

Baum, Lyman Frank *The Wizard of Oz.* New York: Holt Rinehart and Winston, 1982, Numerically stated first printing; 4to., full color pictorial boards, matching full color pictorial dust jacket, as new copy, drawing signed in full by artist, Michael Hague, color illustrations, 292 numbered pages. Jo Ann Reisler, Ltd.   86 - 126   2011 $300

Baum, Lyman Frank *The Wizard of Oz.* New York: Holt, Rinehart & Winston, 1982, Limited to 500 copies; 4to., emerald green cloth, gold lettering on front cover and spine, matching green cloth slipcase, as new copy, full page drawing on blank prelim page, housed in original cardboard mailing box, color illustrations.   Jo Ann Reisler, Ltd.   86 - 125   2011 $450

Baum, Lyman Frank *The Wonderful Wizard of Oz.* West Hatfield: Pennyroyal Press, 1985, Limited to 350 copies; signed by author, 13 x 12 inches, in as new condition, signed and dated pencil drawing on half titlepage, white cloth with elaborate gold decorations on front cover, housed in clamshell box that is covered with wheat cloth that has label on spine, there are two printed booklets laid into volume - "The Wizardry of Barry Moser" (invitation to an exhibition of Moser engravings, also signed in full by Moser) and "Forty-seven Days to Oz" signed by Moser, 62 black and white engravings by Barry Moser, poster for book included,.   Jo Ann Reisler, Ltd. 86 - 17 2011 $2400

Baum, Lyman Frank *Wizard of Oz Waddle Book.* New York: Blue Ribbon, 1934, First edition, first state; cloth fine in slightly frayed dust jacket with few mends, 8 color plates, this copy includes the 6 waddle figures, all of which are unpunched, the Ramp and the original pictorial band that goes around the ramp, enclosed in original pictorial envelope are the ramp and fasteners, few Waddle pieces neatly reinforced at creases.   Aleph-Bet Books, Inc.   95 - 74   2011 $28,500

Baum, Lyman Frank *The Wonderful Wizard of Oz.* Chicago: Geo. M. Hill Co., 1900, First edition, second state of text and second state of the plates; with the following points P. 2, the publisher's ad is not enclosed in a box, page 14, line 1 beings 'low wail of', page 81, the fourth line from bottom has 'pieces', pages (227) line 1 begins "While the Woodman" and colophon on rear pastedown is set in 13 lines and is not enclosed in box, initial letter in black, with broken type in last line of page 100 and page 186, verso of title has copyright notice, plate facing page 34 is in second state, without the two dark blue blots on moon, plate facing page 92 is i second state, without red shading on horizon, quarto, 259, (1), (1, blank) pages, 24 inserted color plates, including title which is included in pagination, original light green cloth, pictorially stamped and lettered in red and darker green (variant C, with publisher's imprint at foot of spine in plain, unserifed type, stamped in red rather than green, with the "C" of "Co" encircling the "o"), color pictorial pastedown endpapers (front pastedown printed in black and gray and rear pastedown printed in black and red), issued without free endpapers, this copy inscribed "To my dear Lyman with Merry Christmas greeting from Aunt Maud 1901", remarkable copy, absolutey fine, totally untouched, housed in velvet lined green cloth clamshell case.   David Brass Rare Books, Inc.   May 26 2011 - 00967   2011 $35,000

Bausch, Richard *Peace.* New York: Knopf, 2008, First edition; fine in very near fine dust jacket, inscribed by author.   Ken Lopez Bookseller   154 - 11   2011 $125

Bawden, Edward *A Book of Cuts.* London: Scolar Press, 1979, First edition; 4to., original cloth, dust jacket, pages 81 lino-cuts, fine.   R. F. G. Hollett & Son Antiquarian Booksellers   General Catalogue Summer 2010 - 41   2011   £120

Bawden, Edward *Edward Bawden A Seventy-fifth Birthday Exhibition 20 Febuary - 10 March 1978.* Curwen Press for the Fine Art Society, 1978, Limited edition, no. 385 of 800 copies; pages (12), title with border in green and 5 illustrations, small 8vo., original wrappers.   R. F. G. Hollett & Son Antiquarian Booksellers   General Catalogue Summer 2010 - 132   2011   £35

Bawden, Edward *Hold Fast by Your Teeth.* Routledge & Kegan Paul, 1963, First edition; (64) pages, 58 pages, colored illustrations, very good in original cloth decorative boards, dust jacket which has some edge wear and chips, scarce.   Ken Spelman Rare Books   68 - 130   2011   £120

Bawden, Edward *Hold Fast by Your Teeth.* London: Routledge & Kegan Paul, 1963, First edition; 4to., original pictorial boards, matching dust jacket, unpaginated, illustrations in color, few faint spots to flyleaf, else near fine.   R. F. G. Hollett & Sons Antiquarian Booksellers   170 - 53   2011   £275

Bawden, William *Dom Bloc. A Translation of the Record Called Domesday, so Far as Relates to the County of York... and to the Counties of Middlesex (et al) and Gloucester.* Doncaster: printed by W. Sheardown, 1809-1812, 2 volumes, 4to., pages (iv) iv, 31, (i), 628, 61, (iii); (iv), 26, 76, (3)-82, 62, 72, 2, 4, 3, i), 4, 6, contemporary tan half calf, spines double rule and single broken rule gilt orange and red lettering and numbering pieces gilt, place and date gilt direct at foot, boards single rule gilt bordered with "nonpareil" marbled sides, matching 'made' endpapers, dark olive green sewn flat endbands, volume I in mid 198's calf reback, little light spotting titlepage toned, some marginal pencil marks, boards bit scuffed, corners and volume 2 spine rubbed, armorial bookplate of Edward Balme Wheatley-Balme, from the collection of Christopher Ernest Weston 1947-2010. Unsworths Booksellers 24 - 68 2011 £300

Baxter, Doreen *Wonderland Tales.* London: J. M. Dent & Sons, 1958, First edition; 12mo., 66 numbered pages of enjoyable stories highlighted with five full color plates and lots of black and white line drawings in text. Jo Ann Reisler, Ltd. 86 - 20 2011 $175

Baxter, Stephen *Raft.* London: Grafton Books a Division of Harper Collins, 1991, First edition; octavo, boards. L. W. Currey, Inc. 124 - 100 2011 $750

Baxter, William *Glossarium Antiquitatum Britannicarum sive Syllabus Etymologicus Antiquitatum Vetris Britannae atque Iberniae Temporibus Romanorum etc.* London: W. Bowyer, 1719, Royal 8vo., (6), xiv, (4), 277, (19) pages, engraved portrait, contemporary russia binding, gilt border on covers, spine gilt, red edges, spine somewhat faded, without list of subscribers, from the library of the Earls of Macclesfield at Shirburn Castle. Maggs Bros. Ltd. 1440 - 27 2011 £600

Bayle, Pierre 1647-1706 *The Dictionary Historical and Critical of Mr. Peter Bayle.* London: J. J. & P. Knapton, 1734-1738, Second edition in English; five volumes, full original dark brown calf, raised gilt ruled bands, gilt stamped modern red leather spine labels, hinges repaired, fine. Jeff Weber Rare Books 163 - 37 2011 $1750

Bayley, Harold *The Lost Language of London.* London: Cape, 1935, First edition; original cloth, gilt, spine rather faded, library label on froot of upper board, pages 287, 31 illustrations, scattered spotting, few marginal ticks, large inked annotation to front pastedown, label removed from rear pastedown, uncommon. R. F. G. Hollett & Son Antiquarian Booksellers 175 - 91 2011 £45

Baylis, Thomas Henry *An Answer to the Attack of the "Daily News" of the 1st July 1856 on the Unity Fire Insurance Association Together with some Remarks on the Position and Progress of the Unity Institutions.* London: Chief Offices, Unity Buildings 8 and 10, Cannon Street, City, July, 1856, First edition; 8vo., 36 pages, preserved in modern wrappers, printed title label on upper cover, very good, rare. John Drury Rare Books 153 - 12 2011 £100

Beagle, Peter Soyer *The Last Unicorn.* New York: Viking Press, 1968, First edition; octavo, cloth backed boards. L. W. Currey, Inc. 124 - 117 2011 $650

Beamish, North Ludlow *The Discovery of America by the Northmen, in the Tenth Century...* London: T. & W. Boone, 1841, First edition; folding frontispiece map, 2 other charts, 2 tables, illustrations, 16 + 4 pages ads, original green cloth, slight rubbing, bookseller's ticket of Nettleton, Plymouth, very good. Jarndyce Antiquarian Booksellers CXCI - 62 2011 £200

Bean, George E. *Turkey's Southern Shore: an Archaeological Guide.* London: Ernest Benn, 1968, First edition; pages 188 with frontispiece, 77 plates, 30 text illustrations and folding map. R. F. G. Hollett & Son Antiquarian Booksellers 177 - 69 2011 £30

Bean, W. J. *The Royal Botanic Gardens Kew.* London: Cassell & Co., 1908, Large paper limited edition; no. 7 of 2100 copies, small folio, original decorated cloth gilt, pages xx, 222, top edge gilt, 60 plates, tipped on to grey card with tissue, front panel of the original dust jacket, laid on to rear pastedown, contemporary large folding colored plan loosely inserted, little foxing to prelim leaves, otherwise handsome, very scarce issue. R. F. G. Hollett & Son Antiquarian Booksellers General Catalogue Summer 2010 - 950 2011 £350

Beard, Dan *Moonblight & Six Feet of Romance.* Trenton: 1904, 238, (2) blank, ads (5) pages, good solid copy, all cover gilt and backstrip gilt bright, cover illustration by Beards, some tiny flecking to covers, dime sized dark spot on front cover, half dollar size white spot on rear cover. Bookworm & Silverfish 669 - 127 2011 $225

Beard, Geoffrey *Craftsmen and Interior Decoration in England 1660-1820.* Bloomsbury Books, 1986, Folio, original cloth, gilt, D (short closed tear to head of spine), pages xxiv, 312, with 16 color plates, 145 illustrations, 3 text figures. R. F. G. Hollett & Son Antiquarian Booksellers General Catalogue Summer 2010 - 42 2011 £45

Beard, Geoffrey *The Work of Robert Adam.* Bloomsbury, 1987, Large 8vo., original cloth, gilt, dust jacket price clipped, pages x, 244, 60 plates, fine. R. F. G. Hollett & Son Antiquarian Booksellers 177 - 70 2011 £40

Beard, John R. *The Life of Toussaint L'Ouverture.* London: Ingram, Cooke and Co., 1853, First edition; 8vo., 11, (1), 335, (1) pages, map and plates, original cloth, spine soiled, half title. M & S Rare Books, Inc. 90 - 34 2011 $350

Beardsley, Aubrey Vincent 1872-1898 *Under the Hill.* London: John Lane, 1904, First edition; 4to., 70 pages, frontispiece, 17 drawings, bright blue cloth with "The Bodley Head" at tail of spine, with gilt design and lettering, cover little worn and bumped at corners and end of spine, otherwise very good, tight copy. Second Life Books Inc. 174 - 30 2011 $800

Beaton, Cecil *Ballet.* London: Wingate, 1951, First edition; original cloth dust jacket, pages 86, color title, plates, line drawings. R. F. G. Hollett & Son Antiquarian Booksellers 175 - 93 2011 £75

Beaton, Cecil *Cecil Beaton's Scrapbook.* London: B. T. Batsford, 1937, First edition; 4to., original publisher's yellow cloth lettered in red on spine, the less common alternative binding (the other floral wallpaper style with similar endpapers), this with plain endpapers, pages (viii), 136, copiously illustrated in black and white, previous owner's neat dedication on front endpaper, clean, very good with very light wear at spine, slight staining at rear and very slight bumping. Any Amount of Books May 29 2011 - A72898 2011 $383

Beaton, K. De P. *Warden's Diary.* Nairobi: East Africa Standard, 1949-1950, Third impression of volume I (1949), first edition volume 2 (1950); 2 volumes, 8vo., pages 114; 120, numerous illustrations, original yellow cloth (volume I), original green cloth (volume 2). J. & S. L. Bonham Antiquarian Booksellers Africa 4/20/2011 - 9013 2011 £35

Beaton, Patrick *Six Months in Reunion: a Clergyman's Holiday and How He Passed It.* London: Hurst & Blackett, 1860, First edition; 2 volumes, 8vo., pages viii, 309; xii, 263, engraved frontispieces, marbled edges, some foxing to endpapers, frontispiece and titlepage, occasional mark internally, 19th century red decorative half calf, little rubbed, gilt library stamp and dark green label on spine, generally very good, rare. J. & S. L. Bonham Antiquarian Booksellers Africa 4/20/2011 - 5930 2011 £400

Beatrice Mary, Princess of England *A Birthday Book.* London: Smith Elder & Co., 1881, 4to., color litho plates, half title, light brown decorated cloth by Burn & Co., little marked, all edges gilt, very good. Jarndyce Antiquarian Booksellers CXCI - 73 2011 £125

Beattie, Ann *Picturing Will.* New York: Random House, 1989, First edition; 8vo., pages 230, nice copy in little scuffed and soiled dust jacket. Second Life Books Inc. 174 - 32 2011 $65

Beattie, Ann *Where You'll Find Me.* New York: Linden Press, 1986, First edition; near fine, spine lightly bumped, frontispiece near fine, light creasing, inscribed to Chris Offutt. Bella Luna Books May 29 2011 - t581 2011 $82

Beattie, George William *Heritage of the Valley. San Bernardino's First Century.* Pasadena: San Pasqual Press, 1939, First edition; xxv, (1), 459 pages, 33 photos, maps, blue cloth lettered in gilt on spine and front cover, light rubbing to extremities, else fine. Argonaut Book Shop Recent Acquisitions Summer 2010 - 179 2011 $350

Beattie, James 1735-1803 *The Minstrel or the Progress of Genius.* Edinburgh: printed by James Ballantyne, 1803, One of a few early editions; engraved frontispiece, first two and last 20 leaves browned, little light foxing, elsewhere, small dampmark in corner of first few leaves and gutter of last few, pages xiv, (2), 147, 4to., modern half biscuit calf with marbled boards, backstrip with few raised bands between gilt fillets, red morocco label in second compartment, rest with small central clover stamps, boards very slightly bowed, good. Blackwell Rare Books B166 - 10 2011 £150

Beattie, James 1735-1803 *The Minstrel.* London: printed for John Sharpe, 1817, contemporary full calf gilt, boards panelled in gilt and blind, central panel in contrasting lther, three broad raised bands, rather rubbed, scratched, pages 176, engraved title and 5 engraved vignettes by Richard Westall, corner of front marble flyleaf defective, some soiling, spotting and creasing to plates. R. F. G. Hollett & Son Antiquarian Booksellers General Catalogue Summer 2010 - 625 2011 £35

Beatty, Bessie *A Political Primer for the New Voter.* San Francsco: Whitaker & Ray-Wiggin, 1912, First edition; 8vo., pages 76, bound in printed paper boards (bent and stained, ex-library stamp on front endpaper, pocket in rear, some marginal waterstain), not a pretty copy, but serviceable and complete, scarce. Second Life Books Inc. 174 - 33 2011 $200

Beaufort, Duke of *Driving.* London: Longman, Green and Co., 1889, First edition; original brown pictorial cloth, pages xvi, 426, (iv), top edge gilt, illustrations. R. F. G. Hollett & Son Antiquarian Booksellers General Catalogue Summer 2010 - 1217 2011 £120

Beaumont, Cyril Winthrop *New Paths.* London: C. W, Beaumont, 1918, First edition, one of 6 copies on Japon specially printed for presentation in addition to the stated 30 copies, with Anne Estelle Rice's illustrations and Edgar Tytgat's frontispiece lithograph, all hand colored; 8vo., pages (xii), 164, complete with frontispiece, illustrations and 18 photogravures, uncut, spotting to endpapers and first and last leaves as often with this title, light offsetting from frontispiece colouring to titlepage, original tan paper boards, printed with illustrations in blue, white paper label printed in blue to spine, some light shelfwear, short crack to lower hinge but holding firm, glassine cover, from the library of John Martin, publisher of Black Sparrow Press. Simon Finch Rare Books Zero - 331 2011   £300

Beaumont, Cyril Winthrop *Sea Magic.* London: John Lane, The Bodley Head, 1928, First edition; original cloth backed decorated boards, pages 120, (vi), frontispiece, text illustrations in colors, flyleaves trifle browned.   R. F. G. Hollett & Sons Antiquarian Booksellers 170 - 500 2011 £30

Beaumont, Francis *Comedies and Tragedies Written by Francis Beaumont and John Fletcher, Gentlemen.* London: printed for Humphrey Robinson and for Humphrey Moseley, 1647, First collected edition; folio, 20th century crimson morocco by Riviere & Sons.   Heritage Book Shop   Booth A12 51st NY International Antiquarian Book Fair April 8-10 2011 - 11 2011 $7500

Beaumont, William 1785-1853 *Experiments and Observations on the Gastric Juice and the Physiology of Digestion.* Plattsburgh: printed by F. P.. Allen, 1833, First edition; 8vo., 280 pages, 3 woodcut illustrations, original tan paper covered boards, purple-brown linen spine, rebacked, retaining 95 per cent of original spine but largely obscuring original printed paper spine label, gathering 2L browned as always, usual scattered foxing, else very good copy of fragile book. Joseph J. Felcone Inc. Fall Miscellany 2010 - 84 2011 $3000

Beaumont, William 1785-1853 *The Physiology of Digestion, with Experiments on the Gastric Juice.* Burlington: Chauncey Goodrich, 1847, Second edition, 1500 copies printed; small 8vo., 303, (1) pages, several text illustrations, original cloth, ends of spine chipped, corners bumped, sound and tight, very good, very scarce. M & S Rare Books, Inc. 90 - 35 2011 $400

Beauvoir, Simone De *Les Belles Images. (The Beautiful Images).* Paris: Gallimard, 1966, Half title, titlepage + dedication page, 5-(258) + leaf - Oeuvres & printer's information, original wrappers, pages just bit browned, otherwise fine.   Athena Rare Books   10 2011 $100

Beauvoir, Simone De *L'Existentialisme et la Sagesse des nations. (Existentialism and the Wisdom of the Nations).* Paris: Nagel, 1948, First edition; half title + titlepage + dedication page 9-(165) + (167) - tables des matieres, small octavo, original publisher's printed wrappers, slightly cocked with pages lightly browned, as usual, overall very good. Athena Rare Books   10 2011 $150

Beauvoir, Simone De *Le Deuxieme Sexe. (The Second Sex).* Paris: Gallimard, 1949, First edition, one of 200 numbered copies (from an edition of 2150) on alfama Marais paper - volume I numbered 1218 and volume 2 numbered 781; bound in original boards with design by Mario Prassinos, publisher's original binding with colorful modern design supplied by Prassinos, carefully protected in original clear wrapping, fine and gorgeous copy.   Athena Rare Books   10 2011 $1800

Beauvoir, Simone De *The Second Sex.* Franklin Center: Franklin Library, 1979, Limited edition reissue; bound in dark blue gilt decorated leather, signed by author, illustrations by Eugene Karlin, fine.   Charles Agvent 2010 Summer Miscellany - 8 2011 $200

Beauvoir, Simone De *Une Mort Tres Douce. (A Very Easy Death).* Paris: Gallimard, 1964, First edition; half title, titlepage + dedication page + quotation page 11-(164) + 1 leaf - oeuvres, 1 leaf - printer's information, original wrapper, signature and date on half title, otherwise fine.   Athena Rare Books   10 2011 $100

Beazley, Samuel *A General View of the System of Enclosing Wastelands with Particular Reference to the Proposed Enclosure at Epsom in Surrey.* London: Printed for C. Chapple, 1812, First edition; 8vo., (4), 51, (1) pages, neat old signature in ink on title (Thos. H. Foxcroft), fine in excellent contemporary style quarter calf over marbled boards, spine lettered in gilt, very rare. John Drury Rare Books 154 - 21 2011 £350

Beccari, Odoardo *Asiatic Palms - Lepidocarveae. Part I. Supplement to Part I, Part II, Part III.* Calcutta: Bengal Secretariat Press and Bengal Secretariat Book Depot, 1908-1921, 4 volumes in 8, including 4 portfolios of plates, 548 plates (mostly photographic), with wormholes, mostly the size of pinholes to plates for volumes I II and supplement, wormholes in volume I affect the back plates in a minor way, occasional foxing, plates toned, few browned, some superficial streaking to several plates for volume III, brown stains to upper margin of 3 plates for volume III, the preliminary pages for plates going with volume I are missing, a plate is faded), folio for text volumes an 21 1/2 x 14 inches for portfolios of plates, pages (5), v, 518; (7), vii, 142, ; (7), 237; viii, 231, 6 plates (tanned), attractive modern cloth (pages browned or tanned, 2 supplement volume with wormholes, mostly the size of pinhole, heavier to margins, not affecting readability, minor worming to margins near fore edges of text in volume II). Raymond M. Sutton, Jr. May 26 2011 - 39395 2011 $2900

Beccari, Odoardo *Asiatic Palms - Lepidocaryeae.* 1908-1921, 3 part in 6 volumes, including 3 volumes of plates, missing plate volume for part II, missing the text section to accompany the plates in supplement for part I, 447 plates (most are toned, few minor marginal wormholes in part I), titlepage to part I is missing, heel of spine bumped, resulting an inch split, prelim pages to supplement are laid down and are with some worming, 2 plates in supplement are laid down, few wormholes, mostly the size of pinholes, to plates in supplement; last plate in supplement soiled and with 3 marginal stains, few minor marginal wormholes to plates in part III, some light brown streaking to few plates in part III, most of which are phototype plates printed in Florence after photos by Beccari, folio, pages (5), iv, 518; (5), 237; (9), 229, unattractive modern cloth over boards (3 original front wrappers are laid down on covers, pages browned or tanned, some pages unopened, occasional foxing, few wormholes not affecting text to part I, last leaf to part I soiled and with some tears, numerous wormholes, mostly to margins near gutter to pages in part II, a page in part II torn, few short tears to pages in part II, edges of prelim page in part III chipped, occasional soiling. Raymond M. Sutton, Jr. May 26 2011 - 33106 2011 $2100

Beccaria, Cesare Bonesana, Marchese Di 1738-1794 *An Essay on Crimes and Punishments.* London: J. Almon, 1797, First edition in English; 8vo., xii, 179, (1), lxxix, (i) pages, little paper browning at beginning and end of volume, rebound fairly recently in half calf over marbled boards, spine with raised bands, gilt lettered label, good. John Drury Rare Books 153 - 13 2011 £950

Becher, Bernhard *Anonyme Skulpturen. Eine Typologie Technischer Bauten.* Dusseldorf: Art Press Verlag, 1970, First edition of Becher's first book; 4to., pages (215) (i) blank, 196 black and white photos, text in German, English and French, original blue cloth, spine and upper side lettered in white, light marks to boards at fore-edge, original dust jacket illustrated with black and white photos, text printed in black, little light soiling, two short closed tears to lower panel and one to upper and light nicks to head of spine, ex-libris of German photographer Michael Ruetz, near fine. Simon Finch Rare Books Zero - 507 2011 £3000

Becher, Bernhard *Anyonyme Skulpturen.* New York: Wittenborn and Co., 1970, First edition; very near fine with slightly splayed boards, very near fine with slightly splayed boards in very near fine dust jacket with couple of closed tears to top corners and one to top of spine, bright. Jeff Hirsch Books ny 2010 2011 $3500

Beck, Conrad *The Microscope.* London: R. & J. Beck, 1921, Original green cloth, little marked, pages 144, 131 illustrations. R. F. G. Hollett & Son Antiquarian Booksellers General Catalogue Summer 2010 - 1085 2011 £45

Beck, Thomas Alcock *Annales Furnesienses. History and Antiquities of the Abbey of Furness.* Payne and Foss, M. A. Nattali and Ulverston: S. Soulby, 1844, First and only edition (250 copies); large 4to., contemporary full pebble grain morocco gilt over heavy bevelled boards, boards panelled and decorated in gilt cathedral style, spine with 5 raised bands and contrasting label, panels decorated overall in blind, few slight old scuffs to boards, pages xii, 403, cxi, all edges gilt and gauffered, engraved title, printed title in red and black, 3 lithographed facsimiles, 1 engraved plan, 18 fine tissue guarded steel engraved plates, 3 tinted lithographs, 11 text woodcuts, occasional spot to plates, handsome, clean, sound copy, rare. R. F. G. Hollett & Son Antiquarian Booksellers 173 - 66 2011 £650

Beckett, Samuel 1906-1989 *Company.* Iowa Center for the Book at the University of Iowa, 1983, First edition thus, one of 52 press numbered copies signed by author and artist, printed by hand on Arches cover paper; folio, 13 full page etchings by Delles Henke, quarter black morocco, black morocco fore-tips and paste paper over boards, speckled endpapers by Bill Anthon, fine in publisher's slipcase which is slightly sunned at edges. James S. Jaffe Rare Books May 26 2011 - 20709 2011 $8500

Beckett, Samuel 1906-1989 *Fin de Partie, Suivi de Acte sans Paroles. (Endgame followed by Act Without Words).* Paris: Les Editions de Minuit, 1957, First edition, first issue on 'grand papier' published Jan. 30 1957, One of 50 copies Printed on 'velin pur fil du Marais", the being #13; 8vo., original printed wrappers, immaculate, unopened copy of this rare issue, preserved in folding linen box with leather spine. James S. Jaffe Rare Books May 26 2011 - 21144 2011 $12,500

Beckett, Samuel 1906-1989 *Imagination Morte Imagines.* Paris: Les Editions de Minuit, 1965, First edition, number 130 of 450; signed, 8vo., pages 24, original white paper wrappers printed in black, pages unopened, author's signature in black ink to titlepage, fine. Simon Finch Rare Books Zero - 208 2011 £350

Beckett, Samuel 1906-1989 *L'Issue.* Paris: Georges Visat, 1968, First Arikha edition and first French edition of Samuel Beckett's text; of a total edition of 151, this exemplar number 15 of 130 on rives paper, 6 original full page color and black and white etchings, each signed by Avigdor Arikha in pencil, 12 x 9.5 inches, about 30 loose leaves, housed in publisher's wrappers, boards, chemise and slipcase, as new. Gemini Fine Books & Arts, Ltd. Art Reference & Illustrated Books: First Editions 2011 $2750

Beckett, Samuel 1906-1989 *Murphy.* London: George Routledge and Sons, 1938, first edition, first issue, one of 1250 copies; original green cloth, spine lettered in gold, 8vo., pages (6), 282, (4) ads, endpapers faintly foxed, small remainder mark to bottom edge, cloth evenly rubbed at spine and corners, spine caps slightly creased, small sticker mark to upper board, previous owner's signature to front free endpaper.   Simon Finch Rare Books   Zero - 206   2011   £1750

Beckett, Samuel 1906-1989 *Nouvelles et Textes Pour Rien.* Paris: Les Editions de Minuit, No. 1071 of a total edition of 1185, 1955, First edition; 8vo., pages 220, (3), uncut, internally fresh and bright, publisher's wrappers, text in blue and black, slightly creased with occasional short nicks to lower edge.   Simon Finch Rare Books   Zero - 207   2011   £150

Beckett, Samuel 1906-1989 *Sans.* Paris: Les Editions de Minuit, 1969, First edition, no. 388 of 550 copies; signed, 8vo., pages 24, original white paper wrappers printed in black, pages unopened, author's signature in black ink, fine.   Simon Finch Rare Books   Zero - 209   2011   £350

Beckett, Samuel 1906-1989 *Sejour.* Paris: Georges Richard, 1970, First edition of Beckett's text (in French); of the total edition of 190, this copy is one of 150 on Rives paper, numbered and signed by Samuel Becket in pen and stamped with Deyrolle's signature, 5 full page original etchings by Louis Maccard after drawings by Jean Deyrolle, small oblong 4to., about 30 pages, loose sheets housed in wrapper folder, cloth chemise and slipcase, in excellent condition.   Gemini Fine Books & Arts, Ltd.   Art Reference & Illustrated Books: First Editions 2011 $1000

Beckford, William 1760-1844 *Vathek.* London: Folio Society, 1958, First edition thus; original cloth backed patterned boards, slipcase, pages 128, 8 color lithographs and color endpapers by Bawden,.   R. F. G. Hollett & Son Antiquarian Booksellers   General Catalogue Summer 2010 - 708   2011   £30

Becon, Thomas *The Reliques of Rome, Contayning All Such Matters of Religion as Have In Times Past Bene Brought into the Church by the Pope and Hi Adherentes.* London: Iohn Day, 1563, Newly corrected and greatly augmented edition; Black letter, woodcut title, author portrait on verso of title, decent, very good copy bound in recent full dark brown leather lettered gilt at spine, author on spine printed as Bacon not Becon, good margins, some pages slighty browned, some slight staining, occasional marginal note in old hand, small repair to last page, text unaffected.   Any Amount of Books   May 26 2011 - A72563   2011 $2097

Bede, the Venerable *Historiae Ecclesiasticae Gentis Anglorum...* Cantabrigiae: Typis Academicis, 1722, Folio, pages (xvi), 823 (xv) + 2 engraved plates and 1 folding map, early 19th century sprinkled an polished calf, spine fully gilt, red lettering piece gilt boards decorative roll gilt bordered, board edges decorative roll gilt, turn-ins decorative roll gilt, "French Shell" "made" endpapers, all edges 'Gloster' marbled, 3 colour (blue, red & white), sewn endbands, early 21st century conservation by Chris Weston, some browning to initial leaves and plates, little minor spotting elsewhere, few old scratched to old boards, signed binding with ticket of Nichols, Wakefield, unidentified armorial bookplate, and below, the later booklabel of Eric Poole, from the collection of Christopher Ernest Weston 1947-2010.   Unsworths Booksellers   24 - 7 2011   £1500

Bedford, Hilory G. *Texas Indian Troubles. The Most Thrilling in the History of Texas.* Dallas: Hargreaves Printing Co., 1905, First edition; 8vo., decorated light gray embossed cloth with black lettering and reddish decoration, decorated endpapers, illustrations, small stains to lower portion of front cover, light wear to spine ends and corners, small rub to edge of rear panel, else very good, tight copy.   Buckingham Books   May 26 2011 - 29547   2011 $1750

Bedini, Silvio *Patrons, Artisans and Instruments of Science 1600-1750.* Aldershot/Brookfield: Ashgate/Variorum, 1999, 8vo., xiv, various pagination, teal cloth, gilt stamped cover and spine titles, fine, from the Bern Dibner reference library, with Burndy bookplate.   Jeff Weber Rare Books   161 - 33   2011 $140

Bedini, Silvio *Science and Instruments in Seventeenth Century Italy.* Aldershot/Brookfield: Variorum, 1994, 8vo., x, various pagination, fine, from the Bern Dibner reference library, with Burndy bookplate.   Jeff Weber Rare Books   161 - 32   2011 $200

The Bee, Fire-Side Companion & Evening Tales... Liverpool: Printed at the Caxton Press by Henry Fisher, 1820, Pages 9-11, 26-1527, columns, ii-viii, engraved frontispiece little spotted, little browning toward beginning, scarce, old full calf gilt.   R. F. G. Hollett & Son Antiquarian Booksellers   General Catalogue Summer 2010 - 643   2011   £65

Beecher, Catherine E. *A Treatise on Domestic Economy for the Use of Young Ladies at Home and At School.* Boston: 1841, 441, (3) blank, 18 ads pages, good only, opaque staining to cover, stitching broken at gathering beginning at page 180 to 192.   Bookworm & Silverfish   678 - 46   2011 $75

Beechey, Frederick William 1796-1856 *Narrative of a Voyage to the Pacific and Beering's Strait...Performed in His Majesty's Ship Blossom... in the Years 1825, 1826, 1827, 1828...* London: Henry Colburn and Richard Bentley, 1831, First edition; 2 volumes, quarto, (iii)-xxi, (1, errata), (1, directions to the binder), (1, blank), 392; (iii)-vii, (1, directions to binder), (393)-742 pages, bound without publisher's ads (2) pages at end volume II and bound without half titles, 3 engraved maps, two of which are folding and 23 engraved plates, contemporary diced calf, rebacked in style, boards ruled in gilt, each volume with red and black, spine labels, spines stamped and lettered in gilt, board edges stamped in gilt, all edges marbled, bit of spotting and offsetting, three quarter inch closed tear to outer margin of b4 in volume I, not affecting text, boards with few light scrapes and spots, overall very good, handsome, the Frank S. Streeter copy with his bookplate.   Heritage Book Shop   Holiday 2010 - 8   2011 $8500

Beehler, William N. *Relief, Work and Rehabilitation.* Charleston: 1934, First edition; 4to., very good, photo illustrated, 208, (3) pages, original binding.   Bookworm & Silverfish   666 - 197   2011 $90

Beer, Arthur *The Origins, Achievement and Influence of the Royal Observatory, Greenwich 1675-1975.* Oxford: Pergamon Press, 1976, Tall 8vo., viii, 272 pages, plates, illustrations, figures, printed wrappers, lightly rubbed, very good, from the Bern Dibner reference library, with Burndy bookplate.   Jeff Weber Rare Books   161 - 35   2011 $185

Beerbohm, Max 1872-1956 *Zuleika Dobson; or an Oxford Love Story.* London: William Heinemann, 1911, Without initial blank, half title printed in brown, title in brown and black, original light brown decorated cloth, spine slightly dulled, contemporary signature and two booksellers' stamps, very good.   Jarndyce Antiquarian Booksellers   CXCI - 64   2011   £120

Beerbohm, Max 1872-1956 *Zuleika Dobson or an Oxford Love Story.* Oxford: Shakespeare Head Press, 1975, 187/750 copies signed by artist; 2 color printed plates, reproductions of 5 pencil character sketches by Beerbohm within prelims, initial letter at beginning of each chapter and shoulder titles printed in dark cerise, titlepage printed in black and cerise, pages xvi, 190, small folio, original quarter Oxford blue morocco, gilt lettered backstrip with gilt blocked Lancester drawing, "Bullingdon" blue and white vertically striped board sides, top edge gilt, blue cotton marker, board slipcase, fine.   Blackwell Rare Books   B166 - 273   2011   £250

Beeton, Isabella *The Book of Household Management.* London: Ward, Lock and Co. circa, 1882, Three hundred and sixty first thousand; thick small 8vo., modern half scarlet levant morocco gilt, pages 1, 1296 (xxiv), 12 color plates, 10 full page woodcut plates, numerous woodcut illustrations in text, frontispiece little defective and laid down, first few leaves little browned, chipped and neatly repaired, little scattered soiling, but very good.   R. F. G. Hollett & Son Antiquarian Booksellers   General Catalogue Summer 2010 - 1088   2011   £150

Beeton, S. O. *Beeton's Famous Voyages, Brigand Adventures, Tales of the Battlefield, Life and Nature.* London: Ward, Lock and Tyler, n.d., Thick 8vo., original blindstamped cloth gilt, neatly recased, pages xiv, 656, 384, 16 with chromolithographed frontispiece (repaired in gutter on reverse) and numerous text woodcuts.   R. F. G. Hollett & Sons Antiquarian Booksellers   170 - 71   2011   £85

Beevor, Charles *The Croonian Lectures on Muscular Movements and Their Representation in the Central Nervous System.* London: Adlard and Son, 1904, First edition; 8vo., original publisher's red cloth lettered gilt at spine, pages xii, 100 with 6 figures, ownership signature of C. S. Sherrington (i.e. Charles Scott Sherrington 1857-1952), tipped in "With the Author's compliments", slight fading at top edge, very slight fading at spine, else very good+.   Any Amount of Books   May 29 2011 - A48318   2011 $213

Begbie, Harold *Great Men.* London: Grant Richards, 1901, First edition; 4to., 51 pages, cloth backed pictorial boards, some cover soil, else very good and clean, full page color illustrations.   Aleph-Bet Books, Inc.   95 - 442   2011 $200

Begley, Louis *Wartime Lies.* New York: Knopf, 1991, First edition; fine in fine dust jacket.   Bella Luna Books   May 29 2011 - 102   2011 $82

Behan, Brendan 1923-1964 *Hold Your Hour and have Another.* London: Hutchinson, 1963, First edition; original cloth gilt, top of upper board faded, dust jacket edges chipped and little stained, pages 192, illustrations by Beatrice Behan.   R. F. G. Hollett & Son Antiquarian Booksellers   General Catalogue Summer 2010 - 725   2011   £35

Behn, Aphra 1640-1689 *All the Histories and Novels Written by the Late Ingenious Mrs. Behn...Together with the History of the Life and Memoirs of Mrs. Behn.* London: for R. Wellington, 1705, Fifth edition; (10), 377 (i.e. 376), 379-401, 442-500, (6) pages including prelim ad leaf, contemporary panelled calf, very skillfully rebacked in period style, tear through several lines of text on S2 repaired, several other minor largely marginal tears neatly repaired and blank corners replaced, marginal staining on last few leaves, very good.   Joseph J. Felcone Inc.   Fall Miscellany 2010 - 12   2011 $2800

Beke, Charles Tilstone *The Sources of the Nile Being a General Survey of the Basin of that River and of Its Head Streams with History of Nilotic Discovery.* London: James Madden, 1860, First edition; 8vo., pages xx, (v), 155, 6 maps and charts, 1 diagram in text, margins very slightly browned or foxed, original brown blindstamped cloth, spine faded and slightly rubbed, but excellent copy, uncommon. J. & S. L. Bonham Antiquarian Booksellers   Africa   4/20/2011 - 5933   2011   £750

Bekoff, Marc *Encyclopedia of Human Animal Relationships: a Global Exploration of Our Connections with Animals.* Westport: Greenwood Press, Sept. 30, 2007, First edition; 4 volumes, large 8vo., illustrated laminated boards, pages 1438, fine.   Any Amount of Books   May 29 2011 - A66217   2011 $272

Belgravia: a London Magazine. London: John Maxwell, 1867, First edition; 6 volumes, bound in half leather, pages 3249, 90 plates, leather worn and rubbed at spine without spine labels, otherwise sound, near very good with clean text.   Any Amount of Books   May 29 2011 - A73016   2011 $340

Belknap, Bill *Gunnar Widforss: Painter of the Grand Canyon.* Flagstaff: 1969, xx, 86 pages, illustrations, dust jacket lightly soiled with short tear, else clean and very good.   Dumont Maps & Books of the West   113 - 26   2011 $150

Bell, A. E. *Christian Huygens and the Development of Science in the Seventeenth Century.* London: Edward Arnold, 1947, First edition; 8vo., 220 pages, frontispiece, plates, figures, brown cloth, silver stamped spine title, dust jacket, jacket chipped, very good, Charles Singer's copy with his small booklabel, from the Bern Dibner reference library, with Burndy bookplate.   Jeff Weber Rare Books   161 - 226   2011 $95

Bell, Charles 1774-1842 *Essays on the Anatomy of Expression in Painting.* London: Longman, Hurst, Rees and Orme, 1806, First edition; large 4to., 12, 186 pages, 6 plates and text illustrations, contemporary three quarter marbled boards, slight foxing, but excellent.   M & S Rare Books, Inc.   90 - 36   2011 $850

Bell, Colin *City Fathers.* Barri & Rockliff: The Cresset Press, 1969, First edition; square 4to., , original cloth, gilt, dust jacket, pages 216, illustrations,.   R. F. G. Hollett & Son Antiquarian Booksellers   177 - 72   2011   £40

Bell, Edward Allen *A History of Giggleswick School from its Foundation 1499 to 1912.* Leeds: Richard Jackson, 1912, Limited large paper edition, no. 40 of 100 copies; original full vellum gilt over bevelled boards, spine trifle rubbed, pages xii, 294 (v), top edge gilt, untrimmed with 44 plates, excellent copy, very scarce deluxe edition, bookplate of A. E. G. Wright, this copy was purchased new by his grandfather T. W. Wright.   R. F. G. Hollett & Son Antiquarian Booksellers   General Catalogue Summer 2010 - 1331   2011   £180

Bell, Elizabeth Turner Bell *Twenty-Five New Figure and Character Dances.* Waverley Book Co., 1927, First edition; 4to., original blue blindstamped cloth, gilt, pages 114, numerous photos and line drawings, 67 page booklet of music under sleeve at end, fine.   R. F. G. Hollett & Son Antiquarian Booksellers   175 - 98   2011   £45

Bell, Henry *An Historical Essay on the Origin of Painting.* Worrall, 1728, First edition; (4), 138, (6) pages table and ads, titlepage printed in red and black, very good expertly bound in recent quarter calf, very scarce.   Ken Spelman Rare Books   68 - 3   2011   £680

Bell, R. C. *Tynside Pottery.* Studio Vista, 1971, First edition; original cloth, gilt, dust jacket, top edges trifle worn, pages 151, illustrations.   R. F. G. Hollett & Son Antiquarian Booksellers   General Catalogue Summer 2010 - 43   2011   £45

Bell, Thomas *A History of British Reptiles.* London: John Van Voorst, 1839, First edition; original green cloth gilt, spine trifle frayed at head and foot, pages xxiv, 142, with over 40 fine text woodcuts, 3 leaves of very neat mss. additions from 1860's tipped in together with exra illustration, few neat additional names on small slips also pasted in, prospectus tipped in at end, scarce.   R. F. G. Hollett & Son Antiquarian Booksellers   General Catalogue Summer 2010 - 951   2011   £150

Bell, Thomas *A History of British Reptiles.* John Van Voorst, 1849, Second edition; 50 wood engravings, 159 pages + ads, half title, good clean, original cloth, covers little faded, signature of 19th century natural history artist F. L. Frohawk at head of titlepage.   Ken Spelman Rare Books   68 - 140   2011   £40

Bell, Whitfield J. *Patriot Improvers: Biographical Sketches of the American Philosophical Society.* Philadelphia: The Society, 1997-1999, Volume one 1743-1768, volume two 1768, 2 volumes, volumes 226-227, tall 8vo., xx, 531; xiii, 425 pages, illustrations, maroon cloth, gilt stamped cover and spine titles, fine, from the Bern Dibner reference library, with Burndy bookplate.   Jeff Weber Rare Books   161 - 36   2011 $70

Bell, William *New Tracks in North America.* Albuquerque: 1965, Reprint of 1869 first edition; near fine in dust jacket. Dumont Maps & Books of the West   111 - 45   2011 $85

Bell, William J. *Cockroaches: Ecology, Behavior and Natural History.* Baltimore: 2007, Quarot, dust jacket, 230 pages, black and white photos, line drawings. Andrew Isles Natural History Books Spring 2010 - 31543 2011 $149

Bellamy, George Anne *An Apology for the Life of George Anne Bellamy, Late of Covent Garden Theatre.* London: for the author, 1785, Third edition; 5 volumes, 12mo., uniformly bound in modern boards, paper labels, half title of first volume frayed at edges and laid down, pages completely untrimmed, causing minor fraying to few corners, dusty to some fore-edges, else contents clean and fresh. Dramatis Personae Booksellers 106 - 17 2011 $300

Belli, Melvin *Modern Trials.* Indianapolis: 1954, 7 volumes, volumes 1-3 have 1966 supplements, volumes 4-6 are 1959 with 1966 supplements, the seventh volume has 1961 supplements to volumes, all fine in brown cloth. Bookworm & Silverfish 665 - 77 2011 $250

Belloc, Hilaire 1870-1953 *The Campaign of 1812 and the Retreat from Moscow.* Thomas Nelson, n.d., Full black morocco gilt, prize binding pages viii, 271, frontispiece, 4 folding maps. R. F. G. Hollett & Son Antiquarian Booksellers General Catalogue Summer 2010 - 591 2011 £35

Belloc, Hilaire 1870-1953 *The Cruise of the "Nona".* London: Constable, 1925, First edition; original blue cloth gilt, two slight marks to upper board, little bubbling to spine and lower board, pages xiv, 347, top edge gilt. R. F. G. Hollett & Son Antiquarian Booksellers General Catalogue Summer 2010 - 1627 2011 £45

Belloc, Hilaire 1870-1953 *Hills and the Sea.* London: Methuen, 1927, First illustrated edition; large 8vo., original blue cloth gilt, pages xvii, 301 with 16 tipped in color plates, signed by Michael Ffinch, poet and author. R. F. G. Hollett & Son Antiquarian Booksellers General Catalogue Summer 2010 - 846 2011 £45

Belloc, Hilaire 1870-1953 *The Historic Thames.* London: J. M. Dent, 1907, First edition; 4to., original green decorated cloth, gilt, pages vii, 224, top edges gilt, 60 color plates, bookplate of John Tricks Spalding. R. F. G. Hollett & Son Antiquarian Booksellers General Catalogue Summer 2010 - 1558 2011 £150

Belloc, Hilaire 1870-1953 *The Road.* British Reinforced Concrete Engineering Co. Ltd., 1923, First edition; original buckram backed cloth, leather spine label, little rubbed, pages (x), 218, 8 plates and 15 maps and diagrams. R. F. G. Hollett & Son Antiquarian Booksellers General Catalogue Summer 2010 - 1332 2011 £35

Bellow, Saul *The Dean's December.* New York: 1982, Proof copy; fine in wrappers. Gemini Fine Books & Arts, Ltd. Art Reference & Illustrated Books: First Editions 2011 $75

Bellow, Saul *Herzog.* London: Weidenfeld & Nicolson, 1964, First British edition; uncorrected proof, author's name on cover, publication date changed in neat hand from November 6th 1964 to January 22nd 1985, orange printed wrappers, very slightly soiled, hinges slightly rubbed, otherwise sound tight, very good. Any Amount of Books May 26 2011 - A70527 2011 $671

Bellow, Saul *More Die of Heartbreak.* New York: Morrow, 1987, Proof copy, 2nd state; brown wrappers fine in custom carton slipcase. Gemini Fine Books & Arts, Ltd. Art Reference & Illustrated Books: First Editions 2011 $75

Bellow, Saul *The Victim.* London: 1948, First British edition; small ownership name, very slight fading, otherwise very clean and in very close to fine dust jacket (very short tear and 2 tiny chips), superior copy. Gemini Fine Books & Arts, Ltd. Art Reference & Illustrated Books: First Editions 2011 $180

Bellwood, Peter S. *South Asia 2005.* London: Europa Publications, 2005, Second edition; 4to., color illustrated map endpapers, 680 pages, very good. Any Amount of Books May 29 2011 - A64361 2011 $340

Bembo, Pietro, Cardinal 1470-1547 *Petri Bembi Patritii Veneti, Scriptoris Omnium Politissimi Disertissimique Quaeccunque Usquam Prodierunt Opera...* Basileae: Michael Isengrin, 1556, 2 parts in one, octavo, (11) 12-624; 229, (23) pages, later engraved portrait inserted facing title, Isengrin's device on titlepage, second part with separate title, index, occasional early underlining, title margin restored, original full calf with four devices stamped on upper and lower corners, floral device in center, neatly rebacked to match, small manuscript title applied to fore-edge (early hand), pencilled signature of John Ashhurst, very good. Jeff Weber Rare Books 163 - 4 2011 $500

Bembo, Pietro, Cardinal 1470-1547 *Rime (followed by Le Stanze). (bound before) De Gli Assolani... ne quali si Ragiona d'Amore Primo (-Terzo) Libro.* Venice: Giovanni Antoni (Nicoloini) da Sabbio and his brothers, 1530, First edition of the Rime; elegantly printed in italic type, guide letters in initials' spaces, some dampstaining, small (blank) piece missing from lower margin of first work, first leaf (here A2) of second work repaired at inner margin, lower outer corner of last leaf signed, pages (216, counting final blank), and (105, but without the three blank leaves), 8vo., 19th century Italian vellum, edges decorated with row of red chevrons, good. Blackwell Rare Books B166 - 11 2011 £3000

Bemelmans, Ludwig *Fifi.* New York: Simon & Schuster, 1940, First edition; 4to., pictorial boards, slightest of edge and tip wear, else near fine in slightly worn, price clipped dust jacket, few close tears on dust jacket, rare title, marvelously illustrated. Aleph-Bet Books, Inc. 95 - 96 2011 $1850

Bemelmans, Ludwig *Madeline in London.* New York: Viking, 1961, First edition; large 4to., red cloth with black lettering on spine and vignette on front cover, full color pictorial dust jacket with some light wear at ends of spine and wrapper, 56 numbered pages, every one of which is illustrated, either in full color or with black and yellow delights. Jo Ann Reisler, Ltd. 86 - 24 2011 $475

Bemelmans, Ludwig *Now I Lay Me Down to Sleep.* New York: Viking Press, 1945, First edition; presentation issue, green cloth with applied illustration and cloth spine label, slight edgewear, front hinge little tender, else near fine, one of a very few copies prepared in this binding for author's use (not to be confused with limited and slipcased edition), wonderfully inscribed by author to Elsie de Wolfe. Between the Covers 169 - BTC343521 2011 $1750

Benavides, Alonso De *The Memorial of Fray Alonso De Benavides.* Chicago: privately printed, 1916, One of a numbered edition of 3000; xiii, 309 pages, plates, light external soil and rubbing, library bookplate on front pastedown, else clean and very good. Dumont Maps & Books of the West 113 - 27 2011 $750

Benchley, Robert *No Poems or Around the World Backwards and Sideways.* New York: Harper, 1932, First edition; illustrations by Gluyas Williams, modest age toning on spine and edge of rear board, tiny tears at crown, very good, without dust jacket, inscribed by author for Adele Lovett. Between the Covers 169 - BTC347389 2011 $950

Bender, Aimee *The Particular Sadness of Lemon Cake.* New York: Doubleday, 2010, First edition; fine in lemon yellow slipcase, includes author interview cards, signed by author. Bella Luna Books May 29 2011 - p3673 2011 $88

Bendixson, Terence *Milton Keynes. Image and Reality.* Granta Editions, 1992, First edition; square 4to., original cloth, gilt, dust jacket, pages 216, illustrations, presentation slip on half title from Milton Keynes Development Corporation. R. F. G. Hollett & Son Antiquarian Booksellers 177 - 73 2011 £45

Benedetti, Giovanni Battista *Resolutio Omnium Euclidis Problematum Aliorumque ad hoc Necessaro Inventrum una Tantummodo...* Venice: Bartolommeo Cesano, 1553, 4to., ff. (12), 57, (1), woodcut diagrams, large device on titlepage, from the library of the Earls of Macclesfield at Shirburn Castle. Maggs Bros. Ltd. 1440 - 28 2011 £5000

Benet, Stephen Vincent 1898-1943 *The Bishop's Beggar.* Flemington: St. Teresa's Press, 1968, First separate edition, one of 200 copies, this #121; 220 x 155mm., 4 p.l., 30 pages, (4) leaves, original hand bound red Strathmore Beau Brilliant mold-made paper, front cover with titling and bishop's miter hot stamped in gold and silver, in publisher's matching paper slipcase with gilt fleurons on sides, with hand lettered capitals on opening page of text, hand tinted line cut on titlepage, and two full page hand tinted line cuts, prospectus laid in at front, pristine. Phillip J. Pirages 59 - 307 2011 $150

Benezet, Anthony *Observations on the Inslaving, Importing and Purchasing of Negores.* Germantown: Christopher Sower, 1760, Second edition; small 8vo. original full leather Saur binding, fine, splendid set (small partial chip on top of spine, contemporary bookplate and signature of John McAllister. M & S Rare Books, Inc. 90 - 37 2011 $2000

Benezet, Anthony *The Potent Enemies of America Laid Open: Being Some Account of the Baneful Effects Attending the Use of Distilled Spirituous Liquours and the Slavery of Negroes.* Philadelphia: Joseph Crukshank, 1774, First edition; 16mo., (2), 48, 83 pages, covers detached, browned, early leaves tending to become loose. M & S Rare Books, Inc. 90 - 38 2011 $1250

Benfield, Eric *Purbeck Shop. A Stoneworker's Story of Stone.* Southampton: Ensign Publication, 1990, First edition; pages 160, well illustrated, original boards gilt, dust jacket. R. F. G. Hollett & Son Antiquarian Booksellers 177 - 74 2011 £30

Bennet, Edward *Shots and Snapshots in British East Africa.* London: Longmans, Green, 1914, First edition; 8vo., pages xii, 312, 2 maps in slipcase, illustrations, original green decorative cloth, gilt vignette, excellent copy. J. & S. L. Bonham Antiquarian Booksellers Africa 4/20/2011 - 9103 2011 £250

Bennet, Thomas *Direction for Studying. I. A General System or Body of Divinity. II. The Thirty Nine Articles of Religion.* London: printed for James and John Knapton, 1727, Third edition; contemporary polished panelled calf, upper hinge cracked, spine label defective, pages (vi), 196, (iv), woodcut head and tailpieces, some light dampstaining. R. F. G. Hollett & Son Antiquarian Booksellers 175 - 101 2011 £140

Bennett, Alan *The Uncommon Reader.* London: Faber & Faber, 2007, First British edition; fine inlike dust jacket, signed by author. Bella Luna Books May 29 2011 - t9042 2011 $82

Bennett, Anna Maria *Viscissitudes Abroad.* London: printed at the Minerva Press for Lane, Newman and Co., 1806, First (only) edition, complete as issued; 6 volumes, large 12mo., full contemporary mottled calf with crimson and black morocco spine labels, gilt rules to spine, minor tear at pages 191-192 of volume five with no loss, small chip to upper fore margin of volume five just touching page number, completely unsophisticated with small loss to spine head of volumes one and four, some occasional spotting, expected wear, armorial bookplate of George M. Knipe, overall, an excellent set, extremely rare, housed in two clamshell boxes.   David Brass Rare Books, Inc.   May 26 2011 - 01475   2011 $8500

Bennett, Arnold *Clayhanger.* London: Methuen, 1910, First edition; 8vo., original publisher's blue cloth lettered and decorated gilt on spine and cover, pages vii, 574, with 32 publisher's catalog at rear, endpapers very slightly foxed, some very slightly faded, very slight rubbing, else near fine, exceptional condition.   Any Amount of Books   May 29 2011 - A76080 2011 $204

Bennett, Arnold *Imperial Palace.* London: Cassell, 1930, First trade edition; 8vo., original publisher's red cloth lettered gilt on spine, pages xi, 630, signed presentation from author, slight lean, very slight rubbing, else very good+ in chipped, nicked and darkened original good only dust jacket.   Any Amount of Books   May 29 2011 - A76739 2011 $238

Bennett, Charles H. *The Nine Lives of a Cat: a Tale of Wonder.* London: Griffith & Farren, 1860, First edition; 4to., frontispiece, engraved title, 20 leaves, 16 page catalog, slightly dusted and marked with odd spot, original green pictorial cloth, following hinge slightly rubbed, spine slightly worn at head.   Jarndyce Antiquarian Booksellers   CXCI - 65   2011   £160

Bennett, Ernest N. *The Downfall of the Dervishes: Being a Sketch of the Final Sudan Campaign of 1898.* London: Methuen, 1898, First edition; 8vo., xii, 255, frontispiece, map, 3 plans, original red decorative cloth.   J. & S. L. Bonham Antiquarian Booksellers   Africa 4/20/2011 - 9018   2011   £40

Bennett, J. A. *The Mathematical Science of Christopher Wren.* Cambridge, et al: Cambridge University Press, 1982, First edition; 8vo., ix, 148 pages, illustrations, index, black cloth, gilt stamped spine title, dust jacket, near fine, from the Bern Dibner reference library, with Burndy bookplate.   Jeff Weber Rare Books   161 - 39   2011 $140

Bennett, Peter *A Very Desolate Position.* Blackpool: Rossall Archives, 1977, First edition; 4to., original pictorial stiff wrappers, pages 146, illustrations, scarce.   R. F. G. Hollett & Son Antiquarian Booksellers   175 - 102   2011   £40

Bennett, Wendell C. *Tarahumara, An Indian Tribe of Northern Mexico.* Chicago: 1935, First edition; xix, 412 pages, illustrations, bookplate, name on titlepage and edges (of noted Pueblo ethnologist Alfonso Ortiz), spine faded, else very good.   Dumont Maps & Books of the West   111 - 56 2011 $125

Benois, Alexander *Ostradoomova-Ljebedeva. The Art of Anna Ostraoomowa.* Moscow and Leningrad: State Press, n.d. mid 1920's, First edition; 4to., pages 89, 18 plates, copious illustrations, some tipped in, illustrated wrappers, edges worn, spine chipped and mostly not present, edges chipped, poorish covers but decent text, good only.   Any Amount of Books   May 29 2011 - A33906   2011 $255

Benson, C. E. *Crag and Hound in Lakeland.* London: Hurst and Blackett, 1902, First edition; pages xvi, 313, 6, with 28 illustrations, original cloth, gilt.   R. F. G. Hollett & Son Antiquarian Booksellers   173 - 72 2011   £60

Benson, Edward Frederic *Visible and Invisibile.* New York: George H. Doran Co., 1924, First US edition; first printing with GHD monogram on verso of title leaf, octavo, original blue green cloth, front and spine panels stamped in dark green.   L. W. Currey, Inc.   124 - 101 2011 $750

Benson, Robert Hugh *The Dawn of All.* London: Hutchinson & Co., 1911, First edition; half title, 32 pages ads (Spring 1911), slight foxing, original blue cloth, slightly marked, inscribed "To the author's mother from him".   Jarndyce Antiquarian Booksellers   CXCI - 66 2011   £85

Benson, Thomas Park *"As I Return to Yesteryear".* Owen Sound: privately published by Fleming Folding Cartons, 1983, Second printing; Original pictorial wrappers, 150 pages, 13 pages of illustrations, stapled in single thick section, scarce.   R. F. G. Hollett & Son Antiquarian Booksellers   173 - 73 2011   £50

Bent, J. Theodore *The Ruined Cities of Mashonaland; Being a Record of Excavation and Exploration in 1891...* London: Longmans Green, 1892, First edition; 8vo., pages xi, 376, ads, 3 folding lithographic maps colored in outline, 12 plates and numerous other woodcut illustrations in text, original blue decorative cloth, gilt vignette on upper cover, gilt, 1 inner hinge cracked, small library stamp on half title only, some crayon underlining but good, sound copy.   J. & S. L. Bonham Antiquarian Booksellers   Africa 4/20/2011 - 3228   2011   £95

Bentham, Jeremy 1748-1832 *Jeremy Bentham to His Fellow Citizens of France, on Death Punishment.* London: Robert Heward, 1831, First edition; 13, (1) pages, recent marbled boards lettered on spine, very good, scarce.   John Drury Rare Books   154 - 23 2011   £275

Bentham, Jeremy   1748-1832   *Official Aptitude Maximized, Expense Minimized as Shown on the Several Papers Comprised in this Volume.*   London: printed for the author and published by Robert Heward, 1830,   First edition of this collection; 8vo., 11 parts with paginations and signatures by Chuo, original boards, neatly rebacked and labelled, partially unopened, very good, old booklabel of W. H. Whinfield.   John Drury Rare Books   154 - 22   2011   £500

Bentham, Jeremy   1748-1832   *Parliamentary Candidate's Proposed Declaration of Principles; or Say a Test Proposed for Parliamentary Candidates.*   London: The Office of the Westminster Review by Robert Heward, 1831, First separate edition; 8vo., (2), 18 pages, recent marbled boards, lettered on spine, very good.   John Drury Rare Books   154 - 24   2011   £275

Bentley, Richard   *Designs by Mr. Bentley for Six Poems by Mr. T. Gray.*   London: for R. Dodsley, 1753,   First edition; large 4to., pages 35 printed recto only apart from illustrations, no front endpaper, first page is half title with words "Drawings &c." indicating the first state, 6 full page engraved plates, engraved vignette on title, 12 vignettes in text, 6 engraved initials by Muller and Grignon, bound in contemporary full brown calf lettered gilt on spine with gilt decoration at spine, 6 raised bands, boards slightly scuffed, bumped at corners with slight incipient splitting at top outer hinge (holding well), very good with slight browning to pages and plates, occasional slight foxing and staining.   Any Amount of Books   May 26 2011 - A70272   2011 $1090

Bentley, Richard   *Designs by Mr. Bentley for Six Poems by Mr. Gray.*   London: printed for R. Dodsley, 1753,   First edition; folio, modern half calf gilt, page (iv), 35, half title, title with vignette, 6 full page copper engraved plates, 12 engraved decorations and 6 engraved initials, half title rather soiled and abraded in places, short tears repaired, little creasing in places, armorial bookplate of Roger Swetenham.   R. F. G. Hollett & Son Antiquarian Booksellers   General Catalogue Summer 2010 - 627   2011   £750

Bentley, Wilder   *The Poetry of Learning.*   Berkeley: Archetype Press, 1973-1985,   20 of 26 letterpress scrolls only, includes scrolls A-S and U, handset in Lutetia type and printed on damp, BFK Rives paper, scrolls A-C are printed on a single sheet, A and B are 14 inches in height, scroll C is 20 1/2 inches in height, remaining scrolls consist of several sheets joined together, longest being nearly 15 feet in length, height 15 1/2 inches, each scroll housed in its own individual storage tube with printed paper labels, storage tube for Scroll C has a woodcut illustration, scroll F with light dust stains, otherwise only a few light fox marks, mostly marginal, overall fine set, very rare; Ward Ritchie's set.   Jeff Weber Rare Books   163 - 107   2011 $1000

Beowulf.   New York: Limited Editions Club, 1952,   First edition, translated by W. E. Leonard and with these illustrations; number 91 of 1500 numbered copies, 18 original full page color lithographs and many smaller lithographic illustrations by Lynd Ward; handmade paper over boards, almost as new, slight binder's imperfection at rear endpaper, in almost fine slipcase, large 4to., 153 pages, book, although numbered, was not signed as issued.   Gemini Fine Books & Arts, Ltd.   Art Reference & Illustrated Books: First Editions 2011 $90

Berendt, Joachim   *Jazzlife.*   Germany: Offenburg, 1961, First edition; photos by William Claxton, simultaneous wrapper issue, about near fine in French style wrappers with some very minor edge wear and small tear to front panel, overall very nice and fresh, uncommon.   Jeff Hirsch Books ny 2010 2011 $400

Beresford, Elisabeth   *The Wandering Wombles.*   London: Ernest Benn, 1970,   First edition; original cloth, gilt, dust jacket, pages 182, illustrations by Oliver Chadwick, fine.   R. F. G. Hollett & Sons Antiquarian Booksellers   170 - 74   2011   £95

Beresford, Elisabeth   *The Wombles.*   London: Ernest Benn, 1968,   First edition; pages 191, illustrations by Margaret Gordon, original cloth, gilt, dust jacket spine rather faded, fine.   R. F. G. Hollett & Sons Antiquarian Booksellers   170 - 75   2011   £95

Beresford, Elisabeth   *The Wombles at Work.*   London: Ernest Benn, 1973,   First edition; original cloth, gilt, dust jacket, price clipped, pages 192, illustrations by Margaret Gordon, fine.   R. F. G. Hollett & Sons Antiquarian Booksellers   170 - 76   2011   £85

Beresiner, Yasha   *British County Maps.*   London: Antique Collectors, 1983,   First edition; 4to., original cloth, gil, dust jacket, pages 295, illustrated with 41 color plates.   R. F. G. Hollett & Son Antiquarian Booksellers   General Catalogue Summer 2010 - 45   2011   £85

Berger, Thomas   *Siamese Twins.*   New York: Harold Matson Co., n.d.,   Apparently unpublished (and unproduced?); corrected typescript, signed by author, 98 pages ribbon copy, heavily corrected by author with numerous changes and deletions in felt tip pen, loose sheets now housed in three ring binder, fine.   Ken Lopez Bookseller   154 - 13   2011 $850

Berggren, J. L.   *Ptolemy's Geography: an Annotated Translation...*   Princeton: Princeton University Press, 2000, 8vo., xii, 192 pages, 20 figures, 7 plates, 8 maps, blue cloth, gilt stamped spine titles, dust jacket, fine, from the Bern Dibner reference library, with Burndy bookplate.   Jeff Weber Rare Books   161 - 41   2011 $100

Bergson, Henri *Duree et Simultaneite A Propos e la Theorie d'Einstein. (Duration and Simultaneity in Einstein's Theory).*   First edition; 2 blank pages + half title, titlepage (v)-viii - preface (1)-245 + 2 blank leaves, small octavo, contemporary green half calf and cloth with marbled endpapers, top edge gilt, pretty copy bound for presentation, spine very lightly faded, bookplate of Newton Hall Cambridge to inside front cover, spine faded, bookplate near fine.   Athena Rare Books   10 2011 $950

Bergson, Henri *Essai sur les Donnees Immediates de la Conscience. (An Essay on the Immediate Data of Consciousness).*   Paris: Felix Alcan, 1889, First edition; half title, titlepage + dedication page (vii)-viii (1)-182 + 1 leaf - table des matieres, octavo, beautifully preserved, original printed green wrappers, spine bit darkened, elegant ink inscription to top right corner of half title "F. Olivier/Lausanne Sept. 94", very pretty and well preserved, untrimmed copy.   Athena Rare Books   10 2011 $1000

Bergson, Henri *Le Rire. Essai sur la Signifcation du Comique. (Laughter, an Essay on the meaning of the Comic).*   Paris: Felix Alcan, 1900, First edition in book form; half title titlepage (v)-vii - avant propos (1)-204 + (205) - Table des matieres + (1)-16 - publisher's ads 1 blank leaf, octavo, wonderfully preserved, original light green wrappers, partially uncut, lovely, near fine.   Athena Rare Books   10 2011 $800

Berkeley, Anthony *Death in the House.*   New York: Doubleday, Doran & Co. for The Crime Club, 1939, First American edition; fine in near fine dust jacket, with few very small nicks and tears.   Between the Covers   169 - BTC 342123   2011 $750

Berkeley, Anthony *Trial and Error.*   Garden City: Doubleday, Doran & Co., 1937, First American edition; corners little bumped and boards trifle soiled, very good or better in very good dust jacket with triangular chip on front panel and other light wear.   Between the Covers   169 - BTC342126   2011 $550

Berkeley, George, Bp. of Cloyne   1685-1753 *Alciphron; or the Minute Philosopher.*   London: Tonson, 1732, 2 volumes, contemporary calf, volume I rubbed, volume II boards detached, some spotting on early leaves volume I, else very good.   C. P. Hyland   May 26 2011 - 256/033   2011 $457

Berkeley, George, Bp. of Cloyne   1685-1753 *A Treatise Concerning the principles of Human Knowledge. Wherein the Chief Causes of Error and Difficulty in the Sciences with the Grounds of Scepticism, Atheism and Irreligion are Inquired Into.*   London: Printed for Jacob Tonson, 1734, Second (first colelcted) edition; 8vo., 355, (1) pages, contemporary calf with raised bands and simple red lettering piece on spine, very slight wear to head and foot of spine, still fine, crisp copy.   John Drury Rare Books   154 - 25   2011   £1500

Berkeley, Grantley F. *Reminiscences of a Huntsman.*   London: Edward Arnold, 1897, New edition; original boards with paper spine label, hinges cracked at head and foot and repaired, pages xix, (iii), 344, top edge gilt, 14 plates.   R. F. G. Hollett & Son Antiquarian Booksellers   General Catalogue Summer 2010 - 1218   2011   £50

Berkenmeyer, Paul Ludolph *Le Curieux Antiquaire ou Recueil Geographique et Historique des Choses les Plus Remarquables qu'on Trouve dans les Quatre Parties de l'Univers...*   Leiden: Pierre Vander Aa, 1729, First and only French edition; 3 volumes in one, 8vo., (22), 385, (2), 386-736, (10), 737-1062 pages, each volume has special titlepage, 2 engraved folding maps, 2 engraved folding plans, 46 engraved plates, title printed in red and black; from the library of the Earls of Macclesfield at Shirburn Castle.   Maggs Bros. Ltd.   1440 - 29   2011   £700

Berman, Robert *A Kind of Rapture.*   New York: Pantheon, 1998, First edition; color photos, signed by Toni Morrison, fine in fine dust jacket.   Ken Lopez Bookseller   154 - 124   2011 $425

Berman, Wallace *Radio/Aether Series 1966/1974.*   Los Angeles: Gemini G. E. L., 1974, First edition, limited to 50 copies with 10 artist's proofs, signed by Berman; very fine, stunning portfolio of 13 two-color offset lithographs, each photographed from an original verifax collage and printed on star-white cover mounted on Gemini rag-board, in original screen printed fabric covered box.   James S. Jaffe Rare Books   May 26 2011 - 20761   2011 $12,500

Bernard, George S. *War Talks of Confederate Veterans.*   Petersburg: 1892, First edition; xxiii, 335 pages, 2 folding maps, patterned endpapers, CSA gray, both inner joints reglued, ownership inscription of Col. Richard L. Maury, very nice, small ripple to right of backstrip.   Bookworm & Silverfish   679 - 40   2011 $150

Bernard, Madame *German Equivalents from English Thoughts.*   London: David Nutt, 1858, First edition; 12mo., text in English and German, errata slip, 8 pages of publisher's ads at end, iv, 306 pages, original embossed cloth, spine faded, short tears on hinges.   Anthony W. Laywood   May 26 2011 - 19496   2011 $76

Berners, Juliana *An Older Form of the Treatyse of Fysshynge with an Angle...*   London: W. Satchell & Co., 1883, First edition; 400 copies, original green cloth gilt, rather marked in places, pages vii, 38, (x), marbled endpapers, few contemporary notes on flyleaves, very scarce.   R. F. G. Hollett & Son Antiquarian Booksellers   General Catalogue Summer 2010 - 1280   2011   £150

Bernhard, Ruth *The Eternal Body. A Collection of Fifty Nudes.* Carmel: Photography West Graphics, 1986, First edition; signed by Bernhard, 4to., pages (114), 28, (2) blank, 51 black an white photos, original pink cloth, spine and upper side lettered in silver, small area of rubbing to bottom edge of upper side at foot of spine, original pink dust jacket, near fine in fine dust jacket. Simon Finch Rare Books   Zero - 508   2011   £400

Bernhard, Ruth *Ruth Bernhard. The Collection of Ginny Williams.* N.P.: Ginny Williams Foundation, 1993, First printing exhibition catalogue; 4to., 43 plates, fine in fine dust jacket. By the Book, L. C.   26 - 24   2011 $525

Bernier, G. R. *Oeil.* Paris: Revue d'Art, Jan., 1955-, Dec. 1975; Nos. 1-245, original wrappers, very good. I. D. Edrich   May 26 2011 - 98565   2011 $2180

Bernier, R. L. *Art in California: a Survey of American Art with Special reference to California Painting, Sculpture and Architecture Past and Present...* San Francisco: R. L. Bernier, 1916, Quarto, 184 pages, 332 plates, original quarter linen backed blindstamped boards, spine label, top edge gilt, spine ends frayed, corners and extremities showing inner hinges cracked, good plus. Jeff Weber Rare Books   163 - 99   2011 $100

Berriman, John *Theos Ephaneros en Sarki (title in Greek).* London: W. Innys and J. Nourse, 1741, First (only) edition; contemporary full speckled sheep, gilt, pages xxviii, 356, Parochial Library label on pastedown, later shelf numbers to flyleaf, but excellent copy of a rare work. R. F. G. Hollett & Son Antiquarian Booksellers   175 - 104   2011   £250

Berry, Geoffrey *Across Northern Hills.* Kendal: Westmorland Gazette, 1975, First edition; square 8vo., original cloth, gilt, dust jacket, pages 151, with 122 photos by author and 10 maps, inscribed by author, scarce. R. F. G. Hollett & Son Antiquarian Booksellers   173 - 75   2011   £45

Berry, Wendell *Another Turn of the Crank.* Washington: Counterpoint, 1995, First edition; 8vo., pages 109, fine in dust jacket, inscribed and dated by author. Second Life Books Inc.   174 - 37   2011 $85

Berry, Wendell *Another Turn of the Crank.* Washington: Counterpoint, 1995, First edition; near fine, light bumping to spine ends, dust jacket fine, signed by author. Bella Luna Books   May 29 2011 - t999   2011 $82

Berry, Wendell *The Broken Ground, Poems.* London: Cape, 1964, First UK edition; 8vo., pages 56, very good in dust jacket, 1 inch closed tear in board and dust jacket on front cover. Second Life Books Inc.   174 - 38   2011 $85

Berry, Wendell *Clearing (Poems).* New York: Harcourt, 1977, Uncorrected page proofs; 8vo. 52 pages, original printed wrappers, fine, scarce. Second Life Books Inc.   174 - 41   2011 $75

Berry, Wendell *Clearing (Poems).* New York: Harcourt, 1977, First edition; 8vo., 52 pages, fine in dust jacket, inscribed by author with good wishes, scarce. Second Life Books Inc.   174 - 40   2011 $125

Berry, Wendell *Findings (Poems).* Iowa City: Prairie Press, 1969, First edition; 8vo., pages 63, fine in dust jacket, scarce, with ownership signature of Marilyn Trumpp, August. 1969, noting it was a gift from book designer Carroll Coleman. Second Life Books Inc.   174 - 44   2011 $300

Berry, Wendell *The Gift of Good Land, Further Essays Cultural and Agricultural.* San Francisco: North Point Press, 1981, First edition; 8vo., 281 pages, fine in dust jacket, scarce. Second Life Books Inc.   174 - 45   2011 $125

Berry, Wendell *The Gift of Gravity...* Deerfield: Deerfield Press: Dublin: The Gallery Press, 1979, First edition, limited to 300 copies; fine in dust jacket, closed tear to rear of dust jacket, brown endpapers, some offsetting from dust jacket, spine title printed in upper and lower case letters, dust jacket state 2, with title on spine in upper and lower case letters, dust jacket has white label covering printed price" The Gallery Press/Bound 6.30 (6.93 inc. vat) limited signed edition this was original issued at 4.20. Second Life Books Inc.   174 - 46   2011 $225

Berry, Wendell *Harlan Hubbard, Life and Work. The Blazer Lectures for 1989.* Lexington: University Press of Kentucky, 1990, First edition; 8vo., pages 108, reproductions, presentation by author on titlepage, fine in dust jacket. Second Life Books Inc.   174 - 47   2011 $95

Berry, Wendell *The Hidden Wound.* Boston: Houghton Mifflin, 1970, First edition; 8vo., pages 145, fine in dust jacket, signed by author. Second Life Books Inc.   174 - 48   2011 $150

Berry, Wendell *The Long-Legged House.* New York: Harcourt, 1969, First edition; 8vo., 213 pages, contemporary inscription, otherwise fine in little soiled dust jacket. Second Life Books Inc.   174 - 49   2011 $275

Berry, Wendell *The Memory of Old Jack.* New York: Harcourt, Brace, 1974, First edition; 8vo., 223 pages, fine in dust jacket. Second Life Books Inc.   174 - 50   2011 $165

Berry, Wendell *Nathan Coulter, a Novel.* Boston: Houghton Mifflin Co., 1960, First edition; nice in little worn dust jacket that has small snag on front cover and little wear at upper tip, scarce. Second Life Books Inc. 174 - 52 2011 $400

Berry, Wendell *November Twenty Six Nineteen Hundred Sixty Three.* New York: George Braziller, 1964, First edition, limited edition, one of 3013 copies; printed on handmade laid paper by Fabriano, tipped in color illustrations, drawings by Ben Shahn, signed by author and artist, housed in publisher's slipcase (little faded as usual), very nice. Second Life Books Inc. 174 - 53 2011 $300

Berry, Wendell *A Part.* San Francisco: North Point Press, 1980, First edition; 12mo., pages 89, fine in dust jacket. Second Life Books Inc. 174 - 54 2011 $75

Berry, Wendell *A Place on Earth.* New York: Harcourt Brace, 1967, First edition; pages 550, 8vo. just about fine in fine dust jacket. Second Life Books Inc. 174 - 55 2011 $500

Berry, Wendell *Collected Poems 1957-1982.* Berkeley: North Point Press, 1985, First edition; 8vo., 268 pages, inscribed by author, fine in dust jacket. Second Life Books Inc. 174 - 42 2011 $250

Berry, Wendell *The Selected Poems of...* Washington: Counterpoint, 1998, First edition; 8vo., 178 pages, fine in dust jacket, signed by author. Second Life Books Inc. 174 - 56 2011 $75

Berry, Wendell *Remembering.* San Francisco: North Point Press, 1988, First edition; fine, dust jacket fine signed by author. Bella Luna Books May 29 2011 - s1007 2011 $82

Berry, Wendell *Sex, Economy, Freedom & Community.* New York: Pantheon Books, 1993, First edition; 8vo., pages 177, signed by author, fine in dust jacket. Second Life Books Inc. 174 - 57 2011 $50

Berry, Wendell *To What Listens.* Crete: The Best Cellar Press, 1975, First edition; printed wrappers, very lightly faded, near fine, scarce. Second Life Books Inc. 174 - 59 2011 $125

Berry, Wendell *Traveling at Home.* Lewisburg: Bucknell University, The Press of Appletree Alley, 1988, First edition, there was one printing of 150 copies, signed by author; 8vo., pages 56, cloth backed boards, fine, issue A of the binding, with spine bound in lighter green cloth, printed on Rives Lightweight mould made paper and set in spectrum type. Second Life Books Inc. 174 - 60 2011 $600

Berry, Wendell *The Unforeseen Wilderness.* Lexington: University Press of Kentucky, 1971, First edition, first printing (with text block on copyright page (p. iv) flushed to right margin); white cloth with flat spine in dust jacket, ex-library with couple of small stamps on titlepage, circulation pocket on rear endpaper, tape holding glassene over dust jacket, 1 of 1500 copies of a total edition of 3000, very good. Second Life Books Inc. 174 - 62 2011 $150

Berry, Wendell *Watch with Me and Six Other Stories of the Yet Remembered Ptolemy Proudfoot and His Wife, Miss Minnie, Nee Quinch.* New York: Pantheon, 1994, First edition; bookplate fine in dust jacket, signed by author. Second Life Books Inc. 174 - 64 2011 $75

Berry, Wendell *Watch With Me.* New York: Pantheon, 1994, First edition; fine in fine dust jacket, signed by author. Bella Luna Books May 29 2011 - t1000 2011 $82

Berry, Wendell *The Wheel.* San Francisco: North Point Press, 1982, First edition; fine in fine dust jacket, signed by author. Bella Luna Books May 29 2011 - s1017 2011 $110

Berry, Wendell *A World Lost.* Washington: Counterpoint, 1996, First edition; fine, dust jacket fine, signed by author. Bella Luna Books May 29 2011 - 4539 2011 $82

Berthoud, Michael *H. & R. Daniel 1822-1846.* Wingham: Micawber Publications, 1980, First edition; tall 8vo., original cloth gilt, dust jacket (head of spine defective), pages 159, 8 pages of color plates and 140 illustrations. R. F. G. Hollett & Son Antiquarian Booksellers General Catalogue Summer 2010 - 49 2011 £45

Bertram, Bonaventure Corneille *Comparatio Grammaticae Hebricae & Aramicae.* Geneva: Apud Eustathium Vignom, 1574, Sole edition; woodcut device to titlepage and verso of errata leaf, printed in italic, Roman and Hebrew characters throughout, pages numbered right to left, little light browning and spotting, tiny dampmark to corner of first three leaves, early marginal notes in Latin and Hebrew (some cropped), underlining, old ownership inscription to title, pages (xxiv), 440, 4to., late 18th century mid brown paneled calf divided by gilt fillets, central panel with blind frame and central cross hatching, recently rebacked, backstrip with four gilt tooled raised bands between double gilt and blind fillets, black morocco label in second compartment, rest plain, hinges relined, touch rubbed at extremities, Chatsworth shelfmark bookplate, good,. Blackwell Rare Books B166 - 12 2011 £800

Bertrand, Louis A. *Memoires d'un Mormon.* Paris: Collection Hetzel, E. Dentu, 1862, First edition; (4), 323 pages, latler half blue morocco, original pale green wrappers bound in, fine, bright copy. Joseph J. Felcone Inc. Fall Miscellany 2010 - 90 2011 $1000

Bertuch, Friedrich Justin *Novus Orbis Pictus Juventuti Instituendae et Oblectandae.* Vienna: Antonii Pichler, 1807, New edition; quarto, bound in contemporary morocco backed boards, 50 hand colored engraved plates, mild aging to text but very clean, near fine.   Charles Agvent   2010 Summer Miscellany - 11   2011 $850

Besant, Annie *The Wisdom of the Upanishads.* Adyar, Madras, India: 1907, First edition; 96 pages, beige cloth age soiled, black lettering on cover and spine, age soiled, left side of backstrip loosening 4 inches, rubber stamps of Theosophical Lodge on first leaf and one other page, pocket vestige on r.f.e.p.   Bookworm & Silverfish   671 - 180   2011 $100

Besant, Walter *The Eulogy of Richard Jefferies.* London: Chatto & Windus, 1888, First edition; frontispiece, uncut in original blue cloth, very good.   Jarndyce Antiquarian Booksellers   CXCI - 224   2011   £35

Beschi, Costantino Giuseppe *Strange Surprising Adventures of the Venerable Goooro Simple and His Five Disciples, Noodle and Doodle, Wiseacre, Zany and Foozle.* London: Trubner & Co., 1861, First edition; half title, hand colored frontispiece, plates, illustrations, 4 pages ads, original blue cloth decorated in gilt and blind, slightly rubbed and marked, leading inner hinge repaired, monogram CSS booklabel, all edges gilt.   Jarndyce Antiquarian Booksellers   CXCI - 67   2011   £50

Besnard, Peter *Observations on the Promotion of the Cultivation of Hemp and Flax...in the South of Ireland.* 1816, First edition; 26 + 16 pages, disbound, light foxing.   C. P. Hyland   May 26 2011 - 259/026   2011 $507

Besse, Joseph *Life and Posthumous Works of Joseph Claridge...* London: printed and sold by Assigns of J. Sowle, 1726, First edition; old calf gilt, rather worn and defective at extremities, hinges cracking, paper spine label, title, A2-a4 (preface, table, etc.) pages 576, Pp1-Qq2 (table etc.), front flyleaf roughly repaired, minor dampstains to final leaves, front joint cracked.   R. F. G. Hollett & Son Antiquarian Booksellers   175 - 105   2011   £140

Best in Children's Books. New York: Nelson Doubleday, 1960, First edition; original cloth backed pictorial boards, dust jacket (odd spot and light mark), pages 160, illustrations by Maurice Sendak.   R. F. G. Hollett & Sons Antiquarian Booksellers   170 - 29   2011   £45

Best, Herbert *The Twenty-Fifth Hour.* New York: Random House, 1940, First edition; octavo, titlepage printed in tan and black, original pictorial red cloth, front and spine panels stamped in black and gold, top edge stained black.   L. W. Currey, Inc.   124 - 220   2011 $125

Bestall, Alfred *The Adventures of Rupert.* Daily Express Annual, 1950, Small 4to., original pictorial boards, spine complete but creased and taped down, pages 120, illustrations in color, inscription on ownership page.   R. F. G. Hollett & Sons Antiquarian Booksellers   170 - 77   2011   £85

Bestall, Alfred *More Adventures of Rupert.* Daily Express, 1947, First edition; Small 4to., original pictorial wrappers, rather worn, one corner creased, pages 120, illustrations in color, inscription on ownership box page, good copy.   R. F. G. Hollett & Sons Antiquarian Booksellers   170 - 79   2011   £150

Bestall, Alfred *More Adventures of Rupert.* Daily Express Annual, 1947, First edition; small 4to., original pictorial wrappers, hinges trifle rubbed, pages 120, illustrations in color, very nice, clean and sound.   R. F. G. Hollett & Sons Antiquarian Booksellers   170 - 78   2011   £220

Bestall, Alfred *The New Rupert Book.* Daily Express, 1938, First edition; small 4to., original cloth backed boards, corners little bumped, pages 126, illustrations in red and black, faint spots to title, small inked ticks to contents leaf, last leaf and lower pastedown trifle marked.   R. F. G. Hollett & Sons Antiquarian Booksellers   170 - 80   2011   £350

Bestall, Alfred *A New Rupert Book.* Daily Express, 1946, Small 4to., original pictorial wrappers, extremities little rubbed, pages 120, illustrations in color, ownership box page filled in, very good, clean copy.   R. F. G. Hollett & Sons Antiquarian Booksellers   170 - 82   2011   £140

Bestall, Alfred *Rupert.* Daily Express, 1948, First edition; small 4to., original pictorial wrappers, extremities little rubbed, pages 120, illustrations in color, inscription on ownership box page, very good.   R. F. G. Hollett & Sons Antiquarian Booksellers   170 - 85   2011   £120

Bester, Alfred *The Demolished Man.* Chicago: Shasta Pub., 1953, First edition; octavo, cloth backed boards.   L. W. Currey, Inc.   124 - 102   2011 $750

Bester, Alfred *Tiger! Tiger!* London: Sidgwick and Jackson, 1956, First edition; octavo, boards.   L. W. Currey, Inc.   124 - 20   2011 $2500

Besterman, Theodore *The Pilgrim Fathers.* Waltham St. Lawrence: Golden Cockerel Press, 1939, One of 300 copies (this copy #65); 255 x 160mm., 3 p.l. (including frontispiece), 7-87, (1) pages, (1) leaf (blank), very inventive gray-green onlaid pictorial crushed morocco by Denise Lubbett, covers and (flat unlettered) spine with large areas of onlaid tan morocco in the shape of a portion of the New England coastline, in felt lined morocco backed folding cloth box with gilt spine titling, box slightly rubbed and faded; with 9 woodcuts by Geoffrey Wales; spine just bit sunned, otherwise in especially fine condition inside and out. Phillip J. Pirages 59 - 115 2011 $2250

Beston, Henry *The Outermost House: a Year of Life of the Great Beach of Cape Cod.* New York: Rinehart & Co., 1949, Twelfth printing; photos by William A. Bradford and others, corners bit bumped, near fine in about fine dust jacket with very short tear, warmly inscribed by author to George Swetman, ALS signed twice by Beston to Mrs. Swetman. Between the Covers 169 - BTC347882 2011 $5000

Bethem-Edwards, Miss *In French Africa.* London: Chapman & Hall, 1912, First edition; 8vo., pages ix, 324, illustrations, original blue cloth, spine faded, covers waterstained. J. & S. L. Bonham Antiquarian Booksellers Africa 4/20/2011 - 4575 2011 £40

Betjeman, John 1906-1984 *Collins Guide to English Parish Churches.* London: Collins, 1958, First edition; original cloth, gilt, dust jacket (little chipped), pages 480, 64 plates and drawings by John Piper. R. F. G. Hollett & Son Antiquarian Booksellers 177 - 80 2011 £50

Betjeman, John 1906-1984 *A Few Late Chrysanthemums.* London: John Murray, 1954, First edition; 8vo., original blue cloth with printed title label onset to cover, pages vii, 95, review copy with publisher's slip loosely inserted, inscribed by author for Leonard Clark, fine in very good, very slightly soiled and spotted dust jacket. Any Amount of Books May 26 2011 - A66497 2011 $461

Betjeman, John 1906-1984 *A Nip in the Air.* London: John Murray, 1984, First edition, number 97 of 175 copies, numbered and signed by author; yellow buckram boards, marbled endpapers, book on handmade paper, uncut at fore and lower edge, top edge gilt, fine, acetate jacket. Any Amount of Books May 29 2011 - A71687 2011 $298

Betjeman, John 1906-1984 *Old Lights for New Chancels.* London: John Murray, 1940, First edition; small 4to., original publisher's black cloth with printed paper label on spine, pages 67, silk marker, very slight lean, otherwise about fine in close to very good dust jacket with few slight marks slight chips and slight soiling. Any Amount of Books May 29 2011 - A71207 2011 $238

Betjeman, John 1906-1984 *Summoned by Bells.* London: John Murray, 1960, First edition; original blind patterned cloth gilt, dust jacket (light crease to front panel), pages 111, with drawings by Michael Tree. R. F. G. Hollett & Son Antiquarian Booksellers General Catalogue Summer 2010 - 726 2011 £75

Bett, Henry *English Legends.* London: Batsford, 1950, First edition; original cloth, gilt, dust jacket by Eric Fraser, pages viii, 150, color frontispiece and text drawings. R. F. G. Hollett & Son Antiquarian Booksellers 175 - 107 2011 £35

Bevan, G. Phillips *A Handbook to the Industries of the British Isles and the United States.* London: David Bogue, 1882, First edition; original cloth, gilt, pages 220, 32, title stamped 'with publisher's compliments', scarce. R. F. G. Hollett & Son Antiquarian Booksellers 175 - 109 2011 £85

Bevans, John *A Brief View of the Doctrines of the Christian Religion as Professed by the Society of Friends...* London: William Phillips, 1810, Old tree calf, edges worn, pages viii, 111, last leaf torn, joints cracked. R. F. G. Hollett & Son Antiquarian Booksellers 175 - 110 2011 £30

Beveridge, William H. *Full Employment in a Free Society.* London: Allen & Unwin, 1944, First edition; original cloth, gilt, spine trifle faded, pages 430, with 62 diagrams, 9 charts, net library label. R. F. G. Hollett & Son Antiquarian Booksellers 175 - 111 2011 £60

Beverland, Adriaan *Peccatum Originale (kat' exochen) sic Nuncupatum Philologice (Problematikos) Elucubratum a Themidis Alumno.* Eleutheropolis (London or Amsterdam): extra plateam obscuram sine privilegio auctoris..., 1678, First edition; 8vo., pages (x) 146 (4), leaves trimmed but crisp, clean, contemporary vellum, lettered in black ink on spine, recased, slightly dusty, old pen annotations to titlepage and page (iii). Simon Finch Rare Books Zero - 107 2011 £950

Bezzerides, A. I. *Long Haul.* New York: Carrick & Evans Inc., 1938, First edition; signed by author, front and rear endpapers lightly toned, else near fine, tight copy in dust jacket with some light professional restoration to spine ends, corners and top edge of rear panel. Buckingham Books May 26 2011 - 27327 2011 $1750

Bianchini, Francesco *De Kalendario et Cyclo Caesaris ac de Paschali Canone S. Hippolyti Martyris Dissertationes Duae...* Rome: A. & F. de Conte, 1703, First edition; handsome copy, 3 parts in 1 volume, folio, 10 engraved plates (of 11), engraved illustrations, contemporary Dutch calf, gilt spine; from the library of the Earls of Macclesfield at Shirburn Castle. Maggs Bros. Ltd. 1440 - 30 2011 £550

Bianco, Margery Williams *Poor Cecco.* New York: George H. Doran Co., 1925, Limited to 105 copies, first edition, deluxe large paper issue; signed by artist, quarto, 175 pages, 7 full page illustrations in color, mounted on white paper, 24 drawings in black and white, original parchment backed light blue paper boards, navy blue lettering label on spine, pictorial endpapers in blue on white, top edge gilt, others uncut, one inch parchment split at top end of bottom joint, not affecting joint integrity, short marginal tear to last blank, upper hinge invisibly restored, otherwise fine,. David Brass Rare Books, Inc. May 26 2011 - 01093 2011 $7500

Biart, Lucien *My Rambles in the New World.* London: Sampson, Low, Marston & Co., n.d. 1890's, Decorative cloth with illustrations in red and various shades of greens, gilt titles to spine and front cover, 8vo., pages (viii), 296, half title, black and white frontispiece, 27 black and white illustrations, very good. Schooner Books Ltd. 96 - 17 2011 $75

Bible Scenes and Sweet Stories of Old. London: Ernest Nister and New York: E. P. Dutton and Co. n.d. circa, 1900, Oblong 4to., original cloth backed pictorial boards, little marked, corners slightly worn, unpaginated, 5 full page chromolithograph plates, each with lift up cut out section, figures, few neat repairs, new cloth guards to leaves, inscription and mss. poem on flyleaf. R. F. G. Hollett & Sons Antiquarian Booksellers 170 - 475 2011 £180

Bible Stories: with Coloured Pictures, of the Most Remarkable Events Therein Recorded. New Testament. London: Dean and Son, n.d. circa 1860's, tall 8vo., original blindstamped blue cloth gilt, little worn and stained and neatly rebacked to match, pages 48, printed on one side of each sheet, with 120 hand colored woodcuts, pastedowns little damaged and repaired, new front flyleaf, few edge repairs in places. R. F. G. Hollett & Son Antiquarian Booksellers 175 - 33 2011 £250

Bible. Arabic - 1616 *Novum D. N. Iesu Christi Testamentum Arabice.* Leiden: Ex typographia Erpentiana Linguarum Orientalium, 1616, Editio princeps; engraved titlepage, head and tailpieces of printer's ornaments, woodcut initials for each book, ink name partially erased from foot of title (partly within engraved area) and at end, very slight spotting or browning here or there, pages (48, including engraved title), 648, 4to., original limp vellum, boldly lettered in ink on spine and with decoration at foot, very good. Blackwell Rare Books B166 - 13 2011 £4500

Bible. Dutch - 1884 *Biblia dat is de Gantsche Heylige Schirfure, Vervattende alle de Canonycke Boecken des Ouden Ende des Nieuwen Testaments.* Amsterdam and Haarlem: Nederlandsche Bibel Compagnie, 1884, Full black morocco gilt, with earlier heavy stamped silver metal clasps and cornerpieces, printed in black letter, full page woodcut plates. R. F. G. Hollett & Son Antiquarian Booksellers 175 - 114 2011 £175

Bible. Dutch - 1884 *Biblia a is de Gantsche Heylige Schrifture...* Amsterdam and Haarlem: Nederlandsche Bijbel Compagnie, 1884, Full black morocco gilt, earlier heavy stamped silver metal clasps and cornerpieces, printed black letter throughout, full page woodcut plates. R. F. G. Hollett & Son Antiquarian Booksellers General Catalogue Summer 2010 - 1157 2011 £175

Bible. English - *The Revelation of Saint John the Divine.* London: Collins, n.d., First edition; folio, original cloth, gilt, dust jacket, edges little chipped, pages 57, with 12 fine full page lithographed color plates. R. F. G. Hollett & Son Antiquarian Booksellers 175 - 438 2011 £65

Bible. English - 1653 *The Holy Bible containing ye Old and New Testaments.... (with, bound at end of volume 2: The Psalms of David in Meeter).* London: printed by Iohn Field, 1653., Edinburgh: i.e. Amsterdam: printed by Evan Tyler, 1653; The first work divided after Dd2, 12mo., ff. (314); (282), 89, (i), contemporary red morocco, unlettered spine panel gilt, boards fully gilt in Scottish 'Herringbone' style, board edges decorative roll gilt, turn-ins decorative roll gilt, 'Dutch floral gilt' endpapers to volume 1, 'dutch-comb' endpapers to volume 2, all edges gilt, pale blue and white sewn endbands, text rubricated throughout, browned, some soiling and staining, one leaf in second work with corner torn away affecting a dozen lines of text, 20th century MS poem to last text leaf in volume 2 signed "Phineas Fletcher", binding rubbed, joints splitting, endpapers worn, spines darkened, old repair to head volume i, ink ownership inscription "MARY ADAMS/1769", from the collection of Christopher Ernest Weston 1947-2010. Unsworths Booksellers 24 - 9 2011 £700

Bible. English - 1750 *The Holy Bible, containing the Old and New Testaments.* Oxford: John Baskett, 1750, 2 volumes, 12mo., contemporary full black calf gilt, boards decorated with cornerpieces and central black, all in gilt, gilt decorated backstrip, little worn, all edges gilt, scarce. R. F. G. Hollett & Son Antiquarian Booksellers 175 - 118 2011 £250

Bible. English - 1790 *The Christian's New and Complete Family Bible.* C. C. Cooke, n.d., 1790, Folio, contemporary full calf, little rubbed, spine slightly defective at head and foot, upper hinge, just cracking, pages 806, engraved frontispiece and over 350 illustrations, complete with Apocrypha which is often omitted from this edition, but with only 2 pages (ex 9) of the general index or concordance and lacks the tables and directions to the binder at the end, few leaves with small stains to top margins, otherwise excellent clean and sound copy, with genealogies on the front flyleaves of Hindle and Cunliffe families of Lancashire. R. F. G. Hollett & Son Antiquarian Booksellers 175 - 123 2011 £180

Bible. English - 1802 *Bible.* London: published for John Reeves, 1802, 241 x 152mm., 9 volumes, very fine dark blue straight grain morocco, handsomely gilt, covers bordered in gilt with angular key roll, raised bands, spines ornately gilt in panels featuring unusual sawtooth and flower roll at head and foot with stippled diapering filling main part of panel, all edges gilt, armorial bookplate of John Pollexfen Bastard; two spines lightly sunned, half dozen boards with light fading at edges, isolated wear to corners and ends of spines, few small indents and flakes, original very decorative bindings extremely well preserved, first volume with noticeable freckled foxing at front and back, isolated gatherings (perhaps a total of six or 8, combined) in the other volumes with less but still apparent foxing, endpapers generally little discolored, otherwise internally in fine condition, almost entirely very bright, fresh and clean. Phillip J. Pirages 59 - 79 2011 $4250

Bible. English - 1812 *The Holy Bible Containing the Old and New Testaments.* London: C. Baldwin, 1812, New edition; 4to., 6 volumes, contemporary diced calf, gilt, boards panelled with broad rolls and fillets in gilt and blind, spines with broad flat raised bands, little worn and recased, some damage to bottom of to backstrips, all edges marbled, excellent clean set. R. F. G. Hollett & Son Antiquarian Booksellers 175 - 131 2011 £250

Bible. English - 1812 *Bible.* London: printed by C. Baldwin published by L. Seeley et al, 1812-1814, 6 volumes, 318 x 254mm., superb contemporary dark purple straight grain morocco, very handsomely gilt, covers panelled with gilt outer frame of triple fillets and wide lobed roll of stylized bunting, blind ruled inner frame with narrow gilt tools at corners and at center gilt octagonal panel of broad and narrow fillets flanked with blind scrolling rolls, flat spines panelled in gilt and blind featuring elaborate gilt scrolling centerpiece with floral and foliate elements and festoons at ends and side, very board turn-ins with designs similar to spine panels, including blind roll of floral festoons and unusual pattern of alternately gilt and blind fleurons, rose colored silk endpapers with blind ruled border, all edges gilt and gauffered; two boards with faint, mottled staining, extremities with very minor rubbing, endpapers little foxed, isolated faint foxing in text, handful of minor tears and stains, binding extremely well preserved with only superficial wear and leaves quite clean, bright and fresh, fine in sumptuous contemporaneous binding. Phillip J. Pirages 59 - 80 2011 $7500

Bible. English - 1830 *The Book of Psalms According to the Authorised Version.* London: Samuel Bagster, 1830, Pages 15, 264, small 8vo., contemporary full black morocco gilt, large stylised lyre with title, all in gilt on each board and spine, extremities little rubbed, upper hinge just cracking at head, all edges gilt. R. F. G. Hollett & Son Antiquarian Booksellers 175 - 115 2011 £95

Bible. English - 1836 *New Testament of Our Lord and Saviour Jesus Christ: Published in 1526.* London: Samuel Bagster, 1836, 8vo., pages iv, 98 ff., ii-ccxvii + engraved titlepage and frontispiece, later calf, spine panelled in blind, lettered in 'Old English' type and dated at foot both in gilt, boards elaborately panelled in blind with rules and decorative rolls, central panel double rule diced board edges decorative roll n blind, turn-ins elaborately decorated with rolls tooled in blind, 'Peacock swirl' 'made' endpapers, all edges gilt & gauffered, 3 color (blue white & pink), sewn flat endbands, maroon silk page marker, frontispiece foxed, spine quite rubbed, joints split and boards loose, armorial bookplate of York Minster /Library / Bequeathed by the Rev. R. A. Talbot 1993" , from the collection of Christopher Ernest Weston 1947-2010. Unsworths Booksellers 24 - 12 2011 £95

Bible. English - 1836 *The Pictorial Bible...* London: Charles Knight & Co., 1836, 1837. 1838; Full maroon morocco gilt, boards panelled in gilt and blind, little light rubbing to extremities and odd mark, but most handsome binding, pages vii, 680; viii, 829; vi, 542, all edges gilt, with 828 text woodcuts, some joints cracking internally, but very good, sound and clean. R. F. G. Hollett & Son Antiquarian Booksellers 175 - 123 2011 £275

Bible. English - 1860 *The Holy Bible.* London: Eyre and Spottiswoode, 1860, Thick small folio, original full brown blind decorated morocco gilt over heavy bevelled boards, brass decoative cornerpieces and clasp (bar lacking), all edges gilt, unpaginated, 20 fine tissue guarded steel engraved plates by W. H. Bartlett. R. F. G. Hollett & Son Antiquarian Booksellers 175 - 117 2011 £180

Bible. English - 1870 *The Illustrated Family Bible Containing the Old and New Testaments...* London: Cassell, Petter & Galpin, n.d. circa, 1870, Thick 4to., publisher's full maroon morocco gilt over heavy bevelled boards, sunken decorations and panels heavily decorated in gilt and blind, little light rubbing to extremities, odd scuff mark, but most handsome binding, pages 1052, 424, all edges gilt, with 12 tissue guarded chromolithographed plates and over 900 text woodcuts and decorations, paper of front joint cracked, some tissues rather browned, very attractive. R. F. G. Hollett & Son Antiquarian Booksellers 175 - 119 2011 £350

Bible. English - 1874 *The Gospel According to St. Matthew.* London: Sampson Low, etc., 1874, Folio, original brown cloth gilt by Burn & Co., over bevelled boards, corners trifle worn, unpaginated, all edges gilt, engraved title with lettering in red title in red and black and 40 magnificent full page etched plates after Alexandre Bida, handsome, clean copy. R. F. G. Hollett & Son Antiquarian Booksellers 175 - 128 2011 £295

Bible. English - 1875 *The Gospel According to St. Mark.* London: Sampson Low, etc., 1875, Folio, original brown cloth, gilt by Burn & Co. over bevelled boards, unpaginated, all edges gilt, complete with engraved title and lettering in red, title in red and black, 24 magnificent full page etched plates after French artist and engraver Alexandre Bida, handsome, clean copy.   R. F. G. Hollett & Son Antiquarian Booksellers   175 - 127   2011   £250

Bible. English - 1877 *The Gospel According to St. Mark.* London: Sampson Low etc., 1877, Folio, original brown cloth gilt by Burn & Co., over bevelled boards, unpaginated, all edges gilt, engraved title with lettering to red, title in red and black and 38 magnificent full page etched plates after French artist and engraver Alexandre Bida, handsome, clean copy.   R. F. G. Hollett & Son Antiquarian Booksellers   175 - 126   2011   £295

Bible. English - 1880 *The Self Interpreting Family Bible, Containing the Old and New Testament.* Heworth: Brooks & Print, n.d. circa, 1880, Thick small folio, good Victorian binding of black morocco gilt extra over bevelled boards, sunken central panel on upper board, neatly recased and lacking clasps, pages lxxxii, 1149, 52, all edges gilt, some 30 chromolithographed plates, few slight edge tears.   R. F. G. Hollett & Son Antiquarian Booksellers   175 - 129   2011   £180

Bible. English - 1881 *New Testament.* Cambridge: 1881, xxv, (1), 606 pages, full morocco, gilt presentation stamps from Merian Committee of revision, all edges gilt, inner dentelles gilt, chocolate coated endpapers, beveled edges, endpapers foxed.   Bookworm & Silverfish   665 - 19   2011 $150

Bible. English - 1881 *The Gospel According to S. John.* Cambridge: Cambridge University Press, circa, 1881, Interleaves with plain rubricated pages, plain red calf, gilt dentelles & edges by Philip Tout, all edges gilt, inscribed "This gift to my father George MacDonald from Miss Violet Cavendish-Bentinck, now offered in much love & gratitude to the Rev. M. C. D'Arcy by Greville MacDonald".   Jarndyce Antiquarian Booksellers   CXCII - 335   2011   £250

Bible. English - 1901 *The Boke off the Revelacion off Sanct John the Devine Done into Englysshe by WilliamTyndale.* Ashendene Press, 1901, One of 54 copies; 218 x 165 mm., 1 p.l., xxx, (i) pages, plus 6 blank leaves at front and three at back, original limp velum dyed dark green, gilt titled flat spine, custom made folding cloth box with gilt titling, initials and chapter headings printed in red, booklabel "From the Books of Crosby Gaige", bookplate of Lord Wardington, little loss of dark green present along fore edges of binding, in all other ways a faultless copy.   Phillip J. Pirages   59 - 74   2011 $4250

Bible. English - 1904 *Wharton Bible.* London: Oxford University Press, 1904, original full black divinity calf, upper board lettered in gilt, one corner trifle worn, pages 607, 176, (viii), all edges gilt, 12 colored maps, presentation slip, excellent clean example.   R. F. G. Hollett & Son Antiquarian Booksellers   175 - 124   2011   £40

Bible. English - 1904 *A Book of Songs and Poems from the Old Testament and The Apocrypha.* Ashendene Press, 1904, One of 150 copies on paper (there were also 25 printed on vellum); 190 x 135mm., 62, (1) pages, original limp vellum, gilt titling on spine, printed in red and black, hand painted blue initials by Graily Hewitt, woodcut bookplate of Edmund Bulkley; vellum binding with usual very slight rumpling and variation in color becasue of grain, fine copy nevertheless, beautiful internally.   Phillip J. Pirages   59 - 75   2011 $2400

Bible. English - 1927 *Ecclesiasticus or the Wisdom of the Jesus the Son of Sirach.* London: John Lane The Bodley Head, 1927, Large 8vo., original decorated cream cloth, gilt, dust jacket with internal tissue liner rather creased, pages xx, 165, top edges gilt, untrimmed with 16 tissue guarded color plates.   R. F. G. Hollett & Son Antiquarian Booksellers   175 - 192   2011   £75

Bible. English - 1928 *Judith.* London: Haymarket Press, 1928, One of 12 copies on vellum, signed by artist (this copy #3); an additional 100 copies issued on paper, original flexible vellum, gilt titling on upper cover and flat spine, green silk ties, four illustrations by W. Russell Flint mounted on vellum, with extra suite of the plates in separate portfolio, head and tail of spine slightly bumped, plates in volume somewhat wrinkled (because of adhesive used when mounting them on the vellum, otherwise very fine copy, binding and text unusually clean and fresh, extra plates in pristine condition.   Phillip J. Pirages   59 - 344   2011 $3000

Bible. English - 1932 *The Revelation of Saint John the Divine.* Gregynog Press, 1932, One of 250 copies; 350 x 210mm., (30) leaves, publisher's red Hermitage calf over bevelled boards, titling in black, 40 striking wood engraved illustrations by Blair Hughes-Stanton, 13 of them full page, text printed in red and black, first 3 words on titlepage wood engraved, with a copy of the prospectus (a reproduction of the first gathering of text from the book, containing four pages after the title) laid in at front; small shallow dent on rear cover, just breath of rubbing here and there, but very fine, easily chafed showing few signs of use and virtually perfect internally.   Phillip J. Pirages   59 - 227   2011 $3500

Bible. English - 1933 *Matthew Merian's Illustrated Bible.* New York: William Morrow & Co., 1933, Large 8vo., original grey cloth, pages (vi), 206, illustrations.   R. F. G. Hollett & Son Antiquarian Booksellers   175 - 130   2011   £50

Bible. English - 1968 *The Oxford Illustrated Old Testament.* London: Oxford University Press, 1968, First edition; tall 8vo., original cloth, gilt, dust jacket, pages 533, illustrations.   R. F. G. Hollett & Son Antiquarian Booksellers   175 - 122   2011   £45

Bible. English - 1977 *The Book of Jonah, Taken from the Authorised Version of King James I.* privately printed at the Rampant Lions Press for Clover Hill Editions, 1977, 60/300 copies (of an edition 470 copies); printed on Barcham Green mouldmade paper, 13 wood engravings, title and fly title printed in green, pages (vi), 22, small folio, original quarter dark green buckram, backstrip gilt lettered, patterned pale green boards, untrimmed, fine.   Blackwell Rare Books   B166 - 271   2011   £400

Bible. English - 1979 *The Book of Jonah Taken from the Authorised Version of King James I.* London: Douglas Cleverdon, 1979, Limited edition, no. 282 of 410 copies; 4to., original cloth backed patterned green boards, gilt, custom made slipcase, pages 22, untrimmed with title spread in green and black and 13 woodcut illustrations, printed on J. Green mould made paper, fine.   R. F. G. Hollett & Son Antiquarian Booksellers   175 - 742   2011   £350

Bible. English - 1982 *The Apocalypse: The Revelation of Saint John the Divine.* Arion Press, 1982, One of 150 copies for sale; an additional 15 copies were printed but not for sale, this copy #32, titlepage signed by artist, 388 x 295mm., (36) leaves (first two and last two blank), publisher's original binding, designed by Jim Dine, featuring honey colored wooden boards with prominent lightning bolt running from top to bottom and backed with flat pigskin spine blindstamped with vertical titling, very fine specially made matching suede lined natural linen clamshell box, wooden lightning bolt design on spine, 29 full page black and white woodblock prints by Jim Dine, colophon signed by printer, Andrew Hoyem, printed on handmade Apta paper, prospectus for this title, relating advertising material and greeting card from press laid in at front, mint.   Phillip J. Pirages   59 - 68   2011 $5000

Bible. English - 2000 *The Holy Bible.* Aron Press, 2000, One of 400 copies for sale; (an additional 26 copies printed for presentation and of the 400, one of 150 special copies with and colored and illuminated abstract decoration of initial letters, 2 volumes, 470 x 350mm., original bindings of violet crushed morocco boards, black morocco spine, thin strip of red morocco between, flat spine with gilt titling, sturdy black buckram box with black morocco label, mint.   Phillip J. Pirages   59 - 67   2011 $12,500

Bible. French - 1843 *Les Saints Evangiles.* Paris: L. Curmer, 1843, First edition thus; the handsomely designed presentation page at the front tells us that this beautiful object was assembled at the order of C. J. T. Tiby and given to his dear wife Anais Duret Tiby on 2 June 1855 as a "Souvenir of 25 years of Happiness", 260 x 184mm., 4 p.l. 552 pages; 2 p.l, 372 pages, 2 volumes bound in one, extremely elegant mid 19th century Neo-gothic presentation binding by Gruel-Engelmann in dark green silk velvet, covers mounted with delicately amd elaborately carved boxwood frames after designs by Martin Riester, upper cover with wooden grapevine cornerpieces forming a large ogival central velvet panel featuring carved wooden vines forming the prominent monogram "A T" (for Anais Tiby) at middle, lower cover with central carved cross twined with grape vines arising from a cluster of leaves, flat spine with carved head and tailpieces, repeating grapevine motif and a carved boxwood banderolle at center on which the title appears in red, blue and gold; two pierced metal clasps at fore edge, saffron yellow moire silk endleaves, morocco hinges, edges very elaborately gauffered with gilt neo-gothic floral pattern on a red background, housed in handsome and very sturdy morocco backed wooden box lined with gold velvet, ornamental borders around text, numerous ornamental headpieces, initials and tailpieces (37 of these illuminated by hand), two chromolithographed titlepages, four woodcut titles for each Gospel, two engraved maps, two steel engraved frontispieces by Lecomte after Decaisne and by Cousin after Meissonier and 17 steel engraved plates after Tony Johannot by Cousin, Fontaine, Revel and others; extra illustrated with 11 steel engraved topographical plates printed on chine, one leaf inscribed in gothic hand with the Prophecies of Isaiah in red, blue and gold inks, a presentation page with calligraphy and a full border with flowers and acanthus leaves of a burnished gold ground, both done by Langlume, in the style of a 15th century Book of Hours, with accompanying original watercolor of the Tiby wedding by Fauquet within an illuminated border by Langlume, with 22 (blank) genealogical pages, printed in colors with ruled centers surrounded by ornamental borders bound in below beginning of text; one barely perceptible chip to one of the grapevine cornerpieces on upper cover, 9 of the Johannot plates rather browned and offset to text, one border slightly soiled, otherwise extraordinarily fine copy of a unique work, text clean, fresh and bright, interior and exterior colors and gold shimmering and quite lovely delicate binding astonishingly well preserved.   Phillip J. Pirages   59 - 105 2011 $15,000

Bible. German - 1927 *Die Bibel Oder die Gange Heilige Schrift Deutsch Von Doctor Martin Luther.* Berlin: 1927, Volume I only (of 2), thick 4to., full blindstamped calf, edges slightly rubbed, neatly recased, pages 967, reproductions in full color.   R. F. G. Hollett & Son Antiquarian Booksellers   175 - 112   2011   £135

Bible. Greek - 1625 *(Greek text) Noveum Testamentum.* Leiden: Elzevier, 1625, First Elzevier Greek New Testament; woodcut printer's device on title, pages (xii), 863, 12mo., contemporary vellum, elaborate gilt arms of Rotterdam supported by lions rampant and surmounted by a crown on both covers, spine with gilt fleuron in each of four compartments, lettered late in English in ink, yapp edges, gilt edges, gauffered frames, traces of green silk ties, vellum somewhat rubbed with loss of some gilt, slightly discolored, very good, prize binding from Rotterdam with inscription dated 1625 on flyleaf presenting it to a young scholar (his name unfortunately crossed out, possibly Franciscus van den Brouck). Blackwell Rare Books B166 - 14 2011 £600

Bible. Greek - 1750 *(Greek). Novum Testamentum.* Glasguae: in Aedibus R. Urie, 1750, Large paper copy, 8vo., pages (iv), 572 i.e. formula (pi)2, A-Bbbb4, Cccc2 = 228 leaves, text in Greek, contemporary crimson morocco, spine panel gilt, black lettering piece gilt, boards broad decorative roll gilt bordered, board edges and turn-ins obliquely broken rule gilt, 'Antique Spot' 'made' endpapers, all edges gilt, pink and white sewn endpapers, little light spotting, joints touch rubbed, spine slightly darkened, armorial bookplate William Johnston Esq, from the collection of Christopher Ernest Weston 1947-2010. Unsworths Booksellers 24 - 10 2011 £300

Bible. Greek - 1812 *Psalterium Graecum E Codice Ms. Alexandrino.* Londini: Ex Prelo Ricardi Taylor et Socii, 1812, One of 17 copies printed on vellum; 356 x 299mm., (1) leaf (blank), xii, (32) leaves, 18 pages, (1) leaf (blank), very handsome contemporary deep blue morocco lavishly gilt, apparently by Charles Lewis, covers with broad elaborately gilt border and simple inner frame, wide gilt decorated raised bands, spine compartments with complex gilt decoration featuring scrolling floral stamps and unusual trapezoidal ornaments on either side of a central stem, very wide and sumptuously gilt inner dentelles, yellow watered silk pastedowns, front and rear free endleaves, made of matching watered silk pasted to vellum sheets, all edges gilt; monogram booklabel and armorial bookplate of William Henry Smith and oval morocco bookplate of Estelle Doheny, subscriber list, slight variation in color of binding and of vellum leaves, but very fine, stunning. Phillip J. Pirages 59 - 340 2011 $15,000

Bible. Hebrew - 1656 *The Hebrew text of the Psalmes and Lamentations....* London: printed for the author and sold by H. Robinson, A Crook, L. Fawn, J. Kirton, S. Thomson..., 1656, 12mo., (12), 266, 149-191, 15, (2) pages, last leaf with errata, contemporary calf, from the library of John Christy 1717, from the library of the Earls of Macclesfield at Shirburn Castle. Maggs Bros. Ltd. 1440 - 32 2011 £450

Bible. Hebrew - 1656 *The Hebrew text of the Psalmes and Lamentations....* London: printed for the author and are to be sold by H. Robinson, A. Crook, L. Fawn, J. Kirton, S. Thomson and G. Sawbridge.., 1656, (8), 248, 22, (2), text in 2 columns printed in vocalised Hebrew and transliterated, last leaf with errata, contemporary English calf over pasteboard, contemporary English calf over pasteboard, upper joint cracking, from the library of the Earls of Macclesfield at Shirburn Castle. Maggs Bros. Ltd. 1440 - 31 2011 £1800

Bible. Hebrew - 1812 *Biblia Hebraica...* London: A. B. R. Goakman, 1812, 2 engraved titles, 2 volumes, old half calf gilt, raised bands, double spine label, rather worn, 2 labels defective or lacking, 2 engraved titles. R. F. G. Hollett & Son Antiquarian Booksellers 175 - 132 2011 £75

Bible. Hebrew - 1822 *Biblia Hebraica...* Londini: Impensis Ogle, Duncan et Sociorum, 1822, 2 volumes, 8vo., pages 35, (i), 559, (i); (ii), 634, contemporary Russia, boards concentrically bordered with alternating blind and gilt decorative rolls, board edges broken hatch gilt at corners, turn-ins decorative roll gilt, 'French Shell' 'made' endpapers, all edges 'French Shell' marbled, blue and white sewn flat endbands, early 21st century calf rebacked by Christ Weston, little faint foxing, board edges just slightly rubbed, 20th century blue ink inscription, "A. G. Widdess" at head of both titlepages, from the collection of Christopher Ernest Weston 1947-2010. Unsworths Booksellers 24 - 11 2011 £200

Bible. Hieroglyphic - 1796 *A New Hieroglyphical Bible for the Amusement & Instruction of Children.* New York: printed for & Published by the Booksellers, 1796, 18mo., 144 pages, extensively illustrated, recent cloth backed boards, engraved titlepage, lacks frontispiece, small replacement at inner margin, top of titlepage, just affecting the "H", corners frayed on a number of early leaves, text browned, sound. M & S Rare Books, Inc. 90 - 204 2011 $1250

Bible. Hieroglyphic - 1847 *The Hieroglyphick Bible; or Selected Passages in the Old and New Testaments, Represented with Emblematical Figures for the Amusement of Youth...* Hartford: S. Andrus & Son, 1847, 12mo., vii, 132 pages, illustrated with nearly five hundred cuts, decorative floral tooled brown cloth on boards, gilt decorative title on upper cover, full page decorative woodcut half title, full page woodcut frontispiece, pencilled signatures on lower endpaper and flyleaf, occasional light spotting and foxing, very good. Hobbyhorse Books 56 - 9 2011 $130

Bible. Latvian - 1704 *Dahwida Dseesmu-Grahmata no Deewa, Sehta Wahrda Grabmatas pa Wahrdu Wahrdeem Insemta. (Pslams). (bound with) Salamana sakkami-wahrdi no deewa sweht̹a Wahrda Grahmatas... (Proverbs).* Riga: G. N. Noller, 1704-1707, 2 works in 1 volume, 8vo., later 18th century English polished calf, gilt spine, red morocco lettering piece, red edges, few headlines slightly shaved, from the library of the Earls of Macclesfield at Shirburn Castle. Maggs Bros. Ltd. 1440 - 33 2011 £550

Bible. Manx - 1819 *Yn Vible Casherick... (Manx Bible).* London: printed by George Eyre and Andrew Strahan for The British and Foreign Bible Society, 1819, First edition thus; 8vo., pages not numbered (about 700+ pages), corners rubbed, spine lightly patterned but not (discernibly) lettered, corners rubbed, spine ends very slightly worn, splitting at front hinge repaired, overall sound decent very good copy with clean text. Any Amount of Books May 26 2011 - A75894 2011 $755

Bible. Polyglot - 1684 *Le Noveau Testament/The New Testament.* Amsterdam: 1684, printed in three columns, in French, Dutch and English, 12mo., pictorial titlepage, pages (4), 601, (1), recently attractively rebound in half brown leather with marbled boards and lettered gilt at spine, 4 raised bands, few small brown stains at blank prelims, otherwise sound, clean, excellent copy. Any Amount of Books May 29 2011 - A39616 2011 $408

Bible. Polyglot - 1809 *Liber Psalmorum Hebraice.* London: Cambridge, 1809, First Printing of any part of the Bible in Hebrew in America; 12mo, (8), (1)-495, (1, blank) pages, with translation and notes in Latin, full contemporary calf, front board attached but loose, lacking part of the backstrip, back cover with some leather lacking, corners and edges chipped, leaves bit toned, some foxing, as usual for American books of this era, old pencil inscription on front free endpaper, very good, extremely scarce, housed in custom calf clamshell, undated gift inscription from Rev. John H. Van Court (1793-1867) to the Rev. John Dorrance (1800-1861). Heritage Book Shop Holiday 2010 - 65 2011 $20,000

Bible. Rarotongan - 1851 *Te Biblia Tapu ra Koia te Koreromotu Taaito e Te Koreromotu ou...* British and Foreign Bible Society, 1851, Scarce first full edition of the Bible in Rarontongan; printed in double columns, pages (iv), (1-) 851, (v), 266, royal 8vo., contemporary (?publisher's) blindstamped calf, rebacked, corners worn, blindstamped of the Glasgow F. C. College Library on gilt, good. Blackwell Rare Books B166 - 15 2011 £1500

Bible. Slovenian - 1968 *Biblia 1584. I. Teil: Text.* Munchen: Dr. Rudolf Trofenik, 1968, Facsimile of 1584 printing; Thick 4to., unpaginated, illustrations, original full hard grain morocco, tooled in blind, centrepiece of brown metal with words "Biblia", ex-library markings, otherwise clean and untouched, very good, scarce. Jeff Weber Rare Books 163 - 5 2011 $125

Bickerton, Derek *The Murders of Boysie Singh - Robber, Arsonist, Pirate, Mass Murderer, Vice and Gambling King of Trinidad.* London: 1962, First edition; very good (endpaper foxed), age soiled, else very good dust jacket. Bookworm & Silverfish 679 - 50 2011 $75

Bickford, Lawrence *Sumo and the Woodblock Print Masters.* Tokyo: Kodansha, 1994, First edition, first printing; 4to. 160 pages, fine in fine dust jacket. By the Book, L. C. 26 - 25 2011 $90

Bicknell, Peter *The Illustrated Wordsworth's Guide to the Lakes.* Webb & Bower, 1984, First edition; small 4to., original cloth, gilt, dust jacket, pages 208, illustrations in color and monochrome. R. F. G. Hollett & Son Antiquarian Booksellers 173 - 78 2011 £35

Bicknell, Peter *The Picturesque Scenery of the Lake District 1752-1855.* Winchester: St. Paul's Bibliographies, 1990, First edition; 4to., original cloth, gilt, dust jacket, pages 198, with 12 pages of plates and other illustrations. R. F. G. Hollett & Son Antiquarian Booksellers 173 - 77 2011 £45

Bidlake, John *A Familiar Introduction to the Study of Geography and to the Use of the Globes...* London: John Murray, 1806, Fourth edition; pages vii, 76, flyleaf removed, little dusty in places, contemporary drab wrappers, rather soiled and chipped, corners creased. R. F. G. Hollett & Sons Antiquarian Booksellers 170 - 86 2011 £65

Bidwell, Paul *Hadrian's Wall 1989-1999.* Carlisle: CWAAS and Soc. Antiquaries Newcastle upon Tyne, 1999, Original glazed pictorial boards, pages vii, 224, with 67 plates and plans, map and text illustrations. R. F. G. Hollett & Son Antiquarian Booksellers 177 - 81 2011 £30

Biffart, M. *Venetia with the Quadrilateral. A Military Geographical Sketch.* London: Topographical and Statistical Dept. War Office, n.d., 1866, First edition; 8vo., modern green cloth lettered gilt at spine with original printed front wrappers (slightly chipped) preserved, pages x, 61, maps, ex-Foreign and Commonwealth Office library with their label and stamps (lightly applied), very good. Any Amount of Books May 29 2011 - A49595 2011 $272

The Big Book of Aeroplanes. London: Henry Frowde and Hodder and Stoughton, 1913, First edition; unpaginated, 1 double page and 11 full page color plates plus drawings in text by H. C. Earnshaw, top of flyleaf creased, otherwise very good, original pale blue cloth, pictorial onlay, few marks and spots and extremities trifle rubbed. R. F. G. Hollett & Sons Antiquarian Booksellers 170 - 214 2011 £35

Bigelow, Jacob 1787-1879 *American Medical Botany, Being a Collection of the Native Medicinal Plants of the United States.* Boston: Cummings and Hilliard, 1817-1820, First edition, mixed state; 60 colored plates (few hand colored, most color printed, foxing to several, occasional light offsetting to plates), tall 8vo., pages xi, (17-) 197, (5); xiv, (15-) 199, (1);x, (11-) 193, contemporary calf, upper corner of back cover bumped, corner to head of spine bumped and with piece missing, scattered foxing, offsetting to some pages, opposite plates, pages 195 through 198 from volume III misbound following page 198 of volume I, inner hinges reinforced, from the Yale College Library, presented by the estate of Benjamin Barrett, M.D., bought from Yale for Dr. Fred. Sumner Smith by his Father.   Raymond M. Sutton, Jr.   May 26 2011 - 39722 2011 $3700

Biggers, Don H. *From Cattle Range to Cotton Patch.. A Series of Historical Sketches.* Abilene: Abilene Printing Co., n.d. circa, 1905, First edition; 8vo., stiff printed wrappers, decorated endpapers, (6), 156 pages, illustrations, plates, ads, rare, moderate wear to spine, but pages still tight, few light corner creases to front and rear panels, else very good, exceedingly rare.   Buckingham Books   May 26 2011 - 26819 2011 $20,000

Biggle, Lloyd *The Metallic Muse.* Garden City: Doubleday & Co., 1972, First edition; octavo, cloth.   L. W. Currey, Inc.   124 - 227 2011 $100

Bigland, John *Letters on Natural History: Exhibiting a View of the Power, Wisdom and Goodness of the Deity, so Eminently Displayed in the Formation of the Universe...* London: James Cundee, 1810, Second edition; pages xvii, (iii), 400, engraved portrait and 100 illustrations on 51 plates, few small patches of browning, excellent copy, old tree calf, edges little worn, nicely rebacked to match with leather spine label.   R. F. G. Hollett & Sons Antiquarian Booksellers   170 - 87 2011   £140

Billingham, Richard *Ray's a Laugh.* Zurich: Scalo, 1996, First edition; 4to., pages (96), 50 color and 2 black and white photos, original endpapers each illustrated with color photo, original peach paper covered boards, text printed in burgundy, original color photo illustrated dust jacket, creasing to top and bottom edge of lower panel with short closed tear at head of spine, fine in very good dust jacket. Simon Finch Rare Books   Zero - 509 2011   £300

Billings, Robert William *Architectural Illustrations, History and Description of Carlisle Cathedral.* London: Thomas and William Boone and R. W. Billings, 1840, First edition; 4to., original black blind ruled cloth, gilt, pages vi, 92, with 45 steel engraved plates on stiff cream paper, vignette on title, exceptionally clean and bright.   R. F. G. Hollett & Son Antiquarian Booksellers   173 - 80 2011   £275

Billings, Robert William *Architectural Illustrations, History and Description of Carlise Cathedral.* London: Thames and William Boone and R. W. Billings, 1840, First edition; 4to., original black blind ruled cloth gilt, pages vi, 92, complete with 45 steel engraved plates on stiff cream paper and vignette on title, exceptionally clean and bright.   R. F. G. Hollett & Son Antiquarian Booksellers   177 - 82 2011   £275

Bingham, Clifton *The Animals' Alpine Club.* London: Nister, n.d. circa, 1913, Oblong 4to., cloth backed pictorial boards, light edge and corner wear and margins toned, else very good+, illustrations by G. H. Thompson with 8 incredible full page chromolithographs and many full and partial page line illustrations and pictorial endpapers.   Aleph-Bet Books, Inc.   95 - 99 2011 $1850

Bingham, Clifton *Dandy Lion.* London: Nister, 1900, 4to., cloth backed pictorial boards, edges rubbed and covers lightly scratched, else very good+, mounted color frontispiece and black and whites by Lois Wain.   Aleph-Bet Books, Inc.   95 - 583 2011 $750

Bingham, Clifton *Funny Doings in Animal Land.* London: Nister, n.d. circa, 1906, Oblong 4to., cloth backed pictorial boards, corners slightly rubbed, else fine in original pictorial dust jacket (lacks backstrip but has both covers), 8 chromolithographed plates, 7 full page and many full and partial page line illustrations, pictorial endpapers, rare in dust jacket.   Aleph-Bet Books, Inc.   95 - 100 2011 $1650

Bingham, Clifton *Proverbs Old Newly Told.* London: Raphael Tuck, n.d. circa, 1900, Folio, cloth backed pictorial boards, 2 archival margin mends, some cover rubbing and paper toning, very good+, 12 full page chromolithographs.   Aleph-Bet Books, Inc.   95 - 432 2011 $400

Bingham, Clifton *With Father Tuck in Playtime.* London: Tuck, circa, 1900, 4to., pictorial boards, neat spine repair, light cover rubbing, very good+, 4 charming fold down scenes that each erect a three dimensional tableau, illustrations in brown line in text by M. Bowley.   Aleph-Bet Books, Inc.   95 - 457 2011 $900

Bingham, Roger *The Church at Heversham.* Milnthorpe: privately published, 1984, First edition; original cloth, gilt, dust jacket, pages 160, illustrations, signed by author, fine, scarce.   R. F. G. Hollett & Son Antiquarian Booksellers   173 - 82 2011   £60

Bingham, Roger *Memories of Milnthorpe for the Millennium.* Milnthorpe: privately published by author, 2000, First edition; square 8vo., original pictorial glazed wrappers, 128 pages, illustrated with over 400 photos, signed, out of print and now scarce.   R. F. G. Hollett & Son Antiquarian Booksellers   173 - 86 2011   £45

Bingley, William *Travels in Africa from Modern Writers.* London: John Sharpe, 1819, 8vo., 346 pages plus ads in front and back, additional titlepage in rear showing that this is volume one of six dated 1823, brown cloth, about good. Barnaby Rudge Booksellers   Travel and Exploration - 019683   2011 $400

Birchall, J. *The Admonitory Task Book.* Manchester: J. Gleave, 1819, Pages 108, woodcut tailpiece, original roan backed marbled boards, paper label, hinges cracking.   R. F. G. Hollett & Sons Antiquarian Booksellers   170 - 90 2011   £180

The Bird-Fancier's Recreation. London: printed for T. Ward, 1735, Third edition; 12mo., 89, (5) pages, engraved frontispiece, very lightly browned, small closed tear to B4, overall good copy, contemporary sheep, front joint cracked, cords firm, from the library of the Earls of Macclesfield at Shirburn Castle.   Maggs Bros. Ltd.   1440 - 34 2011   £450

Birge, John Kingsley *The Bektshi Order of Dervishes.* London: Luzac, 1937, First edition; tall 8vo., original publisher's green cloth lettered gilt at spine, pages 291, 32 illustrations, excellent condition, clean bright, very good+ in used, near very good dust jacket slightly chipped at extremities, some damp marks at edges of boards, otherwise very good.   Any Amount of Books   May 29 2011 - A70952 2011 $340

Birkenhead, Robin *Churchill 1924-1940.* N.P.: privately published, 1989, First edition; 8vo., pages viii, 216, with 19 illustrations, fine in near fine printed dust jacket.   Any Amount of Books   May 29 2011 - A70592 2011 $340

Birkett, Henry F. *The Book of Overton.* J. & E. Bumpus Ltd., 1928, First edition; original cloth, paper spine label, pages ix, 220.   R. F. G. Hollett & Son Antiquarian Booksellers   173 - 91 2011   £35

Birkett, Henry F. *The Story of Ulverston.* Kendal: Titus Wilson, 1949, First edition; large 8vo., original cloth, gilt, pages xv, 182, with 12 plates.   R. F. G. Hollett & Son Antiquarian Booksellers   173 - 93 2011   £65

Birley, Eric *Roman Britain and the Roman Army.* Kendal: Titus Wilson, 1953, First edition; pages xi, 196, original cloth, gilt, dust jacket.   R. F. G. Hollett & Son Antiquarian Booksellers   177 - 83 2011   £30

Birnbaum, Uriel *Der Kaiser und Der Architekt: ein marchn in funzig Bildern. (The Emperor and the Architect: a Tale of Fifty Pictures).* Leipzig und Wien: Thyrsas Verlag, 1924, First edition; large 4to., blue cloth stamped in gold, 82 page, corner of cover faded, else near fine, 50 full page richly color illustrations, this copy inscribed by Birnbaum to Otto Nirenstein Kallir who founded Viennese modern art Neue Galerie in 1923, stunning book quite scarce with nice inscription.   Aleph-Bet Books, Inc.   95 - 101 2011 $800

Birrell, Augustine *The Duties and Liabilities of Trustees. Six Lectures.* London: Macmillan, 1896, First edition; 8vo., original publisher's blue cloth lettered gilt at spine, pages xi, 183, uncut, pencilled ownership signature of historian F. R. Cowell, slight rubbing at hinges slight foxing to prelims, neat oval booksellers stamp, otherwise clean and bright, very good+ with clean text.   Any Amount of Books   May 29 2011 - A49183 2011 $238

Bishop, Elizabeth *Geography III.* New York: Farrar, Straus & Giroux, 1976, First edition, one of 7500 copies printed; inscribed and signed by author on titlepage, fine in fine dust jacket.   Charles Agvent   2010 Summer Miscellany - 12 2011 $2000

Bishop, Elizabeth *Poem.* Phoenix Book Shop, 1973, First edition, copy "L" (for Loren) of 26 lettered copies (Out of a total edition of 126) signed by Bishop on colophon; oblong small 8vo., original string tied unprinted stiff wrappers, marbled outer wrapper, printed paper label, housed in custom green cloth clamshell box with black morocco spine label, with author's presentation for Loren MacIver & Lloyd Frankenberg, laid in is exceptionally interesting TLS from Bishop for MacIver and Frankenberg.   James S. Jaffe Rare Books   May 26 2011 - 20762 2011 $8500

Bishop, George *New England Judged by the Spirit of the Lord.... Containing a Brief Relation of the Sufferings of the People Call'd Quakers in New England...* London: T. Sowle, 1703, 1702. Second edition; (10), 113, 112-141, 152-498, 212, (14) pages, contemporary panelled calf, very skillfully rebacked in handsome period style, gilt, hole in margin of C4, some overall foxing, very attractive copy, contemporary signatures of Jno. Hoyland Jun. and Joseph Stokes, bookplate of Charles Roberts.   Joseph J. Felcone Inc.   Fall Miscellany 2010 - 13 2011 $1800

Bishop, H. H. *Pictorial Architecture in Greece and Italy.* London: SPCK, 1887, First edition; oblong 4to., original pictorial brown cloth, gilt, pages 135, over 100 fine woodcut illustrations, very nice.   R. F. G. Hollett & Son Antiquarian Booksellers   177 - 86 2011   £85

Bishop, H. H. *Pictorial Architecture of the British Isles.* London: SPCK, 1885, Third edition; oblong 4to., original pictorial brown cloth gilt, light marks to upper board, extremities little rubbed, pages 123 with over 180 fine woodcut illustrations.   R. F. G. Hollett & Son Antiquarian Booksellers   177 - 88 2011   £75

Bishop, Zealia B. *The Curse of Yig.* Sauk City: Arkham House, 1953, First edition; octavo, cloth. L. W. Currey, Inc. 124 - 66 2011 $1250

Bissel, Johann *Icaria.* Ingolstadt: C. Haemli, 1637, First edition; 12mo., (24), 343, (17) pages, engraved title, map in text, contemporary vellum, yapp edges, paper shelf labels on spine, from the library of the Earls of Macclesfield at Shirburn Castle, old Macclesfield classmark A IX 23 and number 35 written in ink (slightly dusty). Maggs Bros. Ltd. 1440 - 35 2011 £450

Bisset, Andrew *Memoirs and Papers of Sir Andrew Mitchell, K. B., Envoy Extraordinary and Minsier Plenipotentiary from the Court of Great Britain to the Court of Prussia from 1756 to 1771.* London: Chapman & Hall, 1850, 2 volumes, 8vo., soundly rebound in modern red cloth lettered gilt on spine, pages xviii, 477 & (viii), 524, frontispiece, ex-British Foreign Office library with few library markings, prelims slightly foxed, very good. Any Amount of Books May 29 2011 - A76090 2011 $221

Bixby-Smith, Sarah *Adobe Days: Being the Truthful Narrative of the events in the Life of a California Gilt on a Sheep Ranch and in El Pueblo & de Nuestra Senora de Los Angeles.* Cedar Rapids: Torch Press, 1925, First edition; small octavo, 208 pages, quarter linen boards, dust jacket, few minor tears to jacket, very good plus, scarce in jacket. Jeff Weber Rare Books 163 - 54 2011 $95

Bjorkman, Frances Maule *Where Women Vote.* New York: National American Woman Suffrage Association, 1913, Revised; (72) pages, slender 16mo., original green wrappers, printed in black, stapled as issued, negligible fading to extremities, tiny chip to top of one page, still fine, fragile. Paulette Rose Fine and Rare Books 32 - 166 2011 $325

Bjornson, Val *The History of Minnesota.* West Palm Beach: 1969, First edition; circa 2000 pages, 4 volumes, near fine, volumes 34 and 4 with some full page portraits. Bookworm & Silverfish 671 - 101 2011 $95

Blaauw, Adriaan *History of the IAU: The Birth and the First Half Century of the International Astronomical Union.* Dordrecht: Boston: Kluwer Academic Publishers, 1994, 8vo., xix, 296 pages, figures, printed boards, fine, rare, from the Bern Dibner reference library, with Burndy bookplate. Jeff Weber Rare Books 161 - 43 2011 $150

Black Orpheus. Nigeria: 1958-1976, First edition; Nos. 3-22 and volume 2/1-3, volume 3/2-3, 1958-1976, 24 issues in original pictorial wrappers in very good condition, very good, uncommon. I. D. Edrich May 26 2011 - 84653 2011 $671

Black, Robert *Substance of Two Speeches, Delivered in the General Synod of Ulster at its Annual Meeting in 1812...* Dublin: printed by Stewart and Hopes, King's Inns Quay, n.d., 1812, First edition; 8vo., (2), 77, (1) pages, piece torn away from margin of one leaf of text, but not affecting printed surface, preserved in modern wrappers, printed title label on upper cover, very good, scarce. John Drury Rare Books 153 - 14 2011 £275

Blackburn, Alexander *A Sunrise Brighter Still.* Athens: 1991, Author's Edition, one of 30 signed; xix, 171 pages, hand bound in half leather, gilt spine title trifle faded, else near fine. Dumont Maps & Books of the West 112 - 65 2011 $225

Blackburn, I. W. *Intracranial Tumors Among the Insane: a Study of 29 Intracranial Tumors Found in 1642.* Washington: 1903, 94 (1) pages, 71 plates, green pebbled cloth with some scrapes to front cover. Bookworm & Silverfish 667 - 115 2011 $85

Blackie's Popular Nursery Stories. Blackie & son, n.d., 1921, Small 4to., original cloth backed pictorial boards, edges little worn, unpaginated, 23 full page color plates and numerous drawings, pencilled line on front flyleaves and erasures on first endpapers, otherwise nice, sound copy. R. F. G. Hollett & Sons Antiquarian Booksellers 170 - 309 2011 £35

Blackley, Frederick R. *The Greenland Minstrel...* London: Simpkin and Marshall, 1839, 8vo., pages xxxv, (i) 148 (ii) + engraved frontispiece and 8 other engraved plates, publisher's original brown 'diaper' design book cloth, boards blocked in blind with large curvilinear cornerpieces within ruled border, title lettered in gilt in centre of upper board, lemon coated endpapers early 21st century cloth reback with original plain backskrip relaid, age toned, cloth unevenly faded and worn at edges, from the collection of Christopher Ernest Weston 1947-2010. Unsworths Booksellers 24 - 69 2011 £150

Blackmore, Richard Doddridge 1825-1900 *Erema; or My Father's Sin.* London: Smith, Elder and Co., 1877, First edition; 3 volumes, half titles, later 19th century half dark maroon calf by Kelly & Sons, top edge gilt, very good. Jarndyce Antiquarian Booksellers CXCI - 518 2011 £220

Blackmore, Richard Doddridge 1825-1900 *Lorna Doone: a Romance of Exmoor.* London: Sampson Low, Son & Marston, 1869, First edition, apparently one of 500 copies printed; 3 volumes, octavo, vi, 332; lv, 340; iv, 342 pages, bound without prelim blank leaf in volume I and final blank leaf in volume III, but with 16 page publisher's catalog dated March 1869, at end volume III, bound circa 1960 by Bayntun-Riviere (stamp signed in gilt on front turn-in), full red morocco, covers with gilt double fillet border, spines panelled and lettered in gilt on front turn-in), in full red morocco, covers with gilt double fillet border, spines panelled and lettered in gilt compartments with five raised bands, board edges and turn-ins decoratively tooled in gilt, all edges gilt, marbled endpapers, spines very slightly sunned, few short, expertly repaired margin tears, some occasional minor foxing or soiling, bookplate of J. Hodges, overall, excellent copy, laid in is ALS from author to James Payn, Teddington, Dec. 34d 1877.   David Brass Rare Books, Inc.   May 26 2011 - 00726 2011 $6500

Black's Economical Guide to the English Lakes. Edinburgh: Adam and Charles Black, 1859, Small 8vo., original green blindstamped limp cloth, gilt, fore edge of upper board rather damped, pages 75, (ii), 3 maps, title vignette and 3 woodcut plates.   R. F. G. Hollett & Son Antiquarian Booksellers 173 - 96 2011   £65

Blackstone, William 1723-1780 *Commentaries on the Laws of England.* Oxford: printed at the Clarendon Press, 1765, First edition; with rare 8 page supplement bound at end of first volume, 4 volumes, quarto, uniformly bound in contemporary speckled calf, rebacked in morocco. Heritage Book Shop   Booth A12 51st NY International Antiquarian Book Fair April 8-10 2011 - 12 2011 $20,000

Blackstone, William 1723-1780 *Commentaries on the Laws of England.* Oxford: printed at the Clarendon Press, 1768-1769, Volumes I & II third edition, volumes III & IV first edition; 4to., full contemporary calf, raised bands, red and green gilt labels, joints cracked but firm, surface abrasion to boards, contemporary signature of W. Jeffreys Jr. dated 1769, later bookplate of Fort Augustus Abbey, very good, clean set.   Jarndyce Antiquarian Booksellers   CXCI - 70 2011   £2800

Blackstone, William 1723-1780 *Commentaries on the Laws of England.* London: S. Sweet... A, Maxwell... and Milliken & son, 1836, Nineteenth edition; frontispiece in volume one, 4 volumes, octavo, contemporary half tan calf over marbled boards, maroon calf spine labels, gilt decoration and lettering on spine, edges speckled, very good. Heritage Book Shop   Holiday 2010 - 9 2011 $1500

Blackwell, Antoinette Brown *Sea Drift, or Tribute to the Ocean.* New York: James T. White, 1902, First edition; 8vo., pages 204, green cloth, little dust marked with painted numeral on spine, Library Union printers' Home bookplate, accession numeral and stamp on endpaper, very good, clean, scarce on the market.   Second Life Books Inc.   174 - 66 2011 $350

Blackwell, Elizabeth *The Laws of Life with Special Reference to the Physical Education of Girls.* New York: George P. Putnam, 1852, First edition; 180 pages, slate gray cloth, edges stained red, spine bit faded, few very tiny spots, else remarkably fresh, tight copy, as close to fine as one could hope for, contemporary signature of E. H. Cressey.   Joseph J. Felcone Inc.   Fall Miscellany 2010 - 14 2011 $12,000

Blackwell, K. *The Journal of the Bertrand Russell Archive.* Canada: 1971-1980, Nos. 1-40, VS V. 1/1.2, original wrappers.   I. D. Edrich   May 26 2011 - 82760 2011 $444

Blackwell, Richard J. *Galileo, Bellarmine, and the Bible including a Translation of Foscarini's Letter on the Motion of the Earth.* Notre Dame: University of Notre Dame Press, 1991, 8vo., x, 291 pages, blue cloth, white stamped spine title, dust jacket, fine, from the Bern Dibner reference library, with Burndy bookplate.   Jeff Weber Rare Books   161 - 44 2011 $100

Blackwell, Thomas *Memoirs of the Court of Augustus.* London: printed for A. Millar, 1764, third edition; 3 volumes, 4to., pages (vi) 384 + 9 engraved plates of roundel portraits, viii, 456 + 8 engraved plates of roundel portraits; (vi) 573 (xlix) + 8 engraved plates of roundel portraits, contemporary sprinkled and polished tan calf, spines panel gilt, red and black lettering and numbering pieces gilt, boards double rule gilt bordered, board edges 'zig-zag' decorative roll in blind, turn-ins obliquely striped with dark stain, all edges lightly red sprinkled, red and white sewn endbands, lightly toned and spotted, joints cracking but strong, spine ends bit worn with small repairs to headcaps, armorial bookplate of Jolliffe, from the collection of Christopher Ernest Weston 1947-2010.   Unsworths Booksellers   24 - 70 2011   £300

Blackwood, Algernon *The Doll and One Other.* Sauk City: Arkham House, 1946, First edition; octavo, cloth. L. W. Currey, Inc.   124 - 228 2011 $100

Bladen, Martin *Solon; or Philosophy no Defence Against Love.* London: printed for R. Smith at the Angle and Bible without Temple Bar and sold by J. Nutt near Stationers Hall, 1705, First edition; 4to., without half title, some dampstaining on last 16 leaves, (6), 72 pages, disbound.   Anthony W. Laywood   May 26 2011 - 21758 2011 $67

Blake, Misses *Letters from the Irish Highlands.* London: John Murray, 1825, First edition; xviii, 359 pages, original boards, rebacked, very good.   C. P. Hyland   May 26 2011 - 258/036 2011 $724

Blake, Peter *Marcel Breuer: Architect and Designer.* New York: Museum of Modern Art, 1949, First edition; 4to., original cloth, gilt, pages 128 with 196 illustrations and plans.   R. F. G. Hollett & Son Antiquarian Booksellers   177 - 89 2011   £65

Blake, William 1757-1827 *All Religions are One.* London: Frederick Hollyer, 1926, Small square 8vo. original cloth backed boards, pages (20), printed on reach recto with facsimile of Blake's mss. R. F. G. Hollett & Son Antiquarian Booksellers General Catalogue Summer 2010 - 728 2011 £95

Blake, William 1757-1827 *Songs of Innocence and of Experience.* London: Rupert Hart Davis and Trianon Press, 1967, First edition thus; original cloth, gilt, dust jacket, pages xvii, 54 color plates, fine. R. F. G. Hollett & Son Antiquarian Booksellers General Catalogue Summer 2010 - 729 2011 £40

Blake, William 1757-1827 *William Blake's Water-Colours.* Chicago: J. Philip O'Hara and Paris: Trianon Press, 1972, Large 4to., original cloth gilt, dust jacket closed tear to lower panel, pages xx, 72, 17 color plates and 30 pages of monochrome plates. R. F. G. Hollett & Son Antiquarian Booksellers General Catalogue Summer 2010 - 224 2011 £45

Blakeborough, Ricahrd *Wit, Character, Folklore & Customs of the North Riding of Yorkshire.* London: Oxford University Press, 1898, First edition; original red cloth gilt, pages xxii, 486, (ii), flyleaves rather browned, otherwise fine. R. F. G. Hollett & Son Antiquarian Booksellers 175 - 140 2011 £50

Blakeman, Elisha D'Alembert *The Youth's Guide in Zion and Holy Mother's Promises.* Canterbury: 1842, First edition; 16mo., 35, (1) pages, original plain wrappers, fine. M & S Rare Books, Inc. 90 - 378 2011 $250

Blakemore, Kenenth *The Retail Jeweller's Guide.* London: Butterworths, 1980, Third edition; original boards, dust jacket, pages 323, illustrations. R. F. G. Hollett & Son Antiquarian Booksellers General Catalogue Summer 2010 - 52 2011 £35

Blakesley, Joseph W. *Four Months in Algeria; with a Visit to Carthage.* Cambridge: Macmillan, 1859, First edition; 8vo., pages xii, 441, 2 folding maps, 7 plates, original brown blindstamped cloth, author's presentation copy. J. & S. L. Bonham Antiquarian Booksellers Africa 4/20/2011 - 8235 2011 £180

Blakey, G. Robert *The Plot to Kill the President. Organized Crime Assassinated JFK. The Definitive Story.* New York: 1981, First edition; fine in fine dust jacket, occasional but vigorous underlining, signed by both authors. Bookworm & Silverfish 666 - 132 2011 $75

Blakston, William *The Illustrated Book of Canaries and Cage Birds, British and Foreign.* London: Cassell & Co., circa, 1890, Color chromolithograph frontispiece and plates, illustrations, 1 volume bound in 2, contemporary half maroon calf, slightly rubbed. Jarndyce Antiquarian Booksellers CXCI - 328 2011 £225

Blanchard, Amy E. *My Own Dolly.* London: Griffith & Farran and New York: Dutton & Co., 1906, First edition; square 8vo., original cloth backed pictorial boards, edges very worn and damaged by damp, pages 64, 15 fine chromolithograph plates, all pages with red single rule border, fore edges of 3 pages dampstained, margins of 1 plate little marked. R. F. G. Hollett & Sons Antiquarian Booksellers 170 - 93 2011 £65

Blanchard, Jean Pierre *Exact and Authentic Narrative of M. Blanchard's Third Aerial Voyage.* London: C. Heydigner, 1784, First English edition; small folio, viii, 17, (1, blank) pages, frontispiece, early dark brown paper wrappers, housed in dark blue cloth folder by Sangorski & Sutcliffe for E. P. Dutton, gilt lettering on outside of folder, balloon themed bookplate of previous owner William G. Gerhard on inside front of folder, lacking half title as called for in ESTC, slight offsetting to titlepage from frontispiece and some light foxing to final leaf, very good. Heritage Book Shop Holiday 2010 - 11 2011 $2750

Blanchard, Laman *Life and Literary Remains of L.E.L.* London: Henry Colburn, 1841, First edition; 2 volumes, half titles, engraved frontispiece volume I, contemporary half maroon calf, spines gilt in compartments, dark green leather labels, spines faded to brown, very good. Jarndyce Antiquarian Booksellers CLXC - 82 2011 £225

Blanchard, Laman *Life and Literary Remains of L.E.L.* London: Henry Colburn, 1841, First edition; 2 volumes, half titles, engraved frontispiece, uncut in original brown vertical grained cloth, spines lettered in gilt, lower margin of back board slightly affected by damp volume II, expert minor repairs to heads and tails of spines, small later booklabels of Ian Jack. Jarndyce Antiquarian Booksellers CLXC - 81 2011 £250

Bland, John *The Vale of Lyvennet.* Kendal: Titus Wilson, 1910, First (only) edition; original blue cloth gilt, spine little faded and rubbed, pages xi, 90, frontispiece, illustrations from drawings by author, flyleaves lightly browned, else very good, extremely scarce. R. F. G. Hollett & Son Antiquarian Booksellers 173 - 102 2011 £180

Blanford, W. T. *Observations on the Geology and Zoology of Abyssinia Made During the Progress of the British Expedition to that Country in 1867-1868.* London: Macmillan, 1870, First edition; 8vo., pages xii, (ii), 487, 6 hand colored lithographs by Keuleman, 2 folding colored plates, very clean internally, original green cloth, excellent. J. & S. L. Bonham Antiquarian Booksellers Africa 4/20/2011 - 9148 2011 £750

Blanshard, Frances *Portraits of Wordsworth.* London: Allen & Unwin, 1959, First edition; original cloth, gilt, dust jacket, pages 208, 48 pages of collotype plates. R. F. G. Hollett & Son Antiquarian Booksellers 173 - 103 2011 £40

Blenkinsop, Adam *A Transport Voyage to the Mauritius and Back: Touching at the Cape of Good Hope and St. Helena.* London: John Murray, 1851, First edition; crown 8vo., pages vii, 303, ads, original blue blind stamped cloth, lower inner joint cracked, slightly sprung. J. & S. L. Bonham Antiquarian Booksellers Africa 4/20/2011 - 5140 2011 £360

Blennerhassett, Rose *Adventures in Mashonaland.* London: Macmillan, 1893, Octavo, xii, 340 pages, frontispiece map, original red pictorial cloth stamped in black and gilt, very good plus. Jeff Weber Rare Books 163 - 133 2011 $75

Blewitt, Jonathan *The Matrimonial Ladder.* J. Alfred Novello, circa, 1841, Engraved title by George Cruikshank, few marginal tears, disbound, spine and final leaf repaired with cream tape. Jarndyce Antiquarian Booksellers CXCI - 148 2011 £50

Blezard, Ernst *Lakeland Natural History.* Arbroath: T. Buncle & Co., 1946, Original cloth gilt, pages xi, 149, with 3 illustrations and 2 maps in rear pocket. R. F. G. Hollett & Son Antiquarian Booksellers 173 - 106 2011 £40

Bligh, William 1754-1817 *A Narrative of the Mutiny on Board His Majesty's Ship Bounty.* London: printed for George Nicol, 1790, First edition; large quarto, iv, 88 pages, folding engraved map, 3 engraved charts, 2 folding and printed on blue paper, original blue boards, neatly rebacked at early date, couple of very small expertly repaired marginal tears, some light foxing, browning, offsetting, spectacular and very large copy, housed in quarter brown morocco clamshell case. David Brass Rare Books, Inc. May 26 2011 - 00503 2011 $25,000

Bligh, William 1754-1817 *Reise in das Sudmeer, Welche mit dem Schiffe Bounty Unternommen Worden Ist um Brothaume Nach den Westindischen Inseln zu Verpflanzen.* Berlin: Vossischen Buchandlung, 1793, First German edition; 8vo., xxiv, 362, (1, 1 blank), large folding map, folding engraved plate, 2 engraved plates, contemporary half mottled calf over marbled paper boards, gilt stamped orange leather spine label, paper library spine label, institutional ink stamps on titlepage, fine, rare. Jeff Weber Rare Books 163 - 134 2011 $1000

Blight, J. T. *Ancient Crosses and Other Antiquities in the East of Cornwall.* London: Simpkin Marshall and Co. and Penzance: F. T. Vibert, 1858, First edition; small 4to., original blindstamped blue cloth, gilt, extremities little worn, pages vi, 134, (ii, subscriber), woodcut illustrations. R. F. G. Hollett & Son Antiquarian Booksellers 177 - 90 2011 £120

Blish, James *A Case of Conscience.* London: Faber and Faber Ltd., 1959, First British (and first hardcover) edition; octavo, boards. L. W. Currey, Inc. 124 - 21 2011 $2500

Bliss, Douglas Percy *Edward Bawden.* Pendomer Press, n.d., 1979, Limited deluxe edition, no. 41 of 200 copies; 197 pages, 4to., original morocco backed patterned boards gilt, slipcase, 11 plates in color, lacks separate signed lithograph in slipcase. R. F. G. Hollett & Son Antiquarian Booksellers General Catalogue Summer 2010 - 53 2011 £295

Bliss, Harold C. J. *The Relief of Kumasi.* London: Methuen & Co., 1901, 8vo., 16 illustrations and plans and map, lacking front free endpaper, 8vo., maroon cloth, front hinge loose, good. Barnaby Rudge Booksellers Travel and Exploration - 019689 2011 $95

Blith, Walter *The English Improved or the Survey of Husbandry Surveyed Discovering the Improvableness of all Lands...* London: printed for John Wright at the Kingshead in the Old-Bayley, 1653, Third edition; 4to., engraved pictorial title with small closed tear, ink initials on printed title, 2 folding engraved plates and 2 full page woodcut illustrations, (26), 274, (12) pages, contemporary calf, rebacked, some wear to lower cover, morocco label, nice. Anthony W. Laywood May 26 2011 - 20982 2011 $1593

Bloch, Robert *Pleasant Dreams - Nightmares.* Sauk City: Arkham House, 1960, First edition; octavo, cloth. L. W. Currey, Inc. 124 - 221 2011 $125

Blochman, Lawrence G. *Diagnosis: Homicide the Casebook of Dr. Coffee.* Philadelphia: J. B. Lippincott, 1950, First edition; signed by author, presentation inscription from author for Doc Hease, lightly rubbed at spine ends, else near fine in dust jacket lightly rubbed at spine ends and corners. Buckingham Books May 26 2011 - 27777 2011 $2500

Block, Lawrence *The Burglar in the Library.* Harpenden: No Exit Press, 1997, First British edition, first state with typo on page 1; fine in fine dust jacket.   Bella Luna Books May 29 2011 - t9034 2011 $82

Block, Maurice *The Huntington Art Collections.* San Marino: Huntington Library, 1942, Large 8vo. original pictorial wrappers, pages 96 with numerous illustrations, loosely inserted 4 page ALS from Block to Mary Tout, historian recounting the history of the Huntington collection and its staff during the second world war.   R. F. G. Hollett & Son Antiquarian Booksellers   General Catalogue Summer 2010 - 55 2011   £35

Blocksma, Mary *Ticket to the twenties.* Boston: Little Brown, 1993, First edition; small 4to., pages 64, copiously illustrated by Susan Dennen, about as new in slightly chipped and torn dust jacket.   Second Life Books Inc.   174 - 67 2011 $85

Blomberg, Nancy J. *Navajo Textiles: The William Randolph Hearst Collection.* Tucson: 1988, xii, 257 pages, illustrations, near fine hardcover in like dust jacket, lavishly illustrated.   Dumont Maps & Books of the West 111 - 47 2011 $65

Blome, Richard *L'Amerique Angloise; or Description des Isles et Terres du Roi D'Angleterre, dans L'Amerique.* Amsterdam: Chez Abraham Wolfgang, 1688, First edition in French; 12mo., (4), 331, (1) pages, 7 folding maps, contemporary calf, spine worn and scuffed, chipped at ends, later spine label, inner hinges strengthened, internally few gatherings lightly toned, otherwise fine and fresh.   Joseph J. Felcone Inc.   Fall Miscellany 2010 - 15 2011 $2800

Blomfield, Reginald *A History of French Architecture from the Reign of Charles VIII till the Death of Mazarin.* London: G. Bell & Sons, 1911, First edition; 2 volumes, small 4to., original two tone cloth gilt, few slight marks to backstrips,.   R. F. G. Hollett & Son Antiquarian Booksellers   177 - 91 2011   £75

Blomfield, Reginald *A History of Renaissance Architecture in England 1500-1800.* London: George Bell & Sons, 1897, First edition; 2 volumes, small 4to., original cloth, gilt, spines little faded and rubbed, pages xix, 186; x, 187-432, numerous plates and illustrations.   R. F. G. Hollett & Son Antiquarian Booksellers   177 - 92 2011   £140

Blondel, Nicolas Francois *L'Art de Jetter Les Bombes.* Paris: Chez l'autheur et Nicolas Langlois, 1683, First edition; 251 x 175mm., 5 p.l. (including engraved titlepage), 445, (18) pages (including errata leaf at end) especially elegant late 18th century tree calf, (flat) spine handsomely and elaborately gilt in compartments featuring an intricate interlacing flourish as centerpiece and azured drawer handle ornaments as cornerpieces, along with small floral tools, red morocco labels, yellow edges, added engraved titlepage, large engraved illustration on printed titlepage, woodcut and engraved illustrations, engraved vignette headpieces, engraved and woodcut illustrations (including tables and diagrams), initials and tailpieces, one full page engraved plate, inserted diagram following page 112, as called for, front pastedown of each volume with armorial bookplate of Lt. Gen. G. L. Parker (4th Earl of Macclesfield), first endpaper with similar armorial bookplate of Macclesfield library, first three leaves of each volume with small embossed Macclesfield stamp; isolated gatherings with browning (almost entirely minor, but few leaves with overall darkening), occasional light spot or smudge, but fine copy, most attractive binding, lustrous and virtually unworn, text unusually fresh and clean.   Phillip J. Pirages   59 - 23 2011 $5800

Blore, Edward *The Monumental Remains of Noble and Eminent Persons, Comprising the Sepulchral Antiquities of Great Britain...* Harding, Lepard and Co., 1826, First edition; large 8vo., contemporary half calf, gilt, lower hinge cracking at head, 24 sections, each paginated separately, 30 steel engraved plates by Le Keux and Blore (few rather foxed and 1 text engraving).   R. F. G. Hollett & Son Antiquarian Booksellers   177 - 93 2011   £175

Blount, James *The American Occupation of the Philippines 1898-1912.* New York and London: 1912, First edition; 664 pages, very good, inner joint reglued, 3 maps, one folding.   Bookworm & Silverfish   671 - 128 2011 $175

Blount, Thomas 1618-1679 *Boscobel; or the History of the Most Miraculous Preservation of King Charles II after the Battle of Worcester, September the third 1651.* Birmingham: printed for C. Earl, 1786, Tenth edition; pages 132, uncut, small inkstain to upper part of gutter of some later leaves, modern morocco backed marbled boards, gilt with raised bands.   R. F. G. Hollett & Son Antiquarian Booksellers   175 - 141 2011   £150

Blount, Thomas 1618-1679 *Boscobel.* London: reprinted for Houston and Son, 1832, Small 8vo., finely bound in three quarter morocco gilt with raised bands by Birdsall, pages xix, 91, (i), all edges gilt, engraved frontispiece, folding bird eye view of Boscobel and text woodcut vignette of Boscobel House.   R. F. G. Hollett & Son Antiquarian Booksellers   175 - 142 2011   £120

Bloxam, M. H. *The Principles of Gothic Ecclesiastical Architecture.* London: George Bell & Sons, 1882, Eleventh edition; 8vo., 3 volumes, numerous illustrations on wood, very good, full contemporary olive green morocco, spines faded, all edges gilt. Ken Spelman Rare Books 68 - 81 2011 £85

The Blue Book of Lyon County. Emporia: 1906, (48) pages, illustrations, oblong quarto, original printed paper covers, minor edge chipping to covers, couple of short tears, one page with old tape repair, scarce. Dumont Maps & Books of the West 113 - 17 2011 $225

Blum, Ann Shelby *Picturing Nature: American Nineteenth Century Zoological Illustration.* Princeton: Princeton University Press, 1993, First printing; 4to., xxxiv, 403 pages, 74 color plates, numerous half tone figures, brown cloth, gilt stamped spine title, dust jacket, tiny chip on rear jacket cover, else fine, from the Bern Dibner reference library, with Burndy bookplate. Jeff Weber Rare Books 161 - 45 2011 $72

Blume, Judy *Iggie's House.* Scarsdale: Bradbury Press, 1970, First edition; publisher's reinforced library binding, also issued in un-reinforced binding, child's reasonably neat signature, edgeworn, about very good in very good or better, price clipped dust jacket with light overall wear, very scarce. Between the Covers 169 - BTC347464 2011 $1250

Blundell, R. H. *Trial of Buck Ruxton.* London: William Hodge and Co., 1937, First edition; large 8vo., original cloth gilt, few slight marks, pages xii, 457, 16 plates. R. F. G. Hollett & Son Antiquarian Booksellers 175 - 143 2011 £65

Blundeville, Thomas *M. Blundeville His Exercises Containing Eight Treatises...* London: William Stansby, 1613, Fourth edition; 4to., (16 first leaf blank), 799, (1 (blank) pages, folding table at page 80, folding table at page 695 (loosely inserted), folding woodcut "Mappe of Fraunce" at page 784, folding woodcut of empty globe divided into lines of longitude and latitude at page 798 (loosely inserted), the fifth folding woodcut is a woodcut of a set of compass points linked by thumb lines, it has become detached and is now loosely inserted at page 749, numerous woodcut illustrations, that at page 315 with piece of string as a pointer, that at page 315 a woodcut volvelle with pointer loosely inserted (this has attached to it the semi-circular "file" missing from page 775 (cf. the 1638 edition on EEBO) in place of the circular? Globe found in 1597 and 1638 editions on EEBO; that at page 660 has pointer loosely inserted, a woodcut pointer tipped to margin (?incorrectly) at page 585, that at page 720 has woodcut volvelle and pointer, that at 744 lacks the volvelle, the space for the "Flie" at page 775 is blank as in the Huntington copy on EEBO; mid 17th century calf, gilt spine, marbled edges (joints and spine rubbed, foot of spine torn away exposing the tailband); from the library of the Earls of Macclesfield at Shirburn Castle. Maggs Bros. Ltd. 1440 - 36 2011 £1500

Blunt, Anthony *Art and Architecture in France 1500 to 1700.* Penguin Books, 1953, First edition; small 4to., original cloth, gilt, leather spine label (little chipped), spine slightly rubbed, shelf number at foot, pages xviii, 312, with 192 pages of plates, ex-library with few small stamps and small label on pastedown. R. F. G. Hollett & Son Antiquarian Booksellers 177 - 94 2011 £30

Blunt, John Henry *Dictionary of Doctrinal and Historical Theology.* London: Longman, Green & Co., 1903, Large 8vo., original cloth, gilt, rather stained, little worn, pages 825, endpapers soiled, joints cracked. R. F. G. Hollett & Son Antiquarian Booksellers 175 - 144 2011 £30

Blunt, Wilfred Scawen 1840-1922 *Sonnets and Songs.* London: John Murray, 1875, First edition; foolscap 8vo., pages viii, 112 page 53 misnumbered 5), internally bright and fresh, original yellow sand grain cloth over bevelled boards, upper side with gilt lettering and flaming sun design, dark green endpapers, spine and board edges dust soiled, front hinge cracked by holding, bookseller's ticket and bookplates of H. Bradley Martin and J. O. Edwards, author's presentation inscription, leaf from old bookseller's catalog loosely inserted. Simon Finch Rare Books Zero - 301 2011 £650

Boardman, John *The European and Community in Later Prehistory.* London: Routledge & Kegan Paul, 1971, First edition; large 8vo., original cloth, gilt, dust jacket, pages xv, 294, portrait, 38 plates and 57 figures. R. F. G. Hollett & Son Antiquarian Booksellers 177 - 95 2011 £30

Bobby in Bubbleland. Gale & Polden, n.d., 1913, 4to., original cloth backed pictorial boards, edges rather worn, cloth bubbled, unpaginated 10 superb color plates tipped on to grey captioned card with broad border and text drawings, one or two short tears to very soft paper, few slight marks here and there, small prize label, but excellent copy, rare. R. F. G. Hollett & Sons Antiquarian Booksellers 170 - 58 2011 £450

Bob's School Days. New York: McLoughlin Bros., circa, 1882, Full color pictorial stiff paper covers with some light overall soiling, book has been resewn but is especially clean and bright, 6 full page color illustrations. Jo Ann Reisler, Ltd. 86 - 245 2011 $275

Bodkin, Odds *The Crane Wife.* San Diego: Harcourt Brace, 1998, Stated first edition; signed by artist, illustrations by Gennady Spirin, rarely found signed, fine in fine dust jacket. By the Book, L. C. 26 - 53 2011 $200

Boehn, Max *Modes & Manners of the Nineteenth Century as Represented n the Pictures and Engravings of the Time.* London: J.M. Dent & Co., New York: E. P. Dutton & Co., 1909, 3 volumes, xvi, 178, (1); 164; 157 pages, 8vo., original publisher's decorative cloth in gilt, red and brown, decorated endpapers, color frontispiece in each volume, profusely illustrated throughout with in-text and full page plates in both black and white and color, very fine.   Paulette Rose Fine and Rare Books   32 - 160   2011 $750

Boerio, Giusseppe *Dizionario Del Dialetto Veneziano.* Venice: Andrea Santini E Figlio, 1829, First edition; 4to. pages xiii, 802 (last 2 pages, erratum/corrig.) half white vellum and marbled boards with gilt in gilt on light brown leather label, uncommon, sound, clean very good, attractive example with few pages very slightly creased and endpapers slightly browned.   Any Amount of Books   May 26 2011 - A74383   2011 $1258

Boethius *Opera Omnia.* Basle: Henricpetri, 1570, Second Petri edition; Woodcut printer's device on title and another at end, woodcut initial and numerous woodcut diagrams, occasional light browning and spotting, ff. (24, including final blank), pages 1546, (2), folio, 17th or early 18th century calf, double gilt fillets on sides, rebacked with what was presumably original spine laid down, added gilt decoration and red lettering piece, lower corners repaired, those at top worn, red sprinkled edges, French monastic ownership inscriptions, Vincennes stamp on verso of flyleaf before title, modern bookplate inside front cover of David Skinner of Christ Church, good.   Blackwell Rare Books   B166 - 18   2011   £2000

Bogan, Louise *Body of This Death.* New York: Robert M. McBride, 1923, First edition; very good+ (mild tanning to spine and extremities).   Lupack Rare Books   May 26 2011 - ABE1124943703   2011 $250

Bogardus, Peter *Meskel Demera. The Finding of the True Cross.* New York: Khelcom Press, 2009, Artist's book, one of 52 copies; all on Kochi Mashi paper, each signed by printmaker, photographer -designer - publisher, Peter Bogardus, page size 9 x 6 inches, 60 pages, bound by Gray Parrot in tan linen over boards with original woodblock by Peter Bogardus on front cover within insert endpapers of Kochi Mashi, yellow headbands, binder's ticket on rer left turn-in, housed in custom made matching tan linen clamshell box with title and artist in gold gilt on tan leather label on spine, 16 original copperplate photogravures made and printed by Peter Bogardus, who also carved the 14 woodblocks, text by Selalem Haile Michael was printed by Art Larson at Horton Tank Graphics using Perpetua type cast by Michael Bixler.   Priscilla Juvelis - Rare Books   48 - 11   2011 $3500

Bogg, Edmund *A Thousand Miles in Wharfedale and the Basi of the Wharfe.* London: Simpkin Marshall, etc. n.d., First edition; small 4to., original cloth, gilt, handsomely rebacked in navy blue morocco gilt, pages (xii), (ii), iii, 268, (xx), illustrations.   R. F. G. Hollett & Son Antiquarian Booksellers   General Catalogue Summer 2010 - 1336   2011   £150

Bogg, Edmund *The Vale of Mowbray.* London: Elliot Stock and Leeds: James Miles, 1908, First edition; tall 8vo., original pictorial green cloth, gilt, pages xii, 428, xiii-xvii, numerous illustrations.   R. F. G. Hollett & Son Antiquarian Booksellers   General Catalogue Summer 2010 - 1337   2011   £65

Bogucki, Peter I. *Forest Farmers and Stockherders.* Cambridge: Cambridge University Prss, 1988, First edition; original cloth, gilt, dust jacket, pages xiv, 247, numerous figures and tables.   R. F. G. Hollett & Son Antiquarian Booksellers   177 - 96   2011   £30

Bohny's Neues Bilderbuch. Esslingen: Schreiber Dreizehente, Ganzlich neu Gezeichnete Auflage, 1892, New edition; oblong 4to., cloth backed pictorial boards, slight cover soil, else very good+, 36 chromolithographed plates with nearly 400 objects.   Aleph-Bet Books, Inc.   95 - 252   2011 $850

Bohr, Niels *On the Quantum Theory of Radiation and the Structure of the Atom.* London: Philosophical Magazine, 1915, First separate edition; near fine offprint, original orange printed wrappers, number on front wrapper, mild spine tip wear.   By the Book, L. C.   26 - 93   2011 $600

Boid, Edward *A Description of the Azores; or Western Islands from Personal Observation...* London: Ed Churton, 1835, First edition; 8vo., pages 373, 8, folding map, lithographic frontispiece, illustrations, contemporary brown half calf, marbled boards, handsome copy.   J. & S. L. Bonham Antiquarian Booksellers   Africa 4/20/2011 - 8037   2011   £650

Bokenham, Osbern *Legendys of Hooly Wummen.* Oxford University Press for the Society, 1938, Original cloth, gilt, trifle dusty, pages lxxx, 322, 8 with facsimile frontispiece, armorial library label on pastedown, stamp on reverse of title and few marginal blindstamps.   R. F. G. Hollett & Son Antiquarian Booksellers   175 - 145   2011   £65

Bolingbroke, Henry St. John, 1st Viscount 1678-1751 *Letters on the Study and Use of History.* London: printed for A. Millar, 1752, New edition; 8vo., pages 481, (iii), errata slip pasted at foot of page 481 covering up signature "Hh", contemporary sprinkled calf, boards double rule gilt bordered, board edges zig zag decorative roll in blind, all edges red speckled, red and white sewn endbands, light spotting, small marginal stain to few leaves, corners touch worn, but of scuffing elsewhere, armorial bookplate of Michael Tyson, from the collection of Christopher Ernest Weston 1947-2010. Unsworths Booksellers 24 - 143 2011 £75

Boltanski, Christian *Inventaire des Objets ayant appartenu a une Femme de Bois-Colombes.* Paris: Centre National d'art Contemporain, 1974, First edition; 8vo., pages (48), 310 black and white photos, original brown card wrappers, upper side printed in black, lightly sunned, small light dampstain to top of last few pages, near fine. Simon Finch Rare Books Zero - 510 2011 £500

Bolton, John *Geological Fragments Collected Principally from Rambles among the Rocks of Furness and Cartmel.* London: Whittaker & Co. and Ulverston: D. Atkinson, 1869, First edition; original blindstamped cloth, gilt, few slight marks, pages 264, 5 plates, few spots to frontispiece, scarce original edition. R. F. G. Hollett & Son Antiquarian Booksellers 173 - 109 2011 £95

Bolton, John *Geological Fragments Collected Principally from Rambles Among the rocks of Furness and Cartmel.* Beckermet: Michael Moon, 1978, Limited to 600 copies; original cloth, gilt, dust jacket, pages viii, 272, with 5 plates. R. F. G. Hollett & Son Antiquarian Booksellers 173 - 110 2011 £35

Bonanni, Filippo 1638-1725 *Gabinetto Armonico Pieno d'Istromenti Sonori Indicati e Spiegati.* Rome: Giorgio Placho, 1722, First edition, 2nd issue, with text added to index and additional plates beyond the 136 called for in index; 4to., (8), 177, (9) pages, frontispiece, engraved fore title, 15 full page engraved plates, woodcut ornaments, contemporary mottled vellum, early rebacking in similar vellum (few splits in front hinge, upper cover bit cupped), first gathering slightly loose, lower blank margin of S4 repaired without loss, early repair bottom margin of plate 137, occasional light spotting and soiling, slightly worn, all plates fine and clean, cloth portfolio and slipcase. Joseph J. Felcone Inc. Fall Miscellany 2010 - 93 2011 $7800

Bonaventura, Saint, Cardinal 1221-1274 *Meditationes to Yest Bogosliubna Razmiscglianya od Otaystva Odkupplienya Covicanskogo...* Rome: typis sacr. congreg. de progag fide, 1638, 12mo., (12), 226, (2 blank) pages, 19th century sprinkled calf, gilt fillet on covers, red morocco lettering pieces, red edges, from the library of the Earls of Macclesfield at Shirburn Castle. Maggs Bros. Ltd. 1440 - 38 2011 £700

Bond, Carrie Jacobs *Tales of Little Cats.* Chicago: Volland, 1918, no other printings; square 8vo., pictorial boards, fine in original box (box very slightly worn), beautiful color illustrations by Katherine Sturges Dodge, uncommon. Aleph-Bet Books, Inc. 95 - 141 2011 $350

Bond, Francis *The Chancel of English Churches.* Oxford: Oxford University Press, 1916, First edition; pages ix, 274, 18 with 229 illustrations, flyleaves rather browned, original blue cloth, gilt, spine lettering dulled. R. F. G. Hollett & Son Antiquarian Booksellers 177 - 98 2011 £65

Bond, Francis *Dedications & Patron Saints of English Churches. Ecclesiastical Symbolism, Saints and Their Emblems.* London: Oxford University Press, 1914, First edition; 343 pages + ads, 252 illustrations, very good, original white lettered blue cloth. Ken Spelman Rare Books 68 - 106 2011 £40

Bond, Francis *Dedications of English Churches.* London: Oxford University Press, 1914, First edition; original blue cloth, gilt, spine lettering dulled, pages xvi, 343, 16, with 252 illustrations, flyleaves browned. R. F. G. Hollett & Son Antiquarian Booksellers 177 - 99 2011 £75

Bond, Francis *Fonts and Font Covers.* Oxford University Press, 1908, First edition; original blue cloth, pages xv, 347, with 426 illustrations, endpapers rather browned. R. F. G. Hollett & Son Antiquarian Booksellers 177 - 100 2011 £65

Bond, Francis *Misericords.* London: Oxford University Press, 1910, First edition; original blue cloth gilt, spine lettering dulled, pages xix, 237, (v), with 241 illustrations. R. F. G. Hollett & Son Antiquarian Booksellers 177 - 101 2011 £75

Bond, Francis *Screens and Galleries in English Churches.* London: Oxford University Press, 1908, First edition; original blue cloth gilt, spine rather rubbed, pages xii, 192, with 152 illustrations and measured drawings, endpapers lightly spotted. R. F. G. Hollett & Son Antiquarian Booksellers 177 - 102 2011 £65

Bond, Francis *Stalls and Tabernacle Work.* London: Henry Frowde, Oxford University Press, 1910, First edition; original blue cloth, spine lettering faded, pages xvi, 138, (v), well illustrated, flyleaves lightly browned. R. F. G. Hollett & Son Antiquarian Booksellers 177 - 103 2011 £50

Bond, Frank *Dedications of English Churches.* London: Oxford University Press, 1914, First edition; original blue cloth, spine rather darkened, pages xvi, 343, 16, with 252 illustrations. R. F. G. Hollett & Son Antiquarian Booksellers 175 - 147 2011 £75

Bond, Nelson Slade *Nightmares and Daydreams.* Sauk City: Arkham House, 1968, First edition; octavo, cloth. L. W. Currey, Inc. 124 - 236 2011 $75

Bone, Gertrude *Mr. Paul.* London: Cape, 1921, Signed limited edition, no. 144 of 750 copies; original green cloth, spine label, pages 296, uncut, with full page woodcuts. R. F. G. Hollett & Son Antiquarian Booksellers General Catalogue Summer 2010 - 730 2011 £50

Bone, Gertrude *Of the Western Isles.* London: T. N. Foulis, 1925, First edition; tall small 4to., original cloth backed pictorial boards, spine label, trifle worn, pages 61, with initial letters and title decorations in grey and 40 woodcuts by Stephen Bone, and maps on endpapers, presentation copy inscribed by artist, Stephen Bone to Margaret Gardiner. R. F. G. Hollett & Son Antiquarian Booksellers General Catalogue Summer 2010 - 1340 2011 £120

Boney, Knowles *Liverpool Porcelain of the Eighteenth Century and Its Makers.* Portman Press, 1989, Large 8vo., original cloth, dust jacket, pages viii, 223, 5 plates and map, 50 illustrations. R. F. G. Hollett & Son Antiquarian Booksellers General Catalogue Summer 2010 - 56 2011 £35

Bonham-Carter, Victor *Billy the Bumblebee.* London: Hammond Co., n.d. circa, 1940, Oblong 4to., pictorial boards, fine in slightly worn dust jacket, lovely full page and smaller color illustrations by Weissenborn. Aleph-Bet Books, Inc. 95 - 585 2011 $200

Bonnefoy, Yves *Pierre Ecrite.* Paris: Mercure de France, 1965, 8vo., pages 88, (1) imprint, partly unopened, very bright, clean copy, original printed ivory wrappers as issued, with original protective tissue, blue and black text to upper and lower wrapper and spine, upper hinge detached but text block firm, glassine wrapper, chipped in places, author's presentation inscription for Monsieur et Madame Rene Yasinksi. Simon Finch Rare Books Zero - 302 2011 £350

Bonner, Cindy *Lily.* Chapel Hill: Algonquin, 1992, First edition; fine in fine dust jacket, revie copy with review slip. Bella Luna Books May 29 2011 - 120 2011 $82

Bonnet, Charles *Traite d'Insectologie ou Observations sur les Pucerons.* Paris: Durand, 1745, First edition; 2 volumes, 12mo., pages (iv), xxxii, (6), 228, 4 folding engraved plates; (xii) 232, 4, folding engraved plates, many diagrams in text, woodcut head and tailpieces, occasional spotting, possibly more evident in volume i, barely affecting lower external corner of second plate in first volume, uncut in original drab wrappers, ink titling penned on spine, spines slightly chipped, light traces of water staining only just visible, near spine of volume i, excellent, unsophisticated copy. Simon Finch Rare Books Zero - 115 2011 £750

Bonnet, Charles *Oeuvres d'Histoire Nanturelle et de Philosophie.* Neuchatel: Samuel Fauche, 1779-1783, First collected edition; 8 volumes, 4to., half titles, fine engraved frontispiece, engraved titlepage vignettes, fine engraved head and tailpieces, 2 folding tables, 56 folding engraved plates, wanting 1 leaf of contents in volume VI, pages 423, 424, contemporary tree calf, red and black leather spine labels, richly gilt spines, neat restoration to some spine ends, beautiful stunning set in original tree calf. Jeff Weber Rare Books 161 - 46 2011 $3500

Bonney, T. G. *Abbeys and Churches of England and Wales.* London: Cassell & Co., 1890, 4to. original pictorial cloth gilt over bevelled boards, extremities little worn, pages viii, 274, 8, all edges gilt, numerous full page and other illustrations, upper joint just cracking, free endpapers and frontispiece spotted, very nice. R. F. G. Hollett & Son Antiquarian Booksellers 177 - 104 2011 £50

Bono, James J. *The Word of God and the Languages of Man: Interpreting Nature in Early Modern Science and Medicine. Volume 1: Ficinio to Descartes.* Madison: University of Wisconsin Press, 1995, Volume I only, (all published), 8vo., xi, 317 pages, green cloth, black stamped spine title, fine, from the Bern Dibner reference library, with Burndy bookplate. Jeff Weber Rare Books 161 - 49 2011 $65

Bonser, Wilfrid *Proverb Literature.* William Glaisher for the Folk Lore Society, 1930, First edition; original brown cloth gilt, shelf labels on spine and library name inked on upper board, pages xx, 496, portrait, armorial library label on pastedown, few marginal blindstamps, else very good, clean and tight. R. F. G. Hollett & Son Antiquarian Booksellers General Catalogue Summer 2010 - 369 2011 £40

Bonsor, N. R. P. *North Atlantic Seaway.* Jersey & Channel Islands: Brookside, 1978, Volumes 1 and 2, 237 x 158 mm., 471; 477-868 pages, illustrations, full blue cloth, pinted dust jacket, very good, from the Bern Dibner reference library, with Burndy bookplate. Jeff Weber Rare Books 161 - 50 2011 $60

Bonvalot, Gabriel *Across Thibet Being a Translation of "De Pari Au Tonkin a Travers Le Tibet Inconnu".* London: Cassell, 1891, First edition in English; large 8vo., pages viii, 218 + pages viii, 230, illustrations from photos, large folding map, decent sound set in original publisher's putty green cloth lettered gilt on spine and with gilt heightened illustration on covers, light handling wear, slight rubbing, slight tanning to spines, else very good or better, f.e.p.'s slightly foxed, illustrations very clean. Any Amount of Books May 26 2011 - A74376 2011 $851

Bonwick, James *Port Phillip Settlement.* London: Sampson Low, Marston, Sarle & Rivington, 1883, First edition; octavo, original blue cloth, gilt decoration on front cover, x, 537, (1), (- ads) pages, 4 folding facsimiles of letters, one folding facsimile of handwritten newspaper, folding map, double page plate with numerous facsimile, signatures of Men of the Period, 4 full page lithographed views, 42 half page illustrations on 21 lithographed plates, 4 lithographed portraits, color lithograph frontispiece, pencil signature of H. Britton dated 1884 on front endpaper and below of Rod M. Sutherland dated Nv. 1949, occasional light spotting to text, half inch tear to top of spine, mild rubbing to edges, near fine, uncommon.   Charles Agvent   2010 Summer Miscellany - 13   2011 $350

The Book Collector. Spring, 1952-, Autumn 1987; v.1/1-v.36/1, lacking 1 issue, 142 issues in original wrappers and bound volumes in very good condition.   I. D. Edrich   May 26 2011 - 83859   2011 $1174

The Book of the Household; or Family Dictionary of Everything Connected with Housekeeping and Domestic Medicine. London: London Printing & Publishing Co., 1862-1864, 2 volumes, full sepia plates with some woodcut text illustrations, occasional slight foxing, contemporary half green morocco, purple cloth boards, slight rubbing, nice.   Jarndyce Antiquarian Booksellers   CXCI - 45   2011   £150

The Book of Martyrs, with an Account of the Acts and Monuments of Church and State from the Time of Our Blessed Saviour to the Year 1701. London: privately printed, 1702, First edition; 2 volumes, 8vo., pages x, 376 (xxiv); (iv), 416, (xxxii), 8 copperplates, clean and vivid, some rubbing, some wear, pronounce splitting at hinges, corners worn, spine unlettered, overall near very good with complete text occasionally slightly browned and some worming at edges of pages.   Any Amount of Books   May 29 2011 - 829636   2011 $306

The Book of Princeton Verse. Princeton: 1916, First edition; xviii, (2), 187 pages, cloth, fine in lightly worn dust jacket with small piece out of rear panel.   Joseph J. Felcone Inc.   Fall Miscellany 2010 - 17   2011 $375

The Book of the Knight of La Tour Landry. London: the Verona Society, 1930, One of 7 copies Printed on vellum; 260 x 195mm., xii, 172 pages, publisher's fine alum tawed pigskin with antique style metal clasps raised bands, spine with blind titling, fine large decorative capitals in the style of 16th century crible initials, printed in red and black; slightest hint of smuding and few faint marks to pigskin, inevitable very minor variation in color of vellum on two or three leaves, very fine.   Phillip J. Pirages   59 - 339 2011 $2750

The Book of Trades: or Library of Useful Arts. Tabart and Co., 1810, Part I, 12mo., original roan backed boards, gilt, rather worn, pages 210, (ii), complete with 23 copper engraved plates, few plates little browned, otherwise very nice.   R. F. G. Hollett & Sons Antiquarian Booksellers   170 - 14 2011   £120

Boorman, Derek *At the Going Down of the Sun.* York: privately published, 1988, Second edition; pages 172, 301 illustrations and 8 pages of color plates, tall 4to., original wrappers, spine and lower edges faded, some slight marks and slight surface damage to inside of wrappers, from old tape.   R. F. G. Hollett & Son Antiquarian Booksellers   177 - 105 2011   £35

Boorman, Howard L. *Biographical Dictionary of Republican China.* New York & London: Columbia University Press, 1967, First edition; 4 volumes, pages 1903, 4to., map in each volume, ex-British Foreign Office library with few library markings, else very good.   Any Amount of Books   May 29 2011 - A75346   2011 $272

Booth, Margaret *An Amazon Andes Tour.* London: Edward Arnold, 1910, First edition; pages (viii) 143, photos and extending maps, buckram covers, bookplate, some faint rubbing to covers, very good.   Peter Ellis   May 26 2011 - AMAZON016513   2011 $85

Booth, W. *In Darkest England and the Way Out.* Funk & Wagnalls, 1890, Original cloth, gilt, pages 285, xxxi, folding color frontispiece.   R. F. G. Hollett & Son Antiquarian Booksellers   175 - 150   2011   £45

Booth, W. *Sergeant-Major Do Your Best of Darkington.* Salvation Army Book Department, 1906, First edition; small 8vo., original green cloth, gilt, pages (ii), 287, (v), very scarce.   R. F. G. Hollett & Son Antiquarian Booksellers   175 - 151   2011   £120

Booth, William *The Trial at Large of William Booth and His Associates, George Scot the Three Yates's, John Barrows and Elizabeth Childow for Forgery Coining &c. at the Stafford Summer Assizes 1812 before Mr. Justice Le Blanc.* Wolverhampton: printed and sold by Gower and Smart, 1812, First edition; 8vo., 46 pages, well bound by Morrell, ca. 1900 in half calf over marbled boards, spine lettered in gilt, upper joint and head of spine worn, very good, early 20th century bookplate of numismatist, Samuel Hamer and ms. note in his hand.   John Drury Rare Books   153 - 150   2011   £475

Boothby, William R. *The Olive: Its Culture and Products in the South of France and Italy.* Adelaide: W. C. Cox, Government printer, 1878, First edition; octavo, 42 pages, frontispiece, plus 11 additional lithographic plates bound at rear, 5 mounted albumen photos, publisher's quarter morocco and cloth gilt, bookplate and remnant of small bookseller's ticket, both on front pastedown.   Between the Covers   169 - BTC334035   2011 $5000

Boothroyd, B. *The History of the Ancient Borough of Pontefract.* Pontefract: 1807, xvi, 496 xxiv, frontispiece, folding plan and 4 plates, good, contemporary half calf, marbled boards, joints expertly repaired, some slight browning and foxing as if often case with this title.   Ken Spelman Rare Books   68 - 185   2011   £120

Borcherds, Petrus Borchardus *An Auto-Biographical Memoir.* Cape Town: A. S. Robertson, 1861, First edition; 8vo., pages xxv, 500, frontispiece, tinted plate, original blind stamped cloth, small split at base of spine.   J. & S. L. Bonham Antiquarian Booksellers   Africa 4/20/2011 - 6925   2011   £160

Borde, Charles *Parapilla, et Autres Oeuvres Libres...* Florence: 1784, Small 12mo., pages (iv), 164, 1 plate by Marillier, numerous small wood engraved head and tailpieces, engraved portrait of Borde added as frontispiece, all edges gilt, full green long grain morocco fully gilt decorated in gilt with red dots, by Bozerain, pink silk lined endpieces, bookplate of Bibliotheque Mirault and G. Nordmann, few discrete pencil annotations.   Simon Finch Rare Books   Zero - 411   2011   £1750

Borel, Pierre *Tresor de Recherches et Antiquitez Gauloises et Francoises Reduites en Ordre Alphabetqiue et Renrichies de Beaucoup d'Origines...* Paris: August Courbe, 1655, First edition; 4to., (104), 61 (i.e. 609 pages 73-74 omitted), (23) pages, engraved printer's device, headpiece and initial, all by Jean Picart after F. C. Chauveau?, woodcut headpieces and initials, contemporary speckled calf, spine gilt in compartments, morocco lettering piece, severe worming in bottom right hand corners of 3 quires, affecting text, spine dry, from the library of the Earls of Macclesfield at Shirburn Castle.   Maggs Bros. Ltd.   1440 - 39   2011   £500

Borges, Jorge Luis *Ficciones.* New York: Limited Editions Club, 1984, Limited to 1500 numbered copies; signed by artist, square 4to., full black cowhide, fine in slipcase, Monthly letter laid in, full black cowhide, fine in slipcase, 22 geometric illustrations (silk screens) by Sol Lewitt, strikingly beautiful.   Aleph-Bet Books, Inc.   95 - 333   2011 $650

Born, Ignaz von, Count *Monachologia Figuris Ligno Incisis Illustrata.* Paris: Paulin, 1844, Small 8vo., old boards, edges worn, sometime rebacked, pages 96, woodcut text illustrations, scarce.   R. F. G. Hollett & Son Antiquarian Booksellers   175 - 154   2011   £95

Borrow, George   1803-1881   *The Bible in Spain...* London: John Murray, 1843, Third edition; 8vo., pages (xxiv), 370; viii, 398; viii, 391, (1), bound without half titles in black three quarter calf and marbled boards, spines gilt in compartments, very attractive set, top edge gilt.   Second Life Books Inc.   174 - 68   2011 $263

Borrow, George   1803-1881   *Lavengro; The Scholar- The Gypsy - The Priest.* London: John Murray, 1851, First edition; 8vo., pages xx, 360, 32; xii, 366, 32; xii, 426, bound in three quarter red morocco, gilt on spines in compartments, top edge gilt by Sangorski and Sutcliffe, hinges tnder, lovely set.   Second Life Books Inc.   174 - 70   2011 $563

Borrow, George   1803-1881   *Lavengro; The Scholar- The Gypsy - The Priest.* London: John Murray, 1851, First edition; 8vo., pages xx, 360, 32; xii, 366, 32; xii, 426, publisher's ribbed cloth (worn at extremities of spine, especially on volume three), very good, tight copy.   Second Life Books Inc.   174 - 69   2011 $750

Borrow, George   1803-1881   *The Sleeping Bard; or Visions of the World, Death and Hell by Elis Wyn.* London: John Murray, 1860, Slightly spotted, uncut, original pink paper wrappers, slightly creased.   Jarndyce Antiquarian Booksellers   CXCI - 72   2011   £300

Borrow, George   1803-1881   *The Zincali; or an Account of the Gypsies of Spain...* New York: Wiley and Putnam, 1842, First American edition; 8vo., pages (viii), xii, 323, (1); (iv), 136, 55, (4), 2 volumes in 1, publisher's blind-stamped black cloth, old library bookplate, label on spine, some wear at extremities, very good, some foxing.   Second Life Books Inc.   174 - 71   2011 $244

Borrow, George   1803-1881   *The Zincali, or an Account of the Gypsies of Spain.* London: John Murray, 1843, Third edition; 2 volumes, original cloth, gilt, neatly recased, spine labels worn and browned, pages xxiv, 352; vi, 155.   R. F. G. Hollett & Son Antiquarian Booksellers   175 - 155   2011   £120

Borthwick, John *Observations Upon the Marks of Prosecuting for Libel According to the Law of England.* London: James Ridgway and J. & W. T. Clark and William Tait, Edinburgh, 1830, First edition; apparently pretty rare, 8vo., 44 pages, including half title, recent marbled boards lettered on spine, very good, inscribed by author for Earl of Rosebery.   John Drury Rare Books   154 - 26   2011   £175

Bos, H. J.M. *Studies on Christian Huygens: Invited Papers from the Symposium on Life and Work of Christian Huygens, Amsterdam 22-25 August 1979.* Lisse: Swets & Zeitlinger, 1980, 8vo., v, 321 pages, frontispiece, plates, figures, index, pictorial cloth, near fine, from the Bern Dibner reference library, with Burndy bookplate.   Jeff Weber Rare Books   161 - 227   2011 $275

Boschere, Jean De 1878-1953 *Job le Pauvre.* Paris: Jacques Povolozky & Cie, 1922, First edition, no. 47 of 50 copies on Simili Japon Van Gelder from the tirage de tete,; with Bosschere's presentation inscription to Harry F. Marks, 8vo., pages (iv), 124, (i) contents, (1 blank, frontispiece, 2 sets of 14 plates, fore-edge and lower edge uncut, partly unopened, closed tear to frontispiece at gutter, otherwise exceptionally crisp and fresh, black morocco grain paper covered boards, paper label with black text to spine, bumped, chipped at head and foot of spine, some loss to label, author' presentation inscription. Simon Finch Rare Books Zero - 303 2011 £850

Boschius, Jacobus *Symbolographia sive de Arte Symbolica Sermones Septem.* Augsburg & Eillingen: Johan Kaspar Bencard, 1702, First edition; 5 parts, folio, frontispiece, title vignette, 171 plates, contemporary English calf, spine gilt in compartments, from the library of the Earls of Macclesfield at Shirburn Castle. Maggs Bros. Ltd. 1440 - 40 2011 £5000

Bossut, John *A General History of Mathematics: from the Earliest Times to the Middle of the Eighteenth Century.* London: printed for J. Johnson, St. Paul's Churchyard, By Bye and Law, St. John's Square, Clerkenwell, 1803, First edition; 8vo., pages xxvi, 540; 2 leaves of tables, half dark blue leather lettered gilt at spine with red and brown spine labels and 5 raised bands and marbled boards, sound, clean, very good, some rubbing at spine hinges and extremities, uncommon. Any Amount of Books May 29 2011 - A74586 2011 $383

Boston Athenaeum *Catalogue of the Second Exhibition of Sculpture in the Athenaeum Gallery MCCCCXL.* Boston: Press of J. H. Eastburn, 1840, First edition; 8vo., 15 pages, original printed wrappers. M & S Rare Books, Inc. 90 - 21 2011 $250

Boston Athenaeum *Catalogue of the Eighth Exhibition of Paintings in the Athenaeum Gallery. MDCCCXXXIV.* Boston: Press of J. H. Eastburn, 1834, First edition; 8vo., 8 pages, original printed wrappers. M & S Rare Books, Inc. 90 - 20 2011 $175

Boston, Noel *Church and Chamber Barrel-Organs.* Edinburgh: Lyndesay G. Langwill, 1967, First edition (1000 copies); pages viii, 120, with 28 plates, large 8vo., original cloth, gilt, dust jacket trifle worn. R. F. G. Hollett & Son Antiquarian Booksellers 175 - 156 2011 £40

Boswell, David *Fun with Reid Fleming.* Forestville: Eclipse, 1991, One of 300 copies signed by artist; 4to., 173 pages, nice copy in dust jacket, somewhat scuffed and soiled. Second Life Books Inc. 174 - 72 2011 $125

Boswell, Henry *Historical Descriptions of New and Elegant Picturesque Views of the Antiquities of England and Wales.* Alex. Hogg, n.d., Tall folio, contemporary half green roan gilt with marbled boards, rather rubbed and scraped, pages iv, plus over 400 pages, pagination in contemporary mss., with 290 engraved plates, full page frontispiece (laid down) but lacks maps, many plates cut out and re-inserted or added from other copies, few text leaves soiled or little damaged, the Corby Castle (Cumbria copy). R. F. G. Hollett & Son Antiquarian Booksellers 177 - 106 2011 £450

Boswell, James 1740-1795 *Boswell's Journal of a Tour to the Hebrides with Samuel Johnson.* New York: Viking Press, 1936, very large 8vo., about good, dust jacket has piece missing from spine. Barnaby Rudge Booksellers Travel and Exploration - 019821 2011 $150

Boswell, James 1740-1795 *Boswell's Life of Johnson...* Oxford: Clarendon Press, 1887, 6 volumes in 11, half titles, frontispiece, extra illustrated, additional titlepages, plates as called for + 1293 additional plates, some occasional foxing and offsetting, heavy in places but largely internally, very good, handsomely bound in full crushed red morocco by Riviere & Son, double ruled gilt borders, raised gilt bands, compartments ruled in gilt, bookplates of Edith Bessie Cooke, top edge gilt. Jarndyce Antiquarian Booksellers CXCI - 20 2011 £5800

Boswell, James 1740-1795 *Boswell's Life of Johnson Including Boswell's Journal of a Tour to the Hebrides and Johnson's Diary of a Journey into North Wales.* Oxford: at the Clarendon Press, 1887, 6 volumes, 229 x 152mm., especially pleasing contemporary prize bindings of polished calf, handsomely gilt for H. Sotheran & Co. (stamp signed on front pastedown), boards with gilt double rule border and with gilt scholastic arms on each of the six front covers, raised bands, spines elaborately gilt in compartments featuring scrolling foliate cornerpieces and intricate floral centerpiece, brown morocco labels, ornate gilt turn-ins, marbled endpapers, all edges gilt, with 14 plates as called for (8 of them folding), including facsimiles of Johnson's handwriting, map and chart of Johnson's contemporaries; Latin presentation bookplate to J. Mavrogordato indicating that this set was a prize given to him by the headmaster, William Rutherford of the College of Saint Peter, Westminster, one volume with very minor flaking to one join, odd trivial mark to covers but in exceptionally fine condition, bindings essentially unworn and text probably unread. Phillip J. Pirages 59 - 155 2011 $1800

Boswell, James 1740-1795 *The Life of Samuel Johnson.* London: George Routledge & Sons, circa, 1889, Text in double columns, pages xvi, 526, 8vo., contemporary vellum, double gilt ruled borders on sides, spine richly gilt, very good, inscribed to A. Godfrey James from A. C. Benson, Eton, Xmas 1889. Blackwell Rare Books B166 - 19 2011 £85

The Botanical Magazine; or Flower Garden Displayed. London: printed by Couchman and Fry for W. Curtis, later published by H. D. Symonds, 1790-1808, Engraved portrait (foxed), 1146 engraved hand colored plates (missing plate 120 of Strelitzia reginae, but the famous colored folding plate of the Strelitzia is present), occasional light foxing, small stains, mostly marginal, to few plates, damp ring on 2 plate), most plates fresh and bright, 8vo., modern quarter calf over boards with contemporary marbled paper, overall very nice set, spines with 5 raised bands and gilt decorated panels, volumes 1 and 3 printed in 1790 and 1792 respectively, the Rachel McMaters Miller Hunt copy.   Raymond M. Sutton, Jr.   May 26 2011 - 50252   2011 $12,000

Boteler, Thomas   *Narrative of a Voyage of discovery to Africa and Arabia; Performed in His Majesty's Ships Leven and Barracouta from 1821 to 1826 Under the Command of Captain F. W. Owen, R. N.*   London: Richard Bentley, 1835,   First edition; 2 volumes, 8vo., pages xxiv, 414; viii, 479; with 4 lithographic plates, contemporary brown full polished calf gilt, spine faded, joints rubbed, lower board volume 1 scuffed with small loss of leather in 2 places, Eton binding.   J. & S. L. Bonham Antiquarian Booksellers   Africa 4/20/2011 - 8152   2011   £1450

Bott, Alan   *An Airman's Outings.*   William Blackwood & Sons, 1917,   Fourth impression; original red cloth, gilt, spine little faded, pages xxv, 324.   R. F. G. Hollett & Son Antiquarian Booksellers   General Catalogue Summer 2010 - 592   2011   £40

Botticelli, Sandro   *The Drawings for Dante's Divine Comedy.*   London: Royal Academy of Arts, 2001,   Oblong 4to., original pictorial boards, pages 360, illustrations.   R. F. G. Hollett & Son Antiquarian Booksellers   General Catalogue Summer 2010 - 134   2011   £50

Bottomley, Edwin   *An English Settler in Pioneer Wisconsin: The Letters of Edwin Bottomley 1842-1850.*   Madison: 1918,   1250 copies; 250 pages, original binding, very good, mild ex-library.   Bookworm & Silverfish   665 - 192   2011 $65

Bouch, C. M. L.   *The Lake Counties 1500-1830.*   Manchester: University Press, 1961,   First edition; original cloth gilt, dust jacket, pages xi, 371, with 3 plates and 3 plans, scarce.   R. F. G. Hollett & Son Antiquarian Booksellers   173 - 130   2011   £75

Bouch, C. M. L.   *Prelates and People of the Lake Counties.*   Kendal: Titus Wilson, 1948,   First edition; original cloth, neatly recased, pages xv, 514, 9 illustrations and map.   R. F. G. Hollett & Son Antiquarian Booksellers   173 - 125   2011   £50

Bouchot, Henri   *La Miniature Francaise 1750-1825.*   Paris: Goupil, 1907,   One of 200 copies; 330 x 260 mm., 2 p.l., 245, (1) pages, magnificent sky blue crushed levant, lavishly gilt by Riviere, covers with gilt double fillet border and grand central panel formed by use of 11 plain and decorative rules (as well as small seashell centerpieces), raised bands between richly gilt compartments of rinceaux like decoration around central lozenge elegantly gilt inner dentelles, watered silk endleaves, marbled flyleaves, all edges gilt, with 72 fine plates (containing a total of 154 images, 45 of the plates tinted and 20 fully colored) and 108 illustrations in text, all but two of them tinted, printed tissue guards, even in the case of text illustrations, titlepage in red and black; hint of wear to corners and edges, spine just slightly sun faded, offsetting from two engraved pages, minor dots of foxing in isolated places, otherwise fine, beautifully bound volume, gilt and covers still very bright and text and plates quite clean, bright and fresh.   Phillip J. Pirages   59 - 72   2011 $1600

Boudinot, Elias   1740-1821   *The Second Advent or Coming of the Messiah in Glory, shown to be a Scripture Doctrine and Taught by Divine Revelation from the Beginning of the World.*   Trenton: D. Fenton and S. Hutchinson, 1815,   First edition; 8vo., 19, 570 (of 578) pages, full contemporary speckled calf, leather label, fine, text browned (this copy ends at page 570 and there is no evidence of removal from this fine, tight copy).   M & S Rare Books, Inc.   90 - 5   2011 $400

Bouguer, Pierre   *Pierre Bouguer's Optical Treatise on the Gradiation of Light.*   Toronto: University of Toronto Press, 1961,   First edition; 8vo., xiv, 248 pages, frontispiece, illustrations, tables, blue cloth, silver stamped spine title, dust jacket worn, very good, from the Bern Dibner reference library, with Burndy bookplate.   Jeff Weber Rare Books   161 - 52   2011 $125

Bouguer, Pierre   *Traite d'Optique sur la Gradation de la Lumiere: Ouvrage Posthume de M. Bouguer de l'Acaemie Royale des Scienes &c.*   Paris: H. L. Guerin & L. F. Delatour, 1760,   First edition; 4to., xviii, (2), 368 pages, engraved printer's device on titlepage, 7 engraved folding plates, contemporary full mottled calf, raised bands, gilt stamped spine panels and spine title, few minor covers scars, joints starting, bookplate of Jean Francois Le Boyer and Andras Gedeon, fine, from the Bern Dibner reference library, with Burndy bookplate.   Jeff Weber Rare Books   161 - 51   2011 $2500

Boulenger, G. A.   *The Snakes of Europe.*   London: Methuen, 1913,   First edition; ix, 269 pages, 14 plates, 42 illustrations, very good, red cloth lightly worn, gilt titles, interior clean and tight.   G. H. Mott Bookseller   May 26 2011 - 42937   2011 $450

Boulle, Pierre   *Planet of the Apes.*   New York: Vanguard Press Inc., 1963,   First edition in English; octavo, cloth backed boards.   L. W. Currey, Inc.   124 - 51   2011 $1500

Boulton, David *Early Friends in Dent.* Dent: Dales Historical Monographs, 1986, First edition; original cloth, gilt, spine little faded as usual, pages 113, 1 illustration and map, signed by author, very scarce. R. F. G. Hollett & Son Antiquarian Booksellers 173 - 131 2011 £75

Boulton, W. S. *Practical Coal-Mining by Leading Experts in Mining and Engineering.* Gresham Pub. Co., 1913, 3 volumes, contemporary quarter black morocco, gilt hinges and edges little rubbed, pages x, 348; xi, 404; xi, 459, with 49 plates and over 900 text illustrations, good sound set. R. F. G. Hollett & Son Antiquarian Booksellers General Catalogue Summer 2010 - 1089 2011 £120

Boulton, W. S. *Practical Coal-Mining by Leading Experts in Mining and Engineering.* Gresham Publishing Co., 1913, 6 volumes, original art nouveau decorated cloth, gilt, trifle worn, 46 plates, over 900 text illustrations, good sound set. R. F. G. Hollett & Son Antiquarian Booksellers General Catalogue Summer 2010 - 1090 2011 £140

Boumphrey, R. S. *An Armorial for Westmorland and Lonsdale.* Lake District Museum Trust and CWAAS, 1975, original crimson rexine gilt, leather spine label, pages xxiii, 337, frontispiece and 5 pages of illustrations. R. F. G. Hollett & Son Antiquarian Booksellers General Catalogue Summer 2010 - 370 2011 £40

Bourbaki, Nicolas *Element of the History of Mathematics.* Berlin and New York: Springer Verlag, 1994, 8vo., viii, 301 pages, printed boards, from the Bern Dibner reference library, with Burndy bookplate, fine. Jeff Weber Rare Books 161 - 53 2011 $90

Bourdier De Villemert, Pierre Joseph *The Friend of Women.* London: printed by Knight and Compton for the author, 1802, First edition of this translation; 8vo., (2), v-vii, (1) (5)-164 pages, original boards, little soiled, neatly rebacked with printed spine label, entirely uncut, good, large copy. John Drury Rare Books 153 - 15 2011 £425

Bourdon, Georges *The German Enigma, Being an Inquiry Among Germans as to What They Think, What They Want, What They Can Do.* Paris and London: Georges Cres & J. M. Dent, 1914, First edition; 8vo., pages xiii, 357, rare in dust jacket, original publisher's red cloth lettered gilt at spine, slight sunning at edges, endpapers browned, else very good+ in very good+ clean dust jacket, slightly chipped at head of spine. Any Amount of Books May 29 2011 - A63088 2011 $306

Bourke, John G. *MacKenzie's Last Fight with the Cheyennes: a Winter Campaign in Wyoming & Montana.* London: reprinted from Journal Military Service Institution, 1890, First edition; 8vo., 44 pages, frontispiece, original printed wrappers, top right corner of front panel professionally restored, light wear to fore edges of front and rear panels, else text fine, housed in cloth clamshell case, moderately rubbed along spine panel and corners with leather label on front panel and titles stamped in gold on front cover and spine. Buckingham Books May 26 2011 - 29581 2011 $3500

Bousteau, Fabrice *In the Arab World, Now.* Paris: Galerie Enrico Navarre, 2005, First edition; 4to., 3 volumes in slipcase, pages 1005, copiously illustrated in color and black and white, fine in slipcase. Any Amount of Books May 29 2011 - A73017 2011 $374

Boutet, Henri *Les Modes Feminines Du XIXE Siecle.* Paris: 1900, First edition; 100 colored plates, original canvas backed pictorial boards with original ribbon ties, corners little bumped, cover little rubbed, otherwise very good, bookplate. I. D. Edrich May 26 2011 - 59270 2011 $730

Bowden, Charles *Book Collecting the Last Refuge of the Illiterate.* Salt Lake City: Ken Sanders, 2005, Limited to 100 signed and numbered copies; signed by author, fine. Bella Luna Books May 29 2011 - t7497 2011 $82

Bowden, Charles *Street Signs Chicago.* Chicago: Chicago Review Press, 1981, First edition; fine, near fine dust jacket, light wear and soiling to rear panel, signed by author. Bella Luna Books May 29 2011 - 4037 2011 $82

Bowen, Emanuel *Britannia Depicta; or Ogilby Improv'd: Being a Correct Coppy of Mr. Ogilby's actual Survey of all ye Direct & Principal Cross Roads in England and Wales.* London: printed and sold by Tho. Bowles, 1736, Fourth edition; 4to., pages 5, (iii) 273 + engraved titlepage, contemporary reversed calf, boards double rule bordered in blind with decorative roll adjacent joint border board edges 'zig-zag' roll in blind, all edges lightly red sprinkled, red and white sewn endpapers, green silk page markers, 2009 reversed calf reback with original red lettering piece relaid by Chris Weston, bit of toning and spotting, corners little worn, from the collection of Christopher Ernest Weston 1947-2010. Unsworths Booksellers 24 - 71 2011 £1000

Bowen, Fredric *The Lights in the Sky are Stars.* New York: E. P. Dutton and Co. Inc., 1953, First edition; octavo, boards. L. W. Currey, Inc. 124 - 172 2011 $300

Bowen, Marjorie *Great Tales of Horror: Being a Collection os Strange Stories of Amazement, Horror and Wonder.* London: John Lane, Bodley Head, 1933, First edition; half title, later half calf. Jarndyce Antiquarian Booksellers CXCI - 73 2011 £45

Bower, Samuel *A Sequel to the Peopling of Utopia; or the Sufficiency of Socialism for Human Happiness...* Bradford: printed by C. Wilkinson, 1838, First and only edition; 8vo., 20 pages, recently well bound in blue boards, upper cover lettered.   John Drury Rare Books   153 - 16   2011   £375

Bowle's Practice of Perspective.   1782,   5th or later edition; 150 copper plates, leather covers loose, otherwise excellent, largely free of foxing.   I. D. Edrich   May 26 2011 - 59671 2011 $419

Bowles, Paul   *Let It Come Down.*   London: Lehmann, 1952,   First edition; 320 pages, crown 8vo., original grey cloth, faded backstrip lettered in red within red frame, dust jacket with soiled rear panel, good.   Blackwell Rare Books   B166 - 126   2011   £135

Bowman, James Cloyd   *The Greatest Cowboy of all Time.*   Chicago: Whitman, 1937,   First edition; small 4to., 296 pages, cloth, fine in frayed dust jacket with some chipping, illustrations by Laura Bannon, 6 stunning full page lithographs plus more other striking full and partial black and white lithos, very scarce.   Aleph-Bet Books, Inc.   95 - 70 2011 $275

Bowman, James Cloyd   *John Henry.*   Chicago: Whitman, 1942,   First edition; 8vo., cloth, 288 pages, fine in dust jacket striking full color dust jacket, color pictorial endpapers, color frontispiece, plus profusion of strong black and whites by Roy Lagrone, beautiful copy.   Aleph-Bet Books, Inc.   95 - 105   2011 $250

Bowman, William   *Mr. Bowman's Sermon, Preach'd at Wakefield in Yorkshire...*   London: printed for H. Cook, 1731,   Second edition; pages 32, disbound, title and final page rather browned.   R. F. G. Hollett & Son Antiquarian Booksellers   175 - 158   2011   £180

Bownas, Samuel   *A Description of the Qualifications Necessary to a Gospel Minister...*   London: printed at the Bible in George Yard, 1767,   Second edition; old panelled two tone calf, corners little worn and restored, rebacked in matching calf gilt with raised bands, pages 112, some old pencilled scribbles on front endpapers, few leaves faintly damped, but nice.   R. F. G. Hollett & Son Antiquarian Booksellers   175 - 159   2011   £120

Boxer, C. R.   *The Tragic History of the Sea 1589-1622: Narratives of the Shipwrecks of the Portuguese East Indiamen Sao Thome (1589). Santo Alberto (1593). Sao Joao Baptista (1622) and the Journeys of the Survivors in South East Africa. (with) Further Selections from the Tragic History of the Sea 1559-1565. Narrative of the Shipwrecks of the Portuguese West Indiamen. Aquaia and Garcia (1159). Sao Paulo (1561) and the Misadventures of the Brazil Ship Santo Antonio (1565).*   Cambridge: University Press, 1959-1967,   First editions; 8vo., pages xiv, 297, maps, illustrations, original blue cloth, dust jacket; 8vo., pages x, 170, maps, plates, original blue cloth, dust jacket.   J. & S. L. Bonham Antiquarian Booksellers   Africa 4/20/2011 - 8151   2011   £50

Boxhorn, Marcus Zuerius   *Commentariolus de Statu Confoederatarum Provinciarum Belguii...*   The Hague: A. Vlacq for J. Vlacq, 1668,   12mo., (12 (including engraved title dated 1659), 202, (2 blank) pages, contemporary English calf, gilt fillet on covers, gilt floral cornerpieces, spine gilt, edges gilt, first 2 leaves with slight dampstain, from the library of the Earls of Macclesfield at Shirburn Castle.   Maggs Bros. Ltd.   1440 - 41   2011   £450

Boyd, Alexander   *From the Niger to the Nile.*   London: Ed Arnold, 1907,   First edition; 2 volumes, large 8vo., pages xv, 358; xi, 420, maps and numerous illustrations, original red decorative cloth, backed in recent red half morocco, sound.   J. & S. L. Bonham Antiquarian Booksellers   Africa 4/20/2011 - 8756   2011   £120

Boyd, Thomas   *Poor John Fitch: Inventor of the Steamboat.*   New York: G. P. Putnam's Sons, 1935,   First edition; 8vo., (i), 315 page, illustrations, blue cloth, brown stamped creme spine label, dust jacket worn, very good, rare in jacket, from the Bern Dibner reference library, with Burndy bookplate.   Jeff Weber Rare Books   161 - 55   2011 $100

Boyd, William   *Songs for Children.*   London: Weekes & Co., 1871,   (4), 22, (2) pages, printed music, stamped signature of Boyd.   Jarndyce Antiquarian Booksellers   CXCII - 343   2011   £65

Boyers, Peg   *Honey with Tobacco.*   Chicago: University of Chicago Press, 2007,   First edition; issue in wrappers, inscribed by poet for another writer.   Ken Lopez Bookseller   154 - 14   2011 $100

Boyle, Robert   1627-1691   *An Essay of the Great Effects of Even Languid and Unheeded Motion.*   London: By M. Flesher for Richard Davis, 1685,   First edition; 8vo., (8), 123, (5), 95 pages, including internal blanks 17-8, neat modern calf, antique, retaining original front fyleaf with signature of Mr. Jocelyn, light dust soiling of first few leaves, else fine, clean copy.   Joseph J. Felcone Inc.   Fall Miscellany 2010 - 19   2011 $2800

Boyle, Robert 1627-1691 *The General History of the Air.* London: printed for Awnsham and John Churchill, 1692, First edition; small quarto, contemporary sheep, rebacked to style. Heritage Book Shop Booth A12 51st NY International Antiquarian Book Fair April 8-10 2011 - 15 2011 $7500

Boyle, Robert 1627-1691 *The Sceptical Chymist or Chymico-Physical Doubts and Paradoxes.* London: J. Caldwell for J. Crooke, 1661, First edition; contemporary English speckled calf, lacking first title and final 3 postliminary leaves and final blank. Heritage Book Shop Booth A12 51st NY International Antiquarian Book Fair April 8-10 2011 - 16 2011 $75,000

Boyle, Robert 1627-1691 *The Works of Robert Boyle.* London: Pickering & Chatto, 1999, 14 volumes, 8vo., blue cloth, gilt stamped spine titles, fine, from the Bern Dibner reference library, with Burndy bookplate. Jeff Weber Rare Books 161 - 56 2011 $2650

Boyle, T. Coraghessan *Descent of Man.* Boston: Little Brown, 1979, First edition; fine, near fine dust jacket with light creasing and edgewear, signed by author. Bella Luna Books May 26 2011 - 6406 2011 $302

The Boy's Realm. London: privately published, 1902-1903, First edition; large 4to., June 14 1902-May 30 1903, together 51 issues, well illustrated, large 4to., blue cloth lettered gilt on spine, some wear, slight tear at bottom of spine, slight rubbing, slight edgewear, otherwise sound, very good. Any Amount of Books May 29 2011 - A67971 2011 $374

Boyse, Joseph *A Vindication of the True Deity of Our Blessed Saviour...* London: 1719, 162 pages, early calf, expected scrapes and rubs, top right 3 inces of backstrip loosening. Bookworm & Silverfish 668 - 132 2011 $145

Brabin, Mr. *The Case of Timothy John Evans. Report of an Inquiry.* London: HMSO, 1966, Original blue printed wrappers, pages 158. R. F. G. Hollett & Son Antiquarian Booksellers 175 - 1357 2011 £35

Brackett, Leigh *The Long Tomorrow.* Garden City: Doubleday & Co., 1955, First edition; octavo, boards. L. W. Currey, Inc. 124 - 132 2011 $475

Bradbury, Christopher *Well on the Road.* London: G. Bell & Sons, 1935, First edition; small 4to., original cloth backed pictorial boards, spine little faded at head and foot, matching dust jacket (pieces missing from one corner and head of backstrip lower panel rather torn and creased, lower to inches of backstrip missing), pages 107, illustrations in line by Edward Bawden, excellent copy, remarkably rare. R. F. G. Hollett & Son Antiquarian Booksellers General Catalogue Summer 2010 - 492 2011 £350

Bradbury, Ray *Dandelion Wine.* Garden City: Doubleday & Co., 1957, First edition; octavo, cloth. L. W. Currey, Inc. 124 - 33 2011 $1750

Bradbury, Ray *Dandelion Wine.* New York: Garden City, 1957, First edition; 8vo., pages (2), 281, top edge dyed yellow, fore-edge rough cut, very bright and crisp, original yellow cloth, spine text in blue and gold, original color pictorial dust jacket, adhesive mark to front free endpaper, light soiling to cloth, dust jacket extremities rubbed, spine head and corners with small chips, slight soiling, author's inscription, presentation from author for Stuart. Simon Finch Rare Books Zero - 211 2011 £700

Bradbury, Ray *Dandelion Wine.* Garden City: Doubleday & Co., 1957, First edition; octavo, cloth. L. W. Currey, Inc. 124 - 67 2011 $1250

Bradbury, Ray *Dark Carnival.* Sauk City: Arkham House, 1947, First edition; octavo, cloth. L. W. Currey, Inc. 124 - 28 2011 $2000

Bradbury, Ray *The Golden Apples of the Sun.* Garden City: Doubleday and Co. Inc., 1953, First edition; 8vo., pages 250, drawings by Joe Mugnaini, edges toned, original brown imitation cloth, spine lettered in yellow, head and foot of spine rubbed, original illustrated dust jacket printed in yellow, grey and black, lightly rubbed, spine sunned, price clipped, inscribed "Bill Morgan/(signed) Ray Bradbury/ Oct. 18 1980". Simon Finch Rare Books Zero - 210 2011 £500

Bradbury, Ray *The Illustrated Man.* Garden City: Doubleday & Co. Inc., 1951, First edition; octavo, cloth. L. W. Currey, Inc. 124 - 12 2011 $3500

Bradbury, Ray *The Martian Chronicles.* Garden City: Doubleday & Co., 1950, First edition; octavo, cloth. L. W. Currey, Inc. 124 - 8 2011 $4500

Bradbury, Ray *The Martian Chronicles.* Garden City: Doubleday & Co., 1950, First edition; octavo, cloth. L. W. Currey, Inc. 124 - 6 2011 $5000

Bradbury, Ray *The October Country.* New York: Ballantine Books, 1955, First edition; probable earliest state of hardcover trade binding with publisher's monogram stamped upside down on spine panel (Currey binding B1). L. W. Currey, Inc. 124 - 34 2011 $1750

Bradbury, Ray *R is for Rocket.* Garden City: Doubleday and Co., 1962, First edition; octavo, boards. L. W. Currey, Inc. 124 - 135 2011 $450

Bradbury, Ray *Zen and the Art of Writing and the Joy of Writing. Two Essays.* Santa Barbara: Capra Press, 1973, First edition, of 250 numbered and signed handbound copies, this not numbered but designated "Printer's Copy"; in addition to signing the book Bradbury has added "with thanks!" for the printer, pictorial boards, fine in glassine wrapper.   Charles Agvent 2010 Summer Miscellany - 14 2011 $200

Bradbury, Savile *Dictionary of Light Microscopy.* Oxford Science Publications, 1989, First edition; original glazed boards, pages x, 139 with 10 diagrams, fine.   R. F. G. Hollett & Son Antiquarian Booksellers General Catalogue Summer 2010 - 1091 2011   £65

Bradford Technical College *Rag Times 1936.* Bradford: The College, 1936, Large 8vo., original colored wrappers, 72 pages.   R. F. G. Hollett & Son Antiquarian Booksellers 175 - 163 2011   £30

Bradford Technical College *Rag Times 1938.* Bradford: Bradford Technical College, 1938, Large 8vo., original color wrappers, pages 64, cartoons, etc.   R. F. G. Hollett & Son Antiquarian Booksellers 175 - 164 2011   £30

Bradford, J. S. *Even a Worm.* London: Arthur Barker Ltd., 1936, First edition; octavo, original blue green cloth, spine panel stamped in dark blue.   L. W. Currey, Inc. 124 - 178 2011 $250

Bradley, A. G. *Highways and Byways in the Lake District.* London: Macmillan, 1901, First edition; original cloth, gilt, hinges splitting at head and repaired, pages xii, 332, (4), illustrations by Joseph Pennell, endpapers spotted.   R. F. G. Hollett & Son Antiquarian Booksellers 173 - 137 2011 £35

Bradley, Betsy Hunter *The Works: The Industrial Architecture of the United States.* New York and Oxford: Oxford University Press, 1999, First edition; tall 8vo., xii, 347 pages, photos and illustrations, purple cloth, silver stamped, spine title, dust jacket, fine, from the Bern Dibner reference library, with Burndy bookplate.   Jeff Weber Rare Books 161 - 60 2011 $275

Bradley, Edward *The Adventures of Mr. Verdant Green.* James Blackwood & Co. n.d. early 1870's, Ninety-fourth thousand; original blindstamped cloth, gilt extra, extremities little frayed, pages vi, 112, with woodcut frontispiece and title, text illustrations, joints cracking.   R. F. G. Hollett & Son Antiquarian Booksellers General Catalogue Summer 2010 - 626 2011   £45

Bradley, H. G. *Ceramics of Derbyshire 1750-1975.* Gilbert Bradley, 1978, First edition; tall 4to., original cloth, gilt, dust jacket, pages xvi, 338, (xi), 16 color plates and 470 illustrations.   R. F. G. Hollett & Son Antiquarian Booksellers General Catalogue Summer 2010 - 59 2011   £60

Bradley, Helen *And Miss Carter Wore Pink.* London: Cape, 1971, First edition; oblong 4to., original cloth, gilt, dust jacket, pages 32, illustrations in color, gift inscription on flyleaf (non-authorial).   R. F. G. Hollett & Son Antiquarian Booksellers   General Catalogue Summer 2010 - 731 2011 £35

Bradley, Helen *"In the Beginning" Said Great Aunt Jane.* London: Cape, 1974, First edition; oblong 4to., original cloth, gilt, dust jacket, pages 32, illustrations in color.   R. F. G. Hollett & Son Antiquarian Booksellers   General Catalogue Summer 2010 - 732 2011   £50

Bradley, Helen *Miss Carter Came with Us.* London: Cape, 1973, First edition; oblong 4to., original cloth, gilt, dust jacket, pages 31, illustrations in color.   R. F. G. Hollett & Son Antiquarian Booksellers General Catalogue Summer 2010 - 733 2011   £65

Bradley, J. J. G. *The King of Diamonds.* London: Hogarth House, circa, 1885, Illustrated, some gatherings browned, unopened in original color pictorial wrappers, one worm hole at fore-edge, otherwise very good.   Jarndyce Antiquarian Booksellers CXCI - 74 2011   £40

Bradley, John T. *The History of Seychelles.* Victoria: privately Printed, 1940, First edition; 2 volumes, hardbound by library from paper wrappers using original wrappers as covers, pages (xvi) 173 xvi (x) & (vi) 174-465, with 25 page index and 21 page article "Birds of the Seychelles and other Islands Included Within that Colony" by D. Vesey Fitzgerald, ex-British Foreign Office library with few library markings, covers slightly rubbed and creased and bumped at top corners, else very good.   Any Amount of Books   May 29 2011 - A73271 2011 $204

Bradley, Marion Zimmer *The Mists of Avalon.* New York: Alfred A. Knopf, 1982, i.e. January, 1983, First edition; octavo, cloth backed boards.   L. W. Currey, Inc. 124 - 136 2011 $450

Bradley, Richard *Interpreting the Axe Trade.* Cambridge: Cambridge University Press, 1993, First edition; original cloth, gilt, dust jacket, pages xiv, 236, with 24 plates and numerous figures and tables.   R. F. G. Hollett & Son Antiquarian Booksellers 177 - 108 2011   £40

Bradlow, Edna *Thomas Bowler of the Cape of Good Hope.* Cape Town and Amsterdam: A. A. Balkema, 1955, First edition; no. 1340 of 2000 copies, 4to., original cloth, gilt, dust jacket with color plate tipped on (laid down, lacking lower panel and part of backstrip), pages 248, with 137 tipped in plates.   R. F. G. Hollett & Son Antiquarian Booksellers General Catalogue Summer 2010 - 60 2011   £120

Bradshaw, Peter *18th Century English Porcelain Figures 1745-1795.* Antique Collector's Club, 1981, First edition; 4to., original cloth, gilt, dust jacket, pages 327, 26 color plates and 177 black and white illustrations. R. F. G. Hollett & Son Antiquarian Booksellers   General Catalogue Summer 2010 - 61   2011   £40

Brady, Buckskin *Stories and Sermons.* Toronto: William Briggs, 1905, First edition; 8vo., maroon cloth, portrait label affixed to front cover frontispiece (range scene), 135 pages, illustrations, 19.8cm., scarce, light professional cosmetic restoration to spine ends and some light foxing, else near fine, housed in cloth slipcase with leather label on spine and titles stamped in gold, rare. Buckingham Books   May 26 2011 - 26865   2011 $1875

Brady, William M. *Clerical and Parochial Records of Cork, Cloyne & Ross.* 1863-1864, 3 volumes, volume I in original cloth, volumes 2 and 3 modern rebind (poor quality), titlepages and one page of prelims in each in photocopy, else text good. C. P. Hyland   May 26 2011 - 260/021   2011 $290

Bragg, William L. *Interatomic Distances in Crystals.* N.P.: Philosophical Magazine, 1926, 8vo., pages 258-266, string bound wrappers, mild soil to covers, with TLS by Bragg concerning "Ionic Radii". By the Book, L. C.   26 - 94   2011 $750

Braine, Sheila *To Tell the King the Sky Is Falling.* Blackie & Son, n.d. circa, 1897, Pages xiii, 172, all edges gilt, illustrations by Alice Woodward, original green pictorial cloth, gilt. R. F. G. Hollett & Son Antiquarian Booksellers   General Catalogue Summer 2010 - 500   2011   £50

Braithwaite, Constance *The Voluntary Citizen.* London: Methuen, 1938, First edition; original cloth, dust jacket, pages xix, 344, presentation copy inscribed by author. R. F. G. Hollett & Son Antiquarian Booksellers   175 - 167   2011   £35

Braithwaite, George Foster *The Salmonidae of Westmorland...* Kendal: Atkinson and Pollitt, 1884, First edition; pages (x), 188 with 4 illustrations, original cloth, gilt, trifle marked, head of spine little rucked, very scarce. R. F. G. Hollett & Son Antiquarian Booksellers   173 - 143   2011   £150

Braithwaite, J. W. *Guide to Kirkby Stephen, Appleby, Brough, Warcop, Ravenstonedale, Mallerstang, &c.* Kirkby Stephen: J. B. Braithwaite, 1884, First edition; modern cloth, original yellow printed wrappers laid down, pages 134, (36, local ads), folding colored map and some fine woodcut illustrations, very scarce. R. F. G. Hollett & Son Antiquarian Booksellers   173 - 145   2011   £120

Braithwaite, J. W. *Guide to Kirkby Stephen, Appleby, Brough, Warcop, Ravenstonedale, Mallerstang, &c.* Kirkby Stephen: J. W. Braithwaite, 1938, Original red pictorial wrappers, rather soiled and torn, rebacked with black tape, pages 69, 10 plate on pink paper and 5 page of local ads, little used, scarce. R. F. G. Hollett & Son Antiquarian Booksellers   173 - 146   2011   £65

Braithwaite, John *The History of the Revolutions in the Empire of Morocco Upon the Death of the Late Emperor Muley Ishamel.* London: J. Darby and J. Brown, 1729, First edition; 8vo., pages viii, list of subscribers, 381, facsimile map, contemporary brown full calf, recently rebacked. J. & S. L. Bonham Antiquarian Booksellers   Africa 4/20/2011 - 9125   2011   £250

Braithwaite, William C. *The Second Period of Quakerism.* London: Macmillan, 1919, First edition; original cloth, gilt, trifle rubbed, spine lettering dulled, pages xlvii, 668, joints cracked. R. F. G. Hollett & Son Antiquarian Booksellers   175 - 168   2011   £30

Brakspear, Harold *The Cistercian Abbey of Stanley, Wiltshire.* London: J. B. Nichols, 1907, Pages 24, 2 plates, 9 text figures, large folding colored plan, 4to., original wrappers, rather creased, edges little chipped. R. F. G. Hollett & Son Antiquarian Booksellers   177 - 109 2011   £40

Bramley, Henry Ramsden *Christmas Carols New and Old.* Novello & Co., n.d., Original green cloth, gilt over bevelled boards, pages 184, (ii), all edges gilt, little pencilled annotation. R. F. G. Hollett & Son Antiquarian Booksellers   175 - 169   2011   £45

The Brand New Monty Python Book. London: Eyre Methuen, n.d., 1973, First UK edition; large 8vo., original pictorial boards, dust jacket extremities trifle worn, unpaginated, illustrations. R. F. G. Hollett & Son Antiquarian Booksellers   General Catalogue Summer 2010 - 790   2011   £35

Brandt, Bill *Perspective of Nudes.* London: The Bodley Head, 1916, First edition, signed in year of publication; 4to., pages 120, 90 black and white photos printed in gravure, original decorated paper covered boards, spine and upper side lettered in red, original black and white photo illustrated dust jacket, text printed in red and black, crease to spine fold of upper panel, 2 chips at top and bottom edges of upper and lower panel, tape repairs to both sides, short closed tear to lower panel, tips lightly rubbed, bookseller's ticket to front pastedown, inscription from David Puttnam in black ink to front free endpaper for Julian, fine in very good dust jacket. Simon Finch Rare Books   Zero - 511   2011   £2000

Brandt, Bill *Perspective of Nudes.* New York: Amphoto, 1961, First US edition; fine and tight in very near fine lightly soiled dust jacket with two tears at base of front panel and faint tape repair shadows to verso.   Jeff Hirsch Books   ny 2010 2011 $1250

Brandt, Bill *Shadow of Light.* New York: Viking Press, 1966, First edition; clean and fine in very near fine dust jacket, closed tear that has some associated creasing to top of back panel.   Jeff Hirsch Books   ny 2010 2011 $750

Brangwyn, Frank *The Water-Colours of Sir Frank Brangwyn R.A. 1867-1956.* Leigh-on-Sea: F. Lewis, 1958, First edition; 4to., original publisher's blue cloth lettered gilt on spine and cover, pages 87, 15 black and white plates and 24 color plates tipped in, no. 40 of 100 of the "Special Edition" on Grosvenor Chater Pure White Antique Laid paper, endpapers and fore-edges very slightly foxed, otherwise very good+.   Any Amount of Books   May 26 2011 - A70129 2011 $419

Branschweig-Luneburg, August, Duke of *Gustavi Seleni Cryptomenytices et Cryptographiae Libri IX etc.* Luneburg: J. & H. Stern, 1624, First edition; folio, (36), 493, (1) pages, half title, folding letterpress table, engraved border on titlepage, 3 engraved illustrations, woodcut diagrams, printer's device on final verso, contemporary Dutch vellum, yapp edges, title leaf trimmed at foot and mounted on stub, extremely fine, unspotted copy, from the library of the Earls of Macclesfield at Shirburn Castle.   Maggs Bros. Ltd.   1440 - 17 2011   £7000

Branyan, Lawrence *Worcester Blue and White Porcelain 1751-1790.* Barrie & Jenkins, 1981, First edition; large 8vo., original cloth, dust jacket, pages 367, 400 illustrations, 125 tone drawings, 150 border designs, scarce.   R. F. G. Hollett & Son Antiquarian Booksellers   General Catalogue Summer 2010 - 62 2011   £180

Brassai *The Artists of My Life.* New York: Witken Berley Ltd., 1982, First edition, deluxe edition comprising 'specially selected sheets", this number 11 of 150 copies, signed and numbered by Brassai, issued with hand pulled dust grained photogravure also signed by Brassai of Henri Matisse drawing a nude woman, 19193; large 4to., full page reproductions of photos, pictorial patterned paper covered boards over cloth lettered silver at spine, special presentation folder housing photogravure, in special binding designed by Sage Reynolds and executed at Four Hands Bindery NY, fine in very good plain buff slipcase.   Any Amount of Books   May 26 2011 - A68250 2011 $1845

Brassey, Earl *The Sunbeam RYS. Voyages and Experiences in Many Waters, Naval Reserves and Other Matters.* London: John Murray, 1917, First edition; large 8vo., original cloth, gilt, mast of flags in colors on upper board, neatly recased, pages xvi, 450 with 50 plates.   R. F. G. Hollett & Son Antiquarian Booksellers   General Catalogue Summer 2010 - 1629 2011   £95

Brassey, Lord *The Naval Annual.* Portsmouth: J Griffin & Co., 1886-1889, First edition; 3 volumes, pages xxi, 550 (16 pages ads); xxvi, 784 (4 pages ads); xxiv, 723 (4 pages ads); First 3 volumes, each gift from author to Duke of Bedford, errata slip tipped into volume II, original publisher's royal blue cloth with gilt lettering and decoration, slightly rubbed and bumped at corners, some moderate spotting to prelims including titlepages and tissue guards, otherwise text nice and clean, illustrations bright, not all tissue guards present, overall handsome set.   Any Amount of Books   May 26 2011 - A75246 2011 $1090

Brathwaite, Richard   1588-1673 *Barnabae Itinerarium or Barnabee's Journal.* J. Harding, 1818, Seventh edition; larger cloth with printed spine label, pages 204, engraved frontispiece, 7 engraved plates, old taped repairs to some hinges and torn leaf, engraved armorial bookplate of William Brooke A.M.   R. F. G. Hollett & Son Antiquarian Booksellers   173 - 147 2011   £120

Braudel, Fernand *The Wheels of Commerce. Volume II of Civilization and Capitalism 15th-18th Century.* BCA, 1983, Large 8vo., original cloth, gilt, dust jacket, pages 670, profusely illustrated.   R. F. G. Hollett & Son Antiquarian Booksellers   175 - 171 2011   £30

Braun, Ernst *Novissimum Fundamenturm & Praxis Artilleriae Oder Nachitziger Besten Mannier.* Danzig: J. F. Grafen for the author, 1682, First edition; folio, (4), 197 (7) pages, no dedication, additional engraved title, 24 plates on 22 (of 23) sheets, lacking final double page engraving, annotated in German hand by J. Hopkey with inscription on title and his initials on cover, from the library of the Earls of Macclesfield at Shirburn Castle.   Maggs Bros. Ltd.   1440 - 42 2011   £2800

Braun, Hugh *The English Castle.* London: Batsford, 1936, First edition; original cloth, dust jacket, little wear to one hinge, pages viii, 120, 32 with color frontispiece and 120 illustrations.   R. F. G. Hollett & Son Antiquarian Booksellers   177 - 113 2011   £35

Braun, Hugh *An Introduction to English Mediaeval Architecture.* London: Faber, 1961, First edition; original cloth, gilt, dust jacket, some loss, pages 293, with 215 illustrations and 39 text drawings.   R. F. G. Hollett & Son Antiquarian Booksellers   177 - 114 2011   £65

Brautigan, Richard *A Confederate General from Big Sur.* New York: Grove Press, 1964, First edition; inscribed by author for Shigeyoshi Murao, long-time manager of City Lights Bookstore, foxing to top edge of text block, else fine in near fine dust jacket with strip of foxing to upper rear flap and shallow creasing to upper rear panel.   Ken Lopez Bookseller   154 - 15 2011 $7500

Bray, Anna Eliza *Life of Thomas Sothard.* London: John Murray, 1851, First edition; 217 x 172mm., xxiv, 246 pages, excellent contemporary dark green morocco, handsomely gilt by James Toovey (stamp signed), covers with French fillet border, raised bands, heavily gilt spine compartments featuring scrolling cornerpieces and large and intricate floral centerpiece, turn-ins densely gilt with botanical tools, marbled endpapers, all edges gilt, frontispiece, engraved titlepage frame and more than 50 illustrations in text; spine evenly faded to a pleasing olive brown, covers with just touch of fading and soiling, handful of pages with extensive freckled foxing, trivial to minor foxing in much of the rest of the text, still extremely fresh, in scarcely worn, very attractive decorative binding. Phillip J. Pirages 59 - 328 2011 $550

Brayer, Herbert O. *William Blackmore: the Spanish Mexican Land Grants of New Mexico and Colorado and Early Financing of the Denver & Rio Grande Railway and Ancillary Land Companies.* Denver,: 1949, 1 of 500 copies; 2 volumes, vi, 381 pages, illustrations, map endpapers, vi, 333 pages, illustrations, map endpapers, clean, very good in slipcase. Dumont Maps & Books of the West 111 - 48 2011 $185

Brazil, Angela *A Fourth Form Friendship.* Blackie and Son, n.d. circa, 1925, Original pictorial blue cloth, pages 255, color frontispiece and 4 plates b Frank E. Wiles. R. F. G. Hollett & Son Antiquarian Booksellers General Catalogue Summer 2010 - 501 2011 £30

Brazil, Angela *The Little Green School.* Blackie and Son, n.d., 1931, First edition; original cloth lettered in blue and decorated in green, little marked, spine slightly darkened, pages 320, 6 plates by Frank Wiles, small inscription. R. F. G. Hollett & Sons Antiquarian Booksellers 170 - 103 2011 £65

Brazil, Angela *The Luckiest Girl in the School.* Blackie and Son, n.d. circa, 1925, Original pictorial brown cloth pages 296, 6 plates, flyleaves browned, small scratch to illustrations leaf. R. F. G. Hollett & Son Antiquarian Booksellers General Catalogue Summer 2010 - 502 2011 £30

Brazil, Angela *A Pair of School Girls.* Blackie & Son, n.d. 1920's, Original sage green pictorial cloth, few slight marks to lower board, page 256, with 4 plates, half title little browned. R. F. G. Hollett & Son Antiquarian Booksellers General Catalogue Summer 2010 - 503 2011 £30

Brazil, Angela *The School by the Sea.* Blackie and Son, n.d. circa, 1925, Original pictorial pale blue cloth, pages 256, with 4 plates. R. F. G. Hollett & Son Antiquarian Booksellers General Catalogue Summer 2010 - 504 2011 £30

Breathing in Irrespirable Atmospheres and in Some Cases, Also Under Water, Including A Short History of Gas and Incendiary Warfare from Early Times to the Present Day... London: The St. Catherine Press, n.d., 1948, First edition; 8vo., original publisher's brown cloth lettered gilt on spine and on front cover, pages xi, 386, copiously illustrated in black and white throughout, 4 in color, very good, excellent condition. Any Amount of Books May 29 2011 - A43928 2011 $340

Brecht, Bertoit *The Three Penny Opera.* New York: Limited Editions Club, 1982, First edition with these illustrations; one of 2000 copies signed by Jack Levine and Eric Bentley, plates by Levine include an original full page unsigned color lithograph, monthly letter laid in, fine in original slipcase, large 4to., 155 pages. Gemini Fine Books & Arts, Ltd. Art Reference & Illustrated Books: First Editions 2011 $75

The Breeding Birds of Cumbria. Cumbria Bird Club, 2002, First edition; pages xii, 391, with 33 color plates in text, tinted drawings by Christine Isherwood and others, 8 colored maps, distribution and other maps. R. F. G. Hollett & Son Antiquarian Booksellers 173 - 939 2011 £35

Brehm, A. E. *Thierleben. Allgemeine kunde des Thierreichs.* Leipzig: Bibliographischen Instituts, 1884, 1882. Second edition; 10 volumes, half leather with reinforced cloth backstrips, marbled edges, leather chipped from some corners, edgewear, corners bumped, 1 hinge broken, some toning, else clean, tight, illustrations by Gustav Mutzel, good. G. H. Mott Bookseller May 26 2011 - 34386 2011 $2000

Brentano Clemens *Schoolmaster Whackwell's Wonderful Sons.* New York: Random House, 1962, First edition; 8vo., (88) pages, fine in dust jacket with price intact (few edge chips and some rubbing), illustrations in color by Maurice Sendak, this copy has wonderful 8 line inscription from Sendak to fellow children's book illustrator, very scarce. Aleph-Bet Books, Inc. 95 - 512 2011 $1250

Brereton, F. S. *One of the Fighting Scouts: a Tale of Guerilla Warfare in South Africa.* London: Blackie, 1903, First edition; 8vo., pages 352, ads, illustrations, original red decorative cloth. J. & S. L. Bonham Antiquarian Booksellers Africa 4/20/2011 - 8270 2011 £40

Bresadola, Don Giacopo *Iconographia Mycologica.* Milan and Trento: 1927-1980, 1398 colored plates with descriptive text and 2 portraits, 8vo., most are laid in cloth backed portfolios (some splitting to 3 spines, light spotting to several spines, most internal paper flaps, covering plates, have tears, plates fine, volume 26 little shaken). Raymond M. Sutton, Jr. May 26 2011 - 25553 2011 $3600

Breton, P. N. *Popular Illustrated Guide to Canadian Coins, Medals...* Winnipeg: Canadian Numismatic Publishing Institute, 1963, Copy # 715 of a limited reprint edition of 1894; cloth with gilt titles and decoration on front, pages 195, illustrations, 8vo., cloth stained and worn, interior very good. Schooner Books Ltd. 96 - 275 2011 $60

Brett, Simon *The Engraver's Cut.* printed at the Rampant Lions Press, 1997, 13/135 copies signed by Brett; 28 wood engravings, each illustrated on recto of separate leaf with further 3 engraved headpieces, each printed in brown, all by Brett, title also printed in brown, pages (xvi) 28 (leaves of engravings), (4), 8vo., original brown cloth backed boards, backstrip gilt lettered, yellow boards with overall repeated design in brown by Brett, board slipcase, fine. Blackwell Rare Books B166 - 270 2011 £180

Breuil, Henri *Beyond the Bounds of History.* P. R. Gawthorn, 1949, First edition; original cloth, dust jacket, pages 100 with 31 delicately colored plates and chart and other plates and illustrations, lovely fresh copy. R. F. G. Hollett & Son Antiquarian Booksellers 177 - 119 2011 £40

Brewer, J. M. *The Beauties of Ireland.* 1825-1826, Large paper; 2 volumes, 10 inches tall, lxxx 493; lxxxi-cxliv 501 pages, 24 plates from Petrie originals, original cloth backed marbled boards, many plates have rice paper guards, some foxing, publisher's ads for various publiations of 1822-1825. C. P. Hyland May 26 2011 - 259/041 2011 $1087

Brewer, Roy *Eric Gill. the Man Who Loved Letters.* Frederick Muller, 1973, First edition; large 8vo., original pictorial cloth silvered, price clipped dust jacket, pages x, 86, with 80 illustrations. R. F. G. Hollett & Son Antiquarian Booksellers General Catalogue Summer 2010 - 63 2011 £35

Brewster, Francis *New Essay's on Trade, Wherein the Present State of Our Trade, It's Great Decay in the Chief Branches of It and the Fatal Consequence Thereof to the Nation...* London: H. Walwyn, 1702, First edition; 8vo., (16) 128 pages, folding table between pages 104 and 105, contemporary plain ruled sheep, patches of general surface wear, neatly rebacked and labelled, very good, crisp copy, good margins. John Drury Rare Books 154 - 27 2011 £950

Brewster, John *Practical Reflections on the Ordination Services for Deacons and Priests in the United Church of England and Ireland...* London: F. C. and J. Rivington, 1817, First edition; 8vo., xv, (1), 355, (1) pages, endpapers bit foxed, front free endpaper creased, contemporary half calf over marbled boards, spine gilt and labelled, very good, dedication copy with Bishop Shute Barrington's armorial bookplate on pastedown, scarce. John Drury Rare Books 153 - 17 2011 £175

Brewster, T. C. M. *The Excavation of Staple How.* Malton: East Riding Archaeological Research Committee, 1963, First edition; pages 242, original cloth, gilt, dust jacket, with colored frontispiece and 131 illustrations. R. F. G. Hollett & Son Antiquarian Booksellers 177 - 120 2011 £35

Bridson, Gavin *The History of Natural History: an Annotated Bibliography.* New York and London: Garland, 1994, First edition; 8vo., xxxi, 740 pages, green cloth, gilt stamped cover and spine titles, fine, from the Bern Dibner reference library, with Burndy bookplate. Jeff Weber Rare Books 161 - 64 2011 $250

Briggs, John *The Lonsdale Magazine...* Kendal: J. Briggs, 1820-1822, 3 volumes, modern half levant morocco gilt with contrasting raised bands (volume 2 slightly taller than others and differring a trifle in the leather), pages iv, 566; iv, 476; iv, 476 with 27 aquatints, 1 hand colored map, 1 folding table, 1 engraved plate and text illustrations, 2 plates in volume 2 poorly tinted in red, staining opposing leaves, little light browning in places, very good, sound set. R. F. G. Hollett & Son Antiquarian Booksellers 173 - 153 2011 £395

Briggs, John *The Remains of John Briggs...* Kirkby Lonsdale: printed and sold by Arthur Foster, 1825, First edition; old half calf gilt, neatly recased, original backstrip cracked but laid down, pages 408, complete with half title and subscriber list, excellent copy with near contemporary inscription of Henrietta Harrison. R. F. G. Hollett & Son Antiquarian Booksellers 173 - 152 2011 £395

Briggs, Martin S. *The English Farmhouse.* London: Batsford, 1953, First edition; original cloth, gilt, dust jacket, pages 242, color frontispiece, 131 illustrations. R. F. G. Hollett & Son Antiquarian Booksellers 177 - 121 2011 £35

Briggs, Raymond *Fungus the Bogeyman: Plop-up Book.* Hamilton, 1982, First Pop-up edition; 6 superb color double page concertina pop-ups printed on thick card paper and illustrated by author, each pop-up incorporating moveable elements with tab pulls, wheel and flaps, pages (12), 8vo., original white boards, lettered and illustrated to designs by Briggs, fine. Blackwell Rare Books B166 - 204 2011 £40

Briggs, Richard *The New Art of Cookery; According to the Present Practice; Being a Complete Guide to all Housekeepers...* Boston: for W. Spotswood, 1798, xxiii, (250), 444 pages, contemporary sheep, very skillfully rebacked in period style, retaining original spine label, gathering N very heavily foxed and spotted, few ther gatherings uniformly browned or foxed, due to varying qualities of paper stocks used, otherwise very good. Joseph J. Felcone Inc. Fall Miscellany 2010 - 28 2011 $3800

Brigham, William Tufts *Report of a Journey Around the World to Study Matters Relating to Museums.* Honolulu: Bishop Museum Press, 1913, First edition; wrappers, large 8vo., pages 320, vii page index, 250, illustrations, mostly photos, with loosely inserted printer author's compliments slip, very good solid clean, tight copy, very slight wear, slight staining and slight fading to original publisher's printed faun wrappers. Any Amount of Books May 29 2011 - A40952 2011 $255

Brin, David *The Postman.* New York: Bantam, 1985, First edition; fine, dust jacket very good, few small closed tears and chips, very good, few small closed tears and chips. Bella Luna Books May 29 2011 - t3441 2011 $82

Brin, David *Startide Rising.* West Bloomfield: Phantasia Press, 1985, First hardcover edition; octavo, cloth. L. W. Currey, Inc. 124 - 196 2011 $200

Brin, David *The Uplift War.* West Bloomfield: Phantasia Press, 1987, First edition; octavo, leather. L. W. Currey, Inc. 124 - 79 2011 $1000

Brindley, Charles *Bipeds and Quadrupeds.* T. C. Newby, 1853, First edition; prelims misbound but complete, 2 pages ads, original green cloth, very good, bright. Jarndyce Antiquarian Booksellers CXCI - 75 2011 £150

Brine, Mary D. *Little Lad Jamie.* New York: E. P. Dutton & Co., 1895, First edition; 8vo., grey cloth with elaborate stamping and decorations with gold and blues, 40 numbered pages of text plus 8 toned photogravure reproductions of photos. Jo Ann Reisler, Ltd. 86 - 191 2011 $400

Brinker, Helmut *Chinese Cloisonne. The Pierre Uldry Collection.* Bamboo Pub., 1989, First trade edition; small square 8vo., original cloth, gilt, dust jacket, pages 144 plus 381 illustrations, 12 pages of decorative motifs and bibliography. R. F. G. Hollett & Son Antiquarian Booksellers General Catalogue Summer 2010 - 64 2011 £140

Brinton, Selwyn *Francesco di Giorgi Martini of Sienna: Painter, Sculptor, Engineer, Civil and Military Architect (1439-1502) Part I.* London: Besant, 1934, 8vo., 119 pages, 27 plates, including frontispiece, blue cloth, gilt stamped spine title, extremities rubbed, edges foxed, from the Bern Dibner reference library, with Burndy bookplate, good, rare. Jeff Weber Rare Books 161 - 65 2011 $75

Brinton, Thomas *The Sermons of Thomas Brinton, Bishop of Rochester 1373-1389.* London: Royal Historical Society, 1954, 2 volumes, original cloth, gilt, pages 240; 241-518, few small library stamps. R. F. G. Hollett & Son Antiquarian Booksellers 175 - 369 2011 £30

Brisson, M. *Voyages to the Coast of Africa...* London: G. G. J. and J. Robinson, 1792, First English edition; 8vo., pages viii, 500, large folding map, contemporary brown tree calf, recently rebacked, good, crisp. J. & S. L. Bonham Antiquarian Booksellers Africa 4/20/2011 - 8888 2011 £900

The Bristol Magazine and Western Literary Journal. Henry H. Hodges, Jan. 2, 1841-, Dec. 25, 1841.; 2 volumes in one, 208, 208 pages, comprising 52 issues, each of 8 page, contemporary black half calf, spine gilt and lettered with raised bands, marbled endpapers, front free endpaper renewed, in very good state of preservation. John Drury Rare Books 153 - 109 2011 £375

Bristowe, Sydney, Mrs. *The Oldest Letters in the World.* London: Allen & Unwin, 1923, Revised edition; original cloth, gilt, dust jacket little spotted, pages 96 with frontispiece, small brown patch on title. R. F. G. Hollett & Son Antiquarian Booksellers 177 - 123 2011 £35

Bristowe, W. S. *The World of Spiders.* London: Collins, 1958, First edition; original cloth gilt, dust jacket (spine rather faded and trifle frayed at head, small closed nick to upper panel), pages 304, 4 color and 32 black and white photos, 116 text figures. R. F. G. Hollett & Son Antiquarian Booksellers General Catalogue Summer 2010 - 953 2011 £120

The British History, Briefly Told; and a Description of the Ancient Customs, Sports and Pastimes of the English. London: John Harris, n.d. circa, 1843, Square 12mo., iv, 392, 32 pages, decorative blue sand grained blind embossed cloth with large gilt vignette representing Henry V in armor riding an armored horse on upper cover, gilt title on spine, full page copper engraved frontispiece, large emblematic copper engraved vignette on titlepage, text adorned with 17 full page copper engravings, all engraved printed on heavier paper and on one side of the leaf only, numerous line engravings, new front endpaper and reinforced front hinges. Hobbyhorse Books 56 - 12 2011 $220

The British Journal. London: T. Warner at the Black Boy in Paternoster Row, 1722-1723, 4to, 67 issues, most issues 6 pages, about 400 pages in all, soundly bound in modern grey cloth lettered gilt at spine, red leather label, slight loss at edges of some pages, latter issues fairly closely cropped but text unaffected, very good. Any Amount of Books May 26 2011 - A68252 2011 $922

British Museum *The British Museum Quarterly.* British Museum, 1927, 1960-1961; Volumes I-XXIII, small 4to., original holland backed blue boards, lettered in black, illustrations, original wrappers of earlier numbers bound in, excellent clean and sound. R. F. G. Hollett & Son Antiquarian Booksellers 177 - 845 2011 £450

British Quadrupeds. London: Relgious Tract Society, n.d. circa, 1850, New edition; square 12mo., original cloth, gilt, pages 263, (i), all edges gilt, 24 hand colored woodcut vignette plate, trifle shaken.   R. F. G. Hollett & Sons Antiquarian Booksellers   170 - 108 2011   £85

British Speleological Association   *Bulletin of the.... New Series No.s 1-9.* Settle: The Association, 1970-1973, 9 volumes, 4to. original wrappers side stapled, pages 22-26 per volumes duplicated with inserts, excellent run of this ephemeral journal.   R. F. G. Hollett & Son Antiquarian Booksellers   General Catalogue Summer 2010 - 1341 2011   £120

British Speleological Association *Cave Science. The Journal of the British Speleological Association. Nos. 1-15.* Settle: The Association, 1947-1951, 4to., original wrappers, staples rather rusted, pages 330, duplicated, excellent complete run of the first volume.   R. F. G. Hollett & Son Antiquarian Booksellers   General Catalogue Summer 2010 - 1342 2011   £250

British Speleological Association *Caves and Caving Volume I. No. 5 (November 1938).* The Association, 1938, Large 8vo., original wrappers, pages 161-193, illustrations. R. F. G. Hollett & Sons Antiquarian Booksellers   General Catalogue Summer 2010 - 143 2011   £30

Brittain, F. *Babylon Bruis'd & Mount Moriah mended, Being a Compendious & Authentick Narracioun..* Cambridge: Will Heffer & Sons, 1948, Second edition; Original printed wrappers, pages 16.   R. F. G. Hollett & Son Antiquarian Booksellers   General Catalogue Summer 2010 - 1344 2011   £30

Britten, F. J. *Old Clocks and Watches and Their Makers.* London: Methuen & E. & F. N. Spon, 1982, Ninth edition; 4to., original cloth, gilt, dust jacket rather worn, pages xxi, 700, 388 illustrations, line drawings.   R. F. G. Hollett & Son Antiquarian Booksellers   General Catalogue Summer 2010 - 65 2011   £45

Britton, John *A Brief Memoir of the Life and Writings of John Britton.* London: printed by J. Moyes, 1825, Half title, titlepage, dedication, 44 pages text, 2 page catalog, original boards, paper label on front board, marked and rubbed, hinges splitting, booklabel of Anne and F. G. Renier, inscribed presentation from author to J. Bull.   Jarndyce Antiquarian Booksellers   CXCI - 76 2011   £125

Britton, John *The Union of Architecture, Sculpture & Painting...* London: printed for the author (sold by Longman & Co., 1827, First edition; small 4to., xvi, 60 pages with color aquatint frontispiece and 23 engraved plates, attractively bound in late 19th century full brown leather lettered gilt at spine with gilt decoration at spine and on front and back cover, slight rubbing, very slight foxing to plates, very good.   Any Amount of Books   May 26 2011 - A64419 2011 $1006

Broadbent, Arthur T. *The Minor Domestic Architecture of Gloucestershire.* London: John Tiranti, 1931, Large 4to., original cloth backed blue boards, top corners bumped, pages 19 (iv), 5 pages of drawings, plus 48 plates on stiff card.   R. F. G. Hollett & Son Antiquarian Booksellers   177 - 126 2011   £65

Broch, Hermann *The Death of Virgil.* London: Routledge, 1946, First English edition; 8vo., 494 pages, very good+ in slightly tanned and very slightly soiled dust jacket, otherwise very good or better.   Any Amount of Books   May 29 2011 - A48849 2011 $255

Brock, Alan St. H. *A History of Fireworks.* London. et al: George J. Harrap, 1949, First edition; 8vo., 280 pages, 40 plates, text illustrations, dark blue cloth, gilt stamped spine title, dust jacket worn, very good, from the Bern Dibner reference library, with Burndy bookplate, signed by Cyril Stanley Smith.   Jeff Weber Rare Books   161 - 66 2011 $125

Brock, Alan St. H. *A History of Fireworks.* London: Harrap, 1949, First edition; large 8vo., original cloth, gilt, dust jacket worn and chipped, pages 280 with 8 color plates and 32 half tone plates, occasional mark, signed by author. R. F. G. Hollett & Son Antiquarian Booksellers General Catalogue Summer 2010 - 1093 2011   £120

Brock, Alan St. H. *Pyrotechnics.* Daniel O'Connor, 1922, First edition; small 4to., original pictorial orange cloth, dust jacket rather worn, soiled and chipped, pages xv, 198, 6 color Japanese prints, 20 plates, pictorial endpapers, scattered foxing, mainly to prelim leaves, presentation copy.   R. F. G. Hollett & Son Antiquarian Booksellers   General Catalogue Summer 2010 - 1094 2011   £950

Brockbank, Elisabeth *Richard Hubberthorne of Yealand, Yeoman, Soldier, Quaker 1628-1662.* Friends Book Centre, 1929, Signed limited edition; original cloth, gilt, pages 168, illustrations by author, tipped in color frontispiece, 1 plate and 4 tipped in plates from blocks, little spotting in places. R. F. G. Hollett & Son Antiquarian Booksellers   173 - 154 2011   £45

Brockett, Paul *Bibliography of Aeronautics.* Washington: Smithsonian Institution, 1910, First edition; 8vo., xiv, 940 pages, printed wrappers, worn, small library blindstamp on front cover, very good, from the Bern Dibner reference library, with Burndy bookplate.   Jeff Weber Rare Books 161 - 67 2011 $75

Brocklehurst, H. C. *Game Animals of the Sudan; Their Habits and Distribution.* London: Gurney & Jackson, 1931, First; 8vo, pages xv, 170, folding map, plates, illustrations, original brown cloth, blindstamped vignette on upper cover.   J. & S. L. Bonham Antiquarian Booksellers Africa 4/20/2011 - 6790 2011   £90

Brodovitch, Alexey *Ballet.* New York: J. J. Augustin, 1945, First edition, reportedly only 500 copies printed; clean, very near fine copy, some very minor wear to corners small tear to top of rear corner, lacking scarce slipcase, well preserved copy of an extraordinarily fragile book. Jeff Hirsch Books ny 2010 2011 $9500

Bromley, James *Notes on Some Recent Excavations at Burscough Priory.* Liverpool: Thomas Brakell, 1890, original pebble grained green cloth gilt, pages 27, 11 lithographed plates, scattered rather heavy foxing, joints cracked, stamped "With James Bromley's compliments" on title. R. F. G. Hollett & Son Antiquarian Booksellers 177 - 127 2011 £65

Bronn, Henrich Georg *Die Klassen und Ordnungen des Their-Reichs Wissenshcaftlich Dargestellt in Wort und Bild. Volume 6 part II Amphibien. Part III. Reptilien (I-III).* Leipzig and Heidelberg: C. F. Witner'sche, 1873, 8vo., bound in 4 volumes, 53 + 170 lithographed anatomical plates, 2 blank corners of a plain plate missing, pages 94), 726; (2), 2089, part II is disbound with trimmed original front wrapper included, volumes of part III in contemporary cloth backed boards with original wrappers laid down, good to very good, moderate wear and light soiling to covers, corner bumped, short tear to head of 2 spines, handstamp to front flyleaf and first title of each volume, short tear to title, mostly unopened, minor light foxing to few pages and several plates, part II needs rebound and has several pages browned. Raymond M. Sutton, Jr. May 26 2011 - 48198 2011 $1200

Bronson, Edgar Beecher *The Red Blooded.* Chicago: A. C. McClurg, 1910, First edition; illustrations, original publisher's pictorial cloth, bright, near fine. Lupack Rare Books May 26 2011 - ABE1324086129 2011 $100

Bronte, Anne 1820-1849 *The Tenant of Wildfell Hall.* London: T. C. Newby, 1848, First edition, first issue; 12mo., 3 volumes, (4), 358; (2), 366; (2), 342 pages, excessively rare half title in volume I, but without final leaf of ads in volume I, no half titles called for in volumes II and III, bound circa 1900 by Riviere & Son (stamp signed on verso of front free endpaper) in full tan polished calf, covers with gilt triple fillet border and gilt corner ornaments, spine decoratively tooled in gilt in compartments with two brown morocco gilt lettering pieces, board edges ruled in gilt, turn-ins decoratively tooled in gilt, top edge gilt, others uncut, armorial bookplate of Herbert S. Leon, housed in custom made half tan calf clamshell case with raised bands and two green morocco lettering labels and felt lined dividers, exceptionally copy, minimal foxing and mostly marginal soiling, volume I with tiny dampstain outer margin of P6, volume II with small very neat paper repairs to outer blank margin of D7 and F7, small faint stain in upper corner of G3-G7 and small paper flaw in upper blank margin of H5, volume III with faint stain in upper margin of D4 and D5, tiny tear in outer margin of G3, short tear neatly repaired in upper margin of G6, tiny tear in outer margin of P4. David Brass Rare Books, Inc. May 26 2011 - 00031 2011 $42,500

Bronte, Anne 1820-1849 *The Tenant of Wildfell Hall.* London: Smith, Elder and Co., 1859, New edition; 8vo., original publisher's printed orange cloth, pages 371, slight even soiling, but attractive sond very good. Any Amount of Books May 29 2011 - A49453 2011 $298

Bronte, Charlotte 1816-1855 *Jane Eyre.* London: Smith Elder and Co., 1847, First edition; 3 volumes, octavo, original vertically ribbed cloth. Heritage Book Shop Booth A12 51st NY International Antiquarian Book Fair April 8-10 2011 - 17 2011 $110,000

Bronte, Charlotte 1816-1855 *The Professor.* London: Smith, Elder, 1856, Pages 432, frontispiece (dampstained), some foxing, contemporary half calf, gilt rubbed and scraped, volume 4 of the Pocket edition of the Brontes' Works. R. F. G. Hollett & Son Antiquarian Booksellers General Catalogue Summer 2010 - 630 2011 £30

Bronte, Emily 1818-1848 *Wuthering Heights.* New York: Harper & Bros., 1848, First American edition; octavo, 288 pages, original dark green fine ripple grain cloth, covers blocked in blind and spine lettered and decoratively stamped in gilt, gilt rubbed from small portion of spine, head and tail of spine and corners slightly bumped, some foxing and dampstaining throughout as usual and discoloration to final pastedown, binding very slightly skewed, previous owner's bookplate, beautiful copy, very scarce, particularly in such fine condition. Heritage Book Shop Holiday 2010 - 12 2011 $12,500

Bronte, Emily 1818-1848 *Wuthering Heights.* London: Duckworth, 1931, First edition; 4to., original cloth, gilt, spine lightly faded, pages xvii, 325, with 12 fine page woodcuts by Clare Leighton. R. F. G. Hollett & Son Antiquarian Booksellers General Catalogue Summer 2010 - 835 2011 £120

Bronte, Emily 1818-1848 *Wuthering Heights.* London: Collins, 1955, First edition thus; original cloth backed pictorial boards, spine faded, pages xxx, 331, with 15 fine colored lithographs and triple colored and patterned endpapers by Barnett Freedman, uncommon edition. R. F. G. Hollett & Son Antiquarian Booksellers General Catalogue Summer 2010 - 742 2011 £45

Bronte, The Sisters *The Novels of...* Edinburgh: John Grant, 1907, Thornton edition; 12 volume, 8vo., titlepages printed in red and black, frontispiece portraits and numerous photo plates, bound in dark green three quarter calf and green cloth, spine gilt in compartments, top edge gilt, by Bayntun of Bath, hinge of one volume little tender, fine. Second Life Books Inc. 174 - 73 2011 $2625

Bronte, The Sisters *Poems by Currer, Ellis and Acton Bell.* Philadelphia: Lea and Blanchard, 1848, First American edition; iv, (1), 13-176, (24) pages, original brown paper covered boards, printed paper spine label, outer brown paper worn rom along hinges and at tips of spine revealing lighter paper underneath, scattered foxing, else very nice, very tight in fragile original boards, 1848 ownership signature of A. G. Trafton. Joseph J. Felcone Inc. Fall Miscellany 2010 - 20 2011 $2800

Brook, Richard *New Cyclopaedia of Botany and Complete Book of Herbs: Forming a History and Description of all Plants, British or Foreign.* W. M. Clark, c., 1868, 2 volumes, 8vo., lix, (i), 348; (2), 349-733, (3) pages, color frontispiece, decorative blue and gilt titlepage, and 99 colored plates, fine, clean copy bound by Butler, Ryde, Isle of Wight, in contemporary dark green half calf, raised gilt bands, marbled boards. Ken Spelman Rare Books 68 - 141 2011 £380

Brooke-Hunt, Violet *Lord Roberts.* London: James Nisbet & Co., 1901, pages ix, 346, frontispiece, Full tree calf gilt prize binding,. R. F. G. Hollett & Sons Antiquarian Booksellers 170 - 111 2011 £45

Brooke, Henry *Memoirs of the Life of the Late Excellent and Pious Mr. Henry Brooke, Collected from Original Papers and Other Authentic Sources.* Dublin: printed by R. Napper and sold by M. Keane &c, 1816, 12mo., uncut in original blue boards, brown paper spine, worn paper label, leading hinge weakening, Dublin bookseller's ticket "P. Kennedy, Anglesea Street, Six Doors of College Green". Jarndyce Antiquarian Booksellers CXCI - 91 2011 £85

Brooke, Iris *Western European Costume.* London: Harrap, 1939, First edition; small 4to., original cloth, dust jacket, spine little darkened, pages 151, 16 color plates and 95 text illustrations. R. F. G. Hollett & Son Antiquarian Booksellers 175 - 182 2011 £30

Brooke, Jocelyn *The Birth of a Legend.* London: Bertram Rota, 1964, One of 65 copies signed by author, this "out of series"; 4to., stiff plain card with printed green self wrappers, pages 7, signed presentation from publisher Anthony Rota to writer and activist Yvonne Kapp. Any Amount of Books May 29 2011 - A49029 2011 $383

Brooke, John Hedley *Reconstructing Nature: the Engagement of Science and Religion.* Edinburgh: T&T Clark, 1998, First edition; 8vo. xii, 367 page, illustrations, dark blue cloth, gilt stamped spine title, dust jacket, fine, from the Bern Dibner reference library, with Burndy bookplate. Jeff Weber Rare Books 161 - 68 2011 $75

Brooke, Ralph *A Discoverie of Certaine Errours Published in Print in Much Commended Britannia 1594 to which is added The Learned Mr. Camden's Answer to His Book and Mr. Brooke's Reply (and) A Second Discoverie of Errours.* Woodman & Lyon, 1724, First edition; main titlepage and titlepage to "A Discoverie" printed red and black, titlepage to "A Second Discoverie" printed black, both subsidiary titlepages printed by Woodman and dated 1723, vi, plate (7) 77 (10) 32 196 pages, contemporary calf, 4to., 230 x 170mm., generous margins (large paper?), bookplates of two Norfolk antiquaries, Francis Blomefield & Bryan Hall, very. C. P. Hyland   May 26 2011 - 786 2011 $544

Brooke, Rupert *The Collected Poems of Rupert Brooke.* London: Philip Lee Warner, publisher to the Medici Society, 1919, #595 of 1000 printed on handmade Riccardi paper; Edition leaf, half title, frontispiece, engraved title, uncut in original light blue paper boards, heavy cloth spine, paper labels, boards slightly marked, very good, 2 spare labels tipped in at end. Jarndyce Antiquarian Booksellers CXCI - 92 2011 £225

Brooks, Juanita *John Doyle Lee: Zealot - Pioneer Builder - Scapegoat.* Glendale: The Arthur H. Clark Co., 1961, First edition; limited to 209 copies, 8vo., blue cloth, blue foil stamping on spine and rules, top edge stained blue, 404 pages, frontispiece, illustrations, former owner's bookplate on front free flyleaf, inked name and address on front pastedown sheet, lightly rubbed along edges and corners, else near fine, custom made cloth slipcase with leather label on spine, very scarce. Buckingham Books May 26 2011 - 24726 2011 $2500

Brooks, Shirley *Sooner or Later.* London: Bradbury, Evans & Co., 1868, First edition; 2 volumes, half titles, frontispiece, engraved titlepages, plates, slightly later half green calf, raised bands, decorated in gilt, contemporary signature of Thomas Lambert, handsome copy. Jarndyce Antiquarian Booksellers CXCI - 93 2011 £75

Brooksby, G. *The Hunting Countries of England...* The Field, 1878, First edition; original limp cloth, with paper label (rather defective) boards refixed, pages 122, (ii), pencilled annotation, scarce. R. F. G. Hollett & Son Antiquarian Booksellers General Catalogue Summer 2010 - 1219 2011 £65

Brookshaw, George *Pomona Britannica, or a Collection of the Most Esteemed Fruits at Present Cultivated in Great Britain.* London: printed by Bensley and Son, 1817, First quarto edition; 2 large volumes, quarto, contemporary maroon straight grain morocco. Heritage Book Shop Booth A12 51st NY International Antiquarian Book Fair April 8-10 2011 - 18 2011 $20,000

Brookshaw, George *Pomona Britannica.* Koln: Taschen, 2002, Square 4olio, original boards, dust jacket, pages 200, illustrations in color, with 90 full page reproductions. R. F. G. Hollett & Son Antiquarian Booksellers   General Catalogue Summer 2010 - 954   2011   £30

Broom, Herbert *A Selection of Legal Maxims.* London: A. Maxwell and Son, 1845, First edition; 8vo., pages xl, 469, rebound in plain thin white card, titlepage little soiled with small chip at corner, text otherwise very good, ideal for rebinding.   Any Amount of Books   May 29 2011 - A45458   2011 $340

Broster, Dorothy Kathleen *Couching at the Door.* London: Toronto: William Heinemann, 1942, First edition; octavo, pages 91-6) 1-130, original blue cloth spine panel stamped in gold.   L. W. Currey, Inc.   124 - 127   2011 $500

Brough, John Cargill *The Fairy Tales of Science.* London: Griffith and Farran, 1866, Second edition; small 8vo., original blue cloth, gilt, hinges rather worn, pages xii, 322, 36, all edges gilt, 16 woodcut plates.   R. F. G. Hollett & Sons Antiquarian Booksellers   170 - 112   2011   £130

Brougham and Vaux, Henry Peter Brougham, 1st Baron 1778-1868 *Historical Sketches of Statesmen who Flourished in the Time of George III.* Paris: Baudry's European Library, 1844, Pages xii, iv-viii, 372, old half calf gilt with marbled boards, extremities slightly rubbed and lettering partially dulled, corner torn off front two flyleaves, signature of Edward Stanley Curwen dated 1844.   R. F. G. Hollett & Son Antiquarian Booksellers   175 - 185   2011   £35

Brown, Abner W. *The Infant Brothers.* London: James Nisbet and Co., 1846, Eight thousand; small 8vo., contemporary full polished calf gilt, pages xii, 304.   R. F. G. Hollett & Son Antiquarian Booksellers   175 - 187   2011   £45

Brown, D. K. *Before the Ironclad: Development of Ship Design, Propulsion and Armament in the Royal Navy 1815-1860.* Annapolis: Naval Institute Press, 1990, First US edition; 4to., 217 pages, frontispiece, photos and illustrations, brown paper boards, gilt stamped spine, dust jacket lightly worn along top edge, very good, from the Bern Dibner reference library, with Burndy bookplate.   Jeff Weber Rare Books   161 - 69   2011 $85

Brown, Dan *The Da Vinci Code.* New York: Doubleday, 2003, First Book Club edition; signed by author, fine, dust jacket.   Lupack Rare Books   May 26 2011 - ABE821724122   2011 $125

Brown, Dan *The Da Vinci Code.* New York: Da Vinci Code, 2003, First edition; first state with "Skitoma" on page 243, fine in like dust jacket.   Bella Luna Books   May 29 2011 - t7835   2011 $93

Brown, Dan *The Da Vinci Code.* New York: Doubleday, 2003, First edition; near fine, previous owner's embossing stamp on half titlepage, dust jacket fine, signed by author.   Bella Luna Books   May 26 2011 - t8277   2011 $247

Brown, Dan *Deception Point.* New York: Pocket, 2001, First edition; fine in like dust jacket.   Bella Luna Books   May 26 2011 - t9291   2011 $165

Brown, David *God and Enchantment of Place.* London: Oxford University Press, 2004, First edition; pages xii, 304, small 8vo., contemporary full polished calf gilt.   R. F. G. Hollett & Son Antiquarian Booksellers   175 - 189   2011   £45

Brown, Fredric *And the Gods Laughed: a Collection of Science Fiction and Fantasy.* West Bloomfield: Phantasia Press, 1987, First edition; 2 part black and white leather, spine, front and rear panels stamped in gold.   L. W. Currey, Inc.   124 - 156   2011 $350

Brown, Fredric *Space on My Hands.* Chicago: Shasta Publishers, 1951, First edition; octavo, cloth.   L. W. Currey, Inc.   124 - 137   2011 $450

Brown, G. Baldwin *The Art in Early England.* London: John Murray, 1903, First edition; 2 volumes, original cloth, gilt, spines rather rubbed, pages xiv, 388; xviii, 351, with over 200 illustrations, maps, tables, joints of volume 2 cracked, endpapers rather spotted.   R. F. G. Hollett & Son Antiquarian Booksellers   177 - 130   2011   £75

Brown, Hallie Q. *Homespun Heroines and Other Women of Distinction...* Xenia: Aldine Publishing Co., 1926, First edition; 8vo., pages viii (252), green cloth (little soiled and faded), stamped in gilt, signed by author, previous owner's name "Mrs. J. M. Millon", some pencil underlining of the Harriet Tubman section, front hinge tender, very good.   Second Life Books Inc.   174 - 74   2011 $950

Brown, Henry *The Cotton Fields and Cotton Factories: Being a Familiar View of the Rise and Progress of that Wonderful Branch of Trade..* Darton and Clark n.d., 1840?, 12mo., original cloth, gilt, little worn, head of spine repaired, pages vii, 166, all edges gilt, color printed general title 9 hand colored plates, little shaken, but very good, scarce.   R. F. G. Hollett & Sons Antiquarian Booksellers   170 - 114   2011   £240

Brown, Henry *The History of Illinois from Its First Discovery & Settlement to the Present Time.* New York: 1844, First edition; original brown cloth, head and foot of backstrip with 1/2 inch loss of backstrip, backstrip faded, titlepage and extra large Colton map reglued, otherwise very good.   Bookworm & Silverfish   678 - 89   2011 $450

Brown, Horatio F. *Studies in the History of Venice.* London: John Murray, 1907, First edition; 2 volumes, pages xii, 366 and 49, original publisher's sage green cloth lettered gilt on spine and on front cover, decent copies with little fading at spine, slight nick at head of one spine, slight foxing at prelims, neat name on front endpaper, else sound, about very good+.   Any Amount of Books   May 29 2011 - A61357   2011 $213

Brown, J. *Tourist Rambles in Yorkshire, Lincolnshire, Durham, Northumberland & Derbyshire.* London: Simpkin, Marshall & Co. and York: Pickering and Sampson, 1878, First edition; original decorated blue cloth gilt, spine little dulled and labels stuck on pages viii, 269, uncommon.   R. F. G. Hollett & Son Antiquarian Booksellers   General Catalogue Summer 2010 - 1345   2011   £30

Brown, J. *Tourist Rambles in the Northern and Midland Counties. Second Series.* London: Simpkin Marshall Co. and York: J. Sampson and E. H. Pickering, 1885, Deluxe edition; pages (iv), 308, all edges gilt, 7 photo plates, scattered spots to prelims, original green cloth gilt extra by Potter and Son of York, little rubbed and marked in places. R. F. G. Hollett & Son Antiquarian Booksellers   173 - 158   2011   £150

Brown, J. T. *The Encyclopaedia of Poultry.* Walter Southwood and Co. circa, 1930, 4to., 2 volumes, 105 full page platess, many text illustrations, one plate torn without loss, original red and green cloth, little marked and faded, good set.   Ken Spelman Rare Books   68 - 142   2011   £85

Brown, J. Walter *Carlisle. Three Tracts.* Carlisle: Charles Thurnam, 1904-1912, Original cloth gilt, trifle rubbed, pages 40, 23, 24, folding town plan, plate and 2 pages of music, original wrappers bound in.   R. F. G. Hollett & Son Antiquarian Booksellers   173 - 159   2011   £45

Brown, James S. *California Gold.* Oakland: Pacific Press Pub. Co., 1894, First edition; small 8vo., 20 pages, frontispiece, original printed buff wrappers, minor reinforcement of one corner and spine fold separation, housed in folding chemise an brown morocco slipcase, near fine.   Jeff Weber Rare Books   163 - 56   2011 $3500

Brown, John *The Historical Gallery of Criminal Portraitures Foreign and Domestic.* Manchester: J. Gleave, 1823, First edition; 2 volumes, contemporary half calf, gilt, few slight scrapes, pages xii, 626; (iv), 648, with 2 engraved frontispiece, directions to binder in volume 2 also calls for 16 plates, but these are not included, scarce.   R. F. G. Hollett & Son Antiquarian Booksellers   175 - 190   2011   £150

Brown, John *The North-West Passage and the Plans for the Search for Sir John Franklin a Review.* London: E. Stanford, 1858, First edition; 8vo., pages xii, 463, lithographed frontispiece, 2 folding maps at front and rear, ex-British Foreign Office library with light library markings, else very good, original publisher's ink blue blind patterned cloth with gilt medal vignette on cover, spine renewed and plain matching blue with black gilt lettered spine labels, frontispiece slightly spotted and very slightly worn at edges not affecting image otherwise pleasing, very good, sound example with 2 library stamps and (detachable) library label on f.e.p. Any Amount of Books   May 26 2011 - A73751   2011 $1258

Brown, John Henry *Indian Wars and Pioneers of Texas.* Austin: L. E. Daniel, 1896, First edition; thick quarto, full leather with spine professionally restored in full leather, 762 pages, all edges gilt, illustrations, endpapers replaced, internal spine hinges have been strengthened, else near fine, tight copy, very scarce.   Buckingham Books   May 26 2011 - 30404   2011 $1750

Brown, Larry *Billy Ray's Farm.* Decatur: Wisteria Press, 1997, Limited edition, of a total edition of 287 copies, this one of 250 numbered copies; signed by author and artist, cloth bound, fine, illustrations by Barry Moser.   Ken Lopez Bookseller   154 - 17   2011 $150

Brown, Larry *Facing the Music.* Chapel Hill: Algonquin, 1988, First edition; fine in near fine dust jacket, very light sunning and faint dampstaining on inside top edge.   Bella Luna Books   May 29 2011 - t1506   2011 $137

Brown, Louis *Historical Questions on the Kings of England in Verse.* Boston: Munroe & Francis and David Francis, n.d. circa, 1820, 12mo., 35 page, stiff buff paper covers, upper covered with titlepage and allegorical wood engraved vignette enclosed in decorative printer device, lower cover with publisher ad, each page composed of small wood engraved portrait, printed on handmade provincial paper, inked signature at top edge of titlepage, covers lightly spotted and soiled, some internal spotting, text pages in fine state, page 33 misnumbered as page 14, as issued, rare.   Hobbyhorse Books   56 - 13   2011 $550

Brown, M. Walter *Transactions of Institution of Mining Engineers.* Institute of Mining Engineers, 1894-1911, First edition; Volume 8-Volume 40, lacking 10, 12, 22, 24, 31, 34, 36, plans, elevations, generally very good, spines of three little split along edge and few endpapers missing, half calf marbled boards, 26 volumes generally in very good condition, uncommon.   I. D. Edrich   May 26 2011 - 96354   2011 $1342

Brown, Marcia *Backbone of the King the Story of Poka'a and His Son Ku.* Honolulu: University of Hawaii Press, 1966, 1984; 4to., 180 pages, cloth, fine in dust jacket, inscribed by Brown for Margaret Evans, signed and dated June 1966, , sold with cloth folder holding a complete set of the linoleum block prints used in the book, pulled on Japanese tissue,.   Aleph-Bet Books, Inc.   95 - 117   2011 $5750

Brown, Marcia *Dick Whittington and His Cat.* New York: Charles Scribner's Sons, 1950, First edition; grey pictorial cloth with black lettering on spine, book in nice condition, color pictorial dust jacket with small piece missing from front corner and surface damage to rear of jacket, signed in full by author, every page has powerful linoleum block illustrations.   Jo Ann Reisler, Ltd.   86 - 28   2011 $375

Brown, Margaret Wise *The Noisy Book.* New York: William R. Scott, 1939, First edition; small 4to., pictorial boards, occasional finger soil, else very good-fine in dust jacket, some soil and corner wear, else very good+, illustrations by Leonard Weisgard.   Aleph-Bet Books, Inc.   95 - 119   2011 $1200

Brown, Margaret Wise *The Poodle and the Sheep.* New York: E. P. Dutton, 1941, Stated first edition; oblong 4to., cloth backed pictorial boards, occasional finger soil, else fine in dust jacket (some soil and chips).   Aleph-Bet Books, Inc.   95 - 120   2011 $650

Brown, Margaret Wise *The Steamroller.* New York: Walker and Co., 1974, First edition, first printing (1-10 code); oblong 4to., cloth, fine in dust jacket, illustrations by Evaline Ness, quite hard to find in fine condition.   Aleph-Bet Books, Inc.   95 - 121   2011 $275

Brown, Margaret Wise *Willie's Walk to Grandmama.* New York: William R. Scott, 1944, First edition; 8vo., pictorial boards, near fine in dust jacket with some soil, color lithographs by Lucienne Bloch, rare.   Aleph-Bet Books, Inc.   95 - 122   2011 $850

Brown, Palmer *Hickory.* New York: Harper & Row, 1978, Stated first edition; 8vo., pictorial boards, fine in dust jacket, beautifully illustrated.   Aleph-Bet Books, Inc.   95 - 123   2011 $85

Brown, Paul *Hits and Misses.* New York: Derrydale Press, 1935, Limited to 950 copies, signed, author's copy; 4to., cloth backed color pictorial cloth with staining to edges of cloth, both inside and outside of cover, book clean, pencil drawing with presentation date and full signature on half titlepage by Brown.   Jo Ann Reisler, Ltd.   86 - 29 2011 $1250

Brown, R. J. *English Farmhouses.* London: Robert Hale, 1962, First edition; original cloth, gilt, dust jacket, pages 304 with 174 illustrations.   R. F. G. Hollett & Son Antiquarian Booksellers   177 - 132 2011   £30

Brown, R. P. *Edward Wilson of Nether Levens (1557-1653) and His Kin.* Kendal: Titus Wilson, 1930, Original printed wrappers, pages 104, 7 folding or extending pedigrees.   R. F. G. Hollett & Son Antiquarian Booksellers   173 - 162   2011   £45

Brown, Robert *Letters on the Distressed State of Agriculture, Originally Published in the Edinburgh Courant and Other Newspapers, Under the Signature of "Verus" and Now Reprined with Alterations aand additions.* Edinburgh: printed for the author by David Willison, 1816, First separate edition; 8vo., viii, 72 pages, recently well bound in calf backed marbled boards, spine gilt lettered, uncut, good.   John Drury Rare Books   154 - 32   2011   £250

Brown, Theo *Trojans in the West Country.* St. Peter Port, Guernsey: The Toucan Press, 1970, First edition; small 8vo., original pictorial wrappers, pages 16, map and 4 illustrations.   R. F. G. Hollett & Son Antiquarian Booksellers   175 - 191   2011   £30

Brown, Thomas *An Account of the People Called Shakers: Their Faith, Doctrines and Practice, Exemplified in the Life, Conversations and Experience of the Author During the Time He Belonged to the Society.* Troy: Parker and Bliss, 1812, First edition; 12mo., 372 pages, with one page extract from the Port Folio for Oct. 1812 inserted, full contemporary calf, leather label, rubbed but very good, sheets exceptionally clean.   M & S Rare Books, Inc.   90 - 379   2011 $850

Brown, Thomas *A Manual of Modern Farriery...* London: George Virtue, circa, 1860, 8vo., viii, 920 pages, engraved titlepage, 28 plates, near contemporary half calf, gilt panelled spine, red morocco label, marbled boards, expertly recovered, new endpapers and pastedowns, some slight foxing and blank margin of frontispiece, just little damp-stained, but clear of image.   Ken Spelman Rare Books   68 - 143   2011   £85

Brown, William Wells *A Lecture Delivered Before the Female Anti-Slavery Society of Salem at Lyceum Hall Nov. 14 1847.* Boston: Anti-Slavery Society, 1847, First edition; 16mo., 22 pages, sewn original self wrappers, wrappers soiled, very good.   M & S Rare Books, Inc.   90 - 55   2011 $1750

Browne, Maggie *Pleasant Work for Busy Fingers; or Kindergarten at Home.* London: Cassell & Co., 1896, Half title, illustrations, 4 pages ads, paper browned, original salmon pictorial cloth, little rubbed, slight wear to head of spine.   Jarndyce Antiquarian Booksellers   CXCI - 94   2011   £35

Browne, Maggie *Wanted - a King...* London: Cassell & Co., 1890, Fifth thousand; original green cloth, gilt, surface rather marked, pages (ii), 183, 24, top edges gilt, full page and text drawings by Harry Furniss.   R. F. G. Hollett & Son Antiquarian Booksellers   General Catalogue Summer 2010 - 516   2011   £45

Browne, Peter *Things Divine & Supernatural Conceived by Analogy.* 1733, First edition; 554 pages, modern half calf, ex-library with perforated stamp on titlepage.   C. P. Hyland   May 26 2011 - 259/044   2011 $275

Browne, R. W. *A History of Greek Classical Literature.* London: Richard Bentley, 1853, New edition; full morocco gilt prize binding, arms of King's College, London on upper board, spine and edges little rubbed, pages xii,3 74, all edges gilt, prize label (Dasent Prize awarded to George Austen in 1859).   R. F. G. Hollett & Son Antiquarian Booksellers   General Catalogue Summer 2010 - 374   2011   £85

Browne, R. W. *A History of Roman Classical Literature.* London: Richard Bentley, n.d., 1853, First edition; full morocco gilt prize binding with arms of King's College London on upper board, spine and edges little rubbed, pages xx, 592, all edges gilt, prize label on pastedown (Dasent Prize awarded to George Austen in 1859).   R. F. G. Hollett & Son Antiquarian Booksellers   General Catalogue Summer 2010 - 375   2011   £85

Browne, Thomas   1605-1682   *Pseudodoxia Epidemica: of Unicornes Hornes.* East Hamtpon: Cheloniidae Press, 1984, Limited to 225 copies, signed, with extra, numbered set of 4 plates in pocket inside rear cover; 8vo., gold decorated vellum bound white boards, as new copy, prospectus for the original publication laid into the book, 16 wood engravings by Alan Robinson.   Jo Ann Reisler, Ltd.   86 - 204   2011 $350

Browne, Thomas   1605-1682   *Pseudodoxia Epidemica; of Unicornes Hornes.*   N.P. but Williamsburg: Cheloniidae Press, 1984,   First edition, Artist proof issue, one of 5 copies only; all on obsolete Whatman paper (blue-white laid ca. 1962) from a total issue of 225, all signed by artist, as follows, 5 AP copies (this copy), in elegant full limp vellum non-adhesive binding, title in gilt on spine, frontispiece etching in 2 states, extra suite (14), each signed and numbered, and two extra suites of working proofs (28), each signed and labeled "wp", original drawing, unicorn within an oval border signed in full by Alan J. Robinson, housed in quarter vellum folder with Narwhal 'horn' tooled in gold, gilt on spine, housed in tan cloth over boards with vellum spine stamped with title in gold gilt, with 15 state proof copies, bound in full vellum non-adhesive limp binding with original drawing and an extra suite of prints plus a suite of working proofs of the prints and state proofs of the etching, 60 deluxe copies in vellum binding and extra suite: 150 regular copies on TH Saunders laid, page size 9 1/2 x 7 inches, bound by Gray Parrot with his binder's ticket at lower rear turn-in, full limp vellum, matching quarter vellum sleeve for extra suites all housed in vellum and linen clamshell box, box slightly worn with 2 or 3 minor bumps, book fine; 15 wood engravings and one etching by Robinson, text set and cast in Van Dyck monotype by Winifred and Michael Bixler and printed by Harold Patrick McGrath in black and blue at Hampshire Typothetae, lovely book.   Priscilla Juvelis - Rare Books   48 - 2   2011 $2500

Browne, Thomas Alexander   *Robbery Under Arms.* London: Remington and Co., 1888, First edition; 3 volumes, octavo, (4), 300; (4), 300; (4), 291 (1, blank) pages, original smooth grass green cloth with front covers decoratively stamped in black and spines ruled and lettered in gilt, gray floral patterned endpapers, very slightly skewed, spines very slightly darkened, minor rubbing to corners, few tiny splits to cloth at spine extremities, hinges neatly repaired, free endpapers slightly browned, minimal foxing and soiling, few leaves with tiny black spots (ink splatters?) in upper blank margin; volume I creased, volume III with 84 (page 6/8) creased and tiny paper flaw in upper blank margin of G8 (pages 95/96), overall, excellent copy.   David Brass Rare Books, Inc.   May 26 2011 - 00655   2011 $6500

Brownell, F. R.   *Gunsmith Kinks.* Montezuma: F. Brownell & Son, 1979, Pages viii, 496, illustrations, original cloth, gilt, dust jacket, spine rather browned and worn at head, price clipped.   R. F. G. Hollett & Son Antiquarian Booksellers   General Catalogue Summer 2010 - 1095   2011   £35

Browning, Elizabeth Barrett 1806-1861 *Poems.* London: Chapman & Hall, 1850, Second edition; Barnes's "Second state" with publisher's imprint at foot of titlepage "Chapman & Hall 193 Piccadilly (Late 186 Strand), 2 small octavo, volumes, xii, (1)-362, (2); viii, (1)-480 pages, with half titles in each volume, original publisher's slate blue cloth, covers stamped in blind, spines ruled and lettered in gilt, original pale yellow endpapers, all edges untrimmed, spines lightly sunned, inner hinges of volume I with small crack, rear hinge of volume II professionally repaired, light shelf wear and corners slightly bumped, overall very nice, almost fine set, housed in quarter morocco clamshell. Heritage Book Shop   Holiday 2010 - 13   2011 $11,000

Browning, Elizabeth Barrett 1806-1861 *Two Poems by Elizabeth Barrett and Robert Browning.* London: Chapman & Hall, 1854, First edition; full dark green crushed morocco by Riviere & Son, gilt dentelles, slightly sunned, booklabel and another removed from following pastedown, top edge gilt, very good.   Jarndyce Antiquarian Booksellers   CXCI - 95   2011   £200

Browning, Robert 1812-1889 *Dramatic Idylls. Second Series.* London: Smith, Elder & Co., 1880, First edition; brown cloth with decorative borders, light edgewear, heavier at top and bottom of spine, 1 inch tear along rear joint, some toning, else clean, tight, 147 pages plus ad leaf, very good. G. H. Mott Bookseller   May 26 2011 - 27758   2011 $300

Browning, Robert 1812-1889 *Dramatis Personae.* Doves Press, 1910, One of 250 copies on paper (there were also 15 on vellum); 235 x 170mm., 1 p.l. (2 of them blank), (9)-202 pages, (1) leaf (colophon), original flexible vellum, vertical gilt titling on spine, in sturdy, unworn slipcase, printed in black and red, tail of spine slightly bumped, naturally occurring variations in color of binding, this binding with the pinpoint brown grain predominating), otherwise very fine, text entirely clean, fresh and bright.   Phillip J. Pirages   59 - 177   2011 $550

Browning, Robert 1812-1889 *The Pied Piper of Hamelin.* London: Warne, n.d., First edition thus; original cloth backed pictorial boards, rather scratched, edges very worn, pages 48, illustrations in color, some fingering, two repaired tears, generally very good, illustrations by Kate Greenaway.   R. F. G. Hollett & Sons Antiquarian Booksellers   170 - 293   2011   £85

Browning, Robert 1812-1889 *The Pied Piper of Hamelin.* Harry Quilter, 1898, First edition; small folio, original green decorated cloth gilt, edges little rubbed, 28 leaves interleaved with tissues, printed throughout in fine and intricate detail.   R. F. G. Hollett & Sons Antiquarian Booksellers   170 - 561   2011   £150

Browning, Robert 1812-1889 *The Pied Piper of Hamelin.* London: SPCK, n.d. circa, 1910, First edition; small folio, original cloth backed pictorial boards, edges little worn, pages 47, illustrations in color, trifle loose, very good clean copy, scarce.   R. F. G. Hollett & Sons Antiquarian Booksellers   170 - 705   2011   £150

Browning, Robert 1812-1889 *The Poetical Works.* London: Smith Elder & Co., 1888-1894, First complete edition, one of 250 copies on handmade paper; excellent contemporary purple morocco (stamped Knickerbocker Press on rear turn in), front covers with flourish or gilt monogram (perhaps "G") at center, wide raised bands, spine panels with gilt titling, very broad turn-ins with simple gilt ruling, violet watered silk pastedowns and free endleaves, morocco hinges, edges untrimmed and all but 3 volumes unopened;, 235 x 160mm., 17 volumes, frontispiece and 5 volumes, large paper copy, spines uniformly faded to pleasing chestnut brown, shadow of silk place marker on two pages, otherwise extremely fine set.   Phillip J. Pirages   59 - 156   2011 $3600

Browning, Robert 1812-1889 *The Complete Works of Robert Browning.* New York: Thomas Y. Crowell, 1898, Camberwell edition; 12 volumes, gilt decorated limp red leather, lovely decorated endpapers, top edge gilt, light chipping to extremities of 3 volumes, otherwise about fine, in original cloth covered box with contents displayed on label at top of box, lovely set.   Lupack Rare Books   May 26 2011 - ABE795622079   2011 $250

Browning, Robert 1812-1889 *The Works of Robert Browning.* London: Smith, Elder & Co., 1912, Centenary edition, #273 of 500 copies printed on Antique laid paper, a further 26 were printed on Japanese vellum; half titles, frontispieces, some slight spotting, uniformly bound in original green cloth, attractively decorated and lettered in gilt, spines little dulled, good plus.   Jarndyce Antiquarian Booksellers   CXCI - 2   2011   £420

Brown's South Africa. London: Sampson, Low Marston, 1893, 8vo., 6 colored maps and 2 diagrams, 215 pages plus 87 pages ads, blue cloth, good+.   Barnaby Rudge Booksellers   Travel and Exploration - 019696   2011 $65

Bruce Lockhart, Robert *My Rod My Comfort.* The Flyfisher's Classic Library, 1999, Limited edition, 274 of 500 copies; full grey morocco gilt, slipcase, pages 78, frontispiece, 5 woodcut plates, marbled endpapers, silk marker, fine.   R. F. G. Hollett & Son Antiquarian Booksellers   General Catalogue Summer 2010 - 1221   2011   £50

Bruck, H. A. *The Peripatetic Astronomer: the Life of Charles Piazzi Smyth.* Bristol: Philadelphia: A. Hilger, 1988, 8vo., xii, 274 pages, frontispiece, figures, blue cloth, gilt stamped spine title, dust jacket, fine, from the Bern Dibner reference library, with Burndy bookplate.   Jeff Weber Rare Books   161 - 70   2011 $60

Brunhoff, Jean De 1899-1937 *Babar and His Children.* New York: Random House, 1938, First American edition; small folio, cloth backed color pictorial boards, some edge chipping and wear, especialy along lower edge, full color pictorial dust jacket with chipping along folds and at spine pieces missing along edges on front of jacket, internally clean, lovely copy.   Jo Ann Reisler, Ltd.   86 - 51   2011 $400

Brunhoff, Jean De 1899-1937 *Babar and that Rascal Arthur.* London: Methuen & Co., 1948, First UK edition; folio, original cloth backed pictorial boards, corners and edges little worn and restored, neatly recased, pages 48, illustrations in colors, (some tears mostly fairly short, but one leaf torn across middle), all neatly repaired, few small sellotape stains, mostly in gutters, but nice.   R. F. G. Hollett & Sons Antiquarian Booksellers   170 - 184   2011   £125

Brunhoff, Jean De 1899-1937 *Babar's ABC.* London: Methuen & Co., 1949, Second UK edition; unpaginated, illustrations in color, original cloth backed pictorial boards, few slight scratches.   R. F. G. Hollett & Sons Antiquarian Booksellers   170 - 185   2011   £65

Brunhoff, Jean De 1899-1937 *Babar's Friend Zephir.* London: Methuen & Co., 1937, First UK edition; folio, original cloth backed pictorial boards, edges rather worn and corners bumped and restored, neatly recased, pages 40, illustrations in color, front flyleaf in facsimile, few small tears repaired, few light sellotape marks, very good.   R. F. G. Hollett & Sons Antiquarian Booksellers   170 - 186   2011   £140

Brunhoff, Jean De 1899-1937 *Babar's Travels.* London: Methuen, 1947, Fifth English edition; folio, original cloth backed pictorial boards, rather rubbed and sratches, edges worn, neatly recased, pages 48, illustrations, some short tears repaired, old sellotape stains in places.   R. F. G. Hollett & Sons Antiquarian Booksellers   170 - 187   2011   £120

Brunhoff, Jean De 1899-1937 *The Story of Babar, The Little Elephant.* London: Methuen, 1934, First UK edition; pages 48, illustrations in color, folio, original cloth backed pictorial boards, corners little worn, pages 48, illustrations in colors, few scattered spots and little very light fingering, very good, fresh copy.   R. F. G. Hollett & Sons Antiquarian Booksellers   170 - 188   2011   £220

Brunhoff, Jean De 1899-1937 *The Story of Babar, The Little Elephant.* London: Methuen, 1934, Second edition; original cloth backed pictorial boards, sometime recased by Yuille's Printeries of Trinidad, the upper board restored, blank lower board replaced to match, pages 48, illustrations in colors, fore-edges of flyleaves strengthened, small holes in few other fore-edges, some fingering and creasing.   R. F. G. Hollett & Sons Antiquarian Booksellers   170 - 189   2011   £175

Brunhoff, Jean De 1899-1937 *The Story of Babar, the Little Elephant.* London: Methuen, 1939, Fourth UK edition; folio, original cloth backed pictorial boards, edges and corners little worn, pages 48, illustrations in colors, few scattered marks, but very good.   R. F. G. Hollett & Sons Antiquarian Booksellers   170 - 190   2011   £150

Brunhoff, Jean De 1899-1937 *Les Vacances de Zephir.* Paris: Hachette, 1936, First edition; French text with numerous colour printed illustrations, pages (40), folio, original pale yellow cloth backed boards, illustrated overall, edges of boards lightly rubbed, just little more at corners, very good.   Blackwell Rare Books   B166 - 127   2011   £250

Brunner, A. W. *Cottages or Hints on Economical Building.* New York: William T. Comstock, 1890, Original cloth, gilt, pages 64, 24 lithographed plates.   R. F. G. Hollett & Son Antiquarian Booksellers   177 - 134   2011   £175

Brunner, John *Galactic Storm.* London: printed in Great Britain and Published by Curtis Warren Limited, 1952, First edition; octavo, pictorial wrappers.   L. W. Currey, Inc.   124 - 179   2011 $250

Brunner, John *Stand on Zanzibar.* Garden City: Doubleday & Co., 1968, First edition; octavo, cloth.   L. W. Currey, Inc.   124 - 180   2011 $250

Brunnmark, Gustavus *A Short Introduction to Swedish Grammar...* London: printed for the author by J. Skirven, 1805, First edition; (6), 96 pages, original cloth backed boards, nice.   Anthony W. Laywood   May 26 2011 - 19424   2011 $134

Brunskill, R. W. *English Brickwork.* London: Ward Lock, 1977, First edition; Original cloth, gilt, dust jacket, pages 160 with over 150 illustrations.   R. F. G. Hollett & Son Antiquarian Booksellers   177 - 140   2011   £30

Brunskill, R. W. *Illustrated Handbook of Vernacular Architecture.* London: Faber, 1978, First softback edition; pages 249, original wrappers, illustrations.   R. F. G. Hollett & Son Antiquarian Booksellers   177 - 135   2011   £30

Brunskill, R. W. *Traditional Farm Buildings of Britain.* London: Gollancz, 1982, First edition; large 8vo., original cloth, gilt, dust jacket, pages 160, 111 plates.   R. F. G. Hollett & Son Antiquarian Booksellers   177 - 136   2011   £45

Brunskill, R. W. *Vernacular Architecture of the Lake Counties.* London: Faber, 1974, First edition; original cloth, gilt, dust jacket, pages 164, illustrations, scarce.   R. F. G. Hollett & Son Antiquarian Booksellers   173 - 164   2011   £75

Brunskill, R. W. *Vernacular Architecture of Lake Counties.* London: Faber, 1978, First softback edition; 164 pages, illustrations, original pictorial wrappers, one corner little creased, scarce.   R. F. G. Hollett & Son Antiquarian Booksellers   173 - 165 2011   £35

Bry, Gilles *Historie des Pays et Comte du Perche et Duche d'Alencon etc.* Paris: Pierre Le Mur, 1620, First edition; 4to., (16), 382, (14) pages, title printed in red and black, 18th century English calf, gilt fillets on covers, gilt spine, very handsome copy, from the library of the Earls of Macclesfield at Shirburn Castle.   Maggs Bros. Ltd.   1440 - 43 2011   £650

Bryan, Michael *A Dictionary of Painters and Engravers, Biographical and Critical.*   London: George Bell and Sons, 1886, New edition; 2 volumes, large 8vo., contemporary half morocco, gilt, pages vii, 755; 779; with 5 pages of monograms, handsome, sound set.   R. F. G. Hollett & Son Antiquarian Booksellers   General Catalogue Summer 2010 - 69 2011   £140

Bryant, Jacob *A New System, or an Analysis of Ancient Mythology: Wherein an Attempt is Made to Divest Tradition of Fable.*   London: printed for P. Elmsly, 1774, 1774. 1776; 3 volumes, 4to., pages (iii)-xx (ii) 516 + 8 engraved plates, vii, (i), 537, (i) + 18 engraved plates; (iii)-viii, 601, (i) + 3 engraved maps, 4 engravings included within letterpress, contemporary sprinkled tan calf, spines panel gilt with lozenge and wheel centered compartments alternating, red lettering and numbering pieces, gilt board edges 'milled' decorative roll gilt, pink sewn endbands, spotted and bit toned, plates offset, rubbed, joints worn and splitting, front board of volume 1 lost, armorial bookplate "Eardley" from the collection of Christopher Ernest Weston 1947-2010.   Unsworths Booksellers   24 - 73 2011   £360

Bryant, Jacob *Observations and Inquiries Relating to Various Parts of Ancient History...* Cambridge: printed by J. Archdeacon, printer to the University, 1767, Mixed issue, page 7 has the press figure '2' but page 62 has no press figure and page 63 has '3', errata leaf comes at beginning; 4to., pages (ii) iiii, (v), 324, 7 engraved extending plates, contemporary tan calf, spine panel gilt, red lettering piece gilt, boards double rule gilt bordered, board edges 'zig zag' decorative roll in blind, all edges densely red sprinkled, pink and white sewn endbands, (gathering *1 - 4 leaves of prelims) not bound in this copy (apparently not infrequent error), light toning and spotting, closed tear to one leaf, through but not affecting text, small wormtrack in lower corner at beginning, rubbed at extremities, joints cracked, little loss from headcap, armorial bookplate of "Dacre", from the collection of Christopher Ernest Weston 1947-2010.   Unsworths Booksellers   24 - 72 2011   £300

Bryant, Jacob *Observations and Inquiries Relating to Various Parts of Ancient History...* printed by J. Archdeacon sold by T. and J. Merrill and T. Payne, Cambridge, 1767, First edition; 4to., pages iii, (12), 324, errata leaf, 6 folding engraved maps, 1 engraved plate, maps, full leather tree calf lettered gilt at spine, spine rubbed and front board detached, text and plates very clean, very good.   Any Amount of Books   May 29 2011 - B20293 2011 $408

Bryant, William Cullen   1794-1878 *Picturesque America; or the Land We Live In.* New York: 1872, 2 volumes in 6 books, 568 pages, illustrations, 576 pages, illustrations, with 49 full page steel engraved plates and over 900 wood engravings in all, original publisher's cloth in virtually flawless condition, tops and bottoms of some volumes show slight wear and few plates have offset onto tissue guards, no foxing, bindings tight and gilt titles bright.   Dumont Maps & Books of the West   113 - 28 2011 $1200

Bryant, William Cullen   1794-1878 *Poems.* Cambridge: Hilliard and Metcalf, 1821, First edition; 16mo., 44 pages, original printed boards, neatly rebacked, uncut, the Estelle Doheny copy, housed in morocco backed two part slipcase.   M & S Rare Books, Inc.   90 - 57 2011 $1500

Bryden, Henry Anderson *Gun and Camera in Southern Africa: a Year of Wanderings in Bechuanaland, the Kalahari Desert and the Lake River Country, Ngamiland.*   London: Edward Stanford, 1893, First edition; 8vo., pages xiv, 544, folding map, illustrations, original beige decorative cloth, cockling to upper cover.   J. & S. L. Bonham Antiquarian Booksellers   Africa 4/20/2011 - 9016 2011   £125

Brydson, A. P. *Sidelights on Mediaeval Windermere.* Kendal: Titus Wilson, 1946, First edition; Later green cloth gilt, pages viii, 139, frontispiece.   R. F. G. Hollett & Son Antiquarian Booksellers   173 - 166 2011   £45

Bryson, Bill *The Lost Continent.* London: Secker & Warburg, 1989, First British edition; near fine, light browning to leaves, dust jacket near fine, price partially clipped, pound sign intact.   Bella Luna Books   May 29 2011 - t9550 2011 $82

Bryson, Bill *A Walk in the Woods.* London: Doubleday, 1997, First British edition; near fine, very minor creasing to heel of spine, fine dust jacket.   Bella Luna Books   May 29 2011 - t5938 2011 $82

Buchan, John   1875-1940 *The Long Traverse.* London: Hodder and Stoughton, 1941, First edition; pages 254, (i), 5 plates, original blue cloth, spine patchily stained white, dust jacket worn and chipped,.   R. F. G. Hollett & Sons Antiquarian Booksellers   170 - 115 2011   £45

Buchan, William 1729-1805 *Advice to Mothers on the Subject of Their Own Health and of the Means of Promoting the Health, Strength and Beauty of Their Offspring.* Boston: printed for Joseph Bumstead, 1809, Second American edition; 8vo., (507)-536, 33-64, 569-600, 972-112, 617-629, (3) pages, removed, some foxing, two signatures heavily browned.   M & S Rare Books, Inc.   90 - 58   2011 $425

Buchan, William Paton *Plumbing. A Text-Book to the Practice of the Art of Craft of the Plumber.* Crosby, Lockwood and Co., 1883, Fourth edition; xii, 307 (1) 16 + 30 pages ads, 8vo., very good in original blindstamped and gilt lettered olive green cloth, original paper spine label, back board rather marked by old damp.   Ken Spelman Rare Books   68 - 83   2011   £35

Buchanan, George *Paraphrasis Psalmorum Davidis Poetica Multo Quam Antehac Castigatior.* Antwerp: Christopher Plantin, 1571, First edition thus; 16mo., pages 373, (3), woodcut vignette on titlepage, Italian Latin text, sound copy in full cream vellum now soiled and slightly creased, fore edge and lower edge gilt, small date stamp (1907) at foot of titlepage, older neat initials, light wear, clean text with couple of chips to corners of pages not affecting text or catchwords, near very good.   Any Amount of Books   May 26 2011 - A44442   2011 $545

Buchanan, Joseph *The Philosophy of Human Nature.* Richmond: John A. Grimes, 1812, First edition; 8vo., (7), 336 pages, old plain boards, crudely rebacked, old label laid down, below is handwritten title, minor repair to inner corner of title, some foxing but very good.   M & S Rare Books, Inc.   90 - 59   2011 $950

Buchanan, Joseph *The Philosophy of Human Nature.* Richmond: John A. Grimes, 1812, First edition; 8vo., (7), 336 pages, contemporary calf, leather label, covers worn and front cover detached, many copies erratically printed, wide variations in inking of type, this copy very adequately inked.   M & S Rare Books, Inc.   90 - 60   2011 $750

Buchanan, Robert Williams *Ballads of Life, Love and Humour.* London: Chatto & Windus, 1882, First edition; half title, frontispiece, initial ad leaf, 4 pages ads + 32 page catalog (Feb. 1882), original royal blue cloth, spine slightly faded with very small repair to leading hinge, armorial bookplate.   Jarndyce Antiquarian Booksellers   CXCI - 96   2011   £35

Buchner, Alexander *Mechanical Musical Instruments.* Batchworth Press, n.d. circa, 1959, First edition; large 4to., original black cloth, gilt, dust jacket pages 110, 67 text illustrations, plus 174 plates.   R. F. G. Hollett & Son Antiquarian Booksellers   175 - 196   2011   £65

Buck, Charles *The Close of the Eighteenth Century Improved: a Sermon, Preached at Prince's Street Chapel, Finsbury Square, December 28, 1800...* London: printed by Knight and Compton for the author, 1801?, First edition; 8vo., 48 pages, preserved in modern wrappers, printed title label on upper cover, very good, very rare.   John Drury Rare Books   153 - 23   2011   £125

Bucke, Charles *On the Beauties, Harmonies and Sublimities of Nature.* London: Thomas Tegg & Son, 1837, New edition; 3 volumes, half titles, 8 page catalog (1846) in volume I, volume III lacking leading f.e.p., original red vertical grained cloth by Westley's & Clark, blocked in blind, spines faded, some slight wear to head and tail, booklabels of Charles Ogden, bookseller's ticket of H. Whitmore, Manchester.   Jarndyce Antiquarian Booksellers   CXCI - 329   2011   £110

Bucke, Richard Maurice *Walt Whitman.* Philadelphia: David McKay, 1883, First edition, printing 1, binding A; 8vo., original terra cotta cloth, gilt lettering, frontispiece, cloth little worn and dust soiled, very good, ink stamp of Syracuse Public Library on titlepage, from the collection of Samuel Charters.   The Brick Row Book Shop   Bulletin 8 - 28   2011 $300

Buckland, C. E. *Bengal Under the Lieutenant-Governors: Being a Narrative of the Principal Event and Public Measures During Their Periods of Office from 1854-1898.* Calcutta: Kedarnath Bose, 1902, Second edition; 2 volumes, 8vo., original green cloth lettered gilt at spine, pages xxix, 1130, with 14 plates, volume 2 has slight lean at spine, neat greeting signature at head of titlepage, else very good+, clean set.   Any Amount of Books   May 29 2011 - A47403   2011 $204

Buckle, Henry Thomas *Miscellaneous and Posthumous Works of Henry Thomas Buckle.* London: Longmans, Green and Co., 1872, First edition thus; 3 volumes, 8vo., soundly rebound in light blue buckram lettered gilt on spine, pages lix, 598 & 704 & 708 with 24 page publisher's cataloge at rear, bookplate of Henry Channon (i.e. Chips Channon), very good.   Any Amount of Books   May 29 2011 - A75900   2011 $340

Buckley, James M. *The Wrong and Peril of Woman Suffrage.* New York: Fleming, 1909, First edition; 8vo., 128 pages, original cloth, some underlining in red ink on dozen pages and few ink corrections in margin, lacking some of title stamping on spine, very good, tight copy.   Second Life Books Inc.   174 - 75   2011 $125

Budden, Lionel R. *The Book of the Liverpool School of Architecture.* Liverpool: Liverpool University Press, 1932, Limited edition, no. 218 of 1000 copies; 4to., original cloth, gilt, upper board lightly dampstained, neatly recased, pages 68 frontispiece and 148 plates, some foxing to prelims.   R. F. G. Hollett & Son Antiquarian Booksellers   177 - 143   2011   £95

Budden, Maria Elizabeth Halsey *Always Happy!!! Or, Anecdotes of Felix and His Sister Serena.* London: John Harris, n.d. circa, 1825, Seventh edition; 12mo., vii, 170, 2 pages, original marbled paper on boards, red roan spine with gilt fillets and title, full page copper engraved frontispiece, chipped crown of spine and edges of covers rubbed and rounded, repaired upper corner of front flyleaf, light foxing, short tears at fore-edge of three leaves repaired with no loss of text, one signature lightly sprung, small label of Juvenile Library, Dublin, inside upper cover, despite all defects, scarce, still in very good state.   Hobbyhorse Books   56 - 14   2011 $175

Bude, Guillaume *De Asse et Partibvs Eivs Libri V.* Lvgdvni: Apvd Seb. Gryphivm, 1550, 185 x 120mm., 815, (79) pages, (1) leaf (with errors in pagination), fine contemporary ivory blindstamped pigskin over wooden boards, covers with frames formed by multiple blind rules and foliate roll featuring laurel-wreathed heads in medallions, upper cover with central panel stamp showing Justice with her sword and scales, the letters "C A N" stamped on panel above Justice and date "1566" on panel below, lower cover with central panel stamp depicting virtuous Roman matron Lucretia in act of suicide, raised bands, two fore-edge clasps and front free endpaper missing; printer's device on title, intermittent (presumably early) underlining in brown pencil, front pastedown with modern bookplate showing a ship above mott "Novus Orbis", titlepage with early ink ownership inscriptions and library stamp of Tomaso Luciani of Albona; tip of lower corner of front cover chipped off, adjacent half inch of pigskin missing along tail edge, covers bit smudged, other minor external defects binding very sturdy and still extremely attractive deeply impressed stamps retaining much of their detail and all of their charm, and front cover still rather clean, leaves bit toned with age, occasional minor stains, text quite smooth, few signs of use.   Phillip J. Pirages   59 - 8   2011 $950

Budge, Ernest Alfred Wallis Thompson   1857-1934 *The Dwellers on the Nile.* London: Religious Tract Society, 1891, Third edition; original pictorial brown cloth, gilt, pages 206, (ii), with 22 illustrations.   R. F. G. Hollett & Son Antiquarian Booksellers   177 - 144   2011   £40

Budge, Ernest Alfred Wallis Thompson   1857-1934 *The Egyptian Sudan: Its History and Monuments.* London: Kegan Paul, 1907, First edition; 2 volumes, large 8vo., pages xxviii, 652; x, 618, 66 plates and plans, numerous illustrations, original red decorative cloth, gilt vignette on upper covers, spines little faded.   J. & S. L. Bonham Antiquarian Booksellers   Africa 4/20/2011 - 5757   2011   £320

Budge, Ernest Alfred Wallis Thompson   1857-1934 *From Fetish to God in Ancient Egypt.* Oxford: University Press, 1934, First edition; large thick 8vo., original cloth, gilt, dust jacket, price clipped, pages xii, 45, with 240 illustrations.   R. F. G. Hollett & Son Antiquarian Booksellers   175 - 198   2011   £180

Budge, J. *The Practical Miner's Guide...* London: Longmans, Green and Co., 1866, New edition; original blindstamped cloth, gilt, damped patch on upper board, ink stain on lower board neatly recased, pages xiii, 218, (ii), numerous tables and mine drawings in text.   R. F. G. Hollett & Son Antiquarian Booksellers   General Catalogue Summer 2010 - 1096   2011   £150

Budworth, Joseph *A Fortnight's Ramble to the Lakes in Westmoreland, Lancashire and Cumberland.* printed for J. Nichols, Red Lion Passage, Fleet Street, 1795, Second edition; xxxii, 292 pages, frontispiece, 8vo., slight foxing to frontispiece, recent ownership name on recto, otherwise very good, clean copy, excellently rebound in half sprinkled calf, double gilt ruled spine, red gilt morocco label, marbled boards, fresh contemporary endpapers, with rare frontispiece.   Jarndyce Antiquarian Booksellers   CXCI - 538   2011   £1100

Budworth, Joseph *Windermere, a Poem.* London: T. Cadell, Jun. and W. Davies, 1798, First edition; 8vo., (4), 28 pages, including half title, little very light foxing, preserved in modern wrappers with printed title label on upper cover, very good, very scarce.   John Drury Rare Books   153 - 24   2011   £275

Buffalo Bill's Wild West and Congress of Rough Riders of the World. London: Parthington, n.d., 1903, 4to., chromolithographed pictorial wrappers, little spotting and edge wear to covers, stapled, rusting and wear to backstrip at staples, commercial ads at front and rear, 60 portraits, plates and illustrations, most halftone, complete with insert events flyer.   Dramatis Personae Booksellers   106 - 34   2011 $275

Builders' Supply Company *Modern Building Materials.* Southport: The Company, late 1930's, 4to., original loose leaf folder of cloth backed boards, worn, unpaginated, numerous illustrated sheets.   R. F. G. Hollett & Son Antiquarian Booksellers   177 - 857   2011   £35

Bulfinch, Thomas *Legends of Charlemagne.* New York: Cosmopolitan Book, 1924, First Wyeth edition, 2nd issue with top edge plain; 4to., maroon cloth, pictorial paste-on, top edge gilt, very fine in dust jacket, cover plate, pictorial endpapers and titlepage plus 8 really beautiful color plates, beautiful copy.   Aleph-Bet Books, Inc.   95 - 597   2011 $875

Bullen, A. H. *Lyrics from the Song Books of the Elizabethan Age.* London: Lawrence & Bullen, 1897, First edition; Original decorated cloth, gilt extra, spine little dulled, pages xxxiii, 233, top edge gilt, endpapers lightly spotted.   R. F. G. Hollett & Son Antiquarian Booksellers   175 - 199   2011   £45

Bulloch, John *George Jamesone The Scottish Vandyck.* Edinburgh: David Douglas, 1885, First edition; number 187 of 250 copies initialled by John Bulloch, 8vo., original publisher's green cloth lettered gilt on spine and on front cover, pages 201, uncut, frontispiece, slight marks to cover, slight soiling, else decent, very good.   Any Amount of Books   May 29 2011 - A61722 2011 $255

Bullock, Charles *The Mashona; the Indigenous Natives of S. Rhodesia.* Cape Town: Juta, 1927, First edition; 8vo., pages vi, 400, original red cloth, neatly recased, new endpapers.   J. & S. L. Bonham Antiquarian Booksellers   Africa 4/20/2011 - 5619 2011   £40

Bulmer, George Bertram *Architectural Studies in Yorkshire.* McCorquodale & Co. Ltd., 1887, Limited Jubilee edition (300 copies); small folio, original cloth, gilt, spine little worn at head and foot, some torn chips and wear to fore-edge of upper board, pages ix, xx (iii, subscribers) with tinted map and 20 tinted plates, little shaken, edge of one leaf dusty.   R. F. G. Hollett & Son Antiquarian Booksellers   177 - 147 2011   £85

Bulmer, T., & Co. *History Topography and Directory of East Cumberland.* Manchester: T. Bulmer & Co., 1884, Second edition; old binder's cloth gilt, spine lettering faded, pages 700, xvi, (ii).   R. F. G. Hollett & Son Antiquarian Booksellers   173 - 173 2011   £65

Bulmer, T., & Co. *History Topography and Directory of Furness & Carmel...* Preston: T. Snape, n.d., Second edition; original half red calf gilt, pages (viii) 423, vi, folding pedigree, large folding map loosely inserted.   R. F. G. Hollett & Son Antiquarian Booksellers   173 - 170 2011   £120

Bulmer, T., & Co. *History Topography and Directory of Westmoreland.* Manchester: T. Bulmer & Co., 1885, First edition; modern green cloth gilt pages ii (ad leaf, outer margin repaired), 692, xiii, includes final unpaginated decorative ad leaf for James Douglas, Kendal grocer, which is often lacking.   R. F. G. Hollett & Son Antiquarian Booksellers   173 - 174 2011   £140

Bulow, Ernie *Navajo Taboos.* Gallup: Buffalo Medicine Books, 1991, One of 5 artists proofs signed by Tony Hillerman; full leather, fine, with framed original water color by Franklin.   Bella Luna Books   May 26 2011 - t4196 2011 $495

Bulow, Ernie *Words Weather and Wolfmen.* Gallup: 1989, Limited to 350 copies; xii, 124 pages, (x), illustrations, near fine in like dust jacket, signe by Bulow, Tony Hillerman and Ernest Franklin.   Dumont Maps & Books of the West   113 - 34 2011 $300

Bulwer, John *Chirologia; or the Naturall Language of the Hand.* London: printed by Tho. Harper, 1644, First edition; small 8vo., 2 parts in one volume, (28), 187 (2, 1 blank), (16), 146, (1 errata, 1 blank) pages, 2 engraved additional titlepages, 6 engravings, errata leaf, E^3 supplied in fine facsimile, occasional contemporary pen markings and marginalia, original full gilt ruled calf, green paper ms. spine label, joints rubbed, corners bumped, very good.   Jeff Weber Rare Books   163 - 14 2011 $2300

Bunbury, Henry *Narratives of Some Passages in the Great War with France from 1799 to 1810.* London: Richard Bentley, 1854, First edition; 8vo., sound modern red buckram lettered gilt at spine, pages xxiv, 471, 4 maps, ex-Foreign and Commonwealth Office library with their label and stamps (lightly applied), very good.   Any Amount of Books   May 29 2011 - A47574 2011 $213

Bungener, L. F. *History of the Council of Trent.* Edinburgh: Thomas Constable & Co., 1852, Original cloth gilt, upper board little damped, pages vii, 552, joints just cracking.   R. F. G. Hollett & Son Antiquarian Booksellers   175 - 200 2011   £60

Bunting, Banbridge *Early Architecture in New Mexico.* Albuquerque: 1978, First edition; (x), 122 pages, illustrations, dust jacket shows some soil and rubbing, previous owners' bookplates on front pastedown and endpaper, else clean and very good.   Dumont Maps & Books of the West   112 - 34 2011 $95

Bunyan, John 1628-1688 *A Book for Boys and Girls.* London: Elliot Stock, 1889, Large paper copy; large square 8vo., later quarter levant morocco gilt by Stoakley of Cambridge (but unsigned), pages xxvi, 79, top edge gilt, untrimmed, handsome.   R. F. G. Hollett & Sons Antiquarian Booksellers   170 - 117 2011   £120

Bunyan, John 1628-1688 *Bunyan's Grace Abounding to the Chief of Sinners; Heart's Ease in Heart Trouble: the World to Come or Vision of Heaven and Hell...* Philadelphia: J. Woodward Stereotyped by L. Johnson, 1828, 12mo., x, 409 pages, full speckled leather on boards, black label with gilt title, elaborate gilt decoration on spine, speckled edges, very fine copper engraved full page frontispiece, light rubbing at edges and corners, crown of spine chipped, light browning at edges of endpapers, very good.   Hobbyhorse Books   56 - 15 2011 $120

Bunyan, John 1628-1688 *The Pilgrim's Progress from this World to that which is to Come.* London: printed for Nathanael Ponder, 1682, Eighth edition; 12mo., early 19th century blind tooled sheep.   Heritage Book Shop   Booth A12 51st NY International Antiquarian Book Fair April 8-10 2011 - 19 2011 $40,000

Bunyan, John 1628-1688 *The Pilgrim's Progress.* London: Fisher, Son & Co., 1842, Sixth edition; initial ad leaf, half title, frontispiece, additional engraved title, plates and illustrations, final ad leaf, original full maroon pebble grained calf, borders in blind, corner & central gilt floral decoration with additional floral designs in blind, spine lettered gilt at head, decorated gilt border, lower spine decorated in blind, contemporary gift inscription, dated April 1842, all edges gilt, very good.   Jarndyce Antiquarian Booksellers CXCI - 436 2011   £75

Bunyan, John 1628-1688 *Bunyan's Pilgrim's Progress.* New Haven: E. Barber, n.d. circa, 1855, 12mo., 5 leaves, pictorial title cover with wood engraved vignette, superb full page wood engraving, each panel features two half sheet flaps with additional verse, flap panels folded at top and bottom of main pages and when lifted, form other images in combination with image beneath, for a total of 15 tableaux, very rare, mint state, engravings by John Warner Barber.   Hobbyhorse Books   56 - 106 2011 $1200

Bunyan, John 1628-1688 *The Pilgrim's Progress.* London: Henry G. Bohn, 1856, Eleventh edition; 205 x 145mm., xxxvi, 476 pages, pleasing early 20th century marbled calf by Bayntun, covers framed by an elegant scrolling roll featuring artichokes and strawberry leaves, raised bands, compartments at head and tail of spine filled by three different and pleasing gilt rolls, two compartments with scrolling floral cornerpieces, one dark blue and one green morocco label, turn-ins densely gilt in botanical pattern, marbled endpapers, all edges gilt, in slightly soiled tan linen slipcase; historiated initials, 6 illustrations in text, 17 charming plates by Thomas Stothard, as called for, ours most pleasing colored by a contemporary hand; bit of wear to joints, minor crackling and dulling to spine, isolated foxing, excellent copy, very clean and fresh internally with pretty colored plates, attractive decorative binding that is solid and without any significant defect.   Phillip J. Pirages 59 - 88 2011 $850

Bunyan, John 1628-1688 *The Pilgrim's Progress from this World to that Which is to Come.* New York: Century Co., 1898, very good+, some modest shelfwear to extremities, tight book, nice, clean text and plates, attractive old memorial library bookplate and few unobtrusive blindstamps, very good+.   Lupack Rare Books   May 26 2011 - ABE796733676 2011 $125

Bunyan, John 1628-1688 *The Pilgrim's Progress from this World to that Which is to Come...* London: Faber, 1947, First edition; original cloth, gilt, dust jacket, head of spine chipped, other extremities trifle frayed, prize clipped, pages 320, illustrations by Edward Ardizzone.   R. F. G. Hollett & Son Antiquarian Booksellers   175 - 45 2011   £50

Bunyan, John 1628-1688 *Works. The Pilgrims Progress. The Holy War, A Life of Bunyan by Rev. William Brock.* London: Cassell, Petter and Galpin, n.d., Thick 4to., old half straight grained roan gilt, little scuffed, upper hinge cracking at head, pages xliii, xvi, viii, 400, liii, 364, woodcut illustrations and borders, scattered spotting.   R. F. G. Hollett & Son Antiquarian Booksellers   175 - 202 2011   £45

Bunyan, John 1628-1688 *The Select Works.* London: William Collins Sons & Co., 1869, Thick 4to., publisher's binding of full brown blindstamped and gilt morocco over heavy bevelled boards, each board with four sunken gilt pictorial roundels, pages lxiv, 775, all edges gilt, steel engraved frontispiece, 20 tinted chromolithograph plates and 100 woodcut plates, front flyleaf removed, otherwise excellent copy of a deluxe issue.   R. F. G. Hollett & Son Antiquarian Booksellers   175 - 201 2011   £175

Bunyard, Edward *Old Garden Roses.* London: Country Life, 1936, First edition; small 4to., original cloth, gilt, pages xvi, 163, color frontispiece and 32 plates, scarce.   R. F. G. Hollett & Son Antiquarian Booksellers   General Catalogue Summer 2010 - 955 2011   £35

Buonarroti, Filippo Michele 1761-1837 *Buonarroti's History of Babeuf's Conspiracy for Equality....* London: H. Hetherington, 1836, First edition in English; small 8vo., xxiv, iv, (5), 454 pages (errata), ex-library, rebound with code to spine, library bookplate to front pastedown, usual stamps and marks to interior, cloth little soiled and marked, else sound, near frontispiece with clean text.   Any Amount of Books   May 29 2011 - A61814 2011 $272

Burbank, Luther *Luther Burbank. His Methods and Discoveries and Their Practical Application.* New York and London: Luther Burbank Press, 1914-1915, First edition; 8vo., 12 volumes, 1260 color photo prints, original red cloth, oval photo of Burbank inset on front cover, little staining on two volumes, slight waterstaining in one volume, top of one volume lightly gnawed, very good.   M & S Rare Books, Inc. 90 - 61 2011 $600

Burch, R. M. *Colour Printing and Colour Printers.* Edinburgh: Paul Harris Pub., 1983, Second edition; original cloth, gilt, dust jacket, pages xxii, 281, with 8 illustrations.   R. F. G. Hollett & Son Antiquarian Booksellers   General Catalogue Summer 2010 - 70 2011   £35

Burckhart, John Lewis *Arabic Proverbs or the Manners and Customs of the Modern Egyptians.* London: Bernard Quaritch, 1875, Second edition; pages vii, 283, title little browned, faint library accession stamp on verso and small stamp on front pastedown, original cloth gilt, spine trifle chipped top and base, scarce.   R. F. G. Hollett & Son Antiquarian Booksellers   175 - 203 2011   £225

Burdick, Loraine *The Shirley Temple Scrapbook.* Norwalk: Easton Press, 2002, Easton Press leather bound, signed by Shirley Temple, leather with gold titles and decorations, all edges gilt, silk endpapers and ribbon bookmark, signed certificate of authenticity folded in, bookplate included but not affixed, very clean and tight, 312 pages, fine. G. H. Mott Bookseller May 26 2011 - 37035 2011 $350

Burger, John F. *Contributions to the Knowledge of Diptera.* Gainesville: Associated Publishers, 1999, 8vo., green cloth, gilt titles and fly vignette on front, pages viii, 648, photo illustrations, tables, charts, photo on dedication page, fine, inscribed to previous owners by Elva Fairchild (Sandy's wife). Schooner Books Ltd. 96 - 121 2011 $95

Burges, Tristan *Liberty, Glory and Union or American Independence. An Oration.* Providence: printed at the Office of the Rhode Island American, 1810, First edition; 8vo., 22 pages, removed. M & S Rare Books, Inc. 90 - 362 2011 $150

Burgess, Anthony *The Eve of Saint Venus.* London: Sidgwick & Jackson, 1964, First British edition, true first; near fine, spine ends bumped, dust jacket fine, inscribed to Dwye by author. Bella Luna Books May 26 2011 - t3569 2011 $1045

Burgess, Anthony *Termor of Intent.* London: Heinemann, 1966, First edition; 8vo., pages (viii), 240, signed presentation from author, fine in very good+ complete dust jacket with faint edgewear, very slight marks to rear panel. Any Amount of Books May 29 2011 - A75304 2011 $213

Burgess, Gelett Frank 1866-1951 *Blue Goops and Red Blue.* New York: Stokes, Oct., 1909, First edition; 4to., green pictorial cloth, 81 pages, slightest of cover soil, else near fine, with movable flap, when flap is turned the (good) red Goop illustration is revealed, with short story for each illustration and situation (pictorial endpapers as well). Aleph-Bet Books, Inc. 95 - 126 2011 $875

Burgess, George *Reflections on the Nature and Tendency of the Present Spirit of the Times, in a Letter to the Freeholders of the County of Norfolk. (bound with) Reflections on the Nature and Tendency of the Present Spirit of the Times.* Norwich: printed and sold by Burks and Kinnebrook, 1819, Second edition and first edition respectively; 8vo., iv, 362, (2) pages, including final errata leaf; 8vo., viii, 341, (1) pages, errata on verso of final leaf, minor foxing and paper browning, else very good, from the library of Bryan William James Hall (of Bonningham) with his armorial bookplate. John Drury Rare Books 153 - 25 2011 £325

Burgess, H. W. *Studies of Trees.* J. Dickinson, 1837, Oblong folio, titlepage, dedication leaf and 12 lithograph plates, good copy, original dark green cloth with printed paper label on upper cover, some browning to plates and slight wear to covers. Ken Spelman Rare Books 68 - 32 2011 £220

Burgess, John *Bishop of the Lake Counties.* Carlisle: privately published by author, 1985, Printed in limited edition; Volume I 1860-1864, 4to., original blue wrappers gilt lettered, pages 177, pages of plates, map, family tree. R. F. G. Hollett & Son Antiquarian Booksellers General Catalogue Summer 2010 - 378 2011 £75

Burgess, John *Bishop of the Lake Counties. Letters of Samuel Waldegrave 1860-1869.* Carlisle: privately published by author, 1985-1987, 4 volumes, 4to., original wrappers, gilt lettered by hand, pages 177; 179; 180-462; 446 with numerous photocopied plates, map and family tree, printed on recto early throughout, author's own unique set with his original annotated color photos in volume 3. R. F. G. Hollett & Son Antiquarian Booksellers 175 - 206 2011 £350

Burgess, John *Carlisle Cathedral.* Carlisle: privately published by the author, 1988, 4to., original cloth backed acetate wrappers, pages 18 (20, photo copied plates) all printed on rectos, text cyclostyled. R. F. G. Hollett & Son Antiquarian Booksellers 173 - 177 2011 £35

Burgess, John *The Castles of Cumbria.* Carlisle: privately published by author, n.d. circa, 1985, Volume I: Carlisle and North Cumbria, original cloth backed acetate wrappers, pages 19, (15 photocopies plates) all printed on rectos, text cyclostyled. R. F. G. Hollett & Son Antiquarian Booksellers 173 - 178 2011 £40

Burgess, John *The Country Houses of North West England.* Carlisle: privately published by author, 1989, original cloth backed acetate wrappers, pages 62, (23 photocopied plates) all printed on rectos, text cyclostyled. R. F. G. Hollett & Son Antiquarian Booksellers 173 - 179 2011 £75

Burgess, John *Cumbrian Castles.* Carlisle: privately published by author, 1988, original cloth backed acetate wrappers, pages 37, (17 photocopied plates) all printed on rectos, text cyclostyled. R. F. G. Hollett & Son Antiquarian Booksellers 173 - 180 2011 £50

Burgess, John *Cumbrian Churches: the Architectural Heritage of Cumbrian Palces of Worship.* Carlisle: privately published by author, 1988, Oblong folio, original cloth backed acetate wrappers, pages 97, printed 2 pages to the sheet, (ii), (57, plates), all printed on rectos, text cyclostyled in double columns. R. F. G. Hollett & Son Antiquarian Booksellers General Catalogue Summer 2010 - 1347 2011 £120

Burgess, John *The Georgian Heritage of North West England.* Carlisle: privately published by author, 1989, 4to., original cloth backed acetate wrappers, pages 78, (17 photocopied plates) all printed on rectos, text cyclostyled. R. F. G. Hollett & Son Antiquarian Booksellers 173 - 182 2011 £50

Burgess, John *The Heritage of North West England in the Seventeenth Century.* Carlisle: privately printed by author, 1990, 4to., original cloth backed acetate wrappers, pages 18, (50 photocopied plates) all printed on rectos, text cyclostyled. R. F. G. Hollett & Son Antiquarian Booksellers 173 - 183 2011 £65

Burgess, John *The Historic Ports of North West England.* Carlisle: privately published by author, 1989, 4to., original cloth backed acetate wrappers, pages 62, (7 photocopied plates) all printed on rectos, text cyclostyled. R. F. G. Hollett & Son Antiquarian Booksellers 173 - 184 2011 £75

Burgess, John *The Historic Towns of Cumbria.* Carlisle: privately published by author, n.d. circa, 1988, 4to., original cloth backed acetate wrappers, pages 102, (7 photocopied plates) all printed on rectos, text cyclostyled. R. F. G. Hollett & Son Antiquarian Booksellers 173 - 185 2011 £50

Burgess, John *A History of Keswick.* Carlisle: privately published by author, 1989, 4to., original cloth backed acetate wrappers, pages 35, (15 photocopied plates) all printed on rectos, text cyclostyled. R. F. G. Hollett & Son Antiquarian Booksellers 173 - 186 2011 £50

Burgess, John *The Monasteries of Cumbria.* Carlisle: privately printed, 1987, 7 volumes, oblong folio, original cloth backed stiff blue card, lettered in red, unpaginated, each volume with cyclostyled text, plus same size facsimiles of relevant historical publications and plates, all printed on recto only. R. F. G. Hollett & Son Antiquarian Booksellers 173 - 187 2011 £150

Burgess, John *The Monasteries of Cumbria.* Carlisle: privately published by author, 1987, 4 volumes, oblong folio, original cloth backed stiff blue card, lettered in red, unpaginated, each volume with cyclostyled text, plus same size facsimiles, all printed on recto only. R. F. G. Hollett & Son Antiquarian Booksellers General Catalogue Summer 2010 - 1349 2011 £75

Burgess, John *The Monasteries of Cumbria.* Carlisle: privately published, 1987, 7 volumes, oblong folio, original cloth backed stiff blue card lettered in red, unpaginated, each volume with cyclostyled text. facsimiles, fine set. R. F. G. Hollett & Son Antiquarian Booksellers General Catalogue Summer 2010 - 1347 2011 £120

Burgess, John *The Nobility of North West England.* Carlisle: privately published by author, 1989, 4to., original cloth backed acetate wrappers, pages 79 (16 photocopied plates), all printed on rectos, text cyclostyled. R. F. G. Hollett & Son Antiquarian Booksellers 173 - 189 2011 £75

Burgess, John *Pagan Cumbria.* Carlisle: privately published by author, 1987, 4to., original cloth backed acetate wrappers, pages 35, (32 photocopied plates) all printed on rectos, text cyclostyled. R. F. G. Hollett & Son Antiquarian Booksellers 173 - 190 2011 £75

Burgess, John *Pagan Cumbria.* Carlisle: privately published by author, 1987, Printed in very limited edition; 4to., original wrappers, lettered in gilt, pages 35, cyclostyled text, 32, facsimile plates. R. F. G. Hollett & Son Antiquarian Booksellers General Catalogue Summer 2010 - 1350 2011 £85

Burgess, John *The Roman Heritage in North West England.* Carlisle: privately published by author, 1989, 4to., original cloth backed acetate wrappers, pages 68, (14 photocopied plates) all printed on rectos, text cyclostyled. R. F. G. Hollett & Son Antiquarian Booksellers 173 - 192 2011 £50

Burgess, John *The Victorian Heritage of North West England.* Carlisle: privately published by author, 1989, 4to., original cloth backed acetate wrappers, pages 81, (11 photocopied plates) all printed on rectos, text cyclostyled. R. F. G. Hollett & Son Antiquarian Booksellers 173 - 193 2011 £65

Burgess, John *Westmorland. A Guide.* Carlisle: privately published by author, 2000, 4to., original cloth backed acetate wrappers, pages 59, (18 photocopied plates) all printed on rectos, text cyclostyled. R. F. G. Hollett & Son Antiquarian Booksellers 173 - 194 2011 £50

Burgess, Thornton *Blacky the Crow. Green Forest Series.* London: John Lane, Bodley Head, 1933, First edition; original green cloth with pictorial onlay, little rubbed, pages 206, 8 color plates by Harrison Cady. R. F. G. Hollett & Sons Antiquarian Booksellers 170 - 118 2011 £45

Burgess, Thornton *Lightfoot the Deer.* Boston: Little Brown, April, 1921, First edition; 8vo., blue cloth, slight rubbing, near fine, with 8 color plates, this copy has nice inscription from author. Aleph-Bet Books, Inc. 95 - 127 2011 $450

Burgess, Thornton *Peter Rabbit Puts on Airs.* New York: Eggers, 1914, 1922. 1928; 4to., 8 x 11 inches, stiff pictorial wrappers, 12 pages, including covers, near fine, very stunning scarce Burgess format, illustrations in bold colors by Harrison Cady, with great silhouette borders one very page.   Aleph-Bet Books, Inc.   95 - 129   2011 $150

Burgoyne, Peter *Schoolmaster Spy.* Blackie, 1958, First edition; pages 189, original cloth, dust jacket, head of spine defective, illustrations by Roger Payne.   R. F. G. Hollett & Son Antiquarian Booksellers   General Catalogue Summer 2010 - 744   2011   £30

Burke, Bernard *Burke's Genealogical and Heraldic History of the Landed Gentry of Ireland.* London: Burkes Peerage, 1958, Fourth edition; 8vo., pages xxxvi, 778, ex-British Foreign Office library with few library markings, covers slightly worn and spine little marked and soiled, slight splitting at upper hinge, overall near very good with clean text.   Any Amount of Books   May 29 2011 - A75731   2011 $272

Burke, Bernard *A Genealogical and Heraldic History of the Landed Gentry of Great Britain and Ireland.* London: Harrison & Son, 1898, Ninth edition; 2 volumes, rebound in red buckram lettered gilt at spine, pages 2174 with 18 pages of local ads at rear of each volume, 2 volumes, complete, illustrations, ex-British Foreign Office Library with few library markings, else sound, very good copies.   Any Amount of Books   May 29 2011 - A73018   2011 $340

Burke, Bill *I Want to Take Pictures.* Atlanta: Nexus Press, 1987, First edition, one of only 1000 copies; fine, in illustrated boards.   Jeff Hirsch Books   ny 2010 2011 $1250

Burke, Edmund   1729-1797   *The Correspondence of Edmund Burke.* 1958-1969, Volumes 1-8 (of 10), dust jacket, ex-library, very good.   C. P. Hyland   May 26 2011 - 255/068   2011 $797

Burke, Edmund   1729-1797   *A Philosophical Enquiry into the Origin of Our Ideas of the Sublime and Beautiful.* G. & W. B. Whittaker, 1821, New edition; xv (2) 18-318 pages, most handsome copy in full contemporary dark green calf, wide gilt stamped borders, spine in six compartments, decorated in gilt and with red morocco label, gilt dentelles, marbled endpapers, all edges gilt.   Ken Spelman Rare Books   68 - 21   2011   £120

Burke, Edmund   1729-1797   *The Works of the Right Hon. Edmund Burke.* London: F. & C. Rivington, 1803, (Reflections on the Revolution in France 5th edition, Dodlsey 1790). New edition; 8 volumes + additional volume, slight spotting to prelims, uniformly bound in full mottled calf, dark green morocco labels, spines slightly rubbed, small chip to head of volume III, very good.   Jarndyce Antiquarian Booksellers   CXCI - 3   2011   £680

Burke, James Lee *Black Cherry Blues.* Boston: Little Brown, 1989, First edition; near fine, light shelf wear, dust jacket fine.   Bella Luna Books   May 29 2011 - t3980   2011 $104

Burke, James Lee *Cimarron Rose.* London: Orion, 1997, First British edition; fine in fine dust jacket, signed by author.   Bella Luna Books   May 29 2011 - j1320   2011 $137

Burke, James Lee *The Conflict and Other Stories.* Baton Rouge: LSU Press, 1985, First printing, simultaneous paperback; fine, exceptional, unread copy, pictorial wrappers.   Bella Luna Books   May 29 2011 - t9335   2011 $82

Burke, James Lee *Heaven's Prisoners.* New York: Holt, 1988, First edition; book near fine, minor roughness to cloth at head of spine, looks like manufacturing defect, dust jacket fine.   Bella Luna Books   May 26 2011 - t7041   2011 $330

Burke, James Lee *The Lost Get Back Boogie.* Baton Rouge: LSU Press, 1986, First edition; fine, dust jacket very good, some rubbing, light soiling and wrinkling to front panel, review slips laid in.   Bella Luna Books   May 26 2011 - t7851   2011 $440

Burke, James Lee *The Lost Get Back Boogie.* Baton Rouge: LSU Press, 1986, First edition; fine, near fine dust jacket with evidence of sticker removal from rear panel.   Bella Luna Books   May 26 2011 - t7850   2011 $550

Burke, James Lee *The Lost Get Back Boogie.* Baton Rouge: LSU Press, 1986, First edition; fine in like dust jacket, signed by author.   Bella Luna Books   May 26 2011 - t1259   2011 $825

Burke, James Lee *Sunset Limited.* New York: Doubleday, 1998, First edition; fine, dust jacket fine, also signed by Vine Deloria Jr., inscribed by Burke to same.   Bella Luna Books   May 29 2011 - g2731   2011 $104

Burke, John *Encyclopaedia of Heraldry or a General Armory of England, Scotland and Ireland.* 1884, Third edition; with supplement, half brown morocco, all edges gilt, very good.   C. P. Hyland   May 26 2011 - 259/049   2011 $275

Burke, John *A General and Heraldic Dictionary of the Peerage and Baronetage of the British Empire.* London: Henry Colburn/Richard Bentley, 1833, First edition; 2 volumes, 8vo. soundly rebound in maroon cloth lettered gilt at spine, pages liii, 648 & 729 with 40 page publisher's catalog at rear, copiously illustrated throughout with heraldic devices, ex-British Foreign Office library with few library markings, else very good.   Any Amount of Books   May 29 2011 - A64394   2011 $230

Burke, John *Peter Culler's Boats. The Complete Design Catalog.* Camden: 1984, First edition; 296 pages, 4to., fine in fine dust jacket.   Bookworm & Silverfish   678 - 136   2011 $120

Burke, Thomas *Dark Nights.* Jenkins, 1944, First edition; pages 154, (2) ads, foolscap 8vo., original orange cloth, covers blocked in black, dust jacket little dust soiled and chipped, good.   Blackwell Rare Books   B166 - 128   2011   £70

Burke, Thomas *The Pleasantries of Old Quong.* London: Constable & Co. Ltd., 1931, First edition; octavo, original orange cloth, spine panel stamped in blue.   L. W. Currey, Inc.   124 - 138   2011 $450

Burke, William *The Greek-English Derivative Dictionary showing in English Characters, the Greek Originals of Such Words in the English Language as are Derived from the Greek...* London: J. Johnson, 1806, 8vo., pages 248, 2 neat inscriptions on front endpaper in 19th century handwriting of the Fanny Desborough of Russell Square, also Mary Desborough, Ellen Scholes and Mrs. Geldart, soundly bound in full plain unlettered (but with 7 gold bands at spine), tree calf which is lightly scuffed and slightly marked), very good.   Any Amount of Books   May 29 2011 - A72178   2011 $238

Burkhardt, Frederick *A Calendar of the Correspondence of Charles Darwin 1821-1882.* New York: and London: Garland, 1985, 4to., 690 pages, portrait, red cloth, gilt stamped spine title, fine, from the Bern Dibner reference library, with Burndy bookplate.   Jeff Weber Rare Books   161 - 71   2011 $110

Burl, Aubrey *The Stone Circles of the British Isles.* New Haven: Yale University Press, 1976, Small 4to., original cloth, gilt, dust jacket, pages xxii, 410, with 36 plates and 50 text figures, maps and plans, excellent copy.   R. F. G. Hollett & Son Antiquarian Booksellers   177 - 152   2011   £50

Burleigh, William Henry *The Republican Pocket Pistol. A Collection of Facts for Freeman.* New York: Dayton and Burdick, 1856, First edition; 18mo., 4, (5)-36 pages, original pale yellow printed wrappers, from wrapper chipped with partial loss of 1, text block very nice.   M & S Rare Books, Inc.   90 - 141   2011 $650

Burn, Richard *The Justice of the Peace and Parish Officer.* London: printed by E. Richardson and C. Lintot for A. Millar, 1762, Seventh edition; 3 volumes, contemporary polished calf, backstrips rather dulled, labels renewed, good sound set with booklabel of Calgarth Park (Windermere).   R. F. G. Hollett & Son Antiquarian Booksellers   175 - 208   2011   £350

Burnand, Francis Cowley *Strapmore!* London: Bradbury, Agnew & Co., 1878, Half title, original brown sand grained cloth by Martin of Marylebone, spine lettered in gilt, very good.   Jarndyce Antiquarian Booksellers   CLXC - 707   2011   £75

The Burned Children of America. London: Hamish Hamilton, 2003, First British edition; fine, only issued in wrappers.   Ken Lopez Bookseller   154 - 7   2011 $100

Burnet, Gilbert, Bp. of Salisbury   1643-1715 *Bishop Burnet's History of His Own Time.* London: printed for Thomas Ward, Printed for the editor, by Joseph Downing... and Henry Woodfall, 1724, 1734; Large paper copy, 2 volumes, folio, pages (xvi), 836, (xx); (xxii), 765, (i), Frances Hoffman headpieces in volume 2 on pages i, 1. 139, 309 & 729, later mottled calf, boards gilt double rule bordered, board edges obliquely-broken fillet gilt, 'Dutch-comb' 'made' endpapers, all edges densely red sprinkled, mid 20th century calf reback with original red and green lettering and numbering pieces relaid, bit of light browning, slightly rubbed, old boards little scratched and flaked, all boards have unidentified ducal armorial blindstamped impression (motto" Finem Respice) volume 2 top edge gilt verso has contemporary ink inscription, "The Original Manuscript of both volumes of this/ History will be deposited in the Cotton Library by/ T. Burnett" within red ink double rule border, from the collection of Christopher Ernest Weston 1947-2010.   Unsworths Booksellers   24 - 17   2011   £400

Burnet, Gilbert, Bp. of Salisbury   1643-1715 *Bishop Burnet's History of His Own Time.* London: Thomas Ward, Joseph Downing & Henry Woodfall, 1724-1734, First edition; 2 volumes, folio, contemporary full brown paneled calf, raised bands, gilt stamped black and red leather spine labels, hinges reinforced, bookplates of Samuel Card, fine.   Jeff Weber Rare Books   163 - 33   2011 $375

Burnet, Gilbert, Bp. of Salisbury   1643-1715 *Bishop Burnet's History of His Own Time....* Oxford: at the University Press, 1833, Second edition; 6 volumes, engraved title, pencil notes on endpapers of volume I and occasionally within text, finely bound in full tan calf, gilt borders, raised bands, gilt compartments, red and brown morocco labels, spines slightly tanned, very good.   Jarndyce Antiquarian Booksellers   CXCI - 4   2011   £320

Burnet, Gilbert, Bp. of Salisbury 1643-1715 *An Exhortation to Peace and Union. A Sermon at St. Lawrence - Jury at the Election of Lord Mayor of London on the 29th of September 1681.* London: printed for Richard Chiswell, 1681, Small 4to., pages (iv) 35 (i), disbound, first and last leaves bit soiled, faint dampmark to upper corner, now bound in quarter calf, red moroco lettering piece lettered vertically down, boards sided out with marbled paper by Chris Weston, contemporary (not Burnet's) ink inscription, from the collection of Christopher Ernest Weston 1947-2010. Unsworths Booksellers   24 - 15   2011   £95

Burnet, Gilbert, Bp. of Salisbury 1643-1715 *An Exposition of the Thirty-nine Articles of the Church of England.* London: printed for Ri. Chiswell, 1705, Third edition; contemporary vellum, spine blind ruled, 19th century dark red lettering piece gilt, boards panelled in blind with large open central lozenge centre piece, pink and white sewn endbands, little spotting in places, vellum soiled, slight cracking at joint ends, ink inscription "C. J. Hardey/May 18th 1838", is lightly scored out in ink in favour of "Robt. Hardey Hull 1840", from the collection of Christopher Ernest Weston 1947-2010.   Unsworths Booksellers   24 - 16   2011   £150

Burnet, Gilbert, Bp. of Salisbury 1643-1715 *The Life of William Bedel, D.D. Bishop of Kilmore in Ireland.* (bound with) *An Abstract of the Number of Protestant and Popish Families in the Several Counties and Provinces of Ireland.* Dublin: M. Rhames for R. Gunne, 1736, second edition; 8vo., pages (36) preface and list of subscribers and 423 pages + 15 pages (abstract) and one page publishers ads for Gunne, full brown leather, plain spine with 5 raised bands, lacks spine label but has title in blind stamp, some rubbing, slight marks and scuffing, sound, about very good copy.   Any Amount of Books   May 26 2011 - A72900 2011 $1006

Burnet, Gilbert, Bp. of Salisbury 1643-1715 *Memoires of the Lives and Actions of James and William Dukes of Hamilton and William Dukes of Hamilton and Castleherald... (half title) The History of the Church and State of Scotland, the II Part.* London: J. Grover for R. Royston, 1677, Large paper copy, folio, pages (xxii), 436 (xvi) + 1 engraved plates, 3 engraved portraits within text, contemporary calf boards panelled in blind, central having marbled effect, board edges decorative roll gilt, all edges blue 'swirl' marbled, 'Dutch-comb' 'made' endpapers, early 1990's calf reback and corners by Chris Weston, little dust soiling and browning, old leather scraped and scratched, unidentified armorial bookplate, from the collection of Christopher Ernest Weston 1947-2010.   Unsworths Booksellers   24 - 14   2011   £300

Burnett, Charles *Magic and Divination in the Middle Ages.* Aldershot: Variorum, 1996, 8vo., xii, 370 pages, blue cloth, gilt stamped cover and spine titles, fine, from the Bern Dibner reference library, with Burndy bookplate.   Jeff Weber Rare Books   161 - 73   2011 $125

Burnett, Frances Hodgson *Little Lord Fauntleroy.* Leipzig: Bernhard Tauchnitz, 1887, Copyright edition; 12mo., original decorated cloth, gilt, pages 279.   R. F. G. Hollett & Sons Antiquarian Booksellers   170 - 119 2011 £40

Burnett, Frances Hodgson *A Little Princess.* Philadelphia: J. B. Lippincott Co., 1963, First edition thus, first issue; 8vo., blue grey cloth with gold lettering on spine and gold vignette on front cover, full color pictorial dust jacket of quite clean copy, jacket not price clipped and does have correct, incorrect, death date for Burnett on rear dust jacket flap, this copy signed in full, 240 numbered pages of text and ten full page color plates plus black and white drawings.   Jo Ann Reisler, Ltd.   86 - 253   2011 $300

Burnett, W. R. *Iron Man.* New York: Dial Press, 1930, First edition; 8vo., pages (8), 312, original blue cloth, spine lettered in gold, upper board with publisher's insignia blocked in blind, top edge dyed red and trimmed, original color pictorial dust jacket by Reindel printed in red and black, dust jacket with few short closed tears, slight soiling to spine, corners slightly chipped, author's presentation inscription for Jon Bradshaw.   Simon Finch Rare Books Zero - 212 2011   £300

Burney, Charles *An Account of the Musical Performances in Westminster Abbey and the Pantheon May 26th, 27th, 29th and June the 3d and 5th 1748 in Commemoration of Handel.* London: printed for the Benefit of the Musical Fund and Sold by T. Payne and Son, 1785, First edition; 4to., pages vii (1), xvi, 8 *8, 9-20, *19-*24, 21-56, 21, (6), 46-90, (5), 94-139, (3), frontispiece and 7 other engraved plates, half dark green leather lettered gilt at spine with marbled boards and marbled endpapers, slight rubbing at spine hinges and corners, very slightly occasional foxing, slightly more pronounced at titlepage, else very good, from the library of classical musician Geraint Jones (1917-1998), 3 small drawings by Burney pasted to 2 supplied blanks inserted before title, pencilled beneath 2 drawings are notes, presumably in hand of former owner or past bookseller. Any Amount of Books   May 26 2011 - A46347 2011 $1256

Burney, Charles *General History of Music.* London: printed for the author and sold by T. Beckett, J. Robinson and G. Robinson, 1776, First edition; 4 volumes, large quarto, xx, (12), 522, (1, blank), (4), 597, (1, blank), (1 errata); xi, (1, blank), 622, (11, index) (1, errata); (4), 685, (1, blank), (2 publisher's ads), (12 index), (1, errata), (1 blank) pages, 12 engraved plates, including 4 frontispieces, engraved frontispieces in volumes I-III, 9 additional plates, engraved musical illustrations, contemporary full calf, rebacked to style, green morocco spine labels, spines and labels stamped and lettered in gilt, board edges gilt, gilt dentelles, marbled endpapers, boards rubbed and corners bumped, inner hinges reinforced, some foxing and dampstaining throughout, mainly to prelim pages, previous owner's ink stamp, previous owner R. Sly's old ink signature, he has made ink corrections in accordance with errata throughout each volume, overall very nice. Heritage Book Shop Holiday 2010 - 14 2011 $2500

Burney, James *A Chronological History of the Discoveries in the South Seas or Pacific Ocean.* London: printed by Luke Hansard and sold by G. and W. Nicol, 1803-, 1806-1813. First edition; 12 engraved plates, some foxing, including some charts, 21 engraved maps (missing 1 map from volume 3), separation to lower fold of a map, creases to another map reinforced, offsetting and/or light foxing to some maps, few engravings in text, 4to., pages (10), xii, 391; v, (11), 482; (10) 437, contemporary quarter calf over marbled boards, light rubbing, few small abrasions, heel of spine chipped, one inch split to front edge of spine, near head of volume 2, splitting to calf still solid, on rear edge of spine to volume 1, endpapers foxed, ex-libris Benjamin Silliman, browning to upper margin of 4 pages, offsetting from plates, marginal tear to a page, dampstain to lower corner of 3 leaves, occasional foxing. Raymond M. Sutton, Jr. May 26 2011 - 44145 2011 $3500

Burney, James *A Chronological History of the Discoveries in the South Sea or Pacific Ocean.* London: G and W. Nichol, 1803-1817, First edition; 5 quarto volumes, contemporary half burgundy morocco over marbled boards. Heritage Book Shop Booth A12 51st NY International Antiquarian Book Fair April 8-10 2011 - 20 2011 $20,000

Burney, William *The British Neptune or a History of the Achievements of the Royal Navy, from the Earliest Periods to the Present Time.* London: Richard Phillips, 1807, First edition; 8vo., full leather with red leather spine label lettered gilt, pages vi, 490 and folding world map at rear, frontispiece and 7 plates, occasional marks to text otherwise clean, some rubbing at head and tail of spine and corners, overall sound, very good. Any Amount of Books May 29 2011 - B27636 2011 $204

Burnham, Leavitt *Guide to the Union Pacific Railroad Lands, 12,000,000 Acres, 3,00,00 Acres in Central and Easter Nebraska Now for Sale.* Omaha: Land Union Pacific Railroad Co., 1879, First edition; 8vo., 9 x 6 inch pictorial wrappers with map on back cover, 32 pages, illustrations, maps, light stamp of Union Pacific Railroad on upper portion of front cover, else fine, bright copy. Buckingham Books May 26 2011 - 30999 2011 $1750

Burns, Alan *The Angry Brigade.* London: Allison and Busby, 1973, First edition; small 8vo., original publisher's black cloth lettered gilt at spine, 185 pages, fine in about very good+ complete dust jacket with slight soiling, slight creasing to white covers, very slight wear, one short closed tear and no loss, decent copy of scarce book. Any Amount of Books May 29 2011 - A38415 2011 $213

Burns, Mai *Pssst!* London: Never Limited, 1982, First edition; 10 volumes, complete 4to., color illustrated stapled wrappers, pages 563, cartoon and strip, about fine. Any Amount of Books May 29 2011 - A59929 2011 $272

Burns, Olive Anne *Cold Sassy Tree.* New York: Ticknor & Fields, 1984, Proof copy; printed yellow wrappers, fine. Bella Luna Books May 29 2011 - 1104 2011 $137

Burns, Robert 1759-1796 *Poems, Chiefly in the Scottish Dialect.* Edinburgh: printed for author and sold by William Creech, 1787, First Edinburgh edition, first issue; first issue with "Roxburgh" misprinted "Boxburgh" on page xxxvii in list of subscribers with page 232 correctly printed and with 'skinking' on page 263, line 13, octavo, xlviii, (9)-368 pages, half title, frontispiece, bookplate of Alfred B. Perlman, original blue grey paper boards, uncut, few leaves carelessly opened, bookplate and name in ink on front pastedown, small ink presentation inscription on head of title, chemised within green cloth clamshell box, extraordinary copy, rarely found in original state, quite rare. David Brass Rare Books, Inc. May 26 2011 - 01388 2011 $5500

Burns, Robert 1759-1796 *The Poetical Works.* Chiswick: from the Press of C. Whittingham, 1821, 130 x 85mm., 2 volumes, very attractive contemporary red straight grain morocco, covers with wide gilt leaf border and central panel formed in multipled blind rules, raised bands, spine panels intricately gilt with leaves, acorns, foliage and small tools, gilt turn-ins, all edges gilt, each volume with pleasing fore-edge painting, one of Burns' Birthplace, the Other of His Cenotaph and Brig O'Doon, in (slightly scuffed) rose colored cloth lined linen folding box with gilt titling, extra engraved titlepage with vignette in each volume; covers with touch of soiling, vague scratch across central panel of one board, joints and extremities very slightly rubbed, small spill-over of fore-edge paint onto a couple of leaves at front of each volume, engraved titles bit foxed, other trivial imperfections internally, very pretty set in excellent condition, bindings solid and shining, text fresh and bright, fore-edge paintings quite well preserved. Phillip J. Pirages 59 - 200 2011 $1500

Burns, Robert 1759-1796 *Songs.* Edinburgh: printed by George Robb and Co. for Otto Schulze and Co., 1901, One of 500 copies; 220 x 180mm., 3 p.l. including half title, 99 pages, (3) leaves (index and colophon), lovely contemporary olive brown crushed morocco by Otto Schulze & Co. of Edinburgh (signed on front turn-in), covers with single gilt rule border, upper cover with 11 horizontal bows of gilt and inlaid red morocco thistles, the thistles (numbering 72 in all), separated by small round tools, two raised bands flanked by gilt rules, gilt vertical titling, turn-ins with single gilt rule top edge gilt, woodcut title and frontispiece surrounded by wide, elaborate border of twining thistles and bluebells, large woodcut initials foliated with similar thistles and bluebells at beginning of each poem; spine a definite (pleasing) brown rather than an olive brown, minor offsetting from turn-ins to endleaves, slender trailing two inch marginal (glue?), stain to last two pages of index, occasional thumbing and other trivial imperfections, otherwise fine, text and decorations clean, fresh and bright, handsome binding lustrous and unworn. Phillip J. Pirages 59 - 138 2011 $750

Burns, Robert 1759-1796 *The Works of Robert Burns with an Account of His Life and a Criticism of His Writings.* Philadelphia: William Fairbairn, 1804, First American edition; 16mo., uniform contemporary polished tree calf, spines gilt stamped with leather labels, fine set. M & S Rare Books, Inc. 90 - 62 2011 $275

Burns, Robert 1759-1796 *The Works.* London: James Cochrane and Co., 1834, First printing of this edition; 8 volumes, 165 x 102mm., very attractive contemporary or slightly later dark maroon calf, covers decorated in gilt and blind with border of multiple gilt fillets and blind scrolling roll, gilt thistle cornerpieces, very large lyre centerpiece in blind, raised bands, spines gilt in compartments featuring scrolling foliate cornerpieces an sidepieces an lyre centerpiece, dark green morocco label, all edges gilt, one folding manuscript facsimile and 17 engraved plates, 8 engraved titlepages and frontispieces, armorial bookplate of James Hunter of Hafton; trivial rubbing to bindings, perhaps a score of leaves with minor marginal soiling or isolated faint foxing, few creased corners (one frayed), otherwise, very fine and pretty set, bindings bright and scarcely worn, text quite fresh and smooth. Phillip J. Pirages 59 - 157 2011 $1100

Burnup, Henry *The Carriage Tax. A Letter to the Right Hon. Sir Charles Wood, Bart., Chancellor of the Exchequer.* London: printed by J. King, 1851, First edition; 8vo., 15, (1) pages, preserved in modern wrappers with printed title label on upper cover, very good, apparently very rare. John Drury Rare Books 154 - 35 2011 £125

Burr, Aaron *The Watchman's Answer to the Question, What of the Night &c. A Sermon Preached Before the Synod of New York, Convened at Newark in New Jersey.* Boston: S. Kneeland, 1757, 46 pages, stitched in contemporary blue paper wrappers, then sewn into early (18th century?) homemade covers, stain on both wrappers and first few leaves of text, upper corner of titlepage worn away costing one letter, outer cover chipped at edges, else very good, 18th century ownership signatures of Benjamin Sheldon and Josepha (?) Ely, latter dated 1777. Joseph J. Felcone Inc. Fall Miscellany 2010 - 21 2011 $900

Burr, David H. *The Steamboat, Stage and Canal Register for the Year 1832.* New York: D. H. Burr, 1832, First edition; 18mo., 32 pages, large colored folding map, original calf, breaks in folds, considerable foxing, rare. M & S Rare Books, Inc. 90 - 285 2011 $450

Burrard, Gerald *The Modern Shotgun.* Herbert Jenkins, 1950-1969, 3 volumes, volumes 1 and 2 in original cloth, gilt, dust jackets (little worn) volume 3 in library cloth gilt, numerous plates, tables diagrams, etc., good working set. R. F. G. Hollett & Son Antiquarian Booksellers General Catalogue Summer 2010 - 1222 2011 £85

Burrell, Charles E. *A History of Halifax County, Virginia.* Richmond: 1922, First edition; 408 page, good solid copy with cover soil and flecks, foxing to endpapers. Bookworm & Silverfish 668 - 180 2011 $65

Burrill, Katharine *The Amateur Cook.* London: W. & R. Chambers, n.d., 1905, Original pictorial blue cloth gilt, hinges trifle rubbed, pages viii, 296, pictorial title in red and black, 12 illustrations, decorated and endpapers by Mabel Lucie Attwell, text pages with red ruled borders and cornerpieces. R. F. G. Hollett & Son Antiquarian Booksellers General Catalogue Summer 2010 - 1097 2011 £120

Burroughs, Edgar Rice 1875-1950 *Tarzan of the Apes.* Toronto: McClelland, Goodchild, & Stewart, 1914, True First Canadian edition, first printing (with cancelled title), in first state binding, without acorn above the U.S. publisher's slug on spine; rarest of all editions, astonishing copy, octavo, (2, blank), (8), 400, (1), (5, blank) pages, titlepage illustration, publisher's original dark red cloth, gilt lettering to upper board and spine, gilt rules at spine head and tail, blindstamped panel to upper board, completely untouched, tight, bright and fine copy, housed in quarter red morocco clamshell case. David Brass Rare Books, Inc. May 26 2011 - 01179 2011 $8500

Burroughs, Edgar Rice 1875-1950 *Tarzan Triumphant.* Tarzana: Edgar Rice Burroughs, 1932, First edition; octavo, pages (1-4) 5-6 (7-8) 9-318 (319: ads) (320: blank), five inserted plates with illustrations by Studley O. Bourroughs, original pebbled blue cloth, front and spine panels stamped in orange, top edge stained red. L. W. Currey, Inc. 124 - 128 2011 $500

Burroughs, John *The Writings.* Boston and New York: printed at the Riverside Press for Houghton Mifflin and Co., 1904-1922, One of 750 copies of the special "Autograph edition" signed by publisher and author; 227 x 156mm., 23 volumes, fine contemporary crimson crushed morocco, attractively gilt, covers framed with two sets of triple gilt fillets, raised bands, spines densely gilt in compartments featuring several flowers radiating from a central oval, broad inner gilt dentelles, marbled endpapers, top edge gilt, other edges rough trimmed, vignette on signature leaf and 125 full page plates done on special Japanese paper captioned tissue guards, front pastedown of each volume with bookplate of Mary Howard Gilmour, expert repairs to one short and two long marginal tears but not entering text, half dozen small open tears of no consequence at bottom edge in one index, otherwise exceptionally fine, text consistently very fresh and clean, bindings bright, unfaded and unworn, handsomely bound and well preserved. Phillip J. Pirages 59 - 159 2011 $12,500

Burroughs, Polly *Eisenstaedt Martha's Vineyard.* Birmingham: Oxmoor House, 1988, Stated first edition, first printing; signed by Eisenstaedt, fine in near fine dust jacket with mild sun spine, 4to., vii, 163, (5) pages. By the Book, L. C. 26 - 27 2011 $200

Burroughs, Stephen *Memoirs of Stephen Burroughs.* Hanover: Benjamin True, 1798, Boston: Caleb Bingham 1804. First edition; 2 volumes, original calf, first volume 8vo., (2), vi-vii, (8), 296 pages, errata bottom of page 296, title in red leather on spine, bookplate of William L. Clements Library of American History, University of Michigan, top edge titlepage repaired with old paper, name in ink of Charles Miller, Feb. 14, 1848 on titlepage, small hole on pages 111 and 112 affecting few letters, minor foxing throughout, else very good, exceedingly rare; second volume 16mo., original calf with title in gilt on red leather label on spine, five gilt bands on spine, 202 pages, former owner's name on front pastedown sheet, waterstain to bottom third of front endpapers and titlepage, moderately rubbed to spine ends and extremities, else very good, exceedingly rare. Buckingham Books May 26 2011 - 25797 2011 $6750

Burroughs, William S. *Junkie.* New York: Ace, 1953, Issue d's-a'dos with Narcotic Agent by Maurice Helbrant; pictorial wrappers, rubbed along extremities, hinge starting, good. Second Life Books Inc. 174 - 76 2011 $600

Bursill, Henry *Hand Shadows to be Thrown Upon the Wall: a Series of Novel and Amusing Figures Formed by the Hand...* Griffith and Farran, 1859, Second edition; 4to., modern cloth backed boards, 18 hand colored plates, attractive copy. R. F. G. Hollett & Sons Antiquarian Booksellers 170 - 121 2011 £95

Bursill, Henry *Hand Shadows to be Thrown Upon the Wall.* London: Griffith and Farran, 1860, Fourth edition; 4to., modern three quarter levant morocco gilt by N. A. Hyman, pages 4, with 18 hand colored plates, attractive, coloring probably later, but well done. R. F. G. Hollett & Sons Antiquarian Booksellers 170 - 122 2011 £120

Burton, Isabel *The Life of Captain Sir Richard F. Burton.* London: 1893, 2 volumes, xxiii, 606; viii, 664 pages, small 4to., backstrip lettering bright, modest shelfwear, volume 1 top backstrip with chip at middle and chafing at bottom, volume 2 top of backstrip even less so, front cover volume 2 with 3 small snags concealed amidst the headstone decoration, previous owner bookplate, above 1200 pages. Bookworm & Silverfish 669 - 42 2011 $200

Burton, John *Monasticon Eboracense and the Ecclesiastical History of Yorkshire.* York: printed for the author by N. Nickson, 1758, Large paper copy, folio, pages xii, 448, (xxxvi) + 1 extending engraved map and 2 other engraved plates, contemporary diced Russia, spine single rule gilt with raised bands 'milled' decorative roll gilt, lettered direct to gilt, boards single rule gilt bordered, board edges single rule gilt, turn-ins decorative roll gilt, all edges lemon, red and white sewn endbands, just lightly foxed, bit dusty, joints cracked but strong, corners and spine ends worn, from the collection of Christopher Ernest Weston 1947-2010. Unsworths Booksellers 24 - 74 2011 £500

Burton, John *Trackless Wind.* San Francisco: Johnck & Seeger, 1930, First edition; possibly a presentation issue (also issued in cloth), frontispiece photogravure portrait by Ansel Adams, tall octavo, paper covered boards and endpapers. Between the Covers 169 - BTC342179 2011 $750

Burton, Richard Francis 1821-1890 *Falconry in the Valley of the Indus.* London: John van Voorst, 1852, First edition; 8vo., xii, 107, (ads) 8 pages, 4 half tone lithographic plates, minor marginal stains pages 11-18, frontispiece lightly foxed, original blindstamped brown cloth, gilt spine, spine lightly sunned, spine joint slightly frayed (minor), inner hinges cracking (binding still tight), very good, quite scarce. Jeff Weber Rare Books 163 - 137 2011 $6000

Burton, Richard Francis 1821-1890 *The Kasidah of Haji Adbu El-Yezdi.* Portland: 1913, Limited to 925 copies; yapped pseudo vellum and publisher box (usual wear, missing bottom panel). Bookworm & Silverfish 679 - 27 2011 $75

Burton, Richard Francis 1821-1890 *The Lake Regions of Central Africa, a Picture of Exploration.* New York: Harper & Bros., 1860, First American edition; octavo, xvi, (18)-572, (4 ads) pages, frontispiece illustrations, index, original brown blindstamped publisher's cloth, gilt spine title, head and tail lightly frayed,. Jeff Weber Rare Books 163 - 138 2011 $400

Burton, Richard Francis 1821-1890 *The Lands of Cazembe: Larcerda's Journey to Cazembe in 1798.* London: John Murray, 1873, First edition; 8vo., pages vii, 271, large folding map frontispiece, original blue blind-stamped cloth, near fine.   J. & S. L. Bonham Antiquarian Booksellers   Africa 4/20/2011 - 8656 2011   £195

Burton, Richard Francis 1821-1890 *A Mission to Gelele, King of Dahome: with Notices of the So-called Amazons, the Grand Customs, the Yearly Customs, the Human Sacrifices, the Present State of the Slave Trade and the Negroes Place in Nature.* London: Tinsley Bros., 1864, Second edition; 2 volumes, 8vo., pages xxi, 256; viii, 305, 2 plates, recent purple cloth, very good clean set.   J. & S. L. Bonham Antiquarian Booksellers   Africa 4/20/2011 - 6448 2011   £600

Burton, Richard Francis 1821-1890 *Terminal Essay to The Thousand and One Nights.* privately printed by Leonard Smithers,, 1890, (1901). First separate edition, no. "07" of 50 copies; 8vo., pages 38, x, original deep mauve printed wrappers, slight wear to head and foot of spine, slight fading to edges, otherwise very good.   Simon Finch Rare Books   Zero - 137 2011 £7000

Burton, Richard Francis 1821-1890 *Terminal Essay to The Thousand and One Nights.* London: for private circulation only, 1901, Number 48 of 50 copies; 4to., pages (iv), 57, (3), xxi, (i) blank, purple mimeo-copied text on 'Excelsior' laid paper sheets, sewn into blue-green printed wrappers with paste-over cloth spine, as issued, small chips eroded from top edges of front wrapper and first 6 leaves (not affecting text, some pale whitish staining near spine joint, slight signs of wear to covers due to much handling, previous owner's name in ink top front wrapper), overall acceptable copy, rare.   Simon Finch Rare Books   Zero - 138 2011 £1500

Burton, Richard Francis 1821-1890 *To the Gold Coast for Gold. A Personal Narrative.* London: Chatto & Windus, 1883, First edition; 2 volumes, octavo, xii (1, contents) (1, blank), (1)-354, (2), (32, publisher's ads); (2, blank), (i)-vi,(1)-381, (3) pages, 2 colored folding maps in volume I and colored frontispiece in volume II, publisher's original red cloth, stamped in black and gilt on boards, spines lettered in gilt and stamped in black, black coated endpapers, spines slightly rubbed and sunned, top edges bit foxed, minimal and invisible restoration to inner hinges, bookplate of previous owner John Ralph Willis, very good, handsome.   Heritage Book Shop   Holiday 2010 - 15 2011 $5500

Burton, Richard Francis 1821-1890 *Wanderings in Three Continents.* London: Hutchinson, 1901, First edition; 8vo., pages 313, photogravure frontispiece, illustrations, original red decorative cloth, top edge gilt, spine faded, inner joint cracked, mark on front endpaper where label removed.   J. & S. L. Bonham Antiquarian Booksellers   Africa 4/20/2011 - 7525 2011   £120

Bury, Charlotte *The Exclusives.* London: Henry Colburn, 1830, First edition; 12mo., pages (iv), 312; (iv), 284, (ii) (iv), 334, (ii), bound with half titles and ad leaves in contemporary half calf and marbled boards, morocco spine label, some waterstaining to much of volume one with most of the stains at rear of book, one signature starting in volume 3, otherwise very good, scarce.   Second Life Books Inc.   174 - 77 2011 $850

Busby, Thomas *Costume of the Lower Orders of London.* London: published for T. L. Busby by Messrs. Baldwin, Craddock and Joy, 1820, Quarto, iv, (24) pages, 24 hand colored etched plates, text watermarked 1817, plates watermarked 1822, contemporary quarter green roan over marbled boards, spine decorated and lettered in gilt with raised bands, slight offsetting from some of the plates to text, from the library of Samuel Appleton with his armorial bookplate, excellent.   David Brass Rare Books, Inc.   May 26 2011 - 01625 2011 $5250

Busby, Thomas *The Fishing Costume and Local Scenery of Hartlepool in the County of Durham.* London: J. Nichols and Son, 1819, Large paper copy, early (earliest?) issue; folio, iv, (24) pages, 6 hand colored etched plates, original cloth backed boards with printed paper label on front cover, remarkable and exceedingly scarce copy.   David Brass Rare Books, Inc.   May 26 2011 - 01627 2011 $5500

Bush, James *The Choice or Line of the Beatitudes.* London: R. Sayweel; Cockermouth: Baily & Sons and Carlisle: C.. Thurnam, 1841, square 8vo., full polished calf gilt, edges rubbed, pages 102, engraved frontispiece (foxed), scattered foxing in places, scarce presentation copy , inscribed by author to Mrs. Joshua Stanger.   R. F. G. Hollett & Son Antiquarian Booksellers   173 - 204 2011 £75

Bush, M. L. *Serfdom & Slavery. Studies in Legal Bondage.* London: Longman, 1996, First edition; original cloth, dust jacket, pages vii, 358.   R. F. G. Hollett & Son Antiquarian Booksellers   175 - 211 2011   £45

Bushe-Fox, J. P. *Excavations on the Site of the Roman Town at Wroxeter, Shropshire in 1912.* Oxford: The Society of Antiquaries, 1913, Small 4to., library binding of morocco backed cloth gilt, original wrappers bound in, pages 112, with 33 plates and plans, some folding, title trifle fingered, small library stamps.   R. F. G. Hollett & Son Antiquarian Booksellers   177 - 155 2011   £45

Bushe-Fox, J. P. *Second Report on the Excavation of the Roman Fort At Richborough Kent.* Oxford: University Press for the Society, 1928, Small 4to., library cloth gilt, lower edge of upper board damped, pages viii, 231, with 47 plates and plans, some folding, library accession stamp on verso of title.   R. F. G. Hollett & Son Antiquarian Booksellers   177 - 156 2011   £45

Bushell, W. D. *The Church of St. Mary the Great, The University Church at Cambridge.* Cambridge: Bowes & Bowes, 1948, Original pictorial stiff wrappers, pages xv, 223, with 11 plates. R. F. G. Hollett & Son Antiquarian Booksellers 177 - 157 2011 £30

Busk, Rachel Henriette *Sagas from the Far East; or Kalmouk and Mongolian Traditionary Tales.* London: Griffith & Farran, 1873, First edition; original red cloth, spine slightly dulled, leading inner hinges slightly cracking, signature of Elizabeth Downson. Jarndyce Antiquarian Booksellers CXCI - 100 2011 £120

Busuttil, Vincenzo *Holiday Customs in Malta and Sports, Usages, Ceremonies, Omens & Superstitions of the Maltese People.* Malta: Printed by V. Busuttil, 1894, Paper browned, original printed pink wrappers, carefully respined. Jarndyce Antiquarian Booksellers CXCI - 539 2011 £85

Buswell, Henry F. *The Civil Liability for Personal Injuries Arising Out of Negligence.* Boston: 1899, Second edition; 545 pages, very good in old law calf. Bookworm & Silverfish 667 - 78 2011 $75

Butcher, David *The Whittington Press a Bibliography 1982-1993.* Leonminster: Whittington Press, 1998, No. 224 of 244 copies on Zerkall paper; 4to., quarter green cloth and green leaf patterned boards, copiously illustrated in color and black and white, fine in sound slipcase, slight rubbing, otherwise near fine. Any Amount of Books May 29 2011 - A73501 2011 $366

Butler, Arthur G. *British Birds with Their Nest and Eggs.* Brumby & Clarke, n.d., 1896-1898, First edition; 6 volumes, large 4to., original pictorial cloth, backstrips rather worn at head and foot, pages 208; 192; 175; 219; 178; 252, all edges gilt, 24 color lithographed plates, numerous monochrome plates, very good, sound, bright set. R. F. G. Hollett & Son Antiquarian Booksellers General Catalogue Summer 2010 - 956 2011 £180

Butler, Colin G. *The World of the Honeybee.* London: Collins, 1954, Original cloth, gilt, dust jacket edges little chipped in places, pages 226, 2 color and 87 black and white photos. R. F. G. Hollett & Son Antiquarian Booksellers General Catalogue Summer 2010 - 957 2011 £60

Butler, David M. *Quaker Meeting Houses of the Lake Counties.* Friends Historical Society, 1978, First softback edition; small 4to., original pictorial stiff wrappers, 168 pages, illustrations. R. F. G. Hollett & Son Antiquarian Booksellers 177 - 158 2011 £30

Butler, Eugenia *The Book of Lies Project. Volumes I, II & III.* Fullerton College/Art Gallery/The Artists' (Floating Invisible) Museum of Actual Art/Public Access Press of the Southern California Institute of Architecture, 1996-2004, 1996. First edition, one of 80 numbered copies (entire edition), numbered and signed; quarto, 3 original portfolios, created out of incised and collaged lead, oil paint on vellum, original pencil drawings, photo on platinum paper, polaroid photos, cyanotype, ashes of love letters, hand embroidery and holograph and mechanically reproduced images and texts, with interleaved translucent sheets noting the artist, loose as issued, inserted in paper chemise and cardboard folder (or in a individual folder and laid into a clamshell box), accompanied by spiral bound commentary volume in original printed wrappers, bookplate in two portfolios (small adhesive shelf label on each), set is in fine condition, rare. James S. Jaffe Rare Books May 26 2011 - 21665 2011 $12,500

Butler, Franklin *John Ward or the Victimized Assassin a Narrative of the Facts Connected with the Crime, Arrest, Trial, Imprisonment and Execution of the Willitson Murderer.* Windsor: Vermont Journal print, 1869, First edition; 12mo., 138 pages, original printed wrappers. M & S Rare Books, Inc. 90 - 264 2011 $250

Butler, Gwendoline *Coffin in Malta.* London: Geoffrey Bles, 1964, First edition; 8vo., pages 224, original black cloth lettered gilt on spine, 13/6 price crossed out and 2/6 neatly written in, ownership signature of Richard Hamilton Alexander Cheffins 1945-2011, very good+ in slightly nicked and slightly chipped dust jacket (very good-, slightly nicked and slightly chipped at spine ends and top rear panel). Any Amount of Books May 29 2011 - A76681 2011 $221

Butler, James D. *Poematia. "Blood Drops." Birthday Lines and Other Verses of Society.* Madison: M. J. Dantwell, 1874, First edition; 8vo., 18 pages, disbound. M & S Rare Books, Inc. 90 - 447 2011 $125

Butler, Kenneth B. *Practical Handbook on Display Typefaces.* Mendota: Butler Typo-design Research Center, 1959, First printing; 4to., pages 175, cover little scuffed and soiled, otherwise very good, tight copy. Second Life Books Inc. 174 - 79 2011 $85

Butler, Octavia *Clay's Ark.* New York: St. Martin's Press, 1984, First edition; octavo, boards. L. W. Currey, Inc. 124 - 173 2011 $300

Butler, Octavia *Patternmaster.* Garden City: Doubleday & Co., 1976, First edition; octavo, boards. L. W. Currey, Inc. 124 - 157 2011 $350

Butler, Robert Olen *The Alleys of Eden.* New York: Horizon, 1981, First edition; fine in fine dust jacket, signed by author. Bella Luna Books May 29 2011 - t1177 2011 $137

Butler, Robert Olen *The Alleys of Eden.* New York: Horizon, 1981, First printing; book fine, dust jacket near fine, slight chip to bottom front, author's first book, signed by author.   Bella Luna Books   May 29 2011 - 4192 2011 $110

Butler, Robert Olen *Countrymen of Bones.* New York: Horizon, 1983, First edition; fine, dust jacket near fine, light creasing at top of spine.   Bella Luna Books   May 29 2011 - t1110 2011 $82

Butler, Robert Olen *Countrymen of Bones.* New York: Horizon, 1983, First edition, first printing; fine in near fine dust jacket, little rubbing to spine, signed by author.   Bella Luna Books   May 29 2011 - t1110a 2011 $93

Butler, Robert Olen *Sun Dog.* New York: Horizon, 1982, First edition; fine, near fine dust jacket with light wear to extremities.   Bella Luna Books   May 29 2011 - t1178 2011 $110

Butler, Robert Olen *Sun Dogs.* New York: Horizon, 1982, First edition; fine, dust jacket near fine, some rubbing to front panel, signed by author.   Bella Luna Books   May 29 2011 - 4193 2011 $82

Butler, Samuel 1835-1902   *The Collected Works of Samuel Butler.* London: Jonathan Cape, 1923-1926, Shrewsbury edition; 20 volumes, half titles, frontispiece, uncut and uniformly bound in blue buckram, vellum spines, few spines slightly dulled, top edge gilt, very good.   Jarndyce Antiquarian Booksellers   CXCI - 5 2011   £850

Butler, W. C. *Butler's Modern Practical Confectionary: a Boon to the Trade...* Manchester: Abel Heywood, 1890, small 4to., frontispiece, errata slip, occasional foxing, original light blue cloth, lettered in black and gilt, "With the Author's compliments June 12/94", additional later inscription, fine.   Jarndyce Antiquarian Booksellers   CXCI - 101 2011   £75

Butterfield, Jane *The Trial of Jane Butterfield for the Wilful Murder of William Scawen Esq. at the Assizes held at Croydon for the County of Surry on Saturday the 19th of August 1775....* London: printed for W. Owen at No. 11 and G. Kearsly at No. 46, in Fleet Street, 1775, (4), 53, (1) pages, half title, folio, fine, very nicely rebound in quarter mottled calf, gilt banded spine, red morocco label, marbled boards, vellum cornerpieces.   Jarndyce Antiquarian Booksellers   CXCI - 102 2011   £350

Butterworth, Edwin *Historical Sketches of Oldham.* Oldham: Printed by John Hirst, 1856, Second (first separate) edition; pages 256, (tables) (xlvi, local ads), with engraved frontispiece, woodcut plate and plan on double page and 2 copies, further woodcut plan, scarce.   R. F. G. Hollett & Son Antiquarian Booksellers   General Catalogue Summer 2010 - 1352 2011   £150

Butts, I. R. *The Table Book & Expeditious Calculator Comprising Rules & Tables.* Philadelphia: 1857, (2) pages ads, 88, (4) errata slip, pages, half cloth and patterned paper, missing f.f.e.p., top inch of backstrip stressed, missing the "T" and the "E" in "table", scarce.   Bookworm & Silverfish   676 - 20 2011 $275

Buxbaum, Melvin H. *Critical Essays on Benjamin Franklin.* Boston: G. K. Hall, 1987, 8vo., viii, 214 pages, index, quarter navy cloth with beige cloth sides, silver stamped spine title, fine, from the Bern Dibner reference library, with Burndy bookplate.   Jeff Weber Rare Books   161 - 74 2011 $85

Buxton, Jane *Gate Fever.* London: Cresset Press, 1962, First edition; original cloth, gilt, dust jacket little browned, pages 198 with 7 full page drawings.   R. F. G. Hollett & Son Antiquarian Booksellers   175 - 212 2011   £30

Byers, Richard L. M. *The History of Workington.* Cockermouth: Richard Byers, 1998-2003, First edition; 2 volumes, tall 4to., original pictorial wrappers, pages 246, 228 , illustrations.   R. F. G. Hollett & Son Antiquarian Booksellers   General Catalogue Summer 2010 - 1353 2011   £40

Byfield, Nicolas *Sermons Upon the First Chapter of the First Epistle General of Peter....* London: printed by Edward Griffin for Nathaniel Butter, 1617, First edition; pages (xxvi), 512 joints cracked and endpapers soiled, title rather browned, single wormhole through text, little shaken toward front, few other minor faults, rare.   R. F. G. Hollett & Son Antiquarian Booksellers   175 - 213 2011   £450

Byne, Arthur *Spanish Ironwork.* N.p.: 1915, xxiii, 143 pages, very good, ex-library, no exterior marks, frontispiece.   Bookworm & Silverfish   667 - 82 2011 $75

Byrne, Peter *Religious Studies: an International Journal for the Philosophy of Religion 1994-2003.* Cambridge: Cambridge University Press, 1994-2003, First edition; 37 issues, 8vo., wrappers, complete run from Volume 30 No. 4 Dec. 1994 to volume 39 No. 4 December 2003, circa 4700+ pages in all, all clean, very good.   Any Amount of Books   May 29 2011 - A47863 2011 $238

Byron, George Gordon Noel, 6th Baron   1788-1824
Don Juan. London: printed by Thomas Davison, 1819-1821, (Cantos I-V); John Hunt, 1823-1824 (Cantos VI-XVI), First editions of all 16 cantos; new edition of the extra volume with first two cantos in smaller format; First volume 305 x 232, remaining volumes 233 x 146, half titles in volumes I-II, errata slip in volume VI, ads in volumes III, IV and VI, 16 cantos bound in 7 volumes, original temporary publisher's binding of paper boards, original paper spine labels, edges untrimmed, spine of quarto volume very expertly repaired, retaining label, 7 volumes cleverly and neatly contained in slightly rubbed and faded but extremely sturdy and still handsome half morocco folding box with raised bands and gilt spine titling, bookplate of Edward Whittaker Hennell, tipped in prospectus for Britton's "Cathedral Antiquities", usual edge wear, soiling and staining that come with temporary publisher's bindings but (with exception of one prominent stain on one rear board), octavo first editions in clean and tight, very appealing condition, with considerably less wear than normally seen and virtually no cracking to joints, first two volumes with perhaps half the leaves foxed (usually light, occasionally more noticeable, never severe), other four octavo first edition volumes almost entirely clean and all the volumes still fresh and with very wide margins, extraordinarily appealing set.   Phillip J. Pirages   59 - 160 2011 $17,500

Byron, George Gordon Noel, 6th Baron   1788-1824
English Bards and Scotch Reviewers. London: printed for James Cawthorn, British Library, 1809, Probably a spurious edition; 12mo., pages vi, 54, bound with half title and preface in later, rubbed three quarter morocco, all edges gilt, with earliest, i.e. uncorrected, version of page 5, with line 7 reading "despatch" for "dispatch", also line 159 has uncorrected reading of "crouds" for "crowds", printed on non water marked paper.   Second Life Books Inc.   174 - 80   2011 $250

Byron, George Gordon Noel, 6th Baron   1788-1824
The Genuine Rejected Addresses, Presented to the Committee of Management for Drury Lane Theatre... London: Printed and sold by B. M'Millan, sold also by Hatchard, Sherwood, 1812, First edition; small 8vo., pages ix, (1), 130, later quarter leather with marbled boards lettered gilt at spine, clean very good+ copy.   Any Amount of Books   May 29 2011 - A74568   2011 $238

Byron, George Gordon Noel, 6th Baron   1788-1824
Hebrew Melodies. London: John Murray, 1815, First edition, first issue; 8vo., pages (vii), 53, (ii), bound in later blue drab wrappers, untrimmed, half title and terminal ads, lacking inserted titles and half titles, first issue with verso of Er with ad for Rogers' "Jaqueline" followed by 6 line ad for Campbell's "Selected Beauties of English Poetry".   Second Life Books Inc.   174 - 81   2011 $1500

Byron, George Gordon Noel, 6th Baron   1788-1824
Hours of Idleness. (bound with) English Bards and Scottish Reviewers: a Satire. Newark: S. & J. Ridge, 1807, London Cawthorn, 1810.First edition, first state and third edition of second work; 8vo., recent full dark brown calf lettered and decorated gilt at spine with five raised bands and new marbled endpapers, very slight occasional browning to text, neat small old ownership signature (Theophrania Fairfax), near fine.   Any Amount of Books   May 26 2011 - A69879   2011 $1090

Byron, George Gordon Noel, 6th Baron   1788-1824
Lara, a Tal. Jacqueline, a Tale by Samuel Rogers. London: J. Murray, 1814, First edition; small 8vo., pages (viii), (1), 128, (4), nice, clean copy in original boards, covers and first pages almost separate, some wear to spine, lack label, housed in custom clamshell case.   Second Life Books Inc.   174 - 82 2011 $250

Byron, George Gordon Noel, 6th Baron   1788-1824
Mazeppa, a Poem. London: John Murray, 1819, First edition, 2nd issue with imprint of the printer on verso of page 71, no page 70, bound with 6 pages ads, issued i an edition of 8000 copies; original drab wrappers (worn along spine), some foxing, untrimmed, very good.   Second Life Books Inc.   174 - 84 2011 $800

Byron, George Gordon Noel, 6th Baron   1788-1824
Marino Faliero, Doge of Venice. London: Murray, 1821, First edition; first issue, with 5 line speech of the Doge on page 151, 8vo., pages 261, bound with half titles in original half ribbed cloth and paper boards (little bumped at corners), some light foxing, very good.   Second Life Books Inc.   174 - 83 2011 $250

Byron, George Gordon Noel, 6th Baron   1788-1824
The Prophecy of Dante: a Poem. (bound with) the Two Visions or Byron v. Southey. Philadelphia: M. Carey and Sons, 1821, New York: Wm. Borradale, 1823. First American edition and First edition; 12mo., 2 items bound together in contemporary three quarter calf and marbled boards, name on endpaper.   Second Life Books Inc.   174 - 85 2011 $500

Byron, George Gordon Noel, 6th Baron   1788-1824
Sardanapalus: a Tragedy. The Two Foscari, a Tragedy. Cain, a Mystery. London: John Murray, 1821, First edition; 8vo., pages 439, without ad in front, uncut and unopened, original board, rebacked with new paper spine label partly peeled off, internally nice, little foxing, moderate wear.   Second Life Books Inc.   174 - 86 2011 $450

Byron, George Gordon Noel, 6th Baron 1788-1824 *The Works... with his Letters and Journals and His Life.* London: John Murray, 1832-1833, First edition; 17 volumes, half titles (no in volumes I, IX), engraved frontispiece and titles, illustrations, small repair to half title volume III, original dark green moire cloth, green paper label volume I, gilt little rubbed and bumped, slightly marked, armorial bookplates of William Henry Charlton.   Jarndyce Antiquarian Booksellers   CXCI - 6 2011   £500

Byron, May *Humpty Dumpty.*   New York: Hodder & Stoughton, circa, 1912, 7 1/4 x 7 7/8 inches, boards with pictorial paste-ons, 6 color plates and 8 full page black and whites plus pictorial endpapers by Cecil Aldin, fine.   Aleph-Bet Books, Inc.   95 - 45a 2011 $350

Byron, May *Humpty Dumpty.*   New York: Hodder & Stoughton, circa, 1912, 7 1/4 x 7 7/8 inches, boards with pictorial paste-ons, 6 color plates and 8 full page black and whites plus pictorial endpapers by Cecil Aldin, narrow light stain on 2 inches of spine, otherwise very good+.   Aleph-Bet Books, Inc.   95 - 45b 2011 $225

Byron, May *Master Quack.*   New York: Hodder & Stoughton, circa, 1912, 7 1/4 x 7 7/8 inches, boards with pictorial paste-ons, 6 color plates and 8 full page black and whites plus pictorial endpapers by Cecil Aldin, fine.   Aleph-Bet Books, Inc.   95 - 45c 2011 $350

Byron, May *Peter's Dinner Party.*   New York: Hodder & Stoughton, circa, 1912, 7 1/4 x 7 7/8 inches, boards with pictorial paste-ons, 6 color plates and 8 full page black and whites plus pictorial endpapers by Cecil Aldin, neat paper repair on rear gutter, else fine.   Aleph-Bet Books, Inc.   95 - 45f 2011 $350

Byron, May *Rags.*   New York: Hodder & Stoughton, circa, 1912, 7 1/4 x 7 7/8 inches, boards with pictorial paste-ons, 6 color plates and 8 full page black and whites plus pictorial endpapers by Cecil Aldin, light narrow stain on 2 inches of spine, else very good+.   Aleph-Bet Books, Inc.   95 - 45d 2011 $225

Byron, May *Rufus.*   New York: Hodder & Stoughton, circa, 1912, 7 1/4 x 7 7/8 inches, boards with pictorial paste-ons, 6 color plates and 8 full page black and whites plus pictorial endpapers by Cecil Aldin, narrow spine stain and in margin of one page, else very good+.   Aleph-Bet Books, Inc.   95 - 45e 2011 $225

Bysshe, Edward   *The Art of English Poetry.*   Printed for Sam. Buckley, 1710, Fourth edition; modern full blind panelled calf, gilt, pages (x), 482, viii,3 6, title little dusty and edges little chipped in places, neatly laid down, top corners browned toward end, otherwise most attractive.   R. F. G. Hollett & Son Antiquarian Booksellers   General Catalogue Summer 2010 - 631 2011   £250

Bywater, Hector C.   *The Great Pacific War. A History of the American-Japanese Campaign of 1931-1933.*   London: Constable, 1925, First UK edition; 8vo. pages ix, 317, neat name on first blank, sound clean very good with slight creasing at spine, map front endpapers little browned, slight foxing tp prelims.   Any Amount of Books   May 29 2011 - A40493 2011 $230

C

Cabell, James Branch 1879-1958 *Straws and Prayerbooks.* New York: McBride, 1924, First edition; some age toning to pages, otherwise fine in very good dust jacket with trace edgewear and one small chip.   Ken Lopez Bookseller   154 - 22   2011 $50

Cady, Harrison *Animal Alphabet.* Whitman, n.d. circa, 1930,   4to., pictorial wrapper, tiny nearly invisible repair to top of spine, else near fine, each page has large, rich full color illustration by Cady, very scarce.   Aleph-Bet Books, Inc.   95 - 6   2011 $450

Caesar, Gaius Julius *C. Julii Caesaris quae Extant Accuratissime...* London: Sumptibus & typis Jacobi Tonson, 1712,   Large folio, pages (6), 560, 87 engraved plates and maps, 31 engraved head and tailpieces, vignettes and 17 engraved historiated initials, double page plate of bison, usually lacking, contemporary red straight grain morocco, rebacked, original spine laid down, boards ruled in gilt and borders roll tooled in blind, spine elaborately tooled in gilt and blind in compartments, spine lettered in gilt, board edges stamped in gilt, gilt dentelles, all edges gilt, marbled endpaper, corners with some wear, occasional light toning, four inch closed marginal tear on leaf L11, professionally repaired, not affecting text, 2 previous owner's bookplates of John Jarrett and C. Kalbfleisch, small old bookseller's label, overall excellent copy, very wide margined, clean and in attractive contemporary binding.   Heritage Book Shop   Holiday 2010 - 16   2011 $15,000

Caffin, Charles H. *How to Study Architecture.* New York: Tudor Publishing, 1937,   Pages xv, 540, numerous illustrations, large 8vo., original cloth, gilt, dust jacket, little rubbed.   R. F. G. Hollett & Son Antiquarian Booksellers   177 - 160   2011   £30

Cahun, Claude *Aveux non Avenux.* Paris: Editions du Carrefour, 1930,   First edition, number 268 of 370 copies on velin pur fil Lafuma, from a total edition of 500; 8vo., pages (iv), 238, (3) table, (i) blank, (1) imprint, (1) blank, 10 photographic plates printed in gravure, one illustration in text, uncut, partially unopened, original wrappers printed in black, grey and red, light soiling to wrappers, mild sunning to spine, slip of paper loosely inserted, stamped with copy number, near fine.   Simon Finch Rare Books   Zero - 514   2011   £4500

Cain, James M. *The Moth.* New York: Knopf, 1948, First edition; fine, dust jacket near fine, price clipped but price sticker of .69 affixed to rear flap, light wear.   Bella Luna Books   May 29 2011 - j1337   2011 $82

Caine, Caesar *Capella De Gerardegile or The Story of a Cumberland Chapelry...* Haltwhistle: R. M. Saint, 1908, Limited edition (no. 120); original cloth, gilt, pages xxv, 248, 16 plates and map, 4 text illustrations, excellent, sound copy, scarce.   R. F. G. Hollett & Son Antiquarian Booksellers   173 - 207   2011   £275

Caldecott, Randolph *Jackanapes. Daddy Darwin's Dovecot. Lob Lie-by-the-Fire.* London: SPCK, n.d., Collected edition; large 8vo., original pictorial cloth gilt, extremities minimally rubbed, pages 184, illustrations by Randolph Caldecott.   R. F. G. Hollett & Sons Antiquarian Booksellers   170 - 133   2011   £60

Caldecott, Randolph *The Panjandrum, Picture Book.* London: Warne & co., n.d. c., 1900,   Oblong 8vo., original pictorial cloth, 24 full page color illustrations and line drawings.   R. F. G. Hollett & Sons Antiquarian Booksellers   170 - 125   2011   £45

Caldecott, Randolph *Picture Books.* London: George Routledge, n.d.,   2 volumes, square 8vo. and oblong 8vo., contemporary half crimson roan gilt, rubbed and scraped, one corner very defective an chewed, first volume contains 6 Picture Books, all with original wrappers bound in; second volume contains 8 titles, all bound without wrappers, all illustrated in color, first few titles in second volume with some chewed damage to top corners.   R. F. G. Hollett & Sons Antiquarian Booksellers   170 - 126   2011   £150

Caldecott, Randolph *R. Caldecott's Picture Book No. 3.* London: Frederick Warne and Co., n.d.,   Oblong 12mo., original pictorial boards, little rubbed and soiled, rebacked to match page 88, full page colored plates and sepia illustrations, few slight finger marks in places.   R. F. G. Hollett & Sons Antiquarian Booksellers   170 - 128   2011   £65

Caldecott, Randolph *R. Caldecott's Second Collection of Pictures and Songs.* London: Frederick Warne and Co. n.d., Oblong large 8vo., original pictorial cloth gilt over bevelled boards, dust jacket, edges little torn and chipped, piece missing from head of spine, each title separately paginated and illustrated throughout, numbers color printed plates engraved and printed by Edmund Evans, short closed tear to one text leaf, scarce in jacket.   R. F. G. Hollett & Sons Antiquarian Booksellers   170 - 129   2011   £150

Calderwood, W. L. *The Salmon Rivers and Lochs of Scotland.* Edward Arnold, 1909, First trade edition; large 8vo., original red cloth gilt, handsomely rebacked, matching crimson levant morocco, gilt, with raised bands and spine label, pages x, 442, 16, 4 color plates, 34 other plates, 18 maps, scattered spots, most attractive.   R. F. G. Hollett & Son Antiquarian Booksellers   General Catalogue Summer 2010 - 1224   2011   £195

Caldwell, Erskine Preston 1903-1987 *Say, Is This the U.S.A.* New York: Duell, Sloan and Pearce, 1941, First edition; clean, very near fine copy in near fine dust jacket with little fading to spine and very minor edge wear, photos by Margaret Bourke-White.   Jeff Hirsch Books   ny 2010 2011 $500

Caldwell, Erskine Preston 1903-1987 *Some American People.* New York: McBride, 1935, First edition; review copy, inscribed by author to Stuart Wright, owner signature of Florence Luntz, trace wear to spine ends, very near fine in near fine, slightly dusty dust jacket with tiny tear at upper front spine fold, publisher's review slip laid in, giving publication date Oct. 21 135, very nice association, rare as advance issue, particularly signed.   Ken Lopez Bookseller   154 - 23   2011 $500

Caldwell, Ian *The Rule of Four.* New York: Dial Press, 2004, First edition; near fine, very light bump to heel of spine, fine dust jacket, signed by Ian and co-author Dustin Thomason.   Bella Luna Books   May 29 2011 - t6860   2011 $82

California. A Guide to the Golden State. New York: Hastings House, 1939, First edition; xxxi, (1), 713 pages, plus many photos and maps, including large folding map in rear pocket, light green cloth lettered in dark green, slight offsetting to front endpapers, else fine.   Argonaut Book Shop   Recent Acquisitions Summer 2010 - 246   2011 $75

Callahan, Harry *The Multiple Image.* Chicago: Press of the Institute of Design, 1961, First edition; photos, clean, very near fine copy in photo illustrated wrappers, uncommon.   Jeff Hirsch Books   ny 2010 2011 $450

Callahan, Harry *Water's Edge.* Lyme: Callaway Editions, 1980, First edition; fine in close to near fine price clipped dust jacket that has some very minor wear but overall is much nicer than usual, signed and inscribed by Callahan, very uncommon as such.   Jeff Hirsch Books   ny 2010 2011 $850

Callander, John *Terra Australis Cognita; or Voyages to the Terra Australis or Southern Hemisphere During the Sixteenth, Seventeenth and Eighteenth Centuries.* Edinburgh: printed by A. Donaldson, 1766-1768, First edition; octavo, 3 volumes, contemporary calf.   Heritage Book Shop   Booth A12 51st NY International Antiquarian Book Fair April 8-10 2011 - 21   2011 $22,500

Callaway, Godfrey *Sketches of Kafir Life.* London: A. R. Mowbray, 1905, First edition; 8vo., pages xv, 154, illustrations, original green cloth.   J. & S. L. Bonham Antiquarian Booksellers   Africa 4/20/2011 - 8259   2011   £80

Callcott, Marya Dundas *Three Months Passed in the Mountains East of Rome During the Year 1819.* London: printed for Longman, Hurst, Rees, Orme and Brown, Paternoster Row and A. Constable and Co. Edinburgh, 1820, First edition; frontispiece, 5 plates (all with some browning), vii, (1), 305, (1) pages, contemporary cloth, morocco label,.   Anthony W. Laywood   May 26 2011 - 21026   2011 $419

Callimachus *Hymni (cum Scholiis Graecis) & Epigrammatia Eiusdem Poematium de Coma Berenices...* Geneva: H. Estienne, 1578, 2 parts, 4to., (16), 72, 134, (2 blank) pages, device on titlepage, initials headpieces, Dutch early18th century mottled calf, gilt spine, handsome copy, from the library of the Earls of Macclesfield at Shirburn Castle.   Maggs Bros. Ltd.   1440 - 44   2011   £600

Callimachus *Hymni et Epigrammata, quae Extant...* Basel: Excudebat Leonhardus Ostenius, 1589, Light browning and spotting in places, one gathering heavily foxed, two early ownership inscriptions to title, place of imprint struck through on title and colophon, pages (xlii), 460, (2) 8vo., early vellum, yapp edges, smooth backstrip later lettered in ink two paper labels (one blank and red, other printed shelfmark), ties removed, spot of damage to rear edge, small abraded label to front pastedown, good.   Blackwell Rare Books   B166 - 20   2011   £600

Callimachus *Hymni, Epigrammata et Fragmenta...* Paris: S. Mabre-Cramoisy, 1675, 4to., (20), 262, (56) pages, engraved armorial headpiece to dedication, engraved initial, 19th century olive green morocco by Hatton of Manchester, gilt, from the library of the Earls of Macclesfield at Shirburn Castle, Macclesfield arms on upper cover, edges gilt, title leaf slightly browned, spine slightly faded, extremely handsome, printed on fine paper.   Maggs Bros. Ltd.   1440 - 45   2011   £450

Calmour, Alfred *Rumbo Rhymes.* London and New York: Harper, 1911, First edition; small 4to., green pictorial cloth, 99 pages, printed on heavy coated paper, 24 full color plates by Walter Crane plus several smaller illustrations.   Aleph-Bet Books, Inc.   95 - 173   2011 $750

Calverley, William Slatere *Notes on the Early Sculptured Crosses, Shrines and Monuments in the Present Diocese of Carlisle.* Kendal: T. Wilson, 1899, Original brown cloth gilt, pages xviii, 319, portrait and numerous plates and illustrations, flyleaves browned, scarce.   R. F. G. Hollett & Son Antiquarian Booksellers   177 - 161   2011   £95

Calvino, Italo *The Castle of Crossed Destinies.* New York: Harcourt Brace Jovanovich, 1977, First American edition; 8vo., pages 129, small line drawings with 8 color plates, ex-library with bookplate and pocket removed, edges slightly soiled, very good, tight copy in scuffed dust jacket.   Second Life Books Inc.   174 - 87   2011 $65

Calvino, Italo *Le Cosmicomiche.* Torino: Einaudi, 1965, First edition; 8vo., original pale green cloth, dust jacket, fine, jacket with few short tears, presentation copy inscribed by Calvino to William Weaver, the English translator of Cosmicomics, with a number of discreet pencil annotations by Weaver.   James S. Jaffe Rare Books   May 26 2011 - 20757   2011 $5000

Calvino, Italo *The Path to the Nest of Spiders.* London: Collins, 1956, First English language edition; inscribed by translator, Archibald Colquhoun, in year of publication, tiny corner bumps, near fine in very good dust jacket with slight spine fading, light chipping to corners and crown, small creased, edge tear, scarce.   Ken Lopez Bookseller   154 - 24   2011 $650

The Cambridge History of the British Empire. Cambridge: Cambridge University Press, 1929-1936, First edition; 6 volumes, 8vo., pages 5048, ex-French Embassy, London with minor ex-library attributes otherwise very good.   Any Amount of Books   May 29 2011 - A60843   2011 $238

The Cambridge Quarterly. Cambridge: Cambridge University Press, 1965, First edition; 24 volumes, wrappers, pages 2488, most volumes clean, very good+, occasional slight soiling and tanning to white printed covers.   Any Amount of Books   May 29 2011 - A68979   2011 $340

Cameli, Francesco *Nummi Antiqui Aurei Argentei & Acrei Primae, Secundae, Seu Mediae, Minimae & Maximae Formae.* Rome: G. G. de Buagni, 1690, 4to., 218, (2 blank) pages, French smooth calf c. 1700, spine gilt, engraved bookplate of Nicolas Joseph Foucault, from the library of the Earls of Macclesfield at Shirburn Castle.   Maggs Bros. Ltd.   1440 - 232   2011   £1000

Cameron, Eleanor *Julia's Magic.* New York: E. P. Dutton, 1984, Stated first edition; 8vo., 148 pages, signed and inscribed by Cameron, fine hardback, scarce signed, fine in dust jacket.   By the Book, L. C.   26 - 54   2011 $95

Camm, Dom Bede *Forgotten Shrines. A Account of Some Old Catholic Halls and Families in England and of Relics and Memorials of the English Martyrs.* MacDonald & Evans and St. Louis, B. Herder, 1910, First edition; thick small 4to., original cloth, gilt over bevelled boards, pages xvi, 415, numerous illustrations, joints cracking, else very good.   R. F. G. Hollett & Son Antiquarian Booksellers   177 - 164   2011   £140

Camp, John *Discovering Bells and Bellringing.* Tring: Shire Publications, 1968, First edition; small 8vo., original stiff wrappers, pages 48, illustrations, few annotations by Mary Hudleston (folk song collector), small cutting taped inside front panel.   R. F. G. Hollett & Son Antiquarian Booksellers   175 - 220   2011   £30

Campbell, Alexander *Sketches of Life and Character.* Edinburgh: Edinburgh Printing & Pub. Co., 1842, First edition; original dark green vertically grained cloth, blocked in blind, slightly rubbed, seven line prize inscription.   Jarndyce Antiquarian Booksellers   CXCI - 103   2011   £65

Campbell, George *A Soldier of the Sky.* circa, 1918, First edition; 232 pages, near fine in dust jacket, missing 3/8 inch bottom, top edges ruffled, reasonable reader soil.   Bookworm & Silverfish   678 - 215   2011 $150

Campbell, Guy *Golf for Beginners.* C. Arthur Pearson, 1922, First edition; original pictorial cloth, little soiled and rubbed, pages 124, with 25 diagrams, little pencilled lining.   R. F. G. Hollett & Son Antiquarian Booksellers   General Catalogue Summer 2010 - 1225   2011   £65

Campbell, Helen *Wah Sing Our Little Chinese Friend.* Philadelphia: David McKay, 1906, 8vo., pictorial cloth, bookplate removed from endpaper, else fine and bright, photos.   Aleph-Bet Books, Inc.   95 - 145   2011 $125

Campbell, J. F. *Popular Tales of the West Highlands Orally Collected...* 1860-1862, First editions; 4 volumes, original gilt decorated cloth, needs attention, frontispiece to volume 3 with guard, cxxxv, 353, xiii, 478, xv, 422, viii, 480 pages, text very good.   C. P. Hyland   May 26 2011 - 256/1088   2011 $290

Campbell, John Campbell, 1st Baron 1779-1861 *The Lives of the Chief Justices of England.* Northport: 1894-1899, 5 volumes, large 4to., half beige and crimson cloth, volumes 1 and 2 with library stamps on top and bottom edge, backstrips very mildly rubbed, gilt lettering legible but also mildly rubbed, volumes 1-3 recased, reset into original covers, new endpapers, volumes 1-3 with tear to corners, volumes 4 and 5 damped at top backstrip with most of discoloration concealed beneath publisher's crimson chemise jackets, some volumes unopened, with 2200 pages of text, 126 full page plates, solid set, reasonably good shelf appearance.   Bookworm & Silverfish   665 - 78   2011 $295

Campbell, John Francis *A Short American Tramp in the Fall of 1864.* Edinburgh: Edmonston and Douglas, 1865, Original maroon cloth, gilt to spine, pages (viii), 427, (1) (12 pages ads), half title, frontispiece, illustrated titlepage, numerous tables, 8vo., cloth, slightly worn and sunned.   Schooner Books Ltd.   96 - 23   2011 $125

Campbell, John Gregorson *Superstitions of the Highlands & Islands of Scotland.* Glasgow: James Maclehose and Sons, 1900, pages xx, 319, untrimmed, very good, original blue cloth.   R. F. G. Hollett & Son Antiquarian Booksellers   175 - 222   2011   £150

Campbell, John W. *The Black Star Passes.* Reading: Fantasy Press, 1953, First edition; octavo, cloth. L. W. Currey, Inc. 124 - 139 2011 $450

Campbell, John W. *The Incredible Planet.* Reading: Fantasy Press, 1949, First edition; octavo, original purple cloth, spine panel stamped in gold. L. W. Currey, Inc. 124 - 197 2011 $200

Campbell, John W. *Invaders from the Infinite.* Reading: Fantasy Press, 1961, octavo, boards. L. W. Currey, Inc. 124 - 68 2011 $1250

Campbell, John W. *Islands of Space.* Reading: Fantasy Press, 1956, First edition; octavo, cloth. L. W. Currey, Inc. 124 - 69 2011 $1250

Campbell, John W. *The Mightiest Machine.* Providence: Hadley Pub. Co., 1947, First edition; octavo, original blue pebbled cloth, spine panel stamped in gold. L. W. Currey, Inc. 124 - 237 2011 $75

Campbell, John W. *Who Goes There? Seven Tales of Science Fiction.* Chicago: Shasta Pub., 1948, First edition; octavo, cloth. L. W. Currey, Inc. 124 - 80 2011 $1000

Campbell, Malcolm *My Thirty Years of Speed.* London: Hutchinson, n.d., First edition; original cloth, pages 270, 216, with 50 illustrations, edges rather foxed. R. F. G. Hollett & Son Antiquarian Booksellers General Catalogue Summer 2010 - 1098 2011 £60

Campbell, Marius R. *Guidebook of the Western United States; Part E. The Denver & Rio Grande Western Route.* Washington: 1922, xi, 266 pages, 12 folding maps, illustrations, original printed wrappers, some edgewear to wrappers, bit of paper loss to top of spine, else clean and very good. Dumont Maps & Books of the West 111 - 49 2011 $85

Campbell, Ruth *The Cat whose Whiskers Slipped.* Joliet: Volland, 1925, First edition of this book; 8vo., pictorial boards, fine in publisher's pictorial box, illustrations by Eliazbeth Cadie, beautiful copy. Aleph-Bet Books, Inc. 95 - 140 2011 $400

Campbell, Thomas *Letters from the South.* London: Henry Colburn, 1837, First edition; 2 volumes, 8vo., pages xx, 354; xi, 358; 10 plates, plan, (Algiers) contemporary blue half calf, joints and corners rubbed, small split at head of volume I lacks labels on spine. J. & S. L. Bonham Antiquarian Booksellers Africa 4/20/2011 - 8344 2011 £150

Campbell, Thomas 1733-1795 *A Philosophical Survey of the South of Ireland in a Series of Letters.* Dublin: Watkinson et al, 1778, First Dublin edition; 3 plates, xvi, 478 pages, full contemporary calf, hinges cracked, text good. C. P. Hyland May 26 2011 - 259/056 2011 $362

Campbell, Thomas 1733-1795 *A Philosophical Survey of the South of Ireland. In a Series of Letters.* 1777, First edition; only last plate (folding 'antiquities') of 6, quarter calf, needs rebinding but without plates text good. C. P. Hyland May 26 2011 - 258/070 2011 $391

Campbell, Thomas 1733-1795 *A Philosophical Survey of the South of Ireland. In a Series of Letters.* Dublin: 1778, First Dublin edition; 6 plates, full calf, rebacked, good. C. P. Hyland May 26 2011 - 259/057 2011 $580

Campbell, Thomas 1777-1844 *Gertrude of Wyoming.* London: Longman, Hurst, Rees & Orme, 1809, First edition; original cloth rebacked with spine label added, light foxing to first and last pages, bit of surface soiling. Lupack Rare Books May 26 2011 - ABE4763915092 2011 $100

Campbell, Thomas 1777-1844 *Gertrude of Wyoming and Other Poems.* London: Longman Hurst, Rees, Orme & Brown, 1816, Sixth edition; half title, frontispiece, slightly foxed, uncut in original light brown paper boards, paper label, some very slight wear to lower following hinge, else exceptional copy in its original state; contemporary signature, modern booklabel of Vincent Walmsley and earlier ownership inscription of Lt. Lloyd. Jarndyce Antiquarian Booksellers CXCI - 347 2011 £75

Campbell, Thomas 1777-1844 *Specimens of the British Poets...* London: John Murray, 1819, First edition; 7 volumes, half calf, red and green labels, gilt, slight marking, very good, acttractive. Jarndyce Antiquarian Booksellers CXCI - 7 2011 £620

Camus, Albert *L'Exil et le Royaume (Exile and the Kingdom).* Paris: Gallimard, 1957, First edition, one of 400 copies printed on Alfa Calypso, this copy numbered 799; half title + titlepage + dedication page + half title + (11)-244 (245) - index (247) - Printing information, small octavo, original red boards with gilt lettering on front and spine, spine just little sunned, otherwise lovely. Athena Rare Books 10 2011 $125

Camus, Albert *Lettres a un Ami Allemand. (Letters to a German Friend).* Paris: Gallimard, 1945, First edition; half title + titlepage, quote page + half title + 13-(81) + half title + 1 leaf - contents + 1 leaf - printing information, small octavo, with 3 line inscription and Camus' signature, from a printing of 2250 of which 2000 numbered copies were printed on alfa Navarre paper, this copy #2133, original wrappers with mild darkening to spine, clean and very pretty, fragile. Athena Rare Books 10 2011 $2000

Camus, Albert *Promethee aux Enfers. (Prometheus in Hell).* 1945, First edition, 35 copies printed on Bulle and numbered I-XXXV, another 250 numbered copies printed on white velin, this copy numbered "182; octavo, half title titlepage, (1)-(10) + 1 blank leaf, unbound, two gatherings loosely inserted in card covers, as issued, near fine, but bit of soiling to edges of clear tissue cover. Athena Rare Books 10 2011 $300

Camus, Albert *L'Homme Revolte. (The Rebel).* Paris: Gallimard, 1951, First edition; half title + titlepage + dedication page + quotation page + half title (13)-382 + (383) - Printer's information, octavo, inscribed, original printed paper wrappers, mended tear to front spine fold at head of spine, minor soiling and wear to wrappers, text browned as usual and uncut, preserved in clamshell box, beautiful copy, with 3 line inscription by Camus for Italian philosopher Nicola Chiaramonte, review copy on ordinary paper. Athena Rare Books 10 2011 $2500

Camus, Albert *L'Envers et L'Endroit. (The Wrong Side and the Right Side).* Alger: Editions Edmond Charlot, 1937, First edition; original front wrapper, titlepage + dedication page + half title, 9-(67), original rear wrapper, octavo, original wrappers rebound in modern patterned boards with black morocco spine and gilt lettering, just touch of soiling and some light creasing to original wrappers, else fine in fine modern binding. Athena Rare Books 10 2011 $5000

Camus, Francois Joseph De *Traite des Forces Mouvantes, avec la Description de 23 machines Nouvelles de son Invention.* Paris: C. Jombert and L. Le Cotne, 1722, 8vo., (16), 535, (7) pages, 8 folding engraved plates, woodcut device on title, woodcut initials, head and tailpieces, speckled calf, spine gilt in compartments, red morocco lettering piece, few quires lightly brown, extremities rubbed, red mottled edges, from the library of the Earls of Macclesfield at Shirburn Castle. Maggs Bros. Ltd. 1440 - 46 2011 £800

Caniff, Milton *Terry and the Pirates in Shipwrecked.* Chicago: Pleasure Books, 1935, 4to., pictorial boards, clean and near fine, 3 fabulous color pop-ups and black and whites throughout text, really nice. Aleph-Bet Books, Inc. 95 - 445 2011 $475

Cannell, D. M. *George Green: Mathematician and Physicist 1793-1841: the Background to His Life and Work.* London: Atlantic Highlands: Athlone Press, 1993, 8vo., xxvi, 265 pages, 20 illustrations, blue cloth silver stamped spine title, dust jacket, from the Bern Dibner reference library, with Burndy bookplate, fine. Jeff Weber Rare Books 161 - 76 2011 $90

Cannon, John T. *The Evolution of Dynamics: Vibration Theory from 1687 to 1742.* New York: Springer Verlag, 1981, Thin 8vo., ix, 184 pages, printed boards, fine, from the Bern Dibner reference library, with Burndy bookplate. Jeff Weber Rare Books 161 - 77 2011 $165

Cannon, Peter *Forever Azathoth and Other Horrors.* N.P.: Tartarus Press, 1999, First edition, #166 of 250 copies signed and numbered by author; 8vo., pages viii, 234, frontispiece, fine in fine dust jacket. Any Amount of Books May 29 2011 - A71693 2011 $204

Canot, Theodore *Adventures of an African Slaver.* London: Routledge, 1928, First edition; 8vo., pages xxi, 376, illustrations, original yellow boards. J. & S. L. Bonham Antiquarian Booksellers Africa 4/20/2011 - 8444 2011 £50

Cantor, G. N. *Conceptions of Ether.* Cambridge: Cambridge University Press, 1981, First edition; 8vo., x, 351 pages, near fine, black cloth, gilt lettering. By the Book, L. C. 26 - 95 2011 $300

Capek, Karel *R.U.R. a Play. (Rossum's Universal Robots).* London: Humphrey Milford, Oxford University Press, 1923, First edition; wrappers, small 8vo., pages 102, 2 page publisher's ads, inner hinge very slightly cracked, else very decent copy, scarce, very good. Any Amount of Books May 26 2011 - A39605 2011 $419

Capote, Truman 1924-1985 *Observations.* London: Weidenfeld and Nicholson, 1959, First English edition, with signed letter from photographer, Richard Avedon to Frau Bucher; folio, pages 152, 104 black and white photos printed in gravure, design by Alexey Brodovitch, original white paper covered boards printed in grey, lightly rubbed, original white paper covered board slipcase, printed in red, blue and grey, lightly rubbed and soiled with little wear to edges, with TLS to Frau Bucher. Simon Finch Rare Books Zero - 504 2011 £550

Capote, Truman 1924-1985 *Les Domaines Hantes. (Other Voices, Other Rooms).* Paris: Gallimard, 1949, First French edition; printed wrappers, unopened about fine, Roman numeral copy II (2) of 200 copies on sur velin pur fil Lafuma-Navarre paper (additionally there were 5 lettered copies hors de commerce). Between the Covers 169 - BTC337617 2011 $450

Caprilli, Frederico *The Caprilli Papers: Principles of Outdoor Equitation.* London: J. A. Allen & Co. Ltd., 1967, First edition; frontispiece, pages 40 + 40 illustrations on 26 further pages, original red cloth, white lettering on spine, slightly bumped at lower spine, otherwise very good in very good dust jacket with some ink underlining on 8 pages by former owner, this was Lieut. Col. A. J. B. McFarland, scarce. Any Amount of Books May 26 2011 - A722285 2011 $402

Caradoc, of Llancarvan *The History of Wales.* London: By M. Clark for the author and R. Clavell, 1697, (40) xxiii, (1), 398, (18) pages, contemporary calf, rebacked in period style, later endpapers, very nice.   Joseph J. Felcone Inc. Fall Miscellany 2010 - 124   2011 $450

Caran D'Ache the Supreme. London: Methuen, 1933, First edition; 4to., original pictorial boards, matching dust jacket (tear repaired on reverse, few other short tears and small repaired chips), pages 79, line drawings and cartoons, scarce.   R. F. G. Hollett & Son Antiquarian Booksellers General Catalogue Summer 2010 - 704   2011   £65

Card, Orson Scott *The Folk of the Fringe.* West Bloomfield: Phantasia Press, 1989, First edition; octavo, leather.   L. W. Currey, Inc. 124 - 129   2011 $500

Cardinale, Igino *Papal Rome and Its Influence in the Field of World Politics.* Salzburg: privaely printed, 1959, 4to., pages 42, modern cloth, copy typescript printed on recto only, initial leaves little crease.   R. F. G. Hollett & Son Antiquarian Booksellers   175 - 225   2011   £35

Carey-Hobson, Mary *At Home in the Transvaal.* London: W. Swan Sonnenschein, 1884, 2 volumes, small octavo (iv), 268; (iv), (260)-524 pages, original green cloth, blind rules, gilt spines, speckled edges, titlepage embossed with library stamps, bookplate of R. F. Thorold, very good plus, rare.   Jeff Weber Rare Books   163 - 140   2011 $85

Carey, Charles Henry *History of Oregon.* Chicago: 1922, 3 volumes, large 4to., very good, nearly 3000 pages, volume III shelf skewed, marbled pastedown and all edges.   Bookworm & Silverfish   670 - 120   2011 $165

Carey, H. C. *Past, Present & Future.* Philadelphia: Carey & Hart, 1848, First edition; 8vo., 474 pages, original cloth, stamps and bookplates, light wear to ends of spine, very sound and tight, lacking plate.   M & S Rare Books, Inc. 90 - 68   2011 $450

Carey, H. C. *The Past, The Present and the Future.* London: Longmans, Brown, Green and Longmans, 1848, First edition; 8vo., original publisher' green blind patterned cloth lettered gilt at spine, pages 474, with 32 page publisher's catalog at rear. pencilled ownership signature of historian F. R. Cowell, sound clean copy with unsightly chip at head of spine and loss of about 2 inches of cloth affecting part of lettering, lesser chip at foot of spine, otherwise near very good and text very clean.   Any Amount of Books May 29 2011 - A45215   2011 $340

Carey, Mathew *Carey's American Atlas: Containing Twenty Maps and One Chart.* Philadelphia: Mathew Carey, 1795, First edition; contemporary quarter calf over marbled boards.   Heritage Book Shop   Booth A12 51st NY International Antiquarian Book Fair April 8-10 2011 - 22   2011 $37,500

Carey, Peter *Jack Maggs.* London: Faber & Faber, 1997, First British edition; review copy, fine, in like dust jacket.   Bella Luna Books   May 29 2011 - t9456   2011 $82

Carey, Peter *Theft, a Love Story.* Sydney: Knopf, 2006, First Australian edition; fine in fine dust jacket.   Bella Luna Books   May 26 2011 - t9227   2011 $192

Carisella, P. J. *The Black Swallow of Death...* Boston: Marlbourough House Inc., 1972, 8vo., pages xiv, 271, 22 illustrations in text, one page slightly soiled, otherwise internally fine, publisher's cloth, blue, red lettering to upper board, white lettering and red motif to spine, fine, original color illustrated dust jacket, unclipped, lightly worn with short closed tears to head and foot of spine, presentation letter to Gordon Parks loosely inserted.   Simon Finch Rare Books Zero - 213   2011   £375

Carle, Eric *The Rabbit and the Turtle.* New York: Orchard Books/Scholastic, 2008, Stated first edition; 4to., 28 pages, illustrations by Eric Carle, signed by Carle on titlepage in blue ink, without personalization, fine in fine dust jacket.   By the Book, L. C.   26 - 55   2011 $175

Carlile, Richard *Vice Versus Reason. A Copy of the Bill of Indictment Found at the Old Bailey Sessions, January 16 1819 Against Richard Carlile 1819.* London: printed and published by R. Carlile, 1819, First edition; 8vo., 13 (3) pages, final 3 pages being Carlile's ads for his publications, titlepage rather soiled, brown spot in some inner margins, preserved in modern wrappers with printed title label on upper cover, scarce.   John Drury Rare Books   153 - 153   2011   £275

Carlisle, Nicholas *A Concise Description of the Endowed Grammar Schools in England and Wales; Ornamented with Engravings.* London: Baldwin, Cradock and Joy, 1818, 2 volumes, half titles, engraved illustrations, endpapers foxed, pages xliv, (vi), 858; (iv), 983, thick 8vo., slightly later half calf, backstrips with five raised bands, gilt fillets, red and black morocco labels with gilt lettering, marbled sides, good. Blackwell Rare Books   B166 - 21   2011   £350

Carlyle, Thomas 1795-1881 *History of Friedrich II of Prussia Called Frederick the Great.* London: Chapman & Hall, 1872-1873, 10 volumes in 5, contemporary half calf, gilt, raised bands, double spine labels, edges little rubbed and scraped, folding maps, some colored in outline, tables, scattered spotting, handsome set.   R. F. G. Hollett & Son Antiquarian Booksellers   175 - 226   2011   £275

Carlyle, Thomas 1795-1881 *The Life of John Sterling.* London: Chapman & Hall, 1852, Second edition; half title, initial ad leaf, original green cloth, spine little worn. Jarndyce Antiquarian Booksellers   CXCI - 107   2011   £35

Carlyle, Thomas 1795-1881 *On Heroes, Hero-Worship & the Heroic in History.* London: James Fraser, 1841, First edition in Tarr's primary binding; 2 pages ads, original purple brown cloth, spine gilt, cloth lightly lifting from boards, ownership inscriptions "L.W. 1842" and Carlingford 1878. Jarndyce Antiquarian Booksellers CXCI - 108 2011 £225

Carlyle, Thomas 1795-1881 *Sartor Resartus.* Boston: James Munroe; Philadelphia: James Kay: Pittsburg: John I. Kay, 1837, Excellent rebound in half red brown calf, spine gilt, ownership signature of F. E. (Frances Emma) Wedgwood 11 July 1837". Jarndyce Antiquarian Booksellers CXCI - 109 2011 £480

Carman, Bliss 1861-1929 *Later Poems.* Toronto: McClelland & Stewart, 1921, First edition; inscribed by author in year of publication, lovely decorated cloth, near fine copy. Lupack Rare Books May 26 2011 - ABE3649642564 2011 $100

Carmichael, Alexander *Carmina Gadelica. Hymns and Incantations.* Scottish Academic Press, 1971-1972, Second edition; 6 volumes, large 8vo., original cloth backed boards, gilt, dust jackets price clipped, top edges trifle dusty, otherwise fine, handsome set. R. F. G. Hollett & Son Antiquarian Booksellers 175 - 227 2011 £450

Caro, Annibale 1507-1566 *De Le Lettere Familiari del Commendatore Annibal Caro.* Venice: Bernardo Giunti e Fratelli, 1592, 1591. Later edition; 2 volumes bound together, 8vo., (8), 716; (8), 272 pages, 2 engraved title vignettes, engraved initials, engraved headpieces, early ink marginalia pages 272 (crossed out in early hand), neat marginal repair to page 213-214, early full vellum, early ms. title/author on spine, all edges gauffered in Pointille style with groups of fleur-de-lys in spaces, early ownership rubberstamp of R. P. Knight. Jeff Weber Rare Books 163 - 6 2011 $825

Caroe, W. D. *Sefton. A Descriptive and Historical Account Comprising the Collected Notes and Researches of the late Rev. Engelbert Horley, Together with the Records of the Mock Corporation.* London: Longmans, Green and Co., 1893, First edition; large heavy 8vo., original buckram gilt, uncut, 17 plates, 32 text illustrations and folding pedigree. R. F. G. Hollett & Son Antiquarian Booksellers 177 - 165 2011 £75

Carpenter, George *Golden Rules for Diseases of Infants & Children.* Bristol and London: 1903, 167, (1) pages, original binding, very good. Bookworm & Silverfish 664 - 127 2011 $75

Carpenter, John *Improving Songs for Anxious Children.* New York: Scrhirmer, 1913, Oblong folio, cloth backed decorative boards, 50 pages, corners worn, very good, illustrations in color, quite scarce. Aleph-Bet Books, Inc. 95 - 287 2011 $450

Carpenter, William R. *The Microscope and Its Revelations.* London: John Churchill, 1862, Third edition; thick small 8vo., original cloth, gilt, rather worn, bumped and frayed in places, pages xxiv, 792, with 10 plates and 395 text woodcuts, joints cracked. R. F. G. Hollett & Son Antiquarian Booksellers General Catalogue Summer 2010 - 1099 2011 £140

Carpenter, William R. *The Microscope and Its Revelations.* J. & A. Churchill, 1891, thick 8vo., original cloth, gilt, hinges and corners rather worn, pages xviii, 1009, xvi, with 21 plates, joints cracked. R. F. G. Hollett & Son Antiquarian Booksellers General Catalogue Summer 2010 - 1100 2011 £120

Carr, H. D. *Rosa Mundi.* Paris and London: Renouard & Carr, 1905, First edition, one of 500 copies; folio, pages (8), 16, (4), complete with frontispiece by Rodin, partly unopened, generally bright copy, some light foxing to frontispiece, one leaf torn in upper margin, original rose wrappers, printed in black, spine chipped and cracked along fold, wrappers sunned, worn with traces of old restoration. Simon Finch Rare Books Zero - 310 2011 £500

Carr, John 1772-1832 *The Stranger in Ireland or Tour in the Southern & Western Parts of that Country in the Year 1805.* 1806, First edition; 15 aquatints, tinted map xiv, 530 pages, 2 pages publisher's ad, full calf worn, text good. C. P. Hyland May 26 2011 - 259/063 2011 $1087

Carr, John 1772-1832 *The Stranger in Ireland; or a Tour in the Southern and Western Parts of that Country in the Year 1805.* London: Richard Phillips, 1806, First edition; 4to., xiv, (2), 530, (2) pages, 16 sepia tinted aquatint plates (several folding), engraved map, uncut, modern morocco backed paper covered boards, endpapers bit foxed, internally clean and fresh, large unpressed copy, retaining most of original tissue guards, armorial bookplate of John Towneley, modern booklabel. Joseph J. Felcone Inc. Fall Miscellany 2010 - 64 2011 $2000

Carr, Richard *The Classical Scholar's Guide.* London: printed for the author by John Richardson and Kirkby Lonsdale: Arthur Foster, 1832, First edition; original cloth backed boards with paper spine label, little soiled, pages (xxiv), 299, bound in 6's with some 4, 5 and 8 leaf sections ad little erratic pagination in places, endpapers lightly spotted, few edges and inner margins little stained, but very good, unsophisticated, untrimmed copy. R. F. G. Hollett & Son Antiquarian Booksellers 175 - 228 2011 £125

Carrick, Robert W. *John G. Alden and His Yacht Designs.* Camden: 1983, First edition; fine in near fine, dust jacket, xvii, 445 pages. Bookworm & Silverfish 678 - 137 2011 $100

Carrickford, Richard *This is Television.* London: Frederick Muller, 1967, Third edition; 8vo., 63 pages, illustrations by Ralph Steadman, with cartoons and technical diagrams, dust jacket very good+ in decent, about very good dust jacket slightly nicked at edges and price clipped. Any Amount of Books   May 29 2011 - A44453   2011 $221

The Carrier's Dream and the Broomstick Train. The Carrier Boys of the Carrier Boys of the Salem Gazette and Essex County Mercury to Their Patrons. Salem: 1891, First edition; 8vo., 12 pages, self wrappers, sewn, some uneven browning, oblong dealer's label (?) tipped to title verso, fine, laid in library folder with printed label on spine.   M & S Rare Books, Inc.   90 - 69   2011 $425

Carrington, Wirt J. *A History of Halifax County, Virginia.* Richmond: 1924, 525 pages, extra nice exterior, text bock reseated top edge of first 3 leaves damp ghosted not affecting text.   Bookworm & Silverfish   668 - 180   2011 $65

Carroll, Jonathan *Voice of Our Shadow.* New York: Viking Press, 1983, First edition; octavo, cloth backed boards.   L. W. Currey, Inc.   124 - 198   2011 $200

Carse, Adam *Musical Wind Instruments. A History of the Wind Instruments and In European Orchestras...* London: Macmillan, 1939, First edition; original cloth, gilt, dust jacket, small edge tear, pages xv, 381, with 30 plates showing 183 instruments, 41 drawings and diagrams and 11 fingering charts.   R. F. G. Hollett & Son Antiquarian Booksellers   175 - 230   2011   £65

Carse, Roland *Monarchs of Merrie England.* Leeds: Alf Cooke, n.d., 1910, First edition thus; 4 volumes, 4to., original pictorial stiff card wrappers, some edges little rubbed, unpaginated, 8 full page color plates and numerous line drawings by W. Heath Robinson, very good.   R. F. G. Hollett & Son Antiquarian Booksellers   175 - 1141   2011   £150

Carsley, K. A. *The Deva Pentice. The Journal of the Freemen and Guilds of the City of Chester.* Chester: The Guilds, 1972-1978, Nos. 2-8, 10 & 11 (no. 8 duplicated), 10 volumes, original wrappers, pages 36, illustrations.   R. F. G. Hollett & Son Antiquarian Booksellers   General Catalogue Summer 2010 - 1355   2011   £45

Carson, Rachel *Silent Spring.* Boston: Houghton Mifflin, 1962, First edition; 8vo., 368 pages, nice, dust jacket price clipped and little worn.   Second Life Books Inc.   174 - 88   2011 $600

Carter, Charlotte *Rhode Island Red.* London: Serpent's Tail, 1997, First British edition, true first, preceding the American; warmly inscribed by author, tiny ink dot to fore edge, still fine, without dust jacket, as issued.   Ken Lopez Bookseller   154 - 25   2011 $75

Carter, James *A Lecture on the Primitive State of Man, Read Before the Ipswich Mechanics' Institute on Sept. 15 and Before the Colchester Mechanics' Institute on Sept. 28 1835.* London: Simpkin, Marshall, Taylor, printer, Colchester, 1836, Disbound, 34, (2) pages.   Jarndyce Antiquarian Booksellers   CXCI - 113   2011   £45

Carter, Jimmy *Christmas in Plains.* Norwalk: Easton Press, 2002, Signed by author, leather with gold titles and decorations, all edges gilt, silk endpapers and ribbon bookmark, "A note about card and signed certificate of authenticity folded in, very clean and tight, 155 pages.   G. H. Mott Bookseller   May 26 2011 - 37079   2011 $270

Carter, Jimmy *An Hour Before Daylight: memoirs of a Rural Boyhood.* Norwalk: Easton Press, 2001, Signed by author on limitation page; leather, gold titles and decorations, all edges gilt, silk endpapers and ribbon bookmark, "A note about" card and signed certificate of authenticity folded in, very clean and tight, 284 pages, fine.   G. H. Mott Bookseller   May 26 2011 - 37110   2011 $295

Carter, Jimmy *Keeping Faith.* New York: Bantam, 1982, First edition, limited but not numbered; near fine, light wear to cloth on spine, dust jacket near fine, cloth slipcase, signed on tipped in limitation page, near fine cloth slipcase.   Bella Luna Books   May 26 2011 - t7921   2011 $192

Carter, Jimmy *Keeping Faith: Memoirs of a President.* New York: Bantam, 1982, First edition; limited edition, signed by author, cloth in slipcase, spine very slightly darkened, slipcase with very minor fading at edges, otherwise as new.   Gemini Fine Books & Arts, Ltd.   Art Reference & Illustrated Books: First Editions 2011 $165

Carter, Jimmy *Palestine: Peace Not Apartheid?* New York: Simon & Schuster, 2006, First edition; fine, signed by author, fine dust jacket.   Bella Luna Books   May 26 2011 - 58231   2011 $220

Carter, John 1748-1817 *The Ancient Architecture of England.* London: Henry Bohn, 1845, New improved edition; Parts I and II in one volume, half leather, edge worn, scratched, split at f.f.e.p., else clean, tight, large folio, some spotting, but plates overall are in good condition, etched from drawings.   G. H. Mott Bookseller   May 26 2011 - 43742   2011 $700

Carter, John 1748-1817 *Specimens of Gothic Architecture and Ancient Buildings in England. Volumes I, II and IV.* London: Edward Jeffery and Son, 1824, 3 (of four volumes), 4 x 5 inches, xvi, 132; 148; 157; spines gilt, many sheets loose, very good, etchings.   G. H. Mott Bookseller   May 26 2011 - 43737   2011 $400

Carter, John 1748-1817 *Specimens of the Ancient Sculpture and Painting Now remaining in England from the Earliest Time to the Reign of Henry VIII.* London: Henry Bohn, 1838, 120 plates, several hand colored, binding scuffed and worn, titlepage and frontispiece detached and spotted, prints in good condition with some spotting in margins, large folio.   G. H. Mott Bookseller   May 26 2011 - 53740 2011 $700

Carter, John 1748-1817 *Specimens of the Ancient Sculpture and Painting Now Remaining in England, From the Earliest Period to the Reign of Henry VIII.* London: Henry G. Bohn, 1838, New edition; Atlas folio, contemporary half morocco, gilt, hinges and corners rubbed, pages (iii) 148 vi (index), etched frontispiece and title and 120 full page etched plates.   R. F. G. Hollett & Son Antiquarian Booksellers   General Catalogue Summer 2010 - 74 2011 £495

Carter, Martin *Selected Poems.* Georgetown: Demerara Publishers Ltd., 1989, First edition; 8vo., pages xix, 198, wrappers, slight rubbing, very slight wear at spine, "Guayan Prize 1989 winner" sticker on cover, otherwise sound, clean, very good.   Any Amount of Books   May 29 2011 - A48167 2011 $340

Carter, Susannah *The Frugal Housewife; or Complete Woman Cook.* Philadelphia: 1796, 16mo., 132 pages, 2 plates, 1 table arrangement chart and 12 bills of fare, contemporary quarter calf and marbled boards, front cover detached.   M & S Rare Books, Inc. 90 - 94 2011 $1750

Carter, Susannah *The Frugal Housewife, or Complete Woman Cook.* London: printed for J. Harris and B. Crosby and Co. n.d. circa, 1810, Revised and corrected edition; 12mo., 2 engraved plates, 12 table settings in letterpress, corners of first and last leaves frayed, xx, 184 pages, original printed wrapper at rear only (dust soiled and marked), contained in modern cloth box, morocco label on spine.   Anthony W. Laywood   May 26 2011 - 18298 2011 $579

Cartier-Bresson, Henri *Images a la Sauvette.* Paris: Editions Verve, 1952, First edition; folio, pages (155), 126 black and white photos, printed in yellow, blue, red and black, designed by Joan Miro, head of spine lightly bumped, very light shelfwear to foot of spine and bottom edges, captions bound-in, no dust jacket (as issued), near fine.   Simon Finch Rare Books   Zero - 517 2011   £1250

Cartwright, Bert *The Bible in the Lyrics of Bob Dylan.* Wanted Man, 1985, First edition; 8vo., 65 pages, wrappers, about fine.   Any Amount of Books   May 26 2011 - A68194 2011 $470

Cartwright, David Edgar *Tides: a Scientific History.* Cambridge: Cambridge University Press, 1999, First edition; tall 8vo., xii, 292 pages, frontispiece, illustrations, figures, black cloth, silver stamped spine title, dust jacket, fine, rare in cloth with dust jacket, from the Bern Dibner reference library, with Burndy bookplate.   Jeff Weber Rare Books 161 - 78 2011 $100

Cartwright, Julia *The Early Work of Raphael.* London: Seeley and Co., 1895, First edition; tall 8vo., contemporary half morocco gilt with raised bands, pages 878, top edge gilt, 4 heliogravre plates and 23 text illustrations.   R. F. G. Hollett & Son Antiquarian Booksellers   General Catalogue Summer 2010 - 75 2011   £50

Carver, Raymond *Carver Country.* New York: Scribner's, 1990, First printing; large horizontal 8vo., 159 pages, photos by Bob Adelman, upper corners of few leaves showing slight moisture damage, slight rippling at top of leaves, else nice, dust jacket little scuffed and soiled.   Second Life Books Inc.   174 - 89 2011 $60

Carver, Raymond *Fires.* London: Collins Harvill, 1985, First British edition; inscribed by author to novelist, Robert Stone, uncommon thus, foxing to page edges and endpapers, not affecting inscription, very good in very good dust jacket, lightly edgeworn with foxing, mostly on verso and slight fading to spine title,.   Ken Lopez Bookseller   154 - 26 2011 $2500

Carver, Raymond *The Painter and the Fish.* Concord: William B. Ewert, 1988, Limited edition of 74 numbered signed copies, this is number 58; printed from Janson type on Lana laid paper in blue hand sewn wrappers with gilt lettering front cover, 8vo, fine.   By the Book, L. C. 26 - 1 2011 $150

Carver, Raymond *Where I'm Calling From.* Franklin Center: Franklin Library, 1988, First edition; full burgundy leather binding with raised band spine, gilt lettering and design spine, gilt design covers, all edges gilt, marbled endpapers, silk ribbon bookmark, 8vo., 391 pages, propsectus and letter from Franklin Press laid in.   By the Book, L. C. 26 - 2 2011 $70

Cary, Joyce 1888-1957 *The Moonlight.* London: Michael Joseph, 1946, First edition; 8vo., 307 pages, very good+ in chipped very good- dust jacket, signed presentation from author "Elsie Carlisle/ with author's love".   Any Amount of Books   May 29 2011 - A68504 2011 $255

Carysfort, John Joshua Proby, 1st Earl of *A Serious Address to the Electors of Great Britain on the Subject of Short Parliaments and on Equal Representation.* London: printed for J. Debrett, successor to Mr. Almon, 1782, First edition; 8vo., 31 (1) pages, 19th century dark blue half calf over marbled boards, spine lettered gilt, very good, very scarce.   John Drury Rare Books   153 - 121 2011   £250

Casas, Bartolome De Las, Bp. of Chiapa   1474-1586 *An Account of the First Voyages and Discoveries Made by the Spaniards in America.*   London: J. Darby for D. Brown et al, 1699,   Second English edition; octavo, full contemporary paneled speckled calf, rebacked using original spine.   Heritage Book Shop   Booth A12 51st NY International Antiquarian Book Fair April 8-10 2011 - 23 2011 $7500

Casaux, Charles Le, Marquis De   *Considerations sur quelques Parties du Mechanisme des Societes.*   Londres: de l'imprimerie de T. Spilsbury... se trouve chez P. Elmsley, 1785, First edition; 8vo., viii, (2), 382 pages, half title with errata leaf * inserted after the Table des Matieres and immediately before leaf B1, contemporary mottled half calf, spine fully gilt in compartments with contrasting labels, red edges, silk marker, very good.   John Drury Rare Books   154 - 36 2011   £500

Casey, John   *An American romance.*   New York: Atheneum, 1977,   First edition; fine, dust jacket near fine, light edge wear, one very small chip.   Bella Luna Books   May 29 2011 - m1022 2011 $82

Cash, Johnny   *Cash. The Autobiography.*   San Francisco/ New York: Harper, 1987, First edition; near fine, light creasing to head of spine, dust jacket fine, signed by author on publisher's bookplate which is laid in.   Bella Luna Books   May 26 2011 - t8230 2011 $330

Cash, Johnny   *Cash, The Autobiography.*   San Francisco: Harper, 1997,   First edition; near fine, light bumping to spine ends, dust jacket very good, barely visible 2 inch razor cut on front panel, signed by author on publisher's bookplate, which is laid in.   Bella Luna Books   May 26 2011 - t8914c 2011 $165

Cash, Rosanne   *Cash.*   New York: Crown, 2004, First edition; very good, bumping to bottom corners and top of spine, remainder mark, dust jacket fine, signed by Johnny Cash on bookplate laid in.   Bella Luna Books   May 29 2011 - t8235 2011 $82

Casner, A. James   *Estate Planning.*   Boston: 1961, supplement 1967;   3 volumes, all fine, original binding.   Bookworm & Silverfish   669 - 73 2011 $155

Cassel, Gustav   *The Nature and Necessity of Interest.*   London: Macmillan, 1903, First edition; 8vo., original publisher's brown cloth lettered gilt at spine, pages xii, 189, uncut, covers slightly marked, spine slightly tanned, endpapers slightly browned, otherwise decent, very good.   Any Amount of Books   May 29 2011 - B29340 2011 $213

Cassell & Company   *Historic Houses of the United Kingdom: Descriptive, Historical, Pictorial.*   London: 1891, 330 pages, large 4to., full chocolate cloth, all cover gilt bright, beveled edges, corners good, all edges gilt, missing f.f.e.p., some finger marks to cover, five full page plates.   Bookworm & Silverfish   679 - 64 2011 $68

Cassell & Company   *History of the Boer War 1899-1902.*   London: Cassell, 1903,   Revised edition; 2 volumes, pages viii, 928; viii, 975, numerous illustrations and maps, original green cloth, handsome set.   J. & S. L. Bonham Antiquarian Booksellers   Africa 4/20/2011 - 8299 2011   £80

Cassell & Company   *The Queen's London: a Pictorial and Descriptive Record of the Streets, Buildings, Parks & Scenery... in the 59th year...*   London: 1896,   xii, 370, (4) pages, 9 1/4 x 12 inches, very good in bright blue cloth, corners sharp, gilt bright, about 500 photo illustrations.   Bookworm & Silverfish   679 - 65 2011 $95

Cassell & Company   *Rivers of Great Britain. The Thames...*   London: Cassell & Co., 1891-1892, 2 volumes, large 4to., original half polished green calf gilt, few slight scrapes, pages viii, 366; viii, 376 with 2 engraved frontispieces and numerous full page and text woodcut illustrations and maps, handsome clean and sound pair.   R. F. G. Hollett & Son Antiquarian Booksellers   General Catalogue Summer 2010 - 1356 2011   £150

Cassin, John   *Illustrations of the Birds of California, Texas, Oregon, British and Russian America...*   Philadelphia: J. B. Lippincott & Co., 1853-1856, First edition; 50 hand colored lithographed plates, tanned, light marginal foxing to most, heavier to 5, gutter of 5 plates stained, marginal soiling or smudge to few, small marginal chip to 3, faint dampstain to 1, light offsetting from text to last 10 plates, most tissue guards present, tall 8vo., pages viii, 298, contemporary quarter calf, fair, some rubbing to calf an boards, small marginal dampstain to 90 pages of text including title, larger dampstain to upper third of about 10 pages, foxing to title, prelim pages and last third of text pages, two thirds of text pages, browned, small stains to occasional page, short marginal tears to 2 leaves, vertical crease and sometimes 2 to most pages and plates, gilt decorations to spine (rubbed).   Raymond M. Sutton, Jr.   May 26 2011 - 45546 2011 $1500

Casson, Hugh   *Hugh Casson's London.*   London: Dent, 1983, First edition; large 8vo., original cloth, dust jacket, pages 128, illustrations in color, 2 Christmas cards inscribed by Casson loosely inserted.   R. F. G. Hollett & Son Antiquarian Booksellers   General Catalogue Summer 2010 - 1357 2011   £65

Casson, Mark   *Entrepreneurship and the Industrial Revolution.*   London: Thoemmes Press, 2001,   Reprint; 8vo., over 2000 pages in all, 7 volumes, very good.   Any Amount of Books   May 26 2011 - A69648 2011 $629

Castera, J. H. *The Life of Catharine II Empress of Russia.* London: Printed for T. N. Longman and O. Rees, 1799, Third edition; 3 volumes, 225 x 140mm., original publisher's blue paper boards, original paper labels on spines, untrimmed edges, volumes II and III entirely unopened; with 2 engraved frontispieces, one containing two portrait medallions the other containing five, and a folding "correct map of the Russian empire", inevitable light soiling to covers and faint darkening to paper spines with one leaf with four inch closed tear onto text without loss (apparently incurred during printing because located in middle of one of the unopened gatherings), other trivial imperfections, but exceptionally fine, text consistently clean, fresh and bright, bindings in remarkable condition, completely solid, with much more moderate signs of use than one would normally expect, and even with the always vulnerable paper spine labels entirely intact. Phillip J. Pirages   59 - 24   2011 $1000

Cater, Ian *Marble, a Handbook.* Art Pavements & Decorations Ltd. circa, 1936, 64 pages, 62 illustrations, original cloth backed boards, covers little rubbed, loosely inserted is an 8 page supplement, and a 7 page color catalog for Anselm Odling & Sons Ltd., marble and granite merchants, folio.   Ken Spelman Rare Books   68 - 119   2011 £65

Cather, Willa Sibert   1873-1947   *April Twilights.* Boston: Richard G. Badger/Gorham Press, 1903, First edition; 8vo., pages 52, paper covered boards, paper spine label, uncut, some minor spotting to boards, small tear in lower joint, neatly repaired, otherwise fine internally, untrimmed, better than average copy, scarce.   Second Life Books Inc.   174 - 94   2011 $1400

Cather, Willa Sibert   1873-1947   *Death Comes for the Archbishop.* New York: Alfred A. Knopf, 1927, first edition, one of 175 copies on Borzoi all rag paper, this being number 81; publisher's quarter green cloth over marbled paper boards, signed by author.   Heritage Book Shop Booth A12 51st NY International Antiquarian Book Fair April 8-10 2011 - 24   2011 $3750

Cather, Willa Sibert   1873-1947   *One of Ours.* New York: Knopf, 1922, First edition; of the limited edition of 345 large paper copies, signed by author, this one of 35 on Imperial Japon vellum, signed twice, once on endpaper and again on limitation page, fine, untrimmed copy in custom slipcase, bookplate of collector Efrem Zimbalist.   Second Life Books Inc.   174 - 90   2011 $3750

Cather, Willa Sibert   1873-1947   *The Professor's House.* New York: Knopf, 1925, First edition; 8vo., pages 283, fine in dust jacket that shows little wear at tips and extremities, rare in dust jacket.   Second Life Books Inc.   174 - 91   2011 $1875

Cather, Willa Sibert   1873-1947   *The Professor's House.* New York: Knopf, 1925, First edition; 8vo., pages 283, fine, large paper copy, one of 40 on Imperial Japon vellum, signed by author, top edge gilt, small owner's bookplate on endpaper, housed in custom clamshell case.   Second Life Books Inc.   174 - 92   2011 $3750

Catholic Church. Liturgy & Ritual. Breviary *Breviarium Romanum.* Venetiis: Ex Typographia Balleoniana, 1744, 187 x 112 mm., 4 volumes, very attractive contemporary dark brown crushed morocco, handsomely gilt, covers with simple border of plain and stippled gilt rules and fleuron cornerpieces, raised bands, spines intricately and elegantly gilt in compartments formed by plain and decorative gilt rules and featuring cornerpieces of leaves and volutes framing a central curling lozenge incorporating palmettes with fleur-delys, marbled endpapers, all edges gilt with gauffering on top and bottom edges next to endbands, apparently original elaborate ribbon markers comprised of four silk strands held together at top by large tassel, 14 engravings by M. Beylbrouck, engraved printer's device on titlepages, woodcut tailpieces and floriated initials, printed in red and black, one opening with small wax (?) stain, other very trivial imperfections, nearly flawless copy, binding with only faintest signs of age, clean, fresh and bright text with virtually no signs of use.   Phillip J. Pirages   59 - 7   2011 $1500

Catlin, George   1796-1872   *Letters and Notes of the Manners, Customs and Condition of the North American Indians Written During Eight Years' Travel Amongst the Wildest Tribes of Indians in North America.*   Philadelphia: J. W. Bradley, 1860, 2 volumes in 1, thick 8vo., 792 pages, numerous woodcuts and engravings, recent three quarter leather, marbled boards, 29 plates, nicely hand colored by publisher, outer margin of title carefully repaired, some foxing.   M & S Rare Books, Inc.   90 - 71   2011 $950

Catlin, George   1796-1872   *The Manners, Customs and Condition of the North American Indians...* London: 1841, (but later); 2 volumes, viii, 264 pages, illustrations, folding map, viii, 266 pages, illustrations, original black cloth, pictorial gilt stamped covers, spine gilt lettered, top edge gilt, spines slightly sunned, slight foxing to frontispiece and titlepage volume I, hinges starting, internally clean and plates bright, overall very good set, 3 maps, one folding, 180 chromolithographic plates, very good set.   Dumont Maps & Books of the West   113 - 29   2011 $2500

Catlin, George   1796-1872   *O'Kee-Pa: a Religious Ceremony and Other Customs of the Mandans.* London: Trubner and Co., 1867, First edition; small 4to., vi, (2), 52 pages plus iii page "Folium Reservatum, 13 chromolithographed plates after Catlin by Simonau & Toovey, publisher's purple cloth, gilt, all edges gilt, binding lightly soiled and faded, extremities lightly worn (spine ends more so), occasional minor foxing, very good, fragile to find in fine condition, presentation copy inscribed by publisher Nicholas Trubner to Thomas Scott.   Joseph J. Felcone Inc.   Fall Miscellany 2010 - 22   2011 $20,000

Cauchy, Augustin Louis *Memoire sur La Dispersion De La Lumiere.* Prague: J. G. Calve, 1836, First edition; 4to., pages iv, 236; titlepage and preface to Cauchy's "Novueau Exercises de mathematiques", 1835, pages iv, some foxing at end of volume, otherwise very fresh, half calf and marbled boards, rubbed.   Simon Finch Rare Books   Zero - 129 2011   £650

Caulkins, Frances M. *History of New London, Connecticut from the First Survey of the Coast in 1612 to 1852.* New London: 1852, 724 pages, good to very good, bit white showing at backstrip ends & front fore edge, usual foxing, some damping above text at top edge.   Bookworm & Silverfish   676 - 57 2011 $125

Caulkins, Nehemiah *Narrative of Nehemiah Caulkins, an Extract from "American Slavery As It Is".* New York: American and Foreign Anti-Slavery Society, 1849, 12mo., 22 pages, removed.   M & S Rare Books, Inc.   90 - 391 2011 $450

Caunter, James Hobert *The Fellow Commoner: or Remarkable Escapes of a Predestinated Rogue.* Philadelphia: 1838, 2 volumes, faded half rose sheep footed cloth (well worn) with paper over boards, owner stamps on all 4 pastedowns, foxing as expected, ads dated Dec. 1 1836, untrimmed.   Bookworm & Silverfish   664 - 68 2011 $60

Caussin, Nicholas *The Holy Court in Five Times....* London: printed by William Bentley, 1650, Folio, near contemporary speckled calf with raised bands and spine label, sometime nicely re-cased, rather rubbed, corners restored, pages (xx), 522, (viii) (viii) 319 (i, blank), 13, (vii), half title, printed title in red and black, 6 further titles, engraved head and tailpieces, historiated initials in each section and numerous engraved portraits within text, some 10 leaves in first section have several closed cuts to text, without loss, one leaf fine with lower corner torn off affecting 3 lines of table, otherwise excellent, clean and sound copy, early ownership signatures of John and Jane Comberbach of Barker Street, Nantwich, Cheshire, later armorial bookplate of Sir John Williams of Bodelwyddan Castle in North Wales.   R. F. G. Hollett & Son Antiquarian Booksellers   175 - 233 2011   £350

Cavafy, Constantine P. *Poiemata (1908-1914).* Alexandria: Kasimath & Iona (Print Shop), circa, 1920, Tall 8vo., 29 numbered pages, printed on recto only with table of contents, in beige printed wrapper, very fine, half morocco folding box, presentation from poet to one of his closest friends, Christopher Nomikos.   James S. Jaffe Rare Books   May 26 2011 - 8185 2011 $25,000

Cavally, Frederick L. *Mother Goose's Teddy Bears.* Indianapolis: Bobbs Merrill Co., 1907, First edition; 4to., dark red cloth with gold lettering and color paste label, there is some handling to edges of cloth and faint corner bump of otherwise really nice copy, line drawing borders and decorations.   Jo Ann Reisler, Ltd.   86 - 23 2011 $850

Cave Research Group of Great Britain *Mendip Cave Bibliography ad Survey Catalogue 1901-1963.* Ledbury: Cave Research Group, 1965, 4to. original wrappers, comb bound, pages 164.   R. F. G. Hollett & Son Antiquarian Booksellers   General Catalogue Summer 2010 - 1358 2011   £35

Cave, C. J. P. *The Bosses on the Vault of the Quire of Winchester Cathedral.* Oxford: printed for the Society, 1927, 4to., pages 161-178, 10 pages of plates, modern cloth backed marbled boards, gilt.   R. F. G. Hollett & Son Antiquarian Booksellers   177 - 169 2011   £40

Cave, C. J. P. *Roof Bosses in Medieval Churches.* Cambridge: University Press, 1948, First edition; small 4to., original cloth, pages viii, 235, with 368 illustrations.   R. F. G. Hollett & Son Antiquarian Booksellers   177 - 170 2011   £50

Cave, Francis *Birds of the Sudan: their Identification and Distribution.* Edinburgh: Oliver and Boyd, 1955, First edition; 8vo., pages xxvii, 444, maps, 12 colored plates, illustrations, original blue cloth, dust jacket, very good.   J. & S. L. Bonham Antiquarian Booksellers   Africa 4/20/2011 - 4566 2011   £120

Cave, Henry *Antiquities of York.* London: published by R. Ackermann, York: printed at the Office of G. Peacock, 1813, 1807; 2 works bound together as 1, 4to., pages iv, (ii), 31, (i) + engraved titlepage and 40 engraved plates (iv), iii, (i), 10, (ii) (xxiv) + engraved titlepage and 34 engraved plates, contemporary empanelled calf boards double bordered with decorative roll of consecutive polished pinheads gilt, central 'French Shell' 'made' endpapers, all edges marbled as per outer panels, green & vermillion sewn flat endbands, mid 20th century calf reback, some browning and foxing, few plates significantly but mostly light, old boards scuffed and little rubbed around edges, armorial bookplate of Joseph Robinson Pease, from the collection of Christopher Ernest Weston 1947-2010.   Unsworths Booksellers   24 - 75 2011   £1000

Cave, Roderick *The Private Press.* Bowker, 1983, Second edition; numerous examples, pages xvi, 392, 4to., original orange cloth, backstrip gilt lettered, dust jacket, fine.   Blackwell Rare Books   B166 - 246 2011   £115

Cave, William *Antiquitate Apostolicae; or the History of the Lives, Acts and Martyrdoms of the Holy Apostles of Our Saviour...* London: printed by F. Flesher for R. Royston, 1684, Fifth edition; folio, old full calf gilt with spine label, rather scuffed and bumped, pages (vi), lxviii, (vi), xviii, 238, frontispiece dated 1683 (little soiled, some edge tears and old repair), first title in red and black, second title, double page plate of Church Catholic Tree dated 1679, rather stained, some edge tears partly laid down, 30 engraved plates in pairs within text, later endpapers, few small old repairs and marks, armorial bookplate of William John Renny. R. F. G. Hollett & Son Antiquarian Booksellers 175 - 234 2011 £275

Cecil, Gwendolen *Biographical Studies of the Life and Political, Character of Robert Third Marquis of Salisbury.* London: privately published Hodder & Stoughton, n.d., 1948, Original cream cloth, gilt, pages 96, untrimmed, armorial bookplate of Viscount Bracken of Christchurch on pastedown, another label removed. R. F. G. Hollett & Son Antiquarian Booksellers 175 - 236 2011 £65

Cellini, Benvenuto *The Life of Benvenuto Cellini, a Florentine Artist.* Dublin: printed by John Abbot Husband for Messrs. Sleater, Ewing, Potts (and 12 others in Dublin), 1772, First Dublin edition; 2 volumes in one, slight soiling of title to volume 1, imprint of volume 2 omits list of booksellers, viii, 288; 228, (20) pages, contemporary calf, morocco label, good copy. Anthony W. Laywood May 26 2011 - 19781 2011 $252

Cellini, Benvenuto *The Life of Benvenuto Cellini.* London: printed for the Navarre Society by Riverside Press, 1927, One of 1500 copies; 209 x 140mm., 2 volumes, fine burgundy morocco, handsomely gilt and onlaid by the Harcourt Bindery of Boston (stamp signed on front flyleaf of each volume), boards with triple fillet border each cover with elaborate heraldic frame of gilt and onlaid green morocco around an empty oval, raised bands, very pretty gilt spine compartments featuring looping tendril frame enclosing charming flower centerpiece, densely gilt turn-ins, marbled endpapers, titlepage, double page genealogical table and 62 plates, as called for; one cover with short, vague scratch, but in especially fine condition, fresh, bright and internally, with lustrous bindings with virtually no wear. Phillip J. Pirages 59 - 108 2011 $800

Cendrars, Blaise *La Banlieue de Paris.* Lausanne: Pierre Seghers, 1949, First edition; very near fine in clean, very close to near fine dust jacket, illustrations by Robert Doisneau. Jeff Hirsch Books ny 2010 2011 $3000

Central Society of Education *Papers.* London: printed for Taylor and Walton, 1837, First edition; original cloth gilt, recased with new spine label, pages 414, (xxii). R. F. G. Hollett & Son Antiquarian Booksellers 175 - 237 2011 £140

The Century Magazine. USA: Century Co., 1881-1901, First edition; volumes 1-40, lacking volumes 26 and 27, together 38 volumes in varied bindings, volumes 1-21 similarly bound in green boards, gilt lettering, all in very good condition. I. D. Edrich May 26 2011 - 99070 2011 $956

Ceremonial for the Private Interment of His Late Royal Highness Frederick Duke of York and of Albany in the Road Chapel of St. George at Windsor on Saturday Evening the 20th Day of Jan. 1827. London: printed by S. and R. Bentley, 1827, First edition; folio, printed throughout within black mourning borders, (10) pages, ms. annotations, some minor creasing, sewn but now loose within original black glazed paper wrappers, fore edge of upper wrapper frayed, good, very rare. John Drury Rare Books 154 - 37 2011 £150

Certain Sermons or Homilies Appointed to Be Read in Churches, in the Time of Queen Elizabeth of Famous Memory... London: printed by T. R. for Andrew Croke, Samuel Mearne and Robert Pawlet, 1673, Folio, contemporary blindstamped panelled calf, edges little chipped, top and tail of spine slightly defective, pages (vi), 388, printed in black letter with engraved headpieces and large historiated initials, front flyleaves worn at fore-edges, title little browned and worn at fore-edge, joints cracked, early signature of Hopton, Suffolk. R. F. G. Hollett & Son Antiquarian Booksellers 175 - 1207 2011 £175

Certain Sermons or Homilies Appointed to be Read in Churches in the Time of Queen Elizabeth of Famous Memory... Oxford: printed at the Theatre and are to be sold by Peter Parker at the Leg and Star, 1683, Folio, old calf, scuffed and torn in places, upper hinges cracked, pages (iv), 388, (iv), with woodcut of royal arms on titlepage, fore-edges of first and last leaves frayed and weakened by damp, first few leaves cropped at lower margins with few wormholes, short wormtrack in last few leaves. R. F. G. Hollett & Son Antiquarian Booksellers 175 - 1208 2011 £120

Cervantes Saavedra, Miguel De 1547-1616 *History of the Valorous and Witty Knight Errant, Don Quixote of the Mancha.* London: printed for R. Scot, T. Basset, J. Wright, R. Chiswell, 1675, Early edition of The Thomas Shelton translation in two parts; small folio, (8), 137; (5), 138-214, 216-244, 244-273 leaves, full red morocco, boards and spine tooled and lettered in gilt boards with and attractive art nouveau style tooling with center lozenge containing the gilt initials "FB" (for Fletcher Battershall), gilt dentelles, lower front dentelle with small gilt bat device with initial "B", all edges gilt and rough cut, edges and outer hinges bit rubbed, small bit of splitting to front joint at top and bottom of spine, some minor paper repairs to fore edge margin of titlepage and following leaf as well as final leaf, 2 bookplates belonging to Willis Vickery and binders Fletcher and Maude Battershall, old catalog clippings tipped to front flyleaf by previous owner, overall very good. Heritage Book Shop Holiday 2010 - 18 2011 $5000

Cervantes Saavedra, Miguel De   1547-1616   *The History of the Valorous and Witty Knight Errant, Don Quixote of the Mancha.*   London: R. Scot, T. Basset, J. Wright, R. Chiswell, 1675, 1672. Third English edition; 4to., (8), 173, (5), 138-214, 216-244, 244-273 ff., complete, full calf, blind-stamped Greek key and trifolium border design, gilt stamped red leather spine label, all edges gilt, rebacked, corners showing, signature of Eliz: Burkitt on titlepage, very good.   Jeff Weber Rare Books   163 - 21   2011 $5000

Cervantes Saavedra, Miguel De   1547-1616   *El Ingenioso Hidalgo Don Quixote De La Mancha.*   Madrid: Por Don Joaquin Ibarra, 1780,   Magnificent "Academy Edition"; 4 volumes, quarto, contemporary Spanish mottled calf.   Heritage Book Shop   Booth A12 51st NY International Antiquarian Book Fair April 8-10 2011 - 27   2011 $25,000

Cervantes Saavedra, Miguel De   1547-1616   *The Life and Exploits of the Ingenious Gentleman Don Quixote de La Mancha.*   London: printed for J. Dodsley, 1787,   2 volumes, liii, (4), 280; (vi), 311 pages, 16 engraved plates, pages 304 and 7-8 with short marginal tears (slight loss), modern antique style, full sprinkled calf, elaborately gilt stamped spines, fine.   Jeff Weber Rare Books   163 - 45   2011 $1500

Cervantes Saavedra, Miguel De   1547-1616   *Life and Adventures of Don Quixote de la Mancha.*   London: printed for Hurst, Robinson and Co., 1820,   New edition; 4 small octavo volumes, (2), xx, (1)-371, (1 colophon); (6), (1)-388; (8), (1)-367, (1, colophon); (8), (1)-436 pages, numerous engravings by Richard Westall inserted throughout, full red morocco bound by Bayntun, boards panelled and ruled in gilt with geometric diamond over rectangle design, spines decoratively tooled and lettered in gilt in six compartments with five raised bands, gilt board edges and dentelles, all edges gilt marbled endpapers, previous owner's bookplate on front pastedown of each volume, some very minor occasional foxing to prelim and final leaves, overall about fine.   Heritage Book Shop   Holiday 2010 - 19   2011 $1000

Cervantes Saavedra, Miguel De   1547-1616   *First Part of the History of ... Don Quixote of the Mancha.*   Chelsea: Ashendene Press, 1927,   One of 225 copies on batchelor paper, out of a total edition of 245; 2 large folio volumes, (2, blank), xiii, (1, blank), 268, (1 colophon), (3, blank); (2, blank), x, 256, (1, colophon), (3, blank) pages, printed in red and black in Ptolemy type, text in double columns, border and initials designed by Louise Powell and cut on wood by W. M. Quick and Geo. H. Ford, publisher's quarter cream cloth over printed paper boards, printed paper spine labels, all edges uncut, cloth on spines very slightly soiled, small amount of fraying to head and tail of spines, small hole, slightly larger than pinhole on spine of volume II, few tiny chips to patterned paper of front and back boards, faint mark from removed bookplate on front pastedown of each volume, maroon cloth slipcase, overall very nice, most fragile of binding variants.   Heritage Book Shop   Holiday 2010 - 5   2011 $4500

Cervantes Saavedra, Miguel De   1547-1616   *The First-Second Part of the History of the Valorus and Wittie Knight Errant Don Quixote of the Mancha.*   Chelsea: Ashendene Press, 1927-1928,   One of 225 copies on Batchelor paper; 2 large folio volumes, publisher's quarter cream cloth over printed paper boards.   Heritage Book Shop   Booth A12 51st NY International Antiquarian Book Fair April 8-10 2011 - 3   2011 $4500

Cervantes Saavedra, Miguel De   1547-1616   *The First (and Second) Part of the Histoty of the Various and Wittie Knight-Errant Don Quixote of the Mancha.*   Ashendene Press, 1927-1928,   One of 225 copies; 2 volumes, text in the 1620 English translation of Thomas Shelton, original luxurious white pigskin by W. H. Smith, thick raised bands, gilt titling on spine, sturdy cloth double slipcases (little marked), morocco labels, lovely woodcut initials and borders designed by Louise Powell, cut on wood by W. M. Quick and George H. Ford, bookplate of Vincent Lloyd-Russell in each volume, as well as shadow of another small bookplate now removed; pigskin of first volume, just shade different from second (a common defect as the volumes issued more than a year apart), in all other ways, extremely fine, magnificent binding unusually clean, text in perfect condition.   Phillip J. Pirages 59 - 76   2011 $9500

Cervantes Saavedra, Miguel De   1547-1616   *The Adventures of Don Quixote of La Mancha.*   London: J. M. Dent, 1962,   First edition; original pictorial cloth, extremities little worn, pages xxi, 532, with 43 illustrations, frontispiece and title with red decorated borders, few spots to prelim leaves and final page.   R. F. G. Hollett & Son Antiquarian Booksellers   General Catalogue Summer 2010 - 893   2011   £50

Chabon, Michael   *The Amazing Adventures of Kavalier & Clay.*   New York: Random House, 2000,   Advance uncorrected proof; fine, signed by author.   Bella Luna Books May 26 2011 - 59356   2011 $192

Chabon, Michael   *The Mysteries of Pittsburgh.*   New York: Morrow, 1988,   First edition; fine, dust jacket fine.   Bella Luna Books   May 29 2011 - t9498   2011 $99

Chadwick, John   *The Decipherment of Linear B.*   Cambridge: University Press, 1958,   First edition; original cloth, gilt, dust jacket, little worn, label on foot of spine, pages x, 148, with 2 plates and text figures, including folding chart label removed from pastedown.   R. F. G. Hollett & Son Antiquarian Booksellers   177 - 171   2011   £30

Chaffee, Allen *Zoo Book-Toy.* Springfield: McLoughlin Bros. Inc., 1938, Book housed in original color pictorial box, box about 12 1/4 x 14 1/2 x 1 inches and has some cracking to sides but overall bright and fresh, book laid into box that has spiral binding and 12 pages on stiff paper, concept is to take the book and spread each page so that it is center with dowel (which is included) and you get the sense of animals in the zoo, dowel is inserted into relatively heavy base that holds it all together, base is present, book in nice condition and there is the original flag to put at top of dowl. Jo Ann Reisler, Ltd. 86 - 242 2011 $375

Chagall, Marc *The Biblical Message. Marc Chagall.* New York: Tudor, 1973, First American edition; 4to., 199 pages, fine, near fine dust jacket with minimal edge, original clear plastic dust jacket and original near fine plain slipcase with mild soil and wear, frontispiece original lithograph by Chagall printed by Mourlot. By the Book, L. C. 26 - 42 2011 $265

Chagall, Marc *Derriere Le Miroir. No. 235 Octobre 1979.* Paris: Maeght Editeur, 1979, Limited edition, one of 150 copies, this number 94; folio, 2 original color lithographs by Marc Chagall, unbound in wrappers, uncut. Heritage Book Shop Booth A12 51st NY International Antiquarian Book Fair April 8-10 2011 - 28 2011 $1500

Chalk, Thomas *Journals of the Lives, Travels, and Gospel Labours of Thomas Wilson and James Dickinson.* London: C. Gilpin, 1847, First edition; modern calf gilt, green buckram boards, pages xxx, 217, booklabel of Friends Library, Grangel over Sands Cumbria. R. F. G. Hollett & Son Antiquarian Booksellers 175 - 239 2011 £65

Chalmers, James *Plain Truth.* Philadelphia: R. Bell, 1776, First edition; octavo in fours, 19th century half black calf over marbled boards. Heritage Book Shop Booth A12 51st NY International Antiquarian Book Fair April 8-10 2011 - 29 2011 $10,000

Chalmers, Robert *A History of Currency in the British Colonies.* London: printed for Her Majesty's Government by Eyre & Spottiswoode, 1893, First edition; 8vo., original publisher's red cloth with printed spine label, pages viii, 496, pages uncut, numerous tables, n.d. (1893?), ex-British Foreign Office library with few library markings, sound, near very good with slight soiling and slight tanning to covers, spine label rubbed and chipped with clean text, next name on titlepage. Any Amount of Books May 29 2011 - 73782 2011 $221

Chalmers, Thomas *The Christian and Civic Economy of Large Towns.* London: Chalmers and Collins, 1821, 1823. 1826. First edition; 8vo., 3 volumes, no half titles present, pages (4), 358; (4), 365; (3), xv, (1 blank) 17-408; decent clean set in mid 19th century half brown leather with marbled boards, lettered and decorated gilt at spine, slight scuffing, slight rubbing at corners, slight browning, mostly to prelims, neat contemporary name on front endpapers overall, very good. Any Amount of Books May 26 2011 - A45078 2011 $604

Chalmers, Thomas *The Doctrine of Christian Charity Applied to the Case of Religious Differences.* Glasgow: printed for the Society by Andrew and James Duncan, 1818, Disbound, 52 pages, corner of title and final leaf rather creased, scarce. R. F. G. Hollett & Son Antiquarian Booksellers 175 - 240 2011 £85

Chamberlain, Bernard P. *A Treatise on the Making of Palatable Table Wines.* Charlottesville: 1931, 97 pages, 4to., half cloth (aged) and blue paper (mildy rubbed), paper labels show some age soil, new facsimile label laid in. Bookworm & Silverfish 667 - 73 2011 $65

Chamberlain, Houston Stewart *The Foundations of the Nineteenth Century.* London & New York: John Lane, The Bodley Head,, 1911, First edition; 2 volumes, 8vo., original publisher's Wedgewood blue cloth lettered gilt on spine and cover, pages cii, 578; vii, 580, pages uncut, neat name on front endpaper, endpapers slightly browned, Wedgewood blue covers have one small white mark, otherwise very good+ or better clean set, excellent condition. Any Amount of Books May 29 2011 - A68045 2011 $408

Chamberlain, Houston Stewart *Richard Wagner.* London: J. M. Dent, 1900, Second edition; large 8vo., original publisher's green cloth lettered gilt on spine and cover, pages xvii, 402, copious plates and illustrations, loosely inserted signed card from Houston Stewart Chamberlain dated 1906 to fellow writer Friedrich Poske, clean, very good. Any Amount of Books May 29 2011 - A68665 2011 $255

Chamberlain, John *Letters Written During the Reign of Queen Elizabeth.* Camden Society, 1841, Original blind-stamped cloth, gilt, pages xii, 188, 4, pedigree. R. F. G. Hollett & Son Antiquarian Booksellers General Catalogue Summer 2010 - 379 2011 £45

Chamberlain, Sarah *A Frog He Would A Wooing Go.* Portland: Chamberlain Press, 1981, Limited to 125 copies, signed; square 12mo., color illustrated boards with stitched binding, fine copy, in as new condition, wood engravings. Jo Ann Reisler, Ltd. 86 - 37 2011 $225

Chamberlain, Sarah *The Three Bears.* Portland: The Chamberlain Press, 1983, Limited edition, signed, one of 125 copies; 12mo., bound in patterned paper covered boards with paste label on spine with book title, wood engravings.   Jo Ann Reisler, Ltd.   86 - 38 2011 $275

Chamberlayne, John *Magnae Britanniae Notitia; or the Present State of Great Britain...* London: printed for D. Midwinter etc., 1741, pages (xii) 443, 280, 68, engraved portrait, woodcut ornament and initials, modern half calf gilt with raised bands and spine label.   R. F. G. Hollett & Son Antiquarian Booksellers   175 - 242 2011   £275

Chambers Journal of Popular Literature. W. R. Chambers, 1891-1935, Jan. 1891-June 1925, lacking 8 issues only, over 500 issues in original wrappers, some fraying but generally bright run in very good condition.   I. D. Edrich   May 26 2011 - 99071 2011 $671

Chambers, Ewlyn Whitman *Invasion!* New York: E. P. Dutton & Co., 1943, First edition; cloth.   L. W. Currey, Inc.   124 - 140 2011 $450

Chambers, Robert *The Book of Days.* London: W. & R. Chambers, 1864, 2 volumes, large 8vo., original half crimson morocco, gilt, little scraped, pages (iv), 832; (ii), 840, all edges and endpapers marbled, printed in double columns, red and black pictorial titles, woodcut illustrations, scattered foxing, mainly to flyleaves, but handsome sound set, green morocco presentation label "Mr. & Mrs. Joseph Shorrock from Egerton W. Wood 1865".   R. F. G. Hollett & Son Antiquarian Booksellers   175 - 243 2011   £150

Chambers, Robert *Popular Rhymes of Scotland.* London: W. & R. Chambers, 1870, New edition; Pages 402, engraved vignette on title, ex-library with armorial bookplate, stamp on back of title and marginal blindstamps on first few and final leaves.   R. F. G. Hollett & Son Antiquarian Booksellers   175 - 244 2011   £30

Chambers, S. Allen *Lynchburg (VA): an Architectural History.* Charlottesville: 1981, xiv, 576 pages, 4to., photos, lithos, woodcuts, maps, splendid copy, original binding, near fine in near fine dust jacket, but mildly shelf warped.   Bookworm & Silverfish   662 - 9 2011 $175

Chambers, William *Memoir of Robert Chambers with Autobiographic Reminiscences of William Chambers.* Edinburgh: W. & R. Chambers, 1872, Fourth edition; half title, added engraved title with portraits, blue cloth, slightly dulled, stamps and labels of Bolland Collection.   Jarndyce Antiquarian Booksellers   CXCI - 447 2011   £40

Chambers, William *Memoir of William and Robert Chambers.* Edinburgh: W. & R. Chambers, 1893, Frontispiece, illustrations, portraits, original brown cloth, very good, Renier booklabel.   Jarndyce Antiquarian Booksellers   CXCI - 448 2011   £35

Champernowne, D. G. *Uncertainty & Estimation in Economics.* Edinburgh & San Francisco: Oliver & Boyd/Holden Day, 1969, First edition; 3 volumes, 8vo., pages viii, 280; vi, 426; v, 108, tables, figures, signed presentation from author to Richard Stone, very good+ in like dust jacket (spines slightly tanned).   Any Amount of Books   May 29 2011 - A75931 2011 $204

Champion, Joseph *New and Complete Alphabets in all the Various Hands of Great Britain with the Greek, Hebrew and German Characters.* printed for Carington Bowles, circa, 1764, 21 engraved plates, comprising titlepage and plates numbered 2-21, stitched as issued, some light marginal browning and chipping to lower outer corners and blank leading edge of titlepage, oblong 4to.   Ken Spelman Rare Books   68 - 8 2011   £280

Champneys, Arthur C. *Irish Ecclesiastical Architecture with Some Notice of Similar or Related Work in England, Scotland & Elsewhere.* 1910, First edition; 114 plates, library cloth, ex-library, very good.   C. P. Hyland   May 26 2011 - 255/097 2011 $457

Champneys, Arthur C. *Irish Ecclesiastical Architecture with Some Notice of Similar or Related Work in England, Scotland & Elsewhere.* 1910, First edition; 114 plates, loose insert, from the Irish Builder, Jan. 31st 1914 on Fore Abbey, Co. Westmeath, very good.   C. P. Hyland   May 26 2011 - 255/098 2011 $544

Champneys, Arthur C. *Irish Ecclesiastical Architecture with Some Notice of Similar or Related Works.* 1910, First edition; 114 plates, ex-Prinknash Abbey Library, good.   C. P. Hyland   May 26 2011 - 256/090 2011 $399

Champneys, W. Weldon *Marriage with a Deceased Wife's Sister. Letter in Favour of a Repeal of the Law...* London: Seeleys, 1849, Disbound, 16 pages, slightly dusted.   Jarndyce Antiquarian Booksellers   CXCI - 116 2011   £35

Champollion Le Jeune, J. F. *Grammaire Egyptienne ou Principes Generaux de L'Ecriture Sacree Egyptienne Appliquee a la Representation de la Languae Parlee.* Paris: Didot Freres, 1836, First edition; 2 volumes, folio, pages xxiii, 245; 246-460, numerous hieroglyphics, a page affected by worming in margin, contemporary marbled boards, recently rebacked in brown calf.   J. & S. L. Bonham Antiquarian Booksellers   Africa 4/20/2011 - 9170 2011   £1800

Chandler, George *Four Centuries of Banking. volumes 1 and 2.* London: Batsford, 1963-1968, First edition; pages 572, 608, 2 volumes, large 8vo., original orange cloth gilt, dust jackets, little worn, with 200 illustrations, colored map, few marginal notes and underlining to volume I, excellent set.   R. F. G. Hollett & Son Antiquarian Booksellers   175 - 245 2011   £75

Chandler, George *Four Centuries of Banking as Illustrated by the Bankers, Customers and Staff Associated with the Constituent Banks of Martin Bank Ltd. Volume 2. The Northern Constituent Banks.* London: Batsford, 1968, First edition; large 8vo., original cloth, gilt, dust jacket, rather worn, pages 608, 110 illustrations.   R. F. G. Hollett & Son Antiquarian Booksellers   175 - 246   2011   £35

Chandler, Raymond 1886-1959 *The Little Sister.* Boston: Houghton Mifflin, 1949, First U.S. edition; fine in dust jacket, with light professional restoration to spine ends and corners, exceptional copy.   Buckingham Books   May 26 2011 - 26814   2011 $3000

Chandler, Raymond 1886-1959 *The Little Sister. The Big Sleep. The Smell of Fear. The Long Good-Bye. The Lady in the Lake. Playback. Killer in the Rain. Farewell My Lovely. The High Window.* London: Hamish Hamilton, 1985-1988, First edition thus; 9 volumes, 8vo., attractive dust jackets by Mark Thomas, uncommon set, pages 2521, 9 volumes, all fine in fine dust jackets (one very slight nick on dust jacket of Killer in the Rain).   Any Amount of Books   May 29 2011 - A73480   2011 $340

Chandler, Raymond 1886-1959 *The Long Goodbye.* Boston: Houghton Mifflin Co., 1954, First US edition; fine in dust jacket, lightly rubbed at spine ends and extremities, with tiny crease and closed tear along top edge of front panel, especially nice collector's copy.   Buckingham Books May 26 2011 - 25788   2011 $2000

Chandler, Richard *Travels in Greece, or an Account of a Tour Made at the Expense of the Society of Dilettanti.* Dublin: printed for Messrs Price, Whitestone, Sleater and 31 others, 1776, xvi,3 19, (1) pages, 8vo., few light marks to several pages, otherwise very good, clean copy, full contemporary calf, raised bands, red morocco label, slight wear to head of spine, armorial bookplate of Marquess of Headfort.   Jarndyce Antiquarian Booksellers   CXCI - 540   2011   £320

Chandos, John *In God's Name.* London: Hutchinson, 1971, First edition; thick 8vo., original cloth, gilt, dust jacket, pages xxxi, 586, pencilled annotations to two pages.   R. F. G. Hollett & Son Antiquarian Booksellers   175 - 247   2011   £35

Chapin, Frederick *Pinkey and the Plumed Knight.* Akron: Saalfield, 1909, 4to., pictorial cloth, some normal shelf wear, very good+ illustrations by Merle Johnson, with 8 color plates, pictorial endpapers and many black and whites.   Aleph-Bet Books, Inc.   95 - 235   2011 $300

Chapin, Walter *The Missionary Gazetteer Comprising a View of the Inhabitants and a Geographical Description of the Countries and Places where Protestant Missionaries Have Labored.* Woodstock: David Watson, 1825, 12mo., folding hand colored map, 420 pages, some browning, full leather.   Barnaby Rudge Booksellers   Travel and Exploration - 019371   2011 $150

Chaplin, Jane D. *The Covent & the Manse.* Boston etc.: 1854, 338 pages, good in black embossed cloth, some white showing, backstrip and frayed, one signature reglued.   Bookworm & Silverfish   668 - 139   2011 $150

Chapman, Abel *Wild Spain (Espana Agreste) Records of Sport with Rifle, Rod and Gun, Natural History and Exploration.* London: Gurney and Jackson, 1893, First edition; 8vo., pages xx, 472, original publisher's burgundy cloth lettered gilt on spine, frontispiece map, illustrations, slight lean, front inner hinge, very slightly cracked, slight rubbing and slight shelfwear, otherwise about very good, clean text.   Any Amount of Books   May 29 2011 - A69863   2011 $221

Chapman, Frederic *Proverbs Improved in Twenty Four Coloured Pictures.* London: John Lane, n.d., 1901, Oblong small 8vo., original pictorial glazed boards, edges trifle cracked in places, pages 104 , 24 delicately full page plates.   R. F. G. Hollett & Sons Antiquarian Booksellers   170 - 430   2011   £75

Chapman, Jean *Do You Remember What Happened?* Angus & Robertson, 1969, First edition; original cloth, gilt, dust jacket, pages (400) with 36 two color drawings.   R. F. G. Hollett & Sons Antiquarian Booksellers   170 - 33   2011   £35

Chapman, John Jay *Causes and Consequences.* New York: Charles Scribner's Sons, 1898, First edition; 12mo., 8, 166 pages, original cloth, faded.   M & S Rare Books, Inc.   90 - 72   2011 $150

Chapman, Margaret G. *Lancashire Halls.* Newcastle upon Tyne: Frank Graham, 1971, First edition; 4to., original cloth, gilt, pages 80, illustrations.   R. F. G. Hollett & Son Antiquarian Booksellers   177 - 175   2011   £35

Chapman, R. W. *Johnson's Journey to the Western islands of Scotland and Boswell's Journal of a Tour to the Hebrides with Samuel Johnson.* Oxford University Press, 1924, First edition thus; original blue cloth gilt, light ring mark to upper board, pages xix, 447, xxvii, with 8 plates.   R. F. G. Hollett & Son Antiquarian Booksellers   General Catalogue Summer 2010 - 1359   2011 £35

Chapman, Ronald B. *A History of Queen Elizabeth Grammar School, Wakefield.* Huddersfield: privately printed, 1992, First edition; large 8vo., original cloth, gilt, dust jacket, pages 127, illustrations partly in color, signed by author, scarce. R. F. G. Hollett & Son Antiquarian Booksellers General Catalogue Summer 2010 - 1360 2011 £65

Chapman, William *Copy of the Specification of a Patent, Granted to William Chapman of Murton House in the County of Durham, Civil Engineer, and Edward Walton Chapman of Willington-Ropery, in the Parish of Wallsend in the County of Northumberland...* Newcastle Upon Tyne: printed by Edw. Walker, 1813, First edition; 8vo., 2 folding engraved plates, both little stained and browned, 14, (2) pages, well bound in early 20th century red cloth, spine neatly lettered in gilt, very good, rare. John Drury Rare Books 154 - 38 2011 £350

Chapman's Magazine of Fiction. Chapman, May, 1895-, October 1898; V. 1/1-V.X1/2, 11 volumes in 5 in publisher's blue cloth, all volumes scarce, very good. I. D. Edrich May 26 2011 - 99078 2011 $2264

Chapone, Hester *Letters on the Improvement of the Mind. Addressed to a Lady.* London: printed for Scatcherd and Letterman, etc., 1815, New edition; contemporary tree calf, handsomely rebacked in matching calf gilt, pages xl, 212. R. F. G. Hollett & Son Antiquarian Booksellers 175 - 249 2011 £65

Chapone, Hester *Miscellanies in Prose and Verse.* London: printed for C. Dilly and J. Walter, 1783, New edition; 160 x 105 mm., 6 p.l. (including initial blank), (13)-216 pages, exceptionally pretty contemporary speckled calf, raised bands, spine handsomely gilt in compartments with small foliate cornerpieces and prominent botanical centerpiece, one compartment with unusual olive green morocco onlay decorated with gilt grape cluster and vine, in compartment above it, red morocco title label, early ink signature of Anna Sophia Heathcote, joints with thin crack alongside top compartment, covers faintly marked, verso of final leaf with overall light browning, otherwise quite fine, binding lustrous and little worn, text extraordinarily fresh, clean and bright. Phillip J. Pirages 59 - 25 2011 $1250

Chappe, Ignace *Histoire de la Telegraphie.* Paris: chez l'auteur, 1824, First edition; 8vo., (4), 268 (errata, blank) pages, 34 double page engravings, contemporary quarter green calf over marbled boards, gilt ruled and stamped spine and title, extremities rubbed, presentation inscription by author, fine, from the Bern Dibner reference library, with Burndy bookplate. Jeff Weber Rare Books 161 - 80 2011 $3500

Charas, Moyse *The Royal Pharmacopoea, Galenical and Chymical...* John Starkey and Moses Pitt, 1678, Folio, modern half morocco gilt with raised bands and double spine labels, pages (iv, approbations), (ii, ads), 272, (vi), 245, (iii, explanations of plates), (vi index), 5 engraved plates and engraved table as called for, lacks main title and leaves C2, C3, D3 and D4, some browning and staining, considerable restoration to weakened or torn leaves (mainly at beginning and end), leaf *Hhh2 with some loss to text (now stabilized), 2 plates cut to image and remounted, 2 plates remargined, 1 plate repaired, table rather defective in places and laid down, rare. R. F. G. Hollett & Son Antiquarian Booksellers General Catalogue Summer 2010 - 1101 2011 £750

Charke, Charlotte *A Narrative of the Life of Mrs. Charlotte Charke.* London: printed for W. Reeve, 1755, 12mo., x, (11)-277 pages, half title, heavily wormed throughout, original full calf, rebacked with raised bands, darker brown spine label, bookplate of Sir Frances Baring Bart, good, scarce. Jeff Weber Rare Books 163 - 142 2011 $100

Charles I, King of Great Britain 1600-1649 *Eikon Basilike. (Greek). the Pourtraicture of His Sacred Majestie in His Solitudes and Sufferings with Prayers Used in the Time of His Restraint...* London: reprinted in Reis Memoriam for John Williams, 1649, 24mo., modern full calf gilt, pages (iv), 175, ix), title in red and black and woodcut initials, lacks frontispiece, portrait and leaf, few neat repairs, little staining toward end, rather close cropped. R. F. G. Hollett & Son Antiquarian Booksellers 175 - 250 2011 £250

Charles I, King of Great Britain 1600-1649 *Eikon Basilike. (Greek). The Pourtraicture of His Sacred Majestie in His Solitudes and Sufferings.* London: Elliot Stock, 1880, Reprint of 1648 edition; Pages (xliii), (iii), xii-xiii, 227, folding facsimile page, few spots, publisher's parchment. R. F. G. Hollett & Son Antiquarian Booksellers 175 - 411 2011 £35

Charlestown Female Tract Society *The First Annual Report of the Charlestown Female Tract Society for Evangelizing the West, Presented at a Meeting of the Society June 9 1846.* Boston: Howe's Sheet Anchor Press, 1846, First edition; 8vo., 16 pages, original printed wrappers, (text on both inner wrappers). M & S Rare Books, Inc. 90 - 442 2011 $250

Charlton, Lionel *The History of Whitby and of Whitby Abbey... (with) History and Antiquities of Scarborough and the Vicinity.* York: printed by A. Ward; William Blanchard for E. Bayley, successor to J. Schofield, 1779, 1798; 4to., pages xvii, (i), 379, (i) + engraved extending plan of Whitby as frontispiece and 3 other engraved plates, xi (i), 352, (viii) + engraved frontispiece, 2 engraved plans and 2 other engraved plates, early 19th century marbled half calf, 6 compartmented spine divided by back to back 'acanthus' roll gilt, two black lettering pieces gilt, boards sided with 'French Shell' marbled paper, red and white sewn endbands, early 1970's calf rebacked with old backstrip relaid by John Henderson, intermittent foxing, titlepage creased and spotted, corners touch worn, boards scuffed, from the collection of Christopher Ernest Weston 1947-2010.   Unsworths Booksellers   24 - 76   2011   £600

Charlton, Roy B. *A Lifetime with Ponies.* London: Hodder and Stoughton, 1952, Original cloth, gilt, dust jacket (little worn), pages 160 with 46 illustrations, nice, scarce.   R. F. G. Hollett & Son Antiquarian Booksellers   173 - 226   2011   £45

Charmes, Gabriel *Five Months at Cairo and in Lower Egypt.* London: Richard Bentley, 1883, First edition; 8vo., pages viii, 359, original green decorative cloth, all edges gilt, slight rubbing to extremities, still good copy.   J. & S. L. Bonham Antiquarian Booksellers   Africa 4/20/2011 - 7069   2011   £125

Charters, Ann *The Portable Beat Reader.* New York: Viking, 1992, First edition; 600+ pages, fine in fine dust jacket, exceptional copy, this copy belonged to Nelson Lyon, inscribed to him or signed and dated by William Burroughs, Allen Ginsberg, Gregory Corso, Ed Sanders, Michael McClure and Anne Waldman.   Ken Lopez Bookseller   154 - 12   2011 $1250

Chartier, Alain *Les Oeuvres.* Paris: S. Thiboust, Jan. 25th, 1617, 4to., (16), 868, (20) pages, title printed in red and black, woodcut device, woodcut head and tailpieces, woodcut initials, contemporary calf with triple fillet rule on boards and fleurons in corners, spine gilt in compartments, morocco lettering piece, colored silk page marker, manuscript ex-libris "Normand", manuscript annotations in margins (many trimmed), from the library of the Earls of Macclesfield at Shirburn Castle.   Maggs Bros. Ltd.   1440 - 50   2011   £900

Chase, J. Smeaton *Yosemite Trails: Camp and Pack Train in the Yosemite Region of the Sierra Nevada.* Boston: 1911, First edition; signed by author, x, 354 pages, illustrations, owner's name, extremities rubbed, else very good.   Dumont Maps & Books of the West   111 - 50   2011 $85

Chase, James Hadley *No Orchids for Miss Blandish.* New York: Howell, Soskin Publishers, 1942, First US edition; near fine, tight copy, dust jacket, professionally restored at spine ends, and corners with two small closed tears at bottom edge of rear panel, exceptional copy.   Buckingham Books   May 26 2011 - 24956   2011 $2500

Chastellux, Francois Jean, Marquis De   1734-1788 *Travels in North American in the Years 1780, 1781 and 1782.* London: printed for G. G. J. and J. Robinson, 1787, First English edition; 8vo., (16), 462; (16), 430 pages, 2 folding maps in 1 volume, 3 folding plates in volume II, recent one quarter calf and marbled boards.   M & S Rare Books, Inc.   90 - 73   2011 $1250

Chatham, Russell *The Theory and Practice of Rivers. (Prints only).* Seattle: Winn Books, 1986, First edition, there were supposedly going to be 175 copies, but it appears that they were not all issued, one of 40 artist's proof sets and numbered; 5 print portfolio printed to accompany the book, 13 3/4 x 18 inches, signed by artist, fine.   Bella Luna Books   May 26 2011 - t4293   2011 $1100

Chatterton, Edward Keble *Severn's Saga.* London: Hurst & Blackett, 1938, First edition; 8vo., pages 288, illustrations, map on endpapers, original brown cloth, spine faded.   J. & S. L. Bonham Antiquarian Booksellers   Africa 4/20/2011 - 4569   2011   £60

Chatwin, Bruce *In Patagonia.* London: Cape, 1977, First edition; plates, endpaper and frontispiece maps, pages (iv), 204, crown 8vo., original mid blue boards, backstrip gilt lettered, very faint fading to backstrip panel of dust jacket, much less than usually met with, near fine.   Blackwell Rare Books   B166 - 129   2011   £550

Chatwin, Bruce *On the Black Hill.* London: Jonathan Cape, 1982, First British edition; fine in fine dust jacket.   Bella Luna Books   May 29 2011 - g5467   2011 $137

Chatwin, Bruce *Patagonia revisited.* Salisbury: Michael Russell, 1985, First edition, number 113 of 250 copies signed by Chatwin and Theroux; 8vo., pages 62, (2) blank, original brown cloth, backstrip over grey cloth with man and horse decorative design printed in brown, grey endpapers, original publisher's glassine, lightly rubbed, author's signatures in blue and black ink to limitation page, fine.   Simon Finch Rare Books   Zero - 216   2011   £250

Chatwin, Bruce *The Songlines.* London: London Limited Editions, 1987, One of 150 numbered copies signed by author; mild top edge foxing, else fine in near fine, original glassine dust jacket.   Ken Lopez Bookseller   154 - 28   2011 $750

Chaucer, Geoffrey 1340-1400 *Troilus and Criseyde.* Waltham St. Lawrence: Golden Cockerel Press, 1927, One of 225 numbered copies (first six of which were printed on vellum); 316 x 198mm., xi, (i), 309, (1) pages, (2) leaves (blank and colophon), original publisher's russet quarter morocco by Sangorski & Sutcliffe, patterned paper sides, top edge gilt, others untrimmed, publisher's (only just slightly rubbed and soiled) slipcase, fore margins of every text page with woodcut borders and five full page wood engravings, all by Eric Gill, section titlepages with red or blue lettering, occasional text initials in red or blue; bookplate of the Newton library (begun by Sir Alfred Newton, 1st Baronet and mostly assembled by Sir Harry Newton, 2nd Bart. 1871-1951); some minor spotting or soiling on part of the morocco on front board, otherwise faultless copy, spine unusually bright, corners (which are always rubbed) in virtually perfect condition, text as bright and fresh as new.   Phillip J. Pirages   59 - 219   2011 $19,500

Chaucer, Geoffrey 1340-1400 *Troilus and Criseyde.* Waltham St. Lawrence: Golden Cockerel Press, 1927, First Gill edition, one of 225 numbered copies, this being 13; folio, five full page wood engravings by Eric Gill, publisher's quarter russet morocco over patterned paper boards, near fine.   Heritage Book Shop   Booth A12 51st NY International Antiquarian Book Fair April 8-10 2011 - 62   2011 $9000

Chaucer, Geoffrey 1340-1400 *Workes of Geoffrey Chaucer.* London: Imprinted by Jhon Kyngston for John Wight, 1561, Rare first issue; folio, (14), ccclxxviii leaves (irregular foliation), title within woodcut border, woodcut border, 22 woodcuts, large and small historiated and decorative initials and other ornaments, black letter, fifty-six lines, double columns, early 20th century antique style dark brown calf, expertly and almost invisible rebacked with original spine laid down, covers with double blind fillet border, spine in six compartments with five raised bands, ruled in blind and dated in gilt at foot and with brown morocco gilt lettering label, title lightly soiled with upper blank margin renewed, lower corner of first two leaves strengthened, few tiny holes or paper flaws, occasional foxing or faint dampstaining on few leaves, short (2 inch) repaired tear to lower margin of Mmm6, not affecting text, bookplate with monogram of Dr. George Osborne Mitchell, early ink signature of Anne Abdy and Hercules Holiambe (?) and some additional early ink annotations on title.   David Brass Rare Books, Inc. May 26 2011 - 00642   2011 $48,500

Chaucer, Geoffrey 1340-1400 *The Works of...* London: Folio Society, 2002, First edition thus, number 44 of 1010 copies; full Nigerian white goatskin designed by David Eccles after T. J. Cobden Sanderson; the paper, specially made at James Cropper Mill at Burneside in Cumbria and supplied by John Purcell Paper, binding design redrawn by Eccles from a copy of the Kelmscott Chaucer bound by Coben-Sanderson, elaborate gilt decorated binding by Smith Settle at Otley, Yorkshire, excellent slipcase (bumped at one corner), with gilt goatskin spine label, tipped in at front of slipcase is 15 page booklet with essay by William Peterson on Kelmscott Chaucer.   Any Amount of Books   May 26 2011 - A68251   2011 $1761

Chaudon, Louis Mayeul *Historical and Critical Memoirs of the Life and Writings of M. De Voltaire: Interspersed with Numerous Anecdotes...*   Dublin: White, Wogan, Byrne, Cash, etc., 1786, First edition thus; 8vo., pages viii, 424, 7 page index, disbound, i.e. lacking covers, otherwise in decent sound condition with clean text, suitable for rebinding or reading and reference, discreet library stamp on verso of titlepage.   Any Amount of Books   May 29 2011 - A67944   2011 $230

Chauncey, Charles *Seasonable Thoughts on the State of Religion in New England...*   Boston: Rogers and Fowle, 1743, First edition; 8vo. 30, 18, 424 pages, full contemporary calf, slight chip.   M & S Rare Books, Inc.   90 - 74   2011 $550

Chaundler, Christine *Bunty of the Blackbirds.* London: Nisbet an Co. n.d., 1925, First edition; original red pictorial cloth, pages 255, 4 plates, flyleaves lightly browned.   R. F. G. Hollett & Son Antiquarian Booksellers   General Catalogue Summer 2010 - 506   2011   £30

Checkerboard. New York: Weyhe Gallery, 1930, Limited to 5000 copies; this issued devoted entirely to the work of Wanda Gag, 4 full page and 3 partial page illustrations, wood engravings or linoleum cuts printed directly from blocks.   Aleph-Bet Books, Inc.   95 - 246   2011 $750

Cheetham, F. H. *Haddon Hall.* Sherratt and Hughes, 1904, Original red cloth gilt, pages xiv, 147, (iii), 3 folding plans and numerous illustrations.   R. F. G. Hollett & Son Antiquarian Booksellers   177 - 177   2011   £30

Cheever, Henry *The Whale and His Captors; or the Whaleman's Adventures and the Whale's Biography as Gathered on the Homeward Cruise of the "Commodore Preble".*   London: Thomas Nelson and Sons, 1855, 12mo., original blindstamped blue cloth gilt extra, pages x, 240, all edges gilt, tinted lithograph frontispiece and title, prize label on pastedown.   R. F. G. Hollett & Sons Antiquarian Booksellers   170 - 147   2011   £85

Cheever, John 1912-1984 *Expelled.* Sylvester and Orphanos, 1988, Limited edition of 150 copies signed; miniature book, 70 pages, fine in original slipcase, text set in Baskerville type and paper is Arches mouldmade.   By the Book, L. C.   26 - 3   2011 $250

Cheever, John 1912-1984 *Falconer.* New York: Knopf, 1977, First edition; fine, dust jacket near fine, light sunning to flaps.   Bella Luna Books   May 29 2011 - t9298   2011 $82

Cheever, John 1912-1984 *The Uncollected Stories of John Cheever 1930-1981.* Chicago: Academy Chicago, 1988, Uncorrected proof; fine in wrappers, together with a copy of the later collection and with Anita Miller's book "Uncollecting Cheever" an account of the legal case surrounding the book.   Ken Lopez Bookseller   154 - 29   2011 $950

Cheley, Frank H. *Bettering Boyhood - Boystuff - Home Life and Leadership.* Boston: 1931, First edition; 12mo., fine in good dust jacket, chip at backstrip top affecting title, glue darkening at inner front joint.   Bookworm & Silverfish   667 - 150   2011 $100

Chenu, Jean *Recueil d'Antiquitez et Privileges de la Ville de Bourges et de Plusieurs Autres Villes Capitales du Royaume Divise e Trois Parties.* Paris: Robert Fouet, 1621, First edition; 4to., (4), 503, (9) pages, (page 156 misnumbered 457), engraved portrait by L. Gauthier, mid 17th century French calf with triple fillets on boards and fleurons in corner, spine gilt in compartments, morocco lettering piece, from the library of the Earls of Macclesfield at Shirburn Castle.   Maggs Bros. Ltd.   1440 - 51   2011   £500

Cheronnet, Louis *Algerie.* Paris: Duchartre, 1930, Folio, cloth backed pictorial boards, some cover soil and toning of paper, very good, illustrations.   Aleph-Bet Books, Inc.   95 - 434   2011 $750

Cherry, Peter *Studies in Northern Prehistory.* Kendal: Titus Wilson for the Cumberland and Westmorland Antiquarian & Archaeological Society, 2007, Large 8vo., original cloth, gilt, dust jacket, pages x, 288, illustrations.   R. F. G. Hollett & Son Antiquarian Booksellers   173 - 229   2011   £45

Chesterfield, Philip Dormer Stanhope, 4th Earl of 1694-1773 *The Letters... Including Numerous Letters Now First Published from Original Manuscripts.* London: Richard Bentley, 1845-1853, 5 volumes, 220 x 140mm., very pleasing contemporary rose colored polished calf, attractively gilt, covers bordered with gilt double fillets, raised bands, spines gilt in compartments featuring volute cornerpieces and pineapple lozenge centerpiece, green and maroon morocco labels, marbled edges and endpapers, five engraved plates, backstrips lightly and uniformly faded to pleasing terra cotta color, edges missing a few small flakes, boards with very minor scratches, paper stock, shade less than bright, still quite appealing set, decorative bindings scarcely worn and text virtually pristine.   Phillip J. Pirages   59 - 163   2011 $750

Chesterfield, Philip Dormer Stanhope, 4th Earl of 1694-1773 *Lord Chesterfield's Advice to His Son, on Men and Manners...* Chiswick: from the Press of C. Whittingham, sold by R. Jennings, Poultry, et al, 1823, 12mo., iv, 96 pages, full leather, gilt title on spine, engraved half titlepage with very fine half page copper engraving dated 1820, full tooled black leather with gilt decorative frame on upper and lower cover, elaborate gilt spine with gilt title on red leather, gilt ruling and edges of covers, marbled endpapers and marbled edges, owner label inside front cover, minor light spot on half title, minor rubbing at edges of covers and spine, fine.   Hobbyhorse Books   56 - 141   2011 $140

Chesterton, Gilbert Keith 1874-1936 *The Ball and the Cross.* New York: John Lane Co., 1909, First edition (true first); owner name dated 1911 on front endpaper, light fraying to tips of spine which is darkened with gilt still clear, very good, lacking exceptionally scarce dust jacket.   Charles Agvent   2010 Summer Miscellany - 20   2011 $500

Chesterton, Gilbert Keith 1874-1936 *For Faultless Felons.* London: Cassell and Co. Ltd., 1930, First edition; 8vo., some light foxing to page edges and corners slightly bumped, else near fine, bright, tight copy in bright, crisp dust jacket that has been professionally internally restored along flap folds and spine ends, exceptional copy of scarce book, especially in elusive dust jacket.   Buckingham Books   May 26 2011 - 24907   2011 $2000

Chesterton, Gilbert Keith 1874-1936 *Greybeards at Play.* Brimley Johnson, 1900, First edition; 24 full page line drawings by author, pages 102, (7) (ads), crown 8vo., original white cloth backed boards, backstrip lettered in black, orange boards, soft cover edges trifle rubbed and chipped, front cover with design incorporating lettering by Chesterton, endpapers lightly browned, good.   Blackwell Rare Books   B166 - 130   2011   £385

Chesterton, Gilbert Keith 1874-1936 *The Man Who Was Thursday. A Nightmare.* Bristol: Arrowsmith, 1908, First edition; pages 330, (2) ads, crown 8vo., original first issue red cloth, lightly faded backstrip gilt lettered with "J.W. ARROWSMITH BRISTOL" at tail, front cover blocked in black, light endpaper browning, very good. Blackwell Rare Books B166 - 131 2011 £480

Chevreul, M. E. *The Laws of Contrast of Colour and their Application to the Arts of Painting, Decoration of buildings, Mosaic Work, Tapestry and Carpet Weaving, Calico Printing, Dress, Paper Staining...* London: Routledge, Warne and Routledge, 1860, New edition; illustrations printed in colours, xvi, 237 pages, 17 engraved plates, very good in most striking bright original decorative gilt cloth, expert repair to head of spine, small 8vo. Ken Spelman Rare Books 68 - 71 2011 £120

Chichester, Imogen *The Sad Tale of the Greedy Boy.* London: Collins, 1944, First edition; 8vo., cloth backed color pictorial boards, slight rubbing to corner, else quite clean, 21 numbered pages, each with few color pictures. Jo Ann Reisler, Ltd. 86 - 139 2011 $285

Chiericato, Giovanni Maria *De Ordinis Sacramento Decisiones in Quibus.* Venetiis: Apud Andream Poleti, 1705, Small 4to., (xxiv), 400 pages, index, original full vellum, title with old rubber institutional stamp, very good copy of this rare edition. Jeff Weber Rare Books 163 - 30 2011 $300

The Child's Amusement Primer, Presented to Our Juvenile Friends by Frank A. Robbins' New Shows, Two Ring Circus, Museum and Monster Menagerie. New York: S. Booth, 1887, Original decorative wrappers, mildly toned, engraved illustration to upper cover, numerous vignette illustrations and decorative capital letters to text, light dampstaining at foot, fraying to ends of backstrip. Dramatis Personae Booksellers 106 - 145 2011 $200

The Child's Companion and Juvenile Instructor. London: Religious Tract Society, 1859-1865, 32 numbers, small 8vo., original printed wrappers, upper panels with decorative borders, first wrapper missing, last chipped, numerous full page and other woodcut text illustrations. R. F. G. Hollett & Sons Antiquarian Booksellers 170 - 148 2011 £75

Child's First Peter Rabbit Book. Peter Rabbit. The Little Red Hen. The Owl and the Pussycat. Newark: Charles Graham, n.d. circa, 1920, Large 4to., cloth backed pictorial boards, pictorial paste-on, very good-fine, 16 full page chromolithographs plus numerous full page and partial page illustrations, pictorial endpapers, scarce Potter piracy. Aleph-Bet Books, Inc. 95 - 462 2011 $375

The Child's Keepsake: a Poetical Bouquet for Little Children. New Haven: S. Babcock, 1850, Square 18mo., 8 pages, yellow pictorial paper wrappers, rebacked with matching color paper, trace of stitching inside folders, half page wood engraving, light soiling at wrappers, very good. Hobbyhorse Books 56 - 38 2011 $150

Child, Lydia Maria Frances 1802-1880 *The American Anti-Slavery Almanac for 1839.* New York: American Anti-Slave Society, 1839, First edition; printed wrappers, 48 pages, illustrated wrappers bound in later plain boards, 14 woodcut illustrations, very good plus. Second Life Books Inc. 174 - 95 2011 $225

Childe, V. Gordon *Prehistoric Communities of the British Isles.* London: W. & R. Chambers, 1947, Original cloth gilt, dust jacket piece torn from upper panel, pages xiv, 274, 16 pages of plates and 96 text illustrations. R. F. G. Hollett & Son Antiquarian Booksellers 177 - 179 2011 £30

Childers, Erskine *In the Ranks of the CIV; a Narrative and Diary of Personal Experiences with the CIV Battery in South Africa.* London: Smith, Elder, 1900, Second impression; 8vo., pages 301, frontispiece, original red decorative cloth. J. & S. L. Bonham Antiquarian Booksellers Africa 4/20/2011 - 5638 2011 £60

Childers, Erskine *The Riddle of the Sands.* London: Thomas Nelson and Sons n.d. 1920's, Small 8vo., original pale blue cloth, spine rather worn and darkened, pages 383, 2 charts and 2 maps, all editions scarce. R. F. G. Hollett & Son Antiquarian Booksellers General Catalogue Summer 2010 - 1630 2011 £45

Childhood; or Little Alice. New York: Carlton & Lanahan, 1855, 189 pages, brown cloth, worn, soiled, chipped and torn on spine, hinges weak, endpapers removed, owner's inscription, foxing, few tears and chips to pages, else solid, 189 pages plus ads, good. G. H. Mott Bookseller May 26 2011 - 32600 2011 $400

Childhood's Delight. (Aunt Louisa's London Toy Books number 67). London: Frederick Warne and Co. circa, 1878, 4to., full color pictorial card covers with some dusting and light wear to spine, book has been resewn and is slightly rippled but interior is clean and fresh, 12 pages within (counting inside covers), with 6 offering text and 6 offering full color illustrations with grand gold backgrounds,. Jo Ann Reisler, Ltd. 86 - 243 2011 $225

The Children in the Wood. An Historical Ballad and the Story of Farmer Wilkins. Banbury: J. G. Rusher, n.d. circa, 1825, 16mo., 16 pages (2) pages list inside wrappers, original pictorial paper self wrappers, untrimmed, publisher list on verso of upper wrapper, 2 small wood engravings, wood engraved frontispiece, 6 1/3 page wood engravings, upper wrapper with large vignette of bird and lower wrapper with cut of men in forest, some darkening at edges, near fine. Hobbyhorse Books 56 - 21 2011 $175

Children's Picture Play Book. London: George Routledge and Sons, 1866, 4to., red cloth stamped in blind and gold, 64 pages, light cover soil, rear cover crease, else very good+, 32 full page color lithographs, rare.   Aleph-Bet Books, Inc.   95 - 277   2011 $1500

Childress, Mark   *Crazy in Alabama.*   New York: Putnam, 1993,   First edition; foxing to top edge, near fine in near fine dust jacket, warmly inscribed by author to another writer.   Ken Lopez Bookseller   154 - 31   2011 $100

Childrey, Joshua   *Britannica Baconica; or the Natural Rarities of England, Scotland & Wales.*   London: printed for the author, 1661,   8vo. pages (xxx) 184, early 19th century straight grained dark blue roan, spine single rule gilt, lettered direct in gilt, boards single rule gilt bordered, buff cloth applied endbands, browned and spotted, tiny piece lost from lower corner of titlepage, extremities bit rubbed and corners worn, front joint just cracking at head, from the collection of Christopher Ernest Weston 1947-2010.   Unsworths Booksellers   24 - 77   2011   £300

Childs, Elizabeth Herbert   *The Fun of Being Good...*   New York: Sam Gabriel, 1918,   Oblong 4to., cloth backed pictorial boards, slight cover soil, else near fine in original pictorial box (flap repaired).   Aleph-Bet Books, Inc.   95 - 220   2011 $250

Chilosa, Pseud.   *Venusberg: The Syren City...*   London: Holden & Hardingham, 1913,   First edition thus; 8vo., pages 1-144 and 145-33 (The Sequel), 3 photos, excellent, almost fine copy, scarce, original dark blue cloth lettered in pale blue with draped female figure holding a burning torch on cover (also in pale blue).   Any Amount of Books   May 29 2011 - A71433   2011 $383

Chippindall, W. H.   *A History of the Parish of Tunstall.*   Manchester: for the Society, 1940,   Volume 104 New Series, original mauve cloth gilt, spine trifle frayed at head and foot, pages x, 122, xix, 8 plates and map, some neat marginalia in places but very good, very scarce.   R. F. G. Hollett & Son Antiquarian Booksellers   General Catalogue Summer 2010 - 1362   2011   £150

Chippindall, W. H.   *Memoirs of Lieut.-Colonel Samuel Gledhill Lieutenant Governor of Placentia and Commander-in-Chief of Newfoundland from 1719 to 1727 to which is Prefixed a Connected Narrative of His Life by His Descendant.*   Kendal: Titus Wilson, 8vo., pages vii, 130, folding sheets in rear, red cloth, white titles to front and spine.   Schooner Books Ltd.   96 - 26   2011 $75

Chisenhall, Edward   *A Journal of the Siege of Latham House, in Lancashire Defended by Charlotte de la Tremouille, Countess of Derby against Sir Thomas Fairfax and Other Parliamentary Officers 1644.*   Harding, Mavor & Lepard, 1823,   2 pages ads, uncut in original pink boards, paper label on front board (price 3s), little rubbed and faded, but very good in original state, booksellers ticket of William Whyte, Edinburgh.   Jarndyce Antiquarian Booksellers   CXCI - 348   2011   £75

Chisholm, Hugh   *Several Have Lived.*   New York: Gemor Press, 1942,   First edition, 500 copies printed; large 8vo., unnumbered, about 50 pages, black wrappers, small illustration pasted to cover printed title label at spine, 3 tipped in illustrations in black and white, loosely inserted is rare printed flier for book, very good.   Any Amount of Books   May 29 2011 - A39537   2011 $340

Chisholm, Louey   *The Golden Staircase.*   T. C. & E. C. Jack, 1906,   Large 8vo., original decorated cloth, gilt extra, spine little faded and slightly frayed at head, pages xxxi, 361, top edge gilt, 16 color plates and copper endpapers.   R. F. G. Hollett & Sons Antiquarian Booksellers   170 - 650   2011   £75

Chodsko, Alex   *Fairy Tale of the Slave Peasants & Herdsmen.*   London: 1896,   First edition in English; illustrations by Emily Harding, 353 including plates, very good, top edge gilt, patterned endpapers, original binding, cover gilt quite legible, backstrip better, mild wear to covers.   Bookworm & Silverfish   676 - 108   2011 $75

A' Choisir-Chiuil. The Gaelic Choir. The St. Columba Collection of Gaelic Songs, Arranged for Part Singing.   Paisley: J. and R. Parlane, n.d. early 1900's,   First edition; tall 8vo., original blue cloth, pages 80, scarce.   R. F. G. Hollett & Son Antiquarian Booksellers   175 - 495   2011   £65

Choon, Angela   *Chris Ofili: Devil's Pie.*   New York and Gottingen: Steidl and David Swirner, 2008,   First edition; 4to. original publisher's purple cloth lettered silver on spine and over, signed presentation from Ofili for Louise, illustrations in color, about fine.   Any Amount of Books   May 29 2011 - A7550   2011 $272

Chope, R. Pearse   *The Augustinian Priory of Frithelstock.*   Exeter: A. Wheaton & Co. early 1930's,   Large 8vo. original wrappers, pages 27, with 7 illustrations, site plan and folding plan, inscribed by author.   R. F. G. Hollett & Son Antiquarian Booksellers   177 - 180   2011   £30

Chorier, Nicolas   *L'Academie des Dames.*   A Venise: chez Pierre Arretin but Holland, circa, 1775,   8vo., pages 420, frontispiece, engraved titlepage, 35 engraved erotic plates, some light foxing and browning, contemporary full calf, red morocco lettering piece to spine, lettering in gilt, expertly rebacked, bookplate of Gerard Nordmann.   Simon Finch Rare Books   Zero - 408   2011   £5750

Chorier, Nicolas *Novelle Traduction du Mursius Connu Sous le Nom d'Aloisia ou de L'Academie des Dames...* dans l'Imprimerie de la Volupte, 1749, First edition of the second translation of this work; 2 volumes in one, small 8vo., pages (ii) blank, (iv) xx, 191, (1) blank; (iv), xii, 312, 9 (of 10 etchings, colored), very pretty mid 19th century binding of full tan crushed morocco, marbled endpapers, inner dentelles, 5 raised bands, deep green morocco gilt title labels, elaborately gilt filigrees, front, back and spine, all edges gilt, previous owner's inscription.   Simon Finch Rare Books   Zero - 404 2011   £12,500

Chrimes, Mike *The Civil Engineering of Canals and Railways Before 1850.* Aldershot et al: Ashgate, 1997, 8vo., xxviii, 378 pages, illustrations, tables, red cloth, gilt stamped cover and spine titles, fine, from the Bern Dibner reference library, with Burndy bookplate.   Jeff Weber Rare Books   161 - 85 2011 $100

Christenberry, William *Adam's House in the Black Belt.* Chicago: Landfall Press, 2000, First edition, deluxe edition of 25 copies; massive folio that includes a total of 30 images, including original hand printed lithographs, photogravures and iris prints, fine in fine slipcase, signed and lettered "VIX", includes original color print "Rear of House with Flowers, Alabama 1985".   Jeff Hirsch Books   ny 2010 2011 $7500

Christian Journal. Glasgow: 1837, Volume V #49-60; 666 pages, 12 issues, cloth, later backstrip, covers worn and reattached, some owner notes, scarce.   Bookworm & Silverfish   664 - 173 2011 $60

The Christian Lady's Pocket Book for the Year 1793. London: printed for the Proprietors and sold by J. S. Jorcan, G. Terry and T. Willis, n.d., 1792?, 12mo., engraved frontispiece, (2), 142, (2) pages, original soft calf boards, unlettered and rather worn, stitching strained, complete and pretty good copy nonetheless, diary itself unused.   John Drury Rare Books   153 - 115 2011   £350

Christian, Anne Hait *The Search for Holmes, Robson, Hind, Steele and Graham Families of Cumberland and Northumberland, England.* La Jolla: privately printed, 1984, Number 53 of 1033 copies; small 4to., original blue cloth, gilt, pages (viii), 172, with 75 illustrations, charts, etc., presentation copy inscribed by author to Lorna Carleton.   R. F. G. Hollett & Son Antiquarian Booksellers   General Catalogue Summer 2010 - 381 2011   £65

Christian, Ewan *Architectural Illustrations of Skelton Church, Yorkshire.* London: George Bell, 1846, Folio, viii, 39, (1) pages, 17 plates, very good in original morocco backed blindstamped and gilt lettered cloth boards, corners bumped, attractive, bookplate removed at some stage.   Ken Spelman Rare Books   68 - 39 2011   £120

The Christian's Magazine Designed to Promote the Knowledge and Influence of Evangelical Truth & Order. New York: 1810, 708 pages, small 8vo., half leather, marbled boards, marbled paper rubbed and creased with small section torn away.   Bookworm & Silverfish   662 - 164 2011 $87

Christie, Agatha 1891-1976   *The Murder at the Vicarage.* New York: Dodd, Mead & Co., 1930, First US edition; fine, bright, tight copy in spectacular, fine, bright dust jacket, superb copy.   Buckingham Books   May 26 2011 - 27194 2011 $3750

Christie, Agatha 1891-1976   *The Murder at the Vicarage.* New York: Dodd Mead & Co., 1930, First US edition; cloth moderately soiled and sunned on spine, else very good, in spectacular, fine, bright dust jacket with only minor closed tear and some faint creasing to rear flap, exceptional copy.   Buckingham Books   May 26 2011 - 25491 2011 $300

Christie, Agatha 1891-1976   *The Mysterious Mr. Quinn.* New York: Dodd, Mead & Co, 1930, First US edition; fine in fine, unrestored dust jacket, uncommon, especially in jacket, exceptional copy.   Buckingham Books   May 26 2011 - 25492 2011 $4375

Christisen, D. *Account of the Excavation of Birrens. A Roman Station in Annandale, Scotland by The Society of Antiquities of Scotland in 1895.* The Society, n.d., Square 8vo., modern half maroon levant morocco gilt, pages 119, with 50 text figures and 2 folding colored lithograph plans (little soiled on reverse), little dusty in places.   R. F. G. Hollett & Son Antiquarian Booksellers   177 - 181 2011   £120

Christmas. Pictures by Children. London: J. . Dent & Sons, 1922, First edition; square 4to., original pictorial boards, edges and corners rather worn, pages (iv), with 14 striking colored plates with captioned tissue (2 tissues lacking, 1 plate little torn but complete).   R. F. G. Hollett & Sons Antiquarian Booksellers   170 - 212 2011   £95

Christmas ABC. Akron: Saalfield Pub. Co., 1910, 12 1/2 x 6 inches, cloth covers are in full color and except for light soiling to small section on rear cover, are clean and fresh, each of the cloth pages (there are three cloth leaves, each made up of doubled over material).   Jo Ann Reisler, Ltd.   86 - 41 2011 $350

The Christmas Book. New York: McLoughlin Bros., n.d. circa, 1900, 4to., green pictorial cloth, near fine, illustrations by G. A. Davis with more than 15 full page chromolithographs and marvelous 3 color illustrations on every page of text.   Aleph-Bet Books, Inc.   95 - 149 2011 $800

The Christmas Book. New York: McLoughlin circa, 1905, 4to., green cloth backed full color pictorial boards, wear and soiling to covers, few brown spots on verso of titlepage, illustrations by G. A. Davis.   Jo Ann Reisler, Ltd.   86 - 40   2011 $475

Christmas Stories ABC. Chicago: Donohue, n.d. circa, 1915, Small 4to., pictorial wrappers, rear blank replaced, else very good, illustrations in color.   Aleph-Bet Books, Inc.   95 - 8   2011 $150

Christmas-Tide in Prose and Poetry. London: Ernest Nister, n.d. circa, 1900, Small 8vo., original decorated two-tone cloth gilt, pages 148, illustrations in color and monochrome throughout, inscription.   R. F. G. Hollett & Son Antiquarian Booksellers   General Catalogue Summer 2010 - 671   2011   £45

Christopher, A. B.   *The Word Accomplished.* London: World's End Press, 1974, First edition, number 50 of 75 copies signed by author and artist; 4to., loose pages in illustrated wrappers, 16 embossed etchings, lacks plate VG (6), all plates except final plate signed and numbered by artist, Natalie D'Arbeloff, fine in handsome, near fine drop back box covered in ivory vellum with quarter leather spine, embossed titling.   Any Amount of Books   May 29 2011 - A48590   2011 $340

Christopher, John   *The Death of Grass.* London: Michael Joseph, 1956, First edition; octavo, boards.   L. W. Currey, Inc.   124 - 118   2011 $650

Christopher, John   *The Death of Grass.* London: Michael Joseph, 1956, First edition; 8vo., pages 231, neat name on front endpaper, slightly bumped corner, otherwise very good+ in complete but slightly rubbed and slightly soiled very good+ dust jacket with couple of short closed tears but no loss.   Any Amount of Books   May 29 2011 - A49016   2011 $374

Christy, Cuthbert   *Big Game and Pygmies: Experiences of a Naturalist in Central African Forests in Quest of Okapi.* London: Macmillan, 1924, First edition; 8vo., pages xxxi, 325, folding map, illustrations, original blue pictorial cloth, small wear to head and tail of spine, joints slightly rubbed, inner joints cracked, internally clean.   J. & S. L. Bonham Antiquarian Booksellers   Africa 4/20/2011 - 8859   2011   £70

Christy's Panorama Songster: Containing the Songs as Sung by Christie, Campbell, Pierce's Minstrels and Sable Brothers. New York: William H. Murphy, n.d. citca, 1866, 12mo., original printed yellow wrappers, vignette illustration to upper cover, minor wear to spine ends, contents very good, quite tight, engraved frontispiece, textural wood engraved vignettes.   Dramatis Personae Booksellers   106 - 31   2011 $125

Chubb, Charles   *The Birds of British of Guiana, Based on the Collection of Frederick Vavasour McConnell.* London: Bernard Quaritch, 1916-1921, First edition, limited to 250 numbered copies; portrait, 24 photo plates, 20 color plates by Gronvold, 309 text figures and colored folding map (with small tear), 8vo., pages liii, 528; xcvi, 615, modern half tree calf over black cloth boards, 2 lower corners bumped, inch gouge, covered with cellotape, to cloth on rear cover volume I, small ink stains to fore edge of annotations and revisions made during 1935, 1936 and 1937, abrasion to fore-edge of rear cover, black morocco labels and 4 raised bands, scarce.   Raymond M. Sutton, Jr.   May 26 2011 - 14453   2011 $1250

Chukovski, Kornei   *Barmalei.* Leningrad and Moscow: Raduga, 1929, Fifth printing in smaller format; 8vo., color lithographed self wrappers with some handling and dusting, 10 pages, including inside covers, illustrations by Mstislav Valerianovich Dobuzhinsky.   Jo Ann Reisler, Ltd.   86 - 216   2011 $400

Chukovski, Kornei   *Tarakanische. (The Cockroach).* Leningrad: Raduga, 1925, although cover is dated 1922 when the materials were first published in a magazine but not in book form. first edition; 4to., color pictorial paper wrappers with some light handling, but overall nice copy, 24 numbered pages with black and white illustrations by Sergei Chekhonin.   Jo Ann Reisler, Ltd.   86 - 212   2011 $375

Church of England   *New Week's Preparation for a Worthy Receiving of the Lord's Supper...* London: from the Executors of the late Edw. Wicksteed, c., 1745, 33rd edition; small 8vo., old blind ruled calf, rather worn and rubbed, upper joint cracked but sound, pages ix, (i), 156, 156 with 2 titles and 2 engraved frontispieces, new front endpapers, rear flyleaf with early family notes (repaired).   R. F. G. Hollett & Son Antiquarian Booksellers   175 - 260   2011   £150

Church of England   *The Offices According to the Use of the Church of England, for the Solemnisation of Matrimony...* Oxford: Clarendon Press, 1787, Old blind panelled calf, surface very dulled and cracked, unpaginated, little browned and fingered in places, leaf, G8 repaired without loss, contemporary notes on rear flyleaf, scarce.   R. F. G. Hollett & Son Antiquarian Booksellers   175 - 261   2011   £85

Church of England. Book of Common Prayer *The Book of Common Prayer... together with The Psalter or Psalms of David.* London: engraved and printed by the Permission of Mr. John Baskett, 1717, 206 x 130mm., xxii, 166 pages, (1) leaf of ads, fine contemporary blind tooled somber black morocco, covers with scalloped border accented with leaf and dot ornaments, center panel with field of subtly stamped fleurons, volutes, leafy tools, trefoils and circles arranged in the upper and lower halves as mirror images and at center a large and elaborate lozenge combining these elements, raised bands, double ruled spine compartments decorated in style of boards, gilt turn-ins, marbled endpapers, all edges gilt, attractive modern fleece lined folding cloth box with red morocco spine label; pages ruled in red throughout and volume fully engraved, text in fine tiny italic script, with three, six and 12 line initials, tailpieces, full decorative and historiated borders (10 different designs), volvelle (quite often missing) used to find date of Easter; 125 illustrations, as well as portrait of personages of import, the whole executed by John Strutt; ink inscription Geo(rge) Gill his Book / left him by his mother Mary Gill / who departed this life November 6th / 1765 / Aged 49 years", flyleaf inscribed "Thomas Gill Captain in the Royal / Navy Son of George Gill. This book was presented to T. Gill by his father"; corners bit bumped, just breath of wear here and there to leather, occasional minor marginal stains or thumbing, very fine, original binding tight and especially lustrous and engraved contents unusually fresh and clean. Phillip J. Pirages 59 - 34 2011 $3500

Church of England. Book of Common Prayer *The Book of Common Prayer and Administration of the Sacraments and Other Rites and Ceremonies of the Church.* London: engraved and printed by the permission of John Baskett and sold by John Sturt, 1717, First edition, large issue; pages xxii, 165, (ii, ad leaf), finely engraved throughout with initials, scenes from the life of Jesus and numerous portrait, margins and illustrations etc., ruled in red throughout, complete with volvelle to find moveable Sundays (often lacking), most attractive. R. F. G. Hollett & Son Antiquarian Booksellers 175 - 1093 2011 £850

Church of England. Book of Common Prayer *Book of Common Prayer and Administration of the Sacraments...* Oxford: printed by John Baskett, 1718, Folio, old full calf gilt, edges little worn and chipped in places, spine discolored, two fore-edges little damaged, few marks, but very good. R. F. G. Hollett & Son Antiquarian Booksellers 175 - 1089 2011 £650

Church of England. Book of Common Prayer *The Book of Common Prayer, and Administration of the Sacraments... Together with the Psalter.* Edinburgh: printed by Alexander Kincaid, 1768, 8vo., ff. (ccxiv), contemporary polished green morocco, six compartmented spine panel gilt with three subtly contrasting designs, boards double bordered with two decorative rolls, gilt, board edges and turn-ins obliquely broken fillet gilt, 'Dutch-comb' 'made' endpapers, all edges gilt, red and white sewn endbands, minor spotting, extremities little rubbed, from the collection of Christopher Ernest Weston 1947-2010. Unsworths Booksellers 24 - 30 2011 £150

Church of England. Book of Common Prayer *Book of Common Prayer and Administration of the Sacraments and Other Rites and Ceremonies of the Church, According to the Use of the Church of England.* Oxford: printed by W. Jackson and A. Hamilton, 1784, Unpaginated, 4to., modern half calf gilt with raised bands, very clean and crisp copy. R. F. G. Hollett & Son Antiquarian Booksellers 175 - 1086 2011 £120

Church of England. Book of Common Prayer *Book of Common Prayer and Administration of the Sacraments...* Cambridge: printed by John Archdeacon for John Francis and Charles Rivington, Benjamin White and Charles Dilly and J. & J. Merrill, Thomas Harrison for the Co. of Stationers, 1789, 1787; Unpaginated, all edges gilt, very clean and crisp, nicely printed copy, presentation inscription to James Underwood, brief account of Underwood's life added in pencil by a descendant. R. F. G. Hollett & Son Antiquarian Booksellers 175 - 1088 2011 £250

Church of England. Book of Common Prayer *The Book of Common Prayer.* Paris: printed by P. Didot, Sen. and sold by W. Edwards & Sons, Halifax, 1791, 160 x 100mm., (348) leaves, appealing contemporary vellum, handsomely gilt and painted in style of Edwards of Halifax, covers framed with border featuring a Greek key roll superimposed on blue wash and on inner side of border, each an elegant gilt roll of undulant foliage and flowers, rounded spine (without raised bands) decorated with all over honeycomb pattern in gilt and with blue wash label for title near top and publisher near bottom, marbled endpapers, gilt edges; fore edge with very fine painting depicting the ruins of a medieval English castle; blue wash somewhat faded to places (as almost always), vellum little soiled, otherwise fine example, fresh and clean, internally with painting remarkably well preserved. Phillip J. Pirages 59 - 36 2011 $2400

Church of England. Book of Common Prayer *Book of Common Prayer and Administration of the Sacraments...* London: Gilbert and Rivington, 1830, Fourth edition; 4to., contemporary full tan morocco gilt over heavy boards, upper hinge cracking at head and foot but sound, pages 2, lxxii, 966, all edges gilt, flyleaves foxed, otherwise excellent. R. F. G. Hollett & Son Antiquarian Booksellers 175 - 1085 2011 £150

Church of England. Book of Common Prayer *The Book of Common Prayer According to the Use of the Church of England...* Amsterdam: printed by C. A. Spin, 1838, Full patterned crimson calf gilt, spine and upper hinge cracked and tightened, pages xii, 220, all edges gilt, scattered browning, few leaves slightly proud, uncommon edition.   R. F. G. Hollett & Son Antiquarian Booksellers   175 - 1091   2011   £65

Church of England. Book of Common Prayer *The Book of Common Prayer according to the Use of the Church of England.* Amsterdam: printed by C. A. Spon, 1838, Full patterned crimson calf gilt spine and upper hinge cracked and repaired, pages xii, 220, all edges gilt, scattered browning, few leaves slightly proud, uncommon edition.   R. F. G. Hollett & Son Antiquarian Booksellers   General Catalogue Summer 2010 - 1161   2011   £45

Church of England. Book of Common Prayer *The Book of Common Prayer as Printed in Edinburgh 1637.* London: William Pickering, 1844, Folio, original full panelled vellum with yapp edges, gilt centerpiece to each board, spine with double leather labels, spine trifle soiled, small chips to head, unpaginated, title in red and black.   R. F. G. Hollett & Son Antiquarian Booksellers   175 - 1058   2011   £450

Church of England. Book of Common Prayer *The Book of Common Prayer, printed by Whitchurch March 1549.* London: William Pickering, 1844, Folio, original full panelled vellum with yapp edges, gilt centrepiece to each board, spine with double leather labels, few nicks and tears and little soiled in places, sometime recased and repaired, unpaginated, printed on handmade paper, title in red and back, facsimile of 1552 Prayer book.   R. F. G. Hollett & Son Antiquarian Booksellers   175 - 1059   2011   £450

Church of England. Book of Common Prayer *The Book of Common Prayer printed by Whitchurch 1552.* London: William Pickering, 1844, Folio, original full panelled vellum with yapp edges, gilt centre piece to each board, spine with double leather labels, few nicks and tears and little soiled in places, sometime recased, unpaginated, publisher's title in red and black with Pickering device.   R. F. G. Hollett & Son Antiquarian Booksellers   175 - 1057   2011   £350

Church of England. Book of Common Prayer *Book of Common Prayer and Administration of the Sacraments.* Oxford: University Press, 1861, Small 8vo., original full morocco gilt by Hayday & Mansell over heavy bevelled boards, panelled and tooled in gilt, upper board with ornate central brass cross, boards brass bound with broad clasps (one pin missing), heavily gilt turn-ins with marbled endpapers, unpaginated, all edges gilt, very handsome.   R. F. G. Hollett & Son Antiquarian Booksellers   175 - 1084   2011   £180

Church of England. Book of Common Prayer *Book of Common Prayer and Adminstration of the Sacraments...* London: Eyre and Spottiswoode, n.d. circa, 1920, Square 8vo., original black straight grained morocco, gilt, oval SPCK emblem in blind and gilt stamp of Barrington Prayer Book Fund on upper board, pages 452.   R. F. G. Hollett & Son Antiquarian Booksellers   175 - 1083   2011   £30

Church of England. Book of Common Prayer *Book of Common Prayer and Administration of the Sacraments....* Oxford: University Press, circa, 1960, 12mo., chestnut crushed morocco gilt by Morrell for Mowbray with Cockerell paper marbled boards, all edges gilt, crimson silk markers, printed in red and black throughout.   R. F. G. Hollett & Son Antiquarian Booksellers   175 - 1087   2011   £75

Church of England. Book of Common Prayer *The Booke of Common Praier Noted (1550).* Nottingham Court Press with Magdalene College, Cambridge, 1979, Original black cloth gilt, pages (iv), plus facsimile in red and black.   R. F. G. Hollett & Son Antiquarian Booksellers   175 - 1091   2011   £65

Church, Richard *Observations on an Eligible Line of Frontier for Greece as an Independent State.* London: James Ridgway, 1830, First edition; 8vo., x, 22, (2) pages, including half title and final ad leaf, preserved in modern wrappers, printed title label on upper cover, very good.   John Drury Rare Books   153 - 26   2011   £150

Churchill, Awnsham *A Collection of Voyages and Travels.* London: Lintot & Osborne, 1744-1746, & 1752.. Third edition; 8 volumes, folio, 369 engraved maps, plans and plates, contemporary Scottish binding of full calf.   Heritage Book Shop   Booth A12 51st NY International Antiquarian Book Fair April 8-10 2011 - 30   2011 $35,000

Churchill, Charles *The Candidate. A Poem.* London: printed for the author and sold by W. Flexney, 1764, (2), 38 pages, 4to., disbound.   Jarndyce Antiquarian Booksellers   CXCI - 117 2011   £125

Churchill, Charles *The Duellist.* London: printed for G. Kearsly, 1764, Second edition; (4), 48 pages half title, 4to., disbound.   Jarndyce Antiquarian Booksellers   CXCI - 118 2011   £125

Churchill, Charles *Poems.* London: printed for John Churchill and W. Flexney, 1769, Fourth edition; (4), 369, (1), (2) pages ads, half title; (4), 330 pages, half title, 8vo., full contemporary calf, gilt decorated spines, red and olive green gilt labels, some rubbing to gilt, slight crack to upper joint volume I, signature of J. Churchill at foot of final leaf of text, volume II with armorial bookplates of William Salmon and J. P. Turbervill, very good, attractive.   Jarndyce Antiquarian Booksellers   CXCI - 119 2011   £200

Churchill, Fleetwood *Essays on the Puerperal Fever and Other Diseases Peculiar to Women.* London: Sydenham Society, 1849, First edition; original blindstamped cloth, gilt, little damped, pages viii, 11, front flyleaf removed.   R. F. G. Hollett & Son Antiquarian Booksellers   175 - 262   2011   £140

Churchill, Randolph *Winston S. Churchill.* London: Heinemann, 1966-1986, First edition; 8vo., original publisher's red cloth lettered gilt on spine, 18 volumes, all in dust jackets, a couple of companion volumes are presented to Sir Michael Fraser of Kilmornack with bookplate.   Any Amount of Books   May 26 2011 - A66506   2011 $1006

Churchill, S. Garton *Churchill Natural Bidding Style at Contract Bridge. Bid Successfully Without Artificial Conventions.* privately printed, 1979, Blue cloth torn at spine, hinge cracked, signed with long inscription by author, occasional pencil notes, errata slip laid in, 8vo., 743 pages, good.   G. H. Mott Bookseller   May 26 2011 - 12923   2011 $200

Churchill, Winston Leonard Spencer   1874-1965 *Charles, IXth Duke of Marlborough, K.G.*   Burns, Oates & Washbourne, 1934, First edition; pages 18, (ii), foolscap 8vo., original printed blue gray sewn wrappers, fine.   Blackwell Rare Books   B166 - 132   2011   £100

Churchill, Winston Leonard Spencer   1874-1965 *Into Battle. Speeches.* London: Cassell and Co., 1941, First edition; original blue cloth, gilt, pages viii, 313, frontispiece.   R. F. G. Hollett & Son Antiquarian Booksellers   175 - 265   2011   £50

Churchill, Winston Leonard Spencer   1874-1965 *Lord Randolph Churchill.* London: Macmillan, 1906, First edition; 2 volumes, signed by Churchill, original publisher's red cloth lettered gilt on spine and cover and with gilt heraldic shield at lower right of each cover, page xvii, 564; ix, 531; frontispiece to each volume, 16 plates, signed by author, one letter proof correction likely in his hand on page vii/1 and another in pencil probably by WSC at page 31/2, 2 volumes, Colonial Office Library copy with fairly minimal markings (blindstamp to covers, small stamp on titlepage and small stamp on verso), corners slightly rubbed, edges slightly rubbed, slight edgewear, spine ends slightly frayed, small nick at head of first volume, overall acceptable set, very good.   Any Amount of Books   May 26 2011 - A69558   2011 $4025

Churchill, Winston Leonard Spencer   1874-1965 *My Early Life.* London: Thornton Butterworth, 1930, First edition, first issue; with 11 titles listed on reverse of half title, modern full crimson levant morocco gilt with raised bands, double spine labels, pages 392, 28 maps and illustrations, little faint spotting here and there, handsome copy.   R. F. G. Hollett & Son Antiquarian Booksellers   175 - 264   2011   £450

Churchill, Winston Leonard Spencer   1874-1965 *A Personal Message from the Prime Minister to the Coal Mining Industry.* London: Issued by the Ministry of Fuel and Power, 1942-1943, First edition; pamphlet, illustrated stapled wrappers, pages 16, one illustration, slight edgewear, staples rusted away, covers slightly spotted and creased, overall very good.   Any Amount of Books   May 29 2011 - A72180   2011 $374

Churchill, Winston Leonard Spencer   1874-1965 *The War Speeches of the Rt. Hon. Winston S. Churchill.* London: Cassell, 1951-1952, First edition; 3 volumes, 8vo., pages xv, 483; xv 560; xvi, 578, ex-Foreign and Commonwealth Office library with their label and stamps (lightly applied), slight lean, small white library number on spine, sound clean, very good.   Any Amount of Books   May 29 2011 - A49457   2011 $240

Churchill, Winston Leonard Spencer   1874-1965 *The World Crisis.* London: Folio Society, 2007, First edition; 5 volumes, 8vo., pages xvii, 64; xiii, 453; xiii, 474; xii, 383; xii, 311, original publisher's pale brown cloth lettered gilt on spine, illustrations, maps, fine, slight split bottom corner of red printed slipcase.   Any Amount of Books   May 29 2011 - A70519   2011 $340

Churchyard, Albert *The Arcana of Freemasonry.* London: George Allen, 1915, First edition; very good, inscribed presentation from author with masonic bookplate and typed name slip of E. H. Shackleton, original cloth, rubbed along rear edge of spine with occasional light fading, else very good, uncommon.   I. D. Edrich   May 26 2011 - 98666   2011 $478

Churella, Albert J. *From Steam to Diesel: Managerial Customs and Organizational Capabilitie in the Twentieth Century American Locomotive Industry.*   Princeton: Princeton University Press, 1998, First printing; 8vo., viii, 215 page, charcoal cloth, silver stamped spine title, dust jacket, fine, from the Bern Dibner reference library, with Burndy bookplate.   Jeff Weber Rare Books   161 - 86   2011 $200

Ciampini, Joannis *De Sacris Aedificiis a Constantino Magno Constructi.* Rome: Komarek, 1693, First edition; folio, pages (xvi), 217 (i errata), (ii bookseller's cataloge), allegorical engraved frontispiece by Arnoldo van Westerhout after Giovanni Battista Lenardi, 35 engraved plates, 10 of which are folding, early 18th century full calf with raised bands and gilt decorations, sympathetically rebacked with decorated spine relaid, front endpapers renewed, very good, internally exceptionally clean.   Peter Ellis   May 26 2011 - ARCHITEC016688   2011 $1650

Cicero, Marcus Tullius *The Correspondence of M. Tullius Cicero, Arranged According to Its Chronological Order...* Dublin/London: Hodges, Foster & Figgis/Longmans, Green and Co., 1885, First editions, except volume 1 which is second edition; 6 volumes only, 8vo., approximately 2350 copies with Dublin University Press Services catalog at rear of each volume, and 24 page Longmans catalog at rear volume I, text in English and Latin, all lack half title, sound decent set with some shelfwear, slight rubbing, few marks, clean text.   Any Amount of Books   May 29 2011 - A49584   2011 $306

Cicero, Marcus Tullius *The Letters of Marcus Tullius Cicero to Several of His Friends...*   London: printed for R. Dodsley, 1753, Octavo, (iv), 477, (2); (ii), 468, (iii); (ii), 384, (iv) pages, original full calf, hinges cracked, spine ends worn, corners showing, bookplate of John Somers, Lord, good.   Jeff Weber Rare Books   163 - 144   2011 $125

Cicero, Marcus Tullius *Sebastiani Corradi Commentarius in quo M. T. Ciceronis Declaris Oratoribus Liber..* Florence: Laurentius Torrentinus, 1552, Folio, original limp vellum, sometime washed and rubbed, pages (x), 457, (liii), title trifle dusty with engraved device and 4 fine engraved pictorial initials, one large, to text.   R. F. G. Hollett & Son Antiquarian Booksellers   General Catalogue Summer 2010 - 633   2011   £850

Cicero, Marcus Tullius *Tusculanae Quaestiones.* Paris: Robert Estienne, 1537, 8vo., 223, (15) pages, woodcut printer's device on titlepage, late 17th century calf, spine gilt in compartments, manuscript annotations in margins, nice, from the library of the Earls of Macclesfield at Shirburn Castle.   Maggs Bros. Ltd.   1440 - 53   2011   £450

Cilento, Diane *The Manipulator.* London: Hodder & Stoughton, 1967, First edition; 8vo., pages 190, signed presentation from author to Sheilah from Diane Cilento and Sean Connery, the words are in Connery's hand with "Diane" in Cilento's hand, fine in near fine dust jacket.   Any Amount of Books   May 29 2011 - A68502   2011 $272

Cilia, Daniel *Malta Before History: the World's Oldest Free-Standing Stone Architecture.* Sliema, Malta: Miranda Pub., 2004, First edition; pages 440, 4to., copiously illustrated in color, fine in fine dust jacket with fine color printed firm slipcase.   Any Amount of Books   May 29 2011 - A77052   2011 $272

Cinderella *Adventures of Beautiful Little Maid Cinderella or The History of the Glass Slipper.* York: J. Kendrew, n.d. circa, 1825, 32mo., 31 pages, gray stiff paper wrappers with title on upper wrapper, 8 charming half page woodcuts, light rubbing along spine, fine, lovely well inked cuts.   Hobbyhorse Books   56 - 19   2011 $230

Cinderella *Cinderella.* Hamburg: Gustav W. Seitz, circa 1860's, Shapebook, 7 x 2 1/2 inches, full color pictorial wrappers cut along shape of Cinderella's head, book and been resewn and strengthened within, some wear to spine, 16 attractive pages within, each with full color illustrations on top and bottom of page surrounding text, uncommon.   Jo Ann Reisler, Ltd.   86 - 232   2011 $575

Cinderella *Cinderella.* London: William Heinemann; Philadelphia J. B. Lippincott, 1919, One of 850 copies signed by artist, this # 417 one of 525 on English handmade paper; 285 x 227mm., 110 pages, (1) leaf colophon, very attractive three quarter morocco (stamp signed "Putnam's"), raised bands, spine handsomely gilt in compartments formed by plain and decorative rules, quatrefoil centerpiece, surrounded by densely scrolling, cornerpieces, sides and endleaves of rose colored linen, top edge gilt, with one color plate (frontispiece) mounted within pictorial border, silhouette illustrations by Arthur Rackham, tiny portion of one spine band and of leather at head of spine worn away, very slight hints of wear to corners and joints, faint offsetting from illustrations (never severe, but more noticeable in those openings with facing illustrations), otherwise excellent copy, text very fresh.   Phillip J. Pirages   59 - 284   2011 $1250

Cinderella *Cinderella and Other Tales.* New York: Blue Ribbon Books Inc., 1933, Thick 4to., all edges tinted light green, full color pictorial boards with illustrations on both covers ad spine, some overall light shelf wear to boards, full color pictorial dust jacket with some dusting and bit of rubbing wear to edges, book is perhaps slightly cocked, four pop-ups in fine condition, set within 96 numbered pages.   Jo Ann Reisler, Ltd.   86 - 197   2011 $900

Cinema: The Picture Show. Amalgamated Press, 1919-1921, Volume I no. 13 to volume 4 No. 91, 3 volumes, 4to., original publisher's blue cloth, short tear to head of one spine, illustrations, original wrappers bound in, numerous full page sepia or blue tinted portraits, seveal double page 'art plates', very scarce.   R. F. G. Hollett & Son Antiquarian Booksellers   General Catalogue Summer 2010 - 1167   2011   £850

City of Glasgow Bank Publications. I. Contract of Copartnership. II. List of Shareholders and Trustees. III. Shareholders of Caledonian Bank. IV. The Trustee Test Case in the Court of Session (Muir and Others v. the Liquidators). V. Letter to the Shareholders by George Angus, Accountant, Edinburgh. VI. Report of the Trial of the Manager and Directors. Edinburgh: The Edinburgh Publishing Co., London: Simpkin, Marshall and Co., 1879, First collected edition; very scarce, 6 parts in 1 volume, 8vo., (4), 22 64 55 (1) 115 (1) 16 272 pages, several plates, complete as called for, including double page lithograph of the last meeting of the board of directors, two plates showing the directors in the dock, a sketch of the scene inside the court, photograph of the jury and three further whole page portraits, contemporary green half morocco, raised bands, top edge gilt, gilt lettered, fine.   John Drury Rare Books   153 - 27   2011   £250

Clagett, Marshall *The Science of Mechanics in the Middle Ages.* Madison & London: University of Wisconsin & Oxford University Press, 1959, First edition; large 8vo., xxix, 711 pages, plates, figures, blue cloth, gilt stamped spine title, dust jacket, very good, from the Bern Dibner reference library, with Burndy bookplate. Jeff Weber Rare Books 161 - 88 2011 $125

Clain-Stefanelli, Elvira *Highlights from the Money Collection of the Chase Manhattan Bank.* Washington: 1979, 36 pages, 4to., full custom buckram encasing original wrappers, not a library copy. Bookworm & Silverfish 676 - 132 2011 $75

Clair, Colin *Christopher Plantin.* London: Cassell & Co., 1960, First edition; half title, 24 illustrations, xv, (1), 302 pages, original cloth, dust jacket, nice. Anthony W. Laywood May 26 2011 - 21761 2011 $101

Clairac, Louis Andre De La Mamie De *L'Ingenieur de Campagne, ou Traite de la Fortification Passagere.* Paris: Charles Antoine Jombert, 1749, First edition dedicated to the Comte d'Argenson; 4to., xxiii,(1), 24, (3) pages, 36 folding engraved plates, one engraved headpiece by Cochin contemporary speckled calf, spine gilt in compartments, some light spotting, foxing throughout pages 217-224, fine, Gen. G. L. Parker bookplate, manuscript ex-libris, from the library of the Earls of Macclesfield at Shirburn Castle. Maggs Bros. Ltd. 1440 - 56 2011 £400

Clancy, Tom *Red Storm Rising.* New York: Putnam, 1986, First edition; fine, dust jacket near fine, crease on front flap, very light edge wear, signed by author. Bella Luna Books May 29 2011 - t9650 2011 $82

Clapham, A. R. *Flora of the British Isles - Illustrations.* Cambridge: Cambridge University Press, 1957-1965, First edition; 4 volumes, 4to., original cloth, gilt, dust jackets price clipped, line drawings, excellent set. R. F. G. Hollett & Son Antiquarian Booksellers General Catalogue Summer 2010 - 958 2011 £120

Clapham, Alfred W. *Some Famous Buildings and Their Story.* Technical Journals Ltd., 1913, First edition; original cloth backed boards, pages xi, 275, vii (xv), 108 photos and plans. R. F. G. Hollett & Son Antiquarian Booksellers 177 - 183 2011 £35

Clare, John *The Village Minstrel and Other Poems.* London: printed for Taylor and Hessey, Fleet Street and E. Drury, Stamford, 1821, First edition; 2 volumes, small 8vo., frontispieces, original cloth backed boards with paper spine labels, former owner's neat signature "Edw. Cragg 1843" in upper right hand corner of titlepages and on pastedowns, extremities of boards trifle rubbed, spines and covers bit soiled, but in general exceptionally fine set in original condition, preserved in folding cloth box, the Bradley Martin copy, Carter's variant binding "B". James S. Jaffe Rare Books May 26 2011 - 20616 2011 $8750

Clarendon, Edward Hyde, 1st Earl of 1609-1674 *The History of the Rebellion and Civil Wars in England.* Oxford: Clarendon Press, 1807, New edition; 247 x 154mm., 6 volumes, very attractive contemporary Russia, handsomely decorated in gilt and blind, covers with gilt triple fillet frame and Oxford corners surrounding an inner line tooled border of alternating botanical tools, raised bands, unusual and very appealing gilt decorated spine panels dominated by intricately embellished quadrilateral centerpiece with considerable stippling, marbled edges and endpapers, titlepages with engraved vignette, illegible flourished contemporary signature in upper right corner of each titlepage, verso of title leaves with small round red library stamp of 'fideicomm. Ernesti', front pastedown of each volume with what may be faint shadow of removed bookplate, joints and extremities very lightly rubbed, joints of first volume with bit more wear and with thin, short cracks at top, boards faintly spotted or soiled (not at all serious), variable degrees (though always faint) of offsetting on facing pages of text, but very attractive set in excellent condition, bindings completely sound and generally preserved and text especially smooth, fresh and clean. Phillip J. Pirages 59 - 165 2011 $1900

Clarendon, Edward Hyde, 1st Earl of 1609-1674 *The History of the Rebellion and Civil Wars in England. (and) The Life of Edward Earl of Clarendon.* Oxford: At the Clarendon Press, 1826-1827, 11 volumes, 254 x 160mm., contemporary deep purple hard grain morocco, very lavishly gilt, apparently by Charles Lewis, covers with gilt double fillet border and with central panel formed by a thick band of volutes, large outward facing fleurons as panel cornerpieces, the center of each board with armorial crest, including mottoe "Vincit qui Patitur", gilt decorated raised bands, extremely handsome gilt spine compartments, formed by triple rules and featuring dense masses of fleurons, volutes and dots, attractively gilt turn-ins, marbled endpapers, all edges gilt (over marbling), extra illustrated with 8 frontispiece portraits, from other editions with manuscript letter signed by Charles I tipped in at front volume II, letter lacking its seal, otherwise in excellent condition, apart from some minor foxing (folded over covering sheet with address and notes in contemporaneous hand recording letter's reception torn along folds), sometimes noticeable foxing to endpapers and especially to inserted engraved portraits, along with consequent darkening to titlepages, opposite engraved material, in all other ways, superb set, margins very ample, text smooth, clean and fresh, wonderful binding with only most trivial wear. Phillip J. Pirages 59 - 166 2011 $9500

Clark, C. *An Historical and Descriptive Account of the Town of Lancaster.* Lancaster: C. Clark, 1807, First edition; old cloth, dampstained, pages vii, 118, (ii), complete with half title, 3 folding plans and text engraving, untrimmed, little light dampstaining to upper margins, scarce. R. F. G. Hollett & Son Antiquarian Booksellers General Catalogue Summer 2010 - 1363 2011 £150

Clark, G. T. *Mediaeval Military Architecture in England.* Wyman & Sons, 1884, First edition; 2 volumes, original pictorial cloth, gilt, spines rather faded, neatly recased, pages xii, 491; ix, 548, with numerous illustrations and folding plans, excellent set.   R. F. G. Hollett & Son Antiquarian Booksellers   177 - 187   2011   £150

Clark, Grahame *Prehistoric England.* London: Batsford, 1944-1945, Third edition; original cloth, dust jacket trifle rubbed, pages viii, 120, color frontispiece and 109 illustrations.   R. F. G. Hollett & Son Antiquarian Booksellers   177 - 188   2011   £30

Clark, H. F. *Plants Indoors.* Special Number of Architectural Review, May, 1952, Large 4to., original cloth, pictorial onlay by F. H. Henrion, trifle scratched, pages 287-348, printed on yellow, blue and white paper, illustrations in green and black, with 2 full page plates, 12 pages of photo illustrations at end, uncommon.   R. F. G. Hollett & Son Antiquarian Booksellers   177 - 189   2011   £35

Clark, Henry G. *Outlines of a Plan for a Free City Hospital.* Boston: printed by George C. Rand & Avery, 1860, First edition, one of presumably small number of copies sent out for review and comment; 8vo., 18 pages, original stiff printed paper wrappers, beginning to split along spine, text illustration, this copy interleaved with blank sheets, 2 plates before title, interior tear on title, without loss, stamp of Harvard Medical School Library with neat pencilled note dated March 29 1860 "Gift of Samuel A. Green, M.D. of Boston (Class of 1851), very good, tipped in small leaflet.   M & S Rare Books, Inc.   90 - 47   2011 $275

Clark, J. G. D. *Prehistoric Europe.* London: Methuen, 1952, First edition; 4to., original cloth, gilt, dust jacket little torn and creased, pages xvi, 349, 16 plates and 180 text illustrations.   R. F. G. Hollett & Son Antiquarian Booksellers   177 - 190   2011   £50

Clark, Jeff *Sun on 6.* Calais: Z Press, 2000, First edition, one of 26 lettered copies signed by Jeff Clark on colophon; tipped in original linocut in black, gray and beige, numbered and signed by Jasper Johns in pencil (there were an additional 200 unsigned copies, without linocut), sewn in original wrappers with label on front cover, overall size 9.75 x 6.75 inches, as new, set in Bembo type, printed on handmade papers by Grenfell Press.   Gemini Fine Books & Arts, Ltd.   Art Reference & Illustrated Books: First Editions   2011 $3000

Clark, John B. *The Modern Distributive Process: Studies of Competition and Its Limits, of the Nature and Amount of Profits and of the Determination of Walks in the Industrial Society of To-Day.* Boston: Ginn & Co., 1888, First edition; crown 8vo., pages viii, 69, 1 diagram, original blue cloth lettered gilt on spine and on front cover, bookplate of Edyth Cunliffe and her ownership signature dated 1890, corners slightly bumped, very slight rubbing, else very good+.   Any Amount of Books   May 29 2011 - A46350   2011 $340

Clark, John Willis *The Life and Letters of Rev. Adam Sedgwick...* Cambridge: University Press, 1890, 2 volumes, large 8vo., original brown cloth gilt, pages xiii, 539; vii, 640, untrimmed with 2 frontispiece portraits, 2 colored geological maps and other plates and illustrations, very nice, clean and sound set.   R. F. G. Hollett & Son Antiquarian Booksellers   173 - 233   2011   £250

Clark, John Willis *The Life and Letters of the Rev. Adam Sedgwick...* Gregg International Pub., 1970, Facsimile edition; 2 volumes, original cloth, gilt, pages xiii, 539; vii, 640, 2 frontispiece portraits, 2 folding geological maps and other plates and illustrations.   R. F. G. Hollett & Son Antiquarian Booksellers   173 - 234   2011   £75

Clark, Joseph *Jungle Wedding.* New York: Norton, 1999, First edition; inscribed by author to another writer, with full page handwritten fan letter from Clark laid in, letter folded with corner crease, near fine, book fine in fine dust jacket.   Ken Lopez Bookseller   154 - 32   2011 $100

Clark, Joshua J. *Some Fallacies of Seventh Day Adventism.* Louisville: circa, 1920, 55 pages, wrappers, some spotting.   Bookworm & Silverfish   668 - 138   2011 $125

Clark, Victor S. *History of Manufactures in the United States.* New York: Peter Smith, 1949, Reprint of 1929 edition; 3 volumes, tall 8vo., xi, 607; viii, 566; vi, 467 pages, plates, red cloth, black stamped spine titles, very good, from the Bern Dibner reference library, with Burndy bookplate.   Jeff Weber Rare Books   161 - 90   2011 $135

Clark, Walter Van Tilburg *The Track of the Cat.* New York: Random House, 1949, First edition; near fine, very light shelfwear, dust jacket very good, numerous small chips and creasing to edges, very good, numerous small chips and creasing to edges.   Bella Luna Books   May 29 2011 - t8219C)   2011 $137

Clarke, Arthur C. *Against the Fall of Night.* New York: Gnome Press Inc., 1953, First edition; octavo, boards.   L. W. Currey, Inc.   124 - 53   2011 $1500

Clarke, Arthur C. *Earthlight.* New York: Ballantine Books, 1955, First edition; octavo, cloth.   L. W. Currey, Inc.   124 - 22   2011 $2500

Clarke, Arthur C. *The Nine Billion Names of God: the Best Short Stories of Arthur C. Clarke.* New York: Harcourt Brace & World Inc., 1967, First edition; octavo, cloth. L. W. Currey, Inc. 124 - 94 2011 $850

Clarke, Arthur C. *Reach for Tomorrow.* London: Victor Gollancz Ltd., 1962, First British edition; octavo, boards. L. W. Currey, Inc. 124 - 174 2011 $300

Clarke, Arthur C. *Rendezvous with Rama.* London: Victor Gollancz, 1973, First edition; octavo, boards. L. W. Currey, Inc. 124 - 170 2011 $325

Clarke, Arthur C. *The Sand of Mars.* London: Sidgwick and Jackson Limited, 1951, First edition; octavo, boards. L. W. Currey, Inc. 124 - 181 2011 $250

Clarke, Arthur C. *The Sands of Mars.* New York: Gnome Press Inc., 1952, First US edition; octavo, first binding of red boards stamped in black. L. W. Currey, Inc. 124 - 154 2011 $375

Clarke, Arthur C. *2001: a Space Odyssey.* New York: New American Library, 1968, First edition; octavo, boards. L. W. Currey, Inc. 124 - 35 2011 $1750

Clarke, Arthur C. *2010: Odyssey Two.* Huntington Woods: Phantasia Press, 1982, First edition; octavo, leather. L. W. Currey, Inc. 124 - 52 2011 $1500

Clarke, Francis L. *The Life of the Most Noble Arthur Marquis and Earl of Wellington...with... Professional Anecdotes...* London: printed by and for J. and J. Cundee circa, 1812, 8vo., pages xix, (i) 21-568, vi + engraved titlepage and engraved frontispiece, 2 folding maps and 8 other engraved plates, contemporary tree calf, six compartmented spine divided by quintuple rules gilt compartments alternating between single military emblematic centre piece and massed intersecting broken wave pallets all gilt, lettered direct in gilt, board edges decorative roll gilt, red and white sewn endbands, late 1990's calf reback, backstrip relaid + corners by Chris Weston, plates foxed, some spotting elsewhere, map creased with closed tear to blank margin, old leather scratched, pink paper label with avian heraldic crest surmounting "WC" within an octagon, ruled border on front pastedown, bound in after index in an eleven page ms. narrative, unsigned, from the collection of Christopher Ernest Weston 1947-2010. Unsworths Booksellers 24 - 78 2011 £150

Clarke, H. L. *History of Sedbergh School 1525-1925.* Sedbergh: Jackson & Son, 1925, First edition; original brown buckram gilt, pages ix, 276, top edge gilt, plan of school and a graph, flyleaves little spotted. R. F. G. Hollett & Son Antiquarian Booksellers 173 - 235 2011 £45

Clarke, James *History of Cricket in Kendal from 1836 to 1905.* Kendal: printed by Thompson Brothers, 1906, First edition; original green cloth, gilt, pages 426, (72, ads), illustrations, first few leaves little crinkled in gutters, scarce. R. F. G. Hollett & Son Antiquarian Booksellers 173 - 236 2011 £75

Clarke, James *History of Football in Kendal from 1871 to 1908.* Kendal: printed by Thompson Bros., 1908, First (only) edition; original green cloth gilt, spine lettered in blind, pages 468, (72, local ads), with numerous plates and portraits, two sections shaken rather loose and the edges little chipped, otherwise very good, very scarce. R. F. G. Hollett & Son Antiquarian Booksellers 173 - 237 2011 £95

Clarke, James *A Survey of the Lakes of Cumberland, Westmorland and Lancashire...* printed for the author, 1789, Second edition; tall folio, full diced calf gilt with gilt rule borders, edges rather worn, rebacked in polished calf, gilt, one small scrape, pages xlii, 194, complete with 11 large folding plans and maps, few small creases or repairs to back of the maps as usual, excellent uncut, clean and sound with maps tipped on to guards for easier opening, several printed on heavy paper, armorial bookplate of John Towneley (re-laid). R. F. G. Hollett & Son Antiquarian Booksellers 173 - 239 2011 £1500

Clarke, John *Poems Descriptive of Rural Life and Scenery.* London: printed for Taylor and Hessey, Fleet Street and D. Drury, Stamford, 1820, First edition; small 8vo., original drab boards, printed label on spine, contemporary ownership signature, covers slightly rubbed, rear cover somewhat smudged, but still a superb copy in original and unrestored state, preserved in green half morocco slipcase, with half title and five leaves of publisher's ads bound in at back. James S. Jaffe Rare Books May 26 2011 - 17881 2011 $15,000

Clarke, John Willis *The Observances in Use at the Augustinian Priory of S. Giles and S. Andrew at Barnwell, Cambridgeshire.* Cambridge: Macmillan and Bowes, 1897, Limited edition (300 copies for subscribers); original cloth gilt, trifle marked, pages civ, 254, uncut with double page plan, scarce. R. F. G. Hollett & Son Antiquarian Booksellers 175 - 269 2011 £120

Clarke, L. Lane, Mrs. *Common Seaweeds of the British Coast and Channel Islands; with some Insight into the Microscopic Beauties of their Structure and Fructification.* London: Frederick Warne and Co., 1865, Small 8vo., 140 (4) pages ads, half title, 10 tinted plates, very good in original dark green gilt decorated cloth, all edges gilt, some slight foxing. Ken Spelman Rare Books 68 - 145 2011 £85

Clarke, Samuel *A Paraphrase on the Four Evangelists.* printed for the Booksellers in Cambridge, Oxford and London, 1795, 2 volumes, early 19th century tree calf gilt, pages (ix), 476; 502, (viii).   R. F. G. Hollett & Son Antiquarian Booksellers   175 - 272   2011   £140

Clarke, Susanna *Jonathan Strange and Mr. Norrell.* New York: Bloomsbury, 2004, First edition; illustrations by Portia Rosenberg, book near fine, light bumping to heel of spine, dust jacket fine, this is the first state with the white dust jacket and red endpapers, signed by author.   Bella Luna Books   May 29 2011 - t6865   2011 $110

Clarke, Susanna *Jonathan Strange & Mr. Norrell.* London: Bloomsbury, 2004, First British edition; illustrations by Portia Rosenberg, fine in fine black dust jacket.   Bella Luna Books   May 26 2011 - t7160   2011 $192

Clarke, Susanna *Jonathan Strange & Mr. Norrell.* London: Bloomsbury, 2004, First British edition; illustrations by Portia Rosenberg, fine in like (white) dust jacket).   Bella Luna Books   May 26 2011 - 517134   2011 $192

Clarkson, Christopher *The History of Richmond, in the County of York, Including a Description of the Castle Friary, Easby Abbey and Other Remains of Antiquity in the Neighbourhood.* Richmond: printed by and for T. Bowman at the Albion Press, 1814, 8vo., pages 436 + aquatint frontispiece and 3 other engraved plates, late 19th century dark olive green hard grain half morocco (color fugitive on spine to uniform mid-brown), spine double rule gilt with decorative rolls to flat raised bands and extremities, lettered direct in gilt, 'place & date' gilt direct at foot, boards decorative roll gilt bordered with "Sanspareil" design marbled book cloth sides, "Sanspareil Peacock swirl 'made' endpapers, edges uncut, maroon & primrose multicore made applied endbands, browned and spotted in places, spine and edges faded, just touch rubbed, ink inscription, "Coll & perf. F.C.B. Decr. 1879" (Captain F. C. Brooks of Ufford, Suffolk), ink inscription "James Hutchinson/Brigg/1814", heavily annotated by way of ink marginalia and by sewn-in folding sheets with historical agricultural gleanings, from the collection of Christopher Ernest Weston 1947-2010.   Unsworths Booksellers   24 - 79   2011   £600

Clarkson, Christopher *The History of Richmond, in the County of York.* Richmond: printed for the author by Thomas Bowman, 1821, Large paper copy, 4to., pages iv, 446, cxxxii, + engraved titlepage and extending engraved plan, frontispiece and 16 other engraved plates, contemporary marbled half calf, spine double rule gilt, red lettering piece gilt, date gilt direct at foot, boards double rule bordered in blind with 'French Shell" marbled paper sides, uncut, pink & white sewn flat endbands, calf reback, backstrip relaid & corners by Jenny Aste, decorative 1979, plates foxed, some spotting elsewhere, edges untrimmed, few scratches to boards, contemporary ink inscription from the author, from the collection of Christopher Ernest Weston 1947-2010.   Unsworths Booksellers   24 - 80   2011   £475

Clarkson, Thomas *An Essay on the Slavery and Commerce of the Human Species, Particularly the African.* Georgetown: Published by Rev. David Barrow, J.N. Lyle printer, 1816, Scarce Kentucky imprint; 12mo., xiv, (1 blank) (21)-175 pages, original full calf, gilt ruled spine and leather title label, label chipped, very good, signature of John Bartlett.   Jeff Weber Rare Books   163 - 60   2011 $1100

Clarkson, Thomas *Memoirs of the Public and Private Life of William Penn.* London: G. Gilpin etc., 1849, New edition; pages lx, 367, frontispiece, folding map, further engraved plan, prelims lightly spotted, upper joint just cracking but repaired, otherwise very good, sound, original blind-stamped and diced cloth, gilt spine and upper board rather faded, prelims lightly spotted, upper joint just cracking but repaired, otherwise very good, sound copy.   R. F. G. Hollett & Son Antiquarian Booksellers   175 - 273   2011   £45

Claudianus, Claudius *(Minor Works) Quotquot... extant Opuscula...* Paris: S. de Colines, 1530, 8vo., ff. 185 (=183, ff. 177-178 omitted), (1) (blank), printed in italic, late 17th century French binding of calf, double gilt fillet on covers, spine gilt, beautiful, clean copy, from the library of the Earls of Macclesfield at Shirburn Castle.   Maggs Bros. Ltd.   1440 - 57   2011   £500

Cleary, Jon *Fall of an Eagle.* New York: Morrow, 1964, First edition; 8vo., pages 270 dedication copy, beneath printed words "to Evy and Gordon" on dedication page Cleary has written "who have the gift of making a person feel appreciated - something a writer appreciates - with love Jon", with 3 good signed typed letters loosely inserted, about 4000 words, also loosely inserted a signed titlepage of paperback edition of Sundowners, sound, very good with light handling wear and with 2 bookplates of Gordon and Evy (Featherstone-Witty), the dedicatees and recipients of the letters, slight tape marks to front endpaper.   Any Amount of Books   May 29 2011 - A72358   2011 $383

Clegg, John *The Freshwater Life of the British Isles.* London: Frederick Warne, 1952, First edition; small 8vo., original green cloth, gilt, pages 352, with 67 plates by author, 95 text drawings.   R. F. G. Hollett & Son Antiquarian Booksellers   General Catalogue Summer 2010 - 959   2011   £45

Cleland, John *La Fille De Joie, ou Memoires de Miss Fanny, Ecrits par elle-meme.* Paris: Madame Gourdan, 1786, (1787); Large 8vo., pages (iv), 235, plus frontispiece, 2 supplementary engraved titlepages, 34 engraved plates (numbered 1-33 and 5 bis) by Delcroche (unsigned), all edges gilt, small discrete old repair to titlepage, full mid brown gilt decorated and titled morocco by Hardy, c. 1860, Bookplate of G. Nordmann, fine, stunning copy.   Simon Finch Rare Books   Zero - 413   2011   £9500

Clemens, Samuel Langhorne 1835-1910 *The Adventures of Tom Sawyer.* Toronto: Belford Bros., 1876, First Canadian edition; 12mo., (4), 341, (2) pages, including 4 pages of ads, original cloth, hinges and spine quite rubbed, cover somewhat soiled, shaken, mostly toward front, some edges chipped.   M & S Rare Books, Inc.   90 - 88 2011 $850

Clemens, Samuel Langhorne 1835-1910 *The Adventures of Huckleberry Finn.* London: Chatto & Windus, 1884, First English edition, second state (bound with staples); publisher's red cloth stamped in black and gilt, recased with original spine laid down, repaired at extremities, rear flyleaf in facsimile, when this was recased, it was sewn in conventional manner as the first issue, but this was originally stapled), some discoloring to upper right corner of front board, 32 page catalog of publisher's ad dated Oct. 1884, very good, tight, clean copy.   Second Life Books Inc.   174 - 309 2011 $2400

Clemens, Samuel Langhorne 1835-1910 *The Adventures of Huckleberry Finn.* London: Chatto & Windus, 1884, First edition; 191 x 133mm., xvi, 438 pages, very pleasing red morocco by Bayntun (stamp signed on verso of front free endpaper), covers with two frames formed by simple gilt rules, inner frame with corner-pieces of stylized fleurs-de-lys, raised bands, spine gilt in double ruled compartments with central lily and open dot corners, very pretty intricate floral gilt turn-ins, marbled endpapers, top edge gilt, original red cloth covers bound in at rear, frontispiece and many illustrations in text, spine slightly and evenly a darker red just a breath of rubbing to joints, two small closed tears, other trivial imperfections internally, still fine, difficult to find this good, text clean, fresh and smooth and appealing binding lustrous with only insignificant wear.   Phillip J. Pirages   59 - 167 2011 $2750

Clemens, Samuel Langhorne 1835-1910 *The Adventures of Huckleberry Fine.* New York: Charles L. Webster & Co., 1885, First American edition; later printing with following "traditional" bibliographical points: titlepage is a cancel with copyright notice dated 1884 (BAL second state, with the first state only noted in publisher's prospectuses and advanced sheets), page (13), illustration captioned "Him and another Man" is correctly listed as at page 87 (BAL second state), page 57, the 11th line from bottom reads 'with the saw" (BAL second state), page 283 is a cancel with engraving redone and line indicating the fly on Silas Phelps's trousers a straight vertical line (BAL third state, earliest known to appear in cloth bound copies of the book), page 155, the final "5" in pagination is slightly larger (BAL second state), frontispiece has imprint of the Photo-Gravure Co. NY and the tablecloth, or scarf on which the bust rests not visible (BAL third state), octavo, 366, (2, blank) page, inserted frontispiece, with tissue guard and wood engraved text illustrations, original dark green cloth pictorially stamped and lettered in gilt and black on front cover and spine, original pale peach endpapers, at one time there was a slip of paper inserted between frontispiece and frontispiece portrait, which has left a faint brown mark in gutter, affecting the tissue guard for the portrait and frontispiece, otherwise this is as fine a copy as you could wish for, absolutely bright and fresh, housed in quarter green morocco clamshell case.   David Brass Rare Books, Inc.   May 26 2011 - 00568 2011 $9500

Clemens, Samuel Langhorne 1835-1910 *The Adventures of Huckleberry finn.* New York: Charles Webster, 1885, (1884).First edition; points include: title leaf is bound in with copyright 1884 (3), frontispiece 1st state with cloth visible and heliotype, (1) page 13 1st state incorrectly listing "him and another man" on page 88 (1), page 9 decided (later decides) (1), page 57 1st state 'with the was' (1), page 143 1st state missing "I" (A), page 155 1st state with final 5 absent (1), page 161 1st state with signature mark absent (A), page 283 engraving redone and bound in (D), illustrations by E. W. Kemble with 174 black and white drawings, beautiful copy, 4to., dark green cloth stamped in gold and black, owner name on endpaper, very fine, housed in custom leather slipcase,.   Aleph-Bet Books, Inc.   95 - 559 2011 $18,500

Clemens, Samuel Langhorne 1835-1910 *Adventures of Huckleberry Finn.* New York: Webster, 1885, First edition, later state; 8vo., pages 366, rare blue cloth binding, rubbed at extremities, some darkening and soiling to covers), recased, essentially very good, small water mark to bottom of frontispiece, very good.   Second Life Books Inc.   174 - 310 2011 $3500

Clemens, Samuel Langhorne 1835-1910 *Adventures of Huckleberry Finn.* New York: Charles L. Webster and Co., 1885, First edition, early issue; octavo, frontispiece, original cloth pictorially stamped.   Heritage Book Shop Booth A12 51st NY International Antiquarian Book Fair April 8-10 2011 - 138 2011 $5000

Clemens, Samuel Langhorne 1835-1910 *Adventures of Huckleberry Finn.* New York: Charles L. Webster, 1885, First edition, first issue; with titlepage and page 283/4 as cancel sheets, and with the three required points - "Huck Decided" on page 9, with illustration for page 87 ("Him and Another Man") listed as page 88; and with misprint "with the was" (for "with the saw") on page 57, the book has been bound and signed by Bayntun in full dark green morocco with raised bands, gilt spine decorations, gilt lines to boards, lovely gilt inner dentelles, feathered endpapers and all edges gilt, original cloth covers and spine bound in at end, book housed in green cloth slipcase, book is near fine (light foxing to endpapers, one minor closed tear to one page), binding books fine and attractive.   Lupack Rare Books   May 26 2011 - ABE4707853086   2011 $2100

Clemens, Samuel Langhorne 1835-1910 *Following the Equator.* Hartford: American Publishing Co., 1897, First edition; first state with only "Hartford, Connecticut" on titlepage and with signature mark "11" at bottom of page 161, well illustrated, near fine, only slight shelfwear, nice gilt.   Lupack Rare Books   May 26 2011 - ABE4890170512   2011 $300

Clemens, Samuel Langhorne 1835-1910 *The Jumping Frog.* Easthampton: Cheloniidae Press, 1985, One of 15 State Proof copies; one extra suite of the wood engravings and portrait etching of author, a state-proof suite of prints and copy of regular edition of the book, all signed and numbered by artist and signed on colophon by artist, regular edition as limited to 250 and is bound in green paper wrappers, all editions printed on Saunders paper in Centaur and Arrighi types at Wild Carrot Letterpress with assistance of Arthur Larson - the 15 wood engravings printed by Harold Patrick McGrath, page size 6 x 8.5 inches; bound by Daniel Kelm, full undyed Oasis with onlays of the frog in repose - before the jump on the front panel and after jump on back panel, doublures showing frog in mid-jump, onlays in green oasis of frog jumping are on front and back pastedowns, housed in linen clamshell box with pull-out portfolio for extra suites and book, lovely copy.   Priscilla Juvelis - Rare Books   48 - 6   2011 $3500

Clemens, Samuel Langhorne 1835-1910 *Love Letters of Mark Twain.* New York: Harper & Bros., 1949, Stated first edition, limited to 155 numbered copies, signed twice by author as Twain and as Clemens; tall 8vo, 374 pages, black cloth, as new in green dust jacket, photo frontispiece of Twain, the 15 page introduction and editorial material accompanying each letter help put each letter into context, beautiful copy, rare.   Aleph-Bet Books, Inc.   95 - 560   2011 $5000

Clemens, Samuel Langhorne 1835-1910 *More Tramps Abroad.* London: Chatto & Windus, 1897, First English edition; half title, 32 page catalog (Sept. 1897), original decorated maroon cloth lettered in gilt on front board an spine, slightly marked, top edge gilt.   Jarndyce Antiquarian Booksellers   CXCI - 589   2011   £120

Clemens, Samuel Langhorne 1835-1910 *The Prince in the Pauper.* Leipzig: Bernard Tauchnitz, 1882, Authorized edition; 2 volumes, half titles, 16 page catalog volume II (Dec. 1881), original buff printed wrappers, dated Dec. 1881, small splits at heads of spines, but very good as issued.   Jarndyce Antiquarian Booksellers   CXCI - 590   2011   £125

Clemens, Samuel Langhorne 1835-1910 *The Prince and the Pauper.* Boston: Osgood, 1882, First edition; first edition, first state with Franklin Press imprint on copyright page, original publisher's gold stamped sheep, rebacked with new spine fashioned to closely match original covers, that are rubbed along edges), little soiling to fore edge of leaves, very good.   Second Life Books Inc.   174 - 312   2011 $600

Clemens, Samuel Langhorne 1835-1910 *Mark Twain Sketches.* Hartford: American Publishing Co., 1875, First edition, first state; 8vo., 320 pages, blue cloth stamped in gold, some external stains, hinges loose, good copy, scarce.   Second Life Books Inc.   174 - 311   2011 $750

Clemens, Samuel Langhorne 1835-1910 *The Writings of Mark Twain.* New York: Harper and Brothers, 1929, Stormfield Edition, limited to 1024 numbered sets; 37 volumes, octavo, titlepages printed in red and black, photogravure frontispieces and plates after drawings, paintings, etc., original dark blue fine bead cloth, gilt triple rule border with gilt stencil signature of Mark Twain on front cover, spine lettered in gilt, top edge gilt, others uncut, fine set in original pale blue dust jackets with printed paper labels on spine.   David Brass Rare Books, Inc.   May 26 2011 - 01682   2011 $5500

Clemens, Samuel Langhorne 1835-1910 *The Oxford Mark Twain.* New York/Oxford: Oxford University Press, 1996, Limited, signed edition, one of 300 sets printed; 29 volumes, signed by series editor, Shelley Fisher Fishkin and also signed by the 58 people who provided introductions, and afterwords to each volume, fine in fine dust jackets.   Ken Lopez Bookseller   154 - 219   2011 $3000

Clemenson, George B. *A Manual Relating to Special Verdicts & Special Findings by Juries Based on the Decisions of all the States.* St. Paul: 1905, 350 pages, full law calf, very good, missing f.f.e.p.   Bookworm & Silverfish   669 - 113   2011 $75

Clement, Clara Erskine *Angels in Art.* David Nutt, 1899, First edition; original blue cloth, lettered and decorated in silver, pages 267, top edges silvered, with 34 plates, flyleaves rather browned, scarce.   R. F. G. Hollett & Son Antiquarian Booksellers   General Catalogue Summer 2010 - 78   2011   £75

Clement, Saint *Epistolae Duae ad Corinthios...* Jacob Adamson, 1694, Amended edition; pages 356, (vi), small 8vo., old calf gilt, rather rubbed.   R. F. G. Hollett & Son Antiquarian Booksellers   175 - 276   2011   £140

Clemente, Francesco *Francesco Clemente. Sixteen Pastels.* London: Anthony d'Offay Gallery, 1989, First edition, limited to 1000 copies; signed by Clemente, 10 x 14 inches, original slipcase, paste-on illustration back cover.   By the Book, L. C.   26 - 26   2011 $150

Clenardus, Nicolaus *Institutiones Grammaticae, Latinae.* Lyons: G. & M. Berringen, 1551, 8vo., 155 pages, 18th century mottled calf, spine gilt, second known copy, from the library of the Earls of Macclesfield at Shirburn Castle.   Maggs Bros. Ltd.   1440 - 58   2011   £800

Clenardus, Nicolaus *Institutiones ac Meditationes in Graecum Linguam...* Paris: H. le Be, 1581, (1580); 4to., (108), 414, (2), 23, (1) pages, contemporary brown calf over pasteboards, gilt centerpiece within single gilt fillet, spine gilt in 6 compartments, covers scuffed, handsome copy, from the library of the Earls of Macclesfield at Shirburn Castle.   Maggs Bros. Ltd.   1440 - 59   2011   £800

Clerke, Agnes M. *The Herschels and Modern Astronomy.* London: Paris: Melbourne: Cassell, 1895, 8vo., 224, ads (16) pages, frontispiece, plates, light foxing, green cloth, gilt stamped cover and spine titles, extremities rubbed, light wear to spine ends, inner hinge cracked, else very good, previous owner's inked signature, from the Bern Dibner reference library, with Burndy bookplate.   Jeff Weber Rare Books   161 - 91   2011 $100

Cleveland, Helen M. *Letters from Queer and Other Folk for Boys and Girls to Answer: Book I for Lower Grammar Grades.* New York: 1899, 125 pages, cloth soiled and edge worn with sticker remnants on spine, interior clean and tight.   G. H. Mott Bookseller   May 26 2011 - 42106   2011 $175

Cleveland, John *J. Cleveland Revived: Poems, Oration, Epistles.* London: printed for Natianiel Brooke at the Angel in Cornhil, 1660, Second edition; early calf, one leaf with tear at bottom with loss of 1 and 1/2 words, very good, clean, uncommon.   Lupack Rare Books   May 26 2011 - ABE1357017423   2011 $300

Clifton-Shelton, A. *Nursery Alphabet.* London: Nelson, circa, 1930, 4to., still pictorial wrappers, fine, full color illustrations by Grace Clifton-Shelton.   Aleph-Bet Books, Inc.   95 - 28   2011 $300

Clifton, Mark *They'd Rather Be Right.* New York: Gnome Press, 1957, First edition; octavo, boards.   L. W. Currey, Inc.   124 - 182   2011 $250

Clive-Ross, F. *Studies in Comparative Religion: Metaphysics, Cosmology, Tradition, Symbolism 1967-1968.* Bedfont: Tomorrow Publications, 1967-1968, 8vo., volume 1 #4, Autumn 1967 to volume 17 #1 & 2 Winter 1968 (double issue), one volume missing, volume 3 # 1 Winter 1968, apart from volumes 16 and 17, all are stapled wrappers, circa 4000 pages, clean, very good.   Any Amount of Books   May 29 2011 - A47857   2011 $255

Cloud, C. Carey *Puss in Boots.* New York: Blue Ribbon, 1934, Illustrated Pop-up edition; 4to., pictorial boards, some cover soil, else very good+, 3 fabulous double page color-pop-ups annd several black and whites in text.   Aleph-Bet Books, Inc.   95 - 447   2011 $250

Cloudy, C. H. *Tell Me Why Stories.* New York: McBride Nast, 1912, First edition; tall 8vo, pictorial cloth, 154 pages, very good-fine, illustrations by Norman Rockwell, 8 color plates, rare.   Aleph-Bet Books, Inc.   95 - 493   2011 $850

Clouth, Franz *Rubber, Gutta-Percha and Balata.* Maclaren & Sons, 1903, First English translation; large 8vo., x, (2), 252 pages, 3 maps and charts, 30 text illustrations, good, original gilt lettered plum cloth, slight rubbing to head and tail of spine, titlepage little dusty, with G.E.R. Telegraph superintendents Office stamp on titlepage.   Ken Spelman Rare Books   68 - 100   2011   £50

Clover, Samuel Travers *On Special Assignment, Being the Adventures of Paul Travers: Showing How He Succeeded as a Reporter.* Boston: Lothrop Pub. Co., 1903, First edition; 8vo., small presentation inscription by author, dated Feb. 1911, pictorial colored cloth, frontispiece, 307 pages (blank), plus 4 pages of ads, illustrations by H. G. Laskey, cloth lightly rubbed at top edge of front panel, else very good.   Buckingham Books   May 26 2011 - 26811   2011 $2500

Clutton-Brock, Arthur *Simpson's Choice. An Essay on the Future Life.* London: Omega Workshops, 1915, First edition; folio, pages 16, woodcut initials and 5 woodcut illustrations in text, uncut lower and fore-edge, internally fine, original boards, decorated in black and white, slightly bumped, truce of staining to corner of lower board, endpapers browned.   Simon Finch Rare Books   Zero - 305   2011   £950

Cluverius, Thomas J. *Cluverius My Life, Trial & Conviction.* Richmond: 1887, First edition; 12mo., 112 pages, scarce, wrappers, age soil and staple rust, left margin to wrapper chipped.   Bookworm & Silverfish   668 - 178   2011 $150

Clyne, Geraldine *The Jolly Jump-Ups ABC Book.* Springfield: McLoughlin, 1948, Oblong 4to., pictorial boards, slight edge wear, else very good+, 6 wonderful double page pop-ups (that also have moveable pieces).   Aleph-Bet Books, Inc.   95 - 449   2011 $200

Coakley, Robert W. *Antiwar & Anti-Military Activities in the United States 1846-1954.* Washington: 1970, iv, 148 pages, mimeo, wrappers, some spotting to cover. Bookworm & Silverfish 664 - 133 2011 $75

Coale, Josiah *The Books and Divers Epistles of the Faithful Servant of the Lord Josiah Coale.* London: printed in the year, 1671, 4to., 28, 33-104, 152, 269-343, (i.e. 344), complete as issued, contemporary calf, neatly rebacked and recornered, later (but old) endpapers, modern bookplate. Joseph J. Felcone Inc. Fall Miscellany 2010 - 23 2011 $3000

Coates, Brian J. *Birds of New Guinea and the Bismarck Archipelago: a Photographic Guide.* Alderley: 2001, Octavo, paperback, 272 pages, over 650 color photos, maps. Andrew Isles Natural History Books Spring 2010 - 14733 2011 $60

Coatsworth, Elizabeth *The Cat Who Went to Heaven.* New York: Macmillan, 1930, First edition, first printing; illustrations by Lynd Ward with very beautiful full page wash drawings, quite scarce in dust jacket, 4to., cloth, near fine in dust jacket (mended on back with light stain on joints). Aleph-Bet Books, Inc. 95 - 584 2011 $700

Cobb, Gerald *The Old Churches of London.* London: Batsford, 1942-1943, Second edition; pages x, 116, with 84 pages of plates, 36 text figures, original cloth, gilt, dust jacket head of spine chipped. R. F. G. Hollett & Son Antiquarian Booksellers 177 - 194 2011 £35

Cobbett, William 1763-1835 *Advice to Young Men and (Incidentally) to a Young Women in the Middle and Higher Ranks of Life...* London: Ward, Lock & Tyler, 1874, 24 page catalog, ads on endpapers, original illustrated pale yellow wrappers, slight crease to front wrapper, very good. Jarndyce Antiquarian Booksellers CXCI - 360 2011 £85

Cobbett, William 1763-1835 *A Bone to Gnaw for the Democrats by Peter Porcupine... (bound with) The Life of Thomas Paine...* London: J. Wright, 1797, First British edition; small 8vo., half title, text clean, some slight foxing at prelims, modern quite plain half leather, gilt lettered at spine with marbled boards, both books highly uncommon, very good, text clean and some slight foxing at prelims. Any Amount of Books May 29 2011 - B20839 2011 $272

Cobbett, William 1763-1835 *Cobbett's Manchester Lectures, in Support of His Fourteen Reform Propositions: Which Lectures Were Delivered in the Minor Theatre...* London: published (by the author) at No. 11, Bolt Court, Fleet Street, 1832, First edition; large 12mo., xii, 179, (1) pages, wanting from free endpaper, original boards, spine worn, else very good, uncut. John Drury Rare Books 153 - 28 2011 £250

Cobbett, William 1763-1835 *A Collection of Facts and Observations, Relative to the Peace with Bonaparte Chiefly Extracted from the Porcupine...* London: Cobbett and Morgan, Pall Mall, 1801, First edition; 8vo., pages (iv), lxiii (appendix), ex-British Foreign Office library with 2 small old oval stamps and their library bookplate and a further stamp on verso of new endpaper, later blue cloth lettered gilt at spine, spine faded and slightly chipped at top, rear cover faded, else sound, near very good with clean text, of some rarity. Any Amount of Books May 26 2011 - A49984 2011 $419

Cobbett, William 1763-1835 *A History of the Protestant Reformation in England and Ireland.* Catholic Pub. Co., n.d., Stereotyped edition; old half calf gilt, with raised bands and marbled boards, pages 333, xxxiv, 192, with 12 illustrations. R. F. G. Hollett & Son Antiquarian Booksellers 175 - 279 2011 £75

Cobbett, William 1763-1835 *The Protestant "Reformation" Part Second...* London: William Cobbett, 1827, Old boards rebacked to match, original paper spine label relaid, unpaginated. R. F. G. Hollett & Son Antiquarian Booksellers 175 - 280 2011 £65

Cobbey, J. E. *A Practical Treatise on the Law of Replevin as Administered by the Courts of the United States.* Beatrice: 1890, First edition; scarce, very good, with some age soil in later Judge Adv. General Office cloth. Bookworm & Silverfish 666 - 92 2011 $150

Cobden-Sanderson, Thomas James 1840-1922 *Cosmic Vision.* London: Richard Cobden-Sanderson, 1922, First edition; 8vo., pages 143, (1) imprint, frontispiece with portrait of author, uncut, front and back free endpapers browned, internally fine except for small tear to foot of one leaf, not affecting text, publisher's blue cloth, gilt lettering to spine, dust jacket edges chipped, spine torn with old tape repairs, some loss to head and foot, old tape repairs to upper panel and flap, author's presentation inscription and poem in autograph manuscript to second blank. Simon Finch Rare Books Zero - 306 2011 £475

Cobden-Sanderson, Thomas James 1840-1922 *London: a Paper Read at a Meeting of the Art Workers Guild.... March 6 1891.* Doves Press, presented to the subscribers, 1906, One of 300 copies on paper; there were also five on vellum, 235 x 165mm., 7, (1) pages, original flexible vellum, gilt spine titling, text on final page in black and red, hint of soiling to lower cover, binding vaguely rumpled (as usual), otherwise very fine copy inside and out. Phillip J. Pirages 59 - 179 2011 $275

Coblentz, Stanton A. *Villains and Vigilantes. The Story of James King of William and Pioneer Justice in California.* New York: Wilson Erickson, 1936, First edition; (8), 261 pages, 8 illustrations, green cloth lettered in red, very fine with elusive pictorial dust jacket (very minimal chipping to spine ends and two corners).   Argonaut Book Shop   Recent Acquisitions Summer 2010 - 219   2011 $75

Cochrane, C. B. *Review of Revues & Other Matters.* London: Cape, 1930, First edition; original cloth backed boards with paper label, dust jacket (top edge trimmed, closd tear repaired on reverse, spine rather browned), pages 94, (xxiv calendar), with 2 color illustrations by Bawden and others.   R. F. G. Hollett & Son Antiquarian Booksellers   General Catalogue Summer 2010 - 709   2011   £50

Cochrane, C. B. *Review of Revues and other Matters.* London: Cape, 1930, First edition; original cloth backed boards with paper label, pages 94, (xxiv, calendar), and 2 color illustrations by Bawden and others.   R. F. G. Hollett & Son Antiquarian Booksellers   General Catalogue Summer 2010 - 711   2011   £40

Cock Robin. A Pretty Painted Toy for Either Girl or Boy. London: John Harris, circa, 1830's, 12mo., yellow printed paper wrappers with some light overall soiling and some foxing, mostly on blank endpapers, this copy was Marjorie Moon's and has her bookplate on verso of front cover, 17 numbered pages and page of ads at end of book, half page hand colored engravings.   Jo Ann Reisler, Ltd.   86 - 92   2011 $600

Cockburn, John *A Journey Over Land from the Gulf of Honduras to the Great South Sea. Performed by John Cockburn and Five Other Englishmen.* London: for C. Rivington, 1735,   viii, 349, (3) pages, folding map, contemporary sprinkled calf, very skillfully rebacked with entire original spine and label retained, lovely copy, text clean and fresh and entirely unfoxed, Wolfgang Herz copy with his small booklabel.   Joseph J. Felcone Inc.   Fall Miscellany 2010 - 24   2011 $3500

Cocke, James R. *Blind Leaders of the Blind: The Romance of a Blind Lawyer.* Boston: 1896, 487 pages, very good in cream cloth, mild foxing to backstrip.   Bookworm & Silverfish   679 - 178   2011 $150

Cockerell, Sydney Carlisle *Some German Woodcuts of the Fifteenth Century.* Hammersmith: Sold by the Trustees of the Late William Morris at the Kelmscott Press, 1897, One of 225 paper copies out of a total edition of 233 copies; large quarto, xi pages, 23 leaves, 24-36 pages, 35 reproductions of woodcuts printed on 23 leaves (rectos only), one six line woodcut initial, printed in red and black in Golden type, original holland backed blue paper boards, title printed in black on front cover, tips very lightly bumped, otherwise fine in gray cloth slipcase.   David Brass Rare Books, Inc.   May 26 2011 - 01457   2011 $5500

Cockermouth, Keswick & Penrith Railway *Widening of Line and Additional Lands.* Edinburgh: John Bartholomew, 1894, Oblong atlas folio, original cloth backed printed wrappers, lithographed title and 4 sheets of lithographed plans, fine set.   R. F. G. Hollett & Son Antiquarian Booksellers   173 - 246   2011   £180

Cockroft, Barry *The Dale that Died.* London: J. M. Dent, 1975,   First (only) edition; square 8vo., original cloth, dust jacket, extremities trifle worn, pages 128, illustrations, excellent, scarce.   R. F. G. Hollett & Son Antiquarian Booksellers   173 - 247   2011   £100

Cocteau, Jean *Ceremonial Espagnol Du Phenix Suivi de La Partie D'Echecs.* Paris: Gallimard, 1961, First edition, service de presse copy; 4to., pages 32, (4), uncut, internally bright and clean, publisher's cream wrappers, text in black and red, lightly soiled in places, author's presentation inscription to Andre Marissel (i.e. Jean Marc Pittner) on first half title dated 1961, with 1 leaf, 8 lines autograph MS. signed by Cocteau, defining 'le poete" in envelope addressed to Pittner, 2 news clippings regarding Cocteau, flyer and card advertising Cocteau-Moretti exhibition in Librairie St. Germain des Pres 1967.   Simon Finch Rare Books   Zero - 307   2011   £375

Cocteau, Jean *Le Grand Escart.* Paris: Librairie Stock, 1923,   First edition, one of 250 copies on Japon, number 18 of 25 copies on Japon from a total edition of 575; 8vo., pages (iv), 204, (i) imprint, plus errata slip, uncut, internally fine, publisher's salmon paper wrappers, small loss to foot of spine, lightly sunned at extremities, original glassine, chipped at head and foot.   Simon Finch Rare Books   Zero - 217   2011   £400

Cocteau, Jean *Opium. Journal d'une Desintoxication.* Paris: Librairie Stock, 1930, First edition, deluxe issue, number 16 of 28 copies from the tirage de tete on Japon imperial, froma an edition of 1563 copies; 8vo, pages (2) blank, 264, (i) imprint, (5) blank, complete with all illustrations by author, original wrappers printed in black and brown, light edge wear and soiling, few reading creases and shallow crack to half of spine, bright, very good to near fine copy.   Simon Finch Rare Books   Zero - 218   2011   £1500

Cocteau, Jean *Le Sang D'un Poete.* Paris: Robert Marin, 1948,   First edition, no. IV of 20 "Hors Commerce" copies on velin d'arches; 8vo., pages 106, photos by Sacha Masour, signed presentation from author for Genevieve Marcham, with superb ink drawing by Cocteau, about fine, very faint wear at head of spine.   Any Amount of Books   May 26 2011 - A68702   2011 $2013

Cody, Liza *Dupe.* London: 1980, First edition; 8vo., 238 pages, slight lean at spine, otherwise near fine in very good complete dust jacket with slight edgewear, few very short closed tears, slight creasing.   Any Amount of Books   May 29 2011 - A48554   2011 $238

Coe, Jonathan *The Accidental Woman.* London: Duckworth, 1987, First edition; signed on titlepage, fine in fne dust jacket. Any Amount of Books May 29 2011 - A38068 2011 $298

Coe, Palmer *The Brownie Primer Together with Queerie Queers.* Chicago: George M. Hill, 1901, 4to., cloth backed pictorial boards, some cover rubbing and soil, very good, 12 full page chromolithographed color illustrations, very rare. Aleph-Bet Books, Inc. 95 - 168 2011 $1200

Coel, Margaret *The Eagle Catcher.* Niwot: University Press of Colorado, 1995, First edition; fine in near fine dust jacket with closed tear on bottom of spine, signed by author. Bella Luna Books May 29 2011 - j1414 2011 $137

Coetzee, J. M. *Age of Iron.* London: Secker & Warburg, 1990, First UK edition; fine, dust jacket near fine, very light wear along top rear edge. Bella Luna Books May 29 2011 - t6846 2011 $82

Coetzee, J. M. *The Novel in Africa.* Berkeley: Townsend Center for the Humanities, 1999, No edition stated, presumably first and only edition; uncommon, spine faded, else fine in wrappers. Ken Lopez Bookseller 154 - 33 2011 $100

Coffey, George *Guide to the Celtic Antiquities of the Christian Period Preserved in the National Museum, Dublin, Royal Irish Academy Collection.* Dublin: Hodges, Figgis & Co., 1910, Original cloth, gilt, extremities trifle rubbed, pages ix, 111, 18 plates and 114 text figures, inscribed by Professor W. Boyd Dawkins to Richard Glazier 1917. R. F. G. Hollett & Son Antiquarian Booksellers 177 - 195 2011 £85

Cogniaux Alfred *Dictionnarie Iconographique des Orchidees.* Brussels: 1896-1907, Limited to 250 copies; 803 (of 826) chromolithographed plates, the plate of Maxillaria venusta is chipped and with some pieces missing, an edge of 3 plates chipped, one of which contains a small marginal stain, occasional marginal foxing to Cypripedim plates, light soiling to a plate, ink name on a plate, loose as issued in 15 original green cloth folders with gilt lettering and green ties (occasional foxing to wrappers, tanning or browning to many wrappers, splitting to fold of a few wrappers, soiling to back page of text, staining to a wrappers), good to very good. Raymond M. Sutton, Jr. May 26 2011 - 54635 2011 $10,000

Cohen, David *The Circle of Life - Rituals from the Human Family.* New York: Harper Collins, 1991, First edition; fine in near fine dust jacket, light wear. Bella Luna Books May 29 2011 - t8648 2011 $82

Cohen, I. Bernard *Album of Science: from Leonardo to Lavoisier 1450-1800.* New York: Charles Scribner's Sons, 1980, First printing; tall 8vo., xiii, (306) pages, frontispiece, illustrations, maroon cloth, gilt stamped, black spine label, dust jacket lightly worn, with small chips, very good, from the Bern Dibner reference library, with Burndy bookplate. Jeff Weber Rare Books 161 - 93 2011 $80

Coke, Edward *Complete Copy-Holder Wherein is Contained a Learned Discourse of the Antiquity and Nature of Manors and Copy-holds.* London: for Matthew Walbanck and Richard Best, 1644, Second edition; (4), 16, 13-203 pages, neat modern full calf, period style, worm-trail toward end of text but confined largely to margin, margins close on titlepage, but ample, ele very good. Joseph J. Felcone Inc. Fall Miscellany 2010 - 25 2011 $750

Coke, Gerald *In Search of James Giles.* Broseley: Micawber Publications, 1983, First edition; 4to., original cloth, gilt, dust jacket, pages xiii, 257, 24 color plates and 72 monochrome plates. R. F. G. Hollett & Son Antiquarian Booksellers General Catalogue Summer 2010 - 80 2011 £75

Coke, Henry J. *Tracks of a Rolling Stone.* London: Smith, Elder & Co., 1905, First edition; 8vo., original publisher's red buckram lettered gilt, pages 349, frontispiece, uncut, highly uncommon, bright, very good+, faint marks to cover, very slight foxing to text, neat ownership signature of Bryan Hall of Banningham Hall, Norfolk, heraldic bookplate of one Albemarle Cator. Any Amount of Books May 29 2011 - B21525 2011 $340

Coke, John Estes *Tamawaa Folks.* Macatawa: Tamawaca Press, 1907, First edition; 8vo., green cloth stamped in blue and white, 185 page, fine, quite scarce and beautiful copy. Aleph-Bet Books, Inc. 95 - 87 2011 $2500

Colden, Cadwallader D. *Memoir... at the Celebration of the Completion of the Erie Canal... New York 1826. (an) Narrative of the Festivities Observed in Honor of the Completion of the Grand Erie Canal.* New York: W. A. Davis, 1825, 1826. 1825. First edition; 4to., (8), 408, (2) pages, maps, lithographic plates, portraits, many folding, some in color, old marbled boards, rebacked, presentation inscription from Recorder of New York, Richard Riker. M & S Rare Books, Inc. 90 - 287 2011 $2250

Cole, John *Memoirs of the Life, Writings and Character of the Late Thomas Hinderwell, Esqr. Scarborough.* London: published by John Cole and Longman, Rees, Orme, Brown and Green, 1826, 8vo., pages (ii) 3 (i) 57, (iii) 55, (i) vii (i), engraved frontispiece, publisher's original green canvas, dark green morocco lettering piece gilt by Jenny Aste, late 1980's, some light spotting, especially to title, cloth little spotted and faded, slightly worn at endcaps, contemporary ink inscription to Mrs. Langdell, presented by author, also blue paper ex-libris of John William Clay, from the collection of Christopher Ernest Weston 1947-2010.   Unsworths Booksellers   24 - 82   2011   £125

Coleman, William T. *The San Francisco Vigilance Committee of 1856: Three Views.* Los Angeles: 1971, Limited to 500 copies; quarto, 180 pages, illustrations, blue cloth lettered and decorated in silver, very fine.   Argonaut Book Shop   Recent Acquisitions Summer 2010 - 220 2011 $90

Colenso, John William *Ten Weeks in Natal: a Journal of a First Tour of Visitation among the Colonists and Zulu Kafirs of Natal.* Cambridge: Macmillan, 1855, First edition; 16mo., pages xxxi, 271, 16, folding map, 4 lithographic plates, lacks map, original red decorative cloth, joints split, covers soiled, internally clean.   J. & S. L. Bonham Antiquarian Booksellers   Africa 4/20/2011 - 9019 2011   £40

Coleridge, Samuel Taylor   1772-1834 *Biographia Literaria; or Bibliographical Sketches of My Literary Life and Opinions.* London: Rest Fenner, 1817, Only edition; 2 volumes, royal 8vo., pages (iv), 296; (iv), 309, (3) ads with second half title in volume i, top edge gilt, others uncut, offsetting from bookmark to second blank but fresh and bright copy with occasional slight spotting, later full morocco, raised bands, gilt lettering to spines and gilt edges, gilt decoration to doublures by Tout, with endpapers loosely inserted, in excellent condition, with only very light shelfwear, endpapers browned at edges, portion of both original black labels, rubbed, pasted to rear endpaper loosely inserted into volume i, bookplate of John Whipple Frothingham to initial blank of volume I and loosely inserted front endpaper of volume II, bookplate of Harry Buxton Forman.   Simon Finch Rare Books   Zero - 220   2011   £950

Coleridge, Samuel Taylor   1772-1834 *Biographia Literaria; or Biographical Sketches of My Literary Life and Opinions.* London: Rest Fenner, 1817, First edition; 2 volumes, recently rebound as one in half leather, marbled boards, 5 raised bands, red label lettered gilt on spine; 296; 309 pages, excellent copy, slight creasing to edges of some pages, occasional very slight foxing, very good+.   Any Amount of Books   May 26 2011 - A68509 2011 $503

Coleridge, Samuel Taylor   1772-1834 *The Friend. The Collected Works.* London: Routledge & Kegan Paul, 1969, 2 volumes, original cloth, gilt over bevelled boards, dust jackets slight browning to spines, slipcase with paper label, pages cv, 580; vi, 680 with 5 plates and 4 facsimiles, fine set.   R. F. G. Hollett & Son Antiquarian Booksellers   General Catalogue Summer 2010 - 748   2011   £75

Coleridge, Samuel Taylor   1772-1834 *The Notebooks 1794-1808.* New York: Pantheon Books & Routledge & Kegan Paul, 1957-1962, 4 volumes, large 8vo., original cloth, gilt, dust jackets, some spines little darkened, small hole to one backstrip, first two volumes in slipcase with paper label, pages xlii,5 46; xlv, 615; xx, 478; xxxiv, 548, very good clean and sound set.   R. F. G. Hollett & Son Antiquarian Booksellers   General Catalogue Summer 2010 - 383   2011   £180

Coleridge, Samuel Taylor   1772-1834 *Poems on Various Subjects.* London: G. G. and J. Robinson, 1796, First edition; small octavo, xvi, 188, (4, ads and errata) pages, half title, publisher's ads and errata all present, this title often found without ads and errata, contemporary tree calf in unrestored state, black morocco spine label, spine stamped and lettered in gilt, cover edges stamped in gilt, very small amount of repair to spine, corners slightly bumped, spine label bit rubbed, signatures M and N, bit toned as usual, excellent copy, complete with appropriate binding.   Heritage Book Shop   Holiday 2010 - 20 2011 $7500

Coleridge, Samuel Taylor   1772-1834 *Poems by...* London: 1797, Second edition; small octavo, uncut in quarter parchment over original drab boards.   Heritage Book Shop   Booth A12 51st NY International Antiquarian Book Fair April 8-10 2011 - 32   2011 $2500

Coleridge, Samuel Taylor   1772-1834 *Poems Chosen Out of the Works.* Kelmscott Press, 1896, One of 300 copies on paper (there were also 8 copies on vellum); 210 x 150mm., 4 p.l. (first two blank), 100 pages, original limp vellum, yapp edges, gilt titling on spine, silk ties, edges untrimmed, elaborate woodcut title and border on first page of text, one other page with three quarter border, decorative woodcut initials, woodcut device on final page, printed in red and black; one gathering with dot of foxing on three leaves, otherwise fine, quite clean and fresh inside and out.   Phillip J. Pirages   59 - 241   2011 $3250

Coleridge, Samuel Taylor   1772-1834 *Poems Chosen Out of the Works of Samuel Taylor Coleridge.* Hammersmith: sold by William Morris at the Kelmscott Press, 1896, One of 300 paper copies out of a total edition of 308; octavo, ii, 100 pages, printed in red and black in golden type, decorative borders and initials, original full limp vellum with green silk ties, spine lettered in gilt, fine copy, partially uncut.   David Brass Rare Books, Inc.   May 26 2011 - 01584 2011 $5500

Coleridge, Samuel Taylor 1772-1834 *The Rime of the Ancient Mariner.* New York: Crowell, 1910, First US edition; folio, green gilt pictorial cloth, top edge gilt, others trimmed, gilt on spine dulled, else fine, illustrations by Pogany with pictorial endpapers and titlepage, tipped in color illustrations and full page color illustrations, calligraphic text enclosed within pictorial borders with decorative initials and there are smaller black and whites in text.   Aleph-Bet Books, Inc.   95 - 440 2011 $1600

Coleville, H. E. *A Ride in Petticoats and Slippers.* London: Sampson Low, 1880, First edition; 8vo., pages xvi, 328, ads, frontispiece, folding map, folding plan, original decorative cloth, neatly recased with small wear to head and tail, joints rubbed, new endpapers.   J. & S. L. Bonham Antiquarian Booksellers   Africa 4/20/2011 - 8742 2011 £140

Colfer, Eoin *Artemis Fowl.* London: Viking, 2001, First British edition, true first; fine, in fine dust jacket, includes promotional bookmark and flyer, signed by author.   Bella Luna Books May 26 2011 - t8070 2011 $220

Colfer, Eoin *Artemis Fowl - The Arctic Incident.* London: Puffin Books, 2002, First UK edition, true first; fine in like dust jacket, includes promotional book mark, signed by author.   Bella Luna Books   May 29 2011 - t8071 2011 $137

Colina, Tessa *Ark Full of Animals.* Cincinnati: Standard Publishing Foundation, 1945, Oblong 8vo., spiral backed card covers die cut in shape of Ark, fine, illustrations in full color by Vera Gohman, cut into the illustrations are 40 die-cut windows with surprise pictures underneath.   Aleph-Bet Books, Inc.   95 - 394 2011 $100

Colley, Cibber *The Double Gallant; or the Sick Lady's Cure, a Comedy.* London: printed for Bernard Lintott between the two Temple Gates in Fleetstreet, 1707, Second edition; 4to., small stain on title and following page, without final ad leaf, (8), 80 pages, printed the same year as the first edition, disbound.   Anthony W. Laywood   May 26 2011 - 21747 2011 $126

Collier, J. Payne *The Egerton Papers.* London: Camden Society, 1840, Original blindstamped cloth, gilt, hinges chipped and spine bubbled and frayed, edges little bumped in places, pages viii, 510, endpapers rather soiled and chipped, joints cracking.   R. F. G. Hollett & Son Antiquarian Booksellers   General Catalogue Summer 2010 - 597 2011 £45

Collier, Jane *An Essay on the Art of Ingeniously Tormenting...* London: A. Millar, 1757, Second edition; 8vo., pages (2), iv, 234, little toned around fore edge of titlepage, clean copy with wide margins, bound in contemporary calf, bit worn, rebacked some time ago in brown morocco gilt, large armorial bookplate of Sir William Stirling Maxwell, engraved cat and mouse frontispiece.   Second Life Books Inc.   174 - 101 2011 $450

Collier, Jeremy *Essays Upon Several Moral Subjects in Two Parts.* London: printed for Richard Sare, 1703, Fifth edition; pages (iv), 200, (vi), 279, contemporary blind panelled calf, rebacked in matching calf gilt with raised bands and spine label.   R. F. G. Hollett & Son Antiquarian Booksellers   175 - 284 2011   £180

Colliery Engineer Company *Placer Mining, a Handbook for Klondike and Other Miners and Prospectors.* Scranton: 1897, vi, 146 pages, illustrations, folding map, original printed boards, light wear to boards, private library bookplate on front pastedown, else very good.   Dumont Maps & Books of the West   111 - 51 2011 $150

Collin, Paul Ries *Calling Bridge.* Oxford University Press, 1976, First edition; original cloth, gilt, dust jacket, pages 86, drawings.   R. F. G. Hollett & Sons Antiquarian Booksellers   170 - 356 2011   £35

Collingwood, R. G. *Northumbrian Crosses of the Pre-Norman Age.* London: Faber, 1927, First edition; 4to., original blue cloth gilt, pages (iv), 196, uncut, with 227 text figures, half title lightly spotted, otherwise excellent.   R. F. G. Hollett & Son Antiquarian Booksellers   177 - 198 2011 £225

Collingwood, W. G. *Coniston Tales.* Ulverston: Wm. Holmes, 1899, Original printed patterned boards, slightly marked, spine little cracked, pages (iv) 78, frontispiece and decorated title, scarce.   R. F. G. Hollett & Son Antiquarian Booksellers   173 - 248 2011   £75

Collingwood, W. G. *Elizabethan Keswick.* Kendal: Titus Wilson, 1912, Original printed wrappers, pages viii, 219, few text illustrations, fine, scarce.   R. F. G. Hollett & Son Antiquarian Booksellers   173 - 250 2011   £120

Collingwood, W. G. *The Lake Counties.* London: Frederick Warne, 1932, First edition thus; 4to., original cloth, gilt, dust jacket (top edges and lower hinge chipped and frayed, spine rubbed), pages xvi, 368, with 16 colored plates and large folding map.   R. F. G. Hollett & Son Antiquarian Booksellers   173 - 251 2011   £60

Collingwood, W. G. *The Lake Counties.* London: Dent, 1988, First edition thus; original cloth, gilt, dust jacket, pages xii 243, illustrations, partly in color.   R. F. G. Hollett & Son Antiquarian Booksellers   173 - 252 2011   £35

Collingwood, W. G. *The Memoirs of Sir Daniel Fleming.* Kendal: Titus Wilson, 1928, Original wrappers, pages x, 131, portrait, Kendal Grammar School bookplate, very nice, clean copy.   R. F. G. Hollett & Son Antiquarian Booksellers   173 - 255   2011   £75

Collins, Carl *Pictures of Appalachia, Virginia & Surrounding Areas 1896-1983.* Appalachia: 1963?, First edition; 9 x 12 inches, wrappers in plastic binder, very good.   Bookworm & Silverfish   670 - 188   2011 $150

Collins, Charles Allston *A Cruise Upon Wheels: the Chronicle of Some Autumn Wanderings Among the Deserted Post-Roads of France.* London: Routledge, Warren & Routledge, 1863, Second edition; half title, frontispiece, with marginal mark, little careless opening, original red cloth, blocked in blind, spine slightly faded, endpapers almost imperceptibly replaced, good.   Jarndyce Antiquarian Booksellers   CXCI - 541   2011   £65

Collins, Judith *Winifred Nicholson.* London: Tate Gallery, 1987, Large 8vo. original wrappers, pages 117, with 32 pages of color plates, 69 illustrations.   R. F. G. Hollett & Son Antiquarian Booksellers   General Catalogue Summer 2010 - 136   2011   £50

Collins, Roland *The Flying Poodle.* London: Harvill Press, n.d. circa, 1940, 4to., boards, very good+ in dust jacket with piece off backstrip, illustrations by W. Suschitzky, photos.   Aleph-Bet Books, Inc.   95 - 427   2011 $125

Collins, Samuel *A Systeme of Anatomy, Treating of the Body of Man, Beasts, Birds, Fish, Insects and Plants.* In the Savoy: printed by Thomas Newcomb, 1685, Folio, pages (16), lvi, (14), 52, 49-52, (53-) 678; (10), 679-) 740 739-740, (7451-) 1263, (42), engraved frontispiece, portrait (some light spotting), 74 engraved plates, one or two plates with shaved down fore-edge and just touching engraved border, due to bad setting, both titles printed in red and black (spotting to first), contemporary calf, professionally rebacked and repaired, some scattered marginal wormholes, light dampstaining to several pages in volume 1, with 6 additional dedications (of two leaves each) inserted and extra to collation given above, second volume inscribed "Johannes Morgan E. Coll. Jesus 1718" (possibly John Morgan), very good.   Raymond M. Sutton, Jr.   May 26 2011 - 55971   2011 $10,000

Collins, W. Lucas *Ancient Classics for English Readers.* Edinburgh: William Blackwood & Sons, 1871-1874, Initial ad leaf in volume 1, half titles, publisher's ads, 20 volumes, original light brown cloth, decorated in black, slight rubbing to head and tail of spines, armorial bookplates of Samuel Linder, very good, bookseller's tickets of J. Gilbert, very good.   Jarndyce Antiquarian Booksellers   CXCI - 8   2011   £400

Collins, Wilkie 1824-1889 *After Dark.* London: Gresham Pub. Co., 1900, Frontispiece and plates, original dark olive green cloth, maroon morocco spine decorated in gilt with art nouveau design, spine little faded.   Jarndyce Antiquarian Booksellers   CXCI - 121   2011   £50

Collins, Wilkie 1824-1889 *Antonina, or The Fall of Rome.* London: Chatto & Windus, circa, 1890, New edition; original half tan calf by Mudie, gilt spine, maroon morocco labels, signature of M.D. Baron, very good.   Jarndyce Antiquarian Booksellers   CXCI - 122   2011   £110

Collins, Wilkie 1824-1889 *Armadale.* New York: Harper & Bros., 1866, First American edition; 2 pages initial ads, frontispiece, 36 wood engravings by G. H. Thomas in text, original blue green cloth, blind borders, spine lettered in gilt, slight rubbing, good plus.   Jarndyce Antiquarian Booksellers   CXCI - 123   2011   £225

Collins, Wilkie 1824-1889 *Armadale.* London: Chatto & Windus, 1891, New edition; 32 page catalog (March 1895), some foxing in prelims, original green cloth, blocked and lettered in black and gilt, very good.   Jarndyce Antiquarian Booksellers   CXCI - 124   2011   £120

Collins, Wilkie 1824-1889 *Basil: a Story of Modern Life.* James Blackwood, 1856, First one volume edition; yellowback, original yellow pictorial boards, blacking spine, plainly rebacked, boards slightly dulled and rubbed.   Jarndyce Antiquarian Booksellers   CXCI - 125   2011   £65

Collins, Wilkie 1824-1889 *Basil: a Story of Modern Life.* London: Sampson, Low, Son & Co., 1862, Revised edition; frontispiece, 16 page catalog (May 1863), pencil ownership inscription of George Jones, original mauve cloth by Bone & Son, front board slightly dulled, spine faded to brown.   Jarndyce Antiquarian Booksellers   CXCI - 126   2011   £180

Collins, Wilkie 1824-1889 *The Dead Secret.* London: Chatto & Windus, 1902, New edition; final ad leaf, original light pink original pictorial paper wrappers, odd mark and crease, stationer's stamp of S. Warren, Ipswich.   Jarndyce Antiquarian Booksellers   CXCI - 127   2011   £40

Collins, Wilkie 1824-1889 *The Frozen Deep and Other Stories.* Leipzig: Bernhard Tauchnitz, 1874, Copyright edition; half title, some pencil annotations, original dark green publisher's cloth, recent signature on leading f.e.p.   Jarndyce Antiquarian Booksellers   CXCI - 128   2011   £120

Collins, Wilkie 1824-1889 *Man and Wife; A novel.* London: Chatto & Windus, 1897, Library edition; half title, 4 pages, + 32 page catalog (May 1897), uncut in original maroon cloth, spine faded, leading inner hinge slightly cracked, ownership inscription.   Jarndyce Antiquarian Booksellers   CXCI - 130   2011   £40

Collins, Wilkie 1824-1889 *The Moonstone.* Leipzig: Bernhard Tauchnitz, 1868, (1894). Copyright edition; 2 volumes in 1, half titles, contemporary half dark brown sheep, publisher's binding, rubbed and little worn, good, sound copy, booklabel of Franz Wille, Jerusalem library stamp on half title volume 1.   Jarndyce Antiquarian Booksellers   CXCI - 131   2011   £85

Collins, Wilkie 1824-1889 *The New Magdalen: a Novel.* London: Chatto & Windus, 1893, New edition; contemporary half tan calf by Mudie, gilt spine, maroon morocco labels, booklabel of M. D. Baron, very good.   Jarndyce Antiquarian Booksellers   CXCI - 132   2011   £120

Collins, Wilkie 1824-1889 *No Name.* London: Sampson Low, 1863, New edition; 3 volumes, half titles volumes I-II, some foxing to prelims volume I, binding cracked but firm at pages 240-241, volume III; original orange cloth, spines dulled, slight rubbing to heads and tails, W. H. Smith embossed stamps to endpapers, good plus.   Jarndyce Antiquarian Booksellers   CXCI - 133   2011   £480

Collins, Wilkie 1824-1889 *Poor Miss Finch: a Domestic Story.* London: Chatto & Windus, 1889, New edition; frontispiece and plates, 32 page catalog (Oct. 1889), contemporary signature on leading blank, original green cloth, blocked in black and gilt, very good, bright.   Jarndyce Antiquarian Booksellers   CXCI - 134   2011   £125

Collins, Wilkie 1824-1889 *The Two Destinies: a Romance.* London: Chatto & Windus, 1898, Half title, 32 page catalog (Sept. 1897), uncut in original maroon cloth, decorated in blind, lettered in gilt, spine slightly faded.   Jarndyce Antiquarian Booksellers   CXCI - 135   2011   £60

Collins, Wilkie 1824-1889 *The Woman in White.* Woodstock: Elm Tree Press or the Limited Editions Club, 1964, Signed limited edition, no. 4 of 1500 copies; tall 8vo., original cloth backed marbled boards, gilt, spine trifle faded, slipcase, pages xvi, 574, illustrations in color and signed by Leonard Solomon.   R. F. G. Hollett & Son Antiquarian Booksellers   General Catalogue Summer 2010 - 749   2011   £40

Colomb, Philip Howard *Slave-Catching in the Indian Ocean: a Record of Naval Experience.* London: Longmans Green, 1873, First edition; 8vo., pages 503, 8 engraved plates, including frontispiece, folding map, slight foxing to map and contents page, original red decorative cloth, recased with repair to spine, new endpapers, all edges gilt, very good, rare.   J. & S. L. Bonham Antiquarian Booksellers   Africa 4/20/2011 - 4574   2011   £550

Colonia, Rosina *The Archaeological Museum of Delphi.* Athens: Eurobank Ergasias/John S. Latsis Public Benefit Foundation, 2006, First edition; 4to., copiously in color, fine in dust jacket.   Any Amount of Books   May 29 2011 - A39912   2011 $272

The Colophon. Part one. New York: Colophon, 1930, First edition, 2000 copies; Part one, small 4to., original decorated boards by Edward A. Wilson, flat spine (little darkened), unpaginated, illustrations in line and single colours.   R. F. G. Hollett & Son Antiquarian Booksellers   General Catalogue Summer 2010 - 384   2011   £45

The Colophon. Part Two. New York: the Colophon, 1930, First edition (2000 copies); part two, small 4to., original decorated boards with flat spine, little darkened, torn at foot, unpaginated, illustrations, facsimiles et. tipped in.   R. F. G. Hollett & Son Antiquarian Booksellers   General Catalogue Summer 2010 - 385   2011   £40

The Colophon. Part Four. New York: The Colophon, 1930, First edition 2000 copies; part 4, small 4to., original decorated boards with flat spine, little darkened, unpaginated, illustrations in colors and black and white, facsimiles etc. tipped in.   R. F. G. Hollett & Son Antiquarian Booksellers   General Catalogue Summer 2010 - 386   2011   £50

The Colophon. Part Five. New York: The Colophon, 1931, First edition (300 copies); part 5, small 4to., original decorated boards with flat spine, little darkened, unpaginated, illustrations in colors and black and white, ex-library with small label on front board and labels removed from rear endpapers, lacking the David Milne "Hilltop" print.   R. F. G. Hollett & Son Antiquarian Booksellers   General Catalogue Summer 2010 - 387   2011   £35

The Colophon. Part Seven. New York: The Colophon, 1931, First edition (3000 copies); part 7, small 4to., original decorated boards with flat spine, little darkened, slightly frayed at head, unpaginated, illustrations in colors and black and white.   R. F. G. Hollett & Son Antiquarian Booksellers   General Catalogue Summer 2010 - 389   2011   £35

The Colophon. Part Eight. New York: The Colophon, 1931, First edition (3000 copies); part 8, small 4to., original decorated boards with flat spine, little darkened, unpaginated, illustrations in colors and black and white.   R. F. G. Hollett & Son Antiquarian Booksellers   General Catalogue Summer 2010 - 390   2011   £45

The Colophon. Part Nine. New York: the Colophon, 1932, First edition (3000 copies); part 9, small 4to., original decorated boards with flat spine, little darkened, unpaginated, illustrations in colors and black and white.   R. F. G. Hollett & Son Antiquarian Booksellers   General Catalogue Summer 2010 - 391   2011   £35

The Colophon. Part Ten. New York: The Colophon, 1932, First edition (3000 copies); part 10, small 4to., original decorated boards with flat spine, little darkened, unpaginated, illustrations in colors and black and white.   R. F. G. Hollett & Son Antiquarian Booksellers   General Catalogue Summer 2010 - 392   2011   £30

The Colophon. Part Eleven. New York: The Colophon, 1932, First edition (3000 copies); part 11, small 4to., original decorated boards with flat spine, little darkened, rubbed at head and foot, unpaginated, illustrations in colors and black and white, some Colophon ephemera and 2 page copy typescript review of journal, all loosely inserted. R. F. G. Hollett & Son Antiquarian Booksellers General Catalogue Summer 2010 - 393 2011 £35

Colquhoun, Patrick 1745-1820 *A Treatise on the Police of the Metropolis, Explaining the Various Crimes and Misdemeanors...* London: printed by H. Fry for C. Dilly, 1996, First edition; 8vo., xiii, (2) 6-369 (3) pages, complete with final leaf, which adds a note to page 363 and with folding table bound in between pages 252 and 253, contemporary tree calf, spine neatly restored, gilt and labeled, very good, very scarce. John Drury Rare Books 154 - 40 2011 £950

Coltrane, James *A Good Day to Die.* New York: Norton, 1999, First printing; fine in fine dust jacket, signed by author, review copy with slips laid in. Bella Luna Books May 29 2011 - t1248s 2011 $82

Columbus, Christopher *Select Documents Illustrating the Four Voyages of Columbus...* London: Hakluyt Society, 1933, 8vo., lxxxix, 164 pages, folding frontispiece, plate, maps, blue cloth, gilt stamped cover illustration and spine title, very good, volume II only, from the Bern Dibner reference library, with Burndy bookplate. Jeff Weber Rare Books 161 - 96 2011 $100

Columnis, Guido De *Historia Destructionis Troiae (with Epitaphium Hectoris and Epitaphium Achillis etc.).* Netherlands?: printer of Alexander Magnus, 1477-1479, First edition; fine large copy with "Historia Troiana" written possibly in the atelier of the printer, in red crayon on both first and final blank, chancery folio, ff. (132), first and least leaves blank, lines, type, rubricated, English binding of the first half of the 17th century of brown calf over pasteboard, slightly worn, from the library of the Earls of Macclesfield at Shirburn Castle. Maggs Bros. Ltd. 1440 - 61 2011 £40,000

Colville, Henry *The Land of the Nile Springs.* London: Edward Arnold, 1895, First edition; 8vo., pages xv, 312, folding map, illustrations, original red decorative cloth, gilt vignette on upper cover, covers faded, waterstained but internally clean. J. & S. L. Bonham Antiquarian Booksellers Africa 4/20/2011 - 4584 2011 £150

Combe, William 1742-1823 *The Tour of Doctor Syntax.* London: George Routledge & Sons Ltd. n.d., Ninth edition; 3 volumes, very good, cloth worn at edges, original boards with new spine, corners rubbed, else clean and tight, 80 plates in all, with tissue guards, in very good condition, bookplates of Edgar Guest. G. H. Mott Bookseller May 26 2011 - 43629 2011 $500

Combe, William 1742-1823 *The Second Tour of Doctor Syntax in Search of Consolation.* London: 1903, 12mo., vi, 262 pages, 20 color plates after Thomas Rowlandson, very good. Bookworm & Silverfish 666 - 61 2011 $65

Combe, William 1742-1823 *The Three Tours of Dr. Syntax...* London: R. Ackermann's Repository of Arts, 1812, 1820. 1821. First editions in book form, first issue of the first work with plates in first state; 235 x 146mm., 3 volumes, remarkably pretty sky blue crushed morocco, handsomely gilt by Riviere (signed at foot of front turn-in), covers gilt with double rule border, French fillet center frame and floral cornerpieces, raised bands, spines elaborately gilt in compartments featuring elegant floral tools used for cornerpieces and centerpiece, broad and ornate gilt inner dentelles, all edges gilt, one woodcut illustration, one engraved tailpiece and 80 artfully hand colored aquatint plates by Thomas Rowlandson; engraved bookplate of Douglas Kerr; rear joint of one volume with thin crack along bottom inch or so, two covers with faint soiling, spines evenly faded to very pleasing, blue-grey, otherwise beautiful bindings in lovely condition with bright gilt, leaves opposite plates lightly offset, otherwise very fine internally text clean and with substantial margins, plates finely colored. Phillip J. Pirages 59 - 303 2011 $590

Comber, Thomas *Roman Forgeries in the Councils During the First Four Centuries...* London: Samuel Roycroft for Rover Clavell, 1689, Small 4to., pages (xvi), 175, (i), contemporary sprinkled sheep, spine blind ruled and gilt lettered direct, boards blind double rule bordered with blind decorative roll toward hinges and blind 'tulip' tool in corners, additional gilt and blind tooling indicative of early 19th century decorative update to spine and boards, board edges decorative roll gilt, blue and white sewn endbands, 20th century calf rebacked with old backstrip relaid, little faint spotting, old leather crackled and rubbed, relaid spine heavily worn, from the collection of Christopher Ernest Weston 1947-2010. Unsworths Booksellers 24 - 18 2011 £450

The Comic ABC Painting Book. London: Paris: New York: Raphael Tuck, 1896, Oblong 8vo., pictorial wrappers die-cut in shape of an owl at easel, one small mend, else near fine and unused, illustrations in brown line on every page, 4 fine chromolithographed pages. Aleph-Bet Books, Inc. 95 - 35 2011 $400

Comley, John M. *Cases Argued and Determined in the Supreme Court of Errors of the State of Connecticut.* New York: Banks Law Publishing Co., 1925-1927, First edition; 5 volumes, 101, 102, 103, 104, 105 from June 1924 - March 1927, tan cloth with raised bands and red and black leather labels, near fine set, attractive in appearance. Lupack Rare Books May 26 2011 - ABE1401536327 2011 $100

Commercial Banking Company of Scotland *Articles of Copartnery of the Commercial Banking Company of Scotland.* Edinburgh: Alex. Lawrie & Co., 1810, First edition; 4to., (2), 26 (2) pages, including final blank G2, some dust marking of outer leaves (particularly verso of final blank), recent marbled boards, lettered on spine, good copy. John Drury Rare Books   154 - 41   2011   £450

Commines, Philippe De, Sieur D'Argenton   1445-1511 *The Historie of Philip de Commines, Knight Lord of Argenton.* London: John Bill, 1614, Third edition; folio, (16), 366, blank (3) pages, ornate woodcut title, woodcut headpieces, woodcut initials, woodcut tailpieces, genealogical chart, title marginally trimmed with minor loss of image, G^1 I^6 L^4 Q^2 V^3 marginally scorched with faint waterstains (text bright and readable), early full Cambridge calf, gilt raised bands, red leather spine label, extremities rubbed, bookplate of Earl of Ilchester, very good.   Jeff Weber Rare Books   163 - 9   2011 $500

Commines, Philippe De, Sieur D'Argenton   1445-1511 *Les Memoires.* A Leide: Chez les Elzeviers, 1648, Derniere edition; 140 x 80 mm., 12 p.l., 765, (19) pages, very pretty early 19th century dark green morocco by Thouvenin (stamp-signed at tail of spine), covers with large frame formed by decorative rules and dense, complex cornerpieces in blind, this frame punctuated with a dozen thick gilt dots and enclosing an intricate lozenge in blind and gilt featuring elegant flowers, fronds and seashells, as well as many small tools and curls, raised bands, spine compartments with small, simple gilt lozenge at center of very elaborate quatrefoil fleuron in blind, gilt turn-ins, salmon pink watered silk endpapers, all edges gilt; with four tondo portraits; engraved bookplate of Bibliotheque L. Veydt; spine uniformly sunned to pleasing olive brown, first gathering with quarter inch dampstain to tail edge margin, occasional minor foxing or other trivial imperfections, especially appealing copy in fine condition, clean, fresh leaves, very lustrous binding showing only most superficial wear.   Phillip J. Pirages   59 - 30   2011 $1250

The Complete Peerage of England, Scotland, Ireland and the United Kingdom, Extant, Extinct or Dormant. London: St. Catherine Press Ltd., 1910-1940, Second edition; 13 volumes in 14, 4to., original publisher's green cloth, gilt ruled and decorated, lettering to spines and front covers, first 9 volumes with armorial bookplate of Robert Gordon Gordon-Gilmour of Liberton & Craigmillar, some variance in cloth color due to intervals of publication and possible fading, top edge gilt, very good, partially unopened.   Any Amount of Books   May 26 2011 - A72190   2011 $1384

The Complete Young Mans Companion; or Self Instructor Being an Introduction to all the Various Branches of Useful Learning and Knowledge. Manchester: printed by Russell and Allen, 1811, Second edition; Pages viii, 495, (i), complete with engraved frontispiece and 6 plates, pages 385-408 are supplied from The New Pleasing Instructer, printed by the Same Publisher in c. 1805 and clearly inserted when issued and bound up, extremely scarce.   R. F. G. Hollett & Son Antiquarian Booksellers   175 - 34   2011   £295

Compton-Burnett, Ivy   1892-1969   *Daughters and Sons.* London: Gollancz, 1937, First edition; 8vo., pages 320, blue cloth, owner's bookplate, name on flyleaf, cover slightly soiled, otherwise very good, author Barbara Howes' copy with her signature.   Second Life Books Inc.   174 - 103   2011 $60

Compton-Burnett, Ivy   1892-1969   *Dolores.* Edinburgh: Blackwood, 1911, First edition; 8vo., 330 pages, some foxing on fore edges and staining the blanks and half title, otherwise excellent clean, tight, fine copy, rare.   Second Life Books Inc.   174 - 104   2011 $900

Compton-Burnett, Ivy   1892-1969   *Dolores.* London: William Blackwood & Sons, 1911, First edition; 8vo., pages 330, 64 pages publisher's ads (dated 3/11 and mentioning Dolores), original publisher's blue cloth lettered gilt on spine and on front cover, decent looking, very good copy, slightly tanned and slightly sunned at spine with slight rubbing at extremities.   Any Amount of Books   May 26 2011 - A71689   2011 $755

Comte, Auguste   *The Positive Philosophy of Auguste Comte.* John Chapman, 1853, First edition in English; half titles discarded, pages xxxvi, 480; xvi, 561, (1), 8vo., contemporary half calf, backstrips panelled in gilt, green and tan morocco labels with gilt lettering, marbled edges and endpapers, backstrips sunned, good.   Blackwell Rare Books   B166 - 22   2011   £400

Comte, Auguste   *Systeme de Politique Positive...* Paris: Setier, 1824, First edition; 8vo., pages 8, 289, (i) blank; 84; late 19th century red morocco, marbled boards, panelled spine, filleted and lettered in gilt, preserving original green silk bookmark, tips rubbed, foot of spine bumped and torn, obituary of Auguste Comte mounted between front free endpapers, Comte's autograph inscription to mathematician and politician Dominique Francois Jean Arago, bookplate of Gustave d'Eichthal and manuscript notes of d'Eichthal on half title and front free endpapers.   Simon Finch Rare Books   Zero - 125   2011   £4750

Conard, Howard L.   *Encyclopedia of the History of Missouri, A Compendium of History and Biography for Reference.* New York: Louisville: St. Louis: The Southern History Co., 1901, First edition; quarto, 6 volumes, three quarter leather and cloth, marbled endpapers, all edges gilt, frontispiece, plates, light cosmetic restoration to spine ends and corners, else near fine, rare, exceptionally handsome set.   Buckingham Books   May 26 2011 - DY   2011 $5000

Conder, C. R.   *The Tell Amarna Tablets.* Palestine Exploration Fund, 1892, First edition; original cloth, gilt, rather marked, hinges little rubbed, pages xi, 212, (iv), the copy of Percy F. Kendall (Yorkshire geologist) with his signature, later from the library of Dr. Arthur Raistrick with his bookplate.   R. F. G. Hollett & Son Antiquarian Booksellers   177 - 205   2011   £35

Conder, Josiah *Landscape Gardening in Japan.* Kodansha International, 2002, Small 4to., original pictorial boards, dust jacket, pages 248, with 77 plates and 55 text illustrations, fine.   R. F. G. Hollett & Son Antiquarian Booksellers   General Catalogue Summer 2010 - 960   2011   £65

Condillac, Etienne Bonnot De *The Logic of Condillac.* Philadelphia: printed, 1809, First edition thus; 12mo. in 6's, (6), 136, (2) pages, trifle browned with occasional foxing, early ms. notes in ink on at least 3 leaves, ownership signature of James E. Allen, Lackington Jany 2d 1823, contemporary half calf over marbled boards, spine restored, corners worn, good, sound.   John Drury Rare Books   153 - 29   2011   £375

Cone, Helen *Bonnie Little People.* New York: Stokes, 1890, Folio, cloth backed pictorial boards, light cover soil, edge of frontispiece creased, very good+, printed on rectos only, 6 magnificent full page chromolithographs by Maud Humphrey, rare.   Aleph-Bet Books, Inc.   95 - 298   2011 $1200

Confucius *The Morals of Confucius a Chinese Philosopher.* London: printed for Randal Taylor, 1691, First edition in English; small octavo, (16), 142 pages (A, C-L), contemporary speckled calf, covers ruled in blind, spine ruled in blind and with small leather lettering label, edges sprinkled red, rear endpaper and pastedown have been expertly replaced some time ago, superb copy.   David Brass Rare Books, Inc.   May 26 2011 - 01621   2011 $8750

Conjuring: or, Magic Made Easy. New York: New York Popular Publishing Co. circa, 1880, First edition; 12mo., 30, (2) pages, text illustrations, including two full page, original hand colored printed and pictorial wrappers, vignette portrait above a scene depicting a magician performing on stage, very fine, partly unopened, superb copy.   M & S Rare Books, Inc.   90 - 223   2011 $200

Conley, Robert J. *The Rattlesnake Band and Other Poems.* Muskogee: Indian University Press, 1984, One of 500 numbered copies; apparently only issued in wrappers, bi-lingual, Cherokee/English, illustrations by author, uncommon, inscribed by Conley to La Verne Clarke.   Ken Lopez Bookseller   154 - 134   2011 $350

Connelly, Michael *The Black Echo.* Boston: Little Brown, 1992, First edition; near fine, light bumping at top of spine, dust jacket near fine, corresponding creasing, signed by author.   Bella Luna Books   May 26 2011 - t6179   2011 $247

Connelly, Michael *The Black Echo.* Boston: Little Brown, 1992, First edition; near fine, light bumping to spine ends, dust jacket fine, signed by author.   Bella Luna Books   May 26 2011 - j1423d   2011 $357

Connelly, Michael *The Black Ice.* Boston: Little Brown, 1993, First edition; fine in fine dust jacket.   Bella Luna Books   May 29 2011 - t7830   2011 $137

Connelly, Michael *The Black Ice.* Boston: Little Brown, Little, First edition; fine in like dust jacket, signed by author.   Bella Luna Books   May 26 2011 - t4199   2011 $247

The Connoisseur a Magazine for Collectors. London: 1976, This is the 75th Anniversary issue; 248, viii, (1) pages, large 4to., wrappers, near fine.   Bookworm & Silverfish   679 - 23   2011 $60

Connolly, Cyril   1903-1974 *The Condemned Playground. Essays 1924-1944.* London: Routledge, 1945, First edition; 8vo., pages viii, 287, signed presentation from author for John Lehmann, with card and sheet of paper with notes in Lehmann's hand towards a review for his own purposes, very good.   Any Amount of Books   May 29 2011 - A72088   2011 $340

Connolly, John *The Unquiet.* London: Hodder & Stoughton, 2007, First UK edition; fine, fine dust jacket, includes CD, signed by author.   Bella Luna Books   May 29 2011 - 59424   2011 $82

Conrad, Jack Randolph *The Horn and the Sword.* New York: E. P. Dutton & Co., 1957, First edition; original cloth, gilt, dust jacket (edges rather chipped and creased), pages 222, with 32 plates.   R. F. G. Hollett & Son Antiquarian Booksellers   175 - 295   2011   £30

Conrad, Joseph   1857-1924 *Conrad's Manifesto: Preface to a Career. The History of the Preface to the "Nigger of Narcissus".* Philadelphia: printed for the Rosenbach Foundation by the Gehanna Press, 1966, First edition, one of 1000 copies (of a total edition of 1100); 305 x 241mm., 81 pages, including 15 photographic facsimiles, distinctive marbled paper boards, enclosed in original textured heavy inner folder and matching slipcase, paper labels on volume and case; frontispiece by Leonard Baskin, printed in red and black, very wide margins and elegant Fabriano paper, mint in original cardboard packing container.   Phillip J. Pirages   59 - 216   2011 $90

Conrad, Joseph   1857-1924 *Nostromo A Tale of the Seaboard.* London & New York: Harper's, 1904, First English edition, first issue with page 187 mis-numbered 871; very nice bookplate on front pastedown, light foxing to few pages, early and late, and bit to fore-edges, otherwise fine, tight and bright.   Lupack Rare Books   May 26 2011 - ABE1182026639   2011 $2000

Conrad, Joseph 1857-1924 *An Outcast of the Islands.* London: T. Fisher Unwin, 1896, First edition, first printing with errors mentioned by Cagle on pages 25, 63, 93 and page 356; clean, tight, nearly fine with lovely bright spine and top edge gilt, a beauty in half leather slipcase with raised bands, gilt to spine and boards.   Lupack Rare Books   May 26 2011 - ABE1189054453   2011 $1250

Conrad, Joseph 1857-1924 *The Rescue.* Garden City: Doubleday Page, 1920, First American edition; 8vo., 404 pages, blue cloth stamped in gilt, one hinge tender, cover little scuffed and worn at edges, else very good.   Second Life Books Inc.   174 - 105   2011 $125

Conrad, Joseph 1857-1924 *The Rover.* Garden City: Doubleday, Page, 1923, First American edition; 8vo., 286 pages, dark blue cloth, stamped in gilt, edges of cover and spine little scuffed, otherwise very good.   Second Life Books Inc.   174 - 106   2011 $65

Conrad, Joseph 1857-1924 *The Secret Agent.* London: T. Werner Laurie Ltd., 1923, Limited edition, signed, 1st of this edition, privately printed and limited to 1000 copies (this no. 314) signed by author; parchment backed paper boards, printed paper spine label with extra label tipped in at rear, as called for, wonderful frontispiece portrait photo, printed tissue guard, near fine in slipcase. Lupack Rare Books   May 26 2011 - ABE4707625637   2011 $675

Conrad, Joseph 1857-1924 *The Shadow Line Shadow.* Garden City: Doubleday Page, 1917, First American edition; small 8vo., pages 197, cover little soiled and scuffed at edges, else very good, tight copy.   Second Life Books Inc.   174 - 107   2011 $60

Conrad, Joseph 1857-1924 *The Shadow Line.* London and Toronto: J. M. Dent and Sons Ltd., 1917, First edition, first issue; 8vo., pages (viii), 227, (1) imprint, 18 ads, some light spotting at edges, otherwise internally extremely fresh, top edge and fore edge roughly trimmed, bottom edges uncut, publisher's green cloth, design and lettering in black to upper panel and spine, gilt titling to spine cocked, upper hinge weak, author's presentation inscription. Simon Finch Rare Books   Zero - 222   2011   £1950

Conrad, Joseph 1857-1924 *Typhoon and Other Stories.* London: William Heinemann, 1903, First edition, first issue with windmill device on titlepage and without "Reserved for the colonies only" on verso of half title; front and bottom edges untrimmed, 32 page catalog at end, small neat bookplate on pastedown, light shelfwear, otherwise very nearly fine with bright gilt.   Lupack Rare Books   May 26 2011 - ABE4616668551   2011 $300

Conrad, Joseph 1857-1924 *Within the Tides.* Garden City: Doubleday Page, 1916, First American edition; 8vo., pages 300, dark blue cloth stamped in gilt, cover little scuffed and worn at edges, else very good.   Second Life Books Inc.   174 - 108   2011 $125

Conrad, Joseph 1857-1924 *The Works.* Garden City and New York: Doubleday Page & Co., 1920-1926, Sun Dial edition, one of 735 copies signed by author; 22 volumes, 220 x 150mm., fine and especially flamboyant lilac morocco, elaborately gilt by Stikeman, covers panelled with single and double gilt fillets and intricate scrolling foliate cornerpieces, raised bands, spine attractively gilt in ruled compartments with margin ornaments (seashell or anchor) as centerpiece and with scrolling cornerpieces, crimson morocco doublures, front doublures with central panel to blue morocco, wide turn-ins with alternating floral tools, doublures decorated with very gilt lines and (at corners) floral bouquets, blue central panels with large gilt sailing vessel at middle, watered silk endleaves, morocco hinges, all edges gilt, frontispiece; with APS by author to James Brand Pinker (Conrad's agent) tipped in at front, also with signature of Richard Curle; spines uniformly faded to an even chestnut brown, hint of rubbing to handful of joints and corners (only), one opening in one volume with marginal spots, but quite fine set in very decorative bindings, text virtually pristine, volumes completely solid, covers bright and wear to leather entirely minor.   Phillip J. Pirages   59 - 168   2011 $15,000

Conrad, Joseph 1857-1924 *The Works of Joseph Conrad.* Edinburgh: John Grant, 1925, 20 volumes, half titles, frontispieces, original blue cloth, odd mark, very good. Jarndyce Antiquarian Booksellers   CXCI - 9   2011   £380

Conrat, Maisie *The American Farm.* Scolar Press, 1977, First UK edition; oblong 4to., original cloth, gilt, dust jacket (edges little worn and chipped), pages 256, illustrations. R. F. G. Hollett & Son Antiquarian Booksellers   General Catalogue Summer 2010 - 1631   2011   £30

Conroy, Pat *The Great Santini.* Boston: Houghton Mifflin, 1976, First edition; fine in near fine, price clipped dust jacket with small corner chips, inscribed by author. Ken Lopez Bookseller   154 - 36   2011 $275

Conroy, Pat *The Great Santini.* Boston: Houghton Mifflin, 1976, First edition; fine in fine dust jacket, signed by author and by author's father, Don Conroy.   Between the Covers   169 - BTC34183   2011 $1200

Conroy, Pat *The Lords of Discipline.* Boston: Houghton Mifflin, 1980, First edition; fine in very near fine dust jacket with slightest touch of wear to crown, very nice with nice inscription by author.   Ken Lopez Bookseller   154 - 37 2011 $125

Conroy, Pat *The Prince of Tides.* Boston: Houghton Mifflin, 1986, First edition; little foxing on page edges else fine in fine dust jacket, signed by author.   Between the Covers   169 - BTC343210   2011 $350

Cons, G. J. *The Challenge of Everest: an Introductory Reader to "Climbing Mount Everest" The Official Sound Film Record of the 1933 Expedition.* London: University of London, 1934, First edition; 8vo., original publisher's illustrated wrappers with map on cover, card wrappers sewn at spine, 33 pages, 4 photo illustrations, wrappers very slightly soiled, otherwise sound decent, very good.   Any Amount of Books   May 29 2011 - A64762   2011 $238

Constant, Alphonse Louis *The Mysteries of Magic; a Digest of the Writings of...* London: George Redway, 1886, First edition; half title, (40) page catalog (1886), uncut in original blue cloth, bevelled boards, borders in red decorated in gilt, slightly rubbed and dulled.   Jarndyce Antiquarian Booksellers   CXCI - 256   2011   £450

Contes et Legendes Des Nations Aliees. Paris: H. Piazza, 1917, One of 1000 copies signed by Edmund Dulac; 305 x 241mm., (2 p.l., 149. (3) pages, lovely burgundy morocco by Root and son (signed on rear turn-in), covers framed in gilt with triple fillet border, multiple fillet inner panel with foliate cornerpieces facing outwards, raised bands, spine gilt in compartments formed by concentric plain and stippled rules and featuring ivy leaf cornerpieces, titling compartments with single rule frame and foliate curl cornerpieces, wide gilt ruled turn-ins with ivy leaf cornerpieces, marbled endpapers, top edges gilt, other edges rough trimmed, original paper covers bound in at back, decorative initials, decorative head and tailpieces for all text leaves, decorative and illustrated title and 15 color plates by Dulac (each laid down within ornamental printed frame with captioned tissue guard), bookplate of Joseph H. Haines; printed in green and black throughout (original wrappers printed in blue and black), very small stain in one fore margin, otherwise mint in unworn, very bright and appealing decorative binding.   Phillip J. Pirages   59 - 185   2011 $1750

Contributions to Medical and Biological Research, Dedicated to Sir William Osler in Honour of His Seventieth Birthday July 12 1919 by His Pupils and Co-Workers. New York: Paul B. Hoeber, 1919, Limited to 1600 copies; 2 volumes, 8vo., xix, (xx), 649; xi, (xii), 651-1268 pages, decorative orange title border, frontispiece of Osler with tissue guard (volume I), plates, navy cloth, gilt stamped cover and spine titles, top edge gilt, near fine, from the Medical Library of Dr. Clare Gray Peterson.   Jeff Weber Rare Books   162 - 231   2011 $95

Convention Between His Britannick Majesty and the Empress of Russia, signed at London the 25th of March 1793. London: printed by Edward Johnston, in Warwick Lane, 1793, First published edition; 4to., woodcut of royal arms on title, 8 pages, printed in double columns in parallel French and English texts, preserved in modern wrappers, printed title label on upper cover, very good, rare.   John Drury Rare Books   153 - 30   2011   £175

Convention of Delegates from the Abolition Societies *Minutes of the Proceedings of a Convention of Delegates from the Abolition Societies Established in Different Parts of the United States, Assembled at Philadelphia.* Philadelphia: Zachariah Poulson Junr., 1794-1798, 30 pages, accompanied by proceedings of second through fifth conventions, 32 32, 59, 20 pages, all removed, final leaf of final pamphlet damaged in the margin, with loss of several letters, else all fine copies.   Joseph J. Felcone Inc.   Fall Miscellany 2010 - 26   2011 $3000

Cook, Charles *Personal Experiences in the Prisons of the World, with Stories of Crime, Criminals and Convicts.* London: Morgan and Scott, 1902, Third edition; original pictorial and decorated cloth gilt, trifle rubbed and marked, pages xii 238, v, with woodcut illustrations, endpapers replaced, uncommon.   R. F. G. Hollett & Son Antiquarian Booksellers   175 - 297   2011   £45

Cook, G. & D., & Co's. *Illustrated Catalogue of Carriages and Special Business, Advertiser, New Haven, Connecticut.* New York: Baker & Godwin, 1860, First edition; oblong 4to., 226 pages, mostly illustrated, original cloth, slight fading, cracking of inner hinges, sound and very clean, spotless copy.   M & S Rare Books, Inc.   90 - 420   2011 $2250

Cook, G. H. *The English Mediaeval Parish Church.* Phoenix House, 1954, First edition; original cloth, gilt, dust jacket (little worn and chipped), pages 302 with 180 photos and 54 plans.   R. F. G. Hollett & Son Antiquarian Booksellers   177 - 207   2011   £45

Cook, James 1728-1779 *An Account of the Voyages Undertaken by Order of His Present Majesty for Making Discoveries in the Southern Hemisphere...* London: W. Strahan and T. Cadell, 1773, First edition; 52 engraved maps, charts and plates, including large folding map (not always present), page 139 in volume i misnumbered as usual, first chart of South Seas creased, few closed tears to folding charts at folds and mounts, occasional minor browning and spotting, one or two edges in volume I dampstained, pages (xii) xxxvi, 670; xvi, 410; (vi), 411-710, 4to., modern imitation morocco, backstrips with gilt ruled raised bands, contemporary black and red morocco labels with gilt lettering laid down, good.   Blackwell Rare Books   B166 - 23   2011   £4500

Cook, James 1728-1779 *A Voyage to the Pacific Ocean; Undertaken by Command of His Majesty from Making Discoveries in the Northern Hemisphere.* London: printed for John Stockdale, Scatcherd and Whitaker, John Fielding and John Hardy, 1784, First octavo edition; 4 volumes, 8vo., xii, 370; xii,3 59; xii, 400; xii 310 (2 blank 60) pages, large folding map, folding map, engraved frontispiece, 48 (17 + 11 +16 +4) full page engravings, folding plate, modern half brown calf over marbled boards, gilt stamped spine titles, fine. Jeff Weber Rare Books 163 - 145 2011 $2950

Cook, James 1728-1779 *Voyages du Capitaine Cook, dans la mer du sud aux Deux Poles...* Paris: Lerouge, 1811, Early French edition; 6 volume, 12mo., xxxvi, 363; (4), 419, (4), 360; (4), 328; (4), 394; (4), 386 pages, frontispiece, large folding map, full page engravings, full contemporary speckled calf, gilt stamped black leather spine labels, fine. Jeff Weber Rare Books 163 - 146 2011 $1000

Cook, John R. *The Border and the Buffalo.* Topeka: Crane & Co., 1907, First edition; illustrations, near fine. Lupack Rare Books May 26 2011 - ABE1296792425 2011 $175

Cook, Olive *English Cottages and Farmhouses.* London: Thames & Hudson, 1982, First edition; large 8vo., original cloth, gilt, dust jacket, pages 208 with 177 photos by Edwin Smith. R. F. G. Hollett & Son Antiquarian Booksellers 177 - 208 2011 £30

Cook, Olive *Movement in Two Dimensions.* London: Hutchinson, 1963, First edition; large 8vo., original cloth, gilt, dust jacket little worn and chipped, lacking part of backstrip, pages 143 with 25 illustrations, scarce. R. F. G. Hollett & Son Antiquarian Booksellers 175 - 298 2011 £75

Cook, Theodore Andrea *The Water-Colour Drawings of J. M. W. Turner, R.A. in the National Gallery.* London: Cassell and Co., 1904, Limited edition, no. 217 of 1200 copies; folio, original cloth, gilt folder with linen ties, pages vi, 88, with 5 plates, plus 88 color plates set into mounts, top edges gilt, all loose in folder as issued, scarce, presentation copy from Canon Hardwick Rawnsley. R. F. G. Hollett & Son Antiquarian Booksellers 173 - 256 2011 £450

Cook, Walter *Peggy's Travels.* Blackie & Son, n.d., 1908, Pages 98, 4to., original cloth backed pictorial boards, pages 98, pictorial title, 16 full page color plates and numerous line drawings, pictorial endpapers, prize label on pastedown, very nice, fresh copy, scarce. R. F. G. Hollett & Sons Antiquarian Booksellers 170 - 152 2011 £140

Cooke, J. Y. F. *Stories of Strange Women.* John Long, 1906, First edition; original tan decorated cloth, little dulled with slight nick to front board. Jarndyce Antiquarian Booksellers CXCI - 140 2011 £75

Cooke, Robert *West Country Houses.* London: Batsford, 1957, First edition; 4to., original blue buckram gilt, dust jacket price clipped, pages 184, with 320 illustrations. R. F. G. Hollett & Son Antiquarian Booksellers 177 - 209 2011 £85

Cooke, Thomas *The Universal Letter Writer; or New Art of Polite Correspondence, Containing a Course of Interesting Original Letters...* Gainsborough: Henry Mozley, 1814, Small 8vo., original sheep, pages 215, engraved frontispiece, little spotted. R. F. G. Hollett & Sons Antiquarian Booksellers 170 - 153 2011 £40

Cooley, Thomas M. *A Treatise on the Constitutional Limitations Which Rest Upon the Legislative Power of the States of the American Union.* Boston: 1903, Seventh edition; 1036 pages, very good in full law calf. Bookworm & Silverfish 667 - 44 2011 $75

Cooley, William Desborough *The Negroland of the Arabs Examined and Explained; or an Enquiry into the Early History and Geography of Central Africa.* London: J. Arrowsmith, 1841, First edition; 8vo., pages xvi, 143, large colored folding map, original green blindstamped cloth, recently rebacked. J. & S. L. Bonham Antiquarian Booksellers Africa 4/20/2011 - 6865 2011 £320

Coope, Rosalys *Salomon de Brosse and The Development of Classical Style in French Architecture from 1565 to 1630.* A. Zwememr Ltd., 1972, Large 8vo. 295 pages, 216 illustrations, very good, original cloth. Ken Spelman Rare Books 68 - 134 2011 £85

Cooper, A. N. *Across the Broad Acres.* A. Brown & Sons n.d., 1908, First edition; original green cloth gilt, pages xl, 316, (iv), 8 plates, flyleaves browned, postcard of author loosely inserted. R. F. G. Hollett & Son Antiquarian Booksellers General Catalogue Summer 2010 - 1367 2011 £30

Cooper, F. T. *An Argosy of Fables.* New York: Stokes, 1921, Large thick 4to., 485 pages, blue pictorial cloth, slight wear to end of spine, else fine, inscription from artist March 24 1937, illustrations by Paul Bransom with 24 richly colored and very beautiful color plates plus lovely pictorial endpapers. Aleph-Bet Books, Inc. 95 - 116 2011 $400

Cooper, James Fenimore 1789-1851 *Leatherstocking Tales.* Philadelphia: Lea & Blanchard, 1848, 1848. 1849. 1848. 1849 (but maybe all 1848?). Early reprint of first collected edition; 5 volumes, publisher's uniform brown cloth stamped in blind and titled in gilt, each title is two volumes in one, 3 volumes have ownership signature of Thos. Sackett dated in 1848, corners bumped and worn, some erosion to cloth on spine with minor loss at spine ends considerable foxing, but handsome, about very good set and very uncommon. Between the Covers 169 - BTC3408333 2011 $2200

Cooper, James Fenimore 1789-1851 *The Pioneers or the Sources of the Susquehanna: a Descriptivee Tale.* New York: Charles Wiley, 1823, First edition; first printing of volume I, first state of volume II, 2 volumes, 12mo., 11, (1), 275; 329 pages, original drab boards, uncut, boards detached, most of paper gone from one spine, portions of printed paper labels intact, unsophisticated copy of the first issue, rare found in that state with all the proper readings. M & S Rare Books, Inc. 90 - 100 2011 $1250

Cooper, John Gilbert 1789-1851 *Letters Concerning Taste.* London: printed for R. and J. Dodsley, 1757, Third edition; (16), 220 pages, half title with engraved frontispiece by Grignion, very good in contemporary calf, expertly rebacked, corners repaired, some occasional browning and light foxing. Ken Spelman Rare Books 68 - 5 2011 £395

Cooper, Joseph *The Lost Continent: or Slavery and the Slave Trade in Africa.* London: Longmans, 1875, First edition; 8vo., pages 130, original green cloth, partially unopened, near fine. J. & S. L. Bonham Antiquarian Booksellers Africa 4/20/2011 - 9229 2011 £320

Cooper, Michael *Blinds and Shutters.* Guildford: Genesis/Hedley, 1990, First edition, limited to 5000 copies, this number XXI of 250 copies prepared for contributors; 4to., 368 pages, leather/buckram in yellow and black in matching handmade printed yellow and black solander box, very faint handling wear, otherwise fine, box is slightly rubbed and slightly bumped at corners, else about fine. Any Amount of Books May 26 2011 - A74331 2011 $2264

Cooper, R. Davey *Hunting and Hunted in the Belgian Congo.* London: Smith Elder, 1914, First edition; 8vo., pages xvii, 263, folding map, illustrations, original red cloth, vignette on upper cover, half title foxed, very good. J. & S. L. Bonham Antiquarian Booksellers Africa 4/20/2011 - 7917 2011 £250

Cooper, Thomas 1805-1892 *The Life of Thomas Cooper Written by Himself.* London: Hodder and Stoughton, 1879, Twelfth thousand; original blind decorated cloth gilt, recased, pages viii, 400, engraved portrait, presentation copy inscribed by author for Rev. John Chas. Foster. R. F. G. Hollett & Son Antiquarian Booksellers 175 - 303 2011 £35

Cooper, W. D. *The History of South America...* London: printed for E. Newbery, 1789, First edition; 16mo., frontispiece, (12), pages 168, frontispiece, 5 engraved plates, full brown green calf with plain leather, gilt lettered spine with 7 gold bands, sound, clean very good copy with few marks to leather, front endpaper excised, bookplate of one Cecil Byshopp and a note dated 1791 in neat sepia ink about gifting of book from Katherine Byshopp, first blank has modern neat name, plates and text noticeably clean and bright. Any Amount of Books May 26 2011 - A66548 2011 $587

Cooper, W. Heaton *The Hills of Lakeland.* London: Warne, 1946, First edition; small 4to., original cloth, gilt, rather marked, spine faded, pages xviii, 126, 16 color plates, signed by author. R. F. G. Hollett & Son Antiquarian Booksellers 173 - 262 2011 £50

Cooper, W. Heaton *Lakeland Portraits.* London: Hodder and Stoughton, 1954, First edition; small 4to., original two tone cloth, gilt, dust jacket price clipped, pages 128, 6 fine colored plates, 28 other drawings by author, signed by author. R. F. G. Hollett & Son Antiquarian Booksellers 173 - 263 2011 £95

Cooper, W. Heaton *Lakeland Portraits.* London: Hodder & Stoughton, 1954, First edition; small 4to., original two tone cloth gilt, dust jacket price clipped, pages 128, with 6 fine colored plates, 28 other drawings by author, signed by editor with ALS from author's wife, Ophelia loosely inserted. R. F. G. Hollett & Son Antiquarian Booksellers General Catalogue Summer 2010 - 1368 2011 £100

Cooper, W. Heaton *The Lakes.* London: Frederick Warne and Co., 1966, First edition; 4to., original pictorial cloth, dust jacket, 17 colored plates and 64 drawings by author, 1979 brochure for Heaton Cooper's Log House, Ambleside, loosely inserted, signed. R. F. G. Hollett & Son Antiquarian Booksellers 173 - 265 2011 £75

Cooper, W. Heaton *The Lakes.* London: Frederick Warne & Co., 1966, First edition; 4to., original pictorial cloth, dust jacket, 17 color plates and 64 drawings by author, 1979 brochure for Heaton Cooper's Log House, Ambleside loosely inserted, signed copy. R. F. G. Hollett & Son Antiquarian Booksellers General Catalogue Summer 2010 - 1369 2011 £100

Cooper, W. Heaton *Mountain Painter.* Kendal: Frank Peters, 1984, First edition; large 4to., original cloth, gilt, dust jacket little spotted in upper panel, pages vi, 148, illustrations in color. R. F. G. Hollett & Son Antiquarian Booksellers 173 - 266 2011 £65

Cooper, W. Heaton *The Tarns of Lakeland.* London: Frederick Warne and Co., 1960, First edition; small 4to., original cloth, gilt, dust jacket (spine little darkened and chipped at head and foot), pages xiv, 237, with 16 colored plates. R. F. G. Hollett & Son Antiquarian Booksellers 173 - 267 2011 £85

Cooper, W. Heaton *The Tarns of Lakeland.* London: Frederick Warne and Co., 1960, First edition; small 4to., original cloth, gilt, dust jacket, pages xiv, 237, 16 color plates, signed. R. F. G. Hollett & Son Antiquarian Booksellers General Catalogue Summer 2010 - 1370 2011 £95

Cooper, William *Young People.* London: Macmillan, 1958, First edition; pages (viii), 360, foolscap 8vo., original mid green cloth, faded backstrip gilt lettered, faded backstrip panel to price clipped and chipped dust jacket.   Blackwell Rare Books   B166 - 133   2011   £50

Cooper, William M. *A History of the Rod in all Countries from the Earliest to the Present Time.*   William Reeves, n.d., New edition; original brown blindstamped cloth gilt, spine lettering dulled, pages xii, 544, with 20 plates.   R. F. G. Hollett & Son Antiquarian Booksellers General Catalogue Summer 2010 - 1168   2011   £75

Cooper, William M. *A History of the Rod in all the Countries from the Earliest Period to the Present Time.* London: John Camden Hotten, 1869, First edition; original cloth, gilt, trifle rubbed, pages 544, (32 ads), 20 illustrations, front joint strengthened with tape, rear hinge tender, few leaves of ads slightly torn with little loss to text on one leaf.   R. F. G. Hollett & Son Antiquarian Booksellers   175 - 300   2011   £65

Coots, J. Fred *Santa Claus is Comin' to Town.*   New York: Harper Collins, 2004, First edition; illustrations by Steven Kellogg, signed, inscribed by artist with small drawing, 4to., fine in fine dust jacket,.   By the Book, L. C.   26 - 56   2011 $70

Coover, Robert *The Universal Baseball Association, Inc.* New York: Random House, 1968, First printing; 8vo., 242 pages, very good, tight copy in price clipped and some chipped an soiled dust jacket.   Second Life Books Inc.   174 - 109   2011 $165

Copeia.   New York/Ann Arbor: American Society of Ichthyologists and Herpetologists, 1913-2006, Most first editions, approximately 20 of the earlier issues are reprints; Complete except for 1998 (nos. 1-4), 8vo. (Nos. 1-173 smaller 8vo), numerous photos, text illustrations, folded tables, charts, etc., wrappers beginning with no. 162 (some tears to No. 1), all repaired with cello tape, rest with very modest wear including occasional smudges, tanning, creases, etc, handstamp to front pages or front wrapper, very nice set, issues 1930-1948 with A. C. Taft's name in pencil.   Raymond M. Sutton, Jr.   May 26 2011 - 55023   2011 $1750

Cope's Smoke-Room Booklets.   Liverpool & London: Cope Bros & Co. Ltd., 1889-1896, First or early editions; 8vo., numbers 1-14, complete run, bound in 2 volumes, half leather lettered gilt at spine, top edge gilt, preserving original publisher's illustrated wrappers, with gilt crest of "Society of Writers to the Signet" on marbled boards, original chromolithographed wrappers, gilt highlighting, illustrations in text, 60 to 70 pages each, near fine.   Any Amount of Books   May 26 2011 - A68705   2011 $755

Coppard, Alfred Edgar   1878-1957   *Count Stefan.* Waltham St. Lawrence: Golden Cockerel Press, 1928, First edition; 517/600 copies printed on handmade paper, 4 wood engravings, including frontispiece by Robert Gibbings, pages (v),57, (1)8, 8vo., original quarter lemon yellow buckram, backstrip gilt lettered, blue and green marbled boards, faint partial endpaper browning as usual, untrimmed, faded backstrip panel to dust jacket, fine.   Blackwell Rare Books   B166 - 255   2011   £110

Coppard, Alfred Edgar   1878-1957   *The Hundredth Story.*   Waltham St. Lawrence: Golden Cockerel Press, 1931, First edition; 941/1000 copies printed on English handmade paper, 4 wood engravings by Robert Gibbings, pages (v) (blanks) (iii) 60 (iv) (blanks), royal 8vo. original quarter emerald green morocco, usual fading to gilt lettered backstrip, patterned green and white boards, faint free endpaper browning, top edge gilt, others untrimmed, very good.   Blackwell Rare Books   B166 - 256   2011   £75

Corbett, Bertha   *What's on the Air?*   Topanga: self published?, 1928,   Small 4to., color pictorial stiff card covers with some darkening to edges and some chipping to perfect binding, this copy signed in full with sketch, black and white pictures.   Jo Ann Reisler, Ltd.   86 - 48   2011 $200

Cordiner, Charles   *Remarkable Ruins and Romantic Prospects of North Britain.*   London: published by I. and J. Taylor, 1795,   2 volumes, 4to., pages iv (cxxxvi) + engraved titlepage, engraved frontispiece and another 56 engraved plates (ccxii) + engraved titlepage, 40 engraved plates (of 41), lacking plate "personification of Events etc." in volume 2, contemporary mottled calf, 6 compartmented spine divided up by back to back double rules and polished pinhead decorative roll all gilt compartments, contain 'made'up' central device of gouges and small flowerets, all gilt, black lettering and numbering pieces gilt, place and date gilt direct at foot, boards double rule gilt border with decorative roll within, board edges decorative roll gilt turn-ins, hooded acanthus, roll gilt green 'sugarpaper' 'made' endpapers, all edges pale green "French Shell" marbled, red and pale blue sewn endbands, dark blue silk page markers, slightest bit of rubbing at extremities but very nice, armorial bookplate of "Littlecote" surmounting printed label of "E. W. Leyborne Popham", from the collection of Christopher Ernest Weston 1947-2010.   Unsworths Booksellers   24 - 83   2011   £750

Coridon's Song and Other Verses from Various Sources. London: Macmillan, 1894, First edition; original pictorial cloth, gilt, pages xxiii, 163, all edges gilt, illustrations, fine, bright copy.   R. F. G. Hollett & Son Antiquarian Booksellers General Catalogue Summer 2010 - 680   2011   £45

Corkran, Alice *The Bairn's Annual for 1885-1886. (Volume I).* London: Field & Tuer, 1885, Volume I, small 8vo., original blue paper covered boards, diamond shaped paper labels, spine label little darkened and chipped, corners rather worn, spine rubbed pages (ii), 174, (ii), 4 uncut, frontispiece, 5 pages of music, scarce,. R. F. G. Hollett & Son Antiquarian Booksellers General Catalogue Summer 2010 - 509 2011 £85

Corkran, Alice *Down the Snow Stairs; or from Good Night to Good Morning.* London: Blackie and Son, n.d., 1887, Pages xi, 258, (ii), all edges gilt, 60 woodcut illustrations by Gordon Browne, original brown cloth gilt, one corner little bruised. R. F. G. Hollett & Sons Antiquarian Booksellers 170 - 154 2011 £50

Cormack, Lesley B. *Charting an Empire: Geography at the English Universities 1580-1620.* Chicago and London: University of Chicago Press, 1997, First edition; 8vo., xvi, 281 pages, illustrations, figures, tables, red cloth, gilt stamped spine title, fine, from the Bern Dibner reference library, with Burndy bookplate. Jeff Weber Rare Books 161 - 95 2011 $100

Cornell, F. C. *The Glamour of Prospecting: Wanderings of a South African Prospector in Search of Copper, Gold, Emeralds and Diamonds.* New York: F. A. Stokes, 1920, First edition; 8vo. pages xiv, 334, folding map, illustrations, original decorative maroon blindstamped cloth. J. & S. L. Bonham Antiquarian Booksellers Africa 4/20/2011 - 6939 2011 £60

Corner, Miss *Little Plays for Little People.* London: Dean & Son, n.d., First edition; original blue cloth gilt over bevelled boards, oval central chromolithograph on upper board, extremities little rubbed, pages 46, (ii), all edges gilt, woodcut illustrations by Alfred Crowquill, upper joint cracked, few spots, armorial bookplate of Hugh Cecil Earl of Lonsdale. R. F. G. Hollett & Sons Antiquarian Booksellers 170 - 172 2011 £95

Cornwallis, Charles, 1st Marquis of *Correspondence of Charles, First Marquis Cornwallis.* London: John Murray, 1859, First edition; 3 volumes, 8vo., rebound in red cloth lettered gilt on spine, pages 1786, 20 page publisher's catalog rear volume one, frontispiece volume one, 2 folding maps (foxed) and folding pedigree chart, ex-British Foreign Office library with few library markings, prelims slightly foxed, else very good. Any Amount of Books May 29 2011 - A76086 2011 $204

The Coronation History of the Barnsley British Co-Operative Society Limited 1862-1902. Manchester: Co-operative Society Printing Works, 1903, Original cloth, gilt, pages 207, well illustrated, flyleaves lightly browned, otherwise very good. R. F. G. Hollett & Son Antiquarian Booksellers General Catalogue Summer 2010 - 1328 2011 £35

Corradi, Sebastiano *Commentarius in Quo P. Virgilij Maronis Liber Primus Aeneidos Explicatur.* Florence: L. Torrentino, 1555, First edition; 8vo., 390 (2 blank) pages, device on titlepage, English calf c. 1700, spine gilt, slightly rubbed, from the library of the Earls of Macclesfield at Shirburn Castle. Maggs Bros. Ltd. 1440 - 62 2011 £450

Corry, J. *The History of Lancashire.* London: Geo. B. Whittaker, 1925, First (only) edition; 2 volumes, large 4to., modern half calf gilt, marbled boards, pages (ii), 616, (ii), 726, xliv, 36 engraved plates, odd mark or spot, but nice, clean and sound copy. R. F. G. Hollett & Son Antiquarian Booksellers General Catalogue Summer 2010 - 1371 2011 £395

Corso, Gregory *American Express.* Paris: The Olympia Press, 1961, wrappers, illustrations by author, fine in fine dust jacket, very uncommon thus. Ken Lopez Bookseller 154 - 38 2011 $750

Corso, Gregory *The Happy Birthday of Death.* New York: New Directions, 1960, First edition; wrappers, 8vo., pages 91, with foldout poem (BOMB), signed by author for writer Alan Ansen, reasonable sound very good copy with slight rubbing and slight handling wear. Any Amount of Books May 29 2011 - A84998 2011 $255

Coryate, Thomas *Coryats Crudities Hastily Gobbled Up in Five Moneths Travells in France, Savoy, Italy, Rhetia Comonly Called the Grisons Country, Helvetia Alias Switzerland, some Parts of High Germany and the Netherlands.* London: by William Stansby, 1611, First edition; printed title present, engraved allegorical title by William Hole (shaved very slightly at head), engraved plates, woodcut, text portrait, errata leaf present, many woodcut initials and headpieces, 19th century brown crushed levant morocco, gilt by Bedford, unusually tall, very handsome copy, rare printed title, from the libraries of Ward E. Terry, R. B. Adam, A. Edward Newton, Bois Penrose and Wolfgang A. Herz with their respective bookplates and book labels. Joseph J. Felcone Inc. Fall Miscellany 2010 - 35 2011 $16,000

Cosin, John *Scholastical History of the Canon of the Holy Scripture.* London: E. Tyler and R. Holt for Robert Pawlett, 1672, 4to., pages (xxxvi), 224, (xlviii) + additional engraved titlepage, contemporary speckled calf, boards double ruled in blind, board edges broken ruled gilt, all edges blue 'swirl' marbled blue and white sewn endbands, early 1990's calf reback + corners by Chris Weston, touch of dust soiling, old leather bit flaked and rubbed, ink inscription "J. Lincoln", 20th century ink inscription "This volume belonged to/ John Kaye D.D./Bishop of Lincoln/1827-1853. It belonged to his son/William Frederick John Kaye/Archdeacon of Lincoln/1863-1919", ink inscription "Peter B.G. Binnall/ Barkwith Rectory/Wragby/Lincoln/ (rule) Bought in Lincoln/30 April 1951", 19th century bookseller's ticket "J. Leslie/52 Great Queen Street/Lincoln's Inn Fields/London; from the collection of Christopher Ernest Weston 1947-2010. Unsworths Booksellers 24 - 19 2011 £275

Costanzo, Sam *World of Lugers: Serial Numbers of Lugers Issued to German Agents in the United States 1913-1916.* Wickliffe: privately published, 1975, First edition; 8vo., illustrated wrappers, pages 79, signed by author, very good, covers very slightly marked, otherwise very good. Any Amount of Books May 29 2011 - A76084 2011 $230

Costanzo, Sam *World of Lugers Proof Marks: Complete Listing of Different Variations of Proof Marks on Luger.* Mayfield Heights: privately printed, 1977, First edition; 4to., original publisher's red cloth lettered gilt on spine and with gilt decoration on cover, signed on front endpaper, 432 pages, very good+, very slightly rubbed,. Any Amount of Books May 29 2011 - A76085 2011 $272

Costumi Della Corte Pontificia. Rome: 1846, 30 hand colored plates and color titlepage, last leaf attached to original stiff embossed crimson covers, continuous strip, folding accordion fashion, into 31 leaves, in original matching slip-in case, hinges worn, otherwise excellent. Blackwell Rare Books B166 - 24 2011 £220

Cosway, Richard *Catalogue of a Collection of Miniatures by Richard Cosway.* For Private Circulation Only, 1883, Limited edition, limitation not stated; folio, (32) ff., frontispiece, 26 full page mounted photo plates, original half brown morocco, marbled boards, morocco corners, raised bands, gilt spine title, all edges gilt, bound by J. Leighton, inscribed on titlepage by author, bookplate of John Nolty, fine, rare. Jeff Weber Rare Books 163 - 100 2011 $750

Cotes, Roger *Hydrostatical and Pneumatical Lectures.* London: for the editor and sold by S. Austen, 1738, First edition; (16), 243, (11) pages, 5 engraved folding plates, contemporary sprinkled calf, neatly rebacked, name clipped from top corner of front endpaper and repaired with old paper, very good. Joseph J. Felcone Inc. Fall Miscellany 2010 - 36 2011 $1200

Cott, Jonathan *Stockhausen.* London: Robson Books, 1974, Pages 253, 8 pages of plates, original cloth, gilt, dust jacket. R. F. G. Hollett & Son Antiquarian Booksellers 175 - 310 2011 £30

Cott, Nancy *History of Women in the United States Historical Articles on Women's Lives and Activities.* London: Saur, 1993-1994, 20 books in 28 volumes, bound in green cloth, fine set. Second Life Books Inc. 174 - 110 2011 $1250

Cotton Textile Institute, Inc. *Cotton from Raw Material to Finished Product.* New York: 1947, Fourth edition; 49 pages, 4to., 122 samples, wrappers, ex-library. Bookworm & Silverfish 679 - 191 2011 $61

Coubrough, A. C. *Notes on Indian Piece Goods Trade. Bulletins of Indian Industries & Labour No. 16.* Calcutta: Government Printing, 1921, Original wrappers, pages 16, plus 5 large folding graphs. R. F. G. Hollett & Son Antiquarian Booksellers 175 - 312 2011 £35

Couch, Jonathan *A History of the Fishes of the British Islands...* London: George Bell & Sons, 1877, First edition; 4 volumes, 4to., vii 245, 8 (ads); iv, 265, 8 (ads); iv, 208, 8 (ads); iv, 439, 8 (ads) pages, frontispiece in each volume, 252 color plates, ads dated June 1879, original blue cloth gilt stamped, spines neatly restored, dated 1879 ownership signature of William Lightfoot Harwell, exceptional set, fine. Jeff Weber Rare Books 163 - 148 2011 $2000

The Council of Dogs. Philadelphia: Benjamin Warner, 1821, Reissue of 1809 edition; Square 12mo., 16 pages, original pink salmon stiff paper wrappers, 8 full page wood engravings, frontispiece pasted down inside upper cover, four of the plates uniformly browned, frontispiece spotted, tender at inner fold of upper cover, upper cover with soiling spot, good. Hobbyhorse Books 56 - 41 2011 $170

Country Friends. London: Tuck, n.d. circa, 1890, Folio, stiff pictorial boards, near fine, 16 pages of very fine chromolithographed illustrations, each page mounted on linen. Aleph-Bet Books, Inc. 95 - 565 2011 $250

Courtanvaux, Francois Cesar Letellier, Marquis de *Journal de Voyage de M. le Marquis de Courtanvaux...* Paris: l'Imprimerie Roale, 1768, 4to., viii 316, (3) (1 blank) pages, frontispiece, 5 folding engraved plates, contemporary full polished mottled calf, raised bands, gilt stamped compartments on spine, gilt stamped red morocco spine label, exceptionally clean, fine, from the Bern Dibner reference library, with Burndy bookplate. Jeff Weber Rare Books 161 - 98 2011 $6500

Courtiers and Favourites of Royalty. Paris & New York: Societe des Bibliophiles/Merrill & Baker, Edition deluxe (limited to 500 numbered and registered sets); green cloth with paper spine labels, 20 volumes, full page illustrations, including some frontispieces in color, some mild toning to spines and chipping to spine labels, otherwise very nice, tight, clean set, scarce.   Lupack Rare Books   May 26 2011 - ABE3654383685   2011 $250

Courtney, Thomas P.   *Memoirs of the Life, Works and Correspondence of Sir William Temple.* 1836,   First edition; 2 volumes, frontispiece, folding pedigree, xxiv, 517, vii, 520 pages, fine gilt decorated pale red calf, very good.   C. P. Hyland   May 26 2011 - 258/953   2011 $362

Cousins, Frank W.   *Sundials. A Simplified Approach by Means of the Equatorial Dial.*   London: John Baker, 1969,   First edition; 245 pages, with 166 plates and illustrations, original boards, gilt, dust jacket rather worn, ex-library with front flyleaf removed and stamps on half title and title.   R. F. G. Hollett & Son Antiquarian Booksellers   General Catalogue Summer 2010 - 90   2011   £65

Cousins, Sheila   *To Beg I am Ashamed.*   Allahabad: Kitabistan, 1938,   First Indian edition; 8vo., pages 285, rare, original publisher's crimson cloth, lettered black on spine an cover, some very slight fading at top and bottom of spine, otherwise sound, clean, very good+ copy in slightly chipped and nicked, near very good dust jacket with inch or more loss at lower spine, still handsome example.   Any Amount of Books   May 26 2011 - A64418   2011 $587

Cousins, Sheila   *To Beg I Am Ashamed.*   New York: Vanguard, 1938,   First edition; 8vo., pages 283, original publisher's blue cloth lettered black on spine and cover, some sun fading at top and bottom of spine, otherwise sound, clean, very good in slightly chipped and nicked near very good dust jacket with slight loss at head of spine, not affecting title.   Any Amount of Books   May 29 2011 - A66360   2011 $272

Coussens, Penrhyn W.   *A Child's Book of Stories.*   New York: Duffield & Co., 1911,   First edition; 4to., dark blue ribbed cloth with gold lettering on cover and spine, full color pictorial paste label with some rubbing to edges of label and bit of shelfwear to covers, internally clean, 463 numbered pages with 10 full page color plates by Jessie Wilcox Smith, uncommon.   Jo Ann Reisler, Ltd.   86 - 235   2011 $400

Cowan, John F.   *The You-Ought-To-Buy-Ography of an Ink-Slinger.*   Hohala: 1915,   First edition; heavy wrappers, lower free corner dog eared.   Bookworm & Silverfish   668 - 36   2011 $150

Coward, Noel   1899-1973   *The Noel Coward Song Book.*   London: Michael Joseph, 1953,   First edition; 4to., original cloth gilt, dust jacket, extremities trifle worn, pages 314, color frontispiece, illustrations in color and black and white.   R. F. G. Hollett & Son Antiquarian Booksellers   175 - 320   2011   £75

Coward, Noel   1899-1973   *Qaudrille. A Romantic Comedy in Three Acts.*   London: Heienmann, 1952,   First edition; 8vo., pages 116, signed by 17 members of the English cast and by producer Jack Wilson and by Lynn Fontanne and Alfred Lunt on dedication page (play is dedicated to them), inscribed by Coward to Dorothy Sands (Octavia in the NY production), two more signed cards by Lunt and Fontanne tipped in and 3 notes by Lunt to Sands laid in, with tipped in signed photo of Sands, nice copy in somewhat chipped dust jacket.   Second Life Books Inc.   174 - 111   2011 $700

Coward, Noel   1899-1973   *The Vortex.*   London: Ernest Benn, 1925,   First edition; 8vo., wrappers, pages 106, signed presentation from author for Viola, loosely inserted is short handwritten signed letter from Coward to same, spine mended with tape and with slight loss at lower end covers slightly browned and very slightly creased and slightly fragile, otherwise good only.   Any Amount of Books   May 29 2011 - A75901   2011 $272

Cowboy Jokes and Yarns.   Baltimore: 1922,   64 pages, 12mo., illustrations by author, near fine in wrappers.   Bookworm & Silverfish   666 - 14   2011 $100

Cowe, Martha   *Witchcraft: Catalogue of the Witchcraft Collection in the University Library.*   Millwood: Kto Press, 1977,   First edition; 4to., pages 644, original publisher's crimson cloth lettered git at spine, about fine.   Any Amount of Books   May 26 2011 - A864805   2011 $545

Cowell, Joe, Pseud.   *Thirty Years Passed Among the Players in England and America: Interspersed with Anecdotes and Reminiscences of a Variety of Persons, Directly or Indirectly Connected with the Drama During the Theatrical Life of Joe Cowell...*   New York: Harper & Bros., 1844,   First edition; disbound, separate titlepage for each part, text in double columns, scattered foxing, very light dampstain to head of few leaves.   Dramatis Personae Booksellers   106 - 41   2011 $85

Cowles, Frederick   *Fear Walks the Night: The Complete Ghost Stories of Frederick Cowles.*   London: Ghost Story Press, 1993,   First edition; number 24 of 250 copies, flyer for the Ghost Story Press loosely inserted, 8vo., pages xiv, 361, original red boards, illustrations, fine in fine dust jacket.   Any Amount of Books   May 29 2011 - A69902   2011 $340

Cowley, Abraham 1618-1667 *Poemata Latinia.* Londini: T. Roycroft impensis Jo. Martyn, 1668, First edition; small 8vo., (36), 420 pages, frontispiece, marginal worm trail, pages 271-420, modern brown half morocco over brown cloth, gilt stamped spine title, very good. John Drury Rare Books 154 - 20 2011 $850

Cowley, Malcolm *Exile's Return: a Literary Odyssey of the 1920's.* New York: Limited Editions Club, 1981, One of 2000 copies signed and numbered by Malcolm Cowley and Berenice Abbott; 9.5 x 6.5 inches, 12 reproductions of contemporary photos, cloth, glassine and slipcase, fine, publisher's letter laid in. Gemini Fine Books & Arts, Ltd. Art Reference & Illustrated Books: First Editions 2011 $85

Cowling, Eric T. *Rombalds Way. A Prehistory of Mid Wharfedale.* Otley William Walker and Sons, 1845, First edition; 4to., original cloth, gilt, dust jacket, pages (viii), 173, (xii), with 20 plates and 70 text figures, scarce. R. F. G. Hollett & Son Antiquarian Booksellers 177 - 216 2011 £85

Cowling, Eric T. *Rombalds Way. A Prehistory of Mid Wharfedale.* Otley: William Walker and Sons, 1946, First edition; pages (viii), 173, (xii), with 20 plates, 70 text figures, 4to., original cloth, gilt, dust jacket, loosely enclosed is 4 page ALS from archaeologist J. Romilly Allen regarding cup-markings to Mr. Fison of Otley, pencilled drawings of 10 stones with cup and ring markings loosely inserted. R. F. G. Hollett & Son Antiquarian Booksellers 177 - 215 2011 £120

Cowper, Henry Swainson *Hawkshead.* Bemrose & Sons, 1899, First edition; large 8vo., pages xvi, 580, original buckram gilt over bevelled boards, little rubbed and faded, top edge gilt, 2 colored folding maps and 32 illustrations, lower joints joint cracking, very good, scarce. R. F. G. Hollett & Son Antiquarian Booksellers 173 - 273 2011 £240

Cowper, Henry Swainson *The Hill of the Graces.* London: Methuen, 1897, First edition; original green cloth gilt, pages xxii, 327, 37 (ads), 898 illustrations, folding plan and large folding map, few spots to prelims, presentation copy inscribed by author to Hawkshead Institute, with his armorial bookplate and Institute library labels. R. F. G. Hollett & Son Antiquarian Booksellers 177 - 217 2011 £75

Cowper, William 1731-1800 *The Diverting History of John Gilpin.* Chiswick Press for Sir Allen and Richard Lane, 1952, Limited to 1600 copies; 4to., original card wrappers, integral pictorial dust jacket, pages 46, tinted illustrations by Searle on every page, near fine. R. F. G. Hollett & Son Antiquarian Booksellers General Catalogue Summer 2010 - 900 2011 £60

Cowper, William 1731-1800 *Memoir of the Early Life of William Cowper, Esq./Cowper Illustrated by a Series of Views in or Near the Park of Weston-Underwood and Sketch of Poet's Life.* London: R. Edwards, 1816, 1804. First edition; small 8vo., full brown leather decorated gilt, pages xviii, 126; 53, frontispiece and 12 plates, clean, very good, plates very clean. Any Amount of Books May 29 2011 - A69176 2011 $255

Cowper, William 1731-1800 *Poems.* London: Published by John Sharpe, 1810, New edition; 202 122mm., 432 pages, volume I only, of 2 volumes, once splendid and still pleasing contemporary dark green straight grain morocco, extravagantly gilt, covers with wide gilt frames featuring interlocking circles and arcs accented with leaves and flowers on densely stippled backgrounds, central panel formed by gilt fillet and multiple blindstamped rolls and with foliate spray cornerpieces on stippled ground, board raised bands dividing spine into five panels, three with large animated central gilt fleuron, two with gilt titling, gilt turn-ins and edges, with excellent fore-edge painting of a bustling Regent Street scene in London; with extra engraved titlepage, 21 engraved head and tailpieces designed by Thurston with five engraved plates designed by Richard Westall, R.A., with engraved bookplate of George Ramsay Feilden, with Feilden's ink ownership signature, spine sunned to light olive, joints and extremities somewhat rubbed tiny chip to head of spine, isolated minor foxing, otherwise excellent copy, binding sturdy and retaining its charm, leaves clean and fresh and fore-edge painting generally well preserved. Phillip J. Pirages 59 - 202 2011 $650

Cowper, William 1731-1800 *Poems.* London: printed for J. Johnson and Co., 1812, New edition; 2 volumes, 168 x 107mm., handsome contemporary crimson straight grain morocco elaborately gilt, covers with border of interlacing circles in blind enclosing a broader frame comprised of two parallel rules, flanking a string of floral fleurons emanating in both directions from square cornerpieces featuring a heavily stippled ground, raised bands, spine panels with gilt tilting or else intricately gilt in an all over pattern with floral centerpiece with dense stippling, gilt tooled turn-ins, all edges gilt, 2 volumes with very attractive fore-edge paintings of Ludlow Castle and of Malmsbury, Wiltshire; minor wear, (as expected) to joints, corners with hint of rubbing, cover very slightly soiled, still lovely set, bindings extremely lustrous and text consistently clean, bright and fresh. Phillip J. Pirages 59 - 203 2011 $2500

Cox, C. B. *Critical Quarterly.* 1959-1990, First edition; volume 1/1-volume 32/4, 120 issues in original wrappers in very good condition. I. D. Edrich May 26 2011 - 82809 2011 $1208

Cox, C. B. *Fight for Education. A Black Paper.* The Critical Quartet Society, 1969, 2 volumes, large 8vo., original decorated wrappers, pages 80, 160. R. F. G. Hollett & Son Antiquarian Booksellers 175 - 321 2011 £65

Cox, Edward Godfrey *A Reference Guide to the Literature of Travel...* Seattle: University of Washington, 1935-1949, 3 volumes, (volumes 9, 10, 12), large 8vo., ix, 401; vii, 591, ads, (4), 732 pages, printed wrappers, wrappers and spine worn with pieces missing (volume I and II only), front cover detached on volume I and rear cover missing on volume II, as is, rubber stamps and markings of MIT Libraries, from the Bern Dibner reference library, with Burndy bookplate. Jeff Weber Rare Books 161 - 99 2011 $100

Cox, J. Charles *English Church Fittings, Furniture and Accessories.* London: Batsford, 1923, First edition; pages xii, 320, with 274 illustrations, large 8vo., original cloth, spine faded, little frayed at head and foot. R. F. G. Hollett & Son Antiquarian Booksellers 177 - 220 2011 £40

Cox, J. Charles *The Parish Churches of England.* London: Batsford, 1943-1944, Fourth edition; original cloth, gilt, dust jacket, pages x, 126, color frontispiece and 148 illustrations. R. F. G. Hollett & Son Antiquarian Booksellers 177 - 221 2011 £35

Cox, J. Stevens *Dorset Folk Remedies of the 17th and 18th Centuries.* St. Peter Port, Guernsey: The Toucan Press, 1970, Second edition; small 8vo., original pictorial wrappers, pages 23, frontispiece. R. F. G. Hollett & Son Antiquarian Booksellers 175 - 324 2011 £30

Cox, J. Stevens *The Peasantry of Dorsetshire 1846.* Beaminster: Toucan Press, 1963, Original decorated wrappers, pages 8, 4 illustrations, scarce. R. F. G. Hollett & Son Antiquarian Booksellers 175 - 325 2011 £30

Cox, J. Stevens *Two Dorset Ballads.* St. Peter Port, Guernsey: Toucan Press, 1969, Limited to 200 copies; Large 4to., original wrappers, 8 pages, folded but unbound as issued, printed on fawn paper. R. F. G. Hollett & Son Antiquarian Booksellers 175 - 322 2011 £65

Cox, James *Historical and Biographical Record of the Cattle Industry and Cattlemen of Texas and Adjacent Territory.* published by Woodward & Tiernan Printing Co., 1895, First edition; thick quarto, calf stamped gilt and blind, (1), 743 pages, color frontispiece, illustrations, plates, portraits, indexes, color frontispiece by Gean Smith. Buckingham Books May 26 2011 - 28880 2011 $9000

Cox, Melville Babbage *Remains of Melville B. Cox: Late Missionary to Liberia: with a Memoir.* Boston: Light & Horton, 1835, First edition; 8vo., pages iv, 240, frontispiece, lithographed facsimile plate, original black cloth, some foxing to prelims. J. & S. L. Bonham Antiquarian Booksellers Africa 4/20/2011 - 8841 2011 £135

Cox, Palmer *Another Brownie Book.* New York: Century Co., 1890, 4to., glazed pictorial boards, slight rubbing to spine ends and front hinge (not weak) else fine, original dust jacket (with pieces off at folds and bottom edge), rare in dust jacket, illustrations. Aleph-Bet Books, Inc. 95 - 169 2011 $2000

Cox, Palmer *The Brownies Around the World.* New York: Century Co., 1894, First edition; 4to., glazed pictorial boards, xi, 144 pages, some mild rubbing to spine ends and edges, else near fine, original pictorial dust jacket (lacks flap and is chipped with only 2-3 tiny chips). Aleph-Bet Books, Inc. 95 - 167 2011 $1000

Cox, Palmer *The Brownies at Home.* New York: Century Co., 1893, First edition; 4to., glazed pictorial boards, fine in near fine dust jacket, illustrations on every page, beautiful copy, rare in such nice dust jacket. Aleph-Bet Books, Inc. 95 - 170 2011 $2500

Cox, Palmer *The Brownies Latest Adventures.* New York: Century Co., 1910, First edition; 4to., glazed pictorial boards, fine in near fine dust jacket, illustrations on every page, beautiful copy, rare in such nice dust jacket. Aleph-Bet Books, Inc. 95 - 171 2011 $1500

Cox, Palmer *Brownies Many More Nights.* New York: Century Co., Sept., 1913, 4to., 144 pages, glazed pictorial boards, endpaper rubbed, else fine. Aleph-Bet Books, Inc. 95 - 172 2011 $1500

Cox, Palmer *The Brownies: Their Book.* London: T. Fisher Unwin, n.d. circa, 1890, First UK edition; 4to., original brown pictorial cloth over bevelled boards, extremities little worn, pages xi, 144, illustrations by author, front joint cracking, flyleaf little creased. R. F. G. Hollett & Son Antiquarian Booksellers General Catalogue Summer 2010 - 510 2011 £85

Cox, Richard *Proceedings of the Commons of Ireland in Rejecting the Altered Money Bill 1743 Vindicated.* Cork: Harrison, 1754, 92 pages, modern quarter cloth, very good. C. P. Hyland May 26 2011 - 259/089 2011 $362

Cox, Thomas *Magna Brittainia et Hibernia. Antiqua & Nova. Volume 4.* 1727, Volume 4 (of 6), 4to., full contemporary calf showing signs of its age, binding still sound, good. C. P. Hyland May 26 2011 - 070 2011 $638

Cox, Thomas *Topographical Historical, Ecclesiastical and Natural History of Cumberland...* London: M. Nutt, 1720, First separate edition; square 8vo., old quarter roan gilt with marbled boards, little rubbed, pages 365-422, folding map, text woodcuts and engraved table. R. F. G. Hollett & Son Antiquarian Booksellers 173 - 278 2011 £150

Cox, Thomas *Westmorland.* London: sold by M. Nutt, 1720-1721, Square 8vo., quarter roan gilt hinges little rubbed, pages 46 with folding engraved map, edge of final leaf (folding engraved chart) a trifle dusty.   R. F. G. Hollett & Son Antiquarian Booksellers   173 - 277   2011   £85

Coxe, Daniel *A Description of the English Province of Carolina by the Spaniards Called Florida and by the French La Louisiane.* St. Louis: Churchill and Harris printers, 1840, First American edition; 8vo., 6, 90 pages, large folding engraved map, modern buckram, folds of map weak and one entirely broken, map complete.   M & S Rare Books, Inc.   90 - 134   2011 $600

Coxe, William *Sketches of the Natural, Civil and Political State of Switzerland.* Dublin: printed by George Bonham for the booksellers, 1779, viii, 478, (2) pages, 8vo., with final leaf of postscript, excellent copy, contemporary calf, spine ruled in gilt, red morocco label, bookplate of N. C. Colthurst, Andrum Co. Cork.   Jarndyce Antiquarian Booksellers   CXCI - 543   2011   £520

Crabbe, George *Tales.* J. Hatchard, 1812, First edition; presentation copy, inscribed on half title "The very Reverend The Dean of Lincoln with respects of the Author" (almost certainly George Gordon who held that position between 1810 and his death in 1845), also signed "Isabella Staunton 1848", pages (xxiv), 398, (2) (publisher's catalog), 8vo., contemporary mottled calf, binder's ticket of Johnston, Lincoln, neatly rebacked, backstrip with five flat bands with gilt Greek key-style rolls, black morocco label in second compartment, rest with central blind tools, corners neatly restored, marbled endpapers, hinges neatly relined, very good.   Blackwell Rare Books   B166 - 25   2011   £350

Crabbe, George *Tales of the Hall.* London: John Murray, 1819, First edition; half titles discarded, ownership signature of A. Webb and initials "P.W." on front free endpaper, pages iii-xxiv, 326; iii-viii, 353, (2) (publisher's ad), 8vo., contemporary polished calf, backstrips with darker banding, panels in gilt, central gilt palmettes and gilt lettering, sides with triple gilt fillet and blind borders, gauffered edges, upper joint volume I just starting to crack, still strong, ex-libris of R. W. Chapman, good.   Blackwell Rare Books   B166 - 26   2011   £160

Crabites, Pierre *The Winning of the Sudan.* London: Geo. Routledge, 1934, First edition; 8vo., pages 280, folding map, original red cloth, dust jacket, very good.   J. & S. L. Bonham Antiquarian Booksellers   Africa 4/20/2011 - 9201   2011   £35

Craig, Edward Gordon 1872-1966   *A Living Theatre.* Florence: School of the Art of the Theatre, 1913, Large 8vo., original pictorial orange wrappers, nick to wrapper at top of spine, one folding engraved plate, many line drawings and text illustrations.   Dramatis Personae Booksellers   106 - 42   2011 $175

Craig, Edward Gordon 1872-1966   *Nothing or the Bookplate.* London: Chatto & Windus, 1924, First edition; crown 8vo., original russet buckram lettered gilt on spine and cover, pages vii, 27 and 50 pages of figures, loosely inserted 2 original bookplates by E. C. Craig, limited edition, no. 33 of 280 copies, this with a further bookplate signed by Gordon Craig, bookplates hand colored, from the library of James Lee Wilson with his small neat bookplate by Leo Wyatt, loosely inserted is a compliments slip from London Mercury 1925 with review of book extracted, spine slightly sunned, very good+.   Any Amount of Books   May 26 2011 - A66401   2011 $419

Craig, Edward Gordon 1872-1966   *The Page. Volume Two. Number Four.* Hackbridge: At the Sign of the Rose and printed by Arthur Chilver, 1899, Limited edition, number 2 of 410 copies); large square 8vo., original brown printed wrappers, overlapping edges trifle chipped, backstrip defective, pages (116), 4 woodcuts with hand coloring, other woodcuts, text printed on rectos only, presentation copy, inscribed by Craig for Anthony Thomas.   R. F. G. Hollett & Son Antiquarian Booksellers   175 - 330   2011   £1200

Craig, Edward Gordon 1872-1966   *The Page. Volume Two Number Four.* Hackbridge: At the Sign of the Rose and printed by F.F. of Croyden, 1899, Limited edition, no. 195 of 410 copies; large square 8vo., original brown printed wrappers, overlapping edges trifle torn and creased, pages (68), 2 woodcuts on Japon paper, 2 bookplates and other illustrations by Craig, but lacks hand colored supplement by him, very nice, crisp copy.   R. F. G. Hollett & Son Antiquarian Booksellers   175 - 329   2011   £350

Craig, Edward Gordon 1872-1966   *The Theatre Advancing.* London: Constable, 1921, First edition; original holland backed boards, pages lxxxvii, 290, uncut, tinted frontispiece, half title and flyleaves little browned, very nice.   R. F. G. Hollett & Son Antiquarian Booksellers   175 - 327   2011   £35

Craig, Helen *A Counting Book.* Aurum Press, 1980, First edition; 32mo., original glazed pictorial boards, lower board trifle creased, pictorial slipcase, concertina with 26 glazed sections on board, all illustrated in color on one side.   R. F. G. Hollett & Sons Antiquarian Booksellers   170 - 158   2011   £45

Craig, Helen *The Months of the Year.* Aurum Press, 1981, First edition; 32mo., original glazed pictorial boards, lower board trifle creased, pictorial slipcase (one side panel little damaged), concertina with 26 glazed sections on board, all illustrated in color on one side.   R. F. G. Hollett & Sons Antiquarian Booksellers   170 - 159   2011   £45

Craig, John R. *Ranching with Lords and Commons; or Twenty the Range, Being a Record of Actual Facts and Conditions the Cattle Industry of the Northwest Territories of Canada...* Toronto: William Briggs, 1903, First edition; 8vo., pictorial cloth, 293 pages, illustrations, plates, portraits, former owner's inked name on front fly leaf, white ink to cover is unchipped but white ink on spine panel is moderately chipped, overall in much better condition than most copies, very good tight copy. Buckingham Books May 26 2011 - ATING TO 2011 $2000

Craig, Maurice *Irish Bookbinding 1600-1800.* 1954, First edition; color frontispiece, illustrations, signed by author with his bookplate. C. P. Hyland May 26 2011 - 255/131 2011 $637

Craig, Robert M. *Our Mexicans.* New York: 1904, First edition; 12mo., 101 pages, frontispiece, some external soil, internally very good. Dumont Maps & Books of the West 112 - 36 2011 $85

Craig, W. S. *Child and Adolescent Life in Health and Disease.* Edinburgh: E. & S. Livingstone, 1946, First edition; original red cloth gilt, pages xvi, 667, with 196 illustrations (few in color), fine. R. F. G. Hollett & Son Antiquarian Booksellers 175 - 331 2011 £30

Craik, Dinah Maria Mulock 1826-1887 *About Money and Other Things: a Gift-Book.* London: Macmillan, 1886, First edition; final ad leaf, light foxing in prelims, original olive green cloth, lettered in gilt, small ink mark on front board, spine bit rubbed, good plus. Jarndyce Antiquarian Booksellers CLXC - 554 2011 £75

Craik, Dinah Maria Mulock 1826-1887 *Alice Learmont: a Fairytale.* London: Macmillan and Co., 1884, New edition; half title, frontispiece + illustrations, 2 pages ads, original pale blue cloth, pictorially blocked in gilt, lettered in gilt and maroon, spine slightly darkened, ownership inscription of Sylvia Marguerite Agnes St. George dated August 1892. Jarndyce Antiquarian Booksellers CLXC - 557 2011 £35

Craik, Dinah Maria Mulock 1826-1887 *A Brave Lady.* Leipzig: Bernhard Tauchnitz, 1870, Copyright edition; 2 volumes in 1, contemporary blue binder's cloth, very good. Jarndyce Antiquarian Booksellers CLXC - 557 2011 £35

Craik, Dinah Maria Mulock 1826-1887 *Cola Monti; or the Story of a Genius.* London: W. & R. Chambers, 1898, First edition; half title, frontispiece + 1 plate, original royal blue cloth, blocked in maroon and yellow, lettered in maroon and gilt, Sunday school prize label, very good. Jarndyce Antiquarian Booksellers CLXC - 560 2011 £35

Craik, Dinah Maria Mulock 1826-1887 *Cousin Trix and Her Welcome Tales.* Leipzig: Bernhard Tauchnitz, 1868, Copyright edition; half title, occasional spotting, original blue cloth, blocked in blind and gilt, lettered gilt, spine little dulled and slightly rubbed, good plus. Jarndyce Antiquarian Booksellers CLXC - 561 2011 £50

Craik, Dinah Maria Mulock 1826-1887 *Fair France: Impressions of a Traveller.* London: Hurst & Blackett, 1871, First edition; tall 8vo., half title, 16 page catalog, occasional carless opening, original brown cloth, bevelled boards, blocked in black, spine lettered gilt, very good. Jarndyce Antiquarian Booksellers CLXC - 562 2011 £125

Craik, Dinah Maria Mulock 1826-1887 *The Head of the Family.* London: Chapman and Hall, 1866, Eighth edition; original dark green cloth, inner hinges repaired, all edges gilt. Jarndyce Antiquarian Booksellers CLXC - 564 2011 £35

Craik, Dinah Maria Mulock 1826-1887 *A Hero. Philip's Book.* London: Routledge, Warne & Routledge, 1862, New edition; frontispiece and 3 plates, 10 page catalog, original purple cloth, blocked in blind, lettered gilt, spine slightly faded, but very good. Jarndyce Antiquarian Booksellers CLXC - 566 2011 £45

Craik, Dinah Maria Mulock 1826-1887 *John Halifax, Gentleman.* London: Hurst and Blackett, 1856, First edition; 3 volumes, 3 pages of ads at end of the first volume and two pages at end of the third; extremely pleasing medium green straight grain morocco, attractively gilt by Bayntun stamp signed on front flyleaf), gilt double fillet border on covers, raised bands, gilt spine compartments with filigree lozenge centerpiece and cornerpiece volutes, blue and red morocco labels, heavily gilt turn-ins, marbled endpapers, all edges gilt; joints of first volume bit flaked (with tiny cracks just beginning), two leaves with neatly repaired tear (one in lower fore margin, other into text but without loss), text faintly browned at edges because of inexpensive paper, but still quite appealing set, decorative bindings bright and almost entirely unworn, text very clean and smooth. Phillip J. Pirages 59 - 269 2011 $950

Craik, Dinah Maria Mulock 1826-1887 *John Halifax, Gentleman.* Leipzig: Bernhard Tauchnitz, 1857, Copyright edition; 2 volumes, contemporary green cloth, very good, without half titles. Jarndyce Antiquarian Booksellers CLXC - 567 2011 £40

Craik, Dinah Maria Mulock 1826-1887 *John Halifax, Gentleman.* London: W. Nicholson & Sons, circa, 1890, half title, 10 pages ads, original green cloth, bevelled boards, blocked in black, lettered gilt, very good, bright. Jarndyce Antiquarian Booksellers CLXC - 570 2011 £35

Craik, Dinah Maria Mulock 1826-1887 *John Halifax, Gentleman.* London: Hurst & Blackett, 1897, half title, frontispiece, vignette title, illustrations, final ad leaf, original dark green cloth, pictorially blocked and lettered in gilt, top edge gilt, very good. Jarndyce Antiquarian Booksellers CLXC - 571 2011 £35

Craik, Dinah Maria Mulock 1826-1887 *Little Lizzie and the Fairies and Sunny Hair's Dream.* Boston: Crosby, Nichols and Co. n.d., 1852-1853, Original blindstamped blue cloth gilt, head and foot of backstrip frayed, first title printed in gilt on upper board, pages 6, general title and contents leaf referring to the title "Six Pleasant Companions", frontispiece little soiled, titlepage and contents leaf referring to the present, numerous text woodcut illustrations, early inscription dated Jan. 1st 1853 (probably date of publication) on flyleaf. R. F. G. Hollett & Sons Antiquarian Booksellers 170 - 465 2011 £75

Craik, Dinah Maria Mulock 1826-1887 *Mistress and Maid.* Leipzig: Bernhard Tauchnitz, 1862, Copyright edition; half title, contemporary half dark green morocco, dark green cloth boards, spines rubbed and slightly worn, good, sound copy. Jarndyce Antiquarian Booksellers CLXC - 576 2011 £35

Craik, Dinah Maria Mulock 1826-1887 *A Noble Life.* London: Hurst & Blackett, circa, 1870, Half title, engraved frontispiece, 4 pages ads, one or two gatherings loose, uncut in original purple cloth, blocked in blind, spine blocked and lettered in gilt, slightly dulled and marked, following inner hinge slightly cracked. Jarndyce Antiquarian Booksellers CLXC - 577 2011 £40

Craik, Dinah Maria Mulock 1826-1887 *A Noble Life.* London: Hurst & Blackett, 1891, Half title, frontispiece, 16 page catalog (1891), original purple cloth, lettered gilt, very good. Jarndyce Antiquarian Booksellers CLXC - 579 2011 £35

Craik, Dinah Maria Mulock 1826-1887 *The Ogilvies.* London: Chapman and Hall, 1855, Half title, slightly browned, contemporary half calf, green leather label, spine darkened, slightly rubbed, armorial crest at centre of front board in gilt. Jarndyce Antiquarian Booksellers CLXC - 580 2011 £35

Craik, Dinah Maria Mulock 1826-1887 *The Ogilvies.* London: Chapman and Hall, circa, 1860, Half title, paper slightly browned, original green cloth, blocked and lettered gilt and blind, slightly marked, faded and little rubbed. Jarndyce Antiquarian Booksellers CLXC - 581 2011 £45

Craik, Dinah Maria Mulock 1826-1887 *Olivia.* Paris: Michel Levy Freres, 1870, First French edition; 2 volumes, half titles, uncut, original printed paper wrappers, very slight wear to spines, very good, clean copy. Jarndyce Antiquarian Booksellers CLXC - 582 2011 £68

Craik, Dinah Maria Mulock 1826-1887 *Poems.* London: Hurst & Blackett, 1859, Frontispiece, engraved title, handsomely bound in contemporary full dark green calf, gilt spine and borders, red leather label, ownership inscription, very good. Jarndyce Antiquarian Booksellers CLXC - 583 2011 £80

Craik, Dinah Maria Mulock 1826-1887 *Sermons Out of Church.* London: Macmillan, 1881, New edition; half title, 4 pages ads, largely unopened, original blue cloth, lettered in gilt, very good. Jarndyce Antiquarian Booksellers CLXC - 585 2011 £50

Craik, Dinah Maria Mulock 1826-1887 *Two Women.* Leipzig: Bernhard Tauchnitz, 1881, Copyright edition; 2 volumes in 1, half titles, contemporary half red calf, gilt spine, dark green leather label, very good. Jarndyce Antiquarian Booksellers CLXC - 587 2011 £45

Craik, Dinah Maria Mulock 1826-1887 *A Woman's Thoughts About Women.* London: Hurst & Blackett, circa, 1890, New edition; half title, 8 pages ads, light foxing in prelims, original dark green cloth, bevelled board, lettered in gilt, very good. Jarndyce Antiquarian Booksellers CLXC - 589 2011 £40

Crais, Robert *The Monkey's Raincoat.* London: Piatkus, 1989, First British edition; fine, dust jacket near fine, price clipped, but with publisher's price sticker on front flap. Bella Luna Books May 26 2011 - t8681 2011 $605

Crais, Robert *Stalking the Angel.* New York: Bantam, 1989, First edition; signed by author, fine in near fine dust jacket, mildly rubbed. Ken Lopez Bookseller 154 - 39 2011 $125

Cram, Ralph Adams *Church Building. A Study of the Principles of Architecture in Their Relation to the Church.* Boston: Small, Maynard & Co., 1906, Original cloth, gilt extra, pages xvi, 227, top edge gilt, untrimmed, with 126 illustrations and vignette. R. F. G. Hollett & Son Antiquarian Booksellers 177 - 222 2011 £65

Crane, Stephen 1871-1900 *Maggie.* New York: D. Appleton, 1896, First hardcover edition, first issue with titlepage Printed in upper and lower case; decorated tan buckram stamped in black and red, ownership signature of artist E. C. Burling, very good, little surface spotting, slight darkening of pale cloth, light abrasion to blank spot on titlepage, few dog ears, tight, clean text. Lupack Rare Books May 26 2011 - ABE4707625697 2011 $300

Crane, Stephen 1871-1900 *Maggie, a Girl of the Streets.* New York: Newland Press, circa, 1930, #6 of 100 copies; signed by artist, Bernard Sanders, very good, 8vo., green cloth, with original etching hand signed by Bernard Sanders, few unopened pages split apart carelessly. Barnaby Rudge Booksellers Art & Architecture & Photography - 017328 2011 $150

Crane, Stephen 1871-1900 *War is Kind.* New York: Frederick A. Stokes, 1899, First edition; 8vo., 96 pages, 22 illustrations, uncut paper, original gray pictorial boards by Bradley, original printed paper, spine and portion of book cover moderately sunstruck, unrubbed, fine, early owner's inscription dated Christmas 1900.   M & S Rare Books, Inc. 90 - 101 2011 $1500

Crane, Thomas *Abroad.* Marcus Ward & Co., 1882, Square 8vo., original cloth backed pictorial boards, corners worn, edges rubbed, pages 56, illustrations in color, occasional spot or mark. R. F. G. Hollett & Sons Antiquarian Booksellers 170 - 160 2011   £120

Crane, Thomas *London Town.* London: Marcus Ward & Co., 1883, First edition; square 8vo., original cloth backed pictorial boards, corners worn, edges rather rubbed, pages 56, illustrations in color, couple of short edge tears, very scarce. R. F. G. Hollett & Sons Antiquarian Booksellers 170 - 161 2011   £120

Crane, Walter 1845-1915 *The Baby's Bouquet.* London: Routledge, n.d., 1878, First edition; square 8vo., original cloth backed decorated glazed boards, little soiled, edges slightly rubbed, pages 56, illustrations in color, flyleaves printed. R. F. G. Hollett & Sons Antiquarian Booksellers 170 - 163 2011   £65

Crane, Walter 1845-1915 *The Baby's Bouquet.* London: Frederick Warne and Co. n.d. circa, 1900, Square 8vo., pages 56, illustrations, original cloth backed pictorial boards, corners worn, rear joint cracked and bottom margin of rear flyleaf chipped. R. F. G. Hollett & Sons Antiquarian Booksellers 170 - 164 2011   £45

Crane, Walter 1845-1915 *The Baby's Opera.* London: Frederick Warne and Co. n.d. c., 1900, Square 8vo., original cloth backed pictorial boards, edges rather worn and chipped, pages 56, illustrations. R. F. G. Hollett & Sons Antiquarian Booksellers 170 - 165 2011   £75

Crane, Walter 1845-1915 *The Bases of Design.* London: George Bell, 1902, Second edition; original cloth, rather worn, spine very faded, pages xviii, 381, top edge gilt, text illustrations, endpapers rather browned, upper joint cracked. R. F. G. Hollett & Son Antiquarian Booksellers 177 - 223 2011   £30

Crane, Walter 1845-1915 *Pan-Pipes. A book of Old Songs, Newly Arranged.* London: George Routledge and Sons, 1883, First edition; oblong 4to., original cloth backed decorated boards, few small frayed snags to backstrip, lower corners slightly worn, pages 52, printed in colors, very good. R. F. G. Hollett & Sons Antiquarian Booksellers 170 - 166 2011   £220

Crane, Walter 1845-1915 *Pan-Pipes. A book of Old Songs, Newly Arranged.* London: George Routledge and Sons circa, 1885, Second edition; oblong 4to., original cloth backed decorated boards, edges little worn, pages 52, printed in colors, first few leaves lightly dampstained in gutters. R. F. G. Hollett & Sons Antiquarian Booksellers 170 - 167 2011   £150

Crane, Walter 1845-1915 *Renascence. A Book of Verse.* London: Elkin Mathews, 1891, First edition, no. 6 of 25 copies (plus 3 for author and 15 for America) o Japanese vellum; 4to., pages (xiv) 164 (1) imprint, (19) blank, with errata slip, numerous illustrations, unopened, some light rubbing to margin of titlepage, otherwise internally fine, loosely inserted into original parchment backed folder of drab boards with ties, gold lettering to spine, upper and lower ties worn, folder extremities rubbed, folds cracked in places, old paper tape mend to lower fold, booklabel of Maurice Watting on inner front cover of folder.   Simon Finch Rare Books Zero - 308 2011   £750

Cranstoun, James *Elevations, Sections and Details of the Chapel of Saint Bartholomew near Oxford.* Oxford: Architectural Society, 1844, First edition; folio, original printed stiff wrappers, with vignette, rather dusty, pages (ii), engraved plan frontispiece (little offset on title), 8 finely engraved plates, endpapers rather spotted and damped. R. F. G. Hollett & Son Antiquarian Booksellers 177 - 224 2011   £160

Craven Pothole Club *Records. Nos. 1-92 complete.* Horton-in Ribblesdale: The Craven Pothole Club, 1986-2008, 92 volumes, 4to., original wrappers, mostly side stapled, illustrations, excellent complete run. R. F. G. Hollett & Son Antiquarian Booksellers General Catalogue Summer 2010 - 1373 2011   £450

Crawford, Iain *The Havana Cigar.* Scolar Press for E.P. Publishing for Hunters & Frankau, 1975, Reprinted edition; original cloth, gilt, dust jacket, pages 27, illustrations. R. F. G. Hollett & Son Antiquarian Booksellers 175 - 332 2011   £30

Crawford, O. G. S. *Aspects of Archaeology in Britain and Beyond.* H. W. Edwards, 1951, First edition; small 4to., original cloth, gilt, pages xvii, 386, portrait and 22 pages of plates. R. F. G. Hollett & Son Antiquarian Booksellers 177 - 225 2011   £30

Crawford, O. G. S. *The Sutton Hoo Ship-Burial. Special Number of Antiquity a Quarterly Review of Archaeology.* Gloucester: John Bellows, 1940, Small 4to., library cloth, original wrappers bound in, pages 112, with 24 plates and 6 text figures, few library stamps. R. F. G. Hollett & Son Antiquarian Booksellers 177 - 226 2011 £40

Crawford, Stanley *Gascoyne.* New York: Putnam, 1966, First edition; signed by author, fine in very good, spine faded dust jacket with modest edge wear, uncommon, signed. Ken Lopez Bookseller 154 - 40 2011 $125

Crawford, W. S. *Synesius the Hellene.* London: Rivingtons, 1901, First edition; 8vo., pages xiv, 585, signed presentation from author to Mrs. Willoughby Dominique, original publisher's maroon cloth lettered gilt at spine, faint shelfwear, else very good+ with loosely inserted flyer with quotes from library reviews. Any Amount of Books May 29 2011 - A45131 2011 $221

Crawhall, Joseph *A Beuk O' Newcassel Songs.* Newcastle upon Tyne: Harold Hill, 1965, First edition; pages xiii, 130, woodcuts, original cloth, gilt, front panel and flap of dust jacket preserved. R. F. G. Hollett & Son Antiquarian Booksellers 175 - 334 2011 £45

Crawshay, Richard *The Birds of Tierra Del Fuego.* London: Bernard Quaritch, 1907, First edition, # 138 of 300 copies; 21 hand colored plates (short tear and crease to margin of a plate, marginal foxing to a plate, small stain to corner of another plate), after J. G. Keulemans, 23 photographic plates, woodcut, colored map, 4to., pages xl, 158, later three quarter morocco with raised bands and gilt decorated panels on spine (little tanned, marginal tanning to text plates, occasional marginal foxing, pencil marginalia to few pages). Raymond M. Sutton, Jr. May 26 2011 - 47880 2011 $2500

Crebillon, Claude Prosper Jolyot De *La Nuit et Le Moment ou Les Martines de Cythere Dialogue.* Londres: Paris, 1755, First edition; 12mo., pages (iv), 291, (i) errata, half title, uncut, wide margins, internally extremely crisp and fresh, original wrappers, catalog excerpts to pastedowns, slightly dusty with short tears and chips at foot of spine, still firmly attached to text block, excellent and completely unsophisticated. Simon Finch Rare Books Zero - 223 2011 £1500

Creeley, Robert *Life in Death.* New York: Grenfell Press, 1993, First edition, limited to 70 copies, Printed accordion fold on Arches, signed by Creeley and Clemente; 8vo., seven original photogravures after paintings by Francesco Clemente, gilt stamped Japanese tea chest paper, black paper chemise, mint, preserved in black linen folding box. James S. Jaffe Rare Books May 26 2011 - 1995 2011 $8500

Creeny, W. E. *Illustrations of Incised Slabs on the Continent of Europe from Rubbing and Tracings.* Norwich: privately published, 1891, First edition; pages viii, 76 with 71 photo lithographed facsimile plates, folio, original cloth printed boards, edges worn and bumped. R. F. G. Hollett & Son Antiquarian Booksellers 177 - 227 2011 £180

Crevecoeur, Michel Guillaume St. Jean De, Called Saint John De Crevecoeur 1735-1813 *Letters from an American Farmer...* London: Thomas Davies and Lockyer Davis, 1783, Second edition; 2 engraved folding maps, 8vo., pages (14), 326, modern three quarter leather over marbled boards, wear to corners and ends of spine, an abrasion to upper corner of front cover, small brown stains to 2 pages, few pencil marks, very good plus. Raymond M. Sutton, Jr. May 26 2011 - 55882 2011 $2000

Crevel, Rene *Detours...* Paris: Editions de la Nouvelle revue Francaise, 1924, First edition; 8vo., pages 104, (i) imprint, frontispiece, uncut, prelims unopened, extremely fresh copy, publisher's wrappers, brown, text in black to upper, lower and spine, short closed tear to hinge to upper panel, author's presentation inscription. Simon Finch Rare Books Zero - 224 2011 £500

Crewe, Quentin *Quentin Crewe's Private File of Restaurants.* London: Quentin Crewe, 1972, Large 8vo., 11 issues from beginning Jan 1972 to Nov. 1972, presumably all published; printed on various colors and thicknesses of paper stock, about 150 pages in all, some wear at punch holes at beginning, otherwise decent, very good. Any Amount of Books May 29 2011 - A74694 2011 $255

Crews, Harry *The Gospel Singer.* New York: William Morrow and Co., 1968, first edition, review copy; 8vo., pages 248, (1) (7) blank, original green cloth, spine lettered and ruled in black and white, original blue endpapers, slight bump to head of spine, top edge lightly and evenly toned, front and rear endpapers slightly faded at extremities, original color pictorial dust jacket printed in blue, light blue and green, author's photos to rear panel, very light wear to hinge, rear panel and rear flap, publisher's review slip tipped in, author's inscription, near fine. Simon Finch Rare Books Zero - 225 2011 £800

Crichton, Michael *Five Patients, The Hospital Explained.* New York: Knopf, 1970, First edition; near fine, very light bumping to spine ends, previous owner's name on front free endpapers, dust jacket near fine, small crease on front flap. Bella Luna Books May 29 2011 - t8442 2011 $82

Crichton, Michael *The Lost World.* New York: Alfred A. Knopf, 1995, First trade edition; octavo, cloth backed boards. L. W. Currey, Inc. 124 - 141 2011 $450

Crichton, Michael *Timeline.* New York: Alfred A. Knopf, 1999, First trade edition; octavo, boards. L. W. Currey, Inc. 124 - 222 2011 $125

Crinesius, Christoph *Babel sive, Discursus de Confusione Linguarm tum Orientalium... tum Occidentalium... Statuens Hebraicam Omnium esse Priman & Ispissimam Matricem, etc.* Nurnberg: S. Halbmayer, 1629, 4to., (16), 144, (4), engraved text, small paper repair to recto of last leaf, ff. T1-2 (contents and errata) bound in prelims, 18th century English mottled calf, gilt, some leaves browned, binding slightly rubbed, from the library of the Earls of Macclesfield at Shirburn Castle. Maggs Bros. Ltd. 1440 - 63 2011 £900

Crinitus, Petrus *De Honesta Disciplina lib. xxxv. De Poetis Latinis Lib.* Lyons: S. Gryphe, 1543, 8vo., (48), 585, (5), device on title, last leaf with device on verso (blank recto), woodcut initials, contemporary limp vellum, yapp edges, lacking ties, from the library of the Earls of Macclesfield at Shirburn Castle. Maggs Bros. Ltd. 1440 - 64 2011 £450

Crisp, Stephen *Several Sermons or Declarations.* London: reprinted and sold by J. Sowle, 1707, Third edition; modern half calf gilt, pages 160, 160, 52, 35, (i), top margins little cropped in place, not affecting text, slight worming in title. R. F. G. Hollett & Son Antiquarian Booksellers 175 - 335 2011 £140

Criterion Miscellany. London: Faber, 1929-1935, First edition; nos. 1-43 (lacking 6 issues only, all in original wrappers as issued, in very good condition. I. D. Edrich May 26 2011 - 86376 2011 $646

Critical Quarterly Poetry Supplements. 1960-1975, First edition; No. 1-16, very good. I. D. Edrich May 26 2011 - 81866 2011 $402

Critien, L. *The Malta Almanack and Directory 1870 to 1888 18 Years.* Malta: L. Critien, Strada San Giovanni, Valetta, First edition; small 8vo., 4 volumes, each about 150 pages, ex-British Foreign Office Library with some slight library markings (occasional stamp, gilt numbers on spine), else very good+, clean set in green cloth with clean text, highly uncommon. Any Amount of Books May 26 2011 - A49680 2011 $587

Crockett, S. R. *Sweetheart Travellers.* Wells, Gardner, Darton & Co., 1896, Third edition; original pictorial grey-green cloth, pages xv, 310, (xxiv), top edge gilt, illustrations. R. F. G. Hollett & Son Antiquarian Booksellers General Catalogue Summer 2010 - 634 2011 £45

Crofts, Freeman Willis *Inspector French and the Starvel Tragedy.* London: W. Collins Sons & Co., 1927, First edition; original blue cloth with red lettering, spine little rubbed, pages (iv), 292, (iv), rather foxed in places. R. F. G. Hollett & Son Antiquarian Booksellers 175 - 336 2011 £85

Crofts, Freeman Wills *Golden Ashes.* London: Hodder & Stoughton Limited, 1940, First edition; moderate wear to cover, non-authorial gift inscription, else very good in fine, bright dust jacket, exceptional copy. Buckingham Books May 26 2011 - 25954 2011 $2500

Croly, George *Tales of the Great St. Bernard.* 1828, First edition; 3 volumes, half parchment, half titles to volumes 2 and 3, ownership inscription by Frances Anne Vane Londonderry, very good. C. P. Hyland May 26 2011 - 255/135 2011 $544

Cromar, John *Jock of the Islands.* London: Faber & Faber, 1935, First edition; 16 photo plates and folding map, pages x, 344, 8vo. original cloth, spine bit faded, endleaves foxed, reading copy, sound. Blackwell Rare Books B166 - 100 2011 £55

Cromie, Robert *The Romance of Poisons: Being Weird Episodes from Life.* London: Jarrold & Sons, 1903, Third edition; original purple pebble grained cloth, blocked in blind, spine faded, few small nicks to leading hinge. Jarndyce Antiquarian Booksellers CXCI - 146 2011 £35

Crompton, Richard *Just - William.* London: George Newnes, n.d., 1922, First edition; small 8vo., pages 248, 4 pages unnumbered publisher's ads, 35 illustrations, slight lean at spine, small neat name on pastedown, red cover slightly soiled, slight splitting at top of lower spine hinge, occasional very slight spotting to text, overall very good, sound condition, better than usually found. Any Amount of Books May 29 2011 - B27575 2011 $221

Cronin, Archibald Joseph 1896-1981 *Hatter's Castle.* London: Victor Gollancz, 1931, First edition; 8vo., 627 pages, original publisher's black cloth lettered gilt on spine, bright, clean, very good+ (front endpapers very slightly marked) in very good bright yellow dust jacket with slight fading and few nicks and chips at head of spine and rear flap, decent. Any Amount of Books May 29 2011 - A75942 2011 $238

Cropper, Margaret *The End of the Road.* London: Nelson, 1935, First edition; original boards, dust jacket spine rather faded, pages 106 untrimmed, few faint spots in plates. R. F. G. Hollett & Son Antiquarian Booksellers General Catalogue Summer 2010 - 750 2011 £30

Crosby, Harry *Transit of Venus.* Paris: Black Sun Press, 1929, Second edition, no. 130 of 200 copies on Holland Van Geler Zonen; small 8vo., pages (x, 62, (i) blank, (1) ads, (1) imprint, (1) blank, unopened and uncut, internally very fresh, publisher's ivory wrappers printed in red and black with illustration to lower wrapper, original glassine, silver and gold slipcase, lightly worn at edges, diminutive library ticket of John Martin (publisher of Black Sparrow Press). Simon Finch Rare Books Zero - 309 2011 £500

Crosland, Maurice P. *Studies in the Culture of Science in France and Britain since the Enlightenment.* Aldershot: Variorum, 1995, 8vo., xxii, various pagination, teal cloth, gilt stamped cover and spine titles, fine, from the Bern Dibner reference library, with Burndy bookplate. Jeff Weber Rare Books   161 - 102   2011 $135

Crosland, Thomas W. H. *The First Stone.* London: published by the author, 1912, First edition; half title, stitching weakening, original blue boards, slightly soiled, lacking spine strip.   Jarndyce Antiquarian Booksellers   CXCI - 618   2011   £55

A Cross Section. The Society of Wood Engravers in 1988. Woolley: Fleece Press, 1988, One of 218 copies (of an edition of 225 copies); printed on Zerkall mouldmade paper, wood engraved titlepage, photo portrait of Stanley Lawrence tipped in, 41 wood engravings, pages (110), imperial 8vo., original quarter fawn cloth, backstrip printed in mauve, pale blue-grey boards with repeated wood engraved pattern by Edwina Ellis, rough trimmed, cloth slipcase faded, fine. Blackwell Rare Books   B166 - 249   2011   £250

Cross, David *I Drink for a Reason.* New York: Grand Central publishing, 2009, First edition; dust jacket fine, signed by author.   Bella Luna Books   May 29 2011 - t9311   2011 $82

Cross, M. I. *Modern Microscopy.* Bailliere Tindall and Cox, 1895, Second edition; original maroon cloth gilt, extremities little worn, short creased tear to cloth on lower board repaired, pages 182, (i), 40 illustrations, joints cracking.   R. F. G. Hollett & Son Antiquarian Booksellers   General Catalogue Summer 2010 - 1103   2011   £40

Crossman, Carl L. *The Decorative Arts of the China Trade.* Antique Collector's Club, 1991, First edition; 4to., original cloth, gilt, dust jacket, pages 462, with 461 plates. R. F. G. Hollett & Son Antiquarian Booksellers   General Catalogue Summer 2010 - 95   2011   £45

Croswell, Simon Greenleaf *Handbook on the Law of Executors & Administrators.* St. Paul: 1897, 685, (2) blank (19) ads, pages, endpapers cracked and still sturdy hinge, f.f.e.p. creased.   Bookworm & Silverfish   667 - 93   2011 $75

Crowe, J. A. *History of Painting in Italy. (and) History of Painting in North Italy. (and) Early Flemish Painters.* London: John Murray, 1864-1872, First edition of first two works, second edition of the third; 222 x 144mm., 3 separately published works bound in 6 volumes, uniformly bound in handsome contemporary dark green pebble grain morocco, lavishly gilt, covers with gilt frame formed by multiple plain and decorative rules flanking a central Greek key roll, raised bands, spines heavily gilt in double ruled compartment with Greek key roll at top and bottom, inner dotted frame with scrolling cornerpieces and elongated central fleuron, turn-ins gilt with multiple decorative rules and floral cornerpieces, marbled endpapers, all edges gilt, 148 black and white plates, two of them folding, pencilled ownership inscriptions of C. M. Brewster, fore edge of one upper board just slightly bumped, trivial imperfections internally, but very fine set, sumptuously gilt bindings, especially lustrous and virtually unworn, text and plates showing almost no signs of use.   Phillip J. Pirages   59 - 81   2011 $1500

Crowe, J. A. *A History of Painting in North Italy.* London: John Murray, 1912, 3 volumes, thick 8vo., good sound set in original gilt lettered dark green cloth, slight wear to dust jackets.   Ken Spelman Rare Books   68 - 105   2011   £75

Crowley, Aleister *The Book of the Goetia of Solomon the King.* London: Equinox Press, 4 Holland Street, 1993, First edition thus; 4to., pages ix, 65, some illustrations, original publisher's black cloth closely printed on front and spine in red, fine in very good+ dust jacket slightly dusty and slightly rubbed.   Any Amount of Books   May 29 2011 - A48701   2011 $221

Crown Classics. Grey Walls Press, 1947-1953, First edition; 37 volumes, all in dust jackets, very good.   I. D. Edrich   May 26 2011 - 96705   2011 $713

Croxall, Samuel *Fables of Aesop and Others.* London: T. Longman, B. Law & Son et al, n.d., 1790?, 12mo., (34), 329, (7) pages, frontispiece, 196 engraved vignettes, light foxing, ink date on titlepage, original full dark green calf, gilt stamped spine title and panels, hinges reinforced, ownership signatures on f.f.e.p, very good.   Jeff Weber Rare Books   163 - 44   2011 $375

Croxall, Samuel *The Fables of Aesop; with Instructive Applications.* Halifax: William Milner, 1844, 12mo., original blindstamped cloth gilt, pages xviii, 296 folding frontispiece and over 100 woodcut illustrations.   R. F. G. Hollett & Sons Antiquarian Booksellers   170 - 173   2011   £65

Croxall, Samuel *The Fables of Aesop with Instructive Applications.* Halifax: William Milner, 1844, 12mo., original blindstamped cloth, gilt, pages xviii, 296, folding frontispiece and over 100 woodcut illustrations.   R. F. G. Hollett & Son Antiquarian Booksellers   175 - 338   2011   £65

Croze-Magnan, Simon Celestin *L'Aretin d'Aguustin Carrache, ou Recueil de Postures Erotiques, d'Apres les Gravures a l'eau-forte par cet Artiste Celebre avec le texte Explicatif des sujets.* Paris: A La Nouvelle Cythere, Didot, 1798, First edition; 4to., pages (iv), 12, 80, with 20 dry points and burin engraved plates by J. J. Coiny after Carnach, top edge trimmed, others uncut, very occasional light spotting, otherwise fine, fresh, wide margined copy, red morocco, elaborately gilt, inner gilt decorations and dentelles, silk and marbled endpaper by S. David (mid 20th century), fine, red morocco and marbled paper chemise, red silk lining, matching slipcase, light shelf wear only.   Simon Finch Rare Books   Zero - 419 2011   £9500

Crozier, Gladys Beattie *Children's Games and Children's Parties.* London: Routledge, 1913, Original pictorial cloth gilt, pages xi, 127, top edge gilt, photo text illustrations, flyleaves spotted.   R. F. G. Hollett & Sons Antiquarian Booksellers   170 - 174 2011   £45

Cruden, Alexander *A Complete Concordance to the Old and New Testament or a Dictionary and Alphabetical Index to the Bible.* London: Frederick Warne and Co. n.d., 1970's, Large 8vo., original blue cloth, gilt, dust jacket, pages xvi, 720, excellent copy.   R. F. G. Hollett & Son Antiquarian Booksellers   175 - 339 2011   £45

Cruikshank, George 1792-1878 *Scraps and Sketches.* Published by the artist, 1828, Oblong folio, title and 6 leaves of plates, tear to lower margin of 3rd leaf not affecting image, contemporary half dark brown morocco, marbled paper boards, dark brown morocco label with elaborate gilt borders, extremities, little rubbed, leading inner hinge slightly cracking, presentation inscription on title to Capt. Marryat RN with best compliments, of George Cruikshank; armorial bookplate of Sir Robert Peel.   Jarndyce Antiquarian Booksellers   CXCI - 147 2011   £650

Cruikshankian Momus. London: John Nimmo, 1892, Limited to 520 numbered copies; 136 pages, 4to., gilt, cloth, top edge gilt, corner bumped, else fine, 52 hand colored plates after George, Robert and Isaac Cruikshank, very scarce.   Aleph-Bet Books, Inc.   95 - 174 2011 $1200

Crumley, James *The Collection.* London: Picador/Pan, 1991, Fine in fine dust jacket, laid in is ANS from Crumley to his editor.   Ken Lopez Bookseller   154 - 42 2011 $350

Crumley, James *The Last Good Kiss.* New York: Random House, 1978, First edition; inscribed by author to Andre Dubus, foxing to top edge of text block, else fine in near fine, mildly spine tanned dust jacket with light edgewear.   Ken Lopez Bookseller   154 - 41 2011 $750

Crumley, James *The Last Good Kiss.* New York: Random House, 1978, First edition; near fine, very light wear, dust jacket near fine, small inkstains on front, signed by author.   Bella Luna Books   May 29 2011 - 2191 2011 $82

Crumley, James *The Last Good Kiss.* New York: Random House, 1978, First edition; fine in like dust jacket, signed by author.   Bella Luna Books   May 29 2011 - 2190 2011 $137

Crumley, James *The Muddy Fork & Other Things.* Livingston: Clark City Press, 1991, Limited to 125 numbered copies signed by author; fine in fine dust jacket, missing slipcover.   Bella Luna Books   May 29 2011 - j1479n 2011 $137

Crump, W. B. *Ancient Highways of the Parish of Halifax. Part VII - The York and Chester Highway Part VIII - Sowerby Highways Part IX Heptonstall and Its Highways.* Halifax: Halifax Printing Co., 1929, Original printed wrappers, pages 115 with 2 plates and 2 folding maps, scarce.   R. F. G. Hollett & Son Antiquarian Booksellers   General Catalogue Summer 2010 - 1374 2011   £75

Csoori, Sandor *Memory of Snow.* Barrington: Penmaen Press, 1983, One of 50 signed copies, in an edition of 750, 8vo., pages viii, 67, signed on colophon by author, Nicholas Koluban and Michael McCurdy, woodcut portrait of author in black paper folder at rear, reproduced on title, paper over boards with cloth spine and paper labels, cover little scuffed and worn at edges and top front cover, otherwise nice.   Second Life Books Inc.   174 - 113 2011 $75

Cudworth, R. *The True Intellectual System of the Universe: the First Part; Wherein All the Reason and Philosophy of Atheism is Confuted and Its Impossibility Demonstrated. (bound with) A Discourse Concerning the True Notion of the Lord's Supper, to which are Added Two Sermons.* London: Richard Royston, 1678, London: R. Royston, 1676. First edition; folio, 2 works bound in contemporary folio rebacked at an early date, worn, spine chipped, some foxing, some minor soiling, generally good, sound copy, pages (22), 899, (1, blank), 84 pages, titlepage printed in red and black, pages (ii), 36, 19th century ownership signature, nice clean wide margins.   Second Life Books Inc.   174 - 114 2011 $2000

Cudworth, William *A Letter from a Brother at London to the Society, Belonging to the Tabernacle at Norwich.* Norwich: printed by R. Davy in St. Giles's, 1754, First and only edition; 12mo., 24 pages, each leaf mounted window style in large 4to. volume, all leaves cut close occasionally touching/shaving letters, engraved portrait dated 1824 mounted as frontispiece, bound as a 4to. volume in late 19th century dark blue half roan over marbled boards, morocco gilt title label on upper cover, spine worn, shaken.   John Drury Rare Books   153 - 33 2011   £275

Cudworth, William *Round About Bradford.* Bradfodt: Thomas Brear, 1876, First edition; original green cloth gilt, nicely recased, pages viii, 534, color extending geological section and large folding map, very neat copy. R. F. G. Hollett & Son Antiquarian Booksellers General Catalogue Summer 2010 - 1375 2011 £85

Cujus *Divorce in 1857: the Talbot Case. Letters by "Cujus".* London: Ward and Lock, 1857, First edition; 8vo., iv, 228 pages, contemporary half calf, neatly rebacked and labelled, good, sound copy. John Drury Rare Books 154 - 42 2011 £175

Culverwell, Nathaniel *An Elegant and Learned Discourse of the Light of Nature...* London: printed by T. R. and E. M. for John Rothwell, 1652, First edition; pages (viii), 215, 172, (iv), 28, 197-212, with separate title to "Spiritual Opticks", pagination erratic in places but text continuous, title little dusty and creased and few old shelf numbers lined through, fore-edge neatly reinforced, library label on reverse, some neat contemporary marginal translations of the Greek quotations. R. F. G. Hollett & Son Antiquarian Booksellers 175 - 340 2011 £650

Cumberland and Westmorland Antiquarian & Archaeological Society *Transactions - Old Series. Volumes 1-16.* Kendal: T. Wilson, 1874-1899, 16 volumes matching half morocco gilt by Turnam of Carlisle, with raised bands and marbled boards, stamped in blind "Westminster Public Libraries" in roundel on upper boards, few old scrapes here and there, top edge gilt, uncut, numerous illustrations, diagrams, text drawings, folding pedigrees etc., all wrappers bound in, handsome complete run of this very scarce, each volume with armorial bookplate of Spencer Charles Ferguson and later label (small stamps to back of titles and few other places). R. F. G. Hollett & Son Antiquarian Booksellers 173 - 287 2011 £2500

Cumberland and Westmorland Antiquarian & Archaeological Society *Transactions - Old Series.* Kendal: T. Wilson, 1883-1897, Volumes 6-14, original grey publisher's cloth, gilt, uncut, numerous illustrations, plans, etc., excellent clean and sound run. R. F. G. Hollett & Son Antiquarian Booksellers 177 - 229 2011 £850

Cumberland and Westmorland Antiquarian & Archaeological Society *Transactions - New (Second) and Third Series.* Kendal: Titus Wilson etc. for the Society, 1900-2005, Volumes 1-100 (complete) second series and volumes 1-5 third series, together 105 volumes, 8vo. and large 8vo., original grey or blue cloth or grey wrappers, volumes 18-20 and 40-44, (ethere nver issued in cloth) and volumes 53-56, 58-63, 65, 70-71, 80-18, 87 and 91 are in wrappers, little wear or staining to some earlier volumes but excellent sound and complete set, complete with all illustrations, diagrams, text drawings, folding pedigrees, etc. as called for, also included are index volumes for the second series 13-25 and 60-89. R. F. G. Hollett & Son Antiquarian Booksellers 177 - 232 2011 £1500

Cumberland Association for the Advancement of Literature and Science *Transactions.* Keswick: R. Bailey and Carlisle: G. & T. Coward, 1876-1893, 17 volumes in 4, modern half levant morocco gilt with raised bands and contrasting spine labels, with a separate volume of copies of the contents page of each volume, in modern stiff wrappers, illustrations, original wrappers bound in, fine in handsome binding. R. F. G. Hollett & Son Antiquarian Booksellers 173 - 290 2011 £550

Cumberland, Richard *The Natural Son: a comedy. Performed at the Theatre Royal Drury Lane.* London: printed or C. Dilly, in the Poultry and G. Nicol in the Strand, 1785, First edition; 77 misnumbered 97 in this edition, (4), 84 pages, nice, clean copy. Anthony W. Laywood May 26 2011 - 21759 2011 $67

Cumberland, Richard 1732-1811 *The Observer.* London: printed for C. Dilly, 1785, First edition; 229 x 140mm. 5 p.l., title leaf a singleton, 414 pages, publisher's original blue paper boards, edges untrimmed, woodcut headpieces and initial; lacking backstrip, boards wobbly (though not quite ready to come off), covers somewhat soiled and abraded as expected, half dozen gatherings with dampstaining (sometimes covering much of the page, but always quite faint), two signatures rather foxed, otherwise very clean internally, with all of the spacious margins intact. Phillip J. Pirages 59 - 26 2011 $275

Cumberland's British Theatre with Remarks, Biographical and Critical, Printed from the Acting Copies as Performed at the Theatres Royal London Volume I. London: John Cumberland, 1826, Volume I, small 8vo., old half calf gilt, hinges cracked but sound, frontispiece, armorial bookplate of George Marton. R. F. G. Hollett & Son Antiquarian Booksellers 175 - 341 2011 £65

Cumbria Amenity Trust Mining History Society Cumbria *Newsletter. Nos. 1-48 complete.* 1981-1996, 4to., side stapled, illustrations. R. F. G. Hollett & Son Antiquarian Booksellers 173 - 291 2011 £75

Cuming, E. D. *Squire Osbaldeston: His Autobiography.* London: John Lane, The Bodley Head, 1926, Thick4 to., original cream cloth, pages lv, 249, uncut,16 colored plates, few spots but good sound copy. R. F. G. Hollett & Son Antiquarian Booksellers General Catalogue Summer 2010 - 1234 2011 £50

Cumming, Roualeyn Gordon *Five Years of a Hunter's Life in the Far Interior of South Africa...* London: John Murray, 1850, Second edition; 2 volumes, 8vo., pages xvi, 386; x, 381, with map, 12 plates, original brown decorative cloth, head and tail of spine worn, internally clean. J. & S. L. Bonham Antiquarian Booksellers Africa 4/20/2011 - 8846 2011 £180

Cumming, W. P. *The Exploration of North America 1630-1776.* London: Paul Elek, 1974, First edition; small folio, original cloth, gilt, dust jacket edges rather creased and torn in places, pages 272, illustrations. R. F. G. Hollett & Son Antiquarian Booksellers General Catalogue Summer 2010 - 1633 2011 £30

Cumming, William P. *The Southwest in Early Maps with an Annotated Check List of Printed and Manuscript Regional and Local maps of the Southeastern North America During the Colonial Period.* Chapel Hill: 1962, Later printing of first edition; ix, 284 pages, illustrations, no dust jacket, else clean and very good. Dumont Maps & Books of the West 111 - 97 2011 $75

Cummings, William *A Bibliography of Anti-Masonry.* New York: 1963, Second edition; 79 pages, wrappers, fine. Bookworm & Silverfish 678 - 75 2011 $75

Cummins, George D. *Living for Christ: a Memoir.* London: Selley, Jackson & Halliday, 1859, Final ad leaf, frontispiece, original full olive brown "bible" calf, decorative floral borders in blind and central motif blocked in black with gilt corner crosses, raised bands, compartments decorated with gilt crosses, brown morocco label, all edges red, very good. Jarndyce Antiquarian Booksellers CXCI - 438 2011 £45

Cunard, Nancy *Parallax.* London: Hogarth Press, 1925, First edition, one of about 42 copies; 8vo., pages 24, uncut, some light spotting, original white boards with illustration by Eugene McCown printed in black, slightly soiled and foot of spine bumped with subsequent creasing and slight warping to boards. Simon Finch Rare Books Zero - 311 2011 £375

Cundall, H. M. *Kate Greenaway Pictures from Original Presented by her to John Ruskin and Other Personal Friends...* London: Warne, 1921, First edition; 4to., original two tone cloth gilt over bevelled boards, dust jacket rather worn, pages 11, uncut, tissue guarded portrait frontispiece, 17 tipped in tissue guarded colored plates, fine. R. F. G. Hollett & Sons Antiquarian Booksellers 170 - 175 2011 £350

Cuneo, Terence *The Mouse and His Master. The Life and Work of Terence Cuneo.* New Cavendish Books, 1977, Limited, signed edition, no. 70 of 250 copies; oblong large 4to., original quarter faux morocco gilt with suede boards, matching slipcase, pages 244, illustrations, mostly in color, very special copy, with 3 ALS's from Cueno loosely inserted, a number of signatures laid in against relevant illustrations and portraits, including Lord Leverhulme and Sir Bernard Waley-Cohen, Lord Mayor of London, both with accompanying letters loosely inserted), Co. Sir Richard Glyn, Sir Lionel Denny and Robert Runcie, the letters are all addressed to Harold Ogden, managing Director of Broughton Moor, Slate Quarries, Coniston and signatures assembled by him. R. F. G. Hollett & Son Antiquarian Booksellers General Catalogue Summer 2010 - 96 2011 £1500

Cunliffe, Barry *Iron Age Communities in Britain.* BCA, 1975, Pages xviii, 439, with 28 plates and numerous text figures, poor quality paper slightly and evenly browned, small 4to., original cloth, gilt, dust jacket. R. F. G. Hollett & Son Antiquarian Booksellers 177 - 236 2011 £60

Cunningham, Eugene *Famous in the West.* El Paso: 1926, First edition; 25 pages, illustrated wrappers, archival tissue repair to verso of front wrapper with tiny chip off top corner, pages evenly browned, two inky fingerprints inside, otherwise near fine, scarce, excessively rare. Dumont Maps & Books of the West 112 - 23 2011 $350

Cunningham, John William *The Velvet Cushion.* London: G. Sidney for T. Cadell & W. Davies, 1814, Fourth edition; 12mo., contemporary tree calf, red label, little rubbed, armorial bookplate of Mr. Eardley. Jarndyce Antiquarian Booksellers CXCI - 149 2011 £40

Cunningham, Suzanne *Philosophy and the Darwinian Legacy.* Rochester: University of Rochester Press, 1996, First edition; 8vo., x, 293 pages, sea green cloth, silver stamped spine title, dust jacket, fine, from the Bern Dibner reference library, with Burndy bookplate. Jeff Weber Rare Books 161 - 104 2011 $100

Cunnington, Phillis *Occupational Costume in England from the 11th Century to 1914.* London: Adam and Charles Black, 1967, First edition; large 8vo., original cloth, gilt, dust jacket, pages 427, color frontispiece, 64 pages of plates, uncommon. R. F. G. Hollett & Son Antiquarian Booksellers 175 - 342 2011 £45

Curie, Marie *O Nowych Clalach Promieniotwdrczych.* Cracow: Jagiellonian University Press, 1900, First edition in Polish; 8vo., pages 23, (i) blank, text illustrations, original printed wrappers, protected in glassine wrapper, spine lightly reinforced with tissue paper, small repair to upper cover, author's manuscript corrections in ink to 3 pages, ink stamp removed from verso of title, very good, rare. Simon Finch Rare Books Zero - 136 2011 £7500

Curling, Joseph James *Historical Notes Concerning Queen's College, St. John's Diocese of Newfoundland 1842-1897.* London: Eyre and Spottiswoode, 1898, Blue cloth with gilt titles to front and spine, pages 101, frontispiece, photo illustrations, 8vo., 9 x 6 inches, cloth worn, paper browned, binding starting to separate.   Schooner Books Ltd.   96 - 27   2011 $125

Curll, Edmund *The Life of the Last Honourable Robert Price, Esq. One of the Justices of His Majesty's Court of Common Pleas.* London: printed by the appointment of the family, 1734, First edition; pages xii, 80, 31, 34, (ii), engraved portrait within the title, title tipped in, first leaf of dedication little soiled, small 8vo., old half calf gilt, spine rubbed and scraped, hinges cracking.   R. F. G. Hollett & Son Antiquarian Booksellers   175 - 343   2011   £180

Curly Heads and Long Legs. London: Raphael Tuck, n.d., 1914, 4to., maroon cloth stamped in black and gold, color plate on cover, all edges gilt, margins of 2 plates neatly repaired, else very good+, illustrations by Hilda Cowham and 12 wonderful bright, color plates, pictorial endpapers and black and whites by Hilda Cowham.   Aleph-Bet Books, Inc.   95 - 165   2011 $800

Currie, James *A Letter, Commercial and Political, Addressed to the Rt. Honble. William Pitt in which the Real Interests of Britain in the Present Crisis are Considered...* London: printed for G. G. J. and J. Robinson, Paternoster Row, 1793, Second edition; name torn from upper blank margin of title, but no loss of text, hole on last leaf affecting 3 words of text, (4), 72 pages, disbound, in this issue final sentence is on page 72 (in two lines).   Anthony W. Laywood   May 26 2011 - 21622   2011 $210

Curry, Patrick *Prophecy and Power: Astrology in Early Modern England.* Princeton: Princeton University Press, 1989, First edition; 8vo. ix, 238 pages, blue cloth, gilt stamped spine title dust jacket, fine, from the Bern Dibner reference library, with Burndy bookplate.   Jeff Weber Rare Books   161 - 105   2011 $75

Curtis, B. R. *Executive Power.* Boston: 1862, 34 pages, wrappers (age soil, tear top front).   Bookworm & Silverfish   678 - 1   2011 $100

Curtis, George W. *Nile Notes of Howadji.* New York: 1851, 320, 6, (4) pages, borders fine, cover and backstrip gilt bright, corners with some wear, rose coated endpapers show some wear.   Bookworm & Silverfish   668 - 42   2011 $100

Curtis, George W. *Prue and I.* New York: 1856, First edition; ix, 214 pages, original binding, library shellac and library number on backstrip and library marks on both pastedowns, with ALS by Curtis (1866) tipped in to a stub of f.f.e.p.   Bookworm & Silverfish   665 - 85   2011 $85

Curtis, William *The Botanical Magazine; or Flower Garden Displayed...* London: printed by Stephen Couchman for W. Curtis, 1795, Volume IX and X, octavo, pages 289-360, (4, 2 blank), 73 hand colored plates, original full tree calf, gilt stamped red leather spine label, front hinge splitting, ownership marks, very good.   Jeff Weber Rare Books   163 - 149   2011 $1200

Curwen, John F. *The Ancient Parish of Heversham with Milnthorpe Including the Hamlets of Leasgill, Ackenthwaite and Rowell.* Kendal: Titus Wilson & Son, 1930, First (only) edition; original cloth, patchily faded as usual, pages (iii), 89, uncut, 7 plates and illustrations, scarce, loosely inserted is circular letter regarding Heron Cornmill addressed to John Marsh, Kendall historian and signed by chairman of governors, Lord Paul Wilson of High Wray.   R. F. G. Hollett & Son Antiquarian Booksellers   173 - 306   2011   £150

Curwen, John F. *The Ancient Parish of Heversham with Milnthorpe Including the Hamlets of Leasgill Ackenthwaite and Rowell.* Kendal: Titus Wilson & Son, 1930, First (only) edition; original cloth, rather patchily faded as usual, pages (iii), 89, uncut, 7 plates and illustrations, flyleaves lightly browned, few spots, scarce.   R. F. G. Hollett & Son Antiquarian Booksellers   General Catalogue Summer 2010 - 1377   2011   £120

Curwen, John F. *The Castles and Fortified Towers of Cumberland, Westmorland and Lancashire North of the Sands...* Kendal: Titus Wilson, 1913, First edition; thick 8vo., original brown cloth gilt, neatly recased, boards rather marked, pages xv, 528, with 80 plates, illustrations and plans, very good, extremely scarce.   R. F. G. Hollett & Son Antiquarian Booksellers   173 - 309   2011   £450

Curwen, John F. *A History of the Ancient House of Curwen of Workington in Cumberland and Its Various Branches, Being a Collection of Extracts...* Kendal: Titus Wilson and Son, 1928, First (only) edition; 4to., original red cloth gilt, spine rather faded, pages (viii), 363 with frontispiece arms, 25 plates, map and text plates, illustrations and pedigrees, extremely scarce.   R. F. G. Hollett & Son Antiquarian Booksellers   173 - 316   2011   £450

Curwen, John F. *Kirkbie-Kendall. Fragments Collected relating to Its Ancient Streets and Yards: Church and Castle; Houses and Inns.* Kendal: T. Wilson, 1900, First edition; original cloth, gilt, small 4to., edges and spine rather rubbed and scratched, pages 455, illustrations, very scarce.   R. F. G. Hollett & Son Antiquarian Booksellers   173 - 317   2011   £250

Curwen, John F. *The Later Records Relating to North Westmorland or the Barony of Appleby.* Kendal: Titus Wilson, 1932, Original ribbed green cloth gilt, pages vi, (i), 428, frontispiece, fine, unopened, scarce.   R. F. G. Hollett & Son Antiquarian Booksellers   173 - 321   2011   £150

Cusa, Noel *Tunnicliffe's Birdlife.* Clive Holloway Books, 1985, First edition; square 4to., original cloth, dust jacket, pages 150, illustrations, fine. R. F. G. Hollett & Son Antiquarian Booksellers General Catalogue Summer 2010 - 961 2011 £35

Cushing, Harvey Williams 1869-1939 *Consecratio Medici and Other Papers.* Boston: Little Brown and Co., 1928, First edition; 8vo., 276 pages, minimal cover edge wear, near fine in very good+ dust jacket, price clipped with chips to spine crown tip not affecting lettering and jacket top corners, mild soil, rare in jacket. By the Book, L. C. 26 - 86 2011 $600

Cushing, Harvey Williams 1869-1939 *The Life of Sir William Osler.* Oxford: Clarendon Press, 1925, First edition; 2 volumes, xiii, (2), 685; x, (2), 728 pages, frontispiece (both volumes), 42 plates, index, original navy cloth, gilt stamped spine titles, little tears to spine ends, previous owner's inked signature and rubber stamp, good, from the Medical Library of Dr. Clare Gray Peterson. Jeff Weber Rare Books 162 - 232 2011 $75

Cussler, Clive *Arctic Drift, a Dirk Pitt Novel.* New York: Putnam, 2008, First edition; fine, dust jacket fine, signed by Clive and Dirk Cussler. Bella Luna Books May 29 2011 - t9060 2011 $82

Cussler, Clive *Black Wind.* New York: Putnam, 2004, First edition; fine in fine dust jacket, signed by both authors. Bella Luna Books May 29 2011 - t8517 2011 $82

Cussler, Clive *Fire Ice.* New York: Putnam, 2002, First edition; fine in fine dust jacket, signed by author. Bella Luna Books May 29 2011 - t4355 2011 $82

Cussler, Clive *Iceberg.* New York: Dodd Mead & Co., 1975, First edition; fine in fine price clipped dust jacket with one tiny rub to top front corner. Buckingham Books May 26 2011 - 28696 2011 $1875

Cussler, Clive *The Sea Hunters II.* New York: Putnam, 2002, First edition; signed by author, fine in fine dust jacket. Bella Luna Books May 29 2011 - t4353 2011 $82

Cussler, Clive *Valhalla Rising.* New York: Viking, 2001, First edition; fine, dust jacket fine, signed by author. Bella Luna Books May 29 2011 - t3419 2011 $82

Custance, Olive *Opals.* London & New York: John Lane, Bodley Head, 1897, First edition; small 8vo., pages vi, 76, 20 ads, two tone grey paper backed boards with printed label on spine and letter O stamped decoratively at each corner, elegant titlepage, internally very smart, minor bumps to corners of boards, generally attractive, near fine. Simon Finch Rare Books Zero - 312 2011 £300

Cutler, U. Waldo *King Arthur and His Knights.* London: Harrap, 1933, First edition; large 8vo., original blue pictorial cloth, pages 237, 8 color plates by W. Hatherell, half title and fore edge little spotted. R. F. G. Hollett & Son Antiquarian Booksellers 175 - 345 2011 £30

Cutts, Edward L. *Parish Priests and Their People in the Middle Ages in England.* London: SPCK, 1914, Original cloth, gilt, extremities little worn, pages xvii, 579, (ii), 21 plates, several text illustrations, scarce. R. F. G. Hollett & Son Antiquarian Booksellers 175 - 346 2011 £40

Cuvier, Georges 1769-1832 *Le Regne Animal distribue d'Apres son Organisation, Pour Servir de Base a l'Histoire Naturele des Animaux...* Paris: Chez Deterville, 1817, First edition; 4 volumes, octavo, uncut in original pink wrappers, printed paper spine labels. Heritage Book Shop Booth A12 51st NY International Antiquarian Book Fair April 8-10 2011 - 34 2011 $8500

Czaja, Michael *Gods of Myth and Stone.* New York & Tokyo: Weatherhill, 1974, First edition; 4to., original cloth, gilt, dust jacket, pages 295, with 101 illustrations. R. F. G. Hollett & Son Antiquarian Booksellers 175 - 347 2011 £50

D

D'Ambrosio, Joe *David.* Sherman Oaks: 1993, One of 25 copies; 254 x 330mm, vii columns, (2) leaves, 57 pages, (1) leaf, opening leaves with striking dovetailed bas reliefs of Michelangelo's sculpture of David, text with a variety of decorations and illustrations, binding of cast paper and white Masonic sheepskin in specially fitted side hinged box of black cloth over archival boards, just hint of soiling to case, otherwise faultless copy. Phillip J. Pirages 59 - 172 2011 $2250

D'Aulaire, Ingri *Abraham Lincoln.* New York: Doubleday Doran and Co., 1939, Stated first edition, first issue with errata slip; large 4to., cloth backed pictorial boards, fine in dust jacket, worn at folds, chipped at spine ends, full color lithos, rare. Aleph-Bet Books, Inc. 95 - 179 2011 $1500

D'Aulaire, Ingri *Animals Everywhere.* New York: Doubleday Doran, 1940, Stated first edition; large 4to., cloth, slight fading, else fine in dust jacket (chipped all along bottom edge with 2 inch piece off spine), on one side of the large accordion folded sheet are beautiful full color lithographs, very scarce. Aleph-Bet Books, Inc. 95 - 181 2011 $600

D'Aulaire, Ingri *Don't Count Your Chicks.* New York: Doubleday Doran, 1943, Stated first edition; folio, cloth backed pictorial boards, fine in dust jacket very slightly worn, but also near fine. Aleph-Bet Books, Inc. 95 - 182 2011 $425

D'Aulaire, Ingri *The Magic Rug.* New York: Doubleday Doran & Co., 1931, First edition; oblong 4to., cloth backed pictorial boards, fine in dust jacket with unobtrusive mend on rear panel, magnificent color lithographs, gorgeous copy of rare book. Aleph-Bet Books, Inc. 95 - 180 2011 $1200

D'Israeli, Isaac 1776-1848 *Curiosities of Literature.* (with) *Miscellanies of Literature.* London: Edward Moxon, 1838, 1856. New edition; each volume with engraved additional titlepage, frontispiece in volume one, one folding plate, text in double columns, few fox marks, pages x, 578; xvi 484, 8vo., uniformly bound in later mid brown calf, spines with red and green morocco lettering pieces, other compartments infilled with gilt arches, few minor marks, very good, handsome pair in unsigned binding, but of superior quality. Blackwell Rare Books B166 - 27 2011 £200

D'Israeli, Isaac 1776-1848 *Narrative Poems.* London: John Murray, 1803, First edition; uncut in original grey green boards with printed title, soiled and knocked at edges, spine partly defective, scarce. Jarndyce Antiquarian Booksellers CXCI - 161 2011 £300

D'Oyly, George *The Life of William Sancroft, Archbishop of Canterbury.* London: John Murray, 1821, 2 volumes, 8vo., pages (iii-xvi, 470; (iv) 446 + engraved portrait frontispiece in volume 1, contemporary russia, spines tooled in gilt and in blind with 3 sets of triple raised bands, lettered/numbered/dated in gilt direct, boards alternatively gilt and blind decorative rooled and ruled with central diced panel, board edges 'broken-hatch' gilt at corners, turn-ins 'Grecian Key' roll gilt, 'French Shell' 'made' endpapers and all edges marbled, 3 color (green white & red) patterned 'flat' endbands, some light foxing, frontispiece offset, joints tiny bit rubbed and front joint volume 1 cracking but strong, signed binding, pink ticket "Warren/Bookseller/ & Stationer/ 19 Old Bond St" at top left of front pastedown of both volumes, ink stamp "Bound by Warren Old Bond St.", from the collection of Christopher Ernest Weston 1947-2010. Unsworths Booksellers 24 - 20 2011 £200

Dagliesh, Alice *A Book for Jennifer.* New York: Charles Scribner's Sons, 1941, (1940); 8vo., decorative cloth, 114 page, fine in rubbed and frayed dust jacket, 10 charming full page color illustrations and with 11 cuts taken from old books, this copy inscribed by Dagliesh. Aleph-Bet Books, Inc. 95 - 389 2011 $175

Dahl, Roald *Charlie and the Chocolate Factory.* New York: Alfred A. Knopf, 1964, First edition, first issue; spine lettering rubbed and little soling on boards, else near fine in price clipped, near fine dust jacket with couple of tiny tears and very slight toning, handsome copy. Between the Covers 169 - BTC331941 2011 $4000

Dahl, Roald *Charlie and the Chocolate Factory.* New York: Alfred A. Knopf, 1964, True first edition (preceding the UK edition by three years), first issue with 6 lines of printing information (instead of five) on final page; octavo, (12), 161, (1) (1, blank) (1, colophon) pages, black and white text illustrations, publisher's original red cloth with covers stamped in blind, spine stamped and lettered in gilt, top edge stained chocolate, mustard endpapers, original color pictorial dust jacket, jacket very slightly browned, shallow crease across top edge of jacket, few small chips and some small short closed tears, longest, about an inch, along top front flap, cloth with one small area of wear along bottom edge of front board, overall near fine in very good dust jacket. Heritage Book Shop Holiday 2010 - 22 2011 $2000

Dahl, Roald *Charlie and the Chocolate Factory.* New York: Alfred A. Knopf, 1964, True first edition; first issue with six lines of printing information (instead of five) in colophon on final page, octavo, (12), 161, (1), (1, blank), (1, "About the Author") (six lines of text plus "About the Author") and colophon (6 lines) pages, black and white text illustrations, original red cloth with cover stamped in blind and spine stamped and lettered in gilt, top edge stained chocolate, fine, in original first issue color pictorial dust jacket, with no ISBN number on rear panel and with price $3.95 on front flap, jacket mildly soiled and has a few light creases and tiny closed tears, overall, in excellent condition.   David Brass Rare Books, Inc.   May 26 2011 - 01597 2011 $6500

Dahl, Roald *Charlie and the Chocolate Factory.* New York: Knopf, 1964, First edition; (correct colophon and no isbn#), 8vo., red cloth blindstamped on cover, fine in near fine dust jacket with slight wear at spine ends, beautiful copy.   Aleph-Bet Books, Inc.   95 - 178 2011 $5500

Dahl, Roald *Going Solo.* London: Jonathan Cape, 1986, First British edition, true first; fine, dust jacket near fine, price clipped.   Bella Luna Books   May 29 2011 - t7674 2011 $82

Dahl, Roald *The Gremlins.* New York: Random House, 1943, First edition; large quarto, (52) pages, one double page and 12 full page color illustrations and numerous black and white illustrations in text, original red pictorial boards with red cloth backstrip, yellow and red pictorial endpapers, corners and board edges little rubbed, otherwise fine, original matching color pictorial dust jacket with $1.00 price, jacket chipped at extremities and with some creasing and few closed tears, inside jacket has been reinforced with brown tape which has caused bit of bleed through staining, previous owner's aviation themed bookplate.   Heritage Book Shop   Holiday 2010 - 23 2011 $1750

Dahl, Roald *The Minpins.* London: Cape, 1991, First edition; pages 48, illustrations in color, 4to., original glazed pictorial boards, dust jacket.   R. F. G. Hollett & Sons Antiquarian Booksellers   170 - 179 2011   £40

Dahl, Roald *My Uncle Oswald.* London: Michael Joseph, 1979, First edition; Pages 208, original cloth, gilt, dust jacket price clipped.   R. F. G. Hollett & Sons Antiquarian Booksellers   170 - 180 2011   £45

Dahl, Roald *Tales of the Unexpected.* London: Michael Joseph, 1979, First British edition, true first; fine, dust jacket very good with light creasing to edges and small scuff on front flap from sticker removal, very good, light creasing to edges and small scuff on front flap from sticker removal.   Bella Luna Books   May 29 2011 - t7122 2011 $110

Dahl, Roald *The Witches.* London: Cape, 1983, First edition; original cloth, gilt, dust jacket, pages 208, illustrations by Quentin Blacke, fine.   R. F. G. Hollett & Sons Antiquarian Booksellers   170 - 171 2011   £95

Dahlberg, Edward *Bottom Dogs.* London: G. P. Putnam's Sons, 1929, First edition, for subscriber's only, one of 520 copies, number 461 of 520; 8vo., pages xxi, (i) blank, (ii) half title, 285, (1) blank, (1) imprint, (1 blank, top edge gilt, others uncut, publisher's black cloth, gilt lettering to upper board and spine, original grey dust jacket, printed in black, spine lightly browned, small chips at head and foot of folds, unclipped, John Martin's (publisher of Black Sparrow Press) book ticket, 2 small bookseller's tickets, previous owner's pencil inscription, fine in about very good dust jacket.   Simon Finch Rare Books   Zero - 226 2011   £250

Daiken, Leslie *Children's Toys Throughout the Ages.* London: B. T. Batsford, 1958, First edition; half title, color frontispiece, 115 illustrations (6), 7-207, (1) pages, original purple cloth, dust jacket, good.   Anthony W. Laywood   May 26 2011 - 21632 2011 $81

The Dainty Book.   London: Henry Frowde, Hodder & Stoughton, n.d., 1915, First edition; original embossed pictorial boards, little soiled and rubbed, pages (48), with 12 full page color plates by Millicent Sowerby.   R. F. G. Hollett & Son Antiquarian Booksellers   General Catalogue Summer 2010 - 574 2011   £75

Dalby, Robert *Robert Dalby and His World of Troubles: Being the Early Days of a Connoisseur.*   London: Chapman and Hall, 1865, First edition; 8vo., original publisher's green cloth lettered gilt at spine, pages vii, 324, with 4 page publisher's catalog at rear, uncut, scarce, handsome, very good copy with slight soiling and slight rubbing, otherwise very good.   Any Amount of Books   May 29 2011 - A36784 2011 $213

Dale, Nellie *The Dale Readers. Book 1.*   George Philip & Son, 1902, Original cloth, little rubbed and soiled, pages 94, with 4 full page color plates and color printed illustrations, some fingering, sound.   R. F. G. Hollett & Sons Antiquarian Booksellers   170 - 169 2011   £45

Dalgairns, Mrs. *The Practice of Cookery.*   Edinburgh: Cadell & Co., 1829, Second edition; small 8vo., old half black polished roan, gilt, marbled boards, pages xxix, 532, prelim leaves little spotted, but excellent copy.   R. F. G. Hollett & Son Antiquarian Booksellers   General Catalogue Summer 2010 - 1104 2011   £750

Dali, Salvador *The Biblical Paintings of Dali.*   N.P. n.p., n.d.: circa, 1970, First edition; wrappers, 4to., beige folder printed in blue containing 35 color plates and two pages index of paintings, rare, very good.   Any Amount of Books   May 29 2011 - A61253 2011 $221

Dalrymple, Alexander *An Historical Collection of the Several Voyages and Discoveries in the South Pacific Ocean.* London: printed for the author and sold by J. Nourse, 1770-1771, First edition; 2 volumes in one, quarto, contemporary speckled calf, rebacked with original spine laid down. Heritage Book Shop Booth A12 51st NY International Antiquarian Book Fair April 8-10 2011 - 35 2011 $18,500

Dalrymple, John *Memoirs of Great Britain and Ireland.* Dublin: printed by Boulter, 1771, First edition; 3 volumes, 8vo., pages lxiv, 237; xv, 400, 152; vii, 276, 294, ex-Biritsh Foreign Office library with few library markings, very slight edgewear, spines sunned else very good. Any Amount of Books May 29 2011 - A67372 2011 $255

Dalrymple, John *Memoirs of Great Britain and Ireland from the Dissolution of the Last Parliament of Charles II Until the Sea Battle of La Hogue.* London and Edinburgh: for W. Strahan and T. Cadell and A. Kincaid, J. Bell and J. Balfour, 1771, Second edition; 285 x 215mm., viii, (4) leaves, 509, (1) pages, originally illustrated with separate appendix not present here; handsome contemporary oxblood morocco, gilt, in style of Robert Payne, expertly and sympathetically rebacked, covers with wide and intricate gilt tooled frame composed of closely spaced alternating palm fronds and lancets, cornerpieces composed of 10 different botanical and geometric tools, flat spine divided into compartments by decorative gilt rolls, each compartment with central floral sprig inside a lozenge of stars, circles and other small tools and corners with curling palm fronds, gilt turn-ins, marbled endpapers, all edges gilt; with fine foreedge painting of Limerick and the River Shannon, as seen from the tower of Limerick Cathedral; early 19th century engraved bookplate of Syston Park and with smaller 20th century bookplate of "A.A.H.", with notation in what appears to be late 18th century hand of John Thorold; half dozen small abrasions to covers with minimal loss of gilt, extremities bit rubbed, occasional minor foxing or smudging, other trivial imperfections, excellent copy, binding solidly restored and certainly appealing, text very fresh, quite clean, generous margins, expert fore-edge painting in fine condition, colors soft but clear, composition especially pleasing. Phillip J. Pirages 59 - 41 2011 $2400

Dalrymple, John *Memoirs of Great Britain and Ireland...* 1771-1773, First/second editions; 2 volumes, viii, 59, 232, 211, xiv, 325, 342, 246 pages + erratum/addendum leaf, contemporary calf (rubbed), some foxing but generally very good. C. P. Hyland May 26 2011 - 258/136 2011 $833

Daly, Carroll John *Ready to Burn.* Museum Press, 1951, First edition; pages 224, crown 8vo., original black cloth, backstrip lettered in silver with design in red, light edge foxing, dust jacket with chip to head of front panel, near fine. Blackwell Rare Books B166 - 134 2011 £350

Dalyell, John Graham *Musical Memoirs of Scotland with Historical Annotations and Numerous Illustrative Plates.* London: William Pickering and Edinburgh: Thomas G. Stevenson, 1849, First edition; 4to., plates, original half morocco gilt with marbled boards, hinges and edges rubbed, pages xii, 300, top edge gilt, engraved title and 40 engraved plates, few tinted, engraved armorial bookplate of John Waldie of Hendersyde, fine, clean copy. R. F. G. Hollett & Son Antiquarian Booksellers 175 - 348 2011 £450

Damberger, Christian Frederick *Travels through the Interior of Africa; from the Cape of Good Hope to Morocco in Caffraria...* London: T. N. Longman, 1801, First edition; 8vo., pages xvi, 299, folding map, 3 hand colored aquatint plates, 19th century brown half calf, very good. J. & S. L. Bonham Antiquarian Booksellers Africa 4/20/2011 - 6933 2011 £225

Dame Crump and Her Pig. New York: McLoughlin Brothers, circa, 1882, 4to., full color pictorial paper covers with dusting and little splitting along spine, 6 text pages, black and white drawing on each page, 6 full page full color illustrations (all printed on one side of the page), designs by J. H. Howard. Jo Ann Reisler, Ltd. 86 - 246 2011 $200

Dampier, William James *A Memoir of John Carter.* London: John W. Parker, 1850, First edition; frontispiece, plates, original dark blue cloth, spine faded, very good. Jarndyce Antiquarian Booksellers CXCI - 114 2011 £150

Dana, James D. *Manual of Geology: Treating of the Principles of the Science with Special reference to American Geological History.* Philadelphia: 1863, First US edition; xvi, 798 pages, original cloth, later backstrip and very glassy new label, few pencil notes, embossed library stamp on titlepage cancelled, over 1000 illustrations. Bookworm & Silverfish 665 - 65 2011 $245

Dana, Richarad Henry 1815-1882 *Two Years Before the Mast: a Personal Narrative of Life at Sea.* New York: 1840, First edition, 2nd issue; (without the dot over the "i" on copyright page and with broken type heading on page 9), 483 pages, extraordinarily handsome 20th century half leather with raised bands and tooling on spine, internally clean, without foxing. Dumont Maps & Books of the West 113 - 30 2011 $900

Dance, S. Peter *The Art of Natural History.* Woodstock: Overlook Press, 1978, First edition; folio, original cloth, gilt, dust jacket, pages 224, illustrations in color and black and white. R. F. G. Hollett & Son Antiquarian Booksellers General Catalogue Summer 2010 - 98 2011 £65

Dangell, M. S. *The Cabinet or Philosopher's Masterpiece Containing a Fore-Knowledge of Future Events.* Philadelphia: reprinted from the Dublin edition, 1824, First American edition?; 24mo., 139 pages, illustrated with cyphers, disbound, title loose, soiled & chipped, early ink inscription "Miss L. P. Holland's Book for Rev. F. W.", corners turned and hand soiling in text.   M & S Rare Books, Inc.   90 - 135   2011 $500

Daniel, Gabriel *Histoire De La Milice Francoise.* Paris: Denis Mariette et al, 1721, First edition; 2 volumes, 280 x 204mm., very attractive late 18th century tree calf, handsomely gilt, raised bands, spine compartments with dense gilt field featuring undulant strapwork floral stamps, each spine with two red morocco labels, yellow edges, device on titlepage of both volumes, vignette headpieces, floral tailpieces, foliated initials and 70 full page engraved plates; front pastedown of each volume with armorial bookplate of Lt. Gen. G. L. Parker (4th Earl of Macclesfield), first endpaper with similar armorial bookplate of Macclesfield library, first two leaves of volume I and first three leaves of volume II with small embossed Macclesfield stamp; bit of rubbing where bands intersect with joints, rear joint of first volume with crack just alongside top compartment (and spine end slightly torn), minor wear at extremities, few trivial abrasions, extremely pretty bindings in generally excellent condition, entirely solid with lustrous leather and bright gilt, number of gatherings faintly mottled or with overall light browning, one plate with stain in margin, three marginal tears (one of them, three inches long, neatly mended), handful of other trivial faults, still quite appealing internally, leaves clean and especially fresh, despite flaws, very pleasing set.   Phillip J. Pirages   59 - 27   2011 $2500

Daniel, John W. *A Treatise on the Law of Negotiable Instruments.* New York: 1876, First edition; 2 volumes, large 8vo., full old law calf, about 1500 pages, very good.   Bookworm & Silverfish   665 - 83   2011 $225

Dannreuther, Edward *Musical Ornamentation.* New York: Kalmus, Complete in one volume, 4to., pages 210, 185, paper wrappers, owner's name on cover, edges slightly spotted and spine little worn, else very good, tight copy.   Second Life Books Inc.   174 - 115   2011 $75

Dante Alighieri *The Divine Comedy of Dante Alghieri.* New York: 1915, 4 volumes, extremely good in three quarter leather & chocolate cloth, backstrips extra nice, top edges of backstrip very mildly chafed.   Bookworm & Silverfish   678 - 42   2011 $225

Dante Alighieri *Lo Inferno. (and) Lo Purgatorio. (and) Lo Paradiso.* Ashendene Press, 1902, 1904. 1905. One of 150 copies on paper; (there were also vellum copies of each: 14, 20 and 20 respectively), 200 x 145mm., 3 separately issued volumes, publisher's flexible white vellum, gilt titling on spines, original green silk ties, initials and paragraph marks hand painted in red, blue and green or gold, woodcut device in colophon of each volume, 43 fine woodcut vignettes in text, these cuts copied from a Venetian incunabular edition of Dante; vellum, as always with slight variations in color and with its grain apparent (two of the volume hardly affected but the third with one cover having an overall tan appearance because of the grain), in all other ways, very fine set internally.   Phillip J. Pirages   59 - 77   2011 $22,500

Danziger, James *Beaton.* London: Secker & Warburg, 1980, First edition; 4to., 256 pages, illustrations in black and white, loosely inserted is signed letter in Cecil Beaton's slightly shaky post stroke handwriting for Mr. Ross, about fine in very good+ dust jacket, very slightly rubbed and creased.   Any Amount of Books   May 29 2011 - A48172   2011 $230

Darell, William *The History of Dover Castle.* London: printed for S. Hooper, 1786, 4to., pages (ii), vi, 68 + engraved title, engraved frontispiece, double page engraved plan mounted on stub and another 7 engraved plates, contemporary diced Russia, boards decorative roll gilt (interweaving frond and graded pebbles) bordered, board edges decorative roll gilt, turn-ins decorative roll (alternating metope between quadraglyphs and pearl necklace) gilt, 'Gloster' 'made' endpapers, green silk page marker, early 21st century reback + corners by Chris Weston, some foxing and offsetting, little sunning to spine, from the collection of Christopher Ernest Weston 1947-2010.   Unsworths Booksellers   24 - 84   2011   £200

Darley, Felix Octavius Carr 1822-1888 *Illustrations of the Legend of Sleepy Hollow.* New York: 1849, Folio, 16 (6) plates pages, folio, front wrapper with smoke stains, expected foxing and fraying, two quarter size brown spots begin at front wrapper, diminished by last plate.   Bookworm & Silverfish   676 - 12   2011 $75

Darley, Lionel *Book-binding Then & Now.* London: Faber & Faber, 1959, First edition; pages 126, 19 plates, original cloth, gilt, dust jacket, flyleaves partly and lightly browned, else fine.   R. F. G. Hollett & Son Antiquarian Booksellers   General Catalogue Summer 2010 - 99   2011   £50

Darling, F. Fraser *The Seasons & The Woodman.* Cambridge: University Press, 1945, Large 8vo., original pictorial boards, dust jacket, closed edge tear at foot of spine, pages 70, 50 drawings in black and white.   R. F. G. Hollett & Sons Antiquarian Booksellers   170 - 694   2011   £35

Darlings of the Gods in Music Hall, Revue and Musical Comedy. Alston Rivers, 1929, First edition; pages 80, caricatures printed in monochrome or red and black on card leaves, large 4to., original cloth backed pictorial boards, little soiled, edges of cloth, trifle frayed, the composite cartoon on front endpapers annotated in pencil with numerous names or initials. R. F. G. Hollett & Son Antiquarian Booksellers 175 - 1013 2011 £120

Darrah, H. Z. *Sport in the Highlands of Kashmir.* London: Rowland Ward, 1898, First edition; large 8vo., pages xviii, 506 2 folding maps (in envelope at rear), 52 illustrations, original publisher's maroon cloth lettered gilt at spine, 'Zebra skin' endpapers with ducal Woburn Abbey bookplate, very good, clean. Any Amount of Books May 26 2011 - A74330 2011 $671

Darrell, William *The Lay-Mans Opinion, Sent in a Private Letter to a Considerable Divine of the Church of England.* London: printed in the year, 1687, First edition; 4to., printer's woodcut device on title, 8 pages, disbound. Anthony W. Laywood May 26 2011 - 19360 2011 $109

Darrow, Clarence Seward 1857-1938 *Story of My Life.* New York: Charles Scribners, 1932, First edition, limited to 295 copies signed by author, this being number 143; octavo, color frontispiece after pastel drawing by Leonebel Jacobs and 23 illustrations and photo plates, quarter beige cloth over brown patterned paper boards, red morocco spine label, lettered in gilt, fore-edge and bottom edge uncut, spine lightly browned, new endpapers, previous owner's bookplate, very good, clean, housed in patterned paper slipcase. Heritage Book Shop Holiday 2010 - 24 2011 $1000

Darsi, H. Jackson *Antebellum Virginia Disciples.* Richmond: 1959, First edition; 247 pages, original binding, frontispiece, minor rubbing at edges. Bookworm & Silverfish 662 - 46 2011 $60

Darstellung der Funf Weltheile. Stuttgart: Fried. G. Schutz circa, 1820, 7 x 4 3/4 inches, marbled slipcase with three panel unit has marbled sides and printed pastedown materials on all sides, in the middle is wonderful section that has pull-out panorama, each panel of which is hand colored lithograph, some wear and some of the joints have been taped but basically it is intact, complete. Jo Ann Reisler, Ltd. 86 - 96 2011 $5500

Darton, E. J. Harvey *Tales of The Canterbury Pilgrims...* Wells, Gardner, Darton & Co. n.d., 1904, First edition; original black cloth, gilt, upper board and spine decorated in gilt overall with pilgrim on horseback, pages xxiv, 365, (xxiv), top edge gilt, illustrations, most attractive copy. R. F. G. Hollett & Son Antiquarian Booksellers General Catalogue Summer 2010 - 914 2011 £60

Darwin, Charles Robert 1809-1882 *Charles Darwin's Zoology Notes & Specimen Lists from H.M.S. Beagle.* Cambridge: Cambridge University Press, 2000, 4to., xxxiv, 430 pages, text figures, teal cloth, silver stamped spine title, dust jacket, fine, from the Bern Dibner reference library, with Burndy bookplate. Jeff Weber Rare Books 161 - 107 2011 $130

Darwin, Charles Robert 1809-1882 *The Descent of Man and Selection in Relation to Sex.* London: John Murray, 1871, First edition, 2nd issue (1.297 first word -When; II. titlepage verso - list of titles); no publisher's ads, half leather over marbled boards, matching marbled endpapers and page edges, gilt decoration and lettering on brown and green leather spine labels, slight wear to corners and edges, handful of pages affected by small brown blemishes, but overall excellent clean text, without foxing or annotation, very pleasing set to handle, each volume pastedown bears armorial bookplate of Arthur G. Soames. Any Amount of Books May 26 2011 - A76467 2011 $805

Darwin, Charles Robert 1809-1882 *The Foundations of the Origin of Species, A Sketch Written in 1842...* Cambridge: printed at the University Press, 1909, First printing; 8vo., pages xxii, 53, plus frontispiece and 1 plate, uncut, internally fine, original grey paper covered boards, vellum spine, upper board with text and coat of arms in black, bumped with light shelfwear, presentation copy to Prof. W. H. Bragg, label of H. F. Norman. Simon Finch Rare Books Zero - 141 2011 £450

Darwin, Charles Robert 1809-1882 *Narrative of the Surveying Voyages of His Majesty's Ships Adventure and Beagle Between the Years 1826 and 1836.* London: Henry Colburn, 1839, First edition; 8vo., pages xxviii, (4), 597; xiv, (1), 694, (1); viii, (2), 352; xiv, 629, (609-)615 index, modern navy full morocco with gilt lettering of spines, reminiscent of original gilt lettering, occasional foxing, brown streak on two pages, overall text clean, bindings very attractive, edges of pages and endpapers marbled. Raymond M. Sutton, Jr. May 26 2011 - 36930 2011 $22,000

Darwin, Charles Robert 1809-1882 *A Naturalist's Voyage. Journal of Researches into the Natural History and Geology of the Countries visited During the Voyages of H.M.S. "Beagle" Round the World...* London: John Murray, 1890, Later edition; small 8vo., xi, 500 pages, frontispiece, additional engraved portrait loosely inserted, original green cloth, gilt stamped cover ornament and spine title, ANS by Darwin glued to verso of titlepage and dedication page, ink stamp of D. N. Van Pelt, very good, with Darwin's signature written on slip of paper 200 x 72mm, mounted inside volume, additional engraved portrait of Darwin loosely inserted, from the Bern Dibner reference library, with Burndy bookplate, inscription " to my dear grandson Nevill Forbes, from E.F.". Jeff Weber Rare Books 161 - 106 2011 $5000

Darwin, Charles Robert 1809-1882 *On the Origin of Species by Means of Natural Selection.* New York: D. Appleton and Co., 1860, First American edition, third issue "Revised Edition" on titlepage and 3 quotations on verso of half title; octavo, (1)-432 pages, original pebbled brown cloth with covers decoratively stamped in blind, spine lettered in gilt, yellow coated endpapers, bit of fraying to top and bottom of spine, spine lightly sunned, previous owner's pencil signature on front free endpaper, some light intermittent foxing, overall very nice, better than usual.   Heritage Book Shop   Holiday 2010 - 25   2011 $3500

Darwin, Charles Robert 1809-1882 *The Variation of Animals and Plans Under Domestication.* London: John Murray, 1868, First edition, 2nd issue; 2 volumes, modern full bottle green levant morocco gilt with raised bands and spine label, pages viii, 412; viii, 486; with 43 text woodcuts, lacks ad, most handsome set.   R. F. G. Hollett & Son Antiquarian Booksellers   General Catalogue Summer 2010 - 962   2011   £1200

Darwin, Charles Robert 1809-1882 *The Zoology of the Voyage of H. M. S. Beagle.* Club Internacional del Libro for the Geographical Society, 1994, Facsimile edition, no. 196 of 1000 sets; 4 volumes, 4to., original half morocco gilt extra with marbled boards, presented in oak display case, sides panelled in black and gilt, top bearing brass hinged and ratcheted lectern with shaped sides, whole preserved in original brass bound plywood box, back board of case with slight crack, otherwise excellent condition, fine set, 82 color plates and 85 black and white plates, silk marker to each volume.   R. F. G. Hollett & Son Antiquarian Booksellers   General Catalogue Summer 2010 - 963   2011   £650

Darwin, Erasmus 1731-1802 *Phytologia or the Philosophy of Agriculture and Gardening.* printed for J. Johnson, 1800, 4to., old half calf gilt, corners bruised, pages viii, 89-612, (xii), 12 copper engraved plates (one with short tear) lacks pages 1-88 of text, small piece torn out of P2 affecting 32 lines of text, signature of (Richard) Lovell Edgeworth.   R. F. G. Hollett & Son Antiquarian Booksellers   General Catalogue Summer 2010 - 964   2011   £350

Dasent, George Webbe *The Story of Burnt Nial or Life in Iceland at the End of the Tenth Century.* Edinburgh: Edmonston and Douglas, 1861, First edition; 2 volumes, original decorated cloth, gilt extra, edges trifle bumped in places, pages xxx, cciv, 256; xii, 507, 2 engraved frontispieces and 5 maps and plans, few spots, attractive set.   R. F. G. Hollett & Son Antiquarian Booksellers   175 - 351   2011   £180

Dashwood, Richard Lewes *Chiploquorgan; Or Life by the Camp Fire in the Dominion of Canada and Newfoundland.* London: Simpkin Marshall, 1872, New edition; brown cloth with gold title and vignette on front board, pages (4), 293, half title, frontispiece, 8vo., cloth worn, spine torn along top interior, good.   Schooner Books Ltd.   96 - 284   2011 $125

Dasnoy, Albert *Gods & Men.* London: Harvill Press, 1947, First UK edition; original cloth, dust jacket, pages viii, 122, with line drawings by Charles Lepiae.   R. F. G. Hollett & Son Antiquarian Booksellers   175 - 352   2011   £30

Daumier, Honore *Types Parisiens.* Paris: Chez Bauger for La Charivari, 1838-1843, 2 folio volumes, 50 original black and white lithographed prints 260 x 345mm, numbered 1-50, mounted on stubs, lithography by Chez Aubert, bound ca. 1940 in quarter black calf over faux black morocco cloth, gilt tooled borders, gilt decorated spine, with stamp of the prominent Daumier collector Count Aldo Borletti del'Acqua d'Arosio to the verso of each print, remarkable set in superb condition, with only a few prints exhibiting the lightest of spotting to their margins.   David Brass Rare Books, Inc.   May 26 2011 - 01409   2011 $15,000

Davenant, William 1606-1668 *The Works of Sr. William Davenant Kt. Consisting of those Which were Formerly printed and Those which He Design'd for the Press...* London: by T. N. for Henry Herringman, 1673, First collected edition; folio, (8), 402, (4), 486, 111 pages, portrait, turn-of-the-century red levant morocco, gilt arabesque centerpiece on covers, all edges gilt by Riviere, very skillfully rebacked, though new leather at joints and on cords has uniformly faded, unusually fine, fresh, wide margined copy, fine impression of portrait, leather tipped fleece lined slipcase, edges rubbed, Duke of Beaufort, E. F. Leo, A. E, Newton, with their bookplates.   Joseph J. Felcone Inc.   Fall Miscellany 2010 - 37   2011 $2200

Davenport, Cyril *Cameos.* London: Seeley & Co., 1900, 4to., 8 color plates and 20 monochromes, 6 pages publisher's ads at rear, very good, maroon cloth.   Barnaby Rudge Booksellers   Art & Architecture & Photography - 016616   2011 $85

Davenport, Cyril *The English Regalia.* London: Kegan Paul etc., 1897, Limited edition, number 208 of 500 copies; 4to., original buckram gilt, spine rather faded, 2 small spots to upper board, pages xiii, 66, 12 color plates.   R. F. G. Hollett & Son Antiquarian Booksellers   175 - 352   2011   £120

Davenport, R. A. *A Dictionary of Biography: Comprising the Most Eminent Characters of all Ages, Nations and Professions.* Exeter: 1839, Stated first American edition; 527 pages browned, owner's name, rebound in serviceable cloth, thus tight.   Dumont Maps & Books of the West   111 - 98   2011 $75

Davey, Arthur *The Defence of Ladysmith.* Houghton: The Brenthurst Press, 1983, First edition; 4to., 275 pages, copiously illustrated in color and black and white, fine in very good+ dust jacket with slight edgewear.   Any Amount of Books   May 29 2011 - A45930   2011 $204

David, Rosalie *Evidence Embalmed.* Manchester: Manchester University Press, 1984, First edition; original cloth, gilt, dust jacket price clipped, pages 175, well illustrated, uncommon. R. F. G. Hollett & Son Antiquarian Booksellers 177 - 245 2011 £40

Davidson, D. *The Great Pyramid - Its Divine Message.* London: Williams and Norgate, 1925, Second edition; small folio, original black cloth gilt, neatly rebacked, pages xxxii, 568, double page frontispiece, 70 plates and 67 tables and diagrams, many folding, (1 very heavily annotated by former owner, Rev. Maurice Darwin of Bury St. Edmunds, with relevant ALS from him loosely inserted July 1958). R. F. G. Hollett & Son Antiquarian Booksellers 177 - 246 2011 £140

Davidson, James *The History of Newenham Abbey in the County of Devon.* London: Longman and Co., 1843, v (i) 250 pages + ad leaf, 5 lithograph plates, plan, 8vo., very good in original blind and gilt stamped black cloth, slight wear to joints. Ken Spelman Rare Books 68 - 167 2011 £75

Davies-Shiel, Mike *Watermills of Cumbria.* Dalesman Publications, 1978, First edition; pages 120, over 50 plans and diagrams, half title price clipped, original pictorial stiff wrappers, scarce. R. F. G. Hollett & Son Antiquarian Booksellers 177 - 250 2011 £45

Davies, E. A. *An Account of the Formation and Early Years of the Westminster Fire Office.* London: Country Life, 1952, First edition; large 8vo., original cloth, gilt, dust jacket, pages 90, with 20 plates, including tipped in color frontispiece. R. F. G. Hollett & Son Antiquarian Booksellers 175 - 355 2011 £30

Davies, Edward *Celtic Researches on the Origins, Traditions & Language of the Ancient Britons...* London: printed for the author, 1804, First edition; old full polished tan calf gilt, few small old scrapes, hinges little rubbed, pages lxxiii, 561, 2 engraved plates of runes, 1 leaf torn without loss, otherwise an excellent copy, scarce. R. F. G. Hollett & Son Antiquarian Booksellers 175 - 356 2011 £180

Davies, Edward *The Mythology and Rites of the British Druids.* London: Booth, 1800, First edition; quarter cloth, xvi, 642, 6 pages, untrimmed, plate as frontispiece, owner inscribed by A. Abell, well known Cork Antiquary, very good. C. P. Hyland May 26 2011 - 255/153 2011 $362

Davies, Ellis *The Prehistoric and Roman remains of Denbighshire.* Cardiff: privately printed for th author by William Lewis, 1929, First edition; tall 8vo., original green cloth, gilt, pages xxvi, 464, with 200 illustrations and folding map. R. F. G. Hollett & Son Antiquarian Booksellers 177 - 248 2011 £75

Davies, Hunter *Wainwright. The Biography.* London: Michael Joseph, 1995, First edition; original cloth, gilt, dust jacket, pages xi, 356, well illustrated. R. F. G. Hollett & Son Antiquarian Booksellers 173 - 325 2011 £40

Davies, Hunter *A Walk Around the Lakes.* London: Weidenfeld and Nicolson, 1979, First edition; original cloth, gilt, dust jacket, pages xii, 339, with 21 illustrations, line drawing, scarce. R. F. G. Hollett & Son Antiquarian Booksellers 173 - 327 2011 £60

Davies, Hunter *William Wordsworth. A Biography.* London: Weidenfeld & Nicolson, 1980, First edition; original cloth, gilt, dust jacket, pages xiii, 367, with 26 plates, signed by author. R. F. G. Hollett & Son Antiquarian Booksellers 173 - 328 2011 £35

Davies, Robertson *The Lyre of Orpheus.* London: Limited Editions, 1988, True first edition; one of 150 copies signed by author, cloth, glassine dust jacket, new condition. Gemini Fine Books & Arts, Ltd. Art Reference & Illustrated Books: First Editions 2011 $120

Davies, Robertson *Murther and Walking Spirits.* Franklin Library, 1991, First American edition; signed by author, leather bound, in new condition. Gemini Fine Books & Arts, Ltd. Art Reference & Illustrated Books: First Editions 2011 $95

Davies, W. J. K. *The Ravenglass & Eskdale Railway.* New York: Augustus M. Kelley, 1968, First US edition; original cloth, gilt, dust jacket, extremities trifle rubbed, pages 204 with color frontispiece, 51 illustrations and 18 text drawings and facsimiles. R. F. G. Hollett & Son Antiquarian Booksellers 173 - 330 2011 £35

Davila, Enrico Caterino T *The Historie of the Civill Warres of France.* 1647, First edition; extremely attractive copy, free from foxing, well bound in half calf with hand marbled boards, front board loose, thick folio. I. D. Edrich May 26 2011 - 59106 2011 $419

Davis, Adelle *Optimum Health.* Los Angeles: 1935, First edition; 247 pages, 12mo., very good in orange cloth, modest ex-library, inscribed and signed by author. Bookworm & Silverfish 670 - 91 2011 $150

Davis, F. Hadland *Myths and Legends of Japan.* London: George G. Harrap, 1912, First edition; original blue ribbed cloth gilt, spine and edges little rubbed and cockled, pages 432, top edge gilt, 32 color plates by Evelyn Paul, joints tender. R. F. G. Hollett & Son Antiquarian Booksellers 175 - 357 2011 £35

Davis, George E. *Practical Microscopy.* W. H. Allen and Co., 1889, Revised edition; original pictorial blue cloth gilt, pages viii, 436, tissue guarded color frontispiece and 310 illustrations.   R. F. G. Hollett & Son Antiquarian Booksellers   General Catalogue Summer 2010 - 1105   2011   £50

Davis, Lindsey *The Silver Pigs.* London: Sidgwick & Jackson, 1989, First edition; 8vo., 270 pages, very slight creasing to edges, no sun faint to dust jacket, overall fine in like dust jacket.   Any Amount of Books   May 26 2011 - A72602   2011 $419

Davis, Lindsey *Silver Pigs.* New York: Crown, 1989, First edition; near fine, light bumping to top of spine, dust jacket near fine with corresponding creases.   Bella Luna Books   May 29 2011 - t5981   2011 $77

Davis, Martha Ann *Poems of Laura: an Original American Work.* Petersburg: Whitworth and Yancey, 1818, First edition; 12mo., 106, iv page, contemporary calf, red morocco spine label, early owner's name, label largely chipped away, attractive, very good copy, handsome copy.   Between the Covers   169 - BTC342592   2011 $1750

Davis, Michael Justin *To the Cross. A Sequence of Dramatic Poems for Holy Week.* Marlborough, Wiltshire: Paulinus Press, 1984, 81/75 copies (of an edition of 100 copies); printed on Zerkall mouldmade paper and signed by author and artist, 19 wood engravings in text by Simon Brett, titlepage printed in black and mauve, pages xiv, 58, tall crown 8vo., original quarter mauve cloth, backstrip gilt lettered, boards with overall mauve and white design taken from one of the book's engravings, all edges rough trimmed, fine.   Blackwell Rare Books   B166 - 269   2011   £100

Davis, N. *Carthage and Her Remains...* London: Richard Bentley, 1861, First edition; 8vo., pages xvi 631, folding map, illustrations, contemporary full brown polished calf (Eton binding) spine faded, very clean, crisp copy.   J. & S. L. Bonham Antiquarian Booksellers   Africa 4/20/2011 - 7097   2011   £85

Davis, N. *Carthage and Her Remains: Being an Account of the Excavations and Researches on the Site of the Phoenician Metropolis in Africa and Other Adjacent Places.* London: Richard Bentley, 1861, First edition; large 8vo., original blindstamped cloth, gilt, rather faded, head of spine little frayed in places, gilt stamp of Dunblain Academy on upper board, pages xvi, 632, all edges gilt, complete with half title, 1 folding map (1 repaired on reverse) and 3 plates, several text woodcuts, prize label on pastedown.   R. F. G. Hollett & Son Antiquarian Booksellers   177 - 251   2011   £195

Davis, N. *Ruined Cities within Numidian and Carthaginian Territories.* London: John Murray, 1862, First edition; 8vo., pages xx, 391, map, 8 plates, 4 vignettes, contemporary blue full polished calf (Eton school binding) slight rubbing to head and tail of spine.   J. & S. L. Bonham Antiquarian Booksellers   Africa 4/20/2011 - 6575   2011   £95

Davis, Rebecca Ingersol *Gleanings from Merrimac Valley.* Portland: Hoyt, Fogg & Donham, 1881, First edition; 12mo., pages 128, frontispiece, bound in brown cloth stamped in gilt, some tape remnants on floral endpapers, previous owner's name on endpaper, pink 3 x 5 card with bibliographic information tipped to flyleaf, 1940 note from a bookseller tipped to another black, all edges gilt, very good.   Second Life Books Inc.   174 - 116   2011 $75

Davis, Richard Harding *The Congo and Coasts of Africa.* London: T. Fisher Unwin, 1908, First UK edition; 8vo., pages xi, 220, illustrations, original red brick decorative cloth, very good.   J. & S. L. Bonham Antiquarian Booksellers   Africa 4/20/2011 - 8178   2011   £110

Davis, Richard Harding *The Great Streets of World.* James R. Osgood, McIlvaine, 1892, 4to., illustrations, half title, frontispiece, original dark green cloth.   Jarndyce Antiquarian Booksellers   CXCI - 220   2011   £50

Davy, Gypsy *The Himalayan Letters of Gypsy Davy and Lady B.A.* Cambridge: W. Heffer & Sons, 1927, First British edition; octavo, xii, 280 pages, 4 folding maps, original full olive green pictorial cloth with black and white stamped upper cover, slight hint of rubbing, near fine.   Jeff Weber Rare Books   163 - 150   2011 $125

Davy, John *The Angler in the Lake District; or Piscatory Colloquies and Fishing Excursions in Westmorland and Cumberland.* London: Brown etc., 1857, First edition; original decorated green cloth gilt, spine trifle faded, cloth on boards slightly bubbled, pages viii, 352, 24, presentation copy inscribed "From the author", rear joint cracking, otherwise very nice, scarce.   R. F. G. Hollett & Son Antiquarian Booksellers   173 - 333   2011   £150

Dawe, Donovan *11 Ironmonger Lane. The Story of a Site in the City of London.* London: Hutchinson, 1952, First edition; original cloth, gilt, dust jacket, little worn and chipped, pages 144, colored frontispiece, 15 plates and 4 text plans and diagrams, TLS laid on to pastedown from H. Sanders of Peak, Marwick, Mitchell & Co., the new incumbents of 11 Ironmonger Lane, presenting the book to P. F. Evans of Mackrell, Ward & Knight of 10 Ironmonger Lane, with latter's armorial bookplate.   R. F. G. Hollett & Son Antiquarian Booksellers   177 - 252   2011   £30

Dawes, Manasseh *An Essay on Crimes and Punishments, with a View of and Commentary Upon Beccaria, Rousseau, Voltaire, Montesquieu, Fielding and Blackstone.* London: C. Dilly and J. Debrett, 1782, First and only early edition; 8vo., xxxi (1), 255, (1) pages, 19th century bookplate of "Worcester Library Instituted 1790" and with its blindstamp on titlepage and occasionally elsewhere, contemporary half calf over marbled boards, neatly rebacked an labelled, very good. John Drury Rare Books 154 - 43 2011 £1800

Dawkins, W. Boyd *Cave Hunting, Researches on the Evidence of Caves Respecting the Early Inhabitants of Europe.* London: Macmillan, 1874, First edition; pages vi, xix, 455, with frontispiece and 129 text woodcuts, original cloth, gilt, dust jacket spine faded, tape stains to pastedowns. R. F. G. Hollett & Son Antiquarian Booksellers 177 - 254 2011 £50

Dawson, E. C. *Jame Hannington First Bishop of Eastern Equatorial Africa.* London: Seeley and Co., 1896, Thirty Seventh thousand; pages viii, 39, frontispiece, map and text illustrations, full calf, gilt prize binding, extremities trifle rubbed, scattered foxing, upper hinge just cracking. R. F. G. Hollett & Son Antiquarian Booksellers 175 - 350 2011 £45

Dawson, George M. *Report on an Exploration in the Yukon District, N.W.T. and Adjacent Northern Portion of British Columbia.* Montreal: 1888, First edition; 270 pages, illustrations, large folding map, original printed wrappers, ex-library with bookplate and accession number on front wrapper, dampstain to bottom corner and fore edge, no adhesion or damage. Dumont Maps & Books of the West 112 - 37 2011 $125

Dawson, J. W. *The Origin of the World According to Revelation and Science.* London: Hodder & Stoughton, 1877, Old half calf gilt, little worn, pages vii, 438. R. F. G. Hollett & Son Antiquarian Booksellers 175 - 360 2011 £40

Dawson, Warren R. *The Custom of Couvade.* Manchester: University Press, 1929, First edition; original blue cloth gilt, pages ix, 118, frontispiece, little scattered foxing, scarce. R. F. G. Hollett & Son Antiquarian Booksellers 175 - 361 2011 £65

Day, Adela M. *Sunshine & Rain in Uganda.* London: East Africa, 1932, First edition; small 8vo., pages 160, illustrations, original brown cloth. J. & S. L. Bonham Antiquarian Booksellers Africa 4/20/2011 - 3662 2011 £65

Day, Clarence *Life with Father.* New York: Alfred A Knopf, 1935, First edition; fine in attractive, very good or better, price clipped dust jacket with faint stain on front panel, little nicking at crown, small elegant bookplate of noted collector Frank Hogan, small pencil note on rear pastedown that a previous owner bought this at the Hogan sale in 1945. Between the Covers 169 - BTC344723 2011 $250

Day, David *A Tolkien Bestiary.* Mitchel Beazley, 1979, First edition; 4to., original cloth, dust jacket, pages 287, illustrations. R. F. G. Hollett & Son Antiquarian Booksellers General Catalogue Summer 2010 - 752 2011 £45

Day, Langston *The Life and Art of W. Heath Robinson.* London: Herbert Joseph, 1947, First edition; original cloth, gilt, dust jacket, little worn, price clipped, pages 270, with portrait, 7 color plates and numerous other illustrations, scarce. R. F. G. Hollett & Son Antiquarian Booksellers General Catalogue Summer 2010 - 100 2011 £85

Day, Thomas *The History of Sandford and Merton.* London: J. Wallis and E. Newbery, n.d. circa, 1794, Third edition; 12mo., iv, 173 pages, marbled paper on boards, three quarter green cloth, paper label with title on spine, 6 full page copper engravings, including frontispiece, expertly rebacked, new endpapers with dated ink signature, covers lightly rubbed, very scarce, very fine. Hobbyhorse Books 56 - 43 2011 $320

Day, W. C. *Behind the Footlights or the Stage as I Knew It.* London & New York: 1885, First edition; very good in lime green cloth, designed to encourage the sale of erasers, f.f.e.p. scraped along bottom half of free edge, 8 full page illustrations by G. B. Le Fann. Bookworm & Silverfish 666 - 50 2011 $100

Dayes, Edward *The Works of the Late Edward Dayes, Containing an Excursion through the Principal Parts of Derbyshire and Yorkshire...* by T. Maiden... published by Mr. Davies, 1805, First edition; 4to., xvi, 359 (1) page ad, list of subscribers, engraved frontispiece, general engraved titlepage, 10 other full page engraved plates, large paper in contemporary calf, expertly rebacked, some wear to board edges, new endpapers and pastedowns, some light foxing, few leaves browned. Ken Spelman Rare Books 68 - 17 2011 £120

Daysh, G. H. J. *Cumberland with Special Reference to the West Cumberland Development Area.* Whitehaven: Cumberland Development Council, 1951, First edition; small 4to., original cloth, gilt, pages (viii), 182, 11 maps, 11 figures, maps and sections, 3 plates, 21 photos, presentation from Lord Adams of Ennerdale, Secretary of the Development Council. R. F. G. Hollett & Son Antiquarian Booksellers 173 - 336 2011 £40

De Baye, J., Baron *The Industrial Arts of the Anglo-Saxons.* London: Swan Sonnenschein & Co., 1893, 4to., original decorated cloth gilt over bevelled boards, extremities little worn, pages xii, 135, top edge gilt, with 17 lithographed plates, trifle shaken, but very good.   R. F. G. Hollett & Son Antiquarian Booksellers   177 - 255   2011   £75

De Bernieres, Louis *Birds without Wings.* London: Secker & Warburg, 2004, First edition, limited to 1000 signed and numbered copies; fine, in fine slipcase, signed by author.   Bella Luna Books   May 26 2011 - t7661   2011 $247

De Bernieres, Louis *Labels.* London: One Horse Press, 1993, Limited to 2000 copies; pictorial wrappers, very good, slightly bent at middle, this copy missing the wrap-around band, signed and numbered.   Bella Luna Books   May 29 2011 - p1110   2011 $82

De Bernieres, Louis *Senor Vivo and The Coca Lord.* New York: William Morrow, 1991, First edition; fine in fine dust jacket, signed by author.   Bella Luna Books   May 29 2011 - j1540   2011 $82

De Bernieres, Louis *The War of Don Emmanuel's Nether Parts.* London: Secker and Warburg, 1990, First edition; 8vo., 376 pages, signed and dated on titlepage, fine in fine dust jacket, usual very slight browning at edges of pages.   Any Amount of Books   May 29 2011 - A37458   2011 $213

De Bernieres, Louis *The War of Don Emmanuel's Nether Parts.* New York: William Morrow, 1991, First edition; fine, dust jacket near fine, light creasing to spine and edges.   Bella Luna Books   May 29 2011 - j1542   2011 $82

De Bourdeille, Pierre *The Lives of Gallant Ladies.* Waltham St. Lawrence: Golden Cockerel Press, 1924, 625 copies privately printed for subscribers; quarter cloth, very good, illustrations by Robert Gibbings, tipped in slip signed by Gibbings giving details of publication is present, signed by artist.   C. P. Hyland   May 26 2011 - 255/241   2011 $290

De Camp, L. Sprague *The Carnelian Cube.* New York: Gnome Press, 1948, First edition; octavo, cloth.   L. W. Currey, Inc.   124 - 36   2011 $1750

De Camp, L. Sprague *Divide and Rule.* Reading: Fantasy Press, 1948, First edition; octavo, cloth.   L. W. Currey, Inc.   124 - 183   2011 $250

De Camp, L. Sprague *The Great Monkey Trial.* Garden City: Doubleday, 1968, First edition; 8vo., x, 538 pages, illustrations, black cloth, gilt stamped spine title, dust jacket, fine, from the Bern Dibner reference library, with Burndy bookplate.   Jeff Weber Rare Books   161 - 113   2011 $100

De Camp, L. Sprague *Lest Darkness Fall.* New York: Henry Holt and Co., 1941, First edition; octavo, cloth.   L. W. Currey, Inc.   124 - 103   2011 $750

De Carle, Donald *Practical Clock Repairing.* Ipswich: NAG Press, 1984, Pages x, 244, text illustrations, gift inscription (non-authorial), original cloth, gilt, dust jacket.   R. F. G. Hollett & Son Antiquarian Booksellers   General Catalogue Summer 2010 - 101   2011   £30

De Chair, Somerset *English Lyric Poets. Volume IX. Somerset De Chair.* London: Regency Press, 1970, First edition, no. 18 of limited edition of 50 signed by author on handmade paper; 8vo., pages 108, on page 38 beneath poem "First Morning at Blickling" de Chair has written out a complete poem "The Missing Sonnet" and signed it with note that it was first published by Faber in 1946 in "A Mind on the March", full dark green leather, fine.   Any Amount of Books   May 29 2011 - A64161   2011 $230

De Chair, Somerset *The Golden Carpet.* Waltham St. Lawrence: Golden Cockerel Press, 1943, First edition, one of 500 copies on Arnold's mould made paper; large 8vo., original publisher's quarter green morocco raised bands, lettered gilt, cream linen boards, frontispiece, illustrated endpapers, pages 128, signed presentation copy from author, review from newspaper pasted to rear endpaper, spine slightly sunned, boards slightly soiled, otherwise very good+.   Any Amount of Books   May 29 2011 - A64165   2011 $238

De Chant, John A *Devilbirds. The Story of United States Marine Corps Aviation in World War II.* New York: 1947, First edition; 265 pages, very good mild foxing to cloth, slightly musty, in good + dust jacket, unclipped, some wear to top front and four short tears.   Bookworm & Silverfish   676 - 29   2011 $125

De Garis, Frederic *We Japanese Being Descriptions of Many of the Customs, Manners, Ceremonies, Festivals, Arts & Crafts of the Japanese.* Miyanoshita: Fujiya Hotel, 1935, 8vo., black and white illustrations, green silk covers in very good+ original book case with ivory fastenings, green silk, very good+.   Barnaby Rudge Booksellers   Travel and Exploration - 019647   2011 $150

De Geramb, Marie Joseph *A Pilgrimage to Palestine, Egypt and Syria.* London: Henry Colburn, 1840, First edition; 8vo., 2 volumes bound as one, quarter leather lettered gilt on spine, marbled boards, handsome, very good, bumped at foot of spine, frontispieces to both volumes foxed. Any Amount of Books May 29 2011 - A75433 2011 $213

De Hass, Wills *History of the Early Settlement and Indian Wars of Western Virginia: Embracing an Account of the Expeditions in the West, Previous to 1795...* Wheeling: published by H. Hoblitzell, 1851, First edition; 8vo., original embossed front and rear panels, gold image on front cover, titles stamped in gold on spine, 416 pages, frontispiece, engraved drawing, illustrations, plates, cloth professionally reinforced on spine with original title laid down, little foxing to few pages, light wear to corners and extremities, else very good, tight copy, very rare, housed in cloth slipcase with leather label on spine and titles stamped in gold. Buckingham Books May 26 2011 - 29566 2011 $1750

De La Bedoyere, Guy *Roman Villas and the Countryside.* London: Batsford and English Heritage, 1993, First edition; original cloth, gilt, dust jacket (price clipped), pages 143, with 129 illustrations. R. F. G. Hollett & Son Antiquarian Booksellers 177 - 256 2011 £30

De La Mare, Walter 1873-1956 *Bells & Grass. A Book of Rhymes.* London: Faber, 1941, First edition; original pictorial cloth, dust jacket, pages 155, illustrations. R. F. G. Hollett & Son Antiquarian Booksellers General Catalogue Summer 2010 - 753 2011 £45

De La Mare, Walter 1873-1956 *Down Adown Derry.* London: Constable, 1922, Limited to only 325 numbered copies signed by author; 4to., full vellum like paper over boards, top edge gilt, slightest of cover soil, else fine with little of the usual darkening that seems to affect this title, printed on handmade paper and illustrations by Dorothy Lathrop, 3 magnificent color plates with guards and profusion of truly beautiful black and whites, very scarce. Aleph-Bet Books, Inc. 95 - 319 2011 $850

De La Mare, Walter 1873-1956 *Mr. Bumps and His Monkey.* Philadelphia: John C. Winston, 1942, First edition; 4to., pictorial cloth, fine in nice dust jacket (frayed at spine ends with few closed tears), illustrations by Lathrop, full color lithos. Aleph-Bet Books, Inc. 95 - 321 2011 $200

De La Mare, Walter 1873-1956 *Molly Whuppie Retold by.* London: Faber and Faber, 1983, First edition thus; oblong 4to., full color pictorial boards, as new, full page color illustrations by Errol Le Cain, this copy signed in full. Jo Ann Reisler, Ltd. 86 - 154 2011 $200

De La Mare, Walter 1873-1956 *Peacock Pie.* London: Faber, 1941, First edition; original cloth, dust jacket, pages 128, decorations by Emett. R. F. G. Hollett & Son Antiquarian Booksellers General Catalogue Summer 2010 - 771 2011 £35

De La Mare, Walter 1873-1956 *Songs of Childhood.* London: Longmans, Green and Co., 1902, First edition; 8vo., frontispiece, original half parchment and pale blue linen over boards, top edge gilt, backstrip lightly rubbed along joints, otherwise fine in dust jacket with very small chip out of bottom spine panel and offsetting from two small old cellotape repairs at bottom spine and bottom front flap fold, preserved in half morocco slipcase, booklabel of J. O. Edwards, beautiful copy, inscribed by author "to N./ with his love & all blessings/ from W. J. 1949" and with De La Mare's signature above inscription. James S. Jaffe Rare Books May 26 2011 - 21420 2011 $12,500

De La Mare, Walter 1873-1956 *This Year: Next Year.* London: Faber, 1937, First edition; large 8vo., original pictorial boards, foot of spine and lower corners trifle worn, illustrations in color, front flyleaf trifle spotted, scarce. R. F. G. Hollett & Sons Antiquarian Booksellers 170 - 357 2011 £140

De La Ramee, Louise 1839-1908 *An Altruist.* London: T. Fisher Unwin, 1897, Second edition; ad leaf preceding half title, slight browning, uncut in original olive green cloth, front board lettered in gilt with dark green and brown blocked panel spine lettered in gilt, little dulled, good copy. Jarndyce Antiquarian Booksellers CLXC - 674 2011 £45

De La Ramee, Louise 1839-1908 *Ariadne.* Philadelphia: J. B. Lippincott & Co., 1877, First American edition; Initial ad leaf, original green cloth, blocked in black and gilt, slight rubbing, very good. Jarndyce Antiquarian Booksellers CLXC - 675 2011 £35

De La Ramee, Louise 1839-1908 *Cecil Castlemaine's Gage and Other Novelettes.* London: Chatto & Windus, 1893, 32 page catalog Oct. 1913 slightly browned, yellowback, original printed boards, slight wear to lower leading hinge, very good. Jarndyce Antiquarian Booksellers CLXC - 679 2011 £50

De La Ramee, Louise 1839-1908 *Chandos.* London: Chatto & Windus, 1893, New edition; initial ad leaf, final chromolithograph ad, 32 page catalog (Feb. 1895), ads on endpapers slightly browned, 'yellowback', original printed boards, slight cracking to inner hinges, good plus. Jarndyce Antiquarian Booksellers CLXC - 682 2011 £50

De La Ramee, Louise 1839-1908 *Frescoes etc. Dramatic Sketches.* London: Chatto & Windus, 1890, (1901); half title, initial ad leaf, 32 page catalog (Oct. 1884), original red uniform cloth, very good. Jarndyce Antiquarian Booksellers CLXC - 683 2011 £35

De La Ramee, Louise 1839-1908 *Frescoes etc. Dramatic Sketches.* London: Chatto & Windus, 1890, (1901); half title, initial ad leaf, fine chromolithograph ad, 32 page catalog (Sept. 1901), 'yellowback', original printed boards, endpapers browned, cracking to inner hinges, very good.   Jarndyce Antiquarian Booksellers   CLXC - 684   2011   £60

De La Ramee, Louise 1839-1908 *Guilderoy.* London: Chatto and Windus, 1889, First edition; 3 volumes, half titles, odd spot, contemporary half maroon calf, spines lettered and decorated in gilt, black leather labels, slight rubbing, Mrs. Cuthell's booklabels, good plus.   Jarndyce Antiquarian Booksellers   CLXC - 686   2011   £225

De La Ramee, Louise 1839-1908 *Idalia.* Leipzig: Bernhard Tauchnitz, 1867, Copyright edition; 2 volumes in 1, contemporary half dark green morocco, spine ruled and with devices in gilt, slight rubbing, good plus.   Jarndyce Antiquarian Booksellers   CLXC - 687   2011   £35

De La Ramee, Louise 1839-1908 *In a Winter City: a Sketch.* London: Chatto & Windus, 1903, (1912). New edition; half title, color plate, 4 pages ads and 32 page catalog (1912) slightly browned, 'yellowback', original printed boards, front board slightly marked, otherwise very good.   Jarndyce Antiquarian Booksellers   CLXC - 690   2011   £60

De La Ramee, Louise 1839-1908 *Le Selve.* London: T. Fisher Unwin, 1896, First edition; publisher's monogram preceding half title, 22 page catalog (unopened), slight browning to prelims, uncut in original olive green cloth, front board lettered in green within dark blue and maroon blocked panel, spine lettered in black, little dulled, good plus.   Jarndyce Antiquarian Booksellers   CLXC - 691   2011   £50

De La Ramee, Louise 1839-1908 *Pascarel.* Leipzig: Bernhard Tauchnitz, 1873, 2 volumes in 1, contemporary half vellum, gilt spine and trim, spine dulled, slightly rubbed, good, sound copy, bound without half titles, booklabel of N. Warburton.   Jarndyce Antiquarian Booksellers   CLXC - 695   2011   £35

De La Ramee, Louise 1839-1908 *Pipistrello and Other Stories.* London: Chatto & windus, 1880, First edition; ad preceding half title, 4 pages ads + 32 page catalog (April 1880), uncut in original blue cloth, blocked in black, spine lettered in gilt, spine dulled and little rubbed, armorial bookplate of G.H.R. Dabbs.   Jarndyce Antiquarian Booksellers   CLXC - 695   2011   £55

De La Ramee, Louise 1839-1908 *Pipistrello.* London: Chatto & Windus, 1882, New edition; half title, initial ad leaf, 32 page catalog (Mary 1882), few pencil note in text, 'yellowback', original printed boards, small booklabel of E. Smith, Stratton Strawless, near fine.   Jarndyce Antiquarian Booksellers   CLXC - 697   2011   £85

De La Ramee, Louise 1839-1908 *Princess Napraxine.* Leipzig: Bernhard Tauchnitz, 1884, Copyright edition; 3 volumes, half titles volumes II and III, original pink cloth, front boards lettered "Florence" and with small crown monograms in gilt, dark green leather labels, spines slightly dulled, very good, booklabels of Florence Onslow.   Jarndyce Antiquarian Booksellers   CLXC - 699   2011   £45

De La Ramee, Louise 1839-1908 *Princess Napraxine.* London: Chatto & Windus, 1884, First edition; 3 volumes, half titles, 32 page catalog (March 1884) volume II, inner hinges cracking, original blue cloth, blocked and lettered in black and gilt, spines faded to brown and worn, boards marked, label for Mudie's Circulating Library, poor copy.   Jarndyce Antiquarian Booksellers   CLXC - 698   2011   £125

De La Ramee, Louise 1839-1908 *A Rainy June.* Leipzig: Bernhard Tauchnitz, 1885, Copyright edition; purple morocco, spine faded and little rubbed, bookplate of Edith Bessie Cook, good plus.   Jarndyce Antiquarian Booksellers   CLXC - 701   2011   £40

De La Ramee, Louise 1839-1908 *Ruffino &c.* London: Chatto & Windus, 1890, Half title, colophon leaf, 32 page catalog (April 1890), original red uniform cloth, spine faded and bit rubbed.   Jarndyce Antiquarian Booksellers   CLXC - 702   2011   £40

De La Ramee, Louise 1839-1908 *Strathmore, or, Wrought by His Own Hand.* London: Chatto & Windus, circa, 1880, New edition; contemporary half black sheep, slightly rubbed, first page of text with owner's inscription, Ailsie North of Thurland Castle.   Jarndyce Antiquarian Booksellers   CLXC - 705   2011   £30

De La Ramee, Louise 1839-1908 *Strathmore, or, Wrought by His Own Hand.* London: Chatto & Windus, 1889, New edition; initial and final ad leaves, 32 page catalog (June 1891), yellowback, original printed boards, very good, bright copy.   Jarndyce Antiquarian Booksellers   CLXC - 706   2011   £75

De La Ramee, Louise 1839-1908 *Tricotrin.* London: Chatto & Windus, 1881, New edition; half title, 32 page catalog (Jan. 1881), 'yellowback', original printed boards, very good.   Jarndyce Antiquarian Booksellers   CLXC - 710   2011   £85

De La Ramee, Louise 1839-1908 *Two Little Wooden Shoes.* London: Chatto & Windus, 1877, New edition; 36 page catalog (Nov. 1877), original red cloth, spine lettered in gilt, slightly rubbed.   Jarndyce Antiquarian Booksellers   CLXC - 711   2011   £35

De La Ramee, Louise 1839-1908 *Two Little Wooden Shoes.* London: Chatto & Windus, 1913, New impression; half title, final chromolithograph ad, 32 page catalog (Jan. 1915) slightly browned, yellowback, original printed boards.   Jarndyce Antiquarian Booksellers   CLXC - 713   2011   £60

De La Ramee, Louise 1839-1908 *Two Offenders.* London: Chatto & Windus, 1894, First edition; 32 pages ads (Nov. 1893), half title, original dark green cloth, decorated in black and yellow, spine gilt lettered, George Ryland's small booklabel, nice, fine full page inscription signed by author for Marie Corelli, also pencil inscription "To Dalie with love on his 60th birthday from Tim", loosely inserted typed note by Rylands, "Given me by A. N. L. Munby on my 60th birthday.   Jarndyce Antiquarian Booksellers   CLXC - 714   2011   £600

De La Ramee, Louise 1839-1908 *Under Two Flags.* Leipzig: Bernhard Tauchnitz, 1871, (1885); 2 volumes, half titles, contemporary half maroon calf, green leather labels.   Jarndyce Antiquarian Booksellers   CLXC - 718   2011   £45

De La Ramee, Louise 1839-1908 *Under Two Flags...* London: Chatto & Windus, 1879, New edition; 7 pages ads preceding title, 40 page catalog (July 1879), yellowback, original printed boards, slight wear to edges, otherwise very good.   Jarndyce Antiquarian Booksellers   CLXC - 717   2011   £75

De La Ramee, Louise 1839-1908 *A Village Commune.* Philadelphia: J. P. Lippincott, 1881, First American edition; few notes on endpapers and small booklabel by W. H. Searles, Sing Sing NY, initial ad leaf, original dark green cloth, blocked in black and gilt, leading inner hinge cracking. Jarndyce Antiquarian Booksellers   CLXC - 721   2011   £35

De La Ramee, Louise 1839-1908 *A Village Commune.* London: Chatto & Windus, 1881, First edition; 2 volumes, half titles, 32 page catalog (Oct. 1880) volume 1, 4 pages ads volume II, original blue cloth blocked and lettered in black and gilt, spines dulled and little rubbed, signs of library label removal from front boards.   Jarndyce Antiquarian Booksellers   CLXC - 719   2011   £120

De La Ramee, Louise 1839-1908 *Wanda.* Leipzig: Bernhard Tauchnitz, 1883, Copyright edition; 2 volumes, contemporary half dark brown morocco, spine slightly faded, without distinguishing half titles, very good.   Jarndyce Antiquarian Booksellers   CLXC - 723 2011   £35

De La Ramee, Louise 1839-1908 *Wanda.* London: Chatto & Windus, 1883, First edition; 3 volumes, half titles, few spots, rebound in orange binder's cloth with library nos. 18-20 and 2058-60 on black leather labels, slightly dulled.   Jarndyce Antiquarian Booksellers   CLXC - 722   2011   £120

De La Ramee, Louise 1839-1908 *Wanda.* London: Chatto & Windus, 1893, New edition; half title, initial ad leaf, final chromolithograph ad, 32 page catalog (Sept. 1899), endpapers slightly browned, 'yellowback', original printed boards, spine slightly darkened.   Jarndyce Antiquarian Booksellers   CLXC - 724 2011   £60

De La Ramee, Louise 1839-1908 *Wisdom, Wit and Pathos, Selected from the Works of Ouida.* London: Chatto & Windus, 1889, Second edition; half title, final ad leaf, 32 page catalog (Oct. 1888), 'yellowback', original printed boards, spine slightly rubbed, Renier booklabel, good plus.   Jarndyce Antiquarian Booksellers   CLXC - 726   2011   £50

De Lillo, Don *Americana.* Boston: Houghton Mifflin, 1971, First edition; fine in near fine dust jacket, one small crease to rear panel, several pin holes on rear fold.   Bella Luna Books   May 26 2011 - t9659   2011 $660

De Little, R. J. *The Windmill Yesterday and Today.* London: John Baker, 1975, Large 8vo., original cloth, gilt, dust jacket, pages 104, over 100 illustrations.   R. F. G. Hollett & Son Antiquarian Booksellers   177 - 257 2011   £30

De Mille, James *A Strange Manuscript Found in a Copper Cylinder.* New York: Harper & Bros., 1888, First edition; 8vo., pages viii, 291, (4 publisher's ads), blue cloth boards with gilt to cover and spine with silver and gold design also to spine and front cover, very light wear to edges of binding, otherwise very good to fine.   Schooner Books Ltd.   96 - 140 2011 $75

De Monvel, Maurice Louis Boutet *La Civilite - Puerile et Honnete.* Paris: Plon-Nourrit et Cie circa 1890's, Oblong 4to., all edges tinted red, dark golden boards with some edge and corner rubbing, internally fine, covers have raised color decoration in shape of little boy kissing the land of a young girl in courtly style, this copy is quite special signed it was signed in full by De Monvel, each page with full color illustration.   Jo Ann Reisler, Ltd.   86 - 52 2011 $975

De Pollnitz, Charles Lewis, Baron *The Memoirs of Charles Lewis, Baron De Pollnitz.* London: privately printed, 1738, First edition; 2 volumes, complete, rebound in light brown buckram, leather spine labels lettered gilt, 8vo., pages xx, 431 (xx) & 472 (xxii), ex-British Foreign Office Library with few library markings, else very good.   Any Amount of Books   May 29 2011 - A74024 2011 $306

De Quincey, Thomas 1785-1859 *Confessions of an English Opium-Eater.* London: printed for Taylor and Hessey, 1822, First edition; 12mo., without final leaf of ads and half title, early 20th century full green morocco. Heritage Book Shop   Booth A12 51st NY International Antiquarian Book Fair April 8-10 2011 - 37 2011 $1850

De Regniers, Beatrice Schenk *May I Bring a Friend?* New York: Atheneum, 1964, Stated first edition; 4to., cloth, fine in dust jacket (faint corner stain, price clipped), bright color illustrations, detailed black and whites, beautiful copy, very scarce.   Aleph-Bet Books, Inc.   95 - 369   2011 $600

De Tolnay, Charles *Hieronymus Bosch.* New York: Reynal/William Morrow, 1966, First American edition; 4to., 451 pages, 48 color plates and 364 black and white illustrations, fine in fine dust jacket.   By the Book, L. C.   26 - 31   2011 $80

De Vries, Leonard *Flowers of Delight Culled from the Osborne Collection of Early Children's Books.* Dennis Dobson, 1965, First edition; 4to., original pictorial cloth, gilt, dust jacket, pages 232, over 700 illustrations.   R. F. G. Hollett & Sons Antiquarian Booksellers   170 - 193   2011   £45

De Vries, Peter *The Blood of the Lamb.* Boston: Little Brown Co., 1961, Third printing; near fine in very good dust jacket with couple of tears and rubbing, laid in is 1960 ALS by author.   Between the Covers   169 - BTC344099   2011 $400

De Wald, E. T. *Pietro Lorenzetti.* Cambridge: 1930, Large 4to., viii, 36 (99 plates) pages, wrappers, backstrip abraded top 3 inch, one spot on cover.   Bookworm & Silverfish   676 - 23   2011 $67

Deacon, Margaret *Scientists and the Sea 1650-1900: a Study of Marine Science.* Aldershot and Brookfield: Ashgae, 1997, Second edition; 8vo., xl, 459 pages, illustrations, aqua cloth, silver stamped spine title, dust jacket, fine, from the Bern Dibner reference library, with Burndy bookplate.   Jeff Weber Rare Books   161 - 114   2011 $90

Deak, Gloria Gilda *Picturing America 1497-1899: Prints, Maps and Drawings Bearing on the New World Discoveries and on the Development of the Territory that is now the United States.* Princeton: 1988, 2 volumes, xxx, 657; xix followed by 880 illustrations, near fine in like dust jackets, scarce.   Dumont Maps & Books of the West   113 - 31   2011 $750

Dean, Johnny *The Beatles Book.* Ealing, London: Beat Publications, May, 1976-, Jan. 2003; Complete run of the first issue, 321 monthly issues in all, all in very good clean condition, original 22 red folders issued by Beat Publications lettered gilt at spine.   Any Amount of Books   May 26 2011 - A72990   2011 $1426

Dearden, James S. *Ruskin & Coniston.* Covent Garden Press, 1971, Limited edition, no. 81 of 100 copies, signed; 4to., original quarter calf gilt with yellow cloth boards, pages 69, portrait, 23 plates, scarce.   R. F. G. Hollett & Son Antiquarian Booksellers   173 - 341   2011   £120

Death of Cock Robin. New York: McLoughlin Brothers between, 1858-1862, 5 1/2 x 4 1/2 inches, color pictorial wrappers printed in red and black ink, rather clean, fresh copy with hint of foxing behind pages, 8 pages within, each with half page hand colored wood engravings.   Jo Ann Reisler, Ltd.   86 - 84   2011 $300

Debus, Allen G. *Chemistry, Alchemy and the New Philosophy 1550-1700: Studies in the History of Science and Medicine.* London: Variorum Reprints, 1987, 8vo., xii, 320 pages, frontispiece, illustrations, blue cloth, gilt stamped cover and spine titles, fine, from the Bern Dibner reference library, with Burndy bookplate.   Jeff Weber Rare Books   161 - 115   2011 $125

Decatur, Stephen *Correspondence Between the Late Commodore Stephen Decatur and Commodore James Baron...* Washington: Gales & Seaton, 1820, 8vo., 26 pages, removed, heavily foxed, 1832 news paper article pasted to both sides of blank regarding a review of an essay Shakespeare's test of insanity as pertains to Hamlet.   M & S Rare Books, Inc.   90 - 106   2011 $325

Decker, Duane *Good field, No Hit.* New York: M. S. Mill, 1947, Second edition; dust jacket soiled and worn, some loss on spine, minor smudging to few pages, otherwise clean and tight, 208 pages.   G. H. Mott Bookseller   May 26 2011 - 47096   2011 $650

Decle, Lionel *Three Years in Savage Africa.* London: Methuen, 1900, New edition; 8vo., pages xxxi, 594, frontispiece, maps, illustrations, some small discreet stamps on verso of some plates and maps, original orange decorative cloth.   J. & S. L. Bonham Antiquarian Booksellers   Africa 4/20/2011 - 5635   2011   £220

Dee, John *De Superficerum Divisionibus Liber Machometo Bagdedino Ascriptus Nunc Primum Ioannis Dee...* Pesaro: Hieronymus Concordia, 1570, 4to., pages (viii), 76, woodcut emblems to titlepage, numerous small woodcut diagrams in text, opening leaves slightly foxed but generally very crisp, clean copy, modern vellum, gilt lettering to spine.   Simon Finch Rare Books   Zero - 102   2011   £1500

Defoe, Daniel *The Novels an Selected Writings of Daniel Defoe.* Oxford: Basil Blackwell, 1927-1928, First edition thus; limited to 750 copies, 14 volumes, original publisher's pale blue gilt, top edge gilt, fore-edges untrimmed, spines slightly faded, sound and clean, very good.   Any Amount of Books   May 26 2011 - A72449   2011 $671

Defoe, Daniel *A System of Magick; or a History of the Black Art.* London: printed and sold by Andrew Millar, at Buchana's Head, against St. Clement's Church in the Strand, 1728, Reissue of the first edition of 1727; (8), 403, (1) pages, frontispiece, titlepage in red and black, 8vo., good, clean copy, Aa2 carelessly opened with slight marginal tear not affecting text, contemporary panelled calf, raised bands, red gilt morocco labels, joints cracked but firm, spine rather dry and rubbed, worn at head and tail, near contemporary name of Wallett at head of titlepage and date Jan.. 6th 1737/8. Jarndyce Antiquarian Booksellers CXCI - 150 2011 £750

Defoe, Daniel *A Tour thro' the Whole Island of Great Britain.* London: printed for J. Osborn, S. Birt, D. Browne, A. Millar, F. Cogan, J. Whiston, and J. Robinson, 1738, (2), xiii, (1), 360, (27) index, (5) pages ads; (2), 374, (24) page index; (2), 360, (22) page index, 12mo., some underlinings in pencil, occasionally in red, contemporary calf, double gilt fillet borders, spines gilt in compartments, worn but sound, joints cracked, lacking two labels, sound copy. Jarndyce Antiquarian Booksellers CXCI - 544 2011 £320

Defoe, Daniel *A Tour thro' the Whole Island of Great Britain.* London: printed for S. Birt et al, 1753, Fifth edition; 4 volumes, 12mo., pages viii, 388, (xii); iv, 418, (xviii); iv, 312, (xviii); iv, 371 (xxi), contemporary sprinkled calf, spine double rule gilt, dark red lettering pieces gilt, volume number gilt direct, boards double rule gilt bordered, board edges decorative roll in blind, all edges slightly red sprinkled, red and white sewn endbands, browned and spotted, most so in volume I, dark offsetting from turn-ins, rubbed and worn, especially headcaps, joints cracking, front joint of volume 1 nearly split, labels lost from spines of volumes 1 and 4, armorial bookplate of 'Melville", from the collection of Christopher Ernest Weston 1947-2010. Unsworths Booksellers 24 - 85 2011 £260

Degrevant *Sire Degrevaunt.* Kelmscott Press, 1896, but actually issued November, 1897, One of 350 copies, of an edition of 358 copies; printed in black and red on handmade paper in Chaucer type, woodcut frontispiece designed by Sir E. Burne-Jones, woodcut borders and initials, pages (iv) (blanks), (iv) 82, (8) (blanks), crown 8vo., original holland linen backed pale blue boards, light foxing to linen, title printed on front cover, bookplate, untrimmed, near fine. Blackwell Rare Books B166 - 267 2011 £900

Deineko, Olga *Ot Kauchuka Do Kaloshi. (From Rubber Plants to rubbers).* Moscow: Ogiz, 1931, 4to., pictorial wrappers, cover soil, faint margin stain, very good, illustrations in color. Aleph-Bet Books, Inc. 95 - 499 2011 $1000

Dejob, Charles *Les Femmes dans la Comedie Francaise et Italienne au XVIIIe Siecle.* Paris: Fontemoing, 1899, First edition; (417 pages), 8vo., original yellow wrappers printed in black, wrappers somewhat stained, otherwise fine, unopened. Paulette Rose Fine and Rare Books 32 - 173 2011 $125

Dejong, Meindart *Shadrach.* Lutterworth Press, 1957, First UK edition; original cloth, dust jacket (spine rather faded, edges rubbed and frayed), pages 182, line drawings by Maurice Sendak. R. F. G. Hollett & Sons Antiquarian Booksellers 170 - 619 2011 £60

Delacroix, Eugene *The Journal.* London: Cape, 1938, First edition; 4to., original cloth, gilt, dust jacket rather worn and soiled, spine darkened, pages 731, with 8 color plates 47 duotone plates. R. F. G. Hollett & Son Antiquarian Booksellers General Catalogue Summer 2010 - 106 2011 £120

Delafaye-Brehier, Julie *Les Enfans de la Providence ou Aventures de Trois Jeunes Orphelins.* Paris: Alexis Eymery, 1819, First edition; 4 volumes, (viii), (1), 6-194; 238; 236; 270 pages, 12mo., contemporary three quarter calf over boards, gilt ruled spines, contrasting title labels with gilt decorations, 16 engraved plates, frontispiece in each volume, very fine, pretty copy in original state, scarce. Paulette Rose Fine and Rare Books 32 - 103 2011 $350

Delafaye-Brehier, Julie *Les Petits Bearnais Ou Lecons De Morale Convenables a la Jeunesse.* Paris: A La Librairie d'Education d'Alexis Eymery, 1825, third edition; 140 x 89mm., volumes, contemporary scarlet straight grain morocco gilt, covers bordered with plain and elegant foliate rolls, flat spines with panels formed by gilt and black rules and featuring clustered volute centerpiece, multiple decorative bands at head and foot, marbled endpapers, all edges gilt, 16 charming engraved plates, original tissue guards, one leaf defective at lower corner because of paper flaw, costing perhaps a half dozen letters on each side of leaf, additional trivial imperfections, otherwise exceptionally fine set, remarkably clean, bright and fresh inside and out. Phillip J. Pirages 59 - 164 2011 $875

Delamotte, Freeman Gage *Examples of modern alphabets, Plain and Ornamental...* Crosby, Lockwood & Co., 1884, Ninth edition; occasionally trimmed close to head of page, alphabet printed in variety of colors, original paper wrappers decorated and lettered in blue few small marginal tears. Jarndyce Antiquarian Booksellers CXCI - 361 2011 £75

Delamotte, Freeman Gage *A Primer of the Art of Illumination for the Use of Beginners...* Lockwood, 1874, Printed in black and red, 20 chromolithographed plates of initial letters, pages 44, 20 plates, 1 (ad), (1) (blank), small 4to., original bevel edged maroon cloth, plain backstrip faded, sides with blindstamped double line border and fleur-de-lys corner pieces, upper side elaborately gilt blocked with title and passion flowers, yellow, chalked endpapers, gilt edges, Vivian Ridler's copy with his embossed address on front free endpaper. Blackwell Rare Books B166 - 29 2011 £200

Delaney, Roberta *Perimeter of an Experience of Solitude.* Somerville: Firefly Press, 1995, Artist's book, one of 15 copies only; all on BFK French fold paper, each copy signed and numbered by artist, Roberta Delaney, page size 14 3/4 x 11 1/4 x 8 3/4 inches, 40 pages, 12 of the smaller size pages containing text and 28 of the larger size containing the 10 lithographs, front and rear wrappers, titlepage and colophon also included, housed in grey cloth over boards portfolio with ivory fasteners, the 10 lithographs are each 8 x 8 inches and pulled in black, text by Octavio Paz is set in Optima and repeated, paired with each of the lithographs.   Priscilla Juvelis - Rare Books   48 - 8 2011 $5000

Delaney, Roberta *Plants and Insects from Spring Snow.* Sherborn: 1989, Artist's book, one of 10 copies only; all on French fold Rives heavyweight cream paper, each signed and numbered by artist, page size 9 1/2 x 11 1/2 inches, 2 volumes identically bound by artist in handmade Japanese nacreous paper with various leaves and grasses in paper itself ivory colored background with leaves, etc. in grey/green and buff, handsewn and housed in folding case of handmade green Japanese paper over boards lined with handmade Mexican Bark paper, ivory colored plastic clasps, artist has taken text for Yukio Mishima's "Spring Snow" and illuminated it with hand colored woodcuts, 6 in the volume of "Plants" and 8 in the volume of "Insects", recto page contains the print, verso a graphite rubbing from part of same block, woodcuts printed and hand colored by artist, some printed in color with mica reflecting Edo period techniques, woodcuts were cut from Japanese 5 layered plywood with boxwood exterior surface, enabling artist to print on an etching press (mantle), graphite rubbings on verso wear from a graphite stick, paper laid over block and rubbed in random manner, each print titled by artist in pencil blow print, as each print is hand colored, no two copies the same, delicately beautiful book.   Priscilla Juvelis - Rare Books   48 - 7 2011 $5000

Delany, Samuel Ray *The Einstein Intersection.* London: Victor Gollancz Ltd., 1968, First edition; octavo, boards.   L. W. Currey, Inc.   124 - 29 2011 $2000

Deleuze, Gilles *Emprisime et Subjectivite: Essai sur la Nature Humaine Selon Hume. (Empiricism and Subjectivity: an Essay on Hume's Theory of Human Nature).* Paris: Presses Universitaires de France, 1953, First edition; half title, (1)-152 (153) - table (155) - imprime, squarish octavo, original printed wrappers with light edge wear, pages browned as usual for post-war paper, untrimmed in glassine wrapper, small name unobtrusively stamped to upper corner of titlepage, very good.   Athena Rare Books   10 2011 $450

Deleuze, Gilles *Nietzsche et la Philosophie.* Paris: Presses Universitaires de France, 1962, First edition; half title, titlepage, (1), 232 (233) - Imprime + 1 leaf - ads, original printed wrappers with light edge wear in glassine wrappers, pages bright, very good.   Athena Rare Books   10 2011 $300

Dell, Robert *Burlington Magazine.* 1903-1905, Volume 1/1-Volume 3/32, soft cover, very good,; lacking 6 issues, March 1903-Nov. 1905, no. 2 being limited to 340 numbered copies, profusely illustrated.   I. D. Edrich   May 26 2011 - 98558 2011 $553

Dell, William *The Doctrine of Baptisms Reduced from Its Ancient and Modern Corruptions.* Philadelphia: B. Franklin and D. Hall, 1759, First American edition; 12mo., 43 pages, contemporary plain wrappers.   M & S Rare Books, Inc.   90 - 139 2011 $1000

Demi *The Artist and the Architect.* New York: Henry Holt, 1991, First edition; fine in fine dust jacket, small 4to., signed and inscribed, dated by Demi.   By the Book, L. C.   26 - 57 2011 $75

Demidoff, Anatole De *Voyage dans la Russie Meriodonale & la Crimee.* Paris: Publie par Gihaut Freres, 1838-1848, First edition; large folio, contemporary half red morocco over marbled boards.   Heritage Book Shop Booth A12 51st NY International Antiquarian Book Fair April 8-10 2011 - 39 2011 $45,000

Dempsey, Jack *Championship Fighting: Explosive Punching and Aggressive Defence.* London: Nicholas Kaye, 1950, First UK edition; 8vo., pages 203, illustrations in black and white, neat inscription "A very Happy/Christmas/Jack W. Durnsford", endpapers slightly browned, else very good+ in chipped, nicked (2 inches missing at rear), else very good- dust jacket with good.   Any Amount of Books   May 29 2011 - A47404 2011 $272

Demus, Otto *Byzantine Mosaic Decoration. Aspects of Monumental Art in Byzantium.* London: Kegan Paul, 1947, First edition; pages xiii, 97, plus 64 plates, few spots to front endpapers.   R. F. G. Hollett & Son Antiquarian Booksellers   177 - 258 2011   £45

Denham, Dixon *Narrative of Travels and Discoveries in Northern and Central Africa in the Years 1822 1823, 1824.* London: John Murray, 1826, 2 volumes, octavo, lxxviii, 321, iv, 413 pages, 2 engraved frontispieces, 10 engraved plates, 3 folding maps, original half calf, marbled boards, raised bands, gilt titles on leather labels, very good plus.   Jeff Weber Rare Books   163 - 151 2011 $800

Denham, Dixon *Narrative of Travels and Discoveries in Northern & Central Africa in the Years 1822, 1823 and 1824...* London: John Murray, 1826, First edition; quarto, pages xlviii,335, 269, appendix, maps, 36 plates, contemporary full red brown calf, slight rubbing to corners and head and tail of spine.   J. & S. L. Bonham Antiquarian Booksellers   Africa 4/20/2011 - 5660 2011   £950

Dennis, Charles *Stoned Cold Soldier.* London: Bachman & Turner, 1973, First edition; inscribed by author, fine in near fine dust jacket with short tear at upper rear spine fold, excellent copy, uncommon. Ken Lopez Bookseller 154 - 229 2011 $500

Dennis, George *The Cities and Cemeteries of Etruria.* London: John Murray, 1848, First edition; 2 volumes, old half calf gilt, edges little worn, hinges cracked but sound, pages xx 530, (ii); xiv, 555, (ii), numerous illustrations and 0 maps and plans. R. F. G. Hollett & Son Antiquarian Booksellers 177 - 259 2011 £295

Denshin, Aleksel *Russkaya Narodnaya Igrushka Vypusk 1. Vyatskaya Lepnaya Glinyanaya Ignrushka. (The Russian Folk Toy - Clay Dolls from Vyatka).* Moscow: Moskovskoe Khudozhestvennoe Izdatelstvo, 1929, First edition; oblong 4to., color pictorial paper covers, some wear and corners clipped, edges toned and somewhat brittle, 8 pages (two-sides) of text and titlepage, there are 16 numbered single sided pages of color images. Jo Ann Reisler, Ltd. 86 - 217 2011 $750

Denton, Thomas *A Perambulation of Cumberland 1687-1688.* Boydell Press, 2003, Original cloth gilt, dust jacket, pages (viii) 606 with frontispiece. R. F. G. Hollett & Son Antiquarian Booksellers 173 - 346 2011 £65

Denton, William *Nature's Secrets of Psychometric Researches.* London: Houlston and Wright, 1863, First English edition; half title, index, original brown cloth. Jarndyce Antiquarian Booksellers CXCI - 151 2011 £85

Denver & Rio Grande Railroad *Among the Rockies.* Denver: 1910, 36 pages of photo views, small folio, wrappers. Bookworm & Silverfish 676 - 10 2011 $65

Denwood, J. M. *Red Ike.* Hutchinson & Co. n.d., 1931, First edition; original cloth, dust jacket little worn, pages 288. R. F. G. Hollett & Son Antiquarian Booksellers 173 - 348 2011 £35

Depons, Francois *A Voyage to the Eastern Part of Terra Firma or the Spanish Main in South America During the Years 1801, 1802, 1803, 1804.* New York: Riley, 1806, 3 volumes, 8vo., xxxii, 248, (8); 363, (8); 288, (8) pages, one large folding map, some names and staining to prelim matter, otherwise very good, tight copy, contemporary calf with red morocco labels,. Second Life Books Inc. 174 - 119 2011 $850

Dering, Edward Cholmeley *Poems.* London: George Bubb, 1860, Original blue cloth, bookplate of Cholmeley Edward Dering 1818-1881, very good. Jarndyce Antiquarian Booksellers CXCI - 152 2011 £85

Derleth, August Williams *Dark of the Moon: Poems of Fantasy and the Macabre.* Sauk City: Arkahm House, 1947, First edition; octavo, cloth. L. W. Currey, Inc. 124 - 158 2011 $350

Derleth, August Williams *The Mask of Cthulhu.* Sauk City: Arkham House, 1958, First edition; octavo, cloth. L. W. Currey, Inc. 124 - 184 2011 $250

Derleth, August Williams *100 Books by August Derleth.* Sauk City: Arkham House, 1962, First edition; octavo, pages (1-4) 5-121 (122-124 blank) (note: last leaf is a blank), pictorial boards. L. W. Currey, Inc. 124 - 142 2011 $450

Derleth, August Williams *Someone in the Dark.* Sauk City: Arkham House, 1941, First edition, first issue with binding measuring 17.6 tall and without headband, limited to 1115 copies; near fine in fine facsimile. Lupack Rare Books May 26 2011 - ABE4098457484 2011 $375

Derleth, August Williams *The Trail of Cthulhu.* Sauk City: Arkham House, 1962, First edition; octavo, cloth. L. W. Currey, Inc. 124 - 209 2011 $150

Derrida, Jacques *L'Origine de la Geometrie. (Origin of Geometry).* Paris: Presses Universitaires de France, 1962, First edition; half title, titlepage, 1 leaf - ad, (3)-219, octavo, 3 line inscription and author's signature, very good in printed wrappers, age toned, pages unopened. Athena Rare Books 10 2011 $3000

Derriere Le Miroir 10 Ans D'edition 1946-1956. Paris: Maeght Editeur, 1956, Folio, numerous color and black and white lithographs by Chagall and Miro, original printed wrappers, lettered in black. Heritage Book Shop Booth A12 51st NY International Antiquarian Book Fair April 8-10 2011 - 2 2011 $1250

Desaguliers, John Theophilus *A Course of Experimental Philosophy.* London: printed for John Senex et al, 1734-1744, First edition; 2 volumes, very good++ in contemporary leather with gilt rule, modern leather rebacking, spine labels, covers mildly worn, minimal worming, text, plates fresh and bright with mild scattered marginal foxing, owner name titlepages, complete with 33 folding plates. By the Book, L. C. 26 - 103 2011 $3500

Descartes, Rene *De Homine Figuris.* Leiden: Ex Officina Hackiana, 1664, Second edition; small quarto, (4 blank) (40) 121 (i.e. 123), (1, Nota), (4, blank) pages, text in Latin complete, 10 engraved plates, 2 of which have overlay flaps, first plate facing page 9 with two flaps and plate LIV with one small flap, 55 other intertextual engravings, two of which are folding, 6 full page, one intertextual engraved table, mispagination starting after page 121 as per usual, contemporary full vellum, yapp edges, top half of spine repaired, small chip from vellum on spine, vellum bit soiled, very good.   Heritage Book Shop   Holiday 2010 - 26   2011 $3000

Description of Some Curious and Uncommon Creatures, Omitted in the Description of Three Hundred Animals and Likewise in the Supplement to that Book: Designed as an Addition to those To Treatises for the Entertainment of Young People.   London: printed for Richard Ware, 1739, First edition; 16 x 10cm., pages (iv) 88 (4 page publisher's ads), complete with 16 attractive engraved plates, full contemporary leather, somewhat worn and rubbed covers, rear board loose, very good minus but with sound and clean text and plates.   Any Amount of Books   May 26 2011 - A61864   2011 $671

Desmarets De Saint Sorlin, Jean   *L'Ariane.. Enrichie de Plusieurs Figures.*   Paris: Matthieu Guillemat, 1639,   4to., (8), 775, (1) pages, 17 engraved full page illustrations by Abraham Bosse after Claude Vignon, woodcut head and tailpieces, woodcut initials, 17th century speckled calf, spine gilt in compartments, binding rubbed, fine, from the library of the Earls of Macclesfield at Shirburn Castle.   Maggs Bros. Ltd.   1440 - 66   2011   £500

Detro, Gene   *Patchen: the Last Interview.*   Santa Barbara: Capra Press,   1976,   First edition; copy #56 of 60 numbered and signed copies, fine, pictorial boards.   Charles Agvent   2010 Summer Miscellany - 24   2011 $60

Devastated Halifax.   Halifax: Gerald F. Weir, 1917,   First edition; 14.5 x 22.7 cm., pages 32, with 45 views, decorative light brown card covers and spine split and taped, interior very good.   Schooner Books Ltd.   96 - 160   2011 $75

Devereux, E. C.   *Life's Memoirs of Eton and Eton Colours.*   Eton: E. C. Devereux, circa, 1935,   First edition; original cloth, few tiny spots to upper panel, pages 140 with 98 color plates, scarce.   R. F. G. Hollett & Son Antiquarian Booksellers   175 - 368   2011   £75

Deveria, Johannot   *Moeurs de Paris zeme Livraison.* London: Paris, circa, 1835,   Large 4to., suite of 12 hand colored lithographs, each with overlay flaps, revealing, when lifted, explicit scenes with captions, internally clean with some light spotting, leaves partially loose at gutter, closed tear repeated to one plate not affecting image, light marginal dampstaining to one plate, contemporary maroon quarter morocco, marbled boards and endpapers, spine gilt lettered and decorated with flowers and naked female silhouettes, wrappers bound, leaves untrimmed, wrappers chipped with minor repairs, patch of dampstain to lower board extending through rear endpapers, 2 short typewritten descriptions pasted to front free endpaper.   Simon Finch Rare Books   Zero - 423   2011   £15,000

Devey, Louisa   *Life of Rosina, Lady Lytton, with Numerous Extracts from her MS Autobiography and Other Original Documents...*   London: Swan Sonnenschein, Lowrey & Co., 1887,   First edition; half title, frontispiece, facsimile, prelims little grubby, contemporary half purple cloth, little rubbed, labels of Norfolk & Norwich Library, good, sound copy.   Jarndyce Antiquarian Booksellers   CLXC - 183   2011   £80

Deveze, Jean   *An Enquiry into and Observations Upon the Causes and Effects of the Epidemic Disease, Which Raged in Philadelphia from the Month of August till Towards the Middle of December 1793.*   Philadelphia: Parent, 1794, First edition; 8vo., pages vii, (i) errata, 145, (i) blank, some mild offsetting, uncut in original paper wrappers, with 3 line presentation inscription from author to the initial blank, very good, unsophisticated copy.   Simon Finch Rare Books   Zero - 122   2011   £650

Devonshire, R. L., Mrs.   *Rambles in Cairo.*   Cairo: E. & R. Schindler, 1931,   First edition; 8vo., pages vi, 104, large folding map, 63 plates, original buff boards, joints cracked.   J. & S. L. Bonham Antiquarian Booksellers   Africa 4/20/2011 - 8440   2011   £50

Dewey, Orville   *Discourses on Human Life.*   London: John Green, 1842,   First English edition; 12mo., untrimmed in original drab boards, glazed purple cloth spine, paper label (price 6s), spine faded, few small marks to boards, embossed armorial ownership stamp on titlepage, bookseller's ticket of Waddington's Leicester, very good.   Jarndyce Antiquarian Booksellers   CXCI - 349   2011   £65

Dewey, Thomas F.   *With the Scottish Yeomanry.*   Arbroath: T. Buncle, 1901,   First edition; 8vo., pages 198, original red cloth, lightly stained.   J. & S. L. Bonham Antiquarian Booksellers   Africa 4/20/2011 - 8294   2011   £65

Dexter, Carolyn   *The Cat and the Fox.*   Rochester: Stecher, 1930,   Narrow folio, pictorial card covers, near fine, stunning color lithographs by Byron Culver, very scarce.   Aleph-Bet Books, Inc.   95 - 139   2011 $200

Dexter, Elisha *Narrative of the Loss of whaling Brig. William and Joseph of Martha's Vineyard, and the Sufferings of her Crew for Seven Days...* Boston: 1848, Second edition; 52 pages, 5 full page woodcuts, contemporary printed wrappers, few very faint stains on front wrapper, else remarkably fine, fresh copy. Joseph J. Felcone Inc. Fall Miscellany 2010 - 39 2011 $1800

Di Peso, Charles C. *Casas Grandes. A Fallen Trading Center of the Gran Chichimeca.* Flagstaff: 1974, First edition; 8 volumes, near fine. Dumont Maps & Books of the West 111 - 53 2011 $850

Di Peso, Charles C. *The Sobaipurl Indians of the Upper San Pedro River Valley Southeastern Arizona.* Dragoon: 1953, xii, illustrations, folding map, original printed wrappers, wrappers soiled, edges bent, internally clean and bright. Dumont Maps & Books of the West 111 - 54 2011 $95

Diaz, Junot *The Brief Wondrous Life of Oscar Wao.* New York: Riverhead, 2007, First edition; fine, very good dust jacket, moderate soiling and wrinkling to rear panel, very good dust jacket, moderate soiling and wrinkling to rear panel. Bella Luna Books May 29 2011 - r9703 2011 $82

Diaz, Junot *The Brief Wondrous Life of Oscar Wao.* New York: Riverhead, 2007, First edition; fine, near fine dust jacket, 2 one inch remnants of coffee ring on rear panel. Bella Luna Books May 26 2011 - t9564 2011 $165

Diaz, Junot *The Brief Wondrous Life of Oscar Wao.* New York: Riverhead, 2007, First edition; fine in like dust jacket. Bella Luna Books May 26 2011 - t9704 2011 $275

Dibdin, Charles 1745-1814 *Observations on a Tour through Almost the Whole of England and a Considerable Part of Scotland, in a Series of Letters.* London: published by G. Goulding etc. circa, 1803, 2 volumes bound as 1, 4to., pages 404 + 26 engraved plates; 407 (i) + 34 engraved plates, extending table of distances in Scotland, contemporary straight grained crimson morocco, spine fully gilt in religious sense with cross, chalice and stylised lily tools, lettered direct in gilt and 'dated' at foot, boards double rule gilt bordered with decorative roll (linked looped-leaf), within, board edges decorative roll gilt, turn-ins decorative roll gilt, mauvish brown sugar paper 'made' endpapers, all edges gilt, dark green double core sewn endbands, dark blue silk page marker, offsetting from plates, bit of foxing, spine bit darkened, slightly rubbed at extremities and some scratches to boards, evidence of removal of two early bookplates, armorial bookplate of "Brown", from the collection of Christopher Ernest Weston 1947-2010. Unsworths Booksellers 24 - 86 2011 £550

Dibdin, Thomas Frognall 1776-1847 *The Bibliographical Decameron.* London: printed for the author by W. Bulmer and Co., Shakespeare Press, 1817, First and only edition, evidently limited to 750-800 regular and 50 large paper copies; 3 volumes, 8vo., pages ccxxvi, 410; (iv), 536, (ii); (iv), 544, (iv), 37 engraved plates, two double page page, 35 text illustrations printed on India paper and mounted on pages, one mounted gilt lettered specimen of red panel calf, hundreds of engraved and woodcut text illustrations, several colored, bookplates, later three quarter brown morocco, all edges marbled, some minor foxing, soiling and offsetting, handsome copy. Second Life Books Inc. 174 - 121 2011 $2500

Dibdin, Thomas Frognall 1776-1847 *Bibliotheca Spenceriana; or a Descriptive Catalogue of the Books printed in the Fifteenth Century in the Library of George John Earl Spencer (with) Supplement to the Bibliotheca Spenceriana. (with) Aedes Althorpianae; or an Account of the Mansion, Books and Pictures at Althorp (with) A Descriptive Catalogue of the Books Printed in the Fifteenth Century...* London: for the author by Shakespeare Press, 1814-1815, 1822-1823; 7 volumes, 4to., profusely illustrated with engraved plates, hundreds of facsimiles of early woodcuts and type, some printed in color, modern full tan morocco, richly gilt, covers with central arms and cornerpieces within a two-line fillet, board edges and turn-ins gilt, spines fully gilt in compartments, some engraved plates foxed and few dampstained, offsetting from text illustrations, gathering M in volume 4 heavily foxed, else very good set in very fine, fresh bindings. Joseph J. Felcone Inc. Fall Miscellany 2010 - 40 2011 $2800

Dibdin, Thomas Frognall 1776-1847 *Reminiscenes of a Literary Life.* London: John Major, 1836, First edition; 2 volumes, frontispiece, plates and illustrations, subscriber's list pages xvii-xxxii, plates slightly foxed, some quite heavily, uncut in contemporary or slightly later half maroon calf, slight rubbing, crimson labels, contemporary signatures of J. Holmes Poulter. Jarndyce Antiquarian Booksellers CXCI - 153 2011 £200

Dicey, A. V. *A Digest of the Law of England with Reference to the Conflict of Laws...* London: Stevens & Son/Sweet & Maxwell, First edition; large fat 8vo., pages cvii, 853, sound, very good decent copy, prize binding with slight edgewear, full light brown leather lettered gilt at spine. Any Amount of Books May 29 2011 - A74612 2011 $255

Dick, Philip K. *Counter-Clock World.* London: Sydney and Toronto: White Lion Publishers Ltd., 1977, First hardcover edition; octavo, boards. L. W. Currey, Inc. 124 - 30 2011 $2000

Dick, Philip K. *A Handful of Darkness.* London: Melbourne: Sydney: Auckland: Bombay: Cape Town: New York: Toronto: Rich and Cowan, 1955, First edition; first binding of blue boards with spine panel stamped in silver, octavo. L. W. Currey, Inc. 124 - 23 2011 $2500

Dick, Philip K. *Time Out of Joint.* New York: Lippincott, 1959, First edition; 8vo., pages 221, very good in dust jacket, lacks small chip at upper corner, small adhesion to cover, rear little soiled, very good.   Second Life Books Inc. 174 - 122 2011 $1100

Dickens, Charles 1812-1870 *The Battle of Life.* London: Bradbury & Evans, 1846, First edition, fourth issue; small 8vo., old three quarter blue calf, gilt with marbled boards, pages 176, top edges gilt, illustrated, handsome copy, without 2 ad leaves.   R. F. G. Hollett & Son Antiquarian Booksellers   General Catalogue Summer 2010 - 635 2011   £250

Dickens, Charles 1812-1870 *A Christmas Carol.* Philadelphia: Carey & Hart, 1844, Half title, color frontispiece, plates and illustrations, lager half green crushed morocco by Zaehnsdorf, spine blocked and lettered in gilt, original blue cloth bound in to precede half title, top edge gilt, very good, booklabel of Charles Plumptre Johnson, top edge gilt, very good.   Jarndyce Antiquarian Booksellers CXCI - 154 2011   £1500

Dickens, Charles 1812-1870 *A Christmas Carol. In Prose.* London: Chapman & Hall, 1844, First edition; very rare so called 'trial issue', with titlepage printed in red and green and half title in green, octavo, with "Stave One", 4 color plates, original cinnamon vertically ribbed cloth.   Heritage Book Shop   Booth A12 51st NY International Antiquarian Book Fair April 8-10 2011 - 41 2011 $10,000

Dickens, Charles 1812-1870 *A Christmas Carol.* G. P. Putnam's Sons, 1902, Pages xii, 157, top edges gilt, with 13 photogravure plates and other illustrations by Frederick Simpson Coburn.   R. F. G. Hollett & Son Antiquarian Booksellers   General Catalogue Summer 2010 - 754 2011   £120

Dickens, Charles 1812-1870 *Christmas Books. A Christmas Carol. The Chimes. The Cricket on the Hearth. The Battle of Life. The Haunted Man and the Ghost's Bargain. (with) The Chimes. (with) The Cricket on the Hearth. (with) The Battle of Life. (with) The Haunted Man and The Ghost's Bargain.* London: Chapman and Hall, 1843, London: Chapman and Hall 1845 (i.e. Dec. 1844). London: printed and published for the author by Bradbury and Evans 1846, i.e. Dec. 1845. London: Bradbury & Evans, 1846. London: Bradbury & Evans 1848. First edition, first issue, i.e. "Stave I"; remainder first editions; blue half title, red and blue title, small octavo, (viii), (1) 2-166, (2, publisher's ads) pages, 4 inserted hand colored plates, including frontispiece, in text black and white illustrations, 2 pages of publisher's ads, original green coated endpapers bound in at front, original complete cloth, including front, back and spine, bound in at back; small octavo, (viii), (1) 2-175, (1, colophon), first state additional engraved title and frontispiece, 11 in text black and white illustrations, publisher's prelim ad leaf for tenth edition Christmas Carol, original complete cloth, including front back and spine, bound in at back; small octavo, (viii), (1) 2-174 (2 publisher's ads) pages, engraved title and frontispiece, 12 in text black and white illustrations, with second state of final leaf of publisher's ads for new edition of Oliver Twist, original complete cloth, including front, back and spine bound in at back; small octavo, (viii), (1-3) 4-175, (1, colophon), (2, publisher's ads) pages, second state engraved title and frontispiece, 11 in text black and white illustrations, original complete cloth, including front back and spine, bound in at back; small octavo, (viii), (1) 2-188 pages, prelim leaf of publisher's ads, additional pictorial frontispiece, 15 in text black and white illustrations, original complete cloth, including front back and spine, bound in at back, all books beautifully uniformly bound by Zaehnsdorf in full red morocco, covers ruled in gilt, spines ruled and lettered in gilt in compartments with five raised bands, all edges gilt, gilt board edges and dentelles, marbled endpapers, each volume with original complete cloth (including front back and spine), bound in at back of volume, a Christmas Carol with original coated endpapers bound in at front, slightest rubbing to extremities, superb set, housed in red cloth slipcase.   Heritage Book Shop Holiday 2010 - 27 2011 $12,500

Dickens, Charles 1812-1870 *Dickens Christmas Story of Goblins Who Stole a Sexton.* New York: McLoughlin Bros. circa, 1867, 8vo., hand colored pictorial paper wrappers with some wear and new spine and resewn with some strengthening, 32 numbered pages (including covers with numerous Thomas Nast throughout book).   Jo Ann Reisler, Ltd.   86 - 177 2011 $650

Dickens, Charles 1812-1870 *Dombey and Son.* London: Bradbury & Evans, 1848, First edition in book form, first state following all points in Smith; octavo, xvi, (1, errata), (1, blank), 624 pages, frontispiece, titlepage and 38 plates after Phiz, publisher's variant binding of moderate green fine diaper grain cloth, front and back covers entirely stamped in blind with thin double line border which enclosed a rectangular frame, frame contains a loop-scroll design in each corner and string of 16 beads runs along its inner edge, lineal globe shaped design stamped in center of both covers, spine stamped in blind with thick and thin band at top and thin and thick one at bottom, between which are three decorative rectangular panels, each containing heart shaped flower design in its center, spine lettered in gilt original pale yellow coated endpapers, spine very slightly faded, corners very slightly bumped with just tiny amount of board show through, otherwise binding is as fresh as one could possibly wish for, chemised in half green morocco slipcase with bookplate of William Self on chemise, bookplates of Gilfrid William Hartley and William Self, and Dickens Centenary Testimonial label on front pastedown, signature of original owners Eleanor Trotter September 11th 1859", signature of Kenyon Starling.   David Brass Rare Books, Inc.   May 26 2011 - 01693 2011 $13,500

Dickens, Charles 1812-1870   *The Haunted Man and the Ghost's Bargain.* London: Bradbury & Evans, 1848, First edition; small octavo, lithographic frontispiece and title, unbound in original sheets, uncut and unopened, overall fine.   Heritage Book Shop   Booth A12 51st NY International Antiquarian Book Fair April 8-10 2011 - 42 2011 $10,000

Dickens, Charles 1812-1870   *The Haunted Man and the Ghost's Bargain.* London: Bradbury & Evans, 1848, First edition; small octavo., lithographic frontispiece and title, original red horizontal ribbed cloth, fine.   Heritage Book Shop   Booth A12 51st NY International Antiquarian Book Fair April 8-10 2011 - 43 2011 $1000

Dickens, Charles 1812-1870   *The Holly Tree and Other Christmas Stories.* W. Partridge & Co. n.d., Large 8vo., original tan pictorial cloth, pages 192, color frontispiece and 30 plates by E. H. Shepard, uncommon.   R. F. G. Hollett & Son Antiquarian Booksellers   General Catalogue Summer 2010 - 755 2011   £75

Dickens, Charles 1812-1870   *Letters of Charles Dickens to Wilkie Collins 1851-1870.* London: James R. Osgood, McIlvaine & Co., 1892, Half title, original dark blue cloth, dulled, inner hinges cracking, inscribed by A. J. Watt for George MacDonald.   Jarndyce Antiquarian Booksellers   CXCII - 337 2011   £380

Dickens, Charles 1812-1870   *The Life and Adventures of Nicholas Nickleby.* London: Chapman and Hall, 1839, First edition; bound from parts, 8vo., pages xvi, 624, first state of portrait (with printer's imprint), second issue of page 123, 1. 17, engraved portrait, 39 engraved plates, bound with half title and one cover in later three quarter red morocco, spine gilt, top edge gilt, covers little rubbed, little toning to leaves, but very good, tight clean copy.   Second Life Books Inc.   174 - 123 2011 $800

Dickens, Charles 1812-1870   *The Life and Adventures of Nicholas Nickleby.* London: Chapman and Hall, 1839, First edition; with 30 of Smith's 41 first issue text points, first state frontispiece, and plates with the exception of plates one and two (second state) and plate 31 (fourth state), octavo, xvi, 624 pages, 40 black and white plates, including frontispiece, publisher's full red-brown pebbled morocco, four gilt decorated raised bands, gilt lettered and titled to spine, stamped in gilt at spine foot, blindstamped ruled borders and central panel with blindstamped ruled border, gilt turn-ins, all edges gilt, original pale yellow endpapers, plates untouched with many toned at perimeters and few with spotting, unusual as in bound copies the plates are generally found to have been subsequently washed, rough fore edge to frontispiece, plate at page 386 with loss at lower corner, otherwise excellent, housed in fleece lined custom quarter morocco box.   David Brass Rare Books, Inc.   May 26 2011 - 01064 2011 $10,000

Dickens, Charles 1812-1870   *Life and Adventures of Nicholas Nickleby.* London: Chapman and Hall, 1839, First edition in original monthly parts; 20 numbers bound in 19, mixed issue with first issue "visitor" for "sister" in the Part IV but corrected letter in part V, octavo (i-vii) viii-x (xi) xii-xiv (xv) xvi, (1) 2-624, 39 engraved plates by Phiz, set collates near complete, lacking only first back ad of part VIII "This Day is published... No. 1... Heads of the People", includes very rare and fragile "Hill's Wafer's" ad in part XIX/XX, with all five wax seals intact, this set has very rare "Tilt" slip in part XI, but not the "Mary Ashby" slip in part XVI as usual (Mary Ashby slip in after insertion by publisher and considered a non-essential item), portrait in Part XIX/XX is the first state, with publisher's imprint at bottom, as are plates in Parts I-II, original green printed wrappers generally quite bright, although some have chipping at the spine, some soiling and few have been professionally rebacked, plates very good with some slight browning and foxing, few parts have minor professional repairs, old ink signatures on top of few of the front wrappers, back wrapper of part IX and X stained, part XIX/XX bit foxed, housed in custom half blue morocco clamshell, excellent set.   Heritage Book Shop Holiday 2010 - 28 2011 $3000

Dickens, Charles 1812-1870 *The Life and Adventures of Nicholas Nickleby.* London: Chapman and Hall, 1839, First edition, later issue with "Chapman & Hall" imprint lacking at bottom of plates up to page 45, which Eckel claims were omitted in later impressions, 'visiter' has been corrected to 'sister' in 17th line of page 123, 'letter' has been corrected from 'latter' in sixth line from bottom of page 160; 8vo., pages xvi, 624 pages, 40 black and white plates, including frontispiece, half title, engraved portrait frontispiece by Daniel Maclise in first state with imprint, 39 engraved plates by Phiz, some light browning at page edges of plate pages, otherwise noticeably clean with slight spotting only at frontispiece, original olive green diaper cloth, covers with blindstamped border spine gilt, excellent condition, tight, clean, original publisher's green cloth, blue illustrated cover of part 11 of the parts issue neatly tipped in at half title, covers faintly rubbed, faintly soiled, slight evidence of removal of small press cutting at f.e.p., neat ownership signature of one J.S. Earle dated 1879, slight repaired nick at side of frontispiece with no loss, otherwise near fine and completely unrestored.   Any Amount of Books   May 26 2011 - A49296   2011 $1845

Dickens, Charles 1812-1870 *Little Dorrit.* London: Bradbury and Evans, 1857, First edition; first issue with signature "BB2" signed "B2", without errata slip on page 481, bound in little rubbed red full morocco, bound from parts, 8vo., pages xiv, 625, all edges gilt, original covers (bound out of order) from 18 of the 19 parts (not #17) bound in, lacks one or two rear covers, lacks ads, bound with vignette and illustrated titlepages and 39 plates (little foxed and soiled).   Second Life Books Inc.   174 - 124   2011 $750

Dickens, Charles 1812-1870 *Little Dorrit.* London: Bradbury & Evans, 1857, First edition, Rigaud issue; frontispiece, added engraved title and plates, errata slip, slightly foxed and damp marked, contemporary half calf, marbled boards, well rebacked, black leather, with George Macdonald's bookplate.   Jarndyce Antiquarian Booksellers   CXCII - 336   2011   £500

Dickens, Charles 1812-1870 *Master Humphrey's Clock.* London: Chapman & Hall, 1840-1841, First edition; 3 volumes, tall 8vo., 19th century half morocco gilt with broad raised bands, double contrasting spine labels, edges little rubbed and frayed in places, pages iv, 306; vi, 306; vi, 426, illustrations, very good.   R. F. G. Hollett & Son Antiquarian Booksellers   General Catalogue Summer 2010 - 636   2011   £375

Dickens, Charles 1812-1870 *Mr. Nightingale's Diary.* Boston: James R. Osgood and Co., 1877, First "Collectible" Edition; other than little shelfwear at extremities, this near fine with cover very bright, scarce.   Lupack Rare Books   May 26 2011 - ABE3913285888   2011 $1000

Dickens, Charles 1812-1870 *Mr. Pickwick's Christmas.* London: Cassell & Co., 1907, First UK edition; large 8vo., original embossed green cloth with pictorial onlay, pages xxi, 150, untrimmed 10 color or tinted plates, numerous line drawings by George Alfred Williams, front tissue foxed, short tear to one plate, few marks to endpapers.   R. F. G. Hollett & Son Antiquarian Booksellers   General Catalogue Summer 2010 - 757   2011   £180

Dickens, Charles 1812-1870 *Oliver Twist; or the Parish Boy's Progress.* London: Richard Bentley, 1838, First edition; first state containing rare "Fireside" plate and "Boz" on titles, 3 volumes, octavo, original publisher's reddish brown horizontally ribbed cloth.   Heritage Book Shop   Booth A12 51st NY International Antiquarian Book Fair April 8-10 2011 - 44   2011 $7500

Dickens, Charles 1812-1870 *Our Mutual Friend.* London: Chapman and Hall, 1865, First edition; bound from parts, half titles present, 2 wood engraved frontispieces and 38 plates, original wrappers of part 9 bound in, publisher's ads (found in "some copies") not present, little light foxing and spotting, pages xii, 320; viii, 310; 8vo., early 20th century polished biscuit calf, spine with five gilt milled raised bands, dark olive morocco lettering pieces in second and third compartments, remainder with gilt centre and corner-pieces, marbled endpapers, top edge gilt, just touch rubbed at joints, very good.   Blackwell Rare Books   B166 - 30   2011   £500

Dickens, Charles 1812-1870 *The Personal History of David Copperfield.* London: Bradbury and Evans, 1850, i.e. May 1849-November 1850. First edition in original monthly parts; 20 numbers bound in 19, first issue following all points in Hatton & Cleaver, octavo, (i-vii) viii (ix) x-xii (xiii) xiv (xv-xvi), (1) 2-624, with forty inserted plates, including frontispiece and vignette title part II has small repair to rear wrapper, just touching text, complete with most of ads called for by Hatton and Cleaver except for following, Part VIII lacks Lett's Diary's ad, rear wrapper to part IX is unrecorded variant, part XII possesses a later variant of slip number four, part XIII lacks slip "New Illustrated Weekly Periodical for Ladies", part XVI lacks one leaf of Copperfield Advertiser, Part XVIII has a later variant of green slip following Copperfield Advertiser; parts XIX and XX lack two slips and 20 pages of ads at rear, original blue printed pictorial wrappers, expert restoration to some backstrips, few plates exhibiting some light foxing or toning, Part II possesses a small repair to lower corner of rear wrapper, just touching text, still excellent set that shows well, housed in quarter brown morocco clamshell case.   David Brass Rare Books, Inc.   May 26 2011 - 01255   2011 $5500

Dickens, Charles 1812-1870 *The Personal History of David Copperfield.* London: Bradbury & Evans, 1850, First edition in book form, first state (following all but one of the twenty points listed in Smith), in the primary binding; octavo, xiv, (1, errata), (1, blank), 624 pages, frontispiece, titlepage and 38 engraved plates after Phiz, the single point not in its first state is page 132, line 20 "screamed" for "screwed", publisher's primary binding of moderate green fine diaper grain cloth, front and back covers entirely stamped in blind with thin double line border which encloses a rectangular frame, frame contains a loop-scroll design in each corner and string of 16 beads runs along its inner edge, lineal globe shaped design is stamped in center of both covers, spine stamped in blind with thick and thin band at top and a thin ad thick one at bottom, between which there are three decorative rectangular panels, each containing heart shaped flower design in its center, spine lettered in gilt, original pale yellow coated endpapers, The Kenyon Starling - William Self copy, original owner's signature "Eleanor Trotter/September 1812-1912) to front pastedown endpaper, spine very slightly darkened, few very minor and pale stains on cloth sides, corners very slightly bumped with little show through of boards, chemised in half green morocco slipcase with bookplates of Starling and Self on chemise,. David Brass Rare Books, Inc. May 26 2011 - 01692 2011 $14,500

Dickens, Charles 1812-1870 *The Personal History of David Copperfield.* London: Bradbury & Evans, 1850, First edition in original monthly parts; 20 numbers bound in 19, first issue, following all points in Hatton & Cleaver, octavo, (i-vii), viii, (ix) x-xii (xiii) xiv (xv-xvi), (1) 2-624, with 40 inserted plates, including frontispiece and vignette title, complete with all called for ads, original blue printed pictorial wrappers, expert restoration to some backstrips, few plates exhibits some light foxing or toning, otherwise near fine set, rarely seen in this condition, chemised in green half straight grain morocco slipcase, identical contemporary inked signature to upper margin of front wrapper of several parts. David Brass Rare Books, Inc. May 26 2011 - 01244 2011 $12,500

Dickens, Charles 1812-1870 *Pictures from Italy.* London: published for the author by Bradbury & Evans, 1846, First edition, 2nd issue; half title, vignette title by Samuel Palmer, initial and final ad leaves, original fine blue diaper cloth, slightly marked and dulled, lacking leading f.e.p. Jarndyce Antiquarian Booksellers CXCI - 545 2011 £220

Dickens, Charles 1812-1870 *Sketches by Boz.* London: John Macrone, 1836, First edition; first printing (Whiting), 2 volumes, 12mo., (i-iii) iv-v (vi-vii) viii, (1) 2-348; (i-iv), (1) 2-342, 16 engraved plates by George Cruikshank; bound by Tout in full green morocco, covers decoratively ruled in gilt, spines lettered and decoratively tooled in gilt in compartments, gilt dentelles, all edges gilt, rust color coated endpapers, bit of light browning to plates as usual, still excellent copy,. Heritage Book Shop Holiday 2010 - 29 2011 $2500

Dickens, Charles 1812-1870 *Sketches by Boz.* London: John Macrone, 1836, First edition, first printing (i.e. by Whiting); 2 volumes, 12mo., original dark green leaf patterned cloth, illustrations by George Cruikshank. Heritage Book Shop Booth A12 51st NY International Antiquarian Book Fair April 8-10 2011 - 45 2011 $35,000

Dickens, Charles 1812-1870 *A Tale of Two Cities.* London: Chapman & Hall, 1859, First edition, second state with titlepage still dated 1859 but with corrected pagination on page 213 and no signature 'b' on the list of plates; octavo, (i-vii) viii (ix-x), (1)2-254 pages, 16 inserted plate, including frontispiece and vignette title by Phiz, publisher's secondary binding of moderate olive green fine diaper cloth, covers stamped in blind, spine lettered in gilt, original pale yellow coated endpapers, boards remarkably fresh, text and plates very clean and bright with just minimal scattering of unobtrusive foxing, just tiny amount of wear to top and bottom of spine, inner hinges very expertly and almost invisibly strengthened, armorial bookplate of Sir James Martin, chemised in full green morocco slipcase case, superlative condition. David Brass Rare Books, Inc. May 26 2011 - 00734 2011 $18,500

Dickens, Charles 1812-1870 *A Tale of Two Cities.* London: Chapman & Hall, 1859, First edition, first issue in primary binding with genuine titlepage; octavo, octavo, (i-vii) viii (ix-x), (1)2-254 pages, 16 inserted plate, including frontispiece and vignette title by Phiz, publisher's, each remarkably fine impressions, all 8 of Smith's internal flaws necessary for the first issue present, without the 32 page catalog at rear, primary binding of deep red morocco grain cloth, covers stamped in blind, spine lettered gilt, pale yellow endpapers, joints at upper extreme with one inch cloth split but remain firm, front hinge hints at starting at upper one inch, yet tight, frontispiece with 3 inch split at gutter, otherwise wholly intact and firm in binding, leaves 79-80, 193-194 and 915-196 exhibit 1 x 1/4 inch paper flaws at fore edge or top edge, not affecting text, 1 x 1.5 inch and 1 x 1 inch light stains to rear cloth, mild light soiling to cloth, as expected, withal a superb copy, housed in full crimson morocco clamshell case. David Brass Rare Books, Inc. May 26 2011 - 01088 2011 $19,500

Dickens, Charles 1812-1870 *The Works.* London: Chapman and Hall, 1873-1876, 30 volumes, 220 x 140mm. very pleasing dark blue straight grain morocco, handsomely gilt, by Riviere & Son (stamp signed verso front free endpaper), covers bordered with gilt double rule and wide ornate floral roll incorporating fleuron cornerpieces, raised bands, spines heavily gilt in double ruled compartments with ornate central lozenge, surrounded by small tools and intricate scrolling volute cornerpieces, inner gilt dentelles, marbled endpapers, titlepage (one volume very expertly rebacked using original backstrip), copiously illustrated with 461 plates, plus numerous illustrations in text, half the volumes with shallow chips at head (only noticeable upon close inspection) just hint of wear to joints and extremities, occasional minor foxing, other trivial imperfections internally, but excellent, even with wear at spine ends, text clean and fresh and very decorative bindings quite pleasing, unusually lustrous covers, sumptuously bound.   Phillip J. Pirages   59 - 173 2011 $6500

Dickens, Charles 1812-1870 *The Works of Charles Dickens. (with) The Life of Charles Dickens.* London: Chapman and Hall, 1874-1876, Illustrated Library edition; 32 volumes, octavo, illustrations, contemporary half blue morocco over cloth boards, spines lettered and decorated in gilt, marbled endpapers, top edge gilt, handsome set, excellent condition.   David Brass Rare Books, Inc.   May 26 2011 - 00922   2011 $13,500

Dickens, Charles 1812-1870 *Works.* London: Chapman & Hall, n.d., 1874-1891, Reprint of illustrated library edition; octavo, 30 volumes, plates, late 19th century full tan polished calf by Tout (stamp signed on verso of front free endpaper), covers with gilt triple fillet border with gilt corner ornaments, spines elaborately tooled in gilt in compartments with five gilt dotted raised bands and red and green morocco gilt, others uncut, marbled endpapers, minor rubbing to extremities, headcaps on volumes IX, X, and XXI expertly repaired, small bookseller's ticket on rear pastedown of each volume, near fine, partially unopened.   David Brass Rare Books, Inc.   May 26 2011 - 00785   2011 $20,000

Dickens, Charles 1812-1870 *Charles Dicken's Works.* London: Chapman and Hall, 1881, Edition deluxe, first issue, no. 361 of 1000 numbered copies; 30 volumes, half titles, frontispieces, illustrations with India proofs after original plates, reprint of front wrapper from original part publication, some occasional light foxing, contemporary half maroon morocco by Blunson & Co., spines lettered in gilt, top edge gilt.   Jarndyce Antiquarian Booksellers   CXCI - 10 2011   £4800

Dickens, Charles 1812-1870 *The Works of...* London: Merrill & Baker, 1900, Edition de Grande Luxe, limited to 500 numbered sets; 32 volumes complete, more than 1000 illustrations, the set has been supplemented with aquarelles of Kyd, original cloth, paper spine labels, illustrations with printed tissue guards, top edge gilt, very good set, spines and spine labels slightly darkened with age, some labels have minor spotting or rubbing to paper, one corner chipped, boards show some loss of color at random, overall clean, tight set, handsome and complete.   Lupack Rare Books   May 26 2011 - ABE3654383709 2011 $450

Dickens, Charles 1812-1870 *Works.* London: Merrill & Baker, 1900, Edition des Bibliophiles, one of 26 copies lettered and registered copies, this copy being letter "H"); octavo, 32 volumes, elaborately illustrated with frontispieces and plates, including photogravures, etchings, photo-etchings, descriptive tissue guards, contemporary blue crushed levant morocco, covers decoratively tooled in gilt in floral design within a gilt single fillet border, spines decoratively tooled in gilt in floral design within gilt single fillet border, spines decoratively tooled and lettered in gilt in compartments with five raised bands, gilt dotted board edges, turn-ins decoratively tooled in gilt within an outer border of gilt dotted rule and two gilt fillets, red calf doublures, red watered silk liners, top edge gilt, others uncut, partially unopened, although spines are uniformly faded to green and few leaves poorly opened, this set is in a spectacular binding.   David Brass Rare Books, Inc.   May 26 2011 - 00566   2011 $35,000

Dickey, James *The Eye-Beaters Blood Victory Madness Buckhead and Mercy: New Poems.* Garden City: Doubleday, 1970, Limited edition; number 193 of 250 copies signed by author, fine in slipcase.   Gemini Fine Books & Arts, Ltd.   Art Reference & Illustrated Books: First Editions 2011 $75

Dickinson, Emily Elizabeth 1830-1886 *Poems.* Boston: Roberts Brothers, 1891, First edition; 12mo., 230 pages, silk marker, facsimiles, bevelled edges, original gilt stamped green cloth, top edge gilt, one signature slightly loose, ex-library copy with small stamp on title, bookplate and stamps on front endpapers, spine quite rubbed, library labels in base, extremely scarce.   M & S Rare Books, Inc.   90 - 108 2011 $450

Dickinson, G. Lowes *The Development of Parliament During the Nineteenth Century.* London: Longmans, Green and Co., 1895, First edition; original publisher's green cloth, lettered gilt at spine, pages viii, 183, 24 page publisher's catalogue at rear, uncommon, spine ends and hinges slightly rubbed, corners little bumped and slightly scuffed, otherwise sound, clean, very good+.   Any Amount of Books   May 29 2011 - A49566   2011 $221

Dickinson, H. W. *Richard Trevithick, the Engineer and the Man.* Cambridge: University Press, 1934, First edition; 8vo., xvii, 290 pages, 41 figures, teal cloth, black stamped spine title, dust jacket, lower corner bumped, rear hinge cracked, jacket soiled, very good, rare in dust jacket, from the Bern Dibner reference library, with Burndy bookplate. Jeff Weber Rare Books 161 - 117 2011 $125

Dickinson, H. W. *Robert Fulton, Engineer and Artist.* London: New York: & Toronto: John Lane, The Bodley Head, Bell & Cockburn, 1913, 8vo., xiv, 333, 15 (ads) pages, frontispiece, 32 figures, blue cloth, gilt stamped cover, gilt stamped spine title, dust jacket chipped, soiled, from the Bern Dibner reference library, with Burndy bookplate. Jeff Weber Rare Books 161 - 159 2011 $125

Dickinson, J. C. *The Land of Cartmel. A History.* Kendal: Titus Wilson, 1980, First edition; large 8vo., original cloth gilt, dust jacket, pages xii, 112, with 16 plates 5 text figures, presentation copy, inscribed by author on flyleaf. R. F. G. Hollett & Son Antiquarian Booksellers 173 - 352 2011 £40

Dickinson, Jonathan *God's Protecting Providence. Man's Surest Help and Defence...* Philadelphia: William Bradford, 1751, Fourth edition; 12mo., (8), 80 pages, spine and back cover, front cover present, very browned, piece lacking from outer edge of title, affecting author's surname as indicated, and two or three other words, two leaves (11-12, 41-42) lacking small portions of text, pages 9-10 torn through horizontally without loss. M & S Rare Books, Inc. 90 - 107 2011 $2500

Dickinson, Sally B. *Confederate Leaders.* Staunton: 1937, First edition; 198 pages, very good to fine, without errata, inscribed by author to former VA Governor. Bookworm & Silverfish 666 - 30 2011 $65

Dickinson, William *Cumbriana or Fragments of Cumbrian Life.* London: Whitttaker & Co. and Whitehaven: Callender and Dixon, 1875, First edition; later cloth gilt, pages xii, 327, lower joint cracked. R. F. G. Hollett & Son Antiquarian Booksellers 173 - 359 2011 £35

Dick's Art of Wrestling. New York: Dick and Fitzgerald, 1887, First edition; 12mo., 54 pages, 27 text illustrations, original printed and pictorial wrappers, tiny chip at one corner, trace of wear. M & S Rare Books, Inc. 90 - 403 2011 $425

Dickson, H. R. P. *Kuwait and Her Neighbours.* London: Allen & Unwin, 1956, First edition; 8vo., pages 627, copiously illustrated in color and black and white, 6 folding maps and genealogical tables in pocket at rear, sound, clean, very good with faint mottling to boards in very good, used dust jacket with slight nicks at edges and slight browning. Any Amount of Books May 29 2011 - A68597 2011 $315

Dickson, P. G. M. *The Sun Insurance Office 1710-1960.* London: Oxford University Press, 1960, First edition; pages xiv, 324, color frontispiece, 14 plates, 3 line drawings, original cloth, gilt, dust jacket (trifle dusty), pages xiv, 324, color frontispiece, 14 plates and 3 line drawings, presentation copy inscribed by author for Sir Denys Ford, with 2 page ALS from him to same. R. F. G. Hollett & Son Antiquarian Booksellers 175 - 373 2011 £50

Didion, Joan *A Book of Common Prayer.* Norwalk: Easton Press, 2002, First edition thus; signed by author, leather bound, all edges gilt, as new, certificate of authenticity and note from Easton Press. Gemini Fine Books & Arts, Ltd. Art Reference & Illustrated Books: First Editions 2011 $100

Dilich, Wilhelm *Peribologia.* Frankfurt: A. Humm etc., 1641, Folio, 5-202, 10) pages, engraved title and 7 section titles, 410 plus numbered engravings, contemporary English calf, gilt fillet on covers, spine with gilt ornaments, red edges, from the library of the Earls of Macclesfield at Shirburn Castle, this copy may well stem from the library of John Collins/William Jones, and has the old Macclesfield Library class mark. Maggs Bros. Ltd. 1440 - 68 2011 £2000

Dilich, Wilhelm *Peribologia.* Frankfurt: A. Humm for J. W. Dilich, 1641, Folio, 5-202 (10) pages, engraved title and 7 section titles, 410 plus numbered engravings on c. 240 plates, text and plates mounted on guards, 18th century English calf, gilt, red edges, very handsome, clean copy, from the library of the Earls of Macclesfield at Shirburn Castle. Maggs Bros. Ltd. 1440 - 67 2011 £2000

Dilke, Emilia Frances *The Shrine of Death and Other Stories.* London and New York: Unwin Brothers for George Routledge and Sons, 1886, First edition, large paper issue, no. 62 of 150 copies on handmade paper; 4to., pages (ii), 160, text within black frame, headlines in gothic type, woodcut headpieces, title vignette, initials, front cover design repeated on title verso and final woodcut in text, top edge gilt, others uncut, modern black levant half morocco, spine lettered in gold, five raised bands, marbled sides and endpapers, original blue green front wrapper bound in, with designed printed in blue repeated from title verso, fine, inscribed by author, scarce. Simon Finch Rare Books Zero - 227 2011 £750

Dillard, Annie *Life Class.* Chapel Hill: University of North Carolina Press, 1972, First edition; printed wrapper, very good, shows light foxing and soiling. Bella Luna Books May 29 2011 - t1041 2011 $137

Dillard, Annie *Pilgrim at Tinker Creek.* New York: Harpers Magazine Press, 1974, First edition; near fine, rubbing to cloth on front and rear panel, dust jacket near fine, light ubbing to corners, price of $7.95 on dust jacket and number line on last page with "1" present. Bella Luna Books May 26 2011 - t9413 2011 $192

Dillard, Annie *Pilgrim at Tinker Creek.* Norwalk: Easton Press, 2000, Signed by author, leather with gold titles and decorations, all edges gilt, silk endpapers and ribbon bookmark, "A note about" card and signed certificate of authenticity folded in, very clean and tight, 271 pages, fine.   G. H. Mott Bookseller   May 26 2011 - 37070   2011 $245

Dillon, Richard *Napa Valley Heyday.* San Francisco: Book Club of California, 2004, first edition, one of 450 copies; large quarto, xi, (1), 363 pages, 43 photos, large folding map in color laid in at rear, pictorial endpapers, printed throughout in red and black, full natural linen binding, pictorial inset on front cover, printed paper spine label, very fine.   Argonaut Book Shop   Recent Acquisitions Summer 2010 - 147   2011 $250

Dines, Elaine *Paul Outerbridge a Singular Aesthetic.* Laguna Beach: Laguna Beach Museum of Art, 1981,   4to., wrappers, fine.   Barnaby Rudge Booksellers   Art & Architecture & Photography - 031953   2011 $75

Diogenes Laertius *Diogenis Laertii Clariss Historici De Vitis Ac Moribus Priscorum Philosophorum Librai Decem.* Cologne: ex offinia Eucharii Cervicorni, 1542, contemporary calf, panelled with triple rules and broad fillets with cornerpieces and central emblem, all in blind, extremities rather worn and spine dulled, silk ties worn away, pages 30, 671, (i, blank), title little stained, name scribbled out, label and few old stamps of Treves Cathedral Library, with ownership inscription of Christopher of Kesselstan, Dean of Paderborn, Count Kesselstan.   R. F. G. Hollett & Son Antiquarian Booksellers   General Catalogue Summer 2010 - 637   2011   £450

Dionysius of Halicarnassus *The Roman Antiquities of Dionysius Halicarnassensis.* London: printed and sold by booksellers of London and Westminster, 1758, 4 volumes bound as 2, 4to., pages lviii, 456, (ii); (ii), 439, (iii) + 1 double sided engraved sheet with "The Herodian Inscription" on recto, "The Athenian Inscription" on verso, (ii), 438, (ii); (ii), 516 (ii), contemporary diced Russia, boards 'Grecian Key' gilt bordered, board edges 'milled' decorative roll gilt, turn-ins single rule gilt, 'Antique spot' 'made' endpapers, all edges lemon, early 21st century reback an corners by Chris Weston, age toned and foxed in places, bit of staining including large mark in gutter at end volume 1, old leather rubbed at edges, armorial bookplate of Daniel O'Connell, ink inscription, from the collection of Christopher Ernest Weston 1947-2010.   Unsworths Booksellers   24 - 87   2011   £600

Dionysius, Periegetes *(Greek) Dionysij Orbis Descriptio Arati Astronomicon.* Basel: Thomas Wolf, 1534, Greek texts printed consecutively, and followed by Latin versions, 8vo., ff. (2) 68, (2); (64), last leaf with device etc. on verso, contemporary English brown calf over pasteboard, blind-stamped shield on covers with letters G F & H stamped in blind at sides, spine gilded later with red morocco label, contemporary ms. notes in margins of D3v and D4r, from the library of the Earls of Macclesfield at Shirburn Castle.   Maggs Bros. Ltd.   1440 - 69   2011   £500

Dirac, Paul Adrien Maurice *Spinors in Hilbert Space.* New York: Plenum, 1974,   First edition in dust jacket; 8vo., 91 pages, near fine, very good++ dust jacket with mild chips and short closed tears, uncommon.   By the Book, L. C.   26 - 96   2011 $300

Dircks, Rudolf *Sir Christopher Wren A.D. 1632-1723.* London: Hodder & Stoughton, 1923, First edition; thick 4to., original buckram gilt, very faded, pages xvi, 280, photos and plans, including 13 color plates, joints just cracking part of dust jacket laid on to flyleaf.   R. F. G. Hollett & Son Antiquarian Booksellers   177 - 265   2011   £140

Dirsztay, Patricia *Church Furnishings.* London: Routledge & Kegan Paul, 1978, First edition; 246 pages, illustrations, original cloth, gilt, dust jacket.   R. F. G. Hollett & Son Antiquarian Booksellers   177 - 266   2011   £35

Disch, Thomas M. *The Genocides.* London: Ronald Whiting & Wheaton, 1967,   First British and first hardcover edition; octavo, boards.   L. W. Currey, Inc.   124 - 119   2011 $650

The Discovery and Conquest of Peru. London: Folio Society, 1968, First edition; original cloth, decorated in silver and printed in black, slipcase, pages 271, with 10 full page illustrations in 3 colors by Edward Bawden, fine.   R. F. G. Hollett & Son Antiquarian Booksellers   General Catalogue Summer 2010 - 596   2011   £30

The Discovery of the Lake District. London: Victoria & Albert Museum, 1984,   First edition; large 8vo., original pictorial wrappers, pages 176, well illustrated, rather scarce. R. F. G. Hollett & Son Antiquarian Booksellers   173 - 387 2011   £35

Diseases of Aquatic Organisms. Amelinghausen, Oldendorf/Luhe: Inter-Research, 1985-1998, Numerous photos and text figures, 4to., few issues with minor bump or short tear to paper on spine, small stain to 1 cover. Raymond M. Sutton, Jr.   May 26 2011 - 47082   2011 $1350

Diserens, Corinee *Gordon Matta-Clark.* London: Phaidon Press Limited, 2003, First edition; 4to., 240 pages, copiously illustrated in color and black and white, book spine has been intentionally cut open for 13cm by Phaidon in Matta Clark spirit to show its interior, hardback with cut open spine, fine.   Any Amount of Books   May 29 2011 - A46380   2011 $230

Disher, M. Wilson *Clowns & Pantomimes.* London: Constable and Co., 1925, 4to., orange gilt cloth, spine soiled and cloth at joints torn.   Barnaby Rudge Booksellers Art & Architecture & Photography - 015944   2011 $140

Disher, Maurice William *The Last Romantic.* London: Hutchinson, n.d., First edition; original cloth, gilt, dust jacket little worn, pages 270, frontispiece, 34 plates, 11 text illustrations. R. F. G. Hollett & Son Antiquarian Booksellers 175 - 375 2011 £30

Disney, Walt *The Adventures of Mickey Mouse: Book Number 2.* Philadelphia: David McKay Co., 1932, First edition; full color pictorial boards, slight shelf wear, full color pictorial dust jacket with edge wear and tears along upper edges, every page illustrated in color. Jo Ann Reisler, Ltd. 86 - 56 2011 $1750

Disney, Walt *Bambi.* Paris: Hachette, 1949, First edition; 4to., spiral binding and full color illustrated boards, full color pictorial dust jacket with few closed tears in jacket, 24 numbered pages with five full page color tab activated moveables, all in fine working order, book illustrated in sepia tones and color. Jo Ann Reisler, Ltd. 86 - 65 2011 $475

Disney, Walt *The Cinderella Magic Wand Book.* London: Dean & Son, 1950, Oblong small 4to., original cloth backed pictorial boards, corners worn and edges rubbed, pages 60 (i), 6 color plates and numerous black and white illustrations, complete with 'magic spectacles' in front pocket, 2 examples included. R. F. G. Hollett & Sons Antiquarian Booksellers 170 - 199 2011 £85

Disney, Walt *Father Noah's Ark.* Birn Brothers, circa, 1939, Oblong small 8vo., original pictorial boards, very slight rubbing to extremities, but lovely, bright colors, full black and white illustrations, front joint just splitting at foot, otherwise very nice, clean copy. R. F. G. Hollett & Sons Antiquarian Booksellers 170 - 199 2011 £85

Disney, Walt *Ferdinand the Bull Cut-Outs.* Racine: Whitman Pub, Co., 1938, 16 x 10 1/2 inches, cloth backed full color pictorial stiff card covers with some wear to covers, rear cover offers four punch-outs and there are three pages on stiff card within that also offer lots of full color punch-outs, complete and unpunched, quite scarce. Jo Ann Reisler, Ltd. 86 - 60 2011 $650

Disney, Walt *Mickey Mouse ABC Story.* Racine: Whitman, 1936, 4to., pictorial boards, some edge and tip wear, very good, each page features full color illustration done in shades of orange and black. Aleph-Bet Books, Inc. 95 - 192 2011 $400

Disney, Walt *Mickey Mouse Story Book.* Dean and Son, 1931, First softbound edition; pages 62, illustrated with cartoons and with flip characters in lower corners, original pictorial wrappers, creased, title little spotted with single crease down middle, occasional light fingering, but very scarce. R. F. G. Hollett & Sons Antiquarian Booksellers 170 - 203 2011 £180

Disney, Walt *Nursery Stories from Walt Disney's Silly Symphony.* Racine: Whitman Publishing Co., 1937, 4to., cloth backed illustrated boards with minor edge wear, full color pictorial dust jacket with some overall wear to jacket, internally paper is somewhat browned, 6 full page color plates plus many black and white drawings in text, 212 pages of text and pictures. Jo Ann Reisler, Ltd. 86 - 58 2011 $400

Disney, Walt *Walt Disney's version of Pinocchio.* Collins, 1940, First edition; 4to., original cloth backed pictorial boards, corners little worn, unpaginated, illustrations in color and black and white, small light stain to fore edges, sometimes spending to margins, otherwise very nice. R. F. G. Hollett & Sons Antiquarian Booksellers 170 - 202 2011 £75

Disney, Walt *Walt Disney's Snow White and The Seven Dwarfs adapted from Grimm's Fairy Tales.* New York: Harper Bros, 1937, Stated first edition; folio, cloth backed pictorial boards, 79 pages, fine in worn dust jacket, 32 color illustrations and many black and whites, bold Disney signature - studio signature by one of those authorized to sign. Aleph-Bet Books, Inc. 95 - 195 2011 $750

Disney, Walt *Walt Disney's Snow White & The Seven Dwarfs: a Story Based on a Famous Movie.* Racine: 1938, 94 pages, 4to., cardstock, coloring book, with some crayoning, titlepage loose with large chip at bottom, one leaf tape mended and poor quality paper permits of tears on few other leaves. Bookworm & Silverfish 676 - 63 2011 $75

Disney, Walt *Blanche-Neige et ses Amies Les Betes. (Snow White and Her Firneds the animals).* Paris: Hachette, 1938, First edition; 4to., full color illustrated boards with minor rubbing to edges and along spine, 60 numbered pages with 3 wonderful pop-ups. Jo Ann Reisler, Ltd. 86 - 59 2011 $800

Disney, Walt *Snow White Children's Album. (with) Pinocchio. (with) Gulliver's Travels Children's Album.* London: Chappell & Co., Victoria Music Pub. Co. n.d., circa, 1939, 3 volumes, 4to., original pictorial wrappers, each title 20 pages, illustrations. R. F. G. Hollett & Son Antiquarian Booksellers 175 - 376 2011 £75

Disney, Walt *Walt Disney's the Ugly Duckling adapted from Hans Christian Andersen.* Philadelphia: J. B. Lippincott Co., 1939, First edition thus; oblong 4to., green textured cloth with dark blue and red lettering and full color pictorial paste label, minor shelf wear, full color pictorial dust jacket with some chips at ends of spine, 12 full color illustrations plus line drawings. Jo Ann Reisler, Ltd. 86 - 64 2011 $300

Disraeli, Benjamin 1804-1881 *Novels and Tales by the Earl of Beaconsfield: with Portrait and Sketch of His Life.* London: Longmans, 1881, Hughenden edition; 11 volumes, half titles, frontispiece in volume I, engraved titles, largely unopened in original light brown cloth, oval blue morocco label on front boards, decorated in gilt, spines blocked in black, red and gilt, damp mark to back board of volume I, occasional slight rubbing, booklabels of L. R. Ascott, nice, bookplate of Leopold de Rothschild. Jarndyce Antiquarian Booksellers   CXCI - 11   2011   £280

Disraeli, Benjamin 1804-1881 *The Revolutionary Epick.* Paris: Longman, Green, Longman, Roberts and Green, 1864, First edition; 8vo., original bright copper brown cloth lettered gilt at spine, unopened, pages 176, uncut, very good+, bright clean copy with triangle excised from corner of front endpaper.   Any Amount of Books   May 26 2011 - X47684   2011 $470

Disraeli, Benjamin 1804-1881 *Sybil; or the Two Nations.* London: Henry Colburn, 1845, First edition; 3 volumes, bound without half titles, slight spotting to prelims of volume III, slightly later half red pebble grained morocco, raised bands in gilt, "Stickland" ownership stamp on titlepages, very good.   Jarndyce Antiquarian Booksellers   CXCI - 519   2011   £480

Disraeli, Benjamin 1804-1881 *The Tragedy of Count Alarcos.* London: Henry Colburn, 1839, First edition; titlepage at some time neatly repaired where signature of ownership removed at head, few leaves slightly marked, contemporary half red morocco, spine blocked and lettered in gilt, slightly rubbed, slight worming to one corner, armorial booklabel of Lord Carlingford, good plus copy.   Jarndyce Antiquarian Booksellers   CXCI - 160   2011   £250

Disraeli, Benjamin 1804-1881 *Vindication of the English Constitution in a Letter to a Noble and Learned Lord.* London: Saunders and Otley, 1835, First edition; 8vo., ix, (i), (3)-210 (2) pages, complete with half title, final leaf of ads and rare errata slip, few very minor blemishes and some light marginal soiling, old ink shelf or reference numbers on lower blank margin of one prelim leaf, old probably original, boards, little worn and soiled, rebacked, sometime in maroon patterned cloth, good large copy with generous margins, uncut, scarce.   John Drury Rare Books   153 - 35   2011   £400

Ditchfield, P. H. *The Cottages and the Village Life of Rural England.* London: J. M. Dent, 1912, First edition; original cloth, gilt, lower corners of boards trifle affected by damp, pages xiii, 185, top edge gilt, 52 superb colored plates and 19 line drawings by A. R Quinton, few spots to titlepage, but very nice.   R. F. G. Hollett & Son Antiquarian Booksellers   177 - 720   2011   £220

Ditchfield, P. H. *The Cottages and Village Life of Rural England.* London: J. M. Dent, 1912, First edition; 4to., original cloth, gilt, pages xiii, 185, top edges gilt, with 52 superb colored plates and 19 line drawings by A. R. Quinton, occasional spot, joints little tender.   R. F. G. Hollett & Son Antiquarian Booksellers   General Catalogue Summer 2010 - 1560   2011   £275

Ditchfield, P. H. *The Manor Houses of England.* London: Batsford, 1910, First edition; flyleaves spotted, half title little browned, tall 8vo., original blue pictorial cloth, extremities rather rubbed, spines little discolored, pages 211, (iv), top edge gilt, color frontispiece, full page and text drawings throughout by Sydney Jones.   R. F. G. Hollett & Son Antiquarian Booksellers   177 - 268   2011   £40

Ditchfield, P. H. *Vanishing England.* London: Methuen, 1910, First edition; pages xiv, 403, 32, illustrations, thick 8vo., original cloth, gilt, neatly recased.   R. F. G. Hollett & Son Antiquarian Booksellers   177 - 270   2011   £65

Ditchfield, P. H. *Vanishing England.* London: Methuen, 1911, Second edition; thick 8vo., original cloth, gilt, spine little faded, pages xiv, 403, 30, profusely illustrated by Fred Roe, half title foxed, else very nice.   R. F. G. Hollett & Son Antiquarian Booksellers   177 - 269   2011   £65

Divall, Colin *Suburbanizing the Masses: Public Transport and Urban Development in Historical Perspective.* Aldershot and Burlington: Ashgate, 2003, First edition; 8vo., xvi, 319 pages, figures, tables, pictorial boards, fine, from the Bern Dibner reference library, with Burndy bookplate.   Jeff Weber Rare Books   161 - 119   2011 $150

Divine, A. D. *My Best Secret Service Story.* London: Faber and Faber, 1940, First edition; corners little bumped, else near fine in good plus dust jacket with overall soiling and small chips and tears, scarce especially in jacket.   Between the Covers   169 - BTC322489   2011 $300

Dixie, Florence *In the Land of Misfortune.* London: Richard Bentley and Son, 1882, First edition; octavo, xvi, 434 pages, frontispiece, plates, original lime green pictorial cloth stamped in black and white by Burn, corners showing, rubbed, author's presentation, inscribed to Mr. Maclagan, from author, very good.   Jeff Weber Rare Books   163 - 154   2011 $300

Dixon, E. *Fairy Tales from the Arabian Nights. First and Second Series.* London: J. M. Dent, 1893-1895, 2 volumes, square 8vo., original decorated green cloth gilt, slight crease to one lower board, spines trifle dulled, pages (ii), 268; (ii), 256, with green floral endpapers, titles in red and black, 10 full page plates and 32 other illustrations, half titles and faintly page rather browned, presentation inscription, Welsh boxing bookplate of Harry Arthur James, very good. R. F. G. Hollett & Son Antiquarian Booksellers   175 - 87   2011   £250

Dixon, Joshua *The Literary Life of William Brownrigg...* London: Longman & Rees etc. and Whitehaven: A Dunn, 1801, First edition; original blue boards with paper spine label, very rubbed, pages xiv, 240 (i, errata leaf), very scarce, excellent, uncut, unsophisticated copy. R. F. G. Hollett & Son Antiquarian Booksellers 173 - 362 2011 £375

Dixon, Thomas *The Leopard's Spots.* New York: Doubleday, Page & Co., 1902, First edition; 8vo., 13, 465 pages, 10 plates, gilt stamped cloth backed boards, uncut, binding lightly soiled, text slightly warped and wavy, but little dampstaining, uncut, presentation copy prepared for W. H. Cathcart, general manager of Burrows Brothers in Cleveland, inscribed and signed in full and dated March 21 1902, at end of text "Annotated by author for W. H. Cathcart March 21-25 1902". M & S Rare Books, Inc. 90 - 111 2011 $2500

Dobbs, Betty Jo Teeter *The Foundations of Newton's Alchemy or "The Hunting of the Greene Lyon".* Cambridge: Cambridge University Press, 1975, 8vo., xv, 300 pages, 4 plates index, yellow cloth, gilt stamped spine label, fine, from the Bern Dibner reference library, with Burndy bookplate. Jeff Weber Rare Books 161 - 120 2011 $135

Dobbs, Betty Jo Teeter *The Janus Faces of Genius: The Role of Alchemy in Newton's Thought.* Cambridge: Cambridge University Press, 1991, First edition; 8vo, xii, 359 pages, 11 illustrations, black cloth, copper stamped spine title, dust jacket, near fine, from the Bern Dibner reference library, with Burndy bookplate. Jeff Weber Rare Books 161 - 121 2011 $100

Dobie, James *Memoir of William Wilson of Crummock.* Edinburgh: privately printed, 1896, First edition, number 12 of 60 copies; 8vo., original publisher's quarter leather lettered gilt on spine and on front cover, pages xliii, 238, uncut, slight wear at rear corner, slight splitting at head of spine, otherwise about very good+, with "George Shedden Esq./with the editor's kind regards". Any Amount of Books May 29 2011 - A47872 2011 $340

Dobson, Austin 1840-1921 *Thomas Bewick and His Pupils.* London: Chatto & Windus, 1889, Frontispiece, illustrations, 32 page catalog (Feb. 1889), original blue grey cloth, spine faded, very good. Jarndyce Antiquarian Booksellers CXCI - 68 2011 £50

Dobson, G. *Russia.* London: A. & C. Black, 1913, First edition; original pictorial cloth gilt, pages x, 479 with 48 color and 48 monochrome plates, very nice, clean, sound copy. R. F. G. Hollett & Son Antiquarian Booksellers General Catalogue Summer 2010 - 1637 2011 £150

Dobson, John *A Sermon Preacht at the Funeral of the Honourable the Lady Mary Farmor Relict of Sir William Farmor, Baronet, who Died at London on the 18th Day of July 1670...* London: printed for R. Royston, 1670, Small square 4to., later half straight grained morocco gilt, rather rubbed, pages iv, dedication and imprimatur), 40, title with engraved arms, titlepage and fore edge of final leaf rather dusty. R. F. G. Hollett & Son Antiquarian Booksellers 175 - 379 2011 £95

Dobson, Susanna *The Life of Petarch.* London: T. Bensely, 1797, Third edition; 2 volumes, engraved plates, manuscript poem on front endpaper, few fox marks to plates, half titles discarded, pages xviii, 388, (12); (ii), 410, (8), 8vo., 19th century vellum over boards, backstrips ruled in gilt with brown morocco labels, gilt lettering, boards bowing, marbled endpapers and edges, good, bookplates of Michael Pepper. Blackwell Rare Books B166 - 78 2011 £200

Doctor Comicus, or the Frolics of Fortune. London: B. Blake, 1825?, 210 133mm., 269 pages without printed titlepage, very attractive light tan smooth calf by Sangorski & Sutcliffe/Zaehnsdorf (stamp signed verso of front endpaper), covers bordered with French fillet and fleuron cornerpieces, raised bands, spine gilt in compartments featuring decorative bands, scrolling cornerpieces, fleuron centerpiece and small tools, maroon morocco labels, gilt inner dentelles, marbled endpapers, all edges gilt, 12 plates, all color by hand, bookplate of Robert Marceau; engraved title and two plates, little foxed, three plates slightly trimmed at fore edge, without apparent loss, few leaves with light marginal foxing, or soiling, otherwise excellent, plates bright and well preserved, leaves clean and fresh, sympathetic binding in mint condition. Phillip J. Pirages 59 - 331 2011 $400

Doctorow, E. L. *Billy Bathgate.* New York: 1989, First edition, one of 350 copies signed by author; fine in slipcase. Gemini Fine Books & Arts, Ltd. Art Reference & Illustrated Books: First Editions 2011 $75

Doctorow, E. L. *Lives of the Poets.* New York: 1984, First edition; one of 350 numbered copies, signed by author, fine in slipcase. Gemini Fine Books & Arts, Ltd. Art Reference & Illustrated Books: First Editions 2011 $80

Doctorow, E. L. *Loon Lake.* New York: 1980, First edition, one of 350 numbered copies signed by author; fine in slipcase. Gemini Fine Books & Arts, Ltd. Art Reference & Illustrated Books: First Editions 2011 $60

Document Showing the Testimony Given Before the Judge of the Fifth Judicial Circuit of the State of Missouri in the Trial of Joseph Smith Jr. and Others... Washington: Blair & Rives, 1841, 8vo., 47 pages, sewn as issued. M & S Rare Books, Inc. 90 - 260 2011 $750

Dodd, W. L. *Sketches and Rhymes.* North Shields: T. R. Harrison, 1859, First edition; original blue blindstamped cloth gilt, extremities trifle rubbed, pages (iv), 255, presentation copy by author for Phillis Chisholm, cousin. R. F. G. Hollett & Son Antiquarian Booksellers General Catalogue Summer 2010 - 638 2011 £180

Dodd, William 1729-1777 *An Oration Delivered at the Dedication of Free Masons' Hall, Great Queen Street, Lincoln's-Inn-Fields on Thursday May 23 1776.* London: printed for the Society, and sold by G. Robinson, Richardson and Urquhart... at the Free Mason's Hall, 1776, First edition; 4to., (4), 16, (4) pages, including two final ad leaves, original wrappers, entirely uncut and largely unopened, fine, crisp copy, rare. John Drury Rare Books 154 - 45 2011 £350

Dodd, William 1729-1777 *Thoughts in Prison, in five Parts.* London: printed for J. Mawman etc., 1815, Pages xviii, 212, (iv, ad), untrimmed, modern half levant morocco gilt. R. F. G. Hollett & Son Antiquarian Booksellers 175 - 380 2011 £95

Dodd, William 1729-1777 *The Visitor, by Several Hands, Published by William Dodd...* London: Printed for Edward and Charles Dilly, 1764, First edition; 12mo., 2 volumes, 6.5 x 4 inches, pages (10), 310; (2), 307, index (5), frontispiece in volume 1, contemporary full brown calf, gilt lined with 5 raised bands, spine unlettered, or most probably lacking spine labels, faint gilt volume numbers, hinges slightly tender, neat name at head of titlepages "Ann May Vansittart 1825", overall very good examples of scarce work. Any Amount of Books May 29 2011 - A34287 2011 $255

Dodge, Mary Mapes *Rhymes and Jingles.* New York: Scribner's, 1898, Reprint; 8vo., pages xii, 255, illustrations by various artists, bound in brown cloth, stamped in black and gilt, little rubbing, but near fine, inscribed by author. Second Life Books Inc. 174 - 125 2011 $65

Dodgson, Campbell *The Etchings of James McNeill Whistler.* London: The Studio, 1922, Number 179 of 200 copies; folio, 36 pages, 96 plates, of which 24 are photogravures, fine in original gilt lettered japanese vellum, plain paper protective wrapper, creased an original gilt lettered cloth drop lid case. Ken Spelman Rare Books 68 - 109 2011 £300

Dodgson, Campbell *An Iconography of the Engravings of Stephen Gooden.* London: Elkin Mathews, 1944, Number 215 of 500 copies; small 4to., original blue buckram gilt, trifle marked and bumped, pages xv, 196, with 19 plates, correction/errata slip tipped in. R. F. G. Hollett & Son Antiquarian Booksellers General Catalogue Summer 2010 - 109 2011 £95

Dodgson, Campbell *Prints in the Dotte Manner and Other Metal-Cuts of the XV Century in the Department of Prints and Drawings British Museum.* London: British Museum, 1937, First edition; 34 pages, frontispiece, 43 plates, very good in slightly rubbed original dark green cloth, bookplate of Denis Tegetmeier and note 'gift of Stanley Morison', folio. Ken Spelman Rare Books 68 - 120 2011 £90

Dodgson, Charles Lutwidge 1832-1898 *Alice's Adventures in Wonderland.* London: Ward Lock, n.d., Fourth edition; pages xvi, 332, (xii), 48 color plates by Margaret Tarrant, original cloth, pictorial onlay, little rubbed and marked, slight adhesion damage to 2 leaves, front joint cracked, prize label on flyleaf. R. F. G. Hollett & Sons Antiquarian Booksellers 170 - 665 2011 £45

Dodgson, Charles Lutwidge 1832-1898 *Alice's Adventures in Wonderland. (and) Through the Looking Glass and What Alice Found There.* London: Macmillan and Co., 1866, Second, but first published edition; 183 x 125mm., 2 separately published works bound in 2 volumes, extremely pleasing crimson levant morocco by Root & son (stamp-signed on front turn-in of both volumes), each cover with panels formed by double gilt rules and central gilt medallion, the "Wonderland" medallion depicting Alice holding baby pig, the "Looking-Glass" medallion showing grumpy Red Queen, raised bands, spines gilt in compartments with double ruled frames and small central quatrefoil, gilt ruled turn-ins, marbled endpapers, all edges gilt, with 92 illustrations, letter laid in from bookseller John Newbegin elucidating issue points, bookplate of Florence Magee; spines slightly and evenly a darkened red, handful of leaves with very minor foxing or smudges, one leaf with neat repair to tail edge (no text affected), but fine and attractive set, text clean, fresh, and smooth and bindings lustrous and virtually unworn. Phillip J. Pirages 59 - 176 2011 $11,500

Dodgson, Charles Lutwidge 1832-1898 *Alice's Adventures in Wonderland. (with Through the Looking Glass. (with) Through the Looking Glass and What Alice Found There.* London: MacMillan and Co., 1866-1872, First published edition with inverted 's' on last line of contents page; first edition of Though the Looking Glass and What Alice Found There; octavo, (xii) (1)-192 pages, 42 illustrations by John Tenniel, including frontispiece, original cloth bound in at end; octavo, (xii), (1)-224, (4) pages, with misprint 'wade' instead of 'wabe' on page 21, 50 illustrations by Tenniel including frontispiece, one page publisher's ads, original cloth binding bound in at end; the 2 volumes uniformly bound by Bayntun-Riviere in red calf, boards ruled in gilt, gilt dentelles, all edges gilt, stamped and lettered in gilt, spines stamped and lettered in gilt with blue and green spine label on each volume, marbled endpapers, three quarter inch closed tear professionally repaired to outer margin of K3 of volume I, bit of very light spotting on few pages, otherwise extremely nice housed together in red cloth slipcase. Heritage Book Shop Holiday 2010 - 17 2011 $12,500

Dodgson, Charles Lutwidge 1832-1898 *Alice's Adventures in Wonderland.* New York: Harper & Bros., 1901, First of this edition; 8vo., white imitation vellum boards with gilt decoration, iii-xvii, 1-192 + (1) pages, top edge gilt, fine in original dust jacket with gilt decoration, touch of fading to jacket, else near fine, gravure frontispiece and 40 extrordinary plates by Peter Newell.   Aleph-Bet Books, Inc.   95 - 132   2011 $675

Dodgson, Charles Lutwidge 1832-1898 *Alice's Adventures in Wonderland and Through the Looking Glass.* Chicago and New York: Rand McNally, 1902-1905, 8vo., green cloth stamped in white and blue, 336 pages, cover lettering slightly faded, else fine, illustrations by Fanny Cory with 48 black and whites including 8 full page for Alice and 25 black and whites in text for Looking Glass.   Aleph-Bet Books, Inc.   95 - 130   2011 $400

Dodgson, Charles Lutwidge 1832-1898 *Alice's Adventures in Wonderland.* London: William Heinemann; New York: Doubleday Page & Co., 1907, One of 1130 copies (this #701); 285 x 230mm., xi, (i), 161, (1) pages, (1) leaf (colophon), very attractive red three quarter morocco, raised bands, spine handsomely gilt in compartments formed by plain and decorative rules, quatrefoil centerpiece surrounded by densely scrolling cornerpieces, sides and endleaves of rose colored linen, top edge gilt, pictorial titlepage, four full page black and white illustrations and 13 color plates by Arthur Rackham, each mounted on heavy brown stock and protected by lettered tissue guard; corners rather rubbed, spine with shallow loss of leather across top, overall slight offsetting onto most of the 13 pages opposite brown mounting paper, as typical, otherwise text clean and fresh, binding lustrous.   Phillip J. Pirages   59 - 285   2011 $2250

Dodgson, Charles Lutwidge 1832-1898 *Alice's Adventures in Wonderland.* London: Philip Lee Warner, Publisher to the Medici Society Ltd., 1914, Limited, numbered edition of 1000 copies on handmade Riccardi paper; 8vo., top edge gilt, full leather signed "Birdsall London & Northampton) with color inlay on front cover of the White Rabbit and raised bands and gold lines on spine, slight rubbing to raised bands of otherwise clean, fresh copy, cloth slipcase, at most a touch of rubbing at corners, lovely copy, 131 numbered pages, illustrations by Tenniel.   Jo Ann Reisler, Ltd.   86 - 32   2011 $1500

Dodgson, Charles Lutwidge 1832-1898 *Alice's Adventures in Wonderland.* Boots the Chemists, n.d., 1922, 4to., original pictorial blue cloth gilt, extremities little rubbed, top of lower hinge cracked and repaired, pages (vi), 181, 12 fine tipped in tissue guarded color plates and orange and black text decorations by Gwynedd Hudson, fly-leaves rather spotted.   R. F. G. Hollett & Sons Antiquarian Booksellers   170 - 342   2011   £150

Dodgson, Charles Lutwidge 1832-1898 *Alice's Adventures in Wonderland.* New York: Limited Editions Club, 1932, Limited to 1500 numbered copies; 8vo., full red calf with extensive gilt decorations, fine in original slipcase (case browned around edges), printed by Rudge with beautiful full leather, one of approximately 500 copies signed by Warde and Alice Liddell Hargreaves, illustrations by John Tenniel.   Aleph-Bet Books, Inc.   95 - 137   2011 $2500

Dodgson, Charles Lutwidge 1832-1898 *Alice's Adventures in Wonderland and Through the Looking Glass.* Stockholm/London: Continental Book Co. AB, 1946, First edition of the Peake edition; 12mo., pictorial wrappers, 347 (5) pages, slight leaning, else near fineillustrations by Mervyn Peake, full and partial page black and white drawings, scarce.   Aleph-Bet Books, Inc.   95 - 136   2011 $400

Dodgson, Charles Lutwidge 1832-1898 *Alice's Adventures in Wonderland and through the Looking Glass.* Zephyr Books, 1946, First edition; original printed wrappers, hinges trifle rubbed, head of spine little chipped and creased, pages 352, illustrations by Peake.   R. F. G. Hollett & Sons Antiquarian Booksellers   170 - 507   2011   £120

Dodgson, Charles Lutwidge 1832-1898 *Alice's Adventures in Wonderland and Through the Looking Glass.* Allan Wingate, 1954, First UK edition; original cloth, gilt, dust jacket, head of spine trifle frayed, small piece torn from lower corner of rear panel with few creases, pages 264, with 65 illustrations by Mervyn Peake.   R. F. G. Hollett & Sons Antiquarian Booksellers   170 - 506   2011   £150

Dodgson, Charles Lutwidge 1832-1898 *Alice's Adventures in Wonderland and Through the Looking Glass.* London: Allan Wingate, 1954, First edition printed in England of the Mervyn Peake Alice; 8vo., blue cloth, 264 pages, slight cover wear, else very good+, no dust jacket, illustrations by Peake with 65 full and partial page black and whites plus dust jacket in red, very scarce.   Aleph-Bet Books, Inc.   95 - 135   2011 $250

Dodgson, Charles Lutwidge 1832-1898 *Alice's Adventures in Wonderland.* New York: Delacorte, n.d., 1977, First American edition with Jannson illustrations; 8vo., brown cloth stamped in gold, fine in dust jacket, illustrations by Tove Jannson, scarce.   Aleph-Bet Books, Inc.   95 - 131   2011 $250

Dodgson, Charles Lutwidge 1832-1898 *Alice's Adventures in Wonderland.* New York: Holt, Rinehart and Winston, 1985, Numerically stated first printing; 4to., cloth backed boards with silver lettering on spine, full color pictorial dust jacket, as new, signed in full drawing by artist, Michael Hague on dedication page, 122 numbered pages with lots of full color illustrations.   Jo Ann Reisler, Ltd.   86 - 130   2011 $300

Dodgson, Charles Lutwidge 1832-1898 *The Hunting of the Snark.* London: Macmillan, 1876, First edition; original pictorial cloth, little stained, upper hinge split and sometime repaired, pages xiv, 84, (ii), 9 illustrations by Henry Holliday, joints tightened.   R. F. G. Hollett & Sons Antiquarian Booksellers   170 - 138 2011   £250

Dodgson, Charles Lutwidge 1832-1898 *The Hunting of the Snark an Agony in Eight Fits.... (with) An Easter greeting to every child who loves 'Alice'.* London: Macmillan, 1876, First edition; 4to., pages (14), 86, frontispiece and 9 illustrations, including blank map fine except for occasional spotting, red cloth, border of six lines broken by circles enclosing illustrations on front and back, all gilt, gilt lettering to spine, all edges gilt, dark grey endpapers, hinges cracked but holding, endpapers almost detached, author's presentation inscription to his godson, Clement Rogers, with leaflet 16mo., pages (4) in staining running along outer fold, otherwise fine, disbound with single leaf, presentation inscription from author to Rogers.   Simon Finch Rare Books   Zero - 214 2011   £2750

Dodgson, Charles Lutwidge 1832-1898 *The Hunting of the Snark and Other Poems.* New York: Harper & Bros., 1903, First edition with Peter Newell's illustrations; 8vo., white imitation vellum boards, gilt decoration, titlepage, fine in original cloth backed dust jacket (with some fading, spine fraying and mends on verso, but really very good+), tissue guarded color frontispiece and 39 plates by Peter Newell.   Aleph-Bet Books, Inc.   95 - 133 2011 $500

Dodgson, Charles Lutwidge 1832-1898 *Sylvie and Bruno.* London: Macmillan and Co., 1889, but 1898. People's edition; original green pictorial cloth, spine trifle rubbed, pages xxiii, 400, 46 illustrations by Harry Furniss, endpapers rather spotted.   R. F. G. Hollett & Sons Antiquarian Booksellers   170 - 139 2011   £45

Dodgson, Charles Lutwidge 1832-1898 *Sylvie and Bruno concluded.* London: Macmillan and Co., 1893, First edition; original red cloth gilt, little marked and darkened, pages xxiii, 423 (vi), all edges gilt, 46 illustrations by Harry Furniiss.   R. F. G. Hollett & Sons Antiquarian Booksellers   170 - 140 2011   £85

Dodgson, Charles Lutwidge 1832-1898 *Three Sunsets and Other Poems.* London: Macmillan and Co. Ltd., 1898, First edition; 8vo., pages (x), 67, (1) (4) ads, 12 engraved plates after drawings by Gertrude Thompson, original pale blue green pictorial cloth, lettered and blocked in gilt to upper side, circular gilt design to lower side, edges gilt, light even sunning to spine, much less than usual, near fine.   Simon Finch Rare Books   Zero - 304 2011   £300

Dodgson, Charles Lutwidge 1832-1898 *Three Sunsets and Other Poems.* London: Macmillan, 1898, First edition; small 4to., cloth stamped in gold, all edges gilt, (68) pages, 2 page ads, very slight spine faded and slight wear to spine extremities, very good- fine, illustrations by E. Gertrude Thomson, 12 delicate full page engravings.   Aleph-Bet Books, Inc.   95 - 138 2011 $500

Dodgson, Charles Lutwidge 1832-1898 *Through the Looking Glass and What Alice Found There.* London: Macmillan, 1872, First edition, first issue; original red cloth gilt, rather darkened, neatly recased, pages (vi), 224, (ii), all edges gilt, 50 illustrations by John Tenniel, contemporary inscription dated Xmas 1871, few slight marks but very good.   R. F. G. Hollett & Sons Antiquarian Booksellers   170 - 141 2011   £650

Dodgson, Charles Lutwidge 1832-1898 *Through the Looking Glass and What Alice Found There.* London: Macmillan, 1898, Large 8vo., old binder's cloth gilt, trifle bubbled, pages 126, 50 illustrations by John Tenniel.   R. F. G. Hollett & Sons Antiquarian Booksellers   170 - 142 2011   £35

Dodgson, Charles Lutwidge 1832-1898 *Through the Looking Glass and What Alice Found There.* New York: Harper & Bros., 1902, (Oct. 1902). First edition with these illustrations; 8vo., white imitation vellum boards with gilt decoration, fine in original green cloth backed wrapper and printed inner glassine wrapper as well (green wrapper slightly faded, else near fine glassine wrapper chipped), illustrations by Peter Newell, with gravure frontispiece, 40 full page plates, wonderful copy.   Aleph-Bet Books, Inc.   95 - 134 2011 $650

Dodgson, Charles Lutwidge 1832-1898 *Useful and Instructive Poetry.* London: Geoffrey Bles, 1954, First edition; fine, dust jacket near fine, tears to acetate portion of dust jacket, front flap not affected.   Bella Luna Books   May 26 2011 - t9218 2011 $192

Dods, Margaret *The Cook and Housewife's Manual, Containing the Most Approved Modern Receipts for Making Soups, Gravies, Sauces, Ragouts, Pies, Puddings, Pickles, Preserves and Home Made Wines.* Edinburgh: Oliver and Boyd, 1827, Second edition; half title, wood engraved illustrations in text, 6 leaves of ads, some spotting, mostly in blank margins, uncut, (12), (4), 525, (1), 2 pages, later calf backed boards, spine gilt.   Anthony W. Laywood   May 26 2011 - 21563 2011 $486

Dods, Mary Diana *Tales of the Wild and the Wonderful.* London: Hurst, Robinson and Co., Edinburgh: A. Constable and Co., 1825, First edition; scarce, 8vo., pages xii, 356, extremely bright and fresh, all edges marbled, contemporary calf, upper and lower boards ruled in gilt, spine blind-stamped with gilt spots and decorative pattern at head and foot, green morocco lettering piece with gilt lettering, marbled endpapers, very light shelfwear only, engraved bookplate of Henry Lee Warner and small bookseller's sticker to front pastedown, ownership inscriptions dated 1827 and 1853 to front free endpaper, fine.   Simon Finch Rare Books   Zero - 228   2011   £1200

Dodsley, Robert   1703-1764 *The Art of Preaching: in Imitation of Horcae's Art of Poetry.* London: printed for R. Dodley at Tullys Head in Pall Mall, 1738, First edition; folio, (2), 18 pages, good copy, disbound.   Anthony W. Laywood   May 26 2011 - 21694   2011 $134

Dodsley, Robert   1703-1764 *A Collection of Poems... by Several Hands.* London: For J. Dodsley, 1782, 6 volumes, 173 x 116mm., half titles, superb contemporary sprinkled calf, flat spines, wide gilt bands forming elegantly gilt compartments with scrolling cornerpieces and large sunburst centerpiece, red and green morocco labels, engraved vignette titlepage, engraved and woodcut headpieces and tailpieces, 2 engraved plates; perhaps 20 leaves with moderate foxing, small dent and puncture in fore edge of four gatherings of first volume (text unaffected), frequent offsetting in text, otherwise only insignificant defects internally, leaves quite fresh and clean, covers with only trivial imperfections, especially attractive bindings remarkably well preserved.   Phillip J. Pirages   59 - 10   2011 $1900

Dodsley, Robert   1703-1764 *Select Fables of Aesop and Other Fabulists.* London: William Osborne & J. Mozeley, circa, 1790, New edition; modern calf, gilt, pages xlviii, 228, (xxiv), engraved frontispiece and woodcut illustrations, little spotting and browning.   R. F. G. Hollett & Son Antiquarian Booksellers   175 - 381   2011   £95

Dodsley, Robert   1703-1764 *The Oeconomy of Human Life.* N.P.: n.p., printed in the year, 1772, Faint stain to fore edge, pin prick wormhole in margin of final few leaves, pages 176, 8vo., contemporary sheep, spine with five raised bands between gilt fillets, red morocco lettering pieces, slightest bit worn at corners, but exceptionally well preserved, very good.   Blackwell Rare Books   B166 - 31   2011   £350

Dodsley, Robert   1703-1764 *The Economy of Human Life.* London: Toplis and Benney, 1780, Small 8vo., old full calf, rather rubbed and dulled, spine frayed at head, label chipped, pages xxv, 26-191, complete with half title, edges rather browned, drop title to second part, scarce.   R. F. G. Hollett & Son Antiquarian Booksellers   175 - 382   2011   £175

Dodsley, Robert   1703-1764 *Oeconomy of Human Life.* London: printed by T. Rickaby for S. and E. Harding, 1795, First edition with these illustrations; 272 x 85mm., 2 p.l., (5)-22 pages, (1) leaf, (119 pages (pages 117-119 ads as called for), large paper copy, apparently one of 25 in this format, quite attractive contemporary English crimson straight grain morocco, handsomely gilt, covers with borders of one plain and one decorative gilt rule and small fleuron in each corner, raised bands, spine elegantly gilt in compartments with foliate cornerpieces framing a large cruciform ornament with ribbon outlines enclosing a central starburst on stippled background, turn-ins with gilt Greek key roll, marbled endpapers, all edges gilt; 49 mostly large and always charming engraved emblematic headpieces and tailpieces by Sylvester Harding, typically showing human or angelic figures representing such abstract ideas as contentment, pity, or fortitude; armorial bookplate of Joseph Neeld, modern bookplate of John Porter, handwritten bookseller's? description signed "EB" and dated 1 Feb. 1804 tipped onto front flyleaves; covers slightly marked with minor spotting and soiling, trivial smudges internally, nearly fine and especially pretty copy, original luxury binding lustrous and with virtually no wear, text printed with vast margins extremely fresh and smooth, rare format.   Phillip J. Pirages   59 - 28   2011 $1250

Dodsley, Robert   1703-1764 *A Select Collection of Old English Plays.* London: Reeves and Turner, 1874-1876, Fourth edition; 8vo., 6000+ pages, original publisher's green cloth lettered gilt at spine, boards of few volumes bleached from dampstaining, some shelfwear, but sound, close to very good set.   Any Amount of Books   May 29 2011 - A42288   2011 $340

Dodwell, William *The Sick Man's Companion: or The Clergyman's Assistant in Visiting the Sick.* London: printed for B. White, 1768, Second edition; (8), xlvii, 48-260 pages, 8vo., little waterstaining to foot of final few leaves, contemporary calf, head and tail of spine and first 2 inches of upper joint worn, 19th century bookplate of Rev. John T. H. Le Mesurier, with his pencil notes to endpaper and in several margins; 18th century prayer written in earlier hand on final blank.   Jarndyce Antiquarian Booksellers   CXCI - 162   2011   £90

Dog and Cat Land. London: Raphael Tuck, n.d., circa, 1890, 8vo., pictorial card covers, rear cover soil and light shelfwear, very good, 5 charming full page chromolithographs and in brown line on text pages.   Aleph-Bet Books, Inc.   95 - 144   2011 $250

Doherty, P. C. *A Tournament of Murders.* London: Headline, 1996, First British edition; fine, dust jacket fine, signed by author.   Bella Luna Books   May 29 2011 - t8494   2011 $82

Doig, Ivan *The Sea Runners.* New York: Atheneum, 1982, First edition; vook very good, "not for resale" stamped on edge of leaves, start of foxing to bottom edge, dust jacket very good, price clipped, light creasing and soiling, scarce. Bella Luna Books May 29 2011 - t3407 2011 $137

Doig, Ivan *This House of Sky.* New York: HBJ, 1978, First edition; near fine, previous owner's embossing stamp on front free endpapers, top of spine lightly bumped, dust jacket near fine, creasing and rubbing to spine ends, author's elusive first book. Bella Luna Books May 29 2011 - t1369 2011 $93

Doisneau, Robert *La Banlieue de Paris.* Paris: Pierre Seghers, 1949, Preferred edition; 8vo., pages 56, 135, (5), with 128 black and white photos printed in gravure, original cream paper covered boards, spine and upper board lettered in black, original black and white photo illustrated dust jacket, text printed in black, expertly repaired at head of spine and folds of flaps, near fine. Simon Finch Rare Books Zero - 519 2011 £1250

Doke, Clement M. *The Lambas of Northern Rhodesia; a Study of their Customs and Beliefs.* London: Geo. Harrap, 1931, First edition; 8vo., pages 408, map, 110 illustrations, original blue cloth, dust jacket. J. & S. L. Bonham Antiquarian Booksellers Africa 4/20/2011 - 2236 2011 £60

Dolbey, George W. *The Architectural Expression of Methodism. The First Hundred Years.* Epworth Press, 1964, First edition; original cloth, gilt, dust jacket price clipped, pages x, 195, with 24 pages of plates and plans, edges lightly spotted, presentation copy inscribed by author and signed on title, uncommon. R. F. G. Hollett & Son Antiquarian Booksellers 177 - 271 2011 £45

Dollard, John *Criteria for the Life History with Analyses of Six Notable Documents.* New Haven: Yale University Press for the Institute of Human Relations, 1935, First edition; 8vo., original publisher's grey cloth with printed spine label, pages v, 288, loosely inserted is good 1935 TLS from author to H. G. Wells, spine label very slightly soiled, otherwise very good+. Any Amount of Books May 29 2011 - A45555 2011 $230

Dolling, Robert R. *Ten Years in a Portsmouth Slum.* London: S. C. Brown, 1903, Sixth edition; original cloth, gilt, hinges little rubbed, spine frayed at ead and foot, pages 272, with 18 plates, joints tender, few spots. R. F. G. Hollett & Son Antiquarian Booksellers 175 - 383 2011 £50

Dolly. Boston: De Wolfe Fiske & Co. circa, 1890, 13 1/2 x 6 1/2 inches in size, full color pictorial stiff card covers, shapebook cut around border of this elegantly dressd doll, some light wear overall, 15 pages within (counting inside covers), each with lots of attractive pictures, four of the pages in full color, the rest in sepia tones. Jo Ann Reisler, Ltd. 86 - 233 2011 $275

Donaldson, John William *The Theatre of the Greeks, a Treatise on the History and Exhibition of the Greek Drama...* London: Longman and Co., 1860, Seventh edition; pages xii, 414, all edges and endpapers marbled, 5 engraved plates, full tan calf gilt prize binding over bevelled boards by Bickers, upper hinge cracked, spine rubbed and defective at head. R. F. G. Hollett & Son Antiquarian Booksellers 175 - 384 2011 £50

Donaldson, Lois *In the Mouse's House.* Chicago: Laidlaw, 1930, Printed in Germany; oblong 4to., cloth, pictorial paste on, near fine, full page richly color illustrations, 3 color pictures, all by Mathilde Ritter. Aleph-Bet Books, Inc. 95 - 355 2011 $200

Donellan, John *The Trial of John Donellan, Esq. for the Wilful Murder of Sir Theodosius Edward Allesley Boughton, Bart.* London: sold by George Kearsley, 1781, Second edition; folio, excellently rebound in quarter sprinkled calf, double gilt banded spine, red gilt morocco label, marbled boards, vellum cornerpieces, very good, clean copy. Jarndyce Antiquarian Booksellers CXCI - 163 2011 £250

Donleavy, J. P. *The Ginger Man.* Franklin Library, 1867, Signed edition; bookplate and ownership blindstamp, otherwise fine. Gemini Fine Books & Arts, Ltd. Art Reference & Illustrated Books: First Editions 2011 $65

Donleavy, J. P. *The Ginger Man.* Paris: Olympia Press, 1958, First edition, publisher asserts there were 500 copies Printed, many were allegedly destroyed by British customs; fine, in fine dust jacket. Bella Luna Books May 26 2011 - j1020 2011 $330

Donleavy, J. P. *A Singular Man.* London: Bodley Head, 1965, First UK edition; fin in near fine dust jacket, light soiling to rear panel. Bella Luna Books May 26 2011 - t9231 2011 $165

Donne, John *(Biathanatos). A Declaration of that Paradoxe or Thesis that Selfe-homicide is not so Naturally Sinne, that it my never be otherwise.* London: John Dawson, 1647, First edition; 4to., pages (xviii), 192 '19', 192-218, without initial blank, first three leaves remargined at head, early ink date attribution to title, MS. notes (in another hand) to front free endpaper, some light marginal offsetting from turn-ins onto first and final couple of leaves, contemporary panelled calf, expertly rebacked preserving original spine, new rear free endpaper (original now bound in at front), new spine label lettered in gilt, nice, crisp copy. Simon Finch Rare Books Zero - 103 2011 £3500

Donne, John *Biathanatos. (in Greek).* London: printed for Humphrey Moseley, 1648, First edition of second issue, with cancel titlepage, of original undated edition; small quarto, half 19th century brown morocco over marbled boards.   Heritage Book Shop   Booth A12 51st NY International Antiquarian Book Fair April 8-10 2011 - 46   2011 $2000

Donner, Etta *Hinterland Liberia.* London: Blackie, 1939, First edition; 8vo., pages xiv, 302, maps on endpapers, illustrations, original black cloth.   J. & S. L. Bonham Antiquarian Booksellers   Africa 4/20/2011 - 3556   2011   £35

Donovan, Edward *The Natural History of British Shells, Including Figures and Descriptions of all the Speces Hietherto Discovered in Great Britain...* London: printed for the author and for F. and C. Rivington, 1799-1803, First edition; 180 hand colored engraved plates (brown spots to 2 plates, all other plates virtually fine), with explanatory letterpress for each plate, 8vo., original boards, expertly rebacked with boards covered with paper sympathetic to the period, endpapers tastefully renewed, some of the endpapers foxed, light foxing and marginal stain to title, some splitting to edges of spine to volume I, but solid, plates remarkably clean.   Raymond M. Sutton, Jr.   May 26 2011 - 50534   2011 $4800

Doolittle, Hilda *Hippolytus Temporizes. a Play in Three Acts.* Boston and New York: Houghton Mifflin, 1927, First edition; 8vo, pages (x) 139, uncut, signed prsesentation from author to Murray Constantine (Katherine Burdekin), neat HD obituary press cutting inserted, patterned paper covered boards, slightly mottled, black cloth spine slightly faded/slightly sunned, endpapers slightly foxed, very good in near very good slipcase with printed label.   Any Amount of Books   May 29 2011 - A40498   2011 $221

Doran, Dr. *Monarchs Retired from Business.* London: Richard Bentley, 1857, First edition; 2 volumes, original blindstamped cloth, gilt, extremities rubbed, pages viii, 416; vi, 420, with 2 steel engraved plates.   R. F. G. Hollett & Son Antiquarian Booksellers   175 - 385   2011   £45

Dorn, Edward *Gunslinger Book II.* Los Angeles: Black Sparrow Press, 1969, First edition, one of 250 signed with date and place at rear; 8vo., pages 62, fine, signed to his in-laws on half title.   Any Amount of Books   May 29 2011 - A66646   2011 $213

Dorn, Edward *High West Rendezvous: an Edward Dorn Sampler.* Hay on Wye: Etruscan Books/West House Books, 1996, First edition; 8vo., wrappers, 57 pages, signed by author for Robert and Tatiana Dunbar, fine.   Any Amount of Books   May 29 2011 - A66641   2011 $272

Dorset, Catherine Ann *The Peacock at Home.* London: Harris, 1808, Square 16mo., tan pictorial wrappers, 16 pages, very good+, new edition, illustrations by W. Mulready.   Aleph-Bet Books, Inc.   95 - 280   2011 $600

Dosabhai Sohrabji, Munshi *Help to Conversation in English and Marathi, Embracing Six Parts.* Bombay: printed at the "Indu Prakash" Press, 1864, First edition; lacks front flyleaf, Royal Colonial Library stamp on title, text in English and Marathi in parallel columns, (8), 143, (1) pages, original cloth boards, spine worn, original printed label on upper cover, frayed, label presenting this book to Royal Colonial Institute pasted onto pastedown endpaper.   Anthony W. Laywood   May 26 2011 - 19862   2011 $201

Doten, Dana *The Art of Bundling.* London: Coutnryman Press and Farrar & Rinehart, 1938, Original cloth with paper spine label, dust jacket (little worn and chipped), pages 190, 36 woodcuts.   R. F. G. Hollett & Son Antiquarian Booksellers   175 - 386   2011   £30

Doubleday, Thomas *The Coquet-Dale Fishing Songs.* William Blackwood and Sons, 1852, First edition; original blindstamped green cloth gilt, gilt vignette to upper board, spine rather faded and frayed at head and foot, pages vi, (ii), 168, engraved portrait frontispiece, 9 pages of music, few spots to frontispiece and title, contemporary signature of Geo. Freeman.   R. F. G. Hollett & Son Antiquarian Booksellers   175 - 387   2011   £175

Doudney, Sarah *Thistle-Down.* London: Marcus Ward & Co. n.d. c., 1893, Original cloth backed pictorial boards, pages 32, full page color frontispiece and chromolithographed vignettes, patterned endpapers, nice, fresh copy.   R. F. G. Hollett & Son Antiquarian Booksellers   General Catalogue Summer 2010 - 512   2011   £35

Dougall, John *The Self Instructor of Young Man's Companion...* Halifax: William Milner, 1850, Original blindstamped crimson cloth gilt with pictorial gilt spine, little marked and neatly recased, pages iv, 572, engraved frontispiece and title, 3 folding maps, new endpapers.   R. F. G. Hollett & Sons Antiquarian Booksellers   170 - 205   2011   £85

Douglas, Alfred, Lord *Without Apology.* London: Martin Secker, 1938, First edition; 8vo., 316 pages, original publisher's red cloth lettered gilt on spine, pages 316, slight rubbing, slight soiling, slightly discolored at spine, else sound near very good with clean text.   Any Amount of Books   May 29 2011 - A70913   2011 $238

Douglas, Norman   1868-1952 *Some Antiquarian Notes.* Napoli: R. Tiopografia Francesco Giannini & Figli, 1907, First edition, one of just 250 copies; 8vo., pages 58, bound in printed red wrappers (worn, front detached), rare.   Second Life Books Inc.   174 - 126   2011 $563

Douglas, Robert *The Peerage of Scotland: containing an Historical and Genealogical Account of the Nobility of that Kingdom.* Edinburgh: printed by George Ramsay and Co. for Archibald Constable and Co., 1813, Second edition; 2 volumes, folio, pages xiii, (i), ,759, (i), xiv, 9 engraved plates; iv, 748, xiii, (i), 8 engraved plates, contemporary diced Russia, five flat raised banded spine decorative roll gilt and blind tooled, elaborate symmetrical centerpieces gilt in compartments, lettered and numbered direct in gilt, boards triple rule gilt bordered with decorative roll lozenge in blind, board edges single rule gilt, turn-ins decorative roll gilt, 'French Shell' 'made' endpapers, all edges 'Stormont' marbled, 3 color (fawn, white and blue) symmetrical patterned sewn endbands (toned and foxed in places, rubbed and scratches, spine ends and joints worn and defective in places, board edges sometime renewed in lighter leather, hinges cracked but sound, armorial bookplate of William Gordon Esqr. of Fyvie, signed binding by or produced for A. Brown & Co., with his ticket, from the collection of Christopher Ernest Weston 1947-2010. Unsworths Booksellers 24 - 88 2011 £400

Douglas, William O. *Go East, Young Man, the Early Years.* New York: Random House, 1974, First edition; fine, dust jacket near fine, very light use, laid in is gift letter to Walter Gerash from Lucius Woods dated Feb. 25, 1991. Bella Luna Books May 29 2011 - t9174 2011 $82

Dove, John *Miscellaneous Dissertations on Marriage, Celibacy, Covetousness, Virtue, the Modern System of Education &c.* London: John Millan and S. Bladon, 1769, First edition; 8vo., viii, 68 pages, few old annotations and emphasis marks in text, slight paper flaw on title with displacement of two letters of one word in imprint, but no loss, recent marbled boards lettered on spine, very good. John Drury Rare Books 153 - 36 2011 £275

The Dowie Dens O' Yarrow. London: printed for the members of the Royal Aossition for the Promotion of the Fine Arts in Scotland, 1860, Large folio, original limp green boards, gilt, unpaginated, initials in red and 6 full page engraved plates. R. F. G. Hollett & Son Antiquarian Booksellers General Catalogue Summer 2010 - 672 2011 £85

Dowling, Henry G. *A Survey of British Industrial Arts.* Benfleet: F. Lewis, 1935, First edition; 4to., pages 57 plus 100 plates, ex-library with pocket removed, light embossed stamp on titlepage, cover lightly scuffed at edges, one hinge tender, other beginning, otherwise very good. Second Life Books Inc. 174 - 127 2011 $85

Down Near the Lilly Pond. Chicago: Volland, 1931, Magic roundabout book, illustrations printed on 4 color illustrated wheels attached to wooden paddle, wheels are 9 3/8 inch diameter and it is 12 inches from bottom oof wooden handle to top of wooden handle to top of wheel, triangular window cut into top wheel so that reader can create different versions of text, very rare. Aleph-Bet Books, Inc. 95 - 379 2011 $1500

Downey, Fairfax *Dogs of Destiny.* New York: Scribner, 1949, (A); 8vo., cloth, 186 pages, fine in frayed dust jacket, warmly inscribed to Scribner editor with fine drawing of dog and inscribed by Downey as well, scarce title, special copy inscribed by Brown and Downey with drawing by Brown. Aleph-Bet Books, Inc. 95 - 124 2011 $800

Downs, Dotty *Trailor Family Cut-Out.* Akron: Saalfield, Oblong folio, pictorial wrappers, covers dusty and pinhole in corner of pages, else very good+ and unused, all pages have color lithographed illustrations meant to be cut out to assemble the 4 members of the Trailer family, their auto, their trailer and furniture, very scarce. Aleph-Bet Books, Inc. 95 - 400 2011 $475

Downs, Hugh *My America: What My Country Means to Me by 150 Americans from all Walks of Life.* Norwalk: Easton Press, 2002, Limited edition, number 1159 of 1160 copies; signed by author on limitation page, leather with gold titles and decorations, all edges gilt, silk endpapers and ribbon bookmark, very clean and tight, 266 pages, fine. G. H. Mott Bookseller May 26 2011 - 37093 2011 $180

Dowson, Ernest *The Pierrot of the Minute.* London: Leonard Smithers, 1897, First edition; large 8vo., pages 43, frontispiece, initial letter, vignette and cul-de-lampe by Aubrey Beardsley, chartreuse cloth, stamped in gilt, owner's name and date on flyleaf, cover little worn at corners and ends of spine, otherwise very good, tight copy. Second Life Books Inc. 174 - 28 2011 $950

Doyle, Arthur Conan   1859-1930   *Adventures of Sherlock Holmes.* London: George Newnes, 1892, First edition, first issue with no street name on front cover; "Violent" for "Violet" on page 317, large octavo, (4), 317, (1, printer's imprint) (2, blank) pages, 104 illustrations by Sidney Paget in text, original light blue cloth over beveled boards, front cover and spine blocked and lettered in gilt and black, all edges gilt, gray flower and leaf endpapers, small ink initials to front free endpaper, front hinge professionally and invisibly repaired, back hinge starting but firm, slight bit of shelf wear to top and bottom of spine, some light foxing to few prelim and final pages, else near fine, exceptionally clean and bright, housed in tan cloth clamshell, the fine "Ellery Queen" (Manfred Lee) and "Barnaby Ross" (Frederic Dannay) names in ink on half title. Heritage Book Shop Holiday 2010 - 30 2011 $17,500

Doyle, Arthur Conan   1859-1930   *The Adventures of Sherlock Holmes.* London: George Newnes, 1892, First edition; first issue, large octavo, names in ink on half title, original light blue cloth over bevelled boards, fine Ellery Queen copy, with Manfred Lee and Frederic Dannay names in ink on half title. Heritage Book Shop Booth A12 51st NY International Antiquarian Book Fair April 8-10 2011 - 47 2011 $17,500

Doyle, Arthur Conan 1859-1930   *The Doings of Raffles Haw.* London: Cassell & Co., 1892, First edition; half title, 8 pages ads, slight paper browning, partially uncut in original dark blue cloth, slightly rubbed, top edge gilt.   Jarndyce Antiquarian Booksellers   CXCI - 164   2011   £200

Doyle, Arthur Conan 1859-1930   *The Hound of the Baskervilles.* London: George Newnes Limited, 1902, First edition; 8vo., pages (x), 359, (i) blank, 16 illustrations by Sidney Paget, original red boards, upper and spine with text and illustration in gilt from black, previous owner's presentation inscription dated in year of publication, occasional rust marks and light soiling, stain staining to lower board, overall fresh and bright.   Simon Finch Rare Books   Zero - 221   2011   £1800

Doyle, Arthur Conan 1859-1930   *The Hound of the Baskervilles.* London: George Newnes, 1902, First edition in book form; small octavo, (8), 358, (1) (1, blank) pages, 16 plates, including frontispiece by Sidney Paget, original scarlet cloth pictorially stamped in gilt and black (in a design by Alfred Garth ones) and lettered gilt on front cover and pictorially stamped and lettered in gilt on front cover and pictorially stamped and lettered in gilt on spine, spine slightly faded, minor blistering to cloth on covers near joints, minimal foxing to edges, free endpapers slightly browned from pastedown glue, otherwise excellent copy with gilt bright and fresh.   David Brass Rare Books, Inc. May 26 2011 - 00348   2011 $5500

Doyle, Arthur Conan 1859-1930   *Memoirs of Sherlock Holmes.* London: George Newnes Ltd., 1894, First edition; royal octavo, (vi) (1), 279, (1, blank) pages, frontispiece, 90 illustrations by Sidney Paget, dark blue cloth over heavy beveled boards, front board and spine blocked in black and gilt, lettered in gilt, grey floral patterned endpapers, all edges gilt, faint ownership inscription, inner hinges slightly starting but firm, some wear to extremities, overall very good.   Heritage Book Shop   Holiday 2010 - 31   2011 $1500

Doyle, Arthur Conan 1859-1930   *Our African Winter.* London: John Murray, 1929, First edition; photographic frontispiece, Doyle's presentation inscription on titlepage for friend Nederburgh (possibly author H. G. Nederburgh), very good copy, some wear and rubbing at extremities, especially at top of spine, nice spine gilt, tight.   Lupack Rare Books   May 26 2011 - ABE4707850377   2011 $875

Doyle, Arthur Conan 1859-1930   *The Return of Sherlock Holmes.* London: Smith, Elder & Co., 1908, 8vo., original publisher's blue cloth lettered gilt on spine and cover, pages (viii) 403, all 16 Sidney Paget plates present, very slightly darkened at spine, slight rubbing, faintly nicked, slightly bumped at corners, otherwise clean, very good.   Any Amount of Books   May 29 2011 - A68922   2011 $204

Doyle, Arthur Conan 1859-1930   *The Silver Hatchet. The Gully of Bluemansdyke, Cyprian Overbeck Wells, John Barrington Cowles.* New York: 1896, 223, ads (5 pages), small 8vo., inexpensive paper, original binding.   Bookworm & Silverfish   669 - 135   2011 $125

Doyle, Roddy   *The Commitments.* London: Heinemann, 1988, First British edition; near fine, previous owner's name and one word notation on titlepage, very light use.   Bella Luna Books   May 29 2011 - t3663   2011 $137

Doyle, Roddy   *Paddy Clarke Ha Ha Ha.* London: Viking, 1993, First British edition; fine, dust jacket near fine, light creasing to edges and rear flap.   Bella Luna Books   May 26 2011 - t3561   2011 $192

Doyle, Roddy   *The Van.* New York: Viking, 1992, First edition; fine in near fine dust jacket, price clipped.   Bella Luna Books   May 29 2011 - t1109   2011 $82

Doyle, Roddy   *The Van.* London: Secker & Warburg, 2004, First British edition; book fine, near fine dust jacket, price clipped,.   Bella Luna Books   May 29 2011 - t8029   2011 $80

A Dozen on Denver. Gulden: Fulcrum, 2009, First edition; fine, signed by Connie Willis, Nick Arvin, Robert Greer, Margaret Coel, Manuel Ramos and Arnold Grossman.   Bella Luna Books   May 29 2011 - p3633   2011 $104

Dozois, Gardner   *The Year's Best Science Fiction: Ninth Annual Collection.* New York: St. Martins Press, 1992, First edition; octavo, boards.   L. W. Currey, Inc.   124 - 210   2011 $150

Drabble, Margaret   *A Brief History of My Addiction.* London: Warren Editions, 1974, First separate appearance; one of 150 copies privately distributed for publisher's to celebrate birth of Daisy Victoria Gili, 4 1/2 x 5 1/4 inches, self wrappers, fine, scarce.   Ken Lopez Bookseller   154 - 47   2011 $350

Drabble, Margaret   *A Writer's Britain.* London: Thames & Hudson, 2009, First edition; fine in fine dust jacket, signed by author.   Bella Luna Books   May 29 2011 - t9418   2011 $82

Drake, Daniel *Natural and Statistical View or Picture of Cincinnati and the Miami Country.*   Cincinnati: Looker and Wallace, 1815,   First edition; 2 engraved folding maps (foxed, tear to inside lower corner of each map), 12mo., pages xii, (13)-251, (4), contemporary tree calf, few old abrasions, clear sealant reinforces outer hinges, bookplate removed, browning and soiling to endpapers, 2 old pictures pasted on front blank pages, pages tanned, some foxing to back pages, old clipping glued to rear pastedown, the copy of J. Burgoyne Jr. dated 1855, and H. Hall, Cincinnati with his red stamp.   Raymond M. Sutton, Jr.   May 26 2011 - 55852 2011 $1350

Drake, Francis *Eboracum; or the History and Antiquities of the City of York... together with the History of the Cathedral Church...*   London: printed by William Bowyer for the author, 1736,   Folio, pages (xxviii) 398 (ii) 399-627 (i) cx (xxv) + 59 engraved plates, there are a further 55 engravings among the letterpress, some full page, second half of 18th century diced Russia consummately rebacked & recornered . 1830, seven compartmented spine gilt extra with multi rule bands and massed decorative roll infills, original brown lettering piece gilt relaid, boards decorative roll gilt bordered with cornerpieces, board edges decorative roll gilt, all edges gilt & gauffered, blue and mauve sewn endbands, little light toning, slight dust soiling at beginning, boards touch sunned in places, extra illustrated copy, principally by inclusive of i - mezzotint portrait engraving of Francs. Drake, ii - mezzotint portrait engraving of Mr. Thos. Gent, also 8 minor embellishments at pages 27, 224, 258, 286, 301, 398, additional titlepage and 483, from the collection of Christopher Ernest Weston 1947-2010.   Unsworths Booksellers   24 - 89 2011   £1750

Drake, Francis *The History and Antiquities of the City of York, from its Origin to the Present Times.*   York: printed by A. Ward, 1785,   3 volumes, 12mo., pages (iv), 400 + folding engraved plan frontispiece and 17 other engraved plates; (ii), 402 + 2 other extending engraved plates; (iv), 292 + folding engraved map and one other folding engraved plate, contemporary polished tan calf, spine single rule gilt, red and green lettering and numbering pieces gilt, board edges obliquely broken fillet roll in blind, a lemon, fawn and white sewn endbands, some toning and spotting edges of few folding plates little darkened and frayed, touch of wear to endcaps, front joint of volume I cracked, armorial bookplate of Lord Arundell Wardour, from the collection of Christopher Ernest Weston 1947-2010.   Unsworths Booksellers   24 - 90 2011   £300

Drake, Joseph Rodman *The Croakers.*   New York: Bradford Club, 1860,   First complete edition, limited to 250 copies, this #25 of 100 copies of the Club edition; large 8vo., 8 191 pages, 2 portraits, contemporary three quarter morocco, marbled sides, slight foxing.   M & S Rare Books, Inc.   90 - 114 2011 $300

Drake, Joseph Rodman *The Culprit Fay and Other Poems. (with) Alnwick Castle with Other Poems.*   New York: George Dearborn; New York: George Dearborn, 1835,   First edition; original publisher's cloth, faded.   M & S Rare Books, Inc.   90 - 115 2011 $200

Drake, Leah Bodine *A Hornbook for Witches: Poems of Fantasy.*   Sauk City: Arkham House, 1950,   First edition; octavo, cloth.   L. W. Currey, Inc.   124 - 17 2011 $3000

Drake, Stillman *Essays on Galileo and the History and Philosophy of Science.*   Toronto, Buffalo, London: University of Toronto Press, 1999,   3 volumes, 8vo., xxiii, 473; viii, 380; vi, 392 pages, frontispiece, plates, illustrations, tables, original cloth, gilt stamped cover and spine titles, near fine, from the Bern Dibner reference library, with Burndy bookplate.   Jeff Weber Rare Books   161 - 123 2011 $225

Drake, Stillman *Galileo: Pioneer Scientist.*   Toronto: University of Toronto Press, 1990,   First edition; 8vo., xviii, 261 pages, fine in fine dust jacket, with ANS laid in, book and letter both inscribed to noted British historians of science Rupert and Marie Hall.   By the Book, L. C. 26 - 97 2011 $225

Drayton, Richard *Nature's Government: Science, Imperial Britain and the "Improvement" of the World.*   New Haven and London: Yale University Press, 2000,   First edition; 8vo, xxi 346 pages, frontispiece, 14 plates, 28 illustrations, black cloth gilt stamped spine title, dust jacket, rare, fine, from the Bern Dibner reference library, with Burndy bookplate.   Jeff Weber Rare Books   161 - 125 2011 $100

The Dream of the Rood.   Flemington: St. Teresa's Press, 1966,   One of 150 copies (this #10); 260 x 210mm., 4 p.l., 14 pages, (2) leaves, publisher's pleasing cocoa brown textured paper backed with dark brown polished calf, gilt titling on front cover, hand painted initials, virtually pristine.   Phillip J. Pirages   59 - 308 2011 $325

Dreiser, Theodore 1871-1945   *An American Tragedy.* New York: Limited Editions Club, 1954,   First edition thus; one of 1500 numbered copies, illustrations by Reginald Marsh, fine in slipcase, with LEC letter, artist died just before publication, thus not signed.   Gemini Fine Books & Arts, Ltd.   Art Reference & Illustrated Books: First Editions 2011 $125

Dreiser, Theodore 1871-1945   *The Financier.*   New York: Boni & Liveright, 1927,   Revised edition; spine soiled and bit darkened, good plus without dust jacket, Dwight Macdonald's copy with his bookplate, Macdonald has made a number of slightly insouciant marginal critical notations in pencil in text.   Between the Covers   169 - BTC335183 2011 $450

Dreiser, Theodore 1871-1945 *Sister Carrie.* New York: Limited Editions Club, 1939, First edition, one of 1500 numbered copies; illustrated and signed by Reginald Marsh, book fine, slipcase very close to fine. Gemini Fine Books & Arts, Ltd. Art Reference & Illustrated Books: First Editions 2011 $225

Drew, Bernard *The London Assurance.* London: Curwen Press, 1950, Pages xv, 334, with 53 illustrations, fine, original cloth, gilt, dust jacket. R. F. G. Hollett & Son Antiquarian Booksellers 175 - 388 2011 £35

Drexelius, Jeremias *The Considerations of Drexelius Upon Eternitie.* London: printed by John Redmayne, 1663, 18mo., old splashed calf, nicely rebacked in matching calf gilt with raised bands and lettering piece, pages (xxii), 358, engraved title printed at Cambridge by Roger Daniel and 8 woodcut plates, signature of Matthew Wren on engraved title and some marginal annotations, probably in his hand, some later annotations in another hand (probably that of Lord Torphichen, whose armorial bookplate is on pastedown), few pencilled marginal crosses, originally the copy of Matthew Wren (1585-1667), Christopher Wren's uncle. R. F. G. Hollett & Son Antiquarian Booksellers 175 - 389 2011 £650

Dreyfus, John *Givoanni Mardersteig: an Account of His Work.* Officina Bodoni, 1966, One of 135 copies Printed; very good and tight, 19 pages, printed as a keepsake for Gallery 303 to accompany a lecture given in NY by author 5 Oct. 1966. G. H. Mott Bookseller May 26 2011 - 39674 2011 $300

Drinkwater, John 1882-1937 *Cotswold Characters.* New Haven: 1921, First edition; brown craft paper over boards, paper label very clean, corners sharp, five woodcuts by R. Nash. Bookworm & Silverfish 679 - 160 2011 $75

Drinkwater, John 1882-1937 *A Tribute to the Late C. Lovat Fraser.* N.P.: 1921, 4 pages, stiff wrappers, wrapper stock has shadowed on first and last pages, this shadow accentuated by a tissue over wrapper on which is pencilled a brief title. Bookworm & Silverfish 678 - 74 2011 $150

Driscoli, Jim *The Straight Left and How to Cultivate It.* Athletic Publications, circa, 1943?, Half title, frontispiece, illustrations, 1 page ads, original white pictorial boards, printed in red, very slight wear to head and tail of spine, very good. Jarndyce Antiquarian Booksellers CXCI - 362 2011 £65

Droz, Gustave *Un Ete a La Compagne. Correspondance de Deux Jeunes Parisiennes Receuillie pa un Auteur a la Mode.* Brussels: Poulet Malassis, 1868, First edition; 12mo., pages (iv), 227, frontispiece in 2 states (one black, one in bistre), contemporary citron half morocco, gilt decorated and black spine label lettered within gilt raised band compartments, all edges gilt, clipings from old catalogues to rear free endpaper, slight pale foxing to first and last leaves, as is usual with papier de chine, overall beautiful copy, finely bound. Simon Finch Rare Books Zero - 425 2011 £2950

Druitt, Robert *A Popular Tract on Church Music, with Remarks on Its Moral and Political Importance and a Practical Scheme for Its Reformation.* London: Francis & John Rivington, 1845, First edition; 8vo., 62 (2) pages with some musical notation in text, recent marbled boards lettered on spine, very good, scarce. John Drury Rare Books 154 - 46 2011 £125

Drummond, Henry *The Ascent of Man.* London: Hodder & Stoughton, 1894, First edition; original cloth, gilt, extremities little rubbed, pages xi, 444, (i), upper joint cracked, mss. notes on author on flyleaf. R. F. G. Hollett & Son Antiquarian Booksellers 175 - 392 2011 £30

Drummond, J. C. *The Englishman's Food.* London: Cape, 1957, Revised edition; original cloth, gilt, dust jacket, spine rather darkened and frayed at head and foot, pages 482, 8 plates. R. F. G. Hollett & Son Antiquarian Booksellers General Catalogue Summer 2010 - 1106 2011 £45

Drummond, W. H. *The Large Game: and Natural History of South and South East Africa.* Edinburgh: Edmonston and Douglas, 1875, First edition; large 8vo., pages xxi, 428, map, color frontispiece, tinted illustrations, textual illustrations, margins little browned, rebound in 1936 in black half morocco, small split in base of spine. J. & S. L. Bonham Antiquarian Booksellers Africa 4/20/2011 - 9186 2011 £125

Drusius, Joannes *Animadversionum Libri Duo. (bound with) De Quaesitis per Epistolam.* Leiden: Jan Paets, 1585, Franeker: Gilles van den Rade, 1595; 2 volumes in 1, 8vo., 2 parts, 79, (1); 68 (i.e. 86) (2) pages, printer's device, woodcut head and tailpieces, initials; Oxford contemporary calf, strips of musical manuscript of vellum used as spine liner, extremities slightly rubbed, manuscript notes on prelim leaf and on pasteboard, from the library of the Earls of Macclesfield at Shirburn Castle. Maggs Bros. Ltd. 1440 - 71 2011 £500

Drusius, Joannes *Annotationum in Totum Iesu Christi Testamentum sive Praeteritorum Libri Decem.* (bound with) *Ad Voces Ebraicas Novi Testamenti Commentarius Duplex.* Amsterdam: J. Janssz, 1632, Franeker: F. Heyns for Jan. Jansz, 1616; 2 works in 1 volume, 4to., (8), 456, (12) pages; (8), 226, (10), 138, (8), 1-183, (8), 185-192, 9-52 pages, small clear tear in Ff2 of part I, contemporary English calf, red edges, head of spine slightly worn, from the library of the Earls of Macclesfield at Shirburn Castle.   Maggs Bros. Ltd.   1440 - 70   2011   £400

Dryden, John   1631-1700   *The Medall.* London: Jacob Tonson, 1682, First edition, 2nd issue; small 4to., pages (12), 20, bound in modern thin marbled boards, leaves toned, very good, tight, clean copy.   Second Life Books Inc.   174 - 129   2011 $500

Dryden, John   1631-1700   *Secret-Love; or the Maiden Queen.*   London: for Henry Herringman, 1691, Small 4to., disbound, minute rust hole to two leaves, else very good.   Dramatis Personae Booksellers   106 - 51   2011 $100

Dryden, John   1631-1700   *The Works.* London: printed for William Miller by James Ballantyne, Edinburgh, 1808, 18 volumes, 220 x 145mm., very pleasing polished calf, handsomely gilt, from the first third of the 19th century, sides with simple frame of double gilt fillets, spines densely gilt in compartments featuring many floral and foliate stamps, raised bands with oblique gilt hatching, olive and ochre morocco labels, marbled edges and endpapers, frontispiece, one folding plate, most volumes with at least some foxing, occasional gatherings with noticeable spotting, otherwise excellent internally little wear to some spine ends and to one corner, labels slightly faded, handful of covers lightly scratched or chafed, few other minor defects but quite appealing set, nevertheless, with almost no wear to joints.   Phillip J. Pirages   59 - 184   2011 $1900

Drygalski, Erich Von   *Deutsche Sudpolar-Expedition 1901-1903 in Auftrage des Reichsamtes des Innern.*   Berlin: 1905, Paperback, Volumes I-XX i 83 parts and 5 atlases, 1155 plates (78 colored and some others tinted), some plates folding tinted maps, small marginal dampstain to plate, verso of plate dampstained, lower corner of several plates in Volume VIII(I) dampstained adhesion to a plate), 3 folding colored maps and numerous text figures, in separate parts with original printed wrappers, some wrappers soiled, faded, chipped and/or with tears, while others near fine, backstrip partially perished, 2 front wrappers loose, lower corner of pages and plate from Volume V(IV) dampstained, many lower corners to Atlas II, Erdmagnetismus dampstained, rippling to lower corners of volume VIII(v), an occasional corner to a wrapper missing, plate section to volume XVII detached, small stains to few wrappers, faint marginal dampstaining to pages of 2 other volumes, and atlas on Erdmagnetismus, a volume on botany and 12 volumes on zoology.   Raymond M. Sutton, Jr.   May 26 2011 - 46461   2011 $5000

Du Boccage, Marie Ann Le Page   *La Colombiade.*   Paris: Chez Desaint & Saillant/Durant, 1756, First edition; 8vo., pages viii, 184, (2), frontispiece, portrait of author and 10 engraved plates, engraved vignette on title, headpiece and 10 engraved tailpieces, original uncut marbled wrappers, lacks paper on spine, Swedish bookplate, fine.   Second Life Books Inc.   174 - 130   2011 $750

Du Bois, W. E. Burghardt   *The Souls of Black Folk: Essays and Sketches.*   London: Archibald Constable, 1905, First UK edition (from American sheets); original publisher's black boards lettered gilt at spine, pages 265, uncut, frontispiece with tissue guard, faint browning to endpapers, very slight rubbing at corners, otherwise about fine.   Any Amount of Books   May 26 2011 - A44454   2011 $470

Du Bois, William Pene   *The Forbidden Forest.*   London: Chatto & Windus, 1978, First edition; 4to., original pictorial boards, dust jacket, illustrations in color.   R. F. G. Hollett & Sons Antiquarian Booksellers   170 - 207   2011   £35

Du Bois, William Pene   *The Great Geppy.*   London: Robert Hale, n.d. circa, 1939, First edition; original cloth, dust jacket little worn, top edge creased and chipped, illustrations in color and line.   R. F. G. Hollett & Sons Antiquarian Booksellers   170 - 208   2011   £45

Du Bois, William Pene   *The 21 Balloons.*   New York: Viking, 1947, First edition; tall 8vo., cloth backed patterned boards, fine in very good+ dust jacket very slightly rubbed, many full page and in text illustrations.   Aleph-Bet Books, Inc.   95 - 205   2011 $475

Du Chaillu, Paul Belloni   *Explorations and Adventures in Equatorial Africa with Accounts of the Manners and Customs of the People, and of the Chase of the Gorilla, the Crocodile, Leopard, Elephant Hippopotamus and Other Animals.*   New York: Harper and Brothers, 1861, Octavo, xxii, (23)-531 4 (ads) pages, 80 illustrations, large folding map, few small nicks to fore-edge margin, original full embossed brown cloth with image of African man on upper cover, gilt rubbed, gilt dulled, very good plus.   Jeff Weber Rare Books   163 - 159   2011 $200

Du Chatelet, Marquise De   *Institutions de Physique.*   Paris: Prault, 1740, First edition; (8), 450 pages, (28), 8vo., contemporary marbled calf, gilt decorated spine, all edges gilt, engraved allegoric frontispiece, large vignette on titlepage, 21 engraved vignettes at head of each chapter, 11 folding plates, minor restoration, very attractive.   Paulette Rose Fine and Rare Books   32 - 157   2011 $4500

Du Maurier, Daphne   *The Apple Tree.*   London: Gollancz, 1952, First edition; 264 pages, fools cap 8vo., original pink boards, backstrip gilt lettered, edges lightly foxed, dust jacket, near fine.   Blackwell Rare Books   B166 - 135   2011   £75

Du Maurier, Daphne *The Breaking Point.* London: Gollancz, 1959, First edition; pages 288, foolscap 8vo., original pink boards, faded backstrip gilt lettered, free endpapers lightly browned, dust jacket internally reinforced with tape at head of backstrip panel, backstrip panel browned, good.   Blackwell Rare Books B166 - 136 2011 £50

Du Maurier, Daphne *The Glass Blowers.* London: Gollancz, 1963, First edition; pages 320, crown 8vo., original scarlet boards, backstrip gilt lettered, dust jacket, just trifle rubbed at head, near fine, scarce.   Blackwell Rare Books B166 - 137 2011 £70

Du Maurier, Daphne *The House on the Strand.* London: Gollancz, 1969, First edition; full page map and genealogical table, pages 352, crown 8vo., original scarlet boards, backstrip gilt lettered, dust jacket slightly rubbed, near fine. Blackwell Rare Books B166 - 138 2011 £50

Du Maurier, Daphne *Mary Anne. A Novel.* London: Gollancz, 1954, First edition; pages 380, foolscap 8vo., original scarlet boards, backstrip gilt lettered, dust jacket little soiled, very good.   Blackwell Rare Books B166 - 139 2011 £40

Du Maurier, Daphne *My Cousin Rachel.* London: Gollancz, 1953, First edition; 352 pages, foolscap 8vo. original russet cloth, backstrip blocked in black, dust jacket little soiled, chipped, with few short tears and with internal tape repair, good.   Blackwell Rare Books B166 - 140 2011 £50

Du Maurier, Daphne *The Parasites.* London: Gollancz, 1949, First edition; prelims, final few leaves and edges lightly foxed, pages 352, foolscap 8vo., original limp green cloth, backstrip blocked in maroon, dust jacket, backstrip panel faded, small light glue shadow where label has been removed, very good.   Blackwell Rare Books B166 - 141 2011 £40

Du Maurier, Daphne *Rebecca.* New York: Doubleday Doran & Co. Inc., 1938, First US edition; signed by author on a special page and bound in, fine, bright, tight copy in attractive dust jacket with just bit of rubbing to spine ends and top corner of front panel, exceptional copy.   Buckingham Books May 26 2011 - 25791 2011 $3500

Du Maurier, George Louis Palmella Busson 1834-1896 *Trilby.* Osgood, McIlvaine & Co.,, 1894, Serialised in Harper's Monthly Magazine, Volume LXXXVIII Dec. 1893 to May 1894; Titlepage of the European edition, illustrations, contemporary half maroon morocco, raised bands, gilt compartments, hinges neatly repaired, 6 page news paper article "Trilby" from Publishers' Weekly Aug. 1928 tipped in, 4 page ALS from author to Sir William Morrow, original brown cloth bound in at end of volume, armorial bookplate of Albert Henry Wiggin, very good.   Jarndyce Antiquarian Booksellers CXCI - 166 2011 £150

Du Maurier, George Louis Palmella Busson 1834-1896 *Trilby.* Osgood, McIlvaine & Co., 1894, Second edition; 3 volumes, half titles, partially uncut in early navy blue cloth, some very slight marking in volume III, top edge gilt, very good.   Jarndyce Antiquarian Booksellers CXCI - 520 2011 £150

Du Moulin, Lt. Col. *Two Years on Trek.* London: Murray and Co., 1907, First edition; 8vo., pages vi, 323, 11, folding map, original purple decorative cloth, spine faded.   J. & S. L. Bonham Antiquarian Booksellers Africa 4/20/2011 - 9023 2011 £85

Du Petit-Thouars, Abel Aubert *Voyage Autor Du Monde.* Paris: Gide, 1840-1843, First edition; four octavo text volumes and folio atlas, atlas complete with 68 plates, text in contemporary quarter brown calf over marbled boards, atlas in contemporary quarter black polished calf over blue cloth, rebacked preserving original spine.   Heritage Book Shop Booth A12 51st NY International Antiquarian Book Fair April 8-10 2011 - 48 2011 $30,000

Du Petit-Thouars, Abel Aubert *Voyage Autour Du Monde Sur La Fregate La Venus, Pendnat Lew Annees 1836-1839.* Paris: 1842, First edition of volumes 6 and 7; 3 volumes (volumes 6, 7 and 9 only), 464 pages, untrimmed, paper (age soil), edges shelf worn; 456 pages, untrimmed, paper (age soil), edges shelf worn, missing top half of backstrip; volume 9 454 pages, errata, 2 folding charts and large folding map, backstrip darkened, with 4 page ALS signed at Brest 1836 to Emnangant in Paris.   Bookworm & Silverfish 678 - 23 2011 $2250

Du Ruau, Jean *Cy Commence Une Petite Instruction et Maniere de Viure Pour une Fe(m)e Seculiere...* Paris: Guillaume Merlin, circa, 1650, Small 8vo., pages (48), printed in Gothic type, full page white line metal cut, 2 text woodcuts, wood and metalcut initials, title in four block woodcut frame, woodcut title device, bound in 19th century half green morocco, spine and title gilt, all edges gilt, ruled in red.   Second Life Books Inc. 174 - 131 2011 $6500

Du Toit, S. J. *Rhodesia: Past and Present.* London: Wm. Heinemann, 1897, First edition; 8vo., pages xvii, 218, ads, 16 illustrations, some occasional foxing, original red cloth, spine faded with some flecking.   J. & S. L. Bonham Antiquarian Booksellers Africa 4/20/2011 - 4845 2011 £50

Du Val, Charles *With a Show through Southern Africa and Personal Reminicences of the Transvaal War.* London: Tinsley Bros., 1882, First edition; 8vo., 2 volumes in one, pages viii, 290; vii, 230, frontispiece, original red decorative cloth, all edges gilt, spine faded, armorial crest of St. James' Collegiate School, Jersey on upper cover.   J. & S. L. Bonham Antiquarian Booksellers Africa 4/20/2011 - 4540 2011 £295

Du Verdier, Claude *In Autores Pene Omnes Antiquos Potissimum Censio qua.. Grammaticorum, Potissimum, Censio; Wua.. Grammaticorum, Poetarum....* Lyons: B. Honore, 1586, First edition; 4to., 187, (5) pages, errata on page *188-189), (190-192) blank, device on titlepage, English binding of brown calf, gilt, fillets on covers, gilt spine lettering piece, red, green and white silk maker, from the library of the Earls of Macclesfield at Shirburn Castle. Maggs Bros. Ltd.   1440 - 74   2011   £950

Du Verney, Joseph Guichard *Tractatus de Organo Auditus Continens Structuram Usum et Morbos Omnium Auris Partium.* Nuremberg: Johann Zieger, 1684, First edition in Latin; 4to., (12) 48 pages, 16 engraved folding plates, 19th century paper wrappers, plate 16 neatly backed, title very lightly soiled, else very good, Joseph Friedrich Blumenbach's copy with his signature on verso of titlepage, in fine morocco backed clamshell box.   Joseph J. Felcone Inc.   Fall Miscellany 2010 - 85   2011 $4800

Dubbey, J. M. *The Mathematical Work of Charles Babbage.* Cambridge: Cambridge University Press, 1978, First edition; 8vo., viii, 235 pages, frontispiece, illustrations, black cloth, gilt stamped spine title, dust jacket, near fine, from the Bern Dibner reference library, with Burndy bookplate.   Jeff Weber Rare Books   161 - 124   2011 $165

Dubois, William Edward Burghardt 1868-1963 *The Quest of the Silver Fleece a Novel.* Chicago: McClurg, 1911, First edition; 8vo., pages 434, plates, bound in publisher's blue cloth, some faded and little soiled, very good. Second Life Books Inc.   174 - 133   2011 $550

Dubordieu, John *Statistical Survey of the County of Antrim with Observations on the Means of Improvement....* Dublin: Graisberry & Campbell, 1812, First edition; thick 8vo., xix, 630, 112 pages, 1 engraved folding map, 9 engraved folding plates, 1 engraved folding diary, 7 engraved plates, 1 text engraving, neatly rebacked with original calf boards, gilt decorated spine, fine, rare.   Jeff Weber Rare Books   163 - 158   2011 $750

Dubuisson *Memoire sur les Acides Natifs du Verjus de l'Orange, et du Citron.* Paris: Lambert & Baudouin, 1783, First edition; 8vo., pages iv, (5)-30, (2), title dust soiled and slight stained, old ink inscription, uncut and partly unopened, stab sewn as issued, nice unsophisticated copy, scarce. Simon Finch Rare Books   Zero - 120   2011   £250

Dubus, Andre *The Lieutenant.* New York: Dial, 1967, First edition; near fine, publisher's stamp on front free endpapers, dust jacket very good-, 1 inch chip at top front corner, 2 small closed tears, light soiling, very good-, 1 inch chip at top front corners, 2 small closed tears, light soiling. Bella Luna Books   May 29 2011 - t1180   2011 $82

Dubus, Andre *The Lieutenant.* New York: Dial Press, 1967, First edition; Near fine in very good dust jacket with small chips and tears, signed and inscribed and dated 13 July 1993, slight sunning at spine tips.   Charles Agvent 2010 Summer Miscellany - 26   2011 $600

Ducamp, Emmanuel *Imperial Palaces in the Vicinity of Saint Petersburg: Peterhof, Gachina Pavlovsk...* Paris: Alain De Gourcuff, 1992, First edition; 4 volumes, 4to., pages 438, copiously illustrated in color, all fine in very good+ printed illustrated box, excellent condition.   Any Amount of Books   May 29 2011 - A66648   2011 $272

Duchamp, Marcel *From the Green Box.* New Haven: Readymade Press, 1957, first edition, signed, 400 copies printed; 8vo., pages (62), crisp and clean copy, original black boards patterned with white strips of paper reproducing author's handwriting, some light shelf wear, light offsetting to endpapers, original stone-grey and black dust jacket, couple of nicks along top edge but otherwise extremely well kept, signed by Duchamp and translator George Heard Hamilton dated 1958, near fine.   Simon Finch Rare Books Zero - 213   2011   £950

Ducrest, Georgette *Memoirs of the Court of the Empress Josephine: Being the Secret Memoirs of Madame Ducrest.* Boston: L. C. Page and Co., 1900, Volumes 1 and 2 (of 3), red cloth with gilt decorations, soiled and worn on spines, bookplates, hinge broken, top edge gilt, marginal pencil marks on several pages, otherwise clean and tight, 345, 378 pages, illustrations.   G. H. Mott Bookseller   May 26 2011 - 40749   2011 $200

Ducrot, Nicolas *Andre Kertesz: Sixty Years of Photography 1912-1972.* New York: Grossman Publishers, 1972, First edition; clean, very near fine with small owner name on front free endpaper in fine dust jacket with crease to front flap, signed and inscribed by Keretsz in 1975 on titlepage.   Jeff Hirsch Books   ny 2010   2011 $1000

Dudley, Carrie *My Peek-A-Book Show Book.* Minneapolis: Buzzo a Gordon Volland Book, 1928, Large oblong 4to., cloth backed pictorial boards, very fine in original box, box flaps repaired, 8 thick cardboard scenes with holes cut out in various places, any one of these scenes can be placed over any one of 6 paper pages so reader can change text and illustrations, scarce, rare in box.   Aleph-Bet Books, Inc.   95 - 380   2011 $500

Dudson, Audrey M. *Dudson. A Family of Potters Since 1800.* Stoke-on-Trent: Dudson Brothers, 1985, First privately printed; (2000 copies), pages xiv, 284, with 25 color plates, 91 monochrome plates, 8 plans, 3 maps, and 5 family trees, original cloth, gilt, dust jacket spine rather faded and chipped at head.   R. F. G. Hollett & Son Antiquarian Booksellers   General Catalogue Summer 2010 - 115   2011 £35

Duell, Prentice *The Mastaba of Mereruka Part I. Chambers a 1-10 Plates 1-103.* Chicago: University of Chicago Press, 1938, Elephant folio, boards bowed, edge worn, very clean and tight, 103 plates, part I only, very good. G. H. Mott Bookseller May 26 2011 - 43680 2011 $1100

Duell, Prentice *The Mastaba of Mereruka Part I. Chambers a 1-10 Plates 1-103 Part II. Chambers A 11-13. Doorjambs ad Inscriptions of Chambers A1-21. Tomb Chamber Exterior Plates 104-219 by the Sakarah Expedition.* Chicago: University of Chicago Press, 1938, Very good, elephant folio, boards bowed, edge worn, very clean and tight, 219 plates, in 2 volumes. G. H. Mott Bookseller May 26 2011 - 53679 2011 $3400

Duff, Charles *Spain at War: a Monthly Journal of Facts and Pictures.* London: 1938, First edition; 7 issues, Nos. 1, 3, 4, 5, 6, 7, 8, illustrated wrappers, approximately 272 pages, copiously illustrated in black and white, spines little worn, slightly rubbed, otherwise sound near very good. Any Amount of Books May 29 2011 - A62572 2011 $340

Duffett, Thomas *The Amorous Old-VVoman; or 'tis Vvell If it Take. A Comedy. Acted by His Majesties Servants.* London: printed for Simon Neale at the Three Pidgeons in Bedford Street in Covent Garden and B. Tooth near York House in the Strand, 1674, First edition; 4to., final unpaginated leaf lacks epilogue, some spotting in places in text, (6), 72 pages, disbound. Anthony W. Laywood May 26 2011 - 21751 2011 $134

Dufresne, John *Well Enough Alone: Two Stories and Thirteen Poems.* Candia: Le Bow, 1996, Limited to 10 numbered presentation copies; fine, illustrations by Dina Knapp, fine dust jacket, signed by author and artist. Bella Luna Books May 26 2011 - 2174 2011 $192

Dugdale, Florence E. *The Book of Baby Beasts.* New York: Hodder & Stoughton circa, 1911, First American edition; large 4to., cloth backed boards with brown lettering and circular full color paste label of a cute squirrel, edges of boards rubbed and bump to lower edge of front cover, some minor overall shelf wear, 120 numbered pages with 19 mounted full color plates by Detmold. Jo Ann Reisler, Ltd. 86 - 54 2011 $475

Dugdale, Thomas *England and Wales Delienated.* L. Tallis, n.d. circa, 1860, 8 volumes, original stamped blue cloth gilt, spines little faded overall, 7 engraved frontispieces, 7 engraved titles with vignettes, 53 hand colored double page maps, 176 steel engraved plates, front flyleaf volume I removed, joints of volume 2 cracked, else very good, sound set. R. F. G. Hollett & Son Antiquarian Booksellers General Catalogue Summer 2010 - 1380 2011 £350

Dugdale, Thomas *England and Wales Delienated.* L. Tallis, n.d. circa, 1860, 8 volumes, original stamped blue cloth gilt, spines little faded overall, 7 engraved frontispieces, 7 engraved titles and vignettes, 53 hand colored double page maps and 176 steel engraved plates, front flyleaf of volume 1 removed, joints of volume 2 cracked, else very good, sound set. R. F. G. Hollett & Son Antiquarian Booksellers General Catalogue Summer 2010 - 1379 2011 £85

Dugdale, William 1605-1686 *The Antiquities of Warwickshire Illustrated from Records...* printed by Thomas Warren in the year of our lord God..., 1656, First edition; frontispiece by Hollar (laid down on buff paper), laid down titlepage printed in red and black, slightly trimmed at head with old paper repairs at gutter, woodcut initial letters, head and tailpieces, near contemporary ink presentation inscription at head of first dedication page, 5 double page engraved maps (two laid down), profusely illustrated with numerous engravings in text, upper fore corner of pages 385-6 in ms. facsimile, a considerable number of old paper repairs (some inexpert) mainly to leaf margins and corners, sporadic ink spots and waterstains (mostly not affecting text), pages (16) 232 283-460 471-732, 743, 724-826, (16) pages, (15) leaves of plates, folio, near contemporary reversed calf rebacked with original calf backstrip laid down, backstrip with contemporary gilt lettered red morocco label, gilt dated at foot (modern addition), sides blind panelled (nap worn at extremities and with minor scuff marks), cream endpapers, sound. Blackwell Rare Books B166 - 32 2011 £900

Dugdale, William 1605-1686 *Antiquities of Warwickshire Illustrated...* London: printed by Thomas Warren, 1656, First edition; pages (160, 232, 283-460, 471-732, 743, 724-826, (14) + foldout maps and plates, frontispiece, red and black titlepage, full or part page engravings, frontispiece and titlepage laid onto new sheets, both dedicatory epistle pages archivally repaired with new paper round margins, further occasional paper repairs to page edges, occasional smudging or spotting, almost never affecting text or legibility, 2 neat previous owner inscriptions to front blanks, contemporary full calf leather, soundly rebacked with gilt decoration and red gilt title, label to spine, very good. Any Amount of Books May 26 2011 - A72189 2011 $1174

Dugdale, William 1605-1686 *Monasticon Anglicanum; or the History of the Ancient Abbies, Monasteries, Hosptials...in England and Wales. (with) ... Two Additional volumes to Sir William Dugdale's Monasticon Anglicanum.* London: R. Harbin for D. Browne and J. Smith (et al) for Tho. Taylor..., 1718, 1722-1723; 3 volumes, folio, plates (lacking plates 42-44 in volume 1, contemporary mottled calf, stain darkened, spine panel gilt, red lettering piece gilt, numbered direct in panel gilt compartment, board edges 'zig-zag' roll gilt, all edges 'French Shell' marbled, blue and red sewn endleaves, some damp and mould marking, a few plates loose but present, rather rubbed, joints worn but strong, some loss from endcaps, contemporary ink inscription "Samuel Thomson Esq. of Bradfield Berks", ink stamped armorial of "Samuel Thomson of Bradfield Esqr", armorial bookplates of Honble James Bertie Esqr. of Stanwell in Com. Middx. Second Son to James late/Earle of Abingdon 1702", from the collection of Christopher Ernest Weston 1947-2010.   Unsworths Booksellers   24 - 21   2011   £600

Duhamel Du Monceau, Henri Louis 1700-1781 *Traite des Arbres fruitiers...* Paris and Brussels: J. L. de Boubers, 1782, Second edition, perhaps pirated edition; 178 engraved plates, marginal tear to 2, pages (3), 320; (2), 338; (2), 260; 8vo., contemporary full calf, corners worn, some old scuff marks, head of spines chipped, some abrasions to upper and lower edges of covers, dampstaining and or a few dark spots to lower corner of several pages in each volume, upper corner bumped, some marginal worming to many back pages in volume 2), gilt decorated panels and raised bands on spines.   Raymond M. Sutton, Jr.   May 26 2011 - 37979   2011 $1250

Dujardin, Edouard *Les Lauriers sont Coupes/Avec un Portrait de l'Auteur Grave a l'eau-forte par Jacques E. Blanche.* Paris: Librairie de la revue Indepdendatne, 1888, First edition, no. 42 of 400 copies on velin anglas mecanique, from a total edition of 420; 8vo., pages 139, (5), frontispiece, uncut, sporadic foxing to some leaves, publisher's beige wrappers, text in black, lightly soiled and thumbed, spine creased, author's presentation inscription to limitation page for Gaston Dubreville (?), discreet marginal correction to page 62 (as in other copies).   Simon Finch Rare Books   Zero - 229   2011   £2000

Duke, Donald *Santa Fe... The Railroad Gateway to the American West.* San Marino: Sant, 1995-1997, 2 volumes, 288, illustrations, (290)-540 pages, illustrations, both volumes near fine in like dust jackets, lavishly illustrated.   Dumont Maps & Books of the West   112 - 38   2011 $100

Dulac, Edmund *Lyrics Pathetic and Humorus from A-Z.* London: Frederick Warne & Co., 1908, First edition; 4to., publisher's pictorial paper over cream unlettered buckram, pages 52 (unpaginated), color illustrations, little rubbed at corners, very faint shelfwear, clean bright exceptional copy with very clean text.   Any Amount of Books   May 26 2011 - A68316   2011 $671

Dulcken, H. W. *Domestic Animals and Their Habits.* London: Ward Lock & Tyler, 1865, Folio, original cloth backed pictorial boards, edges little worn, scrapes to lower board, pages 44, 12 superb hand colored double page plates, joints cracked and little shaken, but very good.   R. F. G. Hollett & Sons Antiquarian Booksellers   170 - 213   2011   £350

Dumas, Alexandre *Pictures of Travel in the South of Frances.* London: Offices of the national Illustrated Library, 1851, 10th thousand; half title, frontispiece, vignette title, contemporary half vellum by Fazakerley, Liverpool, dark green label, top edge gilt, very good, attractive.   Jarndyce Antiquarian Booksellers   CXCI - 546   2011   £60

Dumas, Louis *La Biblioteque des Enfans ou Les Premiers Elemens des Lettres, Contenant le Sisteme du Bureau Tipographique... a l'Usage de Monseigneur le Dauphin, et des Augustes Enfans de France.* Paris: Pierre Simon P. Witte, 1733, First edition; 4to., viii, 216, xix, (5), 96, xx, 97-306, 16, (2), vi, 124, 24, woodcut printer's device, etc., contemporary calf, spine gilt in compartments, morocco lettering piece, fine, large copy, uncommon, from the library of the Earls of Macclesfield at Shirburn Castle.   Maggs Bros. Ltd.   1440 - 73   2011   £1500

Dunbaugh, Edwin L. *Night Boat to New England 1815-1900.* New York: Westport: London: Greenwood Press, 1992, First edition; 8vo., xiii, maps, (2), 370 pages, plates, index, creme cloth, navy stamped spine title, dust jacket, fine, from the Bern Dibner reference library, with Burndy bookplate.   Jeff Weber Rare Books   161 - 126   2011 $62

Duncan, David James *The River Why.* San Francisco: Sierra Club Books, 1983, Uncorrected proof; fine, publication date and price handwritten on front cover, printed orange wrappers.   Bella Luna Books   May 26 2011 - t6093   2011 $247

Duncan, David James *The River Why.* San Francisco: Sierra Club Books, 1983, First edition; near fine, blank bookplate affixed to front free endpapers, slight bump to bottom back corner, dust jacket fine, first state of jacket with price of $12.95.   Bella Luna Books   May 26 2011 - t3345   2011 $220

Duncan, Herbert Osbaldeston *The World on Wheels.* Paris: privately published by author, n.d., 1926, 2 volumes, large 4to., original blue cloth gilt, spine lettering of second volume little dulled, pages xxiv, 582; xxxii, 583-1201, profusely illustrated, excellent, clean, sound set.   R. F. G. Hollett & Son Antiquarian Booksellers   General Catalogue Summer 2010 - 1108   2011   £295

Duncan, Malcolm C. *Duncan's Masonic Ritual & Monitor or Guide to the Three Symbolic Degrees.* New York: 1922, Pocket edition with protective flap; 159, (1) ad, 124, (4) pages ads, titlepage reglued, partial label of bookseller on titlepage, very good, 2 parts in one volume. Bookworm & Silverfish 678 - 76 2011 $75

Duncan, Paul *Taxi Driver.* Taschen, 2010, First edition, copy number 610 in edition of 1200 signed on limitation page by Steven Schapiro; 328 pages, folio, black cloth covered boards with black leather spine, color photo onset to front board, yellow printed lettering, all edges stained black, book as new in unopened shrink wrap, black cloth covered clamshell box, also as new, still in original publisher's printed cardboard delivery box. Any Amount of Books May 26 2011 - A73725 2011 $671

Dunham, Curtis *The Golden Goblin.* Indianapolis: Bobbs Merrill, Sept., 1906, First edition; 4to. grey pictorial boards, slight wear, near fine, illustrations by George Kerr with 8 color plates, scarce. Aleph-Bet Books, Inc. 95 - 92 2011 $600

Dunn, Katherine *Geek Love.* New York: Alfred A. Knopf, 1989, First edition; octavo, cloth backed boards. L. W. Currey, Inc. 124 - 238 2011 $75

Dunn, Katherine *Truck.* New York: Harper & Row, 1971, First edition; near fine, foxing along top edge of leaves, near fine dust jacket, one tiny closed tear, very light and bright copy. Bella Luna Books May 29 2011 - j1688 2011 $82

Dunne, J. *Orders, Rules and Regulations and Instructions Framed and Issued for the Government and Guidance of the Cumberland and Westmorland County Police...* Carlisle: Charles Thurnam & Sons, 1857, Original diced roan, upper hinge cracked, pages viii, 124, folding table and pay scales and 12 page 12mo. leaflet on abstracts relating to cruelty to animals, printed on yellow paper tipped in at end, little scattered fingering and spotting, joints strengthened with tape, but very good, extremely scarce. R. F. G. Hollett & Son Antiquarian Booksellers 175 - 400 2011 £350

Dunning, John *Booked to Die.* New York: Scribner, 1992, Later printing; fine, signed by author. Bella Luna Books May 29 2011 - t4208 2011 $82

Dunning, John *Booked to Die.* New York: Scribner, 1992, Uncorrected proof; book near fine, very scarce format, signed by author, printed white wrappers. Bella Luna Books May 26 2011 - t5994 2011 $1540

Dunning, John *Booked to Die.* New York: Scribner, 1992, First edition; fine in fine dust jacket, inscribed by author to Nina and dated 4 - 14 - 92. Bella Luna Books May 26 2011 - t5992 2011 $1320

Dunning, John *Booked to Die.* New York: Scribner, 1992, First printing; fine in fine dust jacket, signed by author, review copy with slip laid in, scarce thus. Bella Luna Books May 26 2011 - 14013 2011 $2750

Dunning, John *Booked to Die.* New York: Scribner, 1992, First edition; fine in like dust jacket, this copy came from Dunning's bookstore and thus the desirable signature date, with bookmark from bookstore, generically inscribed and dated by author on 2/6/92. Bella Luna Books May 26 2011 - t3878 2011 $1650

Dunning, John *The Bookman's Last Fling.* New York: Scribner, 2006, First edition; fine in fine dust jacket, signed and dated by author on titlepage (not tipped in page). Bella Luna Books May 29 2011 - t7470 2011 $137

Dunning, John *The Bookman's Promise.* New York: Scribner, 2004, Advance reading copy; pictorial wrappers, fine, signed by author 1-23-04. Bella Luna Books May 29 2011 - t6323 2011 $82

Dunning, John *The Bookman's Promise.* New York: Scribner, 2004, First edition; fine in fine dust jacket, signed and dated by author on 3-22-04. Bella Luna Books May 29 2011 - p2965L 2011 $110

Dunning, John *The Bookman's Wake.* New York: Scribner, 1994, Advance reading copy; near fine, light bumping to base of spine, signed and dated by author 3-22-95. Bella Luna Books May 29 2011 - t4217 2011 $110

Dunning, John *The Bookman's Wake.* New York: Scribner, 1994, Advance copy, first state; signed by author, fine in pictorial wrappers. Bella Luna Books May 29 2011 - t4220 2011 $137

Dunning, John *The Bookman's Wake.* New York: Scribner, 1995, First edition; fine in fine dust jacket, signed and dated 3-22-95 by author. Bella Luna Books May 29 2011 - 2479 2011 $93

Dunning, John *Bookscout.* Minneapolis: Dinkytown, 1998, First edition; one of 3000 copies signed, sold as a promotion for book fairs, printed wrappers, fine. Bella Luna Books May 29 2011 - t1213 2011 $82

Dunning, John *The Bookwoman's Last Fling.* New York: Scribner, 2006, Advance reading copy; label "Advance Uncorrected Proof", fine, signed and dated by author 2-20-06. Bella Luna Books May 29 2011 - t9263 2011 $82

Dunning, John *Deadline.* London: Gollancz, 1982, First UK edition; 8vo., very slight lean at spine, one edge slightly bumped, else near fine in very close to fine bright clean yellow Gollancz dust jacket with slight creasing to edges.   Any Amount of Books   May 26 2011 - A48700   2011 $537

Dunning, John *Deadline.* Huntington Beach: Cahill, 1995, Limited to 200 numbered copies; signed by author, fine in slipcase.   Bella Luna Books   May 26 2011 - j1690   2011 $192

Dunning, John *Deadline.* Huntington Beach: Cahill, 1995, First US hardcover edition; fine, fine dust jacket, signed and dated by author 3-1-96.   Bella Luna Books   May 29 2011 - j1694   2011 $82

Dunning, John *Deadline.* Japan: Hayakawa Books, 1999, First Japanese edition; pictorial wrappers, fine, with wrap around band, signed by author.   Bella Luna Books   May 26 2011 - t9342   2011 $165

Dunning, John *Denver.* New York: Times Books, 1980, First edition; very good, light dampstaining at top corners, dust jacket very good, creasing to spine ends and scratching to front panel, some bleed through on folds, signed by author, very good, creasing to spine ends and scratching to front panel, some bleed through on folds.   Bella Luna Books   May 26 2011 - t8221w   2011 $275

Dunning, John *On the Air.* New York: Oxford University Press, 1988, First edition; fine in like dust jacket, signed and dated 4-1-98.   Bella Luna Books   May 26 2011 - t4210   2011 $165

Dunning, John *On the Air.* New York: Oxford University Press, 1998, First edition; fine in fine dust jacket, small first printing (6000 copies), signed by author.   Bella Luna Books   May 29 2011 - t4212   2011 $137

Dunning, John *The Sign of the Book.* New York: Scribner, 2005, First edition; fine in fine dust jacket, signed and dated by author 3/2/05.   Bella Luna Books   May 29 2011 - p3205   2011 $82

Dunning, John *Tune in Yesterday.* New York: Prentice Hall, 1976, First edition; near fine, bottom of spine bumped, dust jacket very good, two small chips at top of spine, creasing and rubbing, signed by author.   Bella Luna Books   May 26 2011 - t1191   2011 $330

Dunning, John *Two O'Clock, Eastern Wartime.* New York: Scribner, 2001, Limited to about 2500 copies with signed limitation page and fickle fingerprint by author; near fine, both back free endpaper and back endpaper were cut wrong in production so there is an overlap, dust jacket fine, signed and dated 12-14-00 by author.   Bella Luna Books   May 26 2011 - p2381ff   2011 $440

Dunning, John *Two O'Clock Eastern Wartime.* New York: Scribner, 2001, Limited to about 2500 copies with signed limitation page and index fingerprint by author; copy double signed by author 12-14-00, fine in fine dust jacket.   Bella Luna Books   May 29 2011 - p23391   2011 $82

Duns, Johannes Scotus *Quaestiones Quolibetales Ioannis Duns Scoti (and) Collationes seu Disputationes Feliciter Incipiunt a F. Paulino Berti Lucense.*   Ioannis Salis, 1617, 1618; 478 (2), 210 (3) pages + colophon (there is not titlepage on either of these items, just colphons), worm-traces (with minor text damage) to first three leaves of first item, 17th century vellum (stain to front cover (teapot?), very good.   C. P. Hyland   May 26 2011 - 255/180   2011 $2609

Duns, Johannes Scotus *Quaestiones Quotuor Vluminum Scripti Oxoniensis Super Sententias.*   R. P. Salvatore Bartolucio, published by Haeredes Melchioris Sessae, 1580, (14), 798 (8) pages faint library stamp (English College, Rome) on titlepage, else very good, in 16th century vellum.   C. P. Hyland   May 26 2011 - 255/179   2011 $2174

Dunsany, Edward John Moreton Drax Plunkett   1878-1957   *The Charwoman's Shadow.* London and New York: G. P. Putnams Sons, 1926, First edition; octavo pages (1-2) (i-vi) vii-viii (ix-x) 1-339 (340: printers colophon), first leaf is a blank except for signature mark "A" printed on recto, original blue cloth, front and spine panels stamped in gold, bottom edge untrimmed.   L. W. Currey, Inc.   124 - 89   2011 $950

Dunsany, Edward John Moreton Drax Plunkett   1878-1957   *The Travel Tales of Mr. Joseph Jorkens.* New York and London: G. P. Putnam's Sons, 1931, First US edition; octavo, pages (i-iv) v-vii (viii) (1-2) 3-304, original light brown cloth, front and spine panels stamped in black, top edge stained black.   L. W. Currey, Inc.   124 - 185   2011 $250

Duplessis, Pierre *Histoire Du Marquis De Seligni et De Madame De Luzal.* Londres: et se trouve a Paris: Chez Regnault, 1789, 2 volumes, 165 x 102mm, very pretty contemporary flamed calf, flat spine gilt in compartments with scrolling floral cornerpieces and centerpiece, decorative bands at head and foot of spine, red and green morocco labels, woodcut headpieces and tailpieces, early ownership inscription, joints flaked, small losses of patina on covers, binding very sound, lustrous and quite pleasing, bright gilt; one leaf with small tear at fore edge (just into text, though with only trivial loss), few leaves with isolated rust spots, nearly fine and certainly charming set, text especially fresh and bright. Phillip J. Pirages 59 - 29 2011 $350

Dupont De Nemours, Pierre Samuel 1739-1817 *Memoires sur la Vie et Les Ouvrages De M. (Anne-Robert Jacquest) Turgot Ministre D'Etat.* Philadelphia: (i.e. Paris): Barrois l'aine, 1782, First edition; 8vo., pages viii, 148; (iii), 268, 2 volumes bound in one volume of contemporary calf (rubbed along front hinge, spine gilt), some minor foxing and soiling, but very good. Second Life Books Inc. 174 - 134 2011 $1100

Duport, James *Aabides Emmetros Sive Metaphrasis Libri Psalmorum Graecis Versibus Contexta.* Cantabrigae: 1666, 4to., (1), (972) 431 pages, full early leather, top cover and f.f.e.p. loose, backstrip chipped three quarter inch at both ends. Bookworm & Silverfish 679 - 21 2011 $550

Duppa, R. *Travels in Italy, Sicily and the Lipari Islands.* London: Longman, Rees, Orme and Co., 1828, First edition; 8vo., modern green buckram lettered gilt on spine, pages 224, numerous woodcut illustrations in text by A. J. Morgan and one folding plate, ex-library with usual markings, few stamps and nicks to spine and endpapers, no half title, (text of book has 3 rectangular discreet stamps only one on folding plate). Any Amount of Books May 26 2011 - A76646 2011 $671

Durand, Jean Baptiste Leonard *Voyage au Senegal.* Paris: H. Agasse, 1802, First edition; 2 volumes, 8vo., quarto (Atlas), pages lvi, 359, (1); 383, (1); 67; 16 maps, portrait frontispiece 27 plates in Atlas volume, contemporary brown speckled calf, volume 1 rebacked using original spine, fine French binding, handsome set. J. & S. L. Bonham Antiquarian Booksellers Africa 4/20/2011 - 9238 2011 £1750

Durbin, John Price *Observations in Europe: Principally in France and Great Britiain.* Aberdeen: George Clark & Son, 1848, New edition; 12mo., half title, slight paper browning, original dark purple cloth, spine faded to brown, very good. Jarndyce Antiquarian Booksellers CXCI - 547 2011 £65

Durrell, Lawrence George 1912-1990 *The Alexandria Quartet.* New York: E. P. Dutton, 1962, First printing of the collected edition; fine, clean, nearly fine dust jacket. Lupack Rare Books May 26 2011 - ABE4102581663 2011 $175

Durrell, Lawrence George 1912-1990 *On Seeming to Presume.* London: Faber & Faber, 1948, First edition; 8vo, 60 pages, signed presentation from author for John Waller, poet and literary edition, with his ownership, fine in slightly darkened, otherwise bright, near fine dust jacket. Any Amount of Books May 26 2011 - A68493 2011 $545

Durrell, Lawrence George 1912-1990 *The Plant-Magic Man.* Santa Barbara: Capra Press, 1973, First edition, #54 of 200 numbered and signed copies; handbound by Earle Gray, pictorial boards, fine in glassine dust jacket, illustrated with color blocks by Margaret Wilson and 2 photos. Charles Agvent 2010 Summer Miscellany - 27 2011 $75

Duru, H. *Geographie Illustree.* Paris: Chez tous les Libraires et les Marchands de Nouveautes, n.d. circa, 1845, First edition; 2 volumes, original carmine paper on boards, gilt edges, marbleized endpapers, 16mo., 44 pages each, lithograph decorative hand colored title and half title on each volume, plates printed on heavier paper, inked signature inside front flyleaf volume one, minor chipping at end of spine, very rare. Hobbyhorse Books 56 - 44 2011 $700

Dutcher, John T. *Ballard: the Great American Single Shot Rifle.* Denver: 2002, First edition; vi-xii, 380 pages, open end 4to., fine in fine dust jacket, illustrated endpapers, inscribed and signed by author. Bookworm & Silverfish 676 - 102 2011 $150

Dutton, Clarence Edward *Atlas to Accompany Tertiary History of the Grand Canon District.* Washington and New York: Julius Bien and Co., 1882, First edition; folio, 23 sheets, including titlepage and table of contents (sheet 1), 12 color maps, 10 color or tinted views, minor adhesion damage to first lithographic double page view, original quarter calf over cloth boards, printed paper spine label, covers detached, extremities worn, very good, rare. Jeff Weber Rare Books 163 - 66 2011 $6000

Dutton, E. A. T. *The Basuto of Basutoland.* London: Jonathan Cape, 1923, First edition; 8vo., pages 132, color frontispiece, 41 plates, map, original blue cloth, signed presentation to F. H. D. from Eric A. T. Dutton. J. & S. L. Bonham Antiquarian Booksellers Africa 4/20/2011 - 6674 2011 £110

Dutton, E. A. T. *Lillibullero; or the Golden Road.* Zanzibar: privately printed, 1944, First edition, limited to 100 copies, this being no. 10; 8vo., pages xii, 314, double page map, original green cloth, small indentation on fore edge.   J. & S. L. Bonham Antiquarian Booksellers   Africa 4/20/2011 - 8721 2011   £300

Dutton, E. A. T. *Lillibullero; or the Golden Road.* Zanzibar: Hamish Craigie, 1947, Fourth edition; 8vo., pages xii, 312, double page map, original buff cloth, corners little bumped.   J. & S. L. Bonham Antiquarian Booksellers Africa 4/20/2011 - 9107 2011   £40

Duval, Paul   *The McMichael Canadian Collection.* Kleinburg: The Collection, 1976, Oblong 4to., original wrappers, corners little creased, pages 199, illustrations in color and monochrome.   R. F. G. Hollett & Son Antiquarian Booksellers   General Catalogue Summer 2010 - 116 2011   £40

Dwelly, Edward   *The Illustrated Gaelic-English Dictionary.* Glasgow: Alex MacLaren, 1967, Sixth edition; original cloth, gilt, dust jacket, pages xiv, 1034, with 676 text illustrations. R. F. G. Hollett & Son Antiquarian Booksellers General Catalogue Summer 2010 - 402 2011   £35

Dylan, Bob   *Bob Dylan on Canvas.* London: Halcyon Gallery, 2009, First edition; 4to., pages 51, copiously illustrated in color, very slight scuffing at rear board, otherwise near fine.   Any Amount of Books   May 29 2011 - A6618 2011 $213

E

E. I. Du Pont de Nemours & Company *Colors for Nylon.* Wilmington: 1950, 121 pages, loose leaf binder, extra mild library, 200 color swatch samples 1 x 3 inches. Bookworm & Silverfish 668 - 164 2011 $75

E. I. Du Pont de Nemours & Company *Colors for Wool Yarn.* Wilmington: 1937, 58 (1) pages, nearly 500 actual swatches. Bookworm & Silverfish 668 - 165 2011 $125

Eales, Mary *Mrs. Mary Eales's Receipt. Confectioner to Her Late Majesty Queen Anne.* London: For J. Robson, 1767, Corrected second edition; (8), 106, ii pages, contemporary sheep, neatly rebacked to style, clean, very good, early ownership signature of Ann Clarke. Joseph J. Felcone Inc. Fall Miscellany 2010 - 29 2011 $1500

Earle, G. *The Making & Testing of Portland Cement and Concrete.* Hull: G. & T. Earle Ltd., 1925, First edition; original morocco backed cloth gilt, pages xix, 131, with 56 plates and illustrations. R. F. G. Hollett & Son Antiquarian Booksellers 177 - 274 2011 £35

An Earnest Invitation to all Profane Persons to Repent... Edinburgh: printed by E. Robertson for the Society at Edinburgh for Promoting Religious Knowledge among the Poor, 1757, Small 8vo., old full black calf with leather spine label, neatly rebacked to match, original long lettering piece relaid. R. F. G. Hollett & Son Antiquarian Booksellers General Catalogue Summer 2010 - 1154 2011 £1800

Earnshaw, S. *Description and Use of the Musical Keys...* Novello: Ewer & Co. and Sheffield: Pawson and Brailsford, n.d., Square 12mo., original limp cloth gilt, pages 47, frontispiece, little spotting, some marginal annotations. R. F. G. Hollett & Son Antiquarian Booksellers 175 - 402 2011 £30

Eastlake, C. L. *Contributions to the Literature of the Fine Arts.* London: John Murray, 1848, First edition; xiii, (3), 396 pages + (4) + 16 pages ads, half title, fine in original blindstamped and gilt lettered cloth, armorial bookplate of William Arthur, 6th Duke of Portland. Ken Spelman Rare Books 68 - 42 2011 £180

Eastlake, William *Portrait of an Artist with 26 Horses.* New York: Simon & Schuster, 1963, First edition; near fine, light wear, dust jacket very good with chipping to top of spine, quarter inch closed tear to front by spine, signed by author, very good, chipping to top of spine, quarter inch closed tear to front by spine. Bella Luna Books May 29 2011 - 1118 2011 $137

Eber, Paulus *Vocabula rei Nummariae Ponderum et Mensurarum Graeca, Latina, Ebraica...* Leipzig: J. Rhamba, 1570, 8vo., ff. (112) smooth calf c. 1700, gilt fillet on covers, spine gilt, gilt edges, from the library of the Earls of Macclesfield at Shirburn Castle. Maggs Bros. Ltd. 1440 - 75 2011 £400,

Eberhard, Wolfram *The Chinese Silver Screen. Hong Kong & Taiwanese Pictures in the 1960's.* Taipei: Orient Cultural Service, 1972, First edition; 8vo., pages 241, original publisher's red cloth lettered gilt on spine and on front cover, neat stamped name on pastedown, else very good. Any Amount of Books May 29 2011 - A63568 2011 $230

Eberlein, Harold Donaldson *Historic Houses of the Hudson Valley.* New York: Bonanza Books, 1942, 4to., original cloth, gilt, bottom corners of boards damped, dust jacket, extremities little worn, pages 208, 200 plates. R. F. G. Hollett & Son Antiquarian Booksellers 177 - 275 2011 £45

Eccleston, James *An Introduction to English Antiquities: Intended as a Companion to the History of England.* London: Longman, 1847, First edition; half title, numerous text woodcuts, 32 page Longman catalog (Oct. 1846), original brown cloth, blocked in blind, spine lettered gilt, very slight rubbing, very good. Jarndyce Antiquarian Booksellers CXCI - 168 2011 £60

Eccleston, Robert *Overland to California on the Southwestern Trail 1849. Diary of Robert Eccleston.* Berkeley & Los Angeles: University of California Press, 1950, Limited to 750 copies, this number 95; inscribed by both authors to Reginald Ray and Grace Dell Stuart, with their bookplate, 8vo., xvii, 256 pages, brown cloth, gilt stamped spine title, dust jacket chipped. Jeff Weber Rare Books 163 - 67 2011 $100

Eckenstein, Lina *Comparative Studies in Nursery Rhymes.* London: Duckworth, 1906, First edition; pages 232, original green cloth gilt, scarce. R. F. G. Hollett & Sons Antiquarian Booksellers 170 - 215 2011 £40

Eckfeld, Jacob *A Manual of Gold and Silver Coins of All Nations, Struck Within the Past Quarter Century...* Philadelphia: published at the Assay Office of the Mint, 1842, First edition; 4to., 4, 220 pages, engraved title and 16 plates, original cloth, rubbed and faded, some foxing, very sound and clean. M & S Rare Books, Inc. 90 - 117 2011 $1250

Ecton, John *Thesaurus Rerum Ecclesiasticarum...* London: printed for D. Browne, etc., 1742, Pages xl, 748, (viii), thick 4to., old speckled calf, gilt, little scratched, nicely rebacked to match with raised bands, original spine label preserved, armorial bookplate of Charles Sperling, Dynes Hall.   R. F. G. Hollett & Son Antiquarian Booksellers   175 - 404 2011   £350

Eddy, Mary Baker *A Complete Concordance to Science and Health with Key to the Scriptures.* Boston: First Church of Christ. Scientist, 1931, 4to., original cloth, gilt, pages 1107, printed on india paper, first few leaves little creased.   R. F. G. Hollett & Son Antiquarian Booksellers   175 - 406 2011   £35

Eden, Charles Henry *The Fortunes of the Fletchers: a Story of Life in Canada and Australia.* London: SPCK, 1873, First edition; original green cloth gilt, dampstained, pages 238 (ii), 3 woodcut plates, scattered foxing, joints tender.   R. F. G. Hollett & Sons Antiquarian Booksellers   170 - 216 2011   £45

Eden, Mary *The Philosophy of the Bed.* London: Hutchinson, 1961, First edition; original vellum backed cloth, gilt, 126 pages, with 72 plates.   R. F. G. Hollett & Son Antiquarian Booksellers   175 - 407 2011   £30

Edgar, Marriott *Albert and Balbus and Samuel Small.* London: Francis, Day & Hunter, n.d., 1939, Later issue with price increase overstamped on upper board; large 8vo., original pictorial boards, spine and edges trifle darkened and rubbed, pages 32, illustrations.   R. F. G. Hollett & Son Antiquarian Booksellers   175 - 602 2011   £65

Edgeworth, Anthony *Brandywine: a Legacy of Tradition in Du-Pont-Wyeth Country.* Charlottesville: Thomasson Grant Publishers, Photos, fine, dust jacket, signed by Edgeworth.   Lupack Rare Books   May 26 2011 - ABE1284940946 2011 $100

Edgeworth, Maria 1768-1849 *Belinda.* printed for J. Johnson, 1801, 3 volumes, half titles, discarded, some light browning and spotting, few leaves in volume i little stained in margins, one or two small marginal paper flaws, pages (3)-8, 370; (ii) 387; (ii), 359, (1), 8vo., earl 20th century black and red marbled cloth boards, recently backed with mid brown calf, spines with five raised bands, black lettering pieces, central gilt tools in compartments, hinges relined, touch of wear to corners, bookplate of J. Walpole D'Oyly, good, scarce.   Blackwell Rare Books   B166 - 34 2011   £2000

Edgeworth, Maria 1768-1849 *Practical Education.* New York: George F. Hopkins for Self and Brown and Stansbury, 1801, Providence: Lippitt, Boston, Wait, 1815. First American edition volume I, Second US edition volume II; 8vo., pages vi, 344; 312, contemporary leather, hinges loose, some foxing but good set, nice contemporary binder's ticket on front pastedown of volume I, contemporary ownership signature of Isaac Mills in volume I.   Second Life Books Inc.   174 - 136 2011 $225

Edgeworth, Maria 1768-1849 *Practical Education.* 1798, First edition; quart, 2 volumes in 1, contemporary half calf, gilt decorated, xii, 775 (29) pages, 2 folding plates at end, alphabet plate at page 4to, some faint foxing throughout, generally very good, very scarce.   C. P. Hyland   May 26 2011 - 159/125 2011 $942

Edgeworth, Maria 1768-1849 *Tales and Novels.* London: Baldwin & Cradock, 1832-1833, 18 volumes, each with frontispiece and vignette titlepage, volumes 2-18 are in the more usual reddish brown cloth with gilt decorated spine (in good condition), volume i in alternative publisher's binding of grey buckram, with gilt titling and blind impress decorations with owner inscription on vignette titlepage and some foxing to it and frontispiece.   C. P. Hyland   May 26 2011 - 256/218 2011 $457

Edgeworth, Maria 1768-1849 *Tales and Novels.* London: Whitaker & Co., 1848, 9 volumes, frontispieces, added engraved titles, slightly spotted, ad leaves, original green cloth, elaborately gilt blocked, spines slightly faded, ads on endpapers for William Tegg's publications, good plus set.   Jarndyce Antiquarian Booksellers   CXCI - 12 2011   £250

Edgeworth, Richard Lovell 1744-1817 *Essai Sur La Construction Des Routes et Des Voitures...* Paris: 1827, First printing; xliv, li, 477 pages, 3 tables, 6 plates, modern quarter calf, marbled boards, very good.   C. P. Hyland   May 26 2011 - 255/183 2011 $797

Edgeworth, Richard Lovell 1744-1817 *Essays on Professional Education.* 1809, First edition; quarto, original boards with paper spine, edges untrimmed, (6), 496 pages, boards suffer uusual shelf wear and text is very good.   C. P. Hyland   May 26 2011 - 259/126 2011 $652

Edgeworth, Richard Lovell 1744-1817 *Essays on Professional Education.* 1812, Second edition; 8vo., half calf with gilt decorations, (xiii) 541 pages, early and late pages foxed, else text is very good.   C. P. Hyland   May 26 2011 - 259/127 2011 $507

Edinburgh Almanack, for the Year 1751. Being the Third After Leap Year, with the Greatest Respect, Dedicated Upon the Right Honourable George Drummond Esq. Lord Provost.... (and several others). Edinburgh: printed by R. Fleming and sold by the widow of james Voy in Craig's Close and by the booksellers in town and country, n.d., 1751, 12mo., 24 leaves, 24 pages of which the first leaf is pasted on to front pastedown and 2nd and 3rd leaves pasted back to back (in both cases versos blank), one or two ruled borders just shaved with couple of page numerals cropped, overall very good, complete with red paper duty stamp on titlepage, preserved in original vellum wallet style binding with flap, rare. John Drury Rare Books 154 - 5 2011 £175

Edison Honored Throughout the Entire World. New York: Association of Edition Illuminating Companies, 1929, 4to., 65 pages, illustrations, brown cloth, embossed portrait of Edison on front cover with raised titles, extremity edges lightly rubbed, very good, from the Bern Dibner reference library, with Burndy bookplate. Jeff Weber Rare Books 161 - 128 2011 $75

Edison, Thomas A. *In Nature's Laboratory. (Commemorating Our Vacation Trip of 1916 August 28th to September 9th).* London: n.p., 1916, One of a very small number of copies printed for private distribution by the authors signed by Edison, John Burroughs and Henry Firestone on "Greeting" page; folio, (52) leaves, cover title, printed on brown paper one side only, first and final leaf blank and attached to endpapers, 44 original mounted photographs and facsimile letter tipped in, original suede over padded boards, front cover decoratively stamped and lettered in blind, marbled endpapers, some very expert restoration to board tips, overall very good, scarce, with open end slipcase. Heritage Book Shop Holiday 2010 - 34 2011 $8000

Edmonds, George *Facts and Falsehoods Concerning the War on the South 1861-1865.* Memphis: 1904, (2), (1) viii, (1)-271 pages, issued in wrappers, here in later half leather and marbled boards, new backstrip, f.f.e.p. is pulling, extensive inscription from Berkeley Minor family. Bookworm & Silverfish 678 - 31 2011 $325

Edmonds, Harfield H. *Brook and River Trouting.* Otley: Smith Settle, 1997, Facsimile edition; original brown cloth, gilt, matching slipcase, pages (vi), 106, color shade card, 10 color plates and 10 sepia plates, fine. R. F. G. Hollett & Son Antiquarian Booksellers General Catalogue Summer 2010 - 1239 2011 £85

Edmunds, S. Emma *Nurse and Spy in the Union Army: The Adventures and Experiences of a Woman in Hospitals, Camps and Battle Fields.* Hartford: W. S. Williams, 1864, Octavo, 384 pages, frontispiece, 8 wood engravings, text block stained and foxed, original purple cloth, gilt borders, modern rebacking in black cloth, gilt spine, good plus, rare. Jeff Weber Rare Books 163 - 161 2011 $75

Edwards, Amelia B. *A Thousand Miles Up the Nile.* London: Longmans, Green, 1891, Second edition; 8vo., pages xxvii, 499, frontispiece, illustrations, original brown decorative cloth, vignette (palm trees) on front cover. J. & S. L. Bonham Antiquarian Booksellers Africa 4/20/2011 - 8246 2011 £70

Edwards, George *The True Original Scheme of Human Economy, Applied to the Completion of the Different Interests and Preservation of the British Empire...* Newcastle upon Tyne: printed for the author by S. Hodgson, 1808, First edition; 8vo., xlii, 136 pages, well bound recently in cloth, spine lettered in gilt, very good, early annotations in ink and pencil, single line drawn through the words "an endless sermon" added in ink above and the comment "a most original & able treatise" added in pencil, scarce. John Drury Rare Books 153 - 37 2011 £125

Edwards, Jonathan *A Careful and Strict Enquiry into the Modern Prevailing Notions of that Freedom of Will, Which is Supposed to be Essential to Moral Agency, Vertue and Vice, Reward and Punishment, Praise and Blame.* Boston: S. Kneeland, 1754, First edition; 8vo., (2) 6, (4), 294, (5), (9) pages, full contemporary panelled calf, corners bumped, few early leaves water stained in upper corner, moderate browning throughout, presentation copy from author apparently in recipient's hand "Israel Ashley's Book/ the Gift of the Rev'd? Mr. Jonathan Edwards. M & S Rare Books, Inc. 90 - 1222 2011 $8500

Edwards, Lionel *Huntsmen Past and Present.* London and New York: Eyre and Spottiswoode/Charles Scribner's Sons, 1929, No. 129 of 150 signed copies; 4to., quarter vellum, pages (xviii), 91, with 21 illustrations, slight spotting and discoloration to vellum at spine, otherwise very good + in used slipcase. Any Amount of Books May 29 2011 - A44799 2011 $340

Edwards, Monica *Wish for a Pony.* London: Collins, 1947, First edition; original cloth, spine and edges faded, dust jacket (edges little frayed in places), pages 159, illustrations by Anne Bullen, scarce. R. F. G. Hollett & Sons Antiquarian Booksellers 170 - 217 2011 £85

Edwards, William *The Early History of the North Riding.* A. Brown and Sons, 1924, Deluxe edition; 4to., original full navy blue levant morocco gilt, spine trifle rubbed, pages xvi, 267, top edge gilt, untrimmed, with 55 plates and map. R. F. G. Hollett & Son Antiquarian Booksellers 177 - 279 2011 £95

Edwards, William *The Early History of the North Riding.* A. Brown and Sons, 1924, First edition; 4to., original cloth, gilt, foot of spine little worn, pages xvi, 267, untrimmed, 55 plates and map. R. F. G. Hollett & Son Antiquarian Booksellers General Catalogue Summer 2010 - 1382 2011 £60

Eenberg, Johann *Kort Berattelse af de Markwadigste Saker som for de Frammande are Besee Och Fornimma uti Upsala stad Och Nast om Gransande Orter.* Uppsala: Johann H. Werner, 1704, (1703); Agenda 12mo., (32) 185 pages, pages 185-191, 193-236; 53 (=54) (2(blank) pages, frontispiece (added) and 5 folding woodcut inserted illustrations in part 2, with extra folding titlepage to second part with woodcut of the fire, woodcut illustrations in text, contemporary half calf over marbled boards, most uncommon, from the library of the Earls of Macclesfield at Shirburn Castle. Maggs Bros. Ltd. 1440 - 76 2011 £1500

Egan, Pierce 1772-1849 *Boxiana; or Sketches of Ancient and Modern Puglisim from the Days of the Renowned Broughton and Slack Championship of Cribb.* London: Sherwood Jones & Co., 1823-1829, 5 volumes, small 4to., frontispiece, 32, 9 9 7 12 (i.e. 69) lithographed plates, some plates lightly foxed, full modern black morocco to period style, gilt stamped spine titles, raised bands, fine, booklabel of E. L. Hersey, elegant and complete set with extra illustrations. Jeff Weber Rare Books 163 - 111 2011 $7500

Egan, Pierce 1772-1849 *Life in London; or Day and Night Scenes of Jerry Hawthorn, Esq. and Corinthian Tom, Accompanied by Rob Logic the Oxonian in their Rambles and Sprees through the Metropolis.* Sherwood, Neely & Jones, 1821, First edition, 2nd issue; engraved title and color plates by I. R. & G. Cruikshank, 3 plates folded, engraved music, illustrations, two booksellers' catalog entries laid down on leading pastedown, ink signature on verso of leading f.e.p., slight abrasion to upper margin of titlepage, later 19th century full mottled calf, double gilt borders, raised bands, gilt spine, brown morocco label, slight rubbing to hinges, handsome copy with very good, bright color plates. Jarndyce Antiquarian Booksellers CXCI - 169 2011 £650

Eggers, Dave *A Heartbreaking Work of Staggering Genius.* New York: Simon & Schuster, 2000, First edition; near fine, light bumping to spine ends, dust jacket fine. Bella Luna Books May 29 2011 - t5869 2011 $82

Eggers, Dave *Teachers Have It Easy.* New York: New Press, 2005, First edition; signed by Eggers and co-authors Daniel Moulthrop and Ninive Clements Calegari, fine in fine dust jacket, uncommon. Ken Lopez Bookseller 154 - 48 2011 $200

Eggers, Dave *You Shall Know Our Velocity.* New York: McSweeney's, 2002, First edition; fine, signed and dated by author 10/28/02. Bella Luna Books May 29 2011 - t4156 2011 $110

Eggleston, William *William Eggleston's Guide.* New York: Museum of Modern Art, 1976, First edition; monograph of color images, fine in black leather like cover with color photo, still in original shrinkwrap. Jeff Hirsch Books ny 2010 2011 $950

Egharevba, Jacob U. *Benin Games & Sports.* Sapele: printed by Central Press Ltd., 1951, Second edition; 8vo. 27, (1) pages, small hole in final leaf just touching a single letter, (blank) flyleaf creased and soiled, original printed wrappers, very good. John Drury Rare Books 153 - 38 2011 £50

The Egyptian Struwwelpeter. New York: Stokes, n.d. inscribed, 1897, 4to., cloth backed pictorial boards, title plus (16) leaves, light rubbing and soil, very good+, printed on rectos only, each leaf simulates aged paper an illustrated in color, rare. Aleph-Bet Books, Inc. 95 - 288 2011 $1875

Ehrlich, Gretel *Geode/Rock Body.* Santa Barbara: Capricorn Press, 1970, One of 550 copies of the issue in wrappers, of a total edition of 600 copies; inscribed by author in 1992, mild edge sunning, else fine. Ken Lopez Bookseller 154 - 49 2011 $300

Ehrlich, Gretel *The Solace of Open Spaces.* New York: Viking, 1985, First edition; book near fine, remainder stamp on bottom edge of leaves and boards, dust jacket very good, small closed tears and creases along top edge, slight rubbing to top front fold, author's first book, very good, small closed tears and creases along top edge, slight rubbing to top front fold. Bella Luna Books May 29 2011 - 6413 2011 $82

Ehrlich, Gretel *The Solace of Open Spaces.* New York: Viking, 1985, First edition; fine, dust jacket fine, signed by author. Bella Luna Books May 26 2011 - t1190 2011 $220

Eiseley, Loren *Notes on an Alchemist.* New York: Charles Scribner's Sons, 1972, First edition; signed by author, fine in close to fine dust jacket. Charles Agvent 2010 Summer Miscellany - 28 2011 $100

The Elder Edda. London: Faber, 1969, First edition translated by W. H.Auden and Paul Taylor; original cloth, gilt, dust jacket, pages 175, 2 illustrations, name on flyleaf, else fine. R. F. G. Hollett & Son Antiquarian Booksellers 175 - 64 2011 £60

Elder, Eleanor *Travelling Players. The Story of the Arts League of Service.* London: Frederick Muller, 1939, First edition; original cloth, pages xii, 272, with 26 illustrations. R. F. G. Hollett & Son Antiquarian Booksellers 175 - 412 2011 £40

Elgee, Frank *Early Man in North East Yorkshire.* Gloucester: John Bellows, 1930, First edition; 4to., original green cloth gilt, neatly recased, pages xvi, 260, with 30 plates and 67 figures and maps, 2 long interesting ALS's from author, with 2 additional maps, all loosely inserted. R. F. G. Hollett & Son Antiquarian Booksellers General Catalogue Summer 2010 - 1383 2011 £175

Elgee, Frank *Early Man in North East Yorkshire.* Gloucester: John Bellows, 1930, First edition; 4to, pages xvi, 260, with 30 plates and 67 figures and maps, fine, original cloth, gilt.   R. F. G. Hollett & Son Antiquarian Booksellers   177 - 280   2011   £150

Elgee, Frank *The Moorlands of North Eastern Yorkshire.* A. Brown & sons, 1912, first edition; original cloth gilt over bevelled boards, one corner trifle creased, pages xvi, 361, frontispiece, 70 plates, color folding plate of sections and 2 folding maps, 1 colored, joints cracked, scarce.   R. F. G. Hollett & Son Antiquarian Booksellers   General Catalogue Summer 2010 - 1385   2011   £140

Elias, E. L. *The Book of Polar Exploration.* London: Harrap, 1928, First edition; original striking pictorial cloth, matching dust jacket (rather rubbed), pages 302, numerous plates and illustrations, maps on endpapers, fore edge and prelim leaves little foxed.   R. F. G. Hollett & Sons Antiquarian Booksellers   170 - 218   2011   £75

Elias, Edith L. *The Story of Hiawatha.* London: George G. Harrap & Co. n.d. circa, 1914, First edition thus; square 12mo., original pictorial boards, little rubbed, corners worn and rounded, 32 page (un-numbered) panorama, 16 color plates by Willy Pogany, opening accordion style, odd slight mark but generally nice, clean and sound, scarce. R. F. G. Hollett & Sons Antiquarian Booksellers   170 - 537   2011   £95

Eliot, George, Pseud.   1819-1880   *Adam Bede.* Edinburgh and London: William Blackwood and Sons, 1859, 2 volumes, from Lord Lansdowne's library, half titles, publisher's ads discarded, pages viii, 431; viii, 3-382, 8vo., original wave grain orange brown cloth, backstrips ruled and lettered in gilt, sides with blind decorated panels and paper labels of Lord Lansdowne with his cypher on front covers, slightly rubbed at extremities, joints of volume i skillfully repaired, good.   Blackwell Rare Books   B166 - 35   2011 £180

Eliot, George, Pseud.   1819-1880   *Daniel Deronda.* Edinburgh: Blackwood, 1876, First edition; first issue with misprint on page 83 of volume I, 8 parts in 4 volumes contemporary scuffed three quarter leather and boards, couple of hinges tender, lacking volume labels on spines, small stain from removed scotch tape on titlepage of volume one, very good tight set, bookplate of Augustine Birrell.   Second Life Books Inc.   174 - 137   2011 $700

Eliot, George, Pseud.   1819-1880   *Felix Holt the Radical.* Edinburgh and London: William Blackwood and Sons, 1866, First edition; 3 volumes, octavo, (iv), (1)-303, (1, blank); (2), (1)-290; (iv), (1)-283, (1, blank), (4, publisher's ads), pages, half title present in volume I and III, original reddish brown sand grain cloth with blindstamped borders on covers and spines stamped and lettered in gilt, (Carter's "B" binding), top edges brown, mostly unopened, pale yellow coated endpapers, light shelf wear, light toning to half title volume I, exceptionally bright, clean set, housed in cloth chemise and quarter green morocco slipcase.   Heritage Book Shop   Holiday 2010 - 36   2011 $3500

Eliot, George, Pseud.   1819-1880   *The Mill on the Floss.* Edinburgh: William Blackwood & Sons, 1860, First edition; 3 volumes, half titles, original dark slate grey/blue fine diamond grained cloth, elaborate decorated borders in blind within double ruled borders also in blind, spines lettered in gilt, gilt decorated rules at heads and tails, top edge gilt, very good.   Jarndyce Antiquarian Booksellers   CXCI - 170   2011   £2250

Eliot, George, Pseud.   1819-1880   *Scenes of Clerical Life.* Edinburgh & London: William Blackwood & Sons, 1858, First edition; 2 volumes, half titles, slight foxing in prelims volume II, contemporary half brown crushed morocco by Bayntun, spines with raised gilt bands, and ruled and lettered in gilt, all edges gilt, very good, attractive. Jarndyce Antiquarian Booksellers   CXCI - 171   2011   £850

Eliot, George, Pseud.   1819-1880   *Silas Marner.* London: J. M. Dent, 1905, First deluxe edition thus; original full vellum gilt, spine and upper board decorated in gilt overall, boards trifle bowed, pages xviii, 264, (ii), top edge gilt, untrimmed, 24 color plates by C. E. Brock.   R. F. G. Hollett & Son Antiquarian Booksellers   General Catalogue Summer 2010 - 735   2011   £85

Eliot, Jared   *Thee Two Witnesses; or Religion Supported by Reason and Divine Revelation.*   London: T. Green, 1736,   (4), 79 pages, including half title, untrimmed and stitched as issued, outside of first and last leaf rather soiled and with two small old gummed tape repairs, minor dampstain in margins of last few leaves, else very good.   Joseph J. Felcone Inc.   Fall Miscellany 2010 - 42   2011 $600

Eliot, Thomas Stearns   1888-1965   *Burnt Norton.* London: Faber, 1941, First edition; original wrappers, spine fold faded, pages 16, stapled, neat name on flyleaf, staples trifle rusted in places, very good.   R. F. G. Hollett & Son Antiquarian Booksellers   General Catalogue Summer 2010 - 759   2011   £180

Eliot, Thomas Stearns   1888-1965   *The Elder Statesman.* London: Faber, 1959, First edition; pages 112, crown 8vo., original pink cloth, backstrip gilt lettered, free endpapers lightly browned, very good, inscribed by author and his wife for Mary Harris.   Blackwell Rare Books   B166 - 142   2011   £500

Eliot, Thomas Stearns 1888-1965 *Little Gidding.* London: Faber, 1942, First edition, later issue; pages 16, original wrappers, stapled, edges little faded in places.   R. F. G. Hollett & Son Antiquarian Booksellers   General Catalogue Summer 2010 - 760   2011   £65

Eliot, Thomas Stearns 1888-1965 *Poems 1909-1925.* New York and Chicago: ?, Probably a first edition; 128 pages, original binding, minor shelf wear, very good.   Bookworm & Silverfish   665 - 54   2011 $75

Eliot, Thomas Stearns 1888-1965 *The Waste Land.* London: Faber, 1980, 4to., original cloth, gilt, dust jacket price clipped, pages xxx, 149, transcripts partly in red and black.   R. F. G. Hollett & Son Antiquarian Booksellers   General Catalogue Summer 2010 - 761   2011   £45

Elkin, R. H.   *Children's Corner.*   London & Philadelphia: Augener & McKay, n.d., 1914, Oblong 4to., gilt cloth, pictorial paste-on, fine in repaired dust jacket with 2 pieces off rear panel, illustrations by Le Mair, with 16 magnificent color plates, very scarce.   Aleph-Bet Books, Inc.   95 - 324   2011 $550

Elkin, R. H.   *The Children's Corner.*   London: Augner Ltd., 1914, First edition; oblong 4to., tan cloth with gold lettering and full color oval paste label on front cover, grey paper dust jacket with some marginal chipping but overall quite nice, fold in rear free endpaper, 16 full page mounted color plates (counting titlepage) by Le Mair.   Jo Ann Reisler, Ltd.   86 - 158   2011 $600

Ellacombe, Henry Nicholson   *Shakespeare as an Angler.*   London: Elliot Stock, 1883, Frontispiece, illustrations, uncut in contemporary parchment blocked in red, lettered in gilt, slightly dulled, top edge gilt.   Jarndyce Antiquarian Booksellers   CXCI - 488   2011   £50

Ellegard, Alvar   *Darwin and the General Reader: the Reception of Darwin's Theory of Evolution in the British Periodical Press 1859-1872.*   New York and London: Garland, 1996, First edition; 8vo., 394 pages, tables, diagrams, blue cloth, gilt stamped cover emblem and spine title, dust jacket, near fine, rare in jacket, from the Bern Dibner reference library, with Burndy bookplate.   Jeff Weber Rare Books   161 - 132   2011 $125

Elliot, Daniel Giraud   *A Monogram of the Pittidae; or Family of Ant Thrushes.*   New York: D. Appleton & Co., 1863, First edition; 31 beautiful hand colored lithographed plates, and one unsigned plate after C. P. Tholey, of which 24 are after Elliot, folio, pages 23 and a lettepress for each bird illustrated, modern green three quarter morocco over contemporary marbled boards with matching marbled endpapers (light rubbing to marbled boards, fine copy, plates and text in immaculate, pristine condition, all edges gilt, signature of George N. Lawrence.   Raymond M. Sutton, Jr.   May 26 2011 - 51134   2011 $16,000

Elliot, Daniel Giraud   *A Monograph of the Tetraoninae, or Family of the Grouse.*   New York: published by the author, 1865, 27 hand colored lithographed plates (2 closed marginal tears to first egg plate along with missing lower corner, tip missing from lower corner of second egg plate, some regional dampstaining not touching images to 7 plates), double elephant folio, pages 919) and letterpress for each plate, modern three quarter morocco over marbled boards and a morocco label on front cover (closed tear to margin of 3 pages of letterpress, dampstaining to a margin of 6 pages of letterpress).   Raymond M. Sutton, Jr.   May 26 2011 - 512274   2011 $15,000

Elliot, Frances Minto   *Diary of an Idle Woman in Constantinople.*   London: John Murray, 1893, First edition; (12) (sic), 425 pages, including index, 8vo., contemporary half red calf over marbled boards, gilt decorated spines, contrasting gilt lettered spine, frontispiece, 3 plates, folding map printed in red and black, some rubbing to extremities, small chip to head of spine, upper hinge slightly cracking, unobtrusive light spotting to endpapers, repair to small tear on verso of map, nonetheless attractive copy, from the library of Welsh architect J. Howard Morgan.   Paulette Rose Fine and Rare Books   32 - 175   2011 $480

Elliot, G. F. Scott   *A Naturalist in Mid-Africa. Being an Account of a Journey to the Mountains of the Moon and Tanganyika.*   London: A. D. Innes, 1896, Octavo, xvi 413 pages, frontispiece, 49 figures and plates, 4 maps, original full brown buckram, gilt Wandarobbo sword and scabbard on upper cover, gilt spine, very good.   Jeff Weber Rare Books   163 - 162   2011 $180

Elliotson, John   *Numerous Cases of Surgical Operations without Pain in the Mesmeric State; with Remarks Upon the Opposition of Many Members of the Royal Medical and Surgical Society and Others to the Reception of the Inestimable Blessings of Mesmerism.*   Philadelphia: Lea and Blanchard, 1843, First American edition; 8vo., 56 pages, plus 14 of 16 ad pages, sewn, early leaves, foxed, corners turned, bit weary.   M & S Rare Books, Inc.   90 - 250   2011 $750

Elliott, Bob   *Write If You Get Work: the Best of Bob & Ray.*   New York: Random House, 1975, First edition; this copy inscribed by Elliott and Ray Goulding to Nelson Lyon, small stain to fore edge and shallow sunning to board edges, near fine in very good, spine sunned dust jacket, mild edgewear, very uncommon signed and nice association as well.   Ken Lopez Bookseller   154 - 50   2011 $300

Elliott, Brent   *Flora.*   Scriptum Carago with Royal Horticultural society, 2001, First edition; square folio, original cloth, dust jacket, pages 336, illustrations in color, fine.   R. F. G. Hollett & Son Antiquarian Booksellers   General Catalogue Summer 2010 - 968   2011   £35

Elliott, Charles Boileau *Two Letters Addressed to the Supreme Government of British India, Regarding the Abolition of Suttees, and the Best Means of Ameliorating the Moral and Intellectual Condition of the Natives of India.* Salisbury: Printed by Brodie and Dowding, n.d. but, 1827, First edition; 8vo., (2), 45, (1) pages, recent marbled boards, lettered on spine, very good, presentation copy inscribed by author L. B. Pearson Sept. 1828, very rare. John Drury Rare Books 154 - 47 2011 £175

Elliott, Clark A. *History of Science in the United States: a Chronology and Research Guide.* New York and London: Garland, 1996, 8vo., x, 543 pages, quarter grey cloth with gray paper boards, copper stamped spine title, fine, rare, from the Bern Dibner reference library, with Burndy bookplate. Jeff Weber Rare Books 161 - 133 2011 $85

Elliott, Mary Belson *Precept and Example or Midsummer Holidays.* London: W. Darton Jun. (sic), 1812, 12mo., 188 + 2 pages, original marbled paper on boards, red roan spine, gilt title and fillets, full page copper engraved frontispiece, wood engraved vignette, wanting front free endpaper, covers lightly rubbed including edges and corners, else fine, from the collection of Marjorie Moon and handmade dust jacket with inked title on cover and along spine. Hobbyhorse Books 56 - 45 2011 $300

Elliott, W. G. *Amateur Clubs and Actors.* London: Edward Arnold, 1898, First edition; original blind decorated reen cloth gilt, few slight nicks and scratches, pages 320, uncut, 19 plates, joints cracked, scarce, armorial bookplate of Edward Chevenix Austen Leigh. R. F. G. Hollett & Son Antiquarian Booksellers 175 - 413 2011 £65

Ellis, Brooks F. *Catalogue of Ostracoda.* New York: 1952-1964, 1982; Volumes 1-20 and supplement number 26 for 1980, illustrations, 4to., loose leaf by post in cloth binders (some soiling and some minor stains), binding for volume 18 has come apart, supplement 26 unbound. Raymond M. Sutton, Jr. May 26 2011 - 35337 2011 $2000

Ellis, Howard *The Law and Equity Reporter.* New York: 1876, Volumes 1-3, tall law calf, 2 volumes with old re-enforcement to top panel of backstrip (two volumes need same at bottom), one cover loose. Bookworm & Silverfish 667 - 94 2011 $125

Ellis, Sarah Stickney *Family Secrets.* London: Fisher Son & Co., 1843?, 3 volumes in 1, folio, frontispieces, added engraved title, slight foxing, half red calf, slight rubbing, black label, good, sound copy. Jarndyce Antiquarian Booksellers CXCI - 172 2011 £120

Ellis, W. T. *Memories. My Seventy-Two Years in the Romantic County of Yuba, California.* Eugene: University of Oregon, 1939, First edition; 308 pages, frontispiece, plus illustrations, light brown cloth backed orange boards, printed paper spine label, very fine, bright copy, slightly chipped printed dust jacket. Argonaut Book Shop Recent Acquisitions Summer 2010 - 249 2011 $150

Ellis, William 1794-1872 *Three Visits of Madagascar During the Years 1853-1854-1856...* London: John Murray, 1858, First edition; 8vo., pages xvii, 476, ads, folding frontispiece, plates, woodcut, little light foxing to early pages, original brown half calf, rubbed. J. & S. L. Bonham Antiquarian Booksellers Africa 4/20/2011 - 6370 2011 £140

Ellison, Harlan *Medea: Harlan's World.* Huntington Woods: Phantasia Press, 1985, First edition; octavo, leather. L. W. Currey, Inc. 124 - 81 2011 $1000

Ellison, Harlan *Strange Wine: Fifteen New Stories from the Nightside of the World.* New York: Harper & Row, 1977, First edition; near fine, light bumping of spines, dust jacket near fine, light creasing to spine, signed by author. Bella Luna Books May 29 2011 - p1212 2011 $82

Ellwood, Robert Dun *The Book of the Parish Church of Holy Trinity, Millom, Cumberland.* Millom: Printed by P. C. Dickinson for the Church, 1917, Original oversize printed wrappers, pages 48 with 6 pages of plates, little light spotting, scarce. R. F. G. Hollett & Son Antiquarian Booksellers General Catalogue Summer 2010 - 1386 2011 £45

Ellwood, T. *The Landama Book of Iceland as It Illustrates the Dialect, Places, Names Folk Lore and Antiquities of Cumberland, Westmorland and North Lancashire.* Kendal: T. Wilson, 1894, First edition; very scarce, pages xvii, 69, original blue cloth, gilt, extremities little rubbed. R. F. G. Hollett & Son Antiquarian Booksellers 175 - 415 2011 £150

Ellwood, T. *Leaves from the Annals of a Mountain Parish in Lakeland...* Ulverston: James Atkinson, 1988, First limited edition, 175 copies; pages (ii), 70, pictorial initials and tailpieces, original printed wrappers, slight staining to upper panel from staples. R. F. G. Hollett & Son Antiquarian Booksellers General Catalogue Summer 2010 - 1387 2011 £95

Elstob, Elizabeth *An Anglo-Saxon Homily on the Birthday of St. Gregory.* London: printed for W. Bowyer, 1709, First edition; 8vo., pages (xii) lx (ii) 44 (iv) 49 (vii), engraved frontispiece and titlepage vignette, headpieces and initials by Simon Griblein, contemporary spotted calf, professionally rebacked with matching brown calf, some light foxing and toning, very good. Second Life Books Inc. 174 - 138 2011 $2200

Elstob, Elizabeth *The Rudiments of Grammar for the English-Saxon Tongue.* London: printed by W. Bowyer and sold by J. Bowyer and C. King, 1715, First edition; small 4to., pages (viii), xxxvi, 70, 2 engraved headpieces, contemporary full calf, edges worn, some foxing, joints cracked, upper joint little tender. Second Life Books Inc. 174 - 139 2011 $2250

Elston, Roy *The Traveller's Handbook for Egypt and the Sudan.* London: Simpkin Marshall, 1929, First edition; 2 volumes, 8vo, pages xii, 335; 347, plan as frontispiece, original green decorative cloth, slight rubbing to joints, good, clean set. J. & S. L. Bonham Antiquarian Booksellers Africa 4/20/2011 - 8726 2011 £320

Elsynge, Henry *The Manner of Holding Parliaments in England.* London: printed by Richardson and Clark for Tho. Payne, 1768, 8vo., pages xx, 298, (ii), contemporary tan calf, boards double rule gilt bordered, board edges 'zig-zag' decorative roll in blind, all edges red sprinkled, pink and white sewn endbands, early 21st century calf reback and corners by CEW, little light spotting, old leather marked and scratched, new endpapers, new spine entirely plain and lettering piece unlettered, oval stamp in black ink of "the National Unionst Association, Political Library Reference" dated 9 May 1922, from the collection of Christopher Ernest Weston 1947-2010. Unsworths Booksellers 24 - 91 2011 £75

Elvin, Laurence *Bishop and Son, Organ Builders.* Lincoln: privately published, 1984, Small 4to., original cloth, gilt, dust jacket, pages 356, with 101 illustrations, scarce. R. F. G. Hollett & Son Antiquarian Booksellers 175 - 416 2011 £40

Elvin, Laurence *Family Enterprise.* Lincoln: 1986, Limited to 1000 copies; original cloth, gilt, dust jacket, pages 172, with over 130 illustrations, fine. R. F. G. Hollett & Son Antiquarian Booksellers 175 - 417 2011 £35

Ely, Richard T. *Property and Contract in Their Relations to the Distribution of Wealth.* London: Macmillan, 1914, First edition; 2 volumes, 8vo., pages xlvii, 995, 2 volumes, bright very good+ copies with very slight shelf wear, boards slightly bowed in very good- dust jacket with some soiling and some slight chips and some nicks. Any Amount of Books May 26 2011 - A45291 2011 $629

Emanuel, Walter *The Zoo.* Alston Rivers, 1904, First edition; small 4to., original pictorial boards, little fingered and neatly rebacked, pages 50, with 12 plates in brown, black and white, numerous line drawings, new endpapers, light crayoning to one small drawing, but very good. R. F. G. Hollett & Sons Antiquarian Booksellers 170 - 316 2011 £65

Emboden, William A. *Leonardo da Vinci en Plants and Gardens.* Portland: Dioscorides Press, 1987, Large 8vo., 234 pages, 100 figures, cream cloth, gilt stamped spine title, dust jacket, upper corner of rear cover bumped, very good, from the Bern Dibner reference library, with Burndy bookplate. Jeff Weber Rare Books 161 - 135 2011 $60

Emden, E. *Pesnya o Mame. (song About Mama).* Moscow: GIZ, 1930, First edition; 8vo., color pictorial stiff paper covers, some minor soiling, 10 pages within, including 4 pages of music, illustrations by David Petrovitch Shterenberg. Jo Ann Reisler, Ltd. 86 - 220 2011 $1750

Emerson, P. H. *Wild Life on a Tidal Water. The Adventures of a Houseboat and Her Crew.* London: Sampson Low, Marston, Searle and Rivington, 1890, First and only edition; landscape 4to., original decorative cloth, neatly rebacked, pages xiv, 145, with 29 plates, folding chart, very good, almost no foxing, outer edge little dusty. Any Amount of Books May 26 2011 - A48123 2011 $5870

Emerson, Ralph Waldo 1803-1882 *Compensation.* New York: 1956, vi, 36 pages, warmly inscribed and signed with press's promotional ticket laid in, fine in publisher's slipcase. Bookworm & Silverfish 678 - 158 2011 $100

Emerson, Ralph Waldo 1803-1882 *English Traits.* Boston: Phillips, Sampson & Co., 1856, First Edition; original black cloth, blindstamped with gilt lettering on spine, yellow endpapers, this copy with battered type at bottom of page 230 and the "1" on half titlepage, few small faint stains to cloth, small gouge on spine, not terrible in appearance, otherwise cloth is very nice with spine ends intact and gilt bright, contents very clean, owner name of C. H. A. Carter, housed in cloth chemise and half brown morocco slipcase with gilt lettering on spine, near fine in very good custom made slipcase. Charles Agvent Transcendentalism 2010 - 9 2011 $350

Emerson, Ralph Waldo 1803-1882 *Essays.* Boston: James Munroe and Co., 1841, First edition; contemporary half black morocco and marbled boards, matching morocco corners, recently rebacked with black morocco spine, owner name of George Dickinson on half titlepage, minor internal soiling, covers nice, very good. Charles Agvent Transcendentalism 2010 - 10 2011 $1200

Emerson, Ralph Waldo 1803-1882 *Essays. Second Series.* London: John Chapman, 1844, Stereotype edition; original cloth, gilt, neatly recased, pages vi, (ii), 190, (ii), prelims little spotted. R. F. G. Hollett & Son Antiquarian Booksellers 175 - 418 2011 £75

Emerson, Ralph Waldo 1803-1882   *The Essays of Ralph Waldo Emerson.*   San Francisco: Limited Editions Club, 1934, #196 of 1500 beautifully designed copies, singed by John Henry Nash; folio, cloth backed blue paper boards, bound by John Henry Nash, spine little darkened, slight chipping to spine label, near fine in very good, intact slipcase.   Charles Agvent   Transcendentalism 2010 - 11   2011 $175

Emerson, Ralph Waldo 1803-1882   *Letters and Social Aims.*   Boston: Osgood,, 1876, First edition; original terra cotta cloth, signature mark N present on page 209, Myerson A34.1.a., correct readings on page 308, this copy inscribed and signed by author for J. Elliot Cabot, rear hinge broken, front hinge ready to go with some external splitting there as well, spine tips frayed.   Charles Agvent   Transcendentalism 2010 - 14   2011 $20,000

Emerson, Ralph Waldo 1803-1882   *Letters and Social Aims.*   Boston: Osgood, 1876, First edition; original terra cotta cloth, signature mark N is present on page 209 making it an early copy according to BAL, the "inviolable" reading occurs on page 308, however, which Myerson notes occurs after the first printing, light edgewear, little heavier to spine tips and edges, very good.   Charles Agvent   Transcendentalism 2010 - 13   2011 $125

Emerson, Ralph Waldo 1803-1882   *May-Day and Other Pieces.*   Boston: Ticknor and Fields, 1867, One of only 100 copies bound thus, from a total edition of 2000; original gilt decorated white linen, gift binding, few pages unopened, spine slightly darkened with minor wear to tips, near fine and scarce, signed and inscribed by author for Anna Cabot Lowell.   Charles Agvent   Transcendentalism 2010 - 15   2011 $8500

Emerson, Ralph Waldo 1803-1882   *Miscellanies: Embracing Nature, Addresses and Lectures.*   Boston: Phillips, Sampson, 1856, First edition; original brown cloth, the Stephen H. Wakeman copy with his bookplate, moderate wear to spine tips and corners, few scrapes to spine, numerous pencil markings, very good.   Charles Agvent   Transcendentalism 2010 - 16   2011 $250

Emerson, Ralph Waldo 1803-1882   *Poems.*   Boston: James Munroe and Co., 1847, First American edition; original yellow glazed boards neatly rebacked with most of the original spine laid down on attractive tan morocco, 4 page catalog dated 1 Jan. 1847 inserted at front, pencil signatures of O. B. Frothingham dated 1847, very clean, attractive copy, about fine, housed in cloth chemise and brown half morocco slipcase.   Charles Agvent   Transcendentalism 2010 - 17   2011 $850

Emerson, Ralph Waldo 1803-1882   *The Poems of Ralph Waldo Emerson.*   New York: Limited Editions Club, 1945, #1053 of 1500 copies; tall octavo, full black sheepskin, grained and crushed, with gilt lettering on front cover and spine, 256 pages, 22 lovely watercolor vignettes colored by hand in the Studio of Charlize Brakeley, Monthly letter laid in, mild rubbing to leather, about fine in fine slipcase.   Charles Agvent   Transcendentalism 2010 - 20   2011 $150

Emerson, Ralph Waldo 1803-1882   *The Poems of Ralph Waldo Emerson.*   New York: Limited Editions Club, 1945, Copy 1056 of 1500 signed by artists on colophon page; Tall octavo, bound in full black sheepskin, grained and crushed with gilt lettering on front cover and spine, 256 pages, 22 lovely watercolor vignettes by Richard and Doris Beers colored by hand in the studio of Charlize Brakeley, slipcase with tear at top of backstrip, two tiny nick to leather, about fine, very good.   Charles Agvent   Transcendentalism 2010 - 18   2011 $125

Emerson, Ralph Waldo 1803-1882   *Representative Men: Seven Lectures.*   Boston: Ticknor and Fields, 1863, Contemporary half calf, marbled boards, with calf corners, marbled endpapers and edges, neatly rebacked retaining original spine, signed by author, armorial bookplate of L. Duncan Wood, near fine, scarce.   Charles Agvent   Transcendentalism 2010 - 21   2011 $4500

Emerson, Ralph Waldo 1803-1882   *Complete Works.*   Cambridge: Riverside Press, 1883, Riverside edition, one of 500 copies; 235 x 150m., 11 volumes, very attractive green straight grain morocco (stamp signed "Hatchards of Piccadilly" on front turn-in), covers with border of two gilt fillets, wide raised bands decorated with floral ornaments and three gilt rules, ruled gilt compartments with large fleuron centerpiece, marbled endpapers, top edge gilt, other edges rough trimmed, 2 frontispiece portraits, large paper copy, armorial bookplates of Henry Martin Gibbs of Barrow Court, Flax Bourton, Somerset, backstrips uniformly faded to pleasing caramel color, top of one spine slightly rubbed, three or four joints with trivial wear, three corners bit bumped, endpapers (of a different stock from text), somewhat foxed, otherwise quite appealing set, leather lustrous, wear insignificant and text especially bright, fresh and clean.   Phillip J. Pirages   59 - 189   2011 $2500

Emerson, Ralph Waldo 1803-1882   *The Complete Works.*   Cambridge: printed at the Riverside Press, 1903-1904, Autograph Centenary edition, one of 600 numbered copies, signed by publishers with original leaf (2 pages) of manuscript in Emerson's hand; 12 volumes, 8vo., numerous photogravure illustrations, handsome three quarter morocco, gilt spines, slight chips from top of spines on three volumes, tiny nicks on two more, excellent set.   M & S Rare Books, Inc.   90 - 127   2011 $3500

Emery, Gilbert   *Tarnish: a Play in Three Acts.*   New York: Brentanos, 1924, 82 pages, illustrations, covers soiled and worn at edges, interior clean and tight, very good.   G. H. Mott Bookseller   May 26 2011 - 35650   2011 $200

Emett, Rowland *Buffer's End arrived at by Emett.* London: Faber, 1949, First edition; large 4to., original cloth, gilt, dust jacket trifle dusty, one short closed edge tear, price clipped.   R. F. G. Hollett & Son Antiquarian Booksellers   General Catalogue Summer 2010 - 764   2011   £45

Emett, Rowland *The Emett Festival Railway.* Penguin Books, 1951, First edition; oblong 8vo., original pictorial wrappers, short closed tear to upper edge, pages 30, 12 pages colored cutouts.   R. F. G. Hollett & Sons Antiquarian Booksellers   170 - 219   2011   £85

Emett, Rowland *Far Twittering.* London: Faber, 1949, First edition; large 4to., original cloth, gilt, dust jacket (rather worn with some loss to head of spine and one corner, price clipped), unpaginated, 12 tinted plates and numerous line drawings, light spotting to flyleaves, but very good.   R. F. G. Hollett & Son Antiquarian Booksellers   General Catalogue Summer 2010 - 765   2011   £95

Emett, Rowland *Hobby Horses.* London: Printed by W. S. Cowell for Guinness, n.d., 1958, First edition; 12 pages, illustrations in color on stiff paper, original wrappers, very slight bruising to corners.   R. F. G. Hollett & Son Antiquarian Booksellers   General Catalogue Summer 2010 - 767   2011   £85

Emett, Rowland *Home Rails Preferred.* London: Faber, 1947, First edition; unpaginated, large 8vo., original pictorial cloth, dust jacket rather worn and chipped, some loss to edges of upper panel, cartoons by Emett.   R. F. G. Hollett & Son Antiquarian Booksellers   General Catalogue Summer 2010 - 768   2011   £30

Emett, Rowland *Nellie Come Home.* London: Faber, 1952, First edition; large 4to., original pictorial boards, matching dust jacket (trifle soiled and worn with piece missing from head of upper panel), unpaginated, numerous line drawings, many colored.   R. F. G. Hollett & Son Antiquarian Booksellers   General Catalogue Summer 2010 - 769   2011   £45

Emett, Rowland *Saturday Slow.* London: Faber, 1948, First edition; large 8vo., original pictorial cloth, dust jacket (minimal wear to extremities, price clipped), cartoons by Emett, unpaginated.   R. F. G. Hollett & Son Antiquarian Booksellers   General Catalogue Summer 2010 - 770   2011   £30

Emmens, Stephen Henry *The Philosophy and Practice of Punctuation.* London: Virtue and Co., 1868, First edition; pages viii, 46, 6 x 4.5 inches, original publisher's green cloth lettered gilt on spine and patterned with gilt symbols on cover on front and rear cover, scarce, slight rubbing, otherwise very good, pleasing copy.   Any Amount of Books   May 29 2011 - A63049   2011 $340

Empson, Patience *The Wood Engravings of Robert Gibbings with Some Recollections of the Artist.*   1969, First edition; dust jacket, near fine.   C. P. Hyland   May 26 2011 - 258/292   2011 $290

Encyclopaedia of Connecticut Biography.   Chicago: Century, 1892, 4to., leather, both boards detached (thus fair), leather scratched, torn on spine, worn generally, light stain to top margins, else interior clean and tight, fair.   G. H. Mott Bookseller   May 26 2011 - 9073   2011 $200

Endeavour.   1942-1952, V. 1/1-V.Xi/44, lacking 7 issues, Jan. 1942-Oct. 1952, together 37 issues, excellent condition, signed by authors.   I. D. Edrich   May 26 2011 - 97060   2011 $461

Enfield, William *The Speaker; or Miscellaneous Pieces...* London: printed for Joseph Johnson, 1779, Third edition; contemporary polished calf, gilt, few small scrapes to lower board, spine little frayed at head and cracked at tail, pages xxxiv, 405.   R. F. G. Hollett & Son Antiquarian Booksellers   175 - 420   2011   £75

Engels, Frederick *The Condition of the Working Class in England in 1844.* London: Swan Sonnenschein & Co., 1892, First printing; 8vo., xix, (1), 298 (2) pages, original publisher's red cloth with title in black on upper cover and in gilt on spine, 3 small patch of dampstain on spine and very small marginal stain on lower cover, in all other respects, very good.   John Drury Rare Books   153 - 40   2011   £350

Enger, Leif *Peace Like a River.* New York: Atlantic Monthly, 2001, First edition; fine in fine dust jacket, signed by author.   Bella Luna Books   May 29 2011 - t3237   2011 $82

Englefield, Henry C. *A Description of the Principal Picturesque Beauties, Antiquities and Geological Pheonmena of the Isle of Wight.* London: printed by William Bulmer and Co. for Payne and Foss, 1816, Large paper copy, 4to., pages (viii) vi 238 (iv) (vi)-xxvii, (i) + oval engraved frontispiece, 50 other engraved plates, contemporary russia leather, boards intricately gilt bordered with double triple rules and back to back decorative roll between, within blind tooled acanthus roll and innermost a single rule gilt panel with elaborate made up corner pieces gilt, board edges, 'broken hatch fillet' roll at corners, turn-ins 'composite double rule' gilt, all edges gilt, 3 color double core patterned sewn endbands, orange silk page markers, early 20th century in brown goatskin, spine divided into five compartments by triple raised bands, one flat between two ordinary and tooled in gilt and in blind, lettering gilt direct in two compartments, toned, some foxing to plates, touch of rubbing to extremities, crowned and belted heraldic crest, gilt stamp of Earl of Derby in centre of front board, this copy is extra illustrated by the inclusion of Ordnance Survey sheet 10 of Isle of Wight dated 1810, large folding map bound in, from the collection of Christopher Ernest Weston 1947-2010. Unsworths Booksellers 24 - 92 2011 £1400

English. 1936-1949, Nos. 1-42, Spring 1936-Autumn 1949, 42 issues in original wrappers. I. D. Edrich May 26 2011 - 99146 2011 $503

English as She is Spoke. Lion and Unicorn Press, 1960, Limited edition, no. 195 of 200 copies; oblong 4to., original pictorial boards, pages 101, illustrations in colors by Edward Bawden, very scarce. R. F. G. Hollett & Son Antiquarian Booksellers General Catalogue Summer 2010 - 706 2011 £650

English Fairy Tales. London: Macmillan and Co. Ltd., 1918, One of 500 copies signed by artist, this copy #12; 290 x 230mm., ix, (i), 341, (1) pages, very attractive red three quarter morocco (stamp signed "Putnams" along front turn-in), raised bands, spine handsomely gilt in compartments formed by plain and decorative rules, quatrefoil centerpiece surrounded by densely scrolling cornerpieces and endleaves or rose colored line, top edge gilt, titlepage vignette, numerous black and white illustrations in text, 16 color plates, by Arthur Rackham, as called for, mounted and protected by lettered tissue guards; top of spine worn away to just about headband, corners with hint of rubbing, one tissue guard with minor tear, other trivial imperfections, but nearly fine, binding very lustrous and without significant wear, especially bright, fresh and clean internally. Phillip J. Pirages 59 - 286 2011 $2750

English Studies. Amsterdam: bi-monthly, 1956, Volume 37 1956- Volume 61 1980, lacking only 6 issues, together with index. I. D. Edrich May 26 2011 - 100125 2011 $671

The English Woman's Domestic Magazine. London: S. O. Beeton, 1861, Volume 2 Nos. 1-12, old half calf, marbled boards, rebacked in cloth, lettering piece relaid, rather rubbed, pages 336 with 6 hand colored fashion plates and 5 folding chromo lithographed patterns for needlework and numerous text woodcuts, joints strengthened with marbled paper. R. F. G. Hollett & Son Antiquarian Booksellers 175 - 435 2011 £75

Engvick, William *Lullabies and Night Songs.* London: Bodley Head, 1969, First UK edition; large 4to., original pictorial boards, pages 78, illustrations in color by Maurice Sendak. R. F. G. Hollett & Sons Antiquarian Booksellers 170 - 620 2011 £35

Ennius, Quintus *Quae Supersunt fragmenta ab Hieronymo Columna Conquisita Disposita et Explicata ad Ioannem Filium.* Naples: Ex typographia Horatii Saluiani, 1590, First full separate printing; some light spotting, small library stamp at foot of title, pages (viii), xvi, 505, (43), 4to., late 19th century vellum, backstrip with red morocco label (chipped), front flyleaf removed, ownership inscriptions and prize bookplate on front pastedown, very good. Blackwell Rare Books B166 - 36 2011 £900

Enright, D. J. *The Year of the Monkey.* Kobe: privately Printed, 1956, First edition; number 65 of 400 on handmade paper signed by D. J. Enright under his photo, extra label at rear, slightly browned at lower front edge, else very good+ excellent copy in chipped, near very good glassine wrapper. Any Amount of Books May 29 2011 - A70845 2011 $230

Ensign & Thayer's Travellers' Guide through the States of Ohio, Michigan, Indiana Illinois, Missouri, Iowa and Wisconsin with Railroad Canal State and Steamboat Accompanied with a New Map of Above States. New York: published by Horace Thayer & Co., 1853, First edition; 24mo., original red morocco, front panel has designs of steam train and steamboat in gilt with titles in gilt and frame of floral designs also in gilt, rear panel duplicates front panel except without gilt, 33, (2) pages, map, text moderately foxed ad maps has few minor repairs to few folds, else good, bright, tight copy housed in leather slipcase with leather label on spine and titles stamped in gold. Buckingham Books May 26 2011 - 25415 2011 $2250

Ensign & Thayer's Travellers' Guide through the States of Ohio, Michigan, Indiana Illinois, Missouri, Iowa and Wisconsin with Railroad Canal State and Steamboat Accompanied with a New Map of Above States. New York: Ensign, Bridgman & Fanning, 1855, 24mo., original red morocco, front panel has designs of steam train and steamboat in gilt with titles in gilt and frame of floral designs also in gilt, rear panel duplicates front panel except without gilt, 33, (2) pages, map, folding map has few minor repairs to folds, cosmetic repairs to spine ends and extremities, small chip to fore-edge of front flyleaf, lightly foxed, else near fine, housed in black cloth clamshell case with leather label on spine with titles stamped in gold.   Buckingham Books   May 26 2011 - 25259   2011 $1875

Entick, John   *The General History of the Late War...* London: printed for Edward and Charles Dilly, 1766-1767, First volume third edition, others are second editions; 7 volumes, 8vo., soundly rebound in 20th century beige buckram with black and red leather spine labels, pages 495, 465, 480, 480, 470 and 26 page index, 5 volumes, 8 folding maps, circa 40 portraits, ex-British Foreign Office library with few library markings, else very good, decent sound copy with clean text and excellent plates and maps.   Any Amount of Books   May 26 2011 - A73778 2011 $1510

Envoi. privately printed, 1958-1995, First edition; Nos 2-4, 6, 8-29, 85-111, 54 issues in original wrappers, the issues 2-8 being stencilled, the others printed, loosely inserted comment slips and 3 letters from editor to contributors, all in very good condition.   I. D. Edrich   May 26 2011 - 97611   2011 $587

Epictetus   *Manuale et Sententiae Quibus Accedunt Tabula Cerebtis...* Utrecht: Ex officina Gulielmi Broedelet, 1711, Some browning and spotting in places, one index leaf with 2 small repairs in text area so that a few words are supplied in manuscript, pages (xx), 151, (1), 124, 152, (60), 4to., contemporary unlettered vellum, touch dusty, booklabel of A. A. Land, good.   Blackwell Rare Books   B166 - 37   2011   £250

Epigrammatum. Frankfurt: Apud Andreae Wecheli, 1600, some spotting, title little dusty, pages (iv), 632, 30, (30), folio, late 19th century calf, boards with thick gilt fillet border, rebacked backstrip with five raised bands between gilt rope tools, old green morocco label preserved in second compartment, rest with central blind flower tool, corners worn, some scratches to old leather, good.   Blackwell Rare Books   B166 - 42   2011   £900

Epiphytic Plant Study Group   *Epiphytes: The Epipyhtic Plant Study Group Journal.* Bristol: A. J. S. McMillan, 1968-2001, First edition; 8vo., 100 issues complete in 7 volumes, pages approximately 2500, tipped in full color plates, very good.   Any Amount of Books   May 29 2011 - A40550   2011 $340

Epstein, M.   *The Annual Register: a Review of Public Events at Home and Abroad 1931-1938.* London: Longmans, Green and Co., 1932-1939, First edition; 8 volumes, 8vo., each volume between 450-500 pages, original publisher's purple cloth lettered gilt on spine, new series, all clean, very good copies, slightly sunned at spine, few pastedowns have bookplate of 11th Duke of Bedford, Woburn Abbey.   Any Amount of Books   May 29 2011 - A70517   2011 $306

Epworth and Its Surroundings. the Home of the Wesleys. Epworth Bells Printing Works, n.d., 1900,   Flyleaves lightly browned, otherwise very good, original cloth, gilt, pages 207, well illustrated.   R. F. G. Hollett & Son Antiquarian Booksellers   General Catalogue Summer 2010 - 1328   2011   £35

Equicola, Mario   *Dell'istoria di Mantova Libri Cinque... Riformata Secondo l'Uso Moderne si Scrivere Istorie...* Mantua: F. Osanna, 1607,   4to., (26), 307, (5), Rrl with register and imprint Rr2 with list of errata, English calf, c. 1700, gilt fillet on covers, spine gilt in compartments, green, red silk marker, from the library of the Earls of Macclesfield at Shirburn Castle.   Maggs Bros. Ltd.   1440 - 78   2011   £750

Erasmus, Desiderius   *Colloquia nunc Emendatiora.* Amstelodami: Apud Jodocum Jansonium, 1644,   3 x 5 inches, 743 pages, very good, later quarter leather and marbled boards, lightly soiled, edge worn, page edges soiled, interior very clean and tight.   G. H. Mott Bookseller   May 26 2011 - 45620   2011 $500

Erasmus, Desiderius   *Paraphrasis seu Potius Epitome...in Elegantiarum Libros Laurentii Vallae...* Paris: R. Estienne, October, 1542,   One of 3 editions of 1542; (Lyons and Cologne being the place of printing of the other two), 8vo., 192, (36) pages, last leaf blank, printer's device, 17th century calf, spine gilt in compartments, seems to be extremely uncommon, from the library of the Earls of Macclesfield at Shirburn Castle.   Maggs Bros. Ltd.   1440 - 79   2011   £850

Erasmus, Desiderius   *Paraphrasis seu Potius Epitome...in Elegantiarum Laurentij Vallae.. cum Gallica... Expositione.* Lyons: S. Gryphe, 1547,   8vo., 199, (17) pages, 17th century vellum over pasteboards, bottom edge lettered Erasmus in Vallam, from the library of the Earls of Macclesfield at Shirburn Castle.   Maggs Bros. Ltd.   1440 - 80   2011   £400

Erdrich, Louise   *Jacklight.* New York: Holt Rinehart Winston, 1984,   First edition; wrappers, signed by author on half title, near fine.   Lupack Rare Books   May 26 2011 - ABE3649643652   2011 $125

Erdrich, Louise *Love Medicine.* New York: Holt, Rinehart & Winston, 1984, First edition; inscribed by author, bit of foxing to top edge and mild edge sunning to boards, near fine in very near fine, price clipped dust jacket with just touch of edge wear.   Ken Lopez Bookseller   154 - 135 2011 $150

Erizzo, Sebastiano *Discorso...Sopra le Medaglie de Gli Antichi con la Dichiaratione delle Monete Consulari & Delle Medaglie de Gli Imperadori Romani...*   Venice: Giovanni Varisco & Paganino Paganini, not before, 1584, Splendid copy, 2 parts, 4to., (16), 282, (2 blank); 572 pages, title within woodcut border, woodcut initials and headpieces, woodcut illustrations, 17th century mottled calf, gilt arms of Foucault on covers, spine gilt in compartments, mottled red edges, Y1 torn at head with loss, extremities slightly rubbed, from the library of the Earls of Macclesfield at Shirburn Castle.   Maggs Bros. Ltd.   1440 - 82 2011   £700

Erlich, Bettina *Cocolo's Home.* New York: Harper Bros., 1950, Folio, pictorial boards, fine in dust jacket, illustrations by author.   Aleph-Bet Books, Inc.   95 - 97 2011 $150

Ernst, George *The Law of Married Women in Massachusetts.* Boston: Little Brown and Co., 1897, Second edition; (xxxvi, 285) pages, 8vo., brick colored cloth, gilt lettered spine, some rubbing to extremities, early owner's name on front pastedown, otherwise very nice clean copy.   Paulette Rose Fine and Rare Books   32 - 110 2011 $450

Erpenius, Thomas *Historia Josephi Patriarchae.* Leiden: Ex Typographia Erpentiana Linguarum, 1617, First printed edition of any part of the Koran rinted in its original language, Arabic; small quarto, (2), 141, (1, colophon) pages, title is in an architectural woodcut border, on colophon is woodcut printers device, original brown speckled calf, rebacked to style, boards ruled in blind, spine stamped in blind, four leaves of signature A, with professional repairs to upper inner corners, some marginal dampstaining and contemporary ink marginalia throughout, few leaves in middle of the book have an old foxing type stain, edges at beginning and end, bit browned and crisp and titlepage also bit browned, front and back pastedowns with previous owner's old ink and pencil notes, overall very good.   Heritage Book Shop   Holiday 2010 - 37 2011 $7500

Erpenius, Thomas *Orationes tres, de Linguarum Ebraeae, Atque Arabicae Dignitate.* Leiden: ex typographia auctoris, 1621, 8vo., (12), 132 pages, contemporary English calf, printed pastedowns (Italian text), repaired, from the library of the Earls of Macclesfield at Shirburn Castle.   Maggs Bros. Ltd.   1440 - 83 2011   £1000

Escott, T. H. S. *Anthony Trollope, His Work, Associates and Literary Originals.* London: John Lane, The Bodley Head, 1913, First edition; half title, frontispiece, two other illustrations, original red cloth, slightly dulled, top edge gilt, very good.   Jarndyce Antiquarian Booksellers   CXCI - 586 2011   £50

Espejo, Antonio De *New Mexico: Otherwise the Voiage of Anthony of Espeio...in the Yare 1583.* Lancaster: Privately printed by Frederick Hodge, 1928, Edition of 200 numbered copies, signed by Frederick Hodge; 12mo., 37 pages, tooled leather boards, slightly rubbed, else near fine.   Dumont Maps & Books of the West   113 - 32 2011 $225

Essays & Studies. English Association, 1910-1946, 1948-1984. First edition; v. 1-32, all published in this series, then New Series V. 1-33, 65 volumes in original cloth, 59 of which have dust jackets, all in very good condition.   I. D. Edrich   May 26 2011 - 82435 2011 $2600

Estes, Matthew *A Defence of Negro Slavery, as It Exists in the United States.* Montgomery: Press of the Alabama Journal, 1846, First edition; 18mo., 260 pages, old boards, new calf spine and label, printer's problem on pages 55/56 where small paper tear resulted in a small failure to print completely, affecting perhaps a dozen words.   M & S Rare Books, Inc.   90 - 128 2011 $1500

Ets, Marie Hall *Play with Me.* New York: Viking, 1955, First edition; 4to., cloth, fine in dust jacket with some soil and few edge chips, charming color lithographs on each page.   Aleph-Bet Books, Inc.   95 - 221 2011 $600

Etzler, John Adolphus *Emigration to the Tropical World, for the Melioration of all Classes of People of all Nations.* published at the Concordium Ham Common, Surrey, and sold by J. Watson... J. Cleave... Terington.... London, 1844, First edition; 8vo., 24 pages, paper little browned, last leaf with some foxing and minor staining, sympathetically bound in old style quarter calf gilt, rare.   John Drury Rare Books   153 - 42 2011   £750

Euclides *Geometricorum Elemntorum Libri XV.* Paris: H. Estienne after Jan., 1516-1517, First edition printed outside Italy; folio, ff. 261 (of 262 without final blank), woodcut diagrams in margins, woodcut initials, 19th century calf by Hatton of Manchester, marbled edges, title leaf cut down and remounted, from the library of the Earls of Macclesfield at Shirburn Castle.   Maggs Bros. Ltd.   1440 - 84 2011   £4000

Euclides *Elucidis Phaenomena Posta Zamberti & Maurolyci Editionem...* Rome: G. Martinelli, 1591, First edition of this Latin version; 4to., (22), 89 (=99) pages, woodcut diagrams, ownership inscription of William Charke, from the library of the Earls of Macclesfield at Shirburn Castle.   Maggs Bros. Ltd.   1440 - 85 2011   £1200

Eudora Welty: a Tribute 13 April 1984. Winston Salem: Printed for Stuart Wright, 1984, First edition, one of 75 copies; signed by each of the contributors, 8vo., (32) pages, marbled wrappers over boards, paper title label printed in black on upper cover, fine, as new.   Paulette Rose Fine and Rare Books   32 - 184   2011 $825

European Drawings from the Collections of the Metropolitan Museum of Art II. Flemish, Dutch, German, Spanish, French and British Drawings. New York: Metropolitan Museum of Art, 1943, 10.5 x 14 inch collotype reproductions, portfolio soiled, edgeworn, cloth ties, reproductions in very good condition, softbound, very good.   G. H. Mott Bookseller   May 26 2011 - 33107   2011 $200

Eusebius *(Greek text) De Demonstratione Evangelica. Libri Decem...* Cologne: Mauritii Georg Weidmann, 1688, Bi-lingual edition; folio, (viii), 24, (12), 548, 195, (1 blank) pages, title printed in red and black, engraved titlepage vignette, headpieces, decorative initials, tailpieces, indexes, text printed double column in Greek and Latin, lightly browned, ms. notations on rear endleaves, newly rebound in period style quarter calf, marbled boards, raised bands, orange red gilt stamped spine label, original endleaves preserved, ink ownership signatures, rubber stamps on title of Robert J. Lockart, fine.   Jeff Weber Rare Books   163 - 23   2011 $1200

Eusebius *Eusebius Pamphilius His Ten Books of Ecclesiastical History.* London: printed for George Sawbridge, 1703, First edition; old panelled calf, few light old scrapes to boards, neatly rebacked to match, pages (xiv), 179, (xx), frontispiece little repaired in gutter).   R. F. G. Hollett & Son Antiquarian Booksellers   175 - 1036 2011   £120

Eutropius *Eutropii Historiae Romanae Breviarium...* Parisiis: Apud Viduam Antonii Cellier via Citaraea, 1683, 4to., pages (xiv) 183, (i), this copy lacks engraved half title, found with some copies of the Delphin editions, contemporary vellum, spine fully gilt in compartments, green lettering piece gilt, all edges gilt red and grey sprinkled, green and white sewn endbands, small faint dampmark to upper edge, fore edges of first c. 20 leaves little creased, vellum touch soiled, from the collection of Christopher Ernest Weston 1947-2010.   Unsworths Booksellers   24 - 93 2011   £125

Evanovich, Janet *One for the Money.* New York: Scribner, 1994, First edition; near fine, light bump across top of front board, dust jacket fine.   Bella Luna Books   May 26 2011 - t7956 2011 $192

Evanovich, Janet *Two for the Dough.* New York: Scribner, 1995, First edition; near fine, heel of spine lightly bumped, dust jacket fine, signed on tipped in page and limited to 1000 copies with different ISBN than trade edition, signed by author.   Bella Luna Books   May 29 2011 - j1792 2011 $110

Evans, Arthur *Collectors Guide to Rollei Cameras.* Garden City: 1986, First edition; 271 pages, original binding, dust jacket, fine.   Bookworm & Silverfish   664 - 163   2011 $75

Evans, Daniel *The Life and Work of William Williams M.P. for Coventry 1835-1847, M.P. for Lambeth 1850-1865.* Llandyssul: Gomerian Press, 1939, First edition; pages 372, with 21 plates, large 8vo., original red cloth, gilt, top edge gilt, trifle faded, dust jacket with outer glassine wrapper (edges little chipped and soiled), edges rather spotted.   R. F. G. Hollett & Son Antiquarian Booksellers   175 - 422   2011   £35

Evans, Francis *Furness and Furness Abbey; or a Companion through the Lancashire Part of the Lake District.* Ulverston: D. Atkinson, 1842, First edition; original blind-stamped cloth gilt, spine rather cracked but sound, pages x, 254, (i) complete, 3 engraved plates, plan and hand colored map.   R. F. G. Hollett & Son Antiquarian Booksellers   173 - 382 2011   £175

Evans, Francis *Furness and Furness Abbey...* Ulverston: D. Atkinson, 1842, First edition; original blindstamped cloth gilt, little faded and cockled, spine trifle chipped at head heat and foot, pages x, 254, (ii), 2 engraved plates, land and hand colored map, little shaken.   R. F. G. Hollett & Son Antiquarian Booksellers   General Catalogue Summer 2010 - 1389 2011   £125

Evans, J. Gwenogvryn *Facsimile and Text of the Book of Taliesin.* Llanbedrog: 1910, Number 13 of 100 copies on Japanese vellum (total limitation 350 copies with facsimile); initialled by Evans, half vellum, very good, tight set, untrimmed, signed by author.   C. P. Hyland   May 26 2011 - 255/195 2011 $1232

Evans, James *Small-River Fly Fishing for Trout and Grayling.* London: Adam and Charles Black, 1972, First edition; original cloth, gilt, dust jacket (slight wear to head of spine, price clipped), pages 208, text illustrations and color frontispiece.   R. F. G. Hollett & Son Antiquarian Booksellers   General Catalogue Summer 2010 - 1240 2011   £30

Evans, James *The Speller and Interpreter in Indian and English.* New York: D. Fanshaw, 1837, First edition?; 16mo., quarter contemporary calf over boards, scarce.   Heritage Book Shop   Booth A12 51st NY International Antiquarian Book Fair April 8-10 2011 - 52 2011 $5000

Evans, Joan *Monastic Iconography in France: from the Renaissance to the Revolution.* Cambridge University Press, 1970, First edition; 4to., original cloth, gilt, dust jacket, pages xv, 77, with 117 plates, mint.   R. F. G. Hollett & Son Antiquarian Booksellers   175 - 423   2011   £45

Evans, John *An Address Humbley Designed to Promote a Religious Revival, Amongst the General Baptists.* London: printed and sold by J. Johnson, D. Taylor, J. Marsom, and at the Printing Office No. 31 Fair Street, Horsly Down, n.d., 1793?, First edition; 12mo., 24 pages, minor edge fraying, couple of closed tears in title (but no loss), preserved in modern wrappers with printed title label on upper cover, uncut, good, large copy, very rare.   John Drury Rare Books   153 - 43   2011   £275

Evans, John *English Art 1307-1461.* Oxford: Clarendon Press, 1949, First edition; tall 8vo., original cloth, gilt, dust jacket (little faded, few slight edge chips), pages xxiv, 272 with 96 plates and 13 figures, sporadic light spotting, despite title, the volume deals amost exclusively with early architecture and sculpture.   R. F. G. Hollett & Son Antiquarian Booksellers   177 - 287   2011   £30

Evans, Myfanwy *Diggory Goes to the Never-Never.* London: Collins, 1937, First edition; 4to., original pictorial boards, matching dust jacket (edges little worn and faded), pages (28), illustrations, mostly in shades of blue, pink and brown, front flyleaf lightly spotted, but very nice, scarce.   R. F. G. Hollett & Sons Antiquarian Booksellers   170 - 680   2011   £75

Evans, Myfanwy *The Pavilion.* London: J. T. Publications and Gerald Duckworth, 1946, First edition; pages 80, illustrations, large square 4to., original stiff wrappers, little dusty.   R. F. G. Hollett & Son Antiquarian Booksellers   General Catalogue Summer 2010 - 117   2011   £95

Evans, Nicholas *The Horse Whisperer.* London: Bantam, 1995, First British edition; fine in like dust jacket.   Bella Luna Books   May 26 2011 - t1739   2011 $165

Evans, Nicholas *The Horse Whisperer.* New York: Delacorte Press, 1995, First edition; fine in fine dust jacket, signed and dated 9-14-95.   Bella Luna Books   May 26 2011 - 4238   2011 $192

Evans, Nicholas *The Horse Whisperer.* New York: Delacorte Press, 1995, First edition; fine in like dust jacket, signature dated 9-14-95, with proof of publisher's dust jacket which is erased along spine and has no printing on flaps, signed by author.   Bella Luna Books   May 29 2011 - j1022   2011 $137

Evans, Nicholas *The Horse Whisperer.* London: Bantam, 1995, First British edition; near fine, light bumping to spine ends, dust jacket fine.   Bella Luna Books   May 29 2011 - t7682   2011 $82

Evans, Sebastian *The High History of the Holy Grail.* London: J. M. Dent, 1903, First edition thus; large 8vo., pages xvii, 379, illustrations by Jessie M. King with 23 full page plates, some with red pictorial embellishment + 36 chapter headpieces and gilt black cover and spine illustration on publisher's sky blue cloth, sound decent about very good with slight soiling, slight marks and slight rubbing and slight bumping to covers, endpapers foxed, neat presentation inscription on half title to Duke of Bedford from one J. Bly dated 1903.   Any Amount of Books May 26 2011 - A74369   2011 $755

Evelyn, John   1620-1706 *Acetaria. A Discourse of Sallets.* London: printed for B. Tooke, 1699, First edition; small octavo, (xi), 192, (35, appendix), (13, table), (1, errata) pages, with folded leaf of plates on herbs, vegetables and greens, contemporary calf, expertly rebacked to style, blind-stamped spine compartments, new red morocco gilt spine label, very good.   Heritage Book Shop   Holiday 2010 - 38   2011 $2000

Evelyn, John   1620-1706 *Sylva or a Discourse of Forest Trees.* London: Arthur Doubleday, n.d., 1908, First edition thus, reprint of fourth edition; 2 volumes, tall 8vo., original publisher's green cloth lettered gilt on spine and on front cover, pages cxv, 335 & 287, uncut, 6 plates, uncommon edition, attractive very good+, copies slightly bumped at corners.   Any Amount of Books   May 29 2011 - A39932   2011 $221

Everett, Edward *Inauguration of Washington University at Saint Louis Missouri April 23 1857.* Boston: Little Brown and Co., 1857, First edition; 8vo., 104 pages, removed, presentation inscription from Everett to Rev. Osgood dated 14 Dec. 1857.   M & S Rare Books, Inc.   90 - 437   2011 $150

Everett, Henry *The History of the Somerset Light Infantry (Prince Albert's) 1885-1945.* London: Somerset Light Infantry/Methuen, 1927-1951, First editions,; 3 volumes, mixed set, first volume in half green leather lettered gilt on spine and on front cover (chipped at spine ends, sound but very good-), second volume is in original publisher's green cloth lettered gilt on spine and on front cover, chipped at spine ends, sound but very good-, third volume is in original publisher's green cloth lettered gilt on spine and on front cover, very good+, pages 1000+, 58 illustrations, 73 maps.   Any Amount of Books   May 29 2011 - A34471   2011 $272

Ewald, Alexander Charles *The Right Hon. Benjamin Disraeli Earl of Beaconsfield...* London: William Mackenzie, 1882, 2 volumes, small 4to., original blue decorated cloth, gilt, edges slightly rubbed, few slight scratches, pages 600; 593; all edges gilt, 30 steel engraved portraits and plates, some joints tender, but very good set.   R. F. G. Hollett & Son Antiquarian Booksellers   175 - 425   2011   £75

Ewald, Wendy *Appalachia: a Self Portrait.* Frankfort: 1979, 100 pages, 4to., wrappers, fine. Bookworm & Silverfish 676 - 17 2011 $125

Ewbank, Jane M. *Antiquary on Horseback.* Kendal: Titus Wilson, 1963, First edition; pages xvi, 163, illustrations, original cloth, gilt, dust jacket, scarce. R. F. G. Hollett & Son Antiquarian Booksellers 173 - 383 2011 £85

Ex Ctesia, Agatharchide, Memnone Excerptiae Historiae. Appiani Iberica. Item de Gestis Annibalis... Cum Henrici Stephani Castigationibus. Geneva: ex officina Henrici Stephani Parisiensis typographi, 1557, Editio princeps; 8vo., (16)m., 248, 17th century smooth calf, spine gilt, red edges, extremely handsome, from the library of the Earls of Macclesfield at Shirburn Castle. Maggs Bros. Ltd. 1440 - 65 2011 £1000

The Experienced American Housekeeper, or Domestic Cookery: Formed on Principles of Economy for the Use of Private Families. New York: Nafis & Cornish, Philadelphia: John B. Perry, 1838, 216 pages, 6 plates, contemporary sheep, very skillfully rebacked in period style, original label preserved, occasional spotting and foxing, very nice. Joseph J. Felcone Inc. Fall Miscellany 2010 - 30 2011 $500

Extracts from the Information Received by His Majesty's Commissioners as to the Administration and Operation of the Poor Laws. London: B. Fellowes, 1833, First edition; 8vo., xxi, (1),4 32 pages, original oatmeal linen with title printed in black on spine, very slight fraying to spine, else very good, from the library of W. Jex Blake with his signature dated 1834 on titlepage. John Drury Rare Books 153 - 133 2011 £175

Eyles, Desmond *The Doulton Lambeth Wares.* London: Hutchinson, 1975, 4to., original cloth gilt, dust jacket (head of spine little worn, few closed edge tears), pages 179, 78 color plates, 167 illustrations plus text drawings and numerous marks. R. F. G. Hollett & Son Antiquarian Booksellers General Catalogue Summer 2010 - 149 2011 £65

F

Faber, Michel *The Crimson Petal and the White.* Edinburgh: Cannongate, 2002, First British edition; fine in fine dust jacket, signed by author. Bella Luna Books May 29 2011 - t7193 2011 $110

Fabes, Gilbert H. *The Romance of Bookshop 1904-1929.* Foyles: privately Printed, 1929, Tall 8vo., original black buckram, gilt, few slight marks, pages 56, untrimmed, 10 plates of plates, signed by William and Gilbert Foyle. R. F. G. Hollett & Son Antiquarian Booksellers General Catalogue Summer 2010 - 600 2011 £65

Fabian Society *Fabian Tracts: Numbers 1-242.* 1884-1935, 128 tracts, 2 volumes, cloth, faded and dust marked, ex-library but very good. C. P. Hyland May 26 2011 - 258/209 2011 $580

Fable, Leonard *The Gingerbread Man.* London: George G. Harrap n.d., 1915, First English edition; large 8vo., original cloth backed boards, pictorial onlay, little worn, title in red and black with line drawing, 8 double page color plates, text on reverse, rather loose, scarce. R. F. G. Hollett & Son Antiquarian Booksellers General Catalogue Summer 2010 - 551 2011 £75

Fable, Lionel *The Children at the Pole.* London: George G. Harrap & Co. n.d. circa, 1914, First edition thus; square 12mo., original pictorial boards, little rubbed, corners rather worn and bumped, 14 page panorama, 16 color plates by Willy Pogany, opening accordion style, odd slight finger mark but generally nice, clean and sound copy, very scarce. R. F. G. Hollett & Sons Antiquarian Booksellers 170 - 539 2011 £180

Fabre, Pierre Jean *Sapientia Universalis Quatuor Libris Comprehensa. Videlicet 1. quad sit Sapientia... 2. De Cognitione Hominis. 3. De Medendis Morbis Hominum. 4. De Meliorandis Metallis.* Frankfurt: J. Beyer, 1656, 4to., (2), 418 (=400) , (8) pages, contemporary English calf, ms. index notes at end, slightly browned, hinges weak, from the library of the Earls of Macclesfield at Shirburn Castle. Maggs Bros. Ltd. 1440 - 86 2011 £850

Fabricius, M. Theodosius *Loci Communes D. Martin Lutheri Viri dei et Prophetae Germanici Exscriptis Ipsius Ltinis Forma Gnomolgica & Aphoristica...* Magdeburg: Typis Andreae Genae, impenis Ambosii Kirchneri, 1590, Small square 4to., recent old style blindstamped calf, gilt with raised bands and spine label, pages (xxii), 125, 153, (iv), 206, (iv), 88, (iii), 152, (lxxx), little staining, mostly light, in places, blindstamp to title, some marginal worming to few sections, otherwise very good. R. F. G. Hollett & Son Antiquarian Booksellers 175 - 429 2011 £450

The Facetious History of John Gilpin and the Retired Cat. Newburyport: W. & J. Gilman, 1823, 16mo., rose pink printed wrappers with elaborate border and woodcut on front cover, rear cover has ads and woodcut decorations, some light dusting and bit of wear to spine of rather clean copy, 24 numbered pages counting covers (both inside and out), 3 full page woodcuts and numerous other woodcuts throughout book. Jo Ann Reisler, Ltd. 86 - 80 2011 $300

Fahie, J. J. *Galileo: His Life and Work.* London: John Murray, 1903, 8vo., xvi, 451, ads, (4) pages, frontispiece, plates, figures, index, dark blue cloth, gilt stamped cover decoration and spine title, small tears to top spine end, very good, from the Bern Dibner reference library, with Burndy bookplate. Jeff Weber Rare Books 161 - 137 2011 $200

Fainlight, Ruth *Poems.* London: Rainbow Press, 1971, One of 300 numbered copies; signed by Fainlight, Ted Hughes and Alan Sillitoe, inscribed by Fainlight and Stillitoe as a birthday gift to a friend in 2000, leatherbound, fine in near fine dust jacket. Ken Lopez Bookseller 154 - 51 2011 $300

Fairbrother, Nan *New Lives, New Landscapes.* Architectural Press, 1970, Second impression; tall 8vo., original cloth, gilt, dust jacket, pages viii, 396, illustrations. R. F. G. Hollett & Son Antiquarian Booksellers 177 - 292 2011 £30

Fairclough, Henry Rushton *Some Aspects of Horace.* San Francisco: John Henry Nash, 1935, First edition, one of 262 copies, this copy out of series; original patterned boards, beige cloth spine, edges untrimmed, large decorative initials printed in red, very fine. Phillip J. Pirages 59 - 270 2011 $100

Fairfax-Blakeborough, J. *The Analysis of the Turf.* Philip Allan & Co., 1927, First edition; large tall 8vo., original green cloth gilt, pages xii, 322, with 12 plates, last two leaves rather carelessly opened. R. F. G. Hollett & Son Antiquarian Booksellers General Catalogue Summer 2010 - 1241 2011 £45

Fairfax, John *The Fairy Book.* London: Macmillan, 1913, First edition; large thick 4to., (379) pages, green cloth with extensive and beautiful gilt decoration on cover and spine, top edge gilt, tiny split at head of spine and few spots on title, else near fine, 32 beautiful color plates with lettered tissue guards, scarce in such clean, bright condition. Aleph-Bet Books, Inc. 95 - 257 2011 $975

Fairmont, Ethel *The Lovely Garden.* Chicago: Volland, 1919, First edition, No additional printings; 8vo., pictorial boards, fine in pictorial box, rare, illustrations by John Rae. Aleph-Bet Books, Inc. 95 - 577 2011 $350

Fairmont, Ethel *Rhymes for Kindly Children.* Chicago: Volland, 1916, Later edition; 8vo., pictorial boards, small spine mend, else fine in pictorial box, illustrations by Johnny Gruelle, very scarce, beautiful copy. Aleph-Bet Books, Inc. 95 - 273 2011 $500

Fairmont, Ethel *Rhymes for Kindly Children.* Joliet: P. F. Volland & Co., 1927, Seventeenth edition; 8vo., full color illustrated boards with wrap-around image that is charming, full color pictorial box with some minor cracks along sides of box and bit of dusting to box, almost every page has full color illustrations by Johnny Gruelle, illustrated endpapers. Jo Ann Reisler, Ltd. 86 - 117 2011 $350

Fairy-Land. N.P.: Nelson, n.d., owner dated, 1917, 4to., 32 pages, cloth backed pictorial boards, rear board with some soil and light edge rubbing, very good+, illustrations by Mabel Lucie Attwell, with 8 color plates and 19 charming pen and ink illustrations, scarce. Aleph-Bet Books, Inc. 95 - 55 2011 $650

A Fairy Night's Dream or the Horn of Oberon. Chicago: Laird & Lee, 1900, 4to., cloth backed pictorial boards, 95 pages, light cover rubbing, else very good+, illustrations by Gwynne Price with lovely color frontispiece and 10 nearly full page half tones plus chapter tailpieces. Aleph-Bet Books, Inc. 95 - 224 2011 $200

Fairy Poster Book. Racine: Whitman, 1929, Oblong 4to., stiff pictorial wrappers, some cover wear, else near fine, fine and unused, illustrations M. E. Stout who has inscribed the book. Aleph-Bet Books, Inc. 95 - 397 2011 $250

Fairy Tales. no publication information, circa, 1930, 4to., stiff pictorial wrappers, color plate on cover, minor shelf wear, near fine, 8 color pictorial hankies by Mabel Lucie Attwell, one for each fairy tale, rare. Aleph-Bet Books, Inc. 95 - 54 2011 $2000

Fairy Tales. Christmas Stocking Series. with The Night Before Christmas. Little Black Sambo. Story of Peter Rabbit. Fairy Tales from Grimm. Fairy Tales from Andersen. Cinderella & Sleeping Beauty. Chicago: Reilly & Britton, all dated, 1905, except Peter Rabbit 1911. First edition, 3rd printing of all titles, except Peter Rabbit which is a first printing; 6 volumes, 16mo., pictorial boards stamped in green, pictorial paste-on, spine ends worn on few volumes, overall clean, tight and very good+ in original Christmas Steamer trunk with lid (lid repaired), illustrations in color by John R. Neill and E. S. Hardy. Aleph-Bet Books, Inc. 95 - 114 2011 $3250

Fairy Tales of Other Lands. London: Harrap, 1931, First edition thus; original pictorial cloth, pages 256, with 14 color plates and numerous line illustrations and decorations, fore-edge little spotted, uncommon. R. F. G. Hollett & Sons Antiquarian Booksellers 170 - 536 2011 £85

Fairy Tales. Third Series. Chicago: N. K. Fairbank Co., Makers of Fairy Soap, 1903, 12mo., string bound pictorial wrappers, slightest bit of spine rubbing, else fine, illustrations by Fanny Cory with 10 full page and 1 double page color lithographs highlighted in gold and in 3 color on every page of text, drawings are delicate and absolutely lovely. Aleph-Bet Books, Inc. 95 - 225 2011 $250

Falassi, Alessandro *Folklore by the Fireside.* London: Scolar Press, 1980, First UK edition; original cloth, gilt, dust jacket, pages xix, 379, illustrations, few pencilled annotations. R. F. G. Hollett & Son Antiquarian Booksellers 175 - 430 2011 £30

Falconieri, Ottavio *Inscriptiones Athleticae Nuper Repertae Editae & Notis Illustratae...* Rome: Fabio de Falco, 1668, 4to., (12), 230 pages, engraved illustrations, contemporary vellum with spine gilt in compartments and lettering piece, 2 leaves detached, pages browning within two quires, from the collection of Nicolas Joseph Foucault with his bookplate, from the library of the Earls of Macclesfield at Shirburn Castle. Maggs Bros. Ltd. 1440 - 87 2011 £650

Falkus, Hugh *Salmon Fishing.* London: H. & G. Witherby, 1987, Large 8vo., original cloth, gilt, dust jacket, pages 448, with 9 color plates and numerous photos and diagrams. R. F. G. Hollett & Son Antiquarian Booksellers General Catalogue Summer 2010 - 1242 2011 £50

Falkus, Hugh *Sea Trout Fishing.* H. & G. Witherby, 1987, Large 8vo., original cloth, gilt, dust jacket, pages 448, 5 color plates, 168 photos and numerous diagrams. R. F. G. Hollett & Son Antiquarian Booksellers General Catalogue Summer 2010 - 1243 2011 £35

Family Circle and Parlor Annual. New York: James G. Reed, Sept. and Dec., 1852, First edition; Volume 14, No. 1 and Volume 14, No. 4, pages 38 + 117-148, 2 steel engraved plates and 2 hand colored steel engraved floral costume plates, handsome newer binding of three quarter light brown polished calf, red leather spine label, gilt, front cover with two red leather "shield" inlays, each with gilt pictorial devices, slight foxing to Sacramento image, very fine. Argonaut Book Shop   Recent Acquisitions Summer 2010 - 181 2011 $425

Farber, Paul Lawrence *Finding Order in Nature: the Naturalist Tradition from Linnaeus to E. O. Wilson.* Baltimore: and London: Johns Hopkins University Press, 2000, First edition; 8vo., x, 136 pages, photos and illustrations, green cloth, black stamped spine title, fine, scarce cloth issue, from the Bern Dibner reference library, with Burndy bookplate.   Jeff Weber Rare Books   161 - 138   2011 $60

Farina, Richard *Been Down so Long It Looks Like Up to Me.* New York: Viking, 1983, Reissue of author's first and only novel; issued simultaneously in paperback and hardcover, this is hardcover copy and has bookplate of Pynchon's editor, Ray Roberts, printed on cheap paper which is darkening with age, otherwise fine, near fine dust jacket with couple of small spots of rubbing and closed tear to rear flap fold.   Ken Lopez Bookseller   154 - 188   2011 $100

Farinato, Paolo *Diverses Figures a l'Eau Forte de Petits Amours Anges Vollants et Enfans Propre a Mettre sur Frontons Portes...* Paris: A. Bosse, 1644, Oblong 4to., 30 numbered engraved plates, early 18th century vellum backed boards, acquisition date on fly leaf Jan. 7 1727/8, from the library of the Earls of Macclesfield at Shirburn Castle.   Maggs Bros. Ltd.   1440 - 88   2011   £3500

Farington, Joseph 1747-1821 *The Farington Diary by Joseph Farington, R. A. July 13th 1793 to Dec. 30th 1821.* 1923-1928,   8 volumes, hinge cloth worn on volume I, dust jacket on volumes 2 5-8, very good.   C. P. Hyland   May 26 2011 - 256/227   2011 $333

Farington, Joseph 1747-1821 *Thirty-One Views in Derbyshire. Part VI of Britannia Depicta...* London: Cadell & Davies, 1818, First edition; oblong folio, modern half calf gilt with marbled boards by Period Binders of Bath, original elegant lettering piece relaed on upper band, complete with title, list of plates and 31 tissue guarded steel engraved plates with accompanying leaf of leaves of text, light spotting to few plate margins, but excellent copy, plates in strong impressions.   R. F. G. Hollett & Son Antiquarian Booksellers   General Catalogue Summer 2010 - 1391   2011   £1200

Farjeon, Eleanor *Nuts and May: A Medley for Children.* London: Collins, n.d. circa, 1929, Thick 4to., 264 pages, cloth, pictorial paste on, fine in slightly frayed dust jacket, illustrations by Rosalind Thornycroft, pictorial endpapers, many bold full color illustrations and a profusion of black and whites.   Aleph-Bet Books, Inc.   95 - 236   2011 $375

Farjeon, Eleanor *The Soul of Kol Nikon.* N.P.: (U.K.), n.p., n.d., 1914, First edition; 8vo., pages 107, original publisher's blue cloth lettered gilt on spine, signed presentation copy from author for Maitland Radford, some fading, front and rear covers dampstained, otherwise sound near very good, clean text.   Any Amount of Books   May 26 2011 - A62451   2011 $461

Farleigh, John *Graven Image.* London: Macmillan, 1940, First edition; original pictorial boards, 388 pages, well illustrated.   R. F. G. Hollett & Son Antiquarian Booksellers   General Catalogue Summer 2010 - 151   2011   £95

Farley, Harriet *The Lowell Offering.* Lowell: Misses Curtis & Farley, 1845, First edition; sewn, little foxed and soiled, very good, scarce.   Second Life Books Inc.   174 - 142   2011 $75

Farley, John *The Spontaneous Generation Controversy from Descartes to Oparin.* Baltimore and London: Johns Hopkins University Press, 1977, First edition; 8vo., x, 225 pages, illustrations, index, blue cloth, silver stamped spine title, dust jacket bit worn, very good, from the Bern Dibner reference library, with Burndy bookplate.   Jeff Weber Rare Books   161 - 139   2011 $65

Farley, Walter *The Black Stallion's Sulky Colt.* New York: Random House, 1954, First edition; 8vo., 248 pages, signed by author, scarce thus, illustrations by Harold Eldridge.   By the Book, L. C.   26 - 61   2011 $250

Farm Yard Story. Boston: L. Prang, 1865, 2 1/2 x 4 1/2 inches, pictorial wrappers, slight edge wear, printed on one side and folded accordion style, each of the 12 pages has charming chromolithograph with text below, very scarce. Aleph-Bet Books, Inc.   95 - 410   2011 $400

Farmer, Alec F. *Model Locomotive Boilermaking.* Solihull: privately published, 1996, original wrappers, pages 192, with 302 illustrations, scarce.   R. F. G. Hollett & Son Antiquarian Booksellers   General Catalogue Summer 2010 - 1109   2011   £45

Farmer, Cicely *Dragons & A Bell.* London: Faber, 1931, First edition; original cloth, gilt, dust jacket by Edward Bawden, pages 333, very scarce.   R. F. G. Hollett & Son Antiquarian Booksellers   General Catalogue Summer 2010 - 1638   2011   £120

Farmer, Henry George *Music Making in the Olden Days.* Peters-Henriches Edition, 1950, First edition; large 8vo., original cloth backed boards, gilt dust jacket little creased and torn, pages 122, with 6 plates, scarce. R. F. G. Hollett & Son Antiquarian Booksellers   175 - 433   2011   £65

Farmer, John *A Gazetteer of the State of New Hampshire.* Concord: Jacob B. Moore, 1823, First edition; 12mo., 276 pages, folding map, contemporary calf, sound, some wear and ends of spine, foxed.   M & S Rare Books, Inc.   90 - 280   2011 $200

Farmer, Philip Jose *To Your Scattered Bodies Go.* New York: G. P. Putnam's Sons, 1971, First edition; octavo, cloth.   L. W. Currey, Inc.   124 - 54   2011 $1500

Farmer, Philip Jose *To Your Scattered Bodies Go.* New York: G. P. Putnam's Sons, 1971, First edition; octavo cloth.   L. W. Currey, Inc.   124 - 70   2011 $1250

Farnall, Harry Burrard *The Address of Harry Burrard Farnall, Esq. Inspector of Poor Laws to the Guardians of the Skipton Union, at a Special Meeting Held at the Board Room on Saturday the 22d of November 1851.* Skipton: published by Order of the Guardians of the Union, printed by J. Tasker, bookseller, 1851, First and only edition, very rare; 8vo., 11, (1) pages, extending folding table, sewn as issued in original printed wrappers, very good, very rare. John Drury Rare Books   153 - 45   2011   £150

Farnham, Eliza W. *My Early Days.* New York: Thatcher & Hutchinson, 1859, Small octavo, xi, 13-425 (2 ads) pages, light foxing, original full brown embossed cloth, gilt spine title, almost no sign of wear, inscribed to Nancy Gore from Kate, Eagleswood, NJ 1859, very good plus.   Jeff Weber Rare Books   163 - 163   2011 $75

Farnsworth, Oliver *The Cincinnati Directory, Containing the Names, Profession and Occupation of the Inhabitants of the Town, Alphabetically Arranged with the Number of the Building.* Cincinnati: Published by Oliver Farnsworth Oct., 1819, First edition; 8vo., 185, (1) pages, large engraved folding map, (short tear at gutter), some wrinkling, original printed boards (ads on back), foxed, uncut, spine rubbed and lightly chipped, covers virtually unrubbed, lacks back endpaper, outer front hinge cracking, but sound.   M & S Rare Books, Inc.   90 - 301   2011 $2500

Farnsworth, R. W. C. *Southern California Paradise. (in the Suburbs of Los Angeles).* Pasadena: R. W. C. Farnsworth, 1883, First edition; thin quarto, (2, blank), (i)-vi, (7)-132, (2, blank) pages, numerous illustrations and map, publisher's full blue pebbled cloth, front board elaborately stamped in gilt, black board identically stamped in blind, floral endpapers, cloth slightly rubbed, gilt still very bright, previous owner's old ink inscription, very good, scarce.   Heritage Book Shop   Holiday 2010 - 39   2011 $1100

Farny, Henry F. *"The Lady and the Flea."A Tale of a Tale".* Honolulu: Pretoria and Hammerfest (Cincinnati): published by the Society for the Dissemination of Useless Knowledge and the League for the Propagation of the Castanea Vulgaris, 1897, Only edition; Gershon Legman's copy, 8vo., pages (32), 14 illustrations on tracing paper pasted in, uncut, light offsetting to some pages, centre spread brown at inner margin, pages unattached from boards and bound in single gathering, original brown/green cloth with git lettering to upper panel and gilt decoration to upper and lower panel, some light shelfwear and rubbing, bump to upper hinge.   Simon Finch Rare Books   Zero - 230   2011   £750

Farr & Max *Records of the Federal Convention of 1787.* New Haven: Yale, 1911, First edition, limited to 250 copies; 3 volumes, large thick quarto, quarter vellum & gray paper over boards, nearly 2000 pages.   Bookworm & Silverfish   669 - 13   2011 $1650

Farrar, John *Elements of Electricity, Magnetism & Electromagnetism.. Being the Second Part.* Cambridge: 1826, 395, (1) errata pages, 6 folding plates, poor copy, half paper (abused, title partly legible) and paper (damped) over twisted boards, edges untrimmed, first few leaves and edges of last few leaves damped.   Bookworm & Silverfish   676 - 72   2011 $150

Farrell, J. G. *The Hill Station an Unfinished Novel and an Indian Diary.* London: Weidenfeld and Nicolson, 1981, First edition; pages x, 230, crown 8vo., original biscuit yellow boards, backstrip gilt lettered, dust jacket, fine. Blackwell Rare Books   B166 - 143   2011   £35

Farrow, G. E. *The Missing Prince.* London: Hutchinson, 1896, First edition; original pictorial cloth gilt extra, pages xvi, 197, xi, all edges gilt, full page drawings by Harry Furniss, text vignettes, contemporary signature, otherwise very nice, bright and sound.   R. F. G. Hollett & Son Antiquarian Booksellers   General Catalogue Summer 2010 - 645   2011   £75

Farrow, G. E. *The Wallypug in London.* London: Hutchinson, 1898, First edition; pages xv, 75, 40, full page and text drawings, contemporary signature on half title, dated Xmas 1897, scarce.   R. F. G. Hollett & Son Antiquarian Booksellers   General Catalogue Summer 2010 - 683   2011   £120

Farrow, G. E. *The Wallypug of Why.* London: Hutchinson, n.d., 1895, First edition; contemporary signature on title dated Xmas 1895, otherwise very nice, bright and sound, original pictorial plum cloth gilt extra, spine trifle dulled, pages xii, 202, vi, all edges gilt, full page drawings by Harry Furniss and text vignettes by his daughter Dorothy,.   R. F. G. Hollett & Son Antiquarian Booksellers   General Catalogue Summer 2010 - 646   2011   £120

Farrow, G. E. *What Happened to Ten Little Jappy Chaps.* Chicago: Donohue, n.d. circa, 1908, 8vo., pictorial cloth, slight wear, near fine, 3 full page color illustrations, bright pictorial covers, quite scarce. Aleph-Bet Books, Inc. 95 - 308 2011 $350

Farson, Negley *Going Fishing.* Ashburton: Flyfisher's Classic Library, 1998, Second limited edition; no. 105 of 950 copies, full navy blue crocodile morocco gilt, slipcase, pages 156, top edges gilt, well illustrated, marbled endpapers, silk marker, fine,. R. F. G. Hollett & Son Antiquarian Booksellers General Catalogue Summer 2010 - 1302 2011 £45

Fatio, Louise *Doll for Marie.* New York: Whittlesey House, 1957, First edition; 4to., cloth, fine in slightly soiled dust jacket, wonderfully illustrated in color by Roger Duvoisin, inserted into a pocket in rear of book is smaller version of the book (4 x 5 1/2 inches). Aleph-Bet Books, Inc. 95 - 212 2011 $250

Faulkner, Charles J. *The Speech of Charles Jas. Faulkner (of Berkeley) in the House of Delegates of Virginia on the Policy of the State with Respect to her Slave Population Delivered Jan. 20 1832.* Richmond: Thomas W. White, printer, 1832, First edition; 8vo., 22 pages, removed, fore-edge uncut, foxed. M & S Rare Books, Inc. 90 - 131 2011 $1100

Faulkner, R. O. *The Ancient Eygptian Coffin Texts Volume III Spells 788-1185 & Index.* Warminster: Aris & Phillips, 1978, Large 8vo., original cloth, gilt, dust jacket, pages vii, 204. R. F. G. Hollett & Son Antiquarian Booksellers 177 - 294 2011 £60

Faulkner, William *The Music of Nature.* London: 1832, First edition; xii, 530 pages, illustrations, lacks color frontispiece, original polished cloth, with new backstrip and label. Bookworm & Silverfish 668 - 103 2011 $75

Faulkner, William Harrison 1897-1962 *Fable.* New York: Random House, 1954, First edition, one of 1000 numbered copies signed by author, this #853; octavo, (x), 437, (1, blank) pages, signed limitation leaf inserted at front, publisher's dark blue buckram over bevelled boards, blue and white cross motif on front cover, spine lettered in white and gilt, top edge blue, fore-edge uncut, blue endpapers, original publisher's slipcase with paper spine label, original glassine present at front and back cover, slipcase lightly sunned, book about fine. Heritage Book Shop Holiday 2010 - 40 2011 $1850

Faulkner, William Harrison 1897-1962 *A Fable.* New York: Random House, 1954, First edition; near fine, light scratch on front boards, small crease on front free endpapers, dust jacket near fine, several small rubbed spot, half penny size spot of sticker residue on front panel. Bella Luna Books May 26 2011 - t3790 2011 $550

Faulkner, William Harrison 1897-1962 *The Hamlet.* New York: Random House, 1940, First edition; (8), 421 pages, cloth near fine, spine lettering bit dull as always, in near fine and bright dust jacket with light wear only at corners, lovely copy. Joseph J. Felcone Inc. Fall Miscellany 2010 - 43 2011 $2800

Faulkner, William Harrison 1897-1962 *Intruder in the Dust.* New York: Random House, 1948, First edition; near fine in very good+ dust jacket (light shelfwear). Lupack Rare Books May 26 2011 - ABE4091171628 2011 $275

Faulkner, William Harrison 1897-1962 *Pylon.* New York: Harrison Smith and Robert Haas, 1935, First printing; 8vo., pages 315, blue cloth, stamped in black and gilt, Donor's presentation, cover faded and worn at corners, and ends of spine, else very good, tight copy. Second Life Books Inc. 174 - 143 2011 $75

Faulkner, William Harrison 1897-1962 *Salmagundi... and a Poem.* Milwaukee: The Casanova Press, 1932, First edition, limited to 525 copies; 8vo., original printed wrapper, uncut, tipped in frontispiece, fine in a rubbed publisher's box. Second Life Books Inc. 174 - 144 2011 $600

Faulkner, William Harrison 1897-1962 *Soldier's Pay.* London: Chatto & Windus, 1930, First English edition; 8vo., pages 326 + ad, green cloth stamped in gilt, fine. Second Life Books Inc. 174 - 145 2011 $675

Faulkner, William Harrison 1897-1962 *Speech of Acceptance Upon the Award of the Nobel Prize for Literature, Delivered in Stockholm 10th December 1950.* London: Chatto & Windus for Private Distribution, 1951, First English edition; pages (8) (including covers), crown 8vo., original printed sewn cream wrapper, faint band of dusting to tail of rear cover, very good. Blackwell Rare Books B166 - 144 2011 £60

Faulkner, William Harrison 1897-1962 *Spotted Horses.* Columbia: University of South Carolina, 1989, Limited deluxe edition of 600 copies, this no. 237; signed by Boyd Saunders on colophon page and with original signed color lithograph laid in, fine, quarter brown leather and Holliston sailcloth covered boards with embossed horse design front cover, printed on Mohawk's Artemus genuine felt paper of archival quality using Boyd Saunders' uniquely processed, hand drawn registered, lithographic plates, near fine, original clam shell slipcase with minimal soil, 13 x 71 inches. By the Book, L. C. 26 - 4 2011 $215

Faulkner, William Harrison 1897-1962 *The Town.* New York: Random House, 1957, First edition; fine, very good dust jacket with chipping and creasing to extremities, closed tear on rear fold. Bella Luna Books May 26 2011 - t7994C) 2011 $275

Faulks, Sebastian *Devil May Care.* London: Penguin, 2008, First edition, limited edition, 122 of only 500 copies; signed and numbered by Sebastian Faulks, velvet locking clamshell box with book sitting in black silk, unopened in publisher's original shrinkwrap, with certificate from the Ian Fleming estate, as new.   Any Amount of Books   May 29 2011 - A67618   2011 $340

Fawcett, Henry *Endowed Schools Act Amendment Bill. Speech Delivered in the House of Commons July 20 1874.* London: Unwin Brothers, 1874, First edition; 8vo. 22 pages, preserved in mdoern wrappers with printed title label on upper cover, very good.   John Drury Rare Books   154 - 48   2011   £50

Fay, Bernard *Notes on the American Press at the End of the Eighteenth Century.* New York: Grolier Club, 1927, Limited to 325 copies; tall 4to., (10), 29 pages, 25 folding double page facsimiles of early American newspapers, original blue cloth boards, printed paper cover and spine labels, second cover and spine labels pasted inside rear cover, housed in blue paper slipcase, extremities worn, small piece of box missing, with officer's commission certificate: USN Reserve commission for Stephen Mathew Schuster to the rank of Ensign, signed by secretary of Navy, Frank Knox 6 March 1944, fine.   Jeff Weber Rare Books   163 - 113   2011 $85

Fea, Allan *Rooms of Mystery and Romance.* London: Hutchinson, 1931, First edition; original blue cloth, spine little faded, pages 288, (xii), 33 illustrations, few small annotations.   R. F. G. Hollett & Son Antiquarian Booksellers   175 - 437   2011   £35

Fearn, John Russell *Creature from the Black Lagoon.* London: Dragon Publications Ltd. n.d., 1954, First edition; octavo, boards.   L. W. Currey, Inc.   124 - 24   2011 $2500

Fearnside, Henry Gray *Picturesque Beauties of the Rhine, Displayed in a Series of Eighty Splendid Views....* London: Black and Armstrong, 1860, First edition; 8vo., handsomely rebound in half brown leather, marbled boards, lettered gilt on spine with 5 raised bands at spine, all edges gilt, tissue guards to plates (no date) (186), 80 engravings by Fearnside, neat name on verso of frontispiece, slight foxing to plates almost all at edges of pages, very good.   Any Amount of Books   May 26 2011 - A72601   2011 $604

Featherstonhaugh, T. *Our Cumberland Village.* Carlisle: 1925, First edition; original green cloth, gilt, pages 181, (vi), with 9 illustrations.   R. F. G. Hollett & Son Antiquarian Booksellers   173 - 423   2011   £65

Feaver, William *Frank Auerbach.* New York: Rizzoli, First edition; 4to., pages 359, copiously illustrated in color and black and white, fine in fine illustrated hard slipcase, signed in black felt tip pen by Auerbach.   Any Amount of Books   May 29 2011 - A75491   2011 $374

Federico, P. J. *Descartes on Polyhedra: a Study of the De Solidorum Elementis.* New York: Springer Verlag, 1982, First printing; 8vo., (vii) 145 pages, 36 figures, yellow cloth, black stamped cover and spine titles, fine, from the Bern Dibner reference library, with Burndy bookplate and rubber stamp.   Jeff Weber Rare Books   161 - 141   2011 $70

Fell, Alfred *The Early Iron Industry of Furness and District; an Historical and Descriptive Account from the Earliest Times...* Ulverston: Hume Kitchin, 1908, Limited edition, no. 136 of 157 copies signed; thick large 8vo., modern full black levant morocco, gilt with gilt ruled boards, gilt bordered raised bands, pages xvii, (i), 464, uncut, 20 illustrations, collotypes, drawings, etc. and 2 maps, complete with errata slip, few spots, but excellent copy, exceptionally scarce.   R. F. G. Hollett & Son Antiquarian Booksellers   173 - 397   2011   £450

Fell, Alfred *The Early Iron Industry of Furness and District; an Historical and Descriptive Account from the Earliest Times...* Frank Cass, 1968, Facsimile edition; pages xvii, (i), 461, illustrations, 2 maps, original maroon cloth, gilt.   R. F. G. Hollett & Son Antiquarian Booksellers   173 - 398   2011   £85

Fell, John *Roman and Italic Letter Bequeathed to the University of Oxford (The Fell Types).* Oxford: Oxford University Press, 1950, Limited edition; good in good dust jacket, dust jacket soiled and edge worn, endpapers foxed, otherwise clean and tight, 41 pages, presentation card and menu for a dinner for Batey at the Grolier Club.   G. H. Mott Bookseller   May 26 2011 - 39720   2011 $200

Fell, Ralph *A Tour through the Batavian Republic During the Latter Part of the Year 1800.* R. Phillips, 1801, First edition; contemporary half brown calf, red morocco label, rubbed with loss to gilt on spine, Fasque booklabel, internally exceptional copy.   Jarndyce Antiquarian Booksellers   CXCI - 548   2011   £180

Fellig, Arthur *Naked City.* New York: Essential Books, 1945, First edition; 8vo., pages 3-246 (pagination begins on front free endpaper), 229 black and white photos printed in gravure, original photo illustrated front endpapers, rear endpapers blank, original beige cloth, spine and upper side lettered in blue, light rubbing to tips, page edges lightly toned, original photo illustrated dust jacket, printed in yellow, red and black, lightly edgeworn, chips to tips and foot of spine, thumbnail size piece missing from head of spine red lettering on spine lightly faded.   Simon Finch Rare Books   Zero - 552   2011   £2500

Fellowes, William Dorset *Melancholy Loss of the Lady Hobart Packet, William Dorset Fellows Esq. Which Struck on the Island of Ice in the Atlantic Ocan, June 28 1803 and the Providential Escape of the Crew in the Cutter and Jolly Boat...* London: printed for Thomas Tegg, 111 Cheapside, 1803, 12mo., large folding frontispiece, (3), 8-28 pages, disbound. Anthony W. Laywood May 26 2011 - 21450 2011 $134

Fellowes, William Dorset *A Visit to the Monastery of La Trappe in 1817...* London: Thomas M'Lean, 1820, Third edition; quarto, later green half morocco gilt and cloth, 188 pages, 15 plates, 12 of which are hand colored aquatints, very slight foxing, else fine, handsome copy. Between the Covers 169 - BTC342280 2011 $650

Feltham, Owen *Resolves. A Duple Century.* London: imprinted (by Felix Kyngston?) for Henry Seile and are to be should at the Tygers Head in St. Paules Church yard, 1628, Third edition; 8vo., (6), 448 pages, engraved titlepage, second titlepage, ms. index inside front cover, titlepage laid down on new sheet, leaf A3 remargined, lacks index, contemporary full vellum, rebacked, new front endleaf, very good. Jeff Weber Rare Books 163 - 10 2011 $500

The Female Rebels; Being Some Remarkable Incidents of the Lives, Characters and Families of the Titular Duke and Dutchess of Perth, Lord and Lady Ogilvie and of Miss Florence M'Donald. London: reprinted and sold by L. Gilliver, Mrs. Dodd and G. Woodfall, 1747, 8vo., (2) 5-36 + 33-62 pages, complete as published, recent marbled boards lettered on spine, very good. John Drury Rare Books 154 - 50 2011 £950

Fenelon, Francois Salignac De La Mothe, Abp. 1651-1715 *Les Avatures de Telemaque.* Amsterdam: Wetsteins, 1719, Thick 12mo., lix, 525 pages + 5 page Ode + 22 page table des matieres, contemporary full leather, full page copper engraved half title, one folding map, plus 11 copper engravings in text, all but one signed D. Coster and printed on one side of leaf only with caption beneath, titlepage printed in red and black ink, plus many printer's device engravings, elaborate gilded title and rosettes on five band spine, crack along spine and small tear at lower part, very good, very fine engravings. Hobbyhorse Books 56 - 71 2011 $250

Fenelon, Francois Salignac De La Mothe, Abp. 1651-1715 *Les Aventures de Telemaque.* Paris: Imprimerie de Monsieur (i.e. Pierre-Francois Didot), 1785, 338 x 251mm., 2 volumes, splendid contemporary (or slightly later scarlet straight grain morocco, sumptuously gilt, covers with broad ornate gilt border featuring palmettes, flat spines handsomely gilt in seven compartments (two with titling, two with elegant volutes and pointille decoration and three with large central lozenge enclosing an intricate fleuron), densely gilt turn-ins, azure watered silk endpapers, all edges gilt, engraved titlepage, 96 fine engraved plates, all with handsome frames wrapped in fruited foliage by Jean Baptiste Tilliard after Charles Monnet, 24 of the plates containing chapter summaries and 72 with scenes from the narrative, original tissue guards; bookplates of Rene Choppin and Florencio Gavito (20th century); faint, widely spaced flecks to front cover of second volume, spines ever so slightly sunned, small stain to one endpaper, one page with minor ink spots in bottom margin, two engraved divisional leaves with one other engraving with overall faint mottled foxing, hint of foxing or pale browning in isolated places elsewhere, other trivial imperfections, especially fine set in beautiful binding, leather bright and only insignificant wear, text and plates unusually fresh and bright. Phillip J. Pirages 59 - 47 2011 $11,000

Fenelon, Francois Salignac De La Mothe, Abp. 1651-1715 *Les Aventures de Telemaque.* Paris: Imprimerie de Monsieur (i.e. Pierre Francois Didot, 1785, 340 x 264mm., 4 p.l., 305, (1) pages; 2 p.l., 297, (3) pages, 2 volumes bound in 1; elegant red contemporary straight grain morocco by Staggemeier & Welcher, the covers with wide gilt border, composed of onlaid strips of blue goatskin onlay at corners tooled with a medallion, and with an inner frame composed of onlaid citron goatskin band and large, graceful gilt impressions of flowers, foliage, and ears of wheat; smooth spine divided into four unequal compartments by a strip of onlaid green goatskin tooled with gilt pentaglyph and metope roll, lettered in second compartment on green goatskin label and directly on spine at foot, the first compartment tooled with a face-in-the-sun, third (elongated) compartment featuring a strange figure with winged helmet holding festoons of flowers balancing on top of a flower issuing from a large neoclassical vase, vase in turn perched on a candelabrum, edges of boards and turn-ins tooled with gilt rolls, marbled endpapers, all edges gilt; with fore-edge painting, very probably contemporary, of two boats sailing on a lake with a stately home in background; engraved printer's device on titlepages and two frontispiece portraits of author engraved by Dequevauviller, one in early state before letters, and one printed on India paper and mounted; hint of wear to corners, spine little darkened, slight variation in color of leather covers, other minor defects, but extremely handsome binding entirely solid, nothing approaching a significant fault, covers especially lustrous with bright gilt, intermittent pale foxing in text (few gatherings with faint overall browning or more noticeably foxed), leaves remarkably fresh (they crackle as you turn them), very clean and printed within vast margins. Phillip J. Pirages 59 - 40 2011 $9500

Fenelon, Francois Salignac De La Mothe, Abp. 1651-1715 *Les Aventures De Telmaque.* Paris: De l'Imprimerie De Didot Jeune, 1790, 248 x 165mm., 2 volumes, lovely early 19th century dark blue straight grain morocco, handsomely decorated in blind and gilt by Thouvenin (signed at foot of spine of first volume), covers bordered with wide blind leaf roll framed by single gilt fillets and gilt by Thouvenin signed at foot of spine of first volume, covers bordered with wide blind leaf roll framed by single gilt fillets and with gilt roundel cornerpieces, raised bands, spines with multiple plain and decorative gilt rules at top and bottom and in compartments featuring decorative interlacing bands in blind and intricate gilt diamond centerpiece with fleuron corners, marbled endpapers, turn-ins and all edges gilt, engraved portrait tondo on titlepages and 25 fine engraved plates (with tissue guards), including frontispiece; isolated trivial defects (one gathering with overall faint browning, another lightly foxed), exceptionally fine copy of a beautiful set, elegant bindings unusually bright and virtually without wear, margins ample, plates and text especially fresh, bright and clean and with rich impressions of the plates before letters. Phillip J. Pirages 59 - 45 2011 $3900

Fenelon, Francois Salignac De La Mothe, Abp. 1651-1715 *Fables de Fenelon.* Paris: Ledentu, 1825, 12mo., 196 pages, full brown leather on boards, elaborate gilt decoration and title on spine, gilt dentelles at covers and inside edges of covers, gilt edges, marbled endpapers, half title, titlepage with small decorative vignette, full page copper engravings, restoration along fore edge of page 185, fine. Hobbyhorse Books 56 - 55 2011 $150

Fenelon, Francois Salignac De La Mothe, Abp. 1651-1715 *Instructions for the Education of a Daughter.* London: Jonathan Bowyer, 1721, Fourth edition; pages (x, dedication), v, (iii), 302, typographical decorations, tailpieces and initials, few leaves slightly browned. R. F. G. Hollett & Son Antiquarian Booksellers 175 - 440 2011 £180

Fenelon, Francois Salignac De La Mothe, Abp. 1651-1715 *On the Education of Daughters.* London: W. Darton, Jun., 1812, First edition of this translation signed A. L. L.,; viii, 111 pages, original three quarter maroon roan spine, marbled paper on boards, gilt title along spine, fine large engraved frontispiece folded in three, edges and cover lightly rubbed, minor spotting throughout, damp spots at edges of frontispiece plate, top part of front endpaper repaired, worm damage at inner folding along bottom part of spine, not interfering with text, trace of pencil signatures on endpapers. Hobbyhorse Books 56 - 72 2011 $250

Fenelon, Francois Salignac De La Mothe, Abp. 1651-1715 *Refutation des Erreurs de Benoit de Spinosa.* Brussels (but Amsterdam): chez Francois Foppens, 1731, Half title, blind library stamp to title, cancelled on verso, ink library numeral at head of ad leaf, pages (x), 158, 483, (2), 8vo., modern quarter calf, backstrip ruled in black and gilt with gilt lettering on second compartment, marbled boards, good. Blackwell Rare Books B166 - 38 2011 £600

Fenn, Forrest *The Beat of the Drum and the Whoop of the Dance.* Santa Fe: Fenn, 1983, First edition; 4to., 359 pages, fine in near fine dust jacket with minimal sun covers. By the Book, L. C. 26 - 35 2011 $340

Fenn, William Wilthew *Half Hours of Blind Man's Holiday; or Summer and Winter Sketches in Black and White.* London: Sampson Low, 1878, First edition; 2 volumes, half titles, largely unopened in original dark olive green cloth, armorial bookplate of novelist Edmund Yates, very good. Jarndyce Antiquarian Booksellers CXCI - 174 2011 £180

Fenning, Daniel *The British Youth's Instructor; or New and Easy Guide to Practical Arithmetic.* London: printed for S. Crowder, 1762, Fourth edition; old speckled calf, little scraped, apages xii, 338, (ii), front flyleaf removed. R. F. G. Hollett & Sons Antiquarian Booksellers 170 - 230 2011 £85

Ferber, Edna *Cimarron.* Garden City: Doubleday, Doran and Co., 1930, First edition; small stain on spine, else near fine in modestly age toned, very good or better dust jacket with small chip on rear panel, nice. Between the Covers 169 - BTC347472 2011 $400

Ferchi, Fritz *A Pictorial History of Chemistry.* London: William Heinemann, 1939, First edition in English; 8vo., viii, 214 pages, illustrations, navy cloth, gilt stamped spine title, near fine, from the Bern Dibner reference library, with Burndy bookplate. Jeff Weber Rare Books 161 - 142 2011 $95

Ferguson, Malcom *Fishing Incidents and Adventures with a Descriptive Sketch...* Dundee: & Edinburgh, 1893, First edition; original red cloth, gilt over bevelled boards, panelled in gilt and blind, one corner little bumped, spine little faded, pages 291, with 5 plates, scarce. R. F. G. Hollett & Son Antiquarian Booksellers General Catalogue Summer 2010 - 1245 2011 £140

Ferguson, R. S. *An Accompt of the Most Considerable Estates and Families in the County of Cumberland from the Conquest unto the Beginning of the Reign of K. James (the first) by John Denton of Cardew.* Kendal: T. Wilson, 1887, Original printed wrappers, rather soiled and heavily chipped, edges defective, rebacked in cloth, pages vii, 214, little loose, scarce. R. F. G. Hollett & Son Antiquarian Booksellers 173 - 412 2011 £95

Ferguson, R. S. *The Boke off Recorde or register (of Kirkbie Kendall).* Kendal: T. Wilson, 1892, First edition; original brown cloth, gilt, pages xiv, 437, front joint cracked. R. F. G. Hollett & Son Antiquarian Booksellers 173 - 413 2011 £150

Ferguson, R. S. *Cumberland and Westmorland M.P.s (sic) from the Restoration to the Reform Bill of 1867.* London: Bell and Daldy and Carlisle: C. Thurnam, 1871, First edition; original cloth gilt over bevelled boards, little faded, handsomely rebacked in matching levant morocco with raised bands and contrasting double spine labels, pages xix, 478, frontispiece, very good, scarce.   R. F. G. Hollett & Son Antiquarian Booksellers   173 - 403   2011   £175

Ferguson, R. S. *Cumberland and Westmorland M.P.'s (sic).* London: Bell and Daldy and Carlisle: C. Thurnam, 1871, First edition; original cloth, gilt over bevelled boards, spine little faded, neatly recased, pages xix, 478, frontispiece, very good, scarce.   R. F. G. Hollett & Son Antiquarian Booksellers   General Catalogue Summer 2010 - 409   2011   £150

Ferguson, R. S. *A Cursory Relation of all the Antiquities & Familyes in Cumberland.* Kendal: T. Wilson, 1890, Later plain wrappers, pages (vi), 54, edges marbled, scarce.   R. F. G. Hollett & Son Antiquarian Booksellers   173 - 418   2011   £40

Ferguson, R. S. *Early Cumberland and Westmorland Friends.* F. Bowyer Kitto, 1871, First edition; original brown cloth, gilt, pages 208, front flyleaf removed, scattered spotting or browning, little shaken, scarce.   R. F. G. Hollett & Son Antiquarian Booksellers   173 - 404   2011   £85

Ferguson, R. S. *A History of Cumberland.* London: Elliot Stock, 1890, First edition; pages 312, originalt wo-tone cloth, gilt.   R. F. G. Hollett & Son Antiquarian Booksellers   173 - 405   2011   £65

Ferguson, R. S. *A History of Westmorland.* London: Elliot Stock, 1894, First edition, proof copy; original stiff glazed wrappers, side sewn, pages 312, scattered spotting, author's own proof with his armorial bookplate and neat corrections to text throughout in his hand, annotated "revise 7.5.94".   R. F. G. Hollett & Son Antiquarian Booksellers   173 - 407   2011   £95

Ferguson, R. S. *A History of Westmorland.* London: Elliot Stock, 1894, First edition; original two tone cloth, gilt, rather marked and extremities little worn, pages 312, uncut, endpapers spotted.   R. F. G. Hollett & Son Antiquarian Booksellers   173 - 406   5   £45

Ferguson, R. S. *Miscellany Accounts of the Diocese of Carlisle with the Terriers Delivered in to Me at My Primary Visitation by William Nicolson late Bishop of Carlisle.* London: George Bell and Carlisle: C. Thurnam & Sons, 1877, Original brown cloth gilt, lower board rather marked, pages (iv), 274, very scarce.   R. F. G. Hollett & Son Antiquarian Booksellers   173 - 415   2011   £120

Ferguson, R. S. *Old Church Plate in the Diocese of Carlisle with the Makers and their Marks.* Carlisle: C. Thurnam, 1882, First edition; original brown cloth gilt, neatly recased, pages viii, 327, with 29 lithographed plates and 7 text woodcuts.   R. F. G. Hollett & Son Antiquarian Booksellers   173 - 416   2011   £150

Ferguson, R. S. *The Royal Chapters of the City of Carlise, Printed at the Expense of the Mayor and Corporation.* London: Elliot Stock: Carlisle: C. Turnam; Kendal: T. Wilson, 1894, Original brown cloth gilt, pages xxxi, 348 (iii, subscribers), 5 folding maps, small library stamps on title and backs of plates, very scarce.   R. F. G. Hollett & Son Antiquarian Booksellers   173 - 417   2011   £180

Ferguson, Robert *No Protestant Plot or the Present Pretended Conspiracy of Protestants Against the King and Government Discovered to be a Conspiracy...* London: printed for R. Lett, 1681, First edition; 4to., disbound, 38 pages, title little dusty, some edges dampstained.   R. F. G. Hollett & Son Antiquarian Booksellers   175 - 441   2011   £75

Ferguson, Robert *The Northmen in Cumberland and Westmorland.* London: Longman & Co. and Carlisle: R. & J. Steel, 1856, First edition; original blindstamped brown cloth, gilt, pages (iv), 228, front joint cracking, scarce.   R. F. G. Hollett & Son Antiquarian Booksellers   173 - 422   2011   £85

Fergusson, Bernard *Eton Portrait.* John Miles, 1938, Small 4to., original cloth, gilt, spine and edges little faded, pages xiv, 187, with 58 fine photos.   R. F. G. Hollett & Son Antiquarian Booksellers   175 - 442   2011   £65

Fermi, Enrico *The Decay of Negative Mesotrons in Matter.* N.P.: Physical Review, 1947, Offprint in original green printed wrappers with prior owner's initials on cover.   By the Book, L. C.   26 - 98   2011 $600

Fermor, Patrick Leigh *Roumeli.* London: John Murray, 1966, First edition; original cloth, gilt, dust jacket by John Craxton (two very small spots to lower panel), pages viii, 248, 20 plates and sketch map, near fine.   R. F. G. Hollett & Son Antiquarian Booksellers   General Catalogue Summer 2010 - 1640   2011   £120

Fermor, Patrick Leigh *Mani. Travels in the Southern Peloponnese.* London: John Murray, 1958, First edition; original cloth, gilt, dust jacket, edges trifle rubbed in places, pages xiii, 320, frontispiece, 26 plates and sketch map, near fine.   R. F. G. Hollett & Son Antiquarian Booksellers   General Catalogue Summer 2010 - 1639   2011   £180

Fermor, William *Reflections on the Cow-Pox.* Oxford: printed by Dawson and Co. and sold by Cooke, Hanwell and Parker..., 1800, First edition; slight foxing on title, upper margin of B4 repaired with loss of the page numerals and 5 letters of the text but not the sense, 47, (1) pages, modern printed boards.   Anthony W. Laywood   May 26 2011 - 19808 2011 $587

Fernow, Berthold *The Ohio Valley In Colonial Days.* Albany: 1890, First edition; 299 pages, paper over boards, fore and bottom edges untrimmed, new backstrip. Bookworm & Silverfish   678 - 39 2011 $65

Fertel, Martin Dominique *La Scencie Pratique de l'Imprimerie.* St. Omer: M.D. Fertel, 1723, 4to., (2), 230, (2), 231-292, (10) pages, 5 engraved plates, 2 folding letterpress tables, woodcut diagrams etc., contemporary speckled calf, spine gilt in compartments, slight dampstaining in outer margins and on covers, spine chipped and little rubbed, from the library of the Earls of Macclesfield at Shirburn Castle. Maggs Bros. Ltd.   1440 - 89 2011   £750

Fessenden, Helen May *Fessenden: Builder of Tomorrows.* New York: Coward McCann, 1940, 8vo., vi, 362 pages, frontispiece, 2 color title, printed in blue and black, beige cloth, blue stamped cover and spine titles, dust jacket, jacket worn, else fine, from the Bern Dibner reference library, with Burndy bookplate.   Jeff Weber Rare Books   161 - 143 2011 $110

Fessier, Michael *Fully Dressed and in his Right Mind: a Novel.* New York: Alfred A. Knopf, 1935, First edition; octavo, pages (1-6) (1-2) 3-215 (216-217) (218 colophon), original black cloth, front and some panels stamped in white, top edge stained black.   L. W. Currey, Inc. 124 - 130 2011 $500

Fetters, Thomas T. *The Lustron Home: the History of a Postwar Prefabricated Housing Experiment.* Jefferson: McFarland, 2002, 8vo., xiii, 186 pages, illustrations, printed boards, fine, from the Bern Dibner reference library, with Burndy bookplate.   Jeff Weber Rare Books   161 - 144 2011 $90

Ffinch, Michael *Portrait of the Howgills and the Upper Eden Valley.* London: Robert Hale, 1982, First edition; original cloth, gilt, dust jacket, pages 220 with 35 illustrations and map, fine, scarce.   R. F. G. Hollett & Son Antiquarian Booksellers   General Catalogue Summer 2010 - 1392 2011   £35

Fforde, Jasper *The Eyre Affair.* London: Hodder & Stoughton, 2001, Advance review copy of the first British edition, labeled "Uncorrected Bound Proof"; pictorial wrappers, soft cover, fine, scarce format inscribed by author. Bella Luna Books   May 26 2011 - t5399 2011 $330

Fforde, Jasper *The Eyre Affair.* London: Hodder & Stoughton, 2001, First British edition; fine in near fine dust jacket, very slight wear to top edges.   Bella Luna Books   May 26 2011 - t4657 2011 $275

Fforde, Jasper *The Eyre Affair.* London: Hodder & Stoughton, 2001, First British edition, true first; fine, in like dust jacket, signed by author.   Bella Luna Books   May 26 2011 - t5879 2011 $357

Fforde, Jasper *Lost in a Good Book.* London: Hodder & Stoughton, 2002, First British edition; fine, in like dust jacket.   Bella Luna Books   May 29 2011 - t3955 2011 $104

Fforde, Jasper *Shades of Grey.* London: Hodder & Stoughton, 2010, First UK edition; fine in like dust jacket, signed and limited to 1000 copies.   Bella Luna Books   May 29 2011 - t9431 2011 $137

Ffoulkes, Charles *Armour & Weapons.* Oxford: Clarendon Press, 1909, First edition; 8vo., 112 pages, frontispiece, plates, illustrations, paper boards, black stamped cover title and illustration, very good, signed by former owner, Cyril Stanley Smith, from the Bern Dibner reference library, with Burndy bookplate.   Jeff Weber Rare Books   161 - 145 2011 $60

Ffoulkes, Charles *The Gun-Founders of England.* Cambridge: Cambridge University Press, 1937, First edition; 4to., xvi, 133, (134) pages, 15 plates, 38 text illustrations, red cloth, gilt stamped spine title, dust jacket worn and chipped, corners bumped, very good, from the Bern Dibner reference library, with Burndy bookplate.   Jeff Weber Rare Books   161 - 147 2011 $60

Field, E. M., Mrs. *The Child and His Book.* London: Wells, Gardner, Darton & Co. n.d., 1891, First edition; original green pictorial cloth, gilt, pages vii, 356, frontispiece, front joint trifle tender, otherwise excellent copy.   R. F. G. Hollett & Sons Antiquarian Booksellers   170 - 231 2011   £65

Field, Eugene *Poems of Childhood.* New York: 1904, 199 pages, 4to., applique color cover by Maxfield Parrish, illustrated titlepage and 8 color plates and illustrated endpapers all by Parrish, backstrip gilt bright, few leaves opened carelessly and rough margins have been shaved, 2 leaves have each a tear, mended with what looks like magic mending tape, few scratches on cover.   Bookworm & Silverfish   667 - 128 2011 $165

Field, F. J. *An Armorial for Cumberland.* Kendal: Titus Wilson, 1937, First edition; original brown cloth, gilt, pages xvi 343, with 18 illustrations, fine.   R. F. G. Hollett & Son Antiquarian Booksellers   173 - 428 2011   £175

Field, George *Field's Chromatography. A Treatise on Colours and Pigments for the Use of Artists.* Winsor and Newton, 1885, Fourth edition; 8vo., viii, 207 (i) (4) pages ads, 4 chromolithograph plates, very good, bright original decorative cloth, 19th century embossed 'reward' stamp at head of titlepage. Ken Spelman Rare Books 68 - 84 2011 £75

Field, Horace *English Domestic Architecture of the XVII and XVIIII Centuries.* London: George Bell and Sons, 1905, First edition; large 4to., original two tone cloth gilt, little marked, corners slightly worn, pages xiv, 75 with 71 figures plus 117 pages of plates. R. F. G. Hollett & Son Antiquarian Booksellers 177 - 298 2011 £150

Field, Michael, Pseud. *Stephania: a Trialogue.* London: Elkin Mathews & John Lane, 1892, One of 250 copies; 200 x 150mm., 6 p.l., 1, 100 pages, 4 leaves (colophon and ads), exceptionally attractive modelled goatskin by Mrs. Annie MacDonald of the Guild of Women Binders, front cover with large lobed frame, its upper corner enclosing the binder's initial and the date (1897), lower corners with daffodil blooms, large central panel showing an elaborately detailed scene featuring a woman with long, flowing hair entreating the god Mercury in his signature winged hat and sandals, the two figures, surmounted by an imperial crown through which twines a sprig of mistletoe (a design that appears in the woodcut frame on titlepage), lower cover showing the woman kneeling by a man reclining on a couch, this scene enclosed in an oval beaded frame, flat spine with modelled title flanked by pine cone device at head an tail, green watered silk pastedowns framed in unusual turn-ins, decorated with gilt vines and calf circles painted green and blue, leather hinges, top edge gilt, other edges untrimmed, titlepage with full woodcut border filled with intertwined pine branches and mistletoe, colophon with pine cone device, verso of front flyleaf with engraved bookplate of Charles Williston McAlpin, extra paper title labels tipped onto rear blank; two tiny red (ink?) marks to upper cover, inevitable offsetting from turn-ins to endpapers, one detached front flyleaf tipped onto front free endpaper, other trivial defects, still very attractive copy, binding lustrous and scarcely worn, leaves fresh and clean. Phillip J. Pirages 59 - 107 2011 $4500

Field, Michael, Pseud. *The Tragic Mary.* London: George Bell and Sons, 1890, First edition; 8vo., pages ix, 261, original publisher's light brown boards illustrated with thistles, crowns and carnations by Selwyn Image, slight soiling, slight rubbing at spine ends, little chipped with loss of the O in the 1890 at bottom, otherwise sound, near very good. Any Amount of Books May 29 2011 - A69894 2011 $255

Field, Rachel *Hitty her First Hundred Years.* New York: Macmillan Co., 1929, First edition; 4to., decorated cloth, paste label, some shelfwear at ends of spine, color decorated dust jacket with paste label, some chipping along edges and fading to spine, numerous black and white color illustrations by Dorothy Lathrop. Jo Ann Reisler, Ltd. 86 - 98 2011 $400

Fielder, John *California Images of the Landscape.* Englewood: Westcliffe Publishers, 1985, Folio, green cloth, very good, signed by author and inscribed 11/85, 170 full color photos, dust jacket. Barnaby Rudge Booksellers Travel and Exploration - 016992 2011 $65

Fieldhouse, R. *A History of Richmond and Swaledale.* London: Phillimore, 1978, first edition; original cloth, gilt, dust jacket spine little faded, pages xiv, 520, with 18 plates, 6 maps, 12 figures and 23 tables, scarce. R. F. G. Hollett & Son Antiquarian Booksellers General Catalogue Summer 2010 - 1393 2011 £65

Fielding, Henry 1707-1754 *Amelia.* London: The Navarre Society Ltd. circa, 1900, One of 2000 copies; 180 x 113mm., 3 volumes, very fine burgundy morocco, handsomely gilt and onlaid by the Harcourt Bindery of Boston (stamp signed on front flyleaf), boards with triple fillet border, each cover with elaborate heraldic frame of gilt and onlaid green morocco around an empty oval raised bands, very pretty gilt spine compartments featuring looping tendril frame enclosing a charming flower centerpiece, densely gilt turn-ins, marbled endpapers, top edge gilt, 3 frontispieces by George Cruikshank, showing scenes from the book very fine, bindings especially bright and text with virtually no signs of use. Phillip J. Pirages 59 - 192 2011 $575

Fielding, Henry 1707-1754 *An Apology for the Life of Mrs. Shamela Andrews.* Waltham St. Lawrence: Golden Cockerel Press, 1926, 102/450 copies; printed on Batchelor handmade paper, foolscap 8vo., pages (xi), 80, (1), original quarter white cloth, backstrip gilt lettered, brown boards, untrimmed, fine, bookticket of B. Fairfax Hall. Blackwell Rare Books B166 - 258 2011 £35

Fielding, Henry 1707-1754 *The Journal of a Voyage to Lisbon.* London: Millar, 1755, First published edition, first issue; 12mo., pages (iv), iv, (xviii), (19)-240, 193-228, leather backed contemporary marbled boards, fine, contemporary bookplate of Montague Shearman, bound with half title,. Second Life Books Inc. 174 - 146 2011 $1125

Fielding, Henry 1707-1754 *The Works of Henry Field.* New York: Jenson Society, 1905, Limited edition one of 1000 sets; 12 volumes, complete set, light green cloth with paper spine labels to each volume (fading/soiling to paper spine labels, slight wear/fraying to upper or lower edges of spines), clean text and tight bindings, except for some fading and toning to paper labels, near fine set, tight and clean. Lupack Rare Books May 26 2011 - ABE2942402605 2011 $150

Fielding, T. H. *The Art of Engraving.* Ackermann and Co., 1841, 8vo., vii, (i), 109 + (3) ads, 10 engraved plates, 8 text illustrations, very good in original dark green gilt lettered cloth, some slight toning to paper. Ken Spelman Rare Books 68 - 37 2011 £250

Fields, W. C. *W. C. Fields by Himself.* Englewood Cliffs: Prentice Hall, 1973, Original cloth backed pictorial boards, dust jacket, pages xiv, 510, numerous illustrations and color frontispiece.   R. F. G. Hollett & Son Antiquarian Booksellers   175 - 445   2011   £35

Filhol, Antoine Michel *Galerie Du Musee de France.* Paris: Chez Filhol, 1814-1815, First edition in book form; (with Poussin's "Paysage" in volume VIII misidentified in the contents as plate 557, rather than 577), 305 x 229mm., with half titles, 10 volumes, marvelous contemporary dark green morocco sumptuously gilt in romantic style, covers with complex scrolling and undulant cornerpieces connected by triple gilt rules, raised bands, spine compartments densely and very handsomely gilt with massed scrolling and foliate stamps, very wide turn-ins gilt with thick and thin rules framing a border composed of the same kind of decoration as on spine, all edges gilt, 718 very pleasing engraved plates of famous works of art (numbered 1-720 but with plates #552 and 553 omitted as always), original tissue guards, 4 plates supplied from another copy; large paper copy, more area occupied by margins than by either text or plates; some boards with slightest variation in color, few trivial marks to covers, lovely bindings beautifully preserved, with rich coloring, leather and gilt extraordinarily lustrous, tissue guards and versos of plates normally foxed, variable foxing to plates with only marginal or light foxing, perhaps 30 plates with more noticeable foxing, about as many entirely clean, rest moderately foxed, otherwise in fine condition internally, few signs of use and with fine impressions of engravings.   Phillip J. Pirages   59 - 71   2011 $4800

Fincham, J. R. S. *Genetic Complementation.* New York: Benjamin, 1966, First edition; 8vo., xii, 143 pages, near fine with foxing edges in very good dust jacket (sun spine, mild edgewear, foxing to rear), from the library of Francis Crick.   By the Book, L. C.   26 - 88   2011 $600

Finck, Kaspar *Poetica Latina Nova Methodo Perspicua Tradita Commentariis Luculentis Declarata Exemplis tum Veterum Tum Recentiorum Poetarum Illustrata...* Giessen: N. Hampel, 1607, 8vo., (8), 393, (7) pages, 18th century sprinkled calf, spine gilt, from the library of the Earls of Macclesfield at Shirburn Castle.   Maggs Bros. Ltd.   1440 - 233   2011   £550

Finlay, Michael *English Decorated Bronze Mortars and their Makers.* Carlisle: Plains Books`, 2010, First signed limited edition (600 copies only); 4to., original cloth, gilt, dust jacket, pages 256, with 29 color plates, 330 black and white plates and 280 illustrations.   R. F. G. Hollett & Son Antiquarian Booksellers   General Catalogue Summer 2010 - 153   2011   £50

Finlay, Michael *The Mining and Related Tokens of West Cumberland.* Wetheral: privately published by Palins Books, 2006, Limited signed edition; number 1875 of 500 copies, pages vii, 196, with 275 illustrations, tall 4to., original cloth, gilt, dust jacket.   R. F. G. Hollett & Son Antiquarian Booksellers   173 - 429   2011   £50

Finlinson, J. *Specimens of Penmanship.* Edinburgh: 1834, Engraved title and 12 calligraphic plates engraved by Menzies, oblong folio, original roan backed blue glazed card covers, backstrip worn and some browning and light foxing scarce.   Ken Spelman Rare Books   68 - 28   2011   £220

Finney, Charles G. *The Circus of Dr. Lao.* Grey Walls Press, 1948, First edition; original pictorial yellow cloth, gilt, dust jacket extremities trifle frayed, smaller repairs to reverse, price clipped, pages 151, full page tinted and line 'grotesque' illustrations by Gordon Noel Fish.   R. F. G. Hollett & Son Antiquarian Booksellers   General Catalogue Summer 2010 - 775   2011   £95

Finney, Charles G. *The Circus of Dr. Lao.* Janus Press, 1984, First edition, limited to 150 numbered copies Printed in letterpress on handmade Barcham Green paper and signed by author and artist; large thick 4to., relief etchings and pochoir prints by Claire Van Vliet, vellum backed decorated cloth, folding cloth box, sumptuous work of art.   James S. Jaffe Rare Books   May 26 2011 - 16629   2011 $5000

Finocchiaro, Maurice A. *The Galileo Affair: a Documentary History.* Berkeley: Los Angeles: London: University of California, 1989, First printing; 8vo., xvi 382 pages, beige cloth, silver stamped spine title, dust jacket, fine, rare, from the Bern Dibner reference library, with Burndy bookplate.   Jeff Weber Rare Books   161 - 148   2011 $80

Firbank, Ronald   1886-1926 *Caprice.* 1917, Bookplate and blindstamp on front endpaper, covers very slightly mottled, otherwise very good, frontispiece by Augustus John.   I. D. Edrich   May 26 2011 - 64345   2011 $595

Firbank, Ronald   1886-1926 *Works.* London: Duckworth, 1929, first edition, no. 49 from a total edition of 235; 5 volumes, 8vo., pages (ii), ix, (i) blank, 234; (viii), 248; (viii), 212; (viii), 168; (viii), 152, plus frontispiece in each, top edge tinted blue, others uncut, original yellow buckram, fine, bright set, superb condition.   Simon Finch Rare Books   Zero - 231   2011   £450

The Firelight Book of Nursery Stories. Blackie & Son, n.d., 1924, Small 4to., original cloth backed pictorial boards, edges little rubbed, pages (80), 7 full page color plates, numerous drawings by John Hassall, nice, clean and sound copy.   R. F. G. Hollett & Sons Antiquarian Booksellers   170 - 310   2011   £45

First Lessons in Astronomy. London: Thomas Ward & Co., 1838, Original dust jackets, paper label, printed in black, spine slightly chipped at head and tail, nice, engraved titlepage, 3 pages ads, ownership inscription of Miss Chichester Aug. 1841.   Jarndyce Antiquarian Booksellers   CXCI - 357   2011   £65

First Poems of Childhood. New York: Platt & Munk Publishers, 1967, First edition; 8vo., dark grey cloth spine with grey cloth, gold vignette on front cover and gold lettering on spine, full color pictorial dust jacket with some surface rubbing to rear cover of wrapper, signed in full by Tasha Tudor on titlepage, 46 numbered pages with every page illustrated to enhance verses, illustrations both in black and white in full color for an overall pictorial presentation. Jo Ann Reisler, Ltd. 86 - 254 2011 $275

Fischer, Henry W. *Private Lives of Kaiser William II and His Consort.* New York: J. R. Smith and Co., 1909, Edition deluxe, one of 500 copies, this #7; apparently the first American and first unexpurgated edition, 3 volumes, 228 x 152mm., very pleasing contemporary crimson crushed morocco, covers with gilt French fillet border and central imperial seal in gilt, raised bands, spines gilt in compartments with imperial crown centerpiece, densely gilt turn-ins, marbled endpapers, top edge gilt, other edges rough trimmed, facsimile signatures of Kaiser and Kaiserin on palace note paper and 19 photogravure plates, all with original tissue guards, just hint of shelfwear, minor erosion of some of the gilt, otherwise very fine, bindings lustrous, leaves fresh and bright, set generally showing few signs of use. Phillip J. Pirages 59 - 348 2011 $450

Fish Physiology and Biochemistry. Amsterdam: Dordrecht: Kugler Publications/Kluwer Academic Publishers, 1986-, 2001; volumes 1-25 in 104 issues, issue no. 1 from volume 22 missing, near fine, numerous text figures, 4to., paperbound, occasional minor fading or rubbing to covers. Raymond M. Sutton, Jr. May 26 2011 - 47088 2011 $1125

Fisher, Aileen *We Went Looking.* New York: Thomas Crowell, 1968, (1-10 code), First edition, first printing; oblong 4to., cloth, fine in slightly worn dust jacket, color illustrations by Marie Angel. Aleph-Bet Books, Inc. 95 - 50 2011 $85

Fisher, Anne *The Pleasing Instructor; or Entertaining Novelist.* Newcastle upon Tyne: printed for Thomas Slack, 1756, Second edition; contemporary full calf, rather rubbed, head of spine chipped, pages x, 330, (iv), title printed in red and black, front flyleaf removed. R. F. G. Hollett & Sons Antiquarian Booksellers 170 - 232 2011 £275

Fisher, D. Havelock *Boarding House Reminiscences; or the Pleasures of Living with Others.* London: T. Fisher Unwin, 1896, First edition; half title, frontispiece and illustrations, pages little roughly opened, uncut in original red decorated cloth, slightly dulled, ownership signature and presentation inscription, stamp of W H Smith. Jarndyce Antiquarian Booksellers CXCI - 175 2011 £35

Fisher, F. J. F. *The Alpine Ranunculi of New Zealand.* Wellington: New Zealand Dept. of Scientific and Industrial Research, 1965, 4to., original green cloth, gilt, slight mark to spine, pages 192, color frontispiece, 130 plates, 123 figures, color distribution maps, etc. R. F. G. Hollett & Son Antiquarian Booksellers General Catalogue Summer 2010 - 971 2011 £30

Fisher, George *The Instructor or Young Man's Best Companion.* London: printed for Thomas Martin, 1788, Small 8vo., original plain boards, backstrip lacking but cords just holding, pages xii, 366, 2 plates of calligraphy and few text woodcuts, lacks front flyleaf, perhaps a frontispiece. R. F. G. Hollett & Sons Antiquarian Booksellers 170 - 233 2011 £120

Fisher, M. *Scenes from Scripture and Other Poems.* Carlisle: printed & published by John Irving Lonsdale, 1859, Original pink brown cloth, slightly rubbed, all edges gilt, very good. Jarndyce Antiquarian Booksellers CXCI - 176 2011 £40

Fisher, M. F. K. *Two Kitchens in Provence.* Covelo: Yolla Bolly Press, 1999, Limited edition of 225 numbered copies; signed by artist, Ward Schumaker and Alice Waters, printed on English mouldmade Somerset,. Jeff Weber Rare Books 163 - 119 2011 $600

Fisher, Vardis *In Tragic Life and Passions Spin the Plot and We Are Betrayed and No Villain Need Be.* Caxton: 1932-1936, First edition; 4 volumes, very good + dust jackets with mild soil, edgewear, 8vo., 464, 428, 369, 387 pages. By the Book, L. C. 26 - 5 2011 $425

Fishwick, Henry *Memorials of Old Lancashire.* Bemrose & Sons, 1909, First edition; 2 volumes, string (but attractive) library binding of quarter crimson calf, gilt, page xii, 280; viii, 314, (iv), numerous illustrations, ex-library with numerous small stamps, few spots and marks, generally very good and sound set. R. F. G. Hollett & Son Antiquarian Booksellers General Catalogue Summer 2010 - 1394 2011 £120

Fitch, Samuel S. *Guide to Invalids.* New York: 1848, (1-2) (3)-74, 3-4 pages, wrappers well brown toned and foxed, woodcuts. Bookworm & Silverfish 676 - 127 2011 $100

Fitter, R. S. R. *London's Natural History.* London: Collins, 1945, First edition; original cloth, gilt, spine little faded, dust jacket spine little dulled, trifle frayed at head and foot, small closed nick, pages 282 with 52 color and 41 black and white photos and 12 maps and diagrams, good, clean. R. F. G. Hollett & Son Antiquarian Booksellers General Catalogue Summer 2010 - 973 2011 £35

Fitz-Gerald, Shafto Justin Adair *Drink.* London: Greening & Co., 1903, 8 pages ads, original illustrations, paper wrappers, slightly faded, very good.   Jarndyce Antiquarian Booksellers   CXCI - 376   2011   £45

Fitzgerald, Francis Scott Key   1896-1940   *All the Sad Young Men.* New York: 1926, First edition; (8), 267 pages, cloth, covers moderately spotted, first and last few leaves very slightly foxed, nearly invisible blindstamp on title, good plus.   Joseph J. Felcone Inc.   Fall Miscellany 2010 - 44   2011 $450

Fitzgerald, Francis Scott Key   1896-1940   *The Beautiful and Damned.* New York: Charles Scribner's Sons, 1922, First edition, first state; contemporary pencil owner's name, corners little bumped, near fine, spine easily readable, lacking scarce dust jacket.   Between the Covers   169 - BTC343942   2011 $1000

Fitzgerald, Francis Scott Key   1896-1940   *The Great Gatsby.* New York: Charles Scribner's Sons, 1925, First edition, first printing; octavo, original linen like grain cloth, fine.   Heritage Book Shop   Booth A12 51st NY International Antiquarian Book Fair April 8-10 2011 - 53   2011 $4500

Fitzgerald, Francis Scott Key   1896-1940   *The Great Gatsby.* New York: Scribners, 1925, First edition, first printing; (6), 218 pages, cloth, front free endpaper lacking, covers lightly soiled.   Joseph J. Felcone Inc.   Fall Miscellany 2010 - 45   2011 $1500

Fitzgerald, Francis Scott Key   1896-1940   *The Great Gatsby.* New York: Random House, 1954, First edition; first printing, with the correct issue points as called for by Bruccoli, 'chatter' on page 60, line 16, 'norathern' on page 119, line 22, 'it's' on page 165, line 16, 'away' on page 165 line 29, 'sick in tired' on page 250, lines 9-10 and 'Union Street station' on page 211, lines 7-8, octavo, 218 pages, original green linen like grain cloth with front cover lettered in blind and spine lettered in gilt, top edge trimmed, others uncut, spine gilt quite bright, some very minor foxing, else near fine.   Heritage Book Shop   Holiday 2010 - 41   2011 $4500

Fitzgerald, Francis Scott Key   1896-1940   *Tales of the Jazz Age.* New York: Charles Scribners Sons, 1922, First, first or second printing (not distinguished) with "an" at 232.6; (2), xi, (1), 317 pages, cloth, spine lettering just trifle dulled, front hinge slightly cracked, else very good, without dust jacket.   Joseph J. Felcone Inc.   Fall Miscellany 2010 - 46   2011 $400

Fitzgerald, Francis Scott Key   1896-1940   *Les Efants Du Jazz. (Tales of the Jazz Age).* Paris: Gallimard, 1967, First edition in French; wrappers, 8vo., pages 289, pale blue wrappers slightly faded, else near fine, no. 1 of 47 copies of the tirage de tete on velin por fil Lalfuma-Navarre.   Any Amount of Books   May 29 2011 - B26590   2011 $272

Fitzgerald, Francis Scott Key   1896-1940   *Tender is the Night.* London: Chatto & Windus, 1934, First UK edition; 8vo., original publisher's blue cloth lettered yellow on spine, pages 408, slight lean spine slightly faded, covers slightly marked, corners slightly bumped, otherwise near very good.   Any Amount of Books   May 29 2011 - A75303   2011 $315

Fitzgerald, Francis Scott Key   1896-1940   *Tender is the Night.* New York: Scribner's, 1934, First edition, 2nd printing; (8), 408 pages, cloth, spine lettering very faint, general cover wear, good to very good, Willard Thorp's copy.   Joseph J. Felcone Inc.   Fall Miscellany 2010 - 48   2011 $400

Fitzgerald, Penelope *Human Voices.* London: Collins, 1980, First edition; 8vo., pages 177, appears to be a proof copy in plain blue wrappers but with original dust jacket with price, loosely inserted is good letter to her mother and father, signed with her nickname "Mops", fine in fine dust jacket.   Any Amount of Books   May 29 2011 - A74866   2011 $255

Fitzgerald, W. F. Vesey *Egypt, India and the Colonies.* London: William H. Allen, 1870, First edition; 8vo., pages iv, 246, ads, original red cloth, very good, clean copy.   J. & S. L. Bonham Antiquarian Booksellers   Africa 4/20/2011 - 8227   2011   £50

Fitzgibbon, Maurice *Art Under Arms: an University Man in Khaki.* London: Longman, Green, 1901, First edition; 8vo. pages 232, ads, original beige cloth, all edges gilt, little fading to spine.   J. & S. L. Bonham Antiquarian Booksellers   Africa 4/20/2011 - 8257   2011   £60

Fitzmaurice, R. *Principles of Modern Building. Volume I.* London: HMSO, 1938, First edition; tall 8vo., original cloth, gilt, pages 400, 19 plates, 55 text figures, 44 tables.   R. F. G. Hollett & Son Antiquarian Booksellers   177 - 300   2011   £40

Five Little Pigs. New York: McLoughlin Bros. n.d. circa, 1856, Square 12mo., 4 leaves, 1 page books list on lower wrapper, pictorial paper wrappers, each part illustrated with wood engraved vignette, small spots on fore-edge of upper wrapper, reinforced spine, very good.   Hobbyhorse Books   56 - 99   2011 $120

5 Little Pigs. New York: Akron: Chicago: Saalfield, 1910, Narrow 4to., pictorial card covers die-cut in shape of pig, near fine, printed on stiff card with color covering the entire surface of each page, interior pages have large holes where face would be but face can been seen inside each cover.   Aleph-Bet Books, Inc.   95 - 525   2011 $250

Flake, Sharon G. *The Skin I'm In.* New York: 1998, First edition; 171 pages, fine in fine unclipped dust jacket, inscribed and signed by author.   Bookworm & Silverfish   665 - 5   2011 $75

Flamsteed, John *The Correspondence of John Flamsteed, the First Astronomer Royal.* Bristol and Philadelphia: Institute of Physics, 1995-2002, 3 volumes, large 8vo., xlix, 955; xlvii, 1095; lxvi, 1038 pages, 2 frontispieces in each volume, half tone illustrations, paper boards, gilt stamped cover and spine titles (with small cover and spine portraits of Flamsteed), fine, from the Bern Dibner reference library, with Burndy bookplate.   Jeff Weber Rare Books   161 - 149 2011 $500

Flaubert, Gustave 1821-1880 *Madame Bovary.* Paris: Michel Levy Freres Libraires Editeurs, 1857, First edition, first issue; 2 volumes, 12mo., December 1857 catalog laid in at back of volume I, original pale green printed wrappers and glassine dust jackets, all edges uncut.   Heritage Book Shop   Booth A12 51st NY International Antiquarian Book Fair April 8-10 2011 - 54   2011 $17,500

Flaubert, Gustave 1821-1880 *Madame Bovary.* London: W. W. Gibbings, 1892, Early English edition; decorated mustard cloth, very good, some rubbing and shelfwear, solid, clean text.   Lupack Rare Books   May 26 2011 - 98 2011 $150

Flaubert, Gustave 1821-1880 *Salammbo.* Cambridge: University Press for the Limited Edition Club, 1960, Limited, signed edition, no. 184 of 1550 copies; pages xi, 319, with 8 double page color plates and 50 black and white drawings, original cream cloth gilt, 4to., patterned spine matching patterned slipcase (extremities trifle worn).   R. F. G. Hollett & Son Antiquarian Booksellers   General Catalogue Summer 2010 - 713 2011   £95

Fleetwood, John *The Life of Lord and Saviour Jesus Christ...* London: George Virtue, n.d., 4to., contemporary full black divinity calf gilt, little rubbed, pages xii, 722, engraved title, numerous engraved plates.   R. F. G. Hollett & Son Antiquarian Booksellers   175 - 448 2011   £85

Fleetwood, William *An Essay Upon Miracles.* London: printed for Charles Harper, 1701, Old speckled calf, each board with central panel with broad surround of contrasting plain sheep, decorated and ruled in blind, attractively rebacked to match with heavy raised bands, original spine label preserved, attractive, wide margined copy, very scarce. R. F. G. Hollett & Son Antiquarian Booksellers   175 - 449 2011   £275

Fleischman, Sid *The Whipping Boy.* New York: Greenwillow Books, 1986, First edition; 8vo., cloth backed boards with blindstamped emblem on front cover and silver lettering on spine, full color pictorial dust jacket (not price clipped) of an as new copy, 90 numbered pages with 10 full page black and white illustrations along with vignettes scattered throughout book, illustrations by Pete Sis.   Jo Ann Reisler, Ltd.   86 - 99 2011 $275

Fleming, Alexander *On the Antibacterial Action of Cultures of a Pencillium with Special Reference to their Use in Isolation of B. Influenza.* London: 1929, i.e., 1944, Second separate printing; quarto, self wrappers, stapled as issued.   Heritage Book Shop   Booth A12 51st NY International Antiquarian Book Fair April 8-10 2011 - 55 2011 $10,000

Fleming, Francis *A Geography and Natural History of the Counties.* London: Arthur Hall, Virtue, First edition; 8vo., pages vi, 487, 10 engraved plates, 2 black and white folding maps, additional ms. errata, contemporary decorative half morocco, slightly rubbed, new front endpapers.   J. & S. L. Bonham Antiquarian Booksellers   Africa 4/20/2011 - 7039 2011   £95

Fleming, Ian Lancaster 1908-1964 *From Russia with Love.* London: Jonathan Cape, 1957, First edition; 8vo., recently rebound in full blue calf lettered gilt at spine with gilt raised bands, pages 253.   Any Amount of Books   May 26 2011 - A34143 2011 $470

Fleming, Ian Lancaster 1908-1964 *Thunderball.* London: Cape, 1961, First edition; pages 254, foolscap 8vo., original black boards backstrip gilt lettered, fronr cover blindstamped, two or three small spots to fore-edges, bright, clean dust jacket, near fine.   Blackwell Rare Books   B166 - 145 2011   £735

Fleming, John *The Penguin Dictionary of Decorative Arts.* Viking, 1989, Large thick 8vo., original boards, gilt, dust jacket, pages 937, 67 color plates, fine.   R. F. G. Hollett & Son Antiquarian Booksellers   General Catalogue Summer 2010 - 155 2011   £45

Fleming, John *Robert Adam and His Circle in Edinburgh and Rome.* London: John Murray, 1962, Small 4to., original blue cloth gilt, dust jacket price clipped, pages xxi, 394, 93 plates and 14 text figures.   R. F. G. Hollett & Son Antiquarian Booksellers   177 - 301 2011   £35

Fleming, Vivian M. *Campaigns of the Army of Northern Virginia Including the Jackson Valley Campaign 1861-1865.* Richmond: 1928, 167 pages, fine, folding map, original binding.   Bookworm & Silverfish   665 - 35 2011 $165

Fletcher, J. *A Rational Vindication of the Catholic Faith...* Hull: printed by George Prince, circa, 1790, Pages 223, (i), uncut, old drab wrappers with tick endpapers, side sewn with thick cord, very worn and defective, original stiff sugar paper wrappers preserved, edges little worn, pages 223, (i), uncut, corners little rounded, rare.   R. F. G. Hollett & Son Antiquarian Booksellers   175 - 450 2011   £150

Fletcher, J. S. *The Cartwright Gardens Murder.* New York: Alfred A. Knopf, 1926, First edition; fine in near fine dust jacket with tiny nicks and short tears, scarce in jacket. Between the Covers   169 - BTC316311 2011 $250

Fletcher, J. S. *The History of the St. Leger Stakes 1776-1901.* London: Hutchinson, 1902, First edition; tall 8vo., original green cloth with design of horse shoes in gilt on upper board, extremities trifle rubbed, pages xvi, 504, top edge gilt, 4 color plates, 32 other illustrations. R. F. G. Hollett & Son Antiquarian Booksellers General Catalogue Summer 2010 - 1246 2011 £65

Fletcher, John *Studies on Slavery in Easy Lessons...* Natchez: Jackson Warner et al, 1852, First edition, 4th thousand; 8vo., pages xiv, 637, publisher's sheep, front hinge repaired, little foxed but good. Second Life Books Inc. 174 - 147 2011 $450

Flint, Timothy *Francis Berrigan or the Mexican Patriot.* Boston: Cummings Hilliard and Co., 1826, First edition; 12mo., original tan paper covered boards, printed paper labels, uncut, front covers detached, spines chipped and worn, slight loss of text on labels, text foxed (mostly moderate but some heavy), clamshell box, rare in boards. M & S Rare Books, Inc. 90 - 133 2011 $1750

Florian, Jean Pierre Claris De 1755-1794 *Fables De Florian.* Paris: Remoissenet, 1806, 2 volumes, 4to., original marbled paper on boards, leather spine, gilt fillets and gilt title on red label, full page copper engraved frontispiece, steel engravings, on watermarked handmade paper, line cracks at fold of upper covers, lightly bumped corners of covers, excellent and rare edition. Hobbyhorse Books 56 - 56 2011 $1100

Florian, Jean Pierre Claris De 1755-1794 *Fables de Florian.* Paris: Aug. Renoaurd, 1812, 12mo., 224 + 4 pages, table aphabetque, new boards, taupe papers, original title label on spine, fine full page wood engraved frontispiece, 6 wood engravings, untrimmed edges, inked dated signature, some chipping and folding at fragile edges and light foxing on some engravings, very good. Hobbyhorse Books 56 - 57 2011 $170

Florian, Jean Pierre Claris De 1755-1794 *William Tell, or the Patriot of Switzerland.* London: J. Harris, n.d., 1830, 12mo., 252 pages + 24 page list, marbled paper on boards, red roan spine with gilt title and fillets, 2 half titles, 6 full page very fine copper engravings, engraved vignette on main title, edges and rounded corners rubbed, very good. Hobbyhorse Books 56 - 74 2011 $220

Florian, Jean Pierre Claris De 1755-1794 *Oeuvres de J. P. Florian.* Paris: Lepetit, Berry Dugrit, New edition; 12mo., 212, 207 pages, three quarter leather with corners, marbled paper on boards, red label with gilt title and decorations on spines, full page copper engraved frontispieces, restored front edge of volume II titlepage, transparent brown spont on volume I, very good set. Hobbyhorse Books 56 - 73 2011 $170

Florilegium Diversorum Epigrammatum Veterum, in Septem Libros Diversum... Geneva: E. Estienne, H. Fuggeri typographus, 1566, 4to., (4), 539 (=545, pages 283-288 bis), (35) pages, device on titlepage, later Dutch vellum over pasteboard, yapp edges, fine, clean, large copy, inscription "M. Bruningen 29 June 1657), from the library of the Earls of Macclesfield at Shirburn Castle. Maggs Bros. Ltd. 1440 - 234 2011 £2200

Florus, Lucius Annaeus *A Compendious History of Rome...* York: printed by Thomas Gent for Arthur Bettesworth, 1727, 8vo., pages (vi), 217, (i), contemporary calf, boards panelled in blind, Cambridge style, board edges 'zig-zag' decorative roll in blind, all edges red sprinkled, pink and white sewn endbands, late 20th century calf reback by CEW (some thumbing and soiling, title rehinged, hinge cracked at title), old leather scratched and chipped, substantial portion on front renewed with rebacking, from the collection of Christopher Ernest Weston 1947-2010. Unsworths Booksellers 24 - 94 2011 £175

Flower of Cities. A Book of London. Max Parrish, 1949, First edition; pages 324, with 12 color plates, 27 illustrations, colored maps on endpapers, large 8vo., original cloth, gilt, dust jacket by Barbara Jones, extremities trifle worn,. R. F. G. Hollett & Son Antiquarian Booksellers General Catalogue Summer 2010 - 1465 2011 £35

Floyd, Bryan Alec *The Long War Dead.* New York: Avon, 1976, First edition; intended dedication, this copy inscribed by author to Joe Monda, rubbing and crease to spine, very good in wrappers. Ken Lopez Bookseller 154 - 230 2011 $300

Fludd, Robert *Philosophia Moysaica.* Gouda: Petrus Rammazenius, 1638, First edition; folio, (4), 152 (i.e., 144), 30, (1) leaves, engraved titlepage vignette (repeated in second part), woodcut text illustrations, panelled sprinkled calf, mixed paper stocks, some gatherings lightly browned, some very lightly foxed, lovely, fresh, near fine. Joseph J. Felcone Inc. Fall Miscellany 2010 - 49 2011 $8000

Flynn, John T. *As We Go Marching.* Garden City: 1944, First edition; 272 pages, same date on titlepage and verso, very good in dust jacket with expected wear an small tears at top. Bookworm & Silverfish 671 - 211 2011 $95

Folberg, Neil *And I Shall Dwell Among Them. Historic Synagogues of the World.* New York: Aperture Foundation, 1995, Stated first edition; signed and inscribed by Folberg, 4to., 175 pages, very good++, foxing top edge, in near fine dust jacket with internal foxing. By the Book, L. C. 26 - 28 2011 $90

Folk Songs of the New Palestine: First Series I. New York: Hechalutz Organization and Masada, Youth Zionist Organization of America, 1938, First edition; sheet music, cream colored front cover with black printing pages 8, self wrappers very good.   Second Life Books Inc.   174 - 149   2011 $75

Folk Songs of the New Palestine: First Series 3. New York: Masada, Youth Zionist Organization of America and Hechalutz Organizaton of America, 1938, First edition; sheet music, cream colored front cover with black printing, pages 8, self wrappers, very good.   Second Life Books Inc. 174 - 150   2011 $75

Folkard, Henry Tennyson   *Music and Musicians.*   Wigan: James Starr, 1903,   Limited separate edition (50 copies); large 8vo., original cloth, gilt, top of spine torn, pages 44, flyleaves browned, presentation slip from librarian/author tipped in.   R. F. G. Hollett & Son Antiquarian Booksellers 175 - 452   2011   £30

Folkard, Henry Tennyson   *Painters and Painting.*   Wigan: James Tarr, 1904,   Limited edition (25 copies); large 8vo., contemporary half calf gilt with marbled boards, rather rubbed, page 89, interleaves with ruled leaves throughout. R. F. G. Hollett & Son Antiquarian Booksellers   General Catalogue Summer 2010 - 156   2011   £40

Follett, Barbara Newhall   *The House Without Windows and Eepersip's Life There.*   New York and London: Alfred A. Knopf, 1927, First edition; 8vo., original publisher's decorated cloth with black linen spine lettered gilt, pages (x), 166, endpapers slightly browned, else very good in very good dust jacket, slightly nicked (with no loss) at head of spine and slightly tanned and faintly rubbed at spine, decent condition.   Any Amount of Books   May 26 2011 - A76313 2011 $604

Fontaine, James   *Memoirs of a Huguenot Family.*   New York: 1872,   512 pages, 12mo., inner front joint reglued, also page 511, etc.   Bookworm & Silverfish   679 - 89 2011 $65

Fontaine, James   *A Tale of the Huguenots or Memoirs of a French Refugee Family.*   New York: 1838, First edition; 266 (8) pages, 12mo., Richard L. Maury's copy, endpapes foxed, some foxing to text, patterned cloth with drink ring, signature and bookplate of Col. Richard L. Maury, edges well rubbed, backstrip gilt legible but rubbed.   Bookworm & Silverfish   679 - 196   2011 $225

Fontcuberta, Joan   *Dr. Ameisenhaufen's Fauna.* Gottingen: European Photography, 1988, First edition; 8vo., pages 84, 53 black and white photo and 33 black and white illustrations, text in English, original brown card wrapper, text printed in black, fine.   Simon Finch Rare Books Zero - 522   2011   £400

Fonteyn, Margot   *Autobiography.*   London: W. H. Allen, 1975,   Pages 284, well illustrated, signed by author on title, original gilt dust jacket, irrelevant inscription on back of frontispiece, front flyleaf removed, ticket for Margot Fonteyn gala performance at Darlington 1976 and some related ephemera loosely inserted.   R. F. G. Hollett & Son Antiquarian Booksellers   175 - 453   2011   £40

Foote, George William   *Royal Paupers; Radical's Contribution to the Jubilee.*   Progressive Publishing Co., 1887,   Original wrappers, slightly marked, 31 pages. Jarndyce Antiquarian Booksellers   CXCI - 595   2011   £75

Foote, Horton   *The Screenplay of To Kill A Mockingbird.* New York: Harvest/Harcourt, Brace & World, 1964, Paperback original;   price inked out on front cover, shallow creasing to pages and rear cover, some minor rubbing, very good in wrappers, uncommon.   Ken Lopez Bookseller 154 - 96   2011 $275

Foote, William H.   *Sketches of Virginia Historical and Biographical.*   Richmond: 1850, Second edition; Second Series, 2 volumes, good, solid, corners showing usual shelfwear, backstrip extremities worn, some cover spots, internal foxing, old dampstain to free corners, without frontispiece (as issued, no stubs), volume 2 with normal reader wear to backstrip ends and some wear to shoulders of backstrip. Bookworm & Silverfish   678 - 201   2011 $275

Fooz, Jean Henri Nicolas De   *Fundamental Principles of the Law of Mines.*   San Francisco: J. B. Painter, 1860, First edition;   extremely scarce, contemporary owner's signature (Harmon Bell) on inner cover, repeated on page lxx, (i)-cxlviii, 882 pages, publisher's full sheep, gilt lettered red and black leather labels, contemporary owner's signature, very slight wear to head of spine, fine, extremely scarce. Argonaut Book Shop   Recent Acquisitions Summer 2010 - 132   2011 $2250

Foran, W. Robert   *The Kenya Police 1887-1960.*   London: Robert Hale, 1962,   First edition; 8vo., pages xvi, 237, 2 maps, illustrations, original blue cloth, scarce.   J. & S. L. Bonham Antiquarian Booksellers   Africa 4/20/2011 - 8322 2011   £150

Forbes-Winslow, D.   *Daly's. The Biography of a Theatre.* London: W. H. Allen, 1944,   First edition; Pages 220, illustrations, original late 19th century programme from theatre advertising Bernhardt's performances and original photo postcard of Lily Elsie, both loosely inserted.   R. F. G. Hollett & Son Antiquarian Booksellers   175 - 455   2011 £35

Forbes, Agner *The Rich Men of Massachusetts: Containing a Statement of the Reputed Wealth of About Two Thousand Persons with Brief Sketches of Nearly Fifteen Hundred Characters.* Boston: 1852, Second edition; 224 pages, extra illustrated with 50 portraits and 18 original documents, modern green half morocco, spine slightly and uniformly faded, fine, richly extra illustrated. Joseph J. Felcone Inc. Fall Miscellany 2010 - 50 2011 $850

Forbes, Archibald *Battles of the Nineteenth Century.* London: Cassell and Co. n.d., Special edition; 6 volumes, small 4to., original pictorial green cloth gilt, 36 plates, 12 in color, tissue guarded, numerous other illustrations, few slight marks, excellent set. R. F. G. Hollett & Son Antiquarian Booksellers General Catalogue Summer 2010 - 601 2011 £150

Forbes, Edwin *Life Studies of the Great Army.* New York: Henry J. Johnson sold to subscribers only, 1876, First edition; elephant folio, original cloth portfolio, very worn, descriptive sheet of title and plates pasted inside front cover, mounts generally foxed, plates occasionally foxed, but very bright, chipping to few mount margins, overall fine, each of the plates signed in pencil by Forbes lower left, on the mount. M & S Rare Books, Inc. 90 - 80 2011 $5500

Forbes, Elliot *Thayer's Life of Beethoven.* Princeton: 1967, 2 volumes, xxv, 605-1141 pages, crisp, fine in fine dust jacket, original binding. Bookworm & Silverfish 667 - 22 2011 $100

Forbes, Hugh *Four Lectures Upon recent Events in Italy, Delivered in New York University... March 1851.* New York: printed for the author by D. Fanshaw, 1851, First edition; 12mo., 110 pages, original printed wrappers, front wrapper nearly loose, some minor wear and chipping, library bookplate, faint stain across lower portion of title. M & S Rare Books, Inc. 90 - 56 2011 $750

Forbes, R. J. *Studies in Ancient Technology. Volumes 1-3, 6-9.* Leiden: E. J. Brill, 1953-1964, 7 volumes, 8vo., viii, 194; vi, 215; vi, 268; 196; 253; viii, 288; viii, 295 pages, folding plates, text figures, tan cloth, gilt stamped cover and spine titles, dust jackets, fine, from the Bern Dibner reference library, with Burndy bookplate. Jeff Weber Rare Books 161 - 151 2011 $200

Ford, Brian J. *Images of Science. A History of Scientific Illustration.* New York: Oxford University Press, 1993, 4to., viii, 208 pages, green cloth, gilt stamped spine title, dust jacket, fine, from the Bern Dibner reference library, with Burndy bookplate. Jeff Weber Rare Books 161 - 152 2011 $75

Ford, Charles Henri *Silver Flower Coo.* New York: Kulchur Press, 1968, First edition; large 8vo., pages not numbered, paper wrappers, press release laid in, photos by Andy Fink, cover scuffed, but very good, tight. Second Life Books Inc. 174 - 151 2011 $150

Ford, Gerald R. *A Time to Heal. The Autobiography of Gerald R. Ford.* New York: Harper & Row/Readers Digest, 1979, Fourth printing; photos, signed by Ford and dated 5/7/93, fine in fine dust jacket. Charles Agvent 2010 Summer Miscellany - 31 2011 $400

Ford, James *The Suffolk Garland; or a Collection of Poems, Songs, Tales, Ballads, Sonnets and Elegies, Legendary and Romantic, Historical and Descriptive, Relative to that County...* Ipswich: printed and sold by John Raw, 1818, First edition; pages xv, 404, half title (trifle soiled), title vignette and attractive woodcut vignette head and tailpieces, few marginal blindstamps, accession stamp on verso of title, extensive annotations by early owner on title and few notes in text. R. F. G. Hollett & Son Antiquarian Booksellers 175 - 456 2011 £150

Ford, Paul Leicester *Winnowings in American History - Revolutionary Narratives 1-4.* New York: Historical Printing Club, 1890, Limited edition, 250 copies printed; wrappers soiled and chipped, 3 covers and 2 titlepages detached, interiors clean and tight, some pages uncut. G. H. Mott Bookseller May 26 2011 - 35311 2011 $175

Ford, Richard *A Hand-Book for Travellers in Spain and Readers at Home.* London: John Murray, 1845, First edition; half titles, engraved folding map, pages xii, 1-556; vi, 557-1064, 8vo., recent red buckram, gilt lettered backstrips (titles between gilt rules), gilt dated at foot, ads on laid down yellow chalked endpapers, ink ownership inscription of Arthur C. Mitchell dated Sept. 2nd 1871 at head of titlepages, red sprinkled edges, good. Blackwell Rare Books B166 - 39 2011 £675

Ford, Richard *Independence Day.* New Orleans: B. E. Trice, 1995, Lettered issue of the limited edition, one of 26 lettered copies, signed by author; rarer issue, quarter bound in leather, fine in fine slipcase. Ken Lopez Bookseller 154 - 53 2011 $1500

Ford, Richard *Independence Day.* London: Harvill Press, 1995, First edition; signed by author, light lower corner taps, else fine in very near fine dust jacket. Ken Lopez Bookseller 154 - 54 2011 $125

Ford, Richard *Independence Day.* New York: Knopf, 1995, First edition; fine in fine dust jacket, signed by author. Bella Luna Books May 29 2011 - j1828 2011 $137

Ford, Richard *Independence Day.* New York: Knopf, 1995, First edition; fine in fine dust jacket, signed by author. Bella Luna Books May 29 2011 - t1235 2011 $110

Ford, Richard *Independence Day.* New York: Knopf, 1995, First edition; fine in fine dust jacket. Bella Luna Books May 29 2011 - t1176 2011 $82

Ford, Richard *The Ultimate Good Luck.* Boston: Houghton Mifflin, 1981, First edition; near fine, paper starting to separate at inside of rear hinge in 1 inch area, in fine dust jacket, signed by author. Bella Luna Books May 26 2011 - t9656 2011 $308

Ford, Richard *The Ultimate Good Luck.* Boston: Houghton Mifflin, 1981, First edition; near fine, paper starting to separate at inside of rear hinge in 1 inch area, dust jacket fine. Bella Luna Books May 26 2011 - t9701 2011 $198

Ford, William *A Description of Scenery in the Lake District Intended as a Guide to Strangers.* Carlisle: Charles Thurnam, 1840, Second edition; pages xi, 190, 3 double page fully hand colored maps, each with panoramic view, large folding hand colored map laid on fine linen, original ribbed cloth, gilt, rather faded, engraved paper label with view of waterfall on upper panel. R. F. G. Hollett & Son Antiquarian Booksellers 173 - 433 2011 £195

Ford, Worthington Chauncey *George Washington.* New York: Goupil and Co. and Charles Scribner's Sons, 1900, One of 200 copies of Edition de Luxe; 2 volumes, 270 x 205mm., attractive green crushed morocco, covers with two line gilt frame, raised bands, gilt framed compartments and gilt titling, red morocco doublures surrounded by inch wide green morocco turn-ins, with four gilt fillets, watered silk endleaves, top edges gilt, other edges untrimmed, 8 full page plates in sepia, 42 in black and white and two frontispieces in color, as well as 32 tailpieces, chapter initials in black and red; bookplate of William P. Olds laid in at front of each volume; large paper copy; hint of wear to joints and extremities, spines midly faded to olive green, spine of second volume with just slightly irregular fading, still fine, binding solid and pleasing, text and plates virtually pristine. Phillip J. Pirages 59 - 345 2011 $1500

Forder, John *Hill Shepherd. A Photographic Essays.* Kendal: Frank Peters, 1990, Second edition; oblong 4to., original pictorial boards, dust jacket, pages 157, illustrations in color, signed copy, scarce. R. F. G. Hollett & Son Antiquarian Booksellers 173 - 434 2011 £40

Fordham, Elias Pym *Personal Narrative of Travels in Virginia, Maryland, Pennsylvania, Ohio, Indiana, Kentucky & of a Residence in the Illinois Territory 1817-1818.* Cleveland: 1906, 248 pages, 8vo., very good. Bookworm & Silverfish 668 - 196 2011 $67

Foreign Slave Trade. Abstract of the Information Recently Laid on the Table of The House of Commons on the Subject of the Slave Trade; Being a Report Made by a Committee Specially Appointed for the Purpose to the Directors of the African Institution on the 8th of May 1821 and by them Ordered to be Printed ... London: Printed by Ellerton and Henderson, 1821, First edition; 8vo., 180 pages, recently well bound in watered cloth, spine gilt lettered, very good. John Drury Rare Books 154 - 3 2011 £275

Foreman, Michael *After the War Was Over.* Arcade Publishing, 1966, First US edition; oblong large 8vo., original cloth, dust jacket, pages 96, illustrations in color, fine. R. F. G. Hollett & Sons Antiquarian Booksellers 170 - 237 2011 £35

Foreman, Michael *Michael Foreman's Christmas Treasury.* London: Pavilion, 1999, First edition; 8vo., 121 pages, signed by author, fine in fine dust jacket. By the Book, L. C. 26 - 62 2011 $85

Foreman, Michael *Nursery Rhymes.* Walker Books, 1998, Oblong 4to., original glazed pictorial boards, matching dust jacket, pages 152, (vi), illustrations in color by Michael Foreman. R. F. G. Hollett & Sons Antiquarian Booksellers 170 - 238 2011 £35

Forest Lawn Memorial Park *Pictorial Forest Lawn.* Glendale: Forest Lawn Memorial Park Association, 1955, third edition; large 4to., pages 70, illustrations in color and monochrome, paper wrappers, cover little chipped and creased, otherwise very good, tight copy. Second Life Books Inc. 174 - 152 2011 $75

Forester, Cecil Scott 1899-1966 *Brown on Resolution.* London: Bodley Head, 1929, First edition; 8vo., 272 pages, 8 page publisher's catalog at rear, blue cloth lettered yellow, spine slightly faded and very slightly marked, prelims slightly foxed, sound very good. Any Amount of Books May 29 2011 - B29556 2011 $213

Forester, Cecil Scott 1899-1966 *Josephine, Napoleon's Empress.* London: Methuen & Co., 1925, First edition; 218 x 145mm., vii (i), 246 pages, superb contemporary deep blue morocco by Sangorski & Sutcliffe for Asprey with more than 60 onlays, front cover with center medallion featuring onlaid teal blue crossed "J's", surrounded by gilt wreath and crown as well as onlaid pink flowers, lovely gilt floral sprays with more onlaid pink flowers in corners of both covers, raised bands, spine beautifully gilt and onlaid in same floral vine pattern, doublures of crimson morocco with onlaid blue flowers in corners as well as intricate series of patterned rules against deep blue morocco border, front doublure with fine inset hand painted ivory miniature of Josephine, watered silk free endpapers, gilt edges, in slightly scuffed but sturdy and attractive morocco backed plush-lined folding cloth box, gilt titling on spine; with 12 illustrations, all photos of portraits, as called for, choice binding in immaculate condition. Phillip J. Pirages 59 - 96 2011 $5500

Formes. Le Magazine des Artistes Peintres et Sculpteurs. No. 1. Paris: Art et Photographie, 1950, with photos by Brassai, 4to., pages (12), 16 photos (including recto and verso of wrappers), original stapled black and white photo illustrated wrappers, spine lightly rubbed, scratch with short closed tear to first page, near fine. Simon Finch Rare Books Zero - 513 2011 £350

Fornander, Abraham *Fornander Collection of Hawaiian Antiquities and Folk-Lore, The Hawaiian Account of the Formation of Their Islands and origin of Their Race with the Traditions of Their Migrations etc....* Honolulu: Bishop Museum Press, 1919, First edition; wrappers, large 4to., 217 pages, original publisher's brown printed wrappers, faint rubbing, else near fine, excellent condition with separate supplement, an index to entire volume 6, wrappers xiii pages also in excellent condition.   Any Amount of Books   May 29 2011 - A40950   2011 $255

Forrest, C. *A Ramble on Rumbald's Moor. (bound with) Part 2... Part 3.* Wakefield: W. T. Lamb, 1868-1869, Limited editions (100 copies only); pages 16, 206, 26, uncut, 1 plate and 3 text illustrations, contemporary half calf gilt, spine little rubbed, original wrappers of first and final parts bound in, extremely scarce.   R. F. G. Hollett & Son Antiquarian Booksellers   177 - 305   2011   £140

Forrest, H. E. *The Old Churches of Shrewsbury.* Shrewsbury: Wilding & Son, 1922, Original pictorial stiff wrappers, pages iv, 153, with 28 plates.   R. F. G. Hollett & Son Antiquarian Booksellers   177 - 306   2011   £30

Forrester, Andrew *The Revelations of a Private Detective.* London: Ward & Lock, 1863, Trimmed cloth, original blue green binder's cloth, slightly faded, booklabel of George Rollo.   Jarndyce Antiquarian Booksellers   CXCI - 178   2011   £180

Forskal, Petrus *Descriptiones Animalium, Avium, Amphibiorum, Piscium Insectorum Vermium... (bound with) Icones Rerum Naturalium quad In Itinere Orientali.* Hauniae: Molleri, 1775-1776, Folding engraved map, 4to., pages 19, (1), xxxlv, 164, contemporary quarter calf (some rubbing, wear to edges, small abrasions to spine, front cover detached, text is quite clean), 43 engraved plates (8 are folding, light marginal foxing to last few plates) of which 20 are of plants, 1 of a bird, the remaining plates are of marine animals, from the collection of J. Van der Hoeven, Leon Vaillant the George Vanderbilt Foundation.   Raymond M. Sutton, Jr.   May 26 2011 - 42066   2011 $7000

Forster, Edward Morgan   1879-1970   *Goldsworthy Lowes Dickinson.* London: Edward Arnold, 1934, 8vo., pages xiii, 277, frontispiece, 8 illustrations, small bookplate of Janet Ashbee and C. R. Ashbee and loosely inserted various letters to Janet Ashbee, cuttings and pamphlet, hand written letter signed by Forster tipped in at front, also loosely inserted are two good long TLS's by EL Grant Watson about GLD, pasted in photo of GLD and scarce 4 page pamphlet by Cecil Townsend about GLD's house called "All Soul's Place", some eraseable pencilled linings in margins possibly by Mrs. Ashbee, book slightly bulked by insertions, covers very slightly marked, otherwise decent, very good.   Any Amount of Books   May 29 2011 - A66375   2011 $383

Forster, Edward Morgan   1879-1970   *A Passage to India.* London: Edward Arnold, 1924, First edition; pages 325, (iii, ads), few spots to gutter of title and fore-edge, flyeaves lightly browned or spotted, rear endpapers very neatly replaced, sound, attractive copy, original red ribbed cloth, few faint marks to upper board.   R. F. G. Hollett & Son Antiquarian Booksellers   General Catalogue Summer 2010 - 777   2011   £450

Forster, Edward Morgan   1879-1970   *The Story of the Siren.* Richmond: Hogarth Press, 1920, First edition, one of 500 copies Printed by Leonard and Virginia Woolf; marbled paper wrappers, very good, few archival paper repairs and few small tears.   Lupack Rare Books   May 26 2011 - ABE1162826681   2011 $350

Forster, G. C. F. *Northern History. A Review of the History of the North of England.* Leeds: School of History & Money Publishing, 1967-1999, 29 volumes, original wrappers, illustrations, good broken run, including volumes 2, 4-19, 21-27, 34 and 35.   R. F. G. Hollett & Son Antiquarian Booksellers   General Catalogue Summer 2010 - 602   2011   £250

Forster, Joseph *Studies in Black and Red.* London: Ward & Downey, 1896, First edition; half title, original black decorated cloth, very good.   Jarndyce Antiquarian Booksellers   CXCI - 179   2011   £75

Forster, Westgarth *A Treatise on a Section of the Strata, From Newcastle-upon-Tyne to the Mountains of Cross Fell, in Cumberland...* Alston: printed for the author at the Geological Press and sold by John Pattinson etc., 1821, Second edition; original boards, corners worn, attractively rebacked in pigskin with green lettering piece, pages 422, xvi, (vi, index), (xi, subscribers), (i, errata), uncut, complete with 12 plates, 12 hand colored plates of sections of strata and 8 further hand colored woodcuts, little scattered browning, but excellent wide margined copy, rare title, complete with 12mo. ad leaf tipped in before title, text woodcuts no usually found colored, armorial bookplates of William Henry Brockett, Mayor of Gateshead in 1839, and Edward Joicey of Whinney House (Gateshead).   R. F. G. Hollett & Son Antiquarian Booksellers   173 - 437   2011   £650

Forsythe, William *The State of Prisons in Britain 1775-1895.* London: Routledge, 2000, First edition thus; 7 volumes (of 8) lacks volume 7, over 2000 pages, excellent, clean condition, very good.   Any Amount of Books   May 29 2011 - B30421   2011 $408

Fortescue, J. W. *The Story of a Red-Deer.* London: Macmillan, 1925, First illustrated edition; large 8vo., original green cloth gilt, pages x, 144, with 24 plates.   R. F. G. Hollett & Sons Antiquarian Booksellers   170 - 43   2011   £35

Fortescue, J. W. *The Story of a Red Deer.* London: Macmillan, 1925, First illustrated edition; large 8vo., original green cloth gilt, pages x, 144, 24 plates by G. D. Armour. R. F. G. Hollett & Son Antiquarian Booksellers General Catalogue Summer 2010 - 944 2011 £35

Fortolis, Ludovic *Hantises.* Paris: Bibliotheque De La Critique, 1901, First edition; 8vo., pages 94, (1) imprint (1) blank, 4 plates, numerous small illustrations, uncut, plates browned at edges, otherwise very clean copy, original illustrated wrappers, printed in black, discolored with some light foxing, inscription offset to inner front cover, worn, chipped, spine cracked, but holding, glassine cover chipped, inscribed presentation by author to Monsieur Marches. Simon Finch Rare Books Zero - 314 2011 £500

Foscolo, Ugo *Ultime Lettere di Jacopo Ortis.* Italia: no publisher, 1802, First edition; 8vo., quarter morocco and vellum boards, ownership signature, some light foxing and faint marginal dampstaining, covers trifle worn, otherwise very good, preserved in custom made cloth chemise and quarter morocco and cloth slipcase. James S. Jaffe Rare Books May 26 2011 - 18436 2011 $5500

Foss, Christopher F. *Jane's Armour and Artillery 2006-2007.* Alexandria: Janes Information Group, 2006, First edition; 4to., copiously illustrated in color and black and white, pages 1050, slightly bumped at head and tail of spine with slight nick at lower spine, otherwise sound, very good. Any Amount of Books May 29 2011 - A68112 2011 $323

Foster, G. G. *Gold Regions of California.* New York: Dewit & Davenport, 1849, Third edition; octavo, (i)-80 pages, frontispiece map, third edition sheets with first issue of frontispiece map, modern quarter morocco over marbled boards, spine ruled and lettered in gilt, marbled endpapers, small brown spot on map, otherwise near fine. Heritage Book Shop Holiday 2010 - 43 2011 $1500

Foster, Joseph *The Royal Lineage of Our Noble and Gentle Families Together with their Paternal Ancestry (Volume 3).* Aylesbury: privately published by Hazell, Watson and Viney, n.d., 4to., original blue cloth over bevelled boards, neatly recased with new endpapers, pages (iv, family register), xvi, 367-462, interleaved, register and first 3 blank leaves filled with genealogy of Whitelock and Turner in mss., armorial bookplate of Revd. Henry Whitelock Turner relaid. R. F. G. Hollett & Son Antiquarian Booksellers 175 - 462 2011 £225

Foster, Marcia Lane *Let's Do It.* London: Collins, 1938, First edition; 4to., original cloth, dust jacket price clipped from top edge, pages 112, 4 colored plates and numerous drawings after chalk sketches. R. F. G. Hollett & Sons Antiquarian Booksellers 170 - 240 2011 £35

Foster, Michael *Hornby Dublo Trains. Hornby Dublo 1938-1964.* New Cavendish Books, 1991, Oblong 4to., original cloth, gilt, dust jacket, pages 416, 632 photos and diagrams. R. F. G. Hollett & Sons Antiquarian Booksellers 170 - 241 2011 £40

Foster, Roger *A Treatise on Federal Practice Including Practice in Bankruptcy, Admiralty, Patent Cases, Foreclosure of Railway Mortgages, Suits upon Claims Against the United States...* Chicago: 1901, Third edition; volumes, about 1600 pages, full law calf, very good. Bookworm & Silverfish 678 - 103 2011 $125

Foster, Stephen C. *I Will Be True to Thee.* New York: Waters, 1862, First edition; sheet music, 4to., 3 pages, disbound from a collection, paper cover printed in red and dark blue, little foxing, else very good. Second Life Books Inc. 174 - 153 2011 $65

Fougasse, Pseud. *...And the Gatepost.* London: Chatto & Windus, 1940, First edition; small 8vo., original pictorial boards, matching dust jacket (little rubbed), Pages xiv, with 8 color plates. R. F. G. Hollett & Son Antiquarian Booksellers General Catalogue Summer 2010 - 778 2011 £65

Fougasse, Pseud. *Both Small and Great Beasts.* Universities Federation for Animal Welfare, n.d., 1954, First edition; small 8vo., original pictorial boards, pages 16 illustrations. R. F. G. Hollett & Son Antiquarian Booksellers 175 - 463 2011 £30

Fougasse, Pseud. *The Good Tempered Pencil.* Max Reinhardt, 1956, First edition; original cloth, gilt, dust jacket price clipped, spine little faded, pages 226, cartoons, near fine. R. F. G. Hollett & Son Antiquarian Booksellers General Catalogue Summer 2010 - 158 2011 £50

Fougasse, Pseud. *A School of Purposes.* London: Methuen, 1946, First edition; Pages 48, illustrations in color, original yellow cloth, dust jacket corners trifle worn. R. F. G. Hollett & Son Antiquarian Booksellers General Catalogue Summer 2010 - 159 2011 £45

Foulds, Leonard H. *A Trial of Luck in South Africa.* Stoke-upon-Trent: Vyse & Hill, 1900, First edition; 8vo., pages 192, frontispiece, original black cloth, some slight cockling to lower joint, internally clean. J. & S. L. Bonham Antiquarian Booksellers Africa 4/20/2011 - 8880 2011 £145

A Fowl Alphabet. Easthampton: Cheloniidae Press, 1986, Issued in a regular edition of 150 copies in vellum backed marbled boards, a deluxe edition of 50 signed and numbered copies and a full vellum edition of 50 signed and numbered copies and full vellum edition of 26 copies, this number III of only 5 artist proof copies of the full vellum edition that has each plate signed by artist and numbered "AP III", there is no drawing mentioned in prospectus, printed on Rives paper french fold; 8vo., bound in full vellum by Gray Parrot, includes the alphabet bound in full vellum, seprate suite of proof plates and a blind alphabet housed in vellum backed chemise folder, all housed in vellum backed cloth case, as new with prospectus laid in, 26 wood engravings by Alan James Robinson, magnificent alphabet.   Aleph-Bet Books, Inc.   95 - 7   2011 $2500

Fowler, J. T. *Adamnani Vita S. Columbae.* Oxford: Clarendon Press, 1894, Pages lxxxvii, 202, (ii), 8, original quarter roan gilt, spine rather frayed at head, some pencilled notes and underlinings, distinguished trio of earlier historian owners, Gwilym Peredur Jones, F. Lindstead Downham and Geoffrey Martin.   R. F. G. Hollett & Son Antiquarian Booksellers   175 - 464   2011   £35

Fowler, James *On Mediaveal Representations of the Months and Seasons.*   J. B. Nichols and Sons, 1873, 4to., original roan backed boards, gilt, boards trifle soiled, edges little worn, pages 88, 3 color lithogaphs, few spots in places, scarce.   R. F. G. Hollett & Son Antiquarian Booksellers   175 - 465   2011   £75

Fowles, John *Cinderella.* London: 1974, First edition; illustrations by Sheilah Beckett, fine in prize clipped dust jacket, signed and dated by Fowles, also signed by Beckett.   Gemini   Fine Books & Arts, Ltd.   Art Reference & Illustrated Books: First Editions 2011 $75

Fowles, John *The Collector.* Boston: Little Brown, 1963, First edition; near fine, light bumping to extremities, dust jacket near fine, light edgewear, price clipped.   Bella Luna Books   May 29 2011 - t6387   2011 $82

Fowles, John *The Enigma of Stonehenge.* London: Jonathan Cape, 1980, First edition; fine, dust jacket near fine, small rub on front fold, color plates, inscribed and dated by Fowles for Michael Luveri 8 Oct. 1982.   Bella Luna Books   May 29 2011 - t6805   2011 $82

Fowles, John *The French Lieutenant's Woman.* London: Cape, 1969, First edition; pages 448, crown 8vo., original brown boards, backstrip gilt lettered, lightly faded backstrip panel to dust jacket, overall unusually nice condition, near fine.   Blackwell Rare Books   B166 - 146   2011   £250

Fowles, John *Introduction: Remembering Cruikshank.* Princeton: Princeton University Library Chronicle, 1974, Offprint from the Chronicle, reportedly fewer than 50 copies printed for author's use; signed by author, scarce, fine in stapled wrappers.   Ken Lopez Bookseller   154 - 55   2011 $450

Fowles, John *A Maggot.* Boston: 1985, First American edition; one of 360 copies signed by author, fine in slipcase.   Gemini Fine Books & Arts, Ltd.   Art Reference & Illustrated Books: First Editions 2011 $85

Fowles, John *A Maggot.* London: London Limited Editions, 1985, First edition, one of 500 copies signed by John Fowles; fine in tissue dust jacket.   Gemini Fine Books & Arts, Ltd.   Art Reference & Illustrated Books: First Editions 2011 $100

Fowles, John *Mantissa.* Boston: 1982, First American edition; 1/510 sigend copies, as new in slipcase.   Gemini Fine Books & Arts, Ltd.   Art Reference & Illustrated Books: First Editions 2011 $100

Fowles, John *Mantissa.* London: Jonathan Cape, 1982, First British edition; near fine, previous owner's bookplate, dust jacket fine, signed and dated by author on 7 Oct. 1982.   Bella Luna Books   May 29 2011 - t5461   2011 $82

Fox-Davies, Arthur Charles *A Complete Guide to Heraldry.* Nelson, 1969, Large thick 8vo., original cloth gilt, spine faded and rubbed, pictorial slipcase (edges worn, cracked and taped), pages xii, 513, with 10 color plates and numerous illustrations.   R. F. G. Hollett & Son Antiquarian Booksellers   General Catalogue Summer 2010 - 413   2011   £35

Fox, Carl *The Doll.* New York: Abrams, 1976, First edition; horizontal 4to., pages 343, copiously illustrated in color and black and white, photos, red velvet over boards, stamped in gilt, edges slightly soiled, otherwise nice in soiled dust jacket.   Second Life Books Inc.   174 - 154   2011 $75

Fox, Charles James *Fox and Pitt's Speeches in the House of Commons, on Tuesday, June 8, 1784...* London: printed for J. Debrett, opposite Burlington House, Piccadilly, 1784, First edition; half title, (4), vii, (1), 160 pages, disbound, good.   Anthony W. Laywood   May 26 2011 - 21592   2011 $143

Fox, Ebenezr *The Adventures of Ebenezer Fox in the Revolutionary War.* Boston: 1847, First edition; 12mo., 240 pages, each side of backstrip has repaired a 2 inch split, cover gilt bright, backstrip gilt very good, one leaf with horizontal tear.   Bookworm & Silverfish   669 - 14   2011 $75

Fox, Frank *Switzerland.* Adam and Charles Black, 1917, First re-issue; large 8vo., original pictorial grey cloth, gilt, pages xi, 203, with 64 color plates and map, neat inscription, otherwise very nice, bright copy.   R. F. G. Hollett & Son Antiquarian Booksellers   General Catalogue Summer 2010 - 1641   2011   £75

Fox, George *Gospel Truth Demonstrated in a Collection of Doctrinal Books Given Forth by that Faithful Minister of Jesus Christ George Fox.* London: printed and sold by T. Sowle, 1706, First edition; small folio, contemporary calf with spine label, upper hinge cracked, head and foot of spine rather worn, pages (xii), 1090, (vi), small dampstain to lower corner of page trifle soiled.   R. F. G. Hollett & Son Antiquarian Booksellers   175 - 468   2011   £250

Fox, George *A Journal or Historical Account of the Life, Travels, Sufferings, Christian Experiences...* London: printed by W. Richardson and S. Clark and sold Luke Hinde, 1765, Third edition; folio, modern half calf gilt with raised bands and spine label, pages lix, 679, (xxviii), few spots to title, excellent clean copy.   R. F. G. Hollett & Son Antiquarian Booksellers   175 - 470   2011   £450

Fox, George *A Journal or Historical Account of the Life, Travels, Sufferings, Christian Experiences and Labour of Love in the Work of the Ministry...* London: printed by W. Richardson and S. Clark and sold by Luke Hinde, 1765, Third edition; folio, modern full blind ruled calf, gilt, pages lix, 679, (xxviii), excellent, clean, sound copy with signature of Robert Coleman, inscribed "given to Edwin R. Ransome in 1871...".   R. F. G. Hollett & Son Antiquarian Booksellers 175 - 469   2011   £450

Fox, George *A Journal or Historical Account of the Life, Travels, Sufferings, Christian Experiences and Labour of Love...* Leeds: Anthony Pickard, 1836, 2 volumes, contemporary diced calf gilt, double spine labels, pages 556, 564, neat and attractive set.   R. F. G. Hollett & Son Antiquarian Booksellers   175 - 472   2011   £120

Fox, George E. *Excavations on the Site of the Roma City at Silchester, Hants.* London: printed by Nichols and Sons, 1891-1910, First edition; 19 volumes, 4to. printed blue wrappers, illustrations in black and white, decent set mostly very good or better, some earlier issues have edgewear and slight chipping, later issues (1896-1910) in excellent condition.   Any Amount of Books   May 26 2011 - A49581   2011 $503

Fox, R. Hingston *Dr. John Fothergill and His Friends: Chapters in Eighteenth Century Life.* London: Macmillan, 1919, 8vo., xxiv, 434 pages, frontispiece, 13 illustrations, original blue cloth, gilt stamped spine title, spine ends rubbed, ownership signature of H. Stewart, very good, from the Bern Dibner reference library, with Burndy bookplate. Jeff Weber Rare Books   161 - 153   2011 $85

Fox, Robert *The Culture of Science in France 1700-1900.* Aldershot: Brookfield: Variorum: Ashgate Pub. Co., 1992, 8vo., xii, various pagination, teal cloth, gilt stamped cover and spine tiles, fine,.   Jeff Weber Rare Books   161 - 154 2011 $120

Fox, Uffa *Uffa Fox's Second Book.* London: 1980, First edition; 376 pages, 4to., fine in fine dust jacket, over 300 photo illustrations.   Bookworm & Silverfish   678 - 140 2011 $100

Foy-Vaillant, Jean *Numismata Imperatorum Romanorum Praestantiora a Julio Caesare ad Postumum et Tyrannos...* Paris: Jean Jombert, 1692, 2 volumes, 4to., (12), 256, (8); (8), 397, (35) pages, last leaf blank, numerous engravings, contemporary calf, spine gilt in compartments, binding rubbed, spine gilt erased, lacks lettering piece, from the library of the Earls of Macclesfield at Shirburn Castle. Maggs Bros. Ltd.   1440 - 92   2011   £450

Franchere, Gabriel *Journal of a Voyage on the North West Coast of North America During the years 1811, 1812, 1813, 1814.* Toronto: Champlain Society, 1969, Limited to0 825 copies for members of the Society; large 8vo., very good, red cloth.   Barnaby Rudge Booksellers   Travel and Exploration - 016367   2011 $125

Francis Edwards Co. *Collection of 34 Francis Edwards Catalogs on Africa.* London: 1931-1959, 8vo., 1700 pages, very good.   Bookworm & Silverfish   666 - 1 2011 $450

Francis, Dick *Bonecrack.* London: Michael Joseph, 1971, First British edition; near fine, previous owner's name and address on front free endpapers, dust jacket near fine, no obvious flaws , just shows its age.   Bella Luna Books   May 29 2011 - t2016   2011 $137

Francis, Dick *Break In.* London: Michael Joseph, 1985, First British edition; near fine, heel of spine bumped, near fine dust jacket with light wear.   Bella Luna Books   May 29 2011 - 58664   2011 $82

Francis, Dick *Hot Money.* New York: 1987, First American edition, 1/250 signed copies; fine in fine slipcase. Gemini Fine Books & Arts, Ltd.   Art Reference & Illustrated Books: First Editions 2011 $70

Francis, Dick *Knock Down.* London: Michael Joseph, 1974, First British edition, true first; fine in fine dust jacket. Bella Luna Books   May 29 2011 - g8837   2011 $110

Francis, Dick *Shattered.* London: Michael Joseph, 2000, First British edition, true first, first printing; fine in fine dust jacket, signed by author.   Bella Luna Books   May 29 2011 - t1651   2011 $137

Francis, Grant R. *Scotland's Royal Line.* London: John Murray, 1928, First edition; original blue cloth, gilt, few slight marks, pages xiv, 350, (iv), 29 plates.   R. F. G. Hollett & Son Antiquarian Booksellers   175 - 474   2011   £35

Francis, James B. *Lowell Hydraulic Experiments.* New York: D. Van Nostrand, 1868, Small folio, 11,2 50 pages, 23 double page plates, contemporary three quarter calf and marbled boards, two leather labels, fine, inscribed presentation by author in 1891.   M & S Rare Books, Inc.   90 - 138   2011 $600

Francis, W. F. *Ilam Anastastic Drawing Society. A Series of Sketches to Illustrate Churches, Monastic Ruins, etc.* Ashbourne: 1855-, 1866-1867; 3 parts in 1, 4to., 3 titlepages and 17 plates, contemporary red morocco, spine gilt in compartments, morocco labl on upper cover, all edges gilt, nice.   Anthony W. Laywood   May 26 2011 - 19369   2011 $134

Frank, Elizabeth *True Stories; or Interesting Anecdotes of Children...* York: Longman, Hurst et al, 1810,   192 pages, decorative paper on boards, green morocco spine with blind embossed title, full page copper engraved frontispiece by C. Heath after Carbould, engraved imprint dated Jan 28 1811, some spotting at covers, fine.   Hobbyhorse Books   56 - 75   2011 $210

Frank, George *Ryedale and North Yorkshire Antiquities.* London: Elliot Stock and York: Sampson Bros., 1888, First edition; original decorated maroon cloth, gilt over bevelled boards, corner of top board rather damped, spine little faded, short nick to head, pages xxi 236, 14 text woodcuts, joints cracked, inscribed by author, scarce.   R. F. G. Hollett & Son Antiquarian Booksellers   177 - 309   2011   £85

Frank, Robert *The Americans.* New York: Grove Press Inc., 1959, First American edition; 8vo., pages (iv), vi, 170, 83 black and white photos printed in gravure, edges lightly toned, one gathering pulling but firm, original black cloth, gold lettering to spine, original dust jacket, black and white photo on upper panel and collage by Alfred Leslie on lower panel, toned with closed tears and creasing, loss to head of spine, staining to verso, inscribed by Frank.   Simon Finch Rare Books   Zero - 523   2011   £11,500

Frank, Robert *The Lines of My Hand.* Tokyo: Yugensha, 1972, First edition; one of only 1000 copies, fine in fine slipcase, photos.   Jeff Hirsch Books   ny 2010 2011 $4500

Frankenthal, Herman *Draping. (Window Display of Female Fashions).* Chicago: 1923,   148 pages, 72 full page illustrations, original binding.   Bookworm & Silverfish   678 - 69   2011 $500

Frankenthaler, Helen *Frankenthaler. Valentine for Mr. Wonderful.* New York: Rizzoli, 1996, First trade edition; signed by Frankenthaler, as new in like slipcase with gilt lettering, paste-on color illustration, fine reproductions of seven intaglio prints.   By the Book, L. C.   26 - 29   2011 $225

Franklin, Benjamin   1706-1790 *Experiments and Observations on Electricity.* London: printed for F. Newberry, 1774, Fifth and most complete edition; quarto, (2 blank) (1, half title), (1, blank), v, (1 ad), 514, (16, index) pages, 7 engraved plates, including frontispiece, few text diagrams, 3 of the plates folding, contemporary full calf, rebacked to style, original red morocco spine label lettered in gilt, corners and edges bit rubbed, title and preface leaves with some foxing, previous owner's pencil markings on front free endpapers, old ink signature, overall very good.   Heritage Book Shop   Holiday 2010 - 44   2011 $6750

Franklin, Benjamin   1706-1790 *Experiments and Observations on Electricity, Made at Philadelphia in America...*   London: for F. Newbery, 1774, Fifth and final edition; 4to., v, (1), 514, (16) pages, 7 engraved plates, several woodcut text illustrations, lacks half title, contemporary marbled paper covered boards, calf spine, very skillfully rebacked in period style, later endpapers, occasional foxing of both text and plates, some offsetting from few plates, light stains on H3-4 and 2M3-4, withal good copy.   Joseph J. Felcone Inc.   Fall Miscellany 2010 - 51   2011 $8500

Franklin, Benjamin   1706-1790 *The Writings of Benjamin Franklin.* New York: Haskell House, 1970, Facsimile of the 1905-1907 edition; 10 volumes, plates, charts, red cloth gilt stamped spine title, fore edge of volume II speckled, else near fine, from the Bern Dibner reference library, with Burndy bookplate.   Jeff Weber Rare Books   161 - 155 2011 $150

Franklin, John H. *The Militant Scout 1800-1861.* Cambridge: 1956, First edition; xi, 317 pages, fine in dust jacket with crumples at backstrip ends, few tears and one tape repair at bottom rear panel, inscribed and signed by author.   Bookworm & Silverfish   668 - 149   2011 $275

Franzen, Jonathan *The Corrections.* New York: FSG, 2001, First edition; near fine, light bumping to spine ends, near fine, dust jacket is fine, first state with erratum slip laid in, signed by author.   Bella Luna Books   May 29 2011 - t5741s   2011 $132

Franziska *The Merry Skibook.* New York: Transatlantic Arts, 1939, 4to., boards, light edge soil, else fine in soiled dust jacket, consisting of 17 panels that open to nearly 10 feet, each panel brightly illustrated in color by Franziska.   Aleph-Bet Books, Inc.   95 - 411   2011 $475

Fraser, Craig G. *Calculus and Analytical Mechanics in the Age of Enlightenment.* Aldershot and Brookfield: Variorum, 1997, 8vo., x, 308 pages, frontispiece, figures, light blue cloth, gilt stamped cover and spine titles, fine, from the Bern Dibner reference library, with Burndy bookplate. Jeff Weber Rare Books 161 - 157 2011 $120

Fraser, Donald *Winning a Primitive People: Sixteen Years Work among the Warlike Tribe of the Ngoni and the Senga and Tumbuka Peoples of Central Africa.* London: Seeley Service, 1914, First edition; 8vo., 32 pages, illustrations, 1 plate slightly frayed in margin, original blue decorative cloth. J. & S. L. Bonham Antiquarian Booksellers Africa 4/20/2011 - 6565 2011 £35

Fraser, George MacDonald *The Steel Bonnets.* London: Barrie & Jenkins, 1971, First edition; large 8vo., original cloth, gilt, dust jacket (edges trifle rubbed), pages (viii), 404, with 19 illustrations, maps on endpapers, plan and large folding map at end, few light stains to fore edge. R. F. G. Hollett & Son Antiquarian Booksellers 173 - 439 2011 £225

Fraser, James *A Hand Book for Travellers in Ireland, Descriptive of Its Scenery, Towns, Seats, Antiquities, etc.* Dublin: James McGlashan, 1849, Sixth thousand; xxiii (i) (1)-735 pages, folding map, good copy, original blind-stamped linen cloth with gilt steam engine blocked on upper cover, spine faded and some marking to covers, slight wear to head of spine. Ken Spelman Rare Books 68 - 172 2011 £85

Fraunce, Abraham *The Lawiers Logike, Exemplifying the Praecept of Logike by the Practise of the Common Lawe.* London: by William How for Thomas Gubbin and T. Newman, 1588, First edition; 4to, (1), 151, (i.e. 152) leaves including blank leaf 2A2, folding table, title within type ornament border, woodcut initials, mixed black letter and roman, full red gilt panelled morocco, edges gilt by Bedford, first two leaves lightly washed, short closed tear on table, blank corner of 2K4 replaced, else fine, clean, armorial bookplate of Sir Edward Priaulx and book label of Abel Berland. Joseph J. Felcone Inc. Fall Miscellany 2010 - 52 2011 $8000

Frazer, James *The Golden Bough.* London: Macmillan, 1933, Abridged edition; Pages xiv, 756, 4, original blue cloth, gilt, arms on upper board. R. F. G. Hollett & Son Antiquarian Booksellers General Catalogue Summer 2010 - 1172 2011 £30

Frazer, Lilly *The Singing Wood.* London: A. & C, Black, 1931, First edition; original pictorial pale blue cloth, dust jacket (closed edge tear). R. F. G. Hollett & Sons Antiquarian Booksellers 170 - 109 2011 £35

Frazier, Charles *Thirteen Moons.* New York: Random House, 2006, Limited to 1600 copies; fine, in fine pictorial slipcase, signed and numbered by author. Bella Luna Books May 29 2011 - t8090 2011 $82

Frazier, Ian *Dating Your Mom.* New York: FSG, 1986, First edition; fine in fine dust jacket, signed by author. Bella Luna Books May 29 2011 - t730 2011 $82

Frederic, Harold *The Market Place.* New York: Frederick A Stokes Co., 1899, First edition; half title, frontispiece, plates, original mustard pictorial cloth, spine darkened, slightly dulled, following hinges slightly cracked, Ladies Library Association, Port Huron label. Jarndyce Antiquarian Booksellers CXCI - 180 2011 £45

Frederick III, King of Denmark *The King of Denmark, His Declaration Concenring the English Merchants Ships Lying in Copenhagen.* Printed at Copehagen Anno 1653 and reprinted at London: for Henry Cripps and Lodowick Lloyd, 1653, First edition in English; 4to., 22 (2) pages, including final leaf C4, minute hole in C3 just touching couple of letters on recto, preserved in modern wrappers with printed title label on upper cover, very good, crisp copy. John Drury Rare Books 153 - 47 2011 £300

Freeman, Don *The Seal and the Slick.* New York: Viking Press, 1974, (1-5 code). First edition; oblong 4to., pictorial cloth, fine in slightly worn, near fine dust jacket, this copy has wonderful full page full color drawing of the seal sitting on a rock with water, trees, and mountains in the background, inscribed by author. Aleph-Bet Books, Inc. 95 - 240 2011 $1250

Freeman, Douglas Southall *R. E. Lee. A Biography.* New York & London: 1935, volumes 1 and 2 second edition, volumes 3 and 4 first edition; 4 volumes, volume 1 signed, red cloth over boards, gold spine and cover titles, frontispieces, illustrations, light fading to backstrips, light discoloration to fore edges, light soil to page tips, light foxing to extremities, volume 1 with some mottling to front cover, else very sturdy in good condition, clean content and sound binding. Bookworm & Silverfish 669 - 49 2011 $475

Freeman, Frederic *Mother Goose Comes to Portland.* Portland: Southworth Print Co., 1918, 12mo., cloth backed pictorial boards, nearly as new is original onion skin wrapper, illustrations in line by author. Aleph-Bet Books, Inc. 95 - 373 2011 $200

Freeman, Lydia *Pet of the Met.* New York: Viking, 1953, First edition; oblong 4to., cloth, fine in slightly worn dust jacket, color lithos on every page by Freeman, quite scarce. Aleph-Bet Books, Inc. 95 - 241 2011 $400

Freeman, Mary E. Wilkins *The Wind in the Rose-Bush and Other Stories of the Supernatural.* New York: Doubleday Page and Co., 1903, First edition; octavo, pages (1-8) (1-2) 3-237 (238-240) (note: last leaf blank), 8 inserted plates with illustrations by Peter Newell, original medium green cloth, front and spine panel stamped in dark green and white, pictorial paper inlay affixed to front cover. L. W. Currey, Inc. 124 - 186 2011 $250

Freeman, R. B. *Charles Darwin: a Companion.* Folkstone: Dawson, 1978, 8vo., 309 pages, text figures, green cloth, gilt stamped spine title, dust jacket, fine, from the Bern Dibner reference library, with Burndy bookplate. Jeff Weber Rare Books 161 - 108 2011 $75

Freeman's Address to the North Americans: Proving that Their Present Embarrassments are Owning to Their Federal Union, Their Sovereign States, Their Constitutions and Their Statements and Containing some Propositions for Relief. N.P.: 1846?, First edition; 8vo., 29 pages, uncut, modern wrappers. M & S Rare Books, Inc. 90 - 328 2011 $400

Freese, Stanley *Windmills and Millwrighting.* Cambridge: University Press, 1957, First edition; pages xvii, 168, woodcut title vignette, 35 plates and folding plan (edges little browned and chipped), original cloth, gilt, dust jacket, press cutting removed from flyleaf. R. F. G. Hollett & Son Antiquarian Booksellers 177 - 400 2011 £40

Freitas, Bernardino Jose De Senna *Uma Viagem ao Valle das Furans na Ilha de S. Muguel em Junho e 1840.* Lisboa: 1845, First edition; folio, xvi, 105 pages, 3 lithographed plates, several vignette illustrations in text, later half mottled calf, plates foxed, largely in margins, extremities of binding rubbed. Joseph J. Felcone Inc. Fall Miscellany 2010 - 53 2011 $1200

Freke, John *The Princes of the Several Stocks, Anuuities and Other Publick Securities &c with the Course of Exchange. From Saturday March 26th 1715 to Friday June 22d 1716.* London: sold by author at his office over against Jonathan's Coffee-House in Exchange Alley, 1716, 8vo., general titlepage (blank verso) + dedication leaf (blank verso), followed by 104 + 26 single sheet price lists, each 2 pages on facing leaves, some imprints cropped at foot, some printed on thick paper, contemporary panelled calf, skillfully rebacked and labelled to match, very good, from the 19th century library of Hugh Cecil 5th Earl of Lonsale, with his armorial bookplate, and from the early 20th century library of Harold Charles Drayton, the financier, exceptionally rare. John Drury Rare Books 153 - 49 2011 £3500

Frelinghuysen, Alice Cooney *American Porcelain 1770-1920.* New York: Metropolitan Museum of Art, 1989, First edition; large 4to., original cloth, gilt, dust jacket, pages xv, 320, with 221 illustrations. R. F. G. Hollett & Son Antiquarian Booksellers General Catalogue Summer 2010 - 161 2011 £65

Fremantle, Francis E. *Impressions of a Doctor in Kahki.* London: John Murray, 1901, First edition; 8vo., pages xvi, 549, illustrations, page torn in margin due to careless opening, original red decorative cloth, vignette on front cover, red cross flag, sprung but hinges intact, scarce. J. & S. L. Bonham Antiquarian Booksellers Africa 4/20/2011 - 8318 2011 £120

Fremont, John Charles 1813-1890 *Memoirs of My Life.* Chicago: Belford, Clarke & Co., 1886-1887, First edition, first issue; original pictorial wrappers, issued in 10 parts, 655 pages, 82 full page illustrations, 7 maps, first issue dated Sept. 1 1886 and last Jan. 1887, bound volume, which has been considered the first has a titlepage date of 1887, rare original prospectus laid in, some chipping and light soiling to wrappers, some minor spine repairs, very good, rare issue, protected in custom stiff 4 point case inserted into matching slipcase with gilt stamped morocco label on spine. Buckingham Books May 26 2011 - 23491 2011 $8500

Fremont, John Charles 1813-1890 *Report of the Exploring Expedition to the Rocky Mountains in the Year 1842 and to Oregon and North California in Years 1843-1844.* Washington: Gales and Seaton, 1845, First edition, 2nd issue; early binding for Francis Preston Blair's library of red pebbled buckram with floral wreath designed medallion in gilt on front and rear covers, title in gilt on spine, centered in wreath on front cover and stamped in gilt is "F.P. Blair", 693 pages, 22 lithographed plates, 5 maps, 3 folding with large folding map housed in separate matching red slipcase, professionally rebacked and is now too thick to restore in original volume. Buckingham Books May 26 2011 - 25731 2011 $6250

French Studies. 1966-2001, Volume 20/1-Vol. 55/4; Jan. 1966-Oct. 2001, 144 issues complete, French Studies Bulletin Nos. 1-82 (Winter 81/2-Spring 2002), lacking only no. 24, but including introductory special members issues, these ran to 24 pages each, 226 issues all very good indeed. I. D. Edrich May 26 2011 - 99154 2011 $1518

French, Arthur W. *Stereotomy.* New York: 1902, vii, 155 pages, 22 folding plates, index and 14 page publisher catalog, original brown cloth, very good. Bookworm & Silverfish 667 - 158 2011 $175

Frere, Sheppard *Britannia. A History of Roman Britain.* BCA, 1973, Large 8vo., original cloth, gilt, dust jacket, edges little worn, pages xiv, 432, with 32 pages of plates. R. F. G. Hollett & Son Antiquarian Booksellers General Catalogue Summer 2010 - 603 2011 £35

Freshman, Charles *The Jews and the Israelties: Their Religion, Philosophy, Traditions and Literature, in Connection with their Past and Present Condition, and their Future Prospects.* Toronto: A. Dredge & Co., 1870, First edition; tall 8vo., 26, 456 pages, errata slip, original cloth, one hinge coming open. M & S Rare Books, Inc. 90 - 200 An English and Hebrew $275

Freud, Sigmund 1856-1939 *Aus der Geschichte Einer Infantilen Neuroseaus.* Leipzig: Internationaler Psychoanalytischer Verlag, 1924, First edition in book form; 8vo., pages 131, (1) contents, leaves lightly browned, otherwise unblemished, black half smooth grain cloth and grey boards, gilt lettering to spine, slight rubbing to extremities. Simon Finch Rare Books Zero - 143 2011 £125

Freud, Sigmund 1856-1939 *Drei Abhandlungen zur Sexualtheorie.* Leipzig: and Vienna: Franz Deuticke, 1905, First edition; large 8vo., pages (ii), 84, uncut, original blue grey paper wrappers, lettered in black on front and rear wrappers, slight shelfwear, some restoration to spine excellent copy. Simon Finch Rare Books Zero - 140 2011 £3750

Freud, Tom Seidmann *Das Buch der Dinge: Ein Bilderbuch fur ganz kleine Kinder. (A Book of Things: a Picture Book for Very Young Children).* Berlin: Mauritius, 1922, First edition; oblong 4to., cloth backed pictorial boards, corners worn, binding strengthened, some edge chipping and few mends, due the paper used all copies of this title have some edge chipping, very good, 16 hand colored full page illustrations printed on one side of paper only, rare. Aleph-Bet Books, Inc. 95 - 243 2011 $3500

Frey, Albert R. *Dictionary of Numismatic Names.* New York: Barnes and Noble, 1947, Pages x, 312, 94, 4to., original cloth, gilt. R. F. G. Hollett & Son Antiquarian Booksellers General Catalogue Summer 2010 - 162 2011 £45

Frick, Johann Georg *Commentatio de Druidis Occidentalium Populorum Philosophia...* Ulm: Daniel Bartholomaei & Son, 1744, 4to., (20) 226, (2 blank) pages, engraved frontispiece, contemporary vellum backed decorated paper boards, from the library of the Earls of Macclesfield at Shirburn Castle. Maggs Bros. Ltd. 1440 - 93 2011 £500

Friedman, Mildred *Gehry Talks: Architecture + Process.* New York: Rizzoli, 1999, First edition; signed by Gehry, 4to., 297 pages, fine in like dust jacket. By the Book, L. C. 26 - 30 2011 $295

Friedman, Milton *Income from Independent Professional Practice.* New York: National Bureau of Economic Research, 1945, First edition; 8vo. original publisher's blue cloth lettered gilt at spine, pages xxxiii, 599, tables, charts, from the library of Cambridge economist Sir Richard Stone (1913-1991), slight scuffing to rear boards, else very good+, overall ownership stamp of Stone. Any Amount of Books May 29 2011 - A67478 2011 $255

The Friend of Chastity; or an Inquiry into the Evils of Unchastity and the Means of Its Removal. Dover: F. W. Baptist Printing Estab., 1846, First edition; 16mo., 142, (1) pages, errata, original cloth. M & S Rare Books, Inc. 90 - 377 2011 $325

The Friend of the People: Shewing What Will Be the End of the British Nation and Ought to be Read by Every Man In It. London: printed for the benefit of the people and sold by Smith, Portsmouth Street, Lincoln's Inn Fields and all other booksellers and newscarriers, n.d., 1795?, Fourth edition of first part, first edition of second part; 2 parts in one volume, 8vo., drop-head titles, 12, 12 pages, some dust soiling and minor marginal fraying, neatly bound in old style quarter calf gilt, good, uncut. John Drury Rare Books 153 - 105 2011 £375

The Friendly Bears - Little Boy Blue and Little Bo Peep Fairy Story No. 2. Chicago: John Puhl Products, circa, 1905, 6 x 3 1/2 inches, full color pictorial covers with light dusting and some splitting to spine, four panel panorama that offers full color illustrated story. Jo Ann Reisler, Ltd. 86 - 22 2011 $150

Frisbie, W. A. *ABC Mother Goose.* Chicago: Rand McNally & Co., 1905, First edition; small folio, tan pictorial cloth, rather bright, fresh copy, pictures by Charles L. Bartholomew. Jo Ann Reisler, Ltd. 86 - 5 2011 $475

Frith, W. P. *John Leech, His Wife and Work.* London: Bentley, 1891, First edition; portrait and numerous illustrations, 2 volumes, good copy in contemporary half morocco, raised bands and gilt lettered spines, all edges gilt, joints and corners little rubbed. Ken Spelman Rare Books 68 - 91 2011 £125

Froissart, Jean *Chronicles of England, France and Spain and the Adjoining Countries from the Latter Part of the Reign of Edward II.* London: Henry G. Bohn, 1857, Color lithographed additional titlepage, wood engraved illustrations in text, paper lightly toned, pages xlvii (i.e . xlix), (i), 768; xiv, 733, large 8vo., contemporary olive green calf, boards bordered with double gilt fillet, central gilt stamp of Dulwich College Upper School on front boards, sometime rebacked in brown morocco, backstrip divided by double gilt rules, green morocco label in second compartment and red in fourth, rest with central gilt stamps of armour, marbled endpapers, all edges gilt, some old scrapes and marks, corners renewed, sound. Blackwell Rare Books B166 - 40 2011 £90

From Korti to Khartum. Edinburgh and London: William Blackwood, 1886, 8vo., publisher's original red cloth, worn at top and bottom of spine,. Barnaby Rudge Booksellers Travel and Exploration - 019695 2011 $95

Fronsperger, Leonhard *Kriegsbuch... Jetzt von Neuem Gemehrt und Gebessert Usw.* Frankfurt: J. Feyerabend for the heirs of S. Feyerabend, 1596, 3 parts, folio, engraved plates, woodcuts, late 18th century tree calf, occasional spotting, very handsome, from the library of the Earls of Macclesfield at Shirburn Castle.   Maggs Bros. Ltd. 1440 - 94 2011 £2000

Frost, Robert Lee   1874-1963 *A Boy's Will.* London: David Nutt, 1913, Of approximately 1000 copies, fewer than 350 copies were issued, first edition, first issue; small 8vo., original bronze brown pebbled cloth, very fine, half morocco folding box. James S. Jaffe Rare Books May 26 2011 - 20895 2011 $12,500

Frost, Robert Lee   1874-1963 *A Boy's Will.* London: David Nutt, 1913, First edition; octavo, signed by Frost, with line from poem "Mowing" in author's hand, original beige printed wrappers, lettered in black with four petal flower stamp. Heritage Book Shop Booth A12 51st NY International Antiquarian Book Fair April 8-10 2011 - 57 2011 $3850

Frost, Robert Lee   1874-1963 *Mountain Interval.* New York: Holt, 1924, third edition; signed by Frost and dated Amherst 1927, little wear to corners and spine ends, hinge starting, very good, without dust jacket. Ken Lopez Bookseller 154 - 57 2011 $750

Frost, Robert Lee   1874-1963 *North of Boston.* London: David Nutt, 1914, First edition, one of 350 copies bound in coarse green linen out of a total edition of 1000 copies; 8vo., original green cloth, fine, preserved in black cloth slipcase with chemise, presentation copy from author for Earle Bernheimer. James S. Jaffe Rare Books May 26 2011 - 20897 2011 $15,000

Frost, Robert Lee   1874-1963 *West-Running Brook.* New York: Henry Holt and Co., 1928, First edition, no. 750 of 980 copies; signed by author on colophon page, 8vo., all 4 plates signed in pencil by artist, 58 pages, original publisher's floral printed boards and green cloth spine lettered, gilt, faint rubbing at corners, otherwise about fine. Any Amount of Books May 29 2011 - A75421 2011 $383

Frost, S. Annie *The Ladies' Guide to Needle Work, Embroidery etc.* New York: Ladies' Floral Cabinet Co., n.d. circa, 1877, Pages 158, (ii), with 122 illustrations, original pictorial wrappers (worn and torn, edges very slightly chipped), short edge tear to first leaf of text. R. F. G. Hollett & Son Antiquarian Booksellers General Catalogue Summer 2010 - 163 2011 £45

Fry, Elizabeth *Memoir of the Life of Elizabeth Fry, with Extracts from Her Journal and Letters.* London: Charles Gilpin and John Hatchard and Son, 1847, First edition; pages xii, 495; (iv), viii, 524, (iv), 2 engraved portraits, little stiff in joints from damp, joints of volume I cracking, 2 volumes, original blindstamped cloth, gilt little damped. R. F. G. Hollett & Son Antiquarian Booksellers 175 - 489 2011 £140

Fryer, Jane Eayre *The Mary Frances Cook Book or Adventures Among the Kitten People.* Philadelphia: John C. Winston, 1912, 4to., 175 pages, blue cloth, pictorial paste on, fine in dust jacket, edges frayed, 1 inch piece off spine, illustrations by Jane Allen Boyer with color frontispiece plus a profusion of full page and in text color illustrations by Margaret Hays, great copy in are dust jacket. Aleph-Bet Books, Inc. 95 - 244 2011 $600

Fryer, John *A New Account of East India and Persia in Eight Letters.* New York: William Elliott, 1810, First edition; small folio, with total of 9 engraved plates, full period paneled calf. Heritage Book Shop Booth A12 51st NY International Antiquarian Book Fair April 8-10 2011 - 58 2011 $5000

Fuhrman, Chris *The Dangerous Lives of Altar Boys.* Athens: University of Georgia Press, 1994, First edition; near fine, light bumping to spine, fine in dust jacket. Bella Luna Books May 29 2011 - m1039 2011 $88

Fukukita, Yasunosuke *Cha-No-Yu. Tea Cult of Japan.* Tokyo: Maruzen Co., 1932, First edition; original multi color patterned cloth, gilt, dust jacket, slipcase with pictorial onlay, edges rather rubbed and stained, pages 112, xxxvii, top edge gilt, with 27 plates and illustrations, running heads in green Chinese calligraphy. R. F. G. Hollett & Son Antiquarian Booksellers 175 - 490 2011 £140

A Full and True Account of a Dreadful Fire that Lately Broke Out in the Pope's Breeches. London: J. Baker, 1713, First edition; folio, later brown wrappers, bit worn and soiled, bookplate to inner cover, moderate soiling, short closed tear to foot near gutters (well away from text), untrimmed, wide margins. Dramatis Personae Booksellers 106 - 5 2011 $1250

Fuller, Andrew C. *A Reprint of Legal Notes on Motoring as Published from Time to Time in the Official Journal of the Royal Automobile Club of South Africa.* Cape Town: Edina Press, 1949, Original half calf gilt, pages 412. R. F. G. Hollett & Son Antiquarian Booksellers 175 - 491 2011 £45

Fuller, Emeline L. *Left by the Indians: Story of My Life.* Mt. Vernon: Hawk-eye Steam Print, 1892, First edition; 12mo., original light blue printed wrappers (2), 40, (1) pages, 3 portrait on 2 conjugate leaves on coated stock, tiny chip about quarter inch long to spine panel, else near fine in transparent protective dust jacket, housed in blue quarter leather and cloth slipcase with raised bands and gold stamping on spine panel.   Buckingham Books   May 26 2011 - 20488   2011 $4500

Fuller, Thomas *The Church History of Britain from the Birth of Jesus Christ Until the Year MDCXLVIII.* London: printed for John Williams, 1655, First edition; folio, 20th century full calf gilt over heavy boards, little scratched, pages (vi), 40, (i, blank), 427, (vi), 235, (i, blank), (vi), 237, (i, blank), (v), (i, blank), 172, 22, (xix index), (i, blank), fine folding plan, divisional titles, 4 engraved plates, occasional spot or stain, short worm track to lower margins of few leaves toward end, otherwise excellent, clean and sound copy.   R. F. G. Hollett & Son Antiquarian Booksellers   175 - 492   2011   £950

Fulton, Robert *Torpedo War and Submarine Explosions.* New York: Williamn Elliott, 1810, First edition; oblong folio, 5 plates, first two leaves bit short, issued in marbled wrappers.   Heritage Book Shop   Booth A12 51st NY International Antiquarian Book Fair April 8-10 2011 - 59   2011 $17,500

Fun and Fantasy: a Book of Drawings... London: Methuen, 1927, Limited to 150 numbered copies only; 50 for America (this being #27) signed by artist, printed on handmade paper, 8 lovely color plates plus a profusion of wonderful black and whites by E. H. Shepard, folio, cloth backed decorative boards, fine.   Aleph-Bet Books, Inc.   95 - 532   2011 $850

Funny Things Doughboys Tell. Racine: circa, 1918, Only edition; 64 pages, 12mo., original binding.   Bookworm & Silverfish   666 - 200   2011 $125

Furness & District Year Book for 1924. Barrow in Furness: The Barrow News and Mail, 1924, original cloth backed printed boards, little soiled, edges faded, pages 478 diary section (unused), illustrations and 80 ad pages, scarce.   R. F. G. Hollett & Son Antiquarian Booksellers General Catalogue Summer 2010 - 1411   2011   £95

Furness & District Year Book for 1930. Barrow-in-Furness: The Barrow News and Mail, 1930, Original red wrappers, trifle used, pages 518, illustrations and 80 ad pages, scarce.   R. F. G. Hollett & Son Antiquarian Booksellers   General Catalogue Summer 2010 - 1412   2011   £95

Furness & District Year Book for 1932. Barrow in Furness: Barrow News and Mail, 1932, Modern red cloth gilt, pages 504, illustrations, 72 ad pages, last few leaves rather worn, final leaf taped, scarce.   R. F. G. Hollett & Son Antiquarian Booksellers   General Catalogue Summer 2010 - 1413   2011   £85

Furness and District Year Book for 1934. Barrow-in-Furness: The Barrow News and Mail, 1934, Original red wrappers little worn, pages 460 with illustrations and 66 ad pages, top margins stained towards end, scarce.   R. F. G. Hollett & Son Antiquarian Booksellers   173 - 454   2011   £85

Furness and District Year Book for 1935. Barrow-in-Furness: Barrow News and Mail, 1935, Modern red cloth gilt, pages 7-468, illustrations, numerous ads pages, lacks first 6 leaves and final leaves, top corners worn and defective at beginning and end, very scarce.   R. F. G. Hollett & Son Antiquarian Booksellers   173 - 455   2011   £75

Furness & District Year Book and Directory for 1950-1951. Barrow-in-Furness: Barrow News and Mail, 1950, Modern red cloth, original wrappers bound in, pages 588, illustrations and 90 pages ads, very good, scarce.   R. F. G. Hollett & Son Antiquarian Booksellers   General Catalogue Summer 2010 - 1415   2011   £95

A Furness Military Chronicle. Ulverston: Kitchin & Co., 1937, First (only) edition; very nice, clean copy, tall 8vo., original green cloth gilt, spine and front board lightly faded, pages (vi), 282, (iii, subscribers), uncut with frontispiece, very nice, clean, with original ALS from publishers dated 1944 offering a copy of the book loosely inserted, very scarce.   R. F. G. Hollett & Son Antiquarian Booksellers   173 - 399   2011   £350

Furness Year Book. Fifth Annual. Ulverston: H. W. Mackereth, 1898, Pages 500, 2 folding plans, illustrations and ads, original cloth, gilt, little rubbed and soiled.   R. F. G. Hollett & Son Antiquarian Booksellers   173 - 444   2011   £120

Furness Year Book. Sixth Annual. Ulverston: H. W. Mackereth, 1899, Original cloth gilt, extremities trifle rubbed and faded, pages 505-1000, folding map numerous illustrations and ads, very good.   R. F. G. Hollett & Son Antiquarian Booksellers   General Catalogue Summer 2010 - 1400   2011   £140

Furness Year Book. Eighth Annual. Ulverston: H. W. Mackereth, 1901, Original printed cloth gilt, little bubbled and faded, pages 343, double page map, numerous illustrations and ads.   R. F. G. Hollett & Son Antiquarian Booksellers   General Catalogue Summer 2010 - 1401   2011   £100

Furness Year Book. Ninth Annual. Ulverston: H. W. Mackereth, 1902, Original cloth backed printed boards, pages 313, numerous illustrations and ads, hinges trifle pulled, very good.   R. F. G. Hollett & Son Antiquarian Booksellers   General Catalogue Summer 2010 - 1042   2011   £85

Furness Year Book. Tenth Annual. Ulverston: H. W. Mackereth, 1903, Original cloth backed printed boards, pages 273, numerous illustrations and ads, jonts cracked. R. F. G. Hollett & Son Antiquarian Booksellers   General Catalogue Summer 2010 - 1403   2011   £85

Furness Year Book. Eleventh Annual. Ulverston: H. W. Mackereth, 1904, Original cloth backed printed boards, edges little bruised in places, pages 274, color frontispiece, folding plan and numerous illustrations and ads, excellent copy.   R. F. G. Hollett & Son Antiquarian Booksellers   173 - 448   2011   £80

Furness Year Book. Twelfth Annual. Ulverston: H. W. Mackereth, 1905, Original cloth backed printed boards, pages 266, folding plan folding map, 2 color plates and numerous illustrations and ads, very nice, clean, sound. R. F. G. Hollett & Son Antiquarian Booksellers   General Catalogue Summer 2010 - 1405   2011   £95

Furness Year Book. Fourteenth Annual. Ulverston: W. Holmes, 1907, Original cloth backed printed boards, upper board little faded, pages 271, folding maps, numerous portraits, illustrations and ads, staples rather rusted, excellent copy.   R. F. G. Hollett & Son Antiquarian Booksellers   General Catalogue Summer 2010 - 1406   2011   £75

Furness Year Book. Fifteenth Annual. Ulverston: W. Holmes, 1908, Original cloth backed printed boards, 279 pages, folding map, numerous portraits, illustrations and ads, fore-edge to front flyleaf little worn, joints just cracking. R. F. G. Hollett & Son Antiquarian Booksellers   General Catalogue Summer 2010 - 1409   2011   £85

Furness Year Book. Sixteenth Annual. Ulverston: W. Holmes, 1909, Original cloth backed printed boards, little soiled, 287 pages, folding map, numerous portraits, illustrations and ads, fore-edge of front flyleaf little worn, joints just cracking.   R. F. G. Hollett & Son Antiquarian Booksellers   General Catalogue Summer 2010 - 1410   2011   £75

Furness, William   *History of Penrith from the Earliest Record to the Present Time.*   Penrith: William Furness, 1894, First edition; original maroon limp roan gilt, spine little creased, defective at head and repaired, pages viii, 376, all edges gilt, frontispiece, numerous illustrations.   R. F. G. Hollett & Son Antiquarian Booksellers   173 - 443   2011   £150

Furniss, Harry   *The By Ways and Queer Ways of Boxing.*   London: Harrison & Sons, 1919, First edition; 4to., half title, engraved title, illustrations, date in blue ink on title, endpapers replaced, original green pictorial cloth, bevelled boards, few marks.   Jarndyce Antiquarian Booksellers   CXCI - 182   2011   £160

Furniss, Harry   *Pen and Pencil in Parliament.*   London: Sampson Low Marston & Co., 1897, First edition; large 4to., original pictorial blue cloth, extremities rather worn, pages vii, 198, with frontispiece and illustrations, joints just cracking, but very good.   R. F. G. Hollett & Son Antiquarian Booksellers   175 - 493   2011   £75

Furst, Herbert   *The Modern Woodcut.*   London: John Lane, Bodley Head, 1924, Half title, color frontispiece and plates, illustrations, original light buckram, blocked and lettered in black, very good.   Jarndyce Antiquarian Booksellers   CXCI - 183   2011   £125

Furst, Herbert   *The Modern Woodcut, a Study of the Evolution of the Craft.*   London: John Lane, 1924, First edition; 4to., 271 pages, over 200 illustrations in black and white, 16 plates in color, good, original decorative cloth, covers little rubbed.   Ken Spelman Rare Books   68 - 112   2011   £50

Fyleman, Rose   *Fifty-One New Nursery Rhymes.*   London: Methuen & Co., 1931, First edition; oblong 4to., original cloth backed pictorial boards, corners little bumped, pages viii, 99, illustrations by Dorothy Nurroughes.   R. F. G. Hollett & Sons Antiquarian Booksellers   170 - 244   2011   £40

Fyleman, Rose   *The Merry-Go-Round.*   Blackwell, 1923-1928, First edition; v. 2/1.3-v.4/4.7.10-v.5/10.12v.6/12, together 45 issues, mostly in original pictorial wrappers in very good condition.   I. D. Edrich   May 26 2011 - 99449   2011 $1174

Fyleman, Rose   *The Rainbow Cat and Other Stories.*   London: Methuen, 1922, First edition; original orange cloth gilt, top margins little dusty, pages vii, 120, 6, scarce. R. F. G. Hollett & Sons Antiquarian Booksellers   170 - 245   2011   £50

Fyleman, Rose   *The Sunny Book.*   Oxford University Press, n.d., 1918, First edition; original embossed pictorial boards, top edge gilt of upper board dusty and spotted, head of backstrip torn and bruised pages (48), 12 full page color plates by Millicent Sowerby, scarce.   R. F. G. Hollett & Sons Antiquarian Booksellers   170 - 642   2011   £95

G

Gag, Wanda *Gone is Gone.* New York: Coward McCann, 1935, First edition; 12mo., green cloth, fine in lightly soiled and worn dust jacket, illustrations by Gag, with color frontispiece plus black and whites one very page, very scarce, nice. Aleph-Bet Books, Inc. 95 - 248 2011 $450

Gag, Wanda *Millions of Cats.* New York: Coward McCann, 1928, Limited to 250 numbered copies; signed by author and containing original wood engraving also by Gag, oblong small 4to., pictorial boards, fine in original publisher's slipcase with pictorial label (edges neatly reinforced), rare in limited edition, beautifully illustrated. Aleph-Bet Books, Inc. 95 - 245 2011 $7500

Gage, Andrew Thomas *A Bicentenary History of the Linnean Society of London.* London: Academic Press, 1988, First edition; 8vo., ix, 242 pages, double color frontispiece, illustrations, blue cloth, gilt stamped spine title, dust jacket, fine, from the Bern Dibner reference library, with Burndy bookplate. Jeff Weber Rare Books 161 - 160 2011 $70

Gaier, Claude *Four Centuries of Liege Gunmaking.* Liege: Eugene Wahle, 1985, Second edition; folio original green leather cloth, gilt, dust jacket pages 287, with 135 color plates and 380 illustrations, scarce. R. F. G. Hollett & Son Antiquarian Booksellers General Catalogue Summer 2010 - 164 2011 £195

Gailbraith, John Kenneth *Name Dropping: From F.D.R.* Norwalk: Easton Press, 1999, Limited edition, 451 of 1050 copies; signed by author on limitation page, leather with gold titles and decorations, all edges gilt, silk endpapers and ribbon bookmark, "A note about" card and signed certificate of authenticity folded in, very clean and tight, 194 pages, fine. G. H. Mott Bookseller May 26 2011 - 37085 2011 $275

Gaiman, Neil *Anasi Boys.* New York: William Morrow, 2005, First edition; fine in fine dust jacket, signed and dated Sept. 27, 2005. Bella Luna Books May 29 2011 - k104 2011 $82

Gaiman, Neil *The Graveyard Bone, Adult Version.* London: Bloomsbury, 2008, First edition; fine in fine dust jacket. Bella Luna Books May 29 2011 - t9224 2011 $110

Gaines, Ernest J. *A Lesson Before Dying.* New York: Knopf, 1993, First edition; near fine, light rubbing to cloth, dust jacket near fine, light soiling, small first printing. Bella Luna Books May 29 2011 - t1377 2011 $82

Gale, Elizabeth *Circus Babies.* Chicago: Rand McNally, 1930, Square 4to., cloth, 100 pages, fine full page and partial page color illustrations by John Dukes McKee. Aleph-Bet Books, Inc. 95 - 156 2011 $200

Gale, Norman *Songs for Little People.* London: Constable, 1896, First edition; original pictorial light brown ribbed cloth gilt, corners trifle bruised, pages viii, 111, (ii), top edges gilt with tissue guarded pictorial title in yellow and black and black and white drawings, some full page, scarce. R. F. G. Hollett & Sons Antiquarian Booksellers 170 - 248 2011 £140

Gale, Norman *With Louis Wain in Pussyland.* London: Tuck, n.d. circa, 1919, Folio, stiff pictorial card covers, top die-cut in a cat shape, small rubbing areas to covers, else very good+, illustrations by Lois Wain, 4 large and incredible full page color illustrations, nice copy, rare, fragile Wain item. Aleph-Bet Books, Inc. 95 - 582 2011 $1650

Gale, Roger *Registrum Honoris De Richmond Exhibens Terrarum & Villarum.* Londini: Impensis R. Gosling, 1722, Large paper copy, folio, pages (ii), xxxv, (i), 106, (xxvi), 286, (xxx) + folding engraved map, one extending engraved plate, another 8 engraved plates and 6 extending plates of pedigrees, lacking the list of subscribers leaf, early 19th century calf, boards sided with 'French Shelf' marbled paper, 1970's renewal of leather with half reversed calf by John Henderson (spotted and lightly browned, old boards scuffed), armorial and masonic bookplate of "Robt. Lakeland" and inscription "from Major Sir Edw. Coates' Library", from the collection of Christopher Ernest Weston 1947-2010. Unsworths Booksellers 24 - 95 2011 £400

Galiffe, Jacques Augustin *Italy and His Inhabitants, an Account of a Tour in that Country in 1816 and 1817.* London: John Murray, 1820, First edition; half titles, errata slips in volumes 1 and 2, closed tear on 2 H4 of volume 1, xvi,4 53, (1); xv, 475, (1) pages, 19th century cloth backed marbled boards, spines lettered gilt, bookplates of J. B. and Michael Bury, nice, clean copy. Anthony W. Laywood May 26 2011 - 21007 2011 $461

Galilei, Galileo 1564-1642 *Dialogue on the Great World System: in the Salusbury Translation.* Chicago: University of Chicago Press, 1953, 8vo., lviii, 505 pages, teal cloth, gilt stamped spine title, dust jacket, jacket lightly chipped, very good, from the Bern Dibner reference library, with Burndy bookplate. Jeff Weber Rare Books 161 - 162 2011 $65

Galilei, Galileo 1564-1642 *Mathematical Discourses Concerning Two New Sciences Relating to Mechanicks and Local Motion in Four Dialogues.* London: J. Hooke, 1730, Second edition in English; 4to., xi, (1), 497, (3) pages, red and black titlepage, table, 207 woodcut text figures, errata leaf (contemporaneously struck thru with ink lines), 2 pages of additional titles printed by J. Hooke, pagination error pages 361-368 (as usual) numbers omitted, contemporary full panelled calf, raised bands, gilt stamped spine title, neatly rebacked, corners restored, very good, bookplate of E. N. Da C. Andrade.   Jeff Weber Rare Books   161 - 163   2011 $36,000

Gallagher, Tess *The Lover of Horses.* New York: Harper & Row, 1986, First edition; tiny lower corner bumps, else fine in fine dust jacket, inscribed by author to Raymond Carver's British editor and publisher, laid in is newspaper clipping announcing memorial reading and hand drawn map of Port Angeles WA, tiny lower corner bumps, else fine in fine dust jacket.   Ken Lopez Bookseller   154 - 58   2011 $200

Gallagher, Tess *Moon Crossing Bridge.* St. Paul: Graywolf, 1992, First edition; fine in very near fine dust jacket with mild foxing to verso, inscribed by author to Raymon Carver's British editor and publisher.   Ken Lopez Bookseller   154 - 59   2011 $200

Gallaher, James *The Western Sketch-Book.* New York: 1850, First edition; 408 pages, crimson cloth, all gilt bright, gilt abundant backstrip which has been reglued on right side, all edges gilt.   Bookworm & Silverfish   678 - 5   2011 $72

Gallini, Giovanni Andrea *A Treatise on the Art of Dancing.* London: printed for the author and sold by R. Dodsley (and 2 others)...., 1772, (5), x-xvi, (1), 18-292 pages, fine folding engraved plate, 8vo., slight crease in blank margin, small paper flaw in margin of one leaf not affecting text, very nicely bound in recent quarter sprinkled calf, gilt banded spine, red morocco label, marbled boards, vellum tips, fine, clean copy.   Jarndyce Antiquarian Booksellers   CXCI - 184   2011   £950

Galouye, Daniel Francis *The Lost Perception.* London: Victor Gollancz Ltd., 1966, First edition; octavo, boards.   L. W. Currey, Inc.   124 - 211   2011 $150

Galsworthy, John 1867-1933 *The Forsyte Saga.* London: Heinemann, 1936, Pages 1104, contemporary three quarter calf gilt by Sotheran, corners and edges little rubbed and darkened, extending genealogy, top edge gilt. R. F. G. Hollett & Son Antiquarian Booksellers   General Catalogue Summer 2010 - 784   2011   £45

Galsworthy, John 1867-1933 *A Modern Comedy.* London: Heinemann, 1936, Pages 1088, contemporary three quarter calf gilt by Sotheran, corners and edges little rubbed and darkened, top edge gilt, extending genealogy. R. F. G. Hollett & Son Antiquarian Booksellers   General Catalogue Summer 2010 - 785   2011   £45

Galt, John 1779-1839 *Diary Illustrative of the Times of George the Fourth. Interspersed with Original Letters from the late Queen Caroline, The Princess Charlotte and from Various Other Distinguished Persons.* London: Henry Colburn, 1838-1839, First edition; 4 volumes, soundly rebound in light brown cloth, pages 1619, uncut, frontispiece, ex-British Foreign Office Library with few library markings, else very good.   Any Amount of Books   May 29 2011 - A62805   2011 $213

Galt, John 1779-1839 *George The Third His Court and Family.* London: Henry Colburn, 1821, New edition; 2 volumes, old half calf gilt with marbled boards, spines attractively gilt decorated and lettered, boards little rubbed, pages xvi, 478; 454, 18 engraved plates, few fore-edges little dampstained, attractive set.   R. F. G. Hollett & Son Antiquarian Booksellers   175 - 497   2011   £120

Galt, John 1779-1839 *Ringan Gilhaize or the Covenaters.* Edinburgh: Oliver & Boyd, 1823, First edition; 3 volumes, 12mo., half titles, one in annotation in volume III, uncut in original blue boards, brown paper spines, paper labels, some expert repairs to spines, ownership signatures of H. Hatton, very good.   Jarndyce Antiquarian Booksellers   CXCI - 521   2011   £280

Galt, John 1779-1839 *Sir Andrew Wylie of that Ilk.* Edinburgh: William Blackwood, 1822, First edition; some slight spotting, later 19th century half black roan, marbled boards, slightly rubbed.   Jarndyce Antiquarian Booksellers   CXCI - 522   2011   £120

Galton, Francis 1822-1911 *The Art of Travel; or Shifts and Contrivances Available in Wild Countries.* London: John Murray, 1883, Seventh edition; frontispiece and illustrations, original green cloth limp boards, spine uplettered in gilt, slightly rubbed, inner hinges racked and crudely repaired.   Jarndyce Antiquarian Booksellers   CXCI - 549   2011   £60

Gamble, W. *Penrose Annual.* 1899-1980, Volumes 5, 6, 8 9, 11, 12, 14, 15, 16, 18, 19, 21, 24, 31, 45, 47, 48, 50, 51, 52, 53, 54, 55, 56, 59, 60, 63, 64, 72, together 29 volumes in very good condition.   I. D. Edrich   May 26 2011 - 84667   2011 $1510

Gammer Grethel's Fairy Tales. London: Simpkin Marshall and Hamilton, Kent & Co. n.d. circa, 1925, square 8vo., original blue pictorial cloth, trifle marked, pages x, 359, uncut, two leaves carelessly opened, color frontispiece and numerous line drawings.   R. F. G. Hollett & Sons Antiquarian Booksellers   170 - 339   2011   £85

Gamow, George *The Moon.* New York: Henry Schuman, 1953, First edition; 8vo., 118 page, minimal cover edgewear in very good+ dust jacket with chips, small closed tears, minimal sun spine, scarce.   By the Book, L. C.   26 - 99   2011 $75

Gandee, B. F. *The Artist or Young Ladies's Instructor in Ornamental Painting, Drawing, etc.* London: 1835, 253, ads (3) pages, 6 1/2 x 4 1/2 inches, very good, one tear to top of backstrip, cover gilt sharp, original binding.   Bookworm & Silverfish   665 - 11   2011 $325

Ganzl, Kurt *The British Musical Theatre. Volume I & II 1865 - 1914 & 1915-1984.* Basingstoke: 1987-1988, Reprints; fat 8vo., pages ix, 1258, first volume is very good in very good dust jacket, second also very good+ in dust jacket slightly creased and slightly nicked else very good.   Any Amount of Books   May 29 2011 - A68641   2011 $238

Garcia Marquez, Gabriel 1928- *El Otono Del Patricai. (Autumn of the Patriarch).* Barcelona: Plaza & Janes, 1975, First Spanish edition; near fine, bookstore stamp on titlepage, light shelfwear, dust jacket very good, sunning and light creasing to edges, very good, sunning and light creasing to edges.   Bella Luna Books   May 26 2011 - t1716   2011 $192

Garcia Marquez, Gabriel 1928- *La Maia Hora. (The Evil Hour).* Esso Columiana, 1962, First edition, editor's issue limited to 170 numbered copies specially bound, this copy #4; small 8vo., original full mottled calf with red morocco labels on spine, marbled endpapers, top edge gilt,.   James S. Jaffe Rare Books   May 26 2011 - 13061   2011 $7500

Garcia Marquez, Gabriel 1928- *El Coronel No Tiene Quien la Escriba. (No One Writes to the Colonel).* Medellin: Aguirre Editor, 1961, Small 8vo., original printed wrappers, rare, very fine.   James S. Jaffe Rare Books   May 26 2011 - 13103   2011 $8500

Garcia Marquez, Gabriel 1928- *Of Love and Other Demons.* New York: Knopf, 1995, First American edition, first printing, review copy with review material laid in; fine, 8vo., 147 pages, rare, fine dust jacket.   By the Book, L. C.   26 - 6   2011 $900

Garcia Marquez, Gabriel 1928- *One Hundred Years of Solitude.* London: Jonathan Cape, 1970, First UK edition; 8vo., about fine in complete very good+ dust jacket with 3 tiny closed tears and no loss and slight rubbing at edges and corners.   Any Amount of Books   May 29 2011 - A39554   2011 $315

Gardiner, Dorothy *English Girlhood at School.* London: Oxford University Press, 1929, First edition; original black cloth gilt, pages iii, 501, with 16 plates.   R. F. G. Hollett & Son Antiquarian Booksellers   175 - 498   2011   £35

Gardiner, Howard C. *In Pursuit of the Golden Dream. Reminiscences of San Francisco and the Northern and Southern Mines.* Stoughton: Western Hemisphere, 1970, First trade issue in red cloth; thick quarto, lxv, (1), 390 pages, frontispiece, seven illustrations, 2 maps, red cloth, gilt lettered spine and front cover, fine.   Argonaut Book Shop   Recent Acquisitions Summer 2010 - 138   2011 $125

Gardiner, Robert *Frigates of the Napoleonic Wars.* Annapolis: Naval Institute Press, 2000, First edition; 4to., 208 pages, frontispiece, illustrations, tables, navy blue paper boards, gilt stamped spine title, dust jacket, fine, from the Bern Dibner reference library, with Burndy bookplate.   Jeff Weber Rare Books   161 - 164   2011 $85

Gardiner, Samuel Rawson *Oliver Cromwell.* London and elsewhere: Goupil & Co., 1899, First edition; one of 1475 copies, fine dark plum morocco, simply but elegantly gilt by Riviere (signed on front turn-in), covers with panels formed by triple rules at board edges and double rules closer to center, raised bands, spine compartments defined by triple gilt rules, top edge gilt, other edges rough trimmed, color frontispiece, 2 facsimiles, vignette headpieces and tailpieces, foliated initials and 30 black and white plates, original tissue guards, each with printed text, extra illustrated with more than 150 plates and broadside from 1641, bookplate of Verney family, joints beginning to crack along top two inches, 3 trivial marginal tears, small minority of extra illustrations very lightly foxed (always inoffensively), else in fine condition, simple but dignified binding very bright, text fresh and clean.   Phillip J. Pirages   59 - 171   2011 $3600

Gardner, J. Starkie *English Ironwork of the XVIIth and XVIII Centuries - an Historical Analytical Account of the Development of Exterior Smithcraft.* London: 1911, First edition; xxvi, 336 pages, small 4to., good with repairs to backstrip, corners bumped and worn, with 88 collotype plates, upwards of 150 other illustrations.   Bookworm & Silverfish   670 - 71   2011 $90

Gardner, J. Starkie *Ironwork. In Three Parts.* London: Victoria & Albert Museum, 1922-1930, 3 parts, mixed set, 8vo., xi, 146, plates, 63; xii, 124, plates 44; (vi), 195, plates (48) pages, brown and green cloth, gilt stamped cover and spine titles, very good, from the Bern Dibner reference library, with Burndy bookplate.   Jeff Weber Rare Books   161 - 165   2011 $75

Gardner, John *The Dory Book.* Camden: 1978, First edition; 275 pages, 4to., fine in near fine dust jacket.   Bookworm & Silverfish   678 - 141   2011 $100

Gardner, John *The Poetry of Chaucer.* Carbondale: Southern Illinois University Press, 1978, First edition thus, softcover edition; signed by author, one light corner bump, else fine in wrappers.   Ken Lopez Bookseller   154 - 60   2011 $150

Gardner, Michael *An Old Drama: Three Encounters with Jack the Ripper.* Leicester: Black Knight Press, 1969, First edition; no. 85 of 100 copies signed by printer Duine Campbell on mauve paper, 8vo., illustrated covers, pages 28, illustrations by Deidre Maton.   Any Amount of Books   May 29 2011 - A678866 2011 $255

Garneau, Joseph *Nebraska Her Resources, Advantages & Development.* Omaha: 1893, 24 pages, 7 x 4 inches, original binding.   Bookworm & Silverfish   664 - 147 2011 $65

Garner, Alan *Elidor.* London: Collins, 1965, First edition; octavo, boards.   L. W. Currey, Inc.   124 - 131 2011 $500

Garnett, J. *Views of the English Lakes and Mountains.* London: Hamilton and Co. and Windermere: J. Garnett, n.d., 1859, Oblong 4to., oblong green board folder gilt, little rubbed, silk ties lacking, 8 page 4to. bookplate in original wrappers, plus 8 card leaves loose as issued, each 182 x 271mm., some little spotted, with chromolithograph plate laid on, rare.   R. F. G. Hollett & Son Antiquarian Booksellers   173 - 462 2011   £250

Garnett, Thomas *Popular Lectures on Zoonomia or the Laws of Animal Life in Health and Disease.* Printed by W. Savage Printer to the Royal Institution of Great Britain for the benefit of the author's children by his executors, 1804, First edition; 4to., old half calf, gilt, elegantly tooled spine and Spanish marbled boards, extremities little rubbed and worn, pages xxii, 325, copper enraved portrait frontispiece, 3 text illustrations, few margins little creased, portrait little foxed in margins and slightly offset on to title, contemporary signature of W. Millers, St. John's on title.   R. F. G. Hollett & Son Antiquarian Booksellers   General Catalogue Summer 2010 - 974 2011   £225

Garrard, Lewis H. *Wah-To-Yah and the Taos Trail; or Prairie and Scalp Dances, with a Look at Los Rancheros....* Cincinnati: H. W. Derby & Co., 1850, First edition, first state; from the library of Clint and Dorothy Josey with their bookplate affixed to front pastedown sheep, original black blindstamped cloth with original spine replaced, origina! title in gilt on spine, vi, (2), 349 pages, professionally rebacked with tiny portion of original spine remaining, front and rear endpapers replaced, some pages lightly foxed, else near fine, tight copy, housed in slipcase.   Buckingham Books   May 26 2011 - 28736 2011 $3000

Garrard, Lewis H. *Wah-to-Yah and the Taos Trail; or Prairie and Scalp Dances...* Cincinnati: H. W. Derby & Co., 1850, First edition, first state; original black blindstamped cloth with title in gilt on spine, vi, (2), 349 pages, few pages lightly foxed, else near fine, tight copy, housed in quarter leather and cloth slipcase with titles stamped in gold on spine.   Buckingham Books   May 26 2011 - 28735 2011 $3750

Garrett, Albert *British Wood Engraving of the 20th Century. A Personal View.* London: Scolar Press, 1980, First edition; large 4to., original cloth, gilt, dust jacket, pages 223, woodcuts, slight mark to front flyleaf, else fine.   R. F. G. Hollett & Son Antiquarian Booksellers   General Catalogue Summer 2010 - 165 2011   £45

Garrett, Albert *A History of British Wood Engraving.* Tunbridge Wells: Midas Books, 1978, First edition; pages 407, with 400 illustrations, large 4to., original cloth, gilt, dust jacket, one corner of 3 leaves lightly creased due to binding fault, otherwise excellent.   R. F. G. Hollett & Son Antiquarian Booksellers   General Catalogue Summer 2010 - 166 2011   £75

Garrison, William Lloyd *Sonnets and Other Poems.* Boston: Oliver Johnson, 1843, First edition; 16mo., 96 pages, original cloth, some browning, near fine, inscribed in ink by publisher O(liver) Johnson to his sister.   M & S Rare Books, Inc.   90 - 144 2011 $600

Garrison, William Lloyd *The Spirit of the South Towards the Northern Freemen and Soldiers Defending the American Flag Against Traitors...* Boston: R. F. Wallcut, 1861, First edition; 12mo., 24 pages, sewn.   M & S Rare Books, Inc.   90 - 143 2011 $525

Garth, Will *Dr. Cyclops.* New York: Phoenix Press, 1940, First edition; octavo, pages (1-8) 9-255 (256 blank), original red cloth, front and spine panels stamped in black, top edge stained yellow green, fore and bottom edges rough trimmed.   L. W. Currey, Inc.   124 - 55 2011 $1500

Garvan, Beatrice B. *The Pennsylvania German Collections.* Philadelphia: 1982, First edition; xxviii, 372 pages, with ANS by author tipped in, stiff cardboard covers.   Bookworm & Silverfish   668 - 37 2011 $67

Gascoigne, Bamber *Images of Richmond: a Survey of the Topographical Prints of Richmond in Surrey Up to the Year 1900.* Richmond-upon-Thames: Saint Helena Press, 1978, First edition, number 67 of 200 copies signed by Bamber Gascoigne; 4to., original publisher's full light brown leather lettered gilt on spine and decorated in gilt on front cover, with image of Richmond on cover, pages 237 with many illustrations, full calf bound at Manor Bindery, Fawley, Hants., fine in fine, handsome slipcase, marbled covers and full leather spine lettered gilt.   Any Amount of Books   May 26 2011 - A69200 2011 $503

Gascoigne, Bamber *Images of Richmond: a Survey of the Topographical Prints of Richmond in Surrey Up to the Year 1900.* Richmond-upon-Thames: Saint Helena Press, 1978, First edition, number 161 of 200 signed by Gascoigne; 4to., original publisher's light brown buckram lettered gilt on spine, image of Richmond on cover, pages 237, many illustrations, fine in near fine, handsome slipcase.   Any Amount of Books   May 29 2011 - A69108 2011 $306

Gascoigne, John *Science, Politics and Universities in Europe 1600-1800.* Aldershot: Ashgate, 1998, First edition; 8vo., x, 290 pages, frontispiece, illustrations, blue cloth, gilt stamped cover and spine titles, fine, from the Bern Dibner reference library, with Burndy bookplate.   Jeff Weber Rare Books   161 - 166 2011 $130

Gash, Jonathan *The Judas Pair.* London: Collins, 1977, First edition; 8vo., fine in near fine dust jacket with faint edgewear.   Any Amount of Books   May 29 2011 - A48855 2011 $340

Gask, Lilian *Fairy Tales of Other lands.* London: Harrap, 1931, First edition; original pictorial cloth, pages 256, 14 color plates and numerous illustrations and decorations by Willy Pogany, fore-edge little spotted, uncommon.   R. F. G. Hollett & Son Antiquarian Booksellers   General Catalogue Summer 2010 - 550 2011   £85

Gaskell, Elizabeth Cleghorn 1810-1865 *Cranford.* London: Macmillan, 1894, Original decorated cloth, gilt pages xxx, 298, all edges gilt, contemporary inscription from Knutsford, very nice, fresh sound.   R. F. G. Hollett & Son Antiquarian Booksellers   General Catalogue Summer 2010 - 915 2011   £75

Gaskell, Elizabeth Cleghorn 1810-1865 *Cranford.* London: J. M. Dent, 1904, First edition thus; original green cloth gilt, spine and upper board decorated in gilt overall, pages xv, 256, top edges gilt, untrimmed with 25 color plates by C. E. Brock, flyleaf and final leaf lightly browned, small inscription.   R. F. G. Hollett & Son Antiquarian Booksellers   General Catalogue Summer 2010 - 736 2011   £35

Gaskell, Ernest *Westmorland and Cumberland Leaders. Social and Political.* privately published Queenhithe Printing & Publishing Co. n.d. circa, 1910, 4to., original half morocco gilt, spine trifle faded, all edges gilt, unpaginated, scarce.   R. F. G. Hollett & Son Antiquarian Booksellers   173 - 463 2011   £180

Gaskin, John *The Long Retreating Day.* Leyburn: Tartarus Press, 2006, First limited edition, 450 copies; tall 8vo., original cloth, gilt, dust jacket, pages x, 205, silk marker, signed by author.   R. F. G. Hollett & Son Antiquarian Booksellers   General Catalogue Summer 2010 - 788 2011   £40

Gaster, Theodor H. *Myth, Legend and Custom in the Old Testament.* New York and Evanston: Harper & Row, 1969, First edition; large 8vo., original cloth, dust jacket spine rather faded, stain to top corner of inner flap, pages liii, 899, few slight marks to fore-edges, but excellent copy. R. F. G. Hollett & Son Antiquarian Booksellers   175 - 499 2011   £35

Gates, Barbara T. *Kindred Nature: Victorian and Edwardian Women Embrace the Living World.* Chicago and London: University of Chicago Press, 1998, First edition; 8vo., 293 pages, illustrations, maroon cloth, gilt stamped spine title, fine, rare in cloth, from the Bern Dibner reference library, with Burndy bookplate.   Jeff Weber Rare Books   161 - 167 2011 $100

Gates, Josephine Scribner *The Doll that Was Lost and Found.* Toledo: Franklin Pub. Co., 1903, 8vo., half cloth and patterned paper pictorial paste-on, 137pages, near fine, printed on coated paper and illustrations in black and white by Helen Niles, this copy inscribed by author, scarce. Aleph-Bet Books, Inc.   95 - 197 2011 $300

Gatty, Margaret Scott 1809-1873 *Parables from Nature.* London: George Bell & Sons, 1884-1885, First-fourth Series, 2 volumes, small 8vo., original green cloth gilt, pages xi, 195, ii, 234 with 2 woodcut frontispieces, some spotting to fore-edges, one joint cracked.   R. F. G. Hollett & Sons Antiquarian Booksellers   170 - 252 2011   £50

Gatty, Margaret Scott 1809-1873 *Parables from Nature.* London: George Bell and Sons, 1896, Pages xxviii, 492, original decorated green cloth, trifle rubbed and soiled, all edges gilt, numerous woodcut plates, original decorated green cloth, trifle rubbed and soiled.   R. F. G. Hollett & Sons Antiquarian Booksellers   170 - 251 2011   £75

Gauden, John *A Discourse of Artificial Beauty, in Point of Conscience, Between Two Ladies.* London: printed for R. Royston, 1662, Second edition; pages (ii, blank), (x) 262, (ii, blank), engraved frontispiece, short closed tear to lower margin, small 8vo., contemporary blind ruled and stamped calf, corners worn and rounded, some surface abrasion to lower board, rebacked in modern matching calf gilt, new endpapers.   R. F. G. Hollett & Son Antiquarian Booksellers   175 - 500 2011   £450

Gaudet, Harold *Remembering Railroading on Prince Edward Island.* Prince Edward Island: privately published, 1989, First edition; original wrappers, couple of slight marks, pages 97, illustrations, scarce.   R. F. G. Hollett & Son Antiquarian Booksellers   General Catalogue Summer 2010 - 1110 2011   £45

Gaultier, Bon *The Book of Ballads.* London: Wm. S. Orr and Co., 1849, Pages (vi), 204, (viii), early 20th century full tan calf gilt, original crimson cloth bound in at end, all edges gilt, double page title spread printed in red gilt and black and illustrations by Doyle and Crowquill with ornamental page borders throughout, handsome copy.   R. F. G. Hollett & Son Antiquarian Booksellers   175 - 501 2011   £140

Gaultier, Bon *The Book of Ballads.* William Blackwood & Sons, 1857, Fifth edition; original pictorial blindstamped cloth, gilt, rather faded, neatly recased, pages viii, 256, (ii), all edges gilt, illustrations.   R. F. G. Hollett & Son Antiquarian Booksellers   175 - 502   2011   £65

Gavarni, Paul *Les Debardeurs.* Paris: Baugher & Co., 1841, 66 numbered lithograph plates, some foxing, original royal blue embossed paper boards, dark blue calf spine, elaborately decorated in gilt, rubbed at extremities with small chip to foot of spine.   Jarndyce Antiquarian Booksellers   CXCI - 185   2011   £400

Gavarni, Pseud. *De La Vie Privee (Scenes de la Vie Intime).* Paris: 1837, Folio, 12 original lithographs, original lithographed title on green paper cut down and mounted, green marbled boards, cloth spine, gilt titled on spine, fine, rare.   Simon Finch Rare Books   Zero - 424   2011   £3000

The Gay Book. London: Henry Frowde, Hodder & Stoughton, n.d., 1915, First edition; original emobossed pictorial boards, little marked in places, pages (48), 12 full page color plates by Millicent Sowerby.   R. F. G. Hollett & Son Antiquarian Booksellers   General Catalogue Summer 2010 - 575   2011   £95

Gay, John 1685-1732   *The Beggar's Opera.* London: John Watts, 1729, London: printed for the author, 1729. Third edition; first edition of Polly; 4to., bound together in old full speckled calf, rebacked in matching calf gilt, pages (vi), 60, 46 (engraved music); viii, 72, 31 (engraved music), with 2 titles in red and black, short worm tracks to front margins of last few leaves (some neatly repaired).   R. F. G. Hollett & Son Antiquarian Booksellers   175 - 503   2011   £450

Gay, John 1685-1732   *Fables by the Late Mr. John Gay.* Coventry: Luckman & Suffield, 1798, 16mo., viii, 213, + 3 page publisher list, later straight grained olive green morocco covers, cover edges with gilt fillets and dentelles, gilt edges, gilt title on spine, blue marbled endpapers, full page copper engraved frontispiece, armorial plate and personal calling card pasted inside upper cover and front endpaper, frontispiece foxed, lower cover stained at spine, remarkably well preserved pocket edition in very fine state.   Hobbyhorse Books   56 - 58   2011 $205

Gay, John 1685-1732   *Fables by the Late Mr Gay.* London: J. Johnson, R. Baldwin, Darton and Harvey, J. Harris et al, 1806, 12mo., (2), 924 pages, original full leather on boards, full page wood engraved frontispiece, vignette on titlepage, oval wood engravings by John Bewick, 2 inked signatures on front endpapers, 3 engravings partly hand colored, corners of cover bumped, gold of spine reinforced, excellent copy.   Hobbyhorse Books   56 - 59   2011 $300

Gay, John 1685-1732   *The Fables of Mr. John Gay.* York: T. Wilson and R. Spence, 1806, 12mo., 252 pages, 19th century half red morocco with corners and five raised band with gilt title, date and rosettes on spine, marbled paper on boards, armorial plate inside upper cover, full page copper engraved frontispiece.   Hobbyhorse Books   56 - 61   2011 $320

Gay, John 1685-1732   *Fables by the Late Mr. Gay.* London: C. and J. Rivington, Harvey and Darton, J. Harris and Son et al, 1823, 12mo., (4), 222 pages, original full leather on boards, full page wood engraved frontispiece, wood engravings, repaired corner of one leaf with loss of few letters, covers rubbed at edges, reinforced spine, some signatures sprung but still tightly held, very good, uncommon.   Hobbyhorse Books   56 - 60   2011 $250

Gay, John 1685-1732   *Polly: an Opera.* London: printed for the author, 1729, First edition; quarto, (4), vii, (1), 72, 31, sheet music, (1 blank) pages, engraved sheet music, title printed in red and black, original blue paper wrappers, uncut, some professional repairs to wrappers, new stitching to wrappers, two previous owner's bookplates tipped in to inside front wrapper, chemise and housed, quarter blue morocco slipcase, very good.   Heritage Book Shop   Holiday 2010 - 45   2011 $1750

Gay, John 1685-1732   *Polly: an Opera.* London: for the author, 1729, First edition; 4to., 19th century half red morocco, rather rubbed, marbled boards and endpapers, raised bands, gilt to spine compartments, titlepage in red and black, 31 pages of engraved musical score, minor dusting and foxing, all edges gilt.   Dramatis Personae Booksellers   106 - 74   2011 $400

Gay, John 1685-1732   *Trivia; or the Art of Walking the Streets of London.* London: printed for Bernard Lintott, 1716, First edition; one of 250 large paper copies printed, with vignette title and 3 engraved vignette headpieces with engraved headpiece on page 1 and elaborate engraved ornaments at beginning of book II (page 21) and book III (page 53) in small paper copies, these are printer's ornaments, 8vo., full contemporary calf, covers ruled in gilt with small leaf ornaments in each corner, gilt lines across spine, red morocco gilt tooled spine label, beautiful copy.   James S. Jaffe Rare Books   May 26 2011 - 12557   2011 $8500

Gay, Theresa *James W. Marshall, the Discoverer of California Gold: a Biography.* Georgetown: Talisman Press, 1967, First edition, limited to 250 copies, signed, printed on special paper, specially bound, numbered, boxed; 558 pages, frontispiece, portrait, 25 illustrations from various sources, 5 facsimile inserts (4 in rear pocket), half simulated black morocco over marbled boards, gilt lettered spine, fine with double slipcase (spine of outer slipcase slightly rubbed).   Argonaut Book Shop   Recent Acquisitions Summer 2010 - 123   2011 $175

Gay, Walter *Paintings of French Interiors.* New York: 1920, Limited to 950 copies; small folio, (6), (2), 50 pages, very good in half linen and paper over boards, with 50 full and part page photogravure plates.　Bookworm & Silverfish 679 - 18　2011　$100

Gaya, Louis De *Traite des Armes des Machines de Guerre, Des Feux d'Artifice, des Ensignes & Des Instruments Militaires Anciens & Modernes.* Paris: Sebastien Cramoisy, 1678, 12mo., (6), 172 pages, additional engraved titlepage, 19 engraved plates, woodcut initials and tailpieces, contemporary calf, spine gilt in compartments, spine partly detached, sides rubbed, from the library of the Earls of Macclesfield at Shirburn Castle.　Maggs Bros. Ltd.　1440 - 95　2011　£600

Gaya, Louis De *A Treatise of the Arms and Engines of War of Fire-works, Ensigns, and Military Instruments, both Ancient and Modern...* London: printed for Robert Harford, 1678, 8vo., (16), 143, (1) pages, frontispiece (mounted) and 18 plates, 18th century smooth calf, gilt spine, lacking A the printed title, from the library of the Earls of Macclesfield at Shirburn Castle.　Maggs Bros. Ltd.　1440 - 96　2011 £500

Gaze, Harold *Copper Top.* New York: Harper Brothers, 1924, (B-Y), First American edition; Thick 4to., 338 pages, blue cloth stamped in gold, last illustration slightly out of register, else fine in dust jacket (chipped spine ends), 12 beautiful color plates plus many full and partial page fanciful illustrations, scarce in dust jacket.　Aleph-Bet Books, Inc.　95 - 250　2011　$650

Gebhardt, A. G. *State Papers Relating to the Diplomatic Transactions Bewteen the American and French Governments, From the Year 1793 to the Conclusion of the Convention of the 30th of September 1800.* London: printed by J. E. G. Vogel, 1816, First edition; 3 volumes, half leather lettered gilt at spine, pages 368, 451, 481, English and French text, ex-British Foreign Office Library, few library markings, slight general wear, spine hinges little cracked, otherwise sound.　Any Amount of Books　May 29 2011 - A49589　2011　$340

Geddes, R. Stanley *Burlington Blue-Grey a History of the Slate Quarries.* Kirkby-in-Furness: privately published, 1975, Original cloth, gilt, dust jacket, pages 320, 67 illustrations, 2 maps, 4 folding sections and 19 diagrams.　R. F. G. Hollett & Son Antiquarian Booksellers　173 - 467　2011 £40

Geddes, W. D. *Lavunar Basilicae Sancti Macarii Aberdonensis. The Heraldic Ceiling of the Cathedral Church of St. Machar, Old Aberdeen.* Aberdeen: 1888, 4to., xix, (3), 160, 40 pages, frontispiece, 29 illustrations, very good in original gilt lettered olive green cloth.　Ken Spelman Rare Books　68 - 90　2011　£45

Gee, John *Bunnie Bear.* Minneapolis: Gordon Volland/Buzza, 1928, Fifth edition; 8vo., pictorial boards, fine in publisher's box, illustrations by author.　Aleph-Bet Books, Inc.　95 - 567　2011　$300

Geiger, M. Virginia *Daniel Carroll II, One Man and His Descendants 1730-1978.* Geiger, 1979, 314 pages, pictures, genealogical tables, very good, covers soiled and edgeworn, edges soiled, interior clean and tight.　G. H. Mott Bookseller　May 26 2011 - 41207　2011　$300

Geiger, Maynard *As the Padres Saw Them.* Santa Barbara: 1976, One of an edition of 500; xv, 170 pages, illustrations, near fine.　Dumont Maps & Books of the West 112 - 40　2011　$125

Geikie, Cunningham *The Holy Land and the Bible.* London: Cassell, 1903, Full plum calf gilt prize binding, pages xvi, 432, with 8 plates.　R. F. G. Hollett & Son Antiquarian Booksellers　175 - 504　2011　£30

Geisel, Theodor Seuss 1904-1994 *The Cat in the Hat Comes Back.* New York: Rnadom House, 1958, First edition; original glazed pictorial boards little worn, few scratches, pages 63, illustrations in colors, child's inscription on pastedown.　R. F. G. Hollett & Sons Antiquarian Booksellers　170 - 634　2011　£50

Geisel, Theodor Seuss 1904-1994 *The Cat's Quizzer.* New York: Beginner Books/Random House, 1976, First edition (correct code I-O); 4to., glazed pictorial boards, slight rubbing to bottom of spine, else very good+, illustrations in color.　Aleph-Bet Books, Inc.　95 - 520　2011 $275

Geisel, Theodor Seuss 1904-1994 *The 500 Hats of Bartholomew Cubbins.* New York: Vanguard, 1938, First edition; Large 4to., cloth backed pictorial boards, fine in dust jacket with correct $1.50 price (frayed at spine ends and has few closed tears, otherwise beautiful example), illustrations.　Aleph-Bet Books, Inc.　95 - 519　2011 $7850

Geisel, Theodor Seuss 1904-1994 *How the Grinch Stole Christmas.* New York: Random House, 1957, First edition with following issue points "14 books (up to now) on rear jacket flap and list of 13 books printed at end of book; quarto, illustrations in black and red, original illustrated glossy paper boards, pictorial endpapers, price clipped dust jacket, previous owner's small signature neatly inked out on front free endpaper and half title, jacket spine and corners with some chipping and rubbing, some small crease marks along extremities of jacket, overall near fine, in very good jacket.　Heritage Book Shop　Holiday 2010 - 107　2011 $1250

Geisel, Theodor Seuss 1904-1994 *The Lorax.* New York: Random House, 1971, First edition; 4to., pictorial cloth, light rubbing, very good-fine, illustrations by author. Aleph-Bet Books, Inc. 95 - 513 2011 $1000

Geisel, Theodor Seuss 1904-1994 *Oh, the Places You'll Go!* New York: Random House, 1990, Stated first edition; fine, 4to., fine dust jacket. By the Book, L. C. 26 - 59 2011 $250

Geisel, Theodor Seuss 1904-1994 *On Beyond Zebra.* New York: Random, 1950, First edition; 4to., glazed pictorial boards, touch of rubbing, else fine in dust jacket with price intact, inscribed by author. Aleph-Bet Books, Inc. 95 - 514 2011 $3000

Geisel, Theodor Seuss 1904-1994 *The Seven Lady Godivas.* New York: Random House, 1939, First edition; publisher's original pink cloth, publisher's pictorial dust jacket, inscribed by author. Heritage Book Shop Booth A12 51st NY International Antiquarian Book Fair April 8-10 2011 - 113 2011 $2000

Geisel, Theodor Seuss 1904-1994 *The Tough Coughs as He Ploughs the Dough.* New York: William Morrow/ Remco Worldservice Books, 1987, First edition; small 4to., 143 pages, fine in fine dust jacket. By the Book, L. C. 26 - 60 2011 $600

Geisel, Theodor Seuss 1904-1994 *You're Only Old Once!* New York: Random House, 1986, Limited to 500 copies, signed; green cloth with blindstamped Dr. Seuss on cover and gold lettering on spine, green slipcase, book clean and fresh inside and out, illustrations. Jo Ann Reisler, Ltd. 86 - 231 2011 $500

Geisel, Theodor Seuss 1904-1994 *You're Only Old Once.* New York: Random House, 1986, First edition, limited to 500 copies signed by author; 4to., cloth, as new in slipcase, illustrations. Aleph-Bet Books, Inc. 95 - 515 2011 $850

Gelasius, of Cyzicus *(Greek) ...commentarius Actorum Nicaeni Concilii, cum Corollario Theodori Presbyteri, de Incarnatione Domini...* Paris: F. Morel, 1599, 8vo., 15, (1), 287, (3), device on verso of title, last leaf with imprint, later sprinkled vellum, from the library of the Earls of Macclesfield at Shirburn Castle. Maggs Bros. Ltd. 1440 - 97 2011 £450

Gelleroy, William *The London Cook or the Whole Art of Cookery Made Easy and Familiar.* London: S. Crowder and Co., 1792, First edition; 8vo., soundly rebound in quarter leather with marbled boards, 5 raised bands and red leather label lettered gilt on spine, pages (x), 486, lacks folding frontispiece (as often), slight loss at side of titlepage, not affecting text, otherwise decent, very good+ copy with occasional browning to text. Any Amount of Books May 26 2011 - A68487 2011 $604

Gemmell, David *Lion of Macedon.* London: Random Century Group, 1990, First edition; 9.5 x 6.5 inches, 416 pages, publisher's caramel color cloth with gilt lettering to spine, dust jacket very slightly worn at edges, book itself very good, page edges slightly browned with age and rar endpapers have two very small (under one inch) splash marks, otherwise no defects, inscribed by author for his father. Any Amount of Books May 26 2011 - A40521 2011 $503

The Gems of Song: a Choice Collection of the Newest and Most Popular Copyright Songs. Glasgow: John Cameron, circa, 1860, 8 pages, ads, small 12mo., original yellow pictorial wrappers, printed in red, blue and black, back cover ad, very good. Jarndyce Antiquarian Booksellers CXCI - 370 2011 £55

Genbach, Jean *L'Abbe De L'Abbaye/ Poemes Supernaturalistes.* Paris: Le Tour d'Ivoire, 1927, First edition, no. 332 of 350 on velin de Rives from a total edition of 366; 8vo., pages (ii) blank, xii, 101, (1) blank, (1) limitation, (1) blank, (1) imprint, (1) blank, 16 full page woodcuts, unopened, internally fine, publisher's wrappers partly browned with light shelf wear. Simon Finch Rare Books Zero - 315 2011 £190

Genlis, Stephanie Felicite Ducrest De Saint Aubin, Comtesse De 1746-1830 *Adele et Theodore ou Lettres sur l'Education.* Paris: M. Lambert & F. J. Baudouin, 1782, First edition; 3 volumes, 12mo., 1 + 519-491-536 + (1 page dedication, 1 page Privilege du Roi) contemporary tan calf, flat spine with gilt title on brown leather, number and decorative floral design, gilt fillets at edge of covers, woodcut tailpieces, engraved bookplate inside front cover of each volume, light crack at fold of one volume, inked signature top edge of volume one, very fine set in almost mint state. Hobbyhorse Books 56 - 77 2011 $450

Gent, Thomas *Annales Regioduni Hullini; or the History of the Royal and Beautiful Town of Kingston-upon-Hull from the Original of it... 'till this Present Year 1735.* York: sold at the printing office, 1735, 8vo., pages (iv) xi, (iii), 201, (xxxiv) 4 folding engraved plates (one as frontispiece), 1 extending engraved plate and 1 other engraved plate, additionary at front an engraved plan of York, the plan of Hull has contemporary hand coloring, late 18th century sprinkled and polished calf, spine panel gilt, dark red lettering piece gilt, boards decorative roll bordered in blind with double rule within, all edges red sprinkled, red and yellow sewn endbands, 1970's restoration by John Enderson, browned, edges of frontispiece restored, old leather rubbed at edges, mid 18th century ink inscription referring to an epitaph at Howden on flyleaf facing frontispiece ink inscription quoting the Smyth family epitaph in Howden church and pointing to inaccuracies, on blank verso of last page of postscript, from the collection of Christopher Ernest Weston 1947-2010. Unsworths Booksellers 24 - 98 2011 £600

Gent, Thomas *The Antient and Modern History of the Famous City of Yrok and i a Particular Manner of its Mangificent Cathedral...* York: at the Printing Office in Coffe Yard, 1730, 8vo., pages viii, 256, (viii) + extending engraved frontispiece and one other engraving, contemporary hand colored extending plan, this copy is the first issue with woodcut of framed celestial crown with Latin quotation from Rev. II 10 as a headpiece to page 84, also tall copy, modern (1982) calf by Jenny Aste, browned and spotted, frontispiece and plan rehinged, from the collection of Christopher Ernest Weston 1947-2010. Unsworths Booksellers 24 - 96 2011 £400

Gent, Thomas *The Antient and Modern History of the Loyal Town of Rippon...* York: printed and sold at the Printing Office, 1733, 8vo., pages xvi, (ii) 165, (i), 73, (vii) + folding engraved plan frontispiece, 2 full page woodcuts and 2 extra illustrated engraved plates, modern (March 1982) calf binding by Jenny Aste, some browning and spotting, folding plates rehinged, one extra plate (unflattering portrait of author, bound as frontispiece), substantially smaller and frayed at edge, other copy of folding plate from Gent's "Annales Regioduni Hullini", 2 flyleaves from earlier binding tipped in at end, ink inscription "William Shilleto 1841" and pencil inscription, from the collection of Christopher Ernest Weston 1947-2010. Unsworths Booksellers 24 - 97 2011 £450

Gent, Thomas *Historia Compendiosa Anglicana; or a Compendious History of England.* York: printed and sold by the author, 1741, 2 volumes, 8vo., pages (iv), xvi, (ii), 268, (iv); (iv), 269-376, (ii), 70, xxxviii, later 18th century marbled calf, boards decorative roll gilt bordered, board edges obliquely broken fillet, roll gilt, all edges red speckled, early 20th century calf reback, fully gilt spines, red and black lettering and numbering piece gilt, dark green & purple sewn endbands, some browning, few fore edges cut close and few frayed but no loss of text, little rubbed at extremities, corners sometime, at different times renewed, from the collection of Christopher Ernest Weston 1947-2010. Unsworths Booksellers 24 - 99 2011 £300

Gent, Thomas *The Life of Mr. Thomas Gent, Printer of York.* London: printed for Thomas Thorpe, 1832, Engraved frontispiece, uncut, original pink moire cloth, at some time rebacked, retaining original paper label, faded, cloth slightly creased on back board, Renier booklabel, according to pencil note work was edited by Joseph Hunter. Jarndyce Antiquarian Booksellers CXCI - 449 2011 £150

Gent, Thomas *The Most Delectable, Scriptural and Pious History of the Famous and Magnificent Great Eastern Window .. in St. Peter's Cathedral, York...* York: impress for the author in St. Peter's Gate, 1762, 8vo., pages (iv), xxiii, (i), 196, 12, (iv), 24, (vi) + large folding engraved plates (crudely hand colored) of E. Window and one other engraved plate headed "Pious Contemplations", contemporary sprinkled sheep boards, double rule bordered in blind, all edges red sprinkled, 1970's sheep reback + corners, browned, spotted, few page and plate edges just cropped, folding engraved plate splitting at folds and with handling tear, in places sometime repaired on rear, last leaf cut down, old leather darkened and chipped in places, bound in after titlepage is special presentation leal to Revd. John Mawer from author, from the collection of Christopher Ernest Weston 1947-2010. Unsworths Booksellers 24 - 100 2011 £650

The Gentleman's Diary; or the Mathematical Repository: an Almanack for the Year of Our Lord 1747. London: printed for the Company of Stationers, 1747, (4), (44) pages, 8vo., printed in red and black, small diagrams in text, stitched as issued, titlepage dusted, faint old waterstain to leading edge, inscription dated 1886 at head of titlepage. Jarndyce Antiquarian Booksellers CXCI - 40 2011 £125

Geo. Damon & Sons *Type Borders Ornaments & Brass Rules: Point Line, Point Set, Point Body.* New York: circa, 1915, 72 pages, tall 8vo., wrappers, very good price list present. Bookworm & Silverfish 676 - 154 2011 $115

Geoffrey of Monmouth *Prophetia Anglicana, Merlini Ambrosii Britanni ex Incubo Olim (jut Hominum Fama est) Ante Annos Mille Ducentos Circiter in Anglia Nati...* Frankfurt: Ioachim Brathering, 1603, Small 8vo., (16),269 (3) pages, woodcut portrait on verso of title, mid 18th century English mottled calf, gilt spine, lightly browned, label missing, joints rubbed, from the library of the Earls of Macclesfield at Shirburn Castle. Maggs Bros. Ltd. 1440 - 98 2011 £800

George IV, King of Great Britain *The Letters of King George IV 1812-1830.* Cambridge: Cambridge University Press, 1938, First editions; 3 volumes, 8vo., original publisher's cloth lettered gilt at spine, pages lxxxiv, 525, 554 & 547 2 frontispiece, 3 folding tables, 3 volumes, slight fading, very good, neat stamp of Royal Historical Society. Any Amount of Books May 29 2011 - A61359 2011 $204

George Washington Bicentennial Commission *History of the George Washington Bicentennial Celebration.* Washington: 1932, Volumes 1-3 of 5, large 4to., about 2000 pages, modestly ex-library with later backstrips and labels.   Bookworm & Silverfish   679 - 165   2011 $75

George, B. *Volume: International Discography of the New Wave.* New York: One Ten Records, 1980, First edition; color illustrated wrappers, pages 300, copiously illustrated in black and white throughout, spine very slightly faded, very slight rubbing at edges, otherwise very good+.   Any Amount of Books   May 29 2011 - A44512   2011 $238

George, George Saint *A Saunter in Belgium in the Summer of 1835: with Traits Historical and Descriptive.* F. C. Westley, 1836, First edition; 12mo., frontispiece, plates, original green cloth, some slight wear to head and tail of spine.   Jarndyce Antiquarian Booksellers   CXCI - 530   2011   £85

George, Henry *Read and Think! Henry George to Workingmen. The Protective System... what It Means to American Labor.* Boston: Cupples, Hurd and Co., 1887, First separate edition; 8vo., 40 pages, original front printed wrapper, top edge slightly stained, small chip in fore edge.   M & S Rare Books, Inc.   90 - 145   2011 $200

George, Henry *Read and Think! Henry George to Workingmen. The Protective System...What It means to American Labor.* N.P.: circa, 1888, First separate edition; 8vo., 8 pages, leaflet, sheet browned, two small holes punched in gutter margin.   M & S Rare Books, Inc.   90 - 146   2011 $250

George, Jean Craighead *Julie of the Wolves.* New York: Harper & Row, 1972, First edition; 8vo., color illustrated boards, color dust jacket, fine.   Jo Ann Reisler, Ltd.   86 - 103   2011 $250

George, Prince of Wales *The Correspondence of George, Prince of Wales 1770-1812.* London: Cassell, 1963-1971, First editions; 8 volumes, large 8vo., approximately 400 + pages, tables, illustrations, all very good in like dust jacket, some minor ex-library markings.   Any Amount of Books   May 29 2011 - A61354   2011 $238

Gerarde, John 1545-1612   *The Herball or Generall Historie of Plantes.* London: Adam Islip, Joice Norton and Richard Whitakers, 1633, Second edition; approximately 2800 text woodcuts, woodcut initials, folio, engraved architectural title by John Payne, pages (38), 1-30, 29-30, 29-1630, (2), (1 page of additional illustrations, verso blank), (45), errata, contemporary full calf (professionally rebacked with sympathetic leather, old wear to edges and corners, lacking 1 leaf, H1, 89-90, endpapers renewed, engraved title somewhat soiled and with short marginal tears, some soiling to prelim pages, scattered pages with repairs with no loss to text, tear here and there, some dampstaining, mostly to back third of pages, an old ink annotation to a page, small brown stains to 2 leaves, several index pages soiled, chipped and frayed at fore edges, resulting in partial loss of text to 2 leaves, the copy of John Preston and of John Averill.   Raymond M. Sutton, Jr.   May 26 2011 - 55850   2011 $2400

Gerarde, John 1545-1612   *The Herball or Generall Historie of Plantes.* London: by Adam Islip, Joice Norton and Richard Whitakers, 1633, First printing of the second edition; folio, engraved title, (36), 30, 29-30, 29-1630, (48) pages, over 2500 woodcuts, early 19th century panelled calf, neatly rebacked retaining original fully gilt spine, title lightly soiled, complete and free of any repair, blank fore and bottom edges of A4-5 neatly extended, few marginal tears neatly closed, intermittent faint dampstain in top margin becoming bit more noticeable toward end of text, marginal repair to 7A1 (index) costing several page numbers, blank lower corner of 7B5 replaced, very good, most attractive copy, without extensive repairing and sophistication that nearly always comes with early English herbals, ownership inscription and cost dated 1634.   Joseph J. Felcone Inc.   Fall Miscellany 2010 - 54   2011 $8000

Gerarde, John 1545-1612 *The Herball or Generall Historie of Plantes.* London: printed for Adam Islip, Joice Norton and Richard Whitakers, 1636, Third edition; with errata corrected in text, large folio, (38), 1630 (i.e. 1634), (1) (1, blank), 46, indexes and tables) pages, bound without initial and final blank leaves as usual, engraved allegorical title by John Payne and 2766 woodcut illustrations in text, decorative woodcut head and tailpieces and initials, mid 19th century sprinkled calf, expertly rebacked with original spine laid down, spine decoratively tooled in gilt in compartments with five raised bands and tan morocco gilt lettering label, board edges decoratively tooled in gilt, marbled endpapers, the second edition of Gerarde to be edited by Thomas Johnson, a reprint of 1633 edition with errata corrected, small ink blot on E1 recto (page 53), small paper flaw in upper blank margin of #5 (pages 61/62) just touching one letter on recto, small hole in 14 (pages 107/108) just affecting one woodcut, small piece torn from upper blank margin of Tt1 (pages 497/498), just touching rule, outer margin of Ccc1 (pages 581/582) strengthened on recto, small repair in outer blank margin ov Vuu1 (pages 785/786), short tear (1 inch) in lower blank margin of Ffff1-Ffff2 (pages 893-896) just touching one letter on page 893 small rust hole in Ssssss3 (pages 1593/1594) just affecting a couple of letters, short clean tear in Yyyyyy1 (first leaf of index), not affecting text, some light offsetting from woodcuts, faint dampstain in lower margin of few leaves, few additional small stains or rust spots, few additional minor marginal tears or paper flaws, small bookseller's label.   David Brass Rare Books, Inc.   May 26 2011 - 00641   2011 $8500

Gerhard, H. P. *The World of Icons.* London: John Murray, 1971, First English edition; 4to., original cloth gilt, dust jacket price clipped, pages 232, with 35 color plates and 68 illustrations.   R. F. G. Hollett & Son Antiquarian Booksellers   General Catalogue Summer 2010 - 169   2011   £35

Gershwin, George 1898-1937 *Porgy and Bees. An Opera in Three Acts.* New York: Random House, 1935, First edition, limited to 250 copies signed by authors, this #138; quarto, (xiv), 559, (1, blank) pages, signed limitation page inserted at rear, color frontispiece and titlepage illustrations by George Biddle, publisher's full red morocco, blind-stamped front board and spine, spine with two black morocco spine labels, lettered in silver, original endpapers, publisher's straw covered slipcase, missing black morocco label from front board, spine labels, few pieces missing, still legible and with color filled in, bottom of spine slightly darkened and worn, spot where front board label should be slightly scratched, publisher's slipcase slightly rubbed, very good.   Heritage Book Shop   Holiday 2010 - 46   2011 $8500

Gershwin, Ira *Strike Up the Band.* New York: New York World Music Corp., 1930, Presentation copy inscribed by George and Ira Gershwin, each with small sketch to Newman Levy, quarto, contemporary full red cloth.   Heritage Book Shop   Booth A12 51st NY International Antiquarian Book Fair April 8-10 2011 - 60   2011 $9500

Gerson, Johannes *De Pollutione Nocturna.* Cologne: Johann Guldenschaff, circa, 1480, Rare incunable edition; 8vo., pages (32), including initial blank, some light foxing, two old repairs to initial blank, generally crisp, fresh and wide margined, later paper covered boards, cloth spine and tips rubbed, title to initial blank in early manuscript, sporadic underlining in text, bookplate of Paul Graf von Hoensbroech, his crest stamped to first two leaves.   Simon Finch Rare Books   Zero - 101   2011   £3750

Gerstner, Franz Anton Ritter Von *Early American Railroads: Franz Anton Ritter Von Gerstner's Die Innern Communicationen (1842-1843).* Stanford: Stanford University Press, 1977, Large 4to., vi, 844 pages, plates, tables, burgundy cloth, silver stamped spine title, dust jacket, fine, from the Bern Dibner reference library, with Burndy bookplate.   Jeff Weber Rare Books   161 - 173   2011 $135

Gesner, Konrad 1516-1565 *Historiae Animalium Liber III qui est de Avium Natura.* Francofurti: Henrici Laurentii, 1617, Later edition; over 230 woodcuts, folio, pages (12), 732, (21) contemporary full calf, 6 raised bands and gilt lettered red label on spine (front cover detached, corners showing, one being perished, dampstaining to corner and/or margins of many pages, lower corner of title partly disintegrated, marginal tear to 2 front leaves, ocasional foxing, slight worming to upper corner of few leaves, offsetting to text from woodcuts, many pages misnumbered, although sequence is correct, leaf 413/415 is printed twice, leaf 411/412 omitted), good, the copy of Gilbert R. Regrave, also Aquatic Research Institute.   Raymond M. Sutton, Jr. May 26 2011 - 45718   2011 $2500

Gesualdo, Filippo *Plutosofiae.... Nella Quale si Spiega l'Arte Della Memoria con Altre Crose Notabili Pertinenti Tanto alla Memoria Naturale...* Padua: P. Meietti, 1592, First edition; 4to., ff. (6), 64, device on titlepage, full page woodcut figure of a man on f. (27), very slightly cropped at foot, English binding c. 1700 of brown calf, gilt fillets on covers, gilt spine, morocco lettering piece, from the library of the Earls of Macclesfield at Shirburn Castle.   Maggs Bros. Ltd.   1440 - 99   2011   £3000

Gibb, Robert *Whalesongs.* Berkeley: Turkey Press, 1979, Second edition, #91 of 100 numbered and signed copies of the first hardcover edition; cloth backed boards, printed letterpress on Rives heavy weight paper and bound by Sandra Liddell using Harry Reese's handmade paper on cover inset, illustrations, near fine.   Charles Agvent   2010 Summer Miscellany - 32   2011 $100

Gibbings, Robert *Fourteen Wood Engravings from Drawings Made on Orient Line Cruises.* Waltham St. Lawrence: Golden Cockerel Press, 1932, Wrapper dusty, text very good.   C. P. Hyland   May 26 2011 - 255/225   2011 $580

Gibbings, Robert *Lovely is the Lee.* London: Dent, 1945, First edition; original cloth, gilt, dust jacket top edges rather dusty and frayed, pages vi, 199, woodcuts by author.   R. F. G. Hollett & Son Antiquarian Booksellers   General Catalogue Summer 2010 - 789   2011   £45

Gibbings, Robert *The Wood Engravings of Robert Gibbings with Some Recollections by the Artist.* London: J. M. Dent, 1959, First edition; 4to., original buckram gilt, clear plastic wapper, few slight edge tears, pages 355 with color frontispiece and 100 illustrations of wood engravings.   R. F. G. Hollett & Son Antiquarian Booksellers   General Catalogue Summer 2010 - 170   2011   £150

Gibbon, Edward *The History of the Decline and Fall of the Roman Empire.* London: printed for W. Strahan and T. Cadell, 1777-1781, Third edition volume 1, First editions volumes 2-3; 3 volumes only (of 6), 4to., pages vi, (vi), 704, engraved frontispiece; (xii), 640, (ii) + 1 folding engraved map and 1 extending engraved map (xii), 640, (ii), 1 folding engraved map, contemporary sprinkled tan calf, six compartmented spine fully gilt with 'paterae row' decorative roll bands and 'frond' cornered panels with 'doves and urn' center pieces red & green lettering & numbering pieces gilt, board edges 'obliquely-broken fillet' roll gilt, 'Dutch swirl' 'made' endpapers, all edges lemon, russet and white sewn endbands, green silk page markers, little light spotting, merest touch rubbed at edges, corners gently worn, joints of volumes 1 and 3 cracking a bit at foot, from the collection of Christopher Ernest Weston 1947-2010.   Unsworths Booksellers   24 - 101   2011   £450

Gibbons, A. St. H. *Africa: from South to North through Marotseland.* London: John Lane, 1904, First edition; 2 volumes, 8vo., pages xx, 276; xxi, 297, maps, 2 large folding maps (2 in slipcases), another folding map, frontispieces, numerous illustrations, original blue decorative cloth, inner hinges cracked, very good, clean set.   J. & S. L. Bonham Antiquarian Booksellers   Africa 4/20/2011 - 8764   2011   £600

Gibbons, Kaye *Ellen Foster.* Chapel Hill: Algonquin, 1987, First edition; fine in fine dust jacket.   Bella Luna Books   May 29 2011 - 1149   2011 $110

Gibbons, Kaye *Ellen Foster.* Chapel Hill: Algonquin, 1987, First edition; fine, dust jacket near fine, crease on front flap, 1 inch scratch on front gutter.   Bella Luna Books   May 29 2011 - 1148   2011 $82

Gibbs-Smith, C. H. *Balloons.* London: Ariel Press, 1956, First edition; folio, original wrappers, dust jacket with glassine outer protection, pages xv, color decoration and 12 fine full page color plates.   R. F. G. Hollett & Son Antiquarian Booksellers   175 - 506   2011   £85

Gibson, Alexander Craig *The Folk-Speech of Cumberland and Some Districts Adjaent...* London: John Russell Smith and Carlisle: G. & T. Coward, 1869, First edition; original maroon cloth gilt, spine trifle faded, 232, viii pages, scattered spotting.   R. F. G. Hollett & Son Antiquarian Booksellers   173 - 470   2011   £45

Gibson, Alfred *Association Football & the Men Who Made It.* London: Caxton Publishing Co., n.d., First edition; 4 volumes, large 8vo., original pictorial blue cloth by John Hassall, few slight bumps to edges, corners trifle worn, white printing on one board rather rubbed, pages viii, 224; viii, 215; viii,2 16; viii, 200, numerous sepia and monochrome plates with gold borders and illustrations throughout, very good bright, sound set.   R. F. G. Hollett & Son Antiquarian Booksellers   General Catalogue Summer 2010 - 1249   2011   £750

Gibson, Thomas *Legends and Historical Notes on Places in the East and West Wards, Westmorland.* Manchester: John Heywood, 1877, First edition; pages 95, scarce, original cloth, gilt, little worn.   R. F. G. Hollett & Son Antiquarian Booksellers   175 - 507   2011   £75

Gibson, Thomas *Legends and Historical Notes on Places of North Westmoreland.* London: Unwin Brothers, and Appleby; J. Whitehead & Son, 1887, First edition; original decorated cloth, gilt, spines little darkened and worn, pages xv, 308, lively full page woodcut drawings, frontispiece, scarce.   R. F. G. Hollett & Son Antiquarian Booksellers   175 - 508   2011   £150

Gibson, William *Burning Chrome.* New York: Arbor House, 1986, First edition; near fine, very light shelfwear, dust jacket fine.   Bella Luna Books   May 29 2011 - T7132   2011 $110

Gibson, William Sidney *The History of the Monastery Founded at Tynemouth in the Diocese of Durham to the Honor of God under the invocation of the Blessed Virgin Mary and S. Oswin King & Martyr.* London: published for the author by William Pickering, 1846-1847, 2 volumes, 4to., pages (iv) xxvi (x) xxxiv (xxiv) 251 (i) + chromolithographic frontispiece, 3 plates of facsimiles and 2 other etched plates; viii, (viii), (5)-125, (iii)-ccxii (ii) + chromolithographic frontispiece, 10 etched plates and extending map, contemporary crimson quarter roan, spines double ruled in blind at head and foot, lettered direct between double rules all gilt, boards double ruled in blind with green 'sand' design bookcloth sides, mauvish brown 'coated' endpapers, top edge gilt, bound without endbands, plates bit foxed at edges, leather touch rubbed and conserved/dyed at joints and endcaps, from the collection of Christopher Ernest Weston 1947-2010.   Unsworths Booksellers   24 - 102   2011   £250

Giedion, Sigfried *Space, Time and Architecture.* London: Oxford University Press, 1949, Eighth edition; large 8vo., original black cloth gilt, spine lettering dulled, pages xviii, 665 with 321 illustrations, old tape marks to endpapers. R. F. G. Hollett & Son Antiquarian Booksellers 177 - 410 2011 £75

Giedion, Sigfried *Space, Time and Architecture.* Cambridge: Harvard, 1971, Fifth edition; 8vo., pages liv, 897, copiously illustrations, nice in slightly chipped and soiled dust jacket, 321 black and white photos and plans. Second Life Books Inc. 174 - 157 2011 $200

Gielgud, John *Early Stages.* London: Theatre Book Club, 1953, Original cloth, spine rather faded, pages 269 with 25 illustrations, Gielgud's signature laid on pastedown. R. F. G. Hollett & Son Antiquarian Booksellers 175 - 509 2011 £30

Gierach, John *Dances with Trout.* London: Robinson, 1994, First British edition; fine in fine dust jacket. Bella Luna Books May 29 2011 - t7153 2011 $82

Gierach, John *Fishing Bamboo.* New York: Lyons Press, 1997, First edition; fine in fine dust jacket, illustrations by Barry Glickman. Bella Luna Books May 29 2011 - t9671 2011 $82

Gierach, John *Standing in a River Waving a Stick.* New York: Simon & Schuster, 1999, Limited to 950 copies; fine, slipcase, signed by author and publisher, illustrations by Glenn Wolff. Bella Luna Books May 29 2011 - t4053 2011 $104

Gieryn, Thomas F. *Cultural Boundaries of Science: Credibility on the Line.* Chicago and London: University of Chicago Press, 1999, First edition; 8vo., xiv, 398 pages, map, navy cloth, yellow stamped spine title, fine, from the Bern Dibner reference library, with Burndy bookplate. Jeff Weber Rare Books 161 - 174 2011 $75

Giger, Matthias *Artificium Muniendi Geometricum quo Delineatio Regularium Munimentorum non Solum Absque Omni Calcuo...* Stockholm: H, Kayser, 1650, 4to., ff. (4), woodcut on verso of title, disbound, from the library of the Earls of Macclesfield at Shirburn Castle. Maggs Bros. Ltd. 1440 - 100 2011 £400

Gilb, Dagoberto *Winners on the Pass Line; and Other Stories.* El Paso: Cinco Puntos Press, 1985, First edition; pictorial wrappers, fine, signed by author. Bella Luna Books May 29 2011 - t4405 2011 $137

Gilbert, Anthony *The Woman in Red.* London: Collins Crime Club, 1941, First edition; exceptional copy, some color fading to top edges of cloth, else near fine in price clipped, lightly professionally restored dust jacket at head of spine, lightly sunned on spine. Buckingham Books May 26 2011 - 25920 2011 $3750

Gilbert, John T. *Chartularies of St. Mary's Abbey, Dublin...* 1884, 2 volumes, volume I quarter leather, volume II quarter cloth, ex-library and presented by H. M. Treasury, unopened, very good. C. P. Hyland May 26 2011 - 260/248 2011 $362

Gilbert, William *De Magnete Magnticisque Corporibus et de Magno Magnete Tellure.* London: Excudebat Petrus Short, 1600, First edition; small folio, (16), 240 pages, title with woodcut printer's device on recto and Gilbert's woodcut arms on verso, 88 woodcut diagrams and illustrations in text of which 4 are full page, one folding woodcut plate (with old tidemark down one of fold lines), decorative woodcut head and tailpieces and initial letters, contemporary limp vellum with yapp edges, spine lettered in manuscript, front cover with acronym "IGTCP" stamped in black at top and date '1604' at bottom, all edges blue, lacking ties, endpapers slightly later, title lightly browned, small old university stamp to verso, additional contemporary ink signature on title, some early red ink underlining and shoulder notes in Latin, Publisher's corrections to misprints on pages 11, 22 and 47 as usual, minor dampstains to inner blank margins of first and last few leaves, last leaf repaired at inner margin, intermittent light foxing, pinhole worming to front cover, small sheet of paper bearing catalog description tipped onto inner rear cover, previous owner's bookplate, overall excellent copy, housed in brown cloth clamshell case. Heritage Book Shop Holiday 2010 - 47 2011 $37,500

Gilbert, William Schwenck 1836-1911 *The "Bab" Ballads.* London: John Camden Hotten, 1869, First edition; preface dated October 1868, illustrations by author, 4 pages ads, original green cloth, bevelled boards by W. Bone & Son, decorated and lettered gilt, slightly dulled, all edges gilt. Jarndyce Antiquarian Booksellers CXCI - 186 2011 £250

Gilbert, William Schwenck 1836-1911 *A Colossal Idea.* London and New York: Putnam, 1932, First edition; one of a limited number of copies issued with each of the 9 illustrations hand colored and signed by artist, Townley Searle on limitation page, small 8vo., 62 pages, blue cloth, very nice, tight copy, some illustrations outlined in colors while others fully colored. Second Life Books Inc. 174 - 158 2011 $650

Gilbert, William Schwenck 1836-1911 *Iolanthe; or the Peer and the Peri.* New York: Hitchcock, 1882, Authorized copyright edition; 4to., pages 155, paper wrappers, bookplate, very good. Second Life Books Inc. 174 - 159 2011 $75

Gilbert, William Schwenck 1836-1911 *Songs of a Savoyard.* London: Routledge, 1890, First edition; large 8vo., original pictorial cloth gilt over bevelled boards, pages xi, 142, (ii), all edges gilt, illustrations by author, very nice, clean and sound copy.   R. F. G. Hollett & Son Antiquarian Booksellers   175 - 512   2011   £85

Gilbert, William Schwenck 1836-1911 *Songs of a Savoyard.* London: Routledge, 1891, Large 8vo., original pictorial cloth gilt, little fingered, pages xi, 142, (ii), illustrations by author, flyleaf little spotted.   R. F. G. Hollett & Son Antiquarian Booksellers   175 - 513   2011   £45

Gilchrist, Anne *Mary Lamb.* London: W. H. Allen & co., 1883, Half title, 4 pages ads, original dark green cloth, spine and front board lettered in gilt, slightly rubbed, owner's signature.   Jarndyce Antiquarian Booksellers   CLXC - 70   2011   £25

Gill, Eric 1882-1940 *The Engravings.* Wellingborough: Christopher Skelton, 1983, First edition, 1350 copies; folio, original two-tone cloth gilt by Smith Settle, upper board blindstampd with design by Gill, slipcase, pages xxiv, 545, with over 1000 illustrations, fine.   R. F. G. Hollett & Son Antiquarian Booksellers   General Catalogue Summer 2010 - 172   2011   £450

Gill, Stephen *William Wordsworth.* Oxford University Press, 1989, First edition; original cloth, gilt, dust jacket, pages xix, 525, 20 plates and maps.   R. F. G. Hollett & Son Antiquarian Booksellers   173 - 473   2011   £35

Gillam, Stanley G. *The Building Account of the Radcliffe Camera.* Oxford: Clarendon Press, 1958, Original green cloth, gilt, pages lviii, 189 with 68 plates.   R. F. G. Hollett & Son Antiquarian Booksellers   177 - 413   2011   £75

Gillies, D. M. *Zig Zigs of a Cape Breton Clergyman.* Whycocomagh: 1928, 12mo., pages (4), 5-70, (2), frontispiece, blue cloth with dark blue lettering to front cover, covers badly stained, fraying to spine an edges, interior.   Schooner Books Ltd.   96 - 149   2011 $75

Gillingham, Mitchell & Co. *Catalogue of Fresh Spring Dry Goods and Superfine Cloths to be Sold at Auction...at their Warehouse No. 22 North second Street... January 26th 1830.* Philadelphia: William Brown, 1830, Small folio, 5 pages, disbound, browned and stained but sound.   M & S Rare Books, Inc.   90 - 24   2011 $450

Gilly, William Stephen *Narrative of an Excursion of the Mountains of Piedmont, and Researches Among the Vaudois or Waldenses, Protestant Inhabitants of the Cottian Alps.* London: C. and J. Rivington, 1824, First edition; quarto, xx, (2), 279, (1), ccxxiv pages, 10 lithographic plates, 2 folded maps and 3 facsimile plates, complete, modern period style half calf and marbled paper covered boards, all edges marbled, text pages clean and tight, with few tiny repaired tears, very handsome copy.   Between the Covers   169 - BTC340932   2011 $1500

Gilpin, William 1724-1904 *Observations on Several Parts of England...* London: T. Cadell and W. Davies, 1808, 2 volumes, full contemporary deep green calf gilt, boards with central shaped panel in sage green, decorated in gilt in an elegant simple rococo style, spines with 5 raised bands and double contrasting labels, panels elegantly gilt decorated, little old rubbing and scrapes here and there, pages xlvii, 238, (ii), viii, 264, complete with 30 tinted aquatints, handsome set.   R. F. G. Hollett & Son Antiquarian Booksellers   173 - 477   2011   £350

Gilpin, William 1724-1904 *Observations on Several parts of England, Particularly the Mountains and Lakes of Cumberland and Westmoreland, Relative Chiefly to Picturesque Beauty...* London: T. Cadell and W. Davies, 1808, Third edition; very good, corners rubbed, leather edges worn, some spotting on first few page, else very clean and tight, viii, 264 pages, sepia aquatints, some offsetting.   G. H. Mott Bookseller   May 26 2011 - 43y11   2011 $325

Gilpin, William 1724-1904 *Observations on Several Parts of England...* Richmond Publishing Co., 1973, Original cloth gilt, pages iii, xxxi, xvi, 230, 268, xvi, 30 plates, library labels on front endpapers and stamp to back of title.   R. F. G. Hollett & Son Antiquarian Booksellers   173 - 478   2011   £45

Gilpin, William 1724-1904 *Observations Relative Chiefly to Picturesque Beauty, made in the Year 1776 on Several Parts of Great Britain, Particularly the High Lands of Scotland.* London: Blamire, 1792, Second edition; 2 volumes in one, half leather worn at extremities, library stamp, pencil notes on one page, else very clean and tight, xi, 221; 195, xvi pages, sepia aquatints, some offsetting.   G. H. Mott Bookseller   May 26 2011 - 43610   2011 $300

Gilson, Etienne *The Christian Philosophy of St. Thomas Aquinas.* London: Gollancz, 1957, First UK edition; original cloth, gilt, dust jacket, little browned, tape marks to inner flaps. pages x, 502, library stamp to half title and final leaf.   R. F. G. Hollett & Son Antiquarian Booksellers   175 - 515   2011   £30

Gilson, Etienne *The Unity of Philosophical Experience.* London: Sheed and Ward, 1938, First edition; original cloth, gilt, dust jacket with few short closed tears, light spotting, pages xii, 340, flyleaes lightly spotted. R. F. G. Hollett & Son Antiquarian Booksellers 175 - 517 2011 £35

Gingerich, Owen *God's Universe.* Cambridge: Belknap Press/Harvard University Press, 2006, First edition; 8vo., xi, 139 pages, near fine in fine dust jacket, signed, inscribed and dated by author. By the Book, L. C. 26 - 100 2011 $65

Ginsberg, Allen *Allen Verbatim. Lectures on Poetry, Politics, Consciousness.* US: McGraw Hill Paperbacks, 1975, First paperback edition; 8vo. pages (xvi), 270, internally fine, original pictorial wrappers, crease to upper wrapper corner with slight shelfwear and dust to spine, inscribed by Ginsberg on titlepage to Gregory Corso. Simon Finch Rare Books Zero - 319 2011 £475

Ginsberg, Allen *The Gates of Wrath/Rhymed Poems 1948-1952.* California: Grey Fox Press, 1972, First edition; 8vo., pages (x), 56, (2) blank, clean and fresh, original glassine protected purple, black and white pictorial wrappers with cover photo by poet in March 1949, some minor wear to wrappers, generally fine, inscribed by Ginsberg for Gregory Corso. Simon Finch Rare Books Zero - 317 2011 £675

Ginsberg, Allen *Howl and Other Poems.* San Francisco: City Lights Pocket Bookshop, 1956, First edition; 12mo. pages 44, black wrappers with white printed band, first state with Lucien Carr's name on dedication page, with no printing notice, printed in an edition of only 1500 copies, fine, rare. Second Life Books Inc. 174 - 160 2011 $5000

Ginsberg, Allen *Howl.* New York: Harper & Row, 1986, First edition thus, 30th anniversary original draft facsimile edition; remainder mark lower page edges foxing to top page edges, else fine in near fine dust jacket, inscribed by author to Nelson Lyon in 1992 with drawing. Ken Lopez Bookseller 154 - 62 2011 $750

Ginsberg, Allen *Illuminated Poems.* New York: 4 Walls 8 Windows, 1996, Limited to 300 copies; illustrations by Eric Drooker, book fine, full cloth with gold stamping on book and slipcase, signed by author and artist. Bella Luna Books May 26 2011 - j1887 2011 $440

Ginsberg, Allen *Sad Dust Glories/ Poems During Work Summer in Woods.* Berkeley: The Workingham Press, 1975, First edition; 8vo., pages (iv), 27, (i) imprint, original stapled green pictorial wrappers, some slight discoloration to wrappers, still near fine, inscribed by author for Gregory Corso, with TLS from Gary Wilkie to Corso loosely inserted. Simon Finch Rare Books Zero - 318 2011 £675

Ginsberg, Allen *T.V. Baby Poems.* London: Cape Gilliard Press, 1967, 8vo., pages 936), double page illustration to titlepage, small illustrations to half title and in text, very crisp and clean, original black and white photographic paper wrappers, text in brown to upper panel and spine, lightly soiled and foxed, text in brown to front and spine, author's presentation inscription to W. H. Auden in blue ink to initial blank, several manuscript corrections to text. Simon Finch Rare Books Zero - 316 2011 £600

Ginsberg, Allen *White Shroud.* New York: Harper & Row, 1986, First edition, number 29 of 200 copies signed and numbered by Ginsberg; white cloth in red cloth slipcase, as new. Gemini Fine Books & Arts, Ltd. Art Reference & Illustrated Books: First Editions 2011 $200

Giono, Jean *The Man Who Planted Trees.* Chelsea: Chelsea Green Pub., 1990, Specially packaged presentation including the book and an audio cassette with music composed and performed by Paul Winter consort and narration by Robert J. Lurtsema, both encased in box with illustrations and text, book illustrated with wood engravings by Michael McCurdy, in addition to the package as it was sold in stores, there are also two large illustrated ad posters for the book, both signed in pencil by artist, as well as a collection of 30 wood engravings from the book printed on various types of paper and in various sizes, many of them signed in pencil by artist and often titled with limitation number usually one of 50 or 100 copies, new, still in package, shrinkwrap, occasional minor smudging to art. Charles Agvent 2010 Summer Miscellany - 33 2011 $1000

Giovanni, Nikki *Black Feeling, Black Talk, Black Judgement.* New York: Morrow, 1970, First edition; 8vo, pages vii, 98, nice in scuffed dust jacket. Second Life Books Inc. 174 - 161 2011 $70

Giraldus Cambrensis *Opera.* 1861-1891, 8 volumes, complete, ex-library but very good in modern buckram. C. P. Hyland May 26 2011 - 258/051 2011 $688

Giraldus Cambrensis *Opera.* 1861-1891, Volumes 1-7 (ex 8), ex-library and presented by H. M. Treasury, volume 2 quarter cloth, others quarter leather (some wear to spine tops), else very good. C. P. Hyland May 26 2011 - 280/246 2011 $507

Giraud, S. Louis *Bookano Stories No. 1.* London: Strand, n.d. circa, 1935, 4to., pictorial boards, slight wear to spine, very good+, 5 wonderful double page color pop-ups, illustrations in black and white. Aleph-Bet Books, Inc. 95 - 448 2011 $350

Giraud, S. Louis *Bookano Stories, Series No. 4.* Strand Publications, n.d., 1937, Original pictorial boards, few creases to spine, little wear to extremities, unpaginated, color frontispiece, 5 double page full color pop-ups, line drawings, excellent. R. F. G. Hollett & Sons Antiquarian Booksellers 170 - 257 2011 £150

Giraud, S. Louis *Bookano Stories. Series No. 5.* London: Strand Publications, n.d., 1938, Original pictorial boards, hinges just trifle worn, unpaginated, color frontispiece, 5 double page full color pop-ups, line drawings, excellent, complete with full color ad slip.   R. F. G. Hollett & Sons Antiquarian Booksellers   170 - 258 2011   £175

Giraud, S. Louis *Bookano Stories. Series no. 6.* London: Strand Publications, n.d., 1939, Original pictorial boards, hinges just trifle worn, unpaginated, color frontispiece, 5 double page full color pop-ups, line drawings, excellent copy.   R. F. G. Hollett & Sons Antiquarian Booksellers 170 - 259 2011   £175

Giraud, S. Louis *Bookano Stories. Series No. 12.* Strand Publications, n.d. 1930's, Original pictorial boards, extremities trifle rubbed and bruised, unpaginated, 5 double page full color pop-ups, other color and black and white illustrations, very nice.   R. F. G. Hollett & Sons Antiquarian Booksellers   170 - 256 2011   £180

Giraud, S. Louis *Bookano Stories. 13th Series.* London: Strand Publications, n.d., Sep. 1940, Large 8vo., original pictorial boards, spine creased and little worn, unpaginated, color endpapers, color frontispiece and title, 5 fine colored pop-ups and black and white drawings throughout, inked name to head of title, otherwise good, crisp unused condition.   R. F. G. Hollett & Sons Antiquarian Booksellers   170 - 261 2011   £85

Giraud, S. Louis *Daily Express Children's Annual. No. 3.* Lane Publications, 1930, Pages 95, 6 fine pop-ups all in excellent order, original pictorial boards, spine rather creased.   R. F. G. Hollett & Sons Antiquarian Booksellers 170 - 260 2011   £175

Giraud, S. Louis *The Story of Jesus.* London: Strand Publications n.d. circa, 1930, Large 8vo. original cloth with inset on upper board, hinges trifle rubbed, pages vii, 24, colored endpapers and 8 fine colored pop-ups, one short tear, otherwise in good, crisp unused condition.   R. F. G. Hollett & Sons Antiquarian Booksellers   170 - 263 2011   £85

Girouard, Mark *Life in the Engish Country House. A Social and Architectural History.* BCA, 1979, 4to., original cloth, gilt, dust jacket, pages 344, illustrations.   R. F. G. Hollett & Son Antiquarian Booksellers   177 - 416 2011   £30

Girvin, Brenda *Good Queen Bess 1533-1603.* London: David Nutt, n.d. c., 1907, First edition; oblong 4to., original pictorial boards, rather dusty and marked, edges worn, unpaginated, 23 full page vividly colored plates with title guard with pictorial broder, accompanying text leaf, all printed in red, front joint cracked, flyleaf replaced, half title frayed at fore edge, few edge tears, rear endpapers rather browned.   R. F. G. Hollett & Sons Antiquarian Booksellers 170 - 317 2011   £65

Gisborne, Thomas *An Enquiry into the Duties in the Higher and Middle Classes of Society in Great Britain...* London: printed by J. Davis, 1795, Third edition; 2 volumes, xv, (1), 459, (1) pages; xii, 516 pages, 8vo., small stain to upper corner of final leaves volume II, endpapers lightly foxed, otherwise good, clean copy, contemporary half calf, marbled boards, gilt banded spines, handsome black gilt labels, joints cracked but firm, slight wear to head and tail of spine volume II.   Jarndyce Antiquarian Booksellers CXCI - 187 2011   £110

Gisborne, Thomas *An Enquiry into the Duties of the Female Sex.* London: printed for T. Cadell Jun. and W. Davies, 1797, First edition; octavo, viii, 426 pages, later half calf, marbled boards, gilt and blind rules on spine, gilt title, rubbed, signature of A. Barclay on title, very good. Jeff Weber Rare Books   163 - 167 2011 $150

Gissing, George *The Emancipated.* London: Lawrence & Bullen, 1893, First one volume edition; Half title, 16 pages Laurence & Bullen catalog (Nov. 1893), original maroon cloth, slight rubbing and spine slightly dull, good plus.   Jarndyce Antiquarian Booksellers   CXCI - 188 2011 £120

Gissing, George *New Grub Street; a Novel.* London: Smith, Elder, 1891, Second edition; 3 volumes, half titles, final ad leaf volume I, original dark blue green morocco grained cloth, front boards blocked and lettered in black, spines lettered gilt, slight fading to spines, Cheswick bookabels, bookseller's ticket of Edward Baker, Birmingham, very good, crisp copy.   Jarndyce Antiquarian Booksellers CXCI - 523 2011   £450

Giuseppi, John *The Bank of England.* London: Evans Brothers, 1966, First edition; original cloth, gilt, dust jacket price clipped (top edges trifle frayed), pages xii, 224, 15 pages of plates.   R. F. G. Hollett & Son Antiquarian Booksellers   175 - 520 2011   £35

Give a Show (everything needed is in this book). Chicago: Goldsmith Publishing Co., 1933,   oblong 4to, full color pictorial paper covers with stapled binding, some light dusting and small nick in edge of front cover and spine is partially split, else clean copy, complete and uncut, 6 leaves within offering black and white text as well as full color cut-out masks.   Jo Ann Reisler, Ltd.   86 - 50 2011 $350

Glascock, William Nugent *Land Sharks and Sea Gulls.* London: Richard Bentley, 1838, First edition; frontispiece and plates, small marginal tear to plate facing page 58, volume III, handsomely rebound by J. Larkins in half red morocco, raised bands, decorated lettered in gilt, top edge gilt, very good.   Jarndyce Antiquarian Booksellers   CXCI - 524 2011   £450

Glasgow University *Fortuna Domus.* Glasgow University, 1952, First edition; pages viii, 355, original blue cloth, gilt. R. F. G. Hollett & Son Antiquarian Booksellers 175 - 524 2011 £30

Glasgow, Ellen 1874-1945 *The Deliverance: a Romance of the Virginia Tobacco Fields.* New York: Doubleday Page & Co., 1904, First edition; illustrations by Frank Schoonover, red cloth gilt, fine, signed by author. Between the Covers 169 - BTC347224 2011 $250

Glashow, Sheldon *Interactions.* New York: Warner, 1988, First edition; 8vo., xii, 347 pages, signed and inscribed in year of publication by Glashow. By the Book, L. C. 26 - 101 2011 $200

Glass, I. I. *Shock Waves and Man.* Toronto: University of Toronto Institute for Aerospace Studies, 1974, First edition; 8vo., pages xii, 169, signed presentation from author for John Brunner, with bookplate, very good+ in like dust jacket. Any Amount of Books May 29 2011 - A66971 2011 $255

Glass, Robert C. *Virginia Democracy: a History of the Achievements of the Party and Its Leaders in the Mother of Commonwealths, The Old Dominion.* N.P.: Lyncburg?, 1937, First edition; 3 volumes, large 8vo., very good, heavy text weight has caused some rubbing when volumes are stacked, backstrip ends just tiny bit worn, all cover and backstrip gilt bright, mild foxing to f.e.p. Bookworm & Silverfish 665 - 158 2011 $125

Glasse, Hannah *The Art of Cookery Made Plain and Easy.* Alexandria: Cottom and Stewart, 1805, First American edition; 16mo., 308, (16) pages, contemporary calf, leather label, some wear, slightly shaken, lacking endleaves. M & S Rare Books, Inc. 90 - 98 2011 $1500

Glatigny, Albert *Joyeusetes Galantes et Autres du Vidame Bonaventure de la Braguette.* Luxuriopolis: A l'Ensigne du Beau Triochis l'an du monde ???? Brussels, circa, 1884, Early edition, one of 500 copies on Hollande from a total edition of 510; 8vo., pages 207, 2 half titles, titlepage in red and black with motif of faun and nymph, head and tailpieces, top edge gilt, one leaf chipped, otherwise internally fine, contemporary red half morocco and marbled boards, gilt, light shelf wear, 2 tips bumped, from the Sinclair collection, his cataloging number inscribed to titlepage. Simon Finch Rare Books Zero - 428 2011 £600

Glazier, Richard *A Manual of Historic Ornament.* London: Batsford, 1926, Fourth edition; tall 8vo., original cloth, gilt, dust jacket, pages (iv), 184, 76 plates and numerous text illustrations. R. F. G. Hollett & Son Antiquarian Booksellers 177 - 417 2011 £35

Gleichen, Count *With the Mission to Menelik.* London: Edward Arnold, 1898, First edition; 8vo., pages xi,3 63, 2 folding maps, illustrations, original blue decorative cloth, small nick on fore-edge, corners rubbed. J. & S. L. Bonham Antiquarian Booksellers Africa 4/20/2011 - 9149 2011 £150

Gleig, G. R. *Chelsea Hospital and Its Traditions.* London: Richard Bentley, 1838, First edition; 3 volumes in 1, contemporary half scarlet calf gilt with marbled boards, pages xii, 398, 342, 296 with half titles to volumes 2 and 3, handsome set. R. F. G. Hollett & Son Antiquarian Booksellers General Catalogue Summer 2010 - 605 2011 £150

Glenn, Garrard *The Law Governing Liquidation as Pertaining to Corporations, Partnerships, Individuals, Decedents, Bankruptcy, Receivership & Reorganization.* New York: 1935, 1056 pages, very good in green law cloth, mild shelfwear. Bookworm & Silverfish 667 - 43 2011 $75

Glicksberg, Charles I. *The Literature of Nihilism.* Lewisburg: 1975, First edition; 354 pages, very good in like. Bookworm & Silverfish 670 - 133 2011 $75

Glimsher, Arnold *Louise Nevelson.* New York: Praeger, 1972, First edition; 4to., 172 pages, near fine, in very good++ dust jacket with minimal sun spine, edge wear, chip to dust jacket spine tip. By the Book, L. C. 26 - 46 2011 $300

Glover, Ann *Gloriana's Gass.* Stellar Press, n.d., Limited edition (no. 309 of 1250 copies); original decorated blue and cream cloth, pages 153, uncut and largely unopened printed on Barcham Green paper by Francis Meynell, full page wood engraved portrait. R. F. G. Hollett & Son Antiquarian Booksellers General Catalogue Summer 2010 - 806 2011 £35

Glover, Dorothy *Victorian Detective Fiction. A Catalogue of the Collection Made by Dorothy Glover and Graham Greene Bibliographically Arranged by Eric Osborne...* London: Sydney & Toronto: The Bodley Head, 1966, First edition, number 442 of 500 copies, (of which 25 are not for sale); half title, xviii, (2), 149, (3) pages, dark green cloth lettered in gilt on spine, pictorial endpapers, dust jacket, fine, printed in Ehrhardt types on Strathmore mould-made paper and bound by William Clowes of Beccles, signed by Glover, Grahame Greene and John Carter. Anthony W. Laywood May 26 2011 - 21574 2011 $671

Glover, Richard *Leonidas, a Poem.* London: T. Bensley for F. J. Du Voveray, 1798, Sixth edition according to titlepage; fine contemporary highly polished marbled calf, covers with gilt border of thick and thin rules and central panel formed by gilt fillet with scalloped corners, flat spines divdied into panels by multiple gilt rules, two panels with black morocco labels, other four with central gilt patera, turn-ins with beaded gilt rule, marbled endpapers, frontispiece, 6 more engraved plates, large modern bookplate of Thomas S. Standish from Wigan; very short portions of joints of first volume cracked, just at top, covers slightly marked, margins and versos of plates foxed, otherwise very fine, bindings extremely lustrous and with no signficant wear and text fresh, clean and bright, very ample margins. Phillip J. Pirages   59 - 49   2011 $475

Goblet, Y. M. *A Topographical Index of the Parishes and Towlands of Iceland in Petty's Barony Maps.* IMC, 1932, Only 500 copies printed; very good, ex-libris Horace Jones (Cork genealogist).   C. P. Hyland   May 26 2011 - 259/158   2011 $362

Godcharles, Frederic *Pennsylvania: Political Governmental, Military and Civil.* New York: 1933, 5 volumes, 4to., over 2000 pages, prestige binding in half pseudo black morocco cloth and navy cloth, top edge gilt, fine set.   Bookworm & Silverfish   670 - 123   2011 $175

Goddaeus, Conradus *Laus Ululae. The Praise of Owls. An Oration to the Conscript Fathers and Patrons of Owls.* London: printed by E. Curll in the year, 1727, i.e. 1726. First edition in English; (2), iv, 101 pages, engraved plate, modern calf backed marbled boards, skillfully executed in period style, edges of title trifle chipped, very light overall browning, very good.   Joseph J. Felcone Inc.   Fall Miscellany 2010 - 96   2011 $750

Goddard, T. N. *The Handbook of Sierra Leone.* London: Grant Richards, 1925, First edition; 8vo., pages xvi, 335, maps, illustrations, original decorative cloth.   J. & S. L. Bonham Antiquarian Booksellers   Africa 4/20/2011 - 2678   2011   £65

Godden, Geoffrey A. *British Porcelain.* London: Barrie & Jenkins, 1980, Small 4to., original cloth, gilt, dust jacket, pages 452, 12 color plates and 574 illustrations.   R. F. G. Hollett & Son Antiquarian Booksellers   General Catalogue Summer 2010 - 173   2011   £60

Godden, Geoffrey A. *Caughley & Worcester Porcelains 1775-1800.* London: Herbert Jenkins, 1981, First limited edition, no. 1489 of 1500 copies; large 8vo., original cloth, gilt, dust jacket, pages xxxvii 366 with 327 plates.   R. F. G. Hollett & Son Antiquarian Booksellers   General Catalogue Summer 2010 - 175   2011   £85

Godden, Geoffrey A. *Coalport & Coalbrookdale Porcelains.* Antique Collectors Club, 1981, Limited edition, no. 239 of 1500 copies; small 4to., original cloth, gilt, dust jacket, pages xxxi, 308, with 10 color plates and 237 illustrations.   R. F. G. Hollett & Son Antiquarian Booksellers   General Catalogue Summer 2010 - 176   2011   £50

Godden, Geoffrey A. *Encyclopaedia of British Pottery and Porcelain Marks.* London: Barrie & Jenkins, 1983, Thick small 4to., original cloth, gilt, dust jacket, pages 765, map and 8 plates, facsimiles of marks.   R. F. G. Hollett & Son Antiquarian Booksellers   General Catalogue Summer 2010 - 177   2011   £45

Godden, Geoffrey A. *An Illustrated Encyclopaedia of British Pottery and Porcelain.* London: Barrie and Jenkins, 1982, Second edition; thick small 4to., original cloth gilt dust jacket, pages 390, with 679 illustrations.   R. F. G. Hollett & Son Antiquarian Booksellers   General Catalogue Summer 2010 - 179   2011   £65

Godden, Geoffrey A. *The Illustrated Guide to the Lowestoft Porcelain.* London: Herbert Jenkins, 1969, First edition; tall 8vo., original cloth, gilt, dust jacket, (top edge little chipped), pages xix, 164, with 225 plates, signed copy.   R. F. G. Hollett & Son Antiquarian Booksellers   General Catalogue Summer 2010 - 179   2011   £65

Godden, Geoffrey A. *Mason's China and the Ironstone Wales.* Antique Collector's Club, 1980, Revised edition; 4to., original cloth, gilt, dust jacket, spine rather faded, pages 316, with over 360 illustrations.   R. F. G. Hollett & Son Antiquarian Booksellers   General Catalogue Summer 2010 - 180   2011   £75

Godden, Geoffrey A. *Minton Pottery and Porcelain of the First Period 1793-1850.* London: Barrie & Jenkins, 1978, Large 8vo., original cloth, gilt, dust jacket (two heavy ships to top edge), page xvi, 168, 12 color plates and 161 illustrations.   R. F. G. Hollett & Son Antiquarian Booksellers   General Catalogue Summer 2010 - 181   2011   £35

Godden, Geoffrey A. *Ridgway Porcelains.* Antique Collectors Club, 1985, Second edition; 4to., original cloth, gilt, dust jacket, pages 257, 16 color plates and 218 illustrations, fine.   R. F. G. Hollett & Son Antiquarian Booksellers   General Catalogue Summer 2010 - 182   2011   £75

Godden, Rumer *The Tale of the Tales.* London: Frederick Warne, 1971, First edition; 4to., original cloth, gilt, dust jacket, pages 208, illustrations in color.   R. F. G. Hollett & Sons Antiquarian Booksellers   170 - 264   2011   £45

Godden, Thomas *Catholicks no Idolaters. Or a Full Refutation of Doctor Stillingfleet's Unjust Charge.* London: printed in the year, 1672, 8vo., pages (xxxii), 48, 448, contemporary sprinkled calf, spine double rule panelled in blind, paper label lettered in ink, boards double rule bordered in blind, board edges decorative roll gilt, all edges gilt, densely red sprinkled, white and pink sewn endleaves, just touch marked but very well preserved binding, free endpaper ink stamped angus dei within two leafy springs and underneath "SHEPPARD" (suggestive of heraldic crest), from the collection of Christopher Ernest Weston 1947-2010. Unsworths Booksellers 24 - 22 2011 £275

Godel, Kurt *Kurt Godel on formally Undecidable Propositions of Principia Mathematica and Related Systems.* Edinburgh & London: Oliver & Boyd, 1962, First UK edition; 8vo., pages viii, 72, neat name on titlepage, otherwise very good+ in complete and slightly marked and slightly rubbed dust jacket, near very good. Any Amount of Books May 29 2011 - A72599 2011 $255

Godfrey, Ambrose *A Curious Research in the Element of Water...* London: T. Gardner, 1747, First edition; 4to., (2), 18 pages, disbound, from the library of the Earls of Macclesfield at Shirburn Castle. Maggs Bros. Ltd. 1440 - 101 2011 £850

Godwin, George *Vancouver: a Life 1757-1798.* New York: 1931, xi, 308 pages, illustrations, folding map in back poket, no jacket, bright, very good otherwise. Dumont Maps & Books of the West 112 - 41 2011 $65

Godwin, William 1756-1836 *Enquiry Concerning Political Justice and Its Influence on Morals and Happiness.* Philadelphia: Bioren and Madan, 1796, First American edition; 2 volumes, 12mo., xvi, (1), 22-362 pages; viii, 400 pages, contemporary mottled sheep, spines with red title labels and dark green volume number labels with gilt ovals, quarter sized piece torn from one front endpaper, one gathering slightly pulled, occasional very light scattered foxing, fine, clean copy in lovely period bindings, quite unusual in this condition. Joseph J. Felcone Inc. Fall Miscellany 2010 - 56 2011 $2600

Godwin, William 1756-1836 *Enquiry Concerning Political Justice and Its Influence on Morals and Happiness.* London: J. Watson, 1842, Fourth edition; small 8vo., pages xvi, 286, disbound, i.e. lacks covers, otherwise sound, very good, prelims slightly spotted. Any Amount of Books May 29 2011 - A45532 2011 $204

Godwin, William 1756-1836 *Memoirs of the author of a Vindication of the Rights of Woman.* London: J. Johnson and G. G. and J. Robinson, 1798, First edition; (4) 199 pages and (5) including errata and ad leaf, small 8vo., contemporary half calf, gilt lettered title label, half title, engraved frontispiece, discreet repair to hinges, otherwise nice, complete copy in contemporary binding. Paulette Rose Fine and Rare Books 32 - 187 2011 $3000

Godwin, William 1756-1836 *Memoirs of the author of a Vindication of the Rights of Woman.* Philadelphia: James Carey, 1799, First American edition; 8vo., pages 158, front blank tissued and remounted, bound in new boards with calf spine, some little marginal staining, very good, this copy was owned and annotated by a contemporary American reader, Nathaniel Pendleton Taylor, who signed and dated titlepage. Second Life Books Inc. 174 - 331 2011 $1500

Godwin, William 1756-1836 *Memoirs of Mary Wollstonecraft.* London: Constable and Co., 1927, First edition thus, one of 700 numbered copies; (352) pages, thick 8vo., original cloth, top edge gilt, others uncut, frontispiece, other illustrations, spine trifle faded, still fine, unopened copy. Paulette Rose Fine and Rare Books 32 - 188 2011 $300

Godwin, William 1756-1836 *Of Population. An Enquiry Concerning the Power of Increase in the Numbers of Mankind...* London: printed for Longman, Hurst, Rees, Orme and Brown, 1820, First edition; 235 x 152, xvi, (17)-22, 626 page, publisher's original temporary brown paper boards, paper label, edges untrimmed, text unopened (except for the introduction), folding cloth box with morocco spine label, old armorial bookplate of Jonathan Hargreaves and modern bookplate of John Yudkin; backstrip chipped at head (costing perhaps a square inch of paper), vertical crack at top reaching two-thirds of the way down the spine, loss of paper along half the length of joints (and with short cracks in joints), slight rubbing to corners (as usual), but binding still solid and otherwise well preserved, covers unusually clean, one opening of preface with noticeable ink staining in upper margin, minor foxing and marginal tears, but exceptionally clean and well preserved internally, unopened text obviously unread. Phillip J. Pirages 59 - 217 2011 $3900

Goethe, Johann Wolfgang Von 1749-1832 *Faust.* New York: Dingwall: Rock Limited, 1925, Limited edition of 2000 signed copies; 4to., top edge gilt, grey vellum backed boards, spine with gold lettering and borders, printed dust jacket with few minor chips along lower rear edge, otherwise dust jacket quite nice, original cardboard slipcase with some wear along edges and some minor spotting along spine, very good, 22 full page illustrations in color, black and white line drawings, and black and white with wash, 64 line illustrations by Harry Clarke. Jo Ann Reisler, Ltd. 86 - 46 2011 $1650

Goethe, Johann Wolfgang Von 1749-1832 *Reineke Fuchs. (Reynard the Fox).* Stuttgart and Tubingen: Gottascher, 1846, First edition; folio, 257 pages, all edges gilt, lovely contemporary binding by J. Wright in full crimson morocco with double gilt decorative rules surrounding on elaborate gilt panel on cover, raised bands on spine with beautiful gilt decorations in compartments, gilt dentelles, spine slightly toned with few spots on covers, else fine and clean, free of foxing that is generally found, illustrations by Kaulbach with pictorial titlepage and 36 plates on paper de chine, plus 24 smaller pictorial head and tailpieces.   Aleph-Bet Books, Inc.   95 - 488   2011 $3250

Goethe, Johann Wolfgang Von 1749-1832 *Zur Farbenlehre and Erklarung der Zu Goethe's Fabrenlehre Gehorigen Tafeln and Anzeige und Uebersicht des Goethischen Werkes zur Fabenlehre (the latter two in the plate volume).* Tubingen: J. G. Cotta, 1810, First editions of both text volumes and plate volume; text volumes 200 x 125mm., plate volume 240 x 202mm., 3 volumes, two text volumes and quarto atlas volume as issued), unusual period binding of contemporary paper treated to look like tree calf, paper put on over original half calf, flat spines with plain and decorative gilt rules, orange paper labels, with 17 plates, 12 of them hand colored, bookplate OS?, ink ownership inscription of German painter Ludwig Thiersch; variable foxing because of inferior paper stock, perhaps a dozen gatherings in first volume rather foxed, but problem never severe, the foxing quite minor or absent in many places and plates, done on better paper, almost entirely unaffected, paper covering the binding little worn and chipped at places along joints (revealing gilt decorated leather underneath), corners slightly bumped, atlas volume with two minor scratches to upper cover, still quite an appealing set, original insubstantial board bindings entirely sturdy, remarkably clean and surprisingly bright, text quite fresh and with almost no signs of use.   Phillip J. Pirages   59 - 218   2011 $24,000

Goetz, Hermann *"Mira Bai: Her Life and Times. A Tentative Critical Biography".* Bombay: Journal of the Gujarat Research Society, 1956, Offprint; small 4to., (87-113) pages, stapled paper wrappers, signed with compliments of author, very good, mailfold, small nick to front wrapper, tiny faint dampstain in corner of first signature.   Kaaterskill Books   12 - 259   2011 $95

Goffman, Erving *The Presentation of Self in Everyday Life.* Edinburgh: University of Edinburgh, 1596, First edition; 8vo., wrappers, pages (2) 162, very slight wrinkling at spine, very slight soiling, otherwise very good+.   Any Amount of Books   May 29 2011 - A4755   2011 $204

Goldberg, Benjamin *The Mirror and Man.* Charlottesville: University Press of Virginia, 1985, First edition; 8vo., xii, 260 pages, 38 illustrations, gray cloth with white paper boards, silver stamped spine title, dust jacket, fine, from the Bern Dibner reference library, with Burndy bookplate.   Jeff Weber Rare Books   161 - 176   2011 $115

Goldberg, Jim *Rich and Poor.* New York: Random House, 1985, First edition; photos, near fine in photo illustrated wrappers.   Jeff Hirsch Books   ny 2010 2011 $400

Golden Book of Famous Women. London: Hodder & Stougton, n.d. circa, 1919, First edition; small 4to., original blue pictorial cloth, gilt, pages viii, 200, 16 tipped in tissue guarded color plates, flyleaves lightly browned.   R. F. G. Hollett & Son Antiquarian Booksellers   175 - 173   2011   £150

Golden Book of Songs & Ballads. London: Hodder & Stoughton, n.d. circa, 1919, First edition; small 4to., original green pictorial cloth, gilt, pages 198, with 24 tipped in tissue guarded color plates, flyleaf stamped "Advance Copy Not for Circulation" and with price label of 20/= net.   R. F. G. Hollett & Son Antiquarian Booksellers   175 - 174   2011   £180

Golden Sunbeams. London: Society for Promoting Christian Knowledge, 1896-1897, 4to., Dec. 1896-Nov. 1897, each issue about 16 pages on handmade style uncut paper boards, woodcuts in black and red, stoutly bound in red unlettered cloth, slight wear, very good.   Any Amount of Books   May 29 2011 - B10051   2011 $298

Golden, Arthur *Memoris of a Geisha.* New York: Knopf, 1997, First edition; fine, dust jacket fine, signed by author.   Bella Luna Books   May 26 2011 - T7748   2011 $660

Goldin, Nan *The Devil's Playground.* London: Phaidon, 2003, Special edition, 88 of 100 copies; signed and numbered, small 4to., 448 pages, 460 color illustrations, presented in specially made box, with original large Cibachrome print Valerie in the taxi, Paris 2001, also signed and numbered by Goldin, book placed within larger box with photo in its own compartment and strong dark grey covers, 27 x 18 inches, containing box and print, fine.   Any Amount of Books   May 26 2011 - A73809   2011 $1845

Golding, Harry *Bully Boy: the Story of a Bulldog and His Friend Jock.* London: Ward Lock & Co., n.d. c., 1931, 12mo., original pictorial boards, spine stripped, edges rather rubbed, pages 96, 16 illustrations in color, 8 in black and white by Arthur Cooke, front joint cracked, scarce.   R. F. G. Hollett & Sons Antiquarian Booksellers   170 - 265   2011   £45

Golding, Harry *Fairy Tales.* London: Ward Lock & Co. n.d. circa, 1920, original cloth with oval pictorial onlay, dust jacket (edges trifle rubbed), pages 403, (iv), with 44 colored plates and colored pictorial endpapers by Margaret Tarrant, very nice.   R. F. G. Hollett & Sons Antiquarian Booksellers   170 - 667   2011   £150

Golding, Harry *Zoo Days.* London: Ward Lock & Co., 1919, First edition; original green cloth with oval pictorial onlay, little faded, slight scratch to upper board, pages 344 with 48 color plates and color endpapers, all by Margaret Tarrant, joints tender, but very good.   R. F. G. Hollett & Son Antiquarian Booksellers   General Catalogue Summer 2010 - 580 2011   £75

Golding, Louis *Luigi of Catanzaro.* London: E. Archer, 1926, First edition, limited to 100 copies, numbered and signed by author, this #36; quarto, printed wrappers, 21, (1) pages, covers little soiled, else very good, tight copy, housed in cloth clamshell case with red leather label on spine, titles stamped in gold, rare.   Buckingham Books May 26 2011 - 27900 2011 $3000

Golding, William 1911-1993 *The Inheritors.* London: Faber and Faber Ltd., 1955, First edition; octavo, cloth.   L. W. Currey, Inc.   124 - 95 2011 $850

Golding, William 1911-1993 *Lord of the Flies.* London: Faber and Faber, 1954, Second printing; spine lean, near fine in like dust jacket, slightly dusty with couple of minute edge nicks.   Ken Lopez Bookseller   154 - 64 2011 $450

Golding, William 1911-1993 *The Paper Men.* London: 1984, First edition; fine in fine dust jacket, laid in is publicity photo of William Golding, signed by him.   Gemini Fine Books & Arts, Ltd.   Art Reference & Illustrated Books: First Editions 2011 $95

Golding, William 1911-1993 *The Pyramid.* London: Faber, 1967, First edition; pages 217, foolscap 8vo., original dark blue cloth, cocked backstrip gilt lettered, dust jacket designed by Leonard Rosoman, faint sunning to rear panel, very good.   Blackwell Rare Books   B166 - 147 2011   £50

Golding, William 1911-1993 *The Scorpion God and Other Stories.* London: Faber and Faber, 1971, Advance uncorrected proof copy of the first edition; octavo, printed wrappers.   L. W. Currey, Inc.   124 - 230 2011 $100

Goldsmid, Edmund *Hermippus Revivivus; or the Sage's Triumph Over Old Age and the Grave.* Edinburgh: privately printed, 1885, Limited edition, 1 of 275 small paper copies Printed; blue cloth, corners bumped, spine pastedown darkened, small stain on rear, endpapers foxed, else clean, 1 split to spine but hold, 162 pages, 3 volumes in 1, very good.   G. H. Mott Bookseller   May 26 2011 - 24583 2011 $200

Goldsmid, Edmund *A True Account and Declaration of the Horrid Conspiracy to Assassinate the Late King Charles II at the Rye House.* Edinburgh: privately printed, 1886, Large paper copy; small 8vo., original printed wrappers, little cockled and spine cracked, small label on upper panel, pages 48, few marginal blindstamp accession stamp on verso of title.   R. F. G. Hollett & Son Antiquarian Booksellers   175 - 529 2011   £35

Goldsmith, J. *Geography, on a Popular Plan...* Printed for Richard Phillips, 1806, New edition; modern full polished calf, pages xi-xii 645, (iii), lacks pages i-x and 335-338, 359-360, with 41 maps and woodcut plates (ex 60), map of England torn, with some loss, some wear and fingering, despite being sadly defective, a facsinating work.   R. F. G. Hollett & Son Antiquarian Booksellers   General Catalogue Summer 2010 - 1642 2011   £120

Goldsmith, J. *A Grammar of British Geography...* London: Richard Phillips, n.d., 1812, First edition; small 8vo., soundly rebound in yellow cloth lettered gilt on spine on black spine label, pages viii, 244, 7 maps, ex-British Foreign Office Library, with few library markings, else very good.   Any Amount of Books   May 29 2011 - A64151 2011 $238

Goldsmith, John *An Almanack for the Year of Our Lord MDCCCIX.* London: Company of Stationers, 1809, 64mo., original crimson roan gilt extra, each board with central cream panel decorated with onlaid strips of blue and red leather, gilt tooled overall with broken fillets and rolls, spine defective at head and small piece missing from foot of lower board, matching leather pull off case, extremities trifle rubbed, pages 48, all edges gilt, printed in red an black, almanack pages on verso only, whole printed on stiff paper, marbled endpapers and dusty stamp on reverse of title.   R. F. G. Hollett & Son Antiquarian Booksellers   General Catalogue Summer 2010 - 606 2011   £350

Goldsmith, Oliver 1730-1774 *A History of the Earth and Animated Nature.* London: 1790, Third edition; 8 volumes, 101 plates, full mottled calf, some boards worn but bindings firm, gilt decorated spines, some wear to tops, blank f.e.p.p., half titles lacking, else very good.   C. P. Hyland   May 26 2011 - 256/308 2011 $362

Goldsmith, Oliver 1730-1774 *The Vicar of Wakefield: a Tale Supposed to be Written by Himself.* Salisbury: Printed for B. Collins for F. Newbery, 1766, First edition, variant B; 2 volumes, 172 x 108mm., terminal blank in volume I, beautiful scarlet crushed morocco, heavily gilt by Riviere & Son, covers with French fillet frame, spine with raised bands and handsomely gilt compartments, lovely gilt inner dentelles, all edges gilt, leather book labels of Roderick Terry, (Edgar) Mills and Doris Louise Benz, lower corner of terminal blank in first volume skillfully renewed, artful repair and faint glue stains at inner margin of B3 in second volume, other isolated trivial defects, very fine, text nearly pristine, especially bright and handsome binding.   Phillip J. Pirages   59 - 50 2011 $6500

Goldsmith, Oliver 1730-1774 *The Vicar of Wakefield.*
London: Sampson Low, Son & Co., 1861, Original full purple calf heavily embossed on both boards with borders, floral design & decorated gilt title, spine faded to brown, slight rubbing, ownership signature, illustrations by George Thomas.   Jarndyce Antiquarian Booksellers   CXCI - 437   2011   £60

Goldsmith, Oliver 1730-1774 *The Vicar of Wakefield.*
London: J. M. Dent, 1904, First edition; original green cloth, gilt, spine and upper board decorated gilt overall, pages xvii, 242, top edge gilt, untrimmed, 25 color plates by C. E. Brock.   R. F. G. Hollett & Son Antiquarian Booksellers General Catalogue Summer 2010 - 737   2011   £35

Goldsmith, Oliver 1730-1774 *The Vicar of Wakefield.*
London and New York: Macmillan, 1927, 185 x 125mm., xxxvi, 306 pages, charming contemporary fawn colored pictorial crushed morocco by Riviere and Son, covers with frame formed by multiple gilt rules with onlaid green dot cornerpieces and gilt festoons at head and tail of frame, central pictorial inlay in four colors depicting a vicar pontificating (and in front of him as an indication of shadow, thin penwork lines inscribed into the morocco), raised bands, spine gilt in French fillet compartments with central gilt patera, wide gilt framed turn-ins with ribbon cornerpieces, leather hinges, marbled endpapers, all edges gilt, linen covered slipcase; frontispiece and 181 illustrations in text by Hugh Thomson, spine very slightly and uniformly sunned toward a butterscotch color, but very fine, text clean, fresh and bright and lustrous, appealing binding with only the most insignificant wear.   Phillip J. Pirages   59 - 128   2011 $950

Goldsmith, Oliver 1730-1774 *The Vicar of Wakefield.*
London: Harrap, 1929, First Rackham edition, 4/775 copies signed by artist; 12 color printed plates and other illustrations in text, all by Arthur Rackham, title and Rackham design on titlepage printed in red, prelim leaves foxed, one leaf little creased, pages 232, 4to., original cream parchment, lettering and design on backstrip and lettering on front covers within double rule border, all blocked in gilt, endpapers with designs in green by Rackham, top edge gilt, others untrimmed, board slipcase from The Compleat Angler with printed label to that affect, very good, publisher George Harrap's copy with his bookplate, beneath statement of limitation is pen and ink drawing by Rackham, drawn for Harrap.   Blackwell Rare Books   B166 - 224   2011   £10,000

Goldsmith, Oliver 1730-1774 *The Vicar of Wakefield.*
Philadelphia: David McKay Company, 1929, One of 775 copies signed by artist, including 575 for England (this being #95 of the 200 copies for America); 270 x 205mm., very attractive red three quarter morocco stamp signed "Putnams" along front turn in, raised bands, spine handsomely gilt in compartments formed by plain and decorative rules, quatrefoil centerpiece surrounded by densely scrolling cornerpieces, sides and endleaves of rose colored linen, top edge gilt, other edges untrimmed and mostly unopened, 12 color plates by Arthur Rackham, including frontispiece, several smaller illustrations in text; front board with insignificant small round spot to cloth, but very fine, unusually bright and clean inside and out, almost no signs of use.   Phillip J. Pirages   59 - 287   2011 $2900

Goldsmith, Oliver 1730-1774 *The Vicar of Wakefield.*
London: Harrap, 1929, Limited to 575 copies for England and numbered and signed by artist; 4to., full gilt vellum, top edge gilt, fine, illustrations by Arthur Rackham, 12 very lovely color plates plus text black and whites and pictorial endpapers, beautiful copy.   Aleph-Bet Books, Inc.   95 - 479   2011 $2700

Goldsmith, Oliver 1730-1774 *The Vicar of Wakefield.*
London: George G. Harrap & Co., 1929, First edition; 4to., top edge gilt, publisher's leather with elaborate and lovely inlay on front cover, very nice with no notable faults, 12 full page color plates and line drawings by Arthur Rackham, 232 numbered pages, housed in original publisher's box with title label on one end, box has some wear and side missing, magnificent publisher's inlaid leather binding.   Jo Ann Reisler, Ltd.   86 - 203   2011 $1500

Goldsmith, Oliver 1730-1774 *The Works.* London: John Murray, 1878, 4 volumes, 227 x 148mm; excellent highly polished calf attractively gilt by Root & Son (stamp signed), covers bordered by triple gilt fillet with rosette cornerpieces, raised bands, spines gilt in compartments with trefoil cornerpieces on a stippled ground, each spine with three morocco titling labels (one olive and two burgundy), densely gilt turn-ins, marbled endpapers, top edge gilt, leaves mostly unopened, with extra engraved titlepage (dated 1854), featuring a village vignette; slight wear to joints and extremities, couple of small scratches to covers, but fine set, attractive bindings lustrous and generally well preserved, obviously unread text with virtually no signs of use.   Phillip J. Pirages   59 - 225   2011 $1100

Gole, Susan *Maps of the Mediterranean Regions Published in British Parliamentary Papers 1801-1921.*
Nicosia: Bank of Cyprus Cultural Foundation, 1996, First edition; 4to., copiously illustrated in color and black and white throughout, pages 429, small neat name on front endpaper, otherwise fine.   Any Amount of Books   May 29 2011 - A77032   2011 $272

Gombrich, E. H. *Art and Illusion. A Study in the Psychology of Pictorial Representation.* Pantheon Books, 1960, First edition; large 8vo., very good, hardback, presentation from Herbert Read dated June 1960 to the first Registrar of the University of York.   Ken Spelman Rare Books   68 - 128   2011   £50

Gomme, George Laurence *Folklore as an Historical Science.* London: Methuen, 1908, First edition; original red cloth, gilt, few faint marks to upper board, pages xvi, 371, with 28 illustrations, half title little browned and spotted, otherwise nice, scarce.   R. F. G. Hollett & Son Antiquarian Booksellers   175 - 530   2011   £65

Gontaut-Biron, Marie Josephine Louise, Duchesse De *Memoirs of the Duchesse De Gontaut...* New York: Dodd Mead and Co., 1894, Of this edition on deckle edge paper, 175 copies were printed; 235 x 155mm., 2 volumes, elegant dark green crushed morocco, sumptuously gilt by Chambolle-Duru (stamp signed on front turn-ins), covers ornately gilt with triple ruled borders surrounding a wide internal frame of fleurons, scallops, curls and floral bouquets in urns, raised bands, spine compartments with floral urn centerpiece within a frame of scrolling foliate stamps, elaborate inner gilt dentelles, marbled endpapers, top edge gilt, other edges uncut, each volume with mezzotint color frontispiece and window mount, 12 additional engraved plates with captioned tissue guards, titlepages printed in red and black, joints partly rubbed, front joint of first volume beginning to crack at top and bottom, slight browning at edges of leaves because of acidic paper, still very appealing, especially lovely bindings, solid and bright, text without significant signs of use.   Phillip J. Pirages   59 - 226   2011 $650

The Good Boy. English: no publisher, circa, 1820, 12mo., pictorial buff paper cover, left front flap printed with an alphabet with two words for each letter, right cover flap with half page woodcut, inside left flap and center page printed with two alphabets in upper and lower case and in roman and italic style, inside right flap printed with two woodcuts, small inked name and date at corner of inside first page, very fine battledore in mint state.   Hobbyhorse Books   56 - 8   2011 $340

Good, Gregory *Sciences of the Earth: an Encyclopedia of Events, People and Phenomena.* New York: Garland Pub., 1998, 2 volumes, 8vo., xlv, 407; (409)-901 pages, figures, printed boards, fine, from the Bern Dibner reference library, with Burndy bookplate.   Jeff Weber Rare Books   161 - 177   2011 $70

Goodchild, Laurence *The Lamiae: a Tale of the Roman Conquest.* Newcastle-upon-Tyne: printed at the Daily Journal Office, 1879, First edition; original green pebble grained cloth, slightly rubbed.   Jarndyce Antiquarian Booksellers   CXCI - 189   2011   £75

Goode, G. Brown *The Published Writings of Philip Lutley Sclater 1844-1896.* Washington: GPO, 1896, frontispiece, original dark brown cloth, F. D. Godman bookplate, very good.   Jarndyce Antiquarian Booksellers   CXCI - 341   2011   £75

Goode, James W. *Best Addresses - a Century of Washington's Distinguished Apartment Houses.* Washington: 1988, xxii,597 pages, small folio, very good, some foxing to black cloth, fine dust jacket, endpaper maps, signed by author.   Bookworm & Silverfish   662 - 48   2011 $175

Goode's New Universal Primer. Clerkenwell Green: T. Goode, n.d. circa, 1850, 12mo., 12 pages, pink pictorial paper wrappers, large wood engraved vignette and decorative frame on titlepage, 10 engraved vignettes adorn text, near mint partially uncut.   Hobbyhorse Books   56 - 119   2011 $110

Goodis, David *Behold this Woman.* New York: D. Appleton Century Co., 1947, First edition; fine in fine dust jacket, minor tiny crease to bottom edge of front panel, very scarce book in dust jacket.   Buckingham Books   May 26 2011 - 27092   2011 $2250

Goodrich, Samuel Griswold   1793-1860 *Curiosities of Human Nature.* Boston: Bradbury, Soden & Co., 1843, First edition; small 8vo., vi, 320 pages + 2 page list on lower wrappers, continuous numeration in both volumes, decorative paper wrappers, wood engraved frontispiece, vignette on titlepage and plate guard, half title, many wood engravings, ink signature at top borders of covers, dusted wrappers, tender along spine of first volume, enclosed in modern box, fine set, scarce in such good state.   Hobbyhorse Books   56 - 78   2011 $400

Goodrich, Samuel Griswold   1793-1860 *Peter Parley's visit to London, During the Coronation of Queen Victoria.* London: Charles Tilt, 1838, 12mo., original cloth, gilt extra, neatly recased with new endpapers, pages 116, (ii), pictorial title and 6 hand colored plates, scarce.   R. F. G. Hollett & Son Antiquarian Booksellers   General Catalogue Summer 2010 - 519   2011   £175

Goodrich, Samuel Griswold   1793-1860 *Peter Parley's Visit to London.* London: Charles Tilt, 1946, 12mo., original cloth, gilt extra, neatly recased, new endpapers, pages 116, (ii), complete with pictorial title and 6 hand colored plates, scarce.   R. F. G. Hollett & Sons Antiquarian Booksellers   170 - 272   2011   £175

Goodrich, Samuel Griswold   1793-1860 *Peter Parley's Visit to London During the Coronation of Queen Victoria.* London: Charles Tilt, 1838, 12mo., original cloth, gilt, extra, neatly recased with new endpapers, pages 116, (ii), pictorial title and 6 hand colored plates, scarce.   R. F. G. Hollett & Son Antiquarian Booksellers   175 - 530   2011   £175

Goody Two Shoes' Picture Book. London: George Routledge and Sons, circa, 1880, 4to., dark red embossed cloth with back decorations and gold lettering and decorations on cover and spine, little shelfwear and some minor weakness to hinges 24 pages of full color illustrations by Walter Crane and several pages of black and white text. Jo Ann Reisler, Ltd. 86 - 49 2011 $1200

Goody Two Shoes. New York: McLoughlin Bros., 1898, 4to., 6 leaves, full color pictorial stiff paper wrappers, 6 very fine full page chromolithographs, faint chipping at spine, in all a fine copy. Hobbyhorse Books 56 - 79 2011 $225

Gordimer, Nadine *Burger's Daughter.* London: Cape, 1979, First edition; fading to top stain, one lower corner tapped, near fine in near fine, lightly rubbed, spine faded dust jacket, inscribed by author. Ken Lopez Bookseller 154 - 69 2011 $225

Gordimer, Nadine *Friday's Footprint.* London: Gollancz, 1960, First edition; signed by author, owner name and contemporary date front flyleaf, small ding to upper board edges, near fine in very good, spine tanned dust jacket wth chip to spine base, loss of publisher's name and part of logo. Ken Lopez Bookseller 154 - 67 2011 $75

Gordimer, Nadine *The Lying Days.* London: Gollancz, 1953, Corrected first edition; signed by author, some foxing, small owner name, slight sunning to cloth at spine extremities, foxing to endpages and page edges, still near fine in good, modestly spine tanned dust jacket with shallow loss to edges and folds, but with larger chips to spine ends that have taken four letters, two from title at top and two from publisher's name at bottom. Ken Lopez Bookseller 154 - 65 2011 $100

Gordimer, Nadine *Not for Publication.* London: Gollancz, 1965, First, (true first) edition; signed by author, tape shadows to endpages from previous jacket protector, thus only near fine in very good, spine sunned dust jacket with dampstaining to lower edge and tape shadows to flaps and verso, small set of ink numbers to lower front flap. Ken Lopez Bookseller 154 - 68 2011 $85

Gordimer, Nadine *A World of Strangers.* London: Gollancz, 1958, British edition of true first edition; signed by author, owner name front flyleaf, else fine in very good dust jacket with small chips at corners and crown and 1 1/2 inch tear at upper front spine fold, overall attractive. Ken Lopez Bookseller 154 - 66 2011 $250

Gordon, C. A. *A Concise History of the Antient and Illustrious House of Gordon from the Origin of the Name to the Present Time.* Aberdeen: printed for the author, 1754, 8vo., pages ix (iii) 309, (xi) contemporary crimson sheep, boards double rule gilt bordered with flowerets at corners and in centre black morocco lozenge onlay double rule gilt bordered with flowerets outermost at extremities and 'Scottish Herringbone" design within all gilt, 'Dutch gilt' endpapers, all edges gilt, pale blue and white sewn endbands, early 21st retrospective reback in sheep by Chris Weston, toned and little spotted, old leather bit scratched, ink inscription "Honble Colonel Cosmo Gordon to his friend and relation David Gordon Esre. Abergeldie, further inscriptions signed "Emilia Lucy Gordon/Ivy Lodge August 1873", reverse of loose paper has information about Cosmo Gordon who shot dead a fellow officer, fled abroad for a year then faced a trial at which the jury pronounced him not guilty, from the collection of Christopher Ernest Weston 1947-2010. Unsworths Booksellers 24 - 103 2011 £500

Gordon, Elizabeth *Flower Children - The Little Cousins of the Field and Garden.* Joliet: P. F. Volland Co., 1910, No statement of later printing; 8vo., cloth backed full color pictorial boards with some light sunning to upper edges, else clean, full color pictorial dust jacket with some wear, especially along edges, every page has half page full color illustration. Jo Ann Reisler, Ltd. 86 - 260 2011 $200

Gordon, Elizabeth *Happy Home Children.* Chicago: Volland, 1924, No additional printings; 8vo. pictorial boards, fine in pictorial box, illustrations by Marion Foster, rare. Aleph-Bet Books, Inc. 95 - 570 2011 $375

Gordon, Elizabeth *Wild Flower Children.* Chicago: Volland, 1918, no additional printings; 8vo., green pictorial boards, fine in original box, illustrations by Janet Laura Scott, beautiful copy, extremely scarce. Aleph-Bet Books, Inc. 95 - 579 2011 $600

Gordon, James D. *Great Gunmakers for the Early West.* Santa Fe: 2007, Limited edition of 1000 numbered and signed copies; 3 volumes, oblong folio, (vi), 176 pages, illustrations; (iv), 177-352 pages, illustrations; (iv), 353-50 pages, illustrations, new in slipcase, printed on heavy coated stock. Dumont Maps & Books of the West 112 - 42 2011 $325

Gordon, W. J. *Every-Day Life on the Railroad.* London: Religious Tract Society, 1898, Second edition; original pictorial red cloth, spine little faded, pages 192, 13 plates, flyleaves rather browned, prize label on pastedown, uncommon. R. F. G. Hollett & Son Antiquarian Booksellers General Catalogue Summer 2010 - 1111 2011 £65

Gordon, W. J. *Perseus the Gorgon Slayer.* London: Sampson Low etc., n.d., First edition; small 8vo., original blindstamped cloth gilt, spine mellowed, pages vii, 327 (iv), woodcuts throughout.   R. F. G. Hollett & Sons Antiquarian Booksellers   170 - 273   2011   £65

Gore, Al *Earth in the Balance.* Boston: Houghton Mifflin, 1992, Proof copy; very good, light rubbing, scarce format signed by author.   Bella Luna Books   May 26 2011 - t566 2011 $300

Gore, W. Ormsby *Illustrated Regional Guides to Ancient Monuments Under the Ownership or Guardianship of His Majesty's Office Works.* London: HMSO, 1936-1938, 4 volumes, small 8vo., original cloth, gilt, illustrations.   R. F. G. Hollett & Son Antiquarian Booksellers   177 - 420   2011   £35

Gorey, Edward *Amphigorey - Fifteen Books by Edward Gorey.* New York: G. P. Putnam's Sons, 1972, Limited to 50 copies, signed, with original watercolor; large 4to., color pictorial cloth, lovely copy, color pictorial dust jacket is equally fresh and clean, book housed in original slipcase which has printed paste label on front of slipcase, drawing is pen, ink and watercolor and done on paper, image is about 3 1/4 to 4 inches and signed with his initial monogram.   Jo Ann Reisler, Ltd.   86 - 111   2011 $8500

Gorey, Edward *The Bug Book.* New York: Looking Glass Library, 1959, Limited to 600 copies; 16mo., color printed paper wrappers with some light overall marking, this copy signed in full on titlepage by Gorey, quite uncommon.   Jo Ann Reisler, Ltd.   86 - 109   2011 $1200

Gorey, Edward *The Gilded Bat.* London: Cape, 1967, First UK edition; small square 8vo., original pictorial boards, matching dust jacket price clipped, unpaginated, illustrations.   R. F. G. Hollett & Son Antiquarian Booksellers   175 - 532   2011   £65

Gorey, Edward *Three Books from the Fantod Press. The Chinese Obelisks. The Osbick Bird; and Donald Has a Difficulty.* New York: Fantod Press, 1970, Limited to 500 copies housed inpublisher's printed fuchsia envelpe; oblong 12mo., envelope has slight wear and the 3 books are in lovely condition, books are oblong 12mo. with printed card covers.   Jo Ann Reisler, Ltd.   86 - 110   2011 $1500

Gorham, Maurice *The Local.* London: Cassell, 1939, First edition; 15 color lithographic plates, by Edward Ardizzone, pages xvi, 52, 8vo., original light gray boards little soiled, backstrip and front cover printed in black and red, light browning to endpapers, good, scarce.   Blackwell Rare Books   B166 - 122   2011   £300

The Gorilla Hunters. T. Nelson and Sons, 1870, Pages 422, (ii), woodcut title and plates, slightly shaken, very good, original blindstamped green cloth gilt, hinges rubbed, little frayed, slightly shaken, very good copy of an early edition.   R. F. G. Hollett & Sons Antiquarian Booksellers   170 - 55   2011   £65

Gorman, R. H. *Toyland and Dolldom Moving Pictures.* Chicago: Thompson & Thomas, 1907, 8vo., stiff pictorial wrappers, stain on edge of rear cover, else very good+, two of the pages divided into 6 sections (sliced horizontally) allowing reader to form hundreds of different combinations of pictures.   Aleph-Bet Books, Inc.   95 - 376   2011 $300

Gortz, Johann Eustachius *The Secret History of the Armed Neutrality, together with Memoirs Official Letters and State Papers...* London: printed for J. Johnson, 1792, First edition; 8vo., pages 260, English and French texts, ex-Foreign and Commonwealth Office library with their label and stamps (lightly applied), slight archival repair to titlepage which has 2 stamps, otherwise very good, modern brown cloth.   Any Amount of Books   May 29 2011 - A49986   2011 $238

Gosling, W. G. *Labrador: Its Discovery, Exploration and Development.* London: Alston Rivers Ltd., 1910, First edition; blue cloth with gilt to spine, pages xii 574, half title, index, 10 maps, 34 plates, large 8vo., cloth slightly darkened, interior very good.   Schooner Books Ltd.   96 - 37 2011 $425

Gossage, John *LAMP: Like a Mother Fucker, three Days in Berlin 1987.* N.P.: self published, 1987, First edition, one of only 100 numbered copies; each copy contains a different selection of 28 silver gelatin prints, fine and tight in very near fine dust jacket, jacket has some very tiny edge tears, signed and numbered by Gossage.   Jeff Hirsch Books   ny 2010 2011 $6000

Gosse, Edmund   1849-1928 *On Viol and Flute.* London: Heinemann, 1896, First Selected edition; small 8vo., pages xi, 212, original publisher's green cloth lettered gilt on spine and cover, frontispiece, signed presentation from author to George Moore, from the library of Henry "Chips" Channon with note at rear in his hand "Given me by Lady Cunard, Christmas 1938, slight tanning, slight fading, very small nick at head of spine, otherwise very good.   Any Amount of Books   May 29 2011 - A69860   2011 $255

Gosse, Philip Henry *The Canadian Naturalist: a Series of Conversations on the Natural History of Lower Canada.* London: John Van Voorst, 1840, 8vo., green cloth with gilt titles to spine, pages xii, 372, (2) index, 44 illustrations. Schooner Books Ltd.   96 - 287   2011 $95

Gosse, Philip Henry *Evenings at the Microscope...* London: SPCK, 1895, Original red cloth gilt, microscope stamped in gilt on upper board, hinges little rubbed, pages xvi 434, 6 (ads), with 113 text woodcuts, front flyleaf removed. R. F. G. Hollett & Son Antiquarian Booksellers General Catalogue Summer 2010 - 975 2011 £30

Gosse, Philip Henry *Land and Sea.* London: James Nisbet, 1865, First edition; 15 woodcuts, 10 page catalog + 16 page catalog, slight foxing in prelims, original purple fine pebble grained cloth, bevelled boards, gilt spine slightly dulled, all edges gilt, very good, inscription for Charles Harbin from his wife. Jarndyce Antiquarian Booksellers CXCI - 330 2011 £125

Gosse, Philip Henry *Life in Lower, Intermediate and Higher Forms or Manifestations of the Divine Wisdom in the Natural History of Animals.* London: James Nisbet, 1857, First edition; frontispiece, slightly foxed, 5 plates, original green cloth, borders in blind, lettered and blocked in gilt, spine slightly dulled with slight rubbing to hinges, good plus. Jarndyce Antiquarian Booksellers CXCI - 331 2011 £125

Gosse, Philip Henry *Life in Its Lower, Intermediate and Higher Forms, or Manifestations of the Divine Wisdom in the Natural History of Animals.* London: James Nisbet and Co., 1857, Second edition; original green blindstamped cloth, gilt with large gilt emblem of flyshooter fish, neatly recased, pages viii, 363, with 22 text woodcuts and 6 full page woodcut plates. R. F. G. Hollett & Son Antiquarian Booksellers 175 - 533 2011 £140

Gosse, Philip Henry *Natural History - Birds.* London: SPCK, 1849, First edition; small 8vo., original blind-stamped cloth gilt, spine mellowed, pages vii, 327, (iv) woodcuts. R. F. G. Hollett & Sons Antiquarian Booksellers 170 - 274 2011 £85

Gosse, Philip Henry *Sacred Streams: The Ancient and Modern History of the Rivers of the Bible.* London: Hodder and Stoughton, 1877, Third edition; original pictorial and decorated green cloth gilt, spine little rubbed, pages xii, 435, frontispiece, 44 text woodcuts, front flyleaf removed, little foxing to title and first leaf of preface. R. F. G. Hollett & Son Antiquarian Booksellers 175 - 534 2011 £45

Gosse, Philip Henry *A Year at the Shore.* London: Alexander Strahan, 1865, First edition; half title, color chromolithograph, frontispiece + 35 color plates from drawings by author, final ad leaf, original green cloth, bevelled boards, lettered and with triple ruled border in gilt, some slight rubbing, booklabel, with name erased on leading f.e.p., very good. Jarndyce Antiquarian Booksellers CXCI - 332 2011 £68

Gotch, J. Alfred *The English Home from Charles I to George IV.* London: Batsford, 1919, Second impression; original cloth, gilt, spine little dulled, neatly recased, pages xi, 412, 320 illustrations. R. F. G. Hollett & Son Antiquarian Booksellers 177 - 421 2011 £40

Gother, John *A Papist Mis-represented and Represented; or a Two-Fold Character of Popery.* London: s.n., printed anno domini, 1685, First edition; 4to., title slightly soiled, vignette on title, (10), 79, (1), 8 pages, disbound. Anthony W. Laywood May 26 2011 - 21655 2011 $218

Gottschalk, Paul *The Earliest Diplomatic Documents on America.* Berlin: Paul Gottschalk, 1927, Limited to 172 copies, 150 of which were offered for sale; folio, 89 pages, plus 130 facsimiles, original half vellum an brown cloth, gilt lettered spine, covers slightly boed, Burndy bookplate, fine copy. Jeff Weber Rare Books 163 - 73 2011 $1750

Goudge, Elizabeth *The Little White Horse.* London: University of London Press, 1946, First edition; original cloth, gilt, spine lettering little dulled, dust jacket little worn, spine rather darkened, pages 286, 4 color plates and line drawings by C. Walter Hodges, pictorial endpapers. R. F. G. Hollett & Sons Antiquarian Booksellers 170 - 275 2011 £195

Gough, William *David Blackwood, Master Printmaker.* Buffalo: Firefly Books, 2001, first printing; gray covers with silver spine imprints, very fine in fine dust jacket. Lupack Rare Books May 26 2011 - ABE3439077951 2011 $100

Gould, Chester *The Celebrated Cases of Dick Tracy 1931-1951.* New York: Chelsea House, 1970, First edition; 4to., pages xxviii, 291, nice in slightly scuffed and wrinkled dust jacket. Second Life Books Inc. 174 - 162 2011 $65

Gould, Chester *Dick Tracy: the Capture of Boris Arson.* Chicago: Pleasure Books, 1935, 4to., pictorial boards, covers lightly soiled, else fine, 3 great color pop-ups and many black and whites. Aleph-Bet Books, Inc. 95 - 444 2011 $650

Gould, F. Carruthers *Political Caricatures. 1904.* London: Edward Arnold, 1904, First edition; oblong large 4to., original pictorial cloth, rather marked, corners very worn and rounded, pages viii, 104, political cartoons. R. F. G. Hollett & Son Antiquarian Booksellers 175 - 536 2011 £75

Gould, Robert Freke *The History of Freemasonry.* Edinburgh: T. C. and E. C. Jack, n.d. 1880's, 3 volumes, 4to., publisher's handsome full maroon morocco gilt over heavy bevelled boards, each board decorated in gilt with broad rolls and masonic emblems, corners trifle rubbed and scraped in places, hinges just cracking at some ends but sound, pages 504, 502, 502, all edges gilt, with 41 tissue guarded photo etched portraits and 6 other engraved plates, most attractive, clean, sound set. R. F. G. Hollett & Son Antiquarian Booksellers 175 - 537 2011 £450

Goulden, Shirley *Flak: the Story of a Canine Hero of the War.* London: W. H. Allen, n.d. circa, 1943, 8vo., cloth backed pictorial boards, fine, no dust jacket, illustrations by J. Abbey. Aleph-Bet Books, Inc. 95 - 596 2011 $90

Goulden, Shirley *Tales from Japan.* London: W. H. Allen, 1961, Folio, original pictorial boards, rather worn an soiled, neatly rebacked, pages 64, color illustrations. R. F. G. Hollett & Sons Antiquarian Booksellers 170 - 277 2011 £65

Gourmont, Remy De 1858-1915 *Physique de l'Amour/ Essai sur l'Instinct Sexuel.* Paris: Mercure de France, 1903, 8vo., pages 295, (1) imprint, contemporary niger half morocco, marbled boards and endpapers, top edge gilt, author's presentation inscription to Rene Emery. Simon Finch Rare Books Zero - 139 2011 £200

Gowin, Emmet *Petra. In the Hashemite Kingdom of Jordan.* New York: Pace/MacGill Gallery, 1986, First edition; oversized stiff wrappers in jacket, fine in fine dust jacket, surprisingly uncommon. Jeff Hirsch Books ny 2010 2011 $850

Grabe, Joannes Ernestus *Septuaginta Interpretum. Tomus 1. Continens Octateuchum. Volume IV. Continens Psalmorum...* Oxford: E Theatro Sheldoniano sumptibus Henrici Clementis, 1707-1709, 2 volumes 1 (ex 4), folio, contemporary full panelled calf, worn and scraped, spine rather defective, upper board detached, unpaginated, half title, engraved frontispiece, titles with Sheldonian vignette, several fine engraved pictorial headpieces and initials by Gucht, little marginal worming towards end. R. F. G. Hollett & Son Antiquarian Booksellers 175 - 538 2011 £150

Graber, H. W. *The Life Record of H. W. Graber, a Terry Texas Ranger 1861-1865 Sixty-Two Years in Texas.* N.P.: privately printed by H. W. Graber, 1916, First edition; 8vo., three quarter and cloth, frontispiece, 442 pages, original spine professionally replaced, new front and rear endpapers, typed note dated 1911 to Mrs. Graber and Newspaper review from 1916 laid in, else very good, tight, square copy, rare. Buckingham Books May 26 2011 - 30510 2011 $2250

Grace, Pierce C. *The Unknown. A Prize Tale.* St. Louis: 1849, First edition; 168 pages, very good in blindstamped black cloth, few rub marks and expected opaque spots, endpapers foxed. Bookworm & Silverfish 676 - 131 2011 $75

Graham, Harry *Misrepresentative Women and Other Verses.* London: Edward Arnold, 1906, First edition; pages x, 115, 13 illustrations, library accession stamp on verso of title, few marginal blindstamps, little fingering in places, scarce. R. F. G. Hollett & Son Antiquarian Booksellers 175 - 540 2011 £45

Graham, Henry *The New Coinage.* privately published Civil Service Printing and Publishing Co., 1878, Pages 152, original black cloth, gilt, rather bubbled and stained by damp, pages 152, endpapers rather cockled ad stained, presentation copy inscribed by H. W. Schneider with author's compliments. R. F. G. Hollett & Son Antiquarian Booksellers 173 - 486 2011 £75

Graham, Maria *Letters on India...* London: Longman, 1814, Frontispiece, folding map, 9 plates, final errata leaf, small tear to near margin of titlepage, uncut in contemporary drab boards carefully rebacked, paper spine label, endpapers replaced, some slight rubbing, but very good, title signed "Miss Grahams-Finsbury(?). Jarndyce Antiquarian Booksellers CXCI - 552 2011 £250

Graham, Rigby *Rigby Graham's Leicestershire.* Leicester: Sycamore Press for the Gadsby Galleries, 1980, Limited signed edition, out of series copy, number of 150 copies; oblong folio, original morocco backed green buckram, gilt, slipcase, pages 160, with 160 illustrations, including original lithographs and full color lino blocks, fine, inscribed "Publisher's copy" and signed by John Simpson. R. F. G. Hollett & Son Antiquarian Booksellers General Catalogue Summer 2010 - 1420 2011 £650

Graham, Robert Bontine Cunninghame 1852-1936 *Mogreb-El-Acksa: a Journey in Morocco.* London: Wm. Heinemann, 1898, First edition; 8vo., pages xi, 323, map, photogravure frontispiece, original green decorative cloth, spine faded. J. & S. L. Bonham Antiquarian Booksellers Africa 4/20/2011 - 5069 2011 £65

Graham, T. H. B. *The Barony of Gilsland.* Kendal: Titus Wilson, 1934, Original brown cloth, gilt, pages xv, 164. R. F. G. Hollett & Son Antiquarian Booksellers 173 - 487 2011 £120

Graham, W. S. *The Night Fishing.* London: Faber & Faber, 1955, First edition; 8vo., 76 pages, neat name on front endpaper, slight offsetting to endpapers, else near fine in like dust jacket, very clean with one short closed tear and no loss. Any Amount of Books May 29 2011 - A39928 2011 $213

Graham, William *The One Pound Note in the Rise and Progress of Banking in Scotland and Its Adaptability to England.* Edinburgh: James Thin, 1886, First edition; original cloth, gilt, head of lower hinge frayed, pages ii, 324, 13 plates, scarce, unopened.   R. F. G. Hollett & Son Antiquarian Booksellers   175 - 541 2011   £60

Grahame, Kenneth 1859-1932   *Dream Days.* London: John Lane The Bodley Head n.d., First edition thus; original pictorial green cloth, extremities, rubbed, pages 168, 9 photograuves by Maxfield Parrish, joints cracked.   R. F. G. Hollett & Sons Antiquarian Booksellers   170 - 278 2011   £35

Grahame, Kenneth 1859-1932   *The Dream Days.* London: John Lane, Bodley, 1930, Large paper edition, limited to only 275 copies signed by author and artist; tall 8vo. vellum backed marbled boards, printed on special rag paper and illustrations by E. H. Shepard.   Aleph-Bet Books, Inc.   95 - 262 2011 $1200

Grahame, Kenneth 1859-1932   *The Golden Age.* London: John Lane, The Bodley Head, 1915, 4to., pages viii, 243, 4, 19 colored plates, original pictorial cloth, little rubbed.   R. F. G. Hollett & Sons Antiquarian Booksellers 170 - 222 2011   £75

Grahame, Kenneth 1859-1932   *The Reluctant Dragon.* New York: Holt, Rinehart and Winston, 1983, Limited to 350 copies, special printed illustration by Michael Hague which does not appear in trade edition; lovely copy, still housed in original mailing box, 42 plates, 11 full page color plates plus 8 color images set into text.   Jo Ann Reisler, Ltd.   86 - 127 2011 $300

Grahame, Kenneth 1859-1932   *The Wind in the Willows.* London: Methuen, 1913, First edition with Bransom illustrations; 8vo., green pictorial cloth, slight spotting on fore edge, else near fine, dust jacket with mounted color plate, dust jacket with quarter inch chip across head of spine and few mends, else very good+), illustrations by Paul Bransom with pictorial cover design, pictorial endpapers, tinted pen and ink on title, plus 10 very lovely color plates, nice in rare dust jacket.   Aleph-Bet Books, Inc.   95 - 261 2011 $1250

Grahame, Kenneth 1859-1932   *The Wind in the Willows.* London: Methuen & Co. Ltd., 1931, Limited to 200 copies, signed by author and artist; 4to., green cloth backed boards, printed paste label on spine, clean, fresh copy, 312 pages, plus foldout map at rear of book, housed in leather backed, felt lined case with gold lettering on spine of case.   Jo Ann Reisler, Ltd.   86 - 112 2011 $7000

Grahame, Kenneth 1859-1932   *The Wind in the Willows.* London: Methuen, 1931, Limited to 200 numbered copies signed by author and artist; 4to., 312 pages, cloth backed boards, very slight cover soil, else very good-fine, illustrations by E. H. Shepard printed on handmade paper, rare.   Aleph-Bet Books, Inc.   95 - 260 2011 $9500

Grahame, Kenneth 1859-1932   *The Wind in the Willows.* London: Folio Society, 1995, Large 8vo., original pictorial watered silk, gilt, slipcase, pages 206, illustrations in color by James Lynch.   R. F. G. Hollett & Sons Antiquarian Booksellers   170 - 279 2011   £35

Grainge, William *Fairfax Daemonologia: A Discourse on Witchcraft...* Frederick Muller, 1971, Facsimile edition; pages 189, family trees on endpapers, original cloth, gilt, dust jacket.   R. F. G. Hollett & Son Antiquarian Booksellers General Catalogue Summer 2010 - 1175 2011   £40

Grainge, William *Yorkshire Longevity: or Records and Biographical Anecdotes of Persons Who Have Attained to extreme Old Age Within that County.* Pateley Bridge: printed and published by Thomas Thorpe, London: T. T. Lemare, 1864, First edition; 2 pages ads, original purple brow cloth, little rubbed and faded, small circular ownership label of J. Sunderland Skipton, good sound copy.   Jarndyce Antiquarian Booksellers   CXCI - 191 2011   £35

Granger, James *A Biographical History of England, from the Revolution to the End of George I's Reign...* London: W. Richardson, 1806, 3 volumes, untrimmed in original drab boards, maroon glazed cloth spines, paper labels, spines slightly rubbed and faded to brown, labels worn, armorial bookplates of Sir Kenelm Digby.   Jarndyce Antiquarian Booksellers   CXCI - 192 2011   £120

Grant, C. F. *Twixt Sand and Sea: Sketches and Studies in North Africa.* London: Sampson Low n.d., 1910, First edition; large 8vo., pages xii, 504, map, illustrations, original blue cloth, dust jacket with small loss of paper at head and tail.   J. & S. L. Bonham Antiquarian Booksellers   Africa 4/20/2011 - 7457 2011   £95

Grant, Clara E. *Farthing Bundles.* London: privately published by author, 1931, Second edition; original blue wrappers, glassine dust jacket, pages vii, 180, scarce.   R. F. G. Hollett & Son Antiquarian Booksellers   175 - 542 2011   £140

Grant, James *The Narrative of a Voyage of Discovery, Performed in His Majesty's Vessel The Lady Nelson of Sixty Tons Burthen...* London: printed by C. Rowarth for T. Egerton, 1803, First edition; quarto, pages xxvi, 195, large folding plate, folding chart, 6 plates, with rare leaf of the Encouragers, later dark brown half calf, marbled boards, slightly scuffed, red spine label lettered gilt, folding engraved chart has lengths of coastline colored in red by hand, 2 charts in exceptional clean, unharmed condition, front endpapers slightly spotted, otherwise bright, clean, very good, plates and text in excellent state, superior copy, with generous margins.   Any Amount of Books   May 26 2011 - A69819 2011 $10,902

Grant, U. S. *Coastal Glaciers of Prince William Sound and Kenai Peninsula Alaska.* Washington: 1913, First edition; 75 pages, illustrations, 2 folding maps, viii, original printed wrappers, small chip from front wrapper, back pocket envelope splitting, else tight, near fine.   Dumont Maps & Books of the West   111 - 567   2011 $100

Granta. Ganta Publications by Penguin, 1980-1993, First edition; nos. 2, 3, 5-43, together 41 issues in original wrappers, all very good.   I. D. Edrich   May 26 2011 - 9776 2011 $537

Grattan-Guiness, I. *Companion Encyclopeida of the History and Philosophy of the Mathematical Science.* London and New York: Routledge, 1994, First printing; thick 8vo., xiii, 842; xi, 845-1806 pages, figures, tables, printed green paper boards, fine, from the Bern Dibner reference library, with Burndy bookplate.   Jeff Weber Rare Books   161 - 182   2011 $100

Graves, Algernon *A Dictionary of Artists Who Have Exhibited Works in the Principal London Exhibitions from 1760 to 1880.* Henry Graves and Co., 1884, First edition; large 4to., original quarter calf gilt, spine little scuffed, pages vi, 266, (i), ex-Signet Library with shelf number on pastedown.   R. F. G. Hollett & Son Antiquarian Booksellers General Catalogue Summer 2010 - 184   2011   £120

Graves, C. A. *Virginia Law Register.* Charlottesville: 1895-1915, 33 volumes, old law calf, very good.   Bookworm & Silverfish   665 - 163   2011 $1750

Graves, Robert 1895-1985 *Adam's Rib and Other Anomalous Elements in the Hebrew Creation Myth.* Jura: Trianon Press, 1955, First edition, copy R of 26 lettred copies signed by Graves and artist, James Metcalf; large 8vo., original publisher's red cloth lettered gilt at spine, pages 73, with wood engravings by James Metcalf, signed presentation from books' designer Arnold Fawcus for Audrey, fine in sound slightly browned, very good plain slipcase.   Any Amount of Books   May 26 2011 - A49568 2011 $545

Graves, Robert 1895-1985 *Beyond Giving. Poems.* Privately printed, 1969, First edition, 259/536 copies; signed by author, pages (viii), 40, royal 8vo., original plain white card, untrimmed, dust jacket, fine.   Blackwell Rare Books   B166 - 148 2011   £70

Graves, Robert 1895-1985 *Green Sailed Vessel. Poems.* Privately printed, 1971, First edition; 168/536 copies signed by author, pages viii, 42, royal 8vo., original cinnamon cloth, backstrip gilt lettered, dust jacket, fine.   Blackwell Rare Books   B166 - 149 2011   £70

Graves, Robert 1895-1985 *Letters to Ken (from 1917-1961).* Brunswick Press, Cathedral City, 1997, 116/200 copies; frontispiece, pages (iv), (vi), 54, crow 8vo., original maroon leatherette, backstrip and front cover gilt lettered, fine.   Blackwell Rare Books   B166 - 150 2011   £100

Graves, Robert 1895-1985 *The Penny Fiddle. Poems for Children.* London: Cassell, 1960, First edition; large 8vo., original cloth, gilt, dust jacket price clipped, pages 64, with 42 two color line drawings by Edward Ardizzone.   R. F. G. Hollett & Sons Antiquarian Booksellers   170 - 34 2011   £60

Graves, Robert 1895-1985 *Poems 1929.* London: Seizin Press, 1929, First edition, no. 167 of 225 numbered copies signed by poet; original publisher's olive green buckram lettered gilt at spine, slight browning at spine and edges of covers, endpapers very slightly browned, else very good.   Any Amount of Books   May 29 2011 - A40147 2011 $272

Graves, Robert 1895-1985 *Poems 1930-1933.* London: Arthur Barker, 1931, First edition; 8vo., 38 pages, presentation copy signed on piece of paper pasted to top f.e.p. "Nathaniel with love from Robert. 1933" (Nathaniel Reichenthal, father of Laura Riding), slight browning at edges, head of spine slight chafed, slight soiling, else very good, slight wear, otherwise very good.   Any Amount of Books   May 29 2011 - A36807 2011 $272

Gravesande, Wilhelm Jacob Van S' 1688-1742 *Mathematical Elements of Natural Philosophy.* London: printed for J. Senex and W. Taylor, 1720-1721, First edition; 2 volumes, very good, matching modern half calf, marbled paper boards, spine in compartments, leather spine labels, gilt lettering, 58 folding engraved plates, few pages in volume I remargined, neither text nor images affected, scattered mostly marginal foxing, soil, 8vo., rare.   By the Book, L. C.   26 - 104   2011 $6000

Gravesande, Wilhelm Jacob Van S' 1688-1742
Physices Elementa Mathematica, Experimentis Confirmata. Leiden: Apud Johannen Arnoldum Lanereak Johannem et Hermannum Verbeek, 1742, Third edition; 2 volumes, 4to., titlepage in red and black, 127 folding engraved plates, marginal waterstaining in both volumes, plate XXI torn with loss, plate LIII missing, margins of few plates reinforced, contemporary full calf, raised bands, gilt ruled spines, gilt stamped red leather spine labels, neatly rebacked, institutional bookplates, ink signatures of Isaac Hays on titlepages, very good.   Jeff Weber Rare Books   163 - 38 2011 $1250

Gray, Arthur *Tedious Brief Tales of Granta and Gramarye.* London: Ghost Story Press, 1993, Second edition; octavo, 15 illustrations, pictorial boards.   L. W. Currey, Inc.   124 - 199 2011 $200

Gray, James *How Animals Move.* Cambridge: Cambridge Press, 1953, First edition; original pictorial boards, matching dust jacket (large closed tear to lower panel), both by Bawden, pages xii, 113, with 15 plates and 52 drawings by Bawden.   R. F. G. Hollett & Son Antiquarian Booksellers   General Catalogue Summer 2010 - 949 2011   £30

Gray, John *Dental Practice; or Observations on the Qualification of the Surgeon Dentist - Dental Quackery - Nature & Extent of the Duties of the Dentist.* 1837, First edition; 5 plates, original purple cloth, slightly marked, spine faded.   Jarndyce Antiquarian Booksellers   CXCI - 194 2011   £180

Gray, John 1866-1934 *Silverpoints.* London: Elkin Mathews and John Lane, 1893, First edition, no. 192 of 250 copies on Van Gelder; pages xxviii, (1) imprint, (1) blank, uncut lower and fore-edge, few black ink spots to fore-edge not affecting text, some foxing to endpapers, original green cloth with gilt design by Charles Ricketts, boards worn at top edge, gilt slightly faded, spine bumped, spots of black ink to upper and lower panels, but still very attractive copy, scarce, ownership inscription of S. H. Tinkler.   Simon Finch Rare Books   Zero - 321 2011   £2000

Gray, Robert *A Serious Address to Seceders and Sectarists of Every Description...* London: F. & C. Rivington, 1805, First edition; small 8vo. bound in 12's, original plain wrappers, little creased, pages 48, scarce.   R. F. G. Hollett & Son Antiquarian Booksellers   175 - 543 2011   £75

Gray, Samuel Octavus *British Sea Weeds.* L. Reeve & Co., 1867, First edition; Original green cloth, gilt, extremities little rubbed, pages xxiii, 312, 24, partly unopened with 16 hand colored lithographed plates, joints just starting.   R. F. G. Hollett & Son Antiquarian Booksellers   General Catalogue Summer 2010 - 976 2011   £85

Gray, Thomas 1716-1771 *An Elegy Wrote in a Country Church Yard.* London: printed for R. Dodsley, 1751, First edition first printing; quarto, tall copy, 19th century full calf.   Heritage Book Shop   Booth A12 51st NY International Antiquarian Book Fair April 8-10 2011 - 63 2011 $17,500

Gray, Thomas 1716-1771 *An Elegy Wrote in a Country Church Yard.* London: for R. Dodsley and sold by M. Cooper, 1751, First edition; 4to., 11 pages, full black crushed levant morocco by Zaehnsdorf (very lightly rubbed at extremities), fine, with no loss of punched-through type, bookplates.   Joseph J. Felcone Inc.   Fall Miscellany 2010 - 57 2011 $15,000

Gray, Thomas 1716-1771 *Elegy Written in a Country Church-yard.* London: Limited Editions Club at the Raven Press, 1938, One of 1500 copies signed by artist; 260 x 814mm., xv, (1), 72 pages, (1) leaf, publisher's gray buckram, front cover silvered with raised vignette of moonlit tree between two crypts with stars overhead, flat spine with titling in silver, original blue buckram slipcase slightly worn, titlepage vignette and 32 full page engravings by Agnes Miller Parker; backstrip slightly and evenly faded but very fine, printed on thick, bright paper an with woodcuts.   Phillip J. Pirages   59 - 256 2011 $175

Gray, Thomas 1716-1771 *The Poems.* London: printed by T. Bensley for F. J. Du Roveray, 1800, 190 x 120, xxx, 162, (1) pages, (ads), with half title, extremely pleasing etruscan style calf in the style of quite probably by Edwards of Halifax, very expertly rebacked to style and corners repaired by Courtland Benson, covers with gilt broad and narrow rules and Greek-key roll framing wide inner panel of stencilled palmettes, gilt foliate roll enclosing central flamed panel, raised bands flanked by double blind rules, spine panels with large oval sunburst ornament supported by a floral nest, original black spine label, turn-ins with linked gilt roll, marbled endpapers, all edges gilt, with fore-edge painting of Yarmouth Castle and Harbor, 6 engraved plates, inscription "Frances Maria Phillips June 1824. in remembrance of her grandmother", covers little marked and dried but expertly restored binding solid and pleasing, the painting with a number of very thin parallel uncolored striped where edges of leaves are not quite even or here the fore-edge was not carefully fanned out during painting, one flyleaf with upper corner clipped off, some offsetting from plates, otherwise fine internally with only trivial effects.   Phillip J. Pirages   59 - 195 2011 $800

Gray, Thomas 1716-1771 *A Supplement to the Tour through Great Britain, containing a Catalogue of the Antiquities, Houses, Parks, Plantations, Scenes and Situations in England and Wales...* printed for G. Kearsley, 1787, Small 8vo., (ii) v (1) 119 (i) pages, half title, very good in contemporary half calf, expertly rebacked, corners neatly repaired, contemporary ownership name of Baskerfield on inner front board, who also adds a contents list which reveals that this item must at one stage have been bound with several other guides.   Ken Spelman Rare Books   68 - 166 2011   £850

Graydon, Alexander *Memoirs of a Life, Chiefly Passed in Pennsylvania within the Last Sixty Years.* Edinburgh: William Blackwood, 1822, First English edition; errata slip, uncut in original blue paper boards, brown paper spine, paper label (9s 6d), slight loss to head of spine, neatly repaired, otherwise very good. Jarndyce Antiquarian Booksellers CXCI - 350 2011 £350

Grealey, Shelagh *The Archaeology of Warrington's Past.* Warrington: Development Corporation, 1976, First edition; 4to., original cloth, dust jacket, pages 100 with 37 large folding plates, maps, plans, compliments slip of Warrington & Rucorn Development Corp. loosely inserted. R. F. G. Hollett & Son Antiquarian Booksellers 177 - 422 2011 £30

The Great Southwest - Along the Santa Fe. Kansas City: 1921, Sixth printing; 9 x 11 inches, with full page color photo images, very good, no tears or chips, titlepage and rear of last photo foxed. Bookworm & Silverfish 669 - 16 2011 $75

Great Britain. Laws, Statutes, Etc. - 1695 *The Statutes at Large in Paragraphs and Numbers. Beginning with the Reign of King James I and Continued to the Present Time...* London: printed by Charles Bill and the executrix of Thomas Newcomb, deceas'd and by the assigns of Richard Atkins and Edward Atkins, 1695, Folio, contemporary full blind panelled reversed calf, some chips and surface defects, lower board rubbed, top panel of backstrip mostly lacking, pages 957- 1768 (iv, catalog of titles in table), A-Hhhh (tables), text in black letter throughout, few leaves lightly browned, otherwise very good. R. F. G. Hollett & Son Antiquarian Booksellers 175 - 1486 2011 £350

Great Britain. Laws, Statutes, etc. - 1683 *Acts Made in the First Parliament...of Charles the First. (& First and Third Parliament of Charles the Second. With an index or abridgement of the Acts of Parliament.* Edinburgh: printed by David Lindsay, John Reid, 1683-1685, 12mo., pages 130 (iv) 133-371 (xiii) 373-640, (ii), 292, browned, bit of soiling, titlepage foxed, from the collection of Christopher Ernest Weston 1947-2010. Unsworths Booksellers 24 - 64 2011 £150

Great Britain. Laws, Statutes, Etc. - 1695 *An Acte for Confirmation of the Subsidies Graunted by the Clergie.* no publisher given, 1695, Folio, extract in modern brown paper wrappers, pages (xvi), in black lettered, decorated initial, small wormholes. R. F. G. Hollett & Son Antiquarian Booksellers 175 - 9 2011 £40

Great Britain. Laws, Statutes, Etc. - 1704 *Act of "Queen Anne's Bounty".* London: printed by Charles Bill and the executrix of Thomas Newcomb, 1704, First separately paginated edition; folio, later half calf gilt, marbled boards, pages 11, top of first leaf little soiled, black letter, with floriated initial and royal arms at head, stamp of Patent Office Library on first and final leaves. R. F. G. Hollett & Son Antiquarian Booksellers 175 - 8 2011 £250

Great Britain. Laws, Statutes, Etc. - 1709 *Anno Regni Annae Reginae Magnae Britanniae, Franciae & Hiberniae.* London: printed by Charles Bill and the Executrix of Thomas Newcomb and Others, 1709-1711, Folio, full modern blind ruled calf gilt with raised bands and spine label, pages 277 (iv, table); 560, mostly in black letter with decorated initials, numerous titlepages and folding table, library stamp on reverse of title, rather browned, contemporary manuscript notes of Henry Holland dated 1754. R. F. G. Hollett & Son Antiquarian Booksellers 175 - 3 2011 £350

Great Britain. Laws, Statutes, Etc. - 1734 *The Statutes at Large, Containing all the Public Acts of Parliament Beginning with the Reign of King James the Second, to the Fourth Year of the Reign of Queene Anne.* London: printed by John Baskett and by E. and R. Nutt and R. gosling assigns of Edward Sayer, 1734, Folio, contemporary full blind panelled calf, rubbed and little scraped, spine rather defective at head, gilding rubbed away, lower hinge just cracking, pages (xxviii), 719, printed in black letter throughout, few corners slightly creased, otherwise very nice. R. F. G. Hollett & Son Antiquarian Booksellers 175 - 1485 2011 £295

Great Britain. Laws, Statutes, Etc. - 1766 *An Abstract of the Publick Acts Passed in the Fifth (and Sixth) Session of the Twelfth Parliament of Great Britain and in the Sixth (and Seventh) Years of the Reign of Our Most Gracious Sovereign Lord King George the Third.* London: printed by Marker Baskett, 1766-1768, Modern half calf gilt with raised bands, and contrasting spine labels, pages 171, (iii), 104 (ii), complete with two titles and lists of contents. R. F. G. Hollett & Son Antiquarian Booksellers 175 - 2 2011 £275

Great Britain. Laws, Statutes, Etc. - 1828 *Act for Making the Rivers Mercy and Irwell Navigable from Liverpool to Manchester in the County of Palatine of Lancaster.* London: Eyre and Strahan, 1828, First separately paginated edition; folio, unbound and side sewn as issued, pages 16, royal arms headpiece, sometime folded. R. F. G. Hollett & Son Antiquarian Booksellers 175 - 5 2011 £35

Great Britain. Laws, Statutes, Etc. - 1837 *Act for Registering Births, Deaths, and Marriages in England.* London: George Eyre and Andrew Spottiswoode, 1837, First edition; small 8vo., original printed cloth rather soiled, pages 79, (xi). R. F. G. Hollett & Son Antiquarian Booksellers 175 - 6 2011 £120

Great Britain. Parliament - 1704 *All the Proceedings in Relation to the Aylesbury Men, Committed by the House of Commons and the Report of the Lords Journal and Reports of the Conferences and of the Free Conference.* London: printed for Edward Jones and Timothy Goodwin, 1704, i.e., 1705, First edition; folio, 83, (1) pages, including half title, occasional very minor spots and rust marks, well bound fairly recently in old style half calf over marbled boards with gilt lettered spine label, excellent, large copy. John Drury Rare Books 153 - 6 2011 £275

Great Britain. Parliament - 1798 *A Bill for Making Perpetual, Subject to Redemption and Purchase in the Manner Herein Stated, the Several Sums of Money Now Charged in Great Britain as a Land Tax for One Year from Twenty-Fifty Day of March One Thousand Seven Hundred and Ninety Eight.* London: 1798, First edition; folio, drop head title, docket title, ordered to be printed 19th April 1798, 39, (1) pages, stitched as issued, good copy. Anthony W. Laywood May 26 2011 - 21567 2011 $134

Great Britain. Parliament - 1814 *First and Second Reports from the Committees of the House of Lords Appointed to Inquire into the State of the Growth, Commerce and Consumption of Grain and All Laws Relating Thereto: to Whom Were Referred the Several Petittons Presented to the House in the Session of 1813-1814, Respecting the Corn Laws.* London: James Ridgway, 1814, First 8vo. edition; iv, 343, (1) pages, including several folded tables (all paginated with the text), original boards, neatly rebacked, entirely uncut, very good, crisp copy. John Drury Rare Books 153 - 32 2011 £175

Great Britain. Parliament - 1814 *Report from the Select Committee of the House of Commons on Petitions Relating to the Corn Laws of this Kingdom; Together with the Minutes of Evidence and an Appendix of Accounts.* London: James Ridgway, 1814, First edition; 8vo. iv, 260, xlvi, (2) pages appendix printed in wrong order, original boards with later neat cloth rebacked with printed spine label, uncut and partially unopened, excellent, crisp copy. John Drury Rare Books 153 - 31 2011 £150

Great Britain. Parliament. House of Commons - 1784 *Votes of the House of Commons 1784-1795.* printed for the House of Commons, 1784-1845, 4 volumes, small folio, original half calf, very rubbed and defective, together with large quantity of individual numbers (approximately 150), flat or folded and small collection from 1845. R. F. G. Hollett & Son Antiquarian Booksellers 175 - 671 2011 £450

Great Britain. Parliament. House of Commons - 1794 *Debates in the House of Commons, on the Tenth of March 1794, Upon the Motion of Mr. Adam in Behalf of Muir and Palmer.* Edinburgh: printed and sold by J. Robertson No. 4, Horse Wynd, where may be had, the Trials of Mr. Muir, Mr. Palmer, Mr. Skirving and Mr. Margarot, 1794, First edition; 8vo., 34 pages, recent marbled boards lettered on spine, very good, very scarce. John Drury Rare Books 153 - 34 2011 £250

Great Britain. Parliament. House of Commons - 1810 *Report, together with minutes of Evidence and Accounts from the Select Committee on the High Price of Gold Bullion, and to Take into Consideration the State of the Circulating medium and of the Exchanges Between Great Britain and Foreign Parts.* London: reprinted for J. Johnson and Co. ... and J. Ridgway, 1810, First trade edition; 8vo., x (2), 78 (2) 237 (3) 115 (1) pages, little very minor spotting of titlepage and few other leaves, small blank strip cut away from upper margin of title (partially removing a name), small repair to inner blank margin, occasional emphasis marks in text in pencil, in fine later 19th century binding of half calf over marbled boards, spine with raised bands and crimson label lettered in gilt, handsome copy. John Drury Rare Books 154 - 33 2011 £850

Great Britain. Royal Commission on Historical Manuscripts - 1884 *Reports.* 1884-1917, 8vo., uniform red quarter morocco gilt, some little rubbed at head and foot of spines, handsome set, ex-libris Lloyd Lord Kenyon, Baron of Gredington with his armorial bookplate and family crest in gilt to centre of each upper cover. C. P. Hyland May 26 2011 - 257/249 2011 $5073

Great Britain. Royal Commission on Historical Manuscripts - 1895 *Report on the Manuscripts of the Marquis Of Ormonde.* Historical Manuscripts Commission, 1895, 1909. 1902.1912; together 10 volumes, red quarter morocco gilt, ex-libris, Lloyd, Lord Kenyon, with armorial bookplate and family rest in gilt on each upper cover, slight rubbing at head and foot of spines, 8vo. C. P. Hyland May 26 2011 - 255/338 2011 $1015

Great Britain. Royal Commission on Historical Monuments - 1911 *An Inventory of the Historical Monuments in Hertfordshire.* London: HMSO, 1911, First edition, second thousand; pages xvi, 311 with 43 plates, 2 folding plans and large folding map, little foxing to prelims. R. F. G. Hollett & Son Antiquarian Booksellers 177 - 768 2011 £95

Great Britain. Royal Commission on Historical Monuments - 1916 *An Inventory of the Historical Monuments in The County of Essex.* London: HMSO, 1916-1923, First edition; 4 volumes, 4to., original grey cloth gilt, volume 1 rebound in plain grey cloth gilt, spines little frayed or nicked in places, pages xxxviii, 430; xlii, 335; xl ,274; xlviii, 317, frontispiece, folding map and numerous plates, plans and text figures to each volume, excellent clean and sound set.   R. F. G. Hollett & Son Antiquarian Booksellers   177 - 776   2011   £275

Great Britain. Royal Commission on Historical Monuments - 1924 *An Inventory of the Historical Monuments in London. volume I. Westminster Abbey.* London: RCHM, 1924, First edition; 4to., original grey cloth, gilt, pages xvii, 142, with tissue guarded color frontispiece, 220 pages of plates, numerous text figures and plans, large colored folding plan, few small repairs.   R. F. G. Hollett & Son Antiquarian Booksellers   177 - 771   2011   £75

Great Britain. Royal Commission on Historical Monuments - 1926 *An Inventory of the Historical Monuments in Huntingdonshire.* London: HMSO, 1926, First edition; 4to., original grey cloth, dust jacket (few closed tears), pages xlii, 350, 102 plates ad numerous plans, illustrations, large folding map.   R. F. G. Hollett & Son Antiquarian Booksellers   177 - 767   2011   £75

Great Britain. Royal Commission on Historical Monuments - 1936 *An Inventory of the Historical Monuments in Westmorland.* London: HMSO, 1936, First edition; 4to., original red cloth gilt, dust jacket (few spots), pages lxviii, 302, top edge gilt, with 160 plates and numerous plans and illustrations, folding map in rear pocket, little scattered spotting, otherwise very good, sound and clean copy, signed by N. Drinkwater.   R. F. G. Hollett & Son Antiquarian Booksellers   177 - 769   2011   £250

Great Britain. Royal Commission on Historical Monuments - 1937 *An Inventory of the Historical Monuments in Middlesex.* London: RCHM, 1937, First edition; 4to., original red cloth, gilt, dust jacket, few edge tears, spine trifle soiled, pages xxxv, 176 with 184 pages of plates, numerous text figures and plans and large folding plan in rear pocket.   R. F. G. Hollett & Son Antiquarian Booksellers   177 - 772   2011   £60

Great Britain. Royal Commission on Historical Monuments - 1952 *An Inventory of the Historical Monuments in Dorset. Volume One - West.* London: HMSO, 1952, First edition; pages 1, 353, with 100 plans and plates, 4to., original cloth, gilt, dust jacket, upper panel only remaining.   R. F. G. Hollett & Son Antiquarian Booksellers   177 - 764   2011   £60

Great Britain. Royal Commission on Historical Monuments - 1960 *An Inventory of the Historical Monuments in Caernarvonshire. II.* London: HMSO, 1960, First edition; 4to., original green cloth, gilt, dust jacket, pages lxvi, 287, with 82 pages of plates, numerous plans and maps on endpapers.   R. F. G. Hollett & Son Antiquarian Booksellers   177 - 779   2011   £95

Great Britain. Royal Commission on Historical Monuments - 1962 *An Inventory of the Historical Monuments in The City of York.* London: HMSO, 1962-1981, First editions; 5 volumes, original cloth, 4to., gilt, dust jackets, extremities of volume 1 trifle worn, 3 volumes with top edge gilt, numerous plates, text figures, large folding maps and plans and other illustrations, near fine, complete set.   R. F. G. Hollett & Son Antiquarian Booksellers   177 - 773   2011   £250

Great Britain. Royal Commission on Historical Monuments - 1964 *An Inventory of the Historical Monuments in Newark on Trent.* London: HMSO, 1964, First edition; 4to., original wrappers, pages 108, 17 pages of plates, 20 text figures and maps.   R. F. G. Hollett & Son Antiquarian Booksellers   177 - 778   2011   £45

Great Britain. Royal Commission on Historical Monuments - 1968 *An Inventory of the Historical Monuments in the County of Cambridge. Volume I.* London: RCHM, 1968, First edition; pages lxix, 256, tipped in color frontispiece, 144 plates, numerous text figures and plans, folding map, mint, original cloth, gilt, dust jacket.   R. F. G. Hollett & Son Antiquarian Booksellers   177 - 770   2011   £85

Great Britain. Royal Commission on Historical Monuments - 1970 *An Inventory of the Historical Monuments in Dorset. Volume two - South East.* London: HMSO, 1970, First edition; 3 volumes, 4to., original cloth, gilt, dust jackets, pages lxiv, 188; xviii, 189-417; ix, 418-701, numerous plans, plates and maps, including color frontispiece, bookplate of Richard Sandell, god-son of Sir Emery Walker.   R. F. G. Hollett & Son Antiquarian Booksellers   177 - 765   2011   £140

Great Britain. Royal Commission on Historical Monuments - 1972 *An Inventory of the Historical Monuments in Dorset. Volume Four - North.* London: HMSO, 1972, First edition; pages xxxix, 142, color frontispiece and numerous plans, plates and maps, 4to., original cloth gilt, dust jacket.   R. F. G. Hollett & Son Antiquarian Booksellers   177 - 766   2011   £65

Great Britain. Royal Commission on Historical Monuments - 1975 *An Inventory of the Historical Monuments in the City of York.* London: HMSO, 1975, First edition; 4to., original red cloth, gilt, dust jacket, pages lv, 111, with 132 plates, 82 text figures, 4 large folding maps and plans in rear pocket, 5 maps in text and other illustrations.   R. F. G. Hollett & Son Antiquarian Booksellers   177 - 774   2011   £60

Great Britain. Royal Commission on Historical Monuments - 1980 *An Inventory of the Historical Monuments in the City of Salisbury.* London: HMSO, 1980, First edition; 4to., original red cloth gilt, dust jacket, pages lxiv, 199, with 104 pages of plates, numerous text figures and plans, large folding plan in rear pocket.   R. F. G. Hollett & Son Antiquarian Booksellers   177 - 777   2011   £60

Great Britain. Royal Commission on Historical Monuments - 1987 *Houses of the North York Moors.* London: HMSO, 1987,   Original wrappers, pages xi, 256, 435 illustrations, 4to.   R. F. G. Hollett & Son Antiquarian Booksellers   General Catalogue Summer 2010 - 1574   2011   £45

Great Britain. Royal Commission on Historical Monuments - 1987 *An Inventory of the Historical Monuments in the Houses of the North York Moors.* London: HMSO, 1987, First edition; 4to., original wrappers, pages xi, 256, 435 illustrations.   R. F. G. Hollett & Son Antiquarian Booksellers   177 - 780   2011   £45

Great Britain. Royal Navy - 1801 *A List of the Flag Officers of His Majesty's Fleet with the Dates of Their First Commissions as Admirals, Vice Admirals, Rear Admirals and Captains, Bound with an Alphabetical List of the Post Captains, Commanders and Lieutenants...* London: privately printed, 1801,   First edition; 8vo., full red leather, gilt decorated, pages 137 and 190, binding sound but little rubbed, scuffed and dull and slightly nicked at spine, very good- with very clean, bright text.   Any Amount of Books   May 26 2011 - A73483   2011 $503

The Great Libel Case. Dr. Hunter Versus Pall Mall Gazette. London: C. Mitchell and Co., 1867, First edition; 8vo., 404 pages, 4 large text figures on pages 78-81, titlepage little soiled and with marginal repair, rebound recently in maroon watered cloth, spine gilt and lettered, good copy, very uncommon.   John Drury Rare Books   153 - 158   2011   £275

Greaves, James Pierrepont   *A Brief Account of the First Concordium or Harmonious Industrial College, a Home for the Affectionate, Skilful and Industrious Uncontaminated by False Sympathy...*   Ham Common, Surrey: published at the Concordium, price one penny and sold by all booksellers, n.d., 1840?,   first edition, variant issue; 8vo., caption title, 8 plates, rather foxed and browned, well bound in old style quarter calf, gilt, good, most attractively bound.   John Drury Rare Books   153 - 50   2011   £750

Greedy Ben.   New York: McLoughlin Bros. between, 1868-1874,   16mo., color pictorial cover with some dusting and partial spine splitting, 4 pages of text and four full page color illustrations.   Jo Ann Reisler, Ltd.   86 - 136   2011 $150

Greely, Adolphus W.   *Three Years of Arctic Service.* London: Richard Bentley and Son, 1886,   Second English edition; decorated cloth, plates, in text illustrations, 9 maps, including large folding map tipped into end of volume 2 on a stub, neat bookplates, light shelfwear, otherwise near fine.   Lupack Rare Books   May 26 2011 - ABE4616669070   2011 $300

Green, A. H.   *Geology, Part I: Physical Geology.*   London: 1882,   Third edition; xxiv 728 pages, good solid copy, some shelf ghosting (from adjacent books) in contrasting color, original binding.   Bookworm & Silverfish   665 - 66   2011 $75

Green, Ben K.   *A Thousand Miles of Mustangin'.* Flagstaff: 1972,   First edition; fine in like dust jacket, bright, crisp copy.   Dumont Maps & Books of the West   112 - 43   2011 $75

Green, F. L.   *Odd Man Out.*   London: Joseph, 1945, First edition; pages 224, foolscap 8vo., original black cloth, backstrip gilt lettered, owner's name and date on front free endpaper, dust jacket trifle frayed, rear panel little dust soiled, good.   Blackwell Rare Books   B166 - 151   2011   £500

Green, Lewis H.   *George Mackley Wood Engraver.* Gresham Books, 1981, First edition; tall 4to., original cloth, gilt, dust jacket price clipped, pages 136, illustrated with fine woodcuts, fine.   R. F. G. Hollett & Son Antiquarian Booksellers   General Catalogue Summer 2010 - 186   2011   £75

Green, William   *A Description of a Series of Sixty Small Prints etched by William Green of Ambleside...*   Ambleside: William Green, 1814,   Oblong 8vo., 34 pages, 60 soft ground etchings, very good, recent quarter sheep, moss green paper boards, retaining original tinted label on upper cover, contemporary identification of some of the mountains, neatly added in pencil.   Ken Spelman Rare Books   68 - 174   2011   £480

Green, William *The Tourist's New Guide, Containing a Description of the Lakes, Mountains and Scenery in Cumberland, Westmorland and Lancashire.* Kendal: R. Lough and Co., 1819, 2 volumes, old black half calf, pages 461; ix, 507, lv, with 1 half title, folding map and 33 plates by Green, volume I lacks folding map, preface (pages v-xii), index (iii-viii) and errata leaf, volume 2 lacks half title, errata leaf and 2 aquatints, little spotting in places, small edge tear neatly repaired, good, sound, rarely found complete, labels of Ravenstonedale Reading Room and Library on each pastedown.   R. F. G. Hollett & Son Antiquarian Booksellers   173 - 497   2011   £850

Green, William *The Tourist's New Guide, Containing a Description of the Lakes, Mountains and Scenery in Cumberland, Westmorland and Lancashire.* Kendal: R. Lough and Co., 1819, First edition; 2 volumes, modern full levant morocco gilt, raised bands and contrasting spine labels, boards panelled with blind rules, pages viii, 461 (i); ix, 507 lv, (i, errata with slip advertising Todhunter's Museum), 2 half titles, folding map (neatly repaired) and full complement of 36 plates, contemporary ms. index to plates added to end of each volume, few items added to printed index, titlepage of first volume little soiled, otherwise excellent.   R. F. G. Hollett & Son Antiquarian Booksellers   173 - 498   2011   £1500

Greenaway, Kate   1846-1901   *Almanack for 1883-1895 & Diary for 1897.* London: George Routledge and Sons, Librarie Hachette et Cie, J. M. dent & co., 1882-1897, First editions; 14 volumes, 24mo., almanac for 1887 being oblong 24mo., complete combined set of rare French and British editions, original bindings of glazed pictorial boards with cloth spines, glazed pictorial wrappers (Almanack for 1884) and imitation boards (Almanack & Diary for 1897), Almanack for 1885 with small old bookshop plate on front free endpaper, Almanack & Diary for 1897 with titlepage, overall excellent set, housed together in custom made felt lined half blue morocco clamshell, front hinge of clamshell has been professionally repaired.   Heritage Book Shop   Holiday 2010 - 48   2011 $1850

Greenaway, Kate   1846-1901   *Almanack for 1884.* London: George Routledge & Son, 1884, Large 12mo., original cream pictorial stiff wrappers, trifle soiled and creased illustrated in color.   R. F. G. Hollett & Sons Antiquarian Booksellers   170 - 280   2011   £175

Greenaway, Kate   1846-1901   *Almanack for 1886.* London: George Routledge & Sons, 1886, First edition; 12mo., original publisher's special binding of cream imitation pigskin, green printed borders to board, gilt design by Greenaway on upper board, all edges gilt, illustrations in color, orange endpapers, near fine.   R. F. G. Hollett & Sons Antiquarian Booksellers   170 - 280   2011   £175

Greenaway, Kate   1846-1901   *Almanack for 1887.* London: George Routledge and Sons, 1887, First edition; oblong 12mo., original yellow cloth backed glazed pale yellow pictorial boards, trifle soiled, two tiny edge chips, illustrations in color, with pale blue green endpapers, corners minimally bruised, attractive copy.   R. F. G. Hollett & Sons Antiquarian Booksellers   170 - 282   2011   £220

Greenaway, Kate   1846-1901   *Almanack for 1888.* London: George Routledge & Sons, 1888, First edition; 12mo., original blue cloth backed glazed dark yellow pictorial boards, illustrations in color with olivine edges and endpapers, corners minimally bruised, but fine.   R. F. G. Hollett & Sons Antiquarian Booksellers   170 - 283   2011   £350

Greenaway, Kate   1846-1901   *Almanack for 1895.* London: George Routledge & Sons, 1895, First edition; 12mo., original publisher's special binding of cream imitation pigskin, boards panelled with triple green rules and gilt design, upper hinge cracking, all edges gilt, illustrations in color, olivine endpapers, near fine.   R. F. G. Hollett & Sons Antiquarian Booksellers   170 - 284   2011   £450

Greenaway, Kate   1846-1901   *Baby's Birthday Book.* London: Marcus Ward and Co. Ltd. circa, 1885, Probable first edition; 12mo., all edges tinted pink, cloth backed color pictorial boards, some shelf wear of overall clean copy, every page offers the days of the year surrounded with colorful pictures of happy children.   Jo Ann Reisler, Ltd.   86 - 114   2011 $300

Greenaway, Kate   1846-1901   *Calendar of the Seasons 1881.* London: Marcus Ward & Co., 1881, First edition; 12mo., 4 page booklet, now separated into four leaves, printed in colors on both sides, tiny stab holes from original sewing just visible, two sides, little darkened.   R. F. G. Hollett & Sons Antiquarian Booksellers   170 - 286   2011   £175

Greenaway, Kate   1846-1901   *A Day in a Child's Life.* London: George Routledge and Sons, n.d., First edition; square small 4to., original cloth backed glazed and bevelled boards, edges little rubbed, pages 30, illustrations in color, occasional finger marks but very nice.   R. F. G. Hollett & Sons Antiquarian Booksellers   170 - 287   2011   £180

Greenaway, Kate   1846-1901   *The Kate Greenaway Treasury.* London: Collins, 1978, Large 4to., original cloth backed boards, gilt, dust jacket, pages 320, illustrations in color, a number of additional cards, etc. with Greenaway illustrations and original photo of Hampstead house designed for Greenaway by R. Norman Shaw, all loosely inserted.   R. F. G. Hollett & Sons Antiquarian Booksellers   170 - 295   2011   £45

Greenaway, Kate   1846-1901   *Language of Flowers.* London: George Routledge and Sons, 1888, First edition; square large 12mo., special publisher's binding of imitation cream pigskin gilt, boards panelled with triple rule, gilt on upper and in blind on lower board, small nick to spine, lower hinge just cracking in places, pages 80, all edges gilt, illustrated and printed in color throughout by Edmund Evans, very nice.   R. F. G. Hollett & Sons Antiquarian Booksellers   170 - 289   2011   £350

Greenaway, Kate   1846-1901   *Marigold Garden.* London: Routlege, n.d., 1885, First edition; 4to., original cloth backed glazed boards, top edges and corners bumped, neatly recased, pages 64, illustrations in colors, tear to half title repaired.   R. F. G. Hollett & Sons Antiquarian Booksellers   170 - 290   2011   £140

Greenaway, Kate   1846-1901   *Under the Window.* London: Routledge n.d., First edition; large square 8vo., original glazed pictorial boards, rather worn, pages 64, illustrations in colors, joints strengthened with brown tape, little occasional fingering.   R. F. G. Hollett & Sons Antiquarian Booksellers   170 - 292   2011   £95

Greenaway, Kate   1846-1901   *Under the Window.* London: Routledge, n.d., First edition; large square 8vo., original glazed boards, top edges and corners bumped, neatly recased, pages 64, illustrations in color, tear to half title repaired.   R. F. G. Hollett & Sons Antiquarian Booksellers   170 - 291   2011   £140

Greenaway, Kate   1846-1901   *Under the Window.* London: George Routledge, 1879, 64 pages, 4to., pictorial printed paper on boards, dark blue green endpapers, beautifully illustrated, ex-libris label, inked signatures at half titlepage, residue of decals on flyleaves, light foxing at margins, edges of cover rubbed, internally in good state.   Hobbyhorse Books   56 - 80   2011 $110

Greene, Graham   1904-1991   *Brighton Rock.*   Star Editions, Heinemann, 1947, 16mo., pages (iv), 336, very faint occasional foxing to prelims, original printed light blue wrapper, bound within binder's pale grey cloth, lightly browned backstrip gilt lettered, marbled endpapers, very good, inscribed by Greene for Jacques Duhamel.   Blackwell Rare Books   B166 - 152   2011   £800

Greene, Graham   1904-1991   *The Comedians.* London: Bodley Head, 1966, First British edition; near fine, very minor bump to base of spine, dust jacket is very good, light wear to spine ends, 2 inch closed tear on front panel, very good, light wear to spine ends, 2 inch closed tear on front panel.   Bella Luna Books   May 29 2011 - t7662   2011 $82

Greene, Graham   1904-1991   *The Confidential Agent.* London: Heinemann, 1939, First edition; 8vo., original publisher's blue cloth lettered purple on spine, page 286, neat name on front endpaper, prelims slightly foxed, some slightly rubbed and very slightly dulled, cover faintly marked, otherwise sound, very good.   Any Amount of Books   May 29 2011 - A62412   2011 $383

Greene, Graham   1904-1991   *In Search of a Character. Two African Journals.* London: Bodley Head, 1988, First British edition; fine, dust jacket near fine with very light wear.   Bella Luna Books   May 26 2011 - t5400   2011 $302

Greene, Graham   1904-1991   *It's a Battlefield.*   London: Heinemann, 1934, First edition; final few leaves lightly foxed, pages (viii), 278, crown 8vo., original black cloth, faded backstrip gilt lettered, owner's name on front free endpaper, very good.   Blackwell Rare Books   B166 - 153   2011   £250

Greene, Graham   1904-1991   *The Little Fire Engine.* London: Mac Parrish, 1950, First edition; oblong large 8vo., original pictorial boards, spine little worn, hinges cracking but repaired, one lower corner trifle bruised, pages 46, illustrations in colors by Dorothy Craigie.   R. F. G. Hollett & Sons Antiquarian Booksellers   170 - 296   2011   £250

Greene, Graham   1904-1991   *The Ministry of Fear.* London: William Heinemann Ltd., 1943, First edition; 8vo., original yellow cloth with title, author and publisher stamped in black on spine and windmill device stamped in black at right tail of rear cover, cloth moderately soiled, former owner's inked name on front flyleaf, else very good in professionally restored dust jacket, pasted to rear pastedown sheet is newspaper clipping taken from Sunday supplement of May 29 1943.   Buckingham Books   May 26 2011 - 29296   2011 $3750

Greene, Graham   1904-1991   *Monsignor Quixote.*   New York: 1982, First American edition; 1/250 copies, signed by author, as new in slipcase.   Gemini Fine Books & Arts, Ltd.   Art Reference & Illustrated Books: First Editions 2011 $200

Greene, Graham   1904-1991   *Our Man in Havana.* London: Heinemann, 1958, First edition; pages (vi), 274, crown 8vo., original mid blue cloth backstrip gilt lettered, dust jacket trifle edge rubbed, very good.   Blackwell Rare Books   B166 - 154   2011   £170

Greene, Graham   1904-1991   *The Power and the Glory.* Stockholm: Continental Book Co., 1947, Inscribed by author for Jacques Duhamel, pages (vi), 282, 16mo., original printed cream wrappers bound within binder's pale grey cloth, lightly browned backstrip gilt lettered, marbled endpapers, very good.   Blackwell Rare Books   B166 - 155   2011   £800

Greene, Graham 1904-1991 *Stamboul Train.* London: Heinemann, 1932, First edition, 2nd state with corrected text on page 80; foxing to some pages and to edges, pages (ix), 307, crown 8vo., original black cloth, backstrip gilt lettered, bookplate, very good. Blackwell Rare Books B166 - 156 2011 £300

Greenhill, Thomas *(Nekrokedeia) or the Art of Embalming...* London: for the author, 1705, First and only edition; 4to., pages (6), viii, v, (9), 367, (13), double page engraved frontispiece, unnumbered explication leaf to frontispiece, separate part i title, 13 engraved plates, folding map, list of subscribers, index, contemporary panelled calf, neatly rebacked, worn in places, repair to tear across lower margin of last leaf of text, very good, clean and well margined. Simon Finch Rare Books Zero - 112 2011 £800

Greenleaf, Simon *A Treatise on the Law of Evidence.* Boston: 1883, 1899. 1883. volume 1 is 14th edition, volume 2 is 16th edition; 3 volumes, all leathers, volume 2 with new labels and cosmetic surfacing. Bookworm & Silverfish 664 - 114 2011 $200

Greenleaf, Simon *A Treatise on the Law of Evidence.* 1892, 1892. 1868. Volume I 15th edition, volume 2 15th edition, volume 3 8th edition; 3 volumes, libary buckram, cover wear to volume I, lower label replaced, volumes II and III very good. Bookworm & Silverfish 664 - 115 2011 $175

Greenleaf, Simon *A Treatise on the Law of Evidence.* Boston: 1899, 3 volumes, modestly ex-library (small label), volume 1 and 2 in law cloth, volume 3 in gray cloth, set solid. Bookworm & Silverfish 670 - 79 2011 $225

Greenough, Sarah *Harry Callahan.* Washington: National Gallery of Art, 1996, First edition; 4to., pages 199, copiously illustrated in color and black and white, 2 invites to exhibition at Philadelphia Museum of Art (1986) loosely inserted, signed presentation from author to "Fat Matt", also signed to Fat Matt by Eleanor Callahan on page 95, fine in fine dust jacket. Any Amount of Books May 29 2011 - A75423 2011 $272

Greenwood, Charles *Chester - a Plan for Redevelopment.* Chester: Phillipson & Golder, 1945, First edition; 4to., original cloth, gilt, edges, little faded, dust jacket edges torn and chipped, pages 90, illustrations and colored plates. R. F. G. Hollett & Son Antiquarian Booksellers 177 - 425 2011 £35

Greenwood, Isaac *Arithmetick Vulgar and Decimal with the Application Thereof to a Variety of Cases in Trade and Commerce.* Boston: S. Kneeland and T. Green for T. Hancock, 1729, First edition; 8vo., (10), 158 pages, contents leaves follow title, full new calf, title and next several leaves stained and discolored, moderate foxing and staining thereafter, professionally deacidified, little rebacked, some chipping in last few leaves, affecting few letters, complete copy in sound condition. M & S Rare Books, Inc. 90 - 119 2011 $12,500

Greenwood, James *Curiosities of Savage Life.* London: S. O. Beeton, 1864-1865, Original stamped red and green cloth gilt extra, rather worn, one spine faded, pages xiv, 418; xiv, 418, all edges, 15 color printed plates by W. Dickes and numerous woodcuts, mixed set, 2 leaves refixed their fore edges little worn, joints of volume I cracked. R. F. G. Hollett & Son Antiquarian Booksellers 175 - 547 2011 £150

Greenwood, James *The Philadelphia Vocabulary, English and Latin.* Philadelphia: Carey and Co., 1787, First American edition; 16mo., 8, 123 pages, old calf, crudely rebacked, inner front hinge crudely repaired, some leaves printed faintly, light foxing throughout, small pieces lacking from front end leaf, ink signatures on title. M & S Rare Books, Inc. 90 - 205 2011 $1750

Greenwood, Jeremy *The Wood Engravings of John Nash.* Liverpool: Wood Lea Press, 1987, First edition, limited to 750 copies of the Standard Edition; 4to., 149 pages, tipped in color reproductions, quarter green cloth, floral pattern papering boards, gillt lettered spine, tipped in frontispiece photo portrait of Nash, fine in fine matching green cloth covered slipcase. By the Book, L. C. 26 - 33 2011 $150

Greenwood, Jeremy *The Wood-engravings of Paul Nash, a Catalogue of the Wood Engravings, Pattern Papers, Etchings and an Engraving on Copper.* Woodbridge: Wood Lea Press, 1997, Special limited edition of 60 copies, including matted wood etching; 4to., 141 pages, wood engraved frontispiece, 108 wood engravings, separate matted wood engraved print, quarter gray morocco over geometric color printed boards, gilt stamped spine title, housed in matching grey cloth clamshell box, gilt stamped spine title, fine. Jeff Weber Rare Books 163 - 118 2011 $650

Greenwood, Thomas *Museums and Art Galleries.* London: Simpkin, Marshall and Co., 1888, First edition; xvi, 419, (1) + ads, 25 illustrations, good copy, slightly marked original gilt lettered olive green cloth, scarce. Ken Spelman Rare Books 68 - 88 2011 £95

Gregorius Nazianazenus *Opera nunc Primum Graece Latine Coniunctin Edita.* Lutetiae Parisiorum: Typis Regiis apud Claudium Morellum, 1609, 2 volumes, folio pages (lxviii), 916 (cxvi) (viii), 308, (viii) cols. 1544 (xliv), contemporary calf - an Oxford; spine ruled in blind, boards triple rule panelled in blind with double outer and single inner foliage panelled roll, board edges single ruled in blind, endleaves taken from a 16th century edition of Mesue, all edges rouge, blue and white sewn endbands small paper labels lettered and numbered in ink, lightly browned, titlepage slightly dust soiled, little rubbed and scratched, labels worn, ties removed, headcap of 2 defective, both volumes have inscription "Brentley/Library...", from the collection of Christopher Ernest Weston 1947-2010. Unsworths Booksellers 24 - 23 2011 £1200

Gregory, Franklin *The White Wolf.* New York: Random House, 1941, First edition; octavo, cloth. L. W. Currey, Inc. 124 - 159 2011 $350

Gregory, G. *The Elements of a Polite Education...* London: printed for R. Phillips, 1800, Pages (x), 456, engraved frontispiece, some foxing, very good, contemporary polished tree calf gilt, upper hinge cracking at foot, corners little bumped, pages. R. F. G. Hollett & Son Antiquarian Booksellers 175 - 549 2011 £120

Gregory, Isbaella Augusta Perse 1859-1932 *Irish Folk-History Plays... First Series.... Second Series... (with) Our Irish Theatre/A Chapter of Autobiography.* New York and London: G. P. Putnams Sons, 1912-1913, First edition; First work in 2 volumes, 8vo., pages (ii), vi, 207, (i) blank, (3) ads; (ii), vi, 198, (5) ads, both volumes internally very fresh, short closed tear to one leaf of prelims in volume i, contemporary quarter cloth and blue paper covered boards, labels to spines with text in black, bumped and lightly rubbed, upper hinge volume i repaired, upper hinge volume ii cracked but firmly hold, John Quinn's autograph inscription volume ii, ownership inscription of A. S. Kinkead; second work 8vo., pages (ii), vi, 319, (i) blank, (5) ads, frontispiece and 3 plates, last leaves very slightly spotted otherwise extremely fresh, tight copy, contemporary quarter cloth and blue paper covered boards, label to spine with text in black, slightly bumped, some signs of wear to boards, endpapers lightly spotted, Quinn's presentation inscription to Joseph Conrad, ownership inscription of A. S. Kinkead. Simon Finch Rare Books Zero - 232 2011 £1250

Gregory, J. W. *Livingstone as an Explorer: an Appreciation.* Glasgow: James Maclehose, 1913, First edition; 8vo., pages 38, large folding map, original dark grey wrappers, scarce, presentation copy. J. & S. L. Bonham Antiquarian Booksellers Africa 4/20/2011 - 6466 2011 £65

Gregory, John *The Works of the Reverend and Learned Mr. John Gregory.* London: printed for Richard Royston and Thomas Williams, 1671, Contemporary full calf, edges little worn, few wormholes in upper panel, pages (xviii), 166, (ii), (xxii), 330 with separate titlepages, title vignette ruled in red and hand colored by contemporary hand, rather extensive worming in places, somewhat loose in binding. R. F. G. Hollett & Son Antiquarian Booksellers 175 - 550 2011 £120

Gregory, T. E. *The Westminster Bank through a Century.* London: Oxford University Press, 1936, 2 volumes, large 8vo., original cloth, gilt with leather spine labels, dust jackets, slipcase little repaired, pages xii, 396; vi, 355, with 2 colored frontispieces and 17 plates, fine set, compliments slip of the secretary of the bank loosely inserted. R. F. G. Hollett & Son Antiquarian Booksellers 175 - 551 2011 £85

Greig, Gavin *Folk-Song of the North-East.* Peterhead: printed by P. Scrogie "Buchan Observer" Works, 1914, Limited edition, no. 2 of 12 copies only; tall 8vo., modern quarter green levant morocco gilt, matching original binding, portrait of author at end, 19 page index, little damping of bottom margin toward end. R. F. G. Hollett & Son Antiquarian Booksellers 175 - 552 2011 £350

Grenard, Ross *Requiem for the Narrow Gauge.* Canton: 1985, 125 pages, illustrations, pictorial hardcover, bottom corner bumped else clean and very good, numbered with warm inscription from author to historian Richard Dorman. Dumont Maps & Books of the West 111 - 58 2011 $75

Grenfell, Wilfred *Forty Years for Labrador.* Boston & New York: Houghton Mifflin Co., 1932, Large 8vo., pages (xii), (3)-372, half title, frontispiece, map and 26 black and white photo illustrations, blue cloth with gilt title to spine, some light wear to binding, else very good, first flyleaf with drawing of large walrus with Eskimo in kayak and spear drawn in black ink, signed "With best wishes Wilfred T. Grenfell, Labrador 1934", also written by previous owner "Presented to me by Sir Wilfred Nov. 1935 William Lang", with TLS from Grenfell to Lang. Schooner Books Ltd. 96 - 42 2011 $150

Gresset, Jean Baptiste Louis *Poemes.* Paris: D. Jouaust, 1867, One of 2 copies Printed on vellum, there were also 118 on paper; 215 x 140mm., 6 p.l., (two vellum blanks, half title, title, two frontispieces (on paper), iv, 132 pages, (4) leaves (variants, contents/colophon, two vellum blanks), folio Cii unsigned and misnumbered but copy complete; very attractive contemporary midnight blue crushed morocco handsomely gilt by Thibaron (stamp signed), covers with French fillet border, raised bands, spines ornately gilt in compartments filled with delicately stipped swirling designs accented with small tools, gilt inner dentelles, marbled endpapers, all edges gilt, 9 engraved on (on paper), 2 frontispiece portraits, 7 plates, large paper copy, bookplates of Robert Hoe and Mortimer Schiff, engraved bookplate of Marcellus Schlimovich, library stamp of Sociedad Hebraica Argentina, just hint of wear top and bottom of joints, one side of first and last vellum flyleaf discolored (apparently from a reaction to the gilt on pastedowns(?), plates with variable freckled foxing (never serious), otherwise fine, elegant binding quite lustrous and leaves clean, fresh and bright. Phillip J. Pirages 59 - 343 2011 $3250

Greville, Charles Cavendish Fulke *The Greville Memoirs.* London: Longmans, Green and Co., 1874, Second edition; 3 volumes, contemporary half calf, gilt, spines heavily gilt with 5 raised bands, double contrasting spine labels, pages xvii, 424; ix, 384; x, 432, all edges and endpapers marbled, handsome set. R. F. G. Hollett & Son Antiquarian Booksellers 175 - 553 2011 £175

Grew, Nehemiah 1641-1712 *An Idea of a Phytological History Propounded. Together with a continuation of the Anatomy of Vegetables...* London: Richard Chiswell at the Hosue and Crown in St. Paul's church yard, 1673, First edition; 7 fine folding engraved plates, 8vo., pages (21), 144, (32), contemporary blind tooled calf, rubbed, piece missing from head of spine, front cover nearly detached, rear hinge split but solid, horizontal split to spine near heel, slight browning to covers, old bookplate removed, old owner's signature R. Frevin 1707. Raymond M. Sutton, Jr. May 26 2011 - 28943 2011 $1600

Grew, Nehemiah 1641-1712 *Musaeum Regalis Societatis or a Catalogue & Description of the Natural and Artificial Rarities Belonging to the Royal Society...* London: printed by W. Rawlins for the author, 1681, First edition; folio, pages (12), 386, (4), (2), 43, contemporary tooled full calf professionally rebacked with sympathetic leather, restored tears to corners near spine, bump to fore-edge of front cover, stains to front endpaper, bookplate removal, edges to front blanks chipped, occasional foxing, ink correction to a page, restored tear to rear endpaper, the copy of Francis Willoughby. Raymond M. Sutton, Jr. May 26 2011 - 55886 2011 $2000

Grey, Robert *Journal of the Bishop's Visitation Tour through the Cape Colony in 1848... (with) A Journal of the Bishop's Visitation Tour....1850.* London: SPCK, 1849-1852, First edition and second edition respectively; 12mo., pages vii, 113, folding map, pages iv, 227, folding map, original purple blindstamped cloth, spine faded. J. & S. L. Bonham Antiquarian Booksellers Africa 4/20/2011 - 7328 2011 £125

Grey, Sydney *Story-Land.* London: Religious Tract Society, n.d., Large 8vo., original glazed pictorial boards, rebacked in cloth, corners worn, pages 111, 32 full page and text color illustrations, little light and occasional fingering. R. F. G. Hollett & Sons Antiquarian Booksellers 170 - 297 2011 £45

The Greyfriars Holiday Annual for Boys and Girls. Amalgamated Press, 1927, Original cloth backed pictorial boards, corners trifle worn, pages 300, 4 color plates and illustrations, tear to front flyleaf repaired, very good. R. F. G. Hollett & Son Antiquarian Booksellers General Catalogue Summer 2010 - 561 2011 £30

Gribble, Francis *The Early Mountaineers.* London: T. Fisher Unwin, 1899, First edition; 8vo., pages xiv, 338, uncut, 48 illustrations, neat small name on titlepage, cover very slightly marked otherwise excellent, very good+ clean, sound copy. Any Amount of Books May 29 2011 - A35980 2011 $238

Griffet, Henri *Histoire des Hosties Miraculeuses Ou'on Nomme le Tres-Saint Sacrement De Miracle.* Bruxelles: J. Van de Berghen, 1770, Signed by publisher, 18 x 10.6mm., 124 (7) pages, folding frontispiece, 18 single page and 8 folding plates, on 5 of the single page, part of the outer margin has broken off at the impression edge and another has been professionally repaired, modern half calf with marbled boards and old marbled free endpaper has been retained, good. C. P. Hyland May 26 2011 - 689 2011 $457

Griffin, A. Harry *Adventuring in Lakeland.* Robert Hale, 1980, First edition; original cloth, gilt, dust jacket, pages 189, 40 illustrations, fine. R. F. G. Hollett & Son Antiquarian Booksellers 173 - 501 2011 £50

Griffin, A. Harry *`Freeman of the Hills.* Robert Hale, 1978, First edition; original cloth, gilt, dust jacket, pages 192, photos, scarce. R. F. G. Hollett & Son Antiquarian Booksellers 173 - 502 2011 £60

Griffin, A. Harry *In Mountain Lakeland.* Preston: Guardian Press, 1963, Second impression; original cloth, gilt, dust jacket (upper edges worn and frayed, head of spine chipped), pages 216, numerous illustrations. R. F. G. Hollett & Son Antiquarian Booksellers 173 - 503 2011 £40

Griffin, A. Harry *Inside the Read Lakeland.* Preston: Guardian Press, 1961, First edition; original cloth, gilt, dust jacket (rather worn), page 240, illustrations. R. F. G. Hollett & Son Antiquarian Booksellers 173 - 504 2011 £40

Griffin, A. Harry *A Lakeland Notebook.* Robert Hale, 1975, First edition; original cloth, gilt, dust jacket price clipped, pages 203, photos, scarce. R. F. G. Hollett & Son Antiquarian Booksellers 173 - 505 2011 £50

Griffin, A. Harry *Long Days in the Hills.* Robert Hale, 1974, First edition; original cloth, gilt, dust jacket, pages 188, 46 illustrations, scarce. R. F. G. Hollett & Son Antiquarian Booksellers 173 - 506 2011 £60

Griffin, A. Harry *The Roof of England.* Robert Hale, 1968, First edition; original cloth, gilt, dust jacket (price clipped, few slight tape marks to reverse), pages 192, illustrations, scarce. R. F. G. Hollett & Son Antiquarian Booksellers 173 - 507a 2011 £40

Griffin, A. Harry *Still the Real Lakeland.* London: Robert Hale, 1970, First edition; original cloth gilt, dust jacket, pages 192, color frontispiece and numerous illustrations. R. F. G. Hollett & Son Antiquarian Booksellers 173 - 508 2011 £50

Griffith, George *The Gold-Finder.* London: 1898, 12mo., 312 pages, near fine, cover gilt and cover color all bright, covers mildly bumped as expected, backstrip gilt bright. Bookworm & Silverfish 669 - 78 2011 $125

Griffith, George *The White Witch of Mayfair.* London: F. V. White & Co. Ltd., 1902, First edition, presumed later or variant binding; 8vo., pages (1-8) (1) 2-312, illustrated red cloth, publisher's monogram stamped in black on rear panel, lettered at spine, neat short gift inscription on half title, very faint mottling to spine, bright clean and very good. Any Amount of Books May 29 2011 - A71382 2011 $255

Griffiths, Thomas *The Writing Desk and Contents: Taken as a Text for the Familiar Illustration of Many Important Facts in Natural History and Philosophy.* London: John W. Parker, 1844, Half title, original blue cloth, slightly rubbed, wear to head and tail of spine, contemporary ownership inscription of John Eaton. Jarndyce Antiquarian Booksellers CXCI - 195 2011 £35

Griffiths, William *A Practical Treatise on Farriery, Deduced from the Experience of Above Forty Years, in the Services of the late Sir Watkin Williams Wynn, Bart, the Present Earl Grosvenor and the Present Sir Watkin Williams Wynn, Bart.* Wrexham: printed by R. Marsh, 1784, First edition; 4to., frontispiece, (4), iii, (i) 184 (14) pages, including list of subscribers and errata note generally little soiled, occasional minor foxing, few inoffensive old ink splashed, original tree calf, flat spine gilt in compartments with repeated anchor and cornucopia motifs, crimson morocco lettering piece, some restoration to joints and corners, good copy, handsome late 18th century binding, uncommon. John Drury Rare Books 153 - 51 2011 £450

Grigson, G. *New Verse.* 1933-1939, First edition; volume 1/1-Volume 2/2, all published, 34 numbers in 32 issues, original wrappers. I. D. Edrich May 26 2011 - 82635 2011 $646

Grimaldi, Joseph 1779-1837 *Memoirs.* London: G. Routledge, 1853, New edition; small 8vo., old binder's cloth gilt, pages xvi, 358, with 10 engraved plates by George Cruikshank (rather stained), rear endpapers rather soiled. R. F. G. Hollett & Son Antiquarian Booksellers 175 - 554 2011 £140

Grimm, The Brothers *The Fairy Tales of the Brother Grimm.* London: Constable & Co. Ltd., 1909, One of 750 copies signed by artist, this #732; 297 x 235mm., xv, (i), 325, (1) pages, very attractive red engraved plates morocco (stamp signed "Putnams" along front turn-in), raised bands, spine handsomely gilt in compartments formed by plain and decorative rules, quatrefoil centerpiece surrounded by densely scrolling cornerpieces, sides an endleaves or rose colored linen, top edge gilt (front joint and headcap very expertly repaired by Courtland Benson), top edge gilt with pictorial frame, numerous black and white illustrations and 40 color plates by Arthur Rackham, as called for, mounted on cream stock and protected by lettered tissue guards; front cover with faint minor soiling, just hint of wear to corners, small corner tear to one plate, two tissue guards with minor creasing or chipped edges, otherwise fine, handsome binding lustrous and text and plates clean, fresh and bright. Phillip J. Pirages 59 - 288 2011 $4500

Grimm, The Brothers *Fairy Tales of the Brothers Grimm.* London: Constable, 1909, Limited to 750 copies signed by artist; large thick 4to., 325 pages, full green morocco with gilt pictorial cover and with spine in compartments with gilt decorations, all edges gilt, original cover and spine bound in, very fine, 40 fabulous tipped in color plates with guards plus a profusion of full page and smaller black and whites by Arthur Rackham, very rare, very fine and bright. Aleph-Bet Books, Inc. 95 - 472 2011 $8000

Grimm, The Brothers *Grimm's Fairy Tales.* London: Ernest Nister & P. Dutton, n.d., 1920, Large 8vo., original pictorial cloth gilt over bevelled boards, extremities trifle worn, small frayed nick to upper hinge, pages 208 with 10 colored plates by Ada Dennis and other illustrations. R. F. G. Hollett & Sons Antiquarian Booksellers 170 - 723 2011 £45

Grimm, The Brothers *Fairy Tales.* N.P.: 1931, Limited to 1500 copies signed; 96 pages, full leather, signed by artist, Fritz Kredel, discrete library # on backstrip and top left corner front cover, cancelled library stamps. Bookworm & Silverfish 665 - 84 2011 $60

Grimm, The Brothers *Gammer Grethel's Fairy Tales.* London: Simpkin Marshall & Hamilton, Kent & Co. n.d. circa, 1925, Square 8vo., original pictorial cloth, trifle marked, pages x, 359, uncut, 2 leaves carelessly opened, color frontispiece, numerous line drawings, scarce. R. F. G. Hollett & Son Antiquarian Booksellers General Catalogue Summer 2010 - 527 2011 £85

Grimm, The Brothers *German Popular Stories.* London & Dublin: James Robins and Joseph Robins, volume i dated, 1827, (first issue was 1823) and volume 2 is 1826; 2 volumes, (i-vi) v-xii (1), 2-240, (i-iii) iv (1), 2-256 (2) page, (1 page ads), original pink boards and green cloth spines, boards rubbed, cloth split at joints and at intervals on spine, labels chipped and rubbed, some foxing, 1 plate in volume I trimmed in margins really overall clean, tight and very good, 22 etched plates by George Cruikshank, laid in is one page handwritten ALS by Jacob Grimm written to Mrs. Austin. Aleph-Bet Books, Inc. 95 - 266 2011 $5000

Grimm, The Brothers *Hansel and Grethel & Snow White and Rose Red.* Chicago: Reilly & Britton, 1908, 12mo., 58 pages, red cloth stamped in yellow and black, round pictorial paste-on, fine, 8 full page color illustrations, few smaller illustrations and pictorial endpapers, great copy. Aleph-Bet Books, Inc. 95 - 387 2011 $275

Grimm, The Brothers *Household Tales.* London: Eyre and Spottiswoode, 1946, First edition; original yellow cloth, dust jacket, very worn and chipped, pages 303, with double page color title, 5 color plates and numerous black and white illustrations. R. F. G. Hollett & Sons Antiquarian Booksellers 170 - 511 2011 £65

Grimm, The Brothers *Grimm's Household Tales.* London: Eyre & Spottiswoode, 1946, First Peake edition; small 4to., yellow cloth, 303 pages, fine in dust jacket (very slightly frayed), illustrations by Mervyn Peake. Aleph-Bet Books, Inc. 95 - 418 2011 $300

Grimm, The Brothers *Three Gay Tales.* New York: Coward McCann, 1943, First edition; 8vo. color pictorial boards, lovely copy, pictorial dust jacket, some minor shelf wear, black and white illustrations by Wanda Gag. Jo Ann Reisler, Ltd. 86 - 102 2011 $475

Grimm, The Brothers *Tom Thumb.* Akron: Saalfield, 1929, Small 4to., pictorial boards, some wear to gutters and fraying of spine ends, else tight, clean and very good+, 4 full page color illustrations, rare. Aleph-Bet Books, Inc. 95 - 420 2011 $250

Grimm, The Brothers *The Twelve Dancing Princesses.* New York: Viking Press, 1978, First American edition; oblong 4to., grey cloth backed lavender boards with elaborate blindstamped border design to boards, full color pictorial dust jacket, signed in full presentation from Le Cain, illustrations by Le Cain. Jo Ann Reisler, Ltd. 86 - 153 2011 $200

Grindon, Leo H. *Lancashire. Brief Historical and Descriptive Notes.* London: Seeley, Jackson and Halliday, 1882, First edition; folio, (8), 83, (1) pages, 14 mounted original etchings, 28 vignettes in text, very good, clean copy, some slight foxing, contemporary dark red half morocco, marbled boards, top edge gilt, scarce. Ken Spelman Rare Books 68 - 82 2011 £295

Grinnell, George Bird *American Big Game in Its Haunts: The Book of the Boone & Crockett Club.* New York: 1904, First edition; 497 pages, large 8vo., cover flecked, frontispiece reglued, backstrip lettering oxidized, presentation letter laid in. Bookworm & Silverfish 676 - 143 2011 $100

Grinsell, L. V. *The Ancient Burial-Mounds of England.* London: Methuen, 1936, First edition; original cloth, gilt pages xiii, 240, with 24 plates, 11 plans and diagrams, very nice clean copy. R. F. G. Hollett & Son Antiquarian Booksellers 177 - 426 2011 £30

Griscom, Acton *The Historia Regum Britanniae of Geoffrey of Monmouth.* London: 1929, first edition; xiii, 672 pages, very good, mild foxing to backstrip in good dust jacket. Bookworm & Silverfish 676 - 74 2011 $122

Griset, Ernest *Griset's Grotesques or Jokes Drawn on Wood.* London: George Routledge and Sons, 1867, Small 4to., original green blindstamped cloth gilt over bevelled boards, large embossed gilt oval title inset on upper board with two cutout colored figures laid on, corners trifle worn, pages (iv), 152,(iv), all edges gilt with 100 woodcuts by Griset, joints neatly strengthened with cloth internally. R. F. G. Hollett & Son Antiquarian Booksellers General Catalogue Summer 2010 - 649 2011 £225

Grocer and Producers Bank, Providence *Charter of the Grocers and Producers Bank, Providence, R.I.* Providence: 1853, First edition; 12mo., 8 pages, self wrappers, fine. M & S Rare Books, Inc. 90 - 28 2011 $175

Grolier Club, New York *Catalogue of an Exhibition of Illuminated and Painted Manuscripts Together with a few Early Printed Books with Illuminations...* New York: Grolier Club, 1892, Limited to 350 copies; 8vo., xxxiii, 64 pages, frontispiece, two color title, illustrations, plates, green cloth, gilt stamped cover title, manuscript paper spine label, page uncut, very good, from the Bern Dibner reference library, with Burndy bookplate.   Jeff Weber Rare Books   161 - 183 2011 $125

Gronovius, Johann Friederich *Observationum Libri tres.* Leiden: Daniel and Abraham Gaasbeek, 1662, Additional engraved allegorical titlepage, woodcut vignette on title, slip of paper pasted onto verso of woodcut, obscuring an inscription, pages (xvi, including engraved title), 690, (28), small 8vo., 18th century plain vellum backed boards, red edges, little rubbed, good.   Blackwell Rare Books   B166 - 43   2011   £200

Gronow, Rees Howell 1794-1865   *The Reminiscences and Recollections of Captain Gronow, Being Anecdotes of the Camp Court, Clubs, and Society 1810-1860.* London: John C. Nimmo, 1889, One of 875 copies (this #10); 265 x 170 mm., 2 volumes extended to 4, especially lovely contemporary crimson crushed morocco, very lavishly gilt by Tout (stamp signed) covers with wide, elaborate gilt frames in the style of Derome, this intricate design rich with fleurons, volutes, curls, festoons an small floral tools, raised bands, spine gilt in double ruled compartments with central cruciform ornament sprouting curling leaves and flowers from its head and tail, these swirls accented with dotted rules and small tools filling the compartments, very wide turn-ins with complex curling botanical decoration, silk endleaves with tiny gold floral sprays, all edges gilt, frontispiece, 24 plates, all in two states as called for, one proof before letters on plate paper, other with captions on Whatman paper and colored by hand, extra illustrated with 227 plates, primarily portraits, 18 of these in color, armorial bookplate of William Ewert Baron Camrose pasted over bookplate of William Morris; hint of rubbing to corners, mild shelfwear, occasional minor foxing affecting inserted plates and adjacent leaves (as well as a small handful of other pages), quite handsome set, clean and fresh internally, sumptuous bindings in fine condition, lustrous and virtually unworn.   Phillip J. Pirages   59 - 144   2011 $4800

Groom, Arthur *Edward the Eighth - Our King.* Allied Newspapers, n.d., First edition; 4to., original cloth, gilt, dust jacket, pages 200, well illustrated, "First Broadcast of King Edward VIII" 1936 - 4 pages 4to., loosely inserted.   R. F. G. Hollett & Son Antiquarian Booksellers   175 - 556 2011   £35

Groom, Winston *Better Times than These.* New York: Summit, 1978, First edition; signed by author, remainder stamp and one tiny corner bump, else fine in very good dust jacket with several small edge chips and usual rubbing caused by lack of lamination.   Ken Lopez Bookseller   154 - 231 2011 $100

Grose, Francis 1731-1791   *The Antiquities of England and Wales.* London: S. Hooper, 1773-1776, Supplement 1787; 4 volumes, folio, original or contemporary full leather, plus 2 volumes supplement dated 1787, bookplates of Lord Camden and also bookplates of the Eaton College Library, volume 1 has 53 half page and 13 full page engravings, volume 2 has 87 half page and 7 full page engravings, volume 3 has 105 half page and 13 full page engravings; volume 4 has 89 half page and 10 full page engravings, volume 5 has 18 half page and 17 full page engravings plus 31 half page maps hand colored in outline, volume 6 has 100 half page and 21 full page engravings and 20 half page maps, bindings very good with strong joints and gilt decorations on covers and spines, inside has foxing to some pages and some pages have some light browning, good+.   Barnaby Rudge Booksellers   Travel and Exploration - 019970 2011 $1900

Grose, Francis 1731-1791   *The Antiquities of England and Wales.* circa, 1790, New edition; 8 volumes, engraved title to each volume 571 engraved plates, hand colored folding map, lacks single page maps, pen and ink portrait of Grose to upper pastedown volume I and dated 1788, library stamps to reverse of titles and few pages of text, some foxing mainly to margins and with some staining to first few leaves, uniform contemporary calf, contrasting morocco labels, upper board volume I dampstained and detached, some joints worn, 4to., generally very good.   C. P. Hyland   May 26 2011 - 282 2011 $906

Grose, Francis 1731-1791   *The Antiquities of Scotland.* London: printed for Hooper & Wigstead, 1797, Second edition; large paper copy, folio, pages (iii)-xxiii, (i), iv, 176 + engraved plates and 84 engraved plates; iv, 140 + engraved titlepage and 106 engraved plates, contemporary sprinkled tan calf, four flat raised banded spines fully gilt with triple rules, decorative rolls and centre pieces comprising ogee brackets paired tools and pointille symmetric tool, dark red and green lettering and numbering pieces, gilt, boards single rule gilt bordered board edges decorative roll gilt, all edges brown sprinkled, green sewn endbands, plates bit foxed at edges, some minor spotting elsewhere, joints cracking, bit of wear to spine ends, boards marked and scratched, the issue without continuous pagination, from the collection of Christopher Ernest Weston 1947-2010.   Unsworths Booksellers   24 - 104   2011   £500

Gross, Chaim *Jewish Holidays. A Suite of Eleven Original Lithographs.* Paris and New York: n.p., 1969, Limited, signed first edition, one of 200 copies signed by artist, this being number 159; large oblong folio, 11 full color lithographs on loose sheets, signed and dated by artist, printed on BFK Rives paper, 13 loose signatures, uncut, laid into a publisher's original blue cloth portfolio, portfolio lettered in gilt, all housed in original blue cloth, clamshell, lettered in gilt, fine.   Heritage Book Shop   Holiday 2010 - 49 2011 $1500

Grosvenor, Fredrika *The Noah's Ark ABC.* New York: McLoughlin Bros., 1905, First edition thus; large 4to., red cloth backed full color pictorial boards with some overall wear and light weakness to front hinges, each page illustrated in chromolithographed color.   Jo Ann Reisler, Ltd.   86 - 171 2011 $475

Grote, George *Essentials of Parliamentary Reform.* London: Baldwin and Cradock, 1831, First edition; 8vo., x, (11)-75 + (1) pages, titlepage and verso of final leaf little dust marked, early ownership name in ink at head of title ("Philips - The Park") preserved in modern wrappers with printed title label on upper cover, entirely uncut, scarce. John Drury Rare Books   153 - 52 2011   £350

Grote, George *A History of Greece from the Earliest Period to the Close of the Generation Contemporary with Alexander the Great.* London: John Murray, 1862, 8 volumes, 8vo., xxviii, (1), 581; xvi, 572; xix, 564; xxi, 572; xx, 616; xix, 530; xxvi, 670; xxvii, 732, frontispiece, maps, plans, original golden tan polished calf, double ruled gilt cover borders, elaborately decorated gilt spine with raised bands, dual morocco labels in red and dark olive, gilt turn-ins and inside dentelles, top edge gilt, very good.   Jeff Weber Rare Books   163 - 121 2011 $3500

Grote, George *History of Greece from the Earliest Period to the Close of the Generation Contemporary with Alexander the Great.* London: John Murray, 1862, 223 x 145mm., 8 volumes, handsome contemporary polished calf, ornately gilt, covers with double ruled gilt border raised bands, spines lavishly gilt in compartments formed by plain and decorative rules with swirling volute side and cornerpieces as well as large central floral spray, red and green morocco labels, marbled edges and endpapers; portrait frontispiece, 16 maps; spine bands with minor rubbing, frontispiece and opening leaves bit foxed, occasional minor foxing elsewhere, other trivial imperfections but once beautiful set that is still quite attractive, elaborately decorative contemporary bindings with bright leather and nominal wear only, text almost entirely clean, fresh, bright and smooth.   Phillip J. Pirages   59 - 230 2011 $1500

Grotius, Hugo 1583-1645 *The Truth of the Christian Religion.* London: printed for J. Knapton, 1719, Second edition; 12mo., contemporary blind ruled polished calf with spine label, pages (xxii), 336.   R. F. G. Hollett & Son Antiquarian Booksellers   175 - 558 2011   £140

The Grounds and Danger of Restrictions on the Corn Trade Considered: Together with a Letter on the Substance of Rent. Bath: printed by Richard Cruttwell and sold by Hatchard, London, 1826, Second edition; scarce, 8vo., xi, (1), 134 pages, including half title, half title soiled, otherwise fine, crisp copy, recently well bound in cloth, lettered in gilt. John Drury Rare Books 153 - 53 2011   £250

Grove, Richard H. *Green Imperialism: Colonial Expansion, Tropical Island Edens and the Origins of Enivormentalism 1600-1860.* Cambridge: Cambridge University Press, 1995, First edition; 8vo. xiv, 540 pages, illustrations, green cloth, gilt stamped spine title, dust jacket, fine, from the Bern Dibner reference library, with Burndy bookplate.   Jeff Weber Rare Books   161 - 184 2011 $80

Grover, Eulalie Osgood *The Sunbonnet Babies ABC Book: a Modern Hornbook.* Chicago: Rand. McNally, 1929, First edition; 4to., cloth, 64 pages, pictorial paste-on, some cover soil and slight finger soil, very good, lovely full page color illustrations, very scarce in first edition. Aleph-Bet Books, Inc.   95 - 36 2011 $250

Grove's Dictionary of Music and Musicians. New York: St. Martin's Press, 1962, Fifth edition, fifth printing; 10 volumes, very good set, personal owner name and black cross out on f.f.e.p.'s, some mild (unobtrusive) water marking to lower portions of the volumes which has not left any 'tide' marks in texts, little wear to dust jackets but not chipping. Lupack Rare Books   May 26 2011 - ABE3650944576 2011 $250

Groves, Sylvia *The History of Needlework Tools and Accessories.* London: Country Life, 1968, Second impression; large 8vo, original cloth, gilt, dust jacket (short closed but creased tear to lower panel), pages 136 with 199 plates, 13 text drawings, excellent copy.   R. F. G. Hollett & Son Antiquarian Booksellers   General Catalogue Summer 2010 - 187 2011   £50

Grube, Ernst J. *Islamic Pottery of the Eighth to the Fifteenth Century the Keir Collection.* London: Faber & Faber, 1976, First edition; 4to., pages 378, original publisher's dark green cloth lettered gilt on spine, copiously illustrated in color and black and white, very good in like dust jacket, covers slightly rubbed, dust jacket faintly rubbed and very slightly faded.   Any Amount of Books   May 29 2011 - A69867 2011 $255

Gruelle, Johnny *Friendly Fairies.* Chicago: P. F. Volland & Co., 1919, Nineteenth edition; 8vo., full color pictorial boards, slight wear to spine, full color pictorial box with light wear to sides, quite nice.   Jo Ann Reisler, Ltd.   86 - 115 2011 $385

Gruelle, Johnny *My Very Own Fairy Stories.* Chicago: Volland, 1917, 4to., pictorial boards, fine in original box, light wear to flaps, illustrations by author with pictorial endpapers plus many full page and in text color illustrations, magnificent copy.   Aleph-Bet Books, Inc.   95 - 268 2011 $600

Gruelle, Johnny *Orphant Annie Story Book.* Indianapolis: Bobbs Merrill, 1921, First edition; tall 8vo., cloth, pictorial paste-on, (86) pages, near fine, illustrations.   Aleph-Bet Books, Inc.   95 - 269 2011 $450

Gruelle, Johnny *The Paper Dragon.* Joliet: Volland, 1926, First edition, second issue; 8vo., pictorial boards, wrap around paper spine, as new in fine pictorial box, uncommon.   Aleph-Bet Books, Inc.   95 - 270 2011 $600

Gruelle, Johnny *Raggedy Ann and Andy and the Camel with Wrinkled Knees.* Joliet: Volland, 1924, no additional prints, proper ads; 8vo., cloth backed pictorial boards, minimal wear, near fine in publisher's box, box flap restored, beautiful copy, illustrations in color, laid in is printed Volland ad announcing this title as the "new book" but listing Joliet as the city of publication, not Chicago, beautiful copy.   Aleph-Bet Books, Inc.   95 - 271 2011 $500

Gruelle, Johnny *Raggedy Ann's Magical Wishes.* Joliet: Volland, 1928, First edition; 8vo., cloth backed pictorial boards, fine in publisher's pictorial box, pictorial endpapers. unusually fine.   Aleph-Bet Books, Inc.   95 - 272 2011 $600

Gruger, Heribert *The Sing Song Picture Book.* Philadelphia: Lippincott, 1931, 4to., cloth backed pictorial boards, tips rubbed and covers slightly soiled, else very good, color illustrations by Gruger.   Aleph-Bet Books, Inc.   95 - 53 2011 $350

Grundy, C. Reginald *A Catalogue of the Pictures and Drawings in the Collection of Frederick John Nettlefold.* Bemrose & Sons, 1933, 4 volumes, tipped in plates, good set, original gilt cloth, spines unevenly faded and some marking to boards, folio.   Ken Spelman Rare Books   68 - 118 2011   £120

Guerber, H. A. *Myths of the Norsemen from the Eddas and Sagas.* London: Harrap, 1925, Original imitation leather gilt extra with school crest on upper board, pages xvi, 397, (ii), color frontispiece and 32 plates.   R. F. G. Hollett & Son Antiquarian Booksellers   175 - 559 2011   £30

Guervitch, Jessica *Ecology of Plants.* Sunderland: 2006, Second edition; quarto, laminated boards, 574 pages, color photos, diagrams, other illustrations.   Andrew Isles Natural History Books   Spring 2010 - 30386 2011 $127

Guest, Barbara *The Altos.* Hine Editions/Limestone Press, 1991, First edition, one of 40 Roman numeraled copies Printed by hand on Somerset paper and signed by author and artist, from a total edition of 120 copies; folio, original full white calf stamped in blind on front cover, as new in original mailing glassine and shipping box, illustrations by Richard Tuttle.   James S. Jaffe Rare Books   May 26 2011 - 20646 2011 $9500

Guest, Barbara *The Location of Things.* New York: Tibor De Nagy Editions, 1960, First edition, one of 300 copies; small 8vo., original publisher's present thin green card wrappers, pages 67, slight suning, faint unobtrusive tape mark at lower spine area, very good+.   Any Amount of Books   May 29 2011 - A68053 2011 $238

Gueulette, Thomas Simon *The Thousand and One Quarters of an Hour (Tartarian Tales).* London: H. S. Nichols and Co., 1893, One of 5 copies on Japanese vellum (of an edition of 680 copies); 254 x 159mm, viii, 308 pages, quite pleasing dark green crushed morocco by Morrell (signed), covers bordered in gilt with French fillet elaborate oblique gilt scrolling cornerpieces with blank oval center with raised bands, spine in handsome gilt compartment similarly decorated, wide green morocco turn-ins with simple gilt ornaments and rules, crimson crushed morocco doublures and free endpapers, other edges untrimmed, middle raised band of spine with small expert repair, front endpaper with morocco bookplate of W. A. Foyle, Beeleigh Abbey, titlepage printed in red and black; spine now sunned to uniform warm brown, top and top edge of cover also slightly sunned, few leaves of one gathering with small stain just at fore edge, additional trifling imperfections, otherwise fine, binding lustrous with very little wear, beautifully luxurious paper of text especially fresh and clean.   Phillip J. Pirages   59 - 321 2011 $650

Guevara, Antonio De *Vita Di M. Avrelio Imperadore.* Venice: Bartolomeo Imperador and Francesco Veneziano, 1543, 160 x 103mm., 8 p.l., 132, (2) leaves, fine contemporary Roman red morocco Apollo and Pegasus medallion binding done for Giovanni Battista Grimaldi by Marc Antonio Guillery, (genuine Apollo and Pegasus binding) covers with gilt frame formed by two widely spaced fillets with lobes interlaced at ends and sides, space between fillets decorated with broad foliate curls, small floral tools, inner pane of each board with gilt titling above a horizontal oval Apollo and Pegasus plaquette centerpiece showing Pegasus atop black painted heights of Parnassus and Apollo racing his chariot (drawn by two straining steeds) across steep terrain with reins and whip held aloft and caps fluttering behind, plaquette with gilt motto in Greek in the collar above and below vignette, spine (very expertly rebacked) with four thin and three thick raised bands decorated with gilt rope pattern or plain rules (this being original backstrip?), newer (perhaps 19th century) endpapers, all edges gilt (apparently some remarkably skillful restoration at one or more corners and edges, perhaps some gold added, as well as to the chariot part of the plaquettes); woodcut printer's device on , morocco bookplate and separate gilt monogram of Robert Hoe as well as inscription and vellum bookplate of Swedish collector Thore Virgin, ownership inscription of J. T. Payne dated 1850; covers with half dozen insignificant tiny dark spots, titlepage faintly soiled, thin light brown stain just at top edge of leaves, small wormhole at upper inner margin (text not affected), occasional minor stains, other trivial imperfections, but no defects that are even remotely serious and in general really excellent specimen of a very special binding, text fresh and leather quite lustrous; also from the collection of bibliophile Johannes Gennadius, Liverpool oculist T. Shadford Walker and Swedish collector Rolfe Wistrand. Phillip J. Pirages   59 - 2   2011 $35,000

Guide to the Church Congress and Ecclesiastical Art Exhibition Held in Barrow-in-Furness September 29, October 1, 2, 3, 4 and 5, 1906. Maltravers House, 1906, First edition; original stiff decorated wrappers, neatly rebacked in lettered cloth, new plain card lower panel, pages iii, (ii), 296, (iv-vi), illustrations, scarce.   R. F. G. Hollett & Son Antiquarian Booksellers   173 - 55 2011   £140

A Guide to the English Lake District... London: Simpkin Marshall & Co. and Windermere: J. Garnett, circa, 1865, Second edition; original blindstamped cloth gilt, pages viii, 123, viii, colored frontispiece and 4 folding maps printed in blue, 2 woodcut plates and several tables.   R. F. G. Hollett & Son Antiquarian Booksellers   173 - 511   2011   £65

Guiget, Jean *Virginia Woolf and Her Works.* London: Hogarth Press, 1965, First English translation; (488) page, thick 8vo., blue cloth, gilt lettered spine, very fine in near fine dust jacket.   Paulette Rose Fine and Rare Books 32 - 193   2011 $100

Guilelmus, Abp. of Tyre *The History of Godefrey of Boloyne.* Hammersmith: Kelmscott Press, 1893, One of 300 paper copies, out of a total edition of 306 copies; large quarto, xxii, (2), 450, (2) pages, printed in red and black in Troy and Chaucer types, decorative woodcut title, borders and initials, woodcut printer's device, original full limp vellum with yapp edges, spine lettered in gilt, original brown silk ties, couple of very small areas of rubbing on edges, minimal foxing to edges only, else near fine, gilt on spine bright and fresh, housed in quarter black morocco clamshell case. David Brass Rare Books, Inc.   May 26 2011 - 01472   2011 $7500

Guillard, Rene *Histoire du Conseil du Roy Depuis le Commencement de la Monarchie Jesqu a la fin du Regne de Louis Le Grand...* Paris: A-U Coustelier, 1738, Uncommon, 4to., viii, (4), 855 pages, contemporary sprinkled calf, gilt border on covers, with floral cornerpieces, spine gilt, morocco lettering piece, silk bookmark, from the library of the Earls of Macclesfield at Shirburn Castle. Maggs Bros. Ltd.   1440 - 103   2011   £750

Guiness, H. Grattan *The Approaching End of the Age Viewed in the Light of History, Prophecy & Science.* New York: 1887, Called the tenth edition; 776 pages, good plus, original binding, library bookplate, no other marks. Bookworm & Silverfish   676 - 162   2011   £75

Gunn, Thom *Fighting Terms.* Oxford: Fantasy Press, 1954, First edition; signed copy, one of an unspecified number from first issue with uncorrected error on page 38, line 1, from a total edition of 305 copies only, 8vo., pages (ii) blank, 44, (2) blank, internally clean, original yellow cloth, upper board lettered and tooled in red, cloth extremities rubbed, spine cracked but holding, joint firm, some light soiling.   Simon Finch Rare Books   Zero - 322 2011   £450

Gunther, Albert *The Fishes of Zanzibar.* London: John Van Voorst, 1866, 4to., pages xiv, 153, with 21 lithographed plates (6 hand colored, 2 are loose, dampstain to lower blank corner of most, not affecting images, minor foxing to a few) and 10 engravings in text, 4to., pages xiv, 153, original cloth (faded, 3 corners lightly bumped, tips of corners worn, some splitting to lower front edge and upper rear edge of spine, paper residue to margin of rear cover near spine, minor spotting to heel of spine, short tear to ends of spine, paper on front inner hinge cracked, owner's handstamps to front flyleaf, title and a page, an inner joint partially open, small piece missing from upper blank margin of a page, short marginal tear to a page, rare.   Raymond M. Sutton, Jr.   May 26 2011 - 41459   2011 $2000

Gunther, Albert *The Reptiles of British India.* London: Ray Society by Robert Hardwicke, 1864, First edition; 26 lithographed plates (foxing to first plate, lighter foxing to second state), light thin dampstain to lower margin to first 6 plates, most of the plates virtually clean, folio, pages (1), xxvii, 452, original cloth over flexible boards, soiled, rubbed, edges of boards worn, label of front board partially perished, endpapers foxed, marginal dampstaining to front pastedown ad front free endpaper, foxing to front and back pages, heavier to half title and title, upper corner bumped, ex-libris King's Inns Library, Dublin. Raymond M. Sutton, Jr. May 26 2011 - 44161 2011 $1750

Gunther, Ken *Lilith: a Biography.* N.P.: 2005, First edition; 956 pages, fine in wrappers, this copy inscribed and signed by author to Barbara Kingsolver. Bookworm & Silverfish 671 - 47 2011 $75

Guppy, Henry *A Brief Sketch of the History of the Transmission of the Bible.* Manchester: Manchester University Press, 1926, Pages vii, 75, contemporary half calf gilt with broad raised bands an spine label, top edge gilt, other edges untrimmed, with 20 plates, presentation copy inscribed by author to Mr. Thurlow Baker. R. F. G. Hollett & Son Antiquarian Booksellers General Catalogue Summer 2010 - 417 2011 £65

Guppy, Henry *The History of the Transmission of the Bible.* Manchester: University Press, 1925, Blue library cloth, gilt, pages xii, 133, 20 plates, library label. R. F. G. Hollett & Son Antiquarian Booksellers General Catalogue Summer 2010 - 138 2011 £40

Guppy, Henry *Manuscript and Printed Copies of the Scriptures, Illustrating the History of the Transmission of the Bible.* Manchester: University Press, 1911, Original wrappers, spine faded, pages xiv, 128, with 12 plates, light library stamps to back of title. R. F. G. Hollett & Son Antiquarian Booksellers General Catalogue Summer 2010 - 139 2011 £30

Gurganus, Allan *Breathing Lessons.* Durham: North Carolina Wesleyan College Press, 1981, Printed in an edition of 500 copies, 50 of which were numbered and signed; bit of smudging to inscription, trace rust near staples, else fine in stapled wrappers, this copy unnumbered, lengthily inscribed by author in 1990 to James Freedman, President of Dartmouth College. Ken Lopez Bookseller 154 - 70 2011 $200

Gurney, J. H. *Rambles of a Naturalist in Egypt...* London: Jarrold, n.d., 1876, First edition; 8vo., pages vi, 307, ads, original purple cloth, gilt vignette (ship) on upper cover, spine faded, covers soiled but internally clean. J. & S. L. Bonham Antiquarian Booksellers Africa 4/20/2011 - 6406 2011 £35

Gurney, Joseph John *Observations on the Distinguishing Views and Practices of the Society of Friends.* Norwich: Josian Fletcher, 1842, Eighth edition; original blind-stamped cloth gilt, little worn, top edge of spine slightly chipped, pages xii, 528. R. F. G. Hollett & Son Antiquarian Booksellers 175 - 561 2011 £35

Gursky, Andreas *Montparnasse.* Frankfurt am Main and Stuttgart: Portikus and Oktagon Verlag, 1995, First edition, first printing of this boxed set; long oblong folio, 2 volumes, original publisher's box, mint, rare, complete with separate folded print. James S. Jaffe Rare Books May 26 2011 - 20770 2011 $5500

Gurwood, John *The General Orders of Field Marshal The Duke of Wellington, K. G. &c in Portugal, Spain and France from 1809 to 1814 and the Low Countries and France 1815.* London: William Clowes, 1832, First edition; 8vo. pages xxvii, 460, soundly rebound in modern red cloth lettered gilt on spine, ex-British Foreign Office library with few library markings, slight foxing of prelims and fore-edges, otherwise very good. Any Amount of Books May 29 2011 - A70523 2011 $272

Gutberleth, Tobias *Opuscula.* Franeker: Franciscus Halman, 1704, (1703), Apparently first editions; 4 parts in one volume, 3 folding engraved plates, general half title printed in red and black, engraved portrait of author on verso, additional engraved title to first part, first title printed in red and black, engraved vignette, woodcut printer's device on other titles, engraved headpiece to first part, numerous engravings, pages (xvii, including engraved title, lacking terminal blank of prelims), 170, (22), 187, (13), 8vo., contemporary pencilled vellum over wooden boards, lettered in ink at head of spine, front free endpaper missing, good. Blackwell Rare Books B166 - 44 2011 £275

Guterson, David *The Country Ahead of Us, the Country Behind: Stories.* New York: Harper & Row, 1989, First printing; as new, dust jacket, fine. Lupack Rare Books May 26 2011 - ABE1233855350 2011 $175

Guterson, David *The Country Ahead of Us, The Country Behind.* New York: Harper & Row, 1989, First edition; fine in near fine, dust jacket, price clipped, signed by author. Bella Luna Books May 26 2011 - t091 2011 $247

Guterson, David *Snow Falling on Cedars.* New York: Harcourt Brace, 1994, First edition; fine in fine dust jacket, signed by author. Bella Luna Books May 29 2011 - t8996 2011 $137

Guthrie, Stuart *A Chapbook for Little Chaps.* Flansham, Nr. Bognor: Pear Tree Press, 1920, First edition; 8vo., 25 pages copiously illustrated with colored woodblock prints, calligraphic note "With compliments from The Pear Tree Press, Flansham 1921", rear board slightly tanned and slightly marked head of spine very slightly frayed, otherwise decent, very good copy.   Any Amount of Books   May 29 2011 - A71981   2011 $383

Guthrie, Thomas Anstey *Humour & Fantasy.* London: John Murray, 1931, First edition; octavo, original red cloth, front panel stamped in black, spine panel stamped in gold, top edge stained red.   L. W. Currey, Inc.   124 - 241   2011 $65

Gutman, Walter *The Gutman Letter.* New York: Something Else Press, 1969, First edition; 4to., pages xi, 13-142, photos and few reproductions, some in color, cover little scuffed at corners and ends of spine, otherwise very good, tight copy.   Second Life Books Inc.   174 - 163   2011 $75

H

Hack, Maria Barton *Harry Beaufoy; or the Pupil of nature.* London: Harvey and Darton, 1821, First edition; 12mo., viii, 194, (1) pages, original marbled paper on boards, red roan spine with gilt title and fillets, very fine full page copper engraving, light rubbing at covers and spine, fine. Hobbyhorse Books   56 - 81   2011 $250

Hackel, Sergei *Sobornost: The Journal of the Fellowship of St. Alban and St. Sergius, Incorporating Eastern Churches Review.* London: Fellowship of St. Alban and St. Sergius, 1979-1989, First editions; 17 volumes, 8vo., wrappers, pages 2134, very good+. Any Amount of Books   May 29 2011 - A44130   2011 $298

Haddan, Arthur W. *Councils & Ecclesiastical Documents Relating to Great Britain and Ireland.* 1869-1873, 3 volumes, (xxxii 704, xxiv 361, xv 660 pages), ex-library, mistitled on spine volume II, very good. C. P. Hyland   May 26 2011 - 255/281   2011 $457

Haddon, A. C. *Canoes of Oceania.* Honolulu: 1991, Second complete edition; 884 pages, issued in 3 volumes, crease to rear wrapper and last few leaves, otherwise near fine. Bookworm & Silverfish   678 - 144   2011 $125

Haddon, Mark *The Curious Incident of the Dot in the Night-Time.* London: Cape, 2003, First printing of the scarcer adult issue; original cloth, gilt, dust jacket, 272 pages, illustrations. R. F. G. Hollett & Sons Antiquarian Booksellers   170 - 301   2011   £120

Haddon, Mark *The Curious Incident of the Dog in the Night Time.* London: Cape, 2003, First edition, later edition of adult version; original cloth, gilt, dust jacket, 272 pages, illustrations. R. F. G. Hollett & Sons Antiquarian Booksellers   170 - 302   2011   £35

Haddon, Mark *The Curious Incident of the Dog in the Night Time.* Oxford: Cape, 2003, Adult version of the first British edition; fine in fine dust jacket. Bella Luna Books   May 29 2011 - t6186   2011 $137

Hader, Berta *Jamaica Johnny.* New York: Macmillan, Oct., 1935, First edition; 4to., green pictorial cloth, fine in slightly worn dust jacket, full page color illustrations, with small watercolor drawing, inscription to Elmer's sister Leoto (her book). Aleph-Bet Books, Inc.   95 - 274   2011 $750

Hadfield, Miles *An English Almanac.* London: Dent, 1950, First edition; large 8vo., original cloth gilt, dust jacket (head of spine little frayed), pages 225, over 60 illustrations by author. R. F. G. Hollett & Son Antiquarian Booksellers   175 - 565   2011   £30

Haeckel, Ernst *The Evolution of Man.* London: Watts & Co., 1906, First 1 volume English edition; 2 volumes in 1, original blue cloth, gilt, pages xiv, 364, with 209 illustrations, poor quality paper little browned at edges as usual, ownership label on pastedown, otherwise very nice. R. F. G. Hollett & Son Antiquarian Booksellers   General Catalogue Summer 2010 - 979   2011   £45

Hafen, Leroy R. *The Far West and Rockies Historical Series 1820-1875.* Glendale: Arthur H. Clark Co., 1954-1961, First editions; 15 volumes, all in matching green cloth, gilt on spine, as issued, illustrations, maps,. Buckingham Books   May 26 2011 - 31047   2011 $2000

Hagedorn, Jessica *Pet Food and Tropical Apparitions.* San Francisco: Momo's Press, 1981, Simultaneous issue in wrappers; inscribed by author to another poet, rubbing to spine folds, minor wear, near fine, good association, inscribed by author to another poet. Ken Lopez Bookseller   154 - 71   2011 $75

Hager, Jean *The Grandfather Medicine.* New York: St. Martin's, 1989, First edition; fine in fine dust jacket, signed by author. Bella Luna Books   May 29 2011 - t2628   2011 $82

Haggar, Reginald *Mason Porcelain & Ironstone 1796-1853.* London: Faber, 1977, First edition; original cloth, gilt, dust jacket, pages 133, with 8 color plates and 144 illustrations. R. F. G. Hollett & Son Antiquarian Booksellers   General Catalogue Summer 2010 - 188   2011   £50

Haggard, Henry Rider 1856-1925 *Cetwayo and His White Neighbours; or Remarks on Recent Events in Zululand, Natal & the Transvaal.* London: Trubner & Co., 1882, First edition; half title, followed by leaf printed verso, half red morocco, marbled boards by Mansell, very slight rubbed at head of spine, booklabel of Geo. Evelyn Cower, top edge gilt, fine. Jarndyce Antiquarian Booksellers   CXCI - 197   2011   £450

Haggard, Henry Rider 1856-1925 *King Solomon's Mines.* London: Cassell & Co., 1885, First edition; first issue with "Bamamgwato" for "Bamangwato" on page 10, line 14; "to let twins to live" for "to let Twins live" on page 122, line 27 and "wrod" instead of "word" on page 307, line 29, with publisher's cataloge dated "5G.8.85" and "5B.8.85", small octavo, (4), vi, (7)-320, (16, publisher's catalog) pages, folding color facsimile map inserted as frontispiece, black and white map on page 27, original front cover cloth bound in at back, beautifully bound by Bayntun-Riviere in full red morocco, boards ruled gilt, spine printed and lettered gilt, gilt dentelles, all edges gilt, marbled endpapers, few professional repaired closed tears to folding map, about fine. Heritage Book Shop   Holiday 2010 - 50 2011 $5000

Haggard, Henry Rider 1856-1925 *A Winter Pilgrimage.* London: Longmans, Green and Co., 1901, First edition; half title, frontispiece, illustrations, half red morocco, marbled boards by W. J. Mansell, top edge gilt, fine.   Jarndyce Antiquarian Booksellers   CXCI - 553 2011   £160

Hagman, Larry *Hello Darlin'.* Norwalk: Easton Press, 2001, First edition thus; signed by author, leather, all edges gilt, as new, includes certificate of authenticity and note from Easton Press.   Gemini Fine Books & Arts, Ltd. Art Reference & Illustrated Books: First Editions 2011 $70

Hahemann, Samuel *Organon of Homoeopathic Medicine.* Allentown: Academical Bookstore, 1836, First American edition; 8vo. 23, (9)-212 pages, original cloth, spine worn and cracking at hinges, very sound, clean and tight.   M & S Rare Books, Inc.   90 - 147 2011 $1250

Haigh, A. E. *The Attic Theatre.* Clarendon Press, 1889, First edition; full levant morocco gilt with raised bands and coat of arms gilt on each board, spine little faded, pages xiii, 341, all edges gilt, facsimiles and text illustrations, handsome.   R. F. G. Hollett & Son Antiquarian Booksellers   175 - 567 2011   £75

Haigh, James *The Dier's Assistant in the Art of Dying Wool & Woolen Goods.* Philadelphia: 1810, First US edition; xxi (blank) (23)-311 pages, 12mo., early full leather, new leather backstrip and gilt on red label (text has some old staining).   Bookworm & Silverfish   678 - 194 2011 $285

Haile, Berard *Head and Face Masks in Navajo Ceremonialism.* St. Michaels: 1947, xiv, 122 pages, illustrations, slightly soil and couple of chips to dust jacket, bookplate of ethnologist Bertha Dutton, with her underlining few words and phrases to first 60 or so pages, otherwise nice.   Dumont Maps & Books of the West   113 - 33 2011 $400

Hake, A. Egmont *The Journals of Major-Gen. C. G. Gordon CB at Kartoum...* London: Kegan Paul Trench & Co., 1885, First edition; large 8vo., pages lxviii, 588, portrait, 2 maps, 30 illustrations, original red cloth, spine little faded, joints slightly rubbed.   J. & S. L. Bonham Antiquarian Booksellers   Africa 4/20/2011 - 8673 2011   £45

Halberstam, David *Ho.* New York: Random House, 1971, First edition; signed by author, front free endpaper has been excised in this copy, otherwise fine in near fine dust jacket with tiny nick to front flap fold that has been needlessly tape strengthened on verso, uncommon signed.   Ken Lopez Bookseller   154 - 232 2011 $100

Halberstam, David *The Noblest Roman.* Boston: 1961, 304 pages, very good with opaque spot on front cover, price clipped dust jacket with creases and small tears at bottom of backstrip and creasing to very top, front joint reglued.   Bookworm & Silverfish   671 - 87 2011 $275

Haldane, Henry *The Trial of Lieut. Col. Haldane on an Indictment for Perjury at Kingston in the County of Surrey on the 2d Day of April 1814.* London: J. J. Stockdale, 1814, First edition; 8vo., 49, (1) pages, recent marbled boards lettered on spine, very good, very rare.   John Drury Rare Books   153 - 151 2011   £175

Hale, Kathleen *Orlando the Marmelade Cat Keeps a Dog.* London: Country Life, n.d. circa, 1944, First edition; folio, cloth backed pictorial boards, slightest of edge wear, else fine, frayed dust jacket, increasingly scarce.   Aleph-Bet Books, Inc.   95 - 276 2011 $350

Hale, Kathleen *Orlando's Invisible Pyjamas.* London: John Murray, n.d. c., 1947, Oblong 8vo., original pictorial wrappers, pages 30, lithographed in color and monochrome, some corners little creased.   R. F. G. Hollett & Sons Antiquarian Booksellers   170 - 303 2011   £35

Hale, Sarah *The Countries of Europe, their Manners and Customs.* New York: published by Edward Dunigan, circa, 1843, Square 18mo., 55, (1 blank), pages 16, illustrations on 8 plates, original stiff printed wrappers, worn but sound, text rather spotted.   M & S Rare Books, Inc.   90 - 203 2011 $150

Haley, James Evetts *A Log of the Montana Trail as Kept by Ealy Moore.* Amarillo: Russell Stationery Co., 1932, First edition thus; inscribed by author to C. C. Walsh, printed wrappers (13 pages), fine, housed in imitation leather clamshell case with gold stamping on spine.   Buckingham Books   May 26 2011 - 29752 2011 $2000

Haley, James Evetts *The XIT Ranch of Texas and the Early Days of the Llano Estacado.* Chicago: Lakeside Press, 1929, First edition; 8vo., presentation inscription by author to R. G. Long, also laid in is penned note on Prince George Hotel (NYC) stationery, to Wright Howes advising that they would meet him for breakfast and afterwards, go to a sale together; decorated cloth, xvi, 261 pages, gilt top, frontispiece, fine bright copy in protective transparent dust jacket, exceptional copy.   Buckingham Books   May 26 2011 - 28028   2011 $1875

Halfpenny, Joseph *Gothic Ornaments in the Cathedral Church of York.* York: John and George Todd, 1831, New edition; 105 etched plates, rear cover of final part torn, first cover little dusty, otherwise very good, some occasional foxing.   Ken Spelman Rare Books   68 - 26   2011   £350

Haliburton, R. G. *How a Race of Pygmies was Found in North Africa and Spain.* Toronto: Arbuthnot, 1897, First edition; 8vo., pages 147, 2 plates, later blue cloth, library label on upper pastedowns.   J. & S. L. Bonham Antiquarian Booksellers   Africa 4/20/2011 - 7580   2011   £175

Haliburton, Thomas Chandler   1796-1865   *The Attache; or Sam Slick in England.* London: David Bryce, circa, 1857, Half title, original orange cloth, faded, spine dulled, as on endpapers.   Jarndyce Antiquarian Booksellers   CXCI - 198   2011   £40

The Halifax Catastrophe Showing Effects of Explosion December Sixth 1917... Halifax: Royal Print & Litho Limited, 1917, Oblong 8vo., light brown covers, pages (42), 40 black and white photo illustrations, 1 map, covers worn, spine split and repaired with archival tape, interior good to very good.   Schooner Books Ltd.   96 - 158   2011 $95

Hall, A. Rupert *Science and Society: Historical Essays on the Relations of Science, Technology and Medicine.* Aldershot and Brookfield: Variorum, 1994, 8vo., x, 324 pages, frontispiece, illustrations, blue cloth, gilt stamped cover and spine titles, fine, from the Bern Dibner reference library, with Burndy bookplate.   Jeff Weber Rare Books   161 - 187   2011 $110

Hall, Edward B. *A Lecture on the Pleasures and Vices of the City Delivered... March 30 1856.* Providence: Knowles Anthony & Co., 1856, First edition; 8vo., 31 pages, original printed wrappers, edges chipped.   M & S Rare Books, Inc.   90 - 369   2011 $150

Hall, George Webb *The Origin and Proceedings of the Agricultural Associations in Great Britain in Which their Claims to Protection Against Foreign Produce, Duty-Free, are Fully and Ably Set Forth.* London: printed at the Office of the Farmers' Journal, by Ruffy and Evans, n.d., 1820, First edition, 2nd issue; 8vo., 46 pages, one or two margins cut close by binder (no loss of text), modern boards, spine simply lettered, scarce.   John Drury Rare Books   153 - 54   2011   £100

Hall, Hubert *Court Life Under the Plantagenets (Reign of Henry the Second).* London: Swan Sonnenschein & Co., 1890, Original pictorial cloth, gilt, extremities minimally rubbed, pages 271, with 5 colored plates, many tinted plates and line drawings, armorial bookplate of John Gretton of Stapleford.   R. F. G. Hollett & Son Antiquarian Booksellers   175 - 571   2011   £30

Hall, J. Sparks *The Book of the Feet: a History of Boots and Shoes...* New York: William H. Graham, 1847, First American edition; 16mo, 216 pages, 4 color plates, disbound, sound.   M & S Rare Books, Inc.   90 - 381   2011 $375

Hall, Michael *The English Country House. From the Archives of Country Life 1897-1939.* Mitchell Beazley, 1994, First edition; folio, original cloth, gilt, dust jacket, pages 192, illustrations, fine.   R. F. G. Hollett & Son Antiquarian Booksellers   177 - 430   2011   £60

Hall, R. N. *Great Zimbabwe, Mashonaland, Rhodesia: an Account of Two Years Examination Work in 1902-4 on Behalf of the Government of Rhodesia.* London: Methuen, 1905, First edition; 8vo., pages xliii, 459, maps, plates, illustrations, original red decorative cloth, gilt vignette on upper cover, spine faded, inner hinges racked.   J. & S. L. Bonham Antiquarian Booksellers   Africa 4/20/2011 - 4139   2011   £95

Hallam, Henry *The Constitutional History of England from the Accession of Henry VII to the Death of George II.* London: John Murray, circa, 1860, Tenth edition; 178 x 127mm., 3 volumes, very attractive contemporary polished calf, covers with gilt double fillets and blind stippled border, raised bands, spines elaborately gilt in compartments featuring extensive scrolling floral cornerpieces and very intricate fleuron centerpiece, maroon and brown morocco labels, marbled edges and endpapers; corners of first few leaves slightly creased, isolated light marginal soiling, trivial imperfections to bindings, but fine and handsome, without any perceivable wear and virtually as new internally.   Phillip J. Pirages   59 - 231   2011 $575

Halleck, Firtz-Greene *Fanny.* New York: 1819, First edition; 49 pages, 8vo., original printed wrappers, spine shot, chipped and foxed, lacking blank front end leaf, quite good.   M & S Rare Books, Inc.   90 - 140   2011 $525

Halley, Edmond *Catalouge des Estoilles Australes ou Supplements du Catalgoue Thycho qui Montre les Longitudes & Latitudes...* Paris: J. B. Coignard, 1679, 12mo., (36), 118, (2 blank), contemporary calf, spine gilt, spine worn, lacking map, from the library of the Earls of Macclesfield at Shirburn Castle. Maggs Bros. Ltd. 1440 - 105 2011 £2000

Halliday, Geoffrey *A Flora of Cumbria Comprising the Vice Counties of Westmorland and Furness...* Lancaster University: Centre for North-West Regional Studies, 1997, First hardback edition; large 4to., original cloth, gilt, dust jacket, pages 611, with 113 color plates and 190 colored maps. R. F. G. Hollett & Son Antiquarian Booksellers 173 - 516 2011 £75

Halprin, Lawrence *The RSVP Cycles.* n: 1969, 4to., 207 pages, reglued at interior of backstrip, intact but aged dust jacket (5 inch taped repair). Bookworm & Silverfish 667 - 12 2011 $100

Halsman, Philippe *Halsman" Sight and Insight. Words & Photographs.* Garden City: Doubleday & Co., 1972, First edition; photos, signed and inscribed by Halsman for Peter Pollack. Jeff Hirsch Books ny 2010 2011 $650

Hamady, Walter *The Disillusioned Solipsist and Nine Related Poems.* N.P.: Perishable Press Ltd., 1964, Limited to 60 copies, of which this is marked "Artist's proof, Walter Hamady" on colophon page; small 4to., two original signed etchings, original photography and two drawings by author, original brown paper wrappers, small closed tear in top edge of front wrapper, otherwise very fine, rare. James S. Jaffe Rare Books May 26 2011 - 21070 2011 $9500

Hamady, Walter *The Disillusioned Solipsist an Nine Related Poems.* N.P.: Perishable Press, 1964, Limited to 60 copies, this numbered 36 and signed by author/Printer, Walter Hamady on colophon page; small 4to., 2 original signed etchings, original photo and two drawings by author, original brown paper wrappers, staining from glue used to tip in illustrations, otherwise fine extremely rare. James S. Jaffe Rare Books May 26 2011 - 21197 2011 $7500

Hamady, Walter *Hunkering, the Last Gabberjabb Number Eight and IX/XVIths or Aleatory Annexations.* Mt. Horeb: Perishable Press, 2006, One of 108 copies on various papers (hand, mould, machine-made and even crush or mull) numbered (nine times) and signed by author/publisher/designer/printer, Walter Hamady as well as "augmenters" 8 times; page size 10 1/8 x 7 inches, 160 pages, brown cloth over boards with rondel/cameo in dark blue in middle of binding with silhouette of Hamady within triple ruled frame containing author's name and Perishable Press Ltd., marbled endpapers, new, extraordinary book. Priscilla Juvelis - Rare Books 48 - 17 2011 $3250

Hamer, John L. *The Falls And Caves of Ingleton.* Dalesman Pub. Co., 1946, First edition; original pictorial wrappers, edges trifle dusty, pages 28, 2 illustrations, folding map. R. F. G. Hollett & Son Antiquarian Booksellers General Catalogue Summer 2010 - 1425 2011 £25

Hamerton, J. A. *The New Illustrated.* Amalgamated Press, 1919-1920, Volumes 1 and 2, 4to., publisher's black cloth gilt each number paginated separately, profusely illustrated with numerous full page and tinted photos. R. F. G. Hollett & Son Antiquarian Booksellers 175 - 574 2011 £75

Hamilton, Alexander 1755-1804 *Works of Alexander Hamilton.* New York: G. P. Putnam's Sons, 1903, Constitutional Edition; 12 volumes, octavo, volume on with engraved frontispieces, titlepages printed in red and black, contemporary three quarter brown levant morocco over marbled boards, spines paneled and lettered in gilt in compartments with five raised bands, top edge gilt, others uncut, marbled endpapers, spines lightly sunned, near fine. Heritage Book Shop Holiday 2010 - 51 2011 $2500

Hamilton, Angus *Somaliland.* London: Hutchinson, 1911, First edition; 8vo., pages xvi, 366, ads, folding map, portrait, frontispiece, 24 illustrations, original purple red cloth, top edge gilt. J. & S. L. Bonham Antiquarian Booksellers Africa 4/20/2011 - 8485 2011 £175

Hamilton, Anthony 1646-1720 *Memoires Du Comte De Gramont.* Londres: Chez Edwards, 1793, 299 x 241mm., 5 p.l. (including portrait of Grammont, portrait of author and frontispiece), 313, 77 pages, (3) leaves, once very handsome and still quite pleasing period crimson straight grain morocco, covers with tooled and ruled border in gilt and blind (including very delicate gilt floral tools at corners), raised bands, spine ends with rows of sitppled scales, spine panels with stippled gilt quatrefoil superimposed over elaborate blind tooled centerpiece incorporating various fleurons, all edges gilt, 78 engraved plates (some dated 1792 or 1793), 77 of them portraits, shelf label with motto "Credunt Quod Vient" (identified in pencil on front flyleaf as belonging to the Earl of Minto), large paper copy; joints bit flaked, spine uniformly dulled, but stately binding completely solid and certainly attractive, bright covers, 3 gatherings toward end with prominent (though faint) mottle foxing, intermittent minor foxing elsewhere, light offsetting opposite a number of plates, isolated marginal soiling and other minor imperfections but still quite pleasing, copy internally, leaves extremely fresh and margins vast. Phillip J. Pirages 59 - 51 2011 $1900

Hamilton, Anthony 1646-1720 *Memoirs of Count Grammont.* London and Edinburgh: printed by Jas. Ballantyne & Co. for William Miller and James Carpenter, 1811, 2 volumes, splendid crimson straight grain morocco, elegantly and attractively gilt by Zaehnsdorf (stamp signed and dated 1900 on front turn-ins), covers gilt with double ruled border enclosing a lacy frame formed by drawer handles, fleurons and floral sprays, large fleuron cornerpieces accented with circlets and dots, broad raised bands adorned with six gilt rules, spine compartments with filigree frames echoing cover decoration, densely gilt filigree turn-ins, marbled endpapers, top edge gilt, other edges untrimmed, with a total of 143 engraved portraits, including 64 called for, and extra illustrated with 79 additional portraits apparently take from 1793 edition of the work printed by S. & E. Harding and inserts specially in this copy, large paper copy; noticeable offsetting from portraits whenever there is a facing text page (as opposed to verso of another plate) and rather conspicuous in about a half dozen cases, otherwise extremely fine set, text very fresh and clean, beautiful bindings unworn and extraordinarily bright. Phillip J. Pirages 59 - 147 2011 $1600

Hamilton, Anthony 1646-1720 *Memoirs of Count Grammont.* London: William Miller and James Carpenter, 1811, First edition thus, large paper copy; 64 portraits, 2 volumes, 4to., contemporary half morocco gilt, spines with raised bands and elegantly gilt panelled, rather rubbed, boards scraped, pages xxxvii, 262; 256, complete with 64 fine portrait engravings, some offsetting, foxing or browning to plates, handsome tight set. R. F. G. Hollett & Son Antiquarian Booksellers 175 - 575 2011 £250

Hamilton, Anthony 1646-1720 *Memoirs of Count Grammont.* London: John Lane, The Bodley Head, 1928, Limited to 1000 copies; large 8vo., original two-tone cloth, gilt, pages viii, 231, top edge gilt, untrimmed, woodcuts tipped in by Wilfrid Jones. R. F. G. Hollett & Son Antiquarian Booksellers 175 - 576 2011 £30

Hamilton, Charles Gillingham, Mrs. *The Exiles of Italy.* Edinburgh: Thomas Constable and Co., 1857, First edition with bound-in limitation page signed by artist on fore-edge painting proclaiming, "This is No. 122 of the Books with Fore-edge Paintings by Miss Currie/ The Painting Under the gold is a view of The Temples of Paestrum"; 185 x 125mm., xxxii, (1) leaf (half title), 502 pages, beautiful early 20th century dark blue straight grain morocco sumptuously gilt by Riviere and Son (stamp signed), covers richly decorated in gilt and blind with outer gilt frame featuring pairs of triple fillets flanking a chain roll composed of leaf fronds and then daisy cornerpieces, next to outer frame, blind rolled border in cresting pattern and further in a central panel composed of plain gilt rules and gilt botanical cornerpieces accented with blindstamped daisy tools around outer edge and with tangent dogtooth roll in blind closer to middle of board, raised bands, spine gilt in triple filleted compartments, intricate central lozenge and blind tooled leaf cornerpieces, densely gilt turn-ins, all edges gilt, with fine fore-edge paintings by Miss Currie of the Temple of Hera and the Second Temple of Hera at Paestum; top corners little bumped, mild offsetting to endpapers from gilt turn-ins (as almost always) isolated minor foxing and other trivial imperfections internally, otherwise fine in lovely binding, text clean and fresh binding exceptionally lustrous and virtually unworn and fore-edge painting well preserved. Phillip J. Pirages 59 - 204 2011 $5500

Hamilton, Duke of *Catalogue of the Collection of Pictures, Works of Art and Decorative Objects, the Property of His Grace, The Duke of Hamilton.* London: Christie Manson and Woods, 1882, First edition; 8vo., original publisher's red cloth lettered gilt on front, pages 234, handsome about very good with slight soiling and slight wear at spine. Any Amount of Books May 29 2011 - A35035 2011 $238

Hamilton, Edith *The Greek Way. (and) The Roman Way.* New York: W. W. Norton & Co. Inc., 1942, 1932. First edition of the second work; 211 x 143mm., 2 volumes, excellent dark blue crushed morocco by Frost and Co. (signed on front turn-ins), covers with gilt double fillet border, raised bands, spines gilt in double ruled compartments with central lozenge formed by small leaf tools, turn-ins with gilt rules and volute cornerpieces, marbled endpapers, all edges gilt, slight offsetting as usual from turn-ins onto free endleaves (from binder's glue), but very fine with virtually no signs of use. Phillip J. Pirages 59 - 232 2011 $475

Hamilton, Edmond *The Haunted Stars.* New York: A Torquil Book/Distributed by Dodd, Mead and Co., 1960, First edition; octavo, boards. L. W. Currey, Inc. 124 - 143 2011 $450

Hamilton, Ian *New Review.* 1974-1978, First edition; nos. 1-48, Volume 5/1-2, folio, illustrations, very good, original glossy pictorial wrappers. I. D. Edrich May 26 2011 - 82615 2011 $470

Hamilton, Ian *The Review.* 1962, First edition; nos. 1-30, all in very good condition. I. D. Edrich May 26 2011 - 81014 2011 $587

Hamilton, James Cleland *Famous Algonquins...* Toronto: 1899, Reprint from Canadian Institute Semi Centennial Volume; 27 pages, small 4to., top wrapper loose, well aged, 4 full page plates, scarce. Bookworm & Silverfish 662 - 134 2011 $75

Hamilton, Jane *The Book of Ruth.* New York: Ticknor & Fields, 1988, Review copy with material laid in, first printing; fine in fine dust jacket. Bella Luna Books May 26 2011 - t214 2011 $330

Hamilton, Patrick 1904-1962 *Mr. Stimpson and Mr. Gorse.* London: Constable, 1953, First edition; 8vo., pages vi, 7-356, signed presentation from author to his future wife, Ursula Winifred Chetwynd-Talbot, fore-edges and page edges browned, otherwise very good+ in very good dust jacket with some slight nick at head of spine, slight creasing, closed tear and slight soiling. Any Amount of Books May 26 2011 - A69473 2011 $2516

Hamilton, Patrick 1904-1962 *The West Pier.* London: Constable, 1951, First edition; 8vo., pages 308, spine slightly faded, sound clean, very good, signed presentation by author, likely for his future wife Lady Ursula Winifred Chetwynd-Talbot. Any Amount of Books May 26 2011 - A76991 2011 $2516

Hamilton, William Rowan *Lectures on Quaternions.* Dublin: Hodges and Smith, 1853, First edition; octavo, publisher's plum cloth. Heritage Book Shop Booth A12 51st NY International Antiquarian Book Fair April 8-10 2011 - 64 2011 $5000

Hamley, Edward *The War in the Crimea.* London: Seeley & Co., 1894, Sixth edition; contemporary full plum calf gilt prize binding, spine attractively gilt, pages vii, 312, with 9 illustrations. R. F. G. Hollett & Son Antiquarian Booksellers General Catalogue Summer 2010 - 607 2011 £65

Hamley, W. G. *A New Sea and an Old Hand: Being Papers Suggested by a Visit to Egypt at the end of 1869.* London: Wm. Blackwood, 1871, First edition; 8vo., pages viii, 318, frontispiece, 6 plates, original black decorative cloth, good. J. & S. L. Bonham Antiquarian Booksellers Africa 4/20/2011 - 8226 2011 £75

Hammett, Dashiell *The Thin Man.* New York: Alfred A. Knopf, 1934, First edition; 8vo., cloth lightly mottled as usually the case, else near fine in dust jacket, with light professional restoration to spine ends and corners, housed in two tone quarter leather and cloth clamshell case with titles stamped in gold on spine. Buckingham Books May 26 2011 - 26312 2011 $7500

Hammond, L. M., Mrs. *Trials and Triumphs of an Orphan Girl; or, The Biography of Mrs. Deiadamia Chase, Physician.* Cortland: Van Slyck and Hitchcock, 1859, 230 pages, beaded cloth with floral pattern worn at extremities and torn at joints, one sheet detached, foxing and light dampstains, illustrations. G. H. Mott Bookseller May 26 2011 - 43500 2011 $275

Hammond, Nicholas *Twentieth Century Wildlife Artists.* Croom Helm, 1986, First edition; folio, original cloth, gilt, dust jacket, pages 224, illustrations, bookplate, otherwise fine. R. F. G. Hollett & Son Antiquarian Booksellers General Catalogue Summer 2010 - 190 2011 £50

Hamnett, Nina *Is She a Lady?* Wingate, 1955, First edition; 8 plates, also full page line drawings by author, pages 164, 8vo., original mid blue boards, backstrip gilt lettered, dust jacket with internal tape protection to backstrip panel head and tail showing where head and tail are chipped, good. Blackwell Rare Books B166 - 157 2011 £80

Hamri, Mohamed *Tales of Joujouka.* Santa Barbara: Capra Press, 1975, First edition, #9 of 50 numbered copies signed on pasted-in piece of paper as well as all copies of the limitation; pictorial boards, illustrations by author, fine in glassine dust jacket. Charles Agvent 2010 Summer Miscellany - 36 2011 $75

Hancock, William N. *The Ancient Laws of Ireland: Senchus Mor.* 1865-1879, Volumes 1-4 (ex 6), 3 folding color facsimile plates, volumes 1-3 in quarter leather, volume 4 quarter cloth, ex-library and presented by H.M. Treasury, good. C. P. Hyland May 26 2011 - 260/250 2011 $507

A Hand Book to the Abbey of St. Mary of Furness in Lancashire. Ulverston: Stephen Soulby, 1845, Original quarter roan with printed boards, extremities rather rubbed, boards rather darkened an stained, pages 77, double page steel engraved plan and plate (both rather browned and foxed), lithographed plate by Day & Haghe and woodcut text illustrations and headings, title printed in red and black, scarce. R. F. G. Hollett & Son Antiquarian Booksellers 173 - 1071 2011 £140

Handbooks to the Cathedrals of England and Wales. London: John Murray, 1861-1874, 7 volumes, original blindstamped cloth, gilt extra, head and tail of spines rather chipped and frayed, one lower board affected by damp, illustrated with text and full page woodcut illustrations throughout, some flyleaves rather foxed, two volumes little dampstained in places, but good set, lacking the separate volume St. Pauls, Western Cathedrals volume a presentation copy from publisher to Rev. Francis G. Havergal, with his bookplate and presentation slip loosely inserted. R. F. G. Hollett & Son Antiquarian Booksellers 177 - 168 2011 £180

Handley, John *Catalogue of Plants Growing in the Sedbergh District, Including the Lune Basin, from Middleton to Tebay.* Leeds: Richard Jenkins, 1898, First edition; small 8vo., original printed wrappers, foot of backstrip trifle defective and repaired, pages 48, nice clean copy, scarce. R. F. G. Hollett & Son Antiquarian Booksellers   173 - 518   2011   £40

Hankins, Maude McGehee *Daddy Gander.* Joliet: Volland, 1922, housed in original pictorial box is a printed glassine bag containing a printed envelope of beads, dozens of strips of colored paper of various widths and a pocket of Happiwork paste, also included direction booklet in the form of a story, full color illustration by Wanda Gag.   Aleph-Bet Books, Inc.   95 - 569   2011 $1200

Hankinson, Alan *Camera on the Crags.* London: Heinemann, 1975, First edition; 4to., original cloth, gilt, dust jacket, pages 39, (ii), 105 copies of plates, ex-libris on flyleaf, scarce.   R. F. G. Hollett & Son Antiquarian Booksellers   173 - 519   2011   £95

Hannah, Barry *Nightwatchmen.* New York: Viking, 1973, First edition; edge sunned cloth, near fine in very good dust jacket, spine and edge faded, inscribed by author to Seymour Lawrence.   Ken Lopez Bookseller   154 - 74   2011 $475

Hannaway, Owen *The Chemists and the Word: the Didactic Origins of Chemistry.* Baltimore and London: Johns Hopkins University, 1975, 8vo., xiii, 165 pages, illustrations, red cloth, white stamped spine title, dust jacket, jacket edges are worn, very good, from the Bern Dibner reference library, with Burndy bookplate.   Jeff Weber Rare Books   161 - 191   2011 $100

Hannett, John *The Forest of Arden, Its Towns, Villages and Hamlets: a Topographical and Historical Account of the District Between Around Henley-in-Arden and Hampton in Arden in the County of Warwick.* Birmingham: Charles Lowe, 1894, Second edition; pages xiv, 230, frontispiece map, numerous engravings, quarto, original green cloth lettered in gilt top edge gilt, cover edges just little bruised, very good.   Peter Ellis   May 26 2011 - ARDEN012912   2011 $100

Hanoum, Zeyneb *A Turkish Woman's European Impressions.* London: Seeley, Service & Co., 1913, Octavo, xx, (23)-246 (10) ads, pages 32, illustrated from photos and drawing by Auguste Rodin, red cloth, gilt, printed dust jacket, bookplate, ownership signature, fine.   Jeff Weber Rare Books   163 - 171   2011 $100

Hanrahan, Joyce Y. *Works of Maurice Sendak.* Saco: Custom Communications, 2001, Pages 187, illustrations, original cloth, gilt, spine little faded.   R. F. G. Hollett & Son Antiquarian Booksellers   General Catalogue Summer 2010 - 417   2011   £30

Hansel and Gretel. London: Bancroft, 1961, Oblong 4to., cloth backed pictorial boards, near fine, 8 very fine double page color pop-ups by Kubasta (few of which moveable parts).   Aleph-Bet Books, Inc.   95 - 450   2011 $200

Hansi, Jean Jacque Waltz *Mon Village Ceux qui n'Oublient pas Images et Commentaires par l'Oncle.* Paris: Floury, 1913, First edition; oblong large 4to., all edges tinted red, blue decorated and illustrated cloth covers with maybe a hint of shelf wear, this is a smashing copy, Cockerel patterned endpapers, 32 (plus table of contents) lovely numbered pages (printed on heavy, lustrous paper), each with full color illustrations, full page pictures quite striking.   Jo Ann Reisler, Ltd.   86 - 133   2011 $575

Hanson, James *The Pupil Teacher System and the Instruction of Pupil Teachers, a Paper Read at a Meeting of the Bradford and District Teachers' association Held at Calverley October 19th 1878.* Bradford: Thomas Brear, 1878, Pages 24, sometime lightly folded, original printed wrappers, presentation copy.   R. F. G. Hollett & Son Antiquarian Booksellers   175 - 582   2011   £30

Hanson, John *The Dissection of Owenism Dissected: or a Socialist's Answer to Mr. Frederick R. Lee's Pamphlet entitled "A Calm Examination of the Fundamental Principles of Robert Owen's Misnamed Rational System".* Leeds: printed by J. Hobson, 1838, First edition; 12mo., 34, (2) pages, final leaf blank, original printed wrappers, very good, perhaps fine copy.   John Drury Rare Books   153 - 56   2011   £600

The Happy Rock. A Book About Henry Miller. Berkeley: Bern Porter, 1947, First edition, 1/750 copies for distribution; this copy not numbered, large 8vo., pages 157, printed on color papers, paper over boards, pictorial label and cloth spine, cover bumped at edges, otherwise very good.   Second Life Books Inc.   174 - 135   2011 $75

Harada, Jiro *The Lesson of Japanese Architecture.* London: The Studio, 1936, First edition; 4to., original cloth, gilt, page 192, illustrations.   R. F. G. Hollett & Son Antiquarian Booksellers   177 - 435   2011   £50

The Harbinger, Devoted to Social and Political Progress. New York: Burgess Stringer, Boston: Redding, 1846, First edition; Volume II, #1-26, Dec. 13 1845 to June 6, 1846, 4to., 412 pages, publisher's board, leather spine worn off, certain amount of foxing and staining, but good.   Second Life Books Inc.   174 - 167   2011 $750

The Harbinger, Devoted to Social and Political Progress. New York: Burgess, Stringer, Boston: Redding, 1847, First edition; 4to., 332 pages, bound in publisher's boards, leather spine worn off, certain amount of staining and foxing but good.   Second Life Books Inc.   174 - 167   2011 $750

Harcourt, Edward Vernon *Sporting in Algeria.* Hastings: George Lindridge, 1859, First edition; half title, tinted litho frontispiece, folding map on thin paper, spotting to prelims, unopened in original green pebble grained cloth, spine slightly dulled.   Jarndyce Antiquarian Booksellers   CXCI - 554   2011   £150

Hardie, James *Corderii Colloquia or Cordery's Colloquies, with a Translation of the First Forty to Which is added a Vocabulary.*   New York: 1801, First edition; (i)-(v) vl, (1)-71, blank (72)-174, blank, pages, full early leather, expected age stresses, no label, probably as issued.   Bookworm & Silverfish   671 - 80   2011 $100

Hardwick, Alice *Little Wooden Shoes.* Akron: Saalfield, 1921, 4to., linen like wrappers, slightest bit of cover wear, else rear, fine, color covers plus 2 full pages and 2 almost full page color illustrations by Frances Brundage.   Aleph-Bet Books, Inc.   95 - 125   2011 $100

Hardy, A. L. *The Evangeline Land: made Famous by the Expulsion of the Acadian Farmers by the British Government on Account of Their Fidelity to their French King and afterward immortalized by Longfellow...* Grand Rapids: Kentville:, 1900?, Pages (82), 115 black and white photo views, decorated brown card covers with illustration of Evangeline on upper left corner and title "Evangeline Land" on bottom right corner, red twine through spine and bound with silk string, oblong 8vo., very good.   Schooner Books Ltd.   96 - 161   2011 $75

Hardy, Alister C. *The Open Sea.* London: Collins, 1956, First edition; original cloth, gilt, dust jacket torn and chipped, pages 335, 142 illustrations in color, 67 in black and white, 300 line drawings and maps.   R. F. G. Hollett & Son Antiquarian Booksellers   General Catalogue Summer 2010 - 981   2011   £45

Hardy, Charles Frederick *The Hardys of Barbon an Some Other Westmorland Statesman; their Kith, Kin an Childer.* London: Constable, 1913, First edition; original green cloth gilt, faint shelf numbers on spine, pages xv, 176, top edge gilt, map frontispiece and illustrations.   R. F. G. Hollett & Son Antiquarian Booksellers   173 - 521   2011   £60

Hardy, James Leighton *The House the Hardy Brothers Built.* Ashburton: The Flyfisher's Classic Library, 1998, Limited edition, no. 75 of 950 copies; full navy blue morocco gilt, slipcase, pages xvi, 335, top edge gilt, well illustrated, marbled endpapers and silk marker, fine.   R. F. G. Hollett & Son Antiquarian Booksellers   General Catalogue Summer 2010 - 1251   2011   £150

Hardy, Thomas 1840-1928 *The Dynasts.* London: Macmillan and Co., 1904, First edition, second impression revised (1000 copies). Part Second - London: Macmillan & Co. 1906. Second state. Third Part - London: Macmillan & Co., 1908. First printing; 3 volumes, very good+ (light wear, clean text, bright gilt), 3 volumes, first volume very good+ (some minor dark spotting to spine, clean text, bright gilt; second volume very good (little spotting to spine, clean text, bright gilt), third volume very good+ (light wear, clean text, bright gilt).   Lupack Rare Books   May 26 2011 - ABE4707852855   2011 $350

Hardy, Thomas 1840-1928 *The Famous Tragedy of the Queen of Cornwall at Tintagel in Lyonesse.* London: Macmillan, 1923, First edition; large square 8vo., original pictorial green cloth, gilt, pages 78, frontispiece.   R. F. G. Hollett & Son Antiquarian Booksellers   175 - 585   2011   £75

Hardy, Thomas 1840-1928 *"Far from the Madding Crowd." in The Cornhill Magazine.* 1874, Jan. - Dec.; 2 Volumes bound in 19th century half leather and marbled boards, raised bands, leather spine labels (one of which is new but matching), marbled endpapers, all edges marbled, very good with boards and spines showing some rubbing and wear, scarce.   Lupack Rare Books   May 26 2011 - ABE4616669999   2011 $750

Hardy, Thomas 1840-1928 *Human Shows and Far Phantasies.* London: Macmillan and Co., 1925, First edition; very good plus, little bumping, in very good dust jacket (closed tear, little wrinkling).   Lupack Rare Books   May 26 2011 - ABE4182192005   2011 $125

Hardy, Thomas 1840-1928 *The Mayor of Casterbridge: The Life and Death of a Man of Character.* London: Smith, Elder & Co., 1886, First edition in book form; 2 volumes, octavo, (4), 313, (1, blank), (2, ads); (4), 312, (4, ads) pages, with all ads and half titles called for, beautifully bound by Bayntun in green polished calf, boards and spines printed in gilt, each volume with red and blue spine labels, lettered gilt, gilt dentelles, all edges gilt, marbled endpapers, few pages with minor professionally repaired closed tears and reinforced corners, including title and half title volume I.   Heritage Book Shop   Holiday 2010 - 52   2011 $2500

Hardy, Thomas 1840-1928 *The Mayor of Casterbridge.* New York: Heritage Press, 1964, Original patterned cloth gilt, pages xvi, 318, fine full page and text woodcuts, slipcase.   R. F. G. Hollett & Son Antiquarian Booksellers General Catalogue Summer 2010 - 862   2011   £35

Hardy, Thomas 1840-1928   *A Pair of Blue Eyes.* London: Tinsley Brothers, 1873, First edition in book form, one of presumably 500 copies; 3 volumes, small octavo, (6), 303, (1, blank); (6), 311, (1, blank); (6), 262 pages, complete with half titles, bound circa 1910 by Zaehnsdorf in three quarter green crushed morocco gilt over green cloth boards ruled in gilt, spines lettered and decoratively tooled in gilt, marbled endpapers, top edges gilt, bookplate of Anthony Conyers Surtees on front pastedown, superb copy, very rare.   David Brass Rare Books, Inc.   May 26 2011 - 01306 2011 $9500

Hardy, Thomas 1840-1928   *A Pair of Blue Eyes.* London: C. Kegan Paul & Co., 1880, Rare early edition; 8vo., pages vi, 369, (1) blank, (44) ads, frontispiece, one gathering slightly loose in binding, otherwise fine, contemporary blue cloth, gilt and blindstamped decoration on spine and upper board, blindstamped decoration on lower board, spines slightly rubbed at extremities, signed by author.   Simon Finch Rare Books   Zero - 233 2011   £1200

Hardy, Thomas 1840-1928   *The Patriot.* Edinburgh: Printed for and sold by J. Dickson, London, sold by G. Nicol, 1793, 8vo., (2), 78 pages, contents leaf misbound after A1, late 19th century maroon morocco fully gilt by Birdsall, fine in handsome binding.   John Drury Rare Books   153 - 57 2011   £200

Hardy, Thomas 1840-1928   *Selected Poems of Thomas Hardy.* London: Riccardi Press, 1921, Special reprint of 1916 edition on special paper; limited edition #55 of 1025 copies, portrait and titlepage design engraved on wood by William Nicholson, blue paper covered boards, linen spine, tight, near fine copy.   Lupack Rare Books   May 26 2011 - ABE4310256464 2011 $150

Hardy, Thomas 1840-1928   *Tess of the D'Urbervilles.* London: James R. Osgood, Mcilvaine and Co., 1891, First edition; mixed issued but all dated 1891, 3 voumes, octavo, (8), 263, (1); (8), 277, (1), (2, blank); (8), 277, (1, printer's imprint), (2, blank) pages, original smooth tan cloth, front covers stamped in gilt after design by Charles Ricketts of honeysuckle blossoms on two stems running from top to bottom, spines decoratively stamped and lettered gilt, plain endpapers just slightly skewed, few hinges starting, top outer corner volume I bumped, slight discoloration to front cover of each volume and bit of rubbing, otherwise very good, housed in green cloth open end case, leather spine and green cloth chemise.   Heritage Book Shop   Holiday 2010 - 53 2011 $4500

Hardy, Thomas 1840-1928   *Tess of the D'Urbevilles.* London: Macmillan, 1914, very good, binding with the Hardy monogram on cover, inscribed and signed by Hardy.   Lupack Rare Books   May 26 2011 - ABE 4182255014 2011 $2100

Hardy, Thomas 1840-1928   *The Trumpet Major.* London: Smith Elder & Co., 1880, Half titles, luxuriously bound in full brown crushed morocco by Birdsall of Northampton, gilt spines, borders and dentelles, top edge gilt, very good, handsome.   Jarndyce Antiquarian Booksellers   CXCI - 525 2011   £1250

Hardy, Thomas 1840-1928   *The Well Beloved.* London: Osgood, McIlvaine & Co., 1897, First edition; etching and map, green cloth with the Hardy monogram, light foxing to endpapers, otherwise bright, nearly fine.   Lupack Rare Books   May 26 2011 - ABE4182184886 2011 $200

Hardy, Thomas 1840-1928   *Wessex Tales. Strange, Lively and Commonplace.* London: Macmillan and Co. and New York, 1888, First edition, 750 copies published at 12 shillings each, although only 634 copies were actually bound up to be sold at the time; 2 volumes, 8vo., pages (viii), 248; (viii), 212, (4) ads, publisher's dark green cloth boards, pale green ruled band to top and bottom of front boards and spines, monogram device on backs, gilt lettered spines, both volumes with slight spotting to endpapers, little wear around edges and slight creasing to heads and tails of spines, bookplates of Herbert S. Leon and Frederick Baldwin Adams Jr. in both volumes, very good, clean.   Simon Finch Rare Books   Zero - 234 2011   £2500

Hardy, Thomas 1840-1928   *Thomas Hardy's Works.* London: Osgood, McIlvaine & Co., 1895-1913, 20 volumes, half titles, frontispieces and plates, partially uncut in original dark green cloth, gilt monogram on front boards, final volume slightly rubbed and faded, odd mark, occasional embossed stamp of W. & E. Case, top edge gilt, very good, bright and attractive.   Jarndyce Antiquarian Booksellers   CXCI - 14 2011   £2250

Hardy, Thomas 1840-1928   *Works.* London: Macmillan and Co. Ltd., 1912, Wessex edition; 21 volumes, octavo, photogravure frontispiece, maps, bound by Root & Son in contemporary three quarter blue morocco gilt over blue cloth boards, spines panelled gilt, top edge gilt, blue gray endpapers.   David Brass Rare Books, Inc.   May 26 2011 - 01081 2011 $9500

Hardy, Thomas 1840-1928   *The Works of Thomas Hardy.* London: Macmillan and Co., 1919-1920, Mellstock edition, limited to 500 copies, signed by Hardy in volume 1; 37 volumes, half titles, frontispiece in volume 1, largely unopened in original dark blue buckram, medallion in gilt on front boards, spine decorated and lettered in gilt, marking to boards of volumes XVII, XVIII & XXII, some spines little faded, slight rubbing, good plus.   Jarndyce Antiquarian Booksellers   CXCI - 15 2011   £2750

Hare, Chauncey *Interior America.* Millerton: Aperture, 1978, First edition; fine in very near fine dust jacket with small tear to top of back panel and some small tear to top of back panel and some other very minor wear, uncommon. Jeff Hirsch Books   ny 2010 2011 $750

Hare, E. H. *Mental Health on a New Housing Estate.* London: Oxford University Press, 1965, First edition; tall 8vo., original boards, gilt, dust jacket, pages x, 136, with 70 tables and 9 figures, slip with presentation inscription tipped to flyleaf, fine.   R. F. G. Hollett & Son Antiquarian Booksellers   175 - 587 2011   £50

Hare, Francis *Liber Psalmorum Hebraice.* Cambridge: 1809, First printing of any part of the Bible in Hebrew in America; 12mo., full contemporary calf.   Heritage Book Shop   Booth A12 51st NY International Antiquarian Book Fair April 8-10 2011 - 77   2011 $20,000

Hare, J. *Select Decisions of American Courts, in Several Departments of Law; with Especial Reference to Mercantile Law with Notes.* Philadelphia: 1847, 2 volumes, very good, old law calf with red and black labels.   Bookworm & Silverfish   671 - 82 2011 $175

Hare, Samuel *Memoir of John Sharp.* London: William & Frederick, G. Cash and Darlington: H. Penney, 1857, First edition; original blindstamped cloth, gilt, small label at foot of spine.   R. F. G. Hollett & Son Antiquarian Booksellers   175 - 588 2011   £35

Hargrave, Joseph John *Red River.* Montreal: 1871, 506 pages, early rebinding in half leather and marbled paper boards, text evenly browned, some external rubbing, overall sound.   Dumont Maps & Books of the West   112 - 44 2011 $150

Hargrove, Ely *The History of the Castle, Town and Forest of Knaresborough with Harrogate and Its Medicinal Waters.* York: printed by Wilson, Spence and Mawman, 1798, Fifth edition; 12mo., pages 4, 382, (ii), engraved frontispiece, folding contemporary hand colored map and 7 other engraved plates, original unsophisticated binding of sugar paper over boards, unlettered buff backstrip, blue sides, text uncut, tiny wormhole in gutter throughout, small dampmark to frontispiece, joints and spine ends worn, paper dust soiled, tail of spine defective, housed in modern grey cloth solander box, from the collection of Christopher Ernest Weston 1947-2010.   Unsworths Booksellers   24 - 105 2011   £150

Hargrove, William *History and Description of the Ancient City of York...* York: published and sold by Wm. Alexander, 1818, 2 volumes, 8vo., pages (iii)-xvi, (17)-396 397*-412*, (397)-407 (iii) + engraved frontispiece and 3 other engraved plates; iv, (5)-688, (ii) + engraved frontispiece, an extending hand colored plan and 6 other engraved plates, this copy extra illustrated by the inclusion of Volume I - 16 pages of text and 8 engraved plates between pages xvi and (17) and volume 2 - engraved plate facing page 522 and tipped-in slip with view of gatehouse to Archbishop's palace at Bishopthorpe facing page 518, all additions except the last slip have been taken from James Storer's History and Antiquities of the Cathedral Churches of Great Britain" volume 4 (London 1818), contemporary polished maroon calf, four flat raised band spine ruled in gilt with massed 'intersecting circles' pallet in compartments, lettered and numbered direct in gilt, boards double rule gilt bordered and 'intersecting broken waves' roll within, centrally a large panel 'straight grain' tooled, board edges decorative roll gilt, turn-ins 'intersecting broken waves' roll gilt, 'Spanish' 'made' endpapers, dark blue and white sewn endbands, dark blue silk page markers, some light spotting, split at fold of one extending plate, volume I repaired at head of spine, front joint of volume 2 cracking a bit, little rubbing at extremities, spines lightly sunned, signed binding by Douglas, bookbinder, Blackburn with his paper ticket, printed label of Thomas Butler, from the collection of Christopher Ernest Weston 1947-2010.   Unsworths Booksellers   24 - 106 2011   £450

Harlan, Robert D. *The Two Hundredth Book: a Bibliography of Books Published by Book Club of California 1958-1993.* N.P.: San Francisco, 1993, 1 of 500 following the design of the original; this being number 200, x, 62 pages, folio, near fine.   Dumont Maps & Books of the West   112 - 32 2011 $125

Harland, William, & Sons *Monograms and Heraldic Designs from William Harland and Son.* Merton, Surrey: William Harland and Sons, 1893, First edition; small oblong 8vo., original publisher's red cloth lettered gilt on cover, pages 41, printed recto only, very slight soiling, inner hinge slightly tender, very good or better.   Any Amount of Books   May 29 2011 - A67978   2011 $213

Harling, Robert *Alphabet and Image: 2.* Shenval Press, 1946, large 8vo., original stiff wrappers, light crease to one corner, comb bound, pages 92, illustrations.   R. F. G. Hollett & Son Antiquarian Booksellers   General Catalogue Summer 2010 - 194 2011   £45

Harling, Robert *The Drawings of Edward Bawden.* London: Art and Technics, 1950, First edition; large square 8vo., original orange cloth gilt, dust jacket rather worn and torn, but complete, pages 104, illustrations, very scarce.   R. F. G. Hollett & Son Antiquarian Booksellers   General Catalogue Summer 2010 - 193 2011   £95

Harling, Robert *Image.* Art & Technics, 1952, No. 1-8, illustrations, wood engravings, 8 issues, complete with 6 supplements, original wrappers, very good.   I. D. Edrich   May 26 2011 - 82811   2011 $419

Harlow, Neil *The Maps of San Francisco Bay; From the Spanish Discovery in 1769 to the American Occupation.* Staten Island: 1998,   Facsimile reprint of 1950 Grabhorn Press edition; 153 pages, maps, near fine, issued without dust jacket.   Dumont Maps & Books of the West   111 - 101   2011 $100

Harman, S. W. *Hell on the Border: He Hanged Eighty-Eight Men.* Fort Smith: Phoenix Pub. Co., 1898,   First edition; cloth, 718 pages, numerous illustrations, exceedingly rare, missing corner of pages 717 & 718 resulting in loss of some text and pages 719 &720 not present, however facsimile copies of pages 717-720 have been obtained, they are laid in.   Buckingham Books   May 26 2011 - 25238   2011 $2750

Harmer, F. E. *Anglo Saxon Writs. The Ward Bequest.* Manchester: Manchester University Press, 1952,   First edition; original cloth, gilt, dust jacket spine rather darkened, pages xxii, 604.   R. F. G. Hollett & Son Antiquarian Booksellers   175 - 589   2011   £30

Harmsen, Theodor *Antiquarianism in the Augustan Age: Thomas Hearne 1678-1735.* Oxford: Peter Lang, 2000, 8vo., 336 pages, frontispiece, printed wrappers, near fine, from the Bern Dibner reference library, with Burndy bookplate.   Jeff Weber Rare Books   161 - 192   2011 $70

Harnett, C. M. *In Praise of Dogs.* London: Country Life, 1938,   First edition; 4to., original cloth, gilt, pages 112, with 16 plates.   R. F. G. Hollett & Son Antiquarian Booksellers General Catalogue Summer 2010 - 1055   2011   £30

Harper, Charles G. *Abbeys of Old Romance.* Cecil Palmer, 1930,   First edition; original pictorial cloth, gilt, dust jacket spine rather rubbed and frayed, pages viii, 340, numerous illustrations, fore-edge little spotted.   R. F. G. Hollett & Son Antiquarian Booksellers   177 - 436   2011   £40

Harper, Charles G. *Historic and Picturesque Inns of Old England.* E. J. Burrow & Co. n.d.,   Small 8vo., pages 172, 100 (ads), 47 pen and ink drawings, half title browned, original boards gilt, spine faded.   R. F. G. Hollett & Son Antiquarian Booksellers   177 - 437   2011   £35

Harper, Charles G. *Mansions of Old Romance.* Cecil Palmer, 1930,   First edition; pages ix, 294, with 4 plates and numerous line illustrations, few spots to fore edge, otherwise very nice, original pictorial cloth, gilt.   R. F. G. Hollett & Son Antiquarian Booksellers   177 - 438   2011   £30

Harper, Ida Husted *A Brief History of the Movement for Movement Suffrage in the United States.* New York: National American Woman Suffrage Association, 1913, First edition; (32) pages, 6 x 3 1/4 inches, original purple wrappers printed in black, except for the corner of several leaves turned down, fine.   Paulette Rose Fine and Rare Books   32 - 170   2011 $575

Harris, A. *Cumberland Iron.* Truro: Bradford Barton, 1970,   First edition; original cloth, gilt, dust jacket, pages 122, 2, with 12 pages of plates and 4 figures.   R. F. G. Hollett & Son Antiquarian Booksellers   173 - 526   2011   £35

Harris, Frank *Oscar Wilde/His Life and Confessions.* New York: privately published, 1916, First edition; 2 volumes, 4to., pages (x), vii, 320; (iv), 321-603, top edge gilt, others uncut, original quarter morocco with green paper boards, morocco worn, upper board of volume i detached, lacking spine but textblock firm, joints of volume ii starting, spine partially detached, bookplate of John Quinn, inscribed by author and Quinn, TLS from Quinn laid in.   Simon Finch Rare Books   Zero - 235   2011   £750

Harris, George W. *George W. Harris.* London: Nisbet & Co., 1930,   Limited edition, number 241 of 425 copies; 4to., original two tone cloth, gilt, pages (iv), 23, plus 54 plates and frontispiece, 1 folding with short tear and repair). R. F. G. Hollett & Son Antiquarian Booksellers   175 - 590   2011   £85

Harris, Joanne *Chocolat.* New York: Viking, 1999, First edition; fine in fine dust jacket, signed by author. Bella Luna Books   May 29 2011 - t6014   2011 $137

Harris, Joel Chandler *Uncle Remus. His Songs and Sayings. The Folk-Lore of the Old Plantation.* New York: D. Appleton and Co., 1881,   First edition, BAL first state with 'presumptive' in last line on page 9, and ads on page (233) beginning "New Books. A Treatise on the Practice of Medicine"; 12mo., (2, blank), 231, (1, blank) (8, ads), (2, blank) pages, wood engraved frontispiece and 7 wood engraved plates, wood engraved text illustrations, original green cloth, front cover pictorially stamped in gilt and black, rabbit vingette, back cover ruled in blind, spine stamped and lettered gilt, white endpapers printed in gray with butterfly pattern, about fine and very bright copy, chemise, in quarter green morocco slipcase.   Heritage Book Shop   Holiday 2010 - 54   2011 $5000

Harris, Joel Chandler *Uncle Remus: His Songs and Sayings.* New York: Appleton, 1920,   Deluxe gift edition; large thick 4to., green gilt cloth, 265 pages, V+, 12 plates, in text illustrations and with pictorial borders on each page of text as well.   Aleph-Bet Books, Inc.   95 - 279   2011 $400

Harris, Joel Chandler *Uncle Remus or the Story of Mr. Fox and Brer Rabbit.* Raithby, Lawrence & Co. n.d., 1939, Large 8vo., original cloth, two small dents to lower board, pages 111, with 12 full page color plates by Harry Rountree and 84 text drawings by Rene Bull, one color plate creased, 2 plates with small edge tears, chip and small scribble, trifle shaken, still very good.   R. F. G. Hollett & Son Antiquarian Booksellers General Catalogue Summer 2010 - 524 2011 £120

Harris, Pixie *The "Pixie O. Harris Fairy Book.".* Adelaide: Rigby Ltd., n.d. circa, 1925, First edition; 4to., 63 pages, 2 tipped in color plates including frontispiece, illustrations, original illustrated attached wrappers, modestly worn condition, wrappers little soiled with some chips and wear at spine, gift inscription and name and address on dedication page (dated 1930) and plain rear wrapper little soiled and slightly marked, very good- with text and illustrations clean. Any Amount of Books May 26 2011 - A45446 2011 $587

Harris, Rendel *The Finding of the "Mayflower".* London: Longmans Green and Co. and Manchester: University Press, 1920, First edition; pages 58, uncut with 9 plates, original cloth backed boards, little worn and soiled, joints cracked, scarce.   R. F. G. Hollett & Son Antiquarian Booksellers 177 - 439 2011 £45

Harris, Robert *South Africa: Illustrated by a Series of One Hundred and Four Photographs.* Port Elizabeth: Harris, 1888, First edition; small folio, 104 photos on cards, 13 x 19 cm., 4 photos, 31 x 24 cm., there is an additional large photo of a town taken from hillside, some corners of cards chipped and missing not affecting photos.   J. & S. L. Bonham Antiquarian Booksellers Africa 4/20/2011 - 5615 2011 £1100

Harris, Thaddeus M. *Beauties of Nature Delineated; or Philosophical and Pious Contemplations on the Works of Nature and the Seasons of the Year.* Charlestown: Samuel Etheridge, 1801, Second edition; 12mo., x, 237 pages, red roan on full leather on boards, numerous wood engraved vignette tailpieces, pencilled notes on endpapers, faded owner stamp on table of contents, occasional internal foxing, browning at edges, new red roan backing, covers with light rubbing and fraying at edges, leather staining along edges of first few leaves, one page mended, good copy.   Hobbyhorse Books 56 - 82 2011 $150

Harris, Thomas L. *Brotherhood of the New Life. Its Fact, Law, Method and Purpose Letter...with Passing "Reference to recent Criticisms".* Santa Rosa: Fountaingrove Press, 1891, 8vo., 15, (1) pages, original printed wrappers, volume I No. 2, with slip pasted in indicating events move too swiftly to continue quarterly publication, plus a notice that henceforth a charge with be mad to cover cost of publication.   M & S Rare Books, Inc. 90 - 152 2011 $200

Harris, Thomas L. *The New Republic. A Discourse of the Prospects, Dangers, Duties and Safeties of the Times.* Fountaingrove: 1891, volume I # 1, 8vo., 75, (2), original printed wrappers, uncut, unopened.   M & S Rare Books, Inc. 90 - 65 2011 $300

Harris, W. T. *Educational Theory.* Bristol: Thoemmes Press, 2000, Reprint; 10 volumes, together 3240 pages, about fine.   Any Amount of Books May 26 2011 - B22089 2011 $436

Harris, Walter *Hibernica; or Some Antient Pieces Relating to Ireland.* Dublin: 1770, 2 volumes in one, modern quarter calf with marbled boards, 2 stamps "Bequest of Dean D'Alton, Ballinrobe" otherwise very good.   C. P. Hyland May 26 2011 - 255/287 2011 $507

Harris, William Cornwallis *The Highlands of Aethiopia.* London: Longman Brown, 1844, First edition; 8vo., 3 volumes, pages xvii, 428; xi, 430; xi,4 36; frontispieces, vignette on titlepages, colored dedication plate, folding map (linen lined), clean throughout, later 19th century half red morocco, small wear to head of spines, but handsome set. J. & S. L. Bonham Antiquarian Booksellers Africa 4/20/2011 - 9133 2011 £1000

Harris, William Torrey *The Right of Property and the Ownership of Land.* Boston: Cupples, Hurd & Co., 1887, First separate edition; 8vo., 40 pages, original front printed wrapper, top edge slightly stained, small chip on fore edge. M & S Rare Books, Inc. 90 - 145 2011 $200

Harrison, E. Harris *Rival Ambassadors at the Court of Queen Mary.* Princeton: Princeton University Press, 1940, First edition; original cloth, dust jacket (edges little worn and chipped), pages xiv, 380, plates.   R. F. G. Hollett & Son Antiquarian Booksellers 175 - 583 2011 £45

Harrison, Florence *Elfin Song.* New York: H. M. Caldwell, n.d., 1912, Small 4to., grey gilt pictorial cloth, top edge gilt, 142 pages, scattered foxing, else near fine, pictorial endpapers, 12 magnificent tipped in color plates plus numerous full page and smaller black and whites. Aleph-Bet Books, Inc. 95 - 281 2011 $850

Harrison, Frederic *William the Silent.* London: Macmillan and Co., 1898, Full green calf prize binding, upper board trifle marked, pages vi, 260.   R. F. G. Hollett & Son Antiquarian Booksellers 175 - 591 2011 £40

Harrison, G. B. *Menaphon by Robert Greene and A Margarite of America by Thomas Lodge.* Oxford: Basil Blackwell, 1927, Original holland backed blue boards, pages xii, 234, untrimmed.   R. F. G. Hollett & Son Antiquarian Booksellers General Catalogue Summer 2010 - 804 2011 £30

Harrison, Jesse Burton *Review of the Slave Question... Based on the Speech of Th. Marshall of Fauquier.* Richmond: printed by T. W. White, 1833, First edition; 8vo., 48 pages, sewn as issued, uncut, sheets browned, moderate mousing to outer margin, very good. M & S Rare Books, Inc. 90 - 153 2011 $950

Harrison, Jim *After Ikkyu and Other Poems.* Boston: Shambhala, 1996, First edition; fine in like dust jacket, signed by author. Bella Luna Books May 29 2011 - 3001 2011 $137

Harrison, Jim *Braided Creek. A Conversation in Poetry.* Port Townsend: Copper Canyon Press, 2003, Limited to 250 numbered copies; fine, signed by both authors. Bella Luna Books May 26 2011 - t5862 2011 $275

Harrison, Jim *Just Before Dark.* Livingston: Clark City Press, 1981, Limited to 250 copies; fine, in slipcase, signed by author. Bella Luna Books May 29 2011 - t4505 2011 $110

Harrison, Jim *Livingston Suite.* Boise: Limberlost Press, 2005, One of a handful of series copies from hardcover limited edition; pictorial boards, fine, signed by author and artist. Bella Luna Books May 26 2011 - t7766 2011 $275

Harrison, Jim *Selected and New Poems.* New York: Delacorete Press, 1982, Uncorrected page proof; printed gray wrappers, fine, acetate dust jacket, signed by author. Bella Luna Books May 26 2011 - t19722 2011 $220

Harrison, Jim *The Theory and Practice of Rivers.* Seattle: Winn Books, 1986, First edition; illustrations by Russell Chatham, book fine, signed by author an artist. Bella Luna Books May 26 2011 - t4248 2011 $330

Harrison, Jim *Warlock.* New York: Delacorte Press, 1981, First edition; fine in near fine dust jacket with light edge wear, signed by author. Bella Luna Books May 29 2011 - 6423 2011 $82

Harrison, Jim *Wolf.* New York: Simon & Schuster, 1971, First edition; fine, dust jacket near fine, very light soiling, inscribed by author. Bella Luna Books May 26 2011 - t9698 2011 $275

Harrison, Jim *The Woman Lit by Fireflies.* Boston: Houghton Mifflin, 1990, Limited to 225 copies, this being number 107; fine, signed by author hardcover, with original shrink wrap. Bella Luna Books May 26 2011 - t9721 2011 $220

Harrison, John *Our Tounis Colledge. Sketchs of the History of the Old College of Edinburgh.* William Blackwood and Sons, 1884, First edition; original cloth, gilt, pages (vi), 166. R. F. G. Hollett & Son Antiquarian Booksellers 175 - 592 2011 £35

Harrison, Mary St. Leger 1852-1931 *The History of Sir Richard Calmady.* New York: Dodd, Mead and Co., 1901, First American edition; half title, original pale brown cloth, front board with color pictorial onlay, blocked and lettered in black, red and green, inner hinges slightly cracking, good plus, bright copy. Jarndyce Antiquarian Booksellers CLXC - 201 2011 £40

Harrison, Mary St. Leger 1852-1931 *The History of Sir Richard Calmady.* London: Methuen, 1901, First edition; half title, 48 page catalog, (July 1901), original pink cloth, faded at spine and head, else very good. Jarndyce Antiquarian Booksellers CLXC - 200 2011 £45

Harrison, Mary St. Leger 1852-1931 *Mrs. Lorimer: a Sketch in black and white.* London: Macmillan & Co., 1882-1883, First edition; 2 volumes, endpapers slightly browned, contemporary half red sheep, rubbed and worn, volume I labelled "volume II" on spine and vice versa, good, sound. Jarndyce Antiquarian Booksellers CLXC - 202 2011 £85

Harrison, Mary St. Leger 1852-1931 *The Wages of Sin.* London: Swan Sonnenshein, 1891, First edition; 3 volumes, contemporary half red roan worn, poor copy. Jarndyce Antiquarian Booksellers CLXC - 204 2011 £65

Harrison, Peter *The Bible, Protestation and the Rise of Natural Science.* Cambridge: Cambridge University Press, 1998, First edition; 8vo., 313 pages, dark blue cloth, silver stamped spine title, dust jacket, near fine, from the Bern Dibner reference library, with Burndy bookplate. Jeff Weber Rare Books 161 - 193 2011 $60

Harrison, S. E. *The Tramways of Portsmouth.* The Light Railway Transport League, 1963, First edition; original cloth, dust jacket (few edge tears repaired), pages 175, numerous illustrations and maps, 4 original photographic postcards of trams loosely inserted, all stamped on reverse Portsdown & Horndean Light Rlwy or Portsmouth Corp. Tramways. R. F. G. Hollett & Son Antiquarian Booksellers General Catalogue Summer 2010 - 1113 2011 £30

Harrison, Sarah *The House-Keeper's Pocket-Book and Compleat Family Cook...* London: for J. Rivington and Sons et al, 1777, Ninth edition; (33), 6-208, (8) pages, modern paneled calf, antique, few tiny unobtrusive worm trails in bottom margin, very minor foxing, else very good, clean copy. Joseph J. Felcone Inc. Fall Miscellany 2010 - 31 2011 $1200

Harrison, Susannah *Songs in the Night by a Young Woman Under Heavy.* Ipswich: Punchard & Jermyn, 1788, Fourth edition with supplement; 8vo. pages xiv, 202, bound in contemporary calf, small piece worn from the spine, lightly rubbed, some marginal browning to titlepage and final leaf, contemporary ownership signature of Sara Fox on front endpaper, again on rear.   Second Life Books Inc.   174 - 168   2011 $600

Harrison, T. W. *Wills & Administration. A Discussion of the Devolution of a Decedent's Estate and the Procedure for the Distribution Thereof for Virginia & West Virginia.* Charlottesville: 1927, 2 volumes, average law buckram, one label with chip to author's name.   Bookworm & Silverfish   667 - 197   2011 $125

Harrison, T. W. *Wills & Administration, A Discussion of the Devolution of a Decedent's Estate & the Procedure for the Distribution of Thereof for Virginia & West Virginia.* Charlottesville: 1960, 3 volumes, full law buckram, over 1400 pages with 1975 supplement for each volume.   Bookworm & Silverfish   669 - 112   2011 $75

Harrison, William *An Arachaeological Survey of Lancashire.* London: printed by Nichols Sons, 1896, 4to., pages 26, large colored folding map, original blue wrappers, edges trifle frayed.   R. F. G. Hollett & Son Antiquarian Booksellers   177 - 440   2011   £35

Harrod, R. F. *The Life of John Maynard Keynes.* London: Macmillan, 1951, First edition; large 8vo., original blue cloth gilt, pages xx, 674, with 11 plates, flyleaves faintly browned, otherwise fine.   R. F. G. Hollett & Son Antiquarian Booksellers   175 - 593   2011   £50

Harrowby, Dudley Ryder, 1st Earl of *Substance of the Speech of the Right Honourable the Earl of Harrowby in the House of Lords October 4th 1831 on the Motion that the Reform Will be Read a Second Time.* London: Rooke and Varty, 1831, First separate edition; 8vo., (4), 55 (1) pages, including half title, half title rather stained and marked, several near contemporary ms. annotations and emphasis marks in ink, recent marbled boards, lettered on spine, good, uncommon.   John Drury Rare Books   153 - 131   2011   £125

Harry's Bar, London. London: Harley Pub., n.d., 2005, Members edition; 4to., copiously illustrated in color and black and white, fine in fine dust jacket and box.   Any Amount of Books   May 29 2011 - A67393   2011 $340

Harsell, Olof *The Comparative Anatomy and Histology of the Cerebellum: The Human Cerebellum, Cerebellar Connections and Cerebellar Cortex.* Minneapolis: University of Minnesota Press, 1972, First edition; 4to., ix, (ii), 268 pages, 67 plates, figures, index, original green cloth, gilt stamped spine title, dust jacket, fine, from the Medical Library of Dr. Clare Gray Peterson.   Jeff Weber Rare Books   162 - 185   2011 $125

Hart, Davis *The Lyttelton Hart-Davis Letters: Correspondence of George Lyttelton and Rupert Hart-Davis.* London: John Murray, 1979-1987, Volume 1 reprint, others first editions, volumes 5 and 6 first edition paperback; 8vo, 6 volumes (5 and 6 bound in one book), volume II signed presentation copy from author to Dadie Rylands, 4 volumes have short letters laid in from publisher "Jock" Murray to Dadie Rylands, all very good, clean copies, dust jackets where called for.   Any Amount of Books   May 29 2011 - B9967   2011 $221

Hart, Frances Noyes *The Bellamy Trial.* Garden City: Doubleday, Page and Co., 1927, First edition; former owner's name, else very good in dust jacket with light professional restoration to spine ends and extremities.   Buckingham Books   May 26 2011 - 6892   2011 $1750

Hart, James D. *The Private Press Ventures of Samuel Lloyd Osbourne and R. L. S.* San Francisco: Book Club of California, 1966, First edition; limited to 500 copies, 56 pages, frontispiece, plates, illustrations, 11 facsimiles in rear pocket, pictorial tan cloth stamped in black, very fine.   Argonaut Book Shop   Recent Acquisitions Summer 2010 - 191   2011 $75

Hart, John A. *History of Pioneer Days in Texas and Oklahoma.* N.P. Guthrie: privately printed, n.d. circa, 1906, First edition; 16mo., red cloth, 249 pages, frontispiece, illustrations, non-authorial presentation inscription in pencil, else very good, exceedingly rare, housed in four point folding case with leather label on spine and titles, stamped in gold.   Buckingham Books   May 26 2011 - 26818   2011 $4500

Hart, Joseph *Melodia Divina: Comprising the Most Popular Psalm and Hymn Tunes, Many Original Compositions, Adaptations from Handel, Haydn, Mozart, Beethoven, Mendelssohn...* London: Hart & Co., n.d. circa, 1882, Third edition; folio, original decorated red cloth, gilt over heavy bevelled boards, corners worn, rather stained in places, pages 160, scored throughout, hinges cracking, else very good.   R. F. G. Hollett & Son Antiquarian Booksellers   175 - 594   2011   £120

Harte, Bret *Writings.* Boston: Houghton Mifflin and Co., 1896, Autograph edition, limited to 350 copies; signed by author and artist, dated "Septem. 1896", 19 volumes, octavo, photogravure frontispieces, vignette titles and plates after drawings and paintings, all on India paper mounted, decorative tissue guards, each volume with at least one plate signed by artist, frontispiece of volume V. signed by Frederic Remington, contemporary full dark blue levant morocco, covers elaborately paneled in gilt within double gilt fillet border, spines decoratively paneled in gilt, turn-ins ruled in gilt, red crushed levant morocco doublures ruled in gilt with gilt cornerpieces, red watered silk liners, top edge gilt, others uncut, minimal fading to spines, wonderful set.   David Brass Rare Books, Inc.   May 26 2011 - 00987   2011 $6500

Harte, Negley *The University of London 1836-1986.* Athlone Press, 1986, First edition; large 8vo., original cloth, gilt, dust jacket, pages 303, illustrations.   R. F. G. Hollett & Son Antiquarian Booksellers   General Catalogue Summer 2010 - 1426   2011   £35

Hartley, David *The Budget.* London: printed for J. Almon, Opposite Burlington House in Picadilly, 1764, Fourth edition; 4to., stitched as issued, price on titlepage (price one shilling), 23, (1) pages, good.   Anthony W. Laywood   May 26 2011 - 21568   2011 $101

Hartley, James *History of the Westminster Election, Containing Every Material Ocurrence from Its Commencement on the First of April to the Final close of the Poll on the 17th of May.* London: printed for the editors and sold by J. Debrett and all other booksellers, 1784, 4to., (iii), iv-vii, (2) x-xii (2) 538 pages, including errata leaf inserted between A4 and B1, 18 etched plates (including two color plates not called for), of which 15 folding, repairs to folds of two or three plates, some intermittent old dampstaining, minor marginal soiling of few leaves, rebound fairly recently in very good 18th century style half calf over marbled boards, spine gilt with raised bands and label, uncut, good, complete copy in excellent binding.   John Drury Rare Books   153 - 58   2011   £950

Hartley, L. P. *A History of Greece from the Earliest Times to the Roman Conquest.* London: John Murray, 1902, First edition; 8vo., pages xvi, 614, with 4 page publishers' catalog at rear, frontispiece and 33 illustrations, Hartley's copy with his notes and underlinings, sound, used copy, inner front hinge starting, near very good, sold with a hardbound exercise book from this period, with circa 60 plus pages and in Hartley's hand dated 1915.   Any Amount of Books   May 29 2011 - A26804   2011 $340

Hartley, L. P. *The Travelling Grave and Other Stories.* Sauk City: Arkham House, 1948, First edition; octavo, cloth.   L. W. Currey, Inc.   124 - 26   2011 $2250

Hartley, L. P. *The Travelling Grave and Other Stories.* Sauk City: Arkham House, 1948, First edition; octavo, original black cloth, spine panel stamped in gold.   L. W. Currey, Inc.   124 - 200   2011 $200

Hartley, Marie *The Charm of Yorkshire Churches.* Leeds: Yorkshire Weekly Post, n.d., 1930, Small 4to., original cloth, trifle cockled in joints, pages 200, frontispiece, illustrations, very good, clean, sound.   R. F. G. Hollett & Son Antiquarian Booksellers   General Catalogue Summer 2010 - 1430   2011   £65

Hartley, Marie *Life and Tradition in West Yorkshire.* London: J. M. Dent and Sons, 1976, First edition; 4to., original cloth, gilt, dust jacket, pages 160, 147 photos, 88 drawings and map.   R. F. G. Hollett & Son Antiquarian Booksellers   General Catalogue Summer 2010 - 1427   2011   £45

Hartley, Marie *Life in the Moorlands of North-East Yorkshire.* London: J. M. Dent & Sons Ltd., 1975, Second impression; 4to., original cloth, gilt, dust jacket price clipped, pages xvi, 140, 265 photos, 19 drawings and a map, gift inscription (non-authorial).   R. F. G. Hollett & Son Antiquarian Booksellers   General Catalogue Summer 2010 - 1428   2011   £40

Hartley, Marie *The Old Hand-Knitters of the Dales.* Dalesman, 1951, First edition; original cloth, dust jacket, pages 123, illustrations, near fine, scarce.   R. F. G. Hollett & Son Antiquarian Booksellers   General Catalogue Summer 2010 - 1429   2011   £75

Hartmann, Cyril Hughes *The Story of the Road.* London: George Routledge, 1927, First edition; original green cloth gilt, slight crease to upper board, pages xx, 194, 192 plates, scattered foxing.   R. F. G. Hollett & Son Antiquarian Booksellers   General Catalogue Summer 2010 - 1114   2011   £30

Hartog, Cecile *Barbara's Song Book.* London: George Allen, 1900, Oblong small 4to., original cloth backed boards with pictorial onlay, little rubbed, pages 55 with 17 full and half page color illustrations by John Hassall.   R. F. G. Hollett & Sons Antiquarian Booksellers   170 - 318   2011   £140

Hartree, D. R. *Calculating Machines: Recent and Prospective Developments.* Cambridge: Cambridge University Press, 1947, First edition; 8vo., pages 40, 2 plates, wrappers, very small paperclip mark at rear, otherwise fine.   Any Amount of Books   May 29 2011 - A67386   2011 $272

Hartsoeker, Nicolaas *Suite des Conjectures Physiques.* Amsterdam: H. Desbordes, 1708, First edition; 4to., (8), 147, (1) pages, large paper copy, 5 medical engraved plates, 2 engraved armorial headpieces, woodcut figures, contemporary vellum backed boards, uncut, prelims slightly soiled, particularly titlepage, spine worn, from the library of the Earls of Macclesfield at Shirburn Castle.   Maggs Bros. Ltd.   1440 - 106   2011   £700

Harvey, Alfred *The Castles and Walled Towns of England.* London: Methuen, 1911, First edition; original crimson cloth gilt, pages xix, 276, with 46 illustrations half title and fore-edge rather spotted.   R. F. G. Hollett & Son Antiquarian Booksellers   177 - 441   2011   £30

Harvey, John *English Mediaeval Architects.* London: Batsford, 1954, First edition; pages xxiii, 412, review copy, 16 page supplement of revised edition of 1984 loosely inserted, large 8vo., original cloth, gilt, dust jacket, one small piece chipped from bottom edge.   R. F. G. Hollett & Son Antiquarian Booksellers   177 - 442   2011   £85

Harvey, John *Gothic England.* London: Batsford, 1947, First edition; original cloth, gilt, dust jacket (extremities little worn), pages xiv, 242, with 176 illustrations and charts on endpapers.   R. F. G. Hollett & Son Antiquarian Booksellers   177 - 443   2011   £30

Harvey, John *The Gothic World 1100-1600.* London: Batsford, 1950, First edition; tall 8vo., original cloth, gilt, dust jacket price clipped, little worn, illustrations and maps on endpapers.   R. F. G. Hollett & Son Antiquarian Booksellers   177 - 444   2011   £35

Harwell, Ernie *Turned to Baseball.* South Bend: Diamond Communications, 1985, First edition; near fine, light shelfwear, dust jacket fine, inscribed by author to Danny Freels "A great Tiger fan…".   Bella Luna Books   May 29 2011 - t9296   2011 $82

Hase, Johann Matthias *Regni Davidici et Salomonaei Descripto Geographica et Historica…* Nurnberg: J. H. G. Bieling, prostat in off. Homanniana, 1739, 2 parts, flio, ff. (4), col. 320, ff. (2) ff. (2) (first blank), col. 132, f. (1), title printed in red and black, 6 folding engraved maps, contemporary sprinkled calf, gilt spine, red edges, very handsome, from the library of the Earls of Macclesfield at Shirburn Castle.   Maggs Bros. Ltd.   1440 - 107   2011   £1500

Hase, Karl *Miracles Plays and Sacred Dramas.* London: Trubner and Co., 1880, Original cloth, gilt, spine trifle rubbed and chipped at top, pages x, 273, (iv), few marginal blindstamps, accession stamp verso of title.   R. F. G. Hollett & Son Antiquarian Booksellers   175 - 599   2011   £35

Haskell, L., Mrs. *God is Love.* London: Ernest Nister, n.d. circa, 1880, 4to., original cloth backed pictorial boards, edges rubbed, corners little bruised, unpaginated, 24 fine full page color plates.   R. F. G. Hollett & Son Antiquarian Booksellers   175 - 810   2011   £75

Hasler, H. G. *Practical Junk Rig.* Camden: 1988, First edition; 244 pages, fine in fine dust jacket.   Bookworm & Silverfish   678 - 138   2011 $100

Haslewood, Joseph *Some Account of Life and Publications of the late Joseph Ritson.* Robert Triphook, 1824, Frontispiece with offsetting, original drab boards, brown cloth spine, spine with slight loss to head and tail, ink label, scarce.   Jarndyce Antiquarian Booksellers   CXCI - 467   2011   £180

Hasluck, Paul N. *Portfolio Containing Twenty-Four Plates to Accompany Volume on Carpentry and Joinery.* London: Cassell & Co. n.d., 24 color plates, all loose as issued, in excellent condition, large folio, original cloth backed board folder with linen tie and printed paper label, little dusty.   R. F. G. Hollett & Son Antiquarian Booksellers   177 - 445   2011   £150

Hassell, J. *Beauties of Antiquity; or Remnants of Feudal Splendor and Monastic Times.* London: 1806, Volume 1 (of 2), many aquatints, spotting to margins of some, rebound, edgewear, foxing, some tissue guards detached, owner stamps, 56 pages.   G. H. Mott Bookseller   May 26 2011 - 43773   2011 $250

Hassell, John *Picturesque Rides and Walks, with Excursions by Water Thirty Miles Round the British Metropolis.* London: printed for J. Hassell, 1817-1818, First edition; 163 x 102mm., 2 volumes, quite attractive late 19th century jade green crushed morocco in Arts and Crafts design by Wood of London (stamp signed on front turn-ins), covers with gilt rule border and stippled cornerpieces incorporating drawer handles and three graceful tulips, raised bands, spines gilt in compartments with wide frame formed by drawer handles, heart ornaments and much stippling, turn-ins decorated with charming gilt tulips, marbled endpapers, top edge gilt, other edges rough trimmed; with 120 hand colored aquatint engravings; front joint of one volume with just hint of rubbing at head, faint minor spotting to covers, spines just slightly sunned to richer green trivial imperfections internally, but particularly fine and pretty set, text and plates very clean and fresh, ornate bindings lustrous and with no significant wear.   Phillip J. Pirages   59 - 233   2011 $2900

Hassell, John *Tour of the Isle of Wight.* London: printed by John Jarvis for Thomas Hookham, 1790, 2 volumes, 8vo., pages xxiv, 224 + engraved titlepage and 17 tinted aquatint plates; viii, 248 + engraved titlepage and 13 tinted aquatint plates, contemporary 'Etruscan' calf almost certainly by Edwards of Halifax, spine gilt compartmented with gilt 'coil' cornerpieces and 'classical urn' centre-pieces in blind, black lettering piece gilt, numbered direct in gilt within an open central blind tooled oval, boards 'metope and pentaglyph' roll gilt bordered and concentric borders within (one of palmettes & trident in blind) surrounding a central gilt 'Grecian key' roll edges marbled panel, board edges & turn-ins single rule gilt, vivid pink 'made' endpapers, all edges gilt, brown and white double core sewn endbands, bit foxed in places, neat restoration to endcaps and joints, spines slightly cracked, printed booklabel of John Sparrow at top left of veros of 'made' front endpaper, from the collection of Christopher Ernest Weston 1947-2010.   Unsworths Booksellers   24 - 107   2011   £750

Hassell, John *Tour of the Isle of Wight.* London: T. Hookham, 1790, 2 volumes in one, all leather, spine rebound with 5 raised bands on spine, edgewear, prelims and titlepages foxed, clean, tight, 224, 248 pages, plates (aquatints) in good condition.   G. H. Mott Bookseller   May 26 2011 - 43676   2011 $575

Hasson, Rachel *Early/Later Islamic Jewellery.* Jerusalem: L. A. Mayer Memorial Institute for Islamic Art, 1987, First edition; 2 volumes, 4to., pages 110 and 160, copiously illustrated in color and black and white, very good+ in like dust jacket, (head of jacket on second volume slightly used).   Any Amount of Books   May 29 2011 - A48520   2011 $272

Hastings, A. C. G. *Nigerian Days.* London: John Lane, 1925, First edition; 8vo., pages xxii, 255, map, illustrations, original red cloth, dust jacket. J. & S. L. Bonham Antiquarian Booksellers Africa 4/20/2011 - 7170 2011 £60

Hastings, A. C. G. *Nigerian Days.* London: John Lane, 1925, First edition; 8vo., pages xxii, 255, map, illustrations, original purple cloth. J. & S. L. Bonham Antiquarian Booksellers Africa 4/20/2011 - 4597 2011 £55

Hastings, A. C. G. *The Voyage of the Dayspring: being the Journal of the Late Sir John Hawley Glover...* London: Bodley Head, n.d., 1926, First edition; 8vo, pages x (vi), 230, (2) ads, 21 photogravures, including frontispiece, title in red and black, original turquoise cloth, review copy in fine condition. J. & S. L. Bonham Antiquarian Booksellers Africa 4/20/2011 - 7852 2011 £35

Hastings, James *Encyclopaedia of Religion and Ethics.* Edinburgh: T. & T. Clark, 1908, First edition; 13 volumes, large thick 8vo., original maroon cloth, gilt spines of few volumes trifle sunned, exceptionally good and sound set of original edition. R. F. G. Hollett & Son Antiquarian Booksellers 175 - 604 2011 £650

Hastings, Sally *Poems on Different Subjects.* Lancaster: printed and sold ry (sic) William Dickson...., 1808, First edition; 12mo., pages 220 + 10 page list of subscribers, full contemporary calf, heaf of spine chipped, some rubbing, sheets browned, good tight copy, complete with all blanks, later (1836) owner's inscription. Second Life Books Inc. 174 - 169 2011 $850

Hatch, J. *Morecambe, Lancaster and District.* Oxford University Press, 1909, Original cloth, gilt, rather damp cockled, pages 266, 56, 16 12 (14) a leaves, all edges gilt, frontispiece, numerous text illustrations, rather cockled by damp in places, but good, scarce. R. F. G. Hollett & Son Antiquarian Booksellers 173 - 531 2011 £35

Hatton, Joseph *Newfoundland. Its History, Its Present Condition and its Prospects in the Future.* Boston: Doyle & Whittle, 1883, Reprinted from the English edition; 8vo., half title, black and white frontispiece, black and white illustrations, folding map, brown cloth with gilt to spine, previous owners name in pencil on front pastedown, otherwise clean, bright, very good. Schooner Books Ltd. 96 - 46 2011 $125

Have You Heard the News? An Address to the Freemen of All the Corporations of Great Britain, Upon the Proposed Destruction of Their Rights by the Whig Ministry. London: C. F. Cock, 1835, Second edition; 12mo., 12 pages, preserved in modern wrappers with printed title label on upper cover, uncut, very good, apparently very rare. John Drury Rare Books 153 - 48 2011 £100

Haverfield, F. *Catalogue of the Roman Inscribed and Sculptured Stones in the Grosvenor Museum, Chester.* Chester & N. Wales Arch. & Hist. Soc., 1900, Pages 128, with 29 pages of plates and numerous illustrations, contemporary cloth, gilt, lower board rather marked, original wrappers bound in. R. F. G. Hollett & Son Antiquarian Booksellers 177 - 448 2011 £45

Haverfield, F. *The Romanization of Roman Britain.* Oxford: Clarendon Press, 1923, Fourth edition; original cloth, pages 91, with 28 illustrations. R. F. G. Hollett & Son Antiquarian Booksellers 177 - 449 2011 £30

Havergal, Frances Ridley *Songs of the Master's Love.* London: James E. Hawkins, n.d., Square 8vo., original decorated cloth gilt over bevelled boards, 16 tissue guarded card leaves, chromolithographed throughout, all edges gilt. R. F. G. Hollett & Son Antiquarian Booksellers 175 - 605 2011 £85

Haviland, Virginia *Favorite Fairy Tales told in Czechoslovokia.* Boston: Little Brown, 1966, Stated first edition; 4to., cloth, 90 pages, fine in dust jacket, full page and smaller color illustrations by Trina Schart Hyman. Aleph-Bet Books, Inc. 95 - 302 2011 $200

Hawker, Peter *Instructions to Young Sportsmen in All that Relates to Guns and Shooting.* London: printed for Longman, Hurst, Rees, Orme Brown and Green, 1824, Third edition; 240 x 155mm., xxii, 470 pages; with 10 plates; evidence of bookplate removal; handsome scarlet crushed morocco by Birdsall (stamp signed on front turn-in), covers with double gilt fillet border, raised bands, spine very attractively gilt in compartments with central figure of shooter and his dog framed by tree branch cornerpieces, gilt turn-ins, marbled endpapers, all edges gilt, in felt lined red straight grain morocco slipcase (very slightly marked); spine just shade darker than boards, little faded, with tail compartment bit rubbed, faint soiling to rear cover, trivial imperfections to few plates, isolated minor thumbing, corner creases, marginal stains, still nearly fine and quite attractive, leaves fresh and bright and decorative binding lustrous and virtually unworn. Phillip J. Pirages 59 - 234 2011 $1250

Hawker, Peter *Instructions to Young Sportsmen in all that Relates to Guns and Shooting.* Herbert Jenkins, n.d., 1922, Original green cloth, dust jacket little chipped and creased, pages xxxvi, 340, (ii), with 4 color plates and numerous other illustrations, scattered foxing. R. F. G. Hollett & Son Antiquarian Booksellers General Catalogue Summer 2010 - 1252 2011 £35

Hawkes, C. F. C. *Camulodunum. First Report on the Excavations at Colchester 1930-1939.* Oxford: The Society, 1947, First edition; 4to., original buckram gilt, spine little faded, pages xix, 362, with 112 plates and plans and 66 text figures. R. F. G. Hollett & Son Antiquarian Booksellers 177 - 450 2011 £45

Hawkes, John *The Cannibal.* New York: New Directions, 1949, First edition; small 8vo., original pale grey boards, pages 223, fine in very good yellow and black dust jacket, faintly marked and very slightly chipped at spine ends and with very slight edgewear, signed presentation from author for Richard and Mary Ellman.   Any Amount of Books   May 26 2011 - A75834   2011 $470

Hawking, Stephen *The Large Scale Structure of Timespace.* Cambridge: Cambridge University, 1973, First edition; 8vo., 391 pages, near fine with owner name in near fine dust jacket, mild sun spine, cover edges, minimal soil, rare.   By the Book, L. C.   26 - 102   2011 $750

Hawkins, Frederick *Annals of the French Stage.* London: Chapman and Hall, 1884, First edition; pages viii, 376; 396; 2 portrait frontispieces, 2 volumes, original cloth, gilt, spine little faded and rubbed, small labels removed, pages viii, 376; 396, 2 portrait frontispieces, few marginal blindstamps, accession stamp verso of title, upper joints cracking.   R. F. G. Hollett & Son Antiquarian Booksellers   175 - 606   2011   £75

Hawkins, Joseph *A History of a Voyage to the Coast of Africa and Travels into the Interior of that Country...* Philadelphia: printed for the author by S. C. Ustick & Co., 1797, First edition; 12mo., 179, (1) pages, frontispiece, contemporary mottled sheep, minor paper defect on A2, else pristine, nearly as fresh and bright as the day it was bound. Joseph J. Felcone Inc.   Fall Miscellany 2010 - 58   2011 $4500

Hawkins, Joseph *A History of the Voyage to the Coast of Africa and Travels into the Interior of that Country...* Troy: printed for the author by Luther Pratt, 1797, Second edition; 12mo., 180 pages, lacks engraved frontispiece, full contemporary calf, hinge cracked sound, text browned.   M & S Rare Books, Inc.   90 - 157   2011 $750

Hawley, Frank *Whales and Whaling in Japan.* Kyoto: printed for the author, 1958-1960, One of 125 numbered copies; 18 plates, including color woodblock frontispiece, 4to., pages (7), 354, x, titlepage printed in red and black, quarter undyed Indian goat and paper boards, original handmade slipcase, printed on Japanese handmade paper, printed on handmade kyokushi fabricated of miltsdumata, fine. Raymond M. Sutton, Jr.   May 26 2011 - 36107   2011 $1800

Hawley, James H. *History of Idaho. The Gem of the Mountains.* Chicago: S. J. Clarke Publishing Co., 1920, First edition; thick quarto, green cloth, decorated endpapers, all edges marbled; 895 pages, frontispiece, illustrations; 1008 pages, illustrations, 908 pages, frontispiece, illustrations; light bit of professional cosmetic restoration to spine ends and corners, else near fine set, housed in cloth slipcase with leather label on spine and titles stamped in gold.   Buckingham Books   May 26 2011 - 26275   2011 $1775

Hawthorne, Hildegarde *Arabian Nights.* Philadelphia: Penn Publishing Co., 1928, First edition; large thick 4to., 308 pages, blue gilt cloth, pictorial paste-on, 1 inch rubbed area on gutter, else fine, illustrations by Virginia Sterrett, pictorial endpapers and titlepage, 16 magnificent color plates and 20 partial page black and whites.   Aleph-Bet Books, Inc.   95 - 542   2011 $950

Hawthorne, Nathaniel 1804-1864 *Famous Old People: Being the Second Epoch of Grandfather's Chair.* Boston: E. P. Peabody, 1841, First edition; 12mo., vi, 158 pages, cloth, paper label on front cover, neat owner inscription dated 1851, gilt worn off label, corner one page torn, else very good+.   Aleph-Bet Books, Inc.   95 - 283   2011 $700

Hawthorne, Nathaniel 1804-1864 *Our Old Home.* London: Smith Elder, 1863, First edition; 2 volumes, half titles, 4 pages ads volume II, original dark green wavy grained cloth, front covers marked, some general rubbing & small repairs to inner hinges, good, sound copy.   Jarndyce Antiquarian Booksellers   CXCI - 199   2011   £125

Hawthorne, Nathaniel 1804-1864 *Transformation or the Romance of Monte Beni.* London: Smith, Elder and Co., 1860, First edition; 8vo, 32 page publisher's catalog in volume III, original rose cloth, little wear to ends of spines, bookplates removed from front covers, one hinge cracked and repaired.   M & S Rare Books, Inc.   90 - 159   2011 $1500

Hawthorne, Nathaniel 1804-1864 *Transformation of the Romance of Monte Beni.* Leipzig: Tauchnitz, 1860, Copyright edition; 2 volumes, full leather with raised bands, gilt lines to spine, gilt decorations and "ROMA" on covers, gilt inner dentelles, silken endsheets with fleur-de lis design, original albumen photos, very good, little wear, tight copies. Lupack Rare Books   May 26 2011 - ABE4890-162951   2011 $150

Hawthorne, Nathaniel 1804-1864 *Transformation or the Romance of Monte Beni.* Leipzig: Bernhard Tauchnitz, 1860, First Tauchnitz edition; 12mo., 12, 292; 94), 280, (1) pages, original gilt and red stamped vellum, all edges gilt "The Marble Faun" imprinted on spine, 58 fine photos pasted onto inserted leaves, scratch on front cover but very nice. M & S Rare Books, Inc.   90 - 160   2011 $650

Hawthorne, Nathaniel 1804-1864 *Transformation or the Romance of Monte Beni.* London: Smith, Elder & Co., 1860, Third edition; 3 volumes, slight spotting to prelims, contemporary grained tan calf, gilt borders, raised bands, gilt spine, brown and green morocco labels, booklabels of W. M. Graham, signature of A. Sutherland in volume I, very good.   Jarndyce Antiquarian Booksellers   CXCI - 526 2011   £175

Hawthorne, Nathaniel 1804-1864 *A Wonder Book.* London: New York and Toronto: Hodder & Stoughton Ltd., 1922, One of 600 copies signed by artist, this #370; 290 x 225mm., viii, 206, (2) pages, very attractive red three quarter morocco, raised bands, spine handsomely gilt in compartments formed by plain and decorative rules, quatrefoil centerpiece surrounded by densely scrolling cornerpieces, sides and endleaves of rose colored linen, top edge gilt, 24 colored plates, 16 of them tipped on, other illustrations in text, all by Arthur Rackham; morocco bookplate of W. A. M. Burden; perhaps breath of rubbing to joints and extremities (if one is determined to find it), faint spots on one cover, but exceptionally fine copy in handsome binding, bright, fresh and clean inside and out, volume II the more impressive because its greater thickness provides a larger area to show off its decorative gilt.   Phillip J. Pirages   59 - 289 2011 $2000

Hawthorne, Nathaniel 1804-1864 *A Wonder Book.* London: J. M. Dent & Sons, 1957, Full powder blue calf gilt by Bayntun, contrasting spine labels, spine and top edges of boards little faded, pages x, 195, all edges gilt, 8 colored plates, 4 black and white illustrations.   R. F. G. Hollett & Sons Antiquarian Booksellers   170 - 704 2011   £75

Hawthorne, Nathaniel 1804-1864 *Hawthorne's Works.* Boston: Houghton Mifflin, Riverside Press, copyright, 1879, 12 volumes, half leather and marbled boards and edges, leather torn, chipped and worn on spines and extremities, interiors clean and bright, frontispiece engravings.   G. H. Mott Bookseller   May 26 2011 - 39704 2011 $200

Hawton, Hector *Question.* Bungay, Suffolk: Pemberton Pub., 1968, First edition; 13 volumes, circa 1340 pages, very good, first issue annotated and signed by Rupert Crawshay-Williams, one of the contributors.   Any Amount of Books   May 29 2011 - A48239 2011 $204

Hay, Cynthia *Mathematics from Manuscript to Print 1300-1600.* Oxford: Clarendon Press, 1988, First edition; 8vo., ix, 273 pages, illustrations, navy, red and gilt stamped cover and spine titles, fine, from the Bern Dibner reference library, with Burndy bookplate.   Jeff Weber Rare Books 161 - 197 2011 $100

Hay, Daniel *Whitehaven. A Short History.* Whitehaven: Borough Council, 1966, First edition; original pictorial boards, protected with self-adhesive film, pages 152, illustrations.   R. F. G. Hollett & Son Antiquarian Booksellers 173 - 534 2011   £35

Hay, Ian *The Lighter Side of School Life.* London: T. N. Foulis, 1914, First edition; original brown buckram, pages vi, 227, (xv), , uncut, 12 tipped in color plates by Lewis Baumer. R. F. G. Hollett & Son Antiquarian Booksellers General Catalogue Summer 2010 - 811 2011   £45

Hay, William H. *A Revision of Malaclemmys. A Genius of Turtles.* Washington: 1904, First edition, removed from Bureau of Fisheries; pages 1-20, plates 1-11 (missing plate 12).   Bookworm & Silverfish   679 - 138 2011 $150

Haycock, David Boyd *Quakery and Commerce in Seventeenth Century.*   London: The Wellcome trust Centre for the History of Medicine at UCL, 2005,   8vo., viii, 216 pages, maps, figures, tables, red cloth, gilt stamped cover and spine titles, fine, from the Bern Dibner reference library, with Burndy bookplate.   Jeff Weber Rare Books   161 - 198 2011 $60

Hayden, Ferdinand Vandiveer 1829-1887 *Sun Pictures of Rocky Mountain Scenery.* New York: Julius Bien, 1870, First edition; quarto, viii, 150, (2) pages, 30 black and white photos by A. J. Russell, including frontispiece, photos of views, half dark green morocco over kelly green morocco, rebacked preserving original spine, morocco ruled in gilt, spine stamped and lettered in gilt, all edges gilt, marbled endpapers, some wear along bottom edge of boards, front free endpaper partially detached but holding, previous owner's small bookplate, Old Brigham Young library stamp on verso of titlepage, all photos in great condition, very good, clean copy.   Heritage Book Shop   Holiday 2010 - 55 2011 $9500

Hayden, Joseph *Joseph Hayden: The Complete Symphonies.*   Vienna: Universal Edition/Verlag Doblinger, 1965-1981, First edition; 12 volumes, 8vo., volume 12 is paperback and second edition, text in English and German, but mostly music scores, all very good in like dust jackets with slight occasional chips to jackets, paperback volume very good.   Any Amount of Books   May 29 2011 - A38157 2011 $230

Haydn, Franz Joseph *Haydn's Celebrated Symphones.* Goulding, D. Almaine, Potter & Co., n.d., circa, 1798, First edition thus; 12 symphones bound together, folio, original half scarlet roan gilt, leather worn and defective, pages 28, 13, 16, 18, 13, 15, 21, 21, 18, 17, 23, 19, engraved throughout with 12 titlepages, each numbered in ms. and 3 ad leaves.   R. F. G. Hollett & Son Antiquarian Booksellers 175 - 608 2011   £450

Haydon, Benjamin Robert *Lectures on Painting and Design.*   London: Longman, 1844-1846,   xii, 331, 1 pages including 11 wood engravings; xvi, 295 1 page including 2 wood engravings, 3 lithograph plates, both volumes with errata slips, contemporary cloth rebacked retaining most of the original backstrips, new endpapers, some foxing, sound, very scarce.   Ken Spelman Rare Books   68 - 38 2011   £225

Hayek, F. A. *The Constitution of Liberty.*   London: Routledge and Kegan Paul, 1960, 8vo., pages x, 570, ex-British Foreign Office library with few library markings, slight rubbing and faint markings, else very good.   Any Amount of Books   May 29 2011 - A67624 2011 $238

Hayley, William *A Philosophical, Historical and Moral Essay on Old Maids by a Friend to the Sisterhood.* London: Cadell, 1785, First edition; 8vo., pages 261, 250, 255, 3 volumes, half titles, contemporary calf, rebacked, armorial bookplates, very nice, rare. Second Life Books Inc. 174 - 171 2011 $750

Hayley, William *Posthumous Writings of William Cowper, Esqr.* Chichester: Printed by J. Seagraves for J. Johnson, 1803-1804, First edition; 4to., 3 volumes, pages 413, 422, 436, contemporary calf, neatly rebacked with speckled calf spine and leather labels, some light foxing, generally very nice, wide margins, early bookseller's note on endper says this is "probably" a large paper copy, includes 2 portraits of Cowper, bookplate of Hon. Anne Rushout. Second Life Books Inc. 174 - 172 2011 $825

Hayman, Ronald *John Gielgud.* London: Heinemann, 1971, First edition; original cloth, gilt, dust jacket, head of spine trifle chipped, pages x, 276, 45 plates, signed by Gielgud and inscribed July 1970. R. F. G. Hollett & Son Antiquarian Booksellers 175 - 609 2011 £45

Hays, Mary *Female Biography; or Memoirs of Illustrious and Celebrated Women of All Ages and Countries.* London: Richard Phillips, 1803, First edition; 6 volumes, 12mo., xxvi, 316; (ii), 404; (ii), 444; (ii), 504; (ii), 527; (ii), 476, (ii), bound without half titles, modern calf backed boards, little foxing, ex-library with ink numeral on verso of titlepage, very good, scarce. Second Life Books Inc. 174 - 173 2011 $3500

Hayter, George *A Descriptive Catalogue of the Great Historical Picture Painted by Mr. George Hayter... Representing the Trial of Her Late Majesty Queen Caroline of England...* W. Hersee, 1823, First edition; 16 pages, 5 large folding key plates identifying all characters depicted in picture, scarce, very good, in original drab wrappers. Ken Spelman Rare Books 68 - 22 2011 £225

Hayward, C. *The Courtesan.* London: Casanova Society, 1926, Limited edition No. 905 of 1380 copies; 4to., original cloth backed boards, gilt, dust jacket, pages xxvi, 492, with 8 plates, fine. R. F. G. Hollett & Son Antiquarian Booksellers 175 - 611 2011 £45

Hayward, John *Annals of the First Four Years of the Reign of Queen Elizabeth.* London: Camden Society, 1840, Original blindstamped cloth, gilt, neatly recased, pages 1, 116. R. F. G. Hollett & Son Antiquarian Booksellers General Catalogue Summer 2010 - 608 2011 £40

Hayward, Peter J. *A Natural History of the Seashore.* London: Collins, 2004, First edition; tall 4to., original blue cloth gilt, corners trifle bruised, pages (iv), 22, (viii, index) plus 224 hand colored plates, flyleaves and prelims lightly spotted, otherwise excellent copy. R. F. G. Hollett & Son Antiquarian Booksellers General Catalogue Summer 2010 - 983 2011 £650

Haywood, Carolyn *Here's a Penny.* New York: Harcourt Brace and Co., 1944, (I). First edition; 8vo., pictorial cloth, 158 pages, fine in very good+ dust jacket, full page and half page pen and ink drawings, this copy inscribed by Haywood for fellow artists Violet Oakley and Edith Emerson. Aleph-Bet Books, Inc. 95 - 284 2011 $350

Haywood, Helen *The Helen Haywood Christmas Book.* London: Hutchinson, n.d. mid 1930's, Pages 120, 4to., illustrations in full color, original cloth backed pictorial boards, lovely fresh copy. R. F. G. Hollett & Sons Antiquarian Booksellers 170 - 323 2011 £65

Hazlitt, William 1778-1830 *Sketches of the Principal Picture Galleries in England.* Taylor & Hessey, 1824, Old polished calf gilt, corners rather worn and restored, rebacked in matching calf gilt extra with raised bands and spine label, broad gilt turn-ins and marbled endpapers, pages ix, 195 (v), top edges gilt, complete with half title, two old tape marks to gutter of title. R. F. G. Hollett & Son Antiquarian Booksellers General Catalogue Summer 2010 - 656 2011 £295

Head, Francis Bond *A Faggot of French Sticks: Containing a Series of Descriptive Sketches of Principal Public Institutions of Paris...* London: John Murray, 1855, Third edition; 2 volumes in 1, original red cloth blocked in gilt, slightly rubbed, bookplate, all edges gilt, very good. Jarndyce Antiquarian Booksellers CXCI - 200 2011 £75

Head, George *Forest Scenes and Incidents in the Wilds of North America.* London: 1829, First edition; v, 362 pages, rebound in quarter cloth and marbled paper, light scattered foxing, else very good. Dumont Maps & Books of the West 111 - 59 2011 $150

Head, Richard *The English Rogue Described in the Life of Meriton Latroon, a Witty Extravagant.* New York: Dodd, Mead and Co., 1928, 4to., original blue cloth, 2 dents to upper board, dust jacket, rather torn and repaired, few chips, lower quarter of backstrip replaced, pages viii, 660, 12 plates. R. F. G. Hollett & Son Antiquarian Booksellers 175 - 612 2011 £45

Head, Ruth Mayhew *A History of Departed Things.* London: New York: Kegan, Paul, Trench, Trubner & Co., 1918, First edition; 8vo., pages 242, soundly rebound in quarter green leather, lettered gilt at spine, spine slightly faded, else very good, note on f.e.p. "Felicity Ashbee her book, Hartley Court 1941 i.m. (im=in memory of) Henry and Ruth Head", from the library of Janet Ashbee and C. R. Ashbee and their daughter Felicity with 6 page signed letter loosely inserted from Ruth Head to Janet Ahsbee.   Any Amount of Books   May 29 2011 - A45989 2011 $204

Headlam, Cuthbert *The Three Northern Counties of England.* Gateshead: Northumberland Press, 1939, Limited to 500 copies; small 4to., original full dark blue levant morocco gilt, pages xii, 343, untrimmed, 23 plates and 8 maps and plans, few spots to half title and fore-edge, but most attractive copy, loosely inserted are several letters relating to the production of the book between H. L. Honeyman (one of the contributors), the publishers and others, with press cuttings etc.   R. F. G. Hollett & Son Antiquarian Booksellers   173 - 536 2011   £120

Headlam, Cuthbert *The Three Northern Counties of England.* Gateshead: Northumberland Press, 1939, First Trade edition; small 8vo., original cloth, dust jacket, spine faded, pages xii, 343, 23 plates, 8 maps and plans, prelims and edges lightly spotted.   R. F. G. Hollett & Son Antiquarian Booksellers   173 - 535 2011   £50

Heald, Tim *By Appointment.* Queen Anne Press, 1989, First edition; large 4to., original cloth, gilt, dust jacket, pages 335, illustrations in color.   R. F. G. Hollett & Son Antiquarian Booksellers   175 - 613 2011   £40

Heaney, Seamus *Crediting Poetry.* privately printed, Faber, 1995, First edition; one of 500 copies, pages 32, foolscap 8vo., original plain pale blue stapled wrappers, dust jacket, signed by author.   Blackwell Rare Books   B166 - 160 2011   £175

Heaney, Seamus *Human Chain.* London: Faber, 2010, First edition, 184/300 copies (of an edition of 325) signed by author; pages (x), 8, foolscap 8vo., original brown cloth backed cream boards, printed label, matching boards and cloth slipcase, new.   Blackwell Rare Books   B166 - 161 2011   £350

Heaney, Seamus *Seeing Things.* London: Faber, 1991, First edition; 7/250 coie signed by author, pages 9x), 120, crown 8vo., original black cloth backed pink boards, printed label, matching boards and cloth, slipcase, fine.   Blackwell Rare Books   B166 - 162 2011   £290

Heaney, Seamus *The Sounds of Rain.* Atlanta: Emory University, printed at the Shadowy Waters Press, 1988, First edition; one of 300 copies printed in black and blue, pages (16), 16mo., original pale blue sewn wrappers with faded spine (originally issued with printed envelope no longer present), printed front cover label, untrimmed, near fine.   Blackwell Rare Books   B166 - 163 2011   £140

Heaney, Seamus *The Spirit Level.* London: Faber, 1996, First edition; 150/350 copies signed by author, pages (x), 74, crown 8vo., original black cloth backed grey boards, printed label, matching cloth and board slipcase, fine.   Blackwell Rare Books   B166 - 164 2011   £275

Heaney, Seamus *Ugolino.* Andrew Carpenter, 1979, First edition, limited to 125 copies, signd by poet, artist, and designer and publisher, Andrew Carpenter, only 30 copies were for sale; 4to., 2 lithographs by Louis Le Brocquy, original limp black goatskin, publisher's slipcase, fine, rare.   James S. Jaffe Rare Books   May 26 2011 - 20976 2011 $10,000

Hearn, Lafcadio 1850-1904   *The Boy Who Drew Casts.* Tokyo: Japanese Fairy Tales No. 23, Hasagawa, crepe paper, very good.   C. P. Hyland   May 26 2011 - 337 2011 $406

Hearn, Lafcadio 1850-1904   *Shadowings.* Boston: Little Brown, 1900, First edition; 8vo., pages 268, top edge gilt, other edges uncut, deep blue cloth stamped in light blue and gilt, rather nice in little nicked dust jacket.   Second Life Books Inc.   174 - 174 2011 $600

Hearn, Lafcadio 1850-1904   *Stray Leaves from Strange Literature: Stories from the Anvari-Soheill, Baital, Pachist, Mahabharata, Pntchatantra, Gulistan, Talmud, Kalewala.* Boston: Osgood, 1884, First edition; small 8vo., pages 225, bookplate, bound in brown cloth, stamped in black, little rubbed at extremities, very good, tight copy, one paper browned from laid in news clipping, very scarce in this condition.   Second Life Books Inc.   174 - 175 2011 $750

Hearn, Lafcadio 1850-1904   *Writings.* Boston: Houghton Mifflin Co., 1922, Limited to 750 numbered copies; 16 volumes, octavo, mounted color frontispiece and photograuvre plates, mostly from photos by Charles S. Olcott, several in color and mounted, all on Japanese vellum, with descriptive tissue guards, text illustrations, handsomely bound by Stikeman in contemporary three quarter maroon morocco ruled in gilt over lilac cloth boards, spines with two raised bands decoratively tooled and lettered in gilt, marbled endpapers, top edge gilt, others uncut, fine set.   David Brass Rare Books, Inc.   May 26 2011 - 01581 2011 $5750

Heath, Ambrose *More Good Food.* London: Faber, 1933, First edition; original pictorial cloth by Edward Bawden, matching dust jacket (head of spine rather heavily chipped, price clipped) pages 248, decorations by Bawden, scarce in jacket.   R. F. G. Hollett & Son Antiquarian Booksellers   General Catalogue Summer 2010 - 1082   2011   £65

Heath, H. *Nautical Dictionary.*   1840,   Oblong 4to., pictorial title, 6 numbered etched plates, stitched with plain rear wrapper, but lacking front wrapper, good, clean condition.   Ken Spelman Rare Books   68 - 36   2011   £95

Heath, Henry *The Caricaturist's Scrap Book.* London: Charles Tilt, 1834, Oblong folio, engraved general titlepage, additional engraved title for first suite of plates, + 55 plates, 2 inch tears to two plates neatly repaired with archival tape, occasionally trimmed close, original brown cloth, brown morocco spine loss to head and tail of spine, rubbed and little marked, leading inner hinge cracking, all edges gilt, good, sound.   Jarndyce Antiquarian Booksellers   CXCI - 201   2011   £750

Heath, Sidney *Old English Houses of Alms.* Francis Griffiths, 1910, First edition; small folio, original cloth backed boards, upper board little scraped, pages 148, (iv), untrimmed with 49 plates, 7 text illustrations and 4 plans.   R. F. G. Hollett & Son Antiquarian Booksellers   177 - 455   2011   £75

Heath, Wendy Y. *Book Auction Records.* London: New York. Montreal, Edinburgh & Glasgow, 1962-1992, First edition; volumes 60-89, 30 volumes in total, engravings.   I. D. Edrich   May 26 2011 - 60196   2011 $503

Heath, Wendy Y. *Book Auction Records.* Folkstone: William Dawson & Sons, 1972-1996, 25 volumes, 4to., red cloth, gilt stamped spine titles, very good.   Jeff Weber Rare Books   163 - 109   2011 $550

Heathen Mythology. Willougbhy and Co., 1843, contemporary half calf gilt, little worn and scraped, spine label slightly chipped, pages viii, 194, engraved presentation leaf, nearly 200 engravings, 9 full page and 2 additional woodcut plates laid in scarce.   R. F. G. Hollett & Son Antiquarian Booksellers   175 - 1456   2011   £160

Heath's Book of Beauty 1833. London: Longman, Rees &c, 1833, Engraved frontispiece and title, all plates present, original full dark blue morocco, gilt spine, leading inner hinge cracking, slight rubbing, all edges gilt, good plus.   Jarndyce Antiquarian Booksellers   CLXC - 80   2011   £75

Hebert, Septimus *Whispers of Truth from the Stars.* London: James Nisbet and Co., 1896, First edition; original cloth silvered, spine rather dulled and creased, several indented ring marks to lower board, pages xiv, 214, (iii), 5 diagrams and 2 tables, inserted is 4 page ALS from author to Rev. W. J. Houlgate concerning the book and folded leaflet of "Opinions of the Press", scarce.   R. F. G. Hollett & Son Antiquarian Booksellers   175 - 614   2011   £45

Hecht, Abslam *Instructions for Weaving in all of Its Various branches.* Baltimore: 1849, 28 pages, half leather, worn, with marbled boards, pages 17-22 in facsimile, scarce.   Bookworm & Silverfish   665 - 147   2011 $225

Hector, William *Selections from the Judicial Records of Renfrewshire.* Paisley: J. & J. Cook, 1876, Large paper copy; small 4to., original cloth with paper spine label, trifle defective, pages viii, 358, (11), uncut, 6 plates.   R. F. G. Hollett & Son Antiquarian Booksellers   175 - 615   2011   £120

Heidegger, Martin *Being and Time.*   New York: Harper & Row, 1962, First American edition?; 8vo., pages 589, very good tight copy, no dust jacket.   Second Life Books Inc.   174 - 176   2011 $75

Heinlein, Robert Anson   1907-1988   *Double Star.* Garden City: Doubleday & Co., 1956, First edition; octavo, boards.   L. W. Currey, Inc.   124 - 4   2011 $6500

Heinlein, Robert Anson   1907-1988   *Farnham's Freehold.*   New York: G. P. Putnam's Sons, 1964, First edition; cloth, octavo.   L. W. Currey, Inc.   124 - 96   2011 $850

Heinlein, Robert Anson   1907-1988   *Farnham's Freehold.*   New York: G. P. Putnam's Sons, 1964, First edition; octavo, cloth.   L. W. Currey, Inc.   124 - 71   2011 $1250

Heinlein, Robert Anson   1907-1988   *The Green Hills of Earth.*   Chicago: Shasta Pub., 1951, First edition; octavo, cloth backed boards.   L. W. Currey, Inc.   124 - 144   2011 $450

Heinlein, Robert Anson   1907-1988   *I Will Fear No Evil.* New York: G. P. Putnam's Sons, 1970, First edition; octavo, cloth.   L. W. Currey, Inc.   124 - 37   2011 $1750

Heinlein, Robert Anson   1907-1988   *The Moon is a Harsh Mistress.*   New York: G. P. Putnam's Sons, 1966, First edition; octavo, cloth.   L. W. Currey, Inc.   124 - 72   2011 $1250

Heinlein, Robert Anson 1907-1988 *Methuselah's Children.* Hiksville: Gnome Press, 1958, First edition; first binding of black boards with spine panel lettered in red, octavo.   L. W. Currey, Inc.   124 - 82 2011 $1000

Heinlein, Robert Anson 1907-1988 *The Puppet Masters.* Garden City: Doubleday and Co., 1951, First edition; octavo, cloth.   L. W. Currey, Inc.   124 - 56 2011 $1500

Heinlein, Robert Anson 1907-1988 *The Puppet Masters.* Garden City: Doubleday & Co., 1951, First edition; octavo, cloth.   L. W. Currey, Inc.   124 - 120 2011 $650

Heinlein, Robert Anson 1907-1988 *Red Planet: a Colonial Boy on Mars.* New York: Charles Scribner's Sons, 1949, First edition; octavo, cloth.   L. W. Currey, Inc.   124 - 11 2011 $3750

Heinlein, Robert Anson 1907-1988 *Rocket Ship Galileo.* New York: Charles Scribner's Sons, 1947, First edition; octavo, cloth.   L. W. Currey, Inc.   124 - 27 2011 $2250

Heinlein, Robert Anson 1907-1988 *The Rolling Stones.* New York: Charles Scribner's Sons, 1952, First edition; octavo, cloth.   L. W. Currey, Inc.   124 - 73 2011 $1250

Heinlein, Robert Anson 1907-1988 *Sixth Column.* New York: Gnome Press, 1949, First edition; cloth, octavo.   L. W. Currey, Inc.   124 - 90 2011 $950

Heinlein, Robert Anson 1907-1988 *Sixth Column.* New York: Gnome Press, 1949, First edition; octavo, cloth.   L. W. Currey, Inc.   124 - 104 2011 $750

Heinlein, Robert Anson 1907-1988 *Space Cadet.* New York: Charles Scribner's Sons, 1948, First edition; octavo, cloth.   L. W. Currey, Inc.   124 - 13 2011 $3500

Heinlein, Robert Anson 1907-1988 *Starman Jones.* New York: Charles Scribners Sons, 1953, First edition; octavo, cloth.   L. W. Currey, Inc.   124 - 83 2011 $1000

Heinlein, Robert Anson 1907-1988 *Starship Troopers.* New York: G. P. Putnam's Sons, 1959, First edition; octravo, cloth.   L. W. Currey, Inc.   124 - 14 2011 $3500

Heinlein, Robert Anson 1907-1988 *Stranger in a Strange Land.* New York: G. P. Putnam's Sons, 1961, First edition; octavo, cloth.   L. W. Currey, Inc.   124 - 5 2011 $6000

Heinlein, Robert Anson 1907-1988 *Waldo and Magic, Inc.* Garden City: Doubleday & Co. Inc., 1950, First edition; octavo, cloth.   L. W. Currey, Inc.   124 - 105 2011 $750

Heister, Lorenz 1683-1758 *Chirurgie, in Welcher Alles was Zur Wundarzney Gehoret... Deutlich Vorgesteielt Werden.* Nurnberg: Bey Gabriel Nicolaus Raspe, 1779, 216 x 183mm., 8 p.l. (including frontispiece), 378, (4) pages, 379-1078 (i.e. 1076) pages, 12 leaves, stunning contemporary painted calf, elaborately gilt decorated, covers each with four very large and graceful gilt floral tools within large compartments formed by interlacing strapwork that is painted black, an equally prominent central compartment with dense gilt foliage, flowers and fleurons and much supporting gilt decoration of a similar kind in 20 smaller compartments around the board edges and between the large compartments, raised bands, spine very handsomely gilt with lovely central flower and botanical side pieces, olive green spine label, gilt decorated turn-ins, marbled endpapers, all edges gilt; ornamental headpieces, initial and tailpieces, frontispiece and 38 sometimes startling folding plates, titlepage in red and black, inscribed "Dr. Harald Long 1895"; tiny cracks in label, text printed on inferior paper stock (so not particularly bright), but almost nothing else in the way of a significant defect; superb, even exceptional copy in wonderful binding, text absolutely fresh and leather with virtually no signs of wear.   Phillip J. Pirages   59 - 52 2011 $17,500

Heitman, F. B. *Historical Register of Officers of the Continental Army During the War of the Revolution April 1775 to December 1783.* Washington: 1893, First edition; 525 (8) pages, small 4to., fine in recent blue cloth, all edges rubricated.   Bookworm & Silverfish 665 - 8 2011 $150

Helbig, Wolfgang *Guide to the Public Collections of Classical Antiquities in Rome.* Leipzig: Karl Baedeker, 1895, First edition; 2 volumes, small 8vo., pages xii, 518; 490; lacks front endpaper of both volumes, "Times Office" small label on pastedowns, slight soiling and slight marking, "Discard" stamp to top of titlepage of volume one which is slightly chipped at edge and has additional "Dulau and Company" booksellers label, otherwise very good in original publisher's brick red cloth lettered and patterned in black.   Any Amount of Books   May 29 2011 - A43122 2011 $298

Heldoren, Jan Van *A Nomenclator English and Dutch.* Amsterdam: widow Mercy Bruyning, 1675, 2 volumes, 16mo., pages 48, (1)-64, 67-166 (lacking pages 163-166); 48, 48 pages, ff. (52 (signed A-O in 8's), vellum backed boards, from the library of the Earls of Macclesfield at Shirburn Castle.   Maggs Bros. Ltd.   1440 - 108 2011   £1200

Heliodorus *Aethiopicorum Libri X.* Paris: L. Feburier, 1619, 8vo., (16), 519, (1); 123, 5 (blank) pages, text in Greek and Latin in parallel columns, 17th century Dutch Prize binding of vellum over pasteboard arms of Amsterdam on covers within double gilt fillet with armorial cornerpieces, flat spine gilt, later 18th century red morocco label added at head, lacking green silk ties, from the library of the Earls of Macclesfield at Shirburn Castle. Maggs Bros. Ltd. 1440 - 109 2011 £400

Heller, Joseph *God Knows.* New York: 1984, First edition; 1/350 copies, as new in dust jacket and slipcase. Gemini Fine Books & Arts, Ltd. Art Reference & Illustrated Books: First Editions 2011 $95

Helleu, Paul *A Gallery of Portraits Reproduced from the Original Etchings by Paul Helleu.* London: Edward Arnold, 1907, First edition; folio, 50 x 37 cm., 24 plates, duotone or color, attractive and are book recently finely bound in green half leather with new endpapers and lettered gilt at spine with marbled boards, excellent condition, very slight waving to plates, possibly from damp and couple of slight repaired tears at head of pages in introduction not affecting text in any way. Any Amount of Books May 26 2011 - A32862 2011 $587

Hellman, C. Doris *The Comet of 1577: Its Place in History of Astronomy.* New York: Columbia University Press, 1944, First edition; 8vo., 488 pages, green cloth, blind-stamped cover emblem, gilt stamped spine title, dust jacket worn with tears, very good, rare in jacket, from the Bern Dibner reference library, with Burndy bookplate. Jeff Weber Rare Books 161 - 199 2011 $169

Hellman, Lillian *The Autumn Garden.* Boston: Little Brown, 1951, First edition; 8vo., pages 139, very good in little worn dust jacket (mended on verso), inscribed by author. Second Life Books Inc. 174 - 177 2011 $563

Hellman, Lillian *Candide.* New York: Random House, 1957, First edition; 8vo., 143 pages, fine in little browned dust jacket, inscribed by author. Second Life Books Inc. 174 - 178 2011 $600

Hellmuth, Eckhart *The Transformation of Political Culture; England and Germany in the Late Eighteenth Century.* London: The German Historical Institute/Oxford University Press, 1990, First edition; 8vo., pages 606, from the library of Ian Gilmour (Baron Gilmour of Craigmillar 1926-2006) with his ownership signature and occasional erasable marginal linings and neat notes in pencil, fine in very good+, very slightly sunned dust jacket. Any Amount of Books May 29 2011 - A73534 2011 $213

Helmer-Petersen, Keld *Fragments of a City.* Copenhagen: Hans Reitzel, 1960, First edition; slim paperback with paper label on spine, black and white photos, very bright copy, fine in photo illustrated wrappers. Jeff Hirsch Books ny 2010 2011 $600

Helmont, Franciscus Mercurius Van *Alphabeti vere Naturalis Hebraici Brevissima Delineatio Quae Simul Methodum Suppeditat...* Sulzbach: Abraham Lichtenthaler, 1657, (1667); 12mo., (36 including additional engraved title), 107, (1) pages, 36 engraved plates, 18th century smooth calf, gilt, handsome copy, from the library of the Earls of Macclesfield at Shirburn Castle. Maggs Bros. Ltd. 1440 - 110 2011 £1800

Helvetius *Philosophical Works.* Bristol: Thoemmes Press, 2000, First edition; 8vo., 1460 pages, hardback, 2 volumes. Any Amount of Books May 29 2011 - B15873 2011 $221

Hemingway, Ernest Millar 1899-1961 *Across the River and Into the Trees.* New York: Scribner's, 1950, First printing in first state of dust jacket (title page on spine is in yellow); very good plus, some offsetting to endpapers, especially at rear, little wear to spine gilt, linear indentation to rear cover, very good dust jacket with light shelfwear. Lupack Rare Books May 26 2011 - ABE4102589049 2011 $200

Hemingway, Ernest Millar 1899-1961 *Dateline: Toronto.* New York: 1985, Proof copy; short closed edge tear, otherwise fine in wrappers. Gemini Fine Books & Arts, Ltd. Art Reference & Illustrated Books: First Editions 2011 $70

Hemingway, Ernest Millar 1899-1961 *The First Forty-Nine Stories.* Franklin Station: Franklin Library, 1977, First edition with these illustrations; illustrations by Bernard Fuchs, full gray cloth, publisher's file copy, unstamped but bound in manner of other Franklin Library "record and reference" copies, all edges gilt, silk endpapers and ribbon marker, very slight wear, near fine, presumably one of a very few, or perhaps the only copy bound thus. Between the Covers 169 - BTC335536 2011 $450

Hemingway, Ernest Millar 1899-1961 *For Whom the Bell Tolls.* New York: Limited Editions Club, 1942, One of 1550 numbered copies; illustrations and signed by Lynd Ward, very slight printer's glue residue and very slight fading on spine, otherwise very crisp, unread, slightly discolored crisp slipcase. Gemini Fine Books & Arts, Ltd. Art Reference & Illustrated Books: First Editions 2011 $350

Hemingway, Ernest Millar 1899-1961 *The Old Man and the Sea.* London: Jonathan Cape, 1952, First edition; decorated cloth near fine in near fine dust jacket. Lupack Rare Books May 26 2011 - ABE3762223272 2011 $450

Hemingway, Ernest Millar 1899-1961 *Le Vieil Homme et la Mer. (The Old Man and the Sea).* Paris: Aux Depens de l'Artiste, 1958, First Naly edition; number 48 of 80 copies (total edition of 115), printed on handmade Auvergne paper and illustrated with 19 original black and white etchings, 17 of them full page by Robert Naly, folio, 145 pages text in French, all leaves loose in wrapper folder and clamshell box, fine.   Gemini Fine Books & Arts, Ltd.   Art Reference & Illustrated Books: First Editions 2011 $450

Hemingway, Ernest Millar 1899-1961 *Der Alte Mann und Das Meer. (The Old Man and the Sea).* New York: Knopf, 1961, Limited edition of 500 signed copies, this no. 29; loose sheets in plain cream wrappers, spine lettering in grey green, mild sun spine, soil covers, minimal bump lower spine tip, fine custom made slipcase by Curwen Press, 8 hors texte woodcuts by Frans Masereel, typeset in Janson Antiqua on a special making of Hahnemuhle Butten paper, 8vo., 160 pages.   By the Book, L. C.   26 - 7 2011 $600

Hemingway, Ernest Millar 1899-1961 *The Spanish Earth.* Cleveland: J. B. Savage Co., 1938, First edition; first issue with F. A. I. banner on endpapers, #29 of a limited edition of 1000 numbered copies, small 8vo., pages 60, bound in tan cloth printed in orange and black, covers lightly soiled, otherwise nice, tight, clean copy.   Second Life Books Inc.   174 - 179 2011 $3500

Hemingway, Ernest Millar 1899-1961 *To Have and Have Not.* New York: Charles Scribner's Sons, 1937, First edition; two light tape 'ghosts' to two free endpapers, otherwise fine, in very good dust jacket (some minor, professional restoration at folds, resulting in complete dust jacket, neither chipped nor clipped).   Lupack Rare Books   May 26 2011 - ABE1202783190 2011 $1750

Hemming, George Wirgman *A Just Income Tax How Possible, Being a Review of the Evidence Reported by the Income Tax Committee and an Inquiry into the True Principle of Taxation.* London: John Chapman, 1852, First edition; 8vo., 40 pages, modern wrappers with printed title label on upper cover, very good, scarce.   John Drury Rare Books   153 - 59 2011   £75

Henault, Charles Jean Francois *Nouvel Abrege Chronologique de l'Histoire de France.* Paris: Chez Prault et al, 1756, Fifth edition; 165 x 105mm., 2 volumes with continuous pagination, 5 p.l., (1), 545, (1), 1 blank leaf; (549)-928 pages, (48) leaves, including final blank, second volume with half title but no titlepage, apparently as issued, lovely contemporary olive green morocco, elegantly gilt in style of Derome, covers with plain and stippled fillet border around a frame containing large and graceful gilt floral and botanical stamps as well as dots and circlets, raised bands, spines gilt in compartments featuring charming flower centerpiece and small scrolling foliate cornerpieces, turn-ins with gilt zig-zag decoration, stencilled gilt endpapers, all edges gilt, publisher's device on titlepage, historiated headpieces, foliated initials, ornamental tailpieces; small bookplate of Jean Furstenberg and Henri Beraldi; spines slightly and uniformly faded to an attractive amber, just hint of wear to joints and corners, isolated minor foxing, few trivial stains, but fine, pretty binding sound, lustrous and with only insignificant wear and text, very clean and fresh.   Phillip J. Pirages   59 - 53 2011 $2900

Henderson, Alfred *Latin Proverbs and Quotations.* London: Sampson Low, Son & Marston, 1869, First edition; large 8vo., original cloth, gilt over bevelled boards, closed tear across spine, pages vii, 505, top edges gilt, joints roughly repaired with tape, uncommon.   R. F. G. Hollett & Son Antiquarian Booksellers   General Catalogue Summer 2010 - 422 2011   £75

Henderson, James *Scraps.* James Henderson, 1885, Volume 2 no. 71-Volume 3 No. 123, tall folio, modern brown cloth gilt, cartoons, woodcut illustrations, first leaf creased, chipped and repaired with little loss, other repairs elsewhere but generally very good order.   R. F. G. Hollett & Son Antiquarian Booksellers   General Catalogue Summer 2010 - 657 2011   £350

Henderson, Linda Dalrymple *Duchamp in Context: Science and Technology in the Large Glass and Related Works.* Princeton: Princeton University Press, 1998, large 8vo., xxiii, 374 pages, 189 figures, black cloth, silver stamped spine title, dust jacket, fine, from the Bern Dibner reference library, with Burndy bookplate.   Jeff Weber Rare Books   161 - 200 2011 $95

Henderson, Neville *Failure of a Mission: Berlin 1937-1939.* London: Hodder & Stoughton, 1940, First edition, number 21 of 25 copies signed by author; 8vo., full white vellum lettered gilt on spine on front cover, pages xii-318, very faint soiling, otherwise very good+.   Any Amount of Books   May 29 2011 - A42826 2011 $230

Henley, Pauline *Spenser in Ireland.* 1928, First edition; maps, very good, nice presentation inscription to friend Patrick Tohall, also present are Tohall's two maps 25 x 22 and 13 1/2 x 20 with reduction instructions to printer and a first draft of the map showing Spenser's Grant 14 1/2 x 10 13/4 inches.   C. P. Hyland   May 26 2011 - 258/293 2011 $507

Hennell, Thomas *Lady Filmy Fern or the Voyage of the Window Box.* Hamish Hamilton, 1980, First edition; large oblong 8vo., original glazed pictorial boards, matching dust jacket, unpaginated, illustrations in full color, few slight spots to flyleaves, else fine. R. F. G. Hollett & Sons Antiquarian Booksellers 170 - 65 2011 £35

Hennell, Thomas *Lady Filmy Fern or the Voyage of the Window Box.* London: Hamish Hamilton, 1980, First edition; large oblong 8vo., original glazed pictorial boards, matching dust jacket, unpaginated, illustrations in full color, fine. R. F. G. Hollett & Son Antiquarian Booksellers General Catalogue Summer 2010 - 493 2011 £40

Hennepin, Louis *A New Discovery of a Vast Country in America, Extending Above Four Thousand Miles Between New France and New Mexico.* London: for M. Bentley, J. Tonson, 1698, First edition in English, Tonson issue; (22), 243, (33) 228 pages, engraved fore-title, 5 (of 6) folding plates, lacking two maps and one plate, contemporary calf, early rebacking, hinges and corners worn, text dampstained, imperfect copy. Joseph J. Felcone Inc. Fall Miscellany 2010 - 59 2011 $2200

Hennepin, Louis *A New Discovery of a Vast Country in America.* Chicago: 1903, Reprinted from second London issue of 1698; 2 volumes, lxiv, 353 pages, illustrations, folding map, 358-711 pages, folding map, illustrations, original cloth, some rubbing to exterior, else very good, clean set. Dumont Maps & Books of the West 112 - 45 2011 $225

Hennessy, William M. *The Annals of Ulster 431-1378 A.D.* 1887-1895, Volumes 1-3 only, lacking volume 4, volume 1 quarter leather, others quarter cloth, ex-library and presented by H. M. Tresury, good. C. P. Hyland May 26 2011 - 260/253 2011 $362

Hennessy, William M. *The Annals of Ulster: 431-1378 A.D.* 1887-1895, Volumes 1-3 only, lacking volume 4, quarter cloth, publisher's presentation copy ex-library but very good. C. P. Hyland May 26 2011 - 258/373 2011 $362

Hennessy, William M. *The Annals of Loch Ce: a Chronicle of Irish Affairs 1014-1590.* 1939, 2 volumes, frontispiece, original cloth, ex-Prinknash Abbey Library, very good. C. P. Hyland May 26 2011 - 256/373 2011 $333

Hennessy, William M. *Chronicum Scotorum. A Chronicle of Irish Affairs from the Earliest Times to A. D. 1150.* 1866, Folding frontispiece, quarter cloth, publisher's presentation copy, ex-library, very good; C. P. Hyland May 26 2011 - 258/372 2011 $290

Henniker, Frederick *Notes During a Visit to Egypt, Nubia, the Oasis Mount Sinai and Jerusalem.* London: John Murray, 1823, First edition; 8vo., pages x, 339, 2 folding aquatint plates, plate, small blue stamp in corner of plates, recent half calf, ex-Bradford Library, some occasional light foxing and browning to prelims. J. & S. L. Bonham Antiquarian Booksellers Africa 4/20/2011 - 8394 2011 £350

Henniker, Frederick *Notes During a Visit to Egypt, Nubia, the Oasis Boaris, Mount Sinai and Jerusalem.* London: John Murray, 1824, Second edition; 8vo., pages xi, 352, 3 aquatint plates, soundly rebacked at spine with inner hinges neatly renewed, preserving original yellow endpapers, very good+ tight copy. Any Amount of Books May 29 2011 - B30295 2011 $340

Henriet, Frederic *Le Paysagiste Aux Champs.* Paris: A. Levy, 1876, Limited to 135 copies; 4to., original blue cloth with elaborate gilt design and black stamping, all edges gilt, fine, 20 original etchings and 2 etched reproductions, beautiful copy of beautiful book. Aleph-Bet Books, Inc. 95 - 242 2011 $1850

Henry, Francoise *La Sculpture Irlandaise Pendant les Douze Premiers Siecles de l'ere Chretienne.* Paris: 1933, First and only edition; 2 volumes, 145 figures, 171 plates, original wrappers, almost mint. C. P. Hyland May 26 2011 - 258/374 2011 $1449

Henry, Matthew *A Plain Catechism fro Children. (bound with) A Scripture-Catechism in the Method of the Assembly.* London: printed for J. and B. Sprint etc., 1722, 1720. Fifth and fourth edition respectively; 12mo., modern full calf gilt, pages (ii), 19, (i); 186, (vi, ads), little light browning in places, excellent copy, rare early editions. R. F. G. Hollett & Son Antiquarian Booksellers 175 - 617 2011 £350

Henrywood, R. K. *Relief-Moulded Jugs 1820-1900.* London: Antique Collectors Club, 1984, First edition; 4to., original cloth, gilt, dust jacket, pages 246 with 20 color plates and 278 illustrations. R. F. G. Hollett & Son Antiquarian Booksellers General Catalogue Summer 2010 - 199 2011 £60

Hensman, Howard *Cecil Rhodes: a Study of a Creer.* Edinburgh: Wm. Blackwood, 1901, First edition; 8vo., pages xiii, 382, frontispiece, illustrations, original red cloth. J. & S. L. Bonham Antiquarian Booksellers Africa 4/20/2011 - 8264 2011 £60

Henty, George Alfred   1832-1902   *Bonnie Prince Charlie: A Tale of Fontenoy and Culloden.*   London: Blackie & Son,   8vo., pages 384, plus publisher's catalog, illustrations by Gordon Browne, (one loose) brown cloth with pictorial stamping and lettering in black and gilt, donor's presentation on blank, bookplate, front hinge tender, cover scuffed and soiled, otherwise very good, offered with original pen and ink drawing by Browne of the frontispiece, framed under glass, fine.   Second Life Books Inc.   174 - 180   2011 $650

Henty, George Alfred   1832-1902   *St. Bartholomew's Eve.*   London: Blackie and Son,   1894,   First edition; original pictorial dark green cloth, gilt over bevelled boards, pages 384, 32, with 12 illustrations by H. J. Draper and double page map, scattered foxing.   R. F. G. Hollett & Sons Antiquarian Booksellers   170 - 324   2011   £75

Henty, George Alfred   1832-1902   *With Buller in Natal.*   Blackie and Son,   1901,   First edition; original pictorial blue cloth gilt, rather spotted and little worn, pages 384, 32 with 10 illustrations by W. Rainey and a map, little shaken.   R. F. G. Hollett & Sons Antiquarian Booksellers   170 - 325   2011   £45

Henze, Anton   *Contemporary Church Art.*   New York: Sheed & Ward,   1956,   4to., original cloth, gilt, dust jacket, little chipped, pages 128, illustrations, heavy erasure on flyleaf.   R. F. G. Hollett & Son Antiquarian Booksellers   177 - 458   2011   £85

Henze, Anton   *The Pope and the World.*   London: Sidgwick & Jackson,   1965,   first English edition; large 8vo., original cloth, gilt, dust jacket trifle torn, pages (xii), 133, 189 plates and maps on endpapers.   R. F. G. Hollett & Son Antiquarian Booksellers   175 - 618   2011   £30

Henze, Anton   *La Tourette. The Le Corbusier Monastery.*   Lund Humphries,   1963,   First edition; square 8vo., original cloth, gilt, dust jacket, pages 71, with 68 photos, ex-library, usual labels etc. on front endpapers.   R. F. G. Hollett & Son Antiquarian Booksellers   177 - 457   2011   £30

Hephaestion   *Enchiridion de Metris et Poemate.*   Utrecht: Apud Melchior Leonardum Charlois,   1726,   Light spotting, dampmark to upper margin of few leaves, ownership stamp to title ("Noortheij"), pages (iv), 188, (8), 4to., early 20th century marbled paper boards backed in diaper grain purple paper, sunned backstrip lettered in ink vertically over horizontal gilt, paper worn at front joint and extremities, boards scuffed, good.   Blackwell Rare Books   B166 - 46   2011   £125

Hepplewhite, Alice   *The Cabinet Maker and Upholsterer's Guide.*   London: published I. and J. Taylor,   1789,   Second edition; folio, 127 engraved plates on 126 sheets, bound by Albert Oldach & Son in modern full brown morocco.   Heritage Book Shop   Booth A12 51st NY International Antiquarian Book Fair April 8-10 2011 - 66   2011 $7500

Hepworth, George H.   *Through Armenia on Horseback.*   New York: Dutton,   1898,   First edition; cloth, lightly worn at extremities, corners bumped, library stamp inside front cover, interior clean and tight, xii, 355 pages, photos and foldout map.   G. H. Mott Bookseller   May 26 2011 - 43164   2011 $400

Hepworth, J.   *Resist Much, Obey Little - Some Notes on Edward Abbey.*   Salt Lake City: Dream Garden Press,   1985,   First edition; fine, signed by J. Hepworth and Gary Snyder.   Bella Luna Books   May 26 2011 - 6500   2011 $165

Herben, Beatrice   *Jack O'health and Peg O'Joy: a Fairy tale for Children.*   New York: Scribner,   1921,   8vo., pictorial cloth, very good, 10 full page color illustrations by Frederick Richardson.   Aleph-Bet Books, Inc.   95 - 226   2011 $125

Herbert, A. P.   *A Book of Ballads.*   London: Ernest Benn,   1931,   First edition; original blue cloth gilt, spine trifle faded, pages xi, 488, line drawings.   R. F. G. Hollett & Son Antiquarian Booksellers   General Catalogue Summer 2010 - 812   2011   £35

Herbert, A. P.   *Dolphin Square.*   privately printed for Richard Costain,   1933,   First edition; original stiff wrappers, pages (20), line drawings, printed in red and black, very scarce.   R. F. G. Hollett & Son Antiquarian Booksellers   General Catalogue Summer 2010 - 701   2011   £75

Herbert, Edward, Lord   *A Dialogue Between a Tutor and His Pupil.*   London: printed for W. Bathoe,   1768,   First edition; half title, 18th century calf boards with recent reback, light wear to extremities very clean, tight text.   Lupack Rare Books   May 26 2011 - ABE1920736923   2011 $375

Herbert, Frank   *Chapterhouse: Dune.*   New York: Putnam,   1985,   First edition; fine in near fine dust jacket with light wear and tiny closed tear on rear panel.   Bella Luna Books   May 29 2011 - t9571   2011 $110

Herbert, George   *The Clergyman's Instructor or a Collection of Tracts-on, the Ministerial Duties.*   Oxford: Clarendon Press,   1813,   Second edition; old half black calf, gilt with marbled boards, edges rubbed, pages viii, 427, occasional light browning.   R. F. G. Hollett & Son Antiquarian Booksellers   175 - 621   2011   £65

Herbert, George   *A Priest to the Temple.*   London: printed by T. R. for Benj. Tooke,   1675,   Third impression; small 8vo., old milled calf, rebacked in matching calf gilt with raised bands, pages (xxxvi), 166, (lxx), (viii, ads), imprimatur leaf (contemporary signature of A. Macaulay on recto).   R. F. G. Hollett & Son Antiquarian Booksellers   175 - 620   2011   £395

Herbertson, Agnes Crozier *Tony Sees the World.* Philadelphia: Centaur Press, 1936, One of 300 copies; very good, no dust jacket, cloth soiled and corners bumped, endpapers soiled, otherwise clean and tight, photographs. G. H. Mott Bookseller May 26 2011 - 40479 2011 $225

Herd, Richard *Scraps of Poetry. An Essay on Free Trade.* Sedbergh: Miles Turner, n.d. circa, 1900, 12mo., original brown cloth, gilt, pages ix, 95, lovely copy, extremely scarce. R. F. G. Hollett & Son Antiquarian Booksellers 173 - 537 2011 £120

Herford, Oliver *Peter Pan Alphabet.* New York: Scribner, 1907, 4to., cloth backed pictorial boards, slight cover soil, very good, full page illustrations, quite scarce. Aleph-Bet Books, Inc. 95 - 72 2011 $400

Herivel, John *Joseph Fourier: the Man and the Physicist.* Oxford: Clarendon Press, 1975, First edition; 8vo., xii, 350 pages, frontispiece, plates, navy cloth, gilt stamped spine title, dust jacket, near fine, from the Bern Dibner reference library, with Burndy bookplate. Jeff Weber Rare Books 161 - 201 2011 $175

Hermes Trismegistus *Mercurij Trismegisti Pymander, de Potestate et Sapientia del Eiusdem Asclepius...* Basle: colophon: Michael Isingrin August, 1532, Woodcut printer's device on verso of last leaf, some browning, pages 480 (pages 320-39 omitted in pagination), (4), 8vo., contemporary vellum, lettered in ink on spine, small hole in vellum surface on upper cover, contemporary ownership inscription on flyleaf of Niccolo Franco and two later inscriptions, bookplate, good. Blackwell Rare Books B166 - 47 2011 £3000

Hermes, Gertrude *Funeral Service.* London: Piccadilly, 1983, Large 8vo., pages 3, large vignette woodcut by Hermes on front cover, corners trifle creased. R. F. G. Hollett & Son Antiquarian Booksellers General Catalogue Summer 2010 - 813 2011 £50

Herndon, William Lewis *Exploration of the Valley of the Amazon.* Washington: 1854, 4 volumes (2 volumes text and 2 atlas/maps in folding case). the Herndon illustrations clear and legible with foxing to margins, while the Gibbon (P.S. Duval) plates are of a higher caliber; all 4 volumes have recent backstrips and new labels, Gibbon's fore edge front cover worn, the 2 folding maps in the Gibbon atlas very good, one with 3 inch fold tear with the initial map separated at bottom third (and a few other old stresses), 3 maps in the Herndon Atlas very good and crisp. Bookworm & Silverfish 662 - 5 2011 $450

Herodotus *The History of Herodotus.* London: printed for D. Midwinter et al, 1737, Third edition; 2 volumes, 8vo., pages xvi, 447 (xvii) + 3 extending engraved maps, (ii), 430, (xviii), contemporary orangey tan calf boards triple rule gilt bordered with broad dentelle inner border of individual small tools, board edges decorative roll gilt, late 19th century 'swirl' 'made' endpapers with pale green block cloth, inner joint strengtheners, all edges original blue swirl/marbled pale blue and white sewn endbands, early 21st century retrospective reback + corners by Chris Weston, little toning and marginal dust soiling, some marginal pencil notes, old leather chipped at edges, contemporary ink inscription "Eliza Spencer" at head of titlepages, verso of volume I marbled endpaper has ms. note by Rev. John Bourton/Banningham Rectory/Norfolk referring to early provenance of Sunderland Library and subsequent purchase at Puttick & Simpson's auction in 1882, from the collection of Christopher Ernest Weston 1947-2010. Unsworths Booksellers 24 - 109 2011 £400

Herodotus *Herodoti Halicarnassei Historiarum Libri IX.* Oxonii: Sumtibus J. Cooke et J. Parker et J. Payne et J. Mackinlay, Londini, 1808, 2 volumes, 8vo., pages xxx, 409, (i); (ii), 394, (lvi), contemporary russia, four double raised bands spine, broken rule gilt compartments with blind tooled elaborate centre stars composed of small tools and centered with small circles gilt, lettered, numbered, 'placed & dated' direct in gilt, boards dual single rule intersecting gilt bordered with 'facing drawer handle' roll in blind between rules and 'curtain freize' roll in blind innermost, board edges 'broken-hatch' roll gilt at corners, turn-ins "Grecian Key" roll gilt, "French Shell" 'made' endpapers, all edges marbled thus, pale blue and purple double core sewn endbands, pale blue silk page markers, little light foxing, joints rubbed and cracking, top compartment of volume 2 spine defective, contemporary ink inscription "Henricus Riddell Moody e coll. Oriel", from the collection of Christopher Ernest Weston 1947-2010. Unsworths Booksellers 24 - 108 2011 £40

Heron, Roy *Cecil Aldin. The Story of a Sporting Artist.* Webb & Bower, 1981, First edition; original pictorial boards, dust jacket, pages 208, illustrations in color and tints. R. F. G. Hollett & Son Antiquarian Booksellers General Catalogue Summer 2010 - 200 2011 £65

Herrick, Robert 1591-1674 *A Thanksgiving to God for His Little House.* Flemington: St. Teresa's Press, 1971, One of 200 copies (this No. 172); 180 x 130mm., 2 p.l., 10 pages, (2) leaves, publisher's original fern green Strathmore Beau Brilliant mold made paper, paper label on front cover, in sturdy custom made brown linen folding box with gilt titling on upper cover and spine, 8 charming hand tinted illustrations, prospectus laid in at front, mint. Phillip J. Pirages 59 - 309 2011 $95

Herring, Robert 1591-1674 *Adam and Evelyn at Kew or Revolt in the Garden.* London: Elkin Mathews & Marrot, 1930, No. 1048 of 1060 copies; pages 168, untrimmed, 13 full page plates, head and tailpieces and endpapers all in colors, original cloth backed patterned boards, edges little rubbed and top edges faded.   R. F. G. Hollett & Son Antiquarian Booksellers   General Catalogue Summer 2010 - 714   2011   £120

Hertzog, Carl *The Composing Stick a Paint Brush.* Irving: Quoin Press, n.d., 1970, #15 of 150 copies; not paginated (16) pages, signed, original printed wrappers in paper slipcase which shows some soil and glued flaps have come loose, front wrapper has couple of spots probably form aforementioned flaps, otherwise bright and near fine, miniature book, just 3 1/2 x 3 inches, with ALS from Steve Schuster who was The Quoin Press transmitting the book to New Mexico printer, Jack Rittenhouse.   Dumont Maps & Books of the West   112 - 24   2011 $65

Hertzsprung Kapteyn, Henrietta *The Life and Works of J. C. Kaptyn.* Dordrecht: Boston: and London: Kluwer Academic, 1993, 8vo., xix, 92 pages, 14 illustrations, printed boards, fine, from the Bern Dibner reference library, with Burndy bookplate.   Jeff Weber Rare Books   161 - 203   2011 $100

Hervey, Canon G. A. K. *Natural History of the Lake District.* London: Frederick Warne and Co., 1970, First edition; original cloth, gilt, dust jacket, price clipped, bottom of upper hinge little worn, pages ix, 230, with 8 colored plates, 24 in black and white and maps on endpapers.   R. F. G. Hollett & Son Antiquarian Booksellers   173 - 538   2011   £40

Hervey, James *Meditation and Contemplations.* Coventry: M. Luckman, 1792, New edition; 2 volumes in 1, modern half calf, pages clxxxviii, 370, (iv), 2 engraved plates.   R. F. G. Hollett & Son Antiquarian Booksellers   175 - 622   2011   £175

Hervey, James *Reflections on a Flower Garden.* London: Charles Tilt, 1836, Small 8vo., ix, (i), 202 pages + 1 ad leaf, 12 very attractive hand colored plates, very good in bright original cloth, gilt decorated spine.   Ken Spelman Rare Books   68 - 148   2011   £75

Hervey, M. F. S. *Celebrated Musicians of all Nations.* Stanley Lucas Weber & Co., 1883, Folio, original cloth, gilt, corners trifle frayed, pages (ii, preface and index), 40 with 12 tissue guarded sheet of oval portraits, uncommon.   R. F. G. Hollett & Son Antiquarian Booksellers   175 - 623   2011   £75

Hervey, Thomas *The Writer's Time Redeemed and Speaker's Words Recalled...* Kendal: printed by W. Pennington and sold by J. Smith Bradford, J. Matthews... and Alexander Hogg, London, 1779?, First edition; 8vo., frontispiece, (5) v-xviii (1) 92 (4) pages, 4 engraved plates, contemporary annotations in ink in text, bound with approximately 175 pages of ms. dictionaries and indexes, contemporary blind ruled sheep, neatly rebacked and labelled to match (raised bands), gilt label, very good, crisp, originally belonging to Hervey family member, rare.   John Drury Rare Books   153 - 60   2011   £500

Hervey, Thomas K. *The Book of Christmas, Descriptive of the Customs, Ceremonies, Traditions, Superstitions, Fun, Feeling and Festivities of the Christmas Season.* London: William Spooner, 1837, Small 8vo., original blindstamped cloth, spine rather creased and little frayed at head and foot, pages viii, 344, frontispiece title and 34 plates by R. Seymour, printed on thick paper and rather browned in places, mainly margins.   R. F. G. Hollett & Son Antiquarian Booksellers   General Catalogue Summer 2010 - 658   2011   £150

Herzog, Whitey *You're Missing' a Great Game.* Norwalk: Easton Press, 1999, Limited to 1000 copies, this #972, signed by Herzog; full leather, raised bands, gilt lettered all edges gilt, moire endpapers, silk marker ribbon, note about book and certificate of authenticity laid in.   By the Book, L. C.   26 - 73   2011 $125

Hesiod *Works of Hesiod.* London: printed at the Stanhope Press by Whittingham and Rowland, 1811, 2 volumes, small octavo, (4), 136; (4), 138, (2 blank) pages, frontispiece in each volume, full red straight grain morocco, boards ruled in gilt floral pattern, spine stamped and lettered in gilt, drab grey endpapers, edges lightly rubbed, boards slightly soiled, with double fore-edge painting depicting of St. John's College in Cambridge on one side and King's College Chapel in Cambridge on the other, very good, red cloth slipcase.   Heritage Book Shop   Holiday 2010 - 42   2011 $1500

Hesketh, Phoebe *My Aunt Edith.* Preston: Lancashire County Books, 1992, First illustrated edition; original cloth, gilt, dust jacket, pages 186, with 8 pages of illustrations.   R. F. G. Hollett & Son Antiquarian Booksellers   175 - 625   2011   £35

Hesse, Hermann *Magister Ludi.* London: Aldus Publications Limited, 1949, First edition in English; octavo, cloth.   L. W. Currey, Inc.   124 - 106   2011 $750

Hesse, Hermann *Steppenwolf.* London: Martin Secker, 1929, First English edition; 8vo., original publisher's red cloth lettered black on spine, pages 322, very slightly nicked at head of spine, slight rubbing to corners and edges, covers very slightly marked otherwise sound close, very good.   Any Amount of Books   May 29 2011 - A75305   2011 $306

Hesseltine, William B. *The Blue and the Gray on the Nile.* Chicago: 1961, First edition; 290 pages, near fine, endpapers foxed, in very good unclipped dust jacket. Bookworm & Silverfish 678 - 32 2011 $75

Hetherington, William *Branthwaite Hall. And Other Poems.* Carlisle: printed for the author by Charles Turnam, 1837, First edition; pages xii, 192, complete with half title, original pale green front endpapers preserved, mss. corrections in third line of stanza 6, pages 22, and stanza 6 on page 15, may be in author's hand, scarce. R. F. G. Hollett & Son Antiquarian Booksellers 173 - 540 2011 £250

Hetherington, William *Branthwaite Hall, Canto III.* Cockermouth: printed for the author by Daniel Fidler, 1850, First edition; original cloth, paper spine label, little darkened, extremities minimally worn, pages xii, 194, complete with half title, errata slip and blue sugar paper endpapers. R. F. G. Hollett & Son Antiquarian Booksellers 173 - 541 2011 £140

Heuston, R. F. V. *Lives of the Lord Chancellors 1885-1940.* Oxford: Clarendon Press, 1964, First edition; large 8vo., original green buckram gilt, dust jacket little worn and torn, pages xxiii, 632, with 24 plates. R. F. G. Hollett & Son Antiquarian Booksellers 175 - 626 2011 £35

Heward, Constance *Ameliaranne and the Green Umbrella.* London: Harrap, 1927, Original grey boards with pictorial onlay, illustrations in color and black and white, occasional slight finger marking, very good copy of an early issue. R. F. G. Hollett & Sons Antiquarian Booksellers 170 - 513 2011 £85

Heward, Constance *Ameliaranne Camps Out.* London: Harrap, 1945, First edition; original pictorial boards, dust jacket rather worn in places, head of spine defective, illustrations in color and black and white. R. F. G. Hollett & Sons Antiquarian Booksellers 170 - 514 2011 £35

Heward, Constance *Ameliaranne In Town.* London: Harrap, 1930, First edition; original grey boards with pictorial onlay (slight scratches), illustrations in color and black and white, slight browning to flyleaves. R. F. G. Hollett & Sons Antiquarian Booksellers 170 - 516 2011 £120

Heward, Constance *The Twins & Tabiffa.* London: Harrap, 1933, Original pictorial boards, fragile original glassine dust jacket (edges little chipped), illustrations in color and black and white. R. F. G. Hollett & Sons Antiquarian Booksellers 170 - 517 2011 £45

Heward, S. L. *Simple Bible Stories for the Little Ones.* London: Ernest Nister, n.d., 1902, Large 4to., original cloth backed pictorial boards, extremities little worn, chromolithographed in color, text and smaller drawings in sepia, occasional brown spot or small patch. R. F. G. Hollett & Son Antiquarian Booksellers 175 - 628 2011 £85

Hewitt, Graily *Lettering for Students and Craftsmen.* London: Seeley, Service & Co., 1930, First edition; original decorated cloth, few marks, pages 336, (viii), with 403 illustrations, names and address on slightly browned flyleaf, else very good. R. F. G. Hollett & Son Antiquarian Booksellers General Catalogue Summer 2010 - 201 2011 £35

Hewson, J. B. *A History of the Practice of Navigation.* Glasgow: Brown, Son & Ferguson, 1951, First edition; 8vo., vii, 270 pages, illustrations, dark blue cloth, gilt stamped cover and spine titles, dust jacket worn with pieces missing and tape repair, else very good, rare in jacket, Charles Singer's copy with his bookplate, from the Bern Dibner reference library, with Burndy bookplate. Jeff Weber Rare Books 161 - 204 2011 $125

Hexham, Henry *The Principles of the Art Militarie etc. Parts I-III.* London: M. P(arsons) for M. Symons; Delft: Jan Peterson Waelpte, 1637, London: R Young, 1639. The Hague: F. vander Spruyt, 1640. First, second and First editions; 3 parts in 1 volume, folio, engraved illustrations, engraved volvelles, engraved plates, contemporary red morocco gilt, narrow roll borders, central cartouche formed of sprays of olive, spine gilt in compartments, gilt edges, small hole in text of dedication (paper flaw), tear in pages 15-16 of part I, lacks ties, tear from paper flaw across the top corner of page 19/20 in appendix to part 1, from the library of the Earls of Macclesfield at Shirburn Castle. Maggs Bros. Ltd. 1440 - 111 2011 £10,000

Heyerdahl, Thor *Aku-Aku. the Secret of Easter island.* London: Allen & Unwin, 1958, First UK edition; original cloth, dust jacket (head os spine trifle creased), pages 368, with 58 illustrations, 6 maps and drawings. R. F. G. Hollett & Son Antiquarian Booksellers General Catalogue Summer 2010 - 1644 2011 £35

Heylyn, Peter 1600-1662 *A Help to English History, Containing a Succession of all the Kings of England...* T. Basset and C. Wilkinson, 1680, Armorial and heraldic woodcut throughout, tear to titlepage and Z5, repaired ink ownership signature, manuscript index at end, pages 8, 634, 12mo., contemporary calf, rebacked, gilt lettering to spine, good. Blackwell Rare Books B166 - 48 2011 £180

Heywood, Thomas *The Life of Merlin surnamed Ambrosius.* Carmarthen, 1812, First edition; viii, 324 pages, original boards, rebacked, very good. C. P. Hyland May 26 2011 - 255/298 2011 $544

Hi-Ho Story Box. Akron: Saalfield, circa, 1942, 4 books, Little Black Sambo - Mother Goose - One Happy Day - Baby Animal Stories 9 1/4 x 10 1/4 inches, each book has pictorial wrapper duplicating covers, illustrations by Florence White Williams, Eleanor March, Fern Bisel Peat, Larua Scott and Diana Thorne, rare. Aleph-Bet Books, Inc. 95 - 63 2011 $1250

Hiaasen, Carl *Lucky You.* New Orleans: B. E. Trice, 1997, Limited edition, of a total edition of 176 copies, this one of 26 lettered copies; signed by author, fine in fine slipcase.   Ken Lopez Bookseller   154 - 76   2011 $350

Hiaasen, Carl *Skin Tight.* New York: Putnam, 1989, First edition; fine, dust jacket fine, signed by author.   Bella Luna Books   May 29 2011 - 4302   2011 $110

Hiaasen, Carl *What Dead, Again?* Baton Rouge: Legacy Pub., 1979, First edition; very good, minor offsetting to front endpapers from flap, bump at rear gutter, dust jacket very good, very small closed tears on bottom edge, light soiling, signed by author, very good, several small closed tears on bottom edge, light soiling.   Bella Luna Books   May 26 2011 - t5941   2011 $165

Hibbard, J. R. *Necromancy, or Pseudo Spiritualism, Viewed in the Light of the Sacred Scriptures and the Teachings of the New (Jerusalem) Church.* Chicago: Whitmarsh, Fulton & Co., 1833, First edition; 8vo., 35 pages, original printed wrappers, rare.   M & S Rare Books, Inc.   90 - 75   2011 $200

Hibi, Yuichi *Imprint.* Tucson: Nazareli Press, 2005, First edition, deluxe limited edition of 25 copies; 79 duotone plates, very fine in dust jacket and very near fine cloth clamshell box that has small bump to top of spine, both book and photos signed by Hibi.   Jeff Hirsch Books   ny 2010 2011 $750

Hic-et-Hoc ou l'Eleve des R. R. P.P. Jesuites d'Avignon. Orne de Figures. Berlin: 1798, First edition; 2 volumes in one, 18mo., pages 146, 137, 4 engravings, full deep green long grain morocco, gilt decorated and lettered on spine, within compartments, wine red silk endpapers, , top edge gilt, others untrimmed, printed on blue tinted handmade paper, fine, in attractive and apposite binding (late 19th century), rare.   Simon Finch Rare Books   Zero - 420   2011   £4500

Hickey, Dave *The Works of Edward Ruscha.* New York: Hudson Hills/San Francisco: San Francisco Museum of Modern Art, 1982, First edition; small 4to., 182 pages, near fine in fine dust jacket.   By the Book, L. C.   26 - 45   2011 $300

Hicks, David *David Hicks on Decoration 5.* London: Britwell Books, 1972, First edition; 4to., pages 168, copiously illustrated in color and black and white, fine in near fine dust jacket with very slight creasing, excellent.   Any Amount of Books   May 29 2011 - A67452   2011 $246

Hiemer, Ernst *Der Giftpilz. (The Poisoned Mushroom).* Nurnberg: Sturmer, 1938,   4to., cloth and pictorial boards, some internal margin soil, slight spine wear, very good+, illustrations in full color by Fips.   Aleph-Bet Books, Inc.   95 - 386   2011 $3750

Higginson, Thomas Wentworth *Tales of the Enchanted Islands of the Atlantic.* New York: 1898, 1898, First edition; xv, 259, (2) pages, very good, cover medallion bright, cover gilt bright, foxing to endpapers, smudge bottom of backstrip.   Bookworm & Silverfish   668 - 167   2011 $60

High, James L. *A Treatise on the Law of Junctions.* Chicago: 1880,   Over 1200 pages, 2 volumes, very good in old law calf.   Bookworm & Silverfish   669 - 107   2011 $200

Highsmith, Patricia *Deep Water.* New York: Harper & Brothers, 1957, First edition; fine in dust jacket with light wear to spine ends, small closed tear to top edge of rear panel, couple of small stains to back panel.   Buckingham Books   May 26 2011 - 24571   2011 $2500

Highsmith, Patricia *The Price of Salt.* New York: Coward McCann Inc., 1953, First edition; fine, bright copy in dust jacket with light professional restoration to spine ends, corners and extremities, lovely copy.   Buckingham Books   May 26 2011 - 27091   2011 $4750

Highsmith, Patricia *Strangers on a Train.* London: Cresset Press, 1950, First UK edition; publisher's file copy with slip affixed to front flyleaf, near fine in dust jacket with some light professional restoration to spine ends and corners, exceptional copy.   Buckingham Books   May 26 2011 - 26687   2011 $3750

Highsmith, Patricia *The Talented Mr. Ripley.* New York: Coward McCann Inc., 1955, First edition; some light offsetting to front and rear endpapers, else near fine, tight copy in dust jacket, lightly sunned on spine and with light professional restoration to spine ends and corners.   Buckingham Books   May 26 2011 - 28615   2011 $3750

Hilbersheimer, L. *The Nature of Cities: Origin, Growth and Decline: Pattern and Form: Planning Problems.* Chicago: Paul Theobald, 1955, First edition; quarto, 286 pages, profusely illustrated, endpapers faintly browned, fine in fine dust jacket, slightly faded at spine.   Peter Ellis   May 26 2011 - ARCHITEC010638   2011 $125

Hilfstein, Erna *Science and History: Studies in Honor of Edward Reisen.* Wrocaw: Polish Academy of Sciences Press, 1978, xvi, 80., 353 pages, illustrations, maroon cloth, black and gilt stamped cover and spine titles, dust jacket lightly worn, very good, from the Bern Dibner reference library, with Burndy bookplate.   Jeff Weber Rare Books   161 - 205   2011 $100

Hill, Geoffrey *The Orchards of Syon.* Penguin Books, 2002, First edition; pages (viii), 75, 13 (blanks), foolscap 8vo., original printed white wrappers, fine, inscribed by author.   Blackwell Rare Books   B166 - 165   2011   £40

Hill, Ira *An Abstract of a New Theory of the formation of the Earth.* Baltimore: N. G. Maxwell, 1823, First edition; 12mo., 211 pages, original printed boards, slight soiling, but very fine, uncut, text foxed. M & S Rare Books, Inc. 90 - 162 2011 $400

Hill, M. F. *Permanent Way: the story of the Kenya and Uganda Railway.* Nairobi: East African Railways, 1949, First edition; 2 volumes, quarto, pages xii, 582; xii, 295, numerous maps and illustrations, original green cloth, dust jackets, some slight wear to jacket volume i. J. & S. L. Bonham Antiquarian Booksellers Africa 4/20/2011 - 5641 2011 £160

Hill, Octavia *Homes of the London Poor.* New York: State Charities Aid Association, 1875, First separate edition, first issue; pages 78, original printed wrappers, rather dusty, spine stripped and chipped, corners worn. R. F. G. Hollett & Son Antiquarian Booksellers 175 - 631 2011 £150

Hill, Weldon *One of the Casualties.* New York: Doubleday & Co., 1964, First edition; 8vo., pages 352, fine in near fine dust jacket, rear panel very slightly rubbed and very slightly soiled, sharp copy. Any Amount of Books May 29 2011 - B25399 2011 $204

Hillenbrand, Laura *Seabiscuit.* New York: Random House, 2001, First edition; near fine, light bumping to spine ends, dust jacket near fine, light wear to top corners, first state of jacket, inside back flap does not promote the Random House Audio Book, back panel lists "advance praise" reviews in correct order: Ambrose, Nack, Beyer, Rosenbaum, second bar code reads 52495, front cover does not mention title as being a NY Times bestseller. Bella Luna Books May 26 2011 - t6328 2011 $275

Hillerman, Tony *Buster Mesquite's Cowboy Band.* Gallup: Buffalo Medicine Books, 2001, First edition; illustrations by Ernest Franklin, fine in fine dust jacket, signed by author and artist. Bella Luna Books May 29 2011 - p2772 2011 $88

Hillerman, Tony *Dance Hall of the Dead.* New York: Harper & Row, 1973, First edition; correct numerical sequence appears at bottom of page 168, signed by author on titlepage, laid in is Hillerman's business card from the University of New Mexico which is printed "Tony Hillerman, Assistant to the President" along with telephone number, campus address, etc., fine in dust jacket, exceptional copy. Buckingham Books May 26 2011 - 28626 2011 $2750

Hillerman, Tony *Rio Grande.* Portland: Belding, 1995, First edition; photos by Robert Reynolds, fine in near fine dust jacket, price clipped, very faint moisture stains on rear panel, crease on inside front flap, nice, bright copy. Bella Luna Books May 29 2011 - t4558a 2011 $82

Hillerman, Tony *Sacred Clowns.* New York: Harper Collins, 1993, Limited to 500 copies; fine, signed by author, in illustrated box. Bella Luna Books May 29 2011 - j1114 2011 $82

Hillerman, Tony *The Shape Shifter.* New York: Harper Collins, 2006, First edition; fine in fine dust jacket, signed. Bella Luna Books May 29 2011 - t8227 2011 $82

Hillerman, Tony *Skinwalkers.* New York: Harper & Row, 1986, First edition; fine in fine dust jacket. Bella Luna Books May 29 2011 - t7987 2011 $82

Hillerman, Tony *Talking Mysteries.* Albuquerque: University of New Mexico, 1991, First edition; illustrations by Ernest Franklin, fine, dust jacket fine, with sketch by Franklin on titlepage, this copy signed by Hillerman, Bulow and Franklin. Bella Luna Books May 29 2011 - 2320 2011 $137

Hillerman, Tony *A Thief of Time.* New York: Harper & Row, 1988, First edition; near fine, previous owner's name on front free endpapers, dust jacket fine, signed by author. Bella Luna Books May 29 2011 - t2314 2011 $82

Hills, John Waller *River Keeper.* Ashburton: Flyfisher's Classic Library, 1998, Limited edition, no. 228 of 950 copies; full navy blue morocco gilt, slipcase, pages viii, 175, top edge gilt, with 16 plates, marbled endpapers and silk marker, fine. R. F. G. Hollett & Son Antiquarian Booksellers General Catalogue Summer 2010 - 1253 2011 £65

Hills, Richard Leslie *Power from Steam: a History of the Stationary Steam Engine.* Cambridge: New York: Cambridge University Press, 1989, First edition; 8vo., xv, 338 pages, 80 figures, black cloth, gilt stamped spine title, dust jacket, fine, rare, from the Bern Dibner reference library, with Burndy bookplate. Jeff Weber Rare Books 161 - 206 2011 $150

Hilton, James *Catherine Herself.* London: T. Fisher Unwin, 1920, First edition; signed by author, very scarce, endpapers little toned, light wear on boards, very good, without rare dust jacket. Between the Covers 169 - BTC347538 2011 $2000

Hilton, James *Contango.* London: Ernest Benn, 1932, First edition; fine in very good or better, spine faded dust jacket with modest chip at crown, signed by author, very scarce. Between the Covers 169 - BTC347276 2011 $1000

Hilton, James *Storm Passage.* London: T. Fisher Unwin, 1922, First edition; owner's neat bookshop names on front fly, slight puckering to cloth, else near fine, lacking rare dust jacket, very scarce. Between the Covers 169 - BTC347278 2011 $675

Hinchcliffe, Edgar *Appleby Grammar School - From Chantry to Comprehensive.* Appleby: J. Whitehead & Son, 1974, First edition; original cloth, gilt, dust jacket (price clipped), pages 151, 8 plates. R. F. G. Hollett & Son Antiquarian Booksellers 173 - 548 2011 £50

Hinde, S. L. *The Last of the Masai.* London: Heinemann, 1901, First edition; quarto, pages xix, 180, frontispiece, color plate, illustrations, original green decorative cloth, vignette on upper cover and spine, Mudies library label, cloth faded, corners bumped, internally good, clean copy. J. & S. L. Bonham Antiquarian Booksellers Africa 4/20/2011 - 3779 2011 £240

Hindle, Brooke *David Rittenhouse.* Princeton: Princeton University Press, 1964, First edition; 8vo., xiii, 394 pages, title illustration, plates, charcoal cloth, gilt stamped blue spine label, dust jacket, near fine, from the Bern Dibner reference library, with Burndy bookplate. Jeff Weber Rare Books 161 - 207 2011 $75

Hindley, Charles *The History of the Catnach Press at Berwick Upon Tweed, Alnwick Newcastle Upon Tune and Seven Dials.* London: 1887, Second edition; 308 pages, illustrations, tan buckram with printed title labels, tipped in is excellent ALS in which Hindley discusses Catnach, Bewick cuts for the book, et al, very good, light wear, some spine tanning, small chip to spine label, inscribed by author. Lupack Rare Books May 26 2011 - ABE1269953393 2011 $300

Hindley, Charles *The True History of Tom and Jerry or the Day and Night Scenes of Life in Lond from the Start to the Finish!* London: Charles Hindley, 1890, Uncut, illustrated half title, illustrations, original blue boards, cream paper spine, decorated in black, lettered in gilt, slightly damp marked at spine, lettering slightly faded, otherwise very nice. Jarndyce Antiquarian Booksellers CXCI - 351 2011 £68

Hinds, James Pitcarin *Bibliotheca Jacksoniana.* Kendal: Titus Wilson, 1909, Limited edition; #76; pages viii, 199, flyleaves little browned, others fine, original brown cloth gilt, tall 8vo. R. F. G. Hollett & Son Antiquarian Booksellers General Catalogue Summer 2010 - 424 2011 £85

Hinds, John *The Veterinary Surgeon or Farriery Taught on a New and Easy Plan.* Philadelphia: 1833, xiv 224, (2) pages, 4 plates (first in facsimile) as required, later half cloth, marbled boards and new endpapers and label, text well read. Bookworm & Silverfish 666 - 160 2011 $25

Hine, Darlene Clark *Black Women in United States History.* Brooklyn: Carlson Publishing, 1990, First edition; 8vo., publisher's red cloth, fine set. Second Life Books Inc. 174 - 181 2011 $500

Hine, Joseph *One Hundred Original Tales for Children.* Souter and Law, 1846, First edition; wood engravings, original blindstamped cloth gilt, little rubbed and neatly recased, pages xvi, 324, with 45 text woodcuts, one leaf torn and repaired. R. F. G. Hollett & Sons Antiquarian Booksellers 170 - 328 2011 £95

Hinton, J. O. *Organ Construction.* London: Weekes & Co., 1902, Second edition; 4to., original cloth, gilt, worn at top and base of spine, top of lower hinge split corners bumped, pages 200, frontispiece, 17 plates, several signatures on front free endpaper. R. F. G. Hollett & Son Antiquarian Booksellers 175 - 633 2011 £55

Hinton, James *Life in Nature.* New York: Lincoln MacVeagh/The Dial Press, 1931, First edition; presumably later pencil ownership signature, boards little soiled, very good in good or better dust jacket with couple of small external tape repairs, some faint stains, neatly tipped ot half title is one page ALS from editor, Havelock Ellis to publisher Lincoln MacVeagh returning the proofs for this book (no present), questioning some of the author's premises and inquiring when the book will be released, letter near fine. Between the Covers 169 - BTC335143 2011 $500

Hiroe, Minosuke *Orchid Flowers.* Kyoto: Kyoto-Shoin Co., 1971, First edition; 100 exquisite color photos on fine art paper, folio, red rexine with gilt lettering, upper corners lightly bumped, otherwise fine, publisher's navy cloth slipcase (fine) with gilt lettering, contained in publisher's decorated cardboard shipping carton, text in Japanese and English, exceedingly rare. Raymond M. Sutton, Jr. May 26 2011 - 47540 2011 $5000

Hirsch, Johann Christoph *Bibliotheca Numismatica Exhibens Catalogum Acutorum qui de re Monteraria et Numis tam Antiques quam Recentiorbus Scripsere, Collectra et Indice Rerum Instructa.* Nurenberg: impens Hered, Felseckeri,, 1760, First edition; folio, large engraving on titlepage of interior of rather grand library, (8), 232, (2) pages, including half title and final errata leaf, contemporary German half calf over marbled boards, spine gilt with raised bands, red morocco label lettered in gilt, red edges with just little wear to extremities, else very good. John Drury Rare Books 153 - 61 2011 £500

Hirschfelder, J. O. *The Effects of Atomic Weapons.* Washington: Combat Forces Press, 1950, First edition; slight wear at spine ends, else near fine in fair dust jacket, lacking top inch or so to spine and split at spine fold, Arthur S. Wightman's copy with his ownership signature. Between the Covers 169 - BTC340930 2011 $475

Hirsh, Richard F. *Power Loss: The Origins of Deregulation and Restructuring in the American Electric Utility System.* Cambridge and London: MIT Press, 1999, First edition; 8vo., x 406 pages, illustrations, tables, quarter yellow cloth over beige cloth sides, silver stamped spine title, dust jacket, fine, from the Bern Dibner reference library, with Burndy bookplate. Jeff Weber Rare Books 161 - 208 2011 $165

Hirtenstein, S. A. *Journal of the Muhyddin Ibn 'Arabic Society 1982-2006.* Oxford: Muhyiddin Ibn 'Arabi Society, 1982-2006, First edition; 40 issues, 8vo., wrappers, volume I 1982 to volume 40 2006, missing volume 21 (196/97), circa 4000 pages in all, alll very good+. Any Amount of Books May 26 2011 - A47864 2011 $503

Historical Collections or a Brief Account of the Most Remarkable Transactions of the two Last Parliaments Held and Dissolved at Westminster and Oxford. printed for Simon Neale, 1681, First edition; modern half calf gilt, raised bands, spine label, pages (iv), 302, frontispiece little cropped at foot, running heads in black letter, title rather rubbed. R. F. G. Hollett & Son Antiquarian Booksellers 175 - 634 2011 £150

History of British Educational Theory 1750-1850. London: Thoemmes Press, 2002, reprint; 8vo., 11 volumes, pages 3881, about fine, green hardbacks. Any Amount of Books May 26 2011 - A16285 2011 $419

The History of England from the Conquest to the Death of George II. London: John Wallis, 1800, Tall 24mo., 64 pages, original gray paper on boards, blue printed title label on upper cover, allegorical full page copper engraved frontispiece, plus 31 wood engraved portraits, all crudely hand colored by childish hand, small color spot at two pages, cover soiled, rebacked, very good, rare. Hobbyhorse Books 56 - 84 2011 $120

History of John Gilpin. New York: McLoughlin Bros. n.d. circa, 1860, 12mo., 8 pages + 1 page list on lower wrapper, pictorial pink paper wrappers, decorative, 8 very fine half page hand colored wood engravings, repaired small split at lower part of spine and one page, light spotting along edges of leaves, wrappers lightly dusted, very scarce, very good. Hobbyhorse Books 56 - 100 2011 $325

The History of King William the Third. London: printed for A. Roper, 1703, Second edition; 3 volumes, soundly rebound in modern grey cloth lettered gilt at spine, pages (xx) 1599, 9 illustrations, ex-Foreign and Commonwealth Office library with their label and stamps lightly applied, very good. Any Amount of Books May 29 2011 - A61250 2011 $306

History of Little Tom Tucker. London: printed for the Booksellers, n.d. circa, 1820, 12mo., * + 1 page list on lower wrapper, yellow pictorial paper wrappers, 8 wood engravings, some colored by juvenile hand, from the collection of Marjorie Moon, top edges of pages crudely opened and repaired, good copy. Hobbyhorse Books 56 - 85 2011 $190

The History of Muhammedanism... London: Black, Parbury and Allen, 1817, First edition; 8vo., pages xix, 409, ex-Foreign and Commonwealth Office library with label and stamps (lightly applied), inner hinges reinforced with tape, otherwise very good. Any Amount of Books May 29 2011 - A47940 2011 $272

The History of Origins. London: Sampson Low, 1824, First edition; pages (vi), 244, small 8vo., modern half morocco. R. F. G. Hollett & Son Antiquarian Booksellers 175 - 35 2011 £85

The History of Prince Lee Boo, a Native of the Pelew Islands. London: John Harris, 1832, 12mo., 144 pages, marbled paper on boards, black roan spine with gilt title and fillets, very fine full page copper engraved frontispiece, frontispiece lightly spotted, rubbing at edges of covers, rounded corners, very good. Hobbyhorse Books 56 - 86 2011 $170

The History of Ripon, Comprehending a Civil and Ecclesiastical Account of that Ancient Borough. York: W. Farrer, 1801, Foolscap 8vo., 280 pages + index + errata leaf, very good, uncut and unpressed copy bound in recent quarter calf, marbled boards. Ken Spelman Rare Books 68 - 186 2011 £95

The History of Southern & Central Africa: Its Topography, Geography, Natural Productions. London: Adam & Co., n.d., 1876, First edition; large quarto pages x, 948, colored frontispiece and titlepage, 27 tinted lithographs, light browning to margins of colored plates, all edges gilt, rebound in brown half morocco, very good. J. & S. L. Bonham Antiquarian Booksellers Africa 4/20/2011 - 8755 2011 £150

The History of Southern & Central Africa: Its Topography, Geography, Natural Productions. London: Adam & Co. n.d., 1876, First edition; large quarto, pages x, 948, color frontispiece and titlepage, 27 tinted lithographs, original full black decorative morocco, all edges gilt, gilt decorations on cover, joints slightly rubbed, very good. J. & S. L. Bonham Antiquarian Booksellers Africa 4/20/2011 - 9171 2011 £220

The History of the Abbey, Palace and Chapel-Royal of Holyroodhouse. Edinburgh: J. Hay and Co. for Mrs. John Petrie, 1819, 8vo., pages iv (5)-124 + engraved titlepage and 8 engraved plates, publisher's beige sugar paper covered board, front shewing engraved architectural doorway and titled within, fragmentary remains only of plain sugar paper spine, foxed and spotted, boards soiled, spine paper defective, ink inscription "Mrs. Leveson Douglas Stewart" at head of printed titlepage, earlier ink inscription "Geo. Stewart", from the collection of Christopher Ernest Weston 1947-2010. Unsworths Booksellers 24 - 61 2011 £75

The History of the House that Jack Built. London: Houlston & Son, n.d. circa, 1820, 24mo., pictorial wrappers, 14 pages + 1 page ads, fine,. Aleph-Bet Books, Inc. 95 - 291 2011 $350

A History of the Isle of Anglesey from Its First Invasion by the Romans Until Finally Acceded to the Crown of England Serving as a Supplement to Rowland's Mona Antiqua Restaurata to Which are Added Memoirs of Owen Glendower. London: Dodsley, 1775, First edition; 4to., viii, 88 pages, half title present, recent navy blue half leather with marbled boards, lettered gilt at spine with 5 raised bands, very good, few spots of foxing at prelims, otherwise text generally very clean. Any Amount of Books May 26 2011 - A69883 2011 $461

The History of the Seven Wise Masters of Rome. Hudson: Ashbel Stoddard, 1805, 12mo., 106 pages, original pictorial paper on wood boards with leather spine, protected in custom made acid free phase box with title label, all printed on provincial handmade blue-gray paper, corner of boards chipped and split, soiled and chipped paper on covers is printed in black with woodcut panels, cover worn, text in fine state, very rare. Hobbyhorse Books 56 - 87 2011 $250

History of the Seventh Field Artillery (First Division (A.E.F.) World War 1917-1919. New York: 1929, 257 pages, near fine, foldout maps. Bookworm & Silverfish 667 - 204 2011 $100

The History of Whittington and His Cat: How from a Poor Country Boy, Destitute of Parents or Relations, He Attained Great Riches... York: J. Kendrew, n.d. circa, 1815, 24mo., 31, 1 page book list on lower wrapper, decorative cream paper wrappers, full page woodcut frontispiece, frontispiece and last page pasted down on wrappers, mint state. Hobbyhorse Books 56 - 22 2011 $170

Hitchcock, Henry Russell *Architecture.* Penguin Books, 1958, First edition; small 4to., original cloth, gilt, with leather spine label, slight mark to upper board, pages xxix, 498, 197 plates, piece cut from flyleaf. R. F. G. Hollett & Son Antiquarian Booksellers 177 - 461 2011 £45

Hitler, Adolf *Mein Kampf.* Munich: Franz Eher, 1925-1927, First edition; 2 octavo volumes, original white vellum with yapp edges,. Heritage Book Shop Booth A12 51st NY International Antiquarian Book Fair April 8-10 2011 - 67 2011 $12,500

Hittell, John S. *Yosemite: Its Wonders and Its Beauties.* San Francisco: H. H. Bancroft and Co., 1868, First edition; 12mo., 20 original mounted black and white photos, scarce double page lithographed map, publisher's original green cloth over beveled boards. Heritage Book Shop Booth A12 51st NY International Antiquarian Book Fair April 8-10 2011 - 68 2011 $32,500

Hittorff, J. J. *Les Antiquites Inedites de L'Attique, Les Restes d'Architecture D'Eleusis De Rhammus, De Sunium et De Thoricus.* Paris: Firmin Didot, 1832, Fair, plates by E. Oliver in satisfactory condition, some spotting, binding falling apart, small folio. G. H. Mott Bookseller May 26 2011 - 43794 2011 $2000

Hoare & Co. *Hoare' Bank. A Record 1673-1932.* privately published, 1932, Large 8vo., original cloth, gilt, dust jacket little rubbed and darkened, few short edge tears, pages xi, 88, 33 illustrations, genealogical table, TLS from H. P. R. Hoare to E. A. Jones, presentation copy presented by Bank to Jones. R. F. G. Hollett & Son Antiquarian Booksellers 175 - 636 2011 £40

Hoare, Clement *A Practical Treatise on the Cultivation of the Grape Vine on Open Walls.* London: Longman, Rees, Orme, Brown, Green and Longman; Chichester: Mason and Son, 1835, First edition; 223 x 142mm., 164 pages, original publisher's muslin backed paper boards, original paper spine label, edges untrimmed, text with several drawings of vines, rear pastedown with penned notes in contemporaneous hand; 2 leaves with marginal paper repair; corners and edges somewhat worn (as expected), boards bit soiled, tiny snag at top of front joint, paper spine label little darkened, one gathering with very small wax spot on each page, hint of foxing or yellowing here and there, still quite fine, fragile temporary binding remarkably solid and very appealing as a result, text unusually clean, fresh and bright. Phillip J. Pirages 59 - 349 2011 $550

Hoare, Nicholas *The Life and Adventures of Toby, The Sapient Pig: with His Opinions on Men and Manners.* London: Nicholas Hoare, proprietor & teacher of Toby, circa, 1817?, Frontispiece, little creased, 25 pages, disbound. Jarndyce Antiquarian Booksellers CXCI - 203 2011 £350

Hoatson, A. *Merry Words for Merry Children.* London & New York: W. Hagelberg, n.d. circa, 1890, Oblong 16mo., stiff pictorial card covers, as new in original pictorial dust jacket, 11 full page chromolithographs and one full page drawing in brown line. Aleph-Bet Books, Inc. 95 - 566 2011 $450

Hoban, Russell *Bedtime for Frances.* New York: Harper Brothers, 1960, First edition (correct price and no ads for later titles); 4to., cloth backed pictorial boards, fine in dust jacket with half inch strip off rear top edge and smaller chips of spine, illustrations by Garth Williams, quite scarce. Aleph-Bet Books, Inc. 95 - 590 2011 $325

Hobart, Garret A. Mrs. *Memories.* Carroll Hall: 1930, First edition; 89 pages, full blue leather, near fine, fore edges not trimmed, signed by author. Bookworm & Silverfish 678 - 188 2011 $87

Hobbs, Anne Stevenson *Beatrix Potter's Art. Paintings and Drawings.* London: Warne, 1989, First edition; 4to., original cloth, gilt, dust jacket, pages 192, illustrations in color, related ephemera loosely inserted. R. F. G. Hollett & Son Antiquarian Booksellers 173 - 555 2011 £45

Hobbs, Derek *Bewick's Footsteps.* Newbiggin-by-the-Sea: Rossleigh Music, 1995, First limited edition (500 copies); oblong 8vo., original wrappers, pages 54, illustrations, engravings by Iain Bain. R. F. G. Hollett & Son Antiquarian Booksellers 175 - 637 2011 £30

Hobhouse, Hermione *County Hall. Survey of London Monograph 17.* London: Athlone Press for the RCHME, 1991, First edition; 4to., original cloth, gilt, dust jacket, pages xviii, 151, 48 (plates) with 51 text figures and 2 large extending drawings. R. F. G. Hollett & Son Antiquarian Booksellers 177 - 462 2011 £40

Hodgdon, Frank W. *A Description of Some of the Most Recent Works Executed and in Progress at the Port of Boston, Massachusetts.* Brussels: 1905, 7 pages, 2 folding plates, wrappers, very good. Bookworm & Silverfish 671 - 108 2011 $75

Hodge, Edmund W. *Enjoying the Lakes from Post Chaise to National Park.* Oliver & Boyd, 1957, First edition; pages x, 221, with 32 illustrations, original cloth, dust jacket, maps. R. F. G. Hollett & Son Antiquarian Booksellers 173 - 555 2011 £45

Hodge, Frederick W. *Handbook of American Indians North of Mexico in Two Parts.* Washington: 1907, 1912. Volume 2 is second impression; 2 volumes, nearly 2300 pages, heavy text weight necessitated regluing to volume I, in BAE green cloth with mild yellowish foxing, not easily seen n backstrips. Bookworm & Silverfish 676 - 142 2011 $165

Hodges, C. Walter *Shakespeare's Second Globe.* Oxford University Press, 1973, First edition; 4to., original cloth, gilt, dust jacket, pages 100, 38 illustrations. R. F. G. Hollett & Son Antiquarian Booksellers 175 - 638 2011 £35

Hodges, C. Walter *Shakespeare's Second Globe. The Missing Monument.* Oxford: University Press, 1973, First edition; 4to., original cloth, gilt, dust jacket, pages 100, 38 illustrations. R. F. G. Hollett & Son Antiquarian Booksellers 177 - 463 2011 £35

Hodges, Charles Du Bois *In Search of Young Beauty.* New York: 1968, Third printing; (221) pages, 4to., near fine in dust jacket with chips, tear and creases at top quarter. Bookworm & Silverfish 679 - 155 2011 $95

Hodgkin, Lucy Violet *A Book of Quaker Saints.* Edinburgh: T. N. Foulis, 1918, Second issue; original buckram, pages xiii, 548, uncut, 7 tipped in color plates by F. Cayley Robinson, additional plate of "Fierce Feathers" from original dust jacket loosely inserted, few light spots to endpapers, otherwise fine, bright copy. R. F. G. Hollett & Son Antiquarian Booksellers 175 - 640 2011 £75

Hodgson, Henry *A Bibliography of the History and Topography of Cumberland and Westmorland.* Carlisle: The Record Office, 1968, First edition; large 8vo., original cloth, plain dust jacket (little chipped), pages 301. R. F. G. Hollett & Son Antiquarian Booksellers 173 - 557 2011 £45

Hodgson, J. F. *The Churches of Austin Canons.* Exeter: printed by William Pollard & Co., 1887, Pages 42, 186, contemporary half calf gilt with raised bands and contrasting spine labels little rubbed, scarce. R. F. G. Hollett & Son Antiquarian Booksellers 177 - 464 2011 £75

Hodgson, John *A Topographical and Historical Description of the County of Westmoreland.* printed for Sherwood, Neely and Jones and George Cowie and Co., 1820, Reprint; original publisher's cloth, paper spine label, little rubbed, pages (ii), 245, (vi, index), untrimmed, complete with folding map and engraved title, both little spotted and 6 engraved plates (bound in at end, some upside down, very good. R. F. G. Hollett & Son Antiquarian Booksellers 173 - 558 2011 £140

Hodgson, William *Flora of Cumberland.* Carlisle: W. Meals and Co., 1898, First edition; original green cloth gilt, pages xxvi, 398, geological map. R. F. G. Hollett & Son Antiquarian Booksellers 173 - 561 2011 £85

Hodgson, William Hope *Deep Waters.* Sauk City: Arkham House, 1967, First edition; octavo, cloth. L. W. Currey, Inc. 124 - 223 2011 $125

Hodgson, William Hope *The Ghost Pirates.* London: Stanley Paul, 1909, First edition; 8vo., 276 pages, 12 pages publisher's ads, frontispiece, first state binding, preferred original publisher's red cloth lettered gilt on spine and on front cover, some rubbing at corners, hinges and spine ends, light wear, some light fading at spine, slight marks and darkening on rear board, good, sound used copy with clean text.   Any Amount of Books   May 26 2011 - A73445   2011 $1845

Hodgson, William Hope *The Night Land: a Love Tale.* London: Eveleigh Nash, 1912, First edition; Octavo, pages (i-vi) vii (viii) ix (x) 11-583 (584, printer's imprint) + (16) page undated publisher's catalog inserted at rear, original red cloth, front panel stamped in gold and ruled in blind, spine panel stamped in gold, rear panel ruled in blind.   L. W. Currey, Inc.   124 - 10   2011 $4250

Hodson, Arnold W. *Trekking the Great Thirst.* London: T. Fisher Unwin, 1913, Second edition; 8vo., pages 359, folding maps, illustrations, original green decorative cloth, very good, mounted inscription for Beatrice with author's compliments in memory of Wengen 1923.   J. & S. L. Bonham Antiquarian Booksellers   Africa 4/20/2011 - 8475   2011   £220

Hodson, Arnold W. *Trekking the Great Thirst: Travel and Sport in the Kalahari Desert.* London: T. Fisher Unwin, 1913, Second edition; 8vo., pages 359, folding maps, illustrations, original green decorative cloth, very good.   J. & S. L. Bonham Antiquarian Booksellers   Africa 4/20/2011 - 7396   2011   £200

Hodson, W. S. R. *Twelve Years of a Soldier's Life in India; Being extracts from the letters of Major...* London: John W. Parker and Son, 1859, First edition; 8vo., original publisher's light brick red textured cloth lettered gilt at spine and blind patterned on covers, pages xvi, 365, with 8 page publisher's catalog at rear, frontispiece, slight rubbing, slight shelfwear, prelims slightly foxed, otherwise sound clean, very good uncommon first edition.   Any Amount of Books   May 29 2011 - A49305   2011 $221

Hoe, Richard M. *The Literature of Printing. A Catalogue of the Library Illustrative of the History and Art of Topography, Chalcography and Lithography of Richard M. Hoe.* London: 1877, (4), 149, (2) pages, frontispiece, contemporary cloth, decorated endpapers, front inner hinge open, crown of spine (quarter inch) torn off, presentation copy inscribed by Hoe to his cousin, Samuel J. Barrows, on two front blanks are pasted (bit artlessly) pieces of blue paper containing Hoe family notes in hand of Richard Hoe's great-great granddaughter, who purchased this copy from Warren Howell in 1945.   Joseph J. Felcone Inc.   Fall Miscellany 2010 - 60   2011 $900

Hoe, Robert *A Lecture on Bookbinding as a Fine Art. Delivered Before the Grolier Club February 26 1885.* New York: Grolier Club, 1886, One of 200 copies; 260 x 210mm., 3 p.l., 36 pages, (3) leaves (with plates placed before final leaf), original ivory colored half cloth over matching paper, top edge gilt, other edges untrimmed, 63 plates of fine and historic bindings, boards and spine just bit soiled, gilt spine titling slightly faded, half a dozen plates with extensive (though very fine), sprinkled foxing in margins or on versos, still an excellent copy, text fresh and binding sound.   Phillip J. Pirages   59 - 229   2011 $650

Hoffman, Mary *White Magic.* Rex Collings, 1975, First edition; original cloth, gilt, dust jacket, spine little faded, pages 253.   R. F. G. Hollett & Son Antiquarian Booksellers   175 - 645   2011   £30

Hoffmann-Donner, Heinrich   1809-1894   *The English Struwelpeter or Pretty Stories and Funny Pictures for Little Children.* A. N. Myers & Co., 33rd edition; 4to., original cloth backed pictorial boards, rather rubbed, corners very worn and rounded, pages 24, laid on linen with hand colored woodcuts throughout.   R. F. G. Hollett & Sons Antiquarian Booksellers   170 - 332   2011   £35

Hoffmann-Donner, Heinrich   1809-1894   *The English Struwelpeter or Pretty Stories and Funny Pictures for Little Children.* Frankfurt: Krebs Schmitt, n.d. circa, 1860,   41st edition; pages 24, hand colored throughout, original printed boards little stained and sometime rebacked to match, corners worn, first leaf torn and aid down, few other tears neatly repaired, early hand colored editions now very scarce.   R. F. G. Hollett & Sons Antiquarian Booksellers   170 - 331   2011   £85

Hoffmann-Donner, Heinrich   1809-1894   *The English Struwwelpeter or Pretty Stories and Funny Pictures for Little Children.* London: Agency of the German Literary Society, circa, 1885, Twenty-eighth edition; 4to., stiff orange boards, rebacked, elaborate decorative border surrounding text, some rubbing and soiling to covers, every page mounted on stiff boards and hand colored, pages clean.   Jo Ann Reisler, Ltd.   86 - 134   2011 $285

Hoffmann, Ernst Theodor Amadeus   1776-1822   *Nutcracker.* New York: Crown Publishers Inc., 1984, Signed, limited edition of 250 copies; large square 4to., dark blue cloth with silver lettering on cover and spine, matching slipcase and signed, numbered lithograph (laid into book), illustrations by Maurice Sendak.   Jo Ann Reisler, Ltd.   86 - 229   2011 $1000

Hofland, Barbara *The Son of Genius.* Printed for J. Harris and B. and R. Crosby, 1812, First edition; pages vii, (i, blank), 251, (i, blank), (iv, ads), copper engraved frontispiece, first few leaves damped in top corner, scarce.   R. F. G. Hollett & Son Antiquarian Booksellers   General Catalogue Summer 2010 - 526   2011   £175

Hofmann, Joseph E. *Leibniz in Paris 1672-1676: His Growth to Mathematical Maturity.* London and New York: Cambridge University Press, 1974, Revised English translation of 1949 Munich publication; 8vo., xi, 372 pages, frontispiece, figures, blue cloth, silver stamped spine title, dust jacket, very good, from the Bern Dibner reference library, with Burndy bookplate. Jeff Weber Rare Books 161 - 209 2011 $125

Hofmeyer, Adrian *The Story of My Captivity During the Transvaal War 1899-1900.* London: Edward Arnold, 1900, First edition; 8vo., pages xii, 302, photogravure frontispiece, original red cloth, spine little faded. J. & S. L. Bonham Antiquarian Booksellers Africa 4/20/2011 - 8297 2011 £40

Hogan, Inez *Nicodemus and the Newborn Baby.* New York: E. P. Dutton, 1940, 8vo., pictorial boards, slight wear to spine ends, fine in dust jacket (some soil and rubbing to dust jacket, else very good), sample copy with stamp on dedication page, color lithographs by Hogan, very scarce. Aleph-Bet Books, Inc. 95 - 106 2011 $400

Hogaret, Felix *L'Aretin Francois, par un membre de l'academie des Dames. (second titlepage) Les Epices de Venus ou Pieces Diverses du Meme Academicien.* Londres: Paris: Cazin, 1787, First edition; 8vo., 23 unnumbered leave, frontispiece and 17 erotic engravings, pages (iv), 53, (iii) blank and 1 erotic engraving for second text, 19th century full red morocco, gilt lettered on spine with in compartments, treble gilt rule on covers, marbled endpapers, all edges gilt, light shelfwear, overall near fine. Simon Finch Rare Books Zero - 412 2011 £5000

Hogaret, Felix *L'Aretin Francais par un Membre de l'Academie des Dames: Les Epices de Venus ou Pieces Diverse du Meme Academicien.* Londres: 1788, Unrecorded piracy of the first edition of the previous year; small 12mo., pages (46), 58, (2) blank, frontispiece and 16 erotic engraved plates after Borel for first part, engraved frontispiece for second part, early 19th century red half morocco, marbled boards and endpapers, gilt lettered spine, raised bands, top edge gilt, others untrimmed, bottom corner of lower side rubbed, slight scuff marks to edges. Simon Finch Rare Books Zero - 414 2011 £3250

Hogarth, William *The Analysis of Beauty.* London: by J. Reeves for the author, 1753, First edition; xxii, (2) figures referred to in the book (2) contents & errata 153 (2) price list (1) (2) pages, 2 large folding plates printed on card, very good, expertly bound in recent half calf, marbled boards, red morocco label, some foxing and light browning, old paper repairs to five leaves, without loss. Ken Spelman Rare Books 68 - 7 2011 £650

Hogg, Jabez *The Microscope.* London: George Routledge & Sons, 1911, Fifteenth edition; original red cloth, gilt, pages xxiv, 704, with 20 plates, some 900 illustrations. R. F. G. Hollett & Son Antiquarian Booksellers General Catalogue Summer 2010 - 1115 2011 £65

Hoggarth, James *Echoes from Years Gone By.* Kendal: Thompson Brothers, 1892, Pages x, 168, very scarce, affixed to pastedown is ALS from author soliciting purchase of his book, original brown cloth gilt by Thompson Bros. of Kendal. R. F. G. Hollett & Son Antiquarian Booksellers 173 - 562 2011 £140

Holbrook, G. H. *The Double Suicide. The True History of the Lives of the twin sisters, Sarah and Maria Williams.* New York: H. H. Randall, 1855, 8vo., 63, (1 blank), pages, including 5 full page illustrations, original printed wrappers with engraved vignette within ornamental border, wrappers, text with some light browning, age stains, few leaves crease or torn, fore-edges frayed &c. M & S Rare Books, Inc. 90 - 163 2011 $225

Holbrook, John Edwards *Ichthyology of South Carolina. Volume I (all published).* Charleston: John Russell, 1860, Second edition; 30 hand colored plates, scattered foxing, heavier to 3, a browned 1/2 inch strip near lower margin of first plate in 6 parts, dampstaining to lower blank corner of plate XXIX, 4to., pages vii, 205, original printed wrappers expertly restored, rear wrappers on 3 parts, sympathetically replaced, front wrapper and title to first part foxed, dampspot to first wrapper, few discolored spots to second front wrapper, some foxing to other wrappers, rear wrapper to last part with several creases, housed in custom cloth chemise and quarter morocco clamshell box, extremely rare. Raymond M. Sutton, Jr. May 26 2011 - 51588 2011 $17,000

Holden, Matthew *The Divisible Republic.* New York: Abelard Schuman, 1973, Very good in worn dust jacket, owner's bookplate, interior clean and tight, 284 pages. G. H. Mott Bookseller May 26 2011 - 44950 2011 $225

Holden, William *Cambridge Planning Proposals.* Cambridge: University Press, 1950, 2 volumes, pages xvi, 102, 9 plates, 16 tables and 58 maps, drawings in volume 2, original cloth backed boards, one board slightly marked. R. F. G. Hollett & Son Antiquarian Booksellers 177 - 469 2011 £75

Holden, William Clifford *History of the Colony of Natal, South Africa...* London: Alexander Heylin, 1855, First edition; 8vo., pages viii, 463, 3 maps, tinted lithographs, illustrations, lacks plate on page 331, original green blind-stamped cloth, inner hinge cracked and tender. J. & S. L. Bonham Antiquarian Booksellers Africa 4/20/2011 - 7084 2011 £100

Holden, William Clifford *The Past and Future of the Kaffir Races.* London: Wm. Nichols, 1866, First edition; 8vo., pages xii, 516, frontispiece, folding map, 11 illustrations, some light browning, original green cloth.   J. & S. L. Bonham Antiquarian Booksellers   Africa 4/20/2011 - 4863   2011   £210

Holder, Charles Frederick *The Frozen Dragon and Other Tales: a Story Book of Natural History for Boys and Girls.* New York: Dodd Mead, 1888, Square octavo, vi, 285 pages, illustrations, pages 59-60 badly damaged, original chocolate brown cloth stamped in black, silver and gilt, inner hinges broken, good, scarce.   Jeff Weber Rare Books   163 - 175   2011 $150

Holder, Charles Frederick *Living Lights: a Popular Account of Phosphorescent Animals and Vegetables.* London: Sampson Low, Marston, Searle and Rivington, 1887, First edition; 8vo., original olive cloth lettered gilt on spine, lettered and decorated gilt and black on cover, pages (xvii) 187, with 26 plates, slight edgewear, spine ends slightly bumped, corners rubbed, very slight scuffing, prize label pasted to endpaper, very slightly shaken, otherwise very good.   Any Amount of Books   May 26 2011 - A69402   2011 $470

Holdgate, Martin *Mountains in the Sea: the Story of the Gough Island Expedition.* London: Macmillan, 1958, First edition; 8vo., pages xvi,22, maps, illustrations, original blue cloth, dust jacket (small wear), signed by author.   J. & S. L. Bonham Antiquarian Booksellers   Africa 4/20/2011 - 5307   2011   £85

Hole, Christina *Haunted England.* London: Batsford, 1951, third edition; original cloth, gilt, dust jacket, price clipped, spine little chipped at head and foot, pages viii, 184, illustrations by John Farleigh, few notes on flyleaf and marginal ticks etc., inked ink.   R. F. G. Hollett & Son Antiquarian Booksellers   175 - 648   2011   £65

Hole, Christina *Haunted England.* London: Batsford, 1940, Original cloth gilt, dramatic dust jacket, hea of spine just trifle frayed, pages viii, 184, illustrations by John Farleigh, pencilled ticks to index, otherwise lovely copy, printed on heavy paper.   R. F. G. Hollett & Son Antiquarian Booksellers   General Catalogue Summer 2010 - 1433   2011   £85

Hole, Hugh Marshall *The Passing of the Black Kings.* London: Philip Allan, 1932, First edition; 8vo., pages xi, 322, illustrations, 2 folding maps, foxing to prelims, original blue cloth, spine faded.   J. & S. L. Bonham Antiquarian Booksellers   Africa 4/20/2011 - 5284   2011   £55

Hole, William *Quasi Cursores.* Edinburgh: University Press, 1884, Limited edition, no. 80 of 100 folio copies; original pictorial cloth over bevelled boards, little worn and soiled, hinges trifle frayed in places, pages xvii, 283, uncut, 46 fine etched portraits.   R. F. G. Hollett & Son Antiquarian Booksellers   175 - 651   2011   £120

Holgate, David *New Hall and Its Imitators.* London: Faber, 1971, First edition; original cloth, gilt, dust jacket price clipped, pages xvi, 112, plus 257 illustrations.   R. F. G. Hollett & Son Antiquarian Booksellers   General Catalogue Summer 2010 - 204   2011   £75

Holiday, Henry *Stained Glass as an Art.* London: Macmillan and Co., 1896, First edition; 173 (1) pages, color reproduction of the drawing for "The Creation", 20 collotypes and many illustrations in text, near fine in original gilt lettered cloth, large 8vo.   Ken Spelman Rare Books   68 - 96   2011   £160

The Holidays at Llandudno. London: Cassell, Petter and Galpin, 1868, First edition; original blindstamped cloth gilt, pages viii, 264, woodcut illustrations, endpapers rather browned, joints strained or cracked.   R. F. G. Hollett & Sons Antiquarian Booksellers   170 - 17   2011   £45

Holinshed, Raphael *First-(Laste) Volumes of the Chronicles of England, Scotlande and Irelande.* London: George Bishop (and) John Hunne, 1577, First and best edition; 4 parts in 2, 2 folio volumes, (viii), 124 (i.e. 126) (1, errata) (leaves), 289, (1, blank) (pages), (8), 22, (1, blank) (pages), 1-518, (26) pages, (2), 28 (leaves), 115, (9) pages; (iv), 291-659, 700-981, 990-1592, (2, names of knights), 1593-1876, (100, index) pages, both volumes collate the same as Pforzheimer, titles with woodcut borders, numerous woodcut initials and illustrations of various sizes throughout, many repeated, lacking foldout plate of the Map of Edinburgh which is often the case, Ff4 with publisher's six line paste-over to revise text; original speckled calf, very expertly rebacked preserving original spines, volume II is paneled calf with cover ruled with blind borders, spines elaborately stamped and numbered in gilt, each with red morocco spine label, lettered gilt, while the two volumes look very similar to each other, upon closer inspection they are actually different bindings, all edges speckled red, boards little abraded, but bindings absolutely solid, volumes retaining much of their original appeal, headlines and side notes occasionally trimmed close with slight loss, titlepage of volume II with expert repairs, old ink signatures on titlepage volume I, few stains and tears, none of these serious, tidemark to index in volume II, previous owner's bookplate on front pastedown of each volume, overall excellent copy.   Heritage Book Shop   Holiday 2010 - 56   2011 $30,000

Holland, Elizabeth Vassall, Lady 1770-1845 *A Memoir of the Rev. Sidney Smith.* London: Longmans, Green and co., circa, 1885, Couple of fox spots, pages x, 628, 8vo. contemporary tree calf, spine gilt, second compartment gilt lettered direct by Riviere and Son, slightly sunned, near fine, inscribed by author to Arthur Godfrey James. Blackwell Rare Books B166 - 49 2011 £70

Holland, Henry *Resolutions of the Associated Architects'...* London: 1793, 32 pages, original sugar paper wrappers, side sewn, spine fold of wrappers cracked, few spots, fine, uncut and unpressed copy, rear, especially in this condition. R. F. G. Hollett & Son Antiquarian Booksellers 177 - 470 2011 £140

Holland, Rupert Sargent *Pirate of the Delaware.* Philadelphia: Lippincott, 1925, First edition; 8vo., pages 318, 4 illustrations, author's presentation on flyleaf to poet Barbara Howes, cream cloth with pictorial stamping in dark blue, edges slightly spotted, cover somewhat scuffed and soiled spine little worn at ends, otherwise very good, tight copy. Second Life Books Inc. 174 - 182 2011 $65

Holliday, David *Iota.* privately printed, 1988-1996, First edition; No. 1-33, 33 issues in original wrappers, very good. I. D. Edrich May 26 2011 - 96715 2011 $461

Hollinghurst, Alan *The Line of Beauty.* London: Picador, 2004, First edition; fine in like dust jacket. Bella Luna Books May 26 2011 - t9462 2011 $165

Hollinghurst, Alan *The Line of Beauty.* London: Picador, 2004, First edition; fine in near fine dust jacket, light creasing to top edge. Bella Luna Books May 29 2011 - t7634 2011 $137

Hollinghurst, Alan *The Line of Beauty.* London: Picador, 2004, First edition; fine, dust jacket fine, signed by author. Bella Luna Books May 26 2011 - t7172 2011 $247

Hollings, J. F. *Sketches in Leicestershire, from Original Drawings...* Leicester: printed and published by E. S. Palmer, John Sydney Crossley, 1846, First edition; folio, additional pictorial title and 24 plates, all tinted lithographs, some foxing, mostly marginal, contemporary roan backed cloth with wrappers mounted on covers, upper wrapper with title and panel of views, rubbed, spine rather worn. Anthony W. Laywood May 26 2011 - 21244 2011 $1426

Hollis, Florence *Casework.* New York: Random House, 1966, First edition; original cloth, gilt, dust jacket, slight wear to head and foot of spine, pages xx, 300. R. F. G. Hollett & Son Antiquarian Booksellers 175 - 654 2011 £35

Hollister, O. J. *The Resources and Attractions of Utah.* Salt Lake City: 1882, 96 pages, folding map, original printed wrappers soiled, 1 1/4 x 3 /4 inch chip from corner of front wrapper, smaller chip from back wrapper, overall very good. Dumont Maps & Books of the West 111 - 32 2011 $275

Hollos, Ladislaus *Die Gasteromyceten Ungarns. Im Auftrage der Ungarischen Akademie der Wissenschaften.* Leipzig: Oswald Weigel, 1904, Folio, 31 plates of which 23 are colored, drawn by author, pages 278, original cloth backed printed boards, front and rear joint open, small innocuous handstamp on upper margin of title and foreword, original dust jacket chipped with few tears, original cardboard slipcase, soiled, worn, some splits, pieces missing from spine and lower edge. Raymond M. Sutton, Jr. May 26 2011 - 40372 2011 $1350

Holloway, John *Later English Broadside Ballads.* London: Routledge & Kegan Paul, 1974, First edition, uncorrected proof; original pictorial wrappers, trifle soiled, pages 293, woodcuts. R. F. G. Hollett & Son Antiquarian Booksellers 175 - 655 2011 £50

Holloway, John *Later English Broadside Ballads.* London: Routledge & Kegan Paul, 1975, First edition; original cloth, gilt, dust jacket, spine faded, pages 296, old woodcuts. R. F. G. Hollett & Son Antiquarian Booksellers 175 - 656 2011 £75

Hollowood, Bernard *Pont. An Account of the Life and Work of Graham Laidler 1908-1940.* London: Collins, 1969, First edition; pages 184, with 200 illustrations, 4to., original pictorial boards, dust jacket, fine. R. F. G. Hollett & Son Antiquarian Booksellers General Catalogue Summer 2010 - 205 2011 £40

Holmes, Daniel *Dialogue on Slavery and Miscellaneous Subjects.* Dayton: Gazette Book and Job Rooms, 1854, First edition; 8vo., 29 pages, sewn as issued, original plain back wrapper only, bottom half of rear blank leaf torn away, otherwise good. M & S Rare Books, Inc. 90 - 394 2011 $225

Holmes, Frederic L. *Instruments and Experimentation in the History of Chemistry.* Cambridge and London: MIT Press, 2000, 8vo., xxi, 415 pages, text figures, green cloth, silver stamped spine title, dust jacket, fine, from the Bern Dibner reference library, with Burndy bookplate. Jeff Weber Rare Books 161 - 210 2011 $70

Holmes, Martin *Appleby Castle.* Appleby: Ferguson Industrial Holdings, 1974, First trade softback edition; large 8vo., original pictorial wrappers, pages (iv), 60, illustrations, mostly in color. R. F. G. Hollett & Son Antiquarian Booksellers 173 - 567 2011 £45

Holmes, Martin *Appleby Castle.* Appleby: Ferguson Industrial Holdings, 1974, Limited edition, no. 75 of 250 copies, signed; large 8vo., original parchment backed cloth, gilt, pictorial slipcase, pages (iv), 60, illustrations, mostly in color, scarce. R. F. G. Hollett & Son Antiquarian Booksellers 173 - 566 2011 £120

Holmes, Oliver Wendell 1809-1894 *The Autocrat of the Breakfast Table. (with) The Professor at the Breakfast-Table. (with) The Poet at the Breakfast Table.* London: J. M. Dent & Co., 1907, 1905. 1907. 5th, 3rd and 4th edition respectively; 3 volumes, half titles, frontispiece and illustrations by H. M. Brock, tears repaired to pages 13-14 & 137-8 in third volume, uniformly bound in quarter mustard calf attractively decorated in gilt, brown morocco label at head of spine, top edge gilt, very good. Jarndyce Antiquarian Booksellers CXCI - 204 2011 £35

Holmes, Oliver Wendell 1841-1935 *The Common Law.* Boston: Little Brown and Co. University Press, John Wilson and Son, Cambridge, 1881, First edition; 8vo., 16, 422 pages, index, original brick red cloth, slight soiling, very slight wear on lower spine, inner hinge touch tender, pencilling in text, mostly at front, except for the latter, especially nice. M & S Rare Books, Inc. 90 - 164 2011 $2250

Holmes, Richard R. *Queen Victoria.* London: Longmans, Green and Co., 1901, New edition; full tree calf, gilt prize binding, pages x, 330, frontispiece. R. F. G. Hollett & Son Antiquarian Booksellers 175 - 657 2011 £40

Holmes, Richard R. *Windsor.* London: A. & C. Black, 1908, First edition; pages viii, 117, (vi), top edge gilt, 20 color plates, blindstamped 'presentation copy' on title. R. F. G. Hollett & Son Antiquarian Booksellers 175 - 658 2011 £75

Holt, John *General View of the Agriculture of the County of Lancaster; with Observations on the means of Its Improvement.* G. Nicol, 1795, 8vo., (4), xii 241 (1) pages, folding map and 5 plates, 4 tables and 8 text figures, very good contemporary half red morocco, gilt spine, some slight foxing, considerably enlarged from first edition. Ken Spelman Rare Books 68 - 149 2011 £160

Holt, L. Emmett *The Care and Feeding of Children.* New York: D. Appleton and Co., 1894, First edition; square 16mo., 66 pages plus ads, original cloth, occasional rubbing, owner's signature dated 1895 on front endsheet, notes relative to a baby's weight on back blanks. M & S Rare Books, Inc. 90 - 165 2011 $650

The Holy Land, Syria, Idumea, Arabia, Egypt & Nubia. London: Lithographed, printed and published by Day & Son, 1855-1856, First quarto edition; 6 volumes in 3, 250 tinted lithographed plates by David Roberts, contemporary full dark green morocco. Heritage Book Shop Booth A12 51st NY International Antiquarian Book Fair April 8-10 2011 - 107 2011 $9500

The Home Primer. New York: McLoughlin Bros. n.d. circa, 1865, Square 8vo., 14 leaves, 1 page list on lower wrapper, pictorial orange paper wrappers, half page wood engravings printed in red and black, pencilled name at top of cover, wrapper lightly soiled and creased, fore-edge of one leaf repaired, nick at edges of four pages, rebacked with matching colored paper traces of previous stitching at gutters, very good. Hobbyhorse Books 56 - 101 2011 $125

The Home Companion. London: Frederick Warne & Co., n.d., Unpaginated, 23 full page color plates and accompaying text leaves, all mounted on linen, joints cracked, front flyleaf replaced to match, flyleaf repaired, some fingering and the occasional pencil scribble, scarce. R. F. G. Hollett & Sons Antiquarian Booksellers 170 - 717 2011 £250

Home Games for Little Boys. New York: McLoughlin Bros. n.d. circa, 1870, Oblong 4to., pictorial wrappers, covers somewhat soiled, else very good++, rare. Aleph-Bet Books, Inc. 95 - 346 2011 $600

Home, Gordon *Yorkshire Coast and Moorland Scenes.* A. & C. Black, 1907, Second edition; original decorated green cloth, gilt, pages x, 148, (iv), top edge gilt, untrimmed, 32 color plates and folding map, very good, clean and sound copy. R. F. G. Hollett & Son Antiquarian Booksellers General Catalogue Summer 2010 - 1437 2011 £65

Home, Gordon *Yorkshire Painted and Described.* London: A. & C. Black, 1908, First edition; original decorated cloth, spine trifle dulled, pages xi, 464, 8, top edge gilt, 71 color plates and map, inscription, front joint starting. R. F. G. Hollett & Son Antiquarian Booksellers General Catalogue Summer 2010 - 1436 2011 £85

Homerus *Homer's Hymns to Aphrodite.* London: Fanfrolico Press, 1929, One of 500 copies; 267 x 203mm., p.l., (9) leaves, black cloth, gilt titling on spine, cream colored inset in low relief on cover of the Aphrodite of melos, edges untrimmed, illustrated titlepage and four plates, tiny snag top of front joint, bas-relief slightly abraded, front board slightly soiled, otherwise very fine, quite lovely internally. Phillip J. Pirages 59 - 191 2011 $100

Homerus *Greek text... Homeri Ilias.* Colophon: Venice: 1524, Third Aldine edition; A3-6 incorrectly bound between 11 and 13, full mottled calf, gilt stamped red calf spine label, all edges gilt, neatly repaired, fine. Jeff Weber Rare Books 163 - 2 2011 $5750

Homerus *The Iliad of Homer.* London: Longmans, Green and Co., 1898, First of this edition by Samuel Butler; 8vo., pages xvi (errata/addendum), (1) 421 + publisher's ads, i.e. 1 page of Butler's works and 32 pages general book as dated 3/98; uncommon, with the Beardsley bookplate of Frederick H. Evans, original publisher's maroon cloth lettered gilt at spine, few slight marks, slight scuffing, slight occasional foxing to text, otherwise very good. Any Amount of Books May 29 2011 - A46349 2011 $374

Homerus *Odyssea (and other works).* Venice: Melchiorre Sessa, 1540?, 165 x 108mm., 238, (2) leaves, contemporary olive brown calf over pasteboard, ends of spine repaired (probably late in 19th century), gilt covers framed with two sets of double rules, outer panel with broad foliate curl cornerpieces and sidepieces with trefoil of three rings between each, inner panel with blindstamped horizontal oval centerpiece of Apollo and Pegasus, the gilt collar with Greek motto touching rules at sides, large foliate sprays at head and foot curling to left and right and rising to a fleuron tool at ends, raised bands, spine panelled in gilt featuring broad rules and fleuron centerpiece, brown morocco label; woodcut historiated initials and charming cat and mouse printer's device, leaves at front and back with various marks of ownership, including signature of Francesco Suave at head of titlepage and "proprieta di Carlo Balzi 1884", contemporary marginal annotations in Latin and Greek; joints partly cracked (wormed in two places), corners somewhat worn, some scuffing to leather, binding completely solid, gilt still distinct, plaquettes (not surprisingly) bright and volume altogether pleasing even with its defects, final leaf cropped at fore edge (with loss of first [verso] or last [recto] on two thirds of the lines), upper corner of two gatherings with small, faint dampstain, one minor paper flaw costing half dozen letters, otherwise unusually well preserved internally, text exceptionally bright, fresh and clean, according to Hobson a fraudulent Apollo and Pegasus binding, volume looks absolutely convincing, with usual signs of age and restoration (wheels of Apollo's chariot have four spokes, in the genuine article, they have six. Phillip J. Pirages 59 - 4 2011 $7500

Homerus *The Odyssey.* London: printed an published by Sir Emery Walker, 1932, One of 530 copies; 297 x 210mm., (360) pages; fine original black crushed morocco, raised bands, gilt spine titling, top edge gilt, other edges rough trimmed, original (slightly worn) board slipcase, 26 large and attractive roundels printed in gold and black; with bookplate of Newton library, front flyleaf inscribed by Wilfred Merton to Eric G. Millar Christmas 1932; virtually mint. Phillip J. Pirages 59 - 252 2011 $6500

Homes, Geoffrey *Forty Whacks.* New York: William Morrow and Co., 1941, First edition; 8vo., inscribed by author, front and rear free endpapers beginning to uniformly tan, else fine in dust jacket with light wear to spine ends and to extremities, also along top and bottom edges of inside of jacket are stains caused by removal of old fashioned protective book cover, none of the stain visible on front side of dust jacket,. Buckingham Books May 26 2011 - 24900 2011 $2000

Hone, William *Ancient Mysteries Described, Especially the English Miracles Plays...* London: printed for William Hone, 1823, First edition; pages 299, woodcut frontispiece, 4 full page woodcuts, 8 text woodcuts, fore edge of one leaf repaired, few leaves rather soiled, original blind ruled cloth gilt, little marked and neatly recased. R. F. G. Hollett & Son Antiquarian Booksellers 175 - 662 2011 £45

Hone, William *Works: the Year Book. (With) The Everyday Book.. (with) The Every-Day Book and Table Book.* William Tegg and Co., 1850, 3 volumes, original half calf gilt with marbled, gilding dulled, neatly recased with new lettering pieces, all edges and endpapers marbled, wood engravings, excellent sound set. R. F. G. Hollett & Son Antiquarian Booksellers 175 - 663 2011 £150

Honey, J. R. De S. *Tom Brown's Universe. The Development of the Victorian Public School.* Millington, 1977, First edition; original cloth, gilt, dust jacket, pages xv, 416. R. F. G. Hollett & Son Antiquarian Booksellers 175 - 664 2011 £30

Honorable Society of Cymmrodorion *Transactions of the Honorable Society of Cymmrodorion.* 1945-1977, First edition; a run from 1945-1977, lacking 1952, 1959, 1960, 1964/1 in wrapper and boards as issued, all near fine, illustrations. I. D. Edrich May 26 2011 - 82596 2011 $419

Honorius of Autun *Elucidarius Dvalogicus Theologie Tripertitus: Infinitarum questionum Resolutiuus.* colophon: Landshut: Johann Weyssenburger 20 June, 1514, Title printed in red and below it five vignettes, four within circles and altogether surrounded by a square frame, inner margin of first leaf strengthened, few minor spots and stains, ff., xxvii, (4 index), 4to. in sixes, early 20th century calf backed buckram, spine faded, blindstamped of C. H. Radford on first flyleaf, good, scarce. Blackwell Rare Books B166 - 50 2011 £1500

Hood, Edwin Paxton *Dream Land and Ghost Land: Visits and Wanderings There in the Nineteenth Century.* London: Partridge & Oakey, 1852, 4 page initial ads, half title, 6 pages ads, original brown cloth, slightly rubbed and faded, small tear to lower leading hinge, good plus. Jarndyce Antiquarian Booksellers CXCI - 205 2011 £180

Hood, Thomas *Humorous Poems.* London: Macmillan, 1893, First edition; small 8vo., original decorated green cloth gilt, pages xxxi, 236, all edges gilt, with 130 illustrations by Charles Brock, small light brown mark to 4 pages, otherwise very good. R. F. G. Hollett & Son Antiquarian Booksellers General Catalogue Summer 2010 - 629 2011 £30

Hood, Thomas *Up the Rhine.* London: E. Moxon Son & Co., 1869, Half title, frontispiece, woodcuts by Hood, some slight foxing, original green cloth, decorated and lettered in gilt, bookseller's ticket of J. W. Mason & Son Ltd., St. Leonard on Sea, very good. Jarndyce Antiquarian Booksellers CXCI - 556 2011 £35

Hood, Thomas *"When's & Oddities".* Philadelphia: 1828, 146, (1) pages, 12mo., with 39 full page cartoon illustrations, half leather rubbed at backstrip edges, with enough label chipping to make it illegible, marbled endpapers, mouse chewed starting at back cover into text block affecting two bottom lines of print diminishing so that only last five leaves are affected through bottom edge of previous 100 pages, damage affects rear terminus cover as a diminishing scrape almost at top, bookplate of Col. Richard L. Maury, Plymouth NC. Bookworm & Silverfish 662 - 33 2011 $75

Hood, Tom *The Knight and the Dragon.* London: Eyre and Spottiswoode, n.d. circa, 1870, 4to., original cloth backed pictorial bevelled boards, corners little worn, pages 20, facsimile of mss. text with illustrations, printed in red and black, new endpapers. R. F. G. Hollett & Sons Antiquarian Booksellers 170 - 337 2011 £45

Hood, Tom *The Knight and the Dragon.* London: Eyre and Spottiswoode, n.d. circa, 1870, 4to., original cloth backed pictorial bevelled boards, corners little worn, pages 20, facsimile of mss. text with illustrations, new endpapers. R. F. G. Hollett & Son Antiquarian Booksellers 175 - 665 2011 £45

Hook, Theodore Edward *Love and Pride.* London: Whittaker and Co., 1833, 3 volumes, 12mo., half titles, contemporary full calf, gilt borders raised bands, gilt compartments and dentelles, red and blue morocco label, bookplate of Edward Cunard, very good. Jarndyce Antiquarian Booksellers CXCI - 527 2011 £350

Hooke, Robert 1635-1703 *Micrographia Restaurata; or the Copper-Plates of Dr. Hooke's Wonderful Discoveries by the Microscope...* London: for John Bowles, R. Dodsley and John Cuff, 1745, Folio, iv, 65 (5) pages, 33 engraved plates, contemporary calf, very skillfully rebacked to style retaining original spine label, both text and plates moderately and uniformly foxed, armorial bookplate of Wm. Huskison Esqr. Joseph J. Felcone Inc. Fall Miscellany 2010 - 61 2011 $7500

Hooker, Richard 1554-1600 *Mash.* New York: Morrow, 1968, First printing; near fine, minor creasing to cloth spine ends, dust jacket fine, scarce. Bella Luna Books May 26 2011 - t9700 2011 $660

Hooker, Richard 1554-1600 *The Works of... Mr. Richard Hooker...* London: printed for R.C.S.S. B.W. M.W. G.C., 1705, Folio, pages (x), 553, (I) + engraved portrait frontispiece, contemporary calf (laid on top of original panelled calf), boards panelled in blind Cambridge style (compared with the single panel of binding underneath), board edges decorative roll in blind (previous binding a decorative roll gilt), all edges gilt, all edges red speckled, calf reback, boards restoration and relaying contemporary red lettering piece gilt by Jenny Aste, invoice 4 v 1983£46, touch of minor staining, boards scratched and marked, from the collection of Christopher Ernest Weston 1947-2010. Unsworths Booksellers 24 - 24 2011 £500

Hoole, Barbara *The Son of a Genius.* London: printed for J. Harris and B. and R. Crosby, 1812, First edition; modern half scarlet morocco gilt, pages vii, (i, blank), 251, (i, blank) (iv, ads), copper engraved frontispiece, first few leaves little damped in top corner, scarce. R. F. G. Hollett & Sons Antiquarian Booksellers 170 - 334 2011 £175

Hoole, Barbara *Theodore or the Crusaders.* London: John Harris and Son, c., 1821, First edition?; Small 8vo., original roan backed pictorial boards, vignette of two fighting crusaders on upper board, roundel of John Harris's original Juvenile Library surrounding a vignette of St. Paul's Cathedral on the lower board, little rubbed, head of spine chipped, pages (ii (ad), (iv, contents), 184 with vignette of crusader on title and 24 woodcut illustrations on 12 plates, little spotting to endpapers, some plates trifle offset, excellent sound copy, scarce. R. F. G. Hollett & Sons Antiquarian Booksellers 170 - 335 2011 £175

Hoornbeek, Johanne *Theologiiae Practicae...* Ultrajecti: Johannen & Guiljelmum van de Water, 1689, Second edition; pages (vi), 23, (i), 884, (xvi), title in red and black, 4to., original cloth backed pictorial bevelled board, corners little worn. R. F. G. Hollett & Son Antiquarian Booksellers 175 - 666 2011 £350

Hope, John *Thoughts in Prose and Verse, Started, in His Walks.* Stockton: by R. Christopher and sold by W. Goldsmith etc., 1780, First edition; half title discarded, pages xvi, 349, (1), 8vo., contemporary tree calf, skillfully rebacked, gilt in six compartments and repeated lyre tool, contemporary red morocco label, Greek key pattern borders on sides, minor rubbing, marbled endpapers, good. Blackwell Rare Books B166 - 51 2011 £450

Hope, W. H. St. John *The Abbey of St. Mary in Furness, Lancashire.* Kendal: T. Wilson, 1902, Contemporary half calf gilt, little rubbed, page 82, with 2 folding lithographed plans, 20 plates, scarce. R. F. G. Hollett & Son Antiquarian Booksellers 173 - 570 2011 £120

Hope, W. H. St. John *Architectural Description of Kirkstall Abbey.* Leeds: Thoresby Society, 1907, Pages viii, 150, with 96 figures, photos, plans, etc., lacks large folding plan originally in rear pocket, modern cloth gilt with leather spine label. R. F. G. Hollett & Son Antiquarian Booksellers 177 - 471 2011 £65

Hopkins, John Henry *Essay on Gothic Architecture, with Various Plans and Drawings for Churches, Designed Chiefly for the Use of the Clergy.* Burlington: Smith & Harrington, 1836, First edition; 4to., 6, 46 pages, 13 lithographed plates, plus extra lithographed titlepage, contemporary marbled boards, calf back, hinges weak, cloth wrinkled, occasional browning or stains to plates, very good. M & S Rare Books, Inc. 90 - 17 2011 $1000

Hopper, Dennis *Dennis Hopper: Photographs 1961-1967.* Taschen, 2009, First edition, #AP085/250 in an edition of 1600 copies pus 250 artist's proofs; 546 pages, folio, signed by Hopper in purple ink on limitation page, black and white pictorial cloth covered boards, as new in translucent colored acetate dust jacket with one unobtrusive one inch closed crack at front edge, navy blue cloth covered clamshell box, as new, still in original publisher's printed cardboard delivery box. Any Amount of Books May 26 2011 - A73901 2011 $1342

Horatius Flaccus, Quintus *Horati Carminum Libri IV.* London: Impensis Petr. Davies, 1926, One of 500 copies; 226 x 150m., 2 p.l., 141, (1) pages, handsome contemporary hunter green crushed morocco by Maltby's of Oxford (stamp signed on front turn-in), covers gilt with double ruled border enclosing a large central rectangle formed by strapwork with intersecting lobes in center of each side, raised bands, spine gilt in double ruled compartments with small round tool cornerpieces, gilt ruled turn-ins, top edge gilt, other edges rough trimmed, charming color vignettes by Vera Willoughby; spine uniformly sunned toward pleasing olive brown, but very fine, elegant text clean, fresh and bright, very lustrous binding, only most trivial signs of use. Phillip J. Pirages 59 - 116 2011 $400

Horatius Flaccus, Quintus *Horace: Odes, Epodes and Carmen Saeculare.* London: Simpkin Marshall and Co., 1850, First edition; 8vo., original publisher's blindstamped cloth lettered gilt on cover, pages 120, covers slightly stained (little more so at rear), lightly rubbed, rear board slightly creased, edges very slightly bumped, faint foxing otherwise about very good, pleasing copy, bookplate. Any Amount of Books May 29 2011 - A66673 2011 $238

Horatius Flaccus, Quintus *Opera.* Londini: Iohannes Pine, 1733-1737, First Pine edition, second state of page 108 in volume II with "potest"; tall 8vo., entirely engraved throughout, two volumes bound in 19th century full hard grained red morocco, inner dentelles and marbled endpapers, top edge gilt, little rubbing at edges, darkening to spine and some very minor foxing, generally very clean, fresh copy. Second Life Books Inc. 174 - 183 2011 $1000

Horgan, Paul *Great River: the Rio Grande in North American History.* New York: 1954, Limited to 1000 numbered and signed copies; near fine in slightly shelf worn slipcase, xviii, 447 pages, illustrations; ix, 448-1020 pages, illustrations, maps. Dumont Maps & Books of the West 113 - 35 2011 $275

Horizon: a Review of Literature and Art. London: Horizon, 1940-1950, First edition; Wrappers, 1-120/121, complete run, attractive set, mainly excellent, clean condition, occasional very slight spine wear. Any Amount of Books May 26 2011 - B23079 2011 $839

Hornaday, William T. *Two Years in the Jungle.* New York: Charles Scribner's, 1885, Octavo, xxii, 512 pages, frontispiece, 2 folding maps, plates, index, original tan-mustard pictorial cloth, stamped in black and gilt, spine bottom showing wear, rubbed, ownership signature of E(rwin) W. Webster, Ansonia, Conn. 1886, initials of SJW, very good, scarce. Jeff Weber Rare Books 163 - 177 2011 $400

Hornby, Nick *Contemporary American Fiction.* London: New York: Vision/St. Martin's, 1992, First edition; fine in fine dust jacket, quite uncommon. Ken Lopez Bookseller 154 - 80 2011 $300

Hornby, Nick *Fever Pitch, a Fan's Life.* London: Gollancz, 1992, First British edition; near fine, light bumping to spine ends, dust jacket near fine, price clipped. Bella Luna Books May 26 2011 - T5950 2011 $660

Hornby, Nick *Fever Pitch.* London: Gollancz, 1992, First British edition; near fine, just hint of bumping to spine ends, dust jacket near fine, light creasing to bottom edge, signed by author. Bella Luna Books May 26 2011 - t5922 2011 $825

Hornby, Nick *Fever Pitch, a Fan's Life.* London: Gollancz, 1992, First British edition; book near fine, sunning and shelfwear to edges, faint crease on spine, fine dust jacket, signed by author. Bella Luna Books May 26 2011 - t5842 2011 $1045

Hornby, Nick *High Fidelity.* London: Gollancz, 1995, First edition; inscribed by author, fine in fine dust jacket, beautiful copy with excellent early inscription. Ken Lopez Bookseller 154 - 81 2011 $350

Hornby, Nick *High Fidelity.* London: Victor Gollancz, 1995, First British edition; fine in fine dust jacket. Bella Luna Books May 29 2011 - t8849 2011 $137

Hornby, Nick *Songbook.* New York: McSweeney's, 2002, True First edition; fine, pictorial boards, includes 11 song CD, signed by author. Bella Luna Books May 29 2011 - t5556 2011 $137

Hornby, Nick *Songbook.* New York: McSweeny's, 2002, True first edition; fine, pictorial boards, with 11 song CD, signed and dated by author 13/6/05.   Bella Luna Books   May 26 2011 - t5556d   2011 $192

Horne, Alan *The Dictionary of 20th Century British Book Illustrators.* Antique Collectors Club, 1994, First edition; 4to., original cloth, gilt, dust jacket, pages 456, more than 160 color and 300 black and white illustrations.   R. F. G. Hollett & Son Antiquarian Booksellers   General Catalogue Summer 2010 - 208   2011   £50

Horne, George *Observations on the Case of the Protestant Dissenters with Reference to the Corporation and Test Acts.* Oxford: at the Clarendon Press printed for D. Prince and J. Cooke, sold by G. G. and J. Robinson Pater Noster Row, J. F. and C Rivington, St. Paul's Church Yard and T. Cadell Strand, London, 1790, First edition; title little spotted, most of text clean, (4), 19, (1) pages, disbound.   Anthony W. Laywood   May 26 2011 - 21733   2011 $101

Horne, John Fletcher *The Mirage of Two Buried Cities.* Hazell, Watson and Viney, 1900, First edition; large 8vo., original blue cloth gilt over bevelled boards, pages xii, 355, top edge gilt, tinted plates and text illustrations, presentation from author for Fredk. J. Jackson, good, sound copy.   R. F. G. Hollett & Son Antiquarian Booksellers   177 - 472   2011   £85

Horneman, Frederick *The Journal of Frederick Horneman's Travels from Cairo to Mouzouk...* London: W. Bulmer, 1802, First edition; quarto, pages xxvi, 195 3, folding maps, page and contents list, recent quarter calf, edges of titlepage lightly waterstained very good, clean and crisp.   J. & S. L. Bonham Antiquarian Booksellers   Africa 4/20/2011 - 8700   2011   £650

Horsely, J. E. *Jottings About Old Time Penrith.* Penrith: Reeds, 1926, First edition; original red cloth with leather spine label, pages 158.   R. F. G. Hollett & Son Antiquarian Booksellers   173 - 571   2011   £50

Horsfall, Thomas *Notes on the Manor of Well and Snape in the North Riding of the County of York.* Leeds: J. Whitehead & Son, 1912, First edition; original crimson cloth with silver arms on upper spine rather faded, pages (viii), 305, with 28l, very good, extremely scarce.   R. F. G. Hollett & Son Antiquarian Booksellers   General Catalogue Summer 2010 - 1438   2011   £150

Horsley, J. E. *Jottings about Old-Time Penrith.* Penrith: Reeds, 1926, First edition; original red cloth with leather spine label, pages 158.   R. F. G. Hollett & Son Antiquarian Booksellers   General Catalogue Summer 2010 - 1439   2011   £50

Horsley, John *Britannia Romana; or the Roman Antiquities of Britain...* London: printed for John Osborn and Thomas Longman, 1732, Folio, pages (viii), xxxii, 520, (xl) + 5 extending engraved maps and 100 other engraved plates, early 19th century polished russia, five flat raised banded spine double rule gilt with 'quatrefoil-title' roll gilt bands, compartment with blind tooled elaborate centre pieces composed of stylised plant tools, lettered direct in gilt, boards triple rule gilt bordered with decorative rule in blind within, board edges 'zig-zag' roll gilt, turn-ins decorative roll gilt, 'French Shell' 'made' endpapers, all edges gilt, 3 color (pink, white and green) double core sewn and patterned endbands, dark blue silk page markers, calf reback and relay by John Henderson, some light spotting, unidentified Knight of the Garter armorial gilt stamped on both boards, from the collection of Christopher Ernest Weston 1947-2010.   Unsworths Booksellers   24 - 110   2011   £900

Hort, Dora *Tahiti: the Garden of the Pacific.* London: T. Fisher Unwin, 1891, Octavo, 352 pages, frontispiece, original green gilt stamped cloth, covers freckled, very good, scarce.   Jeff Weber Rare Books   163 - 178   2011 $120

Hose, Charles *Pagan Tribes of Borneo: a Description of Their Physical, Moral and Intellectual Condition with some Discussion of their Ethnic Relations...* London: Macmillan and Co., 1912, First edition; 2 volumes, large octavo, xv, (1, blank), 283, (1, blank), 4, publisher's ads), x, 374 pages, 354 full page photo illustrations, two color frontispieces and numerous text illustrations, 3 folding charts and 4 folding maps at rear second volume, publisher's full dark blue cloth, front boards decoratively stamped in pictorial gilt with vignettes, spines lettered gilt, top edge gilt, small ownership ink stamp on front free pastedown, very bright, about fine, gilt entirely unblemished.   Heritage Book Shop   Holiday 2010 - 57   2011 $1275

Hoskins, G. A. *A Winter in Upper and Lower Egypt.* London: Hurst and Blackett, 1863, First edition; 8vo., pages xiii, 346, frontispiece (foxing in margins), last 100 pages have brown waterstain bottom of page not touching text, recent brown half calf.   J. & S. L. Bonham Antiquarian Booksellers   Africa 4/20/2011 - 8130   2011   £180

Hoskins, W. G. *Fieldwork in Local History.* London: Faber, 1967, First edition; original cloth, gilt, dust jacket, pages 192, with 5 illustrations, Dr. Arthur Raistrick's copy with his bookplate and signature and one or two marginal notes, printed compliments slip from author.   R. F. G. Hollett & Son Antiquarian Booksellers   177 - 474   2011   £30

Hosmer, James K. *History of the Expedition of Captains Lewis and Clark 1804-5-6.* Chicago: A. C. McClurg, 1902, 2 volumes, 8vo., lvi, 500; ix, 586 pages, frontispiece, plates, quarter brown cloth with tan cloth sides, gilt stamped spine title, top edge gilt, inner hinges cracked, very good, some pages uncut, from the Bern Dibner reference library, with Burndy bookplate.   Jeff Weber Rare Books   161 - 212   2011 $140

Hosoe, Eikoh   *Man and Woman. Otoko to Onna.*   Tokyo: CamerArt Inc., 1961,   First edition; 8vo., pages (60), 34 black and white photos printed in gravure, original yellow paper covered boards, upper side lettered in grey, original color pictorial dust jacket, short closed tear and rubbing to foot of spine, original white card slipcase, printed in black and grey, very lightly rubbed, original grey obi, printed in black, light sunning and short closed tear to lower edge, publisher's card tipped onto last page, Hosoe's signature in silver ink to front free endpaper, near fine.   Simon Finch Rare Books   Zero - 528   2011   £2500

Hosseini, Khaled   *The Kite Runner.*   New York: Riverhead, 2003,   First American edition;   near fine, light wear, dust jacket near fine with creasing to top and bottom of spine.   Bella Luna Books   May 26 2011 - t9064   2011 $302

Hotten, John Camden   *Charles Dickens, the Story of His Life.*   London: John Camden Hotten, 1870,   First edition; 193 x 130mm., xvi, 367 pages, (10) leaves (ads), fine butterscotch colored straight grain morocco, handsomely gilt by Morrell (stamp signed verso front free endleaf), covers with French fillet border and rosette cornerpieces, raised bands, spine attractively gilt in double ruled compartments with ornate central lozenge surrounded by small tools and cornerpieces formed by arabesques and volutes, turn-ins heavily gilt in floral design, top edge gilt, other edges rough trimmed, front joint neatly repaired, extra illustrated with 73 portraits and engravings plus 2 folding facsimiles, titlepage with ink ownership inscription of Edmund Ollier, whose neat manuscript marginalia appears occasionally in text; just hint of wear to extremities, one leaf with one inch losed tear to head margin (not affecting text), otherwise only trivial imperfections internally, nearly fine, lustrous and scarcely worn.   Phillip J. Pirages   59 - 174   2011 $950

Houdin, Robert   *The Sharper Detected and Exposed.* London: Chapman & Hall, 1863,   First edition; 12mo., 12, 268 pages, handsome modern three quarter calf.   M & S Rare Books, Inc.   90 - 224   2011 $2500

Houellebecq, Michel   *The Possibility of an Island.* London: Weidenfeld & Nicolson, 2005,   First edition; 8vo., signed on titlepage by author, 345 pages, fine in fine dust jacket.   Any Amount of Books   May 29 2011 - A68049   2011 $306

Hough, Richard   *The BP Book of the Racing Campbells.* Stanley Book, 1960,   First edition; original cloth, gilt, dust jacket (little wear chip to top edge), pages 127, illustrations. R. F. G. Hollett & Son Antiquarian Booksellers   General Catalogue Summer 2010 - 1116   2011   £35

Hough, Romeyn B.   *The American Woods, Exhibited by Actual Specimens and with Copious Explanatory Text.* Lowville: 1910-1928,   Mixed edition, containing 8 sections from the first edition, 4 sections from the second edition and 2 sections from the third edition;   very good, 354 plates containing 1060 wafer thin samples of wood in transverse, radial and tangential sections illustrating 354 species of woody plants, loose window mounted plates, accompanied by text in each volume, are in green cloth bound folders (samples contain some warping and occasional cracks which have occurred naturally over time), 8vo., original gilt lettered wrappers on text volumes, staining, from loose wood samples, to front endpapers of first volume, margin of front cover crease, some wear to front edge of book in volume III, front cover and flyleaf, to text volume VII detached, with paper on spine perished, some spotting to rear wrapper, original green cloth covered slipcase with volume I, original gilt stamped three quarter morocco gilt stamped green cloth on slipcases to volumes II-XIV (6 spines are faded to a natural shade of brown, scuffing and/or rubbing, heavier to 1, to some of the spines, wear to few corners, very good), with metal catches and bosses (catch to volume VIII is detached), overall in remarkably good condition, having slipcases (Volumes II-XIV) in morocco, quite rare, Hough's wooden business cards laid in text of volume I.   Raymond M. Sutton, Jr.   May 26 2011 - 45849   2011 $30,000

Hough, Walter   *The Hopi Indian Collection in the United States National Museum.*   Washington: 1918,   235-296 pages plus 18 pages of plates, title leaf laid in, near fine. Dumont Maps & Books of the West   112 - 46   2011 $100

Houghton, William   *British Fresh Water Fishes.*   London: William Mackenzie, 1879,   2 volumes in 1, very good, 41 chromolithographed plates with colored figure of each species drawn from nature by A. F. Lydon and numerous engravings in text, folio, xxvi, 204,   modern tan three quarter calf over green cloth, occasional light foxing, plate bright, marginal tear to leaf of text.   Raymond M. Sutton, Jr.   May 26 2011 - 51429   2011 $1650

House that Jack Built.   London: Treherne, n.d. circa, 1900, 11 1⁄2 inches tall, pictorial cloth, very good+ with ivory clasp, marvelous full page color illustrations, printed on thick paper on one side of page only.   Aleph-Bet Books, Inc.   95 - 295   2011 $750

The House Jack Built.   London: Darton and Co. between, 1837-1845,   12mo., brown printed stiff paper wrappers and wear and almost detached, the inside covers each have hand colored woodcut, title page, 9 hand colored woodcuts, each on half page along with ever growing text of rhymes. Jo Ann Reisler, Ltd.   86 - 93   2011 $600

House that Jack Built. New York: McLoughlin Bros., n.d. circa, 1860, 12mo., pictorial wrappers, near fine, color cover plus 8 nice half page hand colored illustrations. Aleph-Bet Books, Inc. 95 - 292 2011 $600

House that Jack Built. New York: McLoughlin Bros. n.d. circa, 1910, 8vo., pictorial cloth, some cover wear and soil, very good, cloth book with full color and 2 color illustrations on each page by Charles Robinson (not signed by him, but definitely his work). Aleph-Bet Books, Inc. 95 - 294 2011 $125

House, Homer D. *Wild Flowers.* New York: Macmillan, 1961, original cloth, large square 4to., gilt, dust jacket trifle marked, price clipped, pages 362, 364 color plates, 35 other illustrations. R. F. G. Hollett & Son Antiquarian Booksellers General Catalogue Summer 2010 - 987 2011 £50

Household, Geoffrey *Rogue Male.* Boston: Little Brown and Co., 1939, First US edition; fine, tight, clean copy in especially bright dust jacket with just tract of rubbing at extremities. Buckingham Books May 26 2011 - 27318 2011 $2000

Housman, Alfred Edward 1859-1936 *A Shropshire Lad.* London: Kegan Paul, Trench and Co., 1896, First edition; small 8vo., original parchment backed boards with printed label on spine, spine label and covers rubbed, else very good in navy blue half morocco slipcase, signed copies extremely rare, with spine label in first state (state A), one of fewer than 350 copies in this state, with two ALS's from Housman to Mrs. Beattie. James S. Jaffe Rare Books May 26 2011 - 16628 2011 $17,500

Housman, John *A Descriptive Tour and Guide to the Lakes, Caves, Mountains and Other Natural Curiosities in Cumberland, Westmoreland, Lancashire...* Carlisle: F. Jollie, 1812, Fifth edition; original printed boards, little worn and bumped, pages (iv), 264, complete with 4 engraved maps and plans and 6 plates, several folding, large folding hand colored general map, excellent copy. R. F. G. Hollett & Son Antiquarian Booksellers 173 - 573 2011 £225

Housman, John *A Descriptive Tour and Guide to the Lakes, Caves, Mountains and Other Natural Curiosities in Cumberland, Westmoreland, Lancashire...* Carlisle: F. Jollie, 1814, Sixth edition; old polished half calf, gilt with marbled boards, upon hinge cracking but sound, pages (iv), 226, (ii), folding general map, folding plans, 2 folding sheets of plans (one torn on fold and fore-edge little worn), 6 folding engraved plates, attractive copy. R. F. G. Hollett & Son Antiquarian Booksellers 173 - 574 2011 £275

Housman, Laurence 1865-1959 *Echo de Paris: a Study from Life.* London: Jonathan Cape, 1923, First edition, number 450 of 750 copies; half title, uncut, original grey boards, purple cloth spine, paper label, spine faded, very good. Jarndyce Antiquarian Booksellers CXCI - 209 2011 £65

Housman, Laurence 1865-1959 *Princess Badoura: a Tale from the Arabian Nights.* London: Hodder & Stoughton, n.d., 1913, 4to., white cloth pictorially stamped in blue and gold, fine in publisher's box with color plate on cover (box soiled, slightly worn), illustrations by Edmund Dulac, 10 magnificent tipped in color plates with pictorial guards, excellent condition, rare in box. Aleph-Bet Books, Inc. 95 - 208 2011 $1200

Housman, Laurence 1865-1959 *Rue.* London: At the Sign of the Unicorn, 1899, First edition; 8vo., pages illustrations, figures, tables, (1) 96 + 4 page publisher's ads, pages uncut, original publisher's blue cloth lettered gilt on spine and on front cover, very good+, excellent condition, small bookplate "From the Library of Janet Ashbee and C. R. Ashbee", loosely inserted is signed handwritten 1938 note to Janet Ashbee. Any Amount of Books May 29 2011 - A46831 2011 $221

Housman, Laurence 1865-1959 *Stories from the Arabian Nights.* London: Hodder and Stoughton, 1907, Deluxe edition, limited to 350 copies signed by artist, this being number 82; large quarto, (2), xvi, 133, (3) pages, 50 color plates mounted on dark green paper, including frontispiece, each plate with descriptive tissue guards, original vellum over boards, decoratively stamped in gilt and blue, gold silk ties, top edge gilt, spine with small wrinkle, chemise and housed in blue cloth slipcase, very good. Heritage Book Shop Holiday 2010 - 33 2011 $3000

Housman, Laurence 1865-1959 *Stories from the Arabian Nights Retold by L. Housman.* London & New York: Charles Scribner's Sons & Hodder & Stoughton, 1907, First American edition, identical to the British except for publisher's imprint; Thick 4to., 133 page, gilt decorated cloth, slight bit of rear cover soil and front endpaper rubbed at hinge (not weak), else near fine, 50 tipped in color plates by Edmund Dulac, mounted on dark paper at back of book, fine. Aleph-Bet Books, Inc. 95 - 211 2011 $1500

Houston, Pam *Cowboys Are My Weakness.* New York: W. W. Norton, 1992, First edition; fine in fine dust jacket, signed by author. Bella Luna Books May 26 2011 - 262 2011 $192

Houston, Pam *Cowboys are My Weakness.* New York: W. W. Norton, 1992, First edition; near fine, spine ends bumped, dust jacket near fine, with light use. Bella Luna Books May 29 2011 - t3465 2011 $137

Houston, Pam *Cowboys are My Weakness.* New York: W. W. Norton, 1992, First edition; near fine, top of spine bumped, dust jacket fine. Bella Luna Books May 26 2011 - t3265 2011 $165

Houston, Pam *Cowboys are My Weakness.* London: Virago, 1993, First British edition; fine, dust jacket fine, signed by author. Bella Luna Books May 29 2011 - 2815 2011 $82

How to Be Happy; or the Cottage of Content: The Cottage of Fire and the Water Cress Boy. London: Dean and Munday circa, 1840?, 12mo., tan brown printed card wrappers with some wear to edges and lower half of spine missing, internally rather clean with bright fresh illustrations, 30 numbered pages plus 2 pages of ads at end, a total of 32 pages within wrappers, 13 hand colored engravings. Jo Ann Reisler, Ltd. 86 - 94 2011 $600

Howard, George *Lady Jane Grey and Her Times.* London: Sherwood Neely and Jones, 1822, First edition; (vii 391 pages), 8vo., contemporary three quarter calf, marbled boards, gilt lettered spine, half title, frontispiece, slightly spotted, engraved titlepage and several in text illustrations, some minor work to spine, else nice. Paulette Rose Fine and Rare Books 32 - 99 2011 $150

Howard, J. H. W. *Bond and Free: a True Tale of Slave Times.* Harrisburg: Edwin K. Meyers, 1886, First edition; 12mo., 280 pages, frontispiece, portrait, original cloth, some spotting, spine darkened. M & S Rare Books, Inc. 90 - 172 2011 $950

Howard, J. Jackson *Genealogical Collections Illustrating the History of Roman Catholic Families of England, Based on Lawson Manuscript.* N.P.: printed for private circulation only, 1887, First edition; 2 volumes, folio, soundly rebound with original printed paper covered card covers and new green linen spine, pages 145, covers evenly soiled and slightly marked, more so on volume one, overall sound, about very good. Any Amount of Books May 29 2011 - A36678 2011 $340

Howard, John *The State of the Prisons in England and Wales, with Preliminary Observations and an Account of some Foreign Prisons. (bound with) Appendix to the State of the Prisons in England and Wales...* Warrington: printed by William Eyres and sold by T. Cadell and N. Conant, London, 1777, Warrington: printed by William Eyres, 1784. First edition and second edition of appendix; 4to., 3 engraved plates, with little offsetting as usual, (6), 489, (23) pages, wanting half title; 4to., (8), 286 (10) pages, including both initial blank and half title, 17 engraved plates, well preserved, contemporary calf, sympathetically rebacked, spine gilt lettered, sides rather worn but overall good, sound binding with 19th century armorial bookplate of Bayham. John Drury Rare Books 153 - 63 2011 £1750

Howard, Robert Ervin *The Dark Man and Others.* Sauk City: Arkham House, 1963, First edition; octavo, cloth. L. W. Currey, Inc. 124 - 145 2011 $450

Howard, Robert Ervin *King Conan.* New York: Gnome Press, 1953, First edition; cloth. L. W. Currey, Inc. 124 - 175 2011 $300

Howard, Robert Ervin *Skull-Face and Others.* Sauk City: Arkham House, 1946, First edition; large octavo, cloth. L. W. Currey, Inc. 124 - 57 2011 $1500

Howard, Robert Ervin *Tales of Conan.* New York: Gnome Press Inc., 1955, First edition; octavo, gray cloth lettered in red. L. W. Currey, Inc. 124 - 201 2011 $200

Howard, Seymour *Antiquity Restored: Essays on the Afterlife of the Antique.* Vienna: Irsa Verlag, 1990, 4to., copiously illustrated in black and white, pages 344, fine in slightly creased very good+ dust jacket with very slight edgewear. Any Amount of Books May 29 2011 - A38073 2011 $230

Howell, James *Lustra Ludovici or the late Victorius King of France, Lewis the XIII and his Cardinal de Richelieu.* London: by John Legate II for Humphrey Moseley, 1646, First edition; folio, (12), 188, (8) pages, engraved medallion portrait, woodcut initials and headpieces, rule borders, 17th century red morocco gilt, panelled sides with fleuron at corners, spine gilt in compartments, gilt edges, long tear in P3 with slight loss, occasional other short tears in margins, occasional manuscript notes in margins, small tear on upper cover, from the P. J. Wright collection with note on flyleaf dated September 1720, from the library of the Earls of Macclesfield at Shirburn Castle. Maggs Bros. Ltd. 1440 - 112 2011 £450

Howitt, Anna Mary *An Art Student in Munich.* London: Longman, 1853, First edition; 2 volumes in one, xii, 244; (4), 216 pages, some slight foxing, very good, contemporary half morocco with elaborate gilt tooled spine, marbled boards and edges, some rubbing to boards, inscribed for Isabel Milnes Gaskell, from her sister. Ken Spelman Rare Books 68 - 44 2011 £125

Howitt, William *The Mad War-Planet and Other Poems.* London: Longman, Green, Reader & Dyer, 1871, First edition; half title, 32 page catalog (July 1870), original green cloth, blocked in blind and gilt, spine lettered gilt, bookseller's ticket, W. Hebbett, Nottingham, very good. Jarndyce Antiquarian Booksellers CXCI - 210 2011 £75

Howitt, William *The Rural Life of England.* London: Longman, Orme etc., 1838, First edition; pages xx, 396; ii, 386, (xviii, ads), 2 half titles, engraved title vignettes and 2 engraved headpieces, very nice sound. R. F. G. Hollett & Son Antiquarian Booksellers General Catalogue Summer 2010 - 659 2011 £250

Howitt, William *Visits to Remarkable Places: Old Halls, Battle-Fields and Scenes Illustrative of Striking Passages in English History and Poetry.* London: Longman Brown, Green, Longmans & Roberts, 1856, Third edition; engraved titles, illustrations, original green cloth by Westleys & Co., decorated in gilt, spines slightly faded, hinges slightly cracked, nice. Jarndyce Antiquarian Booksellers CXCI - 557 2011 £75

Howker, Janni *Martin Farrell.* Julia MacRae Books, 1994, First edition; original boards, gilt, dust jacket, pages 86, presentation copy inscribed on dedication page. R. F. G. Hollett & Sons Antiquarian Booksellers 170 - 341 2011 £35

Howley, M. F. *Ecclesiastical History of Newfoundland.* Boston: Doyle & Whittle, 1888, First edition; 8vo., pages (6)-426, black and white frontispiece and 22 black and white maps and illustrations, inner hinge cracking, last flyleaf missing, boards worn, green cloth with blindstamp design to covers and gilt title to spine. Schooner Books Ltd. 96 - 52 2011 $100

Howsam, Leslie *Scientists Since 1660: a Bibliography of Biographies.* Aldershot and Brookfield: Ashgate, 1997, 8vo., vii, 150 pages, burgundy cloth, gilt stamped cover and spine titles, fine. Jeff Weber Rare Books 161 - 214 2011 $90

Hoyle, Edmund 1672-1759 *Mr. Hoyle's Games of Whist, Quadrille, Piquet, Chess and Back Gammon, Complete.* London: printed for Thomas Osborne, Stanley Crowder and Richard Baldwin, n.d., 1775, Twelfth edition; original full speckled calf gilt, little worn, hinges cracked, pages xii, 214, name on pastedown dated 1775, front flyleaf removed, some ink splashes on title, corners torn from 2 leaves with slight loss to text of one, but very good unsophisticated copy. R. F. G. Hollett & Son Antiquarian Booksellers General Catalogue Summer 2010 - 1255 2011 £275

Hoyle, Fred *Frontiers of Astronomy.* London: Heinemann, 1955, First edition; original cloth, gilt, spine and edges rather faded, pages xvi, 360, 59 plates. R. F. G. Hollett & Son Antiquarian Booksellers General Catalogue Summer 2010 - 1118 2011 £35

Hoyningen-Huene, Paul *Reconstructing Scientific Resolutions: Thomas S. Kuhn's Philosophy of Science.* Chicago and London: University of Chicago Press, 1993, 8vo., xx, 310 pages, light yellow cloth, black stamped spine title, fine from the Bern Dibner reference library, with Burndy bookplate. Jeff Weber Rare Books 161 - 217 2011 $60

Hubbard, Arthur John H *Neolithic Dew-Ponds and Cattle-Ways.* London: Longmans, Green and Co., 1916, Third edition; large 8vo., pages xxii, 116, (i), with 29 plates. R. F. G. Hollett & Son Antiquarian Booksellers 177 - 478 2011 £65

Hubbard, Elbert 1856-1915 *Little Journeys to the Homes of Great Musicians. Volume Nine. New Series.* New York: Roycrofters, 1901, Limited edition, no. 76 of 940 copies, signed by author; original limp reverse calf with yapp edges, rather faded, green watered silk pastedown, yellow silk marker, pages 150, top edge gilt, gilt, uncut, 6 portraits, title, decorations and initials hand colored by May Baker. R. F. G. Hollett & Son Antiquarian Booksellers 175 - 674 2011 £125

Hubbard, Elbert 1856-1915 *Little Journeys to the Homes of Great Musicians.* New York: Roycrofters, 1901, 2 volumes, square 8vo., original limp reversed dark brown calf with yapp edges, lettered in blind with green central floral decoration to each board, hand marbled endpapers, pages 150, 159, (iii), uncut, 12 portrait, 12 titles decorated and printed in red and black. R. F. G. Hollett & Son Antiquarian Booksellers 175 - 675 2011 £65

Hubbard, Frank *Three Centuries of Harpsichord Making.* Cambridge: Harvard University Press, 1972, Large 8vo., original cloth gilt, spine trifle rubbed, pages xvi, 371, plus 41 plates. R. F. G. Hollett & Son Antiquarian Booksellers 175 - 676 2011 £40

Hubbard, Hesketh *Architectural Painting in Oils.* Sir Isaac Pitman, 1938, First edition; pages 28, 2 color plates and black and white illustrations, large 8vo., original pictorial boards by Malcolm Easton, scattered spotting, uncommon. R. F. G. Hollett & Son Antiquarian Booksellers 177 - 479 2011 £35

Hubbard, John Gellibrand *How Should an Income tax be Levied?* London: Longman, Brown, Green and Longmans, 1852, First edition; 8vo., 55, (1) pages, preserved in modern wrappers, printed title label on upper cover, very good, uncommon. John Drury Rare Books 153 - 64 2011 £150

Hubbard, John Gellibrand *Reform or Reject the Income Tax.* London: Longman, Brown, Green and Longmans, 1853, First edition; 8vo, 52 pages, modern wrappers, printed title label on upper cover, very good, uncommon. John Drury Rare Books 153 - 65 2011 £150

Hubbell, Rose String *Quacky Doodles' and Danny Daddles' Book.* Chicago: Volland, 1916, Printing statement not legible; 8vo., pictorial boards, fine in original pictorial box, illustrations in color on every page by Gruelle and silhouette endpapers. Aleph-Bet Books, Inc. 95 - 267 2011 $1850

Huddart, Joseph *Memoir of the Late Captain Joseph Huddart.* printed for private circulation W. Phillips, 1821, 4to., old half calf gilt with raised bands and Spanish marbled board, edges little rubbed, spine label defective, vii, 102, lithographed portrait (corner waterstained), woodcut vignette on title and extending engraved plate, very scarce.   R. F. G. Hollett & Son Antiquarian Booksellers   173 - 577 2011   £250

Hudleston, C. Roy *An Armorial for Westmorland and Lonsdale.* Lake District Museum Trust and CWAAS, 1975, Original crimson rexine gilt, pages xxxiii, 337, frontispiece and 5 pages of illustrations, inscribed by author.   R. F. G. Hollett & Son Antiquarian Booksellers   173 - 134 2011   £65

Hudleston, C. Roy *Cumberland Families and Heraldry with a Supplement...* Kendal: Titus Wilson, 1978, Signed limited deluxe edition (no. 13 of 50 copies); original full crimson calf gilt, arms in gilt on boards, pages vi, 429, frontispiece and 5 pages of illustrations, Whittington Hall copy with bookplate of Brian and Enid Greenwood.   R. F. G. Hollett & Son Antiquarian Booksellers   173 - 580 2011   £150

Hudleston, C. Roy *Cumberland Familes and Heraldry...* Kendal: Titus Wilson for the CWAAS, 1978, First edition; (standard edition but with deluxe binding).   R. F. G. Hollett & Son Antiquarian Booksellers   173 - 581 2011   £95

Hudleston, C. Roy *Howard Family Documents.* Durham: The University, 1968-1970, 3 volumes, folio, unbound and side-sewn as issued, pages 219; 216; 125, cyclostyled on each recto.   R. F. G. Hollett & Son Antiquarian Booksellers   173 - 578 2011   £180

Hudleston, C. Roy *Naworth Estate and Household Account 1648-1660.* Durham: Andrew & Co., 1958, Original green cloth, pages vii-xiv, 247, pages i-vi not present as correct.   R. F. G. Hollett & Son Antiquarian Booksellers   173 - 583 2011   £65

Hudson, William Henry   1841-1922   *Far Away and Long Ago.* Buenos Aires: 1943, Limited to 1500 copies; 307 pages, elaborate cowhide, half unscoured (with hair remaining) and half tanned without hair, rawhide endpapers, near fine.   Bookworm & Silverfish   666 - 20 2011 $125

Hudson, William Henry   1841-1922   *Nature in Downland.* London: Longmans, Green and Co., 1900, First edition; half title, frontispiece, engraved titlepage, plates and illustrations, uncut in original green buckram, slightly marked, presentation inscription to Paul Harvey, from friend Henry James.   Jarndyce Antiquarian Booksellers   CXCI - 221 2011   £850

Hudson, William Henry   1841-1922   *153 Letters from W. H. Hudson.* London: Nonesuch Press, 1923, One of 1000 copies; 260 x 172mm., 1 p.l. 191, (1) pages, (1) leaf, original brown buckram over bevelled boards, flat spine with paper label, edges untrimmed, titlepage with photogravure portrait of Hudson, one full page illustration, spare paper label tipped onto rear endpaper, partly torn bookplate of Betty Ricket(ts), boards bit marked and with one small puncture, trivial creasing to few leaves, otherwise nearly fine.   Phillip J. Pirages   59 - 272 2011 $150

Hughes, Edward *North Country Life in the Eighteenth Century. Volume I: The North-East 1700-1750.* Oxford University Press, 1952, First edition; original cloth, gilt, dust jacket, spine little darkened and frayed at head, pages xxi, 435, with 7 illustrations and map.   R. F. G. Hollett & Son Antiquarian Booksellers   General Catalogue Summer 2010 - 1441 2011   £50

Hughes, Edward *North Country Life in the Eighteenth Century. Volume II: Cumberland and Westmoreland 1700-1830.* Oxford University Press, 1965, First edition; original cloth, gilt, dust jacket, pages viii,4 26, 6 illustrations and map.   R. F. G. Hollett & Son Antiquarian Booksellers   173 - 588 2011   £50

Hughes, H. Harold *The Old Churches of Snowdonia.* Bangor: Jarvis & Foster, 1924, First edition; pages xiii, 285, uncut, with 35 plates and numerous text illustrations, original holland backed boards, paper labels, little rubbed. R. F. G. Hollett & Son Antiquarian Booksellers   177 - 481 2011   £85

Hughes, H. Harold *The Old Churches of Snowdonia.* Capel Curig: National Park Society, 1979, Limited edition (1000 copies); pages vii, 75, xxv-xxxviii, 12 plates, numerous text drawings, scarce, original cloth, gilt, dust jacket. R. F. G. Hollett & Son Antiquarian Booksellers   177 - 482 2011   £30

Hughes, H. Harold *The Old Churches of Snowdonia.* Capel Curig: National Park Society, 1984, Limited facsimile edition, number 856 of 2000 copies; pages 16, 309, 35 plates, numerous text illustrations and maps on endpapers. R. F. G. Hollett & Son Antiquarian Booksellers   177 - 483 2011   £35

Hughes, J. E. *Eighteen Years on Lake Bangweulu.* London: Field, 1933, Second impression; quarto, pages xvi, 376, map on front endpapers, numerous illustrations, original orange decorative cloth, small split (repaired) at head of spine, internally very good, clean copy.   J. & S. L. Bonham Antiquarian Booksellers   Africa 4/20/2011 - 8833 2011   £1200

Hughes, John *Itinerary of Provence and the Rhone, Made During the Year 1819.* London: James Cawthorn, 1819, Second edition, only 100 copies printed, large paper copy with india proof plates; large 4to., half title, frontispiece, engraved titlepage vignette and plates, uncut in later half calf, red label, slightly rubbed, corners slightly worn. Jarndyce Antiquarian Booksellers   CXCI - 558   2011   £280

Hughes, Langston *The Big Sea.* New York: 1945, Later printing; (12), 335, (1) pages, cloth, very nice, slightly chipped and creased dust jacket, presentation copy inscribed by author in Akron in 1948.   Joseph J. Felcone Inc. Fall Miscellany 2010 - 62   2011 $375

Hughes, Langston *Fine Clothes to the Jew (poems).* New York: Knopf, 1927, First edition; pages 90, cloth backed boards, spine faded, front hinge tender, very good, scarce.   Second Life Books Inc.   174 - 184   2011 $650

Hughes, Langston *The Weary Blues.* New York: Alfred A. Knopf, 1926, One of 1500 copies printed; small 8vo., original blue cloth backed decorated boards, covers lightly rubbed, lacking rare dust jacket, otherwise in very good condition, presentation copy inscribed by author for George Gershwin.   James S. Jaffe Rare Books   May 26 2011 - 21625 2011 $45,000

Hughes, Langston *The Weary Blues.* New York: Alfred A. Knopf, 1926, First edition, one of 1500 copies; Advance copy with publisher's review slip giving publication date laid in, small 8vo., original blue cloth backed decorated boards, pictorial dust jacket by Covarrubias, extremities of boards slightly rubbed, former owner's signature "Juliette Sessions" on front endpaper, else fine in lightly chipped dust jacket which is faintly darkened along spine, extremely rare in dust jacket.   James S. Jaffe Rare Books   May 26 2011 - 21624   2011 $25,000

Hughes, Richard *A High Wind in Jamaica.* London: Chatto & Windus, 1929, First edition; one of 150 deluxe copies, signed by author, 8vo., 284 pages, fine, buckram backed printed boards, contemporary bookplate of bookseller Herbert F. West, spine trifle faded, some light foxing, very nice, clean copy.   Second Life Books Inc.   174 - 185   2011 $525

Hughes, Stephen *Collieries of Wales.* Royal Commission on the Ancient and Historical Monuments of Wales, n.d., 1994, Large 8vo., original wrappers, pages 76, illustrations. R. F. G. Hollett & Son Antiquarian Booksellers   177 - 486   2011   £75

Hughes, Ted 1930-1998 *Ffangs the Vampire Bat and the Kiss of Truth.* London: Faber, 1986, First edition; numerous line drawings, some full page by Charles Riddell, pages 96, 4to., original black boards, backstrip printed in silver, dust jacket, fine.   Blackwell Rare Books   B166 - 166   2011   £30

Hughes, Ted 1930-1998 *Ffangs the Vampire Bat and the Kiss of Truth.* London: Faber, 1986, First edition; small 4to., original cloth, gilt, dust jacket, pages 96, illustrations.   R. F. G. Hollett & Sons Antiquarian Booksellers 170 - 343   2011   £40

Hughes, Ted 1930-1998 *The Hawk in the Rain.* London: Faber & Faber, 1957, First edition; 8vo., pages (ii), 60, (2), foxing to front and endpages, otherwise crisp and clean, original blue boards, yellow lettering to spine, small bump to lower spine but minimal shelfwear, unclipped, original yellow jacket (minor foxing, tiny fragment chipped from top spine cap and minute tear to lower one).   Simon Finch Rare Books   Zero - 323   2011   £300

Hughes, Ted 1930-1998 *Roosting Hawk.* Grecourt Review, 1959, First edition; 8vo., printed wrappers, offsetting from newspaper insert on inside front cover, otherwise fine, presentation copy inscribed on inside front wrapper by poet to his mother-in-law, Aurelia Plath June 24 1959. James S. Jaffe Rare Books   May 26 2011 - 20984   2011 $7500

Hughes, Ted 1930-1998 *Wolfwatching.* London: Faber & Faber, 1989, First edition; signed presentation to Audrey (Nicholson) the actress, from the author, loosely inserted card signed by Olwyn Hughes, author's sister for Audrey, fine in very good+ dust jacket slightly rubbed at edges.   Any Amount of Books   May 29 2011 - A68490   2011 $272

Hughes, Thomas 1822-1896 *Early Memories for the Children by the Author of Tom Brown's Schooldays.* Thomas Burleigh for Private Circulation only, 1899, First edition; Presentation copy from author's widow, Fanny to Edward Clifford, pages (2), 78, 8vo., uncut, original grey blue card wrappers with title printed in blue on upper cover, olive green paper backstrip, backstrip sometime reinforced with clear tape, but now defective at centre, presentation inscription slightly touched by glue adhering to cover, sound. Blackwell Rare Books   B166 - 52   2011   £275

Hughes, Thomas Francis, Mrs. *Among the Sons of Han.* London: Tinsley Brothers, 1881, First edition; octavo, viii, 314 pages, folding map, later full brick and buckram, ex-library bookplate and markings, very good, rare.   Jeff Weber Rare Books   163 - 179   2011 $100

Hugill, Robert *Castles and Peles of Cumberland and Westmorland.* Newcastle upon Tyne: Frank Graham, 1977, First edition; pages vii, 198, illustrations, original cloth, gilt, dust jacket price clipped.   R. F. G. Hollett & Son Antiquarian Booksellers   177 - 488   2011   £50

Hugo, Thomas *The History of Mynchin Buckland Priory and Preceptory in the County of Somerset.* London: J. R. Smith and Taunton: F. May, 1861, Large paper copy; 4to., modern half levant morocco gilt, pages viii, 112, with 4 lithographed plates, modern half levant morocco gilt. R. F. G. Hollett & Son Antiquarian Booksellers 177 - 489 2011 £130

Hugo, Victor 1802-1865 *Aux Etats Unis d'Amerique.* Octon: Verdigris Press, 2007, One of 4 deluxe copies, each with original pencil and Chinese ink wash painting, double page spread which is preparatory study for the book's mezzotint, from a total edition of 45, all on Rives BFK for text and Hahnemuhle for double page foldout mezzotint, each signed and numbered by artist, Judith Rothchild; page size 7 7/8 x 4 5/8 inches, 14 pages, bound by printer, Mark Lintott, leporello style with brown marbled paper over boards and black cloth showing at spine and edges, title and author in black on spine and front panel, interior guards with tan marbled paper over boards, opening with French text on left and English translation on right, double page mezzotint unfolds across middle, book and special portfolio housing the original painting are both in publisher's custom made black cloth clamshell box with tan and brown marbled papers on spine and front panel with title on front and title, author, artist and press on spine. Priscilla Juvelis - Rare Books 48 - 25 2011 $1250

Hugo, Victor 1802-1865 *(Bug Jargal). The Slave King: a Historical Account of the Rebellion of the Negros in St. Domingo.* London: Simms & M'Intyre, 1852, Last two leaves text with small tear in outer margin with slight loss not affecting text, contemporary half red morocco, green cloth boards, very good. Jarndyce Antiquarian Booksellers CXCI - 211 2011 £65

Hugo, Victor 1802-1865 *Les Contemplations.* Paris: Michel Levy, 1856, First edition; 2 volumes, quarter leather, marbled boards lettered and decorated gilt on spine, pages 359 and 408, some rubbing and spine, otherwise sound, good example with occasional slight foxing. Any Amount of Books May 29 2011 - A61971 2011 $340

Hugo, Victor 1802-1865 *The Hunchback of Notre Dame.* Philadelphia: Carey, Lea and Blanchard, 1834, First American edition; 2 volumes, 12mo., original quarter blue cloth over drab boards, original printed paper spine labels, uncut. Heritage Book Shop Booth A12 51st NY International Antiquarian Book Fair April 8-10 2011 - 70 2011 $5000

Hugo, Victor 1802-1865 *Les Miserables.* New York: Carleton, 1862, First American edition; 5 volumes, 8vo., pages 171, (5); 164, (4); 150, (2); 184; 165, (3), closed tear to first gathering of volume ii, 1 leaf loose, occasional spotting and light soiling in all volumes, generally very clean, all volumes in publisher's cloth, (volume i blue, others purple), blind tooled with lettering and decoration to spines in gilt, volume i chipped at foot of spine, spines of volumes iv and v sunned, all volumes lightly rubbed and bumped, owner's signature, discreet bookseller's stamps. Simon Finch Rare Books Zero - 237 2011 £950

Hugo, Victor 1802-1865 *Notre-Dame De Paris.* New York: Paris: Limited Editions Club, 1930, First edition with these illustrations; one of 1500 copies numbered and signed by Frans Masereel, printed on velin d'Arches, 10 x 8 inches text in English, 310, 376 pages, 11 full page and 11 small woodcuts by Masereel, this copy bound in original wrappers with modern glassine protectors, no slipcase, backstrips with very minor creasing, as usual, tiny stain on top edge of volume one, inside very clean and bright, no foxing, overall close to fine. Gemini Fine Books & Arts, Ltd. Art Reference & Illustrated Books: First Editions 2011 $200

Hugo, Victor 1802-1865 *Toilers of the Sea.* London: Sampson Low, Son & Marston, 1866, First English edition; 3 volumes, 16mo., pages ix, (i) bank, 331, (i) bank; v, (i) blank, 327, (i) imprint; iv, 286, (2) ads, 16 ads, spotted in places and lightly soiled, few leaf tips chipped in volume iii, publisher's cloth, green panels blindstamped, spines with lettering and decoration in gilt, light brownish grey endpapers, all slightly rubbed, rear hinge to volume i cracked, endpapers to volume iii torn along hinge, very good. Simon Finch Rare Books Zero - 238 2011 £1000

Huidekoper, Frederich L. *33rd Division American Expeditionary Forces from Its Arrival in France Until the Armistice with Germany November 11 1918.* Luxembourg: 1919, 32 pages, wrappers, paper age toned. Bookworm & Silverfish 662 - 205 2011 $75

Huie, James *An Abridgment of all the Statutes Now in Force, Relative to the Revenue of Excise in Great Britain...* Edinburgh: printed for the author, 1804, Second edition; contemporary full polished calf with spine label, pages xl, 654, armorial bookplate of Skipness. R. F. G. Hollett & Son Antiquarian Booksellers 175 - 681 2011 £150

Hujar, Peter *Portraits in Life and Death.* New York: Da Capo Press, 1976, First edition; 4to., pages (96), 40 black and white photos, original grey cloth, spine and boards lettered in light gray, original black and white photo illustrated dust jacket, lightly rubbed, tear with some loss to head of spine, chip to foot, fine copy in very good dust jacket. Simon Finch Rare Books Zero - 529 2011 £1000

Hulburd, Percy *Lord Hever.* London: Richard Bentley, 1896, First edition; 2 volumes, 8vo., green cloth lettered gilt, pages viii, 347; vi, 361, neatly rebacked with new endpapers, very good.   Any Amount of Books   May 29 2011 - B28136   2011 $221

Hull, David *Darwin and His Critics: The Reception of Darwin's theory of Evolution by the Scientific Community.* Cambridge: Harvard University Press, 1974, Second printing; 8vo., xii, 473 pages, tan cloth, black stamped spine title, dust jacket lightly rubbed, near fine, from the Bern Dibner reference library, with Burndy bookplate.   Jeff Weber Rare Books   161 - 218   2011 $75

Hull, William *Memoirs of the Campaign of the North Western Army of the United States A.D. 1812.* Boston: True & Greene, 1824, First edition; 8vo., 229, 10 pages, original printed wrappers, uncut, foxed, inscribed presentation by author to Honble. Mr. Nelson.   M & S Rare Books, Inc.   90 - 434   2011 $950

Hullmandel, Charles *The Art of Drawing on Stone, Giving a Full Explanation of the Various Styles of the Different Methods to be Employed to Ensure Success...* London: C. V. Hullmandell and R. Ackermann, 1824, First edition; lithographed titlepage, 6 lithographed plates, including two in colors and one on India paper, occasional minor spotting or browning, uncut, pages xvi, vii, 92, (2, ads, browned and window mounted), royal 8vo., later drab boards, paper lettering piece on spine, but any lettering once thereupon now vanished, trifle worn, original front of printed paper wrapper tipped on to inside front cover, booklabel of Vivian Ridler, good.   Blackwell Rare Books   B166 - 53   2011   £1500

Hulme, F. Edward *Familiar Wild Flowers Series 1 to 5.* London: Cassell, Petter and Galpin, n.d. c., 1878-1884, First edition; 5 volumes, original pictorial green cloth gilt extra over bevelled boards, foot of one spine defective, 200 color plates, good bright and sound set.   R. F. G. Hollett & Son Antiquarian Booksellers   General Catalogue Summer 2010 - 988   2011   £250

Hulsius, Levinus *Chronologia, hoc est Brevis Descriptio Rerum Memorabilium in Provinciis hac Adiuncta Tabula Topographica Comprehensis Gestarum...* Nurnberg: C. Lochner, 1597, 4to., (6), 89 (recte 90) pages large armorial engraving on title (arms of imperial provinces) and of Eberhard, Bishop of Spier on f A2v, contemporary vellum, foot of spine worn, from the library of the Earls of Macclesfield at Shirburn Castle.   Maggs Bros. Ltd.   1440 - 113   2011   £500

Humber, Robert D. *Heversham. The Story of Westmorland School and Village.* Kendal: Titus Wilson, 1968, First edition; original cloth, gilt, dust jacket, pages (vi), 153, frontispiece.   R. F. G. Hollett & Son Antiquarian Booksellers   173 - 596   2011   £35

Humberto. no information whatsoever, possibly circa 1950's?, Large 4to., full color paper covered boards with some light rippling and maybe a hint of browning, wonderful double page pop-up in lovely condition.   Jo Ann Reisler, Ltd.   86 - 196   2011 $485

Hume, Fergus *The Lone Inn. A Mystery.* London: Jarrold, 1894, First edition; 8vo., original publisher's green cloth lettered gilt on spine and on front cover, attractive gilt decoration on cover of an arrow and hearts and masquerade mask, 265 pages, slight foxing to prelims, clean, bright, very good+.   Any Amount of Books   May 29 2011 - A36028   2011 $221

Humphrey, L. B. *Sweet-Girl Goldie: a Wonder Story of Butterfly Time.* New York: Spinney & Perkins, 1884, 4to., stiff pictorial card covers bound with silk ties and die-cut entirely in shape of butterfly, small piece repaired else near fine, beautiful chromolithographs.   Aleph-Bet Books, Inc.   95 - 531   2011 $475

Humphrey, Maud *The Book of Pets.* New York: Frederick A. Stokes, 1893, First edition; 4to., cloth backed color pictorial boards, bit of shelfwear, else lovely condition, 12 full page color plates plus color illustrations, lovely copy.   Jo Ann Reisler, Ltd.   86 - 141   2011 $850

Humphreys, Arthur L. *The Berkshire Book of Song, Rhyme, a Steeple Chime.* London: Methuen & Co., 1935, First edition; pages 267, original cloth backed boards, little soiled and very faded, library numbers on spine, spare spine label at end, few marginal blindstamps.   R. F. G. Hollett & Son Antiquarian Booksellers   175 - 685   2011   £35

Humphreys, Christmas *The Great Pearl Robbery of 1913.* London: Heinemann, 1929, First edition; original cloth, gilt, pages xiii, 300, 12 plate, little spotting to title and fore-edge.   R. F. G. Hollett & Son Antiquarian Booksellers   175 - 685   2011   £35

Hungerford, Edward *The Story of the Baltimore & Ohio Railroad 1827-1927.* New York: and London: G. P. Putnam's Sons, 1928, First edition; 8vo., xii, 372; x, 365 pages, frontispiece, plates, navy cloth, gilt stamped spine title, top edge gilt, dust jackets worn with pieces missing, top spine cloth torn on both volumes, titles affected, good, from the Bern Dibner reference library, with Burndy bookplate.   Jeff Weber Rare Books   161 - 219   2011 $75

Hunt, C. J. *The Book Trade in Northumberland and Durham to 1860.* Newcastle upon tyne: Thorne's Bookshop for the History of the Book Trade in the North, 1975, First edition; original cloth, gilt, dust jacket, pages xviii, 116, with 14 illustrations.   R. F. G. Hollett & Son Antiquarian Booksellers   General Catalogue Summer 2010 - 427   2011   £35

Hunt, Henry *Investigation at Ilchester Gaol, in the County of Somerset, into the conduct of William Bridle, the Gaoler, Before the Commissioners Appointed by the Crown.* London: Thomas Dolby, 1821, First edition in book form; 8vo., fine etched frontispiece by George Cruikshank, viii, 7 (1) 271 (5) 8 pages, absolutely complete including two supplementary addresses found in some copies, contemporary half calf, gilt and marbled boards, some general wear to sides and extremities, nonetheless very good.   John Drury Rare Books   153 - 66   2011   £450

Hunt, Henry *To the Radical Reformers, Male and Female of England, Ireland and Scotland.* Ilchester Gaol: printed by W. Molineux up to 23.12.1820 and thereafter by T. Dolby, June 15th 1820-Feb. 11th 1822, 1820-1822, 28 separate issues, each with caption title, total of approximately 614 pages, variable foxing, bound in one volume in contemporary half calf gilt over marbled boards, neatly rebacked and labelled, in good state of preservation.   John Drury Rare Books   153 - 67   2011   £750

Hunt, Henry *The Trial of Henry Hunt, John Knight, Joseph Johnson, John Thacker Saxton, Samuel Bamford, Joseph Healey, James Moorhouse, Robert Jones, George Swift and Robert Wilde for an Alledged conspiracy to alter the Law by Force and Threats and for Convening and Attending an Illegal Rioutous and Tumultuous Meeting at Manchester...* Manchester: printed by T. J. Evans, 1820, 8vo., iv, 232 pages, titlepage little browned, original boards (soiled), neatly rebacked, entirely uncut, good, large copy, several old related press cuttings tipped in.   John Drury Rare Books   153 - 154   2011   £275

Hunt, Irene *Up a Road Slowly.* Chicago: Follett, 1966, Stated first printed; 8vo., pictorial cloth, fine in very good+ dust jacket with small closed tear, quite scarce.   Aleph-Bet Books, Inc.   95 - 300   2011 $400

Hunt, J. Eric *English and Welsh Crucifixes 670-1550.* London: SPCK, 1956, First edition; large 8vo., original cloth, gilt, dust jacket, pages (viii), 92 with color frontispiece and 39 plates.   R. F. G. Hollett & Son Antiquarian Booksellers   175 - 687   2011   £40

Hunt, Leigh 1784-1859 *Lord Byron and Some of His Contemporaries: With recollections of the Author's Life and of His Visit to Italy.* Colburn, 1828, Second edition; 2 volumes, xi, 450; 449 pages, 6 plates, original boards, hinges weak, occasional foxing, stain on fore corner of much of volume II.   C. P. Hyland   May 26 2011 - 145   2011 $275

Hunt, Rachel McMasters Miller *Catalogue of Botanical Books in the Collection of...* Pittsburgh: Hunt Botanical Library, 1958-1961, Limited to 750 sets; 3 volumes, large 8vo., lxxiv, 517; ccxliv; ix, 655 pages, frontispiece, plates, dark green cloth, gilt stamped cover illustrations and spine titles, fine, from the Bern Dibner reference library, with Burndy bookplate.   Jeff Weber Rare Books   161 - 220   2011 $700

Hunt, Violet *The Last Ditch.* London: Stanley Paul, 1918, First edition; 8vo., original publisher's brown lettered black at spine, pages 309, 27 page publisher's catalog at rear dated 1918 signed presentation from author for Rachel Ferguson, slight wear, slight rubbing, slight marks, else sound, near very good.   Any Amount of Books   May 29 2011 - A67122   2011 $238

Hunter, Andrew *Thornton and Tully' Scientific Books, Libraries and Collectors: a Study of Bibliography and the Book trade in Relation to the History of Science.* Aldershot: Ashgate, 2000, Revision of third 1971 London edition; 8vo., xii, 405 pages, 8 plates, green cloth, silver stamped spine title, dust jacket, fine, from the Bern Dibner reference library, with Burndy bookplate.   Jeff Weber Rare Books   161 - 221   2011 $150

Hunter, John *The Natural History of Human Teeth: Explaining their Structure, Use, Formation, Growth and Diseases.* London: for J. Johnson, 1771, First edition; 4to., (8), 128 pages, 16 engraved plates, with facing letterpress, 19th century half roan, headcap neatly replaced, lightly scuffed, corners worn), just hint of foxing in top margin, else clean, wide margined copy, armorial bookplate of Frederick Symonds.   Joseph J. Felcone Inc.   Fall Miscellany 2010 - 38   2011 $4500

Hunter, Joseph *Hallamshire. The History and Topography of the Parish of Sheffield in the County of York.* London: printed for the author by Richard and Arthur Taylor, published by Lackington, Hughes, Harding, Mavor and Jones, 1819, Large paper copy, folio, pages x, (ii) 299 (I) + engraved frontispiece and 8 other engraved plates, later hard grain purple morocco, spine single ruled in blind, lettered direct in gilt, 'place & date' direct in gilt at foot, turn-ins decorative roll gilt, 'French Shell' 'made' endpapers, all edges gilt, dark blue and pink sewn flat endbands, some foxing to plates and facing leaves, little rubbed at extremities, unidentified Knight of the Gater armorial gilt stamped on both boards, signed binding stamp "Tuckett Binder to the Queen", from the collection of Christopher Ernest Weston 1947-2010.   Unsworths Booksellers   24 - 111   2011   £400

Hunter, Michael *Elias Ashmole 1617-1692: The Founder of the Ashmolean Museum and His World A Tercenteary Exhibition 27 April to 31 July 1983.* Oxford: Ashmolean Museum, 1983, 8vo., xi, 92 pages, color frontispiece, 12 plates, printed wrappers, fine, from the Bern Dibner reference library, with Burndy bookplate.   Jeff Weber Rare Books   161 - 222   2011 $55

Hunter, Monica *Reaction to Conquest: Effects of Contact with Europeans on the Pondo of South Africa.* Oxford: University Press, 1936, First edition; 8vo., pages xx, 582, maps, illustrations, original blue cloth.   J. & S. L. Bonham Antiquarian Booksellers   Africa 4/20/2011 - 5401   2011   £35

Hunter, Robert *The Preservation of Open Spaces and of Footpaths, and of Other Rights of Way.* London: Eyre and Spottiswoode,, 1896, First edition; 8vo., xxii, (2), 424 pages, complete with half title, text followed by several (16) pages of publishers' ads, original green cloth, lettered in gilt, minor rubbing and signs of use to extremities, very good, internally fine.   John Drury Rare Books   153 - 68   2011   £150

Hunter, Robert *The Preservation of Open Spaces and Footpaths and Other Rights of Way.* London: Eyre and Spottiswoode, 1896, First edition; original cloth, gilt, little marked, hinges trifle rubbed, pages xxii, 424, (xiv), scarce.   R. F. G. Hollett & Son Antiquarian Booksellers   175 - 688   2011   £75

Hunter, William S. *Hunter's Ottawa Scenery in the Vicinity of Ottawa City, Canada.* 19 pages, 14 lithographed plates plus lithographed titlepage and folding map, handsomely rebound with original blindstamped title laid down on front board, internally text pages evenly browned, plates have slight edge browning, but otherwise splendidly clean and bright,.   Dumont Maps & Books of the West   113 - 36   2011 $1850

Hurd, Edith Thacher *The Fireman's Friend.* Philadelphia: J. B. Lippincott, 1956, 8vo., pictorial cloth, fine in very slightly soiled dust jacket, illustrations by Clement Hurd with charming color lithographs on every page printed in blue on yellow paper, great copy.   Aleph-Bet Books, Inc.   95 - 301   2011 $125

Hurley, Vic *Men in Sun Helmets.* New York: 1936, Second printing; 252 pages, solid copy, modest rear soil, inscribed and signed by author.   Bookworm & Silverfish   670 - 124   2011 $75

Hurlimann, Bettina *Three Centuries of Children's Books in Europe.* London: Oxford University Press, 1967, First English edition; original cloth, gilt, dust jacket price clipped, pages xviii, 297, 28 plates.   R. F. G. Hollett & Sons Antiquarian Booksellers   170 - 344 2011   £40

Hurt, Freda *Mr. Twink Takes Charge.* Langley: Epworth Press, 1954, First edition; illustrations by Nina Scott Langley, dust jacket unclipped but some chipping top and base of spine, over original green cloth, very good.   C. P. Hyland   May 26 2011 - 821   2011 $435

Hussain, Iqbalunnisa *Purdah and Polygamy. Life in an Indian Muslim Household.* Bangalore: S. R. Zaman, 1944, First edition; original boards, spine and edges faded, spine rather cracked in places, dust jacket, pages 310 compliment slip of Sir C. R. Reddy and authoress tipped in, very scarce.   R. F. G. Hollett & Son Antiquarian Booksellers   175 - 690   2011   £75

Hussey, Christopher *Clarence House. the Home of Her Royal Highness the Princess Elizabeth Duchess of Edinburgh and of His Royal Highness, the Duke of Edinburgh.* London: Country Life, 1949, First edition; 4to., original cloth, gilt, dust jacket, pages 136 with 66 plates, fore-edge little spotted.   R. F. G. Hollett & Son Antiquarian Booksellers   177 - 491   2011   £50

Hussey, Christopher *English Country Houses Open to the Public.* London: Country Life, 1957, Third edition; 4to., original cloth, gilt, dust jacket price clipped, pages 240, with 389 illustrations.   R. F. G. Hollett & Son Antiquarian Booksellers   177 - 492   2011   £40

Hutcheson, F. *An Inquiry into the Original of Our Ideas of Beauty and Virtue....* London: for D. Midwinter, 1738, Fourth edition; xxi, (3), 304 (8) pages, very good in contemporary calf, expertly rebacked, ruled bands, red morocco label, board edges very neatly repaired with fresh contemporary endpapers.   Ken Spelman Rare Books   68 - 4   2011   £395

Hutchings, J. M. *Hutchings' Tourist Guide to the Yosemite Valley.* San Francisco: A. Roman & Co., 1877, First edition; 16mo., (1)-102, (4, blank), frontispiece, map, original brown cloth, rebacked with original spine laid down, board stamped in blind, front board lettered gilt, corners bit bumped and rubbed, cloth slightly wrinkled, very clean inside, very good.   Heritage Book Shop   Holiday 2010 - 58   2011 $1500

Hutchinson, F. E. *Mediaeval Glass at All Souls College.* London: Faber, 1949, First edition; tall 8vo., original cloth, gilt, dust jacket, small edge tear, pages 67 with color frontispiece and 31 plates.   R. F. G. Hollett & Son Antiquarian Booksellers   177 - 492   2011   £40

Hutchinson, George Thomas *From the Cape to the Zambesi.* London: John Murray, 1905, First edition; 8vo., pages xiv, 205, frontispiece, 23 plates, original red cloth, very good, spine lightly faded.   J. & S. L. Bonham Antiquarian Booksellers   Africa 4/20/2011 - 7900   2011   £85

Hutchinson, H. N. *Marriage Customs in Many Lands.* London: Seeley & Co., 1897, Large 8vo., original pictorial cloth, gilt, board edges, little damped and bumped, spine trifle faded, pages xii, 348, with 24 illustrations, lower joint cracking.   R. F. G. Hollett & Son Antiquarian Booksellers   175 - 692   2011   £40

Hutchinson, Horace *Big Game Shooting.* London: Country Life, 1905, First edition; 2 volumes 8vo., pages xiv, 301; x, 356, numerous illustrations, occasional light foxing in margins, original red decorative cloth, small wear to head tail of spines, corners rubbed, nick to head volume I (1 cm.).   J. & S. L. Bonham Antiquarian Booksellers   Africa 4/20/2011 - 8542   2011   £95

Hutchinson, Horace *Big Game Shooting.* London: Country Life, 1905, First edition; 2 volumes, 8vo., pages xiv, 301; x, 356, numerous illustrations, original purple cloth, small rubbing to 1 joint, very good, clean. J. & S. L. Bonham Antiquarian Booksellers Africa 4/20/2011 - 7507 2011 £165

Hutchinson, Horace *The New Book of Golf.* London: Longmans Green and Co., 1912, Original pictorial boards, pages xi, 362, frontispiece and 66 illustrations, flyleaves rather browned, scattered light spotting and little occasional pencilled lining but nice, sound copy, scarce. R. F. G. Hollett & Son Antiquarian Booksellers General Catalogue Summer 2010 - 1256 2011 £150

Hutchinson, Jonathan *Extracts from the Letters with Some Brief Notices of His Life and Character.* London: Harvey and Darton, 1841, Original blindstamped cloth, gilt, pages xxiv, 372. R. F. G. Hollett & Son Antiquarian Booksellers 175 - 693 2011 £35

Hutchinson, Thomas J. *Ten Years Wanderings Among the Ethiopians...* London: Hurst & Blackett, 1861, First edition; 8vo., page xx, 329, ads, color litho frontispiece, vignette on titlepage, original purple cloth, joints and corners rubbed, sprung in middle. J. & S. L. Bonham Antiquarian Booksellers Africa 4/20/2011 - 5544 2011 £280

Hutchinson, Veronica *Fireside Stories.* New York: Minton Balch & co., 1927, First edition; 4to., top edge tinted, brick red cloth with black lettering and vignette on front cover, red and black decorated dust jacket with minor shelf wear, 147 numbered pages, 6 full page color plates, four full page black and white plates and lots of black and white drawings. Jo Ann Reisler, Ltd. 86 - 159 2011 $400

Hutchinson, W. H. *The Life and Personal Writings of Eugene Manlove Rhodes. A Bar Cross Man.* Norman: University of Oklahoma Press, 1965, First edition; xix, 532 pages, 18 illustrations, 2 maps, gray green cloth, very fine in pictorial dust jacket, slightly chipped at head of spine, presentation inscription signed by author. Argonaut Book Shop Recent Acquisitions Summer 2010 - 170 2011 $90

Hutchinson, William *An Excursion to the Lakes in Westmoreland and Cumberland, with a Tour through Part of the Northern Counties in the Years 1773 and 1774.* J. Wilkie and W. Charnley, 1776, First edition; near contemporary half calf with marbled boards, neatly rebacked to match, original spine label re-laid, pages 382, (iv), 2 engraved text vignettes, contemporary inscription of James Waring on title, few pencilled marginalia by later owner William Ball of Glen Rothay. R. F. G. Hollett & Son Antiquarian Booksellers 173 - 603 2011 £295

Hutchinson, William *The History of the County of Cumberland and Some Places Adjacent....* Carlisle: F. Jollie, 1794, First edition; 2 volumes, 4to., modern half levant morocco with raised bands and contrasting double spine labels, pages (ii) 54 (catalogue of Cumberland animals by John Heysham), iv (list of sheriffs, (iv glossary), 600; 688-683-6 (index), 2 engraved titles, folding map (hand colored in outline), 4 folding or double page plans, 50 engraved plates, 1 hand tinted, 4 pages of tables, 1 extending table and over 50 woodcut or engraved illustrations, maps, few neat repairs to folding plates, etc., but handsome, sound set. R. F. G. Hollett & Son Antiquarian Booksellers 173 - 605 2011 £495

Hutchinson, William *The History of the County of Cumberland, and Some Places Adjacent, from the Earliest Accounts ot the Present Time...* Carlisle: F. Jollie, 1794, First edition; 2 volumes, 4to., old half calf gilt, boards rubbed, rebacked in pigskin with original lettering pieces and spine panels relaid, pages 600; 688, iv, 6, 683-6 2 engraved titles, 2 folding or double page plans, 50 engraved plates, 4 pages of tables, 1 extending table and over 50 woodcut or engraved illustrations, maps, etc. in text, lacks general map and plan of Carlisle and section on Cumberland animals by Heysham, some browning and foxing in places, but good, sound set. R. F. G. Hollett & Son Antiquarian Booksellers 173 - 604 2011 £350

Hutton, Hugh *Historical Account of Discoveries and Travels in Africa from the Earliest Ages to the Present Time...* Edinburgh: Archibald Constable, 1818, Second edition; 2 volumes, 8vo., pages 557; 550, 6 maps (browned), foxing in both volumes, recent brown full polished calf. J. & S. L. Bonham Antiquarian Booksellers Africa 4/20/2011 - 7214 2011 £120

Hutton, Ronald *The Pagan Religions of the Ancient British Isles.* BCA, 1991, Original cloth, gilt, dust jacket, pages xii, 397, frontispiece and text illustrations. R. F. G. Hollett & Son Antiquarian Booksellers 175 - 694 2011 £30

Hutton, S. K. *By Eskimo Dog Sled and Kayak a Description of a Missionary's Experiences and Adventures in Labrador.* London: Seeley, Service, & Co. Ltd., 1925, Second edition; beige cloth with red design and lettering to borders of spine and front cover, pages (4 ads), xii, 219, (12 pages of illustrated publisher's ads), half title, color frontispiece, 12 black and white illustrations, plus map, 8vo., mark from removal of previous owner's bookplate on first flyleaf, else very good. Schooner Books Ltd. 96 - 53 2011 $75

Hutton, William *A Trip to Coatham; a Watering Place in the North Extremity of Yorkshire.* John Nichols and Son, 1810, 8vo., vii (i) 317 (1) directions to binder, folding hand colored map, 4 engraved plates, near contemporary black half calf, raised and gilt banded spine, marbled boards, some old waterstaining to paper, not too intrusive. Ken Spelman Rare Books 68 - 197 2011 £120

Huxley, Aldous Leonard 1894-1963 *Adonis and the Alphabet.* London: Chatto & Windus, 1956, First edition; original cloth, gilt, dust jacket, pages 286.   R. F. G. Hollett & Son Antiquarian Booksellers   175 - 695 2011   £35

Huxley, Aldous Leonard 1894-1963 *The Genius and the Goddess.* London: Chatto & Windus, 1955, First edition; minimal cover edge wear, 8vo., 127 pages, near fine in like dust jacket.   By the Book, L. C.   26 - 8 2011 $400

Huxley, Aldous Leonard 1894-1963 *Those Barren Leaves.* London: Chatto & Windus, 1925, First edition; pages (viii), 380, foolscap 8vo., original orange cloth, printed label (spare label tipped in at rear), tail edges rough trimmed, dust jacket with backstrip panel lightly browned, near fine, inscribed by author for Ingle Barr.   Blackwell Rare Books   B166 - 167 2011   £400

Huxley, Elspeth *The Walled City.* London: Chatto & Windus, 1948, First edition; pages xvi, 320, original cloth, dust jacket, light and partial browning to flyleaves, else fine.   R. F. G. Hollett & Son Antiquarian Booksellers   General Catalogue Summer 2010 - 815 2011   £35

Huxley, J. S. *Biology and Human Life.* British Science Guild, 1926, First edition; original wrappers, pages 24, sometime lightly folded vertically, scarce.   R. F. G. Hollett & Son Antiquarian Booksellers   General Catalogue Summer 2010 - 990 2011   £35

Huxley, Leonard *Life and Letters of Sir Joseph Dalton Hooker.* London: John Murray, 1918, First edition; 2 volumes, 8vo., x, 546; vi, 569 pages, frontispiece, blue cloth, gilt stamped cover ornaments, gilt stamped spine titles, recased, new endpapers, fine.   Jeff Weber Rare Books   161 - 211 2011 $600

Huxley, Michael *Geographical Magazine.* 1937-1981, First edition; v.1/1-v.54/12, 1937-Dec. 1981, lacking only 10 issues, well bound in publisher's green cloth, gilt, volumes up to April 1965 with index and errata slips bound in, there after as issues, all profusely illustrated.   I. D. Edrich   May 26 2011 - 82434 2011 $1677

Huxley, Thomas Henry 1825-1895 *A Manual of the Anatomy of Invertebrated Animals.* London: J. and A. Churchill, 1877, First edition; small fat 8vo., original publisher's brown blindstamped cloth lettered gilt at spine, pages viii, 698 with 16 page publisher's catalog at rear, 158 figures, very good.   Any Amount of Books   May 29 2011 - A48853 2011 $272

Huygens, Christiaan *Christiaan Huygens' the Pendulum Clock or Geometrical Demonstrations concerning the Motion of Pendula as Applied to Clocks.* Ames: Iowa State University Press, 1986, 8vo., xxix, 182 pages, with 102 figures, red cloth, gilt stamped spine title, dust jacket, jacket torn without loss, very good, from the Bern Dibner reference library, with Burndy bookplate.   Jeff Weber Rare Books   161 - 225 2011 $125

Huygens, Christiaan *(Cosmotheoros)...* Hagae-Comitum: Adrianum Moetjens, 1698, First edition; small 4to., (2), 144 pages, engraved title vignette, engraved headpieces, engraved tailpiece, engraved initials, 5 folding engraved plates, title margin rebuilt, few pages nicked at margin, light foxing, modern full blind tooled antique style dark brown calf, new endpapers, early rubber stamp on title, very good.   Jeff Weber Rare Books   161 - 223 2011 $8000

Huygens, Christiaan *Opera Varia.* Lugduni Batavvorum: Janssonios Vander Aa, 1724, First collected edition; 4 books in one volume, 4to., (18), (1-4) 5-776, (18) pages, frontispiece, 56 folding plates, contemporary full calf, raised bands, gilt stamped spine panels, gilt stamped red morocco spine label, covers and joints rubbed, hinges beginning to split, very good, bookplate of Andras Gedeon and P. A. Moiroud, with J. B. de Bouvou signature on title dated 1758, very good.   Jeff Weber Rare Books   161 - 224 2011 $5500

Huysmans, Joris Karl *La Bas.* Paris: Tresse & Stock, 1891, First edition; 8vo., pages (iv), 441, (3), top edge gilt, others uncut, 20th century black half morocco, marbled boards and endpapers, spine lettered gilt within raised bands, original printed wrappers and spine bound in, fine.   Simon Finch Rare Books   Zero - 241 2011   £500

Huysmans, Joris Karl *Down There (La Bas).* New York: Albert & Charles Boni, 1924, First edition in English; octavo, cloth.   L. W. Currey, Inc.   124 - 160 2011 $350

Huysmans, Joris Karl *Le Drageoir Aux Epices.* Paris: Librairie Generale, 1875, First edition, number 149 of 300 copies; 12mo., pages (xii, half title), extra leaf bound in extra portrait of author bound in, title, dedication, verse, 115, (3) with 38 original watercolors, initialled to each page of prelims, table and at beginning and end of each chapter, 3 additional leaves bound in with plates or photographic reproductions, top edge gilt, others rough trimmed, original wrappers, lightly dampstained and speckled, bound in full calf, gilt lettered and filleted, gilt dentelles, green decorative endpapers, author's presentations inscription and ALS from him to same recipient bound in, and 38 extra watercolors initialled by P. J., i. e. Le Mlle. Paraf-Javal.   Simon Finch Rare Books   Zero - 239 2011   £3500

Huysmans, Joris Karl *A Rebours.* Paris: Charpentier, 1884, First edition; 18mo., pages (iv), 294, some very light scattered foxing, original yellow printed wrpappers, black morocco backed clamshell box, gilt lettered. Simon Finch Rare Books Zero - 240 2011 £5000

Hyams, Edward *Great Botanical Gardens of the World.* Nelson, 1969, First edition; small folio, original cloth, gilt, dust jacket, pages 288, illustrations in color and monochrome throughout, fine. R. F. G. Hollett & Son Antiquarian Booksellers General Catalogue Summer 2010 - 991 2011 £45

Hyde, H. A. *An Atlas of Airborne Pollen Grains.* London: Macmillan, 1958, First edition; small 4to., original blue cloth silvered, dust jacket few light waterstains in places, spine little frayed at head and foot, pages xvi 112, photomicrographs. R. F. G. Hollett & Son Antiquarian Booksellers General Catalogue Summer 2010 - 992 2011 £45

Hyde, H. Montgomery *John Law. the History of an Honest Adventurer.* London: W. H. Allen, 1969, Revised edition; pages 228, top edge gilt, 9 plates, three quarter crimson levant morocco gilt by Sangorski & Sutcliffe, spine trifle mellowed, original dust jacket bound in at end, author's own copy with his Lamb House bookplate initialled NR 1964. R. F. G. Hollett & Son Antiquarian Booksellers 175 - 698 2011 £85

Hyde, H. Montgomery *Room 3603.* Mayflower-Dell, 1964, Small 8vo., three quarter crimson levant morocco gilt by Sangorski & Sutcliffe, spine rather mellowed, pages 286, (ii), top edge gilt with 9 plates, original paperback wrappers bound in, author's own copy his Lamb House bookplate initialled NR. R. F. G. Hollett & Son Antiquarian Booksellers 175 - 700 2011 £65

Hyde, H. Montgomery *The Trials of Oscar Wilde.* William Hodge and Co., 1948, First edition; pages (x), 384, top edge gilt, 16 plates, three quarter green levant morocco gilt by Sangorski & Sutcliffe, spine little mellowed, author's own copy with his Lamb House bookplate initialled NR 1964. R. F. G. Hollett & Son Antiquarian Booksellers 175 - 701 2011 £140

Hyginus, Caius Julius *Fabularum Liber... Poeticon Astronomicon Libri Quatuor... Arati Phaenomena Graece...* Basel: ex officina Hervagiana, per E. Episcopium August, 1570, Folio, (8), 251, (29) pages, last leaf blank device on titlepage, woodcut illustrations, contemporary vellum over pasteboards, spine slightly cracked, from the library of the Earls of Macclesfield at Shirburn Castle, the Georgius Melchior copy, 1664 with inscription. Maggs Bros. Ltd. 1440 - 114 2011 £1500

Hyginus, Caius Julius *Poeticon Astronomicon.* Venice: Erhard Ratdolt 14 October, 1482, First illustrated edition; chancery 4to., (58) leaves, including blank a1. 31 lines, types 3:91G (text), 7:92G (heading on a2r, title printed in red), woodcut initials, 47 half page woodcuts, probably designed by Santritter, of constellations and planets personified, small wormhole in a1-b1 affecting few letters, stamp washed with lower blank margin of a2, few very faint spots and stains, modern tan goatskin binding, skillfully done in antique style, very good, attractive. Joseph J. Felcone Inc. Fall Miscellany 2010 - 63 2011 $28,000

Hyman, Paula E. *Jewish Women in America.* New York: Routledge, 1997, 2 volumes, 4to., page xxxi, 880; v, 881-1770, portrait, front endpapers little wrinkled in volume 1, dust jacket slightly scuffed, otherwise about as new. Second Life Books Inc. 174 - 186 2011 $325

I

Iamblichus *(Greek)... De Vita Phythagorica Liber... Notisque...* Amsterdam: widow of S. Petzold & C. Petzold, 1707, First separate edition; 2 parts, 4to., (16 (including engraved frontispiece), 219, (17), 93, (1) pages, 2 columns, title printed in red and black, contemporary English panelled calf, gilt spine, red morocco lettering piece, fine, large copy, armorial bookplate of Edward Wake, Christ Church, from the library of the Earls of Macclesfield at Shirburn Castle. Maggs Bros. Ltd. 1440 - 115 2011 £700

Ibsen, Henrik *Brand et Dramatisk Digt.* Kobenhavn: Boghandels, 1866, First edition; 8vo., 271 pages, leather backed cloth little rubbed, name on endpaper, nice clean copy, scarce. Second Life Books Inc. 174 - 188 2011 $1125

Ibsen, Henrik *Et Dukkehjem. (The Doll's House).* Kobenhavn: Boghandels, 1879, First edition; 8vo., 180 pages, publisher's dark green cloth stamped in gilt, near fine, scarce in the US. Second Life Books Inc. 174 - 191 2011 $1000

Ibsen, Henrik *Et Dukkehjem. (Doll's House).* Copenhagen: Gyldendalske Boghandels Forlag, 1879, First edition; 8vo., pages 180, original paper wrappers, printed in black, pages slightly and evenly toned, Frederikke Schmidt's neat ownership signature and Doris Arentz's to half title, chips to spine head and wrappers, front wrappers sometime strengthened, very good. Simon Finch Rare Books Zero - 242 2011 £900

Ibsen, Henrik *A Doll's House.* London: Fisher Unwin, 1889, First English edition; 8vo., pages 123, cream vellum boards little soiled, gilt lettering, untrimmed, top limited to 115 copies, this #45, signed by Unwin, edge gilt, 7 original photos. Second Life Books Inc. 174 - 190 2011 $900

Ibsen, Henrik *Gildet Paa Solhoug. (The Feat at Solhoug).* Christiana: Lonsberge, 1856, First edition; 8vo., pages 88, original printed wrapper cover (top inch of wrapper replaced), very good in modern three quarter morocco and marbled paper covered boards, rare in such nice state with wrapper present. Second Life Books Inc. 174 - 194 2011 $2700

Ibsen, Henrik *Gengangere. (Ghosts).* Kobenhavn: Gyldendalske, 1881, First edition; 12mo., pages 164, paper wrappers, some moisture stain to cover bottom, otherwise very good. Second Life Books Inc. 174 - 193 2011 $1000

Ibsen, Henrik *Hedda Gabler, Skuespil I Fire Akter.* Kobenhavn: Boghandels, 1890, First edition; 8vo., 236 pages, light green cloth elaborately stamped in black and gilt, front hinge loose, all edges gilt, name on endpaper, very nice, clean copy. Second Life Books Inc. 174 - 196 2011 $1500

Ibsen, Henrik *Hedda Gabler.* London: William Heinemann, 1891, First English edition and first edition in English; square 8vo., pages 236, original pictorial wrappers, uncut, fine, fresh copy, quite rare, mounted photogravure as frontispiece. Second Life Books Inc. 174 - 195 2011 $900

Ibsen, Henrik *John Gabriel Borkman.* Kobenhavn: Glydenalske Boghandels Forlag, 1896, First edition; 8vo., 245 pages, light blue publisher's cloth elaborately stamped in black and gilt, all edges gilt, fine. Second Life Books Inc. 174 - 197 2011 $1125

Ibsen, Henrik *Fruen Fra Havet. (The Lady from the Sea).* Kovenhavn: Boghandels, 1888, First edition; 8vo., 223 pages, green cloth, elaborately stamped in black and gilt, all edges gilt, fine, scarce. Second Life Books Inc. 174 - 192 2011 $563

Ibsen, Henrik *Lille Eyolf.* Kobenhavn: Glydendalske F. Hegel & Son, 1894, First edition; 8vo., pages 184, all edges gilt, bright blue cloth, elaborately stamped in black and gilt, dexlue issue, there was also an issue in plain wrappers, bookplate, light wear to top of spine, fine. Second Life Books Inc. 174 - 198 2011 $900

Ibsen, Henrik *Kjaerlinghedens Komedie, Komedie I Tre Ufter. (Love's Comedy).* Christiania: Jensen, 1862, First edition; 8vo., pages 140, lacks rear endpaper, leather backed cloth, some chipping at extremities, very good, tight copy, scarce. Second Life Books Inc. 174 - 187 2011 $1125

Ibsen, Henrik *Bygmester Solness Skuespil I Tre Akter. (Masterbuilder).* Kobenhavn: Gyldendaske, 1892, First edition; 12mo., 263 pages, green cloth elaborately stamped in black and gilt all edges gilt, fine. Second Life Books Inc. 174 - 189 2011 $1500

Ibsen, Henrik *Peer Gynt.* London: Harrap, 1936, Limited only to 460 copies signed by artist; 4to., full vellum decorated in gold, top edge gilt, some natural discoloration of vellum, small areas on endpapers darkened from offsetting, else very fine in original slipcase (case soiled and rubbed some), illustrations by Arthur Rackham, with pictorial endpapers, 12 color plates plus numerous black and whites, beautiful copy, very scarce. Aleph-Bet Books, Inc. 95 - 481 2011 $1850

Ibsen, Henrik *Perry Gynt.* Philadelphia: J. B. Lippincott Co., 1936, First American edition; 4to., top edge tinted red, orange cloth with gold lettering and decorations on cover and spine, perhaps the slightest of bowing to boards, color pictorial dust jacket with few chips, 256 numbered pages, 12 full page color plates and black and white drawings within text, by Arthur Rackham.   Jo Ann Reisler, Ltd.   86 - 201   2011 $450

Ibsen, Henrik *Rosmersholm.* Kobenhavn: Boghandels, 1886, First edition; 8vo., pages 203, all edges gilt, tan cloth elaborately stamped in black, scrape from rear paste down, fine, names on front endpaper.   Second Life Books Inc.   174 - 200   2011 $825

Ibsen, Henrik *Hoermoendene Pan Helgeland. (The Vikings at Helgeland).* Christiania: Zenen, 1858, First edition; 8vo., pages 115, contemporary three quarter leather, some foxed, very good, tipped onto leaf in rear is broadside from a January 30 1876 production of the play at Det Kongelige theater, rare.   Second Life Books Inc.   174 - 202   2011 $1875

Ibsen, Henrik *Nar Vi Dode Vagner. (When We Dead Awake).* Berlin: Fischer, 1899, First edition; 8vo. 202 pages, light brown cloth elaborately stamped in black and brown and gilt, all edges gilt, fine.   Second Life Books Inc.   174 - 199   2011 $675

Ibsen, Henrik *Vildanden. (The Wild Duck).* Kobenhavn: Glydenalske Boghandels Forlag (F. Hegel & Son), 1884, First edition; 8vo., 244 pages, blue cloth elaborately stamped in black and gilt, front hinge broken, otherwise nice, bright copy, name on endpaper, publisher's original deluxe binding.   Second Life Books Inc.   174 - 201   2011 $1125

Illingworth, John L. *Yorkshire's Ruined Castles.* Ed. J. Burrow & co., 1938, First edition; small tall 8vo., original blue cloth gilt, pages xiv, 184, 27 maps and plans, 38 plates, 14 text illustrations, scarce.   R. F. G. Hollett & Son Antiquarian Booksellers   General Catalogue Summer 2010 - 1444   2011   £35

An Illustrated History of New Mexico - Containing History of This Important Section of the Great Southwest.... Chicago: Lewis Pub. Co., 1895, First edition; large quarto, decorated leather with gold stamping on front cover and spine, decorated cloth endsheets, all edges gilt, 671 pages, photos, plates, some cosmetic restoration to corners, else fine, tight, bright copy, clamshell case, handsome copy, rare.   Buckingham Books   May 26 2011 - 21309   2011 $1750

The Illustrated London Instructor. Illustrated London News, 1850, Original blindstamped cloth, gilt, pages viii, 264, woodcut illustrations, endpapers rather browned, joints strained or cracked.   R. F. G. Hollett & Sons Antiquarian Booksellers   170 - 17   2011   £45

Illustrated Primer; or the First Book for Children. New York: George F. Cooledge, n.d. circa, 1848, 12mo., pictorial wrappers, 47 page, neat spine strengthening and stain on bottom edge of some pages, very good, containing 5 aphabets, one of which is a 3 page pictorial ABC with illustrations for each letter, another has letters of alphabet incorporated into a story titled Idle Tom, every page has pictorial border, profusely illustrated on every page of text.   Aleph-Bet Books, Inc.   95 - 15   2011 $150

The Illustrated Primer; or the First Book for Children Designed for Home or Parental Instruction. New York: George F. Cooledge & Brother, n.d. circa, 1865, 12mo., 47 pages, 1 page ad on lower wrapper, pictorial stiff paper wrappers, full page wood engraved frontispiece, wood engravings, near mint, the manner in which the pages have been inked has created ghost offset on facing pages.   Hobbyhorse Books   56 - 120   2011 $120

Imaginative Book Illustration Society *Imaginative Book Illustration Society Newsletter 1995-2005.* Working: Imaginative Book Illustration Society, 1995-2005, First edition; 31 issues, 8vo., stated illustrated wrappers, nos. 1-29 (but missing 27) with 3 extra issues, pages 1000+, copiously illustrated in black and white throughout, all issues fine or near fine.   Any Amount of Books   May 29 2011 - A70294   2011 $340

Imposture unmasked in a Letter to the Labourers & Working People of England on the Schemes of the Church Robbers and Revolutionists with Regard to the Church. London: Roake & Varty, n.d. but, 1831, First edition; uncommon, 12mo., large woodcut illustration on title, 23, (1) pages, preserved in recent plain wrappers, very good.   John Drury Rare Books   153 - 159   2011   £75

The Imprint. 1913, First edition; volume 1/1-6 Jan.-June 1913, bound in one volume, half calf, gilt lettering with composite index, illustrations, excellent condition free from foxing.   I. D. Edrich   May 26 2011 - 99443   2011 $545

Imrie, Anne *Architecture of Guilford Bell 1952-1980.* South Melbourne: Proteus Pub., 1982, First edition; large oblong 4to., 88 pages, illustrations in black and white, neat name on front endpaper, very good+, printed acetate dust jacket in good condition, slightly dusty.   Any Amount of Books   May 26 2011 - A76730   2011 $402

Imrie, David *Lakeland Gamekeeper.* Batchworth Press, 1949, First edition; 203 pages, 17 plates, original cloth, gilt, dust jacket.   R. F. G. Hollett & Son Antiquarian Booksellers   173 - 607   2011   £35

In Nature's Laboratory. N.P.: n.d. circa, 1916, One of a very small number of copies printed for private distribution by authors; folio, 44 original mounted photos, original suede over padded boards, signed by Thomas A. Edison, John Burroughs and Henry S. Firestone.   Heritage Book Shop Booth A12 51st NY International Antiquarian Book Fair April 8-10 2011 - 50 2011 $8000

Incarnate. London: Booth-Clibborn Editions, 1998, First edition; 4to. pages 222 (unpaginated), illustrations in color and black and white, signed by contributor Marc Quinn, loosely inserted post card to Norman Rosenthal, fine in fine dust jacket.   Any Amount of Books May 29 2011 - A45925 2011 $340

Inchbald, Elizabeth *A Simple Story.* London: Richard Bentley, 1833, Half title, bound at Seargeant's Abergavenny in contemporary half dark green calf, armorial bookplate of Edward K. E. Mardon, very good.   Jarndyce Antiquarian Booksellers   CXCI - 216 2011   £40

Incorporation of Merchants in Leith *To the Inhabitants of Scotland.* Edinburgh: 1791, Only printing apparently; 8vo., caption title, 4 pages, large uncut copy, two minute holes in second leaf, some marginal fraying and closed tear at head but with no loss of text, unbound and folded as issued, only printing, apparently very rare.   John Drury Rare Books   153 - 69 2011   £175

Inder, W. S. *On Active Service with St. John Ambulance Brigade South African War 1899-1902.* Kendal: Atkinson, 1903, First edition; pages ix, 321, frontispiece, 24 photos, original green cloth, very good.   J. & S. L. Bonham Antiquarian Booksellers   Africa 4/20/2011 - 8276 2011 £190

Indian Atrocities. Narratives of the Perils and Sufferings of Dr. Knight and John Slover, Among the Indians, During the Revolutionary War, with Short Memoirs of Col. Crawford and John Slover and a Letter from H. Brackinridge on rights of Indians, etc. Cincinnati: U. P. James, 1867, 12mo. 72 pages, original printed wrappers, uncut, superb one of 500 copies.   M & S Rare Books, Inc. 90 - 210 2011 $450

Inge, W. R. *The Idea of Progress. The Romanes Lecture 1920 Delivered in the Sheldonian Theatre 27 May.* Oxford: Clarendon Press, 1920, First edition; original blue printed wrappers, spine chipped and refixed, price torn from corner of upper panel, pages 34, few pencilled marginalia.   R. F. G. Hollett & Son Antiquarian Booksellers   175 - 708 2011 £30

Ingersoll, Edward *Personal Liberty and Martial Law: a Review of Some Pamphlets of the Day.* Philadelphia: April, 1862, First edition; 8vo., (4), 38 pages, removed.   M & S Rare Books, Inc. 90 - 182 2011 $150

Ingersoll, Ernest *Down East Latch Strings.* Boston: Passenger Dept. Boston & Main Railroad, 1887, 6 foldout maps, one of which is missing, original cloth, mild shelfwear to extremities, otherwise near fine, attractive, profusely illustrated, scarce.   Lupack Rare Books   May 26 2011 - ABE3090157185 2011 $250

Ingham, G. Thomas *Digging Gold Among the Rockies or Exciting Adventures of Wild Camp Life.* Philadelphia: 1882, Second edition; 452 pages, good copy, cover gilt rubbed, new backstrip and label, text brown toning, rear cover spotted, 32 woodcut plates.   Bookworm & Silverfish 668 - 97 2011 $95

Ingram, John Henry *The Haunted Homes and Family Traditions of Great Britain.* London: Gibbings & Co., 1897, Half title, frontispiece, plates, original dark grey decorated cloth, slightly dulled.   Jarndyce Antiquarian Booksellers CXCI - 217 2011   £35

Ingrams, Richard *The Tale of Driver Grope.* London: Dennis Dobson, 1969, First edition; 4to., 36 pages, illustrations in color, signed and dated on titlepage by Ralph Steadman, about fine in near very good+, slightly browned and slightly soiled and price clipped dust jacket.   Any Amount of Books   May 29 2011 - A66647 2011 $255

Ingratitude, an Ode and Sir Salvadore, An Allegoric Poem, Canto the First, Salvadore or Gratitude Canto 11. Lincoln: printed by W. Wood, circa, 1780, First edition; slight foxing on title with "Microfiche (d)" stamped on upper bank margin, 4 pages glossary at end with loss of some blank edges but no loss of text, (2), 26 pages (end of Canto 1), 1-38 (End of Canto 11), (6) pages, disbound.   Anthony W. Laywood   May 26 2011 - 21566 2011 $587

Ink and Blood. New York: Heritage Press, 1946, Limited to 1000 numbered copies, Szyk has inscribed each copy to the subscriber by name; 4to., full publisher's black morocco, top edge gilt, fine in publisher's batik slipcase (also fine), 19 pages of explanatory material by Struthers Burt, mounted color frontispiece, 74 plates,.   Aleph-Bet Books, Inc. 95 - 545 2011 $2000

Inkster, Ian *Science and Technology in History: an Approach to Industrial Development.* New Brunswick: Rutgers University Press, 1991, 8vo., xvi, 391 pages, black cloth, gilt stamped spine title, dust jacket, from the Bern Dibner reference library, with Burndy bookplate.   Jeff Weber Rare Books 161 - 228 2011 $125

Inman, Thomas *Ancient Faiths Embodied in Ancient Names...* printed for the author, 1868-1869, 2 volumes, presentation copy inscribed by author for Liverpool Philomathic Society, lithograph frontispiece (touch foxed), 4 further plates in volume I, 8 in volume II, numerous figures in letterpress, little dust soiling in places, purple stamp of Philomathic Society to titles, tissue guards, some leaves, their bylaws pasted to front endpapers and slip recording purchase from Society in March 1925, signed by secretary pasted to flyleaf, pages (viii, 789; 1, 1028, 8vo., original brown cloth by Hanbury & Simpson, boards with frames blocked in blind containing gilt figures blocked in gilt on front, backstrips with gilt figures and titles, just slightly rubbed and darkened at extremities, backstrip ends bumped, hinges almost invisibly reinforced, good. Blackwell Rare Books B166 - 54 2011 £375

Innocent, G. F. *The Development of English Building Construction.* David & Charles, 1971, Tall 8vo., original cloth, gilt, dust jacket, pages (xxii), 294, with 73 illustrations, Dr. Arthur Raistrick's copy with his signature. R. F. G. Hollett & Son Antiquarian Booksellers 177 - 494 2011 £45

Institute of Zoology Academia Sinica *Bulletin of the Institute of Zoology Academia Sinica/Zoological Studies.* Taipei: Institute of Zoology, Academia Simica, 1962-2005, Volumes 1-2 (Nos 1 and 2 complete), volumes 26-43 (nos. 1-4 complete), volume 44 (nos. 1 & 2), together 204 issues total, very good plus, numerous text figures and photo, 8vo., older issues in original wrappers, newer issues paperbound, some older wrappers slightly faded, handstamp to recto and verso of older front wrappers, ink number to first text page in newer issues, occasional bump or minor soiling, newer issues in near fine condition. Raymond M. Sutton, Jr. May 26 2011 - 48661 2011 $1350

An Interesting Appendix to Sir William Blackstone's Commentaries on the Laws of England. Philadelphia: Robert Bell, 1773, Second American edition; 8vo., contemporary calf, crudely rebacked, very good, browned, Institutional name stamped on free endpaper, name erased from title, with John C. Williams bookplate, engraved by Nathaniel Hurd. M & S Rare Books, Inc. 90 - 44 2011 $3500

The Interesting Story of the Children in the Wood, an Historical Ballad. Banbury: J. G. Fusher, n.d. circa, 1820, 16mo., 16 pages including titlepage, paper self wrappers, 7 half page woodcuts, small vignette and full page wood engraving printed at last page with two line caption beneath, mint state. Hobbyhorse Books 56 - 23 2011 $170

International American Conference *Reports of Committees & Discussions Thereon.* Washington: 1890, 4 volumes, three quarter morocco, marbled boards, marbled endpapers, all edges marbled, one volume has leather hinges cracking, one cover loosening but intact, private library # on titlepage, no other marks. Bookworm & Silverfish 670 - 46 2011 $250

International Boundary Commission *Report of the Boundary Commission Upon the Survey and Re-marking of the Boundary Between the United States and Mexico West of the Rio Grande 1891-1896. Album.* Washington: GPO, 1899, First edition; oblong quarto, two title leaves, 258 plates, newly bound in light brown cloth lettered in white on spine, ex-library (withdrawn) with few library stamps to inner cover, fore-edge and top edge of text block, first title leaf soiled and edge repaired with tape, two or three leaves with minor tape repairs to blank borders, else fine and complete copy. Argonaut Book Shop Recent Acquisitions Summer 2010 - 211 2011 $2250

International Fishery Congress *Proceedings of the Fourth International Fishery Congress.* Washington: 1910, 2 volumes, 4to., 10 color plates, some attic dust, some foxing at edges, original binding, G.W. Baird's copy. Bookworm & Silverfish 678 - 71 2011 $175

Ionesco, Eugene *Journeys Among the Dead.* New York: Limited Editions Club, 1987, One of 1000 numbered copies signed by artist; 4 original color lithographs by author, hand bound in traditional French paper wrappers stamped in red and black, just touch of soiling on slipcase, otherwise fine. Gemini Fine Books & Arts, Ltd. Art Reference & Illustrated Books: First Editions 2011 $200

Ireland, William Henry 1777-1835 *The Life of Napoleon Bonaparte.* London: G. Berger (for the first volume) and John Cumberland (for the others), 1828, (this date in Volume II the other volumes undated); 216 x 142mm., bound without half titles in first 3 volumes, 4 volumes, extremely fine 19th century crimson morocco, handsomely gilt by Wood, stamp signed on front turn-ins, coves with single gilt rule border and with gilt springs and Napoleonic bee in each corner, raised bands, spines gilt in compartment repeating the same stamps (but with top compartment featuring the same stamps (but with top compartment featuring instead an "N" surmounted by a crown), marbled endpapers, top edge gilt, other edges rough trimmed, sturdy linen covered slipcase; with one facsimile plate, three black and white plates, 24 hand colored plates, all but two of the folding, plates expertly backed with silk, front pastedown of each volume with modern bookplate; margins of some of the folding plates, little soiled and with few expert repairs without loss (a handful of text also expertly repaired in text), titlepages of second and third volumes as well as a portion of one black and white plate bit soiled, two contents leaves in volume IV gracelessly remargined, other trivial problems with leaves, still very good internally without any fatal flaw, with text still rather fresh and with virtually no foxing, just hint of superficial chafing on covers, lovely decorative bindings in very fine condition especially bright and virtually unworn. Phillip J. Pirages 59 - 237 2011 $4250

Irish University Review. Dublin: University College, 1970-1991, First edition; Volume 1/1-3/1, volume 4/1-5/2, volume 6/2-13/2 volume 14/2-21/2, together 39 of 42 issues, original wrappers, excellent condition. I. D. Edrich May 26 2011 - 83792 2011 $629

Irvine, J. H. *Five Little Pixies. (No. 1 and The Others).* Chicago: Donohue circa, 1900, Oblong 8vo., pictorial cloth, 42 pages, near fine with original ivory clasp, illustrations by Jean Archer with 20 marvelous full page color illustrations.   Aleph-Bet Books, Inc.   95 - 543   2011 $850

Irving, John   1942-   *The Hotel New Hampshire.*   New York: Dutton, 1981, First edition; number 36 of 550 copies signed by John Irving, red morocco, as new in slipcase, likely never opened.   Gemini Fine Books & Arts, Ltd.   Art Reference & Illustrated Books: First Editions 2011 $350

Irving, John   1942-   *My Movie Business.*   New York: Random House, 1999, First edition; near fine, light bumping to head of spine, dust jacket fine, signed by author on tipped in page.   Bella Luna Books   May 29 2011 - t6260   2011 $137

Irving, John   1942-   *A Prayer for Owen Meany.*   New York: Morrow, 1989, First edition; number 16 of 250 copies signed by author, cloth in acetate dust jacket with cloth slipcase, new.   Gemini Fine Books & Arts, Ltd.   Art Reference & Illustrated Books: First Editions 2011 $1300

Irving, John   1942-   *Trying to Save Piggy Sneed.*   Toronto: Knopf, 1993, First Canadian edition; fine in fine dust jacket.   Bella Luna Books   May 29 2011 - 4315   2011 $137

Irving, John   1942-   *Trying to Save Piggy Sneed.*   Toronto: Knopf, 1993, First Canadian edition; near fine, previous owner's inscription and small abrasion on front free endpapers, dust jacket near fine, light wear to corners.   Bella Luna Books   May 29 2011 - t4596   2011 $82

Irving, John   1942-   *Until I Find You.*   London: Bloomsbury, 2005, First British edition; fine in fine dust jacket, signed by author.   Bella Luna Books   May 29 2011 - t7628   2011 $82

Irving, John   1942-   *The Water Method Man.*   New York: Random, 1972, First edition; near fine, light bumping to spine ends and bottom corners, dust jacket is near fine, light creasing and small closed tears to spine ends, sunning to edges.   Bella Luna Books   May 26 2011 - t1183a   2011 $192

Irving, John   1942-   *The Water-Method Man.*   New York: Random, 1972, First edition; fine, dust jacket near fine with just hint of creasing to spine ends.   Bella Luna Books   May 26 2011 - t1183b   2011 $440

Irving, John   1942-   *A Widow for One Year.*   New York: Unicycle, 1998, Limited to 1200 copies; numbered and signed by author, book fine.   Bella Luna Books   May 29 2011 - 2749   2011 $110

Irving, John   1942-   *The World According to Garp.*   New York: Dutton, 1978, First edition; 8vo., pages 437, author's signature on half title, owner's name, very good in little scuffed and chipped dust jacket.   Second Life Books Inc.   174 - 203   2011 $750

Irving, Washington   1783-1859   *The Alhambra.*   London and New York: Macmillan and Co., 1896, One of 500 extra illustrated copies; 263 x 189mm. xx, 436 pages, magnificent contemporary dark green crushed morocco, extravagantly gilt by Bagguley (signed with the firm's ink "Sutherland" patent stamp on verso of front endleaf), covers with borders of multiple plain and decorative gilt rules, lobed inner frame with fleuron cornerpieces, whole enclosing a large and extremely intricate gilt lozenge, raised ands, spine lavishly gilt in double ruled compartments, gilt titling and turn-ins, beautiful vellum doublures elaborately tooled in diapered gilt red, and green moorish pattern, green weathered silk endleaves, top edge gilt, other edges rough trimmed, numerous illustrations in text and 12 inserted lithographs by Joseph Pennell, bookplate of Harold Douthit; in beautiful condition inside and out, lovely bind with lustrous morocco, vellum and gilt, text virtually pristine.   Phillip J. Pirages   59 - 86   2011 $5500

Irving, Washington   1783-1859   *Bracebridge Hall.*   London: Macmillan, 1877, First edition with these illustrations; extremely fine dark green crushed morocco handsomely gilt by the Doves Bindery (stamp signed and dated 1905 on rear turn-in), covers with double gilt fillet border and Tudor rose cornerpieces set among leafy sprays and circlets, raised bands, spine compartments heavily gilt with central Tudor rose framed by trefoil cornerpieces and accented with small tools, gilt turn-ins, all edges gilt, stippled gauffering, illustrations by Randolph Caldecott, including frontispiece, titlepage and five full page plates; engraved bookplate of William F. Gable; edges of free endpaper at front and back with usual (but here rather pronounced) off-setting from turn-ins, otherwise magnificent copy, text with virtually no signs of use, beautiful binding absolutely flawless.   Phillip J. Pirages   59 - 99   2011 $4500

Irving, Washington   1783-1859   *A History of New York.*   New York: Inskeep & Bradford, 1809, First edition; 2 volumes, 12mo., rare folding frontispiece, full red morocco.   Heritage Book Shop   Booth A12 51st NY International Antiquarian Book Fair April 8-10 2011 - 71   2011 $2750

Irving, Washington   1783-1859   *History of New York, from the Beginning of the World to the End of the Dutch Dynasty.*   New York: published by Inskeep & Bradford, 1809, First edition; 2 volumes, 12mo, xxiii, (1, blank), 268, (2, blank); (2 blank), (2) 258, (2, blank) pages, rare folding frontispiece bound in by bottom edge, full red morocco, ruled in gilt on boards and spine, lettered in gilt on spine, bound by Stikeman & Co. NY, all edges gilt, marbled endpapers, small repair to plate at fold, repair to small portion of top edge of titlepage (probably to remove former owner's name), tops of spines very lightly rubbed, pages 140 and 246 volume II, with few ink underlines, very good.   Heritage Book Shop   Holiday 2010 - 59   2011 $2750

Irving, Washington 1783-1859 *The Keeping of Christmas at Bracebridge Hall.* London: J. M. Dent, 1906, First edition thus; original green cloth gilt, spine and upper board decorated in gilt overall, pages xvi 268, top edge gilt, untrimmed, 24 color plates by C. E. Brock.   R. F. G. Hollett & Son Antiquarian Booksellers   General Catalogue Summer 2010 - 738   2011   £35

Irving, Washington 1783-1859 *Legend of Sleepy Hollow.* London: Harrap, 1928, Limited to only 250 numbered copies for UK (125 copies of US) signed by artist; 4to., full gilt vellum, 103 pages, virtually mint in original publisher's box (box slightly scuffed), illustrated with pictorial endpapers, 8 tipped in color plates, numerous wonderful black and whites by Arthur Rackham, exceptionally fine, rare in box.   Aleph-Bet Books, Inc.   95 - 474   2011 $5500

Irving, Washington 1783-1859 *The Legend of Sleepy Hollow.* London: George G. Harrap, 1928, One of 375 copies signed by artist, this copy one of 250 for England (125 copies were Printed for the US); 270 x 205mm., 102, (1) pages, original publisher's gilt titled vellum over stiff boards, top edge gilt, other edges untrimmed, original publisher's box (now very dilapidated and tape reinforced), but worthy of respect for having protected the book so well over time; illustrated titlepage, 30 text illustrations and 8 color plates, all by Arthur Rackham, titlepage printed in green; hint of splaying to boards (as expected), but extremely fine, binding as clean as one could hope for, and text and plates with nothing but most trivial hints of foxing.   Phillip J. Pirages   59 - 290   2011 $2900

Irving, Washington 1783-1859 *Old Christmas.* London: Macmillan, 1856, Original decorated green cloth gilt, pages xiv, 165, all edges gilt, illustrations, joints cracked.   R. F. G. Hollett & Son Antiquarian Booksellers   General Catalogue Summer 2010 - 632   2011   £120

Irving, Washington 1783-1859 *Old Christmas.* Collins Clear-type Press, n.d. circa, 1909, 12mo., original decorated green cloth gilt, pages 150, 8 color plates, title, 2 headpieces and endpapers by Chas. Pears, joints cracking, otherwise good copy.   R. F. G. Hollett & Son Antiquarian Booksellers   General Catalogue Summer 2010 - 816   2011   £30

Irving, Washington 1783-1859 *The Old English Christmas.* London: T. N. Foulis, n.d., 1909, Small 8vo., original decorated blue cloth, gilt, pages 124, untrimmed, 17 color plates by H. M. Brock tipped on to blue paper.   R. F. G. Hollett & Son Antiquarian Booksellers   General Catalogue Summer 2010 - 817   2011   £30

Irving, Washington 1783-1859 *Rip Van Winkle.* London: William Heinemann, 1905, Limited edition, deluxe edition, one of 250 numbered copies signed by artist; first book wholly illustrated by Arthur Rackham, quarto, 57 pages, color frontispiece and 50 color plates mounted on heavy paper with lettered tissue guards, collected at end of text, original gilt pictorial vellum over boards, top edge gilt, others untrimmed, later yellow silk ties, very fine.   David Brass Rare Books, Inc.   May 26 2011 - 01630   2011 $8500

Irving, Washington 1783-1859 *Rip Van Winkle.* London: Heinemann, 1910, Large 8vo., original pictorial green cloth gilt, little marked and faded, few surface tears and dents to upper board, pages viii, 62, plus 51 color plates tipped on to green card with captioned tissue guards, half title and title lightly foxed, little further scattered spotting to few of the text leaves, very good, clean, sound.   R. F. G. Hollett & Sons Antiquarian Booksellers   170 - 564   2011   £180

Irving, Washington 1783-1859 *Rip Van Winkle.* London: Heinemann, 1919, Large 8vo., original decorated brown boards gilt, spine and edges little faded, pages x, 36, frontispiece and 23 tipped in colored plates by Arthur Rackham, endpapers faintly browned, otherwise very nice.   R. F. G. Hollett & Sons Antiquarian Booksellers   170 - 565   2011   £50

Irving, Washington 1783-1859 *Rip Van Winkle.* Philadelphia: David McKay Co., 1921, First edition; 4to., top edge gilt, brown purple cloth with full color pictorial paste label, very clean, bright copy, full color pictorial dust jacket with some spotting to rear of wrapper and touch of edge wear, 86 numbered pages with 8 full page color plates plus black and white drawings,.   Jo Ann Reisler, Ltd.   86 - 266   2011 $850

Irving, Washington 1783-1859 *The Sketch Book of Geoffrey Crayon, Gent.* New York: printed by C. S. Van Winkle, 1819-1820, First edition; 7 original parts, 7 volumes, octavo, all original front wrappers and rear wrappers of parts 1, 2 and 8 trimmed and mounted, with tipped in ALS, full green crushed levant for G. P. Putnam's Sons.   Heritage Book Shop   Booth A12 51st NY International Antiquarian Book Fair April 8-10 2011 - 72   2011 $20,000

Irving, Washington 1783-1859 *The Sketch Book of Geoffrey Crayon.* Dublin: James Duffy, 1850, Small 8vo., contemporary half morocco gilt with marbled boards, pages (ii), 301.   R. F. G. Hollett & Son Antiquarian Booksellers   General Catalogue Summer 2010 - 838   2011   £65

Irving, Washington 1783-1859 *Tales of a Traveller.* New York: Putnam, 1895, First edition, Buckthorne edition; 2 volumes, large 8vo., white cloth with extensive gilt pictorial bindings, signed GWE (George Wharton Edwards), top edge gilt, fine in original printed cloth dust jackets, 5 illustrations in half tone by Arthur Rackham, also illustrated by others.   Aleph-Bet Books, Inc.   95 - 478   2011 $450

Irving, Washington 1783-1859 *Wives: the Henpecked Man.* London: William Heinneman, 1909, First edition; square small 8vo., original boards with pictorial onlay, backstrip rubbed, pages 31, 3 tipped in color plates and line drawings throughout, gift inscription on flyleaf.   R. F. G. Hollett & Son Antiquarian Booksellers   General Catalogue Summer 2010 - 696   2011   £50

Irwin, John *Studies in Indo-European Textile History.* Ahmedabad: 1966, First edition; 124 pages, 4to., wrappers, mild ex-library, mild ripps, without dust jacket.   Bookworm & Silverfish   676 - 186   2011 $75

Irwin, Mabel MacCoy *Whitman: the Poet Liberator of Woman.* New York: published by the author, 1905, First edition, one of 500 numbered copies signed by author; 8vo., original decorated gray cloth (signed "HP"), gilt lettered, tipped in is small promotional borchure about Irwin and her book, stamp of the Syracuse Public Library on titlepage, spine little faded, very good, from the collection of Samuel Charters.   The Brick Row Book Shop   Bulletin 8 - 43   2011 $150

Isherwood, Christopher *How to Know God, The Yoga Aphorisms of Patanjali.* New York: Harper & Brothers, 1953, First US edition; 16mo., 224 pages, faint rubbing, endpapers slightly browned, else fine in very good+ dust jacket with very small inked initials on cover (N,A.B. 1953) faintly rubbed at corners, signed by Isherwood and Swami Prabhavananda, very slight lean otherwise fine in slightly used price clipped, very good dust jacket, neat stamped on pastedown, hidden by dust jacket flap.   Any Amount of Books   May 29 2011 - A66357   2011 $306

Isherwood, Christopher *Lions and Shadows.* London: Hogarth Press, 1938, First edition; first issue binding, very good, in dust jacket.   I. D. Edrich   May 26 2011 - 74021   2011 $545

Isherwood, Christopher *The Memorial. Portrait of a Family.* London: Hogarth Press, 1932, First edition; 294 pages, cloth, very good dust jacket, lightly rubbed at extremities, tiny chip missing from top edge of rear panel.   Joseph J. Felcone Inc.   Fall Miscellany 2010 - 65   2011 $475

Ishiguro, Kazuo *An Artist of the Floating World.* London: Faber & Faber, 1986, First British edition; fine in fine dust jacket.   Bella Luna Books   May 26 2011 - t943   2011 $165

Ishiguro, Kazuo *The Remains of the Day.* London: Faber & Faber, 1989, First edition; 8vo., 245 pages, signed by author, fine in fine dust jacket.   Any Amount of Books   May 26 2011 - A75865   2011 $470

Isocrates *Orationes et Epistolae.* Geneva: H. Estienne, 1593, Folio, (14) ff., 427, 131, XXXIV pages, (1) f. (blank), (4) ff, 31 pages, (9) ff., early 18th century English mottled calf, covers panelled in blind, spine gilt in compartments, red morocco label, printed pastedowns, slight worming, upper joint split at head an foot, inscription on titlepage T. Osborne 17th century and Wm. Robinson (18th century), fine armorial bookplate of William Robinson & Coll. Jes. Soc. Com., from the library of the Earls of Macclesfield at Shirburn Castle.   Maggs Bros. Ltd.   1440 - 116   2011   £900

Ison, Walter *The Georgian Buildings of Bristol.* London: Faber, 1952, First edition; tall 8vo., original cloth, gilt, dust jacket (spine faded), pages 248, 64 pages of plates and plans, 31 line drawings, edges little spotted.   R. F. G. Hollett & Son Antiquarian Booksellers   177 - 495   2011   £30

Isumbras *Syr Ysambrace.* Kelmscott Press, 1897, One of 350 copies on paper (an additional 8 were Printed on vellum); 216 146mm., 2 p.l., 41 pages, original holland backed blue paper boards, edges untrimmed and unopened, wood engraved frontispiece by Sir Edward Burne-Jones, decorative woodcut initials, device in colophon, wide decorative border on first opening of text; bookplate of Carl Edelheim; printed in red and black; spine cloth with minor tears to four plates, fading on rear board along one inch strip next to joint, inevitable (but not severe) wear to corners, else very fine, binding absolutely tight and virtually pristine internally.   Phillip J. Pirages   59 - 248   2011 $1950

Ives, Joseph C. *Report Upon the Colorado River of the West, Explored in 1857 and 1858 by Lieutenant Joseph C. Ives, Corps of Topographical Engineers...* Washington: Government Printing Office, 1861, First edition; quarto, rebound in leather and marbled paper over boards, gold stamped on spine, raised bands, leather corners, 4 maps, including 2 large folding maps, 7 color lithographs, engravings, profile plate are all present, one map has few tears neatly repaired, bottom corner of titlepage has corner clipped but not affecting any of the printing, else near fine, tight copy.   Buckingham Books   May 26 2011 - 25805   2011 $1750

Ives, Joseph C. *Report Upon the Colorado River of the West, Explored in 1857 and 1858...* Washington: Government Printing Office, 1861, First edition; quarto, full leather, new leather spine laid down, gold stamping on spine, raised bands, 4 maps, 7 color lithographs, very faint embossed library stamp on top edge of front cover, else near fine, tight copy.   Buckingham Books   May 26 2011 - 25837   2011 $2250

Ives, Joseph C. *Report Upon the Colorado River of the West, Explored in 1857 and 1858 by Lieutenant Joseph C. Ives, Corps of Topographical Engineers...* Washington: GPO, 1861, First edition; quarto, original gilt pictorial blindstamped cloth, gold stamped on spine, 4 maps, including two large folding maps, all engravings and profile plate present, one map has few tears that have been neatly repaired, lightly soiled on lower portion of front panel, rubbed along front edge, else very good. Buckingham Books   May 26 2011 - 25804 2011 $1750

J

Jabir Ibn Hayyan *The Works of Geber.* London: Toronto: & New York: J. M. Dent & E. P. Dutton, 1928, 8vo., xl, 264 pages, 17 reproductions in black and white from original drawings and diagrams, black cloth, blindstamped cover pentagram, gilt stamped spine title, dust jacket, near fine, from the Bern Dibner reference library, with Burndy bookplate.   Jeff Weber Rare Books   161 - 170 2011 $75

Jack, George S. *History of Roanoke County. (and) History of Roanoke City. (and) History of the Norfolk & Western Railway Co.* Roanoke: 1912, First edition; photo illustrated, cover gilt rubbed, mild fraying to edges, front joint strengthened, small nick to cloth on front cover, some white flecking on covers,.   Bookworm & Silverfish   666 - 168 2011 $225

Jackson Stops (Auctioneers) *Stowe Near Buckingham The Ducal Estate and Contents of the Mansion Nineteen Days' Sale July 1921.* Jackson Stops 5th to 28th, 1921, Catalogue number 318, 232 pages with 58 black and white plates, 5 maps, original printed covers with picture of coat of arms onset, slight edgewear, bump at head of front board, slight scuffing and slight soiling, else very good.   Any Amount of Books   May 26 2011 - A70274 2011 $587

Jackson, Charles *English Goldsmiths and Their Marks.* Dover reprint, 1964, Second edition; 4to., original cloth, little rubbed, pages xvi, 747, with 8 plates and illustrations of marks.   R. F. G. Hollett & Son Antiquarian Booksellers General Catalogue Summer 2010 - 213 2011 £35

Jackson, Charles *The Lost Weekend.* New York: Farrar & Rinehart Inc., 1944, First edition; author's warm contemporary presentation inscription for Dick May Jan. 27 '44, fine, bright copy in dust jacket with some minor professional restoration to spine ends, sharp copy.   Buckingham Books May 26 2011 - 26213 2011 $3750

Jackson, Chevalier *Bronchoscopy an Esophagoscopy.* Philadelphia & London: W. B. Saunders, 1922, First edition; 8vo., 346 pages, 5 plates, numbered figures, index, original black cloth, gilt stamped spine title, ex-library bookplate stamp, spine call number, very good, from the Medical Library of Dr. Clare Gray Peterson.   Jeff Weber Rare Books   162 - 168 2011 $100

Jackson, H. C. *Osman Digna.* London: Methuen, 1926, First edition; 8vo., pages xxiv, 232, map, frontispiece, original brown cloth.   J. & S. L. Bonham Antiquarian Booksellers   Africa 4/20/2011 - 9027 2011 £50

Jackson, Henry *An Examination of the Civil Administration of Governor Jackson in Florida.* Washington: 1828, First edition; 8vo., 48 pages, later cloth backed boards, very browned, ex-library stamp.   M & S Rare Books, Inc.   90 - 186 2011 $400

Jackson, John N. *The Welland Canals and Their Communities: Engineering, Industrial and Urban Transformation.* Toronto: Buffalo: London: University of Toronto Press, 1997, First edition; 8vo., xvi, 535 pages, photos, 13 maps, 11 tables, gray cloth, red stamped spine title, dust jacket, fine, from the Bern Dibner reference library, with Burndy bookplate.   Jeff Weber Rare Books 161 - 234 2011 $100

Jackson, Kate *Around the World to Persia: Letters Written While on the Journey as a Member of the American Persian Relief Commission in 1918.* New York: printed only for Private Circulation Among Friends, 1920, Octavo, 76 pages, quarter cloth backed boards, printed paper cover label, spine label, soiled covers, extremities worn, inscribed by author to Mrs. George R. Carpenter.   Jeff Weber Rare Books   163 - 181 2011 $75

Jackson, LeRoy *Rimskittle's Book.* Chicago: Rand McNally, 1926, Folio, cloth, pictorial paste-on, corner bumped, owner names on endpaper, near fine, profusely illustrated and full page and in text color illustrations by Ruth Caroline Eger, scarce, beautiful copy.   Aleph-Bet Books, Inc. 95 - 433 2011 $275

Jackson, Murray Cosby *A Soldier's Diary in South Africa 1899-1901.* London: Max Goschen, 1913, First edition; 8vo., pages x, 366, frontispiece, text illustrations, original blue cloth.   J. & S. L. Bonham Antiquarian Booksellers Africa 4/20/2011 - 8295 2011 £85

Jackson, Richard *Handbook for Tourists in Yorkshire and Complete History of the County.* Leeds: Richard Jackson, 1891, Original blue cloth gilt, pages xiv, 184, 27 maps and plans, 38 plates and 14 text illustrations, small tall 8vo., scarce.   R. F. G. Hollett & Son Antiquarian Booksellers General Catalogue Summer 2010 - 1446 2011 £85

Jackson, Seguin Henry *Cautions to Women, Respecting the State of Pregnancy; the Progress of Labour and Delivery...* London: J. Robson, n.d., 1801, Second edition; 8vo., neatly rebound in brown buckram with handsome red leather spine label lettered gilt, pages viii, 292, uncut, top one inch of titlepage missing but with no loss of lettering and neatly replaced with plain back paper, some odd marginal linings to text at beginning, otherwise pleasing very good+.   Any Amount of Books   May 29 2011 - A59934 2011 $340

Jackson, Shirley *The Lottery or the Adventures of James Harris.* New York: Farrar Straus and Co., 1949, First edition; first printing with stylized 'fs' on copyright page, octavo, cloth.   L. W. Currey, Inc.   124 - 58 2011 $1500

Jackson, Shirley *The Road through the Wall.* New York: FSG, 1948, First edition; very good, moderate browning to pages, previous owner's name on front free endpapers, dust jacket very good, light chipping and creasing to spine, three 1 inch closed tears. Bella Luna Books May 26 2011 - t3327 2011 $550

Jackson, Thomas *The Life of the Rev. Charles Wesley...* London: John Mason, 1841, from the collection of Christopher Ernest Weston 1947-2010, 2 volumes, 8vo., pages xvi, 592 + engraved frontispiece, viii, 578, (ii) + signed agreement facsimile plate facing page 577, late 1990's retrospective half calf by Chris Weston, frontispiece foxed, otherwise just faint age toning and few tiny spots. Unsworths Booksellers 24 - 25 2011 £180

Jackson, William *Papers and Pedigrees mainly Relating to Cumberland and Westmorland.* Bemrose & Sons, 1892, Volumes V and VI, original cloth, gilt, pages 370, 369, with 20 illustrations, folding pedigrees, very nice, scarce. R. F. G. Hollett & Son Antiquarian Booksellers 173 - 609 2011 £250

Jacob, Alexander *A Complete English Peerage.* London: printed for the author, 1766, 2 volumes, bound as 3, folio, pages (vi), 354 + engraved frontispiece, 25 other engraved plates and 39 plates of pedigrees (ii), 355)-614 (ii) + engraved frontispiece, 36 other engraved plates and 52 plates of pedigrees, 707, (i) + engraved frontispiece, 143 other engraved plates and 1 plate of pedigree, contemporary reversed calf, remains of black morocco spinal onlay panel gilt with compartments 'saltired', red lettering piece gilt, numbering gilt direct, boards panelled in blind, board edges decorative roll in blind, all edges lightly red sprinkled, red and white sewn endbands, green silk page markers, small marginal dampstain to first few leaves of volume 1, little minor spotting elsewhere, joints cracked and spines quite rubbed and cracked, bit of wear to endcaps, boards showing few scratches but relatively well preserved, heraldic stencilled bookplate bearing monograph the letters of which appear to be E.T.H. & C., from the collection of Christopher Ernest Weston 1947-2010. Unsworths Booksellers 24 - 112 2011 £750

Jacob, Giles *The Complete Court-Keeper; or Land-Steward's Assistant...* London: printed by Henry Lintot for T. Woodward etc., 1741, Fourth edition; pages viii, 522, (xxii), small nick to few leaves, little scattered staining and foxing, generally very nice, sound copy of a notable work, old polished blind ruled calf, corners rather worn, some old scrapes and marks, nicely rebacked. R. F. G. Hollett & Son Antiquarian Booksellers 175 - 712 2011 £350

Jacobi, Carl *Portraits in Moonlight.* Sauk City: Arkham House, 1964, First edition; octavo, cloth. L. W. Currey, Inc. 124 - 231 2011 $100

Jacobi, Carl *Revelations in Black.* Sauk City: Arkham House, 1947, First edition; octavo, cloth. L. W. Currey, Inc. 124 - 224 2011 $125

Jacobus De Varagine 1230-1298 *The Golden Legend.* Kelmscott Press, 1892, One of 500 copies; 300 x 215mm., 3 volumes, handsome contemporary burgundy morocco by Fazakerley of Liverpool (stamp signed on front turn-ins), covers with three concentric frames each formed by single gilt rule and one thick and one thin black rule, outer frame with elaborate cascading cornerpieces formed by flowers, leafy volutes and small round tools, middle frame with gilt anular dot at each corner, corners of innermost panel with two entwined gilt leaves, raised bands decorated with gilt fillet and flanked by blood and gilt rule, spine panels with elegant gilt floral centerpiece, gilt turn-in, marbled endpapers, top edges gilt, other edges untrimmed, elaborate woodcut title (first designed by Morris) and first page with full white vine borders, 2 woodcut illustrations and 2 full borders designed by Edward Burne-Jones, large and small decorative woodcut initials, printer's device; decorative bookplate of Samuel Cross, with Tiffany engraved bookplate of Albert May Todd; endpapers (which are ot a part of the collation) with sparse and light mottling, five gatherings with perhaps half of their leaves faintly yellowed (a single leaf only that is more than slightly affected), otherwise only most trivial imperfections, extremely attractive, handsome bindings lustrous and with just negligible signs of use and text virtually immaculate. Phillip J. Pirages 59 - 240 2011 $9500

Jacques, Brian *Redwall.* London: Hutchinson, 1986, First British edition; very good, major bump to top front corner, dust jacket near fine, corresponding creases and light edgewear, signed by author. Bella Luna Books May 26 2011 - t1726 2011 $220

Jacson, Frances *Isabella.* London: Henry Colburn & Co., 1823, First edition; 3 volumes in 2, contemporary half calf by J. Philip of Aberdeen, spines gilt ruled, maroon labels, spines little rubbed at head and tails, good+, armorial bookplates of Alexander Innes. Jarndyce Antiquarian Booksellers CLXC - 1 2011 £225

Jacson, Frances *Rhoda.* London: Henry Colburn & Co., 1816, Second edition; 3 volumes in 4, contemporary full diced calf, gilt spines and borders, maroon labels, slight nick at tail of one spine, good plus, armorial bookplates of Marquess of Headfort. Jarndyce Antiquarian Booksellers CLXC - 2 2011 £200

Jaeger, Werner *Paideia. The Ideals of Greek Culture.* Oxford: Basil Blackwell, 1939-1944, First edition; 2 volumes, original cloth, gilt, dust jackets rather worn and chipped in places, spines darkened, pages xxix, 420; xviii, 442, nice, clean set, third and final volume was published in 1947. R. F. G. Hollett & Son Antiquarian Booksellers 175 - 713 2011 £35

Jafir Barmukee; or Jafir the Barmecide. A Tragedy in Five Acts in Which are Combined and Faithfully Represented, the Real Incidents Which Attended the Fall and Death of that Able and Accomplished Minister of the Khalif Haroon Al Rusheed, in the Year of the Hejira 186 Corresponding with A.D. 802. London: printed by Emily Faithfull & Co., Victoria Press (for the employment of women), 1861, First edition; 8vo., pages 100, recently rebound in thick card boards preserving printed front wrapper which is effectively the titlepage, titlepage also reproduced and pasted on front, some ar and slight chipping to front wrapper and prelims not affecting text, else sound, complete about very good, loosely inserted are 3 good letters to Edith Hunt, second wife of William Holman Hunt.   Any Amount of Books   May 29 2011 - A40829   2011 $238

Jakobsen, Kath   *My New York.*   Boston: Little Brown, 1993,   First edition; 4to., 32 pages, fine in fine dust jacket.   By the Book, L. C.   26 - 63   2011 $75

Jalland, Pat   *Death in the Victorian Family.*   Oxford University Press, 1996,   First edition; large 8vo., original cloth, gilt, dust jacket, pages xii, 464, with 20 plates.   R. F. G. Hollett & Son Antiquarian Booksellers   175 - 714   2011   £45

James and Charles and Other Tales for Children. Providence: Geo. P. Daniels, 1836,   24 mo., 33 pages, original pictorial yellow wrappers, upper wrapper printed with half page engraving, full page frontispiece with 2 half page engravings, small wood engraved vignettes, all engravings hand colored by previous owner, minor waterstain at top margins of some pages, some light soiling at wrapper and upper margins, nice, rare.   Hobbyhorse Books   56 - 24   2011 $220

James II, King of Great Britain   1566-1625   *Papers of Devotion of James II...*   Oxford: printed at the Oxford University Press by Frederick Hall for Presentation to the Members of the Roxburghe Club, 1925,   Apparently First edition; 292 x 229mm., xxx pages, (1) leaf, 173, (5) pages, original Roxburghe binding of maroon half morocco over red textured cloth boards, flat spine with titling in gilt, top edge gilt, other edges untrimmed, one facsimile manuscript plate, this copy originally prepared for Sydney Richardson Christie-Miller (his name printed in red in the Roxburghe list as a way of indicating this), endpapers with hint of foxing, virtually pristine.   Phillip J. Pirages   59 - 304   2011 $525

James Pollock Sons & Co.   *Amazon Vessels of Various Types.*   London: James Pollock Sons & Co. circa, 1911, First edition; text in English and Spanish, copiously illustrated in black and white, with photos, original grey boards with color illustration onset to cover, rather splendid rare trade catalog, sound, clean, very good with slight handling wear. Any Amount of Books   May 26 2011 - A74332   2011 $1258

James, Daniel   *Famous All Over Town.*   New York: Simon & Schuster, 1983,   First edition; this copy has compliments of author card laid in, on which is typed "to supplement your Chicano Studies", card signed by author, spotting to top edge and fore edge, near fine in like dust jacket. Ken Lopez Bookseller   154 - 198   2011 $250

James, E. O.   *From Cave to Cathedral.*   London: Thames and Hudson, 1965,   First edition; large 8vo., original cloth gilt, dust jacket, pages 404 with 152 plates and 48 text figures.   R. F. G. Hollett & Son Antiquarian Booksellers   177 - 498   2011   £40

James, Edwin   *Account of an Expedition from Pittsburgh to the Rocky Mountains. Performed in the Years 1819 and '20.* Philadelphia: H. C. Carey L. Lea, 1822-1823,   First edition; 2 octavo volumes of text, uncut in half red morocco over marbled boards, one small quarto atlas complete with 11 plates in total, atlas in quarter cloth over original drab boards.   Heritage Book Shop   Booth A12 51st NY International Antiquarian Book Fair April 8-10 2011 - 73   2011 $30,000

James, George Payne Rainsford   1799-1860   *Corse de Leon; or the Brigand.*   London: Longman, Orme, Brown, Green and Longmans, 1841,   First edition; 3 volumes, half titles in volumes II & III, contemporary half scarlet calf, gilt bands, compartments decorated in blind, black, morocco labels, fine, handsome copy.   Jarndyce Antiquarian Booksellers   CXCI - 528   2011   £225

James, George Wharton   1799-1860   *Exposition Memories. Panama California Exposition, San Diego, 1916.* Pasadena: The Radiant Life Press, 1917,   Octavo, 216 pages, frontispiece, illustrations, original navy blue gilt stamped cloth, top edge gilt, bookplate, very good.   Jeff Weber Rare Books   163 - 182   2011 $65

James, Gilbert   *Drawings Illustrating Edward Fitzgerald's Translation of the Rubaiyat of Omar Khayyam.*   London: Leonard Smithers & Co., 1898,   First edition; 4to., grey cloth pictorially stamped in gold, beveled edges, very slight cover soil and endpapers toned, else very good+, printed on coated paper on one side of the paper, full page half tone plates by Gilbert James.   Aleph-Bet Books, Inc.   95 - 497   2011 $150

James, H. E. M.   *Extracts from the Pedigrees of James of Barrock. No. 4.*   Exeter: William Pollard & Co., 1913, Thick 4to., original cloth backed boards gilt, rather soiled, edges worn, pages 15 plus 13 large folding pedigrees on stiff paper, uncut.   R. F. G. Hollett & Son Antiquarian Booksellers   173 - 611   2011   £50

James, H. E. M. *Extracts from the Pedigrees of James of Barrock. No. 5.* Exeter: privately printed, William Pollard & co., 1913, 4to., original cloth backed boards, gilt, little fingered, pages 15, 5 (viii, blank ruled leaves for addenda and corrigenda), plus 4 large folding pedigrees on stiff paper, armorial frontispiece, uncut. R. F. G. Hollett & Son Antiquarian Booksellers 173 - 612 2011 £50

James, H. E. M. *Extracts from the Pedigrees of James of Barrock. No. 10.* Exeter: privately printed William Pollard & Co., 1913, 4to., original cloth backed boards, gilt, little fingered, pages 15, 4, 7 (viii, blank ruled leaves for addenda and corrigenda), plus 5 large folding pedigrees on stiff paper, armorial frontispiece, uncut. R. F. G. Hollett & Son Antiquarian Booksellers 173 - 613 2011 £50

James, H. R. *Mary Wollstonecraft. A Sketch.* London: Oxford University Press, 1932, First edition; original cloth, paper spine label, dust jacket spotted, pages xv, 180, color frontispiece and 3 plates. R. F. G. Hollett & Son Antiquarian Booksellers 175 - 717 2011 £40

James, Henry 1843-1916 *English Hours.* London: William Heinemann, 1905, First edition; 4to., half title, frontispiece and illustrations, uncut in original grey cloth, spine slightly dulled. Jarndyce Antiquarian Booksellers CXCI - 218 2011 £75

James, Henry 1843-1916 *The Novels and Tales of Henry James.* New York: Charles Scribner's Sons, 1922, 1920. New York Edition; 28 volumes, half titles, frontispieces, uncut in original maroon cloth, gilt monogram on front boards, spines little faded, boards slightly marked, slight lifting of cloth to front board of volume II, top edge gilt, good plus, bookplate of Clark Prescott Bissett. Jarndyce Antiquarian Booksellers CXCI - 16 2011 £1750

James, Henry 1843-1916 *The Question of Our Speech: The Lesson of Balzac.* Boston: Houghton Mifflin, 1905, First edition, 1/300 copies; small 8vo., pages 116, paper over boards with cloth spine, paper label, cover little worn at edges, one hinge tender, otherwise very good. Second Life Books Inc. 174 - 204 2011 $650

James, Henry 1843-1916 *Stories Revived.* London: Macmillan and Co., 1885, First edition; 3 volumes, octavo, (8), 280; (8, including prelim blank), 280; (8, including prelim blank), 269, (1, blank), (2, publisher's ads) pages, BAL binding C, no priority, full green cloth, boards triple ruled in black ink, spines stamped and lettered in gilt, blue patterned endpapers, top edges green, mostly unopened, each volume with old library bookplate "from Library of the Supreme Council 33... Washington, D.C.", some minor professional restoration to spines of each volume, some glue residue to inner margin of final leaf volume I, back free endpaper of volume II bit chipped along edges, some professional repairs, prelim blank of volume III with one inch closed tear to outer margin and inner hinges with some repair, outer front corners volume III bit bumped, overall very nice set with bright gilt spines. Heritage Book Shop Holiday 2010 - 60 2011 $3500

James, Henry 1843-1916 *The Wings of the Dove.* New York: Charles Scribner's Sons, 1902, First US edition; 2 volumes, original cloth, gilt, spines chipped and frayed at head and foot, few repairs, two board edges badly nibbled, pages 329; 439; with 2 half titles, flyleaf to volume 1 removed, label of Tabard Inn Library, Philadelphia, one partly overlaid with later label, name on flyleaves. R. F. G. Hollett & Son Antiquarian Booksellers General Catalogue Summer 2010 - 819 2011 £150

James, J. *An Essay on the Philosophical Construction of Celtic Nomenclature...* Bristol: 1869, First edition; xii (2) 166 pages, original cloth, very good. Bookworm & Silverfish 671 - 24 2011 $120

James, John Angell *The Family Monitor or a Help to Domestic Happiness.* Frederick Westley and A. H. Davis, 1833, Fifth edition; publisher's full blind panelled and stamped roan gilt, neatly recased, pages ix, 300, all edges gilt. R. F. G. Hollett & Son Antiquarian Booksellers 175 - 718 2011 £35

James, John T. *The Benders in Kansas by John T. James, Attorney for the Defense in the Trial of the "Bender Women" at Labette County in 1889-1890.* Wichita: Kan-Okla Publishing Co., 1913, First edition; 12mo., rebound in quarter leather and marbled paper over boards, brown endpapers, 173 pages, illustrations, rare. Buckingham Books May 26 2011 - 26242 2011 $3750

James, Marian *The Diamond on the Hearth, or the Story of Sister Anne.* Belfast: William Mullan, 1868, Second edition; half title, frontispiece, 7 plates by Dalziel Brothers, some light foxing, original royal blue cloth, bevelled boards, blocked and lettered gilt, slight wear to head and tail of spine, all edges gilt, good plus, bright. Jarndyce Antiquarian Booksellers CLXC - 3 2011 £75

James, Montague Rhodes *Abbeys.* Great Western Railway, 1926, First edition; large 8vo., original cloth backed boards gilt, corners rather bumped, pages x, 154, 7 color plates, 100 illustrations, 56 drawings, 13 plans and folding map in rear pocket.   R. F. G. Hollett & Son Antiquarian Booksellers   177 - 499   2011   £30

James, Montague Rhodes *The Sculpted Bosses in the Roof of the Bauchun Chapel of Our Lady of Pity in Norwich Cathedral.* Norwich: Goose & Son for Norfolk & Norwich Arch. Soc., 1908, Small folio, original printed boards, little soiled, neatly rebacked, pages 7, 5 pages of illustrations.   R. F. G. Hollett & Son Antiquarian Booksellers   177 - 500   2011   £65

James, Montague Rhodes *Thin Ghost.* London: Arnold, 1919, First edition; pages (viii), 152, foolscap 8vo., original grey cloth, backstrip and front cover lettered in blue with blue cobweb design to front cover, contemporary ownership signature of E. L. Kidd, very good.   Blackwell Rare Books   B166 - 168   2011   £200

James, P. D. *The Maul and the Pear Tree: The Ratcliffe Highway.* London: Constable, 1971, First British edition; near fine, in like dust jacket, very light bumping to heel of spine, dust jacket with edgewear.   Bella Luna Books   May 29 2011 - t8490   2011 $137

James, Patricia *Population Malthus. His Life and Times.* London: Routledge & Kegan Paul, 1979, First edition; original cloth, gilt, dust jacket, pages xv, 524, with 8 pages of plates, folding family tree.   R. F. G. Hollett & Son Antiquarian Booksellers   175 - 719   2011   £40

James, Philip *Children's Books of Yesterday.* London: The Studio, 1913, 4to., original wrappers, few slight corner creases, pages iv, 128, illustrated with 8 color plates.   R. F. G. Hollett & Sons Antiquarian Booksellers   170 - 347   2011   £45

James, Philip *Early Keyboard Instruments from their Beginnings to the Year 1820.* London: Peter Davies, 1930, First edition; 4to., original cloth backed boards, gilt extremities trifle worn, pages xviii, 153 with 65 plates, small unobtrusive library stamps on prelim plates.   R. F. G. Hollett & Son Antiquarian Booksellers   175 - 720   2011   £85

James, T. B. *Clarendon Palace.* The Society of Antiquaries of London, 1988, 4to., original cloth, gilt, dust jacket, pages xxiv, 279, 66 pages of plates.   R. F. G. Hollett & Son Antiquarian Booksellers   177 - 501   2011   £50

James, Will   1892-1942   *Home Ranch.* New York: Charles Scribner's Sons, 1935, (A); thick 8vo., 346 pages, some toning on endpapers, else fine with none of the fading that is common with this title, dust jacket not price clipped, lightly soiled and frayed at spine ends, but very good+, 48 full page and half page black and white drawings.   Aleph-Bet Books, Inc.   95 - 305   2011 $650

James, Will   1892-1942   *Lone Cowboy: My Life Story.* New York: Charles Scribner's Sons, 1930, First edition, one of 250 copies with original James drawing bound in on thicker stock; drawing signed and dated, octavo, (i)-xii, 431, (5) pages, photo frontispiece, 2 facsimile letters, 35 James illustrations, original smooth and shiny green cloth with brown cloth spine, original brown morocco spine label lettered gilt, label bit chipped and worn, fore-edge uncut, previous owner's bookplate, previous owner's old inscription, green cloth slipcase with brown paper spine label, label bit chipped, overall excellent copy.   Heritage Book Shop   Holiday 2010 - 61   2011 $4750

James, Will   1892-1942   *Lone Cowboy.* New York: Charles Scribner's Sons, 1930, First edition, one of 250 copies with original James drawing bound in on thicker stock; original green cloth with brown cloth, spine, original brown morocco spine label.   Heritage Book Shop   Booth A12 51st NY International Antiquarian Book Fair April 8-10 2011 - 74   2011 $4750

James, Will   1892-1942   *Smoky.* New York: Charles Scribner's Sons, 1926, First edition; 8vo., green cloth, slight soil and spine slightly faded, else near fine in pictorial dust jacket, dust jacket slightly frayed at spine ends with few mends on verso, profusely illustrated in black and white, this copy signed by James with recipient's name followed by "From the author" and dated 1926.   Aleph-Bet Books, Inc.   95 - 304   2011 $4200

James, William *The Literary Remains of the Late Henry James.* Boston: James R. Osgood and Co., 1885, First edition; 8vo., original publisher's red cloth lettered gilt at spine, pages 469, uncut, frontispiece, pencilled ownership signature of historian F. R. Cowell author of 'Cicero and the Roman Republic", signed presentation by A(lice) J(ames) for friend Constance Maude, slight fading at spine, slight mottling and slight marking, otherwise very good.   Any Amount of Books   May 29 2011 - A47621   2011 $340

James, William *The Naval History of Great Britain.* London: Richard Bentley, 1837, 8vo., 6 volumes, xiv, xxxii, 404; vii, 396; viii, 376; viii, 376; viii, 404; viii, 568 pages, contemporary tan half calf on marbled boards, black spine labels, gilt decoration to spines including ship motifs, from the library of John Chambers White with armorial bookplates, half titles present but without loose charts and abstracts seen accompanying some copies, 24 engraved plates numerous battle plans in text, very little foxing, some occasional light offsetting from plates, slight overall rubbing, withal a still robust, clean handsome set.   Any Amount of Books   May 26 2011 - A63567   2011 $629

James, William *The Naval History of Great Britain: From the Declaration of War by France in 1793 to the Accession of George IV.* London: Macmillan & Co., 1902, New edition; half titles, frontispiece, plates, illustrations, original blue cloth, occasional chips to cloth, most notably to following hinge volume II, spines slightly faded, attractive set. Jarndyce Antiquarian Booksellers CXCI - 17 2011 £250

James, William *The Principles of Psychology.* New York: Henry Holt and Co., 1890, First edition, first impression; 2 volumes, octavo, woodcut text illustrations, original green fine diagonally ribbed cloth. Heritage Book Shop Booth A12 51st NY International Antiquarian Book Fair April 8-10 2011 - 75 2011 $3000

James, William *Talks to Teacher on Psychology and to Students on Some of Life's Ideas.* London: Longmans, Green and Co., 1904, New impression; pages xi, 301, (iv), original cloth, gilt, lower hinge fayed and repaired. R. F. G. Hollett & Son Antiquarian Booksellers 175 - 721 2011 £75

Jameson, Anna Brownell 1794-1860 *Characteristics of Women, Moral, Poetical and Historical.* London: Saunders & Otley, 1836, Third edition; 2 volumes, half titles, illustrations, ad leaf volume 1, uncut in original cream cloth, spine slightly marked, slight nick at head of spine volume II, remarkably good copy in vulnerable binding. Jarndyce Antiquarian Booksellers CLXC - 4 2011 £75

Jameson, Anna Brownell 1794-1860 *Characteristics of Women, Moral, Poetical and Historical.* London: Saunders & Otley, 1846, Fourth edition; 2 volumes half titles, illustrations, final ad leaf volume I, pink endpapers, original blue cloth, blocked in blind and gilt, spines slightly dulled, good plus. Jarndyce Antiquarian Booksellers CLXC - 5 2011 £35

Jameson, Anna Brownell 1794-1860 *Characteristics of Women, Moral, Poetical and Historical.* London: Saunders & Otley, 1858, New edition; 2 volumes, titles in red and black, illustrations, original orange cloth, spines slightly dulled, otherwise fine, bright copy. Jarndyce Antiquarian Booksellers CLXC - 7 2011 £75

Jameson, Anna Brownell 1794-1860 *The Diary of an Ennuyde.* London: Henry Colburn, 1826, New edition; title little spotted, uncut in 20th century marbled boards, paper label, signed Philip H. Ashberry, Sheffield 1876", Skinos booklabel, very good. Jarndyce Antiquarian Booksellers CLXC - 8 2011 £120

Jameson, Anna Brownell 1794-1860 *Legends of the Madonna as Represented in the Fine Arts.* London: Longmans, Green etc., 1864, Third edition; contemporary full polished calf gilt over heavy bevelled boards, boards blind panelled, with central panel tooled overall in blind, with 5 raised ands and spine label, spine trifle worn and scratched, pages lxxv, 344, 27 tinted etchings, 165 woodcuts. R. F. G. Hollett & Son Antiquarian Booksellers 175 - 723 2011 £65

Jameson, Anna Brownell 1794-1860 *Legends of the Madonna as Represented in the Fine Arts.* London: Longmans, 1872, Fifth edition; tall 8vo., frontispiece, plates, illustrations, title in red and black, original pink cloth, spine faded, very good, booklabel of George Ward. Jarndyce Antiquarian Booksellers CLXC - 10 2011 £40

Jameson, Anna Brownell 1794-1860 *Legends of the Monastic Orders as Represented in the Fine Arts.* London: Longman, 1872, Fifth edition; tall 8vo., frontispiece, plates and illustrations, title in red and black, final ad leaf, original pink cloth, spine faded, very good. Jarndyce Antiquarian Booksellers CLXC - 9 2011 £40

Jameson, Anna Brownell 1794-1860 *Letters and Friendships (1812-1860).* London: T. Fisher Unwin, 1915, First edition; half title, frontispiece with tissue guard, title in red and black, plates, foxing in prelims and at end, label partially removed from leading pastedown, uncut in original green cloth, lettered gilt corners little knocked, slight rubbing, top edge gilt, good sound. Jarndyce Antiquarian Booksellers CLXC - 14 2011 £40

Jameson, Anna Brownell 1794-1860 *Memoirs and Essays Illustrative of Art, Literature and Social Morals.* London: Richard Bentley, 1846, First edition; first two leaves of text torn horizontally, old tape repairs, contemporary half blue calf, marbled boards, maroon leather label, boards rubbed, signed "James Clark, Largantogher, Sept. 1866", very good. Jarndyce Antiquarian Booksellers CLXC - 13 2011 £95

Jameson, Anna Brownell 1794-1860 *Memoirs and Essays Illustrative of Art, Literature and Social Morals.* London: Richard Bentley, 1846, First edition; original dark green cloth blocked in blind, spine lettered gilt, good plus. Jarndyce Antiquarian Booksellers CLXC - 12 2011 £120

Jameson, Anna Brownell 1794-1860 *Sacred and Legendary Art.* London: Longmans, 1874, Seventh edition; 2 volumes, half titles, frontispieces, plates, illustrations, titles in red and black, final ad leaf volume II, original pink cloth, spines faded, very good. Jarndyce Antiquarian Booksellers CLXC - 11 2011 £60

Jameson, Anna Brownell 1794-1860 *Shakespeare's Heroines.* London: Ernest Nister, n.d. circa, 1895, Large 8vo., full calf, gilt prize binding by Relfe Brothers, pages 308, all edges gilt, 6 color plates, 70 half tone illustrations by W. Paget.   R. F. G. Hollett & Son Antiquarian Booksellers   175 - 722   2011   £75

Jamieson, Jane H. *Sir John's Ward; or The Heiress of Gladdiswoode.* Edinburgh: Oliphant Anderson & Ferrier, 1889, First edition; half title, frontispiece, original light brown cloth, blocked in maroon and gilt lettered in gilt, contemporary gilt inscription on half title, very good.   Jarndyce Antiquarian Booksellers   CLXC - 16   2011   £60

Jane, Fred T. *Blake of the "Rattlesnake" or the Man Who Saved England.* Tower Publishing Co., 1895, First edition; original pictorial green cloth, neatly recased with new endpapers, pages 269, (ii), 28 illustrations and drawings by author.   R. F. G. Hollett & Sons Antiquarian Booksellers   170 - 348   2011   £120

Jansson, Tove *Sculptor's Daughter.* London: Ernest Benn, 1969, First edition in English; 8vo., pages 175, fine in very slightly sunned, slightly rubbed, near very good+ dust jacket with slight wear at corners and faint edgewear.   Any Amount of Books   May 26 2011 - A63766   2011 $587

Jardine, Nicholas *The Birth of History and Philosophy of Science: Kepler's A Defence of Tycho Against Ursus, with Essays on Its Provenance and Significance.* Cambridge & New York: Cambridge University Press, 1984, 8vo., ix, 301 pages, blue cloth, silver stamped spine title, dust jacket, fine, scarce in cloth, from the Bern Dibner reference library, with Burndy bookplate.   Jeff Weber Rare Books   161 - 235   2011 $125

Jardine, William *The Naturalist's Library.* Edinburgh: W. H. Lizars, 1845-1846, Second edition; 164 x 122mm., 40 volumes, very attractive contemporary half morocco, handsomely gilt, volumes bound in four different colors to reflect various members of the animal Kingdom (the 14 volumes on birds bound in red, 13 volumes on mammals in dark green, seven volumes on insects in dark blue, six volumes on fish in deep purple), all volumes with gilt decorated raised bands, spines uniformly gilt in compartments with lozenge centerpiece composed of drawer handle stamps and enclosing a small flower, the whole surrounded by triangular scrolling cornerpieces, marbled edges (sides and endpapers not uniform-by design, mammals and fish with watered silk covers, birds and insects with buckram, mammals, fish and insects with tartan endpapers, birds with unusual maze like design); with total of 1360 zoological plates, all but few hand colored, along with 40 engraved frontispiece portraits, 40 engraved titlepages, all but very few of the engravings with original tissue guards, front pastedowns with armorial bookplate of Edward Salvin Bowlby; just the most minor rubbing to leather extremities, slight chafing or soiling here and there to cloth boards, trivial imperfections internally, but an extraordinarily appealing set in very fine condition, bindings especially bright, almost without wear and most pleasing on shelf, text remarkably smooth, clean and fresh, virtually no signs of use.   Phillip J. Pirages   59 - 239   2011 $17,500

Jardine, William *The Naturalist's Library.* London: Henry G. Bon, London: W. H. Allen, Edinburgh: W. H. Lizars, various dates most of the printing dates are 1884 and 1885, while some have no dates, 41 portraits, 41 vignettes, 1308 plates, plates 10 and 11 from volume XI of Birds of Western Africa II are missing, small marginal piece missing from plate, occasional soiling and or foxing to plates, most plates clean, few plates trimmed closely, 12mo., original red gilt decorated cloth, spines faded and with some mottled spotting, some soiling, small spots to front cover volume on man; wear to some corners, fraying to few ends of spines, tear near heel of spine of volume on man, offsetting to may vignettes, scattered foxing to several volumes, few pencil notations to text of 2 volumes, marginal tear to 3 leaves of text, pages 161-76 were inadvertently left out of volume XI of birds, paper on 2 inner hinges cracked, lower margin of leaf partly perished, endpaper missing, owner's signature on front blank in each volume, good plus, top edge gilt, later printings.   Raymond M. Sutton, Jr.   May 26 2011 - 47835   2011 $7500

Jarman, Thomas *A Treatise on Wills.* London: 1930, 3 volumes, solid copy, original binding, ex-library, wear to backstrip ends.   Bookworm & Silverfish   668 - 46   2011 $75

Jarrell, Randall *The Animal Family.* Rupert Hart Davis, 1967, First UK edition; small square 8vo., original cloth, gilt, dust jacket, pages 181, black and white decorations.   R. F. G. Hollett & Sons Antiquarian Booksellers   170 - 621   2011   £45

Jarvis, Adrian *Port and Harbour Engineering.* Aldershot: Ashgate, 1998, 8vo., xxxiv, 416 pages, photos and illustrations, red cloth, gilt stamped cover and spine titles, fine, from the Bern Dibner reference library, with Burndy bookplate. Jeff Weber Rare Books 161 - 236 2011 $175

Jarvis, Rupert C. *The Jacobite Risings of 1715 and 1745.* Carlisle: County Council, 1954, First (only) edition; original cloth, gilt, pages xx, 427, illustrations and folding map, scarce. R. F. G. Hollett & Son Antiquarian Booksellers 173 - 615 2011 £120

Jasanoff, Sheila *Handbook of Science and Technology Studies.* Thousand Oaks: Sage Publications, 1995, Thick 8vo., xv, 820 pages, black cloth, gilt stamped spine title, dust jacket, fine, scarce, from the Bern Dibner reference library, with Burndy bookplate. Jeff Weber Rare Books 161 - 238 2011 $100

Jaume Saint Hilaire, J. H. *Traite des Arbres Forestiers, ou Histoire et Description des Arbres Indigenes ou Naturalises...* Paris: Chez l'Auteur, 1824, Large paper edition; 4to., (2), iv, 27, portrait and 80 stipple engraved color printed plates (foxing to 3), retouched by hand, contemporary half calf over marbled boards, boards rubbed, wear to edges of boards, scattered foxing, including titlepage. Raymond M. Sutton, Jr. May 26 2011 - 40263 2011 $1550

Jay, Leonard *Four Parables from the Holy Bible.* Birmingham: Central School of Arts and Crafts, 1927, Tall 4to., original wrappers with design by Webb, sewn with green cord, pages 12, title vignette and 4 fine full page wood engraved plates, few spots to inner margins of centre leaves, otherwise fine. R. F. G. Hollett & Son Antiquarian Booksellers 175 - 1407 2011 £140

Jay, William *Morning Exercises for the Closet; for Every Day in the Year.* Hamilton, Adams & Co., 1833, Eighth edition; 2 volumes, contemporary half calf, gilt with broad raised bands and spine labels, pages xxiv, 446; vi, 542, titlepages rather spotted. R. F. G. Hollett & Son Antiquarian Booksellers 175 - 725 2011 £120

Jayne, Caroline Furness *String Figures.* New York: Charles Scribner's Sons, 1906, First edition; small 4to., original blue cloth, gilt, neatly recased, pages xxiii, 407, with 867 figures, inscribed by author's father to Sir Edward Russell dated 1906, few marginal pencil lines to introduction, otherwise excellent copy. R. F. G. Hollett & Son Antiquarian Booksellers 175 - 726 2011 £250

Jayne, James A. *Tax Income.* New York: Cortland, 1927, 12mo., 136 pages, scarce, wrappers, fine. Bookworm & Silverfish 666 - 56 2011 $75

Jeafferson, John Cordy *A Book About the Table.* London: Hurst and Blackett, 1875, First edition; 2 volumes, original brown cloth, gilt, ruled and decorated in black, little dulled and marked and signs of a label removed from one board, but restored and neatly recased, pages 324, 16; 352; one paragraph underlined in red, but very good, uncommon. R. F. G. Hollett & Son Antiquarian Booksellers 175 - 727 2011 £180

Jean-Aubry, G. *Twenty Letters to Joseph Conrad.* London: Curwen Press for the First Edition Club, 1926, First edition; 12 separately printed pamphlets, each limited to 220 copies, sewn as issued, in double compartment folding case. Second Life Books Inc. 174 - 205 2011 $563

Jeanneret-Gris, Charles Edouard 1887-1965 *The City of Tomorrow and Its Planning.* Architectural Press, 1947, Original cloth, pages 310, illustrations by author. R. F. G. Hollett & Son Antiquarian Booksellers 177 - 540 2011 £30

Jeanneret-Gris, Charles Edouard 1887-1965 *Towards A New Architecture.* John Rodker, 1931, Second to fourth thousand; large 8vo., pages xix, 291, illustrations, original cloth. R. F. G. Hollett & Son Antiquarian Booksellers 177 - 542 2011 £75

Jebb, Bertha *Some Unconventional People.* Edinburgh: William Blackwood & Sons, 1896, half title, plates, final ad leaf, original light blue cloth, very good. Jarndyce Antiquarian Booksellers CLXC - 17 2011 £35

Jebb, Louisa *By Desert Ways to Baghdad.* London: T. Fisher Unwin, 1909, Second impression; octavo, 318 pages, frontispiece, plates, folding color map, original tan cloth, stamped in brown and gilt, gilt spine titles, top edge gilt, very good plus. Jeff Weber Rare Books 163 - 183 2011 $65

Jeeseph, Douglas M. *Squaring the Circle: The War Between Hobbes and Wallis.* Chicago & London: University of Chicago Press, 1999, First edition; 8vo., xiv, 419 pages, figures, black cloth, gilt stamped spine title, fine, from the Bern Dibner reference library, with Burndy bookplate. Jeff Weber Rare Books 161 - 239 2011 $100

Jeffares, A. Norman *A Review of English Literature.* 1960-1967, First edition; v.1/1-v.8/4, together 32 issues in original wrappers. I. D. Edrich May 26 2011 - 97716 2011 $503

Jefferies, Richard 1848-1887 *Field and Hedgerow: Being the Last Essays of Richard Jefferies.* London: Longmans, 1889, First edition; half title, 16 page catalog (June 1888), original grey green decorated cloth, blocked in black and light green, booksellers stamp of F. H. Hutt, very good. Jarndyce Antiquarian Booksellers CXCI - 333 2011 £68

Jefferies, Richard 1848-1887 *Greene Ferne Farm.* London: Smith, Elder & Co., 1880, Half title, 6 pages ads, original olive green cloth, blocked and lettered in gilt, wear to head and tail of spine.   Jarndyce Antiquarian Booksellers   CXCI - 222 2011   £60

Jefferies, Richard 1848-1887 *Red Deer.* London: Longmans, Green and Co., 1889, Second edition; with illustrations, half title, frontispiece, 24 page catalog (coded 10/91), original maroon cloth, blocked and lettered gilt, spine slightly faded, very good, crisp, inserted slip after titlepage spells name of artist correctly as "Tunaley".   Jarndyce Antiquarian Booksellers   CXCI - 336 2011   £40

Jefferies, Richard 1848-1887 *The Scarlet Shawl.* London: Tinsley Bros., 1874, First edition; text slightly spotted, contemporary half blue morocco by Bumpus, raised bands, decorated and lettered gilt on spine, slightly rubbed, armorial bookplate of William Henry Radcliffe Saunders, very good.   Jarndyce Antiquarian Booksellers   CXCI - 223 2011   £420

Jefferies, Richard 1848-1887 *The Toilers of the Field.* London: Longmans, 1892, First edition; half title, frontispiece, 24 page catalog (6.92), original green and white flecked cloth, slightly rubbed paper label, publisher's presentation embossed stamp on titlepage, very good.   Jarndyce Antiquarian Booksellers   CXCI - 337 2011   £50

Jefferson, Geoffrey *Selected Papers.* Springfield: Charles C. Thomas, 1960, First US edition; 8vo., xi, (xii), 563 pages, frontispiece, 51 plates, 69 numbered figures, yellow cloth, gilt stamped orange spine label, dust jacket bit soiled, else fine, previous owner's signature, from the Medical Library of Dr. Clare Gray Peterson.   Jeff Weber Rare Books   162 - 172 2011 $125

Jefferson, Joseph *The Autobiography.* London: T. Fisher Unwin, 1890, Large thick 8vo., original blind pressed cloth gilt over bevelled boards, pages xcv, 501, uncut, 77 plates.   R. F. G. Hollett & Son Antiquarian Booksellers   175 - 729 2011   £30

Jefferson, Samuel *The History and Antiquities of Allerdale Ward Above Derwent...* Carlisle: S. Jefferson, 1842, Large paper edition; old half calf with raised bands, spine label, little rubbed, neatly recased, pages xiii, (v, additional subscribers, contents etc.), 462, (i), complete with 7 steel engraved plates and text engraving.   R. F. G. Hollett & Son Antiquarian Booksellers   173 - 618 2011   £250

Jefferson, Samuel *The History and Antiquities of Allerdale Ward, Above Derwent in the County of Cumberland...* Carlisle: S. Jefferson, 1842, First edition; modern half levant morocco gilt, spine little faded, pages xiii, (iv, additional subscribers, contents, etc.), 462, complete with 7 steel engraved plates.   R. F. G. Hollett & Son Antiquarian Booksellers   173 - 617 2011   £140

Jeffrey, Francis *Contributions to the Edinburgh Review.* London: printed for Longman, Brown, Green and Longmans, 1844, First collected edition; 222, x14mm., 4 volumes, very attractive contemporary purple morocco, boards framed in blind with multiple rules on either side of a decorative roll and featuring complex scrolling floral cornerpieces, raised bands, spines with gilt titling and compartments decorated in blind with scrolling cornerpieces, intricately gilt turn-ins, all edges gilt, armorial bookplate of George William Mason, trivial wear to leather, backstrips lightly and evenly faded, extremely fine set, joints and hinges entirely unworn and virtually as new internally.   Phillip J. Pirages   59 - 187 2011 $750

Jekyll, Gertrude *Home and Garden.* London: Longmans, Green & Co., 1901, Third impression; original cloth, gilt, spine faded, small ink mark to upper board, 301 pages, illustrations, title little foxed.   R. F. G. Hollett & Son Antiquarian Booksellers   General Catalogue Summer 2010 - 995 2011   £50

Jekyll, Gertrude *Wood and Garden.* London: Longmans Green and Co., 1899, Seventh impression; original buckram gilt, spine little faded, pages xvi, 286, 71 plates, nice, clean and sound.   R. F. G. Hollett & Son Antiquarian Booksellers   General Catalogue Summer 2010 - 996 2011   £50

Jemima Placid, or the Advantage of Good Nature, Exemplified in a Variety of Familiar Incidents.   London: John Marshall & Co. circa, 1785-1790, Stated third edition; 4 1/2 x 3 1/4 inches, Dutch floral boards with wear and spine cracked, some damage to frontispiece and titlepage near spine and book has perhaps been trimmed and resewn?, little foxing throughout and some overall dusting to book, 91 numbered pages with frontispiece and 28 woodcuts scattered throughout.   Jo Ann Reisler, Ltd.   86 - 88 2011 $900

Jenkins, Edward *The Blot on the Queen's Head; or How Little Ben, the Head Waiter Changed the Sign of the "Queen's Inn".* London: Strahan and Co., 1876, 100th thousand; frontispiece and plates, without titlepage (as issued, original yellow printed wrappers, trimmed close with partial loss to top and bottom, very good.   Jarndyce Antiquarian Booksellers   CXCI - 596 2011   £50

Jenkins, Rhys *The Collected Papers of Rhys Jenkins, M. I. Mech. E. Comprising Articles in the Professional and Technical Press Mainly Prior to 1920 and a Catalogue of Other Published Work.* Cambridge: Cambridge University Press for the Newcomen Society, 1936, Limited to 300 copies, of which this is 124; signed by author, 4to., x, 247, ads, (1) pages, frontispiece, 7 plates, 26 text figures, index, quarter beige cloth with green cloth sides, gilt stamped spine title (without ruled border), bottom spine end chipped, some light foxing, very good.   Jeff Weber Rare Books   161 - 2347 2011 $90

Jenkinson, Thomas B. *Amazulu: the Zulus, their Past History, Manners...* London: W. H. Allen, 1882, First edition; 8vo., pages xi, 216, ads, tinted frontispiece, original red decorative cloth, covers little soiled in parts. J. & S. L. Bonham Antiquarian Booksellers Africa 4/20/2011 - 8892 2011 £320

Jennings, Bernard *A History of Lead Mining in the Pennines.* London: Longmans, 1965, First edition; original cloth, gilt, dust jacket, spine and edges rather darkened, pages xx, 347, 5 diagrams and plate. R. F. G. Hollett & Son Antiquarian Booksellers General Catalogue Summer 2010 - 1563 2011 £45

Jennings, Hargrave *One of the Thirty: a Strange History, Now for the First Time Told.* London: John Camden Hotten, 1873, First edition; 8vo, pages 359, frontispiece (tissue guarded), signed presentation from author to Frederick J. Hytych dated August 1873, also tipped in at front is good lettered dated Jan. 2nd 1873 where HJ asks the same person discussing the progress of the book, also loosely inserted is signed note of 100+ words possibly to same person, original royal blue cloth, lettered/ruled in gold with silver gilt decorations, covers show little general wear and slight marking, spine tanned, little scuffed with wear at spine ends, overall near very good. Any Amount of Books May 29 2011 - A46391 2011 $398

Jennings, Paul *Dunlopera.* privately published by the Dunlop Rubber Co., 1961, First edition; large 8vo., original coarse weave cloth, gilt, glassine dust jacket, pages 159, 51 plates, 24 two color linocuts and pictorial endpapers, all by Edward Bawden, fine. R. F. G. Hollett & Son Antiquarian Booksellers General Catalogue Summer 2010 - 1083 2011 £75

Jennings, Samuel *Orchids and How to Grow Them in India and Other Tropical Climates.* London: L. Reeve & Co., 1875, 48 beautiful hand colored lithographed plates by F. W. Burbidge (minor foxing to 1 small brown spot to 1, otherwise plates virtually fine), descriptive letterpress, 4to., pages (8), 38, (4 pages index), modern green full morocco with raised bands and gilt decorated panels on spine (mottled browning to half title), owner's signature to upper margin of half title and title, 2 fingerprints to lower margin of dedication page, 2 margins of page of letterpress replaced with recent paper, text pages tanned, marbled endpapers, all edges gilt, Frederick William Burbidge was the artist and lithographer. Raymond M. Sutton, Jr. May 26 2011 - 48517 2011 $5500

Jenyns, Soane *A Free Inquiry into the Nature and Origin of Evil in Six Letters...* London: R. and J. Dodsley, 1758, Third edition; small 8vo., old full polished calf gilt, pages (ii), 195, engraved titlepage, most attractive copy. R. F. G. Hollett & Son Antiquarian Booksellers 175 - 731 2011 £120

Jenyns, Soane *A View of the Internal Evidence of the Christian Religion.* London: 1821, Ninth edition; small 8vo., old full polished calf, gilt, page (ii), 195, engraved title vignette, most attractive copy. R. F. G. Hollett & Son Antiquarian Booksellers 175 - 732 2011 £45

Jephcott, C. M. *The Postal History of Nova Scotia and New Brunswick 1754-1867.* Toronto: Sissons Pub. Limited, 1964, #378 of a limited edition of 400 copies; maroon buckram in dust jacket, pages xx, 393, half title, index, black and white illustrations, frontispiece, maps, 8vo., very good in torn dust jacket, with piece missing from lower front. Schooner Books Ltd. 96 - 290 2011 $250

Jerningham, Hubert E. H. *Norham Castle.* Edinburgh: William Paterson, 1883, First edition; original blue cloth, gilt, spine rather darkened and dulled, pages xvi, 293, with 2 plates and plan, colored arms on title. R. F. G. Hollett & Son Antiquarian Booksellers General Catalogue Summer 2010 - 1449 2011 £85

Jerome, Klapka Jerome *Idle Ideas in 1905.* London: Hurst & Blackett, 1905, First edition; half title, 4 pages, ads, original yellow cloth blocked in red, dulled. Jarndyce Antiquarian Booksellers CXCI - 226 2011 £45

Jerrold, Blanchard 1826-1884 *A Brage-Breaker with the Swedes; or Notes from the North in 1852.* London: Nathaniel Cooke, 1854, First edition; engraved titlepage, frontispiece, illustrations by author, original maroon cloth, gilt, slightly rubbed, spine faded, following f.e.p. slightly torn, very good. Jarndyce Antiquarian Booksellers CXCI - 559 2011 £85

Jervis, H. S. *The 2nd Munsters in France.* 1922, First edition; signed presentation from author, xii, 71 pages, 2 photos, 13 maps, 9 folding sheets, signed by author. C. P. Hyland May 26 2011 - 259/212 2011 $362

Jervis, Henry Jervis White *History of the Island of Corfu and the Republic of the Ionian Islands.* London: Colburn & Co., 1852, First edition; engraved frontispiece and plates, 26 page catalog, corner cut from title, partly unopened in original brown embossed cloth, gilt block on front board, spine slightly faded, ads on endpapers, fine, neat stamps of N.S. Wales Parliamentary Library. Jarndyce Antiquarian Booksellers CXCI - 560 2011 £320

Jervoise, E. *The Ancient Bridges of Mid and Eastern England.* Architectural Press, 1932, First edition; small 8vo., original cloth, pages xi, 164, 80 illustrations, fine. R. F. G. Hollett & Son Antiquarian Booksellers 177 - 506 2011 £30

Jesse, John Heneage *Memoirs of the Court of England During the Reign of the Stuarts Including the Protectorate.* London: Richard Bentley, 1840, First edition; 4 volumes, frontispieces, slightly spotted, finely bound in full tan calf, gilt borders, raised bands, gilt compartments, red and green morocco labels, boards faintly marked, spines slightly sunned, unidentified booklabel on leading pastedowns, very good.   Jarndyce Antiquarian Booksellers   CXCI - 18   2011   £225

Jeter, K. W.   *Wolf Flow.*   New York: St. Martin's Press, 1992, First edition; octavo, quarter leather and cloth.   L. W. Currey, Inc.   124 - 212   2011 $150

Jevons, William Stanley   *Letters and Journals of W. Stanley Jevons.*   London: Macmillan, 1886, First edition; 8vo., pages xii, 473, uncut, unopened, original publisher's russet cloth, lettered gilt at spine, very good.   Any Amount of Books   May 29 2011 - A48860   2011 $306

Jewett, Sarah Orne   1849-1909   *The King of Folly Island and Other People.*   Boston: Houghton Mifflin & Co., 1888, First edition; (lx), 339 pages and 12 pages ads, 8vo., original green cloth, gilt lettered spine, gilt bit dulled, lovely vertical design on front cover, endpapers somewhat darkened, contemporary signature on titlepage, tiny tear to edge of page 77, still very nice, tight, attractive copy.   Paulette Rose Fine and Rare Books   32 - 100   2011 $380

Jewett, Sophie   *The Pilgrim and Other Poems.*   New York: Macmillan, 1896, First edition; 12mo., 99 pages, 2 page publisher's ads, original pictorial grey boards, white cloth spine, top edge gilt, others uncut, light foxing, otherwise nice, inscribed presentation by author to Mary Day Lanier, bookplate indicating that the volume was presented to the Johns Hopkins University Library by Lanier's Son, Charles D. Lanier and subsequently released by that institution.   Paulette Rose Fine and Rare Books   32 - 101   2011 $325

Jewitt, Llewellyn   *The Stately Homes of England.*   London: J. S. Virtue, n.d., Original blue cloth gilt over bevelled boards, trifle marked, pages xi, 399, all edges gilt, 210 woodcut illustrations, nice, clean and tight.   R. F. G. Hollett & Son Antiquarian Booksellers   177 - 507   2011   £75

Jewkes, John   *An Industrial Survey of Cumberland and Furness.*   Manchester: University Press, 1933, Tall 8vo., original wrappers, trifle creased, pages xii, 176, fore edge and last leaves little spotted, few marginalia.   R. F. G. Hollett & Son Antiquarian Booksellers   173 - 620   2011   £65

Jin, Ha   *War Trash.*   New York: Pantheon, 2004, Later printing; inscribed by author to another author, near fine, lacking dust jacket.   Ken Lopez Bookseller   154 - 83   2011 $75

Joan, Natalie   *The Joyous Book.*   Oxford University Press, n.d., 1923, First edition; original embossed pictorial boards, light dustiness to top of upper board, cream dust jacket with line drawing (torn and chipped, a third loss to upper panel), pages (48), 12 full page color plates, illustrations, scarce.   R. F. G. Hollett & Sons Antiquarian Booksellers   170 - 643   2011   £85

Jobson, Richard   *The Golden Trade or a Discovery of the River Gambia and the Golden Trade of the Aethiopians.*   Teignmouth: E. E. Speight, 1904, Limited to 300 copies, this no. 240; 8vo., pages xvii, 209, illustrated titlepage, original linen backed purple boards, upper board sunned in margins, uncut.   J. & S. L. Bonham Antiquarian Booksellers   Africa 4/20/2011 - 8316   2011   £75

Jocelyn, Ada Maria   *The Criton Hunt Mystery.*   London: F. V. White, 1891, First one volume edition; half title, foxing in prelims, original green cloth, slightly marked, front board lettered in black, spine lettered in gilt, cloth slightly marked, otherwise very good.   Jarndyce Antiquarian Booksellers   CLXC - 19   2011   £45

Jodidio, Philip   *Richard Meier.*   New York, etc.: Taschen, Koln, 1995, Limited edition, one of 100 copies; 4to., pages 175, copiously illustrated in color and black and white, including signed and numbered print, 20 30 cm., fine, print also fine, in printed black clam-shell box (very slightly rubbed).   Any Amount of Books   May 26 2011 - A73808   2011 $1090

Joesten, Joachim   *Oswald: the Truth.*   London: Peter Dawnay, 1967, First edition; original cloth, gilt, pages ix, 372, scarce, dust jacket.   R. F. G. Hollett & Son Antiquarian Booksellers   175 - 737   2011   £85

Johnny Headstrong's Trip to Coney Island.   New York: McLoughlin Bros., 1882, Large square 4to., pictorial wrappers (20) pages, including covers, light spine and cover wear and soil, very good, rare, illustrations by W. Bruton.   Aleph-Bet Books, Inc.   95 - 347   2011 $800

Johns, C A.   *Flowers of the Field.*   Society for Promoting Christian Knowledge, n.d., 1853, First edition; 2 volumes, small 8vo., original red blindstamped cloth, gilt, backstrips trifle frayed at head and foot, pages lix, 380; 272; text woodcuts throughout, excellent set, rare.   R. F. G. Hollett & Son Antiquarian Booksellers   General Catalogue Summer 2010 - 997   2011   £150

Johns, W. E.   *Biggles Sees It Through.*   Oxford University Press 1941, but circa, 1942, Pyramid edition with first edition dust jacket (First edition later issue); original blue pictorial cloth, minimal wear to extremities, pages 256, color frontispiece and black and white illustrations by Howard Leigh and Alfred Sindall, some spotting to fore-edge.   R. F. G. Hollett & Sons Antiquarian Booksellers   170 - 350   2011   £450

Johns, W. E. *The Rescue Flight.* London: Oxford University Press, 1939, Pyramid edition; 256 pages, color frontispiece and black and white illustrations, original blue pictorial cloth, minimal wear to extremities, some spotting to fore edge. R. F. G. Hollett & Sons Antiquarian Booksellers 170 - 351 2011 £150

Johnson, Alexander Bryan *A Treatise on Language or the Relation Which Words Bear to Things in Four Parts.* New York: Harper & Bros., 1836, Very rare second edition; 8vo., 26, (33)-274 pages plus 32 page catalog, original cloth, faded, printed paper label (heavily rubbed), lacking one front endleaf, two library stamps on title, foxed,. M & S Rare Books, Inc. 90 - 194 2011 $1500

Johnson, Anna C. *The Cottages of the Alps; or Life and Manners in Switzerland.* London: Sampson Low, 1860, First edition; 2 volumes in 1, half title, color frontispiece, original red cloth blocked and lettered gilt, slightly dulled, Belle Vue House prize label 1864, all edges gilt, very good. Jarndyce Antiquarian Booksellers CLXC - 22 2011 £125

Johnson, Arthur W. *The Thames and Hudson Manual of Bookbinding.* London: Thames & Hudson, 1978, First edition; pages 224, with 270 illustrations, tall 8vo., original cloth, gilt, dust jacket, price clipped. R. F. G. Hollett & Son Antiquarian Booksellers General Catalogue Summer 2010 - 216 2011 £85

Johnson, Audrey *Furnishing Dolls' Houses.* London: G. Bell & Sons, 1972, First edition; pages 284, 19 plates and line drawings, 4to., original cloth, gilt, dust jacket (price clipped), presentation copy inscribed by author. R. F. G. Hollett & Sons Antiquarian Booksellers 170 - 352 2011 £60

Johnson, B. S. *Travelling People.* London: Constable, 1963, First edition; 8vo., pages (i), 304, original black cloth, spine lettered and ruled in gilt, original color pictorial dust jacket, designed by John Holden, light wear to extremities, minor soiling to rear panel, fine, fresh, near fine dust jacket. Simon Finch Rare Books Zero - 243 2011 £175

Johnson, Crockett *Harold's Circus.* New York: Harper & Bros., 1959, First edition; 16mo., plain black cloth spine and pictorial boards, fine in dust jacket with price (dust jacket very good frayed at spine ends, worn along joints and small rub spot on cover), rare. Aleph-Bet Books, Inc. 95 - 309 2011 $1500

Johnson, Cuthbert W. *The Farmer's Encyclopaedia and Dictionary of Rural Affairs.* Philadelphia: Carey & Hart, 1844, large 8vo., 1165 pages + ads, 17 plates, full contemporary sprinkled calf, gilt banded spine with black morocco label, good, sound copy but rather foxed and browned. Ken Spelman Rare Books 68 - 151 2011 £95

Johnson, Denis *Angels.* New York: Knopf, 1983, Uncorrected proof; spine and edge darkened covers, very good in wrappers. Ken Lopez Bookseller 154 - 84 2011 $200

Johnson, Dick *Ted Williams.* Norwalk: Easton, 2000, Collector's edition; 4to., xiv, 225 pages, fine, full leather with raised bands, gilt lettered spine and front cover, gilt decorated spine and front cover, all edges gilt, silk moire endpapers, silk ribbon bookmark. By the Book, L. C. 26 - 76 2011 $150

Johnson, George W. *The Cottage Gardeners' Dictionary.* London: W. Kent & Co., 1860, Fifth edition; illustrations, some slight creasing to corners, endpapers slightly dusted, original wavy grained brown cloth, neatly creased, slightly dulled. Jarndyce Antiquarian Booksellers CXCI - 227 2011 £75

Johnson, H. U. *From Dixie to Canada. Romances and Realities of the Underground Railroad.* Buffalo: Charles Wells Moulton, 1894, First edition; 12mo., 194 pages, frontispiece and 7 plates, original decorated cloth. M & S Rare Books, Inc. 90 - 425 2011 $250

Johnson, Hugh *The Plantsman.* London: The Garden, Journal of the Royal Horticultural Society, 1979-1994, First edition; 15 volumes bound in 8, soundly bound in orange buckram lettered gilt on spine, preserving original green wrappers/covers, unbroken run 1979-1994, 3000+ pages, many illustrations. Any Amount of Books May 29 2011 - A73755 2011 $374

Johnson, James Weldon *The Book of American Negro Poetry.* New York: Harcourt Brace and Co., 1922, First edition; 8vo. 48, 217 page, original cloth backed covered boards, paper label, label slightly rubbed, old newspaper clipping on Negro spirituals printed to front endpaper, with offsetting. M & S Rare Books, Inc. 90 - 196 2011 $200

Johnson, James Weldon *God's Trombones.* New York: Viking Press, 1927, First edition, 5th printing; 8vo., (5), 56 pages, 8 full page deco illustrations, original cloth backed boards, some light rubbing, signed in ink by author. M & S Rare Books, Inc. 90 - 195 2011 $250

Johnson, John B. *Eulogy on General George Washington, a Sermon, Delivered February 22d 1800 in the North Dutch Church, Albany Before the Legislature of the State of New York...* Albany: printed by L. Andrews, Printer to the State, 1800, First edition; inscription, (2), 22 pages, disbound. Anthony W. Laywood May 26 2011 - 21728 2011 $126

Johnson, Joseph *George MacDonald: a Biographical and Critical Appreciation.* London: Sir Isaac Pittman & Sons, 1906, Half title, engraved frontispiece, title in red and black, uncut in original maroon cloth blocked with title and author on front board as well as spine, spine slightly faded, top edge gilt, signature of Wm. R. Barclay and containing 17 manuscript leaves of lecture on MacDonald by Barclay. Jarndyce Antiquarian Booksellers CXCII - 352 2011 £120

Johnson, Joseph *George MacDonald: a Biographical and Critical Appreciation.* Sir Isaac Pitman & Sons, 1906, Half title, engraved frontispiece, title in red and black, uncut in original maroon cloth blocked with gilt and author on front board as well as spine, faded and slightly rubbed with wear to head of spine, top edge gilt. Jarndyce Antiquarian Booksellers CXCII - 351 2011 £40

Johnson, Joseph *George MacDonald: a Biographical and Critical Appreciation.* London: Sir Isaac Pittman & Sons, 1906, Half title, engraved frontispiece, title in red and black uncut in secondary binding of slightly lighter maroon cloth without title and name on front board, spine faded with small splits at head and tail, bookplate of James L. Miller with inscription. Jarndyce Antiquarian Booksellers CXCII - 353 2011 £50

Johnson, Robert *Adventures of Captain Robert Johnson, in the Northern Circars of India, Where He Officiated as Judge Advocate and Chaplain...* London: printed for Thomas Tegg, 111 Cheapside, 1808, 12mo., large folding frontispiece, (3), 8-28 pages, disbound. Anthony W. Laywood May 26 2011 - 21705 2011 $134

Johnson, Robert Flynn *Artist's Books in the Modern Era 1870-2000. The Reva and David Logan Collection of Illustrated Books.* San Francisco: Fine Arts Museums, 2001, 4to., 302 pages, fine in fine dust jacket. By the Book, L. C. 26 - 34 2011 $75

Johnson, Ronald *3 Concrete Poems.* Urbana: Finial Press, 1968, One of 20 numbered copies signed by author (entire edition) this Johnson's own copy, #1; folio, 17 original prints on various colored mat boards silkscreened from hand-cut film by Alvin Doyle Moore, accompanied by a 7 1/2 x 7 1/2 inch book printed in 3 colors and bound in original red Kenent cloth over boards stamped in silver on front cover, all loose, as issued, in publisher's cloth and pastepaper over boards, folding box, with printed paper label on top panel, very fine,. James S. Jaffe Rare Books May 26 2011 - 21661 2011 $6500

Johnson, Samuel 1696-1772 *An English and Hebrew Grammar.* London: W. Faden, 1771, Second edition; 12mo., (1), 4 (1), 58, (2) pages, sewn, original plain back wrapper, light waterstaining but very good. M & S Rare Books, Inc. 90 - 201 2011 $1250

Johnson, Samuel 1709-1784 *Dictionary of the English Language.* London: printed by W. Strahan for J. and P. Knapton, 1755, First edition; 2 volumes, large folio, unpaginated, text in double columns, titlepages printed in red and black, decorative woodcut tailpieces, expertly rebound to style using original full brown calf covers, boards decoratively ruled in blind, spines ruled in gilt in compartments, six raised bands, red and black morocco spine labels, lettered and stamped in gilt, marbled endpapers, volume I with smallest amount of worming along fore-margin, not affecting text, previous owner's pencil inscription and signature to top edge of title volume I, boards lightly scuffed, still handsome, very fine. Heritage Book Shop Holiday 2010 - 63 2011 $27,500

Johnson, Samuel 1709-1784 *Dictionary of the English Language.* London: for F. and C. Rivington, J. Walker et al, 1810, Tenth edition; 2 volumes quarto, engraved frontispiece, contemporary diced calf, ruled in gilt, gilt lettering on spine, marbled endpapers, all edges marbled, 2 former owner's bookplates, neatly rebacked to style, very nice, bright copy. Heritage Book Shop Holiday 2010 - 62 2011 $2500

Johnson, Samuel 1709-1784 *A Dictionary of the English Language.* Philadelphia: Moses Thomas, 1818, First unabridged American edition; 4to., 2 large volumes, unpaginated, full calf, elaborately stamped in gilt, worn at extremities of the spine, weak on hinges, frontispiece, all edges gilt, ownership signature of George Pitt from 1824 and note by his son John that the set was rebound in 1849, waterstain to inner margin of half title and titlepage of volume two, generally very good set. Second Life Books Inc. 174 - 206 2011 $4000

Johnson, Samuel 1709-1784 *A Dictionary of the English Language.* Philadelphia: Moses Thomas, 1818, 1818. 1819. 1819. First American edition; thick 4to., frontispiece, half title in all 4 volumes, full contemporary calf, two leather labels on each volume, all edges marbled, bindings scuffed but sound, occasional waterstaining but unfoxed, very good set. M & S Rare Books, Inc. 90 - 197 2011 $3000

Johnson, Samuel 1709-1784 *A Dictionary of the English Language.* London: printed for G. and J. Offor, W. Allason, 1824, 2 volumes, 4to., frontispiece in volume I, handsomely rebound in half tan calf, gilt bands, red morocco labels. Jarndyce Antiquarian Booksellers CXCI - 156 2011 £750

Johnson, Samuel 1709-1784 *The History of Rasselas, Prince of Abyssinia.* London: Folio Society, 1975, First edition thus; original cloth backed pictorial boards, spine rather faded slipcase, pages 131, with 7 color plates. R. F. G. Hollett & Son Antiquarian Booksellers General Catalogue Summer 2010 - 715 2011 £30

Johnson, Samuel 1709-1784 *Lives of the Most Eminent English Poets, with Critical Observations on their Works...* London: John Murray, 1854, 3 volumes, half titles, scattered fox marks, mostly to endpapers, pages xxxii, 395; vii, 444; xii,456, 8vo., slightly later half calf, backstrips panelled in gilt with green morocco labels with gilt lettering, top edge gilt, marbled endpapers, upper joint volume iii just cracking at head, good.   Blackwell Rare Books   B166 - 55   2011   £160

Johnson, Samuel 1709-1784 *The Prince of Abissinia.* London: printed for R. and J. Dodsley, 1759, First edition, first state of volume II with leaf A2 headed 'CONENTS/VOL. II"; small 8vo., full contemporary calf, gilt ruled borders with minor wear, usual offsetting to endpapers and titlepages, discrete leather booklabel of Blairhame, otherwise unusually attractive copy in original state, with all blanks, preserved in a brown half morocco slipcase.   James S. Jaffe Rare Books   May 26 2011 - 18916   2011 $12,500

Johnson, Samuel 1709-1784 *Prince of Abissinia. a Tale.* London: printed for J. F. and C. Rivington et al, 1790, Eighth edition; 182 x 108mm., viii, 304 pages; extremely pleasing etruscan style calf in style of and quite probably by Edwards of Halifax, covers with gilt metope and pentaglyph border as well as a wide frame of stenciled palmettes enclosing a sprinkled central panel with lightened slats radiating from an oval sunburst and laurel garland at middle, raised bands flanked by plain gilt rules, spine panels with central black urn or ewer framed by gilt floral spray cornerpieces, black morocco label, turn-ins and all edges gilt; with attractive fore-edge painting, quite possibly by Edwards, apparently showing a landscape with Rievaulx Abbey Yorkshire in background; contemporaneous armorial bookplate of "Rycroft", covers with very minor marks and stains, joints and extremities with hint of rubbing (top of spine with very small losses of leather), with no significant wear, only trivial defects internally and with the fore-edge scene very well preserved.   Phillip J. Pirages   59 - 37   2011 $1950

Johnson, Samuel 1709-1784 *The Rambler.* Philadelphia: J. J. Woodward, 1827, New edition; 12mo., v, 257, vii, 230, vii, 259, vii, 235, 2 page list, mottled calf on boards, gilt decorations and titles on spine, presentation label to public library label pasted down inside upper cover of each volume, minor wear and moderate foxing, repaired light splitting at spine, handwritten library pocket and card pasted on inside back cover of each volume, light foxing and offsetting from engraved frontispiece, on titlepages and interspersed in text, some scuffing to spines, restored upper cover of volume four, very good, scarce.   Hobbyhorse Books   56 - 89   2011 $200

Johnson, Samuel 1709-1784 *Rasselas, Prinz von Abyssinien.* Hamburg: Hartwig & Muller, 1826, First edition; 2 volumes in 1, 8vo., half brown leather, pages x, 193, (5); 301 (2), rare, English text and German text, frontispiece, uncommon, half brown leather rubbed at corners and slightly chipped at spine ends, slight splitting at upper spine hinge, otherwise very good, clean pages slightly stained at prelims and with slight 'waving' of pages, possibly from damp at some time.   Any Amount of Books   May 29 2011 - A64756   2011 $306

Johnson, Samuel 1709-1784 *The Works of Samuel Johnson.* London: printed for J. Nichols & Son; F. & C. Rivington &c., 1810, New edition; 12 volumes, 16mo., frontispiece volume 1, half titles in volumes IV, V, VI & VII, contemporary half brown calf, gilt bands, brown morocco labels, marbled paper boards, slight loss to paper to back board volume I, nice set.   Jarndyce Antiquarian Booksellers   CXCI - 19   2011   £485

Johnson, Stephen *Fishing from afar.* Moretonhampstead: Flyfisher's Classic Library, 2004, Limited edition, No. 70 of 150 copies; full navy blue morocco gilt slipcase, pages xvi, (i), 154, (i), top edge gilt, 2 pages of color plates and 25 illustrations, marbled endpapers and silk marker, fine.   R. F. G. Hollett & Son Antiquarian Booksellers   General Catalogue Summer 2010 - 1257 2011   £120

Johnson, T. Broadwood *Tramps Round the Mountains of the Moon and through the Back Gate of the Congo State.* London: T. Fisher Unwin, 1912, Second impression; 8vo., pages xxiii, 36, illustrations, map, original black cloth, inner hinge cracked.   J. & S. L. Bonham Antiquarian Booksellers   Africa 4/20/2011 - 7085   2011   £38

Johnson, Thomas Burgeland *The Mystery of the Abbey; or the Widow's Fire Side.* London: printed for Sherwood, Neely & Jones, Paternoster Row, 1819, Later half calf, gilt bands, compartments blocked in blind, Fasque booklabel, extremely scarce, tipped in rear of volume is single folded sheet with contemporary mss. entitled Widow's Fire Side and with double column list of names.   Jarndyce Antiquarian Booksellers   CXCI - 228   2011   £700

Johnson, Walter *Wimbledon Common.* London: T. Fisher Unwin, 1912, First edition; original cloth, hinges trifle rubbed, pages 304. (i), 4 maps and 25 illustrations by Sydney Harrowing and Jesse Packham.   R. F. G. Hollett & Son Antiquarian Booksellers   General Catalogue Summer 2010 - 1450   2011   £1450

Johnson, William D. *Lincoln University; or the Nation's First Pledge of Emancipation.* Philadelphia: printed for the author, 1867, First edition; 8vo., 32 pages, including frontispiece, original printed paper wrappers, stitched as issued, wrappers lightly dust soiled, some small chips to rear wrapper, small library stamp on verso of title, pencilled correction of typo on page 10 and pencil mark on page 18, good copy. M & S Rare Books, Inc. 90 - 41 2011 $950

Johnston, Alexander Keith *Atlas to Alison's History of Europe.* Edinburgh: William Blackwood & Sons, 1848, frontispiece and 99 mostly hand colored plates, 1 folding map backed on linen, expertly rebound in half brown calf, brown morocco label, very good. Jarndyce Antiquarian Booksellers CXCI - 37 2011 £280

Johnston, Arnid *Animal Families and Where They Live.* London: Country Life, 1939, First edition; large 4to., original cloth, dust jacket, unpaginated, 24 pages of color lithograph illustrations, each with page of text and map, little scattered spotting, mainly to fore edges, but very nice. R. F. G. Hollett & Sons Antiquarian Booksellers 170 - 353 2011 £45

Johnston, Harry Hamilton 1858-1927 *The Kilmanjaro Expedition.* London: Kegan Paul Trench & Co., 1886, First edition; thick 8vo., xv, 572, 34 (ads) pages, 6 maps, engraved frontispiece, 78 illustrations, occasional light foxing, original pictorial cloth boards, over black cloth, gilt stamped cover and spine titles, spine replaced, bookplate of John George Cox, Broxwood Court, very good. Jeff Weber Rare Books 163 - 184 2011 $500

Johnston, Harry Hamilton 1858-1927 *Livingstone and the Exploration of Central Africa.* London: Geo. Philip, 1891, First edition, one of 250 copies; 8vo., pages xii, 372, 7 folding maps, 12 plates with tissue guards, original grey boards, vellum spine, very good. J. & S. L. Bonham Antiquarian Booksellers Africa 4/20/2011 - 9214 2011 £120

Johnston, Harry Hamilton 1858-1927 *The Negro in the New World.* London: Methuen, n.d., 1910, First edition; large 8vo., pages xxix, (i) blank, 499, (1) imprint, half title, color frontispiece, 2 folding maps, numerous text illustrations, original brown cloth lettered in gilt, pictorial endpapers, rather worn, little stained on covers and little loose, library label on lower endpaper, scarce. J. & S. L. Bonham Antiquarian Booksellers Africa 4/20/2011 - 5992 2011 £120

Johnston, John *Diary Notes of a Visit to Walt Whitman and Some of His Friends in 1890.* Manchester: The Labour Press Limited, London: The Clarion Office, 1898, First trade edition; 8vo., original pebbled green cloth, gilt rules and lettering, frontispiece, 10 photo plates, one reduced facsimile, front inner hinge starting, but sound, very good, from the collection of Samuel Charters. The Brick Row Book Shop Bulletin 8 - 40 2011 $125

Johnston, John *Historiae Naturalis de Piscibus et Cetis Libri V. Tabulis Quadraginta Septem ab illo Celeberrimo Mathia Meriano...* Heilbronn: Franciscs Josephus Eckebrecht, 1767, Later edition; 4to., 228, (4) pages, 47 plates, text has some foxing, original paper boards, housed in custom clamshell box, rare, fine. Jeff Weber Rare Books 161 - 240 2011 $2350

Johnston, John *A Report of Special Efforts by the Presbyterian Ministers to Propagate the Gospel in 1851 in the North of Ireland by Means of Open Air Preaching.* Newry: printed by James Henderson, 1852, First edition; 12mo., 22, (2) pages, sewn as issued in original printed wrappers, very good, occasionally rare. John Drury Rare Books 153 - 71 2011 £250

Johnston, Stanley H. *The Cleveland Herbal, Botanical and Horticultural Collections: a Descriptive Bibliography of Pre-1830 Works from the Libraries of the Holden Arboretum, the Cleveland medical Library Association and the Garden Center of Greater Cleveland.* Kent and London: Kent State University Press, 1992, First edition; large 8vo., xviii, 1012 pages, color frontispiece, plates, green cloth, gilt stamped red cover and spine labels, small bump to rear cover, else fine, from the Bern Dibner reference library, with Burndy bookplate. Jeff Weber Rare Books 161 - 241 2011 $95

Johnstone, Christian Isobel *Clan-Albyn: a National Tale.* London: G. Routledge & Co., 1853, Contemporary half green calf, maroon leather label, spine darkened, little rubbed, signed "Bective 1854", good, sound. Jarndyce Antiquarian Booksellers CLXC - 28 2011 £45

Johnstone, Christian Isobel *The Students; or Biography of Grecian Philosophers.* London: John Harris, 1827, First edition; 12mo., 217 pages, contemporary diced olive green calf with gilt rules at cover and gilt title, decorations on red label on spine, marbled endpapers, text in 3 parts, 16 plates, including frontispiece, all printed on heavier paper and one side of leaf only, upper endpaper and verso of frontispiece lightly dampstained, fine. Hobbyhorse Books 56 - 89 2011 $220

Johnstone, James *Antiquitates Celto-Normannicase, Containing the Chronicle of Man & the Isles...* Copenhagen: 1786, First edition; 152 + 296 pages, 4to., full calf, rebacked, very good, very scarce. C. P. Hyland May 26 2011 - 259/214 2011 $797

Johnstone, W. G. *The Nature Printed British Sea Weeds...* London: Bradbury and Evans, 1859, First edition; original publisher's green blind patterned cloth lettered gilt on spine and on front cover, 221 color or tinted plates and one plate uncolored, large gilt vignette on front boards and gilt title and ornaments on spines, clean, sound set, clean text and plates, covers of 3 volumes little sunned and tanned, else very good+. Any Amount of Books May 26 2011 - A74327 2011 $1090

Johnston's Penny Fireside Journal a Magazine of Amusing and Instructive Literature. London: W. Johnston, 1843-1845, 4 volumes (of 5), few spots and stains here and there, 8vo., contemporary maroon half roan, not quite uniform, contemporary signature on each title of Robert Montgomery of ?Conway and his armorial stamp inside front covers, good, rare. Blackwell Rare Books B166 - 56 2011 £400

Jollie, Francis *Cumberland Guide & Directory 1811.* Whitehaven: Michael Moon, 1995, Facsimile edition; original cloth, gilt, dust jacket, pages ii, new foreword, viii, 81, xix, 129 (ix, ads), 3 large folding maps in rear pocket, excellent facsimile reprint. R. F. G. Hollett & Son Antiquarian Booksellers 173 - 624 2011 £45

Jolly Alphabets and Puzzles. London: Blackie, n.d. circa, 1930, 4to., cloth backed pictorial boards, edges slightly rubbed, else fine, illustrated with 3 color cat drawings by A. E. Kennedy, 2 full color plates by Albert Kaye, illustrations in 3-color by C. E. B. Bernard, one color plate by Ruth Cobb. Aleph-Bet Books, Inc. 95 - 21 2011 $275

Jones, Ann *Women Who Kill.* New York: Holt, Rinehart and Winston, 1980, First edition; near fine in near fine dust jacket with half inch tear on front panel, presentation copy, inscribed by James Allan McPherson for Peter Taylor. Between the Covers 169 - BTC336596 2011 $650

Jones, Anson *Memoranda and Official Correspondence Relating to the Republic of Texas, Is History and Annexation.* Chicago: 1966, Limited to 150 copies, this copy not numbered; iv, 24, xiii, 736 pages, folding facsimile letter, folding map, full leather, all edges gilt, light shelfwear, else near fine. Dumont Maps & Books of the West 111 - 62 2011 $100

Jones, Barbara *Follies & Grottoes.* London: Constable, 1953, First edition; original cloth, gilt, dust jacket, slight wear and few short tears to edges, pages xii, 246, colored lithograph title, 28 drawings by author and 17 plates, the copy of engraver poet Laurence Whistler, with his pencilled signature, label removed from flyleaf. R. F. G. Hollett & Son Antiquarian Booksellers 177 - 508 2011 £65

Jones, Barbara *Follies and Grottos.* London: Constable, 1979, Small 4to., original cloth, gilt, dust jacket, spine little faded, pages xx, 459, profusely illustrated. R. F. G. Hollett & Son Antiquarian Booksellers 177 - 509 2011 £50

Jones, Caroline A. *Picturing Science, Producing Art.* New York and London: Routledge, 1998, Tall 8vo., x, 518 pages, frontispiece, illustrations, black cloth, silver stamped spine title, Burndy bookplate, fine, rare in cloth, from the Bern Dibner reference library, with Burndy bookplate. Jeff Weber Rare Books 161 - 241 2011 $150

Jones, Clement *A Tour in Westmorland.* Kendal: Titus Wilson, 1948, First edition; tall 8vo., original green cloth gilt, hinges rubbed and spine little worn and frayed at head, pages xviii, 128, 35 illustrations, folding maps, scarce. R. F. G. Hollett & Son Antiquarian Booksellers 173 - 627 2011 £40

Jones, D. *The Secret History of White Hall, from the Restoration of Charles II, Down to the Abdication of the Late King James.* London: R. Baldwin, 1697, First edition; old speckled blind tooled calf, rather rubbed and surface cracked, rebacked in matching calf gilt with raised bands, pages (xii), 80, 80, 80, 64, 80, 110, edges sprinkled. R. F. G. Hollett & Son Antiquarian Booksellers 175 - 741 2011 £220

Jones, David *In Parenthesis.* London: Faber & Faber, 1937, 8vo., pages xxi, 227, 2 illustrations, one map, lacks front endpaper, else very good, clean copy in otherwise about fine in very good-silver grey dust jacket with some small chips and closed tears, decent copy, no inscriptions. Any Amount of Books May 26 2011 - A70951 2011 $713

Jones, E. Alfred *Catalogue of the Plate of Clare College Cambridge.* Cambridge: University Press, 1938, First edition; large 4to., original plum cloth, gilt, pages xxxvii, 88, with 27 plates, loosely inserted is single sheet TLS from O. Thorshead (Librarian at Windsor Castle) to author. R. F. G. Hollett & Son Antiquarian Booksellers 175 - 744 2011 £250

Jones, Edward *The Bardic Museum of Primitive British Literature Forming the Second Volume of the Musical, Poetical and Historical Relicks of the Welsh Bards and Druids.* London: Strahan, 1802, Ms. amendment to publisher's address, Rowlandson colored frontispiece, modern half leather, very good. C. P. Hyland May 26 2011 - 255/376 2011 $1087

Jones, Edward *A Peep Into the Palace; or a Voice from the House of Correction.* London: J. Pattie, 1841, Seventh edition; some faint damp marking, 64 pages, contemporary half green calf, lacking spine strip, signature of H. T. Jones on titlepage. Jarndyce Antiquarian Booksellers CXCI - 597 2011 £250

Jones, Edward P. *The Known World.* New York: Amistad, 2003, First edition; near fine, spine ends bumped, dust jacket fine. Bella Luna Books May 29 2011 - t6609 2011 $110

Jones, Elizabeth Orton *Big Susan.* New York: Macmillan, 1947, First edition; 8vo., 82, (1) pages, fine in slightly frayed dust jacket, illustrations, very scarce. Aleph-Bet Books, Inc. 95 - 311 2011 $400

Jones, Ernest *Essays in Applied Psychoanalysis Volume I.* London: Hogarth Press, 1951, Second impression; original green cloth, gilt, pages 333. R. F. G. Hollett & Son Antiquarian Booksellers 175 - 745 2011 £35

Jones, Ernest *Swing the Clubhead.* N.P.: Golf Digest Classics, 1996, 8vo., 126 pages, fine, gilt lettered spine and cover, gilt design to cover. By the Book, L. C. 26 - 77 2011 $70

Jones, Frederic Wood *The Principles of Anatomy as Seen in the Hand.* London: J. & A. Churchill, 1920, 8vo., viii, 325 pages, 2 plates, including frontispiece, 123 numbered figures, original brown cloth, gilt stamped spine title, extremities speckled, very good, this copy belonged to C. Elmer Carlson, M.D. Orthopedic Surgery (Oregon) with his signature, from the Medical Library of Dr. Clare Gray Peterson. Jeff Weber Rare Books 162 - 173 2011 $120

Jones, G. D. B. *Roman Manchester.* Manchester University Press, 1974, Tall 4to., original pictorial wrappers, rather creased and used, pages xviii, 198, frontispiece, 32 plates and 62 text drawings and plans. R. F. G. Hollett & Son Antiquarian Booksellers 177 - 510 2011 £30

Jones, Gwyn *The Green Island.* Waltham St. Lawrence: Golden Cockerel Press, 1946, 73/100 specially bound copies (of an edition of 500 copies); printed on Arnold mouldmade paper, 12 wood engravings by John Petts, 2 of which are full page with title printed in green, pages (ii) (blanks), 84, (2) (blanks), royal 8vo., original green and gray moroccos, lettering on faded backstrip and Petts design on front cover all gilt blocked, top edge gilt, others untrimmed, near fine. Blackwell Rare Books B166 - 259 2011 £150

Jones, James *From Here to Eternity.* New York: Scribner, 1951, First edition; signed by author, faint offsetting to front pastedown, lower corners bumped, near fine in like dust jacket with slight edge wear, orange title lettering on spine now yellow, very nice. Ken Lopez Bookseller 154 - 85 2011 $1500

Jones, John Pike *Substance of the Speech of the Rev. J. P. Jones of North Bovey, Delivered at a County Meeting, Held at the Castle of Exeter, on Friday the 16th Day of March 1821...* Exeter: printed by R. Cullum, reprinted from Exeter edition with additional note by Keating and Brown, London, 1821, First edition, 2nd issue; 8vo., 28 pages, some paper browning, preserved in modern wrappers, printed title label on upper cover, good copy. John Drury Rare Books 153 - 72 2011 £125

Jones, Ken *I Was There.* New York: 1953, Called a "Lion" original and marked first edition; 159 pages, paperback, very good. Bookworm & Silverfish 676 - 113 2011 $75

Jones, Oakah L. *Nueva Vizcaya: Heartland of the Spanish Frontier.* Albuquerque: 1988, xx, 342 pages, maps and illustrations, issued without dust jacket, near fine, inexplicably scarce. Dumont Maps & Books of the West 111 - 63 2011 $175

Jones, Owen *The Grammar of Ornament.* London: Bernard Quaritch, 1868, third edition; folio, pages 1 p.l., 157 plus plates, ex-library, bookplate an library pocket on rear, library buckram, a number of the plates have small embossed library identification stamp on fore edge, hard to see but can be felt, chromolithographed title in red and black, 111 chromolithographed plates, many heightened in silver and gold, numerous text illustrations. Second Life Books Inc. 174 - 207 2011 $1000

Jones, Raymond F. *This Island Earth.* Chicago: Shasta, 1952, First edition; octavo, cloth backed boards. L. W. Currey, Inc. 124 - 187 2011 $250

Jones, Rufus M. *The Quakers in the American Colonies.* London: Macmillan, 1923, Original blue cloth, gilt, one corner little bumped, pages xxxii, 603, 4, with 4 folding maps, scattered spotting. R. F. G. Hollett & Son Antiquarian Booksellers 175 - 748 2011 £45

Jones, Rufus M. *Spiritual Reformers in the 16th and 17th Centuries.* London: Macmillan, 1928, Original blue cloth, gilt, pages li, 362. R. F. G. Hollett & Son Antiquarian Booksellers 175 - 747 2011 £35

Jones, S. Walter *A Treatise on the Law of Telegraph and Telephone Companies.* Kansas City: 1906, xxvii, 833 pages, large 8vo., fine in recent green cloth with leather label. Bookworm & Silverfish 662 - 94 2011 $245

Jones, Samuel Arthur *Pertaining to Thoreau.* Detroit: Edwin B. Hill, 1901, First edition, although there is no indication of such, this title was apparently limited to 225 copies according to an issue of The Thoreau Society Bulletin dated July 1949 and original prospectus, not present here; original brown cloth with gilt lettering on spine, xviii, 171 pages, light wear, near fine. Charles Agvent Transcendentalism 2010 - 53 2011 $200

Jones, Stephen *A New Biographical Dictionary or Pocket Compendium: Containing a Brief Account of the Lives and Writings of the Most Eminent Persons in every Age and Nation.* London: printed for G. G. and J. Robinson, J. Wallis, J. Scatcherd and E. Newbery, 1794, First edition; 18mo., 4 pages, circa 425 unnumbered pages, contemporary full red roan on boards, spine with gilt fillets and title, green marbled endpapers, inked name at top edge of titlepage, light chipping at crown and foot of spine, corners lightly bumped, rare copy, internally in fine state. Hobbyhorse Books 56 - 91 2011 $250

Jones, Thomas *James Cropper & Co. Ltd. and Memories of Burneside 1845-1945.* Kendal: Westmorland Gazette, 1945, First edition; original cloth, dust jacket, torn and defective, pages 70, well illustrated, scarce. R. F. G. Hollett & Son Antiquarian Booksellers 173 - 631 2011 £45

Jones, Trevor *Cumbrian Rock. 100 Years fo Climbing in the Lake District.* Pic Publications, 1988, Limited signed edition, no. 164 of 250 copies; large 8vo., original glazed pictorial boards, pages 256, well illustrated, signed by Jones and co-author Geoff Milburn, with short inscription by Milburn. R. F. G. Hollett & Son Antiquarian Booksellers 173 - 632 2011 £95

Jones, William *The Book of Nature; or the True Sense of Things Explained and Made Easy to the Capacity of Children.* London: F. C. and J. Rivington, 1810, Seventh edition; 2 parts, 12mo., xiv, 199 pages, original flamed leather on boards, gilt title on red label and fillets along spine, browning at edges of endpapers, rubbing at fold of spine of covers, text in excellent state, very good, rare. Hobbyhorse Books 56 - 92 2011 $150

Jones, William *Observations in a Journey to Paris by Way of Flanders in the Month of August 1776.* London: printed for G. Robinson, 1777, 2 volumes, 8vo., viii, 196, (4), 200 pages, engraved caricature of Voltaire in volume 1, original blue paper wrappers, volume 2 split, from the library of the Earls of Macclesfield at Shirburn Castle. Maggs Bros. Ltd. 1440 - 117 2011 £550

Jong, Erica *Fruits and Vegetables.* New York: 1971, First edition; slight discoloration on cover, slight traces of glue on endpapers, otherwise fine in dust jacket with small crease, inscribed an signed by author. Gemini Fine Books & Arts, Ltd. Art Reference & Illustrated Books: First Editions 2011 $90

Jonson, Ben *The Masque of Queens.* London: King's Printers, 1930, No. 89 of 188 only for sale in the British Empire, a further 150 were reserved for the USA; Long 4to., original publisher's scarlet cloth lettered gilt on spine and cover, pages 23 text, 16 pages plates and 39 pages reproduction of manuscript, endpapers little browned, bookplate of Sir Lionel Lawson Eaudel-Phillips, corners very slightly rubbed, very slight shelfwear, otherwise near fine. Any Amount of Books May 29 2011 - 169314 2011 $255

Jonson, Ben *Songs of Ben Jonson.* Eragny Press, 1906, One of 175 copies on paper (an additional 10 copies were Printed on vellum); 210 x 140mm., 1 p.l., 59, (3) pages, publisher's quarter grey paper over green 'speedwell' printed paper boards, edges untrimmed, original (slightly frayed) plain tissue dust jacket, very fine frontispiece of lute player printed in four colors, woodcut border on first page of text, decorative woodcut initials in red, printer's device on final page, many pages with printed music in red and black, all by Lucien and Esther Pissarro; original (very slightly foxed) tissue guard, printed in red and black throughout; usual brownish discoloration to front and rear free endpaper (apparently caused by binder's glue under facing pastedown), wrapper with just very minor wrinkling and fraying (as well as small, faint stain to rear panel), but superb copy, text immaculate and publisher's fragile binding in as close to original condition as one is likely to see. Phillip J. Pirages 59 - 190 2011 $1900

Jonson, Ben *The Three Celebrated Plays of the Excellent Poet Ben Jonson...* London: printed for W. Feales, n.d., 12mo., (iv), 96, 96 100, 35, (1) pages, frontispiece, modern antique style calf, gilt, fine. Jeff Weber Rare Books 163 - 47 2011 $125

Jonson, Ben *Volpone or The Fox.* New York: Limited Editions Club, 1952, Limited edition; numbet 91 of 1500 copies, signed by Rene Ben Sussan, illustrations by Sussan with a number of superb original pochoir plates, fine in fine slipcase. Gemini Fine Books & Arts, Ltd. Art Reference & Illustrated Books: First Editions 2011 $60

Jonston, John *Historiae Naturalis de Piscibus et Cetis Libri V. (bound with) Historiae Natralis de Exanguibus Aquaticis Libri IV.* Francofurti ad Moenum: Matthaei Meriani, 1650, First edition; engraved allegorical title (with 1 inch tear), 47 engraved plates (with marginal tears and chipping to margins of a plate, with some loss to margins, marginal stain to 5 pages, minor foxing to margin of few plates), folio, pages 228, 18th century gilt ruled calf, spine replaced later, corners bumped with 1 corner cracked, splitting to edges of spine but solid, spine rubbed, endpapers renewed, marginal stain to first 15 leaves, marginal tear to front leaf, some browning to text; engraved vignette on title and last page and 19 engraved plates, missing plate 18 (torn piece from plate has been restored), folio, pages 78, (12), occasional foxing, some offsetting to text, index pages browned. Raymond M. Sutton, Jr. May 26 2011 - 42560 2011 $3000

Jope, E. M. *The Clarendon Hotel, Oxford.* Oxford: 1958, Large 8vo., original wrappers, one corner little creased, pages 129, with 20 plates and 37 text illustrations. R. F. G. Hollett & Son Antiquarian Booksellers 177 - 512 2011 £40

Joppien, Rudiger   *The Art of Captain Cook's Voyages.* Melbourne: Oxford University Press, 1985, Reprint; 2 volumes, 4to., pages 549, copiously illustrated in color and black and white, neat Australiana collector's blindstamp, otherwise very good+ in like dust jacket, very slight fading and very slight creasing, otherwise excellent.   Any Amount of Books   May 29 2011 - A76751   2011 $281

Joppien, Rudiger   *The Art of Captain Cook's Voyages.* New Haven and London: Yale University Press, 1985-1988,   First edition; 4 volumes, 4to., xv, 247; xiii, 274; xxi, 233; 235-669 pages, illustrations, (ink smeared, text still lightly legible), reddish brown cloth, gilt stamped spine title, dust jacket, near fine, from the Bern Dibner reference library, with Burndy bookplate.   Jeff Weber Rare Books   161 - 244   2011 $675

Jordan, David Starr   *Imperial Democracy. A Study of the Relation of Government by the People Equality Before the Law and Other Tenents of Democracy.*   New York: 1899, (i-vi) vii-ix (x), (1-2) 293 (9) pages, fine, gilt bright, corners sharp, private library # on titlepage (no other marks). Bookworm & Silverfish   679 - 54   2011 $85

Jordanus, Catalani, Bp. of Columbum   *Mirabilia Descripta. The Wonders of the East by Friar Jordanus...* London: printed for the Hakluyt Society, 1863,   (1862). First edition; 4, 8, iv, xvii, 68 pages, 8vo., original blue cloth stamped in blind, gilt vignette of ship on front board, spine ruled in blind, gilt titles, yellow endpapers, spine sunned, small chip to head of spine, small tears to heel, otherwise about very good, institutional bookplate, owner's nautical bookplate.   Kaaterskill Books   12 - 106   2011 $400

Josselyn, John   *An Account of Two Voyages to New England.*   London: Giles Widdows, 1674,   First edition; 12mo., pages (6), 224, (227-)279, (3) G. Widdowes' ads, pages 225-226 ommitted in pagination, page (219) wrongly numbered (223), leaf (A!) recto G. Widdowes' printer's device, verso contains L'Estrange's license dated Nov. 1673, contemporary full calf, worn, outer hinges show some repair, old notations to pastedowns, scattered marginal ink notations, owner's inscriptions on 3 blanks, soiling to many pages, occasional small stain, browning to some front and back pages, chipping to and marginal pieces missing from few pages, ink notations to title for Chronological section, in modern leather backed clamshell box.   Raymond M. Sutton, Jr.   May 26 2011 - 55870   2011 $9000

Jourdain, M.   *The History of English Secular Embroidery.* London: Kegan Paul, 1910,   First edition; xiv, 202 pages, double page frontispiece, illustrations, original gilt lettered, red cloth, spine sunned, scarce.   Ken Spelman Rare Books   68 - 103   2011   £40

The Journal of Industrial Archaeology.   David & Charles, 1965,   1968-1971.; Volumes 5-8 plus 2 earlier numbers (volume 2 nos. 1 dn 3), together 16 numbers plus indices an appendix, original wrappers, numbers for volumes 5 and 6 loose in original publisher's cloth cases, illustrations.   R. F. G. Hollett & Son Antiquarian Booksellers   177 - 493   2011 £45

Journeys.   Rockville: Quill & Brush, 1996,   Limited to 26 lettered copies, this letter D; fine, full leather.   Bella Luna Books   May 26 2011 - t72660   2011 $577

Joutel, Henri   *Journal Historique du Dernier Voyage que feu M. de la Sale fit dans le Golfe de Mexique.*   Paris: Chez Estienne Robinot, 1713,   First edition; 12mo., folding engraved map, contemporary French sprinkled calf. Heritage Book Shop   Booth A12 51st NY International Antiquarian Book Fair April 8-10 2011 - 76   2011 $25,000

Joutel, Henri   *A Journal of the Last Voyage Perform'd by Monsr. De La Sale to the Gulph of Mexico...*   London: for A. Bell, B. Lintott, J. Baker, 1714,   First edition in English; 8vo., (2), xxi, (9), 191, 194-205, (5) pages, engraved folding map, short closed tear, contemporary calf, extremities rubbed, top of spine bit worn, else lovely, untouched copy, text clean and fresh, entirely unfoxed, Peter Porter bookplate and Wolfgang Herz label.   Joseph J. Felcone Inc. Fall Miscellany 2010 - 67   2011 $15,000

Jouve, P.   *Danse Des Morts.*   Geneva: 1917,   First edition, limited to 200 copies; original wrappers rubbed and torn around head and foot of spine, else very good, very scarce, 174 pages.   I. D. Edrich   May 26 2011 - 59043 2011 $461

Jowett, Benjamin   *The Republic of Plato.*   Oxford: Clarendon Press, 1888,   Third edition; half title, original blue cloth, slightly rubbed, very good.   Jarndyce Antiquarian Booksellers   CXCI - 229   2011   £45

Joyce, George Henry   *Some Records of Troutbeck.* Staveley: Kentmere Ltd. circa, 1924,   First edition; original stiff wrappers, pages 76, printed in red and black, tipped in photo portrait, scarce.   R. F. G. Hollett & Son Antiquarian Booksellers   173 - 637   2011   £65

Joyce, James 1882-1941   *Chamber Music.*   Egoist Press, 1923,   Cloth, very good, scarce.   C. P. Hyland May 26 2011 - 258/426   2011 $580

Joyce, James 1882-1941   *Finnegans Wake.*   London: Faber and Faber, 1939,   First edition; 8vo., pages (iv), 628, top edge orange yellow, others uncut, internally fine, publisher's red cloth, gilt lettering to spine, fine, original red and yellow dust jacket, strengthened at head and foot of spine, minor chips and wear to edges, still bright, unclipped. Simon Finch Rare Books   Zero - 244   2011   £1800

Joyce, James 1882-1941 *Giacomo Joyce.* New York: Viking, 1968, First edition; 8vo., circa 80 pages, 4 facsimile pages from manuscript, cloth in slipcase, fine.   Gemini Fine Books & Arts, Ltd.   Art Reference & Illustrated Books: First Editions 2011 $150

Joyce, James 1882-1941 *Pomes Penyeach.* Paris: 1927, First edition; errata slip present, boards (some wear to spine), text very good.   C. P. Hyland   May 26 2011 - 255/379 2011 $580

Joyce, James 1882-1941 *Three Songs for Voice and Piano Set to Poems from "Chamber Music".* New York: Schirmer, 1939, First edition?; without stars in upper right corner, 4to., pages 10, self wrappers, fine.   Second Life Books Inc.   174 - 208 2011 $75

Joyce, James 1882-1941 *Ulysses.* New York: Limited Editions Club, 1935, One of 1500 copies signed by Matisse; (this copy # 976), 305 x 234mm., xv, (iii), 363, (3) pages; publisher's original brown buckram, embossed in gilt and titled on front cover and on flat spine, decorations from a design by LeRoy H. Appleton, housed in original board slipcase with brown titling on spine (slightly worn but generally well preserved), 26 illustrations by Henri Matisse, numbered sticker ("0154") affixed to head edge of slipcase; slipcase with thin crack along one joint and with tiny chips at opening, still absolutely solid and extremely clean, mild offsetting to one page in volume, virtually mint condition.   Phillip J. Pirages   59 - 255 2011 $4900

Joyce, James 1882-1941 *Ulysses.* San Francisco: Arion Press, 1988, Copy #4 of 40 copies with an additional suite of plates (of a total of 175 copies printed, 25 of which were not for sale), signed by artist; 330 x 260mm., 838 pages, "Ulysses" volume plus a companion portfolio of plates (along with related materials); publisher's white alum-tawed half pigskin over boards covered with blue silk flecked with white, flat spine with titling in light blue, untrimmed edges, original matching blue silk slipcase, 40 etchings by Robert Motherwell, plus portfolio of 22 extra prints in publisher's matching blue box, related material, detailed prospectus for this work, an Arion Press price list for May 2007, a copy of the February 1989 issue of "Arts and Antiques" magazine featuring an article on the present book written by Motherwell, and one of 250 copies of "The Ulysses Etchings of Robert Motherwell:, an interview with artist, in mint condition.   Phillip J. Pirages   59 - 58 2011 $45,000

Joyce, Stanislaus *My Brother's Keeper. James Joyce's Early Years.* New York: Viking Press, 1958, Limited to 375 copies; specially bound as Christmas Remembrance for friends of Viking Press, 8vo., xxii, 266 pages, original cloth, beveled edges with gilt lettering spine, near fine.   By the Book, L. C.   26 - 9 2011 $75

Joyce, William *Santa Calls.* New York: Harper Collins, 1993, Limited to 250 numbered copies; fine, signed by author.   Bella Luna Books   May 29 2011 - t4654 2011 $137

Judah, Aaron *The Pot of Gold and Two Other Tales.* London: Faber, 1939, First edition; original pictorial red cloth, dust jacket price clipped and overstamped with decimal price, pages 62 with illustrations by Peake.   R. F. G. Hollett & Sons Antiquarian Booksellers   170 - 509 2011   £60

Judd, John Wesley *The Geology of Rutland and the Parts of Lincoln, Leicester, Northampton, Huntingdon and Cambridge, Included in sheet 64 of the one-inch Map of the Geological Survey.* London: Longmans & Co. E. Stanford, 1875, First edition; folding hand colored sections, 8 tinted lithograph plates, illustrations in text, 3 folding plates (part folding and partly colored including frontispiece), xv, (1), 320 pages, original cloth, spine rather faded, otherwise nice.   Anthony W. Laywood   May 26 2011 - 21245 2011 $184

Judge, Roy *The Jack in the Green.* D. S. Brewer for the Folklore Society, 1979, First UK edition; original cloth, gilt, dust jacket, pages xii, 145, 35 illustrations, scarce.   R. F. G. Hollett & Son Antiquarian Booksellers   175 - 749 2011   £35

Judges, A. V. *The Elizabethan Underworld.* London: Routledge, 1930, First edition; large 8vo., original cloth, gilt, pages lxiv, 543, with 20 illustrations.   R. F. G. Hollett & Son Antiquarian Booksellers   175 - 750 2011   £85

Junck, Oscar Waldemar *Isolated Communities a Study of a Labrador Fishing Village.* New York: American Book Co., 1937, 8vo., pages xxi, 130, photo illustrations, 2 folding charts, red cloth slightly worn, generally very good, inscribed and dated by author to his sister.   Schooner Books Ltd.   96 - 58 2011 $100

Juncken, Johann Helfrich *Chymia Experimentalis Curiosa, sive Medicus Praesenti Seculo Accommodandus per Veram Philosophiam Spagiricam.* Frankfurt: Hermannus a Sande, 1684, Early edition; 8vo., pages (xvi), 840, (8), some light dampstaining and soiling, worming throughout confined to top and bottom of gutter, small tear affecting s4-t2, contemporary vellum, bumped and soiled, crack at foot of spine, still firm, pen marks to front free endpaper, early ownership inscription to initial blank.   Simon Finch Rare Books   Zero - 109 2011   £900

Junius, Hadrianus *Emblemata Eiusdem Aenigmata Libellus.* Leiden: F. Raphelengius ex off. Plantiniana, 1596, 58 woodcuts, mostly unsigned, 16mo., 167 pages, woodcuts, speckled calf, c. 1700, gilt spine, red morocco lettering piece, from the library of the Earls of Macclesfield at Shirburn Castle.   Maggs Bros. Ltd.   1440 - 119 2011   £950

Junius, Pseud. *Junius Stat Nominius Umbra.* London: printed by T. Bensley for Vernor and Hood et al, 1801, 2 volumes, 8vo., pages (ii) xxxiii-xxxii 274 + engraved titlepage (dated 1797), engraved portrait frontispiece and 10 other engraved portrait plates, v, (iii), 318, (ii) + engraved titlepage, engraved portrait frontispiece and 7 other engraved portrait plates, contemporary straight grained dark blue morocco, fully gilt six compartmented spine with 'liberty cap atop oak leaved staff' centerpieces, lettered & numbered direct in gilt, boards full and brown rule gilt bordered with decorative roll (interweaving front and graded pebbles) within, board edges single rule gilt, turn-ins decorative roll gilt, pink 'made' endpapers, all edges gilt, dark green double core sewn endbands, pale blue silk page markers, foxed, bit rubbed at extremities and touched up with blue dye, small printed booklabel of "Gwendolen Brandt", from the collection of Christopher Ernest Weston 1947-2010.   Unsworths Booksellers   24 - 113   2011   £160

Junker, Wilhelm   *Travels in Africa During the Years 1875-1878.*   London: Chapman & Hall, 1890,   First English edition; 3 volumes, 8vo., pages viii, 582; viii, 477, (1) imprint, (2) ads; viii, 586; half titles in volumes 2 and 3, 4 folding maps, numerous textual illustrations, frontispiece in volume 1, original green cloth, vignette in brown on upper covers, marks where library labels remove, library label on pastedowns but no stamps in text, good tight set.   J. & S. L. Bonham Antiquarian Booksellers   Africa 4/20/2011 - 7916   2011   £550

K

Kafka, Franz 1883-1924 *The Metamorphosis.* London: Parton Press, 1937, First edition in English; 8vo., pages (6), 74, original blue cloth backed gray paper boards, blue label printed in black to upper board, spine lettered in black, slightly cocked, spine caps and corners lightly rubbed, minor soiling, acetate jacket, small chip to head of spine and to corners of upper panel. Simon Finch Rare Books Zero - 245 2011 £1400

Kai-Shek, Chiang *General Chiang Kai-Shek - the Account of the Fortnight in Sian when the fate of China Hung in the Balance.* New York: 1937, First edition, first issue dust jacket dated '37'; 187 pages, good, endpapers foxed, tiny bit of white foxing to front cover, price clipped dust jacket damped at both flap folds and top inch of backstrip diminishing to both covers, noticeable from inside and at top 1.5" from outside; rear page with age soil, both ends of backstrip of dust jacket shelfworn, signed Mayling Soong Chiang. Bookworm & Silverfish 679 - 36 2011 $100

Kalep, Elvy *Air Babies.* Denver: Bradford Robinson, 1936, First edition; oblong folio, new cloth spine, printed boards, some edge and tip wear, else very good+, signed by Kalep on endpapers plus 8 line inscription from her signed by Kalep, scarce. Aleph-Bet Books, Inc. 95 - 313 2011 $475

Kallman, Chester *Storm at Castelfranco.* New York: Grove Press, 1956, First edition, one of only 15 copies, signed by Kallman and containing original drawing by Larry Rivers tipped in as frontispiece, signed by author; small 8vo., original cloth backed boards, glassine dust jacket, offsetting to titlepage from original drawing, otherwise very good. James S. Jaffe Rare Books May 26 2011 - 17159 2011 $7500

Kames, Henry Home 1696-1782 *Sketches of the History of Man.* Edinburgh: for W. Creech, Edinburgh: and for W. Strahan and T. Cadell, 1774, First edition; 2 volumes, 4to., (iii)-xii, 519, (1); (2), 507, (1) pages, wanting half titles, titlepage of volume I little soiled and/or foxed, small blank strip cut away from foot (repaired and not near printed surface), intermittent minor soiling and foxing in volume I, two or three leaves with tears (but not with loss), small old ink stain in one leaf causing small hole with loss of few letters on each page, several early (and interesting) annotations in very good 19th century green half calf gilt with raised bands, minor blemishes apart, very good in sound and pleasing binding with mid 19th century ownership inscription in each volume "Wm. G. Mason 3 Bedford Circus, Exeter 1850". John Drury Rare Books 153 - 62 2011 £1250

Kander, Simon, Mrs. *The Settlement Cook Book.* Milwaukee: 1949, Twenty-ninth edition; 623 pages near fine, white cloth very clean, some mottling to fore and bottom edge. Bookworm & Silverfish 676 - 58 2011 $68

Kane, Paul *Paul Kane's Frontier Including Wanderings of an Artist Among the Indians of North America.* Austin: 1971, Limited edition, 1 of 300 numbered copies; xviii, 350 pages, illustrations, oblong quarto, dust jacket with some edgewear and couple of short tears, else near fine. Dumont Maps & Books of the West 111 - 64 2011 $85

Kann, Rodolphe *Catalogue of the Rodolphe Kann Collection Objets d'Art.* Paris: Jules Mannheim, Edouard Rahir, 1907, 2 volumes, folio, 68, 109 pages, 245 photogravure plates, original blue printed wrappers, gilt stamping on upper covers, spines neatly restored to match, fine set, rare. Jeff Weber Rare Books 163 - 102 2011 $200

Kansas *Indian Raid of 1878. The Report of Commission Appointed in Pursuance of the Provisions of Senate Joint Resolution No. 1 Relating to Losses Sustained by Citizens of Kansas by the Invasion of Indians During the Year 1878.* Topeka: Geo. W. Martin, Kansas Pub. House, 1879, First edition; 8vo., original lavender printed wrappers, 58 pages, tables, lightly sunned around perimeters of covers, former owner's name top front cover, else near fine, tight copy, housed in cloth clamshell case with leather label on spine and titles stamped in gold. Buckingham Books May 26 2011 - 26047 2011 $3750

Kant, Immanuel *The Principles of Critical Philosophy...* London: sold by J. Johnson, W. Richardson; Edinburgh: P. Hill, Manners and Miller; Hamburg: B. G. Hoffmann, 1797, First English edition; 8vo., lxxx, 454, (ads 2) pages, occasional light foxing, original full mottled calf, spine with gilt rules, black leather spine label, early ownership signature of Jacob Barker, Glasgow, 14 April crossed out from blank, Sheffield library bookplate, very good, scarce. Jeff Weber Rare Books 161 - 246 2011 $4000

Kant, Immanuel *Zum Ewigen Frieden.* Konigberg: Friedrich Nicolvius, 1795, First edition; pages 104, 8vo., original board, lettered gilt on spine, spine little defective at head, affecting lettering, little worn, frequent underlining in red crayon, good. Blackwell Rare Books B166 - 58 2011 £550

Karma, Ura *Deities, Archers and Planners in the Era of Decentralisation.* Bhutan: Karma Ura, 2004, First edition; 8vo., very uncommon, pages 323, slight bumping, dust jacket has slight edgewear, otherwise very good+ in like dust jacket. Any Amount of Books May 29 2011 - A47524 2011 $221

Karpinski, Louis *Bibliography of Mathematical Works Printed in America through 1850.* Ann Arbor: and London: University of Michigan Press & Oxford University Press, 1940, First edition; 4to., xxvi, 697 pages, illustrations, dark blue cloth, blindstamped cover emblem, gilt stamped spine title, extremities lightly speckled, inner hinge cracked, from the Bern Dibner reference library, with Burndy bookplate. Jeff Weber Rare Books   161 - 247   2011 $400

Kaufman, George S. *Beggar on Horseback.* New York: Boni and Liveright, 1924, First edition; 8vo., 237 pages, two pages in middle of text quite darkened from old news clipping that has been laid in, top edges of boards sunned, otherwise very good, tight copy in very good, bright dust jacket, inscribed by producer Winthrop Ames to George Barbier who played Mr. Cady, splendid association. Second Life Books Inc.   174 - 209   2011 $1500

Kautsky, Karl *Outbreak of the World War.* New York: Oxford University Press, 1924, First edition; 8vo., pages 688, ex-library with label at spine and 2 circular stamp of Pedagogische Hochschule in Potsdam, covers slightly marked and slightly soiled, otherwise sound, near very good.   Any Amount of Books   May 29 2011 - A45045   2011 $340

Kavanagh, Julia *Bessie.* Leipzig: Bernhard Tauchnitz, 1872, bound without half titles, 2 volumes in 1, contemporary half dark green morocco, slightly rubbed, good plus. Jarndyce Antiquarian Booksellers   CLXC - 30   2011   £35

Kavanagh, Julia *Forget-me-Nots.* London: Richard Bentley, 1878, First edition; 3 volumes, leading f.e.p. volume I torn in lower margin with slight loss, repair to pages 15/16 volume 2 without loss, contemporary half dark blue calf, bit rubbed, stamps of Beechworth Public Library, good, sound copy.   Jarndyce Antiquarian Booksellers   CLXC - 31   2011   £110

Kavanagh, Julia *French Women of Letters: Biographical Sketches.* London: Hurst & Blackett, 1862, First edition; 2 volumes, slightly spotted, contemporary half red calf, spines with raised gilt bands, brown leather labels slightly chipped, dulled and little rubbed, small booklabels of Stephen E. Cotton, good, sound copy.   Jarndyce Antiquarian Booksellers   CLXC - 32   2011   £110

Kavanagh, Julia *Rachel Gray.* Leipzig: Bernhard Tauchnitz, 1856, Copyright edition; half title, contemporary half black morocco, slightly rubbed.   Jarndyce Antiquarian Booksellers   CLXC - 33   2011   £35

Kavanagh, Julia *Sybil's Second Love.* Leipzig: Bernhard Tauchnitz, 1867, Copyright edition; 2 volumes, half titles, text slightly browned and slightly marked in prelims volume II, 2 volumes in 1 in contemporary half black morocco, slightly rubbed.   Jarndyce Antiquarian Booksellers   CLXC - 34   2011   £35

Kavanagh, Julia *Two Lilies.* Leipzig: Bernhard Tauchnitz, 1877, Copyright edition; 2 volumes, half titles, contemporary half blue cloth, marbled boards, slightly dulled, very good.   Jarndyce Antiquarian Booksellers   CLXC - 35   2011   £40

Kavanagh, Julia *Women of Christianity, Exemplary for Acts of Piety and Charity.* London: Smith, Elder, 1852, First edition; frontispiece and plates, few internal marks, contemporary full antique 'Bible' calf, bevelled boards, red label, very good.   Jarndyce Antiquarian Booksellers   CLXC - 36   2011   £65

Kavanagh, Ted *Tommy Handley.* London: Hodder & Stoughton, 1949, First edition; pages 255, with 32 pages of sepia plates, original cloth, edges faded, dust jacket, edges little worn.   R. F. G. Hollett & Son Antiquarian Booksellers   175 - 753   2011   £50

Kawauchi, Rinko *Utatane. (Siesta). (with) Hanabi. (Fireworks).* Tokyo: Little More, 2001, First editions, signed copies; Utatane - large 8vo., pages (132), 129 color photos, original wrappers, spine lettered in blue, original color photo illustrated dust jacket, very light rubbing to lower panel, original obi, text printed in black, lightly rubbed, Kawauchi's signature in black ink to half title, fine in near fine dust jacket and obi; Hanabi - large 8vo., pages (72), 69 color photos, original wrappers, spine lettered in pink, head of spine bumped, original color photo illustrated dust jacket, creasing to head of spine, original obi, text printed in black, Kawauchi's signature in black ink to titlepage, near fine. Simon Finch Rare Books   Zero - 530   2011   £750

Kay, Gertrude *The Jolly Old Shadow Man.* Chicago: Volland, 1920, Sixteenth edition; 8vo., pictorial boards, fine in pictorial box (light rubbing, else very good+), illustrations by author.   Aleph-Bet Books, Inc.   95 - 573   2011 $250

Keane, John F. *On Blue-Water. Some Narratives of Sport and Adventure in the Modern Merchant Service.* London: Tinsley, 1883, First edition; half title, 2 pages ads, original blue cloth blocked in black and gilt, spine lettered in gilt, spine little faded and slightly rubbed at head, stamp & initials of B. E. Dunbar Kilburn, nice.   Jarndyce Antiquarian Booksellers   CXCI - 230   2011   £85

Kearton, Richard *The Adventures of Cock Robin and His Mate.* London: Cassell & Co., 1904, First edition; original green pictorial cloth gilt, pages xvi, 240, 8, over 120 illustrations from photos.   R. F. G. Hollett & Son Antiquarian Booksellers   General Catalogue Summer 2010 - 1002   2011   £30

Kearton, Richard *British Birds' Nests.* London: Cassell & Co., 1898, First edition; tall 8vo., original green pictorial cloth, gilt, rather faded, spot to lower board, pages xx, 368 top edge gilt, plates from photos. R. F. G. Hollett & Son Antiquarian Booksellers General Catalogue Summer 2010 - 1004 2011 £75

Kearton, Richard *Nature's Carol Singers.* London: Cassell, 1912, Original pictorial cloth, gilt, dust jacket very worn and defective, pages (x), 252, (iv), well illustrated, little spotting to prelims, uncommon. R. F. G. Hollett & Son Antiquarian Booksellers General Catalogue Summer 2010 - 1000 2011 £30

Kearton, Richard *With Nature and a Camera.* London: Cassell & Co., 1897, First edition; tall 8vo, original pictorial cloth, gilt, spine and edges faded, pages xvi, 368, (iv), top edge gilt, with 180 illustrations from photos, endpapers spotted. R. F. G. Hollett & Son Antiquarian Booksellers General Catalogue Summer 2010 - 1006 2011 £50

Keary, Annie *A Doubting Heart.* London: Macmillan and Co., 1891, Half title, original red cloth lettered in gilt, spine slightly dulled, otherwise very good. Jarndyce Antiquarian Booksellers CLXC - 38 2011 £35

Keary, Annie *Oldbury.* London: Macmillan and Co., 1902, Half title, original red cloth, lettered in gilt, spine slightly dulled, otherwise very good. Jarndyce Antiquarian Booksellers CLXC - 39 2011 £35

Keats, John 1795-1821 *Lamia, Isabella, The Eve of St. Agnes and Other Poems.* London: printed for Taylor and Hessey, 1820, First edition; large duodecimo, (4, blank), (viii), 199, (1, printer's imprint) pages, complete with half title and publisher's ads, publisher's original drab pale brown boards, expertly and near invisibly rebacked with original spine, original printed spine label, few pages with light spots of foxing, otherwise exceptional fresh and fine, housed within full green morocco pull off case. David Brass Rare Books, Inc. May 26 2011 - 01226 2011 $28,500

Keats, John 1795-1821 *Odes, Sonnets & Lyrics.* Oxford: Daniel Press, 1895, 91/250 copies printed on French handmade paper; photogravure frontispiece, tissue guard present, pages (v) (blanks) (ix) 64 (iv) (blanks), royal 8vo., original pale grey projecting wrappers, printed in black on front cover, untrimmed, unopened, fine. Blackwell Rare Books B166 - 248 2011 £270

Keats, John 1795-1821 *Poetical Works and Other Writings.* New York: Charles Scribners Sons, 1938, Hampstead edition, limited to 1050 numbered copies, this being #695 signed by Maurice Buxton Forman and John Masefield; 8 volumes, octavo, photogravure frontispieces with tissue guards, half blue morocco over blue cloth, morocco ruled in gilt, spines stamped and lettered in gilt, top edge gilt, others uncut, blue marbled endpapers, few volumes with small amount of light discoloration to cloth, near fine. Heritage Book Shop Holiday 2010 - 66 2011 $3750

Keble, John *The Christian Year: Thoughts in Verse for the Sundays & Holydays Throughout the Year.* Oxford: James Parker & Co., 1868, Half title, black morocco, slightly rubbed, all edges gilt, very good, signed presentation from Randolph Caldecott, 6th Feb. 1869 for sister Sophia Caldecott. Jarndyce Antiquarian Booksellers CXCI - 439 2011 £150

Keble, John *The Christian Year: thoughts in Verse for the Sundays and Holydays throughout the Year.* London: Bickers & Son, 1875, 24 illustrations, half title, frontispiece, illustrated title, original full dark brown crushed morocco, heavy boards in gilt decorated with diving bird, wings outstretched, in each corner, central gilt design of cross with brown morocco onlay with title, raised bands, compartments ruled and decorated in gilt, contemporary gift inscription facing half title "E.G.S. Hornby with his mother's love July 20 1880", booklabel of Robert J. Hayhurst, all edges gilt, very attractive. Jarndyce Antiquarian Booksellers CXCI - 440 2011 £125

Keen, Graham *Underground Graphics.* London: Academy Editions, 1970, First edition; 4to., original publisher's red cloth lettered gilt on spine, pages xiii, 79 (printed recto only on various colore cartridge papers), covers very slightly marked and slightly dusty, but sound very good+. Any Amount of Books May 29 2011 - A67756 2011 $374

Keenan, Michael *Report of the Trial of Michael Keenan, for Administering an Unlawful oath.* Dublin: printed by J. Exshaw, 1822, First edition; 8vo., (4), 64, (4), 65-111 pages, including half title, very slight foxing at beginning and end, original boards, neatly rebacked, uncut, very good, uncommon. John Drury Rare Books 153 - 155 2011 £300

Keeson, A. *Monts De Piete and Pawnbroking: Containing 1. A Statistical Account of the Operations of the Monts de Piete of Pars, from the French of M. Blaize. 2. Statistics of the Irish Monts de Piete, compiled from Official Documents. 3. A Sketch of Pawnbroking.* 1854, First edition; 12mo., repair to 1 leaf, else very good in original embossed cloth with gilt titling. C. P. Hyland May 26 2011 - 255/401 2011 $637

Keightley, Thomas *The Fairy Mythology Illustrative of the Romance and Supersititon of Various Countries.* London: H. G. Bohn, 1850, New edition; original blindstamped cloth, gilt, neatly recased, pages xvi, 560, etched frontispiece by G. Cruikshank (little spotted). R. F. G. Hollett & Son Antiquarian Booksellers 175 - 755 2011 £150

Keillor, Garrison *Lake Wobegon Summer 1956.* Norwalk: Easton Press, 2001, First edition thus, signed by author; leather bound, all edges gilt, as new, certificate of authenticity and note from Easton Press included. Gemini Fine Books & Arts, Ltd. Art Reference & Illustrated Books: First Editions 2011 $105

Keir, Elizabeth *The History of Miss Greville.* Edinburgh: printed for E. Balfour and W. Creech, Edinburgh and T. Cadell, London, 1787, First edition; 3 volumes, half titles, contemporary half calf, spines with devices in gilt, spines rubbed and lacking labels, engraved bookplates by Bewick for Joseph Cook. Jarndyce Antiquarian Booksellers CLXC - 40 2011 £750

Keith, Arthur *The Antiquity of Man.* London: Williams and Norgate, 1929, Seventh impression; 2 volumes, original cloth, gilt, pages xxxii, 376; xiv, 377-753, with 266 illustrations. R. F. G. Hollett & Son Antiquarian Booksellers 177 - 514 2011 £45

Keith, Thomas *A New Treatise on the Use of the Globes.* London: Longmans, Brown etc., 1845, Original black fine ribbed cloth, gilt, boards panelled in blind, head of spine frayed, pages xxiv, 364, 7 folding copper engraved plates. R. F. G. Hollett & Sons Antiquarian Booksellers 170 - 363 2011 £60

Kekule, L. Bruce *Thailand's Natural Heritage - a Look at some of the Rarest Animals in the Kingdom.* Bangkok: Wkt Publishing, 2004, 4to., pages 223, copiously illustrated in color, fine in fine dust jacket and slightly sunned, very good + printed firm slipcase. Any Amount of Books May 29 2011 - A63570 2011 $238

Kellam, Ian *Where the Snow Lay.* Gryffon Publications, 1990, Limited edition (no. 140 of 250 copies); original cloth decorated in green with paper label inlay, pages 128, illustrations by Arthur Kenne, music on endpapers, presentation copy inscribed by author, signed on front. R. F. G. Hollett & Son Antiquarian Booksellers General Catalogue Summer 2010 - 823 2011 £35

Keller, David H. *Life Everlasting & Other Tales of Science, Fantasy & Horror.* Newark: 1917, First edition; 382 pages, small 8vo., original binding, near fine in very good dust jacket (mild foxing), 12 page bibliography of author's work to date laid in, signed by author. Bookworm & Silverfish 669 - 75 2011 $125

Keller, Helen *The Story of My Life with Her Letters.* New York: Doubleday, 1935, Reprint of 1904 edition; 8vo., pages 441, photos, covers somewhat faded, little soiled, endpapers stained, very good, inscribed by author, laid in paper and stamps from mail wrapper addressed in another hand. Second Life Books Inc. 174 - 210 2011 $750

Kelley, E. G. *The Philosophy of Existence.* London: Chapman & Hall, 1878, First edition; pages xvi, 630, half title and final flyleaf browned, but very good, sound copy, original green cloth, gilt. R. F. G. Hollett & Son Antiquarian Booksellers 175 - 758 2011 £125

Kelley, William *Hon. William D. Kelley.... Speech of... Pennsylvania.* Washington: 1894, 22 pages, printed on letter grade of paper. Bookworm & Silverfish 667 - 58 2011 $75

Kellogg, J. H. *The Art of Massage: Its Physiological Effects and Therapeutic Applications.* Battle Creek: 1895, First edition; xvi, 282 pages, very good in half leather, considerable white showing at shoulders (both sides) of backstrip, corner leather worn, front cover loose, private library number on titlepage, no other library marks. Bookworm & Silverfish 676 - 128 2011 $100

Kelly & Co. *Directory of Cumberland and Westmorland.* Kelly's Directories Ltd., 1938, Small 4to., original crimson cloth gilt, faded, spine little frayed at head and foot, pages 12, xvi, 436, vi, 192, 2 folding colored maps. R. F. G. Hollett & Son Antiquarian Booksellers 173 - 639 2011 £125

Kelly & Co. *Directory of Cumberland and Westmorland.* Kelly & Co., 1897, Small 4to., original blindstamped crimson cloth gilt, corners slightly worn, lower corners rather damped, pages xxiv, 430; 191, 48 (ad), without maps (issued separately). R. F. G. Hollett & Son Antiquarian Booksellers 173 - 638 2011 £120

Kelly, C. M. *The Brocks.* London: Charles Skilton, 1975, First edition; tall 8vo., original cloth, gilt, dust jacket (edges trifle worn), pages 18 with color frontispiece and 46 illustrations and plates, 4 long ALS's and 1 TLS from author, all loosely inserted. R. F. G. Hollett & Son Antiquarian Booksellers General Catalogue Summer 2010 - 222 2011 £40

Kelly, Dollin *New Max Worthies.* Douglas: Manx Heritage Foundation, 2006, First edition; 4to., illustrations in black and white, 504 pages, fine in very good dust jacket with slight edgewear, Frank Kermode's copy with letter to him from Bureau Chief of NY Times and some xeroxs. Any Amount of Books May 29 2011 - A76394 2011 $204

Kelly, George *Behold the Bridegroom.* Boston: Little Brown, 1928, First edition; 8vo., pages 172, frontispiece, blue cloth with paper label, inscribed by author for Jean Dixon who played Constance Peyton. Second Life Books Inc. 174 - 212 2011 $500

Kelly, George *Behold, the Bridegroom.* Boston: Little Brown, 1928, First edition; 8vo., 172 pages, frontispiece, blue cloth with paper label, else near fine in little nicked and soiled dust jacket, rare in dust jacket, inscribed by author to Barrett Clark. Second Life Books Inc. 174 - 211 2011 $500

Kelly, George *Craig's Wife, a Drama.* Boston: Little Brown, 1926, First edition; 8vo., pages 174, very nice tight copy, inscribed by author to Mrs. Lansburg, housed in calf backed cloth slipcase and chemise. Second Life Books Inc. 174 - 214 2011 $1000

Kelly, George *Craig's Wife a Drama.* Boston: Little Brown, 1926, First edition; 8vo., pages 174, very nice, tight copy, inscribed by author to Josephine Williams who played the part of Mrs. Harold in the NY production, also signed by rest of the cast - Annie Sutherland, Crystal Herne, Arthur Shaw, C. Stewart, Eleanor Marsh, Charles Trowbridge, Josephine Hull, J. A. Curtis, Nelan Jaap, Arline Alcine & Mary Gildea, also inscribed by the producer, Rosalie Stewart to whom the play was dedicated. Second Life Books Inc. 174 - 213 2011 $2000

Kelly, George *Philip Goes Forth.* New York: Samuel French, 1931, First edition; 8vo., pages 211, fine in dust jacket that is missing some pieces at edge and corners, inscribed by author to Dorothy Stickney (with her name stamp on endpaper) who played the lead in opening performance, in addition a 'round robin' copy signed by entire cast. Second Life Books Inc. 174 - 216 2011 $750

Kelly, George *The Show-Off.* Boston: Little Brown, 1924, First edition; 8vo., pages 129, frontispiece, fine in little soiled pictorial dust jacket, rare in dust jacket. Second Life Books Inc. 174 - 217 2011 $950

Kelly, George *The Torch Bearers a Satirical Comedy in Three Acts.* New York: American Library Service, 1923, First edition; 8vo., pages 213, publisher's cloth backed boards, very good in nicked and repaired, albeit very rare, dust jacket, scarce. Second Life Books Inc. 174 - 218 2011 $900

Kelly, J. Wells *First Directory of Nevada Territory...and Including Sketches of the Washoe Silver Mines by Henry DeGroot.* Los Gatos: Talisman Press, 1962, Limited to 750 copies, facsimile reprint; pages xvi, (2), xix, (1), 267, (4), 24, numerous ads, folding map, black cloth backed printed boards, gilt lettered spine, very fine in spine darkened dust jacket. Argonaut Book Shop Recent Acquisitions Summer 2010 - 149 2011 $150

Kelly, Thomas *For Advancement of Learning.* Liverpool: University Press, 1981, First edition; large thick 8vo., original cloth, gilt, dust jacket, pages xv, 560, 87 illustrations. R. F. G. Hollett & Son Antiquarian Booksellers 175 - 759 2011 £30

Kelson, George M. *Tips.* Moretonhampstead: The Flyfisher's Classic Library, 2003, Limited edition no. 59 of 150 copies; full black morocco gilt, slipcase, pages (x), 168, (xiv), top edges gilt, 22 illustrations, marbled endpapers, silk marker, fine. R. F. G. Hollett & Son Antiquarian Booksellers General Catalogue Summer 2010 - 1259 2011 £120

Kelton, Elmer *The Art of Howard Terpning.* Trumbull: Greenwich Workshop, 1992, Stated first edition; first printing fine in fine dust jacket with mild edgewear, 4to., 160 pages. By the Book, L. C. 26 - 32 2011 $225

Kelty, Mary Anne *The Favourite of Nature.* London: G. & W. B. Whittaker, 1822, Third edition; 3 volumes, 12mo. contemporary half speckled calf, black leather labels, rubbed, leading hinges weak and repaired, volume I heads and tails of spines slightly worn, Renier booklabels, good, sound copy. Jarndyce Antiquarian Booksellers CLXC - 41 2011 £60

Kemble, Edward W. *The Blackberries and Their Adventures.* London: Kegan Paul, Trench, Trubner & Co., 1897, First English edition; oblong 4to., cloth backed color pictorial boards with edge rubbing and surface handling, all in all, far nicer copy than generally seen, uncommon, 16 full page color plates, as you turn the page after a color plate, there is a blank verso and then a page with half page monocle drawing and short discussion based on color plate topic in heavy stereotypical dialect, rare. Jo Ann Reisler, Ltd. 86 - 25 2011 $2000

Kemble, Frances Anne 1809-1893 *An English Tragedy: a Play in Five Acts.* London: Longman, Green, Longman, Roberts & Green, 1863, First edition; half title, contemporary half calf, marbled boards, dark green leather label, little marked, good plus. Jarndyce Antiquarian Booksellers CLXC - 42 2011 £120

Kemble, Frances Anne 1809-1893 *Far Away and Long Ago.* London: Richard Bentley, 1889, First edition; half title, original grey cloth, spine lettered in gilt, spine slightly dulled, good plus. Jarndyce Antiquarian Booksellers CLXC - 43 2011 £125

Kemble, Frances Anne 1809-1893 *Journal of a Residence on a Georgian Plantation in 1838-1839.* New York: Harper & Brothers, 1863, First edition; first state with word "about" repeated on page 314, line 6, octavo, 337 (10 ads) pages, original publisher's full brown blindstamped cloth, gilt spine title, neat repairs to spine ends, very good. Jeff Weber Rare Books 163 - 186 2011 $70

Kemble, Frances Anne 1809-1893 *Journal of Frances Anne Butler.* London: John Murray, 1835, First edition; 2 volumes, slightly later full green calf, gilt spines, blind borders, gilt dentelles, armorial bookplates of James Bonnell, very good, attractive copy.   Jarndyce Antiquarian Booksellers   CLXC - 44   2011   £350

Kemble, Frances Anne 1809-1893 *Record of a Girlhood.* London: Richard Bentley and Son, 1878-1879, First edition; 3 volumes, half titles, contemporary half gan calf marbled boards, spines with raised gilt bands and gilt devices, brown leather labels, spines worn, labels chipped or missing.   Jarndyce Antiquarian Booksellers   CLXC - 45   2011   £50

Kemble, John M. *Horae Ferales or Studies in the Archaeology of the Northern Nations.* London: Lovell Reeve and Co., 1863, First edition; xii, 251 pages, 4to., 34 lithographic plates by Orlando Jewitt with tissue guards, 11 immaculately hand colored, superbly bound in recent cherry red calf over marbled paper backed boards, gilt lettering and decoration to spine, top edge gilt, new endpapers, superb condition.   Any Amount of Books   May 26 2011 - A75733   2011 $671

Kendal *Bye-Laws Passed by the Local Board of Health of the Borough of Kendal and Allowed and Confirmed by the Secretary of State for the Home Department on the 10th April 1859...* Kendal: printed by James Robinson, 1859, Original plain wrappers, pages 36.   R. F. G. Hollett & Son Antiquarian Booksellers   175 - 764   2011   £35

The Kendalian (The Magazine of Kendal Grammar School) 1900-1908. 1911-1922. Kendal: Atkinson & Pollitt, 1908-1922, 5 volumes, old binder's cloth gilt, remaining volumes in original green cloth gilt with school crest on front board, illustrated throughout with photos.   R. F. G. Hollett & Son Antiquarian Booksellers   173 - 648   2011   £150

Kendall, Edward Augustus *Keeper's Travels in Search of His Master.* Philadelphia: Johnson & Warner, Lydia R. Bailey, 1808, Early American edition; 12mo., 87, (3) pages, wood engraved frontispiece, contemporary marbled paper covered boards, red roan spine, covers rubbed, usual light foxing but tight and lovely, 1809 ownership of Joseph Moore.   Joseph J. Felcone Inc.   Fall Miscellany 2010 - 69   2011 $400

Kendall, George Wilkins *Narrative of the Texan Santa Fe Expedition...* Dallas: 2004, Edition of 500 copies, limited edition reprint; 2 volumes, xxxvi, 252 pages, illustrations, folding map in envelope, xv, 307 pages, issued without dust jackets, near fine.   Dumont Maps & Books of the West   112 - 47   2011 $150

Kendall, John *American Memories: Recollections of a Hurried Run through the United States During the Spring of 1896.* Nottingham: W. Burrows, 1896, First edition; frontispiece, original blue cloth gilt, slightly rubbed.   Jarndyce Antiquarian Booksellers   CXCI - 561   2011   £48

Keneally, Thomas *Schindler's Ark.* London: Hodder & Stoughton, 1982, First British edition, true first; near fine, discrete owner's name on front free endpapers, dust jacket near fine, price clipped and light fading to spine,.   Bella Luna Books   May 29 2011 - t1597   2011 $82

Keneally, Thomas *Schindler's Ark.* London: Hodder & Stoughton, 1982, First British edition, true first; fine, in like dust jacket, publisher's price sticker on front flap.   Bella Luna Books   May 26 2011 - t9250   2011 $275

Kennard, Mary E. *Twilight Tales.* London: F. V. White & Co., 1888, Half title, frontispiece, 5 plates, original green cloth, front board blocked and lettered in black, spine blocked and lettered gilt, very slight rubbing, owner's inscription dated 1890, very good.   Jarndyce Antiquarian Booksellers   CLXC - 47   2011   £35

Kennard, Roy Coleridge *Caresses et Blasphemes.* Paris: Imprimerie de J. Haumont, 1945, First and only edition; 8vo., pages 34, (1), unopened, internally fine, original maize printed wrappers, text in black short slit at top of spine without loss and slight sunning, rare.   Simon Finch Rare Books   Zero - 324   2011   £575

Kennedy-Fraser, Marjory *Songs of the Hebrides.* London: Boosey and Co. n.d. 1920's, Large 4to., original cloth, gilt, rather bumped and marked, backstrip little torn and repaired, pages (xxxix, (i), 164, frontispiece, very scarce.   R. F. G. Hollett & Son Antiquarian Booksellers   175 - 770   2011   £75

Kennedy, Grace *Dunallan; or Know What You Judge: a Story.* Edinburgh: W. Oliiphant, 1825, Second edition; 3 volumes, 12mo., half titles, final ad leaf volume I, contemporary half dark blue calf, armorial bookplate, Cotton & Renier booklabel, very good.   Jarndyce Antiquarian Booksellers   CLXC - 48   2011   £120

Kennedy, Grace *Dunallan.* Edinburgh: W. Oliphant, 1826, Third edition; 2 volumes, 12mo., frontispiece, following errata leaf volume II, contemporary full calf, gilt spines, borders and dentelles, dark brown leather labels, each volume with one gathering slightly proud, otherwise very good.   Jarndyce Antiquarian Booksellers   CLXC - 49   2011   £95

Kennedy, Grace *Dunallan.* Edinburgh: William Oliphant & Son, 1841, Sixth edition; engraved frontispiece with small repaired tear in outer margin, contemporary half black roan, slight rubbing, owner's inscription 1848, good, sound copy.   Jarndyce Antiquarian Booksellers   CLXC - 51   2011   £40

Kennedy, Grace *Dunallan.* Edinburgh: William Oliphant & Son, 1841, Sixth edition; engraved frontispiece, 4 pages ads, untrimmed in original pink brown cloth, blocked in blind, spine lettered in gilt, faded to brown, one or two small marks, good plus.   Jarndyce Antiquarian Booksellers   CLXC - 50   2011   £60

Kennedy, Grace *Father Clement: a Roman Catholic Story.* Edinburgh: W. Oliphant & Son, 1838, Ninth edition; engraved frontispiece slightly spotted, contemporary half calf, gilt spine, maroon leather label, slightly rubbed, ownership signature G. MacDonald, nice.   Jarndyce Antiquarian Booksellers   CLXC - 52   2011   £40

Kennedy, Grace *Willoughby; or Reformation.* London: C. and J. Rivington, 1826, Second edition; 2 volumes, contemporary half green calf, spines with raised gilt bands and decorated in blind, maroon leather labels, nice.   Jarndyce Antiquarian Booksellers   CLXC - 53   2011   £145

Kennedy, J. P. *Address to the Friends of Domestic Industry, Assembled in Convention at New York, October 26 1831 to the People of the United States.* Baltimore: Nov. 10, 1831, First edition; 8vo., 44 pages, original printed wrappers, uncut, removed, stain in upper corner of later leaves, signature in ink of A(lexander) H. Everett on front wrapper.   M & S Rare Books, Inc.   90 - 209   2011 $325

Kennedy, John *A Treatise Upon Planting, Gardening and the Management of the Hot-House.* York: printed by A. Ward for the author, 1776, First edition; 8vo., full brown leather, pages xvi, 420, corner of prelims slightly stained, outer hinges slightly weak, corners bumped, spine ends very slightly worn, else sound, clean, very good, bookplate of Martin Brown Ffolkes.   Any Amount of Books   May 26 2011 - A47678   2011 $419

Kennedy, John Fitzgerald 1917-1963 *As We Remember Joe.* Cambridge: privately printed, 1945, First edition, first issue, one of 300 copies; 3 books in two volumes, with all points as described by Kennedy Library Head, David Powers, titlepage in two colors with sunken panel on front cover, ivory colored paper, caption on page 64, octavo, xii, 75, (1, colophon) pages, 33 black and white photos, including frontispiece, publisher's original full burgundy cloth, front cover stamped in black and gilt on sunken panel, spine lettered gilt, very small about of rubbing to spine and back board, otherwise near fine, publisher's original glassine; with 3 ALS's from head of Kennedy Libary, David Powers to Dr. Maury Bromsen dated Jan. 23, 1978, April 2, 1979 and 1/7/80.   Heritage Book Shop   Holiday 2010 - 68   2011 $3750

Kennedy, Joseph C. G. *Population of the United States in 1860; Compiled from the Original Returns of the Eighth Census.* Washington: 1864, First edition; 694 pages, very good in three quarter leather and marbled boards, errata sheet tipped in.   Bookworm & Silverfish   679 - 33   2011 $150

Kennedy, Kenneth *Studies in the Archaeology and Palaeoanthropology of South Asia.* New Delhi: Oxford & IBH Publishing Co., 1984, Later printing; viii, 144 pages, black and white drawings, plans and maps, small 4to., cloth, boards rubbed, else near fine.   Kaaterskill Books   12 - 110   2011 $75

Kennedy, W. R. *Sport, Travel and Adventure in Newfoundland and the West Indies.* Edinburgh: William Blackwood and Sons, 1885, 8vo., pages x, (2), (1)-399 (24 pages publisher's catalog), half title, color frontispiece, 1 plate, 16 black and white illustrations in text and color folding map at rear, 8vo., blue cloth with gilt to spine and gilt illustration on front cover, wear to edges and whiting to outer edge of front and back covers, interior very good.   Schooner Books Ltd.   96 - 61   2011 $225

Kennedy, William 1928- *The Ink Truck.* New York: Dial Press, 1969, First edition; signed by author, nearly fine in very good+ dust jacket (couple of light coffee stains and light tape residue at spine bottom).   Lupack Rare Books   May 26 2011 - ABE1236479856   2011 $450

Kent Archaeological Society *Archaeologia Cantiana. Volumes LXXII to CXXV.* Kent Archealogical Society, 1959-2005, Volumes LXXII to CXXV, together 52 volumes including 2 index volumes, original blue cloth gilt, illustrations with many folding plates, excellent clean and sound run.   R. F. G. Hollett & Son Antiquarian Booksellers   177 - 517   2011   £650

Kent, Alexander *Stand into Danger.* London: Hutchinson, 1980, First British edition, true first; fine copy, near fine dust jacket with very light wear.   Bella Luna Books   May 29 2011 - t9037   2011 $82

Kent, James *An Address Delivered at New Haven, Before the Phi Beta Kappa Society September 13 1831.* New Haven: Hezekiah Howe, 1831, First edition; 8vo., 48 pages, original printed wrappers, removed, sound.   M & S Rare Books, Inc.   90 - 93   2011 $225

Kentish, Mrs. *The Two Friends; or the Dying Fawn...* London: Dean & Munday, n.d. circa, 1860, 12mo., 26 pages + 1 page ads on back wrapper, decorative maroon stiff wrappers, full page frontispiece, plus eight charming wood engravings, all hand colored, inked name on front endpaper, wrappers spotted, rubbed along edges and chipping on spine, occasional internal foxing and light spotting, upper corner of frontispiece with small chip, good copy, scarce.   Hobbyhorse Books   56 - 93   2011 $250

Kentucky. Laws, Statutes, etc. *Acts Passed at the First Session of the Eighth General Assembly for the Commonwealth of Kentucky.* Frankfort: William Hunter, 1800, (3)-226 pages, lacks title leaf, later cloth backed marbled boards, printed paper spine label, piece torn from corner of K1, side notes cropped on several leaves toward rear, final leaf 2#2 (final page of index) torn and repaired at fore-edge, costing small amount of text, embossed early ex-library blindstamp on covers, James Allen's copy, signed on first page of text. Joseph J. Felcone Inc. Fall Miscellany 2010 - 70 2011 $1400

Kepler, Johann *Prodromus Dissertationum Cosmographicarum...* Frankfurt: Erasmus Kempfer for G. Tampach, 1621-1622, Second edition; folio, (8), 114, 119-163, (1); (50) pages, 4 'tabellae' with woodcut diagrams and with letterpress, (pages 18, IV at p. 54, V at pg. 56), woodcut diagrams, contemporary speckled calf, spine gilt in compartments, some browning, lacking engraved plate numbered III, from the library of the Earls of Macclesfield at Shirburn Castle. Maggs Bros. Ltd. 1440 - 120 2011 £15,000

Ker, Henry *Travels through the Western Interior of the United States, from the Year 1808 up to the Year 1816.* Elizabethtown: the author, 1816, First and only edition; 372 pages, neat modern calf backed marbled paper covered boards, period style, some occasional spotting and light overall toning, unusually nice, printed on inferior quality paper and usually found in poor condition. Joseph J. Felcone Inc. Fall Miscellany 2010 - 71 2011 $1200

Kermode, P. M. C. *Manx Crosses or the Inscribed and Sculptured Monuments of the Isle of Man from about the End of the Fifth to the Beginning of the Thirteenth Century.* 1907, First edition; ex-library, rebound but very good. C. P. Hyland May 26 2011 - 255/404 2011 $457

Kerner Von Marilaun, Anton *The Natural History of Plants Their Forms, Growth, Reproduction and Distribution.* Blackie & Son, 1894-1895, 2 volumes, thick small 4to., contemporary three quarter green levant morocco gilt with marbled boards by Riviere, spines mellowed, top edge gilt, 16 color plates and some 2000 woodcut text illustrations, handsome, bookplate of Sir Henry Francis Redhead Yorke. R. F. G. Hollett & Son Antiquarian Booksellers General Catalogue Summer 2010 - 1008 2011 £220

Kerouac, Jack 1922-1969 *The Dharma Bums.* New York: Viking Press, 1958, First edition; worn, fair only copy, heavily rubbed and frayed at extremities, in very good dust jacket, rubbed, almost certainly married to book (but which came to us thus) in fine custom made quarter morocco clamshell case, inscribed by author to Terry Southern. Between the Covers 169 - BTC346433 2011 $35,000

Kerouac, Jack 1922-1969 *Mexico City Blues.* New York: Grove Press, 1959, First edition; fine in very slightly worn dust jacket, scarce in jacket. Second Life Books Inc. 174 - 219 2011 $3000

Kerouac, Jack 1922-1969 *Mexico City Blues.* New York: Grove Press, 1959, First edition, third printing; 8vo., 244 pages, edges very slightly soiled, else nice in price clipped dust jacket (little soiled). Second Life Books Inc. 174 - 220 2011 $75

Kerouac, Jack 1922-1969 *On the Road.* New York: Viking, 1957, First edition; 8vo., pages 310, fine in dust jacket, little worn and chipped, not price clipped, lacking a quarter inch strip at head of spine, lacking half inch triangle at bottom of front cover, quarter inch tear at top of front cover, lacks half inch square piece at bottom of rear cover, lacks little of paper at bottom of spine. Second Life Books Inc. 174 - 221 2011 $3200

Kerr, Robert *A General History and Collection of Voyages and Travels arranged in systematic Order. Volume IV. (Voyages of Sebastian Cabot and Jacques Cartier to Newfoundland).* Edinburgh, London: William Blackwood and J. Murray, 1812, Half brown calf with marbled boards, pages viii, 506, 8vo., extreme wear to edges of binding and outer hinge cracks, foxing to prelim leaves. Schooner Books Ltd. 96 - 63 2011 $95

Kertesz, Andre *The Manchester Collection.* N.P.: Manchester Collection, 1984, First edition, limited edition, one of only 150 numbered copies; as new in cloth binding, as new dust jacket and new cloth slipcase, signed by Kertesz. Jeff Hirsch Books ny 2010 2011 $1250

Kesey, Ken *One Flew Over the Cuckoo's Nest, a Novel.* New York: Viking, 1962, First edition, first issue with "fool Red Cross woman" on page 9; 8vo., pages 311, fine in price clipped dust jacket that is little nicked, with one closed tear, author's scarce book. Second Life Books Inc. 174 - 222 2011 $5000

Kesey, Ken *One Flew Over the Cuckoo's Nest.* New York: Viking, 1962, First edition; book very good, light soiling to bottom edges and to front free endpapers, front free endpapers top corner clipped, dust jacket very good, creasing to extremities, especially at top of spine, small closed tears on folds that have caused some browning, overall complete and not faded, first state book with 'foot Red Cross Woman' on page 9, first issue dust jacket with one line quote from Kerouac at bottom of front flap, very good, creasing to extremities, especially at top of spine, three small closed tears at folds that have caused some browning, overall complete and not faded. Bella Luna Books May 26 2011 - t6120CO 2011 $1760

Kettilby, Mary *A Collection of Above Three Hundred Receipts in Cookery, Physick and Surgery for the Use of all Good Wives, Tender Mothers and Careful Nurses.* London: for Richard Wilkin, 1714, First edition; (16), 218, (13) pages, contemporary paneled calf, neatly rebacked, light overall toning, minor marginal foxing and dampstaining, upper margin of A3 clipped and neatly restored, just grazing running head on verso, 3 leaves of early owners' recipes bound in at end, early ownership signature of Tho. Tipping, dated at several locations in Hertfordshire 1714-1739, later signature of Elizabeth Randall 1771, modern cookery bookplate, very nice in portfolio and leather backed slipcase. Joseph J. Felcone Inc. Fall Miscellany 2010 - 32 2011 $2800

Kevan, Peter G. *Bees: Biology and Management.* 2007, Octavo, paperback, 345 pages, illustrations. Andrew Isles Natural History Books Spring 2010 - 31332 2011 $138

Key, Ted *So'm I.* New York: 1954, First edition; 70 pages, 4to., original binding, very good, foxing to endpapers, verso of f.f.e.p. and half title page have children's markings & drawings, not ex-library. Bookworm & Silverfish 671 - 74 2011 $122

Keynes, John Maynard, 1st Baron 1883-1946 *Essays in Biography.* London: Macmillan, 1933, First edition; original cloth, gilt, tiny nick to spine, pages x, 318, very nice. R. F. G. Hollett & Son Antiquarian Booksellers 175 - 772 2011 £120

Keynes, John Maynard, 1st Baron 1883-1946 *General Theory of Employment and Interest and Money.* London: Macmillan and Co., 1936, First edition; octavo, (3, blank), (1, ad) xii, 403, (1, blank) pages, original slate blue cloth with covers ruled in blind and spine ruled and lettered in gilt, top edge brown, original gray dust jacket with blue lettering, jacket with price of 5/- net, jacket's spine panel darkened, minimal amount of chipping to head and tail of jacket, book very clean, overall very good. Heritage Book Shop Holiday 2010 - 70 2011 $8000

Keynes, John Maynard, 1st Baron 1883-1946 *The General Theory of Employment Interest and Money.* London: Macmillan and Co., 1936, First edition; octavo, original slate blue cloth, original grey dust jacket with blue lettering. Heritage Book Shop Booth A12 51st NY International Antiquarian Book Fair April 8-10 2011 - 80 2011 $8000

Keynes, John Maynard, 1st Baron 1883-1946 *How to Pay for the War.* London: Macmillan, 1940, First edition; original printed boards, little dusty, pages vii, 88. R. F. G. Hollett & Son Antiquarian Booksellers 175 - 773 2011 £35

Kibble, John *Charming Charlbury.* Charlbury: privately published, 1930, First edition; original printed wrappers, backstrip defective at head, pages 110, text illustrations, and 9 pages of local ads, scarce. R. F. G. Hollett & Son Antiquarian Booksellers General Catalogue Summer 2010 - 1453 2011 £30

Kibble, John *Historical and Other Notes on Charlbury and Its Nine Hamlets.* Oxford: Oxford Chronicle, 1927, First edition; pages 110, few text illustrations and 16 pages of local ads, scarce. R. F. G. Hollett & Son Antiquarian Booksellers General Catalogue Summer 2010 - 1455 2011 £45

Kibble, John *Historical and other Notes on Wychwood Forest and Many of Its Border Places.* Oxford: Oxford Chronicle, 1928, First edition; original printed wrappers, pages (iii), 121, few text illustrations and 13 pages of local ads, fine, scarce. R. F. G. Hollett & Son Antiquarian Booksellers General Catalogue Summer 2010 - 1454 2011 £45

Kickapoo Indian Dream Book. New Haven: Healy & Biegelow, 1892, First edition; 8vo., illustrated with cuts, 32 pages, original chromolithographic wrappers, bit stained and worn, with triangular piece (1" per side) gone from bottom edge of front wrapper at gutter, sheets quite browned, and brittle (as usual) with few marginal chips and tears, withal quite sound. M & S Rare Books, Inc. 90 - 116 2011 $175

Kidd, A. T. *History of the Tin-Plate Workers and Sheet Metal Workers and Braziers Societies.* National Union of Sheet Metal Workers and Braziers, 1949, First edition; small 4to., original cloth, gilt, dust jacket (rather torn and chipped), pages (iv), 335, illustrations, flyleaves lightly browned. R. F. G. Hollett & Son Antiquarian Booksellers 175 - 775 2011 £45

Kidd, Dudley *The Essential Kafir.* London: A. and C. Black, 1925, Second edition; 8vo., pages xiv, 436, map, illustrations. J. & S. L. Bonham Antiquarian Booksellers Africa 4/20/2011 - 4402 2011 £38

Kidd, Dudley *Savage Childhood: a Study of Kafir Children.* London: A. & C. Black, 1906, First edition; 8vo., pages xvi, 314, illustrations, original grey cloth backed boards. J. & S. L. Bonham Antiquarian Booksellers Africa 4/20/2011 - 8209 2011 £35

Kidder, Tracy *The Road to Yuba City.* Garden City: Doubleday, 1974, Uncorrected proof; spot of dampstaining to rear cover, otherwise near fine in tall, ringbound wrappers. Ken Lopez Bookseller 154 - 89 2011 $250

Kiddie-Land. Philadelphia: Geo. Jacobs, 1910, 4to., cloth backed pictorial boards, edges rubbed with slight cover soil, else very good+, 12 color plates plus line illustrations on every page and pictorial endpapers. Aleph-Bet Books, Inc. 95 - 204 2011 $600

Kidner, Michael *Elastic Membrane.* Guildford: The Circle Press, 1979, First edition, one of 300 numbered copies, signed by artist on loose limitation page, from a total edition of 350; handmade, illustrated book with one signed mixed media graph construct of plywood, cloth, paper and pin, three signed and numbered photogravures, three signed and numbered photolithographs an two signed faithful facsimiles of his working spiral notebooks for the project, all of various dimensions housed in 14 x 18 x 3 inch specially crafted plywood case with heavy plastic wraparound, fine as issued. Charles Agvent 2010 Summer Miscellany - 39 2011 $500

Kierkegaard, Soren *Enten-Eller: et Livs-Fragment Udgivat af Victor Cremita (Pseud.).* Kobenhavn: 1849, Second edition; 8vo., 2 volumes in 1, (14), (2), 320; (4), 250 pages, contemporary half morocco, marbled boards, rubbed along edge, rebacked, original spine laid down, text fine. M & S Rare Books, Inc. 90 - 326 2011 $1250

Killip, Christopher *Isle of Man: a Book About the Manx.* London: Arts Council of Great Britain, 1980, First edition; wrappers, 4to., illustrated wrappers, copiously illustrated in black and white, review copy with advance order information sheet loosely inserted, slightly bumped at one corner, white corners slightly tanned, very good. Any Amount of Books May 29 2011 - A72743 2011 $383

Kilner, Joseph *The Account of Pythagoras's School in Cambridge.* Oxford?: n.p. n.d. circa, 1792, Folio, modern half calf gilt, pages v, (i, blank), 5-56, (iv), 59-158, complete with 9 engraved plates, slight offsetting of a few plates, but handsome large copy. R. F. G. Hollett & Son Antiquarian Booksellers 177 - 523 2011 £750

Kimes, William F. *John Muir: a Reading Bibliography.* Palo Alto: William P. Wreden, 1977, First edition, limited to 300 copies, signed by printer and both authors; (11), xviii, (2), 211 pages, illustrations, linen backed decorated boards, gilt lettered spine, very fine, very scarce, signed by printer and both authors. Argonaut Book Shop Recent Acquisitions Summer 2010 - 144 2011 $425

King Albert's Book. A Tribute to the Belgian King and People from Representative Men and Women Throughout the World. London: Daily Telegraph, 1914, First edition; 4to., original decorated cream cloth, trifle marked, pages 188, with 17 tipped in color plates, other illustrations, flyleaves rather browned as usual. R. F. G. Hollett & Son Antiquarian Booksellers 175 - 776 2011 £40

King Albert's Book. London: Daily Telegraph, 1914, First edition; 4to., original decorated cream cloth, pages 188, with 17 tipped colored plates, other illustrations, fine, loosely inserted are two fine sets of art stamps in their original Red Cross folder, each of six stamps to designs by Edmund Dulac and Frank Brangwyn. R. F. G. Hollett & Son Antiquarian Booksellers 175 - 777 2011 £150

King Pole. Bishops Stortford and Butingford: 1974-2005, 2001, one small 8vo. volume and 3 small oblong 4to. volumes, from no. 26 April 1974 to no. 154 June 2005, nos. 26-29, 32, 38-86, 88-137, 139-142, 144-149, 151 and 153, approximately 3350 pages, illustrations in black and white, all very good with very slight creasing. Any Amount of Books May 29 2011 - A35512 2011 $340

King, Alan *Early Pennine Settlement.* Clapham: Dalesman Pub. Co., 1970, First edition; Pages 96, well illustrations, scarce, original pictorial stiff wrappers. R. F. G. Hollett & Son Antiquarian Booksellers 177 - 524 2011 £40

King, Alice *Fettered Yet Free.* London: Hurst & Blackett, 1883, First edition; 3 volumes, half titles, 16 page catalog volume III, uncut in original blue cloth, front boards blocked and lettered in blue, spine lettered in gilt, slightly dulled and marked, spines little rubbed, front board labels for Coombe's Regent Library (partially removed volume I), good plus internally clean. Jarndyce Antiquarian Booksellers CLXC - 55 2011 £150

King, Arthur *Our Sons: How to Start Them in Life.* London: Warne, 1889, Second edition; original green cloth gilt, pages viii, 204, (xii), joints tender. R. F. G. Hollett & Son Antiquarian Booksellers 175 - 778 2011 £30

King, Arthur William *An Aubrey Beardsley Lecture.* London: R. A. Walker, 1924, Limited edition, #223 of 450 copies signed by publisher; 4to., blue cloth, very good. Barnaby Rudge Booksellers Art & Architecture & Photography - 013888 2011 $75

King, Daniel *The Vale Royall of England.* London: printed by John Streater, 1656, folio, pages (x), 99, (v), 239 (x), 55, (vii) 34 + 2 (***) double page engraved maps mounted on stubs, 1 double page plan of Chester and 1 other double page engraving of cathedral, both mounted on their own stubs, 11 plates of armorials and 3 other engraved plates, full page of Beaumont armorials on page (12) in the isle of man section, contemporary sprinkled calf, spine originally double ruled in blind but updated in early 18th century by superimposition of panel gilding, dark orange lettering piece gilt, boards double ruled in blind, board edges originally single rule gilt by superimposed with decorative roll gilt, all edges, dark brown sprinkled pink and white sewn endbands, some spotting in places, boards scratched and marked, joint ends and endcaps sometime restored in a different shade of leather, from the collection of Christopher Ernest Weston 1947-2010.   Unsworths Booksellers   24 - 114 2011   £1600

King, David *The Commissar Vanishes. The Falsification of Photographs and Art in Stalin's Russia.*   New York: 1997, 192 pages, 4to., near fine in fine dust jacket.   Bookworm & Silverfish   666 - 38 2011 $75

King, Frank H. H. *The Hong Kong Bank in the Period of Imperialism and War 1895-1918: Wayfoog. The Focus of Wealth.* Cambridge: Cambridge University Press, 1988, First edition; 8vo., tables, figures, illustrations, 754 pages, ex-British Foreign Office library with few library markings else, very good+ in like dust jacket.   Any Amount of Books   May 29 2011 - A73781 2011 $238

King, Harriet Barbara *The Bridal and Other Poems.* London: Richard Bentley, 1844, First edition; half title, pages 147-154 contain list of subscribers, original pink cloth, spine faded, otherwise very good, inscribed by Lord Ongley, one of the subscribers.   Jarndyce Antiquarian Booksellers   CLXC - 56 2011   £120

King, Jessie *Seven Happy Days.*   London: International Studio Supp. New Year, 1914, 4to., wrappers, some cover soil and tears, very good, magnificent color illustrations heightened with gold and silver, 7 smaller black and white illustrations, laid in is original water color by plus handwritten letter with sketch housed in original mailing envelope,.   Aleph-Bet Books, Inc.   95 - 314 2011 $4250

King, L. W. *Egypt and Western Asia; in the Light of Recent Discoveries.* London: SPCK, 1907, First edition; large 8vo., pages xiv, 480, photogravure frontispiece, numerous illustrations, original red cloth, spine little faded.   J. & S. L. Bonham Antiquarian Booksellers   Africa 4/20/2011 - 4599 2011   £50

King, Laurie R. *The Beekeeper's Apprentice: on the Segregation of the Queen.* New York: St. Martin's Press, 1994, First edition; fine, dust jacket fine, signed by author.   Bella Luna Books   May 26 2011 - p2590 2011 $330

King, Laurie R. *A Grave Talent.* New York: St. Martin's Press, 1993, First edition; fine, dust jacket near fine with very light creasing to corners, signed by author.   Bella Luna Books   May 26 2011 - 2867 2011 $330

King, Laurie R. *A Grave Talent.* London: Harper Collins, 1995, First British edition; fine, dust jacket fine, signed by author.   Bella Luna Books   May 29 2011 - 6200 2011 $82

King, Rufus *Murder by the Clock.* Garden City: Doubleday, Doran & Co., 1929, First edition; professionally rebacked with original spine laid down, former owner's name on front flyleaf, else near fine in professionally restored dust jacket.   Buckingham Books   May 26 2011 - 25303 2011 $2000

King, Stephen 1947-   *Danse Macabre.* London: MacDonald, 1974, First UK edition; 8vo., pages 400, about fine in very good, complete dust jacket with slight rubbing at corners, slight nicks and slight creasing at spine ends, excellent condition, rare.   Any Amount of Books   May 29 2011 - A66372 2011 $340

King, Stephen 1947-   *Dark Tower complete in 7 Books.* Rhode Island, etc.: Donald M. Grant, 1928-2004, First trade editions; first volume signed by King "to Tom...", Gunslinger about fine in near fine jacket slightly rubbed at corners with very minor wear at spine ends, Waste Lands fine/near fine with faint edgewear to jacket, all the fresh fine in fine jacket, excellent condition set.   Any Amount of Books   May 26 2011 - A49171 2011 $1845

King, Stephen 1947-   *Night Shift.* Garden City: Doubleday & Co., 1978, First edition; octavo, cloth backed boards.   L. W. Currey, Inc.   124 - 91 2011 $950

King, Stephen 1947-   *Salem's Lot.* Garden City: Doubleday & Co., 1975, First edition; octavo, cloth backed boards.   L. W. Currey, Inc.   124 - 38 2011 $1750

King, Stephen 1947-   *Salem's Lot.* Garden City: Doubleday, 1975, First edition; inscribed by author Nov. 20 1975 small skinned spot on front free endpaper, near fine, near fine, corner clipped second issue dust jacket with the printed price $7.95 and the reference to "Father Cody" in flap text, with modest corner rubbing and strip of offsetting to rear panel, attractive copy.   Ken Lopez Bookseller   154 - 90 2011 $5000

King, Stephen 1947-   *Salem's Lot.* London: New English Library, 1976, First British edition; octavo, boards.   L. W. Currey, Inc.   124 - 161 2011 $350

King, Stephen 1947- *The Stand.* Garden City: Doubleday & Co. Inc., 1978, First edition; octavo, cloth backed boards. L. W. Currey, Inc. 124 - 15 2011 $3500

King, Stephen 1947- *The Stand.* Garden City: Doubleday and Co., 1978, First edition; ocatavo, cloth backed boards. L. W. Currey, Inc. 124 - 125 2011 $600

King, William *The Dreamer.* London: printed for W. Owen at Homer's Head in Fleet Street, 1754, First edition; no front flyleaf, some unobtrusive blindstamps on few blank margins, 16 pages followed by 2 lines of errata, publisher's ad leaf at end, (4), 240, xxviii, 14, (2) pages, contemporary calf, hinges beginning to crack with bookplate of Bath Public Reference Library, good clean copy. Anthony W. Laywood May 26 2011 - 20006 2011 $461

Kinge, John *Lectures Upon Jonas, Delivered at Yorke in the yeare of Our Lorde 1594.* Oxford: Joseph Barnes, 1599, Small 4to., pages (x), 660, (ii), 661-706, N.B. leaves *1 and 2Y4 are blanks (first except for a fleuron) missing in this copy, early 19th century tan calf, spine gilt, red lettering piece gilt, place and date gilt direct, boards gilt double rule bordered, board edges decorative roll gilt turn-ins decorative roll gilt, "Gloster' 'made' endpapers, all edges red mottled, pink sewn endbands, light age toning and few tiny spots, couple of small marks to leather, headcap slightly worn, early ink inscription of titlepage largely cut off (and undecipherable) and repaired and matching paper, early initials "WPL" on titlepage, healdic bookplate of Marquis of Devonshire, from the collection of Christopher Ernest Weston 1947-2010. Unsworths Booksellers 24 - 26 2011 £500

Kinglake, Alexander William 1809-1891 *Eothen; or Traces of Travel Brought Home from the East.* London: John Ollivier, 1845, Second edition; half title, folding color lithograph frontispiece + 1 color litho plate, some spotting throughout but more heavily to prelims, contemporary half tan calf, raised bands, gilt compartments, red morocco label, little rubbed, bookplate of C. W.R., attractive copy. Jarndyce Antiquarian Booksellers CXCI - 562 2011 £160

Kinglsey, Mary Henrietta *West African Studies.* London: Macmillan, 1899, First Edition; 8vo., pages xxiv, 637, (1) blank, 30 publisher's list, half title, 24 plates, folding map, recent half calf. J. & S. L. Bonham Antiquarian Booksellers Africa 4/20/2011 - 8881 2011 £180

Kingscote, Adeline Georgina *Tales of the Sun; or Folklore of Southern India.* London: W. H. Allen & Co. and at Calcutta, 1890, First edition; half title, some slight careless opening, original blue cloth, front board pictorially blocked and lettered in olive green and brown, spine lettered gilt, bit dulled, leading inner hinges slightly cracked, spine darkened, slightly rubbed, presented to Lydia H. Guest on half title. Jarndyce Antiquarian Booksellers CLXC - 57 2011 £45

Kingsland, Gerald *Curious. The Sex Education Magazine for Men and Women.* London: Rosland Productions, 1969-1975, First edition; 4to., issues 1-31, about 1200 pages in all, wrappers, illustrations in color and black and white, very good+ set. Any Amount of Books May 26 2011 - A40219 2011 $503

Kingsley, Charles 1819-1875 *Glaucus; or the Wonders of the Shore.* Cambridge: Macmillan, 1855, First edition; half title, frontispiece, final ad leaf + 16 page catalog (amy 1855), pencil signature of Annie Cooke on half title, original green cloth, blocked in black and gilt, spine faded, slightly cocked, booksellers ticket of Harold Clever, good plus. Jarndyce Antiquarian Booksellers CXCI - 338 2011 £65

Kingsley, Charles 1819-1875 *Glaucus; or the Wonders of the Shore.* London: Macmillan, 1856, Third edition; half title, frontispiece, ads, 16 page catalog (Feb. 1857), original buff cloth, blocked in black and gilt, slightly marked and dulled, all edges gilt. Jarndyce Antiquarian Booksellers CXCI - 339 2011 £45

Kingsley, Charles 1819-1875 *The Good News of God: Sermons.* London: John W. Parker & Son, 1859, First edition; 4 pages ads, original black cloth, paper label slightly chipped, little rubbed, Carlingford bookplate. Jarndyce Antiquarian Booksellers CXCI - 232 2011 £35

Kingsley, Charles 1819-1875 *Out of the Deep: Words for the Sorrowful.* London: Macmillan, 1880, First edition; half title, final ad leaf, original grey cloth, dulled and rubbed, inner hinges cracking, photo of the Kingsleys laid down on leading pastedown, presentation from Fanny Kingsley. Jarndyce Antiquarian Booksellers CXCI - 234 2011 £65

Kingsley, Charles 1819-1875 *Out of the Deep...* London: Macmillan, 1885, Half title, 4 pages ads, original grey cloth, bevelled boards, spine slightly dulled, all edges gilt, very good, with slip inserted with inscription from Mrs. Kingsley to Fredk Brady. Jarndyce Antiquarian Booksellers CXCI - 235 2011 £60

Kingsley, Charles 1819-1875 *Prose Idylls New and Old.* London: Macmillan, 1884, Half title, frontispiece, added volume title, final ad leaf, unopened in original blue cloth, spine faded and slightly rubbed, inscribed by author's wife for Hugh and Margaret Egerton, with signature of M.A. Egerton. Jarndyce Antiquarian Booksellers CXCI - 233 2011 £35

Kingsley, Charles 1819-1875 *The Water-Babies.* London: Macmillan and Co., 1885, First edition illustrated by Linley Sambourne; small quarto, viii, 371, (1, printers imprint) pages, wood engravings, text illustrations, fine Cosway binding by Riviere & Son (stamp signed in gilt on front turn-in), full red crushed levant morocco, covers with gilt triple fillet border, front cover set a fine rectangular miniature portrait on ivory under bevelled glass 89 x 66mm. of Charles Kingsley by Miss C. B. Currie, within inner gilt double fillet border and wide outer gilt floral and leaf border (in the style of Charles MacLeish), spine in 6 compartments, five raised bands, lettered gilt in two compartments and decoratively tooled in gilt in a similar floral and leaf design in remaining four compartments, with date in gilt at foot, board edges with gilt double fillet, turn-ins ruled in gilt with similar gilt floral corner ornaments, dark green watered silk dobulures and liners, all edges gilt, stamped in gilt on rear doublure "Miniatures by C. B. Currie", additionally stamped in gilt on fore-edges of front and rear boards "Cosway Binding" and "Invented by J. H. Stonehouse", inserted certificate leaf signed by Stonehouse and Currie and numbered in ink identifies the present copy as being "No 951 of the Cosway Bindings invented by J. H. Stonehouse with Miniatures on Ivory by Miss Currie", original front and rear blue cloth covers bound in at end, superb example, housed in velvet lined red cloth clamshell case. David Brass Rare Books, Inc. May 26 2011 - 00892 2011 $11,500

Kingsley, Charles 1819-1875 *The Water Babies.* London: Macmillan, 1891, Pages 330, 100 woodcut illustrations by Linley Sambourne, full scarlet calf gilt prize binding by Relfe Brothers, few slight scratches, pages 330, 100 woodcut illustrations. R. F. G. Hollett & Sons Antiquarian Booksellers 170 - 365 2011 £50

Kingsley, Charles 1819-1875 *The Water Babies.* London: Constable, 1915, First edition thus; original pictorial green cloth gilt, spine partially faded, dust jacket (upper fold and spine torn and frayed at head, but very little loss), pages x, 320, 8 color plates and numerous black and white full page and line drawings by W. Heath Robinson, inscription on flyleaf, otherwise very nice, clean copy in rare dust jacket. R. F. G. Hollett & Sons Antiquarian Booksellers 170 - 596 2011 £450

Kingsley, Charles 1819-1875 *Water Babies.* London: Hodder & Stoughton, n.d., 1919, First English edition; large thick 4to., blue cloth with lovely gold illustrated cover and spine, small rub area on spine and light cover soil, publisher's file copy, so stamped on endpaper and corner of title, illustrations by Jessie Willcox Smith with 12 beautiful tipped-in color plates, plus many lovely green line illustrations. Aleph-Bet Books, Inc. 95 - 539 2011 $600

Kingsley, Charles 1819-1875 *Westward Ho!* Cambridge: Macmillan, 1855, First edition; 3 volumes, half titles, handsomely bound in tan calf by R. D. Steadman, Newcastle upon Tyne, gilt borders, raised bands, gilt compartments & dentelles, brown and dark green morocco labels, some slight marking or darkening to boards, armorial bookplates of Walter Powell Jeffreys, very good, handsome. Jarndyce Antiquarian Booksellers CXCI - 529 2011 £450

Kingsolver, Barbara *Animal Dreams.* New York: Harper Collins, 1990, First edition; fine in fine dust jacket, signed by author. Bella Luna Books May 29 2011 - t142 2011 $82

Kingsolver, Barbara *Another America: Otra America.* Seattle: Seal Press, 1992, First edition; near fine, very minor bump to front corner, in like dust jacket with corresponding creasing, signed by author. Bella Luna Books May 26 2011 - 6112 2011 $165

Kingsolver, Barbara *The Bean Trees.* New York: Harper and Row, 1988, First edition; fine copy in near fine dust jacket, minor creasing at top of spine. Bella Luna Books May 26 2011 - t1410 2011 $302

Kingsolver, Barbara *The Bean Trees.* New York: Harper & Row, 1988, First edition; near fine, small stain on front free endpapers and titlepage, dust jacket near fine, price clipped. Bella Luna Books May 29 2011 - t3332 2011 $137

Kingsolver, Barbara *The Bean Trees.* New York: Harper & Row, 1988, First edition; fine in near fine dust jacket, light foxing at top inside of rear flap. Bella Luna Books May 26 2011 - t3458 2011 $330

Kingsolver, Barbara *The Bean Trees.* London: Virago, 1989, First British edition; fine in fine dust jacket, signed by author. Bella Luna Books May 26 2011 - p2480 2011 $220

Kingsolver, Barbara *The Bean Trees.* London: Virago, 1989, First British edition; fine in like dust jacket. Bella Luna Books May 29 2011 - t4702 2011 $82

Kingsolver, Barbara *High Tide in Tucson.* New York: Harper Collins, 1995, Limited to 150 numbered copies; fine, signed by author, in pictorial slipcase. Bella Luna Books May 26 2011 - p2591 2011 $440

Kingsolver, Barbara *Holding the Line: Women in the Great Arizona Mine Strike of 1983.* Cornell: ILR Press, 1989, First edition; near fine, very light bump to top corner, there were only 816 copies of this book issued, signed by author. Bella Luna Books May 29 2011 - p2145 2011 $137

Kingsolver, Barbara *Holding the Line: Women in the Great Arizona Mine Strike of 1983.* Cornell: ILR Press, 1989, First edition; near fine, minor flaw in cloth on front board, there were 816 copies of this book issued without dust jacket. Bella Luna Books May 29 2011 - t4706 2011 $82

Kingsolver, Barbara *Holding the Line: women in the Great Arizona Mine Strike of 1983.* Cornell: ILR, 1989, First edition; near fine, bottom rear corner bumped, only 816 copies. Bella Luna Books May 29 2011 - t4707 2011 $82

Kingsolver, Barbara *Homeland.* New York: Harper & Row, 1989, First edition; fine in fine dust jacket, inscribed by author. Bella Luna Books May 29 2011 - 51340 2011 $137

Kingston, Elizabeth Hervey Chudleigh, Duchess of *A Plain State of the Case of Her Grace the Duchess of Kingston.* London: printed for Wilkie, 1776, First edition; 4to., pages (vi), 27, disbound half title, uncut, rare. Second Life Books Inc. 174 - 97 2011 $800

Kingston, Elizabeth Hervey Chudleigh, Duchess of *The Trial of Elizabeth (Chudleigh) Duchess Dowager of Kingston for Bigamy before the Right Honourable the House of Peers in Westminster Hall, in Full Parliament on Monday the 15th Tuesday the 16th, Friday the 19th, Saturday the 20th and Monday the 22nd of April.* London: Charles Bathurst in Fleet Street, 1776, First edition; Folio, pages 176, burgundy leather backed marbled boards, raised bands, light shelf/edge wear, chip mid spine, light even toning/soiling to boards, tips through, tiny spot of nibbling at first few leaves, light rubbing to boards, small dampstain at front board, else tight, bright, unmarred. Second Life Books Inc. 174 - 98 2011 $2200

Kingston, William H. G. *The Circassian Chief: a Romance of Russian.* London: David Bryce, n.d., 1854, New edition; small 8vo., full black blind patterned contemporary leather lettered gilt at spine, pages 352, slight uneven gatherings although all edges gilt, some paper creasing at corners, slight wear at head of spine, else very good. Any Amount of Books May 29 2011 - A33909 2011 $255

Kinney, Jay *Gnosis: a Journal of the Western Inner Tradition 1985-1999.* San Francisco: Lumen Foundation, 1985-1999, First edition; wrappers, 40 issues (2 copies of No. 3), 4to., color illustrated stapled wrappers, No. 1- No.25; No. 38-No. 51 (missing Nos. 26-37), circa 3000 pages in all, illustrations in black and white, all clean, very good. Any Amount of Books May 29 2011 - A47862 2011 $221

Kinsella, W. P. *Shoeless Joe.* New York: Houghton Mifflin, 1982, First edition; fine, dust jacket near fine, light creasing and small closed tears at heel of spine. Bella Luna Books May 26 2011 - t9490 2011 $192

Kinsella, William *Dance Me Outside.* Boston: 1986, First American edition; inscribed and signed by William Kinsella, as new in dust jacket. Gemini Fine Books & Arts, Ltd. Art Reference & Illustrated Books: First Editions 2011 $60

Kinsella, William *Red Wolf Red Wolf.* Toronto: 1987, First edition; inscribed and signed by author, as new in dust jacket, laid in photo of Kinsella inscribed and signed. Gemini Fine Books & Arts, Ltd. Art Reference & Illustrated Books: First Editions 2011 $75

Kinsey, Alfred C. Pomeroy *Sexual Behavior in the Human Female.* Philadelphia and London: Saunders, 1953, First edition; 8vo., pages xxx, 842, maroon cloth, cover bumped at corners, somewhat worn at ends of spine and scuffed, otherwise, very good, tight copy. Second Life Books Inc. 174 - 223 2011 $125

Kinsey, Alfred C. Pomeroy *Sexual Behavior in the Human Male.* London: W. B. Saunders Co., 1953, Original two tone cloth, gilt, dust jacket torn and defective, pages xiv, 363, with 1500 illustrations. R. F. G. Hollett & Son Antiquarian Booksellers 175 - 781 2011 £30

Kinsky, Georg *A History of Music In Pictures.* London: Dent, 1937, Small folio, original two tone cloth, gilt, dust jacket torn and defective, pages xvi, 363, 1500 illustrations, including color frontispiece. R. F. G. Hollett & Son Antiquarian Booksellers 175 - 782 2011 £45

Kipling, Rudyard 1865-1936 *Actions and Reactions.* London: Macmillan, 1909, First edition; half title, 12 page catalog, original red cloth gilt, contemporary owner inscription of W. B. Thompson on leading f.e.p. verso, top edge gilt, very good. Jarndyce Antiquarian Booksellers CXCI - 238 2011 £50

Kipling, Rudyard 1865-1936 *All the Mowgli Stories.* London: Macmillan, 1933, 4to., original pictorial pale blue cloth, spine little darkened, page 272, 8 color plates and line drawings, fore edge little spotted. R. F. G. Hollett & Sons Antiquarian Booksellers 170 - 365 2011 £50

Kipling, Rudyard 1865-1936 *An Almanac of Twelve Sports.* London: William Heinemann, 1898, Illustrations, 1 page ad on verso of final leaf, some slight offsetting, original brown pictorial boards, brown cloth spine, small mark to front board, slight rubbing to extremities with small chip to foot of spine, bookplate of Henley Evans, Clifton Bookseller's ticket of William George & Sons, Bristol, nice in original form. Jarndyce Antiquarian Booksellers CXCI - 245 2011 £350

Kipling, Rudyard 1865-1936 *Collected Verse of Rudyard Kipling.* New York: Doubleday Page and Co., 1910, Limited to only 125 numbered copies signed by Rudyard Kipling and printed on handmade paper; 4to., quarter vellum, grey boards, top edge gilt, 392 pages, slight bit of finger soil on covers, else fine, illustrations by W. Heath Robinson, with 8 magnificent mounted color plates with lettered tissue guards plus many full page black and whites, rare. Aleph-Bet Books, Inc. 95 - 492 2011 $1950

Kipling, Rudyard 1865-1936 *Departmental Ditties...* Calcutta: Thacker, Spink, 1891, Sixth edition; half title, 24 page catalog (April 1891), original maroon cloth, bevelled boards, spine slightly faded, very good. Jarndyce Antiquarian Booksellers CXCI - 239 2011 £45

Kipling, Rudyard 1865-1936 *The Elephant's Child.* New York: Garden City Pub. Co., 1942, 4to., pictorial boards, fine in slightly worn dust jacket, illustrations by Feodor Rojankovsky, with color and black and white lithos, inscribed by artist. Aleph-Bet Books, Inc. 95 - 494 2011 $225

Kipling, Rudyard 1865-1936 *The Five Nations.* London: Methuen, 1908, Fourth edition; contemporary three quarter red calf gilt, pages 216, top edge gilt. R. F. G. Hollett & Son Antiquarian Booksellers General Catalogue Summer 2010 - 824 2011 £35

Kipling, Rudyard 1865-1936 *40 Nord 50 Vest. (40 North, 50 West).* Moscow: Leiningrad: Guiz, 1931, First edition thus; 8vo., striking black and white pictorial stiff paper covers, some mild toning to edges, 22 numbered pages within, black and white engravings by David Sherenberg. Jo Ann Reisler, Ltd. 86 - 221 2011 $2000

Kipling, Rudyard 1865-1936 *From Sea to Sea and other Sketches.* Macmillan, 1900, 2 volumes contemporary half polished calf gilt with marbled boards, pages xiv, 498; ix, 438, top edge gilt, attractive copy. R. F. G. Hollett & Son Antiquarian Booksellers General Catalogue Summer 2010 - 825 2011 £95

Kipling, Rudyard 1865-1936 *The Just So Song Book.* London: Macmillan, 1911, 4to., original pictorial cloth gilt, neatly recased, pages 62, excellent, clean copy. R. F. G. Hollett & Son Antiquarian Booksellers 175 - 782 2011 £45

Kipling, Rudyard 1865-1936 *Kim. Just So Stories. Poems. The Jungle Book. The Second Jungle Book. Short Stories. Puck of Pook's Hill.* London: Longmans, Green and Co., 1895, First edition; 8vo. original publisher's green cloth lettered gilt at spine, pages viii, 183, with 24 page publisher's catalog at rear, uncommon first edition, spine ends and hinges slightly rubbed, corners little bumped, and slightly scuffed, otherwise sound, very good+. Any Amount of Books May 29 2011 - A49566 2011 $212

Kipling, Rudyard 1865-1936 *Kim.* New York: Doubleday Page and Co., 1901, First edition, first issue with rhymed chapter headings for chapters VIII (p. 207) and XIII (p. 364) only; 460 pages, illustrations, bound in deep red cloth with gilt titles to spine and cover, small gilt decorations, book is nearly an inch shorter than the published edition in green cloth, a copy in brown cloh has been recorded but this red cloth edition seems unrecorded, binding (which lacks publisher's name on spine), 'might' be a trial binding meant to parallel the London, light shelfwear and article pasted on f.f.e.p., otherwise near fine. Lupack Rare Books May 26 2011 - ABE1269953453 2011 $375

Kipling, Rudyard 1865-1936 *Land and Sea Tales for Scouts and Guides.* London: Macmillan, 1923, First edition; large 8vo., original pictorial cloth, spine faded and few marks to upper board, pages vii, 282, (ii), flyleaves lightly browned. R. F. G. Hollett & Sons Antiquarian Booksellers 170 - 367 2011 £60

Kipling, Rudyard 1865-1936 *The Light that Failed.* 1891, First periodical publication in Lippincott's Monthly Magazine Jan. 1891; 144 pages, without ads, badly chipped, front wrapper bound in at end, half maroon morocco, slight rubbing. Jarndyce Antiquarian Booksellers CXCI - 240 2011 £45

Kipling, Rudyard 1865-1936 *Limits and Renewals.* London: Macmillan, 1932, First edition; half title, original red cloth gilt, top edge gilt, very good. Jarndyce Antiquarian Booksellers CXCI - 241 2011 £40

Kipling, Rudyard 1865-1936 *Rewards and Fairies.* London: Macmillan, 1910, Macmillan's Colonial Library edition; half title, plates by Frank Craig, 8 pages ads, little foxed, pencil signature on leading f.e.p., uncut in original blue cloth, slightly rubbed and marked. Jarndyce Antiquarian Booksellers CXCI - 243 2011 £35

Kipling, Rudyard 1865-1936 *The Seven Seas.* London: Methuen, 1896, First edition; 8vo., pages viii, 230, 37 ads, (i) blank, illustration to titlepage, gilded upper edge, others uncut, internally very clean, original dark red buckram with gilt lettering to spine, some rubbing to boards and bumped edges, matching red, three fold case with quarter leather red slipcase with bands and gilt lettering to spine both near fine, signed by Kipling. Simon Finch Rare Books Zero - 325 2011 £475

Kipling, Rudyard 1865-1936 *Songs of the Sea.* London: Macmillan, 1927, First edition; original blue cloth gilt, 4to., upper board trifle rubbed, pages xi, 100, top edge gilt, 12 color plates and 22 other illustrations, mostly tinted. R. F. G. Hollett & Son Antiquarian Booksellers General Catalogue Summer 2010 - 847 2011 £50

Kipling, Rudyard 1865-1936 *Works.* London: Macmillan and Co. Ltd., 1913, Limited edition signed by author; Bombay edition, 31 volumes, large octavo, printed on handmade paper watermarked RK on each second leaf, handsomely bound in early 1990's in three quarter tan calf over cloth boards ruled in spine labels lettered gilt, top edge gilt, others uncut, fine set,.   David Brass Rare Books, Inc.   May 26 2011 - 01076   2011 $11,500

Kipling, Rudyard 1865-1936 *The Works.* London: Macmillan & Co., 1913-1938, Bombay Edition; 31 volumes, original boards, cloth spines, paper labels, slightly marked, very nice state, complete.   Jarndyce Antiquarian Booksellers   CXCI - 21   2011   £7500

Kirby, Mary *The Discounted Children and How They Were Cured.* London: Grant & Griffith, 1855, First edition; color frontispiece, marginal tear neatly repaired, 3 color plates, 8 page catalog, few spots, later rebound in dark pink binder's cloth, black leather label.   Jarndyce Antiquarian Booksellers   CLXC - 59   2011   £45

Kirby, Mary *The Discontented Children and How They Were Cured.* London: Grant & Griffith, 1855, First edition; color frontispiece and 2 black and white plates, odd spot, half dark green crushed morocco by Bayntun of Bath, green cloth boards, gilt spine, spine faded to brown, booklabel of J. Brocklebank, slightly torn, top edge gilt, very good.   Jarndyce Antiquarian Booksellers   CLXC - 58   2011   £65

Kirby, Mary *The World at Home: Pictures and Scenes from Far-Off Lands.* London: T. Nelson and Sons, 1876, original decorated red cloth gilt over bevelled boards, slightly marked, extremities trifle rubbed and spine lightly faded, pages xii, 296, all edges gilt, woodcut illustrations.   R. F. G. Hollett & Sons Antiquarian Booksellers   170 - 368   2011   £35

Kirby, R. H. *The Rural Deanery of Cartmel in the Diocese of Cartmel, Its Churches and Endowments.* Ulverston: James Atkinson, 1892, Original cloth, gilt, pages 125, 2 illustrations, original cloth, gilt, fine, bright copy.   R. F. G. Hollett & Son Antiquarian Booksellers   173 - 662   2011   £65

Kirby, S. Woodburn *The War Agaisnt Japan.* London: HMSO, 1957, First edition; 5 volumes, pages 2943, copiously illustrated throughout, many folding maps, ex-British Foreign Office library with few library markings, covers rubbed, second volume quite heavily, otherwise sound, very good- copies with clean text.   Any Amount of Books   May 26 2011 - A69024   2011 $545

Kirby, W. F. *Butterflies and Moths of the United Kingdom.* London: George Routledge and Sons, n.d., 1909, First edition; pages lii, 468, 70 color plates, 70 colored plates, original green gilt over bevelled boards.   R. F. G. Hollett & Son Antiquarian Booksellers   General Catalogue Summer 2010 - 1009   2011   £40

Kirk, Robert *The Secret Commonwealth of Elves, Fauns and Fairies.* Stirling: Eneas Mackay, 1933, third edition; original cloth gilt, dust jacket, backstrip little frayed at head and foot, pages 128, frontispiece, excellent copy.   R. F. G. Hollett & Son Antiquarian Booksellers   175 - 784   2011   £150

Kirkland, Caroline Matilda Stansbury 1801-1864 *Western Clearings.* London: George Routledge & Co., 1850, Contemporary half black roan, slight rubbing, signed "Mary Chaytor", good plus.   Jarndyce Antiquarian Booksellers   CLXC - 61   2011   £45

Kirkman, F. B. *British Sporting Birds.* London: T. C. & E. C. Jack, 1936, Thick 4to., original pictorial blue cloth, pages xii, 428, 41 plates, name on label, otherwise lovely bright, clean copy.   R. F. G. Hollett & Son Antiquarian Booksellers   General Catalogue Summer 2010 - 1010   2011   £45

Kirkwood, Edith *Animal Children.* Chicago: Volland, 1913, Later printing; 8vo., pictorial boards, light soil and wear to spine, else near fine, beautiful copy, scarce.   Aleph-Bet Books, Inc.   95 - 578   2011 $175

The Kitbook for Soldiers, Sailors and Marines. Chicago: Consolidated Book Publishers, 1942, First edition; 12mo., 336 pages, cartoons, paper over boards, cover little worn at edges, else very good, tight copy.   Second Life Books Inc.   174 - 24   2011 $700

Kitching, A. L. *On the Back Waters of the Nile: Studies of Some Child Races of Central Africa.* London: T. Fisher, 1912, First edition; 8vo., pages xxiv, 295, folding map, illustrations, original black decorative cloth, near fine.   J. & S. L. Bonham Antiquarian Booksellers   Africa 4/20/2011 - 8313   2011   £90

Kitson, Frank *Gangs and Counter-Gangs.* London: Barrie & Rockliff, 1960, First edition; 8vo., pages xii, 211, frontispiece and 22 illustrations, maps and charts, ex-Foreign and Commonwealth Office Library with their label and stamps (lightly applied), very good, white mark at lower spine hinge, otherwise good, usable copy.   Any Amount of Books   May 29 2011 - 471   2011 $340

Kittchin, C. H. B. *The Sensitive One.* London: Hogarth Press, 1931, First edition; 8vo., original publisher's grey cloth lettered gilt on spine, pages 181, signed presentation copy with drawing, "C.P. from C.H.B.K. 18-2-31", also signed "Pamela Nichola from Clifford Kittchin", spine ends slightly rubbed, very slight shelf wear and bumping to covers, very good in somewhat worn good only, chipped, nicked and soiled dust jacket.   Any Amount of Books   May 29 2011 - A76003   2011 $340

The Kitten Pilgrims or Great Battles and Grand Victories. James Nisbet, n.d. circa, 1897, Original pictorial red cloth gilt, rather soiled, spine little faded, rear panel damped in places, pages 118 8, 17-32 (ads), 9 full page illustrations and numerous text drawings by author, some fingering in places, front joint cracked, scarce. R. F. G. Hollett & Sons Antiquarian Booksellers 170 - 56 2011 £75

Kitton, Frederic G. *Charles Dickens by Pen and Pencil, Including Anecdotes and Reminiscences Collected from his Friends and Contemporaries.* London: Frank T. Sabin, and John F. Dexter, 1890-1892, Large paper edition; 390 x 300 mm., 3 volumes, elegant crimson morocco attractively gilt by Riviere (signed at foot of front turn-in), boards gilt with lozenge centerpiece of scrolled floral tooling around a blind oval center, raised bands, gilt spines with fleuron centerpiece, marbled endpapers, inner gilt dentelles incorporating lovely floral tools, top edge gilt, other edges untrimmed, complete set of th 15 wrappers bound in at back of third volume, text illustrations throughout, 195 fine plates (containing 236 images), all of these added (either as part of the usual Large Paper version, or, in the case of some 70 plates, as inserted, extra illustrations), engraved bookplate of Johannis Neville Cross, titlepage printed in red and black; slight dulling to covers (from leather preservative), trivial soiling, but impressive bindings scarcely worn and very pleasing, dozen of the extra engraved plates and adjacent leaves somewhat foxed, one plate creased in lower corner (not affecting image), few instances of minor marginal soiling, slight offset browning opposite few plates, other trivial defects, generally quite clean and bright. Phillip J. Pirages 59 - 175 2011 $3500

Kitty's Capers. Boston: De Wolfe Fiske, n.d. circa, 1890, Folio, stiff pictorial wrappers, slight creasing on cover, else fine, die-cut in shape of cat, 4 full page chromolithographed pages and in brown line on text pages. Aleph-Bet Books, Inc. 95 - 527 2011 $275

Kjaerbolling, Niels *Ornitholgia Danica. Danmarks Fugle I 304 Afbildninger af de Gamle Hanner. (bound with) Ornithological Danica Danmarks Fugle i 252 Afbildninger af de Dragtskiftende Gamle Hanner...* Copenhagen: Forfatterens Forlag, 1858, Folio, later full leather, some rubbing to spine, gilt decorated spine and boards, 46 hand colored plates (last 11 mounted on stubs), some with marginal soiling and occasional foxing, folio, original front wrappers bound in. Raymond M. Sutton, Jr. May 26 2011 - 30552 2011 $1150

The Kenyon Review. Gambier: Kenyon College, 1979-1982, First edition; first 16 issues of the New Series, these are special issues with loose signatures laid into covers, according to a letter from editor dated 1990, included here, these issues were specially done for a patron who donated $100 per issue in exchange for autographed copies, later note from editorial assistant at the time states the donor actually contributed much more that stated amount per issue, more likely $8000, and only 4 years of signed copies were done, nearly every contribution signed by author, near fine, contributors include Samuel Beckett, Solzhenitsyn, Italo Calvino, Brodsky, Milosz, Harold Pinter, Derek Walcott, Claude Levi-Strauss, Woody Allen, James Merrill, George Crumb, Amy Clampitt, Ursula Le Guin, William Gass, Robert Hass, James Dickey, Sharon Olds, Rita Dove, W. D. Snodgrass, Joyce Carol Oates, Robert Bly, Robert Pinsky, etc. Charles Agvent 2010 Summer Miscellany - 9 2011 $5000

Klare, Normand E. *The Final Voyage of the Central America; The Saga of a Gold Rush Steamship...* Spokane: 1992, Edition of 1042 copies; owner's name on f.f.e.p. else bright and near fine in like dust jacket. Dumont Maps & Books of the West 112 - 48 2011 $125

Klein, Joe *Primary Colors.* New York: Random House, 1996, First edition; original cloth backed boards, gilt, dust jacket, pages 369, fine. R. F. G. Hollett & Son Antiquarian Booksellers 175 - 785 2011 £30

Klein, William *Moscow.* New York: Crown Publishers, Inc., 1964, First edition; folio, pages (xviii), (172), 139 black and white photos printed in gravure, original white cloth, spine lettered in red and black, top and bottom edges lightly sunned, bottom corner of upper side bumped, original white dust jacket printed in black and red, lightly rubbed and toned, closed tears to upper panel at head and foot of spine, couple of nicks to top edge lower panel, blindstamp to front free endpaper. Simon Finch Rare Books Zero - 531 2011 £975

Klein, William *Tokyo.* New York: Crown Publishers Inc., 1964, First edition; folio, (14)-184, with 168 black and white photos printed in gravure, edges lightly foxed, original cloth, spine lettered in red and white, light rubbing to tips and corners, original dust jacket printed in black and red, rubbing to tips, short closed tear in head of upper panel, shallow scratch to lower panel, near fine. Simon Finch Rare Books Zero - 532 2011 £1200

Kleivan, Helge *The Eskimos of Northeast Labrador. A History of Eskimo-White Relations 1771-1955.* Oslo: Norsk Polarinstitutt, 1966, Quarto, pages (8)-195, card covers, 1 map, ex-library with discard stamp and call number label removed. Schooner Books Ltd. 96 - 64 2011 $60

Klemm, Walther *Das Marchen vom Wolf und den Sieben Geislein. (The Story of the Wolf and the Seven Goats).* Weimar: Reiher, 1922, Limited edition of 50 copies, this #30; five matted woodcuts on onion skin paper, each signed and numbered, titlepage contains woodcut and signature, folio soiled, faded edge worn, but tight, plates fine. G. H. Mott Bookseller   May 26 2011 - 43787   2011 $900

Klenman, Allan *Axe Makers of North America.* Victoria: 1990, 112 pages, wrappers, as new photo illustrations. Bookworm & Silverfish   671 - 94   2011 $225

Klickmann, Flora *The Girl's Own Annual. Volume 49.* Girl's Own Annual, n.d., 1928, 4to., original decorated cloth gilt with pictorial onlay over bevelled boards, pages 704, coloured title and plates, illustrations, endpapers by Maude Angell, very good, clean and sound.   R. F. G. Hollett & Sons Antiquarian Booksellers   170 - 370   2011   £65

Klimburg-Salter, Deborah E. *Tabo. A Lamp for the Kingdom. Early Indo-Tibetan Buddhist Art in the Western Himalaya.* New York: Thames and Hudson, 1998, First American edition; signed by author on titlepage, 279 pages, 150 color photos and 90 black and white drawings, 4to., cloth, fine in very near fine dust jacket.   Kaaterskill Books   12 - 112   2011 $75

Klopstock, Freiderich Gottlieb *The Meddiah.* London: printed for R. and J. Dodsley, 1763, First English edition; first and last leaves foxed, 2 volumes bound as one, just little spotting, pages xlviii, 232, (8), 299, 12mo., contemporary mottled sheep, backstrip divided by gilt rules, red morocco label in second compartment, rest with central gilt urn tools surrounded by dots and leaf spears, gilt chain roll along joints, marbled endpapers, lightly rubbed, front joint just cracking at head, tiny gouge at base of front board, one small shallow wormhole at lower joint, good.   Blackwell Rare Books   B166 - 59   2011   £300

Klunzinger, C. B. *Upper Egypt, Its People and Its Products...* London: Blackie, 1878, First edition; 8vo., pages xv, 408, frontispiece, illustrations, original green decorative cloth, very good.   J. & S. L. Bonham Antiquarian Booksellers   Africa 4/20/2011 - 8370   2011   £95

Kneale, Nigel *The Year of the Sex Olympics and Other TV Plays.* London: Ferret Fantasy, 1976, First edition, number 90 of special limited edition of 100 (bound in black buckram) signed by author; fine in fine dust jacket, 8vo., 143 pages.   Any Amount of Books   May 26 2011 - A73443   2011 $470

Kneale, Nigel *The Year of the Sex Olympics and Other TV plays.* London: Ferret Fantasy, 1976, First edition; 8vo., pages 143, original publisher's ochre cloth lettered gilt on spine, ownership signature of S. J. Waytt (i.e. Stephen Wyatt, author of Doctor Who books), about fine in very good, slightly tanned dust jacket (complete, with no nick or tears), excellent condition.   Any Amount of Books   May 29 2011 - A68822   2011 $255

Kneeland, Samuel *Wonders of Yosemite Valley and of California.* Boston: Alexander Moore, 1872, Third edition; octavo, (iii)-xii, 13-98, (2, blank) pages, prelims incorrectly numbered in all editions, 10 mounted albumen photos by Soule, with tissue guards, 3 wood engraved text illustrations, 2 engraved maps, text and photos ruled in red, original publisher's green pebble grain cloth over bevelled boards with front cover and spine decoratively stamped and lettered in gilt and black and rear cover decoratively stamped in blind, all edges gilt, previous owner's small bookplate, over older bookplate that has been partially removed, minimal rubbing to extremities, previous owner's pencil drawings on front and back endpapers dated 1884, pencil lines through paper in small area, very clean and bright copy.   Heritage Book Shop Holiday 2010 - 71   2011 $1500

Knight, Charles   1791-1873 *The Old Printer and the Modern Press.* London: John Murray, 1854, First edition; illustrations, lacking leading f.e.p., original brown cloth by Edmonds & Remnants, decorated in blind, slightly rubbed. Jarndyce Antiquarian Booksellers   CXCI - 450   2011   £75

Knight, Charles   1791-1873 *Passages of a Working Life during Half a Century; with a Prelude of Early Reminiscences.* London: Bradbury & Evans, 1864-1865, First edition; 3 volumes, 8vo., 346 (4) 336 (4) 344 pages, contemporary uniform polished calf gilt with raised bands, fully gilt in compartments with contrasting labels, all edges marbled by Hodgson of Liverpool, fine set in most attractive binding, contemporary unidentified armorial bookplate. John Drury Rare Books   153 - 73   2011   £150

Knight, Charles   1791-1873 *Shadows of the Old Booksellers.* London: Ball & Daldy, 1865, First edition; original brown cloth, slight rubbing, with signature of W. L. Hodson.   Jarndyce Antiquarian Booksellers   CXCI - 451   2011   £75

Knight, E. F. *With the Royal Tour.* London: Longmans Green and Co., 1902, First edition; original pictorial cloth gilt, pages xii, 410, 40, with 16 plates and folding map, 2 opposing text leaves rather stained from an old bookmark. R. F. G. Hollett & Son Antiquarian Booksellers   175 - 787   2011   £30

Knight, Eric *Lassie Come Home.* Philadelphia: John C. Winston, 1940, 8vo., orange pictorial cloth, 248 pages, fine in near fine dust jacket with touch of fraying, corner of rear flap clipped, illustrations by Marguerite Kirmse, with color dust jacket, pictorial endpapers, color frontispiece and 6 full page and several partial page black and whites, beautiful copy.   Aleph-Bet Books, Inc.   95 - 316   2011 $1250

Knight, F. *Knight's Scroll Ornaments, designed for the Use of Silversmiths Chasers, Die-Sinkers, Modellers &c.*   F. Knight, 1833,   4to., engraved titlepage and plates numbered 2-48, contemporary quarter roan, boards detached, contents little dusty, lacks final plate.   Ken Spelman Rare Books   68 - 27   2011   £40

Knight, G. Wilson *The Dynasty of Stowe.*   London: Fortune Press, 1946,   Second edition; original cloth, gilt, dust jacket price clipped, pages 145, untrimmed with 12 plates.   R. F. G. Hollett & Son Antiquarian Booksellers   175 - 788   2011   £35

Knight, H. C. *The Rocket.*   T. Nelson and Sons, 1888, Original pictorial cloth, little rubbed, pages 128, 26 woodcut illustrations, prize label on pastedowns, little marking and fingering in places.   R. F. G. Hollett & Son Antiquarian Booksellers   General Catalogue Summer 2010 - 1120   2011   £30

Knight, William *Through the Wordsworth Country.*   London: Swan Sonnenschein, 1887,   Large paper edition; tall 4to., original decorated green cloth gilt, neatly recased, pages xix, 268, etched frontispiece and 54 plates.   R. F. G. Hollett & Son Antiquarian Booksellers   173 - 482   2011   £150

Knight, William *Through the Wordsworth Country. A Companion to the Lake District.*   London: Swan Sonnenschein & Co., 1906,   original green cloth, pages xix, 268, frontispiece, 16 illustrations, date stamp on flyleaf, little scattered spotting, publisher's slip added to title.   R. F. G. Hollett & Son Antiquarian Booksellers   173 - 663   2011   £40

Knodle, E. A. *A Classifying Word-Book: in Some Parts of Which, Words are Classified According to Ending and In Other Parts...*   Baltimore: 1840,   First edition; 273 pages, half leather and printed paper over boards, paper with some soil and aging, endpapers embrowned and foxed.   Bookworm & Silverfish   676 - 114   2011 $100

Knoop, Johann Hermann *Beschrijving en Afbeeldingen van de Beste Soorten van Appelen en Peeren.* (with) *Beschrijving Van Vruchtboomen en Vruchten die Men in Hoven Plant en Onderhoudt.* (with) *Beschrijving van Plantagie - Gewassen die Men in Hoven Aankwweekt.*   Amsterdam en Dordrecht: Allart Holtrop de Leeuw en Krap, 1790,   Near fine, 39 folding hand colored engraved plates, fold to a plate professionally reinforced on back with archival paper, margin near fore edge of plate soiled and lightly chipped, including 12 plates of apples, 8 plates of pears, 19 plate of miscellaneous fruits, folio, pages viii, 36; (4), 70; (4), 87, (1), (4), recent calf backed marbled boards, small stain to margin of a plate, occasional soiling around lower corner of text pages, 4 raised bands, gilt decorated panels and red label on spine.   Raymond M. Sutton, Jr.   May 26 2011 - 48550   2011 $3600

Knorring, Sofia Margareta, Baroness Von *The Peasant and His Landlord; or Life in Sweden.*   London: Richard Bentley, 1849,   2 volumes in 1, title to volume I is a cancel, original purple remainder cloth, little dulled, good plus.   Jarndyce Antiquarian Booksellers   CLXC - 62   2011   £120

Knowles, David *Monastic Sites from the Air.*   Cambridge: University Press, 1952,   First edition; 4to., original buckram gilt, rather faded, pages xxviii, 283, with 138 photos.   R. F. G. Hollett & Son Antiquarian Booksellers   177 - 527   2011   £60

Knowles, John *A Separate Peace.*   New York: Macmillan, 1960,   First American edition; signed by author, from the collection of Christopher Ernest Weston 1947-2010 owner name stamp and gift inscription noting this is an Autographed copy from a Fairmont Man, minor spine tanning and offsetting to joints from binder's glue, near fine in very good, price clipped, second issue dust jacket,.   Ken Lopez Bookseller   154 - 91   2011 $1500

Knowles, John *A Separate Peace.*   New York: Macmillan Co., 1960,   First edition; in the more commonly encountered second state dust jacket with reviews printed on front and rear panels and with corners of inside front flap clipped, not affecting price, this copy with signature of photographer, Arnold Newman, inscribed and signed to him by author, red ink mark at base of spine of both dust jacket and book, near fine.   Charles Agvent   2010 Summer Miscellany - 40   2011 $6000

Knowles, Laura *The Swallow's Tour.*   No publisher, n.d. circa, 1860-1880, 4to., original blue cloth gilt, corners rather worn, little marked and neatly recased, unpaginated, all edges gilt, monochrome etched plates and decorations, little fingered in places, child's address dated 1898.   R. F. G. Hollett & Sons Antiquarian Booksellers   170 - 371   2011   £75

Knox, Alexander *The New Playground or Wanderings in Algeria.* London: Kegan Paul, 1881, First edition; 8vo., pages viii, original green decorative cloth, spine slightly faded.   J. & S. L. Bonham Antiquarian Booksellers   Africa 4/20/2011 - 8759   2011   £45

Knox, John *The Historie of the Reformation of the Church of Scotland.* London: John Raworth for George Thomason and Octavian Pullen, 1644, Folio, pages (lxxxiv), 276, 279-397, (i) 401-460, 91, (ii), 92-122, contemporary sprinkled calf, boards blind triple ruled, board edges single rule gilt, turn-ins single ruled in blind, all edges rouge, pink and white sewn endbands, calf reback & corners by John Henderson, little light spotting, couple of old scrapes to leather, modern booklabel of Robert J. Hayhurst, from the collection of Christopher Ernest Weston 1947-2010.   Unsworths Booksellers   24 - 27   2011   £950

Knox, Rawle *The Work of E. H. Shepard.* London: Methuen, 1979, First edition; large 8vo., original cloth, gilt, dust jacket, pages 256, over 300 illustrations, fine.   R. F. G. Hollett & Sons Antiquarian Booksellers   170 - 372   2011   £50

Knox, Vicesimus 1752-1821 *Liberal Education or a Practical Treatise on the method of Acquiring Useful and Polite Learning.* London: Charles Dilly, 1781, Third edition; modern half calf gilt with marbled boards, pages xix, 415.   R. F. G. Hollett & Son Antiquarian Booksellers   175 - 790   2011   £160

Koch, Ed *I'm Not Done Yet! Keeping At It. Remaining Relevant and Moving the Time of My Life.* Norwalk: Easton Press, 2000, 196 pages, signed by author, leather with gold titles and decorations, all edges gilt, silk endpapers and ribbon bookmark, "A note about" card and signed certificate of authenticity folded in, very clean and tight.   G. H. Mott Bookseller   May 26 2011 - 37071   2011 $200

Koch, Kenneth *Poems/Prints.* Editions of the Tibor de Nagy Gallery, 1953, First edition, one of 300 numbered copies (entire edition); 4to., original illustrated card wrappers, stapled, very fine, rare in such beautiful condition, none of the offsetting and staining that so often mars this book in half morocco slipcase, scarce, with 4 original linoleum cuts by Nell Blaine, Blaine has signed and dated each of the three large mounted prints in bottom margin, in addition to these large prints, there is one small linoleum cut and five black an white illustrations.   James S. Jaffe Rare Books   May 26 2011 - 21588   2011 $6500

Kocher, Emil Theodor *Text-Book of Operative Surgery.* London: Adam and Charles Black, 1903, Large 8vo., xxv, 440 pages, 255 numbered figures, dark blue cloth, gilt stamped spine title, ex-library bookplate with embossed stamp on title, spine call number painted over, ownership signature of Ernst A. Sommer, very good, from the Medical Library of Dr. Clare Gray Peterson.   Jeff Weber Rare Books   162 - 177   2011 $200

Kohl, Johann Georg *Austria. Vienna, Prague, Hungary, Bohemia and the Danube; Galicia, Styria, Moravia, Bukovina and the Military Frontier.* London: Chapman & Hall, 1843, First edition; half title, untrimmed in original vertical grained black cloth blocked in blind, gilt library number at foot of spine, neat repair to head of spine with horizontal grained cloth, label mostly removed from foot of spine leaving slight chip, nick to upper leading hinge, library stamps and label of Middlesbrough Free Library, good copy.   Jarndyce Antiquarian Booksellers CXCI - 563   2011   £85

Kollman, Paul *The Victoria Nyanza; the Land, the Races and Their Customs with Specimens of Some of the Dialects.* London: Swan Sonnenschein, 1899, First English edition; 8vo., pages ix (i) blank, 254, folding map, numerous illustrations, original maroon decorative cloth, gilt vignette on upper cover, small strip on edge and top edge of upper cover faded.   J. & S. L. Bonham Antiquarian Booksellers   Africa 4/20/2011 - 2976   2011   £295

Komroff, Manuel *The Magic Bow: A Romance of Pagnanini.* New York: Harper & Bros., 1940, First edition; little rubbing at extremities, very good, lacking dust jacket, inscribed by author to publisher, Thomas R. Coward.   Between the Covers   169 - BTC338044   2011 $650

Konigsburg, E. L. *From the Mixed Up File of Mrs. Basil E. Frankweiler.* New York: Atheneum, 1967, Stated first edition; 8vo., cloth, fine in fine dust jacket slightly frayed, but very good, rare.   Aleph-Bet Books, Inc.   95 - 317   2011 $600

Konstam, Gertrude A. *Dreams, Dances and Disappointments.* Thos. de la Rue, n.d. circa, 1890, Large square 8vo., original stiff pictorial wrappers, pages 26 with 8 full page colored plates and other full page and text illustrations.   R. F. G. Hollett & Sons Antiquarian Booksellers   170 - 373   2011   £40

Koons, Jeff *Jeff Koons.* Taschen: 2008, First edition, #1118 in an edition of 1600 signed on limitation page by Koons; lavishly illustrated with hundreds of large format images, clamshell box in paper wrapping, numbered and sealed by publisher, unopened, original publisher's printed cardboard delivery box.   Any Amount of Books   May 26 2011 - A74558   2011 $1593

Koontz, Dean R. *Chase.* London: Arthur Barker, 1974, First UK edition; near fine, shelfwear, not especially tight, dust jacket very good, wear to edges.   Bella Luna Books   May 29 2011 - t6810   2011 $82

Koontz, Dean R. *The Eyes of Darkness.* Essex: Piatkus, Loughton, 1981, First UK edition; near fine, very light shelfwear, dust jacket very good (price clipped, light creasing to edges and wear to corners).   Bella Luna Books   May 29 2011 - t6799   2011 $82

Koontz, Dean R. *Oddkins.* New York: Warner, 1988, First edition; fine in fine dust jacket. Bella Luna Books May 29 2011 - t9364 2011 $82

Koran *L'Alcoran de Mahomet.* Antwerp: J. F. Lucas, 1719, 8vo., (8), 485, (3) pages, title printed in red and black, contemporary speckled calf, spine gilt in compartments, morocco lettering piece, from the library of the Earls of Macclesfield at Shirburn Castle. Maggs Bros. Ltd. 1440 - 174 2011 £300

Koran *The Koran, Commonly Called the Alcoran of Mohammed.* London: Thomas Tegg et., 1825, 2 volumes, contemporary full polished tan calf gilt with gilt coat of arms and emblem "Munificentia Hulmiana" to all boards, edges little marked and rubbed in places, handsomely rebacked to match with broad raised bands and double contrasting labels, pages xxiv, (iv), 255, 214; iv, 536, with 4 engraved plates and maps, most attractive set. R. F. G. Hollett & Son Antiquarian Booksellers 175 - 1171 2011 £250

Kornbluth, Cyril M. *Takeoff.* Garden City: Doubleday & Co., 1952, First edition; octavo, boards. L. W. Currey, Inc. 124 - 239 2011 $75

Kornerup, Andreas *Methuen Handbook of Colour.* London: Methuen, 1963, First edition; small 8vo., pages 224, color charts with loosely inserted Methuen card color finder, small square windows for comparing colors, neat name on front endpaper, slight tape ghost marks to endpapers, otherwise about fine in complete, very good dust jacket with slight rubbing and one slight nick, very decent, clean copy, not price clipped. Any Amount of Books May 26 2011 - A64262 2011 $503

Korthals-Altes, J. *Sir Cornelius Vermuyden: the Lifework of a Great Anglo-Dutchman in Land-Reclamation and Drainage, with Some Notes by the Author on the Present Condition of Drainage in England and a Resume of the Drainage Legislation in Holland.* London/The Hague: Williams & Norgate/W. P. Van Stockum, 1925, First edition; 8vo., original publisher's blue cloth lettered gilt on spine and on front cover, pages xii, 208, 15 illustrations, 6 maps, pencilled ownership signature of historian F. R. Cowell, slight shelfwear, sound, clean very good+. Any Amount of Books May 29 2011 - A49460 2011 $383

Kossak-Szczucka, Zopfja *The Troubles of a Gnome.* London: A. & C. Black, 1928, First English edition; 4to., original cloth backed patterned boards with pictorial label, edges little rubbed, pages viii, 102, (ii), 8 fine color plates and 8 line drawings by Charles Folkard, edges lightly spotted. R. F. G. Hollett & Sons Antiquarian Booksellers 170 - 236 2011 £85

Kountz, William J. *Billy Baxter's Letters.* Harmarville: Duquesne Distributing Co., 1899, Half title, frontispiece and plates, uncut in original light brown decorated cloth, blocked in blue and red, very good. Jarndyce Antiquarian Booksellers CXCI - 247 2011 £35

Kozakiewicz, Stefan *Bernardo Bellotto.* London: Paul Elek, 1972, First edition; 2 volume, copiously illustrated in black and white and color, pages 840, very good+ in very good dust jackets, price clipped and with slight nicks, decent copies. Any Amount of Books May 29 2011 - A69136 2011 $383

Krafft-Ebing, Richard Von *Psychopathia Sexualis.* Stuttgart: Verlag Von Ferdinand Enke, 1886, First edition; large 8vo., pages 110, first and last leaves, slightly spotted, original half chocolate smooth grian cloth, marbled boards and edges, gilt titled on spine, some minor rubbing to fore-edges of boards and outer corners, minor spotting to endpapers, overall very good, occasional pencil annotations in margins, scarce. Simon Finch Rare Books Zero - 133 2011 £750

Krag, Niels *De Republica Lacedaemoniorum Libri III... Opus Politicarum...* Geneva: P. Saintandre, 1593, First edition; 3 parts, 4to., (16), 269, (3 blank), 35, (1), 23 pages, contemporary ?Scandinavian vellum over thin wooden boards, yapp edges, from the library of the Earls of Macclesfield at Shirburn Castle. Maggs Bros. Ltd. 1440 - 121 2011 £400

Krakauer, Jon *Into the Wild.* New York: Villard, 1996, First edition; near fine, previous owner's bookplate, dust jacket fine. Bella Luna Books May 29 2011 - t9545 2011 $110

Krakauer, Jon *Into the Wild.* New York: Villard, 1996, First edition; near fine, very light wear to bottom corners, dust jacket fine. Bella Luna Books May 26 2011 - t9414 2011 $192

Krakauer, Jon *Under the Banner of Heaven.* New York: Doubleday, 2003, First edition; signed and dated by author 21 Sept. 2009, fine in fine dust jacket. Bella Luna Books May 29 2011 - t6506s 2011 $93

Krakauer, Jon *Under the Banner of Heaven.* London: Macmillan, 2003, First UK edition with slips laid in; fine in fine dust jacket, signed by author, review copy. Bella Luna Books May 29 2011 - t6823 2011 $82

Krapf, J. Lewis *Travels, Researches and Missionary Labours During an Eighteen Years Residence in East Africa.* London: Trubner, 1860, First edition; 8vo., pages liii, 566, frontispiece, plates, 12 tinted lithographs, folding maps, later brown half calf, very clean and crisp. J. & S. L. Bonham Antiquarian Booksellers Africa 4/20/2011 - 9145 2011 £980

Krause, Dorothy Simpson *Heretic: Joan of Arc.* Marshfield Hills: Viewpoint Editions, 2009, Artist's book, one of 6 deluxe copies; bound in vellum, from a total issue of 71 (55 regular copies) on Mohawk Via Superfine Eggshell 100# text paper, each signed and numbered in gold ink by author/artist, page size 5 x 7 1/8 inches, 56 pages, bound in vellum wrappers with red suede tie, black paper endpapers, housed in protective box of stiff paper with cloth ties, designed to resemble a well-worn library enclosure for a rare book with "Rare Book Handle with Care" and "Not to Circulate" stamped on front cover, spine with labels, one circular with numbers, rectangular with red board reading "Rare Book Reference" followed by numbers, title and small typeface, fine.   Priscilla Juvelis - Rare Books   48 - 12   2011 $750

Krause, Dorothy Simpson *Losing Ground.* Marshfield Hills: Viewpoint Editions, 2008, Artist's book; one of 6 deluxe copies from a total issue of 106 (100 regular and 6 deluxe), all on Mohawk Options 65 cover made from 100 per cent post consumer content with renewable wind power, each signed and numbered on colophon by artist/author, page size 12 x 12 inches, 40 pages, bound by Harcourt Bindery in aubergine Nigerian goatskin with onlay of copper inset 7 7/8 x 7 7/8 inches that has been manipulated by artist (acid washed with "wrinkles") title blindstamped in center of copper, gold endpapers, housed in matching gold cloth over boards, custom made clamshell box, printed on HP Indigo 5500 Press by Acme Bookbinding that have been manipulated by Ms. Krause with graphite, metallic pigments, gold and silver leaf, text is mainly taken from Intergovernmental Panel on Climate Change, although a notable page spread in text taken from the Holy Bible, Malachi, Chapter 4, Verses 16, beautiful book.   Priscilla Juvelis - Rare Books   48 - 13   2011 $2500

Krause, Johann *Neuer Bucher-Saal der Gelehrten Welt Oder Ausfuhrliche Nachrichten von alelrehand Neuen Buchrern...* Leipzig: Gleditsch & Weidmanishe Buchhandlung, 1710-1711, Issues 1-12 (with index), 8vo., (16), 969, (76) pages, frontispiece and portraits, contemporary vellum backed paper boards, from the library of the Earls of Macclesfield at Shirburn Castle.   Maggs Bros. Ltd.   1440 - 122   2011   £550

Krauss, Ruth *Charlotte and the White Horse.* New York: Harper and Bros., 1955,   12mo., cloth backed pictorial boards, fine in dust jacket with price intact and 1.5" inch piece off top edge, illustrations in color on every page by Sendak, scarce.   Aleph-Bet Books, Inc.   95 - 508   2011 $500

Krauss, Ruth *Charlotte and the White Horse.* London: The Bodley Head, 1977,   First UK edition; small 8vo., original pictorial boards, unpaginated, illustrations in color by Maurice Sendak.   R. F. G. Hollett & Sons Antiquarian Booksellers   170 - 623   2011   £60

Krauss, Ruth *A Hole is to Dig.* London: Hamish Hamilton, 1963,   First UK edition; unpaginated, lettered in brown and illustrations in black and white, small square 8vo., original cloth backed pictorial boards, dust jacket little spotted, some repairs to reverse, unpaginated, lettered in brown, illustrations in black and white by Maurice Sendak, booklabel pasted to pictorial flyleaf, crinkling the paper.   R. F. G. Hollett & Sons Antiquarian Booksellers   170 - 624   2011   £40

Krauss, Ruth *Is This You?* New York: William Scott, 1955,   First edition; 8vo., pictorial boards, slight tip wear, else very good+ in dust jacket with light soil and few small edge mends, illustrations by Crockett Johnson.   Aleph-Bet Books, Inc.   95 - 310   2011 $600

Krauss, Ruth *Open House for Butterflies.* New York: Harper & Bos., 1960,   12mo., cloth backed pictorial boards, fine in slightly worn dust jacket, scarce, illustrations by Maurice Sendak.   Aleph-Bet Books, Inc.   95 - 511   2011 $500

Krieger, Joel *The Oxford Companion to Politics of the World.* Oxford University Press, 1993,   First edition; original cloth, dust jacket, pages xxxi, 1056.   R. F. G. Hollett & Son Antiquarian Booksellers   175 - 792   2011   £30

Krige, E. J. *The Social System of the Zulus.* London: Longmans Green, 1936,   First edition; 8vo., pages xix, 420, maps, illustrations, original green cloth.   J. & S. L. Bonham Antiquarian Booksellers   Africa 4/20/2011 - 2934   2011   £35

Kroeker, Kate Freiligrath *New Fairy Tales from Brentano.* London: T. Fisher Unwin, 1888,   First UK edition; pages 261, large 8vo., original blue cloth gilt, large pictorial onlay to each board, extremities rather worn, 8 colored plates by Carruthers Gould, top third of half title cutt off, little shaken.   R. F. G. Hollett & Sons Antiquarian Booksellers   170 - 375   2011   £45

Krogh, Schack August Steenberg *The Anatomy and Physiology of Capillaries.* New Haven & London: Yale University Press & Oxford University Press, 1922,   First edition; 8vo., xvii, 276 pages, numbered figures, original navy cloth, gilt stamped spine title, previous owner's inked signature and rubber stamp, from the Medical Library of Dr. Clare Gray Peterson.   Jeff Weber Rare Books   162 - 178   2011 $100

Kronheim & Co. *Pictures of English History.* London: George Routledge & Co. n.d. circa, 1869, 4to., original green cloth gilt, little worn, unpaginated, full page frontispiece and 24 plates with 4 illustrations to the page, all printed in colors, each sheet with accompanying page of text, joints tightened, little fingering in places but very good.   R. F. G. Hollett & Son Antiquarian Booksellers   General Catalogue Summer 2010 - 529   2011   £65

Kropotkin, P. *Field, Factories and Workshops or Industry Combined with Agriculture and Brain Work with Manual Work.* London: Swan Sonnenschein, 1907, Fifth impression; small 8vo., original cloth, pages ix, 259, illustrations. R. F. G. Hollett & Son Antiquarian Booksellers 175 - 793 2011 £35

Krudener, Mme. De *Valerie.* Paris: Quantin, 1878, (339) pages, 8vo., three quarter red calf over boards, gilt decorated spine with lettering, top edge gilt, frontispiece, 2 additional plates by Leloir, lovely collectible. Paulette Rose Fine and Rare Books 32 - 194 2011 $125

Krull, Germaine *100 x Paris.* Berlin-Westend: Verlag der Reihe, 1929, First edition; small quarto, 100 photo engraved plates, minor dampstains at extremities, else near fine in tattered, poor dust jacket, housed in cloth custom clamshell case, lengthy inscription by Krull to Stefan Lorant in German, rare in jacket. Between the Covers 169 - STC346670 2011 $5000

Krusenstern, Adam Johann Von *Voyage Round the World in the Years 1803, 1804, 1805 and 1805.* London: for John Murray, 1813, First edition in English; 2 volumes, quarto, two hand colored aquatint and large engraved folding map, contemporary green half calf morocco over marbled boards in Regency Style, the Egremont copy. Heritage Book Shop Booth A12 51st NY International Antiquarian Book Fair April 8-10 2011 - 81 2011 $20,000

Krusenstern, Adam Johann Von *Voyage Round the World in the Years 1803, 1804 , 1805 and 1806.* Amsterdam and New York: 1968, 2 volumes, xxxii, 314 pages, frontispiece, folding map; (x), 404 pages, issued with clear acetate dust covers, minor chipping to one of the covers, else clean, near fine set. Dumont Maps & Books of the West 112 - 50 2011 $150

Krutch, Joseph Wood *Baja California and the Geography of Hope.* San Francisco: Sierra Club, 1967, First edition; 73 color photos by Eliot Porter, large folding map at rear, green cloth gilt, very fine, pictorial dust jacket. Argonaut Book Shop Recent Acquisitions Summer 2010 - 161 2011 $125

Kunos, Ignacz *Turkish Fairy Tales.* London: Lawrence and Bullen, 1806, First edition; original pink cloth, gilt, spine faded and soiled, pages x, 276, top edges gilt, illustrations by Celia Levente, annotated throughout, neatly, but quite heavily in places, by original owner, David Fitzgerald, folklorist. R. F. G. Hollett & Son Antiquarian Booksellers 175 - 795 2011 £65

Kunstadter, Pter *Southeast Asian Tribes, Minorities and Nations.* Princeton: Princeton University Press, 1967, First edition; 2 volumes, xiii, 902 pages + maps, black and white photos and maps, 8vo., cloth, original publisher's review slip laid in loose, fine, very faint soiling, in very good+ to near fine slightly shelfworn dust jacket, handsome set. Kaaterskill Books 12 - 115 2011 $150

Kuroda, Nagamichi *Birds of the Island of Java.* Tokyo: Published by the author, 1933-1936, First edition; volumes I and II, 34 colored plates and 2 folding maps, folio, pages xv, 370; vi, (371)-794, original maroon cloth backed boards, light foxing to 5 prelim pages in volume I, near fine, dust jackets with 3 marginal tears, very good. Raymond M. Sutton, Jr. May 26 2011 - 43262 2011 $2500

Kuttner, Henry *Ahead of Time.* New York: Ballantine Books, 1953, First edition; octavo, boards. L. W. Currey, Inc. 124 - 232 2011 $100

Kwang, Wei-Yuan *Yellow River Cantata.* New York: Leeds Music, 1946, 8vo., pages 48, paper wrappers, map inside front cover, owner bookplate on map, cover little worn an soiled, otherwise very good. Second Life Books Inc. 174 - 224 2011 $65

Kynaston, David *Cazenove & Co. A History.* London: Batsford, 1991, First edition; pages 359, illustrations in color, inscribed "Duff (Hart-Davis) with best wishes John Kemp-Welch (partner, Cazenove & Co.) Oct. 1991". R. F. G. Hollett & Son Antiquarian Booksellers 175 - 796 2011 £35

L

L'Engle, Madeleine *And Both Were Young.* New York: Lothrop Lee and Shepard, 1949, First edition; 8vo., green and yellow cloth, 232 pages , fine in dust jacket (slightly soiled, price clipped), with one page handwritten card by author laid in.   Aleph-Bet Books, Inc.   95 - 328 2011 $950

L'Engle, Madeleine *Small Rain.* New York: Vanguard Press, 1945, First edition; 8vo., cloth, 371 pages, very small strip of fading on spine, else fine in fine dust jacket, one page inscription by author.   Aleph-Bet Books, Inc.   95 - 327 2011 $1850

L'Engle, Madeleine *A Wrinkle in Time.* New York: Farrar, Straus and Cudahy, 1962, Stated first printing; 8vo., blue cloth backed boards, patterned boards, gold and orange lettering on spine, color pictorial dust jacket, book has slight shelf wear and a Christmas presentation on front free endpaper, dust jacket has chips at head and foot of spine and along edges, nice copy, 211 numbered plates, lovely copy.   Jo Ann Reisler, Ltd.   86 - 146 2011 $5000

L'Engle, Madeleine *A Wrinkle in Time.* New York: Ariel, 1962, 8vo., quater cloth, 211 pages, extremely faint soil on rear cover, small spot on endpaper, else fine in dust jacket, dust jacket illustrated by Ellen Raskin, is in beautiful condition with price intact, small amount of soil on rear panel and touch of rubbing at bae of spine but no fraying or tear), exceptionally nice copy, ultra rare.   Aleph-Bet Books, Inc.   95 - 326 2011 $15,500

L'Estrange, A. G. *The Life of Mary Russell Mitford....* London: Richard Bentley, 1870, First edition; 3 volumes, half titles, original brown cloth by Burn & Co., bevelled boards, spines lettered in gilt, inner hinges slightly cracking, very good.   Jarndyce Antiquarian Booksellers   CLXC - 415 2011 £65

L'Estrange, Roger *Fables of Aesop and Other Eminent Mythologists, with Morals and Reflections.* London: for R. Sare, T. Sawbridge, B. Took..., 1692, First L'Estrange edition; (14), 480 pages, 4to., recently bound in half caramel calf over marbled paper backed boards, gilt lettering and date to spine, new endpapers, engraved plates slightly chipped with minor repairs around margins but without loss to image, excellent clean text, without foxing or blemishes and only tiny handful of marginal marks, 18th century sepia hand.   Any Amount of Books   May 26 2011 - A76466 2011 $1174

La Chausse, Michel Ange De *Romanum Museum sive Thesaurus Eruditae Antiquitatis.* Rome: Ex Typographia Joannis Jacobi Komarek Boemi, 1690, First edition; added engraved titlepage, engraved portrait, 160 further engraved plates (in 6 numbered groups of 55, 42, 25, 15, 17 and 6 as called for), engraved head and tailpieces, some browning and spotting (mostly to text rather than plates), one leaf stained, last leaf with blank area of lower inside corner replaced, two other leaves with minor closed tears, pages (xvi), 127, (17) folio, contemporary dark calf, rebacked and recornered with five raised bands, red morocco label in second compartment, rest plain, new endpapers, old leather bit scraped and chipped, sound.   Blackwell Rare Books   B166 - 61 2011   £1250

La Fontaine, Jean De   1621-1695   *Contes et Nouvelles en Vers.* Paris: De l'Imprimerie de P. Didot l'aine, 1795, First printing of the Fragonard edition; 322 x 250mm., 2 volumes, very fine honey brown crushed morocco handsomely gilt by Noulhac (stamp signed and dated 1902 on front turn-ins), covers with French fillet border and sawtooth edging and very elegant large floral ornaments in corners, raised bands, spines very attractively gilt in compartments formed by triple rules and featuring a poppy centerpiece framed by leafy sprays and ribbons, marbled endpapers, all edges gilt, 3 full page portraits of Fragonard, one smaller portrait tondo of La Fontaine, one vignette of Venus, vignette of Cupid on each titlepage and 20 very fine plates "Before Letters" from original edition, 16 of them after Fragonard and, in addition, the 57 etchings "Before Letters? published in 1880 by Roquette based on Fragonard's 57 planned illustrations of the 1795 edition, along with 36 original sepia wash drawings done in 1869 and based on a selection of Fragonard originals (these drawings done in reverse), like images bound next to each other (meaning that sometimes there are three versions of the same illustration bound together); slightest hint of foxing internally (perhaps a half dozen leaves more foxed, but worst being just about negligible), perhaps 10 leaves with expertly repaired short marginal tears (typically less than an inch and never anywhere near text), very special copy in beautiful condition, finely executed lovely bindings lustrous and virtually without wear, margins nothing short of vast, text, plates and inserted material all extraordinarily fresh and clean.   Phillip J. Pirages   59 - 48 2011 $17,500

La Fontaine, Jean De   1621-1695   *Fables Choisies, Mises en Vers.* Paris: Denys Thierry, 31 March, 1668, First edition; 4to., (58), 284 (2) pages, leaf o2 present as both cancellans and cancellandum, roman type, woodcut typographic head and tailpieces, floriated initials, 118 etchings by Francois Chauveau, crushed green morocco, gilt triple rule outer border, spine and wide turn-ins gilt, all edges gilt by Lortic, fils (spine and extremities faded to brown, front hinge worn), neat repair to five leaves (one touching two letters), very light overall toning, Robert Hoe's copy, inscribed in pencil on front flyleaf to his Granddaughter Thyrza Benson.   Joseph J. Felcone Inc.   Fall Miscellany 2010 - 72 2011 $30,000

La Fontaine, Jean De 1621-1695 *Fables Choisies.* Aux depens de la Compagnie, 1749, 2 volumes in 1, 12mo., five raised bands to spine, full leather on boards, elaborate gilt decorations and gilt title on spine, marbled endpapers, red edges, some decorative engraved head and tailpieces, all printed on handmade paper, dated ink dedication on front flyleaf, light shelf wear, else fine and rare. Hobbyhorse Books   56 - 66 2011 $350

La Fontaine, Jean De 1621-1695 *Fables Choisies.* Paris: Chez Desaint & Saillant (et) Durand, De l'Imprimerie de Charles Antoine Jombert, 1755, Oudry edition, large paper copy; Large paper issue, 4 volumes, (4), xxx, xviii, 124; (4), ii, 135, (1, blank); (4), iv, 146; (4), ii, 188 pages, frontispiece, 275 engraved plates after woodcut title vignettes and head and tailpieces, inserted as frontispiece in volume I is portrait of Oudry engraved by J. Tardieu after Nicolas de Largilliere, found in some copies, but not integral, contemporary French red morocco, covers with gilt triple fillet border with tiny gilt corner ornaments enclosing four larger floral/vase ornament in center of each of the five compartments, with 7 raised bands anda two brown morocco gilt lettering labels, board edges ruled in gilt, turn-ins decoratively tooled in gilt, all edges gilt, blue endpapers, binding expertly touched up by James Brockman, very small amount of light margin soiling, very small rough spot affecting text on pages vii-viii i volume I, wonderful extremely large copy.   David Brass Rare Books, Inc.   May 26 2011 - 00494 2011 $60,000

La Fontaine, Jean De 1621-1695 *Fables De La Fontaine.* Paris: P. Didot l'Aine an VII, 1799, Edition Stereotype; 12mo., original three quarter leather with corners, paper on boards, elaborately gilt spines, red and black label with gilt title and number, green edges of leaves, titlepages adorned with monogram of publisher, 2 charming wood engravings, one signed, decorated as headpieces the beginning of the fables in each volume, printed on water marked paper and with original red silk page marker, small owner stamp inside covers, minor spotting at covers and light shelf wear, fine set.   Hobbyhorse Books   56 - 65 2011 $170

La Fontaine, Jean De 1621-1695 *Fables de La Fontaine.* Tours: Alfred Mame et Fils, 1887, Reprint of 1864 edition; 8vo., x, 512 pages, embossed and gilt red cloth on boards, gilt title and decorative motif repeated on spine, gilt edges, gray endpapers, half page engravings, inked and dated signature inside upper endpaper, fine copy. Hobbyhorse Books   56 - 63 2011 $120

La Fontaine, Jean De 1621-1695 *Fables de La Fontaine.* Tours: Alfred Mame et Fils, 1899, 12mo., 400 pages, pictorial paper on boards, red cloth spine with title label, full page wood engraved frontispiece, engraved editor cartouche on titlepage plus numerous very fine third page engraved vignettes in text, engraved vignette on upper and lower boards, enclosed in decorative line border, inked name and date inside upper board, edges and covers rubbed and lightly soiled, one signature sprung, in all very good.   Hobbyhorse Books   56 - 64 2011 $150

La Fontaine, Jean De 1621-1695 *A Hundred Fables of La Fontaine.* London: John Lane, The Bodley Head, 1900, First edition; large 8vo., original pictorial green cloth, pages 202, (ii), numerous full page black and white illustrations, endpapers rather spotted.   R. F. G. Hollett & Sons Antiquarian Booksellers   170 - 88 2011   £95

La Fontaine, Jean De 1621-1695 *Fontaine's Fables.* Racine: Whitman, 1934, Folio, cloth backed pictorial boards, several dedication signatures on endpaper (plain endpapers), some edge rubbing, else near fine in dust jacket (soiled), illustrations by Felix Lorioux.   Aleph-Bet Books, Inc.   95 - 337 2011 $500

La Motte Fouque, Friedrich Heinrich Karl, Freiherr De 1777-1843 *Undine.* London: William Heinemann/New York: Doubleday Page & Co., 1909, One of 1000 copies signed by artist, this #329; 290 x 232mm., viii, 136 pages, very attractive red three quarter morocco (stamp signed "Putnams" along front turn-in), raised bands, spine handsomely gilt in compartments, formed by plain and decorative rules, quatrefoil centerpiece surrounded by densely scrolling cornerpieces, sides and endleaves or rose colored linen, top edge gilt, green woodcut head and tailpieces on titlepage, black and white vignette headpieces for each chapter and 15 color plates by Arthur Rackham, as called for, each mounted on heavy brown stock and protected by lettered tissue guard; top of spine worn away to just above headband, corners with bit of wear, joint just slightly rubbed, with small, thin crack, beginning at top of front joint, spine with hint of darkening, overall slight offsetting onto most of the pages opposite brown mounting paper (as is typical), otherwise bright and clean and generally pleasing, no serious defects.   Phillip J. Pirages   59 - 291 2011 $1750

La Peyrouse, Jean Francois De Galaup, Comte De *A Voyage Round the World; Which was Peformed (sic) in the Years 1785, 1786 1787, 1788.* Edinburgh: printed by J. Moir, 1798, 8vo., (3), vi-xvi, 336 pages, folding engraved map, 3 engraved plates, bound without half title, 8vo., map and plates rather browned, full contemporary tree calf, gilt ship device repeated on spine, dark green morocco label, slight chip to head of spine, also little rubbed, pencil note on f.e.p. with armorial bookplate of Marquess of Headfort. Jarndyce Antiquarian Booksellers   CXCI - 564 2011   £225

La Place, Pierre Simon 1749-1827 *Mecanique Celeste.* Boston: 1829-, 1832-1834-1839. First edition; large and thick quarto, 4 volumes, library buckram, entirely untrimmed and unusual thus, ex-library with small library stamps and ink markings, but y nice.   M & S Rare Books, Inc.   90 - 50 2011 $3500

La Serre, Jean Puget De *The Mirrour Which Flatters Not Concerning the Contempt of the World, or the Meditation of Death, of Philip King of Macedon, Saladine, Adrian and Alexander the Great.* London: E. T. and R. H. for R. Thrale, 1673, 146 x 89mm., 12 p.l., 216 pages, quite pleasing early 19th century vellum in the style of Edwards of Halifax, covers bordered with narrow decorative gilt roll flanked by blue rules and with gilt floral cornerpieces, flat spine with decorative gilt bands forming panels, five of these with charming floral centerpiece, titling and date panels colored blue, unusual additional gilt titling between four pairs of decorative bands, marbled endpapers, woodcut headpieces and five engraved folding plates, including frontispiece, vellum very slightly soiled, front board just barely splayed but binding in excellent condition, completely sound and rather pretty, one plate accidentally cut into at crease (with minor loss of background detail), each plate with small tear in crease near gutter (with no loss), small portion of lower blank fore margin of one leaf cut away, front pastedown very roughened (from lifted bookplate?), leaves slightly browned at edges, bit foxed, text still rather fresh, surprisingly clean, generally well preserved.   Phillip J. Pirages   59 - 12 2011 $650

Labarraque, Antoine Germain *De l'Emploi des Chlorures d'Oxide de Sodium et de Chaux.* Paris: chez l'auteur et Mme Huzard, 1825, First edition; 8vo., 48 pages, little foxing, original printed wrappers, uncut, housed in gray clamshell board box with gilt stamped spine title, fine, presentation copy inscribed by author for M. de Boisrichard, from the Medical Library of Dr. Clare Gray Peterson.   Jeff Weber Rare Books   162 - 180 2011 $1200

Labat, Jean Baptiste *Nouveau Voyage aux Isles de l'Amerique, Contenant l'Histoire Naturelle de Ces Pays, l'Origine, Les Moeurs, La Religion & Le Gouvernement des Habitans Anciens & Modernes...* The Hague: P. Husson et al, 1724, 56 engraved plates, 8 engraved maps, 4to., pages (11), viiii, 168; 184; (185-)-360; (7), 180; (181-)348; (349-) 520, 18, half titles present, modern quarter morocco, slight rubbing to volume, some browning or offsetting to contents, dog earing to few pages in volume 2; upper edge of few pages in volume 2 bumped, resulting in some tears, all but one of which are marginal, few short tears to fore-edge of 3 leaves of index, titlepage printed in red and black.   Raymond M. Sutton, Jr.   May 26 2011 - 36102 2011 $2600

Labillardiere, Jacques Julien Houton De *Relation du Voyage a la Recherche de La Perouse.* Paris: Chez H. J. Jansen, 1799-1800, First edition; 2 quarto text volumes and one folio atlas, atlas with engraved title, double page route map and 43 plates, contemporary French mottled calf by Courteval.   Heritage Book Shop   Booth A12 51st NY International Antiquarian Book Fair April 8-10 2011 - 82 2011 $20,000

Lacan, Jacques *De la Psychose Paranoiaque Dans ses Rapports avec la Personaalite.* Paris: Librairie E. la Francois, 1932, First edition; large 8bo., pages (xx), ix-xiii, (i) blank, 365, (i) blank, (i) errata, (i) blank, 367-381, (i) blank), publisher's wrappers, text and design in black and blue, preserved in quarter morocco slipcase with marbled boards, spine lettered in gilt, fine, letter from author tipped in on front endpaper, author's presentation inscription to half title.   Simon Finch Rare Books   Zero - 144 2011   £9500

Lachapelle, David *Hotel Lachapelle. Photographs.* Boston: Bulfinch Press/Little Brown and Co., 1999, First edition; folio, signed and inscribed by Lachapelle, near fine, mild corners bumped in near fine original color pictorial box.   By the Book, L. C.   26 - 37 2011 $350

Lackington, James *The Confessions of Lackington, Late Bookseller at the Temple of the Muses.* Printed by Richard Edwards for the Author, 1804, First edition; half title, affected by water in margins, uncut, rebound in brown boards, buff paper spine, retaining original label on front board.   Jarndyce Antiquarian Booksellers   CXCI - 452 2011   £75

Laclos, Michel *Bizarre.* Paris: 1953-1968, First series No. 2 (of 2), NS 1-8, 10-12, 15, 17-20, 23, 26-28, 32/32, 36-38, 43/44, 46 (last number), 29 numbers in 24 issues, unusually good condition.   I. D. Edrich   May 26 2011 - 97755 2011 $587

Laclos, Pierre Ambroise Francois Choderlos De 1741-1803 *Dangerous Connections: a Series of Letters, Selected from the Correspondence...* London: Harding and Wright for J. Ebers, 1812, Second English edition; 4 volumes, 12mo., pages xvi, xix, (i) blank, 252; (iv), 243, (i) blank; (iv) 232; (iv), 256, (2) blank, half titles, near contemporary red half morocco, spines lettered and decorated in gilt, marbled boards, excellent set, rare.   Simon Finch Rare Books   Zero - 247 2011   £2500

Laclos, Pierre Ambroise Francois Choderlos De 1741-1803 *Les Liasions Dangereuses.* Brussels: J. Rosez, 1869, 2 volumes bound as one, pages 99; 291, internally clean and bright, minor chip to half title, contemporary blue black quarter morocco, gilt lettered on spine, original lime green printed wrappers bound in, top edge gilt, marbled boards and endpapers, spine and joints expertly repaired, edges of boards slightly rubbed, front endpapers chipped with some restoration also to front wrapper, Aubrey Beardsley's copy with his ink signature at head of titlepage and presentation inscription from his mother to A. W. King, later inscription from his mother, bookplate of Robert Booth.   Simon Finch Rare Books   Zero - 205 2011   £3500

Laclotte, Michel *The Art and Spirit of Paris.* New York/London: Abbeville Press, 2003, First edition; 4to., 2 volumes, original publisher's blue cloth lettered gilt on spine and on front cover with color illustration onset to cover, pages 1654, illustrations in color and black and white, fine in slipcase. Any Amount of Books May 29 2011 - A38594 2011 $230

Lacroix, Jean Francois *Dictionnaire Portatif des Femmes Celebres.* Paris: Chez L. Cellot, 1769, First edition; 3 volumes, 446, 489, 506 pages, 12mo., later 19th century binding, gilt decorated and gilt lettered spines, contrasting title labels in red and green, raised bands, all edges gilt, most attractive set, scarce. Paulette Rose Fine and Rare Books 32 - 105 2011 $1200

Lacroix, Paul *Histoire Naturelle des Quadrupedes des Osieux des Reptiles des Poisson et des Insects...* Paris: Didier, 1841, Square 12mo., 223, 2-257 (2)-291 (2)-268 (2), original three quarter leather with gilt title on red label, gilt numerals on black label and gilt fillets, marbled dark brown paper on boards, each volume includes full page wood engraved half title, 64 pages of superb hand colored copper engravings, including frontispiece, all pages printed on heavier paper and on one side of leaf only. Hobbyhorse Books 56 - 94 2011 $1200

Lacroix, Paul *Ma Republique.* Paris: Librairie L. Conquet, 1902, One of 40 special copies with 2 extra states of the plates and inscribed by publisher to Monsieur L. Rattier (no doubt French bibliophile Leon Rattier; of the limited edition of 100 copies on Japan vellum (of a total edition of 400 copies) 205 x 140mm., 2 p.l., 150, (1) pages, very fine crimson morocco gilt and onlaid by Chambolle-Duru (stamp signed on front doublure), covers with broad border comprised of seven gilt fillets, raised bands, with broad border comprised of seven gilt fillets, raised bands, spine compartments outlined with five concentric gilt rules, doublures of brown crushed morocco featuring stylized flowers of onlaid olive brown morocco on elegant arching gilt stems, cloth and then marbled endleaves, all edges gilt, original printed wrappers bound in, 7 etchings, each in 3 states (for a total of 21 plates), virtually mint. Phillip J. Pirages 59 - 91 2011 $3250

Lactantius, Lucius Coelius Firmianus *Opera quae Exstant... et Commentariis Illustrata a Tho. spark.* Oxonii: E Theatro Sheldoniano, 1684, 8vo., pages (xviii), 912, (ii), 24, 17-38, contemporary speckled calf, boards double rule bordered in blind with stylized 'dahlia' tool in corners, board edges decorative 'zig-zag' roll in blind, turn-ins single ruled in blind, pink and white sewn endbands, early 21st century calf reback by Chris Weston with original decorative red lettering piece gilt relaid, little light spotting, small dampmark in upper corner of first few leaves, old leather scratched and marked, contemporary inscription "E Libris Gui. Brodnag", heraldic bookplate of Montagu George Knight of Chawton, from the collection of Christopher Ernest Weston 1947-2010. Unsworths Booksellers 24 - 28 2011 £250

Lade, Robert *Voyages du Capitaine Robert Lade en Differents Parties de l'Afrique de l'Asie et de l'Amerique.* Paris: Didot, 1744, First edition; 2 volumes, 12mo., pages 370, 360, 2 folding maps, contemporary brown speckled calf, gilt spines with raised bands, slight wear at head of spines, handsome set. J. & S. L. Bonham Antiquarian Booksellers Africa 4/20/2011 - 8765 2011 £800

Ladies' Relief Society of Bridgeport *Report of the Ladies' Relief Society of Bridgeport, Con.., Commenced August 1861 for the Aid of Sick and Wounded Soldiers Belonging to the Army of the United States.* Bridgeport: Standard Steam Press Print, 1865, First edition; 8vo., 8 pages, original pale blue printed wrappers. M & S Rare Books, Inc. 90 - 78 2011 $125

Ladies of the First Congregational Church *Santa Barbara Recipes.* Santa Barbara: 1888, (111) pages, with map, wrappers. Bookworm & Silverfish 676 - 43 2011 $100

The Ladies' Pocket Magazine 1832. Parts 1 and 2. London: Joseph Robins, 1832, Parts 1 and 2, 12mo., modern half calf, pages iv, 244, engraved title to second part, 22 hand colored costume plates and 12 engraved plates, first engraved and dedication leaf in good facsimile, some pencilled scribbles, some engraved plates rather marked. R. F. G. Hollett & Son Antiquarian Booksellers 175 - 36 2011 £95

The Ladies' Treasury: an Illustrated Magazine of Entertaining Literature, Education, Fine Art, Domestic Economy, Needlework and Fashion. London: Ward Lock, 1858-1860, 4 volumes, 4to., frontispiece in color in volume IV, illustrations, contemporary full diced dark blue calf, gilt spines and borders, maroon leather labels, one chipped, one missing, slightly rubbed, all edges gilt. Jarndyce Antiquarian Booksellers CLXC - 63 2011 £150

The Lady's Law; or a Treatise of Feme Converts: containing al the Laws and Statutes Relating to Women Under Several Heads... London: in the Savoy: printed by E. and R. Nutt and R. gosling (assigns of E. Sayer, Esq.) for H. L. and sold by C. Corbett and E. Littleton, 1737, Second edition; 8vo., (iii)-viii 264 (16) pages, wanting initial leaf of ads, contemporary ruled calf, rebacked and labelled, very good, crisp copy, early ownership signature of James Crummer, 20th century bookplate of Richard Pepler. John Drury Rare Books 153 - 75 2011 £850

The Lady's Monthly Museum; or Polite Repository of Amusement and Instruction. London: Vernor, Hood & Sharpe, 1806-1807, 2 volumes, engraved plates, owner's signatures cut from margins of leading f.e.p.'s, contemporary half speckled calf, horizontal gilt rules, black leather labels, good plus, signature of Tho. Guy. Jarndyce Antiquarian Booksellers CLXC - 64 2011 £150

Lafayette, Marie Madeleine Pioche De La Vergne, Comtess De *Memoires de Mme. de la Fayette Publies avec Preface, Notes...* Paris: Librairie des Bibliophiles, 1890, One of 300 numbered copies of total edition of 340; (xxi, 300 pages) 8vo., three quarter blue morocco over marbled board, beautiful gilt decorated spine in compartments, raised bands, top edge gilt, outstanding copy.   Paulette Rose Fine and Rare Books   32 - 106 2011 $250

Lagerlof, Selma *From a Swedish Homestead.* London: William Heinemann, 1901, First English edition; Half title, 32 page catalog, slight foxing to prelims, original grey-green decorated cloth, spine slightly faded, otherwise very good.   Jarndyce Antiquarian Booksellers   CLXC - 65 2011   £45

Lagerlof, Selma *The Girl from the Marsh Croft.* London: T. Werner Laurie, 1911, Half title, original olive green decorated cloth, slightly darkened but good plus.   Jarndyce Antiquarian Booksellers   CLXC - 66 2011   £40

Laidler, Graham *The British at Home.* Collins, 1939, First edition; original cloth, gilt, dust jacket, pages 121, cartoons.   R. F. G. Hollett & Son Antiquarian Booksellers   General Catalogue Summer 2010 - 924 2011   £75

Laird, F. C. *A Topographical and Historical Description of the County of Worcester...* Sherwood, Neely and Jones, circa, 1820, 8vo., 407 (9) pages, folding map, 14 plates, some foxing and light browning, inner margin of titlepage creased, contemporary half calf, gilt spine with red morocco label, joints and corners rubbed, inner front joint loose.   Ken Spelman Rare Books   68 - 196 2011   £50

Lairesse, Gerard De *The Art of Painting in All Its Branches, Methodically Demonstrated by Discourses and Plates...* London: printed for the author and sold by J. Brotherton, 1738, First English edition; old half black calf gilt, pages 654, engraved head and tailpieces, lackings titlepage and plates, fore-edge of final page remargined, good working copy.   R. F. G. Hollett & Son Antiquarian Booksellers   General Catalogue Summer 2010 - 228 2011   £150

Lamarck , Jean Baptiste De *Histoire Naturelle des Animaux Sans Vertebres, Presentant les Caracteres Genereaux et Particuliers de Ces Animaux, Leur Distribution ....* Paris: J. B. Bailliere, 1835-1845, Second edition; 8vo., over 7400 pages, volumes I-VIII are later quarter calf, volumes IX-XI contemporary quarter calf, some rubbing, short splits to 2 ends of a spine, ink number to half title, few corners bumped, tips of several corners worn, scattered foxing to text, sometimes heavy, approximately 250 pages, browned, small hole to lower margin of 6 leaves not affecting text, overall set is very good, gilt decorations on spines.   Raymond M. Sutton, Jr.   May 26 2011 - 42507 2011 $1950

Lamartine, Alphonse Marie Louis De *Graziella.* London: Nonesuch Press, 1929, One of 1600 copies; 210 x 127mm., 2 p.l., 189, (1) page, (1) leaf, original patterned cloth, flat spine with paper label, top edge gilded on rough, all edges untrimmed and unopened, headpieces, decorated titlepage and 30 illustrations, printed in black and green, lower margin of last page with ink smudge (apparently left during printing or during numbering of the colophon), otherwise extremely fine, unread copy.   Phillip J. Pirages   59 - 273 2011 $100

Lamartine, Alphonse Marie Louis De *Graziella.* Paris: Les Heures Claires, 1948, Number 247 in the band 222-421 of the total edition of 999; sur velin pur fil des papeteries de Rives, deluxe printing, 150 (+14) pages + 42 additional suite of illustrations, small 4to., all color illustrations protected by tissue guards, half gree leather over marbled paper backed boards, spine lettered gilt and decorated with brown red inlaid leather, flower and leaf device, top edge gilt, other page edges untrimmed, ribbon book marker stitched in, very good, minimal wear.   Any Amount of Books   May 29 2011 - A77055 2011 $340

Lamartine, Alphonse Marie Louis De *History of the Girondists; or Personal Memoirs of the Patriots of the French Revolution from Unpublished Sources.* New York: 1859, 3 volumes, good solid copies with new backstrips and labels.   Bookworm & Silverfish   669 - 84 2011 $75

Lamb, Caroline 1785-1828 *Glenarvon.* London: Henry Colburn, 1816, First edition; 3 volumes, half titles, volumes I and III, few spots pencil note of inconsistency in volume III pages 104, rebound in quarter calf, marbled boards, with early handwritten key loosely inserted involume I.   Jarndyce Antiquarian Booksellers   CLXC - 68 2011   £950

Lamb, Caroline 1785-1828 *Glenarvon.* London: Henry Colburn, 1816, Second edition; 3 volumes, 12mo., contemporary half calf, crimson labels, slight rubbing, armorial bookplates of Henry Theophilus Clements, very good.   Jarndyce Antiquarian Booksellers   CLXC - 69 2011   £650

Lamb, Charles 1775-1834 *Elia. (Essays Which have Appeared Under that Signature in the London Magazine).* London: Printed for Taylor and Hessey, 1823, First edition; small 8vo., pages (4) 341 (1), soundly rebound in blue cloth lettered gilt at spine, pages 333/334 briefly cropped at corner not affecting text, neat contemporary ownership signature at top of titlepage, else very good, second state with 2 line address on titlepage.   Any Amount of Books   May 29 2011 - A38794 2011 $213

Lamb, Charles   1775-1834   *The Essays of Elia.*   New York: 1851,   (i)-viii (x-xii) (1)-193, blank (iv) 169 pages, embossed cover design, blank circle surrounded by four small and four large ellipses supporting a dodechadron of arches (rose window) centered in a panel surrounded by a plethora of maze-lie squiggles, cornered by (1851) geometrics, diapered backstrip, all this embossment mildly rubbed, but at the right angle, design strikes the eye.   Bookworm & Silverfish   665 - 86   2011 $75

Lamb, Charles   1775-1834   *A Masque of Days.*   London: Cassell & Co., 1901,   First edition; 4to., pages 40, illustrations in color, original cloth backed pictorial boards, edges rubbed, corners little rounded, nice, bright copy.   R. F. G. Hollett & Sons Antiquarian Booksellers   170 - 170   2011   £150

Lamb, Charles   1775-1834   *A Tale of Rosamund Gray and Old Blind Margaret.*   London: Printed for Lee & Hurst, 1798,   First edition, 2nd issue; full brown morocco by Zaehnsdorf, gilt dentelles, all edges gilt, very good, handsome, scarce.   Jarndyce Antiquarian Booksellers   CXCI - 248   2011   £1500

Lamb, Charles   1775-1834   *Tales from Shakespeare.*   London: printed for Thomas Hodgkins, 1807,   First edition, first issue, with printer's imprint on verso of page 235 of volume I and with ad at end of volume II giving the earlier Hanway Street addresss for the Juvenile Library; 172 x 108mm., 2 volumes, very fine citron morocco handsomely gilt by W. Pratt, stamp signed, covers framed in gilt with French fillet border, inner panel with double fillets and outwear extending fleuron cornerpieces, raised bands, spines ornately gilt in compartments featuring scrolling foliate cornerpieces and lozenge centerpiece with black inlaid (?) circle and fleuron elements at ends and sides, blue morocco title and volume labels with scrolling foliate cornerpieces, elaborate gilt inner dentelles, all edges gilt, in suede lined morocco edged marbled paper slipcase, with 20 plates printed on special thick paper after designs by William Mulready and said to have been engraved by William Blake; spines slightly and evenly faded to a pleasant caramel color, front board of first volume with few small spots, breath of foxing in isolated places but a wonderful copy, text and plates clean, fresh and bright, lovely decorative binding unworn.   Phillip J. Pirages   59 - 250   2011 $2500

Lamb, Charles   1775-1834   *Tales from Shakespeare.*   S. T. Fremantle, 1899,   First deluxe edition thus; full vellum gilt with flat spine, pages xxviii, 372, top edge gilt, untrimmed with 15 plates by Robert Anning Bell, silk marker, fine, clean copy.   R. F. G. Hollett & Son Antiquarian Booksellers   General Catalogue Summer 2010 - 826   2011   £180

Lamb, Charles   1775-1834   *Tales from Shakespeare.*   London: Ernest Nister, circa, 1905,   Original pictorial blue cloth gilt over bevelled boards, extremities little worn, pages 320, all edges gilt, gilt with 6 color plates, 70 half tone illustrations by W. Paget, neat inscription, scattered foxing, very good.   R. F. G. Hollett & Sons Antiquarian Booksellers   170 - 377   2011   £45

Lamb, M. C.   *Leather Dressing, Including Dyeing, Staining and Finishing.*   Anglo American Technical Co. Ltd., 1909,   Second edition; large 8vo., xx, 498 pages, frontispiece, plates, text illustrations, 194 swatches of dyed leather samples, very good in original gilt lettered maroon cloth, some slight rubbing to covers, neat repair to inner front hinge, scarce.   Ken Spelman Rare Books   68 - 101   2011   £220

Lamb, Wally   *I Know This Much is True.*   New York: Regan Books, 1998,   First edition; fine in fine dust jacket, signed by author dated 6-11-98.   Bella Luna Books   May 29 2011 - 2237   2011 $110

Lambert, Fred   *Bygone Days of the Old West.*   Kansas City: 1948,   Autograph edition, limited to 200 copies with original pen and ink sketch by Lambert laid in; 487 pages, including 16 page range dictionary and index, over 1300 drawings by author, issued without dust jacket, boards with some rubbing and scratches, internally clean, sketch has crease across bottom corner, warmly inscribed by author and 10 years later inscribed again to recipient's son on her passing.   Dumont Maps & Books of the West   113 - 37   2011 $500

Lammon, Dwight P.   *The Pottery of Zuni Pueblo.*   Santa Fe: 2008,   604 pages, illustrations, near fine in dust jacket, heavy quarto volume, illustrated with 1200 examples reproduced.   Dumont Maps & Books of the West   112 - 53   2011 $175

Lamster, J. C.   *"The Indies" Giving a Description of the Native Population of Netherlands India & Of Its Civilization.*   Haarlem: 1929,   159 (1) errata pages, folio, 144 color pictures laid down, original binding, bit shaken (front joint loosening), bit of edge wear, small chip to front cover.   Bookworm & Silverfish   665 - 71   2011 $75

Lamy, Bernard   *Traitez de Mechanique, de l'Equilibre des Solides et des Liqueurs...*   Paris: Andre Pralard, 1679,   First edition; 12mo., pages (ii) title and permission leaf, 263 (misprinted 163), (1), title with woodcut vignette, numerous woodcut diagrams to text, ornamental head and tailpieces, folding engraved plate , contemporary sprinkled calf, gilt panelled spine, sprinkled edges, minor repair to joints, otherwise excellent copy in contemporary condition, engraved Trotter bookplate, inscription noting purchase at auction in Jan. 1712.   Simon Finch Rare Books   Zero - 108   2011   £800

Lancaster Records or Leaves from Local History. Lancaster: G. C. Clark, 1869, First edition; original blue cloth gilt, pages xv, 338, xviii, all edges gilt, folding plan, folding leaf of illustrations, scattered foxing, scarce.   R. F. G. Hollett & Son Antiquarian Booksellers   General Catalogue Summer 2010 - 1457   2011   £120

Lancaster, J. Y. *The Iron and Steel Industry by West Cumberland.*   Workington & Barrow: British Steel Corporation, 1977, First edition; original cloth, gilt, dust jacket (little worn), pages xii, 198, numerous illustrations and graphs.   R. F. G. Hollett & Son Antiquarian Booksellers   173 - 679   2011   £40

Lancaster, Marie Jaqueline   *Brian Howard. Portrait of a Failure.*   London: Blond, 1968, First edition; portrait, pages xx, 639 16 pages of photos, loosely inserted are 10 signed cards from author to Mrs. Newbury, bookplate of Evy Newbury, she has pasted in flower card on verso of half title and few slight marks to prelims, else book is very good.   Any Amount of Books   May 29 2011 - A70276   2011 $213

Lancaster, Osbert   *Progress at Pelvis Bay.*   London: John Murray, 1936, First edition; original cloth backed pictorial boards, matching dust jacket little rubbed and dusty, pages vi, 70, line drawings by author, pictorial endpapers, from the library of A. J. A. Symons with his small label, part of original wraparound band loosely inserted.   R. F. G. Hollett & Son Antiquarian Booksellers   General Catalogue Summer 2010 - 828   2011   £85

Landacre, Paul   *California Hills.*   Los Angeles: Bruce McCallsiter, 1931, Limited to 500 copies signed by Landacre, this being number 42; large quarto, original blue and orange patterned boards with pictorial paper label on front cover, wood engravings, signed by artist.   Heritage Book Shop   Booth A12 51st NY International Antiquarian Book Fair April 8-10 2011 - 83   2011 $4000

Landacre, Paul   *California Hills and Other Wood Engravings by Paul Landacre from the Original Blocks.*   Los Angeles: Bruce McCallister, 1931, Limited edition, signed by Landacre, no. 138 of 500 copies; 4to., unpaginated, 19ff., 14 woodcut prints, 1 small print on colophon, original orange and gray patterned paper boards, printed and engraved cover title label, housed in custom slipcase, quarter brown morocco over marbled boards, folding chemise, beautiful, fine.   Jeff Weber Rare Books   163 - 115   2011 $6000

Landfall.   New Zealand: Caxton Press, 1947-1974, June 1947-March 1974, virtually complete run, 108 issues, original wrappers, very good, also present are indices for volumes 1-5 1947-1951 and volumes 11-15 1957-1961.   I. D. Edrich   May 26 2011 - 97746   2011 $671

Landman, J. H.   *Human Sterilization: the History of the Sexual Sterilization Movement.*   New York: Macmillan, 1932, First edition; 8vo., pages xviii, 341, original publisher's dark blue boards lettered light blue, very good.   Any Amount of Books   May 29 2011 - A64691   2011 $238

Landon, Letitia Elizabeth   *Ethel Churchill; or the Two Brides.*   London: Henry Colburn, 1837, First edition; 3 volumes, half title volume I, uncut in contemporary drab boards, maroon cloth spines, paper labels, spines faded and slightly darkened, labels little darkened, small booklabels of Lady Mary Stewart and M. F. Montgomery, Convoy, good plus, internally very clean set.   Jarndyce Antiquarian Booksellers   CLXC - 72   2011   £750

Landon, Letitia Elizabeth   *The Golden Violet with Its Tales of Romance and Chivalry and Other Poems.*   London: Longman &c, 1827, First edition; engraved frontispiece, contemporary full calf, boards decorated with elaborate borders in blind within triple ruled gilt borders, spine gilt in compartments, spine worn but sound, label missing, signed Harriet Mackenzie Shettle(?) on leading blank.   Jarndyce Antiquarian Booksellers   CLXC - 73   2011   £110

Landon, Letitia Elizabeth   *The Improvisatrice; and Other Poems.*   London: Hurst, Robinson & Co., 1824, Second edition; frontispiece and engraved title and little spotted, additional printed title, contemporary half calf, spine ruled and with devices in gilt, tan leather label, following inner hinge cracking, bit rubbed and worn, good sound copy, signed presentation copy, pasted to leading pastedown, engraved presentation label completed in ink "to Rosina Lytton Bulwer from L.E.L. 1831", also with later booklabel of Kenneth Rae.   Jarndyce Antiquarian Booksellers   CLXC - 74   2011   £225

Landon, Letitia Elizabeth   *Poetical Works.*   London: Longman &c, 1860, 2 volumes, half title volume I, vignette titles after Richard Doyle, final ad leaf volume II, chocolate brown endpapers with ads on pastedowns, untrimmed in original purple wavy grained cloth, blocked in blind, spines lettered gilt, spines faded, boards slightly marked, good plus, tight copy.   Jarndyce Antiquarian Booksellers   CLXC - 76   2011   £85

Landon, Letitia Elizabeth   *Poetical Works.*   London: Longman, Brown, Greens & Longman, 1844, 4 volumes, half titles, fronts little browned, ads on endpapers, untrimmed in original blue cloth, spines lettered in gilt, spines uniformly faded, slight rubbing, bookeseller's ticket; Godwin, Bath, later booklabels of Ian Jack, very good.   Jarndyce Antiquarian Booksellers   CLXC - 75   2011   £125

Landon, Letitia Elizabeth   *Romance and Reality.*   London: Richard Bentley, 1848, First edition; contemporary half calf, spine with raised gilt bands, maroon leather label, very good.   Jarndyce Antiquarian Booksellers   CLXC - 77   2011   £85

Landon, Letitia Elizabeth *The Troubadour; Catalogue of Pictures and Historical Sketches.* London: Hurst, Robinson & Co., 1825, First edition; engraved title, additional printed title, slight damp staining in prelims, contemporary half vellum by John Jones of Liverpool, spine finely tooled in gilt, maroon leather label, blue paper covered boards, very slight rubbing, good plus, handsome copy.   Jarndyce Antiquarian Booksellers   CLXC - 78 2011   £125

Landon, Letitia Elizabeth *The Venetian Bracelet.* London: Longman &c., 1829, Engraved frontispiece, initial blank creased, uncut in original drab boards, paper label, spine and label little chipped, good plus, internally clean.   Jarndyce Antiquarian Booksellers   CLXC - 79 2011   £150

Lane, E. W. *Arabic-English Lexicon.* Cambridge: Islamic Texts Society, 1984, First edition; 2 volumes, large 8vo., pages xxxii, 3062, very good+ in slightly used and slightly worn, very good dust jackets.   Any Amount of Books   May 29 2011 - A75839 2011 $383

Lanes, Selma G. *The Art of Maurice Sendak.* New York: Harry Abrams, 1980, First edition; pages 78, 261 illustrations, including 94 color plates and 3 folding plates, mint, publisher's original mailing box.   R. F. G. Hollett & Sons Antiquarian Booksellers   170 - 379 2011   £150

Lang, Andrew *The All Sorts of Stories Book.* London: Longmans, Green and Co., 1911, First edition; original purple cloth gilt, spine rather faded, pages xvi, 377, 5 colored plates by H. J. Ford, few spots to endpapers.   R. F. G. Hollett & Sons Antiquarian Booksellers   170 - 387 2011   £65

Lang, Andrew *The Blue Poetry Book.* London: Longman, Green and Co., 1891, First edition; original blue cloth gilt, extremities worn, pages xx, 351, numerous illustrations.   R. F. G. Hollett & Sons Antiquarian Booksellers   170 - 382 2011   £35

Lang, Andrew *The Book of Romance.* London: Longmans, Green and Co., 1902, First edition; original blue pictorial cloth, gilt, extremities worn, spine rather creased and chipped at head, pages xiv, 384, numerous illustrations by H. J. Ford and Lancelot Speed, slight adhesion damage to first plate and its tissue, rear joint cracked.   R. F. G. Hollett & Sons Antiquarian Booksellers   170 - 383 2011   £65

Lang, Andrew *The Book of Romance.* London: Longmans Green and Co., 1902, First edition; original blue pictorial cloth gilt, extremities worn, spine rather creased and chipped at head, pages xiv, 384, numerous illustrations by H. J. Ford and Lancelot Speed, slight adhesion damage to first plate and its tissue, rear joint cracked.   R. F. G. Hollett & Sons Antiquarian Booksellers   170 - 383 2011   £65

Lang, Andrew *The Book of Romance.* London: Longmans, Green and Co., 1903, New impression; Original blue cloth gilt extra, trifle worn, lower board rather marked, pages xiv, 384, all edges gilt with 8 color and 35 black and white plates, 8 text illustrations by H. J. Ford.   R. F. G. Hollett & Sons Antiquarian Booksellers   170 - 388 2011   £120

Lang, Andrew *The Brown Fairy Book.* London: Longmans, Green and Co., 1904, First edition; original brown pictorial cloth gilt, fore-edges pf boards rather damped, pages xiii, 350, all edges gilt, 8 color and numerous other illustrations by H. J. Ford, upper jont cracking, otherwise nice, clean copy.   R. F. G. Hollett & Sons Antiquarian Booksellers   170 - 389 2011   £180

Lang, Andrew *The Crimson Fairy Book.* London: Longmans, Green and Co., 1903, First edition; pages xii, 371, original crimson pictorial cloth gilt, spine rather faded, trifling wear to extremities, pages xii, 371, all edges gilt, 8 color plates and numerous other illustrations by H. J. Ford, tissue to frontispiece, little creased and browned, faintly offset on to title, but very good with series prospectus loosely inserted.   R. F. G. Hollett & Sons Antiquarian Booksellers   170 - 390 2011   £250

Lang, Andrew *The Green Fairy Book.* London: Longmans, Green and Co., 1892, First edition; original green pictorial cloth, gilt, faint spines of wear to extremities, pages xiv, 366, (ii), all edges gilt, numerous illustrations by H. J. Ford, near fine.   R. F. G. Hollett & Sons Antiquarian Booksellers   170 - 391 2011   £450

Lang, Andrew *Johnny Nut and the Golden Goose.* London: Longmans, Green and Co., 1887, Large 4too 8vo., original decorated cloth gilt over bevelled boards, extremities trifle worn, pages 45, top edge gilt, printed on one side of each leaf, illustrations and decorations by A. M. Lynen, little light foxing in places, very nice, tight copy.   R. F. G. Hollett & Sons Antiquarian Booksellers   170 - 384 2011   £175

Lang, Andrew *Prince Charles Andrew.* Paris: 1900, Limited to 350 numbered copies on Japanese paper with two series of plates, one in separate container; very good, soft cover.   I. D. Edrich   May 26 2011 - 76042 2011 $419

Lang, Andrew *The Red Book of Animal Stories.* London: Longmans Green and Co., 1899, First edition; original red pictorial cloth gilt extra, spine little faded and slightly worn at head, pages xvii, 379, all edges gilt, 32 plates by H. J. Ford.   R. F. G. Hollett & Sons Antiquarian Booksellers   170 - 393 2011   £75

Lang, Andrew *The Red Book of Heroes.* London: Longmans, Green and Co., 1908, First edition; original pictorial cloth gilt extra, spine lightly faded, pages xiv, 368, all edges gilt, 8 colored plates, few spots to prelims, lower joint cracked, very good, bright copy.   R. F. G. Hollett & Sons Antiquarian Booksellers   170 - 385 2011   £75

Lang, Andrew *The Red Fairy Book.* London: Longmans, 1890, 8vo., red gilt pictorial cloth, all edges gilt, some cover soil, one leaf frayed and worn on edges, else tight and very good, 1st edition, illustrations by H. J. Ford in black and white.   Aleph-Bet Books, Inc.   95 - 318 2011 $975

Lang, Andrew *The Red Romance Book.* London: Longmans, Green and Co., 1905, First edition; original red pictorial cloth gilt, spine rather faded, fore edges of boards damped, pages xii, 372, 8 color plates and numerous illustrations by H. J. Ford.   R. F. G. Hollett & Sons Antiquarian Booksellers   170 - 386 2011   £45

Lang, Jeanie *Stories from the Iliad or the siege of Troy, Told to the Children.* London: T. C. & E. J. Jack, n.d., 1907?, Small 8vo., original limp cloth, edges trifle frayed, pages vii, 119, with 8 color plates by Charles Robinson, very scarce.   R. F. G. Hollett & Son Antiquarian Booksellers   General Catalogue Summer 2010 - 565 2011   £50

Langdon-Davies, John *A Short History of Women.* London: Jonathan Cape, 1928, First British edition; 8vo., (361) pages, original blue cloth, gilt lettered spine, index, spine sunned, otherwise fine.   Paulette Rose Fine and Rare Books   32 - 107 2011 $95

Langdon, Mary, Pseud. *Ida May: a Story of Things Actual and Possible.* Boston: Phillips, Sampson and Co., 1854, First edition; original purple cloth, slightly faded, very good.   Jarndyce Antiquarian Booksellers   CLXC - 83 2011   £150

Langdon, Mary, Pseud. *Ida May.* London: Ward, Lock and Tyler, 1870, Reissue; small repair to lower margin of title, some foxing, contemporary half black sheep, spine and edges rubbed, good, sound copy.   Jarndyce Antiquarian Booksellers   CLXC - 84 2011   £40

Lange, Jakob E. *Flora Agaricina Danica.* Copenhagen: 1935-1940, 200 chromolithographed plates, 4to., pages (3), xxiv, 90; 105; 96; 119; 105 (12), binder's buckram, fine, plates are superb, the copy of Maurice Walters, inserted A.S. postcard from author to Walters, proof for volume 4 titlepage, order form for subscription and two letters from publication office to Mr. Walters.   Raymond M. Sutton, Jr.   May 26 2011 - 25548 2011 $1500

Langley, John *They Tried to Crucify Me or the Smoke Screen of the Cumberlands.* Pikeville: 1929, 256 pages, very good with library emobssed seal on titlepage.   Bookworm & Silverfish   668 - 128 2011 $75

Langsdorff, Georg Heinrich Von *Voyages and Travels in Various Parts of the World.* London: printed for Henry Colburn, 1813, First English edition; 2 volumes, quarto, frontispiece, folding map, 19 engraved plates, contemporary English sprinkled half calf over marbled boards, frm the library of Sir Robert Peel's First Lord of the Admiralty.   Heritage Book Shop   Booth A12 51st NY International Antiquarian Book Fair April 8-10 2011 - 84 2011 $20,000

Lanier, Sterling E. *Hiero's Journey.* Radnor: Chilton Book Co., 1973, First edition; octavo, cloth backed boards.   L. W. Currey, Inc.   124 - 233 2011 $100

Lankester, Edwin *Half Hours with the Microscope.* London: W. H. Allen & Co., 1890, Seventeenth edition; small 8vo., original red cloth gilt, pages xx, 130, colored frontispiece, 8 lithographed plates and 30 text illustrations.   R. F. G. Hollett & Son Antiquarian Booksellers   General Catalogue Summer 2010 - 1012 2011   £45

Lankester, Mrs. *A Plain and Easy Account of the British Ferns; Together with their Classification, Arrangement of Genera, Structure and Functions...*   Robert Hardwicke, circa, 1860, Small 8vo., xv, (i), 108 (4) pages ads, frontispiece, 8 hand colored plates, very good in original blind and gilt stamped dark green cloth, all edges gilt, some slight foxing and small tear without loss to front endpaper.   Ken Spelman Rare Books   68 - 153 2011   £60

Lansdale, Joe R. *Tight Little Stitches in a Dead Man's Back.* Eugene: Pulphouse Pub., 1992, First separate edition; small octavo, imitation leather.   L. W. Currey, Inc.   124 - 242 2011 $65

Lanting, Frans *Madagascar: a World Out of Time.* New York: Aperture, 1990, First edition; 4to., pages 143, color photos by Lanting, who has signed the half title, fine in fine dust jacket, very slight handling wear.   Any Amount of Books   May 29 2011 - A72289298 2011 $298

Larcom, Lucy *An Idyl of Work.* Boston: James R. Osgood & Co., 1875, First edition, one of 950 copies; ix, 183 pages, 8vo., original brick publisher's cloth with gilt lettered spine, gilt stamped on front panel showing a woman dressed in a classical robe, holding a quill (?), blindstamped on back panel, some wear to extremities, hinges weak, pale contemporary inscription, all in all, decent, good copy.   Paulette Rose Fine and Rare Books   32 - 108 2011 $150

Larder, Fred T. *Thee Ivanhoe Review.* Rotherdam: Advertiser Office, 1898-1899, Volume 1 No. 1 to volume 2 No. 3, small 4to., later binders cloth, pages 144, 36, well illustrated with portraits, photos, titlepage to volume 1 bound in out of order, very scarce.   R. F. G. Hollett & Son Antiquarian Booksellers   General Catalogue Summer 2010 - 1573 2011   £140

Lardner, Ring W. *Bib Ballads.* Chicago: P F. Volland, 1915, One small smudge on page with book's foreword, otherwise very fine in close to fine publisher's box, scarce thus, box notoriously fragile, prone to splitting and fading, and this one, despite three small splits to top edge, the nicest copy we have seen. Ken Lopez Bookseller 154 - 92 2011 $1250

Lardner, Ring W. *Gee! It's a Wonderful Game Song.* New York: Remick, 1911, Popular edition; folio, pages 6, pictorial wrappers, edges somewhat chipped, otherwise very good. Second Life Books Inc. 174 - 225 2011 $300

Larkin, Philip 1922-1985 *The Brynmor Jones Annual Library Reports.* Hull: University Press, 1954-1973, 18 pamphlet (of 19, lacking 1962-63 issue), 8vo., varying from pages 4 to 22, paper or card stapled wrappers, various colors, internally very bright, some light wear to issue 1 an soiling to lower wrapper of issue 18, issue 3 missing wrapper. Simon Finch Rare Books Zero - 326 2011 £700

Larkin, Philip 1922-1985 *The North Ship Poems.* London: Fortune Press, 1945, First edition; light foxing to prelims, final few leaves and edges, pages (iv), 36, foolscap 8vo., original first issue black boards, gilt lettering to backstrip, untrimmed, pink board slipcase, good. Blackwell Rare Books B166 - 169 2011 £450

Larkin, Philip 1922-1985 *The Whitsun Weddings.* London: Faber and Faber, 1971, First edition; 8vo., pages 46, exceptionally clean, original cream printed wrappers, with red and green horizontals of the Faber paper covered edition, carefully proteted in tissue, bumped and lightly discolored at spine, inscribed by Larkin. Simon Finch Rare Books Zero - 328 2011 £350

Larrey, Dominique Jean *Observations on Wounds, and Their Complications by Erysipelas, Gangrene and Tetanus and on the Principal Diseases and Injuries of the Head, Ear and Eye.* Philadelphia: Mielke & Biddle, 1832, Small 4to., viii, 332 pages, 2 plates, original speckled calf, neatly rebacked, gilt spine rules, black morocco spine label, original endleaves preserved, short period inscription on front pastedown and previous owner's inked signature, embossed stamp on title, very good, from the Medical Library of Dr. Clare Gray Peterson. Jeff Weber Rare Books 162 - 182 2011 $650

Larsell, Olof *The Comparative Anatomy and Histology of the Cerebellum from Myxinoids through Birds.* Minneapolis: University of Minnesota Press, 1967, First edition; 4to., viii, (ix-x), 291 pages, 242 numbered figures, index, original red cloth, gilt stamped spine title, dust jacket, fine, from the Medical Library of Dr. Clare Gray Peterson. Jeff Weber Rare Books 162 - 184 2011 $125

Larsell, Olof *The Comparative Anatomy and Histology of the Cerebellum from Monotremes through Apes.* Minneapolis: University of Minnesota Press, 1970, First edition; 4to., v, (ii), 269 pages, 233 numbered figures, original blue cloth, gilt stamped spine title, dust jacket, top jacket edge bit worn, near fine, from the Medical Library of Dr. Clare Gray Peterson. Jeff Weber Rare Books 162 - 184 2011 $125

Larsson, Stieg *The Girl with the Dragon Tattoo.* London: Maclehouse/Quercus, 2008, First British edition and first language edition; fore edge nick to two pages, else fine in very near fine dust jacket with slight scratch to rear panel. Ken Lopez Bookseller 154 - 93 2011 $1250

Larsson, Stieg *The Girl with the Dragon Tattoo.* London: Maclehose/Quercus, 2008, First British edition, advance reading copy; fine in wrappers. Ken Lopez Bookseller 154 - 94 2011 $2500

Lasena, Pietro *Dell'antico Ginnasio Napoletano. Opera Posthuma.* Naples: a spese di C. Porpora, 1688, Second edition; 4to., (20), 229, (3) pages, plus engraved title, titlepage cropped, 17th century mottled calf, gilt fillet on covers, spine gilt in compartments, from the library of the Earls of Macclesfield at Shirburn Castle. Maggs Bros. Ltd. 1440 - 123 2011 £850

Laskey, J. C. *A Description of the Series of Medals Struck at the National Medal Mint by Order of Napoleon Bonaparte Commemorating the most Remarkable Battles and Events During His Dynasty.* London: H. R. Young, 1818, First edition; tall 8vo., neatly rebound in red cloth with leather spine label lettered gilt, pages xiii, 239, frontispiece, engravings in text in style of Bewick, very slight foxing to prelims, otherwise very good+. Any Amount of Books May 29 2011 - A34480 2011 $272

Laski, Harold *A Century of Municipal Progress.* London: Allen & Unwin, 1935, First edition; tall 8vo., original cloth, gilt, pages 512, excellent copy. R. F. G. Hollett & Son Antiquarian Booksellers 175 - 802 2011 £35

Lassay, Madaillan De Lesparre, Marquise De *Histoire de Tullie fille de Ciceron.* Paris: Chez Pierre Prault, 1726, First edition; 12mo., 281 pages, 5 pages, full contemporary calf, gilt decorated spine, bands, contrasting gilt lettered title label, some binding wear, but holding, otherwise very good, scarce. Paulette Rose Fine and Rare Books 32 - 109 2011 $425

Latham, John *A General History of Birds.* Winchester: Jacob and Johnson, 1821-1828, New edition; 193 hand colored copper engraved plates after Latham (minor offsetting from text to some plates, only occasional foxing to plates, plates near fine), 4to., contemporary three quarter leather over marbled boards, spines beautifully replaced with gilt decorated polished calf, rubbing to marbled boards, several corners showing, black stain to inside margin of a page of text, occasional foxing to text, sometimes heavy, ex-libris Thomas Perry, marbled endpapers. Raymond M. Sutton, Jr. May 26 2011 - 50931 2011 $11,000

Lathbury, Thomas *Guy Fawkes; or the Gunpowder Treason, A.D. 1605.* London: John W. Parker, 1840, Second edition; original blindstamped cloth, attractively rebacked in matching levant morocco gilt, pages viii, 150, (vi), folding facsimile. R. F. G. Hollett & Son Antiquarian Booksellers 175 - 803 2011 £120

Lathrop, Harriet Mulford Stone 1844-1924 *Five Little Peppers and How they Grew.* Boston: D. Lothrop and Co., 1880, First edition, first issue; 8vo., pictorial cloth, 410 pages + 4 pages ads, some over soil and scattered foxing, light shelfwear, very good+. Aleph-Bet Books, Inc. 95 - 535 2011 $750

Latimer, Hugh *A Moste Faithfull Sermo(n) Preached Before Kynes Most Excelle(n)te Maiestye and hys most honorable Councels, in his Court at Westminster...* Colophon: Imprinted at London by Iohn Day dwelling over Aldersgate beneth S. Martins..., 1550, First edition; somewhat browned, few tiny stains, final leaf soiled and rather frayed (with loss to outer blank edge), little fraying to bottom blank corner of final few leaves, pages (112), 8vo., modern sprinkled calf, spine with raised bands, good. Blackwell Rare Books B166 - 62 2011 £3500

Laud, William *A Relation of the Conference Between William Lawd...and Mr. Fisher the Jesuite.* London: printed by Richard Badger, 1639, Folio, pages (xxiv), 388, later dark brown turkey, spine panel gilt extra (7 compartments tooled in four designs arranged symmetrically about the centre), boards gilt panelled with double corner pieces out with the elaborately gilt rolled outer frame of centre panel, board edges elaborately decorative roll gilt 'Dutch-comb-swirl' endpapers, all edges gilt, fawn and white sewn endbands, joints and corners conserved, early 21st century by Chris Weston, lightly browned, dust soiled in places, corner of f.e.p. excised, old leather little bit rubbed and chipped, 19th century armorial bookplate of "James Bank M.A./Linc. Coll. Oxon" on front pastedown, from the collection of Christopher Ernest Weston 1947-2010. Unsworths Booksellers 24 - 29 2011 £325

Lauder, T. D. *The Book of Parrots.* Edinburgh: Fraser and London: Smith Elder, 1834, First edition thus; small 8vo., pages x, 170, 24 page publisher's ads, complete 36 plates, 35 of which are hand colored and frontispiece, book very clean with plates in great condition and hand coloring in fine state, bound in later boards covered in scarlet watred silk with leather spine label lettered gilt, all edges gilt, very good. Any Amount of Books May 26 2011 - A75470 2011 $503

Lauderdale, James Maitland, 8th Earl of *An Inquiry into the Nature and Origin of Public Wealth and Into the Means and Causes of Its Increase.* Edinburgh: Archibald Constable & T. N. Longman & O. Rees, 1804, 8vo., (8), 482 pages, folding chart, full contemporary calf, gilt stamped red leather spine label, rebacked, corners showing, edges worn, contemporary notations on final blank, very good. Jeff Weber Rare Books 163 - 42 2011 $700

Laufer, Berthold *Jade.* Chicago: Field Museum of Natural History, 1912, Large 8vo., original black cloth, gilt, pages xiv, 370, top edge gilt, with 68 plates, 204 text figures. R. F. G. Hollett & Son Antiquarian Booksellers 177 - 534 2011 £150

Laufer, Berthold *Jade. A Study in Chinese Archaeology and Religion.* Chicago: Field Museum of Natural Hsitory, 1912, Large 8vo., original black cloth gilt, pages xiv, 370, top edge gilt, 68 plates and 240 text figures. R. F. G. Hollett & Son Antiquarian Booksellers General Catalogue Summer 2010 - 235 2011 £150

Laurent, J. *New Familiar Abenakis and English Dialogues.* Quebec: Printed by Leger Brousseau, 1834, Original edition; disbound, pages 10-230, index, 12mo., 18 x 14 cm., soiling to blank pages in front and rear end edges worn and nicked, pages 33/34 has top corner torn off not affecting text. Schooner Books Ltd. 96 - 5 2011 $200

Lauret, Christophe *La Doctrine des Temps et de l'Astronomie Universelle Contenant la Demonstration du Vray Nombre....* Paris: Cramoisy, 1610, Folio, ff. (8) 133 (=135, several mispaginations etc.) 1), large woodcut printer's device on titlepage, woodcut headpieces, tailpieces, initials, mid 19th century calf by Hatton in Manchester, triple blind fillet on boards, blind fleuron in boards' corner and in spine compartments, morocco lettering piece, red edges, f. 58 stained, small hole with loss of text in f. 126, few manuscript annotations in margin, dedication (signed to Clement VIII by Cayet bound at end), from the library of the Earls of Macclesfield at Shirburn Castle. Maggs Bros. Ltd. 1440 - 124 2011 £6000

Laver, James *Tommy Apple and Peggy Pear.* London: Jonathan Cape, 1936, First edition; 4to., cloth, fine in slightly worn dust jacket. Aleph-Bet Books, Inc. 95 - 429 2011 $150

Lavererie, Raymond De *Alphabet.* Paris: Tolmer editeur, 1923, First edition; 12mo., blank paper wrappers, clean copy with faint fold in first few pages, color paper dust jacket with some dusting, book loose in wrappers, twenty pages within, each with tear and charming pochoir illustrations, text and 10 pochoir pictures work their way through a full 26 letter alphabet, uncommon.   Jo Ann Reisler, Ltd.   86 - 8   2011 $475

Law, Ernest *The History of Hampton Court Palace.* London: George Bell & Sons, 1888-1891, Second edition; 3 volumes, thick square 8vo., original decorated brown cloth gilt, rather faded, spines little frayed at head, pages xxiv, 376, (i), xvi, 312, (iv); xxiii, 566, (ii), frontispiece, plan, map and 24 illustrations, little browning or spotting, mainly to endpapers and prelims, one joint tender, otherwise very good set.   R. F. G. Hollett & Son Antiquarian Booksellers   175 - 806   2011   £120

Law, Ernest *The History of Hampton Court Palace...* London: George Bell & Sons, 1888-1891, Second edition; 3 volumes, thick square 8vo., original decorated brown cloth, gilt, rather faded, spines little frayed at head, pages xxiv, 376, (i); xvi, 312, (iv); xxiii, 566, (ii), frontispiece portrait, plan, map and 124 illustrations, little browning or spotting mainly to endpapers and prelims, one joint tender, otherwise very good set.   R. F. G. Hollett & Son Antiquarian Booksellers   General Catalogue Summer 2010 - 1459   2011   £120

Law, Ernest *The Royal Gallery of Hampton Court Illustrated.* London: George Bell and Sons, 1898, Thick 8vo. original cream buckram gilt with royal arms in gilt on upper board, discolored and soiled, pages xxxviii (ii), 336, top edge gilt, untrimmed with 100 plates, title in red and black, good, sound copy, scarce.   R. F. G. Hollett & Son Antiquarian Booksellers   175 - 807   2011   £150

Law, Ernest *The Royal Gallery of Hampton Court Illustrated.* London: George Bernard Son, 1898, Thick 8vo., original cream buckram gilt, royal arms in gilt on upper board, discolored an soiled, pages xxxviii, ii), 336, top edge gilt, untrimmed with 100 plates, title in red and black, good sound copy, scarce.   R. F. G. Hollett & Son Antiquarian Booksellers   General Catalogue Summer 2010 - 237   2011   £150

Law, William *A Collection of Letters on the Most Interesting and Important Subjects and on Several Occasions.* London: printed for J. Richardson in Pater Noster Row, 1760, First edition; title slightly soiled, editor's ad signed, with two final ad leaves torn across each page and roughly repaired, (4), 220, (4) pages, modern paper wrappers, printed paper label on upper cover,.   Anthony W. Laywood   May 26 2011 - 21745   2011 $92

Law, William *A Short but Sufficient Confutation of the Reverend Dr. Warburton's Protected Defence (as he calls it) of Christianity in his Divine Legation of Moses.* London: printed for J. Richardson, in Pater-noster Row, 1757, First edition; lacks half title, 4 small spots on title, (2), 155, (1) pages, modern paper wrappers, printed paper label on upper cover.   Anthony W. Laywood   May 26 2011 - 21744   2011 $134

Lawless, Emily *With the Wild Geese.* London: Isbister & Co., 1902, First edition; half title, title in red and black, uncut in original olive green cloth, blocked and lettered in light green, lettered in gilt, Preston armorial bookplate, very good, bright.   Jarndyce Antiquarian Booksellers   CLXC - 85   2011   £65

Lawrance, D. M. *The College of Estate Management 1919-1969.* The College, 1969, Original cloth, gilt, dust jacket, pages (vi), 92, (vii), color plate of letters patent and 21 illustrations.   R. F. G. Hollett & Son Antiquarian Booksellers   General Catalogue Summer 2010 - 610   2011   £30

Lawrence, David Herbert   1885-1930 *Amores.* New York: B. W. Huebsch, 1916, First American edition; 8vo., pages (xii), 116, internally fine, original brown cloth boards, spine and upper board lettered in gold, top edge gilt, original cream dust jacket printed in black, dust jacket expertly restored at spine and top edge, small tear not affecting text to upper panel, small bookplate of Charles Edmund Merrill Jr. to pastedown, bookplate of Constance M. and Karl Andrew Muir.   Simon Finch Rare Books   Zero - 329   2011   £500

Lawrence, David Herbert   1885-1930 *Bay.* Westminster: The Beaumont Press, 1919, First edition, in unrecorded trial binding with vignettes uncolored; 8vo., pages 48 plus tipped in dedication leaf, vignettes by Anne Estelle Rice, original decorative paper boards with blue grey paper backstrip, upper cover and spine lettered in gilt, ornaments stamped in gold, fine.   Simon Finch Rare Books   Zero - 332   2011   £700

Lawrence, David Herbert   1885-1930 *Birds, Beasts and Flowers.* London: Martin Secker, 1923, First English edition; 8vo., pages 208, partly unopened, upper edge cut and dyed black, internally bright and clean, black quarter cloth and original yellow paper boards, with yellow paper label printed in black to spine, some shelfwear and bump to upper and lower spine, original green dust jacket printed in black, short tears, wear to extremities, strengthened and chips to top upper cover not affecting text, custom made blue quarter leather slipcase and cloth chemise, fine in very good plus or better dust jacket.   Simon Finch Rare Books   Zero - 334   2011   £375

Lawrence, David Herbert 1885-1930 *England, My England.* London: Martin Secker, 1924, First edition; nearly fine.   Lupack Rare Books   May 26 2011 - ABE1117101872 2011 $100

Lawrence, David Herbert 1885-1930 *Lady Chatterley's Lover.* Florence: printed by the Tipografia Giuntina, 1928, First edition; 232/1000 copies signed by author, pages (iv), 365, (3) (blanks), 8vo., original mulberry boards dust soiled, more so to backstrip, printed backstrip label, front cover with Lawrence's "Phoenix" at centre, short (2 inch) tears to joints at backstrip tail, little rubbed at tail corners, untrimmed, good.   Blackwell Rare Books   B166 - 170 2011   £5000

Lawrence, David Herbert 1885-1930 *Lady Chatterley's Lover.* Florence: printed by the Gipogrfia Giuntina, 1928, First edition; one of 1000 copies signed by author, 232 x 170mm., 2 p.l., 365, (1) pages, (1) leaf (blank), original mulberry colored paper boards, edges untrimmed and unopened, original plain cream colored jacket; two pages with breath of foxing, narrow band inside front flap of jacket bit spotted, just slightest fraying and wrinkling at jacket spine ends, extraordinarily fine, volume itself virtually pristine and jacket in marvelous condition.   Phillip J. Pirages   59 - 251 2011 $24,000

Lawrence, David Herbert 1885-1930 *Love Poems and Others.* London: Duckworth, 1913, First edition; 8vo. original publisher's blue cloth lettered gilt on spine and on front cover, pages lxiii, presentation from Margaret Radford to her brother Maitland Radford, endpapers very slightly browned, covers very faintly rubbed, near fine.   Any Amount of Books   May 26 2011 - A62565 2011 $419

Lawrence, David Herbert 1885-1930 *A Modern Lover.* London: Martin Secker, 1934, First edition; nearly fine.   Lupack Rare Books   May 26 2011 - ABE1117101876 2011 $125

Lawrence, David Herbert 1885-1930 *An Original Poem.* London: Chiswick Polytechnic School of Arts, 1934, First separate edition, number 7 of 12 numbered copies, of a total edition of 150, signed by Catherine Carswell, with an autograph correction to her postscript; 8vo., original mustard yellow wrappers printed in black, small collector's ticket to lower wrap, some minor edge wear, fine.   Simon Finch Rare Books   Zero - 335 2011   £500

Lawrence, David Herbert 1885-1930 *Phoenix.* London: Heinemann, 1936, First edition; tall 8vo., original brown buckram gilt, very short nick to head of spine, pages xxvii, 852, light spotting to prelim leaves and fore edge.   R. F. G. Hollett & Son Antiquarian Booksellers   General Catalogue Summer 2010 - 829 2011   £45

Lawrence, David Herbert 1885-1930 *Rawdon's Roof.* London: Elkin Mathews & Marrot, 1928, First edition, signed limited issue, number 304 of 500 copies signed by Lawrence; 8vo., pages 32, original grey paper boards, printed in blue, decorative endpapers, edges untrimmed, original grey dust jacket printed in blue, author's signature in black ink to limitation page, endpapers slightly browned, from the library of John Martin (publisher of Black Sparrow Press), with his small book ticket to rear pastedown, fine.   Simon Finch Rare Books   Zero - 248 2011   £500

Lawrence, David Herbert 1885-1930 *Rawdon's Roof.* London: Elkin Mathews & Marrot, 1928, First edition, one of 500 copies of a total of 530, signed; 8vo., pages 32, near fine in slightly nicked dust jacket.   Second Life Books Inc.   174 - 226 2011 $650

Lawrence, David Herbert 1885-1930 *Snake.* Edinburgh: Tragara Press, 1984, First edition, one of 12 copies, this one unnumbered; 8vo., pages 4, loosely inserted in printed dust jacket, with first proof of the poems as four separate sheets with printer Alan Anderson's red ink markings, near fine with proof printed on a different handmade paper, neither paper being specified by printer, previous owner's book ticket neatly pasted to limitation page.   Simon Finch Rare Books   Zero - 336 2011   £200

Lawrence, George Alfred *Sword and Gown.* London: John W. Parker & Son, 1859, First edition; author's name written in ink on titlepage, contemporary green morocco grained half calf, lined in gilt, raised bands, gilt compartments, booklabel of S.G. C. with signature of Somerset G. Calthorpe, very good.   Jarndyce Antiquarian Booksellers   CXCI - 250 2011   £125

Lawrence, Heather *Yorkshire Pots and Potteries.* David and Charles, 1974, First edition; original cloth, gilt, dust jacket, spine little faded, pages 294, with 30 plates and 18 text illustrations, scarce.   R. F. G. Hollett & Son Antiquarian Booksellers   General Catalogue Summer 2010 - 238 2011   £60

Lawrence, Jerome *Inherit the Wind.* Norwalk: Easton Press, 2000, Signed by author, leather, gold titles and decorations, all edges gilt, silk endpapers and ribbon bookmark, "a note about" card and signed certificate of authenticity folded in, very clean and tight, 162 pages.   G. H. Mott Bookseller   May 26 2011 - 37046 2011 $675

Lawrence, Thomas Edward 1888-1935 *Correspondence with Bernard and Charlotte Shaw.* Fordingbridge: Castle Hill Press, 2000-2009, First editions, 140/475 sets; 4 volumes, accompanying reproductions of photos of Lawrence and related material, some folded, royal 8vo., original green cloth, backstrips gilt lettered, top edge gilt, dust jackets, matching green cloth case.   Blackwell Rare Books   B166 - 171 2011   £395

Lawrence, Thomas Edward 1888-1935 *The Mint.* London: Jonathan Cape, 1955, Limited to 2000 copies, this #2; fine in moderately soiled slipcase. Bella Luna Books May 26 2011 - t9237 2011 $550

Lawrence, Thomas Edward 1888-1935 *"The Mint" and Later Writings about Service Life.* Fordingbridge: Castle Hill Press, 2009, 112/200 copies (of an edition of 277 copies); tipped in sepia frontispiece, parts 1 and 2 of the diary printed on grey paper, all of the prelims and remainder of text on white paper, pages xiv, 342, royal 8vo., original quarter cream cloth, gilt lettered blue morocco label, light grey board, grey endpapers, matching cream cloth slipcase, new. Blackwell Rare Books B166 - 172 2011 £250

Layard, George Somes *The Life an Letters of Charles Samuel Keene.* London: Sampson Low, 1893, New edition; half title, frontispiece, illustrations, text slightly spotted, original dark blue cloth, gilt, slightly marked and rubbed, inner hinges slightly cracked, loosely inserted printed invitation completed by hand to Charles Keene for a "Punch" supper on 5th July 1871. Jarndyce Antiquarian Booksellers CXCI - 231 2011 £110

Layard, George Somes *Mrs. Lynn Linton: Her Life, Letters and Opinions.* London: Methuen & Co., 1901, First edition; half title, frontispiece, plates, 40 page catalog (May 1903), uncut in original pale blue cloth lettered in black and gilt, little dulled, top edge gilt, good, sound copy. Jarndyce Antiquarian Booksellers CLXC - 157 2011 £50

Lazzaro, Claudia *Italian Renaissance Garden from the Conventions of Planting, Design, and Ornament to the Grand Gardens of Sixteenth Century Central.* New Haven and London: Yale University Press, 1990, First edition; 4to., illustrations in color and black and white, 352, fine in fine dust jacket, in very good slipcase, bookplate of Jeremy Lewis. Any Amount of Books May 29 2011 - A70569 2011 $204

Le Cain, Errol *King Arthur's Sword.* London: Faber and Faber, 1968, First edition; 4to., full color pictorial boards, full color pictorial dust jacket clean and fresh, book fresh with small area of lifted paper on verso of front free endpaper, not affecting text almost every page has full color illustrations. Jo Ann Reisler, Ltd. 86 - 150 2011 $350

Le Carre, John 1931- *A Most Wanted Man.* London: Hodder and Stoughton, 2008, First British edition, limited to 500 copies; fine, in fine slipcase, signed by author. Bella Luna Books May 26 2011 - t9024 2011 $165

Le Carre, John 1931- *The Night Manager.* London: 1993, First edition; as new in dust jacket, signed by author. Gemini Fine Books & Arts, Ltd. Art Reference & Illustrated Books: First Editions 2011 $145

Le Carre, John 1931- *A Perfect Spy.* New York: 1986, First American edition; signed by author, as new in dust jacket. Gemini Fine Books & Arts, Ltd. Art Reference & Illustrated Books: First Editions 2011 $100

Le Carre, John 1931- *The Secret Pilgrim.* New York: 1991, First American edition; signed by author, as new in dust jacket. Gemini Fine Books & Arts, Ltd. Art Reference & Illustrated Books: First Editions 2011 $100

Le Cron, Helen Cowles *Animal Etiquette Book.* New York: Frederick Stokes, 1926, First edition; 8vo., cloth, pictorial paste on, 95 pages, title and frontispiece foxed, else very good, illustrations by Maurice Day with full color frontispiece plus 24 full page black and white line illustrations. Aleph-Bet Books, Inc. 95 - 219 2011 $150

Le Fanu, Joseph Sheridan 1814-1873 *Green Tea and Other Ghost Stories.* Sauk City: Arkham House, 1945, First edition; octavo, cloth. L. W. Currey, Inc. 124 - 146 2011 $450

Le Fanu, Joseph Sheridan 1814-1873 *The House by the Church Yard.* London: Richard Bentley & Son, 1897, New edition; 4 pages ads, original black cloth, blocked in blind, leading hinge slightl weak, embossed stamp of W.H. Smith on leading f.e.p., very good. Jarndyce Antiquarian Booksellers CXCI - 251 2011 £120

Le Fanu, Joseph Sheridan 1814-1873 *The Purcell Papers.* London: Richard Bentley and Son, 1880, First edition; 3 volumes, 8vo., pages xxxi, (1) blank, 236; (iv), 273; (iv), 289, all edges marbled, endpapers and first few leaves of each volume heavily foxed, light foxing throughout, first leaf of volume ii with small chip to bottom edge, contemporary black half morocco, marbled paper boards, spine ruled in compartments, lettered and designed in gilt over red and burgundy labels, marbled edges and endpapers, extremities lightly rubbed, small ticket to front pastedown of each volume, ALS tipped in with envelope to volume i. Simon Finch Rare Books Zero - 248 2011 £3750

Le Fanu, Joseph Sheridan 1814-1873 *Uncle Silas; a Tale of Bartra Haugh.* London: Richard Bentley & Son, 1897, New edition; 2 pages ads, original dark green cloth, blocked in blind, gift inscription, very good. Jarndyce Antiquarian Booksellers CXCI - 252 2011 £75

Le Fanu, Joseph Sheridan 1814-1873 *Willing to Die.* Downey & Co., circa, 1880, half title, illustrated title, original dark green cloth blocked in red, slightly rubbed, inner hinges slightly cracked, embossed library stamp of W. H. Smith. Jarndyce Antiquarian Booksellers CXCI - 253 2011 £85

Le Fanu, Stephen *Random Sketches.* Brisbane: privately published, 1979, Signed limited edition, no. 125 of 300 copies; tall 8vo., original cream boards, gilt, pages (viii), (50), 51 illustrations after pen and ink drawings, printed on super kraft drawing paper and hand colored by artist, plus 3 original hand colored drawings bound in at end.   R. F. G. Hollett & Son Antiquarian Booksellers   General Catalogue Summer 2010 - 830   2011   £130

Le Fanu, Stephen *Random Sketches in Australia.* Perth: privately published, 1985, Limited edition, signed, no. 62 of 300 copies; tall 8vo., original cream boards, gilt, pages (viii), 23, with 23 full page and 3 text illustrations after pen and ink drawings, printed on super kraft drawing paper and hand colored by artist, plus 2 original hand colored drawings by LeFanu bound in at end.   R. F. G. Hollett & Son Antiquarian Booksellers   General Catalogue Summer 2010 - 831   2011   £95

Le Fanu, William *A Catalogue of the Portrait and Other Paintings, Drawings and Sculpture in the Royal College of Surgeons of England.* Edinburgh and London: E. & S. Livingstone, 1960, 8vo., xii, 119, plates, 52 pages, color frontispiece, numerous plates, blue cloth, gilt stamped cover emblem and spine title, dust jacket, very good, signed presentation inscription from author, from the Medical Library of Dr. Clare Gray Peterson.   Jeff Weber Rare Books   162 - 188   2011 $60

Le Feuvre, Amy *The Making of a Woman.* London: RTS, 1909, First edition; half title, frontispiece, 8 pages ads, edges little spotted, original blue cloth, pictorially blocked on pale blue, grey and black, lettered in gilt, prize label, nice, bright copy.   Jarndyce Antiquarian Booksellers   CLXC - 86   2011   £35

Le Guin, Ursula K. *The Lathe of Heaven.* New York: Charles Scribner's Sons, 1971, First edition; octavo, cloth backed boards.   L. W. Currey, Inc.   124 - 107   2011 $750

Le Guin, Ursula K. *The Left Hand of Darkness.* London: MacDonald, 1969, First English edition; slightly cocked, fore edge little foxed tiny tears on two pages, else near fine in near fine, price clipped dust jacket with short tear on front panel and little foxing on rear panel, uncommon.   Between the Covers   169 - BTC343643   2011 $550

Le Maingre De Bouciqualt, Don Luis *Les Amazones Revoltees.* Rotterdam: n.p., 1730, First edition; (1) blank, (4) 274 pages & errata (2) blank), 12mo., modern dark gray cloth a la Bradel, gilt lettered spine with floral ornament in gilt centered, all edges gilt, nice copy, bound by Laurenchet.   Paulette Rose Fine and Rare Books   32 - 113   2011 $1200

Le Prince De Beaumont, Jeanne Marie *Les Americaines ou la Preuve de la Religion Chretienne par les Lumieres Naturelles.* Lyon: Pierre Bruyset Ponthus, 1770, First edition; 12mo., pages vi, 331; (ii), 310, (1); (ii), 310; (ii), 463; (ii), 389; (ii), 287, (viii), full mottled calf, morocco labels, some bumping to some of the corners, yet very good set.   Second Life Books Inc.   174 - 227   2011 $1200

Le Prince De Beaumont, Jeanne Marie *Civan, Roi de Bungo Histoire Japonnoise.* Londres: Jean Nourse, 1754, First edition; 2 volumes in one with separate titlepages, (4), 250; (1) 178 pages, 12mo., contemporary sheepskin, gilt decorated spine, closed tear on page 43, light stain on page 175 (volume II), otherwise very nice, from the library of Chevalier de Leuze with his ex-libris in his hand.   Paulette Rose Fine and Rare Books   32 - 115   2011 $1200

Le Prince De Beaumont, Jeanne Marie *Memoires De Madame La Baronne De Batteville ou la Veuve Parfaite.* Lyon: Pierre Vruyset Ponthus, 1766, First edition; 12mo., pages (2), 324, contemporary French calf, spine gilt in compartments, very nice, clean copy.   Second Life Books Inc.   174 - 228   2011 $900

Le Ros, Christian *Christmas Day and How It Was Spent by Four Persons in the House of Fograss, Fograss, Mowton and Snorton, Bankers.* London: George Routledge, circa, 1873, 2 pages ads, frontispiece and plates, illustrations by Phiz, yellowback, original printed boards, slightly rubbed and dulled, very good, Renier booklabel.   Jarndyce Antiquarian Booksellers   CXCI - 255   2011   £65

Le Sage, Alain Rene   1668-1747   *Les Avantures de Monsieur Robert Chevalier...* Paris: Chez Etienne Ganeau, 1732, First edition; 2 volumes, 12mo., (xvi), 390; (viii), 363, 6 full page engraved plates by Bonnard in contemporary full calf, hinge strengthened at early date, spine gilt, one inch split to lower hinge calf of one volume, contemporary owner's notes at extremities of titlepage, some light foxing and staining, very good, at top of each titlepage is ownership signature of sculptor Pierre Paul David d'Angers.   Second Life Books Inc.   174 - 229   2011 $1200

Le Sage, Alain Rene 1668-1747 *The Adventures of Gil Blas of Santillana.* London: printed for Richard Phillips, 1807, 4 volumes, 203 x 121mm., extremely pleasing contemporary deep blue straight grain morocco handsomely gilt by Samuel Welcher (with his ticket), covers bordered gilt with triple rules and framed with wide palmette roll, inside of which is a rule with small ring and floral tools at corners, raised bands, spines ornately gilt in lobed compartments featuring stippled ground, quatrefoil centerpiece with delicate foliate sprays at sides and fleurons at ends, turn-ins gilt with single rule an fleuron and ring tools at corners, all edges gilt, 100 copperplates by Warner, Tomlinson and others, extra illustrated with 60 plates by Conrad Martin Metz for a total of 160 engravings; armorial bookplate of H. Holland Edwards, Pennant Ereithlyn, North Wales; front joints just little flaked, backstrips slightly sunned, covers with minor variation in color, several plates little foxed, generally only in margins and more frequently on added plates), one leaf with light ink stain in lower margin, light dampstain in margin at head of one plate, isolated very minor marginal soiling, very pleasing set, decorative bindings very well preserved and internally clean, fresh and bright. Phillip J. Pirages 59 - 254 2011 $1800

Leach, A. F. *The Schools of Medieval England.* London: Methuen, 1915, Original cloth gilt, damped patch on spine, backstrip rather darkened, pages xv, 350, with 43 illustrations, scarce. R. F. G. Hollett & Son Antiquarian Booksellers 175 - 813 2011 £55

Leach, Bernard *A Potter's Book.* London: Faber & Faber, 1940, First edition; 8vo., pages xxvii, 293, 4 color plates, 77 half tone illustrations and numerous drawings in text, frontispiece tipped in, neat name on front pastedown (H. & E. Nonnenmacker), inner front hinge slightly cracked, edges of oatmeal boards very slightly stained but nice, bright very good+ in rather tatty worn, good only dust jacket. Any Amount of Books May 29 2011 - B22969 2011 $221

Leacock, Stephen *Canada.* 1941, Limited edition; all edges gilt, ribbon markers, original full red leather, gilt lettered on upper case and spine, internal gilt tooling and multicolored cloth emblem of Canada is very uncommon, near mint in original color matching slipcase which is little rubbed on edges. I. D. Edrich May 26 2011 - 51672 2011 $386

Leaf, Munro *My Book to Help America.* Racine: Whitman, 1942, 4to., pictorial card covers, very good-fine, removable stamp booklet book in pocket in rear that child can use for stamps. Aleph-Bet Books, Inc. 95 - 325 2011 $400

Leaf, Munro *The Story of Ferdinand.* New York: Viking Press, 1938, Stated 17th edition; 8vo., cloth backed color pictorial boards, some light shelf wear, every page illustrated with stunning black and white pictures by Robert Lawson, signed in full with presentation and sketches by Leaf. Jo Ann Reisler, Ltd. 86 - 147 2011 $475

Leaf, Munro *The Story of Simpson and Sampson.* New York: Viking, Oct., 1941, First edition; 4to., red cloth, near fine in slightly worn, very good+ dust jacket, signed by Leaf, illustrations by Robert Lawson, very scarce. Aleph-Bet Books, Inc. 95 - 322 2011 $450

The League: the Exponent of the Principles of Free Trade and the Organ of the National Anti-Corn-Law League. London: published by the Office 67 Fleet street, 1844-1846, Issues no. 1-144 in 3 volumes, large folio, almost complete set but wanting titlepage to volume III and final issue no. 145 fof 4 July 1846, small library stamp on verso of each titlepage, excellent set in contemporary half calf, skillfully rebacked with raised bands, gilt lines and labels. John Drury Rare Books 153 - 110 2011 £900

Lear, Edward *The Book of Nonsense.* London: F. Warne and Co. n.d., 25th edition; pages 115, with 100 illustrations, oblong 4to., original cloth, gilt over bevelled boards, trifle worn, front hinge cracking, few spots, inscription dated 1888. R. F. G. Hollett & Sons Antiquarian Booksellers 170 - 401 2011 £120

Lear, Edward *More Nonsense.* London: Frederick Warne and Cco., 1888, Oblong 4to., original cloth, gilt over bevelled boards, corners little worn, neatly recased, 111 leaves, printed on recto only, Mss. Limerick written in ink with drawing on verso of page 29, slight fingering to one or two leaves, but nice copy. R. F. G. Hollett & Sons Antiquarian Booksellers 170 - 402 2011 £150

Lear, Edward *Nonsense Songs, Stories, Botany and Alpahbets.* Robert John Bush, 1875, Fifth thousand; square 8vo. original pictorial green cloth, gilt over bevelled boards, rather rubbed and neatly recased, unpaginated, illustrations colored by juvenile hand, scattered light fingering. R. F. G. Hollett & Sons Antiquarian Booksellers 170 - 404 2011 £75

Lear, Edward *Nonsense Songs and Stories.* London: Frederick Warne and Co., 1901, Ninth edition; large 8vo., original two tone pictorial cloth gilt, trifle rubbed, pages xviii, 144, illustrations by Lear. R. F. G. Hollett & Sons Antiquarian Booksellers 170 - 403 2011 £65

Lear, Edward *The Pelican Chorus...* London: F. Warne and Co. n.d. 1930's, Square 8vo., original cloth, dust jacket rather torn and chipped, unpaginated, 7 full page color plates, numerous line drawings, endpapers by L. Leslie Brooke. R. F. G. Hollett & Sons Antiquarian Booksellers 170 - 405 2011 £35

Leather, John *Spiritsails and Lugsails.* Camden: 1989, 387 pages, reissue, fine in fine dust jacket. Bookworm & Silverfish 678 - 143 2011 $150

Lebedev, V. *Igrushki Zversushki. (Toys Based on Wild Animals).* N.P.: Detizdat Tsk Vlksm, 1939, First edition; oblong 8vo., color pictorial paper wrappers, 10 pages within (counting inside covers), each with illustration. Jo Ann Reisler, Ltd. 86 - 224 2011 $550

Leckenby, H. *The Collectors Digest.* 1951-1983, Nos. 51-77, 80-86, 88-90, 93-115, 129, 135, 138-438, Feb. 1951-March 1958-June 1983, issues vary between 24 and 60 pages each with different illustrated upper wrapper, together 366 issues, Nos. 169-204 in 3 bound volumes, green cloth with original wrappers bound in, uncommon. I. D. Edrich May 26 2011 - 82609 2011 $1468

Leconte, Carrie E. *Yosemite 1878: Adventures & N. & C. Journal and Drawings by...* San Fransisco: Book Club of California, 1964, Quarto, xviii, 98 pages, frontispiece, illustrations, quarter cloth, decorative paper over boards, plain dust jacket as issued, prospectus included, fine. Jeff Weber Rare Books 163 - 82 2011 $60

Lee, Brian North *Bookplates and Labels by Leo Wyatt.* Wakefield: Fleece Press, 1988, One of 270 copies (of an edition of 300 copies); printed on Zerkall and Mohawk Superfine text, mouldmade papers, 4 duotone photos tipped in as plates, 55 wood engraved booklabels and bookplates reproduced in several colors throughout text and 16 copper engraved bookplates reproduced full page as a suite at end, pages 75 (iv), full page reproductions, (1) colophon, royal 8vo., original quarter brick red cloth, printed label, green patterned Sage Reynolds paste paper boards, untrimmed, cloth, slipcase, fine. Blackwell Rare Books B166 - 253 2011 £150

Lee, Elizabeth *Ouida: a Memoir.* London: T. Fisher Unwin, 1914, First edition; half title, frontispiece, title in red and black, plates, uncut in original pale blue cloth, lettered in dark blue, spine slightly faded, armorial bookplate of Edward Heron-Allen, with signed ALS from author to same. Jarndyce Antiquarian Booksellers CLXC - 729 2011 £40

Lee, Harper *To Kill a Mockingbird.* London: Heinemann, 1960, Uncorrected proof copy of the first British edition; one thumbnail sized spot to upper front edge, else very near fine in plain brown printed wrappers, very nice, uncommon issue. Ken Lopez Bookseller 154 - 95 2011 $2500

Lee, Harper *To Kill a Mockingbird.* Shelton: First Edition Library, 1960, 8vo., 296 pages, fine, near fine dust jacket with mild edge wear and in fine original color printed slipcase, publication information concerning the original first edition laid in. By the Book, L. C. 26 - 10 2011 $80

Lee, Harper *To Kill a Mockingbird.* London: Heinemann, 1960, First English edition; bright, near fine copy in very good dust jacket (2 closed tears to head and foot of spine, a little wrinkle, one minor chip, bright colors). Lupack Rare Books May 26 2011 - ABE4616671862 2011 $750

Lee, Harriet *Herbert, ou Adieu Richesses ou Les Marriages.* Edinbourg et Paris: Chez Buisson, 1788, First edition in French; 3 volumes in one, 264, 275, 282 pages, small 8vo, polished half calf over boards, gilt lettered spine, short tear to inner margin of first page, not affecting text, otherwise very good. Paulette Rose Fine and Rare Books 32 - 111 2011 $650

Lee, Laurie *The Bloom of Candles.* London: John Lehmann, 1947, First edition; 8vo., 22 pages, inscribed by author to poet Leonard Clark, with Clark bookplate, near fine in slightly dusty, very good+ dust jacket. Any Amount of Books May 29 2011 - A68498 2011 $213

Lee, Laurie *Cider with Rosie.* London: Hogarth Press, 1959, First edition; line drawings with a number full page by John Ward, pages (iv), 284, crown 8vo., original mid green boards, backstrip gilt lettered, supplied dust jacket by John Ward, trifle frayed at head, very good. Blackwell Rare Books B166 - 175 2011 £85

Lee, Minnie Mary *The Brown House, at Duffield.* Baltimore: Kelly, Piet & Co., 1876, Half title, original brown moire cloth, bevelled boards, blocked and lettered in black and gilt, little dulled and rubbed, following board with horizontal string mark, good, sound copy. Jarndyce Antiquarian Booksellers CLXC - 96 2011 £40

Lee, Nat *Mithridates King of Pontus a Tragedy...* London: printed for Richard Wellington in St. Paul's Church-yard and sold by Francis Fawcet at the Kings-head and Crown near Durham-yard in the Strand, Paul's Church-yard, 1711, First edition; 4to., (6), 66 pages, some staining at end, disbound. Anthony W. Laywood May 26 2011 - 21748 2011 $101

Lee, Susan P. *Memoirs of William Nelson Pendleton, D. D.* Philadelphia: 1893, First edition; 490 pages, solid copy, some flecking to covers. Bookworm & Silverfish 679 - 41 2011 $137

Leech, John *Pictures of Life and Character. The Collection of Mr. Punch Fifth Series.* London: Bradbury, Evans, 1887, Folio, three quarter leather, some dampstains. Barnaby Rudge Booksellers Art & Architecture & Photography - 015694 2011 $110

Leedy, Walter C. *Fan Vaulting: a Study of Form, Technology and Meaning.* Scolar Press, 1980, First edition; 234 pages, 242 illustrations, very good in dust jacket, scarce, large 8vo. Ken Spelman Rare Books 68 - 137 2011 £50

Leeson, Michael A. *History of Montana 1739-1885. A History of Its Discovery and Settlement...* Chicago: Warner, Beers & Co., 1885, First edition; thick quarto, original three quarter leather and pebbled cloth, gold stamping on front cover and spine, raised bands, all edges marbled, marbled endpapers, 1367 pages, illustrations, wonderful lithograph plates, large color fold-out map has been proved by Rand McNally especially for this volume, with 105 portrait plates and 182 view plates, rebacked with original spine laid down and light cosmetic restoration to corners, else near fine, index bound in cloth with gold stamping on spine and is fine copy. Buckingham Books   May 26 2011 - 28154   2011 $3250

Lefebure, Molly *Cumberland Heritage.* London: Gollancz, 1970, First edition; original cloth, gilt, dust jacket, pages 352, 21 illustrations, signed and dated by author on dedication leaf. R. F. G. Hollett & Son Antiquarian Booksellers   173 - 685   2011   £35

Lefevre D'Etaples, Jacques *Musica Libris Quatuor Demonstrata.* Paris: Guillaume Cavellat, 1551, First separate edition and first illustrated edition; 4to., 44 leave, Cavellat's large woodcut printer's device on title, text diagrams, tables, woodcut initials, early 19th century calf, gilt, neatly rebacked retaining original spine, title very slightly soiled, faint marginal foxing, modern booklabel. Joseph J. Felcone Inc.   Fall Miscellany 2010 - 73   2011 $4800

Lefevre, Raoul *Recuyell of the Historyes of Troye.* Hammersmith: Kelmscott Press, 1892, One of 300 copies; 3 books in 2 volumes, large quarto, xv, (1), 295, (1 blank); (297)-507, (1, blank), (509)-718 pages, printed in red and black in Troy and Chaucer type, decorative woodcut borders and initials, bound by Cedric Chivers in beautiful Art Nouveau "Vellucent" binding, binding elaborately decorated in vivid colors and detail and all boards and spine ruled in gilt, front covers framed by green vines with pink and orange flowers and gilt stamped detail, inside frame of vines stands Helen of Troy on volume I and Cassandra on volume II, title of book shown on a scroll beneath women's feet, spines of both volumes contain similar scroll decoration, also containing title of book on back cover of each volume is image of the towers of Troy in flames, and gauffered, others uncut, marbled endpapers, gilt ruled dentelles, bookplates of former owners Rudloph August Williams and "CKC" Charles C. Kalbfleisch and bookplate of other previous owner on back pastedown of each volume, each volume in its own chemise and quarter calf slipcase, dentelles slightly lifting, otherwise beautiful, near fine set in extraordinary binding. Heritage Book Shop   Holiday 2010 - 67   2011 $22,500

The Legend of Saint Robert the Hermit of Knaresborugh. Knaresborough: G. Wilson, 1838, 12mo., later plain wrappers, pages 8. R. F. G. Hollett & Son Antiquarian Booksellers   175 - 815   2011   £45

Leggot, Michele J. *Reading Zukofsky's 80 Flowers.* Baltimore and London: John Hopkins University Press, 1989, First edition; 8vo., 453 pages, fine in about very good dust jacket slightly nicked and chipped at head of spine. Any Amount of Books   May 29 2011 - A68048   2011 $221

Lehane, Dennis *Mystic River.* Blakeney: Scorpion Press, 2001, Limited to 15 lettered copies, this being G; fine, with acetate protector that has chip at bottom of spine, appreciation by George Pelecanos, Pelecanos had lettered this copy incorrectly and Lehane over wrote the letter with a "G", only the deluxe copies of which there were 15 calls for both signatures. Bella Luna Books   May 26 2011 - t8251   2011 $825

Lehane, Dennis *A Drink Before the World.* New York: HBJ, 1994, First edition; near fine, bottom corners bumped, dust jacket fine, signed by author. Bella Luna Books   May 26 2011 - t668   2011 $220

Lehmann, Rosamond *A Letter to a Sister.* London: Hogarth Press, 1931, (24) pages, 8vo., original cream wrappers printed in red and black, aside from inconsequential scattered foxing, near fine. Paulette Rose Fine and Rare Books   32 - 112   2011 $100

Leiber, Fritz *Two Sought Adventure" Exploits of Fafhrd and the Gray Mouser.* New York: Gnome Press, 1957, First edition; octavo, cloth. L. W. Currey, Inc.   124 - 213   2011 $150

Leigh, Dell *East Coasting.* Curwen Press for the London & North Eastern Railway, 1931, First edition; original orange wrappers, corners trifle creased, short closed tear to one corner pages 64 illustrations and decorations in color and line by Edward Bawden, very scarce. R. F. G. Hollett & Son Antiquarian Booksellers   General Catalogue Summer 2010 - 716   2011   £850

Leigh, Percival *The Comic Latin Grammar.* London: Charles Tilt, 1840, First edition; original blindstamped cloth, gilt, edges rather faded, pages 163, (iii), (ii), complete with 8 etched plates (rather browned and spotted), numerous text drawings, all by John Leech. R. F. G. Hollett & Son Antiquarian Booksellers   General Catalogue Summer 2010 - 661   2011   £65

Leighton, Clare *Country Matters.* London: Victor Gollancz, 1937, First UK edition; 4to., original reddish-brown cloth gilt, dust jacket (spine and edges little darkened) pages 160, woodcuts by author, scarce. R. F. G. Hollett & Son Antiquarian Booksellers   General Catalogue Summer 2010 - 832   2011   £85

Leighton, Clare *Sometime - Never.* London: Fanfare Press for Victor Gollancz, 1939, First edition; original blue cloth, dust jacket spine rather chipped at head and foot, pages 178, illustrations by author. R. F. G. Hollett & Son Antiquarian Booksellers General Catalogue Summer 2010 - 833 2011 £65

Leighton, Clare *Southern Harvest.* London: Victor Gollancz, 1943, First edition; large 8vo., original cloth, gilt, dust jacket, piece torn from foot of lower panel, pages 124, text woodcuts. R. F. G. Hollett & Son Antiquarian Booksellers General Catalogue Summer 2010 - 834 2011 £85

Leighton, Clare *Wood Engraving and Woodcuts.* Studio Publications, 1932, First reprint; pages 96, 11 tipped in photos, 39 illustrations, original cloth backed patterned boards, dust jacket, worn and defective. R. F. G. Hollett & Son Antiquarian Booksellers General Catalogue Summer 2010 - 239 2011 £120

Leinster, Murray *Sidewide in Time and Other Scientific Adventures.* Chicago: Shasta Publishers, 1950, First edition; octavo, cloth. L. W. Currey, Inc. 124 - 162 2011 $350

Leip, Hans *Das Zauberschiff. (The Magic Shop).* Hamburg: Hammerich U. Lesser, 1947, First edition; 4to., stiff pictorial card covers, small corner repair on back cover, else near fine, rare, quite scarce. Aleph-Bet Books, Inc. 95 - 408 2011 $1500

Leiris, Michel *Picasso and the Human Comedy.* New York: Harourt, Brace and Co., 1954, Constitutes the double number 29/30 of Verve in the French Edition, quarto, unpaginated, red and blue pictorial boards, designed by Picasso, original pictorial dust jacket, some browning to intermittent pages, as usual, spine of jacket with small closed tear, about fine. Heritage Book Shop Holiday 2010 - 97 2011 $1750

Leland, Charles G. *The English Gipsies and Their Language.* London: Kegan Paul etc., 1893, Fourth edition; original green cloth gilt, pages 259, flyleaves browned. R. F. G. Hollett & Son Antiquarian Booksellers 175 - 817 2011 £120

Leland, Thomas *The History of Ireland from the Invasion of Henry II.* Dublin: 1773, First edition; 3 volumes, full calf, not matching (volume 3 differs from 1 and 2 but all 18th century and quite good solid copies. C. P. Hyland May 26 2011 - 256/516 2011 $457

Lem, Stanislaw *Solaris.* New York: Walker and Co., 1970, First US edition; octavo, boards. L. W. Currey, Inc. 124 - 39 2011 $1750

Lemery, Louis *A Treatise of all Sorts of Foods, both Animal and Vegetable; also of Drinkables; Giving on Account How to Chuse the Best Sort of All Kinds.* London: printed for T. Osborne in Gray's Inn, 1745, Third edition in English; initial approbation, title in red and black, xii, 572, (24) pages, antique style modern panelled calf, red leather label to spine in compartments, very clean copy. Anthony W. Laywood May 26 2011 - 21681 2011 $922

Lemon, Mark *Mr. Punch: His Origin and Career, with Facsimile of His Original prospectus...* London: printed by Jas. Wade Covent Garden, 1870, First edition; folding facsimile frontispiece on blue paper, 4 pages ads at front, 16 pages ads at back, 1 page with small tear slightly affecting text, original printed wrappers, bound into half tan morocco by Birdsall & Son, Northampton, top edge gilt, very good. Jarndyce Antiquarian Booksellers CXCI - 254 2011 £100

Lemontey, Pierre Edoaurd *Recit exact de ce Qui S'est Passe a la Seance de la Societe des Observateurs da la Femme la Mardi 2 Novembre 1802.* Paris: Chez Deterville, 1803, First edition; xx, 170 pages, 16mo. contemporary speckled brown calf, gilt decorated spine, contrasting black title label, lettered in gilt, attractive copy. Paulette Rose Fine and Rare Books 32 - 114 2011 $1200

Lemore, Clara *A Harvest of Weeds.* London: Griffith, Farran, 1892, New edition; frontispiece, final ad leaf, original crimson cloth, small split at head of spine. Jarndyce Antiquarian Booksellers CLXC - 123 2011 £35

Lemore, Clara *Madge Dale's Marriage Portion.* London: William Stevens, 1891, Half title, original dark green cloth, lettered in black & gilt, very good. Jarndyce Antiquarian Booksellers CLXC - 124 2011 £35

Lenin, Vladimir Il'Ich 1870-1924 *Imperialism. the Highest Stage of Capitalism.* Moscow: Co-operative Publishing Society of Foreign Workers in the USSR, 1934, Limited to 3000 copies; original cloth, gilt, dust jacket, repaired and laid on to stiff paper, pages 123, little damp cockled throughout. R. F. G. Hollett & Son Antiquarian Booksellers 175 - 818 2011 £45

Lennard, Horace *Romps in Town.* London: George Routledge and Sons, n.d., 1885, First edition; large 8vo., original pictorial wrappers, little worn and torn, pages 28, with tinted and colored illustrations, uncommon. R. F. G. Hollett & Son Antiquarian Booksellers General Catalogue Summer 2010 - 517 2011 £30

Lennie, William *A Key to Lennie's Principles of English Grammar...* Edinburgh: printed for the author and sold by Guthrie & Tait and Oliver & Boyd etc., 1824, Sixth edition; 12mo., original full roan gilt, upper hinge cracking, extremities little worn and bumped, pages 190, rather scribbled inscription "presented to Wm. George Jnr in the year 1846 on his 8th birthday". R. F. G. Hollett & Son Antiquarian Booksellers 175 - 819 2011 £45

Lennox, Charles Ramsay *The Female Quixote; or the Adventures of Arabella.* London: printed for F. C. & J. Rivington, W. Otridge & Sons,, 1810, Half titles, contemporary half tan calf, marbled boards, gilt spines, maroon leather labels, armorial bookplate of Rev. G. F. Clarke and signatures of Elizabeth Mary Clarke, very good.   Jarndyce Antiquarian Booksellers   CLXC - 126 2011   £120

Lennox, Sarah *The Life and Letters of Lady Sarah Lennox...Also a Short Political Sketch of the Years 1760 to 1763 by Henry Fox, 1st Lord Holland.* London: John Murray, 1901, First edition; 223 x 143mm., 2 volumes, lovely contemporary loden green crushed morocco, handsomely gilt by J. Larkins (stamp signed on verso of front free endpaper), covers framed with one decorative and two plain gilt rules, raised bands, spines in especially attractive gilt compartments, featuring central pomegranate lozenges and scrolling corner decoration, densely gilt inner dentelles, marbled endpapers, all edges gilt, with 30 photogravures of portraits; spines uniformly sunned to a soft hazel, three very small and hardly noticeable dents in one cover, trivial defects internally but quite handsome set in fine condition, bindings lustrous and virtually unworn, text clean and fresh.   Phillip J. Pirages   59 - 114 2011 $400

Lentz, Harold *The Pop-up Pinocchio.* New York: Blue Ribbon, 1932, Thick 8vo., pictorial boards, normal light cover wear and some spine creasing, very good+, clean and tight, illustrations by Lentz, with 4 marvelous double page color pop-ups, numerous black and white text illustrations and color endpapers.   Aleph-Bet Books, Inc.   95 - 456 2011 $500

Leodhas, Sorche Nic *Always Room for One More.* New York: Holt Rinehart Winston, 1965, First edition; Oblong 8vo., pictorial boards, neat owner inscription, fine in dust jacket with faint ghost of medal, beautifully illustrated by Nonny Hogrogian, scarce.   Aleph-Bet Books, Inc.   95 - 289 2011 $750

Leonard, C. W. *Chronological and Geographical Family Guide to the Holy Bible.* London: C. W. Leonard, n.d. circa, 1870, Full blindstamped calf folder gilt, little rubbed, dissected linen backed chart and map in 15 sections, hand colored, with stitched red cloth edging, attractively printed chart with central map, inset maps.   R. F. G. Hollett & Son Antiquarian Booksellers   175 - 820 2011   £120

Leonard, Elmore *Unknown Man No. 89.* New York: Delacorte, 1977, First edition; bookplate on front fly, spine bit rubbed, very good in near fine dust jacket.   Between the Covers   169 - BTC339023 2011 $300

Leonard, Peter *Records of a Voyage to the Western Coast of Africa; In His Majesty's Ship Dryad...* Edinburgh: Wm. Tait, 1833, First edition; small 8vo., pages iv, 267, 4 pages giving lists of vessels engaged in slave trade 1829, later black buckram very clean internally, rare.   J. & S. L. Bonham Antiquarian Booksellers   Africa 4/20/2011 - 7982 2011   £450

Leonardo Da Vinci 1452-1519 *Leonardo Disegni 1490-1519.* Rome: Trec, 2004, First edition; lavish folio volume, original publisher's full leather lettered gilt on spine and cover, 5 raised bands, pages 463, illustrations, Italian text, very slight handling wear, else fine with fitted wooden case.   Any Amount of Books   May 26 2011 - A68918 2011 $671

Leonardo Da Vinci 1452-1519 *Treatise of Painting.* London: printed for J. Taylor, 1802, Octavo, 23 copperplates, including frontispiece, original marbled boards, rebacked, preserving lightly bumped, very good.   Heritage Book Shop   Holiday 2010 - 72 2011 $1500

Leopold, Johann Friedrich *Relatio Epistolica de Itinere Suo Sueccio Anno MDCCVII Facto ...* London: T. Childe, 1720, First edition; 8vo., viii (vi) (2) 111 pages, fly title, 8 numbered folding engraved plates, and maps, woodcut head and tailpieces, contemporary calf, gilt border on covers, gilt spine, gilt edges, little rubbed, handsome copy, from the library of the Earls of Macclesfield at Shirburn Castle.   Maggs Bros. Ltd.   1440 - 129 2011   £525

Lepsius, Richard *Discoveries Egypt, Ethiopia, and the Peninsula of Sinai in the Years 1842-1845.* London: Richard Bentley, 1853, First edition; 8vo., pages vi, 455, color lithographic frontispiece, folding map, original blue blindstamped cloth, light rubbing to spine.   J. & S. L. Bonham Antiquarian Booksellers   Africa 4/20/2011 - 8423 2011   £240

Leroux, Gaston *The Machine to Kill.* New York: Macauley Co., 1935, First edition in English; octavo, original red boards stamped in black.   L. W. Currey, Inc.   124 - 208 2011 $175

Les-Milne, James *Roman Mornings.* London: Allan Wingate, 1956, First edition; 8vo. pages 148 14 plates, presentation copy, boldly signed by author for Mary(Molly) Montagu Douglas Scott, Duchess of Buccleuch (1990-1993), very good in tatty torn and rubbed very good- dust jacket.   Any Amount of Books   May 29 2011 - A74985 2011 $230

Lesclache, Louis De *La Philosophie Expliquee en Tables par....* Paris: n.p., 1656, Second edition; five parts in one volume, oblong 4to., engraved title, 139 engraved tables, 5 engraved plates, gilt ruled contemporary mottled calf, raised bands, gilt spine ends chipped, small bookplates of Lutley Manor and Fort Hill, manuscript inscription on title, very rare.   Jeff Weber Rare Books   163 - 17 2011 $6500

Leslie, Charles Robert *A Hand-Book for Young Painters.* London: John Murray, 1855, First edition; 8vo., xiii, (1), 313, (i), 32 pages ads, frontispiece and 23 plates, very good, later 19th century half red gilt morocco.   Ken Spelman Rare Books   68 - 45 2011   £60

Leslie, Charles Robert *Life and Letters of John Constable, R.A.* London: Chapman & Hall, 1896, New edition; large 4to., half title, frontispiece, illustrations, original white and blue cloth gilt, slightly marked, nice, bookplate of Freda Blois.   Jarndyce Antiquarian Booksellers   CXCI - 139 2011   £70

Leslie, Charles Robert *Life and Times of Sir Joshua Reynolds.* London: John Murray, 1865, First edition; 222 x 143 mm., 4 volumes, very handsome chestnut brown crushed morocco by Bayntun (signed on turn-in), covers gilt with interlocking strapwork frame and large central lozenge, lancet corner ornaments, spines gilt in compartments of similar design, turn-ins with gilt French fillets ad palmette cornerpieces, marbled endpapers, all edges gilt, housed in brown buckram covered slipcase, upper seams of slipcase neatly reinforced with library tape; extra illustrated with 194 plates, 40 of them in color in addition to the 11 called for; spines lightly but uniformly sunned to pleasing honey brown, one leaf with small neat repair to fore-edge, other trival imperfections but lovely set in very fine condition, leaves and plates fresh, clean and bright, binding nearly pristine. Phillip J. Pirages   59 - 298 2011 $2400

Leslie, Charles Robert *A Short and Easy Method with the Deists... (bound with) The Truth of Christianity Demonstrated...* London: F. and C. Rivington, 1799, New edition; bound together in contemporary full polished tree calf gilt, edges little bumped and cracked, spine rather dulled, engraved roundel bookplate of Jacob Skinner.   R. F. G. Hollett & Son Antiquarian Booksellers   175 - 821 2011   £85

Leslie, Eliza *The Indian Meal Book.* London: Smith, Elder and Co., 1846, First edition; paper little toned, slight marking to title, one blank leaf bound in after title, one blank leaf bound in after this title, pages viii 55, (1), 12mo., modern quarter maroon calf with marbled boards, spine gilt lettered vertically direct, very good, rare.   Blackwell Rare Books B166 - 64 2011   £1200

Lesson, Rene Primevere *Histoire Naturelle des Oiseaux - Mouches: Histoire Naturelle des Colibris, Suivie d'un Supplement a l'Histoire des Oisseaux.* Arthus Bertrand, 1829-1833, 3 volumes, 86 66, 66 hand finished color printed engraved plates (some tanning, light offsetting from text to plates in 2 volumes, light soiling or light foxing to few, many of which have bright iridescence); 8vo., xlvi, 220; x, 196; iv, xliii, 171, matching modern brown half morocco, pages 221-223 of index missing from volume I, occasional foxing, marginal browning to title volume III, half title missing, engraved dedications present in volumes I and II, all edges gilt.   Raymond M. Sutton, Jr.   May 26 2011 - 28608 2011 $5500

Lethem, Jonathan *As She Climbed across the Table.* New York: Doubleday, 1997, First edition; book fine, dust jacket fine, signed by author.   Bella Luna Books   May 29 2011 - t722s 2011 $82

Lethem, Jonathan *Girl in Landscape.* New York: Doubleday, 1998, First edition; fine in fine dust jacket, signed and dated by author Jan 21 2003.   Bella Luna Books   May 29 2011 - t9281 2011 $104

Lethem, Jonathan *Girl in Landscape.* New York: Doubleday, 1998, First edition; fine in fine dust jacket, first printing is incredibly scarce.   Bella Luna Books   May 29 2011 - t8793 2011 $82

Lethem, Jonathan *Gun with Occasional Music.* New York: Harcourt Brace, 1994, First edition; fine, dust jacket fine.   Bella Luna Books   May 29 2011 - 4340 2011 $82

Leto, Giulio Pomponio *Romanae Historiae Compendium etc.* Paris: Jean Dupre 7 May, 1501, 4to. in 6's, ff. (62), woodcut illustration on titlepage, large device at end, 18th century smooth calf, gilt spine, red edges, handsome copy, the copy of Nicolas Maillard of Rouen, from the library of the Earls of Macclesfield at Shirburn Castle.   Maggs Bros. Ltd. 1440 - 130 2011   £1500

A Letter to Ball Hughes Esq. on Club House and Private Gaming, His Dog Hector and Col. B-K-Y, Cribb's Dog and Lord H-R-H and bet with Dean S. and Mr. Lloyd. London: printed and published by J. Evans 20 Wych Street Strand, 1824, Only edition; 8vo., (3)-35 (1) pages, possibly wanting half title, preserved in modern wrappers with printed title label on upper cover, very good, only edition, exceptionally rare.   John Drury Rare Books   154 - 2 2011   £750

A Letter to His Majesty William IV. Paris?: 1830, Only edition; 8vo., (2), 21, (1) pages, generally rather browned and foxed, original printed blue wrappers, contemporary ownership signature of Lord Visct. Althorpe, very rare. John Drury Rare Books   153 - 103 2011   £125

A Letter to John Buxton of Shadwell, Esq. on the Contests Relative to the Ensuing Election for the County of Norfolk. N.P.: Norwich?, 1768, First edition, variant issue; 8vo., 30, (2) pages last leaf blank, titlepage rather browned with old stain, inner margin of titlepage strengthened, preserved in modern wrappers, printed title on upper cover, rare. John Drury Rare Books   153 - 77 2011   £175

A Letter to the Author of a Letter to Mr. Buxton. In which It Is Proved, that the Design of that letter has been enitrely misunderstood and that the author of it is the real friend of Sir Edward Astley and Mr. Coke. Norwich?: printed in the year, 1768, First (only) edition; 8vo., 34 pages, preserved in modern wrappers with printed title label on upper cover, very good, rare.   John Drury Rare Books   153 - 78 2011 £175

A Letter to the Most Noble Thomas, Duke of Newcastle, on Certain Points of the Last Importance to These Nations... London: printed for H. Whitridge, 1746, First and only edition; 8vo., (2), 38 pages, bound fairly recently in marbled card covers with printed label on upper, very good, scarce. John Drury Rare Books   153 - 76   2011   £175

Letters Galantes et Philosophiques De Deux Nones Publiees par un Apotre du Libertinage avec des Notes. Paris: Ipan ile de la republique francaise, 1794, First illustrated edition; 18mo., pages (iv), 172, 4 engravings, first in 2 states, one 'avant la lettre', all edges gilt, some very light spotting and soiling, mid 19th century mid brown full morocco, gilt decorated and titled on spine, bookplate of G. Nordmann, near fine.   Simon Finch Rare Books   Zero - 417   2011   £4000

Lever Brothers   *The "Sunlight" Almanac for 1899.*   Port Sunlight: Lever Brothers, 1899, Original red embossed and decorated leather cloth gilt, edges rather worn, pages 160, printed in red, and blue, numerous illustrations.   R. F. G. Hollett & Son Antiquarian Booksellers   175 - 822   2011   £35

Lever Brothers   *The "Sunlight" Year Book for 1899.*   Port Sunlight: Lever Brothers, 1899, Original red decorated cloth gilt, pages 477, color frontispiece and numerous text illustrations.   R. F. G. Hollett & Son Antiquarian Booksellers   175 - 823   2011   £30

Lever, Charles 1806-1872   *Harry Lorrequer.*   London: Chapman & Hall, 1879, 24 page catalog, original pictorial limp card wrappers, slightly dulled but very good.   Jarndyce Antiquarian Booksellers   CXCI - 366   2011   £75

Lever, Ernest Harry   *Foreign Exchange from the Investor's Point of View.*   London: Charles and Edwin Layton, 1925, First edition; 8vo, original publisher's khaki green cloth lettered gilt on spine and on front cover, pages vii, 106, charts, tables, very slight shelfwear, endpapers very slightly browned, else near fine.   Any Amount of Books   May 29 2011 - A61908   2011 $255

Leverson, Ada   *Bird of Paradise.*   London: Grant Richards, 1914, First edition; half title, color frontispiece, 4 pages ads, original red cloth, blocked in blind, lettered in gilt, small crease in upper margin of front board, spine slightly faded, BGS monogram booklabel, good plus.   Jarndyce Antiquarian Booksellers   CLXC - 129   2011   £200

Leverson, Ada   *Love at Second Sight.*   London: Grant Richards, 1916, First edition; half title, original black cloth, blocked in yellow, lettered in gilt, inner hinges cracking, otherwise very good.   Jarndyce Antiquarian Booksellers   CLXC - 130   2011   £150

Leverson, Ada   *The Twelfth Hour.*   London: E. Grant Richards, 1907, First edition; half title, color frontispiece, 20 page catalog (1907), original green cloth blocked and lettered in gilt, spine slightly faded, inner hinges cracking, good plus.   Jarndyce Antiquarian Booksellers   CLXC - 133   2011   £150

Levi, David   *A Defence of the Old Testament, in a Series of Letters Addressed to Thomas Paine.*   New York: William A. Davis for Naphtali Judah, bookseller, 1797, First American edition; 240 pages, contemporary sheep, very skillfully rebacked in period style with original label retained, lower margin of S3 torn away, costing several words, occasional minor spotting, else very good, attractive copy.   Joseph J. Felcone Inc.   Fall Miscellany 2010 - 68   2011 $900

Levin, Adam   *The Instructions.*   San Francisco: McSweeney's, 2010, First edition thus; fine, signed by author.   Bella Luna Books   May 29 2011 - p3699   2011 $88

Levinson, Orde   *John Piper. The Complete Graphic Works.*   London: Faber, 1987, First edition; tall 4to., original boards, dust jacket, pages 141, with 218 color and 191 black and white illustrations, fine, scarce, etchings and aquatints, wood engravings, lithographs and screenprints.   R. F. G. Hollett & Son Antiquarian Booksellers   General Catalogue Summer 2010 - 240   2011   £275

Levis, H. C.   *Baziliologia. A Booke of Kings.*   New York: Grolier Club, 1913, Limited to 300 copies; 4to., xviii, 188 pages, unopened, original quarter tan cloth over cream paper boards, printed paper spine title label, covers lightly soiled, very good.   Jeff Weber Rare Books   163 - 112   2011 $100

Levitt, Helen   *Mexico City.*   New York: Doubleday & W. W. Norton, 1997, First edition, one of only 200 numbered copies; very fine with tiny publisher creases to top corners of few pages in fine dust jacket and slipcase, signed and numbered by Levitt on limitation page, quite uncommon.   Jeff Hirsch Books   ny 2010 2011 $600

Levitt, Helen   *A Way of Seeing.*   New York: Viking Press, 1965, First edition, cloth issue; very fresh near fine copy in near fine, price clipped dust jacket that has some very minor wear at top of spine and little creasing to top of back panel.   Jeff Hirsch Books   ny 2010 2011 $2500

Levitt, Helen *A Way of Seeing Photographs of New York.* New York: Viking Press, 1965, First edition; signed, oblong 8vo., pages (viii), 8, (65) 73-78, (2) blank, 51 black and white photos reproduced in gravure, original black cloth, spine and upper side lettered in white, original dust jacket printed in black, illustrated with black and white photos on upper and lower panels, small chip to head of spine and also at foot of front of spine, Leavitt's signature to titlepage, fine in near fine dust jacket.   Simon Finch Rare Books   Zero - 533   2011   £3750

Levy, Amy *Miss Meredith.* London: Hodder & Stoughton, 1889, First edition; half title, original cream cloth lettered in black, decorated in blue and black, darkened and little rubbed, good, sound copy.   Jarndyce Antiquarian Booksellers   CLXC - 134   2011   £300

Levy, Deborah *An Amorous Discourse in the Suburbs of Hell.* London: Jonathan Cape, 1990, First edition; 8vo., pages 77, illustrations by Andrzej Borkowski, large format paperback, wrappers, very slight handling wear, but pretty much fine, from the working library of novelist Angela Carter, small attractive bookplate.   Any Amount of Books   May 29 2011 - A63685   2011 $306

Levy, Ferdinand *Flashes from the Dark.* Dublin: Printed at the Sign of the Three Candles, 1941, First edition; number 7 of 12 copies on handmade paper, of an edition of 162, signed presentation from author, spine slightly faded, rear cloth slightly wrinkled, slight rubbing at corners and cover otherwise sound, very good.   Any Amount of Books   May 26 2011 - A76312   2011 $503

Levy, Joseph Hiam *Wealthy and Wise: a Lecture Introductory to the Study of Political Economy.* London: P. S. King, 1879, First separate edition; 8vo., 30 pages, original printed wrappers, good, scarce.   John Drury Rare Books   153 - 79   2011   £35

Lewis, Angelo John   1839-1919 *Card Tricks without Apparatus.* London: Frederick Warne & Co., 1892, Half title, illustrations, 9 pages ads, original white pictorial wrappers, decorated with king of hearts, very good.   Jarndyce Antiquarian Booksellers   CXCI - 364   2011   £40

Lewis, Angelo John   1839-1919 *Later Magic.* London: George Routledge and Sons, 1931, Enlarged edition; original pictorial red cloth, rather faded, pages xviii, 738, portrait, 206 text illustrations.   R. F. G. Hollett & Son Antiquarian Booksellers   175 - 642   2011   £50

Lewis, Angelo John   1839-1919 *More Magic.* Bland's Magical Palace, n.d., Original pictorial green cloth gilt, extremities rubbed, pages x, 457, x, with 140 text illustrations, title with sheet of ads laid in reverse, little damaged. R. F. G. Hollett & Son Antiquarian Booksellers   175 - 644   2011   £50

Lewis, Arthur, Mrs. *Salthurst.* London: Samuel Tinsley, 1878, First edition; 3 volumes, 6 page and 32 page catalog volume III, text slightly browned, facsimile title volume II, original crimson cloth by W. Bone & Son, rubbed and seriously affected by damp, small splits in spine volume III, inner hinges cracking, inscribed by author for her son, Alfred Hartley Lewis.   Jarndyce Antiquarian Booksellers   CLXC - 136   2011   £90

Lewis, Cecil Day *We're Not going to Do Nothing.* The Left Review, 1936, First edition; small 8vo., original wrappers, pages 31.   R. F. G. Hollett & Son Antiquarian Booksellers   175 - 824   2011   £45

Lewis, Clive Staples   1898-1963 *The Allegory of Love: a Study in Medieval Tradition.* Oxford University Press, 1936, First edition; pages (ii), x, 380, 8vo., original dark blue cloth, backstrip gilt blocked, near fine.   Blackwell Rare Books   B166 - 176   2011   £450

Lewis, Clive Staples   1898-1963 *Christian Behavior.* London: Geoffrey Bles, 1943, First edition; small 8vo., original orange cloth, 64 pages.   R. F. G. Hollett & Son Antiquarian Booksellers   175 - 826   2011   £30

Lewis, Clive Staples   1898-1963 *Christian Reflections.* London: Geoffrey Bles, 1967, First edition; original cloth, gilt, dust jacket, pages xiv, 176, label removed from pastedown, otherwise fine.   R. F. G. Hollett & Son Antiquarian Booksellers   175 - 827   2011   £30

Lewis, Clive Staples   1898-1963 *The Four Loves.* London: Geoffrey Bles, 1960, First edition; original cloth, dust jacket, pages 160, slight dustiness and spotting to edges.   R. F. G. Hollett & Son Antiquarian Booksellers   175 - 828   2011   £60

Lewis, Clive Staples   1898-1963 *Letters to Malcolm Chiefly on Prayer.* London: Geoffrey Bles, 1964, First edition; original cloth, gilt, dust jacket price clipped, pages 160, few spots to fore-edge.   R. F. G. Hollett & Son Antiquarian Booksellers   175 - 830   2011   £45

Lewis, Clive Staples   1898-1963 *Miracles. A Preliminary Study.* London: Geoffrey Bles, 1947, First edition; original cloth, gilt, dust jacket (price clipped and trifle dusty, trifling edge wear in places), pages 220, back flyleaf partially browned.   R. F. G. Hollett & Son Antiquarian Booksellers   175 - 831   2011   £120

Lewis, Clive Staples 1898-1963 *Out of the Silent Planet, Perelandra. That Hideous Strength. (C. S. Lewis Space Trilogy - The Ransom Trilogy).* London: John Lane The Bodley Head, 1938, 1943. 1945. First edition; 8vo., 3 volumes, uniformly bound in recent dark blue half morocco with raised bands, gilt titles and gilt to spines, new endpapers, text of "Silent Planet" slightly browned and spotted, other 2 fine. Any Amount of Books May 26 2011 - A69880 2011 $1006

Lewis, Clive Staples 1898-1963 *Reflections on the Psalms.* London: Geoffrey Bles, 1958, First edition; small 8vo., original mauve cloth gilt, dust jacket, pages 151, light spots to fore-edge. R. F. G. Hollett & Son Antiquarian Booksellers 175 - 832 2011 £75

Lewis, Clive Staples 1898-1963 *The Screwtape Letters.* New York: Macmillan, July, 1943, Fifth or later edition, sixth printing; bookplate of Clarence "Clip" Boutell, nearly fine in dust jacket with chips at head and foot of spine. Lupack Rare Books May 26 2011 - ABE1309855976 2011 $250

Lewis, Clive Staples 1898-1963 *The Screwtape Letters.* Bles, 1942, First edition; pages 160, foolscap 8vo., original black cloth, trifle rubbed, printed label, owner's short note on front free endpaper, with rubber stamp, good. Blackwell Rare Books B166 - 177 2011 £300

Lewis, Clive Staples 1898-1963 *Studies in Words.* Cambridge: 1960, 240 pages, 8vo., near fine in like dust jacket (price clipped). Bookworm & Silverfish 668 - 79 2011 $68

Lewis, Clive Staples 1898-1963 *Surprised by Joy.* London: Geoffrey Bles, 1955, First edition; original cloth, gilt, dust jacket (few short edge tears to lower panel), pages 224, few light spots to flyleaves. R. F. G. Hollett & Son Antiquarian Booksellers 175 - 833 2011 £40

Lewis, Clive Staples 1898-1963 *They Asked for a Paper. Papers and Addresses.* London: Geoffrey Bles, 1962, First edition; pages 211, flyleaves faintly browned from dust jacket flaps, original cloth. R. F. G. Hollett & Son Antiquarian Booksellers 175 - 834 2011 £50

Lewis, Clive Staples 1898-1963 *Till We Have Faces.* London: Geoffrey Bles, 1956, First edition; original cloth, gilt, dust jacket, slight spotting to lower panel, pages 320, flyleaves partially and lightly browned. R. F. G. Hollett & Son Antiquarian Booksellers 175 - 835 2011 £180

Lewis, Florence *China Painting.* London: Cassell & Co., 1884, 8vo., three quarter leather, rebacked in modern leather, 16 tipped in chromolithographs. Barnaby Rudge Booksellers Art & Architecture & Photography - 013949 2011 $125

Lewis, G. R. *The Ancient Font of Little Walsingham in Norfolk Drawn and Illustrated with Descriptive Interpretation.* G. R. Lewis, 1843, Folio, original half parchment with marbled boards, crimson straight grained morocco label on upper board, parchment little soiled and defective at head and tail of spine, nick in upper hinge, pages 8 plus 7 lithographed plates, little spotting and staining in places, signature of Earl of Belmore 1884. R. F. G. Hollett & Son Antiquarian Booksellers 177 - 545 2011 £120

Lewis, H. Elvet *Homes and Haunts of the Pilgrim Fathers.* London: Religious Tract Society, 1920, 4to., original red cloth, gilt, corners little bumped, pages 143, 4 color plates and numerous drawings and photos all by Charles Whymper, nice gift inscription (non-authorial). R. F. G. Hollett & Son Antiquarian Booksellers General Catalogue Summer 2010 - 1462 2011 £65

Lewis, John *The History of Great Britain, From the First Inhabitants Thereof...* London: F. Gyles, Woodman & Lyon, C. Davis, 1729, First edition; folio, (6), 71, (1 blank) 251, (1 blank, 22), 52 (i.e. 46) (34) pages, engraved chapter ornament, engraved capitals, full original brown calf, gilt ruled covers, raised bands, gilt stamped spine panels, gilt stamped black leather spine label, covers scratched, corners worn, fine, scarce. Jeff Weber Rare Books 163 - 35 2011 $3000

Lewis, John *The Life of Mayster Wyllyam Caxton etc.* London: printed in the year, 1737, Royal 8vo., xxii (engraved portrait on page (iii), 156, (6) pages, 2 full page woodcut illustrations of watermarks on pages (160-161), contemporary parchment backed blue paper boards, spine completely worn, deckle edges, with Proposals for Printing an Historical Account of that Most Universally Celebrated as well as useful art of typography (The Life of William Caxton) by John Bagford folded in; from the library of the Earls of Macclesfield at Shirburn Castle. Maggs Bros. Ltd. 1440 - 19 2011 £8000

Lewis, John *Pratt Ware. English and Scottish Relief Decorated and Underglaze Coloured Earthenware 1780-1840.* Antique Collectors Club, 1984, First edition; pages 304, with 577 illustrations, original cloth, gilt, dust jacket, fine. R. F. G. Hollett & Son Antiquarian Booksellers General Catalogue Summer 2010 - 243 2011 £85

Lewis, John *Some Account of Suffragan Bishops in England.* London: printed by and for J. Nichols, 1785, 4to., modern blue cloth, gilt, pages 52, with general and specific titles. R. F. G. Hollett & Son Antiquarian Booksellers 175 - 837 2011 £95

Lewis, Leslie Allin *Tales of the Grotesque: a Collection of Uneasy Tales.* London: Ghost Story Press, 1994, Second edition; octavo, cloth. L. W. Currey, Inc. 124 - 163 2011 $350

Lewis, Mathew Gregory 1775-1818 *The Monk: a Romance in Three Volumes.* London: Bell, 1797, 3 volumes, 8vo., pages (vi), 232; (ii), 287; (ii), 315 (page 316 carries ads for 2 recent Bell publications), uncut, old repairs to C7 and C8 of volume i, completely unsophisticated, original pale blue boards, paper spines with spine labels, soiling and spotting to boards, upper board and spine chipped of volume I, ownership name plate to inner pastedown. Simon Finch Rare Books Zero - 250 2011 £1000

Lewis, Meriwether 1774-1809 *Original Journals of the Lewis and Clark Expedition 1804-1806.* New York: Dodd Mead and Co., 1904, One of 200 numbered copies on Van Gelder handmade paper; large quarto, 7 volumes extended to 14 plus atlas volume, with profusion of plates, facsimiles, folding maps &c., green cloth, bindings moderately worn at extremities, cloth lightly discolored as usual, very good, text largely unopened. Joseph J. Felcone Inc. Fall Miscellany 2010 - 74 2011 $15,000

Lewis, Meriwether 1774-1809 *Travels to the Source of the Missouri River and Across the American Continent to the Pacific Ocean.* London: Longman, Hurst, Rees, Orme and Brown, 1814, First British edition; quarto, one large folding engraved map, 5 engraved plans on 3 plates, original full tan polished calf, rebacked to style. Heritage Book Shop Booth A12 51st NY International Antiquarian Book Fair April 8-10 2011 - 85 2011 $27,500

Lewis, Meriwether 1774-1809 *Travels to the Source of the Missouri River and Across the American Continent to the Pacific Ocean Performed... in the Years 1804, 1805 and 1806.* London: for Longman et al, 1817, 3 volumes xxvi, (2) 411; xii, 434; xii, 394 pages, large folding map, 5 plates, modern calf backed marbled paper covered boards, very skillfully executed in period style, plates considerably foxed and offset onto facing pages, old tears to map skillfully remended on verso, otherwise very handsome copy in correct period style binding, contemporary signature "Colonel Forbes" in each copy. Joseph J. Felcone Inc. Fall Miscellany 2010 - 75 2011 $14,000

Lewis, Randle *Reflections on the Causes of Unhappy Marriages, and on Various Subjects Therewith...* London: W. Clarke, 1805, First and only edition; 8vo., (5) iv-vi 160 pages, titlepage little soiled, early 19th century ownership signature at head of title of George Cruikshank, in high quality early 20th century dark green quarter morocco over marbled boards, spine fully gilt and lettered, handsome copy. John Drury Rare Books 153 - 80 2011 £500

Lewis, William 1787-1870 *Chess Problems. Being a Selection of Original Positions...* London: Sampson Low, 1827, First edition; 8vo., (4), 164 pages, 100 illustrations, original blindstamped cloth, spine joints neatly restored, gilt lettered, very good, perhaps fine, most uncommon. John Drury Rare Books 153 - 81 2011 £425

Lewis, Wyndham 1882-1957 *The Jews, Are They Human?* London: Allen & Unwin, 1939, First edition; fine, dust jacket with small tear from top of titlepage not affecting text, otherwise very fine. I. D. Edrich May 26 2011 - 61597 2011 $419

Lewis, Wyndham 1882-1957 *Left Wings Over Europe or How to make a War About Nothing.* London: Cape, 1936, First edition; prelims and final few leaves lightly foxed, pages 336, crown 8vo., original scarlet cloth, backstrip and front cover blocked in black, tail edges rough trimmed, dust jacket soiled (on plain white rear panel), chipped, good. Blackwell Rare Books B166 - 178 2011 £140

LeWitt, Sol *Sol LeWitt 100 Cubes.* Ostfildern: Cantz, 1996, picturing 100 colored cubes, printed recto only, complete with printed band, originals are gouache on paper, fine. By the Book, L. C. 26 - 38 2011 $650

Lewycka, Marina *A Short History of Tractos in Ukrainian.* London: Viking, 2005, First British edition; fine, in like dust jacket, with promotional sticker attached. Bella Luna Books May 29 2011 - t9038 2011 $82

Leybourn, William 1826-1700 *The Ready Reckoner, or Trader's Sure Guide...* London: T. Scollick and York: T. Wilson and R. Spence, 1785, New edition; small 8vo., original roan, rubbed and scraped, unpaginated, printed tables, title with simple decorative typographic border, inner corner torn from front flyleaf. R. F. G. Hollett & Son Antiquarian Booksellers 175 - 839 2011 £180

Leyland, John *Views of Ancient Buildings Illustrative of the Domestic Architecture of the Parish of Halifax.* Halifax: R. Leyland & Son, 1879, First edition; oblong folio, original cloth, gilt, top edges little damped, neatly recased, pages xii, plus 25 photo lithographed plates, few edge tears neatly repaired, title little dusty and spotted, small stamps on title and back of final plate, armorial bookplate of John Theodore Boyle (rather soiled and relaid). R. F. G. Hollett & Son Antiquarian Booksellers 177 - 546 2011 £180

Leymarie, Jean *Chanel.* Geneva/New York: Skira/Rizzoli, 1987, First edition; large 4to., copiously illustrated in color and black and white, 225 pages, fine in fine dust jacket, in very good+ slipcase. Any Amount of Books May 29 2011 - A67816 2011 $204

Lidbetter, Hubert *The Friends Meeting House.* York: Ebor Press, 1961, Limited edition, no. 8; original cloth, gilt, dust jacket, pages xvi, 84, with 72 plates and 47 plans, sections and elevations, Dr. Arthur Raistrick's copy with his stamp. R. F. G. Hollett & Son Antiquarian Booksellers 177 - 548 2011 £35

Lie, Jona *Weird Tales from the Northern Seas from the Danish of Jonas Lie.* London: Kegan Paul etc., 1893, First edition; modern half blue levant morocco gilt, pages vii, 201, 12 plates by Laurence Housman, handsome. R. F. G. Hollett & Son Antiquarian Booksellers General Catalogue Summer 2010 - 624 2011 £150

Life and Death of Cock Robin. New York: McLoughlin Bros., Publishers 30 Beekman Street circa, 1864, 7 1/2 x 4 1/2 inches, dark blue printed paper wrappers with few spots, some clear tape, minor splitting to ends of spine, few spots on pages inside, 8 pages within, each with one or two half page hand colored wood engravings. Jo Ann Reisler, Ltd. 86 - 85 2011 $250

Life in an English Village. London: Penguin Books, 1949, First edition; small 8vo., original decorated boards, upper joint little cracked, pages 32, 16 color plates, 5 full page line drawings. R. F. G. Hollett & Son Antiquarian Booksellers General Catalogue Summer 2010 - 709 2011 £60

The Life of General Zachary Taylor and a History of the War in Mexico. New York: William H. Graham, 1847, First edition; 8vo., 64 pages, original printed and pictorial wrappers (darkened, some wear to extremities), double column, including frontispiece, illustrated title and 5 text illustrations, solid copy, text fairly fresh. M & S Rare Books, Inc. 90 - 252 2011 $250

The Life of Jesus of Nazareth. London: Eyre & Spottiswoode Bible Warehouse, n.d. circa, 1908, Large 8vo., original decorated black cloth gilt over bevelled boards, pages xlv, (80), (22), with 80 color plates. R. F. G. Hollett & Son Antiquarian Booksellers General Catalogue Summer 2010 - 425 2011 £45

The Life of Mohammed Ali: Viceroy of India. London: E. Churton, 1841, First (and only) edition; small 8vo., pages (vi), 96, folding engraved plates, additional engraved title with vignette of Mohammed Ali, 4 pages publishers list bound in at end, original limp blue cloth, lettered in gilt on upper cover, very slight waterstaining of upper endpapers, little foxing of engraved titlepage, very good, most uncommon. J. & S. L. Bonham Antiquarian Booksellers Africa 4/20/2011 - 1982 2011 £480

Light, Golden *Angel's Visits to My Farm in Florida.* New York: United States Book Co., 1892, 8vo, very good, gray cloth. Barnaby Rudge Booksellers Travel and Exploration - 013664 2011 $75

Lightman, Alan *Einstein's Dreams.* New York: Pantheon, 1993, First edition; fine, dust jacket fine, signed by author. Bella Luna Books May 29 2011 - j1913 2011 $82

Ligotti, Thomas *Songs of a Dead Dreamer.* Albuquerque: Silver Scarab Press, 1985, First edition; octavo, illustrations, pictorial wrappers. L. W. Currey, Inc. 124 - 109 2011 $750

Lilford, Thomas Littleton Powys, 4th Baron 1833-1896 *Notes on the Birds of Northamptonshire and Neighbourhood.* London: R. H. Porter, 1893, First edition; original publisher's red cloth lettered gilt on spine, printed for private circulation only, signed presentation from author for Duchess of Bedford, faint mottling to spine, very slight wear to spine ends, otherwise very good, handsome. Any Amount of Books May 29 2011 - A69809 2011 $408

Lillingston, Charles *The Causes of the Present Agricultural Distress Clearly Proved.* Warwick: sold by Merridew, Wrightson and Webb, Birmingham: Tite, Coleshill and Shalders, Ipswich, 1834, First edition; 8vo., (8), 35, (1), 6 (2) pages, including additional (alternative?) titlepage, well bound in linen backed marbled boards lettered, very good, very rare. John Drury Rare Books 153 - 82 2011 £150

Lilly, William *William Lilly's History of His Life and Times from the Year 1602 to 1681.* London: Reprinted for Charles Baldwyn, 1822, 252 x 154mm. 2 p.l., 260 pages, lovely dark brown crushed morocco, lavishly gilt by Zaehnsdorf (stamp signed on front turn-in, and with Zaehnsdorf's gilt oval stamp on rear turn-in), covers with wide lacy filigree border scalloped at inner edge and filled with densely gilt floral tools and sprigs on stippled ground, this border around an inner frame composed of double gilt rules with tiny shamrock at each corner and inside this frame, central panel with ornate cornerpieces filled with flowers, volutes and drawer handles on stippled ground, raised bands, spine densely and handsomely gilt in scallop edged compartments featuring a central quatrefoil containing a rose surrounded by floral sprays, open dots and much stippling, gilt turn-ins, top edge gilt, 12 engraved portraits printed on India paper and mounted, as called for; armorial bookplate of Vincent Lloyd-Russell; leaves faintly toned (no doubt as in all copies because of paper stock used), moderate offsetting from plates, other trivial imperfections, but excellent copy internally text generally clean and fresh, gleaming binding in especially fine condition with no perceptible wear. Phillip J. Pirages 59 - 149 2011 $1250

Limborch, Phil *The History of the Inquisition, As It Has Subsisted in France, Italy, Spain, Portugal, Venice, Sicily, Sardinia, Milan, Poland, Flanders, &c.* London: W. Simpkin and R. Marshall, 1816, First edition; 8vo., wrappers, pages xvi, 542, frontispiece and 2 plates, sound, very good condition in plain brown paper wrappers with title inked on spine, slight foxing to titlepage and to 3 plates. Any Amount of Books May 29 2011 - A32748 2011 $306

Lincoln, Abraham 1809-1865 *Complete Works.* Harrogate: Lincoln Memorial University, 1894, Sponsor's Edition; signed by chancellor of the University (this copy #283 especially prepared for Sylvanus B. Bechtel), 235 x 160mm., 12 volumes, very pleasing publisher's elaborately gilt decorated scarlet morocco, upper boards intricately tooled with entrelac gilt strapwork and twining floral tendrils (in stylized 16th century Italian design), flat spines with similar gilt tooling in an elongated panel, top edge gilt, other edges rough trimmed, mostly unopened, 12 portrait frontispieces, 12 facsimiles of letter and other documents, 32 photo plates; first volume with tipped in letter on onion skin (photographic copy?) from John Hay to unnamed correspondent identifying the two figures in frontispiece with Lincoln as being Hay himself and John Nicolay; spines just bit darkened, printed on inexpensive paper, so leaves little browned at edges (no doubt as in all copies), one leaf with four inch horizontal tear across breadth of text without loss, otherwise quite fine set, text obviously largely unread and with decorative binding showing no significant wear.   Phillip J. Pirages   59 - 257   2011 $3250

Lincoln, Abraham 1809-1865 *The Writings of Abraham Lincoln.* New York: G. P. Putnam's Sons, 1923, Special Constitutional edition; very good plus set (some shading to spines of couple of volumes, tight, clean texts).   Lupack Rare Books   May 26 2011 - ABE3153092429   2011 $200

Lindberg, David C. *Roger Bacon and the Origins of Perspectiva in the Middle Ages.* Oxford: Clarendon Press, 1996, First edition; 8vo., cxi, 411 pages, figures, index, black cloth, gilt stamped cover and spine titles, fine, from the Bern Dibner reference library, with Burndy bookplate.   Jeff Weber Rare Books   161 - 23   2011 $180

Lindbergh, Anne Morrow *North to the Orient.* New York: Harcourt Brace and Co., 1935, First edition; octavo, (1)-255, (1, blank) pages, black and white photo frontispiece and numerous printed maps by Charles Lindbergh, publisher's original blue cloth, spine stamped and lettered in silver, top edge gilt, map printed endpapers, inscription on half title, publisher's dust jacket, jacket bit chipped at extremities and creased along top front edge, fine copy, inscribed by Charles and Anne Lindbergh for Albert H. Ebeling.   Heritage Book Shop   Holiday 2010 - 73   2011 $1500

Lindbergh, Anne Morrow *The Wave of the Future.* New York: Harcourt Brace, 1940, First edition; small 8vo., 41 pages, signed by author, fine in fine dust jacket.   By the Book, L. C.   26 - 11   2011 $500

Lindbergh, Reeve *John's Apples. thirteen Paintings by John Wilde. Twelve Poems by Reeve Lindberg.* Mt. Horeb: Perishable Press, 1995, One of 125 numbered copies; on 10 different papers, this one of the printer's own copies with his pencil notations, page size 9 7/8 x 6 1/4 inches, 102 pages, 78 of which printed, bound by printer in drab paper over boards with rondel cut-out on upper panel showing color image of two Golden Delicious apples (one bitten on), linen spine, printed on Heidelberg CPC and an old Vandercook, 14 pt. Stempel Syntax was set by hand, the unfinished looking front cover is not glued down and two of the 7 signatures are left uncut and untrimmed, replete with colorbars, etc, lovely, intriguing book.   Priscilla Juvelis - Rare Books   48 - 18   2011 $1500

Linden, Eddie *Aquarius.* 1969-1998,   21 numbers in 17 issues, original wrappers, very good.   I. D. Edrich   May 26 2011 - 82144   2011 $419

Lindley, Augustus *After Ophir; or a Search for the South African Gold Fields.* London: Cassell, n.d., 1870, Second edition; small quarto, pages vii,3 12, illustrations, contemporary half red calf, attractive prize copy, gilt stamp of King's College Melbourne.   J. & S. L. Bonham Antiquarian Booksellers   Africa 4/20/2011 - 4663   2011   £175

Lindsay, Caroline Blanche Elizabeth Fitzroy *The Flower Seller and Other Poems.* London: Longman, Green and Co., 1896, First edition; half title, uncut, original olive green cloth, bevelled boards, lettered in gilt, spine slightly dulled, very good.   Jarndyce Antiquarian Booksellers   CLXC - 141   2011   £65

Lindsay, Caroline Blanche Elizabeth Fitzroy *Poems of Love and Death.* London: Kegan Paul, Trench, Trubner & Co., 1907, Half title, 12 pages ads, endpapers little browned, odd spot, original olive green cloth, lettered in gilt, spine slightly faded and slightly rubbed at head and tail, top edge gilt, good plus.   Jarndyce Antiquarian Booksellers   CLXC - 142   2011   £50

Lindsay, John *A View of the History and Coinage of the Parthians.* Cork: 1852, First edition; vii, 250 pages + errata leaf, 12 plates, gathered and stitched ready for binding but never clothed, proof?, very good.   C. P. Hyland   May 26 2011 - 259/253   2011 $290

Lindsay, Lady *About Robins. Facts an Songs and Legends.* London: Frederick Warne, n.d. circa, 1890, 4to., original cloth backed pictorial boards, trifle marked, pages 115, 7 pages in color, numerous drawings, scattered spotting.   R. F. G. Hollett & Son Antiquarian Booksellers   175 - 843   2011   £75

Lindsay, Nicholas Vachel 1879-1931 *The Golden Book of Springfield.* New York: 1920, First edition; iv, 329 pages, near fine, lower free corner bumped, dust jacket with 1 inch splitting top and bottom front crease, one chip at top.   Bookworm & Silverfish   668 - 86   2011 $145

Lindsay, Seymour *Iron and Brass Implements of the English House.* Alec Tiranti, 1964, Revised edition; 4to., pages 88, 473 illustrations, original black cloth.   R. F. G. Hollett & Son Antiquarian Booksellers   General Catalogue Summer 2010 - 245   2011   £30

Linen, James *The Golden Gate.* San Francisco: Edward Bosqui & Co., 1869, Small 8vo., 38 pages, 8 engraved illustrations, original brown cloth, gilt stamped cover title, corners lightly rubbed, ownership marks on f.f.e.p., very good.   Jeff Weber Rare Books   163 - 84   2011 $90

Link, Henry Frederick *Travels in Portugal, and through France and Spain.* London: T. N. Longman & Rees, 1801, Contemporary half calf, excellently rebacked, brown label, very good. Jarndyce Antiquarian Booksellers   CXCI - 565   2011   £250

Linklater, Eric *Sealskin Trousers and Other Stories.* London: Rupert Hart Davis, 1947, First edition; original cloth, gilt, dust jacket edges little worn, spine faded and defective at head and foot, 127 pages, full page and other wood engravings.   R. F. G. Hollett & Son Antiquarian Booksellers   General Catalogue Summer 2010 - 807   2011   £30

Linne, Carl Von 1707-1778 *Genera Plantarum Eorumque Characteres Naturales Secundum Numerum, figuram Situm, et Proportionem Omnium Fructificationis Partium.* Holmiae: Impensis Laurentii Salvii, 1754, Fifth edition; 8vo., pages (3), xxxii, 500, (22), contemporary full calf, corners worn, some old cracks to calf on boards, professionally rebacked in calf, retaining original red morocco label, rear endpapers renewed upper corner to front endpaper, replaced, pages tanned, occasional light marginal foxing, with 5 raised bands.   Raymond M. Sutton, Jr.   May 26 2011 - 51623   2011 $1250

Linne, Carl Von 1707-1778 *Hortus Upsaliensis, Exhibens Plantas Exoticas.* Stockholmiae: Sumtu & Literis Laurentii Salvii, 1748, First edition; 3 folding engraved plates, 8vo., pages (10), 306 (40), 19th century quarter calf, some rubbing to edges, upper edges starting, ex-libris Gustav H. J. Dahl with handstamp on front flyleaf, name blackened out, small ink number on title, 1/8 inch marginal tear to 4 leaves.   Raymond M. Sutton, Jr.   May 26 2011 - 51626   2011 $1600

Linne, Carl Von 1707-1778 *Vollstandiges Natursystem nach der Swolften Lateinischen Ausgabe und Nach Anleituna des Hollandischen Houttuynischen Werks...* Nurnberg: Gabriel Nicolaus Raspe, 1774-1775, Volumes 3, 4, 6, parts 1 and 2 (of 6 volumes), very good, engraved vignette on titles and 60 folding engraved plates (soiling to outer margin of 2), 8vo., pages (14))15-) 64, 350, (16); (16), 400, (16); (16), 638; (14), (641-) 960 (108), early quarter calf with raised bands and gilt decorated panels on spines, rubbing and some abrasions to paper covered boards, titles contain old owner's signature, dated 1801, offsetting from text in volume 4, dampstain to a leaf, occasional foxing, from the library of Leop. Veisz, Vaczi Kegyes'Tanitorendi Haz.   Raymond M. Sutton, Jr.   May 26 2011 - 45686   2011 $1750

Linskill, Mary *Between the Heather and the Northern.* London: Richard Bentley, 1893, New edition; original dark blue embossed cloth, gilt spine, following board slightly marked, inner hinges weakening.   Jarndyce Antiquarian Booksellers   CLXC - 143   2011   £35

Linssen, E. F. *Beetles of the British Isles.* London and New York: Frederick Warne and Co., 1859, First edition; 2 volumes, small 8vo., original publisher's textured maroon cloth lettered gilt on spine and cover, with gilt illustration on cover, pages 295 and 300, 126 plates, numerous text figures and diagrams, volume 1 faintly rubbed at corners, otherwise fine in about very good dust jacket, slightly creased at edges and slightly nicked at head of spine, volume 2 very slightly bumped at corners, otherwise fine in lean, very good dust jacket, both jackets very slightly sunned at spine.   Any Amount of Books   May 29 2011 - A69422   2011 $383

Linstrum, Derek *Historic Architecture of Leeds.* Newcastle upon Tyne: Oriel Press, 1969, First edition; large 8vo., original cloth, gilt, dust jacket, pages 96, illustrations.   R. F. G. Hollett & Son Antiquarian Booksellers   177 - 549   2011   £50

Linton, Eliza Lynn *In Haste and at Leisure.* London: William Heinemann, 1895, Times Reading Club binding of original lime green cloth, lettered in black, spine dulled and little worn at head and tail.   Jarndyce Antiquarian Booksellers   CLXC - 145   2011   £70

Linton, Eliza Lynn *Ione.* Leipzig: Bernhard Tauchnitz, 1884, Copyright edition; 2 volumes, half titles, leading f.e.p. partially removed volume I, slightly later blue binder's cloth, maroon leather labels, good plus copy.   Jarndyce Antiquarian Booksellers   CLXC - 146   2011   £38

Linton, Eliza Lynn *The Lake Country.* London: Smith Elder & Co., 1864, First edition; pages xl, 351, with 100 illustrations by W. J. Linton, map, some scattered light spotting, attractive.   R. F. G. Hollett & Son Antiquarian Booksellers   173 - 689   2011   £180

Linton, Eliza Lynn *The Lake Country.* London: Smith, Elder & Co., 1864, First edition; original red cloth gilt extra, designed by John Leighton, over heavy bevelled boards, corners trifle frayed, pages xl, 351, all edges gilt, with 100 illustrations, double page map, frontispiece lightly spotted, signature of Mary Ogle (wife of Thomas Ogle, Lake District photographer) dated 1863, laid on top of title, handsome tight copy.   R. F. G. Hollett & Son Antiquarian Booksellers 173 - 690 2011   £225

Linton, Eliza Lynn *Lizzie of Greyrigg.* London: Tinsley Bros., 1866, First edition; 3 volumes, half titles, contemporary half maroon sheep, spines faded to brown, worn but sound, each volume signed Sarah A. Dunn in contemporary hand, library shelf numbers on spines.   Jarndyce Antiquarian Booksellers   CLXC - 147 2011   £125

Linton, Eliza Lynn *Patricia Kemball: a Novel.* London: Chatto & Windus, 1875, New edition; contemporary half black roan, head of spine slightly worn, good sound copy.   Jarndyce Antiquarian Booksellers   CLXC - 149 2011   £70

Linton, Eliza Lynn *The Rebel of the Family.* London: Chatto & Windus, circa, 1885, New edition; contemporary half black roan, head of spine slightly worn, good, sound copy.   Jarndyce Antiquarian Booksellers   CLXC - 150 2011   £40

Linton, Eliza Lynn *Sowing the Wind, a Novel.* London: Chatto & Windus, 1895, New edition; half title, 32 page catalog (Dec. 1894), lacks leading f.e.p., original olive green cloth, blocked & lettered in black and gilt, small bookseller's ticket, J. Wheathead of Appleby.   Jarndyce Antiquarian Booksellers   CLXC - 151 2011   £50

Linton, Eliza Lynn *The True History of Joshua Davidson. Christian and Communist.* London: Methuen & Co., 1890, Tenth edition; half title, 4 pages ads, several leaves carelessly opened, original cream boards, printed in black, spine slightly dulled, library label of Incorporation of Architects in Scotland, good plus.   Jarndyce Antiquarian Booksellers CLXC - 152 2011   £40

Linton, Eliza Lynn *Witch Stories.* London: Chatto & Windus, 1883, New edition; half title, original olive green cloth, blocked and lettered in black, very slight rubbing, but very good. Jarndyce Antiquarian Booksellers   CLXC - 154 2011   £75

Linton, Eliza Lynn *With a Silken Thread, and Other Stories.* London: Chatto & Windus, circa, 1885, New edition; original 19th century pink library binding, spine slightly faded, cancelled Bolland collection stamps, good plus.   Jarndyce Antiquarian Booksellers   CLXC - 155 2011   £35

Linton, Eliza Lynn *The World Well Lost.* London: Chatto & Windus, circa, 1884, New edition; half title, frontispiece, plates, 32 page catalog (Oct. 1884), original dark green cloth, blocked and lettered in black and gilt, very slight rubbing to spine, very good.   Jarndyce Antiquarian Booksellers CLXC - 156 2011   £50

Linton, W. J. *The Ferns of the English Lake Country with Tables of Varities.* Windermere: J. Garnett, 1878, Second edition; pages 179, illustrations, small 8vo., original green cloth, gilt, scarce.   R. F. G. Hollett & Son Antiquarian Booksellers   173 - 691 2011   £75

Linton, W. J. *James Watson. A Memoir of the Day of the Fight for a Free Press in England and of the Agitation for the People's Charter (1880).* New York: Augustus M. Kelley, 1971, Facsimile edition; original black cloth, gilt, pages 93, frontispiece.   R. F. G. Hollett & Son Antiquarian Booksellers 175 - 844 2011   £30

Lionni, Leo *Swimmy.* New York: Pantheon, 1963, First edition; 4to., pictorial boards, fine in very good+ slightly soiled dust jacket, illustrations, quite scarce.   Aleph-Bet Books, Inc. 95 - 334 2011 $300

Lipper, J. Heron *History of the Grand Lodge of Free & Accepted Masons of Ireland.* 1952-1957, First edition; 2 volumes, illustrations, lower fore corner volume I damaged (signed presentation from Phillip Crossie, a fellow-Mason), other than that, a very good set.   C. P. Hyland   May 26 2011 - 259/250 2011 $1232

Lister, Maria Theresa *Dacre; a Novel.* London: Longman, 1834, First edition; 3 volumes, contemporary half calf, spines with gilt raised bands, dark green leather labels, armorial bookplates of Thomas Greer with family motto "Memor Est", very good.   Jarndyce Antiquarian Booksellers   CLXC - 159 2011   £320

Lister, Martin *Conchyliorum Bivalvium Utriusque Aquae Exercitatio Anatomica Tertia.* London: Sumptibus authoris impressa, 1696, First edition; 4to., xliii, (1), 173 pages; 51 pages, 10 engraved plates, complete with terminal blank Z4 in first work, Dissertatio has its own titlepage and pagination, contemporary sprinkled calf, very skillfully rebacked to period style, small early shelfmark in red ink on endpaper and on title, minor paper flaw in S2 just grazing catchword, very faint foxing in fore edge, very lovely copy with text and plates, clean and fresh, armorial bookplate of A. Gifford, D.D. of the Museum, presentation copy from Lister for Mr. Dalone.   Joseph J. Felcone Inc.   Fall Miscellany 2010 - 76 2011 $10,000

Lister, Thomas Henry *Arlington.* New York: J. & J. Harper, 1832, First American edition; 2 volumes, 12mo., 2 pages ads, volume i, 4 pages ads, volume ii, some foxing and paper browning, mostly in volume ii which lackings leading f.e.p., tear to head of pages 193-196 volume i, uncut in original cream paper boards, purple cloth spine, paper labels, spines faded to brown, volume i label slightly torn, boards little foxed with slight loss of paper, signatures of Laura M. Kellogg & W. Kellogg with additional signature of D. Kellogg.   Jarndyce Antiquarian Booksellers   CXCI - 352   2011   £150

Litt, Toby *Adventures in Capitalism.* London: Secker & Warburg, 1996, First British edition, true first; fine in fine dust jacket.   Bella Luna Books   May 29 2011 - t5437   2011 $82

Little Bo Peep. New York: McLoughlin Bros. n.d. circa, 1870, 8vo., pictorial wrappers, fine, printed on linen, 6 full page chromolithographs, great copy.   Aleph-Bet Books, Inc.   95 - 348   2011 $250

Little Boy Blue and Other Nursery Rhymes. Blackie and Son, n.d. 1930's, Large 8vo., original card wrappers, glazed pictorial upper board, pages (24), drawings throughout by John Hassall, some brown stains to lower margins in plates, otherwise very good, scarce.   R. F. G. Hollett & Sons Antiquarian Booksellers   170 - 312   2011   £85

Little Deserter. New York: McLoughlin Bros. n.d. circa, 1880, 4to., pictorial wrappers, 12 pages, neat spine mend and one closed tear, very good+, bright and clean, 6 very fine full page chromolithographs on black backgrounds. Aleph-Bet Books, Inc.   95 - 349   2011 $475

The Little Fairy Sister. A. & C. Black, 1923, First edition; small 4to., original cloth backed patterned boards, gilt with paper label, extremities little worn and frayed, pages viii, 92, (iv), 8 color plates, 8 black and white plates and pictorial endpapers, little scattered spotting.   R. F. G. Hollett & Sons Antiquarian Booksellers   170 - 403   2011   £450

Little Folks: a Magazine for the Young. London: Cassell & Co., 1887-1894, 13 bi-annual volumes, large 8vo., contemporary half red roan, gilt, owner's name (Emily Barratt) in gilt on each upper board, some rubbing to extremities, few surface defects to leather in places, each volume with 2 chromolithographs and numerous full page and text illustrations, collections includes parts 1 and 2 for 1887, 1888, 189, 1892 and 1892 and part 2 each for 1889, 1892 and 1893, attractive collection.   R. F. G. Hollett & Son Antiquarian Booksellers   General Catalogue Summer 2010 - 505   2011 £450

The Little Folks' Gift Book. London: Frederick Warne & Co. circa, 1890, 136 pages, 20 color plates and numerous illustrations, fine bright copy, original cloth backed pictorial glazed boards.   Ken Spelman Rare Books   68 - 204   2011 £80

Little Henry and His Bird. New London: John R. Bolles, 1851, 12mo., 8 leaves, decorative paper wrappers, text adorned with 7 half page hand colored wood engravings, titlepage printed with repeat of inside engraving, upper wrapper with designed title enclosed in engraved garland of flowers, lightly dusted, small hole on lower wrapper, rare imprint in very good state.   Hobbyhorse Books   56 - 95   2011 $150

The Little Juggler. New York: Hastings House, 1961, First edition; 8vo., cloth, fine in dust jacket slightly frayed at spine ends, illustrations in color by Barbara Cooney, laid in is 2 page hand written letter from Cooney.   Aleph-Bet Books, Inc.   95 - 164   2011 $350

Little Max. London: Seeley, Jackson and Halliday, 1869, 4to., 15 engravings, original brown cloth gilt, recased, pages 96, plus 15 tinted illustrated pages, new endpapers.   R. F. G. Hollett & Sons Antiquarian Booksellers   170 - 253   2011 £75

Little Nancy, or the Punishment of Greediness. Philadelphia: Morgan & Yeager, n.d. circa, 1824, Square 12mo., 8 pages, 4 leaves, 1 page list on lower wrapper, buff stiff paper wrappers, minor chipping at lower corner of spine, light foxing at last leaf, fine.   Hobbyhorse Books   56 - 96   2011 $220

The Little Ones' Sunday Picture Book. London: 1900, 4to., original cloth backed pictorial boards, lower boards little bruised, unpaginated, titled illustrations without text, chromolithographed throughout.   R. F. G. Hollett & Sons Antiquarian Booksellers   170 - 476   2011   £75

Little Red Riding Hood in Eight Reels. Milwaukee: Craft Novelty Makers, 1921, 4to., pictorial boards, cover soil, else very good+, full page depiction of a movie theatre and where stage woul be is a die-cut hole, moveable wheel beneath hole that tells the story of Little Red as it is turned, rare.   Aleph-Bet Books, Inc.   95 - 378   2011 $600

Little Red Riding Hood. London: Chatto & Windus, 1975, Small 8vo., original glazed pictorial boards, 5 peepshows, illustrations in color by Linda Griffith, elastic tie.   R. F. G. Hollett & Sons Antiquarian Booksellers   170 - 520   2011 £45

Little Red Riding Hood. New York: Blue Ribbon, 1935, 8vo., pictorial boards, fine, illustrations by Harold Lentz, pictorial endpapers, full page and in text black and whites, one double page pop-up.   Aleph-Bet Books, Inc.   95 - 446   2011 $300

The Little Sketch-Book; or Useful Objects Illustrated. New York: Higgins & Kellogg, n.d. cica, 1835, 80 x 50mm., original blue paper wrappers, engraved vignette, full page wood engraved river view frontispiece, plus five half page engravings in text, mint.   Hobbyhorse Books   56 - 107   2011 $90

Little Soldier Boys.   New York: McLoughlin Bros., 1899, 4to., pictorial wrapper, some wear to rear cover, very good+, 6 brilliant full page chromolithographs and with 2 color illustrations in text.   Aleph-Bet Books, Inc.   95 - 350   2011 $375

Little Solider Boys ABC.   New York: McLoughlin Bros., 1900, 4to., pictorial wrappers, some shelf wear, very good+, brightly illustrated with chromolithographs on every page.   Aleph-Bet Books, Inc.   95 - 26   2011 $275

The Little Sportsman's Alphabet (Aunt Louisa's London Toy Books number 95).   London: Frederick Warne & co. circa, 1880, 4to., green paper covers with color decorations and illustrations, some light soiling to covers and bit of minor wear to spine, 12 full page color illustrations by Fred Grey.   Jo Ann Reisler, Ltd.   86 - 4   2011 $650

Little, Arthur D.   *Seaborne Operation Target Bulgaria.*   Cambridge: Arthur D. Little Inc., 1955,   126 pages, very good, plastic comb binding, covers slightly torn, interior clean and tight.   G. H. Mott Bookseller   May 26 2011 - 39961   2011 $200

Little, Elizabeth A.   *Chronicles of Patterdale.*   Penrith: Cumberland and Westmorland Herald, 1961,   First edition; small 4to., original wrappers, spine faded, pages 80, illustrations.   R. F. G. Hollett & Son Antiquarian Booksellers   173 - 692   2011   £50

Little, Henry William   *Madagascar: Its History and People.*   Edinburgh & London: William Blackwood, 1884,   First edition; half title, folding map, initial ad leaf, original brown cloth, spine dulled and slightly marked, small ink number on title.   Jarndyce Antiquarian Booksellers   CXCI - 566   2011   £110

Livingston, William Kenneth   *The Clinical Aspects of Visceral Neurology: with Special Reference to the Surgery of the Sympathetic Nervous System.*   Springfield and Baltimore: Charles C. Thomas, 1935,   First edition; 8vo., xi, 254 pages, 3 color plates, figures, indexes, original blue cloth, gilt stamped spine title, dust jacket, near fine, author's signed presentation to Homer Rush, from the Medical Library of Dr. Clare Gray Peterson.   Jeff Weber Rare Books   162 - 198   2011 $125

Livingstone, David   1813-1873   *The Last Journals of David Livingstone, in Central Africa, from 1865 to his Death.*   London: John Murray, 1874,   First edition; 8vo., 2 volumes, pages xvi, 360, ads; viii, 346, ads, 2 folding maps (1 loose in pocket of lower cover volume I), verso of loose map browned, frontispiece in volume 1 and 2, 20 plates, text illustrations, odd dust mark or spot, original purple decorative cloth, spines faded and chipped, upper edge of cover of volume 1 faded, hinges cracking, upper free endpapers of volume 2 torn away.   J. & S. L. Bonham Antiquarian Booksellers   Africa 4/20/2011 - 5821   2011   £195

Livingstone, David   1813-1873   *The Life and Explorations of David Livingstone.*   London: Adams & Co., n.. circa, 1875,   Quarto, viii, 632 pages, color lithographic frontispiece, lithographic half title, color map, 19 full page tinted lithographic plates, original full black morocco, elaborately stamped in gilt showing a lion on top of Livingstone and a slave with broken chains kneeling, palm trees, all edges gilt, hinges repaired, fine.   Jeff Weber Rare Books   163 - 187   2011 $275

Livingstone, David   1813-1873   *Missionary Travels and Reserarches in South Africa.*   London: John Murray, 1857,   First edition, first state; presentation copy inscribed by author on prelim blank, octavo, illustrations, original light brown morocco grain cloth, presentation copy from David Livingstone to Sir James Watt.   Heritage Book Shop   Booth A12 51st NY International Antiquarian Book Fair April 8-10 2011 - 86   2011 $25,000

Livingstone, David   1813-1873   *Narrative of an Expedition to the Zambesi and Its Tributaries and the Discovery of the Lakes Shirwa and Nyassa 1858-1864.*   New York: Harper and Brothers, 1866,   First American edition; Octavo, xxii, 638, 6 (ads) pages, double page frontispiece, title vignette, 35 engravings, large folding map, later full lime green cloth, gilt spine, soiled covers, spine smudged, rubbed, very good.   Jeff Weber Rare Books   163 - 188   2011 $75

Livius, Titus   *Caroli Sigoni Scholia Quibu T. Livii Patavini Histsoriae et Earum Epistomae Partim.*   Venice: Apud Paulum Manutium Aldi F., 1566,   Second edition; folio, modern marbled stiff wrappers, 104 leaves (lacks final leaf), title with printer's device, fine engraved pictorial initial and engraved headpiece to leaf A2, few wormholes to top inner margins, some browning from damp toward end of work.   R. F. G. Hollett & Son Antiquarian Booksellers   General Catalogue Summer 2010 - 662   2011   £350

Livius, Titus   *Historiarum ab Urbe Condita, Libri Qui Extant XXXV.*   Venice: P. Manutius, 1555,   2 parts, folio, ff. (4), 1-429, 428-430, 433-478; 98, (40), calf, title leaf mounted, scholia bound first, from the library of the Earls of Macclesfield at Shirburn Castle.   Maggs Bros. Ltd.   1440 - 235   2011   £1000

Livius, Titus *Historiarum... Libri Qui Extant XXXV.* Niccolo Bevilaqua for P. Manutius, 1566, 2 parts, folio, (52), 399, (1); 107, (1), later calf, f. 70 with small stain, odd leaf slightly browned, light marginal dampstaining on ff. 140-141, some margins washed near beginning with traces of annotations, from the library of the Earls of Macclesfield at Shirburn Castle.   Maggs Bros. Ltd.   1440 - 236 2011   £1000

Livius, Titus *Titi Livii Patavini Historiarum Libri Qui Extant.* Parisiis: apud Fredericum Leonard, 1679, 5 volumes bound as 6, 4to., pages (lxx) 544 (ix) + engraved half title and 2 engraved maps; (ii) 10 545-876, 3-191, (xix); (viii) 620 (lii) + 1 extending engraved plate and 1 other engraved plate; (viii) 757, (lxv) 678 (xxvi) 776, (xvi), contemporary calf, stain darkened spine panel gilt, brick red lettering piece gilt, numbered direct in gilt boards panelled in blind (Cambridge style), board edges decorative roll gilt, all edges red speckled, blue and white sewn endbands, light toning and some spotting, rubbed at joints and corners, joints cracked, endcaps worn, some labels lost, contemporary armorial bookplate of Sir Robet Clayton , early 19th century armorial bookplate of Stephen Lowdell, from the collection of Christopher Ernest Weston 1947-2010.   Unsworths Booksellers   24 - 115 2011   £450

Llewellyn, Raymond Maude *Occasional Contributions to the Globe.* London: Hamill Watson & Viney, n.d., 1886, First edition; 8vo., pages viii, 370, frontispiece, original blue cloth, unopened.   J. & S. L. Bonham Antiquarian Booksellers   Africa 4/20/2011 - 9121 2011   £65

Lloyd-Williams, Richard *The Village of Churches of Denbigshire.* Architectural Press, 1949, Second edition; pages ix, 487, 888 illustrations, large 4to., modern half green levant morocco, gilt, handsome copy.   R. F. G. Hollett & Son Antiquarian Booksellers   177 - 551 2011   £175

Lloyd, A. L. *Come All Ye Bold Miners. Ballads an Songs of the Coalfields.* London: Lawrence and Wishart, 1978, Revised edition; 384 pages, original cloth, gilt, dust jacket.   R. F. G. Hollett & Son Antiquarian Booksellers   175 - 847 2011   £30

Lloyd, Bertram *The Great Kinship.* London: Allen & Unwin, 1921, First edition; original holland backed boards with leather spine label, pages xviii, 272, untrimmed, etched frontispiece, presentation copy inscribed to Joseph N. Frankland from author, with author's signature from a letter tipped to title.   R. F. G. Hollett & Son Antiquarian Booksellers   175 - 848 2011   £45

Lloyd, Nathaniel *A History of the English House from Primitive Times to the Victorian Period.* Architectural Press, 1949, Corrected edition; numerous illustrations from photos, ownership signature on front pastedown, pages vii, (ii), 487, original green buckram, backstrip and front cover lettered in gilt, backstrip and lower cover sunned, hinges splitting, sound.   Blackwell Rare Books   B166 - 65 2011   £100

Llwyd, Humphrey *Commentarioli Britannicae Descriptionis Fragmentium.* Cologne: J. Birckmann, 1572, First edition; 8vo., ff. (8), 79 (=78) (2(blank), 18th century smooth calf, gilt spine, without final blanks, from the library of the Earls of Macclesfield at Shirburn Castle.   Maggs Bros. Ltd.   1440 - 131 2011   £900

Loades, David *Elizabeth I.* Hambledon & London: 2003, First edition; pages xxii, 410, 16 plates, 3 text illustrations, original cloth, gilt, dust jacket.   R. F. G. Hollett & Son Antiquarian Booksellers   175 - 849 2011   £30

Loccenius, Johan *Antiquitatum Sueo-Gothicarum, cum Huius aevi Moribus, Institutis ac Ritibus Indigenis Pro re Nata Comparaatrum Libri Tres.* Stockholm: Johan Jansson, 1654, 8vo., (8), 168 pages, 17th century English sprinkled calf, very nice, from the library of the Earls of Macclesfield at Shirburn Castle.   Maggs Bros. Ltd.   1440 - 132 2011   £400

Locke, Albyn, Mrs. *Eventide; or the Love To-Day and the Love for Age.* London: Bull, Simmons & Co., 1871, First edition; half titles, 3 volumes in 1, contemporary dark green remainder cloth, borders in blind, spine lettering faded, expertly recased, endpapers replaced, good plus, scarce.   Jarndyce Antiquarian Booksellers   CLXC - 160 2011   £180

Locke, John   1632-1704 *An Abridgment of Mr. Locke's Essay Concerning Humane Understanding.* London: 1700, Second edition; (8) 308 (4) (index) pages, very early leather, equally early stitching to re-attach covers, backstrip deteriorated but sturdy due to stitches, missing rear endpaper and front endpaper shabby, bookplate fragment of John Clayton of Gloucester county.   Bookworm & Silverfish   668 - 123 2011 $100

Locke, John   1632-1704 *An Essay Concerning Humane Understanding.* London: printed by Elizabeth Holt, 1690, First edition, 2nd issue; folio, contemporary brown mottled calf.   Heritage Book Shop   Booth A12 51st NY International Antiquarian Book Fair April 8-10 2011 - 87 2011 $32,500

Locke, John 1632-1704 *Essay Concerning Humane (Human) Understanding.* London: printed for Tho. Basset and sold by Edw. Mory, 1690, First edition, 2nd issue with cancel titlepage containing inverted "SS" of "Essay" the type ornament composed of 23 pieces, and without Elizabeth Holt's name in imprint, dedication undated, errata uncorrected; folio, (12), 362, (22, contents) pages, pages 287, 296 and 303 misnumbered 269, 294, 230 respectively; contemporary brown mottled calf, boards ruled in blind, spine in six compartments, lettered in gilt on brown calf spine label, edges speckled red, expertly rebacked to style with corners repaired, titlepage is short at fore-edge by half an inch due to stub being turned behind A4, marginal paper flaws on D1, P3 and Dd3, not affecting text, very small marginal hole on Hh, not affecting text, errata corrected by contemporary hand with ink and there are two contemporary ink notes on back free endpaper, Locke's name written in contemporary hand on titlepage as John Lock, previous owner's name Brockett, previous owner's name Samuel Gaskell and previous owner's name Roger Gaskell dated 1813, very clean and crisp, excellent contemporary binding. Heritage Book Shop   Holiday 2010 - 74 2011 $32,500

Locke, John 1632-1704 *The Works of John Locke.* London: printed for John Churchill, 1704, Tall 4to., pages 671, (15), volume two only, disbound, i.e. lacking covers, otherwise in decent sound condition (covers marked) with clean text and 2 neat names on titlepage. Any Amount of Books   May 29 2011 - A73752 2011 $340

Lockett, Terence A. *Davenport Pottery and Porcelain 1794-1887.* David Charles, 1972, First edition; large 8vo., original cloth, dust jacket, pages 112, color frontispiece, 103 illustrations, scarce. R. F. G. Hollett & Son Antiquarian Booksellers   General Catalogue Summer 2010 - 247 2011 £180

Lockridge, Ross *Raintree County.* Boston: Houghton Mifflin, 1948, First edition; fine, dust jacket good, price clipped with moderate chipping and creasing. Bella Luna Books   May 26 2011 - 57982 2011 $495

Lockyer, Nicholas *Baulme for Bleeding England and Ireland or Seasonable Instructions for Persecuted Christians.* London: printed by E. G. for John Rothwell an are to be sold at the Shop at the Signe of the Sun in Pauls Church Yard, 1643, First edition; small 8vo., full leather binding unlettered, pages (14), 413, slight browning, slight rubbing at corner and chipping at spine ends, otherwise sound, very good. Any Amount of Books   May 26 2011 - A42245 2011 $403

Loddon, D. L., Pseud. *Do They Remember.* London: Mitre Press, 1933, First edition; 8vo., pages 216, (i), internally fresh and crisp, original puce flowered paper boards, green cloth spine, slight rubbing to outer corners of front cover, slight shelf wear, otherwise very good, sheets still tight in casing, ALS from author. Simon Finch Rare Books   Zero - 251 2011 £750

Lodge, David *Deaf Sentence.* London: Cape: Blackwell Collector's Library, 2008, First edition, one of 100 numbered copies; signed by author, using sheets of first grade edition, pages vi, 298, crown 8vo., original quarter dark blue cloth, backstrip lettered and with design in gilt, white board sides, matching dark blue cloth, slipcase, new. Blackwell Rare Books   B166 - 179 2011 £100

Lodge, Edmund *Portraits of Illustrious Personages of Great Britain...* printed for Harding & Leopard, 1834, 12 volumes, tall 8vo., contemporary full bottle green morocco gilt by W. Nutt, little rubbing to hinges and feet of backstrips, few slight scrapes to one or two boards, all edges gilt, 240 steel engraved portraits, one or two plates little foxed, most handsome set. R. F. G. Hollett & Son Antiquarian Booksellers   General Catalogue Summer 2010 - 436 2011 £1250

Lodge, Edmund *Portraits of Illustrious Personages of Great Britain.* 1835, 12 volumes, full calf, volumes 4 5 and 6 need LCA, set lacks 33 of the 240 portraits. C. P. Hyland   May 26 2011 - 255/424 2011 $362

Lodge, T. *Dictatorship in Newfoundland.* London: Cassell and Co. Ltd., 1939, 8vo., pages (4)-273, half title, index, frontispiece, 8vo., red cloth with gilt title to spine, very good. Schooner Books Ltd.   96 - 67 2011 $75

Loftie, Arthur G. *The Rural Deanery of Gosforth.* Kendal: T. Wilson, 1889, First edition; original blue cloth, lower board little damped, pages 146, plus errata. R. F. G. Hollett & Son Antiquarian Booksellers   173 - 697 2011 £65

Loftie, W. J. *English Lake Scenery from Original Drawings by T. L. Rowlandson...* London: Marcus Ward & Co., 1875, First edition; Square 8vo., original decorated brown pictorial cloth gilt over bevelled boards, rebacked in matching levant morocco gilt, pages 114 (iv), all edges gilt, 6 chromolithographs laid in with gilt ruled borders and 5 text woodcuts. R. F. G. Hollett & Son Antiquarian Booksellers   173 - 698 2011 £175

Lofting, Hugh *Doctor Dolittle's Garden.* London: Cape, 1928, First edition; original cloth, short tears to head and foot of spine, pages 317, color frontispiece and endpapers, drawings. R. F. G. Hollett & Sons Antiquarian Booksellers   170 - 417 2011 £45

Lofting, Hugh *Doctor Dolittle's Return.* New York: Frederick A. Stokes Co., 1933, First edition; 8vo., orange decorated cloth with color paste label, nice, fresh copy, full color pictorial dust jacket with some marginal wear and minor chipping, full color frontispiece and 14 full page black and white plates. Jo Ann Reisler, Ltd.   86 - 163 2011 $475

Lofting, Hugh *Doctor Dolittle's Terugkomst (Return).* Rotterdam: G. W. Elberts circa, 1933-1935, First Dutch edition; 8vo., yellow cloth with green lettering and full color pictorial paste label, spine darkened, book has some overall handling plus some scratch marks to cloth, nice full page presentation and sketch by Lofting.   Jo Ann Reisler, Ltd. 86 - 164   2011 $650

Lofting, Hugh *Doctor Doolittle in the Moon.* London: Cape, 1929, First edition; original cloth, spine rather darkened and frayed at head, upper board marked, pages 320, with brightly colored frontispiece and endpapers, drawings.   R. F. G. Hollett & Sons Antiquarian Booksellers   170 - 416 2011   £45

Lofting, Hugh *The Story of Zingo the Commercial Traveler.* Jersey City: Colgate, 1924, 16mo., pictorial wrappers, fine, illustrations by Lofting, half page drawings in line.   Aleph-Bet Books, Inc.   95 - 336   2011 $150

Lofting, Hugh *Voyages of Doctor Dolittle.* New York: Frederick Stokes, 1922, First edition; 8vo., decorative cloth, pictorial paste on, near fine in dust jacket (mended, chipped at spine ends and corners, 1 inch triangular piece off rear panel), illustrations by Lofting, with color pictorial endpapers, guarded color frontispiece, one other color plate with charming black and whites, scarce, rare in dust jacket. Aleph-Bet Books, Inc.   95 - 335   2011 $1850

Logan, Nick *The Face.* London: Wagadon Ltd., 1980, First issue, May 1980; pages 62, copiously illustrated in color and black and white, slight wear at spine, used but pleasant, very good copy.   Any Amount of Books   May 29 2011 - A35417   2011 $255

Loguen, J. W. *The Rev. J. W. Loguen as a Slave and as a Fireman.* New York: J. G. K. Truair, 1859, First edition; 12mo., x, (11)-444 pages, frontispiece original ful olive green blindstamped cloth, gilt spine title, extremities worn, few signatures sprung from binding, ownership labels of W. M. O'Farrell and David Mc. O'Farrell, good.   Jeff Weber Rare Books   163 - 86   2011 $75

Loisel, Antoine *Memoires des Pays villes Comte et Comies...* Paris: S. Thiboust, 1617, First (and only) edition; 4to., (4), 367, (19) pages, title printed in red and black, woodcut device on titlepage, woodcut head and tailpieces, initials, 1 engraved illustration, 17th century calf, triple fillet gilt with fleuron in each corner on boards, spine gilt in compartments, morocco lettering piece, spine used, slightly waterstained on titlepage, and in upper corner of first pages, manuscript ex-libris on titlepage, from the library of the Earls of Macclesfield at Shirburn Castle.   Maggs Bros. Ltd. 1440 - 133   2011   £700

The London Battledoor (sic). New York: W. B. Gilley not after, 1824, 6 1/2 x 4 inches, printed paper with woodcut on front cover, cover worn with pieces along spine folded back and some splitting to spine internally some dusting but it is not too bad, issued in book format with 8 pages (counting inside covers) printed on stiff card which at least pays homage to usual presentation, book consists mainly of full alphabet with woodcut illustrations of mostly birds but completed with other animals, uncommon.   Jo Ann Reisler, Ltd. 86 - 79   2011 $800

London & North Western Railway *The Ribble Valley District.* 1922,   Pages 116, illustrations, trifle used in places, modern quarter calf, gilt.   R. F. G. Hollett & Son Antiquarian Booksellers   General Catalogue Summer 2010 - 1466   2011   £45

The London Gazette for the year 1950. London: HMSO, 1950, 4 volumes, thick 4to., contemporary library cloth gilt, pages 6508, plus supplements, very good.   R. F. G. Hollett & Son Antiquarian Booksellers   175 - 850   2011   £120

The London Magazine. London: Baldwin, 1747-1752, 12 issues (January March April and June-December 1747 and March and April 1752), original printed sugar paper wrappers, side sewn, each number approximately 56 pages, 8 engraved maps and plans, some edges little chipped, but excellent collection.   R. F. G. Hollett & Son Antiquarian Booksellers   175 - 71   2011   £350

The London Magazine. London: R. Baldwin, 1754, 4 issues (Jan. Feb. May and Oct. 1747), original printed sugar paper wrappers, side sewn, edges chipped, one upper panel defective, one lower panel lacking, each number approximately 56 pages, 2 engraved plates.   R. F. G. Hollett & Son Antiquarian Booksellers   175 - 70   2011   £75

London Magazine. Shenval Press, 1954-1995, First edition; First series V. 1/1-V.8/3, all published, second series v. 1/1-v.35/6.11/12, lacking 5 issues only, v. 41/1/2 April/May 2001 last issue, over 300 issues in original wrappers in excellent condition.   I. D. Edrich   May 26 2011 - 82553 2011 $2684

London, H. Stanford *The Queen's Beasts.* London: Newman Neame, 1953, First edition; 4to., original pictorial boards, top edge rather damped, dust jacket little soiled and creased, few small edge tears, pages 56, fine colored lithographs and other illustrations.   R. F. G. Hollett & Son Antiquarian Booksellers   175 - 89   2011   £35

London, Jack 1876-1916 *Adventure.* New York: Macmillan, 1911, First edition; attractively decorated cloth, very good+, some shelfwear, some loss of white spine print.   Lupack Rare Books   May 26 2011 - ABE1357017505   2011 $300

London, Jack 1876-1916   *The Call of the Wild.*   New York: Macmillan, 1903, First American edition, only issue (vertically ribbed cloth); 231, (2) pages, frontispiece, 17 plates, vertically ribbed green pictorial cloth stamped in white, rust and black, lettering on front cover and spine in gilt, short presentation inscription in pencil by previous owner dated August 1903, bookplate, slightest of rubbing to spine ends, light foxing and stamped name to verso of color frontispiece, lower rear corner just slightly jammed, else very handsome, tipped in bookplate of famous collector Thomas Wayne Norris.   Argonaut Book Shop   Recent Acquisitions Summer 2010 - 118   2011 $1250

London, Jack 1876-1916   *The Game.*   New York: Macmillan, 1905, First edition, 2nd state with (small) Metropolitan stamp on copyright page; bright, near fine. Lupack Rare Books   May 26 2011 - ABE847080747   2011 $250

London, Jack 1876-1916   *Revolution.*   New York: Macmilllan, 1910, First edition; maroon cloth, variant binding with "Macmillan" on spine, very good+, light shelf wear.   Lupack Rare Books   May 26 2011 - ABE806408373 2011 $300

London, Jack 1876-1916   *The Scarlet Plague.*   New York: Macmillan Co., 1915, First American edition, only issue; 181 pages, plus 3 leaves of ads, frontispiece, text illustrations by Gordon Grant, plum red cloth decorated in yellow and light red, lettering in light red on front cover, lettering on spine in gilt, slightest of rubbing to spine ends, less so to corners, overall very fine.   Argonaut Book Shop Recent Acquisitions Summer 2010 - 119   2011 $650

London, Jack 1876-1916   *The Son of the Wolf. Tales of the Far North.*   Boston and New York: Houghton, Mifflin and Co., 1900, First American edition, first issue; with "Houghton Mifflin & Co. at foot of spine and without the "dots" separating the "&", with comma (not a period) after the date on copyright page, frontispiece illustration tipped-in, not sewn; (6), 251 pages, frontispiece, slate gray cloth stamped in silver on cover and spine (silver belt and buckle design), very small spot to front cover, owner's name to flyleaf (M. Hume), slight rubbing, much less than usual, to silver corners on front, overall very fine.   Argonaut Book Shop   Recent Acquisitions Summer 2010 - 120   2011 $3000

Long, Catherine   *Sir Roland Ashton.*   London: James Nisbet & Co., 1844, First edition; 2 volumes, half title, some light foxing, uncut in original blue vertical grained cloth, boards blocked in blind, spines lettered in gilt, spines faded and slightly rubbed, hinges chipped, each volume signed J. E. Lanesborough in contemporary hand, good plus.   Jarndyce Antiquarian Booksellers   CLXC - 161 2011   £150

Long, Charles Chaille   *Central Africa: Naked Truths of Naked People.*   New York: Harper & Brothers, 1877, First American edition; octavo, xv, 328, (2), 6 (ads) pages, frontispiece, 20 plates, folding color map, original brown blind-stamped cloth, gilt spine title and gilt device of an African warrior on upper cover, very good plus.   Jeff Weber Rare Books   163 - 190   2011 $75

Long, Jane   *Conversations in Cold Rooms.*   London: Boydell Press, 1999, First edition; original cloth, gilt, dust jacket, pages xii, 241, with 9 illustrations.   R. F. G. Hollett & Son Antiquarian Booksellers   175 - 853   2011   £35

Long, Richard   *Labyrinth. Local Lane Walks Bristol. 1990.* Frankfurt Am Main: Stadtishe Galerie im Stadel, 1991, First edition; 8vo., pages (108), 100 black and white photos, original black wrappers, spine and upper side lettered in black, Long's presentation in pencil to half title, fine, presentation copy.   Simon Finch Rare Books   Zero - 534   2011 £800

Long, William   *Stonehenge and Its Barrows.*   Devizes: H. F. & E. Bull, 1876, Contemporary half calf gilt, marbled boards, pages v, 244, large folding lithographed plan (little torn), 25 engraved plates and illustrations, scarce.   R. F. G. Hollett & Son Antiquarian Booksellers   177 - 553   2011 £150

Longet, Francois Achille   *Experiences Relatives avec Effets de l'Inhalation de l'ether Suffurique sur le Systeme Nerveux.*   Paris: Victor Masson, 1847, First edition; 8vo., 54 pages, pages lightly foxed, original printed wrappers, uncut, housed in gray cloth clamshell box with gilt stamped black leather spine label, ownership inked signature on front cover, fine, from the Medical Library of Dr. Clare Gray Peterson.   Jeff Weber Rare Books   162 - 199   2011 $3500

Longfellow, Henry Wadsworth 1807-1882   *The Courtship of Miles Standish.*   Boston: 1859, First edition third printing, with correct reading at page 125 and with ads dated Oct. 1858; 215 (11 pages of ads), brown cloth with elaborate dos-a-dos medallion in blind, backstrip gilt bright, few spots of white at backstrip ends, front cover corners rubbed and bruised, very modest shelf wear, owner's date Nov. 2 1858.   Bookworm & Silverfish   669 - 157   2011 $65

Longfellow, Henry Wadsworth 1807-1882   *Hiawatha's Childhood.*   New York: Farrar Straus Giroux, 1984, Stated first American edition; red cloth with gold lettering on spine, full color pictorial dust jacket, as new, signed in full by artist, Errol Le Cain, illustrations by Le Cain.   Jo Ann Reisler, Ltd.   86 - 155   2011 $275

Longfellow, Henry Wadsworth 1807-1882   *Keramos & Other Poems.*   Boston: 1878, First edition; very good in green cloth, gilt bright.   Bookworm & Silverfish   669 - 158 2011 $65

Longfellow, Henry Wadsworth 1807-1882 *The Poetical Works of H. W. Longfellow.* London: T. Nelson & Sons, 1867, Photographic frontispiece, original full maroon morocco, heavily blocked in blind lettered in gilt on boards and spine, spines slightly rubbed, embossed stamp on leading f.e.p., inscription from Madeline Gresley to Lord Henry, all edges gilt, very good.   Jarndyce Antiquarian Booksellers   CXCI - 441   2011   £60

Longfellow, Henry Wadsworth 1807-1882 *The Song of Hiawatha.* London: David Bogue, 1856, New edition; 24 page catalog (March 1855), original blue grey cloth, slightly dulled and slightly marked, good plus, the 316 page edition.   Jarndyce Antiquarian Booksellers   CXCI - 297   2011   £75

Longfellow, Henry Wadsworth 1807-1882 *Tales of a Wayside Inn.* London: Rutledge Warne, 1864, First English edition; half title, frontispiece, 4 page catalog, original green glaced cloth by Burns, lettered in gilt on spine, near fine.   Jarndyce Antiquarian Booksellers   CXCI - 298   2011   £40

Longfellow, Henry Wadsworth 1807-1882 *Voices of the Night.* Cambridge: John Owen, 1840, Third edition, published in an edition of only 200 large paper copies; tall 8vo., 15, 144 pages, gilt tulip motif on each cover, full contemporary green morocco heavily gilt stamped, rebacked with original spine laid down, somewhat darkened but quite handsome, later endpapers.   M & S Rare Books, Inc.   90 - 219   2011 $650

Longinus, Dionysius *On the Sublime.* London: for W. Sandby, 1742, Second edition; 8vo., (16), xxxiv, 189, (1) pages, engraved frontispiece, woodcut head and tailpieces, woodcut initials, contemporary red morocco, wide gilt border on covers, spine gilt in compartments, gilt edges, slight wear to joints, the dedication copy, specially bound for George, second Earl of Macclesfield.   Maggs Bros. Ltd.   1440 - 134   2011   £750

Longus *Les Amours Pastorales de Daphnis et Chloe.* London: Ashendene Press, First edition thus, one of 290 copies; large 8vo., pages 4, iv, 164, including colophon, handset in "Ptolemy" type and printed with marginal notes in red on Batchelor handmade paper, initials and paragraph marks filled in by hand by Graily Hewitt and assistants, 4 full page and 22 other wood engraved illustrations by Gwen Raverat, Viridian green paper covered sides gilt blocked on upper board, vellum spine lettered in gilt with vellum tips at corners, white vellum has very faint handling soiling, otherwise about fine in sound, very good original Curwen decorated slipcase, excellent condition, discreet bookplate of collector done by Marc Severin and signed in plate in pencil by him, very attractive.   Any Amount of Books   May 26 2011 - A65423   2011 $1845

Longus *Daphnis & Chloe.* London: Geoffrey Bles, 1925, First edition thus; large 4to., pages 200, with 12 tipped in colored and 4 black and white full plate illustrations by John Austen, original vellm backed blue cloth, from the Daphnis and Chloe collection of bookplate expert James Wilson with his D&C bookplate (by Mark Severin), hand numbered limitation signed by Austen (number 91), very faint soiling of vellum spine, corners very slightly rubbed, very good or better.   Any Amount of Books   May 26 2011 - A65762   2011 $604

Longus *Daphnis and Chloe.* New York: Braziller, 1977, 4to., pages 222, 58 color lithographs by Marc Chagall, very nice, dust jacket and plain heavy paper slipcase.   Second Life Books Inc.   174 - 231   2011 $150

Lonsdale, Henry *The Howards, Rev. R. Matthews, John Rooke, Captain Joseph Huddart. The Worthies of Cumberland Volume 3.* London: George Routledge, 1872, Original green cloth, gilt, pages vii, 311, 4 photo portraits, little spotting in places.   R. F. G. Hollett & Son Antiquarian Booksellers   173 - 700   2011   £35

Lonsdale, Henry *The Life and Works of Musgrave Lewthwaite Watson, Sculptor.* London: George Routledge, 1866, First edition; large 8vo., original cloth, gilt over bevelled boards, rubbed and damp stained, pages xii, 244, all edges gilt, 12 photo plates, very scarce.   R. F. G. Hollett & Son Antiquarian Booksellers   173 - 701   2011   £140

Lonsdale, Henry *Sir J. R. G. Graham, Bart. of Netherby, The Worthies of Cumberland. Volume 2.* London: Routledge, 1868, Original green cloth, gilt, pages xii, 304, frontispiece and 1 other portrait, few spots.   R. F. G. Hollett & Son Antiquarian Booksellers   173 - 702   2011   £35

Loomes, Brian *Westmorland Clocks and Clockmakers.* David & Charles, 1974, First edition; original cloth, gilt, dust jacket little faded, pages 120, 16 plates, 3 line drawings, scarce.   R. F. G. Hollett & Son Antiquarian Booksellers   173 - 703   2011   £40

Loomes, Brian *White Dial Clocks.* David Charles, 1981, First edition; original cloth, gilt, dust jacket, pages 268, 91 illustrations.   R. F. G. Hollett & Son Antiquarian Booksellers General Catalogue Summer 2010 - 251   2011   £40

Lopez, Barry *Crow and Weasel.* San Francisco: North Point Press, 1990, First edition; illustrations by Tom Pohrt, fine in fine dust jacket, early gold stamping on front cover.   Bella Luna Books   May 29 2011 - 1038   2011 $82

Lopez, Barry *Home Ground. Language for an American Landscape.* San Antonio: Trinity University Press, 2006, Advance copy; this advance copy printers entries for only letters A-C, inscribed by editor, Lopez, fine in wrappers.   Ken Lopez Bookseller   154 - 99   2011 $125

Lopez, Barry *Of Wolves and men.* New York: Scribner, 1978, First edition; near fine, sunning to edges, dust jacket very good, price clipped, one small closed tear to edges, signed by author. Bella Luna Books May 29 2011 - t718 2011 $82

Lopez, Barry *River Notes. The Dance of Herons.* Kansas City: Andrews and McMeel Inc., 1979, First edition; near fine, edges of endpapers sunned, dust jacket near fine, light edge wear, half inch closed tear on rear panel, small printing signed by author. Bella Luna Books May 26 2011 - 1042 2011 $192

Lopez, Barry *River Notes, The Dance of Herons.* Kansas City: Andrews and McMeel Inc., 1979, First edition; book near fine, small quarter inch bulge on front board, looks like a production error, dust jacket near fine, price clipped, light edge wear, elusive title, signed by author. Bella Luna Books May 29 2011 - 1041d 2011 $137

Lopez, Barry *Winter Count.* New York: Scribner, 1981, First edition; fine, near fine dust jacket, price clipped with light wear, signed by author. Bella Luna Books May 29 2011 - j1126 2011 $82

Lorant, Stefan *Lilliput.* Hulton Press, 1937-1959, First edition; July 1937- July 1959, this run includes 6 supplements for 1952/3, 243 out of 265 issues, in bound volumes, annuals and issues beween v. 1/1-v.45/1 in very good condition. I. D. Edrich May 26 2011 - 83766 2011 $2348

Lorca, Federico Garcia *Poema del Cante Jondo.* Madrid: Ediciones Ulises, Compania Iberoamericana de Publicationes, 1931, First edition; 8vo., pages (vi) 8-172, (30) ads, colophon, with half title, upper paper wrapper skillfully repaired at inner margin, very little light marginal fading throughout, contemporary blue quarter morocco, grey marbled sides, spine gilt with cream leather label, lettered in gilt, preserving upper original cream paper wrapper by Mauricio Amster printed in red and black, light rubbing to joints and head and foot of spine, lower board very slightly bowed, extremties very lightly rubbed, author' presentation inscription to Maria E. De Erazuriz,. Simon Finch Rare Books Zero - 337 2011 £12,500

Lorentz, Hendirk Antoon *Versuch Einer Theorie der Electrischen und Optischen Erscheinungen in Bewegten Korpern.* Leiden: E. J. Brill, 1895, First edition; 8vo. 138, (1) pages, modern quarter brown cloth and printed paper boards, gilt stamped black leather spine label, fine, library and release stamp of University of Groningen, from the Medical Library of Dr. Clare Gray Peterson. Jeff Weber Rare Books 162 - 197 2011 $5000

Lorenzini, Carlo 1829-1890 *Pinocchio's Adventures in Wonderland.* Boston: Jordan Marsh, 1898, First edition; 12mo., half blue pictorial cloth, edges and corners rubbed, small hole in one leaf, else very good+, clean and tight, 212 pages, black and white chapter head and tailpieces. Aleph-Bet Books, Inc. 95 - 159 2011 $700

Lorenzini, Carlo 1829-1890 *Pinocchio: Album Di Costruzione.* Milano: Carraccia, n.d. circa, 1940, Square folio, stiff pictorial wrappers, slight bit of soil, else very good+ and unused, 6 leaves of characters, furniture, etc. for the reader to cut out and use to construct Gepetto's studio in intricate detail, rare. Aleph-Bet Books, Inc. 95 - 161 2011 $600

Lorimer, John *A Concise Essay on Magnetism with an Account Declination and Inclination of the Magnetic Needle and an Attempt to Ascertain the Cause of the Variation Thereof.* London: printed for the author and sold by W. Faden, 1795, First edition; inscribed by author to General Melville, from the collection of Harrison D. Horblit with his booklabel, very good, inscribed copy in later half leather, cloth binding with gilt lettering on spine and bottom 1.5" of spine cover chipped, covers edge wear, marbled endpapers with f.f.e.p. clipped, six foldout plates as issued, plates foxed, scattered foxing. By the Book, L. C. 26 - 105 2011 $900

Lorimer, Norma *By the Waters of Africa.* London: Robert Scott, 1917, Octavo, viii, 342 pages, frontispiece, plates, folding map, original blue cloth, printed dust jacket worn, book in fine condition, jacket rare. Jeff Weber Rare Books 163 - 191 2011 $75

Loring, Rosamond B. *Decorated Book Papers.* Cambridge: Harvard College Library, 1973, Third edition; original cloth, gilt, dust jacket, price clipped, pages xxxv, 171, with 16 tinted plates. R. F. G. Hollett & Son Antiquarian Booksellers General Catalogue Summer 2010 - 253 2011 £35

Lorrain, Jean *Le Sang des Dieux.* Paris: Alphonse Lemerre, 1882, First edition; 8vo., pages (iv) initial blank and limitation page, 153, (1) imprint, frontispiece and numerous illustrations, rough cut top edge and uncut lower and fore edge, some light foxing to endpapers and imprint leaf, otherwise internally excellent, original black and red printed ivory wrappers, lightly foxed and rubbed, author's inscription in black ink to initial blank, unnumbered copy of 525. Simon Finch Rare Books Zero - 338 2011 £675

Loss of His Majesty's Ship of Seventy-Four Guns, the 22d of September 1782 and Miraculous Preservation of the Pinnace, with the Captain, Master and Ten of the Crew, also, the Explosion of the French East India Company's Vessel the Prince on the 25th 1752 and Miraculous Preservation of Part of the Crew in the Pinnace. London: printed for Thomas Tegg, 111 Cheapside, 1752, 12mo., large folding frontispiece, (2), 7-28 pages, nice.   Anthony W. Laywood   May 26 2011 - 21690   2011 $168

Loss of the Wager Man of War, One of Commodore Anson's Squadron in the year 1744 and the Consequent Embarassments of the Crew, Separation, Mutinous Disposition... London: printed for Thomas Tegg, 111, Cheaside (sic) circa, 1810, 12mo., large folding frontispiece, (3), 8-28 pages, disbound.   Anthony W. Laywood   May 26 2011 - 21704   2011 $76

Loti, Pierre *From Lands of Exile.* New York: Gottsberger, 1888, First American edition; 12m., pages xix, 301, green cloth, pictorial stamping on front and lettering on front and spine in black, owner's name on flyleaf, spine little sunned, edges slightly scuffed, but nice.   Second Life Books Inc.   174 - 232   2011 $55

Lotka, Alfred J. *Elements of Physical Biology.* Baltimore: Williams & Wilkins Co., 1925, First edition; pages xxx, 460, (2), with 72 illustrations, 36 tables, original blue cloth lettered gilt to spine, head of spine very slightly creased, otherwise very good+ in serviceable repaired tanned and slightly chipped dust jacket, very good-.   Any Amount of Books   May 26 2011 - A67975   2011 $470

Louisiana. (Territory) *The Laws of the Territory of Louisiana.* St. Louis: printed by Joseph Charles printer to the Territory, 1808, First edition; 8vo., 376, (58) pages, index full new morocco, leather label, early leaves with some thumbing and browning in outer margin, slightly frayed to old tape stains on edges, two old signatures on title, near fine.   M & S Rare Books, Inc.   90 - 212   2011 $45,000

Lousley, J. E. *Wild Flowers of Chalk and Limestone.* London: Collins, 1950, First edition; original cloth, gilt, spine faded, dust jacket (spine frayed at head and foot, taped repair to head), pages 254, with 52 color and 29 black and white photos, 20 maps and 15 diagrams.   R. F. G. Hollett & Son Antiquarian Booksellers   General Catalogue Summer 2010 - 1013   2011   £35

Louvet De Couvray, Jean Baptiste *The Life and Adventures of the Chevalier de Faublas....* London: printed for R. Faulder and E. Jeffrey, 1793, First English translation; 4 volumes, 12mo., all edges yellow, occasional scattered light blotching (not foxing, possibly the result of early damp marks dating from before binding), mid 19th century half calf, brown morocco gilt lettered title labels, marbled boards and endpapers, some light rubbing to extremities, upper board volume i cracked but firm.   Simon Finch Rare Books   Zero - 252   2011   £2750

Louys, Pierre *Les Chansons de Bilitis.* Paris: Librairie Charpentier et Fasquelle, 1925, 8vo., pages (iv), xii, 356, plus 12 leaves of manuscript translations bound in, 300 engravings in text, top edge gilt, others uncut, pages lightly browned at edges, contemporary blue cloth, upper board and spine decorated in gilt, gilt lettering to spine, floral endpapers, light shelf wear, tips rubbed, spine darkened, manuscript list of bound in translations to front free endpaper, further manuscript translations to pages 17, 189, 228, 9, 244-5, 256, 330-1, unique Christmas gift from Berta Ruck to "Nony" who is possibly her husband Oliver Onions.   Simon Finch Rare Books   Zero - 339   2011   £350

Louys, Pierre *Mines des Courtisanes De Lucien.* Paris: Ambrose Vollard, 1935, One of 325 copies on Rives paper; original stiff printed wrappers and glassine, illustrations by Edgar Degas.   Heritage Book Shop   Booth A12 51st NY International Antiquarian Book Fair April 8-10 2011 - 38   2011 $3500

Louys, Pierre *Poesies Erotiques d'un Auteur Celebre, Illustrees de Trente-Deuxx Lithographies Originales Destinees par un Artiste Inconnu (Vertes).* Barceloe: Atarazanas (Barrio Chino), L'an I de la Republique Catalane, Paris: Bonnel and Pia, 1932, Special copy of the first edition; 4to., pages (iv) blank, (95), (1) blank, (1), colophon, (iii) blank, 32 hand colored lithographs in text, 3 original preparatory sketches (one pencil, two pencil and ink) by the artist, uncut, internally fine, original white printed wrappers, in original grey board chemise case, with gilt lettered morocco title label on spine, chemise showing signs of rubbing at edges and shelfwear, 2 original manuscript poems in Louy's hand, of 7 and 3 stanzas, not figuring in volume, laid in.   Simon Finch Rare Books   Zero - 442   2011   £3750

Louys, Pierre *Pybrac Illustre de Trente Pointes Seches d'un Artiste Inconnu.* Paris: Aux depens d'un amateur (Marcel Vertes), 1928, Second (first illustrated) edition; 4to., pages (iv), 78, etched frontispiece and 30 erotic dry point etchings (10 hors texte), 2 original aquarelles, 5 original sketches (one foxed), two duplicate suites of 31 engraving (one hand colored, one on Japan nacre), 5 refused plates, 1 original copper plate, red crushed half morocco, spine gilt titled and decorated within raised bands, gilt initialled "A.P."" (i.e. Arpad Pletsch) at base of spine, top edge gilt, others untrimmed, short closed tear to upper hinge at head of spine, bottom edge lightly rubbed, printed wrappers bound in, signed "Jeanne Gazel (c. 1930), presentation inscription and original drawing, choice copy, with original erotic drawing and autograph presentation from Vertes to Pletch, sumptuously bound for collector Pletsch.   Simon Finch Rare Books   Zero - 439   2011   £10,000

Lovecraft, Howard Phillips *Autobiography: Some Notes on a Nonentity.* Sauk City: Arkham House, First edition; 8vo., 17 page, stapled printed white wrappers, very slight rustiness at staples, else clean, near fine.   Any Amount of Books   May 29 2011 - A74570   2011 $204

Lovecraft, Howard Phillips *The Dark Brotherhood and Other Pieces.* Sauk City: Arkham House, 1966, First edition; octavo, cloth.   L. W. Currey, Inc.   124 - 188 2011 $250

Lovecraft, Howard Phillips *Dreams and Fancies.* Sauk City: Arkham House, 1962, First edition; 8vo., pages x, 175, fine in fine dust jacket with very very slight edgewear, excellent condition, signed by introducer August Derleth.   Any Amount of Books   May 26 2011 - A74373 2011 $713

Lovecraft, Howard Phillips *Selected Letters.* Sauk City: Arkham House, 1976, First edition; 5 volumes, 8vo., 46 illustrations, with nice copy of 78 page booklet, very slight shelfwear, otherwise very good+ in very good+ dust jacket (slight sunning to first volume), decent condition.   Any Amount of Books   May 26 2011 - A73839 2011 $503

Lovecraft, Howard Phillips *Marginalia...* Sauk City: Arkham House, 1944, First edition; octavo, cloth.   L. W. Currey, Inc.   124 - 74 2011 $1250

Lovecraft, Howard Phillips *Marginalia.* Sauk City: Arkham House, 1944, First edition; octavo, cloth.   L. W. Currey, Inc.   124 - 121 2011 $650

Lovecraft, Howard Phillips *The Outsider and Others.* Sauk City: Arkham House, 1939, First edition; large octavo, cloth.   L. W. Currey, Inc.   124 - 1 2011 $8500

Lovecraft, Howard Phillips *Something About Cats and Other Pieces.* Sauk City: Arkham House, 1949, First edition; octavo, cloth.   L. W. Currey, Inc.   124 - 189 2011 $250

Lovell, M. S. *The Edible Mollusks of Great Britain and Ireland with Recipes for Cooking Them.* London: Reeve and Co., n.d. 1870's, Second edition; 8vo., original publisher's blue cloth lettered gilt at spine and with gilt illustration on cover, pages (viii), 310, with 6 page publisher's catalog at rear, 12 color plates, ex-Hornsey Public library with occasional stamp in text and labels on f.e.p., attractive plates stamped on back only, slight fading, slight wear and marks, else sound, very good.   Any Amount of Books   May 29 2011 - A49997 2011 $221

Lover, Samuel *The Lyrics of Ireland.* London: Houlston & Wright, 1858, First edition; original blindstamped cloth gilt, edges trifle worn, spine little dulled, pages xxv, 360, with 52 woodcut vignettes, few marginal blindstamps, accession stamp to verso of title.   R. F. G. Hollett & Son Antiquarian Booksellers   175 - 857 2011   £65

Low, D. M. *London is London.* London: Chatto & Windus, 1949, First edition; original cloth gilt, edges little faded, dust jacket little worn and chipped, pages 300, with 32 full page illustrations.   R. F. G. Hollett & Son Antiquarian Booksellers   General Catalogue Summer 2010 - 1329 2011   £35

Low, David *The Best of Low.* London: Cape, 1930, First edition; original cloth backed boards, 4to., edges little worn, repairs to head of lower hinge, pages 212, 100 cartoons, flyleaves spotted, otherwise very good.   R. F. G. Hollett & Son Antiquarian Booksellers   General Catalogue Summer 2010 - 837 2011   £30

Lowe, Constance M. *Hide and Seek Pictures.* London: Ernest Nister, n.d., Folio, original cloth backed glazed pictorial boards, trifle marked and edges slightly rubbed, unpaginated, 10 leaves illustrated, 6 of which bare chromolithographed roundels with silk pull each to transform the page, set under central bar with verse and behind decorated oval border, border defective on first sheet and tear to backing sheet, both pulls missing on second and sixth, one pull missing on fifth, front joint strained, little shaken, but very acceptable, scarce moveable.   R. F. G. Hollett & Son Antiquarian Booksellers   General Catalogue Summer 2010 - 531 2011   £350

Lowe, Joseph *The Present State of England in Regard to Agriculture, Trade and Finance...* London: Longman, Hurst, Rees, Orme and Brown... and J. Richardson, 1822, First edition; 8vo., xxiv, 352, 130 pages, bound without half title, contemporary half calf, spine gilt in compartments with label, very good.   John Drury Rare Books   153 - 84 2011   £200

Lowe, Richard Thomas *History of the Fishes of Madeira.* London: Bernard Quaritch, 1843-1860, Large paper copy; L28 lithographed plates of which 18 are hand colored (minor marginal spotting to 4 plain plates), 4to., pages xvi, 4, (4*-) 196, contemporary half calf (edges rubbed, tips of corners worn, a corner slightly bumped, ink number to a margin of a page, very good), raised bands and gilt decorations on spine, top edge gilt, rare, the copy of Henry A. Sherwin (founder of Sherwin-Williams Co.) and bookplate of R. Harry Jr.   Raymond M. Sutton, Jr.   May 26 2011 - 41582 2011 $2350

Lowe, Robson *The British Postage Stamp.* London: National Postal Museum, 1968, First edition; 4to., original cloth, gilt, edges little faded, dust jacket, few tape marks to reverse, pages viii, 272, with 32 pages of color plates and monochrome illustrations.   R. F. G. Hollett & Son Antiquarian Booksellers   175 - 859 2011   £35

Lowell, Amy *John Keats.* Boston: Houghton Mifflin Co., 1925, First edition; 2 volumes, (xx), 631; 662 pages; thick 8vo., original red cloth, gilt lettered spines, frontispiece in each volume and many additional illustrations, exceptionally fine. Paulette Rose Fine and Rare Books 32 - 117 2011 $300

Lowell, James Russell 1819-1891 *Poems.* Cambridge: John Owen, 1844, First edition; royal 8vo., 12, 279 pages, contemporary full black tooled morocco, gilt gone from outside covers, all edges gilt, marbled endpapers with binder's ticket of MacDonald of Cambridge, inner front hinge trifle weak, despite loss of gilding, very fine in handsome binding, this copy 9 3/8 inches tall. M & S Rare Books, Inc. 90 - 220 2011 $750

Lowell, James Russell 1819-1891 *The Writings.* London: Macmillan and Co., 1890, Riverside edition; 193 x 130mm., 10 volumes beautiful early 20th century olive green textured calf, handsomely gilt by Sangorski & Sutcliffe (stamp signed on verso of front free endpaper), covers with double ruled gilt border and blindstamped in basket weave pattern, raised bands, spines lavishly gilt in compartments with central cruciform ornament framed by wide densely gilt cornerpieces, filled with leaves, flowers and small tools, each with two maroon morocco labels, turn-ins gilt in lacy filigree, marbled endpapers, top edge gilt, other edges rough trimmed, 3 volumes with portrait frontispiece, light rubbing and flaking to one joint (only), spines uniformly sunned to a mellow olive brown, one leaf with triangular tear at upper right just into text (no loss), isolated very minor stains or foxing, otherwise beautiful set in fine condition, handsome bindings very lustrous with no significant wear, text fresh, clean and bright. Phillip J. Pirages 59 - 135 2011 $1750

Lowell, James Russell 1819-1891 *The Complete Writings.* Cambridge: Riverside Press, 1904, Edition de Luxe, one of 1000 copies; 220 x 145mm., 16 volumes, Edition De Luxe, very handsome dark green morocco, extravagently gilt, covers with wavy gilt border and charming floral ornaments at corners, central panel (with square notched corners) formed by six parallel gilt lines, raised bands, spine compartments attractively gilt with scrolling flowers and foliage enclosing a floral fleuron centerpiece, wide turn-ins with elaborate gilt decoration featuring many large and small roses and leaves on stylized lattice work, turn-ins enclosing scarlet colored polished morocco doublures, crimson watered silk free endleaves, top edges gilt, other edges rough trimmed, mostly unopened (6 volumes entirely unopened, and all but one one of the authors largely so), 80 mounted photogravure illustrations on India paper, original tissue guards; front joint of first volume bit worn (rear joint little flaked), half dozen other joints with hint of rubbing, spines evenly sunned to attractive olive brown, one small cover scuff, two leaves roughly opened (with no serious consequences), other isolated trivial imperfections, nearly fine set in quite attractive binding, leather lustrous. Phillip J. Pirages 59 - 258 2011 $3000

Lowerison, Harry *Mother Earth.* London: Walter Scott, 1902, First edition; small 8vo., original pictorial cloth, pages 176, top edge gilt, untrimmed, uncommon. R. F. G. Hollett & Son Antiquarian Booksellers General Catalogue Summer 2010 - 1014 2011 £40

Lowndes, Marie Adelaide Belloc *Good Old Anna.* London: Hutchinson, 1915, First edition; half title, 32 page catalog (Autumn 1915), original pale blue cloth lettered in gilt and white, very good. Jarndyce Antiquarian Booksellers CLXC - 163 2011 £35

Lowry, E. P. *With the Guards Brigade from Bloemfontein to Koomati Poort and Black.* London: Horace Marshall, 1902, First edition; 8vo., 277 pages, frontispiece, illustrations, original red decorative cloth, very good, clean copy. J. & S. L. Bonham Antiquarian Booksellers Africa 4/20/2011 - 8289 2011 £90

Lowther, C. Fallow *Our Journal into Scotland anno Domini 1629 5th of November from Lowther.* Edinburgh: David Douglas, 1894, Original maroon cloth gilt, spine little faded, pages 56, facsimile and text plan, very scarce. R. F. G. Hollett & Son Antiquarian Booksellers 173 - 704 2011 £120

Lowther, John *The Correspondence of Sir John Lowther of Whitehaven 1693-1698.* British Academy, 1983, First edition; thick 8vo., original cloth, gilt, dust jacket, spine little faded, pages xliii, 739, 2 plates and 3 maps. R. F. G. Hollett & Son Antiquarian Booksellers 173 - 513 2011 £75

Luard, John *Views in India, Saint Helena and Car Nicobar. Drawn from Nature and on Stone.* London: J. Graf, printer to her Majesty, 1838, unpaged, lithographic title, 60 lithographic plates mounted on india paper, folio, contemporary crimson morocco over boards, spine tooled and lettered gilt, 5 raised bands, bound by Harrison Bookbinder (Pall Mall, small stamp to front blank), moderate foxing to text leaves and plate mounts, boards rubbed, some discoloration and scuff marks to front board, spine with few minor chips, edgewear, still very good; bookplate of William Backwell Tyringham, neat stamp of A. J. Combridge, Bombay and Madras. Kaaterskill Books 12 - 124 2011 $5250

Lubke, Wilhelm *History of Art.* London: Smith, Elder, 1868, Tall 8vo., 2 volumes, half titles, vignette illustrations in text, 2 pages ads in each volume, original brown cloth, bevelled boards by Burn & Co., decorated in black and gilt, lettered in gilt, very good bright copy. Jarndyce Antiquarian Booksellers CXCI - 299 2011 £75

Lucanus, Marcus Annaeus *Lucan's Pharsalia.* London: for Jacob Tonson, 1718, Large paper copy; subscriber's copy, folio, (6), xxv, (5), 446, 55 pages, frontispiece, double page map, engraved head and tailpieces by Elisha Kirskhall after Cheron, contemporary calf, panelled in blind, gilt spine (upper joint cracked but firm), some light browning, from the library of the Earls of Macclesfield at Shirburn Castle. Maggs Bros. Ltd. 1440 - 136 2011 £600

Lucas, E. V. *Four and Twenty Toilers.* London: Grant Richards, n.d., Oblong 4to., original cloth backed pictorial boards, corners little worn, light surface defect to bottom of lower board, pages 108, with 24 colored plates by Edmund Evans, text and illustrations printed on one side of each sheet, joints strengthened, very nice, clean and bright. R. F. G. Hollett & Sons Antiquarian Booksellers 170 - 68 2011 £220

Lucas, E. V. *Runaways and Castaways.* Wells, Gardner, Darton & Co., 1908, First edition; pages xxx, 310, (xiv), original pictorial red cloth gilt, extremities trifle rubbed, top edge gilt, colored title spread, black and white plates and pictorial endpapers (flyleaves rather browned). R. F. G. Hollett & Sons Antiquarian Booksellers 170 - 70 2011 £45

Lucas, John *History of Warton Parish.* Kendal: Titus Wilson, 1931, First edition; pages xv, 168, facsimile titlepage, original cloth with paper spine label, upper board damped and cockled, front pastedown rather bubbled, very scarce. R. F. G. Hollett & Son Antiquarian Booksellers 173 - 705 2011 £95

Lucas, Joseph *The Yetholm History of the Gypsies.* Kelso: J. and J. H. Rutherfurd, 1882, First edition; original red blindstamped cloth gilt, pages (iv) 152, 8, photo frontispiece, woodcut plate and folding diagram, fore-edges little spotted, corner neatly cut from rear flyleaf, otherwise excellent, bright copy, rare. R. F. G. Hollett & Son Antiquarian Booksellers 175 - 860 2011 £250

Lucas, Thomas J. *Camp Life and Sport in South Africa: Experiences of Kaffir Warfare with Cape Moutned Rifles.* London: Chapman Hall, 1878, First edition; 8vo. pages xiii,2 58, frontispiece, 3 tinted lithographs, original green decorative cloth, recased with new endpapers. J. & S. L. Bonham Antiquarian Booksellers Africa 4/20/2011 - 8860 2011 £240

Luce, Gordon H. *Old Burma - Early Pagan.* New York: Published for the Artibus Asiae and the Institute of Fine Arts, New York University, 1969-1970, 3 volumes, 4to., pages xviii, 422 pages; color frontispiece loosely inserted addenda and errata sheet; pages vii, 337, black and white tipped in frontispiece, folding maps and chart in rear sleeve; volume III 455 black and white plates, color frontispiece, volume one faintly bumped at foot of spine, else close to fine, bright set. Any Amount of Books May 26 2011 - A65117 2011 $629

Luckombe, Philip *The History and Art of Printing.* London: by W. Adlard and J. Browne for J. Johnson, 1771, First edition, 2nd issue with complete titlepage acknowledging Luckombe's authorship; (12), 502, (4) pages, frontispiece, illustrations, facsimiles, contemporary calf, skillfully rebacked in period style, Gathering 2 U a trifle browned, edges of frontispiece lightly smudged, else lovely copy, bookplate. Joseph J. Felcone Inc. Fall Miscellany 2010 - 77 2011 $1100

Ludlum, Robert *The Bourne Identity.* New York: Richard Marek, 1980, First edition; small ownership signature, fore-edge lightly soiled, else near fine in near fine, price clipped dust jacket with edgewear. Between the Covers 169 - BTC337398 2011 $175

Ludolf, Hiob *A New History of Ethiopia.* London: for Samuel Smith, 1682, First edition in English; folio, (8), 88, 151-370, 375-398 pages, 8 engraved plates, engraved plate, folding genealogical table, contemporary or early 18th century calf, front hinge cracked but held by cords, corners worn, some light browning but very good, signatures of Edmund and Rufus Marsden, latter dated 1762, Herz booklabel. Joseph J. Felcone Inc. Fall Miscellany 2010 - 78 2011 $2200

Luer, Carlyle A. *Thesauru Masevalliarum: eine Monographie der Gattung Masdevallia...* Munich: Helga Koniger, 1983-1993, First edition; 270 color plates after watercolor drawings of Anne Marie Techslin, along with maps and drawings, folio, parts with printed front wrappers, in original shipping cartons. Raymond M. Sutton, Jr. May 26 2011 - 48413 2011 $1150

Lugar, Robert *Villa Architecture: a Collection of Views with Plans, of Buildings Executed in England, Scotland &c.* London: J. Taylor, 1828, First edition; folio, (2), x, 34 pages, 42 plates of which 26 are hand colored aquatints and 16 floor plans, modern half red morocco, margins of first two leaves bit soiled, few tiny chips, two leaves of preface moderately foxed, occasional spot of foxing, plates clean and bright, fine, signature of H. Le Roy Newbold, NY 1836. Joseph J. Felcone Inc. Fall Miscellany 2010 - 5 2011 $4500

Lugard, F. D. *The Rise of Our East African Empire: Early Efforts in Nyasaland and Uganda.* London: Wm. Blackwood, 1893, First edition; 2 volumes, 8vo., pages xx, 563, 32 publisher's list; x, 682, with 130 plates, 9 colored maps (2 loose in pockets of volume 1), frontispiece, original decorative red cloth, gilt vignette on upper covers, small repair to base of volume I, very good set. J. & S. L. Bonham Antiquarian Booksellers Africa 4/20/2011 - 8740 2011 £280

Luhan, Mable Dodge *Winter in Taos.* New York: 1935, Stated first edition; publisher's presentation copy with recipient's name in ink on bookplate, viii, 237 pages, illustrations, spine tanned, else very good, no dust jacket. Dumont Maps & Books of the West 111 - 65 2011 $75

Lull, Ramon *Libro dei Ascenso y Decenso del Entendimiento.* Mallorca: La Viuda Frau, 1753, First Vernacular edition; 4to., pages (viii), (2) plates, 252, folding table of contents, and folding woodcut illustration, preceding A1, woodcut vignettes to text, titlepage trimmed and extended at lower margin (probably to erase inscription), couple of pages lightly browned, contemporary Spanish limp vellum, title in ink to spine, lacking ties, very good. Simon Finch Rare Books Zero - 116 2011 £3000

Lull, Ramon *The Order of Chivalry. (with) L'Ordene de Chevalerie.* London: sold by Reeves & Turner, 1893, One of 225 paper copies, out of a total edition of 235 copies; small quarto, (4), 150, (1, colophon), (1, blank) pages, printed in red and black in Chaucer type, wood engraved frontispiece designed by Sir Edward Burne-Jones, decorative woodcut borders and initials, printed by William Morris at the Kelmscott Press, original full limp vellum with red silk ties, spine lettered in gilt, one silk tie little short, small (half inch) tear to lower margin of pages 133/4, otherwise near fine uncut copy, housed in cloth slipcase. David Brass Rare Books, Inc. May 26 2011 - 01473 2011 $5500

Lull, Ramon *Opera ea Quae ad Adinventam ab Ipso Artem Universalem....* Strasbourg: Heirs of Lazarus Zetzner, 1651, 8vo., pages (xvi) 1109 (40) index, (1) colophon, plus final blank, woodcut title device and colophon, woodcut initials and headpieces, 3 folding tables, woodcut diagrams (three with volvelles), all edges red, varying degrees of foxing and offsetting throughout, as usual in German paper of this date, ink staining to top outer margin of last leaves, contemporary vellum over pasteboard, spine lettered in MS ink, early ink inscription to title, now little corroded, 19th century label to front pastedown. Simon Finch Rare Books Zero - 104 2011 £1750

Lumisden, Andrew *Remarks on the Antiquities of Rome and Its Environs...* London: W. Bulmer and Co. for G. and W. Nicol, 1812, Second edition; 4to., modern three quartere calf gilt with raised bands and spine label, pages iv, 478, (xii), complete with engraved frontispiece, large folding map (trifle offset), 5 plates, handsome copy. R. F. G. Hollett & Son Antiquarian Booksellers 177 - 555 2011 £350

Lummis, Charles F. *The Enchanted Burro: Stories of New Mexico and South America.* Chicago: 1897, First edition; (x), 277 pages, illustrations, illustrated cloth, bookplate, light soiling, else very good. Dumont Maps & Books of the West 113 - 39 2011 $600

Lumsden, Harry *History of the Skinners Furriers and Glovers of Glasgow.* Glasgow: Aird & Coghill, 1937, First edition; large 8vo., original blue buckram gilt over bevelled boards, boards trifle marked, pages xxiv, 306, top edge gilt, 9 plates, flyleaves faintly spotted, otherwise very good. R. F. G. Hollett & Son Antiquarian Booksellers 175 - 864 2011 £180

Lundius, Johannes *Die Alten Judischen Heiligthu mer Gottesdienste und Gewohnheiten...* Hamburg: Johann Wolfgang Fictweiler, 1722, Later edition; 4to., (40), 1090, (142) pages, engraved frontispiece, signed by J. G. Mentzel with engraved plate facing red and black titlepage, 29 engraved plates, paper slightly browned, contemporary full vellum, ink signature of Johan Friederich Barth 1732 and notations on f.f.ep., ink stamp of Evangelische Predigerschule, Basel, very good. Jeff Weber Rare Books 163 - 32 2011 $600

Lurie, Alison *Love and Friendship.* London: Heinemann, 1962, First edition; 8vo. pages 319, signed by Lurie, fine in fine dust jacket, very slight sunning to very top of cloth spine, faint browning at rear corners of jacket, excellent condition. Any Amount of Books May 29 2011 - A38817 2011 $213

Luther, Martin 1483-1546 *Ausslegung des hundert and Neundten Psalmen Dixit Dominus Domino Meo.* colophon: Leipzig: Melchior Lotter, 1518, Title within woodcut border, small abrasion on title, slightly affecting woodcut border, minor staining, 17 leaves (ov 18, lacking final blank), small 4to., modern boards, some contemporary annotations (cropped, good). Blackwell Rare Books B166 - 66 2011 £1500

Luther, Martin 1483-1546 *A Commentarie Upon the Fifteene Psalmes, Called Psalmi Graduum... (bound with) A Commentarie of M. Doctor Martin Luther upon the Epistle of S. Paul to the Galathians.* London: by Richard Field, 1616, 4to., (4), 296 leaves, black letter, 2 works bound together in 18th century calf, very neatly rebacked retaining original spine label, titlepage of first work soiled, minor dampstains on first few leaves, else very good, armorial bookplate of John Brogden. Joseph J. Felcone Inc. Fall Miscellany 2010 - 79 2011 $2800

Luther, Seth *An Address to the Working Men of New England on the State of Education and on the Condition of the Producing Classes in Europe and America.* Boston: published by the author, 1832, First edition; 8vo., 39 pages, original printed wrappers, front wrapper slightly wrinkled and nearly detached. M & S Rare Books, Inc. 90 - 221 2011 $1250

Lutyens, Edwin *The Letters of Edwin Lutyens to his Wife Emily.* London: Collins, 1985, First edition; original cloth, gilt, pages (iv), 454, with 21 portraits. R. F. G. Hollett & Son Antiquarian Booksellers 177 - 628 2011 £45

Lyall, Edna *Derrick Vaughan: Novelist.* London: Methuen & Co., 1889, First edition; half title, uncut in original blue cloth, blocked in white and yellow, lettered in gilt and yellow, slightly dulled, R. G. Taylor booklabel, good plus.   Jarndyce Antiquarian Booksellers   CLXC - 166   2011   £75

Lydekker, Richard *A Hand-Book to the British Mammalia.* London: W. H. Allen & Co., 1895, Original cloth backed marbled boards with double leather spine labels, edges little rubbed, pages xvi, 340, with 32 tissue guarded color plates.   R. F. G. Hollett & Son Antiquarian Booksellers   General Catalogue Summer 2010 - 1015   2011   £60

Lydekker, Richard *A Hand-Book to the Carnivora.* Edward Loyd, 1896, original maroon cloth, gilt, pages viii, 312, 32 chromolithographed tissue guarded plates.   R. F. G. Hollett & Son Antiquarian Booksellers   General Catalogue Summer 2010 - 1016   2011   £50

Lydekker, Richard *Life and Rock: Collection of Zoological and Geological Essays.* London: Universal Press, 1894, First edition; original green pictorial cloth gilt, pages xi, 221, 63 text woodcuts, rear flyleaf spotted, otherwise very nice clean and sound, uncommon.   R. F. G. Hollett & Son Antiquarian Booksellers   General Catalogue Summer 2010 - 1017   2011   £45

Lydekker, Richard *Wild Life of the World.* London: Frederick Warne and Co., n.d. circa, 1916, 3 volumes, 4to., original brown cloth gilt, 120 color plates and 600 text engravings, excellent, clean and sound set.   R. F. G. Hollett & Son Antiquarian Booksellers   General Catalogue Summer 2010 - 1018   2011   £250

Lydon, A. F. *English Lake Scenery.* John Walker & Co., 1880, First edition; large 8vo., original decorated green cloth gilt, extra over bevelled boards, pages 48, all edges gilt, 25 chromolithographs, all very bright and clean, few blank leaves loose.   R. F. G. Hollett & Son Antiquarian Booksellers   173 - 706   2011   £185

Lye, Len *No Trouble.* Deya, Majorca: The Seizin Press, 1930, First edition, copy # 156 f 200 handset and hand Printed on handmade paper and signed by author and artist; tall thin quarto, bound with white cloth, gilt stamped spine and boards, decorated in red and brown on gold by Lye, issued as Seizen 4, (vi), 27 pages, some rubbing to gold on covers, as usual, scarce in any condition, just about fine.   Charles Agvent   2010 Summer Miscellany - 42   2011 $750

Lyell, Charles   1797-1875 *Principles of Geology: Being an Inquiry How Far the Former Changes of the Earth's Surface and Referable to Causes Now In Operation.* London: John Murray, 1834, Third edition; plain engraved frontispiece, 3 hand colored engraved maps, 4 plain engraved maps, 6 engraved folding plates, fold to colored plate reinforced, 147 text engravings, 8vo., pages xxx, (1), 420; (2), 453; (2), 426 (ad 2 pages); (2), 393, half titles present, modern black cloth, marginal tanning or browning to pages. marginal tear to 2 pages, light soiling to page, owner's signature to upper corner of titles.   Raymond M. Sutton, Jr.   May 26 2011 - 48898   2011 $1200

Lyell, Charles   1797-1875 *A Second Visit to the United States of North America.* New York: 1849, Volume I only, mildly rubbed, some foxing, missing f.f.e.p.   Bookworm & Silverfish   670 - 86   2011 $125

Lyell, Denis D. *Hunting Trips in Northern Rhodesia; with Accounts of Sport and Travel in Nyasaland and Portuguese East Africa...* London: Horace Cox, 1910, First edition; large 8vo., pages xii, 118, (2) ads, half title, 55 plates, including frontispiece, errata slip tipped to page x, foxing on few sheets, original green patterned cloth vignette of camp mounted on upper cover, very good.   J. & S. L. Bonham Antiquarian Booksellers   Africa 4/20/2011 - 9129   2011   £900

Lyell, Denis D. *Nyasaland for the Hunter & Settler.* London: Horace Cox, 1912, First edition; 8vo., pages xi, 116, map, illustrations, original green decorative cloth, some light fading in corner of upper cover, otherwise very good, very scarce.   J. & S. L. Bonham Antiquarian Booksellers   Africa 4/20/2011 - 8718   2011   £700

Lyle, Robert *The Catacomb.* 1949-1950, April 1949-Summer 1950, nos. 1-7, 13-14, then v.1/1-v.2/2, 14 issues, very good.   I. D. Edrich   May 26 2011 - 97614   2011 $1191

Lyman, George D. *John Marsh, Pioneer. The Life Story of a Trail-Blazer on Six Frontiers.* New York: Charles Scribner's Sons, 1930, First limited edition, one of 150 numbered copies signed by author; quite scarce, pages (xii), (4), 394, four facsimile folding letters tipped in, 24 illustrations, map endpapers, original two-tone red cloth, black leather spine label, very fine, publisher's matching slipcase (spine faded).   Argonaut Book Shop   Recent Acquisitions Summer 2010 - 122   2011 $425

Lyman, Theodore *The Diplomacy of the United States Being an Account of the Foreign Relations of the Country, from the First Treaty with France in 1778 to the Present Time.* Boston: Wlls and Lilly, 1828, Second edition; 2 volumes, 8vo., full leather lettered gilt at spine, pages xii, 470 and xii, 517, ex-Foreign and Commonwealth Office library with their label and stamps, few library marks, covers worn and scuffed, front boards loose on volume one, clean text.   Any Amount of Books   May 29 2011 - A49587 2011 $340

Lynch, Gary *Tom Blake: Surfing 1922-1932.* Santa Barbara: Adler Books, 1999, Deluxe boxed stamped edition, one of 26 lettered copies, this copy lettered F; oblong 4to., quarter black cloth over white illustrated boards, 68 pages, 49 duotone illustrations, stamp of Tom Blake's estate initialled by Lynch on rear colophon as issued, fine in box and beautiful printed hard slipcase, fine.   Any Amount of Books   May 26 2011 - A32986 2011 $545

Lynch, John Gilbert Bohun *Menace from the Moon.* London: Jarrolds Pub. Limited, 1925, First edition; octavo, original decorated black cloth, front and spine panels stamped in red.   L. W. Currey, Inc.   124 - 225 2011 $125

Lynch, Patricia *King of the Tinkers.* London: J. M. Dent, 1948, Second impression; Original cloth, gilt, dust jacket, spine little browned, pages ix, 241, with 7 color plates, line drawings by Katharine C. Lloyd.   R. F. G. Hollett & Son Antiquarian Booksellers   General Catalogue Summer 2010 - 534 2011   £50

Lynch, Patricia *Long Ears. The Story of a Little Grey Donkey.* London: J. M. Dent, 1943, First edition; original pictorial blue cloth silvered, dust jacket rather worn, head of spine chipped, pages vi, 250, color frontispiece and numerous drawings by Kiddell-Monroe.   R. F. G. Hollett & Son Antiquarian Booksellers   General Catalogue Summer 2010 - 535 2011   £60

Lynch, Patricia *The Turf-Cutter's Donkey.* London: J. M. Dent, 1940, Pages viii, 247, original pictorial cream cloth, 5 color plates, 8 line drawings and pictorial endpapers, very good, without dust jacket.   R. F. G. Hollett & Son Antiquarian Booksellers   General Catalogue Summer 2010 - 536 2011   £75

Lynch, Patricia *The Turf-Cutter's Donkey Goes Visiting.* London: J. M. Dent, 1943, Original pictorial cream boards, dust jacket spine lightly browned, pages viii, 229, with 4 color plates, 16 line drawings and pictorial endpapers by George Altendorf.   R. F. G. Hollett & Son Antiquarian Booksellers   General Catalogue Summer 2010 - 537 2011   £35

Lyne, George Maxwell *Balbus. A Latin Reading Book for Junior Forms.* London: Edward Arnold, 1934, First edition; small 8vo., original blue cloth, that on upper board trifle creased, pages 128, line drawings by Charles Robinson, very scarce.   R. F. G. Hollett & Son Antiquarian Booksellers   General Catalogue Summer 2010 - 566 2011   £45

Lynn, Michael *Joy Street.* Blackwell, 1923-1936, First edition; Numbers 1-8.11 1.2.14 1923-1930. 1934. 1936, 11 volumes, overall very good, drawings colored by young owners.   I. D. Edrich   May 26 2011 - 98990 2011 $587

Lynx, J. J. *The Pen is Mightier.* Lindsay Drummond, 1946, Large 8vo., original cloth, spine rather faded, pages 146, cartoons.   R. F. G. Hollett & Son Antiquarian Booksellers   General Catalogue Summer 2010 - 838 2011   £50

Lyon, Danny *The Bikeriders.* New York: Macmillan Co., 1968, First edition,, simultaneous softcover issue; fine and tight in illustrated wrappers, signed by Lyon.   Jeff Hirsch Books   ny 2010 2011 $850

Lyon, George Francis *A Narrative of Travels in Northern Africa in the Years 1818, 1819 and 1820...* London: John Murray, 1821, First edition; quarto, pages xii, 383, map, 17 hand colored aquatints, slight soiling to margins of some of the plates, 2 small marginal tears (1 to a plate and the other to the map, repaired), recent black half morocco, gilt spine, raised bands.   J. & S. L. Bonham Antiquarian Booksellers   Africa 4/20/2011 - 8968 2011   £1000

Lyon, Massey, Mrs. *Etiquette. A Guide to Public and Social Life.* London: Cassell, 1927, First edition; large 8vo., original two tone cloth gilt, pages (iv), 492, 9 plates, fine.   R. F. G. Hollett & Son Antiquarian Booksellers   175 - 866 2011   £30

Lyons, Augusta Louise *Olivia: a Tale for an Hour of Idleness.* London: Simms & M'Intyre, 1848, First edition; half title, contemporary half green calf, maroon leather label, spine slightly darkened, little rubbed, good plus.   Jarndyce Antiquarian Booksellers   CLXC - 176 2011   £50

Lyons, Augusta Louise *Sir Philip Hetherington.* London: Simms & M'Intyre, 1851, First edition; half title, initial 4 pages ads, original green cloth, very good.   Jarndyce Antiquarian Booksellers   CLXC - 178 2011   £65

Lyons, R. S. *Sir Malcolm Campbell's Book of James Motorists.* Blackie, 1937, First reprint; pages 176, with 42 illustrations, large 8vo., original cloth, rather faded and extremities frayed in places, inscriptions (non-authorial), scattered slight spotting.   R. F. G. Hollett & Son Antiquarian Booksellers   General Catalogue Summer 2010 - 1122 2011   £60

Lysons, D. *Cumberland. Volume the Fourth Magna Britannia.* T. Cadell & W. Davies, 1816, First edition; pages ccx, 198, 43 steel engraved plates, plans, etc., occasional patch of light spotting, very nice, clean copy, partially unopened, modern half green levant morocco gilt with raised bands and contrasting spine label.   R. F. G. Hollett & Son Antiquarian Booksellers   173 - 708   2011   £250

Lyster, Annette   *Dora and Nora; or Dreaming and Doing.* London: SPCK, circa, 1886, First edition; frontispiece, 4 pages ads, some light browning, original dark blue green cloth, decorated with peacock feathers in maroon and yellow, lettered in gilt, ownership inscription, very good. Jarndyce Antiquarian Booksellers   CLXC - 179   2011   £45

Lyttelton, R. H.   *Cricket & Golf.*   London: J. M. Dent & Co., 1901, First edition; original green cloth gilt, corners little bruised, pages vii, 252, top edge gilt, 9 plates, endpapers and some chapter headings to Arthur Rackham, library label on pastedown.   R. F. G. Hollett & Son Antiquarian Booksellers   General Catalogue Summer 2010 - 1262   2011   £120

Lytton, Edward George Earle Bulwer-Lytton, 1st Baron 1803-1873   *The Last Days of Pompeii.* London: Richard Bentley, 1834, First edition; 210 x 130mm., volume 1 lacking half title, 3 volumes, publisher's drab paper boards backed with maroon muslin, flat spines with original printed paper labels, edges untrimmed, housed in red buckram chemise, inside very handsome red morocco backed case, its spine designed to appear as three attractively found volumes with raised bands and gilt compartments filled with interlacing floral vines, ALS by apparently written by author's elder brother, the diplomat, Sir Henry Lytton Earle Bulwer to his banker, 19th century armorial bookplate of William Williamson Willink, each volume with morocco bookplate of Estelle Doheny; paper boards bit soiled (one cover with slight dampstain), minor wear at joints and extremities, isolated trivial smudges internally, otherwise excellent unsophisticated set, especially clean and fresh, extremely handsome.   Phillip J. Pirages   59 - 259   2011 $950

Lytton, Rosina, Baroness   *Cheveley; or the Man of Honour.* London: Edward Bull, 1839, First edition; 3 volumes, half titles, contemporary half dark purple calf, gilt spines, dark green leather labels, very slight rubbing, armorial bookplate of Earl of Dundonald and each volume signed "Countess of Dundonald, very good set, extremely scarce. Jarndyce Antiquarian Booksellers   CLXC - 180   2011   £2500

Lytton, Rosina, Baroness   *Unpublished Letters of Lady Bulwer Lytton to A. E. Chalon.* London: Eveleigh Nash, 1914, First edition; half title, frontispiece portrait, plates, 2 + 11 pages ads, lacks following f.e.p., original red cloth lettered in gilt, dulled and rubbed, Harrods Circulating Library label.   Jarndyce Antiquarian Booksellers   CLXC - 181   2011   £38

M

M'Calla, William Latta *Discussion of Universalisms or a Defence of Orthodoxy Against the Heresy of Universalism as Advocated by Mr. Abnery Kneeland.* 1825, 319 (1) errata (1) (ad) pages, new backstrip and paper over boards, all edges untrimmed. Bookworm & Silverfish 670 - 156 2011 $75

M'Clintock, Captain *The Voyage of the "Fox" in the Arctic Seas. A Narrative of the Discovery of the Fate of Sir John Franklin and His Companions.* London: John Murray, 1859, First edition; xxvii, 403, (3) (as), frontispiece, illustrations, 3 folding maps including one in a sleeve at back, as issued, original blue cloth illustrated with ship in gilt on cover, very good plus. Lupack Rare Books May 26 2011 - ABE 4310256498 2011 $450

M'Collum, William *California As I Saw It. Pencillings by the Way of Its Gold and Gold Diggers!* Los Gatos: Talisman Press, 1960, Reprint of extremely rare first edition of 1850, limited to 750 copies; 219 pages, titlepage vignette, 1 illustration, map endpapers, notes, cloth backed pictorial boards, paper spine label, very fine with slightly chipped pictorial dust jacket. Argonaut Book Shop Recent Acquisitions Summer 2010 - 140 2011 $90

M'Dougall, Ellem M. *Songs of the Church with Stories of Their Writers.* London: Robert Culley, circa, 1903, Third thousand; original cloth, spine and edges faded, pages xii, 320, presentation copy inscribed by author for Mr. Endicott. R. F. G. Hollett & Son Antiquarian Booksellers 175 - 874 2011 £35

M'Gibbon, George *Hand-Book for the Study and Discussion of Popery, with a Special Reference to Its Political Relations.* Edinburgh: George M'Gibbon, 1868-1875, First edition; 2 volumes, original blindstamped cloth, gilt, pages lvi, 438; lix, 518, scarce. R. F. G. Hollett & Son Antiquarian Booksellers 175 - 867 2011 £125

M'Intosh, Maria June *Charms and Counter-Charms.* London: George Routledge, 1850, First English edition; frontispiece, engraved title, additional printed title, 8 pages ads, contemporary brown morocco presentation binding, elaborately blocked in gilt, prize inscription, dated 1860, all edges gilt, very good. Jarndyce Antiquarian Booksellers CLXC - 188 2011 £60

M'Intosh, Maria June *Grace and Isabel; or to Seem and to Be.* London: G. Routledge Co., 1852, First English edition; Contemporary half green calf, maroon leather label, spine darkened, slightly worn damage in tail of following hinge, from the Headfort library, signed "Bective 1854). Jarndyce Antiquarian Booksellers CLXC - 190 2011 £45

M'Intosh, Maria June *Louise De La Valliere.* London: T. Nelson & Sons, 1854, First English edition; contemporary half maroon calf, black leather label, spine slightly rubbed, from the Headfort library, signed "Bective 1854". Jarndyce Antiquarian Booksellers CLXC - 191 2011 £45

M'Intosh, Maria June *Praise and Principle; or For What Shall I Live?* London: G. Routledge & Co., 1857, Frontispiece, vignette title, additional printed title, original blue cloth, pictorially blocked and lettered gilt, slightly dulled and rubbed, all edges gilt. Jarndyce Antiquarian Booksellers CLXC - 192 2011 £40

Maberly, Catherine Charlotte *The Love Match.* London: David Bryce, 1856, New edition; contemporary half maroon calf, spine decorated in gilt, black leather label, spine and corners little rubbed, from Headfort library, signed, "Bective 1854", good plus. Jarndyce Antiquarian Booksellers CLXC - 184 2011 £45

Mabey, Richard *Flora Britannica.* Sinclair Stevenson, 1996, First edition; 4to., original cloth, gilt, dust jacket, pages 480, illustrations. R. F. G. Hollett & Son Antiquarian Booksellers General Catalogue Summer 2010 - 1019 2011 £30

Macaulay, Thomas Babington Macaulay, 1st Baron 1800-1859 *Critical and Historical Essays Contributed to the Edinburgh Review.* London: Longman, Brown, Green, Longmans & Roberts, 1858, Ninth edition; 3 volumes, 230 x 150mm., lovely contemporary honey brown full crushed morocco, elegantly gilt by Morrell (signed on front turn-in), covers with double gilt rule frame, raised bands, spine gilt in charming Arts and Crafts design of interlacing flowers and leaves, gilt titling, turn-ins, extra illustrated with 122 engraved plates; upper cover of a third volume with one inch and two three-inch scratches (all shallow and well masked with dye), thin band of offsetting to free endpapers from gilt turn-ins (as usual), some of the plates with minor foxing and bit offset onto facing pages, otherwise quite handsome set in fine condition, text fresh and clean, bindings very lustrous and with virtually no wear to joints or extremities. Phillip J. Pirages 59 - 121 2011 $850

Macaulay, Thomas Babington Macaulay, 1st Baron 1800-1859 *Critical and Historical Essays.* London: Longmans, Green and Co., 1880, New edition; text in double columns, bound as two volumes, half title at beginning of volume ii, pages viii, (ii), 414; (ii), 415-850, 8vo., contemporary dark grey calf, spines gilt, red and green morocco lettering pieces, marbled endleaves and matching edges, bookplates of William Endicott, near fine.   Blackwell Rare Books   B166 - 67   2011   £100

Macaulay, Thomas Babington Macaulay, 1st Baron 1800-1859 *Essays, Critical and Miscellaneous.* Philadelphia: 1849, New edition; 744 pages, half leather rubbed, all edges of backstrip and corners, modest foxing, bookplate of Col. Richard L. Maury with pencil presentation of C. Blackford.   Bookworm & Silverfish   679 - 67   2011 $60

Macaulay, Thomas Babington Macaulay, 1st Baron 1800-1859 *History of England from the Accession of James the Second.* Cambridge: Riverside Press, 1866, Limited edition, 75 copies printed for subscribers; 8 volume set, cloth in slightly soiled and worn at edges, one small tear, spine labels soiled, peeling and chipped, corners bumped, one hinge broken, small hole in one binding, interiors clean and tight, 8vo., 483, 459, 446, 408, 547, 429, 484, 402 pages, very good.   G. H. Mott Bookseller   May 26 2011 - 35384   2011 $200

Macaulay, Zachary *Negro Slavery; or a View of Some of the More Prominent Features of that State of Society as it Exists in the United States of America and in the Colonies of the West Indies, Especially in Jamaica.* London: for Hatchard and Son... and J. and A. Arch, 1823, First edition; (4), 118 pages, attractive modern half calf by Bayntun, fine, fresh copy inside and out, Lord Palmerston's copy with his signature, (Henry John Temple, 3rd Viscount Palmerston).   Joseph J. Felcone Inc.   Fall Miscellany 2010 - 80   2011 $900

MacBride, Mackenzie *Wild Lakeland.* London: A. & C. Black, 1922, First edition; original blue blindstamped cloth, gilt, pages viii, 230, (ii), with 32 colored plates and map.   R. F. G. Hollett & Son Antiquarian Booksellers   173 - 257   2011   £40

MacDermott, K. H. *The Old Church Gallery Minstrels.* London: SPCK, 1948, First edition; pages (iv), 78, 20 plates, uncommon, original cloth, dust jacket, extremities little chipped and torn, uncommon.   R. F. G. Hollett & Son Antiquarian Booksellers   175 - 872   2011   £45

MacDonald, D. *Cape North and Vicinity Including Pioneer Families History and Chronicles including Pleasant Bay, Bay St. Lawrence, Aspy Bay, White Point, New Haven, and Heil's Harbour.* N.P.: n.p., 1933, Blue cloth, 8vo., pages (5)-160, xiv, 20 photo illustrations, covers stained, inner hinge crack.   Schooner Books Ltd.   96 - 180   2011 $95

MacDonald, D. *Cape North and Vicinity Including Pioneer Family History and Chronicles...* N.P.: n.p., 1933, Card covers, pages (5)-160, xiv, 20 photo illustrations, 8vo., covers stained, interior good, previous owner's inscription on titlepage.   Schooner Books Ltd.   96 - 179   2011 $75

MacDonald, Diana Louisa *Villa Verocchio; or the Youth of Leonardo Da Vinci: a Tale.* London: Longmans, 1850, First editions, half title, few spots, 32 page catalog (June 10, 1850); original dark blue cloth by Westleys, small splits at heads of hinges, ads on endpapers.   Jarndyce Antiquarian Booksellers   CLXC - 186   2011   £45

MacDonald, Duff *Africana; or the Heart of Heathen Africa.* London: Simpkin Marshall, 1882, First edition; 2 volumes, 8vo., xvii, 301; xi, 371, illustrations, original buff cloth, spine slightly faded, nevertheless very good set.   J. & S. L. Bonham Antiquarian Booksellers   Africa 4/20/2011 - 7253   2011   £350

MacDonald, George   1824-1905   *Adela Cathcart.* London: Hurst & Blackett, 1864, First edition; 3 volumes, half titles, spotting caused by endpapers, contemporary half dark green roan, rubbed but sound, stamps and booklabels from General Assembly Library, N.Z.   Jarndyce Antiquarian Booksellers   CXCII - 26   2011   £850

MacDonald, George   1824-1905   *Adela Cathcart.* London: Sampson Low, Marston, Searle & Rivington, 1882, Second edition; original red cloth, spine blocked with gilt flowers, leading inner hinge strengthened, slightly rubbed.   Jarndyce Antiquarian Booksellers   CXCII - 27   2011   £150

MacDonald, George   1824-1905   *Adela Cathcart.* London: Sampson Low, Marston, Searle & Rivington, 1887, Colonial edition; original red cloth blocked in black, gilt lettered on spine (style C), blue endpapers printed with ads, staples slight rusting, good.   Jarndyce Antiquarian Booksellers   CXCII - 28   2011   £75

MacDonald, George   1824-1905   *Adela Cathcart.* London: Sampson Low, Marston, Searle & Rivington, 1889, New edition; yellowback with pale blue color pictorial boards, spine darkened, rubbed and cracked, blue endpapers, same ads as the 1887 edition, Renier booklabel.   Jarndyce Antiquarian Booksellers   CXCII - 29   2011   £45

MacDonald, George   1824-1905   *Adela Cathcart.* R. E. King & Co., circa, 1900?, Slight browning, original dark green cloth, elaborate blind design, small gilt coats of arms.   Jarndyce Antiquarian Booksellers   CXCII - 31   2011   £35

MacDonald, George   1824-1905   *Alec Forbes of Howglen.* London: Hurst & Blackett, 1865, First edition; 3 volumes, half titles, rebound in sturdy half red morocco, red cloth boards.   Jarndyce Antiquarian Booksellers   CXCII - 34   2011   £1200

MacDonald, George 1824-1905 *Alec Forbes of Howglen.* London: Hurst & Blackett, 1865, First edition; 3 volumes, half titles, initial a leaf volume I, 14 page catalog volume III (apparently lacking one leaf), original orange cloth, spines little darkened and little rubbed at tails, bookplates of Nigel Ronald, inscription "S. J. Selby in remembrance of Miss Manning Aug. 10th 1905". Jarndyce Antiquarian Booksellers CXCII - 33 2011 £3000

MacDonald, George 1824-1905 *Alec Forbes of Howglen.* London: Hurst & Blackett, 1867, Half title, frontispiece, dated June 15th 1867, rebound in near contemporary half dark green morocco, spine worn at head of spine, stamps and label of General Assembly Library, New Zealand. Jarndyce Antiquarian Booksellers CXCII - 36 2011 £45

MacDonald, George 1824-1905 *Alec Forbes of Howglen.* London: Hurst & Blackett, 1867, First one volume edition; half title, frontispiece, dated June 15th 1867, 4 pages ads, text marked & spotted, original dark green cloth, blind design on boards, gilt lettered spine, small section of cloth removed from back board, gold printed prize label of Barnsbury Park School, Islington. Jarndyce Antiquarian Booksellers CXCII - 35 2011 £65

MacDonald, George 1824-1905 *Alec Forbes of Howglen.* London: Hurst & Blackett, circa, 1875, Half title, frontispiece, bound without ads in half light brown morocco with coronet on spine, armorial bookplate of Duke of Westminster, 1884, very good, handsome copy. Jarndyce Antiquarian Booksellers CXCII - 37 2011 £85

MacDonald, George 1824-1905 *Alec Forbes of Howglen.* London: Hurst & Blackett, circa, 1875?, Later one volume edition; this copy with 1879 inscription, half title, frontispiece, 4 pages ads, ink note on title, original dark green cloth by Leighton, Son & Hodge, slightly damp marked, labels partially removed from pastedowns. Jarndyce Antiquarian Booksellers CXCII - 38 2011 £45

MacDonald, George 1824-1905 *Alec Forbes of Howglen.* London: Hurst & Blackett, circa, 1885?, Half title, frontispiece, 4 pages ads, original dark blue cloth, plain gold borders, very good. Jarndyce Antiquarian Booksellers CXCII - 40 2011 £45

MacDonald, George 1824-1905 *Alec Forbes of Howglen.* London: Hurst & Blackett, 1900, New edition; half title, 4 pages ads, original green cloth, blind design, gilt lettering, very good, inscription. Jarndyce Antiquarian Booksellers CXCII - 42 2011 £35

MacDonald, George 1824-1905 *Alec Forbes of Howglen.* London: Hurst & Blackett, circa, 1907, New edition; half title, 4 pages ads, original green cloth with blind design and gilt lettering, slightly spotted, on rougher paper. Jarndyce Antiquarian Booksellers CXCII - 43 2011 £35

MacDonald, George 1824-1905 *Annals of a Quiet Neighbourhood.* London: Hurst & Blackett, 1867, (1866). First edition; 3 volumes, half titles, 16 page catalog volume III, original green pebble grained cloth, slightly rubbed and marked, lending library copy with labels. Jarndyce Antiquarian Booksellers CXCII - 46 2011 £1250

MacDonald, George 1824-1905 *Annals of a Quiet Neighbourhood.* London: Hurst & Blackett, 1867, (1866). First edition; 3 volumes, half titles, slightly later dark green morocco, bit rubbed, but decent copy, gilt stamps & pressmarks & withdrawn stamped booklabels of General Assembly Library, New Zealand. Jarndyce Antiquarian Booksellers CXCII - 47 2011 £750

MacDonald, George 1824-1905 *Annals of a Quiet Neighbourhood.* Leipzig: Bernhard Tauchnitz, 1867, Copyright edition; 2 volumes in 1, half title, purple binder's cloth, spine faded, armorial bookplate of Fothergill. Jarndyce Antiquarian Booksellers CXCII - 49 2011 £50

MacDonald, George 1824-1905 *Annals of a Quiet Neighbourhood.* Leipzig: Bernhard Tauchnitz, 1867, Copyright edition; 2 volumes in 1, half dark blue morocco, gilt spine, very good, bookplate of Bibliotheque Haut Buisson. Jarndyce Antiquarian Booksellers CXCII - 48 2011 £85

MacDonald, George 1824-1905 *Annals of a Quiet Neighbourhood.* London: Strahan & Co., 1872, First Strahan edition; half title, minor spotting caused by endpapers, original dark green cloth, decorated in black, spine gilt, slightly rubbed & dulled, tipped in slip removed from f.e.p. Jarndyce Antiquarian Booksellers CXCII - 50 2011 £120

MacDonald, George 1824-1905 *Annals of a Quiet Neighbourhood.* London: Daldy, Isbister & Co., 1878, Half title, frontispiece, 7 plates, 4 pages ads, booksellers blindstamp on half title, original royal blue cloth, blocked in black and gilt, slightly rubbed and dulled. Jarndyce Antiquarian Booksellers CXCII - 51 2011 £50

MacDonald, George 1824-1905 *Annals of a Quiet Neighbourhood.* London: Strahan & Co. circa, 1885, New edition; Half title, frontispiece and 7 plates, 4 pages ads, lacking leading f.e.p., original royal blue cloth, blocked in black and gilt. Jarndyce Antiquarian Booksellers CXCII - 52 2011 £45

MacDonald, George 1824-1905 *Annals of a Quiet Neighbourhood.* London: Kegan Paul, Trench, Trubner & Co., 1893, New edition; original red cloth blocked in black and gilt, style G, very good. Jarndyce Antiquarian Booksellers CXCII - 53 2011 £40

MacDonald, George 1824-1905 *Annals of a Quiet Neighbourhood.* London: Kegan Paul, Trench, Trubner & Co., circa, 1895, New edition; Half title, original red cloth blocked in black and gilt, style G, on smooth textured paper with no publishers' ad on titlepage, spine slightly faded. Jarndyce Antiquarian Booksellers CXCII - 54 2011 £40

MacDonald, George 1824-1905 *Annals of a Quiet Neighbourhood.* London: Kegan Paul, Trench, Trubner & Co., circa, 1895, New edition; half title, original red cloth blocked in black and gilt, style G, on rougher textured paper with publishers' address at Dryden House, Gerrard Street on titlepage. Jarndyce Antiquarian Booksellers CXCII - 55 2011 £45

MacDonald, George 1824-1905 *Annals of a Quiet Neighbourhood.* London: Kegan Paul, Trench, Trubner & Co. circa, 1900?, New edition; half title, original orange cloth, blocked in brown, style H, slight dulled, on rougher textured paper with publishers address on titlepage. Jarndyce Antiquarian Booksellers CXCII - 56 2011 £35

MacDonald, George 1824-1905 *At the Back of the North Wind. in Good Words for the Young 1869 & 1870.* London: Strahan & Co., 1869-1870, Color frontispiece and title, 1869, frontispiece & engraved title 1870, plates, illustrations, some browning, 2 volumes in original blue decorated cloth by Burn & Co., 1869 more faded and rubbed, inner hinges cracking, all edges gilt. Jarndyce Antiquarian Booksellers CXCII - 112 2011 £850

MacDonald, George 1824-1905 *At the Back of the North Wind.* London: Strahan & Co., 1871, (1870). First edition; half title, 76 illustrations after Arthur Hughes, 13 page catalog, Sadlier's second binding, original royal blue cloth, blocked in black and gilt, bookseller's ticket of John Pryde, Glasgow, all edges gilt, in dark blue buckram, grey lined box, fine, clean copy. Jarndyce Antiquarian Booksellers CXCII - 113 2011 £5500

MacDonald, George 1824-1905 *At the Back of the North Wind.* London: Strahan & Co., 1872?, 76 illustrations by Arthur Hughes, few spots, rebound in half dark green morocco by Mudie, spine faded and slightly rubbed. Jarndyce Antiquarian Booksellers CXCII - 115 2011 £200

MacDonald, George 1824-1905 *At the Back of the North Wind.* London: Strahan & Co., 1872?, Half title, 76 illustrations by Arthur Hughes, original green cloth in same design as first edition, yellow endpapers, slightly marked and dulled with inner hinges slightly cracking. Jarndyce Antiquarian Booksellers CXCII - 114 2011 £450

MacDonald, George 1824-1905 *At the Back of the North Wind.* London: Strahan & Co., 1882?, Half title, 76 illustrations by Arthur Hughes, original green cloth in same design as first edition, yellow endpapers, slight rubbing, very good, with 1882 inscription on titlepage. Jarndyce Antiquarian Booksellers CXCII - 116 2011 £500

MacDonald, George 1824-1905 *At the Back of the North Wind.* London: Blackie & Son, 1887, Half title, '75' (in fact 76), illustrations by Arthur Hughes, 32 page catalog of books for young people, original decorated brown cloth, maroon endpapers, faded and rubbed with inner hinges splitting. Jarndyce Antiquarian Booksellers CXCII - 117 2011 £45

MacDonald, George 1824-1905 *At the Back of the North Wind.* New York: George Routledge & Sons, circa, 1890?, 76 illustrations by Arthur Hughes, slight spotting, original light blue cloth, 'woman & moon' design blocked in gilt and brown, slightly dulled and marked. Jarndyce Antiquarian Booksellers CXCII - 119 2011 £85

MacDonald, George 1824-1905 *At the Back of the North Wind.* New York: George Routledge & Sons, circa, 1890?, 76 illustrations by Arthur Hughes, original green cloth "branch & basket" design blocked in brown and gilt, very good, ownership signature of Elfridia Roosevelt. Jarndyce Antiquarian Booksellers CXCII - 118 2011 £130

MacDonald, George 1824-1905 *At the Back of the North Wind.* Blackie & Son, 1896, New edition; '75' (in fact 76), illustrations by Arthur Hughes, 32 page catalog of books for young people coded 11, original illustrated brown cloth, grey endpapers, very good bright copy. Jarndyce Antiquarian Booksellers CXCII - 120 2011 £85

MacDonald, George 1824-1905 *At the Back of the North Wind.* Blackie & Son, 1900, New edition; half title, frontispiece, '75' (in fact 76) illustrations by Arthur Hughes, 32 page catalog, original turquoise cloth blocked with brown design of woman & tree on front board, gilt decorated spine, little dulled. Jarndyce Antiquarian Booksellers CXCII - 121 2011 £65

MacDonald, George 1824-1905 *At the Back of the North Wind.* Blackie & Son, circa, 1911, 264 pages, color frontispiece, illustrations by Arthur Hughes, some spotting, original dark blue cloth blocked with green and white art nouveau design and gilt spine title. Jarndyce Antiquarian Booksellers CXCII - 122 2011 £35

MacDonald, George 1824-1905 *At the Back of the North Wind.* Blackie & Son, circa, 1926?, Half title, color frontispiece, illustrations, original maroon cloth blocked with Laurence Housman's cover design, spine slightly faded, very good in slightly torn dust jacket, this copy has inscription dated 1936. Jarndyce Antiquarian Booksellers CXCII - 123 2011 £30

MacDonald, George 1824-1905 *A Book of Strife.* London: printed for the author and to be had by Writing to mr. Hughes 43 Beaufort Street, Chelsea, 1880, First edition; tall 12mo., colophon leaf, partly unopened in original plain red cloth, paper label slightly browned, spine faded, pencil inscription "From M.J.H. May 14th 1880", very good. Jarndyce Antiquarian Booksellers CXCII - 221 2011 £200

MacDonald, George 1824-1905 *A Book of Strife in the Form of the Diary of an Old Soul.* London: printed for the author and to be had by writing to Mr. Hughes 43 Beaufort St. Chelsea, 1880, First edition; tall 12mo., colophon leaf, original plain red cloth, slightly affected by damp, lacking leading f.e.p., slightly worn at head and tail of spine, paper label browned and slightly chipped, inscribed by author for Mrs. David Matheson.   Jarndyce Antiquarian Booksellers CXCII - 220 2011 £1250

MacDonald, George 1824-1905 *A Book of Strife.* London: printed for the author and to be had by Writing to Mr. Hughes 43 Beaufort Street, Chelsea, 1882, Tall 12mo., colophon leaf, original plain red cloth, spine discolored and worn, lacking most of paper label, red cloth box with black leather label, inscribed by author for friend Charles Watson Bond.   Jarndyce Antiquarian Booksellers CXCII - 223 2011 £500

MacDonald, George 1824-1905 *A Book of Strife.* London: printed for the author and to be had by Writing to Mr. Hughes 43 Beaufort Street, Chelsea, 1882, Tall 12mo., colophon leaf, original plain red cloth, slightly dulled, paper label browned with corner clip, ownership inscription of Florrie King, June 1883, good.   Jarndyce Antiquarian Booksellers CXCII - 224 2011 £50

MacDonald, George 1824-1905 *A Book of Strife.* London: printed for the author and to be had by Writing to Mr. Hughes 43 Beaufort Street, Chelsea, 1882, Second edition; tall 12mo., colophon leaf, original plain red cloth, marked, spine faded, inner hinges splitting, paper label browned and chipped, inscribed by author for cousin George MacDonald and with signature of Robt. G. Troup, husband of MacDonald's cousin, Margaret.   Jarndyce Antiquarian Booksellers CXCII - 222 2011 £1200

MacDonald, George 1824-1905 *A Book of Strife.* London: Longman, Green and Co., 1885, New edition; colophon leaf, original plain red cloth, slightly dulled, paper label darkened.   Jarndyce Antiquarian Booksellers CXCII - 225 2011 £85

MacDonald, George 1824-1905 *A Book of Strife.* London: Arthur C. Fifield, 1905, Entirely new edition; half title, frontispiece, portrait, 6 pages ads, original crimson cloth, round bookplate of B. R. M. Hetherington, very good. Jarndyce Antiquarian Booksellers CXCII - 226 2011 £45

MacDonald, George 1824-1905 *A Cabinet of Gems.* London: Elliot Stock, 1891, First edition; 12mo., initial ad leaf, half title, frontispiece plate, stain on pages 22-23 from old insertion, uncut in original dark olive green cloth blocked with gilt fleurs de lys on front board and spine, slightly rubbed, top edge gilt, very good.   Jarndyce Antiquarian Booksellers CXCII - 302 2011 £220

MacDonald, George 1824-1905 *A Cabinet of Gems.* London: Elliot Stock, 1893, 12mo., initial ad leaf, half title, frontispiece, uncut in original light olive green cloth, brown fleurs de lys on front board, gilt on spine, top edge gilt, very good.   Jarndyce Antiquarian Booksellers CXCII - 303 2011 £120

MacDonald, George 1824-1905 *Castle Warlock.* Hamburg: Karl Gradener & J. F. Richter, 1882, Copyright edition; 3 volumes, half titles, uncut in original cream printed wrappers with ads, spies marked and chipped with cracking in volume III, label of Galignani Library, Paris pasted to front wrappers.   Jarndyce Antiquarian Booksellers CXCII - 236 2011 £125

MacDonald, George 1824-1905 *Castle Warlock.* Hamburg: Karl Gardener & J. F. Richter, 1882, Copyright edition; 3 volumes, half titles, slight spotting and browning, tear in last leaf repaired, contemporary half red calf, green label, very good, armorial bookplate of Arthur Hartley Sharpe.   Jarndyce Antiquarian Booksellers CXCII - 237 2011 £125

MacDonald, George 1824-1905 *Castle Warlock: a Homely Romance.* London: Sampson Low, Marston, Searle & Rivington, 1882, First English edition; 3 volumes, half title volume I, final blanks volume I and III, 32 page catalog volume II (Dec. 1881), some spotting, original dark brown fine grained cloth blocked, black borders on boards, gilt lettering on spines, slight rubbed, very good, in this copy a press cutting of a review form Daily News 31 May 82 laid down on half title.   Jarndyce Antiquarian Booksellers CXCII - 235 2011 £2500

MacDonald, George 1824-1905 *Castle Warlock.* London: Kegan Paul, Trench & Co., 1883, Second edition; half title, frontispiece, 47 page catalog (1.83), original red cloth, bevelled boards (style E), spine faded and slightly rubbed.   Jarndyce Antiquarian Booksellers CXCII - 238 2011 £50

MacDonald, George 1824-1905 *Castle Warlock.* London: Kegan Paul, Trench & Co., 1888?, New edition; half title, small tars in pages 95-104, original cream boards with red and black acanthus design by Lewis F. Day 1887, spine strip skillfully replaced with plain paper ads on endpapers.   Jarndyce Antiquarian Booksellers CXCII - 239 2011 £60

MacDonald, George 1824-1905 *Castle Warlock.* London: Kegan Paul Trench and Co., 1888?, New edition; half title, original red cloth blocked with black acanthus (style D), slightly rubbed, inner hinges cracking, initials SMD (Sara MacDonald?).   Jarndyce Antiquarian Booksellers   CXCII - 240   2011   £50

MacDonald, George 1824-1905 *Castle Warlock.* London: Kegan Paul Trench, Trubner & Co., 1892, New edition; original red cloth (style G), spine slightly faded), very good.   Jarndyce Antiquarian Booksellers   CXCII - 241   2011   £40

MacDonald, George 1824-1905 *Castle Warlock.* London: Kegan Paul, Trench, Trubner & Co. circa, 1900, Half title, original red cloth (style G), spine slightly faded, very good, on rougher paper.   Jarndyce Antiquarian Booksellers   CXCII - 242   2011   £40

MacDonald, George 1824-1905 *Cross Purposes and Other Stories.* London: Alexander Strahan, 1884, Reissue with additional title and half title; original grey green cloth blocked with Grolier pattern, spine slightly dulled, with signature of F. W. Troup Mar/1901.   Jarndyce Antiquarian Booksellers   CXCII - 148   2011   £30

MacDonald, George 1824-1905 *David Elginbrod.* London: Hurst and Blackett, 1863, First edition; 3 volumes, viii, 325, (1); vi, 335, (1); vi, 398, original brick red pebble grain cloth with covers ruled in blind and spines ruled in gilt and blind and lettered in gilt, few leaves in gathering N in volume 1 poorly opened at top and few leaves in gathering H in Volume III poorly opened at edge (none affecting any text), front cover volume I shows evidence of lending library label having once been affixed and front and rear pastedowns of volume III shows signs of there once having been a brown paper protective cover, otherwise as near fine as one could ever wish for, with hinges sound and gilt lettering on unfaded spines fresh and bright.   David Brass Rare Books, Inc.   May 26 2011 - 00559   2011 $5500

MacDonald, George 1824-1905 *David Elginbrod.* London: Hurst & Blackett, 1863, First edition; 3 volumes, half titles, original red coarse morocco grained cloth, plain blind borders on boards, gilt lettered spines, dulled with slight wear to spines, inner hinges weakening, endpapers replaced volume I, A. P. Watt's bookplate in each volume.   Jarndyce Antiquarian Booksellers   CXCII - 19   2011   £1650

MacDonald, George 1824-1905 *David Elginbrod.* Leipzig: Bernhard Tauchnitz, 1871, Copyright edition; half titles, 2 volumes, slight browning, green and brown binder's cloth, spines dulled and marked, stamp and shelflabels of Dercsenyi.   Jarndyce Antiquarian Booksellers   CXCII - 20   2011   £65

MacDonald, George 1824-1905 *David Elginbrod.* London: Hurst & Blackett, circa, 1880, 4 pages ads, frontispiece, original dark green cloth blocked in blind and gilt, following f.e.p. removed.   Jarndyce Antiquarian Booksellers   CXCII - 21   2011   £50

MacDonald, George 1824-1905 *David Elginbrod.* London: Hurst & Blackett, circa, 1890, Half title, frontispiece, 4 pages ads, 16 page catalog, original dark blue cloth, plain gilt borders, all edges gilt, with signature of J. N. R. Pim 1881.   Jarndyce Antiquarian Booksellers   CXCII - 22   2011   £40

MacDonald, George 1824-1905 *David Elginbrod.* London: Hurst & Blackett, circa, 1890, Half title, frontispiece, 16 page catalog, original dark blue cloth, plain gilt borders, little rubbed, signature of John S. Allison, Dec. 1891.   Jarndyce Antiquarian Booksellers   CXCII - 23   2011   £30

MacDonald, George 1824-1905 *David Elginbrod.* London: Hurst & Blackett, circa, 1890, Half title, frontispiece, 4 pages ads, 16 page catalog, original dark blue cloth, plain gilt borders, very good.   Jarndyce Antiquarian Booksellers   CXCII - 22   2011   £40

MacDonald, George 1824-1905 *David Elginbrod.* London: Hurst & Blackett, 1897, Half title, frontispiece, 4 pages ads, 24 page catalog (1897), original black cloth, plain gilt borders, slightly rubbed.   Jarndyce Antiquarian Booksellers   CXCII - 24   2011   £45

MacDonald, George 1824-1905 *Dealings with the Fairies.* London: Alexander Strahan, 1867, First edition; half title, frontispiece and plates by Arthur Hughes, 4 pages ads (Dec. 1866), slight stain to page 70-71, few spots, original green cloth blocked in black and gilt, slightly dulled, all edges gilt.   Jarndyce Antiquarian Booksellers   CXCII - 83   2011   £750

MacDonald, George 1824-1905 *Dealings with the Fairies.* London: Arthur Strahan, 1867, First edition; 12mo., green gilt cloth, all edges gilt, 308 pages + 4 pages ads, expertly rebacked with original spine preserved, few mends and light soil, very good+ in cloth slipcase, 12 fine full page illustrations by Arthur Hughes, very scarce.   Aleph-Bet Books, Inc.   95 - 338   2011 $1750

MacDonald, George 1824-1905 *Dealings with the Fairies.* London: Alexander Strahan & Co., 1868, Second edition; half title, frontispiece and plates by Arthur Hughes, 4 pages ads (Dec. 1867), few marks, original green cloth blocked in black and gilt, slightly dulled with small split in leading hinge, all edges gilt, inserted at head of titlepage "Mrs. Pulsford for her ministering children with the author's love & thanks" in author's hand.   Jarndyce Antiquarian Booksellers   CXCII - 84   2011   £2500

MacDonald, George 1824-1905 *The Disciple and Other Poems.* London: Strahan & Co., 1867, First edition; half title, 4 page catalog (Jan. 1868), original dappled dark brown and red cloth, ruled in blind, decorated and lettered in gilt, little rubbed at head and tail of spine and following hinge, monogram of M.E. I., signed presentation copy from author for Alice Caunter.   Jarndyce Antiquarian Booksellers   CXCII - 105 2011   £1800

MacDonald, George 1824-1905 *The Disciple and Other Poems.* London: Strahan and Co., 1867, First edition; half title, 4 page catalog (Jan. 1868), original maroon cloth, ruled in blind and decorated an lettered in gilt, spine faded and slightly worn at head, inner hinge cracking, this is the first issue binding.   Jarndyce Antiquarian Booksellers   CXCII - 104 2011   £380

MacDonald, George 1824-1905 *The Disciple and Other Poems.* London: Strahan & Co., 1868, Second edition; half title, initial ad slip and 4 page catalog (Jan. 1868), original dappled dark brown and red cloth, ruled in blind, decorated and lettered in gilt, faded and slightly rubbed, inscribed by author for Rev. J. Laurie Fogo.   Jarndyce Antiquarian Booksellers   CXCII - 106 2011   £1500

MacDonald, George 1824-1905 *The Disciple and Other Poems.* London: Strahan & Co., 1868, Second edition; half title, initial ad slip and 4 page catalog Jan. 1868, slightly marked, small owner's stamp of Aleck D. Fraser, original dappled dark brown and red cloth, ruled in blind, decorated an lettered in gilt.   Jarndyce Antiquarian Booksellers   CXCII - 107 2011   £200

MacDonald, George 1824-1905 *The Disciple and Other Poems.* London: Chatto & Windus, 1891, New edition; 16mo., half title, original grey green cloth blocked with Grolier pattern, very good.   Jarndyce Antiquarian Booksellers   CXCII - 149 2011   £35

MacDonald, George 1824-1905 *A Dish of Orts.* London: Sampson Low, Marston & Co., 1893, Enlarged edition; half title, frontispiece, title in red and black original plain royal blue cloth, very good, bright.   Jarndyce Antiquarian Booksellers   CXCII - 308 2011   £220

MacDonald, George 1824-1905 *A Dish of Orts.* London: Sampson Low, Marston & Co., 1895, Enlarged edition; half title, original blue cloth with elaborate gilt pattern on spine and left edge of front board, slightly dulled, booklabel, top edge gilt, secondary binding without frontispiece portrait.   Jarndyce Antiquarian Booksellers   CXCII - 310 2011   £50

MacDonald, George 1824-1905 *A Dish of Orts.* London: Sampson Low, Marston & Co., 1895, Enlarged edition; half title, original light blue streaked cloth with horizontal grain, elaborate gilt pattern on spine and left edge of front board, slightly marked, spine slightly faded, top edge gilt.   Jarndyce Antiquarian Booksellers   CXCII - 311 2011   £50

MacDonald, George 1824-1905 *A Dish of Orts.* London: Sampson Low, Marston & Co., 1895, Enlarged edition; original plain royal blue cloth, very good.   Jarndyce Antiquarian Booksellers   CXCII - 309 2011   £85

MacDonald, George 1824-1905 *A Dish of Orts.* London: Edwin Dalton, 1908, Enlarged edition; frontispiece and 3 plates, original red cloth, blocked in black, spine faded and slightly rubbed.   Jarndyce Antiquarian Booksellers   CXCII - 312 2011   £50

MacDonald, George 1824-1905 *Donal Grant.* London: Kegan Paul Trench & Co., 1883, 3 volumes in 1, half title and title volume I, without other titles and half titles, some foxing, contemporary half red calf, spine faded to brown with dark green labels, hinges splitting, preserved in red cloth covered box, brown leather labels, a page proof on thin paper with a number of corrections by MacDonald, inscribed by him to friend William Carey Davies.   Jarndyce Antiquarian Booksellers   CXCII - 261 2011   £4500

MacDonald, George 1824-1905 *Donal Grant.* London: Kegan Paul, Trench & Co.,, 1883, First edition; 3 volumes, half titles, 39 page catalog (10.83) volume 1, original red cloth, spines dulled and slightly rubbed, stitching little loose volume II, inner hinges cracking, ownership inscription of Agnes Coote, Christmas 1883.   Jarndyce Antiquarian Booksellers   CXCII - 262 2011   £2500

MacDonald, George 1824-1905 *Donal Grant.* London: Kegan Paul, Trench and Co., 1883, First edition; 3 volumes, half titles, slightly later half dark brown morocco, stamps and labels of General Assembly Library, New Zealand 1883.   Jarndyce Antiquarian Booksellers   CXCII - 263 2011   £750

MacDonald, George 1824-1905 *Donal Grant.* London: Kegan Paul, Trench & Co., 1890, Fourth edition; half title, frontispiece, pages 90 + 4 page catalog (7.90), original red cloth (style F), bevelled boards, spine dulled.   Jarndyce Antiquarian Booksellers   CXCII - 264 2011   £50

MacDonald, George 1824-1905 *Donal Grant.* London: Kegan Paul, Trench, Trubner & Co. circa, 1891?, Half title, rougher paper text pages, slightly browned, original red cloth (Style G), waterwheel on front board, marked.   Jarndyce Antiquarian Booksellers   CXCII - 265 2011   £50

MacDonald, George 1824-1905 *Donal Grant.* London: Kegan Paul, Trench & Co., 1892, New edition; half title, original red cloth (style D), slightly marked, inscribed S.M.D. (Sara MacDonald).   Jarndyce Antiquarian Booksellers   CXCII - 266 2011   £65

MacDonald, George 1824-1905 *Donal Grant.* London: Kegan Paul, Trench, Trubner & Co. circa, 1895, New edition; half title, original red cloth (style G) with shield on front board, spine slightly faded, on smoother paper with "There and Back" included in titles advertised.   Jarndyce Antiquarian Booksellers   CXCII - 267 2011   £45

MacDonald, George 1824-1905 *Donal Grant.* London: Kegan Paul, Trench, Trubner & Co., 1900, New edition; half title, rougher paper text pages, slightly browned, original red cloth (style G), shield on front board, spine slightly faded, press cutting announcing MacDonald's death in 1905 tipped in on leading f.e.p.   Jarndyce Antiquarian Booksellers   CXCII - 268 2011   £45

MacDonald, George 1824-1905 *The Elect Lady.* London: Kegan Paul, Trench & Co., 1888, First edition sheets but this issue does not have the frontispiece and ads; elaborate inscribed S. MacDonald 23.4.92 on half title and signed Sara MacDonald, half title, original red cloth, Style D, very good.   Jarndyce Antiquarian Booksellers   CXCII - 281 2011   £75

MacDonald, George 1824-1905 *The Elect Lady.* London: Kegan Paul, Trench, Trubner & Co., 1888, First edition; half title, frontispiece, tissue guard spotted, 44 pages + 4 page catalog (11/87), original red cloth, bevelled boards (style F), slightly dulled, very good.   Jarndyce Antiquarian Booksellers   CXCII - 280 2011   £350

MacDonald, George 1824-1905 *The Elect Lady.* London: Kegan Paul, Trench, Trubner & Co. circa, 1895?, Half title, odd spot, original red cloth (style G), spine faded with small tear repaired without loss.   Jarndyce Antiquarian Booksellers   CXCII - 282 2011   £60

MacDonald, George 1824-1905 *England's Antiphon.* London: Macmillan and Co., 1868, First edition; frontispiece, title, red, blue and sepia, plates after Arthur Hughes, contemporary half dark blue roan, slightly rubbed with splits in hinges, plates are bound in wrong order.   Jarndyce Antiquarian Booksellers   CXCII - 110 2011   £125

MacDonald, George 1824-1905 *England's Antiphon.* London: Macmillan & Co., 1868, First edition; frontispiece, color engraved title and plates after Arthur Hughes, original royal blue cloth, borders in blind "The Sunday Library for Household Reading" devices blocked on front board and spine spine dulled, slightly chipped, binder's ticket of Burn & Co., inscribed by author for cousin Margaret MacDonald Troup.   Jarndyce Antiquarian Booksellers   CXCII - 109 2011   £1250

MacDonald, George 1824-1905 *England's Antiphon.* London: Macmillan & Co., 1868?, First edition, later issue?; frontispiece, color engraved title and plates by Arthur Hughes, original royal blue, bevelled boards with borders of gilt rules and crosses to front board, inner hinge cracking, slightly dulled, binder's ticket of Burn & Co, all edges gilt, very good.   Jarndyce Antiquarian Booksellers   CXCII - 111 2011   £200

MacDonald, George 1824-1905 *England's Antiphon.* London: Macmillan & Co., 1868, First edition; frontispiece, color engraved title and plates after Arthur Hughes, original royal blue cloth, binder's ticket of Burn & Co., very good, primary binding, titlepage printed in red, blue and brown, 3 plates in sepia, plain boards have blind borders bearing, on front board and spine, gilt device of "The Sunday Library for Household Reading".   Jarndyce Antiquarian Booksellers   CXCII - 108 2011   £380

MacDonald, George 1824-1905 *Exotics.* London: Strahan & Co., 1876, First edition; half title, original brown cloth, bevelled boards blocked in gilt, slightly dulled, binder's ticket of Seton, Edinburgh, very good.   Jarndyce Antiquarian Booksellers   CXCII - 203 2011   £850

MacDonald, George 1824-1905 *The Flight of the Shadow.* London: Kegan Paul, Trench, Trubner & Co., 1891, First edition; half title, frontispiece by Gordon Browne, rebound in half maroon morocco with stamps and labels of General Assembly Library, New Zealand, slight rubbing.   Jarndyce Antiquarian Booksellers   CXCII - 297 2011   £250

MacDonald, George 1824-1905 *The Flight of the Shadow.* London: Kegan Paul, Trench, Trubner & Co., 1891, First edition; half title, frontispiece by Gordon Browne, 32 page catalog, original red cloth, bevelled boards (style E), spine faded with slight wear at head and tail, inscribed by author for A. P. Watt with Watt's bookplate.   Jarndyce Antiquarian Booksellers   CXCII - 295 2011   £2000

MacDonald, George 1824-1905 *The Flight of the Shadow.* London: Kegan Paul, Trench, Trubner & Co., 1891, First edition; half title, frontispiece, 32 page catalog, original red cloth, bevelled boards (style E), slight wear to head and tail of spine, very good.   Jarndyce Antiquarian Booksellers   CXCII - 296 2011   £350

MacDonald, George 1824-1905 *The Flight of the Shadow.* London: Kegan Paul, Trench, Trubner & Co.1891, circa, 1892?, First edition, later issue; half title, original red cloth (style G), spine slightly faded and rubbed, very good, original sheets bound without frontispiece and ads.   Jarndyce Antiquarian Booksellers   CXCII - 298 2011   £150

MacDonald, George 1824-1905 *The Flight of the Shadow.* London: Kegan Paul, Trench, Trubner & Co., 1894?, New edition; half title, original red cloth (style G), spine faded, very good. Jarndyce Antiquarian Booksellers CXCII - 299 2011 £60

MacDonald, George 1824-1905 *The Flight of the Shadow.* London: Kegan Paul, Trench, Trubner & Co. circa, 1900?, New edition; half title, rougher text paper slightly browned, slightly shorter copy in original orange cloth blocked in brown and gilt (style H), spine slightly faded, slightly torn booklabel of James Slater. Jarndyce Antiquarian Booksellers CXCII - 301 2011 £50

MacDonald, George 1824-1905 *The Flight of the Shadow.* London: Kegan Paul, Trench, Trubner & Co. circa, 1900?, New edition; half title, rougher text paper slightly browned, original deep crimson cloth (Style G), slightly dulled an marked. Jarndyce Antiquarian Booksellers CXCII - 300 2011 £50

MacDonald, George 1824-1905 *Gathered Grace: a Short Selection of George MacDonald's Poems.* Cambridge: W. Heffer & Sons, 1938, Frontispiece and illustrations, original blue cloth, dulled and slightly marked, bookplate with erased name. Jarndyce Antiquarian Booksellers CXCII - 328 2011 £35

MacDonald, George 1824-1905 *George MacDonald: an Anthology.* London: Geoffrey Bles the Centenary Press, 1946, First edition; original yellow cloth with green title panel on spine, very good in torn dust jacket. Jarndyce Antiquarian Booksellers CXCII - 329 2011 £35

MacDonald, George 1824-1905 *The Gifts of the Child Christ.* Leipzig: Bernhard Tauchnitz, 1882, Copyright edition; half title, handsome half dark green calf, black labels, very good. Jarndyce Antiquarian Booksellers CXCII - 249 2011 £250

MacDonald, George 1824-1905 *Guild Court. A London Story. As published in Good Words for 1867.* London: Strahan & Co., 1867, Frontispiece, plates, index, contemporary maroon embossed calf, very good. Jarndyce Antiquarian Booksellers CXCII - 75 2011 £300

MacDonald, George 1824-1905 *Guild Court.* London: Hurst & Blackett, 1868, First edition; 3 volumes, half titles with cover title only for ads in volume III, slightly later half dark green morocco, gilt shelf marks & badges, withdrawn stamped bookabels of General Assembly Library, New Zealand. Jarndyce Antiquarian Booksellers CXCII - 77 2011 £850

MacDonald, George 1824-1905 *Guild Court.* London: Sampson, Low, Marston, Searle & Rivington, 1887, New edition; 32 page Sampson Low catalog (Sept. 1888), original red cloth blocked and lettered in black (style B), very good, signature of young Sara MacDonald 1892. Jarndyce Antiquarian Booksellers CXCII - 78 2011 £85

MacDonald, George 1824-1905 *Guild Court.* London: Sampson Low, Marston, Searle & Rivington, 1890, New and cheaper edition; original pebble grained blue cloth, ruled and lettered in blind, gilt spine very good. Jarndyce Antiquarian Booksellers CXCII - 79 2011 £75

MacDonald, George 1824-1905 *Guild Court.* London: Sampson Low, Marston, Searle & Rivington, 1890, New edition; booklabel of Anne and Fernand Renier, original white boards, printed in blue and red, rubbed with crack in spine, blue endpapers with ads. Jarndyce Antiquarian Booksellers CXCII - 80 2011 £50

MacDonald, George 1824-1905 *Guild Court.* London: Sampson Low, Marston & Co. circa, 1895?, New edition; original blue cloth, ruled and lettered in blind, gilt spine, very good. Jarndyce Antiquarian Booksellers CXCII - 81 2011 £65

MacDonald, George 1824-1905 *Guild Court.* London: Edwin Dalton, 1908, Original maroon cloth with art nouveau design, very good, frontispiece and plates, small brown mark in prelims. Jarndyce Antiquarian Booksellers CXCII - 82 2011 £45

MacDonald, George 1824-1905 *Heather and Snow.* London: Chatto & Windus, 1893, 2 volumes, half titles, 32 page catalog (March 1893), original dark blue morocco grained cloth, slightly dulled and rubbed, signed SMD (Sara MacDonald). Jarndyce Antiquarian Booksellers CXCII - 306 2011 £950

MacDonald, George 1824-1905 *Heather and Snow.* London: Chatto & Windus, 1893, First edition; 2 volumes, half titles, 32 page catalog (March 1893), original dark blue morocco grained cloth, very good, bright copy, inscribed by author for A. P. Watt, with Watt's bookplate. Jarndyce Antiquarian Booksellers CXCII - 305 2011 £2500

MacDonald, George 1824-1905 *Heather and Snow.* London: Chatto & Windus, 1894, (1895), New edition; initial ad leaf, half title, 32 page catalog (Oct. 1895), original maroon cloth, spine slightly faded, very good. Jarndyce Antiquarian Booksellers CXCII - 307 2011 £65

MacDonald, George 1824-1905 *The History of Gutta-Percha Willie. in Good Words for the Young. Annual for 1872.* London: Henry S. King & Co., 1872, Frontispiece, plates, illustrations, spotting, lacking pages 15-16, original blue decorated cloth, rebacked retaining original spine strip, new endpapers.   Jarndyce Antiquarian Booksellers   CXCII - 164 2011   £350

MacDonald, George 1824-1905 *The History of Gutta-Percha Willie...* Blackie & Son, 1887, New edition; 32 page catalog, slightly marked, original blue pictorial cloth, spine slightly rubbed.   Jarndyce Antiquarian Booksellers CXCII - 166 2011   £65

MacDonald, George 1824-1905 *Gutta Percha Willie, The Working Genius.* Blackie & Son, 1887, New edition; half title, frontispiece and 7 plates by Arthur Hughes, 32 page catalog, slightly marked, original blue pictorial cloth, spine slightly rubbed, inscription "Sylvia Kingsley Hunt from Iss Jolly 1875".   Jarndyce Antiquarian Booksellers   CXCII - 166 2011   £65

MacDonald, George 1824-1905 *The History of Gutta Percha Willie.* Blackie & Son, 1901, New edition; half title, frontispiece and 7 plates by Arthur Hughes, 32 page catalog, original olive pictorial cloth, little dulled, School prize label.   Jarndyce Antiquarian Booksellers CXCII - 167 2011   £45

MacDonald, George 1824-1905 *Home Again.* London: Kegan Paul Trench & Co., 1887, First edition; half title, in slightly smaller format in original orange cloth, blocked in brown,.   Jarndyce Antiquarian Booksellers   CXCII - 277 2011   £480

MacDonald, George 1824-1905 *Home Again.* London: Kegan Paul, Trench, Trubner & Co., 1893, New edition; half title, original red cloth (style G), slightly marked, spine slightly faded.   Jarndyce Antiquarian Booksellers   CXCII - 278 2011   £60

MacDonald, George 1824-1905 *The Hope of the Gospel.* London: Ward, Lock, Bowden & Co., 1892, First edition; half title, few marginal marks, original dark green cloth, slight rubbing, small piece torn from leading f.e.p., with touching presentation letter from Caroline Erskine 1931, loosely inserted.   Jarndyce Antiquarian Booksellers   CXCII - 304 2011   £380

MacDonald, George 1824-1905 *The Light Princess and Other Fairy Stories.* Blackie & Son, 1891, First edition in this form; half title, frontispiece, and 2 plates, 32 page catalog, few marks in text, original brown cloth, decorated with bands of black and gilt on front and spine, blind borders to back board, slight rubbing.   Jarndyce Antiquarian Booksellers   CXCII - 86 2011   £120

MacDonald, George 1824-1905 *The Light Princess and Other Fairy Stories.* New York: G. P. Putnam's Sons, 1893, Title in red and black, frontispiece, illustrations by Maud Humphrey, original beige cloth pictorially blocked in black and brown, spine darkened, inner hinge cracking, inscribed presentation form author Christmas Day 1893 for Vera Frances Cremer.   Jarndyce Antiquarian Booksellers CXCII - 87 2011   £1250

MacDonald, George 1824-1905 *The Light Princess and Other Fairy Stories.* Blackie & Son, circa, 1894, 32 page catalog, original beige cloth, blocked in black and gilt, very good, half title, frontispiece, plates by L. L. Brooke.   Jarndyce Antiquarian Booksellers   CXCII - 89 2011   £75

MacDonald, George 1824-1905 *The Light Princess and Other Fairy Stories.* London: Blackie & Son, circa, 1894, Half title, 32 page catalog, frontispiece, plates by L. L. Brooke, original blue cloth blocked in black and gilt, prize inscription from the Calvinistic Methodist Sunday School, 1894.   Jarndyce Antiquarian Booksellers   CXCII - 88 2011   £75

MacDonald, George 1824-1905 *The Light Princess and Other Fairy Stories.* Blackie & Son, circa, 1900, Half title, frontispiece and plates by L. L. Brooke, 32 page catalog on plate paper, few spots, original olive green cloth, blocked in black and grey with gilt title, very good, school prize label Summer 9101.   Jarndyce Antiquarian Booksellers   CXCII - 90 2011   £60

MacDonald, George 1824-1905 *The Light Princess and Other Fairy Stories.* Blackie & Son, circa, 1900, Half title, frontispiece and plates by L. L. Brooke, 32 page catalog on plate paper, few spots, original blue cloth, blocked in black and grey with gilt title, slight rubbing.   Jarndyce Antiquarian Booksellers   CXCII - 91 2011   £60

MacDonald, George 1824-1905 *The Light Princess and Other Fairy Stories.* Blackie & Son circa, 1900, Half title, frontispiece and plates by L. L. Brooke, 32 page catalog on blue paper, few spots, original red cloth, blocked in black and grey with gilt title, bookplate of Lilian Grotrian, very good.   Jarndyce Antiquarian Booksellers   CXCII - 92 2011   £60

MacDonald, George 1824-1905 *The Light Princess and Other Fairy Stories.* London: Arthur C. Fifield, 1904, Half title, title and illustrations by Arthur Hughes, 2 pages ads, original beige cloth blocked in blue and gilt, little dulled, 82, (2) pages.   Jarndyce Antiquarian Booksellers   CXCII - 93 2011   £35

MacDonald, George 1824-1905 *Lilith: a Romance.* London: Chatto & Windus, 1895, First edition; half title, title in red and black, uncut in original vertical grained black cloth, slight splitting at hinges, inscribed by author for Susan Corey.   Jarndyce Antiquarian Booksellers   CXCII - 318 2011   £1500

MacDonald, George 1824-1905 *Lilith: a Romance.* London: Chatto & Windus, 1895, First edition; half title, title in red and black, 32 page catalog (Oct. 1895), original plain black buckram, rather rubbed, signature on titlepage of Robert G. Troup, MacDonald's cousin by marriage. Jarndyce Antiquarian Booksellers   CXCII - 319 2011   £200

MacDonald, George 1824-1905 *Lilith: a Romance.* London: Chatto & Windus, 1896, Second edition; half title, title in red and black, 32 page catalog March 1896, original vertical grained cloth, very good,.   Jarndyce Antiquarian Booksellers   CXCII - 320 2011   £150

MacDonald, George 1824-1905 *Lilith: a Romance.* London: George Allen & Unwin, 1924, Centenary edition; half title with reproduction of MacDonald's bookplate, front plate after F. D. Bedford, few spots, original crimson cloth, spine slightly faded, very good, cutting of the TLS review of the 1962 Gollancz edition laid down on leading f.e.p. Jarndyce Antiquarian Booksellers   CXCII - 321 2011   £45

MacDonald, George 1824-1905   *The Lost Princess; or the Wise Woman.*   Wells, Gardner, Darton & Co., 1895, Half title, frontispiece, illustrations by A. G. Walker, original light olive green cloth blocked in black and gilt, armorial bookplate of Boulton, very good.   Jarndyce Antiquarian Booksellers   CXCII - 185 2011   £120

MacDonald, George 1824-1905   *The Lost Princess; or the Wise Woman.*   Wells Gardner, Darton & Co., 1895, Half title, frontispiece and illustrations, 2 pages ads, original deep olive green cloth blocked in black and gilt, bookplates of Bibliotheca Churchilliana" and George Bernard Rust, very good.   Jarndyce Antiquarian Booksellers   CXCII - 184 2011   £120

MacDonald, George 1824-1905   *Malcolm.* London: Henry S. King & Co., 1875, (1874). Second edition; 3 volumes, half titles, foxing caused by endpapers, slightly later red morocco, stamps and labels of General Assembly Library, New Zealand, inner hinge splitting volume III. Jarndyce Antiquarian Booksellers   CXCII - 168 2011   £380

MacDonald, George 1824-1905   *Malcolm.* London: Kegan Paul, Trench, Trubner & Co., 1892?, New edition; half title, engraved frontispiece, spotting caused by tissue guard original red cloth (style G), spine faded with small splits at head and tail of hinges, with 1897 inscription. Jarndyce Antiquarian Booksellers   CXCII - 169 2011   £45

MacDonald, George 1824-1905   *Malcolm.* London: Kegan Paul, Trench, Trubner & Co., circa, 1900, New edition; half title with partly erased inscription, slight browning to text, original orange cloth (style H).   Jarndyce Antiquarian Booksellers   CXCII - 170 2011   £40

MacDonald, George 1824-1905   *The Marquis of Lossie.* London: Kegan Paul, Trench & Co., 1877, First edition; 3 volumes, without half titles, slight browning caused by endpapers, rebound in half purple roan, red leather label, spines faded, slight rubbing, trace of lot label on front board volume I, armorial bookplates of Thomas Lalor. Cregg (in south Tipperary).   Jarndyce Antiquarian Booksellers   CXCII - 195 2011   £850

MacDonald, George 1824-1905   *The Marquis of Lossie.* London: Kegan Paul, Trench & Co., 1887?, New edition; half title, original red cloth, black acanthus pattern (style D), very good.   Jarndyce Antiquarian Booksellers   CXCII - 197 2011   £50

MacDonald, George 1824-1905   *The Marquis of Lossie.* London: Kegan Paul, Trench & Co., circa, 1887, New edition; half title, final blank, original red cloth, (style G), spine slightly faded, string mark, ownership signature Aug. 1897, on smooth paper with London in large and smaller caps on titlepage.   Jarndyce Antiquarian Booksellers   CXCII - 198 2011   £35

MacDonald, George 1824-1905   *The Marquis of Lossie.* London: Kegan Paul, Trench, Trubner & Co. circa, 1891, New edition; half title, frontispiece, original red cloth, bevelled boards (style F), spine faded with small splits at head and tail of spine.   Jarndyce Antiquarian Booksellers   CXCII - 199 2011   £40

MacDonald, George 1824-1905   *The Marquis of Lossie.* London: Kegan Paul. Trench, Trubner & Co. circa, 1893, New edition; half title, slight browning, original orange cloth style H, very good.   Jarndyce Antiquarian Booksellers   CXCII - 202 2011   £35

MacDonald, George 1824-1905   *Mary Marston.* London: Sampson Low Marston, Searle & Rivington, 1881, Fifth edition; half title, 32 page catalog (Jan. 1881), original red cloth, bevelled boards (Style A) by W. Bone & Son, spine dulled.   Jarndyce Antiquarian Booksellers   CXCII - 230 2011   £65

MacDonald, George 1824-1905   *Mary Marston.* London: Sampson, Low, Marston, Searle & Rivington, 1881, Third edition; 3 volumes, half title volume I, colophon leaf, half dark green morocco, very good.   Jarndyce Antiquarian Booksellers   CXCII - 229 2011   £450

MacDonald, George 1824-1905   *Mary Marston.* London: Sampson Low, Marston, Searle & Rivington, 1892?, New and cheaper edition; half title, original red cloth (style B), spine slightly faded, inner hinge cracking, inscription S.M.D. (Sara MacDonald?).   Jarndyce Antiquarian Booksellers   CXCII - 232 2011   £85

MacDonald, George 1824-1905 *Mary Marston.* London: Sampson Low, Marston & Co., 1894, Half title, 4 pages ads, original royal blue cloth, slight rubbing and marking. Jarndyce Antiquarian Booksellers CXCII - 233 2011 £40

MacDonald, George 1824-1905 *Mary Marston.* London: Sampson Low, Marston & Co. circa, 1896?, Half title, 4 pages ads, original blue cloth, slightly dulled with string mark. Jarndyce Antiquarian Booksellers CXCII - 234 2011 £40

MacDonald, George 1824-1905 *The Miracles of Our Lord.* London: Strahan & Co., 1870, First edition; half title, 16 page catalog (Nov. 1870), original mauve cloth, spine faded, monogram bookplate of M.E.J., signed presentation from author to Uncle, Alexander S. Maccoll. Jarndyce Antiquarian Booksellers CXCII - 129 2011 £2000

MacDonald, George 1824-1905 *Orts.* London: Sampson Low, Marston, Searle & Rivignton, 1882, half title, 2 pages ads + 32 page catalog (Nov. 1882), original brown cloth, bevelled boards blocked in black and gilt with blind ornament on back board, by W. Bone & Son, brown endpapers, inner hinges cracking, good, inscribed by author for Sophia Corey, also signed by MacDonald in pencil with considerable ink alterations. Jarndyce Antiquarian Booksellers CXCII - 255 2011 £3800

MacDonald, George 1824-1905 *Orts.* London: Sampson Low, Marston, Searle & Rivington, 1882, First edition; half title, 2 page catalog (April 1888), original brown cloth, bevelled boards blocked in black and gilt, blind ornament on back board by W. Bone & Sone, brown endpapers, following hinge splitting. Jarndyce Antiquarian Booksellers CXCII - 256 2011 £350

MacDonald, George 1824-1905 *Orts.* London: Sampson Low, Marston, Searle & Rivington, 1882, First edition; half title, original red cloth, bevelled boards, style A, spine slightly faded, very good. Jarndyce Antiquarian Booksellers CXCII - 257 2011 £250

MacDonald, George 1824-1905 *Phantastes: a Faerie Romance for Men and Women.* London: Smith, Elder & Co., 1858, First edition; half title, 16 page catalog (Nov. 1858), half dark brown morocco, red leather label, spine slightly faded, retaining original leading f.e.p., this copy belonged to artist Joseph W. Ebsworth, then of St. John's College Cambridge. Jarndyce Antiquarian Booksellers CXCII - 10 2011 £750

MacDonald, George 1824-1905 *Paul Faber, Surgeon.* London: Hurst & Blackett, 1879, First edition; 3 volumes, half titles, 16 pages catalog volume III, some spotting caused by endpaper, original brown cloth blocked in black and gilt by Leighton Son & Hodge, slightly marked with title wear to heads ad tails of spines, W. H. Smith Library labels marked "sold" on pastedowns. Jarndyce Antiquarian Booksellers CXCII - 208 2011 £2000

MacDonald, George 1824-1905 *Paul Faber, Surgeon.* London: Chatto & Windus, 1883, New edition; initial ad leaf, yellowback in original cream pictorial boards, spine and hinges rubbed, corners knocked, Renier bookplate. Jarndyce Antiquarian Booksellers CXCII - 209 2011 £65

MacDonald, George 1824-1905 *Paul Faber, Surgeon.* London: Kegan Paul, Trench, Trubner & Co., circa, 1890?, New edition; 2 pages ads and colophon leaf, original red cloth blocked with black acanthus (style D), slightly marked, signature of S. MacDonald. Jarndyce Antiquarian Booksellers CXCII - 210 2011 £85

MacDonald, George 1824-1905 *Paul Faber, Surgeon.* London: Kegan Paul, Trench, Turbner & Co. circa, 1891, Sixth edition; half title, final ad and colophon leaf, original red cloth (style G), spine faded, very good. Jarndyce Antiquarian Booksellers CXCII - 211 2011 £75

MacDonald, George 1824-1905 *Phantastes: a Faerie Romance for Men and Women.* London: Chatto & Windus, 1894, New edition; half title, frontispiece, illustrations by John Bell, 32 page catalog (Sept. 1894) odd spot, original sky blue pictorial cloth blocked in black and white, gilt lettered spine, blue edges, spine little dulled, good plus. Jarndyce Antiquarian Booksellers CXCII - 11 2011 £150

MacDonald, George 1824-1905 *Phantastes: a Faerie Romance for Men and Women.* London: Arthur C. Fifield, 1905, New edition; half title, frontispiece, illustrations by Arthur Hughes, uncut in original dark blue cloth, spine slightly dulled, bookplate of George Bernard Rust, top edge gilt. Jarndyce Antiquarian Booksellers CXCII - 12 2011 £85

MacDonald, George 1824-1905 *Phantastes: a Faerie Romance for Men and Women.* London: Arthur C. Fifield, 1905, New edition; half title, frontispiece, illustrations by Arthur Hughes, piece torn from margin pages 221-22 by careless opening, original dark blue cloth, spine dulled, inner hinge cracking, inscribed for Robert Troup from Uncle Edward & Aunt Winifred. Jarndyce Antiquarian Booksellers CXCII - 13 2011 £160

MacDonald, George 1824-1905 *Phantastes and Lilith.* London: Victor Gollancz, 1962, Half title, slight browning caused by endpapers, original blue cloth, very good in slightly torn and dusted dust jacket. Jarndyce Antiquarian Booksellers CXCII - 14 2011 £35

MacDonald, George 1824-1905 *The Pocket George MacDonald: Being a Choice of Passages From Various Works Made by Alfred H. Hayatt.* London: Chatto & Windus, 1907, Half title, title in red and black, final ad leaf, original soft crimson roan, gilt spine slightly worn, top edge gilt, booklabel of George MacDonald Library, the Farm, Huntly.   Jarndyce Antiquarian Booksellers   CXCII - 327   2011   £30

MacDonald, George 1824-1905   *Poems.* London: Longman, Brown, Green, Longmans & Roberts, 1857, March 1856 24 page catalog, original dark brown morocco grained cloth by Edmonds & Remnants, spine marked and worn, following inner hinge cracking, poor copy, but sound.   Jarndyce Antiquarian Booksellers   CXCII - 8 2011   £250

MacDonald, George 1824-1905   *The Poetical Works of Geoge MacDonald.* London: Chatto & Windus, 1893, 2 volumes, half titles, some spotting, original plain crimson buckram, spines faded, volume I slightly marked, with 2 page ALS from author to Alexander Strahan dated only Friday without address.   Jarndyce Antiquarian Booksellers CXCII - 313 2011   £750

MacDonald, George 1824-1905   *The Poetical Works of George MacDonald.* London: Chatto & Windus, 1911, Fine paper edition; 2 volumes, initial ad leaves, half titles, titles in red and black, original dark green cloth blocked in blind with flower pattern gilt spines, top edge gilt, very good.   Jarndyce Antiquarian Booksellers   CXCII - 315   £40

MacDonald, George 1824-1905   *The Portent. in The Cornhill Magazine Volume I-II Jan. - Dec. 1860.* London: Smith, Elder & Co., 1860, 2 volumes in half dark blue calf, bit rubbed, red labels.   Jarndyce Antiquarian Booksellers CXCII - 15 2011   £125

MacDonald, George 1824-1905   *The Portent.* London: Smith, Elder & Co., 1864, First edition; final ad leaf, smooth olive green cloth sides, parchment spine with gilt lettering and ornaments, spine dulled and slightly marked, blue marbled endpapers, good plus.   Jarndyce Antiquarian Booksellers   CXCII - 17 2011   £580

MacDonald, George 1824-1905   *The Portent.* London: Smith Elder & Co., 1864, First Book edition; final ad leaf, uncut in original purple morocco grained cloth with blind borders on boards, spine gilt lettered, cream endpapers, spine slightly faded, inner hinge splitting, bookseller's ticket of Willis & Sotheran, good plus.   Jarndyce Antiquarian Booksellers   CXCII - 16 2011   £680

MacDonald, George 1824-1905   *The Portent and Other Stories.* privately issued, 1924, Centenary edition 1824-1924; half title, spotting caused by endpapers, original cream cloth, impression of MacDonald's bookplate, with gilt lettering, spine dulled, titlepage is a cancel and Shaberman identifies the work as a reissue of 1909 Fisher Unwin edition.   Jarndyce Antiquarian Booksellers   CXCII - 18 2011   £35

MacDonald, George 1824-1905   *The Poetical Works of George MacDonald.* London: Chatto & Windus, 1893, 2 volumes, half titles, some spotting, original plain crimson buckram, spines little faded, very good, tipped into this copy is manuscript rhyming birthday card from recipient's wife and other with initials "A.L.S." and "M.S." Sept. 7 1900.   Jarndyce Antiquarian Booksellers   CXCII - 314 2011   £85

MacDonald, George 1824-1905   *The Princess and Curdie.* Leipzig: Bernhard Tauchnitz, 1883, Half title, 16 page catalog (Feb. 1883), original cream printed wrappers, slightly dusted and creased at corners, split in leading hinge, label of Galignani Library Paris pasted over imprint on front wrapper.   Jarndyce Antiquarian Booksellers   CXCII - 205 2011   £50

MacDonald, George 1824-1905   *The Princess and Curdie.* London: Chatto & Windus, 1883, (1882). First edition; half title, frontispiece and plates, 32 page catalog (Oct. 1882), few spots in text, original olive green cloth, blocked in gilt and brown, yellow edges, spine discolored and slightly rubbed, custom made green morocco box, spine with elaborate gilt block on front board, very good, scarce.   Jarndyce Antiquarian Booksellers   CXCII - 204 2011   £2000

MacDonald, George 1824-1905   *The Princess and Curdie.* Blackie and Son, 1896?, New edition; half title, frontispiece, 7 bi-color plates by James Allen, 32 page catalog, marginal spotting, original pinkish brown pictorial cloth, very slight rubbing, crease in grey f.e.p., very good.   Jarndyce Antiquarian Booksellers   CXCII - 206 2011   £85

MacDonald, George 1824-1905   *The Princess and Curdie.* Blackie & Son, circa, 1908, Frontispiece and illustrations by Helen Stratton, 16 page catalog, original turquoise cloth with design by Laurence Housman, dulled, gilt prize stamp on back board at L.C.C. prize label.   Jarndyce Antiquarian Booksellers   CXCII - 207 2011   £40

MacDonald, George 1824-1905   *The Princess and the Goblin. in Good Words for the Young: Annual for 1871.* London: A. Strahan & Co., 1871, Frontispiece and engraved title, plates, illustrations, some spotting, few pages torn at fore edge, original blue decorated cloth by Burn & Co., spine faded and slightly rubbed, inner hinges cracking, all edges gilt.   Jarndyce Antiquarian Booksellers   CXCII - 137 2011   £300

MacDonald, George 1824-1905 *The Princess and the Goblin.* Philadelphia: J. B. Lippincott & Co., 1872, 12 pages ads, illustrations, some spotting, original maroon pictorial cloth, recased retaining faded original spine strip, new endpapers and blank endleaves. Jarndyce Antiquarian Booksellers CXCII - 138 2011 £250

MacDonald, George 1824-1905 *The Princess and the Goblin.* Blackie & Son, 1888, New edition; half title, 30 illustrations by Arthur Hughes, 32 page catalog, original brown cloth blocked in black and gilt, very good, dated from an inscription Christmas 1889, endpapers are dark blue. Jarndyce Antiquarian Booksellers CXCII - 140 2011 £65

MacDonald, George 1824-1905 *The Princess and the Goblin.* Blackie & Son, 1900?, Half title, frontispiece by Laurence Housman, 30 illustrations by Arthur Hughes, 32 page catalog, original blue cloth blocked in brown and gilt in design by Laurence Housman, very good, inscription May 1904. Jarndyce Antiquarian Booksellers CXCII - 141 2011 £60

MacDonald, George 1824-1905 *The Princess and the Goblin.* Blackie & Son, circa, 1912?, Half title, color frontispiece and plates by Helen Stratton, illustrations by Arthur Hughes, original dark blue cloth with art nouveau design, color onlay on front board, very good. Jarndyce Antiquarian Booksellers CXCII - 142 2011 £60

MacDonald, George 1824-1905 *Princess Rosamond.* Boston: D. Lothrop & Co., 1879, Second American edition of The Wise woman; 4to., frontispiece, plates, illustrations, text in two columns, original green cloth, color printed pictorial boards by Bufford, Boston, slight rubbing at corners. Jarndyce Antiquarian Booksellers CXCII - 182 2011 £300

MacDonald, George 1824-1905 *Ranald Bannerman's Boyhood.* London: Strahan & Co., 1871, First edition; half title, frontispiece, plates, illustrations by Arthur Hughes, some browning and marking, rebound in half maroon calf, raised gilt bands, very good. Jarndyce Antiquarian Booksellers CXCII - 124 2011 £850

MacDonald, George 1824-1905 *Rampolli: Growths from a Long Planted Root: Being Translations, New and Old.* London: Longmans, Green & Co., 1897, First edition; half title, 32 page catalog (5/97), original crimson buckram, spine faded, uneven fading to boards, inscribed by author for cousin Katharine Ling, bookplate and guard of C. H. O. Scaife. Jarndyce Antiquarian Booksellers CXCII - 324 2011 £1200

MacDonald, George 1824-1905 *Rampolli: Growths from a Long Planted Root: Being Translations, New and Old.* London: Longmans, Green and Co., 1897, First edition; half title, 32 page catalog 5/97 lage unopened in original crimson buckram, spine faded to light brown, otherwise very good. Jarndyce Antiquarian Booksellers CXCII - 326 2011 £200

MacDonald, George 1824-1905 *Rampolli: Growths from a Long Planted Root: Being Translations, New and Old.* London: Longmans, Green and Co., 1897, First edition; half title, 32 page catalog (5/97), partly unopened in original crimson buckram, spine faded, some wear and chips from leading free endpaper, inscribed by author for Sophia Corey. Jarndyce Antiquarian Booksellers CXCII - 325 2011 £750

MacDonald, George 1824-1905 *Ranald Bannerman's Boyhood.* Philadelphia: J. B. Lippincott & Co., 1871, Frontispiece and illustrations by Arthur Hughes, 2 pages ads, original maroon cloth, bevelled boards, elaborately gilt spine, blind borders on boards, ornament at centre of front board, hinges slightly rubbed, good. Jarndyce Antiquarian Booksellers CXCII - 125 2011 £300

MacDonald, George 1824-1905 *Ranald Bannerman's Boyhood.* London: Alexander Strahan, 1884, Frontispiece, plates and illustrations by Arthur Hughes, original olive green cloth blocked with "Grolier" design in darker green, brown and gilt, pencil note describes this as the Third English edition, inscription of Sophia B. Corey, Newark, NY. Jarndyce Antiquarian Booksellers CXCII - 126 2011 £120

MacDonald, George 1824-1905 *Ranald Bannerman's Boyhood.* Blackie & Son, 1900, New edition; half title, frontispiece, plates and illustrations by Arthur Hughes, 32 page catalog, slight spotting, original blue cloth blocked in brown and gilt with design by Laurence Housman, Sunday School prize label 1903. Jarndyce Antiquarian Booksellers CXCII - 127 2011 £45

MacDonald, George 1824-1905 *Ranald Bannerman's Boyhood.* Blackie & Son, circa, 1925, Half title, color frontispiece by A. V. Wheelhouse, illustrations after Arthur Hughes, original red-brown cloth blocked with Housman design on front board, slight rubbing, paper pasted over inscription on leading f.e.p. Jarndyce Antiquarian Booksellers CXCII - 128 2011 £30

MacDonald, George 1824-1905 *The History of Robert Falconer as issued in The Argosy, a Magazine of Tales, Travels, Essays and Poems. Midsummer & Christmas volume 1867. (Volume III-IV).* London: Strahan & Co., 1867, First appearance; 2 volumes in 1, original orange cloth, dulled spine slightly worn at head and tail & hinges, leading endpapers replaced, following inner hinge cracking. Jarndyce Antiquarian Booksellers CXCII - 57 2011 £200

MacDonald, George 1824-1905 *Robert Falconer.* London: Hurst & Blackett, 1869, Half title, frontispiece, handsome half brown morocco with coronet, marbled endpapers and edges, bookplate of Hugh, Duke of Westminster 1884 with corner marked. Jarndyce Antiquarian Booksellers CXCII - 59 2011 £150

MacDonald, George 1824-1905 *Robert Falconer.* London: Hurst & Blackett, 1869, First English one volume edition; half title, frontispiece slightly browned, 4 pages ads, original dark green cloth, slightly rubbed, inner hinges cracking. Jarndyce Antiquarian Booksellers CXCII - 58 2011 £160

MacDonald, George 1824-1905 *Robert Falconer.* London: Hurst & Blackett, circa, 1890, Engraved frontispiece, (6) + 4 pages ads, original black cloth, spine slightly worn and dulled, inscription from July 1892. Jarndyce Antiquarian Booksellers CXCII - 60 2011 £35

MacDonald, George 1824-1905 *Robert Falconer.* London: Hurst & Blackett, circa, 1893?, Engraved frontispiece, spotting caused by tissue guard, (6), 4 pages ads, original black cloth, very good, elaborate illuminated calligraphic presentation inscription. Jarndyce Antiquarian Booksellers CXCII - 61 2011 £45

MacDonald, George 1824-1905 *Robert Falconer.* London: Hurst & Blackett, circa, 1895, New edition; frontispiece, contemporary half red morocco, spine slightly faded, bookplate of D. M. L. Urie, very good. Jarndyce Antiquarian Booksellers CXCII - 62 2011 £160

MacDonald, George 1824-1905 *Robert Falconer.* London: Hurst & Blackett, circa, 1900?, New edition; half title, spotted, original dark olive green embossed cloth, lacking leading f.e.p. Jarndyce Antiquarian Booksellers CXCII - 63 2011 £45

MacDonald, George 1824-1905 *Robert Falconer.* London: Hurst & Blackett, circa, 1902?, New edition; half title, 4 pages ads, original light olive green embossed cloth, spine marked. Jarndyce Antiquarian Booksellers CXCII - 64 2011 £30

MacDonald, George 1824-1905 *Robert Falconer.* London: Hurst & Blackett, circa, 1902?, New edition; half title, 4 pages ads, few spots in prelims, original dark olive green embossed cloth, very good, prize inscription Sunday School teacher Dec. 1906. Jarndyce Antiquarian Booksellers CXCII - 66 2011 £35

MacDonald, George 1824-1905 *The Roman Wall in Scotland.* Oxford: Clarendon Press, 1934, Second edition; large 8vo., contemporary half crushed morocco gilt, spine mellowed, pages xvi, 492 with 81 plates and 57 text illustrations, handsome copy. R. F. G. Hollett & Son Antiquarian Booksellers 177 - 558 2011 £150

MacDonald, George 1824-1905 *A Rough Shaking.* New York: George Routledge & Sons, 1890, First American edition; half title, frontispiece and 11 plates, 4 pages ads, original pictorial blue cloth, bevelled boards blocked in gilt, black and green, fine, bright copy, publisher's name blocked at base of spine. Jarndyce Antiquarian Booksellers CXCII - 290 2011 £850

MacDonald, George 1824-1905 *A Rough Shaking, in Atalanta. Volume 3 October 1889 to September 1890.* London: Trischler & Co., 1890, 4to., frontispiece and illustrations, title in red and brown, original olive green cloth blocked in gilt, brown and dark green, little rubbed, inner hinges splitting. Jarndyce Antiquarian Booksellers CXCII - 289 2011 £250

MacDonald, George 1824-1905 *A Rough Shaking.* Blackie & Son, circa, 1894, Half title, frontispiece and plates by William Parkinson, 32 page catalog, original illustrated grey-green cloth, bevelled boards, blocked in gilt, black and dark green, olive green edges, with School Prize label and stamp 1897. Jarndyce Antiquarian Booksellers CXCII - 291 2011 £75

MacDonald, George 1824-1905 *A Rough Shaking.* Blackie & Son, circa, 1897, Half title, frontispiece and plates by William Parkinson, 32 page catalog, original illustrations, red cloth, bevelled boards, blocked in gilt black and dark green, olive green edges. Jarndyce Antiquarian Booksellers CXCII - 292 2011 £75

MacDonald, George 1824-1905 *A Rough Shaking.* Blackie & Son, circa, 1910?, Half title, frontispiece and 11 plates by William Parkinson, 16 page catalog, original blue cloth designed by Laurence Housman, green edges, school prize label 1911 with block on back board, very good, bright. Jarndyce Antiquarian Booksellers CXCII - 294 2011 £50

MacDonald, George 1824-1905 *St. George and St. Michael.* London: Henry S. King & Co., 1876, (1875?). First edition; 3 volumes, half titles, 48 page catalog (Sept. 1875) volume I, few spots, original maroon cloth, plain rule & dotted rule borders in black on volumes I and II, in blind on volume III, gilt lettering on spine, black endpapers, signs of label removal from front boards, signature of William Carey Davies. Jarndyce Antiquarian Booksellers CXCII - 172 2011 £1250

MacDonald, George 1824-1905 *St. George and St. Michael.* London: Kegan Paul Trench & Co., 1883, Fourth edition; half title, frontispiece, 39 page catalog (10.83), original red cloth, bevelled boards (style F), dulled and slightly rubbed, but good, inscribed by author for Francis William Troup, signed twice by Troup. Jarndyce Antiquarian Booksellers CXCII - 173 2011 £850

MacDonald, George 1824-1905 *St. George and St. Michael.* London: Kegan Paul, Trench & Co., 1886, Fifth edition; half title, 41 page catalog (3.89) & Shakespeare catalog (4) pages, original red cloth, bevelled boards, (style F), spine dulled, school prize label 1888.   Jarndyce Antiquarian Booksellers   CXCII - 174   2011   £75

MacDonald, George 1824-1905 *St. George and St. Michael.* London: Kegan Paul, Trench, Trubner & Co., circa, 1890, New edition; half title, frontispiece, 32 page catalog, original red cloth, bevelled boards (style E), spine slightly dulled, very good.   Jarndyce Antiquarian Booksellers   CXCII - 175   2011   £75

MacDonald, George 1824-1905 *St. George and St. Michael.* London: Kegan Paul, Trench & Co., circa, 1893?, New edition; half title, original red cloth (style D), very good, signed MacDonald at head of text page 1 (possibly Sara MacDonald).   Jarndyce Antiquarian Booksellers   CXCII - 177   2011   £75

MacDonald, George 1824-1905 *St. George and St. Michael.* London: Kegan Paul, Trench, Trubner & Co., 1893, New edition; original red cloth (style G), spine slightly faded, very good.   Jarndyce Antiquarian Booksellers   CXCII - 176   2011   £50

MacDonald, George 1824-1905 *St. George and St. Michael.* London: Kegan Paul, Trench, Trubner & Co. circa, 1895, New edition; half title on thicker rougher paper, original red cloth, style G, very good.   Jarndyce Antiquarian Booksellers   CXCII - 178   2011   £50

MacDonald, George 1824-1905 *St. George and St. Michael.* London: Kegan Paul, Trench, Trubner & Co. circa, 1900, Half title, paper slightly browning, original orange cloth (style H), spine slightly faded, booklabel of James Slater.   Jarndyce Antiquarian Booksellers   CXCII - 179   2011   £40

MacDonald, George 1824-1905 *Salted with Fire.* London: Hurst & Blackett, 1897, First edition; half title, 6 page ads, 24 page catalog, original brown purple cloth blocked with thistles in blind on front and gilt lettered, spine unevenly faded and marked, endpapers marked.   Jarndyce Antiquarian Booksellers   CXCII - 322   2011   £120

MacDonald, George 1824-1905 *Salted with Fire.* London: Hurst & Blackett, 1897, First edition; half title 6 pages ads, original dark olive green cloth with blind decoration on front board and spine and gilt lettering.   Jarndyce Antiquarian Booksellers   CXCII - 323   2011   £150

MacDonald, George 1824-1905 *Scotch Songs and Ballads.* Aberdeen: John Rae Smith, 1893, First edition; half title, final colophon leaf, 3 initial and 2 final blanks, original plain blue cloth, gilt blocked, dulled, top edge gilt, with pencil inscription in the hand of F.M. From G. MacD Xmas 1897, F.M.".   Jarndyce Antiquarian Booksellers   CXCII - 317   2011   £200

MacDonald, George 1824-1905 *The Seaboard Parish.* London: Tinsley Bros., 1868, First edition; 3 volumes, contemporary half red roan, well rebacked, ownership inscription in volume I of W. Carey Davies, 1869.   Jarndyce Antiquarian Booksellers   CXCII - 95   2011   £950

MacDonald, George 1824-1905 *The Seaboard Parish.* London: Strahan & Co., 1872, Third edition; half title, some internal spotting, slightly later half green morocco with stamps, shelfmarks and withdrawn label of General Assembly Library, New Zealand, bit rubbed.   Jarndyce Antiquarian Booksellers   CXCII - 96   2011   £120

MacDonald, George 1824-1905 *The Seaboard Parish.* London: Alexander Strahan, 1884, Half title, frontispiece and plates, in slightly taller format in mustard cloth, elaborately decorated in light and dark brown and gilt, very good.   Jarndyce Antiquarian Booksellers   CXCII - 97   2011   £85

MacDonald, George 1824-1905 *The Seaboard Parish.* London: Kegan Paul, Trench & Co., 1886, Fourth edition; half title, frontispiece and plates, 44 page catalog (3.86), original scarlet cloth, bevelled boards, blocked in black and gilt (style E), spine faded, otherwise very good.   Jarndyce Antiquarian Booksellers   CXCII - 98   2011   £65

MacDonald, George 1824-1905 *The Seaboard Parish.* London: Kegan Paul, Trench & Co., 1888, New edition; original red cloth with elaborate decoration black (style D), signature of Sara MacDonald 23.4.92.   Jarndyce Antiquarian Booksellers   CXCII - 99   2011   £65

MacDonald, George 1824-1905 *The Seaboard Parish.* London: Kegan Paul, Trench, Trubner & Co. circa, 1895?, New edition; half title, original scarlet cloth (style G), very good.   Jarndyce Antiquarian Booksellers   CXCII - 101   2011   £60

MacDonald, George 1824-1905 *The Seaboard Parish.* London: Kegan Paul, Trench, Trubner & Co. circa, 1898?, New edition; half title, original orange cloth, style H, slightly buckled with spine faded.   Jarndyce Antiquarian Booksellers   CXCII - 103   2011   £45

MacDonald, George 1824-1905 *Sir Gibbie.* London: Hurst & Blackett, 1879, First edition; 3 volumes, slight foxing to prelims, well rebound in red binder's cloth.   Jarndyce Antiquarian Booksellers   CXCII - 214   2011   £1250

MacDonald, George 1824-1905 *Sir Gibbie.* London: Hurst & Blackett, 1879, First edition; 3 volumes, half titles, few internal marks, handsomely rebound in half maroon morocco. Jarndyce Antiquarian Booksellers CXCII - 213 2011   £1250

MacDonald, George 1824-1905 *Sir Gibbie.* London: Hurst & Blackett, 1879, First edition; 3 volumes, half titles, 16 page catalog volume III, internal mends volume III with occasional torn corners, original brown cloth by Leighton Son & Hodge, neatly recased, little rubbed with traces of label removal on front boards and slight damp marking on brown endpapers. Jarndyce Antiquarian Booksellers   CXCII - 212 2011   £1600

MacDonald, George 1824-1905 *Sir Gibbie.* London: Hurst & Blackett, 1897?, Half title, engraved frontispiece, 6 pages ads, slight spotting caused by endpapers, original dark green cloth, very good, signature dated 1897. Jarndyce Antiquarian Booksellers CXCII - 215 2011 £50

MacDonald, George 1824-1905 *Sir Gibbie.* London: Hurst & Blackett, 1903, New edition; half title, 6 pages ads carelessly opened, some spotting, original olive green cloth, blind blocked panels, gilt lettering, slight rubbing. Jarndyce Antiquarian Booksellers CXCII - 216 2011   £45

MacDonald, George 1824-1905 *Sir Gibbie.* London: Hurst & Blackett, 1909, New edition; half title, 6 pages ads, original dark green cloth, blind blocked panels, gilt lettered, very good. Jarndyce Antiquarian Booksellers CXCII - 217 2011   £40

MacDonald, George 1824-1905 *Sir Gibbie.* London: Cassell & Co., 1927, Half title, original grey blue cloth, slightly sunned, bookplate of Betty Pears. Jarndyce Antiquarian Booksellers CXCII - 219 2011   £30

MacDonald, George 1824-1905 *Stephen Archer and Other Tales.* London: Sampson Low, Marston, Searle & Rivington, 1882, First edition, remainder issue with new titlepage to volume I only; 2 volumes in 1, original red cloth, bevelled boards blocked in red and black, spine dulled. Jarndyce Antiquarian Booksellers CXCII - 250 2011 £1250

MacDonald, George 1824-1905 *Stephen Archer and Other Tales.* London: Sampson Low, Marston, Searle & Rivington, 1883, half title, 2 pages ads, 32 page catalog (Nov. 1882), original red cloth, bevelled boards by W. Bone & Son (style A), spine slightly faded and bukled. Jarndyce Antiquarian Booksellers   CXCII - 251 2011 £65

MacDonald, George 1824-1905 *Stephen Archer and Other Tales.* London: Sampson Low Marston, Searle & Rivington, 1888, New and cheaper edition; half title, original red cloth, style B, spine slightly faded, with signature of Sara MacDonald. Jarndyce Antiquarian Booksellers CXCII - 252 2011   £50

MacDonald, George 1824-1905 *Stephen Archer and Other Tales.* London: Sampson Low, Marston, Searle & Rivington, 1894, New edition; half title, original royal blue cloth, very good. Jarndyce Antiquarian Booksellers CXCII - 253 2011   £65

MacDonald, George 1824-1905 *Stephen Archer and Other Tales.* London: Edwin Dalton, 1908, Reissue of Newnes' edition of 1905; half title, frontispiece and plates, few spots, original crimson cloth with art nouveau design in green & brown lettering gilt, spine slightly dulled.   Jarndyce Antiquarian Booksellers   CXCII - 254 2011   £45

MacDonald, George 1824-1905 *There and Back.* London: Kegan Paul, Trench, Trubner & Co., 1891, First edition; 3 volumes, half titles, final note volume III, original smooth red cloth, spines slightly faded with minor wear at heads and tail of spines and traces of labels at tails of front boards, good plus copy, black endpapers with booklabels of John Kidd and of George MacDonald Library, The Farm, Huntly. Jarndyce Antiquarian Booksellers CXCII - 283 2011   £2000

MacDonald, George 1824-1905 *There and Back.* London: Kegan Paul, Trench, Trubner & Co., 1891, Second edition; half title, frontispiece, original red cloth bevelled boards (Style F), spine faded, otherwise very good, signed presentation from author to A. P. Watt, with Watt's bookplate. Jarndyce Antiquarian Booksellers CXCII - 284 2011   £1500

MacDonald, George 1824-1905 *There and Back.* London: Kegan Paul, Trench, Trubner & Co., 1891, Second edition; half title, frontispiece, few spots, contemporary half brown morocco, gilt stamps and label of General Assembly Library New Zealand, some damage to following endpapers from adhesion. Jarndyce Antiquarian Booksellers   CXCII - 285 2011   £125

MacDonald, George 1824-1905 *There and Back.* London: Kegan Paul, Trench, Trubner & Co., 1893?, Reissue of second edition with the final note still on page v; half title, original red morocco grained cloth (style G), spine slightly faded, very good. Jarndyce Antiquarian Booksellers CXCII - 286 2011   £150

MacDonald, George 1824-1905 *There and Back.* London: Kegan Paul, Trench, Trubner & Co., 1907, Third edition; final leaf with note, slight discoloration at edges, original red cloth (style G variant), very good. Jarndyce Antiquarian Booksellers CXCII - 287 2011   £75

MacDonald, George 1824-1905 *There and Back.* London: Kegan Paul, Trench, Trubner & Co., 1907, third edition; final leaf with note, slight discoloration at edges, original orange cloth (style H), spine slightly dulled. Jarndyce Antiquarian Booksellers CXCII - 288 2011 £50

MacDonald, George 1824-1905 *Thomas Wingfold, Curate.* London: Hurst & Blackett, 1876, First edition; half titles, contemporary half parchment, red cloth boards, red edges, nice except leading hinge weakening volume I. Jarndyce Antiquarian Booksellers CXCII - 186 2011 £950

MacDonald, George 1824-1905 *Thomas Wingfold, Curate.* London: Strahan & Co., 1880, Half title, slight marks caused by binding, contemporary full brown morocco in antique style, bevelled boards, slight rubbing, one gathering slightly proud, all edges gilt, signed presentation from author for William Gellan. Jarndyce Antiquarian Booksellers CXCII - 187 2011 £1250

MacDonald, George 1824-1905 *Thomas Wingfold, Curate.* London: Chatto & Windus, 1883, Half title, colophon leaf, yellowback, rebound in red binder's cloth, cancelled stamp and label of Bolland Collection. Jarndyce Antiquarian Booksellers CXCII - 189 2011 £50

MacDonald, George 1824-1905 *Thomas Wingfold, Curate.* London: Chatto & Windus, 1883, Half title, no ads on endpapers, original yellow printed boards, dullled and little worn. Jarndyce Antiquarian Booksellers CXCII - 188 2011 £50

MacDonald, George 1824-1905 *Thomas Wingfold, Curate.* London: Kegan Paul, Trench & Co., 1887, Fourth edition; half title, frontispiece, final ad leaf, original red cloth, bevelled boards (style E), spine faded with slight mark, else very good. Jarndyce Antiquarian Booksellers CXCII - 190 2011 £40

MacDonald, George 1824-1905 *Thomas Wingfold, Curate.* London: Kegan Paul, Trench and Co., 1889?, New edition; original red cloth (style D), with black acanthus design. Jarndyce Antiquarian Booksellers CXCII - 191 2011 £60

MacDonald, George 1824-1905 *Thomas Wingfold, Curate.* London: Kegan Paul, Trench & Co., 1892, New edition; half title, final blank leaf + later 80 page catalog (1892), slight browning, lacking following f.e.p., original red cloth, slightly faded, very good. Jarndyce Antiquarian Booksellers CXCII - 192 2011 £50

MacDonald, George 1824-1905 *Thomas Wingfold, Curate.* London: Kegan Paul, Trench, Trubner & Co., 1893, New edition; half title, slight spotting caused by endpapers, original scarlet cloth (Style G), spine slightly faded, very good. Jarndyce Antiquarian Booksellers CXCII - 193 2011 £45

MacDonald, George 1824-1905 *Thomas Wingfold, Curate.* London: Kegan Paul, Trench, Trubner & Co., 1906, New edition; half title, original crimson cloth (style G), slight mark, very good. Jarndyce Antiquarian Booksellers CXCII - 194 2011 £40

MacDonald, George 1824-1905 *A Threefold Cord.* not to be had of any bookseller, but by application to Mr. W. Hughes, 43 Beaufort Street, Chelsea, London, 1883, First edition, first issue; colophon leaf, original plain red sand grained cloth, spine rubbed, boards stained, paper label browned and chipped, remains of press cutting on leading pastedown, inscribed by author for Wm. Hanson Palsford. Jarndyce Antiquarian Booksellers CXCII - 259 2011 £850

MacDonald, George 1824-1905 *A Threefold Cord.* not to be had of any bookseller, but by application to Mr. W. Hughes, 43 Beaufort Street, Chelsea, London, 1883, First edition, first issue; original plain red sand grained cloth, printed paper label on spine, dulled and marked on front board, inscribed by author for Sir Baldwyn Leighton. Jarndyce Antiquarian Booksellers CXCII - 258 2011 £1250

MacDonald, George 1824-1905 *A Threefold Cord.* not to be had of any bookseller, but by application to Mr. W. Hughes, 43 Beaufort Street, Chelsea, London, 1883, First edition, 2nd issue?; uncut in original red coarse morocco grained cloth, printed paper label, inserted pink slip, slightly chipped at fore edge, very good. Jarndyce Antiquarian Booksellers CXCII - 260 2011 £300

MacDonald, George 1824-1905 *Unspoken Sermons.* London: Alexander Strahan, 1867, (1866). First edition; half title, title in red and black, original royal blue cloth, little dulled, presentation copy from author for cousin "Robert & Margaret Troup...Dec. 7 1866", with Strahan alone in caps at tail of spine with two heavy rules & publisher's device in gilt on front boards. Jarndyce Antiquarian Booksellers CXCII - 68 2011 £850

MacDonald, George 1824-1905 *Unspoken Sermons. Second Series.* London: Longmans, Green and Co., 1885, First edition; half title, title in red and black, ad leaf, 12 page catalog (Jul 1884), original brown cloth in similar style to First Series, slightly dulled. Jarndyce Antiquarian Booksellers CXCII - 74 2011 £300

MacDonald, George 1824-1905 *Unspoken Sermons. First Series.* London: Longmans, Green & Co., 1897, New edition; half title, title in red and black, 20 page catalog (Aug. 1898), few pencil notes, original grey green cloth blocked in red, black and gilt, slightly dulled. Jarndyce Antiquarian Booksellers   CXCII - 73 2011   £45

MacDonald, George 1824-1905 *Unspoken Sermons.* London: Strahan & Co., 1868, Second edition; half title, title in red and black, original royal blue cloth, slightly marked & dulled, binder's ticket of Virtue & Co. and monogram bookplate of M.E.J., inscribed by author for Alice Caunter, with Strahan & Co. in small caps at tail of spine, rules to front board in blind & without publisher's device. Jarndyce Antiquarian Booksellers   CXCII - 69 2011   £600

MacDonald, George 1824-1905 *Unspoken Sermons.* London: Strahan & Co., 1869, Third edition; half title removed, title in red and black, original royal blue cloth, dulled and slightly rubbed, Renier booklabel, ownership inscription, with Strahan & Co. in large & small caps at tail of spine. Jarndyce Antiquarian Booksellers   CXCII - 70 2011   £85

MacDonald, George 1824-1905 *Unspoken Sermons.* London: Strahan and Co., 1870, Fourth edition; half title, title in red and black, original royal blue cloth, dulled and rubbed, initial printed ad slip for Dora Greenwell's Colloquia Crucis, signature of Alexander Todd 1880. Jarndyce Antiquarian Booksellers   CXCII - 71 2011   £85

MacDonald, George 1824-1905 *Unspoken Sermons.* London: Strahan and Co., 1876?, Undated later edition with no red printing on titlepage; half title removed, 2 pages ads, original royal blue cloth, slightly dulled. Jarndyce Antiquarian Booksellers   CXCII - 72 2011   £60

MacDonald, George 1824-1905 *The Vicar's Daughter.* Leipzig: Bernhard Tauchnitz, 1872, Copyright edition; 2 volumes, slight browning, bound without half titles in half vellum, elaborate gilt spines, red labels, initials of V.C.B., MacDonald's friend Violet Cavendish Bentinck. Jarndyce Antiquarian Booksellers   CXCII - 161 2011   £200

MacDonald, George 1824-1905 *The Vicar's Daughter.* London: Tinsley Bros., 1872, First edition; 3 volumes, half titles, few spots, bound without ads in half dark green roan with stamps and labels for General Assembly Library, New Zealand, spine volume II chipped and rubbed. Jarndyce Antiquarian Booksellers   CXCII - 160 2011   £750

MacDonald, George 1824-1905 *The Vicar's Daughter.* London: Sampson Low, Marston, Searle & Rivinington, 1881, Half title, 32 page catalog (Jan. 1881), original red cloth, bevelled boards (style A), blocked in black and gilt, spine slightly dulled. Jarndyce Antiquarian Booksellers   CXCII - 162 2011   £70

MacDonald, George 1824-1905 *The Vicar's Daughter.* London: Sampson Low, Marston & Co. circa, 1893, Half title, frontispiece, original blue cloth, little dulled. Jarndyce Antiquarian Booksellers   CXCII - 163 2011   £45

MacDonald, George 1824-1905 *Weighed and Wanting. in The Sunday Magazine.* London: Isbister & Co., 1882, Frontispiece and plates, illustrations, some spots, original olive brown decorated cloth, bevelled boards blocked in black and gilt, hinges rubbed, small splits at head and tail of spine, school prize label for 1884 and prize stamp 1885. Jarndyce Antiquarian Booksellers   CXCII - 243 2011   £250

MacDonald, George 1824-1905 *Weighed and Wanting.* London: Sampson Low, Marston, Searle & Rivington, 1882, First edition; 3 volumes, few spots, neatly recased in original red cloth, spines faded and slightly marked, traces of label removed on front boards, still good, cream endpapers. Jarndyce Antiquarian Booksellers   CXCII - 244 2011   £2500

MacDonald, George 1824-1905 *Weighed and Wanting.* London: Sampson Low, Marston, Searle & Rivington, 1883, First one volume edition; 32 page catalog, Nov. 1882, original red cloth, bevelled boards (style A), slightly affected by damp causing red watermarks at heads of few leaves and in catalog, Paris bookseller's ticket. Jarndyce Antiquarian Booksellers   CXCII - 245 2011   £65

MacDonald, George 1824-1905 *Weighed and Wanting.* London: Sampson Low, Marston & Co., 1894?, New edition; original plain blue cloth, slightly dulled. Jarndyce Antiquarian Booksellers   CXCII - 246 2011   £45

MacDonald, George 1824-1905 *Weighed and Wanting.* London: Sidney Kick 22 Paternoter Row, circa, 1900?, Original plain red cloth with imprint, Sampson Low & Co. at tail of spine, Methodist Free Church prize label, titlepage is a cancel of text stereotyped from earlier 183 plates. Jarndyce Antiquarian Booksellers   CXCII - 247 2011   £40

MacDonald, George 1824-1905 *Weighed and Wanting.* London: George Newnes, 1905, Frontispiece, original blue cloth, faded and slightly marked. Jarndyce Antiquarian Booksellers   CXCII - 248 2011   £35

MacDonald, George 1824-1905 *What's Mine's Mine.* London: Kegan Paul, Trench and Co., 1886, First edition; 3 volumes, half titles, 44 page catalog (3.86) volume III, library marks and stamps, original red fine bead grained cloth, black borders and device on back board, gilt spine lettering, spines darkened with traces of label removal at tail, large bookplates of Elizabeth & Arthur Spence, small stamps and reference nos. on initial blank of Wynstone's School, good copy. Jarndyce Antiquarian Booksellers   CXCII - 272 2011   £850

MacDonald, George 1824-1905 *What's Mine's Mine.* London: Kegan Paul, Trench & Co., 1886, First edition; half titles, 44 page catalog (3.86) volume III, some spotting caused by endpapers, original red fine bead grained cloth, black borders and device on back board, gilt spine lettering, slightly dulled, rubbing on leading hinge volume I, but very good, inscribed by author for A. P. Watt", with Watt's bookplate.   Jarndyce Antiquarian Booksellers   CXCII - 271   2011   £2500

MacDonald, George 1824-1905 *What's Mine's Mine.* London: Kegan Paul, Trench & Co., 1886, Second edition; half title, frontispiece by Gordon Browne slightly affected by tissue guard, 44 page catalog (8.86), original red cloth, bevelled boards (style E), darkened on front and spine, rubbed.   Jarndyce Antiquarian Booksellers   CXCII - 273   2011   £50

MacDonald, George 1824-1905 *What's Mine's Mine.* London: Kegan Paul, Trench & Co. circa, 1887?, Half title, original red cloth (style D), spine slightly faded.   Jarndyce Antiquarian Booksellers   CXCII - 274   2011   £60

MacDonald, George 1824-1905 *What's Mine's Mine.* London: Kegan Paul Trench & Co., 1889, Third edition; half title, frontispiece, 89 + 4 page catalog (7.90), original pinkish red cloth, bevelled boards (style E), spine faded.   Jarndyce Antiquarian Booksellers   CXCII - 275   2011   £65

MacDonald, George 1824-1905 *What's Mine's Mine.* London: Kegan Paul, Trench, Trubner & Co., 1892?, Half title, original red cloth (Style G), spine slightly faded, very good.   Jarndyce Antiquarian Booksellers   CXCII - 276   2011   £50

MacDonald, George 1824-1905 *Wilfrid Cumbermede.* London: Hurst & Blackett, 1872, (1871). First edition; 3 volumes, half titles, few spots, slightly later half dark green morocco, stamp & labels of General Assembly Library, New Zealand, hinges rubbed but sound.   Jarndyce Antiquarian Booksellers   CXCII - 130   2011   £950

MacDonald, George 1824-1905 *Wilfrid Cumbermede: an Autobiographical Story.* London: Strahan & Co., 1872, Second edition; half title, frontispiece, odd spot, uncut in original maroon cloth, blocked with gilt & black on spine & ornamental black bands on boards, inscription on endpaper July 12th 1873, bookseller's ticket of Edward White, Doncaster, very good.   Jarndyce Antiquarian Booksellers   CXCII - 131   2011   £200

MacDonald, George 1824-1905 *Wilfrid Cumbermede: an Autobiographical Story.* London: Strahan & Co., 1873, Second edition, but with Daldy, Isbister on spine instead of Strahan & Co; half title, frontispiece by F. A. Fraser, small brown mark at end of text, original maroon cloth, spine blocked in black and gilt ornamental black bands on boards, inner hinges splitting, bookseller's ticket of James Gemmell, Edinburgh.   Jarndyce Antiquarian Booksellers   CXCII - 132   2011   £150

MacDonald, George 1824-1905 *Wilfrid Cumbermede: an Autobiographical Story.* London: Strahan & Co., circa, 1880, Third edition; half title, frontispiece and illustrations, original dark blue cloth blocked in black and gilt, very good.   Jarndyce Antiquarian Booksellers CXCII - 133   2011   £150

MacDonald, George 1824-1905 *Wilfrid Cumbermede: an Autobiographical Story.* London: Kegan Paul, Trench & Co., 1892?, New edition; half title, original red cloth, style D, very good, inscription from Sara MacDonald 23.4.92.   Jarndyce Antiquarian Booksellers   CXCII - 134   2011   £120

MacDonald, George 1824-1905 *Wilfrid Cumbermede: an Autobiographical Story.* London: Kegan Paul, Trench, Trubner, & Co., 1893, New edition; half title, on smooth thinner paper, original red cloth (style G), spine slightly dulled, very good.   Jarndyce Antiquarian Booksellers   CXCII - 135   2011   £65

MacDonald, George 1824-1905 *Wilfrid Cumbermede: an Autobiographical Story.* London: Kegan Paul, Trench, Trubner & Co., 1900?, Half title, title slightly torn without loss and repaired, on thicker tougher paper, slight browning, original red cloth (style G).   Jarndyce Antiquarian Booksellers   CXCII - 136   2011   £45

MacDonald, George 1824-1905 *The Wise Woman.* London: Strahan & Co., 1875, First edition; cut down copy, handsomely rebound in half black morocco gilt, raised bands.   Jarndyce Antiquarian Booksellers   CXCII - 181   2011   £400

MacDonald, George 1824-1905 *The Wise Woman.* London: Strahan & Co., 1875, First edition; half title, original blue cloth, bevelled boards, marked and faded with wear to spine and corners, inner hinges splitting, lacking leading f.e.p., poor copy.   Jarndyce Antiquarian Booksellers   CXCII - 180   2011   £250

MacDonald, George 1824-1905 *The Wise Woman.* London: Cassell & Co., 1883, Fourth edition; half title, 8 page catalog (5R-1083), original royal blue cloth, gilt borders and gilt floral device on front board, spine slightly dulled, 1884 ms. label on leading f.e.p., all edges gilt, very good.   Jarndyce Antiquarian Booksellers   CXCII - 183   2011   £150

MacDonald, George 1824-1905 *Within and Without: a Dramatic Poem.* London: Longman, Brown, Green & Longmans, 1855, First edition; 4 pages ads, 24 page catalog (March 1856), few spots, original brown morocco grained cloth by Edmonds & Remnants, small hole in spine, almost imperceptibly repaired, frontispiece, in this copy grain of cloth is vertical.   Jarndyce Antiquarian Booksellers   CXCII - 1   2011   £950

MacDonald, George 1824-1905 *Within and Without: a Dramatic Poem.* London: Longman, Brown, Green & Longmans, 1855, First edition; 4 pages ads, 24 page catalog (March 1856), few spots, original brown morocco grained cloth, without binder's ticket, slight fading, small splits at head and tail of following hinge, following inner hinge slightly cracking. Jarndyce Antiquarian Booksellers CXCII - 2 2011   £850

MacDonald, George 1824-1905 *Within and Without: a Dramatic Poem.* London: Longman, Brown, Green, Longmans & Roberts, 1857, Second edition; 2 pages ads, original dark brown morocco coarse weave cloth, boards decorated in blind, spine lettered gilt, small splits at head of following hinge and tail of leading hinge, ownership inscriptions of Moira Louis, 61 Eaton Place, good plus. Jarndyce Antiquarian Booksellers CXCII - 4 2011   £350

MacDonald, George 1824-1905 *Within and Without: a Dramatic Poem.* London: Longman, Brown, Green, Longmans & Roberts, 1857, Second edition; contemporary black morocco by Hayday, at some time very neatly recased, all edges gilt. Jarndyce Antiquarian Booksellers CXCII - 5 2011   £200

MacDonald, George 1824-1905 *Within and Without: a Dramatic Poem.* London: Longman, Brown, Green, Longmans & Roberts, 1857, Second edition; 2 pages ads, name cut from upper margin of title, original brown fine dotted diaper cloth, boards decorated in blind, spine lettered in gilt, slight rubbing and marking. Jarndyce Antiquarian Booksellers CXCII - 3 2011   £350

MacDonald, George 1824-1905 *Works of Fancy and Imagination.* London: Strahan & Co., 1871, First edition; volumes I-II, IV, VII-X, 7 volumes only, 16mo., half title, slight spotting caused by endpapers, original red cloth, paper labels, spines dulled, paper label of volume VIII defective, inscribed signed presentation from author for W. Carey Davies. Jarndyce Antiquarian Booksellers CXCII - 145 2011   £750

MacDonald, George 1824-1905 *Works of Fancy and Imagination.* London: Strahan & Co., 1871-1884, Stories Volume II and III are of the 1871 first edition, Stories volume I, Poems Volume III and Portent are undated, remaining volumes are of the 1884 edition with imprint of Alexander Strahan; Uniform set, incorporating mixed editions, 10 volumes, 16mo., original royal blue cloth, black borders and device at tail of spine, all edges gilt, very good, bright set, volumes I & III-V do not have half titles. Jarndyce Antiquarian Booksellers CXCII - 146 2011   £850

MacDonald, George 1824-1905 *Works of Fancy and Imagination.* London: Strahan & Co., 1871, 10 volumes, 16mo., half title, odd spot, original green cloth bevelled boards, eblaborately gilt by Burn, all edges gilt, reasonably good set with spines dulled and some gilt blocking, little rubbed, pencil inscription on half title by recipients "Ellery (?) & L. H. Dothie. The Gift of the Author Decr. 10". Jarndyce Antiquarian Booksellers CXCII - 144 2011   £1600

MacDonald, George 1824-1905 *Works of Fancy and Imagination.* London: Strahan & Co., 1884, 10 volumes, 16mo., made-up set in green Grolier pattern cloth, blocked in gilt, red and black, variously faded and some little worn, some spines darkened. Jarndyce Antiquarian Booksellers CXCII - 147 2011   £125

MacDonald, Greville Matheson *George MacDonald and His Wife.* London: George Allen & Unwin, 1924, First edition; half title with bookplate facsimile, frontispiece, plates, original dark blue cloth, with large part of stamped envelope addressed to Dr. George MacDonald 1877 with Corage, Boscow(en), Bournemouth Hants crossed through and note "Great great grandmother Falconer's letter", Mrs. Falconer with MacDonald's maternal grandmother, with 1298 inscription from Adeline to Miss Bridle. Jarndyce Antiquarian Booksellers CXCII - 354 2011   £50

MacDonald, Greville Matheson *George MacDonald and His Wife.* London: George Allen & Unwin, 1924, First edition; half title with bookplate facsimile, frontispiece, plates, original dark blue cloth, dulled spine slightly creased, armorial bookplate of Violet Cavendish Bentinck. Jarndyce Antiquarian Booksellers CXCII - 355 2011   £50

MacDonald, Greville Matheson *George MacDonald and His Wife.* London: George Allen & Unwin, 1924, First edition; half title with bookplate facsimile, frontispiece and plates, rebound in brown binder's cloth, slightly trimmed but good, clean copy. Jarndyce Antiquarian Booksellers CXCII - 356 2011   £35

MacDonald, Greville Matheson *George MacDonald and His Wife.* London: George Allen & Unwin, 1924, Second edition; half title with bookplate, frontispiece and plates, original dark blue cloth, very good, bright. Jarndyce Antiquarian Booksellers CXCII - 357 2011   £50

MacDonald, Greville Matheson *The Sanity of William Blake.* London: A. C. Fifield, 1908, Half title, frontispiece, plates, 4 pages ads, uncut original grey printed boards, spine slightly sunned, very good. Jarndyce Antiquarian Booksellers CXCII - 358 2011   £40

MacDonald, Philip *Patrol.* New York: Harper & Bros., 1928, First US edition; presentation inscripion by author, fine in professionally restored dust jacket, exceptional copy, scarce, rare in dust jacket. Buckingham Books May 26 2011 - 25705 2011 $3500

MacDonald, Ross *Black Money.* New York: Knopf, 1965, First edition; 8vo., inscribed by author for Bill Gault, fine in fine dust jacket, exceptional copy housed in cloth slipcase with red leather labels on spine, titles and date stamped in gold.   Buckingham Books   May 26 2011 - 25474   2011 $2750

MacDonald, Ross *Black Money.* New York: Alfred A. Knopf, 1966, First edition; 8vo., inscribed by author to poet Donald Davie and his wife Doreen, fine in dust jacket with one tiny rub at head of spine.   Buckingham Books   May 26 2011 - 20957   2011 $2750

MacDonald, Ross *The Chill.* Knopf, 1964, First edition; 8vo., inscribed by author for Paul Nelson, Rolling Stone writer who interviewed author extensively, fine in dust jacket with tiny chip at top edge of rear panel.   Buckingham Books   May 26 2011 - 20958   2011 $2500

MacDonald, Ross *The Doomsters.* New York: Alfred A. Knopf, 1958, First edition; fine in dust jacket with just hint of spine fading to multicolors at base of spine, exceptional copy.   Buckingham Books   May 26 2011 - 25593   2011 $2000

MacDonald, Ross *The Far Side of Dollar.* Columbia/Bloomfield Hills: Bruccoli Clark, 1982, Unpublished "Manuscript Edition"; one of 221 numbered copies (entire edition), this copy being unnumbered and marked "Out of Series", unnumbered copies were used as review copies (publisher's prospectus for the book is laid-in), bound in patterned paper over boards with gilt stamped leather spine, fine, unread copy with one leaf of author's draft affixed to prelim page.   Buckingham Books   May 26 2011 - 27905   2011 $2500

MacDonald, Ross *The Galton Case.* New York: Knopf, 1959, First edition; 8vo., signed by author, fine in price clipped dust jacket with light wear to spine ends and two tiny closed tears to top edge of rear panel, beautiful copy housed in black cloth slipcase with three red leather labels on spine with titles stamped in gilt.   Buckingham Books   May 26 2011 - 25780   2011 $3000

MacDonald, Ross *The Galton Case.* New York: Knopf, 1959, First edition; inscribed by author to his lawyer and friend Harris and Nancy (Seed), fine in dust jacket with light wear to spine ends and with one small closed tear to top edge of rear panel.   Buckingham Books   May 26 2011 - 20956   2011 $3750

MacDougall, J. L. *History of Inverness County, Nova Scotia.* Belleville: Mika Publishing, 1972, Green cloth, gilt to spine and front cover, pages (10), 690, half title, frontispiece, tables, 8vo., very good with wear to edges.   Schooner Books Ltd.   96 - 181   2011 $65

Macedo, Jose *A Meditacao.* Lisboa: 1818, 254, (1) pages, full leather, few scrapes to rear cover, all edges blue, bookplate of John Floyd, fairly scarce.   Bookworm & Silverfish   664 - 168   2011 $150

MacEwen, Ian *Amsterdam.* London: Jonathan Cape, 1998, First British edition, true first; first state of dust jacket with no mention of Booker Prize, fine in fine dust jacket.   Bella Luna Books   May 29 2011 - t8864   2011 $110

MacFadden, Bernard *New Hair Culture.* New York: Physical Culture Pub. Co., 1901, Third edition; small 8vo., original cloth, gilt, rather stained, pages 140, with 15 plates.   R. F. G. Hollett & Son Antiquarian Booksellers   175 - 875   2011   £30

MacFarlane, Alan *Witchcraft in Tudor and Stuart England.* London: Routledge & Kegan Paul, 1970, First edition; tall 8vo., original cloth, gilt, dust jacket, pages xxi, 334, with 10 plates, 9 maps, 5 diagrams, 4 figures and 19 tables.   R. F. G. Hollett & Son Antiquarian Booksellers   175 - 876   2011   £45

MacGill, Thomas *An Account of Tunis; of Its Government, Manners, Customs and Antiquities.* Glasgow: Longman, Hurst, 1811, First edition; 8vo., pages 187, recent boards, some foxing in first section of book, scarce.   J. & S. L. Bonham Antiquarian Booksellers   Africa 4/20/2011 - 2862   2011   £230

MacGregor, John *Commercial Tariffs and Regulations, Resources and Trade of the Several States of Europe and America....* London: printed by Charles Whiting, Beaufort House, Strand, 1847, First edition; folio, (4), 160 pages, large unopened, original printed wrappers, very nice.   Anthony W. Laywood   May 26 2011 - 21687   2011 $168

Machell, Hugh *John Peel, Famous in sport and Song.* Heath Cranton: 1926, First edition; original cloth, boards, mottled by damp, spine rather faded, pages 192, color frontispiece and 30 illustrations, scarce.   R. F. G. Hollett & Son Antiquarian Booksellers   173 - 711   2011   £50

Machell, Hugh *Some Records of Annual Grasmere Sports.* Carlisle: Charles Thurnam and Sons, 1911, Limited edition, no. 140 of 250 copies; 4to., publisher's half morocco gilt, little rubbed, head of spine trifle frayed, pages 80, (ii), , uncut, illustrations from photos.   R. F. G. Hollett & Son Antiquarian Booksellers   173 - 712   2011   £150

Machen, Arthur 1863-1947 *The Great God Pan and the Inmost Light.* London: John Lane and Boston: Roberts Bros., 1894, First edition; 8vo., original publisher's black cloth lettered gilt on spine and lettered and decorated silver on front cover, pages 168 and 16 pages publisher's catalog at rear, pages uncut, light rubbing to spine ends and corners, otherwise very good+, slightly repaired, loss at corner of contents page, not affecting text, neat name on pastedown.   Any Amount of Books   May 26 2011 - A73493   2011 $503

Machen, Arthur 1863-1947 *Tales of Horror and the Supernatural.* New York: Knopf, 1948, First printing of this collection stated; near fine in good dust jacket (quarter size chip to top left of front panel), uncommon.   Lupack Rare Books   May 26 2011 - ABE4633203526 2011 $100

Machiavelli, Niccolo 1469-1527 *The Art of War.* Albany: Henry C. Southwick, 1815, First edition; 8vo., 349 pages, five folding tables, two toned recent hard cover binding, uncut, browned, some tide marks.   M & S Rare Books, Inc.   90 - 142 2011 $425

Machiavelli, Niccolo 1469-1527 *Historie Fiorentine.* Florence: Bernardo di Giunta, 1532, First edition?; The Blado edition was published just two days before the present Giunta edition, octavo, (2, blank), (1)-224, (2, blank) leaves, leaves partly numbered 9-224 with some numbers printed in error, lacking rare four errata leaves found in only few copies, contemporary brown calf, rebacked to style, boards decoratively ruled in blind, spine ornamentally stamped in blind, old printed text visible from underneath front and rear pastedowns, some wear to corners and edges of boards, tail of spine bit weak, tiny bit of worming to inner margin of signatures E-M, not affecting text, , two previous owner's on titlepage, 2 small holes to titlepage, not affecting text, some spotting and dampstains to front and rear blanks, some light tidemarks, overall very good, rare.   Heritage Book Shop   Holiday 2010 - 76 2011 $10,000

Machiavelli, Niccolo 1469-1527 *Historie.* Piacenza: Gli heredi di Gabriel Giolito de Ferrari, i.e. London: John Wolfe, 1587, 12mo., (12), 559, (9) pages, Italic letter, woodcut printer' service on titlepage, woodcut headpiece and initials, 17th century speckled calf binding, spine gilt in compartments, lettering piece, lacking, binding rubbed, spine gilt detaching, small hole on last page, Lt. Gen. George Parker bookplate, from the library of the Earls of Macclesfield at Shirburn Castle.   Maggs Bros. Ltd.   1440 - 137 2011   £700

Machiavelli, Niccolo 1469-1527 *The Florentine Historie.* London: T. C. for W. P., 1595, First English edition; folio, (12), 222 pages, illustrative woodcut border on titlepage, woodcut initials, head and tailpieces, translator's dedication signed Thomas Bedingfield and running titles that read "The Historie of Florence", with Machiavelli's own introduction (Proeme) and table of contents, without final blank, beautifully bound to period in full contemporary calf, boards ruled in blind and elaborately tooled in gilt with black dyed lacework, spine stamped in gilt and black and lettered in gilt, pages very lightly toned, overall very good in lovely binding.   Heritage Book Shop   Holiday 2010 - 75 2011 $6500

Machiavelli, Niccolo 1469-1527 *Tvtte le Opere di Nicolo Machiavelli...* Geneva: Pierre Aubert, 1550, i.e. after, 1649, First "estina" edition; 4to., (4), 351, (1 blank, 4), 116, 14, (2 blank) 304, 16, 170 pages, woodcut portrait on titlepage, double page woodcut, occasional spotting ad toning, small wormhole in lower margin, later half brown levant over marbled boards, gilt stamped spine title, top edge gilt, minor repairs, early ink marginalia on endleaves and titlepage, bookplate, ink signature and notations by Charles Eliot Norton, ex-library ink stamps, monogram ownership mark, fine.   Jeff Weber Rare Books   163 - 15 2011 $2700

MacIvor, J. Smith *Glace Bay Forum.* Glace Bay: Brodie Printing, 1935, Paper wrappers, 52 pages, black and white photo illustrations, paper wrappers almost detached, interior.   Schooner Books Ltd.   96 - 186 2011 $75

Mack, James Logan *The Border Line from the Solway Firth to the North Sea, Along the Marches of Scotland and England.* Oliver & Boyd, 1926, Revised edition; large 8vo., original cloth, gilt, rather marked and faded in places, pages xx, 336, untrimmed, 11 illustrations by Donald Scott and others.   R. F. G. Hollett & Son Antiquarian Booksellers   173 - 718 2011   £60

Mack, Lizzie *A Christmas Tree Fairy.* Griffin, Farran, Obeden & Welsh, n.d., 1887, First edition; original cloth backed glazed pictorial boards, corners trifle bruised, neatly recased, unpaginated, 10 colored plates and tinted text, vignettes throughout, occasional very slight fingering and few faint spots, but very good, scarce.   R. F. G. Hollett & Sons Antiquarian Booksellers   170 - 420 2011   £225

Mack, Robert Ellice *Nister's Holiday Annual.* London: Ernest Nister, 1890, Small 4to., original cloth backed glazed pictorial boards, rather worn, corners bruised and rounded, unpaginated, 6 fine chromolithograph plates and numerous full page and text woodcuts, including full page drawing by Louis Wain, rather shaken and loose.   R. F. G. Hollett & Sons Antiquarian Booksellers   170 - 421 2011   £75

Mackarness, Matilda Planche *The Dream Chintz.* London: W. N. Wright, 1851, First edition; half title, frontispiece, illustrations, 10 pages ads, original mint green glazed boards, lettered in darker green and decorated with elaborate leaf design in gilt, simply rebacked, bookabel of Robert J. Hayhurst, all edges gilt.   Jarndyce Antiquarian Booksellers   CLXC - 193 2011   £65

Mackarness, Matilda Planche *A Peerless Wife.* Leipzig: Bernhard Tauchnitz, 1871, Copyright edition; slight yellowing, 2 volumes in 1, contemporary half dark green morocco, spine ruled and with devices in gilt, slight rubbing, good plus, bound without half titles.   Jarndyce Antiquarian Booksellers   CLXC - 194 2011   £45

MacKay, Charles *The Scenery and Poetry of the English Lakes.* London: Longman, Brown, etc., 1846, First edition; original blindstamped green cloth gilt, pages xvi, 215, 32 (ads), tinted woodcut frontispiece and title, 8 full page vignettes and 52 text illustrations, all from original sketches engraved by Thomas Gilks, upper joint tender, pastedowns trifle stained, but very good.   R. F. G. Hollett & Son Antiquarian Booksellers   173 - 719 2011   £145

MacKenzie, Colin *MacKenzie's Five Thousand Receipts In all the Useful and Domestic Arts.* Philadelphia: 1829, (5), 456 pages, 8vo., full flamed calf with gilt panelled backstrip, really nice, with expected foxing.   Bookworm & Silverfish   679 - 47 2011 $150

MacKenzie, Donald A. *Indian Myth and Legend.* Gresham Pub. Co. n.d., Original decorated green cloth gilt, head of spine little nicked and frayed, pages xlviii, 463, top edge gilt, 8 colored plates by Warwick Goble and 34 monochrome plates, fore-edge rather spotted.   R. F. G. Hollett & Son Antiquarian Booksellers   175 - 880 2011   £35

MacKenzie, Eneas *A Descriptive and Historical Account of the Town and County of Newcastle upon Tyne...* Newcastle upon Tyne: printed & published by Mackenzie & Dent, 1827, 2 volumes bound as 1, 4to., pages x, 414, frontispiece and 10 other engraved plates; (ii), (415)-770, (ii) + engraved frontispiece and 3 other engraved plates, modern half calf by John Henderson, foxed in places, armorial bookplate of Archibald Dawnay, from the collection of Christopher Ernest Weston 1947-2010.   Unsworths Booksellers   24 - 116 2011   £300

MacKenzie, Eneas *A Descriptive and Historical Account of the Town and County of Newcastle upon Tyne, including the Borough of Gateshead.* Newcastle upon Tyne: Mackenzie & Dent, 1827, First edition; 2 volumes, 4to., frontispiece ad plates, uncut in later 19th century half dark green calf, raised bands, compartments in gilt, little rubbed.   Jarndyce Antiquarian Booksellers   CXCI - 300 2011   £125

MacKenzie, Eneas *An Historical, Topographical and Descriptive View of the County Palatine of Durham...* Newcastle upon Tyne: printed and published by MacKenzie and Dent, 1834, 2 volumes, 4to., pages cxxii, 518 + extending engraved map frontispiece and 9 other engraved plates (ii) 450 + engraved frontispiece and 9 other engraved plates, contemporary tan half calf, four flat raised bands, spines double ruled gilt, compartments textured by massed decorative pallets in blind brown lettering pieces, gilt, numbered direct in gilt, 'author' gilt direct at foot, boards decorative roll bordered in blind with 'French Shell' marbled sides, all edges brown sprinkled, pink cloth over core applied endbands, plates foxed, frontispiece onset onto title, from the collection of Christopher Ernest Weston 1947-2010.   Unsworths Booksellers   24 - 117 2011   £350

MacKenzie, Henry *The Letters of Brutus to Certain Celebrated Political Characters.* Edinburgh: printed by Stewart, Ruthven and Co., London: sold by J. Evans, 1791, First separate edition; 8vo., (4) 91 (1) pages, titlepage rather dust marked with marginal tears and fraying (but no loss and printed surface not affected) with contemporary ms. Notes in ink on title verso, original lower wrapper, upper wrapper replaced, entirely uncut.   John Drury Rare Books   153 - 86 2011   £125

MacKenzie, J. *A Woolen Draper's Letter on the French Treaty, to His Friends and Fellow Tradesmen all Over England.* London: printed for the author and sold by J. French, 1786, First edition; half title, signed R. J. Woollen Draper" (i.e. J. Mackenzie), (4), 48 pages, modern paper wrappers, nice.   Anthony W. Laywood   May 26 2011 - 19721 2011 $243

MacKenzie, Mary Jane *Geraldine; or Modes of Faith and Practice.* London: T. Cadell & W. Davies, 1820, First edition; 3 volumes, contemporary full calf, borders in gilt and blind, spines with raised and gilt bands, devices in gilt, leading hinges slightly worn, spine slightly darkened, small labels of Easton Neston Library and Sir Thomas Hesketh, Rufford Hall, good plus.   Jarndyce Antiquarian Booksellers   CLXC - 196 2011   £480

MacKenzie, Therese M. *Dromana: The Memoirs of an Irish Family.* 1907, Deluxe first edition; vellum bound.   C. P. Hyland   May 26 2011 - 259/275 2011 $507

MacKenzie, W. M. *Pompeii.* A. & C. Black, 1910, First edition; original cloth, gilt, spine trifle rubbed, pages xii, 180, top edge gilt, with 20 color plates by Alberto Pisa, flyleaves faintly browned.   R. F. G. Hollett & Son Antiquarian Booksellers   177 - 559 2011   £50

Mackereth, H. W. *Mackereth's Lake District Album.* Ulverston: W. Holmes for H. W. Mackereth, 1902, Original blue cloth, gilt, trifle rubbed, oblong large 8vo., pages (vi), 120, photo illustrations, scarce.   R. F. G. Hollett & Son Antiquarian Booksellers   173 - 720 2011   £85

Mackey, Albert G. *Encyclopadia of Freemasonry and Its Kindred Sciences...* Philadelphia: McClure Pub. Co., 1917, 4to., original cloth, gilt rather damp stained, pages (iv), 1046, color and monochrome plates.   R. F. G. Hollett & Son Antiquarian Booksellers   175 - 882   2011   £65

Mackey, Albert G. *A Manual of the Lodge or Monitorial Instructions in the Degrees of Entered Apprentice, Fellow Craft & Master Mason.* New York: 1870, 254 pages, near fine in publisher's blue cloth over bevelled boards, all gilt bright, corners sharp, 20 plates.   Bookworm & Silverfish   678 - 77   2011 $125

Mackie, Peter Jeffrey *The Keeper's Book.* London: G. T. Foulis & Co., 1929, Sixteenth edition; Thick 8vo, original cloth, spine little rubbed and faded, pages xi, 595, 12 tipped in color plates and 5 text illustrations, front flyleaf removed, half title spotted and with small inscription.   R. F. G. Hollett & Son Antiquarian Booksellers   General Catalogue Summer 2010 - 1264   2011   £45

MacKintosh, James *A Discourse on the Study of the Law of Nature and Nations...* London: printed (by S. Gosnell) for T. Cadell Jun. and W. Davies, in the Strand, J. Debrett, Piccadilly and W. Clarke, Portugal Street, Lincoln's Inn, 1800, Third edition; half title, (4) 72 pages, disbound, very nice.   Anthony W. Laywood   May 26 2011 - 21706   2011 $76

Mackley, George *Engraved in the Wood.* Two Horse Press, 1968, Limited edition, signed, out of series number of 300; large 4to., original cloth solander box, paper label, 22 page booklet in original wrappers plus 68 woodcut plates, loose as issued, fine set, printed on Wookey Hole paper, box handmade by Gray's at Cambridge.   R. F. G. Hollett & Son Antiquarian Booksellers   General Catalogue Summer 2010 - 842   2011   £450

Mackworth-Praed, Cyril Winthrop *African Handbook of Birds. Series One: Birds of Eastern and North Eastern Africa.* London: Longmans, 1952, Second edition; 2 volumes, large 8vo., pages xxvi, 806, index; viii, 1113, index, 96 color plates, maps, numerous illustrations, original grey decorative cloth.   J. & S. L. Bonham Antiquarian Booksellers   Africa 4/20/2011 - 5677   2011   £45

MacLagan, R. C. *Evil Eye in the Western Highlands.* London: David Nutt, 1902, First edition; original brown cloth, gilt, pages vii, 232, near fine.   R. F. G. Hollett & Son Antiquarian Booksellers   175 - 883   2011   £75

MacLauchlan, Henry *The Roman Wall and Illustrations of the Principal Vestiges of the Roman Occupation in the North of England...* printed for private distribution, 1857, First edition; large folio, lithographed title and map on 5 double page sheets, title and map on 6 double page sheets, 2 parts in one volume, contemporary morocco backed cloth, joints rubbed, bookplate of Sir Robert Shafto Adair.   Anthony W. Laywood   May 26 2011 - 21678   2011 $419

MacLean, John S. *The Newcastle and Carlisle Railway 1825-1862.* Newcastle upon tyne: R. Robinson & Co., 1948, First edition; large 8vo., original pictorial boards, spine little worn and chipped at head, pages 121, numerous illustrations, plans and text figures.   R. F. G. Hollett & Son Antiquarian Booksellers   173 - 721   2011   £50

MacLellan, Angus *Stories from South Uist.* London: Routledge and Kegan Paul, 1961, First edition; original cloth, gilt, dust jacket, pages xxix, 254, portrait, presentation copy inscribed by translator, John Lorne Campbell.   R. F. G. Hollett & Son Antiquarian Booksellers   175 - 884   2011   £45

MacLeod, A. C. *Songs of the North.* London: J. B. Cramer & Co., n.d. early 1920's, Sixth and twentieth editions; 2 volumes, small folio, original cloth gilt, few slight marks, extremities trifle rubbed, pages ix, 202; vii, 278, with 2 tissue guarded frontispieces, each volume initialled on title.   R. F. G. Hollett & Son Antiquarian Booksellers   175 - 885   2011   £85

MacLeod, Norman *The Gold Thread.* Edinburgh: Alex Strahan, 1862, Third edition; pages x, 68, with woodcut illustrations, original green cloth, gilt, corners little bumped.   R. F. G. Hollett & Son Antiquarian Booksellers   General Catalogue Summer 2010 - 539   2011   £35

MacLiammoir, Micheal *Oidhcheanna Sidhe: Fairy Nights.* Talbot Press, 1922, First edition; colored stiff wrapper, 93 pages, color frontispiece, black and white text illustrations, cover dull, text very good, very rare.   C. P. Hyland   May 26 2011 - 259/27   2011 $507

MacMichael, William 1784-1839 *The Gold Headed Cane.* London: John Murray, 1828, Second edition; plate and illustrations, uncut in original blue boards, drab paper spine, paper label (10s.6d), expert repairs to spine, very good.   Jarndyce Antiquarian Booksellers   CXCI - 353   2011   £120

MacMillan, Donald B. *Four Years in the White North.* New York: Harper & Bros., 1918, First edition; frontispiece, 65 black and white photo illustrations and 3 maps, signed by author, very good plus (spine little fade, little shelf-wear, nice, tight, clean text), signed by author.   Lupack Rare Books   May 26 2011 - ABE4310256495   2011 $150

MacNeice, Louis *The Sixpence that Rolled Away.* London: Faber, 1956, First edition; pages 24, 5 superb colored lithographs and 7 line drawings by Bawden, little occasional finger, scarce.   R. F. G. Hollett & Son Antiquarian Booksellers   General Catalogue Summer 2010 - 494   2011   £150

Macoun, John *Autobiography of John Macoun.* Ottawa: 1922, x, 305 pages, illustrations, original cloth, extremities rubbed, spine little faded, else clean and very good. Dumont Maps & Books of the West   111 - 66   2011 $85

MacPherson, Earl *Pin-Up Art How to Draw and Paint Beautiful Girls.* Laguna Beach: Foster Art Service circa 1940's, Large 4to., pages 31, illustrations in color and black and white, paper wrappers, cover somewhat soiled and worn, else very good, inscribed by publisher Walter Foster and signed in rear by author.   Second Life Books Inc.   174 - 233   2011 $200

MacPherson, Gerardine *Memoirs of the Life of Anna Jameson.* London: Longman, Green and Co., 1878, First edition; half title, frontispiece, contemporary half calf, marbled boards, black leather label, spine and hinges cracking, label chipped with slight loss, labels of Norfolk and Norwich Library, good, sound copy.   Jarndyce Antiquarian Booksellers   CLXC - 15   2011   £65

MacPherson, H. A. *The Birds of Cumberland Critically Studied...* Carlisle: Chas. Thurman & Sons, 1886, Pages xx, 206, color lithograph frontispiece, folding color map, original cloth, gilt, lower board trifle stained.   R. F. G. Hollett & Son Antiquarian Booksellers   173 - 723   2011   £160

MacPherson, H. A. *A Vertebrata Fauna of Lakeland Including Cumberland and Westmorland with Lancashire North of the Sands.* Edinburgh: David Douglas, 1892, First edition; large 8vo., original ribbed cloth, gilt, spine faded, pages civ, 552, (xx, ads), folding map, 8 plates, 9 text woodcuts, upper joint trifle tender, but excellent, clean and sound copy, armorial bookplate of Sir Thomas G. Glen Coats, Bart.   R. F. G. Hollett & Son Antiquarian Booksellers   173 - 725 2011   £35

MacPherson, H. A. *A Vertebrata Fauna of Lakeland Including Cumberland and Westmorland with Lancashire North of the Sands.* Chichely: Paul M. Minet, 1972, Facsimile edition; original cloth gilt, pages civ, 552, folding map, 8 plates, 9 text woodcuts.   R. F. G. Hollett & Son Antiquarian Booksellers   173 - 725   2011   £35

MacPherson, James   1736-1696 *The Poems of Ossian.* London: Lackington, Allen & Co., 1803, 2 volumes, contemporary quarter calf gilt with marbled boards, spines evenly darkened, one hinge tender, pages xvi, 320; (ii) 363 with 2 engraved frontispieces and 4 engraved plates, scattered foxing, engraved roundel bookplate of Christopher Alexander Markham in each volume.   R. F. G. Hollett & Son Antiquarian Booksellers   General Catalogue Summer 2010 - 664   2011   £120

MacQuer, Pierre Joseph *Dizionario di Chimica del Sig. Pietro Giuseppe Macquer.* Paris: printed at the Monastery of San Salvatore for G. Bianchi, 1783-1784, First edition in Italian; 11 volumes, 8vo., 3 folding tables, 1 plate, all edges sprinkled red, occasional light spotting but generally extremely fresh, contemporary speckled half calf, panelled spines, with four half raised bands, red morocco labels lettered in gilt, small paper library labels to foot of spine of each volume, some small wormholes to upper portion of spines, excellent set.   Simon Finch Rare Books   Zero - 121   2011   £1500

MacRae, David *Book of Blunders; to Which is added a Chapter of Queer Epitaphs.* Douglas, Isle of Man: J. S. Doidge, 1883, Half title, vi pages ads + 16 page catalogue, ownership signature, original green decorated cloth, bevelled boards, little soiled.   Jarndyce Antiquarian Booksellers   CXCI - 303   2011   £38

Macrobius, Ambrosius Theodosius *In Somnium Scipionis Lib. II. Saturnaliorum Lib. VII.* Lyons: S. Gryphe, 1556, 8vo., 567, (73) pages, device on titlepage, contemporary limp vellum, yapp edges, lacking ties, very attractive copy, from the library of the Earls of Macclesfield at Shirburn Castle.   Maggs Bros. Ltd.   1440 - 138   2011   £550

Maddison, A. R. *A Short Account of the Vicars Choral, Poor Clerks, Organists and Choristers of Lincoln Cathedral from the 12th Century to the Accession of Edward 6th.* London: 1878, First edition; 3 page list of subscribers, (4), iii, (1), 95, (1) pages, original cloth, gilt lettering on upper cover, nice.   Anthony W. Laywood   May 26 2011 - 14372   2011 $76

Madeira, Percy C. *Hunting in British East Africa.* Philadelphia: J. b. Lippincott, 1909, First edition; large 8vo. 299, double page frontispiece, 2 folding maps in pocket on lower cover, illustrations, original green decorative cloth, 4 pages of prelims in facsimile.   J. & S. L. Bonham Antiquarian Booksellers   Africa 4/20/2011 - 9241   2011   £85

Madonna *The English Roses. Mr. Peabody's Apples. Yakov and the Seven Theives. The Adventures of Abdi. and Lotsa de Casha.* New York: Callaway Editions, 2005, Limited to 1000 sets, this no. 392; hand signed letter from Madonna and a Giclee digital print signed by artist Loren Long laid in a folder, print is on Somerset fine milled paper suitable for framing, as new, with two disc CD collection of the five books narrated by Madonna plus special CD-ROM with bonus features, entire collection housed in original fine blue printed box with image of Madonna and the colophon for the collection on inside of box, wonderful, scarce production.   By the Book, L. C.   26 - 65   2011 $695

Madox, Thomas *History and Antiquities of the Exchequer of the Kings of England, in Two Periods; To Wit, from the Norman Conquest to the end of the Reign of K. John and from the End of the Reign of K. John to the End of the Reign of K. Edward II...* London: Robert Knaplock, 1711, First edition; folio, contemporary full panelled calf, rather worn, joints cracked, pages xviii, 752, xii, 75, (v), 2 divisional titles, copper engraved head pieces and initials and text illustrations, little light brown spotting to flyleaves and title, armorial bookplate of Thomas Nottidge, excellent copy.   R. F. G. Hollett & Son Antiquarian Booksellers   175 - 898   2011   £650

Madras Tract and Book Society *Twenty-Eighth Annual Report of the Madras Tract and Book Society with list of Subscribers and Benefactors for the Year Ending Dec. 1846 Instituted AD MDCCCXVIII.* Madras: printed by P. R. Hunt, American Mission Press, 1847, First edition; small 8vo., viii, 46 pages, disbound, very good, stitching loose, chip to corner of title, offsetting on 2 leaves, else clean.   Kaaterskill Books   12 - 126   2011 $100

Magee, Alan *Paintings Sculpture Graphics.* New York: Forum Gallery, 2003, First edition; 4to., fine in near fine dust jacket, signed by Magee, uncommon thus.   By the Book, L. C.   26 - 40   2011 $295

Magee, David *The Hundredth Book: a Bibliography of the Publications of the Book Club of California.* N.P.: San Francisco, 1958, One of 400 printed by the Grabhorn Press; xxiii, 80 pages, illustrations, folio, some age toning, else near fine, handsome production.   Dumont Maps & Books of the West   112 - 31   2011 $250

Magnusson, Magnus *Hammer of the North. Myths and Heroes of the Viking Age.* Orbis Publishing, 1976, First edition; 4to., original cloth, gilt, dust jacket, pages 128, illustrations in color.   R. F. G. Hollett & Son Antiquarian Booksellers   175 - 900   2011   £30

Magrath, John Richard *The Flemings in Oxford.* Oxford: Oxford Historical Society, 1924, First edition; Volume III, original blue cloth gilt, hinges little rubbed, pages xxiii, 492, frontispiece.   R. F. G. Hollett & Son Antiquarian Booksellers   173 - 728   2011   £45

Magruder, Julia *Miss Ayr of Virginia & Other Stories.* Chicago: Herbert S. Stone and Co., 1896, First edition; (395, 1 pages, 8 page publisher's Ads dated October 1896), small 8vo., pale green cloth covered pictorial boards, very fine, in most attractive binding designed by F. R. Kimbrough.   Paulette Rose Fine and Rare Books   32 - 119   2011 $200

Maguire, Greogry *Wicked. The Life and Times of the Wicked Witch of the West.* New York: Regan Books, 1995, First edition; fine in like dust jacket.   Bella Luna Books   May 26 2011 - t6857   2011 $275

Mahone, William *An Assassin-Like Blow at the Public Schools by Bourbon Managers.* Petersburg: 1885?, 3 pages.   Bookworm & Silverfish   666 - 182   2011 $600

Mahone, William *The Riddleberger Debt Law Printed by Order of the House of Delegates.* Richmond: 1882, 10 pages,.   Bookworm & Silverfish   666 - 169   2011 $275

Mahone, William *Virginia & Her Debt General Mahone and the Coupon Decision.* Petersburg: 1885?, 23 pages.   Bookworm & Silverfish   666 - 185   2011 $350

Mahr, Adolph *Christian Art in Ancient Ireland.* 1932-1941, First edition, 506 copies of volume I; 2 volumes, 130 plates, folio, covers bubbled but sound set, text and plates very good.   C. P. Hyland   May 26 2011 - 258/572   2011 $797

Maidment, James *A Book of Scotish Pasquils 1568-1715.* Edinburgh: William Paterson, 1868, Modern half morocco gilt with raised bands and spine label, pages xxviii, 438, uncut, few marginal blindstamps, accession stamp on verso of title, edges rather dusty.   R. F. G. Hollett & Son Antiquarian Booksellers   175 - 901   2011   £85

Mailer, Norman   1923-2007 *"An American Dream." in Esquire.* Chicago: Esquire Inc., 1964, Serialized in eight issues of Esquire, Jan.-August 1964 before being published by Dial in 1965, all 8 issues present, signed by Mailer in seven of the eight issues, few cover chips and edge tears, some minor spotting, loss to cover on spine ends on several volumes, overall very good set, uncommon and extremely scarce signed.   Ken Lopez Bookseller   154 - 100   2011 $750

Maillard, Annette Marie *When Other Lips.* London: Remington & Co., 1879, First edition; 3 volumes in 1, some edges little creased, contemporary blue binder's cloth, spine lettered in gilt, dulled and rubbed, poor copy.   Jarndyce Antiquarian Booksellers   CLXC - 197   2011   £85

Maine, Henry Sumner *Lectures on the Early History of Institutions.* London: John Murray, 1914, Seventh edition; original brown cloth, gilt, spine lettered faded, pages x, 412.   R. F. G. Hollett & Son Antiquarian Booksellers   175 - 902   2011   £30

Mais, S. P. B. *Diary of a Public Schoolmaster.* Lutterworth Press, 1940, First edition; original cloth, dust jacket trifle creased, pages 119, illustrations, scarce.   R. F. G. Hollett & Son Antiquarian Booksellers   175 - 903   2011   £30

Maitland, Julia Charlotte *Cat and Dog or Memoirs of Puss and the Captain.* London: Grant & Griffith, 1856, Third edition; frontispiece + 3 plates, 8 pages ads, original olive green morocco cloth, borders in blind, pictorially blocked and lettered in gilt, leading hinges with small neat repairs, bit dulled and slightly affected by damp, signed E. A. Turner in contemporary hand, good.   Jarndyce Antiquarian Booksellers   CLXC - 198   2011   £85

Malahat Review. Canada: 1967-1977, First edition; 38 issues in original wrappers, very good, no. 1-39.41 (lacks nos. 13 & 19).   I. D. Edrich   May 26 2011 - 97731   2011 $503

Malamud, Bernard 1914-1986   *Two Fables.* Banyan Press, 1978, First edition; 1/320 signed copies, without dust jacket, as issued, fine.   Gemini Fine Books & Arts, Ltd.   Art Reference & Illustrated Books: First Editions 2011 $135

Malanga, Gerard   *Autobiography of a Sex Thief.* New York: Lustrum Press, 1984, First edition; large 4to., pages 96, 44 black and white photos, original black and photo illustrated wrappers, spine creased and lightly sunned, near fine, from the library of Alessandro Bertolotti.   Simon Finch Rare Books   Zero - 536   2011   £650

Malcolm, Charles A.   *The Bank of Scotland 195-1945.* Edinburgh: R. & R. Clark, n.d., Tall 8vo., original buckram gilt over bevelled boards, leather spine label, pages viii, 322, with 38 plates ad 2 folding sheets in rear pocket, bookplate of Sir James French.   R. F. G. Hollett & Son Antiquarian Booksellers   175 - 904   2011   £40

Malcolmson, Anne   *Yankee Doodle's Cousins.* Boston: Houghton Mifflin, 1941, First edition; 4to., red cloth with black lettering on cover and spine, color pictorial dust jacket with some browning and wrinkle line that is mainly visible from underneath front cover of jacket, cloth has some minor darking along marginal areas of covers, internally good clean, 268 numbered pages, full page black and white drawings by Robert McCloskey.   Jo Ann Reisler, Ltd.   86 - 165   2011 $450

Malinowski, Bronislaw   *The Sexual Life of Savages in North Western Melanesia.* London: Routledge, 1939, Third edition; large 8vo., original cloth, gilt pages xix, 506, with 91 illustrations, 4 figures, few scattered spots.   R. F. G. Hollett & Son Antiquarian Booksellers   175 - 905   2011   £45

Mallet, David   *The Works of Mr. Mallet: Consisting of Plays and Poems.* London: A. Millar, 1743, Presumed first edition; 8vo. pages (vii) 275, full leather, probably 18th century, lacks f.e.p., some rubbing and scuffing to leather, slight splitting at lower hinge but reasonably sound, near very good with clean text.   Any Amount of Books   May 26 2011 - A4742   2011 $461

Mallinson, Allan   *A Call to Arms.* London: Bantam, 2002, First British edition; near fine, bottom corners lightly bumped, dust jacket fine, signed by author.   Bella Luna Books   May 29 2011 - t8505   2011 $82

Malone, Michael   *Dingley Falls.* New York: Harcourt Brace, 1980, First edition; signed by author, fine in near fine, price clipped dust jacket with small corner chip at lower front spine fold.   Ken Lopez Bookseller   154 - 101   2011 $100

Malone, Michael   *Handling Sin.* Boston: Little Brown, 1986, Small board edge ding, else fine in near fine mildly spine sunned, lightly edgeworn dust jacket.   Ken Lopez Bookseller   154 - 102   2011 $75

Malone, Michael   *Time's Witness.* Boston: Little Brown, 1989, First edition; signed by author, reading creases to spine, near fine in like dust jacket.   Ken Lopez Bookseller   154 - 103 2011 $75

Malory, Thomas   *Morte D'Arthur.* London: David Nutt, 1889, Limited edition; 3 volumes, quarto, uniformly bound by Roger De Coverley in half brown morocco over marbled boards, gilt lettering on spine, titlepage, others uncut, marbled endpapers, previous owner's armorial bookplate to front pastedown of each volume, corners lightly bumped and edges slightly rubbed, folding chart in volume 3 with closed tear, expertly repaired, very good.   Heritage Book Shop   Holiday 2010 - 77   2011 $1350

Malory, Thomas   *Le Morte D'Arthur.* London: published by David Nutt, 1889, One of 100 copies signed by publisher, there were 8 additional copies not for sale; 330 x 260mm. tipped in editor's note at back of first volume, 3 volumes, very appealing dark brown morocco, Jansenist, by Zaehnsdorf (signed), boards panelled with 11 thick and thin gilt and blind fillets, corners of central panel with outward extending gilt fleurons, raised bands, flanked by gilt and blind rules (and with gilt rule across the middle of each), two spine panels with gilt titling and four with arabesque centerpiece, very wide and very intricate gilt scrolling foliate and fleuron inner dentelles, marbled endpapers, top edge gilt, other edges untrimmed, one plate reproducing a page from Caxton, one folding facsimile, 3 folding tables; armorial bookplate of Francis Law Latham, tab at end of volume I with editor's note tipped on, explaining the various typographical alterations from Caxton; titlepages printed in red and black, first initial in red; handful of superficial marks to covers (one very small abrasion), trivial foxing or spotting in perhaps 10 leaves, one table creased, fine, lovely bindings lustrous and virtually unworn and text clean, fresh, bright and with vast margins.   Phillip J. Pirages   59 - 260   2011 $3500

Malory, Thomas *Le Morte D'Arthur.* London: Dent, 1893-1894, First edition, number 257 of the deluxe issue of 300 copies on Dutch handmade paper; 3 volumes, 4to., pages lxiv, 984, photogravure frontispieces, 16 full page and 4 double page wood engravings, 43 borders (some repeated), 288 chapter headings, initial letters and ornaments (many repeated) by Aubrey Beardsley, full page plates printed on French handmade etching paper and the two photogravure frontispieces printed on mounted India paper, in addition, publisher's device on titlepages and 22 initials in text are rubricated, untrimmed, previous owner's signature on front free endpaper, otherwise fine set. Second Life Books Inc. 174 - 26 2011 $10,000

Malory, Thomas *Le Morte D'Arthur.* New York: Dutton, 1909, Second edition, first single volume issue, one of 1000 copies of which 500 were issued for the U.S.; 4to., 624 pages, illustrations by Aubrey Beardsley, untrimmed, green cloth with decorations and lettering in gilt, lacks small piece from fore edge of titlepage, not affecting any text, owner's bookplate, very good. Second Life Books Inc. 174 - 27 2011 $1500

Malory, Thomas *The Noble and Joys Book Entitled Le Morte D'Arthur...* Chelsea: The Ashendene Press, 1913, Limited to 145 copies and the most deluxe format; folio, (6 blank, 4) xxii, 500, (2, 8 blank) pages, 29 woodcut illustrations, 2 full page, initials in red and blue by and after Graily Hewitt, original full dark brown calf designed by Douglas Cockerell and executed by W. H. Smith, binder, raised bands, gilt stamped spine title, neatly rebacked preserving original covers, fine. Jeff Weber Rare Books 163 - 106 2011 $8000

Malory, Thomas *The Romance of King Arthur and His Knights of the Round Table.* London: Macmillan and Co., 1917, Limited to 500 copies numbered and signed by artist; quarto, (2), xxiv, 509, (1 blank) pages, 16 mounted color plates on white textured paper with descriptive tissue guards, 70 drawings in black and white by Arthur Rackham, original full vellum over boards, pictorially stamped and lettered in gilt on front cover and spine, top edge gilt, others uncut, front cover with two inch scratch, otherwise near fine. Heritage Book Shop Holiday 2010 - 103 2011 $3500

Malory, Thomas *The Romance of King Arthur and His Knights of the Round Table.* London: Macmillan and Co., 1917, Limited to 500 copies, numbered and signed by artist; quarto, 16 mounted color plates by Arthur Rackham, original full vellum over boards. Heritage Book Shop Booth A12 51st NY International Antiquarian Book Fair April 8-10 2011 - 105 2011 $3500

Malory, Thomas *The Birth Life and Acts of King Arthur of His Noble Knights of the Round Table.* London: J. M. Dent & Sons, 1927, Third edition, limited to 1600 copies; large quarto, original black cloth over beveled boards, in rare dust jacket, illustrations by Aubrey Beardsley. Heritage Book Shop Booth A12 51st NY International Antiquarian Book Fair April 8-10 2011 - 10 2011 $3850

Malthus, Thomas Robert 1766-1834 *Additions to the Fourth and Former Editions of an Essay on the Principle of Population.* London: John Murray, 1817, First edition; 229 x 152mm., 2 p.l., 327, (1) pages, original blue paper boards, neatly rebacked in buff paper, original printed paper spine label, untrimmed edges, 19th century bookplate; spine label chipped and rubbed, significant loss of legibility, little soil and wear to original sides (as expected), but boards surprisingly well preserved and well restored binding absolutely tight, first few leaves and last three gatherings freckled with foxing, minor foxing elsewhere, few trivial spots, excellent internally, still rather fresh and not at all darkened or browned. Phillip J. Pirages 59 - 261 2011 $1100

Malthus, Thomas Robert 1766-1834 *An Essay on the Principle of Population or a View of Its Past and Present Effects on Human Happiness...* London: printed for J. Johnson by T. Bensley, 1803, Second edition; large 4to., pages viii, (3) contents, (1) errata, 610, contemporary full calf, rebacked at early date with original spine laid down, ownership signature of N. W. Ridley Colborne and Horace W. Baddle 1859, some light intermittent spotting and staining, but nice, clean copy with wide margins. Second Life Books Inc. 174 - 234 2011 $6000

Malthus, Thomas Robert 1766-1834 *An Essay on the Principle of Population.* London: printed for J. Johnson... by T. Bensley, 1803, Second edition; quarto, contemporary calf, rebacked to style, corners renewed. Heritage Book Shop Booth A12 51st NY International Antiquarian Book Fair April 8-10 2011 - 88 2011 $8500

Man Ray *Photographs 1920 Paris 1934.* Hartford: James Thrall Soby, 1934, First edition with rare first issue titlepage; folio, pages (vi) 1-24, (2) 2542, (2), 43-66, (2), 67-84, (2), 85-104, (1) (blank), (i) imprint, 104 black and white photos printed in gravure, original spiral bound color photo illustrated wrappers, some tabs to head and foot of spine detached, light wear to edges, crease to bottom corner of upper side, small piece missing from spiral binding, small stain at foot of spine affects first 11 leaves, corresponding small area of abrasion to titlepage, titlepage previous owner's inscription. Simon Finch Rare Books Zero - 538 2011 £6750

Mandeville, Bernard De *The Fable of the Bees.* London: J. Tonson, 1729, Sixth edition; 8vo., pages (x), 348, half green leather and marbled boards, lettered gilt on spine with 5 raised bands, very slight spotting to text, else near fine. Any Amount of Books May 26 2011 - A69898 2011 $470

Manfredi, Eustachio *Elementi Della Cronologia con Diverse Scritture Appartenenti al Calendario Romano. Opera Postuma.* Bologna: Lelio dalla Volpe, 1744, First edition; 4to., (14), 362, (2 imprimatur) pages, engraved device on titlepage, woodcut initials, woodcut diagrams, engraved headpiece, 19th century half calf by Hatton of Manchester, red morocco lettering piece, red speckled edges, lacking frontispiece, from the library of the Earls of Macclesfield at Shirburn Castle. Maggs Bros. Ltd. 1440 - 139 2011 £450

Manilii, M. *Astronimicon. Liber Secundus.* London: Grant Richards, 1912, First edition; 8vo., original blue thick card paper covered boards, pages xxxii, 123, 11 illustrations, Latin text, spine label missing with white remnants left, slight marking and slight scuffing at corners, otherwise sound, very good. Any Amount of Books May 26 2011 - A43329 2011 $403

Mankoff, Robert *The Complete Cartoons of the New Yorker.* New York: Black Dog & Leventhal, 2004, First edition; signed and dated by Seymour Hersch April 22, 2005, near fine, light shelf wear, in like dust jacket, with occasional scratch, includes two CD's with all 68, 647 cartoons ever published in New Yorker Magazine, includes Damyon Runyon Award Banquet program which is also signed by Mr. Hersch. Bella Luna Books May 26 2011 - t7235 2011 $550

Mankowitz, G. *The Rolling Stones: Out of Their Heads. Photos 1965-1967/1982.* Berlin: Schwarzkopf & Schawarzkopf, 2005, First edition; 2 volumes, illustrated laminated boards, boldly signed by Mankowitz, 2 good large Stones posters loosely inserted, fine in fine pictorial slipcase, in sound, very good, slightly used original packing box. Any Amount of Books May 29 2011 - A75311 2011 $408

Mann, Mary *The Memories of Ronald Love.* London: Methuen & Co., 1907, First edition; half title, 40 page catalog (Oct. 1906), little spotted, original red cloth, lettered in gilt, spine faded, very good. Jarndyce Antiquarian Booksellers CLXC - 206 2011 £35

Mann, Michael *The Rise and Decline of the Nation State.* Oxford/Cambridge: Basil Blackwell, 1990, First edition; 8vo., 233 pages, fine in fine dust jacket. Any Amount of Books May 29 2011 - A61383 2011 $255

Mann, Sally *What Remains.* Boston: Bulfinch, 2003, First edition; 4to., 129 pages, fine in fine dust jacket. By the Book, L. C. 26 - 41 2011 $185

Mann, Thomas *Death in Venice.* London: Ballantyne Press for Martin Secker, 1928, First English edition; 8vo., pages 272, little unobtrusive light foxing to beginning and end, publisher's green cloth with title in gilt to upper cover and spine, dust jacket, light fading to spine and upper edge, head of spine very lightly bumped, dust jacket skillfully repaired with short slit to upper field, very good. Simon Finch Rare Books Zero - 254 2011 £900

Mann, Thomas *Herr und Hund. (Man and His Dog).* Munchen: 1919, Limited to 120 copies signed by author; 8vo., marbled boards with leather spine label, 93 pages, fine, printed on Zanders handmade paper, frontispiece woodcut, woodcuts in text, full page inscription from Mann. Aleph-Bet Books, Inc. 95 - 341 2011 $4000

Mannex, P. & Co. *History & Directory of Furness and Cartmel.* Preston: printed by T. Snape, 1882, New edition; original blindstamped green cloth gilt, pages 375, xxix, fore edges of two leaves little chipped, scarce. R. F. G. Hollett & Son Antiquarian Booksellers 173 - 729 2011 £140

Mannex, P. & Co. *History Gazetteer and Directory of Cumberland, Comprising a General Survey of the County and a History of the Diocese of Carlisle...* printed for the authors by W. B. Johnson, 1847, Modern half levant morocco gilt, pages xvi, 630, (i). R. F. G. Hollett & Son Antiquarian Booksellers 173 - 733 2011 £180

Mannex, P. & Co. *History Gazetteer and Directory of Cumberland, Comprising a General Survey of the County and a History of the Diocese of Carlisle...* printed for authors by W. B. Johnson, 1847, Old cloth backed boards, pages xvi, 630, (i). R. F. G. Hollett & Son Antiquarian Booksellers 173 - 734 2011 £125

Mannex, P. & Co. *History Gazetteer and Directory of Cumberland, Comprising a General Survey of the County and a History of the Diocese of Carlisle...* Beckermet: Michael Moon, 1974, Pages 630, thick 8vo., original cloth, gilt, dust jacket. R. F. G. Hollett & Son Antiquarian Booksellers 173 - 735 2011 £75

Mannex, P. & Co. *History Topography and Directory of Westmorland and Lonsdale North of the Sands, in Lancashire; Together with a Descriptive and Geological View of the Whole of the Lake District.* London: Simpkin Marshall, 1849, First edition; old half calf with marbled boards, nicely rebacked to match, pages xvi, 465, (iii, 2 coach builder's ads), maps mentioned in the title were issued separately and rarely bound in. R. F. G. Hollett & Son Antiquarian Booksellers 173 - 730 2011 £120

Mannex, P. & Co. *History Topography and Directory of Westmorland and Lonsdale North of the Sands, in Lancashire; Together with a Descriptive and Geological View of the Whole of the Lake District.* Whitehaven: Michael Moon, 1978, Facsimile edition; thick 8vo., original cloth, gilt, dust jacket, pages 720, fine. R. F. G. Hollett & Son Antiquarian Booksellers   173 - 731   2011   £85

Mannex, P. & Co. *Topography and Directory of North and South Lonsdale Amounderness.* Preston: printed for the proprietors by J. Harkness, 1866, First edition; original cloth, gilt, extremities little worn and frayed, small paint splash on spine, pages viii, 613, (xxviii), joints cracking, endpapers rather spotted. R. F. G. Hollett & Son Antiquarian Booksellers   173 - 732 2011   £140

Manning, Anne *Deborah's Diary.* London: A. Hall, Virtue and Co., 1858, First edition; half title, initial 4 page catalog, 24 page catalog (Oct. 1858), original maroon embossed cloth, bevelled boards by Westleys, spine faded, slightly worn at head and tail, presentation inscription. Jarndyce Antiquarian Booksellers   CLXC - 208 2011   £45

Manning, Anne *Family Pictures.* London: Arthur Hall, Virtue & Co., 1861, First edition; half title, 24 page catalog (May 1860), original mauve cloth by Westleys, slightly rubbed and discolored, inner hinges cracking, working copy, c. 1900, belonging to publisher Arthur Hall with his notes and revisions. Jarndyce Antiquarian Booksellers   CLXC - 210 2011   £250

Manning, Anne *Family Pictures.* London: Arthur Hall, Virtue and Co., 1861, First edition; slightly later half brown calf, knocked at head of spine, stamps of Beechworth Athenaeum or Public Library. Jarndyce Antiquarian Booksellers   CLXC - 211 2011   £40

Manning, Anne *The Household of Sir Thomas Moore.* London: J. M. Dent, 1906, First edition thus; original green cloth gilt, spine and upper board decorated in gilt overall, page xxiii, 186, top edge gilt, untrimmed, 24 color plates by C. E. Brock. R. F. G. Hollett & Son Antiquarian Booksellers   General Catalogue Summer 2010 - 739 2011   £35

Manning, Anne *The Ladies of Beaver Hollow.* London: Richard Bentley, 1858, First edition; 2 volumes, titles in red and black, contemporary half brown calf, spines with raised gilt bands and red and green leather labels, good plus. Jarndyce Antiquarian Booksellers   CLXC - 212 2011   £120

Manning, Anne *The Maiden & Married Life.* London: Arthur Hall & Co., 1866, Fourth edition; vignette title, original green cloth bevelled boards, front board and spine blocked and lettered in gilt, spine slightly bubbled, all edges gilt. Jarndyce Antiquarian Booksellers   CLXC - 215 2011   £50

Manning, Anne *The Old Chelsea Bun-House.* London: Arthur Hall, Virtue and Co., 1855, First edition; engraved frontispiece, 5 pages ads, red brown endpapers, labels removed from pastedowns, original dark brown cloth by Edmonds & Remnants, bevelled boards, blocked in blind, spine lettered in gilt, very good. Jarndyce Antiquarian Booksellers   CLXC - 217 2011   £75

Manning, Anne *Some Account of Mrs. Clarinda Singleheart.* London: Arthur Hall, Virtue and Co., 1855, First edition; frontispiece, title in red and black, rebound in contemporary half green calf, slight rubbing, booklabel and signature of Courthope, very good. Jarndyce Antiquarian Booksellers   CLXC - 219 2011   £75

Manning, Anne *The Spanish Barber: a Tale.* London: James Nisbet & Co., 1869, First edition; half title, with two color transfers, frontispiece, original green cloth by Burn & Co., front board and spine blocked and lettered in black and gilt, slightly dulled, Morningside school prize label, good plus. Jarndyce Antiquarian Booksellers   CLXC - 229 2011   £40

Manning, Anne *Stories from the History of Italy, In a Connected Series...* London: Baldwin & Cradock, 1831, First edition; engraved frontispiece, vignette title, 4 pages ads, original dark blue green cloth, gilt spine, very slight rubbing, gift inscription, Noel 1841, very good. Jarndyce Antiquarian Booksellers   CLXC - 221 2011   £85

Manning, Anne *Tasso and Leonora. The Commentaries of Ser Pantaleone degli Gambacorti, Gentleman Usher to the August Madama Leonora d'Este.* London: Arthur Hall, Virtue & Co., 1856, First edition; frontispiece, title in red and black, 6 pages ads, 24 page catalog (April 1855), original drab cloth, slightly worn at head and tail of spine, one gathering slightly proud. Jarndyce Antiquarian Booksellers   CLXC - 222 2011   £40

Manning, Robert *England Conversion and Reformation Compared.* Antwerp: printed for R. F. and C. F. i. e. London, by Thomas Howlaatt for Thomas Meighan, 1725, First edition; pages lv, 330, modern half calf gilt with raised bands and spine label, small repair to gutter of title. R. F. G. Hollett & Son Antiquarian Booksellers   175 - 907 2011   £150

Manning, Samuel *Land of the Pharaohs: Egypt and Sinai.* London: RTS, n.d., 1880, First edition; quarto, pages 222, illustrations, original purple decorative cloth, all edges gilt. J. & S. L. Bonham Antiquarian Booksellers   Africa 4/20/2011 - 8768 2011   £35

Manningham, John *Diary of John Manningham of the Middle Temple and of Bradbourne, Kent, Barrister-at-law 1602-1603.* London: Printed by J. B. Nichols and Sons for the Camden Society, 1868, pages xx, 188, facsimile frontispiece, original quarter roan gilt, rubbed, edges scuffed and worn, front joint just cracking, pencilled notes. R. F. G. Hollett & Son Antiquarian Booksellers General Catalogue Summer 2010 - 376 2011 £35

Mannoury D'Ectot, La Marquise *Les Cousines de la Colonelle par Madame la Vicomtesse de Coeur-Brulant.* Lisbon: Antonio de Boa Vista, 1887, Fifth edition; 2 volumes in one, numbered continuously, 8vo., pages 440, plus 3 frontispieces and 6 engraved plates, 11 extra original watercolors in margins, top edge gilt, others roughly trimmed, internally fine, later red morocco, gilt lettering to spine, ex-libris G. Nordmann, his discreet bookplate to front free endpaper, unique copy with 11 extra watercolors added in margins, in superb condition. Simon Finch Rare Books Zero - 430 2011 £3300

Mansbridge, Albert *The Older Universities of England - Oxford & Cambridge.* London: Longmans, Green and Co., 1923, First edition; original cloth backed boards, paper spine label, upper board little stained, pages xxiv, 296. drawings by John Mansbridge. R. F. G. Hollett & Son Antiquarian Booksellers 175 - 909 2011 £45

Mansfield, Brian *Ring of Fire: a Tribute to Johnny Case with CD.* Nashville: Rutledge Hill Press, 2003, First edition; photos by Les Leverett, fine in fine dust jacket, signed by Johnny Cash on book plate laid in, includes CD. Bella Luna Books May 29 2011 - t8236 2011 $137

Mansfield, Edward D. *The Legal Rights, Liabilities and Duties of Women....* Salem: John P. Jewett, Cincinnati: William H. Moore, 1845, Octavo, 369 pages, original green blindstamped cloth, fine, scarce. Jeff Weber Rare Books 163 - 193 2011 $250

Mansfield, Katherine 1888-1923 *Bliss and Other Stories.* New York: Knopf, 1921, First American edition; 8vo., pages 279, green cloth with paper spine label, owner's bookplate, cover scuffed at edges, little soiled, rear hinge tender, otherwise very good. Second Life Books Inc. 174 - 235 2011 $65

Mansfield, Katherine 1888-1923 *The Garden Party and Other Stories.* London: Verona Press, 1939, really, 1947, First illustrated edition, one of 1200 numbered copies (the first 30 were signed); color lithographs by Marie Laurencin, tall octavo, original green pastepaper over boards with printed red paper spine label gilt, slight foxing on front fly, still easily fine, this copy nicely inscribed by Laurencin with elaborate filigree decoration surrounding inscription. Between the Covers 169 - BTC343218 2011 $3500

Mansfield, Katherine 1888-1923 *To Stanislaw Wyspianski.* London: privately printed for Bertram Rota, 1938, First edition in English, 63/100 copies; foxed, pages (8), foolscap 8vo., original stiff grey sewn wrappers, spine little faded, front cover lettered and with linear design, all printed in purple, fore edges untrimmed, very good. Blackwell Rare Books B166 - 180 2011 £150

Manson, James A. *Sir Edwin Landseer, R.A.* London: Walter Scott Publishing Co. Ltd., 1902, First edition; octavo, (i-vi), vii-xvi, 219, (220) pages, titlepage printed in blue and black, 21 engraved plates and photogravure frontispiece, full dark green levant Cosway-stye binding by Riviere & Sons for Sotheran & Co., stamp signed to front turn-in, spine decoratively tooled and lettered in gilt, after floral and leaf design, compartments ruled in gilt, front and back covers ruled and decoratively tooled in a gilt floral and leaf design, surrounding 10 oval-round miniature paintings under glass, 9 miniatures on front cover depict 8 hunting dogs around a stag, miniature on back cover is portrait of Landseer, extremities double ruled in gilt, with turn-ins ruled and decoratively tooled in gilt, green marbled endpapers, joints expertly and totally invisibly repaired, fine, housed in original burgundy roan slipcase,. David Brass Rare Books, Inc. May 26 2011 - 01191 2011 $23,500

Manstein, Cristof Hermann *Memoirs of Russia, Historical, Political and Military from the Year MDCCXXVII to MDCCXLIV.* Dublin: printed for James Williams at No. 5 in Skinner Row, 1770, viii, 424, (8) pages, index, 8vo., few pages little mottled, some worming not affecting text to outer top corner from pages 371 to end, full contemporary calf, raised bands, gilt label, some insect damage to several areas of surface leather and foot of top joint, bookplate of Robert Montgomery of Convoy. Jarndyce Antiquarian Booksellers CXCI - 568 2011 £520

Mant, Alicia Catherine *Caroline Lismore; or the Errors of Fashion.* Southampton: printed by T. Skelton, For Law & Whittaker, London, 1815, First edition; name cut from leading f.e.p., contemporary full marbled calf, spine little worn and slightly chipped at head and tail, good plus, internally clean. Jarndyce Antiquarian Booksellers CLXC - 223 2011 £120

Mant, Alicia Catherine *Montague Newburgh; or the Mother and Son.* London: Law & Whittaker, 1817, First edition; 2 volumes, half titles, engraved frontispieces, some light foxing and browning to prelims, contemporary full tree calf, excellently rebacked, each volume signed "Miss S. J. Arnold July 4th 1822", good plus, scarce. Jarndyce Antiquarian Booksellers CLXC - 224 2011 £380

Mantel, Mickey *All My Octobers: My Memories of 12 World Series When the Yankees Ruled Baseball.* New York: Harper Collins, 1994, First edition; fine in fine dust jacket. Bella Luna Books May 29 2011 - t8750 2011 $137

Manutius, Aldus *De Quaesitis per Epistolam Libri III.* Venice: Aldus Manutius, 1576, First edition; 3 parts, 8vo., (8), 125, (3 (blank); 106, (6 (blank); 103 pages, 17th century German blindstamped pigskin over pasteboard, red edges, very nice, titlepage inscribed "Paulus Johanne?? Patavii MDLXXVII", from the library of the Earls of Macclesfield at Shirburn Castle. Maggs Bros. Ltd. 1440 - 140 2011 £450

Manvell, Roger *Ellen Terry.* London: Heinemann, 1968, First edition; original cloth, gilt, dust jacket little worn, pages x, 390, with 41 illustrations, presentation copy from Manvell for Molly Thomas (curator of Ellen Terry Museum in Smallhythe, Kent). R. F. G. Hollett & Son Antiquarian Booksellers 175 - 911 2011 £30

Marashak, S. *Dom Kotoryi Postroil Dzek (code number 36). (The House that Jack Built).* Petersburg: GIZ, 1923, First edition thus; 8vo., color pictorial covers with perfect binding, slight toning to edges, rather nice copy, 30 numbered pages, each with color illustrations. Jo Ann Reisler, Ltd. 86 - 210 2011 $1800

Marcel, Guillaume *Chronological Tables of Europe from the Nativity of Our Saviour to the Year 1703.* London: printed for B. Barker and C. King, 1707, VIth impression; oblong 12mo., at foot of title is ad by W. Rogers, first 5 leaves are printed on both recto and verso, 2 folding leaves but affixed to inner covers, engraved throughout, (41) leaves, 2 folding leaves included in total, contemporary calf, gilt, hinges cracked, spine rubbed. Anthony W. Laywood May 26 2011 - 19364 2011 $243

Marcellinus, Ammianus *Roman Historie.* London: Adam Islip, 1609, Quarto, (4), 432, (75) (1 blank) pages, full brown speckled calf, ruled in blind, rebacked to stype preserving original brown morocco spine label, lettered in gilt, edges lightly rubbed, light dampstaining throughout, very good. Heritage Book Shop Holiday 2010 - 78 2011 $4000

Marcet, Jane Haldimand *Conversations on Political Economy; in Which the Elements of that Science are Familiarly Explained.* London: Longman, Hurst, Rees, Orme, & Brown, 1827, Sixth edition; 12mo., expertly & sympathetically rebound in half olive green cloth, marbled boards, black leather label, signed F. R. Caffrey in contemporary hand on title, very good. Jarndyce Antiquarian Booksellers CLXC - 225 2011 £85

Marchant, Bessie *Molly Angel's Adventures: a Story of Belgium Under German Occupation.* Blackie & Son, 1915, First edition; half title, color frontispiece and 4 black and white plates by P. B. Hickling, odd spot, original green cloth, pictorially blocked in black and white, spine faded, little dulled, owner's inscription Xmas 1915, good plus copy. Jarndyce Antiquarian Booksellers CLXC - 226 2011 £40

Marchant, Bessie *A V. A. D. in Salonika: a Tale of a Girls Work in the Great War.* Blackie & Son, 1917, First edition; half title, color frontispiece, 4 black and white plates by John E. Sutcliffe, original beige glazed cloth, pictorially blocked in black, white and orange, lettered in black, nice. Jarndyce Antiquarian Booksellers CLXC - 227 2011 £48

Marchbank, Agnes, Pseud. *Ruth Farmer: a Story.* London: Jarrold & Sons, 1896, First edition; half title, 17 pages ads, original dark green cloth, front board lettered in blind, spine lettered in gilt, slight rubbing to spine, very good. Jarndyce Antiquarian Booksellers CLXC - 228 2011 £35

Marchesseau, Daniel *The Intimate World of Alexander Calder.* Paris/New York: Solange Thierry/Abrams, 1989, First edition in English, first printing; 4to., 399 pages, 680 illustrations, fine in fine dust jacket. By the Book, L. C. 26 - 22 2011 $375

Marchmont, Earl *A Selection from the Papers of the Earls of Marchmont, in the Possession of the Right Honble. Sir George Henry Rose, Illustrative of Events from 1685 to 1750.* London: John Murray, 1831, First edition; 3 volumes, soundly rebound in red cloth lettered gilt on spine, pages cxxxiv, 292; viii, 479; viii, 415, ex-British Foreign Office library with few library markings, else very good. Any Amount of Books May 29 2011 - A73932 2011 $213

Marcos, Subcomandante *The Story of Colors.* El Paso: Cinco Puntos Press, 1999, First edition thus; fine in fine dust jacket, this copy has the erratum slip laid in withdrawing thanks to NEA. Bella Luna Books May 29 2011 - t4808 2011 $82

Mardersteig, Hans *The Officina Bodoni.* Editions Officinae Bodoni (at Verona) At the Sign of the Pegasus, Paris, New York, 1929, 191/500 copies printed on Lafuma Rag paper using Arrighi Bodoni and Pastonchi types, with several specimens tipped in of press' work printed on handmade paper and reproductions of number of facsimiles; also with series of 12 full page woodcuts by Frans Masereel, pages (iv) (blanks), 82, (2) (blanks), large 4to., original cream buckram, backstrip gilt lettered, gilt blocked press device on front cover, endpapers lightly foxed, untrimmed, dust jacket, very good, Vivian Ridler's copy with his booklabel. Blackwell Rare Books B166 - 268 2011 £750

Margam Abbey, an Historical Romance of the Fourteenth Century. London: John Green, 1837, Full dark green grained calf, attractively blocked in gilt, rubbed, chip to head and tail of spine, marginal tear to pages 117-1119 without loss to text, inscription "to Miss Steel, March 18th 1849", all edges gilt. Jarndyce Antiquarian Booksellers CXCI - 46 2011 £250

Margary, Ivan D. *Roman Roads in Britain.* Phoenix House, 1955, First edition; 2 volumes, small 4to., original cloth, gilt, dust jackets (rather worn and nicked in places, price clipped), pages 255; 288; with 2 frontispieces, 32 pages of plates and 17 maps, slight foxing to second half title, otherwise very good. R. F. G. Hollett & Son Antiquarian Booksellers General Catalogue Summer 2010 - 1472 2011 £120

Margary, Ivan D. *Roman Roads in the South-East Midlands by the Viatores.* London: Gollancz, 1964, First edition; thick 8vo., original cloth, gilt, dust jacket spine rather darkened, pages 526, with 145 pages of maps, 19 pages of section diagrams and 17 photos. R. F. G. Hollett & Son Antiquarian Booksellers General Catalogue Summer 2010 - 1473 2011 £50

Mariana *Miss Flora McFilmsey and the Little Red Schoolhouse.* New York: Lothrop Lee Shepard, 1957, First edition; 8vo., pictorial cloth, fine in dust jacket, illustrations in color, quite scarce. Aleph-Bet Books, Inc. 95 - 342 2011 $200

Marine Biology. International Journal on Life in Oceans and Coastal Waters. Berlin: Springer-Verlag, 1967-1977, Volumes 1-40 and 41 (nos. 1 and 2 only), together 162 issues numerous text figures and photos, 4to., paperbound, very good to near fine, occasional light soiling or bump, paper to spine torn on several mostly older issues, upper corner of rear cover missing on 1 issue, handstamp to some front covers. Raymond M. Sutton, Jr. May 26 2011 - 47276 2011 $1300

Marine Biological Association of the United Kingdom *Journal of...* Plymouth/Cambridge: Marine Biological Association of the United Kingdom/Cambridge University Press, 1887-2006, First editions and reprint; Old Series Volumes 1 and 2 (of 2) and New Series Volumes 1-84 (complete), volume 85 (Nos. 1, 2, 3, 6) and Volume 86 (nos.1-3) in 112; very good, numerous plates, text figures and some photos, occasional minor soiling, few short tears along folds and tear along fold of a panel in 1, few tears repaired with tape, tall 8vo., some 4to., volumes 1/2, 1-3, 5 an 12-21 contemporary hardbound, volumes, 4, 6-11 and 22-48 recent hardbound, original wrappers bound into volumes 6-11 & 22-48, volumes 49-68 in original printed wrappers, volumes 69-86 paperbound (modest wear to extremities in 6 oldest volumes, spine faded to brown in 3 older volumes and with splitting to cover along edges of spine in 2, some endpapers browned, handstamp to front wrappers and or front endpapers contents and index pages are photocopies in volumes 6 and 10, plates are photocopies in volume 7, occasional tear to soiling to original wrappers or text pages, some pencil notations to text pages, in early issues, occasional bump, short tear or wrinkling to paper on spine, light soiling or pages tanned, recent issues mostly fine; with W(alter) Garstang's signature and handstamp to 3 volumes, A(lister) C(lavering) Hardy's signature to 24 volumes, Lesley D. Wright-Smith's copy with his name on title, numerous dates and some notes on page margins. Raymond M. Sutton, Jr. May 26 2011 - 48790 2011 $2400

Mark, Louis *Books and Bookmen.* Harrison Books, 1955-1980, V.1/1-V.25/9 (no. 297), Oct. 1955-June 1980, lacking only 15 issues for complete run, over 240 issues, all in very good condition. I. D. Edrich May 26 2011 - 99031 2011 $2180

Markham, Clements Robert 1830-1916 *The Voyages of Sir James Lancaster, Kt. to the East Indies with Abstracts of Journals of Voyages to the East Indies During the Seventeenth Century, Preserved in the India Office, and the Voyages of Captain John Knight (1606) to seek the North West Passagev.* London: Hakluyt Society, 1877, First edition; 8vo., xxii, 314 pages, original blue cloth stamped in blind, gilt vignette of ship on front board, spine ruled in blind, gilt titles, yellow endpapers, spine sunned, half inch square chip to head of spine, small insitutional bookplate to front pastedown, owner's nautical bookplate opposite rear hinge split but firm, leaves unopened (uncut), thus overall very good. Kaaterskill Books 12 - 129 2011 $500

Marks, Harrison *Kamera.* London: Kamera Publications, 1957, First edition; 9 issues, 18 x 12 cm., color illustrated wrappers, about 300 pages in all, color and black and white photos, bright, clean condition, very good+. Any Amount of Books May 26 2011 - A46359 2011 $587

Marlantes, Karl *Matterhorn.* Berkeley/New York: El Leon Literary Arts/Atlantic Monthly, 2010, First El Leon/Atlantic Monthly edition; signed by author, fine in fine dust jacket. Ken Lopez Bookseller 154 - 233 2011 $75

Marlborough, John, 1st Duke of *The Letters and Dispatches of John Churchill, First Duke of Marlborough from 1702-1712.* London: John Murray, 1845, First edition; 5 volumes, soundly rebound in red cloth lettered gilt at spine, 3583 pages in all, frontispiece to volume 1, publisher's catalog at rear of volume 4, ex-Foreign and Commonwealth Office library with their label and stamps (lightly applied), very good. Any Amount of Books May 26 2011 - A61243 2011 $419

Marlborough, Sarah Jennings Churchill, Duchess of 1660-1744 *An Account of the conduct of the Dowager Duchess of Marlborough from Her First Coming to Court, to the Year 1710. In a Letter from Herself to My Lord.* London: printed by James Bettenham for George Hawkins, 1742, Octavo, 316 pages, original full calf, rebacked, very good. Jeff Weber Rare Books 163 - 176 2011 $200

Marlitt, E., Pseud. *The Old Maid's Secret.* London: Chapman & Hall, 1873, Yellowback, original printed boards, hinges slightly worn, little loose, good plus. Jarndyce Antiquarian Booksellers CLXC - 230 2011 £45

Marlitt, E., Pseud. *The Owl's Nest.* Philadelphia: J. B. Lippincott, 1889, Blank with ad on verso preceding title, 10 page catalog, original dark olive decorated cloth, very good. Jarndyce Antiquarian Booksellers CLXC - 231 2011 £35

Marlow, Louis *Forth, Beast.* London: Faber and Faber, 1946, First edition; 8vo., pages 200, endpapers slightly foxed, otherwise very good+ in decent about very good dust jacket very slightly soiled and very slightly chipped at head of spine and corners with slight even age toning. Any Amount of Books   May 29 2011 - A66207   2011 $255

Marolles, Michel De *Tableaux Du temple des Muses Representant les Vertus, et les Vices sur les Plus Illustres Fables De l'Antiquite.* Paris: Nicolas Langlois, 1655, First edition; folio, (20), 477, (9) pages, 58 engraved plates and portrait, engraved folding titlepage, woodcut head and tailpieces, initials woodcut, contemporary calf, rubbed, spine gilt in compartments, crackled, waterstained in corners throughout half of book, bookplate of Nicolas Joseph Foucault, from the library of the Earls of Macclesfield at Shirburn Castle.   Maggs Bros. Ltd.   1440 - 141   2011   £900

Marquand, John P. *No Hero.* Boston: Little Brown and Co., 1935, First edition; yellow cloth shows light evidence of foxing, endpapers lightly foxed, minor foxing to fore-edge, else near fine in original yellow cloth dust jacket, light professional restoration to spine ends, corners and extremities, handsome copy.   Buckingham Books   May 26 2011 - 30201   2011 $2500

Marr, James *The City and County of El Paso, Texas, Containing Useful and Reliable Information Concerning the Future Great Metropolis of the Southwest, Its Resources and Advantages for the Agriculturist, Artisan and Capitalist.* El Paso: 1886, 84 pages, folding map, original printed wrappers, some wear and osoil, light vertical crease, small corner chip fro front wrapper, split to map, overall very good, laid in folding case, rare.   Dumont Maps & Books of the West   113 - 18   2011 $950

The Marriage of Cock Robin and Jenny Wren. New York: McLoughlin Bros. n.d. circa, 1870, Small 8vo., 8 leaves + 1 page ad on lower wrapper, pictorial paper wrappers, 7 half page and 1 full page chromolithographs, pencilled signature at top margin of cover, chipped corner, spots along fore edge of cover, internally in very good state.   Hobbyhorse Books   56 - 102   2011 $120

Marriage of Cock Robin and Jenny Wren. New York: T. Nelson and Sons, n.d. circa, 1910, Folio, cloth, pictorial paste-on, slight edge rubbing and finger soil, very good+, printed in blue on coated paper, 12 fine color plates by Scott Rankin, each page of text in large font, also has small color illustration.   Aleph-Bet Books, Inc.   95 - 157   2011 $300

Marriage, Margaret *The Sculptures of Chartres Cathedral.* Cambridge: University Press, 1909, Original cloth, gilt, pages xv, 270, with 120 plates, spine little faded.   R. F. G. Hollett & Son Antiquarian Booksellers   177 - 563   2011   £35

Marriott, Ernest *Jack B. Years, His Pictorial & Dramatic Art.* London: Elkin Mathews, 1911, First edition; 24 pages + 5 pages ads, stiff wrappers, some fading at edges.   C. P. Hyland   May 26 2011 - 259/528   2011 $507

Marriott, John *Poems by John Marriott. To which is Prefixed a Short Account of the Author, Including Extracts from Some of His Letters.* New Bedford: Re-printed by A. Shearman, Jun., 1805, Small 4to., xliii, 141, (1 blanks, 2 ads) pages; pages ii-iv margin chipped, original full dark tree calf, rebacked, corners worn, very good.   Jeff Weber Rare Books   163 - 49   2011 $75

Marrot, H. V. *William Bulmer: Thomas Bensley.* London: The Fleuron, 1930, First edition, one of 300 copies, this unnumbered, printed on handmade paper; prelims and final few leaves lightly foxed, pages (v) (blanks), xi, 84, 4to., original dark green cloth, printer Vivian Ridler's copy with his booklabel and signature.   Blackwell Rare Books   B166 - 246   2011   £115

Marryat, Frank *Mountains and Molehills, or Recollections of a Burnt Journal.* New York: Harper & Brothers, 1855, First American edition; x, (11)-393 pages, frontispiece, plus 25 wood engravings, publisher's blindstamped, royal blue cloth, gilt lettered spine, light and minimal scattered foxing, bit more so to first 10 leaves, early owner's name and date on endpaper (Jos. A. Linton/Aug. 25th 1870), slight darkening to spine, but fine, bright, tight copy.   Argonaut Book Shop   Recent Acquisitions Summer 2010 - 121   2011 $500

Marryat, Frank *Mountains and Molehills or Recollections of a Burnt Journal.* London: Longman, Brown, Green and Longmans, 1855, First edition; octavo, x, (2, list of plates), (1)-443, (1, blank, (24, ads) pages, 8 color plates including frontispiece and 18 black and white woodcuts all drawn by author, 24 pages of publisher's ads, original full pink morocco grain cloth, rebacked preserving original spine, boards ruled in blind, spine lettered in gilt, green coated endpapers, spine slightly sunned, cloth bit soiled, inner hinges cracked but firm, previous owner's small bookplate, very good.   Heritage Book Shop   Holiday 2010 - 79   2011 $1100

Marschak, S. *Dom Kotoryi Postroil Dzhek. (The House that Jack Built).* Leningrad: Giz, 1925, 8vo., pictorial wrappers, fine, color illustrations by Vladimir Konaschevich.   Aleph-Bet Books, Inc.   95 - 498   2011 $1200

Marsh-Caldwell, Anne *Emilia Wyndham.* Paris: Ch. Rinwald, 1851, First edition; 2 volumes, (281 page, 281 pages), 12mo., contemporary quarter deep brown calf beautiful gilt decorated spines with scroll design, all edges marbled, fine and attractive set, from the library of King Ernest of Hanover with his royal ex-libris stamped on verso of titlepages, very fine in lovely binding, uncommon.   Paulette Rose Fine and Rare Books   32 - 120   2011 $750

Marsh, Anne *Adelaide Lindsay.* London: G. Routledge & Co., 1851, Contemporary half green calf maroon leather label, spine darkened, little rubbed, from the Headfort library, signed "Bective 1854", good, sound copy.   Jarndyce Antiquarian Booksellers   CLXC - 232 2011   £60

Marsh, Anne *Adelaide Lindsay.* London: George Routledge & Co., 1852, Contemporary half black roan, slight rubbing, signed "Mary Chaytor" on title, good plus.   Jarndyce Antiquarian Booksellers   CLXC - 233 2011   £50

Marsh, Anne *Castle Avon.* London: Colburn & Co., 1852, First edition; 3 volumes, half title volume I, later blue library buckram, boards slightly damp marked, internally clean, good, sound.   Jarndyce Antiquarian Booksellers   CLXC - 234 2011   £125

Marsh, Anne *Emilia Wyndham.* London: Henry Colburn, 1848, Ad preceding title, uncut in original purple cloth, blocked in blind, spine lettered in gilt, spine faded, slightly rubbed.   Jarndyce Antiquarian Booksellers   CLXC - 236 2011   £45

Marsh, Anne *Father Darcy.* London: Chapman and Hall, 1846, First edition; 2 volumes, half titles, contemporary half dark green calf, spines gilt in compartments, maroon leather labels, slight rubbing, each volume signed by E. A. Wingfield, Digby with associated inscriptions, John Fowles booklabel, good plus.   Jarndyce Antiquarian Booksellers   CLXC - 238 2011   £180

Marsh, Anne *Mount Sorel; or the Heiress of the De Veres.* London: Charles H. Clarke, circa, 1863, Half title, contemporary half green calf, maroon leather label.   Jarndyce Antiquarian Booksellers   CLXC - 239 2011   £50

Marsh, Anne *Ravencliffe.* Leipzig: Bernhard Tauchnitz, 1851, (1892). Copyright edition; 2 volumes, contemporary dark green binder's cloth, maroon leather labels, bound without half titles.   Jarndyce Antiquarian Booksellers   CLXC - 240 2011   £38

Marsh, Anne *The Song of Roland as Chanted Before the Battle of Hastings by the Minstrel Taillefer.* London: Hurst and Blackett, 1854, First edition; frontispiece, rubricated text, original dark blue cloth, borders blocked in blind, lettered in gilt, at some time rebacked retaining most of original spine strip, leading inner hinge strengthened, following endpapers replaced, presentation inscription to Dean of Lichfield from daughters of the authoress, Elaine and Georgina Marsh-Caldwell - Linley Wood Sept 22nd 1879.   Jarndyce Antiquarian Booksellers   CLXC - 241 2011   £110

Marsh, Anne *Tales of the French Revolution.* London: Simms & M'Intyre, 1849, First edition; contemporary half black roan, signed "Mr. R. C. Chaytor", good plus.   Jarndyce Antiquarian Booksellers   CLXC - 242 2011   £85

Marsh, Anne *Tales of the Woods and Fields.* London: Saunders and Otley, 1836, First edition; 3 volumes, half black sheep, slight rubbing, each volume signed "Jane Elizabeth Gibson", very good.   Jarndyce Antiquarian Booksellers   CLXC - 243 2011   £225

Marsh, Anne *Tales of the Woods and Fields.* Belfast: Simms & M'Intyre, 1846, Half title, dedication leaf preceding title, contemporary half green calf, maroon leather label, tail of spine slightly worn, signed "Bective 1856", good sound copy.   Jarndyce Antiquarian Booksellers   CLXC - 244 2011   £45

Marsh, Anne *Two Old Men's Tales. the Deformed and The Admiral's Daughter.* London: Richard Bentley, 1844, Contemporary half olive green morocco by Squires of Woolwich, gilt spine, spine faded to brown, little rubbed at head, bookplate of Colonel William Kemmis of Ballinacor, nice copy.   Jarndyce Antiquarian Booksellers   CLXC - 245 2011   £58

Marsh, Anne *Two Old Men's Tales... Simms & M'Intyre. (with) A Country Vicarage and Love and Duty, or Tales of the Woods and Fields.* London: Darton & Co., 1853-1859, 2 volumes in 1, contemporary half maroon morocco, slightly worn, good, sound copy.   Jarndyce Antiquarian Booksellers   CLXC - 246 2011   £50

Marsh, Anne *The Wilmingtons.* London: Henry Colburn, 1852, Remainder issue of original sheets with cancel titles; 3 volumes in 1, ad on verso of final leaf volume III, original red remainder cloth, repairs to leading hinges and head and tail of spine, slightly darkened, good plus.   Jarndyce Antiquarian Booksellers   CLXC - 247 2011   £150

Marsh, Anne *The Wilmingtons.* London: Thomas Hodgson, 1854, Contemporary half black roan, slight rubbing, signed "Mary Chaytor", good plus.   Jarndyce Antiquarian Booksellers   CLXC - 248 2011   £45

Marsh, George P. *Lectures on the English Language.* New York: Charles Scribner, 1860, First edition; 8vo., 8, 697 pages, original cloth, corners bumped.   M & S Rare Books, Inc.   90 - 231 2011 $225

Marsh, James B. *Four Years in the Rockies or the Adventures of Isaac P. Rose of Shehango Township, Lawrence County...* New Castle: W. B. Thomas, 1884, First edition; 12mo., rebound in full tan morocco with raised bands on spine, with author and title in gilt on red and green morocco labels on spine, 262 pages, frontispiece, very good, cloth clamshell box with leather label stamped in gilt on spine.   Buckingham Books   May 26 2011 - ION 2011 $1750

Marshak, S. *Priklyucheniya Ctola I Ctula. (The Adventures of the Table and Chair).* Leningrad and Moscow: Rainbow, 1928, Second printing of the title but first printing with these illustrations; 8vo., full color pictorial paper covers with some handling and faint staining to rear cover, 10 pages within, counting inside covers. Jo Ann Reisler, Ltd. 86 - 215 2011 $600

Marshak, S. *Bagazh. (Baggage or Luggage).* Leningrad: Moscow: OGIZ, 1934, Stated 7th edition; 12mo., color pictorial paper covers, rather nice, illustrations by V. Lebedev. Jo Ann Reisler, Ltd. 86 - 222 2011 $450

Marshak, S. *Petrushka Inostranets. (Punch and Judy, Puppet Show...).* Leningrad: Detgiz, 1935, Stated 5th edition; 4to., color pictorial paper covers with minor handling, 10 pages within (counting inside covers), illustrations by V. Lebdev. Jo Ann Reisler, Ltd. 86 - 223 2011 $450

Marshall, Alfred *Official Papers.* For the Royal Economic Society by Macmillan, 1926, First edition; ownership signature, pages (viii), 428, 8vo., original green buckram, slightly sunned, good. Blackwell Rare Books B166 - 33 2011 £150

Marshall, Alfred *Principles of Economics.* London: Macmillan and Co., 1890, Scarce first edition; octavo, xxviii, 754, (2, publisher's catalog), original dark green diaper grain cloth with covers ruled in blind and spine ruled and lettered in gilt, dark green coated endpapers, previous owner's signature, corners lightly bumped, some minor repairs to top and bottom of spine, light foxing to half title, otherwise very good, almost always found rebound. Heritage Book Shop Holiday 2010 - 80 2011 $7500

Marshall, Beatrice *Emma Marshall; a Biographical Sketch.* London: Seeley & Co., 1900, First edition; frontispiece, 12 plates, 2 pages ads, uncut in original blue cloth, lettered in gilt, slight rubbing, booklabel of Charles Bidwell, Ely, very good. Jarndyce Antiquarian Booksellers CLXC - 263 2011 £35

Marshall, C. R. *An Introduction to the Theory and Use of the Microscope.* London: George Routledge & Sons, 1928, First edition; original printed boards, spine rubbed, pages viii, 90, (ii), 3 plates and 29 text figures, flyleaves browned. R. F. G. Hollett & Son Antiquarian Booksellers General Catalogue Summer 2010 - 1123 2011 £35

Marshall, Edison *The Doctor of Lonesome River.* New York: Cosmpolitan Book Corp., 1931, First edition; pages (viii), 294, contemporary ownership signature on front pastedown, very good in very good, slightly nicked and dusty dust jacket with brilliant design by F. E. Warren. Peter Ellis May 26 2011 - ALASKANO011315 2011 $65

Marshall, Emma *In the Service of Rachel Lady Russell.* London: Seeley & Co., 1893, First edition; frontispiece and 7 plates, final ad leaf, some light foxing, original maroon cloth, blocked and lettered in gilt, some slight rubbing, good plus. Jarndyce Antiquarian Booksellers CLXC - 252 2011 £45

Marshall, Emma *Lettice Lawson's Legacy and Other Stories.* London: James Nisbet, 1894, First edition; half title, frontispiece and plates, 2 pages ads, 16 page catalog, original green cloth, blocked in gilt, pink and black, very good. Jarndyce Antiquarian Booksellers CLXC - 255 2011 £35

Marshall, Emma *Rose Deane; or Christmas Roses.* Bristol: J. W. Arrowsmith, London: Simpkin, Marshall, Hamilton, Kent & Co., 1899, First edition; half title, frontispiece, original turquoise cloth, front board blocked in brown, lettered in gilt, all edges gilt, very good. Jarndyce Antiquarian Booksellers CLXC - 259 2011 £35

Marshall, Frances *Charlotte Deans (1768-1859).* Kendal: Titus Wilson, 1984, Facsimile edition; original printed wrappers, pages xliv, 111, with 2 folding maps, 3 pages of illustrations, fine. R. F. G. Hollett & Son Antiquarian Booksellers 175 - 913 2011 £30

Marshall, Humphry *Arbustrum Americanum: the American Grove, or an Alphabetical Catalogue of Forest Trees and Shrubs, Natives of the American United States...* Philadelphia: Joseph Cruikshank, 1785, First edition; very good, 8vo., pages xx, 174, modern quarter calf over marbled boards with red morocco label on spine, endpapers renewed, 2 margins to title and last page reinforced, partial browning to few pages, handstamp to a page. Raymond M. Sutton, Jr. May 26 2011 - 55853 2011 $3000

Marshall, J. D. *Furness and the Industrial Revolution. An Economic History of Furness (1711-1900) and the Town of Barrow (1757-1897)...* Barrow-in-Furness: Library and Museum Committee, 1958, First edition; original cloth, gilt, pages xxii, 438, numerous illustrations and maps. R. F. G. Hollett & Son Antiquarian Booksellers 173 - 748 2011 £60

Marshall, J. D. *The Industrial Archaeology of the Lake Counties.* David & Charles, 1969, First edition; original cloth, gilt, dust jacket, pages 287, 27 plates, 25 text illustrations. R. F. G. Hollett & Son Antiquarian Booksellers 173 - 752 2011 £50

Marshall, J. D. *The Industrial Archaeology of the Lake Counties.* Beckermet: Michael Moon, 1977, Original cloth gilt, dust jacket, pages 287, with 27 plates and 25 text illustrations. R. F. G. Hollett & Son Antiquarian Booksellers 173 - 754 2011 £40

Marshall, J. D. *The Lake Counties from 1830 to Mid-Twentieth Century.* Manchester University Press, 1981, First edition; original cloth, gilt, dust jacket, pages xii, 308, with 30 illustrations.   R. F. G. Hollett & Son Antiquarian Booksellers   173 - 757   2011   £40

Marshall, J. D. *The Lake District At Work Past and Present.* David & Charles, 1971, First edition; large 8vo., original cloth, gilt, dust jacket, pages 112, illustrations, color frontispiece.   R. F. G. Hollett & Son Antiquarian Booksellers   173 - 755   2011   £45

Marston, John *The Metamorphosis of Pigmalions Image.* Waltham St. Lawrence: Golden Cockerel Press, 1926, One of 325 copies; 203 x 133mm., 2 p.l., 3-17, (10 pages, (1) leaf (colophon), original buckram backed batik boards, untrimmed edges, printer's device, decorative half borders and two wood engraved plates in three colors by Rene Ben Sussan, spine slightly darkened, otherwise very fine.   Phillip J. Pirages   59 - 222   2011 $100

Marteau, Georges *Miniatures Persanes... Exposees au Musee des Arts Deoratifs Juin-Octobre 1912.* Paris: Bibliotheque d'Art et d'Archeologie, 1913, One of 150 numbered copies (this being copy #100); 410 x 310mm., 2 volumes, unbound sheets as issued in original black cloth covered board portfolios, covers with elaborate blind-stamped design, spines with gilt titling, all three sets of original cloth ties, with 195 mounted reproductions of miniatures and calligraphy from Islamic manuscripts, 21 of these in color, each plate accompanied by descriptive text in French, one portfolio joint starting at head, two inch split to cloth at tail of one spine, boards little chafed and rubbed, half titles with faint soiling, occasional trivial marginal stains or thumbing, couple of fore edges with thin strip of light soil, otherwise fine set, plates very clean and bright, fragile portfolios well preserved.   Phillip J. Pirages   59 - 238   2011 $15,000

Marteau, Robert *Le Ateliers De Chagall.* Paris: Fernand Mourlot, 1976, One of 250 copies for sale (additional 20 'hors commerce' copies produced for artist and collaborators; with color lithograph frontispiece signed and numbered by Marc Chagall (#192), 455 x 355 mm., 116, (6) pages, (2) leaves (blank), unbound as issued in heavy paper portfolio inside gray linen clamshell box with vertical gilt titling on spine, 2 original woodcuts and 7 original lithographs, 3 of these in color, frontispiece signed by author with 40 lithographic reproductions after Chagall, faint show through on verso of plates (never offensive), otherwise very fine with no signs of use.   Phillip J. Pirages   59 - 162   2011 $16,000

Martel, Yann *Life of Pi.* Toronto: Knopf Canada, 2001, True first edition; signed by author, fine in fine dust jacket.   Ken Lopez Bookseller   154 - 104   2011 $1000

Martin, Benjamin *Lingua Britannica Reformata; or a New Universal English Dictionary.* London: printed for C. Hitch & L. Hawes, J. Hodges, &c., 1754, Second edition; with inserted cancel B1 after preface, 6 plates, plate 6 partially defective with large tear to head of page, repaired but with slight loss to image, made good in mss., expertly rebound in half speckled calf, raised bands, gilt compartments, brown morocco label.   Jarndyce Antiquarian Booksellers   CXCI - 157   2011   £380

Martin, Bernardin *Voyages Faits en Divers Temps en Espagne, en Portugal, En Allemagne, En France, En Ailleurs.* Amsterdam: George Gallet, 1700, Second edition; 3 3/4 x 6 inches, contemporary calf, heavily gilt decorated spine, gilt lettered red morocco spine label, vi, 295 pages, engraved frontispiece, 12 engraved plates, slight split to top rear joint, covers tight, near fine.   Charles Agvent   2010 Summer Miscellany - 43   2011 $1000

Martin, Douglas *The Telling Line.* London: Julia MacRae Books, 1989, First edition; small 4to., original cloth, dust jacket, pages 320, with 85 color and 98 monochrome illustrations, fine.   R. F. G. Hollett & Son Antiquarian Booksellers   General Catalogue Summer 2010 - 257   2011   £45

Martin, Francois Xavier *The History of Louisiana from the Earliest Period.* New Orleans: 1882, xxxviii, 469 pages, xvi, frontispiece, folding map, full leather, external wear and rubbing, front hinge weak but holding on, else clean and very good.   Dumont Maps & Books of the West   112 - 54   2011 $175

Martin, Martin *A Description of the Western Islands of Scotland...* London: printed for Andrew Bell, 1703, 8vo., pages (xxxii) 392 + folding engraved map and one other folding engraved plate, early 21st century retrospective panelled calf by Chris Weston, touch of faint spotting, small handling tear to folded map, from the collection of Christopher Ernest Weston 1947-2010.   Unsworths Booksellers   24 - 121   2011   £800

Martin, P. W. *Experiment in Depth.* London: Routledge and Kegal Paul, 1956, Original cloth, gilt, dust jacket price clipped, pages (iv), 275.   R. F. G. Hollett & Son Antiquarian Booksellers   175 - 918   2011   £30

Martin, Robert Montgomery *History of Nova Scotia, Cape Breton, the Sable Islands, New Brunswick, Prince Edward Island, the Bermudas, Newfoundland &c.* London: Whitaker & Co., 1837, Small 8vo., brown cloth with design to front, pages viii 363, (1), 24, frontispiece, 2 folding maps, colored outlines, tables and charts, small 8vo., lending library stickers on inside front and endpaper, cloth worn and sunned along spine, interior very good.   Schooner Books Ltd.   96 - 292   2011 $125

Martin, Theodore *The Life of His Royal Highness the Prince Consort.* London: Smith, Elder, 1879, First volume is sixth edition from 1879 and the second a fourth edition from 1877; stout 8vo., 2 volumes, original publisher's brown cloth lettered gilt at spine, about 1100 pages in all, both very good condition, with one small gathering slightly sprung in first volume, signed presentation from Queen Victoria to George Searle.   Any Amount of Books   May 26 2011 - A39542   2011 $604

Martin, William *The Young Student's Holiday Book: Being Lessons on Architecture, Mechanics, Natural History, Physics, Manufacture of Pottery, etc. Second Series.* James Blackwood and Co. n.d., 1870, Seventh edition; pages viii, 310, (ii), all edges gilt, numerous woodcut illustrations and plates, scattered spotting, small 8vo., original decorated brown cloth gilt over bevelled boards, extremities little rubbed.   R. F. G. Hollett & Sons Antiquarian Booksellers   170 - 429   2011   £45

Martin, William B. *An Index to the Virginia Reports from Jefferson to 33rd Grattan both Inclusive with complete table of Cases.*   Richmond: 1881, 68 pages, full law calf, backstrip reglued, chip at bottom, front hinge repaired. Bookworm & Silverfish   671 - 198   2011 $75

Martin, William C. *Going Texas: the Days of the Houston Livestock Show and Rodeo.*   Houston: Mavis P. Kelsey Jr., 1972, First edition; limited to 500 numbered copies, very near fine, some minor rubbing to photo mounted on front panel in very near fine cloth slipcase, signed by photographer, Geoff Winningham, laid in is original silver gelatin photo that is also signed by Winningham, very uncommon. Jeff Hirsch Books   ny 2010   2011 $1250

Martineau, Alice *The Herbaceous Garden.*   London: Williams & Norgate, 1913, Second impression; half title, color frontispiece, plates, foldout diagram, 8 pages ads, edges slight spotted, original green cloth lettered in gilt, slightly faded, good plus, signed Ellen J. Martineau. Jarndyce Antiquarian Booksellers   CLXC - 353   2011   £45

Martineau, Harriet   1802-1876   *Harriet Martineau's Autobiography.*   Boston: James R. Osgood, 1877, First American edition; 2 volumes, half titles, frontispiece, 4 plates, slight foxing, original pale purple brown cloth, spines lettered in gilt, slight wear to heads and tails of spines, good plus.   Jarndyce Antiquarian Booksellers   CLXC - 348   2011   £85

Martineau, Harriet   1802-1876   *Harriet Martineau's Autobiography.*   London: Smith, Elder & Co., 1877, First edition; 3 volumes, half titles, frontispieces volumes I and II, 4 plates, original purple brown cloth, spines lettered in gilt, slight rubbing, heads and tails of spines bit worn. Jarndyce Antiquarian Booksellers   CLXC - 346   2011   £125

Martineau, Harriet   1802-1876   *Harriet Martineau's Autobiography.*   London: Smith, Elder & Co., 1877, Second edition; 3 volumes, half titles, frontispiece portraits volumes I and II, 4 plates, slight foxing, original purple brown cloth, front boards blocked in black, spines lettered in gilt, slight wear to heads and tails of spines, good plus. Jarndyce Antiquarian Booksellers   CLXC - 347   2011   £110

Martineau, Harriet   1802-1876   *The Billow and the Rock.* London: Charles Knight & Co., 1846, First edition; contemporary half maroon calf, slightly rubbed.   Jarndyce Antiquarian Booksellers   CLXC - 265   2011   £60

Martineau, Harriet   1802-1876   *Biographical Sketches.*   London: Macmillan, 1869, First edition; half title, 2 pages ads, 48 page catalog (July 1868), original blue cloth by Burn & Co., spine lettered in gilt, slightly dulled, rubbed at tail of spine, presentation inscription from author for Ellen Higginson.   Jarndyce Antiquarian Booksellers   CLXC - 266   2011   £200

Martineau, Harriet   1802-1876   *British Rule in India: a Historical Sketch.*   London: Smith, Elder, Bombay: Smith, Taylor, 1857, First edition; small octavo, vi, (1), 356, (4 ads) pages, half title, publisher's ads on endleaves, occasional light foxing, original printed light brown linen cloth, inner hinges tender, very good.   Jeff Weber Rare Books   163 - 194   2011 $75

Martineau, Harriet   1802-1876   *A Complete Guide to te English Lakes.*   Windermere: John Garnett, 1855, First edition; 4to., half title, color frontispiece and 3 color plates on plate paper, illustrations, color foldout map, original morocco grained blue cloth, blocked in blind, lettered in gilt, slightly rubbed, boards slightly affected by damp, all edges gilt, in Rivlin's alternative binding with centre of back board lettered in blind, signed E.K. Martineau on leading f.e.p., family copy.   Jarndyce Antiquarian Booksellers   CLXC - 268   2011   £250

Martineau, Harriet   1802-1876   *A Complete Guide to the English Lakes.*   Windermere: John Garnett, 1858, Second edition; small 8vo., original green blindstamped cloth gilt, spine faded, upper board trifle creased, pages ii, ii, iv, (iii), 210, xviii, xv (ads), engraved frontispiece, large folding map, 12 steel engraved vignettes, 6 outlines ouf mountains and 3 engraved plates.   R. F. G. Hollett & Son Antiquarian Booksellers   173 - 761   2011   £150

Martineau, Harriet   1802-1876   *A Complete Guide to the English Lakes.*   Windermere: John Garnett, 1862, Third edition; engraved frontispiece, vignette title, additional printed title, foldout maps, plates, 15 pages commercial ads, original purple cloth, blocked in blind, lettered in gilt, bit worn, contemporary ownership inscription of H. H. Johnstone, Fairfield.   Jarndyce Antiquarian Booksellers   CLXC - 269   2011   £68

Martineau, Harriet 1802-1876 *Illustrations of Political Economy. VIII. Cousin Marshall.* London: Charles Fox, 1832, First edition; original stiff grey wrappers, printed in black, spine slightly chipped at tail.   Jarndyce Antiquarian Booksellers   CLXC - 296   2011   £40

Martineau, Harriet 1802-1876 *The Crofton Boys.* London: Charles Knight & Co., 1841, First edition; contemporary half maroon calf, spine faded to brown, bit rubbed, inscribed by author to sister Ellen Higginson.   Jarndyce Antiquarian Booksellers   CLXC - 331   2011   £150

Martineau, Harriet 1802-1876 *The Crofton Boys.* London: Charles Knight & Co., 1841, First edition; slightly later half tan pigskin at some time carefully repaired, later paper label, slight rubbing, blindstamp and delicate ms. inscription dated 1856 of Belper Unitarian Sunday School Library, good plus.   Jarndyce Antiquarian Booksellers   CLXC - 332   2011   £50

Martineau, Harriet 1802-1876 *The Crofton Boys.* Addey & Co., 1854, Second edition; half title, frontispiece, original olive green cloth by Bone & Son, blocked in blind, spine lettered in gilt, spine faded and bit worn at head and tail, front board slightly damp marked, little loose, ownership inscription to Charlotte Mary Grimston 1854, good sound copy.   Jarndyce Antiquarian Booksellers   CLXC - 333   2011   £50

Martineau, Harriet 1802-1876 *Dawn Island...* Manchester: J. Gadsby, 1845, First edition; 12mo. engraved frontispiece, vignette title, additional printed title, original blue vertical ribbed cloth, front board decorated with central gilt vignette within blind borders, spine blocked and lettered in gilt, very slight rubbing, all edges gilt, very good.   Jarndyce Antiquarian Booksellers   CLXC - 271   2011   £150

Martineau, Harriet 1802-1876 *Dawn Island.* Manchester: J. Gadsby, 1845, First edition; 12mo., engraved frontispiece, vignette title, additional printed title, odd spot, original blue vertical ribbed cloth, front board decorated with central gilt vignette within blind borders, spine blocked and lettered in gilt, spine very slightly rubbed, all edges gilt, very good, signed by C(harles) E. Martineau (author's great nephew).   Jarndyce Antiquarian Booksellers   CLXC - 270   2011   £180

Martineau, Harriet 1802-1876 *Deerbrook.* London: Edward Moxon, 1839, First edition; 3 volumes, contemporary half calf, bevelled boards, spines with raised bands and devices in gilt, black leather labels, some minor careful repairs to hinges, top edge gilt, signed by author's niece, Jane Martineau.   Jarndyce Antiquarian Booksellers   CLXC - 272   2011   £580

Martineau, Harriet 1802-1876 *Deerbrook.* London: Edward Moxon, 1839, First edition; 3 volumes, contemporary half dark blue calf, spines gilt in compartments, marbled boards, boards bit rubbed, volume 1 signed H. E. Hammond in contemporary hand.   Jarndyce Antiquarian Booksellers   CLXC - 273   2011   £450

Martineau, Harriet 1802-1876 *Deerbrook.* London: Edward Moxon, 1843, New edition; rebound in maroon binder's cloth, paper label.   Jarndyce Antiquarian Booksellers   CLXC - 274   2011   £65

Martineau, Harriet 1802-1876 *Devotional Exercises: Consisting of Reflections and Prayers for the Use of Young Persons.* Boston: Leonard C. Bowles, 1833, frontispiece, some foxing, following f.e.p., torn with loss of half the leaf, original purple cloth, slightly marked, faded to brown, paper label worn.   Jarndyce Antiquarian Booksellers   CLXC - 275   2011   £60

Martineau, Harriet 1802-1876 *Eastern Life, Present and Past.* London: Edward Moxon, 1848, First edition; 3 volumes, half title volume I, occasional light foxing, 19th century half maroon calf, little rubbed, inscription to Mrs. A. Higginson from author (this is married name of author's youngr sister, Ellen).   Jarndyce Antiquarian Booksellers   CLXC - 276   2011   £450

Martineau, Harriet 1802-1876 *Eastern Life, Present and Past.* London: E. Moxon Sons & Co., 1850, New edition; contemporary full vellum, black leather labels, bit discolored, armorial bookplate of Mervyn Marshall.   Jarndyce Antiquarian Booksellers   CLXC - 277   2011   £70

Martineau, Harriet 1802-1876 *England and Her Soldiers.* London: Smith, Elder & Co., 1859, First edition; half title, foldout, color frontispiece, 2 foldout diagrams at end, 2 page ads + 24 page catalog (May 1859), some light browning, original red cloth by Westleys & Co., blocked in blind and gilt spine lettered in gilt, spine little darkened, hinges slightly rubbed, presentation inscription from author to sister Ellen Higginson.   Jarndyce Antiquarian Booksellers   CLXC - 278   2011   £380

Martineau, Harriet 1802-1876 *Feats on the Fiord.* London: Charles Knight & Co., 1841, First edition; half title, original brown cloth, blocked in blind, spine lettered in gilt, bit rubbed, front inner hinge cracking, one or two gatherings slightly proud, inscription "Randolph Mainwaring from Mrs. Foley 1848".   Jarndyce Antiquarian Booksellers   CLXC - 328   2011   £45

Martineau, Harriet 1802-1876 *Feats on the Fiord.* London: Charles Knight Co., 1841, First edition; contemporary half maroon calf, spine faded to brown, bit rubbed, signed presentation from author for sister Ellen Higginson.   Jarndyce Antiquarian Booksellers   CLXC - 327   2011   £200

Martineau, Harriet 1802-1876 *Five Years of Youth; or Sense and Sentiment.* London: Harvey and Darton, 1831, First edition; 12mo., half title, engraved frontispiece, 3 plates, contemporary half tan calf, raised gilt bands, black leather label, spine darkened and little rubbed, hinges carefully repaired, pasted on half tile small piece of paper signed Ellen Martineau. Jarndyce Antiquarian Booksellers CLXC - 279 2011 £225

Martineau, Harriet 1802-1876 *Forest and Game Law Tales.* London: Edward Moxon, 1845-1846, First edition; 3 volumes, original olive green vertical grained cloth, floral borders in blind, spines lettered in gilt, pale yellow endpapers, spines uniformly faded to brown tale of volume I, slightly rubbed, each volume with signature of Caroline Griffiths, in one place dated 1852, very good, tight. Jarndyce Antiquarian Booksellers CLXC - 280 2011 £600

Martineau, Harriet 1802-1876 *Forest and Game-Law Tales.* London: Edward Moxon, 1845-1846, First edition; 3 volumes, contemporary half dark brown calf, gilt spines, brown leather labels, spines and edges rubbed, volumes I and III both signed Martineau, most likely Robert Martineau, Harriet's brother. Jarndyce Antiquarian Booksellers CLXC - 281 2011 £400

Martineau, Harriet 1802-1876 *Health, Husbandry and Handicraft.* London: Bradbury & Evan, 1861, First edition; half title, 12 page catalog (Jan. 1861), uncut in original red pebble grained cloth, blocked in blind, spine lettered in gilt, carefully recased, spine darkened cloth, slightly wormed on following board, signed presentation inscription Catherine Salt, from author, also signed in pencil Margaret Martineau. Jarndyce Antiquarian Booksellers CLXC - 282 2011 £420

Martineau, Harriet 1802-1876 *The History of British Rule in India.* London: Smith, Elder, 1857?, First edition sheets with cancel titlepage; half title, 4 pages ads, ownership inscription 1885 across title, original dark green cloth, slightly marked, inner hinges, slight splitting. Jarndyce Antiquarian Booksellers CLXC - 267 2011 £45

Martineau, Harriet 1802-1876 *The History of England During the Thirty Years' Peace 1816-1846.* London: Charles Knight, 1849-1850, First edition; 2 volumes, foldout maps, plates, half crimson morocco, gilt spines, bit rubbed, all edges gilt, good plus. Jarndyce Antiquarian Booksellers CLXC - 284 2011 £125

Martineau, Harriet 1802-1876 *The History of England During the Thirty Years' Peace 1816-1846. (with) Introduction to the History of the Peace.* London: Charles Knight, 1849-1850, 1851. First edition; foldout maps, plates, half brown morocco, gilt spines, bit rubbed, good plus, this copy presentation copy signed by author for brother in law Alfred Higginson. Jarndyce Antiquarian Booksellers CLXC - 283 2011 £380

Martineau, Harriet 1802-1876 *History of the Peace; Pictorial History of England During the Thirty Years' Peace 1816-1846.* London: W. & R. Chambers, 1858, New edition; large 8vo., color folding map preceding title, illustrations, index, uncut in original brown morocco grained cloth, blocked in blind, spine lettered in gilt, bit rubbed, expert repairs to head and tail of spine, with signature of E. K. Martineau. Jarndyce Antiquarian Booksellers CLXC - 285 2011 £180

Martineau, Harriet 1802-1876 *A History of the Thirty Years' Peace, A.D. 1816-1846.* London: George Bell & Sons, 1877-1878, 4 volumes, half titles, initial and following catalogs in each volume, original dark green uniform cloth, blocked in blind, spines lettered in gilt, carefully repaired split at head of volume IV, Aulae Hypensis library labels, very good. Jarndyce Antiquarian Booksellers CLXC - 286 2011 £50

Martineau, Harriet 1802-1876 *Household Education.* London: Smith, Elder & Co., 1867, Contemporary half maroon morocco, spine with raised gilt bands, corners and leading hinges little rubbed, small booklabel of Henry Gardner, good plus. Jarndyce Antiquarian Booksellers CLXC - 289 2011 £70

Martineau, Harriet 1802-1876 *The Hour and the Man.* London: Edward Moxon, 1841, First edition; 3 volumes, 19th century half calf, bit rubbed, signed "Higginson", probably Alfred Higginson, Harriet's brother-in-law. Jarndyce Antiquarian Booksellers CLXC - 287 2011 £280

Martineau, Harriet 1802-1876 *The Hour and the Man.* London: Edward Moxon, 1843, New edition; original purple cloth, spine faded to brown, slight rubbing, carefully recased retaining original yellow endpapers, very good. Jarndyce Antiquarian Booksellers CLXC - 288 2011 £85

Martineau, Harriet 1802-1876 *Illustrations of Political Economy.* London: Charles Fox, 1832-1833, First editions, except for volumes I-III which are second editions; 20 volumes, uniformly bound in contemporary half green calf, marbled boards, one or two gatherings slightly proud, little rubbed, attractively bound run, spines decorated but not lettered or numbered. Jarndyce Antiquarian Booksellers CLXC - 291 2011 £320

Martineau, Harriet 1802-1876 *Illustrations of Political Economy.* London: Charles Fox, 1832-1834, First edition; 25 parts in 9 volumes in contemporary half dark brown calf, slight rubbing, very good, signed James Martineau, author's younger brother. Jarndyce Antiquarian Booksellers CLXC - 290 2011 £950

Martineau, Harriet 1802-1876 *Illustrations of Political Economy. IV Demerara. A Tale.* London: Charles Fox, 1832, First edition; original stiff grey wrappers, printed in black, spine slightly chipped. Jarndyce Antiquarian Booksellers CLXC - 293 2011 £40

Martineau, Harriet 1802-1876 *Illustrations of Political Economy. V. Ella of Garveloch. * VI. Weal and Woe in Garveloch.* London: Charles Fox, 1832, First edition; 2 volumes in 1 in contemporary full dark green morocco, gilt spine, bit rubbed. Jarndyce Antiquarian Booksellers CLXC - 294 2011 £40

Martineau, Harriet 1802-1876 *Illustrations of Political Economy. IX. Ireland.* London: Charles Fox, 1832, First edition; original stiff grey wrappers, printed in black, spine slightly chipped at tail. Jarndyce Antiquarian Booksellers CLXC - 298 2011 £45

Martineau, Harriet 1802-1876 *Illustrations of Political Economy. XI. For Each and For All.* London: Charles Fox, 1832, First edition; original stiff grey wrappers, printed in black, spine bit worn. Jarndyce Antiquarian Booksellers CLXC - 300 2011 £40

Martineau, Harriet 1802-1876 *Illustrations of Political Economy. XXV. the Moral of Many Fables.* London: Charles Fox, 1834, First edition; contemporary half calf, maroon label, little rubbed. Jarndyce Antiquarian Booksellers CLXC - 315 2011 £35

Martineau, Harriet 1802-1876 *Letters from Ireland.* London: John Chapman, 1852, First edition; 36 page catalog (Dec. 20th 1852), original green morocco grained cloth by Westleys, blocked in blind, spine lettered in gilt, spine slightly darkened and little rubbed, head and tail carefully repaired, good plus, signed "Higginson", almost certainly author's brother-in-law, Alfred Higginson. Jarndyce Antiquarian Booksellers CLXC - 318 2011 £220

Martineau, Harriet 1802-1876 *Letters on Mesmerism.* London: Edward Moxon, 1845, New edition; 4 pages ads + 8 page catalog (Oct. 1844) preceding half title, original pale drab printed wrappers, bound into slightly later olive green cloth, lettered in gilt, wrappers little dusted, family copy signed "Martineau, Birmingham". Jarndyce Antiquarian Booksellers CLXC - 319 2011 £150

Martineau, Harriet 1802-1876 *Life in the Sick Room.* London: Edward Moxon, 1844, Second edition; 8 page catalog (March 1844), preceding half title, spine bit chipped and worn, back hinge with some repairs, following board slightly marked, armorial bookplate of renowned book, collector Robert Washington Oates, good plus. Jarndyce Antiquarian Booksellers CLXC - 320 2011 £220

Martineau, Harriet 1802-1876 *The Martyr Age of the United States of America.* Newcastle upon tyne: Finlay & Charlton, 44 pages, sewn as issued, original cream printed wrappers, single vertical fold, spine worn and partially defective, well preserved copy, scarce, author's personal copy with her signature. Jarndyce Antiquarian Booksellers CLXC - 321 2011 £650

Martineau, Harriet 1802-1876 *Miscellanies.* Boston: Hilliard, Gray and Co., 1836, First edition; 19th century half maroon calf, spines faded to brown, rubbed, this the copy of author's sister, Ellen, signed by Ellen, loosely inserted small sheet of paper listing in contemporary hand 'pencil jottings in Aunt Harriet's copy of Miscellanies". Jarndyce Antiquarian Booksellers CLXC - 322 2011 £200

Martineau, Harriet 1802-1876 *The Peasant and The Prince. A Tale.* London: Charles Knight and Co., 1841, First edition; contemporary half maroon calf, spine faded to brown, slightly rubbed, presentation from author to sister Ellen Higginson. Jarndyce Antiquarian Booksellers CLXC - 325 2011 £150

Martineau, Harriet 1802-1876 *Poor Laws and Paupers Illustrated. I. The Parish. II. The Hamlets.* London: Charles Fox, 1833, First editions; 2 volumes in 1, contemporary green binder's cloth, spine darkened and slightly rubbed at head, signed "Muskett" on initial blank with small bookseller's ticket, C. Muskett of Norwich. Jarndyce Antiquarian Booksellers CLXC - 336 2011 £65

Martineau, Harriet 1802-1876 *Poor Laws and Paupers Illustrated.* London: Charles Cox, 1833-1834, First edition; slightly spotted, 4 volumes in 2, contemporary olive green moire cloth, paper label, spine slightly dulled, signed by Edward Higginson, father-in-law of author's brother James. Jarndyce Antiquarian Booksellers CLXC - 335 2011 £200

Martineau, Harriet 1802-1876 *Retrospect of Western Travel.* London: Saunders & Otley, 1838, First edition; 3 volumes, occasional light spotting, 19th century half maroon calf, spines rubbed, uniformly faded to brown, slight wear to head of spine, volume II, attractive copy, signed presentation inscription by author for sister Ellen. Jarndyce Antiquarian Booksellers CLXC - 338 2011 £400

Martineau, Harriet 1802-1876 *Retrospect of Western Travel.* London: Saunders and Otley, 1838, First edition; 3 volumes, half titles, 2 pages ads volume III (unopened), uncut and partially unopened in original drab boards, labels on spines little browned, very good, signature J. Wyndham 1948. Jarndyce Antiquarian Booksellers CLXC - 337 2011 £380

Martineau, Harriet 1802-1876 *The Settlers at Home.* London: Charles Knight & Co., 1841, First edition; slightly later half tan pigskin, later paper label, slight rubbing, blindstamp and delicate ms. inscription dated 1856, of the Belper Unitarian Sunday School Library, good plus. Jarndyce Antiquarian Booksellers CLXC - 323 2011 £50

Martineau, Harriet 1802-1876 *Sketches from Life.* Whittaker & Co., 1856, First edition; original brown morocco grained cloth by Westleys, bevelled boards, lettered in gilt, head of spine slightly rubbed, half title, vignette title and plates by W. Banks, nice copy, signed presentation by author for her niece, Maria Martineau. Jarndyce Antiquarian Booksellers CLXC - 339 2011 £250

Martineau, Harriet 1802-1876 *Society in America.* London: Saunders & Otley, 1837, First edition; 3 volumes, half titles, contemporary half maroon calf, spines slightly rubbed, faded to brown, this was the copy author's cousin, Frances Anne Martineau. Jarndyce Antiquarian Booksellers CLXC - 340 2011 £500

Martineau, Harriet 1802-1876 *Society in America.* London: Saunders & Otley, 1839, 2nd edition; 3 volumes, 12mo., half titles, contemporary half tan calf, spines gilt in compartments, olive green leather labels, marbled edges and endpapers, hinges slightly rubbed, very good, handsome copy. Jarndyce Antiquarian Booksellers CLXC - 341 2011 £450

Martineau, Harriet 1802-1876 *Society in America.* Paris: Baudry's European Library, 1842, 2 volumes in 1, half title, some slight spotting, contemporary half roan, spine slightly rubbed at head. Jarndyce Antiquarian Booksellers CLXC - 342 2011 £125

Martineau, Harriet 1802-1876 *Suggestions Towards the Future Government of India.* London: Smith, Elder & Co., 1858, First edition; half title, final ad leaf, 16 page catalog (Jan. 1858), original brown cloth, paper label, spine little chipped and slightly worn at head and tail, signed presentation from author to niece, Maria Martineau. Jarndyce Antiquarian Booksellers CLXC - 343 2011 £350

Martineau, Harriet 1802-1876 *Traditions of Palestine.* (bound with) *Devotional Exercises... Reflections and Prayers.* (bound with) *Addresses; with Prayers and Original Hymns.* London: Longman, Rees, Orme, Brown and Green, 1830, London: Rowland Hunter, 1832. London: C. Fox, 1838. First, third and second edition respectively; 3 volumes in 1 in 19th century half maroon calf, spine and edges little rubbed, with presentation by author for sister Ellen. Jarndyce Antiquarian Booksellers CLXC - 344 2011 £280

Martineau, Harriet 1802-1876 *Traditions of Palestine: Times of the Saviour.* London: George Routledge & Sons, 1870, New edition; frontispiece, illustrations, 4 pages ads, original blue cloth, front board with central vignette in gilt, spine lettered in gilt, spine faded and little worn at head and tail, all edges gilt, presentation by author for her nephew, Edward Martineau. Jarndyce Antiquarian Booksellers CLXC - 345 2011 £180

Martineau, James *Endeavours After the Christian Life.* London: John Chapman, 1843-1847, First edition; 2 volumes, half titles, final ad leaves, contemporary half brown morocco, spines lettered and with devices in gilt, spines slightly darkened and bit rubbed, each volume with ownership inscription of Martineau family members, Robt. Martineau, Edwd. K. Martineau, author's representation inscription to R. R. Martineau. Jarndyce Antiquarian Booksellers CLXC - 354 2011 £125

Martineau, James *National Duties and Other Sermons and Addresses.* London: Longmans, Green & Co., 1903, First edition; uncut in original dark blue cloth, spine lettered in gilt, slightly marked, good plus, signed Charles Martin(eau), Harriet' great nephew. Jarndyce Antiquarian Booksellers CLXC - 359 2011 £35

Martineau, James *A Study of Religion, Its Sources and Contents.* Oxford: Clarendon Press, 1889, Second edition; 2 volumes, half titles, 8 page catalog volume II, original blue cloth, spine lettered in gilt, spines slightly rubbed, good plus, presentation from Robert to Ellen Martineau, great niece of Harriet Martineau. Jarndyce Antiquarian Booksellers CLXC - 360 2011 £35

Martineau, Philip Meadows *A Memoir of the Late Philip Meadows Martienau, Surgeon.* Norwich: Bacon & Kinnebrook, Mercury Office, 1831, First edition; 4to., frontispiece, tear in lower margin of leading f.e.p., with slight loss, original blue silk, spine little worn, with presentation inscription from A. D. Martineau for P. E. Elwin. Jarndyce Antiquarian Booksellers CLXC - 362 2011 £350

Martinez, Jose Longinos *Journal of Jose Longinos Martinez.* San Francisco: John Howell Books, 1961, Second edition, limited to 1000 copies; xvii, 114 pages, 3 folding maps, charts, original green cloth, gilt, very fine, uncut. Argonaut Book Shop Recent Acquisitions Summer 2010 - 124 2011 $60

Martinson, Harry *The Road.* London: Jonathan Cape, 1955, First edition in English; very good+ in complete, very good- dust jacket with some soiling, age toning and slight marking and some slight creasing at edges. Any Amount of Books May 29 2011 - A66204 2011 $255

Martyn, William Frederic *A New Dictionary of Natural History or Compleat Universal Display of Animated Nature.* London: for Harrison and Co., 1785-1787, First edition; 2 volumes, folio, unpaginated, 100 engraved hand colored plates with tissue guards, no half titles, 19th century cloth covered boards, green russia leather spines, plates 78 and 84 with marginal tears (not crossing images), tear and separation at bottom of one hinge, another hinge with small split, extremities worn, else clean, entirely unfoxed. Joseph J. Felcone Inc. Fall Miscellany 2010 - 81 2011 $5500

Marvin, Charles *Our Public Offices Embodying an Account of the Disclosure of the Anglo-Russian Agreement and the Unrevealed Secret Treaty of May 31st 1878.* London: Samuel Tinsley, 1879, First edition; 8vo., pages 325, soundly rebound in modern ink blue cloth lettered gilt at spine, handwritten note on titlepage "Foreign Office" and note under author's name where it is printed "Formerly of the Foreign Office", few library markings, else very good. Any Amount of Books   May 29 2011 - A71692 2011 $213

Marx, Erica *Poem in Pamphlet.* Hand and Flower Press, 1951-1952, First edition; 24 booklets in original wrappers with separate index and biographical notes, all in very good condition.   I. D. Edrich   May 26 2011 - 82559 2011 $419

Marx, Karl 1818-1883 *Kritik der Politichen Oekonomie.* Hamburg: Verlag von Otto Meissner, 1867, First edition of volume i and first edition in russian of volume II; 2 volumes, octavo, xii, 784; (i)-xxi, (1, blank), (1)-403, (1, blank) page; volume I contemporary and possibly publisher's terra cotta pebble grain cloth with double blind borders, black spine lettering, expertly rebacked using original spine, cover panels laid down, some expert restoration to outer blank margin of title and dedication leaves, bit of light dampstaining to outer margin of three pages, overall very clean and solid, very scarce, housed in custom cloth clamshell with red spine label, lettered gilt, previous owner's bookplate inside clamshell, volume II - original (?) half red cloth over marbled boards, edges speckled red, green endpapers, boards bit rubbed, head and tail of spine with some wear, previous owner's old ink signature dated 1944, front inner hinge cracked and back inner hinge broken, otherwise very nice, quarter morocco clamshell.   Heritage Book Shop   Holiday 2010 - 81 2011 $42,500

Mary Whitcher's Shaker House-Keeper. Boston: Weeks & Potter, 1882, Variant edition; small 8vo., 32 pages, closed tear on pages 13/14), some stained, lacks rear wrapper, rare.   Second Life Books Inc.   174 - 327 2011 $150

Masefield, John 1878-1967 *Galliopoli.* London: 1916, viii, 183 pages, good with faded backstrip, pages yellowed, large foldout map and two other one page maps, 18 black and white photos.   Bookworm & Silverfish   669 - 195 2011 $154

Masefield, John 1878-1967 *Words Spoken at the Unveiling of the Memorials to the Poets John Keats and Percy Shelley.* N.P.: privately printed, nd., 1940, First edition; wrappers, pages 8 (unpaginated), 8vo., signed by author for Janet Ashbee with short signed letter to Janet Ashbee loosely inserted, very slight browning at edges, else very good.   Any Amount of Books   May 29 2011 - A65713 2011 $238

Masham, Samuel Cunliffe Lister, 1st Baron 1815-1906 *Lord Masham's Inventions.* London: privately published Percy Lund, Humphries & Co. and Bradford: Argus Printing Works, 1905, 4to., original half tan calf gilt over bevelled boards, author's arms in gilt on upper board, pages 88, (v), all edges gilt, tissue guarded frontispiece and 14 plates, very scarce.   R. F. G. Hollett & Son Antiquarian Booksellers   General Catalogue Summer 2010 - 1121 2011   £250

Masks and Faces. (code number 63). no information whatsoever but English, probably circa, 1930, Square 4to., full color pictorial embossed card covers of a clean copy of the book, cover is really neat, since there is discreetly protruding wheel on side edge which when turned, changes the faces within the circle in head of the figure on front cover, 10 pages within, each illustrated in black and red with several lines of text.   Jo Ann Reisler, Ltd.   86 - 176 2011 $450

Mason, Augustus L. *The Pioneer History of America. A Popular Account of the Heroes and Adventures.* Cincinnati: 1884, 1032 pages, massive 8vo., full leather, later backstrip, all edges marbled.   Bookworm & Silverfish   676 - 14 2011 $100

Mason, Bobbie Ann *With Jazz.* Monterey: Larkspur Press, 1994, Limited first printing; one of 50 copies printed on dampened Johannot and hand bound by Carolyn Whitesel, signed by author and artist, fine, illustrated boards, illustrations by LaNelle Mason.   Bella Luna Books   May 29 2011 - p2862 2011 $82

Mason, E. *Practical Coal Mining for Miners.* London: Virtue, 1950, First edition; 2 volumes, 4to., original brown cloth gilt, lettering rather dulled, few markings to one board, pages xv, 346; xii,3 47-787, drawings.   R. F. G. Hollett & Son Antiquarian Booksellers   General Catalogue Summer 2010 - 1124 2011   £35

Mason, George C. *Newport and Its Cottages.* Boston: James R. Osgood & Co., 1875, First edition; folio, 109 hinged leaves printed on rectos only, 45 full page heliotype plates, plus occasional text illustrations, full original black stamped morocco, rebacked, original spine laid down, new endpapers, slight worming in margins of few early leaves, occasional foxing, especially toward front.   M & S Rare Books, Inc.   90 - 294 2011 $2500

Mason, John *J. H. Mason: R. D. I. A Selection from the Notebooks of a Scholar-Printer made by His Son.* Leicester: Twelve by Eight Press for author, 1961, Original linson wrappers, unpaginated, signed by Mason.   R. F. G. Hollett & Son Antiquarian Booksellers   General Catalogue Summer 2010 - 259 2011   £40

Mason, John *Paper Making as an Artistic Craft.* Twelve by Eight Press for the author, 1963, Original cream wrappers gilt, pages 96, illustrations by Rigby Graham with tipped in portrait frontispiece signed by author, text illustrations, 2 original specimens of handmade paper. R. F. G. Hollett & Son Antiquarian Booksellers General Catalogue Summer 2010 - 261   2011   £75

Mason, John Mitchell *The Writings of the Late John Mitchell Mason....* New York: 1832, First edition; about 1600 pages, 4 volumes, all four backstrips shabby, two loose on one side, one cover loose, one attached by threads, bookplate removed. Bookworm & Silverfish 670 - 150   2011 $125

Mason, Lowell *The Boston Glee Book Consisting of an Extensive Collection of Glees, Madrigals and Rounds.* Boston: 1846, Early edition; 264 pages, later cloth backstrip, printed paper over boards, usual wear and age soil, three gatherings loosening, lower free corners on one song diagonally trimmed. Bookworm & Silverfish 679 - 130   2011 $75

Mason, Rupert *Robert of Thespis.* London: Ernest Benn, 1928, First edition; large 4to., original blue cloth gilt extra, dust jacket (rather worn and sometime folded, lower edges defective in places), pages xv, 143, with 109 tissue guarded plates. R. F. G. Hollett & Son Antiquarian Booksellers   175 - 919   2011   £180

Mason, William Monck *History and Antiquities of the... Church of St. Patrick.* for the author, 1819, Lacks second page contents, pages 9, pages 444-478, frontispiece and 5 plates, curious copy, bound in parchment covered boards, subscriber's copy no. 63 and 3 pages ad tipped in at front. C. P. Hyland   May 26 2011 - 259/308   2011 $362

Massam, J. A. *The Cliff Dwellers of Kenya: an Account of a People Driven by Raids, Famine and Droguht...* London: Seeley Service, 1927, First edition; 8vo., 268 pages, ads, maps, illustrations, original decorative cloth, Ex-Munger Africana Library. J. & S. L. Bonham Antiquarian Booksellers   Africa 4/20/2011 - 2943   2011   £68

Massialot, Francois *Nouvelle Insruction Pour les Confitures, Les Liquers, et les Fruits, Nouvelle Instruction Pour Le Confitures, Les Liqueurs of Les Fruits...* Paris: chez la veuve Prudhomme, 1737, New edition; 12mo., 3 folding engraved plates, one plate with tear at fold but no loss, few small stains and waterstains, contemporary speckled calf, richly gilt spine in compartments, head and tail of spine chipped, corners little worn, few light stains, interesting copy. Anthony W. Laywood   May 26 2011 - 21682   2011 $587

Massie, J. W. *A Summer Ramble in Belgium, Germany and Switzerland, Recollections of a Tour.* London: John Snow, n.d., 1845, First edition; 8vo., original publisher's textured red cloth lettered and decorated gilt at spine with gilt fountain image on cover, pages xii, 548, frontispiece and very atttractive steel engraved plates, all edges gilt, handsome, very good with minimal marking. Any Amount of Books   May 29 2011 - B29340   2011 $213

Massingham, H. J. *Downland Man.* Cape, 1927, Large 8vo., original cloth, gilt, spine trifle faded, pages 422, frontispiece, 50 illustrations and 3 maps, flyleaves lightly foxed. R. F. G. Hollett & Son Antiquarian Booksellers   177 - 565   2011   £45

Masson, Irvine *The Mainz Psalters and Canon Missae 1457-1459.* London: Bibliographical Society, 1954, First edition; folio, original holland backed boards, plain dust jacket, pages 72, plus 8 folding tables and 6 folding plates. R. F. G. Hollett & Son Antiquarian Booksellers   175 - 930   2011   £95

Master Henry's Visit at Mrs. Green's and His Return. Troy: Merriam & Moore, n.d. circa, 1835, 12mo., 24 pages + 1 page list on lower wrapper, pictorial brown paper wrappers, wood engraved vignette on titlepage, full page engraved frontispiece and 7 wood engraved vignettes in text, light foxing and rubbing along spine, very good. Hobbyhorse Books   56 - 97   2011 $120

Master Henry's Walk; and the Story of Jenny Crawley. Troy: Merriam & Moore, n.d. circa, 1850, Small 8vo., 24 pages + 1 page list on lower wrapper, pictorial paper wrappers, vignette on titlepage, full page wood engraved frontispiece, six cuts in text and small tailpiece, cover has been crudely hand colored, inked name inside front wrapper and at top of lower wrapper, lightly dampstained internally, light soiling at wrappers, chipping along spine, in all good copy. Hobbyhorse Books   56 - 98   2011 $120

Master J. Straggles - His Version of Robinson Crusoe as narrated and depicted to his School Fellows at Dr. Tickletoby's Academy. New York: McLoughlin Bros. circa, 1867, 4to., pictorial wrappers, 26 pages, light cover soil, owner's name on cover, very good+, 12 full page illustrations in white on black background, rare. Aleph-Bet Books, Inc.   95 - 184   2011 $875

Master Quack and Miss Duck. London: and New York: Nister and Dutton, n.d., circa, 1890, 3 3/4 x 2 5/8 inches, die-cut in shape of ducklings, fine, 4 wonderful chromolithographs. Aleph-Bet Books, Inc.   95 - 528   2011 $225

Masters, Caroline *The Shuttle of Fate.* London: Frederick Warne and Co., 1895, First edition; 32 page catalog, original grey flecked cloth, bevelled boards, pictorially blocked and lettered in black and gilt, spine slightly dulled, prize label 1895, very good. Jarndyce Antiquarian Booksellers   CLXC - 364   2011   £40

Masters, Edgar Lee 1868-1950 *Spoon River Anthology.* New York: Macmillan, 1915, First edition; first state (measures 7/8 inch across top of cloth), 8vo., 248 pages + ads, publisher's gray cloth stamped in black and gilt, little light browning to endpapers, little light soiling to rear board, very nice, tight copy.   Second Life Books Inc.   174 - 236   2011 $600

Masterworks of Children's Literature.   New York: Stonehill Pub. Co./Chelsea House Publishers, 1983-1986, First edition; 7 volumes (of 9), 4to., 2600 + pages, illustrations in black and white, volumes 3 and 9 not present, all clean, very good in very good dust jacket, 3 still unopened in their shrinkwrap.   Any Amount of Books   May 29 2011 - B26223   2011 $213

Mather, G. Leila *Echoes including the Story of John Willy.* Lincoln: privately Printed for author, 1948,   4to., original blue cloth, gilt, fore edges little stained an softened by damp, pages 124, photos and drawings, presentation copy with large inscription and 7 line poem in author's hand dated Christmas 1948.   R. F. G. Hollett & Son Antiquarian Booksellers   General Catalogue Summer 2010 - 441   2011   £120

Mather, Increase 1639-1723   *A Sermon Wherein is Shewed. I. That the Ministers of the Gospel Need.. Preached at Roxbury Oct. 29 1718 when Mr. Thomas Walter was Ordained a Pastor in that Church.* Boston: by S. Kneeland for J. Edwards, 1718, l2), ii, i, 2-35, (1) pages, later full calf, spine label missing, bottom margin cut into, loss of last line of imprint on titlepage and several last lines within text.   Joseph J. Felcone Inc.   Fall Miscellany 2010 - 82   2011 $800

Mather, John C. *The Very First Light.* New York: Basic Books, 1996, First edition; 8vo., xxi, 328 pages, fine in fine dust jacket.   By the Book, L. C.   26 - 106   2011 $300

Mathers, Helen *Cherry Ripe!* London: Richard Bentley and Son, 1878, First edition; 3 volumes, volume II lacks leading f.e.p., volume III with facsimile titlepage, original violet cloth, front boards blocked and lettered in black, spines ruled and lettered in gilt, spines faded to brown and slightly rubbed at edges.   Jarndyce Antiquarian Booksellers   CLXC - 365   2011   £120

Mathers, Helen *A Man of To-day.* London: F. V. White, 1894, First edition; 3 volumes, half titles, 16 page catalog volume III, original dark green cloth, bevelled boards, slightly rubbed with signs of label removal from front boards, stamps of "Willows".   Jarndyce Antiquarian Booksellers   CLXC - 366   2011   £120

Mathers, Helen *Sam's Sweetheart.* London: Hutchinson & Co., 1890, New edition; ad leaf preceding title, ads on endpapers, yellowback, glazed printed boards, bit rubbed, good plus, tight copy.   Jarndyce Antiquarian Booksellers   CLXC - 368   2011   £50

Mathew, Frank *Ireland.* London: A. & C. Black, 1916, New edition; large 8vo., original blue decorated cloth, gilt, pages xix, 212, 50 color plates, neat inscription.   R. F. G. Hollett & Son Antiquarian Booksellers   General Catalogue Summer 2010 - 1632   2011   £95

Mathews, A. E.   *Pencil Sketches of Colorado, Its Cities, Principal Towns and Mountain Scenery.*   Denver: Nolie Mumey, 1961, Number 137 of 350 copies signed by editor; oblong folio, 23 pages of full page color reproductions, printed on rectos only, red cloth, gilt, very fine.   Argonaut Book Shop   Recent Acquisitions Summer 2010 - 126   2011 $400

Mathews, Charles   *Sketches of Mr. Mathews' Invitations.* London: J. Libard, 1826, 12mo., early three quarter tan calf and blue marbled boards, gilt to spine, rubbing to joints and extremities, morocco label to spine, four hand colored engraved portraits to folding frontispiece, light offsetting to plate and titlepage, marbled endpapers.   Dramatis Personae Booksellers   106 - 119   2011 $150

Mathews, John Joseph   *The Osages. Children of the Middle Waters.* Norman: University of Oklahoma, 1961, First edition; over 800 pages, signed by author, bit of play in binding from weight of text block, near fine in good dust jacket with several small edge tears/chips (one internally tape mended), chipping to rear flap fold.   Ken Lopez Bookseller   154 - 138   2011 $150

Mathews, John Joseph   *Talking to the Moon.* Chicago: University of Chicago Press, 1945, First edition; small date stamp to copyright page, light wear to boards, near fine in near fine, lightly edgeworn dust jacket, inscribed by author.   Ken Lopez Bookseller   154 - 137   2011 $450

Mathews, John Lathrop   *Remaking the Mississippi.* Boston: 1909,   265 pages, 8vo., original binding, photos illustrations, white inked titling complete and clean, corners sharp, owner number at top of titlepage.   Bookworm & Silverfish   668 - 99   2011 $74

Matisse, Henri *Jazz.* Paris: Editions Anthese, 2005, First edition thus; one of 1300 copies, not numbered, as issued, folio, 152 leaves and 20 color plates, all printed in hand lithography as facsimile of original copy, loose leaves imprinted wrapper folder, red cloth chemise and matching slipcase, as new.   Any Amount of Books   May 26 2011 - A48705   2011 $1090

Matteucig, Giacinto *Poggio Buco. The Necropolis of Statonia.* University of California Press, 1951, First edition; 4to., original cloth, gilt, dust jacket (few small edge chips), pages xiii, 117, with 24 plates, 2 maps and 20 figures. R. F. G. Hollett & Son Antiquarian Booksellers 177 - 566 2011 £40

Matthews, L. Harrison *South Georgia: The British Empire's Subantarctic Outpost: A Synopsis of the History of the Island.* Bristol and London: John Wright and Sons/Simpkin Marshall, 1931, First edition; 8vo, ex-library rebound with code to spine, library bookplate to front pastedown, usual stamps and marks to interior, pages xii, 163, 20 illustrations, 26 plates, corner slightly rubbed, head of spine slightly worn, otherwise sound, very good. Any Amount of Books May 29 2011 - A61716 2011 $340

Matthiessen, Peter *In the Spirit of Crazy Horse.* New York: Viking, 1983, First edition; fine in near fine, price clipped dust jacket, crease on front flap. Bella Luna Books May 26 2011 - t7980CO 2011 $192

Matthiessen, Peter *The Passionate Seekers.* New York: Avon, 1955, First paperback edition; signed by author, quite uncommon thus, fine. Charles Agvent 2010 Summer Miscellany - 45 2011 $75

Matthiessen, Peter *The Snow Leopard.* New York: Viking, 1978, First edition; cloth mottled, foxing to edges of text block, very good in like dust jacket, mildly spine faded with closed gouge to lower front panel, excellent association, inscribed by author to another author. Ken Lopez Bookseller 154 - 105 2011 $1500

Mattsperger, Melchior *Die Geitstliche Herzens-Einbildungn inn Zweihundert und Funfzig Biblishen Figur-Spruchen Vorgefstellet.* Augsburg: Johann Christian Leopold, n.d. circa, 1720, Oblong folio, (xii), 83, (1) (1) (vii) 83 (1) (1), 2 volumes in one, original heavily decorative embosssed vellum on board covers, four raised bands on spine, red edges, 166 superb full page copper engravings, all printed on water marked hand made paper, light marginal soiling, last three leaves of volume two partly creased, faded pencilled scribble inside lower cover, gatherings separated from spine but held strongly with original sewn binding, very rare. Hobbyhorse Books 56 - 10 2011 $2300

Maturin, Edith *Petticoat Pilgrims on Trek.* London: Eveleigh Nash, 1909, First edition; half title, frontispiece, 12 pages ads, original olive green cloth, pictorially blocked in black and orange, lettered in gilt, spine very slightly faded, very good. Jarndyce Antiquarian Booksellers CLXC - 369 2011 £60

Maubray, John *The Female Physician, Containing All the Diseases Incident to that Sex, in Virgins, Wives and Widows...* London: printed for James Holland, 1724, First edition; 8vo., pages xxiv, 420, (4), initial blank torn, with loss, very occasional spotting or light soiling, but generally very fresh and crisp, contemporary calf, upper and lower panels tooled in blind, spine label with lettering in manuscript, bumped, rubbed, top of spine chipped, lower joint cracked but holding firm, early ownership inscription. Simon Finch Rare Books Zero - 113 2011 £950

Mauchline, Mary *Harewood House.* David & Charles, 1974, First edition; pages 195, with 22 plates and 9 line drawings, original cloth, gilt, dust jacket. R. F. G. Hollett & Son Antiquarian Booksellers 177 - 567 2011 £30

Maud, Constance Elizabeth *An English Girl in Paris.* London: John Lane, The Bodley Head, 1902, 4th edition; half title, final ad leaf, slight browning to edges and prelims, uncut in original olive green glazed cloth, front board pictorially blocked in darker green and maroon, lettered in green and gilt, red wax seal on half title, very good. Jarndyce Antiquarian Booksellers CLXC - 370 2011 £40

Maugham, William Somerset 1874-1965 *Ashenden or the British Agent.* London: Heinemann, 1928, First edition; little light browning to half title and final text page, pages (viii), 304, foolscap 8vo., original mid blue cloth, backstrip and front cover gilt lettered, backstrip trifle darkened, outer tail corners little bumped, front cover trifle marked, Maugham symbol blocked in dark blue on front cover, good, at one the copy of Prime Minister Anthony Eden with his bookplate. Blackwell Rare Books B166 - 183 2011 £300

Maugham, William Somerset 1874-1965 *Cosmopolitans.* London: Heinemann, 1936, First edition, 103/175 copies signed by author; prelims and final few leaves with occasional light foxing, pages xvi, 304, 8vo., original cardinal red bevel edged buckram, gilt lettered black cloth label on faded backstrip, gilt Maugham symbol to front covers, red silk marker, top edge gilt, others untrimmed, tissue jacket, very good. Blackwell Rare Books B166 - 184 2011 £225

Maugham, William Somerset 1874-1965 *Don Fernando.* London: Heinemann, 1935, First edition, 114/175 copies signed by author; pages (viii), 272, 8vo., original apple green bevel edged buckram, gilt lettered black cloth label, lightly faded backstrip, gilt Maugham symbol and small stain to front cover, green silk marker, top edge gilt, others untrimmed, tissue jacket, very good. Blackwell Rare Books B166 - 185 2011 £300

Maugham, William Somerset 1874-1965 *The Moon and Sixpence.* London: Heienmann, 1919, First edition; usual browning to poor quality postwar paper, third issue with two ad leaves inserted and stub of two cancelled leaves still showing, pages (iv), 246, (4) (ads), foolscap 8vo., original sage green cloth, backstrip and front covers with blocking in black, covers trifle soiled, good.   Blackwell Rare Books   B166 - 182 2011   £80

Maugham, William Somerset 1874-1965 *Of Human Bondage.* New York: Doubleday, Doran, 1936, First illustrated edition, one of 751 numbered copies signed by author and artist, this is copy #4; additionally inscribed by author for Doubleday editor Malcolm Johnson, illustrations by Randolph Schwabe, small quarto, full dark blue morocco with raised bands and heavily stamped in gilt, just about fine, laid in is 1936 letter from artist, Schwabe in his calligraphic hand.   Between the Covers   169 - BTC346497 2011 $4250

Maugham, William Somerset 1874-1965 *The Summing Up.* New York: Doubleday, 1954, 153/391 copies signed by author; frontispiece, pages (vi), 284, royal 8vo., original grey bevel edged buckram, backstrip gilt lettered, partly on red ground, top edge gilt, others untrimmed and partly unopened, board slipcase with printed label, fine.   Blackwell Rare Books B166 - 186 2011   £300

Maugham, William Somerset 1874-1965 *The Unconquered.* New York: House of Books, 1944, First edition, 88/300 copies (of an edition of 326); signed by author, pages (ii), 58, foolscap 8vo., original mid blue linen backstrip and front covers gilt lettered, plain tissue jacket, fine.   Blackwell Rare Books   B166 - 187 2011   £300

Maugham, William Somerset 1874-1965 *The Vagrant Mood.* London: Heinemann, 1952, First edition; 105/500 copies signed by author, title printed in red pages (vi), 242, royal 8vo., original quarter mushroom calf just faintly rubbed, black leather label, dark blue calf sides, faint browning to free endpapers, top edge gilt, others untrimmed, tissue jacket, very good.   Blackwell Rare Books   B166 - 188 2011   £225

Maundrell, Henry *A Journey from Aleppo to Jerusalem at Easter, A.D.. 1697. To Which is Now added an Account of the Author's Journey to the Banks of Euphrates at Beer and to the Colony of Mesopotamia....* Oxford: printed at the Theatre for A. Peisley, Bookseller in Oxford and W. Meadows Bookseller in Cornhill, London, 1740, Seventh edition; 8vo., contemporary full calf, pages x, 171, with 15 engraved plates, lacks half title, 8 smaller drawings, text and plates very clean, reasonable sound copy in full leather rubbed at corners with spine soundly held with matching brown linen well applied some time ago with neat hand written title label.   Any Amount of Books   May 29 2011 - B30759 2011 $272

Maupas Du Tour, Henri Couchon De *La Vie du Venerable Serviteur de Dieu, Francois de Sales, etc.* Paris: J. & E. Langlois, 1657, 2 parts, 4to., 411; 53, (3) pages, ruled in red, added engraved plates, 6 engraved plates, engraved headpieces and initials, contemporary French panelled, red morocco, gilt floral cornerpieces, spines gilt, turn-ins, edges gilt, slight damage to upper cover, paper flaw in plate at page 1 with consequent tear, handsome copy, ruled in red and from the Foucault library, De Cohon inscription, from the library of the Earls of Macclesfield at Shirburn Castle.   Maggs Bros. Ltd.   1440 - 142 2011   £850

Mauriceau, A. M. *The Married Woman's Private Medical Companion.* New York: 1850, 16mo., 13, 238 pages, original cloth.   M & S Rare Books, Inc.   90 - 40 2011 $250

Mawe, John 1764-1829 *The Voyager's Companion; or Shell Collector's Pilot...* by the author, 1821, Third edition; xiv, (2), 56 pages, 2 hand colored plates, original boards, backstrip and corners worn, but in good clean condition, apart from some browning to a tissue guard, Enid Marx's copy with inscription on front endpaper, very scarce.   Ken Spelman Rare Books   68 - 155 2011   £225

Mawson, Douglas *Mawson's Antarctic Diaries.* London: 1988, Maps and illustrations, dust jacket rubbed with short tear, book near fine.   Dumont Maps & Books of the West 112 - 55 2011 $150

Maxcy, Jonathan *An Address Delivered to the Graduates of Rhode Island College at the Anniversary Commencement in the Baptist Meeting House in Providence September 5 A.D. 1798.* Providence: Carter and Wilkinson, 1804, First edition; 8vo., 12 pages sewn as issued, some toning, light wear to fore edge, crisp copy, uncut.   M & S Rare Books, Inc.   90 - 243 2011 $125

Maxcy, Jonathan *An Oration. Delivered in the First Congregational Meeting-House in Providence on the Fourth of July 1799.* Providence: John Carter, 1799, First edition; 8vo., 16 pages, sewn, outside leaves browned, fore-edge worn with 1 inch tear throughout, sometimes affecting few words at beginning of line or two, still very good, ample margins in original condition.   M & S Rare Books, Inc.   90 - 136 2011 $250

Maximus Tyrius *The Dissertations of Maximus Tyrius.* London: printed by C. Whittenham, Dean Street for the Translator and sold by R. H. Evans Pall Mall, 1804, First edition; small 8vo., 2 volumes in 1, pages xv, (1) 235, (1); 272 pages, later bottle green cloth (circa 1900), neat label of Pantiles (Tunbridge Wells) Library and Reading Room, no other library markings, booklabel of T. S. Osmond of St. John's College, Oxford (donor of the book), pencilled ownership signature of historian F. R. Cowell, very good, clean text free of foxing, couple of gatherings very slightly protruding but sound attractive copy.   Any Amount of Books   May 26 2011 - A46360 2011 $470

Maxwell, Donald *Adventures Among Churches.* The Faith Press, 1928, First edition; 4to., original blue cloth, gilt, spine and upper edges rather faded, pages (iv), 136 with 24 plates.   R. F. G. Hollett & Son Antiquarian Booksellers   General Catalogue Summer 2010 - 1474   2011   £50

Maxwell, Donald *Adventures with a Sketch Book.* London: John Lane, the Bodley Head, 1914, First edition; small 4to., original two-tone cloth, corners little bumped, pages xii, 124, with 28 illustrations in color and monochrome and 34 line drawings.   R. F. G. Hollett & Son Antiquarian Booksellers   General Catalogue Summer 2010 - 1651   2011   £60

Maxwell, Donald *Colour Sketching in Chalk.* Sir Isaac Pitman, 1934, First edition; original pale blue cloth lettered in silver, spine rather darkened, pages 80, 16 with 47 illustrations.   R. F. G. Hollett & Son Antiquarian Booksellers   General Catalogue Summer 2010 - 263   2011   £45

Maxwell, Donald *The Enchanted Road.* London: Methuen, 1927, First edition; square 8vo., original cloth backed boards, little faded and bumped, pages xiv, 174, with 99 illustrations, flyleaves lightly browned.   R. F. G. Hollett & Son Antiquarian Booksellers   General Catalogue Summer 2010 - 1475   2011   £35

Maxwell, Donald *Excursions in Colour.* London: Cassell, 1927, First edition; original blue cloth, small 4to., dust jacket rather torn, spine defective at head and foot, pages xv, 118 on thick paper, illustrations in colors.   R. F. G. Hollett & Son Antiquarian Booksellers   General Catalogue Summer 2010 - 1652   2011   £65

Maxwell, Donald *The Landscape of Thomas Hardy.* London: Cassell, 1928, First edition; small 4to., original cloth with paper labels, pages xii, 80, 12 fine color plates, numerous drawings in text and maps on endpapers.   R. F. G. Hollett & Son Antiquarian Booksellers   General Catalogue Summer 2010 - 1476   2011   £35

Maxwell, Donald *The Last Crusade.* London: John Lane, The Bodley Head, 1920, First edition; small 4to., original cloth backed boards, one edge little bumped, pages xxii, 144, (iii), illustrations in color and monochrome.   R. F. G. Hollett & Son Antiquarian Booksellers   General Catalogue Summer 2010 - 845   2011   £45

Maxwell, Donald *More Adventures Among Churches.* Faith Press, 1929, First edition; 4to., original red cloth gilt, spine trifle faded, pages (ii), 136, with 30 plates, piece cut from flyleaf, scattered spotting to first and last leaves and fore-edge.   R. F. G. Hollett & Son Antiquarian Booksellers   General Catalogue Summer 2010 - 1477   2011   £45

Maxwell, Donald *The New Lights of London.* Herbert Jenkins, 1926, First edition; small 4to., original blue cloth gilt, dust jacket, spine darkened, pages xvi, 158 on thick paper, 67 color illustrations by author, few spots to front flyleaf and fore-edges, else very nice.   R. F. G. Hollett & Son Antiquarian Booksellers   General Catalogue Summer 2010 - 1478   2011   £45

Maxwell, Donald *A Pilgrimage of the Thames.* The Centenary Press, 1932, First edition; original cloth, rather spotted, spine and edges faded, pages xii, 193, illustrations in monochrome, fine line drawings.   R. F. G. Hollett & Son Antiquarian Booksellers   General Catalogue Summer 2010 - 1479   2011   £30

Maxwell, Donald *Unknown Dorset.* London: John Lane, The Bodley Head, 1927, First edition; large 8vo., original red cloth gilt, gilt and silver arms on front board, spine little faded, pages xii, 208, 6, uncut, 8 color plates and numerous text illustrations, occasional spotting, pencilled plan on rear flyleaf.   R. F. G. Hollett & Son Antiquarian Booksellers   General Catalogue Summer 2010 - 1480   2011   £35

Maxwell, Donald *Unknown Essex.* London: John Lane, The Bodley Head, 1925, First edition; large 8vo., original grey cloth gilt, pages xiii, 204, untrimmed, 30 plates and numerous text illustrations, few spots, very nice.   R. F. G. Hollett & Son Antiquarian Booksellers   General Catalogue Summer 2010 - 1471   2011   £35

Maxwell, Donald *Unknown Kent.* London: John Lane the Bodley Head, 1921, First edition; large 8vo., original blue cloth, gilt, arms in gilt on upper board, spine rather faded, pages xv, 210, 4, untrimmed with 23 color plates, numerous line drawings and maps, prelim leaves spotted.   R. F. G. Hollett & Son Antiquarian Booksellers   General Catalogue Summer 2010 - 1482   2011   £35

Maxwell, Donald *Unknown Norfolk.* London: John Lane The Bodley Head, 1925, First edition; large 8vo., original red cloth, gilt arms on front board, spine trifle faded, pages xiii, 207, untrimmed, 20 color plates and numerous line drawings and maps, prelim leaves spotted.   R. F. G. Hollett & Son Antiquarian Booksellers   General Catalogue Summer 2010 - 1483   2011   £60

Maxwell, Donald *Unknown Somerset.* London: John Lane The Bodley Head, 1928, First edition; large 8vo., original blue cloth, gilt, gilt arms on front board, pages xii, 209, (ii), untrimmed, 24 color plates and numerous line drawings, very nice, clean copy.   R. F. G. Hollett & Son Antiquarian Booksellers   General Catalogue Summer 2010 - 1484   2011   £45

Maxwell, Donald *Unknown Suffolk.* London: John Lane, The Bodley Head, 1926, First edition; large 8vo., original blue cloth gilt, spine little dulled, pages xiii, 202, (vi), untrimmed, 12 plates, numerous text illustrations, very nice, clean copy, signed by author. R. F. G. Hollett & Son Antiquarian Booksellers General Catalogue Summer 2010 - 1485 2011 £35

Maxwell, Donald *Unknown Surrey.* London: John Lane, The Bodley Head, 1924, First edition; large 8vo., original green cloth gilt, dust jacket, stained, stamped on reverse and neatly restored, pages xii, 210, 24 plates, numerous text illustrations, occasional spotting. R. F. G. Hollett & Son Antiquarian Booksellers General Catalogue Summer 2010 - 1486 2011 £65

Maxwell, Donald *Unknown Sussex.* London: John Lane, The Bodley Head, 1929, Third reprint; large 8vo., original red cloth gilt, spine trifle sunned, pages xiii, 207, 4, untrimmed, 21 color plates, 8 black and white illustrations and numerous text drawings. R. F. G. Hollett & Son Antiquarian Booksellers General Catalogue Summer 2010 - 1487 2011 £40

Maxwell, Donald *Wembley in Colour.* London: Longman, Green and Co., 1924, First edition; 4to., original cloth backed boards, pages 112, illustrations in color and monochrome. R. F. G. Hollett & Son Antiquarian Booksellers General Catalogue Summer 2010 - 1488 2011 £50

Maxwell, Gavin *Ring of Bright Water.* London: Longmans, 1960, Second impression; original cloth, gilt, dust jacket edges taped, pages 211, with 69 photos, numerous text illustrations by Peter Scott, line drawings, neat biro address on flyleaf. R. F. G. Hollett & Son Antiquarian Booksellers General Catalogue Summer 2010 - 848 2011 £30

Maxwell, Gordon S. *The Naval Front.* London: A. & C. Black, 1920, Original blue cloth gilt, spine and edges very faded, pages xii, 203, (i), 32 plates. R. F. G. Hollett & Son Antiquarian Booksellers General Catalogue Summer 2010 - 612 2011 £45

Maxwell, William *The Virginia Register & Literary Advertiser.* Richmond: 1848, First editions; volumes 1-6 complete, volumes 1 and 2 in later red cloth, volumes 3 an 4 half leather, covers loose, backstrip very well worn, volume 5 and 6 in half leather, covers loose, backstrip gone,. Bookworm & Silverfish 678 - 8 2011 $100

May, Arthur S. *Marriage A La Mode.* London: John Castle, 1925, First edition; original cloth, gilt, pages ix, 320, (iv), 8 plates. R. F. G. Hollett & Son Antiquarian Booksellers 175 - 922 2011 £30

May, J. Boyer *Trace.* 1952-1970, Nos. 2-5, 8, 10-16, 18 23-73, 65 issues in original wrappers, all very good. I. D. Edrich May 26 2011 - 82531 2011 $654

May, Phil *Phil May's ABC: Fifty Two Original Designs Forming Two Humorous Alphabets from A to Z.* London: Leadenhall Press, 1897, Number 582 of 1050 proof copies; frontispiece and illustrations, final ad leaf, 4 page catalog on blue paper, original green pictorial cloth, very good. Jarndyce Antiquarian Booksellers CXCI - 319 2011 £85

May, Samuel J. *A Discourse on Slavery in the United States, Delivered in Brooklyn (Conn.) July 3 1831.* Boston: Garrison and Knapp, 1832, First edition; 8vo., 29, (1) pages, removed. M & S Rare Books, Inc. 90 - 244 2011 $250

May, Thomas *The Roman Forts of Temple Borough near Rotherham.* Rotherham: Henry Garnett, 1922, First edition; 4to., original cloth, gilt, little soiled, pages ix, 132, plus 61 pages of plates and large folding plan (tear repaired). R. F. G. Hollett & Son Antiquarian Booksellers 177 - 569 2011 £75

Mayer, Marianna *Baba Yaga and Vasilisa the Brave.* New York: William Morrow, 1994, First edition; 4to., 37 pages, fine in fine dust jacket, illustrations by Kinuko Y. Craft, signed. By the Book, L. C. 26 - 66 2011 $120

Mayer, Ralph *The Artist's Handbook of Materials and Techniques.* London: Faber, 1972, Third edition; original cloth, gilt, dust jacket, pages xv, 739, with few illustrations. R. F. G. Hollett & Son Antiquarian Booksellers General Catalogue Summer 2010 - 264 2011 £45

Mayer, Tom *The Weary Falcon.* Boston: Houghton Mifflin, 1971, Uncorrected proof copy; spiralbound proof, printed from galley sheets, covers unevenly sunned, few small stains to rear over, very good, book itself somewhat uncommon, proof is rare. Ken Lopez Bookseller 154 - 236 2011 $250

Mayhall, John *The Annals of Yorkshire from the Earliest Period to the Present Time.* Leeds: Joseph Johnson, 1862-1874, Second edition; 3 volumes, contemporary half polished black calf gilt, pages iv, 768, 732; 706 with 29 steel engraved plates. R. F. G. Hollett & Son Antiquarian Booksellers General Catalogue Summer 2010 - 1489 2011 £175

Mayhall, John *Tradesmen's Guide to the Practice of County Courts... (bound with) A Plain Guide to Landlords, Tenants, and Lodgers.* London: W. Tegg etc., n.d. circa, 1860, Pages 64, 48, small 8vo., original blindstamped cloth, gilt, scarce. R. F. G. Hollett & Son Antiquarian Booksellers 175 - 924 2011 £75

Mayhew, Experience *Indian Converts; or Some Account of the Lives and Dying Speeches of a Considerable Number of the Christianized Indians of Martha's Vineyard...* London: printed for Samuel Gerrish, Bookseller in Boston in New England, 1727, First edition; 8vo., pages xxiv, 310 + 2 pages ads, 20th century calf backed marbled boards, spine gilt, front blank titlepage and first three leaves professionally strengthened along edges, not affecting text, some toning and light staining throughout, 18th century ownership signature on front blank, cropped along top of titlepage, very presentable copy. Second Life Books Inc. 174 - 237 2011 $4500

Mayhew, Experience *Narratives of the Lives of Pious Indian Women who Lived on Martha's Vineyard More than One Hundred Years Since.* Boston: published by James Loring, 1830, First edition thus; 12mo. pages viii, 108, original printed boards, new spine and endpapers, engraved frontispiece, some light foxing and toning, contemporary ownership signature on endpaper and top of titlepage, very good, tight copy. Second Life Books Inc. 174 - 238 2011 $450

Mayhew, The Brothers *Acting Charades or Deeds Not Words.* London: D. Bogue, 1850, First edition; small square 8vo., original red cloth gilt by Bone and Son, stamped in blind and gilt, extremities trifle rubbed, pages x (ii), 158, (ii), all edges gilt, hand colored frontispiece and title and silhouette illustrations in text. R. F. G. Hollett & Sons Antiquarian Booksellers 170 - 431 2011 £120

Mayo, Katherine *Mother India.* London: Cape, 1927, First edition; original cloth, gilt, dust jacket, few slight edge tears and tiny chips, pages 391, flyleaves partially browned from endpapers, otherwise very good. R. F. G. Hollett & Son Antiquarian Booksellers 175 - 926 2011 £250

McCarty's American Primer. Philadelphia: M'Carty & Davis, 1828, 12mo., 36 pages, pictorial blue stiff paper wrappers, large wood engraving in titlepage, 6 pages of large roman alphaet letters, small woodcut, small split at lower edge of wrapper, very fine. Hobbyhorse Books 56 - 121 2011 $150

McCabe, Olivia *The Rose Fairies.* Chicago: Rand McNally, 1911, First edition; Small 4to., cloth, pictorial paste-on, 133 pages, slight cover soil, near fine, 12 beautiful color plates plus black and white in text and pictorial endpapers. Aleph-Bet Books, Inc. 95 - 231 2011 $275

McCaffrey, Anne *Dragonflight.* New York: Walker and Co., 1969, First edition; octavo, boards. L. W. Currey, Inc. 124 - 59 2011 $1500

McCall, H. B. *Richmondshire Churches.* London: Elliot Stock, 1910, First edition; large 8vo., original blue buckram gilt, few light scrapes, pages xxviii, 225, , untrimmed with etched frontispiece and 57 plates, scarce. R. F. G. Hollett & Son Antiquarian Booksellers General Catalogue Summer 2010 - 1469 2011 £50

McCance, S. *History of the Royal Munster Fusiliers 1652-1922.* 1927, First edition; 2 volumes, presentation from H. S. Jervis, for the Old Comrades Association for Sir Barclay Nihill, (8), 254 pages, 5 color plates, 31 photos on 12 plats, 20 maps, ix, 305 pages, 3 color plates, 58 photos on 37 plates, 21 maps, good. C. P. Hyland May 26 2011 - 259/266 2011 $870

McCarthy, Cormac *All the Pretty Horses.* New York: Knopf, 1992, Uncorrected proof; book fine, printed grey wrappers. Bella Luna Books May 26 2011 - 1235 2011 $300

McCarthy, Cormac *All the Pretty Horses.* New York: Knopf, 1992, First edition; fine, near fine dust jacket, price clipped, light creasing top of spine. Bella Luna Books May 26 2011 - t4138 2011 $275

McCarthy, Cormac *Blood Meridian.* New York: Random House, 1985, First edition; review copy with slip laid in, 8vo., two-tone red cloth with red paper over boards, (10), 337, fine, bright, unread copy in fine dust jacket, housed in full imitation leather slipcase with books dust jacket's front panel duplicate on front panel, with spine panel and rear panel also matching dust jacket, exceptional copy. Buckingham Books May 26 2011 - 26129 2011 $5000

McCarthy, Cormac *Child of God.* London: Chatto & Windus, 1975, First British edition; near fine, light foxing to top edge, dust jacket near fine, with light foxing to exposed areas of flaps. Bella Luna Books May 26 2011 - t3566 2011 $440

McCarthy, Cormac *No Country for Old Men.* New York: Knopf, 2005, Advance reading copy; spine slant, thus near fine in wrappers, unread. Ken Lopez Bookseller 154 - 106 2011 $125

McCarthy, Cormac *The Orchard Keeper.* New York: Random House, 1965, First edition; 8vo., 246 pages, crayon mark on front endpaper, very good, tight copy, dust jacket little chipped, soiled, scarce, front flap reattached with scotch tape and rear dust jacket cover soiled, still very good. Second Life Books Inc. 174 - 239 2011 $2000

McCarthy, Cormac *Outer Dark.* London: Andre Deutsch, 1970, First British edition; near fine, light foxing to edges, fine dust jacket. Bella Luna Books May 26 2011 - t993 2011 $825

McCarthy, Cormac *The Sunset Limited.* London: Picador, 2010, Uncorrected proof copy of first British edition; fine in wrappers, uncommon in any advance state or in any first printing. Ken Lopez Bookseller   154 - 107 2011 $200

McCarthy, John C. *Recovery of Damages for Bad Faith.* Kentfield: 1990, Fifth edition; 2 volumes, 1000+ pages, here 1991 supplements in each volume, fine, owner stamp on fore edge.   Bookworm & Silverfish   669 - 109 2011 $75

McCarthy, Mary *Une Jeune Fille Sage. (Memories of a Catholic Girlhood).* Paris: Plon, 1959, First edition, one of 40 numbered copies on alfa; (245 pages) 8vo., original printed wrappers, as new.   Paulette Rose Fine and Rare Books   32 - 121 2011 $100

McCloskey, Robert *Homer Price.* New York: Viking, 1943, First edition; 4to., cloth, 149 pages, fine in dust jacket (light soil and fraying at spine ends but overall very good+, illustrations.   Aleph-Bet Books, Inc.   95 - 343 2011 $750

McCloskey, Robert *Lentil.* New York: Viking Press, 1940, First edition; large 4to., tan yellow cloth with red lettering on spine and vignette on front cover, color pictorial dust jacket with some wear and small pieces missing at corner and ends of spine, there is an extra page laid into book signed by McCloskey.   Jo Ann Reisler, Ltd.   86 - 166 2011 $1200

McCloskey, Robert *One Morning in Maine.* New York: Viking, 1952, First edition; folio, pictorial cloth, 64 pages, fine in very good dust jacket, missing 1 inch at base of spine, illustrations on every page.   Aleph-Bet Books, Inc.   95 - 344 2011 $850

McClure, Michael *The Adept.* New York: Delacorte, 1971, First edition; inscribed by author to another writer, minor foxing to page edges and endpages, near fine in near fine dust jacket with light wear to edges and folds.   Ken Lopez Bookseller   154 - 110 2011 $150

McClure, Michael *Solstice Blossom.* N.P.: Arif Press, 1973, Of a total edition of 130 copies, this is an out-of-series copy labeled as an "Artist's Copy" and signed by author; inscribed by Welsey Tanner who provided an original water color as frontispiece, one small edge tear, else fine in saddle stitched wrappers, attractive, uncommon. Ken Lopez Bookseller   154 - 111 2011 $250

McClure's Magazine Volume IV. December 1894 to May 1895. New York: 1894-1895, 579 pages, large 8vo., full dark green cloth, shelfwear at backstrip ends.   Bookworm & Silverfish   669 - 58 2011 $100

McCoan, J. C. *Egypt as It Is.* London: Cassell, Petter, n.d., 1880, First edition; 8vo., pages xvi, 433, folding map, original green decorative cloth, good, bright copy.   J. & S. L. Bonham Antiquarian Booksellers   Africa 4/20/2011 - 7070 2011   £150

McConnell, James *Presbyterianism in Belfast.* Belfast: Davidson & McCormack, 1912, First edition; original cloth, gilt, pages viii, 167, flyleaves browned.   R. F. G. Hollett & Son Antiquarian Booksellers   175 - 871 2011   £30

McConnochie, Alexander Inkson *The Deer and Deer Forests of Scotland.* London: H. F. And G. Witherby, 1923, First edition; 4to., modern half green levant morocco, gilt roundel from original cloth neatly relaid on upper board, pages 336, untrimmed with 14 plates, occasional faint spotting, but handsome.   R. F. G. Hollett & Son Antiquarian Booksellers   General Catalogue Summer 2010 - 1020 2011   £250

McCosh, James *An Examination of Mr. J. S. Mill's Philosophy being a defence of Fundamental Truth.* London: Macmillan and Co., 1866, First edition; 8vo., vii, (1), 406 (2) pages, original cloth, lettered and ruled in gilt, fine, fresh copy.   John Drury Rare Books   153 - 85 2011   £75

McCosh, James *The Scottish Philosophy, Biographical, Expository, Critical from Hutcheson to Hamilton.* New York: 1875, First edition; vii, 481, (6) ads, pages, very good, one gathering reseated, original binding, bookplate removed. Bookworm & Silverfish   670 - 127 2011 $125

McCourt, Frank *Angela's Ashes.* London: Harper Collins, 1996, First British edition; book fine in like dust jacket.   Bella Luna Books   May 29 2011 - t8012 2011 $137

McCourt, Frank *Angela's Ashes.* London: Harper Collins, 1996, First British edition; near fine, light bumping to spine ends, dust jacket fine.   Bella Luna Books   May 29 2011 - t9248 2011 $82

McCourt, Frank *Angela's Ashes.* London: Harper Collins, 1996, First British edition; fine in like dust jacket, signed by author.   Bella Luna Books   May 26 2011 - t2220 2011 $302

McCourt, Frank *Tis.* London: Flamingo, 1999, First British edition; signed by author, fine in fine dust jacket. Bella Luna Books   May 29 2011 - t2243 2011 $82

McCullin, Donald *The Destruction Business.* London: Open Gate Books, 1971, First edition; 8vo., pages 96, with 81 black and white photos, original black cloth, spine lettered in gold, light rubbing to tips, original black and white photo illustrated dust jacket, printed in black, toned with short closed tears to upper panel, chipping to head and foot of spine and scratches to lower panel, light creasing affects upper edges, McCullin's signature in black, ink to title page, near fine in very good dust jacket. Simon Finch Rare Books Zero - 535 2011 £750

McCully, Emily Arnold *Mirette on the High Wire.* New York: G. P. Putnam's Sons, 1992, Stated first edition,; 4to., full color pictorial boards, full color pictorial dust jacket, signed in full, illustrations. Jo Ann Reisler, Ltd. 86 - 167 2011 $175

McCutchan, Philip *Halfhyde and the Chain Gangs.* New York: St. Martin's Press, 1985, First American edition; near fine, 8vo., 184 pages, near fine dust jacket with mild edge wear, scarce signed volume. By the Book, L. C. 26 - 12 2011 $85

McDougall, Harriette *Sketches of Our Life at Sarawak.* London: SPCK, circa, 1890, Frontispiece, color map, plates, 6 pages ads, original blue green cloth, pictorially blocked and lettered in black and gilt, spine and edges faded, otherwise very good. Jarndyce Antiquarian Booksellers CLXC - 187 2011 £45

McEwan, Ian *Amsterdam.* London: Jonathan Cape, 1998, First British edition; fine, second state of dust jacket, fine jacket. Bella Luna Books May 29 2011 - t5524 2011 $82

McEwan, Ian *Atonement.* London: Cape, 2001, First British edition, true first; near fine, light wear to spine ends, dust jacket near fine, light wear with half inch closed tear at bottom rear fold. Bella Luna Books May 29 2011 - t8833 2011 $82

McEwan, Ian *Fist Love, Last Rtes.* London: Cape, 1975, First edition; signed by author, fine in fine dust jacket. Ken Lopez Bookseller 154 - 112 2011 $1500

McEwan, Ian *First Love, Last Rites.* London: Jonathan Cape, 1975, First edition, first impression; 8vo. 165 pages, signed by author, fine in fine dust jacket. Any Amount of Books May 26 2011 - A37454 2011 $1426

McEwan, Ian *First Love, Last Rites.* London: Jonathan Cape, 1975, First edition; 8vo., pages 165, publisher's black cloth, gilt lettering to spine, dust jacket very slightly creased at extremities, previous owner's signature to front free endpaper, fine. Simon Finch Rare Books Zero - 253 2011 £450

McEwan, Ian *On Chesil Beach.* London: Jonathan Cape, 2007, First British edition; fine in fine dust jacket, signed by author. Bella Luna Books May 29 2011 - t8677s 2011 $82

McEwan, Ian *Other Minds.* London: Bridgewater Press, 2001, One of 12 Roman numeraled copies signed by author; quarter library calf, fine. Ken Lopez Bookseller 154 - 114 2011 $2000

McEwan, Ian *Other Minds.* London: Bridgewater Press, 2001, Of a total of 138 copies, this one of 26 lettered copies signed by author; quarter cloth and marbled boards, fine. Ken Lopez Bookseller 154 - 113 2011 $1500

McFarland, George Bradley *Historical Sketch of Protestant Missions in Siam 1828-1928.* Bangkok: 1928, First edition; good with shelfwear, cover crushed tear to front cover top, endpaper maps, library pocket, bookplate removed, no outside marks. Bookworm & Silverfish 669 - 35 2011 $95

McGahern, John *The Dark.* London: Faber, 1965, First British edition; near fine, light bump to top front corner, dust jacket very good with light 1 inch diameter dampstain to rear panel, light chipping and small closed tears to spine. Bella Luna Books May 26 2011 - t8484 2011 $715

McGill University *Neurological Biographies and Addresses. Foundation Volume.* London: Humphrey Milford, Oxford University Press, 1936, First edition; 8vo. viii 178 pages, frontispiece, plates, navy cloth, gilt stamped spine title, small ownership signature blacked over, fine, scarce, from the Medical Library of Dr. Clare Gray Peterson. Jeff Weber Rare Books 162 - 203 2011 $100

McGowan, Edward *McGowan vs. California Vigilantes.* Oakland: Biobooks, 1946, Reprint of rare 1857 first edition, limited to 675 numbered copies signed by publisher, Joseph A. Sullivan; 205 pages, facsimiles of 2 newspapers in rear pocket, gilt lettered red and black cloth, slight rubbing to spine ends, lower corners just showing, else fine. Argonaut Book Shop Recent Acquisitions Summer 2010 - 221 2011 $75

McGowan, Edward *Narrative...Including a Full Account of the Author's Adventures and Perils while Persecuted by the San Francisco Vigilance Committee of 1856.* San Francisco: published by author, 1857, First edition; 12mo., 248 pages, illustrations, new half calf and marbled boards, corners of text worn and turned, one leaf with marginal replacement. M & S Rare Books, Inc. 90 - 245 2011 $750

McGrandle, Leith *Europe: the Quest for Unity: Speeches and Writings.* London: Ranelagh Editions, 1975, One of 475 numbered copies signed by artist; large folio, frontispiece, publisher's pressmark on titlepage from engraving by Reynolds Stone, printed on Cartiere Magnani paper, fine in full tan leather lettered gilt at spine and cover and in plain woven beige cloth slipcase, as new.   Any Amount of Books   May 29 2011 - A48199   2011 $255

McGrandle, Leith *Europe: the Quest for Unity: Speeches and Writings.* London: Ranelagh Editions, 1975, First edition, one of 475 numbered copies, signed by artist and also signed by Jean Monnet on titlepage; large folio, frontispiece etching by Pietro Annigoni, publisher's press mark on titlepage from engraving by Reynolds Stone, handsome, as new, fine copy in full tan leather lettered gilt at spine and cover and in plain woven beige cloth slipcase.   Any Amount of Books   May 26 2011 - A48127   2011 $604

McGrandle, Leith *Europe: the Quest for Unity: Speeches and Writings.* London: Ranelagh Editions, 1975, First edition, one of 475 numbered copies, signed by artist; large folio, frontispiece etching by Pietro Annigoni, publisher's press mark on titlepage from engraving by Reynolds Stone, printed in Bembo on Cartiere Magnani paper, fine in full tan leather lettered gilt at spine and cover and in plain woven beige cloth slipcase, signed by Winston Churchill's widow (Clementine Spencer Churchill), handsome, as new.   Any Amount of Books   May 29 2011 - A48837   2011 $383

McGraw, DeLoss *Hard Traveling. Etchings and Woodcuts.* San Diego: Brighton Press, 1985, Limited to 100 numbered copies, signed by McGraw; 350 x 287mm., folio, contents loose as issued in clamshell box with original painted binding by McGraw on front cover, 10 full color hand painted etchings and woodcuts, 4 additional 3 dimensional cut-out images in plastic sleeves, hand painted folding case with tie and button, like new.   Jeff Weber Rare Books   163 - 110   2011 $4000

McGuane, Thomas *In the Crazies.* Seattle: Winn Books, 1985, First edition, one of 185 numbered copies, signed by author and artist; there were 5 additional hors commerce copies, very fine, 4to., frontispiece and illustrations tipped-in, original quarter morocco and patterned paper over boards, publisher's cloth slipcase, with matching separate portfolio containing 10 original prints, 8 lithographs and 2 color etchings, each numbered and signed by artist, Russell Chatham.   James S. Jaffe Rare Books   May 26 2011 - 21739   2011 $6500

McGuane, Thomas *The Sporting Club.* New York: Simon & Schuster, 1968, First edition; near fine, light bumping to spine ends, dust jacket near fine-, offsetting or sunning to bottom part of front panel, signed by author.   Bella Luna Books   May 26 2011 - t3385   2011 $192

McIlraith, John *Life of Sir John Richardson.* London: 1868, Frontispiece, xi, 280 pages, original cloth, light wear to extremities, volume slightly cocked, else clean, tight and very good. Dumont Maps & Books of the West   111 - 67 2011 $125

McIntire, Jim *Early Days in Texas: A trip to Hell and Heaven.* Kansas City: McIntire Publishing Co., 1902, First edition; 8vo., green cloth decorated in red and lettered in black, 229 pages, frontispiece, preface, illustrations, plates, portraits, extremely rare, former owner's name on front flyleaf, else near fine, bright, tight copy, housed in clamshell case with titles stamped in gold on spine, exceptional copy, rare.   Buckingham Books   May 26 2011 - 26284   2011 $6250

McIntosh, J. T. *One in Three Hundred.* Garden City: Doubleday & Co., 1954, First edition; octavo, boards.   L. W. Currey, Inc.   124 - 202   2011 $200

McIntyre, Vonda N. *Dreamsnake.* Boston: Houghton Mifflin, 1978, First edition; octavo, cloth.   L. W. Currey, Inc.   124 - 164   2011 $350

McIntyre, Vonda N. *Dreamsnake.* Boston: Houghton Mifflin Co., 1978, First edition; octavo, cloth.   L. W. Currey, Inc.   124 - 203   2011 $200

McInyre, Walter T. *Lakeland and the Borders of Long Ago.* Carlisle: Cumberland News, 1948, First edition; original cloth, gilt, dust jacket (very worn and repaired), pages (vi), 293, (ii), frontispiece.   R. F. G. Hollett & Son Antiquarian Booksellers   173 - 717   2011   £30

McKay, C. D. *The French Garden.* the Daily Mail, n.d., 1908, First edition; original red cloth printed in black, pages 62, (iv), 9 plates.   R. F. G. Hollett & Son Antiquarian Booksellers General Catalogue Summer 2010 - 1021 2011   £30

McKee, Robinson *Tootka. The Little Russian Train.* New York: American Society for Russian Relief, 1945, First edition; 8vo., pages (22), illustrated cloth backed boards, blue papers, illustrations in color, some light wear, but very good, small inscription, scarce.   Second Life Books Inc.   174 - 240   2011 $75

McKelvey, Susan Delano *Botanical Exploration of the Trans-Mississippi West 1790-1850.* Jamica Plain: 1955, First edition; xl, 1144 pages, 11 maps, including two in back pocket, near fine in original glassine jacket.   Dumont Maps & Books of the West   113 - 40   2011 $200

McKenney, Thomas Lorraine *History of the Indian Tribes of North America, with Biographical Sketches and Anecdotes of the Principal Chiefs.* Philadelphia: D. Rice & A. N. Hart, 1858, Fourth edition; 3 volumes, 8vo., pages (2), iv, (3-) 333; xvii, (9-) 290; iv, (17-) 392, 120 hand colored lithographic plates by J. T. Bowen of Philadelphia, most are after Charles Bird King (marginal brown spot to 2 plates), contemporary morocco, elaborately blocked with stylistic foliage in corners and 5 raised bands to spine with 6 tooled panels, 2 of which are gilt lettered, some light scuffing, chipping to head of spine, text virtually clean, worming in gutter of few pages of volume 1, all edges gilt, Prexel copy with coat of arms; Charles Holman copy with coat of arms, very good.   Raymond M. Sutton, Jr.   May 26 2011 - 55944   2011 $25,000

McKim, Alicia *Greetings from California.* Denver: 2009, Artist's book, one of 50 copies; each containing five dioramas of three separate layers each of vintage postcards, printed on an inkjet printer with pigmented ink on neutral ph paper, each copy numbered by author, page size 5 1/2 x 6 1/2 inches, carousel book, bound by artist, paper over boards with blue cloth spine and blue ribbon ties, housed in publisher's stiff white board folding box.   Priscilla Juvelis - Rare Books   48 - 16   2011 $500

McKinley, William *Message from the President of the United States, Transmitting the Report of the Naval Court of Inquiry Upon the Destruction of the United States Battleship Maine in Havana Harbor Feb. 15 1898.* Washington: 1898, 307 pages, three quarter leather and marbled boards, front cover loose, bound without wrappers, many photo and sketch illustrations and two folding plates.   Bookworm & Silverfish   679 - 139   2011 $100

McKitterick, David *Selected Essays on the History of Letter-forms in Manuscript and Print.* Cambridge: Cambridge University Press, 1981, 2 volumes in slipcase, small stains on dust jacket, otherwise very clean and tight, 4to., 416 pages, 126 plates, illustrations, very good.   G. H. Mott Bookseller   May 26 2011 - 39819   2011 $500

McLain, John Scudder *Alaska and the Klondike.* New York: 1905, xiv, 330 pages, illustrations, folding map, original green cloth, light wear to extremities, previous owner's bookplate, else near fine.   Dumont Maps & Books of the West   111 - 68   2011 $125

McLean, Arthur J. *Intercranial Tumors.* Berlin: Julius Springer, 1936, 8vo., (iv), (131-285), errata (1) pages, 138 figures, green cloth, gilt stamped spine title, ownership signature of Lawrence Selling this copy with signed TLS from author to Selling, fine, rare, from the Medical Library of Dr. Clare Gray Peterson.   Jeff Weber Rare Books   162 - 206   2011 $250

McLean, Ruari *Edward Bawden, War Artist and His Letters Home 1940-1945.* London: Scolar Press, 1989, First edition; large 8vo., original cloth, gilt, dust jacket, pages 96 with 40 plates, fine.   R. F. G. Hollett & Son Antiquarian Booksellers   General Catalogue Summer 2010 - 256   2011   £35

McLean, Ruari *Motif 9.* Shenval Press, 1962, Prospectus loosely inserted, pages 102, illustrations, endpapers and 4 color plates by Bawden.   R. F. G. Hollett & Son Antiquarian Booksellers   General Catalogue Summer 2010 - 843   2011   £95

McLeod, Lyons *Travels in Eastern Africa with the Narrative of a Residence in Mozambique.* London: Hurst & Blackett, 1860, First edition; 2 volumes, 8vo., pages viii, 341; vi, 347, (1) imprint, vignette on titlepages, frontispiece, folding map in volume I, colored lithographic frontispiece volume 2, prelims and frontispieces somewhat browned and spotted, contemporary half calf, red and green labels, marbled boards, rubbed, spines neatly repaired, gilt library stamp at foot of spines.   J. & S. L. Bonham Antiquarian Booksellers   Africa 4/20/2011 - 5828   2011   £480

McMurtry, Larry   1936- *All My Friends are Going to Be Strangers.* New York: Simon & Schuster, 1972, First edition; very good, foxing to edges, color from free endpapers has bleed thru along edge of half titlepage bottom corner 1/2 x 1 1/2 inches, dust jacket very good, author's name on spine has faded to yellow, very faint dampstaining to small area of bottom front cover, very good, spine has faded to yellow, very faint dampstaining to small area of bottom front corner.   Bella Luna Books   May 29 2011 - t6137   2011 $82

McMurtry, Larry   1936- *All My Friends are Going to Be Strangers.* New York: Simon & Schuster, 1972, First edition; signed by author, near fine, very light bump to heel of spine, dust jacket near fine, light soiling and wear to extremities, early legible autograph, scarce thus.   Bella Luna Books   May 26 2011 - t7216   2011 $467

McMurtry, Larry   1936- *Anything for Billy.* New York: Simon & Schuster, 1988, First edition; fine in fine dust jacket, signed by author.   Bella Luna Books   May 29 2011 - t4852   2011 $82

McMurtry, Larry   1936- *Lonesome Dove.* New York: Simon & Schuster, 1985, First edition; very good, previous owner's name an damage from sticker removal on front free endpaper, dust jacket very good, creasing and small closed tears to spine ends, all printings of this edition have the error on page 621, there is no point there, very good, creasing and small closed tears to spine ends.   Bella Luna Books   May 29 2011 - t8921   2011 $110

McMurtry, Larry 1936- *Moving On.* New York: Simon & Schuster, 1989, First edition; fine, near fine dust jacket with light general wear with no obvious flaws, signed on front free endpaper in recent scrawl, signed by author.   Bella Luna Books   May 26 2011 - t17221 2011 $275

McMurtry, Larry 1936- *Somebody's Darling.* New York: Simon & Schuster, 1978, First edition; book near fine, light shelf wear, dust jacket near fine, light browning to top edge inside flaps, inscribed by author.   Bella Luna Books   May 26 2011 - 2491A 2011 $192

McMurtry, Larry 1936- *Terms of Endearment.* New York: 1975, First edition; nice clean copy, pages very slightly browned, but less than usual copy, remainder mark on bottom edge, entirely fine dust jacket, overall excellent copy.   Gemini Fine Books & Arts, Ltd.   Art Reference & Illustrated Books: First Editions 2011 $130

McMurtry, Larry 1936- *Terms of Endearment.* New York: Simon & Schuster, 1975, First edition; very good, moderate browning to pages, brief notes inked on pastedown under front flap, dust jacket near fine, fading to edges of front panel, light general wear.   Bella Luna Books   May 26 2011 - t7958b 2011 $275

McNeile, H. C. *The Female of the Species.* Garden City: The Crime Club/Doubleday, Doran & Co., 1928, First American edition; slight soiling, on the boards, else near fine in good or little better, spine faded dust jacket with some very small chips and tears.   Between the Covers   169 - BTC328533 2011 $300

McNickle, D'Arcy *The Surrounded.* New York: Dodd Mead, 1936, Owner name from 1939 on front pastedown, and small bookstore label on rear pastedown, foxing to page edges and dustiness to cloth, still near fine, lacking dust jacket, as is typically the case, very scarce, even without dust jacket.   Ken Lopez Bookseller   154 - 139 2011 $450

McPhee, John *Annals of the Former World.* New York: FSG, 1983, First edition, limited to 450 copies; fine, in slipcase and protective shipping box,.   Bella Luna Books   May 26 2011 - t016 2011 $220

McPhee, John *The Deltoid Pumpkin Seed.* New York: FSG, 1973, First edition; near fine, spine ends sunned and lightly bumped, dust jacket fine, signed by author.   Bella Luna Books   May 29 2011 - g3398 2011 $99

McPhee, John *The Headmaster.* New York: FSG, 1966, First edition; near fine, some creasing to spine, extremely light bumping to top corners, dust jacket is near fine, one small closed tear and light edge wear, very bright.   Bella Luna Books   May 29 2011 - p2490 2011 $137

McPhee, John *Roadkills. A Collection of Prose and Poetry.* Easthampton: Cheloniidae Press, 1981, First edition; one of 5 AP copies, inscribed by artist on first wood engraving in extra suite which is laid in, "for ****", from a total issue of 305. 5 AP copies with original drawing, extra suite of 11 wood engravings, each signed by artist who has signed the colophon as have all the authors, titlepage etching, as well an additional copy of the book, all on white Sakamto paper (text and wood engravings) including all 10 text pages, colophon again signed by all authors and Robinson and 11 wood engravings loose in folder, the 50 deluxe copies were issued (as this copy of the book) with text printed on Sakomoto and Mulberry paper and the prints on Cha-u-ke plus an extra suite of the prints, colophon of text signed by artist and all authors: 250 regular copies with text on Mulberry paper signed by artist on colophon; page size 12 x 8 3/4 inches, 58 pages, bound by Gray Parrot, quarter grey morocco with tire tracks blind tooled across spine and title in blind, matching black chemise, all housed in grey morocco and black cloth clamshell box, tiny bit of sunning to clamshell box morocco spine, else fine, illustrated with 11 wood engravings and one etching, text printed in red and black by Harold Patrick McGrath at Hampshire Typothetae in Bruce Rogers' Centaur and Frederick Warde's Arrighi which was hand set in 18 point by P. Chase Twichell, very rare, Artist's Proof with extra suite each plate signed by artist, colophon with signatures of authors, drawing and extra copy of book on different paper.   Priscilla Juvelis - Rare Books   48 - 3 2011 $3500

McPhee, John *A Roomful of Hovings and Other Profiles.* New York: FSG, 1968, First edition; near fine, light sunning to edges, dust jacket very good, half inch closed tear to top of gutter, light edge wear and some fading to spine, signed by author, very good, half inch closed tear at top of gutter, light edge wear, some fading to spine.   Bella Luna Books   May 29 2011 - 4358 2011 $82

McPhee, John *A Sense of Where You Are.* New York: FSG, 1965, First edition; near fine, very light use, dust jacket very good with light wear to extremities, with two half inch closed tears, one on front panel and one on rear panel, author's fragile first book, signed by author, very good, light wear to extremities with two half inch closed tears, one on front panel and one on rear panel.   Bella Luna Books   May 26 2011 - t7095 2011 $935

McTyeire, H. N. *Duties of Masters to Servants: Three Premium Essays.* Charleston: Southern Baptist Publication Society, 1851, First edition; 16mo., 151, (1) pages, original cloth, spotted, spine faded, stain from old sticker, just touching title leaf.   M & S Rare Books, Inc.   90 - 246 2011 $250

Mead, Kate Campbell Hurd *A History of Women in Medicine.* Haddam: 1938, First edition, one of 250 copies signed; xvi, 569 pages including index, thick 8vo., original red cloth, gilt lettered spine, profusely illustrated with frontispiece and additional full and in text illustrations, inner joints starting but holding, evidence of bookplate removal, otherwise very good, publisher's propsectus laid in.   Paulette Rose Fine and Rare Books   32 - 122   2011 $600

Meade, Elizabeth Thomasina *Bashful Fifteen.* London: Cassell & Co., 1892, First edition; half title, frontispiece + 7 plates by M. E. Edwards, 16 page catalog (coded 5 G 8.92), original lilac cloth, pale green cloth spine, blocked in blue lettered in gilt, slightly dulled, Sunday School prize label dated 1895, good plus.   Jarndyce Antiquarian Booksellers   CLXC - 372   2011   £45

Meade, Elizabeth Thomasina *The Girls of Merton College.* London: W. & R. Chambers, 1911, First edition; half title, color frontispiece + 5 plates, original red cloth, bevelled boards, pictorially blocked in brown, lilac, cream and black, lettered in gilt, slightly dulled, title blindstamped "presentation copy", nice copy.   Jarndyce Antiquarian Booksellers   CLXC - 373   2011   £45

Meade, Elizabeth Thomasina *The Golden Lady.* London: W. & R. Chambers, circa, 1890, 64 pages, frontispiece + 3 plates, original pale green cloth, pictorially blocked in black, red and white, lettered in black and red, very good.   Jarndyce Antiquarian Booksellers   CLXC - 374   2011   £35

Meade, Elizabeth Thomasina *The Honourable Miss: a Story of an Old-Fashioned Town.* London: Methuen & Co., 1891, First edition; original dark green cloth, 2 volumes, half titles, final ad leaves, spines lettered in gilt, spines slightly darkened, slightly rubbed, good plus.   Jarndyce Antiquarian Booksellers   CLXC - 375   2011   £150

Meade, Elizabeth Thomasina *The Medicine Lady.* London: Cassell & Co., 1893, First one volume edition; half title, 16 page catalog (coded 11.94), original dark green cloth, blocked in blind, spine lettered in gilt, spine bit rubbed, several small marks on front board, good, sound copy.   Jarndyce Antiquarian Booksellers   CLXC - 377   2011   £35

Meade, Elizabeth Thomasina *Mother Herring's Chicken.* London: Wm. Isbister, 1881, First edition; half title, frontispiece, 5 plates by R. Barnes, original grey cloth, blocked in black , lettered in gilt, ownership inscription 1882 and 1894, very good.   Jarndyce Antiquarian Booksellers   CLXC - 378   2011   £40

Meade, Elizabeth Thomasina *A Sister of the Red Cross; a Tale of the South African War.* London: Thomas Nelson and Sons, 1901, First edition; half title, frontispiece, engraved title, additional printed title in red and black, illustrations, original brown cloth, pictorially blocked with image of nurse in black, grey and red, lettered in black and gilt, prize label dated 1905, good, sound copy.   Jarndyce Antiquarian Booksellers   CLXC - 379   2011   £45

Meade, Elizabeth Thomasina *A Sweet Girl Graduate.* London: Cassell & Co., 1893, Ninth thousand; frontispiece and plates, 14 pages catalog, original pale brown cloth, outer margin of front board light green cloth, outer margin of front board light green cloth, blocked in gilt and dark green, lettered in gilt, very good.   Jarndyce Antiquarian Booksellers   CLXC - 380 2011   £40

Meade, Elizabeth Thomasina *The Voice of the Charmer.* London: Chatto & Windus, 1896, Half title, frontispiece, 7 plates by Walter Paget, 32 page catalog (Sept. 1896), original brown cloth blocked and lettered in brown and gilt, slightly marked.   Jarndyce Antiquarian Booksellers   CLXC - 382   2011   £40

Meadows, Kenny *Heads of People; or Portraits of English.* London: George Routledge, 1878, 2 volumes, large 8vo., engraved half titles, frontispiece and plates, some foxing to prelims, original brown cloth, blocked in black and gilt, spines slightly rubbed and dulled.   Jarndyce Antiquarian Booksellers   CXCI - 320   2011   £75

Meakin, Budgett *The Moorish Empire: a Historical Epitome + The Moors + The Land of the Moors.* London: Swan Sonnesnschein, 1899-1901, First editions; 3 volumes, original publisher's blue cloth lettered and decorated gilt on spine and cover, 8vo., pages xxiii, 576; xxii, 503; xxxi, 464; with 330 illustrations, signed presentation from author for William Digby, ex-library copies with few labels and stamps but in fairly reasonable condition, slight edgewear, prelims slightly loose, slight lean, inner hinges cracking but holding with clean text, overall apart from this near very good.   Any Amount of Books   May 29 2011 - A73085   2011 $408

Mears, Abraham *The Book of Religion, Ceremonies and Prayers of the Jews as Practised in Their Synagogues and Families on all Occasions.* London: for J. Wilson, 1738, First English adaptation; 8vo., (xiv), 291, (7) pages, fine in contemporary mottled calf, covers ruled with gilt double fillet, gilt spine, slightly rubbed, from the library of the Earls of Macclesfield at Shirburn Castle.   Maggs Bros. Ltd.   1440 - 143   2011   £1500

Mease, James *A Geological Account of the United States...* Philadelphia: Birch & Small, 1807, First edition; 5 engraved plates (marginal dampstain to 1, some foxing to 2), 16mo., (8), 496, xiv, modern cloth, new marbled endpapers, chipped title laid down on later sheet, large library stamp to title small dark stain to 2 leaves, detached corner reset with tape to few tears, mostly marginal, piece missing from a margin with no loss to letters, thin dampstain to upper margin of several pages, last 2 index pages contain marginal chipping, with slight loss to some letters and some tears, pages tanned and somewhat brittle. Raymond M. Sutton, Jr. May 26 2011 - 55884 2011 $1250

Meatyard, Ralph Eugene *Ralph Eugene Meatyard.* New York: Aperture, 1974, First edition; fine in clean, very near fine dust jacket with none of the usual fading to spine, very clean copy, less common cloth copy, author Wright Morris' copy with his ownership signature. Jeff Hirsch Books ny 2010 2011 $350

Mechem, Floyd *Cases on the Law of Agency.* Chicago: 1893, First edition; 748 pages, very good, full cream law cloth, usual finger marks, three coffee splashes to rear cover,. Bookworm & Silverfish 671 - 83 2011 $67

Medhora, Dhunjeebhoy Jamesetjee *The Zoroastrian and Some Other Ancient Systems.* Bombay: printed at the Indian Printing Press, 1886, First edition; 8vo., pages (iv), xlviii, 226, 220-275, 275a, 276-308, with ad tipped on to titlepage, internally fine, contemporary cloth, upper and lower boards decorated in blind, upper board lettered in gilt, spine lightly sunned, some foxing to endpapers, very good, scarce. Simon Finch Rare Books Zero - 132 2011 £350

Meehan, Thomas *Native Flowers and Ferns of the United States in their Botanical, Horticultural and Popular Aspects.* Boston: Prang, 1878, 2 volumes, original three quarter leather, all edges gilt, 192, 200 pages, some rubbing, very occasional soil, very good+, 96 magnificent chromolithographs of flowers after paintings by Alois Lunzer. Aleph-Bet Books, Inc. 95 - 238 2011 $850

Meek, Charles *The Will to Function.* Waltham St. Lawrence: Golden Cockerel Press, 1929, First edition; 8/300 copies printed on handmade paper, pages (iv) (blanks), 135, (5) (blanks), 8vo., original maroon buckram, faded backstrip gilt lettered, top edge gilt, others untrimmed, near fine. Blackwell Rare Books B166 - 254 2011 £50

Meek, Hannah *The Faithful Nurse.* London: Religious Trust Society, circa, 1840, 12mo., contemporary roan backed marbled boards, foot of spine defective, pages 72, 36, 2 engraved frontispieces. R. F. G. Hollett & Sons Antiquarian Booksellers 170 - 434 2011 £35

Megarry, R. E. *Miscellany-At-Law.* London: Stevens & Sons, 1955, First edition; original cloth, pages xvi, 415, patterned endpapers, presentation copy inscribed by author for (Judge) Brian Grant. R. F. G. Hollett & Son Antiquarian Booksellers 175 - 927 2011 £45

Megarry, R. E. *A Second Miscellany at Law.* Stevens & Sons, 1973, Original cloth, dust jacket little worn and faded, pages xviii, 420, patterned endpapers with design by Edward Bawden, presentation copy inscribed by author for Judge Brian Grant. R. F. G. Hollett & Son Antiquarian Booksellers General Catalogue Summer 2010 - 1189 2011 £45

Megaw, J. V. S. *Introduction to British Pre-history from the Arrival of Homo Sapiens to the Claudian Invasion.* Leicester University Press, 1979, First edition; tall 8vo. original cloth, gilt, dust jacket, pages xv, 560, illustrations. R. F. G. Hollett & Son Antiquarian Booksellers 175 - 929 2011 £35

Meggendorfer, Lothar *Der Fidele Onkel.* Esslingen: Schreiber, n.d circa, 1910, 8vo., cloth backed flexible pictorial card covers, near fine, 14 full page full color illustrations, each sliced in thirds enabling reader to made 2000 different illustrations, uncommon, quite scarce. Aleph-Bet Books, Inc. 95 - 353 2011 $1500

Meggendorfer, Lothar *Immer Lustigi.* Munchen: Broun & Schneider, n.d. circa, 1890, Folio, cloth backed pictorial boards, slight edge wear, new spine matching original, tabs extended, very good+, custom clamshell box, 8 fabulous hand colored moveable plates. Aleph-Bet Books, Inc. 95 - 354 2011 $3200

Meigs, Jon Vincent *Tumors of the Female Pelvic Organs.* New York: Macmillan, 1934, First edition; 8vo., xxxiv, 533 pages, color frontispiece, numerous figures and tables, original navy cloth, gilt stamped spine title, previous owner's inked signature and rubber stamp, near fine, from the Medical Library of Dr. Clare Gray Peterson. Jeff Weber Rare Books 162 - 215 2011 $100

Meinertzhagen, Richard *Army Dairy 1899-1926.* London: Oliver and Boyd, 1960, First edition; 8vo., pages viii, 301, 25 maps, 39 plates, illustrations, original red decorative cloth, small crease on upper cover, dust jacket spine faded. J. & S. L. Bonham Antiquarian Booksellers Africa 4/20/2011 - 8677 2011 £75

Meinertzhagen, Richard *Kenya Diary 1902-1906.* Edinburgh and London: Oliver and Boyd, 1957, First edition; 8vo., original publisher's dark brown cloth lettered gilt on spine, pages viii, 347, 30 + illustrations, neat name on front endpaper, slight shelf wear, slight lean at spine, else very good+ in chipped and nicked very good- dust jacket (price clipped but all printed material present). Any Amount of Books May 29 2011 - A62096 2011 $204

Meiselas, Susan *Carnival Strippers.* New York: Steidl/Whitney Museum, 2003, First edition thus, limited, one of 75 numbered copies; fine in fine dust jacket.   Jeff Hirsch Books   ny 2010 2011 $1250

Meitner, Lise *On the Products of Fission of Uranium and Thorium Under Neutron Bombardment.* Copenhagen: Munksgaard, 1939, First separate edition; original red printed wrappers, partially uncut, 8vo., 14 pages.   By the Book, L. C.   26 - 107 2011 $1000

Meksine, Y. *Samodelki. (Home Made Wooden Toys).* Moscow: GIZ, 1930, First edition; 8vo., color pictorial paper covers with some light soiling, 12 numbered pages (counting covers) each with color illustrations by K. Kuznetsov.   Jo Ann Reisler, Ltd.   86 - 219 2011 $550

Meksine, Y. *Kak Alla Khvorala. (How alla suffers).* Moscow: GIZ, 1926, First edition; 4to. color pictorial paper wrappers with maybe hint of toning to edges, really lovely, 20 pages within, each with color illustrations and text, illustrations by Vladimir Konashevich.   Jo Ann Reisler, Ltd.   86 - 213 2011 $2000

Melancholy of His Majesty's Ship the Lieut. Riou, Commander, Which Struck on an Island of Ice, Dec. 24 1780... London: printed for Thomas Tegg, 111, Cheapside, Plummer, printer, Seething Lane, 1789, 12mo., large folding frontispiece (3 inch tear on one fold), (2), 7-28 pages, disbound.   Anthony W. Laywood   May 26 2011 - 21691 2011 $218

Melanchthon, Philipp   1497-1560 *Epistolarum Philipi Melanchtonis Libri IV.* London: M. Flesher & R. Young, 1642, Folio, (6) ff. cols. 968, cols. 116, (9) pages, 2 color title and printer's device printed in red and black, dual column text, rebacked original calf boards, raised gilt decorated bands and orange leather spine label, extremities worn, inner hinges cracked, else very good, ownership signature inked on title with previous signature crossed out.   Jeff Weber Rare Books   163 - 13 2011 $400

Melanchthon, Philipp   1497-1560 *Grammatica Latina.* Paris: R. Estienne, 1550, (1548); 8vo., 368 pages, contemporary French binding of calf, blindstamped panel on covers with central vase of flowers stamp, vellum ms. guards (15th century), binding slightly worn, with note on flyleaf (quotation from Melanchthon) in small neat English hand, from the library of the Earls of Macclesfield at Shirburn Castle.   Maggs Bros. Ltd.   1440 - 144 2011   £550

Mellendy, H. B. *The Governors of California: Peter H. Burnett to Edmund G. Brown.* Georgetown: Talisman Press, 1965, First edition, limited to 1000 copies; 482 pages, portraits, illustrations, black cloth, gilt, very fine, with pictorial dust jacket.   Argonaut Book Shop   Recent Acquisitions Summer 2010 - 128 2011 $150

Mello, J. Magens *The Dawn of Metallurgy.* The Institute, 1889, Original wrappers, pages 26, with 2 pages of illustrations and text drawing, author's copy, so stamped and inscribed by J. Allen Brown to H. Swainston Cowper.   R. F. G. Hollett & Son Antiquarian Booksellers   177 - 572 2011   £30

Melton, Rollan *Nevadanas.* Reno/Las Vegas: University of Nevada Press, 1988, #34 of 100 copies, limited edition; signed by author, specially inscribed by author, 275 pages, slipcase lightly worn, else clean, tight, very good.   G. H. Mott Bookseller   May 26 2011 - 32122 2011 $225

Melvil, James *The Memoirs of Sir James Melvil of Halhill...* Glasgow: printed by Robert Urie, 1751, Third edition; 12mo., pages xx, 21-370 (xxx), contemporary sheep boards 'oblique-hatch fillet' roll in blind, all edges red speckled, red and buff sewn endbands, early 21st century sheep reback and corners by Chris Weston, lightly age toned, few spots, old leather, bit rubbed at edges, early MS. ink annotations cropped by binder, occasional ink annotations in fore margins and occasional manicules, also 19th century ink ownership of Thos. Barclay, from the collection of Christopher Ernest Weston 1947-2010.   Unsworths Booksellers   24 - 122 2011   £150

Melville, Elizabeth *A Residence at Sierra Leone.* London: John Murray, 1849, First edition; small octavo, xii, 335 pages, original full red blindstamped cloth, gilt spine title, covers bit soiled, but in nice shape, previous owner's signature, very good.   Jeff Weber Rare Books   163 - 105 2011 $100

Melville, Herman   1819-1891 *Mardi; and a Voyage Thither.* Boston: Page, 1923, First edition thus; with list of available books by Melville tipped to verso of half title, over a printed list of what appears to be same titles, foxing to boards and top edge, very good, in very good, unevenly sunned dust jacket with edge tear at upper front spine fold, attractive copy, uncommon in dust jacket.   Ken Lopez Bookseller   154 - 115 2011 $75

Melville, Herman   1819-1891 *Moby Dick.* New York: Harper & Bros., 1851, First American edition, first binding with publisher's device blindstamped at center of boards; very good, light shelf wear to head and foot of spine, foxing to endpapers, blanks and less so to titlepage, essentially very clean text, text tight and square, spine gilt has 'two-tone' quality to it with some reddish oxidation and some yellow gold, overall very attractive, pleasing copy.   Lupack Rare Books   May 26 2011 - ABE3422569959 2011 $60,000

Melville, Herman   1819-1891 *Moby Dick.* 1930, First Modern Library edition; 822, (1) blank (1) epilogue pages, good, some darkening to endpapers, few white specks to covers in very good dust jacket, age soil to rear panel, bit musty.   Bookworm & Silverfish   679 - 114 2011 $100

Melville, Herman 1819-1891 *Moby Dick; or, The Whale.* San Francisco: Arion Press, 1979, One of 265 copies of the book (of which 250 were for sale); along with one of 30 extra suites issued of the 100 engravings appearing in the book, the regular 100 in the volume and the extra 100, all signed by artist; with 10 original drawings used for the book's illustrations, each of these signed as well, colophon signed by artist, Barry Moser and with inscription for Becky and Gill Desmarais; 385 x 265mm., 576 pages, (2) leaves, "Moby Dick" volume plus companion portfolio of plates; publisher's fine cerulean crushed morocco, silver vertical titling on spine, in original cloth covered slipcase (hint of fading as usual), extra plates and original drawings in custom made morocco backed folding cloth box with gilt lettering, virtually pristine.   Phillip J. Pirages   59 - 70 2011 $27,500

Melville, Herman 1819-1891 *Selected Poems.* San Francisco: Arion Press, 1995, First edition; number 86 of 250 copies (total edition of 276) with a full page wood engraving by Barry Moser, signed by artist, 10.5 x 7 inches, 130 pages, cloth, matching slipcase, fine.   Gemini Fine Books & Arts, Ltd.   Art Reference & Illustrated Books: First Editions 2011 $550

Melville, Herman 1819-1891 *White Jacket; or the World in a Man-of-War.* New York: Harper and Brothers, 1850, First American edition, first printing; 12mo., (i-v) vi-vii (viii) (9)-465, (1, blank), (6 ads) pages, many text pages unnumbered, no half title called for, original black brown cloth, covers blindstamped with ornate border around center frame lettered "Harper Brothers New York", spine ruled in blind and lettered in bronze, yellow coated endpapers, spine bit sunned, some light foxing throughout and to edges but much less than usual, overall, about fine in original binding.   Heritage Book Shop   Holiday 2010 - 83 2011 $4500

Melville, Herman 1819-1891 *The Works of Herman Melville.* Standard edition, limited to 750 sets; 16 volumes, tall 8vo., original cloth, top edge gilt, dust jackets, exceptionally fine, with all hinges firm and light, no fading to spines and no wear or tear, top edge gilt,.   James S. Jaffe Rare Books   May 26 2011 - 21341 2011 $17,500

Memoir of the Early Campaigns of the Duke of Wellington in Portugal and Spain. London: John Murray, 1820, First edition; 8vo., 234 pages, ex-British Foreign Office library with few library markings, else very good in modern red cloth lettered gilt at spine, presentation copy from author for John Redwell, 1821.   Any Amount of Books   May 26 2011 - A73970 2011 $503

Memorial of Merchants, Ship Owners and Others Against the Establishment by Congress of Additional Lines of Steamships Under Government Contracts. New York: Wm. C. Bryant & Co., 1852, First edition; 8vo., 18 pages, original printed wrappers (light wear), very good.   M & S Rare Books, Inc.   90 - 404 2011 $225

Men Only. 1935,   First edition; Volume I/1-v82/230. V. 1/1-v82/330, Dec. 1935-July 1964, complete run, illustrations, 330 issues in original wrappers, very good, scarce.   I. D. Edrich   May 26 2011 - 96826 2011 $2935

Mencken, Henry L. *The Philosophy of Friedrich Nietzsche.* Boston: Luce & Co., 1908, First edition; original publisher's wine cloth, frontispiece, light shelfwear, else near fine.   Lupack Rare Books   May 26 2011 - ABE422769582 2011 $125

Mencken, Henry L. *Prejudices. First Series.* New York: 1919, First edition; 254 pages, very good, top edge brown, top rear corner bumped, backstrip lettering quite legible.   Bookworm & Silverfish   676 - 115 2011 $75

Mendelsohn, Jane *I Was Amelia Earhart.* New York: Knopf, 1996, Proof copy; fine, signed by author in hand tied brown shipping package stamped "An island somewhere in the Pacific February 1996".   Bella Luna Books   May 29 2011 - 6411 2011 $82

Menen, Aubrey *The Prevalence of Witches.* London: Chatto & Windus, 1947, First edition; pages 272, original pale green cloth, dust jacket by Edward Bawden (piece missing from head of spine), pages 272, near fine.   R. F. G. Hollett & Son Antiquarian Booksellers   General Catalogue Summer 2010 - 849 2011   £60

Menfee, Campbell *Historical and Descriptive Sketch Book of Napa, Sonoma, Lake and Mendocino, Comprising Sketches of their Topography.* Napa City: Reporter Publishing House, 1873, First edition; 356 pages, 13 engraved plates, 1 lithographed plate and 29 quite detailed text engravings, original green cloth with title blindstamped on spine and front cover, upper corners of covers with light spotting, endpapers with light foxing, else fine and clean, collated complete with all engravings, rare.   Argonaut Book Shop   Recent Acquisitions Summer 2010 - 146 2011 $900

Mennens, Frans *Miltitarium Ordinum Origines, Statuta, symbola et Insignia Iconibus, Additis Genuinis.*   Macerata: P. Salvioni for F. Manolessi, 1623, 4to., 12, 120 pages, woodcut illustrations, late 18th century English tree calf, spine gilt, yellow edges, from the library of the Earls of Macclesfield at Shirburn Castle.   Maggs Bros. Ltd.   1440 - 146 2011   £800

Menzies, Robert Henry *Life Assurance Viewed as a Profitable Investment, with Remarks on the System and Practice of Several Offices and Tables in illustration.* Prescot: printed and published by J. Culshaw, Market Place, 1853, Only edition; 8vo., 127, (1) 36 pages, slight foxing on titlepage and occasionally elsewhere, contemporary purple calf gilt, sides embossed with exuberant blind-stamped patterns, spine simply lettered in gilt, all edges gilt, head of spine snagged and worn, very good, contemporary ownership blindstamp of C. E. Driffield, Court coroner, Prescot.   John Drury Rare Books   153 - 95 2011   £275

Mercier, Cardinal *A Manual of Scholastic Philosophy.* London: Kegan Paul, 1938-1950, 2 volumes, original cloth, gilt, dust jackets rather defective in places, pages xxvi, 584; xvi, 542, with facsimile letter frontispiece, library stamps to flyleaves and titles, very good, sound set.   R. F. G. Hollett & Son Antiquarian Booksellers   175 - 931 2011   £65

Merridew, John *The Noble and Renowned History of Guy Earl of Warwick.* Chiswick: printed by C. Whittingham for John Merridew, Warwick: Longman, Hurst et al, 1821, Small 8vo., (2), 146 (2) pages, full page wood engraved frontispiece, titlepage with allegorical engraving, original roan back with printed board, worn and chipped spine, inked and dated signature, very good.   Hobbyhorse Books   56 - 105 2011 $220

Merrifield, Mary Philadelphia *The Art of Fresco Painting, as Practised by the Old Italian and Spanish Masters...* Brighton: Charles Gilpin and Arthur Wallis, 1846, 8vo., (4) lvi (2) 134 pages, half title, very good, original blindstamped gilt lettered dark blue cloth, head and tail of spine expertly repaired, covers little rubbed, scarce.   Ken Spelman Rare Books   68 - 40 2011   £120

Merrill, James *Jim's Book. A Collection of Poems and Short Stories.* New York: privately printed, 1942, First edition; 8vo., original cloth backed boards, tissue dust jacket, no firm figures on the number of copies exist, but most plausbile estimate is about 200 copies, beautiful copy, rare.   James S. Jaffe Rare Books   May 26 2011 - 7678 2011 $6500

Merrill, James *Volcanic Holiday.* New York: Nadja, 1992, First edition, one of 10 Roman numeraled copies with separate suite of original prints, with margins, each signed by Tanning, out of a total of 110 copies Printed on Rives BFK Paper and signed by author and artist; 8vo, 8 original color etchings, by Dorothea Tanning, loose signatures in handmade paper wrappers, enclosed together with a suite of 8 individually signed etchings, enclosed in oblong gray cloth slipcase with printed spine label, this special issue includes a revision of Stanza 5 typed on small piece of cream paper and initialled by Merrill, which was not included with regular issue of the book, portfolio measures 12 1/4 x 16 7/8 inches, prints measure 11 x 15 inches, image size being 7 3/8 x 6 7/ inches.   James S. Jaffe Rare Books   May 26 2011 - 10144 2011 $7500

Merriman, Henry Seton *Dross.* Herbert Stone & Co., 1899, First edition; half title, frontispiece, some slight paper browning to few gatherings, uncut in original maroon decorated cloth, blocked and lettered in white, very good.   Jarndyce Antiquarian Booksellers   CXCI - 322 2011   £40

The Merry Adventures of Robin Hood of Great Renown in Nottinghamshire. New York: printed by Charles Scribner's Sons, 1883, First edition; 245 x 185mm., xx, 296 pages, extremely pleasing modern dark brown crushed morocco, covers with simple gilt rule border, raised bands, spine gilt in double ruled compartments with volute cornerpieces and rosette centerpiece, turn-ins densely gilt with roses and leaves, patterned endpapers, top edge gilt, ornamental flyleaf and titlepage, 24 charming vignette head and tailpieces and 23 full page illustrations by Howard Pyle, bookplate featuring illegible signature of owner, endpaper with same signature; one leaf with small chip to tail edge, 3 other leaves with trivial closed marginal tears (never serious), smudges and thumbing here and there as almost invariably seen in books loved by children, otherwise quite excellent copy.   Phillip J. Pirages   59 - 302 2011 $1650

Merton, Thomas 1915-1968 *Elected Silence. The Autobiography.* London: Hollis & Carter, 1949, First UK edition; pages 381, original cloth, gilt, dust jacket torn and chipped but essentially complete, TLS loosely inserted from the Prioress of the Covent of the Good Shepherd, Edinburgh, apologising for keeping the book for so long.   R. F. G. Hollett & Son Antiquarian Booksellers   175 - 932 2011   £45

Merton, Thomas 1915-1968 *Prometheus/ A Mediation. Pro Manuscripto.* Lexington: King Library Press, 1958, Limited to 150 copies; fine, rare, original boards, 8vo., printed label on spine, presentation copy inscribed by author for Mark and Dorothy Van Doren, superb association.   James S. Jaffe Rare Books   May 26 2011 - 21342 2011 $7500

Merton, Thomas 1915-1968 *The Sign of Jonas.* New York: Harcourt Brace and Co., 1953, First edition; fine in near fine dust jacket with couple of old tape repairs on verso at spine ends, in specially made cloth slipcase, presentation copy inscribed in French by Thomas Merton (as Father Louis) on second endpaper to Dom Preome of the Oka-La Trappe in Quebec, further inscribed by Father James Fox, Merton's Abbot (superior) at Gethsemani at a time to dear Dom Preome with gratitude.   Between the Covers   169 - BTC342154 2011 $1650

Merton, Thomas 1915-1968 *The Waters of Silence.* London: Hollis & Carter, 1950, First edition; original cloth, spine little rubbed, 2 spots on upper board, dust jacket, extremities trifle rubbed.   R. F. G. Hollett & Son Antiquarian Booksellers   175 - 933 2011   £45

Le Merveilleuse De La Voyage Goutte de Vitamine. New York: published by the Coordinating Council of French Relief Societies, 1942, Oblong 8vo., spiral backed pictorial wrappers, very good, text in French with English translation below, rare. Aleph-Bet Books, Inc. 95 - 593 2011 $1200

Merwin, W. S. *Green with Beasts.* London: Rupert Hart Davis, 1956, First British edition, true first; very good with some spotting on boards, dust jacket very good with corresponding spotting. Bella Luna Books May 29 2011 - t5407 2011 $77

Merwin, W. S. *Some Spanish Ballads.* Abelard Schuman, 1961, First edition; original cloth, gilt, dust jacket, edges chipped, pages 128, few illustrations, few marginal ticks. R. F. G. Hollett & Son Antiquarian Booksellers 175 - 934 2011 £35

Mesens, E. L. T. *Troisieme Front/Poemes de Guerre...* London: London Gallery editions, 1944, First edition, no. 31 of 500 copies; 8vo., pages 47, (1) limitation, 6 full page illustrations in text, uncut, crisp, fresh copy, publisher's wrappers, green, text in black to upper side and spine, slightly faded and discolored at edges, dust jacket with light shelfwear, chipped at head and foot of spine, dated presentation inscription for Simon Watson-Taylor to half title and signature to limitation page. Simon Finch Rare Books Zero - 340 2011 £350

Methuen, Paul Cobb *Observations and Reflections Made on His Journey through France and Italy in the Years 1769-1772.* Little Rabbit Book Co., 1978, Limited edition, no. 203 of 300 copies; original marbled boards, paper label, glassine dust jacket, pages 77, illustrations, name on flyleaf, prospectus loosely inserted. R. F. G. Hollett & Son Antiquarian Booksellers General Catalogue Summer 2010 - 1654 2011 £35

Metz, Jerred *The Temperate Voluptuary. Rendered From Platina's Cookbook on Its 500th Anniversary.* Santa Barbara: Capra Press, 1975, First edition, a total of 50 numbered, signed copies; pictorial boards, handbound by Emily Paine, this copy not numbered but rather designated as "Noel Young's copy" in red ink, woodcuts by Thomas Lang, fine in glassine dust jacket. Charles Agvent 2010 Summer Miscellany - 47 2011 $100

Meurdrac, Marie *La Chimie Charitable et Facile, en Faveur des Dames.* Paris: Chez Laurent d'Houry, 1787, (xii), 414 pages and 6 pages, some mispagination, page 336 jumps to page 339, 12mo., contemporary sprinkled calf, all edges sprinkled in red, with tailpieces, ornamental initials, foldout plate with alphabetical listing of chemical symbols, frontispiece, allegorical figure's eyes have been dotted in black ink, some minor repair to extremities, occasional spots, all in all, very nice ex-libris copy from the library of Maurice Villaret and contemporary signature on front free endpaper. Paulette Rose Fine and Rare Books 32 - 156 2011 $875

Meyer, Carl *Bound for Sacramento. Travel Pictures of a Returned Wanderer.* Claremont: Saunders Studio Press, 1938, Limited to 450 numbered copies; xii, (4), 282 pages, facsimile insert, tan cloth printed in dark green, fine with pictorial dust jacket (spine and edges darkened, slight chipping), very good. Argonaut Book Shop Recent Acquisitions Summer 2010 - 131 2011 $150

Meyerowitz, Joel *Wild Flowers.* Boston: New York Graphic Society Book/Little Brown, 1983, Stated first edition; 9 x 10 inches, 63 pages, near fine, mild soil and foxing to edges, owner name, in near fine dust jacket with minimal edgewear. By the Book, L. C. 26 - 43 2011 $90

Meynell, Alice *Poems.* London: Elkin Mathews & John Lane, 1893, Half title, final ad leaf, spotting in text, uncut in original brown buckram, bevelled boards, faded and slightly marked inscribed by author to Pucky (i.e. Florence Kirby). Jarndyce Antiquarian Booksellers CLXC - 390 2011 £45

Meynell, Alice *Poems.* London: Elkin Mathews & John Lane, 1893, Second edition; half title, 7 pages ads, some spots and pencil marginal marks, full contemporary plain green calf by Bumpus, gilt dentelles, slight rubbed, inscribed by author for Florence Kerry Kirby. Jarndyce Antiquarian Booksellers CLXC - 391 2011 £45

Meynell, Alice *Poems.* London: Burns & Oates, 1914, Eleventh thousand; half title, frontispiece by Sargent slightly browned, 2 pages ads, original grey-brown cloth, rubbed, spine darkened, Wilfrid Meynell's presentation copy to Margot Ross, with holograph poem "The Modern Poet" numbered in corner '75' by Alice Meynell on slightly browned lined paper tipped in at end, with 2 cuttings inserted. Jarndyce Antiquarian Booksellers CLXC - 392 2011 £85

Meynell, Alice *The Rhythm of Life and Other Essays.* London: Elkin Mathews & John Lane, 1893, Second edition; half title, 4 pages ads + 7 page catalog, slight spotting, uncut in original light green cloth, spine faded to brown, inscribed by author for Florence Kirby. Jarndyce Antiquarian Booksellers CLXC - 393 2011 £45

Miall, L. C. *The Geology Natural History and Pre-Historic Antiquities of Craven in Yorkshire.* Leeds: Joseph Dodgson, 1878, First separate edition; 4to., original printed wrappers, rather darkened and little rubbed rebacked in matching cloth, pages 42, color map and colored section, few marks in places, library stamps to title, very scarce separate printing.   R. F. G. Hollett & Son Antiquarian Booksellers   177 - 576   2011   £120

Michener, James A. *A Century of Sonnets.* Austin: State House Press, 1997, Limited to 250 copies; fine, spine is in leather with boards in pictorial cloth, signed by author, decorative marbled slipcase.   Bella Luna Books   May 26 2011 - t2891a   2011 $247

Michener, James A. *Literary Reflections.* Austin: State House Press, 1993, Limited to 200 copies; fine, signed by author, slipcase.   Bella Luna Books   May 26 2011 - j1026   2011 $192

Michener, James A. *Literary Reflections.* Austin: State House Press, 1993, First edition; fine in fine dust jacket, signed and stamped by author.   Bella Luna Books   May 29 2011 - t650   2011 $137

Michener, James A. *Modern Japanese Print.* Rutland: & Tokyo: Charles E. Tuttle Co., 1962, First edition, one of 510 numbered copies, this being #46, signed by author and 10 contributing artists; large folio, (1)-55, (1, colophon) pages, 10 original full page prints, each signed by artist, text handset in Perpetua type, printed on handmade kyokushi or Japanese vellum, bound at Okamoto Bindery in original tritone line, stamped in gilt on front boards and spine, uncut, housed in original slipcase of unvarnished spruce or Japanese cedar, Japanese title burned into wood on front panel of slipcase, book fine, slipcase with few minor bumps and scuffs, altogether, lovely, fine copy.   Heritage Book Shop   Holiday 2010 - 84   2011 $4500

Michener, James A. *Tales of the South Pacific.* New York: Macmillan Co., 1947, First edition; octavo, (viii), 326 pages, original orange cloth, spine lettered in blue, price clipped dust jacket, pages slightly browned as usual for this title, otherwise near fine, rare, jacket brighter than usually seen.   Heritage Book Shop   Holiday 2010 - 85   2011 $750

Michie Co. *The Law of Automobiles in Virginia & West Virginia.* Charlottesville: 1947, 3 volumes, very good, each wit 1963 supplements, nearly 3000 pages, original binding.   Bookworm & Silverfish   669 - 37   2011 $75

Middiman, S. *Select Views in Great Britain.* John and Josiah Boydell, n.d., 1810-1812, Oblong small 4to., old full polished chestnut calf gilt, edges rather worn and chipped but restored, rebacked in calf gilt with raised bands and spine label, unpaginated, engraved title and 48 steel engraved plates, each with accompanying leaf of text in English and French, new marbled endpapers, front marbled free endpapers laid on to original rather damp cockled flyleaf, otherwise very nice, clean copy, pages entirely free from foxing or staining.   R. F. G. Hollett & Son Antiquarian Booksellers   173 - 768   2011   £495

Middlemass, Jean *Vaia's Lord.* London: Swan Sonnenschein, 1889, Half title, yellowback, original printed boards, slightly dulled and rubbed, lacking leading f.e.p., good plus.   Jarndyce Antiquarian Booksellers   CLXC - 396   2011   £45

Middleton, Bernard C. *History of English Craft Bookbinding Technique.* London: Holland Press, 1978, Second supplemental edition; tall 8vo., original coarse weave cloth gilt, acetate dust jacket, pages xv, 326, 11 plates, 97 line drawings in text, fine.   R. F. G. Hollett & Son Antiquarian Booksellers   General Catalogue Summer 2010 - 265   2011   £65

Middleton, Charles *A New and Complete System of Geography.* London: 1777-1779, 2 volumes, folio, xviii, 5-546 pages, 58 plates, 6 maps; 548 pages, (x), 44 plates, 15 maps (4 folding), rebound in full leather, contents browned with some marginal staining, one map with some loss to neat line.   Dumont Maps & Books of the West   113 - 41   2011 $5250

Middleton, George *Middleton's Illustrated Escort Guide to Ambleside and District.* Ambleside: G. Middleton, 1891, Small 8vo., old binder's cloth gilt, pages 144 with map frontispiece and woodcut illustrations, folding panorama, 1 leaf of text both in good facsimile, scarce.   R. F. G. Hollett & Son Antiquarian Booksellers   173 - 769   2011   £75

Middleton, Stanley *Brazen Prison.* London: Hutchinson, 1971, First edition; 8vo., 224 pages, signed presentation from author, to Muriel Dumnachie, fine in near fine dust jacket, dust jacket, very slightly creased at inner flap.   Any Amount of Books   May 29 2011 - A38142   2011 $255

Middleton, Stanley *A Place to Stand.* London: Hutchinson, 1992, First edition; 8vo., loosely inserted is good signed letter to a publicity agent, 256 pages, fine in fine dust jacket.   Any Amount of Books   May 29 2011 - A49448   2011 $213

Mikolaycak, Charles *Babushka.* New York: Holiday House, 1984, First edition; inscribed and dated by author, fine, in near fine dust jacket with mild soil, mild edge wear.   By the Book, L. C.   26 - 67   2011 $95

Miles, Sally *Crisis at Crabtree.* Cambridge: Lutterworth Press, 1986, First edition; 8vo., full color pictorial boards, as new, front free endpaper signed in full and dated 1986 by artist, Errol Le Cain, illustrations by Le Cain.   Jo Ann Reisler, Ltd.   86 - 156 2011 $200

Mill, Hugh Robert *The English Lakes...* George Philip & Son, 1895, Original cloth, pages 64, 8 folding colored maps and 20 illustrations in text, title and maps folds foxed, scarce.   R. F. G. Hollett & Son Antiquarian Booksellers   173 - 771 2011   £65

Mill, John Stuart 1806-1873 *Autobiography.* London: 1873, 313, (1) (1) errata (2 pages ads), full green pebbled cloth, corners well bruised.   Bookworm & Silverfish 662 - 150 2011 $85

Mill, John Stuart 1806-1873 *Autobiography.* London: Longmans, Green & Co., 1886, Eighth edition; pages vi, 325, (ii), few light pencilled marginal lines at beginning, name crossed out on flyleaf, otherwise fine, crisp copy, original green cloth gilt, panelled in black.   R. F. G. Hollett & Son Antiquarian Booksellers   175 - 939 2011   £75

Mill, John Stuart 1806-1873 *Principles of Political Economy with Some of Their Applications to Social Philosophy...* London: John W. Parker,, 1852, Third edition; 2 volumes, 8vo., xx, 604, xv, (1), 571, (1) pages, contemporary maroon morocco gilt, double gilt fillets on sides, spines fully gilt in compartments with raised bands and contrasting red and green lettering pieces, marbled edges, fine, late 19th century library of Sir George Bowen, armorial bookplate, ALS presenting this copy to Sir Thomas Jackson.   John Drury Rare Books   153 - 96 2011   £600

Mill, John Stuart 1806-1873 *Subjection of Women.* London: Longmans Green, Reader and Dyer, 1869, First edition; presentation "From the author", octavo, (4), (1)-188 pages, full contemporary tan polished calf gilt stamp decoration on boards and spine, spine with two brown morocco spine labels, lettered in gilt, all edges gilt, blue endpapers, bound by Riviere and Son, some light foxing to endpapers, minor cracking to joints and light wear to tips of spine, very good.   Heritage Book Shop   Holiday 2010 - 86 2011 $4500

Mill, John Stuart 1806-1873 *The Subjection of Women.* London: Longmans, Green Reader and Dyer, 1869, First edition; presentation copy "from the author", octavo, full contemporary tan polished calf by Riviere and Son.   Heritage Book Shop   Booth A12 51st NY International Antiquarian Book Fair April 8-10 2011 - 90 2011 $3500

Mill, John Stuart 1806-1873 *A System of Logic Ratiocinative and Inductive.* London: Longmans, etc., 1868, Seventh edition; 2 volumes, full calf gilt prize bindings, corner of one board little worn, one volume neatly recased, pages xviii, 541, xv, 555, few spots to flyleaves, otherwise excellent set.   R. F. G. Hollett & Son Antiquarian Booksellers   175 - 540 2011   £150

Mill, John Stuart 1806-1873 *A System of Logic Ratiocinative and Inductive.* London: Longmans, Green and Co., 1898, People's edition; original brown cloth gilt, spine trifle faded, pages xvi, 622, 32.   R. F. G. Hollett & Son Antiquarian Booksellers   175 - 941 2011   £30

Millais, John Guille 1865-1931 *Far Away Up the Nile.* London: Longmans, Green, 1924, First edition; royal 8vo., pages xii, 256, frontispiece, 49 plates, map, original red cloth, spine slightly faded.   J. & S. L. Bonham Antiquarian Booksellers   Africa 4/20/2011 - 9185 2011   £90

Millais, John Guille 1865-1931 *Rhododendrons in Which is Set Forth an Account of all Species of the genus Rhododendron (including Azaleas) and the Various Hybrids. First and Second Series.* London: Longmans, Green and Co., 1917-1924, First editions, limited to 550 copies, of which these volumes are numbers 9 and 8; 34 colored plates, 28 collotype plates, 28 half tone plates, 24 photographic plates, folio, pages xi, 268; xii, 2265, original maroon gilt lettered cloth (some wear to ends of spines, light rubbing, scuff marks to rear cover of second volume, and 1 1/2 inch split to upper edge of spine near back cover of second volume, text pages tanned), from the collection of Joseph F. Rock with his attractive bookplates.   Raymond M. Sutton, Jr.   May 26 2011 - 55811 2011 $2000

Millais, John Guille 1865-1931 *Wanderings and Memories.* London: Longmans Green, 1919, Second impression; 8vo., pages xii, 298, 4 collotype plates, 11 illustrations, original purple cloth.   J. & S. L. Bonham Antiquarian Booksellers   Africa 4/20/2011 - 8878 2011   £45

Millar, H. R. *Dreamland Express.* New York: Dodd, Mead and Co., 1927, First American edition; oblong 4to., cloth backed color illustrated boards, edge rubbing, 56 numbered pages, 15 full color illustrations and drawings.   Jo Ann Reisler, Ltd.   86 - 168 2011 $1200

Miller, A. E. Haswell *Military Drawings and Paintings in the Collection of Her Majesty the Queen.* London: Phaidon, 1969, Second edition; 2 volumes in 1, 4to. original red cloth gilt, tissue dust jacket (little creased, short edge tear), pages 20, 279 with 30 tipped in color plates and 169 black and white plates.   R. F. G. Hollett & Son Antiquarian Booksellers   General Catalogue Summer 2010 - 266 2011   £180

Miller, Anna Riggs *Letters from Italy, Describing the Manners, Customs, Antiquities, Paintings &c of that Country in the Years MDCCLXX and MDCCLXXI...* London: Edward & Charles Dilly, 1777, Second edition; 2 volumes, half titles, contemporary full tree calf, spines gilt in compartments, maroon and dark green leather labels, rebacked retaining original spine strips, little rubbed and worn, later bookplates and signatures of M. S. Sorley, good plus, internally very clean. Jarndyce Antiquarian Booksellers CLXC - 398 2011 £285

Miller, Arthur *The Price.* San Francisco: Arion Press, 1999, First Arion Press edition; number 130 of 300 copies (total edition 326), signed by author and artist, full page duotone offset lithographic plates by Stan Washburn, about 11 x 8 inches, 110 pages printed on mouldmade Zerkall paper, cloth in publisher's slipcase, new copy. Gemini Fine Books & Arts, Ltd. Art Reference & Illustrated Books: First Editions 2011 $375

Miller, Arthur *Timebends.* London: Methuen, 1987, First English edition; pages (vi, 618, 8vo. original mid blue boards, backstrip gilt blocked, dust jacket, near fine, signed by author beneath his printed signature. Blackwell Rare Books B166 - 189 2011 £150

Miller, David E. *Hole-in-the-Rock: an Epic in the Colonization of the Great American West.* Salt Lake Cty: 1959, First edition; hardcover, no dust jacket, slightly cocked, else clean and very good. Dumont Maps & Books of the West 112 - 56 2011 $85

Miller, Ellen E. *Alone through Syria.* London: Kegan Paul, Trench, Trubner and Co., 1891, First edition; 8vo., original publisher's copper cloth lettered gilt on spine and on front cover with image of masked Arab woman on cover, pages xxii, 330, frontispiece and 8 plates, unopened, uncut, sound with noticeable dampstains/mottling at edges of boards, else very good-, complete with clean text. Any Amount of Books May 29 2011 - A35410 2011 $221

Miller, George *Latter Struggles in the Journey of Life, or the Afternoon of my Days.* Edinburgh: printed by James Colston for the author, 1833, With 2 page appendix, original brown glazed cloth, corners little worn, paper spine label slightly chipped. Jarndyce Antiquarian Booksellers CXCI - 453 2011 £125

Miller, Henry 1891-1980 *Black Spring.* Paris: Obelisk, June, 1936, First edition; one of 1000 copies, 267 pages, about 7.5 x 5.5 inches, original tan and red wrappers with front cover design by Maurice Kahne, 4 pages in back roughly opened at lower corners, causing very small chips, small collector's label, otherwise in excellent condition, unusually clean, bright and fresh. Gemini Fine Books & Arts, Ltd. Art Reference & Illustrated Books: First Editions 2011 $1100

Miller, Henry 1891-1980 *The Happy Rock. A Book About Henry Miller.* Berkeley: Bern Porter, 1945-1947, First edition, 1/3000 copies; printed on multi color paper, cover illustration in red by Fernand Leger, fine in boards, very slight wear at corners, inscribed by Miller and dated 1960 on piece of paper attached to front endpaper. Gemini Fine Books & Arts, Ltd. Art Reference & Illustrated Books: First Editions 2011 $125

Miller, Henry 1891-1980 *Insomnia or the Devil at Large.* Albuquerque: Loujon Press, 1970, First edition, 1/835 signed by author, edition G; large portfolio, housed in 19 x 34 dark wood box with metal sides, front cover of box (which slides out) has photo of Miller, full set of 12 color plates, sized approximately 12 x 22 inches, and large special titlepage (mounted on cardstock), each image signed and dated in plate (i.e. printed), underneath plates, box is filled with yellow sponge/foam except for square cut-out in centre which is covered with raised decorative paper, inside the cut out is housed the 4to. book, bound in blue and gold foil, fine, signed by author, stamped "Edition G 385 copies, book signed", also inserted is a piece of Chinese/American newspaper possibly as guard to title card, publisher's original engraved gold plate bearing name of original owner on cover, excellent condition, some inevitable oxidizaton to metal sides. Any Amount of Books May 26 2011 - A48887 2011 $713

Miller, Henry 1891-1980 *Maurizius Forever.* San Francisco: Colt Press printed at the Grabhorn Press, 1946, First edition; 1/500 copies with color woodcuts after drawings by Miller, fine in cloth, without the plain brown paper dust jacket. Gemini Fine Books & Arts, Ltd. Art Reference & Illustrated Books: First Editions 2011 $190

Miller, Henry 1891-1980 *To Paint is to Love Again.* Alhambra: Cambria Books, 1960, first edition, this is out-of-series copy of the limited edition and is signed by miller; scarce, trace foxing to page and board edges, one light corner tap, near fine in very near fine dust jacket. Ken Lopez Bookseller 154 - 118 2011 $750

Miller, Henry 1891-1980 *Tropic of Cancer.* Paris: The Obelisk Press, 1939, Fifth printing; printed self wrappers, pages browned, modest tear on front wrapper and first leaf, nice and pleasing copy, very good with no restoration, very scarce. Between the Covers 169 - BTC342980 2011 $950

Miller, Henry 1891-1980 *Tropic of Cancer.* Paris: Obelisk Press, 1934, First edition; 8vo., pages 323, (1) imprint, internally fresh, pale blue grey pictorial wrappers, printed in blue and black from a design by Maurice Kahane, extremities rubbed, spine cracked in places, old repair to upper panel, black morocco backed clamshell box, lettered gilt, amusing pencil inscription, initialled L. (Laurence Vail?), increasingly difficult to find in acceptable original condition. Simon Finch Rare Books Zero - 255 2011 £9500

Miller, Henry 1891-1980 *Tropic of Capricorn.* Paris: The Obelisk Press, 1939, First edition, first issue; 8vo., pages 367, (1) blank, (1) imprint, (3) blank, without errata slip, all edges uncut, internally fine, publisher's wrapper, text and obelisk logo in black, decoration in red and white, edges of wrappers folded with slight chipping and some short tears to foot, occasional spots to spine, excellent copy. Simon Finch Rare Books Zero - 256 2011 £850

Miller, Henry 1891-1980 *What Are You going to Do About Alf?* Paris: Lecram Servant, 1935, First edition; "By Henry Miller" has been penned on first blank, by author, "Miller's name is signed in The First edition but printed in (the second)", there is no printed author name in this volume, slight surface soiling, very near fine in stapled wrappers, approximately 3 3/4 x 5 inches. Ken Lopez Bookseller 154 - 116 2011 $3500

Miller, Henry W. *Address Delivered Before the Philanthropic and Didactic Societies of the University of North Carolina June 3 1857.* Raleigh: Holden & Wilson, 1857, First edition; 8vo, 34, (2 blank) pages, original yellow printed wrappers lightly dust soiled. M & S Rare Books, Inc. 90 - 297 2011 $125

Miller, Hugh *My Schools and Schoolmasters or the Story of My Education.* Edinburgh: William P. Nimmo & Co., 1883, Contemporary half calf gilt, edges of the marbled boards little faded, pages xi, 562, frontispiece. R. F. G. Hollett & Son Antiquarian Booksellers 175 - 946 2011 £75

Miller, Hugh, Mrs. *Stories of the Cat and Her Cousins the Lion, the Tiger and the Leopard.* London: T. Nelson & Sons, 1880, Small 8vo., original brown pictorial cloth gilt over bevelled boards, little soiled an rubbed, pages ix, 132, (xii), chromolithograph frontispiece and 29 woodcuts, frontispiece and title heavily dampstained, endpapers spotted or scribbled upon joints cracked, few spots or finger marks in text, one leaf (pages 79-80) badly defective. R. F. G. Hollett & Sons Antiquarian Booksellers 170 - 436 2011 £120

Miller, Lewis H. *Hogg's Equity Procedure - a Treatise on Practice and Procedure in the Courts of Chancery of Virginia and West Virginia with Approved Forms.* Cincinnati: 1943, Third edition; large 8vo., 2 volumes, xxxii, 864; xxi, 1101-1946 pages, original binding with 1950 supplements to each volume, near fine. Bookworm & Silverfish 679 - 200 2011 $100

Miller, Matthew *Decrees & Judgments in Civil Federal Antitrust Cases (July 2 1890-January 1 1949).* Washington?: 1949?, First edition; 3 volumes, 2700 pages, original binding, very good. Bookworm & Silverfish 665 - 79 2011 $250

Miller, Olive Beaupre *Com Play with me.* Chicago: Volland, 1918, Eighth edition; pictorial boards, fine in pictorial box, illustrations by Carmen Browne, very scarce. Aleph-Bet Books, Inc. 95 - 574 2011 $250

Miller, Olive Beaupre *Whisk Away on a Sunbeam.* Chicago: Volland, 1919, First edition, no additional printings; 8vo., pictorial boards, nearly as new in pictorial box with Volland pictorial ad announcing this title laid in, beautifully illustrated by Maginel Wright Enright. Aleph-Bet Books, Inc. 95 - 575 2011 $550

Miller, Patrick *Anna the Runner.* Waltham St. Lawrence: Golden Cockerel Press, 1937, One of 150 numbered copies; signed, quarter bound niger, almost fine, signed. I. D. Edrich May 26 2011 - 102301 2011 $436

Miller, Philip *An Anthology of British Teapots.* Broseley: Micawber Publications, 1985, First edition; tall 4to., original cloth, gilt, dust jacket, pages xxii, 386, with 16 text illustrations and 2268 plates. R. F. G. Hollett & Son Antiquarian Booksellers General Catalogue Summer 2010 - 267 2011 £65

Miller, S. N. *The Roman Fort at Balmuldby.* Glasgow: Maclehose, Jackson & Co., 1922, First edition; large square 8vo., original cloth, gilt, little rubbed, pages xix, 120, untrimmed, 58 plates. R. F. G. Hollett & Son Antiquarian Booksellers 177 - 578 2011 £65

The Miller's Wife. Greenfield: A. Phelps, 1844, 16mo., 18 pages, yellow pictorial paper wrappers, large wood engraved vignette on titlepage, 11 charming woodcuts, rare, near mint state. Hobbyhorse Books 56 - 26 2011 $200

Millett, Edward, Mrs. *An Australian Parsonage; or the Settler and the Savage in Western Australia.* London: Edward Stanford, 1872, Second edition; half title, uncut in original purple cloth, spine lettered in gilt, little dulled and marked, good, sound. Jarndyce Antiquarian Booksellers CLXC - 399 2011 £150

Milligan, Spike *Pudkoon.* London: Anthony Blond, 1963, First edition; 8vo., pages 153, 5 illustrations, signed presentation from author, very good+ in like dust jacket (very slightly soiled and slightly rubbed at corners), decent copy. Any Amount of Books May 26 2011 - A43809 2011 $419

Milligan, Spike *Small Dreams of a Scorpion. Poems by Spike Milligan.* London: M. & J. Hobbs in association with Michael Joseph, 1972, First edition; 8vo., pages 80, numerous illustrations, very light foxing to extremities and faint stain to pages 46-7, otherwise very crisp and clean copy, original black cloth, spine lettered in silver, scorpion design in silver to upper board, original illustrated dust jacket printed in black and orange, light soiling to inside upper edge of dust jacket, inscribed by author to Robert Graves in blue ink on dedication page, manuscript alterations made by Milligan in blue ink to poem "Mirror, Mirror" on page 75, near fine. Simon Finch Rare Books Zero - 341 2011 £950

Mills, Anson *My Story.* Washington: 1918, 412 pages, illustrations, flexible leather covers, light shelfwear, else near fine. Dumont Maps & Books of the West 111 - 69 2011 $225

Mills, Dorothy *The Arms of the Sun.* London: Duckworth, 1924, First edition; 8vo., pages 284, original publisher's red cloth, lettered black on spine and cover, publisher's monogram blindstamp at rear, second state of binding, first has gilt lettering, sound, decent, about very good with slight marks to cover, endpapers slightly browned, neat name on front endpaper. Any Amount of Books May 29 2011 - A71384 2011 $204

Mills, Herbert V. *Lake Country Romances.* Elliot Stock, 1892, First edition; original cloth, gilt, little soiled, one corner damped, pages (ii), 236, 8 illustrations, scarce. R. F. G. Hollett & Son Antiquarian Booksellers 173 - 772 2011 £45

Mills, John *D'Horsay; or the Follies of the Day.* London: William Strange, 1844, First edition; frontispiece, additional engraved title, plates foxed, some heavily, contemporary half brown calf, green morocco label, slightly rubbed, armorial booklabel of Hastings, laid down on leading pastedown over ink inscription. Jarndyce Antiquarian Booksellers CXCI - 323 2011 £125

Mills, John Fitzmaurice *The Noble Dwellings of Ireland.* London: Thames & Hudson, 1987, First edition; 4to., original cloth, gilt, dust jacket, pages 223 with 158 illustrations. R. F. G. Hollett & Son Antiquarian Booksellers 177 - 579 2011 £30

Mills, W. W. *Forty Years at El Paso.* N.P.: Chicago, 1901, First edition; frontispiece, 166 pages, original red cloth, owner's embossed name stamp on f.f.e.p., else bright and near fine in custom slipcase. Dumont Maps & Books of the West 111 - 70 2011 $400

Millward, Michael *Victorian Landscape.* London: Ward Lock, 1974, First edition; oblong 4to., original cloth gilt, dust jacket, pages 120, with 84 illustrations, 2 copy letters to Brian Coe, and 3 large original photos by him, loosely inserted. R. F. G. Hollett & Son Antiquarian Booksellers 177 - 581 2011 £45

Milne, Alan Alexander 1882-1956 *The Christopher Robin Story Book.* New York: Dutton, 1929, Limited to only 350 numbered copies signed by author and artist; black and white illustrations by E. H. Shepard, 4to., green cloth spine and tips, pink pictorial boards, very fine in original pictorial box (lightly soiled). Aleph-Bet Books, Inc. 95 - 358 2011 $3500

Milne, Alan Alexander 1882-1956 *Christopher Robin Birthday Book.* London: Methuen, 1930, First edition; 12mo., cloth, 215 pages, fine in slightly soiled, near fine dust jacket, illustrations by E. H. Shepard, quite uncommon. Aleph-Bet Books, Inc. 95 - 357 2011 $1500

Milne, Alan Alexander 1882-1956 *The Christopher Robin Story Book.* London: Methuen, 1929, First edition; original blue cloth gilt, trifle worn and bumped, pages x, 172, illustrations by E. H. Shepard. R. F. G. Hollett & Sons Antiquarian Booksellers 170 - 437 2011 £120

Milne, Alan Alexander 1882-1956 *A Gallery of Children.* Stanley Paul & Co., 1925, Second edition; large 4to., original blue cloth gilt with pictorial onlay, trifle marked, extremities little rubbed, pages 106, 12 fine color plates, piece torn from lower corner of one text leaf, not affecting text, otherwise very nice, clean copy. R. F. G. Hollett & Sons Antiquarian Booksellers 170 - 397 2011 £120

Milne, Alan Alexander 1882-1956 *House at Pooh Corner.* London: Methuen, 1928, Deluxe edition; 8vo., full calf with gilt vignettes and floral decoration, all edges gilt, 103 pages, fine in original publisher's box with printed label, box rubbed with light soil, illustrations by E. H. Shepard, scarce in this binding and beautiful copy. Aleph-Bet Books, Inc. 95 - 363 2011 $2700

Milne, Alan Alexander 1882-1956 *The House at Pooh Corner.* London: Methuen, 1928, Limited to only 350 numbered copies; signed by Milne and Shepard, 4to., cloth backed boards, fine in dust jacket only very slightly worn, housed in custom quarter leather box, printed on handmade paper resulting in very sharp reproductions, laid in is 1 page handwritten letter dated 1926 from author presenting the book. Aleph-Bet Books, Inc. 95 - 359 2011 $11,500

Milne, Alan Alexander 1882-1956 *The House at Pooh Corner.* London: Methuen, 1928, First edition; original cloth, gilt, spine trifle faded, lettering dulled, pages xi, 180, top edge gilt, decorations by E. H. Shepard. R. F. G. Hollett & Sons Antiquarian Booksellers 170 - 440 2011 £120

Milne, Alan Alexander 1882-1956   *The House at Pooh Corner.* London: Methuen, 1928, First edition, deluxe issue; original limpred calf gilt, spine and upper board gilt decorated, spine trifle rubbed and canted, all edges gilt, decorations and pink endpapers by E. H. Shepard, very nice, clean copy.   R. F. G. Hollett & Sons Antiquarian Booksellers   170 - 441   2011   £450

Milne, Alan Alexander 1882-1956   *The House at Pooh Corner.* London: Methuen, 1928, First edition; original cloth gilt, head of spine trifle faded, dust jacket (extremities creased and worn, backstrip worn and darkened, pieces msising from head and foot), pages xi, 180, titlepage, decorations by E. H. Shepard, narrow strip lightly browned on each flyleaf.   R. F. G. Hollett & Sons Antiquarian Booksellers   170 - 539   2011   £400

Milne, Alan Alexander 1882-1956   *The King's Breakfast.* London: Methuen, 1928, Third edition; large 8vo., original cloth backed pictorial boards, title soiled, pages vi, 17, flyleaves slightly browned.   R. F. G. Hollett & Son Antiquarian Booksellers   175 - 947   2011   £30

Milne, Alan Alexander 1882-1956   *The Music and Lyrics of Make Believe.* Samuel French, 1925, 4to., original wrappers, pages 65, 10 page lyrics insert, signs of 2 small labels removed from upper wrapper, else fine.   R. F. G. Hollett & Son Antiquarian Booksellers   General Catalogue Summer 2010 - 851   2011   £35

Milne, Alan Alexander 1882-1956   *Now We Are Six.* London: Methuen, 1927, Limited to 200 copies, signed by author and artist; 4to., tan cloth backed brown boards with printed paste label with title and details on front cover, hint of fading to upper covers, printed dust jacket with some soiling and wear, printed on handmade paper.   Jo Ann Reisler, Ltd.   86 - 169   2011 $2000

Milne, Alan Alexander 1882-1956   *Now We Are Six.* London: Methuen, 1927, first edition, deluxe issue; original full limp blue leather gilt, spine little faded, pages x, 104, decorations by Ernest H. Shepard, contents fine.   R. F. G. Hollett & Son Antiquarian Booksellers   170 - 444   2011   £650

Milne, Alan Alexander 1882-1956   *Now We Are Six.* London: Methuen, 1927, First edition; original cloth, gilt, dust jacket (spine little darkened, some loss to head and little wear to foot, short closed tear to lower edge and wear to hinges of flaps), pages x, 104, decorations by E. H. Shepard, slight browning to inner third of half title and final leaf, else contents fine.   R. F. G. Hollett & Sons Antiquarian Booksellers   170 - 443   2011   £500

Milne, Alan Alexander 1882-1956   *Now We Are Six.* London: Methuen, 1927, First edition; original cloth, gilt, dust jacket, spine little darkened, some loss to head and little wear to foot, short closed tear to lower edge and wear to hinges of flaps, pages x, 104, with decorations by E. H. Shepard, slight browning to inner third of half title and final leaf, otherwise contents fine.   R. F. G. Hollett & Son Antiquarian Booksellers   General Catalogue Summer 2010 - 541   2011   £500

Milne, Alan Alexander 1882-1956   *Now We Are Six.* London: Methuen, 1927, First edition, deluxe issue; original full limp blue leather gilt, spine little faded, pages x, 104, decorations by E. H. Shepard, contents fine.   R. F. G. Hollett & Son Antiquarian Booksellers   General Catalogue Summer 2010 - 542   2011   £650

Milne, Alan Alexander 1882-1956   *Now We Are Six.* London: Methuen, 1927, Second edition; original cloth, gilt, spine rather faded, pages x, 104, top edge gilt, decorations by Ernest H. Shepard, half title browned, flyleaves lightly spotted.   R. F. G. Hollett & Sons Antiquarian Booksellers   170 - 445   2011   £85

Milne, Alan Alexander 1882-1956   *Now We Are Six.* London: Methuen, 1927, Third edition; original cloth, gilt, dust jacket (one very short closed edge tear), pages xv, 166, (ii), 8, flyleaves lightly and partially browned, otherwise fine.   R. F. G. Hollett & Sons Antiquarian Booksellers   170 - 450   2011   £350

Milne, Alan Alexander 1882-1956   *Now We Are Six.* London: Methuen, 1927, Third edition; original cloth, gilt, spine rather darkened, dust jacket, spine rubbed and browned, few small edge chips, pages x, 104, top edge gilt, decorations by Ernest H. Shepard, neat name on half title.   R. F. G. Hollett & Sons Antiquarian Booksellers   170 - 446   2011   £180

Milne, Alan Alexander 1882-1956   *(The Four Pooh Books).* London: 1924-1928, First editions; octavo., 4 volumes, decorations by E. H. Shepard, original cloth laid down and uniformly bound in their respective colors.   Heritage Book Shop   Booth A12 51st NY International Antiquarian Book Fair April 8-10 2011 - 92   2011 $5000

Milne, Alan Alexander 1882-1956   *Toad of Toad Hall.* London: Methuen & Co., 1929, Limited to 200 copies; printed on handmade paper, this being number 136, signed by Kenneth Grahame and Milne, quarto, original quarter blue cloth over beige paper covered boards, uncut, publisher's printed dust jacket.   Heritage Book Shop   Booth A12 51st NY International Antiquarian Book Fair April 8-10 2011 - 91   2011 $3000

Milne, Alan Alexander 1882-1956 *Toad of Toad Hall.* London: Methuen & Co., 1929, Limited to 200 copies printed on handmade paper, this being 136; signed by Milne and Kenneth Grahame, quarto, (i)-xv, (1, blank), (1)-166, (1, epilogue), (1, colophon) pages, printed paper label tipped in after colophon, original quarter blue cloth over beige paper boards, printed paper label on front board, uncut, printed on handmade paper, original publisher's printed dust jacket (bit smudged with very minimal chipping to head and tail of spine), overall very good.   Heritage Book Shop   Holiday 2010 - 87   2011 $3000

Milne, Alan Alexander 1882-1956 *Toad of Toad Hall.* London: Methuen, 1929, Limited to only 200 copies, numbered and signed by author and Kenneth Grahame; 4to., cloth backed boards, fine in dust jacket and custom quarter leather box, dust jacket lightly soiled with narrow 1 inch chip off front panel and slight frayed and spine ends, beautiful copy.   Aleph-Bet Books, Inc.   95 - 364   2011 $3500

Milne, Alan Alexander 1882-1956 *When We Were Very Young.* London: Methuen, 1924, First edition; 4to., cloth backed boards, except for a few oxidation marks, very fine in very good+ dust jacket (spine sunned and two small chips off top of spine), housed in custom quarter leather box, #36 of only 100 numbered copies signed by author and artist, rare and beautiful copy.   Aleph-Bet Books, Inc.   95 - 361   2011 $24,000

Milne, Alan Alexander 1882-1956 *When We Were Very Young.* London: Methuen, 1924, Seventh printing; 8vo., publisher's full blue leather deluxe binding, spine ends rubbed and spine slightly faded, owner name on verso of free endpaper, very good-fine, rare.   Aleph-Bet Books, Inc.   95 - 362   2011 $1850

Milne, Alan Alexander 1882-1956 *When We Were Very Young.* London: Methuen, 1924, Second edition; 8vo., pages xi, 100, illustrations by E. H. Shepard, faint rubbing, endpapers very faintly browned, near fine, exceptional condition.   Any Amount of Books   May 29 2011 - A62570   2011 $383

Milne, Alan Alexander 1882-1956 *When We Were Very Young.* London: Methuen, 1924, Fourth edition; original blue cloth gilt, dust jacket, most of backstrip lacking, rather soiled, edges worn, pages x, 100, top edge gilt, decorations by Ernest H. Shepard, inscription on flyleaf, otherwise very good.   R. F. G. Hollett & Sons Antiquarian Booksellers   170 - 451   2011   £150

Milne, Alan Alexander 1882-1956 *When We Were Very Young.* London: Methuen, 1926, Fourteenth edition; pages x, 100, original blue cloth gilt, few slight marks to lower board, top edge gilt, decorations by E. H. Shepard, flyleaves lightly spotted, half title rather browned.   R. F. G. Hollett & Sons Antiquarian Booksellers   170 - 452   2011   £75

Milne, Alan Alexander 1882-1956 *When We Were Very Young.* London: Methuen, 1927, Sixteenth edition; original cloth, gilt, dust jacket (top edge little rubbed and frayed, small chip to head of spine), pages x, 10, top edge gilt, decorations by Ernest H. Shephard, label removed from flyleaf.   R. F. G. Hollett & Sons Antiquarian Booksellers   170 - 453   2011   £95

Milne, Alan Alexander 1882-1956 *A Complete Set of Winnie the Pooh Books. When We Were Very Young. Winnie the Pooh. Now We are Six. The House at Pooh Corner.* London: Methuen, 1924, 1926. 1927. 1928. First editions; crown 8vo., pages xi, 100, original mid blue cloth, illustrations throughout, some full page by E. H. Shepard, pages xi, 100, crown 8vo., original mid blue cloth, backstrip lettering and Shepard designs on covers, all gilt blocked, backstrip little rubbed at head an tail, free endpaper browned, ownership signature, top edge gilt, others rough trimmed, lightly hand soiled, dust jacket frayed, little more so at darkened backstrip panel and tail, good; endpaper designs and decorations throughout, some full page, all by E. H. Shepard, pages xvi, 160, crown 8vo., original mid green cloth, backstrip lettering and Shepard designs on covers, all gilt blocked, usual partial free endpaper browning, top edge gilt, others rough trimmed, dust jacket trifle rubbed and with darkening to backstrip panel, very good; endpaper designs and decorations throughout, some full page by E. H. Shepard, pages xi, 104, crown 8vo., original dark red cloth, backstrip little darkened with lettering and Shepard designs on covers, all gilt blocked partial initial and final page browning as usual, top edge gilt, others rough trimmed, dust jacket with handling soiling, backstrip panel little darkened, chipped at head and lacking half inch at tail, short tear to head of front panel, good; crown 8vo., pages xi, 180, endpaper designs and decorations, by E. H. Shepard, original pink cloth, backstrip lettering and Shepard design on front cover, all gilt blocked, usual partial free endpaper browning, top edge gilt, others rough trimmed, dust jacket trifle darkened at backstrip, panel chipped at head, faint dampstaining fro two inches at tail and on immediately adjacent panels, good.   Blackwell Rare Books   B166 - 190   2011   £4500

Milne, Alan Alexander 1882-1956 *Winnie the Pooh.* London: Methuen & Co., 1926, First edition, one of 350 copies on handmade paper, signed by author and artist; small quarto, xi, (1, blank, (4), 158, (2) pages, folding map at end, text illustrations, original quarter dark blue cloth over light blue boards, printed paper label on front cover, dust jacket, edges uncut, jacket spine and edges lightly browned, with minor wear, some offsetting to endpapers from dust jacket as usual, overall, pleasing, near fine.   Heritage Book Shop   Holiday 2010 - 88   2011 $11,000

Milne, Alan Alexander 1882-1956 *Winnie the Pooh.* London: Methuen, 1926, First edition, deluxe edition; 8vo., full green publisher's morocco, gilt pictorial cover with extensive gilt pictorial spine, all edges gilt, 103 pages, fine, illustrations by E. H. Shepard.   Aleph-Bet Books, Inc.   95 - 360   2011 $4500

Milne, Alan Alexander 1882-1956 *Winnie the Pooh.* London: Methuen, 1936, Sixteenth edition; original cloth, gilt, dust jacket (little rubbed and fingered, piece cut out of front flap), pages xi, 160, decorations by E. H. Shepard, label removed from flyleaf.   R. F. G. Hollett & Sons Antiquarian Booksellers   170 - 454 2011   £45

Milne, Alexander Taylor *A Centenary Guide to the Publications of the Royal Historical Society 1868-1968 and of the former Camden Society 1838-1897.* London: Royal Historical Society, 1968, Original red cloth gilt, upper board rather marked, pages xi, 249.   R. F. G. Hollett & Son Antiquarian Booksellers   General Catalogue Summer 2010 - 442 2011   £30

Milner, Richard *Black Players: The Secret World of Black Pimps.* Boston: Little Brown, 1973, 329 pages, book is very clean and tight, very good, dust jacket worn at edges.   G. H. Mott Bookseller   May 26 2011 - 46749 2011 $250

Milosz, Czeslaw *The View.* Library Fellows of the Whitney Museum of American Art, 1985, First edition, limited to 120 copies signed by author and artist; tall 4to., 4 mezzotints by Vija Celmins, original black leather and paper covered boards, matching slipcase, very fine.   James S. Jaffe Rare Books   May 26 2011 - 5377 2011 $15,000

Milton, John 1608-1674 *Comus.* London: William Heinemann/New York: Doubleday Page, 1921, One of 550 copies; signed by artist, 300 x 233mm., 3 p.l., ix-xviii, 76 pages, (1) leaf, very attractive deep blue morocco by Zaehnsdorf for E. Joseph (stamp signed), upper board with very large gilt pictorial presentation and titling, raised bands, gilt spine titling, densely gilt turn-ins, marbled endpapers, top edge gilt, other edges untrimmed and partly unopened, illustrated titlepages, numerous black and white drawings, and 24 particularly pleasing color plates by Arthur Rackham, mounted on brown paper, original tissue guard, with descriptive letterpress; bookplate of Robert J. Wickenheiser, virtually faultless copy.   Phillip J. Pirages   59 - 292 2011 $3900

Milton, John 1608-1674 *Literae Pseudo-Senatus Anglicani, Cromwellii.* Brussels?: Impressae anno, 1676, First edition of Milton's Latin letters, distinguished by woodcut of fruit on titlepage; 12mo., (4), 234 pages + final blanks K10-12, woodcut of fruit on title, modern full calf, very skillfully executed in period style, original pastedowns retained, fine, lovely copy.   Joseph J. Felcone Inc.   Fall Miscellany 2010 - 89 2011 $900

Milton, John 1608-1674 *Paradise Lost.* London: S. Simons, 1668, First edition, Amory's No. 2 issue (traditional 4th title); small quarto, full modern period style paneled calf, spine decorated in gilt, red morocco spine label with gilt lettering, endpapers replaced, titlepage professionally restored to replace loss of several letters, light ink notations and underlining, overall very good.   Heritage Book Shop   Holiday 2010 - 89 2011 $25,000

Milton, John 1608-1674 *Paradise Lost. A Poem in 12 Books.* London: The Hodgkin for Jacob Tonson, 1695, Sixth edition; pages (8), 343, (30), small folio, frontispiece, 12 superb engravings, superbly bound in recent mocha full calf, front and rear edges decorative blind tooled, spine with five raised bands and gilt lettered, new double endpapers front and rear, tiny (6 x 5MM) chip to edge of first three leaves, nowhere near print, dot sized (2 x 1 mm.) hole in middle of titlepage, foxing/spotting throughout text ranges from negligible to mild with few instances of moderate, occasional closed tear, overall impressive condition.   Any Amount of Books   May 26 2011 - !75495 2011 $1761

Milton, John 1608-1674   *Paradise Lost.* London: Charles Tilt, 1833, Second edition; (10) 373 pages + 24 engraved plates, large 8vo., full black leather lettered gilt at spine, gilt oval decorative device front and rear, all page edges gilt, two and half line 19th century inscription, otherwise excellent clean condition.   Any Amount of Books   May 26 2011 - A76852 2011 $1426

Milton, John 1608-1674   *Paradise Regain'd.* London: printed for J. M. for John Strakey, 1671, First edition, first issue; with licence and errata leaf with error 'loah' on leaf F2 (page 67), line 2 in the corrected state 'loth', small octavo, contemporary brown panelled calf.   Heritage Book Shop   Booth A12 51st NY International Antiquarian Book Fair April 8-10 2011 - 93 2011 $10,000

Milton, John 1608-1674   *Paradise Regain'd. A Poem. in IV Books. To Which is added Samson Agonistes.* London: printed for J. M. for John Starkey, 1671, First edition, first issue; with license leaf and with error "loah" on leaf F2 (page 67), line 2 in the corrected state "loth", (4), 111, (1, blank), 101, (3) pages, small octavo, contemporary brown panelled calf, red calf spine label, lettered in gilt, new endpapers, rebacked, preserving original spine, beautiful copy.   Heritage Book Shop   Holiday 2010 - 90 2011 $10,000

Milton, John 1608-1674   *The Poetical Works...* printed for J. Johnson (and 25 other firms...) by Bye and Law, 1801, First Todd edition; 6 volumes, frontispiece in volume I, one facsimile plate in volume VI, royal 8vo., contemporary Russia, single gilt fillet border on sides, gilt rules on either side of raised bands on spines, lettered in gilt direct, gilt edges, spines little dry and slightly worn at head, bookplate of Shute Barrington, Lord Bishop of Durham, very good.   Blackwell Rare Books   B166 - 68 2011   £900

Milton, John 1608-1674 *The Poems.* New York: printed in Great Britain at the Florence Press by R. & R. Clark of Edinburgh for Brentano's, 1925, 2 volumes, 229 x 152mm., attractively gilt dark blue morocco for Brentano's, one volume skillfully rebacked, retaining original backstrip, other volume artfully rejointed, covers with double gilt ruled border, pretty cornerpieces of entwined vines, terminating in leaves and flowers, raised bands, spines gilt in compartments featuring central floral ornaments and foliate cornerpieces, wide turn-ins with six gilt rules, marbled endpapers, top edge gilt, mostly unopened; spines slightly darkened, covers little dulled from leather preservative, text a shade less than bright, sound and very pleasing copy, well printed scholarly edition, gilt decoration bright and attractive, most of text never having been read. Phillip J. Pirages 59 - 193 2011 $450

Milton, John 1608-1674 *The Poetical Works of John Milton.* London: T. Nelson & Sons, 1855, Frontispiece, additional engraved title, plates, original black morocco heavily blocked in blind, lettered in gilt on boards and spine, all edges gilt, booklabel of Hairlie Lloyd-Jones, fine. Jarndyce Antiquarian Booksellers CXCI - 442 2011 £75

Milton, John 1608-1674 *The Poetical Works with a Life of the Author.* Boston: R. H. Hinkley Co. Printed by D. B. Updike at the Merrymount Press, 1908, One of 555 copies this #132; 250 x 165mm., 4 volumes, publisher's heavily embossed brown pigskin, each cover with deeply impressed ornate central panel of luxuriant flowering vines, raised bands, top edge gilt, other edges untrimmed, titlepages and head and tailpieces, 16 illustrations adapted from John Flaxman; spines uniformly bit lightened, small areas of the heavily blindstamped decoration with residual leather preservative, other trivial defects, but pleasing copy, bindings with no significant wear and text clean, fresh and bright. Phillip J. Pirages 59 - 262 2011 $650

Milton, John 1608-1674 *Prose and Poetical Works.* William Ball, 1838, Thick 4to., original blindstamped cloth, gilt, faded, pages xliv, 963, 14, 192, frontispiece, upper joint cracked. R. F. G. Hollett & Son Antiquarian Booksellers 175 - 949 2011 £65

Milward, John *The Diary of John Milward, Esq. Member of Parliament for Derbyshire September 1666 to May 1668.* Cambridge: University Press, 1938, First edition; original cloth, paper spine label, dust jacket little chipped and rubbed, pages ci, 350, with pedigree. R. F. G. Hollett & Son Antiquarian Booksellers 175 - 1134 2011 £35

Minarik, Else Holmelund *Little Bear's Visit.* Tadworth: The World's Work (1913), 1964, Third impression; original cloth backed pictorial boards, dust jacket (extremities rather worn in places), pages 64, illustrations in green and pink by Maurice Sendak, name on flyleaf. R. F. G. Hollett & Sons Antiquarian Booksellers 170 - 625 2011 £30

Minarik, Else Holmelund *No Fighting. No Bitting!* New York: Harper and Bros., 1958, First edition; 8vo., cloth backed pictorial boards, (63) pages, fine in dust jacket with slight soil and slight fraying at spine ends, quite scarce, illustrations by Maurice Sendak. Aleph-Bet Books, Inc. 95 - 510 2011 $375

Minarik, Else Holmelund *No Fighting No Biting!* New York: Harper and Bros., 1958, First edition; original cloth backed pictorial boards, dust jacket price clipped, pages 62, illustrations in color by Maurice Sendak. R. F. G. Hollett & Sons Antiquarian Booksellers 170 - 626 2011 £50

Mincius Felix, Marcus *Octavius. Cum Integris Woweri, Elmenhorstii Heraldi & Rigaltii notis Aliorumque hinc inde Collectis ex Recensione Jacobi Gronovii...* Leiden: Apud Cornelium Boutestein, Samulem Luchtmans, 1709, One engraved plate, titlepage in red and black little spotting, small shelfmark stamp on title, pages (xx), 496, (24), 8vo., early vellum, red morocco label on smooth backstrip, small shelfmark inked in white to base of backstrip, little soiled, neat monastery bookplate, prize inscription (1728) in verso of flyleaf, good. Blackwell Rare Books B166 - 69 2011 £250

Mintorn, John *The Hand-Book for Modelling Wax Flowers.* London: George Routledge, 1849, Third edition; xi, (i), 82, (2) pages, half title, very good in original blind and gilt stamped cloth, all edges gilt, some slight foxing. Ken Spelman Rare Books 68 - 43 2011 £50

Mirbeau, Octave Henri Marie 1850-1917 *Le Jardin des Supplices avec un desin en Couleur par Auguste Rodin.* Paris: Charpentier et Fasquelle, 1899, First edition, large paper (only large paper copies had initialled frontispiece), no. 124 of 150 on handmade velin de cuve; large 8vo., pages (vi), xxviii, 327, (1) blank, plus original colored lithograph, by Auguste Rodin and initialled in pencil by him, mounted as frontispiece, contemporary crimson half morocco, gilt lettered on spine, marbled boards, marbled endpapers, top edges gilt, others untrimmed, original cream wrappers and spine, lettered in red, bound in, wrappers slightly dust marked, otherwise near fine. Simon Finch Rare Books Zero - 434 2011 £2000

Mirrlees, Helen Hope *Lud-in-the-Mist.* New York: Alfred A. Knopf, 1927, First US edition; octavo, pages (1-2) (1-10) 11-313 (314 blank) (315: "a note on the type...") (316-318 blank) (note: last leaf is a blank), titlepage printed in light blue and black, original decorated boards with green cloth shelf back, printed paper label affixed to spine panel, decorated endpapers, fore and bottom edges rough trimmed. L. W. Currey, Inc. 124 - 75 2011 $1250

Miscellaneous Observations and Opinions on the Continent. London: Longman, Hurst, Rees, Orme, Brown and Green, 1825, First edition; large 8vo., original publisher's grey paper covered boards with printed spine label, pages 214, uncut, half inch chip at head of spine, otherwise sound, clean, very good copy.   Any Amount of Books   May 29 2011 - A49036   2011 $306

Misrach, Richard   *Richard Misrach.*   San Francisco: Grapestake Gallery, 1979, First edition, of a total edition of 100 cloth bound copies, this unnumbered; fine in fine glassine jacket, signed and warmly inscribed in year of publication by Misrach to his friend and fellow photographer Ray McSavaney.   Jeff Hirsch Books   ny 2010 2011 $3500

Missionary Records Greenland, Labrador and Asiatic Russia.   Philadelphia: Presbyterian Board of Publication, n.d. 1850's?, 12mo., pages 279, marbled paper covered boards, cloth spine, gilt titles to spine with call number at top, severely foxed due to poor paper quality, covers and spine worn and bumped, rear endpaper has bottom half missing.   Schooner Books Ltd.   96 - 72   2011 $150

Mr. Stops; or the Guide to Punctuation.   New York: no other information known, circa, 1845, 12mo., blue printed paper wrappers with roughness to edges, marginal tears throughout and lower part of first page missing taking some text with it.   Jo Ann Reisler, Ltd.   86 - 83   2011 $750

Mitchell, David   *Black Swan Green.*   London: Sceptre, 2006, First British edition; fine in fine dust jacket, signed by author.   Bella Luna Books   May 29 2011 - t8847   2011 $137

Mitchell, David   *Cloud Atlas.*   Sceptre, 2004, First edition; pages (vi, 538, 8vo., original maroon boards, backstrip blocked in blue, dust jacket with wrap around hand present, fine, signed by author.   Blackwell Rare Books   B166 - 191   2011   £325

Mitchell, David   *Ghostwritten.*   London: Sceptre, 1999, First edition; pages (x), 438, 8vo., original printed wrappers, no hard cover issue, illustrations, fine.   Blackwell Rare Books   B166 - 192   2011   £120

Mitchell, David   *Number 9 Dream.*   Sceptre, 2001, First edition; pages (x), 422, 8vo., original printed wrappers, no hard cover issue, illustrations, fine, signed and dated by author.   Blackwell Rare Books   B166 - 193   2011   £60

Mitchell, Edmund   *Chickabiddy Stories.*   Wells Gardner: Darton and Co., circa, 1922, Second edition; large 8vo., original pictorial green cloth, pages viii, 110, (i), 4 color plates tipped on to brown card and 26 line drawings by Norman Hardy, contemporary inscription, otherwise very nice.   R. F. G. Hollett & Sons Antiquarian Booksellers   170 - 458   2011   £120

Mitchell, Flora H.   *Vanishing Dublin.*   1966, First edition; 50 superb copper plates from Mithcell's water-colours, dust jacket (some wear), ex-library, discreet stamp on two plates, almost very good.   C. P. Hyland   May 26 2011 - 258/611 2011 $507

Mitchell, Isaac   *A Short Account of the Courtship of Alonzo & Melissa.*   Plattsburgh: printed for the Proprietor, 1811, Second edition; 8vo., 218 pages, contemporary calf backed boards, quite worn, text browned and somewhat shaken, but quite good.   M & S Rare Books, Inc.   90 - 258   2011 $500

Mitchell, John   *The Bottom of the Harbor.*   New York: Limited Editions Club, 1991, First edition with these illustrations, one of 250 copies signed by Mitchell; 5 hors texte hand pulled photogravures by Berenice Abbot, 12 x 10 inches, 250 pages, hand sewn and bound in black Nigerian goatskin and black Irish linen, fit in publisher's cloth slipcase, excellent copy, binder Kim O'Donnell's copy, unnumbered, with extra engraving by Abbot bound in, colophon additionally signed by binder.   Gemini Fine Books & Arts, Ltd.   Art Reference & Illustrated Books: First Editions 2011 $950

Mitchell, John   *The Bottom of the Harbor.*   New York: Limited Editions Club, 1991, First edition with these illustrations, one of 250, signed on justification page by John Mitchell; 5 hors-texte photogravures hand pulled by Jon Goodman after Berenice Abbott, 12 x 10 inches, 250 pages, hand sewn and bound in black quarter Nigerian goatskin and black Irish linen, very slight binder's imperfection on cloth, otherwise excellent copy in publisher's slipcase, this copy additionally inscribed "binder's copy" signed by Kim O'Donnell of the Garthegaat Bindery.   Gemini Fine Books & Arts, Ltd.   Art Reference & Illustrated Books: First Editions 2011 $750

Mitchell, John M.   *The Herring/Its Natural History and National Importance.*   Edinburgh: Edmonston and Douglas and London: Longman, Green, Roberts and Green, 1864, First edition; 8vo., pages xii, 372, folding color lithographed frontispiece, 5 lithographed plates, some foxing, publisher's blue cloth, brown endpapers, bumped spines slightly faded, review pasted to rear endpapers, author's presentation inscription to half title dated 1865, very good; presentation copy to King Leopold I of Belgium dated 1865.   Simon Finch Rare Books   Zero - 131   2011   £400

Mitchell, Margaret 1900-1949   *Eo Vento Levou. (Gone with the Wind).*   Rio de Janeiro: Imaos Pongetti, 1940, First Brazilian edition; 8vo., 854 pages, unopened, small tape mark on half title, printed color wrappers, joints lightly chipped, presentation inscription from author to Atlanta Historical Society, fine.   Jeff Weber Rare Books   163 - 46 2011 $1750

Mitchell, Muriel Moscrip *Adventures of Nip and Tuck.* Joliet: Volland, 1927, Third edition; 8vo., pictorial boards, slight rubbing, else near fine, in publisher's box (some soil and flap repair), illustrations by Mary Ellsworth, very scarce. Aleph-Bet Books, Inc. 95 - 223 2011 $300

Mitchell, Samuel Augustus 1792-1868 *A General View of the World.* Philadelphia: 1846, 828, 4 pages, very good, original embossed leather, some rubbing, backstrip gilt, edges marbled. Bookworm & Silverfish 665 - 145 2011 $325

Mitchell, Samuel Augustus 1792-1868 *A New Universal Atlas Containing Maps of the Various Empires, Kingdoms, State and Republics of the World.* Philadelphia: S. Augustus Mitchell, 1849, Folio, lithographed title with large vignette, letterpress "Table of Contents", hand colored frontispiece, 72 hand colored lithographed maps, charts and city plans, publisher's three quarter red morocco over marbled boards, original red morocco title label on front cover elaborately tooled and lettered in gilt, spine and corners renewed in modern red leather, boards rubbed and scuffed at edges, maps in fine condition, overall fine. Argonaut Book Shop Recent Acquisitions Summer 2010 - 134 2011 $17,500

Mitford, Jessica *The American Way of Death.* London: Hutchinson, 1963, First edition; original cloth, gilt, dust jacket little worn, pages 229, frontispiece. R. F. G. Hollett & Son Antiquarian Booksellers 175 - 952 2011 £40

Mitford, Mary Russell 1787-1855 *Belford Regis; or Sketches of a Country Town.* London: Richard Bentley, 1835, First edition; 3 volumes, contemporary half calf, maroon labels, bit rubbed, good plus, armorial bookplates of William Smith. Jarndyce Antiquarian Booksellers CLXC - 400 2011 £280

Mitford, Mary Russell 1787-1855 *Belford Regis....* London: Richard Bentley, 1846, Engraved frontispiece, original vertical grained purple cloth, blocked in blind, spine lettered gilt, spine slightly faded, very good. Jarndyce Antiquarian Booksellers CLXC - 401 2011 £65

Mitford, Mary Russell 1787-1855 *Country Stories.* London: Seeley & Co., 1896, Half title, illustrations, 4 pages ads (1895), original dark green cloth decorated in gilt, all edges gilt, very good. Jarndyce Antiquarian Booksellers CLXC - 403 2011 £35

Mitford, Mary Russell 1787-1855 *The Dramatic Works of Mary Russell Mitford.* London: Hurst and Blackett, 1854, First edition; 2 volumes, frontispiece, later maroon library binding, inner hinges strengthened with tape, remains of old library stamps, good, sound copy. Jarndyce Antiquarian Booksellers CLXC - 404 2011 £50

Mitford, Mary Russell 1787-1855 *Lights and Shadows of American Life.* London: Henry Colburn and Richard Bentley, 1832, First edition; contemporary half calf, spines with raised bands and devices in gilt, black leather labels, owner's signature "Emily Langley 1847", very good, bright. Jarndyce Antiquarian Booksellers CLXC - 405 2011 £380

Mitford, Mary Russell 1787-1855 *Our Village: Sketches of Rural Character and Scenery.* London: G. & W. B. Whittaker, 1826-1832, 6th/first, 2nd/first, 2nd/second editions; 5 volumes, half titles volumes I-III, neatly trimmed in slightl later drab boards, pale blue cloth spines, black leather labels, little faded, volumes I, III & V. with copious notes on titlepages in contemporary hand. Jarndyce Antiquarian Booksellers CLXC - 406 2011 £380

Mitford, Mary Russell 1787-1855 *Our Village: Sketches of Rural Character and Scenery.* London: G. & w. B. Whittaker, 1828-1832, Sixth, third, third, first, first editions; half titles (not volume v), 3 pages ads volume IV, uncut, contemporary glazed plum cloth, dark green morocco spines, lettered in gilt, boards slightly faded, spines slightly rubbed, volume I signed "Mrs. Ewing" in contemporary hand, Richard Taylor of Liverpool bookseller tickets volumes I & II, good plus, last volume bound slightly later to match volumes I-IV and slightly different blocking with volume number "V" rather than "6". Jarndyce Antiquarian Booksellers CLXC - 407 2011 £420

Mitford, Mary Russell 1787-1855 *Our Village: Sketches of Rural Character and Scenery.* London: Whittaker, Treacher, 1830, Fifth edition of volume I, new edition volume II; 2 volumes, uniformly bound in half calf, blocked in blind, gilt band, red labels, slightly rubbed, splits in hinges, 1 label chipped, booklabel of Louisa Traherne. Jarndyce Antiquarian Booksellers CLXC - 408 2011 £40

Mitford, Mary Russell 1787-1855 *Our Village.* London: Macmillan, 1893, First edition thus; lx, 256 pages, 8vo., original dark green cloth with elaborate gilt decorations showing flowers and leaves on front and spine, all edges gilt, apart from little foxing, unusually bright, fine copy. Paulette Rose Fine and Rare Books 32 - 125 2011 $150

Mitford, Mary Russell 1787-1855 *Our Village: Sketches of Rural Character and Scenery.* London: Macmillan, 1893, Half title, illustrations by Hugh Thomson, original dark green cloth, elaborately blocked with poppies, all edges gilt, very good, bright copy. Jarndyce Antiquarian Booksellers CLXC - 410 2011 £50

Mitford, Mary Russell 1787-1855 *Our Village.* London: J. M. Dent, 1904, First edition thus; original green cloth gilt, spine and upper board decorated in gilt overall, pages xv, 310, top edge gilt, untrimmed, 25 color plates by C. E. Brock. R. F. G. Hollett & Son Antiquarian Booksellers General Catalogue Summer 2010 - 740 2011 £35

Mitford, Mary Russell 1787-1855 *Recollections of a Literary Life; and Selections from My Favourite Poets and Prose Writers.* London: Richard Bentley, 1859, New edition; half title, frontispiece, uncut in original green cloth, gilt spine, slightly rubbed.   Jarndyce Antiquarian Booksellers   CLXC - 411 2011   £45

Mitford, Mary Russell 1787-1855 *Recollections of a Literary Life; and Selections from My Favourite Poets and Prose Writers.* London: Richard Bentley, 1859, New edition; original red cloth, spine faded, back board stained affecting pastedown, armorial bookplate of Earl Fitzwilliam.   Jarndyce Antiquarian Booksellers   CLXC - 412 2011   £35

Mitford, Mary Russell 1787-1855 *Our Village: Sketches of Rural Character and Scenery.* London: Henry G. Bohn, 1852, New edition; first and second series, 2 volumes, frontispiece, engraved titles, additional vignette titles, contemporary half vellum, gilt spines, maroon leather labels, marbled boards and endpapers, spines little darkened, armorial bookplates of Francis Robert Davies, good plus.   Jarndyce Antiquarian Booksellers   CLXC - 409 2011   £120

Mitton, G. E. *Buckingham and Berkshire.* A. & C. Black, 1920, First edition; 8vo., original pictorial cloth, gilt, spine lettering little dulled, pages ix, 232, with 60 color plates and folding map, nice, clean and sound.   R. F. G. Hollett & Son Antiquarian Booksellers   General Catalogue Summer 2010 - 1514 2011   £75

Mitton, Robert *The Lost World of Irian Jaya.* Melbourne: Oxford University Press, 1984, Reprint; 4to., copiously illustrated in color, 235 pages, small Australian collector's blindstamp on front endpaper, else near fine in like dust jacket.   Any Amount of Books   May 29 2011 - A76748 2011 $230

Mo, Timothy *Sour Sweet.* London: Deutsch, 1982, First British edition; 2nd state dust jacket with Booker nomination mention, near fine browning to edges, near fine dust jacket, price clipped.   Bella Luna Books   May 29 2011 - t7671 2011 $110

The Modern Building Record. Volume 3. Charles Jones, 1912, First edition; pages 480, illustrations, 4to., original cloth gilt over bevelled boards, spine little dulled, presentation letter from publisher tipped to pastedown.   R. F. G. Hollett & Son Antiquarian Booksellers   177 - 582 2011   £85

The Modern Family Physician, or the Art of Healing Made Easy, Being a Plain Description of Diseases to Which Persons of Every Age are Most Liable... London: printed for F. Newbery, 1775, First edition; 12mo., viii, 279, (1) pages, first few leaves somewhat creased, old tape mark to gutter of title, some paper browning and very occasional light spotting, well bound in recent quarter calf over plain boards, spine with raised bands, gilt lines and letters, good copy with early 19th century signature of W. M. Nash 1814, rare.   John Drury Rare Books   153 - 97 2011   £350

The Modern Language Review. 1962-1982, First edition; volume 17/1-volume 77/2 Jan 1962-April 1982, over 110 issues in original wrappers and bound volumes.   I. D. Edrich   May 26 2011 - 99450 2011 $755

Modern Packaging. New York: Breskins, Modern Packaging and Latterly McGraw Hill, 1944-1976, First edition; 4to., volumes 18-49 in 54 volumes, most volumes 500+ pages, although 1970's volumes are thinner, one volume has plastic sample of promotional rain bonnet laid in, rebound in red cloth with library labels of ICI Plastics division and their accession numbers on spine and few stamps, sound, very good copies.   Any Amount of Books   May 26 2011 - B10210 2011 $1258

Moeller, B. *Two Years at the Front with the Mounted Infantry.* London: Grant Richards, 1903, First edition; 8vo., pages xxi, 296, frontispiece, 6 plans, 1 plate, original green cloth.   J. & S. L. Bonham Antiquarian Booksellers   Africa 4/20/2011 - 8258 2011   £130

Moffat, Alfred *Little Songs of Long Ago: More Old Nursery Rhymes.* London/Philadelphia: Augener Ltd./David McKay, n.d., 1912, First edition thus,; Oblong 4to., pages 64 (unpaginated), bright, very good+ in bright, quite clean, very good- dust jacket with some nicks and chips.   Any Amount of Books   May 29 2011 - A49309 2011 $238

Mogridge, George *Loiterings Among the Lakes of Cumberland and Westmoreland.* London: Religious Tract Society, circa, 1849, New edition; small square 8vo., original green blindstamped cloth gilt with vignette on upper board, pages viii, 208, (viii, ads), all edges gilt, fine color frontispiece, 6 wood engraved vignettes.   R. F. G. Hollett & Son Antiquarian Booksellers   173 - 789 2011   £120

Mogridge, George *Sergeant Bell and His Raree-Show.* London: printed for Thomas Tegg, 1839, First edition; original red blindstamped cloth, gilt, rather soiled an darkened, neatly recased, new endpapers, pages iii-viii, 447, all edges gilt, title vignette and numerous woodcuts, lacks frontispiece an leaf Ff1, few light spots and finger marks, foreedge of one leaf rather dusty, titlepage vignette and some illustrations by Cruikshank.   R. F. G. Hollett & Son Antiquarian Booksellers   175 - 954 2011   £175

Mohr, Joseph *Silent Night.* New York: E. P. Dutton, 1984, First edition; 4to., fine in near fine dust jacket, illustrations by Susan Jeffers, signed by Jeffers. By the Book, L. C. 26 - 64 2011 $70

Moko and Koko in the Jungle. London: Bancroft, n.d. circa, 1962, Folio, cloth backed pictorial card covers, fine, illustrations in color by Kubasta, large pop-up with moveable pieces as well. Aleph-Bet Books, Inc. 95 - 451 2011 $325

Molesworth, Mary Louisa 1839-1921 *The Blue Baby and Other Stories.* London: W. & R. Chambers, 1904, First Chambers edition; frontispiece and illustrations by Lewis Baumer, final ad leaf, 32 page catalog, original pale ink cloth, pictorially blocked in black, spine darkened, bit dulled, school prize label, 1905. Jarndyce Antiquarian Booksellers CLXC - 419 2011 £45

Molesworth, Mary Louisa 1839-1921 *Carrots; Just a Little Boy.* London: Macmillan, 1879, Tenth thousand; half title, frontispiece and illustrations by Walter Crane, 39 page catalog (May 1879), original red cloth blocked and lettered in black and gilt, little dulled and rubbed. Jarndyce Antiquarian Booksellers CLXC - 422 2011 £35

Molesworth, Mary Louisa 1839-1921 *A Charge Fulfilled.* London: SPCK, 1886, First edition; 4 pages ads (coded 12-8-85), original brown cloth blocked in maroon and green, lettered in gilt, slightly rubbed, prize label 1890. Jarndyce Antiquarian Booksellers CLXC - 425 2011 £40

Molesworth, Mary Louisa 1839-1921 *The Children's Hour.* London: T. Nelson & Sons, 1899, First edition; half title, color frontispiece and plates, illustrations, original purple cloth, pictorially blocked in black and white, lettered in black and gilt, very good. Jarndyce Antiquarian Booksellers CLXC - 427 2011 £45

Molesworth, Mary Louisa 1839-1921 *A Christmas Child.* London: Macmillan, 1880, First edition; half title, color frontispiece and plates, illustrations, original purple cloth, pictorially blocked in black and white, lettered in black and gilt, very good. Jarndyce Antiquarian Booksellers CLXC - 428 2011 £60

Molesworth, Mary Louisa 1839-1921 *A Christmas Posy.* London: Macmillan, 1888, First edition; frontispiece and illustrations by Walter Crane, 32 page catalog (April 1888), original red cloth, blocked and lettered in black and gilt, little dulled and slightly rubbed, bookplate of J. L. R. Hope-Nicholson. Jarndyce Antiquarian Booksellers CLXC - 430 2011 £35

Molesworth, Mary Louisa 1839-1921 *An Enchanted Garden: Fairy Tales.* London: T. Fisher Unwin, 1892, First edition; half title, illustrations by W. J. Hennessy, 8 page catalog, uncut in original green cloth, bevelled boards and lettered in gilt, slightly rubbed, top edge gilt, ownership inscription. Jarndyce Antiquarian Booksellers CLXC - 434 2011 £50

Molesworth, Mary Louisa 1839-1921 *Fairies Afield.* London: Macmillan, 1911, First edition; half title, frontispiece and plates by Gertrude Demain Hammond, original blue cloth, blocked and lettered in gilt, owner's inscription 1911, all edges gilt, very good. Jarndyce Antiquarian Booksellers CLXC - 435 2011 £40

Molesworth, Mary Louisa 1839-1921 *Fairies - Of Sorts.* London: Macmillan, 1908, First edition; half title, frontispiece and plates by Gertrude Demain Hammond, final ad leaf, original blue cloth, blocked and lettered in gilt, inner hinges worn, little dulled and marked, owner's inscription, 1909, all edges gilt. Jarndyce Antiquarian Booksellers CLXC - 436 2011 £35

Molesworth, Mary Louisa 1839-1921 *The February Boys.* W. & R. Chambers, 1909, 8 charming color plates, pages 266, original pink pictorial boards, gilt. R. F. G. Hollett & Sons Antiquarian Booksellers 170 - 51 2011 £85

Molesworth, Mary Louisa 1839-1921 *Five Minutes Stories.* London: SPCK, 1888, Twelfth thousand; half title, color frontispiece and vignette title, illustrations by W.J.M., final ad leaf, small tear in leading f.e.p. neatly repaired, original grey cloth, pictorially blocked in blue, red and gilt lettered in black and red, slightly rubbed, nice. Jarndyce Antiquarian Booksellers CLXC - 438 2011 £50

Molesworth, Mary Louisa 1839-1921 *Four Winds Farm.* London: Macmillan, 1887, (1886). First edition; half title, frontispiece, vignette title, 6 plates, 4 pages ads, original orange cloth blocked and lettered in black, lettered in gilt, prize inscription on half title dated Dec. 1886, very good, bright. Jarndyce Antiquarian Booksellers CLXC - 439 2011 £45

Molesworth, Mary Louisa 1839-1921 *Friendly Joey and Other Stories.* London: SPCK, 1896, First edition; half title, vignette titl, illustrations by W. J. Morgan, original pale pink cloth, pictorially blocked and lettered in red, brown, black and white, ownership inscription May 1899, very good. Jarndyce Antiquarian Booksellers CLXC - 441 2011 £50

Molesworth, Mary Louisa 1839-1921 *The Girls and I: a Veracious History.* London: Macmillan, 1892, First edition; half title, frontispiece and illustrations by L. Leslie Brooke, 44 page catalog (July 1892), original orange pictorial cloth, blocked in black and gilt, very good. Jarndyce Antiquarian Booksellers CLXC - 442 2011 £40

Molesworth, Mary Louisa 1839-1921 *'Grandmother Dear': A Book for Boys and Girls.* London: Macmillan, 1878, First edition; half title, frontispiece and illustrations by Walter Crane, final ad leaf, original red cloth, blocked and lettered in black, spine slightly darkened, good plus. Jarndyce Antiquarian Booksellers CLXC - 443 2011 £45

Molesworth, Mary Louisa 1839-1921 *Great-Uncle Hoot-Toot.* London: SPCK, 1889, First edition; illustrations by Gordon Browne &c., original olive green cloth, pictorially blocked in dark bluee, black and brown, lettered gilt, slightly rubbed. Jarndyce Antiquarian Booksellers CLXC - 445 2011 £40

Molesworth, Mary Louisa 1839-1921 *The Green Casket and Other Stories.* London: W. & R. Chambers, 1890, First edition; half title, illustrations, original green pictorial cloth, blocked and lettered in black and dark green, very good. Jarndyce Antiquarian Booksellers CLXC - 446 2011 £35

Molesworth, Mary Louisa 1839-1921 *Greyling Towers: a Story for the Young.* London: W. & R. Chambers, 1898, First edition; frontispiece and illustrations, 32 page catalog, original pale orange cloth, pictorially blocked in yellow, purple, green, red and black, lettered in black and gilt, prize label Dec. 1898, very good, bright. Jarndyce Antiquarian Booksellers CLXC - 447 2011 £50

Molesworth, Mary Louisa 1839-1921 *The Grim House.* London: James Nisbet & Co., 1899, First edition; half title, frontispiece and plates by Warwick Goble, 6 pages ads, endpapers slightly browned, original blue cloth, lettered in gilt, one corner slightly knocked, otherwise very good, top edge gilt. Jarndyce Antiquarian Booksellers CLXC - 449 2011 £60

Molesworth, Mary Louisa 1839-1921 *Hermy; the Story of a Little Girl.* London: W. & R. Chambers, 1898, 32 page catalog, plates crudely hand colored by previous owner, original pink cloth blocked and lettered in black and gilt, spine dulled and slightly damp marked, slight rubbing. Jarndyce Antiquarian Booksellers CLXC - 451 2011 £35

Molesworth, Mary Louisa 1839-1921 *Hermy...* London: W. & R. Chambers, circa, 1900, Half title, later hand colored frontispiece and illustrations by Lewis Baumer, 32 page catalog, original olive green cloth, blocked and lettered in black and gilt, bit rubbed. Jarndyce Antiquarian Booksellers CLXC - 452 2011 £35

Molesworth, Mary Louisa 1839-1921 *Hoodie.* London: W. & R. Chambers, 1897?, Half title, frontispiece and illustrations by Lewis Baumer, 32 page catalog, original orange cloth, pictorially blocked and lettered in black and gilt, spine very slightly rubbed, otherwise very good. Jarndyce Antiquarian Booksellers CLXC - 454 2011 £40

Molesworth, Mary Louisa 1839-1921 *The House that Grew.* London: Macmillan & Co., 1900, First edition; half title, frontispiece, vignette title, plates by Alice Woodward, final ad leaf, original orange cloth, pictorially blocked and lettered in black, spine lettered in gilt, blind-stamped "presentation copy". Jarndyce Antiquarian Booksellers CLXC - 456 2011 £45

Molesworth, Mary Louisa 1839-1921 *Imogen or Only Eighteen.* London: W. & R. Chambers, circa, 1900?, Frontispiece, illustrations by Lews Baumer, bit foxed, original light blue cloth, blocked and lettered in black, slightly dulled and slightly rubbed,. Jarndyce Antiquarian Booksellers CLXC - 458 2011 £35

Molesworth, Mary Louisa 1839-1921 *Lucky Ducks and Other Tales.* London: SPCK, 1891, First edition; half title, vignette title, illustrations in color and black and white by W. J. Morgan, original pale green cloth, pictorially blocked and lettered in red, yellow, beige, black, white and gilt, very slight rubbing to spine, ownership inscription dated Christmas 1891, very good, bright copy. Jarndyce Antiquarian Booksellers CLXC - 465 2011 £50

Molesworth, Mary Louisa 1839-1921 *Miss Bouverie.* London: W. & R. Chambers, 1901, First edition in 3 volumes; half title, frontispiece and illustrations by Lewis Baumer, 32 page catalog, original cream cloth, bevelled boards, pictorially blocked in green, purple, red and black, lettered in black and gilt, slightly dulled, good plus. Jarndyce Antiquarian Booksellers CLXC - 468 2011 £40

Molesworth, Mary Louisa 1839-1921 *Nurse Heatherdale's Story.* London: Macmillan, 1891, First edition; half title, frontispiece and illustrations by L. Leslie Brooke, 55 page catalog (Aug. 1891), original red cloth, blocked in black, lettered in black and gilt, dulled, spine bit rubbed, owner's signature 1892. Jarndyce Antiquarian Booksellers CLXC - 475 2011 £35

Molesworth, Mary Louisa 1839-1921 *The Old Pincushion.* London: Griffith, Farran, Browne & Co., 1889, First edition; frontispiece, vignette title, illustrations by Mabel & Edith Taylor, originial dark blue cloth, blocked and lettered in gilt, spine slightly rubbed, owner inscription dated 1901, all edges gilt, good plus. Jarndyce Antiquarian Booksellers CLXC - 476 2011 £40

Molesworth, Mary Louisa 1839-1921 *Philippa.* London: W. & R. Chambers, 1896, First edition; frontispiece and plates, 4 pages ads + 32 page catalog, original blue cloth, bevelled boards, pictorially blocked in yellow, green and red, lettering reversed out of gilt, slight rubbing, prize label 1902, very good. Jarndyce Antiquarian Booksellers CLXC - 479 2011 £35

Molesworth, Mary Louisa 1839-1921 *The Red Grange.* London: Methuen & Co., 1891, First edition; half title, frontispiece and plates by Gordon Browne, original olive green cloth, bevelled boards, blocked and lettered in gilt, spine very slightly rubbed at head and tail, owner's inscription, 1894, very good. Jarndyce Antiquarian Booksellers CLXC - 482 2011 £45

Molesworth, Mary Louisa 1839-1921 *The Story of a Spring Morning and Other Tales.* London: Longmans, First edition; half title, frontispiece, illustrations by M. Ellen Edwards, 16 page catalog, original dark blue cloth, blocked in pale blue, lettered in gilt, slight wear to head and tail of spine, owner's inscription dated Christmas 1890, small bookseller's ticket of McKelvie & Sons, very good. Jarndyce Antiquarian Booksellers CLXC - 486 2011 £50

Molesworth, Mary Louisa 1839-1921 *The Story of a Year.* London: Macmillan, 1910, First edition; half title, frontispiece, illustrations by Gertrude Hammond, original blue cloth, decorated and lettered in titlepage, very good, bright. Jarndyce Antiquarian Booksellers CLXC - 488 2011 £50

Molesworth, Mary Louisa 1839-1921 *Sweet Content.* London: Griffith, Farran & Co., 1891, First edition; half title, illustrations by W. Rainey, lacks leading f.e.p., original beige cloth, bevelled boards, pictorially blocked in blue and yellow, lettered in blue and gilt, bit dulled, slight rubbing, all edges gilt. Jarndyce Antiquarian Booksellers CLXC - 489 2011 £35

Molesworth, Mary Louisa 1839-1921 *The Tapestry Room; a Child's Romance.* London: Macmillan, 1879, First edition; half title, frontispiece + 7 plates, few spots in text, original orange cloth, blocked and lettered in black, leading inner hinge slightly cracked, little dulled, contemporary owner's inscription, good, sound copy. Jarndyce Antiquarian Booksellers CLXC - 491 2011 £35

Molesworth, Mary Louisa 1839-1921 *The Thirteen Little Black Pigs and Other Stories.* London: SPCK, 1893, First edition; half title, vignette title, illustrations and black and white, original pink cloth, pictorially blocked and lettered in red, pale blue, black and gilt, slightly dulled, spine darkened, ownership inscription dated Christmas 1894. Jarndyce Antiquarian Booksellers CLXC - 493 2011 £35

Molesworth, Mary Louisa 1839-1921 *This and That: a Tale of Two Tinies.* London: Macmillan, 1899, First edition; half title, frontispiece and illustrations by Hugh Thomson, original orange pictorial cloth, blocked in black and gilt, spine bit dulled, prize inscription Easter 1900, good plus. Jarndyce Antiquarian Booksellers CLXC - 494 2011 £35

Molesworth, Mary Louisa 1839-1921 *Two Little Waifs.* London: Macmillan, 1883, First edition; half title, frontispiece and illustrations by Walter Crane, 32 page catalog (Oct. 1883), original red pictorial cloth, blocked in black and gilt, very good. Jarndyce Antiquarian Booksellers CLXC - 496 2011 £45

Molesworth, Mary Louisa 1839-1921 *Uncanny Tales.* London: Hutchinson & Co., 1896, First edition; half title, engraved title, original dark blue cloth, pictorially blocked, lettered in gilt, very slightly rubbed at head and tail of spine, very good. Jarndyce Antiquarian Booksellers CLXC - 497 2011 £250

Molesworth, Mary Louisa 1839-1921 *"Us." An Old Fashioned Story.* London: Macmillan, 1885, First edition; half title, frontispiece and illustrations by Watler Crane, 28 pages catalog (May 1885), original red pictorial cloth, blocked in black and gilt, very good. Jarndyce Antiquarian Booksellers CLXC - 498 2011 £45

Molesworth, Mary Louisa 1839-1921 *White Turrets.* London: W. & R. Chambers, 1896, First edition; frontispiece and 3 plates, 32 page catalog, original maroon vertical grained cloth lettered in gilt, owner's signature 1896, top edge gilt, very good. Jarndyce Antiquarian Booksellers CLXC - 500 2011 £40

Molineux, T. *An Introduction to Byrom's Universal English Short-Hand.* Macclesfield: printed for the author by E. S. Bayley, 1823, Sixth edition; modern calf backed marbled boards gilt, original engraved label relaid on upper board, pages vii, 94, frontispiece, 6 plates, faint marginal blindstamped on title and final leaf. R. F. G. Hollett & Sons Antiquarian Booksellers 170 - 460 2011 £85

Molnar, Ferenc *The Blue-Eyed Lady.* New York: Viking and Junior Literary Guild, 1942, First edition; 4to., 46 pages, blue cloth, fine in dust jacket, some small chips else very good, illustrations by Helen Sewell, scarce. Aleph-Bet Books, Inc. 95 - 524 2011 $150

Mon Alphabet. Paris: B. Sirven, n.d. circa, 1915, 45o., pictorial card covers, spine lightly rubbed, else very good+, illustrations in color filling every page by P. Laborde. Aleph-Bet Books, Inc. 95 - 40 2011 $250

Monahan, Valerie *Collecting Postcards in Colour 1894-1914; 1914-1930.* Poole: Blandford Press, 1978-1980, First edition; 2 volumes, original boards, gilt, dust jacket, pages 212, 176, each volume with 192 illustrations. R. F. G. Hollett & Son Antiquarian Booksellers General Catalogue Summer 2010 - 268 2011 £50

Moncrieff, A. R. Hope *Bonnie Scotland.* A. & C. Black, 1912, Second reprint; large 8vo., original blue decorated cloth gilt, pages xi, 255, (iv), top edges gilt, 75 color plates, nice clean.   R. F. G. Hollett & Son Antiquarian Booksellers General Catalogue Summer 2010 - 1515 2011   £85

Monk, Maria *Awful Disclosures of Maria Monk...* London: printed for the booksellers, n.d., Original cloth, gilt, extremities trifle rubbed, pages 384, woodcut frontispiece and plates.   R. F. G. Hollett & Son Antiquarian Booksellers 175 - 958 2011   £45

Monk, Maria *Awful Disclosures of Maria Monk...* Philadelphia: T. B. Peterson, n.d., 12mo., original green cloth gilt, few pinpots and marks to upper board, pages 168, woodcut frontispiece, few leaves fingered.   R. F. G. Hollett & Son Antiquarian Booksellers 175 - 959 2011   £35

Monkhouse, William Cosmo *Corn and Poppies.* London: Elkin Mathews, 1890, First edition; half title, uncut in original painted vellum binding. bevelled boards, very slightly dulled, bookplate of Alban Dobson, very good, tipped on to leading f.e.p. a 13 line poem on single sheet of paper signed by author with note by Alban Dobson "found among Austin Dobson's papers".   Jarndyce Antiquarian Booksellers CXCI - 325 2011   £150

Monro, Harold *The Chapbook.* Poetry Bookshop, 1919-1925, First edition; Nos. 1-40, all published in original wrappers and boards as issued, few issues slightly frayed and some staples rusty, very good.   I. D. Edrich May 26 2011 - 99072 2011 $1426

Monro, Thomas Kirkpatrick *Raynaud's Disease Local Syncope, Local Asphyxia, Symmetrical Gangrene): Its History, Causes, Symptoms, Morbid Relations, Pathology & Treatment.* Glasgow: James Maclehose & Sons, 1899, 8vo., xii, 251 pages, frontispiece, 3 tables, green cloth, gilt stamped spine title, very good, inscribed by John F. Fulton to William Livingston, from the Medical Library of Dr. Clare Gray Peterson.   Jeff Weber Rare Books 162 - 218 2011 $150

Monroe, James *Message from the President... to Both Houses of Congress at the Commencement of the First Session of the Eighteenth Congress December 2 1823.* Washington: printed by Gales & Seaton, 1823, First edition; 8vo., full contemporary sheep, lightly shellacked, leather labels, some binding wear, but very nice.   M & S Rare Books, Inc. 90 - 259 2011 $1500

Monson-Fitzjohn, G. J. *Quaint Songs of Olde Inns.* Herbert Jenkins, 1926, First edition; square 8vo., original pictorial cloth spine little darkened, pages 157, illustrations, one tear repaired with tape.   R. F. G. Hollett & Son Antiquarian Booksellers 177 - 583 2011   £35

Montagu, Edward Wortley 1713-1776   *Reflections on the Rise and Fall of the Ancient Republicks.* London: printed for A. Millar and T. Cadell, 1769, 8vo., pages (vi) 392, contemporary sprinkled tan calf, spine fully gilt with massed flowers, board edges 'alternating full and brown hatch fillet' roll gilt, turn-ins as above but in blind, all edges densely red speckled, pink and white sewn endbands, little faint spotting, rubbed at extremities, joints cracking but strong, little wear to endcaps, lettering piece lost, from the collection of Christopher Ernest Weston 1947-2010.   Unsworths Booksellers 24 - 123 2011   £95

Montagu, Mary Pierrepone Wortley 1689-1762   *Letters of the Right Hon. Lady M--y W-----y M-----.* London: printed for T. Cadell, 1784, 2 volumes, small octavo ix, (), 220; (2), 272 pages, some penciling, original full calf, hinges broken, mended, extremities worn, bookplate of F. Murray H. Mayall, signature of F. Mayall.   Jeff Weber Rare Books 163 - 197 2011 $125

Montagu, Mary Pierrepone Wortley 1689-1762   *The Works of the Right Honourable Lady Mary Wortley Montagu.* London: Richard Phillips, 1803, First edition; 5 volumes, engraved frontispiece, portrait and facsimiles volume I, lower corner torn without loss of text page 167/168 volume I, contemporary half red morocco, spines little darkened, slight rubbing, nice set.   Jarndyce Antiquarian Booksellers CLXC - 503 2011   £325

Montaigne, Michel De 1533-1592   *Montaigne's Essays.* London: Folio Society, 2006, First edition thus; 3 volumes, 8vo., pages xiv, 356; vi, 519; 377; original publisher's blue half cloth with marbled boards, lettered gilt on spine, fine in slightly worn, printed very good slipcase.   Any Amount of Books   May 29 2011 - 70522 2011 $238

Montaigne, Michel De 1533-1592   *The Works.* New York: Edwin C. Hill, 1910, Emerson Edition, one of 1050 copies; 225 x 12mm., 10 volumes, very handsome olive brown morocco extravagantly gilt and onlaid, covers with border of three gilt rules, central panel (with square-notched corners), formed by six parallel gilt lines and with large outward pointing floral ornaments as cornerpieces, raised bands, spine compartments attractively gilt in unusual asymmetrical panel design with small fleurs-de-lys in two corners and large inlaid fleur-de-lys of red morocco at center, wide turn-ins with multiple plain and decorative gilt rules, turn-ins framing red crushed morocco doublures, doublures with border of five gilt fillets and with fine large centerpiece of onlaid black morocco in the form of a flower, onlay enclosed by an elegant rococo collar, crimson watered silk free endleaves, top edge gilt, other edges rough trimmed, set entirely unopened with a total of 50 plates, original tissue guards, large paper copy; minor wear to top inch and bottom inch of rear joint of first volume, spines uniformly faded to slightly lighter brown, frontispieces offset onto titlepages, one leaf with one inch tear in fore margin, but very fine, attractive bindings solid, bright and scarcely worn, unopened, text obviously untouched.   Phillip J. Pirages 59 - 266 2011 $5500

Montefiore, Judith Cohen *Notes from a Private Journal of a Visit to Egypt and Palestine.* London: printed by Wertheimer, Lea & Co., 1885, Second edition; (410 pages including appendix), folding table, 8vo., publisher's original royal blue cloth, front panel decorated with coat of arms in gilt, gilt lettered spine, some pages carelessly opened without any loss of text, still very bright and attractive uncut copy. Paulette Rose Fine and Rare Books 32 - 176 2011 $800

Monteiro, Rose *Delagoa Bay: Its Natives and Natural History.* London: George Philip, 1891, First edition; 8vo., pages xii, 274, ads, 6 plates, 12 illustrations, original brown decorative cloth. J. & S. L. Bonham Antiquarian Booksellers Africa 4/20/2011 - 5610 2011 £120

Montgomery, Fanny Charlotte *On the Wing: a Southern Flight.* London: Hurst & Blackett, 1875, First edition; half title, (2), 16 page catalog, original dark green cloth, slight rubbing, armorial bookplate of John Allan Rolls, very good. Jarndyce Antiquarian Booksellers CLXC - 505 2011 £85

Montgomery, Florence *Tony. A Sketch, Being the Account of a Little Incident on a Short Railway Journey.* London: Richard Bentley, 1898, First edition; half title, original cream cloth, blocked with floral design in gilt, very good. Jarndyce Antiquarian Booksellers CLXC - 511 2011 £55

Montgomery, Florence *Wild Mike and His Victim.* London: Richard Bentley & Son, 1875, First edition; half title, 2 pages ads + 24 page catalog (June/July 1875), original brown cloth, blocked in black lettered in gilt, small ink mark on front board, bit dulled, spine slightly worn at head and tail. Jarndyce Antiquarian Booksellers CLXC - 513 2011 £58

Montgomery, Frances Trego *Billy Whiskers in the South.* Akron: Saalfield, 1917, Probably first edition; 4to., cloth backed pictorial boards, 148 pages, fine in dust jacket (edge chipping), exceptionally nice, scarce in wrapper, 6 color plates, many black and whites by Will Fitzgerald. Aleph-Bet Books, Inc. 95 - 104 2011 $250

Montgomery, Frances Trego *Billy Whiskers Out West.* Akron: Saalfield, 1916, Probable first edition; 182 pages, 4to., cloth backed pictorial boards, plus ads, tips rubbed, else near fine in dust jacket (edge chipped), 6 color plates. Aleph-Bet Books, Inc. 95 - 365 2011 $250

Montgomery, James *The World Before the Flood.* London: printed for Longman, Hurst, Rees, Orme and Brown, 1814, Third edition; 168 x 103mm., xvi, (2), 328 pages, attractive and intriguing contemporary calf, heavily gilt by Taylor and Hessey (board edges along fore edge stamp signed in gilt), covers with wide filigree gilt frame, large central panel dominated by an elongated octagon painted in black with gold dot at each of its eight corners, these corners radiating stippled gilt lines that intersect to form 12 triangles of various sizes plus a large central lozenge (lozenge also with gilt dots at its four angles), wide raised bands decorated in blind dividing the spine into four panels, gilt titling, turn-ins with gilt broken cables, all edges gilt, expertly rebacked using original spine, with very pretty fore-edge painting of Pope's Villa at Twickenham, small abrasions to lower spine, bit discolored and with gilt difficult to read, partly because it is so small, tiny nicks here and there in painting, still excellent copy, text unusually clean and fresh, binding solidly restored and with only minor wear, painting generally quite well preserved. Phillip J. Pirages 59 - 197 2011 $950

Montgomery, L. M. *Anne of Avonlea.* Boston: L. C. Page & Co., 1909, Stated first impression; 8vo., green cloth, pictorial pasteon, 367 pages (8) pages ads, fine, color frontispiece by George Gibbs, extremely scarce and beautiful. Aleph-Bet Books, Inc. 95 - 366 2011 $1100

Montgomery, L. M. *Anne of the Island.* Boston: L. C. Page Co., 1915, Stated first impression; 8vo., green cloth, pictorial paste-on, 326 pages + 16 page ads, light rear cover soil, else near fine, frontispiece by H. Weston Taylor. Aleph-Bet Books, Inc. 95 - 367 2011 $1200

Montgomery, L. M. *Rilla of Ingleside.* New York: Frederick Stokes, 1921, First edition; 8vo., purple cloth, pictorial paste-on, slight foxing else, fine in dust jacket with 1 inch piece off top of spine and half inch off bottom of spine, illustrations by Maria Kirk with color frontispiece. Aleph-Bet Books, Inc. 95 - 368 2011 $900

Montherlant, Henri De *Les Jeunes Filles...* Paris: Bernard Grasset, 1936-1939, First edition; 4 volumes, 8vo., pages (iv) blank, (1), original wrappers, (1) imprint, (1) blank, top edge gilt, very clean and bright copy, original wrappers bound into near contemporary red half morocco over marbled sides, spine in compartments with raised bands lettered in gold, marbled sides, marbled endpapers, occasional negligible soiling, fine set. Simon Finch Rare Books Zero - 257 2011 £950

Montolieu, Jeanne Isabelle De *Caroline de Lichtfield.* Londres: et se trouve a Paris: Chez Buisson, 1786, 2 volumes, 292, 257 pages, 12mo., contemporary half calf, gilt decorated spines, some restoration, very nice. Paulette Rose Fine and Rare Books 32 - 126 2011 $800

Moody, F. W. *Lectures and Lessons on Art.* London: George Bell, 1875, Second edition; xvi, 139, (1) pages, frontispiece, 24 plates, good copy, 8vo., contemporary half morocco, prize label from Newcastle School of Art and 'rewear' blindstamp to titlepage, some light marking to cloth boards, rubbing to extremities.   Ken Spelman Rare Books   68 - 80   2011   £65

Moorat, Joseph   *Thirty Old-Time Nursery Songs.* London: T. C. and E. C. Jack, n.d., 4to., original cloth backed pictorial boards, little spotted and marked, corners worn, pages 34, illustrations in color, front joint strengthened, little light fingering here and there, but very good.   R. F. G. Hollett & Sons Antiquarian Booksellers   170 - 737   2011   £75

Moore, A. W.   *The Folk-Lore of the Isle of Man or Its Myth, Legends, Superstitions...* London: D. Nutt an Douglas: Brown & Son, 1891, Original pictorial wrappers, trifle chipped, old tape marks, pages vi, (viii), 192.   R. F. G. Hollett & Son Antiquarian Booksellers   175 - 961   2011   £40

Moore, Brian   *Catholics.* London: Jonathan Cape, 1972, First British edition; fine, dust jacket near fine, 2 closed tears, one of which has been re-enforced with archival tape.   Bella Luna Books   May 29 2011 - t8876   2011 $110

Moore, Christopher   *Bloodsucking Friends.* New York: Simon & Schuster, 1995, First edition; fine in fine dust jacket.   Bella Luna Books   May 29 2011 - t9632   2011 $137

Moore, Christopher   *Coyote Blue.* New York: Simon & Schuster, 1994, First edition; fine, dust jacket fine, signed by author.   Bella Luna Books   May 29 2011 - 4343   2011 $82

Moore, Christopher   *Coyote Blue.* New York: Simon & Schuster, 1994, First edition; book near fine, minor bumping to base of spine, dust jacket fine, signed by author.   Bella Luna Books   May 29 2011 - t4883   2011 $110

Moore, Christopher   *Coyote Blue.* New York: Simon & Schuster, 1994, First edition; signed by author, fine in fine dust jacket.   Ken Lopez Bookseller   154 - 121   2011 $75

Moore, Christopher   *Island of the Sequined Nun.* Avon: 1997, First edition; fine in fine dust jacket, inscribed by author.   Bella Luna Books   May 29 2011 - t9586   2011 $137

Moore, Christopher   *Lamb: the Gospel According to Biff, Christ's Childhood Pal.* New York: William Morrow, 2002, First edition; fine in fine dust jacket.   Bella Luna Books   May 26 2011 - t9610   2011 $324

Moore, Christopher   *Lamb: The Gospel According to Biff, Christ's Childhood Pal.* New York: William Morrow, 2002, First edition; book near fine, light bumping to spine ends, dust jacket fine.   Bella Luna Books   May 26 2011 - t8537   2011 $302

Moore, Christopher   *Practical Demon Keeping.* New York: St. Martin's Press, 1992, First edition; fine, dust jacket fine, signed by author.   Bella Luna Books   May 29 2011 - 4345   2011 $88

Moore, Christopher   *The Stupidest Angel.* New York: Morrow, 2004, First edition; fine, dust jacket fine, signed by author.   Bella Luna Books   May 29 2011 - t6959a   2011 $110

Moore, Clement Clarke   1779-1863   *The Night Before Christmas or a Visit of St. Nicholas.* New York: McLoughlin Bros., 1888, Folio, stiff pictorial wrappers, slight finger soil, else near fine, 12 full page and one double page and 2 partial page fabulous chromolithographs plus color covers as well as color illustrations in text, glorious edition and beautiful copy.   Aleph-Bet Books, Inc.   95 - 150   2011 $1275

Moore, Clement Clarke   1779-1863   *Denslow's Night Before Christmas.* New York: Dillingham (Sept.), 1902, First edition, first issue; 4to., orange pictorial boards, usual edge wear and paper rubbing at joints, else clean and tight, very good++, text done in calligraphy with each page of text illustrated in color by Denslow.   Aleph-Bet Books, Inc.   95 - 185   2011 $2000

Moore, Clement Clarke   1779-1863   *The Night Before Christmas.* Philadelphia: Henry Altemus, 1918, 16mo., cloth backed pictorial boards, pictorial paste on, fine in lightly soiled dust jacket with few small chips, every other page is full page color plate, 28 in all.   Aleph-Bet Books, Inc.   95 - 151   2011 $250

Moore, Clement Clarke   1779-1863   *Night Before Christmas.* Springfield: McLoughlin, n.d. circa, 1925, 10 x 12 inches, cloth backed pictorial boards, spine faded in sports, slight edge wear, very good+, illustrations by Frank Lefevre with pictorial titlepage, 1 double page color spread, 6 full page color illustrations and 7 partial page color illustrations, uncommon, especially nice.   Aleph-Bet Books, Inc.   95 - 154   2011 $400

Moore, Clement Clarke   1779-1863   *The Night Before Christmas.* Racine: Whitman, 1939, Folio, pictorial linen like wrappers, near fine, (24 pages) including covers, very good+, illustrations by Keigh Ward, full and partial page color illustrations.   Aleph-Bet Books, Inc.   95 - 152   2011 $150

Moore, Clement Clarke 1779-1863 *Night Before Christmas.* Racine: Whitman, 1947, Folio, (12) pages, including covers, fine, printed on textured paper, very page wonderfully illustrated by Hilda Miloche and Wilma Kane. Aleph-Bet Books, Inc. 95 - 153 2011 $200

Moore, Clement Clarke 1779-1863 *The Night Before Christmas.* New York: Harper Collins, 2002, Stated first edition; illustrations by Engelbreit, signed and dated in year of publication by Mary Engelbreit, fine in fine dust jacket. By the Book, L. C. 26 - 68 2011 $85

Moore, Clement Clarke 1779-1863 *The Night Before Christmas.* Tarrytown: Marshall Cavendish Children, 2006, Limited to 300 signed and numbered copies, this no. 48; signed by artist with gilt ink, small 4to., 27 pages, illustrations by Gennady Spirin, as new, full green leatherette with gilt lettering to front cover, original beautiful red satin cloth covered clam shell box, paste-on color illustration to front. By the Book, L. C. 26 - 69 2011 $250

Moore, Clement Clarke 1779-1863 *Poems.* New York: Bartlett & Wilford, 1844, First edition; contains the first appearance of his famous poem "A Visit from St. Nicholas", 12mo., xi, (1, blank), (13)-216 pages, uncut in publisher's original brown paper boards, printed paper spine label darkened with ink as the label is bit rubbed, some professional restoration to spine extremities and hinges, bit of rubbing to boards and edges, previous owner's bookplate, previous owner's extensive old ink notes about this edition on front free endpaper, chemise, quarter calf slipcase, overall very nice. Heritage Book Shop Holiday 2010 - 91 2011 $7500

Moore, Edward *The New Ladies' Library.* Philadelphia: M. Carey and Son, 1818, Pages xvi, 276, uncut, engraved frontispiece, small 8vo., original printed boards, little rubbed, spine cracked. R. F. G. Hollett & Son Antiquarian Booksellers 175 - 962 2011 £140

Moore, Francis D. *The Metabolic Response in Surgery.* Springfield: Charles C. Thomas, 1952, Small 4to., xv, 156 pages, figures, tables, black pebbled cloth, gilt stamped cover and spine titles, blue ink underlining on page 136-7, previous owner's inked signature and rubber stamps, signed presentation inscription, from the Medical Library of Dr. Clare Gray Peterson. Jeff Weber Rare Books 162 - 220 2011 $150

Moore, George *Aphrodite in Aulis.* London: 1930, Limited edition to 1825 copies, this #1231, signed by author; vi, 340 pages, full vellum, extra clean, corners sharp, fore edges untrimmed, gilt arch design on cover sharp, in partially worn box. Bookworm & Silverfish 676 - 133 2011 $75

Moore, George *A Communication to my Friends.* London: Nonesuch Press, 1933, One of 1000 copies; 235 x 152mm., 3 p.l. (7)-86 pages, (1) leaf, publisher's grained quarter suede over paper boards, flat spine with titling in gilt along length, all edges untrimmed, original brown printed dust jacket, dust jacket slightly frayed at head and foot, else virtually mint. Phillip J. Pirages 59 - 274 2011 $65

Moore, George *Peronnik the Fool.* Chapelle-Reanville, Eure: Hours Press, 1928, Limited edition, one of 200 copies, numbered (#108) and signed by author; very good+. Lupack Rare Books May 26 2011 - ABE4182184353 2011 $125

Moore, George *Ulick & Soracha.* London: 1926, Limited to 1255 copies (this 866); fine in original dust jacket, untrimmed, unopened, dust jacket half inch shorter than book. Bookworm & Silverfish 668 - 63 2011 $75

Moore, George *Whitehall in Cumberland.* privately published, 1865, Original blindstamped blue cloth, gilt, extremities trifle rubbed, pages 28 with title vignette and 3 color lithographs. R. F. G. Hollett & Son Antiquarian Booksellers 173 - 792 2011 £150

Moore, J. E. S. *To the Mountains of the Moon: being an Account of the Modern Aspect of Central Africa and of some Little Known Regions Traversed by the Tanganyika Expedition in 1899 and 1900.* London: Hurst & Blackett, 1901, First edition; 8vo., pages xvi, 350, color frontispiece, maps, illustrations, original green decorative cloth, top edge gilt, vignette on upper cover, spine faded, corner bumped. J. & S. L. Bonham Antiquarian Booksellers Africa 4/20/2011 - 7817 2011 £200

Moore, John 1729-1802 *A View of Society and Manners in France, Switzerland and Germany.* London: printed by A. Strahan, 1786, Sixth edition; 2 volumes, xvi, 420; xii, 420 pages, 8vo., full contemporary tree calf, gilt spines rubbed, heads and tails worn, joints cracking, but holding, leading inner hinge to volume I reinforced with white tape, modern ownership labels on pastedowns, good, clean copy. Jarndyce Antiquarian Booksellers CXCI - 570 2011 £75

Moore, John 1729-1802 *The Works of John Moore, M.D.* Edinburgh/London: printed for Stirling & Slade/ Longman, Hurst, Rees, Orme & Brown and others, 1820, First edition; 7 volumes, full leather, pages 3473, somewhat used set with some boards detached or loose and some rubbing, text complete and clean with frontispiece in volume one in nice shape, good only. Any Amount of Books May 29 2011 - A49798 2011 $340

Moore, Marianne 1887-1972 *Eight Poems.* New York: Museum of Modern Art, 1962, First edition; number 98 of 195 copies signed by author and artist, 10 printed drawings by Robert Andrew Parker, colored by hand with original watercolors, boards in slipcase, as new.   Gemini Fine Books & Arts, Ltd.   Art Reference & Illustrated Books: First Editions 2011 $800

Moore, Sydney H. *Sursum Corda.* Independent Press, 1956, First edition; pages 127, frontispiece, original cloth, dust jacket, presentation copy inscribed by author, loosely inserted 5 page offprint "Joachim Neander" by the author, inscribed by him and dated 1963.   R. F. G. Hollett & Son Antiquarian Booksellers   175 - 963 2011   £35

Moore, Thomas 1779-1852   *Lalla Rookh, an Oriental Romance.* London: printed for Longman, Hurst, Rees, Orme and Brown, 1817, First edition; 292 x 222mm., 2 p.l., 405, (1) pages, nothing short of spectacular early 20th century dark blue levant morocco extravagantly gilt, richly inlaid and gloriously bejewelled by Sangorski & Sutcliffe (stamp-signed on front doublure), binding with overall Oriental design (befitting the poem) with upper cover featuring a sunken central panel, its unusual nine-sided shape resembling a clump of hanging grapes, within which two birds of paradise, inlaid in lilac, green and brown morocco with two rubies for eyes, perch in a grape arbor, its inlaid leaves with fruit clusters on densely stippled gilt around accented with 19 turquoises, the whole central tableau surrounded by a border of interweaving bands of inlaid brown morocco set with 9 bands of Mother-of-Pearl, the entire sunken panel surrounded by two ornate frames filled with flowering vines of Oriental design composed of hundreds of pieces of inlaid morocco in red, blue, violet and green on a background of brown morocco and heavily stippled gilt, outer frame accented with 20 blue chalcedonies and 20 garnets; lower cover with similar frame and central panel, this one featuring two lovebirds inlaid with multiple colors and with two amethyst eyes, birds in a similar grape arbor above, large Mother-of-Pearl heart, panel further adorned with 3 sapphires, four blue chalcedonies five turquoises, four Carnelians and 10 additional bands of Mother-of-Pearl, raised bands, spine gilt in compartments with large inlaid arabesque in green and brown morocco on a gilt background, gilt titling on inlaid compartments of chestnut brown morocco, glorious front doublure of ivory morocco covered in gilt vines with inlaid violet morocco flowers, the whole framed in green morocco decorated with gilt vines and red morocco posies and berries, at center, a hand painted Cosway-Style portrait of author on ivory surrounded by gilt frame, with 12 flowers composed of no fewer than 72 turquoises and 36 garnets, oval portrait in sunken panel enclosed by wreath of inlaid morocco flowers, rear doublure of similar design, but its medallion featuring 8 amethysts set among sinously curving inlaid lilac strapwork twining around a large (approximately one carat) Mexican fire opal encircled by 12 pearls, the binding containing 226 jewels in all; free endleaves of cream colored watered silk, gilt edges, in original well made (somewhat scuffed), silk and plush lined blue morocco box with shuttered lid; extra illustrated with 12 hand colored engraved plates mounted on lettered Japan vellum bookplate of Charles J. Rosenbloom; two leaves with neatly renewed marginal tears, but magnificent copy of a masterpiece of bookbinding.   Phillip J. Pirages   59 - 111 2011 $65,000

Moore, Thomas 1779-1852   *Melodies Irlandaises.* Paris: 1869, Original wrapper bound under fine half morocco French binding for Chateau de Vertcoeur, top third of half title has been torn off but very skilful graft has been effected, on verso, facing titlepage is shield of printer, J. Claye and underneath, a manuscript"No. 60", a pencil note inside front cover notes "Edition originale sur grand papier, rare, light foxing, early and late, else very good.   C. P. Hyland   May 26 2011 - 258/638 2011 $275

Moore, Thomas 1779-1852 *Paradise and the Peri.* London: 1909, Quarto, beautiful frontispiece with elaborate burnished gold, additional 8 miniatures, beautifully bound by Sangorski & Sutcliffe in full royal blue levant morocco jeweled binding.   Heritage Book Shop   Booth A12 51st NY International Antiquarian Book Fair April 8-10 2011 - 111   2011 $30,000

Moore, Thomas 1779-1852 *A Selection of Popular National Aires, with Symphonies and Accompaniments.* London: J. Power, 1818, Small folio, original half calf with marbled boards, rather worn, engraved tissue guarded frontispiece, engraved tissue guarded title, large vignette (7 cm. tear at foot repaired, not affecting vignette), engraved dedication leaf (similar tear repaired), 2 leaves letterpress (ad and indices) pages 58 (engraved music).   R. F. G. Hollett & Son Antiquarian Booksellers   175 - 964   2011   £75

Moore, Thomas 1779-1852 *Tom Crib's Memorial to Congress.* New York: for Kirk and Mercein, etc., William A. Merein, Pr., 1819, 120 pages, later half morocco, nice tight copy, half title, scarce edition.   Joseph J. Felcone Inc. Fall Miscellany 2010 - 18   2011 $400

Moore, Thomas 1821-1887 *The Octavo Nature Printed British Frns...* London: Bradbury & Evans, 1859-1860, 8vo., pages xvi, 254; xi,3 68, 2 elaborately decorated titles, each with nature printed fern and 122, nature printed ferns, foxing to first plate, occasional minor foxing to rest of plates, 8vo., pages xvi, 254; xi, 368, original green morocco over marbled boards, ex-libris Daniel Hunter Gaskell, elaborate gilt decorated spines with five raised bands, all edges gilt.   Raymond M. Sutton, Jr.   May 26 2011 - 47909   2011 $1350

Moorsom, G. *A Brief Review & Analyses of the Laws for the Admeasurement of tonnage.*   London: 1853, xl, 191 (203 total) pages, 3 large folding plates, very good, cover gilt bright, corners sharp, f.e.p. with minor moisture mark 3/8 inch, some shelf fading, extremely scarce.   Bookworm & Silverfish   676 - 144   2011 $175

Mora, Jo *Californios. The Saga of the Hard Riding Vaqueros, America's First Cowboys.*   New York: Doubleday, 1949, First edition; 175 pages, illustrations by author, brick cloth, lettered and decorated in gilt, very fine, pictorial dust jacket (jacket spine slightly faded).   Argonaut Book Shop   Recent Acquisitions Summer 2010 - 135   2011 $150

Morand, Paul *Paris de Nuit. Paris After Dark.*   Paris: (London): Edition 'Arts et Metiers Graphiques" (B. T. Batsford), 1933, First edition in English; 4to., pages (xii), (2) 2-62, (1), 64 black and white photos printed in gravure, original spiral bound black and white photo illustrated card wrappers, text printed in red and green, light rubbing to extremities, negligible creasing to lower side, top tab on lower side detached binding, price discreetly stamped and written in pencil on lower side, near fine.   Simon Finch Rare Books   Zero - 512   2011   £2500

Morata, Olympia Fulvia *Opera Omnia...*   Basil: P. Perna, 1570, Third edition; 8vo., (16), 511, woodcut printer's device and elaborate woodcut border facing beginning of text, contemporary green velum with red fore-edges which are tooled in blind, 2 small old collection stamps on title and repaired at early time, two blank places where an owner's name was removed, contemporary owner has supplied an index on back pastedown, later owner's inscriptions, some light toning of paper.   Second Life Books Inc.   174 - 241 2011 $6200

More Boners. New York: Viking, 1932, First edition; square 12mo., green blindstamped cloth, 89 pages, near fine in lightly rubbed dust jacket, black and white illustrations by Dr. Seuss.   Aleph-Bet Books, Inc.   95 - 521   2011 $700

More, Hannah 1745-1833 *Bible Rhymes, on The Names of all the Books of the Old and New Testament: with Allusions to Some of the Principal Incidents and Characters.* London: T. Cadell, Hatchard and Son, printed by A. and R. Spottiswoode, 1821, First edition; 8vo., 94 pages, modern blue printed paper wrappers, quarter page woodcuts, untrimmed, ghost square foxing on titlepage caused by card inserted at book, rare, very fine.   Hobbyhorse Books   56 - 110   2011 $150

More, Hannah 1745-1833 *Christian Morals.*   London: T. Cadell & W. Davies, 1813, First edition; 2 volumes, slight spotting, uncut in original blue boards, brown paper spines, slightly chipped with hinges splitting, paper labels, good plus copy as originally issued, inscription "Miss Campbell".   Jarndyce Antiquarian Booksellers   CLXC - 518   2011   £90

More, Hannah 1745-1833 *Coelebs in Search of a Wife.* London: T. Cadell and W. Davies, 1809, Fifth edition; 2 volumes, errata leaf volume II, prelims slightly creased volume I, contemporary half calf, gilt spines, leather labels, hinges and edges rubbed, Marquess of Headfort armorial bookplates, good, sound copy.   Jarndyce Antiquarian Booksellers   CLXC - 520   2011   £125

More, Hannah 1745-1833 *Coelebs in Search of a Wife.* London: T. Cadell and W. Davies, 1809, Eleventh edition; 2 volumes, slight dusting and foxing, pages 151-180 volume II with small nick in outer margin not affecting text, following blank volume II torn in outer margin with slight loss, contemporary full tan calf, gilt and blind spine, hinges slightly worn, each volume signed Kate Roscam in contemporary hand, good plus. Jarndyce Antiquarian Booksellers CLXC - 521 2011 £90

More, Hannah 1745-1833 *Coelebs in Search of a Wife.* London: T. Cadell and W. Daives, 1813, 1810. Fourteenth and thirteenth edition; 2 volumes, expertly and sympathetically rebound in half tan calf, gilt spines, red leather labels, very good, presentation from author to Miss Guillebaud, signatures of Mrs. W. Baynton, 3 Clifton Vale. Jarndyce Antiquarian Booksellers CLXC - 522 2011 £450

More, Hannah 1745-1833 *Hints Towards Forming the Character of a Young Princess.* London: printed for T. Cadell and W. Davies, 1805, First edition; 2 volumes, volume I bound without half title, contemporary full tan calf, gilt spines and borders, dark green leather labels, hinges slightly weakened, good plus. Jarndyce Antiquarian Booksellers CLXC - 523 2011 £150

More, Hannah 1745-1833 *The History of the Two Shoemakers.* Philadelphia: Johnson & Warner, 1811, Parts I, II, III, IV in one, 12mo., 107 pages continuous pagination), gray paper on boards, new spine with colored matching paper, printed on provincial paper, half page woodcuts, shelf wear at edge of covers, expertly rebacked, uniformly tanned paper, very fine, rare. Hobbyhorse Books 56 - 111 2011 $250

More, Hannah 1745-1833 *The History of Tom White, the Postillion.* Bath: sold by S. Hazard, circa, 1795, 24 pages, uncut, sewn as issued, woodcut vignette on titlepage, very good. Jarndyce Antiquarian Booksellers CLXC - 524 2011 £85

More, Hannah 1745-1833 *Moral Sketches of Prevailing Opinions and Manners, Foreign and Domestic.* London: T. Cadell & W. Davies, 1819, Second edition; foxing at end, marbled boards, excellently rebacked in half brown calf, spine tooled in gilt and blind, very good. Jarndyce Antiquarian Booksellers CLXC - 525 2011 £150

More, Hannah 1745-1833 *Poems.* London: T. Cadell & W. Davies, 1816, First edition; engraved title, handsomely bound in contemporary full dark blue calf, spine gilt in compartments, gilt borders and dentelles, red leather label, slight rubbing, small owner's label, Gertrude Selwin, good plus. Jarndyce Antiquarian Booksellers CLXC - 526 2011 £150

More, Hannah 1745-1833 *The Poetical Works.* London: Scott, Webster & Geary, 1836, Frontispiece, added engraved title, initial 12 page catalog, original dark green cloth, very good. Jarndyce Antiquarian Booksellers CLXC - 515 2011 £35

More, Hannah 1745-1833 *The Poetical Works.* Halifax: printed & published by William Milner, 1844, Small 8vo., frontispiece, title, additional printed title, original dark blue cloth, decorated and lettered in blind and gilt, spine very slightly faded, all edges gilt, very good. Jarndyce Antiquarian Booksellers CLXC - 517 2011 £40

More, Hannah 1745-1833 *Sacred Dramas: Chiefly Intended for Young Persons...* London: T. Cadell, 1782, Second edition; contemporary full tree calf, gilt spine, maroon leather label, expertly repaired, presentation to Mary Hamilton (after Dickenson) by author. Jarndyce Antiquarian Booksellers CLXC - 528 2011 £650

More, Hannah 1745-1833 *Sacred Dramas:... Sensibility: an Epistle.* London: T. Cadell and W. Davies, 1817, Twenty-first edition; frontispiece, title vignette, full contemporary calf, gilt spine and borders, green label, very good, attractive copy, inscription to Emma Peyson. Jarndyce Antiquarian Booksellers CLXC - 529 2011 £35

More, Hannah 1745-1833 *The Shepherd of Salisbury Plain.* Bath: sold by S. Hazard, printer to the Cheap Repository for Religious and Moral Tracts &c., 1795, 24 pages, uncut, sewn as issued, woodcut vignette on titlepage, slightly dusted, but very good. Jarndyce Antiquarian Booksellers CLXC - 531 2011 £85

More, Hannah 1745-1833 *Sir Eldred of the Bower and the Bleeding Rock: Two Legendary Tales.* London: T. Cadell, 1776, First edition; 4to., pages (vi), 49, (1), removed from bound volume, little soiled but very good scarce,. Second Life Books Inc. 174 - 242 2011 $1200

More, Hannah 1745-1833 *Strictures on the Modern System of Female Education...* London: Thomas Tegg and Son, 1834, Page xiv, 335, 12mo., original patterned cloth with leather spine label, little stained, upper hinge cracked. R. F. G. Hollett & Son Antiquarian Booksellers 175 - 965 2011 £75

More, Hannah 1745-1833 *The Miscellaneous Works.* London: Thomas Tegg, 1840, 2 volumes, tall 8vo., half titles, initial 8 page catalog (Dec. 1841), volume i, final ad leaf volume II, original black cloth, very good. Jarndyce Antiquarian Booksellers CLXC - 514 2011 £110

More, Henry *An Account of Virtue: or Dr. Henry More's Abridgement of Morals.* London: printed or B. Tooke, 1701, Second edition; 8vo., (16), 264 pages, panelled sheep, from the library of the Earls of Macclesfield at Shirburn Castle, inscription of Bibliothecae Gilberti Walmsley. Maggs Bros. Ltd. 1440 - 148 2011 £400

More, Thomas 1478-1535 *Utopia.* Hammersmith: William Morris at the Kelmscott Press, 1893, One of 300 copies on paper, out of a total edition of 308 copies; octavo, (2, blank), xiv, 282, (1, colophon), (1, blank), pages, printed in red and black in Chaucer and Troy types, decorative woodcut borders and initials, original full limp vellum with yapp edge, spine lettered in gilt, original silk ties, all edges uncut, light bowing to vellum, fine, housed in gray cloth slipcase. David Brass Rare Books, Inc. May 26 2011 - 01251 2011 $6500

More, Thomas 1478-1535 *Utopia.* London: sold by Reeves and Turner, 1893, 1 of 300 copies on paper, out of an edition of 308; octavo, original full limp vellum, yapp edges. Heritage Book Shop Booth A12 51st NY International Antiquarian Book Fair April 8-10 2011 - 78 2011 $4500

More, Thomas 1478-1535 *Utopia.* Waltham St. Lawrence: Golden Cockerel Press, 1929, One of 500 copies; 273 x 203mm., 2 p.l., xiii (1)-137 (1) pages, (1) leaf colophon, light blue buckram, front board with gilt centerpiece titling in gilt on spine, one woodcut, many scrolling foliate decorations and a diagram showing the alphabet of the island country of Utopia, all by Eric Gill, titlepage printed in blue and black; spine and section along top edge of front cover faintly faded to gray, superficial bump near tail of spine, tiny dark spots on front endpapers and 10 leaves, still fine, fresh. Phillip J. Pirages 59 - 220 2011 $525

Moreira, Eduardo *Portuguese East Africa.* London: World Dominion Press, 1936, First edition; 8vo., pages 104, ads, maps, illustrations, original blue cloth, dust jacket. J. & S. L. Bonham Antiquarian Booksellers Africa 4/20/2011 - 5522 2011 £35

Morell, John Reynell *Algeria; the Topography and History, Political, Social and Natural of French Africa.* London: Nathaniel Cooke, 1854, First edition; 8vo., pages 490, illustrations, contemporary red decorative cloth, very good prize binding, fine vignette on upper cover, all edges gilt, spine rubbed at head. J. & S. L. Bonham Antiquarian Booksellers Africa 4/20/2011 - 8176 2011 £75

Morell, W. W. *The History and Antiquities of Selby, in the West Riding of the County of York.* Selby: 1867, 8vo., xxiii, (i), 350 pages, 8 original mounted photos and engraved plates, folding map, good, original cloth, spine little faded and expertly repaired, scarce. Ken Spelman Rare Books 68 - 189 2011 £65

Moreton, C. Oscar *Old Carnations and Pinks.* London: George Rainbird and Collins, 1955, First edition; small folio, original cloth backed pictorial boards, dust jacket, few slight nicks and closed tears, pages xi, 51, 8 color plates by Rory McEwen, flyleaves lightly browned. R. F. G. Hollett & Son Antiquarian Booksellers General Catalogue Summer 2010 - 1026 2011 £85

Morgan, Aubrey Niel *David Morgan 1833-1919.* Newport: Starling Press, 1977, First edition; original cloth, gilt, dust jacket (price clipped), pages 181, (i), illustrated with 2 folding pedigrees. R. F. G. Hollett & Son Antiquarian Booksellers 175 - 966 2011 £30

Morgan, Dale L. *Jedediah Smith and His Maps of the American West.* San Francisco: California Historical Society, 1954, First edition, limited to 350 numbered copies; folio, (6), 86 page, 7 maps, light red cloth, gilt lettered spine, very fine and bright, without usual cover fading, exceptional copy. Argonaut Book Shop Recent Acquisitions Summer 2010 - 185 2011 $900

Morgan, Dale L. *Overland in 1846. Diaries and Letters of the California-Oregon Trail.* Georgetown: Talisman Press, 1963, First deluxe edition, no. 65 of 100 sets of the special edition; printed on Ticonderoga text, bound in half morocco leather and marbled boards, boxed and signed by Morgan on half title, 2 volumes, pages 457, 458-825, folding map, large folding map in rear pocket (4 parts on 2 sheets), publisher's half black morocco leather, gilt lettered spine, marbled boards, very fine set with lightly damaged slipcase. Argonaut Book Shop Recent Acquisitions Summer 2010 - 136 2011 $500

Morgan, Lewis H. *Houses and House-Life of the American Aborigines.* Washington: 1881, First edition; xiv, 281 pages, illustrations, rebound in tan cloth, minor foxing and browning, else very good. Dumont Maps & Books of the West 111 - 71 2011 $165

Morgan, Sydney Owenson 1776-1859 *Florence Macarthy; an Irish Tale.* London: Henry Colburn, 1839, Engraved frontispiece, additional printed title, original maroon patterned cloth, spine lettered in gilt, spine faded to brown, slight rubbing, inner hinges weak, good sound copy. Jarndyce Antiquarian Booksellers CLXC - 533 2011 £65

Morgan, Sydney Owenson 1776-1859 *France in 1829-1830.* London: Saunders & Otley, 1831, Second edition; 2 volumes, frontispiece volume I slightly spotted, uncut in contemporary brown boards, brown cloth spines, paper labels slightly darkened, spines slightly rubbed at head and tail, nice. Jarndyce Antiquarian Booksellers CLXC - 534 2011 £280

Morgan, Sydney Owenson 1776-1859 *Lady Morgan's Memoirs: Autobiography, Diaries and Correspondence.* London: Wm. H. Allen & Co., 1863, Second edition; engraved frontispiece, contemporary full maroon calf, double ruled borders in gilt, spines gilt in compartments, black title labels, lacking volume no. labels, spines faded to brown and slightly rubbed, Eton leaving inscription E. W. Danby to Alexander William Fraser, 19th Lord Saltoun, Saltoun bookplates, good plus.   Jarndyce Antiquarian Booksellers   CLXC - 542 2011   £125

Morgan, Sydney Owenson 1776-1859 *O'Donnel. A National Tale.* London: Henry Colburn, 1815, New edition; 3 volumes, half titles, 9 pages ads volume III, contemporary full tan calf, spines gilt in compartments, green leather labels, spines slightly darkened, slight rubbing, armorial bookplates of Henrietta Burton, good plus.   Jarndyce Antiquarian Booksellers   CLXC - 535 2011   £280

Morgan, Sydney Owenson 1776-1859 *O'Donnel.* London: Henry Colburn, 1835, Revised edition; frontispiece, vignette title, additional printed title, original olive green vertical grained cloth, spine blocked and lettered in gilt, front board with central monogram in gilt and elaborate borders in blind, inner hinges slightly cracked, very good.   Jarndyce Antiquarian Booksellers   CLXC - 536 2011   £75

Morgan, Sydney Owenson 1776-1859 *St. Clair; or the Heiress of Desmond.* London: printed for J. J. Stockdale, 1812, Third edition; 2 volumes, frontispiece volume I, half title volume II, odd small mark, handsomely rebound in half calf, marbled boards, black leather labels, very good.   Jarndyce Antiquarian Booksellers   CLXC - 537 2011   £450

Morgan, Sydney Owenson 1776-1859 *The Wild Irish Girl: a National Tale.* London: Richard Phillips, 1806, First edition; 3 volumes, ad on verso of final leaf volume II, expertly rebound in half brown calf, gilt spine, very good.   Jarndyce Antiquarian Booksellers   CLXC - 538 2011   £1250

Morgan, Sydney Owenson 1776-1859 *The Wild Irish Girl.* London: Richard Phillips, 1806-1807, Volumes I & II first edition, volume III third edition; 3 volums, ad on verso of final leaf volume II, contemporary half calf, plain spines numbered simply 1, 2, 3 with library numbers '254' at heads, little rubbed, good plus copy, unusual library binding.   Jarndyce Antiquarian Booksellers   CLXC - 539 2011   £650

Morgan, Sydney Owenson 1776-1859 *The Wild Irish Girl.* London: Richard Phillips, 1807, Third edition; 3 volumes, 12mo., ad on verso of final leaf volume II, very small tear from bottom corner of following f.e.p. volume II, contemporary half calf, spines ruled in gilt, maroon leather labels slightly chipped, little worn, good plus.   Jarndyce Antiquarian Booksellers   CLXC - 540 2011   £380

Morgan, Sydney Owenson 1776-1859 *Woman; or Ida of Athens.* London: Longman, Hurst, Rees and Orme, 1809, First edition; 4 volumes, contemporary full calf, borders in blind and gilt, gilt spines, black leather labels, spines little dulled and slightly rubbed, good plus, with gift inscription in prelims of each volume, "Mary Wise, the gift of her beloved and affect. husband, 1809".   Jarndyce Antiquarian Booksellers   CLXC - 541 2011   £650

Morgan, William *Illustrations of Masonry, by One of the Fraternity who Has Devoted Thirty Years to the Subject.* New York: printed for the author, 1827, Second edition; 12mo., 84 pages, contemporary plain wrappers, sewn, dust soiled and lightly stained.   M & S Rare Books, Inc. 90 - 233 2011 $600

Morier, James Justinian *Zohrab the Hostage.* London: Richard Bentley, 1833, Third edition; 3 volumes, half titles, contemporary half green calf, maroon and black morocco labels, very good, handsome copy.   Jarndyce Antiquarian Booksellers   CXCI - 530 2011   £225

Morison, Alexander *The Physiognomy of Mental Diseases.* Weiler im Allgau: Editions Medicina Rara, n.d., Limited to 2500 copies, facsimile reproduction of 1843 second edition; 8vo., unpaginated, illustrations, quarter tan leather with black paper boards, blindstamped spine title, housed in paper slipcase, fine, from the Medical Library of Dr. Clare Gray Peterson.   Jeff Weber Rare Books 162 - 221 2011 $95

Morley, Christopher *Mince Pie.* New York: G. H. Doran, 1919, Early printing; very good+, inscribed by author for Hank and Margaret Harris.   Lupack Rare Books May 26 2011 - ABE2464946756 2011 $100

Morley, John *The Struggle for National Education.* London: Chapman and Hall, 1873, First edition; original cloth, gilt, pages viii, 184.   R. F. G. Hollett & Son Antiquarian Booksellers   175 - 967 2011   £45

Morley, Susuan *Throstlethwaite.* London: Henry S. King & Co., 1875, First edition; 3 volumes in 1 in dulled red cloth remainder binding bit dulled and rubbed, inner hinges cracking, Renier booklabel.   Jarndyce Antiquarian Booksellers   CLXC - 545 2011   £60

Morrah, Herbert A. *Highways and Hedges.* Adam and Charles Black, 1911, First edition; original pictorial cloth gilt, pages xv, 144, 20 color plates, endpapers lightly foxed.   R. F. G. Hollett & Son Antiquarian Booksellers   General Catalogue Summer 2010 - 1504 2011   £60

Morrell, J. D. *On the Philosophical Tendencies of the Age: Being Four Lectures Delivered at Edinburgh & Glasgow in January 1848.* London: 1848, Tall 8vo., viii (9) 193 (1) pages, good, some spotting, left side of backstrip, text embrowned, bookplate removed. Bookworm & Silverfish 667 - 130 2011 $87

Morris, Desmond *The Human Zoo.* London: Cape, 1969, First edition; original cloth, gilt, dust jacket spine faded, pages 256. R. F. G. Hollett & Son Antiquarian Booksellers 175 - 968 2011 £35

Morris, Ethelberta *Amerliaranne Bridesmaid.* London: Harrap, 1946, First edition; original pictorial boards, dust jacket, extremities little chipped and worn, illustrations in color and black and white. R. F. G. Hollett & Sons Antiquarian Booksellers 170 - 318 2011 £50

Morris, Francis Orpen 1810-1893 *Country Seats of the Noblemen and Gentlemen of Great Britain and Ireland.* London: William MacKenzie, n.d., Volumes 1, 2, 4 and 6, red cloth with gilt illustrations worn, torn, soiled, all edges gilt, foxing to text, 90, 80, 82, 88 pages, 4to., chromolithographs, some loose, all in very good condition. G. H. Mott Bookseller May 26 2011 - 43738 2011 $500

Morris, Francis Orpen 1810-1893 *A History of the British Birds.* London: George Bell and Sons, 1870, Second edition; 365 hand colored plates, some foxing to few, tall 8vo., over 1600 pages, original green cloth, some wear, mostly to lower corners, partial splitting to cloth on rear edge of 2 volumes, several corners bumped, soiling to some endpapers, few inner joints open, occasional light foxing, Robert Bovil Whitehead armorial bookplates. Raymond M. Sutton, Jr. May 26 2011 - 30708 2011 $1250

Morris, Francis Orpen 1810-1893 *A Natural History of British Moths...* London: Bell and Daldy, 1872, 4 volumes, original blindstamped green cloth, gilt, short tear to head of two spines, with 132 hand colored plates, excellent clean and sound set. R. F. G. Hollett & Son Antiquarian Booksellers General Catalogue Summer 2010 - 1027 2011 £750

Morris, Harrison & Co. *Directory & Gazetteer of Cumberland. 1861.* Whitehaven: Michael Moon, 2000, Facsimile edition; original cloth, gilt, dust jacket, pages 324, (lxxvi, ads), excellent reprint. R. F. G. Hollett & Son Antiquarian Booksellers 173 - 797 2011 £40

Morris, J. P. *A Glossary of the Words and Phrases of Furness.* J. Russell Smith, 1869, First edition; small 8vo., original wrappers, printed label, few light marks, pages xvi, 114, (vi), scarce. R. F. G. Hollett & Son Antiquarian Booksellers 173 - 798 2011 £55

Morris, M. *The Reign of William an Mary.* London & New York: Nister & Dutton, n.d. circa, 1910, Large oblong 4to., cloth backed boards, pictorial paste-on, fine, illustrations by author in bold flat colors with 8 great color plates and many large line illustrations. Aleph-Bet Books, Inc. 95 - 143 2011 $750

Morris, M. C. F. *Francis Orpen Morris. A Memoir by His Son.* London: John C. Nimmo, 1897, First edition; original ribbed green cloth gilt, corners little softened, pages xi, 323, portrait and plates, front joint cracked. R. F. G. Hollett & Son Antiquarian Booksellers General Catalogue Summer 2010 - 444 2011 £65

Morris, W. P. *The Records of Patterdale.* Kendal: T. Wilson, 1903, First edition; original cloth, gilt over bevelled boards, fore edge of upper board little faded, pages 161, with 8 plates, scarce. R. F. G. Hollett & Son Antiquarian Booksellers 173 - 800 2011 £120

Morris, William 1834-1896 *The Defence of Guenevere and Other Poems.* London: Bell and Daldy, 1858, First edition; half title, original brown wavy grained, borders in blind, spine lettered in gilt, very slightly rubbed at head and tail of spine, armorial bookplate of Lord Carlingford on leading pastedown, very good. Jarndyce Antiquarian Booksellers CXCI - 326 2011 £850

Morris, William 1834-1896 *The Earthly Paradise.* Hammersmith: Kelmscott Press, 1896, One of 225 paper copies; 8 volumes, small quarto, woodcut title, decorative woodcut borders and initials, printed in red and black in Golden type, full limp vellum with yapp edges, fine set, housed in cloth slipcase. David Brass Rare Books, Inc. May 26 2011 - 01456 2011 $11,500

Morris, William 1834-1896 *Gothic Architecture: a Lecture for the Arts and Crafts Exhibition Society.* Kelmscott Press, 1893, One of 1500 copies on paper (there were also 45 on vellum); 145 x 110mm., 1 p.., 68 pages, remarkably graceful contemporary calf modelled to an Art Nouveau design by Eva Sparre (signed with her initials at bottom of front cover), upper board dominated by graceful anthhemion of leaves emerging from an intricately tooled base (which resembled stylized feathers, perhaps from a peacock), titling inscribed in blind on either side of this large central object, back covers with floral medallion in middle, flat spine edges untrimmed, woodcut initials and small woodcut decorations in text, headlines and sidenotes printed in red, dozen little spots (perhaps from water droplets) on front cover and two dozen on back, small chip at head of spine, endpapers with offsetting from leather turn-ins, three or four pages with tiny dots of foxing, otherwise excellent, binding with very little wear to joints or extremities, text quite clean and fresh. Phillip J. Pirages 59 - 141 2011 $2500

Morris, William 1834-1896 *Gothic Architecture: a Lecture for the Arts and Crafts Exhibition Society.* Kelmscott Press, 1893, One of 1500 copies on paper, there wer also on 45 on vellum; 145 x 108mm., 1 p.l., 68 pages, original holland backed paper boards, edges untrimmed, woodcut initials and small woodcut decorations in text, headlines and sidenotes printed in red, front flyleaf with pencilled ownership signature of May Morris; covers rather faded and bit soiled, one faint spot of foxing to two leaves, otherwise fine internally, text clean, fresh and bright. Phillip J. Pirages 59 - 242 2011 $500

Morris, William 1834-1896 *The Hollow Land and Other Contributions to the Oxford and Cambridge Magazine.* London: Chiswick Press, 1903, First edition; printed on handmade paper using Morris' Golden typeface, in black with the titles and shoulder titles printed in red, pages (viii) (blanks), iv, 334, (7) (blanks), crown 8vo., original quarter blue grey cloth, printed label (spare label tipped in), pale blue boards lightly soiled and edges rubbed, cloth faded and little worn at backstrip head, free endpapers lightly browned, rough trimmed, front flyleaf inscribed by Emery Walker to Margaret Dickinson. Blackwell Rare Books B166 - 194 2011 £500

Morris, William 1834-1896 *Love is Enough or the Freeing of Pharamond: a Morality.* Kelmscott Press, 1897, One of 300 copies on paper, there were also 8 on vellum; 295 x 215mm., 2 p.l., 90 pages, original vellum, yapp edges, gilt titling on spine, silk ties, two very impressive full page woodcuts by Edward Burne-Jones, elaborate woodcut floral border around frontispiece and first page of text, handsome woodcut initials in black or blue, other charming partial woodcut foliate and floral borders; printed in red, blue and black; upper cover with 4 x 2 inch wrinkled patch, probably from moisture to remove bookplate on pastedown on opposite side, otherwise exceptionally fine, immaculate copy inside and out. Phillip J. Pirages 59 - 243 2011 $4800

Morris, William 1834-1896 *Poems by the Way.* London: Reeves and Turner, 1892, Second edition; square 8vo., original buckram gilt, little soiled and corners bumped, pages (ii), 196. R. F. G. Hollett & Son Antiquarian Booksellers General Catalogue Summer 2010 - 665 2011 £35

Morris, William 1834-1896 *A Prayer for the Opening of the Little League Season.* New York: Harcourt Brace, 1995, Limited to 300 copies, this #4; illustrations by Barry Moser, fine, signed by author and artist. Bella Luna Books May 26 2011 - t3105 2011 $220

Morris, William 1834-1896 *The Saga Library.* London: Bernard Quaritch, 1891, Volume I, old green library cloth, gilt, pages 227, light library stamp to back of titlepage and armorial bookplate on pastedown, otherwise very good, sound and clean. R. F. G. Hollett & Son Antiquarian Booksellers 175 - 971 2011 £35

Morris, William 1834-1896 *Signs of Change. Seven Lectures Delivered on Various Occasions.* Reeves and Turner, 1888, First edition; one leaf of undated ads at front and another at rear, few fox spots and marginal pencil ticks, portrait of Morris from newspaper pasted to verso of half title, another image tipped to verso of contents leaf, pages (ii), viii, (i), 202, (2), 8vo., original dark red cloth, backstrip lettered in gilt, boards with single blind fillet border, booklabel and ownership inscription of Holbrook Jackson to front endpapers, slightly bumped and scuffed at extremities, good. Blackwell Rare Books B166 - 195 2011 £100

Morris, William 1834-1896 *The Story of the Ere-Dwellers (Eyrbyggja Saga) with the Story of the Heath-Layngs...* London: Bernard Quaritch, 1892, First edition; original quarter roan gilt extra, spine little defective at head, pages liii, 410, joints cracked. R. F. G. Hollett & Son Antiquarian Booksellers 175 - 969 2011 £65

Morris, William 1834-1896 *The Story of the Glittering Plain.* London: Sold by Reeves & Turner, 1891, One of 200 paper copies out of a total edition of 206 copies; small quarto, (4), 188 pages, printed in golden type, decorative woodcut border and initials, original stiff vellum with wash leather ties, spine lettered in gilt, armorial bookplate of Lewis Hutchkiss Brittin, near fine, housed in gray cloth slipcase,. David Brass Rare Books, Inc. May 26 2011 - 01308 2011 $7500

Morris, William 1834-1896 *The Sundering Flood.* Kelmscott Press, 1897, One of 300 copies on paper (there were also 10 on vellum); 210 x 148mm., 4 p.l. (3 blank and half title), 507, (1) pages, publisher's blue paper boards expertly rebacked with linen matching original, spine with publisher's paper label at head, edges untrimmed; line block map drawn by H. Cribb, elaborate woodcut border and initial on first page of text and woodcut borders and initials at beginning of each chapter, small woodut initials, printed in black and red; covers bit soiled, corners slightly bruised, spine label bit damaged when relaid, one letter gone and dozen others partly lost, otherwise artfully restored binding entirely sound and not at all dissatisfactory, beautiful copy internally, unusually fresh, clean and bright. Phillip J. Pirages 59 - 244 2011 $1500

Morris, William 1834-1896 *The Water of the Wondrous Isles.* Hammersmith: Kelmscott Press, 1897, One of 250 paper copies of an edition of 256; large quarto, (2), 340, (1) pages, embellished with decorative woodcut borders, ornaments and initials, original rose silk ties, full limp vellum, spine lettered in gilt, armorial bookplate, fine, housed in gray cloth slipcase. David Brass Rare Books, Inc. May 26 2011 - 01485 2011 $6000

Morris, William 1834-1896 *The Wood Beyond the World.* Kelmscott Press, 1894, First edition; one of 350 copies (of an edition of 358) printed in Chaucer typeface in black on handmade paper, chapter and shoulder titles printed in red, wood engraved frontispiece by Edward Burne-Jones, wood engraved border to frontispiece and first page of text and numerous wood engraved half borders and initial letters, pages (viii) (blanks), (iv), 261, (7) (blanks), crown 8vo., original limp cream vellum, backstrip gilt lettered, pink silk ties, untrimmed, near fine. Blackwell Rare Books B166 - 265 2011 £3000

Morris, Wright *Collected Stories 1948-1986.* New York: Harper & Row, 1986, First edition; author's own working copy with his ownership signature and notes, pages detached, pages 249 and forward absent, Morris apparently disassembled the book in order to re-order the stories and create a new selection, titled or subtitled by hand "Origins and Obsessions", his marks to the content page and with two index cards of notes (written on both sides), laid in, existing parts, including jacket are in fine shape. Ken Lopez Bookseller 154 - 122 2011 $350

Morris, Wright *Wright Morris. (Photographs).* Wikin Berley, 1980, First edition, limited to 55 copies; consisting of 5 artist's proofs and 50 numbered sets, with each image signed by Morris on mount, folio, 12 original silver prints, 9 1/2 x 7 1/2 inches, with accompanying printed statement by artist, publisher's tan linen clamshell portfolio with leather label, photos and portfolio fine, rare. James S. Jaffe Rare Books May 26 2011 - 21740 2011 $22,500

Morrison, Toni *Beloved.* New York: Knopf, 1967, First edition; near fine, light bump to bottom front cover, dust jacket near fine, light creasing at top of spine and edges. Bella Luna Books May 29 2011 - t1415 2011 $77

Morrison, Toni *Love.* New York: Knopf, 2003, First edition; fine, near fine dust jacket with occasional minor crease as issued by publisher, signed by author. Bella Luna Books May 29 2011 - t6225 2011 $82

Morritt, J. B. S. *A Vindication of Homer and of the Ancient Poets and Historians who Have Recorded the Siege and Fall of Troy.* York: printed by W. Blanchard for T. Cadell, Jun. and W. Davies, 1798, 4to., pages 124 + 1 double page engraved map and 5 other double page engraved plates all mounted on stubs, contemporary diced Russia, spine double gilt with 'perched peacock' centre-piece gilt in compartments, lettered direct in gilt, boards decorative roll gilt bordered with central gilt ruled panel and quadrant arc corners gilt, board edges decorative roll gilt, turn-ins 'rope-twist' roll gilt, 'French shell' 'made' endpapers, all edges brown speckled, pale blue silk page marker, mid 20th century calf reback, backstrip relaid (partly inserted) + corners, faint dust soiling and toning, little offsetting from plates, old leather darkened around repairs, parts of old spines lost, Devonshire monogrammed heraldic booklabel on front pastedown, from the collection of Christopher Ernest Weston 1947-2010. Unsworths Booksellers 24 - 124 2011 £600

Morrow, Bradford *A Bestiary.* New York: Grenfell Press, 1990, Limited to 100 copies (entire edition) of which only 50 were for sale; original full multi-colored morocco by Claudia Cohen, in morocco and linen slipcase, each copy signed by author and each of the artists, the present copy is accompanied by one of only 3 complete sets of 36 original prints assembled at time of publication, each print is one of an edition of only 10 copies signed by artist, only 10 separate prints of each of the illustrations in book were produced, with the contributing artists receiving 7 copies of each of their prints, remaining 3 copies of the prints were gathered into 3 sets containing the full complement of 36 prints, 2 of these sets were retained by publisher and one by author, folio, 36 original prints by 18 different artists. James S. Jaffe Rare Books May 26 2011 - 5770 2011 $50,000

Morse, Jedidiah 1761-1826 *The American Geography; or a View of the Present Situation of the United States of America.* Elizabeth Town: Shepard Kollock, 1789, xii, 534, (3) pages, 2 folding maps, contemporary sheep, very skillfully rebacked in correct period style, rear endpaper sympathetically replaced, light foxing and occasional browning throughout as usual with early American paper, few short splits and one map tear skillfully mended, 20th century owner's stamp at foot of dedication page and on verso of one map, Rev. Anson Phelps Stokes bookplate. Joseph J. Felcone Inc. Fall Miscellany 2010 - 91 2011 $5500

Morse, Jedidiah 1761-1826 *The American Geography or a View of the present Situation of the United States of America.* Elizabethtown: 1789, First edition; xii, 534 pages, 2 folding maps, errata leaf, original leather, front joint starting, pages browned and foxed, maps repaired with some slight old tape stains, overall very good. Dumont Maps & Books of the West 113 - 42 2011 $4500

Morse, Jedidiah 1761-1826 *The American Geography or a View of the Present Situation of the United States of America.* London: for John Stockdale, 1792, Second edition; xvi, 536 pages, 2 folding maps, folding table, contemporary mottled calf, skillfully rebacked in period style, both maps with few neat and unobtrusive early repairs (fold strengthening) on verso, else fine, clean, entirely unfoxed. Joseph J. Felcone Inc. Fall Miscellany 2010 - 92 2011 $2800

Morshead, Owen *Windsor Castle.* Phaidon, 1951, First edition; 4to., original cloth, dust jacket, pages 54, with 80 plates, neat presentation inscription with list of signatures on flyleaf. R. F. G. Hollett & Son Antiquarian Booksellers 177 - 586 2011 £30

Mortenson, Greg *Three Cups of Tea.* New York: Viking, 2006, First edition; fine in fine dust jacket. Ken Lopez Bookseller 154 - 125 2011 $750

Mortimer, Charles Edward *An Historical Memoir of the Political Life of John Milton.* printed by James Swan, 1805, First edition; half title, text slightly affected by damp, blue sugar paper wrappers, slightly damp affected, rear wrapper chipped. Jarndyce Antiquarian Booksellers CXCI - 324 2011 £50

Mortimer, Favell Lee *Far Off. Asia Described.* Hatchards, 1890, New edition; small 8vo., original pictorial blue cloth gilt, trifle rubbed, pages xx, 562, 28 illustrations, folding colored map. R. F. G. Hollett & Sons Antiquarian Booksellers 170 - 462 2011 £45

Mortimer, Favell Lee *The Peep of Day.* London: Religious Tract Society, n.d., circa, 1920, Original blue cloth gilt, pictorial onlay, pages 310, (x), all edges gilt, gilt in the rough, 8 striking color plates, scarce. R. F. G. Hollett & Sons Antiquarian Booksellers 170 - 461 2011 £35

Mortimer, J. R. *Forty Years' Researches in British and Saxon Burial Mounds of East Yorkshire.* A. Brown and Sons, 1905, First edition; large 4to., original quarter morocco gilt with green cloth boards, pages lxxxvi, 452, (iv), top edge gilt, color frontispiece, color extending plan, 125 plates and over 1000 text figures, etc, flyleaves slightly browned, otherwise fine, handsome copy. R. F. G. Hollett & Son Antiquarian Booksellers 177 - 587 2011 £375

Morton, H. V. *Atlantic Meeting.* London: Methuen, 1943, First edition; original cloth, dust jacket, little chipped, pages 160, with 17 plates. R. F. G. Hollett & Son Antiquarian Booksellers 175 - 973 2011 £30

Morton, Robert Scott *Traditional Farm Architecture in Scotland.* Edinburgh: Ramsay Head Press, 1976, First edition; large 8vo., original cloth, gilt, dust jacket (closed tear to upper panel), pages 96 well illustrated, scarce. R. F. G. Hollett & Son Antiquarian Booksellers 177 - 588 2011 £65

Morus, Cenydd *The Fates of the Princes of Dyfed.* Point Loma: 1914, First edition; illustrations by R. Machell, xvi, 365 pages, very good. C. P. Hyland May 26 2011 - 255/505 2011 $724

Moseley, Henry Nottidge *Notes by a Naturalist.* London: John Murray, 1892, New edition; map, portrait, woodcuts, half title, index, 4 pages ads, tear in half title, pencil notes on endpaper and half title by previous owner, T. Waddington, original dark blue half cloth, lighter blue cloth sides, boards dulled. Jarndyce Antiquarian Booksellers CXCI - 340 2011 £45

Mosher, T. B. *Bibelot.* Mosher, 1895-1914, 236 issues (out of 240), original grey wrappers, very good. I. D. Edrich May 26 2011 - 99026 2011 $461

Mosley, Walter *Devil in a Blue Dress.* New York: W. W. Norton, 1990, First edition; near fine, light bumping to spine ends, dust jacket fine, second state of jacket priced at 19.95, signed by author. Bella Luna Books May 29 2011 - p2277 2011 $82

Mosley, Walter *A Red Death.* New York: W. W. Norton, 1991, First edition; fine, in first state dust jacket with price of $18.95, jacket fine, signed by author. Bella Luna Books May 29 2011 - t3133 2011 $88

Mosley, Walter *A Red Death.* New York: W. W. Norton, 1991, First edition; near fine, crease to cloth at base of spine, dust jacket fine, second state of jacket, priced at $19.95, signed by author. Bella Luna Books May 29 2011 - t4894 2011 $82

Mosley, Walter *White Butterfly.* New York: W. W. Norton, 1992, First edition; fine in fine dust jacket. Bella Luna Books May 29 2011 - p2293 2011 $104

Moss, Fletcher *Pilgrimages to Old Homes.* Didsbury: privately published, 1906, Large 8vo., original cloth, gilt over bevelled boards, rather speckled, pages xii, 392, (i), top edge gilt, profusely illustrated. R. F. G. Hollett & Son Antiquarian Booksellers General Catalogue Summer 2010 - 1506 2011 £35

Mother Goose *The Annotated Mother Goose.* New York: Bramhall House, a Division of Clarkson, N. Potter, 1962, 4to., 350 pages, red paper on boards, cloth spine with red title, decorative endpapers, red and gold glossy dust jacket, mint. Hobbyhorse Books 56 - 124 2011 $100

Mother Goose *Baby's Mother Goose.* N.P.: Peggy Cloth Books, 1947, 8 1/2 x 7 1/4 inches, pictorial cloth, some soil and fraying else very good, illustrations by Charlotte Steiner, scarce. Aleph-Bet Books, Inc. 95 - 370 2011 $200

Mother Goose *The Gay Mother Goose.* New York: Charles Scribner's Sons, 1938, First edition; 4to., color pictorial cloth with few handling marks and little burning to blank endpapers along gutter, 63 numbered pages with black and white drawings and several full color page illustrations by Francoise Seignbosc. Jo Ann Reisler, Ltd. 86 - 100 2011 $200

Mother Goose *Hop o' My thumb.* Cincinnati: Peter G. Thomson, n.d. circa, 1890, 12mo., pictorial wrappers, near fine, 4 charming full page chromolithographs, scarce. Aleph-Bet Books, Inc. 95 - 371 2011 $200

Mother Goose *The Jessie Wilcox Smith Mother Goose.* New York: Dodde, Mead and Co., 1914, First edition, first issue; oblong large 4to., black cloth with white lettering on spine and full color paste label, some minor rubbing to paste label, slight separation at half titlepage, some roughness to edge of one plate, small marginal tear in one page, finger mark in one place, original cardboard box present, little staining to blank bottom of box and some light rubbing to edges of box, but top complete and offers a lovely image from the book, color pictorial endpapers, 173 numbered pages, 12 full page color plates, five black and white plates, numerous drawings. Jo Ann Reisler, Ltd. 86 - 236 2011 $3500

Mother Goose *The Magic Picture Book of Mother Goose Rhymes and Melodies.* New York: Dillingham, 1908, First edition; 4to., cloth, pictorial paste-on, some cover soil and grubbiness, tight and very good, illustrations by Robert Porteos, every page is really a flap that feature a bold vibrant color illustration, when flap is lifted, it reveals a different but related picture beneath it, text pages illustrated in color, rare moveable flap book. Aleph-Bet Books, Inc. 95 - 374 2011 $1250

Mother Goose *Mother Goose.* Boston: Little Brown (Nov.), 1940, 4to., pictorial cloth, (136) pages, fine in slightly rubbed dust jacket, full page and partial page color illustrations, this copy inscribed and dated by Tenggren, uncommon thus. Aleph-Bet Books, Inc. 95 - 547 2011 $1500

Mother Goose *Mother Goose Playhouse.* New York: J.S. Pub. Co., n.d. circa, 1945, Large size pictorial box with great, elaborate pop-up that emerges when the cover is opened (box with normal wear and rubbing), inside are 8 pop-up Mother Goose rhymes, each in its own color pictorial booklet, with illustrations by Geraldine Clyne, quite rare. Aleph-Bet Books, Inc. 95 - 454 2011 $750

Mother Goose *Mother Goose. The Old Nursery Rhymes.* London: William Heineman, 1913, Limited edition, one of 1130 copies; signed by artist, quarto, 13 mounted color plates by Arthur Rackham, original white buckram. Heritage Book Shop Booth A12 51st NY International Antiquarian Book Fair April 8-10 2011 - 104 2011 $3500

Mother Goose *Mother Goose's Rag Book.* London: Dean's Rag Book Co., n.. early 20th century, Square 8vo., original red cloth stitched spine, pages (16), color printed cloth, sometime washed and rather faded, little frayed at head and foot. R. F. G. Hollett & Sons Antiquarian Booksellers 170 - 156 2011 £50

Mothersole, Jessie *Hadrian's Wall.* London: John Lane, The Bodley Head, 1922, First edition; pages xxvii, 248, with 14 illustrations by author, maps and plans, original cloth, gilt, little faded in places. R. F. G. Hollett & Son Antiquarian Booksellers 173 - 803 2011 £35

Motyl, Alexander J. *Encyclopedia of Nationalism: Fundamental Themes.* San Diego: Academic Press, 2001, First edition; 2 volumes, 4to., pages 1557, ex-Foreign and Commonwealth Office library with small label and two small stamps, otherwise fine. Any Amount of Books May 29 2011 - A60713 2011 $298

Moult, Thomas *Best Poems of 1922-1943.* London: J. Cape, 1922, First edition; 22 volumes, very good. I. D. Edrich May 26 2011 - 82835 2011 $503

Mountague, James *The Old Bailey Chronicle; or the Malefactors Register...* London: J. Walker, 1784, First edition; Volume 4 only (of 4), old quarter calf, very worn, corners heavily rounded, pages 340, 441-487, (v), complete with 5 engraved plates, first few leaves rather loose and stained, some fingering in places, very scarce. R. F. G. Hollett & Son Antiquarian Booksellers 175 - 974 2011 £120

Mountford, Arnold R. *The Illustrated Guide to Staffordshire Salt-Glazed Stoneware.* Barrie & Jenkins, 1971, First edition; tall 8vo., original cloth, gilt dust jacket, spine lettering trifle faded, pages xxi, 88, 7 color plates and 244 illustrations. R. F. G. Hollett & Son Antiquarian Booksellers General Catalogue Summer 2010 - 275 2011 £35

Mountfort, William *The Injur'd Lovers; or the Ambitious Father.* London: printed for Sam. Manship at the Black Bull in Cornhill, 1687-1688, First edition; 4to., small stain on title and lesser stain on next leaf, else fest of text clean, errata leaf at end, (8), 72, (2) pages, 19th century half calf, title gilt on spine. Anthony W. Laywood May 26 2011 - 21755 2011 $84

Mouravieff, A. N. *A History of the Church of Russia.* Oxford: St. Tikhon's, n.d., 1985, Facsimile edition; original cloth gilt, pages xix, 448.   R. F. G. Hollett & Son Antiquarian Booksellers   175 - 975   2011   £30

Mowat, Farley   *My Discovery of America.*   Toronto: McClelland & Stewart, 1985, First Canadian edition; fine, dust jacket fine, signed by author.   Bella Luna Books   May 29 2011 - 2263   2011 $82

Moxon, Joseph   *Practical Perspective; or Perspective Made Easie, Teaching by Opticks...*   For Joseph Moxon, 1670, First edition; folio, (4), 66 pages, this copy belonged to artist and drawing master, John Cawse, with his signature and dated 1823, it lacks all plates and has one blank section of a margin cut away, he has pasted a 19th century engraving by Hogarth, the "Perspective" on inside front cover, early half vellum, marbled boards, covers rubbed, some browning and old staining to text, although in imperfect condition, scarce to find treatises actually owned by known drawing masters.   Ken Spelman Rare Books   68 - 1   2011   £280

Moynier   *De La Truffe, Traite Complet de ce Tubercule, Contenant sa Description et son Histoire Naturelle la Plus Detaillee, on Exploitation Commerciale et sa Position dans l'Art Culinaire...*   Paris: Barba an Legrand et Bergougnious, 1836, 8vo., pages 204, uncut, internally excellent with only little light spotting, publisher's wrappers, blue, text in black, worn at spine with some loss, upper panel partially detached, light blue morocco backed clamshell box lined with fine chamois leather by Sangorski & Sutcliffe, bookplate of Eleanor Lowenstein, rare, entirely unsophisticated.   Simon Finch Rare Books   Zero - 128   2011   £2000

Moyse-Bartlett, H.   *The King's African Rifles: a Study in the Military History of East and Central Africa 1890-1945.*   Aldershot: Gale & Polden, 1956, First edition; 8vo., pages xix, 727, maps, illustrations, original black cloth, dust jacket, near fine.   J. & S. L. Bonham Antiquarian Booksellers   Africa 4/20/2011 - 9007   2011   £175

Mozley, Harriet   *The Fairy Bower, or, The History of a Month.*   London: James Burns, 1841, First edition; engraved frontispiece, contemporary half tan calf, black leather label.   Jarndyce Antiquarian Booksellers   CLXC - 548   2011   £45

Mozley, Harriet   *The Lost Brooch, or the History of Another Month.*   London: James Burns and Henry Mozley & Sons, Derby, 1841, First edition; 2 volume, half titles, frontispiece, final ad leaf volume II, owner details crudely removed from upper margin of leading f.e.p. volume I, leading f.e.p. removed volume II, original purple cloth, boards blocked in blind, spines lettered in gilt, spines faded to brown and slight chipped at heads and tails, otherwise good sound copy.   Jarndyce Antiquarian Booksellers   CLXC - 549   2011   £120

Muckley, William J.   *A Handbook for Painters and Art Students on the Character, Nature and Use of Colours...*   Bailliere, Tindall and Cox, 1885, Third edition; original cloth, gilt, slight crack to foot of spine, pages xiv, 126, (ii), prize label on pastedown.   R. F. G. Hollett & Son Antiquarian Booksellers   General Catalogue Summer 2010 - 276   2011   £60

Muhlbach, Luise, Pseud.   *Berlin and Sans-Souci; or Frederick the Great and His Friends.*   New York: D. Appleton & Co., 1867, 4 pages ads, 1 page ad inserted on to leading f.e.p., original green pebble grained cloth, very good.   Jarndyce Antiquarian Booksellers   CLXC - 550   2011   £60

Muhlbach, Luise, Pseud.   *The Daughter of an Empress.*   New York: D. Appleton & Co., 1867, Frontipsiece, 3 full page plates, 1 page ads, original dark blue-green pebble grained cloth, slightly rubbed and dulled, Renier booklabel and "Victoria Library Rules".   Jarndyce Antiquarian Booksellers   CLXC - 551   2011   £50

Muhlbach, Luise, Pseud.   *Joseph II and His Court.*   New York: D. Appleton & Co., 1888, Frontispiece, 2 pages ads, 2 column text, original blue cloth, little rubbed, Renier booklabel.   Jarndyce Antiquarian Booksellers   CLXC - 552   2011   £40

Muir, Edwin   *Poles in Uniform.*   London: Thomas Nelson, 1943, Oblong 4to., original cloth, gilt, few slight marks, pages 128, illustrations, presentation copy inscribed by artist, Aleksander Zyw.   R. F. G. Hollett & Son Antiquarian Booksellers   175 - 1484   2011   £45

Muir, John   1838-1914   *A Thousand-Mile Walk to the Gulf.*   Boston & New York: Houghton Mifflin Co., 1911, First edition; decorated green cloth, drawings by author, interesting owner inscription dated 1911 on front endpaper, light wear to head of spine, very good or better.   Charles Agvent   2010 Summer Miscellany - 52   2011 $200

Muir, John 1838-1914 *The Writings.* Boston and New York: Houghton Mifflin Co., 1916-1924, Manuscript edition, one of 750 copies; 226 x 160mm., 10 volumes, very fine contemporary dark brown morocco, handsomely gilt with front flyleaf in first volume stamped "Bound at the Riverside Press", cover border of triple gilt fillets, large center panel with triangular cornerpieces composed of massed floral and foliate tools, including a Tudor rose, raised bands, spines intricately gilt in compartments, with leaves, flowers and interlacing stems, wide turn-ins, similar gilt decoration framing doublures of white pigskin, dobulures with center panel formed by two gilt rules an featuring circled monogram HMS (Hannah M. Standish), watered silk flyleaves, top edge gilt, other edges untrimmed and unopened, few illustrations in text, 127 plates, mostly on Japanese vellum, 8 of them hand colored, five of them maps; virtually mint, bindings essentially unworn, unopened, text (not surprisingly) without sign of use. Phillip J. Pirages 59 - 268 2011 $10,000

Muir, John 1838-1914 *Yosemite and the Sierra Nevada. Selections from the Works of John Muir.* Boston: Houghton Mifflin Co., 1948, First edition; small 4to., 132 pages, 64 full page photo plates, tan cloth lettered in brown on spine and front cover, lacking dust jacket, very fine. Argonaut Book Shop Recent Acquisitions Summer 2010 - 143 2011 $200

Muir, Percy *English Children's Books 1600 to 1900.* London: Batsford, 1979, Small 4to., original cloth, gilt, dust jacket price clipped, pages 256, 107. R. F. G. Hollett & Sons Antiquarian Booksellers 170 - 463 2011 £50

Muir, Percy *Victorian Illustrated Books.* Portman Books, 1989, Original cloth, gilt, dust jacket, pages xv, 287, 5 color plates, 91 other illustrations. R. F. G. Hollett & Sons Antiquarian Booksellers 170 - 464 2011 £35

Mullaly, John *A Trip to Newfoundland: Its Scenery and Fisheries with an Account of the Laying of the Submarine Telegraph Cable.* New York: T. W. Strong, 1855, Small 8vo., pages (2), (3)-108, chromo frontispiece and 39 engravings in text, red pressed cloth with gilt to spine, some waterstaining to top paper edges, cloth very worn with bad staining to front covers with some loss of cloth at edge, offsetting to some pages, interior good. Schooner Books Ltd. 96 - 73 2011 $200

Muller, Max *Chips from a German Workshop.* New York: 1870, Approxiamtely 1300 pages, 3 volumes, three quarter leather and marbled boards, professional repairs to hinges. Bookworm & Silverfish 676 - 160 2011 $150

Mullion, Mary *The Curate's Daughter; a Tale for Young Persons.* London: G. & B. Whittaker, 1823, First edition; 4 pages ads, contemporary full purple calf embossed with weave pattern, gilt spine and borders, red leather label, spine and edges fading to brown, very good, attractive, prize inscription. Jarndyce Antiquarian Booksellers CLXC - 553 2011 £85

Munari, Bruno *Gigi Cerca Il Suo Berretto.* Mandadori: 1945, 4to., pictorial boards, very good, bold color lithographed illustrations. Aleph-Bet Books, Inc. 95 - 383 2011 $600

Munari, Bruno *Storie Di Tre Uccellini.* Veronase: Mondardori, 1945, Folio, edges of cover toned else fine, brightly colored illustrations. Aleph-Bet Books, Inc. 95 - 384 2011 $600

Munari, Bruno *What I'd Like to Be.* London: Harvill Press, 1945, First edition; folio, flexible card covers, slightly dusty, else near fine, full color illustrations. Aleph-Bet Books, Inc. 95 - 385 2011 $600

Mundell, Frank *Stories of the Coal Mine.* This Sunday School Union, 1895, First edition,; pages 160, 16, with woodcut plates, front flyleaf removed, patterned pastedowns a little spotted, scarce. R. F. G. Hollett & Sons Antiquarian Booksellers 170 - 466 2011 £35

Mundy, James *Echoes from the Realms of Though.* Bradford: Thornton & Pearson, 1891, Pages 188 (iv, subscribers list), frontispiece, original cloth, gilt, fine, scarce. R. F. G. Hollett & Son Antiquarian Booksellers General Catalogue Summer 2010 - 669 2011 £65

Mundy, Talbot *Full Moon.* New York: London: D. Appleton-Century Co. Inc., 1935, First US edition, first printing with "(1)" at base of text on 312; original pictorial yellow cloth, front panel stamped in red and black, spine panel stamped in black, fore edge untrimmed, bottom edge rough trimmed. L. W. Currey, Inc. 124 - 204 2011 $200

Munnings, Alfred J. *The Autobiography.* Museum Press, 1950-1952, First and second edition; 3 volumes, original cloth, gilt, volumes 1 and 3 with dust jackets (rather worn, one spine darkened), pages 328, 368; 378; illustrations, very good sound set. R. F. G. Hollett & Son Antiquarian Booksellers General Catalogue Summer 2010 - 277 2011 £120

Munnings, Alfred J. *Pictures of Horses and English Life.* London: Eyre & Spottiswoode, 1927, First edition; small folio, original cloth over bevelled boards, lettered in black, pages x, 215, all edges gilt, with 29 color plates, with captioned tissues and 109 monochrome illustrations, scattered spots and slight marks, tissues lightly foxed in places, excellent sound copy, from the collection of George Soper RI (1870-1942), signed by him in pencil on title.   R. F. G. Hollett & Son Antiquarian Booksellers   General Catalogue Summer 2010 - 278   2011   £350

Munro, Elsie Smeaton   *Topsy-Turvy Tales.*   London: John Lane The Bodley Head, 1923, First edition; square 8vo., original blue decorated cloth, corners trifle worn, lower edges of boards rather dampstained, pages x, 179, with 6 color plates and 35 line drawings by W. Heath Robinson, contents fine, very scarce.   R. F. G. Hollett & Sons Antiquarian Booksellers   170 - 597   2011   £180

Munro, R. W.   *Scottish Lighthouses.*   Stornoway: Thule Press, 1979, First edition; original boards, gilt, dust jacket, pages 307, illustrations, uncommon.   R. F. G. Hollett & Son Antiquarian Booksellers   177 - 590   2011   £60

Munro, Robert   *Archaeology & False Antiquities.*   London: 1905, First edition; xiii, 292 (4) (38 publisher catalog) pages, photo illustrated plates, original binding, scarce.   Bookworm & Silverfish   670 - 16   2011 $65

Munro, Robert   *Archaeology and False Antiquities.* London: Methuen, 1905, First edition; original cloth, gilt, pages xiii, 292, with 18 plates, 63 illustrations and plan, some occasional spotting especially to endpapers.   R. F. G. Hollett & Son Antiquarian Booksellers   177 - 591   2011 £30

Munro, Robert   *Prehistoric Scotland and Its Place in European Civilisation.*   William Blackwood and Sons, 1899, Large paper limited edition, no. 231 of 100 copies; 4to., original black buckram gilt over bevelled boards, pages xix, 502, (ii), top edge gilt, 18 plates, 262 text woodcuts, most attractive.   R. F. G. Hollett & Son Antiquarian Booksellers 177 - 592   2011   £150

Munro, Robert   *Prehistoric Scotland and Its Place in European Civilisation.*   William Blackwood & Sons, 1899, First edition; original cloth, gilt, little bumped and rubbed, spine rather faded, pages xix, 502, (ii), 18 plates, 262 text woodcut, some patches of spotting, occasionally heavy, lower joint cracked, attractive bookplate of Mary Rose Fitzgibbon.   R. F. G. Hollett & Son Antiquarian Booksellers 177 - 593   2011   £65

Munroe, J.   *More Calcutta Rhymes: Wise, Unwise and Otherwise.*   Calcutta: W. Nemwan & Co., 1931, Initial ad leaf, plates, original stiff decorated card wrappers, spine slightly faded, very good.   Jarndyce Antiquarian Booksellers   CXCI - 367   2011   £38

Murdoch, Iris   *Under the Net.*   London: Chatto & Windus, 1954, First edition; 8vo., half bound in dark green morocco lettered gilt at spine with 5 raised bands and gilt decoration, pages 286, slight spotting to prelims, else about fine.   Any Amount of Books   May 29 2011 - B32153 2011 $213

Murdoch, Iris   *A Year of Birds. Poems.*   Tisbury, Wiltshire: Compton Press, 1978, First edition, 122/350 copies printed on Zerkall mouldmade paper; signed by author and artist, wood engraved title design and 12 other wood engravings by Reynolds Stone, pages (32), foolscap 8vo., original quarter tan cloth, backstrip gilt lettered, blue brown and yellow marbled boards, cloth slipcase, fine.   Blackwell Rare Books   B166 - 196 2011   £300

Murphy, John Nicholas   *Terra Incognita or the Convents of the United Kingdom.*   London: Longmans, Green and Co., 1873, First edition; pages xii, 753, 24, thick 8vo., modern half blue levant morocco gilt with raised bands, gilt spine label.   R. F. G. Hollett & Son Antiquarian Booksellers   175 - 981 2011   £175

Murphy, Samuel   *Grey Gold.*   Tanworth-in-Arden: Moiety Publishing, 1996, First edition; large 8vo., original cloth, dust jacket, pages v, 481, well illustrated, now very scarce. R. F. G. Hollett & Son Antiquarian Booksellers   173 - 807 2011   £150

Murray, Charles Augustus   *The Prairie Bird.*   London: Richard Bentley, 1844, First edition; 3 volumes, 12mo., slightly later half green morocco grained sheep by J. and J. P. Edmond & Spark, Aberdeen, gilt bands, very slightly rubbed, Fasque booklabels, very good, loosely inserted is opened stamped envelope address to H. Magnac (?), Fasque, Lawrencekirk.   Jarndyce Antiquarian Booksellers CXCI - 531   2011   £330

Murray, Edward   *Enoch Restitutus; or an Attempt to Separate from the Books of Enoch the Book Quoted by St. Jude...*   London: J. G. and F. Rivington, 1836, First edition; 8vo., pages viii, 116, all edges gilt, neat inscription (Christmas 1852) on first blank, foxed bookplate, otherwise very good+, bright copy in fine red full leather elaborately decorated gilt at spine, dentelles, 5 raised bands, etc., excellent.   Any Amount of Books   May 29 2011 - A76647 2011 $255

Murray, James A.   *The Avifauna of British India and Its Dependencies.*   London: Richardson & Co., 1887, Volume I parts I-III, Volume II Part I only, small 4to., pages 325; xxiv, 128, 13 color lithographic plates, 14 black and white plates and 39 woodcuts in text, small 4to., green cloth with gilt titles, original wrappers bound in, near fine, rebound, chips to top and fore edge of titlepage and few leaves, leaves faintly browned at edges, plates sharp, prospectus bound in.   Kaaterskill Books   12 - 140 2011 $175

Murray, John *Genuine Memoirs of John Murray, Esq. Late Secretary to the Young Pretender.* London: printed for J. Wilford, 1747, First edition, variant issue; 8vo., (2), 64 pages, mid 19th century green hal roan over marbled boards, spine lettered gilt, minor rubbing of extremities, excellent copy from mid 19th century library of the antiquary James Heywood Markland with his signature and armorial bookplate. John Drury Rare Books 153 - 98 2011 £275

Murray, Lindley *A Compendium of Religious Faith and Practice.* (bound with) *The Duty and Benefit of a Daily Perusal of the Holy Scriptures in Families.* York: printed for W. Alexander, printed by Thomas Wilson and Sons, 1815, 1817. First editions; small 8vo., contemporary half calf, gilt, label at base of spine, pages 90, (i), 43, little spotting, label of Dublin Monthly Meeting on pastedown. R. F. G. Hollett & Son Antiquarian Booksellers 175 - 982 2011 £85

Murray, Lindley *English Exercises.* York: printed by Thomas Wilson and Sons etc., 1813, Eighteenth edition; original speckled sheep gilt, hinges little cracked at head and foot, pages 228, one gathering springing, much contemporary scribbling on endpapers. R. F. G. Hollett & Sons Antiquarian Booksellers 170 - 468 2011 £75

Murry, John Middleton *Moral Man and Immoral Society. A Study in Ethics and Politics.* New York: Charles Scribner's Sons, 1932, 8vo., pages xxv, 284, from the library of Murray with copious pencilled notes and underlinings, with his extra index at rear including a list of misprints, slight wear, some fading at spine, otherwise about very good, with 2 pages of closely written notes loosely inserted. Any Amount of Books May 29 2011 - A40509 2011 $221

Museum d'Historie Naturelle *Memoires du Museum d'Historie Naturelle....* Paris: G. Dufour: A Belin, 1815-1832, Volumes 1-20, complete, small 4to, each volume contains 400-500 pages, 84 pages, 13 are hand colored, 34 are folding, tanning, sometimes marginal, to many of the plates, occasional foxing, small innocuous handstamp, no touching images to many plates, 17 of the volumes in half morocco over marbled boards (worn, but solid, partial splitting to front edge of 2 spines, occasional foxing, marginal ink stain to a page, toning to few pages in volume 1), good to very good, 3 volumes in modern half cloth over marbled boards, very good; from the Athenaeum Liverpool and Aquatic Research Institute. Raymond M. Sutton, Jr. May 26 2011 - 48196 2011 $7000

Mussabini, S. A. *The Complete Athletic Trainer.* London: Methuen, 1913, First edition; 8vo., original publisher's red cloth lettered gilt at spine and blindstamped lettering on cover, pages xii, 264, copiously illustrated, slight shelf wear, corners slightly bumped, very slight nick at head of spine, otherwise sound, clean, very good, scarce. Any Amount of Books May 29 2011 - A61201 2011 $272

Muter, Gladys Nelson *Mother Goose and Her Friends.* Volland, 1923, Oblong small folio, limp pictorial cloth, slight bit of cover fading and rubbing, else very good+, rare Volland printed on cloth and illustrated by Marion Foster. Aleph-Bet Books, Inc. 95 - 372 2011 $500

Muzo, Pio *Considerationi Sopra il Primo Libro di Cornelio Tacito.* Venice: Marco Ginammi, 1642, 4to., (56), 544, (4), (36), 360, (4) pages, 18th century English calf, spine gilt in compartments, red morocco lettering piece, errata and ad leaves for each part are all bound in part 2, from the library of the Earls of Macclesfield at Shirburn Castle. Maggs Bros. Ltd. 1440 - 150 2011 £500

My ABC. Springfield: McLoughlin, 1938, 12mo., pictorial boards, very good+, illustrations by Dorothy Hope Smith. Aleph-Bet Books, Inc. 95 - 27 2011 $125

My Book of Alphabet Rhymes and Jingles. Boston: De Wolfe Fiske, circa, 1880, 4to., cloth backed pictorial boards light shelf wear, very good+, 4 charming full page chromolithographs and photogravures. Aleph-Bet Books, Inc. 95 - 43 2011 $300

My Book of Noble Deeds. Blackie & son, n.d. circa, 1907, Large 8vo., original cloth backed glazed pictorial boards, little soiled, unpaginated, 4 color plates and other plates and illustrations. R. F. G. Hollett & Son Antiquarian Booksellers General Catalogue Summer 2010 - 497 2011 £75

My Picture Book. New York: Gabriel, 1914, Large 4to., stiff linette pictorial wrappers, very good, color illustrations. Aleph-Bet Books, Inc. 95 - 431 2011 $225

Myers, Albert Cook *Immigration of the Irish Quakers into Pennsylvania 1682-1750.* Swathmore, 1902, First edition; beige & indigo cloth, rebacked with beige spine with gilt imprints, light dampstain to extremities of some inner leaves, binding near fine. Lupack Rare Books May 26 2011 - ABE 959220745 2011 $200

Myers, Frederic William Henry *Saint Paul.* London: Macmillan & Co., 1867, First edition; half title, occasional pencil and ink notes, original red cloth by Burn, blocked in black and gilt, slightly rubbed, cloth little lifted in places, label removed from f.e.p., ownership signature of E. W. Gosse, Jan. 1868. Jarndyce Antiquarian Booksellers CXCI - 327 2011 £125

A Mystique of Mummers. London: Gogmagog Press, 1983, First edition; copy number 6 of only 12 sets printed in black, with each linocut individually titled and signed and dated by artist/publisher, quarter cloth solander box with cork lining, printed label on spine by Gemma O'Connor, and monoprint covers on Japanese paper by Cox. James S. Jaffe Rare Books May 26 2011 - 21321 2011 $8500

N

N'Zau, Bula *Travel and Adventures in the Congo Free State and Its Big Game Shooting.* London: Chapman & Hall, 1894, 8vo., xiv, 335 pages, frontispiece, 10 illustrations, folding map, original maroon pebbled cloth, gilt stamped spine title, hinges rubbed, corners bumped, lightly soiled, bookplate removed from inside front cover, very good.   Jeff Weber Rare Books   163 - 200 2011 $1250

N. W. Ayer & Son *In Behalf of Advertising. A Series of Essays Published in National Periodicals from 1919 to 1928.* Philadelphia: Ayer & Son, 1929, First edition; 8vo, pages x, 266, owner's names on pastedown, marbled paper boards with cloth spine stamped in gilt, cover little worn at edges, front hinge beginning tender, otherwise very good.   Second Life Books Inc. 174 - 244 2011 $75

Nabokov, Vladimir   1899-1977   *The Eye.* New York: Phaedra, 1965, First edition; fine, very good dust jacket, exceptional copy of this fragile jacket, light soiling and edge wear, first state with publisher's address on copyright page and Trident Press mentioned to rear flap, very good.   Bella Luna Books   May 29 2011 - t1361 2011 $82

Nabokov, Vladimir   1899-1977   *Look at the Harlequins!* New York: McGraw Hill, 1974, First edition; fine in fine dust jacket, inscribed by author to Gordon Lish, author has corrected several misprint in this copy, housed in chemise and quarter morocco slipcase.   Between the Covers   169 - BTC346457 2011 $14,000

Nabokov, Vladimir   1899-1977   *Poems and Problems.* London: Weidenfeld & Nicolson, 1972, First edition; 8vo., original publisher's maroon cloth lettered gilt on spine, 218 pages, very good+ in very good dust jacket with slight creasing and slight edgewear, decent copy.   Any Amount of Books   May 29 2011 - A73753 2011 $238

Nachtwey, James   *Deeds of War.* New York: Thames & Hudson, 1989, First edition; fine in very near fine dust jacket, signed and inscribed by Nachtwey for Kitty Carlisle Hart.   Jeff Hirsch Books   ny 2010 2011 $1750

Naegeli, Carl   *The Microscope in Theory and Practice.* London: Swan Sonnenschein, Lowrey & Co., 1887, First English edition; original cloth, gilt, extremities trifle rubbed, pages xi, 382, with 210 illustrations.   R. F. G. Hollett & Son Antiquarian Booksellers   General Catalogue Summer 2010 - 1127 2011   £50

Nahm, Milton C.   *Selections from Early Greek Philosophy.* New York: F. S. Crofts, 1945, Second edition, fifth edition; small 8vo., original publisher's cream cloth lettered brown on spine and cover, pages vii, (v) 225, Allen Ginsberg's copy with his name written 3 times on front endpaper twice dated 1955, annotated throughout with short notes in margins, underlinings and maringal linings, covers marked and rubbed, corners and upper spine slightly bumped, inner hinge cracking, otherwise about very good.   Any Amount of Books   May 26 2011 - A71815 2011 $2013

Naipaul, Vidiadhar Surajprasad   *Magic Seeds.* London: Picador, 2004, First British edition; fine in fine dust jacket, signed by author, very difficult autograph.   Bella Luna Books   May 29 2011 - t6797 2011 $82

Naipaul, Vidiadhar Surajprasad   *The Mystic Maseur.* New York: Vanguard, 1959, Uncorrected proof copy; exceedingly scarce proof, spine and bit of lower rear edge darkened, apparently from binder's gule rather than sun, some light dustiness to covers and few gentle turns to page corners, very good in wrappers.   Ken Lopez Bookseller   154 - 129 2011 $2500

Naipaul, Vidiadhar Surajprasad   *The Suffrage of Elvira.* London: A. Deutsch, 1958, First edition, true first, first impression with copyright page stating No Dust Jacket; blue boards, gilt, light edgewear, slight tilt, points intact with no fraying, few stain spots to cover, previous owner's signature inside front, some spine fading, no serious defects, sturdy and well preserved, very scarce, very good.   G. H. Mott Bookseller   May 26 2011 - 57671 2011 $535

Naipaul, Vidiadhar Surajprasad   *The Suffrage of Elvira.* London: A. Deutsch, 1958, First edition; true first, first impression with copyright page state "First Published 1958", blue boards, gilt, light edgewear, points intact with no fraying, few stain spots to cover, previous owner's signature, some spine fading, no serious defects, study and well preserved, solid good +.   G. H. Mott Bookseller   May 26 2011 - B000OPKHH2 2011 $325

Naked Came the Manatee. New York: Putnam, 1996, First edition; fine in fine dust jacket, signed by all authors on single tipped in leaf, including Carl Hiaasen, Elmore Leonard, John Dufresne, Dave Barry, Vicki Hendricks, Edna Buchanan, Les Standiford and James W. Hall, etc.   Ken Lopez Bookseller   154 - 5 2011 $200

Nakhla, Yacoub   *New Manual of English and Arabic Conversation.* Cairo: Neguib Mitri Al-Marref Printing Office, 1910, Second edition; presentation copy, (7), 8-254 pages, contemporary quarter morocco, spine ruled gilt, inscribed by author for Capt. R. B. D. Blakeney.   Anthony W. Laywood   May 26 2011 - 20103 2011 $134

Nameh, Miraj *The Miraculous Journey of Mahomet.* London: Scolar Press, 1977, First edition; small 4to., original glazed boards gilt, pictorial slipcase, pages 158, with 58 double page color plates, sheet of bibliography loosely inserted.   R. F. G. Hollett & Son Antiquarian Booksellers   175 - 1199   2011   £75

Nance, E. Morton *The Pottery & Porcelain of Swansea & Nantgarw.* Haversfordwest: C. I. Thomas & Sons, 1985, Limited, facsimile edition, no. 399 of 500 copies; large thick 8vo., original cloth gilt, dust jacket little worn and creased, pages xviii, 579 with 196 plates, loosely inserted is a 21 page illustrated article on Swansea blue and white pottery by P. D. Pryce and S. H. Williams, 4to., folded.   R. F. G. Hollett & Son Antiquarian Booksellers   General Catalogue Summer 2010 - 280   2011   £120

Nannini, Remigio *Orationi Militari... da Tutti Gli Historici Greci e Latini etc.* Venice: all insegna della concordio (G. A. Bertano), 1585, Second edition; 4to., (40), 1004 pages, italic letter, 18th century tree calf, gilt spine, red morocco lettering piece, red edges, from the library of the Earls of Macclesfield at Shirburn Castle.   Maggs Bros. Ltd.   1440 - 151   2011   £700

Nansen, Fridtjof 1861-1930 *Farthest North.* London: Archibald Constable, 1897, First edition in English; etched frontispiece, photograuvres, maps in color, 16 color plates, many full page and in text illustrations, very good plus set (light shelfwear, some neat repair to inner paper hinge, essentially tight, clean texts, nice bright gilt).   Lupack Rare Books   May 26 2011 - ABE4310256497   2011 $300

Napier, William Francis Patrick *History of the War in the Peninsula and in the South of France, from the Year 1807 to the Year 1814.* London: John Murry/Thomas and William Boone, 1828-1840, Mixed edition; first edition of volume I and II, volume III is third edition, the rest first printings, 6 volumes, full leather, almost all with loose boards, sixth volume lacking boards, otherwise internally clean and bright set, good working copies of candidates for rebinding.   Any Amount of Books   May 29 2011 - A42359   2011 $340

Napier, William Francis Patrick *History of the War in the Peninsula and in the South of France from the Year 1807 to the Year 1814.* London: Thomas William Boone, 1862, New edition; 6 volumes, numerous engraved maps, later 18th century full tan calf, bevelled boards, at some time rebacked, spines gilt in compartments, maroon and black leather labels, hinges and hinges little worn, signed presentation inscription to Maria Martineau from friend, Richd. Napier, with additional signature of Anne Louise Napier, also tipped into prelims volume I is 19 line ALS from Richard Napier to Maria Martineau.   Jarndyce Antiquarian Booksellers   CLXC - 363   2011   £380

Napoleon, Emperor of the French *Maxims of Napoleon.* London: Arthur L. Humphreys, 1903, Small quarto, bound by Riviere & son in full light brown paneled morocco, with two miniature paintings on Ivory by Miss C. B. Currie, almost invisible rebacked with original spine laid down.   Heritage Book Shop   Booth A12 51st NY International Antiquarian Book Fair April 8-10 2011 - 33   2011 $15,000

Naqvi, Ovais *Super Yacht.* London: Gloria Books, 2007, First edition, no. 968 of 1000 copies; folio, 647 pages, copiously illustrated in color and black and white, all edges silver, neat presentation on limitation page to a yacht owner on his 40th birthday, lacks the rare slipcase, covers slightly soiled and slightly marked but sound, decent, attractive, very good copy.   Any Amount of Books   May 26 2011 - A68920   2011 $671

Narayana, Bhatta *Venisamhara: die Ehrenrettung der Konigin. Ein Drama in 6 Akten.* Leipzig: Fue's Verlag, 1871, First edition; xxxvi, 181 pages, small 4to., modern three quarter cloth over marbled paper covered boards, very good+, scattered foxing, leaves crisp.   Kaaterskill Books   12 - 142   2011 $125

Narrative of the North Polar Expedition: U.S. Ship Polaris, Captain Charles Francis Hall Commanding. Washington: 1876, 696 pages, large 4to., half title, frontispiece, titlepage and titlepage verso in facsimiles, cover generally shabby (spots and stains) but price reflects condition, tight and nicely printed with wide margins.   Bookworm & Silverfish   666 - 19   2011 $100

Nash-Williams, V. E. *The Early Christian Monuments of Wales.* Cardiff: University of Wales Press, 1950, First edition; small folio, original green buckram, gilt, dust jacket price clipped, pages xxiii, 258, plus 71 plates, scattered light spotting in places, very good, scarce.   R. F. G. Hollett & Son Antiquarian Booksellers   177 - 596   2011   £180

Nash, Joseph *The Mansions of England in the Olden Time.* London: The Studio, Special Number, 1905-1906, Tall 4to., modern two-tone cloh, gilt, pages vii, plus 104 plates, original wrappers bound in, excellent copy.   R. F. G. Hollett & Son Antiquarian Booksellers   177 - 595 2011   £85

Natesa, Sastri S. M. *Hindu Feasts Fasts and Ceremonies.* Madras: printed at M. E. Publishing House, 1903, First edition; vi, 154 pages, illustrations, 12mo., full calf, with gilt titles, scarce, rebound in black calf with gilt titles, new endpapers, gift inscription, first three and last five leaves heavily taped, tape bit yellowed, overall, good in very good boards.   Kaaterskill Books   12 - 144   2011 $75

Nathusius, Marie *Elizabeth: a Story Which Does Not End in Marriage.* Edinburgh: R. Grant & Son, 1860, First English edition; 2 volumes, original purple cloth, spines lettered in gilt, boards blocked in blind, inner hinges cracking, spines slightly darkened.   Jarndyce Antiquarian Booksellers   CLXC - 592   2011   £125

National Aeronautics & Space Agency *Astronautics & Aeronautics 1969: Chronology on Science, Technology & Policy.* Washington: 1970, vii, 534 pages, wrappers, very good, mild backstrip fading, some crease to backstrip; Bookworm & Silverfish   676 - 181   2011 $75

National Gallery of Canada *A Portfolio of Canadian Paintings.* Ottawa: National Portrait Gallery, 1950, Small 4to., original card portfolio, complete with title, and 24 sheets of colored plates (some two to a sheet), loose as issued, scarce.   R. F. G. Hollett & Son Antiquarian Booksellers   General Catalogue Summer 2010 - 281   2011   £45

National Union Catalog Pre 1956 Imprints. New York: 1968, First edition; 757 volumes, folio, near fine. Bookworm & Silverfish   678 - 20   2011 $7570

Nattes, John Claude *Graphic and Descriptive Tour of the University of Oxford...* London: Albion Press, Published by James Cundee, 1805, First edition; large folio, 8; 9-16 pages, engraved title with tinted aquatint vignette, four tinted aquatint plates engraved by Merigot, one engraved by Pugin, wrappers expertly renewed to style with original brown front printed wrappers laid down, resewn, some minor foxing and edge browning, housed together in blue cloth clamshell case, excellent copy, extremely scarce.   David Brass Rare Books, Inc.   May 26 2011 - 00321   2011 $6500

The Natural Environment of North Walney and Sandscale Haws. Barrow-in-Furness: Borough Council, 1978, Tall 4to., original wrappers, comb bound, few marks, pages 66, xli appendices, few illustrations and maps, all cyclostyled, scarce.   R. F. G. Hollett & Son Antiquarian Booksellers   General Catalogue Summer 2010 - 989   2011   £30

Nature and Art. June 1866-June 1867. Day & Son, circa, 1866-1867, Half title, illustrations, including color chromolithographs, slightly shaken, original purple cloth, bevelled boards, elaborately gilt on front board and spine, slightly rubbed, spine ends slightly worn, all edges gilt, nice.   Jarndyce Antiquarian Booksellers   CXCI - 345   2011   £120

Nature's ABC. London: Universal Text Books, n.d. circa, 1943, 4to., pictorial cloth, fine, color woodcuts by noted artist Eileen Mayo, text in calligraphy.   Aleph-Bet Books, Inc.   95 - 24 2011 $100

The Naval Chronicle. volume 9 Jan. to July 1803. J. Gold, 1803, modern full blind panelled calf gilt, pages viii, 500, (xxviii), engraved title, 14 engraved tissue guarded aquatints and stipple engraved portraits, plan.   R. F. G. Hollett & Son Antiquarian Booksellers   General Catalogue Summer 2010 - 1128   2011   £140

Naylor, Gloria *The Women of Brewster Place.* New York: Viking, 1982, First edition; fine in fine dust jacket, bright, tight copy, signed by author.   Bella Luna Books   May 26 2011 - t9657   2011 $660

Naylor, Robert *From John O'Groats to Land's End; or 1372 Miles on Foot.* London: Caxton Publishing Co., 1916, 4to., half title, frontispiece, photographic plates and illustrations, original olive green cloth blocked in black, lettered in gilt, bookseller's ticket of A. J. Coombes, Surrey, very good.   Jarndyce Antiquarian Booksellers   CXCI - 571   2011   £58

Neal, John *Rachel Dyer.* Portland: Chirley and Hyde, 1828, First edition; 8vo., pages xx, 276, untrimmed, original linen backed boards, rubbed and bumped, some of the paper worn, hinges loose, chipped paper label, one inch of top blank margin of titlepage trimmed off, some foxing and toning, but very good.   Second Life Books Inc.   174 - 245   2011 $975

Neale, Hannah *Amusement Hall: or an Easy Introduction to the Attainment of Useful Knowlede.* T. Gardiner, 1806, Third edition; contemporary full roan, front hinge cracked but cords holding, pages 146, (ii), half title and steel engraved frontispiece.   R. F. G. Hollett & Sons Antiquarian Booksellers   170 - 469   2011   £45

Neale, John Mason   1818-1866   *Good King Wenceslas.* London: 1895, First edition in this state; 4to., not numbered, titlepage, 6 full page woodcuts by Arthur Gaskins, boards in slate gray paper which shows a price sticker ghost on front and some white at backstrip shoulders, endpapers browned.   Bookworm & Silverfish   669 - 128   2011 $150

Neale, John Preston *Views of the Seats of Noblemen and Gentlemen in England, Wales, Scotland and Ireland.* London: published for the proprietors by W. H. Reid, 1818-1823, First edition; 241 x 152mm., 6 volumes, very appealing contemporary dark purple straight grain morocco, covers bordered in gilt with double rules and wide scrolling foliate roll, broad inner frame of a dozen blind concentric rules, raised bands, gilt spines with decorative bands at head and foot, titling in compartments with volute corner-pieces and panels at top and bottom, featuring a large lozenge enclosing a floral centerpiece, turn-ins, all edges gilt, 432 engraved plates; little rubbing to joints and extremities, but bindings solid, with leather and gilt quite bright, persistent but never serious offsetting opposite engraved plates, very small number of plates with hint of foxing, handful of text leaves little browned, extremely pleasing internally, entirely fresh and clean, excellent set in especially attractive decorative bindings.   Phillip J. Pirages   59 - 326   2011 $3500

Neander, Michael *Opus Aureum et Scholasticum in quo Continentur Pythagorae Carmina Aurea, Phocylidis, Theognidius & Aliorum Poemata.* Leipzig: (colophon in volume II: Imprimebat Iohannes Steinman), 1577, 2 volumes, woodcut printer's device on both titles, slight tendency to browning and few spots, blindstamp of Theological Institute of Connecticut fairly liberally bestowed upon prelim and endleaves, pages 789, (3), 268, (16), 191, (1), 4to., early 18th century sprinkled calf over good thick boards, double gilt fillets on sides, enclosing blind roll tooled border, spines with gilt fleuron in each compartment, rebacked, preserving original spines, good.   Blackwell Rare Books   B166 - 72   2011   £1750

Neate, Charles *Three Lectures on Taxation, Especially that of land, Delivered at Oxford in the Year 1860.* Oxford and London: J. H. and Jas. Parker, 1861, First edition; 8vo., 64 pages, titlepage little dusty, preserved in modern wrappers with printed title label on upper cover, very good, surprisingly uncommon.   John Drury Rare Books   153 - 100   2011   £75

Nebraska State Medical Society *Proceedings of the Second Anniversary of the Nebraska State Medical Society Held in Omaha... June 7th and 8th, 1870.* Omaha: Reynolds' Book and Job Print, 1870, First edition; 8vo., 47 pages, removed, retaining original front printed wrapper (one short tear), vertical crease, pencil markings on several leaves, very sound.   M & S Rare Books, Inc.   90 - 273   2011 $200

Necker De Saussure, Albertine Adrienne, Mme. De *Etude et la Vie des Femmes.* Paris: Paulin, Juillet, 1838, First edition; xii, 422 page, 8vo., contemporary quarter calf over boards, gilt lettered and decorated spine, extremities bit rubbed, still nice.   Paulette Rose Fine and Rare Books   32 - 130   2011 $275

Necker, Jacques *De L'Importance Des Opinions Religieuses.* Londres: et se Trouve a Paris, 1788, First edition; 8vo., pages (4), 542, (2), bound with half title in contemporary speckled calf, red morocco spine label, very nice.   Second Life Books Inc.   174 - 246   2011 $600

Needham, Violet *Adventures at Hampton Court.* London: Lutterworth Press, 1954, First edition; 8vo., 160 pages, original publisher's maroon boards lettered gilt on spine, illustrated endpapers, illustrations by Wil Nickless, neat name and erased name on front endpaper, very good in near very good chipped, nicked, creased dust jacket.   Any Amount of Books   May 29 2011 - A76507   2011 $204

Needham, Violet *The Avenue.* London: Collins, 1957, Reprint of 1952 edition; 8vo., pages 221, illustrations by Joyce Bruce, neat name on front endpaper, very good+ in bright, clean colorful, near very good dust jacket (very slightly chipped at edges).   Any Amount of Books   May 29 2011 - A76565   2011 $306

Needham, Violet *The Bell of the Four Evangelists.* London: Collins, 1947, First edition; 8vo., pages 256, illustrations by Joyce Bruce, poor copy, covers worn and used and soiled and marked, text complete and clean.   Any Amount of Books   May 29 2011 - A76576   2011 $304

Needham, Violet *The Great House of Estraville.* London: Collins, 1955, First edition; 8vo., pages 192, original blue boards lettered gilt on spine, illustrations by Joyce Bruce, boards slightly sunned at spin ends and edges, neat name and greeting inscription on front endpaper, small brown mark at lower edge of first 12 pages not affecting text, otherwise very good in chipped and nicked slightly creased very good- dust jacket (chips at corners and head of spine).   Any Amount of Books   May 26 2011 - A76506   2011 $419

Needham, Violet *How Many Miles to Babylon?* London: Collins, 1953, First edition; 8vo., pages 191, original publisher's blue cloth lettered gilt on spine, decent copy, scarce, illustrations by Joyce Bruce, neat name on front endpaper, spine very slightly dull, otherwise near fine in very good dust jacket with slight edgewear and few nicks.   Any Amount of Books   May 26 2011 - A76505   2011 $587

Needham, Violet *The Red Rose of Ruvina.* London: Collins, 1957, First edition; 8vo., blue cloth lettered silver on spine, pages 192, illustrations, neat names on front endpaper, spine ends very slightly bumped, front endpaper slightly browned, otherwise very good+, excellent condition.   Any Amount of Books   May 29 2011 - A76580   2011 $289

Neil, James *Rays from the Realm of Nature or Parables of Plant Life.* London: Cassell, Petter, Galpin & Co., n.d., circa, 1890, Fifth edition; original pictorial green cloth, pages vi, (i), 148, (iii), colored lithograph frontispiece and numerous woodcuts, front flyleaf removed, little pencilled marginal lining, etc.   R. F. G. Hollett & Son Antiquarian Booksellers   175 - 987   2011   £30

Neild, James *An Account of the Rise, Progress and Present State of the Society for the Discharge and Relief of Persons Imprisoned for Small Debts throughout England and Wales. (and) Account of the Various Prisons of England, Scotland and Wales...* London: John Nichols & Son, 1808, Third edition; 8vo., ix, 10-601 pages, engraved frontispiece, engraved portrait plate, large folding plate, full contemporary calf, gilt stamped black leather spine label rebacked, very good, scarce. Jeff Weber Rare Books 163 - 43 2011 $400

Neill, John R. *Lucky Bucky in Oz.* Chicago: Reilly & Lee, 1942, First edition, first state (with buy victory bonds on inside rear flap); 4to., turquoise cloth with full color pictorial paste label, nice copy, single brown spot in margin of "Dear boys and girls page", full color pictorial dust jacket, some marginal wear, complete and bright, 290 numbered pages with lots of black and white drawings by Neill. Jo Ann Reisler, Ltd. 86 - 18 2011 $750

Neill, John R. *Lucky Bucky in Oz.* Chicago: Reilly & Lee, 1942, First edition; 4to., rose cloth, pictorial paste on, 289 pages, near fine, illustrations by Neill. Aleph-Bet Books, Inc. 95 - 79 2011 $475

Neill, John R. *Scalawagons of Oz.* Chicago: Reilly & Lee, 1941, First edition, first state dust jacket (HG-XXXV) (16 page gatherings, hyphenated spine, $1.50, mis-spelling Scallywagons on rear flap of jacket); 4to., rose cloth, pictorial paste-on, 309 pages, very fine in dust jacket (frayed but very good, illustrations by author. Aleph-Bet Books, Inc. 95 - 72 2011 $975

Neilson, George *Annals of the Solway Until A.D. 1307.* Glasgow: James Maclehose, 1899, Limited edition of 200 copies, 150 for sale; large square 8vo., original green ribbed cloyh gilt, pages 74, (ii), 5 maps on 4 plates, flyleaves browned, otherwise fine, scarce. R. F. G. Hollett & Son Antiquarian Booksellers 173 - 809 2011 £150

Neilson, George *Per Lineam Valli: a New Argument Touching the Earthen Rampart Between Tyne and Solway.* Glasgow: William Hodge & Co, 1891, First edition; small 8vo., original cloth, gilt, pages xii, 62, (ii), 8 text diagrams, scarce. R. F. G. Hollett & Son Antiquarian Booksellers 173 - 811 2011 £65

Neiman, Roy *Casey at the Bat.* New York: Harper Collins, 2002, First trade edition, limited to 525 copies; signed on half title by Neiman, fine in fine dust jacket, 4to. By the Book, L. C. 26 - 74 2011 $70

Neinhauser, William H. *The Indiana Companion to Traditional Chinese Literature.* Bloomington: Indiana University Press, 1986, First edition; large fat 8vo., uncommon, very good+ in like dust jacket. Any Amount of Books May 29 2011 - A71204 2011 $255

Nelson, Byron *How I Played the Game.* Dallas: Taylor, 1993, First edition; signed by author, 8vo., vii, 271 pages, fine in fine dust jacket. By the Book, L. C. 26 - 78 2011 $170

Nelson, Robert *A Companion for the Festivals and Fasts of the Church of England...* London: J. & J. Bonwicke S. Brit etc., 1752, Twentieth edition; contemporary full speckled sheep gilt, few slight old tape marks and surface defects, pages (iv), 636, (xvi), engraved frontispiece, prelim leaves slightly creased, sound, clean copy, nice contemporary (1754) inscription in Latin from William Stratford. R. F. G. Hollett & Son Antiquarian Booksellers 175 - 988 2011 £175

Nelson, Robert *A Companion for the Festivals and Fasts of the Church of England...* London: A. Wilson, 1819, Stereotype edition; full polished speckled calf, gilt, spine label, pages xvi, 388, frontispiece. R. F. G. Hollett & Son Antiquarian Booksellers 175 - 989 2011 £45

Nelson, T., & Sons *The English Lakes.* T. Nelson and Sons, 1859, Small 8vo., half black polished calf gilt with marbled boards, pages xxxix, 307, folding map, 24 blue tinted lithographed plates, endpapers and map lightly spotted. R. F. G. Hollett & Son Antiquarian Booksellers 173 - 813 2011 £150

Nelson, T., & Sons *Tourist's Guide to the English Lakes.* T. Nelson and Sons, n.d. circa, 1870, Oblong small 8vo., original blue cloth gilt, pages 61, map, text woodcuts, 12 highly finished chromolithographed plates. R. F. G. Hollett & Son Antiquarian Booksellers 173 - 812 2011 £65

Nelson, T., & Sons *The Union Pacific Railroad: A Trip Across the North American Continent from Omaha to Ogden.* New York: n.d., 1872, 46 pages, illustrations, map, slight wear to extremities, minor foxing, else near fine 4 x 6 34 inches. Dumont Maps & Books of the West 111 - 36 2011 $250

Nelson, Thomas H. *The Birds of Yorkshire.* A. Brown & Sons, 1907, First edition; 2 volumes, original green cloth gilt, pages xlv, 374; xii, 375-843, 2 color frontispieces 2 color titles and numerous monochrome plates, prelims rather foxed in both volumes, otherwise very good. R. F. G. Hollett & Son Antiquarian Booksellers General Catalogue Summer 2010 - 1028 2011 £120

Nemirovsky, Irene *L'Affaire Courilof Roman.* Paris: Bernard Grasset, 1933, First edition, one of 8 numbered copies, this being no. 5 on Montval, of a total edition of 1472; (276) pages, 8vo., original cream self wrappers, lettered in black with publisher's logo beneath title, reading "Pour Mon Plaisir", fine, uncut, scarce. Paulette Rose Fine and Rare Books 32 - 131 2011 $975

Nemirovsky, Irene *Les Mouches d'Automne ou la Femme d'Autrefois.* Paris: Editions Kra, 1931, First edition, one of 50 numbered copies on hollande Van Gelder Zonen, this being no. 39; (142) pages, 10 3/4 x 10 1/2 inches, original printed wrappers, fine in original state, totally uncut, pages varying in length. Paulette Rose Fine and Rare Books 32 - 132 2011 $950

Nepos, Cornelius *De Vita Excellentium Imperatorum. Interpretatione et Notis Illustravit Nicolaus Courtin...* Parisiis: Apud Fredericum Leonard, 1675, 4to., pages (xlii) 163 (lxxvi) + engraved half title, contemporary polished tan calf, spine panel gilt with 'crowned dolphin' centre pieces, green 'Delph' lettering piece gilt, boards single rule gilt bordered, board edges 'exaggerated -wavy' roll gilt, 'Dutch-swirl' endpapers, all edges rouge, early 21st century restoration by Chris Reston, light toning, few spots and faint dampmark in early leaves, old leather little chipped at edges, rebacked preserving spine panel but new red lettering piece, unidentified gilt stamped armorial motto within circular frame, from the collection of Christopher Ernest Weston 1947-2010. Unsworths Booksellers 24 - 125 2011 £225

Nesbit, Edith *Long Ago When I Was Young.* London: Ronald Whiting & Wheaton, 1966, First edition; original cloth, gilt, boards trifle bowed, dust jacket price clipped, pages 127, illustrations by Edward Ardizzone. R. F. G. Hollett & Sons Antiquarian Booksellers 170 - 36 2011 £35

Nesbit, Edith *The New Treasure Seekers.* London: T. Fisher Unwin, 1904, First edition; original red pictorial cloth, gilt, lower board rather marked, spine faded, neatly recased, pages 328, top edge gilt, with 33 illustrations, littler fingering in places. R. F. G. Hollett & Sons Antiquarian Booksellers 170 - 471 2011 £75

Nesbit, Edith *Oswald Bastable and Others.* Wells Gardner Darton & Co., 1905, First edition; pages x, 369, (ix), with 22 plates and pictorial title, address on flyleaf, occasional fox mark but very good, original decorated maroon cloth gilt, faint stains to boards. R. F. G. Hollett & Sons Antiquarian Booksellers 170 - 472 2011 £85

Nesbit, Edith *The Story of the Treasure Seekers, Being the Adventures of the Bastable Children in Search of a Fortune.* London: Fisher Unwin, 1899, First edition; 8vo., pages xii, 296, 12 pages publisher's ads, original green cloth lettered and illustrated gilt on spine and cover, illustrations, all edges gilt, corners slightly bumped, slight rubbing, sound, very good, ownership signature of Daphne Mulholland (1900), i.e. Countess Darnley. Any Amount of Books May 29 2011 - A74864 2011 $340

Nesbit, Wilbur *Holly Kid Book.* Joliet: Volland, n.d. circa, 1920, Large oblong 4to., as new in original box, box flaps rubbed with some wear, printed on thick card stock, stunning full color illustrations by Marie Horne Myers, rare in box. Aleph-Bet Books, Inc. 95 - 572 2011 $650

Nestor, Sarah *Spanish Textile Tradition of New Mexico and Colorado.* Santa Fe: 1979, xii, 264 pages, illustrations, very good in like dust jacket, over 70 annotated color plates and almost 100 black and white photos. Dumont Maps & Books of the West 111 - 73 2011 $85

Neufeld, Charles *A Prisoner of the Khaleefa: Twelve Years Captivity at Omdurman.* London: Chapman & Hall, 1899, First edition; 8vo., pages xiv, 365, 2 maps, plan, 29 plates, original green decorative cloth, spine slightly faded, sprung but clean internally. J. & S. L. Bonham Antiquarian Booksellers Africa 4/20/2011 - 7224 2011 £40

Neuhaus, Eugene *William Keith, the Main and the Artist.* Berkeley: University of California Press, 1938, First edition; quarto, 95 pages, color frontispiece plus 11 black and white reproductions, publisher's dark green cloth decorated and lettered in gilt, very fine. Argonaut Book Shop Recent Acquisitions Summer 2010 - 148 2011 $150

Neumann, Arthur H. *Elephant Hunting in East Equatorial Africa: Being an Account of Three Years Ivory Hunting Under Mount Kenia and Among the Ndorobo Savages of the Lorogi Mountains...* London: Rowland Ward, 1898, First edition; 8vo., pages xix, 447, (16), folding map in pocket at end, frontispiece, color plate, numerous illustrations, recently handsomely bound in red full morocco, clean and crisp throughout. J. & S. L. Bonham Antiquarian Booksellers Africa 4/20/2011 - 8745 2011 £1250

Neumann, Arthur H. *Elephant Hunting in East Equatorial Africa: Being an Account of Three Years Ivory Hunting Under Mount Kenia and Among the Ndorobo Savages of the Lorogi Mountains...* London: Rowland Ward, 1898, First edition; 8vo., pages xix, 447, (16), folding map in pocket at end, frontispiece, color plate, numerous illustrations, original red cloth, very good, clean copy. J. & S. L. Bonham Antiquarian Booksellers Africa 4/20/2011 - 7566 2011 £1850

Neve, Edward De, Pseud. *Barred.* London: Desmond Harmsworth, First edition; 8vo., pages 255, original publisher's black cloth lettered red at spine, covers slightly rubbed, slightly scuffed at spine ends and corners with couple of faint glass or coffee rings on cover, else near very good, sound copy, inscribed by Edward De Neve for Mildred Milligan. Any Amount of Books May 26 2011 - A63905 2011 $755

Neve, Richard *The City and Country Purchaser's and Builder's Dictionary...* London: printed for B. Sprint, D. Browne, J. Osborn, S. Birt, H. Lintot and A, Wilde, 1736, Third edition; 8vo., in 4's, xvi (including frontispiece), ff. (192), contemporary smooth calf, gilt fillet on covers, spine gilt, from the library of the Earls of Macclesfield at Shirburn Castle. Maggs Bros. Ltd. 1440 - 154 2011 £650

Neves, Dioleciano Fernandes Das *A Hunting Expedition to the Transvaal.* London: George Bell, 1879, First English edition; 8vo., pages vii, 280, half title, little foxing at beginning and end, contemporary crimson decorative half morocco, gilt library stamp on upper cover and lower spine, very slight rubbing on corners and spine, otherwise good clean copy. J. & S. L. Bonham Antiquarian Booksellers Africa 4/20/2011 - 5849 2011 £630

Nevill, Ralph *Light Come, Light Go.* London: Macmillan, 1909, First edition; large 8vo., original red cloth, gilt, pages x, 448, 23 plates, scattered spotting, but very good, sound. R. F. G. Hollett & Son Antiquarian Booksellers 175 - 991 2011 £85

Neville, Emily *It's Like This, Cat.* New York: Harper & Row, 1963, Stated first edition; 8vo., pictorial cloth, fine in very good dust jacket with light edge fraying, no award seal, illustrations by Emil Weiss. Aleph-Bet Books, Inc. 95 - 388 2011 $425

Neville, Henry *The Stage, Its Past and Present in Relation to Fine Art.* London: Richard Bentley and Son, 1875, pages vi, 96, errata slip, few faint blindstamps, original cloth, gilt, spine little worn, signs of small label removed. R. F. G. Hollett & Son Antiquarian Booksellers 175 - 991a 2011 £45

Neville, R. *Ink (The Other Magazine).* 1971-1972, First edition; Nos. 1-29 lacking no. 3, for all published, in very good condition. I. D. Edrich May 26 2011 - 99183 2011 $1677

New Directions in Prose and Poetry - Number Eleven. New York: New Directions, 1949, First edition, English issue with '30 shillings' sticker on front flap of dust jacket; 512 pages, near fine in very good dust jacket with one inch tear at lower hinge and some rubbing at edges. Peter Ellis May 26 2011 - ANTHOLOG007051 2011 $65

The New England Primer, Improved; or an Easy and Pleasant Guide to the Art of Reading. Norwich: Russell Hubbard, 1816, 16mo., 71 page, original floral dutch paper wrappers, woodcuts, inked name and date on upper edge of titlepage, light foxing on titlepage, lower corners of wrapper bumped, very fine. Hobbyhorse Books 56 - 122 2011 $520

The New England Primer, Improved... Boston: printed by James Loring, sold wholesale and retail at his bookstore, no. 2 Cornhill, n.d. circa, 1820, 18mo., 32 pages, drab gray paper on wood boards, leather spine, frontispiece, 24 small woodcuts, minor foxing to few leaves, paper covering boards scuffed, particularly at edges, very good. Hobbyhorse Books 56 - 123 2011 $275

New Grammatical Spelling Book being an Easy Introduction to the English Language. New York: printed by David Denniston, 1801, First and probably only edition; 12mo., leather backed paper over wooden boards, 175 pages + 6 page list of subscribers, 1 page of errata, lacks half of free endpaper, endpapers with inked word lists, edges worn, some fraying, overall tight and in typical condition for this book. Aleph-Bet Books, Inc. 95 - 215 2011 $450

The New Handmaid to Arts, Sciences, Agriculture &c...to which is added, The Complete Farriery or Rules for the Management of Horses. Manchester: printed by A. Swindells, Hanging-bridge and sold by J. Sadler and M. Clemnets, 1790?, 96 pages, 8vo., foot of titlepage clipped with loss of price, otherwise very good, disbound. Jarndyce Antiquarian Booksellers CXCI - 47 2011 £420

The New Keepsake for the Year 1921. London and Paris: X. M. Boulestin, Dec., 1920, First edition, number 37 of 50 copies on Japanese vellum, out of a total printing of 620; 8vo., pages 127, (1) imprint, 9 illustrations and 10 pages of musical notation, gilt upper edge, lower and fore edge uncut, some pages unopened, original white cloth in protective tissue, upper side lettered and tooled in gilt, gilt tooling to spine, some slight discoloring to spine, from the library of John Martin, publisher of Black Sparrow Press, fine. Simon Finch Rare Books Zero - 333 2011 £350

The New Manchester Guide; or Useful Pocket Companion... Manchester: J. Leech, 1815, New edition; 204 pages, large folding frontispiece map, large folding ground plan, 3 woodcut plates, very good, uncut, 12mo., recent half calf, gilt banded spine, red label. Ken Spelman Rare Books 68 - 180 2011 £140

New Mexico the Land of Enchantment: Official Souvenir of the State of New Mexico at Panama-California Exposition San Diego 1915. 240, v, (xi) pages, maps and illustrations, quarto, original printed wrappers, some soil and edgewear, internally clean and very good. Dumont Maps & Books of the West 113 - 20 2011 $200

New Numbers. A Quarterly Publication of the Poems of Wilfrid Wilson Gibson, Rupert Brooke, Lascelles Abercrombie, John Drinkwater. Published at Ryton, Dymock, Gloucester, 1914, First edition; pages 60; (iv), 61-108; (iv), 109-152; (iv), 153-212, 4to., original pale grey wrappers printed in black, small stain to head of rear wrappers very good, printed receipt for original purchase of this set filled by Catherine Abercrombie who was secretary and publisher, loosely inserted. Blackwell Rare Books B166 - 197 2011 £250

New Topographics. Rochester: International Museum of Photography at George Eastman House, 1975, 4to., pages 48, 56 black and white photos, original wrappers, text printed in grey to spine and upper side, occasional very light marks to wrappers, foot of spine lightly bumped with light creasing to spine, near fine. Simon Finch Rare Books Zero - 541 2011 £1250

New Year's Gift. New York: Samuel Wood & Sons circa, 1818, 2 5/8 x 4 1/8 inches, plain wrappers, light soil, very good+, small pictorial woodcuts and decorative border. Aleph-Bet Books, Inc. 95 - 17 2011 $150

New York City Humane Society *A Report of a Committee... Appointed to Inquire into the Number of Tavern Licenses; the Manner of Granting Them; Their Effects Upon the Community and Other Sources of Vice and Misery in this City and to Visit Bridwell.* New York: Collins and Perkins, 1810, First edition; 8vo., 15 pages, removed. M & S Rare Books, Inc. 90 - 284 2011 $125

Newberry, John *The Newtonian System of Philosophy Explained by Familiar Objects in an Entertaining Manner for the Use of Young Ladies & Gentlemen...* Philadelphia: Johnson & Warner, Lyrdia R. Railey, Printer, 1808, 16mo., 140 pages, 5 full page plates plus numerous text woodcuts, contemporary calf, leather label, very good. M & S Rare Books, Inc. 90 - 208 2011 $350

Newbigging, Thomas *Sketches and Tales.* London: Sampson Low, Marston & Co. and Bury: W. S. Bartlow, 1883, First edition; small 8vo., original cloth, head of spine little frayed, pages 228. R. F. G. Hollett & Son Antiquarian Booksellers 175 - 992 2011 £35

Newby, George *Pleasures of Melancholy.* Keswick: printed by T. Bailey and Son, 1842, First edition; original patterned cloth with paper spine label, edges faded, pages 114, one or two spots, excellent copy. R. F. G. Hollett & Son Antiquarian Booksellers 173 - 815 2011 £140

Newby, P. H. *The Barbary Light.* London: Faber, 1962, First edition; pages 288, foolscap 8vo., original lemon yellow cloth, backstrip printed in red, faint partial free endpaper browning, dust jacket with light stain to rear panel and backstrip panel little darkened, good. Blackwell Rare Books B166 - 198 2011 £50

Newell, Peter *The Hole Book.* New York: Harper & Brothers, 1908, First edition; 4to., blue cloth with color pictorial paste label, rather clean, fresh copy, full color plates. Jo Ann Reisler, Ltd. 86 - 179 2011 $575

Newell, Peter *Topsys Turveys.* New York: Century Co., 1893, First edition; oblong 8vo., full color pictorial boards, spine has some chipping and light wear, internally clean copy, tan dust jacket with olive lettering and illustrations on front of cover, dust jacket has some chipping along edges and spine with little soiling to cover of jacket, 31 numbered pages of Newell's marvelously inventive mind and artistic skills done early in his career, book shows pictures that transform from one image to another when the book is turned upside down and viewed anew. Jo Ann Reisler, Ltd. 86 - 178 2011 $1250

Newhall, Nancy *Time in New England.* New York: Aperture, 1980, 4to., pages 256, photos by Paul Strand, gray cloth, stamped in silver, remainder mark on bottom, edges slightly soiled, else very good, tight copy in scuffed and soiled dust jacket. Second Life Books Inc. 174 - 247 2011 $100

Newhall, Ruth Waldo *A California Legend. The Newhall Land and Farming Company.* Valencia: Newhall Land and Farming Co., 1992, First edition; x, (2), 324 pages, profusely illustrated with photos, maps, map endpapers, folded chart in rear pocket, cloth backed boards, gilt, very fine, pictorial dust jacket, presentation inscription signed by author. Argonaut Book Shop Recent Acquisitions Summer 2010 - 150 2011 $60

Newman, A. *From a Lover's Garden: More Rondeaux and Other Verses of Boyhood.* London: privately printed, 1924, First edition limited to 200 copies; small 8vo., pages 76, original publisher's green boards with paper labels to spine and cover photo frontispiece, very slight mottling to boards, else very good+. Any Amount of Books May 29 2011 - A73076 2011 $408

Newman, Harold *An Illustrated Dictionary of Jewelry.* London: Thames & Hudson, 1981, First edition; original cloth, gilt, dust jacket, pages 335, with 685 illustrations. R. F. G. Hollett & Son Antiquarian Booksellers General Catalogue Summer 2010 - 283 2011 £65

Newman, John *North East and East Kent.* Penguin, 1969, Original cloth, gilt, dust jacket, edges trifle worn, pages 645, 104 illustrations and map. R. F. G. Hollett & Son Antiquarian Booksellers General Catalogue Summer 2010 - 1541 2011 £30

Newman, William *Sermons Preached at Worsborough.* London: Swan Sonnenschein & Co., 1892, First edition; original blue cloth gilt, small nicks to head of spine, pages iv, 284. R. F. G. Hollett & Son Antiquarian Booksellers 175 - 996 2011 £40

Newmarch, Rosa *Mary Wakefield.* Kendal: Atkinson & Pollitt, 1912, original red cloth gilt, pages 142, frontispiece, 11 illustrations.   R. F. G. Hollett & Son Antiquarian Booksellers   173 - 816 2011   £40

Newmarch, Rosa *Mary Wakefield. A Memoir.* Kendal: Atkinson & Pollitt, 1912, First edition; original red cloth gilt, little used and worn, pages 142, with frontispiece and 11 illustrations, large inscription.   R. F. G. Hollett & Son Antiquarian Booksellers   175 - 907 2011   £35

Newte, Thomas *Prospects and Observations; on a Tour in England and Scotland: Natural, Economical and Literary.* London: printed for G. G. J. and J. Robinson, 1791, 4to., pages viii, 440 + a folding engraved map frontispiece and 23 other engraved plates, contemporary polished tan calf, board edges 'zig-zag' decorative roll in blind, red and white sewn endbands, late 1990's calf reback by Chris Weston, original red lettering piece gilt relaid, some foxing, old leather scratched and bit rubbed at edges, armorial bookplate of C. Kerr Esqr/Calder Bank, ink inscription "Charles Kerr/ Georges Square", from the collection of Christopher Ernest Weston 1947-2010.   Unsworths Booksellers   24 - 126 2011   £350

Newton, Henry *Epistolae, Orationes, et Carmina. (bound with) Orationes quarum Altera Florentiae Anno MDCCV.* Lucca: D. Ciufetti, 1710, Amsterdam: 1710-(1712); 2 works in 1 volume, (6), 250, 115, (3) pages, engraved frontispiece, 58 pages (final quire signed * (pages 51-58) reprinted to include items dated 1711 and 1712, contemporary English panelled calf, spine gilt, rubbed, upper joint slightly cracked, one corner worn, number of small corrections throughout, from the library of the Earls of Macclesfield at Shirburn Castle, bound at end are two manuscript letters from Newton at Florence, one to Jean Le Clerc at Amsterdam and the other to Gisbert Cuper at Deventer, both dated 1710.   Maggs Bros. Ltd.   1440 - 155 2011   £800

Newton, Isaac 1642-1727   *The Chronology of Ancient Kingdoms Amended. (bound with) Observations Upon the Prophecies of Daniel and the Apocalypse of St. John.* London: printed for J. Tonson, 1728, London: printed by J. Darby and T. Browne, 1733. First edition; 2 books in one quarto volume, contemporary full calf.   Heritage Book Shop   Booth A12 51st NY International Antiquarian Book Fair April 8-10 2011 - 95 2011 $4000

Newton, Isaac 1642-1727   *The Chronology of Ancient Kingdoms Amended.* London: printed for J. Tonson &c, 1728, 4to., pages xiv, (ii), 376, 3 extending plates, early 21st century retrospective panelled calf binding by Chris Weston, title washed and repaired at edge, minor spotting elsewhere, from the collection of Christopher Ernest Weston 1947-2010.   Unsworths Booksellers   24 - 31 2011   £950

Newton, Isaac 1642-1727   *Observations upon the Prophecies of Daniel and the Apocalypse of St. John.* London: printed by J. Darby and T. Browne, 1733, 4to., pages vi, (ii), 323, (i), early 21st century retrospective blind tooled calf by Chris Weston, title slightly dusty, otherwise very clean, from the collection of Christopher Ernest Weston 1947-2010.   Unsworths Booksellers   24 - 32 2011   £2250

Newton, Isaac 1642-1727   *Observations Upon the Prophecies of Daniel and the Apocalypse of St. John.* London: J. Darby and T. Browne, 1733, First edition; 4to., (viii), 323, (2 blank) pages, vignette at head of dedication page, occasional light foxing, worming (margins only), few leaves with ink smears or other markings confined mainly to margins, full modern antique style blind paneled calf, raised bands, red leather spine label, gilt spine, ownership signature of White Bates on free endpaper, nice wide margins, very good, rare.   Jeff Weber Rare Books   163 - 36 2011 $4500

Newton, Isaac 1642-1727   *Philosophiae Naturalis Principia Mathematica.* London: Apud Guil. & Joh. Innys, 1726, Third edition; one of 200 large paper copies on 'General Royal Paper with the CC" watermark, quarto, frontispiece and numerous diagrams, bound without rear ad, with initial privilege leaf and half title leaf, contemporary full vellum, front board expertly reattached.   Heritage Book Shop   Booth A12 51st NY International Antiquarian Book Fair April 8-10 2011 - 96 2011 $55,000

Newton, Thomas *Dissertations on the Prophecies, Which have Been Remarkably Fulfilled and are at this Time fulfilling in the World.* London: printed for J. and R. Tonson and S. Draper, 1754-1758, First edition; Volume First(- the Third, and Last), presentation copy, few spots and minor stains, pages (xxvii), 498, (1); (xxiv), xx, 451; (xxiv), 429, (34), 8vo., contemporary sprinkled calf, double gilt fillet borders on sides, spines richly gilt in compartments with twin lettering pieces, spines darkened, three of the labels defective or missing, slightly worn at extremities, volumes I and II inscribed "J. Green from the Author", sound.   Blackwell Rare Books   B166 - 73 2011   £500

Niall, Ian *The Galloway Shepherd, a Story of the Hills.* London: Heinemann, 1970, First edition; 8vo., pages 198, frontispiece and 4 full page illustrations + 21 smaller illustrations, signed presentation from author to a family at Christmas 1970, 6 of the original illustrations, very fine ink drawings by John Fleming, 5 are 4.25 x 5.5. and a later one 8.5 x 5.5 inches, they are on art board, drawings in excellent condition, book clean, tight, very good in slightly used but complete about very good dust jacket.   Any Amount of Books   May 26 2011 - A40508 2011 $503

Niall, Ian *Tunnicliffe's Countryside.* Clive Holloway Books, 1983, First edition; 4to., original cloth, gilt, dust jacket, pages 216, illustrations in color and black and white, fine.   R. F. G. Hollett & Son Antiquarian Booksellers   General Catalogue Summer 2010 - 1029 2011   £40

Nicholls, J. F. *The Remarkable Life, Adventures and Discoveries of Sebastian Cabot of Bristol, The Founder of Great Britain's Maritime Power, Discoverer of America and Its First Colonizer.* London: Sampson Low Son and Marston, 1869, 8vo., pages xv, 190, frontispiece, decorated brown cloth with gilt and black decoration and titles, cloth worn, especially along spine, interior very good. Schooner Books Ltd. 96 - 74 2011 $125

Nicholls, Peter *Foundation.* A Review of Science Fiction, 1972-1999, First edition; Nos. 2-77, unbroken run. I. D. Edrich May 26 2011 - 99060 2011 $503

Nicholls, Robert *Ten Generations of a Potting Family.* Lund Humphries, n.d. circa, 1930, First edition; original buckram gilt, dust jacket, edges little worn, spine rather browned, small nick, pages xxvi, 135, with 54 plates, folding genealogical tree. R. F. G. Hollett & Son Antiquarian Booksellers General Catalogue Summer 2010 - 284 2011 £30

Nicholls, W. *The History and Traditions of Ravenstonedale. Westmorland Volume II.* Manchester: Abel Heywood & Son, n.d. circa, 1910, First edition; original green cloth gilt, little discolored and hinges trifle frayed, pages 184, illustrations. R. F. G. Hollett & Son Antiquarian Booksellers 173 - 823 2011 £120

Nichols, Beverley *Green Grows the City.* London: Cape, 1939, First edition; original cloth, gilt, dust jacket edges rather chipped and frayed, pages 285, illustrations, ownership inscription. R. F. G. Hollett & Son Antiquarian Booksellers General Catalogue Summer 2010 - 856 2011 £30

Nichols, Francis Morgan *Britton: The French Text...* Oxford: Clarendon Press, 1865, First editions; 2 volumes, tall 8vo., original publisher's russet brown cloth lettered gilt at spine, pages lxiv, 419 & 398; bookplate of Sir James Hannen, pencilled ownership signature of historian F. R. Cowell, covers somewhat soiled and marked with staining at spine, otherwise about very good- with very sound, clean text. Any Amount of Books May 29 2011 - A45886 2011 $272

Nichols, John *The Milagro Beanfield War.* New York: Holt Rinehart & Winston, 1975, First edition; fine, dust jacket is near fine-, light sunning and rubbing to spine. Bella Luna Books May 26 2011 - t9166 2011 $275

Nicholson, Cornelius *The Annals of Kendall.* Kendal: Hudson and Nicholson, 1832, First edition; near contemporary full polished calf gilt, boards panelled with broad rolls in gilt, spine faded, pages ix, 260, engraved frontispiece and folding plan of Kendal (defective and partly replaced with modern photocopy taped on), single sheet ALS laid in from author to Henry Swinglehurst, Nicholson's 19 page pamphlet "History and Incidents connected with the grant of the three Royal Charters of Incorporation of the Borough of Kendal (privately published 1876) bound in at end, frontispiece and titlepage laid down, small engraving of Kendal Castle laid down on dedication leaf. R. F. G. Hollett & Son Antiquarian Booksellers 173 - 825 2011 £175

Nicholson, Cornelius *The Annals of Kendal.* Kendal: Hudson and Nicholson, 1832, First edition; original patterned cloth, rebacked in cloth with paper spine label, pages ix, 260, frontispiece, folding plan (little browned and offset as usual), text illustrations, old press cuttings tipped to endpapers, scarce. R. F. G. Hollett & Son Antiquarian Booksellers 173 - 824 2011 £140

Nicholson, Cornelius *The Annals of Kendal...* Whitaker and Co., 1861, Second edition; original blindstamped cloth gilt, extremities trifle rubbed, pages xii, 412, engraved frontispiece (rather spotted), engraved folding plan (some tears, repaired with tape on reverse), numerous text and other illustrations, good copy. R. F. G. Hollett & Son Antiquarian Booksellers 173 - 826 2011 £175

Nicholson, David *Liturgical Music in Benedictine Monasticism, a Post Vatican II Survey. Volume I. The Monasteries of Monks.* printed by five Seasons Press and Fleece Press, 1986, One of 40 copies (of an edition of 350); printed on Zerkall mouldmade paper and the Pax device gilt blocked on front cover, pages xii, 190, royal 8vo., original dark green linen, backstrip gilt lettered and front cover with circular gilt blocked Pax device, marbled endpapers, rough trimmed, glassine jacket. Blackwell Rare Books B166 - 274 2011 £50

Nicholson, Henry Alleyne *An Essay on the Geology of Cumberland and Westmorland.* Hardwicke and Ireland, 1868, First edition; black library cloth, gilt, pages viii, 93, partly unopened, 3 extending plans and numerous text illustrations, library stamp on title, very scarce. R. F. G. Hollett & Son Antiquarian Booksellers 173 - 829 2011 £140

Nicholson, Isa *Dusty Mirrors.* London: Simpkin Marshall & Co. and Manchester: Abel Heywood & son, 1884, First edition; original decorated cloth gilt, neatly recased, pages 176, lower flyleaf replaced, scarce. R. F. G. Hollett & Son Antiquarian Booksellers 173 - 830 2011 £65

Nicholson, Josiah Walker *Crosby Garrett, Westmoreland. A History of the Manor of Crosby Garrett in Westmoreland with Local Customs and Legends.* Kirkby Stephen: J. W. Braithwaite & Son, 1914, First (only) edition; small 8vo., original blue pictorial cloth (extremities trifle rubbed), pages xv, 136, 18 illustrations, flyleaf removed. R. F. G. Hollett & Son Antiquarian Booksellers 173 - 831 2011 £120

Nicholson, Norman *The Lakers. The First Tourists.* Robert Hale, 1955, First edition; original cloth, gilt, dust jacket (little worn), pages (8), 235, with 17 plates. R. F. G. Hollett & Son Antiquarian Booksellers 173 - 835 2011 £45

Nicholson, Norman *Provincial Pleasures.* Robert Hale, 1959, First edition; original cloth, gilt, dust jacket, trifle worn, repaired with tape on reverse, pages 190, illustrations by Biro. R. F. G. Hollett & Son Antiquarian Booksellers 173 - 839 2011 £35

Nicholson, William *Book of Blokes.* London: Faber & Faber, 1929, First edition; 12mo., white boards, green pictorial labels on both covers, fine, printed on one side of paper, each page has line illustration. Aleph-Bet Books, Inc. 95 - 391 2011 $500

Nicholson, William *Clever Bill.* N.P.: New York: Doubleday Page, n.d., 1927, First US edition; 4to., yellow pictorial boards, 23 pages, slight rubbing, near fine in chipped dust jacket, excellent copy, very scarce, wonderful color lithographs. Aleph-Bet Books, Inc. 95 - 390 2011 $3500

Nicholson, William *Slaves of the Mastery.* London: Mammoth, 2001, First British edition; fine in fine dust jacket, signed by author. Bella Luna Books May 29 2011 - t8064 2011 $82

Nicholson, William *The Wind Singer.* London: Mammoth, 2000, First British edition; fine, dust jacket, fine, signed by author. Bella Luna Books May 26 2011 - t8063 2011 $220

Nickel, Douglas R. *Carleton Watkins. The Art of Perception.* San Francisco: Museum of Modern Art, 1999, First edition; small folio, 228 pages, 105 tritone and 20 duotone photos, green cloth lettered in silver, one lower corner slightly jammed, else very fine with pictorial dust jacket. Argonaut Book Shop Recent Acquisitions Summer 2010 - 228 2011 $175

Nickel, Douglas R. *Francis Frith in Egypt and Palestine: a Victorian Photographer Abroad.* Princeton and Oxford: Princeton University Press, 2004, First printing; 4to. 239 pages, frontispiece, 75 duotone plates, 10 black and white plates, quarter brown cloth with pictorial paper boards, gilt stamped spine title, dust jacket, fine, from the Bern Dibner reference library, with Burndy bookplate. Jeff Weber Rare Books 161 - 158 2011 $75

Nickerson, Jackie *Farm.* London: Jonathan Cape, 2002, First edition; 4to., original color illustrated boards, illustrations in color and black and white, fine in near fine dust jacket, faintly creased at spine ends and corners, excellent condition. Any Amount of Books May 26 2011 - A76744 2011 $478

Nicol, James *An Historical and Descriptive Account of Iceland, Greenland and the Faroe Islands...* Edinburgh: Oliver & Boyd, n.d. circa, 1849, Fifth edition; small 8vo., original red blindstamped cloth, rebacked in matching morocco gilt, pages 416, extending map frontispiece, half title with engraved vignette, printed title, plate, map plate, clean and sound, attractive copy. R. F. G. Hollett & Son Antiquarian Booksellers General Catalogue Summer 2010 - 1656 2011 £150

Nicolai, Johann *Disquisitio de Mose Alpha Dicto.* Leiden: H. Teering, 1703, 12mo., 148, (4) pages, last leaf blank, contemporary vellum backed marbled paper boards, from the library of the Earls of Macclesfield at Shirburn Castle. Maggs Bros. Ltd. 1440 - 156 2011 £500

Nicolai, Johann *Tractatus de Siglis Veterum Omnibus Eleganioris Literaturae Amatoribus Utilissimus...* Leiden: Abraham de Swart, 1703, 4to., (22), 314 pages, engraved printer's device on titlepage, titlepage printed in black and red letters, woodcut headpieces, woodcut initials, woodcut illustrations, engraved illustrations in text, contemporary panelled calf, spine gilt in compartments, morocco lettering piece, binding rubbed. from the library of the Earls of Macclesfield at Shirburn Castle. Maggs Bros. Ltd. 1440 - 157 2011 £450

Nicole, Pierre *Discourses.* London: Harvey & Darton, 1928, Later cloth, some foxing, else clean, tight, 239 pages, inscribed and signed by Hancock, very good, the copy of Thomas Hancock. G. H. Mott Bookseller May 26 2011 - 33999 2011 $1500

Nicoll, Allardyce *A History of English Drama 1660-1900.* Cambridge: 1955, circa 2500 pages, 6 volumes, original binding, ex-library, very good. Bookworm & Silverfish 665 - 53 2011 $125

Nicolson, J. *Birdie ABC.* London: Blackie & Son, circa, 1930, 4to., 24 pages, cloth backed pictorial boards, tips rubbed, light cover soil, very good+, printed on French fold paper, each page has very large block letter in color plus illustration of a different bird, absolutely wonderful. Aleph-Bet Books, Inc. 95 - 5 2011 $450

Nicolson, J. *The History and Antiquities of the Counties of Westmorland and Cumberland.* London: W. Strahan and T. Cadell, 1777, First edition; 2 volumes, large 4to., modern full panelled and sprinkled calf ruled in blind, old backstrips relaid with raised bands, heavily gilt compartments and double lettering pieces, pages cxxxiv, 630; 615 (8 index), uncut, complete with 2 large folding maps (short tear repaired), very handsome clean and sound set. R. F. G. Hollett & Son Antiquarian Booksellers 173 - 842 2011 £750

Nicolson, William *The English, Scotch and Irish Historical Libraries.* 1736, Third edition; folio, full contemporary calf, some wear, xviii, 272, 18, xix, 148, xvi, 118 pages, ex-library, plate inside front cover, discreet stamp on rear of main titles, else tight, clean copy. C. P. Hyland May 26 2011 - 259/342 2011 $362

Nicolson, William *The English Scotch and Irish Historical Libraries.* 1776, Corrected, new edition; 4to., library cloth, xii, 241 (2), 116 (2), viii 92 pages, very good. C. P. Hyland May 26 2011 - 255/520 2011 $290

Niebuhr, Carl *The Tel El Amarna Period. The Relations of Egypt and Western Asia in the Fifteenth Century B.C...* David Nutt, 1901, First edition; small 8vo., original brown cloth, gilt, pages 62, untrimmed. R. F. G. Hollett & Son Antiquarian Booksellers 177 - 601 2011 £45

Niebuhr, Reginald *Beyond Tragedy.* London: Nisbet & Co., 1938, First UK edition; original cloth, gilt, dust jacket spine darkened and little rubbed, pages xi, 306, with errata slip. R. F. G. Hollett & Son Antiquarian Booksellers 175 - 1003 2011 £50

Niedecker, Lorine *My Friend Tree. Poems.* Edinburgh: Wild Hawthorn Press, 1961, First edition; oblong 8vo., original wrappers, dust jacket, fine association copy, inscribed by author for her her later publisher, Jonathan Williams. James S. Jaffe Rare Books May 26 2011 - 7948 2011 $7500

Nielsen, Frederik *The History of the Papacy in the XIXth Century.* London: John Murray, 1906, First edition; bookplate of T. J. Hardy and of St. Mary's House Library (partly removed) on each pastedown, 2 volumes, thick 8vo., original cloth, gilt, little marked, extremities slightly frayed in places, pages xiii, 379; 483, endpapers little spotted. R. F. G. Hollett & Son Antiquarian Booksellers 175 - 1004 2011 £75

Niethammer, Wera *Wunderfitchen ein Waldmarchen.* Stuttgart: K. Thienemanns Verlag, n.d., 1914, First edition; oblong 4to., pictorial cloth, 83 pages + 1 page ad, slight darkening of cloth, else near fine, illustrations by Fritz Lang with 14 incredible full page color woodcut plates, many color cuts in text, fine color printing. Aleph-Bet Books, Inc. 95 - 256 2011 $750

Nietzsche, Friedrich *Gotzen-Dammerung, Oder Wie man Mit Dem Hammer Philosophiert.* Leipzig: C. G. Naumann, 1889, First edition; 8vo., pages (vii), 144, later cloth, spine lettered in gilt, original drab wrappers printed in red and black bound in, pencilled note to front pastedown "Ex Biblioth. E. Salin" (Edgar Salin 1892-1974 prominent German sociologist), light wear to wrappers, but excellent, fresh copy. Simon Finch Rare Books Zero - 134 2011 £2250

Niffenegger, Audrey *The Time Traveler's Wife.* London: Jonathan Cape, 2005, Waterstone's limited edition; fine, dust jacket fine, still in original plastic wrapper, signed on publisher's bookplate attached to half titlepage. Bella Luna Books May 26 2011 - k170 2011 $330

The Night Before Christmas. (code number 866). Akron: Saalfield Pub. Co., 1945, Large 4to., full color pictorial boards, full color pictorial dust jacket with some shelf wear to book and edge and surface wear to jacket, some crackling to edge of spine of book itself, inside bright and clean, every page illustrated in full by Ethel Hays, four panel pull-out panorama attached to inside front cover. Jo Ann Reisler, Ltd. 86 - 43 2011 $250

Nightingale, B. *The Ejected of 1662 in Cumberland and Westmorland.* Manchester: 1911, First (only) edition; 2 volumes, thick 8vo., original black cloth, gilt, pages xxiv, 777; 780-1490 (25 ads), top edge gilt, fore-edges and some endpapers, rather spotted, otherwise excellent sound set, very scarce. R. F. G. Hollett & Son Antiquarian Booksellers 173 - 844 2011 £350

Nightingale, Florence *Notes on Nursing; What It Is and What It Is Not.* London: Harrison, 1860, New edition; half title, original maroon wavy grained cloth by Burn & Co., borders blocked in blind, spine lettered in gilt, carefully rebacked, very good, inscribed by author for Harriet Martineau July 1860. Jarndyce Antiquarian Booksellers CLXC - 595 2011 £2500

Nightingale, J. *Memoirs of the Public and Private Life of Her Most Gracious Majesty Caroline, Queen of Great Britain and Consort of King George the Fourth.* London: J. Robins and Co., 1820, Octavo, xiv, iv, (15)-715, (1) pages, frontispiece, engraved half title, 8 (of 9) plates, original full calf, gilt spine, red spine leather label, extremities worn, hinges repaired, ownership signatures inside front cover, very good. Jeff Weber Rare Books 163 - 199 2011 $100

Nihon Fuzoku. Osaka: printed by Oshima Yosuke for Tsujiko Kumatoro, 1890, 2 volumes, 16mo, 26, 27 pages, frenchfold color pictorial paper with sewn bindings in same manner as crepe paper Japanese fairy tale series, housed in original pictorial envelope holder, set in fine condition, every page has lovely woodcut, hand colored or printed color.   Aleph-Bet Books, Inc.   95 - 307   2011 $1250

A Nile Journal. Boston: Roberts Bros., 1876, First edition; 8vo., pages 307, 13 plates, frontispiece has small waterstaining to upper edge, original brown decorative cloth, small split at head of spine.   J. & S. L. Bonham Antiquarian Booksellers   Africa 4/20/2011 - 8766   2011   £35

Nine Niggers More. London & New York: Frederick Warne & Co. n.d. circa, 1885, Square 4to., pictorial wrappers, slight spine wear, else fine, 12 full page color illustrations, printed by the Dalziels, publisher's file company stamped in margin, quite scarce and beautiful copy.   Aleph-Bet Books, Inc.   95 - 112   2011 $1250

Nivedita *Myths of the Hindus & Buddhists.* London: George G. Harrap, 1913, Large 8vo., original limp calf with yapp edges and embossed vignette to upper board, spine lettered in blind, pages xii, 400, top edge gilt, other edges uncut, with 32 tissue guarded color plates, handsome, clean copy.   R. F. G. Hollett & Son Antiquarian Booksellers   175 - 1007   2011   £85

Niven, David *Round the Rugged Rocks.* London: Cresset Press, 1951, First edition; 8vo., original publisher's red cloth lettered gilt on spine and on front cover, pages 263, very good+ in close to very good dust jacket slightly chipped at spine ends and top of rear panel and rubbed at corners, signed presentation from author to the Harrisburgs.   Any Amount of Books   May 29 2011 - A76302   2011 $255

Niven, Larry *The Ringworld Engineers.* Huntington Woods: Phantasia Press, 1979, First edition; octavo, full green goat skin, stamped in gold.   L. W. Currey, Inc.   124 - 110   2011 $750

Niven, Larry *World of Ptavvs.* London: MacDonald & Co., 1968, First British and first hardcover edition; octavo, boards.   L. W. Currey, Inc.   124 - 176   2011 $300

Niven, William *Illustrations of Old Warwickshire Houses.* printed for the author at the Chiswick Press, 1878, Sole edition; frontispiece, engraved vignette on title, 30 copper etchings, pages 37, 4to., original cinnamon cloth, backstrip longitudinally gilt lettered direct, front board gilt titled at centre with gilt ruled border, blue black endpapers, good.   Blackwell Rare Books   B166 - 75   2011   £120

Nixon, John *The Complete Story of the Transvaal from the Great Trek to the Convention of London.* London: Sampson Low, 1885, First edition; 8vo. pages xx, 372, folding map, original grey cloth, worn at head and tail, inner joint cracked, corners bumped and rubbed.   J. & S. L. Bonham Antiquarian Booksellers   Africa 4/20/2011 - 3007   2011   £38

Nixon, Richard Milhous *Real Peace: a Strategy for the West.* New York: privately printed, 1983, First edition; fine in slightly rubbed, near fine dust jacket, signed by author, laid in is printed slip with Nixon's NY address.   Between the Covers   169 - BTC343396   2011 $500

Noakes, Aubrey *The County Fire Office 1807-1957.* London: Witherby, 1957, First edition; large 8vo., original cloth, gilt, dust jacket, pages xv, 189, with 12 plates, presentation slip loosely inserted.   R. F. G. Hollett & Son Antiquarian Booksellers   175 - 1008   2011   £35

Noceti, Caroli *De Iride et Aurora Boreali Carmina...* Rome: N. & M. Pagliarini ex typ. Palladis, 1747, First edition; 4to., (12), 127, (1) pages, printed on thick paper, 2 engraved plates, 18th century English sprinkled calf, gilt spine, morocco lettering piece, first plate slightly torn, from the library of the Earls of Macclesfield at Shirburn Castle.   Maggs Bros. Ltd.   1440 - 158   2011   £400

Nocturnal Revels; or the History of the King's Place and Other Modern Nunneries. London: printed for M. Goadby, 1779, Second and most complete edition; 2 volumes, 12mo., pages (xx), 279; (iv), 192, 193*-252*, 193-270, (2) ad, rebound in full calf expertly to style with spine lettered and decorated in gilt, within raised band compartments, extensively but expertly restored, some worming (restored in binding) to lower fore edge page corners volume 1 (not affecting text).   Simon Finch Rare Books   Zero - 408   2011   £5000

Noel, Augusta *Effie's Friends; or Chronicles of the Woods and Shore.* London: James Nisbet, 1865, Second edition; original blue cloth gilt over bevelled boards, extremities little worn, pages 192 with decorated title and chapter head and tails, joints cracking and rather shaken in places.   R. F. G. Hollett & Son Antiquarian Booksellers   General Catalogue Summer 2010 - 545   2011   £65

Noel, Augusta *From Generation to Generation.* London: Macmillan & Co., 1880, Second edition; 2 volumes, half titles, contemporary half maroon calf, raised gilt bands, little darkened and rubbed, ownership inscription of Constance Elphinstone.   Jarndyce Antiquarian Booksellers   CLXC - 596   2011   £85

Noel, E. B. *First Steps to Rackets.* London: Mills & Boon, 1926, First edition; octavo, 136, 16 ads pages, plates, green cloth, slight bump on front board, very good or better, without dust jacket, inscribed by one of the co-authors, Clarence Bruce for George Standing. Between the Covers 169 - BTC342222 2011 $650

Noguchi, Yone *From the Easter Sea.* London: Unicorn, 1903, 8vo., pages 73, (1) and (4) ads, illustrated titlepage, fore-edge and lower edge uncut, bound in original pictorial cloth with great images of ships and sun, gilt lettering to upper board and spine, green stamp image on lower board, bumped, slightly soiled and sunned but without serious wear, with ALS. Simon Finch Rare Books Zero - 342 2011 £650

The Noisy Boy. New York: McLoughlin Brothers, circa, 1867, 16mo., color pictorial cover with small hole in rear cover, full page color illustrations. Jo Ann Reisler, Ltd. 86 - 135 2011 $150

Nolan, Thomas B. *The Eureka Mining District, Nevada.* Washington: GPO, 1962, First edition; quarto, 2 parts, 78 pages, 15 text figures including photos and maps, 2 tables, 11 folding plates in separate heavy cardboard folder, gray wrappers printed in black, plates in gray folder printed in black, small crack to upper front hinge of folder, fine set. Argonaut Book Shop Recent Acquisitions Summer 2010 - 151 2011 $60

Norden, Greg *Landscapes Under the Luggae Rack.* Northampton: Great Norden Publications, 1997, First edition; oblong 4to., original cloth gilt, dust jacket, pages 192, with 200 color illustrations, scarce. R. F. G. Hollett & Son Antiquarian Booksellers General Catalogue Summer 2010 - 285 2011 £75

Norden, John *Poor Man's Rest.* Kirkby Lonsdale: Arthur Foster, 1826, Twenty-second edition; 12mo., contemporary calf, gilt, hinges cracked, pages viii, 288. R. F. G. Hollett & Son Antiquarian Booksellers 175 - 1009 2011 £35

Nordquist, Myron H. *Current Fisheries Issues and the Food and Agriculture Organization of the United Nations.* The Hague: Boston: London: Martinus Nijhoff, 2000, First edition; large 8vo., 680 pages, fine. Any Amount of Books May 29 2011 - A72625 2011 $213

Norman, George Warde *An Examination of Some Prevailing Opinions as to the Pressure of Taxation in this and Other Countries.* London: T. & W. Boone, 1850, 8vo., 95, (1) pages, recent marbled boards lettered on spine, very good. John Drury Rare Books 153 - 101 2011 £175

Norman, Howard *The Museum Guard.* New York: FSG, 1998, First edition; inscribed by author, slight crown bump, else fine in like dust jacket. Ken Lopez Bookseller 154 - 148 2011 $75

Norman, Howard *The Northern Lights.* New York: Summit Books, 1987, First edition; near fine, light sunning and bumping to bottom of spine, remainder dot, near fine dust jacket, price clipped, light creasing to spine, signed by author. Bella Luna Books May 29 2011 - p1190a 2011 $82

Norman, Philip *London Vanished & Vanishing.* Adam & Charles Black, 1905, First edition; large 8vo., original cloth, gilt, pages xvi, 294, (vi), top edge gilt, 76 color plates, flyleaves lightly browned, otherwise very nice. R. F. G. Hollett & Son Antiquarian Booksellers General Catalogue Summer 2010 - 1510 2011 £195

Norris-Newman, Charles L. *With the Boers in the Transvaal and Orange Free State in 1880-1881.* London: William H. Allen, 1882, First edition; 8vo., pages xvi, 387, folding map, original brown decorative cloth, spine faded and rubbed, small split at head, covers flecked, inner hinges strengthened. J. & S. L. Bonham Antiquarian Booksellers Africa 4/20/2011 - 4849 2011 £95

Norris, Frank 1870-1902 *The Letters of Frank Norris.* San Francisco: Book Club of California, 1956, Limited to 350 copies; 115 pages, frontispiece, 1 facsimile, cloth backed decorated boards, paper spine label, fine. Argonaut Book Shop Recent Acquisitions Summer 2010 - 152 2011 $150

Norris, Frank 1870-1902 *Yvernelle. A Legend of Feudal France.* Philadelphia: Lippincott, 1892, First edition; large 8vo., pages 116, illuminated titlepage, 11 plates inserted in text as well as head and tailpieces by various artists, some in color, original green cloth stamped in gilt, top edge gilt, fine, rare. Second Life Books Inc. 174 - 249 2011 $2625

Norris, Frank 1870-1902 *Yvernelle. A Legend of Feudal France.* Philadelphia: J. B. Lippincott, 1892, First edition; 8vo., 116 pages, text illustrations and inserted plates, original gilt stamped rose cloth, rubbing at extremities of spine and corners, some rubbing of gilt, inner hinges repaired neatly, with very similar replacement paper at front, blank lower portion of title leaf lightly stained, small tear at chip, booklabel of Doxey, Importer, San Francisco. M & S Rare Books, Inc. 90 - 295 2011 $2000

North, Andre *Sargasso of Space: a Dane Thorson-Solar Queen Adventure.* New York: Gnome Press Inc. Pub., 1955, First edition; octavo, boards. L. W. Currey, Inc. 124 - 165 2011 $350

North, Elisha *A Treatise on Malignant Epidemic, Commonly called Spotted Fever, Interspersed with Remarks on the Nature of Fever in General....* New York: T. & J. Swords, 1811, First edition; 12mo., 11, 249 (1), (1) pages, errata leaf and ad leaf, original two toned paper covered boards, portion of printed paper label, spine quite worn, back cover nearly detached, uncut, very good, unusual in original boards. M & S Rare Books, Inc. 90 - 298 2011 $550

North, Marianne *A Vision of Eden.* Webb & Bower, 1980, First edition; large 8vo., original cloth, gilt, dust jacket, pages 240, illustrations in color. R. F. G. Hollett & Son Antiquarian Booksellers General Catalogue Summer 2010 - 1030 2011 £35

Northampton, Henry Howard, Earl of *A Publication of His Majesties Edict and Severe Censure Against Private combats and Combatants.* Robert Parker, 1613, Initial leaf (blank except for signature mark "A"), discarded title soiled, some browning and spotting elsewhere, faint dampmark at foot of some leaves, one with cornertip torn, pages (ii), 119, (1), 4to., modern and morocco, red morocco lettering piece, 2 compartments vertically gilt lettered direct, others plain, older endpapers preserved, front pastedown with old ownership inscription of Charles H. Bayley, good. Blackwell Rare Books B166 - 76 2011 £1250

Norton, Andre *The Defiant Agents.* Cleveland and New York: World Publishing Co., 1962, First edition; octavo, cloth. L. W. Currey, Inc. 124 - 190 2011 $250

Norton, Andre *Galactic Derelict.* Cleveland and New York: World Pub. Co., 1959, First edition; octavo, cloth. L. W. Currey, Inc. 124 - 122 2011 $650

Norton, Andre *Star Born.* Cleveland and New York: World Pub. Co., 1957, First edition; octavo, cloth. L. W. Currey, Inc. 124 - 97 2011 $850

Norton, Andre *Star Guard.* New York: Harcourt Brace and Co., 1955, First edition; octavo, cloth. L. W. Currey, Inc. 124 - 177 2011 $300

Norton, Andre *Star Rangers.* New York: Harcourt Brace and Co., 1953, First edition; cloth, octavo. L. W. Currey, Inc. 124 - 92 2011 $950

Norton, Caroline Elizabeth Sarah *Aunt Carry's Ballads for Children.* London: Joseph Cundall, 1847, First edition; 4to., frontispiece, 7 hand colored plates by John Absolon, original olive green cloth blocked in blind, front board lettered in gilt, slight rubbing, odd small mark, all edges gilt, nice. Jarndyce Antiquarian Booksellers CLXC - 598 2011 £150

Norton, Caroline Elizabeth Sarah *The Lady of La Garaye.* Cambridge & London: Macmillan, 1862, (1861). First edition; half title, frontispiece, 2 plates, 16 page catalog partially unopened, original green glazed cloth, front board elaborately decorated in gilt, back board in blind, spine lettered gilt, very good, inscribed "The Countess of Carnarvon, Xmas 1861". Jarndyce Antiquarian Booksellers CLXC - 599 2011 £50

Norton, Mary *The Borrowers.* New York: Harcourt Brace, 1953, Stated first edition; 8vo., blue pictorial cloth, 180 pages, slight fading on perimeter else fine in near fine dust jacket, there is an extra dust jacket that is slightly frayed at spine ends, special bright copy, illustrations by Beth and Joe Krush. Aleph-Bet Books, Inc. 95 - 396 2011 $600

Norton, Mary *The Borrower's Omnibus.* London: J. M. Dent, 1966, First edition; original cloth, gilt, dust jacket, top edges trifle creased, hinges slightly worn, pages x, 154, color frontispiece and drawings. R. F. G. Hollett & Sons Antiquarian Booksellers 170 - 479 2011 £60

Not Only Possible, but also Necessary: Optimisim in the Age of Global War. Istanbul: Istanbul Foundation for Culture and Arts and Yap Kredi Publications, 2007, First edition; 8vo., wrappers, 666 illustrations, text in Turkish and English, 604 pages, fine in slightly creased, very good+ dust jacket. Any Amount of Books May 29 2011 - A65155 2011 $238

Nouvelle Grammaire Flamnade... Amsterdam: P. Mortier, 1688, 8vo., (4), 156 pages, contemporary calf, upper joint split, from the library of the Earls of Macclesfield at Shirburn Castle. Maggs Bros. Ltd. 1440 - 90 2011 £400

Novok, Daniel A. *The Defense of Personal Injury Actions.* New York?: 1965, 208 pages, original binding. Bookworm & Silverfish 670 - 80 2011 $75

Nowitky, G. I. *Norfolk: the Marine Metropolis of Virginia & the Sound & River Cities of North Carolina.* Norfolk & Raleigh: 1888, (7) 216 (60) ads, pages, black on green cover, rubbed at backstrip edges and corner wear. Bookworm & Silverfish 667 - 188 2011 $125

Noyes, George R. *A New Translation of the Hebrew Prophets, Arranged in Chronological Order.* Boston: 1833, First edition; 3 volumes, bookplate removed, no other marks, 2 volumes, very good, third has 4 inch mend to right of backstrip, all 3 backstrips faded, endpapers foxed. Bookworm & Silverfish 671 - 148 2011 $65

Noyes, John Humphrey *The American Socialist Devoted to the Enlargement and Perfection of Home.* Oneida: 1876-1879, 82 issues, March 30, 1876 to December 18, 1879, folio, unbound, very good broken run. Second Life Books Inc. 174 - 250 2011 $1000

Noyes, John Humphrey *The Circular, Oneida Circular.* 1868-1876, Folio, unbound, 71 issues, Jan. 27 1868 to February 24, 1876.   Second Life Books Inc.   174 - 252   2011 $950

Noyes, John Humphrey *Home-Talks.* Oneida: by the Community, 1875, First edition; volume 1, 8vo., pages 258, brown cloth stamped in gilt, some wear along hinges, tide mark along top of leaves, darker at beginning of book, one leaf loose.   Second Life Books Inc.   174 - 251   2011 $150

Noyes, Pierrepont B. *The Pallid Giant.* New York: Fleming H. Revell Co., 1927, First edition; octavo, cloth.   L. W. Currey, Inc.   124 - 226   2011 $125

Nunn, Kem *Tapping the Source.* New York: Delacorte, 1984, Uncorrected proof copy; light foxing to top edge and tiny spot to fore-edge, near fine in plain yellow printed wrappers.   Ken Lopez Bookseller   154 - 151   2011 $275

Nunn, Kem *Tapping the Source.* New York: Delacorte, 1984, Advance reading copy; faint foxing to top edge, else fine in pictorial wrappers.   Ken Lopez Bookseller   154 - 152   2011 $200

Nunn, Kem *Tapping the Source.* New York: Delacorte, 1984, First edition; review copy, signed by author and dated in 1988, minor foxing to top of text block, several instances of pencil underlinings to text, near fine in very near fine dust jacket with press release and author photo laid in.   Ken Lopez Bookseller   154 - 150   2011 $450

Nunn, Kem *Tapping the Source.* London: Michael Joseph, 1984, First edition; age toning to page edges, else very fine in very near fine dust jacket with hint of crimp to crown.   Ken Lopez Bookseller   154 - 153   2011 $100

Nura *All Aboard We Are Off.* New York: Studio Publications and Junior Literary Guild, 1944, 4to., cloth, fine in dust jacket (very good+, rubbed at folds and frayed at spine ends), color and black and white illustrations.   Aleph-Bet Books, Inc.   95 - 401   2011 $200

Nursery Novelties for Little Masters and Misses. London: J. Harris and Son between, 1819-1824, 7 x 4 1/2 inches, printed stiff paper wrappers with dusting and handling, spine chipped and has been resewn by former owner, titlepage not present and probably missing, since it is the printer listed on verso of title that helps identify the edition so we cannot identify the issue.   Jo Ann Reisler, Ltd.   86 - 91   2011 $600

Nutt, Frederic *The Complete Confectioner; or the Whole Art of Confectionary Made Easy with Receipts for Liqueures, Home Made Wines.* London: J. Smeeton for Mathews and Leight, 1809, Sixth edition; xxiv, 261 pages, (6) pages ads, frontispiece + 10 plates, modern paper covered boards, paper label in period style, untrimmed, considerably foxed.   Joseph J. Felcone Inc.   Fall Miscellany 2010 - 33   2011 $300

O

O'Beirne, H. F. *Leaders and Leading Men of the Indian Territory.* Chicago: American Publisher's Association, 1891, First edition; tall 8vo., 318 (6) pages, original cloth, rubbed, very good, very scarce.   M & S Rare Books, Inc.   90 - 181   2011 $450

O'Brian, Patrick *Capita De mar I Guerra.* Barcelona: Columna Edhasa, 1999, First Catalan edition; this copy signed by author with handwritten letter from author that accompanied the book, fine and unread in European style pictorial wrappers.   Buckingham Books   May 26 2011 - 18303   2011 $2500

O'Brian, Patrick *The Nutmeg of Consolation.* London: Collins, 1991, First edition; 8vo., 315 pages, fine in fine dust jacket.   Any Amount of Books   May 29 2011 - A72738   2011 $221

O'Brian, Patrick *The Road to Samarcand.* London: Rupert Hart Davis, 1954, First edition; pages 255, label removed from flyleaf, leaving slight paste stains, original cloth gilt, dust jacket edges trifle worn and spine slightly dulled.   R. F. G. Hollett & Sons Antiquarian Booksellers   170 - 480   2011   £350

O'Brian, Patrick *The Unknown Shore.* London: Rupert Hart-Davis, 1959, First edition; original cloth, gilt, dust jacket, trifle worn, spine faded, pages 256, scarce.   R. F. G. Hollett & Sons Antiquarian Booksellers   170 - 481   2011   £350

O'Brian, Patrick *The Yellow Admiral.* New York: W. W. Norton, 1996, First edition, first printing; 8vo., 261 pages, fine, fine dust jacket.   By the Book, L. C.   26 - 13   2011 $500

O'Brien, Edna *August is a Wicked Month.* London: Jonathan Cape, 1965, First edition; (221) pages, 8vo., original gray cloth backed boards, gilt lettered spine, very fine with price clipped dust jacket, little dusty, inscribed by author.   Paulette Rose Fine and Rare Books   32 - 133   2011 $125

O'Brien, Henry *The Round Towers of Ireland or The Mysteries of Freemasonry of Sabaism and of Budhism for the First Time Unveiled.* 1834, First edition; half calf, (2), 524 pages, 4 plates, many text illustrations, quarter leather library binding, not a pretty copy, but it has owner inscription of doyen of Cork antiquaries John Windele.   C. P. Hyland   May 26 2011 - 259/350   2011 $362

O'Brien, Michael Fitz-James *The Diamond Lens and Other Stories.* London: Ward & Downey, 1887, Half title, blue cloth blocked in blind and squared pattern, spine faded and worn at head and tail, with George MacDonald's bookplate.   Jarndyce Antiquarian Booksellers   CXCII - 338   2011   £150

O'Brien, Tim *Friends and Enemies.* Teme: Synaesthesia, 2001, Fine, illustrations by Fritz Scholder, fine,.   Bella Luna Books   May 26 2011 - t8273   2011 $192

O'Brien, Tim *Going After Cacciato.* New York: Delacorte Press, 1978, First edition; very good, sunning to edges, spine ends pushed in, dust jacket very good, several 1'8 inch chips along edges, especially at heel of spine, pea size rubbed spot near hinge at top front, very good, several 1/8 inch chips along edges especially at heel of spine.   Bella Luna Books   May 26 2011 - t6482 2011 $192

O'Brien, Tim *If I Die in a Combat Zone.* London: Calder & Boyars, 1973, First British edition; fine, in near fine dust jacket, price clipped, beautiful copy, signed by author.   Bella Luna Books   May 26 2011 - t1736   2011 $577

O'Brien, Tim *If I Die in a Combat Zone/ Box Me Up and Ship Me Home.* NP. but New York: Delacorte Press Seymour Lawrence, 1973, First edition; 8vo., pages (viii), 199, (1) blank, original khaki cloth backstrip over green papered boards, helmet blocked in blind to upper board, spine lettered in black, green endpapers, original color pictorial dust jacket, faint fading to binding edges as often, price clipped dust jacket with shallow crease in bottom edge of rear panel, still fine in very nearly fine dust jacket.   Simon Finch Rare Books   Zero - 258   2011   £900

O'Brien, Tim *In the Lake of the Woods.* Boston: Houghton Mifflin, 1994, Advance reading copy; pictorial wrappers, soft cover, fine, signed by author.   Bella Luna Books   May 29 2011 - t3360   2011 $82

O'Brien, Tim *The Things They Carried.* Boston: Houghton Mifflin, 1990, First edition; fine, dust jacket is fine.   Bella Luna Books   May 29 2011 - 2833   2011 $110

O'Brien, Tim *The Things They Carried.* Franklin Center: Franklin Press, 1990, True first edition; leather, fine copy.   Bella Luna Books   May 26 2011 - t8512   2011 $275

O'Brien, Tim *The Things they Carried.* Boston: Houghton Mifflin, 1990, First edition; near fine, bottom of spine bumped, dust jacket fine.   Bella Luna Books   May 29 2011 - 2836   2011 $99

O'Brien, Tim *The Things They Carried.* Boston: Houghton Mifflin, 1990, First edition; fine in like dust jacket, inscribed by author for John Kirley.   Bella Luna Books   May 29 2011 - t4918   2011 $137

O'Bryen, Denis *Utrum Horum? The Government; or the Country?* London: J. Debrett, 1796, First edition; 8vo., (4), 122, (2) pages, complete with half title and final blank, very small old inkstamp of a Dutch Institution on blank verso of half title, well bound in 18th century style quarter calf, gilt, very good. John Drury Rare Books 153 - 102 2011 £175

O'Connor, Anne *From the Stone Age to the Forty-Five.* Edinburgh: John Donald, 1983, First edition; original cloth, gilt, dust jacket, pages xiii, 621, with portrait and 261 illustrations. R. F. G. Hollett & Son Antiquarian Booksellers 177 - 602 2011 £40

O'Connor, Flannery 1925-1964 *The Violent Bear It Away.* New York: Farrar, Straus & Cudahy, 1960, signed by author in Atlanta on March 18 1960, month after publication; signed copies are rare, fine in near fine dust jacket with some minor spine sunning and trace wear to crown, with faint spotting to rear panel, custom clamshell case, beautiful copy. Ken Lopez Bookseller 154 - 158 2011 $10,000

O'Connor, Flannery 1925-1964 *Wise Blood.* London: Neville Spearman, 1955, First edition; 8vo., original publisher's orange cloth lettered black on spine, pages 232, slight browning to endpapers, else very good+ in complete very good dust jacket with slight soiling on white rear panel and slight sunning at spine, decent collectible copy. Any Amount of Books May 29 2011 - A76081 2011 $230

O'Connor, John *Canals, Barges and People.* London: Art and Technics, 1950, First edition; original cloth backed patterned boards, spine rather faded, pages 96, 24 fine color lithographs, numerous black and white illustrations and maps to endpapers. R. F. G. Hollett & Son Antiquarian Booksellers General Catalogue Summer 2010 - 858 2011 £35

O'Connor, John *The Technique of Wood Engraving.* London: Batsford and New York: Watson Guptill, 1971, First edition; large 8vo., original cloth, gilt, dust jacket, pages 144, with 139 illustrations, fine. R. F. G. Hollett & Son Antiquarian Booksellers General Catalogue Summer 2010 - 286 2011 £35

O'Connor, Robert *Buffalo Soldiers.* New York: Knopf, 1993, First edition; fine in fine dust jacket. Bella Luna Books May 29 2011 - t3368 2011 $82

O'Curry, Eugene *On the Manners & Customs of the Ancient Irish. A Series of Lectures.* 1873, First edition; 3 volumes, (40) cxliv, xix 392, xxiv, 711 pages, original cloth, gilt titling, gilt harp on front boards, blind decorations, corners slightly bumped, some foxing on text, but good tight copy. C. P. Hyland May 26 2011 - 258/687 2011 $797

O'Dell, Scott *Island of the Blue Dolphins.* Boston: Houghton Mifflin, 1960, First edition; 8vo., cloth, fine in very good+ dust jacket, slight chipping to head of spine, no award seal, scarce in first edition. Aleph-Bet Books, Inc. 95 - 402 2011 $400

O'Flaherty, Liam 1897-1984 *The Assassin.* London: Cae, 1928, First edition; 288 pages, crown 8vo., original red cloth, backstrip gilt lettered, with first issue blue and red dust jacket, red on backstrip panel faded to pale pink, near fine. Blackwell Rare Books B166 - 199 2011 £150

O'Flaherty, Liam 1897-1984 *Return of the Brute.* Mandrake, 1929, First edition; pages (ii), 190, foolscap 8vo., original light brown dampstained cloth, backstrip blocked in green, endpapers browned, chipped dust jacket, good, scarce in jacket, signed by author. Blackwell Rare Books B166 - 200 2011 £300

O'Flaherty, Liam 1897-1984 *Thy Neighbours Wife.* 1923, First edition; signed presentation copy, dust jacket slightly chipped, very good, very scarce in this condition, signed by author. C. P. Hyland May 26 2011 - 255/573 2011 $399

O'Flanagan, James R. *The Blackwater in Munster.* 1844, First edition; map, 3 plates, viii, 176 pages, some foxing, original cloth, all edges gilt. C. P. Hyland May 26 2011 - 259/377 2011 $290

O'Flanagan, James R. *Impressions at Home and Abroad; or a Year of Real Life.* London: Smith, Elder, 1837, 2 volumes, xxviii, 324; viii, 347 pages, original quarter cloth, worn, labels still on spine but dull, volume I lacks front flyleaf. C. P. Hyland May 26 2011 - 259/376 2011 $290

O'Halloran, Sylvester *An Introduction to the Study of the History and Antiquities of Ireland.* London: 1772, First edition; 4to., xx (2) 284 pages, missing pages ix-xvi of "Preliminary Discourse" but as the binding is a full calf contemporary, it would appear that the defect lay with the original printed binder, appendices are on different paper to the remainder of the text, and have accumulated foxing not in the remainder, these defects excepted, a very good copy. C. P. Hyland May 26 2011 - 258/721 2011 $652

O'Hara, Frank *A City Winter and Other Poems.* New York: De Nagy Gallery, 1951, One of 20 copies Printed by hand in Bodoni types on Japanese Kochi paper by Ruthven Todd; specially bound with original drawing by Larry Rivers as frontispiece, tall 8vo., reproductions of 2 drawings by Rivers, original cloth backed decorated boards, edges bit rubbed, spine lightly faded, but very good, rare issue, preserved in scarlet half morocco slipcase. James S. Jaffe Rare Books May 26 2011 - 13180 2011 $15,000

O'Hara, Frank *Meditations in an Emergency.* New York: Grove Press, 1957, First edition, one of an unknown number of unnumbered (out of series) hardbound copies, perhaps author's copies, out of a total of 90 cloth bound copies; small 8vo., original green cloth, glassine dust jacket, very fine, lacking slipcase, presentation copy inscribed by author to James Schuyler for Jimmy and Alfred and Guinevere. James S. Jaffe Rare Books   May 26 2011 - 13191 2011 $7500

O'Hara, Frank *Meditations in an Emergency.* New York: Grove Press, 1957, First edition; 8vo., 54 pages, original publisher's grey printed (black) thin card covers, covers faintly marked and slightly toned but overall, sound, clean, very good copy.   Any Amount of Books   May 29 2011 - A74553 2011 $213

O'Hara, John 1905-1970 *Hope of Heaven.* New York: Harcourt Brace, 1938, First edition; near fine, with very light use, very good dust jacket, light creasing and very small chips to extremities,.   Bella Luna Books   May 26 2011 - t8127CO 2011 $220

O'Hara, John 1905-1970 *The Instrument.* New York: 1967, First edition; 1/300 copies signed by author, as new in acetate dust jacket and slipcase.   Gemini Fine Books & Arts, Ltd.   Art Reference & Illustrated Books: First Editions 2011 $150

O'Hara, John 1905-1970 *Lovey Childs.* New York: 1969, First edition, 1/200 copies signed by John O'Hara; as new in acetate dust jacket and slipcase.   Gemini Fine Books & Arts, Ltd.   Art Reference & Illustrated Books: First Editions 2011 $150

O'Hara, John 1905-1970 *Sweet and Sour.* New York: Random House, 1954, First printing; 8vo., pages 162, very tight copy in chipped, rubbed and faded dust jacket. Second Life Books Inc.   174 - 253 2011 $75

O'Hara, John 1905-1970 *Waiting for Winter.* New York: 1966, First edition, 1/300 copies signed by author; cloth, acetate dust jacket, slipcase, as new.   Gemini Fine Books & Arts, Ltd.   Art Reference & Illustrated Books: First Editions 2011 $150

O'Henry Memorial Prize Short Stories. New York: 1919-1964, 1919, 1923, 1925-1926, 1928, 1930, 1933-1936, 1941-1943, 1945-1946, 1948, 1954, 1964, 21 volumes, volume 1 being privately printed presentation copy limited to 400 numbered copies.   I. D. Edrich   May 26 2011 - 99489 2011 $398

O'Meara, James *The Vigilance Committee of 1856.* First edition with 1887 date on titlepage and 1890 date on cover; 12mo., 57 pages, original pink printed wrappers, lightly faded near spine, fine.   Argonaut Book Shop   Recent Acquisitions Summer 2010 - 222 2011 $150

O'Nan, Stewart *Faithful: Two Diehard Boston Red Sox Fans Chronicle the Historic 2004 Season.* New York: Scribner, 2004, First edition; dust jacket fine, signed and dated by O'Nan 12/2/04.   Bella Luna Books   May 29 2011 - t7030 2011 $82

O'Nan, Stewart *In the Walled City.* Pittsburg: University of Pittsburgh Press, 1993, First edition; fine in fine dust jacket, signed by author.   Bella Luna Books   May 29 2011 - t4937 2011 $82

O'Nan, Stewart *Snow Angels.* New York: Doubleday, 1994, Uncorrected proof; book condition is near fine, smudges, one small ink mark, signed by author.   Bella Luna Books   May 26 2011 - p2085 2011 $165

O'Nan, Stewart *Snow Angels.* New York: Doubleday, 1994, Labeled uncorrected proof; pictorial wrappers, near fine, slight creasing to front cover, signed by author.   Bella Luna Books   May 29 2011 - p2086 2011 $137

O'Nan, Stewart *Snow Angels.* New York: Doubleday, 1994, First edition; fine in like dust jacket.   Bella Luna Books   May 29 2011 - 6390 2011 $137

O'Neil, A., Mrs. *A Dictionary of Spanish Painters, Comprehending Simply that Part of their Biography, Immediately Connected with the Arts...*   C. O'Neil, 1834, First edition; Large 8vo., 2 volumes, xv, 1 280; (2) 308 pages, half titles, engraved plates, full contemporary pebble grain morocco with gilt panels, gilt decorated spines, all edges gilt, library stamps on verso of titles and some foxing to plates.   Ken Spelman Rare Books   68 - 29 2011 £220

O'Neil, Owen Rowe *Adventures in Swaziland: the story of a South African Boer.* London: George Allen & Unwin, 1921, First UK edition; 8vo., pages xii, 381, illustrations, original red cloth.   J. & S. L. Bonham Antiquarian Booksellers   Africa 4/20/2011 - 6457 2011   £35

O'Neill, Eugene Gladstone *Days Without End.* New York: Random House, 1934, First edition; limited to 325 copies, signed by author, this #261, leather almost entirely worn off spine and off edges, interior tight and clean, fair. G. H. Mott Bookseller   May 26 2011 - 8437 2011 $200

O'Neill, Rose *The Kewpies their Book.* New York: Stokes, Nov., 1913, First edition; 4to., boards, pictorial paste-on, fine in tattered and worn dust jacket with some pieces off, beautiful copy, rare in dust jacket, illustrations by author.   Aleph-Bet Books, Inc.   95 - 403 2011 $1500

O'Reilly, Eleanor Grace *Sussex Stories.* London: Strahan and Co., 1880, First edition; half titles, 10 illustrations, original pebble grained red/brown cloth, borders in blind, spines lettered in gilt, spine and boards affected by damp volume I, inner hinges cracking with some old tape repairs, good, sound copy, scarce. Jarndyce Antiquarian Booksellers CLXC - 672 2011 £150

O'Riordain, Sean P. *Antiquities of the Irish Countryside.* London: Methuen, 1953, Third edition; Original cloth, gilt, dust jacket (top and base of spine defective), pages xii 108, 88 plates and 5 text illustrations, from the library of Dr. Arthur Raistrick with his bookplate and signature. R. F. G. Hollett & Son Antiquarian Booksellers 177 - 604 2011 £35

O'Shaughnessy, Arthur *Songs of a Worker.* London: Chatto & Windus, 1881, First edition; 8vo., original deep blue cloth lettered gilt on spine, pages xv, 212, pages uncut at edges, very scarce, bookplate of Herbert and Jessie Elkington, prelims slightly foxed, otherwise fine, exceptional condition. Any Amount of Books May 26 2011 - A68492 2011 $419

O'Toole, Judith Hansen *Severin Roesen.* Lewisburg, London & Toronto: Bucknell University Press/Associated University Presses, 1992, First edition; 4to., illustrations in color and black and white, pages 139, sound, very good in like dust jacket, book has very slight marks to covers, dust jacket slightly creased at edges. Any Amount of Books May 26 2011 - A73780 2011 $671

Oakeshott, W. F. *Oxford Stone Restored.* Oxford: Oxford Historic Building Fund, 1975, Tall 8vo., pages viii, 122, with 51 plates, 4 plates of drawings, 12th report of Oxford Historic Buildings Fund pages 12, 1975, loosely inserted, fine. R. F. G. Hollett & Son Antiquarian Booksellers 177 - 605 2011 £45

Oates, George *Interest Tables in Which is Shown the Interest on any Sum From $1 to $10,000 at 6 & 7 Per Centum per Annum.* Philadelphia: 1843, First edition; viii, (105) tables, 18 (tables) pages, 6.75 x 7.25, full suede modest cover bow, gilt on label bright, corners sharp, modest foxing. Bookworm & Silverfish 676 - 30 2011 $275

Oates, George *Tables of Interest & Exchange in Which are Shown the Interest of any Sum.* Philadelphia: 1843, First edition; 4to., good in decorated suede, top cover loose, modest foxing. Bookworm & Silverfish 676 - 32 2011 $150

Oates, Joyce Carol 1938- *Cybele.* Santa Barbara: Black Sparrow, 1979, First edition; number 64 of 300 copies signed by Oates, cloth in acetate dust jacket, as new. Gemini Fine Books & Arts, Ltd. Art Reference & Illustrated Books: First Editions 2011 $60

Obama, Barack *The Audacity of Hope.* New York: Crown, 2006, First edition; near fine, small open tear and coffee stains on titlepage, in fine dust jacket. Bella Luna Books May 29 2011 - t9134d 2011 $137

Obama, Barack *The Audacity of Hope.* New York: Crown, 2006, First edition; near fine, shows very light use, dust jacket fine. Bella Luna Books May 26 2011 - t9058 2011 $302

Obama, Barack *Dreams from My Father.* New York: Random House, 2004, First printing (with a "1" in the number run) of the large print edition; includes president's 2004 keynote address to the Democratic National Convention, near fine in close to fine dust jacket. Lupack Rare Books May 26 2011 - ABE1526785037 2011 $100

Object ABC Book. Akron: Saalfield, 1926, 8 3/4 x 5 3/4 inches, slight fraying and soil, very good+, illustrations in bright colors. Aleph-Bet Books, Inc. 95 - 11 2011 $200

Observations on Modern Gardening. London: T. Payne, 1771, Third edition; 8vo., full brown leather with decorated gilt at spine, raised bands and gilt title on red label, blank (6) 257, ornate armorial bookplate of Agneu (Baronet) of Lochnau, pencilled ownership signature of F. R. Cowell, author of The Garden as a Fine Art, very handsome very good, slightly rubbed at corner, slightly tender at hinges. Any Amount of Books May 29 2011 - A47683 2011 $408

Observations on the Bristol Union Insurance Office: Being a Series of Letters, Which Recently appeared in the Bristol Observer Newspaper. Bristol: printed by H. Savery, 1819, First edition; apparently very rare, 8vo., 21, (1) pages, preserved in modern wrappers with printed title label on upper cover, partially unopened, very good, apparently very rare. John Drury Rare Books 153 - 18 2011 £300

Occo, Adolf *Impp. Romanorum Numismata a Pompeio Magno ad Heraclium... Summa Diligentia & Magno Labhore Collecta ab Adolpho Occone R. P. Aug. medico...* Antwerp: Christopher Plantin for the author, 1579, (1578). First edition; 4to., (16), 398, (10), (5 blank) pages, printer's device on titlepage, initials, contemporary calf, titlepage torn with loss of lower right corner (repaired, first page torn with loss (repaired), both not affecting text, from the library of the Earls of Macclesfield at Shirburn Castle. Maggs Bros. Ltd. 1440 - 159 2011 £500

Odlum, Jerome *Each Dawn I Die.* Indianapolis and New York: Bobbs Merrill Co., 1938, First edition; spine heavily bleached, good only in internally lined, good dust jacket with small chip at crown, inscribed by author to Jennie and Lee Luschier, scarce in jacket, especially signed. Between the Covers 169 - BTC347393 2011 $2200

Oe, Kenzaburo *A Healing Family.* Tokyo: Kodansha, 1995, First American edition; fine, dust jacket in very good++ dust jacket (mild chips). By the Book, L. C. 26 - 14 2011 $70

Official Records Union and Confederate Armies. Series 1 Volume 47 Parts 1-3. Washington: 1895, 3300 pages, 3 volumes, original black cloth, ex-library, books repaired and ready to use. Bookworm & Silverfish 666 - 31 2011 $100

Official Records Union and Confederate Armies. Series 4 volumes 2 and 3 (only). Washington: 1900, 2 volumes, original black cloth, ex-library, book repaired and ready to use,. Bookworm & Silverfish 666 - 35 2011 $75

Offutt, Chris *Kentucky Straight.* New York: Vintage, 1992, First printing, paperback edition; pictorial wrappers, very good, minor creasing and edge wear, scarce, signed by author. Bella Luna Books May 29 2011 - t1285 2011 $110

Offutt, Chris *Tar Pit Love, Lettered.* Bella Luna Books, 2000, First edition; one of 26 lettered copies on handade paper, fine. Bella Luna Books May 29 2011 - t9057 2011 $82

Ogden, Peter Skene *Trait of American Indian Life...* London: Smith, Elder and Co., 1853, First edition; original cloth, pages vii-xiv, 218 pages, 16 pages of ads by publisher, ex-library copy with 1.5 inch library stamp on verso of titlepage and in lower fore corner of 3 other pages, previous owner's name and date at top edge of front free endpaper, some modest sunning to spine and some very slight edgewear, else near fine, rare in exceptional condition, slipcase. Buckingham Books May 26 2011 - 26900 2011 $3000

Ogilvie, William *Early Days on the Yukon & the Story of Its Gold Finds.* Ottawa: 1913, xii, 306 pages, illustrations, original red cloth, some external soil, internally clean and very good. Dumont Maps & Books of the West 111 - 74 2011 $175

Ogilvie, William *Early Days on the Yukon and the Story of Its Gold Finds.* Ottawa: Thorburn & Abbott, 1913, First Canadian edition; small octavo, xii, 306 pages, 26 photo plates, 6 portraits, publisher's red cloth gilt, spine lightly faded, slight foxing to extreme top edge and fore edge of text block, very good. Argonaut Book Shop Recent Acquisitions Summer 2010 - 154 2011 $250

Ohara, Ken *One.* Tokyo: Tsukiji Shokan, 1970, First edition; signed, 4to., pages (500), 500 black and white photos, original black and white photo illustrated wrappers, spine printed red, very light toning to top edge, original black and white photo illustrated dust jacket, spine printed red, inside of dust jacket lightly rubbed with very thin strip of toning to upper edge, price clipped, publisher's ticket laid in, Ohara's signature, near fine. Simon Finch Rare Books Zero - 542 2011 £3000

Ohwi, Jisaburo *Flora of Japan (in English).* Washington: Smithsonian Inst., 1965, Thick 4to., original green cloth gilt, pages ix, 1067, with 16 plates and 17 figures, maps on endpapers, near fine, scarce. R. F. G. Hollett & Son Antiquarian Booksellers General Catalogue Summer 2010 - 1031 2011 £150

Olby, Robert *The Path to the Double.* Seattle: University of Washington Press, 1974, First American edition; 8vo., xxiii, 510 pages, very good++, minimal soil and foxing to edges, cover corners bumped, very good++ dust jacket with mild edge wear, short closed tears, from the library of Erwin Chargaff. By the Book, L. C. 26 - 89 2011 $500

Old Citizen *Hints for the Enlarging and Improvement of the Harbour of Leith.* Edinburgh: 1787, First edition; folio, dated at head of drop-head title, 4 pages, docket title (soiled) on lower part of page 4, text slightly browned, as folded. Anthony W. Laywood May 26 2011 - 21569 2011 $444

Old Dutch Nursery Rhymes. London: Augener, Philadelphia: McKay, 1917, First edition; illustrations on Le Mair, printed on glossy art paper, text and musical notation all printed in pale grey, 15 color printed plates on verso of each leaf, musical notation on each page opposing page, with further color printed plate on titlepage, hinges substantially stained, pages (ii), 32, (2), oblong royal 8vo., original light blue cloth, little waterstained, backstrip and front cover gilt lettered, Le Mair color plate on front cover, rubbed at corners, including backstrip head and tail, good, translator's (R. H. Elkin) presentation. Blackwell Rare Books B166 - 174 2011 £100

Old Father Christmas. London: Ernest Nister circa, 1890, Shapebook cut around outline of giant Christmas tree being carried by Father Christmas, book is 10 x 7 inches, some light wear to covers which are full color pictorial, internally there are 14 pages (counting inside covers), 10 full color chromolithographic illustrations plus some black and whites by C. S. Flint. Jo Ann Reisler, Ltd. 86 - 39 2011 $400

Old Nursery Rhymes with Crimes Collected and Arranged by a Peal of (Bells). London: Bell & Daldy, 1863, Pages 40 of music and verses, the word "Bells" is represented on the title and upper board with picture of three bells, original cloth backed boards, neatly recased. R. F. G. Hollett & Sons Antiquarian Booksellers 170 - 19 2011 £45

The Old Nursery Stories and Rhymes. Blackie & Son, n.d., 4to., original pictorial cloth, gilt, corners trifle bumped, neatly recased, top edges gilt, unpaginated, illustrations in color, old tape removed from gutters, some neat repairs in places and few light pencil scribbles, first few leaves little spotted, generally very good. R. F. G. Hollett & Sons Antiquarian Booksellers 170 - 314 2011 £150

Old Time Fairy Tales and Nursery Rhymes. London: Raphael Tuck & Sons, n.d., 1931, First edition; original red cloth gilt, over bevelled boards with pictorial and lettered paper onlay to upper board, spines faded, pages 248, (viii), 6 color plates and numerous black and white illustrations by Jennie Harbour, scattered spotting. R. F. G. Hollett & Sons Antiquarian Booksellers 170 - 305 2011 £95

Old Time Fairy Tales and Nursery Rhymes. London: Raphael Tuck & Sons, n.d., 1931, Pages 248, (viii), complete with 6 color plates, numerous black and white illustrations, triangular nick cut from fore-edge of some 15 leaves, scattered spotting, variant binding of coarse weave pictorial cloth lettered in red, spine faded, binding indicates that this is a reissue, text and plates identical to those of first edition. R. F. G. Hollett & Sons Antiquarian Booksellers 170 - 306 2011 £35

Oldham, J. Basil *English Blind-Stamped Bindings. The Sandars Lectures 1949.* Cambridge: Cambridge University Press, 1952, First edition (750 copies); tall folio, original blue buckram gilt with leather spine label, dust jacket, few spots in places, pages xiii, 73, plus 61 plates, few spots in fore-edge. R. F. G. Hollett & Son Antiquarian Booksellers General Catalogue Summer 2010 - 287 2011 £180

Oldham, Wilfrid *Britain's Convicts to the Colonies.* Sydney: Library of Australian History, 1990, Original boards, dust jacket, pages xiii, 270, with 7 plates, few spots to front endpapers. R. F. G. Hollett & Son Antiquarian Booksellers 175 - 1019 2011 £30

Oldmixon, John *The History and Life of Admiral Blake; General and Admiral of the Fleets and Naval Forces of England...* London: printed for R. Davis and J. Millan, 1746, Second edition; 12mo., pages (xvi) 128, engraved portrait frontispiece, early 21st century retrospective sheep binding by Chris Weston, some spotting and dust soiling, from the collection of Christopher Ernest Weston 1947-2010. Unsworths Booksellers 24 - 127 2011 £300

Oliphant, Margaret Oliphant Wilson 1828-1897 *The Autobiography and Letters.* Edinburgh: William Blackwood & Sons, 1899, First edition; half title, frontispiece and plate, original dark blue cloth, spine lettered in gilt, very good, bright copy. Jarndyce Antiquarian Booksellers CLXC - 652 2011 £60

Oliphant, Margaret Oliphant Wilson 1828-1897 *A Beleaguered City; Being a Narrative of Certain Recent Events in the City of Semur, in the Department of the Haute Bourgogne.* London: Macmillan, 1892, Half title, 4 pages ads + 55 page catalog (Aug. 1891), original red cloth, spine darkened. Jarndyce Antiquarian Booksellers CLXC - 602 2011 £45

Oliphant, Margaret Oliphant Wilson 1828-1897 *The Cuckoo in the Nest.* London: Hutchinson & Co., 1892, First edition; 3 volumes, half titles removed, original light blue embossed cloth, spines lettered in gilt, little dulled and rubbed, good plus. Jarndyce Antiquarian Booksellers CLXC - 613 2011 £380

Oliphant, Margaret Oliphant Wilson 1828-1897 *The Cuckoo in the Nest.* London: Hutchinson & Co., 1894, Sixth edition; half title, plates, 32 page catalog (Oct. 1893), some light foxing in prelims, little loose, original dark green cloth, spine decorated and lettered in gilt. Jarndyce Antiquarian Booksellers CLXC - 614 2011 £40

Oliphant, Margaret Oliphant Wilson 1828-1897 *The Curate in Charge.* London: Macmillan, 1894, 6 pages ads + 48 page catalog (April 1894), original red brown cloth, slightly dulled and marked, good sound. Jarndyce Antiquarian Booksellers CLXC - 615 2011 £40

Oliphant, Margaret Oliphant Wilson 1828-1897 *The Curate in Charge.* London: Macmillan, 1902, 6 pages ads (10.5.02), original olive green cloth, lettered in blind and gilt, spine faded to brown, boards affected by damp, good, sound copy, signed "Mrs. Jack Canterbury 1902". Jarndyce Antiquarian Booksellers CLXC - 616 2011 £35

Oliphant, Margaret Oliphant Wilson 1828-1897 *The Days of My Life.* London: Ward, Lock and Co., 1882, New edition; half title, 18 page catalog, some light foxing in prelims, original brown cloth blocked in black and cream, lettered in gilt, armorial bookplate and stamp of Sir Alfred Sherlock Gooch, very good. Jarndyce Antiquarian Booksellers CLXC - 617 2011 £60

Oliphant, Margaret Oliphant Wilson 1828-1897 *For Love and Life.* London: Chapman & Hall, 1880, Fourth edition; contemporary half black sheep, slight wear to head and tail of spine, signed "Ailsie North, Thurland Castle". Jarndyce Antiquarian Booksellers CLXC - 618 2011 £40

Oliphant, Margaret Oliphant Wilson 1828-1897 *The Fugitives.* Leipzig: Bernhard Tauchnitz, 1890, Copyright edition; half title, 16 page catalog Feb. 1891, uncut, original printed paper wrappers, signed Adelaide de Reding, Vinzel. Jarndyce Antiquarian Booksellers CLXC - 619 2011 £45

Oliphant, Margaret Oliphant Wilson 1828-1897 *Harry Muir.* London: Chapman & Hall, 1878, Third edition; slightly cut down in contemporary pale blue binder's cloth, very good.   Jarndyce Antiquarian Booksellers   CLXC - 621   2011   £45

Oliphant, Margaret Oliphant Wilson 1828-1897 *He That Will Not When He May.* London: Macmillan, 1880, First edition; 3 volumes, half titles, 4 pages ads, volume III, library labels removed from endpapers, inner hinges glued, original slate grey cloth, rubbed and dulled but sound.   Jarndyce Antiquarian Booksellers   CLXC - 622 2011   £150

Oliphant, Margaret Oliphant Wilson 1828-1897 *Historical Sketches of the Reign of George Second.* Edinburgh & London: William Blackwood and Sons, 1869, First edition; 2 volumes, half titles, original purple cloth, spines lettered in gilt, slight dampmarking in lower margin, otherwise good plus.   Jarndyce Antiquarian Booksellers   CLXC - 623   2011   £110

Oliphant, Margaret Oliphant Wilson 1828-1897 *A House in Bloomsbury.* New York: Dodd, Mead & Co., 1894, First American edition; original grey cloth, blocked with floral design in dark green lettered in gilt, spine slightly dulled, R. G. Taylor booklabel, very good.   Jarndyce Antiquarian Booksellers   CLXC - 624   2011   £120

Oliphant, Margaret Oliphant Wilson 1828-1897 *Innocent: a Tale of Modern Life.* Leipzig: Bernhard Tauchnitz, 1873, Copyright edition; 2 volumes, half titles, contemporary half dark green morocco, green marbled boards, gilt spines, very good.   Jarndyce Antiquarian Booksellers   CLXC - 625 2011   £65

Oliphant, Margaret Oliphant Wilson 1828-1897   *It Was a Lover and His Lass.* Leipzig: Bernhard Tauchnitz, 1883, Copyright edition; 3 volumes, half titles, uncut in original cream printed wrappers, spines slightly darkened, chipped at head (volume I) and tail (volume II), good plus.   Jarndyce Antiquarian Booksellers   CLXC - 626   2011   £45

Oliphant, Margaret Oliphant Wilson 1828-1897 *Jerusalem: Its History and Hope.* London: Macmillan, 1891, First edition; half title, frontispiece, illustrations, contemporary half maroon morocco, rubbed but sound.   Jarndyce Antiquarian Booksellers   CLXC - 627   2011   £45

Oliphant, Margaret Oliphant Wilson 1828-1897 *Kirsteen: the Story of a Scotch Family Seventy Years Ago.* London: Macmillan, 1891, Second edition; half title, 4 pages ads + 47 page catalog (June 1893), original red cloth, spine faded, ownership inscription Christmas 1911 good plus copy.   Jarndyce Antiquarian Booksellers   CLXC - 628   2011   £40

Oliphant, Margaret Oliphant Wilson 1828-1897 *Magdalen Hepburn; a Story of the Scottish Reformation.* London: Ward Lock and Co., 1882, New edition; half title, 16 page catalog, original brown cloth blocked in black and cream, lettered in gilt, slight rubbed, armorial bookplate and stamp of Sir Alfred Sherlock Gooch, very good.   Jarndyce Antiquarian Booksellers   CLXC - 629 2011   £60

Oliphant, Margaret Oliphant Wilson 1828-1897 *The Makers of Florence, Dante, Giotto, Savonarola and their City.* London: Macmillan and Co., 1908, Half title, frontispiece, plates, illustrations, final ad leaf, slight browning to endpapers, original dark green cloth, spine lettered in gilt, very good, bright.   Jarndyce Antiquarian Booksellers   CLXC - 631 2011   £35

Oliphant, Margaret Oliphant Wilson 1828-1897 *The Makers of Modern Rome.* London: Macmillan, 1897, Second edition; half title, frontispiece, plates and illustrations, 2 pages following ads, original dark green cloth, spine lettered in gilt, front board with motif of crossed keys in gilt, evidence of label removed from leading pastedown, very good.   Jarndyce Antiquarian Booksellers   CLXC - 632   2011   £65

Oliphant, Margaret Oliphant Wilson 1828-1897 *Margaret Maitland of Sunnyside.* London: Thomas Hodgson, 1855, Half title, contemporary green binder's cloth, spine lettered in gilt, bit rubbed and marked, stamp of Faithlegg House, good, sound copy.   Jarndyce Antiquarian Booksellers   CLXC - 633 2011   £50

Oliphant, Margaret Oliphant Wilson 1828-1897 *Margaret Maitland of Sunnyside.* New York: G. P. Putnam & Vo., 1856, First American edition; 12 page catalog, original dark green cloth by Davies & Hands, boards blocked in blind, spine lettered gilt, very slight rubbing to tail of spine, very good, bright.   Jarndyce Antiquarian Booksellers   CLXC - 634   2011   £120

Oliphant, Margaret Oliphant Wilson 1828-1897   *The Marriage of Elinor.* London: Macmillan & Co., 1892, Second edition; half title, 4 pages ads (coded 20.7.92) + 44 page catalog (Sept. 1892), original red cloth, spine faded and rubbed.   Jarndyce Antiquarian Booksellers   CLXC - 635   2011   £60

Oliphant, Margaret Oliphant Wilson 1828-1897   *The Marriage of Elinor.* Leipzig: Heinemann and Balestier, 1892, Volumes; 2 volumes, half titles, contemporary half red morocco, spines gilt ruled, spines worn at heads.   Jarndyce Antiquarian Booksellers   CLXC - 636 2011   £35

Oliphant, Margaret Oliphant Wilson 1828-1897   *May.* London: Ward, Lock and Co., 1882, New edition; half title, 22 page catalog, original brown cloth, blocked in black and cream, lettered in gilt, armorial bookplate and stamp of Sir Alfred Sherlock Gooch.   Jarndyce Antiquarian Booksellers   CLXC - 637 2011   £60

Oliphant, Margaret Oliphant Wilson   1828-1897
Memoir of the Life of Laurence Oliphant and of Alice Oliphant, His Wife.   Edinburgh: William Blackwood and Sons, 1891, First edition; 2 volumes, half titles, frontispieces, 24 page catalog, volume I, final ad leaf volume II, original blue cloth, bevelled boards, lettered in gilt, spines slightly dulled, bit rubbed, each volume signed by E. Healey in contemporary hand, with W. H. Smith Circulating library labels.   Jarndyce Antiquarian Booksellers   CLXC - 640   2011   £80

Oliphant, Margaret Oliphant Wilson   1828-1897
Memoir of the Life of Laurence Oliphant and of Alice Oliphant, His Wife.   Edinburgh: William Blackwood and Sons, 1891, Second edition; 2 volumes, half titles, frontispieces, 24 page catalog, volume 1, final ad leaf volume II, original blue cloth lettered in gilt, slight rubbing, good plus.   Jarndyce Antiquarian Booksellers   CLXC - 641   2011   £85

Oliphant, Margaret Oliphant Wilson   1828-1897
Memoir of the Life of Laurence Oliphant and of Alice Oliphant, His Wife.   Edinburgh: William Blackwood, 1892, New edition; 2 pages ads, preceding half title, frontispiece, partially unopened, uncut in original blue cloth, lettered in gilt, spine slightly dulled, some slight rubbing, good plus.   Jarndyce Antiquarian Booksellers   CLXC - 642   2011   £60

Oliphant, Margaret Oliphant Wilson   1828-1897
Memoirs and Resolutions of Adam Graeme of Mossgray.   London: Hurst and Blackett, circa, 1880, Engraved frontispiece, final ad leaf, original fine grained purple cloth, boards blocked in blind, spine blocked and lettered in gilt, slight rubbing.   Jarndyce Antiquarian Booksellers   CLXC - 638   2011   £65

Oliphant, Margaret Oliphant Wilson   1828-1897
Memoirs and Resolutions of Adam Graeme of Mossgray.   London: Hurst and Blackett, circa, 1890?, Half title, lacks leading f.e.p. original red pink cloth, spine lettered in black and gilt, faded and bit dulled.   Jarndyce Antiquarian Booksellers   CLXC - 639   2011   £50

Oliphant, Margaret Oliphant Wilson   1828-1897   *Miss Marjoribanks.*   London: William Blackwood and Sons, circa, 1885, Half title, ads on yellow endpapers, original brick red sand grained cloth, spine lettered in gilt, slight marking to front board.   Jarndyce Antiquarian Booksellers   CLXC - 611   2011   £40

Oliphant, Margaret Oliphant Wilson   1828-1897   *Mrs. Arthur.*   London: George Routledge, 1891, Half title, 6 pages ads, endpapers browned, original red cloth, lettered in gilt and blind, spine slightly faded, good plus.   Jarndyce Antiquarian Booksellers   CLXC - 643   2011   £40

Oliphant, Margaret Oliphant Wilson   1828-1897   *The Mystery of Mrs. Blencarrow.*   London: Richard Edward King, circa., 1895, Half title, browned, original black cloth, front board decorated with floral design in blind, lettered in silver, spine faded and little rubbed at head and tail, inner hinges slightly weak.   Jarndyce Antiquarian Booksellers   CLXC - 644   2011   £35

Oliphant, Margaret Oliphant Wilson   1828-1897   *The Perpetual Curate.*   London: William Blackwood and Sons, 1865, New edition; half title, 4 pages ads + 24 page catalog but misbound, original brick red pebble grained cloth, spine lettered gilt, slightly dulled, blindstamp of Holden Booksellers, Liverpool, nice.   Jarndyce Antiquarian Booksellers   CLXC - 609   2011   £65

Oliphant, Margaret Oliphant Wilson   1828-1897   *The Perpetual Curate.*   New York: Harper and Bros., 1865, First American edition; text in two columns, original brown cloth, spine lettered gilt, spine carefully repaired at head and tail.   Jarndyce Antiquarian Booksellers   CLXC - 610   2011   £120

Oliphant, Margaret Oliphant Wilson   1828-1897
Phoebe, Junior.   Leipzig: Bernhard Tauchnitz, 1876, Copyright edition; 2 volumes, half titles, contemporary half green calf, spines with raised gilt bands, red leather labels, little darkened and slightly rubbed, John Barker booklabels.   Jarndyce Antiquarian Booksellers   CLXC - 612   2011   £45

Oliphant, Margaret Oliphant Wilson   1828-1897   *Royal Edinburgh: Her Saints, Kings, Prophets and Poets.*   London: Macmillan and Co., 1893, Half title, frontispiece, plates and illustrations, original dark green cloth, blocked and lettered in gilt, owner's inscription, top edge gilt, very good.   Jarndyce Antiquarian Booksellers   CLXC - 646   2011   £40

Oliphant, Margaret Oliphant Wilson   1828-1897   *Salem Chapel.*   London: William Blackwood and Sons, 1864, First one volume edition; half title, 20 page catalog, prelims little browned, original brick red pebble grained cloth, spine lettered in gilt, spine little darkened and slightly rubbed, blindstamp of Holden booksellers, Liverpool, good, sound copy.   Jarndyce Antiquarian Booksellers   CLXC - 605   2011   £60

Oliphant, Margaret Oliphant Wilson   1828-1897   *Salem Chapel.*   Leipzig: Bernhard Tauchnitz, 1870, Copyright edition; 2 volumes in 1, contemporary half dark green morocco, very good, bound without half titles.   Jarndyce Antiquarian Booksellers   CLXC - 606   2011   £40

Oliphant, Margaret Oliphant Wilson 1828-1897 *Salem Chapel and The Doctor's Family.* London: William Blackwood & Sons, 1902, New edition; half title, 32 page catalog (coded 6/02), original olive green cloth lettered in black and gilt, spine very slightly rubbed, very good, Renier booklabel.   Jarndyce Antiquarian Booksellers   CLXC - 608   2011   £35

Oliphant, Margaret Oliphant Wilson 1828-1897 *A Son of the Soil.* London: Macmillan and Co., 1894, Half title, final ad leaf, original red cloth, lettered in black, spine dulled and bit marked.   Jarndyce Antiquarian Booksellers   CLXC - 647   2011   £40

Oliphant, Margaret Oliphant Wilson 1828-1897 *Stories of the Seen and Unseen.* London: William Blackwood and Sons, 1902, First English edition; half title, original olive green cloth, blocked with floral design in blind, lettered in gilt, front inner hinge cracking, slightly dulled, top edge gilt, good plus.   Jarndyce Antiquarian Booksellers   CLXC - 648   2011   £200

Oliphant, Margaret Oliphant Wilson 1828-1897 *Thomas Chalmers: Preacher, Philosopher and Statesman.* London: Methuen & Co., 1893, First edition; half title, frontispiece, 16 page catalog (Oct. 1892), uncut in original dark brown buckram, spine lettered in gilt, leading inner hinge slightly cracked, spine darkened and slightly rubbed, old library stamp, mostly erased, good, sound copy.   Jarndyce Antiquarian Booksellers   CLXC - 649   2011   £35

Oliphant, Margaret Oliphant Wilson 1828-1897 *The Victorian Age of English Literature.* London: Percival & Co., 1892, First edition; 2 volumes, half titles, some light foxing, partially unopened in original royal blue cloth, spines lettered in gilt, very good.   Jarndyce Antiquarian Booksellers   CLXC - 653   2011   £75

Oliphant, Margaret Oliphant Wilson 1828-1897 *The Victorian Age of English Literature.* Leipzig: Heinemann and Balestier, 1893, 2 volumes in 1, contemporary dark blue patterned cloth by R. Carswell of Belfast, spine lettered in gilt, very good.   Jarndyce Antiquarian Booksellers   CLXC - 654   2011   £35

Oliphant, Margaret Oliphant Wilson 1828-1897 *Who Was Lost and Is Found.* Edinburgh & London: William Blackwood and Sons, 1894, Second edition; half title, 32 page catalog, uncut in original maroon cloth, lettered in black and gilt, spine faded, little rubbed, good, sound copy.   Jarndyce Antiquarian Booksellers   CLXC - 651   2011   £60

Oliphant, Margaret Oliphant Wilson 1828-1897 *Women Novelists of Queen Victoria's Reign: a Book of Appreciations.* London: Hurst & Blackett, 1897, First edition; half title, uncut, original olive green cloth, lettered in gilt, spine slightly rubbed at head and tail, small nick in cloth, top edge gilt.   Jarndyce Antiquarian Booksellers   CLXC - 655   2011   £75

Oliver Ditson Company *The Ditson Collection: Master Violins of Today and Yesterday.* Boston: Ditson, 1910, Large 8vo., pages (22) plus color illustrations of instruments, paper wrappers, cover slightly yellowed, otherwise nice.   Second Life Books Inc.   174 - 254   2011 $85

Oliver, Chard *Another Kind.* New York: 1953, 170 pages, 12mo., very good, with about 50 pages printed on slightly darker paper, backstrip foxed lower two inches, with correspondence to verso of dust jacket (surface intact, 5/8 inch tear bottom of backstrip, minor ruffle at top).   Bookworm & Silverfish   665 - 58   2011 $300

Oliver, Daniel *Flora of Tropical Africa.* London: L. Reeve, 1868, First edition; 8vo., xiv, sli, 479, original green cloth, spine rubbed, ALS tipped into front pastedown, this is volume 1 of 10 and was presented to Col. James Augustus Grant by HM Office of Works and has been endorsed by him, letter also signed by Grant acknowledging receipt of book.   J. & S. L. Bonham Antiquarian Booksellers   Africa 4/20/2011 - 6976   2011   £150

Oliver, George *The History and Antiquities of the Town and Minister of Beverley in the County of York.* Beverley: printed and sold by M. Turner, 1829, Large paper copy, 4to., pages xxiii (i) 576 + engraved frontispiece, 5 other engraved plates, folding pedigree, contemporary tan calf, boards double rule gilt bordered with triple rule in blind within, board edges single rule gilt, turn-ins single rule gilt, all edges gilt 'peacock swirl' marbled, calf reback by John Henderson (1976) with original red lettering piece gilt relaid, plates foxed and some spotting elsewhere, old leather chipped and scratched, corners worn, from the collection of Christopher Ernest Weston 1947-2010.   Unsworths Booksellers   24 - 128   2011   £250

Oliver, George *Signs and Symbols Illustrated and Explained in a Course of Twelve Lectures on Free Masonry.* Grimsby: printed for the author by Br. Skelton, 1826, First edition; contemporary half calf gilt by Anthony Birdsall of Northampton (with his label), masonic emblem to spine compartments, double spine labels and Spanish marbled boards, extremities little rubbed, pages lx, 248, text illustrations, slight spotting to few leaves, but excellent copy, with ownership inscriptions of Richard Griffiths, architect and William Smith, both of Northampton, 2 small press cuttings relating to death of latter's unmarried daughter in Northampton are tipped to pastedown, S. S. Birdsall of Pomfret Lodge Northampton was a subscriber, rare.   R. F. G. Hollett & Son Antiquarian Booksellers   175 - 1020   2011   £350

Oliver, J. A. *Directory of the City of Los Angeles, California for 1875.* Los Angeles: printed at the Mirror Book and Job Printing House, 1875, First edition of the first separate general directory of the city of LA alone; octavo, (2, blank), 1-80, (2, ad), 81-174, 175 (pastedown), titlepages (i), (3), ads on pastedowns and throughout text, with one leaf of ads inserted between pages 80 and 81, half title (?) inserted and trimmed at upper, lower and fore edge margin and reads "Directory of Los Angeles for 1875", publisher's quarter leather over printed paper boards bearing ads; very light general wear and rubbing, some professional restoration to spine, boards with some soiling, small stain on back cover, altogether a remarkably clean, sound copy, very rare, the copy of noted historian F. B. Houghton. Heritage Book Shop Holiday 2010 - 93 2011 $4000

Oliver, Michel *La Cuisine est un Jeu D'Enfants.* New York: Random House, London and Glasgow: William Collins Sons & Co., 1965, First English language edition; 4to., (96) pages, decorative endpapers, glossy pictorial paper on boards, printed on heavy paper, child like drawings, rebacked with original spine title laid down. Hobbyhorse Books 56 - 40 2011 $100

Oliver, Paul *Conversation with the Blues.* London: Cassell, 1965, First edition; original cloth, gilt, dust jacket, pages xix, 217, with 80 illustrations and 2 maps, part of a menu signed by Count Basie and his vocalist Joe Williams (twice) (April 1960), another (indecipherable) loosely inserted. R. F. G. Hollett & Son Antiquarian Booksellers 175 - 1021 2011 £120

Oliver, Samuel Pasfield *Madagascar and the Malagasy.* London: Day and Son n.d., 1862, First edition; 8vo., pages xi, 150, map, 24 tinted plates, plan, original purple blindstamped cloth, neatly rebacked using original spine, corners rubbed. J. & S. L. Bonham Antiquarian Booksellers Africa 4/20/2011 - 9216 2011 £400

Oliver, William Dudley *Crags and Craters: Rambles in the Island of Reunion.* London: Longmans, Green, 1896, First edition; small 8vo., pages xiv, 213, folding map, frontispiece, 26 illustrations, original green cloth, very good clean, scarce. J. & S. L. Bonham Antiquarian Booksellers Africa 4/20/2011 - 5602 2011 £250

Olliver, G. H. *Notes on the Management of the Gardner-Serpollet Steam Motor Car.* London: Iliffe & Sons Ltd., 1903, Second edition; 8vo., pages 56, original publisher's blue cloth lettered gilt on spine and cover, illustrations, foldout diagram in good shape, covers slightly rubbed, covers slightly bumped, otherwise sound, very good. Any Amount of Books May 29 2011 - A69807 2011 $272

Oman, Charles *Castles.* Great Western Railway, 1926, First edition; pages xii, 232, with 2 colored plates, 105 illustrations, 67 drawings, 5 plans, 2 maps, large 8vo., original cloth backed boards, gilt, lower joint just cracking. R. F. G. Hollett & Son Antiquarian Booksellers 177 - 606 2011 £30

Oman, Charles *English Church Plate 597-1830.* Oxford: 1957, 362 pages, 200 plates, near fine in dust jacket, scarce. Ken Spelman Rare Books 68 - 126 2011 £50

Omar Khayyam *The Rubaiyat of Omar Khayyam.* London: George G. Harrap, 1909, Limited edition of 525 copies, signed; top edge gilt, green cloth with elaborate gold stamping and decorations on cover and spine, some fading to cloth, printed decorated dust jacket with wear and relatively minor pieces missing along edges, 24 full page mounted color plates within seventy five numbered sections plus every page is a graphical delight, illustrations by Wily Pogany. Jo Ann Reisler, Ltd. 86 - 193 2011 $1500

Omar Khayyam *The Rubaiyat of Omar Khayyam.* London: Hodder & Stoughton, n.d., 1909, First edition; 4to., white cloth, elaborate gilt pictorial decoration fine in original box (worn and soiled), illustrations by Edmund Dulac, 20 beautiful tipped in color illustrations with tissue guards, mounted on heavy stock with decorative border plus decorative border on text pages as well, great copy of beautiful book. Aleph-Bet Books, Inc. 95 - 209 2011 $850

Omar Khayyam *Rubaiyat of Omar Khayyam.* London: George Harrap, 1940, Limited to 125 copies, this is 105; small 8vo., pages 63, illustrations by Stephen Gooden with full page frontispiece and 5 plates, each with good distinct plate mark at edge, original publisher's quarter green leather, sunned and evenly faded to brown at spine, else very good in very good pale green firm card printed slipcase. Any Amount of Books May 26 2011 - A74371 2011 $629

On the House that Jack Built. Lees: Corticelli Silk Thread, 1882, Fourth edition; 16mo., pictorial wrappers, fine, 6 full page and 4 half page color lithographs, rare. Aleph-Bet Books, Inc. 95 - 293 2011 $225

Onasch, Konrad *Icons: the Fascination & The Reality.* New York: Riverside Book Co., 1997, First edition; 4to., copiously illustrated in color and black and white, 302 pages, very good+ in like dust jacket, clean, bright, excellent condition. Any Amount of Books May 29 2011 - A7663 2011 $204

Ondaatje, Michael *The Collected Works of Billy the Kid.* New York: Norton, 1974, First American edition; signed by author, top board edges sunned, erasure to front flyleaf, several ink notes in text, thus very good in near fine dust jacket, corner clipped (not price clipped) on lower front flap and with several short closed edge tears. Ken Lopez Bookseller 154 - 157 2011 $175

Ondaatje, Michael *The English Patient.* Toronto: McClelland & Stewart, 1992, First Canadian edition; near fine, previous owner's gift subscription, dust jacket near fine, price clipped.   Bella Luna Books   May 29 2011 - 6470 2011 $137

Ondaatje, Michael *The English Patient.* Toronto: McClelland & Stewart, 1992, First Canadian edition; fine in near fine dust jacket, very light creasing to top edge. Bella Luna Books   May 26 2011 - t3394 2011 $220

Ondaatje, Michael *The English Patient.* Toronto: McClelland & Stewart, 1992, First Canadian edition; near fine, white out over name on front free endpapers, near fine dust jacket, price clipped, one small repaired closed tear. Bella Luna Books   May 29 2011 - t2442 2011 $82

Ondaatje, Michael *The English Patient.* London: Bloomsbury, 1992, First British edition, true first printing; fine in fine dust jacket.   Bella Luna Books   May 26 2011 - t5487 2011 $440

One Hundred and One Ballades. London: Cobden-Sanderson, 1931, First edition; original cloth, gilt, dust jacket by John Nash, backstrip faded, lower half lacking, pages (vi), 108, illustrations by Nash throughout, presentation copy from H. S. MacKintosh.   R. F. G. Hollett & Son Antiquarian Booksellers   General Catalogue Summer 2010 - 854   2011   £60

147 Examples of Armorial Book Plates from Various Collections. (Second Series). London: 1892, 4to., 147 leaves, color frontispiece, very good, recased, resent in original covers, new endpapers.   Bookworm & Silverfish   668 - 22   2011 $295

Onions, C. T. *The Oxford Dictionary of English Etymology.* Oxford: Clarendon Press, 1966, First edition; pages xvi, 1025, large thick 8vo., original cloth, gilt, dust jacket.   R. F. G. Hollett & Son Antiquarian Booksellers   General Catalogue Summer 2010 - 445   2011   £35

Opie, Amelia *Adeline Mowbray, or the Mother and Daughter: a Tale.* London: Longman, 1805, Second edition; 3 volumes, half title and final ad leaf volume I, some occasional light foxing, contemporary full tree calf, spines with gilt devices and black leather labels, little rubbing, hinges slightly cracked, armorial bookplates of William Hales Symons, good plus.   Jarndyce Antiquarian Booksellers CLXC - 656   2011   £450

Opie, Amelia *The Autobiography and Letters.* Edinburgh: William Blackwood & Sons, 1899, First edition; half title, frontispiece and plate, original dark blue cloth, spine lettered in gilt, very good, bright.   Jarndyce Antiquarian Booksellers CLXC - 652   2011   £60

Opie, Amelia *The Father and Daughter, a Tale in Prose.* London: Longman, Hurst, Rees and Orme, 1802, Third edition; engraved frontispiece, very slightly stained in margin, contemporary full calf, spine gilt ruled, red label, hinges little rubbed.   Jarndyce Antiquarian Booksellers   CLXC - 657   2011   £200

Opie, Amelia *The Father and Daughter.* London: Longman, Hurst, Rees, and Orme, 1806, Fifth edition; frontispiece, contemporary full dark blue calf, gilt spine and borders, small maroon leather label, slightly rubbed, armorial bookplate of Marquess of Headfort, good plus.   Jarndyce Antiquarian Booksellers   CLXC - 658   2011   £120

Opie, Amelia *The Father and Daughter.* London: Longman, Hurst, Rees, and Orme, 1809, Sixth edition; frontispiece, contemporary half tan calf, marbled boards, gilt spine, maroon leather label, spines and edges little rubbed, armorial bookplate of Rev. G. F. Clarke and signature of Elizabeth Mary Clarke, good plus.   Jarndyce Antiquarian Booksellers   CLXC - 659   2011   £95

Opie, Amelia *Illustrations of Lying, In All Its Branches.* London: Longman, 1825, Second edition; 2 volumes, 12mo., contemporary half calf, black labels, hinges slightly splitting.   Jarndyce Antiquarian Booksellers   CLXC - 660 2011   £140

Opie, Amelia *Illustrations of Lying, in all Its Branches.* London: Longman, 1825, First edition; 2 volumes, 12mo., contemporary half calf, black labels, hinges slightly splitting. Jarndyce Antiquarian Booksellers   CLXC - 660 2011 £150

Opie, Amelia *Madeline, a Tale.* London: Longman, Hurst, Rees, Orme and Brown, 1822, First edition; 2 volumes, contemporary half maroon calf, black leather labels, spines faded to brown and bit rubbed.   Jarndyce Antiquarian Booksellers   CLXC - 662   2011   £280

Opie, Amelia *Poems by Mrs. Opie.* London: Longman &c., 1808, Fifth edition; frontispiece, contemporary full tan calf, borders finely tooled in blind and with double ruled borders in gilt, spine lettered and with devices in gilt, spine and leading hinges little rubbed, "From the author" on titlepage, good, sound copy, laid in is subscription to an ALS "Yours very respectfully, Amelia Opie".   Jarndyce Antiquarian Booksellers   CLXC - 663   2011   £150

Opie, Amelia *The Warrior's Return and Other Poems.* London: Longman &c, 1808, Second edition; frontispiece, leading f.e.p. stained on verso, contemporary full tan calf, borders finely tooled in blind and with double ruled borders in gilt, spine lettered and with devices in gilt, spine and leading hinges little rubbed, "From the author" on recto of frontispiece, good, sound copy, laid on to leading pastedown is subscription to an ALS "Every truly yours... A. Opie". Jarndyce Antiquarian Booksellers   CLXC - 664   2011 £240

Opie, Iona *A Dictionary of Superstitions.* London: Oxford University Press, 1989, First edition; pages xvi, 494, original cloth, gilt, dust jacket.   R. F. G. Hollett & Son Antiquarian Booksellers   175 - 1022   2011   £30

Opie, Iona *The Lore and Language of School Children.* Oxford: Clarendon Press, 1959, First edition; large 8vo., original cloth, gilt, dust jacket price clipped, pages xx, 418, with 11 distribution maps.   R. F. G. Hollett & Sons Antiquarian Booksellers   170 - 490   2011   £50

Opie, Iona *The Lore and Language of School Children.* Oxford: Clarendon Press, 1961, Large 8vo., original cloth, gilt, dust jacket little worn and torn, price clipped, pages xx, 417, with 11 distribution maps.   R. F. G. Hollett & Sons Antiquarian Booksellers   170 - 491   2011   £40

Opie, Iona *A Nursery Companion.* Oxford University Press, 1980, First edition; 4to., original cloth, gilt, dust jacket price clipped, pages 128, illustrations in color.   R. F. G. Hollett & Sons Antiquarian Booksellers   170 - 484   2011   £40

Opie, Iona *The Oxford Dictionary of Nursery Rhymes.* Oxford: Clarendon Press, 1952, Original cloth, gilt, dust jacket, front edge and inner flap rather defective, pages xxvii, 468, with 24 plates and 13 pages of text illustrations.   R. F. G. Hollett & Sons Antiquarian Booksellers   170 - 486   2011   £50

Opie, Iona *The Oxford Nursery Rhyme Book.* Oxford: Clarendon Press, 1957, Second edition; original cloth, gilt, dust jacket rather defective, pages xiv, 224, 600 illustrations, 150 designs by Joan Hassall, small stain to first few top edges.   R. F. G. Hollett & Sons Antiquarian Booksellers   170 - 489   2011   £65

Opie, Iona *The Oxford Nursery Rhyme Book.* Oxford: Clarendon Press, 1955, First edition; original cloth, gilt, pages xiv, 224, with 600 illustrations, 150 designs by Joan Hassall, flyleaves lightly browned.   R. F. G. Hollett & Sons Antiquarian Booksellers   170 - 488   2011   £50

Opie, Iona *The Treasures of Childhood.* London: Michael Joseph, 1989, First edition; large 4to., original cloth, gilt, dust jacket, pages 192, illustrations in color.   R. F. G. Hollett & Sons Antiquarian Booksellers   170 - 492   2011   £35

Oppenheim, James *Wild Oats.* New York: 1910, 261 pages, 12mo., very good with two scrapes to front, original binding.   Bookworm & Silverfish   662 - 170   2011 $75

Oppenheimer, Lehmann J. *The Heart of Lakeland.* Manchester: Sherratt & Hughes, 1908, First edition; tall 8vo., original cloth, gilt, rather faded, little worn and bumped, frayed nick to lower hinge, pages (x) 196 with 39 plates, scarce.   R. F. G. Hollett & Son Antiquarian Booksellers   173 - 850   2011   £95

Oppian *Alieuticon, Sive de Piscibus, Libri Quinque e Graeco Traducti ad Antonium Imperatorem.* Argenntorati: Jacobus Cammerlander, 1534, 4to., pages (4 ff.) 152ff., woodcut historaited initials and large printer's device on final verso, contemporary vellum, soiled, an abrasion to spine and margin of front cover near spine, 2 short tears to upper end of spine, title written on spine by contemporary hand, old ink inscription "Ex Bibliotheca Tidoniana" and a number to front flyleaf, lower third of title expertly renewed resulting in loss of text, contemporary date & number to title, scattered minor foxing, some pages browned, lower margin of last leaf and a blank corner of page expertly renewed resulting in loss of text, contemporary date and number to title, scattered minor foxing, some pages browned, lower margin of last leaf and a blank corner of page expertly renewed with no loss of text, small dampspot to margin of 3 leaves.   Raymond M. Sutton, Jr.   May 26 2011 - 41479   2011 $3000

Oppian *De Venatione Lib. III. De Piscatu Lib. V. Cum Interpretatione Latina, Commentariis & Indice...* Leiden: ex officina Plantiniana, 1597, (40), 344, 164, (4), 8vo., early vellum, ink lettering faded from spine, yapp edges, slightly soiled, sound, rather browned, some spotting, some underlining and short notes in early ink.   Blackwell Rare Books   B166 - 77   2011   £950

Optic, Oliver *Boat Club; or the Bunkers of Rippleton.* Boston: Brown, Bazin and Co., 1855, First edition; 12mo., brown pictorial cloth with front cover and spine stamped in gold, all edges gilt, spine ends frayed, light and stain on endpaper and next 2 leaves, tight clean and overall very good+, 4 plates.   Aleph-Bet Books, Inc.   95 - 404   2011 $1200

Orange. Los Angeles and Salt Lake Railroad, circa, 1909, Every other page has photo, book is die-cut in shape of an orange 3 3/4 x 3 1/2 inches, fine condition.   Aleph-Bet Books, Inc.   95 - 529   2011 $250

Orbelianski, Sulkhan Saba *The Book of Wisdom and Lies, a Georgian Story Book of the Eighteenth Century.* Kelmscott Press, 1894, One of 250 copies; printed in black in golden type with titles and shoulder titles printed in red, woodcut title, foliated borders and large initials designed by William Morris, pages (iv) (blanks) xvi ii, 256, (4) (blanks), crown 8vo., original limp cream vellum, backstrip gilt lettered, pink silk ties, untrimmed, very good.   Blackwell Rare Books   B166 - 266   2011   £975

Orcutt, Samuel *History of the Town of Wolcott (Connecticut) from 1731 to 1874.* Waterbury: American Printing Co., 1874, First edition; original cloth, gilt to spine, very good, some shelfwear, tape to contents leaf, bright gilt. Lupack Rare Books May 26 2011 - ABE805991442 2011 $150

Orczy, Emmuska, Baroness 1865-1947 *Eldorado: a Story of the Scarlet Pimpernel.* Leipzig: Bernhard Tauchnitz, 1913, Half titles, contemporary half red calf, spine elaborately blocked in gilt, dark green leather labels, top edge gilt, very good. Jarndyce Antiquarian Booksellers CLXC - 668 2011 £75

Orczy, Emmuska, Baroness 1865-1947 *Leatherface: a Tale of Old Flanders.* London: Hodder & Stoughton, 1916, First edition; frontispiece, paper slightly browned, original pale blue cloth, pictorially blocked and lettered in brown, spine faded, little rubbed. Jarndyce Antiquarian Booksellers CLXC - 665 2011 £40

Orczy, Emmuska, Baroness 1865-1947 *The Nest of the Sparrowhawk; a Romance of the 17th Century.* London: Greening and Co., 1909, First edition; ad leaf preceding half title, endpapers little browned, original pale blue cloth, front board pictorially blocked at centre with sparrowhawk in black and white, lettered in gilt, little dulled, good plus copy. Jarndyce Antiquarian Booksellers CLXC - 666 2011 £40

Orczy, Emmuska, Baroness 1865-1947 *The Scarlet Pimpernel.* Leipzig: Bernhard Tauchnitz, 1911, (1920). Copyright edition; half title, paper slightly browned, beige flecked binder's cloth, green leather label, armorial bookplate. Jarndyce Antiquarian Booksellers CLXC - 667 2011 £35

Orczy, Emmuska, Baroness 1865-1947 *Unto Caesar.* Leipzig: Bernhard Tauchnitz, 1914, Copyright edition; 2 volumes, contemporary half red calf, dark green leather labels, top edge gilt, very good, attractive copy. Jarndyce Antiquarian Booksellers CLXC - 671 2011 £75

The Order of Keeping A Court Leet and Court Leet and Court Baron. Manorial Society, 1914, Pages vi, 51, (iii), scattered foxing, mainly to edges, scarce, original cloth backed boards, scarce. R. F. G. Hollett & Son Antiquarian Booksellers 175 - 545 2011 £40

Oribasius *Synopseos ad Evstathivm Filivm Lib. Novem.* Paris: Maurice Meunier for Oudin Petit, 1554, First edition; splendid 16th century Parisian citron morocco, very lavishly gilt for Pietro Duodo, boards with elegant frame of leafy fronds enclosing a large central panel occupied by five horizontal rows of three ovals, each of these ovals enclosing lovely flower tool, covers also with large number of gilt thistles, passion flowers and other small tools, slightly larger central oval on upper cover with armorial crest of Duodo, lower cover with three lilies on hillock as well as a collar containing Duodo's motto "Expectata non eludet", flat spine similarly gilt with two flower medallions above and below a central oval containing author's name, spine ends raised above top and bottom board edges in a la grecque style, all edges gilt, felt lined folding cloth box, woodcut initials and woodcut device on titlepage, ruled in red throughout, green morocco bookplate of Michel Wittock, ink inscription "Cuthell Martin 23 May (18)04" (presumably recording purchase from London Booksellers Cuthell & Martin); hint of uniform darkening to backstrip, two tiny wormholes near tail of spine, corners and joints slightly rubbed, isolated insignificant stains internally, still very fine, text remarkably fresh and clean, exquisite little binding lustrous and generally in especially pleasing state of preservation, minor wear far outweighed by bright, sumptuous gilt. Phillip J. Pirages 59 - 11 2011 $17,500

Orleans, Pierre Joseph De *Histoire des Revolutions D'Angleterre Depuis Le Commencement De La Monarchie.* Paris: Chez Claude Barbin, 1693-1694, First edition; 250 x 193 mm., 3 volumes, splendid and unusual sumptuously gilt early 19th century marbled calf with red morocco spines in the style of Bozerian, covers with gilt borders of two decorative rules and elegant undulating floral vine, flat straight grain morocco spines very handsomely gilt in compartments with pointille ground and central circlet from which radiate four lilies and four leaves on twining stems, turn-ins gilt with plain and decorative rolls, marbled endpapers, all edges gilt, engraved head and tailpieces and 8 engraved portraits, verso of front free endpaper with bookplate of Baron de Mackau, titlepage with ink ownership inscription of Alexander Paul Ludwig Goupy? in contemporary hand; isolated gatherings with variable browning (small handfull rather browned), one leaf in first volume with expert early repair of four inch tear (letters of four words partly obscured or displaced, and text and facing page somewhat discolored), few additional trivial imperfections internally, but text generally quite fresh and clean, one joint with five small wormholes, few hardly noticeable, shallow scratches to covers hint of wear to extremities, lovely bindings in fine condition, lustrous leather and gilt with only minor wear, with their very considerable original visual appeal entirely intact. Phillip J. Pirages 59 - 14 2011 $2250

Orred, Meta *Glamour.* London: John Lane, Bodley Head, 1897, First English edition; half title, 12 pages ads (1897), untrimmed in original pale blue cloth, pictorially blocked and lettered in dark blue, spine faded, slightly dulled, good, sound. Jarndyce Antiquarian Booksellers CLXC - 673 2011 £75

Orrin, J. F. *The Conjurer's Vade Mecum.* London: Stanley Paul, n.d. circa, 1927, Tall 12mo., original cloth, little used, pages 159, (i), with portrait, 80 diagrams and illustrations by author.   R. F. G. Hollett & Son Antiquarian Booksellers   175 - 1025   2011   £30

Orton, Edward *Report on Occurrence of Petroleum Natural Gas & Asphalt Rock in Western Kentucky...* Frankfort: 1891, First edition; 233 pages, very good, few scrapes, plates, map, original binding.   Bookworm & Silverfish   671 - 78   2011 $75

Orton, Harold *The Linguistic Atlas of England.* Croom Helm etc., 1978, First UK edition; folio, original cloth, gilt, slipcase, unpaginated, illustrations, maps.   R. F. G. Hollett & Son Antiquarian Booksellers   General Catalogue Summer 2010 - 446   2011   £120

Orwell, George   1903-1950   *Kolgosp Tvarin. (Animal Farm).* Munich: 1947, First Ukranian edition; full page portrait of author, poor quality paper lightly browned, pages 92, crown 8vo., original cream wrappers, front cover illustrated in shades of red and in cream overall, fine.   Blackwell Rare Books   B166 - 201   2011   £600

Orwell, George   1903-1950   *Homage to Catalonia.* London: Secker & Warburg, 1938, First edition; 8vo., pages 314, original publisher's green cloth lettered gilt at spine, very slight rubbing, few small marks, faint tanning at spine, neat name on front pastedown, otherwise pleasing, very good, bright copy with clean text.   Any Amount of Books   May 26 2011 - A74329   2011 $671

Orwell, George   1903-1950   *Homage to Catalonia.* New York: Harcourt Brace, 1952, First American edition; foxing to boards, otherwise near fine in very good, sun darkened dust jacket with couple of tiny edge chips.   Ken Lopez Bookseller   154 - 159   2011 $175

Orwell, George   1903-1950   *James Burnham and the Managerial Revolution.* London: Socialist Book Centre July, 1946, First edition; 12mo., 19 pages, original printed wrappers, text browned, but fine.   M & S Rare Books, Inc.   90 - 306   2011 $750

Osburn, William *Ancient Egypt, her Testimony to the Truth of the Bible...* London: Samuel Bagster and Sons, 1846, 8vo., pages x, 242, (ii) + color printed frontispiece, additional titlepage and 4 other color printed plates, publisher's original interlinked concentric circle design brown book cloth, spine lettered red on gilt background at head, lemon 'coated' endpapers, early 21st century cloth reback, old backstrip relaid by Chris Weston, corners bit rubbed, from the collection of Christopher Ernest Weston 1947-2010.   Unsworths Booksellers   24 - 129   2011   £50

Oshita, Momoko   *Bernd Greber: a Legendary Snowman.* Bijutsu Shuppan-Sha, 2002,   74 pages, very good, (blx 11), hardcover, white boards, no internal markings, clean pages within, staining to boards, quite scarce.   G. H. Mott Bookseller   May 26 2011 - BOOOSTBAOI 2011 $195

Oskison, John M. *Wild Harvest.* New York: D. Appleton, 1925, First edition; signed by author, small amount of foxing to the book, some general modest signs of wear to cloth, very good, lacks scarce dust jacket.   Ken Lopez Bookseller   154 - 142   2011 $1250

Osler, William   1849-1919   *Bibliotheca Osleriana. A Catalogue of Books Illustrating the History of Medicine and Science.* Mansfield Centre: Maurizio Martino, n.d., Facsimile reprint of 1929 Oxford edition limited to 150 copies; thick 8vo. xxxv, 785 pages, index, light gray cloth, gilt stamped red spine label, fine, from the Medical Library of Dr. Clare Gray Peterson.   Jeff Weber Rare Books   162 - 230   2011 $90

Osler, William   1849-1919   *The Student Life and Other Essays.* London: Constable, 1928, Small 8vo., original cloth gilt, pages xxxvi, 145, frontispiece.   R. F. G. Hollett & Son Antiquarian Booksellers   175 - 1026   2011   £35

Ossoli, Margaret Fuller   1810-1850   *Memoirs of Margaret Fuller Ossoli.* Boston: Phillips Sampson, 1852, Small octavo, 2 volumes, viii, (9)-351; iii (3)-352, (4 ads) pages, original full publisher's blindstamped cloth, gilt spine titles, spine ends worn, extremities shelf worn, corners showing signature in volume I sprung, but complete, good plus, signature of previous owner, Frank A. Doud.   Jeff Weber Rare Books   163 - 92   2011 $85

Oswald, Adrian *English Brown Stoneware 1670-1900.* London: Faber, 1982, First edition; original cloth, gilt, dust jacket, pages 308, 9 color plates, 181 illustrations, 13 figures, fine.   R. F. G. Hollett & Son Antiquarian Booksellers   General Catalogue Summer 2010 - 288   2011   £95

Otis, Job *Memoirs of the Life and Religious Exercises of Job Otis.* New York: Privately printed, Sherwoods, 1861, Good, full leather worn at edges and chipped at top of spine, boards slightly warped, foxing to endpapers, scattered foxing to interior, gift inscription and signature of one of the author's for children, generally clean and tight, 292 pages.   G. H. Mott Bookseller   May 26 2011 - 42517   2011 $200

Otley, Jonathan *A Concise Description of the English Lakes and Adjacent Mountains.* Keswick: privately published and Kirkby Lonsdale: Arthur Foster, 1834, Fifth edition; modern cloth with original paper spine label, rubbed. pages viii, 184, folding map.   R. F. G. Hollett & Son Antiquarian Booksellers   173 - 855   2011   £85

Otley, Jonathan *A Descriptive Guide to the English Lakes and Adjacent Mountains...* Keswick: published by author, 1842, Seventh edition; original blindstamped cloth gilt, little worn and marked, pages viii, 220, folding map, hand colored in outline, 13 outlines of mountains and 33 woodcuts in text.   R. F. G. Hollett & Son Antiquarian Booksellers   173 - 856 2011   £140

Ott, Ludig *Fundamental of Catholick Dogma.* Cork: Mercier Press, 1966, Original black cloth, gilt, small ring mark to upper board, pages xvi, 544.   R. F. G. Hollett & Son Antiquarian Booksellers   175 - 1027 2011   £50

Otto, Whitney *How to Make an American Quilt.* New York: Villard, 1991, First edition; signed and dated by author 5/2/91, review copy, fine in near fine dust jacket, evidence of sticker removal on bar code.   Bella Luna Books   May 29 2011 - t7755 2011 $82

Otway, Thomas 1652-1685 *Don Carlos, Prince of Spain.* London: printed for Jacob Tonson and sold by Tho. Chapman at the Angel in the Pall Mall ove against St. James's Square, 1704, Fifth edition; (8), 54, (2) pages, without final ad leaf, disbound.   Anthony W. Laywood   May 26 2011 - 21749 2011 $84

Ouellette, William *Erotic Postcards.* New York: Excalibur Books, 1977, First edition; 4to., original boards gilt, dust jacket, pages 127, illustrations.   R. F. G. Hollett & Son Antiquarian Booksellers   General Catalogue Summer 2010 - 290 2011   £30

Ould, E. A. *Old Cottages, Farm Houses and Other Half Timber Buildings in Shropshire, Herefordshire and Cheshire.* London: Batsford, 1904, First edition; small 4to., original decorated brown cloth gilt, spine lettering dulled, pages xi, 39, (100, plates), 24, top edge gilt, with 24 text illustrations, excellent, clean and sound set, scarce.   R. F. G. Hollett & Son Antiquarian Booksellers   177 - 608 2011   £150

Our Children: Sketched from Nature in Pencil and Verse. London: Dean & Son, n.d. circa, 1867, Small 4to., original green blindstamped cloth gilt, neatly recased, pages (56), lithographed throughout with pencil drawings, little light spotting to first few leaves, inscription dated July 6th 1867 (British Library gives the date as 1895).   R. F. G. Hollett & Sons Antiquarian Booksellers   170 - 20 2011   £75

Our Four Footed Friends. Cincinnati: Peter G. Thomson, n.d. circa, 1880, 8vo., pictorial wrappers, 14 pages, near fine, 4 lovely full page chromolithographs.   Aleph-Bet Books, Inc.   95 - 550 2011 $200

Our Old Nursery Rhymes. London: Augener, 1911, Limited to 4t0 copies, signed, (the representation in the book notwithstanding, there is no evidence that any copies over number 100 were ever produced so probably limitation is far smaller that it says?); all edges gilt, vellum boards, gold lettering and decoration surrounding a color paste label on front cover, lovely copy with fresh straight boards and original ties, minor foxing to blank endpapers and former owner's name on front free endpaper, full page color illustrations by H. Willebeek Le Mair.   Jo Ann Reisler, Ltd.   86 - 157 2011 $3500

Our Old Nursery Rhymes. London: Augener, 1911, First edition; oblong 4to., original cloth, gilt, oval pictorial onlay to upper board, small repaired snag to lower board, illustrations in soft pastel colors by H. Willebeek Le Mair, each illustration and page of music within oval floral border, upper joint neatly strengthened, occasional slight mark, very nice, scarce.   R. F. G. Hollett & Sons Antiquarian Booksellers   170 - 396 2011   £140

Outbursts from Waterloo(se) House. Being a Sequel to Leakages from Watertight House. London: printed for Private Circulation, 1917, First edition; 4to., original publisher's printed thick card covers with linen spine, pages (6), 41, printed recto only, including one folding plate, some wear and slight soiling to covers and spine, lower spine and slightly frayed, otherwise sound, near very good.   Any Amount of Books   May 26 2011 - A61729 2011 $419

Outhwaite, Ida Rentoul *Blossom: a Fairy Story.* London: A. & C. Black, 1928, First UK edition; 4to., cloth backed patterned boards, 94 pages, 2 pages ads, slightest of rear cover soil, else fine in dust jacket, some soil and some mends, illustrations by author, beautiful copy.   Aleph-Bet Books, Inc.   95 - 407 2011 $2750

Outhwaite, Ida Rentoul *A Bunch of Wild Flowers.* Sydney: Angus & Robertson, 1948, First edition thus; 8vo., blue cloth with gold lettering on cover and spine along with flower vignettes on covers, some white spotting on cloth and dulling to gold on cloth, full color pictorial dust jacket with pieces missing at ends of spine and along edges, there are 22 full page mounted color plates and black and white drawings.   Jo Ann Reisler, Ltd.   86 - 186 2011 $800

Overbury, Thomas *His Wife. With Additions of New Characters...* London: printed or Robert Allot and are to be sold at the signe of the Beare in Paul's Church yard, 1630, Fourteenth impression; full vellum, very good, final few leaves with tissue repair at edges and first two leaves, at top corners, tight book in near fine binding with very good text, bookplate of Clarence "Clip" Boutell.   Lupack Rare Books   May 26 2011 - ABE1296792492 2011 $1500

Overton, Thomas Collins *The Temple Builder's Most Useful Companion.* London: I. Taylor, 1774, First edition; large 8vo., pages 15, (4 pages ads), frontispiece, 50 engraved plates, modern quarter leather lettered gilt at spine with older marbled boards (slightly rubbed), very good, sound, clean with neat contemporary name on titlepage (Ingilby) and small attractive drawings by same on front and rear endpaper, one plate at top with some neat handwritten notes in sepia ink in same hand, presumably to a builder or architect, about construction and cost of the gothic garden building depicted below by Pranker. Any Amount of Books May 26 2011 - A74743 2011 $1761

Ovidius Naso, Publius *Ovid's Epistles: with His Amours.* London: Printed for J. and R. Tonson, 1761, Old full calf gilt, rather rubbed and scraped, spine darkened and hinges cracking, pages (xxii), 309, engraved frontispiece, light pencil scribble to two pages. R. F. G. Hollett & Son Antiquarian Booksellers General Catalogue Summer 2010 - 670 2011 £75

Ovidius Naso, Publius *Opera Quae Vocantur Amatoria... (bound with) Poetae Svlmonensis Fastorum.* Basileae: Per Ioannem Heraugium, 1549, 1543. 1550; 2 volumes, 4to., (16), 528, (32), (28), 355, (5); (8), 793, (10) pages, engraved printer's device on titlepages, volume 1 titlepage restored, titlepage of volume 2 mounted, occasional worming, not affecting text, some contemporary marginal notes, some light marginal waterstains, handcut arrow mounted on page 247 of volume I, full modern morocco to period style, blind ruled covers, raised bands, gilt stamped spines and spine titles, fine. Jeff Weber Rare Books 163 - 3 2011 $1800

Ovidius Naso, Publius *Operum... Tomus Primus (Tertius)...* Frankfurt: C. Marny & Heirs of J. Aubry, typis Wechelianis, 1601, 3 volumes, folio, (4), 500, (16); (2), 388, 116, 244, (12), 340, 199 pages, later 17th century mottled calf, gilt fillet on covers, spines gilt, green silk ties lacking, slightly foxed but highly desirable, handsome copy, from the library of the Earls of Macclesfield at Shirburn Castle, bequeathed by Iosephi Scaliger to D. Heinsius. Maggs Bros. Ltd. 1440 - 160 2011 £3000

Owen, David Dale *Report of a Geological Survey of Wisconsin, Iowa and Minnesota and Incidentally of a Portion of Nebraska Territory.* Philadelphia: 1852, First edition; 638 pages, many illustrations, first 50 pages damped at bottom margin, cover rubbed, bottom 4 inches fron cover damp bowed. Bookworm & Silverfish 679 - 84 2011 $87

Owen, Hugh *The Lowther Family.* Philimore, 1990, First edition; small 4to., original cloth, gilt, dust jacket, pages xx, 476, frontispiece, 100 illustrations, 14 family trees, fine. R. F. G. Hollett & Son Antiquarian Booksellers General Catalogue Summer 2010 - 447 2011 £120

Owen, Hugh *The Lowther Family.* Phillimore, 1990, First edition; small 4to., original cloth, gilt, dust jacket, pages xx, 476, frontispiece, 100 illustrations and 14 family trees, fine, now very good, scarce. R. F. G. Hollett & Son Antiquarian Booksellers 173 - 857 2011 £120

Owen, Richard 1804-1892 *Antiquity of Man as Deduced from the Discovery of a Human Skeleton During the Excavations of the East and West India Dock Extensions at Tilbury, North Bank of the Thames.* John van Voorst, 1884, First edition; original blind ruled cloth gilt, pages 32, 4 folding plates and chart, all lithographed by Hanhart, prelims trifle spotted, excellent, rare. R. F. G. Hollett & Son Antiquarian Booksellers 177 - 609 2011 £180

Owen, Robert 1771-1858 *The Life of Robert Owen. Written by Himself. (with) A Supplementary Appendix to the First volume of the Life of Robert Owen.* London: Effingham Wilson, 1857-1858, Only early edition; 2 volumes, 8vo., (iv) xliv 390 (2); (xviii) (2) blank 358 (2) pages, including final leaf in volume I, advertising the forthcoming volume A!, folding engraved plate, complete with index completion leaf in volume II, each volume entirely unopened, original blindstamped maroon cloth lettered gilt on spines and upper covers, spines slightly faded, else fine, choice, copy in its original state, very scarce. John Drury Rare Books 153 - 107 2011 £2850

Owen, Robert 1771-1858 *Registered for Foreign Transmission. Robert Owen's Millenial Gazette..* London: Effingham Wilson, n.d. but, 1857, First edition; 8vo., caption title, 149 + (5) pages, including 2 final blank leaves, some light paper browning, one or two edge nicks, recently well bound in cloth, spine lettered in gilt, entirely uncut, good. John Drury Rare Books 153 - 106 2011 £375

The Owens College Jubilee. Manchester: Sherratt & Hughes, 1901, 4to., original wrappers, edges little creased, rebacked in matching cloth, pages (iii), 80, (viii), illustrations. R. F. G. Hollett & Son Antiquarian Booksellers 175 - 1028 2011 £75

Owens, Bill *Suburbia.* San Francisco: Straight Arrow Books, 1973, First edition; photos, clean, very near fine copy in illustrated wrappers, some minor rubbing to front and rear panel. Jeff Hirsch Books ny 2010 2011 $550

Owens, Louis *John Steinbeck's Re-vision of America.* Athens: University of Georgia, 1985, First edition; uncommon book, inscribed by author to another writer, fine in near fine, spine faded dust jacket. Ken Lopez Bookseller 154 - 143 2011 $450

Oxenham, Elsie Jeanette *Goblin Island.* London: circa, 1909, 316 pages, blue cloth with gilt titles, pictorial endpapers by A. A. Dixon, with pictorial onlay to front cover, color frontispiece, titlepage and two other plates, all edges gilt, title and frontispiece once damped at edges, each with separation, abrasions not affecting image within printed border, backstrip illustrations has some blue spots from background peeping through, frontispiece illustrations with light rubbing and one small scrape, reglued at rear inner joint and after f.f.e.p.   Bookworm & Silverfish   671 - 76   2011 $100

Oxenham, Elsie Jeanette *Mistress Nanciebel.* Oxford University Press, n.d., 1930,   Original red blindstamped cloth, gilt, dust jacket (bottom third of spine and back panel missing chips to other corners), pages x, 352, color frontispiece and pictorial endpapers, fore-edge little spotted.   R. F. G. Hollett & Sons Antiquarian Booksellers   170 - 495   2011   £85

Oxford and Asquith, Lord *Memories and Reflections 1852-1927.* London: Cassell, 1928,   Second impression; 2 volumes, original cloth, gilt, spines trifle faded, pages xvii, 284; vii, 288, with 16 plates and map, scattered foxing.   R. F. G. Hollett & Son Antiquarian Booksellers   175 - 1029   2011   £40

Oxford Poetry. Blackwells, 1910-1951,   First edition; 22 volumes in original publisher's boards, or original publisher's wrappers as issued in very good condition.   I. D. Edrich   May 26 2011 - 82168   2011 $2851

Oxoniensis *The History of Hibaldstow Derived from Various Published and Manuscript Sources.* Gainsburgh: published by C. Caldicott News Office, 1903,   4to., 22 pages, original printed wrappers, spine worn.   Anthony W. Laywood   May 26 2011 - 21735   2011 $67

P

Paccard, Andre *Traditional Islamic Craft in Moroccan Architecture.* Saint Jorioz: Editions Atelier 74, 1980, First edition; 4to., 508, 582 pages, copiously illustrated in color, neat gift inscription on first blanks page, else excellent condition, very good in like dust jacket. Any Amount of Books May 26 2011 - a7707 2011 $1048

Padgett, Lewis *Tomorrow and Tomorrow and the Fairy Chessmen.* New York: Gnome Press Inc., 1951, First edition; octavo, boards. L. W. Currey, Inc. 124 - 214 2011 $150

Pagan, James *Sketch of the History of Glasgow.* Glasgow: Robert Stuart & co., 1847, 8vo., pages (vi) 198 + engraved titlepage, extending lithographic plan and 22 other lithograph plates, later polished calf by Ramage, signed in gilt above bottom front turn-in, spine panel-gilt, dark orange lettering & 'place & date' pieces gilt, boards panelled in gilt and in blind reinterpreting the 'Cambridge' style, board edges 'broken hatch' roll gilt at corners, turn-ins 'dentelle' roll gilt, 'French Shell' 'made' endpapers, all edges lemon, 3 color double core sewn endbands, replacement lettering piece for author's name, little spotting to plates, pages lightly large toned, from the collection of Christopher Ernest Weston 1947-2010. Unsworths Booksellers 24 - 130 2011 £200

Pagdin, William E. *The Story of the Weathercock.* Stockton-on-Tees: privately published, 1949, Large 8vo., original cloth, dust jacket, pages 103, illustrations. R. F. G. Hollett & Son Antiquarian Booksellers 177 - 610 2011 £45

Page, William *The Victoria History of the Country of Hertford.* London: Constable, 1902, First edition; 4 volumes, 4to., original publisher's half leather lettered gilt on spine with marbled endpapers, pages 1936, copiously illustrated in black and white with plates, maps and line drawings, handsome about very good set with few ex-library stamps and labels, spine rubbed, some rubbing at corners, slight general shelfwear but decent sound set. Any Amount of Books May 26 2011 - A67794 2011 $587

Paget, Violet 1856-1935 *Althea; a Second Book of Dialogues on Aspirations and Duty.* London: Osgood, McIlvaine & Co., 1894, First edition; half title, original dark green cloth, spine lettered in gilt, spine darkened and rubbed at head and tail, inner hinges slightly cracked, armorial bookplate of Elizabeth Kenneys-Tynte (Baroness Wharton). Jarndyce Antiquarian Booksellers CLXC - 98 2011 £40

Paget, Violet 1856-1935 *Ariadne in Mantua; a Romance.* Oxford: B. H. Blackwell, 1903, First edition; uncut in original cream wrappers, decorated in orange and dark blue, paper label, slightly dusted, very good, signed presentation inscription to Nerina Gigliucci. Jarndyce Antiquarian Booksellers CLXC - 99 2011 £160

Paget, Violet 1856-1935 *Baldwin: Being Dialogues on Views and Aspirations.* London: T. Fisher Unwin, 1886, First edition; 8vo., original publisher's dark green cloth lettered gilt on spine and front cover, pages (viii), 375, faint rubbing, slight scuffing, otherwise near fine, excellent. Any Amount of Books May 29 2011 - A66473 2011 $306

Paget, Violet 1856-1935 *The Countess of the Albany.* London: John Lane, The Bodley Head, 1910, Second edition; half title, frontispiece, 2 plates, 12 pages ads, uncut in original olive green cloth, spine lettered gilt, top edge gilt, very good. Jarndyce Antiquarian Booksellers CLXC - 100 2011 £45

Paget, Violet 1856-1935 *Genius Loci: Notes on Places.* London: Grant Richards, 1899, First edition; half title, title in red and black, final ad leaf, uncut in original pale brown buckram, lettered gilt, little dulled, dust jacket, bookplate of collector Mary Hunter. Jarndyce Antiquarian Booksellers CLXC - 101 2011 £110

Paget, Violet 1856-1935 *Genius Loci, and The Enchanted Woods.* Leipzig: Bernhard Tauchnitz, 1906, Copyright edition; contemporary half vellum, label, slightly dulled, bound without half title. Jarndyce Antiquarian Booksellers CLXC - 102 2011 £40

Paget, Violet 1856-1935 *The Golden Keys and Other Essays on the Genius Loci.* London: John Lane, 1925, First edition; half title, 6 pages ads, small brown stain to lower fore edge margins of some pages, uncut in original olive green cloth, spine slightly faded. Jarndyce Antiquarian Booksellers CLXC - 103 2011 £55

Paget, Violet 1856-1935 *Gospels of Anarchy.* London: T. Fisher Unwin, 1900, Half title, slight spotting in prelims, uncut in original green cloth, blocked and lettered in gilt, little faded, slight rubbing, library labels on following endpapers, Joseph M. Gleason bookplate, top edge gilt, good plus. Jarndyce Antiquarian Booksellers CLXC - 105 2011 £75

Paget, Violet 1856-1935 *Gospels of Anarchy and Other Contemporary Studies.* London: T. Fisher Unwin, 1908, First edition; half title, initial ad leaf, few pencil notes, uncut in contemporary half brown calf, top edge gilt. Jarndyce Antiquarian Booksellers CLXC - 104 2011 £120

Paget, Violet 1856-1935 *The Handling of Words and Other Studies in Literary Psychology.* London: John Lane, The Bodley Head, 1923, First edition; half title, 4 pages ads, uncut in original olive green cloth, spine lettered in gilt, very good in slightly worn and repaired dust jacket. Jarndyce Antiquarian Booksellers CLXC - 106 2011 £65

Paget, Violet 1856-1935 *Hauntings: Fantastic Stories.* London: William Heinemann, 1890, First edition; octavo, pages (i-vii viii-xi (xii) (1-2) 3-237 (238: blank) (1) 2-6 ads, original decorated red cloth, front and rear panels stamped in black, spine panel stamped in black and gold, black coated endpapers. L. W. Currey, Inc. 124 - 108 2011 $750

Paget, Violet 1856-1935 *Hortus Vitae: Essays on Gardening of Life.* London: John Lane, 1904, Second edition; half title, 2 pages ads, original light green cloth, very good. Jarndyce Antiquarian Booksellers CLXC - 107 2011 £45

Paget, Violet 1856-1935 *Music and Its Lovers: an Empirical Study of Emotional and Imaginative Responses to Music.* London: George Allen & Unwin, 1932, First edition; half title, original olive green cloth, spine slightly faded, very good. Jarndyce Antiquarian Booksellers CLXC - 108 2011 £50

Paget, Violet 1856-1935 *A Phantom Lover: a Fantastic Story.* London: William Blackwood & Sons, 1886, First edition; contemporary maroon binder's cloth, spine faded and slightly worn at head and tail, signs of label removed from front board, signed "Evelyn Wimbush, 1887" (friend of author). Jarndyce Antiquarian Booksellers CLXC - 109 2011 £650

Paget, Violet 1856-1935 *Pope Jacynth and Other Fantastic Tales.* London: Grant Richards, 1904, First edition, publisher's proof copy with stamps of T. & A. Constable throught, several minor ms. alterations in text; half title, original pale purple binder's cloth, spine lettered in gilt, slightly dulled, top edge gilt, good plus, scarce, signed presentation inscription by author for Violet Hippisley. Jarndyce Antiquarian Booksellers CLXC - 110 2011 £500

Paget, Violet 1856-1935 *The Prince of the Hundred Soups: a Puppet-Show in Narrative.* London: T. Fisher Unwin, 1883, Second thousand; frontispiece, 4 pages ads, original white pictorial boards, blocked and lettered in orange, red and pale green, spine little dulled and slightly rubbed. Jarndyce Antiquarian Booksellers CLXC - 111 2011 £125

Paget, Violet 1856-1935 *Proteus; or the Future of Intelligence.* London: Kegan Paul Trench, Trubner & Co., 1925, First edition; half title, 2 pages ads, original dark purple paper covered boards, white labels, very slight wear to spine, good plus. Jarndyce Antiquarian Booksellers CLXC - 113 2011 £45

Paget, Violet 1856-1935 *Renaissance Fancies and Studies.* London: Smith, Elder & Co., 1895, Half title, final ad leaf, endpapers little browned, original dark green cloth, spine lettered gilt, head and tail of spine rubbed, very good. Jarndyce Antiquarian Booksellers CLXC - 114 2011 £65

Paget, Violet 1856-1935 *The Sentimental Traveller.* London: John Lane, 1908, First edition; half title, 6 pages ads, spots in prelims, original light green cloth, spine dulled. Jarndyce Antiquarian Booksellers CLXC - 115 2011 £65

Paget, Violet 1856-1935 *The Story of a Puppet Show: or Prince of the Hundred Soups.* London: T. Fisher Unwin, 1889, Second thousand; color frontispiece and color plates, 4 pages ads, contemporary half vellum, dark green leather label, slightly dulled, good plus, signed Julia Owering Boit, daughter of American artist Edward Darly Boit. Jarndyce Antiquarian Booksellers CLXC - 112 2011 £65

Paget, Violet 1856-1935 *Studies of the Eighteenth Century in Italy.* London: W. Satchell & Co., 1880, First edition; original dark green cloth, slight rubbing, dark brown endpapers, now rather brittle, inner hinges slight splitting, Paris bookseller's ticket. Jarndyce Antiquarian Booksellers CLXC - 117 2011 £85

Paget, Violet 1856-1935 *The Tower of the Mirrors and Other Essays on the Spirit of Places.* London: John Lane, The Bodley Head, 1914, First edition; half title, 4 pages ads, + 16 page catalog, lacks following f.e.p., original olive green cloth, spine lettered in gilt, very good. Jarndyce Antiquarian Booksellers CLXC - 118 2011 £75

Paget, Violet 1856-1935 *Vanitas; Polite Storie, Including the Hitherto Unpublished Story Entitled "A Frivolous Conversation".* Leipzig: Bernhard Tauchnitz, 1911, Copyright edition; contemporary half vellum, slight dulled, label worn, bound without half title. Jarndyce Antiquarian Booksellers CLXC - 119 2011 £40

Pain, Barry *Playthings and Parodies.* London: Cassell & Co., 1892, First edition; half title, 8 pages and 16 page catalog (8.95), partly uncut in original dark green cloth, elaborately blocked in blind, bookplate of Lionel Lawford Fletcher, very good, bright. Jarndyce Antiquarian Booksellers CXCI - 377 2011 £45

Paine, Albert Bigelow *The Arkansaw Bear.* London: Harrap & Co., 1919, Large 8vo., original pictorial boards, pages 123, with 8 color plates by Harry Rountree. R. F. G. Hollett & Sons Antiquarian Booksellers 170 - 497 2011 £35

Paine, Albert Bigelow *Mark Twain. A Biography.* Harper Brothers, 1912, First edition; 3 volumes, original red cloth, gilt, spines evenly darkened, pages xv, 562; x, 563-1110; x, 1111-1719, with 81 illustrations, very good, sound set.   R. F. G. Hollett & Son Antiquarian Booksellers   General Catalogue Summer 2010 - 448   2011   £150

Paine, James *The Mansion House, Doncaster.* Howden: Hull Academic Press, 2002, Limited facsimile reprint, no. 64 of 200 copies; folio, original brown buckram, gilt, pages (ii), (iv), 3 lus 21 plates, fine.   R. F. G. Hollett & Son Antiquarian Booksellers   177 - 611   2011   £150

Paine, Thomas   1737-1809 *Common Sense.* Philadelphia printed: Providence: John Carter, 1776, First quarto edition; sixth overall, only contemporary large paper quarto edition, uncut, original stitched self wrappers.   Heritage Book Shop   Booth A12 51st NY International Antiquarian Book Fair April 8-10 2011 - 97   2011 $30,000

Paine, Thomas   1737-1809 *Common Sense: Addressed to the Inhabitants of America.* London: for H. D. Symonds, 1792, New edition; 36 pages, removed, very good.   Joseph J. Felcone Inc.   Fall Miscellany 2010 - 97   2011 $400

Paine, Thomas   1737-1809 *The Decline and Fall of the English System of Finance.* Philadelphia: John Page for Benj. Franklin Bache, 1796, 8vo. 33 pages, removed, uncut, half title, neatly disbound, very crisp.   M & S Rare Books, Inc.   90 - 309   2011 $325

Paine, Thomas   1737-1809 *Dissertation on first Principles of Government.* Paris: printed at the English Press, 1795, First edition, 2nd issue; 8vo., 40 pages, removed, uncut, lightly foxed, very nice.   M & S Rare Books, Inc.   90 - 307   2011 $550

Palgrave, Francis Turner   1824-1897 *Amenophis and Other Poems, Sacred And Secular.* London: Macmillan, 1892, First edition; half title, engraved title only, blind-stamped presentation copy, 1 ad leaf, original dark green cloth, fine.   Jarndyce Antiquarian Booksellers   CXCI - 378   2011   £35

Palgrave, Francis Turner   1824-1897 *Palgrave's Golden Treasury of Songs & Lyrics.* London: Hodder & Stoughton, n.d. circa, 1919, First edition; large 8vo., original pictorial orange cloth, pages xv, 459, with 12 tipped in tissue guarded color plates, nice, clean and bright.   R. F. G. Hollett & Son Antiquarian Booksellers   175 - 175   2011   £60

Pall Mall Magazine. Greenwood Press, 1893-1909, First edition; Volumes 1-22, 24, 26, 28?, 30, 32-38, 40-43, 36 volumes, mixed bindings, 29 being in original publisher's binding) generally in very good condition.   I. D. Edrich   May 26 2011 - 100776   2011 $2097

Pallister, Anne *Magna Carta.* Oxford: Clarendon Press, 1971, First edition; original cloth, gilt, dust jacket, pages (viii), 134, with 5 plates, fine, author's compliments slip loosely inserted.   R. F. G. Hollett & Son Antiquarian Booksellers   175 - 1032   2011   £30

Palmer, Agnes L. *The Time Between 1904-1926.* New York: 1926, First edition; 123 pages, 4to., wrappers, very good in Gaylord boards, bookplate removed from board, library pocket on rear wrappers, lower rear corner ruffled.   Bookworm & Silverfish   669 - 176   2011 $75

Palmer, Alicia Tyndal *The Sons of Altringham, a Novel.* London: Lackington, Allen & Co., 1812, Second edition; 3 volumes, half titles, final ad leaves volumes II & III, uncut in original blue boards, drab spines with hand written lettering, corners bit worn volume II, but all in all good plus copy, extremely scarce, with contemporary signatures of Eliza Giffard, Nerquis, Flintshire partially removed in volumes II and III.   Jarndyce Antiquarian Booksellers   CLXC - 734   2011   £600

Palmer, Arnold *Arnold Palmer's Best 54.* Garden City: Doubleday, 1977, First edition; small 4to., xii, 206 pages, very good++ dust jacket with small closed tears, minimal edgewear, signed and inscribed by Palmer.   By the Book, L. C.   26 - 79   2011 $225

Palmer, E. Clephan *The Young Blackbird.* Allan Wingate, 1953, First edition; original cloth, dust jacket trifle dusty, pages 63, illustrations.   R. F. G. Hollett & Sons Antiquarian Booksellers   170 - 510   2011   £65

Palmer, Edwin *History of Hollywood.* Hollywood: 1938, Second printing; near fine, extensively illustrated.   Lupack Rare Books   May 26 2011 - ABE3090157830   2011 $150

Palmer, J. H. *Historic Farmhouses in and Around Westmorland.* Kendal: Westmorland Gazette, 1945, First trade edition; small 4to., original cloth, dust jacket little soiled and chipped, spotted on reverse, pages 126, illustrations, pastedowns little cockled, scarce.   R. F. G. Hollett & Son Antiquarian Booksellers   173 - 862   2011   £85

Palmer, J. H. *Historic Farmhouses in and Around Westmorland.* Kendal: Westmorland Gazette, 1949, Small 4to., original cloth, gilt, small faded patch to top corner of one boards, pages 126, illustrations.   R. F. G. Hollett & Son Antiquarian Booksellers   173 - 863   2011   £45

Palmer, R. Liddesdale *English Monasteries in the Middle Ages.* London: Constable, 1930, First edition; 4to., original cloth, gilt, corners little bumped, library numbers on spine, pages xv, 233, with 74 illustrations, ex-library with few marginal blindstamps, accession stamp on verso of title, blurb from dust jacket laid on to front flyleaf.   R. F. G. Hollett & Son Antiquarian Booksellers   177 - 612   2011   £45

Palmer, Samuel *Moral Essays on Some of the Most Curious and Signfiicant English, Scotch and Foreign Proverbs.* London: printed by Tho. Hodgkin for R. Bonwicke etc., 1710, First edition; contemporary blind panelled calf with spine label, little bumped and scratched, few slight defects, pages xxxi, 384, (xvi), lacks front flyleaf, index leaves little damaged by damp and worn at bottom margin, nowhere affecting text, otherwise very good, scarce. R. F. G. Hollett & Son Antiquarian Booksellers   175 - 1033   2011   £250

Palmer, W. T. *The English Lakes.* A. & C. Black, 1908, Second edition; large 8vo., original blue decorative cloth, gilt, pages ix, 232, 8, top edge gilt, with 75 colored plates, tape stains to corners of flyleaves, edges lightly spotted, otherwise very attractive in scarce dust jacket.   R. F. G. Hollett & Son Antiquarian Booksellers   173 - 259   2011   £140

Palmer, W. T. *The English Lakes.* London: A. & C. Black, 1908, Second edition; large 8vo., original decorative cloth gilt, pages ix, 232, iv, top edge gilt, 75 colored plates, rear endpapers lightly spotted, otherwise very good, fresh copy. R. F. G. Hollett & Son Antiquarian Booksellers   173 - 258   2011   £75

Palmer, W. T. *The Verge of Western Lakeland.* Robert Hale, 1941, Pages 252, with 15 plates, original cloth, gilt, dust jacket rather worn and repaired on reverse but complete.   R. F. G. Hollett & Son Antiquarian Booksellers   173 - 865   2011   £35

Paltock, Robert *The Life and Adventures of Peter Wilkins.* London: J. M. Dent & Sons, 1928, First edition; small 4to., original blue cloth gilt, trifling rubbing to extremities, pages xxii, 342, with 4 double page, 5 full page and 8 half page illustrations stencilled in colours and 23 black and white illustrations, all by Edward Bawden, flyleaves lightly browned but very good.   R. F. G. Hollett & Son Antiquarian Booksellers   General Catalogue Summer 2010 - 718 2011 £95

Paludan-Muller, Frederick *The Fountain of Youth.* London: Macmillan & Co., 1867, First English edition; frontispiece, plates and illustrations, presentation binding in full calf, blocked in gilt on front board, maroon label, presentation label from Glasgow Academy on leading pastedown, nice.   Jarndyce Antiquarian Booksellers   CXCI - 379 2011 £60

Panchaud, Benjamin *Entretiens ou Lecons Mathematiques sur la Maniere d'Etudier Cette Science et su les Principles Utilites...* Lausanne & Geneva: Marc Michel Bousquet, 1743, 2 parts, 12mo., v i, (ii), 372, (2); 250, (2) pages, title printed in black and red, woodcut headpieces and initials, contemporary English blond calf with nice gilt border on boards, spine gilt in compartments, morocco lettering piece, elegant binding, from the library of the Earls of Macclesfield at Shirburn Castle.   Maggs Bros. Ltd.   1440 - 161   2011   £450

Pankhurst, Christabel *Pressing Problems of the Closing Age.* London: Morgan & Scott, 1924, First edition; half titles, frontispiece, 4 pages ads, original grey cloth, spine lettered in gilt, slightly dulled, very good.   Jarndyce Antiquarian Booksellers   CLXC - 735   2011   £35

Pankhurst, Emmeline *My Own Story.* London: Eveleigh Nash, 1914, First edition; half title, frontispiece, 15 plates, erratum slip, original blue cloth lettered in gilt, spine faded, little dulled, good sound copy.   Jarndyce Antiquarian Booksellers   CLXC - 736   2011   £75

Pannell, J. P. M. *The Techniques of Industrial Archaeology.* Phillimore, 1981, Second edition; original cloth, gilt, dust jacket, pages 200 with 14 plates and 59 figures.   R. F. G. Hollett & Son Antiquarian Booksellers   177 - 613   2011   £30

Panshin, Alexei *Rite of Passage.* London: Sidgwick & Jackson, 1969, First British and first hardcover edition; octavo, boards.   L. W. Currey, Inc.   124 - 111   2011 $750

Pantin, William Abel *Chapters of the Black Monks.* London: Royal Horticultural Society, 1931-1937, 3 volumes, volume 2 little faded and scratched, pages xvii, 296; xix, 232, ix, 414.   R. F. G. Hollett & Son Antiquarian Booksellers   175 - 1034   2011   £35

Pantomime and Minstrel Scenes: a Picture Carnival for the Young. London & New York: Geo. Routledge & Sons, 1883, Folio, cloth backed pictorial boards, 2 minor margin mends and slight tip wear, else near fine, 2 huge double page color spreads, 10 other full page color chromolithographs, plus one double page brown illustration, 2 full page brown illustrations and illustrations in brown and orange on every page of text, very rare.   Aleph-Bet Books, Inc.   95 - 108   2011 $2500

Panton, Jane Ellen *Having and Hold a Story of Country Life.* London: Trischler and Co., 1890, First edition; 3 volumes, half title, some browning in prelims, original pale purple cloth, blocked and lettered in black, little dulled, good plus.   Jarndyce Antiquarian Booksellers   CLXC - 738 2011   £250

Paolini, Christopher *Brisinger.* London: Doubleday, 2008, Limited to 100 signed and numbered copies; fine in publisher's slipcase, signed by author.   Bella Luna Books   May 26 2011 - t8822   2011 $165

Papin, Denys *La Maniere d'Amolir les os, et de Faire Cuire Toutes Sortes de Viandes en Fort Peu de Temps & a Peu de Frais.*   Paris: E. Michallet, 1682, First French edition; 12mo., (12), 164, (12), 2 folding engraved plates (first with 8 figures, second with X), contemporary calf, first few leaves slightly stained at head of leaf, spine slightly worn, from the library of the Earls of Macclesfield at Shirburn Castle.   Maggs Bros. Ltd.   1440 - 162   2011   £700

Papworth, John B. 1775-1847 *Select Views of London.* London: printed for R. Ackermann by J. Diggens, 1816, First edition, first issue; with Papworth's name on titlepage, large octavo, (8), 159 pages, 76 hand colored aquatint plates including five double page folding plates, plates watermarked 1815, contemporary Regency calf, neatly rebacked with original spine laid down, covers decoratively bordered gilt, spine decoratively tooled in gilt in compartments with black morocco gilt lettering label, little light off-setting form plates to text, armorial bookplate of Frank Brewer Bemis and bookplate of Gladys Robinson, excellent early copy, housed in tan cloth slipcase.   David Brass Rare Books, Inc.   May 26 2011 - 00640   2011 $8500

Parables of Our Lord.   London: John Mitchell, n.d. c., 1870, Small folio, original full carlet morocco gilt over heavy bevelled boards, each board elaborately tooled in blind, upper board elegantly lettered in gilt, old darkened, scratch across board, extremities little rubbed, unpaginated, all edges gilt and gauffered, 36 leaves mostly of heavy card and attached to guards, text printed in red, some historiated initials in blue with fine steel engraved illustrations, text plates, occasional browned patch or spot, excellent bright copy.   R. F. G. Hollett & Son Antiquarian Booksellers   175 - 477   2011   £250

Pardoe, Julia *The Life of Marie De Medicis Queen of France...*   London: Colburn and Co., 1852, First edition; 3 volumes, original blue blindstamped cloth, gilt, little worn and marked in places, pages xxvi, 443, 16; xvii, 466, 24, (ii); xix, (iii), 578, with 9 steel engraved plates (some rather spotted), joints cracked or strained.   R. F. G. Hollett & Son Antiquarian Booksellers   175 - 1035   2011   £140

Pare, Ambroise 1510-1590 *Ten Books of Surgery and the Magazine of the Instruments Necessary for It.*   Athens: University of Georgia, 1969, First edition; 8vo., xvi, 264 pages, illustrations, brown cloth, gilt ruled cover borders and gilt stamped spine title, near fine, presentation inscription by translator Nathan Womack, from the Medical Library of Dr. Clare Gray Peterson.   Jeff Weber Rare Books   162 - 234   2011 $50

Pare, Ambroise 1510-1590 *Oeuvres Completes d'Ambroise Pare...*   Paris: J. B. Bailliere, 1840-1841, 3 volumes, 8vo., cccli, (1), 459; (4), 811; (4), xxxii, 878 pages, frontispiece in volume I and 217 line engravings by A. Chazal, original printed wrappers, uncut, unopened, fine, near mint set, from the Medical Library of Dr. Clare Gray Peterson.   Jeff Weber Rare Books   162 - 233   2011 $1900

Pare, Ambroise 1510-1599 *The Collected Works of Ambroise Pare.*   Pound Ridge: Milford House, 1968, Facsimile reprint of the 1634 first edition in English; (xii), 1173, table/index 22 pages, brown cloth, black stamped spine title, housed in black paper slipcase with printed cloth label, book in excellent condition, slipcase has bit of wear to extremities, hinges strong and intact, very good+, from the Medical Library of Dr. Clare Gray Peterson.   Jeff Weber Rare Books   162 - 235   2011 $250

The Parental Instructor; or a Father's Present to His Children.   Edinburgh: Oliver and Boyd, sold also by G. and W. B. Whittaker, London and W. Burnbull, Glasgow, n.d. circa, 1820, 12mo., 84 pages, original marbled paper on boards, green morocco spine with gilt fillets, wood engraved frontispiece, 16 half page wood engravings, restored small chip at lower inner corner of frontispiece, light foxing at endpapers and along edges of frontispiece, shelfwear at edges, fine with stunning engravings.   Hobbyhorse Books   56 - 112   2011 $370

Paris, J. A. *Philosophy in Sport.*   London: John Murray, 1861, Ninth edition; original green cloth gilt, pages xxvii, 401, woodcut frontispiece and numerous text illustrations, prelims rather foxed, shaped armorial bookplate of Woodthorpe Brandon.   R. F. G. Hollett & Sons Antiquarian Booksellers   170 - 498   2011   £85

Park, Mungo *Travels in the Interior Districts of Africa. (bound with) The Journal of a Mission to the Interior of Africa in the Year 1805.*   London: G. and W. Nicol, 1799, London, John Murray, 1815. First and second edition respectively; quarto, illustrations, contemporary polished tan calf.   Heritage Book Shop   Booth A12 51st NY International Antiquarian Book Fair April 8-10 2011 - 98   2011 $3500

Park, Mungo *Travels in the Interior Districts of Africa Performed Under the Direction an Patroange of the African Association in the Years 1795, 1796 and 1797...* Philadelphia: printed from the London quarto edition by James Humphreys, 1800, Octavo, xxi, (1), (23)-484 pages, large folding map, original full calf, gilt ruled spine, red spine label, hinges repaired, signature on title of Anna J. M. Randolph 1895, very good "Attleborough Library 6 weeks" on title, very good.   Jeff Weber Rare Books   163 - 203   2011 $300

Park, Mungo *Travels in the Interior Districts of Africa, Performed in the Years 1795, 1796 and 1797.* London: John Murray, 1817, 1816. Second Murray enlarged edition; 2 volumes, 8vo., large folding map, text figures, original half calf over decorative boards, raised bands, gilt stamped spine titles, neatly restored, preserving original spines and endsheets, ink signatures of W. F. Hunt, very good.   Jeff Weber Rare Books   163 - 202   2011 $400

Parke, Thomas Heazle *My Personal Experiences in Equatorial Africa as Medical Officer of the Emin Pasha Relief Expedition.* London: Sampson Low, Marston, 1891, First edition; octavo, xxvi, 526, 32 (ads) pages, frontispiece, 17 illustrations, folding map in rear pocket, index, original olive green cloth stamped in black and gilt, beautiful copy.   Jeff Weber Rare Books   163 - 204   2011 $800

Parker, B. *Cinderella at the Zoo.* London & Edinburgh: W. & R. Chambers, n.d. circa, 1915, Large 4to., pictorial boards, slightest bit of rubbing, else fine in dust jacket (edge chipped), 16 full page chromolithographs, rare in dust jacket.   Aleph-Bet Books, Inc.   95 - 413   2011 $1650

Parker, B. *Cinderella in the Zoo.* London: W. & R. Chambers Limited, circa, 1916, First edition; 4to., color pictorial boards with minor bowing and some corner wear, full color pictorial dust jacket with pieces missing and some edge wear but basically intact, 16 full page color plates by Nancy Parker.   Jo Ann Reisler, Ltd.   86 - 188   2011 $1500

Parker, B. *Funny Bunnies.* London: W. & R. Chambers Limited circa, 1907, Oblong 4to., full color pictorial boards with some light shelf wear and book has been recased, text pages paired with extraordinary full page full color illustrations, text pages and divider sections have charming line drawings.   Jo Ann Reisler, Ltd.   86 - 187   2011 $450

Parker, B. *History of the Hoppers.* London: W. R. Chambers, n.d., 1912, First and probably only edition; Large 4to., pictorial boards, new spine and endpapers, slight edge rubbing, else near fine, color and line illustrations by N. Parker, rare.   Aleph-Bet Books, Inc.   95 - 58   2011 $1500

Parker, B. *The Lays of the Grays.* London and Edinburgh: W. & R. Chambers, n.d circa, 1910, Oblong folio, pictorial boards, light cover rubbing, near fine, full page color illustrations by N. Parker.   Aleph-Bet Books, Inc.   95 - 414   2011 $1200

Parker, B. *Out in the Wood.* London: W. & R. Chambers, n.d. circa, 1910, Oblong folio, pictorial boards, slightest bit of rubbing, else fine, 14 incredible full page color illustrations, pictorial endpapers.   Aleph-Bet Books, Inc.   95 - 415   2011 $1500

Parker, C. A. *The Ancient Crosses at Gosforth, Cumberland.* London: Elliot Stock, 1896, First edition; original cloth, trifle scratched, rebacked in matching brown levant morocco gilt, pages 85, text illustrations.   R. F. G. Hollett & Son Antiquarian Booksellers   173 - 872   2011   £85

Parker, C. A. *The Gosforth District: Its Antiquities and Places of Interest.* Kendal: Titus Wilson, 1904, First edition; original cloth, gilt, few slight marks to lower board, pages 251, illustrations, half title little browned.   R. F. G. Hollett & Son Antiquarian Booksellers   173 - 873   2011   £60

Parker, C. A. *The Gosforth District, Its Antiquities and Places of Interest.* Kendal: Titus Wilson, 1926, Original cloth, gilt, pages 204, illustrations.   R. F. G. Hollett & Son Antiquarian Booksellers   173 - 874   2011   £65

Parker, C. A. *The Story of Shelagh, Olaf Curaran's Daughter.* Kendal: Titus Wilson, 1909, First edition; original cloth, gilt, pages viii, 72, illustrations, folding map, flyleaves lightly browned as usual, scarce.   R. F. G. Hollett & Son Antiquarian Booksellers   173 - 875   2011   £75

Parker, D. C. *Codex Bezae. Studies from the Lumel Colloquium June 1994.* Leiden: E. J. Brill, 1996, First edition; tall 8vo., original cloth, dust jacket, pages xxx, 383, (ii), 19 pages of plates.   R. F. G. Hollett & Son Antiquarian Booksellers   177 - 616   2011   £120

Parker, Eric *Hesketh Prichard DSO, M.C. Hunter: Explorer: Naturalist: Cricketer: Author: Soldier a Memoir.* London: T. Fisher Unwin Ltd., 1924, 8vo., pages (x), 271, (1), half title, index, black and white frontispiece and 8 black and white photo illustrations, red cloth, gilt title to spine, spine and back cover slightly sunned, some foxing to outer margins.   Schooner Books Ltd.   96 - 77   2011 $90

Parker, F. H. M. *The Pipe Rolls of Cumberland and Westmorland 1222-1260.* Kendal: Titus Wilson, 1905, First edition; original brown cloth gilt, pages xliii, 229, folding map.   R. F. G. Hollett & Son Antiquarian Booksellers   173 - 876   2011   £125

Parker, George F. *Recollection of Grover Cleveland.* New York: 1909, First edition; three quarter chocolate morocco and marbled boards and marbled endpapers, top edge gilt, very good.   Bookworm & Silverfish   676 - 54   2011 $75

Parker, J. H. *A Glossary of Terms Used in Grecian, Roman, Italian and Gothic Architecture.* Oxford: John Henry Parker, 1845, 2 volumes, original blindstamped cloth, gilt, fore edges rather damped, neatly recased, pages ix, 416, 16, 23, with 1100 woodcuts in 164 plates, 1 loose, edges little chipped.   R. F. G. Hollett & Son Antiquarian Booksellers   177 - 617   2011   £75

Parker, J. M. *An Aged Wanderer. A Life Sketch of J. M. Parker, A Cowboy on the Western Plains in Early Days.* San Angelo: Elkhorn Wagon Yard, 1923, First edition; original blue pictorial wrappers, portrait verso front wrapper, 32 pages, wrapper title, laid in four point folding case, light wear to bottom edges, else very good, exceedingly rare. Buckingham Books May 26 2011 - 28734 2011 $1875

Parker, John *Who Was Who in the Theatre 1912-1976: a Biographical Dictionary of Actors, Actresses, Directors, Playwrights & Producers of the English Speaking Theatre.* Detroit & London: Gale Research and Pitman, First edition; 4 volumes, 8vo, pages 2663, sound ex-library with few stamps and labels, first volume lacks endpaper, all with clean text, decent, slightly marked covers, sound, about very good. Any Amount of Books May 29 2011 - A76076 2011 $272

Parker, Reuel B. *The New Cold Molded Boat Building from Lofting to Launching.* Camden: 1990, First edition; 320 pages, fine in fine dust jacket. Bookworm & Silverfish 678 - 145 2011 $125

Parker, Samuel *The Ecclesiastical Histories of Eusebius, Socrates, Sozomen and Theodorit.* London: printed for C. Rivington, 1729, Third edition; 4to., pages 16 (viii), 17-368, (i), ccclxii-ccclxviii, 369-651, (xxv) + engraved frontispiece and 4 other plates, contemporary calf, boards panelled in blind Cambridge style, board edges, decorative roll in blind, all edges red sprinkled, contrasting calf reback + corners by W. R. Wiltshire, little light spotting, few early notes in margins and one on tipped in sheet, old leather rubbed and chipped at edges, from the collection of Christopher Ernest Weston 1947-2010. Unsworths Booksellers 24 - 33 2011 £200

Parkman, Francis *Francis Parkman's Works.* Boston: Little Brown & Co., 1899, Frontenac Edition; 16 volumes, 8vo., xcii, 181; x, 311; xii, 280; ix, 309; xxii, 522; xvi 267; viii, 297; xv, 523; xi, 368; vii, 416; xiv, 329; ix, 372; viii, 394; xxi, 31; x, 484; xviii, 479 pages, frontispiece in each volume, illustrations, original blue cloth, printed spine labels, top edge gilt, each volume includes two extra spine labels, fine, as new. Jeff Weber Rare Books 163 - 93 2011 $350

Parkyns, Mansfield *Life in Abyssinia: Being Notes Collected During Three Years Residence and Travels in that Country.* London: John Murray, 1853, First edition; 2 volumes, 8vo., pages xv, (i blank, 425, (1) imprint; iv, 432, engraved frontispiece in each volume (foxing), 16 engraved plates, folding map, some textual illustrations, original blue decorative cloth, small split at head of spine. J. & S. L. Bonham Antiquarian Booksellers Africa 4/20/2011 - 9179 2011 £250

Parmiter, Geffrey De C. *Reasonable Doubt.* London: Arthur Barker, 1938, First edition; original cloth, gilt, dust jacket spine defective, pages xv, 331. R. F. G. Hollett & Son Antiquarian Booksellers 175 - 1037 2011 £30

Parr, Harriet 1828-1900 *Hawksview: a Family History of Our Own Times.* London: James Blackwood, 1859, First edition; half title, name from head of title, original dark green pebbled grained cloth, blocked in blind, spine lettered in gilt, very good. Jarndyce Antiquarian Booksellers CLXC - 91 2011 £60

Parr, Harriet 1828-1900 *Hawksview.* London: Smith Elder, 1862, New edition; contemporary half dark green roan, slight rubbing, slightly foxed. Jarndyce Antiquarian Booksellers CLXC - 92 2011 £35

Parr, Harriet 1828-1900 *Loving and Serving.* London: Smith, Elder, 1883, First edition; 3 volumes, half titles volumes I & II, volume I half title marked with red ink, bound in 2 volumes, without title to volume III in contemporary half calf, inner hinges splitting volume II, stamps of Beechworth Public Library. Jarndyce Antiquarian Booksellers CLXC - 93 2011 £50

Parr, Harriet 1828-1900 *The True, Pathetic History of Poor Match.* London: Smith, Elder & Co., 1863, First edition; half title, frontispiece + 3 plates by Walter Crane, 4 pages ads, new endpapers, uncut in original purple cloth, blocked in blind, pictorially blocked and lettered in gilt, at some time recased, endpapers replaced. Jarndyce Antiquarian Booksellers CLXC - 94 2011 £50

Parr, Harriet 1828-1900 *Tuflongbo's Journey in Search of Ogres; with Some Accounts of His Early Life and How His Shoes Got Worn Out.* London: Smith, Elder & Co., 1862, First edition; half title, frontispiece + 5 plates, hand colored frontispiece, uncut in original green pebble grained cloth, pictorially blocked and lettered in gilt, owner's inscription on leading f.e.p. dated 1864, good plus, scarce. Jarndyce Antiquarian Booksellers CLXC - 95 2011 £85

Parr, Martin *Mexico.* London: Chris Boot, 2006, First edition, one of only 100 copies issued with original numbered photo; fine in boards and in fine slipcase, signed by Parr on verso of photo as well as in the book. Jeff Hirsch Books ny 2010 2011 $650

Parr, Samuel *A Letter from Irenopolis (sic) to the Inhabitants of Eleutheropolis; or a Serious Address to the Dissenters of Birmingham.* Birmingham: printed by John Thompson for C. Dilly, London, 1792, Second edition; 8vo., 40, (2) pages, including half title and final (ad on recto, errata on verso), mid 20th century roan backed marbled boards, spine lettered in gilt, very good, scarce. John Drury Rare Books 153 - 108 2011 £175

Parrhasio, Aulo Giano *Liber de Rebus per Epistola Quaesitis...* Geneva: H. Estienne, 1567, 8vo., (8), 272, (8) pages, English binding circa 1700 of black morocco, panelled in gilt on covers with floral cornerpieces, spine gilt, edges gilt, handsome collection, from the library of the Earls of Macclesfield at Shirburn Castle. Maggs Bros. Ltd. 1440 - 164 2011 £700

Parrish, Anne *The Story of Appleby Capple.* New York: Harper & Bros., 1950, 4to., yellow cloth, 184 pages, very good+ in dust jacket (lightly soiled dust jacket), illustrations in black and white, illustrated color endpapers. Aleph-Bet Books, Inc. 95 - 31 2011 $250

Parrish, Jenni *Abortion Law in the United States Volume I: From Roe V. 1.. Wade to the Present. V. 2. Historical Development of Abortion Law. V. 3. Modern Writings on Abortion.* New York: Garland, 1995, 3 volumes, 8vo., pages xxix, 596; vi, 298; xxix, 596, about as new. Second Life Books Inc. 174 - 256 2011 $125

Parrish, Maxfield *Maxfield Parrish's Four Best Paintings.* New York: P. F. Collier, n.d. circa, 1910, Oblong folio, black boards, printed label, slight edge rubbing, else fine, 4 matted color illustrations, incredibly rare. Aleph-Bet Books, Inc. 95 - 416 2011 $1600

Parry, William Edward 1790-1855 *Journal of a Third Voyage for the Discovery of a North West Passage from the Atlantic to the Pacific, Performed in the Years 1824-25 in His Majesty's Ships Hecla and Fury, Under the Orders of Captain William Edward Parry.* London: John Murray, 1826, First edition; 4to., frontispiece and 10 plates, 1 folding plate with slight tear, otherwise internally very good, uncut, rebound in drab boards, recent paper label, very good. Jarndyce Antiquarian Booksellers CXCI - 572 2011 £1250

Parson, William *History, Directory and Gazetteer of the Counties of Cumberland and Westmorland...* Beckermet: Michael Moon, 1976, Facsimile edition; thick 8vo., original cloth, gilt, dust jacket price clipped, pages 732, xxxiv, (ii), inscription and label on flyleaf. R. F. G. Hollett & Son Antiquarian Booksellers 173 - 878 2011 £75

Parsons, Claudia *Vagabondage.* London: Chatto & Windus, 1941, First edition; 8vo., pages xii, 304, frontispiece, 15 plates, 3 maps, neat name on front endpaper, "K. Coomaraswamy/Segannah/Nov. 11th/ 1941" (possibly Ananda K./Coomaraswamy), loosely inserted is good long signed typed letter from Claudia Parsons to Denis Collings, covers heavily worn and soiled, spine slightly split, contents okay, good only. Any Amount of Books May 29 2011 - A36695 2011 $255

Parsons, Elsie Clews *Pueblo Indian Religion.* Chicago: 1939, First edition; 2 volumes, xviii, 549 pages, illustrations, folding tables (550)-1275 pages, illustrations, folding table, light extremity wear, owner's bookplate in both volumes, else very good. Dumont Maps & Books of the West 112 - 58 2011 $750

Parsons, Elsie Clews *Taos Pueblo.* Menasha: 1936, First edition; 121 pages plus 12 pages of plates, folding plan, original stiff paper printed covers, loss of cloth on spine binding, some external soil, else clean and very good. Dumont Maps & Books of the West 112 - 59 2011 $125

Parsons, George Whitwell *The Private Journal of George Parsons.* Phoenix: Arizona Statewide Archival and Records Project, 1939, First edition; quarto, stiff printed wrappers, vi, (1), 333 pages, all pages photolithographed, re-enforced along fore-edge of front panel and few prelim pages, moderate vertical creases to front panel, else very good, tight copy, housed in quarter leather and cloth folding case with raised bands and gold stamping on spine. Buckingham Books May 26 2011 - 20945 2011 $2500

Partington, Wilfred *Smoke Rings and Roundelays, Blendings from Prose and Verse... (with) Portfolio to Smoke Rings and Roundelays.* London: John Castle, 1924, Portfolio is No. 15 of 25 sets of proofs on Japanese vellum, each proof being signed by artist; woodcuts by Norman Jones, original brown cloth, fine in dust jacket, portfolio 17 17 woodcuts, each proof being signed by artist, brown cloth wrappers, paper label with ties. Jarndyce Antiquarian Booksellers CXCI - 535 2011 £45

Partridge, Eric *The Shaggy Dog Story.* London: Faber, 1953, First edition; inscription from author for Stephen Potter, pages 107, illustrations, original cloth, gilt, dust jacket price clipped. R. F. G. Hollett & Son Antiquarian Booksellers General Catalogue Summer 2010 - 863 2011 £120

Pasha, Colen *Recollections and Reflections.* London: St. Catherine's Press, 1918, First edition; 8vo., pages xv, 208, illustrations, original black cloth. J. & S. L. Bonham Antiquarian Booksellers Africa 4/20/2011 - 8750 2011 £40

Pasternak, Boris 1890-1960 *(In Cyrillic) Doctor Zhivago.* Milan: Feltrinelli, n.d. but late, 1958, or early 1959. First trade or 'official' edition in Russian; (4), 567 pages, pale green laid paper over boards, stamped in black, faint browning of text due to poor quality of paper stock, free endpapers discolored from dust jacket flaps, but very good, dust jacket has some light uniform discoloration on white spine and two very tiny spots and two small closed tears top of back panel. Joseph J. Felcone Inc. Fall Miscellany 2010 - 99 2011 $2500

Pasternak, Boris 1890-1960 *Doktor Zywago (Doctor Zhivago).* Milan: Feltrinelli Editore, 1958, First official edition in Russian; finely bound in full dark green leather lettered gilt and decorated at spine, edges of pages slightly browned, otherwise fine. Any Amount of Books May 26 2011 - A44995 2011 $1006

Patchen, Kenneth *The Memoirs of a Shy Pornographer.* New York: New Directions, 1945, First edition, first impression; clippings on rear endpapers, else near fine, tattered remnants of dust jacket (lacking front panel and front flap), booklabel of Greenwich Village artist Arthur Sturcke on titlepage, inscribed to same by author. Between the Covers 169 - BTC34088 2011 $1500

Patchen, Kenneth *To Say If You Love Someone.* Prairie City: Decker Press, 1948, Unrecorded variant; gray cloth with same design as that of the apparently first issue yellow cloth, in blue dust jacket with gold and black lettering, price of $1 and words THE ARCHIVE of Duke University" in place of "Louis Untermeyer" on dust jacket copy, fine in mildly sunned, else fine dust jacket.   Ken Lopez Bookseller   154 - 161   2011 $2000

Patercullus, Velleius *C. Velleii Paterculi Historiae Romanae and M. Vinicium Cos Libri Duo.* Parisiis: Apud Fredericum Leonard, 1675, 4to., pages (xxviii) 151, (lxxxix) + engraved half title, bound facing title contemporary mottled calf, spine panel gilt, dark red lettering piece gilt, boards double rule bordered in blind with central triple rule panel having fleurons at corners all in blind, board edges decorative roll gilt, all edges red speckled, blue and white sewn endbands, few minor spots, title bit dusty, old leather somewhat scratched, contemporary ink inscription, armorial bookplates of John Peyto Verney/Lord Willoughby de Broke, and of Robert John Verney/Lord Willoughby de Broke, from the collection of Christopher Ernest Weston 1947-2010.   Unsworths Booksellers   24 - 131   2011   £250

Patercullus, Velleius *The Roman History of C. Velleius Paterculus.* Edinburgh: printed for the author by John Mosman and Co., 1722, 8vo., pages (vi) x, 258, contemporary tan calf, untooled spine, red lettering piece gilt, boards panelled in blind 'Cambridge style' board edges decorative roll in blind, all edges gilt lightly red speckled, pink and white sewn endbands, some browning, few marks, touch rubbed at extremities, from the collection of Christopher Ernest Weston 1947-2010.   Unsworths Booksellers   24 - 132   2011   £150

Paternal Advice to Children. To which is Prefixed a Short Narrative of the Awful Event by Which It Was Occasioned. Philadelphia: Clark & Raser, 1818, First American edition; 32mo., 32 pages, original printed wrappers, some soiling and browning, very good.   M & S Rare Books, Inc.   90 - 206   2011 $350

Paterson, A. B. *The Man from Snowy River and Other Verses.* Sydney: Angus and Robertson, 1895, Second edition; 8vo., sound clean copy in original publisher's brown buckram lettered gilt on spine, pages xvi, 184, uncut, endpapers foxed, corners very slightly bumped, very slight marks to covers, very good, pleasing copy.   Any Amount of Books   May 26 2011 - A69020   2011 $671

Paterson, James Laird *Journal of a Tour in Egypt, Palestine, Syria and Greece with Notes and an Appendix on Ecclesiastical Subjects.* New York: Edward Dunigan and Brotehr, 1852, First American edition; folding lithographed frontispiece, 2 double page tinted lithographs, 1 double page and 1 black and white plate, 1 plan and 2 woodcut illustrations in text, occasional light foxing of plates, original blind-stamped cloth, rebacked, printed paper label.   Anthony W. Laywood   May 26 2011 - 19831   2011 $201

Paterson, William *A Narrative of Four Journeys into the Country of the Hottentots and Caffraria in the Yars 1777, 1778 & 1779.* London: J. Johnson, 1790, Second edition; large quarto, pages xii, 176, folding map, 19 engraved plates, some light foxing, recent quarter speckled calf.   J. & S. L. Bonham Antiquarian Booksellers   Africa 4/20/2011 - 7549   2011   £1350

Patmore, Coventry *The Angel in the House. The Betrothal.* London: John W. Parker & Son, 1854, First edition; original brown vertical wavy grained cloth, dulled, slightly buckled and affected by damp, paper label rubbed.   Jarndyce Antiquarian Booksellers   CXCI - 381   2011   £65

Patmore, Coventry *The Children's Garland from the Best Poets.* London: Macmillan, 1862, First edition; original cloth, gilt, little worn and neatly recased, new endpapers, pages xvi, 344, (iv, ads dated Nov. 1862), with half title and vignette on title.   R. F. G. Hollett & Sons Antiquarian Booksellers   170 - 499   2011   £130

Patmore, Coventry *Faithful For Ever.* London: John W. Parker and Son, 1860, First edition; 4 pages ads, original purple brown cloth, slightly faded and damp marked, endpapers replaced in dark blue paper.   Jarndyce Antiquarian Booksellers   CXCI - 382   2011   £50

Patmore, Coventry *How I Managed and Improved my Estate.* London: George Bell & Sons, 1886, First edition; half title, 24 page catalog (July 1883), original salmon pink cloth, boards ruled and lettered in black, spine lettered in gilt, bookplate and signature of Horace Pym, V, scarce.   Jarndyce Antiquarian Booksellers   CXCI - 383   2011   £150

Patmore, Coventry *Poems.* London: George Bell & Son, 1886, Second collective edition; half titles, original blue cloth, spines faded to brown, paper label, volume II chipped.   Jarndyce Antiquarian Booksellers   CXCI - 384   2011   £60

Patmore, Coventry *Religio Poetae etc.* London: George Bell & Sons, 1893, First edition; half title, final ad leaf, pencil signature on leading f.e.p., original olive green cloth slightly marked, paper label slightly rubbed, nice.   Jarndyce Antiquarian Booksellers   CXCI - 385   2011   £40

Patmore, Coventry *Unknown Eros. I - XLVI.* London: George Bell & Sons, 1878, Half title, uncut in original purple brown cloth, spine faded, paper label browned.   Jarndyce Antiquarian Booksellers   CXCI - 386   2011   £50

Paton, Jean A. *The Livewort Flora of the British Isles.* Colchester: Harley Books, 1999, First edition; large 4to., original glazed pictorial boards, pages 626, line drawings, fine.   R. F. G. Hollett & Son Antiquarian Booksellers   General Catalogue Summer 2010 - 1032   2011   £120

Patoun, Archibald *A Complete Treatise of Practical Navigation Demonstrated from its First Principles, Together with all the Necessary Tables.* London: printed for J. Brotherton, J. Hazard (and 9 others in London), 1739, Second edition; lacks front flyleaf, contemporary name on title, folding engraved plates, numerous illustrations in text, with final contents leaf, viii, 525, (3) pages, contemporary calf, slightly rubbed with University of Keele, Turner Collection label.   Anthony W. Laywood   May 26 2011 - 14192   2011 $411

Patten, Brian *The Early Poems of Brian Patten.* Leicester: Transican Books, 1971, First edition, no. 33 of 100 copies signed by author; (32) pages, interleaved with variety of styles and colors of thin handmade papers, one full page colored illustration by Pamela Kindred, other illustrations in text, original black textured faux leather boards, fine exquisitely produced book.   Any Amount of Books   May 26 2011 - A71941   2011 $419

Patterson, R. F. *Mein Rant.* Blackie, 1940, First edition; original cloth, dust jacket extremities minimally frayed, pages x, 70, drawings by Heath Robinson, near fine.   R. F. G. Hollett & Son Antiquarian Booksellers   General Catalogue Summer 2010 - 895   2011   £120

Patteson, Barbe *Chips from Tunis: a Glimpse of Arab Life.* London: Hachette, n.d., 1885, First edition; pages 244, original grey decorative cloth, spine faded with small wear to head.   J. & S. L. Bonham Antiquarian Booksellers   Africa 4/20/2011 - 8760   2011   £45

Pattie, James O. *The Personal Narrative of James O. Pattie of Kentucky.* Chicago: Donnelley, 1930, xliii, 428 pages, frontispiece, illustrations, maroon cloth, gilt, tiny smudge to head of spine, but fine.   Argonaut Book Shop   Recent Acquisitions Summer 2010 - 155   2011 $90

Paucker, Pauline *New Borders. The Working Life of Elizabeth Friedlander.* Oldham: Incline Press, 1998, Limited to 325 copies signed by author; 4to., 92 pages, 2 sizes of leaves 270 x 185mm. and 315 x 185mm., tipped in frontispiece, 74 printing examples tipped in, half cream cloth over yellow and green patterned paper, printed paper cover label, mylar wrappers, housed in green paper slipcase, gilt stamped red leather spine label, fine.   Jeff Weber Rare Books   163 - 114   2011 $275

Paul, C. Kegan *Memories.* London: Kegan Paul, 1899, First edition; half title, uncut in original brown cloth, slightly affected by damp, library label and pressmarks, top edge gilt.   Jarndyce Antiquarian Booksellers   CXCI - 454   2011   £35

Paul, James Balfour *The History of the Royal Company of Archers.* Edinburgh & London: William Blackwood and Sons, 1875, First edition; 250 x 200mm., ix, (i), 393 (1), 78 pages, 20 leaves, very fine contemporary dark green morocco, sumptuously gilt, covers with French fillet border, elaborate gilt picture like central frame around gilt emblem with motto "Dat Gloria Vires" above and "In Peace and War" below, showing figures associated with archery and love, peace, and war, raised bands between compartments with foliate cornerpieces and bow and quiver centerpiece, densely gilt inner dentelles, silk endleaves, gilt edges, in red and black felt lined buckram slipcase, with 6 full page color portraits, six black and white photo plates, and four line drawings, titlepage in red and black, inked note"This book formerly belonged to Lady Louis Mountbatten 4.8.34", bottom 4 inches of front joint just beginning to crack, covers slightly bumped, else beautiful copy, very handsome decorative binding, quite bright, text and plates in perfect state of preservation, luxuriously bound.   Phillip J. Pirages   59 - 66   2011 $750

Paule, George *Life of the Most Reverend and Religious Prelate John Whitgift, Lord Archbishop of Canterbury.* London: printed by Thomas Snodham, 1612, small 4to., pages (viii), 94, (ii), woodcut portrait of Whitgift on titlepage verso, early 21st century retrospective ruled calf binding by CEW, title soiled text block trimmed to printed border and sometimes just inside at top and fore-edge, old f.e.p. corner repaired, early hand has annotated head of blank leaf A1 and final blank leaf N4 armorial bookplate of "James Comerford" on front pastedown, mid 19th century ownership in Philip Bliss's hand on 17th century flyleaf reading "Bodleian Catalogue 1843, p. 62" and at foot of page I signature "P.B.43": and flowery label, presented by William Minet at foot of front pastedown, from the collection of Christopher Ernest Weston 1947-2010.   Unsworths Booksellers   24 - 34   2011   £450

Payn, James *Furness Abbey and Its Neighbourhood.* London: Simpkin Marshall & Co. and Windermere: J. Garnett, circa, 1865, Square 8vo., original blue cloth gilt over bevelled boards, extremities little worn, few slight marks, pages (ii), 54, all edges complete, 14 photo plates (mounts of 2 a little browned and creased), folding plan, text with red ruled borders, trifle shaken, scattered spotting.   R. F. G. Hollett & Son Antiquarian Booksellers   173 - 882   2011   £120

Payn, James *The Lakes in Sunshine.* Windermere: J. Garnett and Simpkin and Marshall & Co., 1867, First edition; 4to., strong quarter morocco gilt library binding, pages x, 105, all edges gilt, pictorial title in red and black, 16 albumen prints, large folding linen backed map 39 wood engravings in text, few slight marks and marginal blindstamps.   R. F. G. Hollett & Son Antiquarian Booksellers   173 - 884   2011   £450

Payne, Humfry *Archaic Marble Sculpture from the Acropolis.* London: Cresset Press, n.d., 1939, First edition; 2 volumes, small folio, original cloth, gilt with leather label on upper boards, acetate wrappers with paper flaps (defective), pages xiv, 75; 139 (plates). R. F. G. Hollett & Son Antiquarian Booksellers 177 - 619 2011 £175

Payton-Smith, D. J. *Oil: A Study of War-Time Policy and Administration.* London: HMSO, 1971, First edition; 8vo, pages xix, 520, 60 tables, 5 color folding maps, ex-British Foreign Office Library with few library markings, else very good. Any Amount of Books May 29 2011 - A76390 2011 $212

Paz, Octavio *Instante Y Revelacion.* Mexico City: Circulo Ediotrial, 1982, First edition; printed in an edition of 2200, elegant black and white photos by Manuel Alvarez Bravo, very near fine in lightly soiled, near fine dust jacket with two tiny internal hotels at rear spine gutter, signed by photographer and additionally signed and inscribed in Spanish by Paz. Jeff Hirsch Books ny 2010 2011 $2500

Paz, Octavo *Marchel Duchamp or the Castle of Purity.* London: Cape Goliard, 1970, First British edition; fine, near fine dust jacket, light creasing on top edge. Bella Luna Books May 26 2011 - t5469 2011 $192

Peabody, Elizabeth P. *Method of Spiritual Culture: Being an Explanatory Preface to the Second edition of Record of a School.* Boston: James Munroe & Co., 1836, First edition; 12mo., 42, (1), pages, sewn and uncut, as issued, library stamp on title, title with modest wrinkling. M & S Rare Books, Inc. 90 - 317 2011 $625

Peabody, Elizabeth P. *Records of School: Exemplifying the General Principles of Spiritual Culture.* Boston: James Munroe and Co.; New York: Leavitt, Lord & Co., Philadelphia: Henry Perkins, 1835, First edition; 12mo., 6, 208 pages, library buckram, half title, fine. M & S Rare Books, Inc. 90 - 316 2011 $500

Peacock, Doug *Grizzly Years.* New York: Holt, 1990, First edition; fine, dust jacket near fine, scratches on rear panel, scarce, signed by author. Bella Luna Books May 29 2011 - t6894 2011 $82

Peacock, Edward *The Army Lists to the Roundheads and Cavaliers.* London: Chatto & Windus, 1874, Second edition; roan backed cloth gilt, head of spine little worn, pages xii, 128, top edges gilt. R. F. G. Hollett & Son Antiquarian Booksellers General Catalogue Summer 2010 - 616 2011 £60

Peacock, Fansie *Pipits of Southern Africa: the Complete Guide to Africa's Ultimate LBJ's.* Pretoria: 2006, Octavo, paperback, 296 pages, color plates, line drwings, maps. Andrew Isles Natural History Books Spring 2010 - 31024 2011 $60

Peacock, Lucy *The Adventures of the Six Princesses of Babylon, in their Travels to the Temple of Virtue: an Allegory.* London: printed for the author by T. Bensley, 1785, xxi, 131 pages, 4to., half leather, marbled boards, covers strengthened, later endpapers, very good, signed in full on last page. Aleph-Bet Books, Inc. 95 - 217 2011 $1200

Peacock, Lucy *The Knight of the Rose: an Allegorical Tale...* London: J. Johnson, J. Harris et al, 1807, 12mo., (ii), 240 pages, original printed pink paper on boards, red roan spine with gilt fillets and title, inked signature at corner of titlepage, pencilled notes inside upper cover, stain at top and lower edge. Hobbyhorse Books 56 - 113 2011 $270

Peacock, Thomas Love *Headlong Hall.* London: printed for T. Hookham Jun. and Co., 1816, First edition; 12mo., 216 pages, half title, 19th century half calf, rubbed at spine, corners and hinges, marbled boards, little scuffed and little chipped, slight loss at head of spine, clean text but slight tear in half title. Any Amount of Books May 26 2011 - A73020 2011 $1342

Peacock, Thomas Love *The Prose Works of ....* London: J. M. Dent & Co., 1891, Large paper edition, only 100 copies printed; 10 volumes, half titles, frontispieces, uncut, uniformly bound in handsome half blue crushed morocco, raised gilt bands, gilt compartments, some occasional slight rubbing, top edge gilt, very good, attractive. Jarndyce Antiquarian Booksellers CXCI - 24 2011 £750

Peacock, Thomas Love *Sir Hornbook; or Childe Launcelot's Expedition.* London: Joseph Cundall, 1843, Square 12mo., 27 pages, + 8 page publisher's book list, decorative green paper on boards, green cloth spine, gilt edges, decorative endpapers, 8 full page hand colored lithographs including frontispiece, printed on one side of leaf and on heavier paper, each one with original plate guard, illustrations after Henry Corbould, corners of leaves chipped, 1 inch section clipped out of book list at end, rubbing at corners of boards, some scuffing at covers, very good, scarce reprint. Hobbyhorse Books 56 - 114 2011 $150

Peake, James *Rudimentary Treatise on Ship Building Parts II and III.* London: 1851, 173, (7) ads, 12 plates, cloth over flexible boards, paper label with age soil. Bookworm & Silverfish 678 - 146 2011 $145

Peake, Mervyn 1911-1968 *Captain Slaughterboard Drops Anchor.* London: Eyre & Spottiswoode, 1945, First edition with color illustrations; 4to., cloth, fine in dust jacket. Aleph-Bet Books, Inc. 95 - 417 2011 $700

Peake, Mervyn 1911-1968 *Captain Slaughterboard Drops Anchor.* London: Thomas Nelson and Sons, 1967, Small 4to., original glazed pictorial boards, matching dust jacket (trifle worn, large chip from bottom corner), unpaginated, illustrations in yellow and black, inscription.   R. F. G. Hollett & Sons Antiquarian Booksellers   170 - 503   2011   £95

Peake, Mervyn 1911-1968 *Captain Slaughterboard Drops Anchor.* London: Macmillan, circa, 1987, First US edition; small 4to., original glazed pictorial boards, matching dust jacket (closed tear and slight surface defect to upper panel), unpaginated, illustrations.   R. F. G. Hollett & Sons Antiquarian Booksellers   170 - 504   2011   £85

Peake, Mervyn 1911-1968 *Letters from a Lost Uncle.* London: Eyre & Spottiswoode, 1948, First edition, 2nd issue;   small 8vo., original pictorial yellow cloth, dust jacket (spine chipped, worn and darkened, chip to upper edge of lower panel, unpaginated, illustrations.   R. F. G. Hollett & Sons Antiquarian Booksellers   170 - 505   2011   £225

Pearce, F. B. *Zanzibar; the Island Metropolis of Eastern Africa.* London: T. Fisher Unwin, 1920, Second impression; large 8vo., pages xii, 431, maps, illustrations, original blue blindstamped cloth, inner hinge cracked but clean.   J. & S. L. Bonham Antiquarian Booksellers Africa 4/20/2011 - 6918   2011   £200

Pearce, Joseph P. *Merseyside to Windermere.* Ormskirk: Advertiser Office, 1931, First edition; 4to., original cloth, pictorial dust jacket, spine rather darkened and rubbed, pages xv, 148, 66 line drawings, scarce.   R. F. G. Hollett & Son Antiquarian Booksellers   173 - 885   2011   £85

Peard, Frances Mary *Near Neighbours.* London: Richard Bentley, 1885, First one volume edition; half title, owner's stamp, 3 pages ads, original dark green cloth.   Jarndyce Antiquarian Booksellers   CLXC - 739   2011   £45

Peard, Frances Mary *The Rose-Garden. (bound with) Unawares: The Story of an Old French Town.* Leipzig: Bernhard Tauchnitz, 1872, Copyright edition; 2 volumes in 1, slight yellow, contemporary half dark green morocco, spine ruled and with devices in gilt, slight rubbing, good plus, without half titles.   Jarndyce Antiquarian Booksellers   CLXC - 741   2011   £45

Pears, Iain *The Rapahel Affair.* New York: HBJ, 1992, First American edition; near fine, remainder mark which has left small dot on bottom of front board, dust jacket fine.   Bella Luna Books   May 29 2011 - t6037   2011 $110

Pearsall, William H. *The Lake District.* Collins, 1973, First edition; original cloth, gilt, dust jacket, pages 320, with 32 plates.   R. F. G. Hollett & Son Antiquarian Booksellers   173 - 888   2011   £75

Pearsall, William H. *The Lake District.* Bloomsbury Books, 1977,   Original cloth gilt, dust jacket, pages 320, with 32 plates.   R. F. G. Hollett & Son Antiquarian Booksellers   173 - 889   2011   £35

Pearson, Alexander *Annals of Kirkby Lonsdale and Lunesdale in Bygone Days.* Kendal: Titus Wilson, 1930, First edition (100 copies); small 4to., original brown buckram gilt, small stain to foot of back board, pages xvi, 272, uncut, 37 illustrations and map on front endpapers, very good, scarce.   R. F. G. Hollett & Son Antiquarian Booksellers   173 - 891   2011   £250

Pearson, Alexander *Annals of Kirkby Lonsdale and Lunesdale in Bygone Days.* Kendal: Titus Wilson, 1930, Limited edition, number 31 of 50 copies, signed; small 4to., original full brown morocco gilt, dust jacket foxed, inkstain on upper panel, pages xvi, 272, uncut, 27 illustrations and map on front endpapers, fine, rare pictorial dust jacket.   R. F. G. Hollett & Son Antiquarian Booksellers   173 - 889   2011   £650

Pearson, Alexander *The Doings of a Country Solicitor.* Kendal: Titus Wilson, 1947, First edition No. 187 of 500 signed copies); tall 8vo., original cloth gilt, little faded as usual, pages xvii, 198 with 32 illustrations.   R. F. G. Hollett & Son Antiquarian Booksellers   173 - 892   2011   £95

Pearson, Alexander *The Doings of a Country Solicitor.* Kendal: Titus Wilson, 1947, First edition, 1000 copies, 1 of 500 unsigned;   tall 8vo., original cloth, gilt, dust jacket, little torn, pages xvii, 198 with 32 illustrations.   R. F. G. Hollett & Son Antiquarian Booksellers   173 - 893   2011   £50

Pearson, G. C. *Overland in 1849 from Missouri to California by the Platte River and the Salt Lake Trail.* Los Angeles: printed at the Cole Holmquist Press, 1961,   First book edition, one of a total edition of 350 copies, this copy being number 148 of 150 copies; 55 pages, frontispiece, illustrations, folding map, original gilt lettered green boards, spine slightly faded, else fine.   Argonaut Book Shop   Recent Acquisitions Summer 2010 - 156   2011 $90

Pearson, John *Bluebird and the Dead Lake.* London: Collins, 1965, First edition; original boards, gilt, dust jacket little rubbed in place, pages 188, 21 illustrations.   R. F. G. Hollett & Son Antiquarian Booksellers   General Catalogue Summer 2010 - 1131   2011   £30

Pearson, John *An Exposition of the Creed.* London: printed by J. F. For Job Williams, 1669, Third edition; folio, contemporary full polished blind ruled calf, little rubbed, one corner rather defective, pages (vi), 398, title ruled in red, very good.   R. F. G. Hollett & Son Antiquarian Booksellers   175   2011   £450

Pearson, Karl *Tables for Statisticians & Biometricians.* London: 1914, First edition; lxxxiii, (1), 143 pages, half cloth, paper with some age soil, modest ex-library. Bookworm & Silverfish 662 - 108 2011 $60

Pearson, Lynn F. *The People's Palaces.* Buckingham: Barracuda Books, 1991, First edition; 4to., original cloth, gilt, dust jacket, pages 112, well illustrated, uncommon. R. F. G. Hollett & Son Antiquarian Booksellers 177 - 624 2011 £65

Pease, Alfred E. *The Book of the Lion.* London: John Murray, 1913, First edition; 8vo., original publisher's red cloth lettered gilt on spine ad front cover, gilt vignette of lion on spine and cover) pages xx, 293, frontispiece, 12 plates, map, text illustrations, 8 pages publisher's ads, excellent condition, f.e.p. very faintly browned, faint handling wear, bright, fresh, near fine. Any Amount of Books May 26 2011 - A70489 2011 $671

Peck, Francis *Desiderata Curiosa; or a Collection of Divers Scarce and Curious Peices.* London: printed, 1732-1735, 2 volumes bound as 1, folio, pages (viii) viii (xii) 66, 26, 52, 50, 44, 56 (xii) + engraved portrait frontispiece and 6 other engraved plates, (xxii), 68, 58, 52, 32, 50, 36, 32, 56, 25 (xix) + engraved portrait frontispiece and 3 other engraved plates, contemporary tan calf over re-used late 16th century, 17th century pasteboards, spine panel gilt, lettered and dated together in gilt direct, boards single rule gilt bordered, board edges decorative roll in blind, all edges red speckled, brown and white sewn endbands, little marginal dust soiling but quite clean, rear joint cracked, front joint sometime restored but now split again with board loose, spine ends and corners worn, old scrapes and scratches to boards, armorial bookplate of Wm. Constable, Esqr, from the collection of Christopher Ernest Weston 1947-2010. Unsworths Booksellers 24 - 133 2011 £450

Peck, George Washington *Aurifordina or Adventures in the Gold Region.* New York: Baker and Scribner, 1849, First edition; 103 pages, original boards, front cover highly decorated and attractively so. M & S Rare Books, Inc. 90 - 318 2011 $1000

Pedley, Charles *The History of Newfoundland from the Earliest Times to the Year 1860.* London: Longman, Green, Longman, Roberts & Green, Spottiswoods and Co. London, 1863, Pages xix, 531, (40 pages of ads and index) brown cloth with gilt to spine, half title, large map in pocket in front, 8vo., expertly rebacked in original cloth, bookplate of Gardiner Green Hubbard and "GBF" in ink front endpaper. Schooner Books Ltd. 96 - 80 2011 $450

Peel, C. V. A. *Somaliland: being an Account of Two Expeditions into the Far Interior, Together with a Complete List of Every Animal and Bird Known to Inhabit that Country...* London: F. E. Robinson, 1900, First edition; 8vo., pages xv, 345, map, illustrations, original green decorative cloth, spine faded, gilt armorial stamp on upper and lower covers, very good, clean copy. J. & S. L. Bonham Antiquarian Booksellers Africa 4/20/2011 - 8929 2011 £750

Peel, C. V. A. *Somaliland: being an Account of Two Expeditions into the Far Interior, Together with a Complete List of Every Animal and Bird Known to Inhabit that Country...* London: F. E. Robinson, 1900, First edition; 8vo., pages xv, 345, map, illustrations, margins of frontispiece foxed, original red cloth, spine and corners rubbed, new endpapers, small scuff mark on upper cover. J. & S. L. Bonham Antiquarian Booksellers Africa 4/20/2011 - 9217 2011 £200

Peel, C. V. A. *Somaliland: being an Account of Two Expeditions into the Far Interior, Together with a Complete List of Every Animal and Bird Known to Inhabit that Country...* London: F. E. Robinson, 1900, First edition; 8vo., pages, xv, 345, map, illustrations, text very clean, original green decorative cloth, spine faded, endpapers lightly spotted. J. & S. L. Bonham Antiquarian Booksellers Africa 4/20/2011 - 9140 2011 £550

A Peep at the World's Fair. London: Paris: New York: Raphael Tuck & sons, n.d. circa, 1893, 4to., cloth backed pictorial boards, corners worn and some normal cover rubbing, else tight, clean and very good+, 11 fabulous chromolithographed plates. Aleph-Bet Books, Inc. 95 - 162 2011 $450

Peirce, B. K. *Life in the Woods; or the Adventures of Audubon.* New York: Carlton and Porter, 1863, 8 illustrations, 18mo., 252 pages 4 page book list, tooled green cloth on boards, gilt decorations and title on spine, full page wood engraved frontispiece, 6 of 8 full page wood engravings printed on heavier paper, missing plates are "Audubon at the Camp of the Runaway" and "The Golden Eagle", scattered foxing, covers rubbed at edges and corners, bumped crowns of spine, trace of bookplate inside upper cover, couple of signatures sprung, fair. Hobbyhorse Books 56 - 115 2011 $110

Pelecanos, George *Down by the River Where the Dead Men Go.* New York: St. Martin's Press, 1995, First edition; fine in fine dust jacket, signed by author. Bella Luna Books May 29 2011 - p3290 2011 $137

Pelecanos, George *Nick's Trip.* New York: St. Martin's, 1993, First edition; fine, dust jacket very good, light wear to extremities with a 1 inch snag on rear panel, signed by author, very good. Bella Luna Books May 26 2011 - t9585 2011 $495

Pellew, Claughton *Five Wood Engravings Printed from Original Wood Blocks with Biographical Note by Anne Stevens.* Wakefield: Fleece Press, 1987, One of 150 sets printed on Zerkal mouldmade paper; pages (15), folio, original plain white sewn wrappers, untrimmed, dust jacket with wood engraving by Pellew reproduced in line block on label on front cover; (with) Five Wood Engravings by Claughton Pellew, each printed on separate sheet and loosely enclosed in pale or mid blue card folder with printed title, book and prints enclosed in grey buckram, card lined, fold down back box, same design of label as that used for book on its front, fine, Anne Stevens' copy, but without mark of ownership. Blackwell Rare Books B166 - 252 2011 £250

Peltier, Jean Gabriel *Periodique Peltier (Jean Gabriel)/ Tableau De L'Europe.* London: W. Glindon, 1794, First edition; 8vo., 14 pieces (livraisons), complete in 2 volumes, ex-British Foreign Office library with minimal library markings else very good+, soundly bound in modern red cloth lettered gilt at spine. Any Amount of Books May 26 2011 - A74693 2011 $1845

Pemberton, J. Despard *Facts and Figures Relating to Vancouver Island and British Columbia showing What to Expect and How to Get there.* London: 1860, ix, 171 pages, 24 ads, 4 folding maps, original embossed cloth, slight external wear and foxing, traces of a bookplate removed from front pastedown, scattered light foxing, repaired tears to one folding map with no loss, overall very good. Dumont Maps & Books of the West 111 - 75 2011 $750

Pemble, William *A Briefe Introduction to Geography Containing a Description of the Grounds and Generall Part Thereof...* Oxford: Iohn Lichfield for Edward Forrest, 1630, First edition; Small 4to., (4), 64 (i.e. 46) pages, 1 folding table, 18 woodcut figures, printer's device on titlepage, 2 woodcut headpieces, very faint waterstain to few pages, modern full vellum, gilt stamped spine, booklabel of John Lawson, fine, rare. Jeff Weber Rare Books 163 - 11 2011 $2500

Penderel, Richard *Dick Wylder: a Romantic Story.* London: Remington & Co., 1894, First edition; 2 volumes, half title volume I, final ad leaf volume II, 2 volumes in 1, contemporary remainder cloth, blocked in black lettered in gilt, bit rubbed, good plus. Jarndyce Antiquarian Booksellers CXCI - 391 2011 £120

Pendlebury, Henry *A Plain Representation of Transubstantiation, as It Is Received in the Church of Rome with the Sandy Foundations It Is Built Upon...* London: printed for J. Johnson, 1687, First edition; 4to., later stiff wrappers, rather chipped and dusty, page (vi "to the reader"), 68, title and final leaf dusty, one leaf creased and corner soiled, few marginal blindstamps. R. F. G. Hollett & Son Antiquarian Booksellers 175 - 1045 2011 £120

Penfield, Wilder Graves *Epilepsy and Cerebral Localization: a Study of the Mechanism, Treatment and Prevention of Epileptic Seizures.* Springfield and Baltimore: Charles C. Thomas, 1941, 8vo., x, 623 pages, illustrations, original navy cloth, gilt stamped cover illustrations, spine title, previous owner's inked signature and rubber stamp, fine, from the Medical Library of Dr. Clare Gray Peterson. Jeff Weber Rare Books 162 - 241 2011 $250

Penfold, John B. *The Clockmakers of Cumberland.* Ashford: Brant Wright Associates, 1977, Limited edition, no. 92, signed; small 4to., original cloth, gilt, pages 284, illustrations, silk marker, 4 page duplicated article on clockmakers of Brampton by Penfold loosely inserted, fine, scarce. R. F. G. Hollett & Son Antiquarian Booksellers 173 - 897 2011 £375

Penhall, Joe *The Road.* N.P.: Productions/Dimension Films, 2009, Paperback original; Penhall's adaptation of the McCarthy novel, perfectbound typescript, two tiny tears upper rear cover, near fine in wrappers. Ken Lopez Bookseller 154 - 109 2011 $85

Penman, Laurie *Clock Design and Construction Including Dial Making.* Alphabooks, 1989, First hardback edition; large 8vo., original glazed pictorial boards, matching dust jacket, pages 144, with 219 text illustrations, fine, scarce. R. F. G. Hollett & Son Antiquarian Booksellers General Catalogue Summer 2010 - 293 2011 £65

Penn, Mary E. *In the Dark and Other Ghost Stories.* Mountain Ash, Wales: Sarob Press, 1999, First edition thus, number 119 of 250 copies,; 8vo., pages xii, 127, illustrations. Any Amount of Books May 29 2011 - A71440 2011 $238

Pennant, Thomas 1726-1798 *Of London.* London: printed for Robt. Faulder, 1790, 4to., pages iii-vi, (ii) 439 (ix) + engraved frontispiece, engraved and 11 other engraved plates, contemporary speckled and polished calf, spine emblematically panel gilt with 'classical urn' centerpieces, cornerpieces, black lettering piece gilt, boards decorative roll gilt bordered, board edges 'alternating full & broken hatch fillet' roll gilt, turn-ins alternating bands of light and dark stain, all edges red and grey sprinkled, green and white sewn endbands, green silk page marker, early 21st century conservation by Chris Weston, few spots, plates lightly foxed, titlepage dusty, from the collection of Christopher Ernest Weston 1947-2010. Unsworths Booksellers 24 - 134 2011 £300

Pennant, Thomas 1726-1798 *A Tour From Downing to Alston Moor.* printed at the Oriental Press by Wilson & Co. for Edward Harding, 1801, First edition, large paper copy; large 4to., recent quarter calf with raised bands and spine label, pages viii, 195, (i), complete with half title (little spotted), 27 engraved plates, some little offset or spotted, very good. R. F. G. Hollett & Son Antiquarian Booksellers 173 - 898 2011 £240

Pennell, Elizabeth Robins 1855-1936 *The Life of James McNeill Whistler.* Philadelphia: Lippincott, 1909, Third impression; 2 volumes, small 4to., pages xxvi, 315; xiv, 327, copiously illustrated in black and white, tan paper over boards, yellow cloth spines, stamped in gilt, brochure about the set laid in, covers little worn at edges and corners, spine little soiled, little foxing at ends, else very good. Second Life Books Inc. 174 - 257 2011 $225

Pennell, Elizabeth Robins 1855-1936 *Lithography and Lithographers.* London: T. Fisher Unwin, 1915, First edition; blindstamped 'presentation copy' on titlepage, xx, 319 pages, 4to., 79 illustrations, good copy in original linen backed boards, corners little worn and slight bump to top edge, ownership note on front free endpaper. Ken Spelman Rare Books 68 - 107 2011 £50

Pennington, Rooke *Notes on the Barrows and Bone Caves of Derbyshire.* Macmillan, 1877, First edition; original brown pebble grain cloth gilt, pages (iv), 124, 36, errata slip tipped in, inscribed "from the author", slight adhesion damage to flyleaf and half title, but very nice, scarce. R. F. G. Hollett & Son Antiquarian Booksellers 177 - 626 2011 £150

Pennington, Sarah *Instructions for a Young Lady, in Every Sphere and Period of Life.* Edinburgh: printed by A. Donaldson and J. Reid for Alex. Donaldson, 1762, 12mo., (4), 240 pages, little minor browning, inscription dated May 12th 176, unsympathetically rebound in quarter calf, raised and gilt bands, red label. Jarndyce Antiquarian Booksellers CXCI - 392 2011 £320

Pennington, Sarah *An Unfortunante Mother's Advice to Her Absent Daughters in a Letter to Miss Pennington.* London: J. Walter, 1770, Fifth edition; pages 158, (i), complete with half title, pencilled notes on half title and ad leaf, contemporary calf gilt, spine panels with overall diced pattern in gilt, little defective at foot, pages 158, (i), complete with half title, pencilled notes on half title and ad leaf. R. F. G. Hollett & Sons Antiquarian Booksellers 170 - 521 2011 £85

Penny, Anne *Poems with a Dramatic Entertainment by....* London: printed for the author..., 1771, First edition; small 4to., (20), 220 pages, engraved headpiece on B2 hand colored, decorative watercolor border by early owner, copper engraved title and other vignettes after Wright, modern calf backed contemporary calf, cover worn and dried, some foxing, minor stains and soiling, generally very good. Second Life Books Inc. 174 - 258 2011 $600

Penny, Marie Prescott *A Treasure Hunt: a Fascinating Game for Boys & Girls.* New York: c., 1935, Folio, original binding, clean, very minor scraping to fore edge, few pencil marks to cover, corner wear, two leaves loose, with 31 of 32 clues intact. Bookworm & Silverfish 662 - 84 2011 $85

Penquer, Augsute *Revelations.* Paris: Didier et c., 1865, First edition; (ii, 348 pages), 8vo., contemporary half red morocco over marbled boards, gilt lettered and gilt decorated spine, all edges gilt, frontispiece, some rubbing to panel, otherwise near fine, inscribed and dated by author. Paulette Rose Fine and Rare Books 32 - 134 2011 $375

Penstone, M. M. *Church Study. Suggestions for a Course of Lessons on the Church Building...* National Society's Depository, 1911, Original cloth gilt, mottled and faded, pages xiii, 416, with 66 illustrations. R. F. G. Hollett & Son Antiquarian Booksellers 175 - 1048 2011 £30

Penzer, N. M. *Poison Damsels and Other Essays in Folklore and Anthropology.* London: privately printed for Chas. J. Sawyer Ltd., 1952, First edition; tall 8vo., original cloth, gilt, spine trifle faded, pages 319. R. F. G. Hollett & Son Antiquarian Booksellers 175 - 1049 2011 £60

Pepper, Charles M. *Pan American Railway.* Washington: 1904, First edition; 75 pages, wrappers, very good, age soil, with folding map. Bookworm & Silverfish 678 - 171 2011 $75

Pepper, John *Cockley Beck.* Element Books, 1984, First edition; original cloth, gilt, dust jacket, 141 pages, drawings by author, presentation copy inscribed by author for Neil Curry. R. F. G. Hollett & Son Antiquarian Booksellers 173 - 902 2011 £45

Pepys, Samuel 1633-1703 *Diary and Correspondence of Samuel Pepys.* London: Henry Colburn, 1854, Fifth edition; 4 volumes, contemporary full tan calf, gilt, spines trifle rubbed, one spine slightly frayed at head, pages xl, 427; 484; 482; 468; with 2 engraved portraits, engraved plate, folding facsimile, folding map, excellent, sound set. R. F. G. Hollett & Son Antiquarian Booksellers General Catalogue Summer 2010 - 453 2011 £250

Pepys, Samuel 1633-1703 *The Diary.* London: G. Bell and Sons Lts., 1924, 188 x 120mm., 8 volumes bound in 3, fine contemporary terra cotta rushed morocco by Sanorski & Sutcliffe (singe don front turn-ins), double gilt fillet border on covers, upper covers with gilt insignia incorporating the initials "S P", crossed anchors and looping ropes with Pepys' (misspelled) motto in Latin on a ribbon above it, raised bands, spines gilt in double ruled compartments with central ornament of either a crown, a sailor's knot, an anchor or crossed quills, turn-ins ruled in gilt, marbled endpapers, all edges gilt, frontispiece, spines slightly and uniformly sunned toward pink, otherwise extremely pleasing set in beautiful condition inside and out. Phillip J. Pirages   59 - 137   2011 $1250

Pepys, Samuel 1633-1703 *Memoires Relating to the State of the Royal Navy of England for Ten Years Determin'd Dec. 1688.* New York: Charles Scribner's Sons, 1925, First edition with the Griffen-Keble imprint; small octavo, (4), 214, (18), (2, blank), pages, frontispiece, large folding sheets of accounts, contemporary mottled calf, rebacked, original spine and recornered edges speckled red, boards tooled in blind, rear hinge professionally repaired, some browning from glue to endpapers, otherwise internally very clean, 1 3/4 inch closed tear to leaf M4, not affecting text, handsomely housed in morocco backed chemise, stamped and lettered in gilt, slipcase with morocco edge.   Heritage Book Shop   Holiday 2010 - 9   2011 $3500

Pepys, Samuel 1633-1703 *Memoirs of Samuel Pepys... Comprising His Diary... and a Selection from His Private Correspondence.* London: Henry Colburn, 1828, Second edition; 229 x 146mm., 5 volumes, especially attractive polished tree calf (stamp signed by Jenkins and Cecil), covers bordered with gilt chain roll, raised band, spine compartments handsomely gilt with knotwork centerpiece surrounded by small tools and with scrolling foliate cornerpieces, decorative rolls on bands and at head and foot of spine, red and blue morocco labels, turn-ins with fine foliate roll marbled edges and endpapers, engraved frontispiece, 6 additional portraits, tailpiece, folding map, two double page views and two page facsimile of Pepys' handwriting, hint of wear to extremities, plates little foxed, very good handsome set in quite fine and bright condition, text especially fresh and clean.   Phillip J. Pirages   59 - 277   2011 $1900

Perceval of Galles *Syr Perecyvelle of Gales.* Kelmscott Press, 1895, One of 350 copies on paper, 8 additional copies were on vellum; 212 x 150mm., 98 pages, without final blank, quite attractive contemporary olive-brown half morocco by W. Launder (stamp signed), flat spine gilt in one long compartment with leafy vines at head and tail, vertical titling in ornate Gothic majuscules, marbled sides and endpapers, top edge gilt, elaborate woodcut frontispiece by Edward Burne-Jones, wide white vine borders on first opening, one page with half border, decorative woodcut initials, device in colophon; spine sunned to a pleasing hazel brown, some irregur fading to leather elsewhere, extremely fine, binding very lustrous and virtually unworn, text immaculate.   Phillip J. Pirages   59 - 247   2011 $1900

Percy, Benjamin *The Wilding.* Minneapolis: Gray Wolf, 2010, First edition; fine in fine dust jacket, gray slipcase, signed with sketch of a person.   Bella Luna Books   May 29 2011 - p3698   2011 $82

Percy, Walker 1916-1990 *Love in the Ruins.* New York: FG, 1971, First edition; fine in fine dust jacket.   Bella Luna Books   May 29 2011 - t4343   2011 $82

Percy, Walker 1916-1990 *The Message in the Bottle.* New York: FSG, 1975, First edition; fine, dust jacket near fine, light soiling to rear panel.   Bella Luna Books   May 29 2011 - t4344   2011 $110

Pereira, Harold B. *The Colour of Chivalry.* Imperial Chemical Industries, 1950, First edition; 4to., original gilded cloth over bevelled boards, printed in black, 141 pages, 30 fine tipped in color plates and pedigrees on endpapers, introductory sheet by Sidney Rogerson loosely inserted. R. F. G. Hollett & Son Antiquarian Booksellers   General Catalogue Summer 2010 - 454   2011   £30

Pereistiany, J. G. *The Social Institutions of the Kipsigis.* London: George Routledge, 1939, First edition; maps, illustrations, 8vo., pages xxxiv, 288, original red cloth, spine faded.   J. & S. L. Bonham Antiquarian Booksellers   Africa 4/20/2011 - 4213   2011   £120

Perelman, S. J. *Dawn Ginsbergh's Revenge.* New York: Horace Liveright, 1929, Third printing (same month as first printing, curiously in the same green plush binding as the first issue); bookplate of Madison Ave. advertising marvel and bibliophile P. K. Thomajan, little wear at bottom of boards, near fine in very good or better third printing dust jacket with shallow chips at top of front panel, inscribed by author at a later date to P. K. Thomajan, rare, some modest wear, still very nice, abrasive plush material of binding tended to rub jacket away to nothing.   Between the Covers 169 - BTC347866   2011 $1600

Peret, Benjamin *1929.* Brussels: 1929, First edition, one of 160 copies on Montval paper from a total edition of 215; folio, pages (28), 4 erotic photolithographs by Man Ray tipped in, uncut in original light grey wrappers '1929' printed in black on front, bottom edge of first and last leaves lightly soiled, near fine.   Simon Finch Rare Books   Zero - 537   2011   £6000

Perez De Mendoza Y Quixada, Miguel *Resumen de la Vera Destreza de las Armas en Treinta y Ocho Asserciones.* Madrid: Francisco Sanz, 1675, 4to., ff. (21), 73, title printed in red and black, engraved portrait frontispiece and armorial title vignette, large folding plate (small tear), bound before f. 69, modern half calf, large engraved bookplate; from the library of the Earls of Macclesfield at Shirburn Castle.   Maggs Bros. Ltd.   1440 - 165   2011   £3000

Perkins, Charles E. *The Phantom Bull.* Boston and New York: Houghton Mifflin Co., 1932, First edition; quarto, small pen and ink drawing on half title and signed "Ed Borein", original decorated red cloth, (6), 70 pages, illustrations very good, tight copy, internally reinforced dust jacket. Buckingham Books   May 26 2011 - 27022 2011 $2000

Perkins, Elisha Douglass *Gold Rush Diary. Being the Journal of... on the Overland Trail in the Spring and Summer of 1849.* Lexington: University of Kentucky Press, 1967, First edition; quarto, xxv, 206 pages, frontispiece, text illustrations, map endpapers, yellow cloth, very fine, pictorial dust jacket.   Argonaut Book Shop   Recent Acquisitions Summer 2010 - 157 2011 $90

Perkins, Jane Gray *The Life of Mrs. Norton.* London: John Murray, 1909, First edition; half title, frontispiece, plates, original olive green cloth, spine faded, small label of Times Book Club, top edge gilt.   Jarndyce Antiquarian Booksellers   CLXC - 600 2011   £45

Perkins, Jane Gray *The Life of the Hon. Mrs. Norton.* New York: Henry Holt & Co., 1909, First American edition; frontispiece, illustrations, original cream decorated cloth, top edge gilt, very good.   Jarndyce Antiquarian Booksellers   CLXC - 601 2011   £50

Perrault, Charles   1628-1703 *Contes De Perrault.* Paris: Theodore Lefevre circa, 1910, 4to., red cloth with elaborate gold and black decorative binding, all edges gilt, 217 pages, near fine, elaborate pictorial border by G. Fraipoint printed in range of colors, steel and wood engravings.   Aleph-Bet Books, Inc.   95 - 424 2011 $175

Perrault, Charles   1628-1703 *Fables de Charles Perrault.* Paris: Eug. Balland, 1827, 12mo., xl, 196 pages, original full leather on boards, gilt rosettes and title along spine, marbled endpapers, full page copper engraved frontispiece, publisher initials on cartouche on titlepage, 12 fine copper engravings, printed on one side of leaf and on handmade heavier paper, each one with engraved title, inked dedication inside upper endpaper, rare work in near mint state.   Hobbyhorse Books   56 - 68 2011 $400

Perrault, Charles   1628-1703 *The Fairy Tales.* New York: Dodge Pub. Co., 1922, First American edition; 4to., blue cloth with white lettering and gold stamping, bright, attractive copy, full color pictorial dust jacket with some marginal tears, few small chips, 12 full page color plates and 12 full page black and white plates and black and white line drawings by Harry Clarke.   Jo Ann Reisler, Ltd.   86 - 47 2011 $1750

Perrault, Charles   1628-1703 *Fairy Garland.* London: Cassell & Co. Ltd., 1928, First edition, limited to 1000 copies signed by artist; this being number 572, large quarto, 251 pages, 12 color plates by Edmund Dulac, quarter vellum over blue cloth, spine lettered in gilt, top edge gilt, others uncut, spine tips very lightly bumped, near fine, signed.   Heritage Book Shop   Holiday 2010 - 32 2011 $1250

Perrault, Charles   1628-1703 *The History of Blue Beard and Little Red Riding Hood.* New York: S. King, 1828, New edition; 6 1/4 x 4 inches, printed stiff paper cover with some handling and light marking but a rather crisp attractive copy, 16 numbered pages plus 8 pages of copper plates ny Solomon King.   Jo Ann Reisler, Ltd.   86 - 81 2011 $1800

Perrault, Charles   1628-1703 *Sleeping Beauty.* Philadelphia: and London: Lippincott & Heinemann, 1920, First edition; 4to., cloth backed pictorial boards, fine in slightly frayed dust jacket, pictorial endpapers, color frontispiece, many full page and in text silhouettes and drawings by Arthur Rackham, nice.   Aleph-Bet Books, Inc.   95 - 476 2011 $750

Perriam, D. R. *The Medieval Fortified Buildings of Cumbria.* Cumberland and Westmorland Antiquarian and Archaeological Society, 1998, Tall 4to., original pictorial wrappers, pages xx, 416, diagrams, plans and photos, now very scarce.   R. F. G. Hollett & Son Antiquarian Booksellers   173 - 904 2011   £60

Perriam, D. R. *The Medieval Fortified Buildings of Cumbria.* Cumberland and Westmorland Antiquarian and Archaeological Society, 1998, Only edition, only 400 copies Printed; Tall 4to., original pictorial wrappers, slight creasing to corners of lower panel, pages xx, 416, diagrams, plans and photos, now very scarce.   R. F. G. Hollett & Son Antiquarian Booksellers   General Catalogue Summer 2010 - 1516 2011   £50

Perriam, D. R. *The Medieval Fortified Buildings of Cumbria.* Cumberland and Westmorland Antiquarian and Archaeological Society, 1998, Only edition, only 400 copies printed; tall 4to., original pictorial wrappers, pages xx, 416, diagrams, plans and photos, prospectuses and related ephemera loosely inserted, now very scarce.   R. F. G. Hollett & Son Antiquarian Booksellers   177 - 629 2011   £65

Perry, Anna M. *Five Thousand Phrases (English-Japanese) for Common Use, Alphabetically Arranged and Indexed for Immediate and Easy Reference.* Tokio & Osaka: Maruzen Kabushik Kaisha (Z.P. Maruya & Co. Ltd.), 1904, Fifth edition; text in English and Japan, 4 pages ads at end, (2), 6, 367, (1) pages, original cloth, little spotted.   Anthony W. Laywood   May 26 2011 - 19948 2011 $84

Persius *The Satires of Persius.* London: printed for A. Millar in the Strand, 1751, Second edition; (2), (iii), iv-xxiv, (2), 3-154, (2) pages ads; 12mo., full contemporary unlettered sprinkled calf, gilt fillet border, raised and gilt banded spine, joints cracked but firm, head and tail of spine chipped, very good, clean copy.   Jarndyce Antiquarian Booksellers   CXCI - 393   2011   £110

Persons, Robert *An Answere to the Fifth Part of Reportes Lately Set Forth by Syr Edward Cooke Knight, the Kinges Attorney Generall.* Saint Omer: imprinted with licence by F. Bellet, 1606, First edition; small 4to., (72), 351, 353-386, (15) pages, contemporary limp vellum, loose in case, covers bit creased, short slit and few small holes in upper cover, ties missing, lightly browned in places, few corners creased, first few leaves cut close at foot, single wormhole through last few leaves, from the library of the Earls of Macclesfield at Shirburn Castle.   Maggs Bros. Ltd.   1440 - 166   2011   £950

Perthshire Illustrated: a Series of Select Views of Its Picturesque and Romantic Scenery, Palaces, Castles and Seats... London: A. Fullerton, 1844, Early edition; 4to., half brown leather decorated spine with raised bands etc., marbled endpapers, pages cxl, 169, engraved title and 63 engraved plates, very slight foxing, internally decent, light wear, somewhat chipped at head of spine, corners rubbed, sound very good-.   Any Amount of Books   May 29 2011 - B32163   2011 $315

Pesaran, M. Hashem *Journal of Applied Econometrics.* London: Wiley, 1988-2003, Volumes 1-18, Jan. 1988 to Feb. 2003 (lacking one issue - last quarter of 1990), with 2 copies of the first issue, very good, wrappers, from the library of economist Sir Richard Stone 1913-1991.   Any Amount of Books   May 26 2011 - A73707   2011 $1342

Peter Parley's Annual. London: Darton & Co., 1849, Pages viii, 376, (xvi, ads), small square 8vo., original blind-stamped cloth, gilt, extremities trifle worn, pages viii, 376 (xvi, ads), all edges gilt, color printed frontispiece and title and numerous woodcut illustrations.   R. F. G. Hollett & Sons Antiquarian Booksellers   170 - 522   2011   £45

Peter Parley's Annual 40th Year 1881. Ben George, 1881, Original decorated red cloth, gilt over bevelled boards, spine rather rubbed, pages 314, (xvi, ads), all edges gilt, 9 chromolithographs, few edges little chipped and soiled.   R. F. G. Hollett & Sons Antiquarian Booksellers   170 - 523   2011   £40

Peter Parley's Annual 43rd Year 1884. Ben George, 1884, Original decorated red cloth gilt over bevelled boards, rather damped, spine label lacking, pages 280 (viii, ads), all edges gilt, 9 chromolithographs and 12 monochrome illustrations, rather shaken.   R. F. G. Hollett & Sons Antiquarian Booksellers   170 - 524   2011   £35

Peter Parley's Annual 44th Year 1885. Ben George, 1885, Original decorated red cloth gilt over bevelled boards, little rubbed, pages 312, (viii, ads), all edges gilt, 9 chromolithographs and 11 monochrome illustrations, upper joint cracked ownership stamp on back of frontispiece.   R. F. G. Hollett & Sons Antiquarian Booksellers   170 - 525   2011   £40

Peter Parley's Annual 45th Year 1886. Ben George, 1886, Original decorated red cloth gilt over bevelled boards, trifle rubbed, page 296 (viii, ads), all edges gilt, 16 chromolithographs, back of frontispiece rather spotted, lower joint tender.   R. F. G. Hollett & Sons Antiquarian Booksellers   170 - 526   2011   £45

Peter Rabbit Hankies. Duenewald, 1950, 8vo., pictorial wrappers, slight cover rubbing, else fine, text printed on rear panel, inside are 2 full page color lithographed pages by Julian Wehr, one has tab operated moveable and other has 2 color illustrated hankies tucked into slots in illustrations, rare.   Aleph-Bet Books, Inc.   95 - 381   2011 $1200

Peter, Thurtan C. *The Old Cornish Drama.* London: Elliot Stock, 1906, Original cloth, gilt over bevelled boards, edges darkened, pages 49, 6 illustrations.   R. F. G. Hollett & Son Antiquarian Booksellers   175 - 1050   2011   £35

Peters, Carl *The Eldorardo of the Ancients.* London: C. Arthur Pearson, 1902, First English edition; 8vo., pages x, 447, (1) imprint, half title, frontispiece, 2 folding maps, 97 illustrations, original brown cloth, upper cover gilt, top edge gilt, spine lightly faded.   J. & S. L. Bonham Antiquarian Booksellers   Africa 4/20/2011 - 8022   2011   £70

Peters, Ellis *The Raven in the Foregate.* New York: Morrow, 1986, First American edition; fine, in like dust jacket, signed by author.   Bella Luna Books   May 26 2011 - t7757   2011 $247

Peters, Ellis *The Raven in the Foregate.* London: Macmillan, 1986, First UK edition; near fine, slightly loose, dust jacket fine.   Bella Luna Books   May 29 2011 - t9429   2011 $82

Peters, Fior *The Organ and Its Music in the Netherlands 1500-1800.* Antwerp: Mercatorfonds, 1971, First edition; square small folio, original vellum backed cloth, gilt, dust jacket, plus vellum backed cloth case, both in cloth gilt slipcase, pages 341, with 66 superb color plates tipped in, over 50 other plates, folding maps, with 2 vinyl records in sleeves in second volume, fine set.   R. F. G. Hollett & Son Antiquarian Booksellers   175 - 1044   2011   £85

Peters, John P. *Body Water: The Exchange of Fluids in Man.* Springfield and Baltimore: Charles C. Thomas, 1935, 8vo., viii, 405 pages, figures, tables, green cloth, gilt stamped spine title, dust jacket, fine, scarce in jacket, bookplate and inkstamp of Ira Albert Manville, Portland, from the Medical Library of Dr. Clare Gray Peterson. Jeff Weber Rare Books 162 - 242 2011 $65

Petersen, Marie *Princess Ilse.* London: pivately printed, 1836, 34 pages, half title, original red cloth, lettered in gilt. Jarndyce Antiquarian Booksellers CLXC - 746 2011 £85

Petersham, Maud *The Rooster Crows: a Book of American Rhymes and Jingles.* New York: Macmillan, 1945, First edition; 4to., tan cloth, fine in dust jacket (chipped, triangular piece off top of spine, not price clipped, no award medal), color and black and white lithos. Aleph-Bet Books, Inc. 95 - 426 2011 $600

Peterson, Clare Gray *Perspectives in Surgery.* Philadelphia: Lea and Febiger, 1972, First edition; 8vo., xvi, 339 pages, frontispiece, 83 numbered figures, blue cloth, gilt stamped cover and spine titles, all edges gilt, fine, author's personal copy and probably a deluxe edition, from the Medical Library of Dr. Clare Gray Peterson. Jeff Weber Rare Books 162 - 243 2011 $75

Peterson, Roger Tory *A Field Guide to the Birds, Giving the Field Marks of all Species Found in Eastern North American.* Boston and New York: Houghton Mifflin, 1934, First edition, first state; 12mo., 36 plates and several drawings, pages xxi, 167, original green silver lettered cloth, some rubbing to edges of spine and corners, owner's signature in pencil, tissue guard to frontispiece partially loose, very good plus. Raymond M. Sutton, Jr. May 26 2011 - 46792 2011 $2000

Peterson, Roger Tory *A Field Guide to the Birds, Giving Field marks of all Species Found in Eastern North America.* Boston and New York: Houghton Mifflin, 1934, First edition, third state; 36 plates, several drawings, 12mo., pages xxi, 167, original green silver printed cloth, near fine, signed inscription, signed in red ink from author to Herman Kitchen. Raymond M. Sutton, Jr. May 26 2011 - 43572 2011 $1200

Peterson, Roger Tory *A Field Guide to the Birds Giving Field Marks of all species Found in Eastern Northern America.* Boston and New York: Houghton Mifflin, 1934, First edition first state; inscription from author to Alice Klund, 36 plates, several drawings, 12mo., pages xxi, 167, original green cloth, wear to corners and edges of spine, short split to front edge of spine, ends of spine frayed, crease to tissue guard. Raymond M. Sutton, Jr. May 26 2011 - 50956 2011 $3000

Peto, Gladys *Twilight Stories.* John F. Shaw & Co n.d., 1932, 4to., original pictorial cloth backed boards, pictorial onlay on upper board, very slight creasing to one corner, unpaginated, 8 full page color plates, numerous drawings, lovely, clean and fresh. R. F. G. Hollett & Sons Antiquarian Booksellers 170 - 527 2011 £175

Petrocokin, A. *Along the Andes in Bolivia, Peru and Ecuador.* London: Gay and Bird, 1903, First edition; 8vo., original red cloth lettered gilt on spine and on front cover and with gilt llama on cover, page viii, 147, uncut, 25 plates, 2 folding maps at rear, folding frontispiece, spine ends very slightly used, otherwise pleasing, very good+, scarce. Any Amount of Books May 29 2011 - A49469 2011 $204

Pettee, W. E. M. *President Lincoln's Funeral March as Played by Shepard's Cornet Band of Providence, R. I. at the Funeral Obsequies of Abraham Lincoln.* Providence: J. R. Cory, 1865, Folio, 5, (1 blank) pages, title printed within black border with decorative cornerpieces, verso of title blank, words and music on pages 3 through 5, removed, sheets detached, left edge little jagged, some other short marginal tears, small shelf number stamped in top margin of title, "Funeral" underlined with blue pencil, foxed, small stain at fore-edge, top, withal, entirely sound and a better copy than description might indicate. M & S Rare Books, Inc. 90 - 218 2011 $200

Petterson, Per *I Curse the River of Time.* Minneapolis: Graywolf, 2010, First American edition; signed on tipped in sheep, fine, black slipcase. Bella Luna Books May 29 2011 - p3684 2011 $88

Pettigrew, Thomas Joseph *A History of Egyptian Mummies and an Account of the Worship and Embalming of the Sacred Animals by the Egyptians.* London: Longman, 1834, First edition; 4to., pages xxi, (i) blank, 264, (i) errata, (i) blank, 13 plates, top edge gilt, slight foxing to titlepage and some plates, 1 plate chipped, faint offsetting from plates, minor wormhole to outer margin of opening leaves, otherwise extremely fresh, half morocco and grey cloth, gilt decoration to boards and spine, lettering to spine in gilt, marbled endpapers, slight bumped and rubbed at extremities, ALS from author laid in, subscription copy. Simon Finch Rare Books Zero - 127 2011 £950

Petty, William *The Economic Writings of Sir William Petty, Together with the Observations upon the Bills of Mortality....* Cambridge: Cambridge University Press, 1899, First edition; 2 volumes, 8vo., pages xci, 313; (314)-700, original publisher's dark blue cloth, black spines with lettered gilt, endpapers slightly browned, otherwise clean, bright, near fine set. Any Amount of Books May 26 2011 - A45369 2011 $419

Pevsner, Nikolaus *The Cathedrals of England.* Viking, 1985, First edition; 4to., original cloth, gilt, dust jacket, pages 399, frontispiece, 200 illustrations and plans, map, fine.   R. F. G. Hollett & Son Antiquarian Booksellers   177 - 683   2011   £60

Pevsner, Nikolaus *Cumberland and Westmorland.* London: Penguin Books, 1967, First edition; original cloth, gilt, dust jacket, pages 341, illustrations.   R. F. G. Hollett & Son Antiquarian Booksellers   177 - 632   2011   £30

Pevsner, Nikolaus *An Enquiry into Industrial Art in England.* Cambridge: University Press, 1937, First edition; small 4to., original cloth, gilt, dust jacket little worn and soiled, piece torn from top of upper panel, pages xiv, 235, with 24 pages of plates.   R. F. G. Hollett & Son Antiquarian Booksellers   General Catalogue Summer 2010 - 294   2011   £65

Pevsner, Nikolaus *Gloucestershire the Cotswolds.* Penguin Books, 1970, First edition; pages 545, 103 illustrations, original cloth, gilt, dust jacket rather worn.   R. F. G. Hollett & Son Antiquarian Booksellers   177 - 696   2011   £30

Pevsner, Nikolaus *Hampshire.* Penguin Books, 1999, Original cloth, gilt, dust jacket, pages 847, 92 illustrations and map.   R. F. G. Hollett & Son Antiquarian Booksellers General Catalogue Summer 2010 - 1528   2011   £30

Pevsner, Nikolaus *London.* New Haven: Yale University Press, 2002-2007, 6 volumes, tall small 8vo., original boards, gilt, dust jacket, pages 702, 813, 804, 810, 864, 872, each volume with over 100 illustrations and maps, fine set.   R. F. G. Hollett & Son Antiquarian Booksellers   177 - 693   2011   £150

Pevsner, Nikolaus *North East and East Kent.* London: Penguin, 1969, First edition; original cloth, gilt, dust jacket, edges trifle worn, pages 645 with 104 illustrations and map.   R. F. G. Hollett & Son Antiquarian Booksellers   177 - 694   2011   £30

Pevsner, Nikolaus *West Kent and the Weald.* London: Penguin, 1969, First edition; original cloth, gilt, dust jacket (little worn), pages 645 with 104 illustrations and map.   R. F. G. Hollett & Son Antiquarian Booksellers   177 - 695   2011   £35

Pevsner, Nikolaus *Yorkshire: the North Riding.* London: Penguin, 1981, Original cloth, gilt, dust jacket, edges faded, chip to upper panel, pages 468, illustrations.   R. F. G. Hollett & Son Antiquarian Booksellers   177 - 671   2011   £30

Pevsner, Nikolaus *Yorkshire: the West Riding.* London: Penguin, 1967, Second edition; pages 652, original cloth, gilt, dust jacket, illustrations.   R. F. G. Hollett & Son Antiquarian Booksellers   177 - 672   2011   £35

Pfeiffer, Ida *Visit to Iceland and the Scandinavian North.* London: Ingram Cooke & Co., 1852, First edition; tinted frontispiece, engraved tinted titlepage, additional printed title, tinted plates, excellently rebound in half dark blue calf, marbled boards, maroon leather label, very good, handsome.   Jarndyce Antiquarian Booksellers   CLXC - 747   2011   £150

Phaedrus *Phaedri Liberti Augusti Fabulae cum Notis Gallicis.* Antonium Molin, n.d. circa, 1785, 28mo., vi, 112 pages, full speckled leather on boards, inked inscription on upper and lower endpaper, both with ragged front edges, cracking along inner hinges repaired edge of upper and lower endpapers, reinforced lower cover fold, very rare, fine. Hobbyhorse Books   56 - 69   2011 $370

Philips, N. G. *Views of the Old Halls of Lancashire and Cheshire.* Henry Gray, 1893, Large paper edition; 28 fine copperplate engravings, large folio, original cloth, gilt, little worn and restored, recased with new matching endpapers, pages xii, 121, top edges gilt with 28 fine tissue guarded copper engraved plates, 3 text woodcut vignettes and folding pedigree.   R. F. G. Hollett & Son Antiquarian Booksellers   177 - 703   2011   £350

Philips, William *Hibernia Freed.* London: for Jonah Bowyer, 1722, First (sole) edition; 8vo., disbound, publisher's ad.   Dramatis Personae Booksellers   106 - 134   2011 $200

Phillippo, James Mursell *Jamaica: its Past and Present State.* London: John Snow, 1843, Second thousand; half title, full page and vignette woodcuts, slightly foxed, original blue cloth, spine lettered in gilt, fine.   Jarndyce Antiquarian Booksellers   CXCI - 573   2011   £400

Phillippo, James Mursell *Jamaica: its Past and Present State.* London: John Snow, 1843, First edition; 8vo., pages xvi, 487, 16 full page woodcut illustrations and woodcut vignettes, inscribed by Rev. Th. H. Clarke/Dry Harbor Jamaica Novb. 1843 for Sam. J. Wilkind.   Any Amount of Books   May 29 2011 - A45552   2011 $255

Phillipps, L. March *With Remington.* London: Edward Arnold, 1901, First edition; 8vo., 219 pages, original red cloth, little fading on lower cover.   J. & S. L. Bonham Antiquarian Booksellers   Africa 4/20/2011 - 8369   2011   £80

Phillips, Anghelen Arrington *Gingerbread Houses: Haiti's Endangered Species.* Port-Au-Prince: Henri Deschamps, 1984, One of 100 copies; full grey leather, signed presentation from Phillips, very good in decent, very good dust jacket, very slightly marked and slightly browned.   Any Amount of Books   May 29 2011 - A70520 2011 $255

Phillips, Catharine *Reasons Why the People Called Quakers Cannot so Fully United with the Methodists in their Missions to the Negroes in the West India Island and Africa...* London: James Phillips, 1792, First edition; modern half calf, gilt, pages 22, (i, ad), complete with half title (rather soiled), few neat and small edge repairs.   R. F. G. Hollett & Son Antiquarian Booksellers   175 - 1487 2011 £950

Phillips, Catherine Coffin *Jessie Benton Fremont, a Woman who Made History.* San Francisco: John Henry Nash, 1935, Tall octavo, vii, 361 pages, frontispiece, plates, index, quarter linen backed brick red boards, paper spine label, bookplate of William Fitzhugh Jr. unusually nice. Jeff Weber Rare Books   163 - 71 2011 $60

Phillips, Charles *Encyclopedia of the American West.* New York: 1996, 4 volumes, lxxvii, 427 pages, illustrations; 428-919 pages, illustrations, 920-1428 pages, illustrations, 1429-1935 pages, illustrations, cloth, near fine, not ex-library.   Dumont Maps & Books of the West   111 - 110 2011 $250

Phillips, Charles *The Speech of Charles Phillips, Esq. in the Case of O'Mullan, V. M'Korkill: delivered in the Court-House of Galway, on the 1st Day of April 1816.* Dublin: printed for Wm. Figgis, 1816, First edition; 8vo., 30 pages, title lightly dust marked, preserved in modern wrappers with printed title label on upper cover, very good, very rare.   John Drury Rare Books   153 - 111 2011   £150

Phillips, Charles *The Speeches of Charles Phillips, Esq. Delivered at the Bar and on Various Public Occasions in Ireland and England.* London: printed for W. Simpkin and R. Marshall... and Millikin, Dublin, 1822, Second edition; 8vo., frontispiece (vi), ii, 304 pages, including half title, occasional light foxing, later 19th century full polished calf gilt with raised bands and crimson spine label, top edge gilt, others uncut, fine, late 19th century library of Earl of Portsmouth with his armorial bookplate and inscription.   John Drury Rare Books   153 - 112 2011   £150

Phillips, J. Arthur *A Treatise on Ore Deposits.* London: 1884, vi,651, (4) publisher's catalog, pages, splendid, unopened, original binding, corners sharp.   Bookworm & Silverfish   679 - 83 2011 $125

Phillips, M. *English Women in Life and Letters.* London: Oxford University Press, 1926, First edition; original cloth, gilt, dust jacket, edges little chipped, pages xviii, 408, well illustrated.   R. F. G. Hollett & Son Antiquarian Booksellers   175 - 1055 2011   £35

Phillips, P. Lee *A List of Maps of America in the Library of Congress.* Washington: 1901, 1137 pages, rebound in cloth thus, tight useable copy.   Dumont Maps & Books of the West   111 - 111 2011 $150

Phillips, Percival *The Prince of Wales's Eastern Book.* London: Hodder & Stoughton for St. Dusntan's, n.d., 1922, First edition; large 8vo., original blue cloth with flat spine, unpaginated, profusely illustrated wit sepia photos and 7 color plates.   R. F. G. Hollett & Son Antiquarian Booksellers   General Catalogue Summer 2010 - 1653 2011   £45

Phillips, R. Randal *Small Family Houses.* London: Country Lfe, 1924, First edition; original cloth, gilt, spine faded, pages 159, with 145 illustrations and plans.   R. F. G. Hollett & Son Antiquarian Booksellers   177 - 705 2011 £30

Phillips, Thomas 1801-1867 *Wales: the Language, Social Condition, Moral Character and Religious Opinions of the People...* London: John W. Parker, 1849, First edition; xvi, 606 pages, 2 pages publisher's ads at end, occasional minor foxing, original black cloth embossed in blind, rebacked, spine lettered, good copy.   John Drury Rare Books   153 - 113 2011   £75

Phillips, W. Alison *The War of Greek Independence 1821 5o 1833.* London: Smith, Elder & Co., 1897, First edition; half title, folding color map, 8 pages unopened catalog, uncut in original green cloth, spine unevenly dulled, inner hinges little weak.   Jarndyce Antiquarian Booksellers   CXCI - 394 2011   £100

Phillpotts, Eden 1862-1960 *My Adventure in the Flying Scotsman: a London and North-Western Railway Shares.* London: James Hogg, 1888, First edition; rainbow colored, cloth front cover and tan rear cover, 63 pages, front cover moderately rubbed, else very good, rare, housed in clamshell case and book's front cover design on front panel.   Buckingham Books   May 26 2011 - 29326 2011 $5000

Phillpotts, Eden 1862-1960 *Nancy Owlett.* London: Raphael Tuck & Sons, 1933, First edition; original cloth, gilt over bevelled boards, spine trifle faded, pages 262, 8 color plates by C. E. Brock, few spots to edges, very nice, clean copy.   R. F. G. Hollett & Son Antiquarian Booksellers   General Catalogue Summer 2010 - 866 2011   £30

Philp, Brian *Excavations at Faversham 1965. the Royal Abbey, Roman Villa and Belgic Famstead.* Kent Archaeological Research Group, 1968, First edition; small 4to., original cloth, gilt, pages vii, 92 with 25 plates, 25 figures and large folding size plan, presentation typescript card signed from author loosely inserted.   R. F. G. Hollett & Son Antiquarian Booksellers   177 - 706 2011   £40

Philp, Kenward *John Brown's Legs.* New York: Norman L. Munro, 1884, Portrait of John Brown, plates, titlepage slightly torn at near margin, later brown paper wrappers, 77 pages.   Jarndyce Antiquarian Booksellers   CXCI - 598   2011   £150

Philp, Robert Kemp *Enquire Within Upon Everything...* Houlston and Co., 1875, 620th thousand; original green cloth gilt, extremities trifle rubbed, pages 412, 8.   R. F. G. Hollett & Son Antiquarian Booksellers   General Catalogue Summer 2010 - 1132   2011   £35

Phipps, Mary *Liza Jane and the Kinkies.* New York: Sears, 1929, 4to., cloth backed pictorial boards, some cover soil and edge rubbing, very good, calligraphic text and color illustrations by author.   Aleph-Bet Books, Inc.   95 - 107   2011 $500

Pickerell, Albert G. *The University of California: a Pictorial History.* Berkeley: University of California Press, 1968, First edition; small folio, 326 pages, profusely illustrated with photos and engravings, blue cloth lettered on spine in gilt, very fine.   Argonaut Book Shop   Recent Acquisitions Summer 2010 - 212   2011 $75

Pickering, Ernest *Architectural Design.* New York: John Wiley & Sons, 1947, Second edition; 4to., original cloth, spine little faded, pages xvii, 329, photographs.   R. F. G. Hollett & Son Antiquarian Booksellers   177 - 707   2011   £40

Pickering, John *A Vocabulary or Collection of Words and Phrases which Have Been Supposed to be Peculiar to the United States of America.* Cambridge: 1816, 206 pages, errata page, rebound in quarter leather and cloth, pages browned with ocasional foxing an staining, serious in places but in no case obscuring text.   Dumont Maps & Books of the West   113 - 44   2011 $500

Pickett, Charles E. *Pickett's Pamphlet on the Railway, Chinese and Presidential Questions.* San Francisco: 1876, 24 pages, original binding, very good.   Bookworm & Silverfish   678 - 47   2011 $100

Picton, Thomas *In the King's Bench. The King Against Picton. Mr. Dallas's Speech on the Motion for a New Trial in the Case of Louisa Calderon, on Thursday Jan. 28 and Thursday, Feburary 4, 1808.* London: James Ridgeway, 1808, First edition; 8vo., (2), 78 pages, recent marbled boards lettered on spine, very good, exceptionally rare.   John Drury Rare Books   153 - 149   2011   £250

Pictorial Comedy. The Humorous Phases of Life Depicted by Eminent Artists. London: James Henderson, 1899-1990, First edition; 3 volumes, beige grained buckram with green cloth, large gilt lettered band across middle, publisher's bound volumes from first issue in September 1899 to September 1900 (12 issues), heavily illustrated with cartoons, minor handling wear, else very good.   Any Amount of Books   May 29 2011 - B26871   2011 $230

Pictorial First Book for Little Boys and Girls. Philadelphia: Presbyterian Board of Publication circa, 1870, 12mo., brown embossed cloth, 64 pages, some wear to spine ends, very good, most pages illustrated.   Aleph-Bet Books, Inc.   95 - 32   2011 $300

Pictorial Handbook to the English Lakes. John Johnstone, 1847, First edition; contemporary half calf gilt, trifle rubbed, pages (ii), 248, (iv), 24, engraved vignettes by Thomas and Edward Gilks, text woodcuts, tables, maps and large folding map at end, scarce.   R. F. G. Hollett & Son Antiquarian Booksellers   173 - 1091   2011   £150

Pictorial Handbook to the English Lakes. Liverpool: George Philip & Son, 1854, New edition; original blind-stamped blue cloth, gilt, rubbed, pages 248, (iv), engraved vignettes, text woodcuts, tables, maps and large folding map at end (torn free but complete), scarce.   R. F. G. Hollett & Son Antiquarian Booksellers   173 - 1092   2011   £150

Picture ABC Book. London & New York: Nister & Dutton, n.d. circa, 1890, 4to., patterned box with pictorial paste-on, flaps strengthened and box rubbed, else very good-fine and complete, housed in original box are 8 fine chromolithographed pages, also 8 wooden jigsaw puzzles.   Aleph-Bet Books, Inc.   95 - 33   2011 $875

Picture Alphabet of Beasts. London and Edinburgh: Thomas Nelson & Sons, n.d. circa, 1880, 4to., 8 leaves, pictorial paper wrappers, each of the four full page chromolithographs are divided into six sections, each one illustrating a different animal with name beneath printed with large red decorative initial letter, facing text page divided into six sections, light soiling to edges of wrappers, excellent copy.   Hobbyhorse Books   56 - 2   2011 $225

The Picture Gallery, Explored; or an Account of Various Ancient Customs and Manners. London: Harvey and Darton, 1824, 12mo., (ii), 200 pages, pictorial buff paper on boards, brown roan spines with gilt fillets and title, 9 very fine full page copper engravings with two images on each plate, printed on heavier handmade paper, owner label inside upper cover and traces of pencil marks, spine reinforced at folds, cover uniformly soiled and rubbed at edges and corners, small chipping at edges of spine, internally in solid state.   Hobbyhorse Books   56 - 116   2011 $270

Pictures of the "Peculiar Institution" as It Exists in Louisiana and Mississippi. Boston: J. R. Yerrington & Son Printers, 21 Cornhill, 1850, First edition; 8vo., 24 pages, removed, last leaf nearly detached, else very good, rare.   M & S Rare Books, Inc.   90 - 399   2011 $550

Picturesque Guide to the English Lakes. London: Adam and Charles Black, 1850, Fourth edition; pages xxiv, 240, 40, folding map frontispiece, 3 woodcut vignette plates, 6 outlines of mountains and 4 maps, original green blind-stamped cloth gilt, rather faded and marked.   R. F. G. Hollett & Son Antiquarian Booksellers   173 - 97   2011   £75

Picturesque Guide to the English Lakes. Adam and Charles Black, 1870, Original pictorial green limp boards, hinges cracked, lower board creased, pages x, 117, 104 with double page map, frontispiece, 1 full page woodcut and 9 text maps.   R. F. G. Hollett & Son Antiquarian Booksellers   173 - 99   2011   £45

Pienkowski, Jan   *Haunted House.*   London: Heinemann, 1982, Large 8vo., original glazed pictorial boards, pages (10), illustrations in color with 6 elaborate pop-ups with tabs, overlays etc.   R. F. G. Hollett & Sons Antiquarian Booksellers   170 - 528   2011   £40

Pierre, D. B. C.   *Vernon God Little.*   London: Faber, 2003, Uncorrected proof; pages 280, crown 8vo., original printed light blue wrappers, fine.   Blackwell Rare Books   B166 - 202   2011   £100

Pierre, D. B. C.   *Vernon God Little.*   London: Faber & Faber, 2003, First British edition; fine in like dust jacket, price on front flap in British pounds, signed by author.   Bella Luna Books   May 29 2011 - t7186   2011 $137

Pierre, D. B. C.   *Vernon God Little.*   New York: Canongate, 2003, First edition; fine in fine dust jacket, signed by author.   Bella Luna Books   May 29 2011 - t7183   2011 $137

Piganiol De la Force, Jean Aimar   *Nouvelle Description De La France Dans Laquelle on Voit Le Gouvernement General De Ce Royaume, Celui De Chaque Province en Particulier...*   Paris: T. Legras fils, 1718, First edition; 6 volumes, 12mo.,(32) 10, 462, (56) pages, engraved frontispiece, 4 engraved folding plates, (18), 304, (62) pages; 7 engraved folding plates, (8), 524, (54) pages, 1 engraved plate, (12), 527, (1 blank), (59) pages, 1 engraved plate, (10), 574, (62) pages; (12), 682, (38) pages, 1 engraved folding map, contemporary speckled calf with fillet gilt on boards and fleurons in corners, spine gilt in compartments, morocco lettering piece, silk page marker, label torn and detaching (2), label detached (6), light patch apparently due to leather treatment that was defective on this upper board (6); from the library of the Earls of Macclesfield at Shirburn Castle.   Maggs Bros. Ltd.   1440 - 167   2011   £550

Pignatorre, Theodore   *The Ancient Monuments of Rome.*   Trefoil Pub. Co. nd., 1932, Large 8vo., original cloth gilt, trifle rubbed and marked, pages xi, 244 with 61 plates, flyleaves and fore-edge spotted.   R. F. G. Hollett & Son Antiquarian Booksellers   177 - 708   2011   £30

Pike, Albert   *A Light Contribution to the History of Cerneallism.*   Washington: circa, 1885, 8vo., self wrappers, this copy bears printed symbol of Pike.   Bookworm & Silverfish   671 - 51   2011 $200

Pike, Albert   *Squirmings.*   Washington: circa, 1889, 21 pages, 8vo., self wrappers.   Bookworm & Silverfish   671 - 52   2011 $200

Pike, Douglas   *Australian Dictionary of Biography.*   Melbourne: Melbourne University Press, 1977-1990, First edition thus; 12 volumes, 8vo., pages 7360, ex-British Foreign Office Library with few library markings else very good, in very good dust jacket, volume 2 lacking jacket.   Any Amount of Books   May 29 2011 - A73757   2011 $340

Pike, Nicolas   *A New & Complete System of Arithmetick Composed for the Use of the Citizens of the United States.*   roy: 1822, Fourth edition; 532 pages, very good, old calf, bit more foxing than average, backstrip leather surface crazed.   Bookworm & Silverfish   676 - 125   2011 $75

Pike, Zebulon Montgomery   1779-1813   *The Expeditions of Zebulon Montgomery Pike.*   New York: 1895, 3 volumes, frontispiece, cxiii 356; vi, 357-855; 857-955, map, 6 folding maps in rear pocket, slight shelfwear, pages browned on edges, one forth of front free endpaper removed from each volume, unsightly but not affecting contents else clean and very good, some of the folding maps weak along folds.   Dumont Maps & Books of the West   113 - 45   2011 $750

Pike, Zebulon Montgomery   1779-1813   *The Expeditions of Zebulon Montgomery Pike to Headwaters of the Mississippi River through Louisiana Territory in New Spain During the Years 1805-6-7.*   New York: Francis P. Harper, 1895, #87 of the Large paper edition of 150 copies; printed on handmade paper, of an edition of 1150 copies, 1000 of which are printed on smaller paper, boards with white cloth spine as issued, cxi, 356 pages; vi, 357-856 pages; (8), 857-956 pages, 7 maps, 6 large folding maps in pocket at rear of volume III, frontispiece, near fine set with only very slightest of edgewear, clean and tight, amazingly, the original 1895 dust jackets are present, jacket for volume I shows cracking and few missing pieces to center of spine (not affecting title), volume II's dust jacket shows some cracking and volume III's dust jacket also shows some cracking, all jackets have some professional internal reinforcement, beautfiul set.   Buckingham Books   May 26 2011 - 26455   2011 $2500

Piketah, Roger *Breks an' Hakes an' Sic Lyk.* London: Simpkin Marshall etc. and Ulverston: W. Holmes, 1902, First edition; original cloth, gilt, pages 177, untrimmed, scarce. R. F. G. Hollett & Son Antiquarian Booksellers 173 - 907 2011 £65

Pilbeam, John *Mammillaria; a Color Supplement.* N.P.: n.p. (Batsford)?, n.d., 1987, 7 volumes, over 250 color prints of photos by Bill Weightman, prepared in 7 stationery volumes (black plastic covers containing 24 clear plastic sleeves, with handwritten label on spine), one or two notes by a cactus scholar in margins, otherwise very good+. Any Amount of Books May 29 2011 - Aa60235 2011 $298

Pilkington, Mary Hopkins *Tales of the Hermitage...* London: Vernor and Hood and E. Newbery, 1800, Small 12mo., 209 pages, 2 page publisher list, original mottled calf on boards, gilt fillets on spine, full page copper engraved frontispiece, line crack at fold of upper cover, inked and dated signature on front endpaper, light foxing at frontispiece. Hobbyhorse Books 56 - 117 2011 $250

Pilnackova Abeceda. Hradec Kralov: n.d. circa, 1925, Complete set of 27 alphabet booklets, each 4 pages, fine, illustrations in bright colors, amazing to find complete set, especially in such nice condition. Aleph-Bet Books, Inc. 95 - 13 2011 $800

Pilpay *The Instructive and Entertaining Fables of Pilpay...* London: printed for J. and F. Rivington, W. Strahan...., 1775, Fifth edition; small 8vo., handsomely rebound in half brown calf, marbled boards, 5 raised bands at spine, lettered gilt on spine, pages xx, 231, passage from Gibbon in contemporary ink on first blank, one short note in text in old hand, few pages slightly stained at corners, otherwise very good+. Any Amount of Books May 29 2011 - A72600 2011 $272

Pimlott, Anne Baker *The Pilgrims of Great Britain: a Centennial History.* London: Profile Books Ltd., 2002, First edition; 8vo., copiously illustrated in black and white, pages 216, fine in fine dust jacket. Any Amount of Books May 29 2011 - A70574 2011 $238

The Pin in the Queen's Shawl, Sketched in Indian ink on "imperial Crown" from a Conservative Standpoint. London: Remington & Co., 1876, Frontispiece, illustrations, original blue pictorial wrappers, slightly dusted, 32 pages. Jarndyce Antiquarian Booksellers CXCI - 593 2011 £85

Pinchard, Elizabeth Sibthorpe *The Blind Child or Anecdotes of the Wyndham Family.* London: printed for E. Newbery, 1795, Third edition; vii, (2), 10-178, (2) pages ads, hand colored frontispiece, 12mo., frontispiece with contemporary coloring, slightly creased with few chips repaired along fore edge, contemporary sheep, gilt banded spine, small neat repairs. Jarndyce Antiquarian Booksellers CXCI - 395 2011 £150

Pinckney, Mary Stead *Letter-Book of Mary Stead Pinckney November 14th 1796 to August 29th 1797.* New York: Grolier Club, 1946, Limited to 300 copies; octavo, vi, 116 pages, bookplate of James Hazen Hyde, fine. Jeff Weber Rare Books 163 - 205 2011 $60

Pink Laffin's Coontown & Other Comedy and Fun. Racine: circa, 1930, 64 pages, 12mo., original binding. Bookworm & Silverfish 664 - 4 2011 $75

Pinkerton, Jon *Walpoliana.* R. Phillips, 1799, Second edition; 2 volumes, engraved titles, 2 pages ads and folding plate in volume I, uncut in original pale blue paper boards, cream cloth spine, slightly dulled pink paper boards, extremely nice. Jarndyce Antiquarian Booksellers CXCI - 356 2011 £150

Pinkerton, Robert *Russia; or Miscellaneous Observations on the Past and Present State of that Country and Its Inhabitants.* London: Seeley & Sons, 169 Fleet Street, Hatchard & Son, Piccadilly, 1833, First edition; lacks half title 8 hand colored lithographs, errata leaf at end, scattered spotting in text, (10), 486, (2) pages, contemporary half calf, rebacked preserving original spine, recased. Anthony W. Laywood May 26 2011 - 21684 2011 $587

Pinkney, Jerry *The Lion and the Mouse.* New York: Little Brown and Co. Books for Young Readers, 1909, Numerically stated first printing; oblong 4to., full color pictorial boards, as new, full color pictorial dust jacket equally fresh and new, signed in full on titlepage. Jo Ann Reisler, Ltd. 86 - 192 2011 $150

Pinn, Keith *Paktong. the Chinese Alloy in Europe 1680-1820.* Antique Collectors Club, 1999, First edition; 4to., original cloth, gilt, dust jacket, pages 190, 18 color plates and over 230 other illustrations, as new. R. F. G. Hollett & Son Antiquarian Booksellers General Catalogue Summer 2010 - 295 2011 £45

Pinney, Charles *Trial of Charles Pinney, Esq. in the Court of King's Bench on an Information filed by His Majesty's Attorney General Charging Him with Neglect in His Office as Mayor of Bristol, During the Riots.* Bristol: printed by Gutch and Martin and published by Cadel (sic), Blackwood, Edinburgh, 1833, First edition; 8vo., xxxviii, (2), 432 pages, ad slip tipped in at end announcing the publication of another account of the Bristol riots, bound in original linen boards, neatly rebacked and labelled to match, entirely uncut, very good. John Drury Rare Books 153 - 157 2011 £125

Pinnock, William *The Golden Treasury.* Shepherd & Sutton, 1843, New edition; original blindstamped red cloth gilt, upper hinge splitting at head, backstrip little frayed at head and foot, pages xxx, 429, frontispiece, 1 woodcut plate and 18 plates each with four panels, one section shaken, scarce. R. F. G. Hollett & Sons Antiquarian Booksellers 170 - 531 2011 £85

Pinnock, William *Whittaker's Improved Editions of Pinnock's Catechisms.* Whittaker & Co., 1820's, Thick small 8vo., original red roan gilt, spine mellowed, 11 separate titles from a series of explanatory and interrogative school books, bound together, each with engraved frontispiece, that on electricity with engraved title and text woodcuts, that on Mental Philosophy with engraved title (rather browned) dated 1822, most titles have 72 pages and thare are 6 pages ads at end.   R. F. G. Hollett & Sons Antiquarian Booksellers   170 - 532   2011   £275

Pinter, Harold *The French Lieutenant's Women.* Boston: Little Brown, 1981, First edition; number 78 of 250 copies signed by Harold Pinter and John Folwes, whose novel this screenplay was based, cloth, slipcase, as new.   Gemini Fine Books & Arts, Ltd.   Art Reference & Illustrated Books: First Editions 2011 $250

Pinter, Harold *The Homecoming.* London: Karnac Curwen, 1968, First edition, 198 out of a limited edition of 200; elephant folio, original publisher's green illustrated cloth with mottling effect, 9 lithographs, scarce, signed by author and artist, 9 original lithographs and cover image have been made by artist and text set in photographically modified version of Bodoni Bold, binding forms an integral part of book, spine slightly darkened, otherwise very good+ in sound, slightly rubbed and slightly marked, very good or better plain slipcase.   Any Amount of Books   May 26 2011 - A47323   2011 $587

Pinter, Harold *No Man's Land.* London: Karnac, 1975, First edition, no. 105 of 150 copies signed by author,; 8vo., pages 96, original publisher's red and black cloth with gilt lining, lettered gilt at spine, fine, fine original publisher's acetate jacket.   Any Amount of Books   May 29 2011 - A71950   2011 $408

Pioneers of the Sacramento: a Group of Letters by and About Johann Augustus Sutter, James W. Marshall & John Bidwell.   San Francisco: Book Club of California, 1953, Limited to 400 copies; pages xii, 34, facsimiles of a broadside and folding map, cloth backed marbled boards, printed paper spine label, very fine, pristine copy.   Argonaut Book Shop   Recent Acquisitions Summer 2010 - 195   2011 $125

Piozzi, Hester Lynch Salusbury Thrale 1741-1821 *Autobiography Letters and Literary Remains of Mrs. Piozzi (Thrale).* London: Longman, Green, Longman & Roberts, 1861, 2 volumes, small octavo, xiii, 375; vi 479 pages, 2 frontispieces, index, later half navy blue morocco, marbled boards, raised bands, gilt spines, top edge gilt by W. Worsford, London, fine.   Jeff Weber Rare Books   163 - 50   2011 $250

Piozzi, Hester Lynch Salusbury Thrale 1741-1821 *Autobiography, Letters and Literary Remains of Mrs. Piozzi Thrale.* London: Longman, Green, Longman and Roberts, 1861, Second edition; 2 volumes, half titles, frontispieces, contemporary green binder's cloth, slightly dulled, good plus.   Jarndyce Antiquarian Booksellers   CLXC - 749   2011   £85

Piozzi, Hester Lynch Salusbury Thrale 1741-1821 *British Synonymy or an Attempt at Regulating the Choice of Words in Familiar Conversation.* London: printed for G. G. and J. Robinson, 1794, First edition; 8vo., pages (2), viii, 424; (2), 416, without half titles in contemporary half calf, stamped in gilt and blind, some rubbed and dried on spine, ownership initials of titlepages, bookplates.   Second Life Books Inc.   174 - 259   2011 $650

Piper, Horace Beame *Four-Day Planet.* New York: G. P. Putnam's Sons, 1961, First edition; octavo, cloth.   L. W. Currey, Inc.   124 - 123   2011 $650

Piper, John *A Painter's Camera.* London: The Tate Gallery, 1985, First edition; oblong 4to., original coarse weave cloth, dust jacket, pages 141, 199 duotone illustrations from photos, near fine.   R. F. G. Hollett & Son Antiquarian Booksellers   General Catalogue Summer 2010 - 1551   2011   £35

Piper, John *Piper's Places. John Piper in England and Wales.* London: Chatto & Windus, 1983, First edition; 4to., original cloth, gilt, dust jacket, pages 184, illustrations in color, near fine.   R. F. G. Hollett & Son Antiquarian Booksellers   General Catalogue Summer 2010 - 296   2011   £95

Pirovano, Carlo *The Graphics of Emilio Greco.* N.P.: Venice: Electa Editrice, 1975, First English edition; folio, original publisher's green cloth lettered gilt on spine and cover, signed presentation from artist, Greco, to Australian art expert Robert Haines, slight rubbing, slight sun fading, otherwise sound, clean, very good.   Any Amount of Books   May 26 2011 - A76883   2011 $503

Pisano, Maria G. *Patterned to the Fabric.* Plainsboro: Memory Press, 2008, Artist's book; one of 10 copies, all on Sekishu and BFK paper, each signed and numbered by artist, page size 5 x 6 inches, 26 pages, bound by artist, accordion fold with intaglio prints in red over boards as covers and endpapers, opening to blue intaglio prints, some with red of blue ground text, printed cyanotype on white Sekishu paper with blue border, Sekishu text pages handsewn with blue thread to Rives pages, housed in red paper publisher's slipcase with label printed in red within black rule on front panel showing title, artist and press.   Priscilla Juvelis - Rare Books   48 - 19   2011 $500

Pisano, Maria G. *Tunnel Vision.* Plainsboro: Memory Press, 2004, Artist's book one of 25 copies; all on Rives BFK paper and Sekishu paper, each signed by artist and numbered in colophon, page size 8 x 8 inches, opening to 80 inches long in form of a tunnel book, bound by artist, housed in clear ocean green plexi hinged box with paper label laid in at spine to show title printed in rondel, artist, press and date below it.   Priscilla Juvelis - Rare Books   48 - 20   2011 $3000

Pitseus, Joannes *Relationum Historicarum de rebus Anglicis tomus Primus (ed. William Bishop).*   Paris: R. Thierry for Joseph Cottereau, 1623, 4to., (20), 990, (2) pages, last leaf blank, title printed in red and black, engraved device, contemporary vellum, lacking ties, motto on titlepage, from the library of the Earls of Macclesfield at Shirburn Castle.   Maggs Bros. Ltd.   1440 - 168   2011   £450

Pitt, William *The Speeches of the Right Honourable William Pitt, in the House of Commons.*   London: Longman, Hurst, Rees and Orme, 1806, First edition; 4 volumes, 8vo., full grain leather, pages 1805, spines faded and worn, 2 lacking spine label, otherwise sound, very good.   Any Amount of Books   May 29 2011 - A70531   2011 $340

Pittiloch, Robert *Oppression Under the Colour of the Law, or My Lord Hercarse His New Pratick...*   Edinburgh: 1827, 4to., old thin boards, spine defective, edges little worn, pages iv, 32, very scarce.   R. F. G. Hollett & Son Antiquarian Booksellers   175 - 1065   2011   £220

Pixie Alphabet Book.   London: Blackie circa, 1930, 4to., cloth backed pictorial boards, near fine, illustrations in full color and 3-color by C. E. B. Bernard.   Aleph-Bet Books, Inc.   95 - 22   2011 $300

Pizzuto, Joseph J. *101 Fabrics.*   New York: 1952, 1961. First edition; 2 volumes, ring binders mildly ex-library, actual swatches 2 x 2 inches.   Bookworm & Silverfish   667 - 168   2011 $875

Planche, James Robinson *Costume of Shakespeare's Comedy of As You Like It...*   London: John Miller, 1825, First edition; 12mo., early half blank calf, minor staining to cloth of upper cover, title gilt to spine, hand colored engraved vignette to titlepage, 18 hand colored plates, marbled endpapers and edges.   Dramatis Personae Booksellers   106 - 136   2011 $500

Planchon, Jules Emile *La Victoria Regia au Point de Vue Horticole et Botanique...*   Ghent: C. Arnoot Braeckman for L. Van Houtte and others, 1850-1851, Very rare large paper offprint with plates unfolded; 7 lithographic plates, occasional light marginal spotting or soiling and 8 uncolored lithographic illustrations, large 4to., pages (5-) 52, original light brown printed wrappers (applied contemporary manuscript label to backstrip, small tears to backstrip with slight loss, light soiling) letterpress title within decorative border on upper cover, list on publishers on lower, modern red box, leather title label on upper cover.   Raymond M. Sutton, Jr.   May 26 2011 - 32288   2011 $2000

Plank, Sam *The Story of the String and How It Grew.*   New York: Artemus Ward, 1916, 8 1/2 x 5 3/4 inches, cloth backed pictorial boards, slightly dusty and tips rubbed, else very good+, illustrations on every page by Crawford Young.   Aleph-Bet Books, Inc.   95 - 399   2011 $400

Plath, Sylvia 1932-1963 *The Colossus. Poems.*   London: Heinemann, 1960, First edition; fine, 8vo., original green cloth, dust jacket, fine, preserved in half morocco slipcase, presentation copy inscribed by author to poet Theodore Roethke.   James S. Jaffe Rare Books   May 26 2011 - 18792   2011 $50,000

Plath, Sylvia 1932-1963 *Crystal Gazer and Other Poems.*   London: Rainbow Press, 1971, First edition; tall 4to., original publisher's quarter black buckram lettered gilt at spine with patterned boards, pages 29, printed on handmade paper, fine in near fine slipcase.   Any Amount of Books   May 29 2011 - A46365   2011 $238

Plato *Dialogues of Plato.*   London: printed for W. Sandby, 1767, First collected edition of Sydenham's translations; 8 (of 13) parts in two volumes, quarto, engraved folding plate in volume II, each part containing special titlepage (except for meno and The Rivals) and separate pagination; contemporary full tan calf, rebacked to style, gilt single rule border on covers, gilt board edges, marbled endpapers, brown calf spine labels, lettered in gilt, corners worn and boards lightly scuffed, occasional light foxing, previous owner's armorial bookplate, very good, crisp copy.   Heritage Book Shop   Holiday 2010 - 98   2011 $4000

Plato *His Apology of Socrates, and Phaedo...*   London: printed by T. R. & N. T. for James Magnes and Richard Bentley, 1675, First English edition; engraved frontispiece, octavo, (4, blank), (40), 300, (4, blank), full modern speckled calf, ruled in blind, red morocco spine label, spine lettered in gilt, all edges speckled, repair to inner bottom corner of titlepage, minimal loss of text, outer blank corner missing from leaf F and I2, very good, complete copy.   Heritage Book Shop   Holiday 2010 - 99   2011 $8500

Platt, A. E. *The History of the Parish and Grammar School of Sedbergh.* London: Longmans, Green and Co., 1876, First (only) edition; original brown cloth, gilt, spine rather faded as usual, small repaired split at top of upper hinge, pages 197, small closed tear to flyleaf, very scarce. R. F. G. Hollett & Son Antiquarian Booksellers 173 - 908 2011 £195

Platt, James *Tales of the Supernatural.* London: Ghost Story Press, 1994, First hardcover edition; octavo, cloth. L. W. Currey, Inc. 124 - 155 2011 $375

Plautus, Titus Maccius *Plauti Comici, Fabulae Superstites XX...* Frankfurt: Apud Nicolaum Hoffmannum Impensis Petri Kopffi, 1610, First Hoffmann Frankfurt edition; 12mo., (16), 804, (7) pages, woodcut printer's device on titlepage, heavily waterstained, original full vellum, yapped edges, ms. spine title, covers bit stained, booklabel and ink notation from Lingenswche Schulbibliothek on titlepage, very good. Jeff Weber Rare Books 163 - 7 2011 $200

Plautus, Titus Maccius *Comedies of Plautus.* London: printed for T. Becket and P. A. De Hondt, 1769-1774, Volumes 1 and 2 are second edition, volumes 3-5 all First editions; 5 volumes, 8vo., full brown leather bindings, hinges bit used, sides dull, slight splitting otherwise reasonable complete near very good set with clean text, pages 1957, volumes 1 and 2 have 2 neat names and dates on front blanks, all have Mirehouse bookplate. Any Amount of Books May 29 2011 - A32674 2011 $306

The Pleasing Toy. Wendell: John Metcalf, 1832, 18mo., 18 pages, original pictorial buff paper wrappers, wood engraved vignette on titlepage, 16 half page oval engravings, chipped corners, mended hole at lower part of page 7, reinforced spine, rare, very good. Hobbyhorse Books 56 - 27 2011 $100

Plevitz, Adolphe De *The Petition of the Old Immigrants of Mauritius presented on the 6th June 1871.* London: R. Barrett, n.d., 1871, First edition; 8vo., 34 pages, original paper stitched pamphlet, rare. J. & S. L. Bonham Antiquarian Booksellers Africa 4/20/2011 - 7182 2011 £150

Plimpton, George *Pet Peeves.* New York: Atlantic Monthly, 2000, Fine in fine dust jacket; inscribed by author to another writer and his wife. Ken Lopez Bookseller 154 - 163 2011 $150

Plimpton, Sarah *Keeping Time.* New York: 2009, Artist's book one of 15 copies all on Tosa Washi paper, each signed and numbered by the artist/author, Sarah Plimpton; page size 15 5/8 x 11 7/8 inches, plus letterpress printed text of poem on small sheet 6 3/8 x 5 3/8 inches, 10 pages, bound loose in grey paper wrappers and housed in custom made cloth over boards clamshell box by Claudia Cohen, label printed in gold gilt on paper on spine with title and author's name, book was set in Filosophia type and printed letterpress by Brad Ewing at the Grenfell Press, 10 reduction woodcuts printed in several shades of grey, black, magenta, blue, brown and chartreuse. Priscilla Juvelis - Rare Books 48 - 21 2011 $1200

Plinius Caecilius Secundus, C. *Caii Plinii Caecilii Secundi Opera.* Glasgow: Robert and Andrew Foulis, 1751, Small 4to., contemporary full polished calf with raised bands, elegantly gilt spine panels and contrasting label, edges little rubbed, page 348 (viii, index), with two titles, separate title and half title for Panegyricus, faint browning to a few margins. R. F. G. Hollett & Son Antiquarian Booksellers General Catalogue Summer 2010 - 673 2011 £250

Plinius Secundus, C. *Historiae Mundi Libri XXXVII ex Postrema ad Vetustos Codices Collatione cum annotationibus...* Parisiis: Apud Audoenum Paruum, 1543, Folio, pages (36), 671, (52), (175), 17th century quarter vellum over marbled boards (worn in places, label on spine chipped, occasional foxing, light dampstaining to a few pages), beautifully printed with 50 lines to a page, many decorative and historiated woodcut and scribble initials, large printer's device on title featuring two griffins. Raymond M. Sutton, Jr. May 26 2011 - 55925 2011 $2250

Plinius Secundus, C. *The Historie of the World.* London: printed by Adam Islip, 1601, First complete edition in English; 2 volumes, folio, without prelim and final blanks, half polished calf over marbled boards, rebacked. Heritage Book Shop Booth A12 51st NY International Antiquarian Book Fair April 8-10 2011 - 100 2011 $7500

Plot, Robert *The Natural History of Oxfordshire...* Oxford: printed at the Theater, 1677, first edition; folio, modern (1993) full 17th century style panelled calf ruled in blind, pages (viii), 358, (ii, errata verso blank) (x index), with folding map by Robert Morden (replacing correct map), engraved title with vignette of Pallas Athene, engraved headpiece of arms of Charles II, engraved initial letter, 14 engraved plates (ex 16 lacks plates 11 and 16), lacks imprimatur leaf, title very browned, worn and laid down some edge wear and browning in places throughout, plates 2 to 7 and 13 more or less defective, some pieces cut out and mostly replaced with blank paper, plate 15 torn without loss. R. F. G. Hollett & Son Antiquarian Booksellers General Catalogue Summer 2010 - 1552 2011 £450

Plowden, Francis *The Case Stated by Francis Plowden, Esq.* printed for the author and sold by P. Keating, 1791, First edition; (2), 5-196 pages, wanting half title and errata leaf (as in most copies), titlepage lightly stained, else good, recently well bound in cloth, spine lettered gilt.   John Drury Rare Books   153 - 114   2011   £175

Pluche, Noel Antoine *Spectacle De La Nature: or Nature Display'd. Being Discourses on Such Particulars of Natural History as Were Thought Most Proper to Excite the Curiosity and Form the Minds of Youth.* London: Pemberton; Franckling, Davies, 1735-1736, Second edition; full paneled calf, octavo, full set of 3 volumes, frontispiece in each volume, with total of 72 copper plates, 58 folding, four plates lacking in third volume, other plates may be lacking in other volumes, there is no guide to the plates in these volumes and we have seen different plate counts from various sources for the set, dampstaining and soiling, primarily to first volume, covers generally firm, spines worn with leather lacking on two volumes, good set.   Charles Agvent   2010 Summer Miscellany - 56   2011 $400

Plunket, Frederica *Here and There Among the Alps.* London: Longmans Green and Co., 1875, First edition; 8vo., original red cloth lettered gilt on spine and on front cover, pages (viii), 195, sound near very good with head of spine slightly chipped, cloth with slight soiling, rubbing and slight marks, internally very clean.   Any Amount of Books   May 29 2011 - A37101   2011 $298

Plunkett, James *Strumpet City.* London: Hutchinson, 1969, First edition; 8vo., signed and dated by author, 578 pages, book very faintly rubbed, dust jacket with slight edgewear, no inscriptions, near fine in like jacket.   Any Amount of Books   May 29 2011 - A68253   2011 $408

Plutarchus *The Live of the Nobel Grecians and Romanes...* Shakespeare Head Press, 1928, One of 500 copies; printed for sale in Great Britain, this copy # 309, another 500 sets were printed for the U.S. and an additional 100 were printed on handmade paper and signed by artist, 233 x 160mm., 8 volumes, quite attractive mid 20th century burgundy half morocco over matching linen, gilt decorated raised bands, spines with large central compartment featuring an intricate gilt filigree lozenge and cornerpieces, marbled endpapers, top edge gilt, other edges untrimmed and largely unopened, engraved headpieces, front flyleaf with tipped on typed note from Harry E. Davis, ABAA describing the book and noting the binding was done by hand for Della Quinn White of Houston Texas in 1952; very small gouge to front cover of volume I (but deep enough to cause a small crack in pastedown), otherwise very fine set, largely unopened, text nearly pristine and handsome bindings lustrous and virtually unworn.   Phillip J. Pirages   59 - 318   2011 $1500

Poe, Edgar Allan 1809-1849 *The Conchologist's First Book.* Philadelphia: Haswell, Barrington and Haswell, 1839, First edition, with plates in second state (uncolored); original printed pictorial boards and leather spine, very good, wear to boards (mostly at corners), some mild, random foxing, owner and seller stamps to f.f.e.p., nice, tight copy in original boards, quite scarce.   Lupack Rare Books   May 26 2011 - ABE 1222942219   2011 $1600

Poe, Edgar Allan 1809-1849 *The Murders in the Rue Morgue: and Other Tales of Horror.* New York: Grosset & Dunlap, n.d., 1932, Later edition; octavo, cloth.   L. W. Currey, Inc.   124 - 76   2011 $1250

Poe, Edgar Allan 1809-1849 *The Raven.* Easthampton: Cheloniidae Press, 1986, Artist's Proof copy; one of a handful of such bound as the state proof edition in full red morocco, with additional two suites of working proofs (21 prints total, 17 wood engravings and 3 states of frontispiece etching), from a total issue of 225 copies, 150 regular edition, 50 deluxe with extra suite of prints, bound in quarter morocco by Claudia Cohen, 25 state proof copies with two extra suites and an original drawing, full morocco binding, all copies on Magnani Letterpress paper and all signed and numbered by Alan James Robinson; page size 6 7/16 x 9 3/8 inches, this is an all new original edition in which the artist revisits the text of the first book of the press, text is letterpress by Dan Keliher at Wild Carrot Letterpress, the 9 original wood engravings and one original etching, frontispiece portrait of Poe, the full red morocco binding is by Daniel Kelm and Sarah Pringle at the Wide Awake Garage, the front panel blindstamped with one of Robinson's wood engravings of a raven, the two additional suites are housed in grey cloth over boards folder with white label printed in black on front "The Raven/Prints" and both housed in grey cloth-over boards clamshell box, red morocco label on spine, blindstamped with title, author and title logo of Cheloniidae Press, both bit worn, book and prints fine.   Priscilla Juvelis - Rare Books   48 - 4   2011 $2000

Poe, Edgar Allan 1809-1849 *Tales of Mystery and Imagination.* London: George G. Harrap & Co., 1935, Half title, color frontispiece, plates by Arthur Rackham, full red crushed morocco by Zaehnsdorf, borders in gilt, raised bands, spine decorated in gilt, gilt dentelles, top edge gilt, fine.   Jarndyce Antiquarian Booksellers   CXCI - 396   2011   £1200

Poe, Edgar Allan 1809-1849 *Tales of Mystery and Imagination.* London: Harrap, 1935, Limited to only 460 numbered copies, signed by artist; thick 4to., full gilt decorated vellum, some slight rubbing and minimal soil, near fine in original slipcase (case worn and scuffed), 12 mounted color plates with lettered tissue guards, plus a profusion of text drawings by Arthur Rackham, beautiful copy.   Aleph-Bet Books, Inc.   95 - 477   2011 $3650

Poe, Edgar Allan 1809-1849 *Tales of Mystery and Imagination.* London: George G. Harrap & Co., 1935, Limited to 460 numbered copies (of which 450 were for sale), One of 10 special copies with original watercolor drawing, signed by artist; containing original watercolor drawing on inserted leaf, signed and dated "Arthur Rackham/1935", large quarto, (2, blank), 317, (1), (2, blank) pages, 12 mounted color plates with descriptive tissue guards, 17 black and white plates, 11 small black and white drawings in text by Arthur Rackham, specially bound by Sangorski Sutcliffe (stamp-signed in gilt) in full green morocco, covers stamped in gilt, top edge gilt, others uncut, "Cockerell" marbled endpapers, original black and white pictorial endpapers bound in at front and back, spine slightly faded, otherwise fine, in original cardboard slipcase with printed spine label, matching limitation number, lower edge of slipcase expertly and almost invisibly replaced, housed in quarter morocco clamshell box.   David Brass Rare Books, Inc.   May 26 2011 - 00267   2011 $37,500

Poeschke, Joachim *Donatello and His World: Sculpture of the Italian Renaissance.*   New York: Harry N. Abrams Inc., 1993, First American edition; quarto, 495 pages, fine in dust jacket, profusely illustrated in color and black and white.   Lupack Rare Books   May 26 2011 - ABE3649630104   2011 $150

Poetry Book Society *Poetry Book Society Bulletin.* Poetry Society, 1958-1993, First edition; Nos. 18-20, 24, 27, 31, 33-35, 37-39 , 56-103, 10, 115, 112, 120, 122, 134-141, 143, 145, 156, together 76 bulletins, all in very good condition.   I. D. Edrich   May 26 2011 - 99884   2011 $503

Poetry of the Bells. Riverside Press printed in Aid of the Cambridge Chime by H. O. Houghton & Co., 1858, First edition; pictorial titlepage, decorative borders to pages, lovely gilt bells stamped on front and rear covers, all edges red, near fine.   Lupack Rare Books   May 26 2011 - ABE2464952325   2011 $200

Pogany, Elaine *The Golden Cockerel.* New York: Thomas Nelson and Sons, 1938, First edition; 4to., original cloth gilt, rather soiled and stained, unpaginated, 12 pages in full color and numerous striking black and white illustrations by Willy Pogany, littler fingering in places, inscriptions on front free endpaper.   R. F. G. Hollett & Sons Antiquarian Booksellers   170 - 540   2011   £95

Pogany, Willy *Willy Pogany's Mother Goose.* London: Thomas Nelson & Sons, 1928, Unpaginated, superbly illustrated in color and black and white in art deco style, couple of small smudges, endpapers lightly browned, bookplate on flyleaf slightly offset onto half title with little adhesion damage, small edge tear, excellent copy.   R. F. G. Hollett & Sons Antiquarian Booksellers   170 - 535   2011   £250

Pohl, Frederik *Gateway.* New York: St. Martin's Press, 1977, First edition; octavo, boards.   L. W. Currey, Inc.   124 - 77   2011 $1250

Pohler, John *Bibliotheca Historico - Militaris.* New York: 1961, Reprint of late 19th century edition; 4 volumes, fine set, original binding, Burt Franklin reprint #28.   Bookworm & Silverfish   679 - 125   2011 $97

Point, Nicolas *Wilderness Kingdom. Indian Life in the Rocky Mountains 1840-1847. The Journals and Paintings of Nicolas Point...* New York: Holt, Rinehart and Winston, 1967, First edition; quarto, 274 pages, 283 reproductions, 232 in full color, navy blue cloth, very fine, pictorial dust jacket.   Argonaut Book Shop   Recent Acquisitions Summer 2010 - 159   2011 $125

Pointer, Larry *Harry Jackson.* New York: Harry N. Abrams, 1981, First edition; large quarto, 308 pages, 397 photo illustrations, light brown cloth lettered in dark brown, very fine, pictorial dust jacket, presentation inscription signed by co-author, Donald Goddard, additionally signed by artist, Harry Jackson.   Argonaut Book Shop   Recent Acquisitions Summer 2010 - 160   2011 $300

Poisonous Plants: Deadly, Dangerous and Suspect. London: Frederick Etchells & Hugh Macdonald, Haslewood Books, 1928, First edition; pages xii, 85, one of 350 copies printed in Walbaum on Renker's Ingres paper at the Curwen Press, 20 full page engravings plus two smaller, quarter green buckram with gilt spine titling, brown cloth sides gold blocked with design by Nash on upper board, endpapers just faintly browned, very good, crisp copy.   Second Life Books Inc.   174 - 260   2011 $950

Poleni, Giovanni, Marchese *Miscellanea. Hoc est. 1. Dissertatio de Barometris & Thermmetris. II. Machinae Aritmeticae, ejusque Usus Descriptio. III. De Sectionibus Comicis Parallerum in Horologiis Solaribus Tractatus.* Venice: Alvise Pavini, 1709, 4to., (8), 56, 9 folding engraved plates, contemporary Italian 'carta rustica', fine, large, clean copy in beautiful condition, from the library of the Earls of Macclesfield at Shirburn Castle.   Maggs Bros. Ltd.   1440 - 169   2011   £4500

Polignac, Melchior De *Anti-Lucretius, Sieu de Deo et Natura, Libri Novem... Opus Posthumum...* Amsterdam: Marc Michel Rey, 1748, 2 volumes in one, titlepages printed in red and black, half title frayed at edges, minor dampstain in lower margins at start, pages (ii, blank), 192, (iv), (193-) 372, small 8vo., contemporary calf, roll tooled border towards spine on upper cover, rebacked, corners worn, sound.   Blackwell Rare Books   B166 - 80   2011   £150

Polk, James Knox *Messages of the President of the United States with the Correspondence.* Washington: Wendell & Van Benthuysen, 1848, First edition; 1277 pages, new three quarter calf, marbled boards, some scattered light foxing, corner crease to titlepage, complete, clean and handsomely bound copy. Argonaut Book Shop Recent Acquisitions Summer 2010 - 129 2011 $1500

Polko, Elise *Musical Tales, Phantasms and Sketches.* London: Samuel Tinsley, 1876, 2 pages ads, original green cloth, spine lettered in gilt, boards and spine blocked in black, later ownership inscription on paper laid on to leading pastedown, very good. Jarndyce Antiquarian Booksellers CLXC - 750 2011 £40

Pollard, Alfred W. *Shakespeare's Fight with the Pirates and the Problems of the Transmission of His Text.* Cambridge: Cambridge University Press, 1920, Second edition; small 8vo., original cloth backed boards, paper spine label, edges little rubbed and darkened, pages xxviii, 111, untrimmed. R. F. G. Hollett & Son Antiquarian Booksellers General Catalogue Summer 2010 - 456 2011 £30

Pollard, Edward A. *Life of Jefferson Davis with a Secret History of the Southern Confederacy Gathered Behind the Scenes in Richmond.* Philadelphia: 1869, First edition; 536 pages, good solid copy, terra cotta pebbled cloth shows few spots, one lower free corner well worn. Bookworm & Silverfish 678 - 33 2011 $60

Pollard, Eliza Fanny *The White Dove of Amritzir.* London: S. W. Partrige, 1896, First edition; half title, frontispiece, 16 page catalog, rather browned, original blue cloth, dulled, endpapers browned. Jarndyce Antiquarian Booksellers CLXC - 751 2011 £50

Pollard, Hugh B. C. *The Gun Room Guide.* London: Eyre & Spottiswoode, 1930, 4to., original green cloth gilt, dust jacket, slight edgewear and fraying in places, pages 183, untrimmed, 12 color plates and 11 black and white illustrations, occasional spot, very nice. R. F. G. Hollett & Son Antiquarian Booksellers General Catalogue Summer 2010 - 1272 2011 £250

Pollard, John Garland *Code of Virginia. Annotated.* Richmond: 1919, 3 volumes, volume 1 very good, labels reglued, volume 2 with both inner joints broken, covers loose, volume 3 very good. Bookworm & Silverfish 678 - 204 2011 $150

Pollard, Percival *Masks and Minstrels of New German.* Boston: John W. Luce, 1911, First American edition; blank leaf bound between pages 4 and 5, title slightly browned, few blue pencil marks in text, uncut in contemporary half dark blue morocco, slight rubbing, top edge gilt. Jarndyce Antiquarian Booksellers CXCI - 397 2011 £35

Pollok, Robert *The Course of Time: a Poem in Ten Books.* Edinburgh: William Blackwood and London: T. Cadell, 1833, 169 x 105mm., 2 p.l. 394 page, charming early 20th century sky-blue crushed morocco, onlaid and gilt, front cover with onlaid red morocco flanked and decorated with gilt, this border expanding into wedge shaped cornerpieces featuring a stylized gilt rosebud with curling gilt stems and onlaid green morocco leaves (veins delicately traced with gilt), border enclosing large center panel featuring prominent round centerpiece of onlaid red morocco containing the same gilt rosebuds and green morocco leaves found in corners (but here seen in graceful interlacing form), back cover repeating same design but entirely in gilt raised bands, heavily gilt spine with rose and leaf patterns repeated wide turn-ins with three gilt fillets, all edges gilt, top of spine with very shallow piece of leather loss approximately half its width, hint of soiling to covers, spine uniformly sunned to pleasing blue green, otherwise fine, quite pretty binding with virtually no wear to joints or hinges and with only trivial problems internally. Phillip J. Pirages 59 - 122 2011 $575

Polyaenus *Strategematum Libri octo Justo Vultejo Interprete.* Leyden: Lugduni Batavorum Johannem Du Vivie & Jordanum Luchtmans, 1691, Second Greek translation; 8vo., (24), 832, (40) pages, added engraved allegorical half title, index, title and text in Greek and Latin, contemporary red calf, gilt ruled cover borders, gilt stamped spine title and decorative compartments with raised bands, all edges gilt, extremities rubbed, corners worn, top spine end chipped (piece missing), bookplate, rubber stamp on title, very good. Jeff Weber Rare Books 163 - 25 2011 $400

Polyaenus *Strategmatum Libri Octo Recensuit Justi Vulteii Versionem Latinam Emandavit et Indicem Graecum adjecit Samuel Mursinna.* Berlin: Sumtibus A. Haude et I. C. Speneri, 1756, Third edition; some foxing, pages (xii), 550, 8vo., 19th century black calf, functionally rebacked, backstrip with five raised bands, label in second compartment, marbled edges and endpapers, old leather chipped and rubbed at edges, crackled around repair, sound. Blackwell Rare Books B166 - 81 2011 £250

Polybius *The General History of Polybius.* London: printed for J. Dodsley, 1772, 2 volumes, 4to., pages xxiv, (viii) 559 (i) + extending engraved map frontispiece and one other extending engraved map, (xvi), 423, (xvii), contemporary sprinkled calf, spines panel gilt with 'Rococo' floral centrepieces, five raised bands and head and foot identically gilt using 'alternating full & broken hatch' pallet, red & black lettering & numbering pieces gilt, board edges decorative roll gilt, all edges lemon, red and white sewn endbands, lightly toned and bit spotted in places, rubbed, joints cracked, spine ends worn, some scapes to boards, armorial bookplate of Thomas Poynder, from the collection of Christopher Ernest Weston 1947-2010. Unsworths Booksellers 24 - 136 2011 £360

Pomey, Francois Antoine *The Pantheon: Representing the Fabulous Histories of the Heathen Gods, and Most Illustrious Heroes...* London: Charles Harper, 1709, 8vo., (6), 410 10 pages, full leather on boards, blind decorative stamping along folds of covers, five raised bands and gilt title on label on spine, full page copper engraved frontispiece, 16 full page copper engravings, inked note inside upper cover, tiny mended chip at lower edge of frontispiece and along front edge, traces of red sealing wax inside covers, spine lightly worn. Hobbyhorse Books 56 - 118 2011 $270

Pond, Oscar L. *A Treatise on the Law of Public Utilities Operating in Citites and Towns.* Indianapolis: 1912, First edition; beige law cloth, some finger marks. Bookworm & Silverfish 669 - 64 2011 $75

Ponsonby, Arthur *The Priory and Manor of Lynchmere and Shulbrede.* Taunton: Barnicott & Pearce, 1920, First edition; original holland backed boards, edges little stained, pages xiv, 207, uncut with 57 illustrations by author, few spots in places, attractive bookplate of William Saunders, 10 line autograph note by author on his headed notepaper tipped on to flyleaf. R. F. G. Hollett & Son Antiquarian Booksellers 175 - 1069 2011 £120

Ponsonby, Emily *Katherine and Her Sisters.* London: Hurst & Blackett, 1861, First edition; 3 volumes, slightly later half purple calf, gilt spines, maroon leather labels, odd small mark, bookplates of Mary Herbert, very good. Jarndyce Antiquarian Booksellers CLXC - 752 2011 £225

Ponsonby, Emily *The Young Lord.* London: Hurst & Blackett, 1856, First edition; 2 volumes, contemporary half green calf, spines gilt in compartments and with brown leather labels, slight rubbing but attractive set. Jarndyce Antiquarian Booksellers CLXC - 753 2011 £225

Ponton, Mungo Melanchthon *Life and Times of Henry M. Turner.* Greenwood Press, 1970, Vey good, very clean and tight, without dust jacket, 173 pages, facsimile reprint. G. H. Mott Bookseller May 26 2011 - 44866 2011 $275

Poole, George Ayliffe *A History of Ecclesiastical Architecture in England.* London: Joseph Masters, 1848, First edition; frontispiece, original dark blue cloth, gilt, fine. Jarndyce Antiquarian Booksellers CXCI - 398 2011 £65

Poole, Reginald Lane *Illustrations of the History of Medieval Thought in the Departments of Theology and Ecclesiastical Politics.* London: Williams and Norgate, 1884, First edition; pages viii, 376, original cloth, gilt. R. F. G. Hollett & Son Antiquarian Booksellers 175 - 1071 2011 £30

Poole, Sophia *The Englishwoman in Egypt: Letters from Cairo, Written During a Residence There in 1842, 3 and 4. (with) Second Series... Letters written 1845-46.* London: Charles Knight & Co., 1844-1846, 3 volumes, half title volume II, frontispiece volume I, plates volumes I & II, original dark green cloth, elaborate borders in blind, spines lettered in gilt, name erased from leading pastedown volume I, otherwise near fine set, bookplates of B. B. Turner. Jarndyce Antiquarian Booksellers CXCI - 574 2011 £1100

Poole, W. *Union Lodge Kendal no. 129 1764-1864.* Kendal: privately printed, n.d. circa, 1932, First edition; original blue cloth, gilt, plain dust jacket (foot of spine defective), pages 96 with 8 plates, scarce, prospectus for 2nd (1949) edition and 2 page transcript of a lecture by Poole loosely inserted. R. F. G. Hollett & Son Antiquarian Booksellers 173 - 909 2011 £45

Poore, Perley *Life of U. S. Grant.* Philadelphia: 1885, First edition; 594 pages, very good, solid copy, all gilt good, bit rubbed on backstrip, backstrip with very small amount of wear at bottom. Bookworm & Silverfish 678 - 34 2011 $125

Pope-Hennessy, James *London Fabric.* London: Batsford, 1941, Second edition; original brown cloth, gilt, dust jacket with striking design by Eric Ravilious (spine little darkened, small chip to foot, few spots to lower panel), pages viii, 184, with 53 plates. R. F. G. Hollett & Son Antiquarian Booksellers General Catalogue Summer 2010 - 1553 2011 £35

Pope-Hennessy, James *Monckton-Milnes: the Years of Promise.* London: Constable, 1949, First edition; 8vo., slight wear, slight sunning, otherwise sound, near very good, signed presentation from author to Janet Ashbee. Any Amount of Books May 29 2011 - A63899 2011 $255

Pope, Alexander 1688-1744 *The Poetical Works of Alexander Pope with His Life by Samuel Johnson.* London: printed by Whittingham and Howard for Sharpe and Hailes, 1811,   222 x 142 mm., 2 volumes, once very striking and still quite handsome contemporary crimson straight grain morocco by Taylor & Hessey (stamp-signed on the narrow board edge of upper cover of each volume), covers with border of thick and thin gilt rules enclosing a fine lacy gilt frame incorporating palmettes and volutes, inner frame formed by single gilt rule terminating at corners in floral sprays, raised bands dividing spine into four large and three small panels, the three narrow panels featuring a gilt rosette flanked by fleurons, the large panels at head and tail with prominent ornate fleuron on a stippled background with scalloped edges, and two middle panels with gilt titling, all edges gilt, the two fore edges with especially attractive paintings of Windsor Castle and Twickenham, frontispiece portraits, 16 engraved plates; contemporary ink ownership inscription of "Miss M(argare)t Rigden", spines uniformly faded to soft rose (with consequent slight muting of gilt), joints and extremities bit rubbed (though well refurbished), considerable foxing to plates as well as foxing and offsetting to adjacent leaves, other trivial imperfections, nevertheless very appealing set in important ways, elegant original bindings entirely sound and with lustrous boards, text almost entirely very smooth and fresh, fore edge paintings in excellent state of preservation.   Phillip J. Pirages   59 - 198   2011 $2900

Pope, Alexander 1688-1744   *The Poetical Works.* London: published by Thomas M'Lean, 1821,   One of 100 copies; 241 x 159mm, 2 volumes, contemporary dark green straight grain morocco, handsomely gilt, covers bordered with various gilt rules flanking a wide roll of llinked drawer handle ornaments, blind floral roll forming a tangent inner frame, wide raised bands decorated in gilt, spines gilt with decorative rolls at head and foot with elaborate all over scrolling foliate design within panels, all edges gilt, designated large paper copy on titlepage and with margins that are quite wide but volume at leas slightly trimmed down, engraved bookplate of Charles Costello (partially removed from first volume), first volume with pencilled ownership signature (perhaps of "Capt. C. Robertson"), hint of wear to leather and of fading to spines, intermittent light foxing, one opening little soiled, additional trivial defects, but quite appealing, decorative bindings bright, clean and very pretty, text quite fresh with nothing approaching a serious problem.   Phillip J. Pirages   59 - 280   2011 $650

Pope, Alexander 1688-1744   *A Supplement to the Works of Alexander Pope Esq. Containing Such Poems, Letters &c as are Omitted in the Edition Published by the Reverend Dr. Warburton...* London: privately Printed for M. Cooper, 1757,   First edition; 8vo., full brown leather, pages viii 206, spine title label missing, some wear and rubbing to leather, otherwise sound, near very good, bookplate of George Lewthwaite and his neat name on endpaper.   Any Amount of Books   May 29 2011 - A32736   2011 $221

Pope, Henry E. *A Winter in Algiers; or the Corsair and His Conqueror.* London: Richard Bentley, 1860,   First edition; 8vo., pages 342, lithograph frontispiece, all edges gilt, original blue decorative cloth, small wear to head and tail of spine.   J. & S. L. Bonham Antiquarian Booksellers   Africa 4/20/2011 - 8326   2011   £110

Popeye and the Pirates. New York: Duenewald, 1945,   4to., pictorial boards, near fine, illustrations in full color by Sagendorf and featuring 4 color moveable plates by Julian Wehr.   Aleph-Bet Books, Inc.   95 - 382   2011 $250

Porley, John   *Mosses & Liveworts.* London: Collins, 2005,   Original cloth, gilt dust jacket, pages 495 with 179 illustrations, mint.   R. F. G. Hollett & Son Antiquarian Booksellers   General Catalogue Summer 2010 - 1035   2011   £65

Portal, Gerald   *My Mission to Abyssina.* London: Edward Arnold, 1892,   First edition; 8vo., pages viii, 261, frontispiece, folding map, 8 plates, original purple decorative cloth, gilt vignette on upper cover, very good, clean.   J. & S. L. Bonham Antiquarian Booksellers   Africa 4/20/2011 - 9144   2011   £300

Porter, Anna Maria   *Don Sebastian; or the House of Braganza.* London: Longman, 1809,   First edition; 4 volumes, 12mo., half titles, contemporary tree calf, gilt spines, bookplates of Robert Firth & "Tavance", very good.   Jarndyce Antiquarian Booksellers   CLXC - 754 2011   £280

Porter, Anna Maria   *The Hungarian Brothers.* London: Longman, 1814,   Third edition; 3 volumes, half titles volumes II and III, uncut in contemporary drab boards, purple spines, paper labels, volumes II and III lettered with title in ink at head of spines, small unobtrusive reparis, paper label with loss volume III, each volume signed Eliza Giffard, Nerquis, Flintshire, very good.   Jarndyce Antiquarian Booksellers   CLXC - 755 2011   £250

Porter, Anna Maria   *The Recluse of Norway.* London: Longman, 1814,   First edition; 4 volumes, slight spotting, handsome contemporary half calf, gilt spines, black labels, armorial bookplates of Eric Carrington Smith, very good, attractive.   Jarndyce Antiquarian Booksellers   CLXC - 756   2011   £380

Porter, Anna Maria   *The Recluse of Norway.* London: G. Routledge & Co., 1852,   Signed Mary Chaytor on title, contemporary half black roan, slight rubbing.   Jarndyce Antiquarian Booksellers   CLXC - 757 2011   £35

Porter, Anna Maria *Roche-Blanche; or the Hunters of the Pyrenees.* London: Longman, 1822, First edition; 3 volumes, 12mo., half titles volumes II & III, inserted 4 pages at front volume I (June 1822), uncut in original blue boards, drab paper spines, paper labels, spines chipped at tails, good copy, 1926 bookplate of Eric Quayle, signatures of Mary Chandos August 1822, tipped in is folded holograph ms. signed by Porter. Jarndyce Antiquarian Booksellers CLXC - 758 2011 £650

Porter, Arthur *The Crosses and Culture of Ireland.* New Haven: Yale University Press, 1931, First edition; xxiv, 143 pages, 276 photo illustrations, very good. C. P. Hyland May 26 2011 - 254/874 2011 $906

Porter, Eugene Stratton 1863-1924 *Homing with the Birds - the History of a Lifetime of Personal Experience with the Birds.* New York: 1919, First edition; 381, (1) pages, very good, original binding, mild wear to backstrip ends, black and white photos by author. Bookworm & Silverfish 665 - 21 2011 $75

Porter, Eugene Stratton 1863-1924 *Laddie, a True Blue Story.* Garden City: Doubleday, Page and Co., 1913, First edition; near fine, light wear to spine ends, dust jacket very good-, several open tears and chips, some tape repairs on verso, first state, without "A True Blue Story" on spine of jacket of book, copyright is 1913, but 1914 appears on titlepage, very good, several open tears and chips, some tape repairs on verso. Bella Luna Books May 26 2011 - t7977CO 2011 $247

Porter, Eugene Stratton 1863-1924 *Moths of the Limberlost.* Garden City: 1912, First edition; with omission and errata slip, 369, (1) pages, large 8vo., very good, one small scrape above title on cover. Bookworm & Silverfish 669 - 141 2011 $125

Porter, J. L. *The Giant Cities of Bashan and Syria's Holy Places.* T. Nelson & Sons, 1865, First edition; original cloth, gilt over bevelled boards, trifle rubbed, top and base of spine lightly worn, pages v, 371, with 8 tinted plates from photos, title faintly dampstained slight adhesion damage to corner of frontispiece and title. R. F. G. Hollett & Son Antiquarian Booksellers 177 - 713 2011 £45

Porter, Jane *The Pastor's Fireside, a Novel.* London: Henry Colburn and Richard Bentley, 1832, 2 volumes, half titles, frontispieces, engraved titles, additional printed titles, binding A - glazed plum colored linen, black labels, spines little faded, labels chipped with some loss volume II, volume II with armorial bookplate of Andrew Arcedeckne, Glevering Hall, good plus. Jarndyce Antiquarian Booksellers CLXC - 759 2011 £60

Porter, Jane *The Pastor's Fire-Side.* London: Longmans, 1817, First edition; publisher's catalogue, 4 pages, dated May 1816, original boards, paper spines worn, all half titles present, very occasional foxing, else very good set in original state. C. P. Hyland May 26 2011 - 739 2011 $544

Porter, Jane *The Scottish Chiefs, a Romance in Five Volumes.* London: Longman et al, 1810, First edition; 12mo., contemporary half calf with gilt stamped spines, some light foxing, very good set, without half titles in volume I and 4, others present, without errata leaf in volume I, small bookplates. Second Life Books Inc. 174 - 261 2011 $850

Porter, Jane *The Scottish Chiefs, a Romance.* London: Longman, 1820, Fourth edition; 5 volumes, lacking pages 1-2 of 12 page catalog volume IV, uncut in original blue boards, brown paper spines, paper labels, spines rubbed and chipped, good plus, as originally issued. Jarndyce Antiquarian Booksellers CLXC - 760 2011 £180

Porter, Jane *The Scottish Chiefs.* Philadelphia: J. B. Lippincott & Co., 1864, Double frontispiece, slight spotting in text, original purple cloth, spine faded, very good. Jarndyce Antiquarian Booksellers CLXC - 761 2011 £40

Porter, Jane *Thaddeus of Warsaw.* London: printed by A. Strahan for T. N. Longman, 1804, Second edition; half titles, contemporary marbled boards, excellently rebacked, retaining original red labels, signature of J. Mansfield 1806, very good, clean copy,. Jarndyce Antiquarian Booksellers CLXC - 762 2011 £420

Porter, Jane *Thaddeus of Warsaw.* London: Richard Bentley, 1835, Frontispiece, engraved title (1831) addtional printed title (1835), leading f.e.p. and frontispiece slightly loose, contemporary full purple calf, single ruled borders in gilt, spine gilt in compartments, maroon leather label, little rubbed, prize label from Ongar Academy, 1838, nice copy. Jarndyce Antiquarian Booksellers CLXC - 763 2011 £50

Porter, Jane *Thaddeus of Warsaw.* London: George Virtue, 1845, New edition; frontispiece, engraved title, additional printed title, frontispiece, plates, full contemporary dark green embossed calf, gilt spine and borders, maroon leather label, very slight rubbing, all edges gilt, very good. Jarndyce Antiquarian Booksellers CLXC - 764 2011 £120

Porter, Jane *Thaddeus of Warsaw.* London: Richard Bentley, 1846, Sadleir style C in brown cloth, spine faded, very good. Jarndyce Antiquarian Booksellers CLXC - 765 2011 £40

Porter, Katherine Anne 1890-1980 *The Leaning Tower.* New York: Harcourt Brace, 1944, First edition; near fine, bumping and soiling to spine ends, dust jacket very good, chippped to spine and corners, two closed tears to front panel, light soiling to rear panel, very good, chipping to spine and corners, two closed tears to front panel, light soiling to rear panel.   Bella Luna Books   May 29 2011 - t6521 2011 $82

Porter, Rufus *A Select Collection of Valuable and Curious Arts and Interesting Experiments.* Concord: published by Rufus Porter, J. b. Moore, printer, 1826, third edition; 16mo., (2), 132 pages, frontispiece and illustrations, contemporary two-toned paper covered boards, uncut, spine shot, front hinge very weak, half title, few leaves disbound.   M & S Rare Books, Inc.   90 - 329 2011 $400

Porter, William D. *State Sovereignty and the Doctrine of Coercion. Together with a Letter from Hon. J. K. Paulding, Former Sec. of Navy (and) The Right to Secede by "States".* Charleston: Evans & Cogswell's Steam Power Presses, 1860, First edition; 8vo., 36 pages, later plain wrappers, title stained, sheets browned, small library blindstamped twice on title and their occasional numeric rubber stamp in text.   M & S Rare Books, Inc.   90 - 85 2011 $250

Porter, William Sydney 1862-1910 *The Complete Writings of O. Henry.* Garden City: Doubleday Page and co., 1917, One of 1075 copies, Memorial edition and edition deluxe; 230 x 150mm., 14 volumes, lavishly gilt by Stikeman, covers with very broad and animated gilt borders of swirling foliage flowers and butterflies in style of Derome, raised bands, spine compartments attractively gilt with antique tools, red morocco doublures with multiple rules and other gilt elaboration, watered silk free endleaves, top edge gilt, other edges untrimmed, entirely unopened; with 90 plates, including colored frontispiece in each volume, the one in volume 1 signed by artist and engraved half title with vignette, signed by publisher; original tissue guards, prelim page of first volume with folding leaf of manuscript, apparently in Porter's hand, tipped in; titlepages and half titles in blue and black; spines evenly sunned, one leaf with minor marginal tear at fore edge, otherwise extraordinarily beautiful set in virtually faultless condition. Phillip J. Pirages 59 - 281 2011 $11,500

Portlock, Nathaniel *A Voyage Round the World.* London: printed for John Stockdale and George Goulding, 1789, First edition; quarto, engraved portrait, 13 engraved plates and 6 folding engraved maps, contemporary blue boards with newer parchment spine, printed paper spine label.   Heritage Book Shop   Booth A12 51st NY International Antiquarian Book Fair April 8-10 2011 - 101 2011 $8500

The Post Office London Directory for 1823. London: Critchett & Woods, 1823, First edition; small 8vo., soundly rebound in half red leather and marbled boards, 5 raised bands, lettered gilt at spine, pages (xii), 1-412 lxxii, titlepage slightly chipped at edges, otherwise sound, clean, very good.   Any Amount of Books   May 26 2011 - A61718 2011 $470

Postgate, Raymond *Fact.* Pelican Press, 1937-1939, First edition; Nos. 1-27, April 1937-June 1939, original wrappers in very good condition.   I. D. Edrich   May 26 2011 - 84522 2011 $453

Postlethwaite, John *The Geology of the English District with Notes on the Minerals.* Carlisle: G. & T. Coward, 1906, Second edition; small 8vo., original decorated boards, neatly rebacked, pages viii, 90, (viii) folding map, 7 plates and a section.   R. F. G. Hollett & Son Antiquarian Booksellers   173 - 914 2011   £65

Postlethwaite, John *Mines and Mining in the (English) Lake District.* Leeds: Samuel Moxon, 1889, Second edition; original green cloth , lower board trifle cockled, pages xi, 101, (xi), 10 plates and sections, folding map.   R. F. G. Hollett & Son Antiquarian Booksellers   173 - 915 2011   £120

Potomac Iron Company *Geological Report of the Potomac Iron Company's Property in the States of Virginia & Maryland.* Philadelphia: 1856, 24 pages, folding map in facsimile, wrappers, front wrapper loose with old chip and usual frays.   Bookworm & Silverfish   668 - 182 2011 $150

Potter, Beatrix 1866-1943 *Cecily Parsley's Nursery Rhymes.* London: Warne, 1922, First edition; frontispiece and 14 other color printed plates by author, pages 54, 16mo., original pink boards trifle finger soiled, backstrip longitudinally lettered in white, front cover lettered in white with rectangular color printed label onlaid depicting a rabbit hurrying down a burrow with a laden wheelbarrow, color printed pictorial endpapers as called for, good.   Blackwell Rare Books   B166 - 212 2011   £500

Potter, Beatrix 1866-1943 *Painting and Drawing Book with Tale of Peter Rabbit.* New York: Platt & Munk (Hurst), 1915, Oblong 4to., cloth backed pictorial boards, corner repair to title, else fine and unused, printed color illustrations faced with illustrations in line for reader to paint, very scarce.   Aleph-Bet Books, Inc.   95 - 461 2011 $400

Potter, Beatrix 1866-1943 *The Pie and the Patty-Pan.* London: Warne, 1905, Early edition; Square 8vo., original light maroon boards with roundel onlay to upper board, trifle faded and rebacked in matching cloth lettered in white, pages 52, 10 color plates and line text illustrations, slight stain to lower corner of pastedowns and last few leaves, otherwise very nice. R. F. G. Hollett & Sons Antiquarian Booksellers   170 - 543 2011   £225

Potter, Beatrix   1866-1943   *The Roly-Poly Pudding.* London: Warne and Co., 1908,   Early issue; square 8vo., original cloth backed pictorial boards, spine and edges little worn and faded, pages 70, with 18 color plates and other illustrations, edges of title little creased and worn, some fingering and light creases, small piece torn from lower margin of 1 leaf (not affecting text), 2 inch tear to another text leaf, early issue.   R. F. G. Hollett & Sons Antiquarian Booksellers   170 - 544   2011   £120

Potter, Beatrix   1866-1943   *The Story of Miss Moppet.* London & New York: Frederick Warne and Co., 1913, First edition in book form; 12mo., 52, (1), (1, blank) pages, color frontispiece and 14 color plates (included in pagination), black and white vignette on titlepage, original gray boards lettered in dark green on front cover and spine, large color pictorial label on front cover within a blind circular panel surrounded by broad dark green border, color pictorial endpapers, very slight foxing to prelims, otherwise very fine in original glazed paper, glassine dust jacket printed in black with price "1/3 NET" at foot of spine with ad on rear panel for "The Peter Rabbit Books" listing the Tale of Pigling Bland and The Tale of Mr. Tod at "1/3 NET" under "Series II New Style" and listing 12 titles already published, jacket has only minimal wear to spine extremities, with no loss, extremely scarce, housed in full dark green morocco gilt clamshell case.   David Brass Rare Books, Inc.   May 26 2011 - 00675   2011 $8500

Potter, Beatrix   1866-1943   *The Tailor of Gloucester.* London: Frederick Warne and Co., 1903,   First trade edition, first printing; 24mo., maroon boards with white lettering and color paste label, slight wear to corners and discreet bookplate on front pastedown, otherwise nice, endpaper design of this, the first issue, is repeated four times, 85 numbered pages, each text page paired with full page full color illustration.   Jo Ann Reisler, Ltd.   86 - 199   2011 $1750

Potter, Beatrix   1866-1943   *The Tailor of Gloucester.* London: F. Warne and Co., 1903,   First edition, 2nd printing; 12mo., original dark green boards with shaped pictorial inlay, rebacked to matching levant morocco lettered in white, pages 86, illustrations in color, very attractive.   R. F. G. Hollett & Sons Antiquarian Booksellers   170 - 545   2011   £350

Potter, Beatrix   1866-1943   *The Tailor of Gloucester.* London: Frederick Warne and Co., 1903,   First published edition, First issue (printed Oct. 1903); with a single page endpaper occurring four times, 12mo., 85, (1, printer's imprint) pages, color frontispiece and 26 color plates, original maroon boards, ruled and lettered in white on front cover and lettered in white on spine, color pictorial label on front cover within blind panel in the shape of a truncate pyramid outlined in blind, color pictorial endpapers, minimal fading to spine, small circular bookseller's label on rear pastedown, otherwise spectacular copy in very fine condition, rare corrected glazed paper glassine dust jacket printed in black with price "1/-NET" at foot of spine.   David Brass Rare Books, Inc.   May 26 2011 - 00665   2011 $17,500

Potter, Beatrix   1866-1943   *The Tale of Benjamin Bunny.* London: Frederick Warne and Co., 1904,   First edition; 12mo., 84, (1), (1, printer's imprint) pages, color frontispiece and 26 color plates, black and white vignette on titlepage, original deluxe binding of tan fine diagonally ribbed cloth, front cover decoratively stamped and lettered in gilt with border of single dots and four-leaf clovers, with stylized rose at each corner, double chain of this border looping down from an oval color pictorial label, spine lettered in gilt, all edges gilt, color pictorial endpapers, fine.   David Brass Rare Books, Inc.   May 26 2011 - 00733   2011 $11,500

Potter, Beatrix   1866-1943   *The Tale of Benjamin Bunny.* London: Frederick Warne and Co., 1904,   First edition; 12mo., 84, (1), (1, printer's imprint) pages, color frontispiece and 26 color plates, black and white vignette on titlepage, original tan boards ruled and lettered in dark green on front cover and lettered in dark green on spine, color pictorial label on front cover within a blind oval panel outlined in blind, correct color pictorial endpapers, minimal darkening to board edges, otherwise near fine, in original glazed paper glassine dust jacket printed in black with vertical lines at top and bottom of spine indicating where the fold should be for the front panel, top 3/8 inch and bottom 7/8 inch of jacket spine (including price) are missing, as well as a piece 1 x 3/4 inch missing on back panel.   David Brass Rare Books, Inc.   May 26 2011 - 00667   2011 $8500

Potter, Beatrix   1866-1943   *The Tale of Johnny Town Mouse.* London: Frederick Warne & Co., 1918,   First edition; 12mo., pages 86, illustrations in color with pictorial endpapers, original grey pictorial boards lettered in white, with shaped onlay.   R. F. G. Hollett & Sons Antiquarian Booksellers   170 - 546   2011   £450

Potter, Beatrix   1866-1943   *The Tale of Little Pig Robinson.* Philadelphia: McKay, 1930,   First US edition; 8vo., green cloth, pictorial paste-on, 141 pages, fine in dust jacket (discolored on part of edges), 6 fine color plates and numerous line illustrations, pictorial endpapers, beautiful copy, scarce in jacket.   Aleph-Bet Books, Inc.   95 - 460   2011 $2000

Potter, Beatrix   1866-1943   *The Tale of Little Pig Robinson.* London: Frederick Warne and Co. Ltd., 1930, First reprint; Large 8vo., original cloth, gilt, spine and edges rather faded, pages 96, 6 colored plates and 22 drawings. R. F. G. Hollett & Sons Antiquarian Booksellers   170 - 547 2011   £65

Potter, Beatrix   1866-1943   *The Tale of Mr. Tod.* New York: Frederick Warne and Co., 1912,   First American edition; 16mo., tan boards with pictorial paste label and dark brown lettering and elaborate spine decoration, clean, tight copy, numerous black and white drawings within text.   Jo Ann Reisler, Ltd.   86 - 200   2011 $385

Potter, Beatrix 1866-1943 *The Tale of Peter Rabbit.* London: Frederick Warne, 1902, First trade edition; this copy has the white dot in the "o's" on cover, leaf patterned endpapers, word 'wept' on page 51 and all other points of first printing; 12mo., brown boards, 97 pages quarter inch rub spot on blank corner of 2 pages, binding tight, clean, fine, housed in beautiful custom clamshell box with leather spine and raised bands, very rare in such fresh condition, text and illustrations engraved and printed by Edmund Evans.   Aleph-Bet Books, Inc.   95 - 458 2011 $16,500

Potter, Beatrix 1866-1943 *The Tale of Peter Rabbit.* London: F. Warne and Co., 1902, First edition, first issue with "wept big tears" on page 51 and other first issue points; 12mo., original brown boards with pictorial onlay, hinges trifle rubbed, pages 98, illustrations in color, leaf patterned endpapers, skillfully resewn, joints neatly repaired, little very slight fingering here and there, but very nice.   R. F. G. Hollett & Sons Antiquarian Booksellers   170 - 548 2011   £2500

Potter, Beatrix 1866-1943 *The Tale of Peter Rabbit.* London and New York: Frederick Warne and Co., 1904, Second published edition; with double page colored endpapers (i.e. seventh or eighth printing), 12mo., 85, (1, printer's slug) pages, color illustrated endpapers, color frontispiece and 26 color illustrations, dark green boards, white lettered with pictorial label in color, original glazed paper glassine dust jacket printed in black with vertical lines at top and bottom of spine indicating where the fold should be for the front panel, with ad on rear panel for "The Peter Rabbit Books" listing five titles, top half inch and part of bottom half inch of jacket spine (including the " of the word net in the price) are missing as well as small piece 5/8 x 1/2 inch missing on top of back panel at spine, overall very bright, fine copy, in very good example of exceptionally are dust jacket, printed glassine jacket is of the utmost rarity, presentation copy inscribed by author for Violet Medcalfe.   David Brass Rare Books, Inc.   May 26 2011 - 01527 2011 $9500

Potter, Beatrix 1866-1943 *The Tale of Peter Rabbit.* New York: Platt & Munk, n.d. circa, 1930, Original pictorial wrappers, 8 line poem (not by Beatrix Potter) on back panel, pages (8), illustrations in color and line, no publisher's imprint inside front panel.   R. F. G. Hollett & Sons Antiquarian Booksellers   170 - 553 2011   £40

Potter, Beatrix 1866-1943 *The Tale of Peter Rabbit.* New York: Platt & Munk, 1932, Original pictorial wrappers, pages (8), illustrations in color and line.   R. F. G. Hollett & Sons Antiquarian Booksellers   170 - 552 2011   £35

Potter, Beatrix 1866-1943 *The Tale of Peter Rabbit.* Ohio: American Crayon Co., 1943, Large 4to., original pictorial wrappers, pages (12), 6 color plates and line drawings by Fern Bisel Peat, very nice, fresh, uncreased and clean.   R. F. G. Hollett & Sons Antiquarian Booksellers   170 - 550 2011   £45

Potter, Beatrix 1866-1943 *The Tale of Peter Rabbit.* New York: Grosset & Dunlap, 1942, Large square 8vo., original pictorial boards, spine little bruised and foot, pages (19), illustrations, colored pictorial endpapers, all by Masha, two booklabels on front pastedown.   R. F. G. Hollett & Sons Antiquarian Booksellers   170 - 549 2011   £35

Potter, Beatrix 1866-1943 *The Tale of Pigling Bland.* London: F. Warne and Co., 1912, First edition; small 8vo., original pale green boards stamped in brown, pictorial onlay, pages 94, color frontispiece and 14 color plates, very nice, fresh copy.   R. F. G. Hollett & Sons Antiquarian Booksellers   170 - 554 2011   £450

Potter, Beatrix 1866-1943 *The Tale of Pigling Bland.* London: F. Warne and Co., 1913, First edition; small 8vo., original pale green board stamped in brown, pictorial onlay, pages 94, color frontispiece and 14 color plates, very nice, fresh copy.   R. F. G. Hollett & Son Antiquarian Booksellers   General Catalogue Summer 2010 - 552 2011   £450

Potter, Beatrix 1866-1943 *The Tale of the Faithful Dove.* London: Frederick Warne, 1971, First edition thus; illustrations by Marie Angel, square 12mo., original pictorial boards, dust jacket, pages 48, 22 color illustrations.   R. F. G. Hollett & Sons Antiquarian Booksellers   170 - 555 2011   £50

Potter, Beatrix 1866-1943 *The Tale of Timmy Tiptoes.* London: Frederick Warne and Co., 1911, First edition; 12mo., 84, (1), (1, blank) pages color frontispiece and 26 color plates, black and white vignette on titlepage, original dark green boards ruled and lettered in white on front cover and lettered in white spine, cover pictorial label (measuring 2 5/8 x 2 1/4 inches) on front cover within a blind arch-shaped panel outlined in blind, color pictorial endpapers, near fine, original glazed paper glassine dust jacket printed in black with price "1/-NET" a foot of spine, with vertical lines at top and bottom of spine indicating where the fold should come for the front panel, with ad for "The Peter Rabbit Books" on rear panel listing The Tale of Timmy Tiptoes under "New Book for 1911".   David Brass Rare Books, Inc.   May 26 2011 - 00687 2011 $6250

Potter, Beatrix 1866-1943 *The Tale of Tom Kitten.* London: F. Warne & Co. Ltd. n.d. early 1920's, 12mo., original brown boards lettered in white with pictorial onlay, two small marks to upper board, spine lettering rather rubbed, little defective and repaired at foot, pages 86, illustrations in color, early inscription (Miss M. Hoggarth of Windermere), signed in full by Potter.   R. F. G. Hollett & Son Antiquarian Booksellers   General Catalogue Summer 2010 - 553 2011   £650

Potter, Beatrix 1866-1943 *The Tale of Tom Kitten.* London: Warne, 1907, First edition; 12mo., boards, slightest bit of edge wear, else fine, color plates by Potter, especially nice.   Aleph-Bet Books, Inc.   95 - 459 2011 $1200

Potter, Beatrix 1866-1943 *The Tale of Two Bad Mice.* London: F. Warne & Co., 1904, First edition; 12mo., original red boards lettered in white with pictorial onlay, edges little rubbed and rebacked in matching levant morocco lettered in white, pages 86, illustrations in color.   R. F. G. Hollett & Sons Antiquarian Booksellers   170 - 557 2011   £250

Potter, Beatrix 1866-1943 *The Tale of Two Bad Mice.* London: Frederick Warne and Co., 1904, First edition; 12mo., 84, (1), (1, printer's imprint) pages, color frontispiece, 26 color plates, black and white vignette on titlepage (expertly hand colored in this copy), original deluxe binding in maroon cloth decoratively stamped and lettered gilt on front cover and spine, color pictorial label on front over within rectangular blind panel outlined in gilt and blind, color pictorial endpapers, all edges gilt, minimal rubbing to spine extremities and covers, very small watercolor stain in margin of titlepage and in lower margin of frontispiece, inscribed "Little Jackie/Feburary 21st 1906/Johannesburg", otherwise excellent, in original plain glazed paper glassine dust jacket.   David Brass Rare Books, Inc.   May 26 2011 - 00668 2011 $6500

Potter, Elisha *A Brief Account of Emissions of Paper Money, Made by the Colony of Rhode Island.* Providence: John E. Brown, 1837, First edition; 8vo., 48 pages, later three quarter calf and marbled boards.   M & S Rare Books, Inc.   90 - 366 2011 $600

Potter, T. W. *Romans in North-West England.* Kendal: Titus Wilson, 1979, First edition; 4to., original stiff wrappers, pages 371, with 26 pages of plates and 149 text figures.   R. F. G. Hollett & Son Antiquarian Booksellers   177 - 714 2011   £35

Potts, Ethelinda Margaretta *Moonshine.* London: Longman, Hurst, Rees, Orme and Brown, 1814, First edition; 2 volumes, 16 pages ads volume I, these have been cut down by binder to fit the text block with loss of some text, index volume II, uncut in contemporary drab boards, paper labels on spines, both spines little worn with roughly an inch of spine strip missing at each tail, labels little dusted and slightly chipped.   Jarndyce Antiquarian Booksellers   CLXC - 766 2011   £225

Potts, Robert *Liber Cantabrigiensis.* London: John W. Parker, Cambridge: University Press, 1855-1863, First editions; 2 volumes, modern half levant morocco, gilt, pages xvi, 554, (vi); xvi, 331, 115, (iii).   R. F. G. Hollett & Son Antiquarian Booksellers   175 - 1079 2011   £175

Poucher, W. A. *Lakeland Holiday.* London: Chapman & Hall, 1942, First edition; 4to., original cloth, dust jacket, corners trifle rubbed, pages 112, illustrations, flyleaves lightly spotted.   R. F. G. Hollett & Son Antiquarian Booksellers   173 - 920 2011   £35

Poucher, W. A. *Lakeland Scrapebook.* London: Chapman & Hall, 1950, First edition; 141 photos, 4to., original cloth, dust jacket (head and tail of spine little worn), pages 136 with 141 plates.   R. F. G. Hollett & Son Antiquarian Booksellers   173 - 923 2011   £35

Poucher, W. A. *Over Lakeland Fells.* London: Chapman & Hall, 1948, First edition; 4to., original cloth, gilt, dust jacket extremities trifle worn, pages 152, with 110 photos by author.   R. F. G. Hollett & Son Antiquarian Booksellers   173 - 924 2011   £35

Poulik, Josef *Prehistoric Art.* Spring Books n.d., Large 4to., original pictorial cloth, dust jacket, edges little worn and frayed, pages 47, plus 22 color plates and 189 monochrome illustrations.   R. F. G. Hollett & Son Antiquarian Booksellers   175 - 1080 2011   £40

Poulson, George *Beverlac; or the Antiquities and History of the Town of Beverley...* London: printed for George Scaum, 1829, 2 volumes bound as 1, large paper copy 4to., pages xx, 510 + engraved frontispiece, 1 extending engraved plate of facsimiles and 3 other plates (ii) (512)-816, 84, tipped in errata slip + 1 engraved plates, vignette "Beverley Foundry" pasted to page 816, folding plan of the "Boundary of the New Borough of Beverley" with hand colored outlines, contemporary purple morocco, four flat raised banded spine, bands and extremities 'paired tool' gilt with connecting gilt rules, compartments blind tooled in concentric panel, green lettering piece gilt, boards panelled in blind, decorative roll between rules all gilt within, quintuple rule with rose head corners innermost panel in blind, board edges single rule gilt, turn-ins 'quintuple zig-zag rules' in blind, 'Spanish' 'made' endpapers (green pasted), all edges 'Spanish' marbled (fawn based), fawn sewn flat endbands, purple silk page marker, plates bit foxed, few offset, spine faded, extremities rubbed, bit of wear to endcaps and top of joints, (?) lettering piece replaced armorial bookplate of Christopher Harrison, from the collection of Christopher Ernest Weston 1947-2010.   Unsworths Booksellers   24 - 137 2011   £250

Poulson, George *The History and Antiquities of the Seigniory of Holderness.* Hull: Robert Brown, 1840, 2 volumes, 4to., xx, 489 pages; (2), 552 pages, 41 plate and maps as repaired and numerous woodcuts in text, very good, clean copy, bound rather unsympathetic half leather cloth with red and green labels, serviceable binding.   Ken Spelman Rare Books   68 - 169 2011   £85

Pound, Ezra Loomis 1885-1972 *ABC of Reading.* New Haven: Yale University Press, 1934, First American edition, one of 1016 copies; minor darkening at edges, otherwise fine in cloth and very good or better dust jacket with tiny edge chips and darkening of spine, unusually nice in dust jacket that is not price clipped.   Gemini Fine Books & Arts, Ltd.   Art Reference & Illustrated Books: First Editions 2011 $200

Pound, Ezra Loomis 1885-1972 *The Cantos of Ezra Pound.* New York: New Directions, 1948, First edition, 2nd printing; presentation copy from author to Russian emigre surgeon Eugene Constantin de Savitsch, 8vo., pages (iv), 150, 56, 46, (2), 168, 118, plus frontispiece with reproduction of photo of author by Arnold Genthe, internally clean and bright, original black cloth with white lettering to spine, faded, very light wear to extremities, original sea gray dust jacket, unclipped, maroon text, Gaudier Breska drawing of Pound to upper panel, chipped, spine sunned.   Simon Finch Rare Books   Zero - 346   2011   £1250

Pound, Ezra Loomis 1885-1972 *Canzoni.* London: Elkin Mathews, 1911, First edition; 8vo., pages (viii), 52, (4) ads, uncut lower and fore edge, some light spotting, original gray cloth, spine and upper board lettered in gilt, spine slightly sunned and light foxing to endpapers, David Garnett's copy with bookplate.   Simon Finch Rare Books   Zero - 344   2011   £400

Pound, Ezra Loomis 1885-1972 *Canzoni.* London: Elkin Mathews, 1911, First edition; 8vo., pages viii, 52 + 4 page publisher's ads, first issue in grey streaky cloth stamped/lettered in gilt at spine and to front board titlepage in black letters with red heraldic device, watermarked laid paper, uncut at side and bottom, sound, decent very good copy with corners slightly bumped, spine ends rubbed, faint marking, slight evidence of a small label removed from spine, no inscriptions, stamps or marks.   Any Amount of Books   May 29 2011 - A44862   2011 $306

Pound, Ezra Loomis 1885-1972 *Cathay.* London: Elkin Mathews, 1915, First edition; 8vo. pages (ii) blank, (iv), 32, (2) blank, partly unopened, occasional spotting and slightly soiled, half little, otherwise very clean, original brown printed wrappers with black text and Chinese calligraphy, minor crease to wrapper, neat ownership inscription.   Simon Finch Rare Books   Zero - 345   2011   £800

Pound, Ezra Loomis 1885-1972 *Cathay.* New York: Limited Editions Club, 1992, First Clemente edition; one of 300 copies, signed and numbered by artist, 7 unsigned original color woodcuts by Francesco Clemente, printed on handmade Japanese Ogawashi paper, 12 x 8.5 inches, spine of book and edges of slipcase faded, otherwise as new, inscribed "binder's copy" and signed by Kim O'Donnell of the Garthegaat Bindery.   Gemini Fine Books & Arts, Ltd.   Art Reference & Illustrated Books: First Editions 2011 $1350

Pound, Ezra Loomis 1885-1972 *A Draft of XXX Cantos.* Paris: Hours Press, 1930, One of 200 numbered copies; printed on Canson Montgolfier paper, 8vo., decorated with woodcut initials by Dorothy Shakespeare, original tan buckram stamped in red, glassine dust jacket, unopened, spine lettering completely unfaded, rare in original glassine dust jacket, preserved in black half morocco slipcase, finest copy we have seen.   James S. Jaffe Rare Books   May 26 2011 - 18910   2011 $8500

Pound, Ezra Loomis 1885-1972 *Drafts and Fragments of Cantos CX-CXVII.* London: Faber & Faber, 1969, First UK edition, signed, no. 243 of 310 copies on Umbria paper, signed by Pound, dated Dec. 1968; folio, pages (viii) bank, (i) half title, (i) blank, 40, (1) imprint, (5) blank, uncut, original red cloth boards with cream label and black initials to spine, slight discoloring to spine, brown slipcase with cream and black label to upper panel, some discoloring and shelfwear, errata slip loose with 7 copy corrections, near fine.   Simon Finch Rare Books   Zero - 347   2011   £375

Pound, Ezra Loomis 1885-1972 *Guide to Kulcher.* Norfolk: New Directions, 1942, First edition, review copy; corners bumped, near fine in like dust jacket (lightly rubbed), review slip laid in, giving publication date (August 29) price and asking for a copy of the review or for the book to be returned if it is not reviewed, nice.   Ken Lopez Bookseller 154 - 164   2011 $125

Pound, Ezra Loomis 1885-1972 *Quia Pauper Amavi.* London: Egoist Ltd., 1919, First edition, number 30 of 100 copies; signed by author, with ink correction by Pound of the misprint on line 24 of page 24, correcting "Wherefore" to "Wherefrom" (some copies were not corrected), printed on handmade paper, one short tear at margin of page 21, five pages have very minor fox marks, back endpapers with very minor waterstain at lower margin, binding with very slight discoloration, overall very crisp and very good.   Gemini Fine Books & Arts, Ltd.   Art Reference & Illustrated Books: First Editions 2011 $2400

Pound, Ezra Loomis 1885-1972 *Ripostes of Ezra Pound.* London: Stephen Swift & Co., 1912, First edition, first issue; 8vo., original gray cloth, covers lightly soiled, spine darkened, some offsetting as usual to endpapers, otherwise very good, presentation copy inscribed to Allen Upward from author Sept. 1913, publisher's ads at end are present in this copy,.   James S. Jaffe Rare Books May 26 2011 - 16359   2011 $6500

Pound, Ezra Loomis 1885-1972 *Umbra: the Early Poems of Ezra Pound.* London: Elkin Mathews, 1920, First edition; 8vo., pages 128, original publisher's printed grey boards with cloth spine, slight soiling slight marks but decent, very good, ownership signature of Humbert Wolfe Jan. 18 1926.   Any Amount of Books   May 29 2011 - A64843   2011 $255

Pourrat, Henry *A Treasury of French Tales.* London: Allen & Unwin, 1953, First edition; original blue cloth silvered, dust jacket (spine little darkened) pages xi, 232, 9 plates and over 40 illustrations. R. F. G. Hollett & Son Antiquarian Booksellers General Catalogue Summer 2010 - 724 2011 £30

Powell Cotton, P. H. G. *A Sporting Trip through Abyssinia...* London: Rowland Ward, 1902, First edition; large 8 vo., pages xxiii, 531, ads, photogravure frontispiece, map in slipcase, illustrations, original pink cloth, spine faded, internally very clean, presentation from author. J. & S. L. Bonham Antiquarian Booksellers Africa 4/20/2011 - 7455 2011 £780

Powell, Dawn *Turn, Magic Wheel.* New York: Farrar & Rinehart, 1936, First edition; couple of pages little roughly opened with corresponding small tears, thus near fine in fine dust jacket, exceptionally scarce. Between the Covers 169 - BTC342146 2011 $6500

Powell, H. M. T. *The Santa Fe Trail to California 1849-1852.* San Francisco: Book Club of California, 1931, One of 300 copies; folio, (16), 272 pages, illustrations, folding maps, half tan calf, slight darkening at head and foot of spine, else near fine. Joseph J. Felcone Inc. Fall Miscellany 2010 - 101 2011 $1800

Powell, Jane *The Girl Next Door and How She Grew.* Norwalk: Easton Press, 2000, Signed by author, leather with told titles and decorations, all edges gilt, silk endpapers and ribbon bookmark, "A note about" card and signed certificate of authenticity folded in, very clean and tight, 253 pages. G. H. Mott Bookseller May 26 2011 - 37111 2011 $300

Powell, Michael *A Life in the Movies: an Autobiography.* London: Heinemann, 1986, First edition; 8vo., pages 705, original green boards lettered gilt on spine, signed by author on titlepage, ownership signature of Stephen Wyatt, playwright, slight lean bumping, otherwise near fine, in like dust jacket (very slight creasing). Any Amount of Books May 26 2011 - A68824 2011 $461

Powell, Michael *200,000 Feet on Foula.* London: Faber & Faber, 1938, First edition; 8vo., original publisher's brown cloth lettered black and blue on spine, pages xii, 334, 32 plates, endpapers slightly browned, cover slightly toned, some rubbing at spine ends, else overall decent, sound, very good. Any Amount of Books May 29 2011 - A75995 2011 $238

Power, Marguerite Agnes *The Letters of a Betrothed.* London: Longman, Brown and Co., 1858, First edition; contemporary full tan calf, spine gilt in compartments, boards double ruled in gilt, maroon leather label, slight rubbing, signed "Robert Gibson 1858" with his armorial bookplate, very good. Jarndyce Antiquarian Booksellers CLXC - 767 2011 £50

Powers, Richard *The Gold Bug Variations.* New York: Morrow, 1991, First edition; 8vo., pages 6420, mustard brown quarter cloth, aqua paper boards, lettered gilt at spine, deckled fore-edges, signed by author on loosely inserted publisher's card "Richard Powers 2004", fine in fine, unclipped dust jacket. Any Amount of Books May 26 2011 - A39561 2011 $922

Powley, Mary *Echoes of Old Cumberland.* Bemrose & Sons and Carlisle: G. and T. Coward, 1875, First edition; original green cloth gilt over bevelled boards, pages vii, 250, (viii ads), fine. R. F. G. Hollett & Son Antiquarian Booksellers 173 - 925 2011 £45

Powys, Theodore Francis *The Left Leg.* London: Chatto & Windus, 1923, First edition; 8vo., pages 311, inscribed presentation from dedicatee, Sylvia Townsend Warner to Angus (Davidson), with a quatrain also inscribed to same, three quarter red morocco, spine gilt in compartments, little browned on fore edge, else fine. Second Life Books Inc. 174 - 262 2011 $713

Pozharskaya, M. N. *The Russian Seasons in Paris: Sketches of the Scenery and Costumes 1908-1929.* Moscow: Iskusstvo Art Publishers, 1988, Oblong 4to., original publisher's blue cloth lettered gilt and purple on spine and cover, pages 292, copiously illustrated in color and black and white, text in Russian and English, very good+ in very good slipcase slightly used at corners. Any Amount of Books May 29 2011 - A64843 2011 $255

Praagh, L. V. *The Transvaal and Its Mines.* London: Praagh & Lloyd, 1906, First edition; quarto, pages 640, numerous illustrations, original red decorative morocco, spine and corners rubbed, very clean internally. J. & S. L. Bonham Antiquarian Booksellers Africa 4/20/2011 - 82811 2011 £225

Pradon, Nicolas *Reponse a la Satire X du Sieur D****.* Paris: Chez Robert J. B. de la Caille, 1694, (1), (11) pages, 12mo., recent blue cloth, gilt lettered spine, from the library of F. Lachevre with his ex-libris, very fine, scarce. Paulette Rose Fine and Rare Books 32 - 135 2011 $700

Praed, Rosa Caroline *The Bond of Wedlock.* London: F. V. White & Co., 1887, Half title, pages 65/66 torn and crudely repaired with tape, odd spot, original orange cloth lettered in black and gilt, slightly rubbed "May/87" in ink on front board, good plus. Jarndyce Antiquarian Booksellers CLXC - 768 2011 £45

Praed, Rosa Caroline *The Romance of a Chalet.* London: F. V. White and Co., 1892, Half title, 10 page catalog, original red cloth lettered in black and gilt, spine faded, dulled and bit marked, good, sound copy. Jarndyce Antiquarian Booksellers CLXC - 769 2011 £50

Praed, Rosa Caroline *Zero, a Story of Monte Carlo.* Leipzig: Bernhard Tauchnitz, 1884, Copyright edition; contemporary half dark blue morocco, spine gilt rubbed, slight rubbing, very good.   Jarndyce Antiquarian Booksellers   CLXC - 770   2011   £50

Pratchett, Terry *Guards! Guards!* London: Gollancz, 1989, First edition; pages 288, 8vo., original light blue boards, backstrip lettered in metallic red, dust jacket, fine, signed by author.   Blackwell Rare Books   B166 - 213   2011   £195

Pratchett, Terry *Lords and Ladies.* London: Gollancz, 1992, First edition; pages 280, 8vo., original mid blue boards, backstrip gilt lettered, ownership inscription, dust jacket, near fine, signed by Terry Pratchett.   Blackwell Rare Books   B166 - 214   2011   £35

Pratchett, Terry *Mort.* London: Gollancz, 1987, First edition; pages 222, crown 8vo., original black boards, backstrip gilt lettered, publisher's price clipping and repricing to dust jacket, fine, signed.   Blackwell Rare Books   B166 - 215   2011   £350

Pratchett, Terry *Moving Pictures.* London: Gollancz, 1990, First edition; pages 280, 8vo., original black boards, backstrip gilt lettered, dust jacket, fine, signed by author.   Blackwell Rare Books   B166 - 218   2011   £200

Pratchett, Terry *Pyramids.* London: Gollancz, 1989, First edition; pages 272, crown 8vo., original black boards, backstrip gilt lettered, dust jacket, fine, signed by author.   Blackwell Rare Books   B166 - 219   2011   £135

Pratchett, Terry *Reaper Man.* London: Gollancz, 1991, First edition; 8vo., 256 pages, original black boards, backstrip gilt lettered, fine, signed by author.   Blackwell Rare Books   B166 - 221   2011   £65

Pratchett, Terry *Wyrd Sisters.* London: Gollancz, 1988, First edition; 252 pages, crown 8vo., original light green boards, backstrip gilt lettered, dust jacket, fine, signed by author.   Blackwell Rare Books   B166 - 222   2011   £150

Pratt, Ambrose *The Living Mummy.* New York: Frederick A. Stokes, 1910, First American edition; octavo, illustrated cloth, illustrations in color by Louis D. Fancher, neat owner's signature on front fly, little edgewear to spine ends, else near fine, exceptionally scarce.   Between the Covers   169 - BTC342149   2011 $1250

Pratt, Anne *Chapters on the Common Things of the Sea Side.* London: SPCK, 1850, First edition; frontispiece, illustrations, original brown cloth, splits at head of spine, inner hinges cracking, stamps of Church of England Young Men's Literary Association and Canterbury Museum Library and label of Canterbury Free Library.   Jarndyce Antiquarian Booksellers   CLXC - 771   2011   £35

Pratt, Anne *The Flowering Plants, Grasses, Sedges & Ferns of Great Britain...* London: Frederick Warne & Co., 1889, 4 volumes, three quarter morocco gilt by Riviere with floral emblems to spine panels and marbled boards, few slight scuffs here and there, top edge gilt, 318 color plates, handsome tall set.   R. F. G. Hollett & Son Antiquarian Booksellers   General Catalogue Summer 2010 - 1036   2011   £750

Pratt, Anne *Wild Flowers.* Society for Promoting Christian Knowledge, n.d., 1853, Unpaginated, title and contents leaves, plus 192 hand colored illustrations, two to a page with text beneath in double columns, scarce.   R. F. G. Hollett & Son Antiquarian Booksellers   General Catalogue Summer 2010 - 1037   2011   £450

Prentiss, Thomas *A Sermon Preached at the Ordination of the Reverend Mr. Henry Wight to the Pastoral Care of the Catholic Congregational Society in Bristol, State of Rhode Island Jan. 5 1785.* Providence: printed by Bennett Wheeler, 1785, First edition; 8vo., 26, (2 blank) pages, including half title, sewn, stains, edges bit frayed and curled, good, with substantial margins, unidentified owner's signature dated June 20 1785.   M & S Rare Books, Inc.   90 - 367 2011 $150

Prescott, J. E. *The Register of the Priory of Wetherhal.* London: Elliot Stock, 1897, Limited edition, c. 200 copies; original cloth, gilt, pages xliii, 552, (iv), frontispiece.   R. F. G. Hollett & Son Antiquarian Booksellers   173 - 927   2011   £220

Prescott, J. E. *The Statutes of the Cathedral Church of Carlisle.* London: Elliot Stock, 1903, Second edition; original cloth, gilt, pages x, 128, with 5 plates, notes on rear endpapers, front flyleaf removed.   R. F. G. Hollett & Son Antiquarian Booksellers   173 - 928   2011   £65

Prescott, William Hickling 1796-1859 *History of the Conquest of Mexico...* London: Richard Bentley, 1844, Second edition; 3 volumes, frontispiece portraits to each volume foxed, 2 engrave maps, one folding, one double page, one engraved plate, pages xxx, 442; xvi, 439; xvi, 455, 8vo., slightly later polished calf, backstrips panelled and elaborately tooled in gilt, russet and olive morocco labels with gilt lettering, sides with triple gilt fillet borders, marbled edges, bookplate, very slightly rubbed, very good.   Blackwell Rare Books   B166 - 82   2011   £280

Prescott, William Hickling   1796-1859   *History of the Conquest of Mexico.*   London: Swan Sonnenschein & Co., 1906,   2 maps, one handwriting facsimile plate, pages xxiv, 713, 8vo., contemporary tree calf, boards with gilt roll border, spine in five compartments with raised bands, green morocco lettering piece, compartments with gilt floral centre pieces and corner vine sprays, marbled edges and endpapers, gilt prize stamp (Cambridge Local Examinations, Southport Centre) to front board, prize bookplate inside, binder's ticket of Edward Howell, Liverpool, spine gently sunned, near fine, award to W. T. Waterhouse of First Class Honours in History and Geography, 1908.   Blackwell Rare Books   B166 - 83   2011   £95

Prescott, William Hickling   1796-1859   *History of the Conquest of Peru.*   London: Swan Sonnenschein & Co., 1907,   New edition;   pages xxiv, 510, (2), 8vo., contemporary tree calf, boards with gilt roll border, spine in five compartments with raised bands, green morocco lettering piece, compartments with gilt floral center-pieces and corner vine sprays, marbled edges and endpapers, gilt prize stamp (Cambridge Local Examinations, Southport Centre) to front board and prize bookplate inside, binder's ticket of Edward Howell, Liverpool, spine gently sunned, near fine, awarded to W. T. Waterhouse for First Class Honours in English, 1908.   Blackwell Rare Books   B166 - 84   2011   £95

Prescott, William Hickling   1796-1859   *The Works of William H. Prescott.*   Philadelphia: J. P. Lippincott, 1904, Aztec edition, number 127 of 250 sets, only a few of which were bound in this deluxe full leather;   printed on fine paper, this set beautifully bound and well illustrated, 22 volumes, hand colored frontispiece in each volume, maps, photogravures after paintings, photos and engravings, beautifully bound in full dark blue crushed morocco, spines ruled in gilt and with floral element between panels, sides with extensive gilt extra, deckle edges at fore edge and foot, top edges gilt, spines ever so slightly faded, stunning set, very fine and clean, stunning set.   Argonaut Book Shop   Recent Acquisitions Summer 2010 - 162   2011 $5000

Preston, Kerrison   *The Blake Collection of W. Graham Robertson.*   London: Faber For William Blake Trust, 1952, First edition;   large 8vo., original cloth, dust jacket (spine rather browned and torn, some loss to head), pages 263, plus 64 plates, flyleaves partially browned.   R. F. G. Hollett & Son Antiquarian Booksellers   General Catalogue Summer 2010 - 298   2011   £60

The Pretty Book.   London: Henry Frowde, Hodder & Stoughton, n.d., 1915,   First edition;   pages (48), 12 full page color plates by Millicent Sowerby, original embossed pictorial boards, little marked in places.   R. F. G. Hollett & Son Antiquarian Booksellers   General Catalogue Summer 2010 - 576   2011   £95

Pretty Rhymes about Birds and Animals for Little Boys and Girls.   New York: Kiggins & Kellogg, n.d. circa, 1835, 24mo., 8 pages, original wrappers, decorative engraved vignette on titlepage, frontispiece, four charming half page wood engravings, brown spots at cover and edges of few leaves, in all good copy.   Hobbyhorse Books   56 - 108   2011 $80

Prevert, Jacques   *Fetes.*   Paris: Maeght Editeur, 1971, One of 200 copies for sale and signed by author and artist; (one of 25 on special handmade papier d'Auvergne, without extra suite of plates, there were also 25 d'Auvergne copies with extra plates, 150 'regular' copies on velin d'arches paper and 25 copies not for sale), unbound as issued in paper portfolio with water color titling by Calder on upper cover, housed in original vermillion linen clamshell box with black vertical titling on spine, cover design and 7 brilliantly colored aquatints by Alexander Calder.   Phillip J. Pirages   59 - 161   2011 $11,000

Prevost, Florent   *Histoire Naturelle d'Oiseaux d'Europe.* Paris: Librairie F. Savy, 1864,   Second edition;   hand colored engraved divisional title, 80 hand colored engraved plates (light foxing to margins of few, not affecting images) and 2 uncolored engraved plates, one double paged, 8vo., pages (3), 132, xii, (32 pages ads), contemporary red cloth with red morocco gilt decorated spine, some rubbing, corners quite worn, light flecking to front cover, some soiling and small stain to covers, front flyleaf loose, front inner hinge open, handstamp on a blank, foxing to some pages, 2 uncolored engravings accompany a supplementary section. Raymond M. Sutton, Jr.   May 26 2011 - 30064   2011 $1200

Prevost, Florent   *Histoire Naturelle des Oiseaux Exotiques.*   Paris: F. Savy, 1864,   Second edition;   very good plus, hand colored engraved part title and 80 hand colored, steel engraved plates, after Pauquet (ink name to 4 otherwise plates virtually fine), 8vo., (4 pages ads), (2), 156, contemporary morocco backed boards, raised bands and gilt decorations on spine, corners and edges rubbed, upper end of spine chipped, bookplate removed, marginal browning and signature to title, scattered light foxing to text. Raymond M. Sutton, Jr.   May 26 2011 - 50883   2011 $4500

Price, Doughbelly   *Doughbelly's Wisdom and Insanity. (with) Short Stirrups: The Saga of Doughbelly (sic) Price.* Taos/Los Angeles: 1954-1960,   2 works, 1110 pages, illustrations, 205 pages, plus ephemera, first work in printed wrappers, light soil else very good, second work is hardcover, very good dust jacket with spine fading.   Dumont Maps & Books of the West   112 - 60   2011 $75

Price, Howell *A Genuine Account of the Life and Transactions of Howell ap David Price, Gentleman of Wales.* London: printed for T. Osborne in Gray's Inn, 1752, First edition; 12mo., viii, 320 (2) pages, including final leaf of ads, flyleaf and endpapers stained, else very good in contemporary sheep, spine with raised bands and gilt lines, joints and head and tail of spine worn. John Drury Rare Books 153 - 117 2011 £1850

Price, Joseph *A Letter to Edmund Burke, Esq. On the Latter Part of the Late Report of the Select Committee of the State of Justice in Bengal.* London: printed for the author and sold by the booksellers of London and Westminster, 1782, First edition; 100, 20, 70 pages, disbound. Anthony W. Laywood May 26 2011 - 21345 2011 $134

Price, Joseph *Some Observations and Remarks on a Late Publication, Intitled Travels in Europe, Asia and Africa...* London: printed for the author and sold by J. Stockdale, Scatchard and Whitaker and all booksellers in London and Westminster, 1782, Second edition; 8vo., 167 (1) pages, titlepage lightly soiled, contemporary half calf over marbled boards, neatly rebacked and gilt lettered, good, scarce. John Drury Rare Books 153 - 118 2011 £250

Price, Nancy *Nettles and Docks.* Allen & Unwin, 1940, First edition; original cloth, dust jacket (price clipped), pages 232, (ii), 8 plates, presentation copy inscribed and with 8 lines of poetry in author's hand. R. F. G. Hollett & Son Antiquarian Booksellers 173 - 931 2011 £35

Price, Nancy *Shadows on the Hills.* London: Gollancz, 1938, Original cloth, dust jacket, pages 320, 16 plates, inscribed with poem by Masefield, all in author's hand. R. F. G. Hollett & Son Antiquarian Booksellers 173 - 932 2011 £35

Price, Reynolds *Blue Calhoun.* New York: Atheneum, 1992, First edition, limited to 350 signed and numbered copies, this no. 68; fine in fine slipcase, original shrink wrap, signed by author. Bella Luna Books May 29 2011 - t7922a 2011 $82

Price, Reynolds *Kate Vaiden.* New York: Atheneum, 1986, First edition; fine, dust jacket near fine, faint crease on front flap. Bella Luna Books May 29 2011 - t7750 2011 $82

Price, Richard *A Discourse on the Love of Our Country, Delivered on Nov. 4 1789, at the Meeting-House in Old Jewry, to the Society for Commemorating the Revolution in Great Britain.* London: T. Cadell, 1789, First edition; 8vo., (2), 51, (1) 13 (1) 24 pages, slight foxing of few leaves, wanting half title and publisher's ads, well bound in old style quarter calf over marbled boards, spine lettered in gilt, very good. John Drury Rare Books 153 - 119 2011 £900

Price, Uvedale *An Essay on the Picturesque, as compared with the Sublime and the Beautiful... (bound with) A Letter to H. Repton, Esq. on the Application as well as the Principles of Landscape Gardening.* London: J. Robson, 1794-1795, First edition; xv, (i), 288; xii, 163, (1) errata, contemporary tree calf, expertly rebacked, gilt banded spine, morocco label, some light foxing. Ken Spelman Rare Books 68 - 15 2011 £480

Prichard, James Cowles 1786-1848 *The Natural History of Man.* London: H. Bailliere, 1855, Fourth edition; 2 volumes, maroon cloth with gilt portraits, titles, cloth scratched and worn at edges, small tear on 1 spine, some foxing to several of the plates, otherwise clean and tight, 720 pages, 8vo., 62 vivid colored plates and 100 woodcuts (all present), very good. G. H. Mott Bookseller May 26 2011 - 35370 2011 $500

Prichard, James Cowles 1786-1848 *Researches into the Physical History of Mankind.* London: Sherwood, Gilbert and Piper, 1847, 1841. Volume I third edition, volumes 2-4 and presumed first (Volume 5); complete in 5 volumes, 376, 373, 507, 631 570 pages, color frontispieces, other illustrations and foldout map, cloth soiled and worn, small tears on spines of two of the volumes, labels on spines soiled and scratched, otherwise clean and tight, owner's name, very good. G. H. Mott Bookseller May 26 2011 - 35324 2011 $325

Prichard, Kate *Flaxman Low, Psychic Detective.* London: Ghost Story Press, 1993, First Edition, no. 78 of 200 numbered copies; 8vo., original publisher's illustrated boards, illustrations in black and white, pages 128, fine. Any Amount of Books May 29 2011 - A75927 2011 $281

Prideaux, Sarah Treverbian *An Historical Sketch of Book Binding.* London: Lawrence & Bullen, 1893, First edition; (303 pages, including bibliography and index), 8vo., original cloth, gilt lettered spine, patterned endpapers, with half title, titlepage printed in red and black, frontispiece with tissue guard, spine lightly rubbed, otherwise fine mostly unopened copy. Paulette Rose Fine and Rare Books 32 - 136 2011 $250

Priest, Christopher *The Prestige.* London: Sydney: New York: Tokyo: Singapore: Toronto: Simon & Schuster Ltd., 1995, First edition; octavo, boards. L. W. Currey, Inc. 124 - 98 2011 $850

Priestley, Joseph 1733-1804 *A Free Discussion of the Doctrines of Materialism and Philosophical Necessity.* London: printed for J. Johnson, 1778, First edition; lightly toned and dust soiled, few fox marks and marginal pencil marks, pages (viii), xliv, (4), 428, (4), 8vo., contemporary sprinkled calf, smartly rebacked with backstrip with five raised bands between double gilt fillets, red morocco label in second compartment, rest plain, later marbled endpapers, light dampmark to lower board, corners renewed, good. Blackwell Rare Books B166 - 85 2011 £600

Priestley, Joseph 1733-1804 *Institutes of Natural and Revealed Religion. Volume III.* London: J. Johnson, 1774, First edition; contemporary full calf gilt, rather worn and darkened, pages xxiv, 248, (iv), first few leaves lightly dampstained in the gutters. R. F. G. Hollett & Son Antiquarian Booksellers 175 - 1097 2011 £250

La Princesse Badourah; Conte Des Mille et Une Nuits. Paris: H. Piazza, 1914, One of 500 copies, signed by Edmund Dulac; 305 x 241mm., 2 p.l. (5)-114 (3) pages, very fine brown crushed morocco by Root and Son (signed on rear turn-in), covers bordered in gilt with French fillet, central panel formed by single rule with foliate branch on stippled ground in each corner of panel raised bands, spine gilt in compartments formed by double rules foliate cornerpieces on stippled ground forming a lobed frame for a floral tool centerpiece, very wide inner gilt dentelles featuring two decorative rolls, each between rules, marbled endpapers, top edge gilt, other edges rough trimmed, original tan front wrapper printed in gilt, blue and white bound in before half title, decorative initials, leaves and decorative border, decorated titlepage and 10 color plates by Edmund Dulac (each laid down with an ornamental frame and with captioned tissue guard), front pastedown with bookplate of Joseph H. Haines, titlepage printed in gilt, muted yellow and blue and leaves throughout in yellow and black, virtually mint, especially bright inside and out. Phillip J. Pirages 59 - 186 2011 $1600

The Principles of the Constitution of England: Including an Account of the Parliament, National Debt and Established Religion. London: J. Debrett, 1797, First and only edition; 8vo., (4), 29. (1) pages, titlepage soiled, with small blank corner torn away (not near printed surface), preserved in modern wrappers with printed title label on upper cover, very rare. John Drury Rare Books 153 - 120 2011 £175

Pringle, Andrew *Practical Photo-Micrography.* Iliffe & Son, 1893, First edition; square 8vo., original pictorial cloth, gilt, pages 169, 29 illustrations. R. F. G. Hollett & Son Antiquarian Booksellers General Catalogue Summer 2010 - 1133 2011 £60

Prior, Herman *Ascents and Passes in the Lake District of England.* London: Simpkin Marshall & Co. and Windermere: J. Garnett, n.d., 1865, First edition; small 8vo., original ribbed cloth gilt, trifle faded, pages x, vi, 269 xv (ads), folding map (slightly torn in corner) and cloth booklet with 4 folding tinted maps in rear pocket, scarce. R. F. G. Hollett & Son Antiquarian Booksellers 173 - 934 2011 £120

Prior, Herman *Ascents and Passes in the Lake District of England...* London: Simpkin Marshall & Co./Windermere: J. Garnett, n.d., 1865, First edition; small 8vo., original ribbed cloth gilt, trifle faded, pages x, vi, 269, xv, (ads), folding map, slightly torn in corner, cloth booklet with 4 folding tinted maps in rear pocket, scarce. R. F. G. Hollett & Son Antiquarian Booksellers General Catalogue Summer 2010 - 1558 2011 £120

Prior, Herman *Guide to the Lake District of England.* Windermere: J. Garnett, n.d. circa, 1865, Fifth (nonpareil) edition; 24mo., original black roan gilt, rubbed and spine rather defective, pages viii, 348, vii, folding colored map in front pocket and numerous woodcut vignettes, illustrations and maps, title supplied in facsimile, lacks double sided map in rear pocket, scarce, bookplate of Emily and Gordon Bottomley bequest on flyleaf. R. F. G. Hollett & Son Antiquarian Booksellers 173 - 935 2011 £85

Prior, Matthew 1664-1721 *The History of His Own Time.* London: printed for the Editor, 1740, Pages viii, 472, (viii, index), engraved frontispiece, few marginal blindstamps, faint library stamp on verso of title, modern full panelled calf, gilt, raised bands. R. F. G. Hollett & Son Antiquarian Booksellers 175 - 1098 2011 £120

Prior, Matthew 1664-1721 *Poems on Several Occasions.* London: Jacob Tonson, 1718, First edition thus; engraved frontispiece (one corner repaired), some light toning, few leaves moderately browned, pages (xl), 506, (6), folio, contemporary dark brown calf, scratched and somewhat dried out, corners worn, recently rebacked, backstrip with 7 raised bands, red morocco label in second compartment, good. Blackwell Rare Books B166 - 86 2011 £600

Pritchard, James A. *The Overland Diary of James A. Pritchard from Kentucky to California in 1849.* Denver: Old West Pub. Co., 1959, First edition, one of 1250 copies; 221 pages, frontispiece, 3 maps, folding chart in rear pocket, red pictorial cloth, gilt, very fine, spine darkened, dust jacket top edge slightly rough. Argonaut Book Shop Recent Acquisitions Summer 2010 - 141 2011 $125

Pritchard, James Cowles *Researches into the Physical History of Mankind.* Houlston and Stoneman, 1851, Fourth edition; 5 volumes, original green cloth, gilt, spine trifle worn at head and foot, labels removed from foot of each volume, 27 engraved plates, partly unopened, scattered spotting, but very good, sound set. R. F. G. Hollett & Son Antiquarian Booksellers 175 - 1099 2011 £350

Pritt, T. E. *North-Country Flies.* Otley: Smith Settle, 1995, First limited edition (500 copies); original green cloth gilt over bevelled boards, matching slipcase, pages xiii, 63, (i), top edges gilt, complete with 12 plates, fine. R. F. G. Hollett & Son Antiquarian Booksellers General Catalogue Summer 2010 - 1273 2011 £60

Private Eye. 1962-1964, First edition; No. 25, 28-53, 55, 68, 73, together 30 issues between 30/11/62 and 2/10/64 with No. 290, 385-563 lacking 505, 572-574, over 200 issues, original wrappers as issued, very good.   I. D. Edrich   May 26 2011 - 99593   2011 $671

Proby, Elizabeth   *Dennes of Daundelyonn.*   London: Smith, Elder & Co., 1859, First edition; 3 volumes, half title volume I, final ad leaf volumes I & III, slight browning, original royal blue sand grained cloth, blocked in blind, spines lettered in gilt, slight wear to heads and tails of spines, small repair to head of leading hinge volume I, nice.   Jarndyce Antiquarian Booksellers   CLXC - 775   2011   £350

Proceedings at the Reception and Dinner in Honor of George Peabody, Esq. of London by the Citizens of the Old Town of Danvers Oct. 9 1856.   Boston: Henry W. Dutton & Son, 1856, First edition; tall 8vo., 6, (1), 195 pages, tinted full page inserted lithographs by Bufford, two initialled by Winslow Homer, original plain stamped brown cloth, slight spinal chipping, inner hinges cracked, some foxing, lacking front endpaper.   M & S Rare Books, Inc.   90 - 166   2011 $225

Proclus Diadochus   *Elementa Theologica et Physica...*   Ferrara: D. Mammarello, 1583, 4to., ff. (3), 69 device at end, modern half calf, with Roldolph Weckherlin manuscript ex-libris, from the library of the Earls of Macclesfield at Shirburn Castle.   Maggs Bros. Ltd.   1440 - 171   2011   £3000

Procopius, of Caesarea   *Historiarum... Libri VIII...*   Augsburg: D. Franck, 1607, Editio princeps of the Greek text; folio, (8), 376; 56, (84) pages, engraved title, dust jacket English (?Oxford) binding of brown calf, double gilt fillet on covers, spine with gilt ornament in compartments, chain mark on upper cover, from the library of the Earls of Macclesfield at Shirburn Castle, this the copy of Thomas Tonkys.   Maggs Bros. Ltd.   1440 - 239   2011   £800

Proctor, Richard A.   *Chance and Luck: a Discussion of the Laws of Luck, Coincidinces, Wagers, Lotteries and the Fallacies of Gambling with Notes on Poker and Martingales.*   London: Longmans, Green and Co., 1891, New edition; 8vo., vi, (2), 263, (1) pages, including half title, followed at end by a 32 page Longmans catalogue, original red cloth lettered in gilt (spine) and black (upper cover), covers just little still but very good, uncut.   John Drury Rare Books   153 - 122   2011   £50

Proctor, Richard A.   *The Expanse of Heaven.*   London: Henry S. King & Co., 1873, First edition; original blue decorated cloth gilt over bevelled boards, pages iv, 305, 36, nice, bright, sound, scarce.   R. F. G. Hollett & Son Antiquarian Booksellers   General Catalogue Summer 2010 - 1135   2011   £65

Proctor, Richard A.   *The Great Pyramid.*   London: Chatto & Windus, 1833, First edition; original pictorial brown cloth, gilt, slight wear to foot of spine, pages vii, 323, 32, with 4 plates, 5 text woodcuts, title lightly spotted.   R. F. G. Hollett & Son Antiquarian Booksellers   177 - 717   2011   £250

Proctor, Richard A.   *The Great Pyramid. Observatory, Tomb and Temple.*   London: Chatto & Windus, 1883, First edition; pages vii, 323, 32, with 4 plates and 5 text woodcuts, gilt lightly spotted, original pictorial brown cloth, gilt, slight wear to foot of spine.   R. F. G. Hollett & Son Antiquarian Booksellers   175 - 1100   2011   £280

Progressive Party   *A Contract with the People - Platform of the Progressive Party.*   Chicago: 1912, 16 pages, very good, self wrappers.   Bookworm & Silverfish   664 - 169   2011 $75

Prokosch, Frederic   *Storm and Echo.*   Garden City: Doubleday & Company Inc., 1948, First edition; copy 379 of only 85 signed copies with leaf of original manuscript bound in, this is the dedication copy, inscribed and signed by author to dedicatee, Russell Hunter, publisher's slipcase with pictorial front reproducing dust jacket art, fine in very good slipcase with edges split but intact.   Charles Agvent   2010 Summer Miscellany - 57   2011 $750

Prosser, Sophie Amelia   *The Cheery Chime of Garth and Other Stories.*   London: R.T.S., 1874, First edition; frontispiece, illustrations, original green cloth by Davison, blocked and lettered in black and gilt, slight rubbing, owner's inscription Christmas 1875, good plus.   Jarndyce Antiquarian Booksellers   CLXC - 776   2011   £35

Prosser, Sophie Amelia   *The Crinkles of Crinklewood Hall.*   London: RTS, 1892, First edition; frontispiece, plates, illustrations, original mustard yellow cloth, pictorially blocked in blue and black, lettered in red and black, Sunday School prize label 1898, very good, bright.   Jarndyce Antiquarian Booksellers   CLXC - 777   2011   £40

Prosser, Sophie Amelia   *Original Fables.*   London: R.T.S., 1870?, Ad leaf preceding frontispiece, illustrations, original brown cloth, bevelled boards, pictorially blocked and lettered in blue and gilt, blocked in black, little rubbed, back board slightly marked, signed H.A. Smith in contemporary hand, all edges gilt, good plus.   Jarndyce Antiquarian Booksellers   CLXC - 785   2011   £40

Prosser, Sophie Amelia   *The Sale of Callowfields.*   London: R.T.S., 1877, First edition; half title, frontispiece, plates 2 pages ads, original maroon cloth, pictorially blocked and lettered in black and gilt, slightly darkened, presentation 1878, G.G. Walmsley bookseller ticket.   Jarndyce Antiquarian Booksellers   CLXC - 787   2011   £40

Proteus: the Mysterious Ruler of Karst Darkness. Ljubljana: Vitrum, 1993, Original pictorial boards, pages 76, illustrations in color. R. F. G. Hollett & Son Antiquarian Booksellers General Catalogue Summer 2010 - 977 2011 £30

Proulx, E. Annie *Close Range: Wyoming Stories.* New York: Scribner, 1999, First edition; fine in fine dust jacket, with color plates, signed by author and artist. Bella Luna Books May 29 2011 - t28795 2011 $137

Proulx, E. Annie *Close Range: Wyoming Stories.* New York: Scribner, 1999, First edition; illustrations by William Matthews, fine, dust jacket fine, signed by author. Bella Luna Books May 26 2011 - t7542 2011 $192

Proulx, E. Annie *Heart Songs.* New York: Scribner, 1988, First edition; fine copy, near fine dust jacket, very light edge wear, with 'not for resale' stamp on top edge of leaves, signed by author. Bella Luna Books May 26 2011 - 6418s 2011 $220

Proulx, E. Annie *Heart Songs.* London: Doueth Estate, 1995, First British hardcover edition; near fine, very minor ding to top rear board, dust jacket is near fine, price inked out on dust jacket flap, signed by author. Bella Luna Books May 29 2011 - 6474 2011 $82

Proulx, E. Annie *Postcards.* London: Fourth Estate, 1993, Proof of first British edition; book fine, signed by author on laid in bookplate, printed matrix wrappers (soft cover). Bella Luna Books May 26 2011 - t2021 2011 $302

Proulx, E. Annie *The Shipping News.* New York: Scribner, 1993, First edition; near fine, previous owner's name on front free endpapers, dust jacket near fine, light creasing at top of spine, signed by author. Bella Luna Books May 26 2011 - t2069 2011 $467

Proulx, E. Annie *That Old Ace in the Hole.* New York: Scribner, 2002, First edition; fine in fine dust jacket, signed and dated by author Jan. 21 2003. Bella Luna Books May 29 2011 - g4629 2011 $104

Proust, Marcel 1871-1922 *In Search of Lost Time. Swann's Way. Within a Budding Grove. The Guermantes Way. Sodom and Gomorrah. The Captive the Fugitive. Time Regained & A Guide to Proust.* London: Chatto & Windus, 1992-1996, First edition thus/second impression; 6 volumes, pages xii, 522; 634; 706; 639; 814; 693; original publisher's white boards lettered black at spines, all second impressions except first two wolumes which are firsts of this translation, fine in near fine dust jacket, jackets faintly sunned at spines. Any Amount of Books May 29 2011 - A71028 2011 $306

Prout, John Skinner *Antiquities of York.* York: W. Hargrove, 1840, Folio, pictorial tinted lithograph titlepage and 20 tinted lithograph plates, some scattered foxing, good copy, original blind embossed and gilt lettered cloth, green roan spine expertly replaced, corners bumped. Ken Spelman Rare Books 68 - 35 2011 £280

Prout, John Skinner *Picturesque Antiquities of Bristol.* Bristol: George Davey, 1835, Folio, titlepage, dedication leaf and 29 lithograph plates, contemporary morocco backed boards, spine repaired, margins of pages foxed and chipped, but india paper plates are mainly unaffected except for some dust marks and streaks across one image, ownership name of Charles Barton 14 York Crescent, Clifton, August 1837 on inner board. Ken Spelman Rare Books 68 - 31 2011 £180

Prowell, Sandra West *By Evil Means.* New York: Walker, 1993, First edition; fine, dust jacket fine, signed by author. Bella Luna Books May 29 2011 - t7047 2011 $82

Prudhomme, Louis *Repertoire Universelle et Historique des Femmes Celebres Mortes ou Vivantes qui se sont Fait Remarquer (sic) dans Toutes les Nations...* Paris: Achille Desauges Libraire, 1826, First edition; 4 volumes, 448 pages, 512 pages, 518 pages, 443 pages, 8vo., contemporary quarter polished calf with lovely gilt decorated spines, all edges speckled, some irregular pagination in volume II but complete, fine and most attractive. Paulette Rose Fine and Rare Books 32 - 139 2011 $1200

Psalmanazar, George *An Historical and Geographical Description of Formosa.* Holden, 1926, Limited to 750 copies, no. 3 signed and presented by editor, N. V. Penzer; xlviii, 288 pages, yellow cloth, parchment spine, near fine, signed by author. C. P. Hyland May 26 2011 - 136 2011 $348

Psalmanazar, George *Memoirs of****.* Dublin: P. Wilson et al, 1765, First Irish edition; 8vo., pages (ii) (ii), 234, bound in contemporary mottled calf, couple of pieces of leather missing from front and rear board, wear along spine, very good, tight copy. Second Life Books Inc. 174 - 264 2011 $600

Psalms of Praise. Flemington: St. Teresa's Press, 1967, One of 100 copies, this #77; 265 x 175mm., 4 p.l., 30 pages, publisher's olive green quarter Oasis Niger goatskin over gold Japanese Kinho paper, leather on upper cover tooled in blind with wisp of smoke issuing from an oil lamp, flat spine with vertical gilt titling, rice paper endleaves; 13 hand painted initials and hand painted miniature of a seagull soaring above the ocean, original tissue guards, prospectus laid in at front, immaculate condition. Phillip J. Pirages 59 - 310 2011 $675

The Public Charities of the Hundred of Lonsdale North of the Sands Reprinted from the Report of the Commissioners (dated Jan. 1820). Ulverston: S. Soulby, 1852, First edition; small 8vo., original half roan gilt, trifle rubbed, pages (ii), 152, signature of J. Maychild Harrison of Flookburgh dated 1852. R. F. G. Hollett & Son Antiquarian Booksellers 173 - 699 2011 £85

The Publisher's Circular. London: Sampson Low, 1837, 30 issues, October 2nd 1837-December 15th 1838, 8vo., 472 pages, disbound (i.e. lacking covers), otherwise in decent sound condition with clean text, slight staining to prelims, red stamp on first page, otherwise sound, about very good. Any Amount of Books May 29 2011 - A74018 2011 $272

Puchowski, Douglas *The Concise Garland Encyclopedia of World Music.* New York: Routledge, 2008, First edition; 2 volumes, 4to., pages xxix, 764; xxi, (765)-1406, printed laminated boards, illustrations, maps, fine. Any Amount of Books May 29 2011 - A69994 2011 $204

Pudney, John *Pick of To-Days Short Stories.* London: Eyre & Spottiswoode, 1948-1963, First edition; nos. 1-14, all in very good condition, 12 of the 14 volumes have dust jackets, all published. I. D. Edrich May 26 2011 - 82782 2011 $419

Puente, Francisco De La *Tratado Breve De La Antiguedad del Linaie de Vera, y Memoria de Personas Senaladas de, que se Hallan en Histoias...* Lima: G. de Contrerars, 1635, 4to., ff. *6), 180 (corrected to 182), 12, marginal notes printed in italic, armorial woodcut on page (ii), contemporary limp velum, lacking ties, minor marginal dampstains to few leaves, handsome, crisp copy, from the library of the Earls of Macclesfield at Shirburn Castle. Maggs Bros. Ltd. 1440 - 172 2011 £6500

Pugh, John *A Treatise on the Science of Muscular Action.* London: Editions Medicina Rara, n.d., Facsimile reprint of original 1794 London edition, limited to 2500 copies (total edition of 2800) bound thus; 330 x 240mm., ix (mis-numbered xi), vi-xvi, 106 pages, 15 plates, each accompanied by duplicate outline plate, three quarter burgundy leather with maroon buckram sides, silver stamped spine title housed in paper slipcase, fine, from the Medical Library of Dr. Clare Gray Peterson. Jeff Weber Rare Books 162 - 246 2011 $100

Pugin, Augustus Welby Northmore 1812-1852
Fifteenth and Sixteenth Century Ornaments. Edinburgh: John Grant, 1904, 4to., engraved color titlepages, plates, original blue cloth, gilt, slightly marked and rubbed. Jarndyce Antiquarian Booksellers CXCI - 460 2011 £200

Puig, Andres *Arithemtca, Especulativa y Practica y Arte de Algebra en la Qual Se Contiene Todo lo Que Pertence al Art Mentor...* Barcelona: A. Lacavalleria vendense e casa del mismo autor, 1672, Second edition; 4to., (16), 576 (8) pages, 19th century English sprinkled calf, gilt spine, red morocco lettering piece, mottled edges, very handsome, from the library of the Earls of Macclesfield at Shirburn Castle. Maggs Bros. Ltd. 1440 - 173 2011 £800

Pullman, Philip *The Amber Spyglass, His Dark Materials III.* London: Scholastic Press, 2000, First British edition; near fine, light bumping to heel of spine, dust jacket near fine, with quarter inch open tear at bottom front fold, one tiny chip (BB size), chip at front hinge, laid in is "The Story is Complete" postcard. Bella Luna Books May 26 2011 - t6625 2011 $357

Pullman, Philip *The Amber Spyglass. His Dark Materials III...* London: Scholastic Press, 2000, First British edition; fine, fine dust jacket, scarce. Bella Luna Books May 26 2011 - t9226 2011 $825

Pullman, Philip *The Amber Spyglass: His Dark Materials III.* New York: Knopf, 2000, First US edition, true first preceding British by three weeks; fine, in like dust jacket. Bella Luna Books May 26 2011 - t9609 2011 $275

Pullman, Philip *The Amber Spyglass, His Dark Materials III.* New York: Knopf, 2000, First US edition; fine in fine dust jacket. Bella Luna Books May 29 2011 - t9154 2011 $110

Pullman, Philip *Lyra' Oxford.* Oxford: David Fickling Books, 2003, First UK edition, true first; fine, signed by author. Bella Luna Books May 29 2011 - t6855 2011 $137

Pullman, Philip *The Northern Lights.* London: Scholastic, 2008, Limited to 3000 copies; fine in fine dust jacket, signed and numbered by author. Bella Luna Books May 29 2011 - t9238 2011 $110

Pulszky, Theresa *Memoirs of a Hungarian Lady.* London: Henry Colburn, 1850, First edition; 2 volumes, 26 page catalog volume I, ads on endpapers, uncut, original blue cloth, blocked in blind, spine lettered in gilt, very good, bright copy. Jarndyce Antiquarian Booksellers CLXC - 792 2011 £200

Pulteney, William *An Enquiry into the Conduct of Our Domestick Affairs from the Year 1721 to the Present Time.* London: printed by H. Haines, 1734, Modern half calf gilt, pages 68. R. F. G. Hollett & Son Antiquarian Booksellers 175 - 1102 2011 £180

Pulteney, William *Mr. Forman's Letter to the Right Honourable William Pulteney, Esq. Shewing How Pernicious the Imperial Company of Commerce and Navigation..* London: printed for and sold by S. Busey, in Ivy Lane,, 1725, First edition; half title, (5), 6-71, (1) pages, in thi edition page 6, line 6 ends 'mercena', disbound.   Anthony W. Laywood   May 26 2011 - 21649   2011 $76

Punch; or the London Charivari.   London: published at the Office, 1841-1920,   Volumes 1-159 in 80 volumes, illustrations, few titlepages slightly browned, uniformly bound in original bright blue cloth, decorated in gilt, bright, attractive run.   Jarndyce Antiquarian Booksellers   CXCI - 26   2011   £850

Puppy Dog's ABC.   London: Tuck, n.d. circa, 1890, Folio, pictorial wrappers, die-cut in shape of dog's head, one small mend else very good+, 4 full page chromos and with line illustrations on other pages.   Aleph-Bet Books, Inc.   95 - 14   2011 $225

Puppy Play House.   N.P.: Polygraphic Co., 1951,   Spiral backed pictorial boards, 9 1/2 x 7 1/2 inches, fine, color lithographs.   Aleph-Bet Books, Inc.   95 - 196   2011 $150

Purcell, Donovan   *Cambridge Stone.*   London: Faber, 1967,   First edition; tall 8vo., original cloth gilt, dust jacket, pages 115, with 48 plates.   R. F. G. Hollett & Son Antiquarian Booksellers   177 - 718   2011   £45

Purcell, Rosamond Wolff   *Illuminations. A Bestiary.*   New York: W. W. Norton, 1986,   First edition; small 4to., 120 pages, signed by Purcell and Stephen Jay Gould, fine in fine dust jacket, scarce signed work.   By the Book, L. C.   26 - 44   2011 $275

Purdon, John   *A Digest of the Laws of Pennsylvania 1700-1872.*   Philadelphia: 1873,   2 volumes, 4to., 2 massive volumes in old full law calf, gilt on both red and black labels bright, very good endpapers with some glue browning, cxxi, 874; ix, 875-1172 pages.   Bookworm & Silverfish   662 - 93   2011 $150

Purdy, James   *63: Dream Palace.*   New York: William Frederick Press, 1956,   First edition; inscribed by author to legendary NY bookseller Roger Richards, one letter rubbed from Purdy's name on spine, else fine in wrappers. Ken Lopez Bookseller   154 - 165   2011 $150

Purey-Cust, A. P.   *Our English Ministers. Second Series.* Isbister & Co. n.d.,   2 volumes, original cloth, gilt, spines little rubbed and darkened, pages 351, 351, illustrations, joints to second volume cracked.   R. F. G. Hollett & Son Antiquarian Booksellers   177 - 719   2011   £60

Pursh, Frederick   *Flora Americae Septentrionalis or a Systematic Arrangement and Description of the Plants of North America.*   London: White Cochrane and Co., 1814, First edition;   24 hand colored engraved plates, light foxing and marginal spot to 1 plate, other plates clean and bright, 8vo., pages xxxvi, 358; (2), (359-) 751 (ad 6 pages), publisher's cloth with original paper labels, faded, especially spines, head of spines reinforced with cloth, front free endpapers missing, some spotting to covers, sticker removed from lower spines, corner and leaf loose, edge of 2 leaves chipped.   Raymond M. Sutton, Jr.   May 26 2011 - 55848   2011 $5000

Purves-Stewart, James   *Intracranial Tumours and Some Errors in Their Diagnosis.*   London, et al: Humphrey Milford, Oxford University Press, 1927,   First edition; 8vo., xiii, 206 pages, illustrations, index, maroon cloth, black stamped cover title and gilt stamped spine title, ex-library bookplate with embossed stamp on title, spine call numbered painted over, rubber stamp of Dr. Ernst A. Sommer, from the Medical Library of Dr. Clare Gray Peterson.   Jeff Weber Rare Books   162 - 247   2011 $65

Purvis, J. B.   *Through Uganda to Mount Elgon.*   London: t. Fisher Unwin, 1909,   First edition; 8vo., 372 pages, folding map, illustrations, original brown decorative cloth, Munger Africana Library stamp.   J. & S. L. Bonham Antiquarian Booksellers   Africa 4/20/2011 - 8069   2011   £90

Purvis, O. W.   *The Lichen Flora of Great Britain and Ireland.*   London: Natural History Museum for the British Lichen Society, 1994,   Thick small 4to., original cloth, dust jacket, pages ix, 710 with 44 text illustrations, fine.   R. F. G. Hollett & Son Antiquarian Booksellers   General Catalogue Summer 2010 - 1038   2011   £120

Pushkin, Aleksandr Sergeevich 1799-1837   *The Golden Cockerel.*   New York: Heritage Press, 1950,   4to., original publisher's blue cloth with cockerel printed in gilt in repeat pattern on covers, spine lettered gilt, pages 42, copiously illustrated in color, signed by artist, Edmund Dulac with presentation from Dulac for Isaac Jones, slight marks, head of spine slightly rubbed, slight soiling otherwise very good+.   Any Amount of Books   May 29 2011 - A43024   2011 $340

Pushkin, Aleksandr Sergeevich 1799-1837   *The Tale of Tsar Saltan.*   New York: Dial Books, 1996,   Stated first edition; 4to., cloth, fine in fine dust jacket, illustrations by Gennady Spirin.   By the Book, L. C.   26 - 70   2011 $95

Puss in Boots.   New York: McLoughlin Bros., 1897, 4to., pictorial wrappers, near fine, 6 stunning full page chromolithographs and with color cover as well.   Aleph-Bet Books, Inc.   95 - 230   2011 $350

Puss in Boots. A Peepshow Book. London: Chatto & Windus, 1977, Small 8vo., original glazed pictorial boards, 5 peepshows, illustrations in color, tie and hanging loop. R. F. G. Hollett & Sons Antiquarian Booksellers   170 - 519   2011   £45

Le Putanisme d'Amsterdam, Livre Contenant les Tours & Les Ruses Don Se Servent les Putains & Les Maquereles... Amsterdam: Elie Jogehemse de Rhin, 1681, First edition; rare, small 12mo., pages (vi), 277, (1) blank, engraved frontispiece and 4 plates, all edges gilt, discreet old repairs to frontispiece and final ad leaf, occasional light spotting early 20th century full black morocco, by Bernasconi, gilt lettering and raised bands to spine, gilt decoration to inside boards, marbled endpapers, bookplate of G. Nordmann.   Simon Finch Rare Books   Zero - 401   2011   £3000

Puydt, Emile De   *Le Orchidees, Histoire Iconographique, Organographie Classification Geographie Collections...* Paris: J. Rothschild, 1880, First edition; 50 hand finished colored lithographed plates (small spot to margin of a plate, plates fine and bright), 244 vignettes, tall 8vo., pages viii, 348, modern quarter morocco (marginal browning and some damp spotting to half title and title, fore-edge of title and next page chipped, tip of lower corner to half title professionally replaced, marginal brown speckling to text pages, chipping and or short tear to fore edge of last 5 leaves, top edge gilt.   Raymond M. Sutton, Jr.   May 26 2011 - 20045   2011 $1250

Puzo, Mario   *The Godfather.* New York: G. P. Putnam's Sons, 1969, First edition; fine with unblemished white boards in near fine dust jacket with two small tears at head of spine and very lightly rubbed at head of spine and corner points, housed in decorated clamshell case, especially attractive, housed in decorated clamshell case. Buckingham Books   May 26 2011 - 27291   2011 $3500

Pyle, Howard   *Howard Pyle's Book of the American Spirit.* New York: Harper Bros., 1923, (b-x). Stated first edition; large thick 4to., cloth backed boards, pictorial paste-on, fine in dust jacket, mounted color plate, dust jacket chipped at spine ends, more than 22 color plates plus a profusion of black and whites.   Aleph-Bet Books, Inc.   95 - 469   2011 $750

Pyle, Howard   *Pepper and Salt; or Seasoning for Young Folk.* New York: Harper and Bros., 1886, Large 4to., brown pictorial cloth, slightest of wear to spine ends and tips, slight cover soil, tight, clean, very good+, very scarce. Aleph-Bet Books, Inc.   95 - 468   2011 $650

Pym, Barbara   *Excellent Women.* New York: Dutton, 1978, First US edition; 8vo. signed presentation from author for Elizabeth Harrison, with pencilled note, slight lean, minimal shelf wear, very good+.   Any Amount of Books   May 26 2011 - A68213   2011 $553

Pym, Barbara   *No Fond Return of Love.* New York: Dutton, 1982, First American edition; (254 pages), 8vo., boards with linen cloth spines gilt lettered, as new in similar dust jacket (not price clipped).   Paulette Rose Fine and Rare Books   32 - 141   2011 $60

Pym, Barbara   *Quartet in Autumn.* London: Macmillan, 1977, First edition; 8vo. pages 218, nice in little chipped and soiled dust jacket.   Second Life Books Inc.   174 - 265   2011 $125

Pym, Barbara   *The Sweet Dove Died.* London: Macmillan, 1978, First edition; (208) pages, 8vo., turquoise boards, silver lettered spine, as new in blue printed dust jacket.   Paulette Rose Fine and Rare Books   32 - 142   2011 $200

Pynchon Notes 1-55. Middletown/Hamilton: Kraft/Tololyan, 1979-2008, 55 issues in 34 volumes, the first 15 issues are fine in stapled wrappers, remaining issues are perfectbound, also fine.   Ken Lopez Bookseller   154 - 192   2011 $1500

Pynchon, Thomas 1937-   *Against the Day.* New York: Penguin, 2006, Review copy; bookplate of Pynchon's editor, Ray Roberts, fine in fine dust jacket with press release laid in, text which appears to be an early draft of front jacket flap, uncommon.   Ken Lopez Bookseller   154 - 186   2011 $450

Pynchon, Thomas 1937-   *The Crying of Lot 49.* Philadelphia: Lippincott, 1966, First edition; minimal tanning to board edges, else fine in very near fine dust jacket with trace rubbing, nice, small bookplate of Ray Roberts (Pynchon's editor).   Ken Lopez Bookseller   154 - 166   2011 $1000

Pynchon, Thomas 1937-   *The Crying of Lot 49.* London: Cape, 1967, First British edition; small bookplate of Ray Roberts, fine in near fine dust jacket with small tear and crease at crown.   Ken Lopez Bookseller   154 - 167   2011 $1000

Pynchon, Thomas 1937-   *Gravity's Rainbow.* N.P.: n.p., n.d., Taiwan piracy; bookplate of Ray Roberts, Tapei bookstore label on rear flyleaf, offsetting to endpages, near fine in good, spine sunned dust jacket with several edge chips and one long tear in upper rear spine fold.   Ken Lopez Bookseller   154 - 171   2011 $300

Pynchon, Thomas 1937-   *Gravity's Rainbow.* London: Cape, 1973, Uncorrected proof of the British edition; fine in wrappers, small bookplate of Pynchon's editor, Ray Roberts.   Ken Lopez Bookseller   154 - 169   2011 $3500

Pynchon, Thomas 1937- *Gravity's Rainbow.* London: Cape, 1973, First British softcover edition; issued simultaneously with hardcover edition, very nice, none of the spine fading typical to this title, quite uncommon, bookplate of Ray Roberts inside front cover. Ken Lopez Bookseller 154 - 170 2011 $350

Pynchon, Thomas 1937- *Gravity's Rainbow.* New York: Viking Press, 1973, Uncorrected proof; tall blue wrappers, pencil number ("7" - all copies seen by us have been numbered), sunning to spine and little offsetting to wrappers, else near fine, on inside front wrapper is small bookplate of Ray Roberts, Pynchon's editor when he went to Little Brown, uncommon issue. Between the Covers 169 - BTC342428 2011 $3750

Pynchon, Thomas 1937- *Gravity's Rainbow.* New York: Viking, 1973, First edition; small hardcover first printing of 4000 copies, the balance of the first edition, 16,000 copies, issued as softcover, small bookplate of Pynchon's editor, Ray Roberts, fine in near fine dust jacket with small creased tear to crown. Ken Lopez Bookseller 154 - 168 2011 $2750

Pynchon, Thomas 1937- *Gravity's Rainbow.* New York: Viking, 1973, First edition; fine in near fine dust jacket, very very faint wear to bottom edge. Bella Luna Books May 26 2011 - 17175 2011 $2200

Pynchon, Thomas 1937- *Mason and Dixon.* New York: Henry Holt, 1997, Of a total of 4 leather bound copies of this title, this one of two copies without topstain; this copy belonged to Pynchon's editor, Ray Roberts, with Roberts bookplate, fine. Ken Lopez Bookseller 154 - 181 2011 $3500

Pynchon, Thomas 1937- *Mason and Dixon.* New York: Henry Holt, 1997, Second issue, uncorrected proof; blue wrappers, tipped in titlepage that adds the ampersand missing in first issue, small bookplate of Ray Roberts, Pynchon's editor, fine, with two dust jackets (bit crimped at crown where they extend past the proof) and fine printed acetate wrapper. Ken Lopez Bookseller 154 - 183 2011 $4000

Pynchon, Thomas 1937- *Mason and Dixon.* New York: Henry Holt, 1997, Uncorrected proof copy; plain blue wrappers, first issue proof, which leaves out the ampersand from "Mason & Dixon" on titlepage, small bookplate of Ray Roberts, Pynchon's editor, inside front cover. Ken Lopez Bookseller 154 - 182 2011 $4500

Pynchon, Thomas 1937- *Mason and Dixon.* New York: Henry Holt, 1997, Advance reading copy; beige wrappers, the number of the copies of each of the two variant issues of the advance reading copy was rumored to be 500, the issues vary only on rear wrapper, this is the one with rear panel featuring publication and promotional data, fine in wrappers, bookplate of Ray Roberts, Pynchon's editor. Ken Lopez Bookseller 154 - 185 2011 $250

Pynchon, Thomas 1937- *Mason and Dixon.* New York: Henry Holt, 1997, Third issue uncorrected proof; blue wrappers, with bound-in titlepage that includes ampersand missing from first issue, small bookplate of Ray Roberts, Pynchon's editor, fine. Ken Lopez Bookseller 154 - 184 2011 $3500

Pynchon, Thomas 1937- *Of a Fond Ghoul.* New York: Blown Litter Press, 1990, One of only 50 numbered copies; fine in stapled wrappers, bookplate of Ray Roberts, Pynchon's editor. Ken Lopez Bookseller 154 - 180 2011 $2000

Pynchon, Thomas 1937- *Slow Learner.* Boston: Little Brown, 1984, Review copy of the first paperback edition; issued simultaneously with hardcover edition, bit of edge sunning to rear cover, else fine in wrappers, with review slip laid in, bookplate of Ray Roberts, Pynchon's editor. Ken Lopez Bookseller 154 - 174 2011 $125

Pynchon, Thomas 1937- *Slow Learner.* Boston: Little Brown, 1984, One of only two leatherbound copies prepared by publisher, one which went to Pynchon; this one belonged to Pynchon's editor, Ray Roberts, small bookplate of Roberts on pastedown, letterhead note card identifying the issue laid in, fine. Ken Lopez Bookseller 154 - 172 2011 $6500

Pynchon, Thomas 1937- *Slow Learner.* Boston: Little Brown, 1984, Advance issue; very small number of folded and gathered signatures were prepared and laid into proof dust jackets and issued as advance copies, the usual number cited for such copies is 'about 10', this is one of those sets of "f&g's" laid into trial binding and dust jacket, the mock-up of the boards is black, bookplate of Pynchon's editor, Ray Roberts on first signature, fine in very good dust jacket, worn where it overlays sheets, probably unique item. Ken Lopez Bookseller 154 - 173 2011 $2500

Pynchon, Thomas 1937- *Slow Learner.* London: Cape, 1985, First British edition; bookplate of Ray Roberts, fine in fine dust jacket. Ken Lopez Bookseller 154 - 175 2011 $125

Pynchon, Thomas 1937- *Slow Learner.* London: Cape, 1985, Uncorrected proof copy of the British edition; bookplate of Ray Roberts, rear pages edge sunned, last blank has corner turn, near fine in wrappers. Ken Lopez Bookseller 154 - 176 2011 $200

Pynchon, Thomas 1937- *V.* Philadelphia: J. B. Lippincott, 1963, Advance reading copy; spine slightly sunned, very nice, near fine in wrappers as issued. Between the Covers   169 - BTC342429   2011 $2500

Pynchon, Thomas 1937- *Vineland.* London: Secker & Warburg, 1990, First British edition; bookplate of Ray Roberts, Pynchon's editor, age toning to pages, else fine in fine dust jacket.   Ken Lopez Bookseller   154 - 179   2011 $125

Pynchon, Thomas 1937- *Vineland.* Boston: Little Brown, 1990, Advance copy in the form of unbound sigantures and with trail bindings; pages uncut, fine, laid into green binding, which has Ray Robert's bookplate and in fine dust jacket.   Ken Lopez Bookseller   154 - 178   2011 $2500

Pynchon, Thomas 1937- *Vineland.* Boston: Little Brown, 1990, First edition; inscribed by author to his editor, Ray Roberts, fine in fine dust jacket.   Ken Lopez Bookseller   154 - 177   2011 $25,000

Pyne, James Barker 1800-1870 *Lake Scenery of England.* London: Day and Sons, 1859, First edition; tall 4to., modern leather effect green cloth gilt, pages vii, plus 25 chromolithographed plates, each with accompanying unpaginated leaf of text, text woodcuts, lower margin of title, little creased with few short tears, few slight defects to one or two margins, generally very good.   R. F. G. Hollett & Son Antiquarian Booksellers   173 - 937   2011   £275

Pyne, William Henry 1767-1843 *The History of the Royal Residences of Windsor Castle, St. James's Palace, Carlton House, Kensington Palace, Hampton Court, Buckingham House and Frogmore.* London: printed for A. Dry, 1819, First edition; 3 volumes, 339 x 270mm., lovely contemporary black straight grain morocco splendidly gilt, covers with square fleuron cornerpieces and wide outer border formed by triple gilt fillets and decorative roll in dense diapered pattern, inner border of single plain gilt rule connecting delicate stylized palmetto cornerpieces, frame with tangent inner border of multiple blind rules, raised bands, spines heavily gilt in alternating wide and narrow compartments, the four smaller compartments with pairs of triple fillets terminating in tulips at either end, two of the wide compartments with gilt titling, others densely gilt with interlacing volutes, floral tools and palmettes, all edges gilt, with 100 fine hand colored plates; covers just slightly marked, majority of the leaves in first two volumes with very light marginal foxing (but not at all distracting), few leaves in volume II with small areas of blotchy foxing (just touching a couple of plates), significant (but not severe) offsetting from one particularly dark plate, occasional faint offsetting from other engravings but majority of pages facing illustrations unaffected and third volume with no appreciable foxing or offsetting at all, in most ways extremely fine set, handsome bindings entirely sound and lustrous, text fresh and smooth, plates richly colored and especially well preserved.   Phillip J. Pirages   59 - 282   2011 $9500

Pyrnelle, Louise Clarke *Diddie, Dumps and Tot; or Plantation Child-Life.* New York: Harper and Brothers, 1882, First edition; frontispiece and illustrations, some spotting, original olive green cloth blocked and lettered in black, spine dulled and little rubbed, good sound copy.   Jarndyce Antiquarian Booksellers   CLXC - 793   2011   £85

Q

Quadri, Antonio *Il Canal Grande Di Venezia Descritto Da Antoni Quadri...* Venezia: Dalla Tipografia Armena Di S. Lazzaro, 1838, Second edition; Oblong folio 48 hand colored engravings, original quarter red morocco and printed boards, aside from some slight rubbing to covers, present copy is in immaculate condition, with pages and colors as fresh as the day they were painted. James S. Jaffe Rare Books   May 26 2011 - 12880   2011 $15,000

Quammen, David *Natural Acts.* New York: Nick Lyons, 1985, First edition; fine, dust jacket near fine, very light wear.   Bella Luna Books   May 29 2011 - t3683   2011 $82

Quarenghi, Giacomo *Fabriche e Disegni di Giacomo Quarenghi Architetto di S. M. ;'Imperatore di Russia, Cavaliere di Malta...* Milano: Presso Paolo Antonio Tosi, 1821, First edition; folio, pages 46 + frontispiece, 59 finely engraved plates, original plain grey boards, rebacked, signs of damp to inner top and bottom corners of leaves, most noticeable towards front and rear of book, one or two plates lightly foxed, covers slightly marked, some mild wear, very good, bright, scarce.   Peter Ellis   May 26 2011 - ARCHITEC008930   2011 $2800

Quarles, Benjamin *Black History's Diversified Clientele.* Washington: 1971, 8vo., wrappers, near fine.   Bookworm & Silverfish   664 - 5   2011 $175

Quartich, Bernard *Contributions Towards a Dictionary of English-Collectors, as Also of Some Foreign Collectors Whose Libraries were Incorporated in English.* London: Bernard Quartich, 1892, Part I-(VIII) of 13, 8vo., numerous plates, original printed wrappers for each part, slight fraying, library blindstamp on wrappers, very nice.   M & S Rare Books, Inc.   90 - 45   2011 $350

The Quarto. 1896, Gilt decorated green cloth, bookplates and stamps of Forbes Library, Northampton, little rubbing, otherwise near fine.   Lupack Rare Books   May 26 2011 - ABE944622488   2011 $175

Quick, Armand James *The Physiology and Pathology of Hemostasis.* Philadelphia: Lea & Febiger, 1951, First edition; 8vo., 188 pages, figures, index, original blue cloth, gilt stamped spine title, previous owner's inked signature and stamp, fine, from the Medical Library of Dr. Clare Gray Peterson.   Jeff Weber Rare Books   162 - 248   2011 $75

Quiller-Couch, Arthur *In Powder and Crinoline.* London: Hodder & Stoughton, n.d., 1913, 4to., laender pictorial cloth, some light foxing, near fine in original publisher's pictorial box with mounted color plate (box soiled, corners strengthened), first trade edition (second issue bound in cloth instead of cloth backed boards), illustrations by Kay Nielsen, with 24 tipped in color plates and pictorial tissue guards, pictorial endpapers plus text decorations, beautiful copy of really magnificent book rarely found with original box.   Aleph-Bet Books, Inc.   95 - 393   2011 $1950

Quincy, John *Lexicon Physico Medicum; or a New Medicinal Dictionary...* London: printed for J. Osborn and T. Longman at the Ship in Pater-Noster Row, 1730, xvi, 480 pages, diagrams in text, ownership inscription dated 1949, 8vo., full contemporary panelled calf, raised bands, early handwritten paper label, joints cracked but firm, head and tail of spine slightly chipped, tinted bookplate of Cholmondely Library, later bookplate ex-libris Nellen, fine, clean copy.   Jarndyce Antiquarian Booksellers   CXCI - 461   2011   £350

Quinn, Elisabeth V. *The Kewpie Primer.* London: George G. Harrap & Co. n.d., 1916, First UK edition; original brown pictorial boards, little faded, spine rubbed and defective at head, pages viii, 118, illustrations in orange and black throughout by Rose O'Neill, flyleaves lightly browned, short closed edge tear to half title, small piece torn from corner of contents leaf, faint fingering to first few leaves, otherwise very nice, clean and sound copy.   R. F. G. Hollett & Sons Antiquarian Booksellers   170 - 482   2011   £95

Quinn, Seabury *The Complete Adventures of Jules De Grandin.* Shelburne and Sauk City: Battered Silicon Dispatch Box/George A. Vanderburgh, 2001, First edition, hardbound issue; 3 volumes, quarto, fine in very slightly rubbed, still easily fine dust jackets, somewhat amateurishly produced (the elaborate color Xeroxed dust jackets have been pieced together with tape, as issued), yet still attractive, very uncommon.   Between the Covers   169 - BTC315979   2011 $750

Quinn, Seabury *Roads.* Sauk City: Arkahm House, 1948, First trade and first hardcover edition; octavo, illustrations by Virgil Finlay, cloth.   L. W. Currey, Inc.   124 - 60   2011 $1500

Quinn, Seabury *Roads.* Sauk City: Arkham House, 1948, First trade (and first hardcover) edition; octavo, illustrations by Virgil Finlay, cloth.   L. W. Currey, Inc.   124 - 40   2011 $1750

Quoy, J. R. C. *Voyage de Decouvertes de l'Astrolabe Execute par Ordre du Roi, Pendant les Annees 1826-1827-1828-1829...* Paris: J. Tastu, 1833, 48 engraved plates (numbered 26; 23 are printed in color and finished by hand, missing plate 14, worming to several, mostly marginal and sometimes reinforced with paper tape, paper tape affects 3 images, stain to upper margin of 1, few short tears to margins of 1 reinforced with paper tape, faint dampstain to lower blank corner of few, 8vo. and folio, pages (3), 390, modern half leather, corner rubbed, head of spine bumped, endpapers renewed, handstamp to half title, worming to a margin of title and few pages of text volume, crudely reinforced with cellotape, minor foxing to few pages of text, raised bands gilt lettering on spines.   Raymond M. Sutton, Jr.   May 26 2011 - 41536 2011 $1500

Qutiman, John A. *Governor's Message Delivered at Called Session of the Legislature of the State of Mississippi, November 18th 1850.*   Jackson: 1850, First edition; 8vo., 8 pages, removed, browned and foxed, but very good.   M & S Rare Books, Inc.   90 - 257 2011 $500

R

Rab, Fordham *Guide to Law of the Sea a Practical Introductory Digest & guide to "Law Everyone Should Know".* New York: 1937, 2 volumes, average ex-library, interior joints mended, original binding. Bookworm & Silverfish 668 - 114 2011 $75

The Rabbit Book. Chicago: Donohue, 1904, Oblong 32mo., pictorial cloth, edge of titlepage rubbed, else very good with original ivory clasp intact, scarce, illustrations in bold colors by Mary Tourtel. Aleph-Bet Books, Inc. 95 - 544 2011 $850

Rabi, I. I. *My Life and Times as a Physicist.* Claremont: Claremont College, 1960, First edition; 8vo., vi, 55 pages, mild foxing to edges, scuff front cover in very good++ dust jacket with minimal sun spine, soil. By the Book, L. C. 26 - 109 2011 $150

Rabier, Benjamin *Gedeon Sportsman.* Paris: Librairie Garnier Freres, n.d., Large 4to., original cloth backed boards, top edges and corners worn and chipped, 23 pages lithographed in colors, upper joint cracked. R. F. G. Hollett & Sons Antiquarian Booksellers 170 - 562 2011 £75

Rackham, Arthur *The Allies' Fairy Book.* London: William Heinemann, n.d., 1916, Limited to 525 numbered copies; signed by author, quarto, 12 mounted color plates, publisher's blue buckram. Heritage Book Shop Booth A12 51st NY International Antiquarian Book Fair April 8-10 2011 - 102 2011 $2000

Rackham, Arthur *Arthur Rackham's Book of Pictures.* London: William Heinemann, 1913, One of 1030 signed, of which 1000 numbered 1-1000 are for sale in Great Britian, Ireland and Colonies, and 30 copies, numbered 1001-1030 for presentation, this number 1030; with 44 mounted color plates mounted on brown paper with descriptive tissue guards, 10 black and white drawings and sketch of a bookplate, original full white cloth stamped in gilt on cover and spine, top edge gilt, others uncut, spine slightly sunned, near fine, very small bookseller label on front pastedown. Heritage Book Shop Holiday 2010 - 101 2011 $2500

Rackham, Arthur *The Arthur Rackham Fairy Book.* London: George G. Harrap & Co., 1933, Limited to 460 numbered copies signed by author; octavo, 8 color plates, original vellum over boards. Heritage Book Shop Booth A12 51st NY International Antiquarian Book Fair April 8-10 2011 - 103 2011 $2000

Rackham, Arthur *Arthur Rackham Fairy Book.* London: George G. Harrap & Co., 1933, Limited to 460 numbered copies signed by artist, this #356; octavo, 286 pages, 8 color plates and numerous drawings in black and white, original vellum over boards, ruled and lettered gilt on front cover and spine, top edge gilt, others uncut, partially unopened, original gold and cream pictorial endpapers, vellum of spine slightly wrinkled, otherwise near fine, housed in original numbered slipcase. Heritage Book Shop Holiday 2010 - 100 2011 $2000

Rackham, Arthur *The Arthur Rackham Fairy Book...* London: Harrap, 1933, Limited to 460 copies (450 for sale) signed by author; small 4to., full vellum stamped in gold, top edge gilt, tiny rub spot on cover and owner inscription on endpaper, else near fine, pictorial endpapers, color plates and black and whites. Aleph-Bet Books, Inc. 95 - 470 2011 $2500

Rackham, Oliver *The Illustrated History of the Countryside.* London: Weidenfeld and Nicolson, 1994, First edition; 4to., original cloth, dust jacket, pages 240, illustrations in color. R. F. G. Hollett & Son Antiquarian Booksellers General Catalogue Summer 2010 - 1039 2011 £30

Radcliffe, Alexander *The Ramble an Anti-Heroick Poem. Together with Some Terrestrial Hymns and Carnal Ejaculations.* London: for the author and to be sold by Walter Davis, 1682, First edition; 8vo., pages (xvi), 128, including initial blank Ai, contemporary black morocco, sides panelled in gilt, spine richly gilt in compartments, marbled pastedowns, gilt edges, lightly rubbed, little marginal browning, fine, the Heber(?) Britwell-Hewyard-Bradley Martin, Edwards copy with modern bookplates of H. Bradley Martin and J. O. Edwards. Simon Finch Rare Books Zero - 348 2011 £2500

Radcliffe, Ann Ward 1764-1823 *L'Italien ou le Confessional.* Paris: Maradan An VI, 1798, 3 volumes, (2), 275 pages; (2), 302 pages; (2), 281 pages, 12mo., contemporary quarter leather, gilt decorated spine (gilt a bit dulled), contrasting title labels, all edges yellow, frontispiece in each volume, the first signed by Gaitte. Paulette Rose Fine and Rare Books 32 - 143 2011 $900

Radcliffe, Ann Ward 1764-1823 *A Journey made in the Summer of 1794 through Holland and the Western Frontier of Germany...* London: G. G. and J. Robinson, 1795, First edition; 4to., pages x, 500, bound in dust jacket sheep backed boards, uncut, shelf worn, spine corroded, some minor stains and soiling, but very good, unsophisticated copy. Second Life Books Inc. 174 - 266 2011 $700

Radcliffe, F. P. Delme *The Noble Science: a Few General Ideas on Fox-Hunting, for the Use of the Rising Generation of Sportsmen and More Especially Those of the Hertfordshire Hunt Club.* London: Rudolph Ackermann, 1839, First edition; large 8vo., original publisher's light blue cloth lettered gilt at spine and decorated gilt on cover with fox motif, all edges gilt, slight bumping at corner, light rubbing at edges, some foxing to prelims, otherwise bright handsome very good+ with plates very clean, neat name on front endpaper.   Any Amount of Books   May 29 2011 - A42890   2011 $247

Radclyffe, William *Graphic Illustrations of Warwickshire.* Birmingham: Beilby, Knott and Beilby, 1829, First edition, large paper copy; frontispiece (tissue guard), 31 engraved proof plates on India paper (each with tissue guard), 12 engraved vignettes in text, very mild foxing to prelim and final leaves, pages (viii) xii, 128, 4to., near contemporary half red morocco, smoth backstrip longitudinally gilt lettered within ornate floral border designs, red moire cloth sides, blindstamped rules on returns, minor shelfwear at board extremities, all edges gilt, yellow chalked endpapers, contemporary steel engraved bookplate of Robert Vaughan Hughes of Wyelands, publisher's ad tipped to front free endpaper, near fine, tipped at front is 4 page publisher's ad with list of subscribers.   Blackwell Rare Books   B166 - 87   2011   £700

Radley, Chris *The Embroidered Silk Postcard.* privately published, 1977, Original wrappers, pages 60, illustrations.   R. F. G. Hollett & Son Antiquarian Booksellers   General Catalogue Summer 2010 - 299   2011   £35

Radley, Chris *The Woven Silk Postcard.* privately published, 1978, Original wrappers, pages 84, illustrations.   R. F. G. Hollett & Son Antiquarian Booksellers   General Catalogue Summer 2010 - 300   2011   £35

Radlov, Nicholas *Stories in Pictures.* Moscow?: USSR, 1937, Original Russian edition; with English titles supplied on small slips, also with info sheet tipped in on f.f.e.p., about very good, wear to extremities, internally near fine.   Lupack Rare Books   May 26 2011 - ABE1256015888   2011 $200

Rae, Colin *Lamaboch; or Notes from my Diary on the Boer Campaign of 1894...* London: Sampson Low, 1898, First edition; 8vo., pages xx, 248, folding map, illustrations, original red decorative cloth, gilt vignette on upper cover, spine little faded.   J. & S. L. Bonham Antiquarian Booksellers   Africa 4/20/2011 - 3079   2011   £135

Rae, Edward *The Country of the Moors: a Journey from Tripoli in Barbary to the City of Karwan.* London: John Murray, 1887, First edition; 8vo., pages xvi, 334, map, 5 plates, 2 plans, original green decorative cloth, very good.   J. & S. L. Bonham Antiquarian Booksellers   Africa 4/20/2011 - 8352   2011   £85

Rae, Gwynedd *All Mary.* London: Routledge, 1942, Original pale blue cloth, spine and edges rather faded, pages 154, illustrations by Irene Williamson.   R. F. G. Hollett & Son Antiquarian Booksellers   General Catalogue Summer 2010 - 554   2011   £30

Rae, Gwynedd *Mary Plain in Town.* London: Routledge, 1941, Fourth impression; original boards, spine trifle faded, pages 118, illustrations by Irene Williamson.   R. F. G. Hollett & Sons Antiquarian Booksellers   170 - 567   2011   £35

Rae, Gwynedd *Mary Plain in Trouble.* London: Routledge, 1940, First edition; original green cloth pages 126, illustrations by Irene Williamson, nice, fresh, clean, scarce.   R. F. G. Hollett & Son Antiquarian Booksellers   General Catalogue Summer 2010 - 556   2011   £45

Rae, Gwynedd *Mary Plain in War-Time.* London: Routledge, 1942, First edition; original green cloth, spine little faded, pages 125, illustrations by Irene Williamson, scarce.   R. F. G. Hollett & Son Antiquarian Booksellers   General Catalogue Summer 2010 - 557   2011   £75

Rae, Gwynedd *Mary Plain on Holiday.* London: Routledge, 1937, First edition; original boards, pages 114, illustrations by Irene Williamson, scarce.   R. F. G. Hollett & Son Antiquarian Booksellers   General Catalogue Summer 2010 - 558   2011   £45

Rae, Gwynedd *Mary Plain's Big Adventure.* London: Routledge, 1944, First edition; original blue cloth, few slight scratches, pages 119, illustrations by Irene Williamson, name on flyleaf.   R. F. G. Hollett & Son Antiquarian Booksellers   General Catalogue Summer 2010 - 559   2011   £45

Rae, John *Grasshopper Green and the Meadow Mice.* Joliet: Volland, 1922, No additional printings; 8vo., cloth backed pictorial boards, fine in publisher's pictorial box, illustrations by Rae, beautiful copy.   Aleph-Bet Books, Inc.   95 - 576   2011 $300

Raferty, Joseph *Prehistoric Ireland.* London: Batsford, 1951, First edition; pages xvi, 228, 16 plates and 267 text illustrations, original cloth, gilt, dust jacket, little spotted and chipped, few slight tape marks to reverse.   R. F. G. Hollett & Son Antiquarian Booksellers   177 - 722   2011   £30

Raff, George Christian *A System of Natural History.* Edinburgh: G. Mudie and Son, 1796, Volume 1 (of 2), contemporary full leather with gilt decoration, front board nearly detached, edges worn, f.f.e.p. detached, remains of bookplate, owner's inscription, name, foxing, else clean, tight, , xxi, iii, xi, 310, iv, frontispiece and 6 plates, excised, the others may appear in volume 2 in this edition, according to table of contents, which covers both volumes, explanation of plates should be in volume 2, so apparently there was at least one printing error. G. H. Mott Bookseller May 26 2011 - 32089 2011 $325

Raffald, Elizabeth *The Experienced English Housekeeper.* London: printed for the author and sold by R. Baldwin, No. 47 in Pater-noster-Row, 1773, Third edition; 3 copper plates, errata, some creasing to plates, 2 pages of ads at end, 12 pages of index, (5), iii, (1), 366, (2), (12), (2) page, modern half calf. Anthony W. Laywood May 26 2011 - 21562 2011 $646

Raffles, Thomas Stamford *A Discourse Delivered to the Literary and Scientific Society at Java on the 10th of September 1815.* London: Pamphleteer, 1816, First edition thus; 8vo., full later brown leather lettered gilt at spine, pamphlet probaby extracted from a collection of such (pagination 68-105) but with its own titlepage, slight rubbing, very good+. Any Amount of Books May 26 2011 - A6803 2011 $419

Rafinesque, Constantine Samuel *Manual of the Medical Botany of the United States...* Philadelphia: published by Professor Rafinesque, A. M, 1841, 12mo., pages (4), xii, 259, 52 plates colored in green (ink notation to upper margin of a plate, foxing and/or offsetting to many plates), original full sheep professionally rebacked with sympathetic calf, corners worn, library label pasted to front pastedown, lower corner to title and next 2 leaves missing with partial loss to 1 letter, some foxing, title is the rare re-issue of volume 1 only of the "Medical Flora', originally issued in 1828. Raymond M. Sutton, Jr. May 26 2011 - 51742 2011 $1250

Ragge, David *Grasshoppers, Crickets and Cockroaches of the British Isles.* London: Frederick Warne and Co., 1965, First edition; original cloth, gilt, dust jacket little worn, pages xiii, 299, 22 color plates, 130 text figures, library stamp to back of title, scarce. R. F. G. Hollett & Son Antiquarian Booksellers General Catalogue Summer 2010 - 1040 2011 £85

Ragusa, Auguste Frederic Louis Viesse Marmont De, Duke of *The Present State of The Turkish Empire.* London: John Olivier, sold by Simpkin, Marshall & Co., 1839, Folding frontispiece map, final ad leaf, original blue green cloth, virtually imperceptible repairs to spine, booklabel of Cathedral Library, Ely, very good. Jarndyce Antiquarian Booksellers CXCI - 569 2011 £750

Raikes, Elizabeth *Dorothea Beale of Cheltenham.* London: Constable, 1908, Second edition; original green cloth gilt over bevelled boards, pages xii, 432, top edge gilt, 10 plates, some foxing to prelim and final leaves. R. F. G. Hollett & Son Antiquarian Booksellers 175 - 1107 2011 £30

Railroad ABC. London: Tuck, 1903, Narrow folio, die-cut in shape of train, several margin mends and one chip, slight soil, very good, every page beautifully illustrated. Aleph-Bet Books, Inc. 95 - 41 2011 $175

Railway ABC. London: Warne, circa, 1870, 4to., pictorial wrappers, very good+, printed on one side of the paper by Kronheim, featuring six fine full page illustrations. Aleph-Bet Books, Inc. 95 - 42 2011 $300

Raine, Matthew *A Sermon Preached at Kingston Upon Thames, on Sunday Feb. 19 1786, Upon the Death of Captain Richard Peirce...* London: printed by C. Macrae and published by G. Kearsley, Messrs. J. and J. Merrill, Cambridge and J. Fletcher, Oxford, 1786, Only edition; 4to., (2) 5-29 (1) pages, marginal perforation in final leaf, fine, uncut and stitched as issued, very rare. John Drury Rare Books 153 - 123 2011 £475

Raistrick, Arthur *Open Fell Hidden Dale.* Kendal: Frank Peters, 1991, Second edition; 4to., original glazed pictorial boards, pages 144, some 95 superb photographs. R. F. G. Hollett & Son Antiquarian Booksellers General Catalogue Summer 2010 - 1395 2011 £30

Rajan, B. *Focus.* Denis Dobson, 1934-1950, First edition; volumes 1-5, all with dust jackets. I. D. Edrich May 26 2011 - 82717 2011 $419

Raleigh, Walter 1552-1618 *The Arts of Empire and Mysteries of State Discabineted.* London: printed by G. Croom for Joseph Watts, 1692, Modern full calf gilt, pages (vi), 238, (ii). R. F. G. Hollett & Son Antiquarian Booksellers 175 - 1108 2011 £450

Ralph, Julian *War's Brighter Side.* London: C. Arthur Pearson, 1901, First edition; 8vo., pages xvi, 421, frontispiece, illustrations, original blue decorative cloth. J. & S. L. Bonham Antiquarian Booksellers Africa 4/20/2011 - 8288 2011 £50

Ralston, W. *Tippoo: a Tale of Tiger.* London: George Routledge and Sons, nd. circa, 1905, Oblong large 8vo., original pictorial wrappers, one short edge tear and chip, pages 28, illustrations. R. F. G. Hollett & Sons Antiquarian Booksellers 170 - 573 2011 £85

Ramazzini, Bernardino *De Morbis Artificum Diatriba.* Modena: Antoni Capponi, 1700, First edition; 8vo., viii, 360 pages, contemporary paste paper boards, paper covered spine with hand lettered paper label, soiled, one tear in backstrip, some mending, uncut, small dampstain in gutter of first few leaves, very faint dampstain in top margin of several quires, very nice, fully untrimmed, cloth clamshell box with leather label.   Joseph J. Felcone Inc.   Fall Miscellany 2010 - 102   2011 $8000

Ramey, Earl *The Beginnings of Marysville.* San Francisco: California Historical Society, 1936, First book edition; (8), 105 pages, frontispiece, titlepage map in color, 4 plates, 2 full page facsimiles, large folding map, reddish brown cloth backed tan boards, printed paper labels on spine and front cover, small surface smudge to bottom of front cover, fine, very scarce.   Argonaut Book Shop   Recent Acquisitions Summer 2010 - 164   2011 $350

Ramm, Agatha *The Political Correspondence of Mr. Gladstone and Lord Granville 1868-1876.* London: Royal Historical Society, 1952, 2 volumes, original cloth, gilt, pages xix, 246; v, 247-518, library label and few stamps.   R. F. G. Hollett & Son Antiquarian Booksellers   175 - 1109   2011   £30

Ramon Y Cajal, Santiago   1852-1934 *Histology of the Nervous System of Man and Vertebrates.* New York: Oxford University Press, 1995, First printing of this edition; thick 8vo., xl, 805; x, 806 pages, 1025 figures, gilt and green stamped pictorial blue cloth, new, from the Medical Library of Dr. Clare Gray Peterson.   Jeff Weber Rare Books   162 - 249   2011 $210

Ramon Y Cajal, Santiago   1852-1934 *Precepts and Counsels on Scientific Imagination: Stimulants of the Spirit.* New York: Oxford University Press, 1951, First edition in English, trade issue; 8vo., xii, 180 pages, frontispiece tipped in, maroon cloth, gilt stamped spine title, ownership signature of John G. Kidd, 1952, fine, from the Medical Library of Dr. Clare Gray Peterson.   Jeff Weber Rare Books   162 - 250   2011 $100

Rand, Ayn *Atlas Shrugged.* New York: Random House, 1957, 1967. Stated Ninth printing, # 68 of 2000 signed by author on limitation page of the Tenth Anniversary edition; some mostly mild staining and fading of covers, slight paper split before titlepage, very good in near fine slipcase.   Charles Agvent   2010 Summer Miscellany - 58   2011 $2000

Rand, Ayn *The Fountainhead.* Indianapolis: Bobbs Merrill Co., 1943, First edition, first issue; octavo, rare first issue dust jacket, with back panel listing 16 Bobbs Merrill books and front flap with with price of $3.00, dust jacket expertly restored, original red cloth.   Heritage Book Shop   Booth A12 51st NY International Antiquarian Book Fair April 8-10 2011 - 106   2011 $25,000

Rand, Edward Sprague *The Rhododendron and "American Plants"...* Boston: 1871, One of 20 presentation copies on large paper; 10 hand colored lithographed plates (one folding & loose), large 8vo., pages xx, 188, contemporary red half morocco (some wear, light foxing to prelim pages, unobtrusive embossed library stamp on title and plates, pages tanned, light marginal dampstaining to 3 pages, modern half morocco clamshell box, the Sondley Reference Library.   Raymond M. Sutton, Jr.   May 26 2011 - 22377   2011 $1700

Randall-MacIver, David *Mediaeval Rhodesia.* London: Macmillan, 1906, First edition; quarto, pages xv, 106, 36 plates, original green decorative cloth with recent reback, small stain on lower cover, inscribed to Frederick Hoppin with author's compliments.   J. & S. L. Bonham Antiquarian Booksellers   Africa 4/20/2011 - 8901   2011   £40

Randles, Marshall *Substitution a Treatise on the Atonement.* London: J. Grose Thomas and Co., 1877, First edition; original green cloth gilt, pages xv, 255, few spots to prelims, scarce.   R. F. G. Hollett & Son Antiquarian Booksellers   175 - 1110   2011   £35

Rankin, Ian *The Flood.* Edinburgh: Polygon, 1986, First edition; signed by author, fine in dust jacket.   Buckingham Books   May 26 2011 - 25118   2011 $2500

Rankin, J. T. *"Dacca Diaries." (From the Journal and Proceedings, Asiatic Society of Bengal. New Series Volume XVI 1920 No. 4 Issued 22nd Nov. 1920).* Bengal: Asiatic Society of Bengal, 1820, Offprint; (91-158) pages, small 4to., stapled paper wrappers torn and chipped, otherwise very good, clean, unmarked.   Kaaterskill Books   12 - 298   2011 $75

Ransome, Arthur *Aladdin and His Wonderful Lamp in Rhyme.* London: Nisbet, n.d., 1919, First edition; 4to., pictorial cloth, near fine, 12 magnificent tipped in color plates with tissue guards an with profusion of stunning black and whites on every page of text, beautiful book.   Aleph-Bet Books, Inc.   95 - 339   2011 $600

Ransome, Arthur *The Big Six.* London: Cape, 1940, First edition; original cloth, gilt, later dust jacket, pages 400, 23 illustrations, 2 maps, 2 color maps on endpapers.   R. F. G. Hollett & Sons Antiquarian Booksellers   170 - 574   2011   £85

Ransome, Arthur *The Book of Love.* London: T. C. & E. C. Jack, n.d., First edition; pages xx, 459, large 8vo., original blue decorated buckram gilt, top edge gilt, title spread and decorations to prelims in black and orange, two contents leaves little carelessly opened, otherwise excellent.   R. F. G. Hollett & Son Antiquarian Booksellers   General Catalogue Summer 2010 - 879   2011   £140

Ransome, Arthur *Coot Club.* London: Cape, 1934, First edition; original cloth, gilt, trifle rubbed, pages 352, with 22 illustrations, 2 colored maps on endpapers, joints cracked, few spots to flyleaves.   R. F. G. Hollett & Sons Antiquarian Booksellers   170 - 575 2011   £65

Ransome, Arthur *Great Northern?* London: Cape, 1947, First edition; original cloth, gilt, pages 352, with 23 illustrations and maps on endpapers.   R. F. G. Hollett & Sons Antiquarian Booksellers   170 - 576 2011   £65

Ransome, Arthur *Mainly About Fishing.* Bovey Tracey: The Flyfisher's Classic Library, 1994, Limited edition 950 copies; quarter crocodile navy blue morocco gilt, slipcase, pages xx, 159, 8 plates, fine.   R. F. G. Hollett & Son Antiquarian Booksellers   General Catalogue Summer 2010 - 1274 2011   £50

Ransome, Arthur *Missee Lee.* London: Cape, 1941, First edition; pages 336, 26 illustrations, colored maps on endpapers, original cloth, gilt.   R. F. G. Hollett & Sons Antiquarian Booksellers   170 - 577 2011   £45

Ransome, Arthur *The Picts and the Martyrs; or Not Welcome at All.* London: Cape, 1943, First edition; original cloth, gilt, faint creasing to upper board, dust jacket extremities trifle rubbed, pages 304, with 20 illustrations and 2 color maps on endpapers.   R. F. G. Hollett & Sons Antiquarian Booksellers   170 - 577a 2011   £325

Ransome, Arthur *Pigeon Post.* London: Cape, 1936, First edition; original cloth, gilt, pages 384, with 23 illustrations and colored maps on endpapers, rear joint cracked, inscription.   R. F. G. Hollett & Sons Antiquarian Booksellers   170 - 579 2011   £65

Ransome, Arthur *We Didn't Mean to Go to Sea.* London: Cape, 1937, First edition; original cloth, gilt, pages 351, with 34 illustrations and maps on endpaper.   R. F. G. Hollett & Sons Antiquarian Booksellers   170 - 582 2011   £120

Rao, C. Hayavadana *Mysore Gazetteer.* Bangalore: printed at the Government Press, 1927-1930, New edition; Six of Eight volumes, volume I, Volume II parts I and II, Volumes III-V, color reproduction, color map, four fold out charts, 8vo., cloth, lacking last two parts of volume II, Volume I, good only, rear board, dampstained, boards wormed, spine worn, leaves clean and very good, volume II part I very good+, volume II Part II very good, tiny wormhole on rear joint, minor staining at fore edge, endpapers offset, volume III boards wormed, tears to head of spine, otherwise binding solid and leaves bright and clean, volume IV very good, wear to one corner and few tiny wormholes to inner margin on few leaves, volume V good, spine rubbed, rear board, endpapers and rear blank dampstained (not affecting leaves which are clean), overall set good to very good.   Kaaterskill Books   12 - 158 2011 $150

Raphael, John N. *The Caillaux Drama.* Max Goschen, 1914, First edition; original blue cloth gilt over bevelled boards, pages (vi), 323, top edge gilt, 25 plates, including gravure frontispiece, some spots to fore edge.   R. F. G. Hollett & Son Antiquarian Booksellers   175 - 1111 2011   £35

Raskin, Ellen *The Westing Game.* New York: Dutton, 1978, Stated first edition; quarter cloth and boards, fine in very good+ dust jacket (slight wear to spine ends, price clipped).   Aleph-Bet Books, Inc.   95 - 482 2011 $350

Raspe, Rudolf Erich   1737-1794   *The Travels and Surprising Adventures of Baron Munchausen.* London: William Tegg, 1868, Five woodcuts by George Cruikshank half title, color frontispiece, plates and illustrations, 4 pages ads, original green cloth blocked in blind, gilt and black, 2 long blue inkstains to back board, slightly affecting spine, otherwise nice.   Jarndyce Antiquarian Booksellers   CXCI - 462 2011   £85

Ratcliffe, Dorthy Una *Island-of-the-Little Yars.* Frederick Muller, 1947, First edition; large 8vo., original patterned cloth, dust jacket little worn and chipped, price clipped, pages 233, illustrations, including tipped in color frontispiece.   R. F. G. Hollett & Sons Antiquarian Booksellers   170 - 584 2011   £30

Ratel, Simonne *Mademoiselle Tarlataine au Pays du Cinema.* Paris: Librarie Plan, 1934, First edition; oblong 4to., cloth backed pictorial boards, 30 pages, light cover wear, very good+, illustrations by Jacqueline Deusche with charming color illustrations.   Aleph-Bet Books, Inc.   95 - 290 2011 $325

Raumer, Frederick Von *England in 1835; Being a Series of Letters Written to Friends in Germany During a Residence in London and Excursions into the Provinces.* London: John Murray, 1836, First English edition; 3 volumes, half title in volume I, 2 pages ads in volume III, uncut, original drab boards, glazed blue green cloth spines, slightly rubbed paper labels, exceptional copy in original binding.   Jarndyce Antiquarian Booksellers   CXCI - 354 2011   £500

Rauthmel, Richard *The Roman Antiquities of Overborough.* Kirkby Lonsdale: Arthur Foster, 1824, First 8vo. edition; contemporary paper covered boards, rebacked in matching cloth with paper spine label, pages vi, 138, aquatint frontispiece (slightly offset on title) and 5 plans and plates, 1 folding, 1 in facsimile, scarce.   R. F. G. Hollett & Son Antiquarian Booksellers   177 - 729 2011   £140

Ravensclough, Arthur *The Journal of Commonwealth Literature.* Leeds: Heinemann/University of Leeds, 1965-1969, First edition; volumes 1-8, September 1965-December 1969, wrappers, pages 1293, sound, very good, slight handling and shelfwear.   Any Amount of Books   May 29 2011 - A35467 2011 $255

Rawle, William H. *A Practical Treatise on the Law of Covenants for Title.* Boston: Little Brown, 1860, Third edition; very good, old law calf. Bookworm & Silverfish 678 - 105 2011 $175

Rawlet, John *A Dialogue Betwixt Two Protestants.* London: printed for Samuel Tidmarsh, 1685, First edition; pages (xx), 262, early full calf, recased, front flyleaf little creased, short thin wormtrack in first few leaves repaired. R. F. G. Hollett & Son Antiquarian Booksellers 175 - 1113 2011 £220

Rawlings, Marjorie Kinnan *Cross Creek.* New York: Scribner's, 1942, First edition; fine, dust jacket very good with wear to extremities, chipping to spine ends and 1 x 1/8 inch piece missing near top of spine, very good, wear to extremities, chipping to spine ends. Bella Luna Books May 26 2011 - t7959CO 2011 $440

Rawlinson, George *History of Ancient Egypt.* London: Longmans Green, 1881, First edition; 2 volumes, original cloth, gilt, hinges trifle rubbed, pages xx, 554, 24; xiii, 567, map, 9 plates and 253 woodcut illustrations. R. F. G. Hollett & Son Antiquarian Booksellers 177 - 730 2011 £140

Rawlinson, George *History of Phoenicia.* London: Longmans, Green and Co., 1889, First edition; large 8vo., original brown cloth, gilt, hinges trifle rubbed, pages xvii, 583, 24, with 1 plates, 2 colored maps and 122 text woodcuts, very good, clean, sound. R. F. G. Hollett & Son Antiquarian Booksellers 177 - 731 2011 £85

Rawnsley, H. D. *Harvey Goodwin, Bishop of Carlisle.* London: John Murray, 1896, First edition; modern full black levant morocco gilt with contrasting spine label and blind ruled panels, pages xi, 372, 28 with 2 etched portraits, handsome copy, scarce. R. F. G. Hollett & Son Antiquarian Booksellers 173 - 943 2011 £175

Rawnsley, H. D. *Henry Whitehead 1825-1896.* Glasgow: James MacLehose, 1898, First edition; original cloth, gilt, pages ix, 250, untrimmed, frontispiece, flyleaves browned. R. F. G. Hollett & Son Antiquarian Booksellers 173 - 944 2011 £60

Rawnsley, H. D. *Literary Associations of the English Lakes. Volume 1 and 2.* Glasgow: James MacLehose and Sons, 1894, First edition; 2 volumes, original green cloth, gilt, extremities trifle rubbed, pages xi, 232; vii, 250, (ii), folding map (little torn), nice, clean set. R. F. G. Hollett & Son Antiquarian Booksellers 173 - 946 2011 £60

Rawnsley, H. D. *Memories of the Tennysons.* Glasgow: MacLehose, 1900, First edition; original cloth, gilt, pages xiv, (i), 254, 16 plates, flyleaves little browned, label on front flyleaf. R. F. G. Hollett & Son Antiquarian Booksellers 173 - 947 2011 £35

Rawnsley, H. D. *Ruskin and the English Lakes.* Glasgow: James MacLehose and Sons, 1901, First edition; contemporary cloth, gilt, extremities trifle rubbed, pages xii, 244, 10 plates, front joint trifle strained, scarce, signatures of T. W. Ogilvie, F. G.S. of Barrow and St. Bees, loosely inserted is autograph postcard initialled from Rawnsley to Ogilvie apologising for being too busy to help him. R. F. G. Hollett & Son Antiquarian Booksellers 173 - 949 2011 £65

Rawnsley, H. D. *A Sonnet Chronicle 1900-1906.* Glasgow: Jame Maclehose, 1906, First edition; original cloth, dust jacket, little defective, pages xii, 84, top edge gilt, uncut. R. F. G. Hollett & Son Antiquarian Booksellers 173 - 950 2011 £35

Rawnsley, H. D. *Valete. Tennyson and Other Memorial Poems.* Glasgow: James MacLehose and Sons, 1893, First edition; pages xv, 176, untrimmed, flyleaves rather browned, otherwise fine. R. F. G. Hollett & Son Antiquarian Booksellers 173 - 951 2011 £45

Rawnsley, Willingham, Mrs. *Country Sketches for City Dwellers.* London: Adam and Charles Black, 1908, First edition; 8vo., pages ix 166, 16 full page illustrations in color, original publisher's green cloth lettered gilt on spine and on front cover and with gilt and dark green leaf illustrations on spine and cover, booksellers label on pastedown, slight browning on endpaper, else fine in fine dust jacket with one short closed tear. Any Amount of Books May 29 2011 - A49306 2011 $238

Ray, Anthony *English Delftware Pottery in the Robert Hall Warren Collection, Ashmolean, Oxford.* Boston: Boston Book & Art Shop, 1968, First US edition; large 8vo., original cloth, gilt, dust jacket, pages 248, with 8 color plates and 110 pages of monochrome plates. R. F. G. Hollett & Son Antiquarian Booksellers General Catalogue Summer 2010 - 302 2011 £85

Ray, Edward *Inland Golf.* London: T. Werner Laurie, n.d., 1913, First edition; 8vo., original publisher's red cloth lettered gilt on spine and on front cover, pages xii, 234, with 10 page publisher's catalog at rear, review copy with publisher's printed note aking for review loosely inseted, dated 1 May 1913, decent, near very good with slight soiling, slight marking and slight looseness to a couple of photos, all 32 plates present. Any Amount of Books May 29 2011 - 43328 2011 $238

Ray, John *A Collection of English Proverbs Digested into a Convenient Method for the Speedy Finding any One Upon Occasion...* Cambridge: printed by John Hayes, printer to the University for W. Morden, 1678, Title printed in red and black, Hebrew proverbs printed in Hebrew, small hole in title with loss of two letters and part of a third, few headlines shaved, bit browned or stained in places, pages (viii), 414, (1, ads), 8vo., old (not contemporary) calf, red lettering piece, rebacked and recornered, contemporary signature on title of one Thomas Goodwin, five proverbs added in manuscript in a contemporary hand (possibly Goodwin's but much messier that the ownership inscription), sound.   Blackwell Rare Books   B166 - 88   2011   £550

Ray, John *Travels through the Low Countries, Germany, Italy and France.*   London: for the various booksellers, 1738, Second edition; 2 volumes, 8vo., (4), iv, 428; 119, (1); 12, 489, (3), 44 pages, title printed in red and black, half titles, 3 engraved plates at volume II pages 4-5, contemporary English half, spines gilt, from the library of the Earls of Macclesfield at Shirburn Castle.   Maggs Bros. Ltd.   1440 - 175   2011   £450

Raymond, Walter *English Country Life.*   London: T. N. Foulis, 1910, First edition; original buckram gilt, spine little faded, pages viii, 444, (iv), top edge gilt, untrimmed, 16 color plates by Wilfrid Ball tipped onto grey card.   R. F. G. Hollett & Son Antiquarian Booksellers   General Catalogue Summer 2010 - 880   2011   £45

Raynal, Guillaume Thomas Francois 1713-1796 *A Philosophical and Political History of the Settlements and Trade of the Europeans in the East and West Indies.*   London: W. Strahan, 1783, First edition; 4 volumes (of 8), volumes 1, 2, 4 and 5, 8vo., full brown tree calf leather, together 1885 pages, some wear to corners, scuffing and rubbing, hinges slightly split but holding, text, frontispiece and folding maps in excellent condition, near very good.   Any Amount of Books   May 26 2011 - A73754   2011 $403

Read-Heimerdinger, Jenny *The Bezan Text of Acts.*   Sheffield Academic Press, 2002, First edition; original cloth, pages xi, 379.   R. F. G. Hollett & Son Antiquarian Booksellers   175 - 1116   2011   £30

Read, Charles Hercules *Catalouge of the Works of Art Bequeathed to the British Museum by Baron Ferdinand Rothschild 1898.*   London: British Museum, 1902, 129 pages, 55 plates, 42 figures in text, few marginal notes to text, good copy in original olive green cloth, top edge gilt, spine sunned.   Ken Spelman Rare Books   68 - 99 2011   £40

Read, Francis *W. G. I. Parson.*   New York: 1945, First and only edition; 117 pages, ex-library with shelf wear to backstrip, missing f.e.p.   Bookworm & Silverfish   679 - 205   2011 $150

Read, Georgia Willis *A Pioneer of 1850. George Willis Read 1819-1880. The Record of a Journey Overland from Independence, Missouri to Hangtown (Placerville), California in the Spring of 1850.*   Boston: Little Brown and Co., 1927, First edition; xxvi, 185 pages, frontispiece, 20 plates, folding map, blue cloth, gilt lettered spine, spine bit darkened, fine, scarce.   Argonaut Book Shop   Recent Acquisitions Summer 2010 - 165   2011 $90

Read, Herbert *The Green Child.*   New York: New Directions, First edition; 8vo., pages 194, light green cloth, cover faded, else very good, tight copy.   Second Life Books Inc.   174 - 267   2011 $65

Read, Herbert *The Green Child.*   London: Heinemann, 1935, First edition; 8vo., original publisher's green cloth lettered gilt on spine and on front cover, pages 256, black endpapers slightly mottled, otherwise clean, very good+, excellent.   Any Amount of Books   May 29 2011 - A38266   2011 $213

Reade, W. Winwood *The Veil of Isis or the Mysteries of the Druids.*   London: Charles J. Skeet, 1861, First edition; 8vo., quarter leather marbled boards lettered gilt at spine, pages vi, 250, uncut, slight wear at foot of spine neat small inked label on spine with number 96, corners rubbed, neat name on front endpaper, else sound, very good, armorial bookplate of Joan Emlyn by W. P. B. on pastedown.   Any Amount of Books   May 29 2011 - A42513   2011 $238

Reamy, Tom *San Diego Lightfoot Sue and Other Stories.*   Kansas City: Earthlight, 1979, First edition; octavo, cloth.   L. W. Currey, Inc.   124 - 205   2011 $200

Reaney, Percy H. *A Grammar of the Dialect of Penrith (Cumberland).*   Manchester: University Press, 1927, Original green cloth gilt, pages xv, 214, scarce.   R. F. G. Hollett & Son Antiquarian Booksellers   173 - 953   2011   £95

Reaney, Percy H. *Records of Queen Elizabeth Grammar School, Penrith.*   Kendal: Titus Wilson, 1915, First edition; original cloth, dust jacket (spine little faded, a short edge tear), pages (ii), 234, 30 pages of plates and numerous diagrams, scarce.   R. F. G. Hollett & Son Antiquarian Booksellers   173 - 954   2011   £60

Recamier, Mme. *Memoirs & Correspondence of Madame Recamier. (with) Madam Recamier and Her Friends.*   Boston: Knight and Miller, 1867, New illustrated edition; (xvi, 408; xviii, 281 pages), thick 8vo., three quarter brown morocco, elaborately gilt decorated spines, compartments. raised bands, all edges gilt, fine, attractive two volume set, both profusely illustrated and mostly unopened.   Paulette Rose Fine and Rare Books   32 - 145   2011 $375

Rede, Alexis Baron De *Alexis. The Memoirs of the Baron De Rede.* Wimborne Minster, Dorset: Privately published, privately published, 2005, 4to., 174 pages, illustrations in color and black and white, fine in fine dust jacket.   Any Amount of Books   May 26 2011 - A77078   2011 $503

Reed, Brian *Crewe to Carlisle.* Ian Allan, 1969, First edition; original cloth, dust jacket, spine little faded, short edge tear, pages (ii), 234, with 30 pages of plates and numerous diagrams, scarce.   R. F. G. Hollett & Son Antiquarian Booksellers   173 - 955   2011   £45

Reed, Jeremy *No Refuge Here.* N.P.: (London): Giles and Jonathan Leman, 1981, First edition, number 257 of 40 copies; 4to., original publisher's green wrappers, pages 4, etching (tissue protected) by Giles Leaman, signed by author and artist, faint creasing, otherwise clean, bright, very good+.   Any Amount of Books   May 29 2011 - A64979   2011 $306

Reed, Langford *The Complete Limerick Book.* Jarrolds, 1924, First edition; small 4to., original yellow pictorial cloth, trifle bumped in places, pages 147, line drawings by Bateman, few scattered spots, 2 mss. limericks on flyleaf.   R. F. G. Hollett & Son Antiquarian Booksellers   General Catalogue Summer 2010 - 702   2011   £30

Reed, Langford *Nonsense Verses. An Anthology.* Jarrolds, 1925, First edition; small 4to., original green pictorial cloth, spine little faded, pages 143, with numerous line drawings, presentation copy inscribed by Reed.   R. F. G. Hollett & Son Antiquarian Booksellers   General Catalogue Summer 2010 - 703   2011   £65

Reed, Walt *Harold Von Schmidt Draws and Paints Old West.* Flagstaff: Northland Press, 1972, First edition, special limited edition of 104 copies, signed; tall quarto, leather and pictorial red cloth, grey endsheets, xvii, (1), 230 pages, numerous illustrations, in handsome slipcase with morocco label, issued joint with Von's first sculpture "The Startled Grizzly" 7 inches high with handsome patina and mounted on light colored marble base, very fine.   Buckingham Books   May 26 2011 - 22478   2011 $2000

Rees, Paul *The Leaving of Liverpool.* Liverpool: Merryside Maritime Museum, 1986, Large 4to., pictorial card folder in original unbroken shrinkwrap plastic, fine set, now scarce.   R. F. G. Hollett & Son Antiquarian Booksellers   General Catalogue Summer 2010 - 617   2011   £40

Refuge, Eustache De *Traicte De La Covr ou Instruction des Courtisans.* Amsterdam: chez les Elzeviers, 1656, Derniere edition; 12mo., pages (viii), 305, (ie. 350), (xxvi), contemporary name on titlepage and later ownership signature on endpaper, contemporary vellum, nice, clean copy.   Second Life Books Inc.   174 - 268   2011 $650

Regnery, Dorothy F. *The Battle of Santa Clara January 2 1847.* San Jose: Smith and McKay Printing Co., 1978, First limited edition, one of 100 copies signed by author; small 4to., vi, 154 pages, reproductions of color sketches and black and white sketches, other illustrations, white linen with gilt lettered spine and cover, very fine with matching white linen slipcase (slightly soiled).   Argonaut Book Shop   Recent Acquisitions Summer 2010 - 166   2011 $150

Rego, Paula *Nursery Rhymes.* London: Folio Society, 1994, First edition thus, one of 100 copies signed by Rego, specially bound; 4to., pages 72, 29 x 22 cm., frontispiece and 35 full page illustrations, quarter bound in Nigerian goatskin with hand marbled sides by Ann Muir and are signed by the artist, printed on Banbury Wove paper, fine in fine slipcase, this copy no. letter C indicates that it is one of a lettered edition (presumably of 26) as other limited edition, fine.   Any Amount of Books   May 26 2011 - A38828   2011 $797

Reichard, Gladys *Navajo Medicine Man.* New York: 1939, xvi, 83 pages, 25 plates, some rubbing to original slipcase, short tears to two prelim pages, else clean and near fine, tissue guards in place.   Dumont Maps & Books of the West   113 - 46   2011 $500

Reid, Forrest *The Spring Song.* London: Edward Arnold, 1916, First edition; pages viii, 312, 8vo., original publisher's green cloth lettered dark green on cover and spine, prelims slightly foxed, bright very good+, slight marks on pastedown, neat non-authorial contemporary inscription.   Any Amount of Books   May 29 2011 - A42076   2011 $255

Reid, James *The Life of Christ in Woodcuts.* London: Elkin Mathews & Marrot, 1930, First UK edition; original three quarter cloth with silver and black patterned boards, pages (158), woodcut half title, title printed in red and black, dedication leaf and chapter heading pages and 71 striking full page woodcuts.   R. F. G. Hollett & Son Antiquarian Booksellers   175 - 1118   2011   £120

Reid, John C. *Reid's Tramp, or a Journal of the Incidents of Ten Months Travel through Texas, New Mexico, Arizona, Sonora and California.* Austin: Steck Co., 1935, Facsimile reprint of rare original journals; (2), 245 pages, publisher's dark green cloth, gilt, one lower corner very slightly jammed, but very fine.   Argonaut Book Shop   Recent Acquisitions Summer 2010 - 167   2011 $90

Reid, Margaret J. C. *The Arthurian Legend.* Oliver & Boyd, 1960, Original cloth, gilt, dust jacket (trifling wear to extremities), pages viii, 277, related ephemeral article loosely inserted.   R. F. G. Hollett & Son Antiquarian Booksellers   175 - 1119   2011   £35

Reid, Mayne 1818-1883 *The Young Voyageurs or Boy Hunters in the North.* London: David Bogue, 1855, Second edition; 12 illustrations by W. Harvey, pages viii, 472, with 12 illustrations by W. Harvey, contemporary full calf gilt prize binding, handsome gilt stamp of the Welsey College Sheffield on upper board.   R. F. G. Hollett & Sons Antiquarian Booksellers   170 - 585   2011   £45

Reigate, Emily *An Illustrated Guide to Lace.* Antique Collectors Club, 1986, First edition; 262 pages, with 12 color plates and 700 illustrations, original cloth, gilt, dust jacket.   R. F. G. Hollett & Son Antiquarian Booksellers General Catalogue Summer 2010 - 303   2011   £45

Reilly, Paul *An Introduction to Regency Architecture.* London: Art and Technics, 1948, First edition; large 8vo., original cloth, gilt, dust jacket trifle torn and chipped, pages 96, 60 plates, 15 text illustrations, from the library of Lake District poet Norman Nicholson, with his bookplate.   R. F. G. Hollett & Son Antiquarian Booksellers   177 - 734   2011   £30

Reilly, Robin *Wedgwood.* Barrie & Jenkins, 1973, First edition; tall 4to., original cloth, gilt, dust jacket spine and edges faded pages 379, illustrations, 16 color plates.   R. F. G. Hollett & Son Antiquarian Booksellers   General Catalogue Summer 2010 - 305   2011   £75

Reilly, Robin *Wedgwood.* Antique Collectors Club, 1996, 4to., original cloth, gilt, dust jacket, 514 pages, illustrations, and with 132 color plates.   R. F. G. Hollett & Son Antiquarian Booksellers   General Catalogue Summer 2010 - 304   2011   £75

Reimann, Guenter *The Vampire Economy: Doing Business Under Fascism.* New York: Vanguard Press, 1939, First edition; near fine in very good or better dust jacket with little toning of spine, scarce, very uncommon in dust jacket.   Between the Covers   169 - BTC339649   2011 $450

Reindorp, James *Selections from the Pioneer, A Manuscript Magazine.* Published at 6, Wine Office Court, 1875, Frontispiece, plates, illustrations, original red brown cloth, blocked in blind, lettered in gilt, little dulled, rubbed.   Jarndyce Antiquarian Booksellers   CXCI - 463   2011   £85

The Relation Betweene the Lord of a Manor and the Coppy Holder His Tenant Delivered in the Learned Readings of the Late Excellent and Famous Lawyer, Char. Calthorpe. London: The Manorial Society, 1917, Pages iii, 76, (vii), original cloth backed boards, scarce.   R. F. G. Hollett & Son Antiquarian Booksellers   175 - 32   2011   £60

A Relation of Three Years Sufferings of Robert Everard Upon the Coast of Affada Near Madagascar in a Voyage to India in the Year 1686. London: Churchill, n.d., 1732, First edition; folio, pages 257-28, disbound but clean.   J. & S. L. Bonham Antiquarian Booksellers   Africa 4/20/2011 - 9284   2011   £35

Religious Tract Society *Tracts. Second Series.* London: Religious Tract Society, n.d. c. 1830's, Old cloth, paper spine label, rather worn, first few leaves lightly dampstained at top edge.   R. F. G. Hollett & Son Antiquarian Booksellers   175 - 1120   2011   £75

Religious Tract Society *The Visitor and Monthly Instructor for 1844.* London: Religious Tract Society, 1844, Contemporary half roan gilt with marbled boards, spine little faded, pages vii, 472, with 26 text woodcuts.   R. F. G. Hollett & Son Antiquarian Booksellers   175 - 1121   2011   £35

Religious Tract Society *The Visitor and Monthly Instructor for 1845.* London: Religious Tract Society, 1845, Contemporary half roan gilt with marbled boards, spine little faded, pages viii, 472, with 25 text woodcuts.   R. F. G. Hollett & Son Antiquarian Booksellers   175 - 1122   2011   £35

Religious Tract Society *The Visitor and Monthly Instructor for 1846.* London: Religious Tract Society, 1846, Contemporary half roan gilt with marbled boards, spine little faded, pages viii, 472, with 24 text woodcuts.   R. F. G. Hollett & Son Antiquarian Booksellers   175 - 1123   2011   £35

Remarks by a Junior to His Senior, on an Article in the Edinburgh Review of January, 1844 on the State of Ireland and the Measures for Its Improvement. London: James Ridgway, 1844, First edition; last 2 leaves slightly foxed, 83, (1) pages, modern boards, printed paper label,.   Anthony W. Laywood   May 26 2011 - 18117   2011 $369

Remarque, Erich Maria *Heaven Has No Favourites.* London: Hutchinson, 1961, First edition; 8vo., pages 254, signed presentation from author to Susan Cabling (?) Porto Rono 4th Sept. 1961, very slight lean, otherwise very good in slightly used and slightly nicked, near very good dust jacket.   Any Amount of Books   May 29 2011 - A75622   2011 $298

Reminiscences of Much Travelled Little Girl "A Fille de (du) Regiment". Delhi: Punjab Herald Press, 1883, 15.5cm., 32 pages, frontispiece with original mounted photo portrait of a young girl, nine tiny ink manuscripts.   Jeff Weber Rare Books   163 - 122   2011 $200

Renard, Jules *Carrots.* Grey Walls Press, 1946, First edition; original cloth, gilt, dust jacket spine little dulled, pages 147, illustrations, near fine.   R. F. G. Hollett & Son Antiquarian Booksellers   General Catalogue Summer 2010 - 881   2011   £50

Rennell, James *The Geographical System of Herodotus, Examined and Explained.* London: printed by W. Bulmer and Co., 1800, First edition; frontispiece (foxed) and 11 engraved plates (all but one folding, all lightly foxed), paper evenly toned throughout, touch of spotting and offsetting from plates in places, pages x, 766, (2), 4to., contemporary dark blue straight grained morocco, boards bordered with triple gilt fillet, spine with five raised bands, compartments bordered with triple gilt fillet, second compartment gilt lettered direct, decorative gilt rolls at head, foot and on hands, marbled edges and endpapers, small gilt armorial stamp on boards, little rubbed at extremities, spine lightly faded, good.   Blackwell Rare Books   B166 - 89   2011   £850

Rennert, Jack *Alphonse Mucha: The Complete Posters and Panels.* Boston: G. K. Hall & Co., 1984, First edition; 4to., illustrations in color and black and white, 405 pages, fine in fine dust jacket.   Any Amount of Books   May 26 2011 - A75544   2011 $411

Renneville, Sophie De Senneterre *La Mere Gouvernante, ou Principes de Politesse Fonde sur les Qualites du Coeur.* Paris: Bellin le Prieur, n.d., 1827, First edition; 12mo., 249 pages, original provincial green drab paper wrapper, rebacked with matching paper and title label on spine, full page copper engraved frontispiece, printed on handmade untrimmed paper, library stamp on verso of frontispiece, some staining at beginning and damp spot at corner of few last pages, not interfering with text, light soiling and chipping at edges of wrappers, browning along edges, rare, good copy.   Hobbyhorse Books   56 - 129   2011 $270

Renouf, Jane *The Lake Artists Society.* Ambleside: Lake Artists Society, 2004, First edition; large 4to., original cloth, gilt, dust jacket, pages xi, 310, illustrations in color, superb work.   R. F. G. Hollett & Son Antiquarian Booksellers   173 - 958   2011   £35

Renton, Andrew *Marc Quinn: Chemical Life Support.* London: White Cube, 2005, First edition; 4to., color illustrated wrappers, illustrations in color, signed presentation from author to Norman Rosenthal, 40 pages, fine.   Any Amount of Books   May 29 2011 - A47541   2011 $204

Rentoul, Annie *Fairyland.* Melbourne: Ramsay Pub., 1926, First edition, limited to 1000 numbered copies signed by Ida Rentoul Outhwaite; folio, blue gilt cloth, top edge gilt, 166 pages, including subscriber list, corner of frontispiece small crease, else fine and bright, pictorial endpapers and 51 mounted plates with tissue guards, 19 plates in color plates and 32 in black and white, especially nice, scarce.   Aleph-Bet Books, Inc.   95 - 405   2011 $7950

Rentoul, Annie *Fairyland of Ida Rentoul Outhwaite.* London: A. & C. Black Ltd., 1931,   First English edition; small folio, blue cloth with dark blue lettering and vignette on front cover and spine, full color pictorial dust jacket with some minor wear along upper edges, 128 numbered pages with 31 full page illustrations, 16 in full color, the rest black and whites, with additional drawings for text by Outhwaite.   Jo Ann Reisler, Ltd.   86 - 185   2011 $3500

Rentoul, Annie *Mollie's Bunyip.* Melbourne: Robert Jolley, 1904, First edition; oblong 4to., string bound pictorial wrappers, (48) pages, edges frayed with some mends, last leaf restored (all blank except for the last two letters of the word 'end') else really very good+, 11 full page black and whites, 11 pages of text in calligraphy, text pages have delicate illustrations in sepia, extremely scarce.   Aleph-Bet Books, Inc.   95 - 406   2011 $4000

Repton, Humphry   1752-1818 *Observations on the Theory and Practice of Landscape Gardening.* London: printed by T. Bensley for J. Taylor at the Architectural Library, High Holborn, 1805, Plates, overlays, contemporary tree calf, gilt spine, red label, slight mark to front board, very good, handsome.   Jarndyce Antiquarian Booksellers   CXCI - 464   2011   £8500

Repton, Humphry   1752-1818 *Observations on the Theory and Practice of Landscape Gardening.* London: J. Taylor, 1805, Second edition; 16, 222, (2) pages, stipple engraved plates frontispiece, 10 hand colored aquatint, including 9 with overlays, four tinted aquatints including one double page, 10 uncolored aquatints including three with overlays, one engraved plate, 2 maps including one colored, additional aquatint or woodcut illustrations, one colored and two with overlays, large quarto, half calf over marbled boards and later rebacking, gilt decoration and lettering on spine, edges and corners worn and endpaper replaced, some light offsetting very minor foxing internally, overall very good.   Heritage Book Shop   Holiday 2010 - 104   2011 $13,500

Residence in Bermuda.   Bermuda: Bermuda Trade Development Board, 1936, First edition; large 4to., 15.5 x 12.5 inches, large attractive book with 52 illustrations, watercolors by Adolph Treidler and photos, bright, clean, near fine with faint shelf wear in original publisher's silver and turquoise cloth.   Any Amount of Books   May 29 2011 - A40933   2011 $340

Return to Oasis. War Poems and Recollections from the Middle East 1940-1946. London: Shepheard-Walwyn/ Editions Poetry London for the Salamander Oasis Trust, 1980, First edition, no. 1 of 100 copies; 8vo. pages xxxiv, 254, frontispiece, illustrations, 3 maps, signed on reverse of titlepage by Lawrence Durrell and all editors and Tambimuttu, fine in fine dust jacket.   Any Amount of Books   May 29 2011 - A40505   2011 $204

Revenflow, Ernst Zu, Count *The Vampire of the Continent.* New York: Jackson Press, 1917, Second American edition; pictorial cloth, light dampstain at bottom of text pages, thus about very good in very good pictorial dust jacket with corresponding stain and some small chips. Between the Covers 169 - BTC347384 2011 $950

Revere, Joseph Warren 1812-1880 *Keel and Saddle: a Retrospect of Forty Years of Military and Naval Service.* Boston: Osgood, 1872, First edition; xiii, (1) 360 pages. original blind and gilt stamped dark green cloth, some light extremity rubbing, primarily at head of spine, owner's name erased from top edge of titlepage, some extremely light foxing to prelim and endleaves, very good, tight and clean. Argonaut Book Shop   Recent Acquisitions Summer 2010 - 169 2011 $300

Revere, Joseph Warren 1812-1880 *A Tour of Duty in California, Including a Description of the Gold Region and an Account of a Voyage Around Cape Horn with Notices of Lower California, the Gulf and Pacific Coasts and Principal Events.* New York & Boston: C.S. Francis & Co. & J. H. Francis, 1849, First edition; 12mo., vi, (2) 305, (1 blank (6 ad), engraved frontispiece, 5 engraved plates, large folding map, modern full brown calf, gilt stamped brown morocco spine label, very good. Jeff Weber Rare Books 163 - 95 2011 $1000

The Review a Bi-Monthly Magazine of Poetry and Criticism. Oxford/London: 1962-1972, No 1 April/May 1962 to No. 29/30 1972, wrappers, 8vo., complete run of 30 issues including three individual three pamphlet series - no. 13 (in original printed envelope) 19 and 21 and supplement is no. 25, all clean, very good copies, some fine, issue 11/12 slightly stained at side. Any Amount of Books May 29 2011 - A66949 2011 $374

Review of Reviews. New York and Great Britain: 1890-1937, First edition; Volume 1-volume 96 Jan. 1890-July 1937, 96 volumes in 93, volumes 1-22 are English editions uniformly bound in blue publisher's cloth gilt, volumes 23-24 English edition bound in leather boards with marbled edges and small bookplates, in excellent condition, volumes 25-95/96 are NY editions, mainly ex-librry, with mixed bindings, with uniform runs and are generally in very good condition, although some (9) have rubbed leather spines and few of the later volumes have neat library bookplates on pastedown, overall very good. I. D. Edrich May 26 2011 - 84961 2011 $1006

The Review of Reviews an International Magazine. New York: Review of reviews, 1893, American edition; 13 volumes, illustrated cloth soiled and edge worn, hinges broken in several of the volumes, interior clean and tight, Volume 7 Feb.-June 1893 8, 10-14, 16-18, 20-22 (July December 1900). G. H. Mott Bookseller May 26 2011 - 39372 2011 $400

Rexford-Welch, S. C. *The Royal Air Force Medical Services.* London: HMSO, 1954, First edition; 3 volumes, 8vo., pages xx, 611; xxiv, 703; xxv, 730, original publishers dark red cloth lettered gilt on spine, plates, maps, figures, ex-British Foreign Office library with few library markings, else very good.   Any Amount of Books   May 29 2011 - A68046 2011 $238

Rey, Margaret *Curious George Flies a Kite.* Boston: Houghton Mifflin, 1958, First edition; 4to., 80 pages, pictorial cloth, fine in dust jacket (3/4" wraparound piece off bottom of spine, fraying at top of spine, some fading of color and spine toned, overall really very good dust jacket, not price clipped), illustrations in color by author.   Aleph-Bet Books, Inc. 95 - 484 2011 $2250

Rey, Margaret *Curious George Goes to the Hospital.* Boston: Houghton Mifflin, 1966, Stated first printing; 8vo., cloth, fine in fine dust jacket, great color illustrations, exceptionally nice, quite scarce.   Aleph-Bet Books, Inc. 95 - 485 2011 $2000

Reynard the Fox *The Most Delectable History of Reynard the Fox. (bound with) The Most Pleasant and Delightful History of Reynard the Fox. The Second Part (and) The Shifts of Reynardine the Son of Reynard the Fox...* London: printed by T. Ilive for Edward Brewster, 1701, London: Printed by A. M. and R. R. for Edward Brewster, 1681. London: Printed by T. J. for Edward Brewster and Thomas Passenger, 1684. Early English edition; 3 parts in one, small quarto, (156), (2 table of contents), (2, publisher's ads); (111), (1, publisher's ads); (8), 160 pages, mostly black letter with titles and side notes in roman letter, 62 woodcuts in first part, printed from 39 blocks and 15 woodcuts in second part, five repeated, all repeats from the first part, wooduct on C1 recto (Part I) printed upside down, contemporary sprinkled sheep, covers ruled and decoratively tooled in blind, spine decoratively tooled in gilt in compartments with two red morocco gilt lettering labels, minor restoration to covers, some browning, occasional light dampstaining and soiling, part I with tiny puncture marks in lower blank margin through gathering 1, just touching one letter in imprint of titlepage, 6 small holes in I3 and one tiny hole in I4, causing loss of a couple of letters, Part III with paper flaw in upper blank corner of A3 and A4, tiny tear (quarter inch) in lower blank margin of F4, and paper flaw in lower blank corner of I2, none affecting text, armorial bookplate of Gloucester on front free endpaper, bookplate of Hugh Cecil Lowther, 5th Earl of Lonsdale (1857-1944), (his sale 12 July 1937 lot 445), excellent copy, housed in quarter morocco clamshell box.   David Brass Rare Books, Inc. May 26 2011 - 00654 2011 $17,500

Reynard the Fox *Reynard the Fox, an Old Story Now Told.* London: Swan Sonnenschein, 1886, Second edition; square 8vo., original decorated blue cloth, gilt over bevelled boards, extremities little worn and frayed, pages viii, 168, top edge gilt, decorative initials, numerous text woodcut vignettes, 40 full page plates by Kaulbach, little shaken.   R. F. G. Hollett & Son Antiquarian Booksellers 175 - 365 2011 £85

Reynard the Fox *The History of Reynard the Foxe.* London: sold by Bernard Quaritch, 1892, One of 300 paper copies, out of a total edition of 310 copies; large quarto, (2, blank), v, (1), 162, (1, colophon), (1, blank) pages, printed in red and black in Troy and Chaucer types, wood engraved title with gothic lettering, decorative woodcut borders and initials, original full limp vellum with yapp edges, spine lettered gilt, original gold silk ties, fine, housed in gray cloth slipcase. David Brass Rare Books, Inc. May 26 2011 - 01312 2011 $8000

Reynolds, A. J. *From the Ivory Coast to the Cameroons.* London: Alfred A. Knopf, 1929, First edition; 8vo., pages 298, folding map, illustrations, original purple cloth, spine faded. J. & S. L. Bonham Antiquarian Booksellers Africa 4/20/2011 - 4642 2011 £45

Reynolds, Barbara *The Cambridge Italian Dictionary.* Cambridge: Cambridge University Press, 1962, First edition; 2 volumes, each slightly different shade of blue, 4to., pages xxxi, 898; ix, 843, ex-British Foreign Office library with few library markings, else sound, very good copy. Any Amount of Books May 29 2011 - A70130 2011 $306

Reynolds, Herbert Edward *Wells Cathedral its Foundation, Constitutional History and Statutes.* Wells: privately printed for the editor, 1881, Small folio, contemporary half calf gilt by Price of Wells with double contrasting spine labels, spine and edges little rubbed, pages (xvi, subscribers and errata), cxcviii (preface, 280, engraved frontispiece, numerous woodcuts, photographic and facsimile plates, folding table little creased, bookplate of Wells Cathedral library. R. F. G. Hollett & Son Antiquarian Booksellers General Catalogue Summer 2010 - 1565 2011 £120

Rhode Island Evangelical Consociation *Minutes of the Annual Meeting of the... and of the Rhode Island Home Missionary Society and Plea, Held at Slatersville June 12th and 13th 1860.* Providence: M. B. Young, 1860, First edition; 8vo., 22, (1) pages, original printed wrappers, corners chipped, some soiling, text very good. M & S Rare Books, Inc. 90 - 371 2011 $85

Rhodes, William Henry *The Case of Summerfield.* San Francisco: Paul Elder & Co., 1907, First separate book edition; 12mo., vi, (2), 54, (2) pages, photogravure frontispiece from painting by Galen J. Perrett, quarter vellum, brown paper boards, beveled edges, gilt lettering to spine and front cover very fine, with slipcase. Argonaut Book Shop Recent Acquisitions Summer 2010 - 171 2011 $175

Rhoscomyl, Owen *Battlement and Tower.* London: Longmans, 1896, First edition; frontispiece, 24 page catalog, original dark blue cloth, bevelled boards, spine faded, boards little marked, presentation inscription. Jarndyce Antiquarian Booksellers CXCI - 465 2011 £50

Rhymer's Club *The Book of the Rhymer's Club.* Cleveland: 1923-1935, 14 volumes, all issues in wrappers except last in paper over boards, complete run, each issue limited from 300 to 500 copies. Bookworm & Silverfish 678 - 164 2011 $275

Rhys, Ernest *Lyrical Poetry from the Bible.* London: Dent, 1895, First edition; 2 volumes, 12mo., original blue cloth gilt extra, pages xxii, 191, xxv-xl, xvi, 200, with 2 tissue guarded engraved frontispiece plates little spotted, 2 pictorial titles in red and black. R. F. G. Hollett & Son Antiquarian Booksellers 175 - 1125 2011 £65

Rhys, John *Studies in the Arthurian Legend.* Oxford: Clarendon Press, 1891, First edition; original cloth, gilt, extremities little worn, pages viii, 411, small labels removed from endpapers. R. F. G. Hollett & Son Antiquarian Booksellers 175 - 1124 2011 £75

Ricardo, David 1772-1823 *Proposals for an Economical and Secure Currency; with Observations on the Profits of the Bank of England as They Regard the Public and the Proprietors of Bank Stock.* London: John Murray, 1816, First edition; 8vo. (2) 126 (2) pages, wanting half title but with final leaf 18 (blank recto/imprint verso), occasional minor spotting, titlepage rather soiled and with small stain, rebound recently in good old style quarter calf over marbled boards, spine gilt and lettered. John Drury Rare Books 153 - 124 2011 £1500

Ricci, Corrado *Pintoricchio (Bernardino di Betto of Perugia). His Life, Work and Time.* London: William Heinemann, 1902, First edition in English; profusely illustrated, plain cloth with gilt lines and imprints to spine, old library bookplate, near fine, plates fine, large folio. Lupack Rare Books May 26 2011 - ABE793015972 2011 $250

Riccoboni, Marie Jeanne Laboras De Mezieres *Histoire du Marquis De Cressy Suivi d'Ernestine.* Paris: Chez P. Didot L'Aine, 1814, (236) pages, 16mo., contemporary three quarter red morocco, gilt lettered and gilt decorated and ruled spines with floral design, raised bands, fine on papier velin. Paulette Rose Fine and Rare Books 32 - 146 2011 $200

Rice, Ann *The Tale of the Body Thief.* New York: Knopf, 1992, First edition; inscribed and signed by Anne Rice, as new in dust jacket. Gemini Fine Books & Arts, Ltd. Art Reference & Illustrated Books: First Editions 2011 $60

Rice, Elmer *Judgment Day.* New York: 1934, First edition (so stated); near fine in extremely good dust jacket, darkened backstrip, inner surface strengthened at both ends of backstrip and both ends of two flap folds, not clipped. Bookworm & Silverfish 669 - 60 2011 $85

Rich, Henry *What Is to be Done? or Past, Present and Future.* London: James Ridgway, 1844, First edition; 8vo., (iv), 123 pages, recent blue boards, lettered on upper cover, paper label on spine, very good, from the contemporary library of Lord William Russell with his signature on titlepage, scarce.   John Drury Rare Books   153 - 125   2011   £100

Rich, R. W. *The Training of Teachers in England and Wales During the Nineteenth Century.* Cambridge: University Press, 1933, First edition; original cloth, gilt, dust jacket, pages (iv), 286, fore edge foxed, presentation copy, inscribed by author.   R. F. G. Hollett & Son Antiquarian Booksellers   175 - 1127   2011   £45

Richards, Alfred Bates *A Sketch of the Career of Richard F. Burton.* London: Waterloo, 1886, First edition; 8vo., pages 96, frontispiece, original black paper covered boards, neatly rebacked, good and clean.   J. & S. L. Bonham Antiquarian Booksellers   Africa 4/20/2011 - 9206   2011   £500

Richards, Anthony *From a Satyric Country.* London: I. M. Imprimit, 1971, First edition, no. 17 of 100 copies signed by Ian Mortimer and Anthony Richards; 4to., wrappers, loose sheets in a box with printed label on cover, text handset in 14 pt. Plantin, on 72lb Barcham Green mould made paper, woodcuts designed and cut by Mortimer and printed by artist, fine in very good box, slightly frayed at top and tail of spine.   Any Amount of Books   May 29 2011 - A48591   2011 $204

Richards, Frank *Billy Bunter Afloat.* London: Cassell, 1957, First edition; original cloth, gilt, dust jacket, spine trifle faded and little chipped at head and foot, pages 223, color illustrations and illustrations, edges little spotted.   R. F. G. Hollett & Sons Antiquarian Booksellers   170 - 587   2011   £50

Richards, J. M. *The Castles on the Ground.* Architectural Press, 1946, First edition; original cloth, gilt, dust jacket spine trifle faded, pages 86, with 8 two-color lithographed plates by John Piper.   R. F. G. Hollett & Son Antiquarian Booksellers   General Catalogue Summer 2010 - 868   2011   £30

Richards, R. D. *The Age. Volume 2 Nos. 35-86.* printed by R. D. Richards for the Age Office, 1838, Folio, old half calf, gilt, hinges cracking, pages 273-688, printed in triple columns, first leaf rather defective and neatly laid down, otherwise excellent state.   R. F. G. Hollett & Son Antiquarian Booksellers   175 - 1129   2011   £140

Richards, Raymond *Old Cheshire Churches.* London: Batsford, 1947, First edition; pages x, 341, with 15 engraved plates, modern half green levant morocco gilt with raised bands.   R. F. G. Hollett & Son Antiquarian Booksellers   177 - 744   2011   £140

Richardson, Charles *A New Dictionary of the English Language.* London: William Pickering, 1839, First one volume edition; prelims foxed, contemporary half brown calf, brown morocco label, rubbed, leading inner hinge slightly cracked but firm, good sound copy.   Jarndyce Antiquarian Booksellers   CXCI - 158   2011   £200

Richardson, Eric *Pennine Lead-Miner.* Dalesman Books, 1979, First edition; original pictorial wrappers, pages 64, illustrations, scarce.   R. F. G. Hollett & Son Antiquarian Booksellers   173 - 964   2011   £35

Richardson, Henry Handel, Pseud. 1870-1946 *The Fortunes of Richard Mahony, Comprising Australia Felix, The Way Home and Ultima Thule.* London: William Heinemann, 1930, First one volume edition; (990) pages, thick 8vo., dark blue cloth, gilt lettered spine, fine in near fine, very slightly chipped, printed dust jacket.   Paulette Rose Fine and Rare Books   32 - 147   2011 $200

Richardson, Henry Handel, Pseud. 1870-1946 *Maurie Guest.* New York: Duffield, 1909, First US edition; 8vo., original publishers blue cloth lettered gilt on spine and cover and with small music notation in gilt, pages 562, spine creased and slightly concave, front inner hinge little cracked, covers slightly marked bu acceptable near very good example of rare book.   Any Amount of Books   May 29 2011 - A66409   2011 $340

Richardson, J. *Furness Past and Present Its History and Antiquities.* Barrow-in-Furness: J. Richardson, 1880, 2 volumes, 4to., old half crimson morocco gilt with double spine labels, both volumes neatly recased, pages xxii, 265; (ii), 316, complete with 1 title and 2 dedication leaves lithographed in colors, 71 tinted colored or steel engraved plates, maps, portraits, arms and numerous text woodcuts, two slight edge tears, excellent set, scarce.   R. F. G. Hollett & Son Antiquarian Booksellers   173 - 965   2011   £650

Richardson, John *A Life of Picasso.* New York: Random House, 1991-1996, First edition; 2 volumes, 4to., original cloth, gilt, dust jacket, pages 548; xii, 500, illustrations, fine.   R. F. G. Hollett & Son Antiquarian Booksellers   General Catalogue Summer 2010 - 308   2011   £180

Richardson, Joseph *A Complete Investigation of Mr. Eden's Treaty, as It May Affect the Commerce, the Revenue or the General Policy of Great Britain.* London: printed for J. Debrett, opposite Burlington House, Piccadilly, 1787, First edition; lacks half title, final errata leaf at end, last numbered page misnumbered, (2), 176 (i.e. 167), (3) pages, clean copy, disbound.   Anthony W. Laywood   May 26 2011 - 21713   2011 $117

Richardson, Samuel 1689-1761 *The Correspondence of Samuel Richardson...* London: Richard Phillips, 1804, 6 volumes, half leather and marbled boards edge worn and scratched, several boards are off, prelims foxed, interiors clean, page 3 of 13 "The Company at Tunbridge Wells" is missing, ccxii, 192; 340; 332; 379; 348; 326 pages. G. H. Mott Bookseller   May 26 2011 - 43630 2011 $900

Richmond, Leigh *The Young Cottager.* London: Religious Tract Society, n.d. circa, 1839, 12mo., original cloth, gilt, little rubbed, pages 124, 13 woodcuts, some fingering in places, front pastedown removed. R. F. G. Hollett & Sons Antiquarian Booksellers   170 - 589 2011 £35

Richmond, Mary E. *The Long View: Papers & Address by Mary E. Richmond.* New York: 1930, First edition; 648 pages, 8vo., original binding, very good, 2 cover spots. Bookworm & Silverfish   662 - 203 2011 $75

Richmond, Maurice *Richmond's Standard Music Guide. Volume I Number 1.* New York: Richmond, 1924, 8vo., pages 67, paper wrappers, cover very slightly chipped and stained, else very good, tight copy.   Second Life Books Inc.   174 - 269 2011 $65

Richter, Edmond *Grammatica Obstetricia.* Paris: P. L. Febvrier, 1607, 8vo., ff. (8), 162, (1 errata), folding table at page 126, device on titlepage, 17th century calf, gilt fillet on covers, gilt spine, top of upper hinge weak, marbled edges, uncommon, from the library of the Earls of Macclesfield at Shirburn Castle.   Maggs Bros. Ltd.   1440 - 177 2011   £550

Richter, Johann Gottfried Ohnefalsch *Ichthyotheolgie Oder; Vernnunft und Schriftmassiger...* Leipzig: Friedrich Lankischens, 1754, First edition; 8 copper engraved plates, folding table, 8vo., pages (32), 912, (32), contemporary goatskin (edges rubbed, dark discoloration to upper third of front cover, also going across upper panel of spine), small paper label to head of spine, 3 small wormholes to edges of spine, bookplate, faint ink inscription to front blank, small stain to upper corner of prelim pages, small dampstain to lower margin of several pages, not affecting text, lower corner of several pages, small dampstain to lower margin of several pages, not affecting text, lower corner of several pages bumped, minor worming to rear pastedown and flyleaf, ex-libris Robert Rofen, good copy.   Raymond M. Sutton, Jr.   May 26 2011 - 42317 2011 $1750

Rickards, George Kettilby *Three Lectures Delivered Before the University of Oxford in Michaelmas term 1852...* Oxford and London: John Henry Parker, 1852, First edition; 8vo., 95, (1) pages recent marbled boards lettered on spine, very good, uncommon.   John Drury Rare Books   153 - 126 2011   £150

Ricketts, Benjamin Merrill *The Surgery of the Heart and Lungs: a History and Resume of Surgical Conditions Found Therein and Experimental and Clinical Research in Man and Lower Animals...* New York: Grafton Press, 1904, First edition; 8vo., xvi 510 pages, 87 photo plates (including frontispiece), navy cloth, gilt stamped spine title, ex-library bookplate and titlepage embossed stamp, spine call numbers, very good, signature of A. A. Rockey.   Jeff Weber Rare Books   162 - 257 2011 $200

Ricketts, W. P. *50 Years in the Saddle.* Sheridan: Star Publishing Co., 1942, First and only edition; 8vo., original green cloth with title stamped in black on front cover and spine, (14), 198 pages, frontispiece, illustrations, map, lightly rubbed at spine ends and corners, else near fine tight copy, very scarce to rare.   Buckingham Books   May 26 2011 - 29587 2011 $2250

Rickman, Thomas *An Attempt to Discriminate the Styles of Architecture in England...* London: Longman Rees etc., 1835, Fourth edition; modern half green levant morocco gilt with raised bands, pages x, 341, 15 engraved plates. R. F. G. Hollett & Son Antiquarian Booksellers   177 - 745 2011   £120

Ride a Cock Horse. Kenasha: Abbott Pub. Co. n.d., circa, 1925, 11 1/2 x 9 inches, stiff pictorial wrapper covers die-cut in shape of rocking horse, slight edge wear, very good+, illustrations by Winifred Pleninger, full color illustrations. Aleph-Bet Books, Inc.   95 - 530 2011 $150

The Ride on the Sled; or the Punishment of Disobedience. Boston: New England Sabbath School Union, 1839, 12mo., original blindstamped cloth gilt, covers little damped, neatly recased with new endpaper, pages 64 with woodcut frontispiece and tailpiece.   R. F. G. Hollett & Sons Antiquarian Booksellers   170 - 23 2011   £85

Rideal, Charles F. *People We Meet.* London: Field & Tuer, 1899, 4to., original drab wrappers, paper label on front cover, slightly chipped.   Jarndyce Antiquarian Booksellers   CXCI - 466 2011   £48

Rider, Fremont *Rider's Bermuda. A Guide Book for Travelers with 4 Maps.* New York: 1924, liv, 158, (24) ads pages, 12mo., very good, one inch rub, top right of backstrip and some scrapes at title, not affecting letters, contains all four maps.   Bookworm & Silverfish   669 - 40 2011 $65

Rider, Fremont *Rider's California: a Guide-Book for Travelers.* New York: Macmillan, 1925, First edition; enlarged issue with extra maps (quite scarce format), 18mo., lxii, (2), 667 pages, plus 48 pages ads, 13 folding color maps, 15 full page black and white maps and plans, full index, original green cloth lettered in gilt, 2 leaves with tiny stain to extreme fore-edge, fine. Argonaut Book Shop Recent Acquisitions Summer 2010 - 172 2011 $250

Riding, Laura *The World and Ourselves.* London: Chatto & Windus, 1938, First edition; 8vo., pages xi, 529, pencilled ownership signature of historian F. R. Cowell, very good+ in like dust jacket with faint edgewear.   Any Amount of Books   May 29 2011 - A48862   2011 $255

Ridley, Guy *The Wood of Treregor.* London: James Nisbet, 1914, First edition; 8vo., original publisher's blue cloth lettered gilt at spine and cover, pages 125, pages uncut, rare, fore-edge very slightly foxed, else about fine, exceptional condition, presentation copy to Denys C. Little from writer.   Any Amount of Books   May 29 2011 - A67184   2011 $255

Rigby, Cuthbert *From Midsummer to Martinmas. A West Cumberland Idyl.* London: George Allen, 1891, First edition; pages x, 353, with 33 illustrations by author, endpapers lightly spotted, otherwise very nice, clean and bright.   R. F. G. Hollett & Son Antiquarian Booksellers   173 - 967   2011   £50

Rigge, Henry Fletcher *Cartmel Priory Church, North Lancashire.* Cartmel: E. Wilson, 1879, First edition; small 8vo., original blue cloth gilt with Earl of Pembroke's arms on upper board, pages 36, all edges gilt, frontispiece, scarce.   R. F. G. Hollett & Son Antiquarian Booksellers   173 - 968   2011   £75

Riley, James Whitcomb   1849-1916 *Out to Old Aunt Mary's.* Indianapolis: Bobbs Merrill, 1904, First edition with Christy illustrations; illustrations by Howard Chandler Christy, binding in mixed state with gilt lettering ("B") but with decorated endpapers ("A"), (printing is by the Charles Francis Press (3rd state of copyright page), book nearly fine, with very scarce dust jacket.   Lupack Rare Books   May 26 2011 - ABE4633203534   2011 $150

Riley, James Whitcomb   1849-1916 *The Raggedy Man.* Indianapolis: Bobbs Merrill, 1907, First edition; large 4to., green cloth, pictorial paste-on, fine, printed on coated paper, illustrations by Ethel Betts with 8 magnificent rich color plates with lovely decorative border and line illustrations on each page of text, nice copy of beautiful book.   Aleph-Bet Books, Inc.   95 - 98   2011 $400

Rimbaud, Arthur *A Season in Hell.* New York: Limited Editions Club, 1986, One of 1000 numbered copies; with 8 original hand rubbed photogravures by Robert Mapplethorpe, signed by translator, Paul Schmidt and by artist, Mapplethorpe, English translation printed en face with the French, hand-sewn and bound in crimson Nigerian Oasis goatskin stamped in black, 12 x 8 inches, 88 pages, as new in slipcase.   Gemini Fine Books & Arts, Ltd.   Art Reference & Illustrated Books: First Editions 2011 $1250

Ringgold, Cadwalader *Series of Charts with Sailing Directions.* Washington: Jno. T. Towers, 1852, Fourth and best edition; small quarto, 48 pages, 8 tinted lithographic plates and 6 folding engraved charts, original full green cloth, front board decoratively stamped and lettered in gilt with seal of California and an eagle standing on an anchor surrounded by gilt border as well as border stamped in blind, back board with same image stamped in blind, cloth bit sunned along edges and spine slightly wrinkled, some foxing as usual, inner hinges cracked but firm, previous owner's small bookplate, very good.   Heritage Book Shop   Holiday 2010 - 105   2011 $3000

Ripley, Hugh *Whisky for Tea.* Lewes: Book Guild, 1991, First edition; 8vo., pages 186, fine in fine dust jacket, signed presentation from author.   Any Amount of Books   May 26 2011 - A69884   2011 $419

Ripley, Hugh *Whisky for Tea.* Lewes: Book Guild, 1991, First edition; 8vo., 186 pages, fine in faintly rubbed, near fine dust jacket.   Any Amount of Books   May 29 2011 - A68052   2011 $298

Riqueti, Honore Gabriel de Mirabeau, Comte *Errotika Bibliion.* Rome: De l'Imprimerie du Vatican, 1783, First edition, scarcest issue; large 8vo., pages iv, 192, titlepage, others untrimmed, light dampstain to margin of two leaves, otherwise internally very fresh, red quarter morocco and marbled boards, gilt lettering and decoration to spine, marbled endpapers, boards slightly rubbed, lacking rear front endpaper.   Simon Finch Rare Books   Zero - 410 2011   £3500

Ritch, John *Jones & Newman's Architectural Publications. First Series. The American Architect Comprising Original Designs of Cheap Country and Village Residence with Details, Specifications, Plans and Directions and an Estimate of the Cost of Each Design.* New York: C. M. Saxton, 1848, First edition; large 4to., 24 leave of text, 48 lithographic plates, full contemporary calf, rubbed, hinges cracked, very nice.   M & S Rare Books, Inc.   90 - 16   2011 $2750

Ritchie, Anne Isabella Thackeray   1837-1919 *Bluebeard's Keys and Other Stories.* London: Smith, Elder & Co., 1874, (x, 512 pages), 8vo., three quarter green morocco over marbled boards, top edge gilt, half title, attractive copy bound by John Bumpus, scarce.   Paulette Rose Fine and Rare Books   32 - 172   2011 $150

Ritchie, Anne Isabella Thackeray   1837-1919 *Records of Tennyson, Ruskin, Browning.* New York: Harper & Brothers, 1893, First edition; original decorated cloth, gilt, extremities little worn, pages (vi), 190, 2, with 27 plates, scarce.   R. F. G. Hollett & Son Antiquarian Booksellers   173 - 972   2011   £75

Ritchie, Leitch *Liber Fluviorum or River Scenery of France.* London: Henry G. Bohn, 1857, 280 x 195mm., lvi, 336 pages, striking contemporary dark brown morocco, elaborately decorated in blind and gilt in a Rennaisance style, covers with multiple frames in blind around a blind-stamped center panel filled with stylized fleurs-de-lys and quatrefoils, four large gilt fleurs-de-lys at corners outside center panel, thick raised double bands, spine in panels repeating large gilt fleur-de-lys as centerpiece surrounded by similar ornaments in blind, edges gilt and elaborately gauffered in a diapered pattern enclosing may wheat sheaf stamps, handsomely decorated gilt turn-ins, marbled endpapers, added engraved titlepage with vignette, 61 engraved plates by J. M. Turner; tiny bit of offsetting from a very small number of plates, but virtually flawless inside and out. Phillip J. Pirages 59 - 338 2011 $1650

Ritchie, Robert Welles *The Hell-Roarin' Forty-Niners.* New York: J. H. Sears & Co. Inc., 1928, First edition; 298 pages, 13 photos, pictorial red cloth stamped in black, very fine, pictorial dust jacket (price clipped, chip at foot of spine). Argonaut Book Shop Recent Acquisitions Summer 2010 - 173 2011 $125

Ritts, Herb *Men and Woman.* Santa Fe: Twin Palms Pub., 1989, First edition; 2 volumes, pages 96 and 96, original publisher's black cloth lettered gilt on spine with illustration onset on each cover, copiously illustrated in black and white, signed by Ritts, both volumes fine in slipcase. Any Amount of Books May 26 2011 - A68262 2011 $503

A Ritual and Illustrations of Freemasonry, Accompanied by Numerous Engravings... London: Reeves and Turner, n.d. 1860's, Pages 30, plates, 254, joints cracked, original green cloth, gilt, trifle marked. R. F. G. Hollett & Son Antiquarian Booksellers 175 - 483 2011 £65

Rivers, John *Greuze and His Models.* London: Hutchinson & Co., 1912, First edition; 225 x 170mm., 9 p.l. including frontispiece, 282 pages, fine contemporary emerald green crushed morocco for Hatchards (done according to a pencilled note at front, by Zaehnsdorf), covers gilt in Arts and Crafts design of interlocking plain rule frames with floral stamps at corners and gilt titling flanked by leaves and berries, raised bands, spine gilt in double ruled compartments, with central floral sprig and three circles to each corner, gilt ruled turn-ins, gray endpapers, all edges gilt, with extra engraved titlepage and 44 plates, 40 with tissue guards (four reproductions of sketches bound in without guards); spine faintly sunned to pleasing slightly darker green, front free endpaper with two small very faint vestiges of tape, but quite fine, handsomely bound, binding unworn and clean, fresh and bright inside and out. Phillip J. Pirages 59 - 151 2011 $500

Riviere, Georges *Renoir et Ses Amis.* Paris: H. Floury, 1921, First edition; quarto, (4), 273, (3) pages, contemporary maroon cloth, gilt spine titles with front wrapper (a color lithograph) bound in with 95 in text gravure illustrations, 56 monotone and color gravure plates (12 in color), one original drypoint etching by Renoir and one color lithograph (the front wrapper), very good with moderate soiling to boards and usual age toning at edges of text pages, plates clean and bright. Between the Covers 169 - BTC342794 2011 $2400

Rivius, Gregorius *Puritani Monastica Historia...* Leipzig: Jo. Christiani Martini, 1737, Pages xxxvi, (ii), 510, (80, index), old half calf gilt with marbled boards, edges and corners worn and chipped, later spine label, upper hinge cracking, pages xxxvi, (ii) 510, (80, index), title in red and black (rather browned), engraved frontispiece and 6 engraved plates, small wormhole in lower margin of index leaves, from Dr. Laing's library. R. F. G. Hollett & Son Antiquarian Booksellers 175 - 1133 2011 £150

Rivoira, G. T. *Lombardic Architecture - Its Origin, Development and Derivatives.* Oxford: Clarendon Press, 1933, 2 volumes, large 4to., original cloth, gilt, dust jackets, little chipped and torn, pages xxviii, 284; xv, 402, with 818 illustrations. R. F. G. Hollett & Son Antiquarian Booksellers 177 - 747 2011 £125

Roach, J. P. C. *Cambridge and the Isle of Ely. Volume Three. Victoria History of the Counties of England Series.* University of London, 1959, First edition; 4to., original cloth, gilt, pages xx, 504, color frontispiece, 55 illustrations and 5 maps, fine. R. F. G. Hollett & Son Antiquarian Booksellers 177 - 748 2011 £95

Robarts, Edith *Robinson Crusoe Retold for Little Folk.* Blackie and Son, n.d. circa, 1910, 4to., original cloth backed pictorial boards, edges and corners worn and rounded, little scratched, pages 80 with 6 full page color plates and fine color centrefold, top quarter of flyleaf cut off. R. F. G. Hollett & Sons Antiquarian Booksellers 170 - 320 2011 £35

The Robber Kitten, Mr. Fox, Simple Simon, Three Little Kittens and The Frog He Would a Wooing. New York: McLoughlin Brothers Manufacturers, 1867, Tall narrow 4to., color pictorial paper covers with small hole in front cover and some minor staining throughout, hand colored woodcuts, black and whites in text and lessons and instructive materials. Jo Ann Reisler, Ltd. 86 - 86 2011 $750

Robbins, Rossell Hope *Historical Poems of the XIVth and XVth Centuries.* New York: Columbia University Press, 1959, 440 pages, very good, light edge wear, very clean and tight. G. H. Mott Bookseller May 26 2011 - 50446 2011 $350

Robbins, Ruth *Baboushka and the Three Kings.* Berkeley: Parnassus Press, 1960, First edition (correct dust jacket price); Oblong 8vo., pictorial cloth, fine in dust jacket, rare, illustrations by Sidjakov.   Aleph-Bet Books, Inc.   95 - 534   2011 $800

Robbins, Tom *Another Roadside Attraction.* Garden City: Doubleday & Co., 1971, First edition; 8vo. pages 400, original green cloth backed black cloth boards, spine lettered in silver, green endpapers, original color pictorial dust jacket, author's photograph to rear panel, small stain to bottom edge of text block, light shelf wear to dust jacket extremities, light soiling to rear panel, author's inscription in blue felt tip pen to first blank, bookplate of Michael T. Norton, presentation from author.   Simon Finch Rare Books   Zero - 260   2011   £450

Robbins, Tom *Even Cowgirls Get the Blues.* Boston: Houghton Mifflin, 1976, Uncorrected proof; exuberantly inscribed by author to his jeweler, one small spot to flyleaf, fine in wrappers, uncommon issue, uncommon signed.   Ken Lopez Bookseller   154 - 194   2011 $1000

Robbins, Tom *Jitterbug Perfume.* New York: Bantam, 1984, Uncorrected proof; inscribed by author to his jeweler, bit dusty, slightest bump to base, very near fine in wrappers, uncommon, especially signed.   Ken Lopez Bookseller   154 - 195   2011 $200

Robbins, Tom *Skinny Legs and All.* New York: Bantam, 1990, Uncorrected proof copy; inscribed by author, above tipped in photocopy of a photo of Robbins, small crease and bump to back upper edge, near fine in wrapper, uncommon signed.   Ken Lopez Bookseller   154 - 196   2011 $200

Robert-Houdin, Jean Eugene *Card-Sharping Exposed.* London: George Routledge and Sons, 1882, Half title, 4 pages ads, few fore-edges slightly dusted, original blue cloth, decorated and lettered in red, black and gilt, very good, bright.   Jarndyce Antiquarian Booksellers   CXCI - 469   2011   £200

Robert, Lewes *The Merchants Map of Commerce.* 1671, Second edition; titlepage, (18), 431, (6), (3) pages, lacking page 57-66 inclusive, some map of Asia present (cracked on folds), contemporary calf, binding in poor condition, text good.   C. P. Hyland   May 26 2011 - 803   2011 $362

Robert, Prior of Shrewsbury *The Admirable Life of Saint Wenefride...* St. Omer: English College Press Superiorum Permissu, 1635, 8vo., (32), 275, (13) pages, plus added engraved titlepage by Martin Baes (loose), text printed within double line border, last leaf blank (here lacking), 18th century English vellum backed boards, signature of James Elcocks and note of his birth on 6 Jan. 1679, from the library of the Earls of Macclesfield at Shirburn Castle.   Maggs Bros. Ltd.   1440 - 178   2011   £500

Roberts, D. Kilham *The Year's Poetry.* 1934-1938, Nos. 1-5, all with dust jackets.   I. D. Edrich   May 26 2011 - 82771   2011 $419

Roberts, Frank H. H. *Archaeological Remains in the Whitewater District Eastern Arizona Part I - House Types/ Part II - Artifacts and Burials.* Washington: 1939-1940, 2 volumes, xii, 276 pages, illustrations; xi, 170 pages, illustrations, original printed wrappers, spine on part II faded, else clean and very good.   Dumont Maps & Books of the West   112 - 61   2011 $75

Roberts, Henry *The Dwellings of the Labouring Classes, Their Arrangement and Construction...* London: published by request and sold for The Benefit of the Society for Improving the Condition of the Labouring Classes, n.d. (last page dated 1855), Third edition; large 8vo., (8), 68 pages, including half title, numerous text figures and whole page illustrations followed by 12 litho plates, original publisher's green flexible cloth lettered gilt on front, slight edgewear, else very good+, bookplate of architect, John Cotton (1844-1934) with his ownership signatures, he has inserted 2 pamphlets, one about an organisation for promoting the enlargement and repair of churches and chapels, the other on improved dwellings for the working classes...   Any Amount of Books   May 26 2011 - A63134   2011 $671

Roberts, Jack *The Wonderful Adventures of Ludo the Little Green Duck.* Paris: Tolmer, 1924, Square small 8vo., pictorial boards, slightest bit of rubbing, else near fine, illustrations by Roberts, very scarce.   Aleph-Bet Books, Inc.   95 - 438   2011 $600

Roberts, Joseph *The Hand-Book of Artillery for the Service of the United States (Army and Militia).* Charleston: Evans & Cogswell, 1862, Second edition; 12mo., 192 pages, index, original flexible cloth with gilt and blue printed paper label, text browned, remarkably nice survival.   M & S Rare Books, Inc.   90 - 91   2011 $2750

Roberts, Keith *The Road to Paradise.* Worcester Park, Surrey: Kerosina Books, 1988, i.e. 26 January, 1989, First edition; octavo, grey cloth with green leather shelf back, lettered and ruled in gold, marbled endpapers.   L. W. Currey, Inc.   124 - 215   2011 $150

Roberts, Kenneth *Trending Into Maine.* Boston: Little Brown and Co., 1938, Limited to 1075 copies; 4to., signed by Wyeth and Roberts, textured cloth backed boards, black and gold paste label on spine, translucent paper dust jacket, original light blue slipcase, former owner's signature on slipcase, minor handling and marking, the copy number written on slipcase label, overall lovely copy, additional suite of plates housed in printed envelope, 14 full page color plates by N. C. Wyeth.   Jo Ann Reisler, Ltd.   86 - 267   2011 $2000

Roberts, Kenneth *Trending into Maine.* Boston: Little Brown, May, 1938, Limited to 1075 numbered copies signed by author and artist; 4to., white cloth spine, blue cloth, spine slightly toned, else fine in publisher's slipcase, slipcase has few small neat repairs on edge, 15 beautiful color plates by N. C. Wyeth, including endpapers, extra suite of color plates in original envelope, great copy,. Aleph-Bet Books, Inc.   95 - 599 2011 $2500

Roberts, Mary *Ruins and Old Trees, Associated with Memorable Events in English History.* London: Harey and Darton, n.d., 1843, First edition; half green calf gilt by Potter and Sons of York, rather rubbed and little scraped.   R. F. G. Hollett & Son Antiquarian Booksellers   177 - 749 2011   £120

Roberts, O. M. *A Description of Texas. Its Advantages and Resources with some Account of Their Development, Past, Present, Future.* St. Louis: Gilbert Book Co., 1881, First edition; 8vo., quarter cloth and decorated boards, (3), x, 17-133 pages, five folding maps in color, 8 colored plates, frontispiece, illustrations, maps, very good, tight copy, rare.   Buckingham Books   May 26 2011 - 23001 2011 $1750

Roberts, William *A Treatise on the Construction of the Statues 13 Eliz. C. 5 & 27 Eliz C. 4 Relating to Voluntary & Fraudulent Conveyances.* Philadelphia: 1807, First US edition; xvi, 668, (10) pages, very good, old law calf with chip to bottom of backstrip.   Bookworm & Silverfish   678 - 102 2011 $125

Robertson, Alexander *The Bible of St. Mark. St. Mark's Church, the Altar & Throne of Venice.* London: George Allen, 1898, First edition; original pictorial red cloth gilt, dust jacket little faded, pages xvi, 376, top edge gilt, with 82 illustrations.   R. F. G. Hollett & Son Antiquarian Booksellers   175 - 1135 2011   £35

Robertson, David *A Tour through the Isle of Man; to Which is Subjoined a Review of all the Manks History.* London: printed for the author by E. Hodson, 1794, Large paper copy, 8vo., pages (xii), 235, (i) + 8 sepia aquatint plates, contemporary straight grained mauve morocco, five flat raised bands spine triple rule and decorative pallet gilt, top and bottom compartment have symmetrical oblong centrepieces, gilt between decorative pallets in blind, 3 other compartments filled with massed French influence 'rolling breakers' decorative pallets gilt, lettered in gilt direct, boards triple rule gilt borders with 'acanthus' roll in blind within, board edges alternating double full and single broken hatch fillet roll in blind, turn-ins similarly tooled, 'French Shell' 'made' endpapers, all edges similarly marbled, blue and white sewn endbands, pink silk page marker, plates bit foxed and few spots to pages, touch scratched, spines little faded and upper joint slightly rubbed, unidentified bookplate, decorative bookplate of Frederick J. G. Montagu, booklabel of John Sparrow, pencil inscription Catherine of Fountayne, pencil annotations in same hand, from the collection of Christopher Ernest Weston 1947-2010.   Unsworths Booksellers   24 - 138 2011   £350

Robertson, Eric *Wordsworthshire.* Kirkby Stephen: Hayloft Pub., 2000, First edition; thick 8vo., original cloth, gilt, spine little faded and hinges trifle rubbed, pages xii, 352, 47 illustrations by Arthur Tucker and maps, endpapers little spotted, presentation copy inscribed by author to Dr. Wilson, Dalston.   R. F. G. Hollett & Son Antiquarian Booksellers   173 - 979 2011   £45

Robertson, Fred W. *An Address Delivered to the Members of the Working Man's Institute at the Town Hall, Brighton... April 18 1850...* Brighton: Henry S. King, 1850, 32 pages, original dark green cloth wrappers, slightly frayed at edges, but good.   Jarndyce Antiquarian Booksellers   CXCI - 470 2011   £35

Robertson, William   1721-1793 *An Historical Disquisition Concerning the Knowledge which the Ancients Had of India and the Progress of Trade with that Country Prior to the Discovery of the Passage to It by the Cape of Good Hope.* London: printed for A. Strahan and T. Cadell and E. Balfour at Edinburgh, 1791, First edition; 4to., half title, 2 folding engraved maps at end, xii, 364, (12) pages, contemporary diced calf, rebacked, label, nice.   Anthony W. Laywood   May 26 2011 - 18226 2011 $327

Robertson, William   1721-1793 *An Historical Disquisition Concerning the Knowledge Which the Ancients Had of India.* London: printed for Cadell and Davies et al, 1812, Sixth edition; 222 x 140mm., 1 p.l., (title), vi, 384, (20) pages, (without half title), handsome contemporary sprinkled calf, flat spine attractively gilt in panels divided by multiple decorative gilt rules, panels with large central fleuron, spine with one red and one green morocco label, two large engraved foldout maps, titles with ink Danish library stamp of Bibliothekaet pap Glorup; joints with short, thin cracks at head, corners little bumped, two inch tear at edge of one map (no loss), occasional minor foxing, smudges or offsetting but really excellent copy, binding solid, lustrous and with only minor wear and text especially clean, bright and fresh.   Phillip J. Pirages   59 - 300 2011 $450

Robertson, William   1721-1793 *The History of America.* London: printed for Cadell and Davies et al, 1812, Twelfth edition; 222 x 140mm., 4 volumes, handsome contemporary sprinkled calf, flat spines attractively gilt in panels, divided by multiple decorative gilt rules, panels with large central fleuron, each spine with one red and one green morocco label, fine engraved folding plates, titles with ink Danish library stamp Bibliotheket paa Glorup; four joints with thin, very short cracks at top, some of the corners little bent, but with especially pretty contemporary bindings entirely solid, very bright and otherwise with only trivial wear, little offsetting on and from maps, isolated minor foxing, affecting primarily opening leaves, but nearly fine internally, text almost entirely clean, fresh and bright.   Phillip J. Pirages   59 - 299 2011 $1500

Robertson, William 1721-1793 *The History of the Reign of the Emperor Charles V, with a View of the Progress of Society in Europe from the Subversion of the Roman Empire.* London and Edinburgh: printed for A. Strahan T. Cadell and J. Balfour, 1792, Seventh edition; 220 x 140mm., with half titles, 4 volumes, fine contemporary tree calf, (flat) spines beautifully gilt in compartments with unusual and elegant interlacing cornerpieces framing a central circle ornament enclosing an eight pointed star, red and green morocco labels, latter with oval red morocco onlay containing volume number and encircled by gilt laurel wreath, 4 engraved plates frontispieces; inkstamp of the Danish Bibliotheket paa Glorup; spines uniformly lighter than the covers (from sunning or perhaps as original), corners with slight wear, frontispieces and facing titles somewhat foxed, minor foxing to final few leaves in each volume as well, otherwise quite handsome set in fine condition, text especially clean and fresh, decorative contemporary bindings very bright and virtually unworn.   Phillip J. Pirages 59 - 57 2011 $1250

Robertson, William 1721-1793 *The History of Scotland During the Reigns of Queen Mary and King James V.* London: printed for Cadell and Davies et al, 1812, Nineteenth edition; 222 x 140mm. handsome contemporary sprinkled calf, flat spines attractively gilt in panels divided by multiple decorative gilt rules, panels with large central fleuron, each spine with one red and one green morocco label, frontispiece, titles with ink Danish library stamp of Bibliothekaet paa Glorup.   Phillip J. Pirages 59 - 301 2011 $950

Robin-Evans, Karyl *Sungods in Exile.* Sudbury: Neville Spearman, 1978, First edition; original cloth gilt, dust jacket, pages 150, fine copy, very scarce.   R. F. G. Hollett & Son Antiquarian Booksellers General Catalogue Summer 2010 - 1195 2011   £175

Robins, F. W *The Smith.* Rider & Co., 1953, First edition; pages 160, 13 plates, 12 line drawings, original cloth, dust jacket.   R. F. G. Hollett & Son Antiquarian Booksellers 175 - 1137 2011   £30

Robins, Joseph *The Ladies Pocket Magazine 1830.* Joseph Robins, 1830, 2 volumes, small 8vo., contemporary half crimson roan, gilt with marbled boards, little rubbed, pages viii, 244, x, 280, 2 engraved frontispiece and titles, 52 engraved plates and text woodcuts.   R. F. G. Hollett & Son Antiquarian Booksellers General Catalogue Summer 2010 - 1196 2011   £120

Robinson, Alan James *Cetacea, The Great Whales.* Easthampton: Cheloniidae Press, 1981, Artist's own copy, artist's proof #1, signed by artist, binders and printer, Harold Patrick McGrath; all on Arches Cover Buff, page size 22 x 15 inches, bound loose as issued with sheets laid in a full black Niger oasis goat folder sculpted in low relief with head of a Right Whale by David Bourbeau at The Thistle Bindery, beautiful folder housed in quarter leather moroccan goat drop back box by Gray Parrot, short split at lower joint of box, else fine; the 7 bleed etchings by Robinson depict the major species of whales, numerous blindstamped line-cut and two wood engravings, text contains biological information, 12 two-color maps showing migration routes and breeding areas printed by Harold McGrath at Hampshire Typothetae; artist printed at Cheloniidae Press.   Priscilla Juvelis - Rare Books 48 - 5 2011 $3000

Robinson, Alfred *Life in California Before the Conquest.* San Francisco: 1925, Limited to 250 numbered, signed by publisher/editor; xxiv, 316 pages, illustrations, 2 ads, quarter cloth, paper over boards, edgewear including some loss of paper exposing boards at extremities, bookplate, internally clean and very good.   Dumont Maps & Books of the West 111 - 76 2011 $300

Robinson, B. W. *Kuniyoshi. The Warrior Prints.* Ithaca: Cornell University Press, 1982, First edition; 4to. 208 pages, fine in fine dust jacket.   By the Book, L. C. 26 - 36 2011 $250

Robinson, Cedric *Sand Pilot of Morecambe Bay.* David & Charles, 1980, First edition; original cloth, gilt, dust jacket (price clipped), pages 157, plates and terxt drawings, scarce.   R. F. G. Hollett & Son Antiquarian Booksellers 173 - 980 2011   £40

Robinson, Charles Henry *Specimens of Hausa Literature.* Cambridge: University Press, 1896, First edition; small quarto, pages 112, numerous Arabic facsimile sheets, original dark green cloth, spine faded.   J. & S. L. Bonham Antiquarian Booksellers Africa 4/20/2011 - 4240 2011 £75

Robinson, Conway *Practice in the Courts of Law and Equity in Virginia.* Richmond: 1832-1839, 1832-1839, 3 volumes, volume one with original leather but backstrip has been remounted and repaired, volume 2 very good, volume 3 backstrip reglued, missing leather above title label. Bookworm & Silverfish 666 - 95 2011 $150

Robinson, Edgar E. *The Evolution of American Political Parties: a Sketch of Party Development.* New York: 1924, First edition; 382 pages, very good in green cloth and gilt lettering.   Bookworm & Silverfish 667 - 135 2011 $65

Robinson, H. Wheeler *The Baptists of Yorkshire.* London: Wm. Byles & Sons and Kingsgate Press, 1912, First edition; pages xiii, 328, with 170 illustrations, original cloth, gilt, scarce.   R. F. G. Hollett & Son Antiquarian Booksellers   175 - 1139   2011   £95

Robinson, J. H. *Silver-Knife, or the Hunter of the Rocky Mountains.* Boston: Hotchkiss and Co., 1850, First edition; tall 8vo., 103 pages, original printed front wrapper, uncut, browning, few stains and chipping of edges, spine shot, but sewn at center, tape on edges, good to very good.   M & S Rare Books, Inc.   90 - 374   2011 $850

Robinson, John *A Guide to the Lakes in Cumberland, Westmorland and Lancashire...* printed for Lackington Hughes, Harding, Mavor and Jones, 1819, First edition; original cloth backed sugar paper covered boards, corners rather worn, backstrip cloth rather defective in places, pages x, 328, folding map, hand colored in outline and 20 uncolored aquatints.   R. F. G. Hollett & Son Antiquarian Booksellers   173 - 981   2011   £250

Robinson, Marilynne *Gilead.* New York: Farrar Straus & Giroux, 2004, First edition; fine in near fine dust jacket, light wear to extremities,.   Bella Luna Books   May 29 2011 - t7546   2011 $110

Robinson, Marilynne *Gilead.* New York: Farrar Staus & Giroux, 2004, First edition; near fine, light bumping to head of spine, dust jacket near fine, light wear to spine ends.   Bella Luna Books   May 29 2011 - t7543   2011 $82

Robinson, Marilynne *Housekeeping.* New York: Farrar Straus Giroux, 1980, First edition; slightest of sunning to boards and touch of foxing on fore-edge, still easily fine in very near fine dust jacket with very slight sunning at spine.   Between the Covers   169 - BTC 342109   2011 $650

Robinson, Marilynne *Housekeeping.* London: Faber and Faber, 1981, First British edition from US sheets; 8vo., original publisher's blue cloth lettered gilt at spine, cloth very slightly tanned, otherwise fine in fine dust jacket.   Any Amount of Books   May 29 2011 - A49701   2011 $340

Robinson, Robert *A Political Catechism.* London: J. Buckland, C. Dilly, J. Mathews, J. Debrett and W. Lepard, 1782, First edition; 8vo., iv, 140 pages, last page little soiled, contemporary ownership inscription (Wm. Newman 1782 No. 6), recently well bound in old style quarter mottled calf over marbled boards, spine with raised bands and label, very good.   John Drury Rare Books   153 - 128   2011   £275

Robinson, Stanford F. H. *Celtic Illuminative Art in the Gospel Books of Durrow, Lindisfarne and Kells.* Dublin: 1908, First edition; ex-library, library cloth, xxx pages, frontispiece, 51 plates, each with an accompanying page of text, frontispiece and 6 plates colored, very good.   C. P. Hyland   May 26 2011 - 256/827   2011 $275

Robinson, W. W. *Land in California.* Berkeley and Los Angeles: University of California Press, 1948, First edition; xiii, 291 pages, 8 pages of illustrations from photos, gray cloth lettered in red, fine.   Argonaut Book Shop Recent Acquisitions Summer 2010 - 176   2011 $60

Robinson, W. W. *Ranchos Become Cities.* Pasadena: 1939, First edition; inscribed by author, 243 pages, map endpapers, very good in dust jacket with slight soil and edgewear.   Dumont Maps & Books of the West   112 - 62   2011 $100

Robinson, William *The Parks and Gardens of Paris Considered in Relation to the Wants of Other Cities and Of Public and Private Gardens.* London: John Murray, 1883, thir edition; 8vo., half dark brown leather, pages xxiv, 548, pencilled ownership signature of historian F. R. Cowell, presentation "From the author/Oct. 27h 1885", endpapers slightly stained, corner and hinges rubbed, one signature slightly protruding, otherwise very good.   Any Amount of Books   May 29 2011 - A47680   2011 $340

Robinson, William Heath *The Adventures of Uncle Lubin.* New York: Brentanos, 1902, First US edition; 8vo., pictorial cloth stamped in blue, green and white, expertly recased, else clean and very good+, color frontispiece, 55 full page black and whites and 72 vignettes plus pictorial endpapers,.   Aleph-Bet Books, Inc.   95 - 491   2011 $3000

Robinson, William Heath *Bill the Minder.* London: Hodder Stoughton, n.d. early 1920s, 4to., original pictorial orange cloth gilt, pages viii, 256, 16 color plates and numerous other illustrations, very good, clean and sound.   R. F. G. Hollett & Son Antiquarian Booksellers   General Catalogue Summer 2010 - 884   2011   £150

Robinson, William Heath *The Light Side of Photography.* Elstree, Herts: Wellington & Ward Ltd., 1925, 8vo., pictorial paper wrappers with few spots and some handling, within there is some light rippling at upper edges of few pages, 16 numbered pages within, black and white illustrations.   Jo Ann Reisler, Ltd.   86 - 208   2011 $600

Robinson, William Heath *Motor Mania.* London: The Motor Owner, 1921, 8vo., printed paper wrappers (stapled binding) with some light wear to covers, internally some light toning to edges of pages, illustrations.   Jo Ann Reisler, Ltd.   86 - 207   2011 $550

Robinson, William Heath *My Line of Life.* Blackie & Son, 1938, First edition; 4to., original pictorial brown cloth, little rubbed and bumped, pages (vi), 198, with 16 plates and numerous drawings. R. F. G. Hollett & Son Antiquarian Booksellers General Catalogue Summer 2010 - 313 2011 £65

Robinson, William Heath *Railway Ribaldry.* Great Western Railway, 1935, First edition; 96 pages, imperial 8vo., original stiff yapped edged wrappers, illustrated overall in green and yellow, very good. Blackwell Rare Books B166 - 227 2011 £95

Robinson, William Heath *Railway Ribaldry.* Great Western Railway, 1935, First edition; small 4to., original pictorial stiff wrappers, yapp edges little chipped and worn, pages 96, illustrations. R. F. G. Hollett & Son Antiquarian Booksellers General Catalogue Summer 2010 - 886 2011 £120

Robinson, William Heath *Some 'Frightful' War Pictures.* London: Duckworth, 1915, First edition; tall folio, original cloth backed pictorial boards, corners little worn, one slightly bumped, unpaginated, 24 full page cartoons, decorations, title illustration and pictorial endpapers all by Heath Robinson. R. F. G. Hollett & Son Antiquarian Booksellers General Catalogue Summer 2010 - 887 2011 £275

Robortello, Francesco *De Artificio Dicendi... Eiusdem Tabulae Oratoriae.* Bologna: Alessandro Benacci, 1567, First edition; extremely handsome, 4to., ff. 52, 20; 32, (18), italic type, large device on titlepage, 9 line woodcut mythological initials, Dutch polished calf, c. 1700, spine gilt, red edges, from the library of the Earls of Macclesfield at Shirburn Castle. Maggs Bros. Ltd. 1440 - 179 2011 £650

Roby, J. *Traditions of Lancashire.* London: Longman, Rees &c., 1829-1831, First edition; 4 volumes, finely bound in half maroon morocco gilt by Hayday, spines with 5 raised bands, marbled boards, top edge gilt, 2 engraved titles, 22 engraved plates, text woodcut vignettes, occasional patch of foxing or finger marking, few inked emendations, handsome, sound set. R. F. G. Hollett & Son Antiquarian Booksellers 175 - 1142 2011 £450

Roby, W. *A Selection of Hymns from Several of the Best Authors...* Manchester: Silburn and Co., 1830, Ninth edition; 12mo., modern full calf gilt, pages (iv), 270. R. F. G. Hollett & Son Antiquarian Booksellers 175 - 1143 2011 £65

Roche, Juliette *Demi Cercle.* Paris: Editions D'Art Le Cible, 1920, First edition, No. 479 of 500 copies; folio, pages (52), internally fresh and bright, gatherings loosely stitched but holding, publisher's mustard colored paper wrappers, upper and lower panels printed in black with design by Alfred Fleizes, spine detached from textblock and torn with some loss to foot, edges chipped, some soiling to lower panel. Simon Finch Rare Books Zero - 351 2011 £1250

Rochester, John, Earl of *The Works of...* London: printed for Jacob Tonson, 1714, First edition thus; 12mo., full 18th century brown calf, pages (xxiv), 312, frontispiece, scuffed on front board, rubbed at hinges and very slightly chipped at head of spine, overall sound, very good with clean text. Any Amount of Books May 26 2011 - A69111 2011 $503

Rochet D'Hericourt, Charles Francois Xavier *Rochet Second Voyage sur les Deux de la Mer Rouge dans la Pays de Adels et la Royame de Choa.* Paris: Arthus Bertrand, 1846, First edition; 15 tinted engraved plates and folding map (inch tear near fold), 8vo., pages xlviii, 406, contemporary quarter mottled calf, corners showing, boards rubbed, edges of boards and spine worn, head of spine abraded, small stain to title, small handstamp to title, institutional handstamp on verso of title, bleeding through title, back page browned, some soiling to front flyleaf, closed tear to errata at back of pages. Raymond M. Sutton, Jr. May 26 2011 - 44605 2011 $1500

Rochfort, Scott *Rambles in Egypt and Candia with Details of the Military Power and Resources of those Countries, and Observations of the Government...* London: Henry Colburn, 1837, First edition; 2 volumes 8vo., pages xx, 348; vii, 358, folding plan, 5 lithographs, recent brown half calf. J. & S. L. Bonham Antiquarian Booksellers Africa 4/20/2011 - 8139 2011 £580

Rochon, Abbe *A Voyage to Madagascar and the East Indies.* London: g. G. J. and J. Robinson, 1792, First edition; 8vo., pages li, 475, folding map, contemporary brown half calf, spine and joints rubbed, internally very clean, crisp copy. J. & S. L. Bonham Antiquarian Booksellers Africa 4/20/2011 - 8137 2011 £550

Rock, Marion Tuttle *Illustrated History of Its Occupation by Spain and France Its Sale to the United States Its Opening to Settlement in 1889 and the Meeting of the First Legislature.* Topeka: C. B. Hamilton & Son, 1890, First edition; thick 8vo., maroon decorated cloth, gold stamping on front cover and spine, decorated endpapers, xii, 277, (1) pages, frontispiece, illustrations, all edges red, some professional restoration to fore-ege of front flyleaf, lightly sunned on spine, light wear to spine ends and corners, else very good, scarce, housed in maroon quarter leather and cloth slipcase, gold stamping on spine and raised bands. Buckingham Books May 26 2011 - 21004 2011 $2500

Rocket Press *Rocket Ephemera.* Blewbury, Oxfordshire: Rocket Press, 1994, One of 80 sets; containing 55 pieces of letterpress printing by Jonathan Stephenson at his Rocket Press, printed in a variety of sizes, colors and on various color papers, small folio, original mid brown drop-down back box, printed labels on backstrip and top and bottom of box, fine. Blackwell Rare Books   B166 - 272 2011   £50

Rockwell, John Arnold *A Compilation of Spanish and Mexican Law, in Relation to Mines and Titles to Real Estate, in force in California, Texas and New Mexico and in the Territories Acquired Under the Louisiana and Florida Treaties.* New York: John S. Voorhies, 1851, First edition; pages (i-iii), iv-xix, (1, blank), (2, errata), (7)-663, (1), period full blindstamped light brown sheep, professionally rebacked with original red and black leather labels, laid down new endpapers, contemporary news clipping on inner cover pertaining to new colonisation laws of Mexico, enacted in 1854, contemporary owner's name (Nathl. Bennett), "volume I (only volume published) erased on title page leaving two small holes and light scarring, some occasional very light foxing, especially to front and endleaves, else fine and fresh, very scarce.   Argonaut Book Shop   Recent Acquisitions Summer 2010 - 133 2011 $2750

Rockwood Pottery Company *Rockwood Pottery Founded in 1880 Its History and Its Aims.* Cincinnati: circa, 1915, 16 pages, 6 x 4 1/2 inches, wrappers, very good, very scarce.   Bookworm & Silverfish   678 - 26 2011 $125

Roe, Charles Francis *Custer's Last Battle.* New York: 1927, 40 pages, maps and illustrations, 12 x 9 inches, pamphlet, original printed wrappers, light soil and edgewear, top corner slightly bumped, else near fine presentation to noted Custer collector Melvin J. Nichols.   Dumont Maps & Books of the West   111 - 38 2011 $100

Roe, F. Gordon *Women in Profile. A Study in Silhouette.* London: John Baker, 1970, First edition; original pictorial two-tone cloth, pages 69 with 42 illustrations. R. F. G. Hollett & Son Antiquarian Booksellers   175 - 1146 2011   £30

Roelands, David *T'magazi oft' pac-huys der loffelycker penn-const.* Vlissingen: letterpress printed at Middleburg by R. Schilders, 1616, (1617); Oblong folio, ff., (47) (44 engraved leaves including title and 3 leaves of letterpress comprising dedication to the Aldermen of Flushing (in French) and "To the reader" (in Dutch), engraved portrait of Roelands, later vellum backed blue paper boards, title leaf creased, few plates very slightly shaved at top edge, just touching swirls, from the library of the Earls of Macclesfield at Shirburn Castle.   Maggs Bros. Ltd.   1440 - 180 2011   £800

Roenau, Ernst *Thousand and One Nights.* Chicago: Julius Wisotzki, n.d. circa, 1920, Folio, cloth backed pictorial boards, 64 pages, fine, illustrations by Rosa with 10 absolutely stunning mounted color plates with detailed black and whites in text, truly a beauty.   Aleph-Bet Books, Inc. 95 - 51 2011 $500

Rogers, Clark *The Husbandman's Aim to Refute the Clergy; Respecting the Decrees of God.* New London: S. Green for the author, 1801, First edition; 8vo., (2), 2, (5)-39 pages, new facsimile printed wrappers, last leaf with five lines of text in printed facsimile, sheets browned, upper corners shaved, uncut, rare.   M & S Rare Books, Inc.   90 - 29 2011 $225

Rogers, David *The Bodleian Library.* Aidan Ellis, 1991, First edition; small 4to., original cloth, gilt, dust jacket, pages 176, illustrations in color.   R. F. G. Hollett & Son Antiquarian Booksellers General Catalogue Summer 2010 - 618 2011   £35

Rogers, George Alfred *The Art of Wood-Carving.* London: Virtue & Co., 1871, Fifth edition; vi (2) 24 (2) pages, 20 plates, good copy, original dark plum cloth, gilt lettered, scarce.   Ken Spelman Rare Books   68 - 79 2011 £85

Rogers, John *Sport in Vancouver and Newfoundland...* Toronto: Musson Book Co., 1912, First Canadian edition; blue cloth with gilt title to spine, pages xii, (2)-275, (1), half title, frontispiece, 7 drawings, 27 black and white photo illustrations and 2 maps, 8vo.,.   Schooner Books Ltd.   96 - 89 2011 $75

Rogers, Nicola *Free Movement of Persons in the Enlarged European Union.* London: Sweet Maxwell, 2005, 8vo., original publisher's illustrated laminated boards, 738 pages, rear cover faintly marked, very good+, excellent condition.   Any Amount of Books   May 29 2011 - A69328 2011 $238

Rogers, Samuel *The Pleasures of Memory with Other Poems.* London: printed for T. Cadell Jun. and W. Davies, 1799, 165 x 102mm., 8 p.l., (9)-188 pages, extremely pleasing etruscan style calf in the style of, and quite probably by, Edwards of Halifax, covers with Greek-key roll border, wide inner frame of stencilled palmettes, and central flamed calf panel formed here by foliate roll, raised bands, spine compartments with gilt wheat and horn centerpiece and foliate corner ornaments, black morocco label, chained gilt turn-ins, marbled endpapers, all edges gilt; with pleasing pastel fore-edge painting of a scene from the (Italian?) countryside, featuring long arched ridge and title roofed villa, 4 engraved plates; joints and extremities just little dried and worn, trivial foxing and offsetting in text, still excellent, unrestored copy, binding entirely sound, with no cracks in joints, text very clean an fresh, bright copy.   Phillip J. Pirages 59 - 38 2011 $1750

Rogers, Samuel *The Pleasures of Memory and Other Poems...* New York: Evert Duyckinck printed by McFarlane & Long, 1808, 12mo., x, 254 pages, full calf, gilt, title label on spine, 7 very fine full page wood engravings, tailpiece vignettes, apparently rebacked, scattered foxing, inked name on titlepage, small corner of one leaf restored, scarce title in very good state. Hobbyhorse Books 56 - 132 2011 $250

Rogers, Samuel *Recollections of the Table Talk of Samuel Rogers to Which is added Porsoniana.* London: Edward Moxon, 1856, Apparently the first edition; 199 x 130 mm., viii, 355 pages, bound with half title with inserted plate as frontispiece, very pleasing later dark brown crushed morocco, attractively gilt, covers with French fillet border and elegant botanical cornerpieces, raised bands, heavily gilt spine in compartments featuring elaborate scrolling cornerpieces, an intricate fleuron centerpiece, and tiny circlets, turn-ins with plain and stippled rules and filigree with gilt decoration at corners and midpoints of two sides, textured (silk?) brown and cream millefleur-patterned endpapers, all edges gilt, extra illustrated with 55 portrait plates, five in color, all with tissue guards, engraved bookplate of Robert B. Lawrence, hint of browning to some of the inserted plates, fine, handsomely bound copy, text especially fresh, clean and smooth, binding bright and virtually unworn; hint of browning to some of the inserted plates, fine, handsomely bound copy, text especially fresh, clean and smooth, binding bright and virtually unworn. Phillip J. Pirages 59 - 131 2011 $650

Rogerson, Ian *Agnes Miller Parker, Wood-engraver and Book Illustrator 1895-1980.* Wakefield: Fleece Press, 1990, One of 251 copies (of an edition of 300 copies); printed in black and blue on Zerkall mouldmade paper in double column, 35 wood engravings and color printed paintings in tempera, all by Agnes Miller Parker, tipped in reproductions of 3 photos and pencil drawing, pages 88 (2), oblong small folio, original quarter mid blue buckram, printed label, multi colored patterned paste paper boards by Claire Maziarczyk, untrimmed, cloth edged board slipcase, printed label, fine. Blackwell Rare Books B166 - 251 2011 £300

Rogerson, Sydney *Both Sides of the Road.* London: Collins, 1949, First edition; 4to., original cloth, dust jacket, pages 183, with 23 full page color plates and numerous black and white illustrations, fine, very scarce in such lovely condition. R. F. G. Hollett & Son Antiquarian Booksellers General Catalogue Summer 2010 - 1069 2011 £120

Rogerson, Sydney *Our Bird Book.* London: Collins, 1949, Third edition; 4to., original cloth, gilt, dust jacket some chips and loss, all neatly repaired and replaced with matching paper, pages 128, with 52 color illustrations and numerous black and white drawings, slight spotting to endpapers. R. F. G. Hollett & Son Antiquarian Booksellers General Catalogue Summer 2010 - 1068 2011 £50

Roland, Mme. De *Memoirs de Madame de Roland.* Paris: Librairie des Bibliophiles, 1884, Onr og 20 numbered copies on Whatman of a total edition of 40 copies; 2 volumes, (xiii, 322 and (1), 328 pages and (2), 16mo., contemporary half brown morocco over marbled boards, richly gilt decorated and gilt lettered spines, frontispiece reproduced in triplicate in each volume, titlepages printed in red and black, original printed wrappers bound in, top edge gilt, front wrapper in second volume reinforced, spines evenly sunned, still a fine and very appealing set with original wrappers bound in. Paulette Rose Fine and Rare Books 32 - 148 2011 $375

Rolfe, Frederick William 1860-1913 *Baron Corvo to Kenneth Grahame.* N.P.: The Peacocks, 1962, First edition, number 20 of 40 copies for private distribution; wrappers, 8vo., 10 pages on handmade paper printed by Alan Anderson of Tragara Press, faint soiling, else very good+ or better. Any Amount of Books May 29 2011 - A45994 2011 $213

Rolfe, Frederick William 1860-1913 *Don Tarquinio.* London: Chatto & Windus, 1905, First edition; half title, title in red and black, colophon leaf, few leaves carelessly opened at end, original red cloth, gilt lettered, spine faded. Jarndyce Antiquarian Booksellers CXCI - 471 2011 £68

Rolfe, Frederick William 1860-1913 *Letter from Baron Corvo.* Reading: Peacocks Press, 1958, First edition, number 4 of 30 copies; large 8vo., pages 8, light blue wrappers, about fine. Any Amount of Books May 29 2011 - B24213 2011 $213

Rolle, Henry *Un Abridgment des Plusieurs Cases et Resolutions Del Common Ley...* A. Crooke etc., 1668, Folio, contemporary full blind ruled calf, edges rather worn, hinges splitting at ends, pages xi, 940, engraved portrait by A. Hertochs, typographical headpiece and 2 decorated initials, text mostly in black letter. R. F. G. Hollett & Son Antiquarian Booksellers 175 - 1148 2011 £450

Rollins, Hyder E. *An Analytical Index to the Ballad Entries (1577-1709) in the Registers of the Company of Stationers of London.* Harboro: Tradition Press, 1967, Original blue cloth gilt, pages xviii, 324. R. F. G. Hollett & Son Antiquarian Booksellers 175 - 1149 2011 £120

Rollinson, William *A History of Man in the Lake District.* London: Dent, 1967, First edition; original cloth, gilt, dust jacket, pages xii, 162, 16 plates and 28 text figures. R. F. G. Hollett & Son Antiquarian Booksellers 173 - 989 2011 £45

Rollinson, William *Life and Tradition in the Lake District.* London: Dent, 1974, First edition; small 4to., original cloth, gilt, dust jacket, spine faded as usual, pages 205, 193 plates. R. F. G. Hollett & Son Antiquarian Booksellers 173 - 992 2011 £40

Roman Roads in the South-East Midlands. London: Gollancz, 1964, First edition; thick 8vo., original cloth, gilt, dust jacket spine rather darkened, pages 526, 145 pages of maps, 19 pages of section diagrams and 17 photos.   R. F. G. Hollett & Son Antiquarian Booksellers   177 - 562 2011   £50

Roman, Alfred   *Military Operations of General Beauregard.* New York: 1884, 2 volumes, nearly 1300 pages, full green cloth with some scrapes, all gilt bright except for two letters, tops of backstrip (above gilt) frayed, top edge gilt, top cover volume 1 very mildly shelf bowed.   Bookworm & Silverfish   676 - 52 2011 $187

Romanus, Adrianus   *Ventorum Secundum Recentiores Distinctorum Usus.* Wurzburg: G. Fleischman, 1596, Small 4to., ff. (9), rebound in half calf, old style, from the library of the Earls of Macclesfield at Shirburn Castle.   Maggs Bros. Ltd.   1440 - 181 2011   £900

Romeo, Francis   *Mirror: Presented to His Sicilian Majesty, Great Britain and the Allied Sovereigns: Reflecting Political Facts of the Utmost Importance, Calculated to Undeceive Them.* London: Printed for author by Dennet Jacques, sold by Brown & Hecker/Simpkin, Marshall, London, 1820, First edition; 8vo., xii, 9-352, frontispiece, sound but disbound (i.e. lacking boards), rear blank slightly soiled chipped, otherwise internally clean.   Any Amount of Books   May 29 2011 - B26422 2011 $238

Romer, C. F.   *The Second Battalion Royal Dublin Fusiliers in the South African War.* London: A. L. Humphrys, 1908, First edition; 8vo., pages xiv, 271, numerous illustrations, original green cloth, very good, presentation copy from Major A. E. Mainwaring.   J. & S. L. Bonham Antiquarian Booksellers   Africa 4/20/2011 - 8300 2011   £175

Romer, F.   *The Bone Caves of Ojcow in Poland.* London: Longmans, Green and Co., 1884, First English edition; large 4to., original cloth, gilt, corners and lower edges rubbed and little worn, pages viii, (iv), 41, with woodburytype frontispiece (mount and tissue lightly foxed), map and 12 lithographed plates, each with leaf of text, scarce.   R. F. G. Hollett & Son Antiquarian Booksellers   177 - 752 2011   £180

Ronalds, Alfred   *Companion to Alfred Ronald's Fly Fisher's Entomology.* London: Longman Green & co. n.d. c., 1890, Brown limp linen fisherman's fly wallet, foldover flap with popper, edges bound in grey linen with internal pockets and leather pocketed needle holder strip, pages 14, printed with 47 descriptions of flies, offsetting of leather strip on to title few pencilled names on first 2 interleaved sheets, else fine, unused copy, scarce.   R. F. G. Hollett & Son Antiquarian Booksellers   General Catalogue Summer 2010 - 1276 2011   £175

Ronalds, Alfred   *The Fly-Fisher's Entomology.* London: Longman, Green and Co., 1877, Eighth edition; original blindstamped green cloth, gilt, extremities little frayed and bumped, lower hinge repaired at foot, pages xiv, (ii), 132, 24, 20 finely hand colored plates, front joint strained and strengthened, armorial bookplates of Thomas Towneley Parker and Reginald Arthur Tatton.   R. F. G. Hollett & Son Antiquarian Booksellers   General Catalogue Summer 2010 - 1277 2011   £195

Ronalds, Alfred   *The Fly-Fisher's Entomology.* Secaucus: Wellfleet Press, 1990, New edition; extra color plates, original boards, gilt with pictorial onlay, pages xvi, 132, 20 color plates, excellent reprint of fifth edition of 1856.   R. F. G. Hollett & Son Antiquarian Booksellers   General Catalogue Summer 2010 - 1278 2011   £35

Rooke, Octavius   *The Life of the Moselle, From Its Source in the Vosges Mountains to Its Junction with Rhine at Coblence.* London: L. Booth, 1858, Half title, frontispiece, illustrations, original maroon cloth, bevelled boards, heavily decorated in gilt and blind, spine slightly faded, prize label laid down on leading pastedown, all edges gilt, very good.   Jarndyce Antiquarian Booksellers   CXCI - 575 2011   £150

Roome, William J. W.   *Can Africa be Won?* London: A. & C. Black, 1927, First edition; 8vo., pages 209, map, illustrations, original blue cloth, spine little faded.   J. & S. L. Bonham Antiquarian Booksellers   Africa 4/20/2011 - 7967 2011   £35

Roosevelt, Eleanor   *A Trip to Washington with Bobby & Betty.* New York: 1935, First edition (so stated); 91 (blank) pages, 4to., full page photo illustrations, very good in clean, red cloth, while ink lettering unblemished, premium copy.   Bookworm & Silverfish   668 - 67 2011 $125

Roosevelt, Theodore 1858-1919   *East of the Sun and West of the Moon.* New York: Scribner's, 1926, First edition; photos, decorated cloth, gilt big horned wild sheep, this copy, signed by Theodore Roosevelt Jr. above his picture in frontispiece, near fine.   Lupack Rare Books   May 26 2011 - 100 2011 $150

Roper, William Oliver   *The Churches, Castles and Ancient Halls of North Lancashire.* Lancaster: E. and A. J. Milner, 1880, First (only) edition; 4to., modern half green calf gilt, few slight marks to bottom of upper board, pages 210, 24, 4 maps and plans and 28 plates, pictorial wrappers, from all of the original five parts bound in at end, together with an invoice to W. Saunders of Wennington Hall from E. and I. L. Milner, extremely scarce.   R. F. G. Hollett & Son Antiquarian Booksellers   173 - 995 2011   £450

Roper, William Oliver *The Churches, Castles and Ancient Halls of North Lancashire.* Lancaster: E. and A. J. Milner, 1880, first edition; 4to., near contemporary half morocco gilt by John Barber of Lancaster, pages 210, 24 with 4 maps and plans and 28 plates. joints strengthened, extremely scarce. R. F. G. Hollett & Son Antiquarian Booksellers General Catalogue Summer 2010 - 1572 2011 £395

Rorer, David *A Treatise on the Law of Judicial and Execution Sales.* Chicago: 1873, First edition; xxxi 411 pages, very good in old law calf, front cover with opaque change to fore edge. Bookworm & Silverfish 667 - 90 2011 $75

Ros, Amanda McKittrick *Irene Iddesleigh.* Belfast: printed by W. & G. Baird, 1897, First edition; half title, original red cloth, spine faded, cutting tipped in prelims. Jarndyce Antiquarian Booksellers CXCI - 472 2011 £90

Ros, Amanda McKittrick *Irene Iddesleigh.* Belfast: 1897, First edition; 189 pages, errata slip, initialled by author, green cloth, spine bit darkened and canted, otherwise nice, Philip Burne-Jones's copy, signed by him on endpaper and later inscribed by him to "Fred. (E.F.?) Benson, tipped in brief one sentence ALS from author to Burne-Jones. Joseph J. Felcone Inc. Fall Miscellany 2010 - 103 2011 $475

Roscoe, John *Twenty-Five Years in East Africa.* Cambridge: University Press, 1921, First edition; 8vo., 288 pages, map, illustrations, original brick red cloth. J. & S. L. Bonham Antiquarian Booksellers Africa 4/20/2011 - 9218 2011 £150

Roscoe, Thomas *The Tourist in Italy.* London: Jennings & Chaplin, 1932, Original green roan gilt, hinges and corners rubbed, crack in top lower hinge repaired, pages (ii), iv, 288, all edges gilt, engraved title, and 25 steel engraved plates, margins rather foxed. R. F. G. Hollett & Son Antiquarian Booksellers General Catalogue Summer 2010 - 1657 2011 £120

The Rose-Posie Book. London: Thomas Nelson, 1920, Pages (48) with 12 full page color plates and 12 monochrome decorated pages of text, printed on oppposing pages, versos blank. R. F. G. Hollett & Son Antiquarian Booksellers General Catalogue Summer 2010 - 485 2011 £85

Rose, Cowper *Four Years in Southern Africa.* London: Henry Colburn, 1829, First edition; 8vo., pages xii, 308, frontispiece, contemporary brown calf, rebacked using original spine. J. & S. L. Bonham Antiquarian Booksellers Africa 4/20/2011 - 6811 2011 £250

Rose, T. *Westmorland, Cumberland, Durham and Northumberland Illustrated.* H. Fisher, R. Fisher and P. Jackson, 1832-1835, 4to., engraved titlepage and 108 leaves with 214 plates, very good, clean, contemporary half calf, most handsomely rebacked, blind lattice decoration with raised and gilt bands, original floral embossed cloth boards, large green morocco label on upper cover. Ken Spelman Rare Books 68 - 177 2011 £295

Rosenbach, Abraham Simon Wolf 1876-1952 *Early American Children's Books.* Portland: Southworth Press, 1933, Limited to 585 copies signed by author, this being number 450; large quarto, lviii, 354, (2), pictorial paper on boards, three quarter leather spine with six compartments and gilt title, cased in original brown paper with green pictorial label and title on upper cover, partially uncut. Hobbyhorse Books 56 - 11 2011 $600

Rosenbach, Abraham Simon Wolf 1876-1952 *Early American Children's Books.* Portland: Southworth Press, 1933, Limited to 585 copies signed by author; large 4to., leather backed pictorial boards, 354 pages, fine in slipcase (solid but shows signs of wear, overall very good), illustrations hand colored after originals, beautiful copy. Aleph-Bet Books, Inc. 95 - 495 2011 $650

Rosenberg-Orsini, Giustiniana Wynne *Del Soggiorno dei Conti del Nord a Venezia in Gennaro del MDCCLXXXII.* Venice: Storti?, 1782, (77 pages), 3 blank, 8vo., contemporary floral "Remondini" wrappers over thin flexible boards, small inkstain in lower margin of pages 26 and 27, otherwise fine, crisp and attractive copy. Paulette Rose Fine and Rare Books 32 - 149 2011 $1750

Rosenfeld, Paul *Musical Portraits.* London: Kegan Paul etc., 1922, First edition; original red cloth gilt, , pages 314, fine. R. F. G. Hollett & Son Antiquarian Booksellers 175 - 1153 2011 £120

Rosenwater, Irving *Sir Donald Bradman. A Biography.* London: Batsford, 1978, First edition; original cloth, gilt, dust jacket, pages 416, 44 plates, presentation from author. R. F. G. Hollett & Son Antiquarian Booksellers General Catalogue Summer 2010 - 1279 2011 £35

Ross, Alexander 1590-1654 *Pansebeia: or a View of all Religions in the World, from the Creation to These Times.* London: printed for John Saywell, 1653, Large 12mo., new full polished calf gilt with raised bands, frontispiece, engraved title with vignette of a greyhound, A1-A12 (contents etc.), pages 578, Dd1-Dd6 (table), 18th century manuscript and scribbles on front endpapers. R. F. G. Hollett & Son Antiquarian Booksellers 175 - 1154 2011 £220

Ross, Alexander 1590-1654 *Der Wunderwurdige Juden-Und Heiden Tempel Darinn Derselben Gottes und Gotzen-Dinst Eroffnet...* Nuremberg: Johann E.. Ernst Adelbulner, 1701, Thick 8vo., (12), 1195, (83) pages, frontispiece, 11 double page engravings, 56 single page engravings, 1 text woodcut left half of frontispiece missing, folding plate at page 254 also missing half of image, original calf, raised bands, gilt stamped spine panels, gilt stamped spine title, corners bumped, corners showing, very good. Jeff Weber Rare Books   163 - 28 2011 $550

Ross, Charles H. *The True Story of Ally Sloper and the Paint Pot.* New York: Art Lithographic Publishing Co., London: Artistic Lithographic Co., circa, 1891, Dated from presentation inscription; Color chromolithograph illustrations, some very slight offsetting, titlepage slightly dusted, original grey cut-out wrappers, chromo lithographs, sewn as issued, very good, (16) pages.   Jarndyce Antiquarian Booksellers   CXCI - 369 2011   £250

Ross, E. Denison *The Art of Egypt through the Ages.* London: The Studio, 1931, First edition; 4to., original blue cloth, gilt over bevelled boards, boards rather damped and spine faded, pages (iv), 354, with 6 color plates and numerous plates.   R. F. G. Hollett & Son Antiquarian Booksellers   177 - 753 2011   £35

Ross, Malcolm *A Climber in New Zealand.* London: Arnold, 1914, First edition; half title, frontispiece with tissue guard, 30 black and white photo plates, pages xx, 316, 8 (publisher's catalog), 8vo., original fine diagonal grain olive green cloth, smooth backstrip lettered gilt, front board blind panelled and lettered gilt, neat ex-libris bookplate, c. 1940's luggage label from "The Hermitage" laid in, scant foxmarks on fore edge, very good.   Blackwell Rare Books   B166 - 71 2011   £350

Ross, Margaret Clunies *Skaldic Poetry of the Scandinavian Middle Ages.* Turnhout: Brepols, 2007, First edition; 2 volumes, 8vo., fine, pages 1109.   Any Amount of Books   May 29 2011 - A70198 2011 $213

Ross, Mr. *Hesitation: or, To Marry or Not to Marry?* New York: 1819, 2 volumes, 12mo., new leather and new labels, probably original marbled boards.   Bookworm & Silverfish   666 - 149 2011 $150

Rosselli, Cosmo *Thesaurus Artificiosae Memorae... Perutilis...* Venice: A. Paduano bibliopola Fiorentino, 1579, First edition; 4to., ff. (16), 145 (errata), printed in italic, 2 leaves with double page, woodcut at centre signed E4 and a similar 2 leaves at R3 with single woodcut on first recto and second verso, full page woodcut, with some repeats, contemporary limp vellum, lacking ties, from the library of the Earls of Macclesfield at Shirburn Castle.   Maggs Bros. Ltd.   1440 - 182 2011   £5000

Rossetti, Christina 1830-1894 *Goblin Market.* London: Macmillan, 1893, First edition thus; slim 8vo., green cloth gilt, boards decorated overall with foliate pattern in gilt, pages (iv), 63, 12 full page woodcut plates and numerous woodcuts, all by Laurence Housman, contemporary gift inscription on flyleaf, endpapers lightly foxed or browned, otherwise very nice, clean and sound copy.   R. F. G. Hollett & Son Antiquarian Booksellers   General Catalogue Summer 2010 - 674 2011   £350

Rossetti, Christina 1830-1894 *Goblin Market.* London: George G. Harrap and Co., 1933, One of 410 copies (400 for sale) signed by artist; 235 x 155mm., 42, (3) pages, original publisher's limp vellum, original(?) tissue dust jacket, original slipcase with printed paper label on top, illustrated endpapers, half title, titlepage, text illustrations and 4 color plates, all by Arthur Rackham, titlepage partly printed in green; slight fraying and tiny chips missing along top of front panel of dust jacket, otherwise almost amazing copy, even slipcase being unusually clean and volume itself virtually printed.   Phillip J. Pirages   59 - 293 2011 $2250

Rossetti, Christina 1830-1894 *Poems Chosen by Walter De La Mare.* Gregynog Press, 1930, One of 25 copies specially bound, of a total edition of 300; 235 x 159mm., 3 p.l., vii-xliii, (1), 107, (1) pages, very fine animated scarlet morocco by Gregynog (signed in gilt by R. Ashwin Maynard and George Fisher on rear turn-in), gilt tooled covers dominated by two large cruciform foliate ornaments elaborated with diagonal blind and gilt decoration (something like evergreen leaves), ornaments on a field of gold dots, covers bordered by gilt and blind rules from which emanate a series of similar gilt and blind evergreen decorations, spine with raised bands, panels outlined in blind, gilt titling, turn-ins with double gilt rule, top edge gilt, other edges untrimmed, original publisher's board slipcase (slightly soiled but sturdy), initial openings and frontispiece after drawings by Dante Gabriel Rossetti, printed in red and black throughout, one page with trivial stain, otherwise virtually pristine.   Phillip J. Pirages   59 - 228 2011 $7500

Rossetti, Dante Gabriel 1828-1882 *Hand and Soul.* Kelmscott Press, 1895, One of 525 copies on paper (an additional 21 copies were Printed on vellum); 145 x 110, 2 p.l. 56 pages, original stiff vellum flat spine with vertical titling, small woodcut text tools, four and six line initials, first text opening with elaborate woodcut full border, printed in red and black; grain of vellum showing slightly, otherwise quite fine, very clean, fresh, bright internally.   Phillip J. Pirages   59 - 245 2011 $1250

Rossetti, Dante Gabriel 1828-1882 *The House of Life.* Boston: Copeland and Day, 1894, First edition; complete edition, small 4to., half leather, lettered and decorated gilt at spine with raised bands, 500 copies, on French handmade paper, pages 120, 3 borders and 114 initial letters designed by Bertram Grosvenor Goodhue, some rubbing and slight wear at spine (more pronounced at covers), neat name on first blank, overall about very good.   Any Amount of Books   May 29 2011 - B25799 2011 $213

Rossetti, Dante Gabriel 1828-1882 *Sonnets and Lyrical Poems.* Kelmscott Press for Ellis & Ivey, 1894, One of 310 copies on paper (6 were issued on vellum); 210 x 143mm., 6 p.l., 197 pages, original flexible vellum with silk ties, gilt titling on spine, edges untrimmed and all but first two gatherings, unopened, lovely large and small woodcut initials, elaborate woodcut frontispiece and border on first page of text, printed in red and black, presentation inscription to Lewis Flower from "SS" dated July 1897; just hint of soil to vellum, but extraordinarily fine, binding unusually lustrous and obviously mostly unread, text virtually pristine. Phillip J. Pirages 59 - 246 2011 $3000

Rosslyn, Earl *The Gram: a Social Magazine Founded by British Prisoners of War in Pretoria.* London: Eyre & Spottiswoode, n.d., 1900, Facsimile edition, no. 2 of a limited edition of 500 and was signed by author; quarto, illustrations, original cream decorative vellum backed boards, photo on upper cover, illustrations, very good and clean. J. & S. L. Bonham Antiquarian Booksellers Africa 4/20/2011 - 8367 2011 £95

Rostand, Edmond *Cyrano de Bergerac.* Paris: Librairie Charpentier et Fasquelle, 1898, First edition; octavo, original light green printed wrappers. Heritage Book Shop Booth A12 51st NY International Antiquarian Book Fair April 8-10 2011 - 108 2011 $2500

Roth, A. *Werk.* 1948, 240 issues, all very good. I. D. Edrich May 26 2011 - 82767 2011 $1510

Rourke, L. *Men Only in the Air.* London: C. Arthur Pearson, 1941, First reprint; original blue stiff wrappers, pages 96, frontispiece, scattered foxing, mainly to half title and final leaf, very scarce. R. F. G. Hollett & Sons Antiquarian Booksellers 170 - 601 2011 £45

Rousseau, Jean Jacques 1712-1778 *Eloisa; or a Series of Original Letters Together with the Sequel of Julia, or the New Eloisa.* Philadelphia: 1796, Stated first edition; 3 volumes, 12mo., vii, 275; 267; 259 pages, 12mo., full sheep, volume 1 top cover loose, backstrip gone, bookplate in each volume. Bookworm & Silverfish 662 - 60 2011 $150

Rousseau, Jean Jacques 1712-1778 *Emile ou De l'Education.* The Hague: i.e. Paris: Chez Jean Neaulme, 1762, First edition; 4 volumes, octavo, 5 engraved plates, contemporary French mottled calf. Heritage Book Shop Booth A12 51st NY International Antiquarian Book Fair April 8-10 2011 - 109 2011 $7500

Rousseau, Jean Jacques 1712-1778 *Emilius or a Treatise on Education.* Edinburgh: printed by A. Donaldson, 1768, 3 volumes, contemporary full speckled calf gilt, hinges just cracking in places but sound, pages 344, 274, (ii), 246, (xlii), titles with ornamental borders, contemporary inscription of James Howson dated 1769 on each flyleaf, very attractive early English edition. R. F. G. Hollett & Son Antiquarian Booksellers 175 - 1156 2011 £450

Rousseau, Josue *Ensayo da Arte Grammatical Portugueza & Franceza, Para Aquelles que Sabendo a Lingua Franceza Querem Aprender a Portugueza Primeira Parte.* Lisbon: A. P. Galram, 1705, First edition; 4to., (8), 176 pages, hand colored woodcut device on titlepage, woodcut illustrations, woodcut initials and headpiece, contemporary vellum over boards, few small tears with slight loss, pages browned, spine cracking, from the library of the Earls of Macclesfield at Shirburn Castle. Maggs Bros. Ltd. 1440 - 183 2011 £500

Roussel, Diana Edwards *The Castleford Pottery 1790-1821.* Wakefield Historical Publications, 1982, First edition; large 8vo., original cloth gilt, dust jacket, spine little faded, pages 78, (57, 7, facsimile pattern book), (x), with 5 color plates and 107 illustrations. R. F. G. Hollett & Son Antiquarian Booksellers General Catalogue Summer 2010 - 316 2011 £75

Roussel, Pierre *Systeme Physique et Moral de la Femme, ou Tableau Philosophique de la Constitution, de l'Etat Organique, Du Temperament, Des Moeurs des Fonctions Propre au Sexe.* Paris: Chez Crapart, Caille et Ravier..., 1803, 8vo., 1-52; (i)-xx; 1-283 pages, including index, 8vo., contemporary tree calf, contrasting red title label, gilt lettered and decorated spine, all edges red, extremities bit rubbed, small and neat shelf mark on spine, otherwise very sound. Paulette Rose Fine and Rare Books 32 - 123 2011 $350

Roustam, Bek *Aerial Russia. The Romance of the Giant Aeroplane.* London: Bodley Head, 1916, First edition; 8vo., original publisher's cloth lettered blue on cover and brown on spine, pages xvi, 154, uncut, frontispiece and 19 plates, signed presentation from Chessborough MacKenzie Kennedy, remains of dust jacket loosely inserted, slight browning to pages, else very good or better. Any Amount of Books May 29 2011 - A39876 2011 $221

Routledge, W. Scoresby *The Akikuyu of British Africa: Being Some Account of the method and Mode of Thought Found Existent Amongst a Nation on Its First Contact with European Civilisation.* London: Edward Arnold, 1910, First edition; large 8vo., pages xxxii, 392, folding map, illustrations, original green decorative cloth, gilt vignette, spine faded, small paper label on base of spine, very good, presentation copy from publishers. J. & S. L. Bonham Antiquarian Booksellers Africa 4/20/2011 - 2614 2011 £165

Rowcroft, Charles *Tales of the Colonies; or the Adventures of an Emigrant.* London: Smith Elder & Co., 1858, New edition; half title, final ad leaf, ads on endpapers, original printed orange glazed cloth, dulled and little marked, presentation "J. Percy Holyoake with his father's best love June 4th 1864". Jarndyce Antiquarian Booksellers CXCI - 476 2011 £35

Rowe, Minnie *Gully Folk.* Melbourne: Melbourne Publishing Co., n.d. circa, 1919, 8vo., boards, pictorial paste-on, 77 pages, very good+ in pictorial dust jacket (with some soil and wear), illustrations by author with 6 fantastic color plates and many line illustrations, rare, especially in dust jacket. Aleph-Bet Books, Inc. 95 - 57 2011 $975

Rowland, Benjamin *The Art and Architecutre of India.* Penguin Books, 1953, First edition; small 4to., original cloth, gilt, dust jacket little chipped and worn, some tears repaired on reverse, pages xvii, 289, with 190 plates. R. F. G. Hollett & Son Antiquarian Booksellers 177 - 755 2011 £85

Rowlandson, T. *Pretty Little Games for Young Ladies & Gentlemen.* 1845, (1872). First edition, few copies only Printed for the artist's friends; small 4to., pages 62 including 10 full page erotic etchings by Rowlandson, each incorporating a short (10 line) obscene verse by artist, etched below each plate, quarter morocco and marbled boards, blue endpapers, gilt lettered on spine, slightly rubbed and bumped, excellent copy, extremely rare. Simon Finch Rare Books Zero - 426 2011 £4500

Rowley, Alexander *Hever le Talmidim.* London: M. Bell for William Larner and George Wittington, 1648, First edition; 8vo., (8), 210, (2), 152, 432 pages, woodcut headpieces and initials, contemporary calf, some headliners and catchwords cut close or shaved, few small wormholes, rust hole in Vvv7, extremities rubbed, from the library of the Earls of Macclesfield at Shirburn Castle. Maggs Bros. Ltd. 1440 - 184 2011 £450

Rowley, Hugh *Gamosagammon or Hints on Hymen.* London: John Camden Hotten, n.d., 1871, First edition; square 8vo., full tan calf gilt by Tout, boards elegantly panelled with triple fillets and cornerpieces, spine with raised bands and contrasting triple lettering pieces, pages xvi, 327, (xviii), all edges gilt, profusely illustrated by author, original cloth laid in at end, handsome copy. R. F. G. Hollett & Son Antiquarian Booksellers 175 - 1157 2011 £180

Rowling, J. K. *Harry Potter and the Chamber of Secrets.* London: Bloomsbury, 1998, First Australian edition; pictorial boards, fine in fine dust jacket. Bella Luna Books May 26 2011 - t5778 2011 $440

Rowling, J. K. *Harry Potter and the Goblet of Fire.* London: Bloomsbury, 2000, First British edition, ture first, first printing errors that were corrected in later copies; fine in near fine dust jacket, light creasing on bottom edge. Bella Luna Books May 29 2011 - t9420 2011 $137

Rowling, J. K. *Harry Potter and the Order of the Phoenix.* London: Bloomsbury, 2003, First UK edition; as new book and dust jacket. Lupack Rare Books May 26 2011 - ABE1927658470 2011 $125

Rowling, J. K. *Harry Potter and the Philosopher's Stone.* London: Bloomsbury, 1997, First edition, uncorrected proof; wrappers, 8vo, 224 pages, original white wrappers, central yellow band with title, very light crease along front and rear joints, very slight handling wear, otherwise near fine. Any Amount of Books May 26 2011 - A67486 2011 $4612

Rowling, J. K. *Harry Potter and the Philosopher's Stone.* London: Ted Smart, 1998, First British edition; near fine, very minor bump to base of spine, pictorial boards, dust jacket near fine, light creasing at base of spine. Bella Luna Books May 26 2011 - t5565 2011 $1375

Rowling, J. K. *Harry Potter and the Philosopher's Stone.* London: Bloomsbury, 1998, First Australian edition; fine in pictorial boards, fine in dust jacket, signed by author on laid in bookplate. Bella Luna Books May 26 2011 - 15564s 2011 $8250

Rowntree, B. Seebohm *English Life and Leisure.* London: Longmans, Green and Co., 1951, Large 8vo., original buckram gilt, few small dents and holes to boards. R. F. G. Hollett & Son Antiquarian Booksellers 175 - 1058 2011 £30

Rowson, Susanna *Slaves in Algiers; or a Struggle for Freedom a Play.* Philadelphia: published by Mathew Carey September 28, 1796, First Carey edition; 12mo., 76, 76; 87, (1); (1), 2, 72, (2) pages, contemporary calf, leather label, very nice. M & S Rare Books, Inc. 90 - 375 2011 $4500

Roy, Arundhati *The God of Small Things.* New York: Random House, 1997, First edition; fine in fine dust jacket. Bella Luna Books May 29 2011 - t3848 2011 $82

Roy, Arundhati *The God of Small Things.* London: Flamingo, 1997, First British edition; near fine, light shelf wear, dust jacket fine. Bella Luna Books May 26 2011 - t2405 2011 $220

Roy, Arundhati *The God of Small Things.* London: Flamingo, 1997, First British edition; fine in near fine dust jacket, 1 inch closed tear at bottom rear fold. Bella Luna Books May 29 2011 - t9441 2011 $137

Roy, Arundhati *The God of Small Things.* London: Flamingo, 1997, First British edition; fine, dust jacket fine, signed by author. Bella Luna Books May 26 2011 - 2021 2011 $302

Roy, Arundhati *The God of Small Things.* London: Flamingo, 1997, First British edition; near fine, light bumping to spine, fine dust jacket. Bella Luna Books May 26 2011 - t2418 2011 $165

Roy, William *The Military Antiquities of the Romans in Britain.* London: printed by W. Bulmer and Co. and sold at the apartments of the Society, in Somerset Place and by Messrs. White, Robson, Nicol, Leigh and Sotheby, Brown and Egerton, 1793, First edition; large folio, 51 plates, all but one engraved, 6 double page including 3 maps, another double page and folding, prelims slightly soiled, mainly in blank margins, last page of list of the Society of Antiquaries discoloured, some of the plates very lightly dampstained at upper inner corner, (10), xvi, (1), 3-206, (6) modern buckram, maroon label on spine, good copy. Anthony W. Laywood May 26 2011 - 21680 2011 $755

Royal Air Force Museum *Reference Book and Catalogue of Royal Air Force Museum and Royal Air Forces Escaping Society Flown Covers.* Hendon: RAF Museum, 1976, Loose leaf edition; original blue plastic coated square 8vo. ring binding, label in plastic, spine sleeve, each section tabbed and paginated separately, illustrations, supplements for 1977 and 1978 bound in , that for 1981 loosely inserted. R. F. G. Hollett & Son Antiquarian Booksellers General Catalogue Summer 2010 - 317 2011 £35

Royal Central Asia Society *Journal of the Royal Central Asian Society.* 1937-1974, First edition; 87 numbers in 72, including complete volumes between volume 24/4 and volume 61/2, original wrappers in very good condition. I. D. Edrich May 26 2011 - 99445 2011 $671

The Royal Illuminated Book of Legends. Edinburgh: William P. Nimmo, n.d. circa, 1870, Later editions; Oblong large 8vo., original cloth backed pictorial boards, edges and corners little worn, 18 colored plates with accompanying text, piece torn from lower margin of one cloth backed pictorial boards, edges and corners little worn, 18 colored plates with accompanying text, piece torn fromn lower margin of one text leaf, lower edge of one leaf rather worn, new endpapers. R. F. G. Hollett & Sons Antiquarian Booksellers 170 - 711 2011 £150

Royal Society of Arts *Journal of the Royal Society of Arts.* 1945-1988, First edition; 400 issues, a continuous run from Feb. 1979-Feb. 1988, the years 1974 and 1975 are also complete, generally very good. I. D. Edrich May 26 2011 - 99459 2011 $545

Royal Society of Arts *Journal of the Royal Society of Arts.* 1961-, Nos. 4-9, 11-15, 18-25, 27-28, 30-33, 35-37, 40-44, 46-78, 81, 84-86, 89, 95-118, New Series 1-12, 14, 17 20, 21, 24-26, 27, 28 + special issue, together 113 issues in original wrappers, very good. I. D. Edrich May 26 2011 - 83732 2011 $587

Royce, Josiah *California from the Conquest in 1846 to the Second Vigilance Committee in San Francisco: A Study of American Character.* Boston and New York: Houghton Mifflin and Co., Riverside Press, 1886, First edition; small octavo, pages (2), xv, (1), 513, (1), (12, ads), double page folded map, printed in color, original gilt lettered dark olive pebbled cloth, top edge gilt, slight rubbing to extremities and upper corners, lower corners just showing, fine. Argonaut Book Shop Recent Acquisitions Summer 2010 - 177 2011 $225

Royse, John *The Geology and Prehistoric Man of Castleton in the High Peak.* London: John Heywood, n.d., First edition; small 8vo., modern buckram with leather spine label, pages 84, frontispiece and 2 diagrams, scarce. R. F. G. Hollett & Son Antiquarian Booksellers 177 - 783 2011 £85

Rozan, S. J. *China Trade.* New York: St. Martin's Press, 1994, First edition; fine in like dust jacket, signed with author's chop for "Snow Flower". Bella Luna Books May 26 2011 - t1291 2011 $275

Rubens, Bernice *Mate in Three.* London: Eyre and Spottiswoode, 1966, First edition; 8vo., original publisher's blue cloth lettered gilt at spine, pages 247, decent copy, scarce, original publisher's blue cloth, about fine in very good dust jacket with slight nick at head of spine and very slight edgewear, decent copy. Any Amount of Books May 29 2011 - A38172 2011 $238

Rucellai, Bernardo *De Bello Italico Commentarius ex authentici Manuscripti Apographo nun Primum in Lucem Editus.* London: William Bowyer for John Rindley, 1724, Large 4to., (8), 102, (2) pages, last leaf blank, small errata slip pasted to pages (vii & viii), contemporary London Harleian style binding of sprinkled calf, by Brindley, from the library of the Earls of Macclesfield at Shirburn Castle. Maggs Bros. Ltd. 1440 - 185 2011 £750

Ruffhead, Owen *A Complete Index to the Statutes at Large, from Magna Charta to the Tenth Year of George III, Inclusive...* London: printed by His Majesty's Statute and Law printer for P. Uriel and B. Tovey, 1772, Contemporary calf, rebacked in matching calf gilt with raised bands and spine label, unpaginated, name partly erased from title, otherwise excellent, clean and sound. R. F. G. Hollett & Son Antiquarian Booksellers 175 - 1162 2011 £180

Ruffhead, Owen *The Life of Alexander Pope Esq...* London: C. Bathurst et al, 1769, First edition; 235 x 152mm., 4 p.l., including frontispiece, 578 pages, publisher's original paper boards, titling in ink on spine and manuscript shelf number at foot, edges untrimmed, frontispiece, joints cracked, backstrip bit frayed at edges, corners somewhat rubbed, temporary binding still firmly intact, generally in surprisingly good condition, one leaf with closed tear at head (extending into text, but without loss), one opening with light sprinkled foxing at foot, occasional faint foxing elsewhere, frontispiece offset onto titlepage, few other minor defects, excellent internally, text quite clean and fresh, very desirable copy.   Phillip J. Pirages   59 - 56   2011 $750

Rules of Discipline of the Yearly Meeting Held on Rhode Island for New England. New Bedford: Abraham Shearman Jun., 1809, 8vo., 156 pages, full contemporary plain calf, interesting annotated copy with tipped in revisions to text (author's?).   M & S Rare Books, Inc.   90 - 334   2011 $125

Rundell, Maria Eliza *A New System of Domestic Cookery, Formed Upon Principles of Economy...* Exeter: Norris and Sawyer, sold also by William Sawyer and Co., Newburyport and Benj. P. Sherriff, Exeter, 1808, (6), xx, 297 pages, contemporary sheep, small piece torn from fore-edge of titlepage, not affecting type, some scattered spotting and foxing, nice solid copy.   Joseph J. Felcone Inc.   Fall Miscellany 2010 - 34   2011 $600

Ruscelli, Girolamo *Kriegs und Archeley Kunst.* Frankfurt: Lukas Jennis (second part: Jakob de Zetter), 1620, First edition in German; 2 parts in one volume, 288 x 188 mm; 6 p.l., 145, (3) pages; 4 p.l., 71, (5) pages, very fine late 18th century tree calf, flat spine handsomely gilt in compartments filled with closely spaced horizontal gilt in compartments filled with closely spaced horizontal rows of alternating strapwork and flowing floral and foliate stamps, reddish orange morocco label, historiated headpieces and tailpieces, both titlepages attractively framed with design of military implements, with 24 double page engraved military plates, 15 accompanying the first section and 9 the second; front pastedown of each volume with armorial bookplate of Lt. Gen. G. L. Parker (4th Earl of Macclesfield), first endpaper with similar armorial bookplate of Macclesfield library, first three leaves with small embossed Macclesfield stamp; bottom of second titlepage just barely touched by binder's knife, three gatherings with inoffensive dampstain at lower inner margin, light offsetting on some of the plates, handful of leaves (including the first title) with light overall browning, additional trivial defects, otherwise really fine, lovely binding lustrous and scarcely worn, text very clean and execptionally fresh.   Phillip J. Pirages   59 - 58   2011 $5500

Ruscha, Ed *Every Building on the Sunset Strip.* Los Angeles: Edward Ruscha, 1966, First edition, one of 1000 copies; 8vo., pages (52), accordion fold sequence of black and white photos, attached to inside of upper wrapper, original wrappers, spine and upper style lettered in silver, faint mark from glue to lower side, original silver paper covered board slipcase, tear, dust and crease to bottom edge, original white paper bands, lightly toned with two short closed tears, fine in near fine slipcase with rare original band.   Simon Finch Rare Books   Zero - 545   2011   £5000

Rush, Anthony *A President for a Prince. Wherein is to be Seene by the Testimonie of Auncient Writers, The Deutie of Kings, Princes and Gouernours.* London: by H. Denham, 1566, First edition; 163 x 113mm., (28) leaves, wonderfully animated and colorful 17th century English brocaded silk binding featuring a gray silk ground embroidered with plaited and crinkled straw in intricate overall pattern incorporating heart tulip and floral designs as well as a crown, the designs done in red, yellow and blue, text block with gilt edges, 19th century green watered silk endleaves, titlepage with woodcut filigree border, foliated initials, bookplate of Cornelius J. Hauck; printed in black letter; minor fraying and small losses to the embroidered border, text perhaps pressed (but probably not washed), titlepage little dark and very slightly stained in top margin, tip of upper corner of final four leaves expertly repaired (three of these leaves, also with flattened creases), still splendid copy, text very clean and smooth and absolutely delightful binding with remarkably bright and scarcely worn stitching.   Phillip J. Pirages   59 - 59   2011 $19,500

Rushdie, Salman *East West.* New York: Pantheon, 1994, First edition; fine, near fine dust jacket with light soiling and minor creasing to edges, signed by author.   Bella Luna Books   May 29 2011 - t1112   2011 $93

Rushdie, Salman *Shalimar the Clown.* London: Jonathan Cape, 2005, First British edition; fine in fine dust jacket.   Bella Luna Books   May 29 2011 - k183   2011 $82

Rushdie, Salman *Two Stories.* London: privately printed, 1989, First edition, one of 12 specially bound copies signed by Rushdie; with separate suite of Khakhar's 8 prints each one signed by artist, entire edition consisted of 72 copies, large 4to., full leather with gilt leather onlays, full cloth folding box.   James S. Jaffe Rare Books   May 26 2011 - 1088   2011 $10,000

Rushworth & Dreaper *Antique Musical Instruments and Historical Manuscripts.* Liverpool: Rushworth and Dreaper, n.d. 1930's, Pages (24), printed in red and dark brown, 20 tipped in photos, plates, together with a later edition of the same, original wrappers, pages 16, illustrations, circa 1950.   R. F. G. Hollett & Son Antiquarian Booksellers   175 - 426   2011   £65

Ruskin, John 1819-1900 *Cambridge School of Art. Mr. Ruskin's Inaugural Address. Delivered at Cambridge Oct. 29 1858.* Cambridge: Deighton Bell & Co., 1858, First edition; small 8vo., (60 40 pages, half title, 19th century half blue morocco, marbled boards, gilt lettered spine, top edge gilt, original printed wrappers bound in, rather dusty and marked, scarce.   Ken Spelman Rare Books   68 - 49   2011 £75

Ruskin, John 1819-1900 *Dame Wiggins of Lee and Her Seven Wonderful Cats.* Sunnyside, Orpington, Kent: George Allen, 1885, Large paper copy, limited to 400 copies issued on fine Whatman paper; 4to., 20 pages, brown gilt pictorial cloth, fine, charming woodcuts by Kate Greenaway, printed on one side of the paper, rare.   Aleph-Bet Books, Inc.   95 - 265   2011 $1000

Ruskin, John 1819-1900 *The Ethics of the Dust: Ten Lectures to Little Housewives on the Elements of Crystallisation.* London: Smith, Elder & Co., 1866, First edition; 191 x 127mm., x, (iv), (3)-244 pages, very fine dark green crushed morocco by Bedford (stamp signed on front turn-in), covers bordered in gilt with French fillet, raised bands, spine handsomely gilt in compartments featuring decorative bands at head and foot, scrolled cornerpieces and thistle centerpiece with surrounding small tools, densely gilt inner dentelles, marbled endpapers, all edges gilt, titlepage with ownership inscription "Walter Macfarlane, Saracen Foundry", boards with hint of soiling, very fine in lovely binding, gilt very bright, text virtually pristine.   Phillip J. Pirages   59 - 90   2011 $500

Ruskin, John 1819-1900 *Ethics of the Dust. Ten Lectures on Little Housewives on the Elements of Crystallisation.* New York: John Wiley & Son, 1866, First edition; from the library of the first woman physician, Elizabeth Blackwell, octavo, (2, blank), (i)-250, (1, publisher's ads), (1, blank) pages, with Blackwell's signature and dated 1866 and her bookplate; publisher's full purple cloth, decoratively ruled in blind, spine lettered in gilt, dampstaining and wrinkling to cloth, spine sunned and soiled, head and tail of spine chipped, some foxing to blanks, otherwise very clean, Blackwell's inscription, housed in custom half morocco clamshell, very good.   Heritage Book Shop   Holiday 2010 - 10   2011 $3500

Ruskin, John 1819-1900 *Fors Clavigera: Letters to the Workmen and Labourers of Great Britain.* Sunnyside, Orpington, Kent: George Allen, 1871-1887, First edition; 9 volumes, frontispieces and illustrations, including one color plate with tissue guard, 8vo., 20th century pale blue paper covered boards with printed paper spine labels, occasional marginal light pencil marks, occasional closed tear due to careless page opening, some pages still unopened, neither conspicuous nor affecting text, overall very nice, clean set.   Any Amount of Books   May 29 2011 - A72535   2011 $306

Ruskin, John 1819-1900 *The King of the Golden River or The Black Brothers.* Boston: Mayhew & Baker, 1860, First American edition; frontispiece, engraved title and vignette illustrations, little browned and marked, original red pebble grained cloth, gilt, carefully recased, all edges gilt.   Jarndyce Antiquarian Booksellers   CXCI - 477   2011   £125

Ruskin, John 1819-1900 *The King of the Golden River or the Black Brothers.* London: Smith Elder & Co., 1863, Fifth edition; 64 pages, half title, frontispiece, decorative titlepages and text engravings, fine in three quarter dark green crushed morocco by Ramage, top edge gilt, marbled boards, original gilt cloth covers bound in at end.   Ken Spelman Rare Books   68 - 50   2011   £125

Ruskin, John 1819-1900 *The King of the Golden River or the Black Brothers.* London: Smith, Elder & Co., 1901, Twenty fourth thousand; square 8vo., original green cloth gilt, pages 64, illustrations by Richard Doyle, very nice, clean copy.   R. F. G. Hollett & Son Antiquarian Booksellers General Catalogue Summer 2010 - 675   2011   £65

Ruskin, John 1819-1900 *Letters Addressed to a College Friend During the Years 1840-1845.* London: George Allen, 1894, First edition, one of 150 copies printed on handmade paper; xiii, (i), 210 pages + ads, half title, good, original cloth, rear board unevenly faded.   Ken Spelman Rare Books   68 - 66   2011   £60

Ruskin, John 1819-1900 *Notes by Mr. Ruskin on His Drawings by the late J. M. W. Turner Exhibited at The Fine Art Society's Galleries.* Fine Art Society, 1878, 101 (1) (6) pages, near contemporary dark blue gilt lettered calf, ruled gilt borders, all edges gilt, very good, some slight foxing.   Ken Spelman Rare Books   68 - 53   2011   £45

Ruskin, John 1819-1900 *Our Fathers Have Told Us.* London: George Allen, 1880-1883, 5 volumes, very good in original printed wrappers which are little foxed.   Ken Spelman Rare Books   68 - 55   2011   £40

Ruskin, John 1819-1900 *The Pleasures of England.* Orpington: George Allen, 1884-1885, First edition; original four parts, pages (ii) 36; (37-)80; (81-122); (123-) 160, (1), 4to., original printed wrappers, some dust staining, especially on spines, very good.   Blackwell Rare Books   B166 - 91   2011   £95

Ruskin, John 1819-1900 *The Pleasures of England.* London: George Allen, 1884-1885, First edition; 4to., very good in original 4 parts, cream printed wrappers, front wrapper of first part little dusty.   Ken Spelman Rare Books   68 - 60   2011   £45

Ruskin, John 1819-1900 *The Political Economy of Art: Being the Substance...* London: Smith, Elder & Co., 1857, First edition; small 8vo., original printed cloth, rather rubbed and neatly recased, pages vii, 248, blindstamp on title of Rev. T. W. Jex-Blake, Headmaster of Rugby School 1874-87, few spots to fore-edge.   R. F. G. Hollett & Son Antiquarian Booksellers   175 - 1164   2011   £65

Ruskin, John 1819-1900 *The Political Economy of Art: Being the Substance...* London: Smith, Elder & Co., 1868, Original green cloth, gilt, pages viii, 248, scattered spotting.   R. F. G. Hollett & Son Antiquarian Booksellers   175 - 1163   2011   £30

Ruskin, John 1819-1900 *Praeterita. Outlines of Scenes and Thoughts Perhaps Worthy of memory in My Past Life.* London: George Allen, 1886-1888, First edition; large paper copy, vii, (2), 432 pages; (4) 442; (2) 182 pages, steel engraved frontispiece, double portrait and one plate, contemporary olive green half calf, gilt lettered spines, marbled boards, some rubbing to joints and corners, one joint cracked.   Ken Spelman Rare Books   68 - 63   2011   £120

Ruskin, John 1819-1900 *The Queen of the Air: Being a Study of the Greek Myths of Cloud and Storm.* London: Smith, Elder and Co., 1869, Second edition; 8vo., pages 199, presentation from author for Mrs. A. J. Scott, decent, clean copy in original publisher's green cloth lettered gilt at spine, top of titlepage has been cut out to reveal the presentation at top of next page (not affecting text), slight rubbing at spine ends, else very good.   Any Amount of Books May 29 2011 - A63060   2011 $374

Ruskin, John 1819-1900 *Seasame and Lillies.* East Aurora: Roycroft Shop, 1897, Limited edition, one of 450 numbered copies initialled by Elbert Hubbard and hand illuminated by Fanny Stiles; quarter cloth and paper covered boards gilt as issued, trifle rubbed, else fine.   Between the Covers   169 - BTC340567   2011 $400

Ruskin, John 1819-1900 *The Seven Lamps of Architecture.* London: Smith, Elder and Co., 1849, First edition; viii, (4), 205 pages, 14 lithograph plates, complete with half title, some occasional foxing, good copy, original blindstamped cloth, expert repairs to joints, inscription dated 1849 on endpaper, bookplate of F. D. Astley.   Ken Spelman Rare Books   68 - 46   2011   £160

Ruskin, John 1819-1900 *The Seven Lamps of Architecture.* London: Smith, Elder and Co., 1855, Second edition; large 8vo., original blindstamped cloth, neatly recased, pages xv (iv), 206 (ii), 14 engraved plates, signs of a label removed from pastedown, few neat marginal lines and notes, but very good.   R. F. G. Hollett & Son Antiquarian Booksellers   177 - 784   2011   £150

Ruskin, John 1819-1900 *The Storm Cloud of the Nineteenth Century.* London: George Allen, 1884, First edition in book form; vi, 152 pages, half title, very good in original gilt lettered cloth, slight wear to head of spine, 4to.   Ken Spelman Rare Books   68 - 61   2011   £50

Ruskin, John 1819-1900 *Studies in Both Arts: Being Ten Subject Drawn and Described.* London: George Allen, 1895, First edition; folio, original decorated cream cloth with design by Edward Burne-Jones on upper board, trifle marked, pages 72, 10 tinted or colored photogravure plates, very nice, neat inscription "Christina Knewstub from J.W.P.L. May 19 1898".   R. F. G. Hollett & Son Antiquarian Booksellers   177 - 785   2011   £180

Ruskin, John 1819-1900 *Time and Tide by Weare and Tyne.* London: George Allen, 1891, Fourth edition; 185 x 125mm., 6 p.l., 235 pages (bound with half title), splendid later maroon morocco lavishly gilt by Zaehnsdorf (with their oval stamped in gilt on rear pastedown), covers with wide gilt border featuring a twining vine with charming little leaves and flowerheads, vine on stippled ground, center panel outlined by single gilt rule with intricate cornerpieces, small flowering vine sprouting from each corner, raised bands, spine sumptuously gilt in pointille, compartments within which four gilt pomegranates spring from the central circle toward the four corners and flowers grow from top and sides of circle, turn-ins with lovely floral garlands extending around corners as well as approaching the hinge at top and bottom, gold dog-tooth roll where pastedowns and turn-ins meet, marbled endpapers, all edges gilt, beautiful volume in very fine condition, binding lustrous and virtually unworn, text immaculate.   Phillip J. Pirages   59 - 152   2011 $850

Ruskin, John 1819-1900 *Unto this Last Four Essays on the First Principles of Political Economy.* Doves Press, 1907, One of 300 copies on paper (additional 12 copies were printed on vellum); 232 x 170mm., xiii, (i), 120, (1) pages, original gilt titled flexible vellum in (lightly soiled), linen clamshell box with brown morocco spine label, Greek type used for occasional words in text and for two lines in appendix; half inch closed tear at fore edge of front free endpaper in all other ways, extraordinarily fine, vellum uniformly white, text pristine.   Phillip J. Pirages   59 - 180   2011 $800

Ruskin, John 1819-1900 *War.* Woolwich: printed for private circulation, 1866, Half title, partially erased pencil notes at end, original red cloth, dulled & rubbed, all edges gilt, good, sound copy, exceedingly scarce, bookplate of military historian Sir Basil Liddell Hart, with 4 page ALS to him from art historian Reginald Wilenski, July 23 1961.   Jarndyce Antiquarian Booksellers   CXCI - 478   2011   £380

Ruskin, John 1819-1900 *The Works.* London: George Allen, 1903, Definitive edition, Library Edition, limited to 2062 copies (of which 2000 are for sale); 39 volumes, large octavo, frontispieces and plates, some tinted blue or sepia and engravings, numerous text illustrations and facsimiles, contemporary three quarter green levant morocco over green cloth boards ruled in gilt, spines with five raised bands decoratively tooled and lettered in gilt, top edges gilt, others uncut, marbled endpapers, several volumes sunned at spine, bookplates of Ernest Ridley Debenham, overall fine set. David Brass Rare Books, Inc. May 26 2011 - 01349 2011 $9500

Russailh, Albert Bernard De *Last Adventure. San Francisco in 1851.* San Francisco: The Westgate Press, 1931, First edition, one of 475 copies; xvii, (96) pages, folding frontispiece facsimile, 5 folding plates, small 12 page facsimile pamphlet bound in, facsimile notation and label on front endpaper, greenish gray cloth spine, marbled boards, printed paper spine label, slight offsetting to free endpapers as usual, fine. Argonaut Book Shop Recent Acquisitions Summer 2010 - 178 2011 $75

Russell, Bertrand Russell, 3rd Earl of 1872-1970 *History of Western Philosophy and Its Connection with Political and Social Circumstances from the Earliest Times to the Present Day.* London: Allen & Unwin, 1954, Fourth impression; original cloth, gilt, dust jacket, edges worn and defective, pages 916. R. F. G. Hollett & Son Antiquarian Booksellers 175 - 1166 2011 £30

Russell, Charles E. B. *Manchester Boys. Sketches of Manchester Lads at Work and Play.* Manchester: University Press, 1905, First edition; half title, frontispiece, illustrations, original red cloth, parchment spine, slightly darkened. Jarndyce Antiquarian Booksellers CXCI - 479 2011 £50

Russell, Eric Frank *Sinister Barrier.* Reading: Fantasy Press, 1948, First US edition; octavo, cloth. L. W. Currey, Inc. 124 - 216 2011 $150

Russell, Mary Doria *The Sparrow.* New York: Villard, 1996, First edition; fine, dust jacket fine, all first issue points with the word Kkarstic" appears instead of Kkarst" on page 16, line 12; "thirty two feet per second" instead of thirty two feet per second per second" on page 95 in second paragraph, first issue dust jacket with photo credited incorrectly to "Dina Ross". Bella Luna Books May 29 2011 - t9472 2011 $99

Russell, Michael *History and Present Condition of the Barbary States.* Edinburgh: Oliver & Boyd, 1835, Second edition; small 8vo., pages 456, folding map, engravings, brown half calf, small wear to head of spine. J. & S. L. Bonham Antiquarian Booksellers Africa 4/20/2011 - 8153 2011 £65

Russo, Richard *Empire Falls.* New York: Knopf, 2001, First edition; near fine, light bumping to spine ends, dust jacket fine, signed by author. Bella Luna Books May 29 2011 - t8436 2011 $110

Russo, Richard *Mohawk.* New York: Vintage, 1986, First edition; paperback original, pictorial wrappers, very good, crease on top front corner, light spotting on first page, signed by author. Bella Luna Books May 29 2011 - t9387 2011 $104

Rusticus, Junicus, Pseud. *Enumeration of the Contributions, Confiscations and Requisitions of the French Nation with an Account of the Countries Revolutionized since the Commencement of the Present War.* London: W. Clarke, 1798, First edition; 8vo., 36 pages, recently well bound in linen backed marbled boards, lettered, very good, scarce. John Drury Rare Books 153 - 129 2011 £175

Rutherford, Samuel *Lex, Rex: the Law and the Prince.* London: printed for John Field, 1644, First edition complete; quarto, full late 18th century calf, sprinkled edges, margins trimmed to side notes with mild intrusion to a few leaves, joints neatly, near invisibly, repaired, headcap restored, very good, rarely found in collectable condition, excessively scarce. David Brass Rare Books, Inc. May 26 2011 - 01539 2011 $9500

Rutland, John Henry Manners, 5th Duke of *Journal of a Tour to the Northern Parts of Great Britain.* London: printed for J. Triphook, 1813, 8vo., pages (iv) 300 + 10 sepia aquatint plates, 2 floor plans for Haddon Hall and 2 plates of room dimensions, contemporary mottled calf with early 20th century reback, spine double rule gilt with 'milled' roll gilt raised bands, compartments with 'covered urn' centre pieces gilt, red lettering piece gilt, number erased from 'open centred' centre piece gilt, boards single rule gilt bordered, board edges 'obliquely-broken fillet' roll gilt turn-ins 'double-rule' gilt, 'French Shell' 'made' endpapers, all edges mottled as per boards, pale blue and white sewn flat endbands, occasional minor spot, bit of chipping to head of spine, small area of surface insect damage at corner of lower board, armorial bookplate of James Comerford, from the collection of Christopher Ernest Weston 1947-2010. Unsworths Booksellers 24 - 120 2011 £150

Rutland, John Henry Manners, 5th Duke of *A Tour Through Part of Belgium and the Rhenish Provinces.* London: printed for Rodwell & Martin, 1822, First edition; plates, later half calf, green label, gilt, couple of plates spotted, otherwise very clean, wide margined crisp copy. Jarndyce Antiquarian Booksellers CXCI - 567 2011 £280

Rutland, John Henry Manners, 5th Duke of *Travels in Great Britain. Journal of a Tour Round the Southern Coasts of England...* London: printed for J. Triphood, 1805, 1813. 1805; 3 volumes, 8vo., pages (viii) 229, (iii) + 2 sepia aquatint plates; (iv), 300 + 10 sepia aquatints, 2 floor plans, 2 plates of room dimensions, (viii), 389, (iii), + 7 sepia aquatint plates, contemporary sprinkled and polished calf, spines triple rule gilt, red lettering and numbering pieces gilt, boards single rule gilt bordered, board edges 'obliquely-broken fillet' roll gilt, turn-ins as above but in blind, all edges blue sprinkled, red and white sewn endbands, touch of faint spotting in places, quite rubbed, little wear to spine ends, some joints cracking, lettering piece of volume I and numbering piece of volume 3 lost, numbering piece of volume 1 upside down, from the collection of Christopher Ernest Weston 1947-2010.   Unsworths Booksellers   24 - 119   2011   £750

Rutter, John *Delineations of Fonthill and its Abbey.* London: (Shaftesbury) Charles Knight for the author, 1893, First edition; xvi, 127 pages; 4to., 13 full page engraved plates, 3 exquisitely hand colored and 20 x 26 inch foldout plan with hand colored walks and further 15 woodcut vignettes in text, additional engraved plate of the abbey from the south west, original endpapers, rear endpaper torn, bookplate of Laurence Ambrose (Larky) Waldron (1858-1823), excellent, clean text, foldout plan, one 3 inch closed tear at fold.   Any Amount of Books   May 26 2011 - A76292   2011 $1426

Ruttledge, Hugh *Everest 1933.* London: Hodder & Stoughton, 1934, First edition; thick 4to., original blue cloth, dust jacket, edges and hinges rubbed, light creases to spine and lower panel, head of spine neatly repaired, pages xv, 390, 59 plates, 3 diagrams and 4 folding maps, scattered light foxing, mainly to prelims and fore-edge.   R. F. G. Hollett & Son Antiquarian Booksellers   General Catalogue Summer 2010 - 938   2011   £180

Ruvigny, Marquis of *The Titles of Nobility of Europe: an International Peerage.* London: Harrison & Sons, 1914, First edition; 4to., soundly rebacked, lettered gilt on spine with gilt crest on cover, original publisher's covers, pages lxxi, 1598, ex-British Foreign Office library with few library markings, mark on titlepage from stamp on verso, else sound, very good copy.   Any Amount of Books   May 29 2011 - A68044   2011 $213

Ruzicka, Rudolph *Studies in Type Design: Alphabets with Random Quotations.* Hanover: 1968, (4) pages and 10 loose signatures, folio, fine in gray grained cloth, all in protective slipcase, bit shelf sunned.   Bookworm & Silverfish   669 - 44   2011 $75

Ryan, Richard *Biographia Hibernica. A Biographical Dictionary of the Worthies of Ireland.* 1821, First edition; 2 volumes, vii, 486 (2), 652 pages, portrait, plate, full diced calf (worn), rebacked, ex-institutional library, good, scarce.   C. P. Hyland   May 26 2011 - 259/429   2011 $725

Ryan, Thomas *The History of Queen Charlotte's Lying in Hospital, From Its Foundation in 1752 to the Present Time with an Account of Its Objects and Present State.* London: privately published, 1885, 4to., pages xv, 70, original publisher's dark green cloth lettered gilt with crest to cover, illustrations, plans, Woburn Abbey bookplate of Francis, Duke of Bedford, scarce, slightly dusty and very faintly marked but bright and clean.   Any Amount of Books   May 29 2011 - A71030   2011 $315

Ryley, Samuel William *The Itinerant; or Memoirs of an Actor. (with) The Itinerant in Scotland.* London: Sherwood Neely & Jones, 1817, 1816. 1827. Second edition of volumes 1-3 and First edition of volumes 4-6 and 7-9; 12mo., in all 9 volumes, three quarter calf, spine gilt, some rubbed along extremities, untrimmed (rear cover separate on volume 1), armorial bookplate of Rodman Wanamaker on each front pastedown.   Second Life Books Inc.   174 - 271   2011 $900

S

Sa'di *Tales from the Gulistan or Rose Garden of the Sheikh Sa'di or Shiraz.* London: 1928, xx, 256 pages, near fine in gilt titling on black cloth, dust jacket with expected defects, dust jacket has separation at left of backstrip, mild shelfwear, text and dust jacket illustrations by Kettlewell.   Bookworm & Silverfish   668 - 91 2011 $75

Sabartes, Jaime *Picasso Lithographe.*   Monte Carlo: Andre Sauret, 1964, First edition, limited to 2500 copies; Volume I being number 795, 4 volumes, large quarto, color and black and white plates, a total of 383, and 8 original lithographs, original black and white lithograph wrappers, volumes III and IV with original onion skin (lightly browned), about fine.   Heritage Book Shop   Holiday 2010 - 96 2011 $4000

Sabuda, Robert *The 12 Days of Christmas.*   New York: Little Simon (an imprint of Simon & Schuster Children's Pub. Division), 1996, Limited to 250 numbered copies; signed, limited edition, square 8vo., green cloth with silver lettering on spine and full color pop-up card set within front cover of book with limitation signature and identification, additional pop-up, cloth slipcase, fresh copy of book and slipcase, 6 double page full color pop-ups, each side offering text.   Jo Ann Reisler, Ltd.   86 - 198 2011 $350

Sacheverell, Henry *The Tryal of Dr. Henry Sacheverell Before the House of Peers for High Courts and Misdemeanors...*   London: printed for Jacob Tonson, 1710, First edition; folio, old blind ruled panelled calf, little bumped and worn, spine trifle defective at head and foot, pages 335 complete with licence leaf before title, small strip cut form head, flyleaves rather creased at edges, little browning in places.   R. F. G. Hollett & Son Antiquarian Booksellers 175 - 1356 2011   £150

Sackville West, Edward *Thomas De Quincey. His Life and Work.*   New Haven: Yale University Press, 1936, First US edition; tall 8vo., original cloth, gilt, small label removed from base of spine, pages xii, 279, with 6 plates. R. F. G. Hollett & Son Antiquarian Booksellers   173 - 1007 2011   £45

Sade, Donatien Alphonse Francois, Comte, called Marquis De 1740-1814   *Justine, ou les Malheurs de la Vertue.*   En Hollande: Paris, 1791, First edition; 2 volumes bound in one, 8vo., pages 283, (iv), 191, etched allegorical frontispiece (supplied separately), mid 19th century navy blue half morocco, navy marbled boards, marbled endpapers, top edge gilt, spine gilt titled and decorated in six compartments, raised bands, slightly rubbed at extremities, scattered foxing and soiling throughout, particularly in volume i, small portion of corner foot of pages 2930 missing (not affecting text), slight creasing and fraying to edge of volume i titlepage, leaf 2 of volume i lacking as usual, stub still visible (torn from al known copies except one in German private collection).   Simon Finch Rare Books   Zero - 416 2011   £9000

Sade, Donatien Alphonse Francois, Comte, called Marquis De 1740-1814   *La Nouvelle Justine, ou les Malheurs de la Vertu; Suivie de l'Histoire de Juliette, sa Soeur.*   Holland: 1797, Paris: 1802. First edition; 4 volumes, 18mo., pages viii, 347; (iv), 356; (iv), 351; (iv), 366, (2) blank, all half titles present, frontispiece and 40 erotic engravings, minor spotting, titles of volumes ii and iii inverted, but withal an excellent copy, binding de l'epoque' of cherry red half calf, gilt titled and volume numbered on black morocco spine labels, edges marbled ("romantique" style), slight rubbing at corners, minor restorations, still in very nice original condition.   Simon Finch Rare Books   Zero - 421 2011   £22,000

Sadler, John *Rights of the Kingdom or Customs of Our Ancestours: Touching the Duty, Power, Election or Succession of Our Kings and Parliaments, Our True Liberty Due Allegiance...*   London: Richard Bishop, 1649, First edition; 4to, (2), (6), 93, 30-191 176-182 (i.e. 198) (4) pages, mid 19th century calf by Hatton of Manchester, panelled in blind, red edges, browned, spine slightly faded, signature of Sum Ashursti, a number of manuscript notes/corrections in text, from the library of the Earls of Macclesfield at Shirburn Castle.   Maggs Bros. Ltd.   1440 - 186 2011 £500

Sage, Juniper *The Man in the Manhole and Fit-it Men.* New York: William R. Scott, 1946, First edition; 4to., fine in excellent dust jacket with just few small closed tears, rare, illustrations in color by Bill Ballantine.   Aleph-Bet Books, Inc.   95 - 118 2011 $1500

Sage, Rufus B. *Scenes in the Rocky Mountains and in Oregon, California, New Mexico, Texas and the Grand Prairies.*   Philadelphia: Carey & Hart, 1846, First edition; 12mo., folding map, original yellow printed wrappers, with ALS NY Oct. 20 1845 written by F. Saunders to Sage. Heritage Book Shop   Booth A12 51st NY International Antiquarian Book Fair April 8-10 2011 - 110 2011 $16.500

Saiki, Tadasu *The World's Peace.* London: Methuen, 1911, First edition; 8vo., original publisher's blue cloth lettered gilt on spine and on front cover, pages vii, 238, with 31 page publisher's catalog at rear, minor wear, else near very good.   Any Amount of Books   May 29 2011 - A35753 2011 $213

Sailor Rumbelow and Britannia. London: Heinemann, 1962, First edition; original cloth, gilt, dust jacket extremities trifle frayed, price clipped, pages 115, illustrations by Edward Ardizzone.   R. F. G. Hollett & Sons Antiquarian Booksellers   170 - 39   2011   £45

Saint John Board of Trade *Report of the Special Committee (St. John Board of Trade) on the Bay of Fundy and Harbor of St. John, N.B.* St. John: J. & A. McMillan, 1887, Blue cloth, gilt title to front cover, pages 56, folding map tipped in at front, 8vo., 21 x 14cm., some wear to edges and darkened spine.   Schooner Books Ltd.   96 - 6   2011 $275

Saint John, Charles *Sketches of the Wild Sports and Natural History of the Highlands.* London: John Murray, 1878, Illustrated edition; old polished half calf gilt, rather rubbed and scuffed, spine mellowed, pages xv, 338, with 71 woodcut illustrations.   R. F. G. Hollett & Son Antiquarian Booksellers   General Catalogue Summer 2010 - 1285   2011   £75

Saint John, Charles *Wild Sports and Natural History of the Highlands.* London: T. N. Foulis, 1919, First edition thus; small 4to., modern half morocco gilt, raised bands and spine label, pages xxx, 472, uncut, 50 plates, handsome. R. F. G. Hollett & Son Antiquarian Booksellers   General Catalogue Summer 2010 - 1286   2011   £150

Saint John, F. E. Molyneux *The Sea of Mountains. An Account of Lord Dufferin's Tour through British Columbia in 1876.* London: 1877, 2 volumes, good to very good in travel green, all cover gilt bright, covers with mild wear, two small cancelled library stamps, very minor stresses to backstrip top, very light rubbing to backstrip edges, laid down photo frontispiece.   Bookworm & Silverfish   669 - 45 2011 $247

Saint John, Percy *The Sailor Crusade.* David Bryce, 1864, Contemporary half crimson roan gilt with marbled boards, little scuffed, pages 384, 4 woodcut plates.   R. F. G. Hollett & Sons Antiquarian Booksellers   170 - 651 2011   £35

Saint Martin, George *Boys Will Be Boys!* New York?: 1966, First edition; 256 pages, very good, 3 small cover spots, wear to bottom of backstrip, original binding. Bookworm & Silverfish   679 - 153   2011 $300

Saint Pierre, Jacques Henri Bernardin De   1737-1814 *Paul and Virginia.* Edinburgh: Oliver & Boyd, 1824, 12mo., 282 pages, three quarter tooled leather with corners, marbled paper on boards, gilt title label on spine, brown endpapers, very fine full page copper engraved frontispiece, ex-libris from the collection of Marjorie Moon, very fine. Hobbyhorse Books   56 - 133   2011 $250

Saint Pierre, Jacques Henri Bernardin De   1737-1814 *A Voyage to the Island of France, The Isle of Bourbon and the Cape of Good Hope...* London: J. Cundee, 1800, First English edition; 8vo., pages xxiv, 334, ads, 2 pages carelessly opened, not affecting text, contemporary quarter brown calf, gilt spine with raised bands, small nick at head of spine.   J. & S. L. Bonham Antiquarian Booksellers Africa 4/20/2011 - 5652   2011   £650

Saint, Fiona *The Yellow Flowers.* London: Dennis Dobson, 1968, First edition; small oblong 4to., pages 20 (printed recto only), illustrations in color, excellent copy, Ralph Steadman's second book boldly signed to "Chen", very good in like dust jacket (edges of pages browned, price clipped but with Dobson £1.50 sticker near corner).   Any Amount of Books   May 29 2011 - A66643   2011 $340

Saintsbury, George *Specimens of English Prose Style from Malory to Macaulay.* London: Kegan Paul, Trench & Co., 1885, First edition; number 1 of 50 copies, signed "Charles Whittingham & Co." (of Chiswick Press), signed in pencil on titlepage (dated Xmas 1887) to Dorothy Cornish, presumably the educationalist and Brighton historian, 8vo., green cloth spine with spine label and marbled boards, pages xlvi, 367, uncut, spine label browned and marked (illegible) edges rubbed, boards quite scuffed at rear, pages uncut with clean text.   Any Amount of Books   May 29 2011 - A47686   2011 $306

Sala, George Augustus *Dutch Pictures: with Some Sketches in the Flemish Manner.* London: Tinsley Brothers, 1861, First edition; half title, 4 page catalog, original mauve cloth, spine blocked in gilt, spine dulled, boards slightly marked, nice.   Jarndyce Antiquarian Booksellers CXCI - 576   2011   £120

Sala, George Augustus *Paris Herself Again in 1878-9.* London: Remington & Co., 1879, First edition; 2 volumes, half titles in volume I, frontispiece in volume I, plates and illustrations, original olive green pictorial cloth, blocked in black, largely inoffensive damp marking to back boards, little rubbed, presentation inscription, "Octobre 1879. A Monsieur L. Gillet. Souvenir de sincere amitie J. Leete", good copy.   Jarndyce Antiquarian Booksellers   CXCI - 577 2011   £150

Sala, George Augustus *A Trip to Barbary by a Roundabout Route.* London: Tinsley, 1866, First edition; 8vo., pages vi, 398, original purple cloth, joint rubbed.   J. & S. L. Bonham Antiquarian Booksellers   Africa 4/20/2011 - 8154   2011   £60

Salame, A. *A Narrative of the Expedition to Algiers in the Year 1816 Under the Command of the Right Hon. Admiral Lord Viscount Exmouth.* London: John Murray, 1819, First edition; 8vo., pages cxli, 230, frontispiece, folding plan, 2 folding plates, contemporary brown full calf, recently rebacked to high standard, browning to titlepage, good.   J. & S. L. Bonham Antiquarian Booksellers   Africa 4/20/2011 - 9173   2011   £500

The Salem Collection of Classical Sacred Musick in Three and Four Parts...   Boston: Manning & Loring for Cushing & Appleton, 1806,   Narrow oblong 4to., 6, (1), 135, (1) pages, contemporary marbled boards, calf back, spine shot, front cover nearly loose, nice, rare.   M & S Rare Books, Inc.   90 - 270   2011 $325

Salem Times Register   *An Historical Record of Roanoke County.*   Salem: 1938,   130 pages, wrappers, fray to free edge and chip (not into text) of first leaf, some age soil to wrappers.   Bookworm & Silverfish   679 - 194   2011 $75

Salensky, W.   *Prjevalsky's Horse.*   London: Hurst and Blackett, 1907,   First edition in English; 8vo., pages xvi, 65, original publisher's reddish brown cloth lettered gilt on spine and cover, folding frontispiece, 28 illustrations and folding table, clean, bright, near fine, very slightly bumped at corner with very slight browning at endpapers.   Any Amount of Books   May 26 2011 - A69861   2011 $503

Salibi, Kamal   *The Bible Came from Arabia.*   London: Cape, 1985,   First edition; pages xvi, 233, original cloth, gilt, dust jacket, scarce.   R. F. G. Hollett & Son Antiquarian Booksellers   175 - 1173   2011   £85

Saliga, Pauline   *The Architecture of Bruce Goff 1904-1932: Design for the Continuous Present.*   Munich and New York: Art Institute of Chicago and Prestel, 1995,   4to. pages 119, copiously illustrated in color and black and white, decent copy, scarce, fine in very good dust jacket with slight wear.   Any Amount of Books   May 29 2011 - A48241   2011 $306

Salim Antonio Dickey   *Harold! Photographs from the Harold Washington Years.*   Evanston: 2007,   First edition; wrappers, fine, signed by author.   Bookworm & Silverfish   676 - 1   2011 $75

Salinger, Jerome David   *Catcher in the Rye.*   Boston: Little Brown, 1951,   Stated first edition; black cloth, bookplate removed from endpaper, else fine in dust jacket with some expert restoration at base of spine and at folds).   Aleph-Bet Books, Inc.   95 - 501   2011 $9500

Salinger, Jerome David   *The Catcher in the Rye.*   Boston: Little Brown, 1951,   First edition; 8vo., pages 277, near fine in unrestored, unclipped dust jacket (showing some nicking at top of spine, little wear at tips, letter marred on rear dust jacket flap because of old removal of tape), name erased from endpaper, first issue jacket with author's photo portrait credited to Lotte Jacobi on rear panel and with "Book-of-the-Month Club" notation bottom of rear flap.   Second Life Books Inc.   174 - 272   2011 $11,500

Sallustius Crispus, Caius   *C. Crispi Sallustii Belli Catilinarii et Jugurthini Historiae.*   Glasguae: in aedibus Robert Urie, 1749,   8vo., pages iv, 250 (ii), rear board only of contemporary polished calf binding remains, board edges being decorative roll gilt, text block edges roughed, late 1980's attempts at rebacking with new front board by Chris Weston, lightly age toned, old leather bit scratched and rubbed, from the collection of Christopher Ernest Weston 1947-2010.   Unsworths Booksellers   24 - 140   2011   £125

Sallustius Crispus, Caius   *C. Crispi Sallustii Belli Catilinarii et Jugurthini Historiae.*   Glasguae: in aedibus Roberti Urie, 1749,   8vo., pages iv, 250, (ii), contemporary polished calf, untooled spine, red lettering piece gilt, boards double rule bordered in blind with extra double rule and decorative roll in blind at joint side, board edges 'zig-zag' decorative roll gilt, all edges red speckled, pink and white sewn endbands, lightly age toned, few stains, rubbed and bit chipped, joints cracking, spine darkened, contemporary ink inscription John Pelch, first name covered by pasted slip and later ink inscription "Wm. Clark, also pencil inscription "From Prof. Henry Jackson's Sale...", from the collection of Christopher Ernest Weston 1947-2010.   Unsworths Booksellers   24 - 139   2011   £50

Sallustius Crispus, Caius   *The History of Catiline's Conspiracy and the Jugurthine War.*   London: printed for D. Browne, A. Millar et al, 1757,   8vo., pages xvi, 253, (iii), contemporary sprinkled calf, spine panel with 'asymetric flowering plant' centrepieces and 'flower head' cornerpieces, red lettering piece gilt, board edges decorative roll gilt, all edges red sprinkled, red and white sewn endbands, little spotting, corners worn, joints cracking but strong, ink ownership stamp "Theo A Moon", from the collection of Christopher Ernest Weston 1947-2010.   Unsworths Booksellers   24 - 141   2011   £150

Salmon, David   *Joseph Lancaster.*   London: Longmans, Green and Co. for the British and Foreign School Society, 1904,   First edition; pages viii, 76, with 5 plates, original limp boards, one corner little creased, scarce.   R. F. G. Hollett & Son Antiquarian Booksellers   175 - 175   2011   £45

Salten, Felix *Bambi.* Berlin: 1923, First edition; historiated initial letter to beginning of each chapter, pages 187, (4) ads, (1), crown 8vo., original pale blue cloth backed boards, backstrip printed in blue, rubbed at head and just trifle so at tail, clean cream boards with lettering and design on front cover, just trifle rubbed at tail corners, red top edges, bookticket, very good.   Blackwell Rare Books   B166 - 228   2011   £800

Saluces, Madame De *Ma Tilette, Manuscrit derobe a une Vieille Femme Suivie de Quatre Novujelles.* Paris: Ridan, 1819, First edition; 2 volumes, (4) 256; (4) 290 pages, 12mo., original pale green wrappers, printed in black, borders on front and back with lovely decoration on back wrappers, half title in each volume, wear to wrappers, half title in each volume, wear to wrappers, one inch lacking on bottom of spine in volume I, scattered spotting, couple of closed tears, all in all, a good, sound uncut copy as it originally appeared, rare.   Paulette Rose Fine and Rare Books   32 - 151   2011 $850

Salvator, Ludwig Louis *Los Angeles in the Sunny Seventies: a Flower from the Golden Land.* Los Angeles: 1929, One of 900 copies, first English translation; xvi, 188 pages, plus notes and index, illustrations, cloth and paper covered boards, extremities rubbed, else clean, very good.   Dumont Maps & Books of the West   112 - 63   2011 $125

Salviani, Hippolito *Aquatillum Animalium Historiae Liber Primus cum Eorumden Formis Aere Excusis.* Rome: Hippolito Salviania, 1554, Folio, pages (16), 256 leaves, early red full sheep (rubbing and wear to edges of boards, few small abrasions to rear cover, professionally rebacked while retaining original ornate gilt decorated spine, vertical crack to spine, small piece missing from lower panel of the spine, corners are vertical crack to spine, small piece missing from lower panel of the spine, corners are professionally restored, light soiling to title, foxing to text is minimal, dampstaining to upper margin or a corner to a few back pages), elaborate gilt decoration with stars to each corner of margin or a corner of few back pages), elaborate gilt decoration with stars to each corner of covers (partial loss of gilt from restoration), with letterpress cancel slips pasted overe three engraved captions, copper engraved allegorical title with architectural frame around a portrait of author and decorated with marine motifs with coat-of-arms of Marcello Cervini, proposed dedicatee, 81 copper engraved plates, scattered foxing, most of which is light, background to a plate browned, 98 drawings of fishes and molluscs, 54 was omitted from all issues and does not exist, include are many woodcut initials and printer's device on last leaf.   Raymond M. Sutton, Jr.   May 26 2011 - 41503   2011 $12,000

Salzman, L. F. *Cambridge and the Isle of Ely. Volume Two. Victoria History of the Counties of England Series.* London: University of London, 1948, First edition; 4to., original cloth, gilt, pages xiii, 419, frontispiece, 36 illustrations, 15 maps, fine.   R. F. G. Hollett & Son Antiquarian Booksellers   177 - 786   2011   £75

Samerius, Henricus *Sacra Chronologia (a) Mundo Condito ad Christum.* Antwerp: Hieronymum Verdussen, 1608, Folio, (4), 67, (i.e. 65) (1) pages, damage to title leaf with loss of word 'a', 19th century crimson hard grained morocco by Hatton of Manchester, from the library of the Earls of Macclesfield at Shirburn Castle, with Macclesfield arms gilt on upper cover, vertical gilt lettering, gilt edges, manuscript annotations (some extensive), white stains on boards, ex-libris William Godolphin, slightly trimmed, from the library of the Earls of Macclesfield at Shirburn Castle.   Maggs Bros. Ltd.   1440 - 187   2011   £750

Sampson, Curt *The Eternal Summer.* Dallas: Taylor, 1992, First edition; 8vo., 214 pages, signed and inscribed, dated in year of publication by Sampson, near fine, minimal foxing to top edge, near fine dust jacket.   By the Book, L. C.   26 - 81   2011 $60

Sampson, Emma Speed *Miss Minerva Goin' Places.* Chicago: 1931, First edition; 327 pages, 12mo., near fine, dust jacket.   Bookworm & Silverfish   678 - 93   2011 $75

Sampson, Emma Speed *Miss Minerva's Baby.* Chicago: 1920, First edition; 12mo., near fine, dust jacket, original binding.   Bookworm & Silverfish   678 - 94   2011 $65

Samuels' Handy Handbook of London. London: Geo. Falkner & Sons, n.d., 1903, Small 8vo., original green decorated cloth, hinges and edges little rubbed, pages 319 with over 100 illustrations, 16 sectional maps, lacks 2 colored maps, very scarce.   R. F. G. Hollett & Son Antiquarian Booksellers   175 - 851   2011   £65

Sanborn, F. B. *The Personality of Thoreau.* Boston: Charles E. Goodspeed, 1901, First edition; #373 of 500 copies on French handmade paper; plate, 2 facsimiles of Thoreau's journal, cloth backed boards, bookplate of noted collector Luther A. Brewer of Cedar Rapids Iowa, tipped to front pastedown, spine label darkened and chipped, mild edgewear, very good.   Charles Agvent   Transcendentalism 2010 - 55   2011 $75

Sancroft, William *The Proceedings and Tryal in the Case of the Most Reverend.* London: printed for Thomas Basset and Thomas Fox, 1689, Later half polished calf gilt, extremities rubbed, 1 corner scraped, pages (iv), 140 with engraved multiple portrait frontispiece (repaired with little loss to one corner just affecting the engraved surface), title rather soiled.   R. F. G. Hollett & Son Antiquarian Booksellers   175 - 1358   2011   £150

Sancroft, William *Proceedings and Tryal in the Case of... William (Sancroft) Lord Archbishop of Canterbury.* London: printed for Thomas Bassett and Thomas Fox, `689, Folio, pages (iv), 140 + engraved frontispiece, disbound, toned and spotted, corner of one leaf excised affecting one letter, from the collection of Christopher Ernest Weston 1947-2010.   Unsworths Booksellers   24 - 39   2011   £75

Sand, George, Pseud. of Mme. Dudevant 1804-1876 *Lelia, Spiridion.* Paris: Perrotin, 1842, New edition; 2 volumes, 372, 444 pages, 12mo., quarter black calf over marbled boards, ornately gilt decorated and lettered spine, fine in handsome 19th century binding.   Paulette Rose Fine and Rare Books   32 - 152 2011 $800

Sandberg, Ryne *Second to Home.* Chicago: Bonus Books, 1995, First edition; 8vo., xi, 313 pages, near fine in like dust jacket.   By the Book, L. C.   26 - 75 2011 $55

Sandburg, Carl 1878-1967 *Abraham Lincoln: the Prairie Years. (and) The War Years.* New York: Harcourt Brace and Co., 1926, 1939. 1940. First edition of the War Years; six volumes (the first work in two volumes, second in four), 240 x 165mm., appealing modern navy blue quarter morocco over light blue linen, raised bands flanked by gilt rules, spine panels with intricate gilt fleuron centerpiece, top edge gilt, leather portion of each front cover with small gilt stamped insignia of binder, just hint of wear to joints, but quite attractive set in fine condition, morocco especially lustrous and text essentially pristine.   Phillip J. Pirages 59 - 312 2011 $1250

Sandburg, Carl 1878-1967 *Abraham Lincoln. The Prairie Years. and The War Years.* New York: Harcourt Brace and Co., 1926-1939, First edition; 6 volumes, large 8vo., original blue buckram gilt, labels removed from pastedowns, but excellent sound set, well illustrated.   R. F. G. Hollett & Son Antiquarian Booksellers   175 - 1176 2011   £300

Sandburg, Carl 1878-1967 *The American Songbag.* New York: Harcourt Brace & Co., 1927, First edition; small 4to., original brown gilt, spine lettering trifle flaked, pages xxi, 495, tailpieces and musical examples.   R. F. G. Hollett & Son Antiquarian Booksellers   175 - 1177 2011   £85

Sandburg, Carl 1878-1967 *Remembrance Rock.* New York: Harcourt Brace & Co., 1948, First edition, limited to 1000 copies numbered and signed by author; near fine, no slipcase.   Lupack Rare Books   May 26 2011 - ABE4890169937 2011 $125

Sandby, William *Thomas and Paul Sandy. Royal Academicians. Some Account of their Lives and Works.* London: Seeley and Co. Limited, Essex Strand, 1892, First edition; 16 plates, xii, 230, (2) pages, original blue cloth, titl in gilt on spine and upper cover.   Anthony W. Laywood   May 26 2011 - 21760 2011 $84

Sander, Allegra *Men. A Dialogue Between Women.* London: Cresset Press, 1955, First edition; small 8vo., original cloth, gilt, spine little faded, dust jacket by Mervyn Peake, pages 95, 3 line drawings by Peake.   R. F. G. Hollett & Son Antiquarian Booksellers   175 - 1178 2011   £45

Sandham, Elizabeth *Sketches of Young People; or a Visit to Brighton.* London: Harvey and Darton, 1822, 12mo., vii, 180, (4) page publisher list, original three quarter maroon roan back, marbled paper on boards, gilt fillets and title on spine, full page engraved frontispiece, engraved label of merit from "Mr. Richard Chambers's Academy, Castle Street, Leicester Square" pasted down on lower cover, small nick at crown and foot of spine, fine.   Hobbyhorse Books   56 - 134 2011 $300

Sandon, Henry *Flight and Barr Worcester Porcelain.* Antique Collectors Club, 1978, First edition; 4to., original cloth, dust jacket, pages 245 with 190 plates, 24 illustrations.   R. F. G. Hollett & Son Antiquarian Booksellers   General Catalogue Summer 2010 - 319 2011   £65

Sandon, Henry *Grainger's Worcester Porcelain.* Barrie & Jenkins, 1989, First edition; large 8vo. original cloth, dust jacket, pages 288, with 8 pages of color plates, 180 black and white photos, over 50 line drawings, with list of 4500 pattern numbers and descriptions.   R. F. G. Hollett & Son Antiquarian Booksellers   General Catalogue Summer 2010 - 322 2011   £95

Sandon, Henry *Royal Worcester Porcelain from 1862 to the Present Day.* New York: Clarkson N. Potter, 1973, Large 8vo., original cloth, gilt, dust jacket, pages xxix, 265, with 19 color plates and 220 illustrations, scarce.   R. F. G. Hollett & Son Antiquarian Booksellers   General Catalogue Summer 2010 - 320 2011   £120

Sandoz, Mari *The Beaver Men: Spearheads of Empire.* New York: Hastings House, 1964, First edition; xv, (1), 335, numerous illustrations, map endpapers, brown cloth, gilt, very fine, pictorial dust jacket.   Argonaut Book Shop Recent Acquisitions Summer 2010 - 180 2011 $75

Santoni-Rugiu, P. *A History of Plastic Surgery.* Berlin: Heidelberg: New York: Springer, 2007, Large 8vo., illustrations in color and black and white, with CD Rom in pocket at rear, about fine.   Any Amount of Books   May 29 2011 - A72610 2011 $221

Sarg, Tony *Who's Who in Tony Sarg's Zoo.* Springfield: McLoughlin, 1937, 4to., cloth backed glazed pictorial boards, slight edge wear, else fine in frayed dust jacket, every page of text with marvelous full page color illustrations, scarce.   Aleph-Bet Books, Inc.   95 - 503 2011 $275

Sargent, Rose Mary *The Diffident Naturalist: Robert Boyle an the Philosophy of Experiment.* Chicago: University of Chicago Press, 1995, 8vo., xi, 355 pages, olive cloth, green stamped spine title, rare in cloth, from the Bern Dibner reference library, with Burndy bookplate.   Jeff Weber Rare Books   161 - 58 2011 $65

Sargisson, Jim *Joe Scoap's Jurneh through Three Wardles: Being a Cumberland Shepherd's Travels in the Old World, the New World and Australasia.* Whitehaven: Smith Brothers, 1881, Original blue cloth, gilt, extremities trifle rubbed, pages vi, 250, scarce. R. F. G. Hollett & Son Antiquarian Booksellers 173 - 1011 2011 £65

Sarpi, Paolo 1552-1623 *Histoire du Concile de Trente de Fra'Paolo Sarpi...* Amsterdam: G. P. & J. Blaeu, 1713, 4to., (48), 800, (46) pages, titlepage printed in red and black, woodcut printer's device, woodcut tailpieces and initials, contemporary calf, spine gilt in compartments, morocco lettering piece, binding rubbed, slight foxing, from the library of the Earls of Macclesfield at Shirburn Castle. Maggs Bros. Ltd. 1440 - 188 2011 £450

Sarton, May *The Fur Person.* New York: Rinehart, 1957, First edition; illustrations by Barbara Knox, near fine, light crease on front of boards, bookplate under flap, dust jacket near fine, light soiling to lighter areas, light wear to extremities. Bella Luna Books May 29 2011 - 6340 2011 $82

Sartorius, Carl Christian *Mexico. Landscapes and Popular Sketches.* London: Trubner & Cie, 1858, First English edition; 4to., vignette title page dated 1859, 6, 202 pages, original gilt stamped cloth, spine neatly replaced, some spotty foxing, but very good, one plate slightly misbound (misplaced). M & S Rare Books, Inc. 90 - 253 2011 $3250

Sassoon, Siegfried Lorraine 1886-1967 *Memoirs of a Fox Hunting Man. Memoirs of an Infantry Officer. Sherston's Progress.* London: Faber, 1928-1936, 126/260 copies/ 275/750 copies; 15/300 copies respectively; 8vo., pages 400, 336, 280, all printed on handmade paper and each signed by author, original light blue buckram, very light bumping to front head corner of Memoirs of an Infantry Officer, backstrips gilt lettered, backstrip to Sherstons Progress unfaded, faint free endpaper browning, that to Memoirs of a Fox Hunting Man more so, top edge gilt, others untrimmed, overall very good. Blackwell Rare Books B166 - 229 2011 £2350

Satow, Ernest *A Guide to Diplomatic Practice.* London: Longmans, Green and Co., 1932, Third edition; fat 8vo., pages x, 519, but stretched to about 1000 pages with interleaved blanks on which Sir Stephen Gaselee has written notes and comments, pencilled ownership signature of historian F. R. Cowell, A S Gow's pamphlet on Life of Fasselee loosely inserted, brown half leather with orange boards and lettered gilt at spine, slight rubbing, minor near, else sound, very good. Any Amount of Books May 26 2011 - A46377 2011 $419

Satterthwait, Walter *The Gold of Mavani, The African Stories of Walter Satterthwait.* Gallup: Buffalo Medicine Books, 1995, One of 250 numbered copies; fine, dust jacket fine, endpapers stamped in silver, signed by Satterthwait, Franklin and Caudwell on limitation page. Bella Luna Books May 29 2011 - 4495s 2011 $82

Sauer, Hans *Ex Africa.* London: Geoffrey Bles, 1937, First edition; 8vo., 336 pages, fold map, illustrations, some occasional light foxing, original purple cloth, spine slightly faded with small nick at head. J. & S. L. Bonham Antiquarian Booksellers Africa 4/20/2011 - 4825 2011 £35

Saunders, Louise *The Knave of Hearts.* New York: Charles Scribner's Sons, 1925, First edition; large quarto, (6), 46, (1) (3, blank) pages, color frontispiece and tissue guards, many full page color illustrations by Maxfield Parrish, laid into this copy is ANS by artist for Mr. Johnson, original black cloth with color pictorial label on front cover, color pictorial endpapers, some very light scuffing of back board, very clean internally, about fine in most of original glassine wrappers, howerever torn quite a bit, original issue cardboard box, box heavily worn, bottom of box intact but cracked at corners, top of box has its sides detached, however this box usually not present at all. Heritage Book Shop Holiday 2010 - 94 2011 $5500

Saunders, Richard *Angelograhia Sive Pneumata Leiturgia Pneumataologia.* London: printed for Thomas Prankhurst, 1701, First edition; 4to., old panelled calf gilt, rather worn at extremities, upper hinge cracking, title (verso blank), 3 leaves (preface and contents), pages 314, 1 (ad leaf), some browned or spotted patches in places, joints tender, rare. R. F. G. Hollett & Son Antiquarian Booksellers 175 - 1180 2011 £350

Saurat, Denis *Death and the Dreamer.* London: John Westhouse, 1946, First edition; original cloth, dust jacket, price clipped, pages 150 with full page illustrations, presentation copy, inscribed for Richard Rowe. R. F. G. Hollett & Son Antiquarian Booksellers General Catalogue Summer 2010 - 719 2011 £120

Savage, Marion W. *The Bachelor of the Albany.* London: Chapman & Hall, 1848, First edition; some internal spots and marks, contemporary half calf, brown label, slight rubbing. Jarndyce Antiquarian Booksellers CXCI - 483 2011 £40

Savaron, Jean *Les Origines de la Ville de Clairmont... Augmentees de Remarques.* Paris: F. Muguet, 1662, Folio, (12), 593, (31) pages, title printed in red and black, engravings in text, 18th century English calf, gilt fillet on covers, spine gilt in compartments, red speckled edges, from the library of the Earls of Macclesfield at Shirburn Castle. Maggs Bros. Ltd. 1440 - 240 2011 £900

Savary, Claude Etienne *Letters on Egypt.* London: G. G. J. & J. Robinson, 1786, First UK edition; 2 volumes, 8vo., pages xxiv 568; xxiv, 596, 2 folding maps, 1 folding plan, contemporary brown full speckled calf, upper cover of volume I tender, light rubbing to head and tail of spines, very good, crisp copy.   J. & S. L. Bonham Antiquarian Booksellers   Africa 4/20/2011 - 9028   2011   £500

Savary, Jacques *Le Parfait Negociant ou Instruction Generale Pour ce Qui Regarde le Commerce des Marchandises de France...* Amsterdam: Etienne Roger, 1717, Eighth edition; 2 volumes in 1, 4to., xx, 651, (25); xxiv, 631 (1) pages, titlepages printed in red and black, 18th century panelled calf, spine gilt in compartments, title piece "parfait negociant", light dampstaining towards centre of volume, scarce, from the library of the Earls of Macclesfield at Shirburn Castle.   Maggs Bros. Ltd.   1440 - 189   2011   £500

Savery, Thomas *The Miner's Friend or an Engine to Raise Water by Fire Described.* London: for S. Crouch, 1702, 8vo., (10), 84 pages, folding engraved plates, contemporary mottled calf gilt, spine gilt in compartments, red edges, without final leaf, plate slightly creased with small tear (repaired), from the library of the Earls of Macclesfield at Shirburn Castle.   Maggs Bros. Ltd.   1440 - 190   2011   £10,000

Saville, Jenny *Closed Contact.* Beverley Hills: Gagosian Gallery, circa, 2002, First edition; folio, beige matt paper covered boards with title embossed in black on front cover and spine, fine copy, pages unmarked, as new, 14 color and 12 black and white plates printed on ultra high gloss finish paper.   Any Amount of Books   May 29 2011 - A63505   2011 $383

Savioli, Lodovico Vittorio *Amri.* Crisopoli (Parma): Co'tipi Bodoniani, 1795, Fine stipple engraved medallion portrait on title just touch of faint dust soiling, pages (viii), 133, (3), 4to., contemporary mottled paper boards backed with mottled sheep, backstrip divided by triple gilt fillets, brown label in second compartment, rest with central gilt portrait tools, marbled pastedowns, stitching strained after title, bit scuffed in places, bookplate of Sir Gore Ouseley, Bt., good.   Blackwell Rare Books   B166 - 93   2011   £400

Sawyer, Eugene T. *The Life and Career of Tiburcio Vasquez, the California Bandit and Murderer...* San Jose: B. H. Cottle printer, 1875, First edition; signed by author July 1875, pictorial wrappers, portrait on cover, 48 pages, illustrations, little wear to fore-edges, else very good, housed in slipcase with gold stamping on spine, very rare and exceptional copy.   Buckingham Books   May 26 2011 - 23657   2011 $4500

Saxby, Argyll *The Gier-an of Burma and Other Adventure Yarns.* Boy's Own Paper, n.d., 1925, First edition; original pictorial boards, pages 245, (x), 7plates by T. W. R. Whitwell.   R. F. G. Hollett & Son Antiquarian Booksellers General Catalogue Summer 2010 - 568   2011   £30

Say, Allen *Grandfather's Journey.* Boston: Houghton Mifflin, 1993, Stated first edition; 4to., 32 pages, fine in fine dust jacket, no medal on jacket.   By the Book, L. C. 26 - 71   2011 $150

Say, Allen *Grandfather's Journey.* Boston: Houghton Mifflin Co., 1993, First edition; 4to., cloth backed blind-stamped boards, full color pictorial dust jacket, as new, signed with drawing by Say, every page illustrated in full color.   Jo Ann Reisler, Ltd.   86 - 225   2011 $200

Say, Jean Baptiste 1767-1832 *A Treatise on Political Economy or the Production, Distribution & Consumption of Wealth.* Philadelphia: 1832, 5th American edition; (2) ads, 455 pages, full sheep, gilt on black label bright, rubbed at top front free corner, endpapers foxed, with expected embrownment.   Bookworm & Silverfish   676 - 70   2011 $225

Sayer, Robert *The Compleat Drawing Book...* printed for and sold by R. Sayer and J. Bennett, 1775, Fourth edition; 8vo., (6) + ad leaf on 119 engravings on 115 numbered sheets, several with 2 separate engravings, but sheet 112 appears not to have been bound in, plates very clean, several with early hand coloring, but text pages dusty and marked with some chipping to lower outer corner, well bound in 19th century red half morocco, gilt banded spine, marbled boards and endpapers.   Ken Spelman Rare Books   68 - 12   2011   £280

Sayers, Dorothy L. *The Documents in the Case.* New York: Brewer & Warner, Inc., 1930, First edition; near fine, tight copy in dust jacket, sunned on spine, near fine, tight copy, dust jacket sunned on spine and with light professional restoration to spine ends and corners, exceptional copy, elusive title.   Buckingham Books   May 26 2011 - 28283   2011 $1750

Sayers, Dorothy L. *Even the Parrot.* London: Methuen, 1944, First edition; small 8vo., original cloth, gilt, dust jacket, spine little rubbed and faded, chipped at head and foot, pages vii, 55, illustrations by Sillince, endpapers little browned in gutters.   R. F. G. Hollett & Sons Antiquarian Booksellers   170 - 605   2011   £75

Scaife, Arthur H. *The War to Date March 1 1900.* London: T. Fisher Unwin, 1900, First edition; 8vo., 372 pages, as, illustrations, original brown decorative cloth.   J. & S. L. Bonham Antiquarian Booksellers   Africa 4/20/2011 - 8268   2011   £65

Scala, Giovanni *Delle Fortificationi etc.* Rome: Giuseppe de Rossi, 1627, Enlarged edition; folio, ff. (64), 18th century half calf, spine gilt, red morocco lettering piece, lacking plan of Macerata, few illustrations shaved, from the library of the Earls of Macclesfield at Shirburn Castle. Maggs Bros. Ltd. 1440 - 1191 2011 £750

Scaliger, Josephus *Collectanea in M. Terentium Varronem de Lingua Latina.* Paris: R. Estienne 22 August, 1565, First edition; 8vo., (8), 221, (3) pages, device on gilt, last leaf blank, contemporary limp vellum, first few leaves, dampstained at head, title leaf little frayed at bottom, from the library of the Earls of Macclesfield at Shirburn Castle. Maggs Bros. Ltd. 1440 - 192 2011 £475

Scaliger, Josephus *(Greek) Proverbiales Graecorum versus los. Scaliger...* Paris: F. Morel, 1594, 2 parts, 8vo., 15, (1), 20 (4), 32 pages, device on royal Greek printer on titlepages, large 'decalogue' device with motto Pietas et Iustitia and Morel's initials on part 2 page (iv), contemporary limp vellum, fine, crisp copy, from the library of the Earls of Macclesfield at Shirburn Castle. Maggs Bros. Ltd. 1440 - 193 2011 £450

Scantlebury, Edward *The Journal of the Fell & Rock Climbing Club of the English Lake District. Volume I 1907-1909.* Ulverston: Fell & Rock Climbing Club, 1909, Contemporary half pebble grain morocco gilt, little rubbed, pages (xvi), 334, well illustrated with plates, diagrams, some in gravure or color. R. F. G. Hollett & Son Antiquarian Booksellers 173 - 1017 2011 £120

Scarff, John E. *Fifty Years of Neurosurgery 1905-1955.* N.P. given: Franklin H. Martin Memorial Foundation, 1955, Reprint from Surgery Gynecology & Obstetrics, Nov. 1955, Volume 101; 8vo., 303-399 pages, 85 numbered figures, printed wrappers, previous owner's inked signature and rubberstamps, title info inked on spine, near fine, signed presentation inscription from author, from the Medical Library of Dr. Clare Gray Peterson. Jeff Weber Rare Books 162 - 270 2011 $75

Scenes and Incidents of Foreign Travel. London: Robert Tyas, circa, 1844, Frontispiece and plates, slightly foxed, small internal tear to leading f.e.p., original dark blue cloth, blocked in blind, spine decorated in gilt, spine slightly faded, signature of Rosa Mayhew, Renier booklabel, all edges gilt, very good. Jarndyce Antiquarian Booksellers CXCI - 536 2011 £58

Schaeffer, Jacob Christian *Elementa Entomolgica....* Regensburg: Gedrukt mit Weissischen Schriften, 1766, First edition; rare, 4to., (186) pages, 140 hand colored engraved plates on 72 leaves, text in Latin and German, modern full calf antique, margins of first few leaves stained from turn-in of original binding, else very good, beautiful, clean plates. Joseph J. Felcone Inc. Fall Miscellany 2010 - 104 2011 $6000

Schaeffer, Jacob Christian *Piscium Bavarico Ratisbonensium Pentas. (bound with) Epistola ad Regio-Borussicam Societatem Litterariam Du'isburgensem de Studii Ichthyologici Facililori...* Ratisbonae: Montagii et Typis Weissianis, 1761, Ratisbonae: Typis Weissianis et Impensis Montagii, 1760; 4to., 4 hand colored engraved plates (light foxing to 1), pages (12), 82; 4to., pages 24, scattered light foxing, contemporary calf backed boards, rubbed, bump to upper edges of covers, 1 inch split to upper edges of spine, old paper label to heel of spine, some worming to upper blank corner of all pages and plates, old ink number to front flyleaf, 3 handstamps on first title, scattered light foxing, from the Musee d'Histoire Naturelle de Geneve, also the copy of H. C. Redeke, P. F. Geiger, and R. Harry, Jr. Raymond M. Sutton, Jr. May 26 2011 - 41627 2011 $1500

Schaeffer, L. M. *Sketches of Travels in South America, Mexico and California.* New York: James Egbert, 1860, First edition; 247 pages, original dark brown blindstamped pebbled cloth, lower corners just starting to show, spine ends with hint of light wear, else fine. Argonaut Book Shop Recent Acquisitions Summer 2010 - 182 2011 $300

Schafer, E. A. *Life: its Nature, Origin and Maintenance.* London: Longmans, Green and Co., 1912, First edition; original green wrappers, pages 36, scarce. R. F. G. Hollett & Son Antiquarian Booksellers General Catalogue Summer 2010 - 1043 2011 £45

Schaller, Charlotte *Histoire d'un Barve Petit Soldat.* Paris: Berger Levrault, 1915, Oblong 4to., cloth backed pictorial boards, covers inside with some finger soil, else very good+, full and partial page color art deco illustrations. Aleph-Bet Books, Inc. 95 - 592 2011 $800

Schapera, I. *The Bantu Speaking Tribes of South Africa.* London: Routledge, 1937, First edition; 8vo., pages xv, 453, illustrations, map, some occasional foxing and knowledgeable notations in text, original red cloth. J. & S. L. Bonham Antiquarian Booksellers Africa 4/20/2011 - 5569 2011 £35

Schealer, John *Zip-Zip Goes Venus.* New York: Dutton, 1958, Stated first edition; 8vo., 125 pages, cloth, fine in dust jacket with few small chips. Aleph-Bet Books, Inc. 95 - 504 2011 $150

Scheips, Paul J. *Army Operational and Intelligence Activities in Civil Disturbances Since 1957.* Washington: 1971, Revised edition; vi, 128 pages, 4to., original binding, author's copy, scarce. Bookworm & Silverfish 664 - 138 2011 $65

Schenk, Peter *Aan Den Hoog-Edel Weigeboren en Gestrengen Heere, Den Heere Joan Baron van Arnhem, Heere van Rozendael tot Harsio...* Amsterdam: P. Schenk, circa, 1700, oblong 4to., engraved titlepage and 15 etched plates, plain wrappers, soiled, 3 short tears to margins, occasional marginal foxing to plates, scarce. Raymond M. Sutton, Jr. May 26 2011 - 34876 2011 $1600

Scherer, Margaret R. *Marvels of Ancient Rome.* Phaidon Press for the Metropolitan Museum of Art, 1956, Large 8vo., original cloth, gilt, dust jacket trifle worn, pages ix, 430, with 222 plates. R. F. G. Hollett & Son Antiquarian Booksellers 177 - 788 2011 £30

Schickard, Wilhelm *Tarich h.e. Series Regum Persiae... Cum Proemio Longiori...* Tubingen: T. Werlin, 1628, 4to., 231 pages, woodcut illustrations, 18th century calf, gilt spine, red edges, last 2 leaves cropped at outer margin with loss of letters, cropped signature at head of title "Nathan Wright of Englefield", from the library of the Earls of Macclesfield at Shirburn Castle. Maggs Bros. Ltd. 1440 - 194 2011 £1800

Schimmelpenninck, Mary Anne *Life of Mary Anne Schimmelpenninck.* Philadelphia: Henry Longstreth, 1859, 2 volumes, (vii, 352; vii, 284 pages) 8vo., original blind-stamped brown cloth, gilt lettered spine, slightly dulled, very little foxing, otherwise very nice. Paulette Rose Fine and Rare Books 32 - 154 2011 $150

Schlich, W. *Schlich's Manual of Forestry.* London: Bradbury Agnew & Co., 1906, Volume 1 is third edition, volume 2 is second, revised edition; 5 volumes, 8vo., pages 2425, copiously illustrated in black and white, Duke of Bedford Woburn Abbey bookplate in 3 volumes, compliments of author label in first volume, original publisher's green cloth lettered gilt on spine and cover, very good, sound, about very good, slight wear and slight mottling to volume 1 and 5, otherwise, decent, sound set. Any Amount of Books May 29 2011 - A75543 2011 $238

Schliemann, Heinrich *Set of the Archaeological Works.* New York: Arno Press, 1976, Facsimile reprints; 5 volumes, original orange cloth gilt, black spine panels, numerous illustrations and plans, some spotting to top edges, otherwise excellent. R. F. G. Hollett & Son Antiquarian Booksellers 177 - 792 2011 £40

Schliemann, Heinrich *Tiryns.* New York: Arno Press, 1976, Facsimile reprint; original cloth, gilt, pages lxiv, 385, with 178 illustrations and 28 plates and plans. R. F. G. Hollett & Son Antiquarian Booksellers 177 - 789 2011 £30

Schliemann, Heinrich *Troja.* New York: Arno Press, 1976, Facsimile reprint; original cloth, gilt, pages xl, 433, with 139 illustrations and 8 plans. R. F. G. Hollett & Son Antiquarian Booksellers 177 - 790 2011 £30

Schmidt, John D. *Ramesses II.* John Hopkins University Press, 1973, First edition; original cloth, large 8vo., pages 216. R. F. G. Hollett & Son Antiquarian Booksellers 177 - 792 2011 £40

Schmiechen, James *The British Market Hall.* New Haven: Yale University Press, 1999, First edition; large 4to., original cloth, gilt, dust jacket, pages xii, 312, illustrations. R. F. G. Hollett & Son Antiquarian Booksellers 177 - 794 2011 £30

Schmitz, James Henry *A Nice Day for Screaming and Other Tales of the Hub.* Philadelphia and New York: Chilton Books, 1965, First edition; octavo, cloth. L. W. Currey, Inc. 124 - 85 2011 $1000

Schmitz, James Henry *The Witches of Karres.* Philadelphia and New York: Chilton Books, 1966, First edition; octavo, cloth. L. W. Currey, Inc. 124 - 99 2011 $850

Schneider, Franz *Letters from Stalingrad.* New York: 1962, First edition; 127 pages, very good in good dust jacket, few rubbed spots. Bookworm & Silverfish 679 - 209 2011 $60

Schnitzler, Arthur *Rhapsody. A Dream Novel.* New York: Simon & Schuster, 1927, First American edition; small 8vo., pages 167, cover little spotted, worn at edge, else very good. Second Life Books Inc. 174 - 273 2011 $65

Schoepf, Johann David *Materia Medica Americana Potissimum Regni Vegetabilis.* Erlangae: Sumtibus Io. Iac. Palmii, 1787, First edition; 8vo., pages (2), xviii, 170, (4), contemporary quarter sheep, some worming to edges of spine, dark stain to lower third of pages and pastedowns, marginal tear to a leaf, ex-libris Johann Thomas Bosch with signature, the Norman copy. Raymond M. Sutton, Jr. May 26 2011 - 51773 2011 $5500

Schomberg, Reginald Charles Francis *Between the Oxus and the Indus.* London: Martin Hopkinson Ltd., 1935, First edition; 270 page, 16 black and white photos, one folding map, 8vo., cloth, very good or better, light scattered foxing, mostly to prelims, binding tight, text clean, folding map near fine, lacking dust jacket, now in clear archival wrapper, nice. Kaaterskill Books 12 - 169 2011 $300

The School of Good Manners. Boston: Manning & Loring, 1808, Third edition; square 16mo., 95 pages, original leather spine, blue gray paper on wood boards, restored, half page wood engraving, inked signature at top edge of titlepage and top edge of first page, scattered worm holes at front leather spine, paper flaw along front edges of titlepage, rare, in very good state. Hobbyhorse Books 56 - 136 2011 $1200

Schoolcraft, Henry Rowe 1793-1864 *Historical and Statistical Information, Respecting the History, Condition and Prospects of the Indian Tribes of the United States...* Philadelphia: Lippincott, Grambo & Co. et al, 1851-1857, First edition; 6 volumes, thick folio, approximately 330 lithographed and steel engraved plates, many tinted, some hand colored or chromolithographed, largely after artist Seth Eastman, original half dark green morocco, marbled sides, reddish brown endpapers, remarkably fine, bright and fresh, engraved fore-titles moderately foxed, black and white plates and tissue guards range from entirely unfoxed to moderately foxed with most lightly foxed in margins, color plates largely unfoxed, few lightly foxed in margins. Joseph J. Felcone Inc.   Fall Miscellany 2010 - 105 2011 $20,000

Schoolcraft, Henry Rowe 1793-1864 *Information, Respecting the History, Condition and Prospects of the Indian Tribes of the United States....* Philadelphia: Lippincott, Grambo & Co., 1852-1857, Mixed set, volume 6 is first edition, remaining 5 volumes are the first reprinted edition; 6 volumes, 6 steel engraved extra titles, steel engraved portrait of Schoolcraft foxed) and 328 plates and maps (engraved or lithographed; numerous plates hand colored or tinted in 2 or more colors, many of the plates from volume 6 are repeated from previous volumes, brown spots to a plate in volume 2; foxing or browning to some of plates in volume 6) after Seth Eastman and others, thick folio, pages xxiv, (13-568; xxiv, (17-) 607; xviii, (19-) 635; xxvi, (19-) 667; xxiv, (25-) 712; xxviii, (25-) 576, all uniformly bound in publisher's cloth with upper boards and spines pictorially stamped in gilt (some fading, especially the spines, some wear to extremities; volume 1 lacks front free endpaper and with previous owner's gift inscription and scattered foxing, marginal dampstain to few plates and pages in volume 3), good.   Raymond M. Sutton, Jr. May 26 2011 - 55945 2011 $12,500

Schoolcraft, Henry Rowe 1793-1864 *Narrative of an Expedition through the Upper Mississippi to Itasca Lake...* New York: Harper & Bros., 1834, First edition; (2), 307, (1) pages, 5 maps, modern half red crushed levant morocco, first leaves neatly washed, old penned number on title and second leaf, else fine.   Joseph J. Felcone Inc. Fall Miscellany 2010 - 106 2011 $1000

Schooling, William *Alliance Assurance 1824-1924.* Alliance Ins. Co., 1924, Pages (iv), 119, with 17 plates, original cloth, gilt.   R. F. G. Hollett & Son Antiquarian Booksellers   175 - 1182 2011   £30

Schoor, Gene *Sugar Ray Robinson World's Greatest Fighter - Pound for Pound.* New York: 1951, First edition; 119 pages, 7 1/2 x 5 inches, photo wrappers, very good, diagonal crease on upper free corner front covers. Bookworm & Silverfish 664 - 187 2011 $85

Schouler, James *A Treatise on the Law of the Domestic Relations Embracing Husband and Wife, Parent & Child, Guardian & Ward, Infancy & Master & Servant.* Boston: 1870, First edition; 670 pages, large 8vo., very good in full old law calf.   Bookworm & Silverfish   665 - 81 2011 $125

Schreiber, T. *Atlas of Classical Antiquities.* London: Macmillan, 1895, First English edition; oblong small folio, later black buckram gilt, pages 203, 100 plates, prelims trifle spotted and creased, edge of one leaf restored.   R. F. G. Hollett & Son Antiquarian Booksellers 177 - 795 2011 £150

Schreiner, Olive 1855-1920 *Dream Life and real Life. A Little African Story.* London: T. Fisher Unwin, 1893, First edition; (12 pages including two prelim ads), 13-93 pages, 8vo., original publisher's flexible beige cloth lettered in dark blue, very fine.   Paulette Rose Fine and Rare Books   32 - 155 2011 $300

Schreiner, Olive 1855-1920 *Woman and Labour.* London: T. Fisher Unwin, 1911, First edition; original blue cloth gilt extra, slight scratch to spine, pages 283, top edge gilt, half title and endpapers rather spotted or browned.   R. F. G. Hollett & Son Antiquarian Booksellers 175 - 1183 2011   £75

Schroder, Miss *The Pictorial Scripture Alphabet.* London: Ackermann & Co., 1851, Original publisher's brown cloth case measuring 3 3/4 x 5 1/4 inches with green printed label contains 26 separate alphabet cards, some normal finger soil, two cards printed in dark blue instead of black else very good-fine, front of each card has fine hand colored illustration.   Aleph-Bet Books, Inc. 95 - 19 2011 $750

Schubler, Johann Jacob *Erste (Beylag zur Ersten Ausgab... Zweyte-Funffzehende). (bound with) Nutzliche Vorstellung, wie man... (bound with) Natzliche Vorstellung und Deutlicher Unterricht von Zierlichen....* Augsburg: Jeremias Wolff, circa, 1715-1730, Nuremberg: L. Bieling for J. C. Weigel, 1730, 1728.; Together 3 works in one volume, folio, woodcut headpieces and initials, contemporary speckled calf, spine gilt in compartments, binding slightly rubbed, tears on both covers, from the library of the Earls of Macclesfield at Shirburn Castle.   Maggs Bros. Ltd. 1440 - 196 2011 £900

Schultz, Christoph *Kurze Fragen Ueber die Christliche Glaubens Lehre... Den Christlichen Glaubens Schulern...* Philadelphia: Carl Cist, 1784, (1), 104 pages, contemporary sprinkled calf, blind roll and fillets on boards and spine, red sprinkled edges, by Christoph Hoffmann, nice, tight copy.   Joseph J. Felcone Inc. Fall Miscellany 2010 - 41 2011 $900

Schulz, Bruno *Cinnamon Shops and Other Stories.* London: Macgibbon & Kee, 1963, First English language edition; owner name front flyleaf, tiny corner bumps, near fine in very good dust jacket with modest surface soiling to rear panel and slight wear to spine extremities. Ken Lopez Bookseller 154 - 200 2011 $750

Schulze, Johann *De Suspecta Poli Declinatione et Eccentricitate Firmamenti vel ruina Cocli, Ultro Citroque Ventilata Materia, Potissimum Tamen hei Contra Domin.* Leipzig: C. Michaelis, 1675, 4to., 239, (1) pages, 18th century English calf, spine gilt uncommon, from the library of the Earls of Macclesfield at Shirburn Castle. Maggs Bros. Ltd. 1440 - 170 2011 £3000

Schumacher, E. F. *Small is Beautiful: a Study of Economics as If People Mattered.* London: Abacus, 1976, Reprint; 8vo., color illustrated wrappers, large format paperback, pages 255, signed by author, rare thus, very good+. Any Amount of Books May 29 2011 - A68921 2011 $272

Schurman, Anna Maria Von *Opuscula Hebraea, Graeca, Latina, Gallica Prosaica & Metrica.* Lud. Batador: Ex Offiicina Elseviriorum, 1648, First edition; 8vo., pages vi, 374, titlepage printed in black and red with engraving of the Elzevir logo of a sage under a tree, some ink writing in old hand on leaf opposite titlepage, few words at top of titlepage, this seems to have been issued both with and without a portrait there is none here, bound in later three quarter morocco and marbled paper, paper little toned but very nice. Second Life Books Inc. 174 - 274 2011 $1750

Schutyser, Sebastian *Flowers of the Moon.* 2007, Quarto, 64 pages, dust jacket, illustrations. Andrew Isles Natural History Books Spring 2010 - 31635 2011 $75

Schwartz, Aubrey *Wild Flowers: Etchings.* 1966, #67 of 100, each numbered and signed by artist; Portfolio of etchings 7 of 10 present, etchings printed by Emiliano Sorini on handmade Italia paper, 11 x 14 inches, very good. G. H. Mott Bookseller May 26 2011 - 31832 2011 $3000

Schweitzer, Albert *Indian Thought and its Development.* London: Hodder and Stoughton, 1936, Second edition; original cloth, dust jacket, little worn, spine faded, pages xii, 272, little pencilled marginalia. R. F. G. Hollett & Son Antiquarian Booksellers 175 - 1196 2011 £30

Schweitzer, George *Emin Pasha: His Life and Work...* London: Archibald Constable, 1898, First UK edition; 2 volumes, 8vo., pages xliv, 330; vii, 339, original blue cloth, spines faded and rubbed, wear to head and tail of spines. J. & S. L. Bonham Antiquarian Booksellers Africa 4/20/2011 - 7155 2011 £135

Schwing, Ned *The Browning Superposed. John M. Browning's Last Legacy.* Iola: Krause Publications, 1996, First edition; 4to., original boards, gilt, dust jacket, pages 496, 48 pages in color, fine, very scarce. R. F. G. Hollett & Son Antiquarian Booksellers General Catalogue Summer 2010 - 323 2011 £350

Scicluna, Hannibal P. *The Church of St. John in Valletta; Its History, Architecture and Monuments with Brief History of the Order of St. John From Its Inception to the Present Day.* San Martin: privately printed, 1955, First edition, one 473 of 2000 copies; 4to., original publisher's red cloth lettered gilt on spine with white Maltese cross on cover, pages liii, 428, with 2 plans and 760 illustrations, ownership signature of Richard Hamilton Alexander Cheffins, slight rubbing, spine slightly sunned, very good or better, decent. Any Amount of Books May 29 2011 - A76512 2011 $383

Sclater, Philip Lutley *Catalogue of a Collection of American Birds.* London: N. Trubner and Co., 1862, Limited to 100 copies; very good, 20 beautiful hand colored lithographed plates, small marginal dampstain to 1, small ink notation on lower blank corner of few, wood engraved vignette on titlepage, 8vo., pages xvi, 368, modern half morocco, endpapers renewed. Raymond M. Sutton, Jr. May 26 2011 - 26205 2011 $1150

Sclauzero, Mariarosa *Narcissism and Death.* Barrytown: Station Hill Press, 1984, First edition; small 4to., wrappers, pages 110, illustrations by Sue Coe, signed presentation from author for Angela Carter, with her posthumous bookplate, very slight rubbing, faint edgewear, very good+. Any Amount of Books May 29 2011 - A64551 2011 $255

Scott, Anna M. *The Flower Babies' Books.* Chicago: Rand McNally, 1914, First edition; moire backed pictorial boards, as new in publisher's pictorial box, light shelf wear to box, illustrations by Penny Ross, with incredible color, very scarce especially in box. Aleph-Bet Books, Inc. 95 - 496 2011 $600

Scott, Colonel *A Journal of a Residence in the Esmailla of Abd-el-Kader and of Travels in Morocco and Algiers.* London: Whittaker, 1842, First edition; 8vo., pages 264, frontispiece, original brown blindstamped cloth, covers faded in parts, spine rubbed. J. & S. L. Bonham Antiquarian Booksellers Africa 4/20/2011 - 8767 2011 £150

Scott, Daniel *Bygone Cumberland and Westmorland.* William Andrews, 1899, First edition; original cloth gilt, little rubbed, neatly recased, pages (xii), 262, (x, ads), illustrations. R. F. G. Hollett & Son Antiquarian Booksellers 173 - 1019 2011 £45

Scott, Daniel *History of Penrith Church. A Bi-Centenary Sketch.* Penrith: R. Scott, 1922, First edition; original blue cloth, gilt, little worn, pages (ii), 128, 6 plates, scarce. R. F. G. Hollett & Son Antiquarian Booksellers 173 - 1020 2011 £85

Scott, Daniel *How Penrith Old Parish Church Was Built.* Penrith: Observer Office, 1903, Author's own copy, original plain limp cloth with silk tie, pages 28.   R. F. G. Hollett & Son Antiquarian Booksellers   173 - 1021 2011   £35

Scott, Edward J. L. *Catalogue of the Stowe Manuscripts in the British Museum.*   1895-1896, First edition; 2 volumes, viii 823, 384 pages, very good.   C. P. Hyland   May 26 2011 - 255/655   2011 $362

Scott, George *The Memoires of Sir James Melhil of Hal-Hill...* London: printed by E. H. For Robert Boulter, 1683, First edition; 4to., (xvi), 204, (26) pages, heavily foxed and browned, title and first 5 leaves chipped at extremities, contemporary full calf, raised bands, leather scuffed, hinges neatly repaired, modern red title spine label, handsomely with gilt rolls, ownership signature of Margaret Jones, Philadelphia, very good.   Jeff Weber Rare Books   163 - 22   2011 $1000

Scott, George Gilbert *Personal and Professional Recollections.* London: Sampson Low, etc., 1879, First edition; original ribbed maroon cloth, gilt, pages xx, 436, some pencilled lining in places, notes on front flyleaf.   R. F. G. Hollett & Son Antiquarian Booksellers   177 - 796 2011   £75

Scott, George Gilbert *Remarks on Secular & Domestic Architecture, Present and Future.* London: John Murray, 1858, Second edition; xii, 290 pages, titlepage in red and black with engraved vignette, very good in elaborately gilt decorated contemporary red morocco prize binding, gilt stamped "Science and Art Department Queens Prize for Art" and with prize label dated 1874, some slight foxing to endpapers.   Ken Spelman Rare Books   68 - 70   2011   £120

Scott, Herbert *English, French and German Banking Terms, Phrases and Correspondence Arranged in Parallel Dictionary From Including an Appendix...* London: Effingham Wilson 16 Copthall Ave, 1926, First edition; half title, (8), 200 pages, original cloth, gilt title on spine slightly faded, good, clean copy.   Anthony W. Laywood   May 26 2011 - 21731   2011 $126

Scott, Janet Laura *Round the World We Sail.* Minneapolis: Gordon Volland/Buzza, n.d. circa, 1930, 4to., cloth backed thick boards, as new in original box, box flaps neatly repaired, each page mounted on thick boards, full color illustrations on every page, rare in box.   Aleph-Bet Books, Inc.   95 - 505   2011 $500

Scott, Joseph *The United States Gazetteer: Containing an Authentic Description of the Several States, Their Situation....* Philadelphia: F. and R. Bailey, 1795, First edition; 12mo., (iii)-vi, (294) pages, engraved title, large engraved folding map, 18 smaller engraved folding maps, contemporary sheep, very skillfully rebacked retaining original spine label, endpapers neatly replaced with period paper, usual light offsetting on maps and on facing text pages, few stray spots, else very good, very attractive, early signature of J. McKnight.   Joseph J. Felcone Inc.   Fall Miscellany 2010 - 107   2011 $10,000

Scott, Michael *Tom Cringle's Log.* London: William Blackwood & Sons, 1863, New edition; half title, frontispiece, plates, original blue cloth, little rubbed, embossed W. H. Smith stamp.   Jarndyce Antiquarian Booksellers   CXCI - 484   2011   £50

Scott, S. H. *A Westmorland Village.* London: Constable & Co., 1904, First edition; original two-tone green cloth, gilt, rebacked to match with paper spine label, pages (iv), 269, with 8 illustrations, good, sound copy, very scarce.   R. F. G. Hollett & Son Antiquarian Booksellers   173 - 1024   2011   £120

Scott, Samuel *A Diary of the Religious Exercises and Experiences of Samuel Scott, Late of Hartford, Deceased.* William Phillips, 1809, Modern half calf gilt, pages xiii, 265, lightly soiled and spotted in places.   R. F. G. Hollett & Son Antiquarian Booksellers   175 - 1190   2011   £85

Scott, Walter   1771-1832 *The Border Antiquities of England and Scotland...* London: Longman, Hurst etc., 1814-1816, First edition; 2 volumes, 4to., contemporary full straight grained dark green russia gilt, boards panelled with broad rolls in gilt and blind, spines with 4 flattened raised bands and richly gilt panels, some heavy scrapes to boards, pages cxxvii, 92, (ii); 209, ci, (xii), 95 steel engraved plates, some spotting to few margins, some plates with modern hand coloring, despite scrapes to boards, still handsome set, armorial bookplate of William Dashwood Fane in each volume.   R. F. G. Hollett & Son Antiquarian Booksellers   173 - 1026   2011   £450

Scott, Walter   1771-1832 *Criminal Trials Illustrative of the Tale Entitled "The Heart of Mid-Lothian"...* Edinburgh: Constable, 1818,   R. F. G. Hollett & Son Antiquarian Booksellers   175 - 1191   2011   £95

Scott, Walter   1771-1832 *Ivanhoe.* Edinburgh: printed for Archibald Constable and Co. Edinburgh: and Hurst, Robinson and Co., London, 1820, First edition, first issue with all points listed by Worthington with one exception; 3 octavo volumes, half titles, uncut in original quarter dark green roan over reddish brown boards.   Heritage Book Shop   Booth A12 51st NY International Antiquarian Book Fair April 8-10 2011 - 112   2011 $10,000

Scott, Walter 1771-1832 *The Lady of the Lake: a Poem.* Edinburgh: John Ballantyne, 1810, First edition; 4to., pages 290, cxxix, copious notes, frontispiece, offsetting to titlepage from portrait, some contemporary notes verso of half title, contemporary full calf, covers separate and first signature separate, armorial bookplate, interior nice and clean with wide margins. Second Life Books Inc. 174 - 275 2011 $1000

Scott, Walter 1771-1832 *Redgauntlet, a Tale of the Eighteenth Century.* Paris: Baudry's Foreign Library, 1832, Half title, 4 pages initial catalog, some spotting, uncut and mostly unopened, original printed wrappers, creased at corners, minor rears to spine. Jarndyce Antiquarian Booksellers CXCI - 485 2011 £55

Scott, Walter 1771-1832 *Waverley Novels.* Edinburgh: Robert Cadell; London: Houslton & Stoneman, 1842-1847, Abbotsford edition; 254 x 184 mm., 12 volumes, second volume lacking one prelim leaf; beautiful polised calf, handsomely gilt by Bedford (stamp signed on verso of front endpapers), covers bordered with French fillets and small roundel cornerpieces, raised bands, spine elegantly gilt in compartments featuring scrolling foliate cornerpieces, floral sidepieces and floral lozenge centerpiece with surrounding small tools, red and green morocco labels, marbled , elaborately gilt turn-ins, all edges gilt, numerous wood engraved illustrations in text, including figured borders on volume and titlepages, and 120 steel engraved plates, monogram book label; slight wear at head of one spine, foot of one joint cracked along bottom compartment, one board with small scuff, few other trivial defects but lovely bindings in fine, bright condition, plates foxed, sometimes noticeably so, leaves adjacent to few plates, little foxed, text otherwise clean, bright and very well preserved. Phillip J. Pirages 59 - 314 2011 $3500

Scott, Walter 1771-1832 *The Works of.* Edinburgh: 1806, 5 volumes, large paper set presented to the Countess of Granard, Mullen's binding is morocco, a gilt tooled red spine, somewhat dull, boards black and red corners, plain but for three line panelling, three edges gilded with typical Mullen tooled panel top, bottom and fore-edge. C. P. Hyland May 26 2011 - 258 2011 $644

Scott, William *Lessons in Elocution; or a Selection of Pieces in Prose and Verse...* Leicester: printed by Hori Brown, 1815, 12mo., viii, 407 pages, full leather on boards, black label with gilt title on spine, inked dated signature on front endpaper, 4 quaint wood engravings, uniformly browned, minor chipping at edges of few leaves, shelfwear at covers, extremely rare title in very good state. Hobbyhorse Books 56 - 137 2011 $190

Scott, William Bell *The Year of the World: a Philosophical Poem on "Redemption from the Fall".* Edinburgh: William Tait, 1846, First edition; original green cloth, lettered in gilt, blocked in blind, inscribed by author for Miss Lucy Madox Brown, further signed presentation inscription from W. M. Rossetti. Jarndyce Antiquarian Booksellers CXCI - 486 2011 £750

Scottish Anthropological Society *Proceedings. Volumes 1 and 2.* Edinburgh: Scottish Anthropological Society, 1934-1937, volumes 1 and 2 in 1, tall 8vo., contemporary blue cloth gilt, pages 32, 24, 24, 48, 32, 50, original wrapper of volume I, no. 1 bound in, scarce. R. F. G. Hollett & Son Antiquarian Booksellers 175 - 1192 2011 £75

Scottish International Quarterly Review. Scottish International, 1968, First edition; Jan. 1968-Dec. 197, lacking 3 issues, together 34 issues in original wrappers, very good. I. D. Edrich May 26 2011 - 06788 2011 $419

Scottish Mountaineering Club *Island of Skye. The Scottish Mountaineering Club Guide. volume III Section A.* Edinburgh: SMC, 1923, First edition; original printed wrappers, pages 126, 37 illustrations, 21 line diagrams, folding map in rear pocket. R. F. G. Hollett & Son Antiquarian Booksellers General Catalogue Summer 2010 - 939 2011 £60

Scribner, J. M. *Scribner's Engineers' & Mechanics' Companion: Comprising United States' Weights and Measures, Mensuration of Superfices & Solids.* New York: 1848, 267 pages, frontispiece, old leather, very good, one f.e.p. mended, new label. Bookworm & Silverfish 662 - 115 2011 $75

Scrope, George Poulett 1797-1876 *Plea for the Abolition of Slavery in England as Produced by an Illegal Abuse of the Poor Law, Common in the Southern Counties.* London: J. Ridgway,, 1829, First edition; 8vo., (iii)-vi, 44 pages, wanting half title, recent marbled boards, lettered on spine, very good, scarce. John Drury Rare Books 153 - 132 2011 £250

Scrutiny: a Quarterly Review. Cambridge: Cambridge University Press, 1963, issued in 20 volumes with index and retrospect, 8vo., original publisher's black cloth lettered gilt at spine, very good in very good dust jackets, slightly tanned at spine. Any Amount of Books May 29 2011 - A65136 2011 $340

Scrymsour, Ella *The Perfect World: a Romance of Strange People and Strange Places.* New York: Frederick A. Stokes, 1922, First US edition; octavo, original blue cloth, front panel stamped in white and ruled in blind, spine panel stamped in white. L. W. Currey, Inc. 124 - 166 2011 $350

Seago, Edward *With Capricorn to Paris.* London: Collins, 1956, First edition; 8vo., pages 141, frontispiece and 7 plates, several illustrations in text, signed presentation from author for Mary (Molly) Montagu Douglas Scott, Duchess of Buccleuch (1900-1993), very good in very good used dust jacket little chipped and nicked at edges with only very minor loss and still presentable. Any Amount of Books May 29 2011 - A72902 2011 $272

Seals, David *The Powwow Highway.* Denver: Sky Books, 1983, First edition; inscribed by author to another writer, small faint abrasion to front cover, else fine in wrappers. Ken Lopez Bookseller 154 - 147 2011 $2500

Seals, David *The Powwow Highway.* Denver: Sky Books, 1983, First edition; signed by author, fine in wrappers. Ken Lopez Bookseller 154 - 146 2011 $1500

Sebald, W. G. *Austerlitz.* Hamilton, 2001, Uncorrected proof copy, 53/100 copies signed by author; illustrations, pages (vi), 358, foolscap 8vo., original cream boards printed in black, white and yellow and illustrated overall on front cover, very light bumping to backstrip tail, near fine. Blackwell Rare Books B166 - 230 2011 £700

Sebald, W. G. *Austerlitz.* New York: Random House, 2001, First edition; fine, in like dust jacket. Lupack Rare Books May 26 2011 - ABE 1269953516 2011 $100

Sebald, W. G. *The Rings of Saturn.* London: Harvill Press, 1998, First English edition; 8vo., pages (viii), 196, numerous photographic reproductions, publisher's cloth, brown lettering to spine in gilt, original color illustrated dust jacket, unclipped, fine. Simon Finch Rare Books Zero - 262 2011 £800

Sebald, W. G. *Unerzahlt" 33 Miniaturen.* Munchen: Carl Hanser Verlag, 2002, One of only 33 numbered copies signed by Hans Magnus Enzenserger who contributes prefatory poem "Abschied von Max Sebald"; small 4to., original half morocco and gray cloth, silk ribbon marker in matching original cloth and cardstock slipcase, as new with acid free box and publisher's shipping carton, unfortunately not signed by Sebald. James S. Jaffe Rare Books May 26 2011 - 20560 2011 $7500

Sebold, Alice *The Lovely Bones.* Boston: Little Brown, 2002, Stated First edition; signed by author and her husband, Glen Gold, dedicatee, fine in first state dust jacket with no mention of "Main Selection of the Book of the Month Club". By the Book, L. C. 26 - 15 2011 $150

Sebold, Alice *The Lovely Bones.* Boston: Little Brown, 2002, First edition; near fine, light bumping to base of spine, dust jacket fine, first state of jacket with Margot Livesey blurb. Bella Luna Books May 29 2011 - t4000 2011 $82

Secker, Thomas *Eight Charges Delivered to the Clergy of the Dioceses of Oxford and Canterbury to Which are Added Instructions to Candidates for Orders and a Latin Speech Intended to Have Been Made at Opening of the Convocation in 1761.* London: printed for John Francis and Charles Rivington and Benjamin White & Son, 1790, Fourth edition; half calf gilt with raised bands, spine panels tooled overall with honeycomb pattern in blind, pages (iv), 376. R. F. G. Hollett & Son Antiquarian Booksellers 175 - 1196 2011 £45

Sedgefield, W. J. *The Place Names of Cumberland and Westmorland.* Manchester: University Press, 1915, First edition; original cloth, gilt, head of spine little frayed, pages xliv, 208, flyleaves lightly spotted. R. F. G. Hollett & Son Antiquarian Booksellers 173 - 1029 2011 £75

Sedgwick, Adam *A Discourse on the Studies of the University.* Cambridge: printed at the Pitt Press by John Smith for J. and J. J. Deighton, 1834, Third edition; original boards, spine label (rather chipped), spine trifle frayed at head, pages viii, 157. R. F. G. Hollett & Son Antiquarian Booksellers 175 - 1197 2011 £275

Seebohm, Henry *The Geographical Distribution of the Family Charadriidae; or the Plovers, Sandpipers, Snipes and Their Allies.* London: Henry Sotheran & Co., 1887-1888, Second issue; 21 hand colored lithographed plates by J. G. Keulemans and numerous other engraved illustrations by Millais, G. E. Lodge, Charles Whymper et al, large 4to., pages xxix, 524, original green gilt stamped cloth, corners worn, small bump to fore-edge of front cover, professionally rebacked with original backstrip laid down, small tear to title reinforced with cellotape, marginal stains to few pages of text, text tanned, some pages of text roughly opened, resulting in few marginal tears, marginal tear to a page, other text pages unopened. Raymond M. Sutton, Jr. May 26 2011 - 30608 2011 $1350

Seebohm, Henry *A Monograph of the Turdidae or Family of Thrushes.* London: Henry Sotheran & Co., 1898-1902, First edition; photogravure portrait of Seebohm and 149 hand colored lithographed plates with small unobtrusive embossed stamp on each plate, by and after Keulmeans, folio, pages xi, 337; i, 250, publisher's three quarter levant morocco (wear to corners volume I, some rubbing to extremities, overall, beautiful set), gilt decorated panels on spine, 5 raised bands, top edge gilt. Raymond M. Sutton, Jr. May 26 2011 - 30623 2011 $6000

Segal, lore *The Juniper Tree and Other Tales from Grimm.* London: Bodley Head, 1974, First UK edition; 2 volumes, small 8vo., original cloth gilt, dust jackets, slipcase, two tiny nicks to top edge of one wrapper, otherwise fine, crisp set, pages (vi), 168; (iv), 169-332, monochrome illustrations by Maurice Sendak. R. F. G. Hollett & Sons Antiquarian Booksellers 170 - 618 2011 £95

Selby, Charles *Maximums and Specimens of William Muggins, Natural Philosopher and Citizen of the World.* London: Routledge, 1846, Plates, bound by Zaehnsdorf in half maroon calf, raised bands, decorated in gilt, black morocco labels, endpapers replaced, original cloth spine, one cloth cover bound in at end, Mexborough armorial bookplate, top edge gilt, handsome. Jarndyce Antiquarian Booksellers CXCI - 487 2011 £140

Selby, Hubert *Last Exit to Brooklyn.* New York: Grove Press, 1964, First edition; 8vo., pages 304, internally fresh, publisher's quarter cloth and red paper boards, red lettering to spine, some light soiling, original dust jacket, dampstained in places, head and foot of spine chipped, old tape repair to upper panel folds rubbed, author's presentation inscription. Simon Finch Rare Books Zero - 263 2011 £950

Selby, Thomas G. *The Theology of Modern Fiction being the 26th Fernley Lecture Delivered in Liverpool July 1896.* London: Charles H. Kelly, 1896, Original black cloth, ownr's name stamped on gilt, very good. Jarndyce Antiquarian Booksellers CXCII - 361 2011 £60

Selden, George *The Cricket in Times Square.* New York: Farrar Straus, 1960, First edition; 8vo., pink cloth, 151 pages, fine in dust jacket, frayed at spine ends and corners, very scarce in first edition. Aleph-Bet Books, Inc. 95 - 591 2011 $550

Selden, John *Titles of Honor.* London: printed by E. Tyler and R. Holt for Thomas Dring, 1672, Third edition; folio, early 20th century half calf with marbled boards, retaining 18th century calf gilt backstrip with blind tooled panels, broad raised bands and spine label, pages (xxxii), 756, engraved portrait frontispiece and numerous text woodcuts, small piece torn off lower corner and two short tears without loss to one leaf, otherwise excellent sound and clean copy. R. F. G. Hollett & Son Antiquarian Booksellers 175 - 1200 2011 £450

Seldes, Gilbert *Movies for the Millions.* London: Batsford, 1937, First edition; original cloth, dust jacket little worn, pages viii, 120 with color frontispiece by Walt Disney and 133 illustrations. R. F. G. Hollett & Son Antiquarian Booksellers 175 - 1201 2011 £30

Select Historical Costumes Compiled from the Most Reliable Sources. New York: Wynkoop & Shwrood, 1868, Text and plates printed on rectos only, publisher's pebble grain cloth with gilt spine and cover vignette, historiated letters, beautiful colored plates, very good (half inch chip at spine top, shelfwear to extremities, light random foxing but not on images). Lupack Rare Books May 26 2011 - ABE3649643602 2011 $200

Seligman, C. G. *Pagan Tribes of the Nilotic Sudan.* London: George Routledge, 1932, First edition; large 8vo., pages xxiv, 565, frontispiece, folding map, 60 plates, illustrations, original red cloth, spine slightly faded. J. & S. L. Bonham Antiquarian Booksellers Africa 4/20/2011 - 7093 2011 £150

Sellman, R. R. *Devon Village Schools in the Nineteenth Century.* London: Davis & Charles, 1967, First edition; original cloth, gilt, dust jacket, pages 171 with 12 plates and 12 diagrams and maps, from the library of Dr. Arthur Raistrick, with his bookplate. R. F. G. Hollett & Son Antiquarian Booksellers 175 - 1203 2011 £35

Selous, Frederick Courteney *African Nature Notes and Reminiscences.* London: Macmillan, 1908, First edition; octavo, xxx, 356 pages, frontispiece, plates, original brick red blindstamped cloth, gilt spine, top edge gilt, covers freckled, top spine showing wear, ownership signatures, very good. Jeff Weber Rare Books 163 - 209 2011 $100

Seltzer, Mark *Henry James & the Art of Power.* Ithaca: 1984, First edition; 200 pages, fine in fine dust jacket. Bookworm & Silverfish 669 - 99 2011 $125

Semonides *De Mulieribus Recensuit atque Animadversionibus Illustravit Georgius David Koeler.* Gottingen: Sumtibus viduae Vandenhoek, 1781, First separate edition; title little dusty, edges entirely untrimmed and bumped as a result, pages xxiv, 103, 8vo., stitched (top stitch loose), original blue paper wrappers, bit soiled and with few small tears at edges, sometime backed with matching paper, this lettered longitudinally in ink, good. Blackwell Rare Books B166 - 94 2011 £350

Semonides *De Mulieribus.* Gottingen: Sumtibus viduae Vandenboek, 1781, Some spotting throughout, small wormtrail to margin of last five leaves, pages xxiv, 103, 8vo., contemporary half sprinkled calf with sprinkled paper boards, backstrip with five raised bands between darkened gilt fillets, dark label in second compartment, joints rubbed and cracking but strong, corners lightly worn, paper bit scuffed, ownership inscription of J. H. Lupton, sound, loosely inserted is letter addressed to (Sir Hugh) Lloyd-Jones dated 14 Feb. (no year). Blackwell Rare Books B166 - 95 2011 £350

Sems, Johan *Practijck des Kantmetens.* Leiden: Jan Bouwensz, 1600, First edition; 2 parts, 4to., (80, 303, (5); (8), 126, (2) pages, 7 engraved plates in part 2, engraving on both titlepages, woodcut diagrams, contemporary vellum, upper hinge split, ms. vellum guards and strengtheners, probably from the library of John Collins, from the library of the Earls of Macclesfield at Shirburn Castle. Maggs Bros. Ltd. 1440 - 197 2011 £3500

Sen, A. K. *Choice of Techniques: an Aspect of the Theory of Planned Economic Development.* Oxford: Basil Blackwell, 1960, First edition; 8vo., pages 122, original publisher's green cloth lettered gilt at spine, fine in close to fine dust jacket, very slightly tanned at spine, excellent condtion.   Any Amount of Books   May 29 2011 - A67480 2011 $238

Sendak, Maurice *Caldecott & Co. Notes on Books and Pictures.* Reinhardt Books and Viking, 1989, First edition; original cloth, gilt, dust jacket, pages 216, fine.   R. F. G. Hollett & Sons Antiquarian Booksellers   170 - 608 2011 £40

Sendak, Maurice *Collection of Books, Posters and Original Drawings.* New York: Justin G. Schiller Ltd., 1984, Original pictorial wrappers, square 4to., pages 245, with 77 illustrations.   R. F. G. Hollett & Sons Antiquarian Booksellers   170 - 609   2011   £35

Sendak, Maurice *Hector Protector and As I Went Over the Water.* New York: Harper & Row, 1965, First edition; oblong 8vo., original cloth backed pictorial boards, dust jacket (price clipped), unpaginated, illustrations in color.   R. F. G. Hollett & Sons Antiquarian Booksellers   170 - 610   2011   £75

Sendak, Maurice *Hector Protector.* New York: Harper & Row, 1965, First edition; oblong 4to., green cloth, pictorial boards, fine in dust jacket, price intact, color illustrations. Aleph-Bet Books, Inc.   95 - 507   2011 $200

Sendak, Maurice *In the Night Kitchen.* New York: Harper & Row, 1965, First US edition; 4to., original cloth, pictorial roundel, dust jacket, illustrations in color, fine, later impression with unpriced wrapper, rear flap printed same as first edition.   R. F. G. Hollett & Sons Antiquarian Booksellers   170 - 611   2011   £180

Sendak, Maurice *Nutshell Library. Alligators All Around. Chicken Soup with Rice. One Was Johnny.* New York: Harper and Row, 1962, First edition; 4 volumes, 12mo., original pink cloth, dust jackets (extremities little worn and chipped in places), pictorial slipcase, later rather worn, taped repair, price sticker torn off damaging surface of one panel, each volume illustrated in color.   R. F. G. Hollett & Sons Antiquarian Booksellers   170 - 612   2011   £75

Sendak, Maurice *Seven Little Monsters.* London: The Bodley Head, 1977, First UK edition; long oblong 8vo., original pictorial boards (no dust jacket issued), unpaginated, illustrations in color, with 6 panel foldout "Leporello" at end (not included in US edition).   R. F. G. Hollett & Sons Antiquarian Booksellers   170 - 614   2011   £75

Sendak, Maurice *Seven Little Monsters.* Harper Collins, 1977, Unpaginated, long oblong 8vo., original plain boards, dust jacket, illustrations in color.   R. F. G. Hollett & Sons Antiquarian Booksellers   170 - 613   2011   £50

Sendak, Maurice *Stories & Pictures.* Harper Collins, circa, 1991, First edition; small square 8vo., original pictorial wrappers, concertina of 16 panels printed in color on stiff coated paper, unfolding to a length of 8 feet, top edges die-cut to shape of illustrations, scarce.   R. F. G. Hollett & Sons Antiquarian Booksellers   170 - 615   2011   £60

Sendak, Maurice *We Are All in the Dumps with Jack and Guy.* Harper Collins, 1993, First edition; oblong large 8vo., original fawn boards, dust jacket, unpaginated, illustrations in color, fine.   R. F. G. Hollett & Sons Antiquarian Booksellers   170 - 616   2011   £60

Sendak, Philip *In Grandpa's House.* New York: Harper and Row, 1985, First edition; original cloth, gilt, dust jacket price clipped, 42 pages, illustrations by Maurice Sendak. R. F. G. Hollett & Sons Antiquarian Booksellers   170 - 627 2011   £45

Seneca, Lucius Annaeas *L. Annai Senecae Philosophi Opera Quae Extant Omnia...* Antwerp: Ex Officina Plantiniana Balthazar Moretus, 1652, Folio, (20), xxxvi, 911 pages, frontisportrait, engraved title with portraits, 2 full page engravings, ornamental tailpieces, full contemporary vellum, gilt stamped arabesques on front and rear covers, gilt stamped red morocco spine label, raised bands, front hinge reinforced, lightly soiled, bookplate of Francis Bourdillon, M.A., fine.   Jeff Weber Rare Books   163 - 16 2011 $1250

Senior, Nassau William 1790-1864 *Statement of the Provision for the Poor and of the Condition of the Labouring Classes, in a Considerable Portion of America and Europe.* London: B. Fellowes Publisher to the Poor Law Commissioners, 1835, First edition; pages vii, (1), 238, (2) final leaf of publisher's ad, bound in modern red half leather lettered gilt at spine with raised bands and marbled boards, half title and first blank not present, prelims slightly creased at corners, otherwise very good.   Any Amount of Books   May 26 2011 - B26989   2011 $503

Senkevitch, Anatole *Soviet Architecture 1917-1962.* Charlottesville: University Press of Virginia, 1974, Original gilt cloth, pages xxxiii, 284, labels removed from front endpapers, light library stamps to title and final leaf.   R. F. G. Hollett & Son Antiquarian Booksellers   177 - 798 2011 £35

A Sequel to the Comic Adventures of Old Mother Hubbard and Her Dog by another Hand. London: published March 1st 1806 by J. Harris...and C. Knight Windsor, 1806, First edition; 16mo., (28) pages, unnumbered comprising 14 leaves each printed on one side only, 12 uncolored engravings, tiny blank corner torn from titlepage, occasional light creasing and soiling, else very good, now preserved in recent marbled card covers** with printed title on upper cover, rare. John Drury Rare Books 153 - 104 2011 £500

Sergeant, Howard *Outposts.* 1944-1993, Nos 2-169 lacking 1 issue only, together with numbers 171 & 174/5, 171 issues in original wrappers. I. D. Edrich May 26 2011 - 82699 2011 $1426

Serjeant, R. B. *The Arabs. A Puffin Picture Book.* Curwen Press for Penguin Books, n.d., 1947, First edition; oblong 8vo., original pictorial boards, edges trifle rubbed and browned, unpaginated, illustrations in color and black and white. R. F. G. Hollett & Sons Antiquarian Booksellers 170 - 66 2011 £45

Serle, Ambrose *The Christian Parent.* V. Griffiths, 1798, Third edition; small 8vo., original tree calf with spine label, small defect and crack to backstrip, pages viii, 126. R. F. G. Hollett & Son Antiquarian Booksellers 175 - 1206 2011 £120

Serling, Rod *Patterns: Four Television Plays.* New York: Simon and Schuster, 1957, First edition; octavo, cloth backed boards. L. W. Currey, Inc. 124 - 61 2011 $1500

Sessions, Frederick *Literary Celebrities of the English Lake District.* London: Elliott Stock, 1905, First edition; original green cloth, few slight marks, pages vii, 238, 21 plates, uncommon. R. F. G. Hollett & Son Antiquarian Booksellers 173 - 1030 2011 £45

Seth, Vikram *A Suitable Boy.* Sixth Chamber Press, 1993, First edition; 61/100 copies of an edition of 126, signed by author, pages (xviii), 1349, 8vo., original quarter tan morocco, backstrip gilt lettered, dark brown boards, fine. Blackwell Rare Books B166 - 231 2011 £350

Seton, Ernest Thompson 1860-1946 *Bannertail. The Story of a Gray Squirrel.* London: Hodder and Stoughton, 1922, First UK edition; original green cloth gilt with pictorial onlay, pages xv, 230, with 8 plates and 100 drawings by author. R. F. G. Hollett & Son Antiquarian Booksellers General Catalogue Summer 2010 - 1045 2011 £35

Seventh Day Baptist Missionary Society *Jubilee Papers... Commemorating the Fiftieth Anniversary of the Seventh Day Baptist Missionary Society.* New York: 1892, 163 pages, original binding, very good, edges rubbed. Bookworm & Silverfish 664 - 176 2011 $78

Sewell, Anna *Black Beauty.* London: Jarrold & Sons, 1877, First edition; octavo, viii, (9)-247, (1) (8) ads, black and white wood engraved frontispiece by C. Hewitt, original publisher's cloth, Carter's variant "C" binding, green cloth blocked in black and gilt, brown coated endpapers, some slight rubbing at extremities and to gilt, inner hinges sympathetically strengthened, some light foxing, mainly to prelim pages and edges, near invisible contemporary ink inscription on front free endpaper and neat pencil inscription to page (iv), very good. Heritage Book Shop Holiday 2010 - 109 2011 $9500

Sewell, Anna *Black Beauty.* London: A. & C. Black, 1936, First edition; original cloth, titlepage spine little faded and marked pages viii, 254, (ii), illustrations by K. F. Barker, top edges little spotted. R. F. G. Hollett & Son Antiquarian Booksellers General Catalogue Summer 2010 - 569 2011 £30

Sewell, Helen *Golden Christmas Manger.* New York: Simon and Schuster, 1948, 2 items housed in original pictorial box 9 1/4 x 10 3/4 inches, first is complete foldout manger that can be erected without paste, second is book containing story of Christmas plus 9 pages of 32 color lithographed bible characters to cut out and arrange on manger to make a Creche, box and flaps have some wear otherwise this is in fine, unused condition, double page color spread and another full page color illustration, rare. Aleph-Bet Books, Inc. 95 - 523 2011 $750

Sexton, Anne *The Death Notebooks.* Boston: Houghton Mifflin, 1974, First printing; 8vo., pages ix, 97, nice somewhat soiled dust jacket. Second Life Books Inc. 174 - 277 2011 $65

Seymour, Henry J. *The Oneida Community.* Kenwood: 1897, First edition; 8vo., 24 pages, self wrappers, very good. Second Life Books Inc. 174 - 278 2011 $85

Seymour, Robert *A Search After the "Comfortable" Being the Adventures of a Little Gentleman of Small Fortune.* London: Thomas McLean, 1829, First edition; oblong folio, original printed upper wrapper, 6 engraved plates, each colored by hand, caption titles on each plate with imprint dated July 1st 1829, minor soiling and finger marking, two plates with old closed tears (no loss), now neatly repaired, original printed card wrappers, rebacked, good, large copy, contemporary ownership signature of Sarah. John Drury Rare Books 153 - 134 2011 £475

Seymour, W. D. *Journal of a Voyage Round the World.* Cork: Guys, 1877, First edition; vii, 169 pages, mounted portrait photo, very good. C. P. Hyland May 26 2011 - 259/437 2011 $1087

Shackleton, Ernest Henry 1874-1922 *Antarctica a New Look.* N.P: circa, 1973, 207, (1) pages, original binding, fine. Bookworm & Silverfish 676 - 15 2011 $75

Shakespeare, William 1564-1616 *All's Well that Ends Well.* London: Jacob Tonson, 1734, First separate edition; crown 8vo., pages 84, bound with engraved frontispiece in modern calf backed boards, nice, tight copy, scarce. Second Life Books Inc. 174 - 279 2011 $700

Shakespeare, William 1564-1616 *Shakespeare's Comedy As You Like It.* London: Hodder & Stoughton, 1909, Limited edition, #217 of 500 signed by artist; large 4to. half title, frontispiece, plates with tipped in illustrations and illustrations, uncut in full vellum, decorated in gilt, 'rust' stain to near margin of front board, foot of spine little darkened. Jarndyce Antiquarian Booksellers CXCI - 489 2011 £125

Shakespeare, William 1564-1616 *Mr. William Shakespeare's Comedies, Histories and Tragedies.* London: printed for H. Herringman, sold by Joseph Knight and Francis Saunders, 1685, Fourth folio; Folio in sixes, pages (xiv), 274, 328, 304, (2) blank, facsimile frontispiece, some light spotting throughout, few small paper flaws, minor repairs, overall generally a crisp and fresh copy, all edges gilt, dark green morocco gilt, rebacked marbled endpapers, light shelfwear, from the library of the Dukes of Northumberland. Simon Finch Rare Books Zero - 264 2011 £65,000

Shakespeare, William 1564-1616 *Tragedy of Cymbeline.* London: printed for H. Herringman, E. Brewster and R. Bentley, 1685, Extracted from Fourth folio; folio, (14) leaves (pages 165-192), modern half tan sheep over cloth, spine lettered in gilt, sheep tooled in blind, edges speckled red, very good. Heritage Book Shop Holiday 2010 - 112 2011 $1750

Shakespeare, William 1564-1616 *The Tragedy of Hamlet.* London: printed for H. Heringman and R. Bentley, 1683, Eighth quarto edition; large quarto, exceptionally large copy, original marbled wrappers. Heritage Book Shop Booth A12 51st NY International Antiquarian Book Fair April 8-10 2011 - 123 2011 $125,000

Shakespeare, William 1564-1616 *Shakespeare's Hamlet: the First Quarto 1603 a Facsimile...* London: W. Griggs, 1880, Final ad leaf, original quarter maroon roan, spine worn and slightly chipped, with George MacDonald's red ink signature and his larger bookplate, at end are extensive pencil notes by MacDonald. Jarndyce Antiquarian Booksellers CXCII - 339 2011 £850

Shakespeare, William 1564-1616 *The Tragedie of Hamlet, Prince of Denmarke...* London: George Allen & Unwin, 1924, Centenary edition; half title, bookplate facsimile, frontispiece, original black cloth blocked in red, small split at head of spine. Jarndyce Antiquarian Booksellers CXCII - 270 2011 £75

Shakespeare, William 1564-1616 *Henry the Sixth the First Part. (together with) Henry the Sixth. The Second Part.* London: printed for R. Bentley and M. Magnes, 1681, First edition, first issue of part 1, first edition, second issue of part II; 2 small quarto volumes, bound without final blank to part 1, modern half blindstamped calf over disparately patterned paper boards. Heritage Book Shop Booth A12 51st NY International Antiquarian Book Fair April 8-10 2011 - 115 2011 $10,000

Shakespeare, William 1564-1616 *Julius Caesar.* London: printed by H. H. Jun. for Hen. Herringman and R. Bentley in Russel-Street in Covent Garden and sold by Joseph Knight and Francis Saunders at the Blew Anchor in the Lower Walk of the Nuw-Exchange in the Strand, n.d. circa, 1684, Early quarto edition; later full brown and tan panelled calf by Ramage. Heritage Book Shop Booth A12 51st NY International Antiquarian Book Fair April 8-10 2011 - 116 2011 $15,000

Shakespeare, William 1564-1616 *The Life of King Henry V.* New York: Limited Editions Club, 1951, No. 91 of 1500 copies; hand mounted color plates by Fritz Kredel, not signed, as issued, spine very slightly spotted, otherwise fine in near fine, very slightly spotted and very slightly scuffed slipcase. Gemini Fine Books & Arts, Ltd. Art Reference & Illustrated Books: First Editions 2011 $70

Shakespeare, William 1564-1616 *Macbeth, a Tragedy.* London: printed for P. Chetwin and are to be sold by most booksellers, 1674, First edition; small quarto, bound without final blank, early 20th century dark blue morocco, exceedingly rare. Heritage Book Shop Booth A12 51st NY International Antiquarian Book Fair April 8-10 2011 - 118 2011 $37,500

Shakespeare, William 1564-1616 *The Merry Wives of Windsor.* London: William Heinemann, 1910, First edition thus; number 183 of 350 numbered copies signed by artist, large quarto, 171 pages, bound in vellum over boards, pictorially tooled in gilt, 40 color plates, including frontispiece mounted on heavy brown paper and protected by lettered tissue guards, untrimmed, top edge gilt, silk ties laid in, front hinge paper starting, still tight, some minor rubbing to covers, very good. Second Life Books Inc. 174 - 282 2011 $650

Shakespeare, William 1564-1616 *A Midsummer Night's Dream.* London: William Heinemann, 1908, First of this edition; 4to., top edge tinted, beige cloth with gold lettering and decoration on front cover and spine, lovely copy with bookplate on front pastedown, signed in full with drawing by the artist, Arthur Rackham, 40 mounted color plates plus black and white decorations within text. Jo Ann Reisler, Ltd. 86 - 202 2011 $3500

Shakespeare, William 1564-1616 *A Midsummer Night's Dream.* London: Constable & Co. Ltd., 1914, First edition; large 4to., elaborate gilt pictorial cloth (most desirable binding) with slight corner bump, color pictorial dust jacket with some overall wear and pieces missing from ends of spine of jacket, 12 mounted color plates and 46 full page and 17 smaller black and white drawings by W. Heath Robinson. Jo Ann Reisler, Ltd. 86 - 205 2011 $1200

Shakespeare, William 1564-1616 *The Late and Much Admired Play Called Pericles, Prince of Tyre.* London: Thomas Cotes, 1635, Sixth edition; octavo in fours, printer's device on titlepage, full 20th century red morocco. Heritage Book Shop Booth A12 51st NY International Antiquarian Book Fair April 8-10 2011 - 117 2011 $75,000

Shakespeare, William 1564-1616 *The Plays and Poems of William Shakespeare.* Philadelphia: Bioren & Madan, 1796, First American edition; Volume 8 of 8 volumes, 12mo., contemporary full brown calf. Heritage Book Shop Booth A12 51st NY International Antiquarian Book Fair April 8-10 2011 - 120 2011 $5000

Shakespeare, William 1564-1616 *The Plays.* London: William Pickering, 1825, 9 volumes, 89 x 57mm., charming contemporary Jansenist-style claret morocco, raised bands, gilt titling on spines, green morocco doublures intricately gilt with outer frames of plain and decorative gilt rules and delicately executed inner frame of ornate fleurons with palmette cornerpieces, marbled flyleaves, top edges gilt, other edges untrimmed, except for two gatherings, entirely unopened in original slipcase (somewhat scuffed but sturdy), touch of wear to joints and extremities, occasional minor foxing, primarily to first half dozen leaves of each volume, other trivial imperfections but fine set, unread text clean, fresh, bright, bindings tight, lustrous and charming. Phillip J. Pirages 59 - 265 2011 $2500

Shakespeare, William 1564-1616 *The Plays.* London: printed for Longman and Co. et al, 1856, 8 volumes, 225 x 140mm., very attractive butterscotch colored polished calf, handsomely gilt fillet and stippled rule in blind, raised bands, spine compartments densely gilt with floral and botanical tools, each spine with green and maroon titling label, marbled edges and endpapers, frontispiece of Shakespeare, rear board of first volume with dozen small blots from intentional but uninspired acid treatment?, very minor wear to joints, handful of trivial marks to covers, still fine set, very decorative bindings solid, bright and without appreciable wear and text immaculate. Phillip J. Pirages 59 - 316 2011 $2750

Shakespeare, William 1564-1616 *The Plays of William Shakespeare. (with) The Poems of William Shakespeare. (and) Shakespeare: a Review and a Preview.* New York: Limited Editions Club, 1941, Plays in 37 folio volumes and limited to 1950 numbered sets and Poems in 2 volumes limited to 1500 copies, signed by designer, Bruce Rogers; together 40 quarto volumes, frontispieces, profusely illustrated with numerous full page color plates, wood engravings, lithographs, hand colored titlepage vignettes, plays bound by Russell Rutter Company in half natural buckram, gold stamped, gilt top edge, paper sides printed in four colors from pattern redrawn by Mr. Rogers after a wall painting in Davenant house at Oxford where Shakesepare is known to have visited, Poems bound by Russell-Rutter Co. in half buckram, gold stamped with decorative paper sides, A review and preview bound in full tan cloth, front cover and spine stamped in red, spines very clean with very slight toning (as usual for this set), overall very good, handsome set. Heritage Book Shop Holiday 2010 - 111 2011 $1250

Shakespeare, William 1564-1616 *The Poems of Shakespeare.* Boston: Oliver and Munroe and Belcher and Armstrong, 1807, First American edition; 12mo., original trade binding, quarter orange paper over marbled boards, uncut, scarce. Heritage Book Shop Booth A12 51st NY International Antiquarian Book Fair April 8-10 2011 - 121 2011 $2750

Shakespeare, William 1564-1616 *The Sonnets of William Shakespeare.* London: Kegan Paul Trench & Co., 1881, First edition thus; 8vo., original publisher's dark brown cloth lettered gilt on spine and on front cover, pages x, 306, with 44 page publisher's catalog at rear, ownership signature of J. M. Robertson with some pencilled notes and marginal linings in his hand, very slight rubbing at spine which has been neatly rebacked, otherwise very good+ with slight lean,. Any Amount of Books May 29 2011 - A49454 2011 $296

Shakespeare, William 1564-1616 *The Sonnets.* London: Medici Society, 1913, Limited edition, no. 330 of 1000 copies; original full vellum gilt, little warped, pages 82, top edge gilt, untrimmed, printed on handmade paper. R. F. G. Hollett & Son Antiquarian Booksellers General Catalogue Summer 2010 - 903 2011 £275

Shakespeare, William 1564-1616 *Shakespeare's Sonnets.* printed by Peter Lord at the Black Swan Press, 1974, One of 190 numbered copies, this #29; 288 x 207mm., 2 p.l., (80) pages, (1) leaf, original scarlet quarter morocco, red buckram sides, gilt spine titling, without slipcase that is sometimes present, bottom corners slightly bumped, otherwise virtually mint. Phillip J. Pirages 59 - 154 2011 $450

Shakespeare, William   1564-1616   *The Tempest.* London: printed by J. Macock for Henry Herringman, 1676, Fourth quarto, the Dryden and Davenant edition, final blank leaf M2, bound in later half maroon morocco over maroon cloth.   Heritage Book Shop   Booth A12 51st NY International Antiquarian Book Fair April 8-10 2011 - 122   2011 $8000

Shakespeare, William   1564-1616   *The Tempest.* London: William Heinemann/New York: Doubleday & Co., 1926, One of 520 copies (this # 341) signed by artist; 290 x 230mm., xiii, (i), 185, (1) pages, very attractive three quarter morocco, raised bands, spine handsomely gilt in compartments formed by plain and decorative rules, quatrefoil centerpiece surrounded by densely scrolling corner pieces, sides and endleaves of rose colored linen, top edge gilt, mostly unopened; with pictorial titlepage, black and white illustrations, 21 color plates, as called for, by Arthur Rackham, all tipped on and with letterpress guards; morocco bookplate of W. A. M. Burden, very slight darkening to spine and leather edges, just hint of shelfwear, otherwise fine, virtually pristine internally.   Phillip J. Pirages   59 - 294   2011 $2250

Shakespeare, William   1564-1616   *Shakespeare's Comedy of Twelfth Night or what you will.* London: Hodder & Stoughton, 1908, First edition; green cloth with elaborate gold lettering and decoration on cover and spine, minor fading to spine, clean, fresh copy, dust jacket with full color pictorial paste label, some light rippling and little edge wear to jacket, dark green endpapers, little wear to jacket, dark green endpapers and plates are on dark green mounts, 144 numbered pages with forty full page mounted color plates by W. Heath Robinson, very nice, unusual in dust jacket.   Jo Ann Reisler, Ltd.   86 - 206   2011 $750

Shakespeare, William   1564-1616   *Venvs and Adonis.* Doves Press, 1912, One of 200 copies on paper; (an additional 15 were printed on vellum), 230 x 170mm., 57, (2) pages, original flexible vellum, gilt titling on spine, printed in black and red, book ticket of Bibliothek H. J. Hiintze; hint of rumpling to covers (as usual), slight smearing of one word on half title (apparently done at time of printing), but very fine, quite clean fresh and bright inside and out.   Phillip J. Pirages   59 - 181   2011 $900

Shakespeare, William   1564-1616   *The Pictorial Edition of the Works of Shakespeare.* London: Charles Knight and Co., 1839-1843, 252 x 170mm., 8 volumes, attractive contemporary rose colored pebble grain morocco, covers with blind ruled border and central gilt armorial crest featuring three stags on an azured escutcheon, whole surrounded by plumes, ribbons and foliage, raised bands flanked by blind rules, elaborate floral gilt turn-ins, marbled endpapers, all edges gilt, approximately 900 steel engravings and woodcuts, many full page, light soiling to bindings, joints and extremities slightly rubbed, one joint with short crack just beginning, but an excellent set, clean with fresh text, in solid appealing bindings showing little wear.   Phillip J. Pirages   59 - 315   2011 $2400

Shakespeare, William   1564-1616   *The Works.* London: Edward Moxon, 1857, 6 volumes, 220 x 143mm., one gathering in third volume with leaves bound out of order, but complete; 6 volumes, beautiful contemporary tree calf by Andrew Grieve of Edinburgh for William Paterson, Edinburgh bookseller (stamp-signed), covers with gilt double fillets and twining leaf border, raised bands, spines very attractively gilt in compartments with graceful floral cornerpieces and elaborate fleuron centerpiece, red and dark green morocco title labels, gilt ruled turn-ins, marbled endpapers and edges, engraved frontispiece, frontispiece and one title leaf bit foxed, isolated very minor foxing elsewhere, couple of very faint scratches to covers, but exceptionally fine, lovely bindings lustrous and virtually unworn, text showing no signs of use.   Phillip J. Pirages   59 - 317   2011 $4800

Shakespeare, William   1564-1616   *Shakespeare's Works.* New York: D. Appleton, 1861, Illustrated edition; 2 volumes, steel engravings, half leather and cloth with raised bands, gilt lines and gilt spine decorations, very good+ (some light shelfwear/scuffing, clean text and plates).   Lupack Rare Books   May 26 2011 - ABE2882733407   2011 $250

Shakespeare, William   1564-1616   *The Works of Shakespeare.* London: Virtue & Co., circa, 1873, Imperial edition; c, 810; (x), 778 pages, 2 volumes, folio, full page steel engravings, leather gilt with gilt lettering to spines and all page edges gilt, very good, slight external fading and handling wear, internally clean, from the library of British songwriter and thespian Ivor Novello with bookplate.   Any Amount of Books   May 26 2011 - A77056   2011 $503

Shakespeare, William   1564-1616   *The Works of William Shakespeare.* London: Swan Sonnenschein & Co., 1891, Sixth edition; 12 volumes, half titles, contemporary half dark green crushed morocco, raised gilt bands and compartments, some occasional slightly rubbed, very good.   Jarndyce Antiquarian Booksellers   CXCI - 27   2011   £1450

Shall We Join the Ladies. Oxford: privately published, 1979, Limited edition 500 copies; 4to., original black cloth, gilt with oval colored floral panel by Joan Hassall on upper cover, glassine wrapper little chipped, pages 102, top edge gilt, illustrations, with Opening address to the exhibition which this book described, by John Dreyfus, 8 pages original wrappers, loosely inserted.   R. F. G. Hollett & Son Antiquarian Booksellers   175 - 268   2011   £75

Shamberger, Hugh A.   *The Story of Goldfield, Esmeralda County, Nevada.* Carson City: by the author and the Nevada Historical Press, 1982, First edition; quarto, xv, (1), 240 pages, profusely illustrated from photos, numerous folding maps, tan cloth, gilt , original gold pictorial wrappers bound in, very fine, presentation inscription signed by author.   Argonaut Book Shop   Recent Acquisitions Summer 2010 - 183   2011 $90

Shand, Alexander Innes *Against Time.* London: Smith Elder, 1870, First edition; 3 volumes, text slightly spotted, contemporary half brown roan, lettered in gilt on spines, some rubbing, small wormhole to spine volume II, ownership stamp of R. S. Copeman.   Jarndyce Antiquarian Booksellers   CXCI - 532   2011   £125

Shapley, Harlow *The View from a Distant Star. Man's Future in the Universe.* New York: Basic Books, 1963, First edition; near fine in very good+ dust jacket with mild chips, soil, edgewear, 8vo., ix, 212 pages.   By the Book, L. C.   26 - 110   2011 $75

Sharp, John *Fifteen Sermons Preached on Several Occasions by... John Lord Arch Bishop of York.* London: printed for Walter Kettilby, 1709, Third edition; 8vo., pages (vi) 472 + engraved frontispiece, contemporary crimson turkey, spine gilt panelled with saltired compartments, lettered direct in gilt, boards panelled in gilt, board edges decorative roll gilt, turn-ins decorative roll gilt, 'Dutch-comb' 'made' endpapers, all edges gilt, blue and white sewn endbands, light spotting, occasional dampmark in lower margin, tidy repairs to headcap with new matching endband, black leather gilt decorative roll bordered label "To Mrs./E.B." ink inscription "Eliz. Battell/Juner", in different hand "The Gift of my Good Aunt Mrs. Eliz Battell to me Anne Hallows junr. May ye 26 1728", in same hand "Anne Leicester", ink inscription "John Roberts No 2 May 14 1792", from the collection of Christopher Ernest Weston 1947-2010.   Unsworths Booksellers   24 - 40   2011   £200

Sharp, Thomas *Oxford Replanned.* Architectural Press for Oxford City Council, 1948, First edition; large 8vo., original blue cloth silvered, city arms on front board, pages 224, numerous plates and folding plans.   R. F. G. Hollett & Son Antiquarian Booksellers   177 - 799 2011   £35

Sharp, William *Prose Poems.* Portland: printed for Thomas B. Mosher, 1906-1908, 145 x 97mm., 3 volumes, each of the volumes in publisher's original sea green stiff paper wrappers, covers with gilt floral design in Arts an Crafts style, original printed tissue dust jackets, edges untrimmed and mostly unopened, each volume in individual paper slipcase covered in floral patterned silk of pale blue green and cream and black letterpress titling on spine, whole contained in publisher's folding stiff paper box covered in same floral silk, box lid with large printed label, engraved printer's device and headpieces; splits in two of the box corners, box bit soiled and faded, one dust jacket with minute snag top edge, otherwise nearly pristine condition, volumes obviously never read and almost untouched. Phillip J. Pirages   59 - 267   2011 $375

Sharpe, Edmund *The Seven Periods of English Architecture Defined and Illustrated.* London: E. & F. N. Spon, 1888, Third edition; small 4to., original decorated red cloth gilt, trifle soiled and neatly recased, pages xiv, 40, (ii) (iv) with 20 finely detailed lithographed plates and few scattered sketches of foxing, but very good.   R. F. G. Hollett & Son Antiquarian Booksellers   177 - 800   2011   £85

Sharpey-Schafer, Edward Albert *The Endocrine Organ: a Introduction to the Study of Internal Secretion.* London, et al: Longmans, Green and Co., 1924-1926, Second edition; 2 volumes, 8vo., ix, 175; xxii, 177-418 pages, 204 numbered figures, indexes, original green cloth, blind-stamped cover title and gilt stamped spine title, previous owner's inked signature and rubber stamp, near fine, from the Medical Library of Dr. Clare Gray Peterson.   Jeff Weber Rare Books   162 - 274   2011 $100

Shaw, George A. *Madagascar and France: with Some Account of the Island, Its People, Its Resources and Development.* London: RTS, 1885, First edition; 8vo., pages 320, folding map, original red decorative cloth, spine faded, small wear to head and tail, slight foxing of prelims and index.   J. & S. L. Bonham Antiquarian Booksellers Africa 4/20/2011 - 3152   2011   £55

Shaw, George Bernard   1856-1950 *Adventures of the Black Girl in Her Search for God.* London: Constable, 1932, First edition; several wood engravings by John Farleigh, final leaves lightly foxed, pages 80, foolscap 8vo., original black boards, illustrated overall and with author and title printed on slightly sunned backstrip and front cover in white, joints trifle worn, good, T. E. Lawrence's copy with gift inscription to him from George Bernard Shaw's wife Charlotte.   Blackwell Rare Books   B166 - 173 2011 £2000

Shaw, George Bernard   1856-1950 *Everybody's Political What's What?* London: Constable, 1944, First edition; original cloth, gilt, dust jacket, edges and lower hinge rather chipped and frayed, neat inscription on flyleaf. R. F. G. Hollett & Son Antiquarian Booksellers 175 - 1212 2011   £45

Shaw, George Bernard   1856-1950 *In Good King Charles's Golden Days: a History Lesson by a Fellow of The Royal Society of Literature.* London: privately printed, 1939, First edition; 8vo., original publisher's printed wrappers designated "First Rehearsal Copy" on cover and "Strictly Private", signed presentation from author to scientist/astronomer James Jeans, few marginal linings in text, presumably in hand of Jeans, clean, very good example with slight creasing to one corner and short split at lower top hinge.   Any Amount of Books   May 26 2011 - A73446 2011 $1845

Shaw, George Bernard 1856-1950 *The Perfect Wagnerite: a Commentary on the Niblung's Ring.* London: Grant Richards, 1898, First edition; quart cloth and silk or linen over boards, sizing under silk little toned, silk worn through a little on edges, very good, small leather bookplate of composer Jerome Kern. Between the Covers 169 - BTC342152 2011 $1000

Shaw, George Bernard 1856-1950 *Complete Plays of Bernard Shaw (and) Prefaces by Bernard Shaw.* London: Constable and Co., Ltd., 1931-1934, First editions; 2 volumes, quarto, pages (viii), 1131; viii, 802, (1 blank) pages, both volumes uniformly bound by Bayntun-Riviere in half red morocco, single rule gilt on covers, spines ruled and lettered in gilt in compartments, five raised bands, top edge gilt, marbled endpapers, fine set. Heritage Book Shop Holiday 2010 - 113 2011 $1250

Shaw, George Bernard 1856-1950 *Prefaces.* London: Constable, 1934, First edition; large thick 8vo., original cloth gilt, dust jacket (spine worn and chipped at head and foot), pages viii, 801 with decorated title, endpapers and edges rather spotted, otherwise very good, sound copy, original bookseller's invoice loosely inserted. R. F. G. Hollett & Son Antiquarian Booksellers 175 - 1214 2011 £75

Shaw, George Bernard 1856-1950 *Saint John.* London: Constable, 1924, Limited edition (1 of 750 copies); small folio, original holland backed decorated boards, small shelf number at foot of spine, dust jacket (few edge tears and piece lacking from foot of spine and lower board, little dusty), pages v, 184, top edge gilt, uncut, 16 tipped in plates by Ricketts, printed on handmade paper, lower corners of few plates slightly creased, neat school library label and very small shelf numbers on pastedown, flyleaf trifle creased but excellent copy. R. F. G. Hollett & Son Antiquarian Booksellers 175 - 1215 2011 £150

Shaw, George Bernard 1856-1950 *Saint Joan.* London: Constable, 1924, First edition; 12mo., pages 114, inscribed by author to Lilian Throckmorton, original silverprint of GBS and recipient posing in a garden, Throckmorton's bookplate, fine. Second Life Books Inc. 174 - 283 2011 $900

Shaw, George Bernard 1856-1950 *Saint Joan.* London: Constable, 1925, Ninth impression; 8vo., pages lxiv, 114, signed presentation from author for Mrs. Diplock, Morrison Davidson's daughter, very good+ in slightly browned about very good, complete jacket. Any Amount of Books May 26 2011 - A74375 2011 $461

Shaw, George Bernard 1856-1950 *The Complete Works of Bernard Shaw.* 1930-1932, Limited to 1025 copies; 30 volumes, a further 3 volumes were added between 1934 & 1938, very good. C. P. Hyland May 26 2011 - 258/870 2011 $507

Shaw, Margaret Fay *Folksongs and Folklore of South Uist.* London: Routledge and Kegan Paul, 1955, First edition; small 4to., original blue cloth gilt, dust jacket (very defective, some three quarter preserved), pages xiv, 290, 32 page of illustrations, double page map and numerous examples of music in text, few notes on front pastedown, otherwise excellent copy. R. F. G. Hollett & Son Antiquarian Booksellers 175 - 1216 2011 £85

Shaw, T. H. *The Mcphersons; or is the Church of Rome Making Progress in England...* Burnes and Oates, 1879, Pages 214, (iv), (vi), 3 lithographed portraits (little stained), original blindstamped cloth, gilt, neatly recased, lower board replaced to match, scarce. R. F. G. Hollett & Son Antiquarian Booksellers 175 - 1217 2011 £85

Shaw, Trevor R. *Foreign Travellers in the Slovene Kartst 1537-1900.* Zalozba ZRC: 2000, First edition; large 8vo., original wrappers, pages 244, color frontispiece and 145 illustrations, scarce. R. F. G. Hollett & Son Antiquarian Booksellers General Catalogue Summer 2010 - 1660 2011 £65

Shaw, Vero *The Illustrated Book of the Dog.* London: Cassell & Co., 1890, 2 volumes, 4to., contemporary half black morocco gilt, pages viii, 664, 28 chromolithographed plates, numerous woodcuts, scattered faint spotting here and there, excellent clean and sound set. R. F. G. Hollett & Son Antiquarian Booksellers General Catalogue Summer 2010 - 1049 2011 £650

Shawn, Wallace *The Designated Mourner.* New York: Noonday Press, 1997, First Noonday Press edition; inscribed by author for Pauline Kael, together with Shawn's interview with Mark Strand in The Paris Review, Volume 40, No. 148 (NY: Paris Review 1998), laid in is APS from Shawn to Kael first book fine in wrappers, second book and card near fine. Ken Lopez Bookseller 154 - 201 2011 $350

Shea & Patten *The "Soapy" Smith Tragedy.* Skagway: Shea & Patten, 1907, First edition; oblong 16mo., red pictorial wrappers, (24) pages, 13 plates, original covers are lightly worn at fore-edges and extremities, however all text is fine, housed in clamshell case with title stamped in gold on spine. Buckingham Books May 26 2011 - 26286 2011 $2250

Shearar, James *Prinkle and His Friends.* London: Tinsley Bros., 1877, First edition; 3 volumes, half titles, original royal blue cloth, spines rubbed and dulled, stitching weakening volumes I and III. Jarndyce Antiquarian Booksellers CXCI - 533 2011 £45

Sheard, Charles *The Tuner's Guide: Containing a Complete Treatise on Tuning the Piano-Forte, Organ, Melodeon and Seraphine...* London: Charles Sheard and Co., n.d. early 1850's, First UK edition; small 8vo., original blue cloth gilt, pages 72, plate, numerous musical examples and diagrams, joints cracking, otherwise excellent copy. R. F. G. Hollett & Son Antiquarian Booksellers 175 - 1218 2011 £350

Shearing, Joseph *Moss Rose.* London: William Heinemann Ltd., 1934, First edition; light foxing to few prelim pages, else near fine in professionally restored dust jacket at spine ends, corners and top edge of rear panel. Buckingham Books May 26 2011 - 26116 2011 $2250

Sheckley, Robert *Immortality Delivered.* New York: Avalon Books, 1958, First edition; octavo, cloth. L. W. Currey, Inc. 124 - 191 2011 $250

Sheldon, Charles *The Wilderness of the Upper Yukon. A Hunter's Explorations for Wild Sheep in Sub-Arctic Mountains.* London: T. Fisher Unwin, 1911, First edition; large 8vo., pages xxii, 354, color frontispiece, 4 maps, 50 photo plates, original publisher's lettered gilt on spine and on front cover, front cover with pictorial gilt ram's head, top edge gilt, sound, clean, very good+ copy, slight browning to endpapers, ownership signature of Duke of Bedford (Woburn Abbey). Any Amount of Books May 29 2011 - 74328 2011 $221

Sheldon, Roy *Consumer Engineering: a New Technique for Prosperity.* London & New York: Harper and Brothers, 1932, First edition; 8vo., original publisher's maroon cloth lettered gilt at spine, pages (viii), 259, about fine in very good+ dust jacket (slightly dusty, faintly marked), excellent condition. Any Amount of Books May 29 2011 - A47873 2011 $340

Sheldon, William *History of the Heathen Gods and Heroes of Antiquity.* Worcester: Isaiah Thomas, Jun. n.d., 1809, First edition; 12mo., xxv, 216 pages, original marbled paper on boards, green leather spine with gilt title and fillets, speckled edges, 29 full page wood engravings, shelf wear at edges, very fine, rare, contemporary wood engraved ownership label. Hobbyhorse Books 56 - 138 2011 $520

Shele, Richard *The Battle of Chevy Chase.* Newcastle: W. Fordyce, n.d. circa, 1830, 12mo., 24 pages, paper self wrappers, reinforced spine, small cuts at edges, very good, scarce. Hobbyhorse Books 56 - 28 2011 $150

Shelley, Mary Wollstonecraft 1797-1851 *The Choice, a Poem.* London: printed for editor for private distribution, 1876, First edition; 8vo., 14 pages, unbound sheets laid into printed wrapper, little soiled, else fine, printed on Whatman laid paper, laid in is engraved portrait of Shelley that is called for. Second Life Books Inc. 174 - 284 2011 $1500

Shelley, Mary Wollstonecraft 1797-1851 *The Last Man.* London: Henry Colburn, 1826, First edition; 8vo., pages (xii) 358 (ii) (88) 12 (1826 ad); (ii), 328; (ii), 352 (with ad for Frakenstein and other works by author at bottom of last leaf of text volume three), all leaves untrimmed (except for titlepage of volume two which has been trimmed along bottom and fore edge), professional marginal repairs on 3 leaves, some minor foxing, stain on two leaves from press flower, but very nice, untrimmed copy, bound in later leather backed marbled boards, raised bands, stamped in gilt. Second Life Books Inc. 174 - 285 2011 $8500

Shelley, Mary Wollstonecraft 1797-1851 *Monsieur Nongtongpaw.* London: Alfred Miller, 1830, First illustrated edition; 12mo., pages 19 (11) (4), 6 engraved plates with contemporary hand coloring, bound in later three quarter morocco and marbled boards by Root and Son (front cover very loose), very clean copy. Second Life Books Inc. 174 - 286 2011 $600

Shelley, Percy Bysshe 1792-1822 *Alastor; or the Spirit of Solitude and Other Poems.* London: printed for Baldwin, Cradock and Joy by S. Hamilton, 1816, First edition; 8vo., pages (viii without half title as issued), 101, (7) blank, gilt edges, some minor spotting to margins of endpapers, otherwise internally very clean, late 19th century navy blue morocco with ornate red, green and gilt decoration, brown fabric to inside of boards and endpapers, gilt lettering to spine, raised bands by Riviere, blue morocco and marbled paper covered slipcase, binding fine with light wear to edges of slipcase, bookplate of John Whipple Frothingham. Simon Finch Rare Books Zero - 352 2011 £4500

Shelley, Percy Bysshe 1792-1822 *The Cenci.* Italy: for C. and J. Olllier, London, 1819, First edition one of 250 copies; 8vo., pages xiv, 104, occasional light spotting, bound without initial blank in later morocco by Ramage, upper and lower boards filleted in gilt, spine with raised bands and compartments delineated in gilt, gilt lettering, inner dentelles, marbled endpapers, top edge gilt, others uncut, bookplate of Joseph Turner. Simon Finch Rare Books Zero - 353 2011 £3500

Shelley, Percy Bysshe 1792-1822 *Epipsychidion.* Officina Bodoni Montagnola, 1923, First edition, one of 220 copies printed on vellum paper; small 4to., 38, ivory paper over boards, uncut and unopened, cover slightly warped, else nice. Second Life Books Inc. 174 - 287 2011 $1500

Shelley, Percy Bysshe 1792-1822 *Notebooks.* Boston: printed for members of the Bibliophile Society, 1911, Limited to 465 copies; 3 volumes, gray boards and white vellum like spine, foxing, otherwise near fine set, housed in double slipcase with spine labels, uncommon. Lupack Rare Books May 26 2011 - ABE4091523450 2011 $150

Shelley, Percy Bysshe 1792-1822 *Poems.* London: Macmillan, 1913, Small 8vo., full crushed scarlet morocco gilt by Ramage, raised bands, pages lxvi, 340, all edges gilt, engraved title vignette, light crayon scribble on flyleaf, otherwise fine.   R. F. G. Hollett & Son Antiquarian Booksellers General Catalogue Summer 2010 - 904 2011   £60

Shelley, Percy Bysshe 1792-1822 *The Poetical Works.* London: Reeves & Turner, 1886, Second edition; 2 volumes, 191 x 135mm., very fine early 20th century olive crushed morocco handsomely gilt by C. and C. McLeish (stamp signed on rear turn-ins), covers bordered with single plain gilt rule, raised bands, spines densely and very attractively gilt in compartments featuring a large centerpiece in the form of a rose with four emanating springs of rose leaves, this quatrefoil design enclosed by a semis field punctuated with trefoil leaves, turn-ins with gilt French fillet border and trefoil cornerpieces, all edges gilt, each volume with frontispiece, engraved armorial bookplate of Douglas and Mary MacEwen; spines lightly sunned, offsetting from frontispieces, isolated minor foxing, otherwise especially fine set in lovely bindings, gilt bright, leather unworn, text with virtually no signs of use.   Phillip J. Pirages 59 - 119 2011 $1950

Shelley, Percy Bysshe 1792-1822 *Queen Mab.* London: W. Clark, 1821, First published edition; 8vo., 182 page, three quarter blue morocco with raised bands and spine gilt by Bayntun, top edge gilt, little worn along hinges, leaves little darkened, very good, bound with the rare dedicatory poem to author's first wife, Harriet, but without ad leaf.   Second Life Books Inc. 174 - 288 2011 $1800

Shelley, Percy Bysshe 1792-1822 *Zastrozzi.* Waltham St. Lawrence: Golden Cockerel Press, 1955, 189/140 copies (of an edition of 200 copies); printed on Japanese vellum, 8 full page wood engravings by Cecil Keeling, pages 132, 8vo., original quarter black morocco, backstrip lettered and decorated in gilt marbled red and black boards, inverted bookplate on rear pastedown, top edge gilt, board slipcase, fine.   Blackwell Rare Books B166 - 260 2011   £140

Shepard, Ernest H. *Drawn from Memory.* London: Methuen, 1957, First edition; 8vo., 190 pages, frontispiece, copious illustrations, loosely inserted by E. H. Shepard and his wife to their daughter Mary Knox, very good in slightly used and slightly rubbed, about very good dust jacket.   Any Amount of Books May 26 2011 - A39617 2011 $503

The Shepherd's Guide 1949. Consett: Ramsden Williams, n.d., 1939?, Original cloth backed printed wrappers, little soiled, pages (x), 656, illustrations.   R. F. G. Hollett & Son Antiquarian Booksellers 173 - 1032 2011   £85

Shepherd, Thomas Hosmer *Metropolitan Improvements or London in the Nineteenth Century.* Jones & Co., 1829, First edition; 4to., contemporary half calf gilt with marbled boards, edges trilfe rubbed, pages vi, 172, (ii), 40, 2 engraved titles, 1 printed title, 198 steel engraved plates on 99 leaves and map, occasional scattered foxing, generally very clean.   R. F. G. Hollett & Son Antiquarian Booksellers General Catalogue Summer 2010 - 1580 2011   £450

The Shepherd's Guide 1960. Consett: Ramsden Williams Publications, 1960, Original cloth backed wrappers, little worn and soiled, pages lxix, 704, illustrations, corners trifle creased.   R. F. G. Hollett & Son Antiquarian Booksellers 173 - 1033 2011   £30

Sheppard, Jill *The "Redlegs" of Barbados: their Origins and History.* Millwood: Kto Press, 1977, First edition; 8vo., 5 illustrations, pages 161, ex-British Foreign Office library with few library markings, else very good.   Any Amount of Books May 29 2011 - A68312 2011 $213

Sheppard, T. *Catalouge of the Mortimer Collection of Prehistoric Remains from East Yorkshire Barrows.* Hull: A. Brown & Son, 1929, Original wrappers, pages viii, 146, illustrations.   R. F. G. Hollett & Son Antiquarian Booksellers 177 - 801 2011   £40

Sherer, Moyle 1789-1869 *Scenes and Impressions in Egypt and in Italy.* London: Longman Hurst, 1824, First edition; 8vo., pages iv, 452, contemporary brown full calf, covers rubbed.   J. & S. L. Bonham Antiquarian Booksellers Africa 4/20/2011 - 8413 2011   £175

Sherer, Moyle 1789-1869 *Scenes and Impressions in Egypt and in Italy.* London: Longman Hurst, 1824, First edition; 8vo., pages iv 452, contemporary brown full calf, covers rubbed.   J. & S. L. Bonham Antiquarian Booksellers Africa 4/20/2011 - 8413 2011   £175

Shergold, M. D. *A History of the Spanish Stage, from Medieval Times Until the End of the Seventeenth Century.* London: 1967, Ex-library, usual marks, 624 pages, 32 black and white plates, cloth pulling away slightly at spine, edges soiled, else very clean and tight, very good.   G. H. Mott Bookseller May 26 2011 - 16896 2011 $200

Sheridan, Louisa Henrietta *The Comic Offering; or Ladies' Melange of Literary Mirth for MDCCCXXXII.* London: Smith, Elder and Co., 1832, Frontispiece, additional engraved title, illustrations, 6 pages ads, original black calf, heavily and pictorially embossed, spine lettered in gilt, slightly rubbed, endpapers replaced, all edges gilt, very good, binding signed "De La Rue & Co. London", superb example.   Jarndyce Antiquarian Booksellers CXCI - 443 2011   £85

Sheridan, Louisa Henrietta *The Comic Offering or Ladies' Melange of Literary Mirth for MDCCCXXXIV.* London: Smith Elder & Co., 1834, Original blindstamped morocco, gilt, boards embossed with elaborate rococo design of laughing figure with cornucopia of flowers, etc., recased, most of original backstrip preserved and relaid, pages xii, 346, frontispiece and title (tear neatly repaired), 60 woodcut illustrations.   R. F. G. Hollett & Son Antiquarian Booksellers   175 - 1221   2011   £85

Sheridan, P. H. *Record of Engagements with Indians Within the Military Division of the Missouri from 1868 to 1882.* Chicago: Headquarters Military Division of the Missouri, 1882, First edition; 8vo., printed wrappers, bound into leather folder, title stamped in gold on front cover, marbled endpapers, 120 pages, fine.   Buckingham Books   May 26 2011 - 2327   2011 $2000

Sheridan, Thomas *Sheridan's and Henderson's Practical Method of Reading and Reciting English Poetry...* London: Printed for E. Newbery, 1796, xii, 264 pages, 12mo., small stain to outer edge of final leaves, paper flaw to page 261-2 with slight loss, missing words being supplied in margin in neat contemporary hand, excellently rebacked in half calf, gilt ruled spine, original marbled boards, ownership label of Rear Admiral Saumarez with note presenting the book to his granddaugther May Snowden.   Jarndyce Antiquarian Booksellers   CXCI - 491   2011   £125

Sheringham, George *Design in the Theatre.* London: The Studio, 1927, 4to., original decorated wrappers, little torn and worn, upper panel very stained, pages viii, 31, plus 120 plates, first a leaves and half title with heavy stain, slight stain to fore-edge of final few leaves.   R. F. G. Hollett & Son Antiquarian Booksellers   175 - 1222   2011   £35

Sherman, Cindy *Untitled Film Stills.* New York: Rizzoli, 1990, First edition, signed; folio, pages 120, with 40 black and white photos, original black cloth, spine lettered in silver, top corner of upper side bumped, bottom tips rubbed, original black and white photo illustrated dust jacket, white, text printed in black, Sherman's signature in black ink to titlepage, almost near fine in fine dust jacket.   Simon Finch Rare Books   Zero - 546   2011   £550

Sherman, Edwin A. *Fifty Years of Masonry in California.* San Francisco: George Spaulding & Co., 1898, First edition; 2 volumes, folio, pages 534 (535)-802, 218, xvi, (6 index), profusely illustrated with engraved portraits, group photos, plates, exterior and interior images, publisher's pictorial blindstamped morocco, decorated and lettered in gilt on spines and front covers, two or three ownership stamps, few minor surface scratches to rear cover of volume one, magnificent set.   Argonaut Book Shop   Recent Acquisitions Summer 2010 - 125   2011 $750

Sherrington, Charles Scott *The Integrative Action of the Nervous System.* New York: Charles Scribner's Sons, 1906, First American edition; 8o., xvi, 411 pages, 85 text figures, original blue cloth, gilt stamped spine title, fine, from the Medical Library of Dr. Clare Gray Peterson.   Jeff Weber Rare Books   162 - 276   2011 $2700

Sherrington, Charles Scott *The Integrative Action of the Nervous System.* New Haven: Yale University Press, 1947, Reprint; 8vo., xxiv, 433 pages, frontispiece, 85 numbered figures, beige cloth, black stamped spine title, previous owner's inked signature, very good, from the Medical Library of Dr. Clare Gray Peterson.   Jeff Weber Rare Books   162 - 277   2011 $75

Sherwood, Mary Martha Butt   1775-1851   *The Fawns.* London and Wellington, Salop: printed for Houlston and Son, 1831, Third edition; 16mo., 15 pages, 1 page list, printed paper wrappers, full page wood engraved frontispiece signed O. Jewitt, plus 4 half page wood engraved vignettes in text, small inked name at titlepage, very fine.   Hobbyhorse Books   56 - 29   2011 $110

Sherwood, Mary Martha Butt   1775-1851   *The History of the Fairchild Family or the Child's Manual...*   T. Hatchard, 1854, Twentieth, sixth and third editions; 3 volumes, original blindstamped cloth gilt, little worn and faded, hinges of volume 3 frayed and splitting, corners rather bumped, pages viii, 294, (ii), 32 page smaller insert of ads dated April 1857, 334, (ii), 32 page insert dated 1859; 352, (iv), 32 page insert dated 1859, each with engraved tissue guarded frontispiece, joints cracking.   R. F. G. Hollett & Sons Antiquarian Booksellers   170 - 637   2011   £120

Sherwood, Mary Martha Butt   1775-1851   *The Two Sisters.* London: Houlston and Wright, n.d. circa, 1855, 12mo., 34 + 1 page book list on lower wrapper, decorative pink paper wrappers, full page wood engraved frontispiece, fine.   Hobbyhorse Books   56 - 139   2011 $100

Shetelig, Haakon *Scandinavian Archaeology.* Oxford: Clarendon Press, 1937, First edition; original cloth, gilt, pages xx, 459, with 63 pages of plates and 33 text figures, fine.   R. F. G. Hollett & Son Antiquarian Booksellers   177 - 802   2011   £65

Shields, Carol *Happenstance.* Toronto: McGraw-Hill Ryerson, 1980, First Canadian edition, true first; fine copy, near fine dust jacket with two half inch closed tears.   Bella Luna Books   May 29 2011 - t1010   2011 $82

Shields, Carol *The Orange Fish.* Toronto: Random House, 1989, First Canadian edition, true first; fine in near fine dust jacket with small ding and creases to bottom of rear panel, signed by author.   Bella Luna Books   May 29 2011 - 2371   2011 $137

Shields, Carol *The Stone Diaries.* Toronto: Random House, 1983, First Canadian edition; near fine, small spot of sticker residue on front free endpapers, dust jacket near fine, with light wear to extremities.   Bella Luna Books   May 26 2011 - t685   2011 $330

Shimmin, A. N. *The University of Leeds. The First Half Century.* Cambridge: University Press, 1954, First edition; 4to., original cloth, gilt, dust jacket, pages xv, 230, with drawings by Maurice de Sausmarez and plates.   R. F. G. Hollett & Son Antiquarian Booksellers   175 - 1224   2011   £30

Shinn, Charles Howard *Graphic Description of Pacific Coast Thrilling Exploits of Their Arch-Enemy Sheriff Harry N. Morse for Many Years the Terror of the Brigands of California - a Man of Courage wonderful Skill and Splendid Leadership...* San Francisco: R. Patterson, n.d. circa, 1890, First edition; 16mo., original printed wrappers, 32 pages, frontispiece, very rare, shows evidence of light waterstaining to top cover and page edges but does not extend into text, which is unaffected, small 1 inch closed tear to bottom of spine, else very good; accompanying this copy is a fine copy of the 1958 reprint edition (with former owner's bookplate affixed to verso of front flyleaf, else near fine in price clipped jacket), both copies housed in maroon leather clamshell case with raised bands and titles stamped in gold on front cover and spine.   Buckingham Books   May 26 2011 - 25237   2011 $3750

Shipley, Arthur E. *Hunting Under the Microscope.* Ernest Benn, 1928, First edition; original blue cloth gilt, spine little faded, dust jacket (head of spine trifle frayed), pages 184, frontispiece, 34 illustrations.   R. F. G. Hollett & Son Antiquarian Booksellers   General Catalogue Summer 2010 - 1050   2011   £65

Shiras, Wilmar H. *Children of the Atom.* New York: Gnome Press Inc., 1953, First edition; octavo, cloth.   L. W. Currey, Inc.   124 - 240   2011 $75

Shire, Helena Mennie *Song, Dance and Poetry of the Court of Scotland Under King James VI.* Cambridge: University Press, 1969, First edition; small 4to., original cloth, gilt, pages xi, 286, with 4 plates and 16 illustrations. R. F. G. Hollett & Son Antiquarian Booksellers   175 - 1226   2011   £45

Shoberl, Frederic *Excursions in Normandy, Illustrative of the Character, Manners, Customs and Traditions of the People.* London: Henry Colburn, 1841, First edition; 2 volumes, 12mo., final ad leaf, 4 page catalog (May 1841), volume I, 6 pages ads in volume II, original fine grained blue cloth, blocked in blind, lettered in gilt, spines slightly faded, very atractive.   Jarndyce Antiquarian Booksellers   CXCI - 578   2011   £150

Shore, Stephen *Uncommon Places.* New York: Aperture/A New Images Book, 1982, First edition; 4to., pages 63, (i) blank, 49 color photos, original maroon cloth, spine and upper side lettered in brown, original maroon cloth, spine and upper side lettered in brown, original color photo illustrated dust jacket, light sunning to spine and small portion of upper panel, ISBN sticker to lower panel, Shore's signature, fine in near fine dust jacket.   Simon Finch Rare Books Zero - 547   2011   £1200

Shore, W. Teignmouth *Kent.* London: Adam and Charles Black, 1907, First edition; original decorated cloth gilt, short tear to head of spine, pages x, 240, top edges gilt, 73 color plates, folding map.   R. F. G. Hollett & Son Antiquarian Booksellers   General Catalogue Summer 2010 - 1581   2011   £95

A Short History of Birds & Beasts for the Amusement and Instruction of Children. Wellington: F. Houlston and Son, n.d. circa, 1830, 24mo., 23 pages, 1 page ad on back cover, printed brown stiff paper wrappers, frontispiece pasted down on cover, woodcuts, woodcut tailpieces, scarce, mint.   Hobbyhorse Books   56 - 30   2011 $200

Short, Bob *Hoyle Abridged or Short Rules for Short Memories at the Game of Whist.* London: printed for B. Reynolds and John Stacy, 1818, Thirtieth edition; 108 x 57mm., 24 pages, extraordinarily fine and charming contemporary green morocco very lavishly gilt, covers with multiple plain and decorative rules at edges around two decorative frames, outer one with closely spaced fleurons pointing inward, inner one filled with row of interlocking floral loops, these two frames enclosing an elongated central panel with attenuated stems reaching toward and flowering at the corner of the board, flat spine with two panels of massed scrolling tools and one panel with titling, full morocco doublures very richly gilt in panelled design similar to (but even more intricate than) that on covers, gilt edges, early signature of Henry Bell, Woolsington; tiny tear in fore edge of one leaf, just slightest of rubbing to joints and extremities, in remarkably fine condition, binding bright and beautiful, text clean and fresh.   Phillip J. Pirages   59 - 264   2011 $750

Short, Ernest *A History of Religious Architecture.* London: Eyre & Spottiswoode, 1951, Third edition; original cloth, gilt, dust jacket, pages xix, 306 with 65 illustrations an 19 plans.   R. F. G. Hollett & Son Antiquarian Booksellers   177 - 893   2011   £45

Shortridge, G. C. *The Mammals of South West Africa.* London: William Heinemann, 1934, First edition; 8vo., 2 volumes, pages xxiii, 437; ix, 439-779, maps, illustrations, original green cloth, dust jacket (worn).   J. & S. L. Bonham Antiquarian Booksellers   Africa 4/20/2011 - 8836   2011   £75

The Shoso-In bulletin: an International Sherlockian Magazine. Tokyo: Men with the Twisted Konjo, 1993-2002, All numbered and limited editions; Unbroken run from volume 3 (August 1993) to volume 12 (2002), total 1919 pages, copiously illustrated in black and white, all in very good+ condition with some very slight minor wear (volume 3 has slight wear at spine end, volume 5 very slightly creased at top of spine, volume 6 has neat presentation on titlepage. Any Amount of Books May 29 2011 - A36182 2011 $340

Shreve, Susan Richards *Warm Springs.* Boston/New York: Houghton Mifflin, 2007, First edition; inscribed by author to another writer, fine in very near fine dust jacket with lamination peeling at one corner. Ken Lopez Bookseller 154 - 202 2011 $75

Shrinivasacharyah, G. C. V. *Harischandra. The Martyr to Truth.* Madras: Srinivasa Varadachari & Co., 1897, First edition; 153 pages, small 4to., paper covered boards, good copy, joints split, worn and chipped at edges of boards, repair at tail of spine, worm holes on boards mainly to edges, with some loss at upper fore corner and leaves, primarily to first few and last few, then one of two tiny holes, but in all cases marginal and not affecting text. Kaaterskill Books 12 - 174 2011 $100

Shuffrey, William Arthur *Lessons from the Dale.* Skeffington, 1911, First edition; original blue cloth gilt over bevelled boards, few slight marks, pages viii, 93, frontispiece of Armcliffe Vicarage and 5 plates of local views, scarce. R. F. G. Hollett & Son Antiquarian Booksellers 175 - 1227 2011 £35

Shute, Nevil *On the Beach.* London: Heinemann, 1957, First edition, uncorrected proof copy "Not for sale"; wrappers, 8vo., 312 pages, slightly creased at corners, very slight soiling, otherwise very good. Any Amount of Books May 29 2011 - A32601 2011 $204

Shvarts, Evgenil *The Little Crow.* Moscow: Raduga, 1925, First edition; 4to., color pictorial paper covers with slight handling but overall very nice, illustrated pages within, illustrations by E. D. Belukhi and Konstantin Rudakov. Jo Ann Reisler, Ltd. 86 - 211 2011 $2000

Siang, Song Ong *One Hundred Years' History of the Chinese in Singapore.* Singapore: Oxford University Press, 1984, First edition thus; , 8vo., pages xxii, 602, copiously illustrated, clean very good+. Any Amount of Books May 29 2011 - A66775 2011 $255

Sibree, James *Madagascar Before the Conquest; the Island the Country and the People.* London: T. Fisher, 1896, First edition; 8vo., pages xiii, 382, folding map, plates, lacks plate 6, rebound in blue cloth, presentation copy from author. J. & S. L. Bonham Antiquarian Booksellers Africa 4/20/2011 - 8678 2011 £85

Sidgwick, Alfred, Mrs. *Children's Book of Gardening.* London: Adam and Charles Black, 1909, First edition; 8vo., gilt decorative cloth, pictorial paste-on, 235 pages + ads, top edge gilt, near fine, 12 beautiful color plates by Mrs. Cayley-Robinson, great copy, quite scarce. Aleph-Bet Books, Inc. 95 - 249 2011 $325

Sidney, Philip 1554-1586 *Astrophel and Stella. The Sonnets of Sir Philip Sidney.* London: Hacon and Ricketts (Vale Press), 1898, First edition, 10 copies only; 8vo., green and white patterned paper covered boards, olive green matt spine with printed paper label, pages 67, corners rubbed, spine very slightly stained, spine label slight chipped, endpapers slightly browned red inkstain to corner of rear cover, bookplate of Evan Morgan (Lord Tredegar) overall sound, near very good with bright clean text and illustrations. Any Amount of Books May 29 2011 - B27468 2011 $238

Sidonius Apollinaris, Saint *Opera Castigata & Restituta.* Lyons: Joan de Tournes, 1552, 8vo., 360 pages, device on titlepage, ruled in red, English calf c. 1700, gilt fillet on covers, spine gilt, red edges, from the library of the Earls of Macclesfield at Shirburn Castle. Maggs Bros. Ltd. 1440 - 198 2011 £450

Siegel, Jules *Limeland. Mortality and Mercy on the Internet' Pynchon-L@Waste.Org Discusson List.* Philadelphia: Intangible Assets Manufacturing, 1997, First edition; fine in wrappers, bookplate of Ray Roberts, together with bound galleys of the book, 8 1/2 x 11 inches, velobound, lower inch of binding broken, else fine in acetate cover. Ken Lopez Bookseller 154 - 191 2011 $200

Siemienowicz Kazimierz *(Grand art d'Artillerie) Ausfuhrliche Beschreibung der Grossen Feuerwercks.* Frankfurt: J. D. Zunner, 1676, Reissue of 1651 French edition; folio, (2), 410, (6) pages, text in French, engraved title (in German) and 22 plates, contemporary English calf, lacking 4 leaves of printed prelims, the copy of R. Andersson, from the library of the Earls of Macclesfield at Shirburn Castle. Maggs Bros. Ltd. 1440 - 199 2011 £550

Sigourney, Lydia *Selections from Various Sources.* Worcester: John H. Turner, 1863, First edition; (240) pages, 8vo., original blindstamped purple cloth with gilt design on front panel, gilt decorated spine envely faded with gilt lettering, some wear to head and foot, faint waterstain in margins of first and final pages, all in all, tight, sound copy, signed presentation copy in year of publication to Mr. Curtis. Paulette Rose Fine and Rare Books 32 - 158 2011 $350

Sigourney, Lydia *Sketches.* Philadelphia: Key & Biddle, 1834, First edition; 8vo., pages 216, little toning to titlepage, some light foxing to endpaper, little soiling to cover, nick to spine, very good, inscribed by author for Caroline Griffin, brown cloth, page 146 correctly paged. Second Life Books Inc. 174 - 289 2011 $600

Sike, Hernicus *Evangelium Infante...* Utrecht: Franciscusm Halman-Guillaume Vande Water, 1697, First edition; small 8vo., 16 x 10 cm., full leather rather rubbed and scuffed, lacking spine leather with loose, detached boards, text block sound and clean and complete, Arabic text facing Latin text.   Any Amount of Books   May 26 2011 - A74870   2011 $671

Silliman, Augustus E. *A Gallop Among American Scenery; or Sketches of American Scenes and Military Adventure.* New York: D. Appleton, 1843, First edition; original cloth, very good, light but consistent foxing, shelfwear to extremities, tight copy, bright spine gilt.   Lupack Rare Books   May 26 2011 - ABE1189054406   2011 $175

Silliman, Benjamin *Manual on the Cultivation of the Sugar Cane and the Fabrication and Refinement of Sugar.* City of Washington: printed by Francis Preston Blair, 1833, First edition; tall 8vo., 122 pages, four folding plates, contemporary plain wrappers, uncut, moderate staining scarce.   M & S Rare Books, Inc.   90 - 407   2011 $350

Silva, Tony *A Monograph of Endangered Parrots.* Pickering: Silvio Mattacchione and Co., 1989, Remarque Edition of which only 26 lettered copies were produced, this copy lettered T and signed by Tony Silva and Gracia Bennish and contains original full page drawing by Bennish; 28 colored and 15 plain plates by Gracia Bennish, folio, pages xviii, 356, gilt decorated green full morocco (fine), green cloth slipcase lined with matching suede/luxe (minor scuff to side panel).   Raymond M. Sutton, Jr.   May 26 2011 - 46176   2011 $2000

Silverstein, Shel *Different Dances.* New York: Harper and Row, 1979, First edition; near fine, small ownership name on front pastedown, dust jacket near fine, price clipped.   Bella Luna Books   May 26 2011 - t7964   2011 $247

Simak, Clifford D. *All Flesh is Grass.* Garden City: Doubleday & Co., 1965, First edition; octavo, cloth.   L. W. Currey, Inc.   124 - 192   2011 $250

Simenon, Georges *Les 13 Coupagles. (with) Les 13 Enigmes. (with) Les 13 Mysteres.* Paris: Artheme Fayard & Co., 1932, First editions; 3 volumes, original photo wrappers, exceedingly rare, small bookseller's label on bottom edge of front cover and with partial sticker over original price on spine, else very good, second volume has light wear to spine ends and lightly creased on bottom edge of front cover, else very good, all volumes housed in cloth slipcase with titles stamped in black contrast on spine.   Buckingham Books   May 26 2011 - 26815   2011 $2500

Simmons, Amelia *American Cookery, or the Art of Dressing Viands, Fish, Poultry, and Vegetables and the Best Modes of Making Pastes, Puffs Pies, Tarts, Puddings, Custards...* Brattleborough: William Fessenden, 1814, 24mo., 69 pages, contemporary paper covered boards, spine shot, covers nearly detached, two leaves slightly torn, foxed, fairly crisp and nice enough.   M & S Rare Books, Inc.   90 - 97   2011 $950

Simmons, Owen *The Book of Bread.* London: MacLaren & Sons, 1903, First edition; 4to., pages 360, 12 chromolithographic plates and 10 mounted (on green card) black and white photo plates, 4 reproductions in text, original publisher's green cloth lettered black on spine and gilt on front cover, ex-library, 2 plates slightly chipped at one corner, one bound upside down, overall sound, near very good, complete.   Any Amount of Books   May 26 2011 - A12942   2011 $839

Simms, Jeptha R. *The American Spy or Freedom's Early Sacrifice.* Albany: J. Munsell, 1857, Reprint of 1846 edition; 8vo., 63 pages, original printed and pictorial wrappers, front wrapper with two chips in top margin, crude celo tape repair to lower corners with some marginal paper loss, internally clean and very sound overall.   M & S Rare Books, Inc.   90 - 386   2011 $150

Simms, William G. *Life in America or the Wigwam and the Cabin.* Aberdeen: 1848, First Aberdeen edition; 311 pages, extremely good, original binding, backstrip gilt oxidized.   Bookworm & Silverfish   667 - 153   2011 $225

Simon, John *English Sanitary Institutions.* London: Cassell, 1890, First edition; pages xv, 496, 16 page publisher's catalog at rear, original publisher's maroon cloth lettered gilt at spine, mark on front endpaper, else very good+.   Any Amount of Books   May 29 2011 - A33502   2011 $213

Simon, Kathleen *Slavery.* London: Hodder & Stoughton, 1929, First edition; original black cloth, gilt, pages xiii, 284, portrait frontispiece, fore-edge lightly spotted.   R. F. G. Hollett & Son Antiquarian Booksellers   175 - 1232   2011   £35

Simon, Neil *The Heartbreak Kid.* New York: Palomar Pictures, 1971, First draft screenplay for the movie based on Bruce Jay Friedman story "A Change of Plan"; bradbound in near fine studio wrappers at edges and folds.   Ken Lopez Bookseller   154 - 203   2011 $250

Simple Simon and His Friends. Greening and Co. n.d., 1906, Oblong folio, original cloth backed boards, unpaginated, 12 superb full color plates by Charles Crombie, staples little rused, otherwise lovely, clean, fresh and tight copy.   R. F. G. Hollett & Sons Antiquarian Booksellers   170 - 171   2011   £375

Simple Stories for Little Readers Interspersed with Moral and Religious Reflections. Yarmouth: printed by and for F. Skill, 1835, Second edition; 18mo., (2), 101 pages, three quarter leather with corners, marbled paper on boards, gilt title and fillets on spine, full page copper engraved frontispiece, half page wood engravings, two ink signatures, almost mint.   Hobbyhorse Books   56 - 140   2011 $850

Simpson, George   *Peace River. A Canoe Voyage from Hudson's to Pacific by the Late Sir George Simpson in 1828...*   Published by J. Durie & Son, 1872, First edition; 8vo., original blindstamped brown cloth, orange endpapers, xix (blank), 119 pages, preface, addendum, folding map bound in at rear, tables, errata sheet affixed before titlepage.   Buckingham Books   May 26 2011 - 26810   2011 $4000

Simpson, John   *Oxford English Dictionary Additions Series.*   Oxford: Clarendon Press, 1993-1997, 3 volumes, original cloth, gilt, dust jackets, pages xiii, 329, (iv); viii, 336, 39; xii, 352, 54.   R. F. G. Hollett & Son Antiquarian Booksellers   General Catalogue Summer 2010 - 460   2011   £65

Simpson, John Palgrave   *Letters from the Danube.*   London: Richard Bentley, 1847, First edition; 2 volumes, 12mo., half titles, bound in contemporary full tan calf, gilt borders, raised gilt bands, gilt compartments, dark green and brown morocco labels, presentation inscription for Robert Peel, 4th Baronet from friend Henry James Vansittart Neale, on leaving Eton, Election 1860, fine.   Jarndyce Antiquarian Booksellers   CXCI - 579   2011   £350

Simpson, John W.   *Essays and Memorials by John W. Simpson...*   Architectural Press, 1923, First edition; original cloth backed boards, paper spine label (little chipped), pages (viii), 174, untrimmed, etched frontispiece, 10 plates and 90 text figures.   R. F. G. Hollett & Son Antiquarian Booksellers   177 - 806   2011   £30

Sims, George R.   *Ballads and Poems.*   London: John P. Fuller, 1883, First edition; 3 parts, frontispiece, original lime green decorated cloth, inner hinges cracking, all edges gilt.   Jarndyce Antiquarian Booksellers   CXCI - 492   2011   £38

Sims, George R.   *Living London. Its Work and Its Play, Its Humour and Its Pathos, Its Sights and Its Scenes.*   London: Cassell and Co., n.d., 1890, First edition; 3 volumes, 4to., original green cloth, gilt, pages viii, 384; viii, 384; viii, 384; profusely illustrated, over 1450 illustrations, titles in red and black, one section trifle strained, otherwise, excellent, clean and sound.   R. F. G. Hollett & Son Antiquarian Booksellers   General Catalogue Summer 2010 - 1582   2011   £350

Sims, Orlando L.   *Gun-toters I Have Known.*   Austin: 1967, Limited to 750 numbered copies; ix, 57 pages, frontispiece, spine slightly faded, else near fine, signed.   Dumont Maps & Books of the West   111 - 77   2011 $95

Sinclair, Colin   *Thatched Houses.*   Oliver & Boyd, 1953, First edition; small 8vo., original cloth, gilt, dust jacket, pages 80, plus 32 pages of plates, scarce.   R. F. G. Hollett & Son Antiquarian Booksellers   177 - 809   2011   £40

Sinclair, Upton   1878-1968   *The Gnomobile.*   New York: Farrar Rinehart, 1936, First edition; 8vo., tan cloth stamped in red, 181 pages, fine in dust jacket, chipped at spine end and top of rear panel, illustrations in black and white, very scarce, rare in fragile dust jacket.   Aleph-Bet Books, Inc.   95 - 536   2011 $275

Singer, Charles   *A History of Technology.*   New York and London: 1954, First edition; 5 volumes, near fine in dust jackets - volume 1 chipped 2 x 4 inch horizontal rear panel, volumes I-III with small chips atop of backstrip volumes IV and V show dampness to jacket at heel of backstrip, inked owner name bottom edge volume IV and on dust jacket at top of front panel, later expanded to 8 volumes.   Bookworm & Silverfish   662 - 180   2011 $250

Singer, Isaac Bashevis   *The Magician of Lublin.*   New York: Limited Editions Club, 1984-1985, First edition with these illustrations; one of 1500 copies signed by Singer and Larry Rivers who illustrated the book with 3 original color lithographs, book is hand bound in quarter blue goatskin stamped in gold, with linen sides, pages 236, cloth, slipcase, as new.   Gemini Fine Books & Arts, Ltd.   Art Reference & Illustrated Books: First Editions 2011 $250

Singh, Khushwant   *The Mark of Vishnu and Other Stories.*   London: Saturn Press, 1950, First edition; 122 pages, 8vo., cloth, bump to tail of spine, else very good.   Kaaterskill Books   12 - 175   2011 $75

Sint Nicolaas en Zijn Knecht.   Amsterdam: J. Vlieger, circa, 1900, Folio, stiff pictorial wrappers, slight cover and spine rubbing, very good+, 16 full page color illustrations.   Aleph-Bet Books, Inc.   95 - 147   2011 $750

Siodmak, Curt   *Donovan's Brain.*   New York: Alfred A. Knopf, 1943, First edition; octavo, cloth.   L. W. Currey, Inc.   124 - 124   2011 $650

Siringo, Charles Angelo   1855-1928   *Riata and Spurs. The Story of a Lifetime Spent in the Saddle as Cowboy and Detective.*   Boston and New York: Houghton Mifflin Co., 1927, First edition; 8vo., 14, (1), 276 pages, original cloth, dust jacket, complete and present, but one flap detached, fine, presentation by author to Miss Catherine Kingman, on half title is photo of Siringo taken in Pasadena by Spencer Kingman, with long pencil written explanation above.   M & S Rare Books, Inc.   90 - 387   2011 $850

Sisam, Kenneth *Fourteenth Century Verse & Prose.* Oxford: Clarendon Press, 1933, Original cloth, gilt, pages xlvii, 292, unpaginated glossary.   R. F. G. Hollett & Son Antiquarian Booksellers   General Catalogue Summer 2010 - 906   2011   £65

Sisson, J. L. *Historic Sketch of the Parish Church, Wakefield.* Wakefield: Richard Nichols, 1824, One of 75 large paper copies; 120 pages, half title, frontispiece, titlepage woodcut, 2 plates, several text illustrations, original roan backed printed boards, covers rubbed, spine and corners worn, clean copy internally.   Ken Spelman Rare Books   68 - 23   2011   £40

Sitwell, Edith   1887-1964   *The Collected Poems of Edith Sitwell.* London: Gerald Duckworth, 1930, First edition, no. 310 of 320 copies; 8vo., pages x, 278, frontispiece, Reynolds Stone bookplate of a collector, covers very slightly soiled, else very good or better.   Any Amount of Books   May 29 2011 - A80780   2011 $221

Sitwell, H. D.   *The Crown Jewels and Other Regalia in the Tower of London.* London: Dropmore Press, 1953, Limited, signed edition, no. 13 of 99 copies; folio, original three quarter red crushed morocco gilt, gilt crown on upper board, dust jacket (short closed tear to spine neatly repaired on reverse), cloth slipcase, pages 115, all edges gilt, with 8 superb tissue guarded color plates and 28 pages of monochrome illustrations, fine copy.   R. F. G. Hollett & Son Antiquarian Booksellers   175 - 1235   2011   £275

Skelton, John   1460-1529   *Pithy Pleasaunt and Profitable Workes of Maister Skelton, Poete Laureate to King Henry the VIIIth.* London: C. Davis, 1736, First edition thus, small blindstamp on titlepage "Harvard College Library"; and 2 small round stamps verso of same library and note "Welsh Fund", slight repair to edge of titlepage, otherwise, clean, very good+ in recent half dark blue leather and marbled boards, lettered gilt at spine.   Any Amount of Books   May 29 2011 - A44877   2011 $340

Sketch of the Life, Personal Appearance, Character and Manners of Charles S. Stratton, the Main in Miniature, Known as General Tom Thumb... London: Thomas Brettell, 1856, 12mo., printed wrappers, lacking rear wrapper, front wrapper creased and torn, some loss at fore-edge, front cover repaired to verso, vignette illustrations, minor finger soiling and dusting.   Dramatis Personae Booksellers   106 - 155   2011 $65

Skidmore, Thomas   *The Rights of Man to Property! Being a Proposition to make It Equal Among the Adults of the Present Generation.* New York: printed for the author by Alexander Ming Jr., 1829, First edition; 12mo., 405, (1) pages, original calf, sides stamped "Rights of Man to Property!", binding rubbed and slightly worn, some foxing, very good, early bookplate of Eli West of Carthage, Jefferson County NY.   M & S Rare Books, Inc.   90 - 388   2011 $7500

Skinner & Co. *A Catalogue of the Portland Museum Lately the Property of the Duchess Dowager of Portland...* London: 1786, 4to., viii, (3)-194 pages, frontispiece, neat modern quarter calf, lightly foxed, bit heavier on first and last few leaves, very good.   Joseph J. Felcone Inc.   Fall Miscellany 2010 - 100   2011 $5500

Skinner, Robert P. *Abyssinia of To-Day.* London: Edward Arnold, 1906, First edition; 8vo., pages xiv, 227, frontispiece, map illustrations, original red decorative cloth, gilt vignette on upper cover, spine faded, ex-library with stamps on titlepage and verso of some plates, partially unopened.   J. & S. L. Bonham Antiquarian Booksellers   Africa 4/20/2011 - 4665   2011   £50

Slade, Dorothea *Gutter Babies.* London: Heinemann, 1912, First edition; original blue cloth gilt with pictorial onlay to upper board, spine rather faded, pages viii, 342, 16 with 12 color plates by Lady Stanley, titlepage stamped "presentation copy".   R. F. G. Hollett & Sons Antiquarian Booksellers   170 - 638   2011   £35

Slater, Don *Tangents: 11 Odd Issues 1966-1969.* Hollywood: Tangent Group, 1966-1969, First edition; wrappers, 11 issues, some light dampstaining and some crinkling from damp but reasonable, very good- set, scarce.   Any Amount of Books   May 29 2011 - A76087   2011 $306

Slaughter, Philip *A Brief Sketch of the Life of William Green, LL.D.* Richmond: 1883, First edition; 131 pages, pencil signature of Col. R. L. Maury, good, rear 1/8" of free edge has lost it's cloth and same amount on inner fear free edge, one other small scrape.   Bookworm & Silverfish   678 - 82   2011 $95

Slovenly Peter's Story Book. New York: McLoughlin Bros., n.d. inscribed, 1877, 12mo., cloth stamped in black and gold, pictorial paste-on, few minor mends, paper worn on one page and finger soil throughout, tight and overall very good, 48 chromolithographs, rare.   Aleph-Bet Books, Inc.   95 - 286   2011 $1750

Slythe, R. Margaret *The Art of Illustration 1750-1900.* The Library Association, 1970, First edition; large 8vo., original cloth, gilt, dust jacket, pages 144 with color frontispiece and 42 illustrations.   R. F. G. Hollett & Son Antiquarian Booksellers   General Catalogue Summer 2010 - 325   2011   £45

Small, Tunstall *English Brickwork Details 1450-1750.* Architectural Press, n.d., Original printed board folder with linen ties, spine rubbed, label at foot, pages iv, plus 20 card sheet of drawings, loose as issue, School library label etc. on pastedown.   R. F. G. Hollett & Son Antiquarian Booksellers   177 - 813   2011   £35

Smalley, Janet *The Animals Came in 1 x 1, 2 x 2.* New York: 1930, Half cloth and printed paper over boards, extremity wear, inner joint mended.   Bookworm & Silverfish   669 - 103   2011 $60

Smart, Ninian *Atlas of the World's Religions.* Oxford University Press, 1999, First edition; folio, original cloth, gilt, dust jacket, pages 240, illustrations in color.   R. F. G. Hollett & Son Antiquarian Booksellers   175 - 1236   2011   £30

Smeaton, John *The Report of John Smeaton, Engineer, Concerning the Drainage of the North Level of the Fens and the Outfall of the Wisbeach River.* London?: 1768, First edition; 4to., large folding plate, 24 pages, original blue wrappers, stitched as issued, fine.   Anthony W. Laywood   May 26 2011 - 21737   2011 $243

Smelt, Leonard *The Speech of Leonard Smelt, Esq. Delivered by Him at the Meeting of the County of York December 3 1779.* York: printed by A. Ward and sold by all booksellers in York, and by R. Faulder, Londin, 1780, First edition; 4to., (4), 28 pages, preserved in modern wrappers with printed title label on upper cover, very good, very scarce.   John Drury Rare Books   153 - 135   2011   £375

Smelt, Leonard *The System Occasioned by the Speech of Leonard Smelt, Esq. Late Sub-Govenror to their Royal Highnesses the Prince of Wales and Bishop of Osnabrugh, at the Meeting at York December 30 1779.* London: J. Almon, 1780, Second edition; 8vo., 23, (1) page, with ad on verso of final leaf, preserved in modern wrappers with printed title label on upper cover, good, crisp copy, very scarce.   John Drury Rare Books   153 - 136   2011   £175

Smiles, Samuel *Duty.* Skeffington, 1897, New edition; pages xv, 430, 6, original maroon cloth gilt over bevelled boards, spine trifle faded, front flyleaf removed, joint cracked.   R. F. G. Hollett & Son Antiquarian Booksellers   175 - 1238   2011   £30

Smiles, Samuel *The Life of Thomas Telford, Civil Engineer.* London: John Murray, 1867, New edition; original maroon cloth gilt, spine rather faded and trifle frayed, pages xiv, 331, 6, numerous text and full page woodcuts, front joint little tender, scarce.   R. F. G. Hollett & Son Antiquarian Booksellers   General Catalogue Summer 2010 - 462   2011   £65

Smiley, Jane *Barn Blind.* New York: Harper & Row, 1980, First edition; near fine, light bump to top front corner and top of spine, dust jacket fine, inscribed and dated by author for Aunt Ginny.   Bella Luna Books   May 26 2011 - t7174   2011 $605

Smiley, Jane *The Life of the Body.* Minneapolis: Coffee House Press/Espresso Editions, 1990, One of 17 numbered copies signed by author and artist; 6 linoleum cut illustrations, couple of small faint stains to spine cloth, else fine in boards, publisher's ribbon tied plexiglass case, attractive production.   Ken Lopez Bookseller   154 - 206   2011 $950

Smiley, Jane *A Thousand Acres.* New York: Knopf, 1991, Uncorrected proof; near fine, one very tiny soiled spot on rear panel, printed orange wrappers.   Bella Luna Books   May 29 2011 - t5276   2011 $137

Smiley, Jane *A Thousand Acres.* New York: Knopf, 1991, First edition; fine in fine dust jacket.   Bella Luna Books   May 29 2011 - t1213a   2011 $82

Smith, A. H. *The Place Names of the North Riding of Yorkshire. English Place Name Society Volume 5.* Cambridge: Cambridge University Press, 1928, First edition; original cloth, gilt, very faded, pages xlvi, 352, large folding map in rear pocket.   R. F. G. Hollett & Son Antiquarian Booksellers   General Catalogue Summer 2010 - 1584   2011   £30

Smith, A. H. *The Place-Names of Westmorland, E.P.N.S. Volumes 42 and 43.* Cambridge: University Press, 1967, First edition; 2 volumes, original cloth, gilt, dust jackets price clipped, pages lxxv, 212; xiv, 367.   R. F. G. Hollett & Son Antiquarian Booksellers   173 - 1059   2011   £85

Smith, Adam   1723-1790   *An Inquiry into the Nature and Causes of the Wealth of Nations.* London: for A. Strahan and T. Cadell, 1789, Fifth edition; 3 volumes, 8vo., x, 499, (1) (1) and vi 518 (6) and v (1), 465 (51) pages, contemporary uniform calf gilt, sides with gilt borders, almost imperceptibly rebacked, spines fully gilt tooled in compartments with contrasting crimson and black lettering pieces by Trevor Lloyd, superb set of presentation quality.   John Drury Rare Books   153 - 137   2011   £3500

Smith, Adam   1723-1790   *An Inquiry into the Nature and Causes of the Wealth of Nations...* Edinburgh: printed for Oliphant, Waugh, & Innes and John Murray, London, 1814, 4 volumes, 8vo., complete with all half titles, contemporary uniform diced russia, simply gilt and lettered, marbled edges, very minor wear to bindings but very good, near contemporary presentation inscription recording (in Latin) presentation prize of this copy on 9th April 1820 to William Lillie at King's College, Aberdeen by Andrew Alexander, the professor of moral philosophy.   John Drury Rare Books   153 - 138   2011   £850

Smith, Alan *The Illustrated Guide to Liverpool Herculaneum Pottery 1796-1840.* Barrie & Jenkins, 1970, First edition; original cloth, gilt, dust jacket (spine lettering rather faded), pages xvi, 142, with 7 color plates, 191 monochrome illustrations, 4 maps and plans. R. F. G. Hollett & Son Antiquarian Booksellers General Catalogue Summer 2010 - 326 2011 £30

Smith, Alexander *City Poems.* Cambridge: Macmillan, 1857, First edition; half title, final ad leaf + 24 page catalog Feb. 1857, original blue cloth, slightly rubbed, embossed W. H. Smith stamp, contemporary signature of J. E. Jackson. Jarndyce Antiquarian Booksellers CXCI - 494 2011 £35

Smith, Alexander McCall *La's Orchestra Saves the World.* Edinburgh: Polygon, 2008, First British edition; fine in like dust jacket, signed by author. Bella Luna Books May 29 2011 - t9031 2011 $82

Smith, Ali *The Accidental.* London: Hamish Hamilton, 2005, First British edition; fine, in fine dust jacket. Bella Luna Books May 29 2011 - t7635 2011 $82

Smith, Ali *It Don't Mean a Thing.* London: Birkbeck University, 2004, First edition; signed by author, fine in stapled wrappers. Ken Lopez Bookseller 154 - 208 2011 $125

Smith, Ali *Like.* London: Virago, 1997, British first edition; fine in fine dust jacket, signed by author. Bella Luna Books May 29 2011 - t7678 2011 $137

Smith, C. Fox *Thames Side Yesterdays.* Leigh-on-Sea: F. Lewis, 1945, First edition; large 8vo., original red cloth, gilt, pages 45, 10 plates in yellow and black, text vignettes. R. F. G. Hollett & Son Antiquarian Booksellers General Catalogue Summer 2010 - 1585 2011 £30

Smith, Charles *The Ancient & Present State of the County & City of Waterford.* 1746, First edition; folding views, (386) pages, shaky, needs rebinding. C. P. Hyland May 26 2011 - 260/277 2011 $435

Smith, Clark Ashton *The Dark Chateau and Other Poems.* Sauk City: Arkham House, 1951, First edition; octavo, cloth. L. W. Currey, Inc. 124 - 25 2011 $2500

Smith, Clark Ashton *Genius Loci and Other Tales.* Sauk City: Arkham House, 1948, First edition; octavo, cloth. L. W. Currey, Inc. 124 - 62 2011 $1500

Smith, Clark Ashton *Genius Loci and Other Tales.* Sauk City: Arkham House, 1948, First edition; octavo, cloth. L. W. Currey, Inc. 124 - 167 2011 $350

Smith, Clark Ashton *Other Dimensions.* Sauk City: Arkham House, 1970, First edition; octavo, cloth. L. W. Currey, Inc. 124 - 217 2011 $150

Smith, Clark Ashton *Selected Poems.* Sauk City: Arkham House, 1971, First edition; octavo, cloth. L. W. Currey, Inc. 124 - 218 2011 $150

Smith, Clark Ashton *Tales of Science and Sorcery.* Sauk City: Arkham House, 1964, First edition; octavo, cloth. L. W. Currey, Inc. 124 - 206 2011 $200

Smith, Dodie *Call It a Day.* London: Victor Gollancz, 1936, First edition; 8vo., 151 pages, very good in slightly tanned and slightly marked decent and very good dust jacket, signed presentation form author to Ann Wilton. Any Amount of Books May 29 2011 - A71753 2011 $408

Smith, Dodie *Dear Octopus.* London: Heinemann, 1938, 8vo., original publisher's red cloth lettered gilt on spine, pages (viii), 124, frontispiece and 7 plates, signed presentation from author for Emmie Allen, near fine in slightly soiled and very slightly creased about very good dust jacket slightly chipped at head of spine, fore-edges slightly foxed. Any Amount of Books May 26 2011 - A68501 2011 $604

Smith, Dodie *Dear Octopus.* London: Heinemann, 1938, First edition; 8vo., pages (xi) 124, frontispiece and 7 plates, signed presentation from author to actress Angela Baddeley who played Grace Fenning in the play, very slight shelf wear, very good+. Any Amount of Books May 26 2011 - A69112 2011 $545

Smith, Dodie *The Hundred and One Dalmations.* London: Heinemann, 1956, First edition; 8vo., pages (viii), 391, illustrations, signed presentation from author for C. Henry Warren, with shipboard photo of author with husband Alec Beesley on RMS Queen Mary + Christmas card signed by Smith loosely inserted, very slight edgewear, faint mottled patch at rear lower corner, very slight foxing to prelims, otherwise very good+ in near very good dust jacket, price clipped and slightly darkened at edges, short closed tear at top of spine with slight loss and some foxing. Any Amount of Books May 26 2011 - A70716 2011 $2013

Smith, Dodie *I Capture the Castle.* Boston: Little Brown, 1948, First edition; 8vo., 343 pages, illustrations by Ruth Steed, signed presentation from author to friend C. Henry Warren, full dark blue morocco titles and decoration to spine gilt, rule to boards gilt, marbled endpapers, 5 raised bands at spine, excellent condition. Any Amount of Books May 26 2011 - A71762 2011 $1761

Smith, E. Boyd *Chicken World.* New York: G. P. Putnam, 1910, First edition; oblong 4to., cloth backed pictorial boards, tips rubbed, else near fine, scarce, printed on every heavy coated stock, color illustrations. Aleph-Bet Books, Inc. 95 - 537 2011 $475

Smith, Edward Elmer *Second Stage Lensmen.* Reading: Fantasy Press, 1953, First edition; octavo, cloth. L. W. Currey, Inc. 124 - 147 2011 $450

Smith, Edward Elmer *Triplanetary: a Tale of Cosmic Adventure.* Reading: Fantasy Press, 1948, First edition; octavo, cloth. L. W. Currey, Inc. 124 - 148 2011 $450

Smith, Edwin *The Ila-Speaking Peoples of Northern Rhodesia.* London: Macmillan, 1920, First edition; 2 volumes, 8vo., pages xxviii, 423; xvl, 433, folding map, illustrations, original green cloth, spines faded, small wear to heads and tails, fading to fore-edges. J. & S. L. Bonham Antiquarian Booksellers Africa 4/20/2011 - 7171 2011 £75

Smith, Edwin *The Mabilles of Basutoland.* London: Hodder & Stoughton, 1939, First edition; 8vo., 382 pages, maps on endpapers, illustrations, original light green cloth, some light foxing to fore edges. J. & S. L. Bonham Antiquarian Booksellers Africa 4/20/2011 - 4482 2011 £38

Smith, Elias *A Discourse Delivered at Jefferson Hall.... November 15 1802 the Subject Nebuchadnezzar's Dream.* Portsmouth: printed by N. S. & W. Peirce, 1803, First edition; 8vo., 40 pages, removed, foxed. M & S Rare Books, Inc. 90 - 400 2011 $150

Smith, Elias *An Essay on the Fall of Angels and Men with Remarks on Dr. Edward's Notion of the Freedom of the Will and the System of University.* Boston: True & Rowe, 1812, Third edition; 35 pages, 12mo., sewn and uncut, slight fraying, some soiling and few tears in early leaves, text intact. M & S Rare Books, Inc. 90 - 124 2011 $175

Smith, Ernest Bramah *The Wallet of Kai Lung.* Boston: L. C. Page and Co., 1900, First US edition; octavo, original pictorial green cloth, front panel stamped in black, yellow and gray, spine stamped in black. L. W. Currey, Inc. 124 - 229 2011 $100

Smith, F. D. *Parsons and Weavers.* Skeffington, 1897, First edition; original blue cloth gilt, pages (vi), 120, uncut, flyleaves and final pages rather browned, scarce. R. F. G. Hollett & Son Antiquarian Booksellers 175 - 1239 2011 £45

Smith, F. R. *Bookbinding.* London: Sir Isaac Pitman, 1957, First edition; small 8vo., original boards, dust jacket, extremities little chipped, pages xiv, 113, 16, 32 plates,. R. F. G. Hollett & Son Antiquarian Booksellers General Catalogue Summer 2010 - 327 2011 £35

Smith, Frank *A History of English Elementary Education 1760-1902.* University of London Press, 1931, First edition; tall 8vo., original red cloth, gilt, spine rather faded, pages viii, 360. R. F. G. Hollett & Son Antiquarian Booksellers 175 - 1243 2011 £30

Smith, Frank *The Life and Work of Sir James Kay-Shuttleworth.* London: John Murray, 1923, First edition; original blue cloth gilt, faint ring mark to upper board, pages xiii, 365, (iv), with 4 plates, prelims and fore-edge foxed, presentation copy from a later Lord Shuttleworth, inscribed "To Elsie Coope from Shuttleworth (in very shaky hand) Nov. 1938", later unrelated inscription and date on endpapers, scarce. R. F. G. Hollett & Son Antiquarian Booksellers 175 - 1244 2011 £75

Smith, Frank Meriweather *San Francisco Vigilance Committee of '56 with some Interesting Sketches of Events Succeeding 1846.* San Francisco: Barry, Baird, 1883, First edition; 83 pages, original printed wrappers, head and foot of spine show light wear or chipping, slight scratch to lower fore-edge of text block, small bookseller's label on front cover, very good, internally fine. Argonaut Book Shop Recent Acquisitions Summer 2010 - 223 2011 $250

Smith, Frank Meriweather *San Francisco Vigilance Committee of '56...* San Francisco: Barry, Baird, 1883, First edition; new full cloth, leather spine label, very fine. Argonaut Book Shop Recent Acquisitions Summer 2010 - 224 2011 $350

Smith, G. E. Kidder *Switzerland and Builds. Its Native and Modern Architecture.* London: Architectural Press, 1950, First edition; 4to., original cloth, spine faded, pages 234, illustrations, partly in color. R. F. G. Hollett & Son Antiquarian Booksellers 177 - 814 2011 £30

Smith, George *A Collection of Fifty-Three Prints, consisting of etchings and engravings...* John Boydell, 1770, First and only edition; letterpress titlepage and 53 plates on 29ff. (some one to a page, mostly two to a page and one leaf with three plates), contemporary marbled boards, expertly rebacked with new calf spine, gilt label and vellum cornerpieces, some light foxing, mainly marginal and few corners little chipped, but very good, very scarce. Ken Spelman Rare Books 68 - 11 2011 £1800

Smith, George *The Conversion of India from Pantaenus to the Present time A.D. 193-1893.* New York: Fleming H. Revell Co., 1894, First edition; (vii)-xvi, (3), 258 pages, 2 folding plates, small 8vo., cloth, wear to spine at head and tail, some soiling on rear board and endpapers, tiny tears to lower margin of first few leaves, otherwise text clean, binding solid, overall about very good. Kaaterskill Books 12 - 176 2011 $100

Smith, George Washington *Description of the Eastern Penitentiary of Pennsylvania.* Philadelphia: C. G. Childs, 1829, First edition; 8vo., 8 pages, full page engraved view and full page plan, of the prison, removed, sheets nearly loose, browned and somewhat brittle, some marginal chips and tears, good only. M & S Rare Books, Inc. 90 - 322 2011 $175

Smith, H. Clifford *The Panelled Rooms. IV The Inlaid Room from Sizergh Castle.* London: HMS), 1915, Small 4to., original boards, trifle marked, pages 34, plus 15 plates. R. F. G. Hollett & Son Antiquarian Booksellers 173 - 1061 2011 £45

Smith, H. G. *Minerals and the Microscope.* Thomas Murby & Co., 1919, Second edition; pages xi, 116, (viii), tissue guarded color frontispiece and 12 plates, small 8vo., original green cloth, gilt. R. F. G. Hollett & Son Antiquarian Booksellers General Catalogue Summer 2010 - 1139 2011 £35

Smith, H. Shirley *The Worlds Great Bridges.* Phoenix House, 1964, Original cloth gilt, dust jacket, pages 9x), 250, with 48 plates and 28 drawings. R. F. G. Hollett & Son Antiquarian Booksellers 177 - 815 2011 £30

Smith, Helena Huntington *The War on Powder River. The History of an Insurrection.* New York: McGraw Hill, 1966, First edition; 320 pages, illustrations from photos, brown cloth, gilt, fine, lightly chipped pictorial dust jacket. Argonaut Book Shop Recent Acquisitions Summer 2010 - 184 2011 $75

Smith, Henry, Mrs. *The Female Disciple of the First Three Centuries of the Christian Era: Her Trials and Her Mission.* London: Longman, Brown, Green & Longmans, 1845, Small octavo, xii, 297 pages, original full black morocco, blind and gilt stamped, all edges gilt, raised bands, gilt spine, rubbed, very good, scarce, inscribed to Miss Margaret Fitzgerald. Jeff Weber Rare Books 163 - 210 2011 $65

Smith, Horace *Love & Mesmerism.* New York: 1846, First edition; 168 pages, very good in half leather and marbled boards, foxing. Bookworm & Silverfish 676 - 42 2011 $75

Smith, Horatio *Festivals, Games and Amusements, Ancient and Modern.* London: Henry Colburn and Richard Bentley, 1831, First edition; half green calf gilt with raised bands and spine label, pages viii, 382, all edges gilt, all edges and endpapers marbled, engraved frontispiece and 2 folding plates (rather foxed), scarce. R. F. G. Hollett & Son Antiquarian Booksellers 175 - 1247 2011 £140

Smith, J. Sutcliffe *The Music of the Yorkshire Dales.* Leeds: Richard Jackson, 1930, first edition; 248 pages, musical examples, signed by author, original pale green boards, scarce. R. F. G. Hollett & Son Antiquarian Booksellers General Catalogue Summer 2010 - 1586 2011 £35

Smith, J. Sutcliffe *A Musical Pilgrimage in Yorkshire.* Leeds: Richard Jackson, 1928, First edition; large 8vo., original blue cloth gilt, pages xix, 340, with 68 illustrations. R. F. G. Hollett & Son Antiquarian Booksellers 175 - 1248 2011 £65

Smith, James *A Pilgrimage to Egypt: an Account of a Visit to Lower Egypt.* Aberdeen: John Avery, 1897, First edition; 8vo., pages x, 341, 2 maps, illustrations, original green decorative cloth, all edges gilt, lacks back free endpaper, repairs to front free endpaper, upper hinge cracked. J. & S. L. Bonham Antiquarian Booksellers Africa 4/20/2011 - 7072 2011 £60

Smith, John 1580-1631 *The True Travels, Adventures and Observations of Captaine John Smith in Europe, Asia, Africke and America...* Richmond: Franklin Press, 1819, First American edition; 2 volumes, octavo, (xiv), 247; xi, (1), 282 pages, frontispiece, 3 large folding engraved plates, volume II with heraldic frontispiece, full contemporary tree calf, rebacked, very good. Jeff Weber Rare Books 163 - 211 2011 $1200

Smith, John 1752-1809 *A Hebrew Grammar.* Boston: David Carlisle for John West, 1803, First edition; 8vo., 56 pages, contemporary calf backed marbled boards, front hinge cracked, crisp copy, very scarce. M & S Rare Books, Inc. 90 - 202 2011 $375

Smith, John William *A Compendium of Mercantile Law.* Stevens and Sons etc., 1871, Eighth edition; large thick 8vo., full calf gilt, little worn and scratched, pages lviii, 700, cccxxvii. R. F. G. Hollett & Son Antiquarian Booksellers 175 - 1249 2011 £85

Smith, Kenneth M. *Mumps Measles and Mosaics.* London: Collins, 1954, First edition; original cloth, gilt, upper board lightly damped at one corner, dust jacket edges little frayed and chipped in places, spine and folds slightly darkened, pages 160, color frontispiece, 25 photos and 10 diagrams. R. F. G. Hollett & Son Antiquarian Booksellers General Catalogue Summer 2010 - 1051 2011 £450

Smith, Leslie N. S. *The Stained Glass in the Churches of the Anglican Diocese of Carlisle.* Cumberland and Westmorland Antiquarian and Archaeological Society, 1994, small 4to., original cloth, gilt, dust jacket, pages viii, 180, plus 34 colored plates on 16 pages, fine. R. F. G. Hollett & Son Antiquarian Booksellers 173 - 1062 2011 £50

Smith, Logan Pearsall 1865-1946 *Songs and Sonnets.* London: Elkin Mathews, 1909, First edition; small 8vo., uncut, pages 64, tipped in 4 page publisher's ads dated Dec. 1909, signed presentation from author for Mary Craik, very good, prelims and edges little browned, spine slightly rubbed. Any Amount of Books May 29 2011 - A68491 2011 $204

Smith, Matthew *Memoirs of Secret Service.* Printed for A. Baldwin near the Oxford Arms, 1699, First edition; endpapers foxed, few spots, pages 160, 24, 8vo., early sprinkled calf, rebacked, backstrip with five raised bands, green morocco lettering piece, touch rubbed at extremities with slight wear to one corner, bookplate of Henry Massingberd of Gunby, good. Blackwell Rare Books B166 - 97 2011 £695

Smith, P. G. L. *Notes on Building Construction Arranged to Meet the Requirements of the Syllabus of the Board of Education, South Kensington Part II.* London: Longmans, Green and Co., 1904, New edition; large 8vo., original plum cloth, gilt, spine and edges rather faded, extremities little worn, pages xviii, 422, with 496 illustrations. R. F. G. Hollett & Son Antiquarian Booksellers 177 - 816 2011 £35

Smith, Patti *The Night.* London: Aloes Books, 1976, First edition, #13 of 22 hand numbered copies with a Rimbaud piece signed by Smith bound in, colophon indicates that there were 25 copies signed by Smith and Tom Verlaine, but Verlaine signed none, handwritten limitation seems to indicate that there were 22 copies rather than the 25 stated or the 20 we've heard speculated; octavo, string-tied red printed wrappers, fine, rare. Between the Covers 169 - BTC347388 2011 $2500

Smith, Pauline *The Little Karoo.* New York: Vanguard, 1952, 8vo., pages 188, black cloth stamped in red and gilt, poet Barbara Howes' bookplate, edges and endpapers little spotted, else very good, tight copy. Second Life Books Inc. 174 - 290 2011 $75

Smith, Roger K. *Patented Transitional & Metallic Planes in America 127-1927.* Lancaster: 1981, First edition; 336 pages, largre 4to., fine in fine dust jacket, signed and inscribed by author. Bookworm & Silverfish 671 - 183 2011 $250

Smith, S. D. *"An Exact and Industrious Tradesman". The Letter Book of Joseph Symson of Kendal 1711-1720.* Oxford University Press for the British Academy, 2002, Large 8vo., original cloth, gilt, dust jacket, pages cxxxi,794, (ii), frontispiece, map and 8 plates. R. F. G. Hollett & Son Antiquarian Booksellers 173 - 1064 2011 £75

Smith, Samuel *The History of the Colony of Nova Caesaria or New Jersey...* Burlington: James Parker, 1765, First edition; x, 573, (1) pages, modern calf backed marbled paper covered boards, very skillfully executed in period style, noticeably foxed as usual, few blank corners torn away without loss, contemporary ownership signatures of Burlington County residents Saml. Black and Abner Wright. Joseph J. Felcone Inc. Fall Miscellany 2010 - 108 2011 $2000

Smith, Stevie *The Holiday.* London: Chapman & Hall, 1949, First edition; pages 202, (2), foolscap 8vo., original pale grey cloth, backstrip lettered in silver on pink ground, few small chips to dust jacket, very good. Blackwell Rare Books B166 - 232 2011 £100

Smith, Sydney *Ballot.* London: Longman, Orme, Brown, Green and Longmans, 1839, First edition; 8vo., 46 pages, preserved in modern wrappers with printed title label on upper cover, very good. John Drury Rare Books 153 - 139 2011 £100

Smith, Sydney *The Works.* London: Longman, 1840, Second edition; 3 volumes, frontispiece volume I, contemporary full calf, red and green labels, gilt, slightly rubbed, very good, attractive set. Jarndyce Antiquarian Booksellers CXCI - 495 2011 £125

Smith, Sydney *The Works.* London: Longman, Green etc., 1860, 2 volumes in 1, modern half levant morocco gilt, pages x, 368, 356, edges marbled. R. F. G. Hollett & Son Antiquarian Booksellers 175 - 1252 2011 £85

Smith, Thomas 1513-1577 *De Republica Anglorum Libri Tres.* Leiden: Ex Officina Elzeviriana Lugdunum Batavorum, 1641, Second issue; 24mo., 428, (12) pages, engraved title, index, later full blindstamped English calf, raised bands, gilt and blindstamped spine, maroon leather spine label by Lambert, Hull, hinges just starting, very good. Jeff Weber Rare Books 163 - 12 2011 $175

Smith, Thornley *South Africa Delineated; or Sketches, Historical and Descriptive...* London: John Mason, 1850, First edition; 8vo., pages xii, 216, with 6 plates, original black blindstamped cloth, spine worn with small loss to top and tail. J. & S. L. Bonham Antiquarian Booksellers Africa 4/20/2011 - 8330 2011 £125

Smith, W. H., Mrs. *The Children's Japan.* Tokyo: T. Hasegawa, 1911, (based on address); 8vo., full color pictorial crepe paper book with silk tied binding, some light staining throughout, 20 numbered pages.   Jo Ann Reisler, Ltd.   86 - 144   2011 $225

Smith, W. W. *Honor Roll of Cabell County West Virginia.* Chicago: 1920,   First edition; 434 pages, large 4to., flexicord cover, recased with enw paper label, frontispiece and titlepage in facsimile.   Bookworm & Silverfish   666 - 199   2011 $150

Smith, Watson *Kiva Mural Decorations at Awatovi and Kawaika-A: with a Survey of Other Wall paintings in Pueblo Southwest.* Cambridge: 1952, xxi, 363 pages plus plates, originally in wrappers, this nicely rebound in cloth, near fine.   Dumont Maps & Books of the West   111 - 78   2011 $175

Smith, William *A New & Compendious History, of the County of Warwick, from the Earliest Period to the Present Time...* Birmingham: W. Emans, 1830, Sole edition; engraved map as frontispiece, engraved titlepage (with vignette), 60 engraved plates on steel, pages (4), 379, 4, 4to., near contemporary half green morocco rebacked (with original spine laid on) to match, backstrip divided into six compartments by raised bands between gilt rules, gilt lettered direct in second compartment, remainder plain, gilt rules on turn-ins, morocco grain green cloth sides, marbled endpapers, bookplate of John Ireland Blackburne dated 1874, all edges gilt.   Blackwell Rare Books   B166 - 98   2011   £200

Smith, William *A Smaller Classical Dictionary of Biography, Mythology and Geography.* London: John Murray, 1866, Ninth edition; bound into earlier and slightly larger fine full vellum case, originally intended for a copy of Greogrius' De Dialectis, with spine label to that effect, both boards with foliate borders in gilt an ornate gilt stamped Dutch armorial on each board with text "Pallas Minerva sospitatrix urbium", pages 464, printed in double columns with text illustrations, blindstamp on half title, little spotting, slightly amateurish new endpapers.   R. F. G. Hollett & Son Antiquarian Booksellers   General Catalogue Summer 2010 - 464   2011   £65

Smith, William Cusack *Review of a Publication Entitled, The Speech of the Right Honourable John Foster, Speaker of the House of Commons of Ireland in a Letter Addressed to Him.* Dublin: printed and sold by Marchbank, 1799, First edition; 8vo., iv, 63, (1) pages, very good, recently in linen backed marbled boards lettered.   John Drury Rare Books   153 - 140   2011   £100

Smith, Zadie *White Teeth.* London: Hamish Hamilton, 2000, First British edition; true first edition, fine in fine dust jacket.   Bella Luna Books   May 29 2011 - t8738   2011 $110

Smithson, Peter *Course of the Exchange &c.* London: published, Tuesdays and Fridays by Peter Smithson broker and the sister of the late John Castaing, Tuesday Jan. 3, 1764-, Tuesday Dec. 31, 1765; Tall 8vo., with a total of 230 (of 207) issues, printed on rectos only, all leaves stabbed at head, presumably for office filing, many issues cropped at foot with varying loss to imprint, several leaves cropped at fore margin, sometimes affecting final letters, some old ink marks and annotations, usually on versos, four issues missing, one issue with about one third cut away, original calf backed marbled boards with remains of printed label on upper cover, binding very worn, upper joint broken, now securely preserved in specially made book-box suitably labelled, remarkable survival with late 19th century inkstamp of Chancellor & White stockbrokers, 7 Tokenhouse Yard, London, E.C., 1894, of exceptional rarity.   John Drury Rare Books   153 - 141   2011   £2000

Smollett, Tobias George   1721-1771 *The Adventures of Covent Fathom.* London: Navarre Society Ltd. circa, 1902, One of only 2000 copies; 180 x 113mm., 2 volumes, very fine burgundy morocco, handsomely gilt and onlaid by the Harcourt Bindery of Boston (stamp-signed), boards with triple fillet border, each cover with elaborate heraldic frame of gilt and onlaid green morocco, around an empty oval, raised bands, very pretty gilt spine compartments featuring looping tendril frame enclosing a charming flower centerpiece, densely gilt turn-ins marbled endpapers, top edge gilt, two frontispieces by George Cruikshank; very fine, bindings especially bright and text with virtually no signs of use.   Phillip J. Pirages   59 - 322   2011 $400

Smollett, Tobias George   1721-1771 *The Adventures of Ferdinand Count Fathom.* London: W. Johnston, 1753, First edition; 12mo., pages (ii), viii, 262; (ii), 315, contemporary calf, red spine labels with blanks fore and aft, housed in half morocco clamshell box (rubbed), some minor rubbing, browning and soiling, very good.   Second Life Books Inc.   174 - 291   2011 $1100

Smollett, Tobias George   1721-1771 *The Adventures of Peregrine Pickle.* London: The Navarre Society Ltd. circa, 1902, One of 2000 copies; 180 x 113mm., 4 volumes, very fine burgundy morocco, handsomely gilt and onlaid by the Harcourt Bindery of Boston (stamp signed), boards with triple fillet border, each cover with elaborate heraldic frame of gilt and onlaid green morocco around an empty oval, raised bands, very pretty gilt spine compartments featuring looping tendril frame enclosing a charming flower centerpiece, densely gilt turn-ins, marbled endpapers, top edges gilt, 4 frontispiece drawings by George Cruikshank, very fine, bindings especially bright and text virtually with no signs of use.   Phillip J. Pirages   59 - 323   2011 $600

Smollett, Tobias George 1721-1771 *The Adventures of Roderick Random.* London: Navarre Society Ltd. circa, 1902, One of 2000 copies; 3 volumes, 180 x 113mm., very fine burgundy morocco, handsomely gilt and onlaid by Harcourt Bindery of Boston (stamp signed), boards with triple fillet border, each cover with elaborate heraldic frame of gilt and onlaid green morocco around an empty oval, raised bands, very pretty gilt spine compartments featuring looping tendril fame enclosing charming flower centerpiece, densely gilt turn-ins, marbled endpapers, top edge gilt, 3 frontispiece drawings by George Cruikshank, very fine, bindings especially bright and text with virtually no signs of use. Phillip J. Pirages 59 - 324 2011 $550

Smollett, Tobias George 1721-1771 *The Works of Tobias Smollett.* New York: Jenson Society, 1905, Limited to 1000 set; very good+ set (some shelfwear, little spotting, tight, clean texts). Lupack Rare Books May 26 2011 - ABE2942402607 2011 $200

Smyth, Alexander *An Explanation of the Apocalypse or Revelation of St. John.* Washington City: Way & Gideon, 1825, First edition; 12mo., 59 pages, uncut as issued, but stitching broken, browned. M & S Rare Books, Inc. 90 - 6 2011 $225

Smyth, Henry De Wolf *A General Account of the Development of Methods of Using Atomic Energy for Military Purposes Under the Auspices of the United States Government 1940-1945.* United States Army publication authorized as of August, 1945, Pre-publication copy; 263 x 197mm., pages 198, single sheets of litho printed typescript, diagrams in text, original cream wrappers, stapled, signature of E. L. Brady, fine. Simon Finch Rare Books Zero - 145 2011 £2500

Smyth, Henry De Wolf *A General Account of the Development of Methods of Using Atomic Energy for Military Purposes Under the Auspices of the United States Government 1940-1945.* Washington: Adjutant General's Office August, 1945, Rare lithoprint version; 10 3/8 x 7 7/8 inches, (193) pages (97 leaves), diagrams, printed by lithoprint from stencils made by multiple typewriters, stapled in cream textured stiff paper covers, pristine signed by author. Joseph J. Felcone Inc. Fall Miscellany 2010 - 109 2011 $4200

Smyth, Henry De Wolf *A General Account of the Development of Methods of Using Atomic Energy for Military Purposes Under the Auspices of the United States Government 1940-1945.* Washington: printed at the Pentagon, 1945, First edition; advance publisher copy for press use, cyclostyled pages, stapled, original cream wrappers, quarter morocco clamshell. Heritage Book Shop Booth A12 51st NY International Antiquarian Book Fair April 8-10 2011 - 125 2011 $3000

Smythies, Susan *Les Freres ou Histoire de Miss Osmond.* Amsterdam: Prault, 1766, First edition; 4 parts in 2 volumes, 12mo., (viii 176; 176; 187; 173 pages, contemporary full calf, gilt decorated spine, contrasting labels in red and green morocco, half titles present, fine, extremely rare. Paulette Rose Fine and Rare Books 32 - 159 2011 $650

Snape, Andrew *The Anatomy of an Horse.* M. Flesher for J. Hindmarsh at the Golden Ball, against the Royal Exchange i Cornhill, 1686, Third edition; engraved portrait, 49 copper engraved plates, dampstaining to nearly half the plates, 4to., pages (12), 237, (1), 45, (6), contemporary full calf, corners worn, ends of spine perished, professionally rebacked with leather, first 2 blank sheets loose, dampstaining to text in second half of book, heavier towards last one fourth, rear endpapers missing. Raymond M. Sutton, Jr. May 26 2011 - 55752 2011 $4000

Snape, Andrew *The Anatomy of an Horse, Containing an exact and Full Description of the Frame Situation and Connexion of all His Parts (with their Actions and Uses) Exprest in Forty Nine Copper-Plates.* M. Flesher for J. Hindmarsh at the Golden Ball against the Royal Exchange in Cornhill, 1686, Third edition; very good, engraved portrait, 49 copper engraved plates, folio, pages (12) 237 (1) 45, (6), 19th century three quarter morocco over marbled boards, some wear and abrasions to spine, old notations to title dated 1702, 2 brown stains to a leaf of text, pages 235-237 appear to have been supplied from another copy, scattered light marginal soiling. Raymond M. Sutton, Jr. May 26 2011 - 55751 2011 $6000

Snead, Sam *The Game I Love.* New York: Ballantine Books, 1997, First edition; signed by author, fine in fine dust jacket, small 8vo., xvi, 223 pages. By the Book, L. C. 26 - 82 2011 $125

Snell, Willebrord *Tiphys Batavus sive Histriodromice de Navium Cursibus et re Navali.* Leiden: Officinana Elzeviriana, 1624, 4to., (56), 109, (3), 62, (2) pages, last leaf with errata, 2 engraved plates, woodcut diagrams, contemporary turkey morocco, gilt and blind fillet borders, spine gilt in compartments, blue edges, binding rubbed, spine crackling and chipped at head, on front endpapers are 3 pages of manuscript followed by page of tables, the copy of Christophorus Plass, Leiden 1671 who gave it to Benjamin de Munchausen, the Hague 1675, from the library of the Earls of Macclesfield at Shirburn Castle. Maggs Bros. Ltd. 1440 - 200 2011 £950

Snelling, John *Fifty Years of Rhodesian Verse.* Oxford: B. H. Blackwell, 1939, second edition; 8vo., pages 128, frontispiece, illustrations, original blue cloth, spine little faded. J. & S. L. Bonham Antiquarian Booksellers Africa 4/20/2011 - 4784 2011 £40

Snicket, Lemony, Pseud. *A Series of Unfortunate Events.* Egmont, 2001-2006, First UK edition; 13 volumes, small 8vo., original pictorial matt glazed boards, illustrations by Brett Helquist, 3 volumes have child's name on printed ex-libris on flyleaf, else fine, unmarked, complete set. R. F. G. Hollett & Sons Antiquarian Booksellers 170 - 640 2011 £250

Snodgrass, W. D. *These Trees Stand.* New York: Carol Joye, 1981, One of two artist's proofs signed by poet ad photographer (of a total of 12 copies, 10 of them for sale); 238 x 285mm., 15 French-fold leaves, memorable original pictorial maroon morocco with molded onlays and gilt highlights by Carol Joyce binding featuring a molded cream colored onlaid calf tree its trunk occupying almost all of the flat spine, its bare limbs spread across both covers with wrinkling gilt stars visible between its branches, trunk dividing in two at head of spine with author's name in gilt appearing in fork, original matching burgundy cloth clamshell box with morocco spine label, with 12 black and white photos of poet by Robert Mahon, virtually mint. Phillip J. Pirages 59 - 140 2011 $6000

The Snow-Storm; or an Account of the Nature, Properties, Dangers and Uses of Snow in Various Parts of the World. London: SPCK, 1852, 8vo., 116 pages, frontispiece, plate, text illustrations, very good in original blindstamped and gilt lettered cloth, spine little faded, some foxing. Ken Spelman Rare Books 68 - 158 2011 £60

Snow White. London: Bancroft, 1960, Oblong 4to., cloth backed pictorial card covers, fine, 8 fabulous and detailed pop-up scenes one of which has moveable tab part and with moveable cover, all by Kubasta. Aleph-Bet Books, Inc. 95 - 452 2011 $200

Snow, Jack *The Shaggy Man of Oz.* Chicago: Reilly & Lee Co., 1949, First edition; 4to., grey cloth with greenish cast, color paste label and spine with publisher's name in semi script letters, pictorial endpapers, full color dust jacket with light marginal wear, overall nice, slight bump to one corner. Jo Ann Reisler, Ltd. 86 - 19 2011 $600

Snowden, Richard *The Columbiad; or a Poem on the American War in thirteen Cantos.* Philadelphia: Jacob Johnson & Co., 1795, First edition; many lower edges uncut, though two such leaves stained in lower margin, few spots, pages iv, 46, 8vo., bound with blank leaves at end, modern boards, top edge gilt, good. Blackwell Rare Books B166 - 99 2011 £950

Snoy, Raynerius *Psalterium Paraphrasibus Illustratum...* Lovanii: typis G. Stryckwant, 1704, Small 6vo., (xii), 52, (6) pages, 3 small woodcut devices as chapter headings, original full speckled calf, gilt spine, modern title label, minor wear to extremities, bookplates, fine. Jeff Weber Rare Books 163 - 29 2011 $200

Snyder, Gary *Mountains and Rivers without End.* Washington: Counterpoint, 1996, First edition; limited to 150 copies, fine, signed by author, slipcase. Bella Luna Books May 26 2011 - p2647 2011 $192

Snyder, Gary *Three on Community.* Boise: Limberlost Press, 1996, Limited to 100 signed and numbered copies; signed by all 3 authors, fine, issued in handmade foldover Japanese style box of green cloth, beautiful hand stitched production. Bella Luna Books May 26 2011 - t7765 2011 $825

Society for Medieval Archaeology *Journal of the Society for Medieval Archaeology.* London: Society for Medieval Archaeology, 1957-1978, First edition; large 8vo., each issue about 200 to 300 pages with photos and illustrations, volume I-XXII 1957-1978 + Index of volumes I-V, VI-X, XI-XV, XVI-XX, together 20 volumes, wrappers, numerous text figures and plates, lacks volume II, Volume II page 215 torn, volume XVI slightly waterstained. Any Amount of Books May 29 2011 - A49994 2011 $374

Society for the Diffusion of Useful Knowledge *Penny Magazine of the Society for the Diffusion of Useful Knowledge Volume 3.* London: Charles Knight, 1834, Volume 3, 4to., contemporary half calf gilt with marbled boards, little rubbed, pages (iii), 511, (i), with 231 woodcut illustrations, very good copy. R. F. G. Hollett & Son Antiquarian Booksellers 175 - 1254 2011 £95

Society of Antiquaries of London *The Journal of the Society of Antiquaries of London.* Oxford University, 1976-1990, Volumes LVI Part 2 to LXX part 2, plus general indices for volumes XLI-L and volumes LI-LX; original wrappers, 4to., plates and diagrams, fine run. R. F. G. Hollett & Son Antiquarian Booksellers 177 - 818 2011 £150

Society of Antiquaries of Scotland *Proceedings.* Edinburgh: printed for the Society, 1951-2003, Volume 83 (seventh series volume II) to volume 133, together 57 volumes, large 8vo., original cloth, gilt or cloth backed boards gilt, well illustrated, one or two of the earlier spines trifle marked, few volumes with slightly dusty top edges, excellent clean and sound run. R. F. G. Hollett & Son Antiquarian Booksellers 177 - 819 2011 £650

Society of California Pioneers *Quarterly of The Society of California Pioneers.* San Francisco: 1924-1933, and 1941-1947. First editions; complete run of the first 10 years, Volume I no. 1 to Volume 10, plus annuals for 1941 to 1947, together 44 issues, illustrations, portraits, maps, original light blue wrappers printed in black, spines faded, minor spotting to few volumes, fine set. Argonaut Book Shop Recent Acquisitions Summer 2010 - 186 2011 $750

Society of the Fifth Division *The Official History of the Fifth Division USA.* Washington: 1919, 423 pages, 4to., 11 folding map, very good, modest cover soil suede and khaki cloth.   Bookworm & Silverfish   671 - 208   2011 $75

Society of the Plastics Industry, Composites Institute *Composites Institute's 51st Annual Conference & Expo.* New York: 1996, c. 600 pages, 4to., wrappers, modest ex-library, near fine copy.   Bookworm & Silverfish   667 - 36   2011 $75

Soifer, M. *Arabian Nights (Golden Tales From).* New York: Simon & Schuster, 1957, First edition; folio, pictorial boards, fine, full page and smaller color lithographs by Gustaf Tenggren, inscribed and dated by Tenggren.   Aleph-Bet Books, Inc.   95 - 546   2011 $1200

Solly, N. N. *Memoir of the Life of David Cox.* London: Chapman & Hall, 1875, xii, 339 (i) pages, vignette titlepage and 21 plates, very good, original gilt decorated plum cloth, titlepage, large 8vo., some occasional foxing.   Ken Spelman Rare Books   68 - 79   2011   £85

Solomon, Alan *New York: the New Art Scene.* New York: Holt Rinehart & Winston, 1967, First edition; photos by Ugo Mulas, very near fine with small bookplate, close to near fine dust jacket with some very minor edge wear and few small tears.   Jeff Hirsch Books   ny 2010 2011 $2750

Some Account of the conduct of the Religious Society of Friends Towards the Indian Tribes in the Settlement of the Colonies of East and West Jersey and Pennsylvania... London: Edward Marsh, 1844, First edition; color map as frontispiece, large folding color map, (iv), x, (11)-247, (1) pages, original blindstamped cloth, nice.   Anthony W. Laywood   May 26 2011 - 19085   2011 $419

Some British Ballads. London: Constable & Co. Ltd., 1919, First printing of this edition, one of 575 copies signed by artit, this #379; 8, (2), 170 pages, 285 x 225mm., very attractive red three quarter morocco (stamp signed "Putnams"), raised bands, spine handsomely gilt in compartments formed by plain and decorative rules, quatrefoil centerpiece surrounded by densely scrolling cornerpieces, sides and endleaves of rose colored linen, top edge gilt, with titlepage vignette, black and white illustrations in text, 17 color plates by Arthur Rackham, as called for, all tipped on with letterpress guards, bookplate of W. A. M. Burden; only most trivial signs of use externally, exceptionally fine inside and out, in exceptionally fine copy inside and out.   Phillip J. Pirages   59 - 295   2011 $1800

Some Imagist Poets, 1916: An Annual Anthology. Boston and New York: Houghton Mifflin Co., Riverside Press, Cambridge, 1916, 8vo., pages (k), (i) ads, xvi, 96, (i) blank, (1), imprint, uncut, lower and fore-edge, crease to upper fore-edge, otherwise very crisp and clean, original leaf green paper wrappers, spine lettered in black, upper wrapper printed in black with decoration, shelfwear and discoloring, some small cracks and rubbing to spine, from the library of John Martin, publisher of Black Sparrow Press with his small book ticket.   Simon Finch Rare Books   Zero - 330   2011   £150

Somervell, Arthur *Singing Time.* Elkin & C., n.d. circa, 1900, 4to., original cloth baked pictorial boards, unpaginated, black and white illustrations, joints cracking, little loose.   R. F. G. Hollett & Sons Antiquarian Booksellers   170 - 110   2011   £45

Somervell, John *Some Westmorland Wills 1686-1738.* Kendal: Titus Wilson, 1928, First edition; pages 119, uncut, 9 plates, slight stain to gutter of flyleaf, bookplates of George Charles Williamson and Helen Mary Garnett.   R. F. G. Hollett & Son Antiquarian Booksellers   173 - 1068 2011   £60

Somervell, John *Water Power Mills of South Westmorland on the Kent, Bela and Gilpin and Their Tributaries.* Kendal: Titus Wilson, 1930, First edition; original cloth, gilt, pages xiv, 138, with 4 plates, very scarce.   R. F. G. Hollett & Son Antiquarian Booksellers   173 - 1069   2011   £175

Somerville, Boyle T. *Ocean Passages for the World.* Somerset: 1973, Third edition; folio, near fine in very good slipcase, folding map data laid in.   Bookworm & Silverfish   678 - 147   2011 $125

Somner, William *The Antiquities of Canterbury.* London: by I. L(egat) for Richard Thrale, 1640, First edition; 4to., (16), 516, (12) pages, full page woodcut cut of arms of William Laud, Archbishop of Canterbury on verso of title, folding engraved plan of Canterbury, folding engraved plan of the High altar and surrounding chapels in the cathedral, folding engraved plate, contemporary sprinkled calf, covers panelled in gilt and with gilt lozenge in centre, smooth spine divided into 11 panels by gilt rules (headcap broken, front flyleaf loose, occasional light browning/spotting, outer margin of page 411/2 and 425/8 spotted by damp, light purple, otherwise good, presentation copy inscribed in ink to unidentified recipient, from the library of the Earls of Macclesfield at Shirburn Castle.   Maggs Bros. Ltd.   1440 - 201 2011   £950

Somner, William *A Treatise of Gavelkind Both Name and Thing.* London: printed by Rand W. Leybourne for the author and are to be sol by John Crooke an Daniel White, 1660, First edition; pages (xxii), 216, (viii), woodcut decorations, very good unpressed copy, small 4to., dust jacket blind ruled polished calf, nicely rebacked in matching calf gilt with raised bands, original spine label, relaid.   R. F. G. Hollett & Son Antiquarian Booksellers   175 - 1257 2011 £650

Songs for Gentlemen, Patriotic, Comic and Descriptive. New Haven: Sidney's Press, 1820, First edition; 24mo., 156, (4) pages, frontispiece, contemporary three quarter calf, plain boards, rubbed.   M & S Rare Books, Inc.   90 - 314 2011 $150

Sonnini De Manoncourt, Charles Nicolas Sigisbert *Voyage Dans la Haute et Basse Egypte...* Paris: F. Buisson An VII, 1788-1799, First edition; 8vo. and 4to., pages 94, vii, (1), 425, (3); (4), 417; (4), 424; engraved portrait, 2 folding tables, 39 engraved plates with tissue guards (half inch marginal tear to folding plate, some marginal tanning and foxing to plain plates, colored plates clean and fresh), folding map with 1 1/2 inch and shorter tear, marginal tanning near 2 edges, light chipping to margin, contemporary calf backed boards, edges of text volumes rubbed, edges of atlas worn, boards of atlas rubbed, few corners bumped, calf near 3 ends of spines perished, upper end of spine chipped, light cracking to calf on spines, front edge of spine split but hinge solid, few shorter splits to other edges of spines, dampstain to lower corner of rear cover and margin of few leaves, not affecting text, small marginal stain or dampspot to few pages in volume I, light marginal tanning to some pages, 2 inch tear to leaf and shorter tear to another, 2 page gatherings in volume 3 are bound out of border, with black leather labels (1 chipped) and floral gilt decorations (rubbed and with some loss of gilt) on spines, bookplates of Hermann Frankl, handstamp of George Vanderbilt Foundation.   Raymond M. Sutton, Jr.   May 26 2011 - 43952 2011 $2000

Sontag, Susan *Women.* New York: Random House, 1999, First edition; photographs by Annie Leibovitz, fine in very near fine dust jacket with some minute wear, signed and inscribed by Leibovitz to another photographer and additionally signed by Sontag, genuinely uncommon signed by both.   Jeff Hirsch Books   ny 2010 2011 $450

Sophocles (Greek) *Sophoclis Tragoediae Septem.* Paris: Simon de Colines 16 December, 1528, 8vo., ff. (200), last leaf blank, device on titlepage, late 17th century sprinkled calf, gilt spine, few (cropped), marginal notes on first 2 leaves of Ajax, from the library of the Earls of Macclesfield at Shirburn Castle.   Maggs Bros. Ltd.   1440 - 202 2011 £850

Sorenstam, Annika *Golf Annika's Way.* New York: Gotham, 2004, First edition; 8vo., 271 pages, fine in near fine dust jacket with minimal edgewear.   By the Book, L. C. 26 - 83 2011 $225

Sorrento, Jerome Merolla Da *A Voyage to Congo and Several Other Countries, Chiefly in Southern-Africk.* London: Churchill, 1704, First UK edition; folio, pages 655-756, recent brown speckled quarter calf.   J. & S. L. Bonham Antiquarian Booksellers   Africa 4/20/2011 - 9063 2011 £180

Soth, Alec *Niagara.* Gottingen: Steidl, 2006, First edition; signed by Soth, 4to., 94 pages, full black embossed leatherette with paste-on cloth photo front cover, 39 full page full color photos.   By the Book, L. C.   26 - 47 2011 $190

Souder, Casper *The Mysteries and Miseries of Philadelphia as Exhibited and Illustrated by a Late Presentment of the Grand Jury, and by a Sketch of the Condition of the Most Degraded Classes in the City.* Philadelphia: 1853, First edition; 8vo, 20 pages, rebacked with paper.   M & S Rare Books, Inc.   90 - 324 2011 $450

Southern Exposure. Durham: 1978+, 23 issues, all 4to., wrappers, photos illustrations.   Bookworm & Silverfish 669 - 186 2011 $75

South Carolina. General Assembly *Reports & Resolutions of.... 1848. (with) Journal of the Senate 1848 (and) Journal of the House of Representatives... 1848.* Columbia: 1848, Approximately 800 pages, original binding, recent new backstrip, label.   Bookworm & Silverfish 664 - 184 2011 $60

South Indian Ocean Pilot: Islands Westward of Longitude 92° East Including Madagascar and the Comoro Islands. Washington: GPO, 1917, First edition; 8vo., pages xxxii, 578, large folding map, original brown cloth.   J. & S. L. Bonham Antiquarian Booksellers   Africa 4/20/2011 - 8988 2011 £65

South, R. *The Moths of the British Isles.* London: F. Warne & Co. Ltd., 1948, 2 volumes, small 8vo., original cloth, gilt, pages 360, 399, with 318 plates.   R. F. G. Hollett & Son Antiquarian Booksellers   General Catalogue Summer 2010 - 1052 2011   £40

South, Robert *Musica Incantans, Sive Poema Exprimens Musicae Vires, Juvenem in Ansaniam Adigentiis, et Musici Inde Periculum.* Oxford: printed by W. H. for G. West, 1667, Second edition; small 4to., old boards, little rubbed, pages 20 with typographical decoration and initial, rare.   R. F. G. Hollett & Son Antiquarian Booksellers   175 - 1259 2011   £250

Southam, A. D. *From Manuscript to Bookstall.* Southam and Co., n.d., original blue cloth gilt over bevelled boards, lower board little scratched, small label on upper board, pages vi 107, (vi, ads), with frontispiece and blue stamp affixed to titlepage as required, scarce.   R. F. G. Hollett & Son Antiquarian Booksellers   175 - 1260   2011   £65

Southern Excursions.   N.P.: Fellowship of Southern Writers, 1997,   Limited edition, there were 150 copies outside the numbered sequence, this being number VII as handwritten on colophon and signed by all contributors; scarce.   Ken Lopez Bookseller   154 - 6   2011 $200

Southern Nights: Epigraphs....   Chapel Hill: The Mud Puppy Press, 1988,   First edition, complete set of 8 limited edition chapbooks; complete set, printed color wrappers, with original printed paper wraparound band, of a total edition of 126, these are one of 26 lettered copies, each chapbook is lettered "E" and signed by its author, entire set quite scarce, fine.   Charles Agvent   2010 Summer Miscellany - 5   2011 $1000

Southern, Terry *Candy.* Paris: Olympia Press, 1958, 2 volume edition in orange wrappers and printed in black with inner text printed in blue, unknown variant edition, although it is indicated as being in the Traveler's Companion Series, it is in a smaller format and different color than that series, there is no record of there having been a two volume edition published by Olympia, very good set, spines faded and part 2 has diagonal cover crease, both volumes have been used as coasters, but only from the back, rings to rear covers, with slight bleed through to final page of text on final volume, completely legible, in all very good set.   Ken Lopez Bookseller   154 - 209   2011 $4500

Southey, Robert   1774-1843   *The Life of Nelson.* Bickers and Son, 1902,   12 woodburytype plates and one folding map, one illustration, pages xiv, (ii), 351, 8vo., contemporary green polished calf, prize binding of Southport Centre Cambridge Local Examinations (awarded to W. T. Waterhouse in 1907), spine gilt just slightly faded, red morocco lettering piece by B. Howell, Liverpool, near fine.   Blackwell Rare Books   B166 - 101   2011   £125

Southey, Robert   1774-1843   *Oliver Newman: a New England Tale (Unfinished) with Other Poetical Remains.* London: Longman, Brown etc., 1845,   First edition; modern full blind panelled calf gilt with raised bands and contrasting spine label, pages (xvi), 116, half title and dedication leaf to William and Mary Wordsworth, very nice, clean copy, scarce.   R. F. G. Hollett & Son Antiquarian Booksellers   General Catalogue Summer 2010 - 676   2011   £180

Southgate, Richard   *Sermons Preached to Parochial Congregations....*   London: F. and C. Rivington, 1799, Third edition; 2 volumes, old half calf gilt, double spine labels, xix, (viii), 395; (viii), 412, with engraved title (offset on to title), few spot to fore-edges.   R. F. G. Hollett & Son Antiquarian Booksellers   175 - 1262   2011   £65

Southwart, Elizabeth   *Bronte Moors & Villages from Thornton to Haworth.*   London: John Lane, The Bodley Head, 1923,   Limited edition (no. 39 of 75 copies);   Square 8vo., original cream cloth gilt, spine lettering little faded, pages x, 190, top edge gilt, other edges untrimmed, original etching of Wuthering Heights by Thomas Mackenzie, signed in pencil as frontispiece and 36 color or tinted plates, also by MacKenzie, tissue to frontispiece torn and repaired, gift inscription (non-authorial, but very nice, extremely scarce.   R. F. G. Hollett & Son Antiquarian Booksellers   General Catalogue Summer 2010 - 1587   2011   £180

Southwold, Stephen   *The Children's Play-Hour Book.* London: Longman Green and Co., 1929,   Small 4to., original pictorial boards, spine trifle faded and rubbed at foot, pages 184, color plates, both tipped in and in text, other illustrations and pictorial endpapers, few spots and marks, very nice, bright copy.   R. F. G. Hollett & Son Antiquarian Booksellers   General Catalogue Summer 2010 - 570   2011   £30

Souvenir of Scotland. Its Cities, Lakes and Mountains. London: Edinburgh and New York: T. Nelson and Sons, 1889,   First edition;   half title, 120 chromolithograph views on 60 plates, each with tissue guard, original decorated cloth, spine slightly rubbed, all edges gilt, good.   Anthony W. Laywood   May 26 2011 - 19825   2011 $184

Souvenir and Guide to Ullswater. The Official Guide... Bemrose and Sons, 1903,   Second edition (24th thousand);   pages 136, 5 folding colored maps and numerous plates, original stiff marbled wrappers, gilt with rounded corners.   R. F. G. Hollett & Son Antiquarian Booksellers   173 - 1141   2011   £45

Souvestre, Emile   *Brittany and La Vendee.*   Edinburgh: Thomas Constable & Co., 1855,   4 pages ads, initial and 2 pages final ads, text unopened, original beige cloth, very good.   Jarndyce Antiquarian Booksellers   CXCI - 581   2011   £45

Souza, Adelaide Marie Emilie   *Oeuvres Completes.* Paris: Alexis Eymery, 1821-1822,   First collected edition; 6 volumes, 8vo., contemporary half tan calf, richly gilt decorated and gilt lettered spines, all edges speckled with red, 12 engraved plates, most attractive, scarce set.   Paulette Rose Fine and Rare Books   32 - 162   2011 $1000

Sowell, A. J.   *History of Fort Bend County, Containing Sketches of Many Noted Characters.*   Houston: W. H. Coyle & Co., 1904,   First edition; thick 8vo., red cloth, black printing on front cover and spine, xii, 373 pages, former owner has put his comments in pencil on front flyleaf of this book regarding what will happen if you borrow the book and don't return it, front and rear spine has been internally reinforced with matching archival tape, old water stains to few endpages, covers stained and soiled, however entire text block is very good and tight, very serviceable copy.   Buckingham Books   May 26 2011 - 31046   2011 $1875

Sowerby, A. De C. *The Naturalist in Manchuria.* Tientsin: Tientsin Press Ltd., 1922-1930, Large 8vo., 5 volumes in 3, 3 tipped in colored plates, 2 folding maps, 87 black and white plates, several line drawings and folding chart, original decorated green cloth, wear to cloth, soiled, some tears to cloth on 4 edges of spines, short tears to ends of spine to 2nd volume, a label on lower spines removed, leaving stains, occasional light foxing, some soiling to endpapers, few institutional handstamps to prelim pages, few pencil notations to a chapter, pages tanned.   Raymond M. Sutton, Jr.   May 26 2011 - 12349   2011 $2000

Sowerby, Gita A. *The Bright Book.* London: Henry Frowde, Hodder & Stoughton, n.d, 1915, First edition; pages (48), 12 full page color plates by Millicent Sowerby, scarce, original embossed pictorial boards, little marked, spine slightly worn.   R. F. G. Hollett & Sons Antiquarian Booksellers   170 - 645   2011   £75

Sowerby, Gita A. *The Bumbletoes.* London: Chatto & Windus, 1907, First edition; original parchment backed boards, trifle worn and darkened, pages 62, with 12 color plates by Millicent Sowerby, front flyleaf removed, odd spot.   R. F. G. Hollett & Sons Antiquarian Booksellers   170 - 644   2011   £45

Sowerby, Gita A. *The Dainty Book.* London: Henry Frowde, Hodder & Stoughton, n.d., 1915, First edition; original embossed pictorial boards, little soiled and rubbed, pages (48), with 12 full page color plates by Millicent Sowerby, scarce.   R. F. G. Hollett & Sons Antiquarian Booksellers   170 - 646   2011   £75

Sowerby, Gita A. *The Pretty Book.* London: Henry Frowde, Hodder and Stoughton, n.d., 1915, First edition; original embossed pictorial boards, little marked in places, pages (48), 12 full page color plates, text by Millicent Sowerby, scarce.   R. F. G. Hollett & Sons Antiquarian Booksellers   170 - 648   2011   £95

Sowerby, R. R. *Historical Kirkby Stephen and North Westmorland.* Kendal: Titus Wilson, 1950, Second edition; original cloth, gilt, dust jacket, pages 116, 5 maps and 65 illustrations, scarce.   R. F. G. Hollett & Son Antiquarian Booksellers   173 - 1073   2011   £75

Spanheim, Ezechiel *Dissertationes de Praestantia et Usu Numismatum Antiquorum.* London: R. Smith, Amsterdam: Rodolph & Gerhard Wetstein, 1717, 2 volumes, folio, (36), 1 f. pl.), 656 (50) pages, (1 f. pl.); (6), xxviii, 726, (42), engraved frontispiece, engraved folding portrait of author, title printed in red and black, engraved illustrations in text, contemporary calf, spine gilt in compartments, binding extremely rubbed, from the library of the Earls of Macclesfield at Shirburn Castle.   Maggs Bros. Ltd.   1440 - 203   2011   £450

Spark, Muriel *The Bachelors.* Macmillan, 1960, First edition; pages (vi), 242, foolscap 8vo., original red cloth, backstrip gilt lettered, dust jacket with two short tears, very good, inscribed by author to Mrs. John Bennett.   Blackwell Rare Books   B166 - 233   2011   £300

Spark, Muriel *The Hothouse by the East River.* London: Macmillan, 1973, First edition; from the Rolland Comstock collection, with author's autograph on Comstock's bookplate, fine book and dust jacket.   Lupack Rare Books   May 26 2011 - ABE1314281545   2011 $125

Sparks, Nicholas *A Bend in the Road.* New York: Warner Books, 2001, First edition; fine in fine dust jacket, inscribed by author.   Bella Luna Books   May 29 2011 - t9547   2011 $82

Sparks, Nicholas *Nights in Rodanthe.* New York: Warner Books, 2002, First edition; fine in fine dust jacket, inscribed by author.   Bella Luna Books   May 29 2011 - t9548   2011 $137

Sparrman, Anders 1748-1820 *Voyage au Cap de Bonne-Esperance, et Autour du Monde avec le Capitaine Cook...* Paris: Buisson, 1787, First edition in French; 16 engraved plates and large folding engraved map, 4to., pages (3), xxi, (3), 478; (3), 462, contemporary sheep, worn, head of pine to volume 1 partially perished and frayed, occasional foxing, minimally affecting plates, several small worm holes to last 9 plates, gilt decorated spines.   Raymond M. Sutton, Jr.   May 26 2011 - 36103   2011 $1250

Sparrow, Anthony *A Rationale Upon the Book of Common Prayer of the Church of England...* London: printed for Robert Pawlet, 1672, 12mo., pages (viii), 353 (xxvii) 52 + engraved frontispiece, two engraved titles and 3 engraved portrait plates, contemporary speckled calf, boards double rule bordered in blind, board edges 'zig-zag' decorative roll gilt, all edges blue 'swirl' marbled, early 21st century re-sew and calf reback by Chris Weston, edges of frontispiece and first engraved title repaired, little spotting elsewhere, old leather a touch rubbed and chipped, contemporary ink inscription, from the collection of Christopher Ernest Weston 1947-2010.   Unsworths Booksellers   24 - 41   2011   £250

Sparrow, John *A Day with Myself.* Burford - Cygnet Press, 1979, One of 100 copies; pages (8) 16mo., original black wrappers, printed front cover label, fine, inscribed by John Sparrow for Bent J(uel) J(ensen).   Blackwell Rare Books   B166 - 247   2011   £50

Sparrow, Walter Shaw 1862-1940 *The English House.* Eveleigh Nash, 1908, First edition; original cloth, gilt, spine trifle rubbed and darkened, pages xiv, 348, top edge gilt, 66 illustrations, occasional spotting.   R. F. G. Hollett & Son Antiquarian Booksellers   177 - 822   2011   £50

Speakman, Colin *The Nut Brown Maid and Other Dales Stories.* Pudsey: Allenwood Books, 1986, First edition; 163 pages, illustrations by Geoffrey Cowton, original cloth, gilt, dust jacket.   R. F. G. Hollett & Son Antiquarian Booksellers   175 - 1264   2011   £30

Specimens of the Early English Poets. London: printed for Edwards, 1790, First edition; 190 x 127mm., 5 p.l., 323 pages, extremely pleasing etruscan style calf in the style of and quite probably by, Edwards of Halifax, covers with gilt metope and pentaglyph border, wide inner frame of stencilled palmettes, sprinkled central panel featuring at middle a stained obelisk tool draped with four slender fronds on either side, this centerpiece painted over in red, recently and beautifully rebacked by Courtland Benson to replicate original (flat) spine with all over gilt lattice design, black titling label, marbled endpapers, turn-ins and all edges gilt; with attractive fore-edge painting, very probably by Edwards, apparently showing Walton Hall near Wakefield; large paper copy, armorial bookplate of Thomas Walker, that bookplate as well as verso of endpaper inscribed in ink "Wm. Walker", former dated August 1848 and later "Wilsick, July 1848", titlepage with painted armorial laid down beneath imprint; minor pitting (as inevitable with acid treated calf), few leaves with small faint stains, otherwise fine, expertly restored binding with lustrous covers and bright gilt, text especially clean, fresh and bright with very spacious margins.   Phillip J. Pirages   59 - 39   2011 $1400

The Spectator. London: printed by H. Baldwin for Longman, Dodsley, et al, 1797, 264 x 165mm., 8 volumes, excellent contemporary light green straight grain morocco sides with gilt double fillet, raised bands decorated with stippled rule an flanked by plain rules, second and third panels of each spine gilt lettered, marbled endpapers, all edges gilt, in two modern fleece lined matching cloth slipcases; each of the 8 volumes with beautiful fore-edge painting; engraved vignette on each titlepage, large paper copy, ownership signature of Mary Erskine dated 1803 with inscription "This book was given her when she married by her cousin Lord Wodehouse"; spines somewhat darkened and gilt titling consequently dulled, leather slightly varied in color (due partly to refurbishing), soiled and marked, bindings nevertheless in remarkably good condition, entirely sound and with little wear to joints, each volume with isolated openings just bit foxed in (typically upper) margins (one volume with slightly more foxing), three or four leaves with frayed corner or minor tear in margin at foot, other trivial imperfections, still fine internally, almost entirely very clean, bright and fresh.   Phillip J. Pirages   59 - 42   2011 $11,000

Spedding, James *Publishers and Authors.* London: printed for the author, published by John Russell Smith, 1867, Original dark green cloth covered boards, slightly rubbed, very good.   Jarndyce Antiquarian Booksellers   CXCI - 457   2011   £60

Speedy, Thom *Sport in the Highlands and Lowlands of Scotland with Rod and Gun.* William Blackwood and Sons, 1886, Second edition; original pictorial green cloth gilt neatly recased, pages xx, 444, 32, 52 woodcut illustrations.   R. F. G. Hollett & Son Antiquarian Booksellers   General Catalogue Summer 2010 - 1283   2011   £120

Speer, Helen *Helen Speer Book of Children's White Pine Toys & Furniture.* New York: Helen Speer, 1915, Oblong 8vo., pictorial wrappers, 24 pages, fine, 4 full pages in color and others in line, scarce.   Aleph-Bet Books, Inc.   95 - 218   2011 $200

Speidel, Frederick G. *The York Rite of Freemasonry... a History & Handbook.* Chicago: 1989, First edition; 78, (1) colophon on wrappers, fine.   Bookworm & Silverfish   676 - 93   2011 $100

Speke, John Hanning *Journal of the Discovery of the Source of the Nile.* Edinburgh: William Blackwood, 1864, Second edition; 8vo., pages xxxi, 658, ads, folding map, plates, illustrations, contemporary brown morocco, spine and corners rubbed, internally clean and crisp.   J. & S. L. Bonham Antiquarian Booksellers   Africa 4/20/2011 - 9226   2011   £320

Speke, John Hanning *What Led to the Discovery of the Source of the Nile.* Edinburgh: William Blackwood, 1864, First edition; 8vo., pages x, 372, 3 maps, frontispiece, original brown cloth, slight rubbing to joints, very good, clean copy.   J. & S. L. Bonham Antiquarian Booksellers   Africa 4/20/2011 - 9209   2011   £1250

The Speleologist. Exeter: Speleologist, 1965-1968, Volumes I nos. 1-4 and volume 2 Nos. 6-14, 15 numbers, 4to. and large 8vo., original wrappers, illustrations.   R. F. G. Hollett & Son Antiquarian Booksellers   General Catalogue Summer 2010 - 1379   2011   £85

Spelman, Henry *Reliquiae Spelmannianade. The Posthumous Works of...* Oxford: printed at the Theater for Awnsham and John Churchill, 1698, First edition; engraved frontispiece and large titlepage vignette, 2 folding tables, title dusty, light browning elsewhere, final two leaves of text transposed, pages (xxxii), 214, (12), folio, later calf, boards with double gilt fillet border, neatly rebacked with spine with five raised bands between blind fillets, red morocco label in second compartment, old leather flaked, corners renewed, good.   Blackwell Rare Books   B166 - 102   2011   £300

Spence, Basil *Phoenix at Coventry.* London: Geoffrey Bles, 1962, First edition; large 8vo., original cloth, gilt, dust jacket, pages 141, 45 plates.   R. F. G. Hollett & Son Antiquarian Booksellers   177 - 823   2011   £30

Spence, Joseph   1699-1768   *Polymetis or an Enquiry Concerning the Agreement Between the Works of the Roman Poets and the Remains of the Ancient Artists.*   London: printed for R. and J. Dodsley, 1755,   Second edition; folio, pages vi, 361, (i) + engraved frontispiece and 41 other engraved plates, contemporary calf, spine fully gilt with 'sun-spot filled lattice' compartments, boards single rule gilt bordered with elaborate stencil design of interlocking 'eared' ovoids and quatrefoil corners, board edges decorative roll gilt, 'Dutch swirl' 'made' endpapers, all edges lemon, some minor spotting, frontispiece offset onto title, joints and corners skillfully repaired, old leather bit rubbed and scratched, contemporary engraved armorial bookplate lettered "southouse" pasted to verso of first plain flyleaf signed "Timbrell & Harding" later armorial bookplate of Strathallan, from the collection of Christopher Ernest Weston 1947-2010.   Unsworths Booksellers   24 - 142 2011   £675

Spence, Lewis   *Myth and Ritual in Dance, Game and Rhyme.*   London: Watts & Co., 1947,   Second impression; original cloth, gilt, dust jacket, pages 163, illustrations by Geoffrey Cowton.   R. F. G. Hollett & Son Antiquarian Booksellers   175 - 1265 2011   £30

Spencer, Herbert   *The Data of Ethics.*   London: 1884, Fourth thousand; original blindstamped cloth, gilt, little faded, head of spine frayed, pages x, 320, 16, library label on pastedown.   R. F. G. Hollett & Son Antiquarian Booksellers   175 - 1267 2011   £65

Spencer, J. L.   *The Royal Grammar School Lancaster.*   Edinburgh: Neill & Co., 1969,   First edition; original boards, gilt, dust jacket, spine faded, pages xii, 123, 11 plates, rather scarce.   R. F. G. Hollett & Son Antiquarian Booksellers   General Catalogue Summer 2010 - 1590   2011   £35

Spencer, Raine   *The Spencers on Spas.*   London: Weidenfeld and Nicolson, 1983,   First edition; 4to., original cloth, gilt, dust jacket, pages 160, illustrations in color and monochrome by John Spencer, two TLS's loosely inserted from Christina Foyle to Russell Harty asking him to be a Guest of Honour at a luncheon to celebrate publication of the book.   R. F. G. Hollett & Son Antiquarian Booksellers   177 - 824 2011   £30

Spender, Brender E.   *Important People.*   London: Country Life, 1931,   4to., original cloth backed boards, pages vi, 78, illustrations by J. H. Dowd.   R. F. G. Hollett & Son Antiquarian Booksellers   General Catalogue Summer 2010 - 758 2011   £30

Spender, Stephen   *Three Versions from the German.*   London: privately published, 1956,   First edition, no. 50 of 100 copies; inscribed by author for Winnie and Geraint Jones, also signed by author's wife Natasha Spender, 8vo., original gold paper wrappers, titles to pink label on upper wrapper in black, gold wrappers in very good order, but creased at lower front and rear corner.   Any Amount of Books   May 29 2011 - A46011 2011 $272

Spenser, Edmund   1552-1599   *The Faerie Queen. The Shepheards Calendar; With Other Works of England's Arch-Poet, Edm. spenser.*   London: printed for H. L. for Mathew Lownes, 1611,   First colleted edition, first issue; five parts in one volume, folio, woodcut illustrations and ornamental borders, contemporary full mottled calf, rebacked to style, boards double ruled in gilt with gilt lion and cannon device on front and back boards, spine stamped and lettered in gilt, red morocco spine label, lettered in gilt, some light browning to pages and few spots throughout, generally very clean, Mother Hubberd's Tale with some wear to edges, previous owner's bookplate, very good, overall.   Heritage Book Shop   Holiday 2010 - 115 2011 $7500

Spenser, Edmund   1552-1599   *The Faerie Queen: The Shepheards Calendar; together with the Other Works of England's Arch Poet.*   London: by H(umphrey) L(ownes) for Mathew Lownes, 1611,   Folio (4), 363, (19); (10), 56, (2); (136) pages, title within woodcut border, 12 woodcut vignettes, woodcut head and tailpieces, complete with all blanks, 2I4 (para) 8 and 2F4, contemporary blind ruled calf, central gilt stamped ornament on covers and smaller ornaments on spine, very skillfully rebacked retaining most of original spine, Leaf 2B2 soiled, final leaf creased, lower blank corner torn away without loss, occasional very light soiling, lovely, crisp copy, from the library of Henry Dethick with his signature and that of George Dethick, 2 modern booklabels.   Joseph J. Felcone Inc.   Fall Miscellany 2010 - 111 2011 $7000

Spenser, Edmund   1552-1599   *The Faerie Queen (with Prosopopoia Or Mother Hubberds Tale inserted after The Shepheards Calendar.*   London: 1611,   First collected edition; folio, contemporary full mottled calf, rebacked to style.   Heritage Book Shop   Booth A12 51st NY International Antiquarian Book Fair April 8-10 2011 - 126 2011 $7500

Spenser, Edmund   1552-1599   *The Faerie Queen. The Shepheards Calendar.*   London: printed for H. L. Lownes, 1617,   Early reprint of 1611 first collected edition; here with magnificent fore-edge painting by John Beer "Shepheard's Pastoral", tall quarto in sixes, (iv), 363, (1); (x), 56, (2, blank); 16, (14), (2, blank; (136) pages, decorative woodcut title, woodcut head - tailpieces, initials, colophon misprinted "16012", with an additional four pages in manuscript at rear as index, contemporary full oxblood morocco, gilt tooled panels, corner tulips, gilt ruled border, neatly rebacked with original spine laid down, new spine label to style, all edges gilt, later endleaves, small mid leaf burr chip to colophon, occasional small stain, beautiful copy,.   David Brass Rare Books, Inc.   May 26 2011 - 01595 2011 $6500

Spenser, Edmund 1552-1599 *Spenser's Minor Poems, Containing the Shepheardes Calender, Complaints, Daphnaida, Colin Clovts, Come Home Again, Amoretti, Hymnes, Epithalamion, Prothalamion, Sonnets and Svndrie Other Verses.* Ashendene Press, 1925, One of 200 copies; 175 of them for sale (there were also 15 copies on vellum, 12 of them for sale), 437 x 310mm., 2 p.l., 216 pages, original calf backed thick vellum boards, raised bands, gilt spine titling, printed in black, red and blue with numerous large and small roman style initials by Graily Hewitt; hint of splaying, joints bit rubbed and flaked with two inch cracks at head and tail of front joint, vellum on covers curling just slightly (as often), where it meets spine leather, spine little marked, vellum lightly soiled, binding nevertheless entirely solid and a flawless copy internally. Phillip J. Pirages 59 - 78 2011 $1900

Spenser, Edmund 1552-1599 *The Works.* London: Bell and Daldy, 1862, 5 volumes, 230 x 150mm., very attractive deep blue pebble grain morocco handsomely gilt, covers with frames of one dogtooth and three plain rules, raised bands, spines in antique style compartments with delicate scrolling cornerpieces and intricate central fleuron surrounded by small tools, densely gilt floral turn-ins, marbled endpapers, all edges gilt, frontispiece portrait of Spender in volume I, front pastedown with armorial bookplate of Herbert Lionel Bashford, M.A. Dibon Lodge Godalming, spines just shade darker than covers, corners with hint of rubbing, extremely fine set in very attractive bindings, text fresh and bright with leather especially lustrous and with only the most insignificant wear. Phillip J. Pirages 59 - 325 2011 $1500

Spewack, Samuel *Kiss me Kate: a Musical Play.* New York: Alfred A. Knopf, 1953, First edition; fine in modestly spine faded, else near fine dust jacket. Between the Covers 169 - BTC344100 2011 $750

Spice, R. P. *The Wanderings of the Hermit of Westminster Between New York & San Francisco in the Autumn of 1881.* London: Metchim & Son, n.d. circa, 1882, First edition; 84 pages, engraved titlepage vignette, one engraved text vignette, 2 engraved plates, cloth backed printed boards, boards lightly soiled and with light wear to extremities, inner hinges cracked, contemporary owner's name and date on endpaper (Sept. 1882), very good, extremely scarce. Argonaut Book Shop Recent Acquisitions Summer 2010 - 187 2011 $425

Spicer, Jack *After Lorca.* San Francisco: White Rabbit Press, 1957, One of 26 lettered copies signed by Spicer with drawing by poet out of a total edition of 500 copies typed on an Olivetti Lexikon 80 by Robert Duncan; 8vo., original pictorial wrappers with cover drawing by Jess, covers somewhat foxed, some portion rubbed, otherwise very good, rare, although not noted, this copy belonged to poet and Jargon Press publisher, Jonathan Williams. James S. Jaffe Rare Books May 26 2011 - 21279 2011 $6500

Spiegel, Fritz *Slavers and Privateers.* Liverpool: Scouse Press, 1972, Oblong folio self sealing plastic sleeve containing a pictorial title sheet, folding sheet of general text and 38 different facsimiles and copies of documents, mss. and other items relating to slave trade and Liverpool some printed in color, some copied on color paper. R. F. G. Hollett & Son Antiquarian Booksellers General Catalogue Summer 2010 - 619 2011 £45

Spielmann, Marion Harry *Hugh Thomson: His Art, His Letters, His Humour and His Charm.* London: A. & C. Black, 1931, First edition; half title, color frontispiece, plates, illustrations, original scarlet cloth, very good in dust jacket, inscribed to Dorothy from Kitty and Alban (Dobson). Jarndyce Antiquarian Booksellers CXCI - 515 2011 £110

Spiers, R. Phene *The Orders of Architecture Greek, Roman and Italian.* London: Batsford, 1902, Fourth edition; folio, original cloth, neatly recased, pages 20, plus 27 plates. R. F. G. Hollett & Son Antiquarian Booksellers 177 - 825 2011 £120

Spinckes, Nathaniel *The Sick Man Visited and Furnish'd with Instructions, Meditations and Prayers for Putting Him in Mind of His Change...* London: C. Rivington, 1731, Fourth edition; modern full calf gilt with raised bands and spine label, pages (vi), xl, 409, (viii), engraved frontispiece. R. F. G. Hollett & Son Antiquarian Booksellers 175 - 1268 2011 £350

The Spirit Lamp. Oxford: James Thornton, 1892-1893, First edition; wrappers, 8vo., 8 issues, No. II May 13 1892 chipping to front and back covers, now detached, No. III May 20 1892 minimal chipping, front cover lifting at top and bottom from spine; No. IV May 27 1892 with slight chipping at bottom of front and rear covers; Nov. VI June 10 1892 with chipping front and rear covers; volume II no. II 4 Nov. 1892 very good, volume III no. III 10 March 1893 very good, Volume IV no. I May 1893 very good, volume IV June 1893 small tears and chipping on front cover, not affecting text, back cover mostly torn away, else clean, good condition. Any Amount of Books May 26 2011 - A68762 2011 $1090

The Spirit of Love: a Novel. London: Henry & Co., 1893, First edition; 3 volumes, half titles, final ad leaf volume 1, 6 pages ads volume II carelessly opened, original green cloth, browning in prelims caused by endpapers, slightly dulled and rubbed. Jarndyce Antiquarian Booksellers CXCI - 48 2011 £150

Spizelius, Theophilus *Vetus Academia Jesu Christi in Qua XXII Priscae Sinceraeque Pietatis Professorum Icones Exhibentur etc.* Augsburg: apud Gottlieb Goebelium Augustae Vindelic, 1671, First edition; pages (xxiv), 221, (vii), 8vo., full page copperplate portraits, engraved titlepage plus engraved frontispiece, recent bound in brown half calf gilt with new endpapers, few light property stamp of Norfolk & Norwich Archaelogical Society, Inc. to titlepage, neat previous owner inscription dated 1778 facing second titlepage, otherwise excellent, clean condition. Any Amount of Books May 26 2011 - A75897 2011 $671

Splatt, Cynthia *Isadora Duncan and Gordon Craig.* Book Club of California, 1988, Limited to 450 copies; large 8vo, original cloth, plain dust jacket, pages xvii, 138, with 8 illustrations. R. F. G. Hollett & Son Antiquarian Booksellers 175 - 1269 2011 £75

Spofford, Harriet Elizabeth Prescott 1835-1921 *In Titian's Garden and Other Poems.* Boston: Little Brown and Co., 1903, Reissue; (iv, 108) pages, 8vo., original green cloth, dark blue floral decorated front cover, gilt titled front and spine, very good, inscribed by author to Mr. Knapp (who wrote "Female Biography"). Paulette Rose Fine and Rare Books 32 - 163 2011 $100

Spooner, Brian *Fungi.* London: Collins, 2005, Pages 594, with 164 color illustrations, original cloth, gilt, dust jacket, mint. R. F. G. Hollett & Son Antiquarian Booksellers General Catalogue Summer 2010 - 1054 2011 £85

Spooner's Protean Views No. I. Alloway Kirk and Burn's Monument. London: W. Spooner circa, 1840, Oblong 4to., full color transformation sheet with little dusting and few minor spots, card describes its transformation as Changing tot he Scene of Tam O'Shanter & Witches. Jo Ann Reisler, Ltd. 86 - 182 2011 $575

Spottiswood, John *The History of the Church of Scotland, Beginning the Year of Our Lord 203 and Continued to the End of the Regn of King James the VI.* London: J. Flesher for R. Royston, 1655, Folio, pages (xx), 546, (xiv), engraved frontispiece and engraved portrait dedication leaf, contemporary calf, spine double ruled in blind, boards double rule double bordered connected by stylised mitre pieces at corners, board edges, single rule gilt, all edges red sprinkled and with black ink handwritten "Spotiswood" on fore edge, bit of spotting and dust soiling, rubbed and marked, some surface damage at extremities, recent amateur red lettering piece gilt, touch of wear to corners and front joint, booklabel "Abrahamus Francke, now detached and loosely inserted, ink inscription "Affrancke/ A.M. / T.C.C. of Soc./ Ecc. de W. D,. Paul/1716", later ink inscription "Little Horksley Library" at inner head, from the collection of Christopher Ernest Weston 1947-2010. Unsworths Booksellers 24 - 42 2011 £400

Spragg, Mark *An Unfinished Life.* New York: Knopf, 2004, First edition; fine in fine dust jacket, signed by author. Bella Luna Books May 29 2011 - t7005 2011 $82

Spragg, Mark *Where Rivers Change Direction.* London: Jonathan Cape, 2000, First British edition; fine, dust jacket fine. Bella Luna Books May 29 2011 - t8889 2011 $82

Sproxton, Judy *The Women of Muriel Spark.* London: Constable, 1992, First edition, uncorrected proof; original wrappers, super proof dust jacket, pages 155. R. F. G. Hollett & Son Antiquarian Booksellers 175 - 1270 2011 £30

Squire, J. C. *London Mercury.* The Field Press, 1919-1939, First edition; V. 1/1-V.39/234, 234 issues in all, complete set, original wrappers, with cloth bound index for first 10 years, very scarce, very good. I. D. Edrich May 26 2011 - 82764 2011 $2935

Squire, John *A Plain Exposition Upon the First Part of the Second Chapter of Saint Paul His Second Epistle to the Thessalonians.* London: printed by M. Flesher for Philip Waterhouse, 1630, Small 4to., modern full blind panelled calf, gilt, pages (xvi), 383, 390-768 (complete), title little dusty and chipped, some corners rounded and worn, some contemporary notes and scribbles at beginning and end, rare. R. F. G. Hollett & Son Antiquarian Booksellers 175 - 1272 2011 £450

Stackhouse, Thomas *The Life of Our Lord and Saviour Jesus Christ.* printed by C. Sympson, 1765, Third edition; old full calf, extremities little chipped or worn, spine label dulled, pages viii, 584, engraved frontispiece and 12 plates, titlepage in red and black, typographic head and tailpieces and initials, very good, clean and sound, scarce. R. F. G. Hollett & Son Antiquarian Booksellers 175 - 1278 2011 £250

Stackhouse, Thomas *A New and Practical Exposition of the Apostles Creed...* London: Thomas Longman, Thomas Shewell and Charles Hitch, 1747, First edition; folio, contemporary full polished calf with raised ands, few old surface scratches and small defects, pages (ii), xxviii (ii, analysis, verso blank), 208, 217-421, (i, ad), (xiv, index and table, final leaf blank), text and signature complete despite pagination, nice contemporary inscription on flyleaf in Latin from William Stratford, Commissary of the Archdeaconry of Richmond, presenting the book to the Curate of Dent, Mark Rumney and his successors. R. F. G. Hollett & Son Antiquarian Booksellers 175 - 1277 2011 £350

Stackhouse, Thomas *A System of Practical Duties, Moral and Evangelical.* London: J. Hinton, 1760, First separate edition; full polished calf, gilt, pages vi, 329, (i), title little dusty, scarce. R. F. G. Hollett & Son Antiquarian Booksellers 175 - 1279 2011 £120

Stael Holstein, Anne Louise Germaine Necker, Baronne De 1766-1817 *Corinne ou L'Italie.* Paris: A La Librairie Stereotype chez H. Nicolle, 1807, First edition; uncut in original wrappers, hinges loose with paper labels, half title in each volume, first leaves adhering at inner margin a bit, not affecting any letterpress, first signature loose in volume 3, very good set.   Second Life Books Inc.   174 - 117 2011 $750

Stael Holstein, Anne Louise Germaine Necker, Baronne De 1766-1817 *Oeuvres de Mm. La Baronne de Stael-Holstein.* Paris: Chez Lefevre, 1858, 3 volumes, 882 pages and table of contents, 857 pages including table of contents, 755 pages, including table of contents, 8vo., contemporary full aubergine calf, elaborate gilt decorated spines with gilt border on front and back panels, all edges marbled, half titles in each volume, publisher's gift binding for College Royal de Louis Le Grand stamped in gilt with floral design on front panel of each volume, small defect to bottom of spine on volume II, otherwise most attractive set with very readable print.   Paulette Rose Fine and Rare Books   32 - 164 2011 $500

Stael Holstein, Auguste Louis, Baron De *Letters on England.* Treuttel and Wurtz, Treuttel, Jun. and Richter, 1825, Little bit of foxing at either end, frontispiece offset onto title, pages viii, including frontispiece, 339, (4 ads), 8vo., contemporary half green calf, spine gilt, black lettering piece, spine darkened, very good.   Blackwell Rare Books   B166 - 28 2011   £200

Stafford, Magdalen *The Romance and Its Hero.* London: Bell & Daldy, 1859, 2 volumes, 12mo., 2 pages ads, volumes I and II, original yellow stiff cloth wrappers, blocked in black and red on front, lettered in black on spine, little dulled and marked, booklabels of Henry L. Hammond.   Jarndyce Antiquarian Booksellers   CXCI - 497 2011   £125

The Stages of Human Life. New York: C. Shepard, between, 1835-1837, 12mo., green printed paper wrappers with few spots of surface rubbing and some light dusting, 16 numbered pages.   Jo Ann Reisler, Ltd.   86 - 82 2011 $675

Stainforth, Gordon *Lakeland. Landscape of Imagination.* London: Constable, 1992, First edition; large 4to., original cloth, gilt, dust jacket, pages 192, illustrations in color, fine, scarce.   R. F. G. Hollett & Son Antiquarian Booksellers 173 - 1077 2011   £65

Stainton, Lindsay *British Landscape Watercolours 1600-1860.* Cambridge: Cambridge University Press, 1985, First edition; 8.5 x 10 inches, 8 pages + plates, with 144 color plates and 7 black and white photos, fine in fine dust jacket.   By the Book, L. C.   26 - 48 2011 $75

Stanesby, Samuel *The Bridal Souvenir.* London: Griffith & Farran, circa, 1866, Small 4to., original heavily decorated and panelled cloth gilt over bevelled boards, little dulled and bubbled and neatly recased, 4 prelim leaves and 1 final leaf, all printed on one side, 15 leaves of text printed on both side, all in colors and gilt on stiff card, all edges gilt, few gutter margins spotted from old gutta percha binding, generally very nice, inscribed in neat calligraphic hand "October 2d Mrs. John Harcombe Cox from Mrs. William Castell".   R. F. G. Hollett & Son Antiquarian Booksellers 175 - 1281 2011   £180

Stanhope, Eugenia *The Deportment of a Married Life Laid Down in a Series of Letters...* London: printed for Mr. Hodges Pall Mall and sold by C. Mason, 1798, Second edition, but first edition using sheets of the 1790 first edition with new prelims; 8vo., pages (iii)-xi (i) 281, (1), all edges gilt, full 19th century polished calf, couple of minor spots but very nice, rare.   Second Life Books Inc.   174 - 293 2011 $1000

Stanhope, Philip Henry Stanhope, Earl of *Life of William Pitt...* London: John Murray, 1879, New edition; 3 volumes, half titles, frontispieces in volumes I and II, finely bound by Riviere & Son in full tree calf, gilt borders and dentelles, raised bands, gilt compartments, maroon and brown morocco labels, spines slightly sunned, armorial bookplates of John Warren, very handsome set.   Jarndyce Antiquarian Booksellers   CXCI - 25 2011   £165

Stanke, Julian *The Saviours and Liberators.* N.P.: privately printed, 1950, First edition; small oblong 4to., pages iv, 262, mimeographed text, mounted photos, soundly rebound, couple of ex-Foreign and Commonwealth Office library stamps, otherwise very good.   Any Amount of Books May 29 2011 - A65219 2011 $255

Stanley, Henry Morton 1841-1904 *The Congo and the Founding of Its Free State: a Story of Work and Exploration.* New York: Harper and Brothers, 1885, First American printing; 2 volumes, octavo, xxvii, 528; x, 483, 12 (ads) pages, 2 frontispieces, over 100 full page and smaller illustrations, 2 large maps, plus several smaller maps, original full lime green cloth with Belgium emblem stamped in black, olive, red, silver and gilt, apart from minor soiling, superb copy of the set, near fine.   Jeff Weber Rare Books   163 - 213 2011 $350

Stanley, Henry Morton   1841-1904   *In Darkest Africa.* New York: Charles Scribner's Sons, 1890, Edition de luxe, limited to 250 numbered copies signed by author, this being number 93, first American edition; 2 volumes, large quarto, (4, blank), (2) xv, (1, blank), 529, (1, printer's imprint), (2, blank); (4, blank), (2), xv, (1, blank), 472, (2, blank), pages, 41 plates on India paper mounted (including two engraved frontispiece portraits, two heliogravure portraits, 37 wood engraved plates, 6 original etchings, signed in pencil, 105 wood engravings in text on India paper mounted, 3 folding color maps, two backed with line, one color plan, one facsimile plate (as issued) and one folding table, titlepages printed in red and black, original half dark brown morocco gilt over vellum boards, front cover decoratively stamped and lettered in gilt, spines lettered in gilt with raised bands, top edge gilt, others uncut, some minor rubbing and staining to vellum, small bit of browning to endpapers and final leaves volume I, near fine set.   Heritage Book Shop   Holiday 2010 - 116   2011 $7500

Stanley, Henry Morton   1841-1904   *In Darkest Africa.* London: Sampson Low, Marston, Searle & Rivington, 1890, Edition Deluxe, one of only 250 copies signed by author; this being no. 243, 2 volumes, large quarto, photogravures as frontispieces, 6 etchings signed in pencil by G. Montbard, 37 mounted woodcut plates on india paper, with tissue guards, 113 woodcuts, 3 foldout color maps (two line backed), publisher's three quarter dark green crushed morocco decoratively ruled over vellum sides, front covers decorated and lettered in gilt, spines with five raised bands lettered in gilt, bevelled edges, top edge gilt, others uncut, minor soiling to vellum sides and some foxing to plate margins, despite marginal foxing, this a very good set.   David Brass Rare Books, Inc.   May 26 2011 - 01688   2011 $8500

Stanley, Henry Morton   1841-1904   *In Darkest Africa of the Quest, Rescue an Retreat of Emin Governor of Equatoria.* New York: Charles Scribner's Sons, 1891, 2 volumes, octavo, xiv, 547; xvi, 540 pages, 2 steel engravings, 150 illustrations and maps, 3 maps located in rear pockets, one map has repaired tear, two smaller maps have chips at corner folds, generally in very good condition, original full green cloth with black stamped image of Africa on upper cover, gilt titles and reproduction of author's signature, gilt spine titles, rubbed, bookplate of George W. McIntosh, Doylestown, PA.   Jeff Weber Rare Books   163 - 214   2011 $75

Stanley, Henry Morton   1841-1904   *In Darkest Africa.* London: Sampson Low Marston etc., 1907, Forty eighth thousand; contemporary half calf, gilt, few slight scrapes, pages xviii, 686, 150 full page and text woodcut illustrations and large folding color map, prize label of Storey Institute, Girls' Grammar Schook, Lancaster.   R. F. G. Hollett & Son Antiquarian Booksellers   General Catalogue Summer 2010 - 1662   2011   £45

Stanley, Henry Morton   1841-1904   *Through the Dark Continent or the Sources of the Nile Around the Great Lakes of Equatorial Africa and Down the Livingstone River to the Atlantic Ocean.* New York: Harper & Brothers, 1879, 2 volumes, octavo, xiv, 522; ix, 566, 2 (ads) pages, 10 maps, 150 woodcuts, index, 2 large folding maps found in rear pockets, their condition very nice with only small breaks in paper at corner fold, original full dark green pictorial cloth stamped in red and black, gilt, bookplate of Sacred Heart School of Education, Fall River, Mass., unusually fine set.   Jeff Weber Rare Books   163 - 215   2011 $225

Stanley, William Owen   *Memoirs on Remains of Ancient Dwellings in Holyhead Island...*   London: printed for the author by James Bain, 1871, Original cloth, gilt, rather faded and rubbed, neatly recased, pages v, 33, 29, 15, with 2 folding or double page lithographed plans, 6 steel engraved plates, 34 woodcut plates and numerous woodcut diagrams and illustrations, signed by author, woodcut bookplate of Isaac Evans of Meani Bridge.   R. F. G. Hollett & Son Antiquarian Booksellers   177 - 826   2011   £120

Stansbury, Howard   *Exploration and Survey of the Valley Great Salt Lake of Utah...*   Philadelphia: Lippincott, Gambo & Co., 1852, First edition; 2 volumes, cloth, 487 pages, 2 large folding maps in separate portfolio volume, 58 plates, including folding panoramic views, many appendices, charts, tables, index, former owner's inscription "Robley Doughton presented by Col. Albert, Washington", wear to spine ends and extremities, else very good, map volume missing backstrip, however maps are in very good condition with usual splitting at some of the folds, both volumes complete with all plates and maps present, very scarce in original cloth.   Buckingham Books   May 26 2011 - 25961   2011 $2000

Stanton, Elizabeth Cady   *History of Woman Suffrage.* Paris: Susan B. Anthony, Charles Mann, 1887, 3 volumes, octavo, 878, iii-vii, 952; xix, 1013 pages, 3 frontispieces, 11, 11, 22 engravings, volume II lacks a titlepage, original maroon blindstamped cloth, gilt spine titles, spines faded, remarkably well preserved, fine.   Jeff Weber Rare Books   163 - 216   2011 $400

Stanyon, Ellis   *Conjuring with Cards: A Practical Treatise on How to Perform Modern Card Tricks.*   L. Upcott Gill, 1898, Initial ad leaf, half title, illustrations, 14 page catalog + 2 pages ads, original pictorial wrappers, printed in red, black , back cover ad, very good.   Jarndyce Antiquarian Booksellers   CXCI - 371   2011   £45

Stapledon, William Olaf   *Sirius: a Fantasy of Love and Discord.*   London: Secker & Warburg, 1944, First edition; first impression, octavo, cloth.   L. W. Currey, Inc.   124 - 149   2011 $450

Stark, Archibald G. *The South of Ireland in 1850: Being the Journal of a Tour of Leinster and Munster.* Dublin: Duffy, 1850, First and only edition; numerous illustrations by M. Angelo Hayes, xii, 214 pages, original cloth, faded at edges, some wear at spine base, text very good. C. P. Hyland May 26 2011 - 259/459 2011 $362

Starkey, James *Twenty-Five Lyrics.* Flansham, Bognor Regis, Sussex: Pear Tree Press, 1933, First edition one of 150 numbered copies; 229 x 152mm., 2 p.l., v, 27 (1) pages, (1) leaf, original thin boards, linen spine, printed paper label on front cover, edges untrimmed and mostly unopened, printed in black and green title within green decorative frame, first page of text in white on green decorative background, headpiece and tailpiece in green, binding slightly bumped and splayed, otherwise fine, especially clean. Phillip J. Pirages 59 - 275 2011 $100

Starkie, Thomas *A Treatise on the Law of Slander & Label & Incidentally of Malicious Prosecutions.* Hartford: 1858, 2 volumes bound as one, 494, 451, very good in old law calf with usual wear, top three inches of backstrip with linen repair above the top label. Bookworm & Silverfish 667 - 100 2011 $65

A Statement Showing the Location, Connections and Importance of the Indianapolis, Bloomington and Western Railway of Indiana and Illinois, April 27th 1870. New York: Turner Brothers, 1870, First edition; 8vo., 31 pages, large folding map, wrappers wrinkled and lightly soiled, text damp wrinkled and tidemark throughout, folding map in fine ste. M & S Rare Books, Inc. 90 - 338 2011 $375

Statham, E. C. F. *Coal Mining Practice.* Caxton Pub. Co., 1960, 4 volumes, 4to., original black cloth gilt, pages x, 448; ix, 516; iii, 468; 438 946 index), illustrations, library stamp on each flyleaf and title, else excellent set. R. F. G. Hollett & Son Antiquarian Booksellers General Catalogue Summer 2010 - 1141 2011 £85

Statham, H. Heathcote *A Short Critical History of Architecture.* London: Batsford, 1927, Second edition; 3 volumes, original cloth, gilt, small shelf labels at base of spines, pages 563, with some 600 text illustrations. R. F. G. Hollett & Son Antiquarian Booksellers 177 - 827 2011 £60

Stead, W. T. *Books for the Bairns.* Review of Reviews, Mawbray House, Books for the Bairns, etc., n.d. circa, 1895-1903, Small thick 8vo., original binder's cloth gilt, 11 titles bound together, paginated separately, illustrations. R. F. G. Hollett & Sons Antiquarian Booksellers 170 - 654 2011 £65

Stead, W. T. *The First Birdie Book.* Review of Reviews Office, n.d. circa, 1900, Small 8vo., original pictorial wrappers, pages 60, with 48 wood engravings. R. F. G. Hollett & Sons Antiquarian Booksellers 170 - 653 2011 £30

Steadman, F. Cecily *In the Days of Miss Beale.* Ed. J. Burrow, 1931, First edition; small 4to., original cloth, boots label on upper board, pages xv, 194, untrimmed with 9 plates and 16 line drawings, little spotting to half title and title. R. F. G. Hollett & Son Antiquarian Booksellers 175 - 1288 2011 £60

Steadman, Ralph *Ralph Steadman's Jelly Book.* London: Dennis Dobson, 1967, First edition; small oblong 4to., bright and clean, original publisher's orange cloth, pages 32, illustrations in color, boldly signed and dated 14/4/78 by Steadman, very good+ in very good, complete dust jacket, browned and tanned, largely at edges and rear cover. Any Amount of Books May 29 2011 - A66644 2011 $408

Steedman, Amy *Legends & Stories of Italy for Children.* New York & London: 1909, First edition; 188 pages, near fine with 12 tipped in color plates by Katharine Cameron, original binding, top edge gilt, all cover and little gilt, highly ornate endpaper. Bookworm & Silverfish 665 - 73 2011 $65

Steedman, Andrew *Wanderings and Adventures in the Interior of Southern Africa.* London: Longman, 1835, First edition; 2 volumes, 8vo., pages x, 330, v, 358, folding map, 2 vignettes, 12 plates, foxed but text clean, contemporary brown half calf. J. & S. L. Bonham Antiquarian Booksellers Africa 4/20/2011 - 7000 2011 £450

Steegman, John *A Survey of Portraits in Welsh Houses. Volume I: North Wales.* Cardiff: National Museum of Wales, 1957, First edition; large 8vo., original cloth, gilt, dust jacket, pages xi, 362, with 46 plates, scarce. R. F. G. Hollett & Son Antiquarian Booksellers General Catalogue Summer 2010 - 329 2011 £120

Steel, Flora Annie *English Fairy Tales.* New York: Macmillan, 1918, First American edition, later issue with top edge plain instead of gilt; thick 8vo., red cloth, 363 pages + ads, neat hinge strengthening, edge soil on endpaper and some finger soil on cover, very good+ in beautiful custom half leather box with raised bands, illustrations by Arthur Rackham, 16 magnificent color plates plus 41 black and whites ad pictorial endpapers, charming 3 inch pen drawing of a crow signed and dated 1919 by Rackham. Aleph-Bet Books, Inc. 95 - 480 2011 $2750

Steel, Flora Annie *Tales of the Punjab told by the People.* London: Macmillan, 1894, First edition; original pictorial green cloth, gilt, neatly recased, pages xvi, 395, all edges gilt, illustrations by J. Lockwood Kipling. R. F. G. Hollett & Son Antiquarian Booksellers 175 - 1289 2011 £85

Steele, Francesca M. *Monasteries and Religious Houses of Great Britain and Ireland.* London: R. & T. Washborne, 1903, First edition; original green cloth gilt, spine little marked, pages xv, 267, 3 with 26 illustrations. R. F. G. Hollett & Son Antiquarian Booksellers 175 - 1290 2011 £40

Steele, Isobel *Enchanted Capital of Scotland.* Edinburgh: Plaid Pub., 1945, First edition; 4to., gilt cloth, fine in dust jacket, 4 double page color illustrations and many lovely line illustrations by Jessie King.   Aleph-Bet Books, Inc.   95 - 315   2011 $575

Steele, John *Across the Plains in 1850.* Chicago: printed for the Caxton Club, 1930, First edition, limited to 350 copies; small octavo, xxxvii, (1), 234 pages, frontispiece, 6 photogravures, folding map, original decorative brown German cloth with design stamped in gilt, red Interlake vellum, gilt lettered, very fine, publisher's plain slipcase.   Argonaut Book Shop   Recent Acquisitions Summer 2010 - 189   2011 $425

Stegner, Wallace *Beyond the Hundredth Meridian: John Welsey Powell and the Second Opening of the West.* Boston: Houghton Mifflin, 1954, First edition; large folding color frontispiece, xxiii, 438 pages, illustrations, 6 text maps, cloth, dust jacket extremities rubbed with few short nicks, very good.   Jeff Weber Rare Books   163 - 217   2011 $100

Stegner, Wallace *The Big Rock Candy Mountain.* Franklin Center: Franklin Library, 1978, Limited edition; Signed by author, full brown leather binding with raised bands, gilt lettering and decorated spine, gilt decorated covers, all edges gilt, silk moire endpapers, silk ribbon bookmark, 8vo., 733 pages.   By the Book, L. C.   26 - 17   2011 $95

Stegner, Wallace *Crossing to Safety.* Franklin Center: Franklin Library, 1987, Limited First edition, First printing; signed by author, fine blue leather, raised bands, gilt lettering and decoration spine and cover, all edges gilt, marbled endpapers, silk ribbon bookmark, 8vo., 289 pages, letter from publisher laid in.   By the Book, L. C.   26 - 16   2011 $70

Stein, Aurel   1862-1943 *Archaeological Reconnaissances in North Western India and South Eastern Iran...* London: Macmillan, 1937, First edition; small folio, pages xix, 267, 34 plates, 88 illustrations, 22 maps and plans, 2 large folding maps in rear pocket, ex-library in original publisher's red buckram lettered gilt at spine and cover with beveled boards, library bookplate on pastedown, discreet stamps on verso of title and at head of preface page and reverse of plates, small white number at lower spine, very good, few marks to covers and slight rubbing.   Any Amount of Books   May 26 2011 - A78501   2011 $1426

Stein, Gertrude   1874-1946 *Geography and Plays.* Boston: Four Seas Co., 1922, First edition; 2nd state binding, first state dust jacket, superior copy in boards that are just very slightly rubbed at crown and heel, spine label and cloth like new, dust jacket somewhat age toned at spine, one tear at inner fold and a shallow chip at top of spine, very clean, near fine, scarce.   Gemini Fine Books & Arts, Ltd.   Art Reference & Illustrated Books: First Editions 2011 $165

Stein, Gertrude   1874-1946 *In Savoy, or Yes is for a Very Young Man.* London: Pushkin Press, 1946, First edition; small 8vo., fine in wrappers, illustrated dust jacket with slight soiling, word Savoy stamped on front fly as usual, scarce in this condition.   Gemini Fine Books & Arts, Ltd.   Art Reference & Illustrated Books: First Editions 2011 $80

Stein, Gertrude   1874-1946 *Three Lives. Stories of the Good Anna, Melanctha and Gentle Lena.* London: John Rodker, 1927, First edition; 8vo., pages 279, original publisher's blue cloth lettered black on cover and spine, slight bumping at lower spine, else very good+ in slightly nicked and slightly chipped, very good dust jacket that is slightly browned.   Any Amount of Books   May 29 2011 - A38818   2011 $306

Stein, Gertrude   1874-1946 *The World is Round.* New York: William Scott, Stated first edition; 4to., cloth backed pictorial boards, fine in slightly worn frayed dust jacket, printed on rose color paper, illustrations by Clement Hurd, nice.   Aleph-Bet Books, Inc.   95 - 540   2011 $600

Stein, Gertrude   1874-1946 *The World is Round.* New York: William R. Scott, 1939, First edition; very good, signed by Stein and artist, Clement Hurd, covers are soiled with light wear at edges, interior clean and tight, 67 (pink) pages, slipcase worn at edges and torn along back.   G. H. Mott Bookseller   May 26 2011 - 45565   2011 $300

Steinbeck, John Ernst   1902-1968 *America and Americans.* New York: Viking, 1966, First edition; first issue binding with author and title in gilt running down the spine, 136 pages of color and black and white photos, nearly fine in near fine, price clipped dust jacket.   Lupack Rare Books   May 26 2011 - ABE4091524406   2011 $100

Steinbeck, John Ernst   1902-1968 *Burning Bright.* New York: Viking, 1950, First edition; very near fine in near fine dust jacket (small closed tear at spine top).   Lupack Rare Books   May 26 2011 - ABE1368418426   2011 $225

Steinbeck, John Ernst   1902-1968 *Cannery Row.* New York: Scribner's, 1945, First edition, fiirst binding in light buff cloth (second binding was in bright yellow cloth); nearly fine, bright and clean, complete, very good plus dust jacket (repaired ear on blank area of rear panel and little rubbing to extremities).   Lupack Rare Books   May 26 2011 - ABE4707853083   2011 $1500

Steinbeck, John Ernst 1902-1968 *Cannery Row.* New York: Viking, 1945, First edition in first issue (buff colored) cloth; near fine in nearly fine dust jacket neither chipped nor clipped. Lupack Rare Books May 26 2011 - ABE1202783237 2011 $2750

Steinbeck, John Ernst 1902-1968 *The Grapes of Wrath.* New York: Viking Press, 1939, 8vo., 619 pages, tan cloth, brown stamped cover vignette and spine title, original dust jacket, fine, flawless. Jeff Weber Rare Books 163 - 51 2011 $10,000

Steinbeck, John Ernst 1902-1968 *The Grapes of Wrath.* New York: Viking Press, 1939, First edition; octavo, (vi0, 619, (3, blank) pages, publisher's original beige cloth, boards and spine pictorially stamped and lettered in reddish brown, top edge yellow, endpapers with portion of "The Battle Hymn of the Republic" printed in reddish brown, top edge of spine and book, little darkened, very small smudge on bottom edge, otherwise near fine, bright, near fine dust jacket, dust jacket price clipped with price of $2.75 stamped directly below where price should be, spine completely unfaded. Heritage Book Shop Holiday 2010 - 117 2011 $7500

Steinbeck, John Ernst 1902-1968 *In Dubious Battle.* New York: Covici Friede, 1936, First edition; fine, bright copy with red top stain very bright, in very nearly fine dust jacket (just tiny paper niggling to very bottom right of front panel), dust jacket fresh, bright, housed in half leather clamshell box, this is a beautiful copy. Lupack Rare Books May 26 2011 - ABE1368418458 2011 $7500

Steinbeck, John Ernst 1902-1968 *The Moon is Down.* New York: 1942, First edition, with all points; 188 pages, very good (glue dark at gutter), dust jacket, rubbed at extremities, rear panel age soiled. Bookworm & Silverfish 678 - 70 2011 $175

Steinbeck, John Ernst 1902-1968 *The Moon is Down.* New York: Viking, 1942, First edition, first issue; with the dot on page 112, L.11 and without printer's name on copyright page, near fine with bright silver on spine, in very good plus dust jacket (slight shelfwear, price clipped). Lupack Rare Books May 26 2011 - ABE24030-4074 2011 $200

Steinbeck, John Ernst 1902-1968 *Of Mice and Men.* New York: Covici Friede Publishers, 1937, First edition; first issue with lines 20 and 21 on page 9 reading "and only moved because the heavy hands were pendula" and with a bullet between the eights of the page numbers on page 88, small octavo, (1)-186, (b, blank) pages, original full beige cloth stamped in terra cotta and black on front cover and spine, original dust jacket, some very minor small closed tears to edges of jacket and some tiny chipping to extremities of jacket and spine and corners, book spine and edge bit darkened, overall very good to fine in very bright jacket. Heritage Book Shop Holiday 2010 - 118 2011 $2500

Steinbeck, John Ernst 1902-1968 *Positano.* Salerno: Ente Provinciale Per Il Turismo, 1959, Second English language issue; near fine, light soiling and wear, stiff yellow wrappers. Bella Luna Books May 29 2011 - t7550 2011 $137

Steinbeck, John Ernst 1902-1968 *Sweet Thursday.* New York: Viking, 1954, Intermediate edition, with red and black titlepage, unstained top edge red dot at lower corner rear cover and testimonials under the Halsman photo on dust jackets rear panel; x, 273 pages, cloth, spine canted, dust jacket price clipped, light chipping at spine ends and corner, few dampstains, inscribed George "Sonny Boy" Velis, Velis operated the restaurant and bar in Montgomery that is the subject of the entire chapter 23 in Sweet Thursday as well as a paragraph in Travels with Charley. Joseph J. Felcone Inc. Fall Miscellany 2010 - 112 2011 $450

Steinbeck, John Ernst 1902-1968 *Tortilla Flat.* New York: Covici Friede Publishers, 1935, First edition; octavo, vi,(2), (9)-(317), (blank) pages, with inter textual illustrations by Ruth Gannett, original tan cloth, front board and spine ruled and lettered in blue, top edge blue, price clipped dust jacket, spine sunned and faded, jacket chipped at extremities and corners, book spine and edges bit browned, previous owner's name in ink on front free endpaper, overall very good. Heritage Book Shop Holiday 2010 - 119 2011 $3500

Steinbeck, John Ernst 1902-1968 *The Wayward Bus.* New York: Viking, 1947, First edition, first binding (with blindstamped bus showing up lighter than the rest of the binding); fine in very nearly fine dust jacket (very minor shelfwear), dust jacket neither chipped or clipped. Lupack Rare Books May 26 2011 - ABE1368418431 2011 $500

Steinbeck, John Ernst 1902-1968 *Zapata.* London: Heinemann, 1991, First British edition; fine in fine dust jacket. Bella Luna Books May 29 2011 - t5306 2011 $137

Steiner, Charlotte *Birthdays and for Everyone.* Garden City: Doubleday & Co., 1964, Stated first edition; 12mo., pictorial cloth, fine in dust jacket slightly rubbed, charming color illustrations by Steiner. Aleph-Bet Books, Inc. 95 - 541 2011 $125

Steinert, Otto *Subjektive Fotographie & Subjektive Fotographie 2.* Bonn: Bruder Auer, 1952-1955, First edition; 2 volumes, photos, volume I clean, very near fine with crease to foldout index page, about near fine dust jacket with thumbnail size chip from head of spine and some other minor wear to spine as well as a number of tears, volume 2 is a fine and tight copy in fine dust jacket, very nice set. Jeff Hirsch Books ny 2010 2011 $2000

Stephanapoulous, George *All To Human: a Political Education.* Norwalk: Easton Press, 1999, Limited edition Easton Press, number 220 of 1200 copies; signed by author, leather with gold titles and decorations, all edges gilt, silk endpapers and ribbon bookmark, "A note about" card and signed certificate of authenticity folded in, very clean and tight, pages 456, fine.   G. H. Mott Bookseller   May 26 2011 - 37136   2011 $240

Stephanides, Theodore *The Microscope and the Practical Princples of Observations.* London: Faber, 1947, First edition; original cloth, gilt, dust jacket, spine little browned, few repairs to reverse, pages 160, with 20 illustrations.   R. F. G. Hollett & Son Antiquarian Booksellers   General Catalogue Summer 2010 - 1142   2011   £35

Stephens, James 1882-1950 *Irish Fairy Tales.* London: Macmillan, 1924, Original red cloth, gilt, extremities trifle rubbed, pages x, 318, with 16 color plates by Arthur Rackham.   R. F. G. Hollett & Son Antiquarian Booksellers   175 - 1106   2011   £85

Stephens, Thomas *The Literature of the Kymry...* Landovery: William Rees, 1849, Original cloth, gilt, spine little torn at top, lettering rather faded, pages xii, 512, few faint stamps.   R. F. G. Hollett & Son Antiquarian Booksellers   175 - 1293   2011   £60

Stephenson, George *Repairs, How to Measure and Value Them.* London: Batsford, 1901, Third edition; original red cloth, gilt, spine rather faded, pages 99, 10.   R. F. G. Hollett & Son Antiquarian Booksellers   177 - 830   2011   £45

Stephenson, Mill *Appendix to a List of Monumental Brasses in the British Isles.* privately Printed by Hadley Brothers, 1938, Original blue cloth gilt, pages 719-849.   R. F. G. Hollett & Son Antiquarian Booksellers   General Catalogue Summer 2010 - 330   2011   £45

Stephenson, Mill *A List of Monumental Brasses in the British Isles and Appendix.* Ashford and London: privately printed by Headley Brothers, 1926-1938, 8vo., original publisher's blue cloth lettered gilt on spine and front cover, pages xvi, 849, ownership signature of Professor G. H. Bushnell, clipped signature of Stephenson tipped in, and 1 page signed letter from him to G. H. S. Busnell loosely inserted, faint rubbing, very good+.   Any Amount of Books   May 29 2011 - A49466   2011 $272

Stephenson, Neal *The Confusion.* New York: Morrow, 2004, First edition; fine in fine dust jacket.   Bella Luna Books   May 29 2011 - t8539   2011 $82

Sterling, George *A Wine of Wizardry and Other Poems.* San Francisco: A. M. Robertson, 1909, First edition; 8vo., 137 pages, signed presentation from author for Frank McConnors, original publisher's burgundy red cloth lettered gilt on spine, gilt illustration on front cover, slight fading at spine, otherwise bright, very good+ copy.   Any Amount of Books   May 26 2011 - A39601   2011 $503

Sterne, Emma Gelders *Little Boy Blue Gift Box.* New York: Cupples & Leon, 1924, 1917. 1924.; 3 volumes, all books 16mo., pictorial boards with pictorial paste-ons, all are in fine condition in fine dust jackets, 8 color plates and line drawings, illustrations by Johnny Gruelle and Thelma Gooch, rare boxed set.   Aleph-Bet Books, Inc.   95 - 46   2011 $800

Sterne, Laurence 1713-1768 *A Sentimental Journey through France and Italy.* London: Navarre Society, circa, 1926, One of 200 copies; 180 x 113mm., 2 p.l. (including frontispiece), 147 pages, very fine burgundy morocco, handsomely gilt and onlaid by the Harcourt Bindery of Boston (stamp-signed), boards with triple fillet border, each cover with elaborate heraldic frame of gilt and onlaid green morocco, around an empty oval, raised bands, very pretty gilt spine compartments featuring looping tendril frame enclosing a charming flower centerpiece, densely gilt turn-ins marbled endpapers, top edge gilt, frontispiece by George Cruikshank; very fine.   Phillip J. Pirages   59 - 327   2011 $375

Sterne, Laurence 1713-1768 *The Works.* Printed at the Shakespeare Head Press for Houghton Mifflin Co., 1926, One of 500 copies (this #65); 238 x 162, 7 volumes, quite attractive original dark blue three quarter morocco over blue linen at Riverside Press (signed on verso), raised bands, spines gilt in compartments with corner curls and ornate scrollwork, top edge gilt, other edges untrimmed, unopened, 12 pleasing plates by George Cruikshank, isolated pencilled marginalia, occasional minor foxing, especially to leaves at beginning and end of volumes, otherwise nearly mint set, bindings with no perceivable wear, unopened text obviously with no signs of use.   Phillip J. Pirages   59 - 319   2011 $1900

Sternfeld, Joel *American Prospects.* New York: Times Books, 1987, First edition; fine, tight copy in very near fine dust jacket with some minor fading to spine and rear panel.   Jeff Hirsch Books   ny 2010 2011 $1250

Stevens, C. E. *The Building of Hadrian's Wall.* Kendal: Titus Wilson, 1966, Volume XX, original cloth, gilt, pages ix, 141, folding chart.   R. F. G. Hollett & Son Antiquarian Booksellers   177 - 831   2011   £45

Stevens, E. S. *My Sudan Year.* London: Mills & Boon, 1912, First edition; 8vo., pages x, 305, illustrations, original red cloth, spine worn and rubbed.   J. & S. L. Bonham Antiquarian Booksellers   Africa 4/20/2011 - 4247   2011   £50

Stevens, Wallace 1879-1955 *Esthetique du Mal. A Poem by Wallace Stevens...* Cummington: Cummington Press, 1945, First edition, one of 300 copies printed on Pace paper, one of One of 300 copies Printed on Pace paper, one of only a few copies bound in the rose Natsume; 8vo., original quarter black morocco, and rose Natsume paper covered boards (original?) glassine dust jacket, very fine copy, preserved in cloth folding box.   James S. Jaffe Rare Books   May 26 2011 - 21107 2011 $7500

Stevens, Wallace 1879-1955 *Ideas of Order.* New York: Alcestis Press, 1935, First edition; one of 10 review copies from a total edition of 165, author's signature to limitation page, 8vo., pages (iv) 5-63, (i) blank, (i) limitation (7) blank, sporadic light spotting but generally clean, top edge trimmed, others uncut, original ivory paper wrapper, text in black to upper side and spine, lightly soiled and rubbed, without glassine and slipcase, previous owner's presentation inscription to front free endpaper.   Simon Finch Rare Books   Zero - 354 2011   £1500

Stevens, Wallace 1879-1955 *The Palm at the End of the Mind.* New York: Knopf, 1971, First edition; pages (iv), xvi, 404, xxiv, 8vo., original tan cloth blocked in blind, backstrip printed in silver, rubber stamp on front free endpaper, dust jacket trifle rubbed, very good.   Blackwell Rare Books   B166 - 234 2011   £40

Stevens, Wallace 1879-1955 *Poems.* San Francisco: Arion Press, 1985, Limited edition, one of 300 numbered copies for sale out of a total edition of 326 copies, this being number 20; small folio, xxviii, (1)-249, (1, blank), (1), (3, blank) pages, frontispiece which is original etching by Jasper Johns, signed by artist in pencil, titles and initial letters are handset in Dante Titling, text composed in monotype Bembo on English mould made paper by T. Edmonds, bound by Schuberth Bookbindery of San Francisco in publisher's half blue morocco over blue and white linen, foreedge and bottom edge uncut, spine lettered in silver, some slight darkening to top of spine, otherwise near fine.   Heritage Book Shop   Holiday 2010 - 120 2011 $4500

Stevenson-Hamilton, J. *The Low Veld: Its Wild Life and Its People.* London: Cassell, 1929, First edition; 8vo, pages xvi, 287, map on endpapers, illustrations, original brown cloth, some light flecking to head.   J. & S. L. Bonham Antiquarian Booksellers   Africa 4/20/2011 - 6738 2011   £45

Stevenson, Robert Louis 1850-1894 *A Child's Garden of Verses.* London: John Lane, The Bodley Head, 1913, Original decorated green cloth, corner third of lower board rather badly damped, pages xix, 144, 16 (ads dated 1895), all edges gilt, illustrations by Charles Robinson, flyleaves partly browned.   R. F. G. Hollett & Son Antiquarian Booksellers   General Catalogue Summer 2010 - 563 2011   £30

Stevenson, Robert Louis Balfour 1850-1894 *The Black Arrow.* New York: Charles Scribner's Sons, 1936, Large 8vo., original black cloth gilt with pictorial onlay, spine lettering dulled, pages ix, 328, with title, 9 color plates and color endpapers by N. C. Wyeth.   R. F. G. Hollett & Son Antiquarian Booksellers   General Catalogue Summer 2010 - 577 2011   £30

Stevenson, Robert Louis Balfour 1850-1894 *A Child's Garden of Verses.* London: John Lane, The Bodley Head, 1896, First edition thus; small 8vo., original decorated green cloth, corner third of lower board rather badly damped, pages xiv, 144, 16 (ads dated 1895), all edges gilt illustrations by Charles Robinson, several name stamps on front pastedown.   R. F. G. Hollett & Son Antiquarian Booksellers   General Catalogue Summer 2010 - 562 2011   £45

Stevenson, Robert Louis Balfour 1850-1894 *A Child's Garden of Verses.* London: John Lane The Bodley Head, 1896, First edition thus; small 8vo., original decorated green cloth gilt, corner third of lower board rather badly damped, pages xiv, 144, 16 (ads dated 1895), all edges gilt, illustrations by Charles Robinson, several name stamps on front pastedown.   R. F. G. Hollett & Sons Antiquarian Booksellers   170 - 591 2011   £45

Stevenson, Robert Louis Balfour 1850-1894 *A Child's Garden of Verses.* London: Harrap, 1931, First edition thus; oblong small folio, original cloth backed pictorial boards, trifle marked and bubbled in places, pages 72, 12 color plate, top edge of title little dusty, otherwise nice, clean copy.   R. F. G. Hollett & Sons Antiquarian Booksellers   170 - 400 2011   £180

Stevenson, Robert Louis Balfour 1850-1894 *The Childrens' Year.* England: Modern Art Society n.d., Small 8bo., original blue boards, pictorial onlay by artist on upper board, unpaginated, double page title with line drawing in blue, full page color illustrations.   R. F. G. Hollett & Sons Antiquarian Booksellers   170 - 670 2011   £75

Stevenson, Robert Louis Balfour 1850-1894 *The Dynamiter.* London: Longmans, Green and Co., 1885, First edition; original wrappers, very good, spine rebacked with green linen, very slight shelfwear, tight, clean copy.   Lupack Rare Books   May 26 2011 - ABE1196217660 2011 $350

Stevenson, Robert Louis Balfour 1850-1894 *Pentland Rising: a Page of History 1666.* Edinburgh: Andrew Elliot, 1866, First edition; 12mo., publisher's printed green wrappers.   Heritage Book Shop   Booth A12 51st NY International Antiquarian Book Fair April 8-10 2011 - 130 2011 $5000

Stevenson, Robert Louis Balfour 1850-1894 *Poems.* London: printed at the Florence Press for Chatto & Windus in association with Longmans Green & Co., 1913, One of 500 numbered copies on handmade paper (this being copy #472); 225 x 185mm., xvi, 399, (1) pages, stunning contemporary rose colored morocco, elaborately onlaid and inlaid as well as lavishly tooled in gilt by Riviere (stamp signed on front turn-in), covers with frame composed of two parallel borders, outer one featuring a curving gilt vine bearing green inlaid morocco blossom, the inner one with small inlaid black morocco circles connected by single gilt rule, two borders joined by interlacing strapwork cornerpieces inner border interrupted at center of each side with very intricate strapwork, each lobe containing three red onlaid morocco roses and connected on its inside tip, with prominent central mandorla featuring a beautiful onlaid composition of four lilies and four acanthus leaves in ivory, red and green morocco, the panel surrounding the centerpiece filled in with some 200 gilt leaves and flowers on twining stems, entire surface of boards covered with gilt stippling (sidepieces, cornerpieces and mandorla very densely stippled), raised bands, spine elaborately gilt in double ruled compartments of a complex design, each with four inlaid black morocco flowers, central inlaid circle and much stippling, extremely pretty white morocco doublures with very flamboyant floral gilt cornerpieces, doublure framed by very wide and unusually lovely turn-ins heavily gilt in repeating floral pattern, moss green watered silk endleaves, top edges gilt, other edges untrimmed, in binder's original (rather worn) folding morocco box with one defective metal closure, title printed in blue and black, front doublure with ivory morocco bookplate with monogram of "ABJ (apparently Annie Burr Jennings) above motto from Seneca "Otium sine litteris ors est", bookplate of Mrs. A. H. Ely, bookplate faintly discolored upper corner of front free endpaper just slightly crumpled, front flyleaf with two small stains, very short closed fore-edge tear, one leaf with rust spot, remarkably fine, unusually bright text pristine, dazzling binding with virtually no signs of wear.   Phillip J. Pirages   59 - 127   2011 $15,000

Stevenson, Robert Louis Balfour 1850-1894 *R. L. S. to J. M. Barrie: A Vailima Portrait.* San Francisco: Book Club of California, 1962, First edition, limited to 475 copies; (42) pages, 4 sketches by Isobel Strong, page of facsimile manuscript, cloth backed decorated boards, paper spine label, very fine.   Argonaut Book Shop   Recent Acquisitions Summer 2010 - 190   2011 $90

Stevenson, Robert Louis Balfour 1850-1894 *Strange Case of Dr. Jekyll and Mr. Hyde.* London: Longmans, Green and Co., 1886, First English edition; octavo, (8), 141, (1, blank), (1, ads), (1, blank) pages, original buff paper wrappers printed in blue and red, with 1885 date on front wrapper altered in ink to 1886 (as always), ads for Longman's Magazine on inner front wrapper and ads for J. G. Whyte Melville's works on inner rear wrapper, overall excellent copy of fragile item.   Heritage Book Shop   Holiday 2010 - 122   2011 $6000

Stevenson, Robert Louis Balfour 1850-1894 *Strange Case of Dr. Jekyll and Mr. Hyde.* London: Longmans, Green and Co., 1886, First English edition; octavo, original buff paper wrappers printed in blue and red.   Heritage Book Shop   Booth A12 51st NY International Antiquarian Book Fair April 8-10 2011 - 131   2011 $6500

Stevenson, Robert Louis Balfour 1850-1894 *Strange Case of Dr. Jekyll and Mr. Hyde.* London: Longmans, Green and Co., 1886, First UK and first hardcover edition; fine, bright, square copy, housed in green quarter leather and cloth clamshell case with raised bands on spine and titles stamped in gold gilt, exceptional copy.   Buckingham Books   May 26 2011 - 22471   2011 $6000

Stevenson, Robert Louis Balfour 1850-1894 *Treasure Island.* London: Cassell & Co., 1883, First edition, first issue; frontispiece printed in three colors, with tissue guard, original olive green diagonal fine ribbed cloth with covers ruled in blind and spine ruled and lettered in gilt, original black coated endpapers, absolute minimum of wear to corners and extremities, rear hinge expertly and almost invisibly repaired, some very occasional browning and soiling, previous owner's neat ink inscription, exceptionally fresh, bright and fine, chemised in quarter green morocco slipcase, the Bradley Martin copy, bookplate of Mildred Greenhill on front pastedown, in this copy the "7" in the pagination on page 127 has been hand stamped in larger font and darker ink, and, as with other copies of the first issue, the "8" is not present in the pagination on page 83 (copies are known with the "8" present on page 83 and with the "7" missing from pagination on page 127),.   David Brass Rare Books, Inc.   May 26 2011 - 00036   2011 $32,500

Stevenson, Sarah Hackett *Wife and Mother or Information for Every Woman...* Chicago & Philadelphia: H. J. Smith, 1887, First edition?; 8vo., 526 pages, maroon cloth stamped in black and gilt with 20 page plate pamphlet with illustrations in rear pocket, nice, bright copy.   Second Life Books Inc.   174 - 294   2011 $125

Stevenson, W. H. *Royal Charters Granted to the Burgesses of Nottingham A.D. 1155-1712.* London: Bernard Quaritch 15 Piccadilly Nottingham: Thomas Forman & Sons, 1890, First edition; half title, viiii, 155, (1) pages, original cloth, calf backed, spine slightly worn, title in gilt on spine, bookplate of Jesse Hind, nice clean copy.   Anthony W. Laywood   May 26 2011 - 21700   2011 $76

Stewart, Cecil *Serbian Legacy.* London: Allen & Unwin, 1959, First edition; large 8vo., original cloth, dust jacket, pages 136, 81 plates, numerous text illustrations.   R. F. G. Hollett & Son Antiquarian Booksellers   177 - 832   2011   £40

Stewart, Cecil *Topiary, an Historical Diversion.* Waltham St. Lawrence: Golden Cockerel Press, 1954, 327/400 copies (of an edition of 500 copies; printed on handmade paper, 13 fanciful topiary designs, pages (iv), 40, imperial 8vo., original quarter bright orange cloth, backstrip gilt lettered, pale grey boards, patterned overall in green to designs by Barker Mill and with matching orange cloth fore-edges, untrimmed, fine.   Blackwell Rare Books   B166 - 261   2011   £100

Stewart, D. J. *On the Architectural History of Ely Cathedral.*   John Van Voorst, 1868, 8vo., viii, 296 + (10) pages ads, 8 plates, folding plan, original cloth, spine faded and inner joints worn.   Ken Spelman Rare Books   68 - 74   2011   £45

Stewart, Dugald   1753-1828   *Elements of Philosophy of the Human Mind. (with) Elements of the Philosophy of the Human Mind.*   London: printed for A. Strahan and T. Cadell and W. Creech, 1792, 1814. First edition; 2 volumes, 4to., xii, 569 (mis-numbered 566), (1 errata), xiv, 554, (1 ads, 1 blank, 1 errata, 1 blank) pages, occasional light foxing, contemporary calf, raised bands, gilt ruled, gilt stamped red morocco spine label, rebacked to style preserving covers, Kelson Library in contemporary ink and shelfmarks on front pastedown, bookseller tickets of Archibald Rutherfurd in both volume, fine.   Jeff Weber Rare Books   163 - 41   2011 $2200

Stewart, Dugald   1753-1828   *Elements of the Philosophy of the Human Mind.*   Edinburgh: A. Strahan and T. Cadell, W. Creech, 1792, First edition; 4to., contemporary polished tree calf, sometime rebacked in matching calf gilt, hinges little worn, pages xii, 567, very clean and sound.   R. F. G. Hollett & Son Antiquarian Booksellers   175 - 1294   2011   £375

Stewart, George Rippley   *Earth Abide.*   New York: Random House, 1949, First edition; octavo, cloth.   L. W. Currey, Inc.   124 - 78   2011 $1250

Stewart, K. J.   *The Freemason's Manual a Companion for the Initiated through all the Degrees of Freemasonry.*   Philadelphia: 1852, New edition; 359 pages, very good, backstrip gilt bright, corners good, top extremity of backstrip frayed, original binding.   Bookworm & Silverfish   678 - 80   2011 $87

Stewart, Mary   *Wildfire at Midnight.*   London: Hodder & Stoughton, 1956, First reprint; original cloth, dust jacket (rather worn), pages 191, plan.   R. F. G. Hollett & Sons Antiquarian Booksellers   170 - 657   2011   £45

Stewart, Paul   *Stormchaser/Edge Chronicles.*   London: Doubleday, 1999, First edition, first impression; illustrations by Chris Riddell, 394 pages, fine in fine dust jacket. Any Amount of Books   May 29 2011 - 827016   2011 $238

Stewarton   *The Female Revolutionary Plutarch.*   London: printed for John Murray, 1806, 1805. First editions; 196 x 11mm., 3 volumes, publisher's original blue paper boards, paper title labels on flat spines, edges untrimmed, frontispiece portraits, page one of each volume with lightly written signature of Lt. Col. Pepper(?), some (surprisingly minor) chafing and soiling to covers and spines, upper corner of one leaf torn off by rough opening (no loss of text), insignificant tiny round wormhole in gutter margin of first two gatherings of volume III, but exceptionally fine set, bindings all completely sound and showing no serious wear, text especially clean, bright and fresh.   Phillip J. Pirages   59 - 351   2011 $1900

Stiff, Peter   *Nine Days of War and South Africa's Final Days in Namibia.*   Galago Pub. Ltd., 1991, 304 pages, appears to be signed by author on titlepage, light browning to edges of pages, light rips to bottoms of 4 pages within, text not impacted, out of print, quite scarce, 42 black and white illustrations/photos.   G. H. Mott Bookseller   May 26 2011 - 062014878   2011 $225

Stigand, Chauncy Hugh   *The Game of British East Africa.*   London: Horace Cox, 1909, First edition; quarto, pages xi, 310, ads, numerous illustrations, some marginal light foxing, original green decorative cloth, vignette on front cover, joints rubbed, small wear to head and tail of spine.   J. & S. L. Bonham Antiquarian Booksellers   Africa 4/20/2011 - 9187   2011   £280

Stigand, Chauncy Hugh   *The Game of British East Africa.*   London: Horace Cox, 1909, Second edition; quarto, pages xi, 310, ads, numerous illustrations, original green decorative cloth, vignette on front cover, very good.   J. & S. L. Bonham Antiquarian Booksellers   Africa 4/20/2011 - 9199   2011   £140

Stigand, Chauncy Hugh   *Hunting the Elephant in Africa and Other Recollections of Thirteen Years Wanderings.*   New York: Macmillan, 1913, First edition; 8vo., pages xvi, 379, frontispiece, 22 plates, original blue cloth, top edge gilt, very slight rubbing to joint.   J. & S. L. Bonham Antiquarian Booksellers   Africa 4/20/2011 - 8855   2011   £400

Stigand, Chauncy Hugh   *The Land of Zinj: Being an Account of British East Africa...*   London: Constable, 1913, First edition; 8vo., pages xii, 351, large folding map, illustrations, some light occasional foxing, original blue cloth, head of spine little worn.   J. & S. L. Bonham Antiquarian Booksellers   Africa 4/20/2011 - 9153   2011   £190

Stigand, Chauncy Hugh *To Abyssinia Through an Unknown Land: an Account of a Journey through Unexplored Regions of British East Africa...* London: Seeley & Co., 1910, First edition; large 8vo., pages ix, 352, ads, maps, illustrations, lacks plate (camels drinking at Maidahad), original orange decorative cloth, titlepage, small brown spot on titlepage, very good, signed by author.   J. & S. L. Bonham Antiquarian Booksellers   Africa 4/20/2011 - 9150 2011   £180

Stiles, Robert *Four Years Under Marse Robert.* New York and Washington: 1903, Second edition; CSA gray with applique image on front, cover gilt bright, backstrip gilt not bright, but not dull, CSA gray is considerably foxed, reglued at half title, two leaves with bottom interior corner dog eared.   Bookworm & Silverfish   678 - 35 2011 $75

Stillingfleet, Edward *An Answer to Some Papers... Concerning the Authority of the Catholick Church in Matters of Faith and the Reformation of the Church of England.* London: printed for Ric. Chiswel, 1686, 4to., (iv), 72, (ii) late 1990's half calf by Chris Weston, few minor spots, some early ink annotations, from the collection of Christopher Ernest Weston 1947-2010.   Unsworths Booksellers   24 - 48 2011   £95

Stillingfleet, Edward *A Defence of the Discourse Concerning the Idolatry Practised in the Church of Rome.* London: Robert White for Henry Nortlock, 1676, 8vo., pages (xxxii), 877, (i), contemporary calf, spine panel gilt, boards double ruled in blind, board edges 'zig-zag' decorative roll gilt, all edges red and grey sprinkled, pink and white sewn endbands, small inkmark to half title and titlepage, endcaps worn, old leather scratched and conserved, recent replacement red lettering piece gilt, dust jacket ink inscription "JJ.20", from the collection of Christopher Ernest Weston 1947-2010.   Unsworths Booksellers   24 - 46 2011   £250

Stillingfleet, Edward *A Discourse Concerning the Doctrine of Christ's Satisfaction...* London: J. Heptinstall for Henry Mortlock, 1696, 8vo., pages xlvi, (ii) 35, (i), contemporary sprinkled calf, spine double ruled in blind, red lettering piece, boards double rule bordered in blind with stylized plant at corners, board edges decorative roll gilt, all edges gilt, lightly red speckled, blue and white sewn endbands, little thumbsoiling, front joint just cracking at foot, slight rubbing to extremities, contemporary ink printing, ink inscription, from the collection of Christopher Ernest Weston 1947-2010. Unsworths Booksellers   24 - 50 2011   £200

Stillingfleet, Edward *Origines Sacrae, or a Rational Account of the Grounds of Christian Faith.* London: R. W. for Henry Mortlock, 1663, Small 4to., pages (xxxvi), 619, (i), contemporary calf, unlettered spine double ruled in blind, boards double ruled in blind, board edges single rule gilt, inner face of boards exposed all edges rouge, browned and spotted, some dust soiling, rubbed and scratched, front board detached, rear joint splitting, endcaps worn, early ink inscription "Robert Whitaker" on front endpaper, also "George Stead/Book May 16 1833" reading downwards at fore-edge of same leaf, from the collection of Christopher Ernest Weston 1947-2010.   Unsworths Booksellers   24 - 43 2011   £150

Stillingfleet, Edward *The Unreasonableness of Separation; or an Impartial Account of the... Present.* London: T. N. for Henry Mortlock, 1681, 4to., pages (ii), xciv, (xvi), 450, contemporary calf, boards double rule bordered in blind, board edges 'zig-zag' decorative roll gilt, all edges blue 'swirl' marbled, mid 1980's calf rebacked and corners by Chris Weston, some spotting and toning, first few leaves soiled, titlepage touch worn at fore-edge, old leather scratched and crackled, early ink inscriptions "Christopher Metcalfe" (reading across) and in a different hand "Christopher Metcalfe book" reading upwards, contemporary ink inscription "C.M.", also printed booklabel of Revd. Richard Gibbons Binnall, from the collection of Christopher Ernest Weston 1947-2010.   Unsworths Booksellers   24 - 47 2011   £275

Stillwell, Margaret Bingham *General Hawkins as He Revealed Himself to His Librarian.* Providence: 1923, First separate edition; 8vo., 39 pages, frontispiece, original cloth backed boards, light foxing, inscribed by author 1924.   M & S Rare Books, Inc.   90 - 406 2011 $150

Stirk, David *Carry Your Bag, Sir? A History of Golf Caddies.* London: H. F. and G. Witherby, 1989, First edition; 8vo., 128 pages, signed, inscribed and dated in year of publication by Stirk, fine in fine dust jacket.   By the Book, L. C.   26 - 84 2011 $100

Stirling, James Hutchinson *Philosophy and Theology.* Edinburgh: T. & T. Clark, 1890, First edition; original cloth, gilt, pages xvi, 407, (xvi), scattered spotting, very good, largely unopened.   R. F. G. Hollett & Son Antiquarian Booksellers   175 - 1295 2011   £90

Stock, Charles *Clavis Linguae Veteris (& Novi) Testamenti Vocabularum.* Leipzig: Weidmann, 1752-1753, Fifth and sixth edition; pages (xii), 1414, (vii); (xii), 1190, (xl), with 2 engraved portrait frontispieces, vignette on each title, 2 engraved headpieces, occasional brown patch stamp of Baptist Union of Scotland, but very good.   R. F. G. Hollett & Son Antiquarian Booksellers   175 - 1296 2011   £220

Stockdale, James *Annales Caermoelenses; or Annals of Cartmel.* Ulverston: William Kitchin, 1872, First edition; thick 8vo., modern full maroon morocco gilt over bevelled boards with raised bands and double spine labels by J. P. J. Smith of Cartmel, with matching slipcase, pages (ii), 595, (iii), 2, vii, top edge gilt, complete with engraved frontispiece, 4 photos plates, genealogical table printed in red and black, gilt ruled dentelles and patterned endpapers, few neat repairs, scattered foxing, very scarce.   R. F. G. Hollett & Son Antiquarian Booksellers 173 - 1080 2011 £350

Stocks, Michael *Report of the Trial of Michael Stocks, Esq. for Wilful and Corrupt Perjury at the Yorkshire Lent Assizes 1815 Before the Honourable Sir Alexander Thompson, Knight...* Huddersfield: printed for the editor by J. Lancashire and sold by Longman, Hurst, Rees and Co. London and the booksellers of York, Leeds, Bradford, Huddersfield, Halifax, Sheffield, Wakefield, Rochdale, Manchester &c, 1815, Only edition; 8vo., (4), 109, (1) pages, list of errata on verso of final leaf, contemporary half calf over marbled boards, neatly rebacked and gilt lettered, very good.   John Drury Rare Books   153 - 152 2011 £450

Stockton, Frank *The Bee-Man of Orn.* Holt, Rhinehart & Winston, 1964, First edition; square 8vo., original cloth backed boards with pictorial onlay, dust jacket price clipped, spine little chipped at head and foot, pages 48, illustrations in color, inscription, few slight finger marks to final leaf of text.   R. F. G. Hollett & Sons Antiquarian Booksellers 170 - 628 2011 £120

Stockton, Frank *Griffin and the Minor Cannon.* New York: Holt Rinehart Winston, 1963, Stated first edition; 4to., cloth backed boards, fine in slightly worn dust jacket, illustrations in color by Sendak, inscribed and dated 1963 by Maurice Sendak and includes color illustrated greeting card by Sendak, uncommon.   Aleph-Bet Books, Inc. 95 - 509 2011 $500

Stockton, R. F. *Letter of Commodore Stockton on the Slavery Question.* New York: S. W. Benedict 10 Spruce St., 1859, First edition; 12mo., 23, (1) (blank) pages, removed, contemporary signature and two old library stamps on title, lightly stained, otherwise sound.   M & S Rare Books, Inc. 90 - 390 2011 $200

Stockwell, A. H. *The Baptist Churches of Lancashire.* London: Arthur H. Stockwell, n.d. circa, 1910, First edition; original blue cloth gilt over bevelled boards, pages 256 with numerous illustrations, little light spotting, scarce.   R. F. G. Hollett & Son Antiquarian Booksellers   175 - 1297 2011 £75

Stoddard, Lathrop *Scientific Humanism.* New York: Charles Scribner's Sons, 1926, First edition; original blue cloth, pages 177, fore-edges spotted, presentation copy, inscribed to Dr. A. J. Toynbee (historian) by the author and dated 1926, with compliments slip of publisher loosely inserted.   R. F. G. Hollett & Son Antiquarian Booksellers 175 - 1298 2011 £35

Stoddard, Lothrop *A Gallery of Jewish Types.* N.P. circa: 1962, Reprint; (2) 314-332 (2) pages, wrappers, surface vermining along front wrapper, top margin.   Bookworm & Silverfish 664 - 102 2011 $75

Stoker, Bram 1847-1912 *Dracula.* New York: Grosset & Dunlap, n.d., 1931, Later edition; octavo, pages (1-2) (i-vi) vii-ix (x) 1-354 (355-356: ads), 4 inserted plates with film stills, original red cloth, front and spine panels stamped in black, top edge stained black.   L. W. Currey, Inc. 124 - 86 2011 $1000

Stoker, Bram 1847-1912 *The Lady of the Shroud.* London: William Heinemann, 1909, First edition; red cloth gilt, faint stain on copyright page and facing dedication page, else very near fine, lovely copy, uncommon.   Between the Covers 169 - BTC341023 2011 $2500

Stokes, G. Vernon *A Town Dog in the Country.* London & Edinburgh: W. & R. Chambers, n.d., 1924, First edition; large 4to., original publisher's illustrated boards, lettering slightly rubbed and slightly chipped at spine, corners slightly rubbed, inner hinge slightly broken, overall bright, very good.   Any Amount of Books May 26 2011 - A69335 2011 $503

Stokes, Margaret *Early Christian Architecture in Ireland.* 1878, First edition; 52 plates, original cloth, good.   C. P. Hyland May 26 2011 - 255/725 2011 $507

Stokes, Margaret *Early Christian Architecture in Ireland.* 1887, First edition; 52 plates, rebound, ex-library, very good.   C. P. Hyland May 26 2011 - 255726 2011 $457

Stone, Reynolds *Boxwood. Sixteen Engravings by Reynolds Stone.* Monotype Corporation, 1957, First edition; scarce first issue, 37, (1) pages, fine, gilt stamped cloth with clear plastic over wrapper.   Ken Spelman Rare Books 68 - 127 2011 £40

Stone, Robert *Children of Light.* New York: Knopf, 1986, Uncorrected proof copy of the first American edition; some dustiness and rubbing to covers, bit of spine fading, very good in wrappers, custom folding chemise and slipcase, inscribed by author for another writer.   Ken Lopez Bookseller 154 - 214 2011 $750

Stone, Robert *A Flag for Sunrise.* New York: Knopf, 1981, First edition, review copy; signed by author, one page corner turned, little foxing to spine cloth and page edges, near fine in very near fine, mildly rubbed black dust jacket, although there is no explicit indication of it, this was purchased from author's own library, letter of provenance indicating that can be provided.　Ken Lopez Bookseller　154 - 211　2011　$150

Stone, Robert *A Flag for Sunrise.* New York: Knopf, 1981, First edition; review copy, inscribed by author, cocked, spotting to top edge, very good in near fine dust jacket with light wear at spine ends, review slip laid in, not an uncommon book, but uncommon as an advance copy and with a warm personal inscription.　Ken Lopez Bookseller　154 - 213　2011　$125

Stone, Robert *A Flag for Sunrise.* New York: Knopf, 1981, First edition; signed by author, bit of foxing to spine cloth, very near fine in near fine dust jacket, price clipped, from author's library.　Ken Lopez Bookseller　154 - 212　2011　$125

Stone, Robert *Outerbridge Beach.* New York: Ticknor & Fields, 1992, First trade edition; signed by author, foxing to top edge and mild concavity to spine, near fine in near fine dust jacket, foxed on verso, from author's own library.　Ken Lopez Bookseller　154 - 215　2011　$65

Stone, Robert *Outerbridge Ridge.* Boston: 1992, First edition, 1/300 numbered and signed copies; fine in slipcase.　Gemini Fine Books & Arts, Ltd.　Art Reference & Illustrated Books: First Editions 2011　$150

Stone, Robert *Outerbridge Reach.* New York: Ticknor & Fields, 1992, First edition, signed, limited edition, 1/300 numbered copies; black cloth in blue card slipcase, fine book and case, signed by authors.　Lupack Rare Books　May 26 2011 - ABE878652151　2011　$100

Stone, William L. *Life of Joseph Brant-Thayendanegea. Including the Indian Wars of the American Revolution.* New York: 1838, First edition; 2 volumes, full calf, front hinge volume 1 repaired neatly, backstrip gilt bright, marbled endpapers, all edges marbled, fore edge of text (volume 1) mildly damped, previous owner's name incised into cover of one volume, the set has 2 small spots with some cosmetic efforts, set has all 8 plates, including 2 folding plates, one plan and five portraits.　Bookworm & Silverfish　678 - 11　2011　$250

Stoppard, Tom *Rock 'n' Roll.* London: Faber & Faber, 2006, First edition thus; 8vo., wrappers, signed by Stoppard, Rufus Sewell, Brian Cox and Sinead Cusak, pages 128, fine.　Any Amount of Books　May 29 2011 - A68668　2011　$340

Storey, David *Radcliffe.* London: Longmans, 1963, First edition; 376 page, crown 8vo., original lime green boards, gilt lettered backstrip lightly faded, dust jacket rubbed, good.　Blackwell Rare Books　B166 - 235　2011　£30

Stories Selected from the History of Scotland for Children, Intended as a Companion to the Stories Selected from the History of England. London: Harris and Son, 1820, First edition; 12mo., ii, 212 pages, marbled paper on boards, red roan, spine with gilt title and fillets, small engraved bookseller label inside upper cover, lacking front endpaper, near mint.　Hobbyhorse Books　56 - 142　2011　$175

The Story of Jesus. London: Strand Publications, n.d. circa, 1930, Large 8vo., original cloth, inset on upper board, hinges trifle rubbed, pages vii, 24, color endpapers and 8 fine color pop-ups, one short tear, otherwise good, crisp unused edition.　R. F. G. Hollett & Son Antiquarian Booksellers　175 - 518　2011　£85

The Story of Old Mother Hubbard and Her Dog. Blackie & Son, n.d. circa, 1930, Large 4to., original cloth backed boards with pictorial onlay, little surface abrasion to corners and edges, pages (32), 12 full page color illustrations, numerous black and white drawings by Frank Adams, two color pictorial endpapers, very nice.　R. F. G. Hollett & Son Antiquarian Booksellers　General Catalogue Summer 2010 - 484　2011　£65

The Story of Robin-Hood. New York: McLoughlin Bros., 1895, Full color pictorial card covers cut around shape of Robin blowing his horn and holding his bow, book is 12 x 6 inches in size, some light handling and spine rubbed off but intact with stapled binding, 14 pages (counting inside covers), 6 have full color illustrations, rest with line drawings.　Jo Ann Reisler, Ltd.　86 - 234　2011　$175

The Story of Robinson Crusoe with Surprise Pictures. London: Dean & Son Publishers &c, 1874, 8vo., color pictorial board covers with some edge rubbing and light overall handling, book is clean and lovely within, 12 pages of text and six full page transformation plates.　Jo Ann Reisler, Ltd.　86 - 173　2011　$2200

The Story of the Kings of Judah and Israel. Edinburgh: William P. Nimo, 1868, Third edition; small square 8vo., original green pictorial cloth, gilt extra, pages 133, (iii), all edges gilt, chromolithographed frontispiece, additional title, lovely copy, very scarce.　R. F. G. Hollett & Son Antiquarian Booksellers　175 - 65　2011　£120

Story, Joseph *Commentaries on Equity Jurisprudence as Administered in England and American.* Boston: 1861, Eighth edition; 2 volumes, lxxix, (blank), 768; v, (blank), 856 pages, old law calf with few scrapes, very good, two inch separation to one side of one backstrip.　Bookworm & Silverfish　665 - 82　2011　$150

Story, Thomas *A Journal of the Life of Thomas Story...* Newcastle upon Tyne: Isaac Thompson and Co., 1747, First edition; folio, contemporary blind panelled calf, little rubbed attractively rebacked in matching calf gilt extra with raised bands, pages (ii), iv, 768, 8, exceptionally good, tall, wide margined copy.   R. F. G. Hollett & Son Antiquarian Booksellers   175 - 1299   2011   £425

Stowe, Calvin E. *The Prussian System of Public Instruction with Its Applicability to the United States.* Cincinnati: Truman & Smith, 1836, First edition; original floral decorated cloth and paper label, some foxing throughout, but overall, near fine.   Lupack Rare Books   May 26 2011 - ABE2882733777   2011 $200

Stowe, Charles Edward *The Life of Harriet Beecher Stowe.* Boston and New York: Houghton Mifflin And Co., 1889, First edition; xii, 530 pages, including index and 3 page List of Works of Harriet Beecher Stowe, royal 8vo., three quarter black morocco over marbled boards, gilt lettered spine, top edge gilt, frontispiece, 13 plates and 2 facsimiles, touch of wear to extremities, otherwise very fine.   Paulette Rose Fine and Rare Books   32 - 165   2011 $200

Stowe, Harriet Elizabeth Beecher   1811-1896   *The Key to Uncle Tom's Cabin...* London: 1853, Early printing of London issue; viii, 508 pages, white backstrip lettered in third format, blue ink on white endpaper, very good, recased, laid into original covers, better than original, covers bit rubbed.   Bookworm & Silverfish   666 - 155   2011 $75

Stowe, Harriet Elizabeth Beecher   1811-1896   *Sketches of American Life a Companion to the Mayflower.* London: 1855, First edition in this form; xxxii, 256, 7 (1) pages, 16mo., extremely nice, cover gilt sharp, backstrip rubbed but legible, very scarce.   Bookworm & Silverfish   666 - 11   2011 $150

Stowe, Harriet Elizabeth Beecher   1811-1896   *Uncle Tom's Cabin or Life Among the Lowly.* Boston: John P. Jewett & Co., 1852, First edition; 2 volumes, 12mo., six black and white plates, BAL's rare extra gilt gift binding C, publisher's original red cloth with extra gilt.   Heritage Book Shop   Booth A12 51st NY International Antiquarian Book Fair April 8-10 2011 - 132   2011 $16,000

Strachan, James *Early Bible Illustrations.* Cambridge: University Press, 1957, First edition; original cloth, gilt, dust jacket, pages viii, 170, frontispiece and 126 illustrations, author's compliments slip loosely inserted.   R. F. G. Hollett & Son Antiquarian Booksellers   175 - 1301   2011   £65

Strachan, James *A New Set of Tables for Computing the Weight of Cattle by Measurement...*   Edinburgh: Oliver & Boyd, n.d. circa, 1860, Sixteenth edition; Modern cloth backed marbled boards, gilt, pages 116, 24, uncommon.   R. F. G. Hollett & Son Antiquarian Booksellers   175 - 1302   2011   £75

Strachey, Lytton   1880-1932   *Elizabeth and Essex.* London: Chatto & Windus, 1928, First edition; original cloth, gilt, pages 288, with 6 plates.   R. F. G. Hollett & Son Antiquarian Booksellers   175 - 1203   2011   £30

Strachey, Lytton   1880-1932   *Queen Victoria.* London: Chatto & Windus, 1921, First edition; pages (viii), 314, with 9 plates, half title very lightly spotted, original blue cloth with paper spine label.   R. F. G. Hollett & Son Antiquarian Booksellers   175 - 1304   2011   £30

Strada, Famiano *Histoire de la Guerre de Flandre.* Leiden: B. & A. Elzevier, 1652, 2 volumes, 8vo., (12), 768, (36); (12), 881, (65) pages, titles printed in red and black, engraved portraits in text, late 18th century English tree calf, spines gilt, joints little weak, bookplate of Hon. Lieut Gen. G. L. Parker, from the library of the Earls of Macclesfield at Shirburn Castle.   Maggs Bros. Ltd.   1440 - 204   2011   £500

Strang, Herbert, Mrs. *ABC and 123.* London: Oxford University Press, 1942, 4to., pictorial cloth, fine, illustrations in pen and ink.   Aleph-Bet Books, Inc.   95 - 4   2011 $125

Stratton, Arthur *The Orders of Architecture. Greek, Roman and Renaissance with Selected Examples of their Application Shown on 80 Plates.* London: Batsford, 1931, First edition; large 4to., original black cloth, gilt, pages viii, 16, 34, 49, (i), with 80 plates.   R. F. G. Hollett & Son Antiquarian Booksellers   177 - 835   2011   £75

Stratton, Clarence *Swords and Statues.* Philadelphia: John C. Winston, 1937, First edition; 8vo., blue cloth stamped in gold, 254 pages, offsetting on title, else fine, in slightly worn dust jacket, uncommon title.   Aleph-Bet Books, Inc.   95 - 323   2011 $175

Straus, Ralph *The Unspeakable Curll.* New York: R. M. McBride & London: Chapman & Hall, 1928, First edition, limited to 525 copies; top edge gilt, very good, spine lettering faded away.   Lupack Rare Books   May 26 2011 - ABE1256702459   2011 $100

Streatfeild, Noel *Curtain Up.* London: J. M. Dent, 1944, First edition; original cloth, dust jacket trifle worn, pages 288 with color frontispiece and line drawings.   R. F. G. Hollett & Sons Antiquarian Booksellers   170 - 660   2011   £60

Street Scene, American Opera. New York: Chappell, 1948, First edition; 4to., pages 173, printed wrappers, bit of edgewear at top of spine, ownership signature of pianist-composer Margaret Bonds.   Second Life Books Inc.   174 - 295   2011 $500

Strickland, Agnes *Fisher's Juvenile Scrap Book.* Fisher Son & Co., 1839, Original blindstamped cloth gilt, spine rather faded, pages 112, all edges gilt, steel engraved title, 15 engraved plates (some little foxed). R. F. G. Hollett & Sons Antiquarian Booksellers 170 - 661 2011 £65

Strickland, Agnes *The Rival Crusoes or the Shipwreck.* London: J. Harris, 1826, First edition; 12mo., 191 pages, contemporary dark brown calf, blind and gilt embossing, six gilt compartments and title along spine, marbled endpapers, gilt edges, large wood engraved vignette, corner of one leaf restored, light cracking at folds of cover, fine. Hobbyhorse Books 56 - 143 2011 $325

Stromholm, Christer *Till Minnet av mig sjalv. (In Memory of Myself).* Stockholm: Foto Expo, 1965, First edition; pages (32), (8), 12mo., 38 black and white photos, original black and white photo illustrated wrappers, fine, inscribed by Stromholm for Tore Falk. Simon Finch Rare Books Zero - 548 2011 £3500

Stromholm, Christer *Poste Restante.* Stockholm: P. A. Norstedt & Soners Forlag, 1967, First edition; 8vo., pages (xviii) (100), 96 black and white photos, original brown cloth, spine and upper side lettered in silver, original black and white photo illustrated dust jacket, very lightly rubbed, minor abrasions to upper edge, short closed tear to upper and lower panels, Stromholm's business card attached by a paperclip to front flap, inscription to Tore Falk, fine in near fine dust jacket. Simon Finch Rare Books Zero - 548 2011 £5000

Strong, Leonard Alfred George *The Hansom Cab and the Pigeons, Being Random Recollections upon the Silver Jubilee of King George.* Waltham St. Lawrence: Golden Cockerel Press, 1935, First edition, 142/212 special issue copies (of an edition of 1212 copies; printed on Arnold handmade paper and signed by author, wood engraved frontispiece and 16 other engravings in text by Eric Ravilious, pages 52, 8vo., original quarter royal blue crushed morocco, silver gilt lettered backstrip faded as usual, boards marbled in various shades of blue on cream ground, top edge silver, others untrimmed, near fine. Blackwell Rare Books B166 - 262 2011 £350

Strong, Leonard Alfred George *Sixteen Portraits of People.* The Naldrett Press for the National Trust, 1951, First edition; Original cloth, dust jacket (spine little browned and trifle frayed at head and foot, price clipped), pages 245, 16 plates by Hassall, flyleaves partly browned. R. F. G. Hollett & Son Antiquarian Booksellers General Catalogue Summer 2010 - 420 2011 £35

Stroud, Dorothy *Humphrey Repton.* London: Country Life, 1962, First edition; 4to., original cloth, gilt, dust jacket, pages 182, illustrations, slight stain to fore-edge of last few pages, otherwise very nice, scarce. R. F. G. Hollett & Son Antiquarian Booksellers 177 - 837 2011 £150

Stroud, Jonathan *The Amulet of Samarkand (The Bartimaeus Trilogy. Book 1).* London: Doubleday, 2003, First UK edition; fine in fine dust jacket, wrap around band from Pan Bookshop, signed by author. Bella Luna Books May 29 2011 - t9427 2011 $82

Strouse, Norman H. *C-S The Master Craftsman. (and) A Letter from Stella by Stella Cobden-Sanderson.* Harper Woods: printed by Leonard F. Bahr at The Adagio Press, 1969, One of 12 copies with two original leaves Printed on vellum (and of these, one of 10 with gilt initial) of 329 copies printed total; signed by printer, 394 x 160mm., 54, (1) leaf blank; 10 leaves, publisher's vellum backed, marbled paper boards, gilt titling on spine, second work in original stitched paper wrapper, both works in fine heavy folding felt lined cloth box covered in gray linen and with gilt lettered spine label, mounted photo of Emery Walker and Cobden-Sanderson laid in at front, with typed letter from David Magee describing this copy, first work printed in brown, blue and black, second work printed in green and black, virtually mint. Phillip J. Pirages 59 - 183 2011 $3500

Strube, Sidney *War Cartoons from the Daily Express 1939 to 1944.* Daily Express, 1944, Oblong 8vo., original pictorial wrappers, trifle used, unpaginated, cartoons. R. F. G. Hollett & Son Antiquarian Booksellers General Catalogue Summer 2010 - 907 2011 £45

Struther, Jan *The Modern Struwwelpeter.* London: Methuen and Co., 1936, Cloth backed color pictorial boards with slight darkening but overall nice copy, 38 pages, illustrations. Jo Ann Reisler, Ltd. 86 - 137 2011 $750

Struther, Jan *Sycamore Square an Other Verses.* London: Methuen, 1932, First edition; original green pictorial cloth gilt, pages viii, 64, illustrations by E. H. Shepard. R. F. G. Hollett & Son Antiquarian Booksellers General Catalogue Summer 2010 - 908 2011 £30

Strutt, Samuel *An Essay Towards Demonstrating the Immateriality and Free Agency of the Soul.* London: printed for J. Shuckburg at the Sun, next to the Inner-Temple Gate, in Fleet Street MDCCLX, 1760, First edition; date in imprint error for (1760) (1740), xvi 136 pages, disbound. Anthony W. Laywood May 26 2011 - 21569 2011 $184

Strype, John *The History of the Life and Acts of... Edmund Grindal...* London: printed for John Wyat and John Hartley, 1710, Folio, pages (i), xviii, 314, 108, (vi) + engraved frontispiece, contemporary calf, untooled spine, red lettering piece gilt, boards panelled in blind (Cambridge style) board edges decorative roll gilt, all edges red sprinkled, blue and white sewn endbands, lightly browned and spotted, rubbed and chipped, corners worn, joints cracking at ends, strong, contemporary inscription "Ant. Johnson, ink inscriptions crossed out on both pastedowns, from the collection of Christopher Ernest Weston 1947-2010. Unsworths Booksellers 24 - 51 2011 £250

Stuart, J. M. *The Ancient Gold Fields of Africa from the Gold Coast to Mashonaland.* London: Express Printing Co., 1891, First edition; quarto, pages 312, maps, plates, illustrations, original olive green cloth, neatly recased. J. & S. L. Bonham Antiquarian Booksellers Africa 4/20/2011 - 6791 2011 £280

Stuart, Ruth McEnery *Daddy Do-Funny's Wisdom Jingles.* New York: Century, 1913, First edition; 8vo., cloth, 95 pages, edges of covers soiled else very good, illustrations on every page in line, very scarce. Aleph-Bet Books, Inc. 95 - 109 2011 $225

Stuart, Simon *Threatened Amphibians of the World.* Barcelona: Lynx Editions, 2008, First edition; large 8vo., illustrated laminated boards, copiously illustrated in color, fine. Any Amount of Books May 29 2011 - A66246 2011 $306

Stubbins, Thomas Alva *The Patriot.* Chicago: 1908, First edition; 287 pages, large 12mo., nearly very good, silver gilt cover and backstrip design quite legible but mildly rubbing. Bookworm & Silverfish 669 - 185 2011 $145

Stubbs, Horace *Sketching through Cumberland.* Seacastle: privately published, 1971, Large 8vo., original cloth, gilt, dust jacket, 51 pages, profusely illustrated. R. F. G. Hollett & Son Antiquarian Booksellers 173 - 1081 2011 £35

Studd, Will *Chalk and Cheese.* South Melbourne: Purple Egg, 1999, First edition; 4to., illustrations in color, fine in fine dust jacket. Any Amount of Books May 29 2011 - A69493 2011 $272

The Studio. 1948-1963, First edition; Jan. 498-Dec. 1963 (lacking 10 issues), color plates, photo illustrations, over 180 issues in original wrappers with 2 earlier issues Jan. 1944 & Nov. 1947. I. D. Edrich May 26 2011 - 97799 2011 $671

The Studio: a Bibliography of the First Fifty Years 1893-1943. London: Sims & Reed, 1978, First edition; tall 8vo., original wrappers, trifle worn, pages 142, with 12 pages of illustrations, uncommon. R. F. G. Hollett & Son Antiquarian Booksellers General Catalogue Summer 2010 - 206 2011 £45

Stukeley, W. *Copy of a Letter, Containing a Description of a Roman Pavement found Near Grantham, Lincolnshire with the Economy of the Roman Times in that Part of England.* Lincoln: W. Brooke, 1801, First edition; folio, 3, 1) pages, very nice. Anthony W. Laywood May 26 2011 - 21712 2011 $587

Sturgis, Russell *A History of Architecture.* London: Batsford, 1907-1910, Small 4to., 2 volumes only (of 4), original cloth, gilt, one spine trifle creased, pages xxvi, 425; xxiii, 448; with 728 illustrations. R. F. G. Hollett & Son Antiquarian Booksellers 177 - 838 2011 £75

Sturluson, Snorri *The Heimskringla: the Stories of the Kings of Norway Called the Round World.* London: Bernard Quaritch, 1893, 4 volumes, old green library cloth gilt, pages 410, 484, 505, 518, with large folding map and 14 extending genealogies, light library stamps to backs of titlepages, armorial bookplate, otherwise very good, sound, clean. R. F. G. Hollett & Son Antiquarian Booksellers General Catalogue Summer 2010 - 666 2011 £150

Sturm, C. C. *Reflections on the Works of God and Of His Providence throughout all Nature.* London: printed for Walker and Edwards, 1817, 2 volumes, contemporary full calf gilt with spine labels, pages xiv, 376; (viii), 412, engraved frontispiece and title to each volume. R. F. G. Hollett & Son Antiquarian Booksellers 175 - 1306 2011 £65

Sturm, Leonhard Christoph *Prodomus Architecturae Goldmannianae oder Betreue und Grundliche Anweisung.* Augsburg: Peter Detleff for Jermias Wolff, 1714, Oblong folio, bound as upright folio, ff. (10), engraved illustration in text, 22 (of 25) plates, bound as 29 engraved double page plates, contemporary calf backed, spine gilt in compartments, lacking plate VI, bookplate of Hon. Lieut. Gen. G. L. Parker, from the library of the Earls of Macclesfield at Shirburn Castle. Maggs Bros. Ltd. 1440 - 205 2011 £450

Styan, K. E. *A Short History of Sepulchral Cross-Slabs with Reference to Other Emblems found Thereon.* London: Bemrose & Son, 1902, First edition; original cloth, gilt, trifle marked, pages (vi), 45, plus 71 plates. R. F. G. Hollett & Son Antiquarian Booksellers 177 - 839 2011 £35

Styles, Philip *The Borough of Stratford-Upon-Avon and the Parish of Alveston.* Oxford University Press, 1946, Tall 8vo., original wrappers, pages 72, plates and text figures. R. F. G. Hollett & Son Antiquarian Booksellers 177 - 840 2011 £35

Styron, William *Admiral Robert Penn Warren and the Snows of Winter.* Palaemon, 1977, First edition; one of 26 copies, signed by author, as new in wrappers. Gemini Fine Books & Arts, Ltd. Art Reference & Illustrated Books: First Editions 2011 $170

Styron, William *Against Fear.* Palaemon, 1981, First edition; one of 50 copies signed by William Styron, as new in wrappers. Gemini Fine Books & Arts, Ltd. Art Reference & Illustrated Books: First Editions 2011 $150

Styron, William *The Confessions of Nat Turner.* New York: Random House, 1967, First trade edition; signed by author on blank sheet following f.f.e.p., fine in near fine, first printing dust jacket (price clipped but with correct date bottom of front flap). Lupack Rare Books May 26 2011 - ABE4890170510 2011 $150

Styron, William *The Confessions of Nat Turner.* Norwalk: Easton Press, 2000, First edition thus; signed by author, leather bound, all edges gilt, as new, includes certificate of authenticity and note from Easton Press. Gemini Fine Books & Arts, Ltd. Art Reference & Illustrated Books: First Editions 2011 $120

Styron, William *Lie Down in Darkness.* Indianapolis: Bobbs Merrill, 1951, First edition; near fine in very good+ dust jacket. Lupack Rare Books May 26 2011 - ABE3658730120 2011 $175

Styron, William *This Quiet Dust and Other Writings.* New York: 1982, First edition, 1/250 signed copies; fine in slipcase. Gemini Fine Books & Arts, Ltd. Art Reference & Illustrated Books: First Editions 2011 $90

Styron, William *This Quiet Dust.* New York: Random House, 1982, First edition, one of 250 numbered copies; signed by author, fine in fine publisher's slipcase. Lupack Rare Books May 26 2011 - ABE1663490765 2011 $200

Styron, William *A Tidewater Morning.* New York: Random House, 1993, First edition; signed on half title, fine in fine dust jacket. Lupack Rare Books May 26 2011 - ABE1503305695 2011 $125

Styron, William *A Tidewater Morning.* New York: Random House, 1993, First edition, limited, signed, one of 200 copies specially bound; fine in like slipcase and (opened) shrinkwrap still present, signed. Lupack Rare Books May 26 2011 - ABE4890169943 2011 $125

Suckling, John *Fragmenta Aurea. A Collection of all the Incomparable Pieces.* London: for Humphrey Moseley, 1646, First edition; first state of title with "FRAGMENTA AVREA" in upper case, a period after "Churchyard" in imprint and rule under date; A3v: 16 reads "allowed", second state of frontispiece, re-incised with heavier lines around leaves of garland and bulge in left sleeve; (6), 119, (7), 82, 64, (4), 52 pages, engraved portrait by William Marshall, contemporary calf, gilt fillet and cornerpieces, red morocco spine label, portrait and first two leaves with two very tiny holes at gutter, worm trail in lower margin of first three gatherings, else very nice, contemporary binding, bookplate of C. Pearl Chamberlain and booklabel of Abel Berland; fine red morocco pull-off case, ALS of John Suckling (1659-1627) father of the poet, Goodfathers 29 July 1625 to unnamed recipient seeking information on his election as a burgess in Yarmouth. Joseph J. Felcone Inc. Fall Miscellany 2010 - 113 2011 $6000

Sucksmith, Harvey Peter *Those Whom the Old Gods Love and Other Ghostly Tales of Vision and Dread.* London: Ghost Story Press, 1994, First edition; octavo, boards. L. W. Currey, Inc. 124 - 150 2011 $450

Sudek, Josef *Praha Panoramaticka.* Prague: Statni Nakladateistva Krasne Literary, Hudby a Umeni, 1959, First edition; beautifully printed book with 284 gravure images, near fine in close to near fine dust jacket with some moderate soiling and a number of tears, very nice, fragile. Jeff Hirsch Books ny 2010 2011 $1250

Sue, Eugene 1804-1857 *The Works.* Boston: printed for Francis A Niccolls & Co., circa, 1899-1900, Edition des Amateurs, limited to 50 copies, this designated as "Publisher's Copy" on limitation page; 230 x 154mm., 20 volumes, very fine contemporary honey-brown morocco, lavishly gilt, covers with all over Art Nouveau design of tendrils swirling around a central strapwork panel, lower corners outside the panel as well as the four corners inside panel with flowers of inlaid red or white morocco, decorated raised bands, spines elegantly gilt in compartments, featuring slender stems, lush foliage and an inlaid red or white morocco flower, very wide turn-ins framing navy blue morocco doublures, the center of the doublure with an elaborate emblem of gilt and inlaid purple and brown morocco, turn-in frame with several gilt fillets. leafy foliage and four more inlaid morocco flowers in red (a total of 23 floral inlays per volume, or 460 for the set), watered silk flyleaves, top edge gilt, other edges rough trimmed, with total of 190 plates, virtually perfect set with only most trivial imperfections, lovely bindings very bright and immaculate internally. Phillip J. Pirages 59 - 329 2011 $7500

Suetonius Tranquillus, Caius *XII Caesares.* Antwerp: Ex officina Plantiniana, 1591, 4to., titlepage engraved, outer edges occasionally soiled and bumped, first and last few just slightly frayed, small dampmark to few margins, pages (iv), 407, (23), 4to., early vellum, backstrip divided by blind fillets, top compartment lettered in ink, yapp edges, bit rumpled an rather soiled, ties removed, no flyleaves, hinges cracked, ownership inscription of Eduard Fraenkel (and some other marks) to front pastedown, sound. Blackwell Rare Books B166 - 103 2011 £750

Suetonius Tranquillus, Caius *(Opera).* Paris: Typographia Regia, 1645, 12mo., (12), 558, (30) pages, engraved title, engraved medallion portraits, engraved head and tailpiece, contemporary French calf, gilt fleurs de lys on covers within double gilt fillet, spine gilt in compartments, marbled edges, signature of Vincent Loger 1667, from the library of the Earls of Macclesfield at Shirburn Castle. Maggs Bros. Ltd. 1440 - 206 2011 £700

Suffer Little Children. London: Ernest Nister, n.d. circa, 1897, 4to., original cloth backed pictorial boards, edges worn, some dampstaining, 14 chromolithographed plates and sepia illustrations, rather shaken and loose in places, little fingering. R. F. G. Hollett & Sons Antiquarian Booksellers 170 - 477 2011 £45

Sugden, Edward Burtenshaw 1781-1875 *A Practical Treatise of the Law of Vendors Purchasers of Estates.* Philadelphia: 1820, Called the second American edition; large 8vo., lxx, 588, 49, 83 pages, full law calf, mild shelf twist. Bookworm & Silverfish 662 - 90 2011 $125

Sulivan, G. L. *Dhow Chasing in Zanzibar Waters; and on the Eastern Coast of Africa.* London: Sampson Low, 1873, Second edition; 8vo., pages xi, 453, map, illustrations, contemporary half calf, very good, clean copy. J. & S. L. Bonham Antiquarian Booksellers Africa 4/20/2011 - 6853 2011 £1100

Sullivan, Arabella *Recollections of a Chaperon.* London: Richard Bentley, 1849, First issue of this title; (428) pages, 8vo., original dark brown morocco grain cloth, blindstamped front and back, spine gilt lettered, glazed yellow endpapers, printed with titles in the Standard Novels series to No. 121, frontispiece dated 1848, fine with booklabel of Fothergill on front pastedown. Paulette Rose Fine and Rare Books 32 - 171 2011 $150

Sullivan, J. *Cumberland & Westmorland, Ancient and Modern...* Whittaker & Co. and Kendal: John Hudson, 1837, First edition; original blindstamped cloth, gilt, pages iii, 171, scarce, James Parker's copy. R. F. G. Hollett & Son Antiquarian Booksellers 173 - 1082 2011 £95

Sultan, Larry *Evidence.* Greenbrae: Clatworthy Colorvues, 1979, First edition; just about fine copy with ownership signature of Boston photographer Mark Goodman, increasingly uncommon in this condition. Jeff Hirsch Books ny 2010 2011 $2250

Summer Rambles Illustrative of the Pleasures Derived from the Study of Natural History. London: Hamilton, Adams and Co. and Liverpool: D. Marples & Co., date erased, 1834, 12mo., original watered cloth gilt, hinges cracked and repaired, pages viii, 184, (ii), 8, all edges gilt, steel engraved frontispiece, dated May 1834 (month partly erased), 8 finely hand colored tissue guarded plates, front flyleaf stuck to pastedown, otherwise very nice, clean and sound, scarce. R. F. G. Hollett & Sons Antiquarian Booksellers 170 - 24 2011 £150

Summerhayes, V. A. *Wild Orchids.* London: Collins, 1951, First edition; original cloth, gilt, rather faded, dust jacket spine frayed at head and foot, pages 366, 61 color and 39 black and white photos, 19 text figures, 43 distribution maps, label removed from and ownership inscription. R. F. G. Hollett & Son Antiquarian Booksellers General Catalogue Summer 2010 - 1056 2011 £75

Summers-Smith, J. D. *The House Sparrow.* London: Collins, 1963, First edition; original cloth, gilt, dust jacket spine very slightly browned, pages 269 color frontispiece, 32 photos and 36 text figures. R. F. G. Hollett & Son Antiquarian Booksellers General Catalogue Summer 2010 - 1057 2011 £95

Summers, Montague *Covent Garden Drollery.* Fortune Press, 1927, Limited edition, no.530 of 575 copies; original buckram backed boards, gilt, dust jacket, half of spine lacking, pages vi, 123, (i), untrimmed, frontispiece and tailpiece by Paul Rotha. R. F. G. Hollett & Son Antiquarian Booksellers General Catalogue Summer 2010 - 909 2011 £65

Summerson, Henry *Lanercost Priory, Cumbria.* Kendal: CWAAS, 2000, First edition; tall 4to., original wrappers, pages xii, 219, with 109 plates, plans and illustrations, very scarce. R. F. G. Hollett & Son Antiquarian Booksellers 177 - 841 2011 £85

Summerson, John *Architecture in Britain 1530-1830. Pelican History of Art.* Penguin Books, 1953, First edition; thick small 4to., original cloth, gilt, leather spine label, dust jacket rather defective, pages xviii, 373, with 192 pages of plates and 48 text figures. R. F. G. Hollett & Son Antiquarian Booksellers 177 - 842 2011 £45

Sumner, Charles *The Crime Against Kansas. The Apologies for the Crime. The True Remedy. Speech...in the Senate of the United States 19th and 20th May 1856.* Washington: Buell & Blanchard printers, 1856, 8vo., 32 pages, as issued, uncut, inscribed in ink by author on titlepage to E. W. Kin(g)sley (sic). M & S Rare Books, Inc. 90 - 408 2011 $3000

Sumner, Helen *Equal Suffrage, the Results of an Investigation in Colorado Made for the Collegiate Equal Suffrage League of NY State.* New York: Harper and Brothers, 1909, First edition; 8vo., pages 282, label removed from spine, very good tight copy. Second Life Books Inc. 174 - 296 2011 $125

The Sunday Scholar. London: Religious Tract Society, n.d. circa, 1840, 16mo., 16 pages, pictorial buff paper wrappers, small wood engraved vignette on titlepage, 4 large wood engraved vignettes, fine. Hobbyhorse Books 56 - 31 2011 $70

Suri, Manil *The Death of Vishnu.* London: Bloomsbury, 2001, First British edition; fine in fine dust jacket, signed by author. Bella Luna Books May 29 2011 - t5492 2011 $82

Surtees, Robert Smith 1803-1864 *Ask Mamma; or the Richest Commoner in England.* London: Bradbury and Evans, Subscribers edition; pages xii, 423, 13 hand colored plates by John Leech, original pictorial crimson cloth, gilt over bevelled boards, spine rather faded. R. F. G. Hollett & Son Antiquarian Booksellers General Catalogue Summer 2010 - 1290 2011 £95

Surtees, Robert Smith 1803-1864 *Handley Cross; or Mr. Jorrock's Hunt.* London: Bradbury, Agnew & co. n.d., Subscriber's edition; Original crimson pictorial cloth gilt over bevelled boards, spine faded pages xiv, 578, (ii), complete with 17 hand colored plates and 100 text woodcuts.   R. F. G. Hollett & Son Antiquarian Booksellers   General Catalogue Summer 2010 - 1292 2011   £95

Surtees, Robert Smith 1803-1864 *Handley Cross.* London: Bradbury Agnew & Co. n.d., Original crimson pictorial cloth gilt over bevelled boards, spine faded and frayed at head, lower board rather faded in vertical bars, pages xiv, 578, (ii) complete with 16 hand colored plates and 100 text woodcuts.   R. F. G. Hollett & Son Antiquarian Booksellers General Catalogue Summer 2010 - 1291 2011   £85

Surtees, Robert Smith 1803-1864 *Handley Cross; or Jorrock's Hunt.* Bradbury Agnew, circa, 1880, Hand colored frontispiece, title vignette and 16 hand colored plates, one or two foxmarks, pages viii, 550, 8vo., full polished calf, spine panelled in gilt, central haunting emblems and morocco labels, with gilt lettering, upper cover with running fox in gilt and triple gilt fillet borders, top edge gilt, by Hatchards, with their stamp on endpaper, very good.   Blackwell Rare Books   B166 - 104 2011   £250

Surtees, Robert Smith 1803-1864 *Handley Cross.* London: Edward Arnold, 1912, First edition with these illustrations; one of 250 copies signed by artist, this is copy #34, 2 volumes, 249 x 190mm., especially pleasing modern scarlet highly polished calf, handsomely gilt "stamp signed" "Bound by Brentanos" on verso of front free endpaper, covers with gilt double fillet, raised bands, spine attractively gilt in a hunting theme, double ruled compartments featuring a fox head, hunter's horn or riding hat and crop as centerpieces, each framed by ornate scrolling cornerpieces, each spine with one tan and one dark brown morocco label, turn-ins with intricate gilt floral vine, marbled endpapers, all edges gilt, titlepage vignettes, 97 illustrations in text, 24 tipped-on color plates, all by Cecil Aldin, one tiny scratch to one title label, one leaf with upper corner and narrow portion of top half of fore-edge margin expertly renewed (perhaps after rough opening?), but very fine and quite pretty set with only trivial imperfections in text, especially fresh, clean and bright, plates in pristine condition, very attractive decorative bindings unusually lustrous and virtually unworn.   Phillip J. Pirages   59 - 143 2011 $950

Surtees, Robert Smith 1803-1864 *Hawbuck Grange: or the Sporting Adventures of Thomas Scott Esq.* London: Bradbury Agnew & Co. n.d. circa, 1885, Original pictorial crimson cloth gilt over bevelled boards, spine faded, worn at head, lower board rather faded at top edge, pages (iv), 329, 16, 8 hand colored plates and numerous text woodcuts by Phiz.   R. F. G. Hollett & Son Antiquarian Booksellers General Catalogue Summer 2010 - 1293 2011   £85

Surtees, Robert Smith 1803-1864 *Hunts with Jorrocks.* London: Hodder & Stoughton, n.d., Small 4to., original crimson cloth, little faded and damped, pages (viii), 215, with 25 tissue guarded color plates tipped on to grey card.   R. F. G. Hollett & Son Antiquarian Booksellers   General Catalogue Summer 2010 - 1214 2011   £75

Surtees, Robert Smith 1803-1864 *Jorrocks's Jaunts and Jollities.* London: George Routledge and Sons, n.d. circa, 1901, New edition; original pictorial crimson cloth, gilt, spine faded and trifle frayed at head, lower board rather damped, pages viii, 272, 16 color plates, numerous other illustrations.   R. F. G. Hollett & Son Antiquarian Booksellers General Catalogue Summer 2010 - 1295 2011   £35

Surtees, Robert Smith 1803-1864 *Mr. Romford's Hounds.* Bradbury Agnew & Co., n.d., Subscribers edition; Original pictorial cloth gilt, spine little faded, pages xii, 405, 24 hand colored plates, numerous text woodcuts.   R. F. G. Hollett & Son Antiquarian Booksellers   General Catalogue Summer 2010 - 1296 2011   £85

Surtees, Robert Smith 1803-1864 *Mr. Sponge's Sporting Tour.* Bradbury, Agnew & Co. n.d., Subscriber's edition; original pictorial cloth gilt, spine rather faded, pages (viii), 450, 13 hand colored plates and numerous text woodcuts by John Leech, half title spotted.   R. F. G. Hollett & Son Antiquarian Booksellers   General Catalogue Summer 2010 - 1297 2011   £65

Surtees, Robert Smith 1803-1864 *Mr. Sponge's Sporting Tour.* London: Bradbury & Evans, 1853, First edition; half title, frontispiece, hand colored steep engraved plates, illustrations, original brown cloth, borders in blind, pictorially blocked in gilt, neatly recased, little dulled, inscribed by author to F. D. Johnson, all edges gilt, tipped in 3 page ALS from author to Johnson.   Jarndyce Antiquarian Booksellers   CXCI - 501 2011   £280

Surtees, Robert Smith 1803-1864 *Plain or Ringlets?* Bradbury & Evans, n.d., Original scarlet pictorial cloth gilt, spine rather faded, pages x, (ii), 398, hand colored title and 12 hand colored plates.   R. F. G. Hollett & Son Antiquarian Booksellers   General Catalogue Summer 2010 - 1298 2011   £85

Surtees, Robert Smith 1803-1864 *Plain or Ringlets?* London: 1860, viii, 406 pages, 13 hand colored illustrations by John Leech, original cloth cover with finger marks, gilt design replicate of titlepage, backstrip (missing ends), reseated professionally on later cloth, new endpapers.   Bookworm & Silverfish   667 - 110 2011 $125

Sutermeister, Edwin *Casein and its Industrial Applications.* New York: 1939, 433 pages, very good, modest library marks.   Bookworm & Silverfish   668 - 125 2011 $60

Sutherland, Douglas *Tried and Valiant. The History of the Border Regiment (the 34th and 55th Regiment of Foot) 1702-1959.* Leo Cooper, 1972, First edition; original cloth, gilt, dust jacket, pages 239, color frontispiece and 37 illustrations. R. F. G. Hollett & Son Antiquarian Booksellers 173 - 1084 2011 £50

Sutherland, Elihu J. *Meet Virginia's Baby... History of Dickenson County.* Kingsport?: circa, 1955, First edition; original binding, very good, embossed cover design, photo illustrated, endpaper maps. Bookworm & Silverfish 670 - 189 2011 $175

Sutherland, Graham *Sutherland, Apollinaire: le Bestiaire ou Cortege d'Orphee.* London: Milan: Marlborough Fine Art/2 RC Editrice, 1979, Deluxe edition of the catalogue with original color aquatint of the device created as a hallmark for this edition by Sutherland and numbered 18/45, laid in; volume itself signed andf dated in pencil in year of publication by Sutherland, fine first edition in original fine printed dust jacket over wrappers, 4to., scarce. By the Book, L. C. 26 - 49 2011 $400

Sutherland, James *The Adventures of an Elephant Hunter.* London: Macmillan & Co., 1912, First edition, first issue; 8vo., xviii, 324 (2 ads) pages, frontispiece, 52 illustrations, original blue cloth, gilt stamped cover ornament and spine title, top edge gilt, extremities rubbed, corners bumped, library card inside rear cover, bookplate of Charles Atwood Kofoid, very good, rare. Jeff Weber Rare Books 163 - 218 2011 $600

Sutherland, Millicent, Duchess of *Wayfarer's Love: Contributors from Living Poets.* London: Archibald Constable & Co., 1904, First edition, limited print run of 100 copies, this number 48, hand numbered and signed by author; large 8vo., pages 80, vellum covers, decorated gilt by Walter Crane, endpapers browned, edges and covers rather mottled but gilt decorated, unscratched, clear and attractive, interior bright and unmarked, very good. Any Amount of Books May 29 2011 - A76952 2011 $212

Sutter, John A. *New Helvetia Diary: a Record of Vents - at New Helvetia, California from September 9 1845 to May 25 1848.* San Francisco: Society of California Pioneers, 1939, First edition; limited to 950 copies, xxiii, 138 pages, color frontispiece, 2 plates, map, cloth backed decorated boards, paper spine label, very fine and clean. Argonaut Book Shop Recent Acquisitions Summer 2010 - 194 2011 $175

Sutton, Adah Louise *Teddy Bears.* Akron: Saalfield, 1907, 4to., pictorial boards, 154 pages + ads, paper spine neatly strengthened, else very good+, 6 color plates, many line illustrations, pictorial covers by A. J. Schaffer, very scarce. Aleph-Bet Books, Inc. 95 - 94 2011 $600

Sutton, Graham *North Star.* Collins, 1949, Original cloth gilt, dust jacket, edges little worn, pages 352, maps on endpapers, scarce. R. F. G. Hollett & Son Antiquarian Booksellers 173 - 1088 2011 £40

Suvern, Johann W. *Essay on "The Birds" of Aristophanes. (bound with) Two Essays on "The Clouds" and "The (Greek)" of Aristophanes.* London: John Murray, 1835, First editions; Half calf and marbled boards, extremities rubbed, spine ends chipped, light scattered foxing to first leaves, heavily annotated and footnoted. Dramatis Personae Booksellers 106 - 156 2011 $75

Swailes, Alec *Kirkby Stephen Grammar School 1566-1966.* Appleby: J. Whitehead & Son, n.d., 1966, First edition; original wrappers, pages 114, illustrations, flyleaf lightly spotted, scarce. R. F. G. Hollett & Son Antiquarian Booksellers 173 - 1089 2011 £45

Swallow, G. C. *Geological Report of the Country Along the Line of the South-Western Branch of the Pacific Railroad, State of Missouri.* St. Louis: 1859, xvii, 93 pages, 2 plates, errata, illustrations, folding map, original stamped boards, spine faded, loss of cloth to top and bottom of spine, edges of first few pages noticeably foxed, scattered foxing, else good. Dumont Maps & Books of the West 111 - 79 2011 $175

Swammerdam, Jan *Historie Generale des Insectes.* Utrecht: Jean Ribbius, 1685, Second edition in French; 4to., (8), 215 pages, 13 engraved plates, folding table, later hald calf, antique, extremities of spine bit rubbed, else very good. Joseph J. Felcone Inc. Fall Miscellany 2010 - 114 2011 $1200

Swann, Alfred J. *Fighting the Slave-Hunters in Central Africa: a Record of Twenty-Six Years of Travel and Adventure Round the Great Lakes...* London: Seeley Service, 1910, First edition; large 8vo., pages 359, folding map, illustrations, original blue decorative cloth, gilt vignette, top edge gilt, very good. J. & S. L. Bonham Antiquarian Booksellers Africa 4/20/2011 - 9156 2011 £450

Swannell, Mildred *Paper Silhouettes.* George Philip & Son, 1929, Small 4to., original boards, little rubbed, lower board spotted, pages 58, color frontispiece and 150 diagrams in black and white, uncommon. R. F. G. Hollett & Sons Antiquarian Booksellers 170 - 663 2011 £35

Swaysland, W. *Familiar Wild Birds.* London: Cassel & Co., 1903, 4 volumes in 1, modern quarter red calf gilt with raised bands, top edge gilt, 160 color plates, very attractive set. R. F. G. Hollett & Son Antiquarian Booksellers General Catalogue Summer 2010 - 1058 2011 £120

Swedenborg, Emanuel *De Coelo et Eius Mirabilibus et de Inferno.* London: by John Lewis of Hyde, 1758, First edition; 4to., pages 272, without final errata leaf sometimes present, woodcut title vignette, decorative woodcut head and tailpieces, contemporary sprinkled calf, gilt ruled raised bands, red sprinkled edges, from the Hurstbourne Park Library of Earl of Portsmouth, with gilt shelf mark '2303' in top compartment, inserted slip, inscribed in contemporary manuscript "from the author", upper joint repaired, chipping to head and foot of spine, some stripping to lower cover, wormhole at inner margin of last few leaves, internally very crisp and clean, extremely good, large copy.   Simon Finch Rare Books   Zero - 118   2011   £1600

Swedenborg, Emanuel *De Nova Hierosolyma et Ejus Doctrina Coelesti.* London: by John Lewis of Hyde, 1758, First edition; 4to., pages 156, (2) errata, verso blank, woodcut title vignette, decorative woodcut head and tailpieces, light dampstains on corners of few leaves, generally very crisp and clean, contemporary sprinkled calf, raised bands with later gilt shelfmark '2304' in top compartment, red sprinkled edges, hinges repaired, very good, from the library of the Earls of Portsmouth at Hurstbourne Park.   Simon Finch Rare Books   Zero - 117   2011   £1600

Sweetser, M. F. *The Maritime Provicnes: a Handbook for Travellers. A Guide.* Boston: James R. Osgood and Co., 1884, Third edition; red cloth, gilt titles to front and spine, ads on endpapers, pages ix, 336, 4 maps and 4 plans, ads at rear, small 8vo., cloth, slightly worn, generally very good. Schooner Books Ltd.   96 - 299   2011 $75

Swett, Morris *Fort Sill, a History.* Fort Sill: privately printed, 1921, First edition; 8vo., original printed wrapper (66 pages), photos, very good copy, housed in cloth folding case with titles stamped in gold on spine, scarce. Buckingham Books   May 26 2011 - 25695   2011 $2500

Swift, Graham *Last Orders.* London: Picador, 1996, First British edition; fine, dust jacket fine.   Bella Luna Books   May 29 2011 - t1696   2011 $82

Swift, Jonathan   1667-1745 *Miscellaneous Poems.* Waltham St. Lawrence: Golden Cockerel Press, 1928, One of 375 copies; 273 x 203mm., viii, 67, (2) pages, original quarter vellum over marbled paper boards, titling in gilt on spine, publisher's orange printed dust jacket, woodcut printer's device, 12 wood engravings by Robert Gibbings, titlepage printed in red and black; two prelim leaves, embossed ownership stamp of Robert Hess; edges of volume little faded, one leaf slightly torn at top as result of uncareful opening, otherwise fine in very good dust jacket, with clean covers, but with darkened, torn and chipped spine and with fraying along upper edge of cover panels. Phillip J. Pirages   59 - 223   2011 $300

Swift, Jonathan   1667-1745 *The Prose Writings of Jonathan Swift.* All first editions, except volumes 10 and 11 which are revised editions of 1959; 13 volumes, lacking 14th - index, first 3 volumes (no dust jacket) have dull cloth, else very good 8 volumes with dust jackets.   C. P. Hyland May 26 2011 - 255/741   2011 $1087

Swift, Jonathan   1667-1745 *Travels into Several Remote Nations of the World.* printed for Benj. Motte, 1726, Mixed set, the first volume being from the AA (second) edition and the second volume from the B (third edition); frontispiece in second state and 6 further plates, soiled and spotted in places, occasional staining, 19th century ownership stamp of James Bubb on two leaves and one plate in volume i, early ink sketch of Gulliver's ship on another place in that volume, pages xii, 148, (6), 164; (vi) 154 (8), (155)-353, (1), 8vo., modern sprinkled calf, spines with five raised bands, black and green lettering pieces, sound.   Blackwell Rare Books   B166 - 105   2011   £2500

Swift, Jonathan   1667-1745 *Gulliver's Voyages to Lilliput and Bobdingnag.* London: Folio Society, 1948, First edition; original cloth backed marbled boards, gilt dust jacket by Edward Bawden, edges little chipped in places, pages xx, 153, 12 fine full page color plates by Bawden. R. F. G. Hollett & Son Antiquarian Booksellers   General Catalogue Summer 2010 - 911   2011   £35

Swift, Jonathan   1667-1745 *The Works of...* 1760-1769, Small 8vo., 23 volume, 2 contemporary calf bindings (1-17 and 18-23), spines of 1-17 dried, else mainly very good set.   C. P. Hyland   May 26 2011 - 255/750   2011 $906

Swift, Jonathan   1667-1745 *The Works of the Rev. Jonathan Swift.* Edinburgh: 1801, New edition; volumes 1-6 and 8-12 (11 volumes) of 19, full diced calf, two spines damaged, portrait and text good.   C. P. Hyland   May 26 2011 - 256/934   2011 $275

Swinburne, Algernon Charles   1837-1909 *Astrophel and Other Poems.* London: Chatto & Windus, 1894, First edition; 190 x 130mm., 4 p.l., 228 pages, exquisite garnet red crushed morocco beautifully gilt by Doves Bindery, signed on rear turn-in and dated 1894), covers with gilt border accented with small tools enclosing a center panel framed by a single gilt rule, roseleaf cornerpieces, raised bands, spine lavishly gilt in compartments with large central Tudor rose (Doves tool 1h) surrounded by leaves and stippling, gilt titling, turn-ins adorned with gilt rules and roseleaf cornerpieces, all edges gilt, housed in suede lined black straight grain morocco pull-off case (slightly scuffed), front pastedown with faint evidence of bookplate removal, minor offsetting to endpapers from turn-ins (as usual), old bookseller's description taped to front free endpaper causing two small adhesive stains, otherwise really beautiful book, text clean and fresh, splendid binding in superb condition. Phillip J. Pirages   59 - 102   2011 $6500

Swinburne, Algernon Charles 1837-1909 *Bothwell.* London: Chatto and Windus, 1874, First edition; very good, light shelfwear at extremities. Lupack Rare Books May 26 2011 - ABE4182184354 2011 $125

Swinburne, Algernon Charles 1837-1909 *Notes on Poems and Reviews.* London: John Camden Hotten, 1866, First edition; half title, contemporary half green morocco, marbled boards, spine uplettered gilt, slightly rubbed, 23 pages. Jarndyce Antiquarian Booksellers CXCI - 503 2011 £200

Swinburne, Algernon Charles 1837-1909 *Notes on Poems and Reviews.* London: John Camden Hotten, 1866, Second edition; half title, contemporary half orange morocco, marbled boards, slightly dulled and little rubbed, perfectly nice. Jarndyce Antiquarian Booksellers CXCI - 504 2011 £120

Swinburne, Algernon Charles 1837-1909 *Pasiphae.* Waltham St. Lawrence: Golden Cockerel Press, 1950, One of 100 specially bound volumes with an extra engraving; (of a total of 500 printed), 229 x 152mm., 2 p.l., 5-40 pages, beet colored vellum, stamp signed on front pastedown by Sangorski & Sutcliffe, gilt titling on spine, head of a bull in gilt on cover, top edge gilt, other edges untrimmed, buckram slipcase (just slightly worn), 7 charming copper engravings by John Buckland Wright (including titlepage), spine slightly and uniformly sunned, cover slightly faded, with color lost on corners and right at fore edges, otherwise fine. Phillip J. Pirages 59 - 224 2011 $375

Swinburne, Algernon Charles 1837-1909 *Pomes and Ballads. (with) Poems and Ballads. Second Series.* London: Edward Moxon and Co., 1866, London: Chatto & Windus 1878. First editions; 2 volumes, 8vo., (first series 164 x 100mm, second series 180 xm), pages viii, 344; x, 240, internally very crisp and fresh, uniformly bound in contemporary green half morocco, marbled boards and endpapers, all edges marbled, some rubbing to extremities, ALS from D. G. Rossetti for John Skelton, presenting the book with envelope tipped into volume i, address panel of letter from Swinburne to Shelton tipped into volume ii, numerous pencil notes throughout volume i by Skelton, with presentation letter from Rossetti to Skelton. Simon Finch Rare Books Zero - 355 2011 £1800

Swinburne, Algernon Charles 1837-1909 *The Springtime of Life.* London: William Heinemann, 1918, One of 76 copies signed by author (this copy #369); 287 x 2 30mm., ix, (i), 132, (2) pages, very attractive red leather morocco, raised bands, spine handsomely gilt in compartments formed by plain and decorative rules, quatrefoil centerpiece surrounded by densely scrolling cornerpieces, sides and endleaves of rose colored linen, top edge gilt, numerous black and white illustrations, 9 color plates by Arthur Rackham, as called for, all tipped onto brown paper with letterpress guards, morocco bookplate of W. A. M. Burden; just hint of offsetting from brown mounting paper, otherwise very fine, bright, fresh and clean, inside and out, only most trivial imperfections. Phillip J. Pirages 59 - 296 2011 $1600

Swinburne, Algernon Charles 1837-1909 *The Tragedies.* London: Chatto & Windus, 1905, First collected edition; one of 110 large paper copies, this #6, 230 x 150mm., especially fine contemporary burgundy crushed morocco by Bumpus (signed on front turn-in), covers and board edges with double gilt rule, spines with attractively and densely gilt in compartments, filled with massed stippled volutes, enclosing a quatrefoil at center, elegant inner gilt dentelles, top edge gilt, other edges rough trimmed, entirely unopened, photograuvre frontispiece in final volume, titles printed in red and black; one spine just barely darker than the others, couple of mild corner bumps, otherwise beautifully bound set in splendid condition. Phillip J. Pirages 59 - 330 2011 $1250

Swinburne, Algernon Charles 1837-1909 *Tristram of Lyonesse.* Portland: Thomas B. Mosher, 1904, Limited edition; original paper spine and blue boards, erasure of a name at top of titlepage has resulted in some thinning and tiny holes, otherwise fine, fresh copy. Lupack Rare Books May 26 2011 - ABE4313999490 2011 $125

Swinburne, Henry *The Courts of Europe at the Close of the Last Century.* London: Henry Colburn, 1841, First edition; 2 volumes, original blindstamped olive green cloth gilt, little bumped, backstrips sometime torn and partially laid down, pages xxxii, 400; 396, engraved frontispiece (lightly foxed). R. F. G. Hollett & Son Antiquarian Booksellers 175 - 1311 2011 £180

Swire, Herbert *The Voyage of the Challenger. A Personal Narrative of the Historic Circumnavigation of the Globe in the Years 1872-1876.* London: Golden Cockerel, 1938, One of 300 numbered copies; printed in Eric Gill's Perpetua type on Van Gelder paper, 2 volumes, small folio, colored plates, text illustrations, blue cloth boards, white cloth spines, gilt, fine, publisher's cloth slipcase, lightly rubbed at extremities. Joseph J. Felcone Inc. Fall Miscellany 2010 - 115 2011 $1000

Swisher, Mary *The Stones of Mani. Views of the Southern Peloponnese.* Sacramento: Stalwart Press, 2008, Limited edition, one of 50 copies, signed; text on Rives Heavyweight paper and each of the 12 platinum-palladium photograph on Crane's 90-lb. business card stock with preceding legend for each photo on Wyndstone vellum, each copy signed and numbered by author/photographer, who has also signed and numbered each of her photos, pages size 11 3/4 x 10 inches, text volume 72 pages, print volume 24 leaves, bound by L. J. Dillon, text volume in tan linen over boards with stitched binding in natural linen thread using Greek key design, plate volume is loose as issued housed in tan linen portfolio identical in trim size to text volume, both housed in publisher's slipcase of same tan linen with blue Hahnemuhle Bugra papers on front and back, title and author in black with cross and lion motifs used also as decorations in text, same blue Hahnemuhle paper used as endsheets in text volume and to line plate portfolio case. Priscilla Juvelis - Rare Books   48 - 22   2011 $3000

The Swiss Family Robinson Retold for Little Folk. Blackie & son, n.d., 1909, Small 4to., original pictorial cloth, pages with 29 full page illustrations, numerous other illustrations, odd mark or spot, very nice, clean and sound. R. F. G. Hollett & Sons Antiquarian Booksellers   170 - 321   2011   £35

Sword, Wiley *Embrace an Angry Wind.* New York: 1992, First edition; 499 pages, fine in dust jacket (laminated), original binding, inscribed and signed by author. Bookworm & Silverfish   679 - 42   2011 $65

Sykes, J. B. *The Concise Oxford Dictionary of Current English.* Oxford University Press, 1957, First edition; pages viii, 170, frontispiece and 126 illustrations, author's compliments slip loosely inserted, original cloth, gilt, dust jacket. R. F. G. Hollett & Son Antiquarian Booksellers General Catalogue Summer 2010 - 466   2011   £65

Symington, Andrew *The Duty of Stated and Select Private Christian Fellowship Briefly Inculcated and Directed.* Paisley: printed by Stephen Young, 1823, First edition; 8vo., 44 pages, couple of short closed marginal tears, near contemporary ink inscription on upper margin of titlepage, rebound recently in cloth, spine lettered gilt, original blue upper wrapper preserved on which is early 19th century ownership inscription of Rev. Gilbert McMaster (of) Duanesburgh (i.e Duanesbury in Schenactady County, NY). John Drury Rare Books   153 - 144   2011   £175

Symington, Noel Howard *The Night Climbers of Cambridge.* London: Chatto & Windus, 1937, Second edition; original black cloth, spine lettering dulled, small mark to front board, corners little bumped, pages viii, 184, with 55 illustrations, rear hinge cracking, label removed from rear pastedown. R. F. G. Hollett & Son Antiquarian Booksellers General Catalogue Summer 2010 - 940   2011   £180

Symonds, John *The Isle of Cats.* London: Wenrer Laurie, 1955, First edition; original cloth, top inner corners of boards rather faded, dust jacket trifle soiled, price clipped, pages 49, 6 color plates and numerous drawings by Gerard Hoffnung. R. F. G. Hollett & Sons Antiquarian Booksellers   170 - 333   2011   £65

Symonds, John Addington *The Life of Benvenuto Cellini.* London: 1888, First edition published by Nimmo; 2 volumes, frontispiece and 8 plates, top edge gilt, good set, half leather, age crazed but gilt legible, with foxing to prelim leaves. Bookworm & Silverfish   669 - 34   2011 $125

Symonds, John Addington *Miscellanies by John Addington Symonds.* London: 1871, First edition; xxxii, 416 pages, electric blue cloth, very few bubbles, very good, 8 text plates and folding chart, plate edges mildly frayed. Bookworm & Silverfish   667 - 159   2011 $75

Symons, Arthur *A Study of Thomas Hardy.* London: Charles J. Sawyer, 1927, Limited edition, no. 4 of 100 copies; printed on handmade paper, signed by author on limitation page and by photographer on frontispiece, nearly fine, signed by author. Lupack Rare Books   May 26 2011 - ABE4310256467   2011 $150

Symons, G. J. *The Floating Island in Derwent Water, Its History and Mystery...* E. Stanford & Simpkin & Marshall & Co., 1888, First edition; original green blindstamped cloth gilt, pages xii, 166, (ii, errata, verso blank), (24, ads), hand colored folding map, engraved title (little spotted) and 41 fine etched plates (foxed, few scattered spots elsewhere). R. F. G. Hollett & Son Antiquarian Booksellers   173 - 1095   2011   £120

Synge, John Millington 1871-1909 *The Complete Works of...* Maunsel, 1910, First collected edition; 4 volumes, ex-library, some wear to cloth, text very good. C. P. Hyland   May 26 2011 - 255/764   2011 $348

Synge, John Millington 1871-1909 *The Complete Works.* Maunsel, 1910, First collected edition; 4 volumes, covers dull, else good. C. P. Hyland   May 26 2011 - 258/945   2011 $399

Synge, John Millington 1871-1909 *The Complete Works of...* Maunsel, 1910, First collected edition; 4 volumes, volume II ex-library, else very good. C. P. Hyland   May 26 2011 - 256/947   2011 $377

Szechenyi, Zsigmond *Land of Elephants: Big Game Hunting in Kenya, Taganyika and Uganda.* London: Putnam, 1935, First English edition; 8vo., 208 pages, frontispiece, 47 plates, original black cloth, dust jacket, small loss to head and tail of spine. J. & S. L. Bonham Antiquarian Booksellers   Africa 4/20/2011 - 8780   2011   £580

T

Ta Ra Ra Boom De Ay (code number 832). London: Raphael Tuck & Sons, circa, 1900, 6 x 4 inches, full color pictorial paper covers of rather clean copy of the book, four pages within, each with full color illustration printed on one side of the page which is folded in such a way that the image transforms when you unfold the edge of the page. Jo Ann Reisler, Ltd. 86 - 175 2011 $250

Taaffe, Nicholas, Viscount *Observations on Affairs in Ireland from the Settlement in 1691 to the Present Time.* London: Griffin, 1766, First edition; 438 pages, loose in stiff wrappers, neat 19th century insert suggests this is the first literary effort on behalf of the Irish Roman Catholics during the penal times, very scarce, bordering on rare. C. P. Hyland May 26 2011 - 258/949 2011 $457

Le Tableau des Piperies des Femmes Mondaines ou Par Plusieurs Histoires, se Vyent les Ruses dont Elles se Servent. Cologne: Piere (sic) du Marteau, Utrecht: R. Van Zyll, 1685, Third edition; (1), 2-284 pages, 12mo., contemporary full calf, gilt decorated spine with floral design, raised bands, inside dentelles, all edges red, wear to head of spine, otherwise fresh, tight and very attractive copy, uncommon, rare. Paulette Rose Fine and Rare Books 32 - 124 2011 $2500

Tacitus, Gaius Cornelius *Annales of Cornelius Tacitus.* London: printed by John Bill, 1622, Fifth edition; small folio, pages (vi) 271, (vii), 12, 228, (ii), the second page 213 is a full page engraving, this copy lacks initial blank, contemporary speckled calf, spine double ruled in blind, unlettered, boards double rule bordered in blind with smaller double rule central panel fleurons outermost at corners and smaller stylised flower, innermost all in blind, board edges decorative roll in blind, all edges red speckled, pink and white sewn endbands, little spotting, dampmark in upper corner, excisions to title repaired, rubbed, corners and endcaps worn, joints cracked, upper just holding, original ownership inscription cut out, but may have been same as "Fran: Cornwallis" at head fore corner of first page 1 or may have been same as "Richard Rowlandson" verso front blank, 19th century unidentified circular armorial bookplate, from the collection of Christopher Ernest Weston 1947-2010. Unsworths Booksellers 24 - 145 2011 £300

Tacitus, Gaius Cornelius *Five Books of the History of C. Cornelius Tacitus with his Treatise on the Manners of the Germans and His Life of Agricola.* Hartford: 1826, 315 pages, full leather, rubbed at edges, top edge of backstrip abraded. Bookworm & Silverfish 679 - 103 2011 $75

Tacitus, Gaius Cornelius *C. Cornelii Taciti Opera quae exstant...* Antwerpiae: Ex Officina Plantiniana Balthasaris Moreti, 1648, Folio, pages (xvi) 547 (xxxiii) 36 84 (xvi), contemporary Dutch blind panelled vellum, spine lettered in MS. ink, all edges red sprinkled, green sewn endbands, green ties, early 21st century conservation by Chris Weston, lightly soiled, vellum dusty, little bit ruckled, from the collection of Christopher Ernest Weston 1947-2010. Unsworths Booksellers 24 - 144 2011 £600

Tacitus, Gaius Cornelius *The Works of...* London: printed for G. G. J. and J. Robinson, 1793, 4 volumes, 4to., engraved maps, contemporary densely speckled calf, spine fully gilt with triple rules, interweaving front and graded pebbles' roll and 'sun-burst brooche' centerpieces, red and black lettering and numbering pieces gilt, board edges decorative roll gilt, all edges blue sprinkled, red and white sewn endbands, plates somewhat foxed, rubbed at corners, endcaps worn, joints cracking, labels lost from volumes 1 and 2 and partly lost on volume 3, stipple engraved booklabel of Theo. Leigh/Toft", ink ownership Theodosia Leigh, from the collection of Christopher Ernest Weston 1947-2010. Unsworths Booksellers 24 - 146 2011 £300

Tager, E. *Veichiki Bubeichiki. (Little Bells).* Leningrad: Raduga, 1929, First edition; oblong 12mo., color pictorial paper wrappers with some dusting, 10 pages within (counting inside covers), each with color illustrations. Jo Ann Reisler, Ltd. 86 - 218 2011 $500

The Tailor and the Elephant. Cincinnati: Peter G. Thomson, 1882, 12mo., pictorial wrappers light edge wear, very good+, 4 charming full page color illustrations, scarce. Aleph-Bet Books, Inc. 95 - 551 2011 $175

Taken by Design: Photographs from The Institute of Design 1937-1971. Chicago: University of Chicago Press, 2002, First edition; very fine in photo illustrated boards, issued without dust jacket, signed by a large number of photographers and some of the editors, among the signatures are Yasuhiro Ishimoto, Marvin E. Newton (twice), Barbara Crane, Ray K. Metzker, Joseph Jachna, Joseph Sterling (twice), Kenneth Josephson, David Travis, Keith Davis and quite a few others, unique copy. Jeff Hirsch Books ny 2010 2011 $750

Talbot, P. Amaury *Life in Southern Nigeria: the Magic Beliefs and Customs of the Ibibio Tribe.* London: Macmillan, 1923, First edition; 8vo., pages xvi, 356, folding map, illustrations, original blue decorative cloth. J. & S. L. Bonham Antiquarian Booksellers Africa 4/20/2011 - 6772 2011 £100

Talbot, P. Amaury *Some Nigerian Fertility Cults.* London: Oxford University Press, 1927, First edition; 8vo., pages xi, (i) blank, 140, frontispiece, 15 plates, text diagrams, original green cloth. J. & S. L. Bonham Antiquarian Booksellers Africa 4/20/2011 - 4249 2011 £65

Talbot, P. Amaury *Woman's Mysteries of a Primitive People; the Ibibios of Southern Nigeria.* London: Cassell, 1915, First edition; 8vo., 252 pages, illustrations, original decorative blue cloth, spine creased with wear to head and tail of spine.   J. & S. L. Bonham Antiquarian Booksellers Africa 4/20/2011 - 3111   2011   £90

Tales of Cumberland: Containing a Miscellaneous Collection of Historical Stories &c.   Whitehaven: Callander & Dixon, circa, 1900, Frontispiece, original blue paper wrappers, printed in black, slight rust marks, very good.   Jarndyce Antiquarian Booksellers   CXCI - 358   2011   £40

Tallack, William *The California Overland Express.* Los Angeles: Historical Society of Southern California, 1935, First Book edition, limited to 150 copies; 85 pages, long folding frontispiece map, 9 illustrations, 1 photo plate, printed in red and black, cloth backed boards, lettered in black on spine, slight fading to top edge of front board, two smudges to rear cover, one lower corner worn, near fine, internally fine and clean.   Argonaut Book Shop   Recent Acquisitions Summer 2010 - 196   2011 $175

Tallent, Elizabeth *Married Men and Magic Tricks: John Updike's Erotic Heroes.* Berkeley: Creative Arts Book Co., 1982, First edition; uncommon hardcover issue, fine in fine dust jacket.   Ken Lopez Bookseller   154 - 223   2011 $65

The Tame Goldfinch; or The Unfortunate Neglect. Philadelphia: Jacob Johnson, 1808, 16mo., 36 pages, original marbled boards, full page copper engravings, including frontispiece, printed on heavier handmade paper and on one side of leaf only, very fine, rare in almost mint state.   Hobbyhorse Books   56 - 149   2011 $570

Tan, Amy *The Hundred Secret Senses.* New York: Putnam, 1995, One of an unspecified number of copies signed by her on tipped in leaf; inscribed by author to Kaye Gibbons, stains to front board, else near fine in fine dust jacket.   Ken Lopez Bookseller   154 - 61   2011 $125

Tan, Amy *The Hundred Secret Senses.* New York: Putnam, 1995, Limited to 175 copies; fine, slipcase, signed by author.   Bella Luna Books   May 29 2011 - t6590   2011 $93

Tan, Amy *The Joy Luck Club.* New York: Putnam, 1989, First edition; near fine, light wear, dust jacket near fine with light edge wear and creasing, very nice first state which is usually quite worn.   Bella Luna Books   May 29 2011 - t4256   2011 $137

Tan, Amy *The Joy Luck Club.* New York: Putnam, 1989, Advance reading copy; spine faded, near fine in wrappers.   Ken Lopez Bookseller   154 - 216   2011 $150

Tan, Amy *The Joy Luck Club.* New York: Putnam, 1989, First edition; near fine, very faint beginnings of yellowing around edges of pages, dust jacket near fine, small closed tears and rubbing to extremities, first state of jacket.   Bella Luna Books   May 26 2011 - t3884   2011 $192

Tan, Amy *The Joy Luck Club.* New York: Putnam, 1989, First edition; fine, in like (first state) dust jacket, exceptional unread copy.   Bella Luna Books   May 26 2011 - t9321   2011 $247

Tan, Amy *The Moon Lady.* New York: Macmillan, 1992, First edition; illustrations by Gretchen Schields, fine in fine dust jacket signed by author and artist, with author's Chinese wood block stamp.   Bella Luna Books   May 29 2011 - j2242   2011 $137

Tanner, Robin *Double Harness.* Impact Books, 1987, First edition; large 8vo., original cloth, gilt, dust jacket (red spine lettering faded), pages (iv), 215, 7 etchings and 10 pen drawings, fine, label signed by Robin and Heather Tanner and dated July 1987 laid on flyleaf.   R. F. G. Hollett & Son Antiquarian Booksellers   General Catalogue Summer 2010 - 912   2011   £45

Tanner, Robin *Wiltshire Village.* London: Collins, 1939, First edition; small 4to., original green buckram gilt, dust jacket price clipped, small tape mark, extremities trifle frayed, pages 179, numerous full page and text illustrations after etchings and woodcuts, scattered light spotting, but very good.   R. F. G. Hollett & Son Antiquarian Booksellers   General Catalogue Summer 2010 - 913   2011   £75

Tans'ur, William *A Musical Grammar and Dictionary: or a General Introduction to the Whole Art of Music.* Stokesley: W. Pratt, n.d. circa, 1840, Old half calf, gilt, rubbed and worn, pages xiv, 239, engraved portrait frontispiece (edges little defective), numerous musical and notational examples, illustrations throughout, some fingering and soiling, one or two tears, upper joint cracked, scarce.   R. F. G. Hollett & Son Antiquarian Booksellers   175 - 1312   2011   £120

Taplin, William *A Compendium of Practical and Experimental Farriery... for the Convenience of the Gentleman, the Farmer the Groom and the Smith... to Insure the Prevention, as Well as to Ascertain the Cure of Disease.* Richmond: Pace, 1803, First edition; 24mo., 184 (of 190) pages, contemporary calf backed marbled boards.   M & S Rare Books, Inc.   90 - 130   2011 $125

Tappan, Lewis *Narrative of the late Riotous Proceeding Against the Liberty of the Press, in Cincinnati.* Cincinnati: 1836, First edition; 8vo., 48 pages, original printed wrappers (soiled), some fraying but very good.   M & S Rare Books, Inc.   90 - 39   2011 $1250

Tapping, Thomas *A Treatise on the Derbyshire Mining Customs and Mineral Court Act 1852 (15 & 16 Vict. CCLXIII) Analytically and Practically Arranged...*   Shaw and Sons, 1854, First edition; pages xi, 166, original printed boards, rather rubbed, spine and corners worn, scarce, signature of Arthur G. Taylor and W. B. Brooke-Taylor, successive stewards and barmasters of the Marmote Court.   R. F. G. Hollett & Son Antiquarian Booksellers   175 - 1313 2011   £220

Taraval, Sigismundo, Father *The Indian Uprising in Lower California 1734-1737.*   Los Angeles: Quivira Society, 1931, First edition, number 661 of 665 copies; xii, 298 pages, facsimiles, maps, plates, white simulated parchment backstrip, brown boards with gilt cover vignette, exquisite, uncut copy, in plain paper dust jacket.   Argonaut Book Shop   Recent Acquisitions Summer 2010 - 197 2011 $325

Tarde, Jean Gabriel De *Underground Man.*   London: Duckworth & Co., 1905, First edition in English; octavo, original maroon cloth, front panel stamped in gold and ruled in blind, spine panel stamped in gold, publisher's device stamped in blind on rear panel.   L. W. Currey, Inc.   124 - 193 2011 $250

Tarpon Tales: Lost Stories and Research.   Sanibel Island: Lost Stories, 1990, Paperback original, first printing; pictorial wrappers, fine, scarce, signed.   Bella Luna Books   May 29 2011 - 3770 2011 $137

Tartt, Donna *The Secret History.*   New York: Knopf, 1992, First edition; fine in fine dust jacket.   Bella Luna Books   May 29 2011 - t7298 2011 $137

Tasso, Torquato 1544-1595 *Jerusalem Delivered.*   London: printed for J. Dodsley, 1787, Sixth edition; 214 x 130mm., 2 volumes, handsome contemporary flamed calf, backstrips with wide Greek key roll at head and tail and with six compartments formed by decorative rolls, two of these with a central urn and graceful dangling fronds, two with unusual oval ornament composed of a central floral lozenge encircled first by a garland of leaves and then by a string of beads, each spine with two red morocco labels, one of them a circular volume label, engraved frontispiece by Thomas Stothard in each volume; late 19th century(?) bookplate of Harvey Bonnell (and with evidences of removed bookplate); gift inscription in pencil to Christopher Carter from Herbert Hudson at Wickham Bishops in Essex, dated June 1946, recto of front free endpaper of volume II with two newspaper cuttings about this work dated in 1830's tipped in; vaguest hint of rubbing to joints and corners, occasional minor smudges and other trivial imperfections internally, fine contemporary copy, text remarkably fresh, clean and bright, most attractive bindings especially lustrous and scarcely worn.   Phillip J. Pirages   59 - 60 2011 $750

Taswell-Langmead, Thomas P. *English Constitutional History from the Teutonic Conquest to the Present Time.*   London: 1881, called 2nd edition; xxiv, 803 pages, rebound in Library of Congress maroon cloth, call# on backstrip, interior library stamps.   Bookworm & Silverfish   665 - 41 2011 $75

Tate Gallery *John Piper.*   London: Tate Gallery, 1983, 4to., original stiff wrappers, pages 152, illustrations, fine.   R. F. G. Hollett & Son Antiquarian Booksellers   General Catalogue Summer 2010 - 123 2011   £45

Tate, Allen *The Hovering Fly and Other Essays.*   Cummington: Cummington Press, 1949, One of only 12 copies on Van Gelder paper with original drawing and woodcuts hand colored, specially bound and signed by author and artist, out of a total edition of 245; 8vo., woodcuts by Wightman Williams, full russet morocco with inlaid hand colored panel on front cover by Arno Werner, very fine, in half morocco folding box, binder's copy, signed by Arno Werner.   James S. Jaffe Rare Books   May 26 2011 - 11551 2011 $15,000

Tattersall, George *The Lakes of England.*   Sherwood and Co. and Hudson and Nicholson, Kendal, 1836, First edition; 8vo., xii, 165 (3) + 24 pages ads, half title, folding colored map, titlepage vignette and 41 engraved plates, very good in bright original blindstamped and gilt lettered cloth.   Ken Spelman Rare Books   68 - 178 2011   £160

Taupenot, M. J. *Lusotte et Les Histoires qu-on Lui Raconte.*   Paris: A La Belle Edition, 1917, Limited to 1000 numbered copies printed on verge paper in large readable font,; folio, pictorial wrappers, covers slightly dusty, else fine, 10 full page and more than 50 smaller charming hand colored illustrations by author.   Aleph-Bet Books, Inc.   95 - 234 2011 $1350

Taylor, Ann *My Mother, a Poem.*   New York: Mahlon Day, 1833, 16mo., 17 pages, large wood engraved vignette on titlepage, 2 small vignettes, pagination misnumbered as published, but text is correct, inked signature on top portion of titlepage, reinfored fold of first two pages, protective modern floral paper folder, very good, uncommon early American edition.   Hobbyhorse Books   56 - 144 2011 $120

Taylor, Ann *Select Rhymes for the Nursery.*   London: Darton and Harvey, 1808, Second edition; 6 x 3 1/2 inches, buff printed paper wrappers, some wear and soiling and some wear along spine, internally some dusting and foxing, 48 numbered pages with copper engraved titlepage and 22 copper engravings.   Jo Ann Reisler, Ltd.   86 - 90 2011 $1000

Taylor, Bayard 1825-1878 *Eldorado; or Adventures in the Path of Empire, Comprising a Voyage to California, via Panama...* New York: George P. Putnam, London: Richard Bentley, 1850, First edition; first issue with list of plates in volume 2 giving the plate "Mazatlan" at page 8 rather than page 80 and with the 23 leaves of publisher's ads, 2 volumes, pages 3 leaves, (vii)-xii, 251 + 1 leaf, (1)-3, (1) (1 leaf), (5)-247, (248) blank, 23 numbered leaves of ads, 8 full page tinted lithographs, original blind and gilt stamped green cloth, very slight wear to corners and head of spines, light cover soiling, spines slightly faded, scattered light foxing to text and plates (as usual), light dampstain to extreme upper corners of volume I, front free endpaper lacking in volume I, very good, collectable set in original publisher's cloth. Argonaut Book Shop   Recent Acquisitions Summer 2010 - 199 2011 $1750

Taylor, Benjamin F. *Between the Gates.* Chicago: S. C. Griggs and Co., 1878, First edition; 12mo., pages 292, (8), frontispiece, text illustrations, green cloth, covers decoratively stamped in black, gilt lettered spine, light wear to spine ends and corners, name in ink on inner cover, very good, presentation inscription signed and dated by author. Argonaut Book Shop   Recent Acquisitions Summer 2010 - 201 2011 $200

Taylor, Captain *Secrets of the Deep or the Perfect Yachtsman.* Essomarine, 1934, 8vo., pictorial wrappers, 34 pages, spine slightly soiled, else very good+, illustrations. Aleph-Bet Books, Inc.   95 - 516 2011 $600

Taylor, Deems *The Nutcracker Suite from Walt Disney's Fantasia.* London: Collins, n.d. early 1940s, First English edition; large square 8vo., original cloth backed decorated boards, edges little worn, one corner slightly creased, unpaginated, illustrations in color and monochrome. R. F. G. Hollett & Son Antiquarian Booksellers   175 - 1316 2011   £65

Taylor, Deems *Peter Ibbetson. Lyric Drama in Three Acts from the Novel by George du Maurier.* New York: J. Fischer & Bro., 1930, Deluxe limited edition, one of 12 presentation copies out of a total of 110 copies, this being letter "K"; inscribed by Taylor to publisher George Fischer, x, 329, (1, blank) pages, additional colored titlepage, laid in is ALS by Taylor to Fischer, also laid in is list of both typed and hand-written of who each of the 12 deluxe lettered copies are to go to, original quarter teal morocco over marbled boards, spine lettered gilt, top edge gilt, others uncut, marbled endpapers, extremities of spine bit chipped, 2 3/4 inch crack bottom of outer hinge, spine hinges have had restoration boards with some staining, overall very good. Heritage Book Shop   Holiday 2010 - 123 2011 $1250

Taylor, Deems *Walt Disney's Fantasia.* New York: Simon & Schuster, 1940, First edition; folio, tan cloth, 158 pages, few light marks on cover, else fine in frayed but very good+ dust jacket, pictorial endpapers plus many tipped in color plates in addition to illustrations throughout, text in color and black and white. Aleph-Bet Books, Inc.   95 - 193 2011 $2250

Taylor, H. M. *Anglo-Saxon Architecture.* Cambridge: Cambridge University Press, 1965, First edition; 2 volumes, 4to., pages xxx, 734 with 362 illustrations in text and 642 illustrations at rear, loosely inserted pamphlet by Taylors (Problems of the Dating of Pre-Conquest Churches), with note on cover reading "Please see pages 69-72/Please excuse my pencilled markings/made when I used this copy for preparing/an independent lecture/H.T", also loosely inserted 2 letters to Professor Bushnell (one from Harold Taylor) and another pamphlet (North Elham: a Saxon Town in Norfolk" by Peter Wade Martins), very good+ in slightly nicked clean, very good dust jacket. Any Amount of Books May 29 2011 - A49553 2011 $238

Taylor, H. V. *The Apples of England.* Crosby Lockwood & Son, 1948, Third edition; 4to., original cloth, gilt, dust jacket, very worn and defective, pages 206, xxiii, 36 color plates. R. F. G. Hollett & Son Antiquarian Booksellers   General Catalogue Summer 2010 - 1060 2011   £30

Taylor, Isaac *Words and Places or Etymological Illustrations of History, Ethnology and Geography.* London: Macmillan, 1896, Original red cloth, gilt, small torn dent to lower board, pages xii, 376, 5 folding maps. R. F. G. Hollett & Son Antiquarian Booksellers   General Catalogue Summer 2010 - 469 2011   £35

Taylor, J. Golden *A Literary History of the American West.* Fort Worth: 1987, xiii, 1353 pages, quarter cloth and marbled boards, slight fading to spine area, else near fine, clean, bright copy.   Dumont Maps & Books of the West 111 - 80 2011 $125

Taylor, Jane 1783-1824 *City Scenes or a Peep into London.* London: Darton, Harvey & Darton, 1818, 12mo., 72 pages, marbled paper on boards, red roan spine with gilt rulers and title, full page copper engraved titlepage, 73 superb numbered copper engravings, small brown spot at gutter of page 47, crown of spine chipped, shelf wear at covers, gilt title on spine, printed upside down, very good. Hobbyhorse Books   56 - 145 2011 $470

Taylor, Jane 1783-1824 *City Scenes or a Peep Into London.* Harvey and Darton, 1828, Fourth edition; Original blind panelled cloth gilt, rebacked in matching cloth, pages 80, copper engraved title and 87 copper engraved illustrations on 28 leaves. R. F. G. Hollett & Sons Antiquarian Booksellers   170 - 675 2011   £450

Taylor, Jane 1783-1824 *Hymns for Infant Minds.* London: Jackson and Walford, 1840, Thirty-second edition; 12mo., original roan backed marbld boards, gilt, edges and corners little rubbed or worn, pages (iv), 98, (ii), woodcut vignette frontispiece, some early leaves little fingered, some contemporary annotations, this copy inscribed "Master W. B. Willyams Oct. 1841". R. F. G. Hollett & Sons Antiquarian Booksellers 170 - 676 2011 £45

Taylor, Jane 1783-1824 *Little Ann and Other Poems.* London: George Routledge & Son, n.d., 1883, Tall 8vo., original cloth backed pictorial boards, scratched and soiled, pages 64, with 39 color illustrations and numerous endpieces all by Kate Greenaway, front flyleaf little creased and slightly marked, otherwise contents fine and clean. R. F. G. Hollett & Son Antiquarian Booksellers General Catalogue Summer 2010 - 522 2011 £140

Taylor, Jane 1783-1824 *Meddlesome Matty and Other Poems for Infant Minds.* London: John Lane, The Bodley Head, 1925, First edition; original cloth backed pictorial boards, pages xii, 55, colored illustrations, flyleaves lightly spotted, prize label on front pastedown. R. F. G. Hollett & Sons Antiquarian Booksellers 170 - 678 2011 £45

Taylor, Jane 1783-1824 *Original Poems for Infant Minds.* London: Harvey and Darton, 1836, New edition; 12mo., 2 volumes, original red blindstamped cloth gilt, both volumes neatly recased, pages viii, 130; viii, 100, 2 engraved frontispieces, nice, clean set. R. F. G. Hollett & Sons Antiquarian Booksellers 170 - 677 2011 £120

Taylor, Jane 1783-1824 *Rhymes for the Nursery.* Boston: G. W. Cottrell, n.d., copyright by Munroe & Francis, 1837, Square 12mo., 112 + 1 page book list on lower wrapper, three quarter brown morocco with corners and marbled paper, four raised bands spine with gilt title and date, bound with original pictorial paper wrappers, original upper cover printed in red and blue, titlepage with half page wood engraved vignette, enclosed in decorative frame, illustrations, one corner of original wrappers lightly trimmed, rare, clean and tight. Hobbyhorse Books 56 - 146 2011 $270

Taylor, Jane 1783-1824 *Rural Scenes or a Peep into the Country.* London: Darton Harvey & Darton, 1818, 12mo., 58 pages, red roan spine, marbled paper on boards, 2 large hand colored engravings on titlepage, 87 numbered copper engravings on 29 plates, lacking endpapers and pages 24, 31, 32 and 59, but engravings complete, 3 plates crudely repaired at edges, lacking endpapers, chipping at edges, spots throughout, large inked name inside lower cover, flawed copy. Hobbyhorse Books 56 - 147 2011 $120

Taylor, Jane 1783-1824 *Wouldst Know Thyself! or the Outline of Human Physiology...* New York: George F. Cooledge, n.d. circa, 1860, 12mo., 64 + 4 pages ads, decorative paper on boards, maroon paper spine, full page wood engraved frontispiece, 2 vignettes on titlepage framed by decorative borders, covers spotted and browned, very good. Hobbyhorse Books 56 - 148 2011 $170

Taylor, Jeremy *The Architectural Medal.* London: British Museum, 1978, First edition; 4to., original cloth, gilt, dust jacket price clipped, pages xiii, 244, illustrations. R. F. G. Hollett & Son Antiquarian Booksellers 177 - 843 2011 £30

Taylor, Jeremy 1613-1667 *The Rule and Exercise of Holy Living and Holy Dying...* London: Miles Flesher for Richard Royston, 1680, Twelfth edition; 2 volumes, 8vo., pages (xiv), 335, (i) + engraved titlepage and 1 double page engraved plates stub-mounted; (xiv), 259, (v) + engraved titlepage and 1 double page engraved plate stub mounted, contemporary black polished turkey, spines multi rule panelled in blind with contrasting stylised flower centerpieces, boards entirely blind tooled with triangular and rectangular densely ruled blocks, tulip & carnation heads, gouges and small 5 pointed stars, board edges and turn-ins decorative roll gilt, "Dutch-comb swirl" "made" endpapers, all edges gilt, 3 color pink, white and pale blue 2 core-sewn endbands, pink silk page markers, wholly unrestored "Sombre" bindings (age toned, few small stains, edges trimmed close, joints and edges rubbed, spines slightly faded, contemporary ink inscription M. Mcqueen", armorial bookplate of Shute Barrington, from the collection of Christopher Ernest Weston 1947-2010. Unsworths Booksellers 24 - 52 2011 £950

Taylor, Jeremy 1613-1667 *The Rule and Exercise of Holy Living... (bound with) The Rules and Exercises of Holy Dying...* printed by J. Heptinstall and J. L. for John Meredith, 1703, Second edition; modern half calf, gilt, pages 239, (iii), engraved frontispiece and title vignette, scattered spotting or browning, scarce. R. F. G. Hollett & Son Antiquarian Booksellers 175 - 1319 2011 £295

Taylor, John *Reminiscences of Isaac Marsden of Doncaster.* London: Charles H. Kelly, 1902, Ninth thousand; original blue cloth gilt, pages xii, 194, (ii) with portrait. R. F. G. Hollett & Son Antiquarian Booksellers General Catalogue Summer 2010 - 470 2011 £35

Taylor, Joseph *Mirabilia; or the Wonders of Nature and Art.* London: F. J. Mason, 1829, First edition; 12mo., frontispiece and plates, untrimmed in original pink glazed cloth by Wareing Webb, Manchester, slightly chipped paper label (7s 6d), cloth faded mostly to brown, little rubbed, inscriptions and embossed stamp of James Smith, Darley Dale Nurseries, nice. Jarndyce Antiquarian Booksellers CXCI - 507 2011 £125

Taylor, Joseph H. *Sketches of Frontier and Indian Life on the Missouri and Great Plains Embracing the Author's Personal Recollections of Noted Frontier Characters and some Wild Indian Life During a "Twenty-Five Years' Residence in the Two Dakotas and Other Territories Between the Years 1864 and 1889.* Pottstown: printed and published by the author, 1989, First edition; 12mo., original publisher's deluxe quarter leather and marbled paper, 200 pages, frontispiece, illustrations, rebacked in maroon leather with original spine laid down, light wear to fore-edges of boards, else very good, housed in cloth slipcase. Buckingham Books   May 26 2011 - 29564 2011 $2000

Taylor, Michael Waistell *The Old Manorial Halls of Westmorland and Cumberland.* Kendal: T. Wilson, 1892, First edition; original brown cloth, gilt, head of spine little frayed, one corner bumped, pages xxi, 384, with 54 illustrations, 27 folding plans, joints tender, scarce.   R. F. G. Hollett & Son Antiquarian Booksellers   177 - 844 2011   £180

Taylor, Peter *Eudora Welty.* N.P.: Stuart Wright, 1984, Offprint from the limited edition "Eudora Welty: a Tribute", one of 500 numbered copies, signed by author, this being copy #2; scarce, fine in wrappers, signed by Taylor.   Ken Lopez Bookseller   154 - 217 2011 $475

Taylor, R. H., Mrs. *The Airedale Fairy Stories.* Keighley: Keighley Printers, 1926, First edition; original pictorial boards, pages 115, illustrations and decorations by B. M. Cass, scarce.   R. F. G. Hollett & Sons Antiquarian Booksellers   170 - 679 2011   £50

Taylor, Samuel *Cartmel, People and Priory.* Kendal: Titus Wilson, 1955, First edition; original cloth, gilt, dust jacket (edges torn and chipped), pages x, 181, 17 illustrations, edges and flyleaf little spotted.   R. F. G. Hollett & Son Antiquarian Booksellers   173 - 1099 2011   £35

Taylor, Tom *Life of Benjamin Robert Haydon, Historical Painter...* London: Longman, Brown and Longmans, 1853, First edition; 3 volumes, original blindstamped brown cloth, gilt, little soiled and faded, spines little worn and frayed at head and foot, pages vi, 386, (vi); 368; 358, 32, endpapers little spotted, very good set, Roger Senhouse's set with his label and pencilled notes on first pastedown and neat signature in each volume.   R. F. G. Hollett & Son Antiquarian Booksellers   General Catalogue Summer 2010 - 471 2011   £140

Teachwell, Timothy, Pseud. *Pretty Tales, Containing Five Entertaining Stories for the Amusement and Instruction of Little Children.* Chelmsford: I. Marsden, n.d. circa, 1815, 18mo., 23 pages, original green paper wrappers, 7 quaint full page woodcuts, frontispiece, rebacked with matching color paper, rare, fine.   Hobbyhorse Books   56 - 32 2011 $220

Teasley, D. O. *Every-Day Dont's or the Art of Good Manners.* Anderson: 1918, 267 pages, good to very good in publisher's green cloth, cover gilt bright, backstrip gilt quite eligible, missing f.f.e.p., library number on backstrip, expected rubbing to backstrip ends, small ding to bottom edge of rear cover.   Bookworm & Silverfish   671 - 44 2011 $115

Teeling, William *The Nearby Thing: or Living with Our Unemployed and How They are Solving Their Own Problems.* London: Herbert Jenkins, 1933, First edition; pages xii, 232, frontispiece, original green cloth, scarce.   R. F. G. Hollett & Son Antiquarian Booksellers   175 - 1323 2011   £45

Tegetmeier, W. B. *The Poultry Book..* London: George Routledge, 1873, Additional chromolithographed title and 29 chromolithographed plates by Harrison Weir, 17 uncolored plates and numerous wood engraved illustrations in text, ink ownership signature, pages viii, 390, (2), large 8vo., original quarter red roan, rebacked preserving most of original spine, gilt lettering, mid green cloth sides, yellow endpapers, owner's name on front free endpaper, top edge gilt.   Blackwell Rare Books   B166 - 106 2011   £450

Tegg, William *The Knot Tied.* London: William Tegg & Co., 1877, Original decorated red cloth gilt over bevelled boards, rather soiled, pages 410, (iv), all edges gilt, tinted frontispiece and title few pencilled marginalia.   R. F. G. Hollett & Son Antiquarian Booksellers   175 - 1324 2011   £45

Tegner, Esaias *Frithiof's Saga.* London: Black and Armstrong and Stockholm: A Bonnier, 1839, First edition; modern half calf gilt with raised bands and contrasting spine labels, pages xlvi, 302, (ii, errata) with 17 engraved plates and 12 examples of music, marginal blindstamp on title, library stamp on verso, short tear repaired.   R. F. G. Hollett & Son Antiquarian Booksellers   175 - 1325 2011   £180

The Temperance Volume Embracing the Temperance Tracts of the American Tract Society. New York: to the Society, 1834, First edition; 8vo., 17 tracts, each individually paginated, original leather backed boards, front cover very loose, some light pencil holograph on endpaper, little toning but good.   Second Life Books Inc.   174 - 297 2011 $225

Temple, F. J. *Vesuvius.* Kent: Volair/Capra, 1979, Limited to 275 signed copies with original etchings by Arthur Secunda; signed titlepage etching by Arthur Secunda, 8vo., hand bound in quarter black leather, marbled board covers, gilt lettered spine, very good++ original glassine dust jacket with mild sun spine, mild chips, original slipcase, text printed on Arches paper.   By the Book, L. C.   26 - 50 2011 $200

Temple, Richard *Journals Kept in Hyderabad, Kashmir, Sikkim and Nepal.* London: W. H. Allen, 1887, First edition; xxvii, 314 pages; 303, (1) pages, 2 (ads), 7 maps, 5 chromolithographic plates, 2 folding panoramas, 6 further plates and 1 mounted, woodburytype portrait, 8vo., green cloth stamped in black lettered in gilt, very good or better, first volume unopened (uncut), boards rubbed, spines dulled, small oval Jesuit institutional stamp on free endpaper, small inked numerals to corner of endpapers, some minor foxing, mostly marginal, otherwise plates and maps brilliant, small inner marginal tear not affecting image on one map.   Kaaterskill Books   12 - 190   2011 $1350

Temple, Richard *The World Encompassed and Analogous Contemporary Documents Concerning Sir Francis Drake's Circumnavigation of the World.* New York: Cooper Square, 1969, Reprint; tall 8vo., x, 235 pages, maps, illustrations, blue cloth, silver and gilt stamped spine title, near fine, from the Bern Dibner reference library, with Burndy bookplate.   Jeff Weber Rare Books   161 - 122   2011 $65

Temple, William *The Works of Sir William Temple Bart.* 1757, New edition; 4 volumes, library cloth, ex-library, very good.   C. P. Hyland   May 26 2011 - 255/768   2011 $457

Ten Little Colored Boys. New York: Howell Soskins, 1942, Oblong 4to., spiral backed boards, light soil and wear, very good+, attached to top of very page is cardboard cut-out head in color, illustrations in color and black and white by Emery Gondor.   Aleph-Bet Books, Inc.   95 - 110   2011 $400

Z'ah Chylni Neegerli. (Ten Little Colored Boys). Zurich: Neue Bucher A. G. Verlagsbuchhandlung, n.d. circa, 1945, Oblong 4to., pictorial boards, near fine, attached to top of every page is cardboard cut-out head in color of a little Black boy, so that as each page is turned, the number decreases according to the text of counting rhyme, 8 full page rich color illustrations by unknown hand.   Aleph-Bet Books, Inc.   95 - 113   2011 $475

Ten Little Niggers. New York: McLoughlin Bros. n.d. circa, 1895, 4to., pictorial wrappers, slight soiling to covers, else very good+, 12 full page chromolithographed illustrations, very scarce.   Aleph-Bet Books, Inc.   95 - 111   2011 $1100

Ten Little Pussy Cats. no publishing information, circa, 1890, Small 4to., chromolithographed die cut covers in scalloped design, small margin mends and spine slightly rubbed, else very good, rare Victorian counting book, 4 full page chromolithographed pages and brown line illustrations on other pages.   Aleph-Bet Books, Inc.   95 - 142   2011 $375

Ten Tales. Huntington Beach: Cahill, 1994, Limited to 250 copies; book fine, signed by all ten authors as well as by Lawrence Block and Poppy Z. Brite.   Bella Luna Books   May 26 2011 - j1032   2011 $495

Tennyson Turner, Charles *Sonnets and Fugitive Pieces.* Cambridge: B. Bridges, 1830, Half title, green crushed morocco by Zaehnsdorf, gilt spine borders and dentelles, bookplate of Robert Pinkney, top edge gilt, inscribed with author's compliments, for T. H. Rawnsley.   Jarndyce Antiquarian Booksellers   CXCI - 509   2011   £500

Tennyson, Alfred Tennyson, 1st Baron   1809-1892
The Death of Oenone, Akbar's Dream and Other Poems. London: 1892, First edition; vi, 111 pages, very good, endpaper foxing, backstrip gilt bright, corners sharp, original binding.   Bookworm & Silverfish   669 - 159   2011 $65

Tennyson, Alfred Tennyson, 1st Baron   1809-1892
The Devil and the Lady. London: Macmillan, 1930, First edition, one of 1500 copies; printed on Whatman handmade paper, pages xvi, 72, 8vo., original quarter white boards, gilt lettered backstrip, trifle browned, fawn and brown marbled batik boards, untrimmed, partly unopened, fragile, dust jacket little defective at head of backstrip panel, very good.   Blackwell Rare Books   B166 - 107   2011   £35

Tennyson, Alfred Tennyson, 1st Baron   1809-1892
Guinevere. New York: Geo. Routledge, 1868, Large folio, green gilt decorated cloth, all edges gilt, slight wear to tips and spine ends, hinges neatly strengthened, very good+, 9 exquisitely detailed engraved plates by Gustave Dore, rare and excellent copy.   Aleph-Bet Books, Inc.   95 - 203   2011 $800

Tennyson, Alfred Tennyson, 1st Baron   1809-1892
The Holy Grail. New Rochelle: George D. Sproul, 1902, One of 30 copies (18 for America)) of the Saint Dunstan edition; this copy #5 especially prepared for socialite and philanthropist Elizabeth Stauffer Moore and signed by publisher and illuminator, 267 x 207mm., 52 unnumbered leaves, printed on one side only, all printed on vellum, arresting neo-gothic crushed morocco by Trautz-Bauzonnet (stamp signed), covers with outer frame of dark red flanked by onlaid green morocco adorned with gilt dots, each of the four sides of this frame with centered green framed roundel containing either a stylized gilt cross or a Christogram, frame enclosing a central panel of scarlet morocco with large central cross inlaid in white vellum decorated in Celtic pattern, red morocco square at center featuring a gilt chalice and inlaid white vellum Host, four small roundels (where the arms of the cross meet) with onlaid gilt and green shamrocks raised bands, vertical gilt titling inside dotted gilt frame, very pleasing onlaid white morocco doublures, surrounded and embellished by red and green morocco as well as gilt, repeating the cover frame and host and shamrock designs, vellum endleaves, all edges gilt; in original white silk box (fraying) with brass clasp, gilt titling along fore edge and padded satin interior, handsomely illuminated by W. Formilli in colors and gold, inevitable offsetting form doublure frame to vellum endleaves, some slight variation in whiteness of vellum, most leaves with hint of rumpling, otherwise handsome production in fine, creamy vellum leaves, bright colors and gold, lustrous, unworn binding.   Phillip J. Pirages   59 - 341   2011 $5000

Tennyson, Alfred Tennyson, 1st Baron 1809-1892
Maud a Monodrama. Kelmscott Press, 1893, One of 500 copies on paper (there were also five vellum copies not for sale; first state of text, without corrections later made on page 16, 19, 26 and 69); original limp vellum, vertical gilt titling on spine, silk ties, original (slightly soiled but generally well preserved) green cardboard slipcase with gilt tilting on front, initial opening with elaborate woodcut initials with decorative marginal extensions, device at end, printed in red and black, gift inscription "Winifred Lord/with her Uncle's love/and best wishes/may 20, 1895", half inch closed tear to fore edge of one leaf, otherwise virtually pristine, extraordinarily clean, fresh and bright inside and out.   Phillip J. Pirages   59 - 249 2011 $2750

Tennyson, Alfred Tennyson, 1st Baron 1809-1892
Poems, Chiefly Lyrical. London: Effingham Wilson, 1830, First edition; 191 x 114mm., 2 p.l., 154 pages, (1) leaf ads), original brown paper boards, flat spine with paper label, buckram chemise and contained in quarter morocco slipcase with raised bands, gilt titling, morocco bookplate of "Blairhame" (used by Natalie K. (Mrs. J. Insley) Blair 1887-1952), the "Blairhame" referring to her magnificent Tudor style home in Tuxedo Park NY, titlepage with 19th century ink presentation inscription "William Rowan Hamilton from Francis Beaufort Edgeworth"; joints with thin cracks, backstrip and label little torn and soiled, extremities with expected wear, leaves bit foxed and soiled, but surprisingly well preserved, nevertheless quite solid, covers very clean and text still fresh.   Phillip J. Pirages   59 - 332 2011 $1250

Tennyson, Alfred Tennyson, 1st Baron 1809-1892
The Poetical Works. Collins' Clear-Type Press, n.d. circa, 1914, Full polished tree calf gilt, pages xxxii, 720, all edges gilt, numerous full page plates.   R. F. G. Hollett & Son Antiquarian Booksellers   General Catalogue Summer 2010 - 677 2011   £50

Tennyson, Alfred Tennyson, 1st Baron 1809-1892
The Princess. Bobbs Merrill, 1911, First edition; 4to., pages, not numbered, illustrations in color and black and white, olive cloth with pictorial printing, gilt lettering, somewhat scuffed, little foxing at front, else very good.   Second Life Books Inc.   174 - 298 2011 $75

Tennyson, Alfred Tennyson, 1st Baron 1809-1892
Queen Mary. Henry S. King & Co., 1875, First edition; pages 278, old full scarlet calf gilt, little rubbed and marked. R. F. G. Hollett & Son Antiquarian Booksellers   General Catalogue Summer 2010 - 678 2011   £45

Tennyson, Alfred Tennyson, 1st Baron 1809-1892
Seven Poems of Two Translations. Doves Press, 1902, One of 325 copies on paper; (there were also 25 on vellum), 235 x 165 mm., 55, (1) pages, original flexible vellum with gilt titling on spine, very slight variation in color of vellum, quite fine binding text clean, fresh and bright with virtually no splaying or foxing.   Phillip J. Pirages   59 - 182 2011 $500

Tennyson, Alfred Tennyson, 1st Baron 1809-1892
Unpublished Early Poems. Macmillan, 1931, First edition, one of 1500 copies; printed on Whatman handmade paper, pages xvi, 88, 8vo., original quarter white boards, lightly foxed, backstrip gilt lettered, blue and grey marbled boards, untrimmed and partly unopened, fragile dust jacket chipped, very good.   Blackwell Rare Books   B166 - 108 2011   £35

Tennyson, Alfred Tennyson, 1st Baron 1809-1892 *A Welcome to Her Royal Highness the Princess of Wales; from the Poet Laureate.* London: Day & Son, 1863, 4to., color lithograph titlepage with 7 further lithographic plates by Owen Jones, some slight foxing, original maroon cloth, bevelled boards, embossed with vellum blocked in gilt, lettered on front board and spine, slightly rubbed and faded, bookplate of Charles Edward Fewster, Hull.   Jarndyce Antiquarian Booksellers   CXCI - 508 2011   £225

Tennyson, Alfred Tennyson, 1st Baron 1809-1892
(The Works of). London: Macmillan & Co., 1907, Eversley edition; 9 volumes, half titles, frontispiece in volume 1, some foxing, contemporary half vellum, spines decorated in gilt, maroon leather labels, pink cloth spines, small numbered ticket on front board volume VI, spines dulled and odd mark, top edge gilt.   Jarndyce Antiquarian Booksellers   CXCI - 28 2011   £180

Tennyson, Lionel *Lionel Tennyson.* London: privately printed, 1891, 8vo., original publisher's dark blue cloth lettered gilt on spine, pages xiii,225, pages uncut at edges, very slightly rubbed at corners of spine ends, else very good+, excellent condition.   Any Amount of Books   May 29 2011 - A68925 2011 $238

Tennyson, The Brothers *Poems by Two Brothers.* London: printed for W. Simpkin and J. and J. Jackson, Louth, 1827, First edition; 197 x 127mm., xii, 228 pages, especially attractive apple green crushed morocco by Bedford (signed on inside front dentelle), covers bordered with gilt French fillet, raised bands, compartments handsomely gilt with double bands and decorative rolls, scrolled floral cornerpieces and floral centerpiece surround by small tools, elaborately gilt inner dentelles, top edge gilt, spine uniformly faded to a pleasing sea green, cover with uneven fading (browned at top and fore edge), just hint of rubbing to joints, isolated faint foxing, otherwise fine, pretty binding still pleasing because still bright and without any significant wear, text clean and fresh, no real signs of use.   Phillip J. Pirages   59 - 333 2011 $3500

Terentius Afer, Publius *Comoediae Sex.* Lvgd. Batavorvm: Ex Officina Elzeviriana, 1635, 122 x 70mm, 1 p.l., 304, (8) pages, (lacking (23 prefatory leaves, apparently never bound in), excellent contemporary maroon morocco elaborately gilt covers with blind rule border, flat spine gilt in single compartment with densely repeated scrolling foliate tools at either end and titling in panel at center, marbled endpapers, turn-ins, all edges gilt; with woodcut initials, headpiece, portrait tondo and Medusa tailpiece, engraved titlepage by C. C. Duysend, morocco bookplate of H. V. Ingram; a sliver of leather worn away at bottom of backstrip, corners little rubbed, infrequent light foxing, one or two small stains, excellent copy in pretty binding, leather lustrous, text very fresh and pleasing.   Phillip J. Pirages   59 - 31   2011 $375

Teriade, E. *Fernand Leger.* Cahier D'art, 1928, One of 800 copies onlly; 93 full page illustrations, very good, original stiff wrappers, little used, inscription.   I. D. Edrich   May 26 2011 - 61383   2011 $922

Terrell, John Upton *War for the Colorado River.* Glendale: Arthur H. Clark Co., 1965, First edition, limited to 1604 and 1597 copies respectively; 2 volumes, 325, 323 pages, frontispiece map in each volume, fine set with dust jackets.   Argonaut Book Shop   Recent Acquisitions Summer 2010 - 202   2011 $125

The Territory of Wyoming. Its History, Soil, Climate, Resources etc.   Laramie City: Dailey Sentinel Print Dec., 1874, 83, (1) pages, blue printed wrappers, long diagonal tear in lower corner of titlepage has been neatly closed with strip of cellophane tape on either side (touching one letter of type), spine ends bit chipped, else very good, clean, wrapper in lovely condition.   Joseph J. Felcone Inc.   Fall Miscellany 2010 - 131   2011 $4500

Terry, Ezekiel *Narrative of the Adventures and Sufferings of Samuel Patterson, Experienced in the Pacific Ocean and Many Other Parts of the World, with an Account of the Feegee and Sandwich Islands.*   Palmer: May 1, 1817, First edition, 2nd issue?; 16mo., 144 pages, contemporary calf, leather label, binding worn but sound.   M & S Rare Books, Inc.   90 - 315   2011 $950

Testino, Mario *Kate Moss.* Taschen, 2010, first edition, copy #AP0093 (i.e. artist's proof no. 93 of 250) in an edition of 1500 plus 250 artist's proofs, signed on limitation page by Testino; photos, silver paper covered boards in dust jacket all page edges silver, as new, dark crimson translucent acrylic box, also as new, packaged in black and folding box only opened twice, hardly touched, still in original publisher's printed delivery box.   Any Amount of Books   May 26 2011 - A74557   2011 $1761

Tevis, A. H. *Beyond the Sierras; or Observations on the Pacific Coast.*   Philadelphia: J. B. Lippincott, 1877, First edition; 12mo. 259 pages, numerous engraved plates, vertically folding plate, publisher's dark green cloth, gilt lettered spine, fine, bright copy, scarce in this condition.   Argonaut Book Shop   Recent Acquisitions Summer 2010 - 203   2011 $250

Tew, David *The Oakham Canal.*   Wymondham: Brewhouse Press, 1968, 146/450 copies; double page color printed plate, 11 full page illustrations printed in one or more colors, 28 other black and white text illustrations, all by Rigby Graham, several facsimiles of maps and ephemeral pieces, titlepage printed in black and red, pages 116, (1), small folio, original mid green cloth, backstrip lettering and Rigby Graham design on front cover, all gilt blocked, pale green and white illustrated endpapers, fine.   Blackwell Rare Books   B166 - 244   2011   £70

Texas. Laws, Statutes, etc. *Laws of the Republic of Texas Passed at the First Sesson of the third Congress. (bound with) Laws of the Republic.... Fourth Congress.*   Houston: Telegraph Power Press, 1839-1840, (2), 145, (1) v.p. + addenda slip pasted to verso of final page of index, 280, (2), vii, (1) page including errata leaf, 2 work bound in modern law cloth, red and black leather spine labels, line endings in gathering I of second work, slightly cropped, scattered light foxing and overall light browning, else very good.   Joseph J. Felcone Inc.   Fall Miscellany 2010 - 116   2011 $750

Texas. Laws, Statutes, etc. *Laws Passed by the Eighth Congress of the Republic of Texas.*   Houston: Cruger & Moore, 1844, 120, viii, vii pages, later marbled paper covered boards, cloth spine, printed paper spine label, library stamps on titlepage, embossed stamp (barely noticeable) on each cover, stamps aside, very good.   Joseph J. Felcone Inc.   Fall Miscellany 2010 - 117   2011 $250

Thacher, James   1754-1844   *Observations on Hyrdrophobia, Produced by the Bite of a Mad Dog, or Other Rabid Animal.*   Plymouth: Joseph Avery, 1812, First edition; 301, (1) pages, hand colored plate, contemporary mottled sheep, foxed as always with this book very attractive, binding particularly nice.   Joseph J. Felcone Inc.   Fall Miscellany 2010 - 86   2011 $500

Thackeray, William Makepeace   1811-1863   *Ballads.* London: Smith, Elder & Co., 1879, Illustrated edition; this edition was given to C. R. Ashbee by family friend and bibliophile, Robert Samuel Turner, 8vo., pages 323, illustrations, pasted on reverse of frontispiece is 5 x 5 inch square of light blue paper upon which are written just over 12 lines of prose in blue ink and underneath which, in Ashbee's hand, are pencilled the words "Autograph of Thackeray", original publisher's cloth little used, snagged at head of spine, slightly shaken and scuffed, very good.   Any Amount of Books   May 26 2011 - A49450   2011 $587

Thackeray, William Makepeace 1811-1863 *Etchings by the late William Makepeace Thackeray, While at Cambridge, Illustrative of University Life etc.* Sotheran & Co., 1878, First edition; illustrations slightly spotted, original drab boards printed in black, brown cloth spine, marking to front board.   Jarndyce Antiquarian Booksellers CXCI - 510 2011 £55

Thackeray, William Makepeace 1811-1863 *The Kickleburys on the Rhine.* New York: Stringer & Townsend, 1851, First American edition; 12mo., 69, (3 (publisher's ads) page, original pictorial front wrapper only, corners chipped, foxed.   M & S Rare Books, Inc. 90 - 414 2011 $175

Thackeray, William Makepeace 1811-1863 *The Kickleburys on the Rhine.* London: Smith Elder, 1866, Half title, color frontispiece, vignette title and plates by author, 12 pages ads, text slightly browned, original scarlet cloth, pictorially blocked and lettered in gilt, spine little faded and slightly rubbed at head and tail, top edge gilt, good, sound.   Jarndyce Antiquarian Booksellers CXCI - 511 2011 £35

Thackeray, William Makepeace 1811-1863 *The Letters and Private Papers of William Makepeace Thackeray.* Oxford University Press, 1945-1946, Letters; 4 volumes, half titles, illustrations, original pink cloth, spines slightly faded, odd mark.   Jarndyce Antiquarian Booksellers CXCI - 513 2011 £85

Thackeray, William Makepeace 1811-1863 *Notes of a Journey from Cornhill to Grand Cairo by Way of Lisbon, Athens, Constantinople and Jerusalem.* London: Chapman and Hall, 1846, Second edition; 12mo., pages 221, ads, color frontispiece, vignette on titlepage, original red decorative cloth, 1 joint split, spine faded with wear to head and tail of spine, some light foxing to prelims.   J. & S. L. Bonham Antiquarian Booksellers Africa 4/20/2011 - 3108 2011 £85

Thackeray, William Makepeace 1811-1863 *The Rose and the Ring.* New York: Limited Editions Club, 1942, First edition with these illustrations; large 4to., 120 pages, one of an unspecified number of copies designed by George Macy and illustrated by Fritz Kredel with 8 hand colored plates and many black and white illustrations by Michael Angelo Titmarsh, blue buckram stamped in red, green, gilt and silver, fit in chemise an slipcase, small owner's name, otherwise fine, well preserved in moderately worn slipcase, this edition, although numbered in red ink, was not signed.   Gemini Fine Books & Arts, Ltd. Art Reference & Illustrated Books: First Editions 2011 $80

Thackeray, William Makepeace 1811-1863 *Vanity Fair.* London: Bradbury & Evans, 1848, First edition, 2nd issue; frontispiece, engraved title, plates and illustrations by author, full crushed royal blue morocco, double border in gilt, raised bands, gilt compartments lettered "Works of Thackeray" & "Vanity Fair" in gilt on spine, slight wear to head of leading hinge, top edge gilt, bound without initial ad leaf.   Jarndyce Antiquarian Booksellers CXCI - 512 2011 £380

Thackeray, William Makepeace 1811-1863 *The Works.* London: Smith, Elder & Co., 1898, 26 volumes, near contemporary three quarter calf gilt by Sotheran with raised bands and double spine labels, top edge gilt, endpapers marbled, illustrations by author, handsome, sound set.   R. F. G. Hollett & Son Antiquarian Booksellers General Catalogue Summer 2010 - 679 2011 £750

Thackeray, William Makepeace 1811-1863 *The Works of...* Jenson Society, 1907, Limited to 1000 sets; 30 volumes, illustrations, original buff buckram, very good, out of series, unnumbered.   C. P. Hyland May 26 2011 - 001 2011 $406

Thatcher, Margaret *The Downing Street Years.* London: Harper Collins, 1933, First edition, first impression; 8vo., copiously illustrated in black and white, boldly signed on titlepage by Thatcher.   Any Amount of Books May 29 2011 - A48286 2011 $340

Thaxter, Celia *An Island Garden.* Boston: Houghton Mifflin, 1894, First edition; 4to., white cloth with extensive gilt, Art Nouveau design, 126 pages, titlepage, slightest of toning on spine ends, else fine with original plain paper wrapper (tattered), full page chromolithographs and chapter heads in color by Childe Hasssam.   Aleph-Bet Books, Inc. 95 - 282 2011 $3750

Theal, George McCall *Records of South Eastern Africa.* N.P.: (London)? Government of the Cape Colony, 1964, Reprint; 9 volumes, 8vo., pages 4651, text in English, French and Portuguese, about fine complete set, endpapers slightly browned.   Any Amount of Books May 26 2011 - A56885 2011 $713

The Theatre. A Monthly Review and Magazine New Series Volume II. Wyman & Sons and Carson & Comerford, 1879-1886, New series, volumes I-VII, 8 volumes, small 4to., half morocco or roan gilt, lt 6 volumes matching little scraped or rubbed in places, with 151 woodburytypes from photos, bookplate and signature in each volume of Henry P. Greenhow.   R. F. G. Hollett & Son Antiquarian Booksellers 175 - 1327 2011 £350

Theatre Miniature IIeme Volume. La Kermesse Villageoise. Grande Fete Foraine en Quatare Parties. Paris: Guerin Muller et Cie, circa, 1890, 4to., cloth backed color pictorial boards with some edge chipping and overall dusting, outer edges of some pages within are similarly chipped, four scenes within, each activated by lifting a tab that reveals a multi-plane stage setting, each setting is like a popup peepshow with four or five levels, each with full color characters and settings. Jo Ann Reisler, Ltd. 86 - 195 2011 $3000

Theodore Metochites *Annalium Liber III Theodori Metochitae Historiae Romanae a Iulio Caesare ad Constantinum Magnum Liber Singularius.* Leiden: J. Colster, 1618, 4to., ff. (22), 103, (5), Greek text printed in Plantin's large Greek font, last leaf with short list of errata, mid 17th century English binding of brown calf over pasteboard, blindstamped fillets, red edges, very nice, from the library of Thomas Smith (1638-1710), from the library of the Earls of Macclesfield at Shirburn Castle. Maggs Bros. Ltd. 1440 - 207 2011 £450

Theognis *Theognis Restitutus. the Personal History of the Poet Theognis Deduced from an Analysis of His Existing Fragments.* Malta: Privately printed, 1842, First edition; small 4to., pages 117, appears to be original unlettered blue moire patterned cloth, slight dampstaining/mottling to edges of front and back boards, edges slightly worn and endpapers slightly foxed, else sound, near frontispiece. Any Amount of Books May 29 2011 - A40517 2011 $306

Thisted, Valdemar Adolf *Letters from Hell...* London: Richard Bentley & Son, 1892, 26th thousand; half title, original dark grey fine diaper cloth, blind borders on boards and spine, publisher's device on back board, gilt lettered on spine. Jarndyce Antiquarian Booksellers CXCII - 269 2011 £50

Thoby-Marcelin, Philippe *The Beast of the Haitian Hills.* New York: Rinehart & Co., 1946, First edition; fine in near fine, mildly spine dullled dust jacket, with slight edge wear, very nice, scarce signed, inscribed by author to Barbara Howes, with Howes/Smith bookplate. Ken Lopez Bookseller 154 - 73 2011 $450

Thoby-Marcelin, Philippe *Canape-Vent.* New York: Farrar & Rinehart, 1994, First edition; fine in good, price clipped dust jacket with small corner chips but splitting at flap folds, inscribed by author to poet Barbara Howes in 1971, nice association, scarce signed. Ken Lopez Bookseller 154 - 72 2011 $450

Thomajan, P. K. *The White Lie.* Philadelphia: Rittenhouse, 1940, First edition; illustrations by Leo Manso, glazed illustrated boards, small nick on front gutter, else near fine, probably issued without dust jacket, this copy inscribed by Manso for the author. Between the Covers 169 - BTC340320 2011 $750

Thomas Pynchon. Modern Critical Views. New York: Chelsea House, 1986, First edition; fine in fine dust jacket, bookplate of Ray Roberts, Pynchon's editor. Ken Lopez Bookseller 154 - 189 2011 $75

Thomas A Kempis 1380-1471 *The Christian Pattern.* Oxford: Jas. Parker & Co., n.d. 1870's, Full limp scarlet morocco gilt, extremities rubbed and head of spine frayed, pages xii, 354, all edges gilt, 2 titles in red and black (one with small photo roundel laid on) and 13 mounted albumen photo plates, text leaves all bordered with red rule, decorated initials to chapter heads, silk marker. R. F. G. Hollett & Son Antiquarian Booksellers 175 - 763 2011 £120

Thomas A Kempis 1380-1471 *The Christian Pattern.* London: William Rayner, 1738, Old full calf gilt with raised bands and spine label, rubbed and dulled, upper hinge cracked, pages (vi), 518, title in red and black, 22 engraved plates, little occasional browning, very good, armorial bookplate of William Brodie. R. F. G. Hollett & Son Antiquarian Booksellers 175 - 760 2011 £275

Thomas A Kempis 1380-1471 *The Christian Pattern.* London: printed in the year, 1757, Pages (x), 335, endpapers browned and stained, contemporary calf, worn. R. F. G. Hollett & Son Antiquarian Booksellers 175 - 761 2011 £65

Thomas A Kempis 1380-1471 *The Christian's Pattern; or a Treatise of The Imitation of Jesus Christ.* London: privately printed by T. C. Hansard, 1831, First edition thus; 8vo., 261 pages, full brown leather with gilt lettered spine label, interesting copy, long handwritten note in 1832 on tips to verso of front endpaper presents the book from printer of the book, T. C. Hansard, to Rev. Christopher Benson, Master of the Temple, London, signed with flourish by Hansard, Rev. Benson has signed the front endpaper, book further presented in 1939 from Desmond and Molly Macarthy to L. P. Hartley, head of spine chipped, front outer hinges cracked but holding, very good. Any Amount of Books May 29 2011 - A36006 2011 $340

Thomas A Kempis 1380-1471 *Of the Imitation of Christ.* London: printed for John Nicholson, Robert Kanplock and Jonah Bowyer, 1707, 20th century blue blind ruled library style morocco with raised bands, pages (x), xlviii (iv, 402), (vi), 5 steel engraved plates, old repair to back of title, frontispiece plate little darkened. R. F. G. Hollett & Son Antiquarian Booksellers General Catalogue Summer 2010 - 1185 2011 £120

Thomas A Kempis 1380-1471 *Opera Thomae a Campis Cognometo Milleoli...* Paris: Iodous Badius Ascensius, 1523, 2nd collected edition; folio, contemporary London binding of blindstamped panelled calf over wooden boards. Heritage Book Shop Booth A12 51st NY International Antiquarian Book Fair April 8-10 2011 - 134 2011 $10,000

Thomas Magister *(Greek) Thomae Magistri Dictionum Atticarum Collectio.* Paris: M. Vascosan, 1532, 2 parts, 8vo., ff. (128); (148), Greek letter, French 17th century calf, gilt fillet on covers, gilt spine, red edges, binding slightly worn, from the library of the Earls of Macclesfield at Shirburn Castle.   Maggs Bros. Ltd.   1440 - 209   2011   £450

Thomas N. Fairbanks Company *A Series of text Papers Mould made from the Famous Mills of Marais France, Miliani, Italy, Portals, England, Rives, France.* New York: circa, 1930, (60) pages, large 8vo. 11 pages paper samples, wrappers, very good untrimmed.   Bookworm & Silverfish   671 - 123   2011 $75

Thomas, Ann Van Wynen *Non-Intervention: the Law and Its Import in the Americas.* Dallas: 1956, First edition; xvi, 476 pages, fine in dust jacket with chip at bottom of backstrip and some other frazzles.   Bookworm & Silverfish   676 - 61   2011 $150

Thomas, David *Travels through the Western Country in the Summer of 1816...* New York: David Rumsey, 1819, First edition; 16mo., (2), 320 pages, crisp folding map, second errata slip pasted in, full contemporary tree calf, leather label, fine.   M & S Rare Books, Inc.   90 - 416   2011 $1750

Thomas, Dylan Marlais 1914-1953   *Deaths and Entrances.* London: Dent, 1946, First edition; very good, dust jacket with small closed tear at head of spine and small loss (half inch square) on upper top edge otherwise very good.   I. D. Edrich   May 26 2011 - 62347   2011 $587

Thomas, Dylan Marlais 1914-1953   *Deaths and Entrances.* London: J. M. Dent, 1946, First edition; 12mo., 66 pages, neat name on front endpaper, else about fine in complete dust jacket, very good+ (very slightly rubbed at spine ends and slightly soiled at edges), superb example.   Any Amount of Books   May 29 2011 - A39732   2011 $255

Thomas, Dylan Marlais 1914-1953   *18 Poems.* London: Sunday Referee and The Parton Bookshop, 1934, First edition; 8vo., pages (ii), 36, (4), occasional light spotting, overall very crisp and fresh, black cloth, gilt lettering to spine, slightly bumped, light shelfwear, dust jacket, unclipped, soiled and chipped in several places, some loss of text on spine, ownership inscription of Wilfred Gibson dated 1936.   Simon Finch Rare Books   Zero - 358   2011   £2000

Thomas, Dylan Marlais 1914-1953   *The Map of Love.* London: J. M. Dent, 1939, First edition, first issue; original publisher's smooth mauve cloth lettered gilt at spine, pages viii, 116, frontispiece by Augustus John, 7/6 price on first state dust jacket, neat name on front endpaper, else fine in very good dust jacket with very slight soiling, spine little browned with small 1 cm. chip at top of spine slightly affecting "H" and "E" of "THE".   Any Amount of Books   May 29 2011 - A39762   2011 $272

Thomas, Dylan Marlais 1914-1953   *The Mouse and the Woman.* San Diego: Brighton Press, 1988, Limited to 180 numbered copies signed by artist; octavo, 27 pages, woodcuts by James Renner, printed on Rives heavyweight paper, full hand painted cloth covers, slipcase, fine.   Jeff Weber Rare Books   163 - 220   2011 $225

Thomas, Dylan Marlais 1914-1953   *Twenty-Six Poems.* N.P. London: Jams Laughlin & J. M. Dent & Sons Ltd., 1949, One of only 10 copies printed on Japan vellum, out of a total edition of 150 Printed by Hans Mardersteig at the Officina Bodoni in Verona and signed by author, this copy #2 of the vellum issue; 4to, full black French morocco gilt with inner dentelles, matching chemise and slipcase by Patrick Loutrel of Rouen, very fine, extremely rare issue.   James S. Jaffe Rare Books   May 26 2011 - 17107   2011 $25,000

Thomas, Edward *The Chessplayer and Other Essays.* Andoversford: Whittington Press, 1981, First edition, 54/350 copies (of an edition of 375); printed on Heritage laid paper, 2 wood engravings by Hellmuth Weissenborn, printed in black with title fyl titles and engraving above colophon printed in brown, pages (x), x, 32, 8vo., original quarter black cloth, backstrip gilt lettered, marbled blue and brown boards, untrimmed, fine.   Blackwell Rare Books   B166 - 275   2011   £80

Thomas, Edward *Selected Poems of Edward Thomas.* Newtown: Gregynog Press, 1927, First edition; 8vo. original publisher's yellow buckram lettered gilt on spine, pages xx, 96, no. 53 of 275 copies, slight general even dust soiling, slight abrasion at lower spine, sound clean, very good, with clean text.   Any Amount of Books   May 29 2011 - A69337   2011 $306

Thomas, Edward *Richard Jefferies. His Life & Work.* London: Hutchinson & Co., 1909, First edition; half title, frontispiece, illustrations, map at end, original blue cloth, slightly rubbed, 4 contemporary reviews from newspapers.   Jarndyce Antiquarian Booksellers   CXCI - 225   2011   £40

Thomas, Frank *Disney Animation. The Illusion of Life.* New York: Abbeville, 1981, First edition; fine in fine dust jacket, inscribed by Thomas and Ollie Johnston.   Bella Luna Books   May 26 2011 - t6520   2011 $247

Thomas, Lately *The Vanishing Evangelist (the Aimee Semple McPherson Kidnapping Affair).* New York: Viking Press, 1959, First edition; xiv, 334 pages, plus 16 pages of illustrations, two-tone cloth, slight stain to lower cover, else fine in spine faded pictorial dust jacket.   Argonaut Book Shop   Recent Acquisitions Summer 2010 - 204 2011 $60

Thomas, M. G. Lloyd *Travellers' Verse.* London: Frederick Muller, 1946, First edition; original pictorial boards, matching dust jacket (closed tear to lower fold), pages viii, 120, with 16 fine colored lithographs by Edward Bawden.   R. F. G. Hollett & Son Antiquarian Booksellers   General Catalogue Summer 2010 - 721 2011   £95

Thomas, Owen *Agricultural and Pastoral Prospects of South Africa.* London: Archibald Constable, 1904, First edition; 8vo., pages viii, 335, one folding map at rear, ghosted to a great extent by Baron Corvo, sound, clean, very good+ copy, green cloth lettered in darker green, prelims foxed, endpapers browned, sharp copy, dust jacket.   Any Amount of Books   May 29 2011 - B29614 2011 $340

Thomas, S. *The Banker's Sure Guide or Monied Man's Assistant.* London: printed for G. & J. Robinson, 1803, Eighth edition; square 12mo., full mottled calf with brass clasp, pages (iiii), xxvi, (ii), 328 (table, label of Gaythorpe Booksellers, attractive copy.   R. F. G. Hollett & Son Antiquarian Booksellers   175 - 1331 2011   £150

Thomas, W. Cave *Mural or Monumental Decoration: its Aims and Methods.* Winsor and Newton, circa, 1870, 8vo., viii, 314, 1 32 pages of illustrated ads for artists' supplies, very good, original gilt stamped cloth, some foxing.   Ken Spelman Rare Books   68 - 75 2011   £65

Thomas, William S. *Trails and Tramps in Alaska and Newfoundland.* New York and London: G. P. Putnam's Sons, Knickerbocker Press, 1913, 8vo., beige cloth with gilt titles on spine and front cover, with black and white photo illustration attached to front cover, 8vo., pages (xvi), 330, (6 pages of publisher's ads), half title, index, black and white frontispiece and numerous black and white photo illustrations, 8vo., previous owner's bookplate, very good.   Schooner Books Ltd.   96 - 96 2011 $75

Thomassin, Simon *Recueil des Figures, Groupes, Thermes, Fontaines, Vases et Autres ornemens tels qu'ils se Voyent a Present dans le Chateau et Par de Versailles...* Paris: S. Thomassin, 1694, First edition; (6), 7-23 (1) (4) page table, engraved titlepage, engraved portrait and 218 engraved plates, recent full calf, gilt banded spine, red black gilt labels, some slight old waterstain to several text pages, otherwise very good, clean.   Ken Spelman Rare Books   68 - 2 2011   £650

Thompson, A. Hamilton *Military Architecture in England During the Middle Ages.* Oxford University Press, 1912, First edition; original pale blue cloth, pages xxi, 34, (viii), with 200 illustrations, drawings, and plans.   R. F. G. Hollett & Son Antiquarian Booksellers   177 - 848 2011   £85

Thompson, Albert W. *The Story of Early Clayton, New Mexico.* Clayton: Clayton News, 1933, First edition; 8vo., brief inscription by Earl Vandale, a book collector, fine, housed in cloth four point clamshell case with leather label on spine with titles stamped in gold.   Buckingham Books   May 26 2011 - 26281 2011 $2500

Thompson, Archibald *Interesting Narrative of the Shipwreck and Captivity of Dr. Archibald Thompson, who Served as Surgeon on Board the Sympathy 1777....* London: printed for Thomas Tegg, 111 Cheapside, 1777, 12mo., large folding frontispiece, (3), 4-28 pages, slight browning of title, disbound.   Anthony W. Laywood   May 26 2011 - 21703 2011 $117

Thompson, B. L. *Some Westmorland Villages Including the County Town of Appleby.* Kendal: Titus Wilson, 1957, First (only) edition; original cloth, gilt, dust jacket (rather worn), pages (vi), 211, illustrations,.   R. F. G. Hollett & Son Antiquarian Booksellers   173 - 1106 2011   £45

Thompson, Charles *Evidences in Proof of the Book of Mormon.* Batavia: D. D. Waite, 1841, First edition; original plain muslin, outer hinges, cracking (repaired), rubbed, later endpapers, printing on title somewhat faint, light foxing but very good.   M & S Rare Books, Inc.   90 - 417 2011 $9500

Thompson, Francis *Sister Songs: an Offering to Two Sisters.* London: John Lane, 1895, First edition; half title, frontispiece and decorated title printed in orange by Laurence Housman, uncut in original green buckram, bevelled boards, with gilt leaf design, slight fading, very good.   Jarndyce Antiquarian Booksellers   CXCI - 514 2011   £45

Thompson, Hunter S. *Fear and Loathing in Las Vegas, a Savage Journey to the Heart of the American Dream.* New York: Random House, 1971, First edition; 8vo., 206 page, illustrations by Ralph Steadman, fine in dust jacket little soiled.   Second Life Books Inc.   174 - 299 2011 $750

Thompson, Hunter S. *Hell's Angels.* New York: Random House, 1967, First edition; this copy inscribed by author, few small spots of soiling at fore edge, near fine in very good dust jacket.   Ken Lopez Bookseller   154 - 218 2011 $7500

Thompson, Hunter S. *The Proud Highway.* New York: Villard, 1997, Stated first edition, first printing; 8vo., xxxii, 683 pages, fine in fine dust jacket, signed.   By the Book, L. C.   26 - 18 2011 $240

Thompson, J. *A Commentary on the Dresden Codex. A Maya Hieroglyphic Book.* Philadelphia: 1972, First edition; 156 pages, open end folio, fine in fine dust jacket (one crease).   Bookworm & Silverfish   669 - 140   2011 $195

Thompson, Jim *Child or Rage.* Los Angeles: Blood and Guts Press, 1991, Limited to 500 numbered copies, first printing; fine, in fine, very tight slipcase, signed by introducer, Gerald Petievich.   Bella Luna Books   May 29 2011 - t6140   2011 $82

Thompson, Jim *Fireworks: the Lost Writings of Jim Thompson.* New York: Donald I. Fine, 1988, First edition; very good, light bumping to extremities, dust jacket near fine, corresponding creasing, signed note signed by Polito laid in, signed by editors Robert Polito and Michael McCauley.   Bella Luna Books   May 29 2011 - t6144   2011 $82

Thompson, Jim *Nothing More than Murder.* New York: Harper & Bros., 1949, First edition; fine in dust jacket with light professional internal restoration to spine ends and corners and some minor light rubbing to front fore-edge, attractive copy.   Buckingham Books   May 26 2011 - 23290   2011 $2500

Thompson, Jim *Nothing More than Murder.* New York: Dell, 1949, First edition, first paperback issue; pictorial wrappers, very good, wear to corners and wrinkling to spine, bright and complete,.   Bella Luna Books   May 29 2011 - t6147   2011 $82

Thompson, Jim *Recoil.* New York: Lion, 1953, Paperback original, first printing; pictorial wrappers, good, creasing and soiling, pages darkened.   Bella Luna Books   May 29 2011 - t6165   2011 $82

Thompson, Jim *Roughneck.* New York: Lion Library, 1954, First printing; Paperback original, pictorial wrappers, very good, light creasing.   Bella Luna Books   May 29 2011 - t6156   2011 $82

Thompson, John *The Tale Breakers. The Story of the California Dredge.* Stockton: Stockton Corral of Westerners and The University of the Pacific, 1983, First trade edition, one of 2450 copies; signed by co-author, Edward Dutra, oblong quarto, xiv, 368, (2) pages, photos, maps and plans, very fine, as new, pictorial dust jacket.   Argonaut Book Shop   Recent Acquisitions Summer 2010 - 205   2011 $90

Thompson, Robert *The Gardener's Assistant.* Gresham Pub., 1906, 2 volumes, thick small 4to., original half green calf gilt, spines little faded, cloth little bubbled, 18 fine color lithograph plates and numerous full page and text woodcuts throughout.   R. F. G. Hollett & Son Antiquarian Booksellers   General Catalogue Summer 2010 - 1061   2011   £150

Thompson, Ruth Plumly *The Gnome King of Oz.* London: Reilly & Lee, 1927, First edition; 4to., green cloth, pictorial paste-on, slight soil and rubbing, near fine, illustrations by J. R. Neill and 12 color plates (coated on both sides) plus black and whites, beautiful copy.   Aleph-Bet Books, Inc.   95 - 78   2011 $600

Thompson, Ruth Plumly *Pirates in Oz.* Chicago: Reilly & Lee, 1931, First edition, first state (H-G XXV); 4to., blue green cloth, pictorial paste-on, mint in dust jacket (dust jacket not price clipped, frayed with ads through this title), illustrations by J. R. Neill with cover plate, pictorial endpapers, 12 beautiful color plates plus black and whites in text, inscribed by author, beautiful and special copy.   Aleph-Bet Books, Inc.   95 - 81   2011 $3000

Thompson, Ruth Plumly *Silver Princess in Oz.* Chicago: Reilly & Lee, 1938, First edition, first state with pictorial endpaper and 16 page gathers (H-GXXXII); illustrations by J. R. Neill, 4to., red cloth, slight rubbing, else near fine, beautiful copy.   Aleph-Bet Books, Inc.   95 - 83   2011 $500

Thompson, Ruth Plumly *Wonder Book.* Chicago: Reilly & Lee, 1929, 4to., cloth, pictorial paste on, 217 pages, cover plate rubbed, else very good+, 8 color plates and hundreds of full and partial page black and whites.   Aleph-Bet Books, Inc.   95 - 549   2011 $850

Thompson, T. W. *Wordsworth's Hawkshead.* Oxford University Press, 1970, First edition; original cloth, gilt, frontispiece, 15 plates, extending map on rear endpaper.   R. F. G. Hollett & Son Antiquarian Booksellers   173 - 1108   2011   £50

Thompson, W. *Sedbergh, Garsdale and Dent.* Leeds: Richard Jackson, 1892, 8vo., 280 pages, ads, well illustrated, original cloth gilt, spine and board edges rubbed.   Ken Spelman Rare Books   68 - 188   2011   £60

Thompson, W. *Sedbergh Garsdale and Dent.* Leeds: Richard Jackson, 1892, First edition, large paper copy, no. 16 of 150 copies; pages xiv, 280, (ii), complete with 47 illustrations, 4to., original quarter morocco gilt, handsomely rebacked in straight grained crimson morocco gilt.   R. F. G. Hollett & Son Antiquarian Booksellers   173 - 1112   2011   £350

Thompson, W. *Sedbergh Garsdale and Dent.* Leeds: Richard Jackson, 1892, First edition; original pictorial brown cloth gilt, extremities trifle rubbed and corners little bumped, pages xiv, 280, (iv, ads), 47 illustrations from drawings by J. A. Symington, joints just cracking in plates, but very nice, clean copy.   R. F. G. Hollett & Son Antiquarian Booksellers   173 - 1113   2011   £180

Thompson, W. *Sedbergh Garsdale and Dent.* Leeds: Richard Jackson, 1910, Second edition, special limited edition (1 of 500 copies); modern half levant morocco gilt, pictorial title panel from original cloth laid on to upper board, pages xx, 291, (viii, ads), top edges gilt, uncut, color frontispiece, 43 photo plates, little damping toward end. R. F. G. Hollett & Son Antiquarian Booksellers 173 - 1114 2011 £125

Thompson, Will L. *Thompson's Class and Concert Containing a Complete Elementary Course & Music for Singing Schools, Conventions & Social Singing Societies.* East Liverpool: circa, 1885, 163, (1) pages, open end tune book, very good. Bookworm & Silverfish 664 - 143 2011 $75

Thomson, Cyrus *Dr. Thomson's Materia Medica; a Book for Everybody; Comprising a Complete Treatise Upon the Laws of Life and Health, the Pathology of Disease...* Geddes: Doctor Cyrus Thomson, 1863, First edition; 8vo., 624 pages, index, extensively illustrated, original cloth, additional printed leaf pasted to rear endleaf for "Nervous Liniment" and "Diabetes Powders", slip with text for "Nervous Liniment" pasted over text on page 550. M & S Rare Books, Inc. 90 - 49 2011 $425

Thomson, G. P. *Electronic Waves. Nobel Lecture Delivered at Stockhom on June 7th 1938.* Stockholm: Kungl. Boktryckeriet, P. A. Norstedt & Soner, 1938, First edition; 8vo., 7 pages, inscribed and signed with initials, original printed wrappers with minimal soil to covers. By the Book, L. C. 26 - 111 2011 $300

Thomson, James 1700-1748 *The Seasons.* London: printed by and for T. Chapman, 1795, 224 x 140mm., 1 p.l. (frontispiece), xiv, 233, (1) pages, (1) leaf (ads), pleasing contemporary mottled calf expertly rebacked using original spine leather, covers with wide border of stippled, knotted and Greek key rolls, flat spine in panels formed by bands of massed plain and decorative rules, simple gilt floral ornament used as panel centerpiece, marbled endpapers, all edges gilt, immensely pleasing fore-edge painting showing a snowy skating scene on a wooded canal; engraved frontispiece, engraved vignette titlepage, large and attractive engraved head and tailpieces and with four full page engravings, early ink ownership inscription of Cathe Cassin; leather little dry and pitted (as always with early mottled calf), small losses of gilt on spine, minor foxing to initial leaves and to plates and adjacent leaves, otherwise fine, carefully restored binding quite solid and still attractive, text generally clean, fresh and bright with especially pleasing fore-edge painting exceptionally bright and fresh. Phillip J. Pirages 59 - 43 2011 $1800

Thomson, James 1700-1748 *The Seasons.* London: printed for John Sharpe, 1821, 170 x 105mm., 215, (1) pages, extremely pleasing etruscan style calf in the style of and quite probably by Edwards of Halifax, covers with gilt Greek key border, wide inner frame of stencilled palmettes, central panel of tree calf framed by a gilt broken cable, flat spine gilt in compartments separated by Greek key roll and with a lyre centerpiece framed by foliate cornerpieces, with black morocco label, marbled endpapers, all edges gilt, very attractive fore-edge painting of an English stately home, perhaps Stourhead House, extra engraved titlepage with vignette and fine engraved plates, inscription "Mary Williams/The last gift of her affectionate Aunt/Mary Hoyle, July 31st 1826"; extremities and joints bit dry and rubbed, rear joint just starting at tail, gilt eroded from head and tail of spine, half a dozen small patches of lost patina in frame around outside of stencilled central panel, plates little foxed, one more noticeably but still quite pleasing copy, appealing unrestored original binding entirely sound, text clean and smooth and rich colors of painting beautfully preserved. Phillip J. Pirages 59 - 196 2011 $1100

Thomson, James 1700-1748 *The Works.* London: printed by A. Strahan for J. Rivington and Sons, 1788, 227 x 145mm., 3 volumes, once elegant and still pleasing contemporary scarlet straight grained morocco simply gilt, covers with single gilt fillet border, raised bands flanked by plain gilt rules, gilt titling, turn-ins with gilt chain roll, marbled endpapers, all edges gilt; with fine fore-edge paintings of Folkestone, Dublin and Worcester; volumes in recent sturdy buckram slipcase with marbled paper sides; frontispiece portrait, 10 engraved plates; 19th century armorial bookplate of Richard Davies, morocco bookplate of Estelle Doheny and modern engraved bookplate of John Taylor Reynolds, titlepage with ink ownership inscription of Mihill Slaughter 1811 (Secretary of the Railways Department); hint of soil to covers, joints and extremities with little rubbing (but well refurbished), leaves with intermittent minor foxing, engravings bit more foxed (half of them rather browned), offset onto facing page, text with general light browning and occasional trivial soiling, four leaves with short marginal or paper flaw tears (no loss); although not without problems, set nevertheless appealing, internal flaws never really unsightly, bindings all solid and paintings where it really matters, entirely well preserved. Phillip J. Pirages 59 - 45 2011 $4500

Thomson, Joseph *Through Masai Land: a Journey of Exploration Among the Snow Clad Volcanic Mountains and Strange Tribes of Eastern Equatorial Africa.* London: Sampson Low, 1885, First edition; 8vo., pages xii, 576, 2 folding maps, frontispiece, illustrations, no stamps inside, original green decorative cloth, neatly recased, gilt stamp on upper cover. J. & S. L. Bonham Antiquarian Booksellers Africa 4/20/2011 - 9134 2011 £1000

Thomson, Richard *An Historical Essay on the Magna Charta of King John...* London: John Major and Robert Jennings, 1829, Old boards, corners rubbed and rounded, sometime rebacked in calf with raised bands and spine label, pages xxxiii, 612, engraved title, decorative borders with arms throughout, frontispiece lightly spotted, first few leaves little damped at foot. R. F. G. Hollett & Son Antiquarian Booksellers 175 - 1334 2011 £85

Thomson, Robert *Treatise on the Progress of Literature, and Its Effects on Society...* Edinburgh: Adam & Charles Black, 1834, Half title, odd spot, few repairs in inner margins with sellotape by previous owner, uncut in original drab boards, purple cloth, recased, paper label chipped and faded, inscribed presentation from author to T. F. Kennedy. Jarndyce Antiquarian Booksellers CXCI - 516 2011 £35

Thomson, Samuel *New Guide to Health or Botanic Family Physician.* Boston: printed for the author by E. G. House No. 13 Merchants Hall, 1822, First edition; 12mo., (4), (183), 300, (2) pages, stippled engraved frontispiece, contemporary calf backed plain boards, portrait, once loose, has been taped at inner margin but fine. M & S Rare Books, Inc. 90 - 418 2011 $1250

Thorburn, Archibald *British Birds.* London: Longmans Green and Co., 1915-1918, First edition; 82 colored plates, including 80a and 80b, plates are fine, with about 500 figures after A. Thorburn, 4to., pages viii, 143; vi, 72; vi, 87; vii, 107, 11, original red gilt lettered cloth with gilt line border on front covers (spines faded and rubbed, some dampspots to 2 spines, vertical dampstain to spine of volume III, some wear to ends of spines, red stain to margin of aa text page, light foxing to endpapers of volume I, occasional marginal foxing to text, 2 small spots to covers of volume IV, text in volume IV tanned, top edges gilt), original wrappers on supplement (mildy ex-library), a piece missing from top edge of wrappers soiled, some separation of wrappers at spine, pages tanned, good. Raymond M. Sutton, Jr. May 26 2011 - 44805 2011 $1250

Thorburn, Archibald *Game Birds & Wild-Fowl of Great Britain and Ireland.* London: Longmans, Green and Co., 1923, First edition; 30 colored plates, each protected with original tissue, 4to., red cover with gold line border, spine being little sunned, gilt lettering, top edge gilt, edges and corners lightly rubbed, neat presentation inscription "Septimus J. Beck January 12th 1924 form LCB & A D", 3 front and rear endpapers and in each case the one nearest the cover little foxed with foxing getting progressively lighter on other two, no foxing on any of the text of plates. I. D. Edrich May 26 2011 - 59010 2011 $1174

Thorburn, Grant *The Correspondence Between Thomas Paine and William Carver.* New York: S. Gould, 1831, First separate edition; 8vo., 18 pages, contemporary drab blue wrappers, torn along spine, folded in quarters at some point, text lightly soiled, corners curled &c., withal very sound with good margins. M & S Rare Books, Inc. 90 - 310 2011 $225

Thoreau, Henry David 1817-1862 *Cape Cod.* Boston: Ticknor and Fields, 1865, First edition; original purple Z cloth, binding D, no priority, catalog dated December 1864, modern bookplate on front free endpaper, internally quite clean, spine gilt bright with some fraying to tips and edges, very good. Charles Agvent Transcendentalism 2010 - 29 2011 $500

Thoreau, Henry David 1817-1862 *Cape Cod.* Boston: Ticknor & Fields, 1865, First edition; original brown cloth, binding C, no priority, light to moderate foxing, spine touch rubbed but gilt still sharp, bright, near fine. Charles Agvent Transcendentalism 2010 - 27 2011 $1000

Thoreau, Henry David 1817-1862 *Cape Cod.* Boston: Ticknor & Fields, 1865, First edition; original brown cloth, binding A, no priority, light to moderate foxing, some early pencil writing on endpapers, spine gilt bright, some fraying to tips and edges, very good. Charles Agvent Transcendentalism 2010 - 28 2011 $600

Thoreau, Henry David 1817-1862 *Cape Cod.* Boston: Ticknor & Fields, 1865, First edition; 8vo., pages 252 and 25 pages ads (dated Dec. 1864) bound in purple cloth, spine faded, title wear at extremities of spine, very good plus tight, clean copy, bookplate, excellent. Second Life Books Inc. 174 - 300 2011 $1250

Thoreau, Henry David 1817-1862 *Civil Disobedience.* Boston: David R. Godine, 1969, Copy #XIV of only 50 numbered copies bound by hand; morocco backed marbled boards, of a total edition of 650 printed in red and black, darkening at head and heel of gutters from binder's glue with slight effect on few pages just about fine. Charles Agvent Transcendentalism 2010 - 30 2011 $350

Thoreau, Henry David 1817-1862 *Excursions.* Boston: Ticknor & Fields, 1863, First edition; original blue green z cloth, portrait frontispiece, one signature pulled, scattered foxing and staining, covers lightly soiled, minor wear to spine, gilt bright, very good, early owner name of Edward L. Temple, early bookplate of Rutland High School. Charles Agvent Transcendentalism 2010 - 31 2011 $850

Thoreau, Henry David 1817-1862 *Excursions.* Boston: Ticknor & Fields, 1863, First edition; 8vo., pages 319, frontispiece (offset to titlepage), green cloth, some worn at top of spine and some minor wear along extremities, spine stamped in gold, dark brown endpapers, near fine, bookplate. Second Life Books Inc. 174 - 301 2011 $1250

Thoreau, Henry David 1817-1862 *Excursions.* Boston: Ticknor & Fields, 1863, First edition; original blue green z cloth, frontispiece, fairly clean clopy with very minor wear, spine gilt bright, near fine, owner name of Charles(?) Davis. Charles Agvent Transcendentalism 2010 - 32 2011 $1250

Thoreau, Henry David 1817-1862 *Letters to Various Persons.* Boston: Ticknor & Fields, 1865, First edition; original purple cloth, binding A, very light wear to spine tips, few faint spots to front cover, near fine. Charles Agvent Transcendentalism 2010 - 34 2011 $750

Thoreau, Henry David 1817-1862 *Letters to Various Persons.* Boston: Ticknor and Fields, 1865, First edition; original brown cloth, binding A, small chip to front endpaper, bit rubbed but spine still readable, frayed at head and heel, very good. Charles Agvent Transcendentalism 2010 - 33 2011 $500

Thoreau, Henry David 1817-1862 *The Maine Woods.* Boston: Ticknor & Fields, 1864, First edition; original purple Z cloth, true first printing with list of Thoreau's books priced, catalog dated 1864 with last leaf advertising "The Thirteenth Volume", contents clean, spine pleasantly sunned, tips bit frayed, gilt clear, near fine and scarce in this condition. Charles Agvent Transcendentalism 2010 - 35 2011 $3500

Thoreau, Henry David 1817-1862 *The Maine Woods.* Boston: Ticknor & Fields, 1864, First edition; original plum TR cloth, true first printing with list of Thoreau's books priced, no catalog bound into this copy, from the library of John Shepard Keyes with his ownership signature, contents clean, spine sunned, gilt little dull and frayed at tips and along edges, large vertical piece missing but not affecting lettering. Charles Agvent Transcendentalism 2010 - 36 2011 $2000

Thoreau, Henry David 1817-1862 *The Maine Woods.* Portland: Ascensius Press, 1998, Copy #44 of only 45 total copies; folio, bound by Gray Parrot in full dark green morocco, gilt lettered and ruled brown morocco spine label inlay, author's signature stamped in black on front cover, frontispiece and several illustrations by Jon Luoma, printed on paper handmade in Maine, laid into the book is sheet of paper presenting the book from the nature Conservancy to a Maine Environmentalist fine in about fine slipcase made of solid Maine white pine. Charles Agvent Transcendentalism 2010 - 37 2011 $2000

Thoreau, Henry David 1817-1862 *Of Friendship. An Essay from a Week on the Concord and Merrimack Rivers.* Boston: New York: Chicago: Riverside Press, 1901, #482 of 500 printed in red and black; cloth backed charcoal gray boards with gilt lettering on the front cover and spine, vi, 88, (2) pages, woodcut ornament on titlepage, designed by Bruce Rogers, owner inscription dated 1902 on front endpaper, spine gilt dull, near fine. Charles Agvent Transcendentalism 2010 - 38 2011 $85

Thoreau, Henry David 1817-1862 *A Plea for Captain John Brown.* Boston: David R. Godine, 1969, First separate book printing; copy XXIX of only 50 numbered copies, bound by hand in morocco backed boards, total edition of 75, fine. Charles Agvent Transcendentalism 2010 - 39 2011 $350

Thoreau, Henry David 1817-1862 *The Transmigration of the Seven Brahmans.* New York: William Edwin Rudge, 1932, Limited to 1200 copies, this one of 1000 of the trade issue; quarto, cloth backed boards, tasteful bookplate, fine in near fine dust jacket. Charles Agvent Transcendentalism 2010 - 40 2011 $60

Thoreau, Henry David 1817-1862 *Walden; or Life in the Woods.* Boston: Ticknor & Fields, 1854, First edition; rebound around the turn of the twentieth century by Crombie & Lamothe in three quarter brown morocco and marbled paper boards, five raised bands, gilt ruling and lettering, matching marbled paper used as pastedowns and endpapers, original cloth covers and spine in very nice condition, gilt still bright, bound at rear, 8 page publisher's catalog not bound in, engraved titlepage and map inserted, marginal dampstain in outer top and bottom corners throughout, except on map, rarely just touching text, but mostly not affecting any text, small neat bookplate of Abram Joseph Abeloff, very minor rubbing to joints, very good or better. Charles Agvent Transcendentalism 2010 - 41 2011 $6500

Thoreau, Henry David 1817-1862 *Walden or Life in the Woods.* New York: Limited Editions club, 1936, limited to 1500 copies, signed by photographer, #468 of 1500 copies; quarto, black linen and blue-green paste paper covered boards, photos by Edward Steichen, contents fine, boards fine, spine mildly sunned with some dust spotting and crinkling at head where there is a quarter inch closed tear and slightly smaller closed tear, slipcase lacking three quarter inch piece top outside edge, otherwise quite nice, very good in slipcase with small piece missing on top front edge. Charles Agvent Transcendentalism 2010 - 42 2011 $550

Thoreau, Henry David 1817-1862 *Walden or Life in the Woods.* New York: Limited Editions Club, 1936, Limited to 1500 copies, signed by photographer; #431 of 1500 copies, quarto, black linen and blue-green paste paper covered boards, photos by Edward Steichen, contents fine, boards with bump to upper front corner, spine with some of the black rubbed off in few spots but not badly sunned or worn, slipcase with one bottom edge neatly repaired, length with sympathetic brown tape, otherwise quite nice, very good in like slipcase. Charles Agvent Transcendentalism 2010 - 43 2011 $650

Thoreau, Henry David 1817-1862 *Walden or Life in the Woods.* New York: Limited Editions Club, 1936, Limited to 1500 copies signed by photographer; #1208 of 1500 copies, quarto, black linen and blue-green paste paper covered boards, photos by Edward Steichen, Monthly Letter laid in, mild bumping to spine tips, small adhesive stain on front pastedown from bookplate once tipped in, about fine in near fine slipcase. Charles Agvent Transcendentalism 2010 - 44 2011 $1000

Thoreau, Henry David 1817-1862 *A Week on the Concord and Merrimack Rivers.* Boston and Cambridge: James Munroe and Co., 1849, First edition, first printing, first issue; 12mo., 413, (1, blank), [1, publisher's ads ("Will Soon be Published, "Walden, or Life in the Woods. By Henry D. Thoreau")], (1, blank) pages, original brown cloth, BAL binding variant A, Trade binding) with five rule border stamped in blind on covers, spine lettered in gilt with rules and decorative leaf design stamped in blind, original buff endpapers, some wear to spine extremities, contemporary ink signatures on first prelim blank, armorial bookplate of Jacob Chester Chamberlain, with his acquisition slip tipped in between rear endpapers: From "Che Col." (filled in in pencil) Through "Dodd Mead & Co." (filled in in pencil) and date "Dec. 27/00" (filled in in pencil) "J.CC." Sold at the Chamberlain Sale First Editions of Ten American Authors, The Anderson Auction Company, February 16 and 17, 1909, with note by late owner inserted discussing its purchase from Seven Gables Bookshop in NY 1951, some neat marginal pencil notes and underlining, 3 lines of type dropped by printer on page 396 are provided in pencil, with Chamberlain's note concerning this textual point, spectacular copy, totally untouched, gilt on spine bright and fresh, chemised in full dark green straight grain morocco pull-off case by Bradstreet. David Brass Rare Books, Inc. May 26 2011 - 00541 2011 $19,500

Thoreau, Henry David 1817-1862 *A Week on the Concord and Merrimack Rivers.* Boston: Ticknor & Fields, 1862, First edition; original green Z cloth, binding D, no priority, large skimmed spot at center of front blank with slight effect on titlepage is the only defect, gorgeous copy, spectacular example of scarce book. Charles Agvent Transcendentalism 2010 - 45 2011 $7500

Thoreau, Henry David 1817-1862 *A Week on the Concord and Merrimack Rivers.* Bosston: Ticknor and Fields, 1862, First edition; original brown z cloth, binding D, no priority, owner name of Elizabeth dated 1865 on front along with ink name "E. B. Simpkins on dark brown front endpaper, possibly a relation to Emerson's publisher Samuel G. Simpkins, contents clean, couple of signatures slightly pulled, spine tips frayed with about a quarter inch piece lacking at head not affecting any lettering, gilt quite dull but readable, light wear to corners, good to very good. Charles Agvent Transcendentalism 2010 - 46 2011 $2000

Thoreau, Henry David 1817-1862 *A Week on the Concord and Merrimack Rivers.* Lunenburg: Limited Editions Club, 1975, One of 2000 numbered copies, signed by artist; 352 pages, octavo, bound in green buckram and green marbled paper, drawings by Raymond Holden, fine in fine slipcase. Charles Agvent Transcendentalism 2010 - 47 2011 $75

Thoreau, Henry David 1817-1862 *The Winged Life The Poetic Voice of Henry David Thoreau.* Covelo: Yolla Bolly Press, 1986, Limited to 85 numbered copies signed by editor, Robert Bly and artist, Michael McCurdy; folio, 134 pages, wood engravings, decorative linen cloth, paper spine label, slipcase, fine, scarce. Jeff Weber Rare Books 163 - 120 2011 $1500

Thoreau, Henry David 1817-1862 *Winter: From the Journal of Henry D. Thoreau.* Boston & New York: Houghton Mifflin and Co., 1892, Early reprint of 1888 edition; original beveled green cloth, with Thoreau's signature in gilt on front cover, contemporary owner name on front blank, rear hinge cracked, but covers tight, some spotting and rubbing to cloth, good or better. Charles Agvent Transcendentalism 2010 - 48 2011 $50

Thoreau, Henry David 1817-1862 *The Writings.* Boston and New York: Houghton Mifflin and Co., 1906, One of 600 copies; 228 x 158mm., 20 volumes, fine dark green three quarter morocco, marbled sides and endpaper, spines very handsomely gilt in animated compartments filled with floral stamps and stars, top edges gilt, other edges rough trimmed, most of the volumes unopened, with 104 black and white and 20 color plates, mostly photogravures, with portion of manuscript in Thoreau's hand, as called for; spines faded uniformly and very slightly to a pleasing brown (just a hint of fading to perimeter of covers), total of four leaves with expertly repaired tears (one tear of four inches entering text, others smaller and marginal and no loss in any case), otherwise very fine set, bindings quite bright and virtually unworn, leaves without any significant signs of use, majority of text obviously never having been read. Phillip J. Pirages 59 - 334 2011 $18,000

Thoreau, Henry David 1817-1862 *A Yankee in Canada, with Anti-Slavery and Reform Papers.* Boston: Ticknor and Fields, 1866, First edition; original green C cloth, binding C, no priority given, bookplate of Julian La Pierre, M.D. dated 1904, scattered light foxing, cloth with no wear, but old staining to spine, especially rear cover, still very good. Charles Agvent Transcendentalism 2010 - 50 2011 $900

Thoreau, Henry David 1817-1862 *A Yankee in Canada, with Anti-Slavery and Reform Papers.* Boston: Ticknor & Fields, 1866, First edition; contemporary half dark green morocco and marbled boards with matching morocco corners, internally fine in fine, attractive binding. Charles Agvent Transcendentalism 2010 - 52 2011 $900

Thoreau, Henry David 1817-1862 *A Yankee in Canada, with Anti-Slavery and Reform Papers.* Boston: Ticknor & Fields, 1866, First edition; original purple C cloth, binding A, no priority given, front flyleaf lacking though brown endpapers are present, contents quite clean, spine sunned, but gilt still bright, minor fraying to spine tips, very good. Charles Agvent   Transcendentalism 2010 - 51   2011 $800

Thoreau, Henry David 1817-1862 *A Yankee in Canada, with Anti-Slavery and Reform Papers.* Boston: Ticknor & Fields, 1866, First edition; original green C cloth, binding A, no priority given, evidence of removal of small bookplate on front pastedown, pencil owner name and notes on front endpaper, front hinge cracked, covers tight, contents quite clean, some edgewear to front board, else little wear, very good.   Charles Agvent   Transcendentalism 2010 - 49   2011 $1000

Thoresby, Ralph *Ducatus Leodiensis; or the Topography of the Ancient and Populous Town and Parish of Leedes and Parts Adjacent in the West Riding of the County of York...* London: printed for Maurice Atkins, 1715, Folio, pages iv (ii) v-xii 628 (xii), frontispiece, folding engraved map, 4 extending engraved plates and 7 other engraved plates, mid 18th century sprinkled and polished tan calf spine panel gilt with made-up centre pieces, 'frond' corner-pieces, six raised bands and head and foot identically tooled using 'opposing multi rule triangles' pallet, orange lettering piece gilt, boards double rule gilt bordered, board edges 'exaggerated-wavy' roll in blind, all edges red sprinkled, pink and white sewn endbands, browned and spotted in places, little surface damage to boards, small loss from headcap, corners slightly worn, 19th century armorial bookplate of Montagu George Knight of Chawton, from the collection of Christopher Ernest Weston 1947-2010.   Unsworths Booksellers   24 - 147 2011   £1000

Thornber, John James *The Fantastic Clan. The Cactus Family.* New York: Macmillan Co., 1932, First edition; xiv, (2), 194 pages, 4 color plates, numerous photo illustrations, line drawings, endpaper map, brown pictorial cloth stamped in gilt, spine and upper edge of rear cover with slight fading, else fine.   Argonaut Book Shop   Recent Acquisitions Summer 2010 - 206   2011 $60

Thorndike, Russell *Jet and Ivory.* London: Rich and Cowan, 1934, First edition; pages viii, 9-443, 8vo., original publisher's black cloth lettered white on spine, with 36 page publisher's catalog at rear, signed presentation from author to Mildred Pratt, prelims very slightly foxed, white lettering at spine very slightly flaked, but title legible, slight rubbing, slight shelfwear, otherwise sound very good.   Any Amount of Books   May 29 2011 - A70325 2011 $230

Thornhill, Bonnie *The Road to North River - an Rathad Gu Abhainu-A-Tuath: a Community History and Genealogical Sketches of Pioneer Families and Their Descendants, North River, Victoria County, Nova Scotia.* St. Ann's Baddeck Waipu Twining Society, City Publisher's, Sydney, 2006, Pages 352, card covers, black and white photo illustrations, quarto, fine, signed by author. Schooner Books Ltd.   96 - 250 2011 $75

Thornhill, Bonnie *The Road to St. Ann's - An Rathad gu Bagh Naoimh Anna: a Community History and Genealogical Sketches.*   St. Ann's Baddeck Waipu Twinning Society, City Publisher's, Sydney, 2007,   quarto, card covers, pages 394, black and white photo illustrations, fine, signed by editor.   Schooner Books Ltd.   96 - 252 2011 $75

Thornhill, Bonnie *The Road to Tarbot an Rathad Do Thairbeart A Community History and Genealogical Sketches of Pioneer Families and Their Descendants, Tarbot, Victoria County, Nova Soctia.* Sydney: City Printers, 2004, Pages 323, 10.5 x 8.5 inches, card covers, black and white photo illustrations, quarto, fine, signed by Thornhill.   Schooner Books Ltd.   96 - 251 2011 $75

Thornton, Jessy Quinn *Oregon and California in 1848...* New York: Harper and Brothers, 1864,   Third edition; large hand colored folding map, 2 volumes, pages ix, (3), 13-393 + ix, (3), (13)-379, 12 plates, large hand colored folding map, newly bound in maroon cloth, gilt leather spine label, fine set.   Argonaut Book Shop   Recent Acquisitions Summer 2010 - 207   2011 $550

Thornton, Richard H. *An American glossary, Being an Attempt to Illustrate Certain Americanism Upon Historical Principles.*   Philadelphia and London: 1912,   2 volumes, polished cloth with modest rubbing, foxing to endpaper.   Bookworm & Silverfish   671 - 79 2011 $175

Thorp, John *Letters of the Late John Thorp of Manchester...* Manchester: printed by Henry Smith, 1828, Second edition; contemporary half calf gilt, label little rubbed, pages xlvii, 216.   R. F. G. Hollett & Son Antiquarian Booksellers   175 - 1336 2011   £60

Thorpe, Mary *London Church Staves.* London: Elliot Stock, 1895, Large 8vo., original cloth, gilt, little soiled, pages xiii, 76, uncut, illustrations.   R. F. G. Hollett & Son Antiquarian Booksellers   177 - 850 2011   £30

The Three Bears. London: George G. Harrap & Co. n.d. circa, 1914, First edition thus; square 12mo., original pictorial boards, little rubbed, corners worn and rounded, 32 page (unnumbered) panorama with 16 color plates by Willy Pogany and text below, main text on reverse (with line decorations, some rather childishly colored) opening accordion style, odd slight mark but generally nice, clean and sound copy, scarce.   R. F. G. Hollett & Sons Antiquarian Booksellers   170 - 538 2011   £120

The Three Bears Cutouts. Racine: Whitman, 1939, Oblong 4to., stiff pictorial card wrappers, fine and unused, 6 pages of sturdy, brightly colored die-cut cardboard cut-outs in color.   Aleph-Bet Books, Inc.   95 - 95   2011 $250

Thring, Edward   *Theory and Pratice of Teaching.* Cambridge: University Press, 1910,   Small 8vo., original green cloth gilt, pages xiv, 264, 8, name and neat stamp on pastedown.   R. F. G. Hollett & Son Antiquarian Booksellers   175 - 1337   2011   £30

Thulie, Henri   *La Femme. Essai de Sociologie Physiologique.*   Paris: Delahaye et Lecrosnier, 1885, First edition; (iv 520 pages), thick 8vo., contemporary half blue morocco over marbled boards, gilt lettered spine, raised bands.   Paulette Rose Fine and Rare Books   32 - 174   2011 $300

Thunberg, Carl Peter   *Resa Uti Europa Africa, Asia, Forrattad Aren 1770-1779.*   Upsala: Joh. Edman, 1788-1793,   First edition; Small 8vo., pages (26), 390; (32), 384; (14), 414; (36), 341, 4 volumes, contemporary quarter sheep, some wear, scattered stains at beginning and end of volume 4, good.   Raymond M. Sutton, Jr.   May 26 2011 - 33437   2011 $1750

Thurber, James   *The Beast in Me and Other Animals: a New Collection of Pieces and Drawings About Human Beings and Less Alarming Creatures.*   New York: Harcourt Brace and Co., 1948,   First edition; 8vo., original green cloth lettered black on spine, pages xi, 340, illustrations, signed presentation by author for Margot Hall, slightly bumped, very slight fading and slight shelfwear, else sound, clean, very good.   Any Amount of Books   May 26 2011 - A69301   2011 $461

Thurley, Simon   *Abbeys, Castles and Ancient Halls of England and Wales.*   London: Frederick Warne and Co. n.d., 3 volumes, original cloth, gilt, little worn, one hinge splitting at top, 12 plates, top edge gilt, fore-edges little spotted, one flyleaf removed.   R. F. G. Hollett & Son Antiquarian Booksellers   177 - 853   2011   £35

Thurley, Simon   *Abbeys, Castles and Ancient Halls of England and Wales.*   London: Frederick Warne and Co. n.dd. circa, 1883, 3 volumes, pages xii, 477; x, 576; xi, 574, with 12 woodcut plates, contemporary half calf gilt, marbled boards, all edges and endpapers marbled, most attractive set.   R. F. G. Hollett & Son Antiquarian Booksellers   177 - 852   2011   £150

Thurley, Simon   *The Royal Palaces of Tudor England.* Yale University Press for the Paul Mllon Centre, 1993, First edition; square 4to., original cloth, gilt, dust jacket, pages ix, 283, illustrations in color and black and white, 15 ground plans, fine.   R. F. G. Hollett & Son Antiquarian Booksellers   175 - 1338   2011   £65

Thurston, Clara Bell   *The Jingle of a Jap.*   Boston: Caldwell, 1906,   Small 4to., elaborately illustrated pictorial cloth with Oriental design, fine in original box (soiled but some but sound and very good+), complete with original real Japanese doll in cloth dress that ties to cover of book, pictorial endpapers, full page color illustrations, very rare with doll and box.   Aleph-Bet Books, Inc.   95 - 306   2011 $1250

Tibbles, Percy Thomas   *The Magician's Handbook: a Complete Encyclopaedia of the Magic Art for Professional and Amateur Entertainers.*   London: Marshal and Brookes and Dawbarn & Ward, n.d., 1901,   First edition; 8vo., original publisher's green cloth with illustration, pages 188 with 10 pages ads at rear, signed presentation from author to Robert Elsley 21/10/01, slight soiling and slight wear to covers, appears to lack front endpaper, slight foxing to prelims otherwise near very good.   Any Amount of Books   May 29 2011 - A49177   2011 $340

Ticehurst, N. F.   *The Mute Swan in England.*   Cleaver Home Press, 1957,   First edition; small 4to., original cloth, gilt, top edges trifle dusty, dust jacket, pages xiii, 136, 32 pages of plates, 31 line and 3 half tone illustrations.   R. F. G. Hollett & Son Antiquarian Booksellers   175 - 1340   2011   £40

The Tickler or Monthly Compendium of Good Things, In Prose and Verse...   London: printed by J. White, 1818-1819,   First edition; issues 1-13, lacking no. 4, original printed brown wrappers, pages 208, generally in very good or better condition, although no. 1 is somewhat worn at edges and slightly soiled.   Any Amount of Books   May 29 2011 - Aa47495   2011 $340

Tierney, George   *Two Letters Addressed to Right Hon. Henry Dundas and the Hon. Henry Hobart on the Conduct Adopted Respecting the Colchester Petition.*   London: J. Debrett, 1791, 4to., 22 (2) pages with half title and final blank outer leaves dust marked, but good, uncut copy, sewn as issued, only edition and very rare.   John Drury Rare Books   153 - 145   2011   £175

Tillotson, John   *Sermons on Several Subjects and Occasions. Volume the Eleventh.*   B. Ware etc., 1744, Old boards, worn and sometime rebacked in parchment darkened, pages 4709-5180, (v).   R. F. G. Hollett & Son Antiquarian Booksellers   175 - 1341   2011   £35

Timbs, John   *Abbeys, Castles and Ancient Halls of England and Wales.*   London: Frederick Warne & Co., n.d., circa, 1883, 3 volumes, contemporary half calf, gilt, marbled boards, pages xii, 477; x, 576; xi, 574, 12 woodcut plates, all edges and endpapers marbled.   R. F. G. Hollett & Son Antiquarian Booksellers   General Catalogue Summer 2010 - 1594   2011   £150

Timbs, John *English Eccentrics and Eccentricities.* London: Chatto and Windus, 1875, Frontispiece, illustrations, 40 page catalog, original brown decorated cloth, very good.   Jarndyce Antiquarian Booksellers   CXCI - 534   2011   £45

Timbs, John *Things Not Generally Known. Mysteries of Life, Death, and Futurity... (with) Things Not Generally Known. Predictions Realized in Modern Times.* Crosby, Lockwood & Co., 1766, New edition; frontispiece, 24 page catalog, bound for publisher in half red morocco grained sheep, spine elaborately decorated in gilt, green cloth boards, slight rubbed, very good.   Jarndyce Antiquarian Booksellers   CXCI - 444   2011   £58

Timlin, William *The Ship that Sailed to Mars.* London: Harrap, n.d., Large 4to., gilt decorated vellum backed boards, fine in dust jacket chipped at spine ends, few closed tears, each page of calligraphic text individually mounted on heavy paper (47 pages of text), 48 mounted color plates by Timlin.   Aleph-Bet Books, Inc.   95 - 552   2011 $5750

Timlin, William *The Ship that Sailed to Mars.* New York: Frederick A. Stokes, 1923, First American edition; large thick 4to., cloth decorated vellum backed boards, grey printed paper dust jacket has some chipping at ends of spine and at corners, clean, bright copy with few minor nicks in edges of some of the tipped in plates, elaborate and elegant red cloth box with slipcase, etc., book consists of 48 mounted decorated pages of text, 48 mounted color plates.   Jo Ann Reisler, Ltd.   86 - 241   2011 $4500

Timrod, Henry *The Poems of Henry Timrod.* New York: 1873, New edition; 232 pages, small 8vo. full green cloth, gilt decoration, very good, few scrapes to cloth.   Bookworm & Silverfish   662 - 153   2011 $60

Timrod, Henry *The Poems of Henry.* New York: 1873, First edition; 205 pages, small 8vo., terra clotta cloth, with replicated signification as noted per BAL 20327, gilt decoration, very good, few scrapes and some reader soil.   Bookworm & Silverfish   662 - 154   2011 $60

Tinley, George F. *Colour Planning of the Garden.* London: T. C. & E. C. Jack, 1924, First edition; 4to., original green cloth gilt, boards little marked and rubbed, pages xv, 288, 53 plates, address on flyleaf.   R. F. G. Hollett & Son Antiquarian Booksellers   General Catalogue Summer 2010 - 1063   2011   £65

Tiny Tots' ABC. (Aunt Louisa's Playtime Toy Books code number 94). London: Frederick Warne & Co., 1919, Large 4to., full color pictorial stiff card covers, some dusting, wear at edges, split along spine, Warne File copy, stamps and notes on first two pages inside, 14 pages within, four in full color and rest in two color (red and black).   Jo Ann Reisler, Ltd.   86 - 6   2011 $225

Tip and Top and Tap Look at Ships. London: Bancroft, 1964, Large square 4to., stiff pictorial card covers, near fine, 6 double page pop-up pages, illustrations in color and pop-ups designed by Kubasta.   Aleph-Bet Books, Inc.   95 - 453   2011 $475

Tipping, Henry Avray *English Homes.* London: Country Life, 1921-1926, Mostly first editions; 9 volumes, folio, copiously illustrated with black and white photos, photo frontispiece to each volume, original blue publisher's cloth lettered gilt on spine and front cover, some with jackets, slight fading, else very good+.   Any Amount of Books   May 26 2011 - A45203   2011 $4025

Tirrell, Albert *The Authentic Life of Mrs. Mary Ann Bickford, Who was Murdered in... Boston, on the 27th of October 1845.* Boston: published by the Compiler, 1846, First edition; 12mo., 48 pages, original printed wrappers, portrait, tiny chip to rear wrapper, some light staining in text, very nice.   M & S Rare Books, Inc.   90 - 263   2011 $475

Tissot, Samuel Auguste *L'Onanisme.* Lausanne: Marc Chapuis, 1764, Third edition; 12mo., pages xxii (2), 264, light dampstain to lower margin of some leaves, otherwise fresh copy, contemporary calf, spine decorated and lettered in gilt, lettered on spine label, slightly rubbed with chip and short crack to upper joint.   Simon Finch Rare Books   Zero - 119   2011   £250

Titus, Eve *Basil of Baker Street.* New York: McGraw Hill, 1958, 8vo., pages 96, illustrations by Paul Galdone, edges and cover little soiled, otherwise very good, tight copy in worn dust jacket.   Second Life Books Inc.   174 - 302   2011 $75

Tizac, H. D'Ardenne De *Animals in Chinese Art.* London: Benn Brothers, 1923, Limited edition, no. 174 of 250 copies; pages (vi), uncut with 50 finely printed photogravure plates, printed on handmade paper, very good, folio, original cloth, gilt, light scratch to upper board, extremities trifle rubbed or bumped.   R. F. G. Hollett & Son Antiquarian Booksellers   General Catalogue Summer 2010 - 332   2011   £350

Tizard, T. H. *Gibraltar: Report on Proposed Eastern Harbour and Dock.* London: HMSO, 1903, Folio, original printed wrappers, edges little chipped, pages 11, 5 folding colored charts.   R. F. G. Hollett & Son Antiquarian Booksellers   177 - 854   2011   £40

Tobie, Harvey *No Man Like Joe. The Life and Times of Joseph L. Meek.* Portland: Binfords & Mort, 1949, First edition; 320 pages, frontispiece and 5 illustrations, brick cloth lettered in black on spine and front cover, fine with lightly worn and spine faded pictorial dust jacket.   Argonaut Book Shop   Recent Acquisitions Summer 2010 - 208   2011 $90

Tocque, Philip *Kaleidoscope Echoes.* Roronto: Hunter Rose Co., 1895, Pressed cloth, blindstamped floral decorations and gilt titles and author's name on front board and spine, pages vi, 300, 4 black and white illustrations, 8vo., very good, paper browning due to poor quality.   Schooner Books Ltd.   96 - 98   2011 $100

Tocqueville, Alexis Charles Henri Maurice Clerel De 1805-1859 *De la Democratie en Amerique.* Paris: Librairie de Charles Gosselin, 1835-1840, First edition of volumes I and II, 2nd edition of volumes III and IV; presentation copy inscribed by author, 4 small volumes, octavo, uniformly bound in contemporary quarter dark blue calf over marbled boards, with presentation inscription by author.   Heritage Book Shop   Booth A12 51st NY International Antiquarian Book Fair April 8-10 2011 - 135   2011 $65,000

To-Day: a Weekly Magazine Journal. London: W. A. Dunkerley, 1894, First edition; volume 3 May 12 1894 to August 4 1894, 4to., illustrations, original publisher's beige cloth, pages 416, some modest even soiling, otherwise handsome, very good.   Any Amount of Books   May 29 2011 - A61832   2011 $340

Todd, Hugh *Some Municipal Records of the City of Carlisle.* Carlisle: C. Thurnam & Sons, 1887, Original brown cloth, gilt, pages 340, with extending frontispiece, 2 colored lithographs and 9 illustrations, very scarce.   R. F. G. Hollett & Son Antiquarian Booksellers   173 - 421   2011   £180

Todd, James H. *Descriptive Remarks on Illuminations in Certain Ancient Irish Manuscripts.* 1869, First edition; 16 pages, 4 (magnificent) reproductions, original printed wrappers, 48 x 40cm., mint.   C. P. Hyland   May 26 2011 - 259/484   2011 $362

Todd, John *California and Its Wonders.* London: 1884, New edition; 208 pages, illustrations, decorative boards, some spotting to back board, spine faded, front board bright, owner's name, overall tight, very good copy.   Dumont Maps & Books of the West   112 - 64   2011 $85

Todd, John M. *The Lanercost Cartulary.* Gateshead: printed for the Societies, 1997, Pages (vi) 476, small text illustrations, 3 maps, original cloth, gilt, dust jacket.   R. F. G. Hollett & Son Antiquarian Booksellers   173 - 1120   2011   £50

Todd, Mabel Loomis *Corona and Coronet.* Boston: Houghton Mifflin and Co., The Riverside Press, Cambridge, 1898, First edition; (xxxviii, 383 pages), thick 8vo., original publisher's dark green cloth decorated in gilt, with crowns, similarly gilt decorated spine, top edge gilt, with 34 black and white illustrations including two maps, one of which spans two facing pages, expert repair to front and rear inner hinges, tear to upper corner of titlepage, otherwise fine.   Paulette Rose Fine and Rare Books   32 - 177   2011 $300

Toibin, Colm *Brooklyn.* Dublin: Tuskar Rock Press, 2009, First edition; 8vo., pages 251, full grained yellow leather, gilt lettered to spine in firm mustard colored cloth slipcase as issued, XVI of 25 copies signed and dated 1 May 2009 by author, book and slipcase fine.   Any Amount of Books   May 26 2011 - A74372   2011 $503

Toklas, Alice B. *What Is Remembered.* London: Michael Joseph, 1963, First edition; original cloth, gilt, dust jacket head and foot of spine trifle frayed, pages 192, illustrations.   R. F. G. Hollett & Son Antiquarian Booksellers   175 - 1343   2011   £75

Toland, John *A Critical History of the Celtic Religion and Learning: Druids...* London: Lackington, Hughes, n.d. circa, 1820, 254 page, original boards, rebacked, text age browned, but very good.   C. P. Hyland   May 26 2011 - 255/772   2011 $362

Tolkien, John Robert Reuel 1892-1973 *The Hobbit.* London: George Allen & Unwin, 1959, Eleventh impression; 315, (1) pages, illustrations, color frontispiece, green cloth blocked in black, dust jacket, fine in just about fine dust jacket with just two tiny edge tears, signed by author, armorial bookplate, lovely copy.   Joseph J. Felcone Inc.   Fall Miscellany 2010 - 118   2011 $10,000

Tolkien, John Ronald Reuel 1892-1973 *The Hobbit or There and Back Again.* London: Allen & Unwin, 1937, True first edition; 8vo., pages 310, illustrations by author, superb full green leather, lettered gilt at spine with 5 raised bands, decorated gilt, inner gilt dentelles and marbled endpapers, very good.   Any Amount of Books   May 26 2011 - B29630   2011 $6709

Tolkien, John Ronald Reuel 1892-1973 *The Hobbit or there and Back Again.* Boston: Houghton Mifflin Co., 1984, Numerically stated first printing thus; 4to., green patterned boards with gold lettering on spine and vignette on front cover, full color pictorial dust jacket of an as new copy, signed in full by Michael Hague illustrated bookplate laid into book, 290 numbered pages, 48 full page full color illustrations.   Jo Ann Reisler, Ltd.   86 - 129   2011 $175

Tolkien, John Ronald Reuel 1892-1973 *Pictures.* Boston: Houghton Mifflin, 1979, First US edition; square folio, original cloth, gilt, slipcase edges trifle faded and rubbed, unpaginated, color portrait, 48 color plates and many illustrations by Tolkien.   R. F. G. Hollett & Son Antiquarian Booksellers   General Catalogue Summer 2010 - 916   2011   £150

Tolkien, John Ronald Reuel 1892-1973 *The Road Goes ever On.* London: Allen & Unwin, 1968, First UK edition; small 4to., original boards, dust jacket, pages ix, 68, with decorations in red and grey by Tolkien, near fine.   R. F. G. Hollett & Son Antiquarian Booksellers   175 - 1344   2011   £120

Tolleth, Ann *Recommended by the Rev. J. Newton.* Philadelphia: Sunday and Adult School Union, 1821, 16mo., 26 pages, original blue gray paper wrappers, wood engraved vignette on titlepage, owner ink signature vero of titlepage, lightly spotted at edges of few leaves, spine reinforced with matching paper, good, rare.   Hobbyhorse Books   56 - 34   2011 $110

Tolstoi, Lev Nikolaevich   1828-1910   *Voina i Mir. (War and Peace).*   Moscow: 1868-1869, First edition; 7 parts in 6 octavo volumes, all half titles present, contemporary Russian green pebble grain cloth boards, recent black morocco spine and tips.   Heritage Book Shop   Booth A12 51st NY International Antiquarian Book Fair April 8-10 2011 - 136   2011 $37,500

Tolstoi, Lev Nikolaevich   1828-1910   *War and Peace.* New York: William S. Gottsberger, 1886,   First edition in English, first printing, all titlepages dated 1886 and with proper Gottsberger imprint on versos; 6 volumes, small octavo, original dark brown cloth with front cover decoratively stamped in black and gilt, lettered in gilt back cover decoratively stamped in black and spine ruled in black and gilt and decoratively stamped and lettered in gilt, original brown coated endpapers, hinges of some volumes professionally restored, top and bottom of spines of some volumes professionally repaired, staining to back board of volume III, back free endpaper of volume I creased, very small part of upper right corner torn off, exceptionally nice and bright. Heritage Book Shop   Holiday 2010 - 125   2011 $8500

Tolstoi, Lev Nikolaevich   1828-1910   *War and Peace.* New York: William S. Gottsberg, 1886-1887,   First edition in English, mixed issue; 6 small octavo volumes, original dark brown cloth.   Heritage Book Shop   Booth A12 51st NY International Antiquarian Book Fair April 8-10 2011 - 137   2011 $5000

Tomasini, Giacomo Filippo   *Elogia Virorum Literis & Sapientia Illustrium ad Vivum Expressis Imaginibus Exornata.*   Padua: S. Sardi, 1644,   Handsome copy, 4to., (12), 411, (1) pages, device on titlepage, engraved portraits, contemporary vellum over pasteboard, from the library of the Earls of Macclesfield at Shirburn Castle.   Maggs Bros. Ltd. 1440 - 210   2011   £550

Tommy Tatters.   New York: McLoughlin Bros. n.d. circa, 1880,   square 16mo., 8 leaves + 1 page list on lower wrapper, pictorial stiff paper wrappers, 4 very fine full page chromolithographs, small spit at lower part of wrapper, very good.   Hobbyhorse Books   56 - 104   2011 $100

Tompkins, Leslie J.   *Trial Evidence. the Chamberlayne Handbook ...*   Albany: 1936,   1259 pages, very good in blue law cloth.   Bookworm & Silverfish   676 - 117   2011 $75

Tonna, Charlotte Elizabeth   *Mesmerism. a Letter to Miss Martineau.*   London: Seeley, Burnside and Selley, 1844, First edition; 16 pages text leaves sometime folded vertically resulting in consequential wear on final leaf (but no loss of printed surface), slip of paper with (apparently) R. M. Ballantyne's signature, affixed to blank part of titlepage, bound fairly recently in boards with printed label on upper cover, very rare.   John Drury Rare Books   153 - 146   2011 £350

Tooke, John Horne   1736-1812   *Ptereonta or the Diversions of Purley.*   London: 1798,   1805. Volume I is second edition, volume II is first edition; 2 volumes, large 4to., very free of foxing, text with wide margins, three quarter diced morocco and marbled boards, shelfwear, surface of leather at front edge of backstrip of volume I wearing but still tight, volume II has 3 inch split to right side of backstrip (marbling shelf rubbed), chip to backstrip extremities, bookplate of John Lowe.   Bookworm & Silverfish   670 - 77 2011 $295

Toole, John Kennedy   *A Confederacy of Dunces.*   Baton Rouge: LSU Press, 1980,   First edition; fine, dust jacket very good, with several closed tears, wear to spine ends, first state of dust jacket with Percy blurb on rear panel and price of $12.95 on front flap, very presentable copy, very good, several closed tears, wear to spine ends.   Bella Luna Books   May 26 2011 - t19280   2011 $1925

Topham, John   *Libri Censualis Vocati Domesday Book Indices.*   N.P. (UK): n.p., 1811,   First edition; folio, pages 570, part of 4 volume set of Domesday book but complete in itself, sound, disbound copy with slightly worn original printed label on spine which otherwise lacks its backstrip, first page is titlepage with small neat stamps of Brentford Free Library, several other pages have this stamp but no other ex-library properties, first and last page slightly foxed, else very good.   Any Amount of Books   May 29 2011 - B31430 2011 $213

Topham, W. F.   *The Lakes of England.*   Billing, Guildford for... T. J. Allman, 1869,   Square 8vo., 18 color etchings, 40 pages, 18 attractive hand colored etchings, good, original decorated blue gilt cloth, all edges gilt, head and tail of spine and corners little worn.   Ken Spelman Rare Books 68 - 179   2011   £220

Topham, W. F.   *The Lakes of England.*   T. J. Allman, 1869,   First edition; 18 color etchings, original blind-stamped blue cloth gilt extra over bevelled boards, pages 40, all edges gilt, lovely bright and clean copy, plates with original tissues.   R. F. G. Hollett & Son Antiquarian Booksellers   173 - 1121   2011   £250

Topinard, Paul   *Anthropology.*   London: Chapman and Hall, 1890,   New edition; tall 8vo., original cloth, gilt, pages xvi, 548, 40, with 49 text woodcuts.   R. F. G. Hollett & Son Antiquarian Booksellers   175 - 1345   2011   £45

Toplis, Frederick Henry *Popular Patter for Prestidigitateurs Part I.* London: London Magical Co., n.d., 1920?, Second edition; original wrappers, spine worn, pages 16 plus ad leaves, little used, one leaf rather stained, stapled rusted, very scarce, no other parts appear to have been issued.   R. F. G. Hollett & Son Antiquarian Booksellers   175 - 1346   2011   £35

Topliss, Helen *Tom Roberts 1856-1931: a Catalogue Raisonne.* Melbourne: Oxford University Press, 1985, First edition; 2 volumes, large 8vo., pages xvii, 261; (xvi), 270 (pages in volume 2 unpaginated), illustrations in color and black and white, neat Australian collectors blindstamp in both volumes, otherwise fine in very good+ dust jackets, slightly sunned at spine.   Any Amount of Books   May 29 2011 - A76885   2011 $315

Toriiyama, Toyoki *To You.* N.P. (Japan): n.p., 1999, First edition; 8vo., 97 pages, copiously illustrated in color and black and white, fine in very good+ dust jacket which is slightly scuffed at edges and faintly marked.   Any Amount of Books   May 29 2011 - A39919   2011 $255

Torr, James *The Antiquities of York City and the Civil Government Thereof...* York: printed by G. White for F. Hildyard, 1719, 8vo., pages (viii), 148, (v), late 19th/early 20th century half sheep, cloth sides, text block uncut, height 210mm., some browning and soiling to page edges, spine and corners sunned, from the collection of Christopher Ernest Weston 1947-2010.   Unsworths Booksellers   24 - 148   2011   £200

Torre, Filippo Del, Bp. of Adria *Moumenti Veteris Antii hoc est Inscriptio M. Aquilii et Tabula Solis Mithrae...* Rome: Gaetano Zenobi & G. Placho, 1700, First edition; 4to., (16), 400, (32) pages, 4 engraved plates at page 6, 159, 161, 257, contemporary smooth French calf, gilt stamp of N. J. Foucault on covers, gilt spine, red edges, some occasional marginal dampstaining, from the library of the Earls of Macclesfield at Shirburn Castle.   Maggs Bros. Ltd.   1440 - 211   2011   £1100

Torrend, J. *Specimens of Bantu Folk-Lore from Northern Rhodesia.* London: Kegan Paul, 1921, First edition; 8vo., pages iv, 187, original blue cloth.   J. & S. L. Bonham Antiquarian Booksellers   Africa 4/20/2011 - 3124   2011   £50

Torrey, John *A Flora of the State of New York...* Albany: Carroll and Cook, Printers to the Assembly, 1843, Volume 1, large 4to., original blindstamped cloth gilt, part of upper board damaged by damp, spine chipped and repaired, pages xii, 484, engraved title and 72 lithographed plates by Endicott of NY, some foxing to text and plates, occasionally heavy, contemporary signature of John Clapp.   R. F. G. Hollett & Son Antiquarian Booksellers   General Catalogue Summer 2010 - 1064   2011   £150

The Tourist's Illustrated Handbook for Ireland...   London: Great Exhibition Year, John Cassell, 1853, Deluxe copy; gilt decorated calf with silk endpapers, all edges gilt, ex-Malahide Castle (60), 248, (83) pages, bracketed pages and ads, text interleaved throughout with rice paper guards, sadly, the foldover of the Plan of the Building has been torn-off from the crease.   C. P. Hyland   May 26 2011 - 259/487   2011 $290

Tourtel, Mary *The Little Bear and the Ogres.* Thomas Nelson and Sons, n.d., 1922, First edition; small square 8vo., original pictorial boards, upper board trifle creased, patch of surface abrasion at foot, corners rounded and backstrip lacking, pages 84, orange and black, few spots and marks, little light fingering to some lower margins, otherwise very good.   R. F. G. Hollett & Sons Antiquarian Booksellers   170 - 685   2011   £350

Tourtel, Mary *Margot the Midget and Little Bear.* Thomas Nelson and Sons, n.d., 1922, First edition; small square 8vo., original pictorial boards, trifle soiled, corners rounded, backstrip lacking, pages 68, illustrations in orange and black, final 4 pages rather stained with brown patches, otherwise very good.   R. F. G. Hollett & Son Antiquarian Booksellers   General Catalogue Summer 2010 - 586   2011   £295

Tourtel, Mary *The Monster Rupert.* London: Sampson Low, Marston & Co., 1948, 4to., original cloth backed pictorial boards, edges little worn, pages 158, illustrations, first illustrations neatly colored in with crayon, ownership box on pastedown filled in.   R. F. G. Hollett & Sons Antiquarian Booksellers   170 - 687   2011   £50

Tower, Wells *Everything Ravaged, Everything Burned.* New York: FSG, 2009, First edition; dust jacket fine, signed by author.   Bella Luna Books   May 29 2011 - t9391   2011 $82

Towers, Edward *Harlequin King Crystal and the Princess of the Silver Maze; or the Good Fairy at the Bottom of the Well.* London: E. J. Bath, n.d. circa, 1864, Small 8vo., original decorative yellow wrappers, signs of removal from a bound volume to backstrip, vignette illustration to upper cover.   Dramatis Personae Booksellers   106 - 161   2011 $80

Towner, Donald C. *The Leeds Pottery.* Cory, Adams & MacKay, 1963, First edition; large 8vo., original cloth, gilt, slight staining to top of upper board, dust jacket chipped and torn, spine rather soiled, pages x, 180, with 4 color plates, 10 line drawings, 102 page facsimile pattern book and 48 pages of plates.   R. F. G. Hollett & Son Antiquarian Booksellers   General Catalogue Summer 2010 - 333   2011   £60

Townsend, Hannah *The Anti-Slavery Alphabet.* Philadelphia: printed for the Anti-Salvery Fair, 1847, First edition; printed on facing pages (others blank), illustrations, original printed wrappers (soiled), burn mark on front wrapper has left sizeable hole, but no loss of text, stain on following blank page, later(?0 owner's stamp on wrappers front and back, fair to good copy only, but intact, 12mo., (3), 5-15 pages, scarce.   M & S Rare Books, Inc.   90 - 395   2011 $650

Townsend, John Rowe *Written for Children.* Middlesex: Kestrel Books, 1983, New edition; 8vo., 284 pages, green cloth on boards, title printed along spine, pictorial green paper dust jacket, dust jacket printed in red, black and white with reproductions from five internal illustrations, negligible rubbing at corner of dust jacket, fine.   Hobbyhorse Books   56 - 128   2011 $70

Townshend, F. *A Cruise in Greek Waters with a Hunting Excursion in Tunis.* London: Hurst & Blackett, 1870, First edition; 8vo., pages xv, 286, vignette, frontispiece, original red decorative cloth, head and tail of spine rubbed.   J. & S. L. Bonham Antiquarian Booksellers   Africa 4/20/2011 - 8944   2011   £175

Toy Store ABC. Newark: Charles Graham circa, 1900, 12mo., pictorial cloth, near fine, charming linen alphabet, 2 full page color illustrations and 4 full pages of brown line illustrations.   Aleph-Bet Books, Inc.   95 - 38   2011 $150

Toy, Sidney *A History of Fortification from 3000 BC to AD 1700.* London: Heinemann, 1955, First edition; original cloth, gilt, dust jacket price clipped, edges little faded, pages xxiv, 262, profusely illustrated with plates and diagrams.   R. F. G. Hollett & Son Antiquarian Booksellers   177 - 856   2011   £60

Toynbee, Arnold *An Historian's Approach to Religion.* Oxford University Press, 1956, First edition; original cloth, gilt dust jacket, head of spine trifle rucked, price clipped, pages ix, 316, top edges little dusty.   R. F. G. Hollett & Son Antiquarian Booksellers   175 - 1349   2011   £35

The Tragi-Comic History of the Burial of Cock Robin; with the Lamentation of Jenny Wren; The Sparrow's Apprehension and the Cuckoo's Punishment. Philadelphia: Benjamin Warner, 1821, Square 12mo., 17 pages, pink paper on board, full page frontispiece and 7 charming copper engravings, plates printed on one side of leaf, good copy, cover spotted, pages foxed and uniformly browned.   Hobbyhorse Books   56 - 39   2011 $125

Traill, H. D. *Social England. A Record of the Progress of the People in Religion, Laws, Learning, Arts, Industry, Commerce, Science, Literature and Manners from the Earliest Times to the Present Day.* London: Cassell, 1901, First edition thus; specially illustrated edition, 6 volumes of 2 parts each, 8vo., approximately 5400 pages total, with 2370+ illustrations, some foxing to endpapers, else bright, very good+.   Any Amount of Books   May 29 2011 - B22873   2011 $221

Transatlantic Review. New York: 1959-1976, First edition; no. 1-60, 60 issues in original wrappers, all in very good condition, cover of first issue being little foxed, separate index for issues 1-60 included.   I. D. Edrich   May 26 2011 - 96801   2011 $1208

Transition. Paris: 1927, Issue 2 and 3, 250+ pages, issue 2 h as wrappers chipped & loose, issue 3 missing front wrapper and rear wrapper as above, all edges untrimmed, leaves unopened, all plates present, 7 1/2 x 5 1/2 inches, library stamp on half title, title and rear wrapper.   Bookworm & Silverfish   669 - 114   2011 $225

Transition. Paris: Transition, 1929, First edition; 8vo., pages 291, 15 plates, pages uncut, original publisher's illustrated wrappers, some general soiling, spine slightly chipped at ends, slight edgewear otherwise near very good.   Any Amount of Books   May 29 2011 - A66991   2011 $238

Transition. Paris: Transition, 1930, First edition; large 8vo., original publisher's illustrated wrappers/paper back, pages 398, 21 plates, ownership signature of surrealist Roger Roughton, sound, near very good, decent copy with slight soiling, slight wear at spine hinge and slight browning.   Any Amount of Books   May 29 2011 - A66993   2011 $306

Transition. Uganda: 1961-1968, Volume 1-33, 35, 37, 38, 40, 41, together 38 issues in original wrappers, very good.   I. D. Edrich   May 26 2011 - 82759   2011 $637

Transon, Abel Louise Etienne *Charles Fourier's Theory of Attractive Industry and Moral Harmony of the Passions.* London: published at the office of the London Plananx, 1841, First edition in English; 8vo., 120 pages, original blindstamped dark green cloth, spine darkened and chipped at extremities, stitching rather shaken, else good copy.   John Drury Rare Books   153 - 147   2011   £450

Trask, Willard R. *The Unwritten Song.* London: Cape, 1969, First edition; 2 volumes, original cloth, gilt, dust jackets, pages xxix, 287; xxxv, 316.   R. F. G. Hollett & Son Antiquarian Booksellers   175 - 1350   2011   £40

Traubel, Horace *In Re Walt Whitman.* Philadelphia: David McKay, 1893, First edition; 8vo., 10, 452, (2) pages, recent half leather and marbled boards.   M & S Rare Books, Inc.   90 - 421   2011 $950

Traubel, Horace *With Walt Whitman in Camden (March 28-July 14 1888).* Boston: Small Maynard, 1906, First edition; royal 8vo., original decorated green cloth, gilt lettered, folding facsimile frontispiece and 32 plates, cloth little rubbed and worn, good copy, from the collection of Samuel Charters.   The Brick Row Book Shop   Bulletin 8 - 44   2011 $100

The Traveller or an Entertaining Journey Round the Habitable Globe Being a Novel and Easy Method of Studying Geography.   London: J. Harris & Son, n.d. circa, 1821, Second edition; 12mo., viii, 204 pages, pictorial paper on boards, red roan spine with gilt title and fillets, half page wood engraved allegorical vignette on titlepage, 42 very fine engraved plates on 22 leaves, on handmade heavier paper and on one side of leaf only, inked signature on front endpaper, covers lightly soiled and rubbed at edges, minor chipping at crown of spine, good.   Hobbyhorse Books   56 - 150   2011 $180

The Traveller's Miscellany and Magazine of Entertainment. (with) The Tourist's Guide Book...   London: W. J. Adams, 1855, 12mo., double frontispiece, engraved title, illustrations, 3 pages ads, frontispieces foxed; original blue cloth, limp boards, marked and dulled, leading inner hinge slightly cracking.   Jarndyce Antiquarian Booksellers   CXCI - 582   2011   £38

Traven, B. *The Death Ship.*   London: Cape, 1940, 8vo., pages 388, tan cloth, owner's bookplate, name on flyleaf, spine browned, endpapers little stained, else very good, tight copy.   Second Life Books Inc.   174 - 303   2011 $65

Traven, B. *The Rebellion of the Hanged.*   New York: Knopf, 1952, First American edition; fine in near fine dust jacket, price clipped with minor rubbing and fading to spine. exceptionally bright.   Bella Luna Books   May 29 2011 - j2198   2011 $137

Traven, B. *Trozas.*   Chicago: Ivan R. Dee, 1994, First edition; 8vo., 265 page, about as new, dust jacket.   Second Life Books Inc.   174 - 304   2011 $65

Traver, Robert *Trouble-Shooter. The Story of a Northwoods Prosecutor.*   New York: 1943, First edition; (6), 294 pages, 8vo., cream cloth shoes reader soil, very good.   Bookworm & Silverfish   666 - 96   2011 $75

Travers, P. L. *Mary Poppins from A-Z.*   London: Collins, 1963, First edition; 8vo., cloth, fine in slightly worn dust jacket, illustrations by Mary Shepard.   Aleph-Bet Books, Inc.   95 - 553   2011 $250

Tredrey, F. D. *The House of Blackwood 1804-1954: the History of Publishing Firm.*   Edinburgh: William Blackwood & Son, 1954, half title, frontispiece and plates, original dark blue cloth, 4to., very good.   Jarndyce Antiquarian Booksellers   CXCI - 445   2011   £45

Trelawny, Edward *Records of Shelley, Byron and the author.*   London: Basil Montague Pickering, 1878, First edition thus; 2 volumes, 8vo., pages (xxvi), 214; (xiv), 245, portrait and 3 other illustrations, bound in publisher's cloth, stamped in gilt, some modest wear, very good, tight, clean copy.   Second Life Books Inc.   174 - 305   2011 $600

Tremearne, A. J. N. *Hausa Superstitions and Customs: an Introduction to the Folk-lore and the Folk.*   London: John Bale, 1913, First edition; large 8vo., pages xv, 548, map, plates, illustrations, original red decorative blindstamped cloth, lower hinge cracked, very good.   J. & S. L. Bonham Antiquarian Booksellers   Africa 4/20/2011 - 7544   2011   £85

Tressell, Robert *The Ragged Trousered Philanthropists.* New York and London: 1962, First complete edition; 633 pages, wrappers with normal wear.   Bookworm & Silverfish   678 - 98   2011 $75

Trevelyan, G. M.   *The Life of John Bright.*   London: Constable, 1913, First edition; original cloth, gilt, pages xii 480, with 21 plates.   R. F. G. Hollett & Son Antiquarian Booksellers   175 - 1351   2011   £30

Trevor, William *Marrying Damian.*   London: Colophon Press, 1985, First edition, one of 207 copies, this unnumbered; large 8vo., pages 22, the dedication copy, signed presentation from author to poet and dedicatee James Michie, loosely inserted is good handwritten postcard from Trevor to same, book with some soiling and staining (at rear) and what may be a coffee ring on pale orange covers, very good-.   Any Amount of Books   May 29 2011 - A40216   2011 $374

Trial of Abraham Lincoln by the Great Statesmen of the Republic.   New York: Office of the Metropolitan Record, 1863, First edition; 8vo., 29 pages, original printed wrappers, blank portions of outer front wrapper and title chipped.   M & S Rare Books, Inc.   90 - 215   2011 $375

Trial of the Taunton Election Petition Before a Committee of the House of Commons February 23rd 1831.   Taunton: printed and published by W. Bragg, 1831, First and only edition; apparently very rare, 8vo., (2), 298, (2) pages, including errata leaf, contemporary handwritten index of names on front endpapers, one or two gatherings strained, contemporary dark green half roan, spine gilt and lettered, little wear to binding, but good, apparently very rare.   John Drury Rare Books   153 - 156   2011   £450

The Trials of James, Duncan and Robert M'Gregor, Three Sons of the Celebrated Rob Roy, Before the High Court of Justiciary in the years 1752, 1753 and 1754. Edinburgh: printed by J. Hay & Co. for Baldwin, Cradock and Joy, 1818, First (only) edition; original boards with paper spine label, backstrip defective at head and foot, hinges cracked but cords holding, pages cxxix, 244, uncut, scarce. R. F. G. Hollett & Son Antiquarian Booksellers 175 - 1355 2011 £150

Triggs, H. Inigo *Formal Gardens in England and Scotland: Their Planning and Arrangement, Architectural and Ornamental Features.* London: B. T. Batsford, 1902, First edition; 3 volumes with 122 plates loose in portfolios, lacks 3 plates pages xxiv, 63 and 122 plates, spine and hinges worn and covers and some page edges worn and little soiled, very good-. Any Amount of Books May 29 2011 - A70559 2011 $255

Trimble, Isaac P. *A Treatise on the Insect Enemies of Fruit and Fruit Trees.* New York: William Wood & Co., 1865, First edition; 4to., 139 pages, 11 full page plates, 9 in color, 2 tinted, original green cloth, scuffed, foxed, very good. M & S Rare Books, Inc. 90 - 423 2011 $850

Trimmer, Sarah Kirby *Fabulous Histories.* London: N. Hailes, 1818, Twelfth edition; 12mo., viii, 164 pages, full tooled leather on boards, gilt fillets at faces of covers and gilt edges, rebacked, gilt title and rulers, brown endpapers, original silk page marker, first edition with these illustrations, wood engravings repaired small cut at fore-edge of a leaf, fine. Hobbyhorse Books 56 - 151 2011 $450

Trip, Tom *The History of Giles Gingerbread, a Little Boy.* York: J. Kendrew, n.d. circa, 1820, 24mo., 31 + 1 page, rebound maintaining original blue paper wrappers, three quarter green leather with corners, marbled paper on board, gilt title along spine, frontispiece, 10 beautiful and quaint half page woodcuts, fine, well preserved by handsome binding. Hobbyhorse Books 56 - 35 2011 $250

Tripp, Barlett *My Trip to Samoa.* Cedar Rapids: the Torch Press, 1911, Small octavo, 182 pages, frontispiece, plates, quarter cloth backed paper over boards, gilt on upper cover, gilt spine, very good plus, scarce. Jeff Weber Rare Books 163 - 221 2011 $75

Trismosin, Solomon *Splendor Solis Alchemical Treatises of Solomon Trismosin.* London: Kegan Paul, Trench, Trubner, circa, 1920, Small 4to., pages 103, pictures in black and white, some leaves slightly ripped, cover little scuffed at edges, else very good, tight copy. Second Life Books Inc. 174 - 306 2011 $150

Tristram, William Outram *Coaching Days and Coaching Ways.* London: Macmillan and Co., 1924, 185 x 125mm., green pictorial crushed morocco by Riviere & Son, covers with frames formed by multiple gilt rules with onlaid red dot cornerpieces and gilt festoons at head and tail of frame, front cover with central pictorial inlay in five colors depicting a mounted groom holding another horse by its reins, raised bands, spine gilt in French fillet compartments with central gilt ornament of horseshoe, bridle, or riding hat, gilt ruled turn-ins with horseshoe with bridle cornerpieces, leather hinges, marbled endpapers, all edges gilt, 214 illustrations in text by Hugh Thomson and Herbert Railton, joints little worn (though rubbing well masked with dye), spine slightly darkened and with four tiny abrasions at bottom, still excellent copy, attractive inlaid binding solid and lustrous and text virtually pristine. Phillip J. Pirages 59 - 130 2011 $750

Troeltsch, Ernst *The Social Teaching of the Christian Churches.* London: Allen & Unwin, 1931, First edition; 2 volumes, large 8vo., original cloth, gilt, little faded, pages 455, 456-1019, (iii), flyleaves rather spotted. R. F. G. Hollett & Son Antiquarian Booksellers 175 - 1359 2011 £45

Trojan, J. *Struwwelpeter.* London: Jarrolds, n.d., 1893, First English edition; 4to., color illustrated pages, pages 24, illustrations mostly in color, boards little soiled, chipped at corners, text slightly loose, used and slightly worn, otherwise very good, of considerable rarity. Any Amount of Books May 26 2011 - A62579 2011 $419

Trollope, Anthony 1815-1882 *The Barchester Novels (and) An Autobiography.* Stratford-upon-Avon: printed at the Shakespeare Head Press and published for the Press by Basil Blackwell, Oxford and Houghton Mifflin Co. Boston and New York, 1929, Apparntly one of 500 copies of the large paper library edition; 240 x 160mm., 14 volumes, publisher's orange paper boards backed with brown linen, flat spine with orange morocco label, edges untrimmed and mostly unopened, 72 plates from photos, few of the labels just slightly chafed or faded, otherwise very fine set, bindings showing almost no signs of use and interior obviously never read (because unopened). Phillip J. Pirages 59 - 320 2011 $1250

Trollope, Anthony 1815-1882 *Can You Forgive Her?* Oxford University Press, 1948, First edition thus; 2 volumes, original cloth, gilt, dust jacket, edges minimally worn, price clipped, pages xxii, 424; ix, 428, 18 tinted plates an 29 text illustrations. R. F. G. Hollett & Son Antiquarian Booksellers General Catalogue Summer 2010 - 827 2011 £35

Trollope, Anthony 1815-1882 *Castle Richmond.* 1860, First edition; 3 volumes, moern cloth, it may be in th process of this rebind, the corners of fore-edge where shaved (to prevent 'dog-ears'?), otherwise good scarce. C. P. Hyland May 26 2011 - 259/494 2011 $435

Trollope, Anthony 1815-1882 *The Chronicles of Barsetshire.* London: Chapman & Hall, 1879, Collected edition; 8 volumes, half titles, frontispieces, volume titles, slight splash marks to volume I of The Small House, uniformly bound in decorated dark olive green cloth, some occasional slight rubbing, odd mark, W. H. Smith embossed stamps, very good.   Jarndyce Antiquarian Booksellers   CXCI - 29 2011   £450

Trollope, Anthony 1815-1882 *An Editor's Tales.* London: Strahan & Co., 1870, First edition; half title, original brown cloth, expertly recased with spine strip slightly trimmed at head and tail, binder's ticket of Burn & Co., inscribed by publisher, A. Strahan for George MacDonald, with MacDonalds bookplate.   Jarndyce Antiquarian Booksellers   CXCII - 340 2011   £450

Trollope, Anthony 1815-1882 *How the "Mastiffs" Went to Iceland.* London: Virtue and Co., 1878, First edition; 4to., half title, frontispiece map and full page illustrations, 2 silver print photos, original blue cloth, bevelled boards, gilt, slight rubbing but nice, tight copy, all edges gilt, inscribed "R. Admiral A. Phillimore with Mr. John Burns' kind regards, from Castle Wemyss Jany 21 1874".   Jarndyce Antiquarian Booksellers   CXCI - 583 2011   £750

Trollope, Anthony 1815-1882 *North America.* London: Chapman and Hall, 1862, First edition; 2 volumes, 8vo., pages viii, (2), 488, viii, 496, original blind patterned pink/red cloth lettered gilt at spine, very early issue with publisher's ads at rear of volume one dated May 1862, complete very good- copies somewhat worn and shaken but clean text, folding map slightly torn at side with map itself complete.   Any Amount of Books   May 29 2011 - A45822 2011 $374

Trollope, Anthony 1815-1882 *Phineas Redux.* London: Chapman and Hall, 1874, First edition; 8vo., uncommon, 2 volumes in one, original decorated green cloth lettered gilt on spine and on front cover, pages vi (2), 339, 329 (contents page of volume 2 bound with contents page of volume I at front), frontispiece and 23 plates, slightly chipped at head of spine, slightly larger chip at bottom of spine, slight edgewear, otherwise very good, slight foxing to prelims.   Any Amount of Books   May 29 2011 - A45761 2011 $340

Trollope, Frances Milton 1780-1863 *Italy and the Italians.* London: Richard Bentley, n.d., 1842, First edition; 8vo., 2 volumes in one, early state, original publisher's red cloth lettered and decorated gilt on spine and on front cover, very good, solid, clean tight copy, very short nick at head of spine, slight foxing to prelims, faint tape ghosts to yellow endpapers.   Any Amount of Books   May 29 2011 - A58761 2011 $408

Trollope, Frances Milton 1780-1863 *Jessie Phillips.* London: Henry Colburn, 1844, First one volume edition; (352) pages, 8vo., later three quarter dark red morocco over marbled boards, gilt lettered and gilt decorated spines, raised bands, 6 compartments, , frontispiece, 11 additional full page engraved illustrations by John Leach, very fine and handsome copy bound by Zaehnsdorf.   Paulette Rose Fine and Rare Books   32 - 178 2011 $625

Trollope, Frances Milton 1780-1863 *The Life and Adventures of a Clever Woman.* London: Chapman and Hall, 1866, Third edition; (397) page, 8vo., original paper covered pictorial boards, royal arms on spine, some rubbing along edges and hinges, Paris bookseller's ticket, good plus, scarce.   Paulette Rose Fine and Rare Books   32 - 179 2011 $700

Trollope, Frances Milton 1780-1863 *The Widow Barnaby.* London: Richard Bentley, 1839, First edition; 3 volumes, (iv) 348 pages (iv) 380 pages; (iv) 368 pages; 8vo., original green cloth over boards, black printed title labels, half title in each volume, wear to corners, scattered light foxing, some staining to boards, all in all, very good set, scarce in trade.   Paulette Rose Fine and Rare Books   32 - 180 2011 $1000

Trollope, Thomas Adolphus 1810-1892 *The Papal Conclaves as They Were and a They Are.* London: Chapman and Hall, 1876, First edition; original cloth, gilt, spine and corners rather worn, pages xviii, 434, 36, untrimmed, joints cracked, fine decorative bookplate of Alfred Austin, poet laureate.   R. F. G. Hollett & Son Antiquarian Booksellers   175 - 1360 2011   £60

Trollope, Thomas Adolphus 1810-1892 *A Summer in Brittany.* London: Henry Colburn, 1840, 2 volumes, hand colored engraved frontispiece, engraved titles, 10 plates drawn and etched by A. Herviue, 2 pages ads, volume I and II, uncut in original olive green cloth by Westleys and Clark, blocked in blind, sympathetically rebacked in plain cloth.   Jarndyce Antiquarian Booksellers   CXCI - 583 2011   £150

Trotter, Alexander *Observations by Alexander Trotter... (bound with) A Plan of Communication Between the New and Old Town of Edinburgh, in the Line of the Earthen Mound...* Edinburgh: for Laing & Forbes and R. Ackermann, London, 1834, Edinburgh: Oliver & Boyd; Simpkin & Marshall, London and Robertson & Atkinson, Glasgow, 1829. Second edition; 4to., engraved frontispiece and plan, 24 pages, 6 folding plates, 16 + 2 pages, original straight grained red morocco gilt, slightly rubbed with 4 small abrasions to front board, attractive copy, author's own copy with armorial bookplate with two extracts from Edinburgh Advertiser Jan. 31 and Edinburgh Courant Feb. 25 1834.   Jarndyce Antiquarian Booksellers   CXCI - 587 2011   £850

Trotter, J. K. *The Niger Sources an the Borders of the New Sierra Leon Protectorate.* London: Methuen, 1898, First edition; 8vo., pages 238, 4 plates, large folding map with small tear, original cloth, spine faded. J. & S. L. Bonham Antiquarian Booksellers Africa 4/20/2011 - 1642 2011 £55

Trotter, Lionel James *The History of the British Empire in India from the Appointment of Lord Hardinge to the Political Extinction of the East India Company 1844 to 1862...* London: William H. Allen, 1866, xvi, 407 pages, xvi, 443 pages, 8vo., three quarter red morocco over marbled boards, five raised bands bordered in gilt, four compartments with gilt florets, two with brown morocco spine labels, top edge gilt, marbled endpapers, very good, boards and spine scuffed, some edgewear, leaves lightly browned. Kaaterskill Books   12 - 197   2011 $175

Troup, Robert *The Missionary Kirk of Huntly.* Edinburgh & Glasgow: John Menzies & Co., 1901, Frontispiece, original turquoise cloth, slightly dulled, Dunbar's ticket. Jarndyce Antiquarian Booksellers   CXCII - 363   2011   £45

Troyat, Henri *Les Ponts De Paris.* Paris: Flammarion, 1946, 14 watercolors of bridges of Paris by Kuder, mounted on heavy paper, 26 page French text, unopened, all in a folder, glassine dust jacket torn, yellowed, stained, edgewear, light stains to cover, some darkening to margins, not affecting text or pictures, 12 x 16 inches, softbound, good. G. H. Mott Bookseller   May 26 2011 - 16597   2011 $350

True Stories of the Olden Days. Blackie & Son, n.d. circa, 1907, Large 8vo., original cloth backed glazed pictorial boards, upper board little soiled, especially at one corner, unpaginated, 4 color plates and other plates and illustrations. R. F. G. Hollett & Son Antiquarian Booksellers General Catalogue Summer 2010 - 498   2011   £65

Truhart, Peter *Regents of Nations: Systematic Chromology of States and Their Political Representatives in Past and Present.* Munich: New York: London: Paris: K. G. Saur, 1984, First edition; 2 volumes, pages xxx, 2275, ex-British Foreign Office library with few library markings, else very good.   Any Amount of Books   May 29 2011 - A70718   2011 $255

Trusler, John *The London Adviser and Guide: Containing Every Instruction and Information Useful and Necessary to Persons Living in London and Coming to Reside There...* London: printed for the author no. 14 Red Lion Street, Clerkenwell, 1786, First edition; 12mo., xx, 191, (1) pages, original paper flaw in leaf C2, endpapers foxed, contemporary half calf over marbled boards, neatly rebacked with gilt lines and label, very good.   John Drury Rare Books   153 - 160   2011   £950

Truths about Whisky. London: printed by Sutton Sharpe and Co., 1878, First edition; 8vo., 4 fine folding tinted lithographed plates, vi, (2), 103, (7) pages, original green cloth embossed in black and lettered in gilt, good copy with fine impressions of the plates, scarce.   John Drury Rare Books   153 - 70   2011   £475

Tryon, Thomas *The New Art of Brewing, Ale and Other Sorts of Liquors.* London: printed for Tho. Salusbury, 1691, 12mo., (6), 138 pages with ad leaf and contents leaf immediately following titlepage, general paper browning throughout, gutter of titlepage frayed (not touching printed surface), numeral entered in red ink in early hand on title, ms. inscription in ink on flyleaf, signed by Henry Cope recording the gift of the book to him by Sir Harry Fane (Vane) on January 4th 1699 with 4 pages of ms. notes" in ink apparently by Henry Cope on prelim blanks and 19th century armorial bookplate of Alfred Chadwick, contemporary ruled sheep, neatly appropriately rebacked and labelled, good copy.   John Drury Rare Books   153 - 161   2011   £1250

Tsa Toke, Monroe *The Peyote Ritual: Visions and Descriptions of Monroe Tsa Toke.* San Francisco: 1957, Limited to 325 copies; folio, xvii, 67 pages, 14 color plates, original plain paper wrappers soiled and chipped, owner's name on f.f.e.p. book near fine.   Dumont Maps & Books of the West   113 - 47   2011 $500

Tubbs, Colin R. *The New Forest.* London: Collins, 1986, First edition; original cloth, gilt, dust jacket (spine lightly faded), pages 300, with 20 color and over 100 black and white photos and diagrams, small name inscribed on half title, otherwise fine.   R. F. G. Hollett & Son Antiquarian Booksellers   General Catalogue Summer 2010 - 1066   2011   £250

Tucker, Elizabeth *Baby Folk.* New York: Frederick Stokes, 1898, 4to., cloth backed pictorial boards, edges rubbed, margin of one plate strengthened, else tight and very good+, 6 exceptionally magnificent full page chromolithograph illustrations by Maud Humphrey.   Aleph-Bet Books, Inc.   95 - 297   2011 $950

Tucker, Elizabeth *Book of Pets.* New York: Stokes, 1893, 4to., cloth backed pictorial boards, edges and corners rubbed, else tight, very good-fine, 12 fine full page chromolithographs by Maud Humphrey, very scarce. Aleph-Bet Books, Inc.   95 - 299   2011 $1000

Tucker, John T. *Angola: the Land of the Blacksmith Prince.* London: World Dominion Press, 1933, First edition; tall 8vo., 180 pages, maps, illustrations, original blue cloth, dust jacket. J. & S. L. Bonham Antiquarian Booksellers   Africa 4/20/2011 - 3159   2011   £75

Tucker, Mark *A Discourse Preached on Thanksgivng Day at the Beneficent Congregational Meeting House, Providence, July 21 1842.* Providence: Benjamin F. Moore, 1842, First edition; 8vo., 16 pages, original printed wrappers, light wear, dust soiling, splitting along spine, very good, contemporary owner's signature on front wrapper. M & S Rare Books, Inc. 90 - 359 2011 $225

Tucker, William *The Family Dyer and Scourer.* Hartford: Andrus & Judd, 1831?, 12mo., 15, 123 pages, one woodcut, original linen, printed paper label (chipped), some stains in inner margin, foxed, lacks front endleaves. M & S Rare Books, Inc. 90 - 424 2011 $275

Tuckey, James Kingston *Narrative of an Expedition to Explore the River Zaire.* London: John Murray, 1818, First edition; quarto, pages lxxxii, 498, folding map, 13 plates, some plates foxed as always, red half morocco with later grey boards, joints rubbed, very good. J. & S. L. Bonham Antiquarian Booksellers Africa 4/20/2011 - 9167 2011 £750

Tudor, Tasha *A is for Annabelle.* New York: Oxford University Press, 1954, First edition; oblong 4to., green cloth, fine in dust jacket with some soil and slight fraying to spine ends, illustrations in color and black and white. Aleph-Bet Books, Inc. 95 - 557 2011 $375

Tudor, Tasha *Amanda and the Bear.* New York: Oxford University Press, 1951, First edition; 12mo., light blue textured cloth with color paste label and red orange lettering on spine, quite nice, full color pictorial dust jacket, clean, fresh copy, front free endpaper signed in full with presentation for Marion Smith. Jo Ann Reisler, Ltd. 86 - 251 2011 $1000

Tudor, Tasha *The County Fair.* New York: Oxford University Press, 1940, First edition; 24mo., red cloth with white dots and border decorations surrounding title block on front cover, clean copy, full color pictorial dust jacket with some dusting and closed tears to upper edges, reinforced with tape from underneath, signed in full with presentation from Tudor. Jo Ann Reisler, Ltd. 86 - 247 2011 $950

Tudor, Tasha *The Doll's Christmas.* New York: Oxford University Press, 1950, First edition; square 8vo., red cloth with color paste label on cover and black lettering on spine, full color pictorial dust jacket with picture of two dolls within a wreath decoration, bright copy of book and wrapper, wrapper image does not appear in the book, this copy signed in full with presentatoin by Tudor. Jo Ann Reisler, Ltd. 86 - 250 2011 $450

Tudor, Tasha *Dorcas Porkus.* New York: Oxford University Press, 1942, First printing; 16mo., yellow cloth with white dots, lovely clean copy color pictorial dust jacket with dusting to point of being darkened, this copy signed and dated on front free endpaper by Tudor, along with presentation to Marion Smith. Jo Ann Reisler, Ltd. 86 - 249 2011 $1000

Tudor, Tasha *Edgar Allan Crow.* New York: Oxford University Press, 1953, First edition; 12mo., dark blue textured boards (with gold lettering on spine), color decorated paste label, full color pictorial dust jacket, quite fresh, clean copy, signed in fulll by Tudor with presentation for Marion Smith, full page color illustrations. Jo Ann Reisler, Ltd. 86 - 252 2011 $1000

Tudor, Tasha *Edgar Allan Crow.* New York: Oxford University Press, 1953, First edition, first printing; 8vo., cloth, paste-on, near fine in dust jacket (lightly foxed), illustrations in color. Aleph-Bet Books, Inc. 95 - 556 2011 $975

Tudor, Tasha *Snow Before Christmas.* New York: Oxford University Press, 1941, First edition; square 8vo., grey cloth with color paste label with decorated title on front cover, bright fresh copy, color pictorial dust jacket with little spot to rear cover, otherwise nice, presentation by Tudor signed in full on front free endpaper for Marion Smith. Jo Ann Reisler, Ltd. 86 - 248 2011 $950

Tudor, Tasha *White Goose.* New York: Oxford University Press, 1943, First edition, first printing; 8vo., blue cloth, fine in fine dust jacket, signed by Tudor, full page color illustrations. Aleph-Bet Books, Inc. 95 - 558 2011 $850

Tuer, Andrew White 1838-1900 *The Follies & Fashions of Our Grandfathers.* London: Field & Tuer, 1887, First edition; drab boards and embroidered linen labels, decorated linen backed endpapers, embroidered ribbon marker, very good+ ex-library, with tape on spine (linen label laid on), neat old "Curtis Memorial Library" bookplate and blindstamps, great plates in color and monotone. Lupack Rare Books May 26 2011 - ABE903626204 2011 $175

Tuer, Andrew White 1838-1900 *Old London Street Cries and Cries of Today.* London: Field & Tuer, The Leadenhall Press, 1885, 12mo., original marbled boards, tie and printed label, cloth backstrip lacking, pages 137, (vii), hand colored woodcut frontispiece and numerous full page and text woodcut and illustrations. R. F. G. Hollett & Son Antiquarian Booksellers 175 - 1362 2011 £65

Tuer, Andrew White 1838-1900 *Stories from Old Fashioned Children's Books.* Leadenhall Press, 1899-1900, First edition; new endpapers, original blue cloth, gilt extra, little worn and marked, pages xvi, 440, (i), xxx, top edges gilt, untrimmed, with 250 illustrations, new endpapers. R. F. G. Hollett & Sons Antiquarian Booksellers 170 - 691 2011 £50

Tufnell, Edward Carlton *Character, Object and Effects of Trades' Unions: with Some Remarks on the Law Concerning them.* London: James Ridgway and Sons, 1834, First and only edition; 8vo., (2), 140 pages, recently well bound in cloth lettered in gilt, very good, very scarce.   John Drury Rare Books   153 - 162   2011   £475

Tugay, Emine Foat *Three Centuries: Family Chronicles of Turkey and Egypt.* London: Oxford University Press, 1963, First edition; 8vo., pages xi 324, 8 tables at rear, 11 plates, very good in slightly used, very good dust jacket.   Any Amount of Books   May 29 2011 - A71205   2011 $255

Tuit, J. E. *The Tower Bridge; Its History and Construction from the Date of the Earliest Project to the Present Time.* London: 1894, First edition; 4to., frontispiece, pages 106, 6 folding plates at rear, 62 figures, original publisher's green cloth lettered gilt on spine and on front cover, spine slightly rubbed with slight wear at spine ends, covers very slightly marked, otherwise very good or better.   Any Amount of Books   May 29 2011 - A67468   2011 $255

Tunbelly, Tim, Pseud. *The Letters of Tim. Tunbelly, Gent. Free Burgess, Newcastle Upon Tyne on the Tyne, the Newcastle Corporation, the Freemen, The Tolls &c.* Newcastle upon Tyne: printed and published by W. A. Mitchell, 1823, First edition; 8vo., engraved frontispiece, (2), xx, 155, (1) pages, errata on verso of final leaf, bound fairly recently in boards with printed spine label, entirely uncut, very good, rare.   John Drury Rare Books   153 - 163   2011   £275

Tunnicliffe, Charles F. *Mereside Chronicle.* London: Country Life, 1948, First edition; large 4to., original cloth, gilt, dust jacket (foot of spine chipped), few old tape shadows, pages 200, superb two tone illustrations.   R. F. G. Hollett & Son Antiquarian Booksellers   General Catalogue Summer 2010 - 1067   2011   £120

Tupper, John Lucas *Hiatus: the Void in Modern Education, Its Cause and Antidote.* London: Macmillan, 1869, First edition; 8vo., disbound, pages 251 with 51 page publisher's catalog at rear, presentation copy on verso of front endpaper to W. M. Rossetti from the author, last page has note about errata on 3 pages, possibly in hand of Rossetti, disbound, otherwise in decent, sound condition with clean text.   Any Amount of Books   May 26 2011 - A62731   2011 $419

Tupper, Martin Farquhar   1810-1889 *Proverbial Philosophy: a Book of Thoughts and Arguments Originally Treated.* London: Joseph Rickerby, 1838, First edition; tall 8vo., 4 page catalog, original dark green cloth, rubbing to hinges, scarce first edition, this copy stamped Marchioness of Donegal.   Jarndyce Antiquarian Booksellers   CXCI - 588   2011   £150

Turberville, A. S. *Johnson's England: an Account of the Life and Manners of His Age.* London: 1952, 2 volumes, blue cloth, second volume has faded spine and half inch of top front and back cover, corners bumped, top and bottom of spine rubbed, free edge of pages uncut, numerous black and white illustrations in each volume, interior clean.   Bookworm & Silverfish   667 - 67   2011 $90

Turgenieff, Ivan   1818-1883 *The Jew and Other Stories.* New York: Charles Scribner's Sons, 1904, 213 x 145mm., viii, (2), 357 pages; lovely contemporary dark rose colored morocco, ornately gilt by Sickles (stamp signed), covers with border of double gilt rules enclosing an Art Nouveau style frame of wavy rules connecting large cornerpieces, these with small oval medallion of onlaid black morocco, enclosed by gilt drawer handle tools and leafy sprays, upper cover with circular stylized monogram of "CEB" at center, raised bands, spines gilt in double ruled compartments decorated with drawer handles and circlets, wide turn-ins with gilt frame featuring pretty fleuron cornerpieces, ivory watered silk pastedowns and free endleaves, top edge gilt, frontispiece; spine evenly faded to soft rose, 3 leaves with uneven fore edges from rough opening, half a dozen leaves with corner creased, other trival imperfections but fine, text clean, fresh and bright, handsome binding lustrous and virtually unworn.   Phillip J. Pirages   59 - 335   2011 $375

Turgenieff, Ivan   1818-1883 *Phantoms and Other Stories.* New York: Charles Scribner's Sons, 1904,   213 x 145mm., ix, (3), 321 pages, lovely contemporary dark rose colored morocco, ornately gilt by Sickles (stamp signed), covers with border of double gilt rules enclosing an Art Nouveau style frame of wavy rules connecting large cornerpieces, these with small oval medallion of onlaid black morocco enclosed by gilt drawer handle tools and leafy sprays, upper cover with circular stylized monogram of "CEB" at center, raised bands, spines gilt in double ruled compartments, decorated with drawer handles and circlets, wide turn-ins with gilt frame featuring pretty fleuron cornerpieces, ivory watered silk pastedowns and free endleaves, top edge gilt, frontispiece, except for even fading of spine, very fine, pretty copy.   Phillip J. Pirages   59 - 336 2011 $350

Turgenieff, Ivan 1818-1883 *A Reckless Character and Other Stories.* New York: Charles Scribner's Sons, 1904, 213 x 1455mm., 8 p.l., 385 pages, lovely contemporary dark rose colored morocco, ornately gilt by Sickles (stamp signed), covers with border of double gilt rules enclosing an Art Nouveau style frame of wavy rules connecting large cornerpieces, these with small oval medallion of inlaid black, morocco enclosed by gilt drawer handle tools and leafy sprays, upper cover with circular stylized monogram of "CEB" at center, raised bands, spines gilt in double ruled compartments decorated with drawer handles and circlets, wide turn-ins with gilt frame featuring pretty fleuron cornerpieces, ivory watered silk pastedowns and free endleaves, top edge gilt, frontispiece; spine evenly faded, very small dark spot on upper cover, otherwise very attractive decorative binding in fine condition, first half of book with very faint dampstain in upper quarter of page (front leaves with slightly larger and darker dampstain), four leaves with cellotape mends to short marginal tears (none touching text), one page with three marginal inkspots, otherwise excellent internally.   Phillip J. Pirages   59 - 337   2011 $125

Turnbull, Peter Evan *Austria.* London: John Murray, 1840, First edition; 2 volumes, tall 8vo., half brown leather lettered gilt at spine, raised bands, marbled boards, etc., xx, 394; x, 448, highly uncommon, slight foxing to prelims, bookplate of Sir Norton Joseph Knatchbull, minor rubbing and scuffing, else close to very good+.   Any Amount of Books   May 26 2011 - A65104   2011 $419

Turner, A. Logan *History of the University of Edinburgh 1833-1933.* Edinburgh: Oliver & Boyd, 1933, First edition; large 8vo., original cloth, gilt, dust jacket, little creased and chipped, pages xxxi 452, top edge gilt, untrimmed, illustrations.   R. F. G. Hollett & Son Antiquarian Booksellers   175 - 1364   2011   £35

Turner, A. Logan *Story of a Great Hospital. The Royal Infirmary of Edinburgh 1729-1929.* Edinburgh: Oliver & Boyd, 1937, First edition; large 8vo., original blue cloth gilt, pages xvi, 406, top edge gilt, untrimmed, etched frontispiece and 32 plates.   R. F. G. Hollett & Son Antiquarian Booksellers   General Catalogue Summer 2010 - 1598   2011   £40

Turner, Elizabeth *The Daisy or Cautionary Stories.* London: Griffith and Farran, n.d. circa, 1860, Small 12mo., 66 pages + 6 pages ads, green cloth with decorative gilt title and blind motif, 29 (of 30) half page beautifully hand colored very fine woodcuts, binding worn, light foxing internally, missing page 23-4, few blisters on front cover, inked owner name, merit label pasted inside front cover, good book.   Hobbyhorse Books   56 - 152   2011 $100

Turner, Gerard L'E. *Collecting Microscopes.* London: Studio Vista, 1981, First edition; large 8vo., original cloth, gilt, dust jacket, page 120, illustrations in color and monochrome.   R. F. G. Hollett & Son Antiquarian Booksellers   General Catalogue Summer 2010 - 335   2011   £40

Turner, Gerard L'E. *The Great Age of the Microscope and the Practical Principles of Observation.* Bristol: Adam Hilger, 1989, First edition; large 8vo., original cloth, gilt, dust jacket, pages ix 379, 600 illustrations, fine.   R. F. G. Hollett & Son Antiquarian Booksellers   General Catalogue Summer 2010 - 1144   2011   £150

Turner, Graham *Fishing Tackle.* London: Ward Lock, 1989, First edition; large 4to., original cloth, gilt, dust jacket, pages 384 with 32 pages of color plates and 750 black and white illustrations, very good.   R. F. G. Hollett & Son Antiquarian Booksellers   General Catalogue Summer 2010 - 336   2011   £120

Turner, Richard *An Introduction to the Art and Sciences...* London: printed for F. C. and J. Rivington, G. Wilkie et al, 1811, Fourteenth edition; 16mo., xii, 276, modern full calf on boards, gilt rulers and gilt title on red leather label on spine, new endpapers, 3 full page copper engraving, 21 half page wood engravings, 19 quaint woodcuts, very fine, scarce.   Hobbyhorse Books   56 - 153   2011 $170

Turner, Steve *The Man Called Cash.* Nashville: W. Publishing, 2004, First edition; signed by author on bookplate laid in, fine dust jacket fine.   Bella Luna Books   May 29 2011 - t8234   2011 $82

Turner, W. J. *The Duchess of Popocatapetl.* London: Dent, 1939, original cloth, silvered, dust jacket by Edward Bawden, head of spine chipped, price clipped, pages 316, very scarce.   R. F. G. Hollett & Son Antiquarian Booksellers   General Catalogue Summer 2010 - 919   2011   £150

Turner, W. J. *Mozart. The Man and His Works.* London: Victor Gollancz, 1938, Uncorrected proof copy; original printed wrappers, edges little stained, pages 391, 16 plates, some edges little dampstained, TLS from Victor Gollancz to Compton MacKenzie loosely inserted.   R. F. G. Hollett & Son Antiquarian Booksellers   175 - 1368   2011   £45

Turton, Keith *Private Owner Wagons.* Lydney: Lightmoor Press, 2003, First edition; 7 volumes, 4to., illustrated laminated boards, issued without dust jacket, pages 1280, very clean, very good.   Any Amount of Books   May 29 2011 - A69333   2011 $272

Tuthill, Franklin *The History of California.* San Francisco: H. H. Bancroft, 1866, First edition; xvi, 657 pages, index, publisher's brown cloth, gilt spine lettered, spine faded and worn at spine ends, some spotting to covers, minimal foxing to extreme fore-edge of text block, overall very good, internally clean.   Argonaut Book Shop   Recent Acquisitions Summer 2010 - 209   2011 $275

Tutin, T. G. *Flora Europaea.* Cambridge: Cambridge University Press, 1964-1972, First edition; 3 volumes, 4to., pages xxxiii, 465; xxix, 455; xxxi, 370, very good+ in very good dust jackets (slight edgewear). Any Amount of Books May 29 2011 - A40096 2011 $255

Tweedie, Alec *Mexico As I Saw It.* London: Hurst and Blackett Ltd., 1901, First edition; half title, color frontispiece, title in red and black, 71 plates, marks on upper margins of 6 leaves, xii, 472 pages, contemporary half calf, spine gilt, label, top edge gilt, good copy. Anthony W. Laywood May 26 2011 - 19271 2011 $185

The 20th Century Art Book. London: Phaidon, 1966, 4to., pages 512, color illustrations, near fine in slightly chipped and soiled dust jacket, extremely heavy. Second Life Books Inc. 174 - 13 2011 $65

The Twigs or Christmas at Ruddock Hall. Printed on Bavaria for Castell Brothers, n.d. circa, 1890, Oblong small 8vo., original stiff card pictorial wrappers with tasselled silk cord ties, pages (20) with 8 chromolithographs and other illustrations by Robert Dudley, scattered foxing, but very sound, rare. R. F. G. Hollett & Son Antiquarian Booksellers General Catalogue Summer 2010 - 639 2011 £95

Twisleton, Edward *The Tongue Not Essential to Speech...* London: John Murray, 1873, First edition; original cloth, gilt, pages iv, 232, (iv), joints cracking, tear to upper margin of B1, lower margins lightly stained toward end, scarce. R. F. G. Hollett & Son Antiquarian Booksellers 175 - 1370 2011 £75

Twitchell, Ralph Emerson *The Leading Facts of New Mexico History.* Albuquerque: 1963, 2 volumes, xx, 506 pages, illustrations, 2 folding maps; xxi, 631 pages, illustrations, 6 folding maps, full red leather, near fine and almost completely unopened, wonderful bright set. Dumont Maps & Books of the West 113 - 48 2011 $300

Twitchett, John *Landscapes on Derby and Worcester to Porcelain.* Henderson & Stirk, 1984, First edition; small 4to., original cloth, dust jacket (spine rather faded), page 80, 20 color plates and numerous illustrations. R. F. G. Hollett & Son Antiquarian Booksellers General Catalogue Summer 2010 - 337 2011 £35

Twopenny, William *Extracts from Various Authors...* privately printed at the Chiswick Press, 1868, Half title, original brown cloth, borders blocked in blind, upper board blocked in gilt, few small marks, armorial bookplate of Charlotte, Duchess of Norfolk with inscription, presented by her to Thomas Henry Foley, 4th Baron Foley. Jarndyce Antiquarian Booksellers CXCI - 591 2011 £50

Tyler, Anne 1941- *The Clock Winder.* London: Chatto & Windus, 1973, First English edition; near fine in very good dust jacket, wrinkle at bottom of rear panel, neither chipped nor clipped, scarce. Lupack Rare Books May 26 2011 - ABE2935950029 2011 $300

Tyler, Anne 1941- *Morgan's Passing.* New York: Knopf, 1980, First edition; near fine, light bumping to corners, near fine dust jacket, small rubbed spots near tp and bottom front corners. Bella Luna Books May 29 2011 - g6527 2011 $110

Tyler, Anne 1941- *The Tin Can Tree.* London: Macmillan, 1966, First English edition; signed on titlepage, near fine in very good+ dust jacket. Lupack Rare Books May 26 2011 - ABE2935951799 2011 $500

Tyler, Anne 1941- *Tumble Tower.* New York: Orchard Books, 1993, First edition; illustrations by Mitra Modarressi, near fine, spine ends bumped, dust jacket fine, inscribed by author and signed by artist. Bella Luna Books May 29 2011 - t5321 2011 $82

Tyler, Ian *Seathwaite Wad and Other Mines of the Borrowdale Valley.* Carlisle: Blue Rock Publications, 1995, First edition; pages 220, well illustrated, original wrappers, large 4to. R. F. G. Hollett & Son Antiquarian Booksellers General Catalogue Summer 2010 - 1603 2011 £30

Tyler, J. E. A. *The Tolkien Companion.* London: Macmillan, 1976, First British edition, true first edition; fine, dust jacket near fine, light wear ont op edge. Bella Luna Books May 29 2011 - t9045 2011 $82

Tyler, Robert Ogden *Memoir of Brevet Major General Roberg Ogden Tyler, U.S. Army Together with his Journal of Two Months' Travel in British and Farther India.* Philadelphia: 1878, 120 pages, folio, terra cotta cloth, cover gilt bright, backstrip dull, some scrapes to front cover, backstrip reglued, photo frontispiece, endpapers ghosted, very mild ex-library. Bookworm & Silverfish 670 - 64 2011 $150

Tyndall, John *Lectures on Light Delivered in the United States in 1872-1873.* New York: 1873, First American edition; 194, (11 pages of ads), original wrappers, top wrapper loose, edges worn, corners creased. Bookworm & Silverfish 678 - 160 2011 $100

Tyrell-Green, E. *Parish Architecture.* London: SPCK, 1931, Pages 247, with 64 illustrations, map, half title foxed, some scattered spotting elsewhere, original cloth gilt, dust jacket rather soiled and chipped. R. F. G. Hollett & Son Antiquarian Booksellers 177 - 861 2011 £30

Tyrwhitt, R. St. John *A Handbook of Pictorial Art.* Oxford: Clarendon Press, 1868, 8vo., xi, (5), 480 pages, 37 illustrations, very good in contemporary full morocco prize binding.   Ken Spelman Rare Books   68 - 73   2011   £65

Tyson, Edward *Orang-Outang sive Homo Sylvestris; or the Anatomy of a Pygmie, Compared with that of a Monkey, an Ape and a Man.* London: Thomas Bennet and Daniel Brown, 1699, First edition; 8 folding engraved plates (plates trimmed by binder resulting in some loss to image on 2 plates, few repairs, some soiling, light spotting to 2, upper corner of 3 plates stained), 4to., pages (12), 108, (2), 58, (ad, 2 pages), new three quarter calf over marbled boards (endpapers renewed, old marginal notations to title and back page, scattered minor foxing, slight worming to lower margin of many pages).   Raymond M. Sutton, Jr.   May 26 2011 - 55810   2011 $9000

Tyson, James L. *Diary of a Physician in California.* Oakland: Biobooks, 1955, Limited to 500 copies; 124 pages, index, printed in red and black, red cloth, fine. Argonaut Book Shop   Recent Acquisitions Summer 2010 - 210   2011 $60

Tyson, John *Dalton-in-Furness District Local Board Abstract of Account for the Year Ending 2th March 1887.* Dalton-in-Furness: 1887, Pages 224, folding tables, compiler's printed presentation slip tipped in, redated Feb. 1892, scarce, bookplate of Edward Sergeant.   R. F. G. Hollett & Son Antiquarian Booksellers   173 - 1140   2011   £120

Tyson, Lyle *Pueblo Art of America's Southwest.*   Santa Fe?: 1977, Folio, one page text, 4 plates, colophon, approximately 14 x 11 inches, signed by artist and graced with first day cover stamp of related ceramic, all in attractive presentation folder, some spots to cover.   Bookworm & Silverfish   678 - 133   2011 $1500

Tyssot De Patot, Simon *Voyages et Avantures de Jaques Masse.* Bourdeaux (i.e. The Hague): James L'Aveugle 1710 i.e., 1714, First edition; pages viii, 508, contemporary calf, neatly rebacked in antique style, little rubbed, some minor foxing, soiling, very good.   Second Life Books Inc.   174 - 313   2011 $3000

Tytler, Sarah *Childhood a Hundred Years Ago.* London: Marcus Ward & Co. n.d., 1877, Original decorated cloth gilt over bevelled boards, extremities trifle worn, pages 150 (ii), 6 chromolithographs laid in, prize label on pastedown, very nice.   R. F. G. Hollett & Sons Antiquarian Booksellers   170 - 698   2011   £40

Tzara, Tristan *Terre sur Terre/ Dessins d'Andre Masson.* Geneva and Paris: Trois Collines, 1946, First edition; 8vo., pages (iv) (blank), (5)-66, (2) blank, (2) contents, (2) blank, 10 illustrations, uncut, original wrappers very slightly rubbed at bottom edge, number 3067 of total print run 3160, inscription from Tzara for Pierre Goetschel.   Simon Finch Rare Books   Zero - 357   2011   £375

U

Udall, Brady *The Lonely Polygamist.* New York: Norton, 2010, First edition; fine, dust jacket fine, pictorial slipcase, includes cars with author interview, signed by author.   Bella Luna Books   May 29 2011 - t9549   2011 $93

Ude, Louise Eustache *The French Cook.* Philadelphia: Lea and Carey, 1828, First American edition; octavo, 8 plates depicting table settings, contemporary half red morocco over marbled boards.   Heritage Book Shop Booth A12 51st NY International Antiquarian Book Fair April 8-10 2011 - 139   2011 $1500

Uncle Frank's Select Fables for Good Boys and Girls. New York: Wm. H. Murphy n.d. circa, 1845, 12mo., 2 34 pages, pictorial yellow paper wrappers, text composed of 25 fables, each one with a reflection, illustrated with 17 charming half page woodcuts enclosed in decorative printer device, upper wrapper with engraving of a tree, pagination is continuous with this volume starting at page 69, restored edge of lower wrappers, rare copy in excellent state. Hobbyhorse Books   56 - 70   2011 $300

Uncle Gus's Farm. Boston: Houghton Mifflin, 1942, Folio, cloth backed pictorial wrappers, small closed margin tear, else near fine and unused, cut-out and play book with paper dolls and farm machinery that require no pasting to use, unusually fine, rare.   Aleph-Bet Books, Inc.   95 - 487   2011 $1750

Underwood, Isaac Fletcher *The Diary of Isaac Fletcher of Underwood, Cumberland 1756-1781.* Cumberland and Westmorland Antiquarian and Archaeological Society, 1994, Large 8vo., original cloth, gilt, dust jacket, pages xlii, 518, frontispiece, 4 text figures.   R. F. G. Hollett & Son Antiquarian Booksellers   173 - 1230   2011   £45

The United States Magazine and Democratic Review Volumes 1-15. Washington: Langtree & O'Sullivan, 1838-1844, 1848. First edition; 15 volumes, octavo, bound in 14 volumes, half calf and marbled boards with calf corners, contents mostly clean with just a few pages foxed, including portraits, leather dry on some spines and has not been treated but all covers tight, very little flaking, very good, with 51 (of 53) engraved portraits and two tinted lithographs of the Yucatan, the set lack four issues from the last volume, 1844 and includes issue 95 from volume 22, 1848. Charles Agvent   Transcendentalism 2010 - 26   2011 $2500

United States Magazine & Democratic Review. Volume VI. Philadelphia: 1839, First edition in book form; 540 pages, half leather, bottom 4 inch backstrip reglued, top 1.5 inch missing, marbled boards, some volumes report from one to four plates, this volume with no plates.   Bookworm & Silverfish   678 - 13   2011 $60

United States. Commerce Department - 1917 *Circular of the Bureau of Standards #70: Materials for the Household.* Washington: 1917, 259 pages, original binding, some stains and few small chips, some waffles, no dampstains to text.   Bookworm & Silverfish   665 - 51   2011 $75

United States. Congress - 1835 *Acts of the 23rd Congress. (Second Session) 1835.* Washington: 1835, First edition; plain contemporary wrappers, stitched, very good+ (mild dampstaining to several leaves, minor chipping at spine, solid copy).   Lupack Rare Books   May 26 2011 - ABE442585234   2011 $125

United States. Congress - 1913 *Hearing Before the Committee on Rules...on Resolution Establishing a Committee on Woman Suffrage 63rd Congress 2nd Sessions Document 754.* Washington: Dec. 3, 4, 5, 1913, 8vo., pages 214, removed from bound volume, very good. Second Life Books Inc.   174 - 102   2011 $125

United States. Congress. House of Representatives - 1792 *Journal of the House of Representatives of the United States at the First (-Second) Session of the Second Congress.* Philadelphia: Francis Childs and John Swaine, 1792-1793, Folio, 2 volumes in 1, 245 pages; 267 (i.e. 167), (25) pages, modern calf backed marbled boards, very skillfully executed in period style, several gatherings in second volume foxed, else near fine, from the library of James Mott, treasurer of New Jersey during this period.   Joseph J. Felcone Inc.   Fall Miscellany 2010 - 119   2011 $2000

United States. Congress. Senate - 1908 *A Company for Breeding Horses on the Crow Indian Reservations, Montana. The Survey & Allotment of Indian Lands Within the Limits of the Crow.* Washington: 1908, First edition; 794 (4) pages, original binding, inner joints reglued, top 3 inch backstrip damped.   Bookworm & Silverfish   667 - 122   2011 $125

United States. Continental Congress - 1777 *Journals of Congress. Containing the Proceedings in the Year 1776 Published by Order of Congress. Volume II.* Philadelphia: R. Aitken, 1777, First edition; (2), 513 (22) pages, modern full mottled sheepskin, superbly executed in exact facsimile of original binding, spine with red morocco title label and "1776" tooled on black oval onlay, some internal dampstaining and browning particularly toward end of text, else very handsome volume, signature of Samuel McCraw Gunn, dated 1822 on titlepage, enclosed in four flap chemise and morocco backed slipcase.   Joseph J. Felcone Inc.   Fall Miscellany 2010 - 120   2011 $20,000

United States. Department of the Interior - 1866 *Statistics of the United States in 1860.* Washington: 1866, 584 pages, large 4to., very good, three quarter leather and marbled boards, some rubbing at edges. Bookworm & Silverfish 679 - 34 2011 $225

United States. General Land Office - 1867 *Report of the Commissioner of General Land Office for the Year 1867...* Washington: 1867, 191 pages, with 32 60 inch folding map, very good with few holes to right side of backstrip, bottom to inches rear cover dusty and quarter inch tide mark to first 30 pages, errata slip tipped in. Bookworm & Silverfish 679 - 8 2011 $250

United States. Laws, Statues, etc. - 1828 *Acts of the 20th Congress. (2 Sessions).* Washington: 1828-1829, First edition; plain contemporary wrappers, stitched, first session is in very good- condition (mild dampstaining to first and last few sheets), second session in similar condition. Lupack Rare Books May 26 2011 - ABE4425849551 2011 $175

United States. Laws, Statutes, Etc. - 1813 *Acts of the 13th Congress (3 Sessions).* Washington: 1813-1815, First edition; plain contemporary wrappers, stitched, first session in very good- condition (mild dampstaining to first and last several sheets), second session very good plus (little random foxing, mild tanning to text), third session poor with paper loss at top and bottom of first several sheets, very little text is lost, but it is unsightly. Lupack Rare Books May 26 2011 - ABE4425836551 2011 $200

United States. Laws, Statutes, Etc. - 1815 *Acts of the 14th Congress (2 Sessions).* Washington: 1815-1816, First edition; plain contemporary wrappers, stitched, first session very nice (little dampstaining to bottom right corner of first few pages), second session has nice clean pages and little paper loss at spine. Lupack Rare Books May 26 2011 - ABE4425845886 2011 $250

United States. Laws, Statutes, Etc. - 1817 *Acts of the 15th Congress (2 Sessions) 1817/1819.* Washington: 1817-1819, First edition; plain contemporary wrappers, stitched, first session very good (some chipping to spine paper), second session good (some dampstaining through first 25 pages, some chipping at spine). Lupack Rare Books May 26 2011 - ABE442584954 2011 $250

United States. Laws, Statutes, etc. - 1819 *Acts of the 16th Congress (2 sessions 1819/1921).* Washington: 1819-1821, First edition; plain contemporary wrappers, stitched, scarce, first session in good condition (dampstaining and browning to text), second session is very good (no dampstain but uniform paper tanning). Lupack Rare Books May 26 2011 - ABE4425849543 2011 $200

United States. Laws, Statutes, etc. - 1837 *Acts of the 24th Congress (Second Session) 1837.* Washington: 1837, First edition; plain contemporary wrappers, stitched, scarce, very good, some mild tanning, chipping along front edge of paper wrapper, solid copy. Lupack Rare Books May 26 2011 - ABE4425852036 2011 $125

United States. War Department - 1825 *Military Laws of the United States to which is Prefixed the Constitution of the United States.* Washington: Edward De Krafft, 1825, First edition; xxxi, (1), 279 pages, contemporary sheep, foxed, binding scuffed but very tight and solid, William G. McNeill's copy, signed and dated 1827 on titlepage and with his name neatly lettered ink on front cover, portfolio and fine morocco backed slipcase. Joseph J. Felcone Inc. Fall Miscellany 2010 - 121 2011 $2200

United States. War Department - 1855 *Reports of Explorations and Surveys, to Ascertain the Most Practicable and Economical Route Railroad from the Mississippi River to the Pacific Ocean, made in the Direction of the Secretary of War in 1853-4, According to Acts of Congress March 3 1953 May 31 1854 and August 5 1854.* Washington: A. O. P. Nicholson, Printer, 1855-1861, Each volume has been rebound in black buckram, signatures resewn, titles stamped in gold on spine panel, while each volume is stamped with word "Senate" on spine, five of the volumes are actually for House of Representatives; flaws as noted - volume I with small stamp of Library of Washington and Jefferson College and word 'withdrawn', else very good, tight copy; volume IV with presentation inscription to Irving Holcomb from Hon. F. E. Sprimer (?) dated Nov. 1857, small waterstain to bottom edges of front flyleaf which continues lightly to page 3, else very good, tight copy; volume X - light foxing to first 8 pages in front of volume and last 8 pages in rear of volume, else very good, tight copy; volume XI - moderate foxing and two small waterstains that diminish over first 16 pages, else very good, tight copy, a majority of the color lithographic plates are in fine condition as are the majority of black and white plates; volume XI contains maps and plates, including desirable large folding map done by Lt. Warren, all maps and plates in this volume are tightly secured. Buckingham Books May 26 2011 - 26611 2011 $15,000

United States. War Department - 1860 *Report of Explorations and Surveys to Ascertain the Most Practicable and Economical Route for a Railroad from the Mississippi River to the Pacific Ocean.* Washington: 1860-, 1855; 12 volumes in 13 books consisting of both House and Senate issues, complicated collation, uniformly rebound in blue buckram, overall condition very good, but not without occasional flaws. Dumont Maps & Books of the West 113 - 43 2011 $9500

United States. War Department - 1886 *Annual Report of the Secretary of War for the Year 1886. Volume 1 Apache Wars.* Washington: Government Printing Office, 1886, First edition; thick 8vo., cloth, 837 pages, illustrations, tables, maps, one foldout chart, one large foldout map, surplus copy from the Office of the Army's Quartermaster General with their neat bookplate and small stamp, else very good, tight copy. Buckingham Books May 26 2011 - 29073 2011 $2750

The Universal Songster or Museum of Mirth Forming the Most Complete, Extensive and Valuable Collection of Ancient and Modern Songs in English Language with Copious and Classified Index. London: Routledge, 1840, First edition; 3 volumes, large 8vo., original publisher's red cloth lettered and decorated gilt on spines and with gilt and black illustration on cover, n.d. (1840?), attractive mid 19th century edition, engraved titles by George Cruikshank and woodcut illustrations by him, sound, very good copies, slightly tanned at spine, slight wear at heads of spines, slight soiling. Any Amount of Books May 29 2011 - A67976 2011 $238

Unna, Warren *The Coppa Murals. A Pageant of Bohemian Life in San Francisco at the Turn of the Century.* San Francisco: Book Club of California, 1952, First edition, one of 350 copies; oblong octavo, (11), 2-61, (2) pages, 8 full page illustrations, black cat chapter heading designs, cloth backed decorative boards, printed paper spine label, spine faded, else fine, very scarce. Argonaut Book Shop Recent Acquisitions Summer 2010 - 213 2011 $200

An Unsophisticated Genealogy of Her Majesty, Queen Victoria from William the Bastard alias the Conqueror. York: Henry Roberts, circa, 1838, 26 pages disbound. Jarndyce Antiquarian Booksellers CXCI - 594 2011 £200

Updike, John *Getting the Words Out.* Northridge: Lord John, 1988, One of 250 numbered copies, of a total edition of 300; signed by author, fine without dust jacket, as issued. Ken Lopez Bookseller 154 - 221 2011 $100

Updike, John *Howells as Anti-Novelist.* Kittery Point: William Dean Howells Memorial Committee, 1987, One of 150 copies; approximately 40 pages of text, fine in self wrapper with complimentary slip from publisher laid in. Ken Lopez Bookseller 154 - 220 2011 $2000

Updike, John *January.* Concord: W. B. Ewert, 1997, First edition, number 1 of 10 ad personam 'gold thread' copies; signed by author, printed on special paper at Firefly Press and illustrated with reproduction from a Thomas Bewick engraving, as new in wrappers. Gemini Fine Books & Arts, Ltd. Art Reference & Illustrated Books: First Editions 2011 $250

Updike, John *Rabbit Redux.* New York: Alfred A. Knopf, 1971, Limited to 350 copies, this no. 161; blue cloth spine and red and blue patterned cloth covers with gilt lettering to spine, original paper covered mildly worn slipcase with red and blue lettered pattern, 8vo., 406 pages. By the Book, L. C. 26 - 20 2011 $165

Updike, John *A Rabbit Omnibus. Rabbit, Run, Rabbit Redux, Rabbit is Rich.* London: Andre Deutsch, 1990, First British edition, first printing; 8vo., 700 pages, signed by author on bookplate tipped in, fine, fine dust jacket, mild age darkening page edges. By the Book, L. C. 26 - 19 2011 $150

Updike, John *Rabbit Run.* New York: Knopf, 1960, First edition; in first state dust jacket with 16 line blurb on front flap, housed in half leather clamshell box, near fine in very good+ dust jacket (little rubbing at extremities, minor, nickel-size dampstain more visible on verso than on recto, spine colors still nice and bright, dust jacket neither chipped nor clipped). Lupack Rare Books May 26 2011 - ABE3067464712 2011 $1250

Updike, John *Radiators.* Concord: W. B. Ewert, 1998, First edition; 1 of 15 ad personam copies signed by author, printed on special paper at Firefly Press, as new in wrappers. Gemini Fine Books & Arts, Ltd. Art Reference & Illustrated Books: First Editions 2011 $275

Updike, John *S.* New York: Knopf, 1988, First edition; number 338 of 350, signed by author, fine in acetate and slipcase. Gemini Fine Books & Arts, Ltd. Art Reference & Illustrated Books: First Editions 2011 $125

Upfield, Arthur W. *The House of Cain.* Philadelphia: Dorrance and Co., 1929, First US edition; very good, tight copy in dust jacket with some minor restoration to head and toe of spine and fold points but not visible outside, slipcase,. Buckingham Books May 26 2011 - 13083 2011 $3750

Upton, Bertha *Adventures of Two Dutch Dolls and a Golliwog.* Boston: De Wolfe Fiske, n.d., 1895, First American edition; Oblong 4to., cloth backed pictorial boards, 68 pages, edges and corners worn, few archival marginal mends, very good full page chromolithographs plus brown illustrations in text by Florence Upton. Aleph-Bet Books, Inc. 95 - 562 2011 $700

Upton, Bertha *Golliwogg in the African Jungle.* London: Longmans, Green and Co., 1909, First edition; oblong small 4to., original cloth backed pictorial boards, boards rubbed, corners rather worn, pages 64, illustrations in color, contents very clean, free of any tears or markings, nice, scarce. R. F. G. Hollett & Sons Antiquarian Booksellers 170 - 699 2011 £450

Upton, Bertha *The Golliwogg's Air-Ship.* London: Longmans, Green & Co. n.d., First edition; Oblong small 4to., original cloth backed pictorial boards, little rubbed and soiled, edges an corners worn and repaired, nicely rebacked to match, pages 66, illustrations in color, contents clean and untorn throughout.   R. F. G. Hollett & Sons Antiquarian Booksellers   170 - 700 2011   £450

Upton, Bertha *Golliwogg's "Auto-go-Cart".* London: Longmans, Green & Co., 1901, First edition; original cloth backed pictorial boards, oblong small 4to., little soiled, edges and corners worn, pages 66, illustrations in color, joints cracked, few short edge tears, spots and marks, but very good.   R. F. G. Hollett & Sons Antiquarian Booksellers 170 - 701 2011   £350

Upton, Bertha *The Golliwogg's Bicycle Club.* London: Longmans, Green & Co., 1903, New edition; oblong small 4to., original cloth backed pictorial boards, little soiled, corners rather worn, pages 63, illustrations in color, little spotting and small pencilled name to title, otherwise contents very clean and free of any tears or markings.   R. F. G. Hollett & Sons Antiquarian Booksellers 170 - 702 2011 £350

Upton, Bertha *The Golliwogg's Christmas.* London: Longmans, Green and Co., 1907, First edition; oblong 4to., green cloth backed color illustrated boards, particularly nice, elusive, especially in this condition, illustrations printed lithographically.   Jo Ann Reisler, Ltd. 86 - 258 2011 $2500

Upton, Bertha *The Golliwogg's Desert Island.* London: Longmans,, Green and Co., 1906, First edition; oblong 4to., cloth backed illustrated boards with some soiling and edge rubbing, quite nice internally, 64 pages of color plates by Florence Utpon.   Jo Ann Reisler, Ltd. 86 - 257 2011 $775

Upton, Florence *The Golliwogg's Bicycle Club.* London: Longmans, 1896, First edition; Oblong 4to., cloth backed pictorial boards, corner bumped, edges rubbed and usual cover rubbing, tight and very good, wonderful color illustrations.   Aleph-Bet Books, Inc. 95 - 561 2011 $900

Upton, Francis H. *The Law of Nations Affecting Commerce During War...* New York: 1961, First edition; good in law calf, top and bottom 2 inch of backstrip with cloth, not ex-library, title label chipped, loss of one letter.   Bookworm & Silverfish 667 - 47 2011 $75

Upward, Edward *Journey to the Border.* London: Hogarth Press, 1938, Pages 256, 8vo., original publisher's blue cloth, neat name on front endpaper, very slight foxing to endpapers, else near fine in first state Vanessa Bell dust jacket, complete but with very slight soilng, little darkening and little staining at spine, overall very good+.   Any Amount of Books May 29 2011 - A39761 2011 $340

Uris, Leon *The Angry Hill.* New York: Random House, 1958, First edition; near fine, gift inscription and staple holes on front free endpapers, dust jacket near fine, creasing to top edge, signed by author.   Bella Luna Books   May 26 2011 - t3590 2011 $275

Uris, Leon *Trinity.* Norwalk: Easton Press, 1999, Signed by author, leather, 751 pages, gold titles and decorations, all edges gilt, silk endpapers and ribbon, bookmark "A note about" card an signed certificate of authenticity folded in, very clean and tight.   G. H. Mott Bookseller May 26 2011 - 37097 2011 $475

Urquhart, Fred *W.S.C. A Cartoon Biography.* London: Cassell, 1955, First edition; large 8vo., original cloth, gilt, dust jacket, extremities trifle chipped, pages xiii, 242, cartoons.   R. F. G. Hollett & Son Antiquarian Booksellers 175 - 1372 2011   £35

Urquhart, George *The Experienced Solicitor in Proceedings under the Appellant Jurisdiction of...the House of Lords on Appeals and Writs in Error...* London: W. Strahan and M. Woodfall etc., 1773, Large paper copy; pages (xiv), 155, (1), folio, contemporary mottled calf, backstrip lettered vertically in gilt on red morocco label, gilt borders on sides, upper joint just starting to crack, still strong, marbled endpapers, good, scarce.   Blackwell Rare Books B166 - 112 2011 £500

Urrea, Luis Alberto *Across the Wire.* New York: Anchor, 1990, Uncorrected proof with slip laid in; fine, signed by author, blue printed wrappers, paperback original.   Bella Luna Books   May 26 2011 - t3331 2011 $302

Urrea, Luis Alberto *Across The Wire.* Anchor: 1990, First printing; paperback original, very good, shows light use, signed by author.   Bella Luna Books May 29 2011 - t3310 2011 $137

Urrea, Luis Alberto *By the Lake of Sleeping Children.* London: Anchor, 1996, First printing, paperback original; fine, signed by author, pictorial wrappers.   Bella Luna Books   May 29 2011 - t9127 2011 $99

Urrea, Luis Alberto *The Devil's Highway.* Boston: Little Brown, 2004, Advance reading copy; fine, signed and dated by author 3/20/04.   Bella Luna Books   May 29 2011 - t6405 2011 $82

Urrea, Luis Alberto *The Hummingbird's Daughter.* New York: Little Brown, 2005, Advance reading copy; pictorial wrappers, fine, promotional postcard picturing Teresita and signed by author laid in, signed and dated 6/10/05.   Bella Luna Books   May 29 2011 - t7165 2011 $137

Urrea, Luis Alberto *Nobody's Son.* Tucson: University of Arizona Press, 1998, Advance reading copy; printed wrappers, fine, signed by author.   Bella Luna Books   May 29 2011 - t095 2011 $82

Urrea, Luis Alberto *Nobody's Son.* Tucson: University of Arizona Press, 1998, First edition; fine in fine dust jacket. Bella Luna Books   May 29 2011 - t437 2011 $82

Ursinus, Johann Heinrich *De Zoroastre Bactriano, Hermete Trismegito Sanchoniathone Phoenicio Eorumque Sriptis...* Nuremberg: Michael Endterus, 1661, First edition; small 8vo., pages (xvi), 240, 71, uniformly browned with some foxing throughout, later speckled paper covered boards, bumped, rubbed, 4 lines of early manuscript notes to front free endpaper, bookseller's label to front pastedown, partially erased.   Simon Finch Rare Books   Zero - 108 2011   £950

Usher, Roland G. *The Rise and Fall of the High Commission.* Oxford: Clarendon Press, 1913, First edition; Original cloth, gilt, spine rather faded, few marks, pages 380.   R. F. G. Hollett & Son Antiquarian Booksellers 175 - 1373 2011   £45

Ussher, James *A Body of Divinity, or the Summe and Substance of Christian Religion...* London: M. F. for Tho. Downes and Geo. Badger, 1648, Third edition; folio, pages (xii) 3-451, (xv), 24 + engraved portrait frontispiece, signed "W. Marshall Sculpist 1647", contemporary sprinkled calf, boards double ruled in blind, board edges single rule gilt, all edges rouge with black ink hand written "Ussher" at head of fore-edge, pink & white sewn endbands, evidence of chaining staple at head of fore-edge of upper board, also evidence of later ties, early 1990's calf reback by Chris Weston, spotting and staining (mostly light), small tear to titlepage border repaired with sellotape, old leather marked and bit chipped at edges, near contemporary ink inscription "Roger Mostyn Anno 1685" at head of titlepage and underneath later ink inscription, booklabel of Gloddaeth Library, also ex-libris of Rev. John F. Brencher, his MS mini biography of Ussher on f.e.p. and his signature on reverse, from the collection of Christopher Ernest Weston 1947-2010. Unsworths Booksellers   24 - 54 2011   £450

Ussher, James *A Speech Delivered in the Castle-Chamber at Dublin the XXII of November Anno 1622 at the Censuring of Certain Officers Who Refused to Take the Oath of Supremacie.* London: printed by R. Y. for the Partners of the Irish Stocke, 1631, Small 4to., pages (ii), 12, (ii) disbound, age toned, soiled an spotted, now bound in quarter calf, red lettering piece lettered vertically down, boards sided out with marbled paper by Chris Weston, from the collection of Christopher Ernest Weston 1947-2010. Unsworths Booksellers   24 - 53 2011   £75

Ussher, Richard J. *The Birds of Ireland: an Account of the Distribution, Migrations and Habits of Birds as Observed in Ireland...* London: Gurney and Jackson, 1900, First edition; 8vo., pages xxxii, 419, original publisher's blue cloth lettered gilt on spine with map of Ireland in black on cover, color frontispiece, illustrations, two folding color maps, faint rubbing, clean, bright, very good.   Any Amount of Books May 29 2011 - A69862 2011 $408

An Utilitarian Catechism. London: Effingham Wilson, 1830, First and only edition; 8vo., vi, (2), 64 pages, title lightly spotted and soiled, recently well bound in cloth, spine lettered in gilt, good.   John Drury Rare Books   153 - 165 2011   £275

Uttley, Alison *The Knot Squirrel Tied.* London: Collins, 1937, First edition; 8vo., light grey boards with maroon lettering and border about full full color paste label, few faint finger marks on boards, 101 numbered pages with lots of full page color pictures.   Jo Ann Reisler, Ltd.   86 - 259 2011 $200

V

V. Muller & Co. *A Comprehensive Guide to Purchasing Hospital Professional Instruments-Equipment-Supplies.* Chicago: V. Mueller, 1956, 8vo., 611 pages, illustrations, stiff leatherette wrappers, top spine bit worn, previous owner's inked signature, very good, from the Medical Library of Dr. Clare Gray Peterson. Jeff Weber Rare Books 162 - 296 2011 $75

Vad, Poul *Vilhelm Hammershoi and Danish Art at the Turn of the Century.* New Haven and London: Yale University Press, 1992, First edition; 4to., pages 463, illustrations in color and black and white, slightly bumped and abrasion to cover, dust jacket little chipped and nicked dust jacket, very good in like dust jacket. Any Amount of Books May 29 2011 - A75938 2011 $238

Valerius Flaccus *Argonautica.* Venice: Aldus and Andrea Asulani, May, 1523, First and only Aldine edition; small 8vo., 148 leaves, Aldine dolphin and anchor woodcut device on titlepage and colophon leaf, 19th century red pebble grain morocco, fully gilt (upper hinge splitting), very occasional marginal dampstaining, else fine, A. A. Renouard's copy. Joseph J. Felcone Inc. Fall Miscellany 2010 - 1 2011 $4500

Valerius Maximus *Dictorum Factorumque Memorabilium Libri IX.* Amstelodami: Juxta Exemplar Elzeviriorum, 1690, 127 x 70mm., 4 p.l., 328 pages, fine 18th century burgundy morocco, covers with border of thick and thin gilt rules, flat spine handsomely gilt with rows of tangent ovals, each surrounded with four dots, board edges and turn-in with oblique plain and broken gilt rules, gilt edges, blue painted endpapers, engraved titlepage, minor flaking on corners and head of spine, leaves just shade less than bright, but fine, pretty copy with only trivial imperfections and very tall with especially wide margins and several leaves untrimmed at bottom. Phillip J. Pirages 59 - 32 2011 $275

Valery, Paul *Le Cimetiere Martin.* Paris: Emile Paul Freres, 1920, First edition; 8vo., pages (18), top edge cut, others uncut, minor dampstain to fore edge of two leaves, original wrappers, upper side with text and decorative border printed in black, slightly thumbed, some spotting, small dampstain to upper side, text block loose in wrapper but internally firm, author's presentation inscription. Simon Finch Rare Books Zero - 358 2011 £4750

Vallance, Aymer *Greater English Church Screens.* London: Batsford, 1947, First edition; 4to., original cloth, dust jacket, little chipped and torn, pages viii 184, color frontispiece and 154 illustrations. R. F. G. Hollett & Son Antiquarian Booksellers 177 - 863 2011 £75

Vallance, Aymer *Old Crosses and Lychgates.* London: Batsford, 1920, First edition; small 4to., original cloth, gilt, dust jacket (defective, parts of spine and upper edge lacking), pages xvii, 198, with 237 plates. R. F. G. Hollett & Son Antiquarian Booksellers 177 - 864 2011 £65

Vallance, Aymer *Old Crosses and Lychgates.* London: Batsford, 1933, New issue; small 4to., original cloth, gilt, spine little darkened, pages xvii, 198, with 237 plates, fine. R. F. G. Hollett & Son Antiquarian Booksellers 177 - 865 2011 £75

Valuable Secret Concerning Arts and Trades; or, Approved Directions from the Best Artists for the Various Methods of Engraving on Brass Copper or Steel. Norwich: Thomas Hubbard, 1795, First American edition, one of 2 editions published in 1795; 12mo., (2), xxii, 240 pages, contemporary full brown sheep, red leather spine label, lettered in gilt, boards with few scuffs and dents, spine and outer hinges rubbed, corners bit rubbed and bumped, head of spine slightly chipped, some toning to pages as usual, leaf A2 with small paper flaw, barely affecting text, very good. Heritage Book Shop Holiday 2010 - 21 2011 $1000

Valuable Secrets Concerning Arts and Trades or Approved Directions from the Best Artists with an Appendix. Boston: J. Bumstead, 1798, Second edition; 12mo., 264 pages, contemporary calf, leather label, hinges repaired. M & S Rare Books, Inc. 90 - 96 2011 $850

Valuable Secrets in Arts, Trades &c. Selected from the Best Authors and Adapted to the Situation of the United States. New York: Everet Duyckinck, 1809, First edition; 16mo., 380, 20 pages, contemporary calf, split in spine repaired. M & S Rare Books, Inc. 90 - 95 2011 $650

Van Allsburg, Chris *Jumanji.* Boston: Houghton Mifflin, 1981, First edition, first printing; oblong 4to., cloth, fine in fine dust jacket, illustrations by author. Aleph-Bet Books, Inc. 95 - 563 2011 $850

Van Allsburg, Chris *Polar Express.* Boston: Houghton Mifflin, 1985, First edition, first printing; oblong 4to., as new in as new dust jacket, magnificent color illustrations, with Houghton Mifflin's 1985 Seasons greetings card in envelope laid in. Aleph-Bet Books, Inc. 95 - 564 2011 $650

Van De Water, Frederic *The Real McCoy.* Garden City: Doubleday, Doran and Co., 1931, First edition; fine in near fine dust jacket but for small chip on spine, inscribed by subject of the book "To Bob Davis, the man who suggested that this yarn be put in print. Bill McCoy", scarce either in jacket or signed. Between the Covers 169 - BTC342132 2011 $950

Van Der Leeuw, J. J. *The Fire of Creation.* Chicago: 1926, First edition; 220 pages, very good, few small cover spots, bookplate on front pastedown. Bookworm & Silverfish 671 - 159 2011 $100

Van Dyke, Theodore S. *Flirtation Camp; or the Rifle, Rod and Gun in California.* New York: Fords, Howard & Hulbert, 1881, First edition; small octavo, (6), 299 pages, original dark green pictorial cloth stamped and lettered in gilt on spine and front cover, covers with beveled edge, owner's bookplate, slightest of bubbling to small portion of cloth on rear cover, fine. Argonaut Book Shop Recent Acquisitions Summer 2010 - 214 2011 $90

Van Gulik, Robert *Dee Goong An: Three Murder Cases solved by Dee, an Old Chinese Detective...* Tokyo: privately printed, 1949, First edition; one of 100 numbered copies, signed by author, this #672, illustrations, fine, bright copy, lacking original plain kraft paper unprinted dust jacket in which the book was mailed to subscribers and housed in custom made clamshell case with design of book's front cover and on front panel, book's rear cover design on back panel, author's name, title and publication date on spine panel, exceptional copy. Buckingham Books May 26 2011 - 23679 2011 $5000

Van Gulik, Robert *New Year's Eve in Lan-Fang.* Beirut: Imprimerie Catholique, 1958, First edition; limited to 200 copies, generic inscription by author, fine in printed wrappers, unusually sharp copy, very scarce title, housed in four point case that is inserted into cloth slipcase with leather labels on spine and titles stamped in gold. Buckingham Books May 26 2011 - 26901 2011 $3250

Van Gundy, John C. *Reminicences of Frontier Life on the Upper Neosho in 1855 and 1856.* Topeka: 1925, 41 pages, wrappers, very good. Bookworm & Silverfish 666 - 90 2011 $100

Van Maele, Martin *La Grande Danse Macabre Des Vifs.* Paris: circa, 1909, First edition; 8vo., 40 engraved black and white plates and 4 sepia engraved titles, top edge gilt, others uncut, bound on stubs in later crimson half morocco, marbled boards, spine lettered gilt, raised bands, marbled endpapers, extremities very slightly rubbed, otherwise excellent, finely bound set. Simon Finch Rare Books Zero - 437 2011 £11,000

Van Nostrand, Jeanne *California Pictorial: a History in Contemporary Pictures 1786 to 1859.* Berkeley and Los Angeles: University of California Press, 1948, First edition; signed by both authors, 4to., 159 pages, frontispiece plus 69 plates, 10 in color, fine with lightly worn pictorial dust jacket. Argonaut Book Shop Recent Acquisitions Summer 2010 - 216 2011 $125

Van Nostrand, Jeanne *California Pictorial: a History in Contemporary Pictures 1786 to 1859.* Berkeley and Los Angeles: University of California, 1948, First edition; 4to., 159 pages, frontispiece, plus 69 plates, 10 in color, small bookplate on inner cover, fine, without dust jacket. Argonaut Book Shop Recent Acquisitions Summer 2010 - 217 2011 $90

Van Nostrand, Jeanne *San Francisco 1806-1906 in Contemporary Paintings, Drawings and Watercolors.* San Francisco: Book Club of California, 1975, First edition, limited to 500 copies; quarto, 23 pages, plus 53 plates, tan cloth, decorated in red and stamped in gilt, very fine. Argonaut Book Shop Recent Acquisitions Summer 2010 - 215 2011 $225

Van Vogt, Alfred Elton *The Book of Ptath.* Reading: Fantasy Press, 1947, First edition; octavo, cloth. L. W. Currey, Inc. 124 - 151 2011 $450

Van Vogt, Alfred Elton *The Mixed Men.* New York: Gnome Press, 1952, First edition; octavo, probable first binding of blue boards with spine panel lettered in orange. L. W. Currey, Inc. 124 - 234 2011 $100

Van Vogt, Alfred Elton *The World of A.* New York: Simon and Schuster, 1948, First edition; octavo, cloth. L. W. Currey, Inc. 124 - 168 2011 $350

Vanbrugh, John *The Relapse; or Virtue in Danger: Being the Sequel of the Fool of Fashion.* London: For Richard Wellington, 1708, Third edition; small 4to., disbound, sporadic foxing, publisher's ads to terminal leaf and, unusually, foot of titlepage, early ink excisions to two leaves. Dramatis Personae Booksellers 106 - 164 2011 $85

Vancouver, George *Voyage of Discovery in the North Pacific Ocean and Round the World... Performed in the years 1791, 1792, 1793, 1794 and 1795 in the Discovery Sloop of War and Armed Tender Chatham...* London: printed for G. G. and J. Robinson and J. Edwards, 1798, First edition; quarto, 3 volumes, plus folio atlas volume, (8), xxix, (1, blank), (2, ads), (4, contents), (2, list of plates), 432; (10, 504; (10), 505, (3, errata) pages, 18 engraved plates one of which is a map in text, 10 folding maps and 6 plates of profiles in atlas volume, complete with half titles and errata, text volumes bound in contemporary tan polished calf with double gilt borders, spines stamped and lettered in gilt, gilt board edges and dentelles, marbled endpapers, edges stained yellow, previous owner's bookplate, plates with some light foxing, volume I with some slight cracking to front outer hinge, still firm, atlas bound in modern tan calf to match 3 volumes, overall, excellent set, tall, clean and complete.   Heritage Book Shop   Holiday 2010 - 126   2011 $65,000

Vancouver, George *A Voyage of Discovery to the North Pacific Ocean and Round the World 1791-1795.* London: Hakluyt Society, 1984, First edition; 4 volumes, 8vo., pages 1752, 46 plates, 10 maps, corners slightly bumped and with slight edgewear, else sound very good in near very good dust jackets which are rubbed and slightly creased at edges, few very small chips and nicks at spine ends, one short closed tear to cover volume I.   Any Amount of Books   May 29 2011 - A75684   2011 $221

Vandeleur, Seymour *Campaigning on the Upper Nile and Niger.* London: Methuen, 1898, First edition; 8vo., pages xxvii, 320, folding map, illustrations, original blue decorative cloth, near fine, Vandeleur calling card attached to front endpaper.   J. & S. L. Bonham Antiquarian Booksellers   Africa 4/20/2011 - 8314   2011   £135

Vanderbilt School of Law *Race Relations Law Reporter.* Nashville: 1956+, 4to., 6 issues, volume ! #2-5, volume 4 # 3, Volume 5 #1, about 1300 pages, wrappers, very good.   Bookworm & Silverfish   676 - 116   2011 $65

Vansleb, Felix *The Present State of Egypt; or a New Relation of a Late Voyage into the Kingdom. Performed in the Years 1672 and 1673.* London: John Starkey, 1678, First edition; small 8vo., pages 253, stain on page 5, some light occasional foxing, contemporary brown speckled calf, rebacked in 19th century brown calf, some cropping.   J. & S. L. Bonham Antiquarian Booksellers   Africa 4/20/2011 - 8404   2011   £650

Varigny, Charles De *La Femme aux Etats Unis.* Paris: Armand Colin, 1893, First edition; (322) pages, 8vo., original yellow wrappers, printed in black, uncut and some pages unopened, few spots on cover, spine skillfully rebacked, very good to fine.   Paulette Rose Fine and Rare Books   32 - 181   2011 $125

Varnhagen, K. A. *Uber Rahels Religiositat Von einem Ihrer Altern Freunde.* Leipzig: Gebruder Reichenbach, 1836, First edition?; (79) pages, 12mo., original black lettered grey wrappers, ruled borders on front and rear, some age wear and small chip on lower right side of front cover, scattered light foxing, still overall good copy, extremely rare, fragile title.   Paulette Rose Fine and Rare Books   32 - 102   2011 $850

Vatsyayana *The Kama Sutra of Vatsyayana.* Benares: printed for the Hindoo Kama Shastra Society for private circulation only, 1883, First edition; large 8vo., pages 198, titlepage in red black , half niger crushed morocco, marbled boards and endpapers, top edge gilt, spine gilt titled and dated within raised bands.   Simon Finch Rare Books   Zero - 427   2011   £3500

Vaughan, Henry *The Poems of Henry Vaughan, Silurist.* London: Lawrence & Bullen, 1896, 2 volumes, series and half titles, titles in red and black, uncut in original blue cloth, slightly sunned, top edge gilt, signed presentation from George MacDonald to Lady Ottoline Morrell.   Jarndyce Antiquarian Booksellers   CXCII - 341   2011   £650

Veblen, Thorstein *The Theory of the Leisure Class.* New York: Macmillan, 1989, First edition; 8vo., pages viii, 400, 2 pages ads, uncommon, top edge gilt, original publisher's dark green cloth lettered gilt, light edgewear and slight rubbing at spine, slight chip at spine and spine ends slightly frayed, used very good copy with name in ink on pasted own and half title, f.e.p. lacking and some ink underlinings on 3 pages.   Any Amount of Books   May 26 2011 - A72901 2011 $805

Venegas, Miguel *Juan Maria de Salvatierra of the Company of Jesus: Missionary in the Province of New Spain and Apostolic Conqueror of the Californias.* Cleveland: Arthur H. Clark Co., 1929, First edition, one of 755 copies; 350 pages, illustrations, maps, facsimiles, portraits, red cloth, gilt, slight rubbing to spine ends, fine, presentation copy signed by editor, Marguerite Eyer Wilbur to author Lindley Bynum.   Argonaut Book Shop   Recent Acquisitions Summer 2010 - 218   2011 $275

Veniard, John *Fly Dressers' Guide.* Adam and Charles Black, 1964, Fifth impression; 4to., original cloth, gilt, dust jacket, slipcase (rather worn), pages 256, 14 color plates, 160 photos, numerous drawings.   R. F. G. Hollett & Son Antiquarian Booksellers   General Catalogue Summer 2010 - 1303   2011   £40

Venn, H. *The Complete Duty of Man, or a System of Doctrinal and Practical Christianity.* S. Crowder and G. Robinson and Carnan and Newbery, 1779, Third edition; pages xiv, 500, short wormtracks to lower margin of first few leaves, lacks all before title, old full calf, very rubbed, scraped and defective, hinges cracked and upper board sometime sewn back.   R. F. G. Hollett & Son Antiquarian Booksellers   175 - 1377   2011   £45

Venturi, Ken *The Venturi Analysis.* New York: Atheneum, 1981, First edition; 8vo., 160 pages, signed and inscribed by Venturi, near fine in like dust jacket, price clipped with minimal edge wear.   By the Book, L. C.   26 - 85 2011 $95

Veresaev, Vikenty Vikentevich *In the War - Memoirs of V. Veresaev.* New York: Mitchell Kennerley, 1917, Red cloth faded on spine, edgeworn, edges soiled, owner's name in pencil on f.e.p., interior tight and clean, good.   G. H. Mott Bookseller   May 26 2011 - 16180 2011 $250

Vergilius Maro, Publius *The Nyne Fyrst Bookes of the Eneidos of Virgil...* London: by Rouland Hall for Nicholas Englande, 1562, Rare early edition in English; 4to., (220) pages, woodcut on title, text in black letter, 19th century morocco, ruled in gilt, edges gilt, extremities lightly worn, minor scuffing, first quire washed and neatly extended at top edge, possibly supplied from another copy, few internal repairs, else very good, excellent full margins, Rubislaw House bookplate of John Morgan.   Joseph J. Felcone Inc.   Fall Miscellany 2010 - 122 2011 $11,000

Vergilius Maro, Publius *Bucolica, Georgica et Aeneis.* Birmingham: John Baskerville, 1757, First Baskerville edition; glorious copy, 4to., (10), 432 pages, contemporary English or Irish green morocco, gilt floral borders on covers, spine richly gilt with floral and ornamental tools, red morocco lettering piece, fine, beautifully, 18th century engraved bookplate of Thomas Kelly, contemporary signature of Hen. Gore.   Joseph J. Felcone Inc.   Fall Miscellany 2010 - 11   2011 $3800

Vergilius Maro, Publius *The Georgicks of Virgil.* London: printed for the editor by Richard Reilly in Little Britain, 1741, First edition; 4to., light brown mark on inner margin of title, list of subscribers, index, 13 colored plates, xxii, 403, (1), 3, (11) pages, contemporary calf, hinges cracked, upper cover almost detached, original gilt spine replaced, morocco label.   Anthony W. Laywood   May 26 2011 - 21425 2011 $503

Vergilius Maro, Publius *Opera.* Venice: Apud Iuntas, 1544, Folio in sixes, lacking final blank D6, the Aeneid with separate titlepage and 1543 imprint, early 18th century half vellum over marbled boards.   Heritage Book Shop   Booth A12 51st NY International Antiquarian Book Fair April 8-10 2011 - 140 2011 $7500

Vergilius, Polydorus *De Rerum Inventoribus Libri Octo.* Basel: apud Isingrinium, 1546, Final blank discarded, dampmarking to lower outer corner and upper inner corner appearing intermittently, small neat repair to blank area of title, little faint browning elsewhere, pages (xliv), 524 12mo., 18th century mottled sheep, rebacked, backstrip with five raised bands between double gilt fillets, red morocco label in second compartment, joints and bands rubbed, area of surface abrasion on lower cover, marbled endpapers, a.e.r., sound.   Blackwell Rare Books   B166 - 113 2011   £650

Verity, Robert *Changes Produced in the Nervous System by Civilsation...* London: S. Highley, 1837, First edition; original cloth with paper label to upper board, neatly recased, pages 79, first third of text rather dampstained at head, few other marks but good, rare.   R. F. G. Hollett & Son Antiquarian Booksellers   General Catalogue Summer 2010 - 1147 2011   £195

Verlaine, Paul   1844-1896 *Amour.* Paris: Leon Vanier, 1888, First edition; presentation from author to Leon Deschamps, 18mo., pages (viii) including initial blank, 174, (2) back, top edge gilt, others uncut, publisher's wrappers, text in black, spine tipped in, bound in half morocco and gold and silver sprinkled paper, spine with 5 bands, elaborate decorated compartments and lettering in gilt, fine.   Simon Finch Rare Books   Zero - 359 2011   £3750

Verlaine, Paul   1844-1896 *Clair de Lune.* Octon: Verdigris Press, 2009, Artist's book, one of 4 deluxe copies, from a total issue of 24 copies; (4 deluxe with original copperplate and 20 regular), all on Hahnemuhle paper, each signed and numbered by artist, Judith Rothchild, page size 7 3/4 x 4 inches, 14 pages, bound by Mark Lintott, leporello style laid into bordeaux paper over boards folder, title in black on front panel, laid into matching paper over boards clamshell box with original copperplate laid into back of box, protected by paper over boards folder with ribbon pull, paper are original serigraph prints made by Ms Rothchild with darker bordeaux printing in pattern of sunflowers and tendril border, matching label on spine with title, author, artist and press printed in black; Mr. Lintott has handset and printed Verlaine's poem in Vendome romain, taken from his Fetes Galantes.   Priscilla Juvelis - Rare Books   48 - 26 2011 $1250

Verlaine, Paul   1844-1896 *Hombres.* Paris: Imprime sous le Maneau et ne se vend nul part, 1904, First edition, number 261 of 500 copies on Hollande Van Glder (total edition of 525); 8vo., pages (iv), 48, (4) contents, as issued in light brown mottled printed wrappers, in glassine over wrappers, fine.   Simon Finch Rare Books   Zero - 435 2011   £1250

Verlaine, Paul   1844-1896 *Parallelement.* Paris: Leon Vanier, 1889, First edition; 8vo., modern half dark green leather, marbled boards, lettered gilt at spine, pages 116, excellent condition, clean text.   Any Amount of Books   May 26 2011 - A76718 2011 $470

Verne, Jules   1828-1905 *The Archipelago on Fire.* London: Sampson Low, Marston & Co., n.d. , about, 1910, New edition; 8vo., original publisher's red pictorial cloth showing 3 ships, pages vi, 198, covers faintly tanned, else very good+.   Any Amount of Books   May 26 2011 - A67385 2011 $537

Verne, Jules 1828-1905 *For the Flag.* London: Sampson Low, Marston and Co., 1897, First edition; 8vo., original publisher's printed brown cloth lettered gilt on spine and cover, pages viii, 312, exceptional bright, clean, fresh, very good, but lacks 6 plates.   Any Amount of Books   May 26 2011 - A67381 2011 $587

Verne, Jules 1828-1905 *Michael Strogoff.* New York: Scribner, 1927, First edition of this Scribner Classic illustrated by Wyeth; 4to., black cloth, pictorial paste-on, fine in publisher's box with pictorial label pasted on, box slightly rubbed, else near fine, 9 color plates plus titlepage, magnificent copy, rarely found in publisher's box.   Aleph-Bet Books, Inc. 95 - 598 2011 $1350

Verner, Willoughby *Sketches in the Souodan.* London: R. H. Porter, 1885, First edition; oblong folio, 39 tinted lithographs, original grey decorative cloth, corners rubbed, spine faded with small wear to head and tail, upper cover rubbed around edges, internally very clean and crisp.   J. & S. L. Bonham Antiquarian Booksellers   Africa 4/20/2011 - 7363 2011   £400

Verneuil, Maurice Pillard *Images d'une Femme/Vingt Quatre Etudes De Nu.* Paris: Editions Denoel et Steele, 1931, First edition; folio, pages 1-8, 9-16, 24 black and white photo plates, unbound, original black cloth backed red paper covered board portfolio, white label to front cover printed in black and red, black ribbon tie to fore edge, lightly rubbed, fine set in near fine portfolio, from the library of Alessandro Bertolotti.   Simon Finch Rare Books   Zero - 544 2011   £650

Vernon, C. W. *Cape Breton, Canada at the Beginning of the Twentieth Century.* Toronto: Nation Publishig Co., 1903, Quarto, blue cloth, gilt titles to front and spine, pages 337, (3), index, photo illustrations, cloth sunned, interior good, long inscription by previous owner.   Schooner Books Ltd. 96 - 253 2011 $75

Vernon, W. V. *A Second Letter to Viscount Milton on the Restoration of York Minster and the Proposed Removal of the Choir Screen.* W. Hargrove for John and George Todd, 1830, 8vo., 62 pages, engraved plate, large uncut copy in later gilt lettered blue cloth, outer leaves rather dusty, contemporary signature of J. P. Tempest.   Ken Spelman Rare Books 68 - 24 2011   £75

Vertur, George *Anecdotes of Painting in England: with Some Account of the Principal Artists; and Incidental Notes on Other Arts.* London: printed for J. Dodsley, 1782, Mostly third editions; volume 4 is second edition, bookplate of Sir Claude Alexander at front of each volume, with his neat ownership signature at top of titlepages (dated 1828), 4 volumes, full tree calf decorated gilt at spine, pages 1300+, text clean and complete, boards somewhat worn and loose, good+.   Any Amount of Books   May 29 2011 - A62201 2011 $306

Verve, an Artistic and Literary Quarterly. Paris: Verve, 1937, Volume 1 No. 1 (December 1937), first edition of the premier issue; small folio, 36cm., 128 pages, original color pictorial wrappers, illustrations, photos, very good, bookplate of Vance Gerry.   Jeff Weber Rare Books   163 - 104 2011 $475

Verwandlungs Bilderbuch. Metamorphoses Picture Book. no publishing information except made in Germany circa, 1895, 12mo., pictorial wrappers, inconspicuous repair at fold, else very good+, 6 pages in 3 sections folded to size, chromolithographs.   Aleph-Bet Books, Inc. 95 - 377 2011 $500

Very, Jones *Essays and Poems.* Boston: Charles C. Little & James Brown, 1839, First edition; 12mo., 7, (1), 175 pages, original cloth, faded, paper label, rubbed, bottom of spine chipped, title foxed.   M & S Rare Books, Inc. 90 - 432 2011 $650

Very, Lydia L. *Goody Two Shoes.* Boston: L. Prang n.d. circa, 1863, 12mo., pictorial wrappers, fine, die cut in shape of Little Goody Two Shoes, every page delicately illustrated in color by Very, rare.   Aleph-Bet Books, Inc. 95 - 526 2011 $750

Vettriano, Jack *Jack Vettriano.* London: Pavilion, 2004, First edition; 4to., 192 pages, lavishly illustrated in color, signed presentation from author for Mariella Frostrup, fine in fine dust jacket.   Any Amount of Books   May 29 2011 - A40514 2011 $213

Viardot, Louis *Masterpieces of French Art.* Philadelphia: 1883, 20 parts with all front and most rear wrappers present, has all 81 photogravure images and all 93 woodcut illustrations and with 18 (of 19) woodcuts, about a fourth of the images with noticeable foxing and like number with marginal waterstaining, this set never bound, with consignment fraying to edges of wrappers, while margins of images remain generally undisturbed, wrappers dated 1881 while text dated 1883.   Bookworm & Silverfish 676 - 24 2011 $175

Victoria, Queen of Great Britain 1819-1901 *Leaves from the Journal of the Highlands from 1848 to 1861.* London: Smith, Elder & Co., 1868, Illustrated edition; 4to., original cloth, gilt extra over bevelled boards, upper board elaborately decorated in gilt within shaped panels with central title panel of a stag in highland landscape, signed De Lacy, neatly recased, pages xvii, 198, all edges gilt, engraved frontispiece, 2 chromolithographs and numerous vignettes, short tear to lower margin of title repaired, otherwise most attractive.   R. F. G. Hollett & Son Antiquarian Booksellers 175 - 1381 2011   £275

Victoria, Queen of Great Britain 1819-1901 *Leaves from the Journal of the Highlands from 1848 to 1861.* London: Smith, Elder and Co., 1868, First edition; original green cloth, gilt over bevelled boards, few light creases to head of spine, pages xv, (iii), 316, 2 engraved plates.   R. F. G. Hollett & Son Antiquarian Booksellers   175 - 1380   2011   £75

Victoria, Queen of Great Britain 1819-1901 *Leaves from the Journal of Our Life in the Highlands from 1848 to 1861.* London: Smith, Elder and Co., 1868, First edition thus; 4to., pages xvii, 198, frontispiece, 6 engraved plates and 2 color chromolithographs and numerous vignettes, original publisher's red cloth highly decorated and illustrated on covers and spine in gilt with some black patterning, illustrations, inscribed by Queen Victoria for Captain Waller, R.E, sound, clean attractive about very good copy with slight wear at lower hinge of spine and spine ends with corners rubbed.   Any Amount of Books   May 26 2011 - A66337   2011 $604

Victoria, Queen of Great Britain 1819-1901 *The Letters of Queen Victoria.* London: John Murray, 1908, 3 volumes, small 8vo., original red cloth, gilt, pages xii, 512; xi, 472; vii, 520, 16 plates.   R. F. G. Hollett & Son Antiquarian Booksellers   175 - 1382   2011   £85

Vidal, Gore *Romulus.* New York: Grove Press, 1966, First edition; signed by author, fine in near fine, rubbed dust jacket with creased edge tear at upper front panel, uncommon signed.   Ken Lopez Bookseller   154 - 227   2011 $200

Vidal, Gore *Weekend.* New York: Dramatists Play Service, 1968, First edition; sheet laid in printing three dialogue changes to be made to text, in response to the assassination of Bobby Kennedy, covers heavily edge sunned, thus very good in stapled wrappers, scarce.   Ken Lopez Bookseller   154 - 227   2011 $200

Vieuchange, Jane *Smara: the Forbidden City, Being the Journal of Michel Vieuchange While Travelling Among the Independent Tribes of South Morocco and Rio De Oro.* London: Methuen, 1933, First UK edition; 8vo., pages xii, 276, ads, map, illustrations, original red cloth, dust jacket worn.   J. & S. L. Bonham Antiquarian Booksellers   Africa 4/20/2011 - 5584   2011   £75

Views of the Parish Churches in York; with a Short Account of Each. York: A. Barclay, 1831, large 8vo., (4) pages, 23 mounted india paper lithograph plates by R. B. each with leaf of descriptive text, some foxing, rather heavy in places, little chipping to fore-edges of some leaves, recent wrappers with original printed front wrapper bound in, scarce.   Ken Spelman Rare Books   68 - 25   2011   £120

Vigfusson, Gudbrand *Icelandic Sagas.* 1887-1894, 4 volumes, folding colored lithograph frontispiece, 2 plates, liii,4 26, xlv, 473, lxiii,470, xxxvii, 491 pages, unopened, quarter cloth, ex-library presented by H.M. Treasury, very good.   C. P. Hyland   May 26 2011 - 260/271 2011 $290

Viljoen, Ben *My Reminiscences of the Anglo-Boer War.* London: Hood Douglas, 1902, First edition; 8vo., 542 pages, ads, maps, illustrations, original red cloth, rebacked using original spine and new endpapers.   J. & S. L. Bonham Antiquarian Booksellers   Africa 4/20/2011 - 5583 2011   £85

Villedieu, Marie Catherine Desjardins, Madame De *Recveil De Poesies De Mademoiselle Desjardins.* Paris: Chez Clavde Barbin, 1662, First edition; 12mo., (xiv), 99, (iii), bound in contemporary calf, spine gilt, neatly rebacked with spine laid down, leaves little toned, but very good, author's first book, rare.   Second Life Books Inc.   174 - 316 2011 $2200

Villon, Francois *Les Ballades.* Eragny Press, 1900, One of 226 copies (of which 200 were for sale); 198 x 128mm., 2 p.l., 88, (4) pages, lovely contemporary olive green crushed morocco by Sarah Prideaux (stamp signed "STP" and dated 1901 on rear turn-in), covers with wide double ruled gilt frame filled with curling tendrils, 12 of these terminating in leaves, six more connected to large pomegranates located at each corner and at midpoint of the left and right side, frame with interspersed large and small dots, raised bands, spine panels with single leaf on a curling vine, gilt turn-ins, edges gilt on the rough, with woodcut printer's device on opening page, titlepage with woodcut vignette surrounded by full border of leaves and berries, 37 woodcut foliate initials all by Lucien Pissarro, printed in red and black, isolated spots of foxing, spine perhaps just a shade darker than covers, but very fine, text especially clean, fresh and smooth, lustrous binding without perceptible wear.   Phillip J. Pirages   59 - 123   2011 $7500

Vinge, Joan D. *The Snow Queen.* New York: Dial Press, 1980, First edition; octavo, cloth backed boards.   L. W. Currey, Inc.   124 - 194   2011 $250

Virchow, Rudolf *Die Cellularpathologie in Ihrer Begrundung auf Physiologische und Patholgische Gewebelehre.* Berlin: August Hirschwald, 1858, First edition; 4to., pages xvi, 440, with half title, 144 woodcut illustrations, very light barely noticeable even browning, contemporary marbled boards, flat spine ruled in gilt, green morocco label, some wearing or rubbing to extremities, lower corner of label torn.   Simon Finch Rare Books   Zero - 130   2011   £3750

Virginia *Journal, Acts & Proceedings of a General Convention of the State of Virginia.* Richmond: 1850, ca. 800 pages, worn and damped copy, top cover with threads only, backstrip loose on one side, internal foxing.   Bookworm & Silverfish   671 - 188   2011 $200

Virginia Cavalcade Magazine. 1951-1981, Volume I summer 1951 to volume 30 # 4 (spring 1981), total of 120 issues, (missing 20, largely volumes 2-6), one cover damaged, else very good, few issues creased.   Bookworm & Silverfish   678 - 198   2011 $550

Virginia Republican Party   *Platform & Address of the Republican Party of Virginia Adopted July 15 1885.* Petersburg?: 1885?,   8 pages.   Bookworm & Silverfish   666 - 194   2011 $450

Virginia Republican Party   *Whig, New Virginia.* Richmond: 1885, 95 pages, last leaf frayed below bottom of text.   Bookworm & Silverfish   666 - 188   2011 $350

Virginia State Library   *Virginia Cavalcade.*   Richmond: 1962-1987,   60 volumes, issues all fine, but 3 with paper residue.   Bookworm & Silverfish   668 - 195   2011 $175

Virginia. Laws, Statutes, etc.   *Acts of the General Assembly of Virginia.*   Richmond: 1848,   First edition; 420 pages, half law leather and marbled boards, bottom 2 inch of backstrip mended, top of backstrip chipped and frayed. Bookworm & Silverfish   667 - 171   2011 $75

Virginia. Laws, Statutes, Etc.   *A Collection of All Such Acts of the General Assembly of Virginia.*   Richmond: 1803,   First edition; 454, (2) blank, 72 (index) pages, early law calf, 2 inch surface crack top right and bottom left of backstrip, most presentable copy with signature of John Roane.   Bookworm & Silverfish   671 - 194   2011 $195

Visiak, E. H.   *Medusa. A Story of Mystery and Ecstasy and Strange Horror.*   London: Victor Gollancz, 1929,   First edition; 8vo., 286 pages, endpapers slightly browned, else very good+ in chipped and slightly soiled, very good- dust jacket neatly restored by previous owner, words Medusa and Gollancz inked in excellent facsimile), signed presentation from author for Sidney and Olive.   Any Amount of Books   May 26 2011 - A74374   2011 $1048

A Visit to Aunt Agnes.   London: Religious Tract Society, n.d. circa, 1868,   Pencilled signature dated 1868, square small 8vo., original blindstamped cloth gilt extra, spine and edges faded, pages 80, all edges gilt, text woodcuts, 4 Kronheim color plates, pencilled signature date 1868 on flyleaf.   R. F. G. Hollett & Sons Antiquarian Booksellers   170 - 25   2011   £85

A Visit to the Tower.   London: Religious Tract Society, n.d. circa, 1890,   Large 8vo., original picctorial wrappers, little soiled, pages 6 plus 6 colored plates, all linen backed, edges little frayed, little fingered in places.   R. F. G. Hollett & Sons Antiquarian Booksellers   170 - 26   2011   £45

Vitruvius Pollio, Marcus   *I Dieci Libri dell'Architettura.* Venice: Appresso Francesco d'Franceschi Senese & Giovanni Chrieger, 1567,   Second edition; Woodcut titlepage, 2 folding woodcuts, numerous others in text, (121 in total, 14 printed full page on 7 leaves), foxed (mostly lightly), little staining, intermittent light dampmark to upper corner, first three leaves with small marginal repairs and gutters reinforced, few early ink annotations, pages (viii), 506, 4to., 19th century Italian sponge mottled paper boards backed in vellum, backstrip divided by gilt rolls, green gilt lettered label in second compartment, corners tipped in velum, paper just slightly chipped at edges, no flyleaves, modern bookplate to front pastedown and verso of title, sound.   Blackwell Rare Books   B166 - 115   2011   £1750

Vizetelly, Ernest Alfred   *With Zola in England.*   London: Chatto & Windus, 1899,   First edition; original pictorial brown cloth, lower board dampstained, pages (ii), xviii, 219, with 4 plates, label removed from pastedown, first few leaves rather creased, few spots, uncommon.   R. F. G. Hollett & Son Antiquarian Booksellers   General Catalogue Summer 2010 - 473   2011   £45

Vizetelly, Henry   *Facts About Sherry, Gleaned in the Vineyards and Bodegas of the Jerez, Seville, Moguer & Montilla Districts During the Autumn of 1875.*   London: Ward Lock & Tyler, 1876,   6 page initial ads, frontispiece, plates, illustrations, original yellow pictorial wrappers, slightly rubbed, small chip to head and tail of spine.   Jarndyce Antiquarian Booksellers   CXCI - 372   2011   £150

Vlacq, Adriaan   *Ephemerides of the Celestiall Motions for the Yeeres of the Vulgar Era 1633, 1634, 1635, 1636.* London: by William Iones, 1635,   4to., (2), 22, (104) (tables) pages closely shaved, cropping some signatures and catchwords and part of the one rule border, text itself untouched, in first part (A-C4) and in the tables touching a few signatures with some slight damage to extreme upper outer corners on few leaves, affecting a few dates, rebound in half calf, old style, from the library of the Earls of Macclesfield at Shirburn Castle.   Maggs Bros. Ltd.   1440 - 222   2011   £4000

Vogel, Hermann   *The Chemistry of Life and Photography.* New York: 1875,   xi (1) 288 (12) pages, of 6 plates, 3 have laid down photo prints, very good, missing f.f.e.p., red cloth, slight rub on backstrip.   Bookworm & Silverfish   662 - 179   2011 $150

The Voice of the Prophets.   Flemington: St. Teresa's Press, 1970,   One of 125 copies this copy #65; 270 x 210mm., 4 p.l., 31, (1) pages, (1) leaf (colophon), publisher's quarter black morocco over marbled boards, gilt titling on spine, 22 hand illuminated initials in 23 carat gold, metallic silver and colors all with original tissue guards, printed on handmade English paper in uncial type, virtually pristine.   Phillip J. Pirages   59 - 311   2011 $950

Volcyre De Serouville, Nicolas *L'Histoire & Recueil de (la Triumphante et Glorieuse Victoire Obtenue Contre les Seduyctz et (Abusez) Lutheriens Mescreans du Pays Daulsays et Autres...* Paris: for Galliot du Pre, 1526, First edition; folio, ff., (10), xcviii, text in 2 columns, woodcut illustration on titlepage, woodcut of a scribe, 5 woodcut illustrations, 18th century calf with triple fillet gilt, spine gilt in compartments, red speckled edges, 3 colored silk markers, first 4 leaves torn with loss, H-3-H4 transposed, last leaf torn in margin, occasional slight staining, despite heavily damaged first leaves (woodcut on titlepage untouched), overall good copy, rare, from the library of the Earls of Macclesfield at Shirburn Castle. Maggs Bros. Ltd. 1440 - 223 2011 £2500

Vollmann, William T. *Butterfly Stories.* London: Andre Detusch, 1993, Limited to 100 copies, true first edition; book fine, in slipcase. Bella Luna Books May 26 2011 - 6201 2011 $330

Vollmann, William T. *You Bright and Risen Angels.* New York: Atheneum, 1987, First edition; fine copy, in near fine dust jacket with very light edge wear, drawing by author, inscribed by author. Bella Luna Books May 29 2011 - 2510 2011 $137

Vollmann, William T. *You Bright and Risen Angels.* London: Andre Deutsch, 1987, First British edition, true first; fine in fine dust jacket. Bella Luna Books May 26 2011 - j2149 2011 $165

Voltaire, Francois Marie Arouet De 1694-1778 *Candide...* Geneva: 1759, 12mo., full contemporary mottled French calf, spine expertly repaired at foot, tear to lower blank corner of A3 (pages 5/6) and lower blank corner of Ar (page 7/8) expertly repaired, tear to D7, just touching catchword, also repaired, these minor blemishes notwithstanding, remarkably fine, in contemporary binding of correct first edition. James S. Jaffe Rare Books May 26 2011 - 14139 2011 $85,000

Voltaire, Francois Marie Arouet De 1694-1778 *Candide ou l'Optimisme: Zadig: Jeannot Et Colin.* Paris: Editions Nilsson, n.d., 1928, 4to., 217 pages, pictorial wrappers, spine ends frayed, else fine and partially unopened, 6 stunning mounted pochoir plates highlighted in metallic silver by Robert Polack. Aleph-Bet Books, Inc. 95 - 437 2011 $200

Voltaire, Francois Marie Arouet De 1694-1778 *Letters Concerning the English Nation.* London: for C. Davis and A. Lyon, 1733, First edition; 8vo., (16), 253, (19) pages, fine, contemporary calf, gilt spine, small dampstain in upper inside corner of title, fading away over next few leaves, from the library of the Earls of Macclesfield at Shirburn Castle. Maggs Bros. Ltd. 1440 - 224 2011 £600

Voltaire, Francois Marie Arouet De 1694-1778 *Poem Upon the Lisbon Disaster.* Lincoln: Penmaen Press, 1977, First edition; quarto, copy #162 of 200 numbered copies of the special edition illustrated with 6 wood engravings by Lynd Ward, signed by artist, Lynd Ward, translator, Anthony Hecht, the translator and Arthur Wilson who wrote the introduction, wood engravings struck from blocks, there were also 100 deluxe copies and 200 trade copies, near fine in very good slipcase with light spotting. Charles Agvent 2010 Summer Miscellany - 62 2011 $125

Voltaire, Francois Marie Arouet De 1694-1778 *La Pucelle D'Orleans.* Londres: Paris, 1775, First enlarged edition; large 8vo., pages xv, (1), 447, (1), frontispiece and 21 engraved plates, all edges gilt, very crisp, fresh copy, contemporary full deep green morocco, red morocco spine lettering piece lettered in gilt, within gilt decorative compartments, triple gilt borders on each panel with fleur-de-lis devices at each corner, royal blue floral endpapers, slight signs of wear at head and foot of spine and outer corners, bookplate of George, Second Marquis of Milford Haven. Simon Finch Rare Books Zero - 407 2011 £3500

Voltaire, Francois Marie Arouet De 1694-1778 *Romances, Tales and Smaller Pieces.* London: printed for P. Dodsley, 1794, First edition; 2 volumes, pages (4) vii, (1) 9-340; (iv), 341, frontispiece, 23 engraved plates, all edges gilt, extremely bright, crisp copy, brown morocco, gilt ruled, gilt decoration and lettering to spine, red endpapers by Riviere, light spotting to boards. Simon Finch Rare Books Zero - 265 2011 £600

Voltaire, Francois Marie Arouet De 1694-1778 *Therese. A Fragment.* Cambridge: for Presentation to members of the Roxburghe Club, 1981, 286 x 210mm., 4 p.l., 20 pages, maroon morocco over light brown cloth boards, top edge and titling on spine in gilt, four facsimiles leaves (printed recto and verso), bookplate of Frederick Baldwin Adams, Jr., and this copy originally prepared for Adams (his name printed in red in the Roxburghe list a way of indicating this), extremely fine. Phillip J. Pirages 59 - 305 2011 $125

Voltaire, Francois Marie Arouet De   1694-1778
Oeuvres Completes.   Kehl: De L'Imprimerie de la Societe Litteraire Typographique, 1784,   230 x 145mm., 69 volumes, exceptionally attractive contemporary flamed calf, covers with gilt braided border, flat spines with six compartments, each compartment with bands above and below consisting of gilt Greek key roll flanked by triple gilt rules, 3 compartments with large sunburst centerpiece within a circular wreath, other compartments with morocco labels, two conventional titling labels of red and olive green and circular volume number label of dark blue within a beaded collar, turn-ins with leafy foliate gilt stamps, marbled endpapers, edges painted yellow, 2 engraved portraits and 14 plates, front pastedown of each volume with at least faint vestiges of removed bookplate (usually hardly noticeable), front flyleaf of each volume with modern two-line ownership stamp of Silke Montague; 2 volumes with hints of now erased pencil annotations on many leaves (3 other volumes with lesser numbers of such erased penciled notes), 3 consecutive leaves in one volume slightly discolored by minor spill, occasional gatherings with very slight overall browning (isolated signatures bit more noticeably affected, but never seriously so), final volume with light browning and foxing, other trivial imperfections, outstanding copy, bindings extraordinarily bright and virtually without wear, text remarkably fresh and clean.   Phillip J. Pirages   59 - 61 2011 $16,000

Von Breitschwert, Wilhelm Carl   *Neues Verwandlungs Bilderbuch: zur Unterhalltung und Belustigung der Heiteren Jugend.*   Esslingen: J. F. Schreiber, n.d. owner inscription, 1879, 4to., printed on rectos only, each page has full page color lithograph, cloth backed pictorial boards, writing on top margin of cover and some cover soil and edge rubbing, else very good, printed on rectos only, each page has full page color lithograph, there is an extra flap that when lifted and folded over, the consequences of bad behavior is revealed, rare.   Aleph-Bet Books, Inc. 95 - 285 2011 $1500

Von Mises, Ludwig   *Socialism: an Economic and Sociological Analysis.* London: Jonathan Cape, 1936, First edition; 8vo., pages 528, original publisher's black cloth lettered gilt at spine, handsome, very good or better copy with faint marking to boards.   Any Amount of Books May 26 2011 - A45450 2011 $461

Von Reuter, Florizel   *The Master from Afar.*   New York: Carlton Press, 1972, First edition; original cloth, dust jacket, extremities little worn, pages 400, presentation copy with 6 line inscription in author's hand on flyleaf dated 1972. R. F. G. Hollett & Son Antiquarian Booksellers   175 - 13 83 2011   £35

Von Vogt, Alfred Edward   *Empire of the Atom.* Chicago: Shasta Publishers, 1957, First edition; octavo, boards. L. W. Currey, Inc.   124 - 195 2011 $225

Vonnegut, Kurt   *Cat's Cradle.*   New York: Chicago: San Francisco, Holt, Rinehart and Winston, 1963, Advance copy (uncorrected proof) of the First edition; octavo, blue wrappers printed in black, spiral bound with white plastic spine.   L. W. Currey, Inc.   124 - 2 2011 $7500

Vonnegut, Kurt   *Cat's Cradle.*   New York: Holt, Rinehart and Winston, 1963, First edition, first issue; signed by author, octavo, (4), (1-233, (3, blank) pages, original full green cloth with blue panel along fore-edge of front board, stamped and lettered in gilt and blue on front board and spine, top edge green, publisher's original, pictorial dust jacket, slightest amount of chipping and rubbing to spine and top edge of jacket, small one inch closed fold tear on back panel, overall about fine in very good or better dust jacket.   Heritage Book Shop   Holiday 2010 - 127 2011 $4500

Vonnegut, Kurt   *Cat's Cradle.*   New York: Chicago: San Francisco: Holt, Rinehart and Winston, 1963,   First edition; octavo, three quarter cloth and boards.   L. W. Currey, Inc. 124 - 18 2011 $3000

Vonnegut, Kurt   *Welcome to the Monkey House: A Collection of Short Works.*   New York: A. Seymour Lawrence Book Delacorte Press, 1968, Advance copy, uncorrected proof of first edition; tall octavo, salmon wrappers printed in black, spiral bound with white plastic spine, advance.   L. W. Currey, Inc.   124 - 9 2011 $4500

Voorsanger, Jacob   *The Chronicles of Emanu-El: Being an Account of the Rise and Progress...* San Francisco: George Spaulding, 1900, First edition; very scarce, pages 169, (1), xxi, frontispiece, 24 photo plates, handsomely rebound in full polished calf, gilt, very fine.   Argonaut Book Shop Recent Acquisitions Summer 2010 - 226 2011 $750

Vostell, Wolf   *Fantastic Architecture.*   Something Else Press, 1969, First English edition; 8vo., near fine in dust jacket, scarce.   Ken Spelman Rare Books   68 - 133 2011   £40

Vredenburg, Edric   *Tinker, Tailor.* London: Tuck, 1914, 4to., cloth backed pictorial boards, pictorial paste-on (144), cloth backed pictorial boards, pictorial paste on, (144) pages, tips rubbed, near fine, 12 fabulous color plates, very scarce.   Aleph-Bet Books, Inc. 95 - 581 2011 $1875

Vreeland, Frank   *Dishonoured.* London: Readers Library Publishing Co., n.., 1931, First British edition; small 8vo., pages 253, patterned boards slightly rubbed, faintly marked otherwise very good in very good dust jacket with few small closed tears, excellent condition, neat name on front pastedown.   Any Amount of Books   May 29 2011 - A44801 2011 $255

W

Waagen, Gustav Friedrich *Works of Art and Artists in England.* London: John Murray, 1838, First edition; 3 volumes, 12mo., slight spotting to prelims, very occasional red ink underlining in volume III, attractively bound in slightly later half dark blue calf, red morocco labels, marbled boards, booklabels of J. M. Mackie, student of Christ Church, very good. Jarndyce Antiquarian Booksellers CXCI - 599 2011 £250

Waddington, George *Journal of a Visit to Some Parts of Ethiopia.* London: John Murray, 1822, First edition; quarto, pages (vi) (i) blank, 333, (1) imprint, (2) ads, 16 lithographic plates and plans, 2 folding engraved maps (slight foxing), contemporary brown diced calf, recently rebacked with raised boards and red morocco labels. J. & S. L. Bonham Antiquarian Booksellers Africa 4/20/2011 - 5580 2011 £550

Waddy, Edith *The Father of Methodism. A Sketch of the Life and Labours of the Rev. J. Wesley.* Wesleyan Conference Office, n.d. circa, 1872, First edition; small 8vo., original brown blindstamped cloth gilt, pages viii, 120, with full page woodcut plates, very scarce. R. F. G. Hollett & Son Antiquarian Booksellers General Catalogue Summer 2010 - 474 2011 £65

Wade, John *The Extraordinary Black Book, an Exposition of Abuses in Church and State, Courts of Law, Representation, Municipal and Corporate Bodies...* London: published by Effingham Wilson, 1832, 8vo., engraved frontispiece, xxx, 683, (1) pages, contemporary dark blue half calf, spine gilt with raised bands and label, fine. John Drury Rare Books 153 - 166 2011 £150

Wade, John *The Extraordinary Black Book: an Exposition of Abuses in Church and State...* London: Effingham Wilson, 1832, Pages xxxii, 684, engraved frontispiece rather spotted, joints just cracking, title little browned, otherwise very good. R. F. G. Hollett & Son Antiquarian Booksellers 175 - 21385 2011 £150

Wade, John *History of the Middle & Working Classes.* New York: Augustus M. Kelley, 1966, Facsimile edition; original cloth, gilt, pages xx, 640, frontispiece. R. F. G. Hollett & Son Antiquarian Booksellers 175 - 1386 2011 £35

Wafer, Lionel *A New Voyage and Description of the Isthmus of America, giving an Account of the Author's Abode there...* London: for James Knatpon, 1699, First edition; (8), 224, (16) pages, engraved folded map, 3 folding plates, 19th century morocco, hinges and extremities scuffed, very faint toning to edges of text, else excellent internally, Wolfgang Herz bookabel. Joseph J. Felcone Inc. Fall Miscellany 2010 - 123 2011 $2400

Wagner, Anthony *Medieval Pageant.* London: by Bernard Quaritch Ltd. for the Roxburghe Club, 1993, 470 x 356mm., 5 p.l., xiii-xxi, (i) 100 pages, (1) leaf, tan quarter morocco over blue buckram boards, vellum tips, top edge and titling on spine in gilt, with 79 mostly full page illustrations, bookplate of Frederick Baldwin Adams Jr. and this copy originally prepared for Adams (his name printed in red in the Roxburghe list as a way of indicating this), very fine. Phillip J. Pirages 59 - 306 2011 $950

Wagner, Henry Raup 1862-1957 *The Cartography of the Northwest Coast of America to the Year 1800.* Mansfield Center: Maurizio Martino, 1999, Second reprint edition; 543 pages, quarto, 2 volumes in one, 40 maps, including 11 foldouts, original cloth, mint. Argonaut Book Shop Recent Acquisitions Summer 2010 - 227 2011 $125

Wagner, Henry Raup 1862-1957 *Henry R. Wagner's the Plains and The Rockies...* San Francsico: 1937, Limited to 600 copies, fourth edition; (viii, 299 pages, illustrations, spine and title block faded, small owner's name on front pastedown, else very good. Dumont Maps & Books of the West 111 - 85 2011 $95

Wagner, Henry Raup 1862-1957 *Spanish Explorations in the Strait of Juan De.* Santa Ana: Fine Arts Press, 1933, First edition, #7 of special illustrated edition of 25 signed copies, from a total first printing of 425; original vellum, 323 pages, 13 maps and plans of which 6 are large folding plates or maps, Special Illustrated Edition has 12 extra illustrations, 6 of which are reproduced from Atlas of the Viage and Repertorio of the Museo Naval, minor professional repair to top of spine and small spot on rear panel, else clean, near fine, rare, custom slipcase. Buckingham Books May 26 2011 - 28354 2011 $3250

Wagstaffe, William *The Character of Richard St-le Esq. with Some Remarks.* London: printed for J. Morphew near Stationers Hall, 1713, First edition; (4), 32, 1 f. blank, with half title, engraved frontispiece, 8vo. in fours, fine, clean, crisp, frontispiece very slightly shaved, full polished calf by Riviere, gilt fillet borders, gilt panelled spine, red gilt morocco labels, all edges gilt. Jarndyce Antiquarian Booksellers CXCI - 498 2011 £280

Wagstaffe, William *The State and Condition of our Taxes, Considered or a Proposal for a Tax Upon Funds.* London: John Morphew, 1714, First edition; 8vo. in half sheets, 46 pages, including half title, light waterstain in gutter of a few leaves, recently bound in cloth backed marbled boards, gilt green morocco label on upper board, very good.   John Drury Rare Books   153 - 167 2011   £250

Wailes, Rex *The English Windmill.* London: Routledge & Kegan Paul, 1954, First edition; tall 8vo., original blue cloth gilt, trifle marked, dust jacket (little faded, tear taped, price clipped), pages xxiii, 246, with 32 pages of plates and 65 figres.   R. F. G. Hollett & Son Antiquarian Booksellers   177 - 872 2011   £35

Wain, Louis *Cat's Cradle. A Picture Book for Little Folk.* London: Blackie, n.d. circa, 1908, Small 4to., grey pictorial paper boards, dark grey endpapers, 6 full page color Wain illustrations, backstrip worn, paper separated from boards slightly at spine and is slightly chipped, else sound near very good copy, rubbed at corners and lower edges but with very clean text and illustrations.   Any Amount of Books   May 29 2011 - A72284 2011 $408

Wain, Louis *Des Chats a Travers Le Monde. (Cats Across the World - issued in English as Cats of Many Lands).* Paris: Rapahel Tuck & Fils, circa, 1912, Tall 4to., full color pictorial limp boards, some dusting and light wear along spine, 14 pages within (counting inside covers), 8 of the pages in full color and others in two color (black and blue).   Jo Ann Reisler, Ltd.   86 - 261 2011 $2000

Wain, Louis *Flossy and Fluffy.* London: Valentine & Sons, Ltd., 1919, 11 x 6 1/2 inches, full color stiff paper covers cut around shape of pussy cats, slight folds but in overall nice condition, 16 pages of text and illustrations in black and red, seven full pages of illustrations in black and red and one black and white chapter heading.   Jo Ann Reisler, Ltd.   86 - 262 2011 $750

Wake, Robert *Southwold and Its Vicinity, Ancient and Modern.* Yarmouth: F. Skill, 1839, First edition; 8vo., half red leather marbled boards, attractively bound with gilt decoration at spine and 5 raised bands, pages xviii, 420, 5 folding illustrations, cover sound and clean, very good+, endpapers slightly spotted, occasional tape repair to charts, overall excellent condition.   Any Amount of Books   May 29 2011 - A61720 2011 $383

Wake, William *The Excellency and Benefits of a Religious Education. (bound with) The Methods Used for Erecting Charity Schools...* printed by J. Downing for R. Sare, 1715, First edition and fourteenth edition; modern half calf gilt with marbled boards, pages 43; 16, 33-36, (iv), typographic head and tailpieces and initials, uncut.   R. F. G. Hollett & Son Antiquarian Booksellers   175 - 1388 2011   £175

Wakefield, D. R. *Alphabet of Extinct Mammals.* Poole, East Yorkshire: Chevington Press, 2009, One of 55 copies; all on Somerset satin white mould made paper, each copy signed and numbered by Wakefield, page size 11 x 15 inches, 70 pages, 4 of which are double page foldouts etching of extinct mammal, bound by Gray Parrot, gold morocco spine with fabulous green and gold pastepaper over boards, title in gilt on spine, binder's ticket on lower rear turn-in, Wakefield has printed in color 26 etchings plus frontispiece etching with accompanying text, hand set in 12 pt. Plantin, on an early Ullmer and Watts Ablion Press.   Priscilla Juvelis - Rare Books   48 - 27 2011 $3000

Wakefield, Dan *Island in the City.* Boston: Houghton Mifflin, 1959, First printing; 8vo., pages 278, very good in chipped and soiled dust jacket.   Second Life Books Inc.   174 - 317 2011 $75

Wakefield, Gilbert *An Examination of the Age of Reason by Thomas Paine.* London: sold by Kearsley and Shepperson and Reynolds, 1794, 8vo., (2), 72, (3), 60-66 pages, paper generally little age browned, very slight foxing on last couple of leaves, well bound recently in linen backed marbled boards, lettered, good.   John Drury Rare Books   153 - 168 2011   £125

Wakefield, Herbert Russell *The Clock Strikes Twelve.* Sauk City: Arkham House, 1946, First US edition; octavo, cloth.   L. W. Currey, Inc.   124 - 41 2011 $1750

Wakefield, Priscilla *An Introduction to Botany, in a Series of Familiar Letters...* London: printed by and for Darton & Harvey, 1803, Third edition; 12mo., xi plates, uncut in original turquoise glazed paper boards, slightly rubbed, slight cracking to lower corner of front board, booklabel removed, otherwise very nice.   Jarndyce Antiquarian Booksellers   CXCI - 355 2011 £75

Wakeman, Geoffrey *English Marbled Papers: a Documentary History.* Loughborough: Plough Press, 1978, First edition, no. 83 of 112 copies; 8vo., original publisher's quarter dark blue leather lettered gilt on spine, pages 27 (text) and 26 samples tipped in, faint soiling, very slight marks, otherwise fine.   Any Amount of Books   May 29 2011 - 64760 2011 $383

Walbran, Francis M. *Grayling and How to Catch Them and Recollections of a Sportsman.* Flyfisher's Classic Library, 2004, Full crimson morocco gilt, slipcase, pages xxviii, (ii), 142, (i), top edge gilt, with 8 illustrations, marbled endpapers and silk marker, fine.   R. F. G. Hollett & Son Antiquarian Booksellers   General Catalogue Summer 2010 - 1304 2011   £65

Waldor, Melanie *Poesies du Coeur.*   Paris: Louis Janet, 1835, First edition; (315 pages, including errata), 8vo., contemporary quarter brown calf over matching marbled boards, gilt decorated spine with floral design, contrasting gilt lettered title label, half title, scarce wood engraved frontispiece and title vignette by Jean Gigoux, except for light waterstain on margin to some sheets and small chip to lower spine edge, near fine copy, with ALS to Edouard Monnais.   Paulette Rose Fine and Rare Books   32 - 1182   2011 $400

Walford, Cornelius *Fairs, Past and Present: a Chapter in the History of Commerce.*   London: Elliot Stock, 1883, Deluxe edition; original quarter roan gilt, head of spine trifle frayed, pages x, 318, (ii), top edge gilt gilt in rough, untrimmed.   R. F. G. Hollett & Son Antiquarian Booksellers   175 - 1389   2011   £140

Walker, Alice   1944-   *Possessing the Secret of Joy.*   New York: HBJ, 1992, Limited to 250 numbered copies; book is fine, signed by author.   Bella Luna Books   May 29 2011 - j2140   2011 $137

Walker, Alice   1944-   *The Complete Stories.*   London: Women's Press, 1994, First British edition; near fine, light bumping to spine ends, dust jacket is near fine, corresponding creasing.   Bella Luna Books   May 29 2011 - t6847   2011 $110

Walker, Alice   1944-   *The Third Life of Grange Copeland.*   New York: Harcourt Brace, 1970, First edition; near fine, light wear, no major defects, dust jacket fine, signed by author.   Bella Luna Books   May 26 2011 - t3874   2011 $770

Walker, Eric A.   *W. P. Schreiner: a South African.*   Oxford: University Press, 1937, First edition; 8vo., pages xii, 386, 6 plates, original red cloth, spine slightly faded, presentation copy to A. F. Russell from author's son.   J. & S. L. Bonham Antiquarian Booksellers   Africa 4/20/2011 - 5166   2011   £45

Walker, J.   *The History of Penrith from the Earliest Period to the Present Time.*   Penrith: B. T. Sweeten, 1858, Third edition; pages (viii), 243, engraved frontispiece, half pebble grained morocco gilt with marbled boards.   R. F. G. Hollett & Son Antiquarian Booksellers   173 - 1153   2011   £120

Walker, J.   *The History of Penrith, from the Earliest Period to the Present Time.*   Penrith: Hodgson, circa, 1870, Second edition; (4), 180 pages, folding frontispiece and plates, contemporary dark blue half calf, marbled boards, gilt bands, red morocco label, some browning and foxing to contents.   Ken Spelman Rare Books   68 - 184   2011   £50

Walker, J. U.   *History of Wesleyan Methodism in Halifax an Its Vicinity.*   Halifax: Hartley & Walker, 1836, First edition; original watered cloth with paper spine label, rather rubbed, head of spine little chipped, pages viii, 279, scarce.   R. F. G. Hollett & Son Antiquarian Booksellers   General Catalogue Summer 2010 - 1204   2011   £120

Walker, John   *A Critical Pronouncing Dictionary and Expositor of the English Language.*   New York: 1839, 609, 103 pages, pages well browned but completely legible, rebound in serviceable cloth, thus tight, bound with A Key to the Classical Pronunciation of Greek, Latin and Scripture Proper Names by the same author.   Dumont Maps & Books of the West   111 - 118   2011 $65

Walker, Margaret   *For My People.*   New York: Limited Editions Club, 1992, First edition; one of 400 numbered copies signed by author and artist, 6 bound in unsigned hors-texte original color lithographs by Elizabeth Catlett, housed in handsome folding cloth box, overall size 22.5 x 18.5 inches, new condition, LEC letter laid in.   Gemini Fine Books & Arts, Ltd.   Art Reference & Illustrated Books: First Editions 2011 $1700

Walker, Mary Willis   *The Red Scream.*   New York: Doubleday, 1994, First edition; fine, signed by author, dust jacket fine.   Bella Luna Books   May 29 2011 - j1262   2011 $82

Walkingame, Francis   *The Tutor's Assistant: Being a Compendium of Arithmetic and a Complete Question Book.*   Gainsborough: Henry Mozley, 1801, New edition; contemporary full blindstamped calf, little worn and hinges cracking, pages (vi), 172, folding table frontispiece (edges rather worn), joints cracked.   R. F. G. Hollett & Sons Antiquarian Booksellers   170 - 709   2011   £45

Wall, Bernard   *Colosseum.*   J. Miles, then Sheed & Ward, 1934-1939, First edition; nos. 1-15, 17, 18, 20, together 18 issues in original wrappers, very good.   I. D. Edrich   May 26 2011 - 98034   2011 $419

Wallace, Alfred Russel   1823-1913   *Australasia.* London: Edward Stanford, 1879, First edition; 8vo., pages xix, 672, copiously illustrated in black and white, many folding color maps, original publisher's green cloth lettered and decorated gilt on spine and cover, endpapers appear to be stuck down, so half title is first page, inner front hinge slightly cracked, covers little mottled and scuffed, otherwise sound, decent, very good, folding maps in good condition.   Any Amount of Books   May 29 2011 - A67625   2011 $374

Wallace, Alfred Russel 1823-1913 *Contributions to the Theory of Natural Selection.* London: Macmillan & Co., 1870, 43 page catalog (Jan. 1870), small tear to upper edge of titlepage, one or two gatherings slightly loose, pencil signature, original green cloth, slightly rubbed, inner hinges little weak.   Jarndyce Antiquarian Booksellers   CXCI - 342   2011   £750

Wallace, Edgar *The Four Just Men.* Tallis Press, 1905, First edition; folding frontispiece, the competition slip (no. 7013) present at end, owner's name and date "Xmas 1905" on half title, pages 224 (slip), frontispiece 8vo., original pale yellow cloth, faded backstrip and front cover printed in black, covers slightly soiled, hinges cracked, good.   Blackwell Rare Books   B166 - 236   2011   £100

Wallace, Robert *Elements of Geometry or a New and Compendious Demonstration of the First six books of Euclid...* Glasgow: Richard Griffin and Co. and London: Thomas Tegg, 1825, First edition; 12mo., pages (iv) blank, viii, 88, 2 folding plates, (4) blank, blue ribbon bookmark attached, occasional spotting but fresh copy, red morocco, upper and lower boards decorated in gilt with gilt lettering and decoration to spine and all edges gilt, blue endpapers, slightly rubbed at extremities, slight dampstaining to front endpapers, bookplate and label to front pastedown and traces of bookplate to front free endpaper, presentation inscription to initial blank, news cutting about Henry Brougham, loosely inserted, excellent copy.   Simon Finch Rare Books   Zero - 126   2011   £225

Wallace, W. *Alton Moor: Its Pastoral People: its Mines and Miners, from the Earliest Periods to Recent Times.* Newcastle upon Tyne: Davis Books, 1986, Facsimile edition; original cloth, gilt, dust jacket, pages viii, 213, (vii), folding map, illustrations.   R. F. G. Hollett & Son Antiquarian Booksellers   173 - 1155   2011   £35

Wallenstein, Abraham *Jews & Germanism.* London: 1918, First edition; original binding, 14 pages.   Bookworm & Silverfish   664 - 106   2011 $75

Waller, Erik *Bibliotheca Walleriana.* Stockholm: Almqvist & Wiksell, 1955, Limited to 100 copies; 2 volumes 8vo., xi, (xii), 471; 494 pages, frontispiece with facsimile signature, two color title printed in brown and black, 55 plates, original printed wrapper, like new in original shipping box, from the Medical Library of Dr. Clare Gray Peterson.   Jeff Weber Rare Books   162 - 266   2011 $150

Waller, George *Kidnap. The Story of the Lindberg Case.* New York: Dial Press, 1961, First edition; original two-tone cloth, pages 597, 31 illustrations, 2 plans.   R. F. G. Hollett & Son Antiquarian Booksellers   175 - 1390   2011   £30

Waller, J. F. *Inauguration Ode Performed at the Opening of the National Exhibiton Cork 1852.* Cork: Bradford, 1852, Titlepage, 4 pages text, 32 pages music, quarter cloth, signed by Robert Stewart.   C. P. Hyland   May 26 2011 - 259/84   2011 $507

Waller, S. E. *Six Weeks in the Saddle: a Painter's Journal in Iceland.* London: Macmillan, 1874, Small octavo, 177 pages, frontispiece, title vignette, 14 illustrations, modern full calf, fine, rare.   Jeff Weber Rare Books   163 - 223   2011 $100

Walling, Henry F. *New Atlas of the State of Pennsylvania with Descriptions Historical, Scientific and Statistical.* Philadelphia: Stedman, Brown & Lyon, 1872, First edition; folio, original cloth, gilt lettering on cover, 110 (28) pages, marbled endpapers, maps, cover blind tooled except for front title which is gilt stamped, pages rebacked with new leather spine laid down, some page edges and corners professionally reinforced, leather corners replaced, else very good, tight copy.   Buckingham Books   May 26 2011 - 22633   2011 $1750

Wallis, Isaac Henry *Frederick Andrews of Ackworth.* London: Longmans, Green and Co., 1924, First edition; original blue cloth gilt, pages ix, 325, 26 plates.   R. F. G. Hollett & Son Antiquarian Booksellers   General Catalogue Summer 2010 - 475   2011   £30

Wallis, John *Operum Mathematicorum Pars Prima Qua Contenentur, Oratio Inauguralis. Mathesis Universalis sive Arithemeticum Opus Integrum, tum Numerosam Arithemticam.* Oxford: Leon. Lichfield for Tho(mas) Robinson, 1657, First edition; 3 parts in one volume, small 4to., pages (40); 1-119, 122-398 (complete but misnumbered after 119; O3 misprinted as P3); (ii), 50, 62, (2), numerous woodcut diagrams in text, sporadic light soiling, otherwise very clean, contemporary vellum, title in early manuscript to spine, upper hinge slightly weakened, excellent, unsophisticated copy.   Simon Finch Rare Books   Zero - 105   2011   £2750

Wallis, John *A Treatise of Algebra, Both Historical and Practical.* London: printed by John Playford for Richard Davis, 1685, First edition; folio, pages (xx), 33, 36-374 (some misnumbered), (iv), 17, (1) blank; (ii), 176 (last two pages misnumbered 75 and 76), extra leaf (repetition of 93-4); (ii), 17 (leaf 5-6 out of sequence), (i) blank, 10 folding plates, title to part 1 foxed, trimmed at foot with loss of inscription, light waterstaining to part 2, clean tear to one leaf with no loss, occasional spotting throughout but nonetheless a bright, crisp copy, sprinkled calf, worn at extremities, some rubbing, joints repaired, 3 leaves of early notes, very good.   Simon Finch Rare Books   Zero - 110   2011   £6000

Walpole, Horace 1719-1797 *A Catalogue of the Royal and Noble Authors of England.* Twickenham: printed at Strawberry Hill, 1758, First edition, second state (A2 verso, line 3 reads "to have a bias" rather than "to be partial"; 8vo., 2 volumes, vignette titlepage and Grignion frontispiece very slightly browned, otherwise clean but disbound, wide margins, rubbed leather spines preserved, ideal for rebinding.   Any Amount of Books   May 29 2011 - A72899   2011 $374

Walpole, Horace 1719-1797 *The Letters of Horace Walpole, Earl of Orford.* London: Richard Bentley, 1858-1859, First edition; 9 volumes, 8vo., sound modern red cloth lettered gilt on spine, pages 5049, with 40 plates, ex-Foreign and Commonwealth Office Library, very good.   Any Amount of Books   May 29 2011 - A60910   2011 $874

Walpole, Horace 1719-1797 *Letters to Sir Horace Mann British Envoy at the Court of Tuscany...* London: Richard Bentley, 1833, Second edition; 3 volumes, original boards with paper spine labels, backstrips rather defective and cracked, pages lvi, 400; 450; 434, complete with 3 half titles and engraved portrait (foxed).   R. F. G. Hollett & Son Antiquarian Booksellers   175 - 1392   2011   £150

Walsh, J. H. *British Rural Sports: Comprising Shooting, Hunting, Coursing, Fishing, Hawking, Racing, Boating, Pedestrianism with all Rural Games an Amusements.* London: Routledge Warne & Routledge, 1859, Fourth edition; thick small 8vo., original roan backed boards, spine chipped and torn at head, pages x, vi, 720, numerous full page woodcut plates and text illustrations, joints cracked.   R. F. G. Hollett & Son Antiquarian Booksellers   General Catalogue Summer 2010 - 1305   2011   £180

Walsh, John Evangelist *The Bones of St. Peter.* London: Gollancz, 1983, First edition; original cloth, gilt, dust jacket, pages (xii), 195, with 32 plates and 13 text illustrations, fine.   R. F. G. Hollett & Son Antiquarian Booksellers   175 - 1393   2011   £50

Walsh, William *Dialogue Concerning Woman, Being a Defence of the Sex.* London: R. Bentley and J. Tonson, 1691, First edition; 8vo., pages (viii) 1-134, (2 blank), contemporary calf, neatly speckled, worn along hinge, spine stamping worn off.   Second Life Books Inc.   174 - 318   2011 $7500

Walsh, William *Discours sur Les Femmes, Addresse a Eugenie et Suivi d'un Dialogue Philosophique & Moral sur le Bonheur.* Amsterdam: et se trouve Paris: Chez la Veuve Duchesne, 1768, First French edition; 8vo., pages (iii) 3-179, contemporary French calf, spine gilt, may lack front flyleaf, some light waterstain to margins, very nice tight copy.   Second Life Books Inc.   174 - 319   2011 $650

Walter L. Main's Great Circus Songster.   New York: New York Popular Publishing circa, 1887, Small 8vo., pink pictorial wrappers, stapled, moderate creasing to covers, two very short closed tears to fore-edge margins.   Dramatis Personae Booksellers   106 - 115   2011 $65

Walter, William *A Discourse Delivered before the Humane Society of Massachusetts at the Semi-annual Meeting Twelfth of June 1798.* Boston: printed by John & Thomas Fleet, 1798, First edition; small 4to., 48, (2) (blank leaf) pages, half title, sewn as issued, small blank piece missing from half title, edges slightly frayed, contemporary signature of Joseph Peirce at top of half title.   M & S Rare Books, Inc.   90 - 433   2011 $325

Walters, Eurof *The Serpent's Presence.* Waltha St. Lawrence: Golden Cockerel Press, 1954, 45/60 copies (of an edition of 290 copies); printed on mouldmade paper, 8 wood engravings, (v) (blanks), 106, (6) (blanks), 8vo., original quarter apple green morocco, pink buckram sides, lettering to faded backstrip and Webb design on front cover all gilt blocked, matching apple green morocco fore edges, top edge gilt, others untrimmed, near fine.   Blackwell Rare Books   B166 - 263   2011   £100

Walters, H. B. *Church Bells of England.* London: Oxford University Press, 1912, First edition; original blue cloth gilt, spine lettering rather dulled, pages xx, 400, (iv), with 170 illustrations.   R. F. G. Hollett & Son Antiquarian Booksellers   177 - 873   2011   £95

Walters, H. B. *Select Bronzes, Greek, Roman and Etruscan in the Departments of Antiquities.* London: Trustees of the British Museum, 1915, First edition; fat 4to., original publisher's brown moire cloth lettered gilt on spine and on front cover, pages 9, 73 plates with accompanying text and tissue guards, sound, clean, bright, near fine.   Any Amount of Books   May 29 2011 - A47325   2011 $340

Walters, Minette *The Sculptress.* London: Macmillan, 1993, First British edition; fine, fine dust jacket.   Bella Luna Books   May 26 2011 - j1001   2011 $192

Walton, Izaak 1593-1683 *The Compleat Angler; or Contemplative Man's Recreation...* London: by Henry Kent, 1759, Seventh edition; xxiv, 340, (8) pages, woodcuts in text, 10 engraved plates by H. Burgh contemporary mottled calf, very skillfully rebacked in period style retaining original spine label, offsetting from plates, else fine, fresh and quite handsome copy, armorial bookplate.   Joseph J. Felcone Inc.   Fall Miscellany 2010 - 125   2011 $1400

Walton, Izaak 1593-1683 *The Complete Angler.* London: Bell and Daldy, 1864, old half calf, gilt, trifle marked and scuffed, pages xvi, 304, top edges gilt, 2 engraved plates and 13 text woodcuts.   R. F. G. Hollett & Son Antiquarian Booksellers   General Catalogue Summer 2010 - 1306   2011   £65

Walton, Izaak 1593-1683 *The Compleat Angler or the Contemplative Man's Recreation.* London: Hodder & Stoughton, 1911, Hodder's first trade edition; quarto, xvi, 166, (1) pages, 25 plates tipped in on green paper, each plate with descriptive tissue guards, original green cloth from front cover bound in at back, beautifully bound by Bayntun Riviere for Asprey in full black morocco, boards ruled in gilt, inner rule with floral corners, front board with mutiple colors of morocco inlays to create shape of a fisherman, rear board with central gilt device, spine elaborately stamped and lettered gilt, all edges gilt, gilt dentelles, marbled endpapers, Bayntun Riviere stamped in blind on dentelles, Asprey stamped in gilt on lower edge of back pastedown, some very light foxing to text, plates very clean, previous owner's small leather bookplate, near fine, green cloth slipcase. Heritage Book Shop   Holiday 2010 - 124 2011 $2000

Walton, Izaak 1593-1683 *The Compleat Angler or the Contemplative Man's Recreation.* London: George G. Harrp, 1931, One of 775 copies signed by artist; 207 x 200mm., 223, (1) pages, original vellum covered boards, gilt titling and decoration on front cover an spine, top edge gilt, other edges untrimmed, unopened, illustrated titlepage and endpapers, 24 illustrations in text and 12 color plates (including frontispiece) all by Arthur Rackham, 3 miniscule dots near top of spine, else virtually faultless copy, rare thus, especially because vellum soils so easily. Phillip J. Pirages   59 - 297   2011 $2100

Walton, Izaak 1593-1683 *Universal Angler, Made so by Three Books of Fishing.* London: 1676, 3 volumes bound as one, small 8vo., early leather with new backstrip and endpaper, all edges gilt circular bookplate of Edward Utterson remounted on new endpaper, music and pictorial copper plates (in text) are complete and book is very free of foxing, titlepage to part one mended chip to free margin not affecting text, bottom edge clipped below "London", free edge with some fraying and precedes "Universal" titlepage, top edge of some leaves ahved to touch running titles, page 195 with small chip affecting extreme letter of bottom line, this copy enchanced with two inserted folding maps (Hampshire & Derbyshire). Bookworm & Silverfish 671 - 175 2011 $4500

Walworth, Jeanette H. *Southern Silhouetttes.* New York: 1887, First edition; good in CSA gray cloth, backstrip darkened, backstrip ends chafed, 38" top and bottom. Bookworm & Silverfish   668 - 151   2011 $75

Wandrei, Donald *Strange Harvest.* Sauk City: Arkham House, 1965, First edition; octavo, cloth. L. W. Currey, Inc.   124 - 235   2011 $100

Wandrei, Donald *The Web of Easter Island.* Sauk City: Arkham House, 1948, First edition; octavo, cloth. L. W. Currey, Inc.   124 - 169   2011 $350

Wanley, Nathaniel *The Wonders of the Little World; or a General History of Man.* London: printed for W. J. and J. Richardson, Otridge & Son, &c, 1806, 2 volumes, frontispiece and plates, text in two columns, index, handsome plain contemporary calf, gilt borders, armorial bookplates of W. S. & Wyndham Portal, very good. Jarndyce Antiquarian Booksellers   CXCI - 601 2011   £180

Wantrup, Jonathan *Australian Rare Books 1788-1900.* Sydney: Hordern House, Potts Point, 1987, First edition, limited to 125 numbered copies signed by Jonathan Wantrup; 8vo., pages x, 468, 32, copiously illustrated in black and white with color frontispiece tipped in, 2 volumes, printed slipcase, excellent, about fine condition with discreet collectors blindstamp in both volumes. Any Amount of Books   May 29 2011 - A76717 2011 $238

Ward, Elizabeth Stuart Pehlps *The Master of the Magicians.* London: William Heinemann, 1890, First edition; half title, 16 page catalog (May 1890), original dark green cloth blocked and lettered in gilt, slight rubbing to spine, H.P.B. Lodge library label and stamp, very good. Jarndyce Antiquarian Booksellers   CLXC - 748 2011   £40

Ward, Elizabeth Stuart Phelps 1815-1852 *The Silent Partner.* London: Sampson Low, Son & Marston, 1871, First UK edition; original blue decorated cloth, gilt extra over bevelled boards, corners trifle rubbed, pages 304, 16, all edges gilt, rear flyleaf removed, very scarce. R. F. G. Hollett & Son Antiquarian Booksellers   175 - 1054 2011 £85

Ward, Herbert *My Life with Stanley's Rear Guard.* London: Chatto & Windus, 1891, First edition; small 8vo., pages viii, 163, ads, map, original dark blue, decorative cloth, vignette (tropical tree) on upper cover, very good, rare. J. & S. L. Bonham Antiquarian Booksellers   Africa 4/20/2011 - 7436 2011   £850

Ward, Herbert *My Life with Stanley's Rear Guard.* London: Chatto & Windus, 1891, First edition; small 8vo., pages viii, 163, ads, map, recent red quarter morocco, original paper upper cover bound in at end of book. J. & S. L. Bonham Antiquarian Booksellers   Africa 4/20/2011 - 8694 2011   £550

Ward, James Arthur *The Man Haupt: a Biography of Herman Haupt.* Baton Rouge: Louisiana State University Press, 1973, 8vo., xvi, 278 pages, brown cloth, gilt stamped spine title, dust jacket, fine, from the Bern Dibner reference library, with Burndy bookplate. Jeff Weber Rare Books   161 - 195 2011 $75

Ward, Jean *The Medical Casebook of William Brownrigg, MD. FRS (1712-1800) of the Town of Whitehaven in Cumberland.* Wellcome Inst., 1993, First edition; large 8vo., original cloth, pages xxii, 176, 4 plates. R. F. G. Hollett & Son Antiquarian Booksellers   173 - 1160 2011 £35

Ward, John *Romano-British Buildings and Earthworks.* London: Methuen, 1911, First edition; original red cloth gilt, trifle worn, upper board creased, pages xi, 320, 8 (ads), numerous illustrations, scarce. R. F. G. Hollett & Son Antiquarian Booksellers 177 - 876 2011 £45

Ward, Lynd *Madman's Drum: a Novel in Woodcuts.* New York: Jonathan Cape, 1930, First edition; 8vo., pages not numbered, donor's presentation on blank, printed paper over boards, black cloth spine, very good in somewhat worn dust jacket. Second Life Books Inc. 174 - 320 2011 $400

Ward, Robert Plummer *Illustrations of Human Life.* London: Henry Colburn, 1837, First edition; pages viii, 359; viii, 324; (iv), 301, 8vo., contemporary dark green half morocco, backstrips panelled with gilt fillets and repeated leafy and drawer handle tools, marbled boards, slightly rubbed, all edges gilt, bookplates of Thomas Smith, good. Blackwell Rare Books B166 - 116 2011 £300

Ward, Rowland *A Naturalist's Life Study in the Art of Taxidermy.* London: Rowland Ward, 1913, First edition; 8vo., pages 227, frontispiece, 62 plates, original tan decorative cloth, label on upper board, rare. J. & S. L. Bonham Antiquarian Booksellers Africa 4/20/2011 - 9196 2011 £1100

Ward, Samuel *A Modern System of Natural History.* London: printed for F. Newbery, 1775-1776, First edition; 12 volumes in 6, 12mo. (printed in 6s) collating either (A)-(P6) or (b)-(Q6), 118 engraved plates, contemporary uniform half calf over marbled boards, red spine labels, bindings generally rather worn, joints cracked, spine of volume 6 with recent restoration, internally in good state of preservation, complete set. John Drury Rare Books 153 - 169 2011 £650

Warden, Florence, Pseud. *The Disappearance of Nigel Blair.* London: Ward Lock & Co., 1912, Half title, frontispiece and plate, 4 pages ads, original pictorial wrappers, very good. Jarndyce Antiquarian Booksellers CXCI - 373 2011 £45

Warden, Florence, Pseud. *The Visitor's Guide to Cambridge.* Cambridge: Metcalfe & Co., circa, 1898, Half title, frontispiece, plate, 2 pages ads, original pictorial wrappers, tear with slight loss to lower corner of front wrapper, slight mark to back wrapper, bright copy. Jarndyce Antiquarian Booksellers CXCI - 374 2011 £50

Wardle, Thomas *Select Works of the British Poets, from Falconer to Sir Walter Scott.* Thomas Wardle, 1838, First edition; half leather, marbled boards, gilt lines to spine, very good, light shelfwear, some foxing to endpapers and prelims, nice, tight copy. Lupack Rare Books May 26 2011 - ABE4633207498 2011 $100

Ware, Henry *Papers on the Diaries of William Nicolson, Sometime Bishop of Carlisle.* Kendal: Titus Wilson, 1905, Volumes 1, 2, 3, 4, and 5, contemporary full blind ruled roan gilt, head of spine little frayed, pages (ii), 236, 67, 78, 37 with separate title, 2 plates and 2 pages of facsimiles, very scarce. R. F. G. Hollett & Son Antiquarian Booksellers 173 - 1163 2011 £140

Warhol, Andy *Andy Warhol's Index (Book).* New York: Random House, 1967, First edition; quarto, black and white photo reproductions with pop-ups and fold-outs, most in color, black cloth over pictorial boards, front board with holographic design, spine printed in silver, book fine, as new, complete, having never been opened, publisher's "dust jacket" plastic bag, bag with original price sticker $12.95, bag with bit of wear and few small holes. Heritage Book Shop Holiday 2010 - 128 2011 $3500

Waring, George *The Squirrels and Other Animals; or Illustrations of the Habits and Instincts of Many of the Smaller British Quadrupeds.* London: Harvey and Darton, n.d. circa, 1840, Square 12mo., original cloth gilt, spine trifle rubbed and faded, neatly recased, pages 268, (iv), frontispiece (top margin repaired), title vignette and 6 full page woodcut vignettes (little spotting). R. F. G. Hollett & Sons Antiquarian Booksellers 170 - 714 2011 £65

Warner, Rex *Greeks and Trojans.* MacGibbon & Kee, 1951, First edition; original cloth, gilt, dust jacket price clipped, spine defective at head, taped on reverse, pages 192, with 9 full page line drawings by Bawden. R. F. G. Hollett & Son Antiquarian Booksellers General Catalogue Summer 2010 - 722 2011 £35

Warner, Susan B. *The Hills of the Shatemuc.* New York: 1856, First US edition; issue A (Juno) and binding 2 (author's last name), 516 (8 ads) pages, tight copy, embossed cloth, backstrip gilt legible, top edge frayed quarter inch, backstrip has one paper wafer at top and wafer ghost at bottom, missing two leaves of ads, ink # on titlepage. Bookworm & Silverfish 669 - 119 2011 $65

Warnow, Joan N. *Images of Einstein: a Catalog.* New York: Center for Physics American Institute of Physics, 1979, Second edition; oblong 8vo., 77 pages, printed wrappers, corners creased, very good, from the Bern Dibner reference library, with Burndy bookplate. Jeff Weber Rare Books 161 - 130 2011 $200

Warren, Edward *The Life of John Warren, M.D.* Boston: Noyes, Holmes and Co., 1874, First edition; 8vo., 15, 568 pages, index, frontispiece, original cloth, very scarce. M & S Rare Books, Inc. 90 - 436 2011 $250

Warren, G. K. *Explorations in the Country in the Year 1855.* Washington: A. O. P. Nicholson, Senate Printer, 1856, First edition; 8vo., bound in red quarter leather and red and black marbled paper over boards, titles stamped in gold on spine, raised bands, 79 pages (blank), vi pages of index, (blank), plus 3 folded maps, illustrations, appendices, index, the maps complete to detail with only minor wear, both text and maps in very good condition in fine binding. Buckingham Books   May 26 2011 - 28009 2011 $1875

Warren, Robert Penn   1905-1989   *Audubon: A Vision.* New York: Random House, 1969, First edition; number 212 of 250 copies signed by Robert Penn Warren, book fine, dust jacket very crisp and bright, with very slight corner crease, slipcase very close to fine.   Gemini Fine Books & Arts, Ltd.   Art Reference & Illustrated Books: First Editions 2011 $125

Warren, Robert Penn   1905-1989   *Selected Poems 1923-1975.* New York: Random House, 1975, First edition, number 23 of 250 copies; signed by author, fine in slipcase.   Gemini Fine Books & Arts, Ltd.   Art Reference & Illustrated Books: First Editions 2011 $75

Warren, Robert Penn   1905-1989   *New and Selected Poems 1923-1985.* New York: Random House, 1985, First edition; number 279 of 350 copies signed by Robert Penn Warren, fine in slipcase.   Gemini Fine Books & Arts, Ltd.   Art Reference & Illustrated Books: First Editions 2011 $70

Warren, Samuel   *The Works of Samuel Warren.*   William Blackwood & Sons, 1854, 5 volumes, title and frontispiece in volumes I, II & IV, uniformly bound in red morocco, gilt spines, brown morocco labels, red moire cloth boards, some slight rubbing, nice attractive set.   Jarndyce Antiquarian Booksellers   CXCI - 30 2011   £125

Warton, Thomas   *The Oxford Sausage.*   London: Longman, Hurst Rees, 1815, New edition; half title, frontispiece, vignette woodcuts, uncut in original drab boards carefully rebacked, little worn on corners.   Jarndyce Antiquarian Booksellers   CXCI - 602 2011   £65

Wascher-James, Sande   *In Your Hands.* Whidbey Island: 2010, Artist's book, one of 18 copies; all hand painted and digitally printed on Lutradur, designed and bound by Sande Wascher-James, signed and numbered by her on colophon, page size in shape of a hand 8 x 5.5 inches, hand shaped pages cut with Graphtec Robo cutter, 32 pages including covers, handsewn by artist in blue thread matching the Liberty of London floral fabric on which text and stamp images of women, especially Eleanor Roosevelt were collaged, scanned and then printed, housed in custom made box of pale blue handmade paper over boards with collage of stamp of Eleanor Roosevelt on lid.   Priscilla Juvelis - Rare Books   48 - 28 2011 $850

Washington, Booker T.   *The Future of the American Negro.* Boston: Small Maynard & Co., 1900, Second edition; spine slightly dulled, otherwise near fine, frontispiece.   Lupack Rare Books   May 26 2011 - ABE 3658730373 2011 $125

Wason, J. Cathcart   *East Africa and Uganda or Our Last Land.* London: Francis Griffiths, 1905, First edition; 8vo., pages 111, frontispiece, illustrations, original red cloth, very good.   J. & S. L. Bonham Antiquarian Booksellers Africa 4/20/2011 - 8274 2011   £100

Waterfield, Gordon   *Layard of Nineveh.* London: John Murray, 1963, First edition; original cloth, gilt, dust jacket, pages x, 535, with 59 illustrations, Mss. Layard genealogy on front pastedown.   R. F. G. Hollett & Son Antiquarian Booksellers   177 - 879 2011   £35

Waterhouse, Benjamin   *Cautions to Young Persons Concerning Health in a Public Lecture Delivered at the Close of the Medical Course in... Cambridge No. 20 1804....* Cambridge: University Press by W. Hilliard, 1805, 32 pages, contemporary marbled paper covers, printed paper label on upper cover, neatly bound in later cloth, light mostly marginal foxing, some spotting on label, else very good, wide margined copy.   Joseph J. Felcone Inc.   Fall Miscellany 2010 - 126 2011 $650

Waterhouse, John   *The Stone Circles of Cumbria.* London: Phillimore, 1985, First edition; small 4to., original cloth, gilt, dust jacket, pages xx, 167, 2ith 21 plates and numerous text figures, scarce.   R. F. G. Hollett & Son Antiquarian Booksellers   177 - 880 2011   £40

Waterland, Daniel   *A Critical History of the Athanasian Creed.* Cambridge: University Press for Corn. Crownfield, 1724, 8vo., pages xxiv, 533, (xi), Francis Hoffman headpiece on page 1, contemporary calf untooled spine, boards panelled in blind (Cambridge style), board edges decorative roll gilt, all edges red speckled, pale blue and white sewn endbands, replacement lettering piece, dampstain to lower corner at beginning and end, touch of wear to corners, repairs to spine ends, later ink inscription "Richard Troyle his book 1774" and below "Elizabeth Troyle" on final f.e.p. (inverted), from the collection of Christopher Ernest Weston 1947-2010.   Unsworths Booksellers   24 - 56 2011   £250

Waterland, Daniel   *Scripture Vindicated: in Answer to Book Intituled, Christianity as Old as the Creation.* London: printed for W. Innys, Cambridge printed for Cornelius Crownfield and John Crownfield, 1730-1731, 2 parts bound as 1, with collective half title, 8vo., pages (iv), 96, (iv), 160, disbound and subsequently (late 1980's) calf bound by Chris Weston, few minor spots, lower corner of first leaf worn, from the collection of Christopher Ernest Weston 1947-2010.   Unsworths Booksellers   24 - 57 2011   £150

Waterland, Daniel *A Second Vindication of Christ's Divinity or a Second Defense of Some Queries Relating to Dr. Clarke's Scheme of the Holy Trinity...* London: for W. and J. Innys and Corn. Crownfield, 1723, 8vo., pages xxiv, 533, (xi), headpiece on p. 1, contemporary calf, boards panelled in blind (Cambridge style), board edges decorative roll gilt, all edges sprinkled red, early 21st calf reback and corners by Chris Weston, touch of marginal dust soiling, old leather slightly rubbed at edges.   Unsworths Booksellers   24 - 55   2011   £150

The Waters of the Earth. London: Religious Tract Society, circa, 1840, First edition; 12mo., original blindstamped cloth, gilt, pages, 160, all edges gilt, woodcut title and numerous full page and vignette woodcuts, fine.   R. F. G. Hollett & Sons Antiquarian Booksellers   170 - 27   2011   £65

Waters, Frank *Brave Are My People.* Santa Fe: Clear Light Press, 1993, First edition; fine in like dust jacket, this copy signed by author and introducer, Vine Deloria Jr.   Bella Luna Books   May 29 2011 - j2120   2011 $82

Waters, Sarah *Fingersmith.* London: Virago, 2002, First British edition, true first; fine in fine dust jacket, with promotional book mark.   Bella Luna Books   May 29 2011 - t5525   2011 $82

Waterson, Merlin *The National Trust. The First Hundred Years.* BB and the National Trust, 1994, First edition; large 8vo., original cloth, gilt, dust jacket, pages 288, illustrations in color and monochrome.   R. F. G. Hollett & Son Antiquarian Booksellers   General Catalogue Summer 2010 - 1607   2011   £30

Watin, Jean Felix *L'Art de Faire et d'Employer le Vernis, ou l'Art de Vernisseur...* Paris: Chez Quillau & Chez L'Auteur, 1772, 8vo., xvi, 249 (1 errata), 6 (table/privilege), 8 (supplement), contemporary English half calf, marbled boards, red morocco label, from the library of the Earls of Macclesfield at Shirburn Castle.   Maggs Bros. Ltd.   1440 - 225   2011   £750

Watkins-Pitchford, D. J. *Meeting Hill.* Hollis & Carter, 1948, First edition; 4to., original cloth, head of spine little faded, dust jacket price clipped, extremities chipped, pages vii, 141, with 15 color plates, few spots to flyleaves, but very nice.   R. F. G. Hollett & Sons Antiquarian Booksellers   170 - 717   2011   £250

Watkins, Alfred *The Old Straight Track: its Mounds, Beacons, Moats, Sites and Mark Stones.* London: Methuen, 1925, First edition; 8vo., original publisher's light blue cloth lettered gilt on spine, pages xx, 234, with 8 page publishers' catalog at rear, 40 illustrations, pages uncut at edges, faint rubbing, very light wear, endpapers very slightly browned, otherwise near fine, exceptional condition.   Any Amount of Books   May 29 2011 - A68507   2011 $213

Watkins, John *A Biographical Memoir of His late Royal Highness Frederick Duke of York and Albany, Commander-in-Chief of the Forces of Great Britain...* London: Henry Fisher Son & Co., 1827, First edition; finely bound in contemporary full straight grained maroon morocco gilt, boards panelled with multiple rules with rococo corner fillets within 2 single rules and broad rule, centre with a pattern of crossed triple rules bounded with fine wave pattern roll in blind, spine with 4 broad flattened raised bands decorated with 10 parallel rules, the compartments panelled with seven fine rules, pastedowns in same morocco with highly elaborate overall gilt design, blue watered silk opposing flyleaves with gilt roll borders and central arabesque in gilt, pages 600, all edges gilt, complete with 2 plates of facsimile signatures and 13 engraved plates, 1 hand colored, 1 extending, neatly repaired in one fold with small amount of loss, little browning to some plates, still very nice in superb and elaborate binding.   R. F. G. Hollett & Son Antiquarian Booksellers   175 - 1397   2011   £450

Watkins, T. H. *Gold Rush Country.* San Francisco: California Historical Society, 1981, First edition; large quarto, 96 pages, 63 high gloss black and white photos, map photo endpapers, brown cloth, gilt over dark green pictorial boards, stamped in brown, spine very slightly faded, else very fine.   Argonaut Book Shop   Recent Acquisitions Summer 2010 - 230   2011 $60

Watkins, William *Was There a Real Belle Starr?* N.P.: circa, 1990, 15 pages, wrappers, photo illustrations.   Bookworm & Silverfish   662 - 6   2011 $65

Watney, Bernard *Longton Hall Porcelain.* London: Faber, 1957, First edition; original cloth, gilt, dust jacket, pages xvi, 72, with 4 color plates, 80 pages monochrome illustrations.   R. F. G. Hollett & Son Antiquarian Booksellers   General Catalogue Summer 2010 - 339   2011   £40

Watson-Jones, Reginald *Fractures and Joint Injuries.* Baltimore: Williams and Wilkins, 1944, Third edition; 2 volumes, 4to. xi, 407; vii, 409-960 pages, numerous figures, original navy cloth, gilt stamped spine titles, extremities lightly rubbed, ownership signature stamp of Clare Gray Peterson, near fine, signed and inscribed to Peterson by author.   Jeff Weber Rare Books   162 - 307   2011 $500

Watson, Douglas S. *California in the Fifties. Fifty Views of Cities and Mining Towns in California and the West.* San Francisco: John Howell, 1936, First edition, limited to 850 copies (of an edition of 1000); oblong folio, (113) pages, 50 full page reproductions with accompanying text on facing page, wine cloth, gilt lettered paper label on front cover, half inch dent to center of spine, else very fine, presentation inscription signed by publisher, John Howell, to bibliographer, Robert Cowan.   Argonaut Book Shop   Recent Acquisitions Summer 2010 - 232   2011 $400

Watson, Douglas S. *The Spanish Occupation of California: Plan for the Establishment of a Government. Junta or Council Held at San Blas May 16 1768.* San Francisco: Grabhorn Press, 1934, First edition; one of 550 copies, quarto, (xiii), (64) pages, 2 woodcut portraits, folding facsimile map, decorative boards, light green cloth spine, paper spine label, very fine, with elusive plain orange dust jacket (lightly worn).   Argonaut Book Shop   Recent Acquisitions Summer 2010 - 231   2011 $175

Watson, E. L. Grant *Departures.* Pleiades Books, 1948, First edition; pages 131, 9 full page woodcuts, large 8vo., original cloth, gilt, dust jacket, inscription on flyleaf, else fine.   R. F. G. Hollett & Son Antiquarian Booksellers   General Catalogue Summer 2010 - 859   2011   £40

Watson, Elizabeth L. *Houses for Science. (with) Landmarks in Twentieth Century Genetics.* Plainview: Cold Spring Harbor Laboratory Press, 1991, First edition; 4to., xiii, 351 pages, fine in near fine dust jacket, signed and inscribed and dated by Elizabeth Watson and James Watson.   By the Book, L. C.   26 - 90   2011 $275

Watson, Geoffrey G. *Early Man in the Halifax District.* Halifax Scientific Society, 1952, First edition; Original cloth, gilt, dust jacket, pages xiii, 102, with 6 illustrations and 7 maps and diagrams.   R. F. G. Hollett & Son Antiquarian Booksellers   177 - 881   2011   £65

Watson, George *Anne Clifford, Countess of Pembroke.* 1886, Original printed wrappers, spine sometime taped, pages 89-113, couple of small alterations, probably in author's hand.   R. F. G. Hollett & Son Antiquarian Booksellers   173 - 1166   2011   £35

Watson, James D. *Genes, Girls, and Gamow. After the Double Helix.* New York: Alfred A. Knopf, 2001, Stated first edition; 8vo., xxix, 259 pages + 22 pages, as new in like dust jacket.   By the Book, L. C.   26 - 91   2011 $180

Watson, James D. *A Passion for DNA.* Cold Springs Harbor: Cold Springs Harbor Laboratory, 2000, First edition; signed by Watson, 8vo., xx, 250 pages, as new in like dust jacket.   By the Book, L. C.   26 - 92   2011 $400

Watson, John *The English Lake District Fisheries.* London: T. N. Foulis, 1925, Original cloth backed boards, gilt, pages xiv, 271, with 12 illustrations.   R. F. G. Hollett & Son Antiquarian Booksellers   173 - 1170   2011   £45

Watson, John *The English Lake District Fisheries.* London: George Routledge & Sons, 1899, First edition; original decorated cloth, gilt, recased, pages xi, 271, 12 illustrations, folding map.   R. F. G. Hollett & Son Antiquarian Booksellers   173 - 1169   2011   £75

Watson, Nigel *Around the Coast and Across the Seas.* Leyburn: St. Matthew's Press, 2000, First edition; large 8vo., original cloth, gilt, dust jacket, pages 178, illustrations in color and monochrome.   R. F. G. Hollett & Son Antiquarian Booksellers   173 - 1171   2011   £45

Watson, Richard *Anecdotes of the Life of Richard Watson, Bishop of Landaff.* London: printed for T. Cadell and W. Davies, 1818, 2 volumes, 8vo., pages (ii), 476, contemporary polished dark blue half calf, spines decoratively gilt in six compartments, lettered direct in gilt numbered direct within a geometrical frame gilt, boards, single rule with 'tight French shell' marbled sides, all edges densely red sprinkled, pink and white patterned sewn endbands, titlepages foxed, light foxing elsewhere, boards little scuffed touch of rubbing at spine ends, from the collection of Christopher Ernest Weston 1947-2010.   Unsworths Booksellers   24 - 58   2011   £120

Watson, Richard *A Letter to His Grace the Archbishop of Canterbury.* London: printed for T. Evans, 1783, First published edition; 4to., modern half calf gilt, pages 54, complete with half title, some corners little creased, last leaf slightly soiled and neatly repaired at edges.   R. F. G. Hollett & Son Antiquarian Booksellers   175 - 1401   2011   £120

Watson, Richard *Two Apologies, One for Christianity...* Scatcherd and Letterman etc., 1806, First combined edition; pages 470, (ii), with half title, modern half green levant morocco, gilt, raised bands and contrasting spine label.   R. F. G. Hollett & Son Antiquarian Booksellers   175 - 1400   2011   £140

Watson, Robert *The History of the Reign of Philip the Second, King of Spain.* London: printed for W. Strahan, 1777, 2 volumes, 4to., pages (iv) 443, (i); (iv) 437 (xix), contemporary 'Antique Spot' sided boards, original ultra worn quarter sheep renewed in 1990s by Chris Weston, all text uncut, bit of light spotting, boards scuffed and corners worn, ink ownership inscription "Anketell Singleton", from the collection of Christopher Ernest Weston 1947-2010. Unsworths Booksellers   24 - 149   2011   £200

Watson, William   1858-1935   *The Eloping Angels.* London: Elkin Mathews & John Lane, 1893, First edition; original green buckram gilt, spine faded to brown, very good.   Jarndyce Antiquarian Booksellers   CXCI - 605   2011   £35

Watson, William   1858-1935   *Odes and Other Poems.* London: John Lane, 1894, First edition; half title, 16 page catalog (1894), original green buckram gilt, spine faded to brown, very good.   Jarndyce Antiquarian Booksellers   CXCI - 606   2011   £35

Watson, William 1858-1935 *Wordsworth's Grave and other Poems.* London: T. Fisher Unwin, 1890, First edition; half title, frontispiece, original blue boards, printed in black, rubbed and slightly marked, spine slightly darkened. Jarndyce Antiquarian Booksellers CXCI - 607 2011 £35

Watts, Alan W. *The Way of Zen.* New York: Pantheon, 1957, First edition; fine in near fine dust jacket with mild sunning to spine and edges, inscribed by author to Mai-Mai Sze. Ken Lopez Bookseller 154 - 237 2011 $1500

Watts, Diana *The Renaissance of the Greek Ideal.* London: Heinemann, 1914, First edition; 4to., original cloth, gilt, pages (iv), 186, illustrations, endpapers lightly spotted. R. F. G. Hollett & Son Antiquarian Booksellers 175 - 1403 2011 £120

Watts, Isaac *Logic or the Right Use of Reason in the Enquiry after Truth.* London: printed for Thomas Tegg, 1811, 12mo., pages (ii), 234, frontispiece (rather stained), some pencil scribbles to flyleaves, original sheep gilt, rubbed. R. F. G. Hollett & Sons Antiquarian Booksellers 170 - 718 2011 £35

Watts, Isaac *The Psalms of David. (bound with) Hymns and Spiritual Songs.* London: printed by and for J. W. Pasham, 1778, 123 x 70mm., 2 p.l., 240 pages, (10) leaves; 4 p.l., 216 pages, (12) leaves (index leaves for "Hymns and Spiritual Songs" bound out of order but all present), 2 parts in one volume, superb hand painted and gilt decorated vellum by Edwards of Halifax, both covers with very prominent oval paintings, front covers depicting a statue in grisaille of a female figure, probably representing Faith, casting her eyes upward to heaven, one arm aloft, other holding a cross, whole against a sky blue oval, back cover with very dynamic grisaille painting of the Resurrection, with Christ flying upward from the tomb amidst brilliant light, three soldiers beneath shielding themselves in protective wonderment and presiding angel supplying adoration at right, both covers bordered by gilt chain motif, flat spine divided by blue wash bands into compartments featuring gilt lyres and swirling gilt cornerpieces, blue wash label, all edges gilt in original soft green leather slipcase bordered by gilt chain matching that of binding, this in turn housed in modern morocco backed folding box with raised bands and gilt titling, bookplate of James Gordon, Esquire, Moor Place; inscription "Harriot Whitbread/The Gift of John Howard Esq(ui)re/ Cardington/ 1785", similar inscription to Harriot from M. Howard of Cardington dated 1787; blue spine label trifle faded, blue cover background on front board showing little soil, small ink blot on three pages, wonderful binding in very fine condition, text nearly pristine, original slipcase bit worn and faded but remarkable survival. Phillip J. Pirages 59 - 13 2011 $6900

Watts, Louisa *Pretty Little Poems for Pretty Little People...* Halifax: William Milner, 1846, Pages viii, 146, all edges gilt, woodcut frontispiece (rather foxed), 12mo., original blindstamped cloth gilt. R. F. G. Hollett & Sons Antiquarian Booksellers 170 - 719 2011 £65

Watts, R. M. *ABC's of Forest Fire Prevent.* Ottawa: Cloutier, 1950, 8vo., pictorial wrappers, near fine, illustrations in color on every page. Aleph-Bet Books, Inc. 95 - 20 2011 $200

Wauchope, Robert *Handbook of Middle American Indians.* Austin: University of Texas Press, First editions; small 4to., volumes 1-16, al but 5 and 6 have jackets, clean, very good+ copies in mostly very good dust jackets, some with slight rubbing and toning and occasional light wear, 6000+ pages, illustrations, maps, plans, diagrams, from the library of Professor G. H. Bushnell, Curator of the Cambridge University Museum of Archaology and Ethnology. Any Amount of Books May 26 2011 - A49503 2011 $587

Waugh, Alec *Public School Life.* London: Collins, 1922, First edition; original black cloth, gilt, hinges trifle rubbed, pages viii, 272, (ii). R. F. G. Hollett & Son Antiquarian Booksellers 175 - 1405 2011 £35

Waugh, Edwin *Rambles in the Lake Country and Other Travel Sketches.* John Heywood, n.d., original blue cloth, gilt, pages (ix), 290, with 26 illustrations and map. R. F. G. Hollett & Son Antiquarian Booksellers 173 - 1173 2011 £35

Waugh, Evelyn 1903-1966 *The Holy Places.* Queen Anne Press, 1952, First edition; 488/900 copies (of an edition of 950), printed on Spicers' mouldmade cream wove paper, wood engravings by Reynolds Stone, titlepage printed in red and black, short tear to front free endpaper, pages (x), 42, 8vo., original red buckram, blocked and lettered in gilt, untrimmed, very good, dust jacket. Blackwell Rare Books B166 - 237 2011 £200

Waugh, Evelyn 1903-1966 *Ninety-Two Days.* London: Duckworth, 1934, First edition; 24 plates, folding map printed in black and red, little creased at one edge, usual darkening to initial and final page of text block, pages 238, (2) (ads), 8vo., original mid blue cloth, gilt lettered backstrip, good. Blackwell Rare Books B166 - 238 2011 £385

Waugh, Evelyn 1903-1966 *Scott-King's Modern Europe.* London: Chapman & Hall, 1947, First edition; small 8vo., pages 88, frontispiece, slight foxing, upper corner of flyleaf removed, cover little worn at edges, else very good, tight copy. Second Life Books Inc. 174 - 321 2011 $60

Waugh, Frederick J. *The Clan of Munes.* New York: Charles Scribner's Sons, 1916, First edition; oblong large 4to., color decorated cloth, some light scratching to cloth of an otherwise clean copy. Jo Ann Reisler, Ltd. 86 - 264 2011 $475

Way, Albert *Promptorium Parvulorum Sive Clericum, Dictionarius Anglo-Laitnus Princeps.* London: Camden Society, 1865, 3 parts bound in one volume, 2 colored, 1 black and white plate, 2nd plate has been bound to face (xiii), rather than, as instructed, xxxviii, 536 pages + instructions to binder leaf, quarter cloth, modern rebacking, very good.   C. P. Hyland   May 26 2011 - 690 2011 $275

Wayland, John Walter *The Political Opinions of Thomas Jefferson an Essay by...* New York: 1907, First edition; 98 pages, 12mo., near fine, top edge gilt, fore edge not trimmed, one leaf with horizontal 2 inch tear from free edge. Bookworm & Silverfish   662 - 155 2011 $100

Weatherley, F. E. *Told in the Twilight.* New York: E. P. Dutton & Co. n.d. circa, 1884, Original cloth backed pictorial boards, corners little worn, pages 64, illustrations.   R. F. G. Hollett & Sons Antiquarian Booksellers   170 - 720   2011   £65

Weatherley, Frederic *Punch & Judy and Some of Their Friends.* London: Marcus Ward, circa, 1880, Square 8vo., cloth backed pictorial boards, slight edge rubbing else very good+, chromolithographs by Patty Townsend.   Aleph-Bet Books, Inc.   95 - 466 2011 $600

Weaver, Lawrence *English Leadwork Its Art and History.* London: Batsford, 1909, First edition; 4to., pages xv, 268, 441 illustrations, new endpapers, original grey cloth gilt, signs of label removed from foot of spine, excellent copy.   R. F. G. Hollett & Son Antiquarian Booksellers   177 - 885 2011   £250

Weaver, Lawrence *Houses and Gardens by E. L. Lutyens.* Antique Collectors' Club, 1922, Facsimile of original 1913 edition; large 4to., original cloth, gilt, dust jacket price clipped, pages xl, 344, 580 illustrations.   R. F. G. Hollett & Son Antiquarian Booksellers   177 - 886 2011   £50

Weaver, Lawrence *The Scottish National War Memorial. The Castle, Edinburgh.* London: Country Life, n.d., Folio, original stiff wrappers, pages 20, with 63 illustrations.   R. F. G. Hollett & Son Antiquarian Booksellers   177 - 887 2011   £45

Weaver, R. *Monumenta Antiqua or the Stone Monuments of Antiquity Yet Remaining in the British Isles...* London: J. B. Nichols and Son, 1840, First edition; original green cloth, gilt, pages xvi, 199 (i, ad), uncut, complete with 4 wood engraved plates, excellent, clean and sound copy.   R. F. G. Hollett & Son Antiquarian Booksellers   177 - 888   2011   £120

Webb, Benjamin *Sketches of Continental Ecclessiology or Church Notes in Belgium, Germany and Italy.* London: Joseph Masters, 1848, First edition; original blindstamped cloth, gilt, rather faded and neatly recased, pages xviii, 595.   R. F. G. Hollett & Son Antiquarian Booksellers   177 - 889   2011   £120

Webb, Maria *The Penns & Pennigtons of the Seventeenth Century.* E. Hicks Junr., 1891, Second edition; original green cloth, gilt, small label at foot of spine, pages viii, 343, 5 plates, edges spotted, library label on pastedown.   R. F. G. Hollett & Son Antiquarian Booksellers   173 - 1175 2011   £45

Webb, Marion St. John *The Littlest One.* London: George G. Harrap, 1922, Pages 46. original boards, dust jacket (edges defective), 4 color plates.   R. F. G. Hollett & Sons Antiquarian Booksellers   170 - 671 2011   £35

Webb, Marion St. John *The Littlest One.* London: George G. Harrap, 1928, 4to. original cloth backed pictorial boards, upper board little marked, signs of label removed, pages 118, 4 color plates by Margaret Tarrant.   R. F. G. Hollett & Sons Antiquarian Booksellers   170 - 673 2011   £65

Webb, Marion St. John *The Littlest One Again.* London: George G. Harrap, 1926, 4to., original cloth backed pictorial boards, upper board little soiled, pages 96. 4 colored plates by Margaret Tarrant.   R. F. G. Hollett & Sons Antiquarian Booksellers   170 - 672 2011   £45

Webb, Mary *Jane's Urban Transport Systems.* Coulsdon: Jane's Information Group, 2005, First edition; 4to., copiously illustrated in black and white, pages 877, House of Commons library stamps and label on endpapers, otherwise very good+.   Any Amount of Books   May 29 2011 - A64753 2011 $340

Webb, Sidney *The History of Trade Unionism 1666-1920.* privately printed by the authors, 1920, Original limp green boards, upper board creased, edges trifle frayed, pages xviii, 784, (vi), endpapers rather browned and spotted.   R. F. G. Hollett & Son Antiquarian Booksellers   175 - 1408 2011   £45

Webb, Sidney *Industrial Democracy.* printed by the authors for the Seaham Divisonal Labour Party, 1920, Fourteenth thousand; Original boards, pages xxxix, 899, (iv), edges trifle browned.   R. F. G. Hollett & Son Antiquarian Booksellers   175 - 1409 2011   £30

Webber, F. R. *Church Symbolism.* Cleveland: J. H. Jansen, 1927, First edition; large 8vo., original black cloth gilt, little rubbed and recased, pages ix, 395, numerous half tone illustrations, little fingering in places, new endpapers and front joint strengthened.   R. F. G. Hollett & Son Antiquarian Booksellers   175 - 1410 2011   £65

Weber, Bruce *Gentle Giants: a Book of Newfoundlands.* New York: Bulfinch Press, 1994, First edition; photos, fine, some very minute rubbing to bottom front corner, issued without dust jacket. Jeff Hirsch Books ny 2010 2011 $600

Weber, Bruce *O Rio de Janeiro. A Photographic Journal.* New York: Alfred A. Knopf, 1986, First edition; folio, pages (196) (two gatefold), 130 black and white photos, drawings by Richard Giglio, original black and white photo illustrated wrappers, printed in purple, shallow crease and light rubbing to spine, near fine. Simon Finch Rare Books Zero - 551 2011 £400

Weber, David J. *The Californios Versus Jedediah Smith 1826-1827.* Spokane: Arthur H. Clark Co., 1990, First edition; 8vo., (8), 82, (1) pages, map, red cloth, gilt lettered spine very fine. Argonaut Book Shop Recent Acquisitions Summer 2010 - 142 2011 $90

Webster, Daniel 1782-1852 *An Address Delivered Before the New York Historical Society February 23, 1852.* New York: Press of the Historical Society, 1852, First edition; octavo, pamphlet bound in printed wrappers, 57 pages, moderate age toning, minor wear to wrappers, front wrapper neatly detached, vertical crease down center, very good, inscribed and signed by Webster for Mrs. (Harriette Story) Page. Charles Agvent 2010 Summer Miscellany - 64 2011 $950

Webster, F. A. M. *Sports Grounds and Buildings.* Sir Isaac Putnam, 1940, First edition; 4to., original cloth, gilt, pages xviii, 305, (xiii), 136 illustrations and 4 folding plans. R. F. G. Hollett & Son Antiquarian Booksellers 177 - 890 2011 £65

Weeden, Howard *Bandanna Ballads Including "Shadows on the Wall".* New York: 1899, xvi, 90 pages, front cover gilt bright, backstrip bit dull but legible, front joint strengthened, ex-library (private). Bookworm & Silverfish 665 - 7 2011 $125

Weedon, Lucy L. *Fine Fun for Everyone.* London: Ernest Nister, n.d., 1898, First edition; small folio, original cloth backed glazed pictorial boards, cracked and scratched in places, edges rather worn, unpaginated, illustrations in color and line. R. F. G. Hollett & Sons Antiquarian Booksellers 170 - 722 2011 £120

Weeks, Edward P. *A Treatise on the Law of Depositions Comprising Abstracts of the Statutory Law Pertaining Thereto.* San Francisco: 1880, First edition; xx, 714 pages, later law cloth, wafer on backstrip and internal stamps, ex-library U.S/ Judge Advocate General Office. Bookworm & Silverfish 667 - 106 2011 $75

Weeks, John H. *Among the Primitive Bakongo a Record of Thirty Years Close Intercourse with the Bakongo and Other Tribes of Equatorial Africa.* London: Seeley Service, 1914, First edition; 8vo., 318 pages, map, 40 illustrations, original red decorative cloth. J. & S. L. Bonham Antiquarian Booksellers Africa 4/20/2011 - 6767 2011 £125

Weever, John *Antient Funeral Monuments of Great Britain, Ireland and the Islands Adjacent.* London: printed by W. Tooke for the editor, 1767, 4to., pages (x) clxxvii (i) 608 + engraved portrait frontispiece and 5 other engraved plates, extending table, contemporary calf much worn, board edges 'milled' decorative roll gilt, pink & white, sewn endbands, removal of amateur reback, revealed fragment of a once fully gilt spine with massed decorative pallets, awaiting restoration, now with early 21st century reback to corners by Chris Weston, light toning and some spotting, frontispiece offset, old leather somewhat scratched and bit rubbed at extremities, ink ownership inscription "Robt. Entwisle", from the collection of Christopher Ernest Weston 1947-2010. Unsworths Booksellers 24 - 150 2011 £400

Weihnacht: Vierzehn Fabirge Original Steinzeich. Wien: Richter & Zollner, 1922, 4to., cloth backed pictorial boards, cover edges rubbed, some finger soil, very good, exceptionally stunning, 14 original color stone engravings printed on rectos only plus pictorial endpapers and pictorial cover designs. Aleph-Bet Books, Inc. 95 - 155 2011 $950

Weir, Harrison William *Stories About Animals.* London: Darton & Co., Thin 8vo., 4 leaves, original pictorial wrappers on beige, tan and yellow papers, full page chromolithograph frontispiece, light soiling and dusting at wrappers, minor splits at reinforced spines, very good. Hobbyhorse Books 56 - 155 2011 $425

Weir, Jean B. *Rich in Interest and Charm. the Architecture of Andrew R. Cobb.* Art Gallery of Nova Scotia, 1990, Stapled wrappers worn, owner's name, interior clean and tight, 65 pages, photos and plans, 10 x 8 inches. G. H. Mott Bookseller May 26 2011 - 47146 2011 $175

Weir, Robert *Riding - Polo. Badminton Library Series.* London: Longmans, Green & Co., 1902, New edition; Original pictorial brown cloth gilt, nick to head of spine, pages xiii, 423, numerous illustrations, front joint cracking, prelims little spotted. R. F. G. Hollett & Son Antiquarian Booksellers General Catalogue Summer 2010 - 1308 2011 £75

Weiseenburger, Steven *A Gravity's Rainbow Companion.* Athens: University of Georgia Press, 1988, Review copy; simultaneous issue in wrappers, near fine, review slip and press release laid in, bookplate of Ray Roberts, Pynchon's editor. Ken Lopez Bookseller 154 - 190 2011 $75

Welch, Denton *I Left My Grandfather's House.* Lion & Unicorn Press, 1958, First edition; limited to 100 numbered copies, illustrations by L. Jones, pictorial endpapers and 12 pages of colored plates. I. D. Edrich May 26 2011 - 62224 2011 $444

Welch, James *Fool's Crow.* New York: Viking, 1986, First edition; fine, near fine dust jacket, small chip at top of spine, signed by author increasingly scarce thus. Bella Luna Books May 29 2011 - t3804 2011 $82

Welch, James *The Heartsong of Charging Elk.* New York: Doubleday, 2000, First edition; fine in fine dust jacket, signed and dated by author on 8/24/0. Bella Luna Books May 29 2011 - p2176 2011 $82

Welch, James *Riding the Earthboy 40.* New York: World Publishing, 1971, First edition; dust jacket near fine, 1 inch closed tear on rear panel, signed by author. Bella Luna Books May 26 2011 - p1134 2011 $247

Welch, James *Winter in the Blood.* New York: Harper & Row, 1974, First edition; near fine, soiling to edges, light use, dust jacket very good, small chip at base of front panel, light sunning and creasing to front flap, very good dust jacket, small chip at base of front panel. Bella Luna Books May 29 2011 - t3043 2011 $82

Weldon, Fay *Darcys Utopia.* London: Collins, 1990, First British edition; fine, in fine dust jacket, signed by author. Bella Luna Books May 29 2011 - t3646 2011 $77

Wellbeloved, Charles *Some Account of the Ancient and Present State of the Abbey of St. Mary, York and the Discoveries Recently Made in Excavating the Ground... (bound with) Some Remarks on the Pillar, or Obelisk at Forres...* London: published by the Society of Antiquaries, 1829, Large folio, pages 17 (i) 10 lithographic engraved plates numbered LI-LX (plus) extra illustration "Details of St. Mary's Abbey York" a tinted lithograph plate by F. Bedford, 2 + 2 lithographic engraved plates, contemporary half calf, boards triple rule bordered in blind, 'French Shell' sides, awaiting restoration, plates foxed, some dust soiling, rubbed, worn at edges, spine perished, boards detached, from the collection of Christopher Ernest Weston 1947-2010. Unsworths Booksellers 24 - 151 2011 £250

Welles, C. M. *Three Years' Wanderings of a Connecticut Yankee in South America, Africa, Australia and California...* New York: American Subscription Pub. House, 1859, Second edition; 358 pages, extra engraved title, frontispiece, 8 steel engravings, publisher's brown cloth with elaborate gilt decoration on covers and spine, spine lettered in gilt, spine ends show just bit of light wear, bookplate, covers slightly dulled, but fine copy of book often found in atrocious condition. Argonaut Book Shop Recent Acquisitions Summer 2010 - 233 2011 $250

Wellesley Club *Favorite Recipes Recommended by the Colorado Wellesley Club.* Denver: 1907, 55 pages, 6 3/4 x 5 inches, cloth, very good. Bookworm & Silverfish 679 - 45 2011 $75

Wellington, Arthur Wellesley, 1st Duke of 1769-1852 *The Life of His Grace the Duke of Wellington.* London: T. Allman, 1839, 12mo., contemporary half calf gilt with marbled boards, little rubbed, pages xii, 432, engraved portrait, 5 woodcut plates, few marks and small annotations, but very good, nice. R. F. G. Hollett & Son Antiquarian Booksellers General Catalogue Summer 2010 - 477 2011 £45

Wellman, Paul I. *Broncho Apache.* New York: Macmillan Co., 1936, First edition; 8vo., laid in to this copy is 1943 TLS from author to a newspaper editor, exceptional and lovely copy. Buckingham Books May 26 2011 - 23335 2011 $2750

Wells, Edward *The Young Gentleman's Astronomy, Chronology, and Dialling...* London: printed for James, John and Paul Knapton, 1736, (8), 148 pages, 16 engraved plates, (8), 86 pages; (8), 54 pages, 9 folding engraved plates, 8vo., some offset browning from turn-ins, pencil doodle on front endpaper, full contemporary calf, raised bands, red morocco label, joints cracked but firm, corners bumped, label chipped with slight loss. Jarndyce Antiquarian Booksellers CXCI - 608 2011 £175

Wells, Herbert George 1866-1946 *The Adventures of Tommy.* London: George G. Harrap & Co., 1929, First edition; 4to., half title, color illustrations, original orange boards, brown cloth spine, very good. Jarndyce Antiquarian Booksellers CXCI - 610 2011 £45

Wells, Herbert George 1866-1946 *Ann Veronica. A Modern Love Story.* London: T. Fisher Unwin, 1909, First edition; original cloth, gilt, upper board little marked, pages 352, scattered foxing mainly to fore edge. R. F. G. Hollett & Son Antiquarian Booksellers 175 - 1418 2011 £60

Wells, Herbert George 1866-1946 *The Shape of Things to Come.* London: Hutchinson & Co., 1933, First edition; ix, 13-432 pages (+ 12 page catalog), large 8vo., inscribed by author for Elizabeth Bruce, original blue cloth in dust jacket, spine slightly rubbed and 4 inch closed crack and small chip, dust jacket rather worn with chipping at folds and some loss, also some poorly executed restoration of original color. Any Amount of Books May 26 2011 - A76605 2011 $461

Wells, Herbert George 1866-1946 *The Time Machine.* London: William Heinemann, 1895, First English edition; first two gatherings expertly reattached, last page bit browned, offset from wrapper, pages (viii), 152, foolscap 8vo., original light blue paper wrappers, lettered in darker blue and with device of sphinx on upper cover, upper cover faded, edges frayed, spine mostly defective, not a great copy but rare in fragile original wrappers, now preserved in solander box.   Blackwell Rare Books   B166 - 239 2011 £2000

Wells, Herbert George 1866-1946 *The War of the Worlds.* New York: Harper, 1898, Reprint; 8vo., pages 291, several illustrations on glossy paper, red cloth, blind-stamped and lettered gilt, cover little faded and slightly soiled, edges scuffed front hinge tender, otherwise very good.   Second Life Books Inc.   174 - 325 2011 $100

Wells, Herbert George 1866-1946 *When the Sleeper Wakes.* Leipzig: Bernhard Tauchnitz, 1899, Copyright edition; contemporary half black calf, maroon morocco label, slightly rubbed, ownership signature.   Jarndyce Antiquarian Booksellers   CXCI - 611 2011 £45

Wells, Herbert George 1866-1946 *The Works of...* London: T. Fisher Unwin, 1924-1927, One of 620 hand numbered copies for the UK; signed by author, this being set 313, 28 volumes, octavo, photogravure frontispieces with tissue guards, printed on pure rag paper watermarked "HGW", publisher's original dark red buckram, gilt lettering, top edge gilt, beveled edges, very fine set in original cream dust jackets printed in red, extremely scarce in original printed dust jackets in fine condition.   David Brass Rare Books, Inc.   May 26 2011 - 01407 2011 $7750

Wells, J. M., Mrs. *Darling Bright Eyes Living Nursery Rhymes Newly Treated with Moving Pictures.* London: Dean & Sons circa 1870's, 8vo., cloth backed color pictorial boards with nick in front cover lower edge and there is small corner missing from rear cover, bump that is in lower corner that extends from rear of book a few pages within, 6 full page, full color tab activated moveables with charm and directness that is especially appealing for the nursery rhymes, all movables in lovely condition and in full working order.   Jo Ann Reisler, Ltd.   86 - 172 2011 $3750

Wells, Louisa Susannah *The Journal of a Voyage from Charlestown, S.C. to London Undertaken During the American Revolution by a Daughter of an Eminent American Loyalist.* New York: New York Historical Society, 1906, Limited numbered edition of 200 copies; octavo, 121 pages, frontispiece, 1 plate, original full maroon cloth stamped in black and gilt, top edge gilt, spine rubbed or discolored, very good.   Jeff Weber Rare Books   163 - 224 2011 $175

Wells, Ruth *A to Zen. A Book About Japanese Culture.* Saxonville: Picture Book Studio, 1992, First edition; 4to., pictorial boards, as new in dust jacket, illustrations by Yoshi, this copy inscribed by Yoshi.   Aleph-Bet Books, Inc.   95 - 23 2011 $100

Wells, Samuel *The Revenue and the Expenditure of the United Kingdom.* London: James Ridgway, 1835, First edition; pages ix, 491, uncut, unopened, 8vo., original green boards, printed spine label, corners bumped, spine ends slightly worn, nicked, otherwise about very good with slight foxing to endpapers.   Any Amount of Books   May 29 2011 - A47676 2011 $306

Wells, Seth Y. *Millennial Praises, Containing a Collection of Gospel Hymns.* Hancock: 1813, Second edition; 12mo., 8, 288, (4) pages, full contemporary calf (very plain), some rubbing but very nice, text moderately browned, very scarce edition.   M & S Rare Books, Inc.   90 - 380 2011 $1250

Wells, William Charles *An Essay on Dew and Several Appearances Connected With It.* London: printed for Taylor and Hessey, 1815, Second edition; 12mo., (4), 150 pages, contemporary gilt and blindstamped calf, minor rubbing.   M & S Rare Books, Inc.   90 - 441 2011 $1250

Welter, Gerhard *Cleaning and Preservation of Coins and Medals.* New York: Sanford J. Durst, 1976, Original cloth gilt pages ix, 118, with few illustrations.   R. F. G. Hollett & Son Antiquarian Booksellers   General Catalogue Summer 2010 - 340 2011 £45

Welty, Eudora *The Eye of the Story. Selected Essays and Reviews.* New York: Random House, 1978, First edition, one of 300 unnumbered copies, signed by author; some rubbing to spine with light dampstain to heel, near fine in slipcase, as issued.   Charles Agvent   2010 Summer Miscellany - 65 2011 $200

Welty, Eudora *The Golden Apples.* New York: 1949, Stated first edition; 244 pages, original binding, unclipped dust jacket (very good, with some foxing beneath dust jacket), half inch tear top of back panel and just bit darker on backstrip.   Bookworm & Silverfish   662 - 104 2011 $175

Welty, Eudora *Losing Battles.* New York: Random House, 1970, First edition, 2nd printing; (x) 436, (1) pages, 8vo., original publisher's green cloth, very slight fading to edges of boards as usual, gilt lettered spine and decorations, top edges dark yellow, half title, fine immaculate copy in fine dust jacket.   Paulette Rose Fine and Rare Books   32 - 183 2011 $175

Welty, Eudora *The Optimist's Daughter.* New York: Random House, 1972, First edition; #250 of 300 numbered and signed copies, fine in fine slipcase, issued without dust jacket. Charles Agvent 2010 Summer Miscellany - 66 2011 $600

Welty, Eudora *The Robber Bridegroom.* Pennyroyal Press, 1987, One of 150 copies signed by author and artist (#115); 237 x 160, 8 p.l., 134 pages, (1) leaf (colophon), publisher's rich maroon morocco, covers with blind ruled border, upper cover with blindstamped medallion depicting a raven in profile, flat spine with gilt titling, marbled endpapers, titlepage vignette, tailpiece, printer's device, 20 full page woodcuts by Barry Moser, mint. Phillip J. Pirages 59 - 276 2011 $950

Wemys, Thomas *Beth-Hak-Kodesh. Or the Separation and Consecration of Places in God's Publick Service and Worship.* London: printed for Thomas Dring, at the Harrow, over agaisnt the Inner Temple-gate in Fleet Street, 1674, First and only edition; 12mo., (24) 164 pages, complete with initial imprimatur leaf (A1), wormtracks affect lower margins throughout, occasionally with loss of single letter of text, small tear in margin of leaf F4 with loss of single letter on recto, contemporary sheep, unlettered, spine and corners rather worn but sound, from the 17th century library of John Rawlett with his signature and shelfmark on tag affixed to lower board, scarce. John Drury Rare Books 153 - 170 2011 £650

Wendel, C. H. *150 Years of International Harvester.* Sarasota: 1981, First edition; 416 pages, large 4to., fine with cover gilt bright, corners sharp, original binding. Bookworm & Silverfish 676 - 6 2011 $167

Wendingen The Life Work of the American Architect Frank Lloyd Wright. Santpoort: 1925-1926, First English language edition; numbers I-VII of the magazine Wendingen, inscribed by the artist on titlepage, oblong folio, publisher's full beige cloth, inscribed by Frank Lloyd Wright. Heritage Book Shop Booth A12 51st NY International Antiquarian Book Fair April 8-10 2011 - 142 2011 $4000

Wenham, Leslie P. *The Romano-British Cemetry at Trentholme Drive York.* London: HMSO, 1968, 4to., original cloth, gilt, dust jacket, card slipcase, pages xii, 223, with 53 plates and 45 text figures, mint. R. F. G. Hollett & Son Antiquarian Booksellers 177 - 893 2011 £75

Wentworth-Sheilds, Peter *Clarice Cliff.* L'Odeon, 1976, Numbered edition; 81 pages, color and black and white illustrations, very good in slightly worn dust jacket, scarce. Ken Spelman Rare Books 68 - 135 2011 £40

Wentz, W. Y. Evans *The Fairy Faith in Celtic Countries.* Rennes: 1909, First (and only) edition; 22, 314 pages, original wrappers under fine full crushed morocco by Hatchards (rubbing on pressure points), very good. C. P. Hyland May 26 2011 - 258/1083 2011 $1305

Werfel, Franz *Hearken Unto the Voice.* New York: Viking, 1938, First American edition; warmly inscribed by author for Edith Snow, minor fore edge foxing and offsetting to hinges, very good in very good dust jacket with mild edgewear, books signed by author scarce. Ken Lopez Bookseller 154 - 239 2011 $500

Werndly, Georg Henrik *Maleische Spraakkunst uit de Eige Schriften der Malaiers Opgemaakt...* Amsterdam: R. & G. Wetstein op kosten va de E. A. Heren Bewindhebberen der oost indische maatschappye, 1736, First edition; 8vo., (120, lxviii, (23) pages, 18th century English polished calf, spine gilt in compartments, morocco lettering piece lacking, from the library of the Earls of Macclesfield at Shirburn Castle. Maggs Bros. Ltd. 1440 - 226 2011 £1400

Wesley, John 1703-1791 *A Compendium of Natural Philosophy..* London: Thomas Tegg and Son, 1835-1838, 3 volumes, small 8vo., original printed cloth, spines little darkened with few small snags and chips, pages xvi, 384; iv, 376; viii, 376; complete with 3 engraved frontispieces, good sound. R. F. G. Hollett & Son Antiquarian Booksellers 175 - 1419 2011 £275

Wesley, John 1703-1791 *Explanatory Notes Upon the New Testament.* London: printed by William Bowyer, 1755, First edition; 4to., contemporary full straight grained calf gilt, boards little rubbed, corners worn, hinges cracked and repaired, pages vi, 762, (page 759 misnumbered 765), front flyleaf removed, lacks portrait, near contemporary mss. transcription of epitaph on Welsey's tombstone laid on to pastedown, very scarce. R. F. G. Hollett & Son Antiquarian Booksellers 175 - 1420 2011 £450

Wesley, John 1703-1791 *Graces, Before Meat.* London?: 1770?, 12mo., drop head title, some browning on lower margin occasionally touching text, (1), ii-xii pages, disbound. Anthony W. Laywood May 26 2011 - 21734 2011 $126

Wesley, John 1703-1791 *The Journal.* London: J. M. Dent and Sons, 1938, 4 volumes, small 8vo., original cloth, gilt, dust jackets edges and spines little darkened, pages xvi, 576; 508; 516; 598, excellent set. R. F. G. Hollett & Son Antiquarian Booksellers 175 - 1421 2011 £95

Wesley, John 1703-1791 *Primative (sic) Physic; or an Easy and Natural Method of Curing Most Diseases.* Trenton: Quequelle and Wilson, 1788, 12mo., 125 pages, modern full sheep, superbly executed in period style, title leaf washed and very skillfully laid down, lower corner neatly replaced, random dampstaining and few chipped corners, correctly restored copy of very scarce book. Joseph J. Felcone Inc. Fall Miscellany 2010 - 127 2011 $1800

Wesley, L. *Air Guns and Air Pistols.* London: Cassell, 1974, Revised edition; original cloth, gilt, dust jacket spine little faded, price clipped, pages xiv, 224, 24 plates. R. F. G. Hollett & Son Antiquarian Booksellers General Catalogue Summer 2010 - 1150 2011 £30

West, John *Cathedral Organists Past and Present.* London: Novello and Co., 1899, First edition; original cloth, gilt, pages 141, few leaves rather carelessly opened, scarce. R. F. G. Hollett & Son Antiquarian Booksellers 175 - 1425 2011 £95

West, Michael *Bilingualism (With Special Reference to Bengal).* Calcutta: Government of India Central Publication Branch, 1926, First edition; original cloth backed printed boards, little soiled, corners bumped, pages xiii, 354, (ii), with 1 plate, 10 diagrams and graphs, upper corner rather creased and little bent throughout. R. F. G. Hollett & Son Antiquarian Booksellers 175 - 1426 2011 £75

West, Michael *Clair De Lune and Other Troubadour Romances.* St Albans: Camperfield Press for Brentano's of New York, n.d., Original pictorial cloth, gilt, dust jacket, pages 140, top edges gilt, color plates and full and two color decorations throughout. R. F. G. Hollett & Son Antiquarian Booksellers 175 - 1427 2011 £75

West, Nathaniel *The Day of the Locust.* New York: Random House, 1939, First edition; bit of darkening to spine cloth and endpages, likely from binder's glue, near fine in near fine dust jacket, lightly rubbed. Ken Lopez Bookseller 154 - 240 2011 $12,000

West, Thomas *The Antiquities of Furness; or, an Account of the Royal Abbey of St. Mary, in the Vale of Nightshade near Dalton in Furness...* 4to., old full speckled calf, gilt, elegantly gilt decorated spine, a little worn, corners bumped, pages (xvi), (ii), lvi, 288, 3A-3R4 (appendices), complete with folding engraved map (slightly torn in folds), folding plan, 2 engraved plates, armorial bookplate of Richard Henry Roundell, good, clean and sound. R. F. G. Hollett & Son Antiquarian Booksellers General Catalogue Summer 2010 - 1612 2011 £295

West, Thomas *The Antiquities of Furness; or an Account of the Royal Abbey of St. Mary...* printed for the author by T. Spilsbury, 1774, First edition; 4to., contemporary full polished calf gilt, edges rather rubbed, rebacked in matching calf gilt with raised bands, original spine label retained, pages (xx) lvi, 288, 3A-3R4 (appendices), folding engraved map, folding plan, 2 engraved plates, attractive copy, pictorial bookplate of James Frothingham Hunnewell. R. F. G. Hollett & Son Antiquarian Booksellers 173 - 1179 2011 £350

West, Thomas *The Antiquities of Furness; or, An Account of the Royal Abbey of St. Mary.* 1774, First edition; folding diagram, 1 plate, 1 folding view, (18), lvi, 288 (137) pages, full contemporary calf, needs rebacking, very good. C. P. Hyland May 26 2011 - 330 2011 $507

West, Thomas *The Antiquities of Furness; or an Account of the Royal Abbey of St. Mary...* Ulverston: George Ashburner, 1805, First 8vo. edition; pages (xxii), 426, (vi), engraved map, 5 aquatint plates, 3 hand colored plans and 2 engraved plates, title trifle dusty. R. F. G. Hollett & Son Antiquarian Booksellers 173 - 1180 2011 £140

West, Thomas *A Guide to the Lakes in Cumberland, Westmorland and Lancashire.* for W. J. and J. Richardson, 1799, Seventh edition; x 311 (1) pages ads, 2 engraved plates, folding engraved map, very good in contemporary half calf, marbled boards, vellum tips, gilt banded spine and red morocco label, corner clipped on final ad leaf, but without loss of text. Ken Spelman Rare Books 68 - 173 2011 £140

West, Thomas *A Guide to the Lakes in Cumberland, Westmorland and Lancashire.* Kendal: W. Pennington, 1802, Eighth edition; modern half blue calf gilt, pages vi, (ii), 311, (i) complete with extending hand colored map frontispiece. R. F. G. Hollett & Son Antiquarian Booksellers 173 - 1182 2011 £125

West, Thomas *A Guide to the Lakes in Cumberland, Westmorland and Lancashire.* Kendal: W. Pennington, 1812, Tenth edition; old half calf gilt, rather worn, hinges cracked, pages vi, (ii), 311, uncut, complete with extending hand colored map frontispiece (little browned), armorial bookplate of Rev. Ley Brooks (of Mayfield, Derby). R. F. G. Hollett & Son Antiquarian Booksellers 173 - 1184 2011 £85

West, Thomas *A Guide to the Lakes in Cumberland, Westmorland and Lancashire.* Kendal: W. Pennington, 1821, Eleventh edition; v (3) 312 pages, fine hand colored frontispiece and double page hand colored map, uncut, original boards, joints expertly repaired and paper on boards neatly restored in 3 places, spine rubbed. Ken Spelman Rare Books 68 - 175 2011 £140

West, Thomas *A Guide to the Lakes in Cumberland, Westmorland and Lancashire.* Kendal: W. Pennington, 1821, Eleventh edition; 20th century full calf gilt, spine little dulled, neatly repaired at head, few old scrapes to lower board, pages v (iii), 312, uncut, complete with finely hand colored aquatint frontispiece and extending hand colored map, endpapers little foxed. R. F. G. Hollett & Son Antiquarian Booksellers General Catalogue Summer 2010 - 1613 2011 £175

West, William *Fifty Years' Recollections of an Old Bookseller; Consisting of Anecdotes, Characteristic Sketches and Original Traits and Eccentricities of authors, Artists, Actors, Books, Booksellers...* Cork: printed by and for the author, 1836, Frontispiece, plates, illustrations, few spots, uncut and rebound in fairly recent half calf, marbled boards, maroon label. Jarndyce Antiquarian Booksellers CXCI - 459 2011 £280

Westbrook, Kate *The Moneypenny Diaries.* London: John Murray, 2005, First edition; fine in fine dust jacket. Bella Luna Books May 29 2011 - t9242 2011 $110

Westbrook, Kate *The Moneypenny Diaries.* London: John Murray, 2005, First British edition; fine, dust jacket fine, signed by author. Bella Luna Books May 29 2011 - t8215 2011 $137

Westell, W. Percival *Fifty-Two Nature Rambles.* London: Religious Tract Society, 1917, Fifth impression; full black calf gilt prize binding, pages xx, 237, 5 colored plates and 160 illustrations, scattered spotting. R. F. G. Hollett & Sons Antiquarian Booksellers 170 - 725 2011 £35

Western Primer or Introduction to Webster's Spelling Book. Cincinnati: Corey and Fairbanks, 1834, (1833); 3 1/2 x 5 1/2 inches, 35 pages, cloth on spine, occasional fox spot, very good+, 50 progressive lessons illustrated with 77 woodcuts. Aleph-Bet Books, Inc. 95 - 216 2011 $150

Westmorland Gazette. Directory, Year Book and Diary. Kendal: Atkinson & Pollitt, 1930, Tall 8vo., original cloth, upper board faded and stained, extremities rather worn. R. F. G. Hollett & Son Antiquarian Booksellers 173 - 1193 2011 £85

The Westmorland Natural History Record. A Quarterly Magazine. Elliot Stock and Kendal: Edward Gill, 1890, Volume I (March 1888-December 1889), contemporary half calf gilt with raised bands and contrasting spine labels, little scraped, pages iv, 188, all edges marbled, folding colored map, portrait of Thomas Gough, very scarce. R. F. G. Hollett & Son Antiquarian Booksellers 173 - 1187 2011 £180

The Westmorland Note-Book. Volume I 1888-1889. Elliot Stock and Kendal: Edward Gill, n.d. circa, 1890, First (only) edition; pages 382, complete with tinted engraved frontispiece, modern half green levant morocco gilt with raised bands. R. F. G. Hollett & Son Antiquarian Booksellers 173 - 1188 2011 £180

Westrup, E. Kate *A Hunting Alphabet.* London: Blackie and Son, n.d. circa, 1906, Oblong 8vo., original cloth backed pictorial boards, edges rather worn and bumped, unpaginated and french folded, 24 colored plates, few Victorian scraps pasted to the flyleaves and one to upper board, joints cracked, very good, rare. R. F. G. Hollett & Sons Antiquarian Booksellers 170 - 726 2011 £375

Wethey, Harold E. *Titian.* New York: Phaidon, 1975, First edition; 3 volumes, 4to., pages viii, 390 plus one color and 1 black and white plate; pages xiv, 426 plus pages 4 of color plates; pages vii, 480 plus pages 8 of color plates, copiously illustrated in black and white, volume I very good in like dust jacket, slightly scuffed and marked, very slightly bumped and creased at edges; volume II slightly marked, else very good in slightly creased, chipped and rubbed and scratched at back, else very good dust jacket, slightly misaligned with book; volume III very slightly creased at tp of spine and corner of page else very good in slightly creased, rubbed and marked dust jacket, otherwise very good, slightly misaligned with book, text and plates all clean and in excellent condition. Any Amount of Books May 26 2011 - A74689 2011 $1258

Weule, Karl *Native Life in East Africa; the Results of an Ethnological Research Expedition.* New York: D. Appleton, 1909, First American edition; 8vo., pages xxiv, 431, frontispiece, 4 colored plates, folding map, numerous text illustrations, pages 289 little torn in margin, map slightly foxed, recent brown decorative quarter morocco. J. & S. L. Bonham Antiquarian Booksellers Africa 4/20/2011 - 5914 2011 £150

Weule, Karl *Native Life in East Africa: the Results of an Ethnological Research Expedition.* London: Pitman, 1909, First UK edition; 8vo., pages xxiv, 431, ads, frontispiece, numerous illustrations, folding map, original red cloth, spine little faded, joint rubbed at base of spine. J. & S. L. Bonham Antiquarian Booksellers Africa 4/20/2011 - 4223 2011 £350

Whaite, H. C. *St. Christopher in Mediaeval Wallpainting.* London: Ernest Benn, 1929, First edition; small 4to., original cloth backed boards, gilt, dust jacket very soiled and torn, pages xvi, 44 plus, 36 plates. R. F. G. Hollett & Son Antiquarian Booksellers 177 - 894 2011 £35

Whaley, Nathaniel *A Preparatory Discourse of Death.* Oxford: printed at the Theater for Jo. Stephens, 1708, Contemporary full panelled polished calf gilt, leather little defective in places, pages (iv), 101, (ii). R. F. G. Hollett & Son Antiquarian Booksellers 175 - 1429 2011 £120

Wharton, Edith 1862-1937 *Italian Villas and Their Gardens.* New York: Century, 1904, First and only edition; heavily illustrated with photos, drawings, 26 full color plates by Maxfield Parrish, with 3 page ALS from Wharton tipped in, written to Mrs. Sage, with two page ALS from Maxfield Parrish, written in his elegant calligraphic hand, owner's small tasteful bookplate adorns front pastedown. Ken Lopez Bookseller 154 - 241 2011 $10,000

Wharton, Francis *A Treatise on Criminal Law.* Philadelphia: 1880, Eighth edition; full law calf, 2 volumes, some rubbing. Bookworm & Silverfish 678 - 101 2011 $158

Wharton, Francis *A Treatise on Criminal Pleading and Practice.* Philadelphia: 1880, 834 pages, first 48 pages misaligned, very good, old law calf. Bookworm & Silverfish 678 - 108 2011 $75

Wharton, Francis *A Treatise on Criminal Pleading & Practice.* Philadelphia: 1880, 834 pages, very good in old law calf, inner front joint strengthened. Bookworm & Silverfish 678 - 109 2011 $95

Wharton, Henry *The History of the Troubles and Tryal of the Most Reverend Father in God and Blessed Martyr, William Laud, Lord Archbishop of Canterbury.* London: R(ichard) Chiswell, 1694-1695, First edition; 4to., (22), 616 (2 ads) pages, frontispiece, titlepage in red and black in, full contemporary brown calf, gilt stamped red leather spine label, raised bands, rebacked, preserving original spine, signature of Will: Boothby and ownership marks on titlepage, bookplate and ink stamp of Spring Hill College Library, very good. Jeff Weber Rare Books 163 - 26 2011 $500

Wharton, Henry *The History of the Troubles and Tryal of.... William Laud...to which is prefixed the Diary of His Own Life.* London: printed for Ri. Chiswell, 1695, Folio, pages (xx) 616, (ii), engraved frontispiece, contemporary speckled calf, spine double ruled in blind decorative red lettering piece gilt, boards blind double ruled with decorative roll out with the supplementary ruling, board edges decorative roll gilt, all edges lightly red sprinkled, pink and white sewn endbands, title bit dusty, few minor spots elsewhere, touch rubbed joints cracking but strong, front joint bit defective at head, some scratches to boards, ink inscription "W. Danby", armorial 18th century bookplate "William Danby Esqr.", from the collection of Christopher Ernest Weston 1947-2010. Unsworths Booksellers 24 - 59 2011 £400

Wharton, Thomas *Memoirs of the Life of the Most Noble Thomas, Late Marquess of Wharton.... (with) A True Copy of the Last Will and Testament of the Most Honourable Thomas, Late Marquis of Wharton.* London: printed for J. Roberts, 1715, First edition; Pages (iv), 106, 22, with 2 titlepages, original front pastedown with pencilled notes retained, old panelled calf, rather darkened and worn, rebacked to match, raised bands, spine label. R. F. G. Hollett & Son Antiquarian Booksellers 173 - 1194 2011 £225

Wharton, William *Franky Furbo.* New York: Henry Holt, 1989, First edition, one of 250 copies signed; fine book and dust jacket. Lupack Rare Books May 26 2011 - ABE922173660 2011 $100

What Did You do in the War Daddy? A Visual History of Propaganda Posters. Melbourne: Oxford University Press, 1983, 4to., unpaginated, 1 page detached, else clean, tight, good in very good dust jacket (edgeworn). G. H. Mott Bookseller May 26 2011 - 33426 2011 $200

What the Children Like. London: Nister, n.d. circa, 1897, Folio, cloth backed pictorial boards, margins of few pages repaired, neat strengthening, else very good+, 5 very fine large double page chromolithographed pop-ups gorgeous illustrations. Aleph-Bet Books, Inc. 95 - 455 2011 $1200

Whately, Mary L. *Letters form Egypt to Plain Folks at Home.* London: Seeley, 1879, First edition; small 8vo., pages 259, 4 colored illustrations, small marginal foxing of illustrations not affecting images, original blue decorative cloth, spine split at head. J. & S. L. Bonham Antiquarian Booksellers Africa 4/20/2011 - 4714 2011 £55

Wheat, Carl Irving *Mapping the Transmississippi West 1540-1861.* San Francisco: 1957-1963, First edition; five volumes in six, folio, (xiv), 264; xiii, 281; xiii, 349; xiii, 260; xviii, 222; 223-487 pages, each volume profusely illustrated with map reproductions, many folded, all volumes clean and near fine. Dumont Maps & Books of the West 111 - 86 2011 $3500

Wheater, W. *Old Yorkshire. Second Series.* London: Hamilton, Adams & Co. and Leeds: Goodall & Suddick, 1885, Large paper copy; 4to., original blue cloth gilt over bevelled boards, extremities rather worn, pages x, 324, etched frontispiece and text illustrations, joints cracking. R. F. G. Hollett & Son Antiquarian Booksellers General Catalogue Summer 2010 - 1615 2011 £50

Wheatley, Charles *A Rational Illustration of the Book of Common Prayer.* London: printed for A. Bettesworth, W. & J. Innys and C. Rivington, 1720, Third edition; folio, contemporary full plain calf gilt with raised bands and spine label, few small surface defects, pages xxvi, (xxii, index), 548, engraved frontispiece, title in red and black, woodcut head and tailpieces, old tape stain to fore edge of recto of frontispiece and gutter of title, very short worm track to inner margin of few leaves, otherwise excellent unpressed copy, nice contemporary inscription from William Stratford, presenting the book to Curate of Dent, Mark Rumney and his successors.   R. F. G. Hollett & Son Antiquarian Booksellers   175 - 1431   2011   £250

Wheatley, Vera *The Life and Work of Harriet Martineau.* London: Secker & Warburg, 1957, First edition; original cloth, gilt, dust jacket, top edges trifle worn, pages 421, with 12 illustrations, inscribed by author.   R. F. G. Hollett & Son Antiquarian Booksellers   173 - 1196   2011   £40

Wheeler, Joseph L. *The American Public Library Building...* Chicago: American Library Association, 1941, 4to., original cloth, gilt, pages (x), 484, illustrations and plans, endpapers little browned and stained.   R. F. G. Hollett & Son Antiquarian Booksellers   177 - 895   2011   £75

Wheeler, Marshal *The Earth --- Its Third Motion. An Open Letter to the Scientific and Learned World.* Eugene: Harrison R. Kincaid, Oregon Sate Journal, 1889, First edition; small 4to., laflet comprising title, text on pages (2-3) page (4) blank, signed in type at conclusion and dated June 1889, near fine, rare.   M & S Rare Books, Inc.   90 - 23   2011 $225

Wheeler, Mortimer *Still Digging.* London: Michael Joseph, 1955, First edition; original cloth, gilt, dust jacket, pages 236, 17 plates, relevant press cuttings laid on to front endpapers and half title, more loosely inserted.   R. F. G. Hollett & Son Antiquarian Booksellers   177 - 897   2011   £30

Wheeler, Owen *The War Office Past and Present.* London: Methuen, 1914, First edition; original red cloth gilt, spine rather faded, light creasing to upper board, pages xii, 314, with 14 plates, uncommon.   R. F. G. Hollett & Son Antiquarian Booksellers   175 - 1432   2011   £45

Wheeler, R. E. M. *Verulamium. A Belgic and Two Roman Cities.* Oxford: University Press for the Society, 1936, First edition; small 4to., library buckram, gilt, pages xi, 244, 120 plates and plans, 49 text figures, few small library stamps.   R. F. G. Hollett & Son Antiquarian Booksellers   177 - 898   2011   £65

Wheelwright, Mary C. *Emergence Myth According to the Hanelthnayhe or Upward-Reaching rite.* Santa Fe: 1949, (x), 186 pages, illustrations, dust jacket with some light edge wear and faded spine, book near fine.   Dumont Maps & Books of the West   111 - 89   2011 $225

Wheelwright, Mary C. *Hail Chant and Water Chant.* Santa Fe: 1946, (vi), 237 pages, illustrations, near fine in dust jacket with some light edge wear.   Dumont Maps & Books of the West   111 - 88   2011 $450

Wheelwright, Mary C. *The Myth and Prayer of the Great Star Chant and Myth of the Coyote Chant.* Santa Fe: 1956, (viii), 190 pages, original cloth, lacking dust jacket, book spine faded, else near fine, 22 color serigraph plates.   Dumont Maps & Books of the West   111 - 90   2011 $225

Wheelwright, Mary C. *Navajo Creation Myth. The Story of the Emergence.* Santa Fe: 1942, Limited to 1000 copies; 237 pages, illustrations, near fine in dust jacket.   Dumont Maps & Books of the West   111 - 87   2011 $375

Whellan, William   1794-1866   *The History and Topography of the Counties of Cumberland and Westmoreland.* Pontefract: W. Whellan & Co., 1860, First edition; thick 4to., original half black morocco gilt with decorated spine, extremities rubbed, damped patch on cloth of lower board, pages vi, 896, viii scattered spotting, very good.   R. F. G. Hollett & Son Antiquarian Booksellers   173 - 1197   2011   £175

Where Shall We Go? A Guide to the Healthiest and Most Beautiful Watering Places in the British Islands... Edinburgh: Adam and Charles Black, 1864, Third edition; xvi, 279 (1) page, frontispiece, 2 plates, 3 folding maps, very good, contemporary half morocco, marbled boards, gilt lettered spine, additional tipped in slip provides information on Salburn-by-the-Sea, small 8vo.   Ken Spelman Rare Books   68 - 195   2011   £45

Whewell, William   1794-1866   *Of a Liberal Education in General: and with Particular Reference to the Leading Studies of the University of Cambridge.* London: John W. Parker, 1845, First edition; 8vo., pages xviii, 248, 15, (1), pages, original publisher's paper covered boards, with green linen spine and spine label, now somewhat faded and hard to read, corners scuffed and worn, front inner hinge cracked but holding well, slight soiling, else sound, near very good, pencilled ownership signature of historian F. R. Cowell.   Any Amount of Books   May 29 2011 - A46028   2011 $306

Whewell, William   1794-1866   *On the Principles of English University Education.* London: John W. Parker, 1837, First edition; 8vo., original publisher's blindstamped dark green cloth lettered gilt at spine, pages iv, 186, 16 page publisher's catalog at rear, slight wear at spine ends, ele very good+, excellent condition.   Any Amount of Books   May 29 2011 - A48352   2011 $204

While, J. H. Ernest *Ode on the Coronation of Their Majesties King George V and Queen Mary 1911.* Birmingham: printed at the Shakespeare Press for Siegle Hill & Co., 1911, Square 8vo., original decorated parchment, upper panel little dusty at top, 2 cm. circular stain at foot, pages (28) printed in red, black and gold, illustrated and decorated throughout by Edward Morton and H. Foster Newey. R. F. G. Hollett & Son Antiquarian Booksellers 175 - 1433 2011 £35

Whistler, Laurence *The Imagination of Vanbrugh and His Fellow Artists.* London: Art & Technics, 1954, First (only) edition; 4to., original decorated black cloth gilt, little rubbed, pages xv, 269, text decoration and illustration in green and black by Rex Whistler, 5 text illustrations and 140 plates. R. F. G. Hollett & Son Antiquarian Booksellers 177 - 900 2011 £180

Whistler, Rex *Designs for the Theatre. Part Two.* Curtain Press, 1947, First edition; 8 color plates and 17 sepia illustrations, original wrappers. R. F. G. Hollett & Son Antiquarian Booksellers 175 - 1434 2011 £30

Whitaker, Fess *History of Corporal Fess Whitaker.* Louisville: 1918, First edition; 152 pages, considerable insect spotting, one drink ring. Bookworm & Silverfish 676 - 18 2011 $85

Whitaker, Joseph I. S. *The Birds of Tunisia: Being a History of the Birds Found in the Regency of Tunis.* London: R. H. Porter, 1905, Unnumbered copy from an edition of 250 copies; 2 photo frontispieces, 2 plates, 15 hand colored plates, 2 folding colored maps, tall 8vo., pages xxxii, 294; xviii, 410, later buckram, this copy unnumbered. Raymond M. Sutton, Jr. May 26 2011 - 43264 2011 $1150

Whitaker, Thomas Dunham *Ducatus Leodiensis or the Topography of the Ancient and Populous Town and Parish of Leedes.* Leeds: printed by B. Dewhirst for Robinson, Son and Holdsworth etc. Printed by T. Davison for Robinson Son and Holdsworth etc., 1816, 2 works together as issued in 2 volumes, large paper copy, folio, pages (iv), xvii, (i), xvii, (i), 268, (ii) 123, (i), 159, 11, (i), engraved frontispiece and 10 other engraved plates, (vi), 404, 2, 88 + engraved portrait frontispiece and 52 other engraved plates, original grey sugar paper covered boards, white paper printed title labels with "Vol. 1" for the Ducatus volume and "vol. II" for the Loidis vol., all edges uncut, toned and spotted, rubbed and soiled, spine ends worn and rumpled, label edges and joints chipped, unidentified armorial bookplates, contemporary ink inscription Hallen Edge 1844, from the collection of Christopher Ernest Weston 1947-2010. Unsworths Booksellers 24 - 153 2011 £900

Whitaker, Thomas Dunham *History and Antiquities of the Deanery of Craven in the County of York.* London: printed by Nichols and sold, 1805, Folio, pages xii, 437, (i) 16 + engraved frontispiece and 36 other engraved plates, early 20th century marbled half leather, maroon bookcloth (watered design) sides, all edges uncut, toned and bit spotted, some foxing in plates, spine rubbed and faded, front joint bit worn, from the collection of Christopher Ernest Weston 1947-2010. Unsworths Booksellers 24 - 152 2011 £250

Whitaker, Thomas Dunham *The History and Antiquities of the Deanery of Craven in the County of York.* Leeds: Joseph Dodgson, 1878, Third edition; portrait, 59 plates, 29 genealogical tables, numerous text illustrations, very good, contemporary half morocco with handsome blind tooled spine and green gilt label, thick 4to. Ken Spelman Rare Books 68 - 198 2011 £295

White, Arthur Silva *The Expansion of Egypt: under Anglo-Egyptian Condominium.* London: Methuen, 1899, First edition; 8vo., pages xv, 438, ads, 4 maps, original red decorative cloth, presentation copy to Sir George Tabuman-Goldie in 1899. J. & S. L. Bonham Antiquarian Booksellers Africa 4/20/2011 - 8260 2011 £100

White, E. B. *Charlotte's Web.* New York: Harper Brothers, 1952, Stated first edition; 8vo., tan cloth, fine in fine dust jacket, illustrations by Garth Williams, more than 40 black and white plates plus color jacket, magnificent copy. Aleph-Bet Books, Inc. 95 - 586 2011 $2250

White, Edward Lucas *Lukundoo and Other Stories.* New York: George H. Doran, 1927, First edition; octavo (pages (1-8) 9-328, original decorated blue cloth, front and spine panels stamped in gold, fore edge untrimmed, bottom edge rough trimmed. L. W. Currey, Inc. 124 - 87 2011 $1000

White, Gilbert 1720-1793 *Natural History and Antiquities of Selborne, in the County of Southampton.* London: printed by T. Bensley for B. Shite and Son, 1789, First edition; quarto, v, (1, blank), 468 (i.e. 466), (12, index) (1, errata), (1 blank) pages, folding engraved frontispiece, 2 engraved title vignettes, 6 engraved plates, engravings by Peter Mazell and Daniel Lerpinire after drawing by Samuel Grimm, bound by Riviere & Son in full olive morocco, boards ruled in gilt, spine decoratively stamped and lettered in gilt, marbled endpapers, all edges gilt, very good. Heritage Book Shop Holiday 2010 - 129 2011 $2750

White, Gilbert 1720-1793 *The Natural History and Antiquities of Selborne.* London: J. & A. Arch; Longman, etc., printed at the Chiswick Press, 1833, Half title, some woodcut illustrations in text, slightly later dark green calf, green cloth boards, maroon label, very good. Jarndyce Antiquarian Booksellers CXCI - 343 2011 £125

White, Gilbert 1720-1793 *The Natural History and Antiquites of Selborne.* London: Printed at the Chiswick Press for J. and A. Arch, etc., 1833, First Rennie eition; pages 378, all edges an endpapers marbled, illustrated with text woodcuts, prize label of Windermere Grammar School on pastedown.   R. F. G. Hollett & Son Antiquarian Booksellers   General Catalogue Summer 2010 - 1071 2011   £120

White, James *Treatise on Veterinary Medicine.* London: Longman, Hurst etc., 1822-, 1823-1825. Various editions; 4 volumes, small 8vo., contemporary full tree calf, gilt, pages xlvi, 348; xii , 329; xii, 384; xvi, 331, with 24 engraved plates, scattered foxing but attractive set.   R. F. G. Hollett & Son Antiquarian Booksellers   General Catalogue Summer 2010 - 1151   2011   £375

White, James *A Treatise on Veterinary Medicine.* London: Longman, Hurst (and others), 1820-1821, Mixed edition, volume i 12th edition, volume ii new edition, volume iii third edition, volume iv first edition; 19 plates, very good in uniform 19th century half calf, 12mo.   Ken Spelman Rare Books   68 - 161 2011   £225

White, Jim *A Crow's Story of Deer.* Santa Barbara: Capra Press, 1974, first edition; pictorial boards, copy #42 of 75 numbered and signed copies with additional small drawing by author, fine.   Charles Agvent   2010 Summer Miscellany - 67   2011 $75

White, John *Three Letters to a Gentleman Dissenting form the Church of England.* London: printed for C. Davis, 1748, Pages lx, 277, (iii), contemporary calf, gilt, rubbed.   R. F. G. Hollett & Son Antiquarian Booksellers   175 - 1435   2011   £150

White, John Pagen *Lays and Legends of the English Lake Country with Copious Notes.* John Russell Smith & Carlisle: G. & T. Coward, 1873, Original cloth gilt over bevelled boards, spine rather faded, recased, pages xvi, 334, (viii, ads).   R. F. G. Hollett & Son Antiquarian Booksellers   173 - 1199   2011   £45

White, John W. *Jubilee History of West Stanley Co-Operative Society Limited 1876 to 1926.* Pelaw-on-Tyne: Co-operative Wholesale Society's printing Works, 1926, Original cloth, gilt, pages 226 with 45 plates, contemporary address on pastedown.   R. F. G. Hollett & Son Antiquarian Booksellers   General Catalogue Summer 2010 - 1617   2011   £50

White, Leslie A. *The Pueblo of Santa Ana, New Mexico.* New York: 1969, Reprint of 1942 first edition; 360 pages, illustrations, original printed wrappers lightly soiled, else near fine.   Dumont Maps & Books of the West   112 - 66   2011 $65

White, Minor *Mirrors Messages Manifestations.* New York: Aperture, 1969, First edition; several hundred photographs, fine, small owner signature and date from a student of White's on front free endpaper copy, text booklet in bright, very near fine dust jacket with none of the usual fading to spine, signed and inscribed by White to this student, very uncommon signed.   Jeff Hirsch Books   ny 2010 2011 $1250

White, Randy Wayne *Batfishing in the Rainforest.* New York: Lyons & Burford, 1991, First edition; near fine, very light use, dust jacket near fine, hint of creasing to spine.   Bella Luna Books   May 26 2011 - t152   2011 $165

White, Randy Wayne *Captive.* New York: Putnam, 1996, First edition; fine, dust jacket fine, signed by author.   Bella Luna Books   May 29 2011 - j1251   2011 $82

White, Walter *A Month in Yorkshire.* London: Chapman and Hall, 1861, Fourth edition; original blindstamped cloth gilt, spine little faded and marked, pages xv, 272, folding map.   R. F. G. Hollett & Son Antiquarian Booksellers   General Catalogue Summer 2010 - 1618   2011   £65

White, William *The Visitor's Guide to Cambridge.* Cambridge: Metcalfe & Co., circa, 1880, Second edition; 10 pages initial ads, folding map, illustrations, 6 pages ads, original pictorial wrappers, printed in red and blue, back cover ad, very good.   Jarndyce Antiquarian Booksellers   CXCI - 375   2011   £75

The Whitehead Catalogue. James and Charles Whitehead, Manufacturers, Hanley, Staffordshire. Bletchley: D. B. Drakard, n.d., 1970, 4to., original cloth, gilt, pages (vi), 25, 30, 4 (facsimiles).   R. F. G. Hollett & Son Antiquarian Booksellers   General Catalogue Summer 2010 - 189   2011   £50

Whitehead, Henry *Talks About Brampton in the Olden Times.* Selkirk: James Lewis, 1907, First edition; original green cloth, upper board rather spotted, pages (vi), 240, text illustrations, front flyleaf removed, otherwise very good, scarce.   R. F. G. Hollett & Son Antiquarian Booksellers   173 - 1204   2011   £120

Whitehead, Henry *West India Lights.* Sauk City: Arkham House, 1946, First edition; octavo, original black cloth, spine panel stamped in black.   L. W. Currey, Inc.   124 - 219   2011 $150

Whitehead, R. B. *The Pre-Mohammedan Coinage of Northwestern India.* New York: American Numismatic Society, 1922, First edition; 56 pages + plates, black and white photos, 16mo., paper wrappers, very good,.   Kaaterskill Books   12 - 209   2011 $75

Whitehead, Roberta *Five and Ten.* Boston: Houghton Mifflin, 1943, First edition; 8vo., red pictorial cloth, fine in dust jacket mended on verso, full page color illustrations by Lois Lenski, quite uncommon. Aleph-Bet Books, Inc. 95 - 332 2011 $250

Whitehead, Thomas *History of the Dales Congregational Churches Sedbergh, Dent, Ravenstonedale and Kirkby Lonsdale.* Keighley: Feather Bros., 1932, Original wrappers, edges little faded, pages 73, with numerous illustrations and double page map, scarce. R. F. G. Hollett & Son Antiquarian Booksellers General Catalogue Summer 2010 - 1619 2011 £45

Whitelocke, Bulstrode *A Journal of the Swedish Embassy in the Years 1653 and 1654.* London: Longman, Brown, Green and Longmans,, 1855, New edition; 2 volumes, 8vo., soundly rebound with title inked on plain white label on spine, slightly stained and faded, boards very good with clean text, pages xlvii, 451 & 468 with 24 page publisher's catalog at rear, ex-British Foreign Office library with few library markings, else very good. Any Amount of Books May 29 2011 - A70590 2011 $238

Whiteside, J. *Shappe in Bygone Days.* Kendal: Titus Wilson, 1904, First edition; original green cloth, gilt over bevelled boards, pages xvi, 395, uncut, frontispiece, 21 plates, odd spot, excellent copy, scarce. R. F. G. Hollett & Son Antiquarian Booksellers 173 - 1205 2011 £195

Whitfield, Christopher *Together and Alone.* Waltham St. Lawrence: Golden Cockerel Press, 1945, First edition, 76/100 copies (of an edition of 500); signed by author and John O'Connor, the artist, printed on Arnold mouldmade paper, 10 wood engravings by O'Connor, pages (ii) (blanks), 110, (2) (blanks), 8vo., original cream morocco, backstrip gilt lettered, faintly rubbed Cockerell marbled cloth sides, morocco bookplate, top edge gilt, others untrimmed, cloth slipcase, very good. Blackwell Rare Books B166 - 264 2011 £150

Whitier, Leonard *Spode. A History of the Family, Factory and Wares from 1733 to 1833.* New York: Praeger, 1970, First edition; 4to., original coarse weave cloth gilt, dust jacket (few slight edge tears), pages xiii, 246, with 9 color plates, 302 monochrome illustrations and numerous other illustrations, examples of marks, etc. R. F. G. Hollett & Son Antiquarian Booksellers General Catalogue Summer 2010 - 343 2011 £35

Whiting, Sydney *Memoirs of a Stomach.* W. E. Painter, 1853, Third edition; text slightly browned with largely inoffensive damp mark to upper margin, contemporary half blue cloth, booklabel and stamp of Norfolk & Norwich Library. Jarndyce Antiquarian Booksellers CXCI - 616 2011 £40

Whiting, W. *Report on the Excavation of the Roman Cemetery at Ospringe Kent.* Oxford University Press for the Society, 1931, Small 4to., library binding of quarter calf gilt, little rubbed, original wrappers bound in pages 107 with 64 plates and plans, some folding, 5 text figures, few small library stamps. R. F. G. Hollett & Son Antiquarian Booksellers 177 - 901 2011 £45

Whitling, Henry John *Pictures of Nuremberg; and Rambles in the Hills and Valleys of Franconia.* London: Richard Bentley, 1850, First edition; 2 volumes, half titles, frontispiece, illustrations, slight foxing to illustrations, original orange cloth, slightly dulled, small armorial booklabels of Etherington Welch Rolls, very good, crisp copy. Jarndyce Antiquarian Booksellers CXCI - 584 2011 £280

Whitman, Walt 1819-1892 *After All, Not to Create Only.* Boston: Roberts Brothers, 1871, First trade edition; 8vo., original green flexible cloth, gilt lettering, cloth little worn, very good, from the collection of Samuel Charters. The Brick Row Book Shop Bulletin 8 - 15 2011 $750

Whitman, Walt 1819-1892 *Autobiographia or the Story of My Life.* New York: Charles L. Webster, 1892, First edition, issue A; 8vo., original decorated olive green cloth, gilt lettered, frontispiece, cloth little darkened, ink signature lettered dated 1901 across titlepage, very good, from the collection of Samuel Charters. The Brick Row Book Shop Bulletin 8 - 37 2011 $125

Whitman, Walt 1819-1892 *Calamus: a Series of Letters Written During the Years 1868-1880...* Boston: Small, Maynard, 1897, Trade edition, issue B; 8vo., original green cloth, gilt lettered, frontispiece and one plate, spine slightly faded to blue, fine, from the collection of Samuel Charters. The Brick Row Book Shop Bulletin 8 - 39 2011 $350

Whitman, Walt 1819-1892 *Calamus. A Series of Letters Written During the Years 1868-1880.* Boston: published by Laurens Maynard at 287 Congress Steeet, 1897, First (trade) edition, first issue, following a limited edition of 35 large paper copies signed by Dr. Bucke, of which 243 were for sale; small 8vo., frontispiece and facsimile, original yellow green cloth with blindstamped covers, usual discoloration of illustrations and page margins, head of spine trifle rubbed, otherwise fine, presentation copy inscribed at top of front free endpaper "Patrick Dougherty with the regards of Pete Doyle". James S. Jaffe Rare Books May 26 2011 - 13860 2011 $17,500

Whitman, Walt 1819-1892 *Dirge for Two Veterans.* New York: Edward Schuberth, 1880, First edition; folio, original printed self wrappers, 8 pages, very good, from the collection of Samuel Charters. The Brick Row Book Shop Bulletin 8 - 19 2011 $850

Whitman, Walt 1819-1892   *Drum-Taps.* New York: published by the author, 1865,   First edition, first issue; 12mo., original brown cloth, round gilt decoration on upper board, repeated in blind on lower board, some minor discoloration on edges of prelims and endpapers, cloth slightly worn, very good, from the collection of Samuel Charters.   The Brick Row Book Shop   Bulletin 8 - 11   2011 $17,500

Whitman, Walt 1819-1892   *Drum-Taps.* New York: published by author, 1865,   First edition, first printing, second issue; 12mo., original brown cloth, round gilt decoration on upper board, repeated in blind on lower board, contemporary inscription on front free endpaper and notes in pencil on rear free endpaper, paper little browned, cloth slightly worn, good, sound, from the collection of Samuel Charters.   The Brick Row Book Shop   Bulletin 8 - 12   2011 $4500

Whitman, Walt 1819-1892   *Drum-Taps. (with) Sequel to Drum-Taps.* New York & Washington: 1865-1866,   First edition, 2nd issue; small 8vo., original plum cloth, dust jacket inscription on front free endpaper, hint of wear to spine and extremities, otherwise exceptionally fine bright copy, in black half morocco slipcase, rare in this condition.   James S. Jaffe Rare Books   May 26 2011 - 13036 2011 $17,500

Whitman, Walt 1819-1892   *The Earlier Poems and Fiction.* New York: New York University Press, 1963, First edition; 4to. original red half cloth, gilt lettered, very good, printed dust jacket, from the collection of Samuel Charters.   The Brick Row Book Shop   Bulletin 8 - 48 2011 $75

Whitman, Walt 1819-1892   *Franklin Evans or the Inebriate...* New York: Random House, 1929,   Second edition, one of 700 copies; 8vo., original patterned blue cloth, printed paper label, cloth slightly stained, very good, from the collection of Samuel Charters.   The Brick Row Book Shop   Bulletin 8 - 47 2011 $125

Whitman, Walt 1819-1892   *The Gathering of the Forces.* New York and London: G. P. Putnam's Sons, 1920,   First edition, one of 1250 sets; 2 volumes, 8vo., gray paper boards, brown leather labels, gilt lettered, untrimmed, 2 frontispiece portraits, 6 plates, one folding facsimile, fine copies in original printed dust jackets (little chipped and worn, with piece missing from one spine), from the collection of Samuel Charters.   The Brick Row Book Shop   Bulletin 8 - 45 2011 $500

Whitman, Walt 1819-1892   *Gems from Walt Whitman.* Philadelphia: David McKay, 1889,   First edition; oblong 12mo., original maroon cloth, gilt lettering, top edge gilt, edges slightly rubbed, fine, from the collection of Samuel Charters.   The Brick Row Book Shop   Bulletin 8 - 35 2011 $250

Whitman, Walt 1819-1892   *Good-Bye My Fancy: 2nd Annex to Leaves of Grass.* Philadelphia: David McKay, 1891,   First edition; 8vo. original maroon cloth, beveled edges, gilt lettered, top edge gilt, frontispiece, from the library of A. J. A. Symons, with his Brick House bookplate, small nick in spine, edges little rubbed and faded, good, from the collection of Samuel Charters.   The Brick Row Book Shop   Bulletin 8 - 36 2011 $400

Whitman, Walt 1819-1892   *Leaves of Grass.* Brooklyn: published by author, 1855,   First edition, 2nd issue binding, second state of page iv; the 795 copies were bound in different stages, and this one of the 262 bound between Dec. 1855 and Jan. 1856, 4to., original decoratively blindstamped green cloth, gilt lettering, engraved frontispiece, 8 pages of extracts of reviews and notices tipped in before frontispiece, bookplate of Arthur B. Spingarn (1878-1971), from the collection of Samuel Charters.   The Brick Row Book Shop   Bulletin 8 - 5   2011 $125,000

Whitman, Walt 1819-1892   *Leaves of Grass.* Brooklyn: published by the author, 1856,   Second edition; 12mo., original grey-green cloth, decoratively blindstamped, gilt decorations and lettering, engraved frontispiece by Samuel Hollyer, bookplates of E. M. Cox and Michael Sadleir, cloth slightly rubbed, some light to moderate foxing, fine, from the collection of Samuel Charters.   The Brick Row Book Shop   Bulletin 8 - 6   2011 $22,500

Whitman, Walt 1819-1892   *Leaves of Grass.* Boston: Thayer and Eldridge, 1860-1861,   Third edition, first printing; 12mo., original reddish orange cloth, blindstamped decorations and gilt lettering, frontispiece, cloth skillfully repaired at edges, spine somewhat soiled, very good, from the collection of Samuel Charters.   The Brick Row Book Shop   Bulletin 8 - 9   2011 $1800

Whitman, Walt 1819-1892   *Leaves of Grass.* New York: published by the author, 1867,   Fourth edition, 2nd issue without "Drum-Taps" present but with "Songs Before Departing"; 12mo., black quarter calf, marbled paper sides, gilt lettering, spine skillfully rebacked, paper little browned, endpapers and few margins with paper repairs at edges, very good, from the collection of Samuel Charters.   The Brick Row Book Shop   Bulletin 8 - 13 2011 $2250

Whitman, Walt 1819-1892   *Leaves of Grass.* Washington: 1872, for London: John Camden Hotten, 1873,   Sixth edition; 8vo., original dark green cloth, gilt lettering, untrimmed, edges somewhat worn, cloth slightly stained, very good, from the collection of Samuel Charters.   The Brick Row Book Shop   Bulletin 8 - 17 2011 $1250

Whitman, Walt 1819-1892 *Leaves of Grass.* Camden: Author's Edition, 1876, Fifth edition, third printing, second issue, one of 600 copies signed by author; 8vo., original cream quarter calf and corners, marbled boards, gilt lettering, 2 portraits, this copy inscribed to English botanist Sidney H. Vines, from the author, binding little soiled and rubbed, some slight foxing, very good, much nicer than usual for this fragile binding, from the collection of Samuel Charters.   The Brick Row Book Shop   Bulletin 8 - 18 2011 $9000

Whitman, Walt 1819-1892 *Leaves of Grass.* Boston: Thayer and Eldridge, 1860-1861 (but New York: Richard Worthington,, 1879, or after). Later issue of the 1860-61 third edition using original plates but printed about 1879 or after; 8vo., dark maroon brown cloth, gilt lettering, frontispiece, cloth little worn and faded, edges slightly stained, chip in upper corner of front free endpaper, good, from the collection of Samuel Charters.   The Brick Row Book Shop   Bulletin 8 - 10 2011 $150

Whitman, Walt 1819-1892 *Leaves of Grass.* Boston: James R. Osgood, 1881-1882, Seventh edition, first printing, also known as the "suppressed" edition; 8vo., original mustard yellow cloth, gilt decorated and lettered, engraved portrait, cloth somewhat stained and worn, inner hinges starting, sound, good copy, from the collection of Samuel Charters.   The Brick Row Book Shop   Bulletin 8 - 20 2011 $350

Whitman, Walt 1819-1892 *Leave of Grass.* Philadelphia: Rees, Welsh and Co., 1882, Seventh edition, fourth printing; 8vo., original dark mustard yellow cloth, gilt decorated and lettered, portrait, cloth little worn and soiled, very good, from the collection of Samuel Charters.   The Brick Row Book Shop   Bulletin 8 - 22 2011 $375

Whitman, Walt 1819-1892 *Leaves of Grass.* Philadelphia: David McKay, 1883, Seventh edition, 10th printing; original cabinet photo of Whitman by Frank Parsall, which is laid down to front blank, 8vo., original dark mustard yellow cloth, gilt decorated and lettered, good, from the collection of Samuel Charters.   The Brick Row Book Shop   Bulletin 8 - 27 2011 $450

Whitman, Walt 1819-1892 *Leaves of Grass.* Philadelphia: David McKay, 1883, Seventh edition, 10th printing; 8vo., original dark mustard yellow cloth, gilt decorated and lettered, edges little rubbed, particularly at bottom near spine and soiled, lacking front free endpaper, good, from the collection of Samuel Charters.   The Brick Row Book Shop   Bulletin 8 - 26 2011 $150

Whitman, Walt 1819-1892 *Leaves of Grass. The Poems of Walt Whitman.* London: Walter Scott, 1886, Eighth edition, first printing, binding B; small 8vo., original navy blue cloth, printed paper label, frontispiece, label and cloth somewhat worn, good, from the collection of Samuel Charters.   The Brick Row Book Shop   Bulletin 8 - 29 2011 $100

Whitman, Walt 1819-1892 *Leaves of Grass.* Philadelphia: David McKay, 1888, Seventh edition, 12th printing; 8vo., original mustard cloth, gilt decorations and lettering, top edge gilt, others untrimmed, engraved portrait, edges rubbed, hinges repaired, few pages little roughly opened, some light foxing, very good, from the collection of Samuel Charters.   The Brick Row Book Shop   Bulletin 8 - 33 2011 $375

Whitman, Walt 1819-1892 *Leaves of Grass with Sands at Seventy & A Backward Glance O'er Travel'd Roads.* Philadelphia: Ferguson Bros. & Co., 1889, Seventh edition, 14th printing of Leaves of Grass in Myerson's presumed second binding with double laid paper flyleaves but varying from bibliographer's description of the second binding in having accordion flaps on sides connected at bottom as in first binding, limited to 300 copies printed on India paper and signed on titlepage by Whitman; 8vo., original photo frontispiece, 5 additional portraits throughout text, original wallet style black leather, over flexible boards, head of spine lightly worn, small three quarter inch split to leather at spine fold, light scuffing to leather covers, but very good, very scarce, presentation copy inscribed by author to Mr. Bancroft.   James S. Jaffe Rare Books   May 26 2011 - 13858 2011 $10,000

Whitman, Walt 1819-1892 *Leaves of Grass.* Philadelphia: McKay, 1891-1892, Deathbed edition; 8vo., portrait inserted, original heavy grey wrappers, printed yellow spine label The Garden copy, front lower wrapper split approximately 2 1/2 inches at joint, otherwise fine, unopened in half morocco slipcase, inscribed in Horace Traubel's hand "To Warren Fitzinger Jan. 7 1892 given by direction of Walt Whitman from his sick bed. H.L.T.".   James S. Jaffe Rare Books   May 26 2011 - 21628 2011 $35,000

Whitman, Walt 1819-1892 *Leaves of Grass. Including Sands a Seventy, Good-Bye My Fancy, A Backward Glance O'er the Travel'd Roads and Portraits from Life.* Philadelphia: David McKay, 1894, Seventh edition; 8vo., original green cloth, gilt lettered, top edge gilt, others untrimmed, engraved portrait, some slight browning to endpapers and prelims, edges lightly rubbed, fine, from the collection of Samuel Charters.   The Brick Row Book Shop   Bulletin 8 - 38 2011 $475

Whitman, Walt 1819-1892   *Leaves of Grass.* Philadelphia: David McKay, 1900, Edition not determined, but tenth or so; 8vo., original decorated green cloth, gilt lettering, top edge gilt, others untrimmed, spine little dull, very good, from the collection of Samuel Charters.   The Brick Row Book Shop   Bulletin 8 - 42 2011 $75

Whitman, Walt 1819-1892   *November Boughs.* Philadelphia: David McKay, 1888, First edition, third printing, binding C, but in cloth color not recorded; 4to., original green cloth, gilt lettering, top edge gilt, others untrimmed, one leaf of publisher's terminal ads for other Whitman titles, large copy, edges little worn, inner hinges broken, good, from the collection of Samuel Charters.   The Brick Row Book Shop   Bulletin 8 - 31 2011 $200

Whitman, Walt 1819-1892   *November Boughs.* Philadelphia: David McKay, 1888, First edition, first printing, binding D; 4to., original maroon cloth, gilt lettering, top edge gilt, frontispiece, cloth little worn, some slight smudges in text, very good, from the collection of Samuel Charters. The Brick Row Book Shop   Bulletin 8 - 30 2011 $500

Whitman, Walt 1819-1892   *November Boughs.* Philadelphia: David McKay, 1888, First edition, 3rd printing, binding C but in cloth color not recorded; 4to., original green cloth, gilt lettered, top edge gilt, others untrimmed, large copy, beveled edges, cloth slightly worn, very good, from the collection of Samuel Charters.   The Brick Row Book Shop   Bulletin 8 - 32 2011 $500

Whitman, Walt 1819-1892   *November Boughs.* Philadelphia: David McKay, 1888, First edition, large paper issue (only 400 issued); in green cloth binding with beveled edges and top edges gilt, some repair to (inner) paper hinge, otherwise near fine, signed by Thomas B. Harned, Literary Executor of Walt Whitman.   Lupack Rare Books   May 26 2011 - ABE4633235541 2011 $375

Whitman, Walt 1819-1892   *Complete Poems & Prose of Walt Whitman 1855.... 1888.* Camden: Published by the author, 1888, Seventh edition, 13th printing, number 213 of 600 numbered copies, signed by Whitman; large 8vo., original olive brown buckram, top edge gilt, gilt lettered, illustrated titlepage, gilt lettered, illustrated titlepage, 3 inserted portraits, edges little rubbed, recased, edges little rubbed, recased with new endpapers, very good, enclosed in clamshell box, from the collection of Samuel Charters.   The Brick Row Book Shop   Bulletin 8 - 34 2011 $4250

Whitman, Walt 1819-1892   *Specimen Days & Collect.* Philadelphia: Rees Welsh, 1882-1883, First edition, first printing; 8vo., original mustard yellow cloth, gilt lettered, photographic portrait of Whitman with butterfly on his finger, one terminal leaf of publisher's ads; portrait from magazine tipped to front free endpaper; spine slightly darkened and worn at head and foot, very good, from the collection of Samuel Charters.   The Brick Row Book Shop   Bulletin 8 - 24 2011 $450

Whitman, Walt 1819-1892   *Specimen Days & Collect.* Philadelphia: David McKay, 1882-1883, First edition, 2nd printing; 8vo., original dark mustard yellow cloth, gilt decorations and lettering, photo portrait, cloth somewhat soiled, slight dampstaining to few margins, good, from the collection of Samuel Charters.   The Brick Row Book Shop   Bulletin 8 - 25 2011 $150

Whitman, Walt 1819-1892   *Walt Whitman's Blue Book. The 1860-61 Leaves of Grass Containing His Manuscript Additions and Revisions.* New York: New York Public Library, 1968, First edition; 2 volumes, 8vo., blue cloth, gilt lettered, fine, publisher's slipcase, from the collection of Samuel Charters.   The Brick Row Book Shop   Bulletin 8 - 49 2011 $250

Whitman, Walt 1819-1892   *The Complete Writings.* New York: G. P. Putnam's Sons, 1902, Paumanok Edition, limited to 300 numbered sets; printed on Ruisdael handmade paper (of which this is #92), signed by publisher, 10 volumes, large octavo, etched and photogravure frontispieces and plates with decorative tissue guards, publisher's three quarter dark green morocco over marbled boards, ruled in gilt, spines lettered and decoratively tooled in gilt in compartments in a floral design, top edge gilt, others uncut, marbled endpapers, fine set.   David Brass Rare Books, Inc.   May 26 2011 - 00912 2011 $12,500

Whitman, Walt 1819-1892   *The Wound Dresser: a Series of Letters Written from the Hospitals in Washington During the War of the Rebellion.* Boston: Small Maynard, 1898, First edition; trade issue, second issue, 8vo., original red cloth, gilt lettered, frontispiece, one plate, spine little dull, very good, from the collection of Samuel Charters. The Brick Row Book Shop   Bulletin 8 - 41 2011 $200

Whitman, Walt 1819-1892   *The Complete Writings of Walt Whitman.* New York: G. P. Putnam's Sons, 1902, Paumanok Edition, limited to 300 numbered sets, this being number 21; printed on Ruisdael handmade paper, 10 volumes, large octavo, aquatint etched and photogravure frontispieces and plates with descriptive tissue guards, titlepages printed in red and black, additional engraved titlepages, printed in red and green, handsomely bound in full burgundy morocco, covers decoratively ruled and stamped in gilt, spines decoratively paneled and lettered in gilt in compartments, five raised bands, top edge gilt, others uncut, gilt dentelles, green suede doublures and liners, professional and near invisible repairs to some head-caps and tailpieces, overall superb set.   Heritage Book Shop   Holiday 2010 - 130 2011 $8500

Whitney, Adeline Dutton *A Golden Gossip. Neighborhood Story Number Two.* Boston and New York: Houghton Mifflin and Co., Riverside Press, Cambridge, 1892, First edition; (iv, 348) pages, 12mo., light green cloth with smooth dark green and gilt lettered spine with elongated dahlia running straight down spine, front cover stamped in dark green, gray coated endpapers, except for touch of wear on extremities and Brentano's book ticket inside rear cover, fine in very handsome Whitman binding.   Paulette Rose Fine and Rare Books   32 - 185   2011 $100

Whitney, Josiah Dwight *The Yosemite Book.* New York: Julius Bien, 1868, First edition, one of 250 copies; quarto, (5), 116 pages, plus 28 mounted albumen photos and 2 maps, photos measure 6 x 8 inches, publisher's three quarter brown morocco, marbled endpapers, spine gold tooled, gold stamping to cloth, light foxing to text pages, photos, very good to very fine.   Argonaut Book Shop   Recent Acquisitions Summer 2010 - 229   2011 $17,500

Whittier, John Greenleaf 1807-1892 *Moll Pitcher, a Poems.* Boston: Carter and Hendee, 1832, First edition; 8vo., original printed blue wrappers, uncut, slight chipping of spine, Massachusetts library stamp at top of verso of titlepage, great rarity in wrappers.   M & S Rare Books, Inc.   90 - 444   2011 $15,000

Whittier, John Greenleaf 1807-1892 *Moll Pitcher, and the Minstrel Girl. Poems.* Philadelphia: Joseph Healy, 1840, First complete edition; 18mo., 44 pages, original printed wrappers, light soiling, slight chipping.   M & S Rare Books, Inc.   90 - 445   2011 $750

Whittier, John Greenleaf 1807-1892 *The Poetical Works.* Oxford University Press, 1909, Full crimson padded morocco gilt with repeated art nouveau design of triple flowers on upper board, backstrip trifle faded, pages xv, 598, all edges gilt, frontispiece.   R. F. G. Hollett & Son Antiquarian Booksellers   General Catalogue Summer 2010 - 682   2011   £45

Whittier, John Greenleaf 1807-1892 *Works (bound with) Life and Letters of John Greenleaf Whittier.* Boston and New York: printed at the Riverside Press for Houghton Mifflina and Co., 1892-1894, Artist's edition, one of 750 copies; 223 x 150mm., seven volume set of the works and 2 volume biography, bound in 9, 223 x 150mm., beautiful ochre crushed morocco elegantly gilt (stamp signed)), covers with border of two thin gilt fillets and with cornerpieces, composed of three gilt leaves on interlacing sinuous tendrils, raised bands, spine compartments with more scrolling gilt tendrils and leaves, wide turn-ins, striking burgundy crushed morocco doublures, slender stems and leaves recurring at corners here and with elaborate variation of this motif at center of doublures, watered silk endleaves, top edge gilt, other edges untrimmed and the set entirely unopened, vignette titlepages and 81 plates (etchings and photogravures), including frontispieces in two states (black and white and colored) and specimen of Whittier's hand, tissue guards with printed captions, ALS by Whittier tipped in, spines uniformly faded to a pleasing butterscotch color, some slight fading extending onto a few of the covers, one cover with shadow of a bookend, minor scratches on cople of boards, another cover with some faintly dull spots, still very fine set in lovely bindings, leather with virtually no wear, unopened, text not surprisingly without any signs of use.   Phillip J. Pirages   59 - 346   2011 $3250

Whittington-Egan, Richard *A Casebook On Jack the Ripper.* London: Wildy & Sons, 1975, First edition; 8vo, red gilt decorated Rexine covers, pages xviii, 174, loosely inserted is handwritten letter from author making offer on some "Dougal Case papers" and flyer for book showing that it is limited to 700 copies, endpapers very slightly foxed, otherwise fine in glassine dust jacket.   Any Amount of Books   May 29 2011 - A73487   2011 $315

Whittington, Stephen *Bones of the Maya.* Smithsonian Institution Press, 1997, First edition; small 4to., original cloth, dust jacket, pages x, 290, well illustrated.   R. F. G. Hollett & Son Antiquarian Booksellers   177 - 902   2011   £30

Whittle, G. *The Newcastle & Carlisle Railway.* David & Charles, 1979, First edition; original cloth, gilt, dust jacket, 208 pages, well illustrated.   R. F. G. Hollett & Son Antiquarian Booksellers   173 - 1206   2011   £40

Who Killed Cock Robin. London: Tuck, n.d. circa, 1890, 4to., pictorial wrappers, fine, 6 fine full page chromolithographs plus many brown illustrations.   Aleph-Bet Books, Inc.   95 - 158   2011 $275

Who Owns Whom. London: Ap Information Services, 2006, First edition; 3 volumes, illustrated laminated boards, pages 6196, may show some very slight shelfwear, but contents fine and unread, exceptional condition.   Any Amount of Books   May 29 2011 - A73092   2011 $408

Who Was Who. London: Adam & Charles Black, 1966-1991, 9 volumes, 8vo., all very good or better in like dust jackets, first 6 volumes presentation from Roy Jenkins to Ian Gilmour.   Any Amount of Books   May 26 2011 - A70295   2011 $419

The Whole Duty of Man, Laid Down in a Plain and Familiar Way, for the Use of All... London: printed for John Eyres, William and John Mount and Thomas Page, 1748, Contemporary calf, gilt, little worn, pages xvi, 503, (ix), engraved frontispiece and title.   R. F. G. Hollett & Son Antiquarian Booksellers   175 - 38   2011   £65

Who's Who in Cumberland and Westmorland. 1937, Limited edition, number 30; tall 8vo., original two tone cloth, gilt, pages 246, uncut, very nice, clean and bright.   R. F. G. Hollett & Son Antiquarian Booksellers   173 - 1207   2011   £85

Who's Who in France 2005-2006. Levallois Perret: Jacques Lafitte, 2005, First edition; large fat 4to., original publisher's red cloth lettered gilt on spine and on front cover, pages 2351 copiously illustrated in color and black and white, French text, ex Foreign and Commonwealth Office library with their label and stamps lightly applied, otherwise very good+.   Any Amount of Books   May 29 2011 - A48255   2011 $306

Whymper, F.   *The Sea.*   London: Cassell Petter & Galpin, n.d., 4 volumes in 2, contemporary half calf gilt with raised bands and spine labels, slight wear to short length of one fore-edge, pages viii,3 20, viii, 320; viii, 320, viii, 320, viii, 320, colored plate and 400 full page and text woodcut illustrations, excellent set.   R. F. G. Hollett & Sons Antiquarian Booksellers   170 - 727   2011   £180

Wiedemann, A.   *Religion of the Ancient Egyptians.*   H. Grevel & Co., 1897, First edition; original cloth, gilt, pages xvi, 324, 16, top edge gilt with 73 illustrations.   R. F. G. Hollett & Son Antiquarian Booksellers   177 - 904   2011   £120

Wiesel, Elie   *The Judges.*   Norwalk: Easton Press, 1999, Number 619 of 1250 copies; signed by author on limitation page, leather with gold titles and decorations, all edges gilt, silk endpapers and ribbon bookmark, "a note about" card and signed certificate of authenticity folded in, very clean, and tight, 209 pages, bookplates included but not affixed, signed first edition, fine.   G. H. Mott Bookseller   May 26 2011 - 37045   2011 $260

Wiesner, David   *Flotsam.*   New York: Clarion, 2006, First edition; fine, in fine dust jacket, inscribed by author "say cheese!".   Bella Luna Books   May 29 2011 - p3371   2011 $82

Wiggin, Kate Douglas   *Penelope's English Experiences.*   Gay & Bird, 1900, First edition thus; original decorated green cloth gilt, pages xii, 174, 16, all edges gilt, illustrations.   R. F. G. Hollett & Son Antiquarian Booksellers General Catalogue Summer 2010 - 741   2011   £35

Wiggin, Kate Douglas   *Penelope's Experiences in England. Penelope's Progress In Scotland and Penelope's Irish Experiences.*   Boston: Houghton Mifflin, 1901, 1902.; 3 volumes, 8vo., green cloth elaborately stamped in gold, top edge gilt, fine, each volume illustrated with beautiful black and white illustrations by C. E. Brock, lengthy inscription from Wiggin to Irish Singer Tom Dobson in each of the Three books, marvelous set.   Aleph-Bet Books, Inc.   95 - 587   2011 $650

Wiggin, Kate Douglas   *Penelope's English Experiences.*   London: Gay and Bird, 1903, First edition; pages xii, 174, original decorated green cloth, gilt, all edges gilt, illustrations by Charles Brock.   R. F. G. Hollett & Son Antiquarian Booksellers   General Catalogue Summer 2010 - 925   2011   £30

Wiggin, Kate Douglas   *Penelope's Irish Experiences.*   Gay and Bird, 1902, First edition thus; original decorated green cloth gilt, pages xiv, 334, 16, all edges gilt, illustrations by Charles Brock.   R. F. G. Hollett & Son Antiquarian Booksellers   General Catalogue Summer 2010 - 926   2011   £35

Wilberforce, Albert Basil Orme   *Sermons in the Parish Magazine of St. John', Kensington.*   St. John's Parish, 1905-1916, Small 4to., contemporary binder's cloth, gilt, unpaginated.   R. F. G. Hollett & Son Antiquarian Booksellers   175 - 1440   2011   £75

Wilbur, Richard   *Things of this World.*   New York: Harcourt Brace, 1956, First edition; signed by William S. Burford with a few of his notes in text, small stain front flyleaf, near fine in very good dust jacket with some rubbing, sunning and wear.   Ken Lopez Bookseller   154 - 242   2011 $150

Wilcox, E. G.   *The Lost Plum Cake/A Tale for Tiny Boys.*   Tenby: J. MacLaren, 1927, 16mo., pages (x) 101, 9 full page illustrations, first and last leaves slightly foxed, thumbed at edges but otherwise very fresh, original grey paper wrappers, original dust jacket, paper panel illustrated, flaps pasted to wrappers, head and foot of spines slightly chipped, short closed tear to upper panel, browned and soiled, very good, ownership inscription, presentation inscription to first page.   Simon Finch Rare Books   Zero - 215   2011   £750

Wild, John *Tetney Lincolnshire. A History.* Grimsby: printed for the author by Albert Gait, 1901, First edition; inscribed by Florence L. Baker, frontispiece, plate, 2 photographic plates, 7 page list of subscribers, (14), 112, (4) pages, original maroon cloth, gilt, nice. Anthony W. Laywood   May 26 2011 - 19904   2011 $201

Wilde, John *The Story of Jane and Joan.* Mt. Horeb: Perishable Press, 1977, First edition, one of only 25 copies Printed (entire edition); 4to., 12 hand colored etchings by Wilde, original quarter blue oasis leather tipped paste paper boards, folding cloth box, fine, rare, box faded as usual.   James S. Jaffe Rare Books   May 26 2011 - 21272   2011 $7500

Wilde, Oscar 1854-1900   *After Berneval. Letters of Oscar Wilde to Robert Ross.* Beaumont Press, 1922, First edition, one of 75 copies on Japanese vellum of the edition De Luxe signed by publisher and artist (of a total of 475 copies); 223 x 154mm., 65, (1) pages, (3) leaves original vellum backed decorative boards, woodcuts printed in blue on front and rear endpapers, two color titlepage woodcut, one plate with three additional woodcuts at back, prospectus and order form laid in at front, spine vellum pitted in six small areas, with 10 gilt letters partly (though never entirely) lost, otherwise very fine.   Phillip J. Pirages   59 - 347   2011 $550

Wilde, Oscar 1854-1900   *The Ballad of Reading Gaol.* Stelton: published and printed by Joseph Ishill, Ferrer Colony, 1916, (4), v, (5), 9-39 pages, paper covered boards, printed label on front cover, muslin spine, covers soiled and worn at extremities, good copy only.   Joseph J. Felcone Inc.   Fall Miscellany 2010 - 128   2011 $400

Wilde, Oscar 1854-1900   *De Profundis.* London: Methuen & Co., 1905, First edition; half title, 40 page catalog (Feb. 1905), uncut in original cloth, very good. Jarndyce Antiquarian Booksellers   CXCI - 617   2011   £60

Wilde, Oscar 1854-1900   *The Happy Prince and Other Tales.* London: Duckworth & Co., 1913, First edition thus; 4to., original pictorial purple cloth, gilt, pages 136, 12 tipped in tissue guarded color plates, line drawings, flyleaves lightly browned, occasional faint spot, but lovely, bright and clean.   R. F. G. Hollett & Son Antiquarian Booksellers   General Catalogue Summer 2010 - 883   2011   £375

Wilde, Oscar 1854-1900   *A House of Pomegranates.* London: James Osgood, McIlvaine, 1891, First edition one of 1000 copies; small quarto (8), 157, (1) (1 printers imprint) (1, blank) pages, 4 full page inserted illustrations, original quarter moss green linen over cream colored linen boards, front cover printed in light red and stamped with gilt designs of a peacock, running fountain and basket of split pomegranates, spine decoratively stamped and lettered in gilt, decorative endpapers printed in olive green all edges uncut, minimal rubbing to extremities, light soiling to covers small bookplates on endpapers, repair to front endpaper, binding starting to loosen, very good, book usually found in poor condition.   Second Life Books Inc.   174 - 329   2011 $1600

Wilde, Oscar 1854-1900   *Picture of Dorian Gray.* London: Petersburg Press, 1968, Limited, signed and numbered by artist; this number 29 of 200 in Edition A, folio, 12 lithographs in color by Jim Dine, with set of an additional 6 loose lithographs issued in a portfolio, each annotated "Edition A" on reverse and numbered 29/200 and signed by artist, original full fuchsia (red) velvet boards, front board lettered in silver, pictorial patterned endpapers, housed in black cloth slipcase, additional black cloth portfolio fine. Heritage Book Shop   Holiday 2010 - 131   2011 $4500

Wilde, Oscar 1854-1900   *Poems.* Boston: Roberts Brothers, 1881, First American edition; pages (ii), viii, 232, (2), foolscap 8vo., original variant issue of mid brown cloth, author's name and title blocked on backstrip, backstrip and front cover with sunflower designs within black rule boxes, minor spotting to front cover, decorated floral tan endpapers, top edge gilt, others rough trimmed, very good. Blackwell Rare Books   B166 - 240   2011   £300

Wilde, Oscar 1854-1900   *Salome.* London: Limited Editions Club, 1938, One of 1500 numbered copies; pages 106, maroon cloth, lettering and decorative stamping in gilt, boxed set with Salome, drame en un acte, in original French, with gouache drawings on black paper by Andrew Derain, signed by artist, Aubrey Beardsley, paper wrappers, slight foxing on endpapers and title, nice set in scuffed box. Second Life Books Inc.   174 - 29   2011 $750

Wildenstein, Daniel *Monet, or the Triumph of Impressionism.* Koln: Tashcen, 1996, First edition; 2 volumes, 4to., pages 479 and 359, illustrations in color and black and white, 2 volumes, slight wear, sound, clean, very good.   Any Amount of Books   May 29 2011 - A64352   2011 $213

Wilder, Alex *Lullabies and Night Songs.* New York: Harper & Row, 1965, First edition; large 4to., black cloth with gold lettering on spine and within decorated box on front cover, full color pictorial dust jacket with some wear and tear on front wrappers, charming drawing with presentation signed in full and dated by the artist, Maurice Sendak. Jo Ann Reisler, Ltd.   86 - 228   2011 $975

Wilder, Laura Ingalls *Little Town on the Prairie.* New York: Harper Brothers, 1941, Stated first edition; 8vo. 288 pages, fine in very good+ dust jacket which is slightly frayed at spine ends, color dust jacket and color frontispiece by Helen Sewell and in line by Mildred Boyle, very scarce. Aleph-Bet Books, Inc. 95 - 588 2011 $2250

Wilder, Laura Ingalls *These Happy Golden Years.* New York: Harper & Bros., 1943, Stated first edition; 8vo., pictorial cloth, 299 pages, slight covers soil, near fine in slightly frayed and soiled dust jacket, illustrations by Helen Sewell and Mildred Boyle with color dust jacket, color frontispiece plus full page black and whites, rare. Aleph-Bet Books, Inc. 95 - 589 2011 $1750

Wildlife Society *The Journal of Wildlife Management. (with) Wildlife Monographs.* Bethesda: Washington. Menasha: The Wildlife Society, 1937, First edition; very good plus, 8vo., volumes 1-66 (missing 3 issues, volume 35 (No. 4) 36 (1) and 49 (1), includes indies for volumes 40 and with Wildlife Monographs Nos. 1-2, 8-51 and 142-150; volumes 1-29 bound in red cloth by year, remaining volumes as published by number in original wrappers, occasional minor scuff, short tear smudge, light bump, Fred R. Zimmerman's handstamp and or signature to early volumes, very nice. Raymond M. Sutton, Jr. May 26 2011 - 55375 2011 $1200

Wildman, Thomas Coote *The General Orders and Minutes of the Board of Customs Consolidated by their Directions to the 30th June 1854...* London: HMSO, 1854, Large 8vo., contemporary full polished calf gilt, little scuffed and corners rather worn, pages xvi, 290, interleaved, volume 1 (only, of 2). R. F. G. Hollett & Son Antiquarian Booksellers 175 - 1441 2011 £120

Wilhelm, Kate *Where Late the Sweet Birds Sang.* New York: Evanston: San Francisco: London: Harper & Row, 1976, First edition; octavo, cloth backed boards. L. W. Currey, Inc. 124 - 152 2011 $450

Wilkes, Charles *Narrative of the United States Exploring Expedition During the Years 1838, 1839, 1840, 1841, 1842.* Philadelphia: Lea & Blanchard, 1845, First trade edition, Haskell's 'unofficial issue' 2B limited to 1000 copies; Imperial 8vo., pages lx, 434; xvi, 476; xvi, 438; xvi, 539; xvi, 558, 64 steel engraved plates with tissue guards, 2 of which are portraits, 47 steel engraved vignettes, 248 woodcuts and 9 double page copper engraved maps, separate atlas contains 5 large folding copper engraved maps, 1 is hand colored, all in near fine condition; original brown cloth, straight grained pattern, front and back cover have blindstamped three rule border, enclosing blind stamped scroll work rectangular covers have blindstamped three rule border enclosing blindstamped scroll work rectangular border containing blindstamped decorations at top and bottom and having eagle standing on shield with sailing ship in background stamped in center in gold leaf, spine has five blindstamped bands enclosing four panels, fourth having, stamped in gilt, female figure with staff surmounted by liberty cap and holding in one hand an unrolled chart lettered at top, sailing ship in background, lettered in second panel in gold leaf (corners worn, fraying to some ends of spines, cloth unfaded, gilt bright and text mostly very clean, light foxing to plates, offsetting to some double page maps, occasional splits to cloth on edges of spines, volumes solid and with no splitting to hinges, faint blindstamp of the Maidstone Museum & Public Library to titlepages, no other markings, exceptional copy, maps in nearly perfect condition, the copy of Julius Brenchley. Raymond M. Sutton, Jr. May 26 2011 - 49406 2011 $7500

Wilkes, George *McClellan: from Ball's Bluff in Antietam.* New York: Sinclair Tousey, 1863, First separate edition; 8vo., 40 pages, removed, vertical crease. M & S Rare Books, Inc. 90 - 87 2011 $225

Wilkes, Wetenhall *A Letter of Genteel and Moral Advice to a Young Lady...* London: printed for C. Hitch and L. Hawes at the Red Lion in Pater-noster row, 1760, Seventh edition; 12mo., (6), 198 pages, large uncut copy, light browning and slight foxing, contemporary quarter calf, marbled boards, ruled and banded spine, joints cracked, foot of spine slightly chipped, corners little worn, contemporary ownership name of Ann Berney 1760. Jarndyce Antiquarian Booksellers CXCI - 619 2011 £380

Wilkins, John *An Essay Towards a Real Character and a Philosophical Language.* London: printed for S. Gellilbrand and for J. Martin printer to the Royal Society, 1668, First edition; 5 folded plates, 2 engraved tables and engravings in text, includes section title for the alpahbetic dictionary, errata and approbation leaves, pages (xx), 454 (2 blank), (158), folio, contemporary calf, hinges and corners skillfully repaired, crisp, clean copy, very good. Blackwell Rare Books B166 - 117 2011 £1800

Wilkins, John *Of the Principles and Duties of Natural Religion... to which is added A Sermon Preach'd at his Funeral by William Lloyd.* London: printed for R. Chiswell, W. Battersby and C. Brome, 1699, 8vo., pages (ii), vii, (v) 410 (iv) 55 (i) engraved frontispiece, contemporary speckled calf, boards double rule bordered to blind with triangular cornerpieces within, board edge decorative roll in blind, all edges red sprinkled, blue and white sewn endbands, early 21st century calf reback, original dark red lettering piece relaid + corners by Chris Weston, browned and spotted, intermittent oil stain to lower corner, contemporary ink inscription, from the collection of Christopher Ernest Weston 1947-2010.   Unsworths Booksellers   24 - 60   2011   £200

Wilkins, John *Sermons Preach'd Upon Several Occasions Before the King at White Hall...* London: printed by A. M. and R. R. for John Gellibrand, 1680, Second Edition; contemporary full panelled calf, spotted and rubbed, corners worn, head and foot of spine defective, pages (vi), 176, engraved frontispiece, lacks front flyleaf, some worming to lower margins in places.   R. F. G. Hollett & Son Antiquarian Booksellers   175 - 1442   2011   £175

Wilkinson, Charlotte *Noah's Ark and All that Were Therein.* Cleveland: Harter, 1935, Large oblong folio, pictorial card covers, fine and unused, 8 leaves of die-cut figures illustrated with rich color lithographs by Ruth Williams, they include 110 pieces to punch out and use to assemble the Ark, Noah and his wife and sons and their wives plus all animals, each animal has a stand printed with name of the animal and country where it can be found, very scarce.   Aleph-Bet Books, Inc.   95 - 395   2011 $1200

Wilkinson, Frederick *Antique Firearms.* Guinness Superlatives, 1977, Original cloth gilt, dust jacket, pages 276 with 33 color plates and 202 text illustrations.   R. F. G. Hollett & Son Antiquarian Booksellers   General Catalogue Summer 2010 - 346   2011   £35

Wilkinson, J. Gardiner *The Manners and Customs of the Ancient Egyptians.* London: John Murray, 1878, 3 volumes, early 29th century three quarter scarlet levant morocco gilt by Hatchards with broad flattened raised bands, hinges rather rubbed and cracked in places but sound, pages xxx, 510; xii,5 16; xi, 528, top edge gilt, complete with 74 plates, 643 text figures and woodcut vignettes, handsome clean set.   R. F. G. Hollett & Son Antiquarian Booksellers   177 - 906   2011   £650

Willans, John *Marc Bolan: Wilderness of the Mind.* London: Xanadu, 1992, First edition; 8vo., pages 176, illustrations in black and white, signed by Willans and Caron Thomas, fine in very good dust jacket with slight edgewear, stamp with note "This edition signed by authors is limited to one thousand copies, of which this is number 179".   Any Amount of Books   May 29 2011 - A66474   2011 $238

Willard, Emma *Last Leaves of American History: Comprising Histories of the Mexican War and California.* New York: George P. Putnam, 1849, First edition; Small octavo, 230 pages plus 5 leaves of publisher's ads, large folding map, foxing, publisher's blind and gilt stamped green cloth, some spotting to covers, spine faded to brown, 2 inch tear to gutter of map, overall very good, tight copy. Argonaut Book Shop   Recent Acquisitions Summer 2010 - 235   2011 $475

Willard, Joseph *An Address to the Members of the Bar of Worcester County, Massachusetts, Octobr 2 1829.* Lancaster: Carter, Andrews & Co., 1830, First edition; 8vo., 144 pages, plus errata slip (detached, neatly torn in half), removed, spotting foxing, outer pages little dust colored.   M & S Rare Books, Inc.   90 - 213   2011 $150

Willem, Bernhard *Forty Dirty Drawings.* Amsterdam: Thomas Rap, 1969, First edition; 16mo. near fine in printed pink wrappers with some fading and small hole on front wrapper, very rude drawings.   Between the Covers   169 - BTC339721   2011 $450

Willey, Samuel H. *Thirty Years in California.* San Francisco: A. L. Bancroft & Co., 1879, First edition; 76 pages, newer half leather, gilt, brown cloth sides, original wrappers bound in, 2 minor smudges to front cover, fine copy.   Argonaut Book Shop   Recent Acquisitions Summer 2010 - 237   2011 $325

Willey, Samuel H. *The Transition Period of California from a Province of Mexico in 1846 to a State of the American Union in 1850.* San Francisco: Whitaker and Ray Co., 1901, First edition; small octavo, xii, 160 (4, ads) pages, red cloth lettered in black on front cover, spine slightly faded, else fine.   Argonaut Book Shop   Recent Acquisitions Summer 2010 - 236   2011 $175

William Morris Society *Journal of the William Morris Society.* 1962-1996, First edition; volume 1/1-volume 12/1, winter 1962-Aug. 1996 (volume 1/1 is photocopy), illustrations, photos, 45 issues in original wrappers.   I. D. Edrich   May 26 2011 - 99454   2011 $402

Williams Ellis, Clough *On Trust for the Nation.* Paul Elek, 1947, First edition; large 8vo., original cloth backed pictorial boards, rather rubbed, pages 172, numerous plates, color drawings by Barbara Jones and large folding map. R. F. G. Hollett & Son Antiquarian Booksellers   General Catalogue Summer 2010 - 1622   2011   £30

Williams, Benjamin Samuel *Hints on the Cultivation of British and Exotic Ferns and Lycopodiums, with Descriptions...* London: Chapman and Hall, 1852, First edition; 8vo., (8), 67 (1) pages, very good in original blind-stamped and gilt lettered dark green cloth, scarce.   Ken Spelman Rare Books   68 - 162 2011   £45

Williams, Charles *The Descent of the Dove.* London: Longman, Green and Co., 1939, First edition; original cloth, gilt, dust jacket little spotted and marked, spine little darkened, (price of 8/6 on inner flap blacked out and overprinted 7/6 net), pages ix, 245, frontispiece, few spots to endpapers, signature of Margaret Cropper, Cumbrian poet. R. F. G. Hollett & Son Antiquarian Booksellers 175 - 1445 2011 £65

Williams, Charles *James I.* Arthur Barker, 1934, First edition; original cloth, gilt, hinges minimally rubbed, pages vii, 304, frontispiece. R. F. G. Hollett & Son Antiquarian Booksellers 175 - 1446 2011 £30

Williams, Charles *Silvershell; or the Adventures of an Oyster.* Judd & Glass, 1857, Second edition; original green blindstamped cloth, gilt, spine and edges mellowed to brown, pages viii, 184, viii, frontispiece, 18 text woodcuts, scarce. R. F. G. Hollett & Sons Antiquarian Booksellers 170 - 729 2011 £160

Williams, Charles *Three Plays.* Oxford: University Press, 1931, First edition; original pictorial boards, nearly fine, spare spine label. Lupack Rare Books May 26 2011 - ABE4313993819 2011 $125

Williams, Charles *War in Heaven.* London: Gollancz, 1930, First edition; pages 288, crown 8vo., original black cloth, backstrip lettered in green, free endpapers lightly browned, edges foxed. Blackwell Rare Books B166 - 241 2011 £95

Williams, Charles *The Zoological Gardens, Regent's Park.* London: C. Tilt, n.d. circa, 1838, 78 x 64 mm., 191, 1 page list, blind tooled green cloth on boards, gilt title enclosed in decorative frame on upper cover, repeated gilt title and floral decorations and rosettes on spine, gilt edges, frontispiece, small vignette, full page engravings, first signature lightly sprung, else fine, scarce. Hobbyhorse Books 56 - 109 2011 $325

Williams, Ellen *Three Years and a Half in the Army...* New York: Published for the author by Fowler & Wells Co., 1885, First edition; original gilt stampd red cloth, decorated endpapers, (8), 178 pages plus 8 pages of ads, frontispiece, near fine, bright, tight copy. Buckingham Books May 26 2011 - 23276 2011 $2750

Williams, Emlyn *Emlyn. An Early Autobiography.* London: The Bodley Head, 1973, First edition; original cloth, gilt, dust jacket, little worn, pages 424, presentation copy, inscribed to Anthony Thomas with author's affection Jan. 1974. R. F. G. Hollett & Son Antiquarian Booksellers 175 - 1447 2011 £30

Williams, Emlyn *George. An Early Autobiography.* London: Hamish Hamilton, 1961, Original two tone cloth, dust jacket rather creased, torn and repaired on reverse, pages 461, presentation copy inscribed to Molly and Anthony Thomas, from author, with single sheet ALS from author taped to pastedown to Anthony Thomas. R. F. G. Hollett & Son Antiquarian Booksellers 175 - 1448 2011 £35

Williams, Gwyn *An Introduction to Welsh Poetry.* London: Faber, 1953, First edition; original cloth, gilt, dust jacket, few slight marks, backstrip little browned and frayed at head, pages xiii, 271. R. F. G. Hollett & Son Antiquarian Booksellers General Catalogue Summer 2010 - 927 2011 £30

Williams, Harcourt *Tales for Ebony.* Nattali & Maurice, 1947, New edition; original cloth gilt, dust jacket, some edge tears and pieces lost from extremities, price clipped, pages 167, with 33 fine color plates and black and white head and tailpieces, name on flyleaf, scarce. R. F. G. Hollett & Sons Antiquarian Booksellers 170 - 697 2011 £75

Williams, Helen Maria *A Residence in France, During the Years 1792, 1793, 1794 and 1795...* Elizabeth-town: printed by Shepard Kollock for Cornelius Davis, 1798, Octavo, xx, (21) - 517 pages, original full calf, maroon spine label, rubbed, front hinge broken, corners worn, signature of Theodore (?) Dwight, good. Jeff Weber Rare Books 163 - 226 2011 $150

Williams, Henry Lionel *A Guide to Old American Houses 1700-1900.* Thomas Yoseloff, 1967, Small 4to., original cloth, gilt, bottom edges trifle damped and bumped, dust jacket, pages 168 with 198 illustrations. R. F. G. Hollett & Son Antiquarian Booksellers 177 - 907 2011 £30

Williams, Iolo A. *The Firm of Cadbury 1831-1931.* London: Constable, 1931, First edition; original blue cloth, gilt, pages ix 295, with 16 plates. R. F. G. Hollett & Son Antiquarian Booksellers 175 - 1450 2011 £40

Williams, John *Barddas; or a Collection of Original Documents. Illustrative of the Theology, Wisdom and Usages of the Bardo-Druidic System.* Llandovery: 1862, Volume I only (volume 2 did not appear until 1874), lxxxv 425 pages, original cloth, needs recasing, good, very scarce. C. P. Hyland May 26 2011 - 255/817 2011 $457

Williams, John *First Annual Industrial Directory of New York State 1912.* Albany: State Department of Labor, 1913, 562 pages, fair, hinges broken, edges soiled, inteiror clean and tight. G. H. Mott Bookseller May 26 2011 - 41584 2011 $195

Williams, John G. *The Adventures of a Seventeen Year Old Lad.* Boston: Collins Press, 1894, First edition; little soiling, otherwise nice, tight, near fine copy. Lupack Rare Books   May 26 2011 - ABE2618205375   2011 $150

Williams, Jonathan *Sharp Tools for Catullan Gardens. Poems by...* Fine Arts Department University of Indiana, 1968, First edition, one of only 36 copies (entire edition) signed by Williams and McGarrell; large folio, loose sheets in fabricoid portfolio, fine, rare, lithographs by James McGarrell, each lithograph individually signed by artist. James S. Jaffe Rare Books   May 26 2011 - 1343   2011 $5000

Williams, Margery *The Velveteen Rabbit.* New York: Holt, Rinehart and Winston, 1983, First edition thus; 4to., green textured boards with gold lettering on spine, full color pictorial dust jacket, as new copy, charming signed in full drawing by artist, Michael Hague, 33 numbered pages with 12 full page color plates (three are double page spreads), plus full color illustrations in text.   Jo Ann Reisler, Ltd.   86 - 128   2011 $300

Williams, O. W. *Pioneer Surveyor, Frontier Lawyer, the Personal Narrative of O. W. Williams 1877-1902.* El Paso: 1966, xii, 350 pages, original binding, fine in very good dust jacket, cloth of book has been offset on inside of dust jacket.   Bookworm & Silverfish   668 - 8   2011 $100

Williams, Otho Holland *Calendar of the General Otho Holland Williams Papers in the Maryland Historical Society.* Baltimore: 1940, First edition; 454 pages, 4to., mimeo, wrappers, front wrapper loosening with 4 inch closed tear, modestly ex-library.   Bookworm & Silverfish   678 - 6   2011 $150

Williams, Robert *Lexicon Cornu-Birtannicum: a Dictionary of the Ancient Celtic Language of Cornwall...* Llandover: Roderic/London: Trubner, 1865, First edition; 4to., pages (4), 398 (4 subscriber list), half dark blue leather lettered gilt at spine, 4 raised bands, some rubbing at extremities, dab of paint at lower spine, unobjectionable, sound, very good. Any Amount of Books   May 26 2011 - A42062   2011 $461

Williams, Tennessee 1911-1983 *Eight Mortal Ladies Possessed: a Book of Stories.* New York: New Directions, 1974, Trade paperback edition; 8vo., pages 100, boldly signed by Tennessee Williams across front endpaper (half title), clean, bright, very good+.   Any Amount of Books   May 29 2011 - A48208   2011 $221

Williams, Tennessee 1911-1983 *Five Plays: Cat on a Hot Tin Roof. The Rose Tattoo. Something Unspoken. Suddenly Last Summer. Orpheus Descending.* London: Secker & Warburg, 1962, First English collected edition; pages xvi, 376, 8vo., original pale blue cloth, backstrip gilt lettered, dust jacket, fine, authorial gift inscription to Angus Stewart, novelist.   Blackwell Rare Books   B166 - 242   2011   £600

Williams, Tennessee 1911-1983 *The Kingdom of Earth with Hard Candy: a Book of Stories.* New York: New Directions, 1954, First edition, limited to 100 copies and a few for presentation; signature and conjugate pages plus title leaf, title leaf, 20 pages (paginated as in the book), fine, rare.   Between the Covers   169 - BTC337569   2011 $1250

Williams, Terry Tempest *Pieces of White Shell.* New York: Scribner, 1984, First edition; fine, near fine- dust jacket with 1 inch closed tear on rear panel, light rubbing to extremities, signed by author.   Bella Luna Books   May 26 2011 - g3803   2011 $357

Williams, Terry Tempest *Pieces of White Shell.* New York: Scribner, 1984, First edition; dust jacket near fine with life edge wear, signed by author, book fine.   Bella Luna Books   May 26 2011 - 2228   2011 $440

Williams, Terry Tempest *Refuge.* New York: Pantheon, 1991, First edition; near fine, light sunning to top of spine near fine dust jacket, small closed tear at top front corner, creasing to top edge, signed by author.   Bella Luna Books   May 29 2011 - t3578   2011 $82

Williams, Ursula Moray *Jean Pierre.* A. & C. Black, 1931, First edition; original pictorial cloth, pictorial dust jacket (price clipped), pages 32, with 4 striking color plates and black and white drawings by author.   R. F. G. Hollett & Sons Antiquarian Booksellers   170 - 730   2011   £65

Williams, W. M. *The Sociology of an English Village - Gosforth.* London: Routledge & Kegan Paul, 1956, First edition; original cloth, gilt, dust jacket, pages 245, 16 with 12 maps and text figures, scarce, library address stamped on flyleaf and crossed out.   R. F. G. Hollett & Son Antiquarian Booksellers   173 - 1215   2011   £40

Williams, W. M. *The Sociology of an English Village - Gosforth.* London: Routledge & Kegan Paul, 1956, First edition; original cloth, gilt, dust jacket, few small chips and tears to extremities, pages 245, 16 with 12 maps, text figures, scarce, Norman Nicholson's copy with his bookplate, loosely inserted 2 postcards of Gosforth an 2 different 3 sided typescript reviews by Nicholson for the work, with alterations and corrections throughout both typescripts in his hand, much pencilled lining of text by Nicholson throughout. R. F. G. Hollett & Son Antiquarian Booksellers   173 - 1214   2011   £150

Williams, William *The Duty and Interest of a People Among Who Religion Has Been Planted, to Continue Steadfast and Sincere...* Boston: printed and sold by S. Kneeland and T. Green, 1736, First edition; 12mo., (2), 8, 120, (2), 38, 19 pages, contemporary blindstamped sheep over wooden boards, with lines, flowers and leaves, highly appealing contemporary binding, very slight cracking to outer hinges, top and bottom, lower outer corners lacking from front endleaves, slight break in lower edge of title, occasional staining of text, but remarkably good, tight and sound, ownership signature of John How 1770.   M & S Rare Books, Inc.   90 - 123   2011 $3000

Williams, William Carlos   1883-1963   *Kora in Hell.* San Francisco: Arion Press, 1998, First Arion Press edition, number 134 of 300 copies (total edition of 326); signed on colophon and with 21 black and white woodcuts by Mel Kendrick, circa 13.5 x 10 inches, about 80 pages printed on handmade Fabriano paper, quarter black goatskin with wooden boards, both covers of which is design by Kendrik, new copy, handsome edition.   Gemini Fine Books & Arts, Ltd.   Art Reference & Illustrated Books: First Editions 2011 $450

Williamson, Duncan   *The Horseiman. Memories of a Traveller 1928-1958.* Edinburgh: Canongate Press, 1994, First edition; original cloth, gilt, dust jacket, pages xii, 276, 8 pages of plates and maps on endpapers.   R. F. G. Hollett & Son Antiquarian Booksellers   175 - 1452   2011   £45

Williamson, George Charles   1858-1942   *George Third Earl of Cumberland 1558-1605. His Life and Voyages.* Cambridge: University Press, 1920, First edition; original cloth, gilt, pages xix, 336, with 21 plates, original cloth, gilt.   R. F. G. Hollett & Son Antiquarian Booksellers   173 - 1216   2011   £65

Williamson, George Charles   1858-1942   *Lady Anne Clifford. Countess of Dorset, Pembroke & Montgomery 1590-1676.* Kendal: Titus Wilson, 1923, Limited signed edition, number 108 of 250 copies; small 4to., original vellum backed boards, corners rather worn and rounded, pages xxii, 547, uncut, 53 plates, very scarce, fine large armorial bookplate of Lionel Cresswell of Middle Temple and Burley in Wharfedale, later of Ruth Cresswell of Crackenthorpe Hall, Appleby.   R. F. G. Hollett & Son Antiquarian Booksellers   173 - 1217 2011   £350

Williamson, Henry   *Tarka the Otter, His Joyful Waterlife & Death in the Country of the Two Rivers.* Putnam's, 1927, First edition, one of 1000 copies (of an edition of 1100 copies); printed in black and brown, pages xii, 256, 8vo., original quarter maize buckram, gilt lettered brown leather label, brown linen sides, usual darkening to backstrip, top edge gilt, others untrimmed, very good.   Blackwell Rare Books   B166 - 243 2011   £400

Williamson, Jack   *Darker than You Think.*   Reading: Fantasy Press, 1948,   First edition; octavo, cloth.   L. W. Currey, Inc.   124 - 153   2011 $450

Williamson, Jack   *Seetee Shock.*   New York: Simon and Schuster, 1950,   First edition; octavo, boards.   L. W. Currey, Inc.   124 - 207   2011 $200

Willis, A. Parker   *Summer Cruise in the Mediterranean.*   T. Nelson and Sons, 1853,   First UK edition; original blindstamped red cloth gilt, pages xvii, 300 (iv), 16 with engraved vignette frontispiece and title, small prize label on pastedown.   R. F. G. Hollett & Son Antiquarian Booksellers   General Catalogue Summer 2010 - 1665   2011   £65

Willis, Alfred E.   *Illustrated Physiognomy.*   Chicago: n.p., 1882,   Numerous illustrations, contemporary half blue cloth, label of Alfred Bresslauers Bucherei.   Jarndyce Antiquarian Booksellers   CXCI - 620 2011   £40

Willis, Connie   *Doomsday Book.*   New York: Bantam Books, 1992,   First edition; octavo, cloth backed boards. L. W. Currey, Inc.   124 - 42   2011 $1750

Willis, Robert   *The Architectural History of Glastonbury Abbey.*   Cambridge: Deighton Bell and Co., 1866,   First edition; original cloth, gilt, edges faded, head of spine little chipped, pages viii, 91 with 7 lithographed plates, few spots. R. F. G. Hollett & Son Antiquarian Booksellers   177 - 909   2011   £40

Willis, Robert   *The Architectural History of the University of Cambridge and of the Colleges of Cambridge and Eton.* Cambridge: University Press, 1886,   4 volumes, large 8vo., original buckram backed cloth gilt, spine little stained in places, some little frayed at head, pages 630, 776, 722, profusely illustrated with text drawings and plans, plus 29 double page plates on stubs, many with glassine overlays (partly hand colored), in final volume, labels removed from endpapers.   R. F. G. Hollett & Son Antiquarian Booksellers   177 - 910 2011   £350

Willis, Robert   *The Architectural History of the University of Cambridge and of the Colleges of Cambridge and Eton.* Cambridge: Cambridge University Press, 1886,   First edition thus; 4 volumes including the slimmer atlas/plans volume, small 4to., cxxiv, (4), 630 pages, 19 plates, 5 folding, illustrations; xiii, (4), 726 pages, 32 plates, 18 folding, 2 colored, illustrations; xi, 722 pages, 5 plates, 2 folding illustrations; vi pages, 29 pans, 27 folding, 12 with overlays, some hand colored, clean, sound, very good set with very slight rubbing, corners slightly bumped and faint shelf wear, original publisher's quarter buckram and green cloth lettered gilt at spine, bookplate of Professor G. H. Bushnell (1903-1978) Curator of the Cambridge University Museum of Archaeology and Ethnology.   Any Amount of Books   May 26 2011 - A49502   2011 $503

Willison, John *The Afflicted Man' Companion.* Glasgow: printed by J. and M. Robertson, 1789, Pages xxiv, 25-288, rather fingered and browned in places, contemporary sheep, rubbed. R. F. G. Hollett & Son Antiquarian Booksellers 175 - 1455 2011 £120

Willoughby De Broke, Lord *The Sport of Our Ancestors.* London: Constable, 1921, First edition; 4to. original red cloth gilt, spine trifle faded, pages xi, 280, top edge gilt, untrimmed, 20 tipped in plates. R. F. G. Hollett & Son Antiquarian Booksellers General Catalogue Summer 2010 - 1213 2011 £85

Willoughby, Francis *De Historica Piscium Libri Quatuor. totum Opus Recognovit Coaptavit Supplevit...* Oxford: at the Sheldonian Theatre, 1686, First edition; Folio, engraved vignette to title, headpieces, engraved allegorical title to plates by Paul van Somer and 817 engraved plates (occasional foxing, mostly marginal), light offsetting to some plates, small stain to plate, some soiling to 2 plates, last plate detached, folio, pages (6), 343; 30, (1), (11, contemporary full calf, 6 raised bands, covers and endpapers detached, vertical crack to calf on spine, title soiled and with old owner's signature, dampstain to lower inside corner of several front leaves, scattered foxing, few leaves browned. Raymond M. Sutton, Jr. May 26 2011 - 415156 2011 $5000

Willoughby, Francis *The Ornithology of Francis Willoughby of Middleton, in the County of Warwick Esq.* London: A. C. for John Martyn, 1678, First edition in English; folio, title printed in red and black, 2 engraved plates of bird trapping and 78 engraved plates of birds, pages (12), 441, (index, 6 pages), contemporary panelled calf with elaborate gilt decorated spine with 7 compartments including brown morocco label (some soiling to title, creases and partial soiling to a chart, 3 marginal spots to a plate, partial loss to a margin of a plate, light dampstaining to upper margin of 2 plates, 2 marginal spots and some overall foxing to last plate), text and most plates remarkably clean, old scuffs to covers, professionally rebacked at earlier time while retaining compartments from original spine), bookplate of Rev. Sir Thomas Gerry Cullum Barr, very good copy. Raymond M. Sutton, Jr. May 26 2011 - 54388 2011 $6000

Willson, Beckles *The Tenth Island Being Some Account of Newfoundland, Its People, Its Politics, Its Problems and Its Peculiarities.* London: Grant Richards, 1897, First edition; light green cloth with dark green lettering to spine and front cover, pages xix, 208, half title, folding map in rear, 8vo., spine browned an covers slightly soiled, front hinge cracked. Schooner Books Ltd. 96 - 103 2011 $125

Willyams, Cooper *A Voyage up the Mediterranean in His Majesty's Ship the Swiftsure...* London: by T. Bensley for J. White, 1802, First edition; 4to., xxiii, (1), 309 pages, engraved dedication leaf with colored arms, double page aquatint map and 41 aquatint plates, contemporary straight grain red morocco, skillfully rebacked at an early date retaining entire original spine with gilt sailing ship ornaments within compartments, edges gilt, other than light offsetting from plates, and an occasional marginal spot or tiny stain, clean, lovely copy. Joseph J. Felcone Inc. Fall Miscellany 2010 - 129 2011 $4500

Wilson-Haffenden, J. R. *The Red Men of Nigeria: An Account of a Lengthy Residence Among the Fualni or Red Men...* London: Seeley Service, 1930, First edition; 8vo., 318 pages, folding map, plates, original red cloth, dust jacket. J. & S. L. Bonham Antiquarian Booksellers Africa 4/20/2011 - 6848 2011 £75

Wilson, Albert *The Flora of Westmorland.* Arbroath: T. Buncle, 1938, First edition, privately printed for the author; original green cloth gilt, pages 413, 37 illustrations, folding colored map in rear pocket, fine. R. F. G. Hollett & Son Antiquarian Booksellers 173 - 1219 2011 £100

Wilson, Alfred P. *Yorkshire Moors and Dales.* A. Brown & Son, 1910, First edition; large 8vo., original cloth backed pictorial boards, rather rubbed, pages 172, numerous plates, color drawings by Barbara Jones, large folding map. R. F. G. Hollett & Son Antiquarian Booksellers General Catalogue Summer 2010 - 1623 2011 £45

Wilson, Arnold T. *The Suez Canal: Its Past, Present and Future.* Oxford: University Press, 1939, Second edition; 8vo. pages xvii, 224, folding map, original black cloth. J. & S. L. Bonham Antiquarian Booksellers Africa 4/20/2011 - 3164 2011 £70

Wilson, Augusta Evans *Devota.* New York: 1907, first edition; 122 pages, near fne in stained, but very scarce dust jacket with small chips at top. Bookworm & Silverfish 671 - 171 2011 $65

Wilson, Augustus, Mrs. *Parsons' and Historical Library Magazine, Opening Session of the First Cattle Browers' Convention.* St. Louis: Becktold & Co., 1885, First edition thus; quarto, presentation inscription from author, pictorial decorated cloth, gold stamping on front cover and spine, xiii, (1), 409 pages, frontispiece, illustrations, plates, portraits, double column, ads, very good, tight copy. Buckingham Books May 26 2011 - 27376 2011 $1750

Wilson, C. J. *The Story of the East African Mounted Rifles.* Nairobi: East African Standard, 1938, First edition; 8vo., pages 136, illustrations, maps on endpapers, very good, scarce. J. & S. L. Bonham Antiquarian Booksellers Africa 4/20/2011 - 8751 2011 £120

Wilson, Charles W. *From Koriti to Khartum: a Journal of the Desert March from Korti to Gubat and of the Ascent of the Nile in General Gordon's Steamers.* Edinburgh: William Blackwood, 1885, First edition; 8vo., pages xxvii, 311, folding map, original red cloth cloth.   J. & S. L. Bonham Antiquarian Booksellers   Africa 4/20/2011 - 8277   2011   £100

Wilson, Colin   *The Outsider.*   London: Victor Gollancz, 1957, First edition, 11th impression; 8vo. 288 pages, signed presentation from author, neat name on front endpaper, very good+ in later laminated dust jacket.   Any Amount of Books   May 29 2011 - A37453   2011 $238

Wilson, David M.   *The Northern World. the History and Heritage of Northern Europe AD 400-1100.*   London: Thames & Hudson, 1980, First edition; large 4to., original cloth, gilt, dust jacket, pages 248, with 340 illustrations, 258 photos, drawings and maps.   R. F. G. Hollett & Son Antiquarian Booksellers   177 - 912   2011   £35

Wilson, Dermot   *Fishing the Dry Fly.*   London: Adam and Charles Black, 1974, Original cloth gilt, dust jacket, few closed edge tears, pages x, 217, with 12 plates, inscribed by author.   R. F. G. Hollett & Son Antiquarian Booksellers   General Catalogue Summer 2010 - 1311   2011   £30

Wilson, Edmund   *The Scrolls from the Dead Sea.*   London: W. H. Allen, 1955, First edition; original cloth, gilt, dust jacket (extremities trifle worn), pages 159.   R. F. G. Hollett & Son Antiquarian Booksellers   177 - 913   2011   £45

Wilson, Elijah Nicholas   *Among the Shoshones.*   Salt Lake City: Skelton Pub. Co., 1910, First edition, first issue; original dark green cloth, hand written titles on orange labels affixed to front cover and spine, 222 pages, frontispiece, illustrations, variant binding when compared side-by-side with actual trade edition, this copy 23cm. in height compared to 21cm. for trade edition.   Buckingham Books   May 26 2011 - 28498   2011 $2750

Wilson, Elijah Nicholas   *Among the Shoshones.*   Salt Lake City: Skelton Pub. Co., 1910, First edition; first issue, 8vo., presentation inscription by publisher and signed by him (rare thus), original dark green decorated cloth, titles on front cover and spine stamped in black ink, 222 pages, frontispiece, illustrations, some light professional restoration to spine ends and corners, else near fine, bright, tight copy, housed in decorated cloth clamshell case with titles stamped in black on spine, rare with rare unexpurgated tale.   Buckingham Books   May 26 2011 - 24796   2011 $7500

Wilson, George Herbert   *The History of the Universities Mission to Central Africa.*   London: Universities Mission, 1936, First edition; 8vo., pages xvi, 278, map on endpaper, illustrations, original blue blindstamped cloth.   J. & S. L. Bonham Antiquarian Booksellers   Africa 4/20/2011 - 2688   2011   £35

Wilson, H. A.   *A British Borderland: Service and Sport in Equatoria.*   London: John Murray, 1913, First edition; 8vo., pages xxi, 347, map, 18 illustrations, original green decorative cloth, gilt vignette on upper cover, spine faded with small mark, but very good.   J. & S. L. Bonham Antiquarian Booksellers   Africa 4/20/2011 - 4647   2011   £160

Wilson, J. Leighton   *Western Africa: its History, Condition and Prospects.*   London: Sampson Low, 1856, First UK edition; 8vo, pages 527, double page map, 14 plates, some marginal browning, later brown half calf.   J. & S. L. Bonham Antiquarian Booksellers   Africa 4/20/2011 - 4768   2011   £95

Wilson, J. Oliver   *Birds of Westmorland and the Northern Pennines.*   London: Hutchinson, 1933, First edition; original black cloth gilt, spine trifle faded, pages 319, 153 illustrations, signed by ornithologist, James Fisher, joints strained.   R. F. G. Hollett & Son Antiquarian Booksellers   173 - 1223   2011   £85

Wilson, James   *The Inclosure of Moors, Commons and Waste Lands of Dalston, Cumberland.*   Dalston: W. R. Beck, 1898, Original printed wrappers, roughly rebacked, rather worn and stained, piece torn from upper margin of upper panel, lower panel badly torn and laid down, but complete, pages x, 108, fore-edge little worn, extremely scarce. R. F. G. Hollett & Son Antiquarian Booksellers   173 - 1228   2011   £180

Wilson, James   *The Register of the Priory of St. Bees.*   London: Bernard Quaritch and Durham: Andrews & Co., 1915, Thick 8vo., original cloth, gilt, pages xxxix, 663.   R. F. G. Hollett & Son Antiquarian Booksellers   173 - 1226   2011   £180

Wilson, James   *Rose Castle.*   Carlisle: Charles Thurnam and Sons, 1912, First edition; large 8vo., original brown cloth gilt, pages xv, (ii), 270, uncut, 15 plates, flyleaves slightly browned as usual, scarce.   R. F. G. Hollett & Son Antiquarian Booksellers   173 - 1227   2011   £120

Wilson, James   *Zendelings-reis naar den Stillen Ocean, oder bet Bevel van James Wilson.*   Dordrecht & Amsterdam: Blusse & Allart, 1801-1802, 3 volumes, 8vo., (34), 371; 414; (4), 314 pages, 4 folding maps, five engraved folding plates, one plate waterstained, quarter tan calf over marbled boards, gilt stamped tan leather spine labels, new endpapers small holes on rear hinge of volume I, very good.   Jeff Weber Rare Books   163 - 228   2011 $1700

Wilson, James Grant *The Life and Letters of Fitz-Greene Halleck.* New York: D. Appleton and Co., 1869, First trade edition; 8vo., 607 pages, plus ads, portrait, later blue half morocco, spine gilt stamped, blue cloth covered endpapers, very good, tipped in note by General Wilson noting he purchased the volume "at the sale of the Sedgwick Library" in 1877, with Halleck Book contract tipped in, also inserted letters to General Wilson from Horatio Gates Jones and fine two page letter from journalist W. L. Stone.   M & S Rare Books, Inc.   90 - 150   2011 $950

Wilson, Laura *Avedon at Work in the American West.* Austin: University of Texas Press, 2003, First edition; signed by author and Avedon, fine in fine dust jacket.   Jeff Hirsch Books   ny 2010 2011 $650

Wilson, Lucy Sarah Atkins *Amusing Anecdotes of Various Animals: Intended for Children.* London: J. E. Evans, n.d. circa, 1830, 12mo. 2 + 35 pages, pictorial light green paper wrappers, upper wrapper with engraved vignette, full page frontispiece and small vignette on titlepage, 8 half page wood engravings, fine, elegant custom made folder cased in slipcase with three quarter red leather back, five raised bands and gilt fillets and title on spine.   Hobbyhorse Books   56 - 156   2011 $475

Wilson, Lynn Winfield *History of Fairfield County, Connecticut 1639-1928.* Chicago: S. J. Clarke, 1929, 3 volumes, 699, 615, 629 pages, photos and other illustrations, very good, three quarter cloth and marbled boards, small price sticker on cover of volume I, rubbed at edges, some toning, otherwise clean and tight, top edges gilt.   G. H. Mott Bookseller   May 26 2011 - 38115   2011 $225

Wilson, Marcius *The Drawing Guide: a Manual of Instruction in Industrial Drawing Designed to Accompany the Industrial Drawing Series.* New York: 1873, First edition; 205 pages (8 plates), very good, marbled edges, titlepage reseated, bottom of backstrip frayed.   Bookworm & Silverfish   668 - 38   2011 $87

Wilson, Margaret *The Able McLaughlins.* New York: Harper and Bros., 1923, First edition; spine gilt slightly tarnished else very near fine in attractive very good or better dust jacket with short internally repaired split, thin chip along edge of spine fold and some small chips at crown, exceptionally scarce title in jacket.   Between the Covers   169 - BTC347395   2011 $9500

Wilson, Paul F. *The Christmas Thingy.* Baltimore: 2000, One of 350 copies, 26 lettered copies also issued; large 4to., signed by author and artist, Alan M. Clark, fine in fine dust jacket, fine slipcase.   Bookworm & Silverfish   669 - 48   2011 $200

Wilson, Richard *Creating Paradise. The Building of the English Country House 1660-1880.* Hambledon and London: 2000, First edition; large 8vo., original cloth, gilt, dust jacket, pages xvi, 428, with 134 illustrations, 5 figures and 21 tables.   R. F. G. Hollett & Son Antiquarian Booksellers   177 - 915   2011   £35

Wilson, Robert A. *Mexico and Its Religion; with Incidents of Travel in that Country During Parts of the Years 1851-52-53-54 and Historical Notices of Events Connected with Places Visited.* New York: Harper and Bros., 1855, First edition; 12mo., xiii, (2), 16-406 pages, wood engraved frontispiece, 8 plates, 5 text illustrations, publisher's light purple elaborately blindstamped cloth, gilt lettered spine, spine faded with two short vertical scratches, else fine and clean.   Argonaut Book Shop   Recent Acquisitions Summer 2010 - 239   2011 $275

Wilson, Sloan *The Man in the Gray Flannel Suit.* New York: Four Walls Eight Windows, 2002, First edition thus; paperback reissue, signed by author, fine in wrappers.   Ken Lopez Bookseller   154 - 56   2011 $100

Wilson, T. *An Archaeological Dictionary or Classical Antiquities of the Jews, Greeks and Romans, Alphabetically Arranged...* London: T. Cadell, 1783, First edition; 8vo., full brown leather, lettered gilt at spine on red label, approximately 440 pages (unpaginated), boards cracked and held by sewing with consequent loose, some rubbing and scuffing, slightly browning to text, otherwise decent, near very good condition.   Any Amount of Books   May 29 2011 - A35755   2011 $246

Wilson, Thomas *The Knowledge and Practice of Christianity Made Easy to the Meanest Capacity.* London: B. Dod, 1759, Ninth edition; small 8vo., contemporary speckled calf gilt, few tape marks from old labels and slight surface scratches, pages (ii, dedication and contents), iv, xvi, 300, with half title (ad on reverse) parochial library label and library shelf numbers, some foxing to flyleaf, otherwise excellent, sound copy.   R. F. G. Hollett & Son Antiquarian Booksellers   175 - 1460   2011   £250

Wilson, William *Newfoundland and Its Missionaries.* Halifax: printed by Dakin & Metcalf sold at the Wesleyan Book Room, Cambridge, 1866, First edition; 8vo., original black cloth with blindstamp design in front and rear boards and gilt titles to spine, corners worn, top and bottom of spine frayed and first blank fly leaf missing.   Schooner Books Ltd.   96 - 104   2011 $350

Wilson's Almanacks 1872-1885 1887-1910. no publisher, 1872-1910, 2 volumes, binder's cloth gilt, unpaginated.   R. F. G. Hollett & Son Antiquarian Booksellers   173 - 19   2011   £85

Wiltsee, Ernest A. *Gold Rush Steamers (of the Pacific).* San Francisco: Grabhorn Press, 1938, First edition, limited to 500 copies; x, (2), 367, (1) pages, title printed in red and black, colored frontispiece, 14 full page reproductions of ships, 2 full page portraits and nine pages with 33 reproductions of cancelled envelopes, endpaper maps, original brick red cloth, tan cloth backstrip, printed paper label on spine, very fine.   Argonaut Book Shop   Recent Acquisitions Summer 2010 - 240 2011 $350

Wiltsee, Ernest A. *The Truth About Fremont: an Inquiry.* San Francisco: printed by John Henry Nash, 1936, First edition, limited to 1000 copies, signed by author; vi, 54 pages, frontispiece, original cloth backed boards, paper spine label, bookplate, ink not top edge of blank flyleaf, very fine, printed dust jacket (slight chip to foot of jacket spine). Argonaut Book Shop   Recent Acquisitions Summer 2010 - 241 2011 $150

Windham, Donald *Stone in the Hourglass.* Verona: 1981, First edition; number 24 of 50 copies, signed by author (out of a total edition of 750), printed on Magnani paper by Stamperia Valdonega under supervision of Martino Mardersteig, 8vo., stiff wrappers in slipcase, as new (original Scribner price label affixed to slipcase).   Gemini Fine Books & Arts, Ltd. Art Reference & Illustrated Books: First Editions 2011 $155

Windham, Joan *The King's Christmas Present.* London: Sheed and Ward, 1936, Square 4to., 57 pages, cloth backed pictorial boards, light wear, illustrations by Jeanne Hebbelynck with 5 charming color plates highlighted in gold. Aleph-Bet Books, Inc. 95 - 148 2011 $200

Wing, Donald *Short-Title Catalogue of Books printed in England, Scotland, Ireland, Wales and British America and of English Books Printed in Other Countries 1641-1700.* New York: Index Committee of the Modern Language Association of America, 1972, Second edition; volume 1 (of only 3), 4to., original maroon cloth gilt, edges trifle rubbed, pages xx, 622.   R. F. G. Hollett & Son Antiquarian Booksellers General Catalogue Summer 2010 - 480 2011 £30

Wingate, Ealan *Hiroshi Sugimoto.* New York: Gregosian Gallery, 2008, First edition; oblong 4to., 18 pages folded accordion style, illustrations in black and white, 18 pages, fine.   Any Amount of Books   May 29 2011 - A67902 2011 $204

Wingate, F. R. *Mahidism and the Egyptian Sudan; Being an Account of the Rise and Progress Of Mahidism and of Subsequent Events in the Sudan...* London: Macmillan, 1891, First edition; 8vo., pages xxviii 617 30 maps and plans, 1 map in slipcase, original red cloth, spine slightly faded, inner hinge cracked, internally clean.   J. & S. L. Bonham Antiquarian Booksellers   Africa 4/20/2011 - 8298 2011   £350

Wingfield, Lewis *Notes on Civil Costume in England from the Conquest to the Regency.* London: 1884, First edition; 4to., xxxiv, 38 (24 chromolitho plates) pages, library stamp, good missing 2 inches of backstrip, foot of backstrip reglueed, edges frayed, new endpapers, few plates loose, some with micro chipping at free margin and most with a 3/16" dampstain at top margin.   Bookworm & Silverfish 667 - 68 2011 $75

Wingfield, Lewis *Under the Palms in Algeria and Tunis.* London: Hurt & Blackett, 1868, First edition; 8vo., 2 volumes, pages xiv, 318; vii, 295, frontispieces and vignettes, contemporary full blue polished prize calf, spines gilt, joints and head and tail of spines slightly rubbed.   J. & S. L. Bonham Antiquarian Booksellers   Africa 4/20/2011 - 5586 2011   £275

Winkles, B. *French Cathedrals.* London: Charles Tilt, 1837, First edition; viii, 169 (1) errata + index, engraved titlepage and 49 engraved plates, contemporary half calf, neatly rebacked, marbled paper covering on boards rather rubbed, some scattered foxing, oval stamp of Llanbedr Hall Library.   Ken Spelman Rare Books 68 - 33 2011   £60

Winkles, H. *Winkles's Architectural and Picturesque Illustrations of the Cathedral Churches of England and Wales.* London: Tilt and Bogue, 1836-1838, 2 volumes (ex 3), tall 8vo., modern half levant morocco, gilt, pages (ii), xx, 144; viii, 40, engraved titles (2 rather heavily foxed) and 120 steel engraved plates (rather foxed).   R. F. G. Hollett & Son Antiquarian Booksellers 177 - 918 2011   £95

Winship, George Parker 1871-1952 *Cabot Bibliography.* London: Henry Stevens, Son & Stiles, 1900, maroon cloth, gilt titles and vignettes to front and spine, decorated endpapers, pages lii, 180, half title, 8vo., spine slightly sunned, generally very good.   Schooner Books Ltd. 96 - 105 2011 $75

Winship, George Parker 1871-1952 *William Caxton: a Paper Read at a Meeting of the Club of Odd Volumes.* Doves Press, 1909, One of 54 numbered copies printed for members of Club of Odd Volumes (this #47); there were 246 additional copies printed on paper as well as 15 on vellum, 240 x 170mm., 25, (1) pages, (1) leaf (colphon), original vellum backed blue paper boards, gilt device of Club of Odd Volumes on upper cover, gilt titling on spine, printed in black and red, tipped-in slip reading "With compliments of the Club of Odd Volumes", covers bit soiled, two one inch pink stains to lower cover, faint freckled foxing to one gathering, otherwise fine.   Phillip J. Pirages 59 - 178 2011 $275

Winslow, Forbes E. *The Children's Fairy History of England.* David Stott, 1889, Large 8vo., original pictorial green cloth gilt, few stains to lower board, pages xxviii, 308, (iv), with 200 woodcut illustrations by Ernest Marillier.   R. F. G. Hollett & Sons Antiquarian Booksellers 170 - 731 2011 £50

Winter, C. J. W. *Illustrations of the Rood-Screen at Randworth.* Norwich: Miller and Leavins for the Norfolk and Norwich Arch. Soc., 1867, Small folio, original printed thick card wrappers, neatly rebacked in cloth, pages 8, chromolithographed frontispiece and 26 lithographed plates, mostly printed in sepia, text in red and black, some mostly light foxing to plates.   R. F. G. Hollett & Son Antiquarian Booksellers   177 - 919   2011   £85

Winter, William *Life & Art of Richard Mansfield With Selections from His Letters.* New York: 1910, 2 volumes, approximately 700 pages, many illustrations, very good with frew ripples to cloth, top edge gilt, with two cabinet photos by Pach Bros. circa 1880.   Bookworm & Silverfish   669 - 61   2011 $100

Winterson, Jeanette *Oranges are Not the Only Fruit.* London/ Boston: Pandora Press, 1985, First edition; 8vo., color illustrated wrappers, pages 176, clean bright near fine copy little browned at page edges as is almost inevitable.   Any Amount of Books   May 29 2011 - A47346   2011 $298

Winterson, Jeanette *Sexing the Cherry.* London: Bloomsbury, 1989, First British edition, true first; near fine, light bumping to spine ends, dust jacket fine.   Bella Luna Books   May 29 2011 - t3508   2011 $88

Wirt, Elizabeth Washington *Flora's Dictionary.* Baltimore: Fielding Lucas Jr., 1837, First complete edition; 4to., 136, 87 pages, double column text, 58 fine color plates, both covers in matching design and quite spectacular, original dark brown morocco, elaborately stamped in gilt, quite good, minor wear and some scuffing at edges and joints, several leaves and one plate partially detached with slight wear at edges and joints.   M & S Rare Books, Inc.   90 - 446   2011 $4000

Wirth-Miller, Denis *Heads Bodies & Legs.* London: Penguin Books, 1951, Tall small 8vo., original pictorial wrappers, pages 14, lithographed in colors, uncut.   R. F. G. Hollett & Son Antiquarian Booksellers   General Catalogue Summer 2010 - 929   2011   £65

Wisden, John *John Wisden's Cricketers' Almanack for 1897.* London: John Wisden & Co. Ltd., 1897, First edition; 16mo., pages lxxx, 416 + 30 pages of illustrated ads, with photographic plate, soundly bound in fairly recent plain dark green cloth lettered gilt at spine, bound without back printed wrapper, front wrapper preserved, photo plate with tissue guard only slightly faded and very clean, occasional very slight foxing, else sound, clean, very good.   Any Amount of Books   May 29 2011 - A45085   2011 $383

Wisdom in Miniature: or the Young Gentleman and Lady's Magazine. Philadelphia: John Adams, 1805, 16mo., 16 leaves, original buff paper wrappers, full page woodcut frontispiece, 12 very fine half page woodcuts, reinforced spine, very fine.   Hobbyhorse Books   56 - 36   2011 $250

Wise, Daniel *The Young Lady's Counselor or Outlines & Illustrations of the Sphere, The Duties & The Dangers of Young Women.* Cincinnati: 1855, 255 pages, 12mo., original binding, backstrip reglued, corners abraded.   Bookworm & Silverfish   662 - 202   2011 $75

Wise, John *System of Aeronautics.* Philadelphia: Joseph A. Speel, 1850, First edition; 8vo., (2, blank), (i)-310, (4, blank) pages, errata slip, engraved frontispiece, 12 lithographic plates, original brown vertically ribbed blindstamped cloth, spine lettered in gilt, corners and ends of spine slightly chipped, occasional very light soiling or browning, previous owner's light old ink signature on front free endpaper, very good.   Heritage Book Shop   Holiday 2010 - 132   2011 $1250

Wise, John S. *Conrad Cornered and Crushed... reply of Hon. John S. Wise.* Petersburg?: 1883, 16 pages, original binding.   Bookworm & Silverfish   670 - 201   2011 $750

Wise, John S. *Hon. John S. Wise. Speech of John S. Wise of Virginia (Young Republicans of Philadelphia).* N.P.: 1887, 37 pages, original binding.   Bookworm & Silverfish   667 - 136   2011 $250

Wise, Larry *Playette Phone Book.* New York: Playette Corp., 1945, 4to., spiral backed boards, covers rubbed, else very good+, through a circle cut into all pages and front cover merges a metal phone dial, attached by a string is removable phone cradle, bright color lithos.   Aleph-Bet Books, Inc.   95 - 398   2011 $275

Wiseman, Richard *Eight Chirurgical Treatises on these Following Heads.* London: for B. T. and L. M. and sold by W. Keblewhite and J. Jones, 1697, Third edition; folio, (14), 563, (14) pages, including half title A1, 18th century paneled calf, very skillfully rebacked retaining original gilt spine, period style label, tiny (half inch) repaired tear in lower margin of third leaf, else remarkably fine, fresh copy, contemporary ownership signature of Stewart Sparkes.   Joseph J. Felcone Inc.   Fall Miscellany 2010 - 87   2011 $3200

Wissmann, Hermann Von *My Second Journey through Equatorial Africa from the Congo to the Zambesi in the Years 1886 and 1887.* London: Chatto & Windus, 1891, First edition; 8vo., pages xiv, 326, portrait frontispiece, map, 92 illustrations, original brown decorative cloth, small crack to inner joint of lower cover, otherwise very good.   J. & S. L. Bonham Antiquarian Booksellers   Africa 4/20/2011 - 8873   2011   £275

Wister, Owen   1860-1938 *How Doth the Simple Spelling Bee.* New York: Macmillan, 1907, First edition; signed in 1907 on half title very good+ (light surface soiling),.   Lupack Rare Books   May 26 2011 - ABE46332335608   2011 $100

Wister, Owen 1860-1938 *When West was West.* New York: Macmillan, 1928, First edition; (8), 449 pages, blindstamped blue cloth, gilt lettered spine, gilt rule on front cover, small spot to contents page, else fine. Argonaut Book Shop   Recent Acquisitions Summer 2010 - 242   2011 $90

Wither, George *Carmen Expostulatorium or a timely Expostulation with Those both of the City of London and the Present Armie...* London: printed in the Yeere, 1647, First edition; scarce, 4to., (24) pages, well bound in old style quarter calf over marbled boards, spine gilt lettered, fine, crisp copy, fine, scarce.   John Drury Rare Books   153 - 172   2011   £750

Withering, William *A Botanical Arrangement of all the Vegetables Naturally Growing in Great Britain, with Descriptions of the Genera and Species...* Birmingham: M. Swinney for T. Cadell and P. Elmsley, 1776, First edition; 12 engraved plates (some foxing, light offsetting to some), 8vo., pages (1), xcvi, 838, modern full calf (endpapers renewed, some offsetting to first title), marginal browning to title and half title in volume 2.   Raymond M. Sutton, Jr.   May 26 2011 - 36293   2011 $1300

Wittgenstein, Ludwig *On Certainty.* Oxford: Basil Blackwell, 1969, First edition; original cloth, gilt, dust jacket, spine trifle rubbed, pages 90, parallel texts in German and English.   R. F. G. Hollett & Son Antiquarian Booksellers   175 - 1462   2011   £45

Wittigenstein, Ludwig *On Certainty/ Uber Gewissheit.* San Francisco: Arion Press, 1991, Limited to 3000 copies signed by artist, Mel Bochner, this is no. 112; first edition thus, planographic prints, folio, fine, original blue and grey cloth with black lettering and red geometric design on cover and black lettering on spine, original fine grey cloth covered slipcase, printed on Rives heavyweight, Plantin French mould made paper.   By the Book, L. C.   26 - 51   2011 $975

Wittkower, Rudolf *Art and Architecture in Italy 1600 to 1750. the Pelican History of Art Series.* London: Penguin Books, 1958, First edition; small 4to., original cloth, gilt, leather spine label (trifle chipped), pages xxiii, 428, with 192 pages of plates.   R. F. G. Hollett & Son Antiquarian Booksellers   177 - 920   2011   £75

Woas, Lee *Self-Steering Without a Windvane.* Newport: 1982, First edition; 173 pages, 4to., fine in fine dust jacket.   Bookworm & Silverfish   678 - 148   2011 $125

Wodehouse, Pelham Grenville 1881-1975 *The Head of Kay's.* London: A. & C. Black, 1924, Original red cloth, spine little faded, tiny nick to edge of upper board, pages (iv), 280, color frontispiece, prize label on flyleaf.   R. F. G. Hollett & Sons Antiquarian Booksellers   170 - 732   2011   £45

Wodehouse, Pelham Grenville 1881-1975 *Mike: a Public School Story.* London: Adam and Charles Black, 1910, Reprint; 8vo., original publisher's olive green illustrated covers, one illustration missing (page 164), otherwise plates decent, illustrated covers worn and used, good only with names on front endpaper, text very good.   Any Amount of Books   May 29 2011 - A75836   2011 $255

Wojcik, Jan W. *Robert Boyle and the Limits of Reason.* New York: Cambridge University Press, 1997, 8vo., xvi, 243 pages, navy cloth, gilt stamped spine title, dust jacket, fine, from the Bern Dibner reference library, with Burndy bookplate.   Jeff Weber Rare Books   161 - 59   2011 $90

Wolfe, Humbert *The Craft of Verse.* New York: Crosby Gaige, 1928, One of 395 copies signed by author; 299 x 203mm., 3 p.l., (5)-45, (1)pages, original patterned cloth, paper spine label, untrimmed edges, light sprinkled foxing on several text pages, otherwise fine,.   Phillip J. Pirages   59 - 215   2011 $50

Wolfe, Thomas *The Crisis in Industry.* Chapel Hill: University of North Carolina, 1919, First edition, one of 300 copies; pamphlet, pages (iv), 5-14, (2) blank, original grey wrappers printed in black, green cloth chemise with bookplate of H. Bradley Martin, green cloth slipcase, spine with lettering and filleting in gilt and with morocco lettering piece in gilt, fine.   Simon Finch Rare Books   Zero - 142   2011   £4000

Wolfe, Tom *From Bauhaus to Our House.* London: Cape, 1981, First UK edition; original cloth, gilt, dust jacket, pages 143, illustrations in text, mint copy.   R. F. G. Hollett & Son Antiquarian Booksellers   177 - 921   2011   £30

Wolfe, Tom *Of Time and the River.* New York: Charles Scribner's Sons, 1935, First edition, 6th Printing; 8vo., pages (12), 912, uncut, publisher's cloth, blue-grey, lettering on upper board and spine in gilt, with green background, faded on spine and slightly rubbed on upper board, dust jacket, green design with white text, author's photo on back, slightly rubbed at extremities, presentation inscription, near fine.   Simon Finch Rare Books   Zero - 266   2011   £1250

Wolfenden, J. F. *The Public Schools of To-Day.* London: University of London Press, 1948, First edition; original cloth, dust jacket (rather worn and chipped), pages 111.   R. F. G. Hollett & Son Antiquarian Booksellers   175 - 1464   2011   £30

Wolff, Robert Lee *The Golden Key: a Study of the Fiction of George MacDonald.* New Haven: Yale University Press, 1961, First edition; half title, plates, original black cloth, very good in dust jacket.   Jarndyce Antiquarian Booksellers   CXCII - 365   2011   £35

Wolff, Tobias *Back in the World.* Boston: Houghton Mifflin, 1985, First edition; near fine, previous owner's name on front free endpapers, dust jacket near fine with very light edgewear. Bella Luna Books May 29 2011 - t5805 2011 $88

Wolff, Tobias *Back in the World.* Boston: Houghton Mifflin, 1985, First edition; near fine, minor bumping to top of spine, dust jacket near fine, light rubbing, signed by authot. Bella Luna Books May 29 2011 - t3335 2011 $82

Wolff, Tobias *Back in the World.* Boston: Houghton Mifflin, 1985, First edition; near fine, light ink mark on front free endpapers, dust jacket near fine, light edge wear, signed by author. Bella Luna Books May 29 2011 - 6081 2011 $82

Wolff, Tobias *In the Garden of the North American Martyrs.* New York: Ecco Books, 1981, First edition; near fine, previous owner unobtrusive embossing stamp on half titlepage, dust jacket near fine, very small closed tear at bottom foot of spine, first state with price of $10.95. Bella Luna Books May 26 2011 - t9495 2011 $825

Wolff, Tobias *In the Garden of North American Martyrs.* New York: Ecco, 1981, First edition; scarce first issue, with dust jacket with "$14.95" price, price was lowered to $10.95 prior to publication and later jacket was printed with lower price, signed by author, faint foxing to cloth, near fine in near fine, lightly spine tanned dust jacket with closed edge tear at upper front spine fold. Ken Lopez Bookseller 154 - 243 2011 $1500

Wolhuter, Harry *Memories of a Game Ranger.* Johannesburg: Wild Life Protection Sciety of South Africa, 1948, First edition; large 8vo., original cloth, slight edge fading in places, dust jacket rather chipped, worn and torn, pages (xii), 313, (iii), 17 plates, numerous line drawings, maps on endpapers, flyleaves trifle cockled. R. F. G. Hollett & Son Antiquarian Booksellers General Catalogue Summer 2010 - 1666 2011 £45

Wollaston, A. F. R. *From Ruwenzori to the Congo: a Naturalist's Journey Across Africa.* New York: E. P. Dutton, 1908, Octavo, xxv, 315 pages, frontispiece, numerous plates, 2 maps, half brown morocco, cloth, raised bands, gilt spine top edge gilt by Himebauch & Browne, front hinge repaired, very. Jeff Weber Rare Books 163 - 230 2011 $400

Wollaston, A. F. R. *Letters and Diaries of A. F. R. Wollaston.* Cambridge: University Press, 1933, First edition; 8vo., pages xv, 261, frontispiece, 3 portraits, original blue cloth, slight rubbing to joints. J. & S. L. Bonham Antiquarian Booksellers Africa 4/20/2011 - 5581 2011 £75

Wolle, Muriel Sibell *Stampede to Timberline - The Ghost Towns & Mining Camps of Colorado.* Boulder: 1949, First edition; (5) blank (5) 544 pages, 4to., very good, some foxing, signed by author, illustrations, endpaper maps, original binding. Bookworm & Silverfish 671 - 30 2011 $75

Wollstonecraft, Mary 1759-1797 *Letters Written During a Short Residence in Sweden, Norway and Denmark.* London: J. Johnson, 1802, Second edition; small 8vo., pages (iv) 262, vi, 12, contemporary calf, later rebacking, worn along extremities of covers and along hinges, scarce. Second Life Books Inc. 174 - 332 2011 $750

Wollstonecraft, Mary 1759-1797 *Maria, ou le Malheur d'etre Feme Ouvrage Posthume.* Paris: Chez Maradan An VI, 1798, First French edition; (151) pages, 12mo., original wrappers, half title, original engraved frontispiece, very small piece torn to top edges of first four pages, negligible pale waterstain on lower corner of prelims, still near fine, uncut, preserved in beige linen box, gilt lettered title label, rarely seen in original state. Paulette Rose Fine and Rare Books 32 - 186 2011 $3500

Woloshuk, Nicholas *E. Irving Couse 1866-1936.* Santa Fe: 1976, Numbered and signed edition of 3000; viii, 115 pages, illustrations, original cloth issued without dust jacket, near fine. Dumont Maps & Books of the West 113 - 50 2011 $250

Wolstenholme, G. *Over 900 Things to Know About Postcard Collecting.* Mirfield: West Yorkshire Postcard Centre, n.d. 1970's, First edition; original wrappers, pages (60), illustrations. R. F. G. Hollett & Son Antiquarian Booksellers General Catalogue Summer 2010 - 350 2011 £35

The Woman Citizen. A Weekly Chronicle of Progress. New York: published by the Woman Citizen Corporation March 6, 1920, (30) pages, 12 1/2 x 9 1/2 inches, pictorial wrappers, printed in black, little wear to wrappers, still good. Paulette Rose Fine and Rare Books 32 - 169 2011 $75

Women's Club of Carpinteria *Carpenteria Cook Book - Selected Recipes 1925.* Santa Barbara: 1925, 112 (1) pages, wrappers, covers loose, backstrip shabby. Bookworm & Silverfish 676 - 44 2011 $65

Wonder ABC Book: Three Jolly Alphabets. London: Collins, circa, 1930, 4to., cloth backed pictorial boards, some rubbing, very good+, illustrations in color. Aleph-Bet Books, Inc. 95 - 39 2011 $175

Wood, Christopher *The Dictionary of Victorian Painters.* Antique Collectors' Club, 1971, First edition; 4to., original cloth, gilt, dust jacket, pages xv, 435, with 300 illustrations and index to artists' monograms, price review for 1973 loosely inserted.   R. F. G. Hollett & Son Antiquarian Booksellers   General Catalogue Summer 2010 - 351   2011   £45

Wood, Ellen Price 1814-1887 *Anne Hereford.* London: Tinsley Bros., 1868, First edition; 3 volumes, octavo, (6), 295, (1, printer's imprint); (6), 319, (1, printer's imprint); (6), (7)-316 (1, ad), (1, blank) pages, original violet vertically ribbed moire cloth with covers decoratively stamped in blind and spines decoratively stamped and lettered in gilt, original cream colored endpapers, spine with slight cock, otherwise excellent copy, extremely scarce.   David Brass Rare Books, Inc.   May 26 2011 - 01395   2011 $8500

Wood, George W. *Report Of Mr. Wood's Visit To the Choctaw and Cherokee Missions 1865.*   Boston: 1865, First edition; 24 pages,.   Bookworm & Silverfish   671 - 106 2011 $75

Wood, Harvey *Personal Recollections of Harvey Wood.* Pasadena: Grant Dahlstrom at the Castle Press, 1955, Second edition, number 2 of 200 copies signed by John Goodman; pages xxiv, (4), 27, (5), 2 folding facsimiles, illustrations, cloth backed printed boards, slight offsetting to endpapers, else very fne.   Argonaut Book Shop   Recent Acquisitions Summer 2010 - 243   2011 $150

Wood, Horatio Charles *A Treatise on Therapeutics, Comprising Materia Medica and Toxiology...* Philadelphia: J. B. Lippincott, 1876, Second edition; thick 8vo., 674 (ads), 12 pages, figures, pencil marginalia, original full sheepskin, black leather spine label, gilt spine, lightly rubbed, ownership signature and rubber stamp, very good, from the Medical Library of Dr. Clare Gray Peterson.   Jeff Weber Rare Books   162 - 311   2011 $100

Wood, John D., & Co. *Byram Hall Estate, West Riding, Yorkshire. An Elaborate Catalogue for the Sale of the Estate Auction by John D. Wood & Co. On July 4th & 5th 1922.* London: John D. Wood, 1922, 34 pages, 2 plates, 3 large colored folding plans, conditions of sale at end have numerous corrections and note on upper reads 'revised conditions, see end', small mark on upper wrapper, otherwise very good.   Ken Spelman Rare Books   68 - 111   2011   £50

Wood, John George *The Boy's Own Book of Natural History.* London: George Routledge & Sos, n.d., Full crimson calf gilt, few light scratches and marks to the boards, pages 378, all edges and endpapers marbled, illustrated with text woodcuts, prize label of Windermere Grammar School on pastedown.   R. F. G. Hollett & Son Antiquarian Booksellers   General Catalogue Summer 2010 - 1072   2011   £35

Wood, John George *The Field Naturalist's Handbook.* London: Casell, Petter, Galpin & Co., 1883, Third edition; original green cloth gilt corners trifle bumped, pages 167, (iv), uncommon.   R. F. G. Hollett & Son Antiquarian Booksellers   General Catalogue Summer 2010 - 1075   2011   £35

Wood, John George *Insects at Home.* London: Longmans, Green and Co., 1872, First edition; contemporary strong half morocco gilt, hinges and edges rubbed, pages xx, 670, all edges gilt, color frontispiece and 20 woodcut plates.   R. F. G. Hollett & Son Antiquarian Booksellers   General Catalogue Summer 2010 - 1074   2011   £120

Wood, John George *Six Lectures on the Principles and Practice of Perspective, as Applicable to Drawing from Nature...* Bye and Law, 1804, First edition; xi, (1), 77 pages, 8 engraved plates (all but one folding and one with moveable slip), very good, large uncut and unpressed copy in original marbled boards, paper spine label, slight marginal waterstain in outer margins at beginning and at end, otherwise unusually freh, clean state, minor very neat repairs to paper backstrip, scarce.   Ken Spelman Rare Books   68 - 16   2011   £420

Wood, Joseph Garbett *Through Matabeleland; the Records of a Ten Months Trip in an Ox-Wagon...* London: Richards Glanville, 1893, First edition; 8vo., pages iv, 198, folding map, illustrations, original red cloth, very good.   J. & S. L. Bonham Antiquarian Booksellers   Africa 4/20/2011 - 7937   2011   £250

Wood, Lawson *The Lawson Wood Nursery Rhyme Book.* Thomas Nelson, n.d. circa, 1930, Small 4to., original cloth backed glazed pictorial boards, little scratched, edges slightly worn, 7 thick board leaves with rounded corners, 16 color plates.   R. F. G. Hollett & Sons Antiquarian Booksellers   170 - 734 2011   £75

Wood, Lawson *The Lawson Wood Nursery Rhyme Book.* Thomas Nelson, n.d. c., 1930, First edition; small 4to., original cloth backed glazed pictorial boards, scratched and worn, corners very rounded, 7 thick board leaves with rounded corners and 16 color plates.   R. F. G. Hollett & Sons Antiquarian Booksellers   170 - 735   2011   £45

Wood, Margaret *The English Mediaeval House.* Ferndale Editions, 1981, Small 4to., original cloth, gilt, dust jacket, pages xxxi, 448, frontispiece, 60 pages of half tone plates, 32 pages of engravings and 117 text illustrations.   R. F. G. Hollett & Son Antiquarian Booksellers   177 - 923   2011   £40

Wood, Margaret *The English Mediaeval House.* London: Studio Editions, 1994, Small 4to., original cloth, gilt, dust jacket, pages xxxi, 448, frontispiece, 60 pages of half tone plates, 32 pages of engravings and 117 text illustrations. R. F. G. Hollett & Son Antiquarian Booksellers 177 - 924 2011 £35

Wood, Mary Anne Everett *Letters of Royal and Illustrious Ladies of Great Britain.* London: Henry Colburn, 1846, First edition; 3 volumes, xx, 372; x, 378; x, 352 pages, 8vo., contemporary black half calf, marbled boards, gilt decorated spines contrasting title labels with gilt lettering, hinges on volumes I and II reinforced, still very good. Paulette Rose Fine and Rare Books 32 - 189 2011 $375

Wood, Raymund F. *California's Agua Fria: the Early History of Mariposa County.* Fresno: Academy Library Guild, 1954, First edition; 112 pages, frontispiece, numerous black and white illustrations, map endpapers tan cloth, fine. Argonaut Book Shop Recent Acquisitions Summer 2010 - 244 2011 $60

Wood, Richard Coke *Calaveras, the Land of Skulls.* Sonora: The Mother Lode Press, 1955, First edition; vii, (1), 158 pages, 16 photos, tan cloth lettered in brown on spine and front cover, very fine. Argonaut Book Shop Recent Acquisitions Summer 2010 - 245 2011 $75

Wood, Robert *Six Great Events in British History and Six Famous Stories from English History.* London: Stead's Publishing House, 1909-1912, 12mo., 64 + 2 page list on upper and lower wrapper; 2, 58 8 list and ad, pictorial green paper wrappers, wood engraved vignettes, printed on provincial paper, wrappers lightly sunned with small chipping at edges, very good set. Hobbyhorse Books 56 - 157 2011 $150

Wood, Robin *Claude Chabrol.* New York: Praeger, 1970, First edition; small 4to., pages 144, copiously illustrations in black and white, signed by author on titlepage, loosely inserted note on card signed by Claude Chabrol, very good+ in slightly used, nicked and rubbed, else near very good dust jacket. Any Amount of Books May 29 2011 - A72809 2011 $238

Wood, Thomas *The Monster Telescopes.* Parsonstown: Sheilds & Son, 1844, Second edition; (iii) 54 pages, frontispiece, 3 plates, 2 pages, publisher's ad, original cloth, some wear on spine, not affecting the tight binding), some spotting in text but not enough to distract the reader, good copy, very scarce. C. P. Hyland May 26 2011 - 259/516 2011 $580

Woodall, Joy *From Hroca to Anne.* Solihull: privately printed for the author, 1974, Pages xix, 188, with 7 maps (2 in rear pocket), 12 tables, 39 full page illustrations, 69 text drawings, fine, 4to., original boards, gilt, dust jacket. R. F. G. Hollett & Son Antiquarian Booksellers General Catalogue Summer 2010 - 1625 2011 £45

Woodforde, James *The Diary of a Country Parson: The Reverend James Woodforde 1758-1781.* Oxford University Press, 1974, Original cloth gilt, paper spine label, browned and little chipped, pages xii, 364, frontispiece, spare label tipped in. R. F. G. Hollett & Son Antiquarian Booksellers General Catalogue Summer 2010 - 481 2011 £65

Woodhouselee, Alexander Fraser Tytler, Lord 1747-1813 *Plan and Outlines of a Course of Lectures on University History, Ancient and Modern, Delivered in the University of Edinburgh.* Edinburgh: William Creech, 1782, First edition; small 4to., (iv) 216 (2) (217)-250 pages, full contemporary black calf, gilt ruled covers and spine, gilt stamped spine title, contemporary ink inscription by John Gordon to Christopher Stannard, 1795, fine. Jeff Weber Rare Books 163 - 50 2011 $850

Woodleigh House or the Happy Holidays. T. Nelson and Sons, 1852, 12mo., original blindstamped crimson cloth gilt, hinges trifle rubbed, pages 288, engraved title and 6 engraved vignette plates (rather foxed). R. F. G. Hollett & Sons Antiquarian Booksellers 170 - 28 2011 £35

Woodruff, Elizabeth *Stories from a Magic World.* Springfield: McLoughlin, 1938, Large 4to., cloth pictorial paste-on, slight tip and spine end wear, very good-fine, printed on coated paper and illustrated by Tenggren with 5 incredible color plates, plus 13 full page black and whites by Gustaf Tenggren. Aleph-Bet Books, Inc. 95 - 548 2011 $600

Woodward, G. L. *English Play 1641-1700.* Chicago: The Newbury Library, 1945, Full leather with lovely gilt decorations to covers and spine, as well as matching inner gilt, decorations, very nearly fine, inscribed by co-compiler, J. G. McManaway for Mary Morley Crapo, Viscountess Eccles. Lupack Rare Books May 26 2011 - ABE345163586 2011 $100

Woodwark, T. H. *The Crosses on the North York Moors.* Whitby: Lit. & Phil. Soc., 1924, Pages 38, original wrappers, 17 illustrations. R. F. G. Hollett & Son Antiquarian Booksellers 177 - 926 2011 £30

Woolf, Virginia 1882-1941 *Congenial Spirits. The Selected Letters of Virginia Woolf.* London: Hogarth Press, 1989, First edition; xviii, 472 pages, including index, large 8vo., publisher's blue cloth, gilt lettered spine, as new in original dust jacket. Paulette Rose Fine and Rare Books 32 - 192 2011 $115

Woolf, Virginia 1882-1941 *The Letters of Virginia Woolf.* London: Hogarth Press, 1975-1980, First edition; 8vo., 3000+ pages, fine in close to fine dust jackets with very slight sunning at spines (as usual). Any Amount of Books May 29 2011 - A69202 2011 $408

Woolf, Virginia 1882-1941 *Reviewing.* London: Hogarth Press, 1939, First edition; (31) pages, 8vo., stiff blue paper wrappers, lettered in purple, sewn at spine as issued, fine.   Paulette Rose Fine and Rare Books   32 - 191 2011 $175

Woolf, Virginia 1882-1941 *A Room of One's Own.* New York: and London: Hogarth Press, 1929, Limited to 492 copies of which 450 were for sale, this copy being number 340; signed by Woolf, octavo, publisher's full cinnamon cloth.   Heritage Book Shop   Booth A12 51st NY International Antiquarian Book Fair April 8-10 2011 - 141 2011 $6500

Woolf, Virginia 1882-1941 *A Room of One's Own.* London: Hogarth, 1931, Second edition; 8vo., 172 pages, green cloth, owner's bookplate, name on flyleaf, edges slightly spotted, few pencil notations in margins, cover slightly spotted, otherwise very good, poet Barbara Howes' copy with her bookplate and signature.   Second Life Books Inc.   174 - 333 2011 $135

Woolley, A. E. *35MM Nudes.* New York: 1966, First edition; 160 pages, large 4to., very good, some white on blue cover (might be part of design), very good in dust jacket.   Bookworm & Silverfish   679 - 154 2011 $75

Woolman, John *A Journal of the Life, Gospel, Labours and Christian Experience of that Faithful Minister of Jesus Christ, John Woolman, Late of Mount Holly in the Province of New Jersey, North America.*   Dublin: printed by R. M. Jackson, 1794, Pages xv, 464, modern half calf gilt.   R. F. G. Hollett & Son Antiquarian Booksellers   175 - 1467 2011   £150

Woolrich, Cornell *Black Alibi.* New York: Simon & Schuster, 1942, First edition; near fine in bright dust jacket with some very light professional restoration to spine ends and corners, handsome, bright copy.   Buckingham Books   May 26 2011 - 27079 2011 $3000

Woolrich, Cornell *The Black Angel.* Garden City: Doubleday, Doran and Co. Inc., 1943, First edition; near fine in dust jacket, tight, clean copy with minor offsetting to front and rear pastedown sheets, adjacent to spine hinge, dust jacket shows light rubbing to spine ends with one small (half inch) closed tear to top edge of front panel.   Buckingham Books   May 26 2011 - 27084 2011 $2750

Woolrich, Cornell *The Black Angel.* Garden City: Doubleday, Doran and Co. Inc., 1943, First edition; fine in dust jacket, some minor professional restoration to spine ends and corners.   Buckingham Books   May 26 2011 - 29809 2011 $2750

Woolrych, Humphry William *A Treatise on the Criminal Statutes of 7 Will IV & I Vict. cc. 84-91.* London: A. Maxwell, 1837, First edition; 12mo., xviii, 186 pages, original boards, neatly rebacked with printed label on spine, uncut, presentation copy inscribed "from the author", good, surprisingly scarce.   John Drury Rare Books   153 - 173 2011   £175

Worcester, Edward Somerset, Marquis of *A Century of the Names and Scantlings of Such Inventions as a Present I Can Call to Mind...* London: J. Grismond, 1663, First edition; 12mo., (24), 72, (12), (2), 34 pages (A1 blank (here lacking), A11v, E5v, E6r blank, woodcut royal arms on Flv, 18th century speckled calf, spine gilt in compartments, red morocco lettering piece, hinges cracked, binding rubbed, rare, from the library of the Earls of Macclesfield at Shirburn Castle.   Maggs Bros. Ltd.   1440 - 230 2011   £4500

Worcester, G. R. G. *The Junks & Sampans of the Yangtze.* Annapolis: 1971, First edition; 626 pages, folio, fine in near fine dust jacket.   Bookworm & Silverfish   678 - 149 2011 $200

Worcester, Samuel *An Address on Sacred Musick, Delivered Before the Middlesex Musical Society and the Handel Society of Dartmouth College.* Boston: Manning and Loring, 1811, 8vo., pages 22, sewn self wrappers, inscribed by author to William Cunningham, very slight foxing in places, edges of leaves little chipped, else very good.   Second Life Books Inc.   174 - 334 2011 $75

Wordsworth, Dorothy *Journals of Dorothy Wordsworth.* London: Macmillan, 1941, First edition; 2 volumes, original cloth, gilt, dust jackets (trifle frayed at head of spines), pages xxv, 443; vii, 434 with 11 plates and 7 maps, excellent set.   R. F. G. Hollett & Son Antiquarian Booksellers   173 - 338 2011   £140

Wordsworth, William 1770-1850 *The Excursion Being a Portion of the Recluse.* London: printed for Longman, Hurst, Rees, Orme and Brown, Paternoster-Row, London, 1814, One of 500 copies, First edition with errata leaf and with Y1 cancelled as usual; 4to., full contemporary green morocco, elaborately gilt tooled with thistles and lyres, all edges gilt, magnificent contemporary presentation binding, expertly rebacked by James Brockman with original spine laid down, preserved in green half morocco slipcase, inscribed by author to Allan Cunningham.   James S. Jaffe Rare Books   May 26 2011 - 13825 2011 $25,000

Wordsworth, William 1770-1850 *Guide to the Lakes.* Henry Frowde, 1906, Fifth edition; small 8vo., original cloth, gilt, pages xxxii, 204, map and 8 illustrations.   R. F. G. Hollett & Son Antiquarian Booksellers   173 - 1240 2011   £60

Wordsworth, William 1770-1850 *The Letters of William and Dorothy Wordsworth.* Oxford University Press, 1935-1939, First edition; 6 volumes, original cloth, dust jackets (trifle worn), 2 facsimiles and map in first volume, excellent clean and sound set. R. F. G. Hollett & Son Antiquarian Booksellers 173 - 339 2011 £350

Wordsworth, William 1770-1850 *The Letters of William and Dorothy Wordsworth III. The Middle Years Part 2 1812-1820.* Oxford: Clarendon Press, 1970, Original cloth gilt, dust jacket, pages xx, 692, frontispiece, roundel library stamp on title. R. F. G. Hollett & Son Antiquarian Booksellers 173 - 340 2011 £60

Wordsworth, William 1770-1850 *The Letters of William and Dorothy Wordsworth. III. The Later Years Part I 1821-1828.* London: Oxford University Press, 1978, Second edition; pages xxxii, 730, 3 plates, original cloth, gilt, dust jacket, fine. R. F. G. Hollett & Son Antiquarian Booksellers 173 - 545 2011 £60

Wordsworth, William 1770-1850 *Memorials of a Tour on the Continent 1820.* London: Longman Hurst Rees, Orme and Brown, 1822, First edition; tall 8vo., pages viii, 103, 4 pages ads dated March 1822, untrimmed and bound with half title in contemporary boards, rebacked with later cloth and leather label, contemporary ownership signature of Hannah Hoare. Second Life Books Inc. 174 - 335 2011 $1250

Wordsworth, William 1770-1850 *My Dearest Love. Letters of William and Mary Wordsworth 1810.* Grasmere: Dove Cottage, 1981, Limited edition (no. 196 of 300 copies; large 4to., original quarter morocco gilt with marbled boards, oval leather label, gilt monogram, cloth slipcase with matching marbled boards, pages 81, untrimmed, 25 facsimile plates, loosely inserted prospectus with 1 page (folded as issued), original invoice with 4 line autograph postcard from Jonathan Wordsworth (St. Catherine's College, Oxford '81), fine. R. F. G. Hollett & Son Antiquarian Booksellers 173 - 1241 2011 £400

Wordsworth, William 1770-1850 *Poems.* London: printed for Longman, Hurst, Orme, 1807, First edition, one of 500 copies Printed; with cancels D11-12 in volume I and B2 in volume II, volume I has half title and erratum leaf H8, volume II has half title, sectional half title leaf B1 and first state of sheet F9(i) in volume 2 with misprint "Thy fnuction" on page 98, last line; 2 volumes 8vo., original drab boards with pink paper covered spines as issued, contemporary ownership inscription to Anne Watson in volume I, with pencil ownership signature on titlepage, bookplates of Simon Nowell-Smith and his wife, light foxing, covers slightly chipped and worn but very good. James S. Jaffe Rare Books May 26 2011 - 21014 2011 $27,500

Wordsworth, William 1770-1850 *Poems.* London: Macmillan, 1911, Small 8vo., full crushed scarlet morocco gilt by Ramage (although unsigned), with raised bands, pages xxxi, 331, all edges gilt, engraved title vignette portrait, fine in lovely little gift binding. R. F. G. Hollett & Son Antiquarian Booksellers General Catalogue Summer 2010 - 930 2011 £75

Wordsworth, William 1770-1850 *The Poetical Works.* London: Edward Moxon, 1849-1851, New edition; 7 volumes, half titles, frontispiece volume I, initial 8 page catalog, May 1853 in volume I, uniform black cloth, slightly rubbed, spines volumes II and III slightly worn at head, very good set. Jarndyce Antiquarian Booksellers CXCI - 31 2011 £300

Wordsworth, William 1770-1850 *The Poetical Works of Wordsworth.* London: Frederick Warne and Co. c., 1880, Elaborate birthday gift inscription in purple ink on initial blank, pages xxxix, 600, 8vo., contemporary half calf, marbled boards, spine with five raised bands, black morocco lettering piece, gilt corner and centerpieces in other compartments, marbled edges and endpapers, rubbed at extremities, very good. Blackwell Rare Books B166 - 118 2011 £40

Wordsworth, William 1770-1850 *Yarrow Revisited and Other Poems.* London: Longman, Rees, Orme, Brown, Green and Longman, Paternoster Row and Edward Moxon, Dover Street, 1835, First edition; small 8vo., full contemporary cranberry calf gilt, marbled edges, green morocco label on spine and with Earl of Lonsdale's coat of arms on front cover, extremities of calf trifle rubbed, otherwise superb copy in unusually fine contemporary binding, preserved in maroon half morocco slipcase, presentation copy to poet's patron, William Lowther, Earl of Lonsdale, with bookplate of recipients descendant, Hugh Cecil, Fifth Earl of Lonsdale. James S. Jaffe Rare Books May 26 2011 - 13824 2011 $7500

The Working Man's Friend and Family Instructor. Volume the First. London: John Cassell, 1850, Small hole in 1 leaf affecting few lines of text, contemporary half roan gilt, pages 412. R. F. G. Hollett & Son Antiquarian Booksellers 175 - 1468 2011 £35

Workman, Fanny Bullock *Ice-Bound Heights of the Mustagh...* London: Archibald Constable and Co., 1908, First edition; 8vo., pages xvi, 444, original publisher's green cloth lettered gilt on spine and cover with cover illustration of mountain scene, 170 illustrations, 2 folding maps, color frontispiece and 3 other color plates and 3 photogravures, bookplate of Duchess of Bedford, faint rubbing to cover and head of spine, very slight marks, lettering bright covers, not faded, very good, maps, plates, text clean and bright. Any Amount of Books May 26 2011 - A69805 2011 $1132

Worlds Columbian Exposition 1893 *Catalogue of the Russian Section.* St. Petersburg: Imperial Russian Commission, 1893, First edition; small 4to., 572 pages, cloth and decorated boards, decorative color litho to front cover, very good with rubbing to boards and some soiling to rear cover, quite scarce. Lupack Rare Books May 26 2011 - ABE1169611649 2011 $600

Wortham, Louis J. *A History of Texas from Wilderness to Commonwealth.* Fort Worth: 1924, 5 volumes, xiv, 430, illustrations; (vi0, 432 pages, illustrations; (vi) 448 pages, illustrations; (vi), 400 pages, illustrations; (vi), 377 pages, illustrations, original half leather and green cloth, some external rubbing and spine fading, two bookplates on endpapers of each volume, internally tanned, overall very good. Dumont Maps & Books of the West 111 - 91 2011 $225

Worthington, John *A Systeme of Christian Doctrine: Being a Commentary Upon the Scripture-Catechism Composed by the Pious and Learned Dr. John Worthington...* Joseph Downing, 1723, 12mo., contemporary blind ruled speckled sheep, some wormholes in lower board, pages (ii), 116, woodcut headpiece, fore-edge spotted, Parochial Library label on pastedown, later shelf numbers to flyleaf, very good, rare. R. F. G. Hollett & Son Antiquarian Booksellers 175 - 1470 2011 £175

Worthington, S. *Inland Waters of Africa; The Result of Two Expeditions to the Great Lakes of Kenya and Uganda...* London: Macmillan, 1933, First edition; 8vo., pages xix, 259, maps, 40 plates, original red cloth, dust jacket torn. J. & S. L. Bonham Antiquarian Booksellers Africa 4/20/2011 - 5540 2011 £90

Worthy, Alfred N. *A Treatise on the Botanic Theory and Practice of Medicine...* Forsyth: printed by C. R. Hanleiter, 1842, First edition; 8vo., 8 631, (1) pages, errata leaf, full contemporary calf, leather label, very good, rare. M & S Rare Books, Inc. 90 - 450 2011 $825

Wragg, Arthur *Alice through the Paper Mill.* Birmingham: privately published for C. H. Foyle of Boxfoldia, 1940, Large 8vo., original cloth backed boards, lower corners little rounded, back board slight marked, pages 57, with 12 striking full page woodcut plates and vignette, uncommon. R. F. G. Hollett & Son Antiquarian Booksellers General Catalogue Summer 2010 - 931 2011 £95

Wragg, Arthur *"Jesus Wept".* London: Selwyn & Blount, n.d., 1935, tall 8vo. original black cloth silvered, dust jacket, unpaginated, illustrated with black and white drawings. R. F. G. Hollett & Son Antiquarian Booksellers General Catalogue Summer 2010 - 932 2011 £65

Wragg, Arthur *Thy Kingdom Come.* London: Selwyn & Blount, 1939, First edition; Tall 8vo., original cream coarse weave pictorial cloth, dust jacket, unpaginated, illustrations in black and white. R. F. G. Hollett & Son Antiquarian Booksellers General Catalogue Summer 2010 - 933 2011 £45

Wrangham, C. E. *Journey to the District from Cambridge 1779.* Oriel Press, 1983, First edition; original cloth, gilt, dust jacket, price clipped, pages 96, well illustrated. R. F. G. Hollett & Son Antiquarian Booksellers 173 - 1242 2011 £40

Wraxall, L. *Life in the Sea; or Nature and Habits of Marine Animals.* London: Houlston & Wright, 1860, First edition; frontispiece and illustrations, original purple wavy grained cloth by Leighton, Son & Hodge, spines slightly faded, armorial bookplate of Llangattock, very good. Jarndyce Antiquarian Booksellers CXCI - 344 2011 £68

Wraxall, N. William *Memoirs of the Courts of Berlin, Dresden, Warsaw and Vienna in the Years 1777, 1778 and 1779.* London: T. Cadell and W. Davies, 1806, Third edition; 2 volumes, contemporary full calf gilt with gilt spines and double spine labels, few slight stains and defects, hinges just cracking in places, but sound, pages xii, 418; xii, 510. R. F. G. Hollett & Son Antiquarian Booksellers 175 - 1471 2011 £85

Wray, Mary *The Ladies' Library.* London: printed for Jacob Tonson, 1714, First edition; 3 volumes, 12mo., rebound in the period in quarter sprinkled calf over marbled boards, gilt ruled and raised bands, contrasting red morocco title labels, vellum tips, engraved frontispiece in each volume, small stamp of Hampstead Public Library on each titlepage, smaller stamp to edge of page 95 and final text leaf in each volume, contemporary signature "Chester" at head of each titlepage, else very nice, clean and attractive, scarce. Paulette Rose Fine and Rare Books 32 - 194 2011 $4000

Wright, D. *X.* 1960-1961, Volume 1/1-4, Volume 2/1-3, all issued, 7 issues in original wrappers, very good. I. D. Edrich May 26 2011 - 99168 2011 $461

Wright, Elizabeth Mary *The Life of Joseph Wright.* London: Oxford University Press, 1932, First edition; 2 volumes, half titles, frontispiece, original light blue cloth, spines slightly faded, very good. Jarndyce Antiquarian Booksellers CXCI - 621 2011 £110

Wright, Ernest Vincent *Gadsby: a Story of Over 50,000 Words Without using the Letter "E".* Los Angeles: Wetzel Pub. Co., 1939, First edition; 8vo., pages 267, original publisher's red cloth lettered black at spine and on cover, clean sound very good copy with slight creasing at head of spine and two slight marks to covers, decent copy, scarce. Any Amount of Books May 26 2011 - A68218 2011 $1342

Wright, Ethel *Saturday Walk.* New York: William R. Scott, 1941, (1954). First edition of the revised version; oblong 4to., pictorial cloth, fine in dust jacket, scarce, illustrations by Richard Rose. Aleph-Bet Books, Inc. 95 - 506 2011 $200

Wright, G. N. *China, in a Series of Views Displaying the Scenery, Architecture and Social Habits of that Ancient Empire, Drawn from Original and Authentic Sketches...* London: and Paris: Fisher, Son and Co., 1843, 4 volumes bound as 2, 4to., pages 96, 72; 68, 56 72 + engraved vignette title and 31 steel engraved plates in each volume, contemporary tan half calf, spines panel gilt extra, green and black lettering and numbering pieces gilt, green 'publisher & date' piece gilt at foot, boards double rule gilt bordered with broken rule in blind within, 'pin head' design blue bookcloth sides, orange 'coated' endpapers, all edges gilt, multi core made red and yellow applied endbands, plates little foxed at edges, spine chipped at ends, numbering pieces mostly lost, joints cracking, ink inscription, from the collection of Christopher Ernest Weston 1947-2010. Unsworths Booksellers 24 - 154 2011 £1000

Wright, G. N. *Ireland Illustrated from Original Drawings by G. Petrie, W. H. Bartlett & T. M. Baynes.* 1831, First edition; 80 views on 40 plates, rice guards on all plates, still some foxing, owner inscribed by Anna Maria Hall, St. Ives, Cornwall, Feb. 1812, full mottled calf, worn. C. P. Hyland May 26 2011 - 259/519 2011 $507

Wright, Joseph *Old English Grammar.* Oxford University Press, 1934, Third edition; pages xvi, 372, original cloth, gilt. R. F. G. Hollett & Son Antiquarian Booksellers General Catalogue Summer 2010 - 483 2011 £30

Wright, Lewis *The Microscope.* London: Religious Tract Society, 1927, Pages 293, 195 illustrations, original blue cloth gilt. R. F. G. Hollett & Son Antiquarian Booksellers General Catalogue Summer 2010 - 1153 2011 £40

Wright, Richard 1908-1960 *Native Son.* New York: Harper Bros., 1940, Second state with grey cloth and grey spine; near fine, light bumping to spine ends and bottom coroners, dust jacket very good, creasing and chipping to corners, flap corners clipped, rubbing to spine, very good, creasing and chipping to corners, flap corners clipped, rubbing to spine. Bella Luna Books May 26 2011 - t6388 2011 $192

Wright, Sydney Fowler *The Throne of Saturn.* Sauk City: Arkham House, 1949, First U.S. edition expanded; octavo, pages (i-vi) vii-viii (1-2) 3-186 (187: colophon) (188: blank) publisher's black cloth spine panel stamped in gold. L. W. Currey, Inc. 124 - 63 2011 $1500

Wright, Thomas *Dictionary of Obsolete and Provincial English, Containing Words from the English Writers Previous to the Nineteenth Century...* London: Henry G. Bohn, 1857, First edition; 2 volumes, ads preceding titles and ends of both volumes, original blue glazed cloth, elaborately blocked in blind, spines faded, hinges strengthened, very good. Jarndyce Antiquarian Booksellers CXCI - 159 2011 £150

Wright, Thomas *Essays on Subjects Connected with the Literature, Popular Superstitions and History of England in the Middle Ages.* London: John Russell Smith, 1846, First edition; 2 volumes, half titles, titles in red and black, uncut in original brown cloth, spines darkened, minor splits, cloth little dusted and marked, inscribed. Jarndyce Antiquarian Booksellers CXCI - 622 2011 £95

Wrighte, William *Grotesque Architecture or Rural Amusement...* London: printed for Henry Webley, 1767, First edition; 8vo., 14 pages + (2) page publisher's list, engraved frontispiece, 28 pages engraved plates, very good, uncommon, older marbled boards and leather corners, newer leather spine and leather spine label, text slightly browned, plates also faintly browned, but very good. Any Amount of Books May 26 2011 - A70271 2011 $1258

Wroblewski, David *The Story of Edgar Sawtelle.* New York: Ecco, 2008, First edition, true first edition with ISBN ending in 4227; fine in near fine dust jacket, color on front flap has run slightly, first state of dust jacket (not laminated). Bella Luna Books May 29 2011 - t8924r 2011 $82

Wydnham, John *Planet Plane.* London: Newnes, 1936, First edition, first impression; 8vo., pages 248, original publisher's yellow cloth, titles to spine in black, spine slightly marked with few darker damp marks, slight soiling, slight rubbing, otherwise very good-, sound, with clean text. Any Amount of Books May 29 2011 - A71764 2011 $340

Wynne, W. Arnold Smith *St. Olave's Priory and Bridge, Herringfleet, Suffolk.* Norwich: Goose and Son, 1914, First edition; Tall 8vo., original cloth, gilt, pages v, 101, with plan frontispiece and numerous photo illustrations. R. F. G. Hollett & Son Antiquarian Booksellers 177 - 928 2011 £85

Wyoming. State Board of Live Stock Commissioners *Official Brand Book of the State and a Compilation of Laws Affecting Live Stock.* Cheyenne: Issued by the State Board of Live Stock Commissioners of Wyoming, 1916, First edition; 12mo., original full maroon calf, title in gilt on front cover, (4), 450 pages, brands, name index, Thomas W. Streeter's copy with his bookplate, scarce, minor cosmetic restoration to spine ends and covers, else fine, housed in quarter leather and cloth clamshell case with raised bands and titles stamped in gold on spine. Buckingham Books May 26 2011 - 25798 2011 $3750

Wyss, Johann David 1743-1818 *The Swiss Family Robinson or Adventures of a Father and Mother and Four Sons on a Desert Island...* New York: J. & J. Harper, 1832, First American edition; 2 volumes, 16mo., frontispiece and vignette title in volume 1, original printed and pictorial boards, heavily foxed, small pieces lacking from frontispiece and vignette title, both volumes rebacked, most of original spine laid down on volume 1, cloth printed labels made for volume II, not terribly attractive but sound set.   M & S Rare Books, Inc.   90 - 208   2011 $850

X Y Z

Yanase, Masamu *Shogaku Kagaku Ehon. (Something about Growing Rice).* Tokyo: Tokyo-sha Showa 12, circa 1920-1930's, 8vo., pictorial cloth, rather clean copy, original pictorial dust jacket, minor handling to wrapper, each page illustrated in either color or black and white. Jo Ann Reisler, Ltd. 86 - 145 2011 $750

Yang, H. H. *Aromatic High Strength Fibers.* New York: 1989, First edition; xiii, 873 pages, 4to., original cloth, very good in like dust jacket. Bookworm & Silverfish 671 - 179 2011 $345

Yanker, Gary *Prop Art.* Studio Vista, 1972, First edition; large 4to., original cloth, gilt, dust jacket, pages 256, illustrations. R. F. G. Hollett & Son Antiquarian Booksellers 175 - 1475 2011 £40

Yarbrough, Steve *Two Dogs.* Candia: LeBow, 2000, Limited to 26 signed, lettered copies; fine, signed by introducer John Dufresne and Ewa Yarbrough who did the charcoal sketch. Bella Luna Books May 29 2011 - t1107 2011 $82

Yashima, Taro *The Youngest One.* New York: Viking, 1962, Oblong 4to., cloth, edge of one page creased, else fine in dust jacket, beautiful color lithographs, inscribed by Yashima with watercolor drawing, scarce. Aleph-Bet Books, Inc. 95 - 600 2011 $600

Yate, Walter Honywood *Political, Historical and Analytical Arguments, Proving the Necessity of a Parliamentary Reform and Pointing Out the Means of Effecting that Important Measure without Injuring Individuals or Convulsing the Nation.* London: printed for the author and sold by Longman &c, 1825, Second edition; 2 volumes in one, 8vo., cxviii, 252; xii,3 40 pages, contemporary half calf, spine gilt and labelled with raised bands, light wear to extremities, else excellent copy, very scarce. John Drury Rare Books 153 - 174 2011 £275

Yazdani, Ghulam *Ajanta. The Colour and Monochrome Reproductions of the Ajanta Frescoes Based on Photography Part I. Text.* London: Oxford University Press, 1930, First edition; Volume I (of 4 text volumes), xix, 55 pages, folding black and white map, 4to., cloth, top edge gilt, about very good with tears to top of spine, wear at tail, spine darkened. Kaaterskill Books 12 - 215 2011 $75

Year's Work in English Studies. 1919-1969, Volumes 1-50, first few volumes have small rubber stamp of Cambridge Union Society "Cancelled" on bookplate. I. D. Edrich May 26 2011 - 96371 2011 $1258

Yearsley, Ann Cromartie *Poems on Several Occasions by Ann Yearsley.* London: printed for T. Cadell, 1785, First edition; (xxx, 237 pages), 4to., mid 20th century half tan calf, contrasting red morocco gilt lettered title label, new endpapers, good, attractive copy. Paulette Rose Fine and Rare Books 32 - 195 2011 $1500

Yearsley, MacLeod *The Folklore of Fairy Tale.* London: Watts & Co., 1924, First edition; original cloth, gilt, spine rather faded, trifle marked, pages xiii, 240, edges and flyleaves foxed. R. F. G. Hollett & Son Antiquarian Booksellers 175 - 1476 2011 £30

Yeats, Jack Butler *A Little Fleet.* London: Elkin Mathews, circa, 1909, 17 pages, 5 pages ads, stiff wrappers, cracked, else good, signed presentation with extra watercolor added. C. P. Hyland May 26 2011 - 259/523 2011 $7247

Yeats, Jack Butler *The Treasure of the Garden. (One of Jack B. Yeats Plays for the Miniature Stage).* London: Elkin Mathews, 1902, First edition; 29 x 22.5 cm., 11 pages + 7 plates colored by author, printed wrapper with color vignette, unusual in this condition. C. P. Hyland May 26 2011 - 259/520 2011 $2899

Yeats, William Butler 1865-1939 *Essays 1931-1936.* Dublin: Cuala Press, 1937, One of 300 copies; Uncut and unopened, original blue boards, cream cloth spine, paper label, original glassine wrappers, slightly chipped, fine, from the library of the grandfather of John Rolls who was the Rolls of Rolls-Royce. Jarndyce Antiquarian Booksellers CXCI - 623 2011 £250

Yeats, William Butler 1865-1939 *Irish Fairy Tales.* 1892, Fourth impression; 2 illustrations by Jack B. Yeats, in specially made box, very good. C. P. Hyland May 26 2011 - 259/532 2011 $870

Yeats, William Butler 1865-1939 *Per Amica Silentia Lunae.* London: Macmillan, 1918, First edition; 8vo., original publisher's blue cloth lettered gilt on spine and cover, gilt illustration on cover, pages vi, 95, slight rubbing, covers little toned and darkened, neat name on front endpaper and date 1918), sound, about very good with clean text. Any Amount of Books May 29 2011 - A66645 2011 $272

Yeats, William Butler 1865-1939 *Poems.* Dublin: Cuala Press, 1935, First edition, one of 30 copies; small 8vo., frontispiece by Victor Brown, hand colored and heightened with gold, hand drawn ornaments by Elizabeth Corbet Yeats, original light blue paper wrappers, some very minor spotting, gatherings slightly pulled at gutter, otherwise fine. James S. Jaffe Rare Books   May 26 2011 - 20776 2011 $17,500

Yeats, William Butler 1865-1939 *The Poems of W. B. Yeats.* London: Macmillan, 1949, Limited to 375 numbered sets printed on specially made Glastonbury Ivory Toned Antique Laid paper and signed by author; large 8vo., 2 volumes, original olive green buckram with gilt lettering on front cover and spine, top edge gilt, slipcase, fine in original slipcase.   James S. Jaffe Rare Books   May 26 2011 - 21139 2011 $6000

Yeats, William Butler 1865-1939 *Variorum Edition of the Poems of W. B. Yeats.* New York: Macmillan Co., 1957, First edition, limited to 825 numbered copies signed by author; this being number 660, octavo, xxxv, (1, blank), 884 pages, signed limitation page inserted after half title, original quarter orange buckram over beige buckram boards, spine ruled and lettered in gilt, top edge stained gray, fine, original cardboard slipcase (bit chipped at corners), very good.   Heritage Book Shop   Holiday 2010 - 134 2011 $2000

Yeats, William Butler 1865-1939 *Collected Works in Verse and Prose of William Butler Yeats.* Stratford-on-Avon: imprinted at the Shakespeare Head Press, 1908, First collected edition, limited to 1060 copies; 8 volumes, octavo, photograuvre frontispiece portraits, titles in red and black, original quarter vellum over gray linen boards, front cover and spine lettered in gilt, top edge gilt, others uncut, cloth covers of volumes I, III, IV, VII and VIII with minor staining, not affecting inside text, previous owner's ink signature, very nice set.   Heritage Book Shop   Holiday 2010 - 133 2011 $4500

Yee, Chiang *Chin-Pao and the Giant Pandas.* London: Country Life, 1939, First edition; original cloth gilt, dust jacket little torn and soiled, pages 84, color frontispiece and text illustrations, endpapers lightly spotted.   R. F. G. Hollett & Sons Antiquarian Booksellers   170 - 738 2011   £30

Yee, Chiang *Chin-pao at the Zoo.* London: Methuen, 1941, First edition; original cloth, gilt. dust jacket with few short closed edge tears, spine little darkened, pages 96, color frontispiece and text illustrations, presentation copy inscribed by author, scarce.   R. F. G. Hollett & Sons Antiquarian Booksellers   170 - 739 2011   £45

Yee, Chiang *Dabbitse.* Transatlantic Arts, 1945, Second edition; large 8vo., original cloth, gilt, dust jacket, pages 64, 4 colored plates, numerous illustrations, scarce. R. F. G. Hollett & Sons Antiquarian Booksellers   170 - 740 2011   £40

The Yellow Book. London: Mathews & Lane, 1894-1897, Complete run of the magazine from April 1894 to April 1897, first 5 volumes have some illustrations by Aubrey Bearsley, volume I stained on back cover, spines rippled on some volumes, otherwise very good tight.   Second Life Books Inc. 174 - 31 2011 $2500

Yellow Dwarf. New York: McLoughlin Brothers, n.d. circa, 1880, 8vo., pictorial wrappers, near fine, illustrations by Howard with 4 full page and 1 double page chromolithograph.   Aleph-Bet Books, Inc.   95 - 351 2011 $300

Yepes, Lopez Joaquin *Catecismo y Declaraction de la Doctrina Cristiana en Jengua Otomi, con un Vocabulario del Misimo Idioma.* Mexico City: Alejandro Valdes, 1826, First edition; small 4to., 254, (2) pages, small perforated stamp on titlepage, period tree calf, paper labels on spine, neatly restored, Library of Congress bookplate, very good. Jeff Weber Rare Books   163 - 201 2011 $2500

The Yes! Capra Chapbook Series. Santa Barbara: Capra Press, 1972-1977, First edition, issued with limitations between 50 and 250 copies, this set is made up of different limitation numbers, volume one is numbered and signed by author; 41 volumes, complete set, pictorial paper covered boards with clear (original?) glassine wrappers, fine. Charles Agvent   2010 Summer Miscellany - 48 2011 $3000

Yilma, Asfa, The Princess *Haile Selassie Emperor of Ethiopia with a brief Account of the History of Ethiopia.* London: Sampson Low, 1935, First edition; 8vo., pages xiv, 305, folding map, illustrations, original black cloth.   J. & S. L. Bonham Antiquarian Booksellers   Africa 4/20/2011 - 8672 2011   £60

Yokley, E. C. *Zoning Law & Practice.* Charlottesville: 1967, 4 volumes, with 1979 supplements for each volume, very good.   Bookworm & Silverfish   667 - 109 2011 $250

Yokley, E. C. *Zoning Law & Practice.* Charlottesville: 1978, 8 volumes, fine, about 3000 pages, each with 1984 supplement, original binding.   Bookworm & Silverfish   669 - 129 2011 $275

Yonge, Charlotte Mary 1823-1901 *Aunt Charlotte's Stories of German History.* London: Marcus Ward and Co., 1878, Original decorated cloth gilt, neatly recased, pages 338, 32, all edges gilt, chromolithograph frontispiece and title, woodcut illustrations.   R. F. G. Hollett & Sons Antiquarian Booksellers   170 - 743 2011   £65

Yonge, Charlotte Mary 1823-1901 *The History of Sir Thomas Thumb.* London: Hamilton Adams and Co. and Edinburgh: Thomas Constable and Co., 1855, First edition; original cloth, gilt, little rubbed and marked, pages vii, 142, (ii), all edges gilt, full page and other drawings by J. Blackburn, occasional finger mark, but very good. R. F. G. Hollett & Sons Antiquarian Booksellers 170 - 742 2011 £160

Yonkers Military Institute. A Boarding School for Boys, Benjamin Mason, Principal. Yonkers: n.p. circa, 1863, First edition; 8vo., 20 pages, illustrations, original printed and pictorial wrappers, some light soiling, creased vertically. M & S Rare Books, Inc. 90 - 254 2011 $225

Young & Minns *The Defence of Young and Minns, Printers to the State.* Boston: Gilbert & Dean, March, 1805, First edition; 8vo., 68 pages, removed, foxed, half title present but detached. M & S Rare Books, Inc. 90 - 140 2011 $375

The Young Cottager... New York: J. Seymour, 1817, 12mo., 36 pages, pictorial blue paper wrappers, upper wrapper with half page wood engraving, reinforced spine and light spotting at inner edges, wrapper lightly faded, very nice, rare. Hobbyhorse Books 56 - 37 2011 $220

The Young Ladies' Faithful Remembrancer of Obligations Responsibilities and Duties... York: printed for the author by W. Pickwell, 1850, 12mo., viii, (1), 10-82 pages, original printed card covers, upper cover just bit dust soiled, else good copy, internally fine. John Drury Rare Books 153 - 175 2011 £95

The Young Lady's Own Book: a Manual of Intellectual Improvement and Moral Deportment. Philadelphia: Thomas Cowperthwaite & Co., 1839, 12mo., modern cloth, gilt, pages xi, 320, with engraved frontispiece and title, little browning and marking in places, but very good, sound. R. F. G. Hollett & Son Antiquarian Booksellers 175 - 39 2011 £65

Young Learner's Pictorial Primer or, First Lessons in Spelling and Reading. New York: George F. Cooledge, n.d. circa, 1848, 12mo., pictorial wrappers, 26 pages, neat spine strengthening else fine, containing 4 alphabets, profusely illustrated. Aleph-Bet Books, Inc. 95 - 18 2011 $200

Young, Andrew *Quiet as Moss.* London: Rupert Hart-Davis, 1959, First edition; large 8vo., original cloth, dust jacket, pages 40, with woodcut decorations by Hassall. R. F. G. Hollett & Son Antiquarian Booksellers General Catalogue Summer 2010 - 808 2011 £65

Young, Andrew McLaren *Charles Rennie MacKintosh 1868-1928.* Edinburgh: Scottish Arts Council, 1968, Square 4to., original pictorial wrappers, pages 72, plus 32 plates. R. F. G. Hollett & Son Antiquarian Booksellers 177 - 291 2011 £40

Young, Ann Eliza *Wife No. 18 or the Story of a Life in Bondage.* Dustin: Gilman & Co., 1875, First edition; octavo, 605 pages, frontispiece, illustrations, original full sheep, crudely repaired preserving original spine, new endpapers, opens rather tightly, very good, scarce. Jeff Weber Rare Books 163 - 231 2011 $225

Young, Art *Socialist Primer.* Chicago: Socialist Party of America, 1930, 12mo., pictorial wrappers, normal shelfwear, paper toning on edges, very good+, black and white cartoons. Aleph-Bet Books, Inc. 95 - 464 2011 $275

Young, Arthur 1741-1820 *An Enquiry into the State of the Public Mind Amongst the Lower Classes...* London: W. and J. and J. Richardson, 1798-1819, First edition; 8vo., modern half red leather, marbled boards lettered gilt on spine, 5 raised bands, pages 37-1798, bound with 9 other tracts on education, very good set, slightly soiled and foxed, otherwise very good. Any Amount of Books May 26 2011 - A75312 2011 $2013

Young, Christie T. *The Black Princess and Other Fairy Tales from Brazil.* London: Simpkin Marshall, Hamilton, Kent & Co. n.d. circa, 1917, First edition; original cloth with pictorial roundel on upper board, little soiled, pages viii, 160, 12 striking color plates and text line drawings, flyleaves lightly browned very scarce. R. F. G. Hollett & Son Antiquarian Booksellers General Catalogue Summer 2010 - 486 2011 £140

Young, Dennis *Furniture in Britain Today.* London: Alec Tiranti, 1964, First edition; 4to., original publisher's blue cloth lettered gilt at spine, pages 10 (unpaginated), 310 illustrations, neat name on front endpaper, otherwise very good+. Any Amount of Books May 29 2011 - A62728 2011 $204

Young, Edward *Night Thoughts on Life, Death and Immortality.* London: Nuttall, Fisher and Dixon, n.d., Stereotype edition; Modern half levant moroco gilt, pages 418, engraved portrait and 6 plates (little browned, frontispiece neatly repaired in gutter). R. F. G. Hollett & Son Antiquarian Booksellers 175 - 1479 2011 £65

Young, Edward *Night Thoughts and a Paraphrase on Part of the Book of Job.* London: printed at the Chiswick Press by C. Whittingham for Taylor and Hessey, 1812, 240 x 145mm., lxvi, (2), 353, (1) pages, striking contemporary black morocco elaborately tooled in blind and gilt by Taylor & Hessey (board edges at middle on either side of painting stamped in gilt "Taylor and Hessey/Booksellers London"), covers with frame outlined by gilt rules and with cornerpieces in form of a stylized gilt satire, frame also featuring a chain of blindstamped oval medallions connected by palm fronds of an unusual ground of blind stippling, the whole enclosing a large central panel ornately tooled in blind, with cornerpieces composed of shells, leaves and volutes and with intricate sunburst medallion centerpiece, central panel further decorated in blind with complex of elaborate strapwork between the centerpiece and cornerpieces, highlighted by botanical and other tools, raised bands, spine with rows of gilt tools at head and tail, three spine panels tooled in blind and highlighted with gilt lancets with flowers, gilt turn-ins in Greek key style, all edges gilt, with exceptionally fine fore-edge painting depicting Westminster Bridge and Westminster Hall; with engraved frontispiece, armorial bookplate of David Gill, ink presentation inscription "Eliza Gill/the gift of her attached and affectionate Husband/Decem(ber) 3rd 1812", joints and extremities with touch of rubbing (though well marked with dye), offsetting to titlepage from frontispiece, occasional trivial imperfections internally, exceptionally pleasing copy, binding especially lustrous, text unusually clean, fresh and bright, painting beautifully preserved.   Phillip J. Pirages   59 - 199   2011 $2500

Young, Francis Brett *Marching on Tanga; with General Smuts in East Africa.* London: W. Collins, 1917, Third impression; 8vo., pages xii, 265, folding map, illustrations, original blue cloth, spine faded, two original photos included.   J. & S. L. Bonham Antiquarian Booksellers   Africa 4/20/2011 - 4486   2011   £85

Young, William *Botanica Neglecta.* Philadelphia: 1916, One of 50 copies on large paper quarto, numbered and signed by editor; 4to., xi, (4), 55 pages, unopened, cloth backed boards, printed paper endpapers discolored from glue migration, extremities bit rubbed, very good.   Joseph J. Felcone Inc.   Fall Miscellany 2010 - 132   2011 $300

Younger, Helen *Dr. Seuss: a Guide to First Editions.* New York: 2002, Only 1000 copies printed; 8vo., pictorial boards, 200 pages, index, signed by Helen and Marc Younger, full color reproductions of dust jackets.   Aleph-Bet Books, Inc.   95 - 522   2011 $150

Younghusband, Eileen *Social Work in Britain.* Dunfermilne: Carnegie UK Trust, 1951, 4to., original wrappers, little dusty and marked, pages viii, 256.   R. F. G. Hollett & Son Antiquarian Booksellers   175 - 1482 2011 £30

Younghusband, Ethel *Glimpses of East Africa and Zanzibar.* London: Jong Long, 1910, First edition; 8vo., pages xvi, 17-320, half title, title in red and black, folding map, 36 plates, original blue cloth, top edge gilt, some fading on upper cover, inner joint cracked, author's presentation copy.   J. & S. L. Bonham Antiquarian Booksellers   Africa 4/20/2011 - 5676   2011 £175

Yule, Henry *Narrative of the Mission to the Court of Ava in 1855, Together with the Journal of Arthur Phayre.* Kuala Lumpur: London: New York: Oxford University Press, 1968, First edition thus; 4to., pages xlvi, iii-vii, 391, 29 color plates, 49 figures, one folding map at rear, crease to front board which is slightly bowed, tear to rear hinge, else sound, very good in slightly nicked and chipped, very good dust jacket.   Any Amount of Books   May 29 2011 - A64552   2011 $255

Zaehnsdorf, Joseph W. *The Art of Bookbinding.* Gregg International Publishers, 1969, Facsimile of second edition; original green cloth gilt by Zaehnsdorf, pages ii, new introductory note), xix, 190, (i), illustrations.   R. F. G. Hollett & Son Antiquarian Booksellers   General Catalogue Summer 2010 - 353   2011   £45

Zafon, Carlos Ruiz *The Angel's Game.* London: Weidenfeld & Nicolson, 2009, Limited to 1000 signed and numbered copies; fine.   Bella Luna Books   May 26 2011 - t9233   2011 $165

Zeier, Franz *Book, Boxes and Portfolios.* New York: Design Press, 1983, First edition; large 8vo., original boards, dust jacket, pages 304, line drawings, 28 pagaes in color.   R. F. G. Hollett & Son Antiquarian Booksellers   General Catalogue Summer 2010 - 354   2011   £35

Zelazny, Roger *Creatures of Light and Darkness.* Garden City: Doubleday & Co. Inc., 1969, First edition; octavo, cloth.   L. W. Currey, Inc.   124 - 64   2011 $1500

Zelazny, Roger *The Doors of His Face, the Lamps of His Mouth and Other Stories.* Garden City: Doubleday & Co., 1971, First edition; octavo, cloth.   L. W. Currey, Inc.   124 - 112   2011 $750

Zelazny, Roger *Lord of Light.* Garden City: Doubleday & Co., 1967, First edition; octavo, cloth.   L. W. Currey, Inc.   124 - 16   2011 $3500

Zelazny, Roger *Madwand.* Huntington Wood: Phantasia Press, 1981, First edition; octavo, cloth.   L. W. Currey, Inc.   124 - 88   2011 $1000

Zelazny, Roger *Nine Princes in Amber.* Garden City: Doubleday & Co., 1970, First edition; cloth, octavo.   L. W. Currey, Inc.   124 - 19   2011 $2750

Zelazny, Roger *This Immortal.* London: Rupr Hart-Davis, 1967, First edition; octavo, boards.   L. W. Currey, Inc.   124 - 93   2011 $950

Zempel, Edward *Book Prices: Used and Rare.* Peoria: The Spoon River Press, 1995, 1996. 1997. 1998. 1999; Folio, 798 798 800 796 800 pages, red cloth on boards, gilt title repeated along spine, mint.   Hobbyhorse Books   56 - 125   2011 $200

Zimara, Marco Antonio *Questio de Primo Cognito.* Lyon: Venundantur apud Scipionem de Gabiano (colophon): Impressum per Jacobi Myt, 1530, Scarce separate printing; title printed in red and black within woodcut border, first leaf little frayed at edges, bit browned in first half, ff., lxxv (lacking final blank), 8vo., 19th century German sheep backed boards, newer endleaves, good.   Blackwell Rare Books   B166 - 119   2011   £1500

Zionitischer Weyrauchs Hugel Oder: Myrrhen Berg, Worinnen Allerley Liebliches und Wohl Riecehendes Nach Apotheker-Kunst Zubereitets... Germantown: Christoph Sauer, 1739, 8vo., (12), 1792, (14) pages, contemporary calf over wooden boards, clasps lacking, very skillfully rebacked in period style, free endpapers neatly replaced with old paper, original pastedowns present and with contemporary notes in a German hand, few very tiny ink-burn holes in title, last 8 leaves with small neat strengthening at fore-edge just touching few letters, usual light browning and staining to text, very good, quite attractive copy, cloth portfolio and morocco backed slipcase.   Joseph J. Felcone Inc. Fall Miscellany 2010 - 55   2011 $6500

Zola, Emile *Abbe Mouret's Transgression.* Vizetelly & Co., 1886, First English edition; original green cloth, decorated in red, black and silver and lettered in gilt, spine lettering dulled, extremities rather rubbed, one corner bumped, pages viii, 350, 32 (ads), 8 woodcut plates, half title, lightly browned, very good, scarce.   R. F. G. Hollett & Son Antiquarian Booksellers   General Catalogue Summer 2010 - 684   2011   £180

Zola, Emile *La Bete Humaine.* Paris: G. Charpentier et Cie, 1890, First edition on grand papier, no. 127 of 250 copies on papier de Hollande,; 12mo., pages (iv), 415, (1) blank, 8 publisher's catalog, top edge gilt, others uncut, internally fine, 20th century deep blue crushed morocco, marbled boards and endpapers, original wrappers bound in with minor old repair to upper panell, near fine.   Simon Finch Rare Books   Zero - 287   2011   £1750

Zola, Emile *The Downfall.* London: Chatto & Windus, 1893, third edition; original decorated black cloth, gilt, spine chipped at head, hinges tightened, pages xiv, 535, 32 (ads, dated April 1893) and 2 plans, patterned endpapers, joints cracked.   R. F. G. Hollett & Son Antiquarian Booksellers   General Catalogue Summer 2010 - 686   2011   £45

Zola, Emile *The Downfall.* London: Chatto & Windus, 1896, New edition; original decorated back cloth, gilt, rather bubbled in places, light ring mark to lower board, pages xiv, 535, 32 (ads dated Jan. 1898), 2 plans, patterned endpapers.   R. F. G. Hollett & Son Antiquarian Booksellers   General Catalogue Summer 2010 - 685   2011   £30

Zola, Emile *His Excellency Eugene Rougon.* London: Vizetelly & Co., 1887, First English edition; original blue cloth, lettered and ruled in red and gilt, very slight rubbing to head and foot of spine, pages 400, slip tipped to title "Vizetelly's original 5s non-illustrated edition", joints just cracking, flyleaves lightly browned, otherwise very good, tight.   R. F. G. Hollett & Son Antiquarian Booksellers   General Catalogue Summer 2010 - 688   2011   £180

Zola, Emile *Lourdes.* London: Chatto & Windus, 1896, Third English edition; original maroon decorated cloth, faint ring-mark and light crease to upper board, spine trifle faded, pages xii, 491, 32 (ads dated Sept. 1896), some biro notes to rear endpapers, lower joint cracking.   R. F. G. Hollett & Son Antiquarian Booksellers   General Catalogue Summer 2010 - 689   2011   £40

Zola, Emile *Money (L'Argent).* Scott & Co. n.d. circa, 1910, Pages xv, 428, photogravure frontispiece, modern inscription on back of frontispiece, little spotting mainly toward end, original reddish brown cloth gilt, spine little faded and slightly frayed at head and foot.   R. F. G. Hollett & Son Antiquarian Booksellers   General Catalogue Summer 2010 - 690   2011   £35

Zola, Emile *Paris.* London: Chatto & Windus, 1898, Second English edition; original blue decorated cloth, spine rather worn at head and little rubbed at foot, pages xvi, 488, 32 (ads dated March 1898), patterned endpapers, joints trifle tender.   R. F. G. Hollett & Son Antiquarian Booksellers   General Catalogue Summer 2010 - 691   2011   £50

Zola, Emile *Rome.* London: Chatto & Windus, 1896, First English edition; original light brown cloth, upper board and spine decorated with pattern of crossed keys, spine little darkened and spotted, pages viii, 587, 32 (ads dated March 1896), light crease to first few leaves.   R. F. G. Hollett & Son Antiquarian Booksellers   General Catalogue Summer 2010 - 693   2011   £60

Zola, Emile *Stories for Ninon.* London: William Heinemann, 1895, First English edition; original maroon cloth, gilt, few light marks and edge bumps to boards, spine little faded and dulled, slightly rubbed and nicked at head and foot, pages vi, 344, 24 (ads dated March 1895), frontispiece, scattered spotting, mainly to first and last few pages and endpapers, otherwise very good.   R. F. G. Hollett & Son Antiquarian Booksellers   General Catalogue Summer 2010 - 694 2011   £180

Zola, Emile *Work. (Travail).* London: Chatto & Windus, 1901, First English edition; original decorated orange and brown cloth gilt, rather soiled and little frayed and bumped in places, pages (iv), vii, 500, 32, endpapers rather soiled and joints cracked, edges little spotted, still good, scarce.   R. F. G. Hollett & Son Antiquarian Booksellers   General Catalogue Summer 2010 - 695   2011   £50

Zoological Society of London   *The Zoological Record.* London: Butterworths Scientific Publications, 1854, 1954-2000. Reprints published by Butterworths Scientific Publications (London) or Johnson Reprint Corporation; 8vo. volumes 1-106 and 4to. volumes 107-136, in binder's buckram, original cloth or original printed wrappers (8 laid into publisher's hard portfolio), original cloth, original front wrappers bound into 12 volumes, endpapers renewed in 7 volumes, light rubbing to covers, especially older volumes, edges of pages spotted or soiled in several, wobbly handstamp to some front flyleaves, few titles, occasional text page, scattered pencil markings to margins in 6 volumes, reprints - (a scratch to 1 cover, short tear to head of spine in dampstain to upper end of spine in 1 section of 1 volume, 1 portfolio bumped, bent and creased but intact, handstamp ink number to front wrapper of first page.   Raymond M. Sutton, Jr.   May 26 2011 - 47527   2011 $4000

Zosimus   *(Greek) Historiarum Libri VIII.*   Geneva: H. Estienne, 1581, 2 parts in 1, (8), 182, (2); 79, (1 (blank) pages, small burn holes in margins on pages 35-40 (part I), affecting odd letter of printed marginal notes, late 17th century English panelled calf, somewhat rubbed, from the library of the Earls of Macclesfield at Shirburn Castle.   Maggs Bros. Ltd.   1440 - 231   2011   £750

Zurher, F.   *Volcanoes and Earthquakes.*   Philadelphia: J. B. Lippincott & Co./London: Richard Bentley, 1869, First American edition; lacks front free endpaper, frontispiece, title in red and black 23 plates, 38 illustrations in text, viii,2 53, (1) pages, original cloth, spine gilt, head and tail of spine worn.   Anthony W. Laywood   May 26 2011 - 15208   2011 $84

Association Copies

Association – Abdy, Anne

Chaucer, Geoffrey 1340-1400 *Workes of Geoffrey Chaucer.* London: Imprinted by John Kyngston for John Wight, 1561. Rare first issue; folio, (14), ccclxxviii leaves (irregular foliation), title within woodcut border, woodcut border, 22 woodcuts, large and small historiated and decorative initials and other ornaments, black letter, fifty-six lines, double columns, early 20th century antique style dark brown calf, expertly and almost invisible rebacked with original spine laid down, covers with double blind fillet border, spine in six compartments with five raised bands, ruled in blind and dated in gilt at foot and with brown morocco gilt lettering label, title lightly soiled with upper blank margin renewed, lower corner of first two leaves strengthened, few tiny holes or paper flaws, occasional foxing or faint dampstaining on few leaves, short (2 inch) repaired tear to lower margin of Mmm6, not affecting text, bookplate with monogram of Dr. George Osborne Mitchell, early ink signature of Anne Abdy and Hercules Holiambe (?) and some additional early ink annotations on title. David Brass Rare Books, Inc. May 26 2011 - 00642 2011 $48,500

Association – Abell, A.

Davies, Edward *The Mythology and Rites of the British Druids.* London: Booth, 1800. First edition; quarter cloth, xvi, 642, 6 pages, untrimmed, plate as frontispiece, owner inscribed by A. Abell, well known Cork Antiquary, very good. C. P. Hyland May 26 2011 - 255/153 2011 $362

Association – Abeloff, Abram Joseph

Thoreau, Henry David 1817-1862 *Walden; or Life in the Woods.* Boston: Ticknor & Fields, 1854. First edition; rebound around the turn of the twentieth century by Crombie & Lamothe in three quarter brown morocco and marbled paper boards, five raised bands, gilt ruling and lettering, matching marbled paper used as pastedowns and endpapers, original cloth covers and spine in very nice condition, gilt still bright, bound at rear, 8 page publisher's catalog not bound in, engraved titlepage and map inserted, marginal dampstain in outer top and bottom corners throughout, except on map, rarely just touching text, but mostly not affecting any text, small neat bookplate of Abram Joseph Abeloff, very minor rubbing to joints, very good or better. Charles Agvent Transcendentalism 2010 - 41 2011 $6500

Association – Adair, Robert Shafto

MacLauchlan, Henry *The Roman Wall and Illustrations of the Principal Vestiges of the Roman Occupation in the North of England...* printed for private distribution, 1857. First edition; large folio, lithographed title and map on 5 double page sheets, title and map on 6 double page sheets, 2 parts in one volume, contemporary morocco backed cloth, joints rubbed, bookplate of Sir Robert Shafto Adair. Anthony W. Laywood May 26 2011 - 21678 2011 $419

Association – Adam, R. B.

Coryate, Thomas *Coryats Crudities Hastily Gobbled Up in Five Monenths Travells in France, Savoy, Italy, Rhetia Comonly Called the Grisons Country, Helvetia Alias Switzerland, some Parts of High Germany and the Netherlands.* London: by William Stansby, 1611. First edition; printed title present, engraved allegorical title by William Hole (shaved very slightly at head), engraved plates, woodcut, text portrait, errata leaf present, many woodcut initials and headpieces, 19th century brown crushed levant morocco, gilt by Bedford, unusually tall, very handsome copy, rare printed title, from the libraries of Ward E. Terry, R. B. Adam, A. Edward Newton, Bois Penrose and Wolfgang A. Herz with their respective bookplates and book labels. Joseph J. Felcone Inc. Fall Miscellany 2010 - 35 2011 $16,000

Association – Adams, Frederick Baldwin

Hardy, Thomas 1840-1928 *Wessex Tales. Strange, Lively and Commonplace.* London: Macmillan and Co. and New York, 1888. First edition, 750 copies published at 12 shillings each, although only 634 copies were actually bound up to be sold at the time; 2 volumes, 8vo., pages (viii), 248; (viii), 212, (4) ads, publisher's dark green cloth boards, pale green ruled band to top and bottom of front boards and spines, monogram device on backs, gilt lettered spines, both volumes with slight spotting to endpapers, little wear around edges and slight creasing to heads and tails of spines, bookplates of Herbert S. Leon and Frederick Baldwin Adams Jr. in both volumes, very good, clean. Simon Finch Rare Books Zero - 234 2011 £2500

Voltaire, Francois Marie Arouet De 1694-1778 *Therese. A Fragment.* Cambridge: for Presentation to members of the Roxburghe Club, 1981. 286 x 210mm., 4 p.l., 20 pages, maroon morocco over light brown cloth boards, top edge and titling on spine in gilt, four facsimiles leaves (printed recto and verso), bookplate of Frederick Baldwin Adams, Jr., and this copy originally prepared for Adams (his name printed in red in the Roxburghe list a way of indicating this), extremely fine. Phillip J. Pirages 59 - 305 2011 $125

Wagner, Anthony *Medieval Pageant.* London: by Bernard Quaritch Ltd. for the Roxburghe Club, 1993. 470 x 356mm., 5 p.l., xiii-xxi, (i) 100 pages, (1) leaf, tan quarter morocco over blue buckram boards, vellum tips, top edge and titling on spine in gilt, with 79 mostly full page illustrations, bookplate of Frederick Baldwin Adams Jr. and this copy originally prepared for Adams (his name printed in red in the Roxburghe list as a way of indicating this), very fine. Phillip J. Pirages 59 - 306 2011 $950

Association – Adams, Lord

Daysh, G. H. J. *Cumberland with Special Reference to the West Cumberland Development Area.* Whitehaven: Cumberland Development Council, 1951. First edition; small 4to., original cloth, gilt, pages (viii), 182, 11 maps, 11 figures, maps and sections, 3 plates, 21 photos, presentation from Lord Adams of Ennerdale, Secretary of the Development Council. R. F. G. Hollett & Son Antiquarian Booksellers 173 - 336 2011 £40

Association – Adams, Mary

Bible. English - 1653 *The Holy Bible containing ye Old and New Testaments.... (with, bound at end of volume 2: The Psalms of David in Meeter).* London: printed by Iohn Field, 1653. Edinburgh: i.e. Amsterdam: printed by Evan Tyler, 1653; The first work divided after Dd2, 12mo., ff. (314); (282), 89, (i), contemporary red morocco, unlettered spine panel gilt, boards fully gilt in Scottish 'Herringbone' style, board edges decorative roll gilt, turn-ins decorative roll gilt, 'Dutch floral gilt' endpapers to volume 1, 'dutch-comb' endpapers to volume 2, all edges gilt, pale blue and white sewn endbands, text rubricated throughout, browned, some soiling and staining, one leaf in second work with corner torn away affecting a dozen lines of text, 20th century MS poem to last text leaf in volume 2 signed "Phineas Fletcher", binding rubbed, joints splitting, endpapers worn, spines darkened, old repair to head volume i, ink ownership inscription "MARY ADAMS/1769", from the collection of Christopher Ernest Weston 1947-2010. Unsworths Booksellers 24 - 9 2011 £700

Association – Affleck, James

Barwick, Peter *The Life of the Reverend Dr. John Barwick, D.D.* London: printed by J. Bettenham, 1724. Large paper copy, 8vo., pages (xxiv), 552, (xl) + 2 engraved portrait frontispieces, contemporary calf, gilt panelled spine, orange lettering piece gilt, boards panelled in blind (Cambridge style), board edges decorative roll gilt, 'Dutch-comb' 'made' endpapers, all edges red and grey sprinkled green and white sewn endbands, rubbed at extremities, spine darkened, joints cracked but strong, endcaps worn "James Affleck" book label, contemporary ink inscription "Eliz. Dolben" and above "James Affleck", mid 20th century provenance note by Peter B. G. Binnall, from the collection of Christopher Ernest Weston 1947-2010. Unsworths Booksellers 24 - 6 2011 £200

Association – Albert, Colonel

Stansbury, Howard *Exploration and Survey of the Valley Great Salt Lake of Utah...* Philadelphia: Lippincott, Gambo & Co., 1852. First edition; 2 volumes, cloth, 487 pages, 2 large folding maps in separate portfolio volume, 58 plates, including folding panoramic views, many appendices, charts, tables, index, former owner's inscription "Robley Doughton presented by Col. Albert, Washington", wear to spine ends and extremities, else very good, map volume missing backstrip, however maps are in very good condition with usual splitting at some of the folds, both volumes complete with all plates and maps present, very scarce in original cloth. Buckingham Books May 26 2011 - 25961 2011 $2000

Association – Alcine, Arline

Kelly, George *Craig's Wife a Drama.* Boston: Little Brown, 1926. First edition; 8vo., pages 174, very nice, tight copy, inscribed by author to Josephine Williams who played the part of Mrs. Harold in the NY production, also signed by rest of the cast - Annie Sutherland, Crystal Herne, Arthur Shaw, C. Stewart, Eleanor Marsh, Charles Trowbridge, Josephine Hull, J. A. Curtis, Nelan Jaap, Arline Alcine & Mary Gildea, also inscribed by the producer, Rosalie Stewart to whom the play was dedicated. Second Life Books Inc. 174 - 213 2011 $2000

Association – Alexander, Andrew

Smith, Adam 1723-1790 *An Inquiry into the Nature and Causes of the Wealth of Nations...* Edinburgh: printed for Oliphant, Waugh, & Innes and John Murray, London, 1814. 4 volumes, 8vo., complete with all half titles, contemporary uniform diced russia, simply gilt and lettered, marbled edges, very minor wear to bindings but very good, near contemporary presentation inscription recording (in Latin) presentation prize of this copy on 9th April 1820 to William Lillie at King's College, Aberdeen by Andrew Alexander, the professor of moral philosophy. John Drury Rare Books 153 - 138 2011 £850

Association – Alexander, Claude

Vertur, George *Anecdotes of Painting in England: with Some Account of the Principal Artists; and Incidental Notes on Other Arts.* London: printed for J. Dodsley, 1782. Mostly third editions; volume 4 is second edition, bookplate of Sir Claude Alexander at front of each volume, with his neat ownership signature at top of titlepages (dated 1828), 4 volumes, full tree calf decorated gilt at spine, pages 1300+, text clean and complete, boards somewhat worn and loose, good+. Any Amount of Books May 29 2011 - A62201 2011 $306

Association – Allen, Emmie

Smith, Dodie *Dear Octopus.* London: Heinemann, 1938. 8vo., original publisher's red cloth lettered gilt on spine, pages (viii), 124, frontispiece and 7 plates, signed presentation from author for Emmie Allen, near fine in slightly soiled and very slightly creased about very good dust jacket slightly chipped at head of spine, fore-edges slightly foxed. Any Amount of Books   May 26 2011 - A68501 2011 $604

Association – Allen, James

Condillac, Etienne Bonnot De *The Logic of Condillac.* Philadelphia: printed, 1809. First edition thus; 12mo. in 6's, (6), 136, (2) pages, trifle browned with occasional foxing, early ms. notes in ink on at least 3 leaves, ownership signature of James E. Allen, Lackington Jany 2d 1823, contemporary half calf over marbled boards, spine restored, corners worn, good, sound.   John Drury Rare Books   153 - 29 2011   £375

Kentucky. Laws, Statutes, etc. *Acts Passed at the First Session of the Eighth General Assembly for the Commonwealth of Kentucky.* Frankfort: William Hunter, 1800. (3)-226 pages, lacks title leaf, later cloth backed marbled boards, printed paper spine label, piece torn from corner of K1, side notes cropped on several leaves toward rear, final leaf 2#2 (final page of index) torn and repaired at fore-edge, costing small amount of text, embossed early ex-library blindstamp on covers, James Allen's copy, signed on first page of text.   Joseph J. Felcone Inc.   Fall Miscellany 2010 - 70 2011 $1400

Association – Allison, John

MacDonald, George 1824-1905 *David Elginbrod.* London: Hurst & Blackett, circa, 1890. Half title, frontispiece, 16 page catalog, original dark blue cloth, plain gilt borders, little rubbed, signature of John S. Allison, Dec. 1891.   Jarndyce Antiquarian Booksellers   CXCII - 23 2011 £30

Association – Althorpe, John Charles Spencer, Viscount

A Letter to His Majesty William IV. Paris?: 1830. Only edition; 8vo., (2), 21, (1) pages, generally rather browned and foxed, original printed blue wrappers, contemporary ownership signature of Lord Visct. Althorpe, very rare.   John Drury Rare Books   153 - 103 2011   £125

Association – Ames, Winthrop

Kaufman, George S. *Beggar on Horseback.* New York: Boni and Liveright, 1924. First edition; 8vo., 237 pages, two pages in middle of text quite darkened from old news clipping that has been laid in, top edges of boards sunned, otherwise very good, tight copy in very good, bright dust jacket, inscribed by producer Winthrop Ames to George Barbier who played Mr. Cady, splendid association.   Second Life Books Inc.   174 - 209 2011 $1500

Association – Andersson, R.

Siemienowicz Kazimierz (*Grand art d'Artillerie*) *Aussfuhrliche Beschreibung der Grossen Feuerwercks.* Frankfurt: J. D. Zunner, 1676. Reissue of 1651 French edition; folio, (2), 410, (6) pages, text in French, engraved title (in German) and 22 plates, contemporary English calf, lacking 4 leaves of printed prelims, the copy of R. Andersson, from the library of the Earls of Macclesfield at Shirburn Castle.   Maggs Bros. Ltd.   1440 - 199 2011 £550

Association – Andrade, E. N. Da C

Galilei, Galileo 1564-1642 *Mathematical Discourses Concerning Two New Sciences Relating to Mechanicks and Local Motion in Four Dialogues.* London: J. Hooke, 1730. Second edition in English; 4to., xi, (1), 497, (3) pages, red and black titlepage, table, 207 woodcut text figures, errata leaf (contemporaneously struck thru with ink lines), 2 pages of additional titles printed by J. Hooke, pagination error pages 361-368 (as usual) numbers omitted, contemporary full panelled calf, raised bands, gilt stamped spine title, neatly rebacked, corners restored, very good, bookplate of E. N. Da C. Andrade.   Jeff Weber Rare Books   161 - 163 2011 $36,000

Association – Ansen, Alan

Corso, Gregory *The Happy Birthday of Death.* New York: New Directions, 1960. First edition; wrappers, 8vo., pages 91, with foldout poem (BOMB), signed by author for writer Alan Ansen, reasonable sound very good copy with slight rubbing and slight handling wear.   Any Amount of Books   May 29 2011 - A84998 2011 $255

Association – Appleton, Samuel

Busby, Thomas *Costume of the Lower Orders of London.* London: published for T. L. Busby by Messrs. Baldwin, Craddock and Joy, 1820. Quarto, iv, (24) pages, 24 hand colored etched plates, text watermarked 1817, plates watermarked 1822, contemporary quarter green roan over marbled boards, spine decorated and lettered in gilt with raised bands, slight offsetting from some of the plates to text, from the library of Samuel Appleton with his armorial bookplate, excellent.   David Brass Rare Books, Inc.   May 26 2011 - 01625 2011 $5250

Association – Arago, Dominique Francois Jean

Comte, Auguste *Systeme de Politique Positive...* Paris: Setier, 1824. First edition; 8vo., pages 8, 289, (i) blank; 84; late 19th century red morocco, marbled boards, panelled spine, filleted and lettered in gilt, preserving original green silk bookmark, tips rubbed, foot of spine bumped and torn, obituary of Auguste Comte mounted between front free endpapers, Comte's autograph inscription to mathematician and politician Dominique Francois Jean Arago, bookplate of Gustave d'Eichthal and manuscript notes of d'Eichthal on half title and front free endpapers.   Simon Finch Rare Books   Zero - 125 2011   £4750

Association – Arcedeckne, Andrew

Porter, Jane *The Pastor's Fireside, a Novel.* London: Henry Colburn and Richard Bentley, 1832. 2 volumes, half titles, frontispieces, engraved titles, additional printed titles, binding A - glazed plum colored linen, black labels, spines little faded, labels chipped with some loss volume II, volume II with armorial bookplate of Andrew Arcedeckne, Glevering Hall, good plus. Jarndyce Antiquarian Booksellers CLXC - 759 2011   £60

Association – Arentz Doris

Ibsen, Henrik *Et Dukkehjem. (Doll's House).* Copenhagen: Gyldendalske Boghandels Forlag, 1879. First edition; 8vo., pages 180, original paper wrappers, printed in black, pages slightly and evenly toned, Frederike Schmidt's neat ownership signature and Doris Arentz's to half title, chips to spine head and wrappers, front wrappers sometime strengthened, very good.   Simon Finch Rare Books   Zero - 242 2011   £900

Association – Arnold, S. J.

Mant, Alicia Catherine *Montague Newburgh; or the Mother and Son.* London: Law & Whittaker, 1817. First edition; 2 volumes, half titles, engraved frontispieces, some light foxing and browning to prelims, contemporary full tree calf, excellently rebacked, each volume signed "Miss S. J. Arnold July 4th 1822", good plus, scarce.   Jarndyce Antiquarian Booksellers CLXC - 224 2011   £380

Association – Arvin, Nick

A Dozen on Denver. Gulden: Fulcrum, 2009. First edition; fine, signed by Connie Willis, Nick Arvin, Robert Greer, Margaret Coel, Manuel Ramos and Arnold Grossman. Bella Luna Books   May 29 2011 - p3633 2011 $104

Association – Ascott, L. R.

Disraeli, Benjamin 1804-1881 *Novels and Tales by the Earl of Beaconsfield: with Portrait and Sketch of His Life.* London: Longmans, 1881. Hughenden edition; 11 volumes, half titles, frontispiece in volume I, engraved titles, largely unopened in original light brown cloth, oval blue morocco label on front boards, decorated in gilt, spines blocked in black, red and gilt, damp mark to back board of volume I, occasional slight rubbing, booklabels of L. R. Ascott, nice, bookplate of Leopold de Rothschild. Jarndyce Antiquarian Booksellers   CXCI - 11 2011   £280

Association – Ashbee, Charles Robert

Andersen, Hans Christian 1805-1875 *Wonderful Stories for Children.* New York: Wiley and Putnam, 1847. Early US edition; 12mo., pages 144, frontispiece and one other illustration, with author's name spelled Anderson on spine and titlepage, original publisher's green cloth lettered and decorated gilt on spine and on front cover, small bookplate of Janet and C. R. Ashbee and pictorial bookplate of Janet Ashbee designed by C. R. Ashbee, sound, clean, very good with slight wear at head of spine, slight foxing, very slight shelf wear, some family notes, press cutting on blank prelims.   Any Amount of Books   May 29 2011 - A46337 2011 $340

Head, Ruth Mayhew *A History of Departed Things.* London: New York: Kegan, Paul, Trench, Trubner & Co., 1918. First edition; 8vo., pages 242, soundly rebound in quarter green leather, lettered gilt at spine, spine slightly faded, else very good, note on f.e.p. "Felicity Ashbee her book, Hartley Court 1941 i.m. (im=in memory of) Henry and Ruth Head", from the library of Janet Ashbee and C. R. Ashbee and their daughter Felicity with 6 page signed letter loosely inserted from Ruth Head to Janet Ahsbee.   Any Amount of Books   May 29 2011 - A45989 2011 $204

Housman, Laurence 1865-1959 *Rue.* London: At the Sign of the Unicorn, 1899. First edition; 8vo., pages illustrations, figures, tables, (1) 96 + 4 page publisher's ads, pages uncut, original publisher's blue cloth lettered gilt on spine and on front cover, very good+, excellent condition, small bookplate "From the Library of Janet Ashbee and C. R. Ashbee", loosely inserted is signed handwritten 1938 note to Janet Ashbee.   Any Amount of Books   May 29 2011 - A46831 2011 $221

Thackeray, William Makepeace 1811-1863 *Ballads.* London: Smith, Elder & Co., 1879. Illustrated edition; this edition was given to C. R. Ashbee by family friend and bibliophile, Robert Samuel Turner, 8vo., pages 323, illustrations, pasted on reverse of frontispiece is 5 x 5 inch square of light blue paper upon which are written just over 12 lines of prose in blue ink and underneath which, in Ashbee's hand, are pencilled the words "Autograph of Thackeray", original publisher's cloth little used, snagged at head of spine, slightly shaken and scuffed, very good.   Any Amount of Books   May 26 2011 - A49450   2011 $587

Association – Ashbee, Felicity

Head, Ruth Mayhew *A History of Departed Things.* London: New York: Kegan, Paul, Trench, Trubner & Co., 1918. First edition; 8vo., pages 242, soundly rebound in quarter green leather, lettered gilt at spine, spine slightly faded, else very good, note on f.e.p. "Felicity Ashbee her book, Hartley Court 1941 i.m. (im=in memory of) Henry and Ruth Head", from the library of Janet Ashbee and C. R. Ashbee and their daughter Felicity with 6 page signed letter loosely inserted from Ruth Head to Janet Ahsbee.   Any Amount of Books   May 29 2011 - A45989   2011 $204

Association – Ashbee, Janet

Andersen, Hans Christian 1805-1875 *Wonderful Stories for Children.* New York: Wiley and Putnam, 1847. Early US edition; 12mo., pages 144, frontispiece and one other illustration, with author's name spelled Anderson on spine and titlepage, original publisher's green cloth lettered and decorated gilt on spine and on front cover, small bookplate of Janet and C. R. Ashbee and pictorial bookplate of Janet Ashbee designed by C. R. Ashbee, sound, clean, very good with slight wear at head of spine, slight foxing, very slight shelf wear, some family notes, press cutting on blank prelims.   Any Amount of Books   May 29 2011 - A46337   2011 $340

Head, Ruth Mayhew *A History of Departed Things.* London: New York: Kegan, Paul, Trench, Trubner & Co., 1918. First edition; 8vo., pages 242, soundly rebound in quarter green leather, lettered gilt at spine, spine slightly faded, else very good, note on f.e.p. "Felicity Ashbee her book, Hartley Court 1941 i.m. (im=in memory of) Henry and Ruth Head", from the library of Janet Ashbee and C. R. Ashbee and their daughter Felicity with 6 page signed letter loosely inserted from Ruth Head to Janet Ahsbee.   Any Amount of Books   May 29 2011 - A45989   2011 $204

Housman, Laurence 1865-1959 *Rue.* London: At the Sign of the Unicorn, 1899. First edition; 8vo., pages illustrations, figures, tables, (1) 96 + 4 page publisher's ads, pages uncut, original publisher's blue cloth lettered gilt on spine and on front cover, very good+, excellent condition, small bookplate "From the Library of Janet Ashbee and C. R. Ashbee", loosely inserted is signed handwritten 1938 note to Janet Ashbee.   Any Amount of Books   May 29 2011 - A46831 2011 $221

Masefield, John 1878-1967 *Words Spoken at the Unveiling of the Memorials to the Poets John Keats and Percy Shelley.* N.P.: privately printed, nd., 1940. First edition; wrappers, pages 8 (unpaginated), 8vo., signed by author for Janet Ashbee with short signed letter to Janet Ashbee loosely inserted, very slight browning at edges, else very good.   Any Amount of Books   May 29 2011 - A65713   2011 $238

Pope-Hennessy, James *Monckton-Milnes: the Years of Promise.* London: Constable, 1949. First edition; 8vo., slight wear, slight sunning, otherwise sound, near very good, signed presentation from author to Janet Ashbee.   Any Amount of Books   May 29 2011 - A63899   2011 $255

Association – Ashberry, Philip

Jameson, Anna Brownell 1794-1860 *The Diary of an Ennuyde.* London: Henry Colburn, 1826. New edition; title little spotted, uncut in 20th century marbled boards, paper label, signed Philip H. Ashberry, Sheffield 1876", Skinos booklabel, very good.   Jarndyce Antiquarian Booksellers   CLXC - 8 2011   £120

Association – Ashhurst, John

Bembo, Pietro, Cardinal 1470-1547 *Petri Bembi Patritii Veneti, Scriptoris Omnium Politissimi Disertissimique Quaeccunque Usquam Prodierunt Opera...* Basileae: Michael Isengrin, 1556. 2 parts in one, octavo, (11) 12-624; 229, (23) pages, later engraved portrait inserted facing title, Isengrin's device on titlepage, second part with separate title, index, occasional early underlining, title margin restored, original full calf with four devices stamped on upper and lower corners, floral device in center, neatly rebacked to match, small manuscript title applied to fore-edge (early hand), pencilled signature of John Ashhurst, very good.   Jeff Weber Rare Books   163 - 4 2011 $500

Association – Ashley, Israel

Edwards, Jonathan *A Careful and Strict Enquiry into the Modern Prevailing Notions of that Freedom of Will, Which is Supposed to be Essential to Moral Agency, Vertue and Vice, Reward and Punishment, Praise and Blame.* Boston: S. Kneeland, 1754. First edition; 8vo., (2) 6, (4), 294, (5), (9) pages, full contemporary panelled calf, corners bumped, few early leaves water stained in upper corner, moderate browning throughout, presentation copy from author apparently in recipient's hand "Israel Ashley's Book/ the Gift of the Rev'd? Mr. Jonathan Edwards. M & S Rare Books, Inc. 90 - 1222 2011 $8500

Association – Ashursti, Sum

Sadler, John *Rights of the Kingdom or Customs of Our Ancestours: Touching the Duty, Power, Election or Succession of Our Kings and Parliaments, Our True Liberty Due Allegiance...* London: Richard Bishop, 1649. First edition; 4to, (2), (6), 93, 30-191 176-182 (i.e. 198) (4) pages, mid 19th century calf by Hatton of Manchester, panelled in blind, red edges, browned, spine slightly faded, signature of Sum Ashursti, a number of manuscript notes/corrections in text, from the library of the Earls of Macclesfield at Shirburn Castle. Maggs Bros. Ltd. 1440 - 186 2011 £500

Association – Astley, F. D.

Ruskin, John 1819-1900 *The Seven Lamps of Architecture.* London: Smith, Elder and Co., 1849. First edition; viii, (4), 205 pages, 14 lithograph plates, complete with half title, some occasional foxing, good copy, original blindstamped cloth, expert repairs to joints, inscription dated 1849 on endpaper, bookplate of F. D. Astley. Ken Spelman Rare Books 68 - 46 2011 £160

Association – Attwell, Mabel Lucy

Barrie, James Matthew 1860-1937 *Peter Pan and Wendy.* London: Hodder & Stoughton, n.d. circa, 1921. Thick 4to., blue cloth, slight fade spots on covers, else very good+, 12 beautiful tipped in color plate and many black and whites in text by Mabel Lucy Attwell, this copy inscribed by Attwell with lovely full page watercolor of baby mermaid playing with bubbles, exceedingly scarce. Aleph-Bet Books, Inc. 95 - 71 2011 $2750

Association – Auden, Wystan Hugh

Ginsberg, Allen *T.V. Baby Poems.* London: Cape Gilliard Press, 1967. 8vo., pages 936), double page illustration to titlepage, small illustrations to half title and in text, very crisp and clean, original black and white photographic paper wrappers, text in brown to upper panel and spine, lightly soiled and foxed, text in brown to front and spine, author's presentation inscription to W. H. Auden in blue ink to initial blank, several manuscript corrections to text. Simon Finch Rare Books Zero - 316 2011 £600

Association – Auerbach, Frank

Feaver, William *Frank Auerbach.* New York: Rizzoli, First edition; 4to., pages 359, copiously illustrated in color and black and white, fine in fine illustrated hard slipcase, signed in black felt tip pen by Auerbach. Any Amount of Books May 29 2011 - A75491 2011 $374

Association – Austen, George

Browne, R. W. *A History of Greek Classical Literature.* London: Richard Bentley, 1853. New edition; full morocco gilt prize binding, arms of King's College, London on upper board, spine and edges little rubbed, pages xii,3 74, all edges gilt, prize label (Dasent Prize awarded to George Austen in 1859). R. F. G. Hollett & Son Antiquarian Booksellers General Catalogue Summer 2010 - 374 2011 £85

Browne, R. W. *A History of Roman Classical Literature.* London: Richard Bentley, n.d., 1853. First edition; full morocco gilt prize binding with arms of King's College London on upper board, spine and edges little rubbed, pages xx, 592, all edges gilt, prize label on pastedown (Dasent Prize awarded to George Austen in 1859). R. F. G. Hollett & Son Antiquarian Booksellers General Catalogue Summer 2010 - 375 2011 £85

Association – Austin, Alfred

Trollope, Thomas Adolphus 1810-1892 *The Papal Conclaves as They Were and a They Are.* London: Chapman and Hall, 1876. First edition; original cloth, gilt, spine and corners rather worn, pages xviii, 434, 36, untrimmed, joints cracked, fine decorative bookplate of Alfred Austin, poet laureate. R. F. G. Hollett & Son Antiquarian Booksellers 175 - 1360 2011 £60

Association – Austin, Mrs.

Grimm, The Brothers *German Popular Stories.* London & Dublin: James Robins and Joseph Robins, volume i dated, 1827. (first issue was 1823) and volume 2 is 1826; 2 volumes, (i-vi) v-xii (1), 2-240, (i-iii) iv (1), 2-256 (2) page, (1 page ads), original pink boards and green cloth spines, boards rubbed, cloth split at joints and at intervals on spine, labels chipped and rubbed, some foxing, 1 plate in volume I trimmed in margins really overall clean, tight and very good, 22 etched plates by George Cruikshank, laid in is one page handwritten ALS by Jacob Grimm written to Mrs. Austin. Aleph-Bet Books, Inc. 95 - 266 2011 $5000

Association – Avedon, Richard

Capote, Truman 1924-1985 *Observations.* London: Weidenfeld and Nicholson, 1959. First English edition, with signed letter from photographer, Richard Avedon to Frau Bucher; folio, pages 152, 104 black and white photos printed in gravure, design by Alexey Brodovitch, original white paper covered boards printed in grey, lightly rubbed, original white paper covered board slipcase, printed in red, blue and grey, lightly rubbed and soiled with little wear to edges, with TLS to Frau Bucher. Simon Finch Rare Books Zero - 504 2011 £550

Association – Averill, John

Gerarde, John 1545-1612 *The Herball or Generall Historie of Plantes.* London: Adam Islip, Joice Norton and Richard Whitakers, 1633. Second edition; approximately 2800 text woodcuts, woodcut initials, folio, engraved architectural title by John Payne, pages (38), 1-30, 29-30, 29-1630, (2), (1 page of additional illustrations, verso blank), (45), errata, contemporary full calf (professionally rebacked with sympathetic leather, old wear to edges and corners, lacking 1 leaf, H1, 89-90, endpapers renewed, engraved title somewhat soiled and with short marginal tears, some soiling to prelim pages, scattered pages with repairs with no loss to text, tear here and there, some dampstaining, mostly to back third of pages, an old ink annotation to a page, small brown stains to 2 leaves, several index pages soiled, chipped and frayed at fore edges, resulting in partial loss of text to 2 leaves, the copy of John Preston and of John Averill. Raymond M. Sutton, Jr. May 26 2011 - 55850 2011 $2400

Association – Baddeley, Angela

Smith, Dodie *Dear Octopus.* London: Heinemann, 1938. First edition; 8vo., pages (xi) 124, frontispiece and 7 plates, signed presentation from author to actress Angela Baddeley who played Grace Fenning in the play, very slight shelf wear, very good+. Any Amount of Books May 26 2011 - A69112 2011 $545

Association – Baddle, Horace

Malthus, Thomas Robert 1766-1834 *An Essay on the Principle of Population or a View of Its Past and Present Effects on Human Happiness...* London: printed for J. Johnson by T. Bensley, 1803. Second edition; large 4to., pages viii, (3) contents, (1) errata, 610, contemporary full calf, rebacked at early date with original spine laid down, ownership signature of N. W. Ridley Colborne and Horace W. Baddle 1859, some light intermittent spotting and staining, but nice, clean copy with wide margins. Second Life Books Inc. 174 - 234 2011 $6000

Association – Baines, Florence

Barrie, James Matthew 1860-1937 *When a Man's Single.* London: Hodder & Stoughton, 1888. Half title, final ad leaf, partially uncut, original navy blue buckram, bevelled boards, slight string mark to leading edge of spine, signature of Florence A. Baines 1890 on half title, top edge gilt, very good in custom made half dark blue morocco slipcase. Jarndyce Antiquarian Booksellers CXCI - 61 2011 £180

Association – Baird, G. W.

International Fishery Congress *Proceedings of the Fourth International Fishery Congress.* Washington: 1910. 2 volumes, 4to., 10 color plates, some attic dust, some foxing at edges, original binding, G.W. Baird's copy. Bookworm & Silverfish 678 - 71 2011 $175

Association – Baker, Thurlow

Guppy, Henry *A Brief Sketch of the History of the Transmission of the Bible.* Manchester: Manchester University Press, 1926. Pages vii, 75, contemporary half calf gilt with broad raised bands an spine label, top edge gilt, other edges untrimmed, with 20 plates, presentation copy inscribed by author to Mr. Thurlow Baker. R. F. G. Hollett & Son Antiquarian Booksellers General Catalogue Summer 2010 - 417 2011 £65

Association – Ball, William

Hutchinson, William *An Excursion to the Lakes in Westmoreland and Cumberland, with a Tour through Part of the Northern Counties in the Years 1773 and 1774.* J. Wilkie and W. Charnley, 1776. First edition; near contemporary half calf with marbled boards, neatly rebacked to match, original spine label re-laid, pages 382, (iv), 2 engraved text vignettes, contemporary inscription of James Waring on title, few pencilled marginalia by later owner William Ball of Glen Rothay. R. F. G. Hollett & Son Antiquarian Booksellers 173 - 603 2011 £295

Association – Balzi, Carlo

Homerus *Odyssea (and other works).* Venice: Melchiorre Sessa, 1540? 165 x 108mm., 238, (2) leaves, contemporary olive brown calf over pasteboard, ends of spine repaired (probably late in 19th century), gilt covers framed with two sets of double rules, outer panel with broad foliate curl cornerpieces and sidepieces with trefoil of three rings between each, inner panel with blindstamped horizontal oval centerpiece of Apollo and Pegasus, the gilt collar with Greek motto touching rules at sides, large foliate sprays at head and foot curling to left and right and rising to a fleuron tool at ends, raised bands, spine panelled in gilt featuring broad rules and fleuron centerpiece, brown morocco label; woodcut historiated initials and charming cat and mouse printer's device, leaves at front and back with various marks of ownership, including signature of Francesco Suave at head of titlepage and "proprieta di Carlo Balzi 1884", contemporary marginal annotations in Latin and Greek; joints partly cracked (wormed in two places), corners somewhat worn, some scuffing to leather, binding completely solid, gilt still distinct, plaquettes (not surprisingly) bright and volume altogether pleasing even with its defects, final leaf cropped at fore edge (with loss of first [verso] or last [recto] on two thirds of the lines), upper corner of two gatherings with small, faint dampstain, one minor paper flaw costing half dozen letters, otherwise unusually well preserved internally, text exceptionally bright, fresh and clean, according to Hobson a fraudulent Apollo and Pegasus binding, volume looks absolutely convincing, with usual signs of age and restoration (wheels of Apollo's chariot have four spokes, in the genuine article, they have six. Phillip J. Pirages 59 - 4 2011 $7500

Association – Bancroft, Mr.

Whitman, Walt 1819-1892 *Leaves of Grass with Sands at Seventy & A Backward Glance O'er Travel'd Roads.* Philadelphia: Ferguson Bros. & Co., 1889. Seventh edition, 14th printing of Leaves of Grass in Myerson's presumed second binding with double laid paper flyleaves but varying from bibliographer's description of the second binding in having accordion flaps on sides connected at bottom as in first binding, limited to 300 copies printed on India paper and signed on titlepage by Whitman; 8vo., original photo frontispiece, 5 additional portraits throughout text, original wallet style black leather, over flexible boards, head of spine lightly worn, small three quarter inch split to leather at spine fold, light scuffing to leather covers, but very good, very scarce, presentation copy inscribed by author to Mr. Bancroft. James S. Jaffe Rare Books May 26 2011 - 13858 2011 $10,000

Association – Bank, James

Laud, William *A Relation of the Conference Between William Lawd...and Mr. Fisher the Jesuite.* London: printed by Richard Badger, 1639. Folio, pages (xxiv), 388, later dark brown turkey, spine panel gilt extra (7 compartments tooled in four designs arranged symmetrically about the centre), boards gilt panelled with double corner pieces out with the elaborately gilt rolled outer frame of centre panel, board edges elaborately decorative roll gilt 'Dutch-comb-swirl' endpapers, all edges gilt, fawn and white sewn endbands, joints and corners conserved, early 21st century by Chris Weston, lightly browned, dust soiled in places, corner of f.e.p. excised, old leather little bit rubbed and chipped, 19th century armorial bookplate of "James Bank M.A./Linc. Coll. Oxon" on front pastedown, from the collection of Christopher Ernest Weston 1947-2010. Unsworths Booksellers 24 - 29 2011 £325

Association – Barbier, George

Kaufman, George S. *Beggar on Horseback.* New York: Boni and Liveright, 1924. First edition; 8vo., 237 pages, two pages in middle of text quite darkened from old news clipping that has been laid in, top edges of boards sunned, otherwise very good, tight copy in very good, bright dust jacket, inscribed by producer Winthrop Ames to George Barbier who played Mr. Cady, splendid association. Second Life Books Inc. 174 - 209 2011 $1500

Association – Barclay, A.

Gisborne, Thomas *An Enquiry into the Duties of the Female Sex.* London: printed for T. Cadell Jun. and W. Davies, 1797. First edition; octavo, viii, 426 pages, later half calf, marbled boards, gilt and blind rules on spine, gilt title, rubbed, signature of A. Barclay on title, very good. Jeff Weber Rare Books 163 - 167 2011 $150

Association – Barclay, William

Johnson, Joseph *George MacDonald: a Biographical and Critical Appreciation.* London: Sir Isaac Pittman & Sons, 1906. Half title, engraved frontispiece, title in red and black, uncut in original maroon cloth blocked with title and author on front board as well as spine, spine slightly faded, top edge gilt, signature of Wm. R. Barclay and containing 17 manuscript leaves of lecture on MacDonald by Barclay. Jarndyce Antiquarian Booksellers CXCII - 352 2011 £120

Association – Barker, Jacob

Kant, Immanuel *The Principles of Critical Philosophy...* London: sold by J. Johnson, W. Richardson; Edinburgh: P. Hill, Manners and Miller; Hamburg: B. G. Hoffmann, 1797. First English edition; 8vo., lxxx, 454, (ads 2) pages, occasional light foxing, original full mottled calf, spine with gilt rules, black leather spine label, early ownership signature of Jacob Barker, Glasgow, 14 April crossed out from blank, Sheffield library bookplate, very good, scarce.   Jeff Weber Rare Books   161 - 246   2011 $4000

Association – Barker, John

Oliphant, Margaret Oliphant Wilson   1828-1897 *Phoebe, Junior.* Leipzig: Bernhard Tauchnitz, 1876. Copyright edition; 2 volumes, half titles, contemporary half green calf, spines with raised gilt bands, red leather labels, little darkened and slightly rubbed, John Barker booklabels. Jarndyce Antiquarian Booksellers   CLXC - 612   2011   £45

Association – Baron, M. D.

Collins, Wilkie   1824-1889 *Antonina, or The Fall of Rome.* London: Chatto & Windus, circa, 1890. New edition; original half tan calf by Mudie, gilt spine, maroon morocco labels, signature of M.D. Baron, very good. Jarndyce Antiquarian Booksellers   CXCI - 122   2011   £110

Collins, Wilkie   1824-1889 *The New Magdalen: a Novel.* London: Chatto & Windus, 1893. New edition; contemporary half tan calf by Mudie, gilt spine, maroon morocco labels, booklabel of M. D. Baron, very good. Jarndyce Antiquarian Booksellers   CXCI - 132   2011   £120

Association – Barr, Ingle

Huxley, Aldous Leonard   1894-1963 *Those Barren Leaves.* London: Chatto & Windus, 1925. First edition; pages (viii), 380, foolscap 8vo., original orange cloth, printed label (spare label tipped in at rear), tail edges rough trimmed, dust jacket with backstrip panel lightly browned, near fine, inscribed by author for Ingle Barr.   Blackwell Rare Books   B166 - 167   2011   £400

Association – Barr, Thomas Gerry Cullum

Willoughby, Francis *The Ornithology of Francis Willoughby of Middleton, in the County of Warwick Esq.* London: A. C. for John Martyn, 1678. First edition in English; folio, title printed in red and black, 2 engraved plates of bird trapping and 78 engraved plates of birds, pages (12), 441, (index, 6 pages), contemporary panelled calf with elaborate gilt decorated spine with 7 compartments including brown morocco label (some soiling to title, creases and partial soiling to a chart, 3 marginal spots to a plate, partial loss to a margin of a plate, light dampstaining to upper margin of 2 plates, 2 marginal spots and some overall foxing to last plate), text and most plates remarkably clean, old scuffs to covers, professionally rebacked at earlier time while retaining compartments from original spine), bookplate of Rev. Sir Thomas Gerry Cullum Barr, very good copy. Raymond M. Sutton, Jr.   May 26 2011 - 54388   2011 $6000

Association – Barrett, Benjamin

Bigelow, Jacob   1787-1879 *American Medical Botany, Being a Collection of the Native Medicinal Plants of the United States.* Boston: Cummings and Hilliard, 1817-1820. First edition, mixed state; 60 colored plates (few hand colored, most color printed, foxing to several, occasional light offsetting to plates), tall 8vo., pages xi, (17-) 197, (5); xiv, (15-) 199, (1);x, (11-) 193, contemporary calf, upper corner of back cover bumped, corner to head of spine bumped and with piece missing, scattered foxing, offsetting to some pages, opposite plates, pages 195 through 198 from volume III misbound following page 198 of volume I, inner hinges reinforced, from the Yale College Library, presented by the estate of Benjamin Barrett, M.D., bought from Yale for Dr. Fred. Sumner Smith by his Father.   Raymond M. Sutton, Jr.   May 26 2011 - 39722   2011 $3700

Association – Barrington, Shute

Brewster, John *Practical Reflections on the Ordination Services for Deacons and Priests in the United Church of England and Ireland...* London: F. C. and J. Rivington, 1817. First edition; 8vo., xv, (1), 355, (1) pages, endpapers bit foxed, front free endpaper creased, contemporary half calf over marbled boards, spine gilt and labeled, very good, dedication copy with Bishop Shute Barrington's armorial bookplate on pastedown, scarce.   John Drury Rare Books   153 - 17   2011   £175

Milton, John   1608-1674 *The Poetical Works...* printed for J. Johnson (and 25 other firms...) by Bye and Law, 1801. First Todd edition; 6 volumes, frontispiece in volume I, one facsimile plate in volume VI, royal 8vo., contemporary Russia, single gilt fillet border on sides, gilt rules on either side of raised bands on spines, lettered in gilt direct, gilt edges, spines little dry and slightly worn at head, bookplate of Shute Barrington, Lord Bishop of Durham, very good. Blackwell Rare Books   B166 - 68   2011   £900

Taylor, Jeremy   1613-1667   *The Rule and Exercise of Holy Living and Holy Dying...*   London: Miles Flesher for Richard Royston, 1680.   Twelfth edition; 2 volumes, 8vo., pages (xiv), 335, (i) + engraved titlepage and 1 double page engraved plates stub-mounted; (xiv), 259, (v) + engraved titlepage and 1 double page engraved plate stub mounted, contemporary black polished turkey, spines multi rule panelled in blind with contrasting stylised flower centerpieces, boards entirely blind tooled with triangular and rectangular densely ruled blocks, tulip & carnation heads, gouges and small 5 pointed stars, board edges and turn-ins decorative roll gilt, "Dutch-comb swirl" "made" endpapers, all edges gilt, 3 color pink, white and pale blue 2 core-sewn endbands, pink silk page markers, wholly unrestored "Sombre" bindings (age toned, few small stains, edges trimmed close, joints and edges rubbed, spines slightly faded, contemporary ink inscription M. Mcqueen", armorial bookplate of Shute Barrington, from the collection of Christopher Ernest Weston 1947-2010.   Unsworths Booksellers   24 - 52   2011   £950

Association – Barrows, Samuel

Hoe, Richard M.   *The Literature of Printing. A Catalogue of the Library Illustrative of the History and Art of Topography, Chalcography and Lithography of Richard M. Hoe.*   London: 1877.   (4), 149, (2) pages, frontispiece, contemporary cloth, decorated endpapers, front inner hinge open, crown of spine (quarter inch) torn off, presentation copy inscribed by Hoe to his cousin, Samuel J. Barrows, on two front blanks are pasted (bit artlessly) pieces of blue paper containing Hoe family notes in hand of Richard Hoe's great-great granddaughter, who purchased this copy from Warren Howell in 1945.   Joseph J. Felcone Inc.   Fall Miscellany 2010 - 60   2011 $900

Association – Barry, Dave

Naked Came the Manatee.   New York: Putnam, 1996.   First edition; fine in fine dust jacket, signed by all authors on single tipped in leaf, including Carl Hiaasen, Elmore Leonard, John Dufresne, Dave Barry, Vicki Hendricks, Edna Buchanan, Les Standiford and James W. Hall, etc.   Ken Lopez Bookseller   154 - 5   2011 $200

Association – Bart, Frances Baring

Charke, Charlotte   *A Narrative of the Life of Mrs. Charlotte Charke.*   London: printed for W. Reeve, 1755.   12mo., x, (11)-277 pages, half title, heavily wormed throughout, original full calf, rebacked with raised bands, darker brown spine label, bookplate of Sir Frances Baring Bart, good, scarce.   Jeff Weber Rare Books   163 - 142   2011 $100

Association – Barth, Johan Friederich

Lundius, Johannes   *Die Alten Judischen Heiligthu mer Gottesdienste und Gewohnheiten...*   Hamburg: Johann Wolfgang Fictweiler, 1722.   Later edition; 4to., (40), 1090, (142) pages, engraved frontispiece, signed by J. G. Mentzel with engraved plate facing red and black titlepage, 29 engraved plates, paper slightly browned, contemporary full vellum, ink signature of Johan Friederich Barth 1732 and notations on f.f.ep., ink stamp of Evangelische Predigerschule, Basel, very good.   Jeff Weber Rare Books   163 - 32   2011 $600

Association – Bartlett, John

Clarkson, Thomas   *An Essay on the Slavery and Commerce of the Human Species, Particularly the African.*   Georgetown: Published by Rev. David Barrow, J.N. Lyle printer, 1816.   Scarce Kentucky imprint; 12mo., xiv, (1 blank) (21)-175 pages, original full calf, gilt ruled spine and leather title label, label chipped, very good, signature of John Bartlett.   Jeff Weber Rare Books   163 - 60   2011 $1100

Association – Barton, Charles

Prout, John Skinner   *Picturesque Antiquities of Bristol.*   Bristol: George Davey, 1835.   Folio, titlepage, dedication leaf and 29 lithograph plates, contemporary morocco backed boards, spine repaired, margins of pages foxed and chipped, but india paper plates are mainly unaffected except for some dust marks and streaks across one image, ownership name of Charles Barton 14 York Crescent, Clifton, August 1837 on inner board.   Ken Spelman Rare Books   68 - 31   2011   £180

Association – Bashford, Herbert Lionel

Spenser, Edmund   1552-1599   *The Works.*   London: Bell and Daldy, 1862.   5 volumes, 230 x 150mm., very attractive deep blue pebble grain morocco handsomely gilt, covers with frames of one dogtooth and three plain rules, raised bands, spines in antique style compartments with delicate scrolling cornerpieces and intricate central fleuron surrounded by small tools, densely gilt floral turn-ins, marbled endpapers, all edges gilt, frontispiece portrait of Spender in volume I, front pastedown with armorial bookplate of Herbert Lionel Bashford, M.A. Dibon Lodge Godalming, spines just shade darker than covers, corners with hint of rubbing, extremely fine set in very attractive bindings, text fresh and bright with leather especially lustrous and with only the most insignificant wear.   Phillip J. Pirages   59 - 325   2011 $1500

Association – Basie, Count

Oliver, Paul *Conversation with the Blues.* London: Cassell, 1965. First edition; original cloth, gilt, dust jacket, pages xix, 217, with 80 illustrations and 2 maps, part of a menu signed by Count Basie and his vocalist Joe Williams (twice) (April 1960), another (indecipherable) loosely inserted. R. F. G. Hollett & Son Antiquarian Booksellers 175 - 1021 2011 £120

Association – Baskerfield

Gray, Thomas 1716-1771 *A Supplement to the Tour through Great Britain, containing a Catalogue of the Antiquities, Houses, Parks, Plantations, Scenes and Situations in England and Wales...* printed for G. Kearsley, 1787. Small 8vo., (ii) v (1) 119 (i) pages, half title, very good in contemporary half calf, expertly rebacked, corners neatly repaired, contemporary ownership name of Baskerfield on inner front board, who also adds a contents list which reveals that this item must at one stage have been bound with several other guides. Ken Spelman Rare Books 68 - 166 2011 £850

Association – Bastard, John Pollexfen

Bible. English - 1802 *Bible.* London: published for John Reeves, 1802. 241 x 152mm., 9 volumes, very fine dark blue straight grain morocco, handsomely gilt, covers bordered in gilt with angular key roll, raised bands, spines ornately gilt in panels featuring unusual sawtooth and flower roll at head and foot with stippled diapering filling main part of panel, all edges gilt, armorial bookplate of John Pollexfen Bastard; two spines lightly sunned, half dozen boards with light fading at edges, isolated wear to corners and ends of spines, few small indents and flakes, original very decorative bindings extremely well preserved, first volume with noticeable freckled foxing at front and back, isolated gatherings (perhaps a total of six or 8, combined) in the other volumes with less but still apparent foxing, endpapers generally little discolored, otherwise internally in fine condition, almost entirely very bright, fresh and clean. Phillip J. Pirages 59 - 79 2011 $4250

Association – Bates, White

Newton, Isaac 1642-1727 *Observations Upon the Prophecies of Daniel and the Apocalypse of St. John.* London: J. Darby and T. Browne, 1733. First edition; 4to., (viii), 323, (2 blank) pages, vignette at head of dedication page, occasional light foxing, worming (margins only), few leaves with ink smears or other markings confined mainly to margins, full modern antique style blind paneled calf, raised bands, red leather spine label, gilt spine, ownership signature of White Bates on free endpaper, nice wide margins, very good, rare. Jeff Weber Rare Books 163 - 36 2011 $4500

Association – Battell, E.

Sharp, John *Fifteen Sermons Preached on Several Occasions by... John Lord Arch Bishop of York.* London: printed for Walter Kettilby, 1709. Third edition; 8vo., pages (vi) 472 + engraved frontispiece, contemporary crimson turkey, spine gilt panelled with saltired compartments, lettered direct in gilt, boards panelled in gilt, board edges decorative roll gilt, turn-ins decorative roll gilt, 'Dutch-comb' 'made' endpapers, all edges gilt, blue and white sewn endbands, light spotting, occasional dampmark in lower margin, tidy repairs to headcap with new matching endband, black leather gilt decorative roll bordered label "To Mrs./E.B." ink inscription "Eliz. Battell/Juner", in different hand "The Gift of my Good Aunt Mrs. Eliz Battell to me Anne Hallows junr. May ye 26 1728", in same hand "Anne Leicester", ink inscription "John Roberts No 2 May 14 1792", from the collection of Christopher Ernest Weston 1947-2010. Unsworths Booksellers 24 - 40 2011 £200

Association – Battershall, Fletcher

Cervantes Saavedra, Miguel De 1547-1616 *History of the Valorous and Witty Knight Errant, Don Quixote of the Mancha.* London: printed for R. Scot, T. Basset, J. Wright, R. Chiswell, 1675. Early edition of The Thomas Shelton translation in two parts; small folio, (8), 137; (5), 138-214, 216-244, 244-273 leaves, full red morocco, boards and spine tooled and lettered in gilt boards with and attractive art nouveau style tooling with center lozenge containing the gilt initials "FB" (for Fletcher Battershall), gilt dentelles, lower front dentelle with small gilt bat device with initial "B", all edges gilt and rough cut, edges and outer hinges bit rubbed, small bit of splitting to front joint at top and bottom of spine, some minor paper repairs to fore edge margin of titlepage and following leaf as well as final leaf, 2 bookplates belonging to Willis Vickery and binders Fletcher and Maude Battershall, old catalog clippings tipped to front flyleaf by previous owner, overall very good. Heritage Book Shop Holiday 2010 - 18 2011 $5000

Association – Battershall, Maude

Cervantes Saavedra, Miguel De 1547-1616 *History of the Valorous and Witty Knight Errant, Don Quixote of the Mancha.* London: printed for R. Scot, T. Basset, J. Wright, R. Chiswell, 1675. Early edition of The Thomas Shelton translation in two parts; small folio, (8), 137; (5), 138-214, 216-244, 244-273 leaves, full red morocco, boards and spine tooled and lettered in gilt boards with and attractive art nouveau style tooling with center lozenge containing the gilt initials "FB" (for Fletcher Battershall), gilt dentelles, lower front dentelle with small gilt bat device with initial "B", all edges gilt and rough cut, edges and outer hinges bit rubbed, small bit of splitting to front joint at top and bottom of spine, some minor paper repairs to fore edge margin of titlepage and following leaf as well as final leaf, 2 bookplates belonging to Willis Vickery and binders Fletcher and Maude Battershall, old catalog clippings tipped to front flyleaf by previous owner, overall very good. Heritage Book Shop Holiday 2010 - 18 2011 $5000

Association – Bayham

Howard, John *The State of the Prisons in England and Wales, with Preliminary Observations and an Account of some Foreign Prisons. (bound with) Appendix to the State of the Prisons in England and Wales...* Warrington: printed by William Eyres and sold by T. Cadell and N. Conant, London, 1777. Warrington: printed by William Eyres, 1784. First edition and second edition of appendix; 4to., 3 engraved plates, with little offsetting as usual, (6), 489, (23) pages, wanting half title; 4to., (8), 286 (10) pages, including both initial blank and half title, 17 engraved plates, well preserved, contemporary calf, sympathetically rebacked, spine gilt lettered, sides rather worn but overall good, sound binding with 19th century armorial bookplate of Bayham. John Drury Rare Books 153 - 63 2011 £1750

Association – Bayley, Charles

Northampton, Henry Howard, Earl of *A Publication of His Majesties Edict and Severe Censure Against Private combats and Combatants.* Robert Parker, 1613. Initial leaf (blank except for signature mark "A"), discarded title soiled, some browning and spotting elsewhere, faint dampmark at foot of some leaves, one with cornertip torn, pages (ii), 119, (1), 4to., modern and morocco, red morocco lettering piece, 2 compartments vertically gilt lettered direct, others plain, older endpapers preserved, front pastedown tih old ownership inscription of Charles H. Bayley, good. Blackwell Rare Books B166 - 76 2011 £1250

Association – Baynton, W., Mrs.

More, Hannah 1745-1833 *Coelebs in Search of a Wife.* London: T. Cadell and W. Daives, 1813. 1810. Fourteenth and thirteenth edition; 2 volumes, expertly and sympathetically rebound in half tan calf, gilt spines, red leather labels, very good, presentation from author to Miss Guillebaud, signatures of Mrs. W. Baynton, 3 Clifton Vale. Jarndyce Antiquarian Booksellers CLXC - 522 2011 £450

Association – Beardsley, Aubrey

Laclos, Pierre Ambroise Francois Choderlos De 1741-1803 *Les Liasions Dangereuses.* Brussels: J. Rosez, 1869. 2 volumes bound as one, pages 99; 291, internally clean and bright, minor chip to half title, contemporary blue black quarter morocco, gilt lettered on spine, original lime green printed wrappers bound in, top edge gilt, marbled boards and endpapers, spine and joints expertly repaired, edges of boards slightly rubbed, front endpapers chipped with some restoration also to front wrapper, Aubrey Beardsley's copy with his ink signature at head of titlepage and presentation inscription from his mother to A. W. King, later inscription from his mother, bookplate of Robert Booth. Simon Finch Rare Books Zero - 205 2011 £3500

Association – Beardsley, Ellen A. Pitt

Laclos, Pierre Ambroise Francois Choderlos De 1741-1803 *Les Liasions Dangereuses.* Brussels: J. Rosez, 1869. 2 volumes bound as one, pages 99; 291, internally clean and bright, minor chip to half title, contemporary blue black quarter morocco, gilt lettered on spine, original lime green printed wrappers bound in, top edge gilt, marbled boards and endpapers, spine and joints expertly repaired, edges of boards slightly rubbed, front endpapers chipped with some restoration also to front wrapper, Aubrey Beardsley's copy with his ink signature at head of titlepage and presentation inscription from his mother to A. W. King, later inscription from his mother, bookplate of Robert Booth. Simon Finch Rare Books Zero - 205 2011 £3500

Association – Beaton, Cecil

Danziger, James *Beaton.* London: Secker & Warburg, 1980. First edition; 4to., 256 pages, illustrations in black and white, loosely inserted is signed letter in Cecil Beaton's slightly shaky post stroke handwriting for Mr. Ross, about fine in very good+ dust jacket, very slightly rubbed and creased. Any Amount of Books May 29 2011 - A48172 2011 $230

Association – Beattie, Mrs.

Housman, Alfred Edward 1859-1936 *A Shropshire Lad.* London: Kegan Paul, Trench and Co., 1896. First edition; small 8vo., original parchment backed boards with printed label on spine, spine label and covers rubbed, else very good in navy blue half morocco slipcase, signed copies extremely rare, with spine label in first state (state A), one of fewer than 350 copies in this state, with two ALS's from Housman to Mrs. Beattie. James S. Jaffe Rare Books May 26 2011 - 16628 2011 $17,500

Association – Beaufort, Duke of

Davenant, William 1606-1668 *The Works of Sr. William Davenant Kt. Consisting of those Which were Formerly printed and Those which He Design'd for the Press...* London: by T. N. for Henry Herringman, 1673. First collected edition; folio, (8), 402, (4), 486, 111 pages, portrait, turn-of-the-century red levant morocco, gilt arabesque centerpiece on covers, all edges gilt by Riviere, very skillfully rebacked, though new leather at joints and on cords has uniformly faded, unusually fine, fresh, wide margined copy, fine impression of portrait, leather tipped fleece lined slipcase, edges rubbed, Duke of Beaufort, E. F. Leo, A. E, Newton, with their bookplates. Joseph J. Felcone Inc. Fall Miscellany 2010 - 37 2011 $2200

Association – Bechtel, Sylvanus

Lincoln, Abraham 1809-1865 *Complete Works.* Harrogate: Lincoln Memorial University, 1894. Sponsor's Edition; signed by chancellor of the University (this copy #283 especially prepared for Sylvanus B. Bechtel), 235 x 160mm., 12 volumes, very pleasing publisher's elaborately gilt decorated scarlet morocco, upper boards intricately tooled with entrelac gilt strapwork and twining floral tendrils (in stylized 16th century Italian design), flat spines with similar gilt tooling in an elongated panel, top edge gilt, other edges rough trimmed, mostly unopened, 12 portrait frontispieces, 12 facsimiles of letter and other documents, 32 photo plates; first volume with tipped in letter on onion skin (photographic copy?) from John Hay to unnamed correspondent identifying the two figures in frontispiece with Lincoln as being Hay himself and John Nicolay; spines just bit darkened, printed on inexpensive paper, so leaves little browned at edges (no doubt as in all copies), one leaf with four inch horizontal tear across breadth of text without loss, otherwise quite fine set, text obviously largely unread and with decorative binding showing no significant wear. Phillip J. Pirages 59 - 257 2011 $3250

Association – Beck, Septimus

Thorburn, Archibald *Game Birds & Wild-Fowl of Great Britain and Ireland.* London: Longmans, Green and Co., 1923. First edition; 30 colored plates, each protected with original tissue, 4to., red cover with gold line border, spine being little sunned, gilt lettering, top edge gilt, edges and corners lightly rubbed, neat presentation inscription "Septimus J. Beck January 12th 1924 form LCB & A D", 3 front and rear endpapers and in each case the one nearest the cover little foxed with foxing getting progressively lighter on other two, no foxing on any of the text of plates. I. D. Edrich May 26 2011 - 59010 2011 $1174

Association – Bective

Johnstone, Christian Isobel *Clan-Albyn: a National Tale.* London: G. Routledge & Co., 1853. Contemporary half green calf, maroon leather label, spine darkened, little rubbed, signed "Bective 1854", good, sound. Jarndyce Antiquarian Booksellers CLXC - 28 2011 £45

M'Intosh, Maria June *Grace and Isabel; or to Seem and to Be.* London: G. Routledge Co., 1852. First English edition; Contemporary half green calf, maroon leather label, spine darkened, slightly worn damage in tail of following hinge, from the Headfort library, signed "Bective 1854). Jarndyce Antiquarian Booksellers CLXC - 190 2011 £45

M'Intosh, Maria June *Louise De La Valliere.* London: T. Nelson & Sons, 1854. First English edition; contemporary half maroon calf, black leather label, spine slightly rubbed, from the Headfort library, signed "Bective 1854". Jarndyce Antiquarian Booksellers CLXC - 191 2011 £45

Maberly, Catherine Charlotte *The Love Match.* London: David Bryce, 1856. New edition; contemporary half maroon calf, spine decorated in gilt, black leather label, spine and corners little rubbed, from Headfort library, signed, "Bective 1854", good plus. Jarndyce Antiquarian Booksellers CLXC - 184 2011 £45

Marsh, Anne *Adelaide Lindsay.* London: G. Routledge & Co., 1851. Contemporary half green calf maroon leather label, spine darkened, little rubbed, from the Headfort library, signed "Bective 1854", good, sound copy. Jarndyce Antiquarian Booksellers CLXC - 232 2011 £60

Marsh, Anne *Tales of the Woods and Fields.* Belfast: Simms & M'Intyre, 1846. Half title, dedication leaf preceding title, contemporary half green calf, maroon leather label, tail of spine slightly worn, signed "Bective 1856", good sound copy. Jarndyce Antiquarian Booksellers CLXC - 244 2011 £45

Association – Bedford, Duchess of

Lilford, Thomas Littleton Powys, 4th Baron 1833-1896 *Notes on the Birds of Northamptonshire and Neighbourhood.* London: R. H. Porter, 1893. First edition; original publisher's red cloth lettered gilt on spine, printed for private circulation only, signed presentation from author for Duchess of Bedford, faint mottling to spine, very slight wear to spine ends, otherwise very good, handsome. Any Amount of Books May 29 2011 - A69809 2011 $408

Workman, Fanny Bullock *Ice-Bound Heights of the Mustagh...* London: Archibald Constable and Co., 1908. First edition; 8vo., pages xvi, 444, original publisher's green cloth lettered gilt on spine and cover with cover illustration of mountain scene, 170 illustrations, 2 folding maps, color frontispiece and 3 other color plates and 3 photogravures, bookplate of Duchess of Bedford, faint rubbing to cover and head of spine, very slight marks, lettering bright covers, not faded, very good, maps, plates, text clean and bright. Any Amount of Books May 26 2011 - A69805 2011 $1132

Association – Bedford, Duke of

The Badminton Library. London: Longmans, Green and Co., 1891-1898. Early editions; 29 volumes, octavo, standard trade edition, bound in illustrated brown cloth with gilt titles and decoration to spines, patterned endpapers, slight rubbing and occasional tiny splits to heads of spines, overall clean, very good, internally very good, occasional light foxing to some pages, partly unopened, each volume with armorial Woburn Abbey bookplate of Duke of Bedford. Any Amount of Books May 26 2011 - A76291 2011 $2348

Brassey, Lord *The Naval Annual.* Portsmouth: J Griffin & Co., 1886-1889. First edition; 3 volumes, pages xxi, 550 (16 pages ads); xxvi, 784 (4 pages ads); xxiv, 723 (4 pages ads); First 3 volumes, each gift from author to Duke of Bedford, errata slip tipped into volume II, original publisher's royal blue cloth with gilt lettering and decoration, slightly rubbed and bumped at corners, some moderate spotting to prelims including titlepages and tissue guards, otherwise text nice and clean, illustrations bright, not all tissue guards present, overall handsome set. Any Amount of Books May 26 2011 - A75246 2011 $1090

Epstein, M. *The Annual Register: a Review of Public Events at Home and Abroad 1931-1938.* London: Longmans, Green and Co., 1932-1939. First edition; 8 volumes, 8vo., each volume between 450-500 pages, original publisher's purple cloth lettered gilt on spine, new series, all clean, very good copies, slightly sunned at spine, few pastedowns have bookplate of 11th Duke of Bedford, Woburn Abbey. Any Amount of Books May 29 2011 - A70517 2011 $306

Evans, Sebastian *The High History of the Holy Grail.* London: J. M. Dent, 1903. First edition thus; large 8vo., pages xvii, 379, illustrations by Jessie M. King with 23 full page plates, some with red pictorial embellishment + 36 chapter headpieces and gilt black cover and spine illustration on publisher's sky blue cloth, sound decent about very good with slight soiling, slight marks and slight rubbing and slight bumping to covers, endpapers foxed, neat presentation inscription on half title to Duke of Bedford from one J. Bly dated 1903. Any Amount of Books May 26 2011 - A74369 2011 $755

Ryan, Thomas *The History of Queen Charlotte's Lying in Hospital, From Its Foundation in 1752 to the Present Time with an Account of Its Objects and Present State.* London: privately published, 1885. 4to., pages xv, 70, original publisher's dark green cloth lettered gilt with crest to cover, illustrations, plans, Woburn Abbey bookplate of Francis, Duke of Bedford, scarce, slightly dusty and very faintly marked but bright and clean. Any Amount of Books May 29 2011 - A71030 2011 $315

Sheldon, Charles *The Wilderness of the Upper Yukon. A Hunter's Explorations for Wild Sheep in Sub-Arctic Mountains.* London: T. Fisher Unwin, 1911. First edition; large 8vo., pages xxii, 354, color frontispiece, 4 maps, 50 photo plates, original publisher's lettered gilt on spine and on front cover, front cover with pictorial gilt ram's head, top edge gilt, sound, clean, very good+ copy, slight browning to endpapers, ownership signature of Duke of Bedford (Woburn Abbey). Any Amount of Books May 29 2011 - 74328 2011 $221

Association – Bell, Harmon

Fooz, Jean Henri Nicolas De *Fundamental Principles of the Law of Mines.* San Francisco: J. B. Painter, 1860. First edition; extremely scarce, contemporary owner's signature (Harmon Bell) on inner cover, repeated on page lxx, (i)-cxlviii, 882 pages, publisher's full sheep, gilt lettered red and black leather labels, contemporary owner's signature, very slight wear to head of spine, fine, extremely scarce. Argonaut Book Shop Recent Acquisitions Summer 2010 - 132 2011 $2250

Association – Bell, Henry

Short, Bob *Hoyle Abridged or Short Rules for Short Memories at the Game of Whist.* London: printed for B. Reynolds and John Stacy, 1818. Thirtieth edition; 108 x 57mm., 24 pages, extraordinarily fine and charming contemporary green morocco very lavishly gilt, covers with multiple plain and decorative rules at edges around two decorative frames, outer one with closely spaced fleurons pointing inward, inner one filled with row of interlocking floral loops, these two frames enclosing an elongated central panel with attenuated stems reaching toward and flowering at the corner of the board, flat spine with two panels of massed scrolling tools and one panel with titling, full morocco doublures very richly gilt in panelled design similar to (but even more intricate than) that on covers, gilt edges, early signature of Henry Bell, Woolsington; tiny tear in fore edge of one leaf, just slightest of rubbing to joints and extremities, in remarkably fine condition, binding bright and beautiful, text clean and fresh. Phillip J. Pirages 59 - 264 2011 $750

Association – Bemis, Frank Brewer

Papworth, John B. 1775-1847 *Select Views of London.* London: printed for R. Ackermann by J. Diggens, 1816. First edition, first issue; with Papworth's name on titlepage, large octavo, (8), 159 pages, 76 hand colored aquatint plates including five double page folding plates, plates watermarked 1815, contemporary Regency calf, neatly rebacked with original spine laid down, covers decoratively bordered gilt, spine decoratively tooled in gilt in compartments with black morocco gilt lettering label, little light offsetting form plates to text, armorial bookplate of Frank Brewer Bemis and bookplate of Gladys Robinson, excellent early copy, housed in tan cloth slipcase. David Brass Rare Books, Inc. May 26 2011 - 00640 2011 $8500

Association – Bennett, John, Mrs.

Spark, Muriel *The Bachelors.* Macmillan, 1960. First edition; pages (vi), 242, foolscap 8vo., original red cloth, backstrip gilt lettered, dust jacket with two short tears, very good, inscribed by author to Mrs. John Bennett. Blackwell Rare Books B166 - 233 2011 £300

Association – Bennett, N.

Rockwell, John Arnold *A Compilation of Spanish and Mexican Law, in Relation to Mines and Titles to Real Estate, in force in California, Texas and New Mexico and in the Territories Acquired Under the Louisiana and Florida Treaties.* New York: John S. Voorhies, 1851. First edition; pages (i-iii), iv-xix, (1, blank), (2, errata), (7)-663, (1), period full blindstamped light brown sheep, professionally rebacked with original red and black leather labels, laid down new endpapers, contemporary news clipping on inner cover pertaining to new colonization laws of Mexico, enacted in 1854, contemporary owner's name (Nathl. Bennett), "volume I (only volume published) erased on title page leaving two small holes and light scarring, some occasional very light foxing, especially to front and endleaves, else fine and fresh, very scarce.   Argonaut Book Shop   Recent Acquisitions Summer 2010 - 133 2011 $2750

Association – Benson, A. C.

Boswell, James 1740-1795 *The Life of Samuel Johnson.* London: George Routledge & Sons, circa, 1889. Text in double columns, pages xvi, 526, 8vo., contemporary vellum, double gilt ruled borders on sides, spine richly gilt, very good, inscribed to A. Godfrey James from A. C. Benson, Eton, Xmas 1889.   Blackwell Rare Books   B166 - 19 2011   £85

Association – Benson, F.

Ros, Amanda McKittrick *Irene Iddesleigh.* Belfast: 1897. First edition; 189 pages, errata slip, initialled by author, green cloth, spine bit darkened and canted, otherwise nice, Philip Burne-Jones's copy, signed by him on endpaper and later inscribed by him to "Fred. (E.F.?) Benson, tipped in brief one sentence ALS from author to Burne-Jones.   Joseph J. Felcone Inc.   Fall Miscellany 2010 - 103 2011 $475

Association – Benson, Thyrza

La Fontaine, Jean De 1621-1695 *Fables Choisies, Mises en Vers.* Paris: Denys Thierry, 31 March, 1668. First edition; 4to., (58), 284 (2) pages, leaf o2 present as both cancellans and cancellandum, roman type, woodcut typographic head and tailpieces, floriated initials, 118 etchings by Francois Chauveau, crushed green morocco, gilt triple rule outer border, spine and wide turn-ins gilt, all edges gilt by Lortic, fils (spine and extremities faded to brown, front hinge worn), neat repair to five leaves (one touching two letters), very light overall toning, Robert Hoe's copy, inscribed in pencil on front flyleaf to his Granddaughter Thyrza Benson.   Joseph J. Felcone Inc.   Fall Miscellany 2010 - 72 2011 $30,000

Association – Benz, Doris Louise

Goldsmith, Oliver 1730-1774 *The Vicar of Wakefield: a Tale Supposed to be Written by Himself.* Salisbury: Printed for B. Collins for F. Newbery, 1766. First edition, variant B; 2 volumes, 172 x 108mm., terminal blank in volume I, beautiful scarlet crushed morocco, heavily gilt by Riviere & Son, covers with French fillet frame, spine with raised bands and handsomely gilt compartments, lovely gilt inner dentelles, all edges gilt, leather book labels of Roderick Terry, (Edgar) Mills and Doris Louise Benz, lower corner of terminal blank in first volume skillfully renewed, artful repair and faint glue stains at inner margin of B3 in second volume, other isolated trivial defects, very fine, text nearly pristine, especially bright and handsome binding.   Phillip J. Pirages 59 - 50 2011 $6500

Association – Beraldi, Henri

Henault, Charles Jean Francois *Nouvel Abrege Chronologique de l'Histoire de France.* Paris: Chez Prault et al, 1756. Fifth edition; 165 x 105mm., 2 volumes with continuous pagination, 5 p.l., (1), 545, (1), 1 blank leaf; (549)-928 pages, (48) leaves, including final blank, second volume with half title but no titlepage, apparently as issued, lovely contemporary olive green morocco, elegantly gilt in style of Derome, covers with plain and stippled fillet border around a frame containing large and graceful gilt floral and botanical stamps as well as dots and circlets, raised bands, spines gilt in compartments featuring charming flower centerpiece and small scrolling foliate cornerpieces, turn-ins with gilt zig-zag decoration, stencilled gilt endpapers, all edges gilt, publisher's device on titlepage, historiated headpieces, foliated initials, ornamental tailpieces; small bookplate of Jean Furstenberg and Henri Beraldi; spines slightly and uniformly faded to an attractive amber, just hint of wear to joints and corners, isolated minor foxing, few trivial stains, but fine, pretty binding sound, lustrous and with only insignificant wear and text, very clean and fresh.   Phillip J. Pirages   59 - 53 2011 $2900

Association – Berland, Abel

Fraunce, Abraham *The Lawiers Logike, Exemplifying the Praecept of Logike by the Practise of the Common Lawe.* London: by William How for Thomas Gubbin and T. Newman, 1588. First edition; 4to, (1), 151, (i.e. 152) leaves including blank leaf 2A2, folding table, title within type ornament border, woodcut initials, mixed black letter and roman, full red gilt panelled morocco, edges gilt by Bedford, first two leaves lightly washed, short closed tear on table, blank corner of 2K4 replaced, else fine, clean, armorial bookplate of Sir Edward Priaulx and book label of Abel Berland.   Joseph J. Felcone Inc.   Fall Miscellany 2010 - 52 2011 $8000

Suckling, John *Fragmenta Aurea. A Collection of all the Incomparable Pieces.* London: for Humphrey Moseley, 1646. First edition; first state of title with "FRAGMENTA AVREA" in upper case, a period after "Churchyard" in imprint and rule under date; A3v: 16 reads "allowred", second state of frontispiece, re-incised with heavier lines around leaves of garland and bulge in left sleeve; (6), 119, (7), 82, 64, (4), 52 pages, engraved portrait by William Marshall, contemporary calf, gilt fillet and cornerpieces, red morocco spine label, portrait and first two leaves with two very tiny holes at gutter, worm trail in lower margin of first three gatherings, else very nice, contemporary binding, bookplate of C. Pearl Chamberlain and booklabel of Abel Berland; fine red morocco pull-off case, ALS of John Suckling (1659-1627) father of the poet, Goodfathers 29 July 1625 to unnamed recipient seeking information on his election as a burgess in Yarmouth.   Joseph J. Felcone Inc. Fall Miscellany 2010 - 113   2011 $6000

Association – Berney, Ann

Wilkes, Wetenhall *A Letter of Genteel and Moral Advice to a Young Lady...* London: printed for C. Hitch and L. Hawes at the Red Lion in Pater-noster row, 1760. Seventh edition; 12mo., (6), 198 pages, large uncut copy, light browning and slight foxing, contemporary quarter calf, marbled boards, ruled and banded spine, joints cracked, foot of spine slightly chipped, corners little worn, contemporary ownership name of Ann Berney 1760.   Jarndyce Antiquarian Booksellers   CXCI - 619   2011   £380

Association – Bernheimer, Earle

Frost, Robert Lee   1874-1963   *North of Boston.* London: David Nutt, 1914. First edition, one of 350 copies bound in coarse green linen out of a total edition of 1000 copies; 8vo., original green cloth, fine, preserved in black cloth slipcase with chemise, presentation copy from author for Earle Bernheimer.   James S. Jaffe Rare Books   May 26 2011 - 20897   2011 $15,000

Association – Bertie, James

Dugdale, William   1605-1686   *Monasticon Anglicanum; or the History of the Ancient Abbies, Monasteries, Hospitals...in England and Wales.* (with) ... *Two Additional volumes to Sir William Dugdale's Monasticon Anglicanum.* London: R. Harbin for D. Browne and J. Smith (et al) for Tho. Taylor..., 1718. 1722-1723; 3 volumes, folio, plates (lacking plates 42-44 in volume 1, contemporary mottled calf, stain darkened, spine panel gilt, red lettering piece gilt, numbered direct in panel gilt compartment, board edges 'zig-zag' roll gilt, all edges 'French Shell' marbled, blue and red sewn endleaves, some damp and mould marking, a few plates loose but present, rather rubbed, joints worn but strong, some loss from endcaps, contemporary ink inscription "Samuel Thomson Esq. of Bradfield Berks", ink stamped armorial of "Samuel Thomson of Bradfield Esqr", armorial bookplates of Honble James Bertie Esqr. of Stanwell in Com. Middx. Second Son to James late/Earle of Abingdon 1702", from the collection of Christopher Ernest Weston 1947-2010.   Unsworths Booksellers   24 - 21 2011   £600

Association – Bertolotti, Alessandro

Attali, Marc   *Les Erotiques du Regard.* Paris: Andre Balland, 1968. First edition; folio, pages (112), 64 black and white photos, original black and white photo illustrated paper covered boards, tinted pink, text and spine printed in black, rubbing to tips and to head and foot of spine, short closed tear to lower panel at foot of spine, horizontal crease towards foot of spine, near fine, from the library of Alessandro Bertolotti.   Simon Finch Rare Books   Zero - 503 2011   £900

Malanga, Gerard   *Autobiography of a Sex Thief.* New York: Lustrum Press, 1984. First edition; large 4to., pages 96, 44 black and white photos, original black and photo illustrated wrappers, spine creased and lightly sunned, near fine, from the library of Alessandro Bertolotti.   Simon Finch Rare Books   Zero - 536 2011   £650

Verneuil, Maurice Pillard   *Images d'une Femme/Vingt Quatre Etudes De Nu.* Paris: Editions Denoel et Steele, 1931. First edition; folio, pages 1-8, 9-16, 24 black and white photo plates, unbound, original black cloth backed red paper covered board portfolio, white label to front cover printed in black and red, black ribbon tie to fore edge, lightly rubbed, fine set in near fine portfolio, from the library of Alessandro Bertolotti.   Simon Finch Rare Books   Zero - 544 2011   £650

Association – Best, Frida

Austen, Jane 1775-1817 *Pride and Prejudice.* London: printed for T. Egerton, Military Library, Whitehall, 1813. First edition, following all points in Gilson and Keynes and complete with all half titles present; 12mo., 3 volumes, (iv), 307, (1, blank); (iv), 239, (1, blank); (v), (323), (1, blank) pages, contemporary speckled calf, blind tooled board edges, edges sprinkled red, original light brown endpapers, expertly rebacked with original spines laid down, later green morocco gilt lettering labels on spines, gilt stamped "Charleton" to upper boards of each volume (possibly that of Charleton House, Montrose), from the library of German artist and music historian Frida Best (1876-1964) with her bookplate in each volume, edges to few leaves professionally and near invisibly repaired, occasional light foxing, excellent and complete copy in original and contemporary binding, housed in modern half red morocco clamshell case with 3 individual spines decoratively lettered and tooled in gilt, Regency binders typically removed half titles, those with half titles rare. David Brass Rare Books, Inc. May 26 2011 - 01651 2011 $75,000

Association – Bidwell, Charles

Marshall, Beatrice *Emma Marshall; a Biographical Sketch.* London: Seeley & Co., 1900. First edition; frontispiece, 12 plates, 2 pages ads, uncut in original blue cloth, lettered in gilt, slight rubbing, booklabel of Charles Bidwell, Ely, very good. Jarndyce Antiquarian Booksellers   CLXC - 263 2011   £35

Association – Binnall, Peter

Barwick, Peter *The Life of the Reverend Dr. John Barwick, D.D.* London: printed by J. Bettenham, 1724. Large paper copy, 8vo., pages (xxiv), 552, (xl) + 2 engraved portrait frontispieces, contemporary calf, gilt panelled spine, orange lettering piece gilt, boards panelled in blind (Cambridge style), board edges decorative roll gilt, 'Dutch-comb' 'made' endpapers, all edges red and grey sprinkled green and white sewn endbands, rubbed at extremities, spine darkened, joints cracked but strong, endcaps worn "James Affleck" book label, contemporary ink inscription "Eliz. Dolben" and above "James Affleck", mid 20th century provenance note by Peter B. G. Binnall, from the collection of Christopher Ernest Weston 1947-2010.   Unsworths Booksellers 24 - 6 2011   £200

Cosin, John *Scholastical History of the Canon of the Holy Scripture.* London: E. Tyler and R. Holt for Robert Pawlett, 1672. 4to., pages (xxxvi), 224, (xlviii) + additional engraved titlepage, contemporary speckled calf, boards double ruled in blind, board edges broken ruled gilt, all edges blue 'swirl' marbled blue and white sewn endbands, early 1990's calf reback + corners by Chris Weston, touch of dust soiling, old leather bit flaked and rubbed, ink inscription "J. Lincoln", 20th century ink inscription "This volume belonged to/ John Kaye D.D./Bishop of Lincoln/1827-1853. It belonged to his son/William Frederick John Kaye/Archdeacon of Lincoln/1863-1919", ink inscription "Peter B.G. Binnall/ Barkwith Rectory/Wragby/Lincoln/ (rule) Bought in Lincoln/30 April 1951", 19th century bookseller's ticket "J. Leslie/52 Great Queen Street/Lincoln's Inn Fields/London; from the collection of Christopher Ernest Weston 1947-2010.   Unsworths Booksellers   24 - 19 2011   £275

Association – Binnall, Richard Gibbons

Stillingfleet, Edward *The Unreasonableness of Separation; or an Impartial Account of the... Present.* London: T. N. for Henry Mortlock, 1681.   4to., pages (ii), xciv, (xvi), 450, contemporary calf, boards double rule bordered in blind, board edges 'zig-zag' decorative roll gilt, all edges blue 'swirl' marbled, mid 1980's calf rebacked and corners by Chris Weston, some spotting and toning, first few leaves soiled, titlepage touch worn at fore-edge, old leather scratched and crackled, early ink inscriptions "Christopher Metcalfe" (reading across) and in a different hand "Christopher Metcalfe book" reading upwards, contemporary ink inscription "C.M.", also printed booklabel of Revd. Richard Gibbons Binnall, from the collection of Christopher Ernest Weston 1947-2010.   Unsworths Booksellers   24 - 47 2011   £275

Association – Birrell, Augustine

Eliot, George, Pseud. 1819-1880 *Daniel Deronda.* Edinburgh: Blackwood, 1876. First edition; first issue with misprint on page 83 of volume I, 8 parts in 4 volumes contemporary scuffed three quarter leather and boards, couple of hinges tender, lacking volume labels on spines, small stain from removed scotch tape on titlepage of volume one, very good tight set, bookplate of Augustine Birrell.   Second Life Books Inc.   174 - 137 2011 $700

Association – Bissett, Clark Prescott

James, Henry 1843-1916 *The Novels and Tales of Henry James.* New York: Charles Scribner's Sons, 1922. 1920. New York Edition; 28 volumes, half titles, frontispieces, uncut in original maroon cloth, gilt monogram on front boards, spines little faded, boards slightly marked, slight lifting of cloth to front board of volume II, top edge gilt, good plus, bookplate of Clark Prescott Bissett.   Jarndyce Antiquarian Booksellers   CXCI - 16 2011   £1750

Association – Black, Samuel

Smith, Samuel *The History of the Colony of Nova Caesaria or New Jersey...* Burlington: James Parker, 1765. First edition; x, 573, (1) pages, modern calf backed marbled paper covered boards, very skillfully executed in period style, noticeably foxed as usual, few blank corners torn away without loss, contemporary ownership signatures of Burlington County residents Saml. Black and Abner Wright.   Joseph J. Felcone Inc.   Fall Miscellany 2010 - 108   2011 $2000

Association – Blackburne, John Ireland

Smith, William *A New & Compendious History, of the County of Warwick, from the Earliest Period to the Present Time...* Birmingham: W. Emans, 1830. Sole edition; engraved map as frontispiece, engraved titlepage (with vignette), 60 engraved plates on steel, pages (4), 379, 4, 4to., near contemporary half green morocco rebacked (with original spine laid on) to match, backstrip divided into six compartments by raised bands between gilt rules, gilt lettered direct in second compartment, remainder plain, gilt rules on turn-ins, morocco grain green cloth sides, marbled endpapers, bookplate of John Ireland Blackburne dated 1874, all edges gilt.   Blackwell Rare Books   B166 - 98   2011   £200

Association – Blackford, C.

Macaulay, Thomas Babington Macaulay, 1st Baron 1800-1859 *Essays, Critical and Miscellaneous.* Philadelphia: 1849. New edition; 744 pages, half leather rubbed, all edges of backstrip and corners, modest foxing, bookplate of Col. Richard L. Maury with pencil presentation of C. Blackford.   Bookworm & Silverfish   679 - 67   2011 $60

Association – Blackwell, Elizabeth

Ruskin, John   1819-1900 *Ethics of the Dust. Ten Lectures on Little Housewives on the Elements of Crystallisation.* New York: John Wiley & Son, 1866. First edition; from the library of the first woman physician, Elizabeth Blackwell, octavo, (2, blank), (i)-250, (1, publisher's ads), (1, blank) pages, with Blackwell's signature and dated 1866 and her bookplate; publisher's full purple cloth, decoratively ruled in blind, spine lettered in gilt, dampstaining and wrinkling to cloth, spine sunned and soiled, head and tail of spine chipped, some foxing to blanks, otherwise very clean, Blackwell's inscription, housed in custom half morocco clamshell, very good.   Heritage Book Shop   Holiday 2010 - 10   2011 $3500

Association – Blair, Francis Preston

Fremont, John Charles   1813-1890 *Report of the Exploring Expedition to the Rocky Mountains in the Year 1842 and to Oregon and North California in Years 1843-1844.* Washington: Gales and Seaton, 1845. First edition, 2nd issue; early binding for Francis Preston Blair's library of red pebbled buckram with floral wreath designed medallion in gilt on front and rear covers, title in gilt on spine, centered in wreath on front cover and stamped in gilt is "F.P. Blair", 693 pages, 22 lithographed plates, 5 maps, 3 folding with large folding map housed in separate matching red slipcase, professionally rebacked and is now too thick to restore in original volume.   Buckingham Books   May 26 2011 - 25731   2011 $6250

Association – Blair, Natalie

Tennyson, Alfred Tennyson, 1st Baron   1809-1892 *Poems, Chiefly Lyrical.* London: Effingham Wilson, 1830. First edition; 191 x 114mm., 2 p.l., 154 pages, (1) leaf ads), original brown paper boards, flat spine with paper label, buckram chemise and contained in quarter morocco slipcase with raised bands, gilt titling, morocco bookplate of "Blairhame" (used by Natalie K. (Mrs. J. Insley) Blair 1887-1952), the "Blairhame" referring to her magnificent Tudor style home in Tuxedo Park NY, titlepage with 19th century ink presentation inscription "William Rowan Hamilton from Francis Beaufort Edgeworth"; joints with thin cracks, backstrip and label little torn and soiled, extremities with expected wear, leaves bit foxed and soiled, but surprisingly well preserved, nevertheless quite solid, covers very clean and text still fresh.   Phillip J. Pirages   59 - 332   2011 $1250

Association – Blake, W. Jex

Extracts from the Information Received by His Majesty's Commissioners as to the Administration and Operation of the Poor Laws. London: B. Fellowes, 1833. First edition; 8vo., xxi, (1),4 32 pages, original oatmeal linen with title printed in black on spine, very slight fraying to spine, else very good, from the library of W. Jex Blake with his signature dated 1834 on titlepage.   John Drury Rare Books   153 - 133   2011   £175

Association – Blakeney, R. B. D.

Nakhla, Yacoub *New Manual of English and Arabic Conversation.* Cairo: Neguib Mitri Al-Marref Printing Office, 1910. Second edition; presentation copy, (7), 8-254 pages, contemporary quarter morocco, spine ruled gilt, inscribed by author for Capt. R. B. D. Blakeney.   Anthony W. Laywood   May 26 2011 - 20103   2011 $134

Association – Bliss, Philip

Paule, George *Life of the Most Reverend and Religious Prelate John Whitgift, Lord Archbishop of Canterbury.* London: printed by Thomas Snodham, 1612. small 4to., pages (viii), 94, (ii), woodcut portrait of Whitgift on titlepage verso, early 21st century retrospective ruled calf binding by CEW, title soiled text block trimmed to printed border and sometimes just inside at top and fore-edge, old f.e.p. corner repaired, early hand has annotated head of blank leaf A1 and final blank leaf N4 armorial bookplate of "James Comerford" on front pastedown, mid 19th century ownership in Philip Bliss's hand on 17th century flyleaf reading "Bodleian Catalogue 1843, p. 62" and at foot of page I signature "P.B.43": and flowerly label, presented by William Minet at foot of front pastedown, from the collection of Christopher Ernest Weston 1947-2010.   Unsworths Booksellers   24 - 34   2011   £450

Association – Blois, Freda

Leslie, Charles Robert *Life and Letters of John Constable, R.A.* London: Chapman & Hall, 1896. New edition; large 4to., half title, frontispiece, illustrations, original white and blue cloth gilt, slightly marked, nice, bookplate of Freda Blois.   Jarndyce Antiquarian Booksellers   CXCI - 139   2011   £70

Association – Blomefield, Francis

Brooke, Ralph *A Discoverie of Certaine Errours Published in Print in Much Commended Britannia 1594 to which is added The Learned Mr. Camden's Answer to His Book and Mr. Brooke's Reply (and) A Second Discoverie of Errours.* Woodman & Lyon, 1724. First edition; main titlepage and titlepage to "A Discoverie" printed red and black, titlepage to "A Second Discoverie" printed black, both subsidiary titlepages printed by Woodman and dated 1723, vi, plate (7) 77 (10) 32 196 pages, contemporary calf, 4to., 230 x 170mm., generous margins (large paper?), bookplates of two Norfolk antiquaries, Francis Blomefield & Bryan Hall, very.   C. P. Hyland   May 26 2011 - 786   2011 $544

Association – Blumenbach, Joseph Friedrich

Du Verney, Joseph Guichard *Tractatus de Organo Auditus Continens Structuram Usum et Morbos Omnium Auris Partium.* Nuremberg: Johann Zieger, 1684. First edition in Latin; 4to., (12) 48 pages, 16 engraved folding plates, 19th century paper wrappers, plate 16 neatly backed, title very lightly soiled, else very good, Joseph Friedrich Blumenbach's copy with his signature on verso of titlepage, in fine morocco backed clamshell box.   Joseph J. Felcone Inc.   Fall Miscellany 2010 - 85   2011 $4800

Association – Bly, J.

Evans, Sebastian *The High History of the Holy Grail.* London: J. M. Dent, 1903. First edition thus; large 8vo., pages xvii, 379, illustrations by Jessie M. King with 23 full page plates, some with red pictorial embellishment + 36 chapter headpieces and gilt black cover and spine illustration on publisher's sky blue cloth, sound decent about very good with slight soiling, slight marks and slight rubbing and slight bumping to covers, endpapers foxed, neat presentation inscription on half title to Duke of Bedford from one J. Bly dated 1903.   Any Amount of Books May 26 2011 - A74369   2011 $755

Association – Boit, Julia Owering

Paget, Violet   1856-1935   *The Story of a Puppet Show: or Prince of the Hundred Soups.* London: T. Fisher Unwin, 1889. Second thousand; color frontispiece and color plates, 4 pages ads, contemporary half vellum, dark green leather label, slightly dulled, good plus, signed Julia Owering Boit, daughter of American artist Edward Darly Boit.   Jarndyce Antiquarian Booksellers   CLXC - 112   2011   £65

Association – Bolland

Chambers, William *Memoir of Robert Chambers with Autobiographic Reminiscences of William Chambers.* Edinburgh: W. & R. Chambers, 1872. Fourth edition; half title, added engraved title with portraits, blue cloth, slightly dulled, stamps and labels of Bolland Collection.   Jarndyce Antiquarian Booksellers   CXCI - 447   2011   £40

MacDonald, George   1824-1905   *Thomas Wingfold, Curate.* London: Chatto & Windus, 1883. Half title, colophon leaf, yellowback, rebound in red binder's cloth, cancelled stamp and label of Bolland Collection.   Jarndyce Antiquarian Booksellers   CXCII - 189   2011   £50

Association – Bond, Charles Watson

MacDonald, George   1824-1905   *A Book of Strife.* London: printed for the author and to be had by Writing to Mr. Hughes 43 Beaufort Street, Chelsea, 1882. Tall 12mo., colophon leaf, original plain red cloth, spine discolored and worn, lacking most of paper label, red cloth box with black leather label, inscribed by author for friend Charles Watson Bond.   Jarndyce Antiquarian Booksellers   CXCII - 223   2011   £500

Association – Bonds, Margaret

Street Scene, American Opera. New York: Chappell, 1948. First edition; 4to., pages 173, printed wrappers, bit of edgewear at top of spine, ownership signature of pianist-composer Margaret Bonds.   Second Life Books Inc.   174 - 295   2011 $500

Association – Bone, Stephen

Bone, Gertrude *Of the Western Isles.* London: T. N. Foulis, 1925. First edition; tall small 4to., original cloth backed pictorial boards, spine label, trifle worn, pages 61, with initial letters and title decorations in grey and 40 woodcuts by Stephen Bone, and maps on endpapers, presentation copy inscribed by artist, Stephen Bone to Margaret Gardiner.   R. F. G. Hollett & Son Antiquarian Booksellers General Catalogue Summer 2010 - 1340   2011   £120

Association – Bonnell, Harvey

Tasso, Torquato 1544-1595 *Jerusalem Delivered.* London: printed for J. Dodsley, 1787. Sixth edition; 214 x 130mm., 2 volumes, handsome contemporary flamed calf, backstrips with wide Greek key roll at head and tail and with six compartments formed by decorative rolls, two of these with a central urn and graceful dangling fronds, two with unusual oval ornament composed of a central floral lozenge encircled first by a garland of leaves and then by a string of beads, each spine with two red morocco labels, one of them a circular volume label, engraved frontispiece by Thomas Stothard in each volume; late 19th century(?) bookplate of Harvey Bonnell (and with evidences of removed bookplate); gift inscription in pencil to Christopher Carter from Herbert Hudson at Wickham Bishops in Essex, dated June 1946, recto of front free endpaper of volume II with two newspaper cuttings about this work dated in 1830's tipped in; vaguest hint of rubbing to joints and corners, occasional minor smudges and other trivial imperfections internally, fine contemporary copy, text remarkably fresh, clean and bright, most attractive bindings especially lustrous and scarcely worn.   Phillip J. Pirages   59 - 60   2011 $750

Association – Bonnell, James

Kemble, Frances Anne 1809-1893   *Journal of Frances Anne Butler.* London: John Murray, 1835. First edition; 2 volumes, slightly later full green calf, gilt spines, blind borders, gilt dentelles, armorial bookplates of James Bonnell, very good, attractive copy.   Jarndyce Antiquarian Booksellers   CLXC - 44   2011   £350

Association – Bonnelle, F. J.

Barnum, Phineas Taylor 1810-1891   *Life of P. T. Barnum Written by Himself. Brought up to 1886.* Buffalo: Courier Co., 1886. First edition; original brick cloth, 361 pages, engravings, this copy inscribed and signed by author to F. J. Bonnelle, near fine, minor fraying to spine tips.   Charles Agvent   2010 Summer Miscellany - 4   2011 $1000

Association – Booth, Robert

Laclos, Pierre Ambroise Francois Choderlos De 1741-1803   *Les Liasions Dangereuses.* Brussels: J. Rosez, 1869. 2 volumes bound as one, pages 99; 291, internally clean and bright, minor chip to half title, contemporary blue black quarter morocco, gilt lettered on spine, original lime green printed wrappers bound in, top edge gilt, marbled boards and endpapers, spine and joints expertly repaired, edges of boards slightly rubbed, front endpapers chipped with some restoration also to front wrapper, Aubrey Beardsley's copy with his ink signature at head of titlepage and presentation inscription from his mother to A. W. King, later inscription from his mother, bookplate of Robert Booth.   Simon Finch Rare Books   Zero - 205   2011   £3500

Association – Boothby, Will

Wharton, Henry   *The History of the Troubles and Tryal of the Most Reverend Father in God and Blessed Martyr, William Laud, Lord Archbishop of Canterbury.* London: R(ichard) Chiswell, 1694-1695. First edition; 4to., (22), 616 (2 ads) pages, frontispiece, titlepage in red and black in, full contemporary brown calf, gilt stamped red leather spine label, raised bands, rebacked, preserving original spine, signature of Will: Boothby and ownership marks on titlepage, bookplate and ink stamp of Spring Hill College Library, very good.   Jeff Weber Rare Books   163 - 26   2011 $500

Association – Borein, Ed

Perkins, Charles E.   *The Phantom Bull.* Boston and New York: Houghton Mifflin Co., 1932. First edition; quarto, small pen and ink drawing on half title and signed "Ed Borein", original decorated red cloth, (6), 70 pages, illustrations very good, tight copy, internally reinforced dust jacket.   Buckingham Books   May 26 2011 - 27022   2011 $2000

Association – Borletti Del'Acqua D'Arosio, Aldo, Count

Daumier, Honore   *Types Parisiens.* Paris: Chez Bauger for La Charivari, 1838-1843. 2 folio volumes, 50 original black and white lithographed prints 260 x 345mm, numbered 1-50, mounted on stubs, lithography by Chez Aubert, bound ca. 1940 in quarter black calf over faux black morocco cloth, gilt tooled borders, gilt decorated spine, with stamp of the prominent Daumier collector Count Aldo Borletti del'Acqua d'Arosio to the verso of each print, remarkable set in superb condition, with only a few prints exhibiting the lightest of spotting to their margins.   David Brass Rare Books, Inc.   May 26 2011 - 01409   2011 $15,000

Association – Bosch, Johann Thomas

Schoepf, Johann David *Materia Medica Americana Potissimum Regni Vegetabilis.* Erlangae: Sumtibus Io. Iac. Palmii, 1787. First edition; 8vo., pages (2), xviii, 170, (4), contemporary quarter sheep, some worming to edges of spine, dark stain to lower third of pages and pastedowns, marginal tear to a leaf, ex-libris Johann Thomas Bosch with signature, the Norman copy.   Raymond M. Sutton, Jr.   May 26 2011 - 51773   2011 $5500

Association – Bottomley, Emily

Prior, Herman *Guide to the Lake District of England.* Windermere: J. Garnett, n.d. circa, 1865. Fifth (nonpareil) edition; 24mo., original black roan gilt, rubbed and spine rather defective, pages viii, 348, vii, folding colored map in front pocket and numerous woodcut vignettes, illustrations and maps, title supplied in facsimile, lacks double sided map in rear pocket, scarce, bookplate of Emily and Gordon Bottomley bequest on flyleaf.   R. F. G. Hollett & Son Antiquarian Booksellers   173 - 935   2011   £85

Association – Bottomley, Gordon

Prior, Herman *Guide to the Lake District of England.* Windermere: J. Garnett, n.d. circa, 1865. Fifth (nonpareil) edition; 24mo., original black roan gilt, rubbed and spine rather defective, pages viii, 348, vii, folding colored map in front pocket and numerous woodcut vignettes, illustrations and maps, title supplied in facsimile, lacks double sided map in rear pocket, scarce, bookplate of Emily and Gordon Bottomley bequest on flyleaf.   R. F. G. Hollett & Son Antiquarian Booksellers   173 - 935   2011   £85

Association – Boulton

MacDonald, George   1824-1905 *The Lost Princess; or the Wise Woman.* Wells, Gardner, Darton & Co., 1895. Half title, frontispiece, illustrations by A. G. Walker, original light olive green cloth blocked in black and gilt, armorial bookplate of Boulton, very good.   Jarndyce Antiquarian Booksellers   CXCII - 185   2011   £120

Association – Bourdillon, Francis

Seneca, Lucius Annaeas *L. Annai Senecae Philosophi Opera Quae Extant Omnia...* Antwerp: Ex Officina Plantiniana Balthazar Moretus, 1652. Folio, (20), xxxvi, 911 pages, frontisportrait, engraved title with portraits, 2 full page engravings, ornamental tailpieces, full contemporary vellum, gilt stamped arabesques on front and rear covers, gilt stamped red morocco spine label, raised bands, front hinge reinforced, lightly soiled, bookplate of Francis Bourdillon, M.A., fine.   Jeff Weber Rare Books   163 - 16   2011 $1250

Association – Bourton, John

Herodotus *The History of Herodotus.* London: printed for D. Midwinter et al, 1737. Third edition; 2 volumes, 8vo., pages xvi, 447 (xvii) + 3 extending engraved maps, (ii), 430, (xviii), contemporary orangey tan calf boards triple rule gilt bordered with broad dentelle inner border of individual small tools, board edges decorative roll gilt, late 19th century 'swirl' 'made' endpapers with pale green block cloth, inner joint strengtheners, all edges original blue swirl/marbled pale blue and white sewn endbands, early 21st century retrospective reback + corners by Chris Weston, little toning and marginal dust soiling, some marginal pencil notes, old leather chipped at edges, contemporary ink inscription "Eliza Spencer" at head of titlepages, verso of volume I marbled endpaper has ms. note by Rev. John Bourton/Banningham Rectory/Norfolk referring to early provenance of Sunderland Library and subsequent purchase at Puttick & Simpson's auction in 1882, from the collection of Christopher Ernest Weston 1947-2010.   Unsworths Booksellers   24 - 109   2011   £400

Association – Boutell, Clarence

Lewis, Clive Staples   1898-1963 *The Screwtape Letters.* New York: Macmillan, July, 1943. Fifth or later edition, sixth printing; bookplate of Clarence "Clip" Boutell, nearly fine in dust jacket with chips at head and foot of spine.   Lupack Rare Books   May 26 2011 - ABE1309855976   2011 $250

Overbury, Thomas *His Wife. With Additions of New Characters...* London: printed or Robert Allot and are to be sold at the signe of the Beare in Paul's Church yard, 1630. Fourteenth impression; full vellum, very good, final few leaves with tissue repair at edges and first two leaves, at top corners, tight book in near fine binding with very good text, bookplate of Clarence "Clip" Boutell.   Lupack Rare Books   May 26 2011 - ABE1296792492   2011 $1500

Association – Bowen, George

Mill, John Stuart   1806-1873 *Principles of Political Economy with Some of Their Applications to Social Philosophy...* London: John W. Parker,, 1852. Third edition; 2 volumes, 8vo., xx, 604, xv, (1), 571, (1) pages, contemporary maroon morocco gilt, double gilt fillets on sides, spines fully gilt in compartments with raised bands and contrasting red and green lettering pieces, marbled edges, fine, late 19th century library of Sir George Bowen, armorial bookplate, ALS presenting this copy to Sir Thomas Jackson.   John Drury Rare Books   153 - 96 2011   £600

Association – Bowlby, Edwin Salvin

Jardine, William *The Naturalist's Library.* Edinburgh: W. H. Lizars, 1845-1846. Second edition; 164 x 122mm., 40 volumes, very attractive contemporary half morocco, handsomely gilt, volumes bound in four different colors to reflect various members of the animal Kingdom (the 14 volumes on birds bound in red, 13 volumes on mammals in dark green, seven volumes on insects in dark blue, six volumes on fish in deep purple), all volumes with gilt decorated raised bands, spines uniformly gilt in compartments with lozenge centerpiece composed of drawer handle stamps and enclosing a small flower, the whole surrounded by triangular scrolling cornerpieces, marbled edges (sides and endpapers not uniform-by design, mammals and fish with watered silk covers, birds and insects with buckram, mammals, fish and insects with tartan endpapers, birds with unusual maze like design); with total of 1360 zoological plates, all but few hand colored, along with 40 engraved frontispiece portraits, 40 engraved titlepages, all but very few of the engravings with original tissue guards, front pastedowns with armorial bookplate of Edward Salvin Bowlby; just the most minor rubbing to leather extremities, slight chafing or soiling here and there to cloth boards, trivial imperfections internally, but an extraordinarily appealing set in very fine condition, bindings especially bright, almost without wear and most pleasing on shelf, text remarkably smooth, clean and fresh, virtually no signs of use. Phillip J. Pirages 59 - 239 2011 $17,500

Association – Boyle, John Theodore

Leyland, John *Views of Ancient Buildings Illustrative of the Domestic Architecture of the Parish of Halifax.* Halifax: R. Leyland & Son, 1879. First edition; oblong folio, original cloth, gilt, top edges little damped, neatly recased, pages xii, plus 25 photo lithographed plates, few edge tears neatly repaired, title little dusty and spotted, small stamps on title and back of final plate, armorial bookplate of John Theodore Boyle (rather soiled and relaid). R. F. G. Hollett & Son Antiquarian Booksellers 177 - 546 2011 £180

Association – Bracken, Viscount

Cecil, Gwendolen *Biographical Studies of the Life and Political, Character of Robert Third Marquis of Salisbury.* London: privately published Hodder & Stoughton, n.d., 1948. Original cream cloth, gilt, pages 96, untrimmed, armorial bookplate of Viscount Bracken of Christchurch on pastedown, another label removed. R. F. G. Hollett & Son Antiquarian Booksellers 175 - 236 2011 £65

Association – Bradley, Bill

Archer, Jeffrey *A Prison Diary.* London: Macmillan, 2003-2004. First editions; Volume two and three only, corners little bumped, thus near fine in near fine or better dust jackets, both volumes inscribed to basketball player and former US Senator Bill Bradley and his wife Ernestine. Between the Covers 169 - BTC 343394 2011 $400

Association – Bradley, Ernestine

Archer, Jeffrey *A Prison Diary.* London: Macmillan, 2003-2004. First editions; Volume two and three only, corners little bumped, thus near fine in near fine or better dust jackets, both volumes inscribed to basketball player and former US Senator Bill Bradley and his wife Ernestine. Between the Covers 169 - BTC 343394 2011 $400

Association – Bradshaw, Jon

Burnett, W. R. *Iron Man.* New York: Dial Press, 1930. First edition; 8vo., pages (8), 312, original blue cloth, spine lettered in gold, upper board with publisher's insignia blocked in blind, top edge dyed red and trimmed, original color pictorial dust jacket by Reindel printed in red and black, dust jacket with few short closed tears, slight soiling to spine, corners slightly chipped, author's presentation inscription for Jon Bradshaw. Simon Finch Rare Books Zero - 212 2011 £300

Association – Brady, E. L.

Smyth, Henry De Wolf *A General Account of the Development of Methods of Using Atomic Energy for Military Purposes Under the Auspices of the United States Government 1940-1945.* United States Army publication authorized as of August, 1945. Pre-publication copy; 263 x 197mm., pages 198, single sheets of litho printed typescript, diagrams in text, original cream wrappers, stapled, signature of E. L. Brady, fine. Simon Finch Rare Books Zero - 145 2011 £2500

Association – Brady, Frederick

Kingsley, Charles 1819-1875 *Out of the Deep...* London: Macmillan, 1885. Half title, 4 pages ads, original grey cloth, bevelled boards, spine slightly dulled, all edges gilt, very good, with slip inserted with inscription from Mrs. Kingsley to Fredk Brady. Jarndyce Antiquarian Booksellers CXCI - 235 2011 £60

Association – Bragg, W. H.

Darwin, Charles Robert 1809-1882 *The Foundations of the Origin of Species, A Sketch Written in 1842...* Cambridge: printed at the University Press, 1909. First printing; 8vo., pages xxii, 53, plus frontispiece and 1 plate, uncut, internally fine, original grey paper covered boards, vellum spine, upper board with text and coat of arms in black, bumped with light shelfwear, presentation copy to Prof. W. H. Bragg, label of H. F. Norman. Simon Finch Rare Books Zero - 141 2011 £450

Association – Brandon, Woodthorpe

Paris, J. A. *Philosophy in Sport.* London: John Murray, 1861. Ninth edition; original green cloth gilt, pages xxvii, 401, woodcut frontispiece and numerous text illustrations, prelims rather foxed, shaped armorial bookplate of Woodthorpe Brandon. R. F. G. Hollett & Sons Antiquarian Booksellers 170 - 498 2011 £85

Association – Brandt, Gwendolen

Junius, Pseud. *Junius Stat Nominius Umbra.* London: printed by T. Bensley for Vernor and Hood et al, 1801. 2 volumes, 8vo., pages (ii) xxxiii-xxxii 274 + engraved titlepage (dated 1797), engraved portrait frontispiece and 10 other engraved portrait plates, v, (iii), 318, (ii) + engraved titlepage, engraved portrait frontispiece and 7 other engraved portrait plates, contemporary straight grained dark blue morocco, fully gilt six compartmented spine with 'liberty cap atop oak leaved staff' centerpieces, lettered & numbered direct in gilt, boards full and brown rule gilt bordered with decorative roll (interweaving front and graded pebbles) within, board edges single rule gilt, turn-ins decorative roll gilt, pink 'made' endpapers, all edges gilt, dark green double core sewn endbands, pale blue silk page markers, foxed, bit rubbed at extremities and touched up with blue dye, small printed booklabel of "Gwendolen Brandt", from the collection of Christopher Ernest Weston 1947-2010. Unsworths Booksellers 24 - 113 2011 £160

Association – Bransom, Paul

Cooper, F. T. *An Argosy of Fables.* New York: Stokes, 1921. Large thick 4to., 485 pages, blue pictorial cloth, slight wear to end of spine, else fine, inscription from artist March 24 1937, illustrations by Paul Bransom with 24 richly colored and very beautiful color plates plus lovely pictorial endpapers. Aleph-Bet Books, Inc. 95 - 116 2011 $400

Association – Brencher, John

Ussher, James *A Body of Divinity, or the Summe and Substance of Christian Religion...* London: M. F. for Tho. Downes and Geo. Badger, 1648. Third edition; folio, pages (xii) 3-451, (xv), 24 + engraved portrait frontispiece, signed "W. Marshall Sculpist 1647", contemporary sprinkled calf, boards double ruled in blind, board edges single rule gilt, all edges rouge with black ink hand written "Ussher" at head of fore-edge, pink & white sewn endbands, evidence of chaining staple at head of fore-edge of upper board, also evidence of later ties, early 1990's calf reback by Chris Weston, spotting and staining (mostly light), small tear to titlepage border repaired with sellotape, old leather marked and bit chipped at edges, near contemporary ink inscription "Roger Mostyn Anno 1685" at head of titlepage and underneath later ink inscription, booklabel of Gloddaeth Library, also ex-libris of Rev. John F. Brencher, his MS mini biography of Ussher on f.e.p. and his signature on reverse, from the collection of Christopher Ernest Weston 1947-2010. Unsworths Booksellers 24 - 54 2011 £450

Association – Brenchley, Julius

Wilkes, Charles *Narrative of the United States Exploring Expedition During the Years 1838, 1839, 1840, 1841, 1842.* Philadelphia: Lea & Blanchard, 1845. First trade edition, Haskell's 'unofficial issue' 2B limited to 1000 copies; Imperial 8vo., pages lx, 434; xvi, 476; xvi, 438; xvi, 539; xvi, 558, 64 steel engraved plates with tissue guards, 2 of which are portraits, 47 steel engraved vignettes, 248 woodcuts and 9 double page copper engraved maps, separate atlas contains 5 large folding copper engraved maps, 1 is hand colored, all in near fine condition; original brown cloth, straight grained pattern, front and back cover have blindstamped three rule border, enclosing blind stamped scroll work rectangular covers have blindstamped three rule border enclosing blindstamped scroll work rectangular border containing blindstamped decorations at top and bottom and having eagle standing on shield with sailing ship in background stamped in center in gold leaf, spine has five blindstamped bands enclosing four panels, fourth having, stamped in gilt, female figure with staff surmounted by liberty cap and holding in one hand an unrolled chart lettered at top, sailing ship in background, lettered in second panel in gold leaf (corners worn, fraying to some ends of spines, cloth unfaded, gilt bright and text mostly very clean, light foxing to plates, offsetting to some double page maps, occasional splits to cloth on edges of spines, volumes solid and with no splitting to hinges, faint blindstamp of the Madistone Museum & Public Library to titlepages, no other markings, exceptional copy, maps in nearly perfect condition, the copy of Julius Brenchley. Raymond M. Sutton, Jr. May 26 2011 - 49406 2011 $7500

Association – Brewer, Luther

Sanborn, F. B. *The Personality of Thoreau.* Boston: Charles E. Goodspeed, 1901. First edition, #373 of 500 copies on French handmade paper; plate, 2 facsimiles of Thoreau's journal, cloth backed boards, bookplate of noted collector Luther A. Brewer of Cedar Rapids Iowa, tipped to front pastedown, spine label darkened and chipped, mild edgewear, very good. Charles Agvent Transcendentalism 2010 - 55 2011 $75

Association – Brewster, C. M.

Crowe, J. A. *History of Painting in Italy. (and) History of Painting in North Italy. (and) Early Flemish Painters.* London: John Murray, 1864-1872. First edition of first two works, second edition of the third; 222 x 144mm., 3 separately published works bound in 6 volumes, uniformly bound in handsome contemporary dark green pebble grain morocco, lavishly gilt, covers with gilt frame formed by multiple plain and decorative rules flanking a central Greek key roll, raised bands, spines heavily gilt in double ruled compartment with Greek key roll at top and bottom, inner dotted frame with scrolling cornerpieces and elongated central fleuron, turn-ins gilt with multiple decorative rules and floral cornerpieces, marbled endpapers, all edges gilt, 148 black and white plates, two of them folding, pencilled ownership inscriptions of C. M. Brewster, fore edge of one upper board just slightly bumped, trivial imperfections internally, but very fine set, sumptuously gilt bindings, especially lustrous and virtually unworn, text and plates showing almost no signs of use.   Phillip J. Pirages   59 - 81   2011 $1500

Association – Briggs, John

Adams, Charlotte *Boys at Home.* London: Routledge, 1857. New edition; original red blindstamped cloth gilt extra, pages 414, with 8 full page tissue guarded woodcuts by John Gilbert, nice, bright copy, contemporary school prize inscription (Wesleyan School, Ulverston: presented to John Briggs, Christmas 1857).   R. F. G. Hollett & Sons Antiquarian Booksellers   170 - 1   2011   £45

Association – Brittin, Lewis Hutchkiss

Morris, William   1834-1896   *The Story of the Glittering Plain.* London: Sold by Reeves & Turner, 1891. One of 200 paper copies out of a total edition of 206 copies; small quarto, (4), 188 pages, printed in golden type, decorative woodcut border and initials, original stiff vellum with wash leather ties, spine lettered in gilt, armorial bookplate of Lewis Hutchkiss Brittin, near fine, housed in gray cloth slipcase,.   David Brass Rare Books, Inc.   May 26 2011 - 01308   2011 $7500

Association – Britton, H.

Bonwick, James *Port Phillip Settlement.* London: Sampson Low, Marston, Sarle & Rivington, 1883. First edition; octavo, original blue cloth, gilt decoration on front cover, x, 537, (1), (- ads) pages, 4 folding facsimiles of letters, one folding facsimile of handwritten newspaper, folding map, double page plate with numerous facsimile, signatures of Men of the Period, 4 full page lithographed views, 42 half page illustrations on 21 lithographed plates, 4 lithographed portraits, color lithograph frontispiece, pencil signature of H. Britton dated 1884 on front endpaper and below of Rod M. Sutherland dated Nv. 1949, occasional light spotting to text, half inch tear to top of spine, mild rubbing to edges, near fine, uncommon.   Charles Agvent   2010 Summer Miscellany - 13   2011 $350

Association – Britwell

Radcliffe, Alexander   *The Ramble an Anti-Heroick Poem. Together with Some Terrestrial Hymns and Carnal Ejaculations.* London: for the author and to be sold by Walter Davis, 1682. First edition; 8vo., pages (xvi), 128, including initial blank Ai, contemporary black morocco, sides panelled in gilt, spine richly gilt in compartments, marbled pastedowns, gilt edges, lightly rubbed, little marginal browning, fine, the Heber(?) Britwell-Hewyard-Bradley Martin, Edwards copy with modern bookplates of H. Bradley Martin and J. O. Edwards.   Simon Finch Rare Books   Zero - 348   2011   £2500

Association – Brockett

Locke, John   1632-1704   *Essay Concerning Humane (Human) Understanding.* London: printed for Tho. Basset and sold by Edw. Mory, 1690. First edition, 2nd issue with cancel titlepage containing inverted "SS" of "Essay" the type ornament composed of 23 pieces, and without Elizabeth Holt's name in imprint, dedication undated, errata uncorrected; folio, (12), 362, (22, contents) pages, pages 287, 296 and 303 misnumbered 269, 294, 230 respectively; contemporary brown mottled calf, boards ruled in blind, spine in six compartments, lettered in gilt on brown calf spine label, edges speckled red, expertly rebacked to style with corners repaired, titlepage is short at fore-edge by half an inch due to stub being turned behind A4, marginal paper flaws on D1, P3 and Dd3, not affecting text, very small marginal hole on Hh, not affecting text, errata corrected by contemporary hand with ink and there are two contemporary ink notes on back free endpaper, Locke's name written in contemporary hand on titlepage as John Lock, previous owner's name Brockett, previous owner's name Samuel Gaskell and previous owner's name Roger Gaskell dated 1813, very clean and crisp, excellent contemporary binding.   Heritage Book Shop   Holiday 2010 - 74   2011 $32,500

Association – Brocklebank, J.

Kirby, Mary *The Discontented Children and How They Were Cured.* London: Grant & Griffith, 1855. First edition; color frontispiece and 2 black and white plates, odd spot, half dark green crushed morocco by Bayntun of Bath, green cloth boards, gilt spine, spine faded to brown, booklabel of J. Brocklebank, slightly torn, top edge gilt, very good.   Jarndyce Antiquarian Booksellers   CLXC - 58   2011   £65

Association – Brodie, William

Thomas A Kempis   1380-1471   *The Christian Pattern.* London: William Rayner, 1738. Old full calf gilt with raised bands and spine label, rubbed and dulled, upper hinge cracked, pages (vi), 518, title in red and black, 22 engraved plates, little occasional browning, very good, armorial bookplate of William Brodie.   R. F. G. Hollett & Son Antiquarian Booksellers   175 - 760   2011   £275

Association – Brodnag, G.

Lactantius, Lucius Coelius Firmianus *Opera quae Exstant... et Commentariis Illustrata a Tho. spark.* Oxonii: E Theatro Sheldoniano, 1684. 8vo., pages (xviii), 912, (ii), 24, 17-38, contemporary speckled calf, boards double rule bordered in blind with stylized 'dahlia' tool in corners, board edges decorative 'zig-zag' roll in blind, turn-ins single ruled in blind, pink and white sewn endbands, early 21st century calf reback by Chris Weston with original decorative red lettering piece gilt relaid, little light spotting, small dampmark in upper corner of first few leaves, old leather scratched and marked, contemporary inscription "E Libris Gui. Brodnag", heraldic bookplate of Montagu George Knight of Chawton, from the collection of Christopher Ernest Weston 1947-2010. Unsworths Booksellers 24 - 28 2011 £250

Association – Brogden, John

Luther, Martin 1483-1546 *A Commentarie Upon the Fifteene Psalmes, Called Psalmi Graduum... (bound with) A Commentarie of M. Doctor Martin Luther upon the Epistle of S. Paul to the Galathians.* London: by Richard Field, 1616. 4to., (4), 296 leaves, black letter, 2 works bound together in 18th century calf, very neatly rebacked retaining original spine label, titlepage of first work soiled, minor dampstains on first few leaves, else very good, armorial bookplate of John Brogden. Joseph J. Felcone Inc. Fall Miscellany 2010 - 79 2011 $2800

Association – Brooke, William

Brathwaite, Richard 1588-1673 *Barnabae Itinerarium or Barnabee's Journal.* J. Harding, 1818. Seventh edition; larger cloth with printed spine label, pages 204, engraved frontispiece, 7 engraved plates, old taped repairs to some hinges and torn leaf, engraved armorial bookplate of William Brooke A.M. R. F. G. Hollett & Son Antiquarian Booksellers 173 - 147 2011 £120

Association – Brooke-Taylor, W. B.

Tapping, Thomas *A Treatise on the Derbyshire Mining Customs and Mineral Court Act 1852 (15 & 16 Vict. CCLXIII) Analytically and Practically Arranged...* Shaw and Sons, 1854. First edition; pages xi, 166, original printed boards, rather rubbed, spine and corners worn, scarce, signature of Arthur G. Taylor and W. B. Brooke-Taylor, successive stewards and barmasters of the Marmote Court. R. F. G. Hollett & Son Antiquarian Booksellers 175 - 1313 2011 £220

Association – Brooks, F. C.

Clarkson, Christopher *The History of Richmond, in the County of York, Including a Description of the Castle Friary, Easeby Abbey and Other Remains of Antiquity in the Neighbourhood.* Richmond: printed by and for T. Bowman at the Albion Press, 1814. 8vo., pages 436 + aquatint frontispiece and 3 other engraved plates, late 19th century dark olive green hard grain half morocco (color fugitive on spine to uniform mid-brown), spine double rule gilt with decorative rolls to flat raised bands and extremities, lettered direct in gilt, 'place & date' gilt direct at foot, boards decorative roll gilt bordered with "Sanspareil" design marbled book cloth sides, "Sanspareil Peacock swirl 'made' endpapers, edges uncut, maroon & primrose mutilcore made applied endbands, browned and spotted in places, spine and edges faded, just touch rubbed, ink inscription, "Coll & perf. F.C.B. Decr. 1879" (Captain F. C. Brooks of Ufford, Suffolk), ink inscription "James Hutchinson/Brigg/1814", heavily annotated by way of ink marginalia and by sewn-in folding sheets with historical agricultural gleanings, from the collection of Christopher Ernest Weston 1947-2010. Unsworths Booksellers 24 - 79 2011 £600

Association – Brooks, Ley

West, Thomas *A Guide to the Lakes in Cumberland, Westmorland and Lancashire.* Kendal: W. Pennington, 1812. Tenth edition; old half calf gilt, rather worn, hinges cracked, pages vi, (ii), 311, uncut, complete with extending hand colored map frontispiece (little browned), armorial bookplate of Rev. Ley Brooks (of Mayfield, Derby). R. F. G. Hollett & Son Antiquarian Booksellers 173 - 1184 2011 £85

Association – Brougham, Henry

Wallace, Robert *Elements of Geometry or a New and Compendious Demonstration of the First six books of Euclid...* Glasgow: Richard Griffin and Co. and London: Thomas Tegg, 1825. First edition; 12mo., pages (iv) blank, viii, 88, 2 folding plates, (4) blank, blue ribbon bookmark attached, occasional spotting but fresh copy, red morocco, upper and lower boards decorated in gilt with gilt lettering and decoration to spine and all edges gilt, blue endpapers, slightly rubbed at extremities, slight dampstaining to front endpapers, bookplate and label to front pastedown and traces of bookplate to front free endpaper, presentation inscription to initial blank, news cutting about Henry Brougham, loosely inserted, excellent copy. Simon Finch Rare Books Zero - 126 2011 £225

Association – Brown

Dibdin, Charles 1745-1814 *Observations on a Tour through Almost the Whole of England and a Considerable Part of Scotland, in a Series of Letters.* London: published by G. Goulding etc. circa, 1803. 2 volumes bound as 1, 4to., pages 404 + 26 engraved plates; 407 (i) + 34 engraved plates, extending table of distances in Scotland, contemporary straight grained crimson morocco, spine fully gilt in religious sense with cross, chalice and stylised lily tools, lettered direct in gilt and 'dated' at foot, boards double rule gilt bordered with decorative roll (linked looped-leaf), within, board edges decorative roll gilt, turn-ins decorative roll gilt, mauvish brown sugar paper 'made' endpapers, all edges gilt, dark green double core sewn endbands, dark blue silk page marker, offsetting from plates, bit of foxing, spine bit darkened, slightly rubbed at extremities and some scratches to boards, evidence of removal of two early bookplates, armorial bookplate of "Brown", from the collection of Christopher Ernest Weston 1947-2010. Unsworths Booksellers 24 - 86 2011 £550

Association – Brown, J. Allen

Mello, J. Magens *The Dawn of Metallurgy.* The Institute, 1889. Original wrappers, pages 26, with 2 pages of illustrations and text drawing, author's copy, so stamped and inscribed by J. Allen Brown to H. Swainston Cowper. R. F. G. Hollett & Son Antiquarian Booksellers 177 - 572 2011 £30

Association – Brown, Lucy Madox

Scott, William Bell *The Year of the World: a Philosophical Poem on "Redemption from the Fall".* Edinburgh: William Tait, 1846. First edition; original green cloth, lettered in gilt, blocked in blind, inscribed by author for Miss Lucy Madox Brown, further signed presentation inscription from W. M. Rossetti. Jarndyce Antiquarian Booksellers CXCI - 486 2011 £750

Association – Brown, Paul

Downey, Fairfax *Dogs of Destiny.* New York: Scribner, 1949. (A); 8vo., cloth, 186 pages, fine in frayed dust jacket, warmly inscribed to Scribner editor with fine drawing of dog and inscribed by Downey as well, scarce title, special copy inscribed by Brown and Downey with drawing by Brown. Aleph-Bet Books, Inc. 95 - 124 2011 $800

Association – Brownlee, Leigh

Andrea De Nerciat, Andre Robert *Felicia ou Mes Fredaines, Orne de Figures en taille Douce.* Londres: Paris: Cazin, 1782. First edition; 4 parts bound in 2, 18mo., pages (iv), 160, (iv), 161-352; (iv), 204, (iv), 205-396, with 24 plates by Elluin after Borel, one supplied from another, slightly later copy, apres la lettre, the others all avant la lettre, initial blanks to parts 1 and 3, short tear to margin of volume II A1, otherwise internally fine, all edges gilt, mid 19th century full morocco, gilt filleting to boards, gilt decoration and lettering to spines, marbled endpapers by Hardy, firm, bright with very light negligible shelfwear, bookplates of Leigh D. Brownlee to each volume. Simon Finch Rare Books Zero - 409 2011 £5000

Association – Bruce, Clarence

Noel, E. B. *First Steps to Rackets.* London: Mills & Boon, 1926. First edition; octavo, 136, 16 ads pages, plates, green cloth, slight bump on front board, very good or better, without dust jacket, inscribed by one of the co-authors, Clarence Bruce for George Standing. Between the Covers 169 - BTC342222 2011 $650

Association – Bruce, Elizabeth

Wells, Herbert George 1866-1946 *The Shape of Things to Come.* London: Hutchinson & Co., 1933. First edition; ix, 13-432 pages (+ 12 page catalog), large 8vo., inscribed by author for Elizabeth Bruce, original blue cloth in dust jacket, spine slightly rubbed and 4 inch closed crack and small chip, dust jacket rather worn with chipping at folds and some loss, also some poorly executed restoration of original color. Any Amount of Books May 26 2011 - A76605 2011 $461

Association – Bruningen, M.

Florilegium Diversorum Epigrammatum Veterum, in Septem Libros Diversum... Geneva: E. Estienne, H. Fuggeri typographus, 1566. 4to., (4), 539 (=545, pages 283-288 bis), (35) pages, device on titlepage, later Dutch vellum over pasteboard, yapp edges, fine, clean, large copy, inscription "M. Bruningen 29 June 1657), from the library of the Earls of Macclesfield at Shirburn Castle. Maggs Bros. Ltd. 1440 - 234 2011 £2200

Association – Brunner, John

Asimov, Isaac 1920-1992 *Isaac Asimov, First Visit to Britain 1974.* London: Aardvaark House/Steve Odell, First edition; wrappers, 8vo., pages 18, photos, illustrated wrappers, fine, signed presentation from author for Margery and John Brunner. Any Amount of Books May 29 2011 - A66921 2011 $408

Association – Brunner, Margery

Asimov, Isaac 1920-1992 *Isaac Asimov, First Visit to Britain 1974.* London: Aardvaark House/Steve Odell, First edition; wrappers, 8vo., pages 18, photos, illustrated wrappers, fine, signed presentation from author for Margery and John Brunner.   Any Amount of Books   May 29 2011 - A66921 2011 $408

Association – Bubb, James

Swift, Jonathan 1667-1745 *Travels into Several Remote Nations of the World.* printed for Benj. Motte, 1726. Mixed set, the first volume being from the AA (second) edition and the second volume from the B (third edition); frontispiece in second state and 6 further plates, soiled and spotted in places, occasional staining, 19th century ownership stamp of James Bubb on two leaves and one plate in volume i, early ink sketch of Gulliver's ship on another place in that volume, pages xii, 148, (6), 164; (vi) 154 (8), (155)-353, (1), 8vo., modern sprinkled calf, spines with five raised bands, black and green lettering pieces, sound.   Blackwell Rare Books   B166 - 105 2011   £2500

Association – Buccleuch, Mary Montagu Douglas Scott, Duchess of

Les-Milne, James *Roman Mornings.* London: Allan Wingate, 1956. First edition; 8vo. pages 148 14 plates, presentation copy, boldly signed by author for Mary(Molly) Montagu Douglas Scott, Duchess of Buccleuch (1990-1993), very good in tatty torn and rubbed very good- dust jacket.   Any Amount of Books   May 29 2011 - A74985 2011 $230

Seago, Edward *With Capricorn to Paris.* London: Collins, 1956. First edition; 8vo., pages 141, frontispiece and 7 plates, several illustrations in text, signed presentation from author for Mary (Molly) Montagu Douglas Scott, Duchess of Buccleuch (1900-1993), very good in very good used dust jacket little chipped and nicked at edges with only very minor loss and still presentable.   Any Amount of Books   May 29 2011 - A72902 2011 $272

Association – Buchanan, Edna

Naked Came the Manatee. New York: Putnam, 1996. First edition; fine in fine dust jacket, signed by all authors on single tipped in leaf, including Carl Hiaasen, Elmore Leonard, John Dufresne, Dave Barry, Vicki Hendricks, Edna Buchanan, Les Standiford and James W. Hall, etc. Ken Lopez Bookseller   154 - 5 2011 $200

Association – Bucher, Frau

Capote, Truman 1924-1985 *Observations.* London: Weidenfeld and Nicholson, 1959. First English edition, with signed letter from photographer, Richard Avedon to Frau Bucher; folio, pages 152, 104 black and white photos printed in gravure, design by Alexey Brodovitch, original white paper covered boards printed in grey, lightly rubbed, original white paper covered board slipcase, printed in red, blue and grey, lightly rubbed and soiled with little wear to edges, with TLS to Frau Bucher.   Simon Finch Rare Books   Zero - 504 2011   £550

Association – Bucherei, Alfred Bresslauers

Willis, Alfred E. *Illustrated Physiognomy.* Chicago: n.p., 1882. Numerous illustrations, contemporary half blue cloth, label of Alfred Bresslauers Bucherei.   Jarndyce Antiquarian Booksellers   CXCI - 620 2011   £40

Association – Bulkley, Edmund

Bible. English - 1904 *A Book of Songs and Poems from the Old Testament and The Apocrypha.* Ashendene Press, 1904. One of 150 copies on paper (there were also 25 printed on vellum); 190 x 135mm., 62, (1) pages, original limp vellum, gilt titling on spine, printed in red and black, hand painted blue initials by Graily Hewitt, woodcut bookplate of Edmund Bulkley; vellum binding with usual very slight rumpling and variation in color becasue of grain, fine copy nevertheless, beautiful internally.   Phillip J. Pirages   59 - 75 2011 $2400

Association – Bull, J.

Britton, John *A Brief Memoir of the Life and Writings of John Britton.* London: printed by J. Moyes, 1825. Half title, titlepage, dedication, 44 pages text, 2 page catalog, original boards, paper label on front board, marked and rubbed, hinges splitting, booklabel of Anne and F. G. Renier, inscribed presentation from author to J. Bull.   Jarndyce Antiquarian Booksellers   CXCI - 76 2011   £125

Association – Bulwer Lytton, Rosina

Landon, Letitia Elizabeth *The Improvisatrice; and Other Poems.* London: Hurst, Robinson & Co., 1824. Second edition; frontispiece and engraved title and little spotted, additional printed title, contemporary half calf, spine ruled and with devices in gilt, tan leather label, following inner hinge cracking, bit rubbed and worn, good sound copy, signed presentation copy, pasted to leading pastedown, engraved presentation label completed in ink "to Rosina Lytton Bulwer from L.E.L. 1831", also with later booklabel of Kenneth Rae.   Jarndyce Antiquarian Booksellers   CLXC - 74 2011   £225

Association – Bulwer, Henry Lytton Earle

Lytton, Edward George Earle Bulwer-Lytton, 1st Baron 1803-1873 *The Last Days of Pompeii.* London: Richard Bentley, 1834. First edition; 210 x 130mm., volume 1 lacking half title, 3 volumes, publisher's drab paper boards backed with maroon muslin, flat spines with original printed paper labels, edges untrimmed, housed in red buckram chemise, inside very handsome red morocco backed case, its spine designed to appear as three attractively found volumes with raised bands and gilt compartments filled with interlacing floral vines, ALS by apparently written by author's elder brother, the diplomat, Sir Henry Lytton Earle Bulwer to his banker, 19th century armorial bookplate of William Williamson Willink, each volume with morocco bookplate of Estelle Doheny; paper boards bit soiled (one cover with slight dampstain), minor wear at joints and extremities, isolated trivial smudges internally, otherwise excellent unsophisticated set, especially clean and fresh, extremely handsome. Phillip J. Pirages 59 - 259 2011 $950

Association – Burd, L.

Airay, Christopher *Fasciculus Praeceptorum Logicorum: In Gratiam Juventutis Academiae (sic)...* Oxford: Henry Hall, 1660. Title within arched woodcut border, woodcut Porphyrian Tree on verso of *4, lacking initial leaf, probably blank, fore-edge of title brittle, pages (vi), 224, 12mo. in 8s, contemporary sheep, worn, loss to surface leather, rebacked, some contemporary underlinings and few emendations to text, author's name added in MS. on title and date altered to 1679, this being date of an ownership inscription at inside front cover but name indecipherable thanks to wormhole, below this name of L. Burd dated 1890 with his large armorial bookplate below stamp of Repton School. Blackwell Rare Books B166 - 1 2011 £750

Association – Burdekin, Katherine

Doolittle, Hilda *Hippolytus Temporizes. a Play in Three Acts.* Boston and New York: Houghton Mifflin, 1927. First edition; 8vo, pages (x) 139, uncut, signed presentation from author to Murray Constantine (Katherine Burdekin), neat HD obituary press cutting inserted, patterned paper covered boards, slightly mottled, black cloth spine slightly faded/ slightly sunned, endpapers slightly foxed, very good in near very good slipcase with printed label. Any Amount of Books May 29 2011 - A40498 2011 $221

Association – Burden, W. A. M.

Hawthorne, Nathaniel 1804-1864 *A Wonder Book.* London: New York and Toronto: Hodder & Stoughton Ltd., 1922. One of 600 copies signed by artist, this #370; 290 x 225mm., viii, 206, (2) pages, very attractive red three quarter morocco, raised bands, spine handsomely gilt in compartments formed by plain and decorative rules, quatrefoil centerpiece surrounded by densely scrolling cornerpieces, sides and endleaves of rose colored linen, top edge gilt, 24 colored plates, 16 of them tipped on, other illustrations in text, all by Arthur Rackham; morocco bookplate of W. A. M. Burden; perhaps breath of rubbing to joints and extremities (if one is determined to find it), faint spots on one cover, but exceptionally fine copy in handsome binding, bright, fresh and clean inside and out, volume II the more impressive because its greater thickness provides a larger area to show off its decorative gilt. Phillip J. Pirages 59 - 289 2011 $2000

Shakespeare, William 1564-1616 *The Tempest.* London: William Heinemann/New York: Doubleday & Co., 1926. One of 520 copies (this # 341) signed by artist; 290 x 230mm., xiii, (i), 185, (1) pages, very attractive three quarter morocco, raised bands, spine handsomely gilt in compartments formed by plain and decorative rules, quatrefoil centerpiece surrounded by densely scrolling corner pieces, sides and endleaves of rose colored linen, top edge gilt, mostly unopened; with pictorial titlepage, black and white illustrations, 21 color plates, as called for, by Arthur Rackham, all tipped on and with letterpress guards; morocco bookplate of W. A. M. Burden, very slight darkening to spine and leather edges, just hint of shelfwear, otherwise fine, virtually pristine internally. Phillip J. Pirages 59 - 294 2011 $2250

Swinburne, Algernon Charles 1837-1909 *The Springtime of Life.* London: William Heinemann, 1918. One of 76 copies signed by author (this copy #369); 287 x 2 30mm., ix, (i), 132, (2) pages, very attractive red leather morocco, raised bands, spine handsomely gilt in compartments formed by plain and decorative rules, quatrefoil centerpiece surrounded by densely scrolling cornerpieces, sides and endleaves of rose colored linen, top edge gilt, numerous black and white illustrations, 9 color plates by Arthur Rackham, as called for, all tipped onto brown paper with letterpress guards, morocco bookplate of W. A. M. Burden; just hint of offsetting from brown mounting paper, otherwise very fine, bright, fresh and clean, inside and out, only most trivial imperfections. Phillip J. Pirages 59 - 296 2011 $1600

Association – Burford, William

Wilbur, Richard *Things of this World.* New York: Harcourt Brace, 1956. First edition; signed by William S. Burford with a few of his notes in text, small stain front flyleaf, near fine in very good dust jacket with some rubbing, sunning and wear. Ken Lopez Bookseller 154 - 242 2011 $150

Association – Burgoyne, J.

Drake, Daniel *Natural and Statistical View or Picture of Cincinnati and the Miami Country.* Cincinnati: Looker and Wallace, 1815. First edition; 2 engraved folding maps (foxed, tear to inside lower corner of each map), 12mo., pages xii, (13)-251, (4), contemporary tree calf, few old abrasions, clear sealant reinforces outer hinges, bookplate removed, browning and soiling to endpapers, 2 old pictures pasted on front blank pages, pages tanned, some foxing to back pages, old clipping glued to rear pastedown, the copy of J. Burgoyne Jr. dated 1855, and H. Hall, Cincinnati with his red stamp. Raymond M. Sutton, Jr. May 26 2011 - 55852 2011 $1350

Association – Burkitt, E.

Cervantes Saavedra, Miguel De 1547-1616 *The History of the Valorous and Witty Knight Errant, Don Quixote of the Mancha.* London: R. Scot, T. Basset, J. Wright, R. Chiswell, 1675. 1672. Third English edition; 4to., (8), 173, (5), 138-214, 216-244, 244-273 ff., complete, full calf, blind-stamped Greek key and trifolium border design, gilt stamped red leather spine label, all edges gilt, rebacked, corners showing, signature of Eliz: Burkitt on titlepage, very good. Jeff Weber Rare Books 163 - 21 2011 $5000

Association – Burling, E. C.

Crane, Stephen 1871-1900 *Maggie.* New York: D. Appleton, 1896. First hardcover edition, first issue with titlepage Printed in upper and lower case; decorated tan buckram stamped in black and red, ownership signature of artist E. C. Burling, very good, little surface spotting, slight darkening of pale cloth, light abrasion to blank spot on titlepage, few dog ears, tight, clean text. Lupack Rare Books May 26 2011 - ABE4707625697 2011 $300

Association – Burne-Jones, Philip

Ros, Amanda McKittrick *Irene Iddesleigh.* Belfast: 1897. First edition; 189 pages, errata slip, initialled by author, green cloth, spine bit darkened and canted, otherwise nice, Philip Burne-Jones's copy, signed by him on endpaper and later inscribed by him to "Fred. (E.F.?) Benson, tipped in brief one sentence ALS from author to Burne-Jones. Joseph J. Felcone Inc. Fall Miscellany 2010 - 103 2011 $475

Association – Burns, John

Trollope, Anthony 1815-1882 *How the "Mastiffs" Went to Iceland.* London: Virtue and Co., 1878. First edition; 4to., half title, frontispiece map and full page illustrations, 2 silver print photos, original blue cloth, bevelled boards, gilt, slight rubbing but nice, tight copy, all edges gilt, inscribed "R. Admiral A. Phillimore with Mr. John Burns' kind regards, from Castle Wemyss Jany 21 1874". Jarndyce Antiquarian Booksellers CXCI - 583 2011 £750

Association – Burroughs, John

In Nature's Laboratory. N.P.: n.d. circa, 1916. One of a very small number of copies printed for private distribution by authors; folio, 44 original mounted photos, original suede over padded boards, signed by Thomas A. Edison, John Burroughs and Henry S. Firestone. Heritage Book Shop Booth A12 51st NY International Antiquarian Book Fair April 8-10 2011 - 50 2011 $8000

Association – Burroughs, William

Charters, Ann *The Portable Beat Reader.* New York: Viking, 1992. First edition; 600+ pages, fine in fine dust jacket, exceptional copy, this copy belonged to Nelson Lyon, inscribed to him or signed and dated by William Burroughs, Allen Ginsberg, Gregory Corso, Ed Sanders, Michael McClure and Anne Waldman. Ken Lopez Bookseller 154 - 12 2011 $1250

Association – Burton, Henrietta

Morgan, Sydney Owenson 1776-1859 *O'Donnel. A National Tale.* London: Henry Colburn, 1815. New edition; 3 volumes, half titles, 9 pages ads volume III, contemporary full tan calf, spines gilt in compartments, green leather labels, spines slightly darkened, slight rubbing, armorial bookplates of Henrietta Burton, good plus. Jarndyce Antiquarian Booksellers CLXC - 535 2011 £280

Association – Bury, J. B.

Galiffe, Jacques Augustin *Italy and His Inhabitants, an Account of a Tour in that Country in 1816 and 1817.* London: John Murray, 1820. First edition; half titles, errata slips in volumes 1 and 2, closed tear on 2 H4 of volume 1, xvi,4 53, (1); xv, 475, (1) pages, 19th century cloth backed marbled boards, spines lettered gilt, bookplates of J. B. and Michael Bury, nice, clean copy. Anthony W. Laywood May 26 2011 - 21007 2011 $461

Association – Bury, Michael

Galiffe, Jacques Augustin *Italy and His Inhabitants, an Account of a Tour in that Country in 1816 and 1817.* London: John Murray, 1820. First edition; half titles, errata slips in volumes 1 and 2, closed tear on 2 H4 of volume 1, xvi,4 53, (1); xv, 475, (1) pages, 19th century cloth backed marbled boards, spines lettered gilt, bookplates of J. B. and Michael Bury, nice, clean copy. Anthony W. Laywood May 26 2011 - 21007 2011 $461

Association – Bushnell, G. H.

Allen, Frank J. *The Great Church Towers of England.* Cambridge: Cambridge University Press, 1932. First edition; 4to., xi, 305 pages, 52 monochrome plates, original publisher's brown cloth lettered gilt at spine, handsome very good+ copy wit minor rubbing, ownership signature of Professor G. H. Bushnell (1903-1978), with his bookplate and 2 substantial signed handwritten letters from Allen to him loosely inserted.   Any Amount of Books   May 29 2011 - A675761 2011 $213

Stephenson, Mill *A List of Monumental Brasses in the British Isles and Appendix.* Ashford and London: privately printed by Headley Brothers, 1926-1938. 8vo., original publisher's blue cloth lettered gilt on spine and front cover, pages xvi, 849, ownership signature of Professor G. H. Bushnell, clipped signature of Stephenson tipped in, and 1 page signed letter from him to G. H. S. Bushnell loosely inserted, faint rubbing, very good+.   Any Amount of Books   May 29 2011 - A49466 2011 $272

Wauchope, Robert *Handbook of Middle American Indians.* Austin: University of Texas Press, First editions; small 4to., volumes 1-16, al but 5 and 6 have jackets, clean, very good+ copies in mostly very good dust jackets, some with slight rubbing and toning and occasional light wear, 6000+ pages, illustrations, maps, plans, diagrams, from the library of Professor G. H. Bushnell, Curator of the Cambridge University Museum of Archeology and Ethnology.   Any Amount of Books   May 26 2011 - A49503 2011 $587

Willis, Robert *The Architectural History of the University of Cambridge and of the Colleges of Cambridge and Eton.* Cambridge: Cambridge University Press, 1886. First edition thus; 4 volumes including the slimmer atlas/plans volume, small 4to., cxxiv, (4), 630 pages, 19 plates, 5 folding, illustrations; xiii, (4), 726 pages, 32 plates, 18 folding, 2 colored, illustrations; xi, 722 pages, 5 plates, 2 folding illustrations; vi pages, 29 pans, 27 folding, 12 with overlays, some hand colored, clean, sound, very good set with very slight rubbing, corners slightly bumped and faint shelf wear, original publisher's quarter buckram and green cloth lettered gilt at spine, bookplate of Professor G. H. Bushnell (1903-1978) Curator of the Cambridge University Museum of Archaeology and Ethnology.   Any Amount of Books   May 26 2011 - A49502 2011 $503

Association – Butler, Thomas

Hargrove, William *History and Description of the Ancient City of York...* York: published and sold by Wm. Alexander, 1818. 2 volumes, 8vo., pages (iii)-xvi, (17)-396 397*-412*, (397)-407 (iii) + engraved frontispiece and 3 other engraved plates; iv, (5)-688, (ii) + engraved frontispiece, an extending hand colored plan and 6 other engraved plates, this copy extra illustrated by the inclusion of Volume I - 16 pages of text and 8 engraved plates between pages xvi and (17) and volume 2 - engraved plate facing page 522 and tipped-in slip with view of gatehouse to Archbishop's palace at Bishopthorpe facing page 518, all additions except the last slip have been taken from James Storer's History and Antiquities of the Cathedral Churches of Great Britain" volume 4 (London 1818), contemporary polished maroon calf, four flat raised band spine ruled in gilt with massed 'intersecting circles' pallet in compartments, lettered and numbered direct in gilt, boards double rule gilt bordered and 'intersecting broken waves' roll within, centrally a large panel 'straight grain' tooled, board edges decorative roll gilt, turn-ins 'intersecting broken waves' roll gilt, 'Spanish' 'made' endpapers, dark blue and white sewn endbands, dark blue silk page markers, some light spotting, split at fold of one extending plate, volume I repaired at head of spine, front joint of volume 2 cracking a bit, little rubbing at extremities, spines lightly sunned, signed binding by Douglas, bookbinder, Blackburn with his paper ticket, printed label of Thomas Butler, from the collection of Christopher Ernest Weston 1947-2010.   Unsworths Booksellers   24 - 106 2011   £450

Association – Bynum, Lindley

Venegas, Miguel *Juan Maria de Salvatierra of the Company of Jesus: Missionary in the Province of New Spain and Apostolic Conqueror of the Californias.* Cleveland: Arthur H. Clark Co., 1929. First edition, one of 755 copies; 350 pages, illustrations, maps, facsimiles, portraits, red cloth, gilt, slight rubbing to spine ends, fine, presentation copy signed by editor, Marguerite Eyer Wilbur to author Lindley Bynum.   Argonaut Book Shop   Recent Acquisitions Summer 2010 - 218 2011 $275

Association – Byshopp, Cecil

Cooper, W. D. *The History of South America...* London: printed for E. Newbery, 1789. First edition; 16mo., frontispiece, (12), pages 168, frontispiece, 5 engraved plates, full brown green calf with plain leather, gilt lettered spine with 7 gold bands, sound, clean very good copy with few marks to leather, front endpaper excised, bookplate of one Cecil Byshopp and a note dated 1791 in neat sepia ink about gifting of book from Katherine Byshopp, first blank has modern neat name, plates and text noticeably clean and bright.   Any Amount of Books   May 26 2011 - A66548 2011 $587

Association – Byshopp, Katherine

Cooper, W. D. *The History of South America...* London: printed for E. Newbery, 1789. First edition; 16mo., frontispiece, (12), pages 168, frontispiece, 5 engraved plates, full brown green calf with plain leather, gilt lettered spine with 7 gold bands, sound, clean very good copy with few marks to leather, front endpaper excised, bookplate of one Cecil Byshopp and a note dated 1791 in neat sepia ink about gifting of book from Katherine Byshopp, first blank has modern neat name, plates and text noticeably clean and bright. Any Amount of Books   May 26 2011 - A66548   2011 $587

Association – Cabling, Susan

Remarque, Erich Maria *Heaven Has No Favourites.* London: Hutchinson, 1961. First edition; 8vo., pages 254, signed presentation from author to Susan Cabling (?) Porto Rono 4th Sept. 1961, very slight lean, otherwise very good in slightly used and slightly nicked, near very good dust jacket.   Any Amount of Books   May 29 2011 - A75622   2011 $298

Association – Cabot, J. Elliot

Emerson, Ralph Waldo   1803-1882   *Letters and Social Aims.* Boston: Osgood,, 1876. First edition; original terra cotta cloth, signature mark N present on page 209, Myerson A34.1.a., correct readings on page 308, this copy inscribed and signed by author for J. Elliot Cabot, rear hinge broken, front hinge ready to go with some external splitting there as well, spine tips frayed.   Charles Agvent Transcendentalism 2010 - 14   2011 $20,000

Association – Caffrey, F. R.

Marcet, Jane Haldimand *Conversations on Political Economy; in Which the Elements of that Science are Familiarly Explained.* London: Longman, Hurst, Rees, Orme, & Brown, 1827. Sixth edition; 12mo., expertly & sympathetically rebound in half olive green cloth, marbled boards, black leather label, signed F. R. Caffrey in contemporary hand on title, very good.   Jarndyce Antiquarian Booksellers   CLXC - 225   2011   £85

Association – Caldecott, Randolph

Keble, John   *The Christian Year: Thoughts in Verse for the Sundays & Holydays Throughout the Year.* Oxford: James Parker & Co., 1868. Half title, black morocco, slightly rubbed, all edges gilt, very good, signed presentation from Randolph Caldecott, 6th Feb. 1869 for sister Sophia Caldecott.   Jarndyce Antiquarian Booksellers   CXCI - 439   2011   £150

Association – Caldecott, Sophia

Keble, John   *The Christian Year: Thoughts in Verse for the Sundays & Holydays Throughout the Year.* Oxford: James Parker & Co., 1868. Half title, black morocco, slightly rubbed, all edges gilt, very good, signed presentation from Randolph Caldecott, 6th Feb. 1869 for sister Sophia Caldecott.   Jarndyce Antiquarian Booksellers   CXCI - 439   2011   £150

Association – Calegari, Ninive Clements

Eggers, Dave   *Teachers Have It Easy.* New York: New Press, 2005. First edition; signed by Eggers and co-authors Daniel Moulthrop and Ninive Clements Calegari, fine in fine dust jacket, uncommon.   Ken Lopez Bookseller   154 - 48   2011 $200

Association – Callahan, Eleanor

Greenough, Sarah   *Harry Callahan.* Washington: National Gallery of Art, 1996. First edition; 4to., pages 199, copiously illustrated in color and black and white, 2 invites to exhibition at Philadelphia Museum of Art (1986) loosely inserted, signed presentation from author to "Fat Matt", also signed to Fat Matt by Eleanor Callahan on page 95, fine in fine dust jacket.   Any Amount of Books   May 29 2011 - A75423   2011 $272

Association – Calthorpe, Somerset G.

Lawrence, George Alfred   *Sword and Gown.* London: John W. Parker & Son, 1859. First edition; author's name written in ink on titlepage, contemporary green morocco grained half calf, lined in gilt, raised bands, gilt compartments, booklabel of S.G. C. with signature of Somerset G. Calthorpe, very good.   Jarndyce Antiquarian Booksellers   CXCI - 250   2011   £125

Association – Camden, Lord

Grose, Francis   1731-1791   *The Antiquities of England and Wales.* London: S. Hooper, 1773-1776. Supplement 1787; 4 volumes, folio, original or contemporary full leather, plus 2 volumes supplement dated 1787, bookplates of Lord Camden and also bookplates of the Eaton College Library, volume 1 has 53 half page and 13 full page engravings, volume 2 has 87 half page and 7 full page engravings, volume 3 has 105 half page and 13 full page engravings; volume 4 has 89 half page and 10 full page engravings, volume 5 has 18 half page and 17 full page engravings plus 31 half page maps hand colored in outline, volume 6 has 100 half page and 21 full page engravings and 20 half page maps, bindings very good with strong joints and gilt decorations on covers and spines, inside has foxing to some pages and some pages have some light browning, good+.   Barnaby Rudge Booksellers   Travel and Exploration - 019970   2011 $1900

Association – Campbell, H. D.

Addresses, Petitions, etc. from the Kings and Chiefs of Sudan (Africa) and the Inhabitants of Sierra Leone to His Late Majesty, King William the Fourth and His Excellency. London: privately printed, 1838. First edition; 8vo., pages ii 59, original green textured cloth boards, paper label to upper board showing a few marks and light fading, little dust soiling (heavier to front endpapers), and faint age browning, tiny tear to margin of title, binding loosening just slightly, sides rubbed, upper hinge cracking, gilt stamps of BMS Library to upper board, sellotaped shelf label to spine, inscription presented by Lt. Colonel H. D. Campbell, presented to Lord Bishop of London.   J. & S. L. Bonham Antiquarian Booksellers   Africa 4/20/2011 - 8065 2011   £250

Association – Campbell, John Lorne

MacLellan, Angus *Stories from South Uist.* London: Routledge and Kegan Paul, 1961. First edition; original cloth, gilt, dust jacket, pages xxix, 254, portrait, presentation copy inscribed by translator, John Lorne Campbell.   R. F. G. Hollett & Son Antiquarian Booksellers   175 - 884 2011   £45

Association – Campbell, Miss

More, Hannah 1745-1833 *Christian Morals.* London: T. Cadell & W. Davies, 1813. First edition; 2 volumes, slight spotting, uncut in original blue boards, brown paper spines, slightly chipped with hinges splitting, paper labels, good plus copy as originally issued, inscription "Miss Campbell".   Jarndyce Antiquarian Booksellers   CLXC - 518 2011   £90

Association – Camrose, William Ewert, Baron

Gronow, Rees Howell 1794-1865 *The Reminiscences and Recollections of Captain Gronow, Being Anecdotes of the Camp Court, Clubs, and Society 1810-1860.* London: John C. Nimmo, 1889. One of 875 copies (this #10); 265 x 170 mm., 2 volumes extended to 4, especially lovely contemporary crimson crushed morocco, very lavishly gilt by Tout (stamp signed) covers with wide, elaborate gilt frames in the style of Derome, this intricate design rich with fleurons, volutes, curls, festoons an small floral tools, raised bands, spine gilt in double ruled compartments with central cruciform ornament sprouting curling leaves and flowers from its head and tail, these swirls accented with dotted rules and small tools filling the compartments, very wide turn-ins with complex curling botanical decoration, silk endleaves with tiny gold floral sprays, all edges gilt, frontispiece, 24 plates, all in two states as called for, one proof before letters on plate paper, other with captions on Whatman paper and colored by hand, extra illustrated with 227 plates, primarily portraits, 18 of these in color, armorial bookplate of William Ewert Baron Camrose pasted over bookplate of William Morris; hint of rubbing to corners, mild shelfwear, occasional minor foxing affecting inserted plates and adjacent leaves (as well as a small handful of other pages), quite handsome set, clean and fresh internally, sumptous bindings in fine condition, lustrous and virtually unworn.   Phillip J. Pirages   59 - 144 2011 $4800

Association – Canterbury, Jack, Mrs.

Oliphant, Margaret Oliphant Wilson 1828-1897 *The Curate in Charge.* London: Macmillan, 1902. 6 pages ads (10.5.02), original olive green cloth, lettered in blind and gilt, spine faded to brown, boards affected by damp, good, sound copy, signed "Mrs. Jack Canterbury 1902".   Jarndyce Antiquarian Booksellers   CLXC - 616 2011   £35

Association – Card, Samuel

Burnet, Gilbert, Bp. of Salisbury 1643-1715 *Bishop Burnet's History of His Own Time.* London: Thomas Ward, Joseph Dowming & Henry Woodfall, 1724-1734. First edition; 2 volumes, folio, contemporary full brown paneled calf, raised bands, gilt stamped black and red leather spine labels, hinges reinforced, bookplates of Samuel Card, fine.   Jeff Weber Rare Books   163 - 33 2011 $375

Association – Carleton, Lorna

Christian, Anne Hait *The Search for Holmes, Robson, Hind, Steele and Graham Families of Cumberland and Northumberland, England.* La Jolla: privately printed, 1984. Number 53 of 1033 copies; small 4to., original blue cloth, gilt, pages (viii), 172, with 75 illustrations, charts, etc., presentation copy inscribed by author to Lorna Carleton.   R. F. G. Hollett & Son Antiquarian Booksellers   General Catalogue Summer 2010 - 381 2011   £65

Association – Carlingford, Lord

Carlyle, Thomas 1795-1881 *On Heroes, Hero-Worship & the Heroic in History.* London: James Fraser, 1841. First edition in Tarr's primary binding; 2 pages ads, original purple brown cloth, spine gilt, cloth lightly lifting from boards, ownership inscriptions "L.W. 1842" and Carlingford 1878. Jarndyce Antiquarian Booksellers   CXCI - 108   2011   £225

Disraeli, Benjamin 1804-1881 *The Tragedy of Count Alarcos.* London: Henry Colburn, 1839. First edition; titlepage at some time neatly repaired where signature of ownership removed at head, few leaves slightly marked, contemporary half red morocco, spine blocked and lettered in gilt, slightly rubbed, slight worming to one corner, armorial booklabel of Lord Carlingford, good plus copy.   Jarndyce Antiquarian Booksellers   CXCI - 160   2011   £250

Kingsley, Charles 1819-1875 *The Good News of God: Sermons.* London: John W. Parker & Son, 1859. First edition; 4 pages ads, original black cloth, paper label slightly chipped, little rubbed, Carlingford bookplate.   Jarndyce Antiquarian Booksellers   CXCI - 232   2011   £35

Morris, William 1834-1896 *The Defence of Guenevere and Other Poems.* London: Bell and Daldy, 1858. First edition; half title, original brown wavy grained, borders in blind, spine lettered in gilt, very slightly rubbed at head and tail of spine, armorial bookplate of Lord Carlingford on leading pastedown, very good.   Jarndyce Antiquarian Booksellers   CXCI - 326   2011   £850

Association – Carlisle, Elsie

Cary, Joyce 1888-1957 *The Moonlight.* London: Michael Joseph, 1946. First edition; 8vo., 307 pages, very good+ in chipped very good- dust jacket, signed presentation from author "Elsie Carlisle/ with author's love".   Any Amount of Books   May 29 2011 - A68504   2011 $255

Association – Carlson, C. Elmer

Jones, Frederic Wood *The Principles of Anatomy as Seen in the Hand.* London: J. & A. Churchill, 1920. 8vo., viii, 325 pages, 2 plates, including frontispiece, 123 numbered figures, original brown cloth, gilt stamped spine title, extremities speckled, very good, this copy belonged to C. Elmer Carlson, M.D. Orthopedic Surgery (Oregon) with his signature, from the Medical Library of Dr. Clare Gray Peterson.   Jeff Weber Rare Books   162 - 173   2011 $120

Association – Carlyon, Horatio

Bacon, Francis, Viscount St. Albans 1561-1626 *The Twoo Bookes of Francis Bacon. Of the Proficience and Advancement of learning, Divine and Humane.* London: for Henrie Tomes, 1605. First edition; 4to., (1), 45, 118 (i.e. 121), leaves, lacks final blank 3H2 an, as always, the rare two leaves of errata at end, late 18th century half calf and marbled boards, extremities of boards worn, very skillfully and imperceptively rebacked retaining entire original spine, small worm trail in bottom margin of quires 2D-2F, occasional minor marginalia in an early hand, else lovely, early signature of Row'd Wetherald on title, signature of Horatio Carlyon 1861, Sachs bookplate and modern leather booklabel, calf backed clamshell box.   Joseph J. Felcone Inc. Fall Miscellany 2010 - 8   2011 $7500

Association – Carnarvon, Evelyn Stanhope, Countess of

Norton, Caroline Elizabeth Sarah *The Lady of La Garaye.* Cambridge & London: Macmillan, 1862. (1861). First edition; half title, frontispiece, 2 plates, 16 page catalog partially unopened, original green glazed cloth, front board elaborately decorated in gilt, back board in blind, spine lettered gilt, very good, inscribed "The Countess of Carnarvon, Xmas 1861".   Jarndyce Antiquarian Booksellers   CLXC - 599   2011   £50

Association – Carpenter, George, Mrs.

Jackson, Kate *Around the World to Persia: Letters Written While on the Journey as a Member of the American Persian Relief Commission in 1918.* New York: printed only for Private Circulation Among Friends, 1920. Octavo, 76 pages, quarter cloth backed boards, printed paper cover label, spine label, soiled covers, extremities worn, inscribed by author to Mrs. George R. Carpenter.   Jeff Weber Rare Books   163 - 181   2011 $75

Association – Carter, Angela

Levy, Deborah *An Amorous Discourse in the Suburbs of Hell.* London: Jonathan Cape, 1990. First edition; 8vo., pages 77, illustrations by Andrzej Borkowski, large format paperback, wrappers, very slight handling wear, but pretty much fine, from the working library of novelist Angela Carter, small attractive bookplate.   Any Amount of Books   May 29 2011 - A63685   2011 $306

Sclauzero, Mariarosa *Narcissism and Death.* Barrytown: Station Hill Press, 1984. First edition; small 4to., wrappers, pages 110, illustrations by Sue Coe, signed presentation from author for Angela Carter, with her posthumous bookplate, very slight rubbing, faint edgewear, very good+.   Any Amount of Books   May 29 2011 - A64551   2011 $255

Association – Carter, C. H. A.

Emerson, Ralph Waldo 1803-1882 *English Traits.* Boston: Phillips, Sampson & Co., 1856. First Edition; original black cloth, blindstamped with gilt lettering on spine, yellow endpapers, this copy with battered type at bottom of page 230 and the "1" on half titlepage, few small faint stains to cloth, small gouge on spine, not terrible in appearance, otherwise cloth is very nice with spine ends intact and gilt bright, contents very clean, owner name of C. H. A. Carter, housed in cloth chemise and half brown morocco slipcase with gilt lettering on spine, near fine in very good custom made slipcase. Charles Agvent Transcendentalism 2010 - 9 2011 $350

Association – Carter, Christopher

Tasso, Torquato 1544-1595 *Jerusalem Delivered.* London: printed for J. Dodsley, 1787. Sixth edition; 214 x 130mm., 2 volumes, handsome contemporary flamed calf, backstrips with wide Greek key roll at head and tail and with six compartments formed by decorative rolls, two of these with a central urn and graceful dangling fronds, two with unusual oval ornament composed of a central floral lozenge encircled first by a garland of leaves and then by a string of beads, each spine with two red morocco labels, one of them a circular volume label, engraved frontispiece by Thomas Stothard in each volume; late 19th century(?) bookplate of Harvey Bonnell (and with evidences of removed bookplate); gift inscription in pencil to Christopher Carter from Herbert Hudson at Wickham Bishops in Essex, dated June 1946, recto of front free endpaper of volume II with two newspaper cuttings about this work dated in 1830's tipped in; vaguest hint of rubbing to joints and corners, occasional minor smudges and other trivial imperfections internally, fine contemporary copy, text remarkably fresh, clean and bright, most attractive bindings especially lustrous and scarcely worn. Phillip J. Pirages 59 - 60 2011 $750

Association – Cassin, Cathe

Thomson, James 1700-1748 *The Seasons.* London: printed by and for T. Chapman, 1795. 224 x 140mm., 1 p.l. (frontispiece), xiv, 233, (1) pages, (1) leaf (ads), pleasing contemporary mottled calf expertly rebacked using original spine leather, covers with wide border of stippled, knotted and Greek key rolls, flat spine in panels formed by bands of massed plain and decorative rules, simple gilt floral ornament used as panel centerpiece, marbled endpapers, all edges gilt, immensely pleasing fore-edge painting showing a snowy skating scene on a wooded canal; engraved frontispiece, engraved vignette titlepage, large and attractive engraved head and tailpieces and with four full page engravings, early ink ownership inscription of Cathe Cassin; leather little dry and pitted (as always with early mottled calf), small losses of gilt on spine, minor foxing to initial leaves and to plates and adjacent leaves, otherwise fine, carefully restored binding quite solid and still attractive, text generally clean, fresh and bright with especially pleasing fore-edge painting exceptionally bright and fresh. Phillip J. Pirages 59 - 43 2011 $1800

Association – Cathcart, W. H.

Dixon, Thomas *The Leopard's Spots.* New York: Doubleday, Page & Co., 1902. First edition; 8vo., 13, 465 pages, 10 plates, gilt stamped cloth backed boards, uncut, binding lightly soiled, text slightly warped and wavy, but little dampstaining, uncut, presentation copy prepared for W. H. Cathcart, general manager of Burrows Brothers in Cleveland, inscribed and signed in full and dated March 21 1902, at end of text "Annotated by author for W. H. Cathcart March 21-25 1902". M & S Rare Books, Inc. 90 - 111 2011 $2500

Association – Cator, Albermarle

Coke, Henry J. *Tracks of a Rolling Stone.* London: Smith, Elder & Co., 1905. First edition; 8vo., original publisher's red buckram lettered gilt, pages 349, frontispiece, uncut, highly uncommon, bright, very good+, faint marks to cover, very slight foxing to text, neat ownership signature of Bryan Hall of Banningham Hall, Norfolk, heraldic bookplate of one Albermarle Cator. Any Amount of Books May 29 2011 - B21525 2011 $340

Association – Caunter, Alice

MacDonald, George 1824-1905 *The Disciple and Other Poems.* London: Strahan & Co., 1867. First edition; half title, 4 page catalog (Jan. 1868), original dappled dark brown and red cloth, ruled in blind, decorated and lettered in gilt, little rubbed at head and tail of spine and following hinge, monogram of M.E. I., signed presentation copy from author for Alice Caunter. Jarndyce Antiquarian Booksellers CXCII - 105 2011 £1800

Association – Cavendish-Bentinck, Violet

Bible. English - 1881 *The Gospel According to S. John.* Cambridge: Cambridge University Press, circa, 1881. Interleaves with plain rubricated pages, plain red calf, gilt dentelles & edges by Philip Tout, all edges gilt, inscribed "This gift to my father George MacDonald from Miss Violet Cavendish-Bentinck, now offered in much love & gratitude to the Rev. M. C. D'Arcy by Greville MacDonald". Jarndyce Antiquarian Booksellers CXCII - 335 2011 £250

MacDonald, George 1824-1905 *The Vicar's Daughter.* Leipzig: Bernhard Tauchnitz, 1872. Copyright edition; 2 volumes, slight browning, bound without half titles in half vellum, elaborate gilt spines, red labels, initials of V.C.B., MacDonald's friend Violet Cavendish Bentinck. Jarndyce Antiquarian Booksellers CXCII - 161 2011 £200

MacDonald, Greville Matheson *George MacDonald and His Wife.* London: George Allen & Unwin, 1924. First edition; half title with bookplate facsimile, frontispiece, plates, original dark blue cloth, dulled spine slightly creased, armorial bookplate of Violet Cavendish Bentinck. Jarndyce Antiquarian Booksellers CXCII - 355 2011 £50

Association – Cawse, John

Moxon, Joseph *Practical Persective; or Perspective Made Easie, Teaching by Opticks...* For Joseph Moxon, 1670. First edition; folio, (4), 66 pages, this copy belonged to artist and drawing master, John Cawse, with his signature and dated 1823, it lacks all plates and has one blank section of a margin cut away, he has pasted a 19th century engraving by Hogarth, the "Perspective" on inside front cover, early half vellum, marbled boards, covers rubbed, some browning and old staining to text, although in imperfect condition, scarce to find treatises actually owned by known drawing masters. Ken Spelman Rare Books 68 - 1 2011 £280

Association – Chabrol, Claude

Wood, Robin *Claude Chabrol.* New York: Praeger, 1970. First edition; small 4to., pages 144, copiously illustrations in black and white, signed by author on titlepage, loosely inserted note on card signed by Claude Chabrol, very good+ in slightly used, nicked and rubbed, else near very good dust jacket. Any Amount of Books May 29 2011 - A72809 2011 $238

Association – Chadwick, Alfred

Tryon, Thomas *The New Art of Brewing, Ale and Other Sorts of Liquors.* London: printed for Tho. Salusbury, 1691. 12mo., (6), 138 pages with ad leaf and contents leaf immediately following titlepage, general paper browning throughout, gutter of titlepage frayed (not touching printed surface), numeral entered in red ink in early hand on title, ms. inscription in ink on flyleaf, signed by Henry Cope recording the gift of the book to him by Sir Harry Fane (Vane) on January 4th 1699 with 4 pages of ms. notes" in ink apparently by Henry Cope on prelim blanks and 19th century armorial bookplate of Alfred Chadwick, contemporary ruled sheep, neatly appropriately rebacked and labeled, good copy. John Drury Rare Books 153 - 161 2011 £1250

Association – Chamberlain, C. Pearl

Suckling, John *Fragmenta Aurea. A Collection of all the Incomparable Pieces.* London: for Humphrey Moseley, 1646. First edition; first state of title with "FRAGMENTA AVREA" in upper case, a period after "Churchyard" in imprint and rule under date; A3v: 16 reads "allowred", second state of frontispiece, re-incised with heavier lines around leaves of garland and bulge in left sleeve; (6), 119, (7), 82, 64, (4), 52 pages, engraved portrait by William Marshall, contemporary calf, gilt fillet and cornerpieces, red morocco spine label, portrait and first two leaves with two very tiny holes at gutter, worm trail in lower margin of first three gatherings, else very nice, contemporary binding, bookplate of C. Pearl Chamberlain and booklabel of Abel Berland; fine red morocco pull-off case, ALS of John Suckling (1659-1627) father of the poet, Goodfathers 29 July 1625 to unnamed recipient seeking information on his election as a burgess in Yarmouth. Joseph J. Felcone Inc. Fall Miscellany 2010 - 113 2011 $6000

Association – Chamberlain, Houston Stewart

Chamberlain, Houston Stewart *Richard Wagenr.* London: J. M. Dent, 1900. Second edition; large 8vo., original publisher's green cloth lettered gilt on spine and cover, pages xvii, 402, copious plates and illustrations, loosely inserted signed card from Houston Stewart Chamberlain dated 1906 to fellow writer Friedrich Poske, clean, very good. Any Amount of Books May 29 2011 - A68665 2011 $255

Association – Chamberlain, Jacob Chester

Thoreau, Henry David 1817-1862 *A Week on the Concord and Merrimack Rivers.* Boston and Cambridge: James Munroe and Co., 1849. First edition, first printing, first issue; 12mo., 413, (1, blank), [1, publisher's ads ("Will Soon be Published, "Walden, or Life in the Woods. By Henry D. Thoreau")], (1, blank) pages, original brown cloth, BAL binding variant A, Trade binding) with five rule border stamped in blind on covers, spine lettered in gilt with rules and decorative leaf design stamped in blind, original buff endpapers, some wear to spine extremities, contemporary ink signatures on first prelim blank, armorial bookplate of Jacob Chester Chamberlain, with his acquisition slip tipped in between rear endpapers: From "Che Col." (filled in in pencil) Through "Dodd Mead & Co." (filled in in pencil) and date "Dec. 27/00" (filled in in pencil) "J.CC." Sold at the Chamberlain Sale First Editions of Ten American Authors, The Anderson Auction Company, February 16 and 17, 1909, with note by late owner inserted discussing its purchase from Seven Gables Bookshop in NY 1951, some neat marginal pencil notes and underlining, 3 lines of type dropped by printer on page 396 are provided in pencil, with Chamberlain's note concerning this textual point, spectacular copy, totally untouched, gilt on spine bright and fresh, chemised in full dark green straight grain morocco pull-off case by Bradstreet. David Brass Rare Books, Inc. May 26 2011 - 00541 2011 $19,500

Association – Chandos, Mary

Porter, Anna Maria *Roche-Blanche; or the Hunters of the Pyrenees.* London: Longman, 1822. First edition; 3 volumes, 12mo., half titles volumes II & III, inserted 4 pages at front volume I (June 1822), uncut in original blue boards, drab paper spines, paper labels, spines chipped at tails, good copy, 1926 bookplate of Eric Quayle, signatures of Mary Chandos August 1822, tipped in is folded holograph ms. signed by Porter. Jarndyce Antiquarian Booksellers CLXC - 758   2011   £650

Association – Channon, Henry

Buckle, Henry Thomas *Miscellaneous and Posthumous Works of Henry Thomas Buckle.* London: Longmans, Green and Co., 1872. First edition thus; 3 volumes, 8vo., soundly rebound in light blue buckram lettered gilt on spine, pages lix, 598 & 704 & 708 with 24 page publisher's cataloge at rear, bookplate of Henry Channon (i.e. Chips Channon), very good.   Any Amount of Books   May 29 2011 - A75900   2011 $340

Gosse, Edmund   1849-1928   *On Viol and Flute.* London: Heinemann, 1896. First Selected edition; small 8vo., pages xi, 212, original publisher's green cloth lettered gilt on spine and cover, frontispiece, signed presentation from author to George Moore, from the library of Henry "Chips" Channon with note at rear in his hand "Given me by Lady Cunard, Christmas 1938, slight tanning, slight fading, very small nick at head of spine, otherwise very good.   Any Amount of Books   May 29 2011 - A69860   2011 $255

Association – Chapman, R. W

Crabbe, George   *Tales of the Hall.*   London: John Murray, 1819. First edition; half titles discarded, ownership signature of A. Webb and initials "P.W." on front free endpaper, pages iii-xxiv, 326; iii-viii, 353, (2) (publisher's ad), 8vo., contemporary polished calf, backstrips with darker banding, panels in gilt, central gilt palmettes and gilt lettering, sides with triple gilt fillet and blind borders, gauffered edges, upper joint volume I just starting to crack, still strong, ex-libris of R. W. Chapman, good.   Blackwell Rare Books   B166 - 26   2011   £160

Association – Chargaff, Erwin

Olby, Robert   *The Path to the Double.*   Seattle: University of Washington Press, 1974. First American edition; 8vo., xxiii, 510 pages, very good++, minimal soil and foxing to edges, cover corners bumped, very good++ dust jacket with mild edge wear, short closed tears, from the library of Erwin Chargaff.   By the Book, L. C.   26 - 89   2011 $500

Association – Charke, William

Euclides   *Elucidis Phaenomena Posta Zamberti & Maurolyci Editionem...*   Rome: G. Martinelli, 1591. First edition of this Latin version; 4to., (22), 89 (=99) pages, woodcut diagrams, ownership inscription of William Charke, from the library of the Earls of Macclesfield at Shirburn Castle.   Maggs Bros. Ltd.   1440 - 85   2011   £1200

Association – Charleton

Austen, Jane   1775-1817   *Pride and Prejudice.* London: printed for T. Egerton, Military Library, Whitehall, 1813. First edition, following all points in Gilson and Keynes and complete with all half titles present; 12mo., 3 volumes, (iv), 307, (1, blank); (iv), 239, (1, blank); (v), (323), (1, blank) pages, contemporary speckled calf, blind tooled board edges, edges sprinkled red, original light brown endpapers, expertly rebacked with original spines laid down, later green morocco gilt lettering labels on spines, gilt stamped "Charleton" to upper boards of each volume (possibly that of Charleton House, Montrose), from the library of German artist and music historian Frida Best (1876-1964) with her bookplate in each volume, edges to few leaves professionally and near invisibly repaired, occasional light foxing, excellent and complete copy in original and contemporary binding, housed in modern half red morocco clamshell case with 3 individual spines decoratively lettered and tooled in gilt, Regency binders typically removed half titles, those with half titles rare.   David Brass Rare Books, Inc.   May 26 2011 - 01651   2011 $75,000

Association – Charlton, William Henry

Byron, George Gordon Noel, 6th Baron   1788-1824 *The Works... with his Letters and Journals and His Life.* London: John Murray, 1832-1833. First edition; 17 volumes, half titles (no in volumes I, IX), engraved frontispiece and titles, illustrations, small repair to half title volume III, original dark green moire cloth, green paper label volume I, gilt little rubbed and bumped, slightly marked, armorial bookplates of William Henry Charlton.   Jarndyce Antiquarian Booksellers   CXCI - 6   2011   £500

Association – Charters, Samuel

Whitman, Walt   1819-1892   *Good-Bye My Fancy: 2nd Annex to Leaves of Grass.*   Philadelphia: David McKay, 1891. First edition; 8vo. original maroon cloth, beveled edges, gilt lettered, top edge gilt, frontispiece, from the library of A. J. A. Symons, with his Brick House bookplate, small nick in spine, edges little rubbed and faded, good, from the collection of Samuel Charters.   The Brick Row Book Shop   Bulletin 8 - 36   2011 $400

Whitman, Walt 1819-1892 *Leaves of Grass.* Brooklyn: published by author, 1855. First edition, 2nd issue binding, second state of page iv; the 795 copies were bound in different stages, and this one of the 262 bound between Dec. 1855 and Jan. 1856, 4to., original decoratively blindstamped green cloth, gilt lettering, engraved frontispiece, 8 pages of extracts of reviews and notices tipped in before frontispiece, bookplate of Arthur B. Spingarn (1878-1971), from the collection of Samuel Charters.   The Brick Row Book Shop   Bulletin 8 - 5   2011 $125,000

Whitman, Walt 1819-1892 *Leaves of Grass.* Brooklyn: published by the author, 1856. Second edition; 12mo., original grey-green cloth, decoratively blindstamped, gilt decorations and lettering, engraved frontispiece by Samuel Hollyer, bookplates of E. M. Cox and Michael Sadleir, cloth slightly rubbed, some light to moderate foxing, fine, from the collection of Samuel Charters.   The Brick Row Book Shop   Bulletin 8 - 6   2011 $22,500

Whitman, Walt 1819-1892 *Leaves of Grass.* Camden: Author's Edition, 1876. Fifth edition, third printing, second issue, one of 600 copies signed by author; 8vo., original cream quarter calf and corners, marbled boards, gilt lettering, 2 portraits, this copy inscribed to English botanist Sidney H. Vines, from the author, binding little soiled and rubbed, some slight foxing, very good, much nicer than usual for this fragile binding, from the collection of Samuel Charters.   The Brick Row Book Shop   Bulletin 8 - 18   2011 $9000

Association – Chatsworth Library

Bertram, Bonaventure Corneille *Comparatio Grammaticae Hebricae & Aramicae.* Geneva: Apud Eustathium Vignom, 1574. Sole edition; woodcut device to titlepage and verso of errata leaf, printed in italic, Roman and Hebrew characters throughout, pages numbered right to left, little light browning and spotting, tiny dampmark to corner of first three leaves, early marginal notes in Latin and Hebrew (some cropped), underlining, old ownership inscription to title, pages (xxiv), 440, 4to., late 18th century mid brown paneled calf divided by gilt fillets, central panel with blind frame and central cross hatching, recently rebacked, backstrip with four gilt tooled raised bands between double gilt and blind fillets, black morocco label in second compartment, rest plain, hinges relined, touch rubbed at extremities, Chatsworth shelfmark bookplate, good,.   Blackwell Rare Books   B166 - 12   2011   £800

Association – Chaytor, Mary

Kirkland, Caroline Matilda Stansbury 1801-1864 *Western Clearings.* London: George Routledge & Co., 1850. Contemporary half black roan, slight rubbing, signed "Mary Chaytor", good plus.   Jarndyce Antiquarian Booksellers   CLXC - 61   2011   £45

Marsh, Anne *Adelaide Lindsay.* London: George Routledge & Co., 1852. Contemporary half black roan, slight rubbing, signed "Mary Chaytor" on title, good plus.   Jarndyce Antiquarian Booksellers   CLXC - 233   2011   £50

Marsh, Anne *The Wilmingtons.* London: Thomas Hodgson, 1854. Contemporary half black roan, slight rubbing, signed "Mary Chaytor", good plus.   Jarndyce Antiquarian Booksellers   CLXC - 248   2011   £45

Porter, Anna Maria *The Recluse of Norway.* London: G. Routledge & Co., 1852. Signed Mary Chaytor on title, contemporary half black roan, slight rubbing.   Jarndyce Antiquarian Booksellers   CLXC - 757   2011   £35

Association – Chaytor, W. R. C.

Marsh, Anne *Tales of the French Revolution.* London: Simms & M'Intyre, 1849. First edition; contemporary half black roan, signed "Mr. R. C. Chaytor", good plus.   Jarndyce Antiquarian Booksellers   CLXC - 242   2011   £85

Association – Cheffins, Richard Hamilton Alexander

Scicluna, Hannibal P. *The Church of St. John in Valletta; Its History, Architecture and Monuments with Brief History of the Order of St. John From Its Inception to the Present Day.* San Martin: privately printed, 1955. First edition, one 473 of 2000 copies; 4to., original publisher's red cloth lettered gilt on spine with white Maltese cross on cover, pages liii, 428, with 2 plans and 760 illustrations, ownership signature of Richard Hamilton Alexander Cheffins, slight rubbing, spine slightly sunned, very good or better, decent.   Any Amount of Books   May 29 2011 - A76512   2011 $383

Association – Chesterton

Aristoteles *Commentarii Colegii Conimbricensis Societatis Iesu in Tres Libros de Anima Aristotelis Stagiritae.* Cologne: Impensis Lazari Zetzneri, 1609. Some light browning and spotting, few marginal paper flaws and touch of marginal worming near end (never affecting text) pages (viii), columns 694, pages (19), 4to., contemporary Oxford blind tooled dark calf boards, outer border of triple blind fillet, frame of triple blind fillet with cornerpieces and central decorative blind lozenge, spine with four raised bands between blind fillets, hatched at top and bottom, little rubbed in places, bit of wear to corners and head of spine, pastedowns lifted and early printed binder's waste exposed to front, ownership inscription of "Chesterton", good.   Blackwell Rare Books   B166 - 17   2011   £950

Association – Chetwynd-Talbot, Ursula Winifred

Hamilton, Patrick 1904-1962 *Mr. Stimpson and Mr. Gorse.* London: Constable, 1953. First edition; 8vo., pages vi, 7-356, signed presentation from author to his future wife, Ursula Winifred Chetwynd-Talbot, fore-edges and page edges browned, otherwise very good+ in very good dust jacket with some slight nick at head of spine, slight creasing, closed tear and slight soiling.   Any Amount of Books   May 26 2011 - A69473 2011 $2516

Association – Chevalier de Leuze

Le Prince De Beaumont, Jeanne Marie *Civan, Roi de Bungo Histoire Japonnoise.* Londres: Jean Nourse, 1754. First edition; 2 volumes in one with separate titlepages, (4), 250; (1) 178 pages, 12mo., contemporary sheepskin, gilt decorated spine, closed tear on page 43, light stain on page 175 (volume II), otherwise very nice, from the library of Chevalier de Leuze with his ex-libris in his hand.   Paulette Rose Fine and Rare Books   32 - 115 2011 $1200

Association – Chiang, Mayling Soong

Kai-Shek, Chiang *General Chiang Kai-Shek - the Account of the Fortnight in Sian when the fate of China Hung in the Balance.* New York: 1937. First edition, first issue dust jacket dated '37'; 187 pages, good, endpapers foxed, tiny bit of white foxing to front cover, price clipped dust jacket damped at both flap folds and top inch of backstrip diminishing to both covers, noticeable from inside and at top 1.5" from outside; rear page with age soil, both ends of backstrip of dust jacket shelfworn, signed Mayling Soong Chiang.   Bookworm & Silverfish   679 - 36 2011 $100

Association – Chiaramonte, Nicola

Camus, Albert *L'Homme Revolte. (The Rebel).* Paris: Gallimard, 1951. First edition; half title + titlepage + dedication page + quotation page + half title (13)-382 + (383) - Printer's information, octavo, inscribed, original printed paper wrappers, mended tear to front spine fold at head of spine, minor soiling and wear to wrappers, text browned as usual and uncut, preserved in clamshell box, beautiful copy, with 3 line inscription by Camus for Italian philosopher Nicola Chiaramonte, review copy on ordinary paper.   Athena Rare Books   10 2011 $2500

Association – Chichester, Miss

First Lessons in Astronomy. London: Thomas Ward & Co., 1838. Original dust jackets, paper label, printed in black, spine slightly chipped at head and tail, nice, engraved titlepage, 3 pages ads, ownership inscription of Miss Chichester Aug. 1841.   Jarndyce Antiquarian Booksellers   CXCI - 357 2011   £65

Association – Chisholm, Phillis

Dodd, W. L. *Sketches and Rhymes.* North Shields: T. R. Harrison, 1859. First edition; original blue blindstamped cloth gilt, extremities trifle rubbed, pages (iv), 255, presentation copy by author for Phillis Chisholm, cousin.   R. F. G. Hollett & Son Antiquarian Booksellers   General Catalogue Summer 2010 - 638 2011   £180

Association – Cholmondely

Quincy, John *Lexicon Physico Medicum; or a New Medicinal Dictionary...* London: printed for J. Osborn and T. Longman at the Ship in Pater-Noster Row, 1730. xvi, 480 pages, diagrams in text, ownership inscription dated 1949, 8vo., full contemporary panelled calf, raised bands, early handwritten paper label, joints cracked but firm, head and tail of spine slightly chipped, tinted bookplate of Cholmondely Library, later bookplate ex-libris Nellen, fine, clean copy.   Jarndyce Antiquarian Booksellers   CXCI - 461 2011   £350

Association – Choppin, Rene

Fenelon, Francois Salignac De La Mothe, Abp. 1651-1715 *Les Aventures de Telemaque.* Paris: Imprimerie de Monsieur (i.e. Pierre-Francois Didot), 1785. 338 x 251mm., 2 volumes, splendid contemporary (or slightly later scarlet straight grain morocco, sumptuously gilt, covers with broad ornate gilt border featuring palmettes, flat spines handsomely gilt in seven compartments (two with titling, two with elegant volutes and pointille decoration and three with large central lozenge enclosing an intricate fleuron), densely gilt turn-ins, azure watered silk endpapers, all edges gilt, engraved titlepage, 96 fine engraved plates, all with handsome frames wrapped in fruited foliage by Jean Baptiste Tilliard after Charles Monnet, 24 of the plates containing chapter summaries and 72 with scenes from the narrative, original tissue guards; bookplates of Rene Choppin and Florencio Gavito (20th century); faint, widely spaced flecks to front cover of second volume, spines ever so slightly sunned, small stain to one endpaper, one page with minor ink spots in bottom margin, two engraved divisional leaves with one other engraving with overall faint mottled foxing, hint of foxing or pale browning in isolated places elsewhere, other trivial imperfections, especially fine set in beautiful binding, leather bright and only insignificant wear, text and plates unusually fresh and bright.   Phillip J. Pirages   59 - 47 2011 $11,000

Association – Christie-Miller, Sydney Richardson

James II, King of Great Britain 1566-1625 *Papers of Devotion of James II...* Oxford: printed at the Oxford University Press by Frederick Hall for Presentation to the Members of the Roxburghe Club, 1925. Apparently First edition; 292 x 229mm., xxx pages, (1) leaf, 173, (5) pages, original Roxburghe binding of maroon half morocco over red textured cloth boards, flat spine with titling in gilt, top edge gilt, other edges untrimmed, one facsimile manuscript plate, this copy originally prepared for Sydney Richardson Christie-Miller (his name printed in red in the Roxburghe list as a way of indicating this), endpapers with hint of foxing, virtually pristine. Phillip J. Pirages 59 - 304 2011 $525

Association – Christy, John

Bible. Hebrew - 1656 *The Hebrew text of the Psalmes and Lamentations....* London: printed for the author and sold by H. Robinson, A Crook, L. Fawn, J. Kirton, S. Thomson..., 1656. 12mo., (12), 266, 149-191, 15, (2) pages, last leaf with errata, contemporary calf, from the library of John Christy 1717, from the library of the Earls of Macclesfield at Shirburn Castle. Maggs Bros. Ltd. 1440 - 32 2011 £450

Association – Churchill, Clementine Spencer

McGrandle, Leith *Europe: the Quest for Unity: Speeches and Writings.* London: Ranelagh Editions, 1975. First edition, one of 475 numbered copies, signed by artist; large folio, frontispiece etching by Pietro Annigoni, publisher's press mark on titlepage from engraving by Reynolds Stone, printed in Bembo on Cartiere Magnani paper, fine in full tan leather lettered gilt at spine and cover and in plain woven beige cloth slipcase, signed by Winston Churchill's widow (Clementine Spencer Churchill), handsome, as new. Any Amount of Books May 29 2011 - A48837 2011 $383

Association – Churchill, J.

Churchill, Charles *Poems.* London: printed for John Churchill and W. Flexney, 1769. Fourth edition; (4), 369, (1), (2) pages ads, half title; (4), 330 pages, half title, 8vo., full contemporary calf, gilt decorated spines, red and olive green gilt labels, some rubbing to gilt, slight crack to upper joint volume I, signature of J. Churchill at foot of final leaf of text, volume II with armorial bookplates of William Salmon and J. P. Turbervill, very good, attractive. Jarndyce Antiquarian Booksellers CXCI - 119 2011 £200

Association – Clapp, John

Torrey, John *A Flora of the State of New York...* Albany: Carroll and Cook, Printers to the Assembly, 1843. Volume 1, large 4to., original blindstamped cloth gilt, part of upper board damaged by damp, spine chipped and repaired, pages xii, 484, engraved title and 72 lithographed plates by Endicott of NY, some foxing to text and plates, occasionally heavy, contemporary signature of John Clapp. R. F. G. Hollett & Son Antiquarian Booksellers General Catalogue Summer 2010 - 1064 2011 £150

Association – Clark, Barrett

Kelly, George *Behold, the Bridegroom.* Boston: Little Brown, 1928. First edition; 8vo., 172 pages, frontispiece, blue cloth with paper label, else near fine in little nicked and soiled dust jacket, rare in dust jacket, inscribed by author to Barrett Clark. Second Life Books Inc. 174 - 211 2011 $500

Association – Clark, James

Jameson, Anna Brownell 1794-1860 *Memoirs and Essays Illustrative of Art, Literature and Social Morals.* London: Richard Bentley, 1846. First edition; first two leaves of text torn hofizontally, old tape repairs, contemporary half blue calf, marbled boards, maroon leather label, boards rubbed, signed "James Clark, Largantogher, Sept. 1866", very good. Jarndyce Antiquarian Booksellers CLXC - 13 2011 £95

Association – Clark, La Verne

Conley, Robert J. *The Rattlesnake Band and Other Poems.* Muskogee: Indian University Press, 1984. One of 500 numbered copies; apparently only issued in wrappers, bi-lingual, Cherokee/English, illustrations by author, uncommon, inscribed by Conley to La Verne Clarke. Ken Lopez Bookseller 154 - 134 2011 $350

Association – Clark, Leonard

Betjeman, John 1906-1984 *A Few Late Chrysanthemums.* London: John Murray, 1954. First edition; 8vo., original blue cloth with printed title label onset to cover, pages vii, 95, review copy with publisher's slip loosely inserted, inscribed by author for Leonard Clark, fine in very good, very slightly soiled and spotted dust jacket. Any Amount of Books May 26 2011 - A66497 2011 $461

Lee, Laurie *The Bloom of Candles.* London: John Lehmann, 1947. First edition; 8vo., 22 pages, inscribed by author to poet Leonard Clark, with Clark bookplate, near fine in slightly dusty, very good+ dust jacket. Any Amount of Books May 29 2011 - A68498 2011 $213

Association – Clark, William

Sallustius Crispus, Caius *C. Crispi Sallustii Belli Catilinarii et Jugurthini Historiae.* Glasguae: in aedibus Roberti Urie, 1749. 8vo., pages iv, 250, (ii), contemporary polished calf, untooled spine, red lettering piece gilt, boards double rule bordered in blind with extra double rule and decorative roll in blind at joint side, board edges 'zip-zag' decorative roll gilt, all edges red speckled, pink and white sewn endbands, lightly age toned, few stains, rubbed and bit chipped, joints cracking, spine darkened, contemporary ink inscription John Pelch, first name covered by pasted slip and later ink inscription "Wm. Clark, also pencil inscription "From Prof. Henry Jackson's Sale...", from the collection of Christopher Ernest Weston 1947-2010. Unsworths Booksellers 24 - 139 2011 £50

Association – Clarke, Ann

Eales, Mary *Mrs. Mary Eales's Receipt. Confectioner to Her Late Majesty Queen Anne.* London: For J. Robson, 1767. Corrected second edition; (8), 106, ii pages, contemporary sheep, neatly rebacked to style, clean, very good, early ownership signature of Ann Clarke. Joseph J. Felcone Inc. Fall Miscellany 2010 - 29 2011 $1500

Association – Clarke, Elizabeth Mary

Lennox, Charles Ramsay *The Female Quixote; or the Adventures of Arabella.* London: printed for F. C. & J. Rivington, W. Otridge & Sons,, 1810. Half titles, contemporary half tan calf, marbled boards, gilt spines, maroon leather labels, armorial bookplate of Rev. G. F. Clarke and signatures of Elizabeth Mary Clarke, very good. Jarndyce Antiquarian Booksellers CLXC - 126 2011 £120

Opie, Amelia *The Father and Daughter.* London: Longman, Hurst, Rees, and Orme, 1809. Sixth edition; frontispiece, contemporary half tan calf, marbled boards, gilt spine, maroon leather label, spines and edges little rubbed, armorial bookplate of Rev. G. F. Clarke and signature of Elizabeth Mary Clarke, good plus. Jarndyce Antiquarian Booksellers CLXC - 659 2011 £95

Association – Clarke, G. F.

Lennox, Charles Ramsay *The Female Quixote; or the Adventures of Arabella.* London: printed for F. C. & J. Rivington, W. Otridge & Sons,, 1810. Half titles, contemporary half tan calf, marbled boards, gilt spines, maroon leather labels, armorial bookplate of Rev. G. F. Clarke and signatures of Elizabeth Mary Clarke, very good. Jarndyce Antiquarian Booksellers CLXC - 126 2011 £120

Opie, Amelia *The Father and Daughter.* London: Longman, Hurst, Rees, and Orme, 1809. Sixth edition; frontispiece, contemporary half tan calf, marbled boards, gilt spine, maroon leather label, spines and edges little rubbed, armorial bookplate of Rev. G. F. Clarke and signature of Elizabeth Mary Clarke, good plus. Jarndyce Antiquarian Booksellers CLXC - 659 2011 £95

Association – Clarke, T. H.

Phillippo, James Mursell *Jamaica: its Past and Present State.* London: John Snow, 1843. First edition; 8vo., pages xvi, 487, 16 full page woodcut illustrations and woodcut vignettes, inscribed by Rev. Th. H. Clarke/Dry Harbor Jamaica Novb. 1843 for Sam. J. Wilkind. Any Amount of Books May 29 2011 - A45552 2011 $255

Association – Clay, John William

Cole, John *Memoirs of the Life, Writings and Character of the Late Thomas Hinderwell, Esqr. Scarborough.* London: published by John Cole and Longman, Rees, Orme, Brown and Green, 1826. 8vo., pages (ii) 3 (i) 57, (iii) 55, (i) vii (i), engraved frontispiece, publisher's original green canvas, dark green morocco lettering piece gilt by Jenny Aste, late 1980's, some light spotting, especially to title, cloth little spotted and faded, slightly worn at endcaps, contemporary ink inscription to Mrs. Langdell, presented by author, also blue paper ex-libris of John William Clay, from the collection of Christopher Ernest Weston 1947-2010. Unsworths Booksellers 24 - 82 2011 £125

Association – Clayton, John

Locke, John 1632-1704 *An Abridgment of Mr. Locke's Essay Concerning Humane Understanding.* London: 1700. Second edition; (8) 308 (4) (index) pages, very early leather, equally early stitching to re-attach covers, backstrip deteriorated but sturdy due to stitches, missing rear endpaper and front endpaper shabby, bookplate fragment of John Clayton of Gloucester county. Bookworm & Silverfish 668 - 123 2011 $100

Association – Clayton, Robert

Livius, Titus *Titi Livii Patavini Historiarum Libri Qui Extant.* Parisiis: apud Fredericum Leonard, 1679.   5 volumes bound as 6, 4to., pages (lxx) 544 (ix) + engraved half title and 2 engraved maps; (ii) 10 545-876, 3-191, (xix); (viii) 620 (lii) + 1 extending engraved plate and 1 other engraved plate; (viii) 757, (lxv) 678 (xxvi) 776, (xvi), contemporary calf, stain darkened spine panel gilt, brick red lettering piece gilt, numbered direct in gilt boards panelled in blind (Cambridge style), board edges decorative roll gilt, all edges red speckled, blue and white sewn endbands, light toning and some spotting, rubbed at joints and corners, joints cracked, endcaps worn, some labels lost, contemporary armorial bookplate of Sir Robert Clayton , early 19th century armorial bookplate of Stephen Lowdell, from the collection of Christopher Ernest Weston 1947-2010.   Unsworths Booksellers   24 - 115 2011   £450

Association – Clements, Henry Theophilus

Lamb, Caroline 1785-1828   *Glenarvon.* London: Henry Colburn, 1816.   Second edition; 3 volumes, 12mo., contemporary half calf, crimson labels, slight rubbing, armorial bookplates of Henry Theophilus Clements, very good.   Jarndyce Antiquarian Booksellers   CLXC - 69 2011   £650

Association – Clifford, Edward

Hughes, Thomas 1822-1896   *Early Memories for the Children by the Author of Tom Brown's Schooldays.* Thomas Burleigh for Private Circulation only, 1899.   First edition; Presentation copy from author's widow, Fanny to Edward Clifford, pages (2), 78, 8vo., uncut, original grey blue card wrappers with title printed in blue on upper cover, olive green paper backstrip, backstrip sometime reinforced with clear tape, but now defective at centre, presentation inscription slightly touched by glue adhering to cover, sound.   Blackwell Rare Books   B166 - 52 2011   £275

Association – Coates, E.

Gale, Roger *Registrum Honoris De Richmond Exhibens Terrarum & Villarum.* Londini: Impensis R. Gosling, 1722.   Large paper copy, folio, pages (ii), xxxv, (i), 106, (xxvi), 286, (xxx) + folding engraved map, one extending engraved plate, another 8 engraved plates and 6 extending plates of pedigrees, lacking the list of subscribers leaf, early 19th century calf, boards sided with 'French Shelf' marbled paper, 1970's renewal of leather with half reversed calf by John Henderson (spotted and lightly browned, old boards scuffed), armorial and masonic bookplate of "Robt. Lakeland" and inscription "from Major Sir Edw. Coates' Library", from the collection of Christopher Ernest Weston 1947-2010.   Unsworths Booksellers   24 - 95 2011   £400

Association – Cobden-Sanderson, Annie

Arts & Crafts Exhibition Society *Art and Life and the Building and Decoration of Cities...* Rivington, Percival & Co., 1897.   Half title, recent ownership inscription, uncut, original red brown publisher's gilt monogram on front board, worn paper label on spine, little sunned, presentation inscription for Elie Reclus, from T. J. and Annie Cobden-Sanderson, 5 volumes.   Jarndyce Antiquarian Booksellers   CXCI - 53 2011   £250

Association – Cobden-Sanderson, Thomas James

Arts & Crafts Exhibition Society *Art and Life and the Building and Decoration of Cities...* Rivington, Percival & Co., 1897.   Half title, recent ownership inscription, uncut, original red brown publisher's gilt monogram on front board, worn paper label on spine, little sunned, presentation inscription for Elie Reclus, from T. J. and Annie Cobden-Sanderson, 5 volumes.   Jarndyce Antiquarian Booksellers   CXCI - 53 2011   £250

Association – Coe, Brian

Millward, Michael *Victorian Landscape.* London: Ward Lock, 1974.   First edition; oblong 4to., original cloth gilt, dust jacket, pages 120, with 84 illustrations, 2 copy letters to Brian Coe, and 3 large original photos by him, loosely inserted.   R. F. G. Hollett & Son Antiquarian Booksellers   177 - 581 2011   £45

Association – Coel, Margaret

A Dozen on Denver. Gulden: Fulcrum, 2009.   First edition; fine, signed by Connie Willis, Nick Arvin, Robert Greer, Margaret Coel, Manuel Ramos and Arnold Grossman.   Bella Luna Books   May 29 2011 - p3633 2011 $104

Association – Colborne, N. W. Ridley

Malthus, Thomas Robert 1766-1834   *An Essay on the Principle of Population or a View of Its Past and Present Effects on Human Happiness...* London: printed for J. Johnson by T. Bensley, 1803.   Second edition; large 4to., pages viii, (3) contents, (1) errata, 610, contemporary full calf, rebacked at early date with original spine laid down, ownership signature of N. W. Ridley Colborne and Horace W. Baddle 1859, some light intermittent spotting and staining, but nice, clean copy with wide margins.   Second Life Books Inc.   174 - 234 2011 $6000

Association – Coleman, Carroll

Berry, Wendell *Findings (Poems).* Iowa City: Prairie Press, 1969.   First edition; 8vo., pages 63, fine in dust jacket, scarce, with ownership signature of Marilyn Trumpp, August. 1969, noting it was a gift from book designer Carroll Coleman.   Second Life Books Inc.   174 - 44 2011 $300

Association – Coleman, Robert

Fox, George *A Journal or Historical Account of the Life, Travels, Sufferings, Christian Experiences and Labour of Love in the Work of the Ministry...* London: printed by W. Richardson and S. Clark and sold by Luke Hinde, 1765. Third edition; folio, modern full blind ruled calf, gilt, pages lix, 679, (xxviii), excellent, clean, sound copy with signature of Robert Coleman, inscribed "given to Edwin R. Ransome in 1871...". R. F. G. Hollett & Son Antiquarian Booksellers 175 - 469 2011 £450

Association – Collett, Oliver

Acton, John *An Essay on Shooting.* London: printed for T. Cadell, 1789. First edition in English; 192 x 133mm., xiii, (i), 303 pages (missing A1, blank), original publisher's boards, blue paper sides, plain paper spine with ink titling, untrimmed edges, very nice folding cloth box with leather label on spine, armorial bookplate of Oliver Collett over early ink signature; paper on covers and spine and bit soiled and chafed, as expected, small portion of backstrip perished at bottom, isolated minor foxing internally, extremely desirable copy, binding entirely sound, text clean and fresh and bright. Phillip J. Pirages 59 - 54 2011 $1250

Association – Collins, John

Dilich, Wilhelm *Peribologia.* Frankfurt: A. Humm etc., 1641. Folio, 5-202, 10) pages, engraved title and 7 section titles, 410 plus numbered engravings, contemporary English calf, gilt fillet on covers, spine with gilt ornaments, red edges, from the library of the Earls of Macclesfield at Shirburn Castle, this copy may well stem from the library of John Collins/William Jones, and has the old Macclesfield Library class mark. Maggs Bros. Ltd. 1440 - 68 2011 £2000

Sems, Johan *Practijck des Kantmetens.* Leiden: Jan Bouwensz, 1600. First edition; 2 parts, 4to., (80, 303, (5); (8), 126, (2) pages, 7 engraved plates in part 2, engraving on both titlepages, woodcut diagrams, contemporary vellum, upper hinge split, ms. vellum guards and strengtheners, probably from the library of John Collins, from the library of the Earls of Macclesfield at Shirburn Castle. Maggs Bros. Ltd. 1440 - 197 2011 £3500

Association – Colquhoun, Archibald

Calvino, Italo *The Path to the Nest of Spiders.* London: Collins, 1956. First English language edition; inscribed by translator, Archibald Colquhoun, in year of publication, tiny corner bumps, near fine in very good dust jacket with slight spine fading, light chipping to corners and crown, small creased, edge tear, scarce. Ken Lopez Bookseller 154 - 24 2011 $650

Association – Colthurst, N. C.

Coxe, William *Sketches of the Natural, Civil and Political State of Switzerland.* Dublin: printed by George Bonham for the booksellers, 1779. viii, 478, (2) pages, 8vo., with final leaf of postscript, excellent copy, contemporary calf, spine ruled in gilt, red morocco label, bookplate of N. C. Colthurst, Andrum Co. Cork. Jarndyce Antiquarian Booksellers CXCI - 543 2011 £520

Association – Comberbach, Jane

Caussin, Nicholas *The Holy Court in Five Times....* London: printed by William Bentley, 1650. Folio, near contemporary speckled calf with raised bands and spine label, sometime nicely re-cased, rather rubbed, corners restored, pages (xx), 522, (viii) (viii) 319 (i, blank), 13, (vii), half title, printed title in red and black, 6 further titles, engraved head and tailpieces, historiated initials in each section and numerous engraved portraits within text, some 10 leaves in first section have several closed cuts to text, without loss, one leaf fine with lower corner torn off affecting 3 lines of table, otherwise excellent, clean and sound copy, early ownership signatures of John and Jane Comberbach of Barker Street, Nantwich, Cheshire, later armorial bookplate of Sir John Williams of Bodelwyddan Castle in North Wales. R. F. G. Hollett & Son Antiquarian Booksellers 175 - 233 2011 £350

Association – Comberbach, John

Caussin, Nicholas *The Holy Court in Five Times....* London: printed by William Bentley, 1650. Folio, near contemporary speckled calf with raised bands and spine label, sometime nicely re-cased, rather rubbed, corners restored, pages (xx), 522, (viii) (viii) 319 (i, blank), 13, (vii), half title, printed title in red and black, 6 further titles, engraved head and tailpieces, historiated initials in each section and numerous engraved portraits within text, some 10 leaves in first section have several closed cuts to text, without loss, one leaf fine with lower corner torn off affecting 3 lines of table, otherwise excellent, clean and sound copy, early ownership signatures of John and Jane Comberbach of Barker Street, Nantwich, Cheshire, later armorial bookplate of Sir John Williams of Bodelwyddan Castle in North Wales. R. F. G. Hollett & Son Antiquarian Booksellers 175 - 233 2011 £350

Association – Combridge, A. J.

Luard, John *Views in India, Saint Helena and Car Nicobar. Drawn from Nature and on Stone.* London: J. Graf, printer to her Majesty, 1838. unpaged, lithographic title, 60 lithographic plates mounted on india paper, folio, contemporary crimson morocco over boards, spine tooled and lettered gilt, 5 raised bands, bound by Harrison Bookbinder (Pall Mall, small stamp to front blank), moderate foxing to text leaves and plate mounts, boards rubbed, some discoloration and scuff marks to front board, spine with few minor chips, edgewear, still very good; bookplate of William Backwell Tyringham, neat stamp of A. J. Combridge, Bombay and Madras.   Kaaterskill Books   12 - 124   2011 $5250

Association – Comerford, James

Paule, George *Life of the Most Reverend and Religious Prelate John Whitgift, Lord Archbishop of Canterbury.* London: printed by Thomas Snodham, 1612. small 4to., pages (viii), 94, (ii), woodcut portrait of Whitgift on titlepage verso, early 21st century retrospective ruled calf binding by CEW, title soiled text block trimmed to printed border and sometimes just inside at top and fore-edge, old f.e.p. corner repaired, early hand has annotated head of blank leaf A1 and final blank leaf N4 armorial bookplate of "James Comerford" on front pastedown, mid 19th century ownership in Philip Bliss's hand on 17th century flyleaf reading "Bodleian Catalogue 1843, p. 62" and at foot of page I signature "P.B.43": and flowerly label, presented by William Minet at foot of front pastedown, from the collection of Christopher Ernest Weston 1947-2010.   Unsworths Booksellers   24 - 34   2011   £450

Rutland, John Henry Manners, 5th Duke of *Journal of a Tour to the Northern Parts of Great Britain.* London: printed for J. Triphook, 1813. 8vo., pages (iv) 300 + 10 sepia aquatint plates, 2 floor plans for Haddon Hall and 2 plates of room dimensions, contemporary mottled calf with early 20th century reback, spine double rule gilt with 'milled' roll gilt raised bands, compartments with 'covered urn' centre pieces gilt, red lettering piece gilt, number erased from 'open centred' centre piece gilt, boards single rule gilt bordered, board edges 'obliquely-broken fillet' roll gilt turn-ins 'double-rule' gilt, 'French Shell' 'made' endpapers, all edges mottled as per boards, pale blue and white sewn flat endbands, occasional minor spot, bit of chipping to head of spine, small area of surface insect damage at corner of lower board, armorial bookplate of James Comerford, from the collection of Christopher Ernest Weston 1947-2010.   Unsworths Booksellers   24 - 120   2011   £150

Association – Comstock, Rolland

Spark, Muriel *The Hothouse by the East River.* London: Macmillan, 1973. First edition; from the Rolland Comstock collection, with author's autograph on Comstock's bookplate, fine book and dust jacket.   Lupack Rare Books   May 26 2011 - ABE1314281545   2011 $125

Association – Conrad, Joseph

Gregory, Isbaella Augusta Perse   1859-1932 *Irish Folk-History Plays... First Series.... Second Series... (with) Our Irish Theatre/A Chapter of Autobiography.* New York and London: G. P. Putnams Sons, 1912-1913. First edition; First work in 2 volumes, 8vo., pages (ii), vi, 207, (i) blank, (3) ads; (ii), vi, 198, (5) ads, both volumes internally very fresh, short closed tear to one leaf of prelims in volume i, contemporary quarter cloth and blue paper covered boards, labels to spines with text in black, bumped and lightly rubbed, upper hinge volume i repaired, upper hinge volume ii cracked but firmly hold, John Quinn's autograph inscription volume ii, ownership inscription of A. S. Kinkead; second work 8vo., pages (ii), vi, 319, (i) blank, (5) ads, frontispiece and 3 plates, last leaves very slightly spotted otherwise extremely fresh, tight copy, contemporary quarter cloth and blue paper covered boards, label to spine with text in black, slightly bumped, some signs of wear to boards, endpapers lightly spotted, Quinn's presentation inscription to Joseph Conrad, ownership inscription of A. S. Kinkead.   Simon Finch Rare Books   Zero - 232   2011   £1250

Association – Conroy, Don

Conroy, Pat *The Great Santini.* Boston: Houghton Mifflin, 1976. First edition; fine in fine dust jacket, signed by author and by author's father, Don Conroy.   Between the Covers   169 - BTC34183   2011 $1200

Association – Constable, William

Peck, Francis *Desiderata Curiosa; or a Collection of Divers Scarce and Curious Peices.* London: printed, 1732-1735. 2 volumes bound as 1, folio, pages (viii) viii (xii) 66, 26, 52, 50, 44, 56 (xii) + engraved portrait frontispiece and 6 other engraved plates, (xxii), 68, 58, 52, 32, 50, 36, 32, 56, 25 (xix) + engraved portrait frontispiece and 3 other engraved plates, contemporary tan calf over re-used late 16th century, 17th century pasteboards, spine panel gilt, lettered and dated together in gilt direct, boards single rule gilt bordered, board edges decorative roll in blind, all edges red speckled, brown and white sewn endbands, little marginal dust soiling but quite clean, rear joint cracked, front joint sometime restored but now split again with board loose, spine ends and corners worn, old scrapes and scratches to boards, armorial bookplate of Wm. Constable, Esqr, from the collection of Christopher Ernest Weston 1947-2010.   Unsworths Booksellers   24 - 133   2011   £450

Association – Constantine, Murray

Doolittle, Hilda *Hippolytus Temporizes. a Play in Three Acts.* Boston and New York: Houghton Mifflin, 1927. First edition; 8vo, pages (x) 139, uncut, signed prsesentation from author to Murray Constantine (Katherine Burdekin), neat HD obituary press cutting inserted, patterned paper covered boards, slightly mottled, black cloth spine slightly faded/slightly sunned, endpapers slightly foxed, very good in near very good slipcase with printed label.   Any Amount of Books   May 29 2011 - A40498   2011 $221

Association – Cook, Edith Bessie

De La Ramee, Louise   1839-1908   *A Rainy June.* Leipzig: Bernhard Tauchnitz, 1885. Copyright edition; purple morocco, spine faded and little rubbed, bookplate of Edith Bessie Cook, good plus.   Jarndyce Antiquarian Booksellers   CLXC - 701   2011   £40

Association – Cook, Joseph

Keir, Elizabeth   *The History of Miss Greville.*   Edinburgh: printed for E. Balfour and W. Creech, Edinburgh and T. Cadell, London, 1787. First edition; 3 volumes, half titles, contemporary half calf, spines with devices in gilt, spines rubbed and lacking labels, engraved bookplates by Bewick for Joseph Cook.   Jarndyce Antiquarian Booksellers   CLXC - 40   2011   £750

Association – Cooke, Annie

Kingsley, Charles   1819-1875   *Glaucus; or the Wonders of the Shore.*   Cambridge: Macmillan, 1855. First edition; half title, frontispiece, final ad leaf + 16 page catalog (May 1855), pencil signature of Annie Cooke on half title, original green cloth, blocked in black and gilt, spine faded, slightly cocked, booksellers ticket of Harold Clever, good plus.   Jarndyce Antiquarian Booksellers   CXCI - 338   2011   £65

Association – Cooke, Edith Bessie

Boswell, James   1740-1795   *Boswell's Life of Johnson...* Oxford: Clarendon Press, 1887. 6 volumes in 11, half titles, frontispiece, extra illustrated, additional titlepages, plates as called for + 1293 additional plates, some occasional foxing and offsetting, heavy in places but largely internally, very good, handsomely bound in full crushed red morocco by Riviere & Son, double ruled gilt borders, raised gilt bands, compartments ruled in gilt, bookplates of Edith Bessie Cooke, top edge gilt.   Jarndyce Antiquarian Booksellers   CXCI - 20   2011   £5800

Association – Coomaraswamy, K.

Parsons, Claudia   *Vagabondage.*   London: Chatto & Windus, 1941. First edition; 8vo., pages xii, 304, frontispiece, 15 plates, 3 maps, neat name on front endpaper, "K. Coomaraswamy/Segannah/Nov. 11th/ 1941" (possibly Ananda K./Coomaraswamy), loosely inserted is good long signed typed letter from Claudia Parsons to Denis Collings, covers heavily worn and soiled, spine slightly split, contents okay, good only.   Any Amount of Books   May 29 2011 - A36695   2011 $255

Association – Coope, Elsie

Smith, Frank   *The Life and Work of Sir James Kay-Shuttleworth.*   London: John Murray, 1923. First edition; original blue cloth gilt, faint ring mark to upper board, pages xiii, 365, (iv), with 4 plates, prelims and fore-edge foxed, presentation copy from a later Lord Shuttleworth, inscribed "To Elsie Coope from Shuttleworth (in very shaky hand) Nov. 1938", later unrelated inscription and date on endpapers, scarce.   R. F. G. Hollett & Son Antiquarian Booksellers   175 - 1244   2011   £75

Association – Coote, Agnes

MacDonald, George   1824-1905   *Donal Grant.*   London: Kegan Paul, Trench & Co.,, 1883. First edition; 3 volumes, half titles, 39 page catalog (10.83) volume 1, original red cloth, spines dulled and slightly rubbed, stitching little loose volume II, inner hinges cracking, ownership inscription of Agnes Coote, Christmas 1883.   Jarndyce Antiquarian Booksellers   CXCII - 262   2011   £2500

Association – Cope, Henry

Tryon, Thomas   *The New Art of Brewing, Ale and Other Sorts of Liquors.*   London: printed for Tho. Salusbury, 1691. 12mo., (6), 138 pages with ad leaf and contents leaf immediately following titlepage, general paper browning throughout, gutter of titlepage frayed (not touching printed surface), numeral entered in red ink in early hand on title, ms. inscription in ink on flyleaf, signed by Henry Cope recording the gift of the book to him by Sir Harry Fane (Vane) on January 4th 1699 with 4 pages of ms. notes" in ink apparently by Henry Cope on prelim blanks and 19th century armorial bookplate of Alfred Chadwick, contemporary ruled sheep, neatly appropriately rebacked and labelled, good copy.   John Drury Rare Books   153 - 161   2011   £1250

Association – Cope, John

Astell, Mary *Some Reflections Upon Marriage.* Printed for William Parker, 1730. Fourth edition; Complete with prelim and terminal ad leaves, pages (viii), 180, (4), 8vo., contemporary sheep, gilt roll tooled borders on sides, unlettered spine with gilt rules on either side of raised bands, joints cracked, bookplate inside front cover of Sir John Cope, good.   Blackwell Rare Books   B166 - 5 2011   £350

Association – Copeman, R. S.

Shand, Alexander Innes *Against Time.* London: Smith Elder, 1870. First edition; 3 volumes, text slightly spotted, contemporary half brown roan, lettered in gilt on spines, some rubbing, small wormhole to spine volume II, ownership stamp of R. S. Copeman.   Jarndyce Antiquarian Booksellers   CXCI - 532 2011   £125

Association – Corby Castle

Boswell, Henry *Historical Descriptions of New and Elegant Picturesque Views of the Antiquities of England and Wales.* Alex. Hogg, n.d., Tall folio, contemporary half green roan gilt with marbled boards, rather rubbed and scraped, pages iv, plus over 400 pages, pagination in contemporary mss., with 290 engraved plates, full page frontispiece (laid down) but lacks maps, many plates cut out and re-inserted or added from other copies, few text leaves soiled or little damaged, the Corby Castle (Cumbria copy). R. F. G. Hollett & Son Antiquarian Booksellers   177 - 106   2011   £450

Association – Corelli, Marie

De La Ramee, Louise   1839-1908 *Two Offenders.* London: Chatto & Windus, 1894. First edition; 32 pages ads (Nov. 1893), half title, original dark green cloth, decorated in black and yellow, spine gilt lettered, George Ryland's small booklabel, nice, fine full page inscription signed by author for Marie Corelli, also pencil inscription "To Dalie with love on his 60th birthday from Tim", loosely inserted typed note by Rylands, "Given me by A. N. L. Munby on my 60th birthday.   Jarndyce Antiquarian Booksellers   CLXC - 714   2011   £600

Association – Corey, Sophia

MacDonald, George   1824-1905 *Orts.* London: Sampson Low, Marston, Searle & Rivignton, 1882. half title, 2 pages ads + 32 page catalog (Nov. 1882), original brown cloth, bevelled boards blocked in black and gilt with blind ornament on back board, by W. Bone & Son, brown endpapers, inner hinges cracking, good, inscribed by author for Sophia Corey, also signed by MacDonald in pencil with considerable ink alterations.   Jarndyce Antiquarian Booksellers   CXCII - 255 2011   £3800

MacDonald, George   1824-1905 *Rampolli: Growths from a Long Planted Root: Being Translations, New and Old.* London: Longmans, Green and Co., 1897. First edition; half title, 32 page catalog (5/97), partly unopened in original crimson buckram, spine faded, some wear and chips from leading free endpaper, inscribed by author for Sophia Corey.   Jarndyce Antiquarian Booksellers   CXCII - 325 2011   £750

MacDonald, George   1824-1905 *Ranald Bannerman's Boyhood.* London: Alexander Strahan, 1884. Frontispiece, plates and illustrations by Arthur Hughes, original olive green cloth blocked with "Grolier" design in darker green, brown and gilt, pencil note describes this as the Third English edition, inscription of Sophia B. Corey, Newark, NY. Jarndyce Antiquarian Booksellers   CXCII - 126 2011   £120

Association – Corey, Susan

MacDonald, George   1824-1905 *Lilith: a Romance.* London: Chatto & Windus, 1895. First edition; half title, title in red and black, uncut in original vertical grained black cloth, slight splitting at hinges, inscribed by author for Susan Corey.   Jarndyce Antiquarian Booksellers   CXCII - 318   2011   £1500

Association – Cornish, Dorothy

Saintsbury, George *Specimens of English Prose Style from Malory to Macaulay.* London: Kegan Paul, Trench & Co., 1885. First edition; number 1 of 50 copies, signed "Charles Whittingham & Co." (of Chiswick Press), signed in pencil on titlepage (dated Xmas 1887) to Dorothy Cornish, presumably the educationalist and Brighton historian, 8vo., green cloth spine with spine label and marbled boards, pages xlvi, 367, uncut, spine label browned and marked (illegible) edges rubbed, boards quite scuffed at rear, pages uncut with clean text.   Any Amount of Books   May 29 2011 - A47686 2011 $306

Association – Cornwallis, F.

Tacitus, Gaius Cornelius *Annales of Cornelius Tacitus.* London: printed by John Bill, 1622. Fifth edition; small folio, pages (vi) 271, (vii) 12, 228, (ii), the second page 213 is a full page engraving, this copy lacks initial blank, contemporary speckled calf, spine double ruled in blind, unlettered, boards double rule bordered in blind with smaller double rule central panel fleurons outermost at corners and smaller stylised flower, innermost all in blind, board edges decorative roll in blind, all edges red speckled, pink and white sewn endbands, little spotting, dampmark in upper corner, excisions to title repaired, rubbed, corners and endcaps worn, joints cracked, upper just holding, original ownership inscription cut out, but may have been same as "Fran: Cornwallis" at head fore corner of first page 1 or may have been same as "Richard Rowlandson" verso front blank, 19th century unidentified circular armorial bookplate, from the collection of Christopher Ernest Weston 1947-2010. Unsworths Booksellers   24 - 145   2011   £300

Association – Corso, Gregory

Charters, Ann *The Portable Beat Reader.* New York: Viking, 1992. First edition; 600+ pages, fine in fine dust jacket, exceptional copy, this copy belonged to Nelson Lyon, inscribed to him or signed and dated by William Burroughs, Allen Ginsberg, Gregory Corso, Ed Sanders, Michael McClure and Anne Waldman.   Ken Lopez Bookseller   154 - 12   2011 $1250

Ginsberg, Allen *Allen Verbatim. Lectures on Poetry, Politics, Consciousness.* US: McGraw Hill Paperbacks, 1975. First paperback edition; 8vo. pages (xvi), 270, internally fine, original pictorial wrappers, crease to upper wrapper corner with slight shelfwear and dust to spine, inscribed by Ginsberg on titlepage to Gregory Corso.   Simon Finch Rare Books   Zero - 319   2011   £475

Ginsberg, Allen *The Gates of Wrath/Rhymed Poems 1948-1952.* California: Grey Fox Press, 1972. First edition; 8vo., pages (x), 56, (2) blank, clean and fresh, original glassine protected purple, black and white pictorial wrappers with cover photo by poet in March 1949, some minor wear to wrappers, generally fine, inscribed by Ginsberg for Gregory Corso.   Simon Finch Rare Books   Zero - 317   2011   £675

Ginsberg, Allen *Sad Dust Glories/ Poems During Work Summer in Woods.* Berkeley: The Workingham Press, 1975. First edition; 8vo., pages (iv), 27, (i) imprint, original stapled green pictorial wrappers, some slight discoloration to wrappers, still near fine, inscribed by author for Gregory Corso, with TLS from Gary Wilkie to Corso loosely inserted.   Simon Finch Rare Books   Zero - 318   2011   £675

Association – Costello, Charles

Pope, Alexander   1688-1744   *The Poetical Works.* London: published by Thomas M'Lean, 1821.   One of 100 copies; 241 x 159mm, 2 volumes, contemporary dark green straight grain morocco, handsomely gilt, covers bordered with various gilt rules flanking a wide roll of linked drawer handle ornaments, blind floral roll forming a tangent inner frame, wide raised bands decorated in gilt, spines gilt with decorative rolls at head and foot with elaborate all over scrolling foliate design within panels, all edges gilt, designated large paper copy on titlepage and with margins that are quite wide but volume at least slightly trimmed down, engraved bookplate of Charles Costello (partially removed from first volume), first volume with pencilled ownership signature (perhaps of "Capt. C. Robertson"), hint of wear to leather and of fading to spines, intermittent light foxing, one opening little soiled, additional trivial defects, but quite appealing, decorative bindings bright, clean and very pretty, text quite fresh with nothing approaching a serious problem.   Phillip J. Pirages   59 - 280   2011 $650

Association – Cotton

Kennedy, Grace *Dunallan; or Know What You Judge: a Story.* Edinburgh: W. Oliphant, 1825. Second edition; 3 volumes, 12mo., half titles, final ad leaf volume I, contemporary half dark blue calf, armorial bookplate, Cotton & Renier booklabel, very good.   Jarndyce Antiquarian Booksellers   CLXC - 48   2011   £120

Association – Cotton, John

Roberts, Henry *The Dwellings of the Labouring Classes, Their Arrangement and Construction...* London: published by request and sold for The Benefit of the Society for Improving the Condition of the Labouring Classes, n.d. (last page dated 1855), Third edition; large 8vo., (8), 68 pages, including half title, numerous text figures and whole page illustrations followed by 12 litho plates, original publisher's green flexible cloth lettered gilt on front, slight edgewear, else very good+, bookplate of architect, John Cotton (1844-1934) with his ownership signatures, he has inserted 2 pamphlets, one about an organisation for promoting the enlargement and repair of churches and chapels, the other on improved dwellings for the working classes...   Any Amount of Books   May 26 2011 - A63134   2011 $671

Association – Cotton, Stephen

Kavanagh, Julia *French Women of Letters: Biographical Sketches.* London: Hurst & Blackett, 1862. First edition; 2 volumes, slightly spotted, contemporary half red calf, spines with raised gilt bands, brown leather labels slightly chipped, dulled and little rubbed, small booklabels of Stephen E. Cotton, good, sound copy.   Jarndyce Antiquarian Booksellers   CLXC - 32   2011   £110

Association – Courthope

Manning, Anne *Some Account of Mrs. Clarinda Singleheart.* London: Arthur Hall, Virtue and Co., 1855. First edition; frontispiece, title in red and black, rebound in contemporary half green calf, slight rubbing, booklabel and signature of Courthope, very good.   Jarndyce Antiquarian Booksellers   CLXC - 219   2011   £75

Association – Cowan, Robert

Watson, Douglas S. *California in the Fifties. Fifty Views of Cities and Mining Towns in California and the West.* San Francisco: John Howell, 1936. First edition, limited to 850 copies (of an edition of 1000); oblong folio, (113) pages, 50 full page reproductions with accompanying text on facing page, wine cloth, gilt lettered paper label on front cover, half inch dent to center of spine, else very fine, presentation inscription signed by publisher, John Howell, to bibliographer, Robert Cowan.   Argonaut Book Shop   Recent Acquisitions Summer 2010 - 232   2011 $400

Association – Coward, Thomas

Komroff, Manuel *The Magic Bow: A Romance of Pagnanini.* New York: Harper & Bros., 1940. First edition; little rubbing at extremities, very good, lacking dust jacket, inscribed by author to publisher, Thomas R. Coward.   Between the Covers   169 - BTC338044   2011 $650

Association – Cowell, F. R.

Birrell, Augustine *The Duties and Liabilities of Trustees. Six Lectures.* London: Macmillan, 1896. First edition; 8vo., original publisher's blue cloth lettered gilt at spine, pages xi, 183, uncut, pencilled ownership signature of historian F. R. Cowell, slight rubbing at hinges slight foxing to prelims, neat oval booksellers stamp, otherwise clean and bright, very good+ with clean text.   Any Amount of Books   May 29 2011 - A49183   2011 $238

Carey, H. C. *The Past, The Present and the Future.* London: Longmans, Brown, Green and Longmans, 1848. First edition; 8vo., original publisher' green blind patterned cloth lettered gilt at spine, pages 474, with 32 page publisher's catalog at rear. pencilled ownership signature of historian F. R. Cowell, sound clean copy with unsightly chip at head of spine and loss of about 2 inches of cloth affecting part of lettering, lesser chip at foot of spine, otherwise near very good and text very clean.   Any Amount of Books   May 29 2011 - A45215   2011 $340

James, William *The Literary Remains of the Late Henry James.* Boston: James R. Osgood and Co., 1885. First edition; 8vo., original publisher's red cloth lettered gilt at spine, pages 469, uncut, frontispiece, pencilled ownership signature of historian F. R. Cowell author of 'Cicero and the Roman Republic", signed presentation by A(lice) J(ames) for friend Constance Maude, slight fading at spine, slight mottling and slight marking, otherwise very good.   Any Amount of Books   May 29 2011 - A47621   2011 $340

Korthals-Altes, J. *Sir Cornelius Vermuyden: the Lifework of a Great Anglo-Dutchman in Land-Reclamation and Drainage, with Some Notes by the Author on the Present Condition of Drainage in England and a Resume of the Drainage Legislation in Holland.* London/The Hague: Williams & Norgate/W. P. Van Stockum, 1925. First edition; 8vo., original publisher's blue cloth lettered gilt on spine and on front cover, pages xii, 208, 15 illustrations, 6 maps, pencilled ownership signature of historian F. R. Cowell, slight shelfwear, sound, clean very good+.   Any Amount of Books   May 29 2011 - A49460   2011 $383

Maximus Tyrius *The Dissertations of Maximus Tyrius.* London: printed by C. Whittenham, Dean Street for the Granslator and sold by R. H. Evans Pall Mall, 1804. First edition; small 8vo., 2 volumes in 1, pages xv, (1) 235, (1); 272 pages, later bottle green cloth (circa 1900), neat label of Pantiles (Tunbridge Wells) Library and Reading Room, no other library markings, booklabel of T. S. Osmond of St. John's College, Oxford (donor of the book), pencilled ownership signature of historian F. R. Cowell, very good, clean text free of foxing, couple of gatherings very slightly protruding but sound attractive copy.   Any Amount of Books   May 26 2011 - A46360   2011 $470

Nichols, Francis Morgan *Britton: The French Text...* Oxford: Clarendon Press, 1865. First editions; 2 volumes, tall 8vo., original publisher's russet brown cloth lettered gilt at spine, pages lxiv, 419 & 398; bookplate of Sir James Hannen, pencilled ownership signature of historian F. R. Cowell, covers somewhat soiled and marked with staining at spine, otherwise about very good- with very sound, clean text.   Any Amount of Books   May 29 2011 - A45886   2011 $272

Observations on Modern Gardening. London: T. Payne, 1771. Third edition; 8vo., full brown leather with decorated gilt at spine, raised bands and gilt title on red label, blank (6) 257, ornate armorial bookplate of Agneu (Baronet) of Lochnau, pencilled ownership signature of F. R. Cowell, author of The Garden as a Fine Art, very handsome very good, slightly rubbed at corner, slightly tender at hinges. Any Amount of Books   May 29 2011 - A47683   2011 $408

Riding, Laura *The World and Ourselves.* London: Chatto & Windus, 1938. First edition; 8vo., pages xi, 529, pencilled ownership signature of historian F. R. Cowell, very good+ in like dust jacket with faint edgewear. Any Amount of Books May 29 2011 - A48862 2011 $255

Robinson, William *The Parks and Gardens of Paris Considered in Relation to the Wants of Other Cities and Of Public and Private Gardens.* London: John Murray, 1883. thir edition; 8vo., half dark brown leather, pages xxiv, 548, pencilled ownership signature of historian F. R. Cowell, presentation "From the author/Oct. 27h 1885", endpapers slightly stained, corner and hinges rubbed, one signature slightly protruding, otherwise very good. Any Amount of Books May 29 2011 - A47680 2011 $340

Satow, Ernest *A Guide to Diplomatic Practice.* London: Longmans, Green and Co., 1932. Third edition; fat 8vo., pages x, 519, but stretched to about 1000 pages with interleaved blanks on which Sir Stephen Gaselee has written notes and comments, pencilled ownership signature of historian F. R. Cowell, A S Gow's pamphlet on Life of Fasselee loosely inserted, brown half leather with orange boards and lettered gilt at spine, slight rubbing, minor near, else sound, very good. Any Amount of Books May 26 2011 - A46377 2011 $419

Whewell, William 1794-1866 *Of a Liberal Education in General: and with Particular Reference to the Leading Studies of the University of Cambridge.* London: John W. Parker, 1845. First edition; 8vo., pages xviii, 248, 15, (1), pages, original publisher's paper covered boards, with green linen spine and spine label, now somewhat faded and hard to read, corners scuffed and worn, front inner hinge cracked but holding well, slight soiling, else sound, near very good, pencilled ownership signature of historian F. R. Cowell. Any Amount of Books May 29 2011 - A46028 2011 $306

Association – Cower, G. E.

Haggard, Henry Rider 1856-1925 *Cetwayo and His White Neighbours; or Remarks on Recent Events in Zululand, Natal & the Transvaal.* London: Trubner & Co., 1882. First edition; half title, followed by leaf printed verso, half red morocco, marbled boards by Mansell, very slight rubbed at head of spine, booklabel of Geo. Evelyn Cower, top edge gilt, fine. Jarndyce Antiquarian Booksellers CXCI - 197 2011 £450

Association – Cowper, H. Swainston

Mello, J. Magens *The Dawn of Metallurgy.* The Institute, 1889. Original wrappers, pages 26, with 2 pages of illustrations and text drawing, author's copy, so stamped and inscribed by J. Allen Brown to H. Swainston Cowper. R. F. G. Hollett & Son Antiquarian Booksellers 177 - 572 2011 £30

Association – Cox, Brian

Stoppard, Tom *Rock 'n' Roll.* London: Faber & Faber, 2006. First edition thus; 8vo., wrappers, signed by Stoppard, Rufus Sewell, Brian Cox and Sinead Cusak, pages 128, fine. Any Amount of Books May 29 2011 - A68668 2011 $340

Association – Cox, E. M.

Whitman, Walt 1819-1892 *Leaves of Grass.* Brooklyn: published by the author, 1856. Second edition; 12mo., original grey-green cloth, decoratively blindstamped, gilt decorations and lettering, engraved frontispiece by Samuel Hollyer, bookplates of E. M. Cox and Michael Sadlier, cloth slightly rubbed, some light to moderate foxing, fine, from the collection of Samuel Charters. The Brick Row Book Shop Bulletin 8 - 6 2011 $22,500

Association – Cox, John George

Johnston, Harry Hamilton 1858-1927 *The Kilmanjaro Expedition.* London: Kegan Paul Trench & Co., 1886. First edition; thick 8vo., xv, 572, 34 (ads) pages, 6 maps, engraved frontispiece, 78 illustrations, occasional light foxing, original pictorial cloth boards, over black cloth, gilt stamped cover and spine titles, spine replaced, bookplate of John George Cox, Broxwood Court, very good. Jeff Weber Rare Books 163 - 184 2011 $500

Association – Cragg, E.

Clare, John *The Village Minstrel and Other Poems.* London: printed for Taylor and Hessey, Fleet Street and E. Drury, Stamford, 1821. First edition; 2 volumes, small 8vo., frontispieces, original cloth backed boards with paper spine labels, former owner's neat signature "Edw. Cragg 1843" in upper right hand corner of titlepages and on pastedowns, extremities of boards trifle rubbed, spines and covers bit soiled, but in general exceptionally fine set in original condition, preserved in folding cloth box, the Bradley Martin copy, Carter's variant binding "B". James S. Jaffe Rare Books May 26 2011 - 20616 2011 $8750

Association – Craik, Mary

Smith, Logan Pearsall 1865-1946 *Songs and Sonnets.* London: Elkin Mathews, 1909. First edition; small 8vo., uncut, pages 64, tipped in 4 page publisher's ads dated Dec. 1909, signed presentation from author for Mary Craik, very good, prelims and edges little browned, spine slightly rubbed. Any Amount of Books May 29 2011 - A68491 2011 $204

Association – Crane, Barbara

Taken by Design: Photographs from The Institute of Design 1937-1971. Chicago: University of Chicago Press, 2002. First edition; very fine in photo illustrated boards, issued without dust jacket, signed by a large number of photographers and some of the editors, among the signatures are Yasuhiro Ishimoto, Marvin E. Newton (twice), Barbara Crane, Ray K. Metzker, Joseph Jachna, Joseph Sterling (twice), Kenneth Josephson, David Travis, Keith Davis and quite a few others, unique copy.   Jeff Hirsch Books   ny 2010 2011 $750

Association – Crawshay-Williams, Rupert

Hawton, Hector   *Question.*   Bungay, Suffolk: Pemberton Pub., 1968. First edition; 13 volumes, circa 1340 pages, very good, first issue annotated and signed by Rupert Crawshay-Williams, one of the contributors.   Any Amount of Books   May 29 2011 - A48239   2011 $204

Association – Cremer, Vera Frances

MacDonald, George   1824-1905   *The Light Princess and Other Fairy Stories.*   New York: G. P. Putnam's Sons, 1893. Title in red and black, frontispiece, illustrations by Maud Humphrey, original beige cloth pictorially blocked in black and brown, spine darkened, inner hinge cracking, inscribed presentation form author Christmas Day 1893 for Vera Frances Cremer.   Jarndyce Antiquarian Booksellers   CXCII - 87   2011   £1250

Association – Cressey, E. H.

Blackwell, Elizabeth   *The Laws of Life with Special Reference to the Physical Education of Girls.*   New York: George P. Putnam, 1852. First edition; 180 pages, slate gray cloth, edges stained red, spine bit faded, few very tiny spots, else remarkably fresh, tight copy, as close to fine as one could hope for, contemporary signature of E. H. Cressey.   Joseph J. Felcone Inc.   Fall Miscellany 2010 - 14   2011 $12,000

Association – Cresswell, Lionel

Williamson, George Charles   1858-1942   *Lady Anne Clifford. Countess of Dorset, Pembroke & Montgomery 1590-1676.*   Kendal: Titus Wilson, 1923. Limited signed edition, number 108 of 250 copies; small 4to., original vellum backed boards, corners rather worn and rounded, pages xxii, 547, uncut, 53 plates, very scarce, fine large armorial bookplate of Lionel Cresswell of Middle Temple and Burley in Wharfedale, later of Ruth Cresswell of Crackenthorpe Hall, Appleby.   R. F. G. Hollett & Son Antiquarian Booksellers   173 - 1217   2011   £350

Association – Cresswell, Ruth

Williamson, George Charles   1858-1942   *Lady Anne Clifford. Countess of Dorset, Pembroke & Montgomery 1590-1676.*   Kendal: Titus Wilson, 1923. Limited signed edition, number 108 of 250 copies; small 4to., original vellum backed boards, corners rather worn and rounded, pages xxii, 547, uncut, 53 plates, very scarce, fine large armorial bookplate of Lionel Cresswell of Middle Temple and Burley in Wharfedale, later of Ruth Cresswell of Crackenthorpe Hall, Appleby.   R. F. G. Hollett & Son Antiquarian Booksellers   173 - 1217   2011   £350

Association – Crick, Francis

Fincham, J. R. S.   *Genetic Complementation.*   New York: Benjamin, 1966. First edition; 8vo., xii, 143 pages, near fine with foxing edges in very good dust jacket (sun spine, mild edgewear, foxing to rear), from the library of Francis Crick.   By the Book, L. C.   26 - 88   2011 $600

Association – Cropper, Margaret

Williams, Charles   *The Descent of the Dove.*   London: Longman, Green and Co., 1939. First edition; original cloth, gilt, dust jacket little spotted and marked, spine little darkened, (price of 8/6 on inner flap blacked out and overprinted 7/6 net), pages ix, 245, frontispiece, few spots to endpapers, signature of Margaret Cropper, Cumbrian poet. R. F. G. Hollett & Son Antiquarian Booksellers   175 - 1445   2011   £65

Association – Cross, Johannis Neville

Kitton, Frederic G.   *Charles Dickens by Pen and Pencil, Including Anecdotes and Reminiscences Collected from his Friends and Contemporaries.*   London: Frank T. Sabin, and John F. Dexter, 1890-1892. Large paper edition; 390 x 300 mm., 3 volumes, elegant crimson morocco attractively gilt by Riviere (signed at foot of front turn-in), boards gilt with lozenge centerpiece of scrolled floral tooling around a blind oval center, raised bands, gilt spines with fleuron centerpiece, marbled endpapers, inner gilt dentelles incorporating lovely floral tools, top edge gilt, other edges untrimmed, complete set of the 15 wrappers bound in at back of third volume, text illustrations throughout, 195 fine plates (containing 236 images), all of these added (either as part of the usual Large Paper version, or, in the case of some 70 plates, as inserted, extra illustrations), engraved bookplate of Johannis Neville Cross, titlepage printed in red and black; slight dulling to covers (from leather preservative), trivial soiling, but impressive bindings scarcely worn and very pleasing, dozen of the extra engraved plates and adjacent leaves somewhat foxed, one plate creased in lower corner (not affecting image), few instances of minor marginal soiling, slight offset browning opposite few plates, other trivial defects, generally quite clean and bright.   Phillip J. Pirages 59 - 175   2011 $3500

Association – Crossie, Phillip

Lipper, J. Heron *History of the Grand Lodge of Free & Accepted Masons of Ireland.* 1952-1957. First edition; 2 volumes, illustrations, lower fore corner volume I damaged (signed presentation from Phillip Crossie, a fellow-Mason), other than that, a very good set. C. P. Hyland May 26 2011 - 259/250 2011 $1232

Association – Cruikshank, George

Lewis, Randle *Reflections on the Causes of Unhappy Marriages, and on Various Subjects Therewith...* London: W. Clarke, 1805. First and only edition; 8vo., (5) iv-vi 160 pages, titlepage little soiled, early 19th century ownership signature at head of title of George Cruikshank, in high quality early 20th century dark green quarter morocco over marbled boards, spine fully gilt and lettered, handsome copy. John Drury Rare Books 153 - 80 2011 £500

Association – Crummer, James

The Lady's Law; or a Treatise of Feme Converts: containing al the Laws and Statutes Relating to Women Under Several Heads... London: in the Savoy: printed by E. and R. Nutt and R. gosling (assigns of E. Sayer, Esq.) for H. L. and sold by C. Corbett and E. Littleton, 1737. Second edition; 8vo., (iii)-viii 264 (16) pages, wanting initial leaf of ads, contemporary ruled calf, rebacked and labelled, very good, crisp copy, early ownership signature of James Crummer, 20th century bookplate of Richard Pepler. John Drury Rare Books 153 - 75 2011 £850

Association – Culpepper, Nick

Anger, Kenneth *Hollywood Babylon.* London: Arrow Books Ltd., 1986. First Arrow Books edition; wrappers, small 4to., illustrations in black and white, signed presentation from author for Nick Culpepper, 305 pages, slight rubbing, else sound, very good+. Any Amount of Books May 29 2011 - A73504 2011 $306

Association – Cunard, Edward

Hook, Theodore Edward *Love and Pride.* London: Whittaker and Co., 1833. 3 volumes, 12mo., half titles, contemporary full calf, gilt borders raised bands, gilt compartments and dentelles, red and blue morocco label, bookplate of Edward Cunard, very good. Jarndyce Antiquarian Booksellers CXCI - 527 2011 £350

Association – Cunard, Lady

Gosse, Edmund 1849-1928 *On Viol and Flute.* London: Heinemann, 1896. First Selected edition; small 8vo., pages xi, 212, original publisher's green cloth lettered gilt on spine and cover, frontispiece, signed presentation from author to George Moore, from the library of Henry "Chips" Channon with note at rear in his hand "Given me by Lady Cunard, Christmas 1938, slight tanning, slight fading, very small nick at head of spine, otherwise very good. Any Amount of Books May 29 2011 - A69860 2011 $255

Association – Cunliffe, Eadyth

Clark, John B. *The Modern Distributive Process: Studies of Competition and Its Limits, of the Nature and Amount of Profits and of the Determination of Walks in the Industrial Society of To-Day.* Boston: Ginn & Co., 1888. First edition; crown 8vo., pages viii, 69, 1 diagram, original blue cloth lettered gilt on spine and on front cover, bookplate of Eadyth Cunliffe and her ownership signature dated 1890, corners slightly bumped, very slight rubbing, else very good+. Any Amount of Books May 29 2011 - A46350 2011 $340

Association – Cunningham, Allan

Wordsworth, William 1770-1850 *The Excursion Being a Portion of the Recluse.* London: printed for Longman, Hurst, Rees, Orme and Brown, Paternoster-Row, London, 1814. One of 500 copies, First edition with errata leaf and with Y1 cancelled as usual; 4to., full contemporary green morocco, elaborately gilt tooled with thistles and lyres, all edges gilt, magnificent contemporary presentation binding, expertly rebacked by James Brockman with original spine laid down, preserved in green half morocco slipcase, inscribed by author to Allan Cunningham. James S. Jaffe Rare Books May 26 2011 - 13825 2011 $25,000

Association – Cunningham, William

Worcester, Samuel *An Address on Sacred Musick, Delivered Before the Middlesex Musical Society and the Handel Society of Dartmouth College.* Boston: Manning and Loring, 1811. 8vo., pages 22, sewn self wrappers, inscribed by author to William Cunningham, very slight foxing in places, edges of leaves little chipped, else very good. Second Life Books Inc. 174 - 334 2011 $75

Association – Cuper, Gisbert

Newton, Henry *Epistolae, Orationes, et Carmina. (bound with) Orationes quarum Altera Florentiae Anno MDCCV.* Lucca: D. Ciufetti, 1710. Amsterdam: 1710-(1712); 2 works in 1 volume, (6), 250, 115, (3) pages, engraved frontispiece, 58 pages (final quire signed * (pages 51-58) reprinted to include items dated 1711 and 1712, contemporary English panelled calf, spine gilt, rubbed, upper joint slightly cracked, one corner worn, number of small corrections throughout, from the library of the Earls of Macclesfield at Shirburn Castle, bound at end are two manuscript letters from Newton at Florence, one to Jean Le Clerc at Amsterdam and the other to Gisbert Cuper at Deventer, both dated 1710. Maggs Bros. Ltd. 1440 - 155 2011 £800

Association – Curle, Richard

Conrad, Joseph 1857-1924 *The Works.* Garden City and New Yorj: Doubleday Page & Co., 1920-1926. Sun Dial edition, one of 735 copies signed by author; 22 volumes, 220 x 150mm., fine and especially flamboyant lilac morocco, elaborately gilt by Stikeman, covers panelled with single and double gilt fillets and intricate scrolling foliate cornerpieces, raised bands, spine attractively gilt in ruled compartments with margin ornaments (seashell or anchor) as centerpiece and with scrolling cornerpieces, crimson morocco doublures, front doublures with central panel to blue morocco, wide turn-ins with alternating floral tools, doublures decorated with very gilt lines and (at corners) floral bouquets, blue central panels with large gilt sailing vessel at middle, watered silk endleaves, morocco hinges, all edges gilt, frontispiece; with APS by author to James Brand Pinker (Conrad's agent) tipped in at front, also with signature of Richard Curle; spines uniformly faded to an even chestnut brown, hint of rubbing to handful of joints and corners (only), one opening in one volume with marginal spots, but quite fine set in very decorative bindings, text virtually pristine, volumes completely solid, covers bright and wear to leather entirely minor. Phillip J. Pirages 59 - 168 2011 $15,000

Association – Curry, Neil

Pepper, John *Cockley Beck.* Element Books, 1984. First edition; original cloth, gilt, dust jacket, 141 pages, drawings by author, presentation copy inscribed by author for Neil Curry. R. F. G. Hollett & Son Antiquarian Booksellers 173 - 902 2011 £45

Association – Curtis, J. A.

Kelly, George *Craig's Wife a Drama.* Boston: Little Brown, 1926. First edition; 8vo., pages 174, very nice, tight copy, inscribed by author to Josephine Williams who played the part of Mrs. Harold in the NY production, also signed by rest of the cast - Annie Sutherland, Crystal Herne, Arthur Shaw, C. Stewart, Eleanor Marsh, Charles Trowbridge, Josephine Hull, J. A. Curtis, Nelan Jaap, Arline Alcine & Mary Gildea, also inscribed by the producer, Rosalie Stewart to whom the play was dedicated. Second Life Books Inc. 174 - 213 2011 $2000

Association – Curtis, Mr.

Sigourney, Lydia *Selections from Various Sources.* Worcester: John H. Turner, 1863. First edition; (240) pages, 8vo., original blindstamped purple cloth with gilt design on front panel, gilt decorated spine evenly faded with gilt lettering, some wear to head and foot, faint waterstain in margins of first and final pages, all in all, tight, sound copy, signed presentation copy in year of publication to Mr. Curtis. Paulette Rose Fine and Rare Books 32 - 158 2011 $350

Association – Curwen, Edward Stanley

Brougham and Vaux, Henry Peter Brougham, 1st Baron 1778-1868 *Historical Sketches of Statesmen who Flourished in the Time of George III.* Paris: Baudry's European Library, 1844. Pages xii, iv-viii, 372, old half calf gilt with marbled boards, extremities slightly rubbed and lettering partially dulled, corner torn off front two flyleaves, signature of Edward Stanley Curwen dated 1844. R. F. G. Hollett & Son Antiquarian Booksellers 175 - 185 2011 £35

Association – Curzon-Herrick, Kathleen

Barrie, James Matthew 1860-1937 *Rosalind.* New York: Charles Scribner's Sons, 1914. 190 x 130mm., 1 p.l., 89-151 pages, very pleasing dark green pebble grain morocco, attractively gilt by J. S. H. Bates of Leicester (stamp signed on rear turn-in), covers with border of plain and broken gilt fillets around a central rectangular panel formed by the same broken rule (four flap-like panels surrounding the central rectangle in an arrangement resembling fold-over closures) large and very attractive cornerpieces of five grouped tulips on leaves stems, spine with two raised bands, large gilt tulips at either end, vertical titling in middle, gilt turn-ins, top edge gilt, gilt stamped presentation "To Lady Kathleen Curzon-Herrick/ A Memento of June 1918/ from Mr. and Mrs. A. Laxton-Hames", spine faded (as always with green morocco) to a pleasing olive green, hint of wear to extremities, still quite fine, especially attractive, very bright and clean inside and out. Phillip J. Pirages 59 - 87 2011 $850

Association – Cusack, Sinead

Stoppard, Tom *Rock 'n' Roll.* London: Faber & Faber, 2006. First edition thus; 8vo., wrappers, signed by Stoppard, Rufus Sewell, Brian Cox and Sinead Cusak, pages 128, fine.   Any Amount of Books   May 29 2011 - A68668   2011 $340

Association – Cussler, Dirk

Cussler, Clive *Arctic Drift, a Dirk Pitt Novel.* New York: Putnam, 2008. First edition; fine, dust jacket fine, signed by Clive and Dirk Cussler.   Bella Luna Books   May 29 2011 - t9060   2011 $82

Association – D'Alton, Dean

Harris, Walter *Hibernica; or Some Antient Pieces Relating to Ireland.* Dublin: 1770. 2 volumes in one, modern quarter calf with marbled boards, 2 stamps "Bequest of Dean D'Alton, Ballinrobe" otherwise very good.   C. P. Hyland   May 26 2011 - 255/287   2011 $507

Association – D'Angers, Pierre Paul David

Le Sage, Alain Rene   1668-1747   *Les Avantures de Monsieur Robert Chevalier...*   Paris: Chez Etienne Ganeau, 1732. First edition; 2 volumes, 12mo., (xvi), 390; (viii), 363, 6 full page engraved plates by Bonnard in contemporary full calf, hinge strengthened at early date, spine gilt, one inch split to lower hinge calf of one volume, contemporary owner's notes at extremities of titlepage, some light foxing and staining, very good, at top of each titlepage is ownership signature of sculptor Pierre Paul David d'Angers.   Second Life Books Inc.   174 - 229   2011 $1200

Association – D'Arcy, M. C.

Bible. English - 1881   *The Gospel According to S. John.*   Cambridge: Cambridge University Press, circa, 1881. Interleaves with plain rubricated pages, plain red calf, gilt dentelles & edges by Philip Tout, all edges gilt, inscribed "This gift to my father George MacDonald from Miss Violet Cavendish-Bentinck, now offered in much love & gratitude to the Rev. M. C. D'Arcy by Greville MacDonald".   Jarndyce Antiquarian Booksellers   CXCII - 335   2011   £250

Association – D'Eichthal, Gustave

Comte, Auguste   *Systeme de Politique Positive...*   Paris: Setier, 1824. First edition; 8vo., pages 8, 289, (i) blank; 84; late 19th century red morocco, marbled boards, panelled spine, filleted and lettered in gilt, preserving original green silk bookmark, tips rubbed, foot of spine bumped and torn, obituary of Auguste Comte mounted between front free endpapers, Comte's autograph inscription to mathematician and politician Dominique Francois Jean Arago, bookplate of Gustave d'Eichthal and manuscript notes of d'Eichthal on half title and front free endpapers.   Simon Finch Rare Books   Zero - 125   2011   £4750

Association – D'Oyly, J. Walpole

Edgeworth, Maria   1768-1849   *Belinda.*   printed for J. Johnson, 1801. 3 volumes, half titles, discarded, some light browning and spotting, few leaves in volume i little stained in margins, one or two small marginal paper flaws, pages (3)-8, 370; (ii) 387; (ii), 359, (1), 8vo., earl 20th century black and red marbled cloth boards, recently backed with mid brown calf, spines with five raised bands, black lettering pieces, central gilt tools in compartments, hinges relined, touch of wear to corners, bookplate of J. Walpole D'Oyly, good, scarce.   Blackwell Rare Books   B166 - 34   2011   £2000

Association – Dabbs, G. H. R.

De La Ramee, Louise   1839-1908   *Pipistrello and Other Stories.*   London: Chatto & windus, 1880. First edition; ad preceding half title, 4 pages ads + 32 page catalog (April 1880), uncut in original blue cloth, blocked in black, spine lettered in gilt, spine dulled and little rubbed, armorial bookplate of G.H.R. Dabbs.   Jarndyce Antiquarian Booksellers   CLXC - 695   2011   £55

Association – Dacre

Bryant, Jacob   *Observations and Inquiries Relating to Various Parts of Ancient History...*   Cambridge: printed by J. Atchdeacon, printer to the University, 1767. Mixed issue, page 7 has the press figure '2' but page 62 has no press figure and page 63 has '3', errata leaf comes at beginning; 4to., pages (ii) iiii, (v), 324, 7 engraved extending plates, contemporary tan calf, spine panel gilt, red lettering piece gilt, boards double rule gilt bordered, board edges 'zig zag' decorative roll in blind, all edges densely red sprinkled, pink and white sewn endbands, (gathering *1 - 4 leaves of prelims) not bound in this copy (apparently not infrequent error), light toning and spotting, closed tear to one leaf, through but not affecting text, small wormtrack in lower corner at beginning, rubbed at extremities, joints cracked, little loss from headcap, armorial bookplate of "Dacre", from the collection of Christopher Ernest Weston 1947-2010.   Unsworths Booksellers   24 - 72   2011   £300

Association – Dahl, Gustav H. J.

Linne, Carl Von 1707-1778 *Hortus Upsaliensis, Exhibens Plantas Exoticas.* Stockholmiae: Sumtu & Literis Laurentii Salvii, 1748. First edition; 3 folding engraved plates, 8vo., pages (10), 306 (40), 19th century quarter calf, some rubbing to edges, upper edges starting, ex-libris Gustav H. J. Dahl with handstamp on front flyleaf, name blackened out, small ink number on title, 1/8 inch marginal tear to 4 leaves. Raymond M. Sutton, Jr. May 26 2011 - 51626 2011 $1600

Association – Dalone, Mr.

Lister, Martin *Conchyliorum Bivalvium Utriusque Aquae Exercitatio Anatomica Tertia.* London: Sumptibus authoris impressa, 1696. First edition; 4to., xliii, (1), 173 pages; 51 pages, 10 engraved plates, complete with terminal blank Z4 in first work, Dissertatio has its own titlepage and pagination, contemporary sprinkled calf, very skillfully rebacked to period style, small early shelfmark in red ink on endpaper and on title, minor paper flaw in S2 just grazing catchword, very faint foxing in fore edge, very lovely copy with text and plates, clean and fresh, armorial bookplate of A. Gifford, D.D. of the Museum, presentation copy from Lister for Mr. Dalone. Joseph J. Felcone Inc. Fall Miscellany 2010 - 76 2011 $10,000

Association – Danby, E. W.

Morgan, Sydney Owenson 1776-1859 *Lady Morgan's Memoirs: Autobiography, Diaries and Correspondence.* London: Wm. H. Allen & Co., 1863. Second edition; engraved frontispiece, contemporary full maroon calf, double ruled borders in gilt, spines gilt in compartments, black title labels, lacking volume no. labels, spines faded to brown and slightly rubbed, Eton leaving inscription E. W. Danby to Alexander William Fraser, 19th Lord Saltoun, Saltoun bookplates, good plus. Jarndyce Antiquarian Booksellers CLXC - 542 2011 £125

Association – Danby, William

Wharton, Henry *The History of the Troubles and Tryal of.... William Laud...to which is prefixed the Diary of His Own Life.* London: printed for Ri. Chiswell, 1695. Folio, pages (xx) 616, (ii), engraved frontispiece, contemporary speckled calf, spine double ruled in blind decorative red lettering piece gilt, boards blind double ruled with decorative rollout with the supplementary ruling, board edges decorative roll gilt, all edges lightly red sprinkled, pink and white sewn endbands, title bit dusty, few minor spots elsewhere, touch rubbed joints cracking but strong, front joint bit defective at head, some scratches to boards, ink inscription "W. Danby", armorial 18th century bookplate "William Danby Esqr.", from the collection of Christopher Ernest Weston 1947-2010. Unsworths Booksellers 24 - 59 2011 £400

Association – Dannay, Frederic

Doyle, Arthur Conan 1859-1930 *The Adventures of Sherlock Holmes.* London: George Newnes, 1892. First edition; first issue, large octavo, names in ink on half title, original light blue cloth over bevelled boards, fine Ellery Queen copy, with Manfred Lee and Frederic Dannay names in ink on half title. Heritage Book Shop Booth A12 51st NY International Antiquarian Book Fair April 8-10 2011 - 47 2011 $17,500

Doyle, Arthur Conan 1859-1930 *Adventures of Sherlock Holmes.* London: George Newnes, 1892. First edition, first issue with no street name on front cover; "Violent" for "Violet" on page 317, large octavo, (4), 317, (1, printer's imprint) (2, blank) pages, 104 illustrations by Sidney Paget in text, original light blue cloth over beveled boards, front cover and spine blocked and lettered in gilt and black, all edges gilt, gray flower and leaf endpapers, small ink initials to front free endpaper, front hinge professionally and invisibly repaired, back hinge starting but firm, slight bit of shelf wear to top and bottom of spine, some light foxing to few prelim and final pages, else near fine, exceptionally clean and bright, housed in tan cloth clamshell, the fine "Ellery Queen" (Manfred Lee) and "Barnaby Ross" (Frederic Dannay) names in ink on half title. Heritage Book Shop Holiday 2010 - 30 2011 $17,500

Association – Darnley, Daphne Mulholland, Countess

Nesbit, Edith *The Story of the Treasure Seekers, Being the Adventures of the Bastable Children in Search of a Fortune.* London: Fisher Unwin, 1899. First edition; 8vo., pages xii, 296, 12 pages publisher's ads, original green cloth lettered and illustrated gilt on spine and cover, illustrations, all edges gilt, corners slightly bumped, slight rubbing, sound, very good, ownership signature od Daphne Mulholland (1900), i.e. Countess Darnley. Any Amount of Books May 29 2011 - A74864 2011 $340

Association – Darwin, Maurice

Davidson, D. *The Great Pyramid - Its Divine Message.* London: Williams and Norgate, 1925. Second edition; small folio, original black cloth gilt, neatly rebacked, pages xxxii, 568, double page frontispiece, 70 plates and 67 tables and diagrams, many folding, (1 very heavily annotated by former owner, Rev. Maurice Darwin of Bury St. Edmunds, with relevant ALS from him loosely inserted July 1958). R. F. G. Hollett & Son Antiquarian Booksellers 177 - 246 2011 £140

Association – Davidson, Angus

Powys, Theodore Francis *The Left Leg.* London: Chatto & Windus, 1923. First edition; 8vo., pages 311, inscribed presentation from dedicatee, Sylvia Townsend Warner to Angus (Davidson), with a quatrain also inscribed to same, three quarter red morocco, spine gilt in compartments, little browned on fore edge, else fine.   Second Life Books Inc.   174 - 262   2011 $713

Association – Davie, Donald

MacDonald, Ross *Black Money.* New York: Alfred A. Knopf, 1966. First edition; 8vo., inscribed by author to poet Donald Davie and his wife Doreen, fine in dust jacket with one tiny rub at head of spine.   Buckingham Books   May 26 2011 - 20957   2011 $2750

Association – Davie, Doreen

MacDonald, Ross *Black Money.* New York: Alfred A. Knopf, 1966. First edition; 8vo., inscribed by author to poet Donald Davie and his wife Doreen, fine in dust jacket with one tiny rub at head of spine.   Buckingham Books   May 26 2011 - 20957   2011 $2750

Association – Davies, Francis Robert

Mitford, Mary Russell   1787-1855   *Our Village: Sketches of Rural Character and Scenery.*   London: Henry G. Bohn, 1852. New edition; first and second series, 2 volumes, frontispiece, engraved titles, additional vignette titles, contemporary half vellum, gilt spines, maroon leather labels, marbled boards and endpapers, spines little darkened, armorial bookplates of Francis Robert Davies, good plus.   Jarndyce Antiquarian Booksellers   CLXC - 409   2011   £120

Association – Davies, Richard

Thomson, James   1700-1748   *The Works.*   London: printed by A. Strahan for J. Rivington and Sons, 1788. 227 x 145mm., 3 volumes, once elegant and still pleasing contemporary scarlet straight grained morocco simply gilt, covers with single gilt fillet border, raised bands flanked by plain gilt rules, gilt titling, turn-ins with gilt chain roll, marbled endpapers, all edges gilt; with fine fore-edge paintings of Folkestone, Dublin and Worcester; volumes in recent sturdy buckram slipcase with marbled paper sides; frontispiece portrait, 10 engraved plates; 19th century armorial bookplate of Richard Davies, morocco bookplate of Estelle Doheny and modern engraved bookplate of John Taylor Reynolds, titlepage with ink ownership inscription of Mihill Slaughter 1811 (Secretary of the Railways Department); hint of soil to covers, joints and extremities with little rubbing (but well refurbished), leaves with intermittent minor foxing, engravings bit more foxed (half of them rather browned), offset onto facing page, text with general light browning and occasional trivial soiling, four leaves with short marginal or paper flaw tears (no loss); although not without problems, set nevertheless appealing, internal flaws never really unsightly, bindings all solid and paintings where it really matters, entirely well preserved.   Phillip J. Pirages   59 - 45   2011 $4500

Association – Davies, William Carey

MacDonald, George   1824-1905   *Donal Grant.*   London: Kegan Paul Trench & Co., 1883. 3 volumes in 1, half title and title volume I, without other titles and half titles, some foxing, contemporary half red calf, spine faded to brown with dark green labels, hinges splitting, preserved in red cloth covered box, brown leather labels, a page proof on thin paper with a number of corrections by MacDonald, inscribed by him to friend William Carey Davies.   Jarndyce Antiquarian Booksellers   CXCII - 261   2011   £4500

MacDonald, George   1824-1905   *St. George and St. Michael.*   London: Henry S. King & Co., 1876. (1875?). First edition; 3 volumes, half titles, 48 page catalog (Sept. 1875) volume I, few spots, original maroon cloth, plain rule & dotted rule borders in black on volumes I and II, in blind on volume III, gilt lettering on spine, black endpapers, signs of label removal from front boards, signature of William Carey Davies.   Jarndyce Antiquarian Booksellers   CXCII - 172   2011   £1250

MacDonald, George   1824-1905   *The Seaboard Parish.*   London: Tinsley Bros., 1868. First edition; 3 volumes, contemporary half red roan, well rebacked, ownership inscription in volume I of W. Carey Davies, 1869.   Jarndyce Antiquarian Booksellers   CXCII - 95   2011   £950

MacDonald, George 1824-1905 *Works of Fancy and Imagination.* London: Strahan & Co., 1871. First edition; volumes I-II, IV, VII-X, 7 volumes only, 16mo., half title, slight spotting caused by endpapers, original red cloth, paper labels, spines dulled, paper label of volume VIII defective, inscribed signed presentation from author for W. Carey Davies.   Jarndyce Antiquarian Booksellers   CXCII - 145   2011   £750

Association – Davis, Bob

Van De Water, Frederic *The Real McCoy.* Garden City: Doubleday, Doran and Co., 1931. First edition; fine in near fine dust jacket but for small chip on spine, inscribed by subject of the book "To Bob Davis, the man who suggested that this yarn be put in print. Bill McCoy", scarce either in jacket or signed.   Between the Covers   169 - BTC342132   2011 $950

Association – Davis, Charles

Thoreau, Henry David 1817-1862 *Excursions.* Boston: Ticknor & Fields, 1863. First edition; original blue green z cloth, frontispiece, fairly clean clopy with very minor wear, spine gilt bright, near fine, owner name of Charles(?) Davis.   Charles Agvent   Transcendentalism 2010 - 32   2011 $1250

Association – Davis, Harry

Plutarchus *The Live of the Nobel Grecians and Romanes...* Shakespeare Head Press, 1928. One of 500 copies; printed for sale in Great Britain, this copy # 309, another 500 sets were printed for the U.S. and an additional 100 were printed on handmade paper and signed by artist, 233 x 160mm., 8 volumes, quite attractive mid 20th century burgundy half morocco over matching linen, gilt decorated raised bands, spines with large central compartment featuring an intricate gilt filigree lozenge and cornerpieces, marbled endpapers, top edge gilt, other edges untrimmed and largely unopened, engraved headpieces, front flyleaf with tipped on typed note from Harry E. Davis, ABAA describing the book and noting the binding was done by hand for Della Quinn White of Houston Texas in 1952; very small gouge to front cover of volume I (but deep enough to cause a small crack in pastedown), otherwise very fine set, largely unopened, text nearly pristine and handsome bindings lustrous and virtually unworn.   Phillip J. Pirages   59 - 318   2011 $1500

Association – Davis, Keith

Taken by Design: Photographs from The Institute of Design 1937-1971. Chicago: University of Chicago Press, 2002. First edition; very fine in photo illustrated boards, issued without dust jacket, signed by a large number of photographers and some of the editors, among the signatures are Yasuhiro Ishimoto, Marvin E. Newton (twice), Barbara Crane, Ray K. Metzker, Joseph Jachna, Joseph Sterling (twice), Kenneth Josephson, David Travis, Keith Davis and quite a few others, unique copy.   Jeff Hirsch Books   ny   2010 2011 $750

Association – Dawkins, W. Boyd

Coffey, George *Guide to the Celtic Antiquities of the Christian Period Preserved in the National Museum, Dublin, Royal Irish Academy Collection.* Dublin: Hodges, Figgis & Co., 1910. Original cloth, gilt, extremities trifle rubbed, pages ix, 111, 18 plates and 114 text figures, inscribed by Professor W. Boyd Dawkins to Richard Glazier 1917.   R. F. G. Hollett & Son Antiquarian Booksellers   177 - 195   2011   £85

Association – Dawnay, Archibald

MacKenzie, Eneas *A Descriptive and Historical Account of the Town and County of Newcastle upon Tyne...* Newcastle upon Tyne: printed & published by Mackenzie & Dent, 1827. 2 volumes bound as 1, 4to., pages x, 414, frontispiece and 10 other engraved plates; (ii), (415)-770, (ii) + engraved frontispiece and 3 other engraved plates, modern half calf by John Henderson, foxed in places, armorial bookplate of Archibald Dawnay, from the collection of Christopher Ernest Weston 1947-2010.   Unsworths Booksellers   24 - 116   2011   £300

Association – De Bouvou, J. B.

Huygens, Christiaan *Opera Varia.* Lugduni Batavvorum: Janssonios Vander Aa, 1724. First collected edition; 4 books in one volume, 4to., (18), (1-4) 5-776, (18) pages, frontispiece, 56 folding plates, contemporary full calf, raised bands, gilt stamped spine panels, gilt stamped red morocco spine label, covers and joints rubbed, hinges beginning to split, very good, bookplate of Andras Gedeon and P. A. Moiroud, with J. B. de Bouvou signature on title dated 1758, very good.   Jeff Weber Rare Books   161 - 224   2011 $5500

Association – De Cohon

Maupas Du Tour, Henri Couchon De *La Vie du Venerable Serviteur de Dieu, Francois de Sales, etc.* Paris: J. & E. Langlois, 1657. 2 parts, 4to., 411; 53, (3) pages, ruled in red, added engraved plates, 6 engraved plates, engraved headpieces and initials, contemporary French panelled, red morocco, gilt floral cornerpieces, spines gilt, turn-ins, edges gilt, slight damage to upper cover, paper flaw in plate at page 1 with consequent tear, handsome copy, ruled in red and from the Foucault library, De Cohon inscription, from the library of the Earls of Macclesfield at Shirburn Castle. Maggs Bros. Ltd. 1440 - 142 2011 £850

Association – De Erazuriz, Maria

Lorca, Federico Garcia *Poema del Cante Jondo.* Madrid: Ediciones Ulises, Compania Iberoamericana de Publicationes, 1931. First edition; 8vo., pages (vi) 8-172, (30) ads, colophon, with half title, upper paper wrapper skillfully repaired at inner margin, very little light marginal fading throughout, contemporary blue quarter morocco, grey marbled sides, spine gilt with cream leather label, lettered in gilt, preserving upper original cream paper wrapper by Mauricio Amster printed in red and black, light rubbing to joints and head and foot of spine, lower board very slightly bowed, extremities very lightly rubbed, author' presentation inscription to Maria E. De Erazuriz,. Simon Finch Rare Books Zero - 337 2011 £12,500

Association – De Reding, Adelaide

Oliphant, Margaret Oliphant Wilson 1828-1897 *The Fugitives.* Leipzig: Bernhard Tauchnitz, 1890. Copyright edition; half title, 16 page catalog Feb. 1891, uncut, original printed paper wrappers, signed Adelaide de Reding, Vinzel. Jarndyce Antiquarian Booksellers CLXC - 619 2011 £45

Association – De Rolland De Lastous, F.

Andrea De Nerciat, Andre Robert *Le Doctorat In-Promptu.* (bound with) *Les Religieuses au Serail.* (with) *Les Progres du Libertinage Historiette Trouvee das le Porte-Feuille d'un Carme Reforme.* Paris: Cazin, 1788. Paris: Au ouvent des Filles du Sauveur,1790. Paris: L'Imprimerie de l'Abbesse du Mont-Martre...1794; First editions of first two titles, second edition of third; 3 works in one volume, 12mo., pages (iv), iv, 120, 2 erotic engravings; xii, 13-58, engraved frontispiece, 108 engraved frontispiece (lacking the 3 plates called for by Gay-Lemmonyer), all edges gilt, sporadic light spotting, frontispiece third text expertly remargined, otherwise very crisp and fresh copy, full glazed tan calf, early 19th century, gilt decorated and lettered on spine, endpapers browned in margin, bookplate of F. de Rolland de Lastous. Simon Finch Rare Books Zero - 415 2011 £4500

Association – De Stift, Baron

Adams, William *Practical Observations on Ectropium or Eversion of the Eyelids with the Descriptions of a New Operation for the Cure of that Disease and the Description of a Series of New and Improved Operations for the Cure of the Different Species of Cataract.* (bound with) *Official Papers Relating to Operations Performed by Order of the Directors of the Royal Hospital for Seamen at Greenwich on Several of the Pensioners Belonging Thereto for the Purpose of Ascertaining the General Efficacy of the New Modes of Treatment of Dr. Adams...* (and with) *Report Made by Order of the Philomathic Society of Paris, by Drs. Magendie and Blainville on the Subject of the New Operations and Instruments Invented by Sir William Adams for the Cure of Various Diseases of the Eye...* London: J. Callow, 1814. London: W. Winchester, 1814. London: Richard and Arthur Taylor, 1814; 3 works in one volume, 8vo., pages xvi 252 (131-136 misbound after 126), (i) errata, (i) (blank); (iv), 21, (5) blank, 8. 3 stipple engraved plates, included 2 printed in color, all edges gilt, some light sporadic spotting, elaborate contemporary straight grain red morocco, raised bands, decorated in gilt, gilt ruled and decorated border to sides, with blind rolls inside border, gilt inner dentelles, author's presentation inscription to verso of initial blank, his autograph note on inserted leaf bound after the second work, excellent copy, presentation copy inscribed by author to Baron de Stift, Counsellor of the State in the Service of His Majesty the Emperor of Austria. Simon Finch Rare Books Zero - 123 2011 £1800

Association – De Wolfe, Elsie

Bemelmans, Ludwig *Now I Lay Me Down to Sleep.* New York: Viking Press, 1945. First edition; presentation issue, green cloth with applied illustration and cloth spine label, slight edgewear, front hinge little tender, else near fine, one of a very few copies prepared in this binding for author's use (not to be confused with limited and slipcased edition), wonderfully inscribed by author to Elsie de Wolfe. Between the Covers 169 - BTC343521 2011 $1750

Association – Debenham, Ernest Ridley

Ruskin, John 1819-1900 *The Works.* London: George Allen, 1903. Definitive edition, Library Edition, limited to 2062 copies (of which 2000 are for sale); 39 volumes, large octavo, frontispieces and plates, some tinted blue or sepia and engravings, numerous text illustrations and facsimiles, contemporary three quarter green levant morocco over green cloth boards ruled in gilt, spines with five raised bands decoratively tooled and lettered in gilt, top edges gilt, others uncut, marbled endpapers, several volumes sunned at spine, bookplates of Ernest Ridley Debenham, overall fine set. David Brass Rare Books, Inc. May 26 2011 - 01349 2011 $9500

Association – Deloria, Vine

Burke, James Lee *Sunset Limited.* New York: Doubleday, 1998. First edition; fine, dust jacket fine, also signed by Vine Deloria Jr., inscribed by Burke to same. Bella Luna Books   May 29 2011 - g2731 2011 $104

Waters, Frank *Brave Are My People.* Santa Fe: Clear Light Press, 1993. First edition; fine in like dust jacket, this copy signed by author and introducer, Vine Deloria Jr. Bella Luna Books   May 29 2011 - j2120 2011 $82

Association – Derby, Earl of

Englefield, Henry C. *A Description of the Principal Picturesque Beauties, Antiquities and Geological Pheonmena of the Isle of Wight.* London: printed by William Bulmer and Co. for Payne and Foss, 1816. Large paper copy, 4to., pages (viii) vi 238 (iv) (vi)-xxvii, (i) + oval engraved frontispiece, 50 other engraved plates, contemporary russia leather, boards intricately gilt bordered with double triple rules and back to back decorative roll between, within blind tooled acanthus roll and innermost a single rule gilt panel with elaborate made up corner pieces gilt, board edges, 'broken hatch fillet' roll at corners, turn-ins 'composite double rule' gilt, all edges gilt, 3 color double core patterned sewn endbands, orange silk page markers, early 20th century in brown goatskin, spine divided into five compartments by triple raised bands, one flat between two ordinary and tooled in gilt and in blind, lettering gilt direct in two compartments, toned, some foxing to plates, touch of rubbing to extremities, crowned and belted heraldic crest, gilt stamp of Earl of Derby in centre of front board, this copy is extra illustrated by the inclusion of Ordnance Survey sheet 10 of Isle of Wight dated 1810, large folding map bound in, from the collection of Christopher Ernest Weston 1947-2010. Unsworths Booksellers   24 - 92 2011   £1400

Association – Dercsenyi

MacDonald, George 1824-1905   *David Elginbrod.* Leipzig: Bernhard Tauchnitz, 1871. Copyright edition; half titles, 2 volumes, slight browning, green and brown binder's cloth, spines dulled and marked, stamp and shelflabels of Dercsenyi.   Jarndyce Antiquarian Booksellers   CXCII - 20 2011   £65

Association – Derleth, August

Lovecraft, Howard Phillips *Dreams and Fancies.* Sauk City: Arkham House, 1962. First edition; 8vo., pages x, 175, fine in fine dust jacket with very very slight edgewear, excellent condition, signed by introducer August Derleth. Any Amount of Books   May 26 2011 - A74373 2011 $713

Association – Desborough, Fanny

Burke, William *The Greek-English Derivative Dictionary showing in English Characters, the Greek Originals of Such Words in the English Language as are Derived from the Greek...* London: J. Johnson, 1806. 8vo., pages 248, 2 neat inscriptions on front endpaper in 19th century handwriting of the Fanny Desborough of Russell Square, also Mary Desborough, Ellen Scholes and Mrs. Geldart, soundly bound in full plain unlettered (but with 7 gold bands at spine), tree calf which is lightly scuffed and slightly marked), very good.   Any Amount of Books   May 29 2011 - A72178 2011 $238

Association – Desborough, Mary

Burke, William *The Greek-English Derivative Dictionary showing in English Characters, the Greek Originals of Such Words in the English Language as are Derived from the Greek...* London: J. Johnson, 1806. 8vo., pages 248, 2 neat inscriptions on front endpaper in 19th century handwriting of the Fanny Desborough of Russell Square, also Mary Desborough, Ellen Scholes and Mrs. Geldart, soundly bound in full plain unlettered (but with 7 gold bands at spine), tree calf which is lightly scuffed and slightly marked), very good.   Any Amount of Books   May 29 2011 - A72178 2011 $238

Association – Deschamps, Leon

Verlaine, Paul 1844-1896   *Amour.* Paris: Leon Vanier, 1888. First edition; presentation from author to Leon Deschamps, 18mo., pages (viii) including initial blank, 174, (2) back, top edge gilt, others uncut, publisher's wrappers, text in black, spine tipped in, bound in half morocco and gold and silver sprinkled paper, spine with 5 bands, elaborate decorated compartments and lettering in gilt, fine. Simon Finch Rare Books   Zero - 359 2011   £3750

Association – Desmarais, Becky

Melville, Herman 1819-1891   *Moby Dick; or, The Whale.* San Francisco: Arion Press, 1979. One of 265 copies of the book (of which 250 were for sale); along with one of 30 extra suites issued of the 100 engravings appearing in the book, the regular 100 in the volume and the extra 100, all signed by artist; with 10 original drawings used for the book's illustrations, each of these signed as well, colophon signed by artist, Barry Moser and with inscription for Becky and Gill Desmarais; 385 x 265mm., 576 pages, (2) leaves, "Moby Dick" volume plus companion portfolio of plates; publisher's fine cerulean crushed morocco, silver vertical titling on spine, in original cloth covered slipcase (hint of fading as usual), extra plates and original drawings in custom made morocco backed folding cloth box with gilt lettering, virtually pristine.   Phillip J. Pirages   59 - 70 2011 $27,500

Association – Desmarais, Gill

Melville, Herman 1819-1891 *Moby Dick; or, The Whale.* San Francisco: Arion Press, 1979. One of 265 copies of the book (of which 250 were for sale); along with one of 30 extra suites issued of the 100 engravings appearing in the book, the regular 100 in the volume and the extra 100, all signed by artist; with 10 original drawings used for the book's illustrations, each of these signed as well, colophon signed by artist, Barry Moser and with inscription for Becky and Gill Desmarais; 385 x 265mm., 576 pages, (2) leaves, "Moby Dick" volume plus companion portfolio of plates; publisher's fine cerulean crushed morocco, silver vertical titling on spine, in original cloth covered slipcase (hint of fading as usual), extra plates and original drawings in custom made morocco backed folding cloth box with gilt lettering, virtually pristine.   Phillip J. Pirages 59 - 70 2011 $27,500

Association – Dethick, George

Spenser, Edmund 1552-1599 *The Faerie Queen: The Shepheards Calendar; together with the Other Works of England's Arch Poet.* London: by H(umphrey) L(ownes) for Mathew Lownes, 1611. Folio (4), 363, (19); (10), 56, (2); (136) pages, title within woodcut border, 12 woodcut vignettes, woodcut head and tailpieces, complete with all blanks, 2I4 (para) 8 and 2F4, contemporary blind ruled calf, central gilt stamped ornament on covers and smaller ornaments on spine, very skillfully rebacked retaining most of original spine, Leaf 2B2 soiled, final leaf creased, lower blank corner torn away without loss, occasional very light soiling, lovely, crisp copy, from the library of Henry Dethick with his signature and that of George Dethick, 2 modern booklabels.   Joseph J. Felcone Inc.   Fall Miscellany 2010 - 111   2011 $7000

Association – Dethick, Henry

Spenser, Edmund 1552-1599 *The Faerie Queen: The Shepheards Calendar; together with the Other Works of England's Arch Poet.* London: by H(umphrey) L(ownes) for Mathew Lownes, 1611. Folio (4), 363, (19); (10), 56, (2); (136) pages, title within woodcut border, 12 woodcut vignettes, woodcut head and tailpieces, complete with all blanks, 2I4 (para) 8 and 2F4, contemporary blind ruled calf, central gilt stamped ornament on covers and smaller ornaments on spine, very skillfully rebacked retaining most of original spine, Leaf 2B2 soiled, final leaf creased, lower blank corner torn away without loss, occasional very light soiling, lovely, crisp copy, from the library of Henry Dethick with his signature and that of George Dethick, 2 modern booklabels.   Joseph J. Felcone Inc.   Fall Miscellany 2010 - 111   2011 $7000

Association – Devonshire, Marquis of

Kinge, John *Lectures Upon Jonas, Delivered at Yorke in the yeare of Our Lorde 1594.* Oxford: Joseph Barnes, 1599. Small 4to., pages (x), 660, (ii), 661-706, N.B. leaves *1 and 2Y4 are blanks (first except for a fleuron) missing in this copy, early 19th century tan calf, spine gilt, red lettering piece gilt, place and date gilt direct, boards gilt double rule bordered, board edges decorative roll gilt turn-ins decorative roll gilt, "Gloster" 'made' endpapers, all edges red mottled, pink sewn endbands, light age toning and few tiny spots, couple of small marks to leather, headcap slightly worn, early ink inscription of titlepage largely cut off (and undecipherable) and repaired and matching paper, early initials "WPL" on titlepage, heraldic bookplate of Marquis of Devonshire, from the collection of Christopher Ernest Weston 1947-2010.   Unsworths Booksellers   24 - 26 2011   £500

Morritt, J. B. S. *A Vindication of Homer and of the Ancient Poets and Historians who Have Recorded the Siege and Fall of Troy.* York: printed by W. Blanchard for T. Cadell, Jun. and W. Davies, 1798. 4to., pages 124 + 1 double page engraved map and 5 other double page engraved plates all mounted on stubs, contemporary diced Russia, spine double gilt with 'perched peacock' centre-piece gilt in compartments, lettered direct in gilt, boards decorative roll gilt bordered with central gilt ruled panel and quadrant arc corners gilt, board edges decorative roll gilt, turn-ins 'rope-twist' roll gilt, 'French shell' 'made' endpapers, all edges brown speckled, pale blue silk page marker, mid 20th century calf reback, backstrip relaid (partly inserted) + corners, faint dust soiling and toning, little offsetting from plates, old leather darkened around repairs, parts of old spines lost, Devonshire monogrammed heraldic booklabel on front pastedown, from the collection of Christopher Ernest Weston 1947-2010.   Unsworths Booksellers   24 - 124 2011   £600

Association – Di Palma, Ray

Auster, Paul *Living Hand 1-8.* V.P.: Living Hand, 1973-1976. First edition; 8 chapbooks in printed color wrappers, from the library of poet Ray di Palma with two books inscribed to him, uncommon to fine complete set, occasional sunning to spines, about fine.   Charles Agvent   2010 Summer Miscellany - 2   2011 $1500

Association – Dibner, Bern

Adas, Michael 1805-1882 *Technology and European Overseas Enterprise: Diffusion, Adaption and Adoption.* Aldershot & Brookfield: Variorum & Ashgate, 1996. 8vo., xxvi, 433 pages, illustrations, tables, navy cloth, gilt stamped cover and spine titles, fine, from the Bern Dibner reference library, with Burndy bookplate.   Jeff Weber Rare Books 161 - 1 2011 $100

Adelmann, Howard B. *The Correspondenve of Marcello Malpighi.* Ithaca and London: Cornell University Press, 1975. 5 volumes, 4to., maroon cloth, gilt stamped spine title, inner hinge cracked (volume V only), very good, from the Bern Dibner reference library with Burndy bookplate. Jeff Weber Rare Books   161 - 2   2011 $100

Alden, John Doughty *The American Steel Navy: a Photographical History of the U.S. Navy from the Introduction of the Steel Hull in 1883 to the Cruise of the Great White Fleet 1907-1909.* Annapolis & New York: Naval Inst. Press & American Heritage Press, 1972. Square 4to., ix, 396 pages, heavily illustrated with photos, creme cloth, gray stamped spine title, dust jacket, very good, from the Bern Dibner reference library, with Burndy bookplate. Jeff Weber Rare Books   161 - 3   2011 $75

Alexander, Amir R. *Geometrical Landscapes: The Voyages of Discovery and the Transformation of Mathematical Practice.* Stanford: Stanford University Press, 2002. First printing; 8vo., xv, 293 pages, illustrations, index, blue cloth, white stamped spine title, dust jacket, fine, rare in jacket, from the Bern Dibner reference library, with Burndy bookplate. Jeff Weber Rare Books   161 - 4   2011 $100

Alexander, J. A. *The Life of George Chaffey; a Story of Irrigation Beginnings in California and Australia.* Melbourne & London: Macmillan, 1928. 8vo., xv, 381 page, frontispiece, large folding map, 35 illustrations, pale green cloth, gilt stamped spine title, spine ends frayed, very good, from the Bern Dibner reference library, with Burndy bookplate. Jeff Weber Rare Books   161 - 5   2011 $90

Allibone, S. Austin *A Critical Dictionary of English Literature and British and American Authors, Living and Deceased...* Philadelphia: J. B. Lippincott, 1886-1898. 5 volumes, large 8vo., green cloth, gilt stamped spine title, extremities rubbed, some volumes waterstained, some hinges cracked, still strong, very good, from the Bern Dibner reference library, with Burndy bookplate. Jeff Weber Rare Books   161 - 7   2011 $275

Anderson, Lorin *Charles Bonnet and the Order of the Known.* Dordrecht, Boston, London: D. Reidel, 1982. 8vo., x, 159 pages, frontispiece, brown cloth, gilt stamped spine title, dust jacket, fine, from the Bern Dibner reference library, with Burndy bookplate. Jeff Weber Rare Books   161 - 9   2011 $75

Appel, Toby A. *The Cuvier-Geoffroy Debate: French Biology in the Decade before Darwin.* New York and Oxford: Oxford University Press, 1987. First edition; 8vo., 305 pages, plates, navy cloth, gilt stamped cover and spine titles, dust jacket, fine, from the Bern Dibner reference library, with Burndy bookplate. Jeff Weber Rare Books   161 - 11 2011 $150

Aristoteles *The Basic Works of Aristotle.* New York: Random House, 1941. Thick 8vo., xxxix, 1487 pages, frontispiece, beige cloth, gilt stamped black spine label, dust jacket worn along top edge, else very good, scarce in jacket, from the Bern Dibner reference library, with Burndy bookplate. Jeff Weber Rare Books   161 - 14 2011 $95

Asimov, Isaac 1920-1992 *Asimov's Chronology of Science and Discovery.* New York: Harper Collins, 1994. First edition; thick 8vo., 790 pages, illustrations, quarter gray cloth with black paper boards, silver stamped spine title, dust jacket, from the Bern Dibner reference library, with Burndy bookplate. Jeff Weber Rare Books   161 - 17 2011 $80

Atkinson, Dwight *Scientific Discourse in Sociohistorical Context: The Philosophical Transactions of the Royal Society of London 1675-1975.* Mahwah and London: Lawrence Erlbaum, 1999. First printing; 8vo., xxxi, 208 pages, figures, pictorial boards, fine, from the Bern Dibner reference library, with Burndy bookplate. Jeff Weber Rare Books   161 - 18 2011 $75

Babbage, Charles 1792-1871 *Science and Reform: Selected Works of Charles Babbage Chosen with Introduction and Discussion by Anthony Hyman.* Cambridge et al: Cambridge University Press, 1989. First edition; tall 8vo., vii 336 pages, 18 plates, figures, index, dark blue cloth, gilt stamped spine title, dust jacket, fine, scarce, from the Bern Dibner reference library, with Burndy bookplate. Jeff Weber Rare Books   161 - 21 2011 $100

Babbage, Charles 1792-1871 *The Works of Charles Babbage.* New York: New York University Press, 1989. 11 volumes, 8vo., 456, 223, 253, 217, 192, 129, 133, 280, 118, 173, 425 pages, blue cloth, gilt stamped spine titles, fine, from the Bern Dibner reference library, with Burndy bookplate. Jeff Weber Rare Books   161 - 20 2011 $700

Bacon, Francis, Viscount St. Albans 1561-1626 *The New Organon.* Cambridge: Cambridge University Press, 2000. First edition; 8vo., xxxv, 252, (2) pages, pictorial boards, fine, from the Bern Dibner reference library, with Burndy bookplate. Jeff Weber Rare Books   161 - 22 2011 $85

Bacon, Roger *Roger Bacon's Philosophy of Nature.* Oxford: Clarendon Press, 1983. First edition; 8vo., lxxxi, 420 pages, figures, navy cloth, gilt stamped cover and spine titles, fine, from the Bern Dibner reference library, with Burndy bookplate. Jeff Weber Rare Books   161 - 24 2011 $120

ASSOCIATION COPIES

Baer, Karl Ernst Von *Autobiography of Dr. Karl Ernst von Baer.* Canton: Science History Publications, 1986. 8vo., xiv, 389 pages, frontispiece, gray paper boards, black stamped spine title, dust jacket, very good, from the Bern Dibner reference library, with Burndy bookplate.   Jeff Weber Rare Books   161 - 25 2011 $100

Bailey, Stephen A. *L. L. Nunn: a Memoir.* Ithaca: Telluride Association, 1933. First edition; 8vo. 180 pages, frontispiece, plates, navy cloth, gilt stamped cover and spine titles, fine, scarce, from the Bern Dibner reference library, with Burndy bookplate.   Jeff Weber Rare Books 161 - 26 2011 $100

Bedini, Silvio *Patrons, Artisans and Instruments of Science 1600-1750.* Aldershot/Brookfield: Ashgate/Variorum, 1999. 8vo., xiv, various pagination, teal cloth, gilt stamped cover and spine titles, fine, from the Bern Dibner reference library, with Burndy bookplate.   Jeff Weber Rare Books   161 - 33 2011 $140

Bedini, Silvio *Science and Instruments in Seventeenth Century Italy.* Aldershot/Brookfield: Variorum, 1994. 8vo., x, various pagination, fine, from the Bern Dibner reference library, with Burndy bookplate.   Jeff Weber Rare Books 161 - 32 2011 $200

Beer, Arthur *The Origins, Achievement and Influence of the Royal Observatory, Greenwich 1675-1975.* Oxford: Pergamon Press, 1976. Tall 8vo., viii, 272 pages, plates, illustrations, figures, printed wrappers, lightly rubbed, very good, from the Bern Dibner reference library, with Burndy bookplate.   Jeff Weber Rare Books   161 - 35 2011 $185

Bell, A. E. *Christian Huygens and the Development of Science in the Seventeenth Century.* London: Edward Arnold, 1947. First edition; 8vo., 220 pages, frontispiece, plates, figures, brown cloth, silver stamped spine title, dust jacket, jacket chipped, very good, Charles Singer's copy with his small booklabel, from the Bern Dibner reference library, with Burndy bookplate.   Jeff Weber Rare Books 161 - 226 2011 $95

Bell, Whitfield J. *Patriot Improvers: Biographical Sketches of the American Philosophical Society.* Philadelphia: The Society, 1997-1999. Volume one 1743-1768, volume two 1768, 2 volumes, volumes 226-227, tall 8vo., xx, 531; xiii, 425 pages, illustrations, maroon cloth, gilt stamped cover and spine titles, fine, from the Bern Dibner reference library, with Burndy bookplate.   Jeff Weber Rare Books   161 - 36 2011 $70

Bennett, J. A. *The Mathematical Science of Christopher Wren.* Cambridge, et al: Cambridge University Press, 1982. First edition; 8vo., ix, 148 pages, illustrations, index, black cloth, gilt stamped spine title, dust jacket, near fine, from the Bern Dibner reference library, with Burndy bookplate.   Jeff Weber Rare Books   161 - 39 2011 $140

Berggren, J. L. *Ptolemy's Geography: an Annotated Translation...* Princeton: Princeton University Press, 2000. 8vo., xii, 192 pages, 20 figures, 7 plates, 8 maps, blue cloth, gilt stamped spine titles, dust jacket, fine, from the Bern Dibner reference library, with Burndy bookplate.   Jeff Weber Rare Books   161 - 41 2011 $100

Blaauw, Adriaan *History of the IAU: The Birth and the First Half Century of the International Astronomical Union.* Dordrecht: Boston: Kluwer Academic Publishers, 1994. 8vo., xix, 296 pages, figures, printed boards, fine, rare, from the Bern Dibner reference library, with Burndy bookplate. Jeff Weber Rare Books   161 - 43 2011 $150

Blackwell, Richard J. *Galileo, Bellarmine, and the Bible including a Translation of Foscarini's Letter on the Motion of the Earth.* Notre Dame: University of Notre Dame Press, 1991. 8vo., x, 291 pages, blue cloth, white stamped spine title, dust jacket, fine, from the Bern Dibner reference library, with Burndy bookplate.   Jeff Weber Rare Books   161 - 44 2011 $100

Blum, Ann Shelby *Picturing Nature: American Nineteenth Century Zoological Illustration.* Princeton: Princeton University Press, 1993. First printing; 4to., xxxiv, 403 pages, 74 color plates, numerous half tone figures, brown cloth, gilt stamped spine title, dust jacket, tiny chip on rear jacket cover, else fine, from the Bern Dibner reference library, with Burndy bookplate.   Jeff Weber Rare Books 161 - 45 2011 $72

Bono, James J. *The Word of God and the Languages of Man: Interpreting Nature in Early Modern Science and Medicine. Volume 1: Ficinio to Descartes.* Madison: University of Wisconsin Press, 1995. Volume I only, (all published), 8vo., xi, 317 pages, green cloth, black stamped spine title, fine, from the Bern Dibner reference library, with Burndy bookplate.   Jeff Weber Rare Books   161 - 49 2011 $65

Bonsor, N. R. P. *North Atlantic Seaway.* Jersey & Channel Islands: Brookside, 1978. Volumes 1 and 2, 237 x 158 mm., 471; 477-868 pages, illustrations, full blue cloth, printed dust jacket, very good, from the Bern Dibner reference library, with Burndy bookplate.   Jeff Weber Rare Books   161 - 50 2011 $60

Bos, H. J.M. *Studies on Christian Huygens: Invited Papers from the Symposium on Life and Work of Christian Huygens, Amsterdam 22-25 August 1979.* Lisse: Swets & Zeitlinger, 1980. 8vo., v, 321 pages, frontispiece, plates, figures, index, pictorial cloth, near fine, from the Bern Dibner reference library, with Burndy bookplate. Jeff Weber Rare Books 161 - 227 2011 $275

Bouguer, Pierre *Pierre Bouguer's Optical Treatise on the Gradation of Light.* Toronto: University of Toronto Press, 1961. First edition; 8vo., xiv, 248 pages, frontispiece, illustrations, tables, blue cloth, silver stamped spine title, dust jacket worn, very good, from the Bern Dibner reference library, with Burndy bookplate. Jeff Weber Rare Books 161 - 52 2011 $125

Bouguer, Pierre *Traite d'Optique sur la Gradation de la Lumiere: Ouvrage Posthume de M. Bouguer de l'Acaemie Royale des Scienes &c.* Paris: H. L. Guerin & L. F. Delatour, 1760. First edition; 4to., xviii, (2), 368 pages, engraved printer's device on titlepage, 7 engraved folding plates, contemporary full mottled calf, raised bands, gilt stamped spine panels and spine title, few minor covers scars, joints starting, bookplate of Jean Francois Le Boyer and Andras Gedeon, fine, from the Bern Dibner reference library, with Burndy bookplate. Jeff Weber Rare Books 161 - 51 2011 $2500

Bourbaki, Nicolas *Element of the History of Mathematics.* Berlin and New York: Springer Verlag, 1994. 8vo., viii, 301 pages, printed boards, from the Bern Dibner reference library, with Burndy bookplate, fine. Jeff Weber Rare Books 161 - 53 2011 $90

Boyd, Thomas *Poor John Fitch: Inventor of the Steamboat.* New York: G. P. Putnam's Sons, 1935. First edition; 8vo., (i), 315 page, illustrations, blue cloth, brown stamped creme spine label, dust jacket worn, very good, rare in jacket, from the Bern Dibner reference library, with Burndy bookplate. Jeff Weber Rare Books 161 - 55 2011 $100

Boyle, Robert 1627-1691 *The Works of Robert Boyle.* London: Pickering & Chatto, 1999. 14 volumes, 8vo., blue cloth, gilt stamped spine titles, fine, from the Bern Dibner reference library, with Burndy bookplate. Jeff Weber Rare Books 161 - 56 2011 $2650

Bradley, Betsy Hunter *The Works: The Industrial Architecture of the United States.* New York and Oxford: Oxford University Press, 1999. First edition; tall 8vo., xii, 347 pages, photos and illustrations, purple cloth, silver stamped, spine title, dust jacket, fine, from the Bern Dibner reference library, with Burndy bookplate. Jeff Weber Rare Books 161 - 60 2011 $275

Bridson, Gavin *The History of Natural History: an Annotated Bibliography.* New York and London: Garland, 1994. First edition; 8vo., xxxi, 740 pages, green cloth, gilt stamped cover and spine titles, fine, from the Bern Dibner reference library, with Burndy bookplate. Jeff Weber Rare Books 161 - 64 2011 $250

Brinton, Selwyn *Francesco di Giorgi Martini of Sienna: Painter, Sculptor, Engineer, Civil and Military Architect (1439-1502) Part I.* London: Besant, 1934. 8vo., 119 pages, 27 plates, including frontispiece, blue cloth, gilt stamped spine title, extremities rubbed, edges foxed, from the Bern Dibner reference library, with Burndy bookplate, good, rare. Jeff Weber Rare Books 161 - 65 2011 $75

Brock, Alan St. H. *A History of Fireworks.* London. et al: George J. Harrap, 1949. First edition; 8vo., 280 pages, 40 plates, text illustrations, dark blue cloth, gilt stamped spine title, dust jacket worn, very good, from the Bern Dibner reference library, with Burndy bookplate, signed by Cyril Stanley Smith. Jeff Weber Rare Books 161 - 66 2011 $125

Brockett, Paul *Bibliography of Aeronautics.* Washington: Smithsonian Institution, 1910. First edition; 8vo., xiv, 940 pages, printed wrappers, worn, small library blindstamp on front cover, very good, from the Bern Dibner reference library, with Burndy bookplate. Jeff Weber Rare Books 161 - 67 2011 $75

Brooke, John Hedley *Reconstructing Nature: the Engagement of Science and Religion.* Edinburgh: T&T Clark, 1998. First edition; 8vo. xii, 367 page, illustrations, dark blue cloth, gilt stamped spine title, dust jacket, fine, from the Bern Dibner reference library, with Burndy bookplate. Jeff Weber Rare Books 161 - 68 2011 $75

Brown, D. K. *Before the Ironclad: Development of Ship Design, Propulsion and Armament in the Royal Navy 1815-1860.* Annapolis: Naval Institute Press, 1990. First US edition; 4to., 217 pages, frontispiece, photos and illustrations, brown paper boards, gilt stamped spine, dust jacket lightly worn along top edge, very good, from the Bern Dibner reference library, with Burndy bookplate. Jeff Weber Rare Books 161 - 69 2011 $85

Bruck, H. A. *The Peripatetic Astronomer: the Life of Charles Piazzi Smyth.* Bristol: Philadelphia: A. Hilger, 1988. 8vo., xii, 274 pages, frontispiece, figures, blue cloth, gilt stamped spine title, dust jacket, fine, from the Bern Dibner reference library, with Burndy bookplate. Jeff Weber Rare Books 161 - 70 2011 $60

ASSOCIATION COPIES

Burkhardt, Frederick *A Calendar of the Correspondence of Charles Darwin 1821-1882.* New York: and London: Garland, 1985. 4to., 690 pages, portrait, red cloth, gilt stamped spine title, fine, from the Bern Dibner reference library, with Burndy bookplate. Jeff Weber Rare Books 161 - 71 2011 $110

Burnett, Charles *Magic and Divination in the Middle Ages.* Aldershot: Variorum, 1996. 8vo., xii, 370 pages, blue cloth, gilt stamped cover and spine titles, fine, from the Bern Dibner reference library, with Burndy bookplate. Jeff Weber Rare Books 161 - 73 2011 $125

Buxbaum, Melvin H. *Critical Essays on Benjamin Franklin.* Boston: G. K. Hall, 1987. 8vo., viii, 214 pages, index, quarter navy cloth with beige cloth sides, silver stamped spine title, fine, from the Bern Dibner reference library, with Burndy bookplate. Jeff Weber Rare Books 161 - 74 2011 $85

Cannell, D. M. *George Green: Mathematician and Physicist 1793-1841: the Background to His Life and Work.* London: Atlantic Highlands: Athlone Press, 1993. 8vo., xxvi, 265 pages, 20 illustrations, blue cloth silver stamped spine title, dust jacket, from the Bern Dibner reference library, with Burndy bookplate, fine. Jeff Weber Rare Books 161 - 76 2011 $90

Cannon, John T. *The Evolution of Dynamics: Vibration Theory from 1687 to 1742.* New York: Springer Verlag, 1981. Thin 8vo., ix, 184 pages, printed boards, fine, from the Bern Dibner reference library, with Burndy bookplate. Jeff Weber Rare Books 161 - 77 2011 $165

Cartwright, David Edgar *Tides: a Scientific History.* Cambridge: Cambridge University Press, 1999. First edition; tall 8vo., xii, 292 pages, frontispiece, illustrations, figures, black cloth, silver stamped spine title, dust jacket, fine, rare in cloth with dust jacket, from the Bern Dibner reference library, with Burndy bookplate. Jeff Weber Rare Books 161 - 78 2011 $100

Chappe, Ignace *Histoire de la Telegraphie.* Paris: chez l'auteur, 1824. First edition; 8vo., (4), 268 (errata, blank) pages, 34 double page engravings, contemporary quarter green calf over marbled boards, gilt ruled and stamped spine and title, extremities rubbed, presentation inscription by author, fine, from the Bern Dibner reference library, with Burndy bookplate. Jeff Weber Rare Books 161 - 80 2011 $3500

Chrimes, Mike *The Civil Engineering of Canals and Railways Before 1850.* Aldershot et al: Ashgate, 1997. 8vo., xxviii, 378 pages, illustrations, tables, red cloth, gilt stamped cover and spine titles, fine, from the Bern Dibner reference library, with Burndy bookplate. Jeff Weber Rare Books 161 - 85 2011 $100

Churella, Albert J. *From Steam to Diesel: Managerial Customs and Organizational Capabilitie in the Twentieth Century American Locomotive Industry.* Princeton: Princeton University Press, 1998. First printing; 8vo., viii, 215 page, charcoal cloth, silver stamped spine title, dust jacket, fine, from the Bern Dibner reference library, with Burndy bookplate. Jeff Weber Rare Books 161 - 86 2011 $200

Clagett, Marshall *The Science of Mechanics in the Middle Ages.* Madison & London: University of Wisconsin & Oxford University Press, 1959. First edition; large 8vo., xxix, 711 pages, plates, figures, blue cloth, gilt stamped spine title, dust jacket, very good, from the Bern Dibner reference library, with Burndy bookplate. Jeff Weber Rare Books 161 - 88 2011 $125

Clark, Victor S. *History of Manufactures in the United States.* New York: Peter Smith, 1949. Reprint of 1929 edition; 3 volumes, tall 8vo., xi, 607; viii, 566; vi, 467 pages, plates, red cloth, black stamped spine titles, very good, from the Bern Dibner reference library, with Burndy bookplate. Jeff Weber Rare Books 161 - 90 2011 $135

Clerke, Agnes M. *The Herschels and Modern Astronomy.* London: Paris: Melbourne: Cassell, 1895. 8vo., 224, ads (16) pages, frontispiece, plates, light foxing, green cloth, gilt stamped cover and spine titles, extremities rubbed, light wear to spine ends, inner hinge cracked, else very good, previous owner's inked signature, from the Bern Dibner reference library, with Burndy bookplate. Jeff Weber Rare Books 161 - 91 2011 $100

Cohen, I. Bernard *Album of Science: from Leonardo to Lavoisir 1450-1800.* New York: Charles Scribner's Sons, 1980. First printing; tall 8vo., xiii, (306) pages, frontispiece, illustrations, maroon cloth, gilt stamped, black spine label, dust jacket lightly worn, with small chips, very good, from the Bern Dibner reference library, with Burndy bookplate. Jeff Weber Rare Books 161 - 93 2011 $80

Columbus, Christopher *Select Documents Illustrating the Four Voyages of Columbus...* London: Hakluyt Society, 1933. 8vo., lxxxix, 164 pages, folding frontispiece, plate, maps, blue cloth, gilt stamped cover illustration and spine title, very good, volume II only, from the Bern Dibner reference library, with Burndy bookplate. Jeff Weber Rare Books 161 - 96 2011 $100

Cormack, Lesley B. *Charting an Empire: Geography at the English Universities 1580-1620.* Chicago and London: University of Chicago Press, 1997. First edition; 8vo., xvi, 281 pages, illustrations, figures, tables, red cloth, gilt stamped spine title, fine, from the Bern Dibner reference library, with Burndy bookplate. Jeff Weber Rare Books 161 - 95 2011 $100

Courtanvaux, Francois Cesar Letellier, Marquis de *Journal de Voyage de M. le Marquis de Courtanvaux...* Paris: l'Imprimerie Roale, 1768. 4to., viii 316, (3) (1 blank) pages, frontispiece, 5 folding engraved plates, contemporary full polished mottled calf, raised bands, gilt stamped compartments on spine, gilt stamped red morocco spine label, exceptionally clean, fine, from the Bern Dibner reference library, with Burndy bookplate. Jeff Weber Rare Books 161 - 98 2011 $6500

Cox, Edward Godfrey *A Reference Guide to the Literature of Travel...* Seattle: University of Washington, 1935-1949. 3 volumes, (volumes 9, 10, 12), large 8vo., ix, 401; vii, 591, ads, (4), 732 pages, printed wrappers, wrappers and spine worn with pieces missing (volume I and II only), front cover detached on volume I and rear cover missing on volume II, as is, rubber stamps and markings of MIT Libraries, from the Bern Dibner reference library, with Burndy bookplate. Jeff Weber Rare Books 161 - 99 2011 $100

Crosland, Maurice P. *Studies in the Culture of Science in France and Britain since the Enlightenment.* Aldershot: Variorum, 1995. 8vo., xxii, various pagination, teal cloth, gilt stamped cover and spine titles, fine, from the Bern Dibner reference library, with Burndy bookplate. Jeff Weber Rare Books 161 - 102 2011 $135

Cunningham, Suzanne *Philosophy and the Darwinian Legacy.* Rochester: University of Rochester Press, 1996. First edition; 8vo., x, 293 pages, sea green cloth, silver stamped spine title, dust jacket, fine, from the Bern Dibner reference library, with Burndy bookplate. Jeff Weber Rare Books 161 - 104 2011 $100

Curry, Patrick *Prophecy and Power: Astrology in Early Modern England.* Princeton: Princeton University Press, 1989. First edition; 8vo. ix, 238 pages, blue cloth, gilt stamped spine title dust jacket, fine, from the Bern Dibner reference library, with Burndy bookplate. Jeff Weber Rare Books 161 - 105 2011 $75

Darwin, Charles Robert 1809-1882 *A Naturalist's Voyage. Journal of Researches into the Natural History and Geology of the Countries visited During the Voyages of H.M.S. "Beagle" Round the World...* London: John Murray, 1890. Later edition; small 8vo., xi, 500 pages, frontispiece, additional engraved portrait loosely inserted, original green cloth, gilt stamped cover ornament and spine title, ANS by Darwin glued to verso of titlepage and dedication page, ink stamp of D. N. Van Pelt, very good, with Darwin's signature written on slip of paper 200 x 72mm, mounted inside volume, additional engraved portrait of Darwin loosely inserted, from the Bern Dibner reference library, with Burndy bookplate, inscription " to my dear grandson Nevill Forbes, from E.F.". Jeff Weber Rare Books 161 - 106 2011 $5000

Darwin, Charles Robert 1809-1882 *Charles Darwin's Zoology Notes & Specimen Lists from H.M.S. Beagle.* Cambridge: Cambridge University Press, 2000. 4to., xxxiv, 430 pages, text figures, teal cloth, silver stamped spine title, dust jacket, fine, from the Bern Dibner reference library, with Burndy bookplate. Jeff Weber Rare Books 161 - 107 2011 $130

De Camp, L. Sprague *The Great Monkey Trial.* Garden City: Doubleday, 1968. First edition; 8vo., x, 538 pages, illustrations, black cloth, gilt stamped spine title, dust jacket, fine, from the Bern Dibner reference library, with Burndy bookplate. Jeff Weber Rare Books 161 - 113 2011 $100

Deacon, Margaret *Scientists and the Sea 1650-1900: a Study of Marine Science.* Aldershot and Brookfield: Ashgate, 1997. Second edition; 8vo., xl, 459 pages, illustrations, aqua cloth, silver stamped spine title, dust jacket, fine, from the Bern Dibner reference library, with Burndy bookplate. Jeff Weber Rare Books 161 - 114 2011 $90

Debus, Allen G. *Chemistry, Alchemy and the New Philosophy 1550-1700: Studies in the History of Science and Medicine.* London: Variorum Reprints, 1987. 8vo., xii, 320 pages, frontispiece, illustrations, blue cloth, gilt stamped cover and spine titles, fine, from the Bern Dibner reference library, with Burndy bookplate. Jeff Weber Rare Books 161 - 115 2011 $125

Dickinson, H. W. *Richard Trevithick, the Engineer and the Man.* Cambridge: University Press, 1934. First edition; 8vo., xvii, 290 pages, 41 figures, teal cloth, black stamped spine title, dust jacket, lower corner bumped, rear hinge cracked, jacket soiled, very good, rare in dust jacket, from the Bern Dibner reference library, with Burndy bookplate. Jeff Weber Rare Books 161 - 117 2011 $125

Dickinson, H. W. *Robert Fulton, Engineer and Artist.* London: New York: & Toronto: John Lane, The Bodley Head, Bell & Cockburn, 1913. 8vo., xiv, 333, 15 (ads) pages, frontispiece, 32 figures, blue cloth, gilt stamped cover, gilt stamped spine title, dust jacket chipped, soiled, from the Bern Dibner reference library, with Burndy bookplate. Jeff Weber Rare Books   161 - 159   2011 $125

Divall, Colin *Suburbanizing the Masses: Public Transport and Urban Development in Historical Perspective.* Aldershot and Burlington: Ashgate, 2003. First edition; 8vo., xvi, 319 pages, figures, tables, pictorial boards, fine, from the Bern Dibner reference library, with Burndy bookplate.   Jeff Weber Rare Books   161 - 119   2011 $150

Dobbs, Betty Jo Teeter *The Foundations of Newton's Alchemy or "The Hunting of the Greene Lyon".* Cambridge: Cambridge University Press, 1975. 8vo., xv, 300 pages, 4 plates index, yellow cloth, gilt stamped spine label, fine, from the Bern Dibner reference library, with Burndy bookplate.   Jeff Weber Rare Books   161 - 120   2011 $135

Dobbs, Betty Jo Teeter *The Janus Faces of Genius: The Role of Alchemy in Newton's Thought.* Cambridge: Cambridge University Press, 1991. First edition; 8vo, xii, 359 pages, 11 illustrations, black cloth, copper stamped spine title, dust jacket, near fine, from the Bern Dibner reference library, with Burndy bookplate.   Jeff Weber Rare Books   161 - 121   2011 $100

Drake, Stillman *Essays on Galileo and the History and Philosophy of Science.* Toronto, Buffalo, London: University of Toronto Press, 1999. 3 volumes, 8vo., xxiii, 473; viii, 380; vi, 392 pages, frontispiece, plates, illustrations, tables, original cloth, gilt stamped cover and spine titles, near fine, from the Bern Dibner reference library, with Burndy bookplate.   Jeff Weber Rare Books   161 - 123   2011 $225

Drayton, Richard *Nature's Government: Science, Imperial Britain and the "Improvement" of the World.* New Haven and London: Yale University Press, 2000. First edition; 8vo, xxi 346 pages, frontispiece, 14 plates, 28 illustrations, black cloth gilt stamped spine title, dust jacket, rare, fine, from the Bern Dibner reference library, with Burndy bookplate.   Jeff Weber Rare Books   161 - 125   2011 $100

Dubbey, J. M. *The Mathematical Work of Charles Babbage.* Cambridge: Cambridge University Press, 1978. First edition; 8vo., viii, 235 pages, frontispiece, illustrations, black cloth, gilt stamped spine title, dust jacket, near fine, from the Bern Dibner reference library, with Burndy bookplate.   Jeff Weber Rare Books   161 - 124   2011 $165

Dunbaugh, Edwin L. *Night Boat to New England 1815-1900.* New York: Westport: London: Greenwood Press, 1992. First edition; 8vo., xiii, maps, (2), 370 pages, plates, index, creme cloth, navy stamped spine title, dust jacket, fine, from the Bern Dibner reference library, with Burndy bookplate.   Jeff Weber Rare Books   161 - 126   2011 $62

Edison Honored Throughout the Entire World. New York: Association of Edition Illuminating Companies, 1929. 4to., 65 pages, illustrations, brown cloth, embossed portrait of Edison on front cover with raised titles, extremity edges lightly rubbed, very good, from the Bern Dibner reference library, with Burndy bookplate.   Jeff Weber Rare Books   161 - 128   2011 $75

Ellegard, Alvar *Darwin and the General Reader: the Reception of Darwin's Theory of Evolution in the British Periodical Press 1859-1872.* New York and London: Garland, 1996. First edition; 8vo., 394 pages, tables, diagrams, blue cloth, gilt stamped cover emblem and spine title, dust jacket, near fine, rare in jacket, from the Bern Dibner reference library, with Burndy bookplate.   Jeff Weber Rare Books   161 - 132   2011 $125

Elliott, Clark A. *History of Science in the United States: a Chronology and Research Guide.* New York and London: Garland, 1996. 8vo., x, 543 pages, quarter grey cloth with gray paper boards, copper stamped spine title, fine, rare, from the Bern Dibner reference library, with Burndy bookplate.   Jeff Weber Rare Books   161 - 133   2011 $85

Emboden, William A. *Leonardo da Vinci en Plants and Gardens.* Portland: Dioscorides Press, 1987. Large 8vo., 234 pages, 100 figures, cream cloth, gilt stamped spine title, dust jacket, upper corner of rear cover bumped, very good, from the Bern Dibner reference library, with Burndy bookplate.   Jeff Weber Rare Books   161 - 135   2011 $60

Fahie, J. J. *Galileo: His Life and Work.* London: John Murray, 1903. 8vo., xvi, 451, ads, (4) pages, frontispiece, plates, figures, index, dark blue cloth, gilt stamped cover decoration and spine title, small tears to top spine end, very good, from the Bern Dibner reference library, with Burndy bookplate.   Jeff Weber Rare Books   161 - 137   2011 $200

Farber, Paul Lawrence *Finding Order in Nature: the Naturalist Tradition from Linnaeus to E. O. Wilson.* Baltimore: and London: Johns Hopkins University Press, 2000. First edition; 8vo., x, 136 pages, photos and illustrations, green cloth, black stamped spine title, fine, scarce cloth issue, from the Bern Dibner reference library, with Burndy bookplate.   Jeff Weber Rare Books   161 - 138   2011 $60

Farley, John *The Spontaneous Generation Controversy from Descartes to Oparin.* Baltimore and London: Johns Hopkins University Press, 1977. First edition; 8vo., x, 225 pages, illustrations, index, blue cloth, silver stamped spine title, dust jacket bit worn, very good, from the Bern Dibner reference library, with Burndy bookplate. Jeff Weber Rare Books 161 - 139 2011 $65

Federico, P. J. *Descartes on Polyhedra: a Study of the De Solidorum Elementis.* New York: Springer Verlag, 1982. First printing; 8vo., (vii) 145 pages, 36 figures, yellow cloth, black stamped cover and spine titles, fine, from the Bern Dibner reference library, with Burndy bookplate and rubber stamp. Jeff Weber Rare Books 161 - 141 2011 $70

Ferchi, Fritz *A Pictorial History of Chemistry.* London: William Heinemann, 1939. First edition in English; 8vo., viii, 214 pages, illustrations, navy cloth, gilt stamped spine title, near fine, from the Bern Dibner reference library, with Burndy bookplate. Jeff Weber Rare Books 161 - 142 2011 $95

Fessenden, Helen May *Fessenden: Builder of Tomorrows.* New York: Coward McCann, 1940. 8vo., vi, 362 pages, frontispiece, 2 color title, printed in blue and black, beige cloth, blue stamped cover and spine titles, dust jacket, jacket worn, else fine, from the Bern Dibner reference library, with Burndy bookplate. Jeff Weber Rare Books 161 - 143 2011 $110

Fetters, Thomas T. *The Lustron Home: the History of a Postwar Prefabricated Housing Experiment.* Jefferson: McFarland, 2002. 8vo., xiii, 186 pages, illustrations, printed boards, fine, from the Bern Dibner reference library, with Burndy bookplate. Jeff Weber Rare Books 161 - 144 2011 $90

Ffoulkes, Charles *Armour & Weapons.* Oxford: Clarendon Press, 1909. First edition; 8vo., 112 pages, frontispiece, plates, illustrations, paper boards, black stamped cover title and illustration, very good, signed by former owner, Cyril Stanley Smith, from the Bern Dibner reference library, with Burndy bookplate. Jeff Weber Rare Books 161 - 145 2011 $60

Ffoulkes, Charles *The Gun-Founders of England.* Cambridge: Cambridge University Press, 1937. First edition; 4to., xvi, 133, (134) pages, 15 plates, 38 text illustrations, red cloth, gilt stamped spine title, dust jacket worn and chipped, corners bumped, very good, from the Bern Dibner reference library, with Burndy bookplate. Jeff Weber Rare Books 161 - 147 2011 $60

Finocchiaro, Maurice A. *The Galileo Affair: a Documentary History.* Berkeley: Los Angeles: London: University of California, 1989. First printing; 8vo., xvi 382 pages, beige cloth, silver stamped spine title, dust jacket, fine, rare, from the Bern Dibner reference library, with Burndy bookplate. Jeff Weber Rare Books 161 - 148 2011 $80

Flamsteed, John *The Correspondence of John Flamsteed, the First Astronomer Royal.* Bristol and Philadelphia: Institute of Physics, 1995-2002. 3 volumes, large 8vo., xlix, 955; xlvii, 1095; lxvi, 1038 pages, 2 frontispieces in each volume, half tone illustrations, paper boards, gilt stamped cover and spine titles (with small cover and spine portraits of Flamsteed), fine, from the Bern Dibner reference library, with Burndy bookplate. Jeff Weber Rare Books 161 - 149 2011 $500

Forbes, R. J. *Studies in Ancient Technology. Volumes 1-3, 6-9.* Leiden: E. J. Brill, 1953-1964. 7 volumes, 8vo., viii, 194; vi, 215; vi, 268; 196; 253; viii, 288; viii, 295 pages, folding plates, text figures, tan cloth, gilt stamped cover and spine titles, dust jackets, fine, from the Bern Dibner reference library, with Burndy bookplate. Jeff Weber Rare Books 161 - 151 2011 $200

Ford, Brian J. *Images of Science. A History of Scientific Illustration.* New York: Oxford University Press, 1993. 4to., viii, 208 pages, green cloth, gilt stamped spine title, dust jacket, fine, from the Bern Dibner reference library, with Burndy bookplate. Jeff Weber Rare Books 161 - 152 2011 $75

Fox, R. Hingston *Dr. John Fothergill and His Friends: Chapters in Eighteenth Century Life.* London: Macmillan, 1919. 8vo., xxiv, 434 pages, frontispiece, 13 illustrations, original blue cloth, gilt stamped spine title, spine ends rubbed, ownership signature of H. Stewart, very good, from the Bern Dibner reference library, with Burndy bookplate. Jeff Weber Rare Books 161 - 153 2011 $85

Franklin, Benjamin 1706-1790 *The Writings of Benjamin Franklin.* New York: Haskell House, 1970. Facsimile of the 1905-1907 edition; 10 volumes, plates, charts, red cloth gilt stamped spine title, fore edge of volume II speckled, else near fine, from the Bern Dibner reference library, with Burndy bookplate. Jeff Weber Rare Books 161 - 155 2011 $150

Fraser, Craig G. *Calculus and Analytical Mechanics in the Age of Enlightenment.* Aldershot and Brookfield: Variorum, 1997. 8vo., x, 308 pages, frontispiece, figures, light blue cloth, gilt stamped cover and spine titles, fine, from the Bern Dibner reference library, with Burndy bookplate. Jeff Weber Rare Books 161 - 157 2011 $120

Freeman, R. B. *Charles Darwin: a Companion.* Folkstone: Dawson, 1978. 8vo., 309 pages, text figures, green cloth, gilt stamped spine title, dust jacket, fine, from the Bern Dibner reference library, with Burndy bookplate. Jeff Weber Rare Books 161 - 108 2011 $75

Gage, Andrew Thomas *A Bicentenary History of the Linnean Society of London.* London: Academic Press, 1988. First edition; 8vo., ix, 242 pages, double color frontispiece, illustrations, blue cloth, gilt stamped spine title, dust jacket, fine, from the Bern Dibner reference library, with Burndy bookplate. Jeff Weber Rare Books 161 - 160 2011 $70

Galilei, Galileo 1564-1642 *Dialogue on the Great World System: in the Salusbury Translation.* Chicago: University of Chicago Press, 1953. 8vo., lviii, 505 pages, teal cloth, gilt stamped spine title, dust jacket, jacket lightly chipped, very good, from the Bern Dibner reference library, with Burndy bookplate. Jeff Weber Rare Books 161 - 162 2011 $65

Gardiner, Robert *Frigates of the Napoleonic Wars.* Annapolis: Naval Institute Press, 2000. First edition; 4to., 208 pages, frontispiece, illustrations, tables, navy blue paper boards, gilt stamped spine title, dust jacket, fine, from the Bern Dibner reference library, with Burndy bookplate. Jeff Weber Rare Books 161 - 164 2011 $85

Gardner, J. Starkie *Ironwork. In Three Parts.* London: Victoria & Albert Museum, 1922-1930. 3 parts, mixed set, 8vo., xi, 146, plates, 63; xii, 124, plates 44; (vi), 195, plates (48) pages, brown and green cloth, gilt stamped cover and spine titles, very good, from the Bern Dibner reference library, with Burndy bookplate. Jeff Weber Rare Books 161 - 165 2011 $75

Gascoigne, John *Science, Politics and Universities in Europe 1600-1800.* Aldershot: Ashgate, 1998. First edition; 8vo., x, 290 pages, frontispiece, illustrations, blue cloth, gilt stamped cover and spine titles, fine, from the Bern Dibner reference library, with Burndy bookplate. Jeff Weber Rare Books 161 - 166 2011 $130

Gates, Barbara T. *Kindred Nature: Victorian and Edwardian Women Embrace the Living World.* Chicago and London: University of Chicago Press, 1998. First edition; 8vo., 293 pages, illustrations, maroon cloth, gilt stamped spine title, fine, rare in cloth, from the Bern Dibner reference library, with Burndy bookplate. Jeff Weber Rare Books 161 - 167 2011 $100

Gerstner, Franz Anton Ritter Von *Early American Railroads: Franz Anton Ritter Von Gerstner's Die Innern Communicationen (1842-1843).* Stanford: Stanford University Press, 1977. Large 4to., vi, 844 pages, plates, tables, burgundy cloth, silver stamped spine title, dust jacket, fine, from the Bern Dibner reference library, with Burndy bookplate. Jeff Weber Rare Books 161 - 173 2011 $135

Gieryn, Thomas F. *Cultural Boundaries of Science: Credibility on the Line.* Chicago and London: University of Chicago Press, 1999. First edition; 8vo., xiv, 398 pages, map, navy cloth, yellow stamped spine title, fine, from the Bern Dibner reference library, with Burndy bookplate. Jeff Weber Rare Books 161 - 174 2011 $75

Goldberg, Benjamin *The Mirror and Man.* Charlottesville: University Press of Virginia, 1985. First edition; 8vo., xii, 260 pagess, 38 illustrations, gray cloth with white paper boards, silver stamped spine title, dust jacket, fine, from the Bern Dibner reference library, with Burndy bookplate. Jeff Weber Rare Books 161 - 176 2011 $115

Good, Gregory *Sciences of the Earth: an Encyclopedia of Events, People and Phenomena.* New York: Garland Pub., 1998. 2 volumes, 8vo., xlv, 407; (409)-901 pages, figures, printed boards, fine, from the Bern Dibner reference library, with Burndy bookplate. Jeff Weber Rare Books 161 - 177 2011 $70

Gottschalk, Paul *The Earliest Diplomatic Documents on America.* Berlin: Paul Gottschalk, 1927. Limited to 172 copies, 150 of which were offered for sale; folio, 89 pages, plus 130 facsimiles, original half vellum an brown cloth, gilt lettered spine, covers slightly bowed, Burndy bookplate, fine copy. Jeff Weber Rare Books 163 - 73 2011 $1750

Grattan-Guiness, I. *Companion Encyclopedia of the History and Philosophy of the Mathematical Science.* London and New York: Routledge, 1994. First printing; thick 8vo., xiii, 842; xi, 845-1806 pages, figures, tables, printed green paper boards, fine, from the Bern Dibner reference library, with Burndy bookplate. Jeff Weber Rare Books 161 - 182 2011 $100

Grolier Club, New York *Catalogue of an Exhibition of Illuminated and Painted Manuscripts Together with a few Early Printed Books with Illuminations...* New York: Grolier Club, 1892. Limited to 350 copies; 8vo., xxxiii, 64 pages, frontispiece, two color title, illustrations, plates, green cloth, gilt stamped cover title, manuscript paper spine label, page uncut, very good, from the Bern Dibner reference library, with Burndy bookplate. Jeff Weber Rare Books 161 - 183 2011 $125

Grove, Richard H. *Green Imperialism: Colonial Expansion, Tropical Island Edens and the Origins of Enviorenmentalism 1600-1860.* Cambridge: Cambridge University Press, 1995. First edition; 8vo. xiv, 540 pages, illustrations, green cloth, gilt stamped spine title, dust jacket, fine, from the Bern Dibner reference library, with Burndy bookplate. Jeff Weber Rare Books   161 - 184   2011 $80

Hall, A. Rupert *Science and Society: Historical Essays on the Relations of Science, Technology and Medicine.* Aldershot and Brookfield: Variorum, 1994. 8vo., x, 324 pages, frontispiece, illustrations, blue cloth, gilt stamped cover and spine titles, fine, from the Bern Dibner reference library, with Burndy bookplate. Jeff Weber Rare Books   161 - 187   2011 $110

Hannaway, Owen *The Chemists and the Word: the Didactic Origins of Chemistry.* Baltimore and London: Johns Hopkins University, 1975. 8vo., xiii, 165 pages, illustrations, red cloth, white stamped spine title, dust jacket, jacket edges are worn, very good, from the Bern Dibner reference library, with Burndy bookplate. Jeff Weber Rare Books   161 - 191   2011 $100

Harmsen, Theodor *Antiquarianism in the Augustan Age: Thomas Hearne 1678-1735.* Oxford: Peter Lang, 2000. 8vo., 336 pages, frontispiece, printed wrappers, near fine, from the Bern Dibner reference library, with Burndy bookplate. Jeff Weber Rare Books   161 - 192   2011 $70

Harrison, Peter *The Bible, Protestation and the Rise of Natural Science.* Cambridge: Cambridge University Press, 1998. First edition; 8vo., 313 pages, dark blue cloth, silver stamped spine title, dust jacket, near fine, from the Bern Dibner reference library, with Burndy bookplate. Jeff Weber Rare Books   161 - 193   2011 $60

Haycock, David Boyd *Quakery and Commerce in Seventeenth Century.* London: The Wellcome trust Centre for the History of Medicine at UCL, 2005. 8vo., viii, 216 pages, maps, figures, tables, red cloth, gilt stamped cover and spine titles, fine, from the Bern Dibner reference library, with Burndy bookplate. Jeff Weber Rare Books   161 - 198   2011 $60

Hellman, C. Doris *The Comet of 1577: Its Place in History of Astronomy.* New York: Columbia University Press, 1944. First edition; 8vo., 488 pages, green cloth, blindstamped cover emblem, gilt stamped spine title, dust jacket worn with tears, very good, rare in jacket, from the Bern Dibner reference library, with Burndy bookplate. Jeff Weber Rare Books   161 - 199   2011 $169

Henderson, Linda Dalrymple *Duchamp in Context: Science and Technology in the Large Glass and Related Works.* Princeton: Princeton University Press, 1998. large 8vo., xxiii, 374 pages, 189 figures, black cloth, silver stamped spine title, dust jacket, fine, from the Bern Dibner reference library, with Burndy bookplate. Jeff Weber Rare Books   161 - 200   2011 $95

Herivel, John *Joseph Fourier: the Man and the Physicist.* Oxford: Clarendon Press, 1975. First edition; 8vo., xii, 350 pages, frontispiece, plates, navy cloth, gilt stamped spine title, dust jacket, near fine, from the Bern Dibner reference library, with Burndy bookplate. Jeff Weber Rare Books   161 - 201   2011 $175

Hertzsprung Kapteyn, Henrietta *The Life and Works of J. C. Kaptyn.* Dordrecht: Boston: and London: Kluwer Academic, 1993. 8vo., xix, 92 pages, 14 illustrations, printed boards, fine, from the Bern Dibner reference library, with Burndy bookplate. Jeff Weber Rare Books   161 - 203   2011 $100

Hewson, J. B. *A History of the Practice of Navigation.* Glasgow: Brown, Son & Ferguson, 1951. First edition; 8vo., vii, 270 pages, illustrations, dark blue cloth, gilt stamped cover and spine titles, dust jacket worn with pieces missing and tape repair, else very good, rare in jacket, Charles Singer's copy with his bookplate, from the Bern Dibner reference library, with Burndy bookplate. Jeff Weber Rare Books   161 - 204   2011 $125

Hilfstein, Erna *Science and History: Studies in Honor of Edward Reisen.* Wrocaw: Polish Academy of Sciences Press, 1978. xvi, 80., 353 pages, illustrations, maroon cloth, black and gilt stamped cover and spine titles, dust jacket lightly worn, very good, from the Bern Dibner reference library, with Burndy bookplate. Jeff Weber Rare Books   161 - 205   2011 $100

Hills, Richard Leslie *Power from Steam: a History of the Stationary Steam Engine.* Cambridge: New York: Cambridge University Press, 1989. First edition; 8vo., xv, 338 pages, 80 figures, black cloth, gilt stamped spine title, dust jacket, fine, rare, from the Bern Dibner reference library, with Burndy bookplate. Jeff Weber Rare Books   161 - 206   2011 $150

Hindle, Brooke *David Rittenhouse.* Princeton: Princeton University Press, 1964. First edition; 8vo., xiii, 394 pages, title illustration, plates, charcoal cloth, gilt stamped blue spine label, dust jacket, near fine, from the Bern Dibner reference library, with Burndy bookplate. Jeff Weber Rare Books   161 - 207   2011 $75

Hirsh, Richard F. *Power Loss: The Origins of Deregulation and Restructering in the American Electric Utility System.* Cambridge and London: MIT Press, 1999. First edition; 8vo., x 406 pages, illustrations, tables, quarter yellow cloth over beige cloth sides, silver stamped spine title, dust jacket, fine, from the Bern Dibner reference library, with Burndy bookplate.   Jeff Weber Rare Books   161 - 208 2011 $165

Hofmann, Joseph E. *Leibniz in Paris 1672-1676: His Growth to Mathematical Maturity.* London and New York: Cambridge University Press, 1974. Revised English translation of 1949 Munich publication; 8vo., xi, 372 pages, frontispiece, figures, blue cloth, silver stamped spine title, dust jacket, very good, from the Bern Dibner reference library, with Burndy bookplate.   Jeff Weber Rare Books   161 - 209 2011 $125

Holmes, Frederic L. *Instruments and Experimentation in the History of Chemistry.* Cambridge and London: MIT Press, 2000. 8vo., xxi, 415 pages, text figures, green cloth, silver stamed spine title, dust jacket, fine, from the Bern Dibner reference library, with Burndy bookplate.   Jeff Weber Rare Books   161 - 210 2011 $70

Hosmer, James K. *History of the Expedition of Captains Lewis and Clark 1804-5-6.* Chicago: A. C. McClurg, 1902. 2 volumes, 8vo., lvi, 500; ix, 586 pages, frontispiece, plates, quarter brown cloth with tan cloth sides, gilt stamped spine title, top edge gilt, inner hinges cracked, very good, some pages uncut, from the Bern Dibner reference library, with Burndy bookplate.   Jeff Weber Rare Books   161 - 212 2011 $140

Hoyningen-Huene, Paul *Reconstructing Scientific Resolutions: Thomas S. Kuhn's Philosophy of Science.* Chicago and London: University of Chicago Press, 1993. 8vo., xx, 310 pages, light yellow cloth, black stamped spine title, fine from the Bern Dibner reference library, with Burndy bookplate.   Jeff Weber Rare Books   161 - 217 2011 $60

Hull, David *Darwin and His Critics: The Reception of Darwin's theory of Evolution by the Scientific Community.* Cambridge: Harvard University Press, 1974. Second printing; 8vo., xii, 473 pages, tan cloth, black stamped spine title, dust jacket lightly rubbed, near fine, from the Bern Dibner reference library, with Burndy bookplate.   Jeff Weber Rare Books   161 - 218 2011 $75

Hungerford, Edward *The Story of the Baltimore & Ohio Railroad 1827-1927.* New York: and London: G. P. Putnam's Sons, 1928. First edition; 8vo., xii, 372; x, 365 pages, frontispiece, plates, navy cloth, gilt stamped spine title, top edge gilt, dust jackets worn with pieces missing, top spine cloth torn on both volumes, titles affected, good, from the Bern Dibner reference library, with Burndy bookplate.   Jeff Weber Rare Books   161 - 219 2011 $75

Hunt, Rachel McMasters Miller *Catalogue of Botanical Books in the Collection of...* Pittsburgh: Hunt Botanical Library, 1958-1961. Limited to 750 sets; 3 volumes, large 8vo., lxxiv, 517; ccxliv; ix, 655 pages, frontispiece, plates, dark green cloth, gilt stamped cover illustrations and spine titles, fine, from the Bern Dibner reference library, with Burndy bookplate.   Jeff Weber Rare Books   161 - 220 2011 $700

Hunter, Andrew *Thornton and Tully' Scientific Books, Libraries and Collectors: a Study of Bibliography and the Book trade in Relation to the History of Science.* Aldershot: Ashgate, 2000. Revision of third 1971 London edition; 8vo., xii, 405 pages, 8 plates, green cloth, silver stamped spine title, dust jacket, fine, from the Bern Dibner reference library, with Burndy bookplate.   Jeff Weber Rare Books   161 - 221 2011 $150

Hunter, Michael *Elias Ashmole 1617-1692: The Founder of the Ashmolean Museum and His World A Tercentenary Exhibition 27 April to 31 July 1983.* Oxford: Ashmolean Museum, 1983. 8vo., xi, 92 pages, color frontispiece, 12 plates, printed wrappers, fine, from the Bern Dibner reference library, with Burndy bookplate.   Jeff Weber Rare Books   161 - 222 2011 $55

Huygens, Christiaan *Christiaan Huygens' the Pendulum Clock or Geometrical Demonstrations concerning the Motion of Pendula as Applied to Clocks.* Ames: Iowa State University Press, 1986. 8vo., xxix, 182 pages, with 102 figures, red cloth, gilt stamped spine title, dust jacket, jacket torn without loss, very good, from the Bern Dibner reference library, with Burndy bookplate.   Jeff Weber Rare Books   161 - 225 2011 $125

Inkster, Ian *Science and Technology in History: an Approach to Industrial Development.* New Brunswick: Rutgers University Press, 1991. 8vo., xvi, 391 pages, black cloth, gilt stamped spine title, dust jacket, from the Bern Dibner reference library, with Burndy bookplate.   Jeff Weber Rare Books   161 - 228 2011 $125

Jabir Ibn Hayyan *The Works of Geber.* London: Toronto: & New York: J. M. Dent & E. P. Dutton, 1928. 8vo., xl, 264 pages, 17 reproductions in black and white from original drawings and diagrams, black cloth, blindstamped cover pentagram, gilt stamped spine title, dust jacket, near fine, from the Bern Dibner reference library, with Burndy bookplate. Jeff Weber Rare Books 161 - 170 2011 $75

Jackson, John N. *The Welland Canals and Their Communities: Engineering, Industrial and Urban Transformation.* Toronto: Buffalo: London: University of Toronto Press, 1997. First edition; 8vo., xvi, 535 pages, photos, 13 maps, 11 tables, gray cloth, red stamped spine title, dust jacket, fine, from the Bern Dibner reference library, with Burndy bookplate. Jeff Weber Rare Books 161 - 234 2011 $100

Jardine, Nicholas *The Birth of History and Philosophy of Science: Kepler's A Defence of Tycho Against Ursus, with Essays on Its Provenance and Significance.* Cambridge & New York: Cambridge University Press, 1984. 8vo., ix, 301 pages, blue cloth, silver stamped spine title, dust jacket, fine, scarce in cloth, from the Bern Dibner reference library, with Burndy bookplate. Jeff Weber Rare Books 161 - 235 2011 $125

Jarvis, Adrian *Port and Harbour Engineering.* Aldershot: Ashgate, 1998. 8vo., xxxiv, 416 pages, photos and illustrations, red cloth, gilt stamped cover and spine titles, fine, from the Bern Dibner reference library, with Burndy bookplate. Jeff Weber Rare Books 161 - 236 2011 $175

Jasanoff, Sheila *Handbook of Science and Technology Studies.* Thousand Oaks: Sage Publications, 1995. Thick 8vo., xv, 820 pages, black cloth, gilt stamped spine title, dust jacket, fine, scarce, from the Bern Dibner reference library, with Burndy bookplate. Jeff Weber Rare Books 161 - 238 2011 $100

Jeeseph, Douglas M. *Squaring the Circle: The War Between Hobbes and Wallis.* Chicago & London: University of Chicago Press, 1999. First edition; 8vo., xiv, 419 pages, figures, black cloth, gilt stamped spine title, fine, from the Bern Dibner reference library, with Burndy bookplate. Jeff Weber Rare Books 161 - 239 2011 $100

Johnston, Stanley H. *The Cleveland Herbal, Botanical and Horticultural Collections: a Descriptive Bibliography of Pre-1830 Works from the Libraries of the Holden Arboretum, the Cleveland medical Library Association and the Garden Center of Greater Cleveland.* Kent and London: Kent State University Press, 1992. First edition; large 8vo., xviii, 1012 pages, color frontispiece, plates, green cloth, gilt stamped red cover and spine labels, small bump to rear cover, else fine, from the Bern Dibner reference library, with Burndy bookplate. Jeff Weber Rare Books 161 - 241 2011 $95

Jones, Caroline A. *Picturing Science, Producing Art.* New York and London: Routledge, 1998. Tall 8vo., x, 518 pages, frontispiece, illustrations, black cloth, silver stamped spine title, Burndy bookplate, fine, rare in cloth, from the Bern Dibner reference library, with Burndy bookplate. Jeff Weber Rare Books 161 - 241 2011 $150

Joppien, Rudiger *The Art of Captain Cook's Voyages.* New Haven and London: Yale University Press, 1985-1988. First edition; 4 volumes, 4to., xv, 247; xiii, 274; xxi, 233; 235-669 pages, illustrations, (ink smeared, text still lightly legible), reddish brown cloth, gilt stamped spine title, dust jacket, near fine, from the Bern Dibner reference library, with Burndy bookplate. Jeff Weber Rare Books 161 - 244 2011 $675

Karpinski, Louis *Bibliography of Mathematical Works Printed in America through 1850.* Ann Arbor: and London: University of Michigan Press & Oxford University Press, 1940. First edition; 4to., xxvi, 697 pages, illustrations, dark blue cloth, blindstamped cover emblem, gilt stamped spine title, extremities lightly speckled, inner hinge cracked, from the Bern Dibner reference library, with Burndy bookplate. Jeff Weber Rare Books 161 - 247 2011 $400

Lindberg, David C. *Roger Bacon and the Origins of Perspectiva in the Middle Ages.* Oxford: Clarendon Press, 1996. First edition; 8vo., cxi, 411 pages, figures, index, black cloth, gilt stamped cover and spine titles, fine, from the Bern Dibner reference library, with Burndy bookplate. Jeff Weber Rare Books 161 - 23 2011 $180

Nickel, Douglas R. *Francis Frith in Egypt and Palestine: a Victorian Photographer Abroad.* Princeton and Oxford: Princeton University Press, 2004. First printing; 4to. 239 pages, frontispiece, 75 duotone plates, 10 black and white plates, quarter brown cloth with pictorial paper boards, gilt stamped spine title, dust jacket, fine, from the Bern Dibner reference library, with Burndy bookplate. Jeff Weber Rare Books 161 - 158 2011 $75

Sargent, Rose Mary *The Diffident Naturalist: Robert Boyle an the Philosophy of Experiment.* Chicago: University of Chicago Press, 1995. 8vo., xi, 355 pages, olive cloth, green stamped spine title, rare in cloth, from the Bern Dibner reference library, with Burndy bookplate. Jeff Weber Rare Books 161 - 58 2011 $65

Temple, Richard *The World Encompassed and Analogus Contemporary Documents Concerning Sir Francis Drake's Circumnavigation of the World.* New York: Cooper Square, 1969. Reprint; tall 8vo., x, 235 pages, maps, illustrations, blue cloth, silver and gilt stamped spine title, near fine, from the Bern Dibner reference library, with Burndy bookplate. Jeff Weber Rare Books 161 - 122 2011 $65

Ward, James Arthur *The Man Haupt: a Biography of Herman Haupt.* Baton Rouge: Louisiana State University Press, 1973. 8vo., xvi, 278 pages, brown cloth, gilt stamped spine title, dust jacket, fine, from the Bern Dibner reference library, with Burndy bookplate. Jeff Weber Rare Books 161 - 195 2011 $75

Warnow, Joan N. *Images of Einstein: a Catalog.* New York: Center for Physics American Institute of Physics, 1979. Second edition; oblong 8vo., 77 pages, printed wrappers, corners creased, very good, from the Bern Dibner reference library, with Burndy bookplate. Jeff Weber Rare Books 161 - 130 2011 $200

Wojcik, Jan W. *Robert Boyle and the Limits of Reason.* New York: Cambridge University Press, 1997. 8vo., xvi, 243 pages, navy cloth, gilt stamped spine title, dust jacket, fine, from the Bern Dibner reference library, with Burndy bookplate. Jeff Weber Rare Books 161 - 59 2011 $90

Association – Dickenson, Mary Hamilton

More, Hannah 1745-1833 *Sacred Dramas: Chiefly Intended for Young Persons...* London: T. Cadell, 1782. Second edition; contemporary full tree calf, gilt spine, maroon leather label, expertly repaired, presentation to Mary Hamilton (after Dickenson) by author. Jarndyce Antiquarian Booksellers CLXC - 528 2011 £650

Association – Dickinson, George

Emerson, Ralph Waldo 1803-1882 *Essays.* Boston: James Munroe and Co., 1841. First edition; contemporary half black morocco and marbled boards, matching morocco corners, recently rebacked with black morocco spine, owner name of George Dickinson on half titlepage, minor internal soiling, covers nice, very good. Charles Agvent Transcendentalism 2010 - 10 2011 $1200

Association – Dickinson, Margaret

Morris, William 1834-1896 *The Hollow Land and Other Contributions to the Oxford and Cambridge Magazine.* London: Chiswick Press, 1903. First edition; printed on handmade paper using Morris' Golden typeface, in black with the titles and shoulder titles printed in red, pages (viii) (blanks), iv, 334, (7) (blanks), crown 8vo., original quarter blue grey cloth, printed label (spare label tipped in), pale blue boards lightly soiled and edges rubbed, cloth faded and little worn at backstrip head, free endpapers lightly browned, rough trimmed, front flyleaf inscribed by Emery Walker to Margaret Dickinson. Blackwell Rare Books B166 - 194 2011 £500

Association – Digby, Kenelm

Granger, James *A Biographical History of England, from the Revolution to the End of George I's Reign...* London: W. Richardson, 1806. 3 volumes, untrimmed in original drab boards, maroon glazed cloth spines, paper labels, spines slightly rubbed and faded to brown, labels worn, armorial bookplates of Sir Kenelm Digby. Jarndyce Antiquarian Booksellers CXCI - 192 2011 £120

Association – Digby, William

Meakin, Budgett *The Moorish Empire: a Historical Epitome + The Moors + The Land of the Moors.* London: Swan Sonnesnschein, 1899-1901. First editions; 3 volumes, original publisher's blue cloth lettered and decorated gilt on spine and cover, 8vo., pages xxiii, 576; xxii, 503; xxxi, 464; with 330 illustrations, signed presentation from author for William Digby, ex-library copies with few labels and stamps but in fairly reasonable condition, slight edgewear, prelims slightly loose, slight lean, inner hinges cracking but holding with clean text, overall apart from this near very good. Any Amount of Books May 29 2011 - A73085 2011 $408

Association – Dixon, Jean

Kelly, George *Behold the Bridegroom.* Boston: Little Brown, 1928. First edition; 8vo., pages 172, frontispiece, blue cloth with paper label, inscribed by author for Jean Dixon who played Constance Peyton. Second Life Books Inc. 174 - 212 2011 $500

Association – Dobson, Alban

Spielmann, Marion Harry *Hugh Thomson: His Art, His Letters, His Humour and His Charm.* London: A. & C. Black, 1931. First edition; half title, color frontispiece, plates, illustrations, original scarlet cloth, very good in dust jacket, inscribed to Dorothy from Kitty and Alban (Dobson). Jarndyce Antiquarian Booksellers CXCI - 515 2011 £110

Association – Dobson, Austin

Monkhouse, William Cosmo *Corn and Poppies.* London: Elkin Mathews, 1890. First edition; half title, uncut in original painted vellum binding. bevelled boards, very slightly dulled, bookplate of Alban Dobson, very good, tipped on to leading f.e.p. a 13 line poem on single sheet of paper signed by author with note by Alban Dobson "found among Austin Dobson's papers". Jarndyce Antiquarian Booksellers CXCI - 325 2011 £150

Association – Dobson, Kitty

Spielmann, Marion Harry *Hugh Thomson: His Art, His Letters, His Humour and His Charm.* London: A. & C. Black, 1931. First edition; half title, color frontispiece, plates, illustrations, original scarlet cloth, very good in dust jacket, inscribed to Dorothy from Kitty and Alban (Dobson). Jarndyce Antiquarian Booksellers   CXCI - 515   2011   £110

Association – Dobson, Tom

Wiggin, Kate Douglas *Penelope's Experiences in England. Penelope's Progress In Scotland and Penelope's Irish Experiences.* Boston: Houghton Mifflin, 1901. 1902.; 3 volumes, 8vo., green cloth elaborately stamped in gold, top edge gilt, fine, each volume illustrated with beautiful black and white illustrations by C. E. Brock, lengthy inscription from Wiggin to Irish Singer Tom Dobson in each of the Three books, marvelous set.   Aleph-Bet Books, Inc.   95 - 587   2011 $650

Association – Doheny, Estelle

Bryant, William Cullen   1794-1878   *Poems.* Cambridge: Hilliard and Metcalf, 1821. First edition; 16mo., 44 pages, original printed boards, neatly rebacked, uncut, the Estelle Doheny copy, housed in morocco backed two part slipcase.   M & S Rare Books, Inc.   90 - 57   2011 $1500

Bible. Greek - 1812   *Psalterium Graecum E Codice Ms. Alexandrino.*   Londini: Ex Prelo Ricardi Taylor et Socii, 1812. One of 17 copies printed on vellum; 356 x 299mm., (1) leaf (blank), xii, (32) leaves, 18 pages, (1) leaf (blank), very handsome contemporary deep blue morocco lavishly gilt, apparently by Charles Lewis, covers with broad elaborately gilt border and simple inner frame, wide gilt decorated raised bands, spine compartments with complex gilt decoration featuring scrolling floral stamps and unusual trapezoidal ornaments on either side of a central stem, very wide and sumptuously gilt inner dentelles, yellow watered silk pastedowns, front and rear free endleaves, made of matching watered silk pasted to vellum sheets, all edges gilt; monogram booklabel and armorial bookplate of William Henry Smith and oval morocco bookplate of Estelle Doheny, subscriber list, slight variation in color of binding and of vellum leaves, but very fine, stunning.   Phillip J. Pirages   59 - 340   2011 $15,000

Lytton, Edward George Earle Bulwer-Lytton, 1st Baron 1803-1873   *The Last Days of Pompeii.*   London: Richard Bentley, 1834. First edition; 210 x 130mm., volume 1 lacking half title, 3 volumes, publisher's drab paper boards backed with maroon muslin, flat spines with original printed paper labels, edges untrimmed, housed in red buckram chemise, inside very handsome red morocco backed case, its spine designed to appear as three attractively found volumes with raised bands and gilt compartments filled with interlacing floral vines, ALS by apparently written by author's elder brother, the diplomat, Sir Henry Lytton Earle Bulwer to his banker, 19th century armorial bookplate of William Williamson Willink, each volume with morocco bookplate of Estelle Doheny; paper boards bit soiled (one cover with slight dampstain), minor wear at joints and extremities, isolated trivial smudges internally, otherwise excellent unsophisticated set, especially clean and fresh, extremely handsome.   Phillip J. Pirages   59 - 259   2011 $950

Thomson, James   1700-1748   *The Works.*   London: printed by A. Strahan for J. Rivington and Sons, 1788. 227 x 145mm., 3 volumes, once elegant and still pleasing contemporary scarlet straight grained morocco simply gilt, covers with single gilt fillet border, raised bands flanked by plain gilt rules, gilt titling, turn-ins with gilt chain roll, marbled endpapers, all edges gilt; with fine fore-edge paintings of Folkestone, Dublin and Worcester; volumes in recent sturdy buckram slipcase with marbled paper sides; frontispiece portrait, 10 engraved plates; 19th century armorial bookplate of Richard Davies, morocco bookplate of Estelle Doheny and modern engraved bookplate of John Taylor Reynolds, titlepage with ink ownership inscription of Mihill Slaughter 1811 (Secretary of the Railways Department); hint of soil to covers, joints and extremities with little rubbing (but well refurbished), leaves with intermittent minor foxing, engravings bit more foxed (half of them rather browned), offset onto facing page, text with general light browning and occasional trivial soiling, four leaves with short marginal or paper flaw tears (no loss); although not without problems, set nevertheless appealing, internal flaws never really unsightly, bindings all solid and paintings where it really matters, entirely well preserved.   Phillip J. Pirages   59 - 45   2011 $4500

Association – Dolben, Eliz

Barwick, Peter   *The Life of the Reverend Dr. John Barwick, D.D.*   London: printed by J. Bettenham, 1724. Large paper copy, 8vo., pages (xxiv), 552, (xl) + 2 engraved portrait frontispieces, contemporary calf, gilt panelled spine, orange lettering piece gilt, boards panelled in blind (Cambridge style), board edges decorative roll gilt, 'Dutch-comb' 'made' endpapers, all edges red and grey sprinkled green and white sewn endbands, rubbed at extremities, spine darkened, joints cracked but strong, endcaps worn "James Affleck" book label, contemporary ink inscription "Eliz. Dolben" and above "James Affleck", mid 20th century provenance note by Peter B. G. Binnall, from the collection of Christopher Ernest Weston 1947-2010.   Unsworths Booksellers   24 - 6   2011   £200

Association – Donegall, Marchioness

Tupper, Martin Farquhar 1810-1889 *Proverbial Philosophy: a Book of Thoughts and Arguments Originally Treated.* London: Joseph Rickerby, 1838. First edition; tall 8vo., 4 page catalog, original dark green cloth, rubbing to hinges, scarce first edition, this copy stamped Marchioness of Donegall. Jarndyce Antiquarian Booksellers CXCI - 588 2011 £150

Association – Dorman, Richard

Grenard, Ross *Requiem for the Narrow Gauge.* Canton: 1985. 125 pages, illustrations, pictorial hardcover, bottom corner bumped else clean and very good, numbered with warm inscription from author to historian Richard Dorman. Dumont Maps & Books of the West 111 - 58 2011 $75

Association – Dorrance, John

Bible. Polyglot - 1809 *Liber Psalmorum Hebraice.* London: Cambridge, 1809. First Printing of any part of the Bible in Hebrew in America; 12mo, (8), (1)-495, (1, blank) pages, with translation and notes in Latin, full contemporary calf, front board attached but loose, lacking part of the backstrip, back cover with some leather lacking, corners and edges chipped, leaves bit toned, some foxing, as usual for American books of this era, old pencil inscription on front free endpaper, very good, extremely scarce, housed in custom calf clamshell, undated gift inscription from Rev. John H. Van Court (1793-1867) to the Rev. John Dorrance (1800-1861). Heritage Book Shop Holiday 2010 - 65 2011 $20,000

Association – Dothie, Ellery

MacDonald, George 1824-1905 *Works of Fancy and Imagination.* London: Strahan & Co., 1871. 10 volumes, 16mo., half title, odd spot, original green cloth bevelled boards, elaborately gilt by Burn, all edges gilt, reasonably good set with spines dulled and some gilt blocking, little rubbed, pencil inscription on half title by recipients "Ellery (?) & L. H. Dothie. The Gift of the Author Decr. 10". Jarndyce Antiquarian Booksellers CXCII - 144 2011 £1600

Association – Dothie, L. H.

MacDonald, George 1824-1905 *Works of Fancy and Imagination.* London: Strahan & Co., 1871. 10 volumes, 16mo., half title, odd spot, original green cloth bevelled boards, elaborately gilt by Burn, all edges gilt, reasonably good set with spines dulled and some gilt blocking, little rubbed, pencil inscription on half title by recipients "Ellery (?) & L. H. Dothie. The Gift of the Author Decr. 10". Jarndyce Antiquarian Booksellers CXCII - 144 2011 £1600

Association – Doud, Frank

Ossoli, Margaret Fuller 1810-1850 *Memoirs of Margaret Fuller Ossoli.* Boston: Phillips Sampson, 1852. Small octavo, 2 volumes, viii, (9)-351; iii (3)-352, (4 ads) pages, original full publisher's blindstamped cloth, gilt spine titles, spine ends worn, extremites shelf worn, corners showing signature in volume I sprung, but complete, good plus, signature of previous owner, Frank A. Doud. Jeff Weber Rare Books 163 - 92 2011 $85

Association – Doughton, Robley

Stansbury, Howard *Exploration and Survey of the Valley Great Salt Lake of Utah...* Philadelphia: Lippincott, Gambo & Co., 1852. First edition; 2 volumes, cloth, 487 pages, 2 large folding maps in separate portfolio volume, 58 plates, including folding panoramic views, many appendices, charts, tables, index, former owner's inscription "Robley Doughton presented by Col. Albert, Washington", wear to spine ends and extremities, else very good, map volume missing backstrip, however maps are in very good condition with usual splitting at some of the folds, both volumes complete with all plates and maps present, very scarce in original cloth. Buckingham Books May 26 2011 - 25961 2011 $2000

Association – Douthit, Harold

Irving, Washington 1783-1859 *The Alhambra.* London and New York: Macmillan and Co., 1896. One of 500 extra illustrated copies; 263 x 189mm. xx, 436 pages, magnificent contemporary dark green crushed morocco, extravagantly gilt by Bagguley (signed with the firm's ink "Sutherland" patent stamp on verso of front endleaf), covers with borders of multiple plain and decorative gilt rules, lobed inner frame with fleuron cornerpieces, whole enclosing a large and extremely intricate gilt lozenge, raised ands, spine lavishly gilt in double ruled compartments, gilt titling and turn-ins, beautiful vellum doublures elaborately tooled in diapered gilt red, and green moorish pattern, green weathered silk endleaves, top edge gilt, other edges rough trimmed, numerous illustrations in text and 12 inserted lithographs by Joseph Pennell, bookplate of Harold Douthit; in beautiful condition inside and out, lovely bind with lustrous morocco, vellum and gilt, text virtually pristine. Phillip J. Pirages 59 - 86 2011 $5500

Association – Downham, F. Lindstead

Fowler, J. T. *Adamnani Vita S. Columbae.* Oxford: Clarendon Press, 1894. Pages lxxxvii, 202, (ii), 8, original quarter roan gilt, spine rather frayed at head, some pencilled notes and underlinings, distinguished trio of earlier historian owners, Gwilym Peredur Jones, F. Lindstead Downham and Geoffrey Martin. R. F. G. Hollett & Son Antiquarian Booksellers 175 - 464 2011 £35

Association – Downson, Elizabeth

Busk, Rachel Henriette *Sagas from the Far East; or Kalmouk and Mongolian Traditionary Tales.* London: Griffith & Farran, 1873. First edition; original red cloth, spine slightly dulled, leading inner hinges slightly cracking, signature of Elizabeth Downson. Jarndyce Antiquarian Booksellers CXCI - 100 2011 £120

Association – Drayton, Harold Charles

Freke, John *The Princes of the Several Stocks, Anuuities and Other Publick Securities &c with the Course of Exchange. From Saturday March 26th 1715 to Friday June 22d 1716.* London: sold by author at his office over against Jonathan's Coffee-House in Exchange Alley, 1716. 8vo., general titlepage (blank verso) + dedication leaf (blank verso), followed by 104 + 26 single sheet price lists, each 2 pages on facing leaves, some imprints cropped at foot, some printed on thick paper, contemporary panelled calf, skillfully rebacked and labelled to match, very good, from the 19th century library of Hugh Cecil 5th Earl of Lonsale, with his armorial bookplate, and from the early 20th century library of Harold Charles Drayton, the financier, exceptionally rare. John Drury Rare Books 153 - 49 2011 £3500

Association – Drinkwater, N.

Great Britain. Royal Commission on Historical Monuments - 1936 *An Inventory of the Historical Monuments in Westmorland.* London: HMSO, 1936. First edition; 4to., original red cloth gilt, dust jacket (few spots), pages lxviii, 302, top edge gilt, with 160 plates and numerous plans and illustrations, folding map in rear pocket, little scattered spotting, otherwise very good, sound and clean copy, signed by N. Drinkwater. R. F. G. Hollett & Son Antiquarian Booksellers 177 - 769 2011 £250

Association – Dubreville, Gaston

Dujardin, Edouard *Les Lauriers sont Coupes/Avec un Portrait de l'Auteur Grave a l'eau-forte par Jacques E. Blanche.* Paris: Librairie de la revue Indepdendante, 1888. First edition, no. 42 of 400 copies on velin anglas mecanique, from a total edition of 420; 8vo., pages 139, (5), frontispiece, uncut, sporadic foxing to some leaves, publisher's beige wrappers, text in black, lightly soiled and thumbed, spine creased, author's presentation inscription to limitation page for Gaston Dubreville (?), discreet marginal correction to page 62 (as in other copies). Simon Finch Rare Books Zero - 229 2011 £2000

Association – Dubus, Andre

Crumley, James *The Last Good Kiss.* New York: Random House, 1978. First edition; inscribed by author to Andre Dubus, foxing to top edge of text block, else fine in near fine, mildly spine tanned dust jacket with light edgewear. Ken Lopez Bookseller 154 - 41 2011 $750

Association – Dufresne, John

Naked Came the Manatee. New York: Putnam, 1996. First edition; fine in fine dust jacket, signed by all authors on single tipped in leaf, including Carl Hiaasen, Elmore Leonard, John Dufresne, Dave Barry, Vicki Hendricks, Edna Buchanan, Les Standiford and James W. Hall, etc. Ken Lopez Bookseller 154 - 5 2011 $200

Association – Duhamel, Jacques

Greene, Graham 1904-1991 *Brighton Rock.* Star Editions, Heinemann, 1947. 16mo., pages (iv), 336, very faint occasional foxing to prelims, original printed light blue wrapper, bound within binder's pale grey cloth, lightly browned backstrip gilt lettered, marbled endpapers, very good, inscribed by Greene for Jacques Duhamel. Blackwell Rare Books B166 - 152 2011 £800

Greene, Graham 1904-1991 *The Power and the Glory.* Stockholm: Continental Book Co., 1947. Inscribed by author for Jacques Duhamel, pages (vi), 282, 16mo., original printed cream wrappers bound within binder's pale grey cloth, lightly browned backstrip gilt lettered, marbled endpapers, very good. Blackwell Rare Books B166 - 155 2011 £800

Association – Dulac, Edmund

Pushkin, Aleksandr Sergeevich 1799-1837 *The Golden Cockerel.* New York: Heritage Press, 1950. 4to., original publisher's blue cloth with cockerel printed in gilt in repeat pattern on covers, spine lettered gilt, pages 42, copiously illustrated in color, signed by artist, Edmund Dulac with presentation from Dulac for Isaac Jones, slight marks, head of spine slightly rubbed, slight soiling otherwise very good+. Any Amount of Books May 29 2011 - A43024 2011 $340

Association – Dumnachie, Muriel

Middleton, Stanley *Brazen Prison.* London: Hutchinson, 1971. First edition; 8vo., 224 pages, signed presentation from author, to Muriel Dumnachie, fine in near fine dust jacket, dust jacket, very slightly creased at inner flap. Any Amount of Books May 29 2011 - A38142 2011 $255

Association – Dunbar, Robert

Dorn, Edward *High West Rendezvous: an Edward Dorn Sampler.* Hay on Wye: Etruscan Books/West House Books, 1996. First edition; 8vo., wrappers, 57 pages, signed by author for Robert and Tatiana Dunbar, fine. Any Amount of Books May 29 2011 - A66641 2011 $272

Association – Dunbar, Tatiana

Dorn, Edward *High West Rendezvous: an Edward Dorn Sampler.* Hay on Wye: Etruscan Books/West House Books, 1996. First edition; 8vo., wrappers, 57 pages, signed by author for Robert and Tatiana Dunbar, fine.   Any Amount of Books   May 29 2011 - A66641   2011 $272

Association – Dundonald, Earl of

Lytton, Rosina, Baroness *Cheveley; or the Man of Honour.* London: Edward Bull, 1839. First edition; 3 volumes, half titles, contemporary half dark purple calf, gilt spines, dark green leather labels, very slight rubbing, armorial bookplate of Earl of Dundonald and each volume signed "Countess of Dundonald, very good set, extremely scarce.   Jarndyce Antiquarian Booksellers   CLXC - 180   2011   £2500

Association – Dunn, Sarah

Linton, Eliza Lynn *Lizzie of Greyrigg.* London: Tinsley Bros., 1866. First edition; 3 volumes, half titles, contemporary half maroon sheep, spines faded to brown, worn but sound, each volume signed Sarah A. Dunn in contemporary hand, library shelf numbers on spines.   Jarndyce Antiquarian Booksellers   CLXC - 147   2011   £125

Association – Duodo, Pietro

Oribasius *Synopseos ad Evstathivm Filivm Lib. Novem.* Paris: Maurice Meunier for Oudin Petit, 1554. First edition; splendid 16th century Parisian citron morocco, very lavishly gilt for Pietro Duodo, boards with elegant frame of leafy fronds enclosing a large central panel occupied by five horizontal rows of three ovals, each of these ovals enclosing lovely flower tool, covers also with large number of gilt thistles, passion flowers and other small tools, slightly larger central oval on upper cover with armorial crest of Duodo, lower cover with three lilies on hillock as well as a collar containing Duodo's motto "Expectata non eludet", flat spine similarly gilt with two flower medallions above and below a central oval containing author's name, spine ends raised above top and bottom board edges in a la grecque style, all edges gilt, felt lined folding cloth box, woodcut initials and woodcut device on titlepage, ruled in red throughout, green morocco bookplate of Michel Wittock, ink inscription "Cuthell Martin 23 May (18)04" (presumably recording purchase from London Booksellers Cuthell & Martin); hint of uniform darkening to backstrip, two tiny wormholes near tail of spine, corners and joints slightly rubbed, isolated insignificant stains internally, still very fine, text remarkably fresh and clean, exquisite little binding lustrous and generally in especially pleasing state of preservation, minor wear far outweighed by bright, sumptuous gilt.   Phillip J. Pirages   59 - 11   2011 $17,500

Association – Durnsford, Jack

Dempsey, Jack *Championship Fighting: Explosive Punching and Agressive Defence.* London: Nicholas Kaye, 1950. First UK edition; 8vo., pages 203, illustrations in black and white, neat inscription "A very Happy/Christmas/ Jack W. Durnsford", endpapers slightly browned, else very good+ in chipped, nicked (2 inches missing at rear), else very good- dust jacket with good.   Any Amount of Books   May 29 2011 - A47404   2011 $272

Association – Dutra, Edward

Thompson, John *The Tale Breakers. The Story of the California Dredge.* Stockton: Stockton Corral of Westerners and The University of the Pacific, 1983. First trade edition, one of 2450 copies; signed by co-author, Edward Dutra, oblong quarto, xiv, 368, (2) pages, photos, maps and plans, very fine, as new, pictorial dust jacket.   Argonaut Book Shop   Recent Acquisitions Summer 2010 - 205   2011 $90

Association – Dutton, Bertha

Haile, Berard *Head and Face Masks in Navajo Ceremonialism.* St. Michaels: 1947. xiv, 122 pages, illustrations, slightly soil and couple of chips to dust jacket, bookplate of ethnologist Bertha Dutton, with her underlining few words and phrases to first 60 or so pages, otherwise nice.   Dumont Maps & Books of the West   113 - 33   2011 $400

Association – Dwight, Theodore

Williams, Helen Maria *A Residence in France, During the Years 1792, 1793, 1794 and 1795...* Elizabeth-town: printed by Shepard Kollock for Cornelius Davis, 1798. Octavo, xx, (21) - 517 pages, original full calf, maroon spine label, rubbed, front hinge broken, corners worn, signature of Theodore (?) Dwight, good.   Jeff Weber Rare Books   163 - 226   2011 $150

Association – Eardley

Arbousset, T. *Narrative of an Exploratory Tour to the North East of the Colony of the Cape of Good Hope.* London: John C. Bishop, 1852. First London edition; small 8vo., pages 455, folding map, original blue cloth, little wear to head and tail of spine, rubbing to joints, some light foxing to prelims, inscribed by author to Miss Eardley.   J. & S. L. Bonham Antiquarian Booksellers   Africa 4/20/2011 - 5355   2011   £350

Bryant, Jacob *A New System, or an Analysis of Ancient Mythology: Wherein an Attempt is Made to Divest Tradition of Fable.* London: printed for P. Elmsly, 1774. 1774. 1776; 3 volumes, 4to., pages (iii)-xx (ii) 516 + 8 engraved plates, vii, (i), 537, (i) + 18 engraved plates; (iii)-viii, 601, (i) + 3 engraved maps, 4 engravings included within letterpress, contemporary sprinkled tan calf, spines panel gilt with lozenge and wheel centered compartments alternating, red lettering and numbering pieces, gilt board edges 'milled' decorative roll gilt, pink sewn endbands, spotted and bit toned, plates offset, rubbed, joints worn and splitting, front board of volume 1 lost, armorial bookplate "Eardley" from the collection of Christopher Ernest Weston 1947-2010. Unsworths Booksellers   24 - 73   2011   £360

Cunningham, John William *The Velvet Cushion.* London: G. Sdney for T. Cadell & W. Davies, 1814. Fourth edition; 12mo., contemporary tree calf, red label, little rubbed, armorial bookplate of Mr. Eardley.   Jarndyce Antiquarian Booksellers   CXCI - 149   2011   £40

Association – Earle, J. S.

Dickens, Charles   1812-1870   *The Life and Adventures of Nicholas Nickleby.* London: Chapman and Hall, 1839. First edition, later issue with "Chapman & Hall" imprint lacking at bottom of plates up to page 45, which Eckel claims were omitted in later impressions, 'visiter' has been corrected to 'sister' in 17th line of page 123, 'letter' has been corrected from 'latter' in sixth line from bottom of page 160; 8vo., pages xvi, 624 pages, 40 black and white plates, including frontispiece, half title, engraved portrait frontispiece by Daniel Maclise in first state with imprint, 39 engraved plates by Phiz, some light browning at page edges of plate pages, otherwise noticeably clean with slight spotting only at frontispiece, original olive green diaper cloth, covers with blindstamped border spine gilt, excellent condition, tight, clean, original publisher's green cloth, blue illustrated cover of part 11 of the parts issue neatly tipped in at half title, covers faintly rubbed, faintly soiled, slight evidence of removal of small press cutting at f.e.p., neat ownership signature of one J.S. Earle dated 1879, slight repaired nick at side of frontispiece with no loss, otherwise near fine and completely unrestored.   Any Amount of Books   May 26 2011 - A49296   2011 $1845

Association – Easton Neston Library

MacKenzie, Mary Jane   *Geraldine; or Modes of Faith and Practice.* London: T. Cadell & W. Davies, 1820. First edition; 3 volumes, contemporary full calf, borders in gilt and blind, spines with raised and gilt bands, devices in gilt, leading hinges slightly worn, spine slightly darkened, small labels of Easton Neston Library and Sir Thomas Hesketh, Rufford Hall, good plus.   Jarndyce Antiquarian Booksellers   CLXC - 196   2011   £480

Association – Eaton, John

Griffiths, Thomas   *The Writing Desk and Contents: Taken as a Text for the Familiar Illustration of Many Important Facts in Natural History and Philosophy.* London: John W. Parker, 1844. Half title, original blue cloth, slightly rubbed, wear to head and tail of spine, contemporary ownership inscription of John Eaton.   Jarndyce Antiquarian Booksellers   CXCI - 195   2011   £35

Association – Eaudel-Phillips, Lionel Lawson

Jonson, Ben   *The Masque of Queenes.* London: King's Printers, 1930. No. 89 of 188 only for sale in the British Empire, a further 150 were reserved for the USA; Long 4to., original publisher's scarlet cloth lettered gilt on spine and cover, pages 23 text, 16 pages plates and 39 pages reproduction of manuscript, endpapers little browned, bookplate of Sir Lionel Lawson Eaudel-Phillips, corners very slightly rubbed, very slight shelfwear, otherwise near fine.   Any Amount of Books   May 29 2011 - 169314   2011 $255

Association – Ebeling, Albert

Lindbergh, Anne Morrow   *North to the Orient.* New York: Harcourt Brace and Co., 1935. First edition; octavo, (1)-255, (1, blank) pages, black and white photo frontispiece and numerous printed maps by Charles Lindbergh, publisher's original blue cloth, spine stamped and lettered in silver, top edge gilt, map printed endpapers, inscription on half title, publisher's dust jacket, jacket bit chipped at extremities and creased along top front edge, fine copy, inscribed by Charles and Anne Lindbergh for Albert H. Ebeling.   Heritage Book Shop   Holiday 2010 - 73   2011 $1500

Association – Eberhard

Hulsius, Levinus   *Chronolgoia, hoc est Brevis Descriptio Rerum Memorabilium in Provinciis hac Adiuncta Tabula Topographica Comprehensis Gestarum...* Nurnberg: C. Lochner, 1597. 4to., (6), 89 (recte 90) pages large armorial engraving on title (arms of imperial provinces) and of Eberhard, Bishop of Spier on f A2v, contemporary vellum, foot of spine worn, from the library of the Earls of Macclesfield at Shirburn Castle.   Maggs Bros. Ltd.   1440 - 113   2011   £500

Association – Ebsworth, Joseph

MacDonald, George   1824-1905   *Phantastes: a Faerie Romance for Men and Women.* London: Smith, Elder & Co., 1858. First edition; half title, 16 page catalog (Nov. 1858), half dark brown morocco, red leather label, spine slightly faded, retaining original leading f.e.p., this copy belonged to artist Joseph W. Ebsworth, then of St. John's College Cambridge.   Jarndyce Antiquarian Booksellers   CXCII - 10   2011   £750

Association – Eccles, Mary Morley Crapo, Viscountess

Woodward, G. L. *English Play 1641-1700.* Chicago: The Newbury Library, 1945. Full leather with lovely gilt decorations to covers and spine, as well as matching inner gilt, decorations, very nearly fine, inscribed by co-compiler, J. G. McManaway for Mary Morley Crapo, Viscountess Eccles. Lupack Rare Books   May 26 2011 - ABE345163586 2011 $100

Association – Edelheim, Carl

Isumbras *Syr Ysambrace.* Kelmscott Press, 1897. One of 350 copies on paper (an additional 8 were Printed on vellum); 216 146mm., 2 p.l., 41 pages, original holland backed blue paper boards, edges untrimmed and unopened, wood engraved frontispiece by Sir Edward Burne-Jones, decorative woodcut initials, device in colophon, wide decorative border on first opening of text; bookplate of Carl Edelheim; printed in red and black; spine cloth with minor tears to four plates, fading on rear board along one inch strip next to joint, inevitable (but not severe) wear to corners, else very fine, binding absolutely tight and virtually pristine internally. Phillip J. Pirages   59 - 248 2011 $1950

Association – Eden, Anthony

Maugham, William Somerset   1874-1965   *Ashenden or the British Agent.* London: Heinemann, 1928. First edition; little light browning to half title and final text page, pages (viii), 304, foolscap 8vo., original mid blue cloth, backstrip and front cover gilt lettered, backstrip trifle darkened, outer tail corners little bumped, front cover trifle marked, Maugham symbol blocked in dark blue on front cover, good, at one the copy of Prime Minister Anthony Eden with his bookplate.   Blackwell Rare Books   B166 - 183 2011 £300

Association – Edgeworth, Francis Beaufort

Tennyson, Alfred Tennyson, 1st Baron   1809-1892 *Poems, Chiefly Lyrical.* London: Effingham Wilson, 1830. First edition; 191 x 114mm., 2 p.l., 154 pages, (1) leaf ads), original brown paper boards, flat spine with paper label, buckram chemise and contained in quarter morocco slipcase with raised bands, gilt titling, morocco bookplate of "Blairhame" (used by Natalie K. (Mrs. J. Insley) Blair 1887-1952), the "Blairhame" referring to her magnificent Tudor style home in Tuxedo Park NY, titlepage with 19th century ink presentation inscription "William Rowan Hamilton from Francis Beaufort Edgeworth"; joints with thin cracks, backstrip and label little torn and soiled, extremities with expected wear, leaves bit foxed and soiled, but surprisingly well preserved, nevertheless quite solid, covers very clean and text still fresh.   Phillip J. Pirages   59 - 332 2011 $1250

Association – Edison, Thomas A.

In Nature's Laboratory. N.P.: n.d. circa, 1916. One of a very small number of copies printed for private distribution by authors; folio, 44 original mounted photos, original suede over padded boards, signed by Thomas A. Edison, John Burroughs and Henry S. Firestone.   Heritage Book Shop Booth A12 51st NY International Antiquarian Book Fair April 8-10 2011 - 50 2011 $8000

Association – Edwards, H. Holland

Le Sage, Alain Rene   1668-1747   *The Adventures of Gil Blas of Santillana.* London: printed for Richard Phillips, 1807. 4 volumes, 203 x 121mm., extremely pleasing contemporary deep blue straight grain morocco handsomely gilt by Samuel Welcher (with his ticket), covers bordered gilt with triple rules and framed with wide palmette roll, inside of which is a rule with small ring and floral tools at corners, raised bands, spines ornately gilt in lobed compartments featuring stippled ground, quatrefoil centerpiece with delicate foliate sprays at sides and fleurons at ends, turn-ins gilt with single rule an fleuron and ring tools at corners, all edges gilt, 100 copperplates by Warner, Tomlinson and others, extra illustrated with 60 plates by Conrad Martin Metz for a total of 160 engravings; armorial bookplate of H. Holland Edwards, Pennant Ereithlyn, North Wales; front joints just little flaked, backstrips slightly sunned, covers with minor variation in color, several plates little foxed, generally only in margins and more frequently on added plates), one leaf with light ink stain in lower margin, light dampstain in margin at head of one plate, isolated very minor marginal soiling, very pleasing set, decorative bindings very well preserved and internally clean, fresh and bright.   Phillip J. Pirages   59 - 254 2011 $1800

Association – Edwards, J. O.

Blunt, Wilfred Scawen   1840-1922   *Sonnets and Songs.* London: John Murray, 1875. First edition; foolscap 8vo., pages viii, 112 page 53 misnumbered 5), internally bright and fresh, original yellow sand grain cloth over bevelled boards, upper side with gilt lettering and flaming sun design, dark green endpapers, spine and board edges dust soiled, front hinge cracked by holding, bookseller's ticket and bookplates of H. Bradley Martin and J. O. Edwards, author's presentation inscription, leaf from old bookseller's catalog loosely inserted.   Simon Finch Rare Books   Zero - 301 2011   £650

De La Mare, Walter 1873-1956 *Songs of Childhood.* London: Longmans, Green and Co., 1902. First edition; 8vo., frontispiece, original half parchment and pale blue linen over boards, top edge gilt, backstrip lightly rubbed along joints, otherwise fine in dust jacket with very small chip out of bottom spine panel and offsetting from two small old cellotape repairs at bottom spine and bottom front flap fold, preserved in half morocco slipcase, booklabel of J. O. Edwards, beautiful copy, inscribed by author "to N./ with his love & all blessings/ from W. J. 1949" and with De La Mare's signature above inscription.   James S. Jaffe Rare Books   May 26 2011 - 21420   2011 $12,500

Radcliffe, Alexander *The Ramble an Anti-Heroick Poem. Together with Some Terrestrial Hymns and Carnal Ejaculations.* London: for the author and to be sold by Walter Davis, 1682. First edition; 8vo., pages (xvi), 128, including initial blank Ai, contemporary black morocco, sides panelled in gilt, spine richly gilt in compartments, marbled pastedowns, gilt edges, lightly rubbed, little marginal browning, fine, the Heber(?) Britwell-Hewyard-Bradley Martin, Edwards copy with modern bookplates of H. Bradley Martin and J. O. Edwards.   Simon Finch Rare Books   Zero - 348   2011   £2500

Association – Egerton, Hugh

Kingsley, Charles 1819-1875 *Prose Idylls New and Old.* London: Macmillan, 1884. Half title, frontispiece, added volume title, final ad leaf, unopened in original blue cloth, spine faded and slightly rubbed, inscribed by author's wife for Hugh and Margaret Egerton, with signature of M.A. Egerton.   Jarndyce Antiquarian Booksellers   CXCI - 233   2011   £35

Association – Egerton, Margaret

Kingsley, Charles 1819-1875 *Prose Idylls New and Old.* London: Macmillan, 1884. Half title, frontispiece, added volume title, final ad leaf, unopened in original blue cloth, spine faded and slightly rubbed, inscribed by author's wife for Hugh and Margaret Egerton, with signature of M.A. Egerton.   Jarndyce Antiquarian Booksellers   CXCI - 233   2011   £35

Association – Egremont

Krusenstern, Adam Johnann Von *Voyage Round the World in the Years 1803, 1804, 1805 and 1805.* London: for John Murray, 1813. First edition in English; 2 volumes, quarto, two hand colored aquatint and large engraved folding map, contemporary green half calf morocco over marbled boards in Regency Style, the Egremont copy.   Heritage Book Shop   Booth A12 51st NY International Antiquarian Book Fair April 8-10 2011 - 81   2011 $20,000

Association – Elcocks, James

Robert, Prior of Shrewsbury *The Admirable Life of Saint Wenefride...* St. Omer: English College Press Superiorum Permissu, 1635. 8vo., (32), 275, (13) pages, plus added engraved titlepage by Martin Baes (loose), text printed within double line border, last leaf blank (here lacking), 18th century English vellum backed boards, signature of James Elcocks and note of his birth on 6 Jan. 1679, from the library of the Earls of Macclesfield at Shirburn Castle.   Maggs Bros. Ltd.   1440 - 178   2011   £500

Association – Elkin, R. H.

Old Dutch Nursery Rhymes. London: Augener, Philadelphia: McKay, 1917. First edition; illustrations on Le Mair, printed on glossy art paper, text and musical notation all printed in pale grey, 15 color printed plates on verso of each leaf, musical notation on each page opposing page, with further color printed plate on titlepage, hinges substantially stained, pages (ii), 32, (2), oblong royal 8vo., original light blue cloth, little waterstained, backstrip and front cover gilt lettered, Le Mair color plate on front cover, rubbed at corners, including backstrip head and tail, good, translator's (R. H. Elkin) presentation.   Blackwell Rare Books   B166 - 174   2011   £100

Association – Elkington, Herbert

O'Shaughnessy, Arthur *Songs of a Worker.* London: Chatto & Windus, 1881. First edition; 8vo., original deep blue cloth lettered gilt on spine, pages xv, 212, pages uncut at edges, very scarce, bookplate of Herbert and Jessie Elkington, prelims slightly foxed, otherwise fine, exceptional condition.   Any Amount of Books   May 26 2011 - A68492   2011 $419

Association – Elkington, Jessie

O'Shaughnessy, Arthur *Songs of a Worker.* London: Chatto & Windus, 1881. First edition; 8vo., original deep blue cloth lettered gilt on spine, pages xv, 212, pages uncut at edges, very scarce, bookplate of Herbert and Jessie Elkington, prelims slightly foxed, otherwise fine, exceptional condition.   Any Amount of Books   May 26 2011 - A68492   2011 $419

Association – Ellis, Havelock

Hinton, James *Life in Nature.* New York: Lincoln MacVeagh/The Dial Press, 1931. First edition; presumably later pencil ownership signature, boards little soiled, very good in good or better dust jacket with couple of small external tape repairs, some faint stains, neatly tipped ot half title is one page ALS from editor, Havelock Ellis to publisher Lincoln MacVeagh returning the proofs for this book (no present), questioning some of the author's premises and inquiring when the book will be released, letter near fine.   Between the Covers   169 - BTC335143   2011 $500

Association – Ellman, Mary

Hawkes, John *The Cannibal.* New York: New Directions, 1949. First edition; small 8vo., original pale grey boards, pages 223, fine in very good yellow and black dust jacket, faintly marked and very slightly chipped at spine ends and with very slight edgewear, signed presentation from author for Richard and Mary Ellman.   Any Amount of Books   May 26 2011 - A75834   2011 $470

Association – Ellman, Richard

Hawkes, John *The Cannibal.* New York: New Directions, 1949. First edition; small 8vo., original pale grey boards, pages 223, fine in very good yellow and black dust jacket, faintly marked and very slightly chipped at spine ends and with very slight edgewear, signed presentation from author for Richard and Mary Ellman.   Any Amount of Books   May 26 2011 - A75834   2011 $470

Association – Elphinstone, Constance

Noel, Augusta *From Generation to Generation.* London: Macmillan & Co., 1880. Second edition; 2 volumes, half titles, contemporary half maroon calf, raised gilt bands, little darkened and rubbed, ownership inscription of Constance Elphinstone.   Jarndyce Antiquarian Booksellers   CLXC - 596   2011   £85

Association – Elsley, Robert

Tibbles, Percy Thomas *The Magician's Handbook: a Complete Encyclopaedia of the Magic Art for Professional and Amateur Entertainers.* London: Marshal and Brookes and Dawbarn & Ward, n.d., 1901. First edition; 8vo., original publisher's green cloth with illustration, pages 188 with 10 pages ads at rear, signed presentation from author to Robert Elsley 21/10/01, slight soiling and slight wear to covers, appears to lack front endpaper, slight foxing to prelims otherwise near very good.   Any Amount of Books   May 29 2011 - A49177   2011 $340

Association – Elwin, P. E.

Martineau, Philip Meadows *A Memoir of the Late Philip Meadows Martineau, Surgeon.* Norwich: Bacon & Kinnebrook, Mercury Office, 1831. First edition; 4to., frontispiece, tear in lower margin of leading f.e.p., with slight loss, original blue silk, spine little worn, with presentation inscription from A. D. Martineau for P. E. Elwin.   Jarndyce Antiquarian Booksellers   CLXC - 362   2011   £350

Association – Ely, Josepha

Burr, Aaron *The Watchman's Answer to the Question, What of the Night &c. A Sermon Preached Before the Synod of New York, Convened at Newark in New Jersey.* Boston: S. Kneeland, 1757. 46 pages, stitched in contemporary blue paper wrappers, then sewn into early (18th century?) homemade covers, stain on both wrappers and first few leaves of text, upper corner of titlepage worn away costing one letter, outer cover chipped at edges, else very good, 18th century ownership signatures of Benjamin Sheldon and Josepha (?) Ely, latter dated 1777.   Joseph J. Felcone Inc. Fall Miscellany 2010 - 21   2011 $900

Association – Emerson, Edith

Haywood, Carolyn *Here's a Penny.* New York: Harcourt Brace and Co., 1944. (I). First edition; 8vo., pictorial cloth, 158 pages, fine in very good+ dust jacket, full page and half page pen and ink drawings, this copy inscribed by Haywood for fellow artists Violet Oakley and Edith Emerson.   Aleph-Bet Books, Inc.   95 - 284   2011 $350

Association – Emery Rene

Gourmont, Remy De   1858-1915   *Physique de l'Amour/ Essai sur l'Instinct Sexuel.*   Paris: Mercure de France, 1903. 8vo., pages 295, (1) imprint, contemporary niger half morocco, marbled boards and endpapers, top edge gilt, author's presentation inscription to Rene Emery.   Simon Finch Rare Books   Zero - 139   2011   £200

Association – Endicott, Mr.

M'Dougall, Ellem M. *Songs of the Church with Stories of Their Writers.* London: Robert Culley, circa, 1903. Third thousand; original cloth, spine and edges faded, pages xii, 320, presentation copy inscribed by author for Mr. Endicott. R. F. G. Hollett & Son Antiquarian Booksellers   175 - 874   2011   £35

Association – Endicott, William

Macaulay, Thomas Babington Macaulay, 1st Baron 1800-1859   *Critical and Historical Essays.*   London: Longmans, Green and Co., 1880. New edition; text in double columns, bound as two volumes, half title at beginning of volume ii, pages viii, (ii), 414; (ii), 415-850, 8vo., contemporary dark grey calf, spines gilt, red and green morocco lettering pieces, marbled endleaves and matching edges, bookplates of William Endicott, near fine.   Blackwell Rare Books   B166 - 67   2011   £100

Association – Entwisle, Robert

Weever, John *Antient Funeral Monuments of Great Britain, Ireland and the Islands Adjacent.* London: printed by W. Tooke for the editor, 1767. 4to., pages (x) clxxvii (i) 608 + engraved portrait frontispiece and 5 other engraved plates, extending table, contemporary calf much worn, board edges 'milled' decorative roll gilt, pink & white, sewn endbands, removal of amateur reback, revealed fragment of a once fully gilt spine with massed decorative pallets, awaiting restoration, now with early 21st century reback to corners by Chris Weston, light toning and some spotting, frontispiece offset, old leather somewhat scratched and bit rubbed at extremities, ink ownership inscription "Robt. Entwisle", from the collection of Christopher Ernest Weston 1947-2010. Unsworths Booksellers 24 - 150 2011 £400

Association – Ernest, King of Hanover

Marsh-Caldwell, Anne *Emilia Wyndham.* Paris: Ch. Rinwald, 1851. First edition; 2 volumes, (281 page, 281 pages), 12mo., contemporary quarter deep brown calf beautiful gilt decorated spines with scroll design, all edges marbled, fine and attractive set, from the library of King Ernest of Hanover with his royal ex-libris stamped on verso of titlepages, very fine in lovely binding, uncommon. Paulette Rose Fine and Rare Books 32 - 120 2011 $750

Association – Erskine, Caroline

MacDonald, George 1824-1905 *The Hope of the Gospel.* London: Ward, Lock, Bowden & Co., 1892. First edition; half title, few marginal marks, original dark green cloth, slight rubbing, small piece torn from leading f.e.p., with touching presentation letter from Caroline Erskine 1931, loosely inserted. Jarndyce Antiquarian Booksellers CXCII - 304 2011 £380

Association – Erskine, Mary

The Spectator. London: printed by H. Baldwin for Longman, Dodsley, et al, 1797. 264 x 165mm., 8 volumes, excellent contemporary light green straight grain morocco sides with gilt double fillet, raised bands decorated with stippled rule an flanked by plain rules, second and third panels of each spine gilt lettered, marbled endpapers, all edges gilt, in two modern fleece lined matching cloth slipcases; each of the 8 volumes with beautiful fore-edge painting; engraved vignette on each titlepage, large paper copy, ownership signature of Mary Erskine dated 1803 with inscription "This book was given her when she married by her cousin Lord Wodehouse"; spines somewhat darkened and gilt titling consequently dulled, leather slightly varied in color (due partly to refurbishing), soiled and marked, bindings nevertheless in remarkably good condition, entirely sound and with little wear to joints, each volume with isolated openings just bit foxed in (typically upper) margins (one volume with slightly more foxing), three or four leaves with frayed corner or minor tear in margin at foot, other trivial imperfections, still fine internally, almost entirely very clean, bright and fresh. Phillip J. Pirages 59 - 42 2011 $11,000

Association – Evans, Frederick

Homerus *The Iliad of Homer.* London: Longmans, Green and Co., 1898. First of this edition by Samuel Butler; 8vo., pages xvi (errata/addendum), (1) 421 + publisher's ads, i.e. 1 page of Butler's works and 32 pages general book as dated 3/98; uncommon, with the Beardsley bookplate of Frederick H. Evans, original publisher's maroon cloth lettered gilt at spine, few slight marks, slight scuffing, slight occasional foxing to text, otherwise very good. Any Amount of Books May 29 2011 - A46349 2011 $374

Association – Evans, Margaret

Brown, Marcia *Backbone of the King the Story of Poka'a and His Son Ku.* Honolulu: University of Hawaii Press, 1966. 1984; 4to., 180 pages, cloth, fine in dust jacket, inscribed by Brown for Margaret Evans, signed and dated June 1966, , sold with cloth folder holding a complete set of the linoleum block prints used in the book, pulled on Japanese tissue,. Aleph-Bet Books, Inc. 95 - 117 2011 $5750

Association – Everett, Alexander

Kennedy, J. P. *Address to the Friends of Domestic Industry, Assembled in Convention at New York, October 26 1831 to the People of the United States.* Baltimore: Nov. 10, 1831. First edition; 8vo., 44 pages, original printed wrappers, uncut, removed, stain in upper corner of later leaves, signature in ink of A(lexander) H. Everett on front wrapper. M & S Rare Books, Inc. 90 - 209 2011 $325

Association – Ewing, Mrs.

Mitford, Mary Russell 1787-1855 *Our Village: Sketches of Rural Character and Scenery.* London: G. & w. B. Whittaker, 1828-1832. Sixth, third, third, first, first editions; half titles (not volume v), 3 pages ads volume IV, uncut, contemporary glazed plum cloth, dark green morocco spines, lettered in gilt, boards slightly faded, spines slightly rubbed, volume I signed "Mrs. Ewing" in contemporary hand, Richard Taylor of Liverpool bookseller tickets volumes I & II, good plus, last volume bound slightly later to match volumes I-IV and slightly different blocking with volume number "V" rather than "6". Jarndyce Antiquarian Booksellers CLXC - 407 2011 £420

Association – Fairchild, Elva

Burger, John F. *Contributions to the Knowledge of Diptera.* Gainesville: Associated Publishers, 1999. 8vo., green cloth, gilt titles and fly vignette on front, pages viii, 648, photo illustrations, tables, charts, photo on dedication page, fine, inscribed to previous owners by Elva Fairchild (Sandy's wife). Schooner Books Ltd. 96 - 121 2011 $95

Association – Fairfax, Theophrania

Byron, George Gordon Noel, 6th Baron 1788-1824 *Hours of Idleness. (bound with) English Bards and Scottish Reviewers: a Satire.* Newark: S. & J. Ridge, 1807. London Cawthorn, 1810.First edition, first state and third edition of second work; 8vo., recent full dark brown calf lettered and decorated gilt at spine with five raised bands and new marbled endpapers, very slight occasional browning to text, neat small old ownership signature (Theophrania Fairfax), near fine. Any Amount of Books May 26 2011 - A69879 2011 $1090

Association – Falk, Tore

Stromholm, Christer *Poste Restante.* Stockholm: P. A. Norstedt & Soners Forlag, 1967. First edition; 8vo., pages (xviii) (100), 96 black and white photos, original brown cloth, spine and upper side lettered in silver, original black and white photo illustrated dust jacket, very lightly rubbed, minor abrasions to upper edge, short closed tear to upper and lower panels, Stromholm's business card attached by a paperclip to front flap, inscription to Tore Falk, fine in near fine dust jacket. Simon Finch Rare Books Zero - 548 2011 £5000

Association – Fane, William Dashwood

Scott, Walter 1771-1832 *The Border Antiquities of England and Scotland...* London: Longman, Hurst etc., 1814-1816. First edition; 2 volumes, 4to., contemporary full straight grained dark green russia gilt, boards panelled with broad rolls in gilt and blind, spines with 4 flattened raised bands and richly gilt panels, some heavy scrapes to boards, pages cxxvii, 92, (ii); 209, ci, (xii), 95 steel engraved plates, some spotting to few margins, some plates with modern hand coloring, despite scrapes to boards, still handsome set, armorial bookplate of William Dashwood Fane in each volume. R. F. G. Hollett & Son Antiquarian Booksellers 173 - 1026 2011 £450

Association – Farrer, James

Akerman, John Yonge *Remains of Pagan Saxondom.* John Russell Smith, 1855. First edition; 4to., original quarter polished roan gilt extra, odd scratch to boards, corners trifle softened, pages xxviii, 84, (ii), top edge gilt, 40 tissue guarded chromolithographed plates, many with additional hand coloring, little scattered foxing, but excellent copy, signature of James Farrer, 19th century Yorkshire archaeologist. R. F. G. Hollett & Son Antiquarian Booksellers 177 - 5 2011 £275

Association – Fasque

Fell, Ralph *A Tour through the Batavian Republic During the Latter Part of the Year 1800.* R. Phillips, 1801. First edition; contemporary half brown calf, red morocco label, rubbed with loss to gilt on spine, Fasque booklabel, internally exceptional copy. Jarndyce Antiquarian Booksellers CXCI - 548 2011 £180

Murray, Charles Augustus *The Prairie Bird.* London: Richard Bentley, 1844. First edition; 3 volumes, 12mo., slightly later half green morocco grained sheep by J. and J. P. Edmond & Spark, Aberdeen, gilt bands, very slightly rubbed, Fasque booklabels, very good, loosely inserted is opened stamped envelope address to H. Magnac (?), Fasque, Lawrencekirk. Jarndyce Antiquarian Booksellers CXCI - 531 2011 £330

Association – Fawcus, Arnold

Graves, Robert 1895-1985 *Adam's Rib and Other Anomalous Elements in the Hebrew Creation Myth.* Jura: Trianon Press, 1955. First edition, copy R of 26 lettred copies signed by Graves and artist, James Metcalf; large 8vo., original publisher's red cloth lettered gilt at spine, pages 73, with wood engravings by James Metcalf, signed presentation from books' designer Arnold Fawcus for Audrey, fine in sound slightly browned, very good plain slipcase. Any Amount of Books May 26 2011 - A49568 2011 $545

Association – Featherstone-Witty, Evy

Cleary, Jon *Fall of an Eagle.* New York: Morrow, 1964. First edition; 8vo., pages 270 dedication copy, beneath printed words "to Evy and Gordon" on dedication page Cleary has written "who have the gift of making a person feel appreciated - something a writer appreciates - with love Jon", with 3 good signed typed letters loosely inserted, about 4000 words, also loosely inserted a signed titlepage of paperback edition of Sundowners, sound, very good with light handling wear and with 2 bookplates of Gordon and Evy (Featherstone-Witty), the dedicatees and recipients of the letters, slight tape marks to front endpaper.   Any Amount of Books   May 29 2011 - A72358   2011 $383

Association – Featherstone-Witty, Gordon

Cleary, Jon *Fall of an Eagle.* New York: Morrow, 1964. First edition; 8vo., pages 270 dedication copy, beneath printed words "to Evy and Gordon" on dedication page Cleary has written "who have the gift of making a person feel appreciated - something a writer appreciates - with love Jon", with 3 good signed typed letters loosely inserted, about 4000 words, also loosely inserted a signed titlepage of paperback edition of Sundowners, sound, very good with light handling wear and with 2 bookplates of Gordon and Evy (Featherstone-Witty), the dedicatees and recipients of the letters, slight tape marks to front endpaper.   Any Amount of Books   May 29 2011 - A72358   2011 $383

Association – Feilden, George Ramsay

Cowper, William   1731-1800 *Poems.* London: Published by John Sharpe, 1810. New edition; 202 122mm., 432 pages, volume I only, of 2 volumes, once splendid and still pleasing contemporary dark green straight grain morocco, extravagantly gilt, covers with wide gilt frames featuring interlocking circles and arcs accented with leaves and flowers on densely stippled backgrounds, central panel formed by gilt fillet and multiple blindstamped rolls and with foliate spray cornerpieces on stippled ground, board raised bands dividing spine into five panels, three with large animated central gilt fleuron, two with gilt titling, gilt turn-ins and edges, with excellent fore-edge painting of a bustling Regent Street scene in London; with extra engraved titlepage, 21 engraved head and tailpieces designed by Thurston with five engraved plates designed by Richard Westall, R.A., with engraved bookplate of George Ramsay Feilden, with Feilden's ink ownership signature, spine sunned to light olive, joints and extremities somewhat rubbed tiny chip to head of spine, isolated minor foxing, otherwise excellent copy, binding sturdy and retaining its charm, leaves clean and fresh and fore-edge painting generally well preserved.   Phillip J. Pirages   59 - 202 2011 $650

Association – Fell, William

Atkinson, George *The Worthies of Westmorland; or Notable Persons Born in the County Since the Reformation.* London: J. Robinson, 1849.   First edition; 2 volumes, original blindstamped red cloth, gilt, few marks to boards, pages 320; 360, steel engraved frontispiece (little spotted), joints tender, very good set, volume 2 inscribed By William Fell to Bernard Gilpin, Belle Vue House Ulverstone.   R. F. G. Hollett & Son Antiquarian Booksellers   173 - 36 2011   £140

Association – Fenton

Allen, George Loscomb, Mrs. *The Views and Flowers from Guzerat and Rajpootana.* Paul Jerrard & Son, circa, 1860. 4to., 12 color plates with text on verso, 1 page ads, apparently lacking frontispiece, some leaves neatly strengthened at hinge, original cream wavy grained cloth, blocked elaborately in gilt on front board and blind on back board, heavily spotted, small nick to upper margin with slight loss of cloth, little rubbed, inner hinges with some slight repair, armorial bookplate of Fenton, internally nice and bright.   Jarndyce Antiquarian Booksellers   CXCI - 38   2011   £220

Association – Ferguson, Rachel

Hunt, Violet *The Last Ditch.* London: Stanley Paul, 1918.   First edition; 8vo., original publisher's brown lettered black at spine, pages 309, 27 page publisher's catalog at rear dated 1918 signed presentation from author for Rachel Ferguson, slight wear, slight rubbing, slight marks, else sound, near very good.   Any Amount of Books   May 29 2011 - A67122 2011 $238

Association – Ferguson, Spencer Charles

Cumberland and Westmorland Antiquarian & Archaeological Society *Transactions - Old Series. Volumes 1-16.* Kendal: T. Wilson, 1874-1899. 16 volumes matching half morocco gilt by Turnam of Carlisle, with raised bands and marbled boards, stamped in blind "Westminster Public Libraries" in roundel on upper boards, few old scrapes here and there, top edge gilt, uncut, numerous illustrations, diagrams, text drawings, folding pedigrees etc., all wrappers bound in, handsome complete run of this very scarce, each volume with armorial bookplate of Spencer Charles Ferguson and later label (small stamps to back of titles and few other places).   R. F. G. Hollett & Son Antiquarian Booksellers   173 - 287   2011   £2500

Association – Fewster, Charles Edward

Tennyson, Alfred Tennyson, 1st Baron 1809-1892 *A Welcome to Her Royal Highness the Princess of Wales; from the Poet Laureate.* London: Day & Son, 1863. 4to., color lithograph titlepage with 7 further lithographic plates by Owen Jones, some slight foxing, original maroon cloth, bevelled boards, embossed with vellum blocked in gilt, lettered on front board and spine, slightly rubbed and faded, bookplate of Charles Edward Fewster, Hull. Jarndyce Antiquarian Booksellers CXCI - 508 2011 £225

Association – Ffinch, Michael

Belloc, Hilaire 1870-1953 *Hills and the Sea.* London: Methuen, 1927. First illustrated edition; large 8vo., original blue cloth gilt, pages xvii, 301 with 16 tipped in color plates, signed by Michael Ffinch, poet and author. R. F. G. Hollett & Son Antiquarian Booksellers General Catalogue Summer 2010 - 846 2011 £45

Association – Ffolkes, Martin Brown

Kennedy, John *A Treatise Upon Planting, Gardening and th Management of the Hot-House.* York: printed by A. Ward for the author, 1776. First edition; 8vo., full brown leather, pages xvi, 420, corner of prelims slightly stained, outer hinges slightly weak, corners bumped, spine ends very slightly worn, else sound, clean, very good, bookplate of Martin Brown Ffolkes. Any Amount of Books May 26 2011 - A47678 2011 $419

Association – Field, Cecil

Bacon, Frederick T. *Bibliography of the Writings of William Somerset Maugham.* Unicorn Press, 1931. First edition, 628/950 copies (of an edition of 1000); pages (ii), 82, 8vo., , original red cloth, backstrip gilt lettered on faded backstrip, front cover stamped in blind and with press device in gilt, untrimmed, good, inscribed by bibliographer on dedication page to fellow Maugham enthusiast Cecil Field and note to fellow admirer. Blackwell Rare Books B166 - 181 2011 £50

Association – Finden, Frederick

Austin, William *A Specimen of Sketching Landscapes in a Free and Masterly Manner with a Pen or Pencil; Exemplified in thirty Etchings done from original drawings of Lucatelli after the Life in and about Rome.* by the author in George Street, Hanover Square..., 1781. 4 pages, 30 etchings, some signed Austin F (or Fecit) Lucatelli, inscribed by Frederick Finden for Catherine Ward, very good, contemporary half calf with red morocco label, dark blue glazed paper boards which are rubbed and marked, marginal stain to one plate but clear of image and little old and faint waterstaining the inner lower corner, again not affecting images. Ken Spelman Rare Books 68 - 13 2011 £2200

Association – Findlay, J. N.

Aristotelian Society *Aristotelian Society Proceedings.* London: Methuen/Compton Press/Aristotelian Society, 1969-1987. First edition; 13 volumes, 8vo., most books about 300 pages, from the library of philosophy professor J. N. Findlay, but with no sign of his ownership apart from train times written in his hand on endpaper of 1938 volume, all about very good and complete. Any Amount of Books May 29 2011 - B26238 2011 $298

Association – Firestone, Henry S.

In Nature's Laboratory. N.P.: n.d. circa, 1916. One of a very small number of copies printed for private distribution by authors; folio, 44 original mounted photos, original suede over padded boards, signed by Thomas A. Edison, John Burroughs and Henry S. Firestone. Heritage Book Shop Booth A12 51st NY International Antiquarian Book Fair April 8-10 2011 - 50 2011 $8000

Association – Firth, Robert

Porter, Anna Maria *Don Sebastian; or the House of Braganza.* London: Longman, 1809. First edition; 4 volumes, 12mo., half titles, contemporary tree calf, gilt spines, bookplates of Robert Firth & "Tavance", very good. Jarndyce Antiquarian Booksellers CLXC - 754 2011 £280

Association – Fischer, George

Taylor, Deems *Peter Ibbetson. Lyric Drama in Three Acts from the Novel by George du Maurier.* New York: J. Fischer & Bro., 1930. Deluxe limited edition, one of 12 presentation copies out of a total of 110 copies, this being letter "K"; inscribed by Taylor to publisher George Fischer, x, 329, (1, blank) pages, additional colored titlepage, laid in is ALS by Taylor to Fischer, also laid in is list of both typed and handwritten of who each of the 12 deluxe lettered copies are to go to, original quarter teal morocco over marbled boards, spine lettered gilt, top edge gilt, others uncut, marbled endpapers, extremities of spine bit chipped, 2 3/4 inch crack bottom of outer hinge, spine hinges have had restoration boards with some staining, overall very good. Heritage Book Shop Holiday 2010 - 123 2011 $1250

Association – Fisher, James

Wilson, J. Oliver *Birds of Westmorland and the Northern Pennines.* London: Hutchinson, 1933. First edition; original black cloth gilt, spine trifle faded, pages 319, 153 illustrations, signed by ornithologist, James Fisher, joints strained. R. F. G. Hollett & Son Antiquarian Booksellers 173 - 1223 2011 £85

Association – Fitzgerald, David

Kunos, Ignacz *Turkish Fairy Tales.* London: Lawrence and Bullen, 1806. First edition; original pink cloth, gilt, spine faded and soiled, pages x, 276, top edges gilt, illustrations by Celia Levente, annotated throughout, neatly, but quite heavily in places, by original owner, David Fitzgerald, folklorist. R. F. G. Hollett & Son Antiquarian Booksellers 175 - 795 2011 £65

Association – Fitzgerald, Margaret

Smith, Henry, Mrs. *The Female Disciple of the First Three Centuries of the Christian Era: Her Trials and Her Mission.* London: Longman, Brown, Green & Longmans, 1845. Small octavo, xii, 297 pages, original full black morocco, blind and gilt stamped, all edges gilt, raised bands, gilt spine, rubbed, very good, scarce, inscribed to Miss Margaret Fitzgerald. Jeff Weber Rare Books 163 - 210 2011 $65

Association – Fitzgibbon, Mary Rose

Munro, Robert *Prehistoric Scotland and Its Place in European Civilisation.* William Blackwood & Sons, 1899. First edition; original cloth, gilt, little bumped and rubbed, spine rather faded, pages xix, 502, (ii), 18 plates, 262 text woodcut, some patches of spotting, occasionally heavy, lower joint cracked, attractive bookplate of Mary Rose Fitzgibbon. R. F. G. Hollett & Son Antiquarian Booksellers 177 - 593 2011 £65

Association – Fitzhugh, William

Phillips, Catherine Coffin *Jessie Benton Fremont, a Woman who Made History.* San Francisco: John Henry Nash, 1935. Tall octavo, vii, 361 pages, frontispiece, plates, index, quarter linen backed brick red boards, paper spine label, bookplate of William Fitzhugh Jr. unusually nice. Jeff Weber Rare Books 163 - 71 2011 $60

Association – Fitzinger, Warren

Whitman, Walt 1819-1892 *Leaves of Grass.* Philadelphia: McKay, 1891-1892. Deathbed edition; 8vo., portrait inserted, original heavy grey wrappers, printed yellow spine label The Garden copy, front lower wrapper split approximately 2 1/2 inches at joint, otherwise fine, unopened in half morocco slipcase, inscribed in Horace Traubel's hand "To Warren Fitzinger Jan. 7 1892 given by direction of Walt Whitman from his sick bed. H.L.T.". James S. Jaffe Rare Books May 26 2011 - 21628 2011 $35,000

Association – Fitzwilliam, Earl

Mitford, Mary Russell 1787-1855 *Recollections of a Literary Life; and Selections from My Favourite Poets and Prose Writers.* London: Richard Bentley, 1859. New edition; original red cloth, spine faded, back board stained affecting pastedown, armorial bookplate of Earl Fitzwilliam. Jarndyce Antiquarian Booksellers CLXC - 412 2011 £35

Association – Fletcher, Phineas

Bible. English - 1653 *The Holy Bible containing ye Old and New Testaments.... (with, bound at end of volume 2: The Psalms of David in Meeter).* London: printed by Iohn Field, 1653. Edinburgh: i.e. Amsterdam: printed by Evan Tyler, 1653; The first work divided after Dd2, 12mo., ff. (314); (282), 89, (i), contemporary red morocco, unlettered spine panel gilt, boards fully gilt in Scottish 'Herringbone' style, board edges decorative roll gilt, turn-ins decorative roll gilt, 'Dutch floral gilt' endpapers to volume 1, 'dutch-comb' endpapers to volume 2, all edges gilt, pale blue and white sewn endbands, text rubricated throughout, browned, some soiling and staining, one leaf in second work with corner torn away affecting a dozen lines of text, 20th century MS poem to last text leaf in volume 2 signed "Phineas Fletcher", binding rubbed, joints splitting, endpapers worn, spines darkened, old repair to head volume i, ink ownership inscription "MARY ADAMS/1769", from the collection of Christopher Ernest Weston 1947-2010. Unsworths Booksellers 24 - 9 2011 £700

Association – Flower, Lewis

Rossetti, Dante Gabriel 1828-1882 *Sonnets and Lyrical Poems.* Kelmscott Press for Ellis & Ivey, 1894. One of 310 copies on paper (6 were issued on vellum); 210 x 143mm., 6 p.l., 197 pages, original flexible vellum with silk ties, gilt titling on spine, edges untrimmed and all but first two gatherings, unopened, lovely large and small woodcut initials, elaborate woodcut frontispiece and border on first page of text, printed in red and black, presentation inscription to Lewis Flower from "SS" dated July 1897; just hint of soil to vellum, but extraordinarily fine, binding unusually lustrous and obviously mostly unread, text virtually pristine. Phillip J. Pirages 59 - 246 2011 $3000

Association – Floyd, John

Macedo, Jose *A Meditacao.* Lisboa: 1818. 254, (1) pages, full leather, few scrapes to rear cover, all edges blue, bookplate of John Floyd, fairly scarce. Bookworm & Silverfish 664 - 168 2011 $150

Association – Fogo, J. Laurie

MacDonald, George   1824-1905   *The Disciple and Other Poems.*   London: Strahan & Co., 1868.   Second edition; half title, initial ad slip and 4 page catalog (Jan. 1868), original dappled dark brown and red cloth, ruled in blind, decorated and lettered in gilt, faded and slightly rubbed, inscribed by author for Rev. J. Laurie Fogo.   Jarndyce Antiquarian Booksellers   CXCII - 106   2011   £1500

Association – Foley, Mrs.

Martineau, Harriet   1802-1876   *Feats on the Fiord.* London: Charles Knight & Co., 1841.   First edition; half title, original brown cloth, blocked in blind, spine lettered in gilt, bit rubbed, front inner hinge cracking, one or two gatherings slightly proud, inscription "Randolph Mainwaring from Mrs. Foley 1848".   Jarndyce Antiquarian Booksellers   CLXC - 328   2011   £45

Association – Foley, Thomas Henry, 4th Baron

Twopenny, William   *Extracts from Various Authors...*   privately printed at the Chiswick Press, 1868.   Half title, original brown cloth, borders blocked in blind, upper board blocked in gilt, few small marks, armorial bookplate of Charlotte, Duchess of Norfolk with inscription, presented by her to Thomas Henry Foley, 4th Baron Foley.   Jarndyce Antiquarian Booksellers   CXCI - 591   2011   £50

Association – Folk, Tore

Stromholm, Christer   *Till Minnet av mig sjalv. (In Memory of Myself).*   Stockholm: Foto Expo, 1965.   First edition; pages (32), (8), 12mo., 38 black and white photos, original black and white photo illustrated wrappers, fine, inscribed by Stromholm for Tore Falk.   Simon Finch Rare Books   Zero - 548   2011   £3500

Association – Fontanne, Lynn

Coward, Noel   1899-1973   *Qaudrille. A romantic Comedy in Three Acts.*   London: Heienmann, 1952.   First edition; 8vo., pages 116, signed by 17 members of the English cast and by producer Jack Wilson and by Lynn Fontanne and Alfred Lunt on dedication page (play is dedicated to them), inscribed by Coward to Dorothy Sands (Octavia in the NY production), two more signed cards by Lunt and Fontanne tipped in and 3 notes by Lunt to Sands laid in, with tipped in signed photo of Sands, nice copy in somewhat chipped dust jacket.   Second Life Books Inc.   174 - 111   2011 $700

Association – Foot, Michael

An Authentic Narrative of the Events of the Westminster Election Which Commenced on Saturday, February 13th and Closed on Wednesday March 3rd 1819...   London: R. Stodart, 1819.   First edition; 8vo., engraved portrait frontispiece (torn and repaired - no loss), vii, (1), 412 pages, early to mid 19th century half cloth over marbled boards, spine simply lettered in gilt, slightly worn at head and foot, good copy from the library of Michael Foot, the British labour Party politician with his ownership signature.   John Drury Rare Books   154 - 11   2011   £250

Association – Forbes, Colonel

Lewis, Meriwether   1774-1809   *Travels to the Source of the Missouri River and Across the American Continent to the Pacific Ocean Performed... in the Years 1804, 1805 and 1806.*   London: for Longman et al, 1817.   3 volumes xxvi, (2) 411; xii, 434; xii, 394 pages, large folding map, 5 plates, modern calf backed marbled paper covered boards, very skillfully executed in period style, plates considerably foxed and offset onto facing pages, old tears to map skillfully remended on verso, otherwise very handsome copy in correct period style binding, contemporary signature "Colonel Forbes" in each copy.   Joseph J. Felcone Inc.   Fall Miscellany 2010 - 75   2011 $14,000

Association – Forbes, Nevill

Darwin, Charles Robert   1809-1882   *A Naturalist's Voyage. Journal of Researches into the Natural History and Geology of the Countries visited During the Voyages of H.M.S. "Beagle" Round the World...*   London: John Murray, 1890.   Later edition; small 8vo., xi, 500 pages, frontispiece, additional engraved portrait loosely inserted, original green cloth, gilt stamped cover ornament and spine title, ANS by Darwin glued to verso of titlepage and dedication page, ink stamp of D. N. Van Pelt, very good, with Darwin's signature written on slip of paper 200 x 72mm, mounted inside volume, additional engraved portrait of Darwin loosely inserted, from the Bern Dibner reference library, with Burndy bookplate, inscription " to my dear grandson Nevill Forbes, from E.F.".   Jeff Weber Rare Books   161 - 106   2011 $5000

Association – Ford, Denys

Dickson, P. G. M.   *The Sun Insurance Office 1710-1960.* London: Oxford University Press, 1960.   First edition; pages xiv, 324, color frontispiece, 14 plates, 3 line drawings, original cloth, gilt, dust jacket (trifle dusty), pages xiv, 324, color frontispiece, 14 plates and 3 line drawings, presentation copy inscribed by author for Sir Denys Ford, with 2 page ALS from him to same.   R. F. G. Hollett & Son Antiquarian Booksellers   175 - 373   2011   £50

Association – Ford, George

Cervantes Saavedra, Miguel De 1547-1616 *The First (and Second) Part of the History of the Various and Wittie Knight-Errant Don Quixote of the Mancha.* Ashendene Press, 1927-1928. One of 225 copies; 2 volumes, text in the 1620 English translation of Thomas Shelton, original luxurious white pigskin by W. H. Smith, thick raised bands, gilt titling on spine, sturdy cloth double slipcases (little marked), morocco labels, lovely woodcut initials and borders designed by Louise Powell, cut on wood by W. M. Quick and George H. Ford, bookplate of Vincent Lloyd-Russell in each volume, as well as shadow of another small bookplate now removed; pigskin of first volume, just shade different from second (a common defect as the volumes issued more than a year apart), in all other ways, extremely fine, magnificent binding unusually clean, text in perfect condition. Phillip J. Pirages 59 - 76 2011 $9500

Association – Forman, Harry Buxton

Coleridge, Samuel Taylor 1772-1834 *Biographia Literaria; or Bibliographical Sketches of My Literary Life and Opinions.* London: Rest Fenner, 1817. Only edition; 2 volumes, royal 8vo., pages (iv), 296; (iv), 309, (3) ads with second half title in volume i, top edge gilt, others uncut, offsetting from bookmark to second blank but fresh and bright copy with occasional slight spotting, later full morocco, raised bands, gilt lettering to spines and gilt edges, gilt decoration to doublures by Tout, with endpapers loosely inserted, in excellent condition, with only very light shelfwear, endpapers browned at edges, portion of both original black labels, rubbed, pasted to rear endpaper loosely inserted into volume i, bookplate of John Whipple Frothingham to initial blank of volume I and loosely inserted front endpaper of volume II, bookplate of Harry Buxton Forman. Simon Finch Rare Books Zero - 220 2011 £950

Association – Foster, John

Cooper, Thomas 1805-1892 *The Life of Thomas Cooper Written by Himself.* London: Hodder and Stoughton, 1879. Twelfth thousand; original blind decorated cloth gilt, recased, pages viii, 400, engraved portrait, presentation copy inscribed by author for Rev. John Chas. Foster. R. F. G. Hollett & Son Antiquarian Booksellers 175 - 303 2011 £35

Association – Foster, Walter

MacPherson, Earl *Pin-Up Art How to Draw and Paint Beautiful Girls.* Laguna Beach: Foster Art Service circa 1940's, Large 4to., pages 31, illustrations in color and black and white, paper wrappers, cover somewhat soiled and worn, else very good, inscribed by publisher Walter Foster and signed in rear by author. Second Life Books Inc. 174 - 233 2011 $200

Association – Foucault, Nicolas Joseph

Cameli, Francesco *Nummi Antiqui Aurei Argentei & Acrei Primae, Secundae, Seu Mediae, Minimae & Maximae Formae.* Rome: G. G. de Buagni, 1690. 4to., 218, (2 blank) pages, French smooth calf c. 1700, spine gilt, engraved bookplate of Nicolas Joseph Foucault, from the library of the Earls of Macclesfield at Shirburn Castle. Maggs Bros. Ltd. 1440 - 232 2011 £1000

Erizzo, Sebastiano *Discorso...Sopra le Medaglie de Gli Antichi con la Dichiaratione delle Monete Consulari & Delle Medaglie de Gli Imperadori Romani...* Venice: Giovanni Varisco & Paganino Paganini, not before, 1584. Splendid copy, 2 parts, 4to., (16), 282, (2 blank); 572 pages, title within woodcut border, woodcut initials and headpieces, woodcut illustrations, 17th century mottled calf, gilt arms of Foucault on covers, spine gilt in compartments, mottled red edges, Y1 torn at head with loss, extremities slightly rubbed, from the library of the Earls of Macclesfield at Shirburn Castle. Maggs Bros. Ltd. 1440 - 82 2011 £700

Falconieri, Ottavio *Inscriptiones Athleticae Nuper Repertae Editae & Notis Illustratae...* Rome: Fabio de Falco, 1668. 4to., (12), 230 pages, engraved illustrations, contemporary vellum with spine gilt in compartments and lettering piece, 2 leaves detached, pages browning within two quires, from the collection of Nicolas Joseph Foucault with his bookplate, from the library of the Earls of Macclesfield at Shirburn Castle. Maggs Bros. Ltd. 1440 - 87 2011 £650

Marolles, Michel De *Tableaux Du temple des Muses Representant les Vertus, et les Vices sur les Plus Illustres Fables De l'Antiquite.* Paris: Nicolas Langlois, 1655. First edition; folio, (20), 477, (9) pages, 58 engraved plates and portrait, engraved folding titlepage, woodcut head and tailpieces, initials woodcut, contemporary calf, rubbed, spine gilt in compartments, crackled, waterstained in corners throughout half of book, bookplate of Nicolas Joseph Foucault, from the library of the Earls of Macclesfield at Shirburn Castle. Maggs Bros. Ltd. 1440 - 141 2011 £900

Maupas Du Tour, Henri Couchon De *La Vie du Venerable Serviteur de Dieu, Francois de Sales, etc.* Paris: J. & E. Langlois, 1657. 2 parts, 4to., 411; 53, (3) pages, ruled in red, added engraved plates, 6 engraved plates, engraved headpieces and initials, contemporary French panelled, red morocco, gilt floral cornerpieces, spines gilt, turn-ins, edges gilt, slight damage to upper cover, paper flaw in plate at page 1 with consequent tear, handsome copy, ruled in red and from the Foucault library, De Cohon inscription, from the library of the Earls of Macclesfield at Shirburn Castle. Maggs Bros. Ltd. 1440 - 142 2011 £850

Torre, Filippo Del, Bp. of Adria *Moumenti Veteris Antii hoc est Inscriptio M. Aquilii et Tabula Solis Mithrae...* Rome: Gaetano Zenobi & G. Placho, 1700. First edition; 4to., (16), 400, (32) pages, 4 engraved plates at page 6, 159, 161, 257, contemporary smooth French calf, gilt stamp of N. J. Foucault on covers, gilt spine, red edges, some occasional marginal dampstaining, from the library of the Earls of Macclesfield at Shirburn Castle. Maggs Bros. Ltd. 1440 - 211   2011   £1100

Association – Fowles, John

Marsh, Anne *Father Darcy.* London: Chapman and Hall, 1846. First edition; 2 volumes, half titles, contemporary half dark green calf, spines gilt in compartments, maroon leather labels, slight rubbing, each volume signed by E. A. Wingfield, Digby with associated inscriptions, John Fowles booklabel, good plus. Jarndyce Antiquarian Booksellers CLXC - 238   2011   £180

Association – Fox, James

Merton, Thomas 1915-1968 *The Sign of Jonas.* New York: Harcourt Brace and Co., 1953. First edition; fine in near fine dust jacket with couple of old tape repairs on verso at spine ends, in specially made cloth slipcase, presentation copy inscribed in French by Thomas Merton (as Father Louis) on second endpaper to Dom Preome of the Oka-La Trappe in Quebec, further inscribed by Father James Fox, Merton's Abbot (superior) at Gethsemani at a time to dear Dom Preome with gratitude. Between the Covers   169 - BTC342154   2011 $1650

Association – Fox, Sara

Harrison, Susannah *Songs in the Night by a Young Woman Under Heavy.* Ipswich: Punchard & Jermyn, 1788. Fourth edition with supplement; 8vo. pages xiv, 202, bound in contemporary calf, small piece worn from the spine, lightly rubbed, some marginal browning to titlepage and final leaf, contemporary ownership signature of Sara Fox on front endpaper, again on rear. Second Life Books Inc.   174 - 168   2011 $600

Association – Foxcroft, Thomas

Beazley, Samuel *A General View of the System of Enclosing Wastelands with Particular Reference to the Proposed Enclosure at Epsom in Surrey.* London: Printed for C. Chapple, 1812. First edition; 8vo., (4), 51, (1) pages, neat old signature in ink on title (Thos. H. Foxcroft), fine in excellent contemporary style quarter calf over marbled boards, spine lettered in gilt, very rare. John Drury Rare Books   154 - 21   2011   £350

Association – Foyle, Christina

Spencer, Raine *The Spencers on Spas.* London: Weidenfeld and Nicolson, 1983. First edition; 4to., original cloth, gilt, dust jacket, pages 160, illustrations in color and monochrome by John Spencer, two TLS's loosely inserted from Christina Foyle to Russell Harty asking him to be a Guest of Honour at a luncheon to celebrate publication of the book. R. F. G. Hollett & Son Antiquarian Booksellers 177 - 824   2011   £30

Association – Foyle, W. A.

Gueulette, Thomas Simon *The Thousand and One Quarters of an Hour (Tartarian Tales).* London: H. S. Nichols and Co., 1893. One of 5 copies on Japanese vellum (of an edition of 680 copies); 254 x 159mm, viii, 308 pages, quite pleasing dark green crushed morocco by Morrell (signed), covers bordered in gilt with French fillet elaborate oblique gilt scrolling cornerpieces with blank oval center with raised bands, spine in handsome gilt compartment similarly decorated, wide green morocco turn-ins with simple gilt ornaments and rules, crimson crushed morocco doublures and free endpapers, other edges untrimmed, middle raised band of spine with small expert repair, front endpaper with morocco bookplate of W. A. Foyle, Beeleigh Abbey, titlepage printed in red and black; spine now sunned to uniform warm brown, top and top edge of cover also slightly sunned, few leaves of one gathering with small stain just at fore edge, additional trifling imperfections, otherwise fine, binding lustrous with very little wear, beautifully luxurious paper of text especially fresh and clean. Phillip J. Pirages   59 - 321   2011 $650

Association – Francke, Abraham

Spottiswood, John *The History of the Church of Scotland, Beginning the Year of Our Lord 203 and Continued to the End of the Reign of King James the VI.* London: J. Flesher for R. Royston, 1655. Folio, pages (xx), 546, (xiv), engraved frontispiece and engraved portrait dedication leaf, contemporary calf, spine double ruled in blind, boards double rule double bordered connected by stylised mitre pieces at corners, board edges, single rule gilt, all edges red sprinkled and with black ink handwritten "Spotiswood" on fore edge, bit of spotting and dust soiling, rubbed and marked, some surface damage at extremities, recent amateur red lettering piece gilt, touch of wear to corners and front joint, booklabel "Abrahamus Francke, now detached and loosely inserted, ink inscription "Affrancke/ A.M. / T.C.C. of Soc./ Ecc. de W. D,. Paul/1716", later ink inscription "Little Horksley Library" at inner head, from the collection of Christopher Ernest Weston 1947-2010. Unsworths Booksellers   24 - 42   2011   £400

Association – Franco, Niccolo

Hermes Trismegistus *Mercurij Trismegisti Pymander, de Potestate et Sapientia del Eiusdem Asclepius...* Basle: colophon: Michael Isingrin August, 1532. Woodcut printer's device on verso of last leaf, some browning, pages 480 (pages 320-39 omitted in pagination), (4), 8vo., contemporary vellum, lettered in ink on spine, small hole in vellum surface on upper cover, contemporary ownership inscription on flyleaf of Niccolo Franco and two later inscriptions, bookplate, good. Blackwell Rare Books B166 - 47 2011 £3000

Association – Franenkel, Eduard

Suetonius Tranquillus, Caius *XII Caesares.* Antwerp: Ex officina Plantiniana, 1591. 4to., titlepage engraved, outer edges occasionally soiled and bumped, first and last few just slightly frayed, small dampmark to few margins, pages (iv), 407, (23), 4to., early vellum, backstrip divided by blind fillets, top compartment lettered in ink, yapp edges, bit rumpled an rather soiled, ties removed, no flyleaves, hinges cracked, ownership inscription of Eduard Fraenkel (and some other marks) to front pastedown, sound. Blackwell Rare Books B166 - 103 2011 £750

Association – Frankenberg, Lloyd

Bishop, Elizabeth *Poem.* Phoenix Book Shop, 1973. First edition, copy "L" (for Loren) of 26 lettered copies (Out of a total edition of 126) signed by Bishop on colophon; oblong small 8vo., original string tied unprinted stiff wrappers, marbled outer wrapper, printed paper label, housed in custom green cloth clamshell box with black morocco spine label, with author's presentation for Loren MacIver & Lloyd Frankenberg, laid in is exceptionally interesting TLS from Bishop for MacIver and Frankenberg. James S. Jaffe Rare Books May 26 2011 - 20762 2011 $8500

Association – Frankl, Hermann

Sonnini De Manoncourt, Charles Nicolas Sigisbert *Voyage Dans la Haute et Basse Egypte...* Paris: F. Buisson An VII, 1788-1799. First edition; 8vo. and 4to., pages 94, vii, (1), 425, (3); (4), 417; (4), 424; engraved portrait, 2 folding tables, 39 engraved plates with tissue guards (half inch marginal tear to folding plate, some marginal tanning and foxing to plain plates, colored plates clean and fresh), folding map with 1 1/2 inch and shorter tear, marginal tanning near 2 edges, light chipping to margin, contemporary calf backed boards, edges of text volumes rubbed, edges of atlas worn, boards of atlas rubbed, few corners bumped, calf near 3 ends of spines perished, upper end of spine chipped, light cracking to calf on spines, front edge of spine split but hinge solid, few shorter splits to other edges of spines, dampstain to lower corner of rear cover and margin of few leaves, not affecting text, small marginal stain or dampspot to few pages in volume I, light marginal tanning to some pages, 2 inch tear to leaf and shorter tear to another, 2 page gatherings in volume 3 are bound out of border, with black leather labels (1 chipped) and floral gilt decorations (rubbed and with some loss of gilt) on spines, bookplates of Hermann Frankl, handstamp of George Vanderbilt Foundation. Raymond M. Sutton, Jr. May 26 2011 - 43952 2011 $2000

Association – Frankland, Joseph

Lloyd, Bertram *The Great Kinship.* London: Allen & Unwin, 1921. First edition; original holland backed boards with leather spine label, pages xviii, 272, untrimmed, etched frontispiece, presentation copy inscribed to Joseph N. Frankland from author, with author's signature from a letter tipped to title. R. F. G. Hollett & Son Antiquarian Booksellers 175 - 848 2011 £45

Association – Fraser, Aleck

MacDonald, George 1824-1905 *The Disciple and Other Poems.* London: Strahan & Co., 1868. Second edition; half title, initial ad slip and 4 page catalog Jan. 1868, slightly marked, small owner's stamp of Aleck D. Fraser, original dappled dark brown and red cloth, ruled in blind, decorated an lettered in gilt. Jarndyce Antiquarian Booksellers CXCII - 107 2011 £200

Association – Freedman, James

Gurganus, Allan *Breathing Lessons.* Durham: North Carolina Wesleyan College Press, 1981. Printed in an edition of 500 copies, 50 of which were numbered and signed; bit of smudging to inscription, trace rust near staples, else fine in stapled wrappers, this copy unnumbered, lengthily inscribed by author in 1990 to James Freedman, President of Dartmouth College. Ken Lopez Bookseller 154 - 70 2011 $200

Association – Freels, Danny

Harwell, Ernie *Turned to Baseball.* South Bend: Diamond Communications, 1985. First edition; near fine, light shelfwear, dust jacket fine, inscribed by author to Danny Freels "A great Tiger fan...". Bella Luna Books May 29 2011 - t9296 2011 $82

Association – Freeman, G.

Doubleday, Thomas *The Coquet-Dale Fishing Songs.* William Blackwood and Sons, 1852. First edition; original blindstamped green cloth gilt, gilt vignette to upper board, spine rather faded and frayed at head and foot, pages vi, (ii), 168, engraved portrait frontispiece, 9 pages of music, few spots to frontispiece and title, contemporary signature of Geo. Freeman. R. F. G. Hollett & Son Antiquarian Booksellers 175 - 387 2011 £175

Association – French, James

Malcolm, Charles A. *The Bank of Scotland 195-1945.* Edinburgh: R. & R. Clark, n.d., Tall 8vo., original buckram gilt over bevelled boards, leather spine label, pages viii, 322, with 38 plates ad 2 folding sheets in rear pocket, bookplate of Sir James French. R. F. G. Hollett & Son Antiquarian Booksellers 175 - 904 2011 £40

Association – Frevin, R.

Grew, Nehemiah 1641-1712 *An Idea of a Phytological History Propounded. Together with a continuation of the Anatomy of Vegetables...* London: Richard Chiswell at the Hosue and Crown in St. Paul's church yard, 1673. First edition; 7 fine folding engraved plates, 8vo., pages (21), 144, (32), contemporary blind tooled calf, rubbed, piece missing from head of spine, front cover nearly detached, rear hinge split but solid, horizontal split to spine near heel, slight browning to covers, old bookplate removed, old owner's signature R. Frevin 1707. Raymond M. Sutton, Jr. May 26 2011 - 28943 2011 $1600

Association – Frohawk, F. L.

Bell, Thomas *A History of British Reptiles.* John Van Voorst, 1849. Second edition; 50 wood engravings, 159 pages + ads, half title, good clean, original cloth, covers little faded, signature of 19th century natural history artist F. L. Frohawk at head of titlepage. Ken Spelman Rare Books 68 - 140 2011 £40

Association – Frostrup, Mariella

Vettriano, Jack *Jack Vettriano.* London: Pavilion, 2004. First edition; 4to., 192 pages, lavishly illustrated in color, signed presentation from author for Mariella Frostrup, fine in fine dust jacket. Any Amount of Books May 29 2011 - A40514 2011 $213

Association – Frothingham, John Whipple

Coleridge, Samuel Taylor 1772-1834 *Biographia Literaria; or Bibliographical Sketches of My Literary Life and Opinions.* London: Rest Fenner, 1817. Only edition; 2 volumes, royal 8vo., pages (iv), 296; (iv), 309, (3) ads with second half title in volume i, top edge gilt, others uncut, off-setting from bookmark to second blank but fresh and bright copy with occasional slight spotting, later full morocco, raised bands, gilt lettering to spines and gilt edges, gilt decoration to doublures by Tout, with endpapers loosely inserted, in excellent condition, with only very light shelfwear, endpapers browned at edges, portion of both original black labels, rubbed, pasted to rear endpaper loosely inserted into volume i, bookplate of John Whipple Frothingham to initial blank of volume I and loosely inserted front endpaper of volume II, bookplate of Harry Buxton Forman. Simon Finch Rare Books Zero - 220 2011 £950

Shelley, Percy Bysshe 1792-1822 *Alastor; or the Spirit of Solitude and Other Poems.* London: printed for Baldwin, Cradock and Joy by S. Hamilton, 1816. First edition; 8vo., pages (viii without half title as issued), 101, (7) blank, gilt edges, some minor spotting to margins of endpapers, otherwise internally very clean, late 19th century navy blue morocco with ornate red, green and gilt decoration, brown fabric to inside of boards and endpapers, gilt lettering to spine, raised bands by Riviere, blue morocco and marbled paper covered slipcase, binding fine with light wear to edges of slipcase, bookplate of John Whipple Frothingham. Simon Finch Rare Books Zero - 352 2011 £4500

Association – Frothingham, O. B.

Emerson, Ralph Waldo 1803-1882 *Poems.* Boston: James Munroe and Co., 1847. First American edition; original yellow glazed boards neatly rebacked with most of the original spine laid down on attractive tan morocco, 4 page catalog dated 1 Jan. 1847 inserted at front, pencil signatures of O. B. Frothingham dated 1847, very clean, attractive copy, about fine, housed in cloth chemise and brown half morocco slipcase. Charles Agvent Transcendentalism 2010 - 17 2011 $850

Association – Fulton, John Farquhar

Monro, Thomas Kirkpatrick *Raynaud's Disease Local Syncope, Local Asphyxia, Symmetrical Gangrene): Its History, Causes, Symptoms, Morbid Relations, Pathology & Treatment.* Glasgow: James Maclehose & Sons, 1899. 8vo., xii, 251 pages, frontispiece, 3 tables, green cloth, gilt stamped spine title, very good, inscribed by John F. Fulton to William Livingston, from the Medical Library of Dr. Clare Gray Peterson. Jeff Weber Rare Books 162 - 218 2011 $150

Association – Furstenberg, Jean

Henault, Charles Jean Francois *Nouvel Abrege Chronologique de l'Histoire de France.* Paris: Chez Prault et al, 1756. Fifth edition; 165 x 105mm., 2 volumes with continuous pagination, 5 p.l., (1), 545, (1), 1 blank leaf; (549)-928 pages, (48) leaves, including final blank, second volume with half title but no titlepage, apparently as issued, lovely contemporary olive green morocco, elegantly gilt in style of Derome, covers with plain and stippled fillet border around a frame containing large and graceful gilt floral and botanical stamps as well as dots and circlets, raised bands, spines gilt in compartments featuring charming flower centerpiece and small scrolling foliate cornerpieces, turn-ins with gilt zig-zag decoration, stenciled gilt endpapers, all edges gilt, publisher's device on titlepage, historiated headpieces, foliated initials, ornamental tailpieces; small bookplate of Jean Furstenberg and Henri Beraldi; spines slightly and uniformly faded to an attractive amber, just hint of wear to joints and corners, isolated minor foxing, few trivial stains, but fine, pretty binding sound, lustrous and with only insignificant wear and text, very clean and fresh.   Phillip J. Pirages   59 - 53   2011 $2900

Association – Gable, William

Irving, Washington   1783-1859   *Bracebridge Hall.* London: Macmillan, 1877.   First edition with these illustrations; extremely fine dark green crushed morocco handsomely gilt by the Doves Bindery (stamp signed and dated 1905 on rear turn-in), covers with double gilt fillet border and Tudor rose cornerpieces set among leafy sprays and circlets, raised bands, spine compartments heavily gilt with central Tudor rose framed by trefoil cornerpieces and accented with small tools, gilt turn-ins, all edges gilt, stippled gauffering, illustrations by Randolph Caldecott, including frontispiece, titlepage and five full page plates; engraved bookplate of William F. Gable; edges of free endpaper at front and back with usual (but here rather pronounced) offsetting from turn-ins, otherwise magnificent copy, text with virtually no signs of use, beautiful binding absolutely flawless.   Phillip J. Pirages   59 - 99   2011 $4500

Association – Gaige, Crosby

Bible. English - 1901   *The Boke off the Revelacion off Sanct Jhon the Devine Done into Englysshe by WilliamTyndale.*   Ashendene Press, 1901.   One of 54 copies; 218 x 165 mm., 1 p.l., xxx, (i) pages, plus 6 blank leaves at front and three at back, original limp velum dyed dark green, gilt titled flat spine, custom made folding cloth box with gilt titling, initials and chapter headings printed in red, booklabel "From the Books of Crosby Gaige", bookplate of Lord Wardington, little loss of dark green present along fore edges of binding, in all other ways a faultless copy. Phillip J. Pirages   59 - 74   2011 $4250

Association – Gardiner, Margaret

Bone, Gertrude *Of the Western Isles.* London: T. N. Foulis, 1925. First edition; tall small 4to., original cloth backed pictorial boards, spine label, trifle worn, pages 61, with initial letters and title decorations in grey and 40 woodcuts by Stephen Bone, and maps on endpapers, presentation copy inscribed by artist, Stephen Bone to Margaret Gardiner.   R. F. G. Hollett & Son Antiquarian Booksellers General Catalogue Summer 2010 - 1340 2011   £120

Association – Gardner, Henry

Martineau, Harriet   1802-1876   *Household Education.* London: Smith, Elder & Co., 1867. Contemporary half maroon morocco, spine with raised gilt bands, corners and leading hinges little rubbed, small booklabel of Henry Gardner, good plus.   Jarndyce Antiquarian Booksellers CLXC - 289   2011   £70

Association – Garnett, David

Pound, Ezra Loomis   1885-1972   *Canzoni.* London: Elkin Mathews, 1911. First edition; 8vo., pages (viii), 52, (4) ads, uncut lower and fore edge, some light spotting, original gray cloth, spine and upper board lettered in gilt, spine slightly sunned and light foxing to endpapers, David Garnett's copy with bookplate.   Simon Finch Rare Books Zero - 344   2011   £400

Association – Garnett, Helen Mary

Somervell, John   *Some Westmorland Wills 1686-1738.* Kendal: Titus Wilson, 1928. First edition; pages 119, uncut, 9 plates, slight stain to gutter of flyleaf, bookplates of George Charles Williamson and Helen Mary Garnett.   R. F. G. Hollett & Son Antiquarian Booksellers   173 - 1068 2011 £60

Association – Garstang, Walter

Marine Biological Association of the United Kingdom *Journal of...* Plymouth/Cambridge: Marine Biological Association of the United Kingdom/Cambridge University Press, 1887-2006. First editions and reprint; Old Series Volumes 1 and 2 (of 2) and New Series Volumes 1-84 (complete), volume 85 (Nos. 1, 2, 3, 6) and Volume 86 (nos.1-3) in 112; very good, numerous plates, text figures and some photos, occasional minor soiling, few short tears along folds and tear along fold of a panel in 1, few tears repaired with tape, tall 8vo., some 4to., volumes 1/2, 1-3, 5 an 12-21 contemporary hardbound, volumes, 4, 6-11 and 22-48 recent hardbound, original wrappers bound into volumes 6-11 & 22-48, volumes 49-68 in original printed wrappers, volumes 69-86 paperbound (modest wear to extremities in 6 oldest volumes, spine faded to brown in 3 older volumes and with splitting to cover along edges of spine in 2, some endpapers browned, handstamp to front wrappers and or front endpapers contents and index pages are photocopies in volumes 6 and 10, plates are photocopies in volume 7, occasional tear to soiling to original wrappers or text pages, some pencil notations to text pages, in early issues, occasional bump, short tear or wrinkling to paper on spine, light soiling or pages tanned, recent issues mostly fine; with W(alter) Garstang's signature and handstamp to 3 volumes, A(lister) C(lavering) Hardy's signature to 24 volumes, Lesley D. Wright-Smith's copy with his name on title, numerous dates and some notes on page margins. Raymond M. Sutton, Jr. May 26 2011 - 48790 2011 $2400

Association – Gaselee, Stephen

Satow, Ernest *A Guide to Diplomatic Practice.* London: Longmans, Green and Co., 1932. Third edition; fat 8vo., pages x, 519, but stretched to about 1000 pages with interleaved blanks on which Sir Stephen Gaselee has written notes and comments, pencilled ownership signature of historian F. R. Cowell, A S Gow's pamphlet on Life of Fasselee loosely inserted, brown half leather with orange boards and lettered gilt at spine, slight rubbing, minor near, else sound, very good. Any Amount of Books May 26 2011 - A46377 2011 $419

Association – Gaskell, Daniel Hunter

Moore, Thomas 1821-1887 *The Octavo Nature Printed British Frns...* London: Bradbury & Evans, 1859-1860. 8vo., pages xvi, 254; xi,3 68, 2 elaborately decorated titles, each with nature printed fern and 122, nature printed ferns, foxing to first plate, occasional minor foxing to rest of plates, 8vo., pages xvi, 254; xi, 368, original green morocco over marbled boards, ex-libris Daniel Hunter Gaskell, elaborate gilt decorated spines with five raised bands, all edges gilt. Raymond M. Sutton, Jr. May 26 2011 - 47909 2011 $1350

Association – Gaskell, Roger

Locke, John 1632-1704 *Essay Concerning Humane (Human) Understanding.* London: printed for Tho. Basset and sold by Edw. Mory, 1690. First edition, 2nd issue with cancel titlepage containing inverted "SS" of "Essay" the type ornament composed of 23 pieces, and without Elizabeth Holt's name in imprint, dedication undated, errata uncorrected; folio, (12), 362, (22, contents) pages, pages 287, 296 and 303 misnumbered 269, 294, 230 respectively; contemporary brown mottled calf, boards ruled in blind, spine in six compartments, lettered in gilt on brown calf spine label, edges speckled red, expertly rebacked to style with corners repaired, titlepage is short at fore-edge by half an inch due to stub being turned behind A4, marginal paper flaws on D1, P3 and Dd3, not affecting text, very small marginal hole on Hh, not affecting text, errata corrected by contemporary hand with ink and there are two contemporary ink notes on back free endpaper, Locke's name written in contemporary hand on titlepage as John Lock, previous owner's name Brockett, previous owner's name Samuel Gaskell and previous owner's name Roger Gaskell dated 1813, very clean and crisp, excellent contemporary binding. Heritage Book Shop Holiday 2010 - 74 2011 $32,500

Association – Gaskell, Samuel

Locke, John 1632-1704 *Essay Concerning Humane (Human) Understanding.* London: printed for Tho. Basset and sold by Edw. Mory, 1690. First edition, 2nd issue with cancel titlepage containing inverted "SS" of "Essay" the type ornament composed of 23 pieces, and without Elizabeth Holt's name in imprint, dedication undated, errata uncorrected; folio, (12), 362, (22, contents) pages, pages 287, 296 and 303 misnumbered 269, 294, 230 respectively; contemporary brown mottled calf, boards ruled in blind, spine in six compartments, lettered in gilt on brown calf spine label, edges speckled red, expertly rebacked to style with corners repaired, titlepage is short at fore-edge by half an inch due to stub being turned behind A4, marginal paper flaws on D1, P3 and Dd3, not affecting text, very small marginal hole on Hh, not affecting text, errata corrected by contemporary hand with ink and there are two contemporary ink notes on back free endpaper, Locke's name written in contemporary hand on titlepage as John Lock, previous owner's name Brockett, previous owner's name Samuel Gaskell and previous owner's name Roger Gaskell dated 1813, very clean and crisp, excellent contemporary binding. Heritage Book Shop Holiday 2010 - 74 2011 $32,500

Association – Gault, William Campbell

MacDonald, Ross *Black Money.* New York: Knopf, 1965. First edition; 8vo., inscribed by author for Bill Gault, fine in fine dust jacket, exceptional copy housed in cloth slipcase with red leather labels on spine, titles and date stamped in gold. Buckingham Books May 26 2011 - 25474 2011 $2750

Association – Gavito, Florencio

Fenelon, Francois Salignac De La Mothe, Abp. 1651-1715 *Les Aventures de Telemaque.* Paris: Imprimerie de Monsieur (i.e. Pierre-Francois Didot), 1785. 338 x 251mm., 2 volumes, splendid contemporary (or slightly later scarlet, straight grain morocco, sumptuously gilt, covers with broad ornate gilt border featuring palmettes, flat spines handsomely gilt in seven compartments (two with titling, two with elegant volutes and pointille decoration and three with large central lozenge enclosing an intricate fleuron), densely gilt turn-ins, azure watered silk endpapers, all edges gilt, engraved titlepage, 96 fine engraved plates, all with handsome frames wrapped in fruited foliage by Jean Baptiste Tilliard after Charles Monnet, 24 of the plates containing chapter summaries and 72 with scenes from the narrative, original tissue guards; bookplates of Rene Choppin and Florencio Gavito (20th century); faint, widely spaced flecks to front cover of second volume, spines ever so slightly sunned, small stain to one endpaper, one page with minor ink spots in bottom margin, two engraved divisional leaves with one other engraving with overall faint mottled foxing, hint of foxing or pale browning in isolated places elsewhere, other trivial imperfections, especially fine set in beautiful binding, leather bright and only insignificant wear, text and plates unusually fresh and bright. Phillip J. Pirages 59 - 47 2011 $11,000

Association – Gedeon, Andras

Bouguer, Pierre *Traite d'Optique sur la Gradation de la Lumiere: Ouvrage Posthume de M. Bouguer de l'Acaemie Royale des Scienes &c.* Paris: H. L. Guerin & L. F. Delatour, 1760. First edition; 4to., xviii, (2), 368 pages, engraved printer's device on titlepage, 7 engraved folding plates, contemporary full mottled calf, raised bands, gilt stamped spine panels and spine title, few minor covers scars, joints starting, bookplate of Jean Francois Le Boyer and Andras Gedeon, fine, from the Bern Dibner reference library, with Burndy bookplate. Jeff Weber Rare Books 161 - 51 2011 $2500

Huygens, Christiaan *Opera Varia.* Lugduni Batavvorum: Janssonios Vander Aa, 1724. First collected edition; 4 books in one volume, 4to., (18), (1-4) 5-776, (18) pages, frontispiece, 56 folding plates, contemporary full calf, raised bands, gilt stamped spine panels, gilt stamped red morocco spine label, covers and joints rubbed, hinges beginning to split, very good, bookplate of Andras Gedeon and P. A. Moiroud, with J. B. de Bouvou signature on title dated 1758, very good. Jeff Weber Rare Books 161 - 224 2011 $5500

Association – Geiger, P. F.

Schaeffer, Jacob Christian *Piscium Bavarico Ratisbonensium Pentas. (bound with) Epistola ad Regio-Borussicam Societatem Litterariam Du'isburgensem de Studii Ichthyologici Facililori...* Ratisbonae: Montagii et Typis Weissianis, 1761. Ratisbonae: Typis Weissianis et Impensis Montagii, 1760; 4to., 4 hand colored engraved plates (light foxing to 1), pages (12), 82; 4to., pages 24, scattered light foxing, contemporary calf backed boards, rubbed, bump to upper edges of covers, 1 inch split to upper edges of spine, old paper label to heel of spine, some worming to upper blank corner of all pages and plates, old ink number to front flyleaf, 3 handstamps on first title, scattered light foxing, from the Musee d'Histoire Naturelle de Geneve, also the copy of H. C. Redeke, P. F. Geiger, and R. Harry, Jr. Raymond M. Sutton, Jr. May 26 2011 - 41627 2011 $1500

Association – Geldart, Mrs.

Burke, William *The Greek-English Derivative Dictionary showing in English Characters, the Greek Originals of Such Words in the English Language as are Derived from the Greek...* London: J. Johnson, 1806. 8vo., pages 248, 2 neat inscriptions on front endpaper in 19th century handwriting of the Fanny Desborough of Russell Square, also Mary Desborough, Ellen Scholes and Mrs. Geldart, soundly bound in full plain unlettered (but with 7 gold bands at spine), tree calf which is lightly scuffed and slightly marked), very good. Any Amount of Books May 29 2011 - A72178 2011 $238

Association – Gennadius, Joannes

Guevara, Antonio De *Vita Di M. Avrelio Imperadore.* Venice: Bartolomeo Imperador and Francesco Veneziano, 1543. 160 x 103mm., 8 p.l., 132, (2) leaves, fine contemporary Roman red morocco Apollo and Pegasus medallion binding done for Giovanni Battista Grimaldi by Marc Antonio Guillery, (genuine Apollo and Pegasus binding) covers with gilt frame formed by two widely spaced fillets with lobes interlaced at ends and sides, space between fillets decorated with broad foliate curls, small floral tools, inner pane of each board with gilt titling above a horizontal oval Apollo and Pegasus plaquette centerpiece showing Pegasus atop black painted heights of Parnassus and Apollo racing his chariot (drawn by two straining steeds) across steep terrain with reins and whip held aloft and caps fluttering behind, plaquette with gilt motto in Greek in the collar above and below vignette, spine (very expertly rebacked) with four thin and three thick raised bands decorated with gilt rope pattern or plain rules (this being original backstrip?), newer (perhaps 19th century) endpapers, all edges gilt (apparently some remarkably skillful restoration at one or more corners and edges, perhaps some gold added, as well as to the chariot part of the plaquettes); woodcut printer's device on , morocco bookplate and separate gilt monogram of Robert Hoe as well as inscription and vellum bookplate of Swedish collector Thore Virgin, ownership inscription of J. T. Payne dated 1850; covers with half dozen insignificant tiny dark spots, titlepage faintly soiled, thin light brown stain just at top edge of leaves, small wormhole at upper inner margin (text not affected), occasional minor stains, other trivial imperfections, but no defects that are even remotely serious and in general really excellent specimen of a very special binding, text fresh and leather quite lustrous; also from the collection of bibliophile Johannes Gennadius, Liverpool oculist T. Shadford Walker and Swedish collector Rolfe Wistrand. Phillip J. Pirages   59 - 2   2011 $35,000

Association – Gensler, Lewis

Adams, Franklin P. *Something Else Again.* Garden City: Doubleday, Page, 1920. First edition; bookplate and ownership signature of Lewis Gensler, boards little soiled, very good in very good dust jacket with some shallow chipping around crown, inscribed by author to Gensler, scarce in jacket.   Between the Covers   169 - BTC347699   2011 $225

Association – George, William

Lennie, William *A Key to Lennie's Principles of English Grammar...* Edinburgh: printed for the author and sold by Guthrie & Tait and Oliver & Boyd etc., 1824. Sixth edition; 12mo., original full roan gilt, upper hinge cracking, extremities little worn and bumped, pages 190, rather scribbled inscription "presented to Wm. George Jnr in the year 1846 on his 8th birthday".   R. F. G. Hollett & Son Antiquarian Booksellers   175 - 819   2011   £45

Association – Gerash, Walter

Douglas, William O. *Go East, Young Man, the Early Years.* New York: Random House, 1974. First edition; fine, dust jacket near fine, very light use, laid in is gift letter to Walter Gerash from Lucius Woods dated Feb. 25, 1991. Bella Luna Books   May 29 2011 - t9174   2011 $82

Association – Gerhard, William

Blanchard, Jean Pierre *Exact and Authentic Narrative of M. Blanchard's Third Aerial Voyage.* London: C. Heydigner, 1784. First English edition; small folio, viii, 17, (1, blank) pages, frontispiece, early dark brown paper wrappers, housed in dark blue cloth folder by Sangorski & Sutcliffe for E. P. Dutton, gilt lettering on outside of folder, balloon themed bookplate of previous owner William G. Gerhard on inside front of folder, lacking half title as called for in ESTC, slight offsetting to titlepage from frontispiece and some light foxing to final leaf, very good.   Heritage Book Shop Holiday 2010 - 11   2011 $2750

Association – Gerry, Vance

Verve, an Artistic and Literary Quarterly. Paris: Verve, 1937. Volume 1 No. 1 (December 1937), first edition of the premier issue; small folio, 36cm., 128 pages, original color pictorial wrappers, illustrations, photos, very good, bookplate of Vance Gerry.   Jeff Weber Rare Books   163 - 104   2011 $475

Association – Gershwin, George

Gershwin, Ira *Strike Up the Band.* New York: New York World Music Corp., 1930. Presentation copy inscribed by George and Ira Gershwin, each with small sketch to Newman Levy, quarto, contemporary full red cloth. Heritage Book Shop   Booth A12 51st NY International Antiquarian Book Fair April 8-10 2011 - 60   2011 $9500

Hughes, Langston *The Weary Blues.* New York: Alfred A. Knopf, 1926. One of 1500 copies printed; small 8vo., original blue cloth backed decorated boards, covers lightly rubbed, lacking rare dust jacket, otherwise in very good condition, presentation copy inscribed by author for George Gershwin.   James S. Jaffe Rare Books   May 26 2011 - 21625   2011 $45,000

Association – Gibbs, Henry Martin

Emerson, Ralph Waldo 1803-1882 *Complete Works.* Cambridge: Riverside Press, 1883. Riverside edition, one of 500 copies; 235 x 150m., 11 volumes, very attractive green straight grain morocco (stamp signed "Hatchards of Piccadilly" on front turn-in), covers with border of two gilt fillets, wide raised bands decorated with floral ornaments and three gilt rules, ruled gilt compartments with large fleuron centerpiece, marbled endpapers, top edge gilt, other edges rough trimmed, 2 frontispiece portraits, large paper copy, armorial bookplates of Henry Martin Gibbs of Barrow Court, Flax Bourton, Somerset, backstrips uniformly faded to pleasing caramel color, top of one spine slightly rubbed, three or four joints with trivial wear, three corners bit bumped, endpapers (of a different stock from text), somewhat foxed, otherwise quite appealing set, leather lustrous, wear insignificiant and text especially bright, fresh and clean.   Phillip J. Pirages   59 - 189 2011 $2500

Association – Gibson, Jane Elizabeth

Marsh, Anne *Tales of the Woods and Fields.* London: Saunders and Otley, 1836. First edition; 3 volumes, half black sheep, slight rubbing, each volume signed "Jane Elizabeth Gibson", very good.   Jarndyce Antiquarian Booksellers   CLXC - 243 2011   £225

Association – Gibson, Ralph

Baltz, Lewis *The New Industrial Parks Near Irvine, California.* New York: Castelli Graphics, 1974. First edition, one of 960 copies; 4to., pages (10&0, (5) blank, 51 black and white photos, edges lightly toned, original grey boards, spine and upper side lettered in black, corners lightly rubbed, bottom corner of lower side bumped, original black and white photo illustrated dust jacket, text printed in black, lightly tone, creasing to flaps, rubbing to tips and to head and foot of spine, 3 short closed tears internally, strengthened, spotting to verso, dampstain to verso of lower panel, Ralph Gibson's ex-libris stamp in black, ink to front free endpaper, laid in are two postcards from Baltz to Gibson, one signed, the other initialled, near fine in very good dust jacket.   Simon Finch Rare Books   Zero - 506 2011   £2250

Association – Gibson, Robert

Power, Marguerite Agnes *The Letters of a Betrothed.* London: Longman, Brown and Co., 1858. First edition; contemporary full tan calf, spine gilt in compartments, boards double ruled in gilt, maroon leather label, slight rubbing, signed "Robert Gibson 1858" with his armorial bookplate, very good.   Jarndyce Antiquarian Booksellers   CLXC - 767 2011   £50

Association – Gibson, Wilfred

Thomas, Dylan Marlais 1914-1953 *18 Poems.* London: Sunday Referee and The Parton Bookshop, 1934. First edition; 8vo., pages (ii), 36, (4), occasional light spotting, overall very crisp and fresh, black cloth, gilt lettering to spine, slightly bumped, light shelfwear, dust jacket, unclipped, soiled and chipped in several places, some loss of text on spine, ownership inscription of Wilfred Gibson dated 1936.   Simon Finch Rare Books   Zero - 358 2011   £2000

Association – Gielgud, John

Hayman, Ronald *John Gielgud.* London: Heinemann, 1971. First edition; original cloth, gilt, dust jacket, head of spine trifle chipped, pages x, 276, 45 plates, signed by Gielgud and inscribed July 1970.   R. F. G. Hollett & Son Antiquarian Booksellers   175 - 609 2011   £45

Association – Giffard, Eliza

Palmer, Alicia Tyndal *The Sons of Altringham, a Novel.* London: Lackington, Allen & Co., 1812. Second edition; 3 volumes, half titles, final ad leaves volumes II & III, uncut in original blue boards, drab spines with hand written lettering, corners bit worn volume II, but all in all good plus copy, extremely scarce, with contemporary signatures of Eliza Giffard, Nerquis, Flintshire partially removed in volumes II and III.   Jarndyce Antiquarian Booksellers   CLXC - 734 2011   £600

Porter, Anna Maria *The Hungarian Brothers.* London: Longman, 1814. Third edition; 3 volumes, half titles volumes II and III, uncut in contemporary drab boards, purple spines, paper labels, volumes II and III lettered with title in ink at head of spines, small unobtrusive reparis, paper label with loss volume III, each volume signed Eliza Giffard, Nerquis, Flintshire, very good.   Jarndyce Antiquarian Booksellers   CLXC - 755 2011   £250

Association – Gifford, A.

Lister, Martin *Conchyliorum Bivalvium Utriusque Aquae Exercitatio Anatomica Tertia.* London: Sumptibus authoris impressa, 1696. First edition; 4to., xliii, (1), 173 pages; 51 pages, 10 engraved plates, complete with terminal blank Z4 in first work, Dissertatio has its own titlepage and pagination, contemporary sprinkled calf, very skillfully rebacked to period style, small early shelfmark in red ink on endpaper and on title, minor paper flaw in S2 just grazing catchword, very faint foxing in fore edge, very lovely copy with text and plates, clean and fresh, armorial bookplate of A. Gifford, D.D. of the Museum, presentation copy from Lister for Mr. Dalone.   Joseph J. Felcone Inc.   Fall Miscellany 2010 - 76 2011 $10,000

Association – Gigliucci, Nerina

Paget, Violet 1856-1935 *Ariadne in Mantua; a Romance.* Oxford: B. H. Blackwell, 1903. First edition; uncut in original cream wrappers, decorated in orange and dark blue, paper label, slightly dusted, very good, signed presentation inscription to Nerina Gigliucci.   Jarndyce Antiquarian Booksellers   CLXC - 99   2011   £160

Association – Gildea, Mary

Kelly, George *Craig's Wife a Drama.* Boston: Little Brown, 1926. First edition; 8vo., pages 174, very nice, tight copy, inscribed by author to Josephine Williams who played the part of Mrs. Harold in the NY production, also signed by rest of the cast - Annie Sutherland, Crystal Herne, Arthur Shaw, C. Stewart, Eleanor Marsh, Charles Trowbridge, Josephine Hull, J. A. Curtis, Nelan Jaap, Arline Alcine & Mary Gildea, also inscribed by the producer, Rosalie Stewart to whom the play was dedicated.   Second Life Books Inc.   174 - 213   2011 $2000

Association – Gill, David

Young, Edward *Night Thoughts and a Paraphrase on Part of the Book of Job.* London: printed at the Chiswick Press by C. Whittingham for Taylor and Hessey, 1812. 240 x 145mm., lxvi, (2), 353, (1) pages, striking contemporary black morocco elaborately tooled in blind and gilt by Taylor & Hessey (board edges at middle on either side of painting stamped in gilt "Taylor and Hessey/Booksellers London"), covers with frame outlined by gilt rules and with cornerpieces in form of a stylized gilt satire, frame also featuring a chain of blindstamped oval medallions connected by palm fronds of an unusual ground of blind stippling, the whole enclosing a large central panel ornately tooled in blind, with cornerpices composed of shells, leaves and volutes and with intricate sunburst medallion centerpiece, central panel further decorated in blind with complex of elaborate strapwork between the centerpiece and cornerpieces, highlighted by botanical and other tools, raised bands, spine with rows of gilt tools at head and tail, three spine panels tooled in blind and highlighted with gilt lancets with flowers, gilt turn-ins in Greek key style, all edges gilt, with exceptionally fine fore-edge painting depicting Westminster Bridge and Westminster Hall; with engraved frontispiece, armorial bookplate of David Gill, ink presentation inscription "Eliza Gill/the gift of her attached and affectionate Husband/Decem(ber) 3rd 1812", joints and extremities with touch of rubbing (though well marked with dye), offsetting to titlepage from frontispiece, occasional trivial imperfections internally, exceptionally pleasing copy, binding especially lustrous, text unusually clean, fresh and bright, painting beautifully preserved.   Phillip J. Pirages   59 - 199   2011 $2500

Association – Gill, Eliza

Young, Edward *Night Thoughts and a Paraphrase on Part of the Book of Job.* London: printed at the Chiswick Press by C. Whittingham for Taylor and Hessey, 1812. 240 x 145mm., lxvi, (2), 353, (1) pages, striking contemporary black morocco elaborately tooled in blind and gilt by Taylor & Hessey (board edges at middle on either side of painting stamped in gilt "Taylor and Hessey/Booksellers London"), covers with frame outlined by gilt rules and with cornerpieces in form of a stylized gilt satire, frame also featuring a chain of blindstamped oval medallions connected by palm fronds of an unusual ground of blind stippling, the whole enclosing a large central panel ornately tooled in blind, with cornerpieces composed of shells, leaves and volutes and with intricate sunburst medallion centerpiece, central panel further decorated in blind with complex of elaborate strapwork between the centerpiece and cornerpieces, highlighted by botanical and other tools, raised bands, spine with rows of gilt tools at head and tail, three spine panels tooled in blind and highlighted with gilt lancets with flowers, gilt turn-ins in Greek key style, all edges gilt, with exceptionally fine fore-edge painting depicting Westminster Bridge and Westminster Hall; with engraved frontispiece, armorial bookplate of David Gill, ink presentation inscription "Eliza Gill/the gift of her attached and affectionate Husband/Decem(ber) 3rd 1812", joints and extremities with touch of rubbing (though well marked with dye), offsetting to titlepage from frontispiece, occasional trivial imperfections internally, exceptionally pleasing copy, binding especially lustrous, text unusually clean, fresh and bright, painting beautifully preserved.   Phillip J. Pirages   59 - 199   2011 $2500

Association – Gill, George

Church of England. Book of Common Prayer *The Book of Common Prayer... together with The Psalter or Psalms of David.* London: engraved and printed by the Permission of Mr. John Baskett, 1717. 206 x 130mm., xxii, 166 pages, (1) leaf of ads, fine contemporary blind tooled somber black morocco, covers with scalloped border accented with leaf and dot ornaments, center panel with field of subtly stamped fleurons, volutes, leafy tools, trefoils and circles arranged in the upper and lower halves as mirror images and at center a large and elaborate lozenge combining these elements, raised bands, double ruled spine compartments decorated in style of boards, gilt turn-ins, marbled endpapers, all edges gilt, attractive modern fleece lined folding cloth box with red morocco spine label; pages ruled in red throughout and volume fully engraved, text in fine tiny italic script, with three, six and 12 line initials, tailpieces, full decorative and historiated borders (10 different designs), volvelle (quite often missing) used to find date of Easter; 125 illustrations, as well as portrait of personages of import, the whole executed by John Strutt; ink inscription Geo(rge) Gill his Book / left him by his mother Mary Gill / who departed this life November 6th / 1765 / Aged 49 years", flyleaf inscribed "Thomas Gill Captain in the Royal / Navy Son of George Gill. This book was presented to T. Gill by his father"; corners bit bumped, just breath of wear here and there to leather, occasional minor marginal stains or thumbing, very fine, original binding tight and especially lustrous and engraved contents unusually fresh and clean. Phillip J. Pirages 59 - 34 2011 $3500

Association – Gill, Mary

Church of England. Book of Common Prayer *The Book of Common Prayer... together with The Psalter or Psalms of David.* London: engraved and printed by the Permission of Mr. John Baskett, 1717. 206 x 130mm., xxii, 166 pages, (1) leaf of ads, fine contemporary blind tooled somber black morocco, covers with scalloped border accented with leaf and dot ornaments, center panel with field of subtly stamped fleurons, volutes, leafy tools, trefoils and circles arranged in the upper and lower halves as mirror images; at center a large elaborate lozenge combining elements, raised bands, double ruled spine compartments decorated in style of boards, gilt turn-ins, marbled endpapers, all edges gilt, attractive modern fleece lined folding cloth box with red morocco spine label; pages ruled in red and volume fully engraved, text in fine tiny italic script, with three, six and 12 line initials, tailpieces, full decorative and historiated borders (10 different designs), volvelle (quite often missing) used to find date of Easter; 125 illustrations, as well as portrait of personages of import, the whole executed by John Strutt; ink inscription Geo(rge) Gill his Book / left him by his mother Mary Gill / who departed this life November 6th / 1765 / Aged 49 years", flyleaf inscribed "Thomas Gill Captain in the Royal / Navy Son of George Gill. This book was presented to T. Gill by his father"; corners bit bumped, just breath of wear here and there to leather, occasional minor marginal stains or thumbing, very fine, original binding tight and especially lustrous and engraved contents unusually fresh and clean. Phillip J. Pirages 59 - 34 2011 $3500

Association – Gill, Thomas

Church of England. Book of Common Prayer *The Book of Common Prayer... together with The Psalter or Psalms of David.* London: engraved and printed by the Permission of Mr. John Baskett, 1717. 206 x 130mm., xxii, 166 pages, (1) leaf of ads, fine contemporary blind tooled somber black morocco, covers with scalloped border accented with leaf and dot ornaments, center panel with field of subtly stamped fleurons, volutes, leafy tools, trefoils and circles arranged in the upper and lower halves as mirror images and at center a large and elaborate lozenge combining these elements, raised bands, double ruled spine compartments decorated in style of boards, gilt turn-ins, marbled endpapers, all edges gilt, attractive modern fleece lined folding cloth box with red morocco spine label; pages ruled in red throughout and volume fully engraved, text in fine tiny italic script, with three, six and 12 line initials, tailpieces, full decorative and historiated borders (10 different designs), volvelle (quite often missing) used to find date of Easter; 125 illustrations, as well as portrait of personages of import, the whole executed by John Strutt; ink inscription Geo(rge) Gill his Book / left him by his mother Mary Gill / who departed this life November 6th / 1765 / Aged 49 years", flyleaf inscribed "Thomas Gill Captain in the Royal / Navy Son of George Gill. This book was presented to T. Gill by his father"; corners bit bumped, just breath of wear here and there to leather, occasional minor marginal stains or thumbing, very fine, original binding tight and especially lustrous and engraved contents unusually fresh and clean. Phillip J. Pirages 59 - 34 2011 $3500

Association – Gillet, L.

Sala, George Augustus *Paris Herself Again in 1878-9.* London: Remington & Co., 1879. First edition; 2 volumes, half titles in volume I, frontispiece in volume I, plates and illustrations, original olive green pictorial cloth, blocked in black, largely inoffensive damp marking to back boards, little rubbed, presentation inscription, "Octobre 1879. A Monsieur L. Gillet. Souvenir de sincere amitie J. Leete", good copy. Jarndyce Antiquarian Booksellers CXCI - 577 2011 £150

Association – Gilmour, Caroline

Ayer, A. J. *Part of My Life.* London: Collins, 1977. First edition; 8vo., pages 318, illustrations, signed presentation by author to Lady Caroline Gilmour, very good+, price clipped, very good dust jacket with slight edgewear. Any Amount of Books May 29 2011 - A74370 2011 $298

Association – Gilmour, Ian

Who Was Who. London: Adam & Charles Black, 1966-1991. 9 volumes, 8vo., all very good or better in like dust jackets, first 6 volumes presentation from Roy Jenkins to Ian Gilmour. Any Amount of Books May 26 2011 - A70295 2011 $419

Association – Gilpin, Bernard

Atkinson, George *The Worthies of Westmorland; or Notable Persons Born in the County Since the Reformation.* London: J. Robinson, 1849. First edition; 2 volumes, original blindstamped red cloth, gilt, few marks to boards, pages 320; 360, steel engraved frontispiece (little spotted), joints tender, very good set, volume 2 inscribed By William Fell to Bernard Gilpin, Belle Vue House Ulverstone. R. F. G. Hollett & Son Antiquarian Booksellers 173 - 36 2011 £140

Association – Ginsberg, Allen

Charters, Ann *The Portable Beat Reader.* New York: Viking, 1992. First edition; 600+ pages, fine in fine dust jacket, exceptional copy, this copy belonged to Nelson Lyon, inscribed to him or signed and dated by William Burroughs, Allen Ginsberg, Gregory Corso, Ed Sanders, Michael McClure and Anne Waldman. Ken Lopez Bookseller 154 - 12 2011 $1250

Nahm, Milton C. *Selections from Early Greek Philosophy.* New York: F. S. Crofts, 1945. Second edition, fifth edition; small 8vo., original publisher's cream cloth lettered brown on spine and cover, pages vii, (v) 225, Allen Ginsberg's copy with his name written 3 times on front endpaper twice dated 1955, annotated throughout with short notes in margins, underlinings and marginal linings, covers marked and rubbed, corners and upper spine slightly bumped, inner hinge cracking, otherwise about very good. Any Amount of Books May 26 2011 - A71815 2011 $2013

Association – Glazier, Richard

Coffey, George *Guide to the Celtic Antiquities of the Christian Period Preserved in the National Museum, Dublin, Royal Irish Academy Collection.* Dublin: Hodges, Figgis & Co., 1910. Original cloth, gilt, extremities trifle rubbed, pages ix, 111, 18 plates and 114 text figures, inscribed by Professor W. Boyd Dawkins to Richard Glazier 1917. R. F. G. Hollett & Son Antiquarian Booksellers 177 - 195 2011 £85

Association – Gleason, Joseph

Paget, Violet 1856-1935 *Gospels of Anarchy.* London: T. Fisher Unwin, 1900. Half title, slight spotting in prelims, uncut in original green cloth, blocked and lettered in gilt, little faded, slight rubbing, library labels on following endpapers, Joseph M. Gleason bookplate, top edge gilt, good plus. Jarndyce Antiquarian Booksellers CLXC - 105 2011 £75

Association – Gloucester

Reynard the Fox *The Most Delectable History of Reynard the Fox. (bound with) The Most Pleasant and Delightful History of Reynard the Fox. The Second Part (and) The Shifts of Reynardine the Son of Reynard the Fox...* London: printed by T. Ilive for Edward Brewster, 1701. London: Printed by A. M. and R. R. for Edward Brewster, 1681. London: Printed by T. J. for Edward Brewster and Thomas Passenger, 1684. Early English edition; 3 parts in one, small quarto, (156), (2 table of contents), (2, publisher's ads); (111), (1, publisher's ads); (8), 160 pages, mostly black letter with titles and side notes in roman letter, 62 woodcuts in first part, printed from 39 blocks and 15 woodcuts in second part, five repeated, all repeats from the first part, woodcut on C1 recto (Part I) printed upside down, contemporary sprinkled sheep, covers ruled and decoratively tooled in blind, spine decoratively tooled in gilt in compartments with two red morocco gilt lettering labels, minor restoration to covers, some browning, occasional light dampstaining and soiling, part I with tiny puncture marks in lower blank margin through gathering 1, just touching one letter in imprint of titlepage, 6 small holes in I3 and one tiny hole in I4, causing loss of a couple of letters, Part III with paper flaw in upper blank corner of A3 and A4, tiny tear (quarter inch) in lower blank margin of F4, and paper flaw in lower blank corner of I2, none affecting text, armorial bookplate of Gloucester on front free endpaper, bookplate of Hugh Cecil Lowther, 5th Earl of Lonsdale (1857-1944), (his sale 12 July 1937 lot 445), excellent copy, housed in quarter morocco clamshell box. David Brass Rare Books, Inc. May 26 2011 - 00654 2011 $17,500

Association – Goddard, Donald

Pointer, Larry *Harry Jackson.* New York: Harry N. Abrams, 1981. First edition; large quarto, 308 pages, 397 photo illustrations, light brown cloth lettered in dark brown, very fine, pictorial dust jacket, presentation inscription signed by co-author, Donald Goddard, additionally signed by artist, Harry Jackson. Argonaut Book Shop Recent Acquisitions Summer 2010 - 160 2011 $300

Association – Goddard, Jefry

Addison, Joseph 1672-1719 *The Evidences of the Christian Religion.* Oxford: Clarendon Press, 1809. 165 x 100 mm., 354 pages, very attractive dark green straight grain morocco, handsomely gilt, covers with border of multiple blind rules as well as intricate scrolling gilt cornerpieces, wide raised bands, spine compartments densely gilt cornerpieces, wide raised bands, spine compartments densely gilt with many floral and foliate tools emanating from central flower, all edges gilt, excellent fore-edge painting showing Eton College, front flyleaf with signature of Jefry Goddard dated 1819; joints just slightly rubbed, covers bit marked, isolated very minor foxing, generally in quite attractive condition, binding bright and scarcely worn, text fresh and clean. Phillip J. Pirages 59 - 194 2011 $1100

Association – Godman, F. D.

Goode, G. Brown *The Published Writings of Philip Lutley Sclater 1844-1896.* Washington: GPO, 1896. frontispiece, original dark brown cloth, F. D. Godman bookplate, very good.   Jarndyce Antiquarian Booksellers   CXCI - 341   2011   £75

Association – Godolphin, William

Samerius, Henricus *Sacra Chronologia (a) Mundo Condito ad Christum.* Antwerp: Hieronymum Verdussen, 1608. Folio, (4), 67, (i.e. 65) (1) pages, damage to title leaf with loss of word 'a', 19th century crimson hard grained morocco by Hatton of Manchester, from the library of the Earls of Macclesfield at Shirburn Castle, with Macclesfield arms gilt on upper cover, vertical gilt lettering, gilt edges, manuscript annotations (some extensive), white stains on boards, ex-libris William Godolphin, slightly trimmed, from the library of the Earls of Macclesfield at Shirburn Castle.   Maggs Bros. Ltd.   1440 - 187   2011   £750

Association – Goetschel, Pierre

Tzara, Tristan *Terre sur Terre/ Dessins d'Andre Masson.* Geneva and Paris: Trois Collines, 1946. First edition; 8vo., pages (iv) (blank), (5)-66, (2) blank, (2) contents, (2) blank, 10 illustrations, uncut, original wrappers very slightly rubbed at bottom edge, number 3067 of total print run 3160, inscription from Tzara for Pierre Goetschel.   Simon Finch Rare Books   Zero - 357   2011   £375

Association – Gold, Glen

Sebold, Alice *The Lovely Bones.* Boston: Little Brown, 2002. Stated First edition; signed by author and her husband, Glen Gold, dedicatee, fine in first state dust jacket with no mention of "Main Selection of the Book of the Month Club".   By the Book, L. C.   26 - 15   2011 $150

Association – Gollancz, Victor

Turner, W. J. *Mozart. The Man and His Works.* London: Victor Gollancz, 1938. Uncorrected proof copy; original printed wrappers, edges little stained, pages 391, 16 plates, some edges little dampstained, TLS from Victor Gollancz to Compton MacKenzie loosely inserted.   R. F. G. Hollett & Son Antiquarian Booksellers   175 - 1368   2011   £45

Association – Gooch, Alfred Sherlock

Oliphant, Margaret Oliphant Wilson   1828-1897   *The Days of My Life.* London: Ward, Lock and Co., 1882. New edition; half title, 18 page catalog, some light foxing in prelims, original brown cloth blocked in black and cream, lettered in gilt, armorial bookplate and stamp of Sir Alfred Sherlock Gooch, very good.   Jarndyce Antiquarian Booksellers   CLXC - 617   2011   £60

Oliphant, Margaret Oliphant Wilson   1828-1897   *Magdalen Hepburn; a Story of the Scottish Reformation.* London: Ward Lock and Co., 1882. New edition; half title, 16 page catalog, original brown cloth blocked in black and cream, lettered in gilt, slight rubbed, armorial bookplate and stamp of Sir Alfred Sherlock Gooch, very good.   Jarndyce Antiquarian Booksellers   CLXC - 629   2011   £60

Oliphant, Margaret Oliphant Wilson   1828-1897   *May.* London: Ward, Lock and Co., 1882. New edition; half title, 22 page catalog, original brown cloth, blocked in black and cream, lettered in gilt, armorial bookplate and stamp of Sir Alfred Sherlock Gooch.   Jarndyce Antiquarian Booksellers   CLXC - 637   2011   £60

Association – Goodman, Mark

Sultan, Larry *Evidence.* Greenbrae: Clatworthy Colorvues, 1979. First edition; just about fine copy with ownership signature of Boston photographer Mark Goodman, increasingly uncommon in this condition.   Jeff Hirsch Books   ny 2010 2011 $2250

Association – Goodwin, Thomas

Ray, John *A Collection of English Proverbs Digested into a Convenient Method for the Speedy Finding any One Upon Occasion...* Cambridge: printed by John Hayes, printer to the University for W. Morden, 1678. Title printed in red and black, Hebrew proverbs printed in Hebrew, small hole in title with loss of two letters and part of a third, few headlines shaved, bit browned or stained in places, pages (viii), 414, (1, ads), 8vo., old (not contemporary) calf, red lettering piece, rebacked and recornered, contemporary signature on title of one Thomas Goodwin, five proverbs added in manuscript in a contemporary hand (possibly Goodwin's but much messier that the ownership inscription), sound.   Blackwell Rare Books   B166 - 88   2011   £550

Association – Gordon, Cosmo

Gordon, C. A. *A Concise History of the Antient and Illustrious House of Gordon from the Origin of the Name to the Present Time.* Aberdeen: printed for the author, 1754. 8vo., pages ix (iii) 309, (xi) contemporary crimson sheep, boards double rule gilt bordered with flowerets at corners and in centre black morocco lozenge onlay double rule gilt bordered with flowerets outermost at extremities and 'Scottish Herringbone" design within all gilt, 'Dutch gilt' endpapers, all edges gilt, pale blue and white sewn endbands, early 21st retrospective reback in sheep by Chris Weston, toned and little spotted, old leather bit scratched, ink inscription "Honble Colonel Cosmo Gordon to his friend and relation David Gordon Esre. Abergeldie, further inscriptions signed "Emilia Lucy Gordon/Ivy Lodge August 1873", reverse of loose paper has information about Cosmo Gordon who shot dead a fellow officer, fled abroad for a year then faced a trial at which the jury pronounced him not guilty, from the collection of Christopher Ernest Weston 1947-2010.   Unsworths Booksellers   24 - 103   2011   £500

Association – Gordon, David

Gordon, C. A. *A Concise History of the Antient and Illustrious House of Gordon from the Origin of the Name to the Present Time.* Aberdeen: printed for the author, 1754. 8vo., pages ix (iii) 309, (xi) contemporary crimson sheep, boards double rule gilt bordered with flowerets at corners and in centre black morocco lozenge onlay double rule gilt bordered with flowerets outermost at extremities and 'Scottish Herringbone" design within all gilt, 'Dutch gilt' endpapers, all edges gilt, pale blue and white sewn endbands, early 21st retrospective reback in sheep by Chris Weston, toned and little spotted, old leather bit scratched, ink inscription "Honble Colonel Cosmo Gordon to his friend and relation David Gordon Esre. Abergeldie, further inscriptions signed "Emilia Lucy Gordon/Ivy Lodge August 1873", reverse of loose paper has information about Cosmo Gordon who shot dead a fellow officer, fled abroad for a year then faced a trial at which the jury pronounced him not guilty, from the collection of Christopher Ernest Weston 1947-2010.   Unsworths Booksellers   24 - 103   2011   £500

Association – Gordon, Emilia Lucy

Gordon, C. A. *A Concise History of the Antient and Illustrious House of Gordon from the Origin of the Name to the Present Time.* Aberdeen: printed for the author, 1754. 8vo., pages ix (iii) 309, (xi) contemporary crimson sheep, boards double rule gilt bordered with flowerets at corners and in centre black morocco lozenge onlay double rule gilt bordered with flowerets outermost at extremities and 'Scottish Herringbone" design within all gilt, 'Dutch gilt' endpapers, all edges gilt, pale blue and white sewn endbands, early 21st retrospective reback in sheep by Chris Weston, toned and little spotted, old leather bit scratched, ink inscription "Honble Colonel Cosmo Gordon to his friend and relation David Gordon Esre. Abergeldie, further inscriptions signed "Emilia Lucy Gordon/Ivy Lodge August 1873", reverse of loose paper has information about Cosmo Gordon who shot dead a fellow officer, fled abroad for a year then faced a trial at which the jury pronounced him not guilty, from the collection of Christopher Ernest Weston 1947-2010.   Unsworths Booksellers   24 - 103   2011   £500

Association – Gordon, George

Crabbe, George *Tales.* J. Hatchard, 1812. First edition; presentation copy, inscribed on half title "The very Reverend The Dean of Lincoln with respects of the Author" (almost certainly George Gordon who held that position between 1810 and his death in 1845), also signed "Isabella Staunton 1848", pages (xxiv), 398, (2) (publisher's catalog), 8vo., contemporary mottled calf, binder's ticket of Johnston, Lincoln, neatly rebacked, backstrip with five flat bands with gilt Greek key-style rolls, black morocco label in second compartment, rest with central blind tools, corners neatly restored, marbled endpapers, hinges neatly relined, very good.   Blackwell Rare Books   B166 - 25   2011   £350

Association – Gordon, James

Watts, Isaac *The Psalms of David. (bound with) Hymns and Spiritual Songs.* London: printed by and for J. W. Pasham, 1778. 123 x 70mm., 2 p.l., 240 pages, (10) leaves; 4 p.l., 216 pages, (12) leaves (index leaves for "Hymns an Spiritual Songs" bound out of order but all present), 2 parts in one volume, superb hand painted and gilt decorated vellum by Edwards of Halifax, both covers with very prominent oval paintings, front covers depicting a statue in grisaille of a female figure, probably representing Faith, casting her eyes upward to heaven, one arm aloft, other holding a cross, whole against a sky blue oval, back cover with very dynamic grisaille painting of the Resurrection, with Christ flying upward from the tomb amidst brilliant light, three soldiers beneath shielding themselves in protective wonderment and presiding angel supplying adoration at right, both covers bordered by gilt chain motif, flat spine divided by blue wash bands into compartments featuring gilt lyres and swirling gilt cornerpieces, blue wash label, all edges gilt in original soft green leather slipcase bordered by gilt chain matching that of binding, this in turn housed in modern morocco backed folding box with raised bands and gilt titling, bookplate of James Gordon, Esquire, Moor Place; inscription "Harriot Whitbread/The Gift of John Howard Esq(ui)re/ Cardington/ 1785", similar inscription to Harriot from M. Howard of Cardington dated 1787; blue spine label trifle faded, blue cover background on front board showing little soil, small ink blot on three pages, wonderful binding in very fine condition, text nearly pristine, original slipcase bit worn and faded but remarkable survival.   Phillip J. Pirages   59 - 13   2011 $6900

Association – Gordon, John

Woodhouselee, Alexander Fraser Tytler, Lord   1747-1813   *Plan and Outlines of a Course of Lectures on University History, Ancient and Modern, Delivered in the University of Edinburgh.*   Edinburgh: William Creech, 1782. First edition; small 4to., (iv) 216 (2) (217)-250 pages, full contemporary black calf, gilt ruled covers and spine, gilt stamped spine title, contemporary ink inscription by John Gordon to Christopher Stannard, 1795, fine.   Jeff Weber Rare Books   163 - 50   2011 $850

Association – Gordon, William

Douglas, Robert   *The Peerage of Scotland: containing an Historical and Genealogical Account of the Nobility of that Kingdom.*   Edinburgh: printed by George Ramsay and Co. for Archibald Constable and Co., 1813.   Second edition; 2 volumes, folio, pages xiii, (i), ,759, (i), xiv, 9 engraved plates; iv, 748, xiii, (i), 8 engraved plates, contemporary diced Russia, five flat raised banded spine decorative roll gilt and blind tooled, elaborate symmetrical centerpieces gilt in compartments, lettered and numbered direct in gilt, boards triple rule gilt bordered with decorative roll lozenge in blind, board edges single rule gilt, turn-ins decorative roll gilt, 'French Shell' 'made' endpapers, all edges 'Stormont' marbled, 3 color (fawn, white and blue) symmetrical patterned sewn endbands (toned and foxed in places, rubbed and scratches, spine ends and joints worn and defective in places, board edges sometime renewed in lighter leather, hinges cracked but sound, armorial bookplate of William Gordon Esqr. of Fyvie, signed binding by or produced for A. Brown & Co., with his ticket, from the collection of Christopher Ernest Weston 1947-2010.   Unsworths Booksellers   24 - 88   2011   £400

Association – Gordon-Gilmour, Robert Gordon

The Complete Peerage of England, Scotland, Ireland and the United Kingdom, Extant, Extinct or Dormant.   London: St. Catherine Press Ltd., 1910-1940.   Second edition; 13 volumes in 14, 4to., original publisher's green cloth, gilt ruled and decorated, lettering to spines and front covers, first 9 volumes with armorial bookplate of Robert Gordon Gordon-Gilmour of Liberton & Craigmillar, some variance in cloth color due to intervals of publication and possible fading, top edge gilt, very good, partially unopened.   Any Amount of Books   May 26 2011 - A72190   2011 $1384

Association – Gore, H.

Vergilius Maro, Publius   *Bucolica, Georgica et Aeneis.* Birmingham: John Baskerville, 1757.   First Baskerville edition; glorious copy, 4to., (10), 432 pages, contemporary English or Irish green morocco, gilt floral borders on covers, spine richly gilt with floral and ornamental tools, red morocco lettering piece, fine, beautifully, 18th century engraved bookplate of Thomas Kelly, contemporary signature of Hen. Gore.   Joseph J. Felcone Inc.   Fall Miscellany 2010 - 11   2011 $3800

Association – Gore, Nancy

Farnham, Eliza W.   *My Early Days.*   New York: Thatcher & Hutchinson, 1859.   Small octavo, xi, 13-425 (2 ads) pages, light foxing, original full brown embossed cloth, gilt spine title, almost no sign of wear, inscribed to Nancy Gore from Kate, Eagleswood, NJ 1859, very good plus.   Jeff Weber Rare Books   163 - 163   2011 $75

Association – Gosse, E. W.

Myers, Frederic William Henry *Saint Paul.* London: Macmillan & Co., 1867. First edition; half title, occasional pencil and ink notes, original red cloth by Burn, blocked in black and gilt, slightly rubbed, cloth little lifted in places, label removed from f.e.p., ownership signature of E. W. Gosse, Jan. 1868.   Jarndyce Antiquarian Booksellers   CXCI - 327   2011   £125

Association – Goulding, Ray

Elliott, Bob *Write If You Get Work: the Best of Bob & Ray.* New York: Random House, 1975. First edition; this copy inscribed by Elliott and Ray Goulding to Nelson Lyon, small stain to fore edge and shallow sunning to board edges, near fine in very good, spine sunned dust jacket, mild edgewear, very uncommon signed and nice association as well.   Ken Lopez Bookseller   154 - 50   2011 $300

Association – Goupy, Alexander Paul Ludwig

Orleans, Pierre Joseph De *Histoire des Revolutions D'Angleterre Depuis Le Commencement De La Monarchie.* Paris: Chez Claude Barbin, 1693-1694. First edition; 250 x 193 mm., 3 volumes, splendid and unusual sumptuously gilt early 19th century marbled calf with red morocco spines in the style of Bozerian, covers with gilt borders of two decorative rules and elegant undulating floral vine, flat straight grain morocco spines very handsomely gilt in compartments with pointille ground and central circlet from which radiate four lillies and four leaves on twining stems, turn-ins gilt with plain and decorative rolls, marbled endpapers, all edges gilt, engraved head and tailpieces and 8 engraved portraits, verso of front free endpaper with bookplate of Baron de Mackau, titlepage with ink ownership inscription of Alexander Paul Ludwig Goupy? in contemporary hand; isolated gatherings with variable browning (small handfull rather browned), one leaf in first volume with expert early repair of four inch tear (letters of four words partly obscured or displaced, and text and facing page somewhat discolored), few additional trivial imperfections internally, but text generally quite fresh and clean, one joint with five small wormholes, few hardly noticeable, shallow scratches to covers hint of wear to extremities, lovely bindings in fine condition, lustrous leather and gilt with only minor wear, with their very considerable original visual appeal entirely intact.   Phillip J. Pirages   59 - 14   2011 $2250

Association – Graham, W. M.

Hawthorne, Nathaniel 1804-1864 *Transformation or the Romance of Monte Beni.* London: Smith, Elder & Co., 1860. Third edition; 3 volumes, slight spotting to prelims, contemporary grained tan calf, gilt borders, raised bands, gilt spine, brown and green morocco labels, booklabels of W. M. Graham, signature of A. Sutherland in volume I, very good.   Jarndyce Antiquarian Booksellers   CXCI - 526   2011   £175

Association – Granard, Countess of

Scott, Walter 1771-1832   *The Works of.* Edinburgh: 1806. 5 volumes, large paper set presented to the Countess of Granard, Mullen's binding is morocco, a gilt tooled red spine, somewhat dull, boards black and red corners, plain but for three line panelling, three edges gilded with typical Mullen tooled panel top, bottom and fore-edge.   C. P. Hyland   May 26 2011 - 258   2011 $644

Association – Grant, Brian

Megarry, R. E.   *Miscellany-At-Law.*   London: Stevens & Sons, 1955. First edition; original cloth, pages xvi, 415, patterned endpapers, presentation copy inscribed by author for (Judge) Brian Grant.   R. F. G. Hollett & Son Antiquarian Booksellers   175 - 927   2011   £45

Megarry, R. E.   *A Second Miscellany at Law.*   Stevens & Sons, 1973. Original cloth, dust jacket little worn and faded, pages xviii, 420, patterned endpapers with design by Edward Bawden, presentation copy inscribed by author for Judge Brian Grant.   R. F. G. Hollett & Son Antiquarian Booksellers   General Catalogue Summer 2010 - 1189   2011   £45

Association – Grant, James Augustus

Oliver, Daniel   *Flora of Tropical Africa.*   London: L. Reeve, 1868. First edition; 8vo., xiv, sli, 479, original green cloth, spine rubbed, ALS tipped into front pastedown, this is volume 1 of 10 and was presented to Col. James Augustus Grant by HM Office of Works and has been endorsed by him, letter also signed by Grant acknowledging receipt of book.   J. & S. L. Bonham Antiquarian Booksellers   Africa 4/20/2011 - 6976   2011   £150

Association – Greco, Emilio

Pirovano, Carlo   *The Graphics of Emilio Greco.* N.P.: Venice: Electa Editrice, 1975. First English edition; folio, original publisher's green cloth lettered gilt on spine and cover, signed presentation from artist, Greco, to Australian art expert Robert Haines, slight rubbing, slight sun fading, otherwise sound, clean, very good.   Any Amount of Books   May 26 2011 - A76883   2011 $503

Association – Green, J.

Newton, Thomas *Dissertations on the Prophecies, Which have Been Remarkably Fulfilled and are at this Time fulfilling in the World.* London: printed for J. and R. Tonson and S. Draper, 1754-1758. First edition; Volume First(- the Third, and Last), presentation copy, few spots and minor stains, pages (xxvii), 498, (1); (xxiv), xx, 451; (xxiv), 429, (34), 8vo., contemporary sprinkled calf, double gilt fillet borders on sides, spines richly gilt in compartments with twin lettering pieces, spines darkened, three of the labels defective or missing, slightly worn at extremities, volumes I and II inscribed "J. Green from the Author", sound.   Blackwell Rare Books   B166 - 73   2011   £500

Association – Green, Samuel

Clark, Henry G. *Outlines of a Plan for a Free City Hospital.* Boston: printed by George C. Rand & Avery, 1860. First edition, one of presumably small number of copies sent out for review and comment; 8vo., 18 pages, original stiff printed paper wrappers, beginning to split along spine, text illustration, this copy interleaved with blank sheets, 2 plates before title, interior tear on title, without loss, stamp of Harvard Medical School Library with neat pencilled note dated March 29 1860 "Gift of Samuel A. Green, M.D. of Boston (Class of 1851), very good, tipped in small leaflet.   M & S Rare Books, Inc.   90 - 47   2011 $275

Association – Greenhill, Mildred

Stevenson, Robert Louis Balfour 1850-1894 *Treasure Island.* London: Cassell & Co., 1883. First edition, first issue; frontispiece printed in three colors, with tissue guard, original olive green diagonal fine ribbed cloth with covers ruled in blind and spine ruled and lettered in gilt, original black coated endpapers, absolute minimum of wear to corners and extremities, rear hinge expertly and almost invisibly repaired, some very occasional browning and soiling, previous owner's neat ink inscription, exceptionally fresh, bright and fine, chemised in quarter green morocco slipcase, the Bradley Martin copy, bookplate of Mildred Greenhill on front pastedown, in this copy the "7" in the pagination on page 127 has been hand stamped in larger font and darker ink, and, as with other copies of the first issue, the "8" is not present in the pagination on page 83 (copies are known with the "8" present on page 83 and with the "7" missing from pagination on page 127),.   David Brass Rare Books, Inc.   May 26 2011 - 00036   2011 $32,500

Association – Greenwood, Brian

Hudleston, C. Roy *Cumberland Families and Heraldry with a Supplement...* Kendal: Titus Wilson, 1978. Signed limited deluxe edition (no. 13 of 50 copies); original full crimson calf gilt, arms in gilt on boards, pages vi, 429, frontispiece and 5 pages of illustrations, Whittington Hall copy with bookplate of Brian and Enid Greenwood.   R. F. G. Hollett & Son Antiquarian Booksellers   173 - 580   2011   £150

Association – Greenwood, Enid

Hudleston, C. Roy *Cumberland Families and Heraldry with a Supplement...* Kendal: Titus Wilson, 1978. Signed limited deluxe edition (no. 13 of 50 copies); original full crimson calf gilt, arms in gilt on boards, pages vi, 429, frontispiece and 5 pages of illustrations, Whittington Hall copy with bookplate of Brian and Enid Greenwood.   R. F. G. Hollett & Son Antiquarian Booksellers   173 - 580   2011   £150

Association – Greer, Robert

A Dozen on Denver. Gulden: Fulcrum, 2009. First edition; fine, signed by Connie Willis, Nick Arvin, Robert Greer, Margaret Coel, Manuel Ramos and Arnold Grossman.   Bella Luna Books   May 29 2011 - p3633   2011 $104

Association – Greer, Thomas

Lister, Maria Theresa *Dacre; a Novel.* London: Longman, 1834. First edition; 3 volumes, contemporary half calf, spines with gilt raised bands, dark green leather labels, armorial bookplates of Thomas Greer with family motto "Memor Est", very good.   Jarndyce Antiquarian Booksellers   CLXC - 159   2011   £320

Association – Gresley, Madeline

Longfellow, Henry Wadsworth 1807-1882 *The Poetical Works of H. W. Longfellow.* London: T. Nelson & Sons, 1867. Photographic frontispiece, original full maroon morocco, heavily blocked in blind lettered in gilt on boards and spine, spines slightly rubbed, embossed stamp on leading f.e.p., inscription from Madeline Gresley to Lord Henry, all edges gilt, very good.   Jarndyce Antiquarian Booksellers   CXCI - 441   2011   £60

Association – Gretton, John

Hall, Hubert *Court Life Under the Plantaginets (Reign of Henry the Second).* London: Swan Sonnenschein & Co., 1890. Original pictorial cloth, gilt, extremities minimally rubbed, pages 271, with 5 colored plates, many tinted plates and line drawings, armorial bookplate of John Gretton of Stapleford.   R. F. G. Hollett & Son Antiquarian Booksellers   175 - 571   2011   £30

Association – Griffin, Caroline

Sigourney, Lydia *Sketches.* Philadelphia: Key & Biddle, 1834. First edition; 8vo., pages 216, little toning to titlepage, some light foxing to endpaper, little soiling to cover, nick to spine, very good, inscribed by author for Caroline Griffin, brown cloth, page 146 correctly paged.   Second Life Books Inc.   174 - 289   2011 $600

Association – Griffiths, Caroline

Martineau, Harriet 1802-1876 *Forest and Game Law Tales.* London: Edward Moxon, 1845-1846. First edition; 3 volumes, original olive green vertical grained cloth, floral borders in blind, spines lettered in gilt, pale yellow endpapers, spines uniformly faded to brown tale of volume I, slightly rubbed, each volume with signature of Caroline Griffiths, in one place dated 1852, very good, tight. Jarndyce Antiquarian Booksellers   CLXC - 280 2011 £600

Association – Griffiths, Richard

Oliver, George *Signs and Symbols Illustrated and Explained in a Course of Twelve Lectures on Free Masonry.* Grimsby: printed for the author by Br. Skelton, 1826. First edition; contemporary half calf gilt by Anthony Birdsall of Northampton (with his label), masonic emblem to spine compartments, double spine labels and Spanish marbled boards, extremities little rubbed, pages lx, 248, text illustrations, slight spotting to few leaves, but excellent copy, with ownership inscriptions of Richard Griffiths, architect and William Smith, both of Northampton, 2 small press cuttings relating to death of latter's unmarried daughter in Northampton are tipped to pastedown, S. S. Birdsall of Pomfret Lodge Northampton was a subscriber, rare.   R. F. G. Hollett & Son Antiquarian Booksellers   175 - 1020 2011 £350

Association – Grimaldi, Giovanni Battista

Guevara, Antonio De *Vita Di M. Avrelio Imperadore.* Venice: Bartolomeo Imperador and Francesco Veneziano, 1543. 160 x 103mm., 8 p.l., 132, (2) leaves, fine contemporary Roman red morocco Apollo and Pegasus medallion binding done for Giovanni Battista Grimaldi by Marc Antonio Guillery, (genuine Apollo and Pegasus binding) covers with gilt frame formed by two widely spaced fillets with lobes interlaced at ends and sides, space between fillets decorated with broad foliate curls, small floral tools, inner pane of each board with gilt titling above a horizontal oval Apollo and Pegasus plaquette centerpiece showing Pegasus atop black painted heights of Parnassus and Apollo racing his chariot (drawn by two straining steeds) across steep terrain with reins and whip held aloft and caps fluttering behind, plaquette with gilt motto in Greek in the collar above and below vignette, spine (very expertly rebacked) with four thin and three thick raised bands decorated with gilt rope pattern or plain rules (this being original backstrip?), newer (perhaps 19th century) endpapers, all edges gilt (apparently some remarkably skillful restoration at one or more corners and edges, perhaps some gold added, as well as to the chariot part of the plaquettes); woodcut printer's device on , morocco bookplate and separate gilt monogram of Robert Hoe as well as inscription and vellum bookplate of Swedish collector Thore Virgin, ownership inscription of J. T. Payne dated 1850; covers with half dozen insignificant tiny dark spots, titlepage faintly soiled, thin light brown stain just at top edge of leaves, small wormhole at upper inner margin (text not affected), occasional minor stains, other trivial imperfections, but no defects that are even remotely serious and in general really excellent specimen of a very special binding, text fresh and leather quite lustrous; also from the collection of bibliophile Johannes Gennadius, Liverpool oculist T. Shadford Walker and Swedish collector Rolfe Wistrand. Phillip J. Pirages   59 - 2 2011 $35,000

Association – Grimm, Jacob

Grimm, The Brothers *German Popular Stories.* London & Dublin: James Robins and Joseph Robins, volume i dated, 1827. (first issue was 1823) and volume 2 is 1826; 2 volumes, (i-vi) v-xii (1), 2-240, (i-iii) iv (1), 2-256 (2) page, (1 page ads), original pink boards and green cloth spines, boards rubbed, cloth split at joints and at intervals on spine, labels chipped and rubbed, some foxing, 1 plate in volume I trimmed in margins really overall clean, tight and very good, 22 etched plates by George Cruikshank, laid in is one page handwritten ALS by Jacob Grimm written to Mrs. Austin. Aleph-Bet Books, Inc.   95 - 266 2011 $5000

Association – Grimston, Charlotte Mary

Martineau, Harriet 1802-1876 *The Crofton Boys.* Addey & Co., 1854. Second edition; half title, frontispiece, original olive green cloth by Bone & Son, blocked in blind, spine lettered in gilt, spine faded and bit worn at head and tail, front board slightly damp marked, little loose, ownership inscription to Charlotte Mary Grimston 1854, good sound copy.   Jarndyce Antiquarian Booksellers   CLXC - 333   2011   £50

Association – Grossman, Arnold

A Dozen on Denver. Gulden: Fulcrum, 2009. First edition; fine, signed by Connie Willis, Nick Arvin, Robert Greer, Margaret Coel, Manuel Ramos and Arnold Grossman.   Bella Luna Books   May 29 2011 - p3633   2011 $104

Association – Guest, Edgar

Combe, William 1742-1823 *The Tour of Doctor Syntax.* London: George Routledge & Sons Ltd. n.d., Ninth edition; 3 volumes, very good, cloth worn at edges, original boards with new spine, corners rubbed, else clean and tight, 80 plates in all, with tissue guards, in very good condition, bookplates of Edgar Guest.   G. H. Mott Bookseller   May 26 2011 - 43629   2011 $500

Association – Guest, Lydia

Kingscote, Adeline Georgina *Tales of the Sun; or Folklore of Southern India.* London: W. H. Allen & Co. and at Calcutta, 1890. First edition; half title, some slight careless opening, original blue cloth, front board pictorially blocked and lettered in olive green and brown, spine lettered gilt, bit dulled, leading inner hinges slightly cracked, spine darkened, slightly rubbed, presented to Lydia H. Guest on half title.   Jarndyce Antiquarian Booksellers   CLXC - 57   2011   £45

Association – Guettard, Jean Estienne

Axtius, Johann Conrad *Tractatus de Arboribus Coniferis et Pice Conficienda.* Jena: Samuel Krebs for Joann Bielcken, 1679. 16mo., engraved titlepage and 5 plates, 16mo., pages (2), 131, contemporary full mottled calf, corners worn, covers scuffed, some losses to spine, institutional handstamp on a blank, old notations on blanks, occasional foxing, ownership signature of Jean Estienne Guettard, geologist.   Raymond M. Sutton, Jr.   May 26 2011 - 28947   2011 $2000

Association – Guillebaud, Miss

More, Hannah 1745-1833 *Coelebs in Search of a Wife.* London: T. Cadell and W. Daives, 1813. 1810. Fourteenth and thirteenth edition; 2 volumes, expertly and sympathetically rebound in half tan calf, gilt spines, red leather labels, very good, presentation from author to Miss Guillebaud, signatures of Mrs. W. Baynton, 3 Clifton Vale.   Jarndyce Antiquarian Booksellers   CLXC - 522   2011   £450

Association – Gunn, Samuel McCraw

United States. Continental Congress - 1777 *Journals of Congress. Containing the Proceedings in the Year 1776 Published by Order of Congress. Volume II.* Philadelphia: R. Aitken, 1777. First edition; (2), 513 (22) pages, modern full mottled sheepskin, superbly executed in exact facsimile of original binding, spine with red morocco title label and "1776" tooled on black oval onlay, some internal dampstaining and browning particularly toward end of text, else very handsome volume, signature of Samuel McCraw Gunn, dated 1822 on titlepage, enclosed in four flap chemise and morocco backed slipcase.   Joseph J. Felcone Inc.   Fall Miscellany 2010 - 120   2011 $20,000

Association – Guy, T.

The Lady's Monthly Museum; or Polite Repository of Amusement and Instruction. London: Vernor, Hood & Sharpe, 1806-1807. 2 volumes, engraved plates, owner's signatures cut from margins of leading f.e.p.'s, contemporary half speckled calf, horizontal gilt rules, black leather labels, good plus, signature of Tho. Guy.   Jarndyce Antiquarian Booksellers   CLXC - 64   2011   £150

Association – Hader, Leoto

Hader, Berta *Jamaica Johnny.* New York: Macmillan, Oct., 1935. First edition; 4to., green pictorial cloth, fine in slightly worn dust jacket, full page color illustrations, with small watercolor drawing, inscription to Elmer's sister Leoto (her book).   Aleph-Bet Books, Inc.   95 - 274   2011 $750

Association – Hague, Michael

Baum, Lyman Frank *The Wizard of Oz.* New York: Holt Rinehart and Winston, 1982. Numerically stated first printing; 4to., full color pictorial boards, matching full color pictorial dust jacket, as new copy, drawing signed in full by artist, Michael Hague, color illustrations, 292 numbered pages.   Jo Ann Reisler, Ltd.   86 - 126   2011 $300

Dodgson, Charles Lutwidge 1832-1898 *Alice's Adventures in Wonderland.* New York: Holt, Rinehart and Winston, 1985. Numerically stated first printing; 4to., cloth backed boards with silver lettering on spine, full color pictorial dust jacket, as new, signed in full drawing by artist, Michael Hague on dedication page, 122 numbered pages with lots of full color illustrations.   Jo Ann Reisler, Ltd.   86 - 130 2011 $300

Association – Haines, Joseph

Contes et Legendes Des Nations Aliees. Paris: H. Piazza, 1917. One of 1000 copies signed by Edmund Dulac; 305 x 241mm., (2 p.l., 149. (3) pages, lovely burgundy morocco by Root and son (signed on rear turn-in), covers framed in gilt with triple fillet border, multiple fillet inner panel with foliate cornerpieces facing outwards, raised bands, spine gilt in compartments formed by concentric plain and stippled rules and featuring ivy leaf cornerpieces, titling compartments with single rule frame and foliate curl cornerpieces, wide gilt ruled turn-ins with ivy leaf cornerpieces, marbled endpapers, top edges gilt, other edges rough trimmed, original paper covers bound in at back, decorative initials, decorative head and tailpieces for all text leaves, decorative and illustrated title and 15 color plates by Dulac (each laid down within ornamental printed frame with captioned tissue guard), bookplate of Joseph H. Haines; printed in green and black throughout (original wrappers printed in blue and black), very small stain in one fore margin, otherwise mint in unworn, very bright and appealing decorative binding.   Phillip J. Pirages   59 - 185 2011 $1750

La Princesse Badourah; Conte Des Mille et Une Nuits. Paris: H. Piazza, 1914. One of 500 copies, signed by Edmund Dulac; 305 x 241mm., 2 p.l. (5)-114 (3) pages, very fine brown crushed morocco by Root and Son (signed on rear turn-in), covers bordered in gilt with French fillet, central panel formed by single rule with foliate branch on stippled ground in each corner of panel raised bands, spine gilt in compartments formed by double rules foliate cornerpieces on stippled ground forming a lobed frame for a floral tool centerpiece, very wide inner gilt dentelles featuring two decorative rolls, each between rules, marbled endpapers, top edge gilt, other edges rough trimmed, original tan front wrapper printed in gilt, blue and white bound in before half title, decorative initials, leaves and decorative border, decorated titlepage and 10 color plates by Edmund Dulac (each laid down with an ornamental frame and with captioned tissue guard), front pastedown with bookplate of Joseph H. Haines, titlepage printed in gilt, muted yellow and blue and leaves throughout in yellow and black, virtually mint, esecially bright inside and out.   Phillip J. Pirages   59 - 186 2011 $1600

Association – Haines, Robert

Pirovano, Carlo *The Graphics of Emilio Greco.* N.P.: Venice: Electa Editrice, 1975. First English edition; folio, original publisher's green cloth lettered gilt on spine and cover, signed presentation from artist, Greco, to Australian art expert Robert Haines, slight rubbing, slight sun fading, otherwise sound, clean, very good.   Any Amount of Books May 26 2011 - A76883 2011 $503

Association – Hall, Anna Maria

Wright, G. N. *Ireland Illustrated from Original Drawings by G. Petrie, W. H. Bartlett & T. M. Baynes.* 1831. First edition; 80 views on 40 plates, rice guards on all plates, still some foxing, owner inscribed by Anna Maria Hall, St. Ives, Cornwall, Feb. 1812, full mottled calf, worn.   C. P. Hyland May 26 2011 - 259/519 2011 $507

Association – Hall, Arthur

Manning, Anne *Family Pictures.* London: Arthur Hall, Virtue & Co., 1861. First edition; half title, 24 page catalog (May 1860), original mauve cloth by Westleys, slightly rubbed and discolored, inner hinges cracking, working copy, c. 1900, belonging to publisher Arthur Hall with his notes and revisions.   Jarndyce Antiquarian Booksellers   CLXC - 210 2011   £250

Association – Hall, B. Fairfax

Fielding, Henry 1707-1754 *An Apology for the Life of Mrs. Shamela Andrews.* Waltham St. Lawrence: Golden Cockerel Press, 1926. 102/450 copies; printed on Batchelor handmade paper, foolscap 8vo., pages (xi), 80, (1), original quarter white cloth, backstrip gilt lettered, brown boards, untrimmed, fine, bookticket of B. Fairfax Hall.   Blackwell Rare Books   B166 - 258 2011   £35

Association – Hall, Bryan

Brooke, Ralph *A Discoverie of Certaine Errours Published in Print in Much Commended Britannia 1594 to which is added The Learned Mr. Camden's Answer to His Book and Mr. Brooke's Reply (and) A Second Discoverie of Errours.* Woodman & Lyon, 1724. First edition; main titlepage and titlepage to "A Discoverie" printed red and black, titlepage to "A Second Discoverie" printed black, both subsidiary titlepages printed by Woodman and dated 1723, vi, plate (7) 77 (10) 32 196 pages, contemporary calf, 4to., 230 x 170mm., generous margins (large paper?), bookplates of two Norfolk antiquaries, Francis Blomefield & Bryan Hall, very.   C. P. Hyland   May 26 2011 - 786 2011 $544

Burgess, George *Reflections on the Nature and Tendency of the Present Spirit of the Times, in a Letter to the Freeholders of the County of Norfolk.* (bound with) *Reflections on the Nature and Tendency of the Present Spirit of the Times.* Norwich: printed and sold by Burks and Kinnebrook, 1819. Second edition and first edition respectively; 8vo., iv, 362, (2) pages, including final errata leaf; 8vo., viii, 341, (1) pages, errata on verso of final leaf, minor foxing and paper browning, else very good, from the library of Bryan William James Hall (of Bonningham) with his armorial bookplate. John Drury Rare Books 153 - 25 2011 £325

Coke, Henry J. *Tracks of a Rolling Stone.* London: Smith, Elder & Co., 1905. First edition; 8vo., original publisher's red buckram lettered gilt, pages 349, frontispiece, uncut, highly uncommon, bright, very good+, faint marks to cover, very slight foxing to text, neat ownership signature of Bryan Hall of Banningham Hall, Norfolk, heraldic bookplate of one Albermarle Cator. Any Amount of Books May 29 2011 - B21525 2011 $340

Association – Hall, H.

Drake, Daniel *Natural and Statistical View or Picture of Cincinnati and the Miami Country.* Cincinnati: Looker and Wallace, 1815. First edition; 2 engraved folding maps (foxed, tear to inside lower corner of each map), 12mo., pages xii, (13)-251, (4), contemporary tree calf, few old abrasions, clear sealant reinforces outer hinges, bookplate removed, browning and soiling to endpapers, 2 old pictures pasted on front blank pages, pages tanned, some foxing to back pages, old clipping glued to rear pastedown, the copy of J. Burgoyne Jr. dated 1855, and H. Hall, Cincinnati with his red stamp. Raymond M. Sutton, Jr. May 26 2011 - 55852 2011 $1350

Association – Hall, James

Naked Came the Manatee. New York: Putnam, 1996. First edition; fine in fine dust jacket, signed by all authors on single tipped in leaf, including Carl Hiaasen, Elmore Leonard, John Dufresne, Dave Barry, Vicki Hendricks, Edna Buchanan, Les Standiford and James W. Hall, etc. Ken Lopez Bookseller 154 - 5 2011 $200

Association – Hall, Margot

Thurber, James *The Beast in Me and Other Animals: a New Collection of Pieces and Drawings About Human Beings and Less Alarming Creatures.* New York: Harcourt Brace and Co., 1948. First edition; 8vo., original green cloth lettered black on spine, pages xi, 340, illustrations, signed presentation by author for Margot Hall, slightly bumped, very slight fading and slight shelfwear, else sound, clean, very good. Any Amount of Books May 26 2011 - A69301 2011 $461

Association – Hall, Marie

Drake, Stillman *Galileo: Pioneer Scientist.* Toronto: University of Toronto Press, 1990. First edition; 8vo., xviii, 261 pages, fine in fine dust jacket, with ANS laid in, book and letter both inscribed to noted British historians of science Rupert and Marie Hall. By the Book, L. C. 26 - 97 2011 $225

Association – Hall, Rupert

Drake, Stillman *Galileo: Pioneer Scientist.* Toronto: University of Toronto Press, 1990. First edition; 8vo., xviii, 261 pages, fine in fine dust jacket, with ANS laid in, book and letter both inscribed to noted British historians of science Rupert and Marie Hall. By the Book, L. C. 26 - 97 2011 $225

Association – Hallows, Anne

Sharp, John *Fifteen Sermons Preached on Several Occasions by... John Lord Arch Bishop of York.* London: printed for Walter Kettilby, 1709. Third edition; 8vo., pages (vi) 472 + engraved frontispiece, contemporary crimson turkey, spine gilt panelled with saltired compartments, lettered direct in gilt, boards panelled in gilt, board edges decorative roll gilt, turn-ins decorative roll gilt, 'Dutch-comb' 'made' endpapers, all edges gilt, blue and white sewn endbands, light spotting, occasional dampmark in lower margin, tidy repairs to headcap with new matching endband, black leather gilt decorative roll bordered label "To Mrs./E.B." ink inscription "Eliz. Battell/Juner", in different hand "The Gift of my Good Aunt Mrs. Eliz Battell to me Anne Hallows junr. May ye 26 1728", in same hand "Anne Leicester", ink inscription "John Roberts No 2 May 14 1792", from the collection of Christopher Ernest Weston 1947-2010. Unsworths Booksellers 24 - 40 2011 £200

Association – Hamer, Samuel

Booth, William *The Trial at Large of William Booth and His Associates, George Scot the Three Yates's, John Barrows and Elizabeth Childow for Forgery Coining &c. at the Stafford Summer Assizes 1812 before Mr. Justice Le Blanc.* Wolverhampton: printed and sold by Gower and Smart, 1812. First edition; 8vo., 46 pages, well bound by Morrell, ca. 1900 in half calf over marbled boards, spine lettered in gilt, upper joint and head of spine worn, very good, early 20th century bookplate of numismatist, Samuel Hamer and ms. note in his hand. John Drury Rare Books 153 - 150 2011 £475

Association – Hamilton, George Heard

Duchamp, Marcel *From the Green Box.* New Haven: Readymade Press, 1957. first edition, signed, 400 copies printed; 8vo., pages (62), crisp and clean copy, original black boards patterned with white strips of paper reproducing author's handwriting, some light shelf wear, light offsetting to endpapers, original stone-grey and black dust jacket, couple of nicks along top edge but otherwise extremely well kept, signed by Duchamp and translator George Heard Hamilton dated 1958, near fine. Simon Finch Rare Books Zero - 213 2011   £950

Association – Hamilton, William Rowan

Tennyson, Alfred Tennyson, 1st Baron 1809-1892 *Poems, Chiefly Lyrical.* London: Effingham Wilson, 1830. First edition; 191 x 114mm., 2 p.l., 154 pages, (1) leaf ads), original brown paper boards, flat spine with paper label, buckram chemise and contained in quarter morocco slipcase with raised bands, gilt titling, morocco bookplate of "Blairhame" (used by Natalie K. (Mrs. J. Insley) Blair 1887-1952), the "Blairhame" referring to her magnificent Tudor style home in Tuxedo Park NY, titlepage with 19th century ink presentation inscription "William Rowan Hamilton from Francis Beaufort Edgeworth"; joints with thin cracks, backstrip and label little torn and soiled, extremities with expected wear, leaves bit foxed and soiled, but surprisingly well preserved, nevertheless quite solid, covers very clean and text still fresh. Phillip J. Pirages 59 - 332 2011 $1250

Association – Hammond, H. E.

Martineau, Harriet 1802-1876 *Deerbrook.* London: Edward Moxon, 1839. First edition; 3 volumes, contemporary half dark blue calf, spines gilt in compartments, marbled boards, boards bit rubbed, volume 1 signed H. E. Hammond in contemporary hand. Jarndyce Antiquarian Booksellers CLXC - 273 2011   £450

Association – Hammond, Henry

Stafford, Magdalen *The Romance and Its Hero.* London: Bell & Daldy, 1859. 2 volumes, 12mo., 2 pages ads, volumes I and II, original yellow stiff cloth wrappers, blocked in black and red on front, lettered in black on spine, little dulled and marked, booklabels of Henry L. Hammond. Jarndyce Antiquarian Booksellers CXCI - 497 2011   £125

Association – Hannen, James

Nichols, Francis Morgan *Britton: The French Text...* Oxford: Clarendon Press, 1865. First editions; 2 volumes, tall 8vo., original publisher's russet brown cloth lettered gilt at spine, pages lxiv, 419 & 398; bookplate of Sir James Hannen, pencilled ownership signature of historian F. R. Cowell, covers somewhat soiled and marked with staining at spine, otherwise about very good- with very sound, clean text. Any Amount of Books   May 29 2011 - A45886 2011 $272

Association – Harbin, Charles

Gosse, Philip Henry *Land and Sea.* London: James Nisbet, 1865. First edition; 15 woodcuts, 10 page catalog + 16 page catalog, slight foxing in prelims, original purple fine pebble grained cloth, bevelled boards, gilt spine slightly dulled, all edges gilt, very good, inscription for Charles Harbin from his wife. Jarndyce Antiquarian Booksellers CXCI - 330 2011   £125

Association – Hardey, C. J.

Burnet, Gilbert, Bp. of Salisbury 1643-1715 *An Exposition of the Thirty-nine Articles of the Church of England.* London: printed for Ri. Chiswell, 1705. Third edition; contemporary vellum, spine blind ruled, 19th century dark red lettering piece gilt, boards panelled in blind with large open central lozenge centre piece, pink and white sewn endbands, little spotting in places, vellum soiled, slight cracking at joint ends, ink inscription "C. J. Hardey/May 18th 1838", is lightly scored out in ink in favour of "Robt. Hardey Hull 1840", from the collection of Christopher Ernest Weston 1947-2010. Unsworths Booksellers 24 - 16 2011 £150

Association – Hardey, Robert

Burnet, Gilbert, Bp. of Salisbury 1643-1715 *An Exposition of the Thirty-nine Articles of the Church of England.* London: printed for Ri. Chiswell, 1705. Third edition; contemporary vellum, spine blind ruled, 19th century dark red lettering piece gilt, boards panelled in blind with large open central lozenge centre piece, pink and white sewn endbands, little spotting in places, vellum soiled, slight cracking at joint ends, ink inscription "C. J. Hardey/May 18th 1838", is lightly scored out in ink in favour of "Robt. Hardey Hull 1840", from the collection of Christopher Ernest Weston 1947-2010. Unsworths Booksellers 24 - 16 2011 £150

Association – Hardy, Alister Clavering

Marine Biological Association of the United Kingdom *Journal of...* Plymouth/Cambridge: Marine Biological Association of the United Kingdom/Cambridge University Press, 1887-2006. First editions and reprint; Old Series Volumes 1 and 2 (of 2) and New Series Volumes 1-84 (complete), volume 85 (Nos. 1, 2, 3, 6) and Volume 86 (nos.1-3) in 112; very good, numerous plates, text figures and some photos, occasional minor soiling, few short tears along folds and tear along fold of a panel in 1, few tears repaired with tape, tall 8vo., some 4to., volumes 1/2, 1-3, 5 an 12-21 contemporary hardbound, volumes, 4, 6-11 and 22-48 recent hardbound, original wrappers bound into volumes 6-11 & 22-48, volumes 49-68 in original printed wrappers, volumes 69-86 paperbound (modest wear to extremities in 6 oldest volumes, spine faded to brown in 3 older volumes and with splitting to cover along edges of spine in 2, some endpapers browned, handstamp to front wrappers and or front endpapers contents and index pages are photocopies in volumes 6 and 10, plates are photocopies in volume 7, occasional tear to soiling to original wrappers or text pages, some pencil notations to text pages, in early issues, occasional bump, short tear or wrinkling to paper on spine, light soiling or pages tanned, recent issues mostly fine; with W(alter) Garstang's signature and handstamp to 3 volumes, A(lister) C(lavering) Hardy's signature to 24 volumes, Lesley D. Wright-Smith's copy with his name on title, numerous dates and some notes on page margins. Raymond M. Sutton, Jr. May 26 2011 - 48790 2011 $2400

Association – Hardy, T. J.

Nielsen, Frederik *The History of the Papacy in the XIXth Century.* London: John Murray, 1906. First edition; bookplate of T. J. Hardy and of St. Mary's House Library (partly removed) on each pastedown, 2 volumes, thick 8vo., original cloth, gilt, little marked, extremities slightly frayed in places, pages xiii, 379; 483, endpapers little spotted. R. F. G. Hollett & Son Antiquarian Booksellers 175 - 1004 2011 £75

Association – Hargreaves, Jonathan

Godwin, William 1756-1836 *Of Population. An Enquiry Concerning the Power of Increase in the Numbers of Mankind...* London: printed for Longman, Hurst, Rees, Orme and Brown, 1820. First edition; 235 x 152, xvi, (17)-22, 626 page, publisher's original temporary brown paper boards, paper label, edges untrimmed, text unopened (except for the introduction), folding cloth box with morocco spine label, old armorial bookplate of Jonathan Hargreaves and modern bookplate of John Yudkin; backstrip chipped at head (costing perhaps a square inch of paper), vertical crack at top reaching two-thirds of the way down the spine, loss of paper along half the length of joints (and with short cracks in joints), slight rubbing to corners (as usual), but binding still solid and otherwise well preserved, covers unusually clean, one opening of preface with noticeable ink staining in upper margin, minor foxing and marginal tears, but exceptionally clean and well preserved internally, unopened text obviously unread. Phillip J. Pirages 59 - 217 2011 $3900

Association – Harrap, George

Goldsmith, Oliver 1730-1774 *The Vicar of Wakefield.* London: Harrap, 1929. First Rackham edition, 4/775 copies signed by artist; 12 color printed plates and other illustrations in text, all by Arthur Rackham, title and Rackham design on titlepage printed in red, prelim leaves foxed, one leaf little creased, pages 232, 4to., original cream parchment, lettering and design on backstrip and lettering on front covers within double rule border, all blocked in gilt, endpapers with designs in green by Rackham, top edge gilt, others untrimmed, board slipcase from The Compleat Angler with printed label to that affect, very good, publisher George Harrap's copy with his bookplate, beneath statement of limitation is pen and ink drawing by Rackham, drawn for Harrap. Blackwell Rare Books B166 - 224 2011 £10,000

Association – Harris, Hank

Morley, Christopher *Mince Pie.* New York: G. H. Doran, 1919. Early printing; very good+, inscribed by author for Hank and Margaret Harris. Lupack Rare Books May 26 2011 - ABE2464946756 2011 $100

Association – Harris, Margaret

Morley, Christopher *Mince Pie.* New York: G. H. Doran, 1919. Early printing; very good+, inscribed by author for Hank and Margaret Harris. Lupack Rare Books May 26 2011 - ABE2464946756 2011 $100

Association – Harris, Mary

Eliot, Thomas Stearns 1888-1965 *The Elder Statesman.* London: Faber, 1959. First edition; pages 112, crown 8vo., original pink cloth, backstrip gilt lettered, free endpapers lightly browned, very good, inscribed by author and his wife for Mary Harris. Blackwell Rare Books B166 - 142 2011 £500

Association – Harrisburg

Niven, David *Round the Rugged Rocks.* London: Cresset Press, 1951. First edition; 8vo., original publisher's red cloth lettered gilt on spine and on front cover, pages 263, very good+ in close to very good dust jacket slightly chipped at spine ends and top of rear panel and rubbed at corners, signed presentation from author to the Harrisburgs. Any Amount of Books May 29 2011 - A76302 2011 $255

Association – Harrison, Christopher

Poulson, George *Beverlac; or the Antiquities and History of the Town of Beverley...* London: printed for George Scaum, 1829. 2 volumes bound as 1, large paper copy 4to., pages xx, 510 + engraved frontispiece, 1 extending engraved plate of facsimiles and 3 other plates (ii) (512)-816, 84, tipped in errata slip + 1 engraved plates, vignette "Beverley Foundry" pasted to page 816, folding plan of the "Boundary of the New Borough of Beverley" with hand colored outlines, contemporary purple morocco, four flat raised banded spine, bands and extremities 'paired tool' gilt with connecting gilt rules, compartments blind tooled in concentric panel, green lettering piece gilt, boards panelled in blind, decorative roll between rules all gilt within, quintuple rule with rose head corners innermost panel in blind, board edges single rule gilt, turn-ins 'quintuple zig-zag rules' in blind, 'Spanish' 'made' endpapers (green pasted), all edges 'Spanish' marbled (fawn based), fawn sewn flat endbands, purple silk page marker, plates bit foxed, few offset, spine faded, extremities rubbed, bit of wear to endcaps and top of joints, (?) lettering piece replaced armorial bookplate of Christopher Harrison, from the collection of Christopher Ernest Weston 1947-2010. Unsworths Booksellers 24 - 137 2011 £250

Association – Harrison, Elizabeth

Pym, Barbara *Excellent Women.* New York: Dutton, 1978. First US edition; 8vo. signed presentation from author for Elizabeth Harrison, with pencilled note, slight lean, minimal shelf wear, very good+. Any Amount of Books May 26 2011 - A68213 2011 $553

Association – Harrison, Henrietta

Briggs, John *The Remains of John Briggs...* Kirkby Lonsdale: printed and sold by Arthur Foster, 1825. First edition; old half calf gilt, neatly recased, original backstrip cracked but laid down, pages 408, complete with half title and subscriber list, excellent copy with near contemporary inscription of Henrietta Harrison. R. F. G. Hollett & Son Antiquarian Booksellers 173 - 152 2011 £395

Association – Harrison, J. Maychild

The Public Charities of the Hundred of Lonsdale North of the Sands Reprinted from the Report of the Commissioners (dated Jan. 1820). Ulverston: S. Soulby, 1852. First edition; small 8vo., original half roan gilt, trifle rubbed, pages (ii), 152, signature of J. Maychild Harrison of Flookburgh dated 1852. R. F. G. Hollett & Son Antiquarian Booksellers 173 - 699 2011 £85

Association – Harry, R.

Lowe, Richard Thomas *History of the Fishes of Madeira.* London: Bernard Quaritch, 1843-1860. Large paper copy; L28 lithographed plates of which 18 are hand colored (minor marginal spotting to 4 plain plates), 4to., pages xvi, 4, (4*-) 196, contemporary half calf (edges rubbed, tips of corners worn, a corner slightly bumped, ink number to a margin of a page, very good), raised bands and gilt decorations on spine, top edge gilt, rare, the copy of Henry A. Sherwin (founder of Sherwin-Williams Co.) and bookplate of R. Harry Jr. Raymond M. Sutton, Jr. May 26 2011 - 41582 2011 $2350

Schaeffer, Jacob Christian *Piscium Bavarico Ratisbonensium Pentas. (bound with) Epistola ad Regio-Borussicam Societatem Litterariam Du'isburgensem de Studii Ichthyologici Facililori...* Ratisbonae: Montagii et Typis Weissianis, 1761. Ratisbonae: Typis Weissianis et Impensis Montagii, 1760; 4to., 4 hand colored engraved plates (light foxing to 1), pages (12), 82; 4to., pages 24, scattered light foxing, contemporary calf backed boards, rubbed, bump to upper edges of covers, 1 inch split to upper edges of spine, old paper label to heel of spine, some worming to upper blank corner of all pages and plates, old ink number to front flyleaf, 3 handstamps on first title, scattered light foxing, from the Musee d'Histoire Naturelle de Geneve, also the copy of H. C. Redeke, P. F. Geiger, and R. Harry, Jr. Raymond M. Sutton, Jr. May 26 2011 - 41627 2011 $1500

Association – Hart, Kitty Carlisle

Nachtwey, James *Deeds of War.* New York: Thames & Hudson, 1989. First edition; fine in very near fine dust jacket, signed and inscribed by Nachtwey for Kitty Carlisle Hart. Jeff Hirsch Books ny 2010 2011 $1750

Association – Hart-Davis, Duff

Kynaston, David   *Cazenove & Co. A History.*   London: Batsford, 1991.   First edition; pages 359, illustrations in color, inscribed "Duff (Hart-Davis) with best wishes John Kemp-Welch (partner, Cazenove & Co.) Oct. 1991".   R. F. G. Hollett & Son Antiquarian Booksellers   175 - 796   2011   £35

Association – Hartley, Gilfrid William

Dickens, Charles   1812-1870   *Dombey and Son.*   London: Bradbury & Evans, 1848.   First edition in book form, first state following all points in Smith; octavo, xvi, (1, errata), (1, blank), 624 pages, frontispiece, titlepage and 38 plates after Phiz, publisher's variant binding of moderate green fine diaper grain cloth, front and back covers entirely stamped in blind with thin double line border which enclosed a rectangular frame, frame contains a loop-scroll design in each corner and string of 16 beads runs along its inner edge, lineal globe shaped design stamped in center of both covers, spine stamped in blind with thick and thin band at top and thin and thick one at bottom, between which are are three decorative rectangular panels, each containing heart shaped flower design in its center, spine lettered in gilt original pale yellow coated endpapers, spine very slightly faded, corners very slightly bumped with just tiny amount of board show through, otherwise binding is as fresh as one could possibly wish for, chemised in half green morocco slipcase with bookplate of William Self on chemise, bookplates of Gilfrid William Hartley and William Self, and Dickens Centenary Testimonial label on front pastedown, signature of original owners Eleanor Trotter September 11th 1859", signature of Kenyon Starling.   David Brass Rare Books, Inc.   May 26 2011 - 01693   2011 $13,500

Association – Harty, Russell

Spencer, Raine   *The Spencers on Spas.*   London: Weidenfeld and Nicolson, 1983.   First edition; 4to., original cloth, gilt, dust jacket, pages 160, illustrations in color and monochrome by John Spencer, two TLS's loosely inserted from Christina Foyle to Russell Harty asking him to be a Guest of Honour at a luncheon to celebrate publication of the book.   R. F. G. Hollett & Son Antiquarian Booksellers   177 - 824   2011   £30

Association – Harvey, Paul

Hudson, William Henry   1841-1922   *Nature in Downland.*   London: Longmans, Green and Co., 1900.   First edition; half title, frontispiece, engraved titlepage, plates and illustrations, uncut in original green buckram, slightly marked, presentation inscription to Paul Harvey, from friend Henry James.   Jarndyce Antiquarian Booksellers   CXCI - 221   2011   £850

Association – Harwell, William Lightfoot

Couch, Jonathan   *A History of the Fishes of the British Islands...*   London: George Bell & Sons, 1877.   First edition; 4 volumes, 4to., vii 245, 8 (ads); iv, 265, 8 (ads); iv, 208, 8 (ads); iv, 439, 8 (ads) pages, frontispiece in each volume, 252 color plates, ads dated June 1879, original blue cloth gilt stamped, spines neatly restored, dated 1879 ownership signature of William Lightfoot Harwell, exceptional set, fine.   Jeff Weber Rare Books   163 - 148   2011 $2000

Association – Hastings

Mills, John   *D'Horsay; or the Follies of the Day.*   London: William Strange, 1844.   First edition; frontispiece, additional engraved title, plates foxed, some heavily, contemporary half brown calf, green morocco label, slightly rubbed, armorial booklabel of Hastings, laid down on leading pastedown over ink inscription.   Jarndyce Antiquarian Booksellers   CXCI - 323   2011   £125

Association – Hatton, H.

Galt, John   1779-1839   *Ringan Gilhaize or the Covenaters.*   Edinburgh: Oliver & Boyd, 1823.   First edition; 3 volumes, 12mo., half titles, one in annotation in volume III, uncut in original blue boards, brown paper spines, paper labels, some expert repairs to spines, ownership signatures of H. Hatton, very good.   Jarndyce Antiquarian Booksellers   CXCI - 521   2011   £280

Association – Hauck, Cornelius

Rush, Anthony   *A President for a Prince. Wherein is to be Seene by the Testimonie of Auncient Writers, The Deutie of Kings, Princes and Gouvernours.*   London: by H. Denham, 1566.   First edition; 163 x 113mm., (28) leaves, wonderfully animated and colorful 17th century English brocaded silk binding featuring a gray silk ground embroidered with plaited and crinkled straw in intricate overall pattern incorporating heart tulip and floral designs as well as a crown, the designs done in red, yellow and blue, text block with gilt edges, 19th century green watered silk endleaves, titlepage with woodcut filigree border, foliated initials, bookplate of Cornelius J. Hauck; printed in black letter; minor fraying and small losses to the embroidered border, text perhaps pressed (but probably not washed), titlepage little dark and very slightly stained in top margin, tip of upper corner of final four leaves expertly repaired (three of these leaves, also with flattened creases), still splendid copy, text very clean and smooth and absolutely delightful binding with remarkably bright and scarcely worn stitching.   Phillip J. Pirages   59 - 59   2011 $19,500

Association – Havergal, Francis

Handbooks to the Cathedrals of England and Wales. London: John Murray, 1861-1874. 7 volumes, original blindstamped cloth, gilt extra, head and tail of spines rather chipped and frayed, one lower board affected by damp, illustrated with text and full page woodcut illustrations throughout, some flyleaves rather foxed, two volumes little dampstained in places, but good set, lacking the separate volume St. Pauls, Western Cathedrals volume a presentation copy from publisher to Rev. Francis G. Havergal, with his bookplate and presentation slip loosely inserted.   R. F. G. Hollett & Son Antiquarian Booksellers   177 - 168 2011   £180

Association – Hay, John

Lincoln, Abraham   1809-1865   *Complete Works.* Harrogate: Lincoln Memorial University, 1894. Sponsor's Edition; signed by chancellor of the University (this copy #283 especially prepared for Sylvanus B. Bechtel), 235 x 160mm., 12 volumes, very pleasing publisher's elaborately gilt decorated scarlet morocco, upper boards intricately tooled with entrelac gilt strapwork and twining floral tendrils (in stylized 16th century Italian design), flat spines with similar gilt tooling in an elongated panel, top edge gilt, other edges rough trimmed, mostly unopened, 12 portrait frontispieces, 12 facsimiles of letter and other documents, 32 photo plates; first volume with tipped in letter on onion skin (photographic copy?) from John Hay to unnamed correspondent identifying the two figures in frontispiece with Lincoln as being Hay himself and John Nicolay; spines just bit darkened, printed on inexpensive paper, so leaves little browned at edges (no doubt as in all copies), one leaf with four inch horizontal tear across breadth of text without loss, otherwise quite fine set, text obviously largely unread and with decorative binding showing no significant wear.   Phillip J. Pirages   59 - 257 2011 $3250

Association – Hayhurst, Robert

Keble, John   *The Christian Year: thoughts in Verse for the Sundays and Holydays throughout the Year.*   London: Bickers & Son, 1875. 24 illustrations, half title, frontispiece, illustrated title, original full dark brown crushed morocco, heavy boards in gilt decorated with diving bird, wings outstretched, in each corner, central gilt design of cross with brown morocco onlay with title, raised bands, compartments ruled and decorated in gilt, contemporary gift inscription facing half title "E.G.S. Hornby with his mother's love July 20 1880", booklabel of Robert J. Hayhurst, all edges gilt, very attractive.   Jarndyce Antiquarian Booksellers   CXCI - 440 2011   £125

Knox, John   *The Historie of the Reformation of the Church of Scotland.*   London: John Raworth for George Thomason and Octavian Pullen, 1644. Folio, pages (lxxxiv), 276, 279-397, (i) 401-460, 91, (ii), 92-122, contemporary sprinkled calf, boards blind triple ruled, board edges single rule gilt, turn-ns single ruled in blind, all edges rouge, pink and white sewn endbands, calf reback & corners by John Henderson, little light spotting, couple of old scrapes to leather, modern booklabel of Robert J. Hayhurst, from the collection of Christopher Ernest Weston 1947-2010.   Unsworths Booksellers   24 - 27 2011   £950

Mackarness, Matilda Planche   *The Dream Chintz.* London: W. N. Wright, 1851. First edition; half title, frontispiece, illustrations, 10 pages ads, original mint green glazed boards, lettered in darker green and decorated with elaborate leaf design in gilt, simply rebacked, booklabel of Robert J. Hayhurst, all edges gilt.   Jarndyce Antiquarian Booksellers   CLXC - 193 2011   £65

Association – Hays. Isaac

Gravesande, Wilhelm Jacob Van S'   1688-1742 *Physices Elementa Mathematica, Experimentis Confirmata.* Leiden: Apud Johannen Arnoldum Lanereak Johannem et Hermannum Verbeek, 1742. Third edition; 2 volumes, 4to., titlepage in red and black, 127 folding engraved plates, marginal waterstaining in both volumes, plate XXI torn with loss, plate LIII missing, margins of few plates reinforced, contemporary full calf, raised bands, gilt ruled spines, gilt stamped red leather spine labels, neatly rebacked, institutional bookplates, ink signatures of Isaac Hays on titlepages, very good.   Jeff Weber Rare Books   163 - 38 2011 $1250

Association – Headfort, Marquess of

Chandler, Richard   *Travels in Greece, or an Account of a Tour Made at the Expense of the Society of Dilettanti.* Dublin: printed for Messrs Price, Whitestone, Sleater and 31 others, 1776. xvi,3 19, (1) pages, 8vo., few light marks to several pages, otherwise very good, clean copy, full contemporary calf, raised bands, red morocco label, slight wear to head of spine, armorial bookplate of Marquess of Headfort.   Jarndyce Antiquarian Booksellers   CXCI - 540 2011   £320

Jacson, Frances   *Rhoda.*   London: Henry Colburn & Co., 1816. Second edition; 3 volumes in 4, contemporary full diced calf, gilt spines and borders, maroon labels, slight nick at tail of one spine, good plus, armorial bookplates of Marquess of Headfort.   Jarndyce Antiquarian Booksellers   CLXC - 2 2011   £200

La Peyrouse, Jean Francois De Galaup, Comte De *A Voyage Round the World; Which was Peformed (sic) in the Years 1785, 1786 1787, 1788.* Edinburgh: printed by J. Moir, 1798. 8vo., (3), vi-xvi, 336 pages, folding engraved map, 3 engraved plates, bound without half title, 8vo., map and plates rather browned, full contemporary tree calf, gilt ship device repeated on spine, dark green morocco label, slight chip to head of spine, also little rubbed, pencil note on f.e.p. with armorial bookplate of Marquess of Headfort. Jarndyce Antiquarian Booksellers   CXCI - 564   2011   £225

M'Intosh, Maria June *Grace and Isabel; or to Seem and to Be.* London: G. Routledge Co., 1852. First English edition; Contemporary half green calf, maroon leather label, spine darkened, slightly worn damage in tail of following hinge, from the Headfort library, signed "Bective 1854). Jarndyce Antiquarian Booksellers   CLXC - 190   2011   £45

M'Intosh, Maria June *Louise De La Valliere.* London: T. Nelson & Sons, 1854. First English edition; contemporary half maroon calf, black leather label, spine slightly rubbed, from the Headfort library, signed "Bective 1854". Jarndyce Antiquarian Booksellers   CLXC - 191   2011   £45

Maberly, Catherine Charlotte *The Love Match.* London: David Bryce, 1856. New edition; contemporary half maroon calf, spine decorated in gilt, black leather label, spine and corners little rubbed, from Headfort library, signed, "Bective 1854", good plus. Jarndyce Antiquarian Booksellers   CLXC - 184   2011   £45

Marsh, Anne *Adelaide Lindsay.* London: G. Routledge & Co., 1851. Contemporary half green calf maroon leather label, spine darkened, little rubbed, from the Headfort library, signed "Bective 1854", good, sound copy. Jarndyce Antiquarian Booksellers   CLXC - 232   2011   £60

More, Hannah   1745-1833   *Coelebs in Search of a Wife.* London: T. Cadell and W. Davies, 1809. Fifth edition; 2 volumes, errata leaf volume II, prelims slightly creased volume I, contemporary half calf, gilt spines, leather labels, hinges and edges rubbed, Marquess of Headfort armorial bookplates, good, sound copy. Jarndyce Antiquarian Booksellers   CLXC - 520   2011   £125

Opie, Amelia *The Father and Daughter.* London: Longman, Hurst, Rees, and Orme, 1806. Fifth edition; frontispiece, contemporary full dark blue calf, gilt spine and borders, small maroon leather label, slightly rubbed, armorial bookplate of Marquess of Headfort, good plus. Jarndyce Antiquarian Booksellers   CLXC - 658   2011   £120

Association – Healey, E.

Oliphant, Margaret Oliphant Wilson   1828-1897 *Memoir of the Life of Laurence Oliphant and of Alice Oliphant, His Wife.* Edinburgh: William Blackwood and Sons, 1891. First edition; 2 volumes, half titles, frontispieces, 24 page catalog, volume I, final ad leaf volume II, original blue cloth, bevelled boards, lettered in gilt, spines slightly dulled, bit rubbed, each volume signed by E. Healey in contemporary hand, with W. H. Smith Circulating library labels. Jarndyce Antiquarian Booksellers   CLXC - 640   2011   £80

Association – Hease, Doc

Blochman, Lawrence G. *Diagnosis: Homicide the Casebook of Dr. Coffee.* Philadelphia: J. B. Lippincott, 1950. First edition; signed by author, presentation inscription from author for Doc Hease, lightly rubbed at spine ends, else near fine in dust jacket lightly rubbed at spine ends and corners. Buckingham Books   May 26 2011 - 27777   2011 $2500

Association – Heathcote, Anna Sophia

Chapone, Hester *Miscellanies in Prose and Verse.* London: printed for C. Dilly and J. Walter, 1783. New edition; 160 x 105 mm., 6 p.l. (including initial blank), (13)-216 pages, exceptionally pretty contemporary speckled calf, raised bands, spine handsomely gilt in compartments with small foliate cornerpieces and prominent botanical centerpiece, one compartment with unusual olive green morocco onlay decorated with gilt grape cluster and vine, in compartment above it, red morocco title label, early ink signature of Anna Sophia Heathcote, joints with thin crack alongside top compartment, covers faintly marked, verso of final leaf with overall light browning, otherwise quite fine, binding lustrous and little worn, text extraordinarily fresh, clean and bright. Phillip J. Pirages   59 - 25   2011 $1250

Association – Heber

Radcliffe, Alexander *The Ramble an Anti-Heroick Poem. Together with Some Terrestrial Hymns and Carnal Ejaculations.* London: for the author and to be sold by Walter Davis, 1682. First edition; 8vo., pages (xvi), 128, including initial blank Ai, contemporary black morocco, sides panelled in gilt, spine richly gilt in compartments, marbled pastedowns, gilt edges, lightly rubbed, little marginal browning, fine, the Heber(?) Britwell-Hewyard-Bradley Martin, Edwards copy with modern bookplates of H. Bradley Martin and J. O. Edwards. Simon Finch Rare Books   Zero - 348   2011   £2500

Association – Hendricks, Vicki

Naked Came the Manatee. New York: Putnam, 1996. First edition; fine in fine dust jacket, signed by all authors on single tipped in leaf, including Carl Hiaasen, Elmore Leonard, John Dufresne, Dave Barry, Vicki Hendricks, Edna Buchanan, Les Standiford and James W. Hall, etc. Ken Lopez Bookseller 154 - 5 2011 $200

Association – Henry, Lord

Longfellow, Henry Wadsworth 1807-1882 *The Poetical Works of H. W. Longfellow.* London: T. Nelson & Sons, 1867. Photographic frontispiece, original full maroon morocco, heavily blocked in blind lettered in gilt on boards and spine, spines slightly rubbed, embossed stamp on leading f.e.p., inscription from Madeline Gresley to Lord Henry, all edges gilt, very good. Jarndyce Antiquarian Booksellers CXCI - 441 2011 £60

Association – Hensius, D.

Ovidius Naso, Publius *Operum... Tomus Primus (Tertius)...* Frankfurt: C. Marny & Heirs of J. Aubry, typis Wechelianis, 1601. 3 volumes, folio, (4), 500, (16); (2), 388, 116, 244, (12), 340, 199 pages, later 17th century mottled calf, gilt fillet on covers, spines gilt, green silk ties lacking, slightly foxed but highly desirable, handsome copy, from the library of the Earls of Macclesfield at Shirburn Castle, bequeathed by Iosephi Scaliger to D. Heinsius. Maggs Bros. Ltd. 1440 - 160 2011 £3000

Association – Herbert, Mary

Ponsonby, Emily *Katherine and Her Sisters.* London: Hurst & Blackett, 1861. First edition; 3 volumes, slightly later half purple calf, gilt spines, maroon leather labels, odd small mark, bookplates of Mary Herbert, very good. Jarndyce Antiquarian Booksellers CLXC - 752 2011 £225

Association – Herne, Crystal

Kelly, George *Craig's Wife a Drama.* Boston: Little Brown, 1926. First edition; 8vo., pages 174, very nice, tight copy, inscribed by author to Josephine Williams who played the part of Mrs. Harold in the NY production, also signed by rest of the cast - Annie Sutherland, Crystal Herne, Arthur Shaw, C. Stewart, Eleanor Marsh, Charles Trowbridge, Josephine Hull, J. A. Curtis, Nelan Jaap, Arline Alcine & Mary Gildea, also inscribed by the producer, Rosalie Stewart to whom the play was dedicated. Second Life Books Inc. 174 - 213 2011 $2000

Association – Heron-Allen, Edward

Lee, Elizabeth *Ouida: a Memoir.* London: T. Fisher Unwin, 1914. First edition; half title, frontispiece, title in red and black, plates, uncut in original pale blue cloth, lettered in dark blue, spine slightly faded, armorial bookplate of Edward Heron-Allen, with signed ALS from author to same. Jarndyce Antiquarian Booksellers CLXC - 729 2011 £40

Association – Hersch, Seymour

Mankoff, Robert *The Complete Cartoons of the New Yorker.* New York: Black Dog & Leventhal, 2004. First edition; signed and dated by Seymour Hersch April 22, 2005, near fine, light shelf wear, in like dust jacket, with occasional scratch, includes two CD's with all 68, 647 cartoons ever published in New Yorker Magazine, includes Damyon Runyon Award Banquet program which is also signed by Mr. Hersch. Bella Luna Books May 26 2011 - t7235 2011 $550

Association – Herz, Wolfgang

Cockburn, John *A Journey Over Land from the Gulf of Honduras to the Great South Sea. Performed by John Cockburn and Five Other Englishmen.* London: for C. Rivington, 1735. viii, 349, (3) pages, folding map, contemporary sprinkled calf, very skillfully rebacked with entire original spine and label retained, lovely copy, text clean and fresh and entirely unfoxed, Wolfgang Herz copy with his small booklabel. Joseph J. Felcone Inc. Fall Miscellany 2010 - 24 2011 $3500

Coryate, Thomas *Coryats Crudities Hastily Gobbled Up in Five Moneths Travells in France, Savoy, Italy, Rhetia Comonly Called the Grisons Country, Helvetia Alias Switzerland, some Parts of High Germany and the Netherlands.* London: by William Stansby, 1611. First edition; printed title present, engraved allegorical title by William Hole (shaved very slightly at head), engraved plates, woodcut, text portrait, errata leaf present, many woodcut initials and headpieces, 19th century brown crushed levant morocco, gilt by Bedford, unusually tall, very handsome copy, rare printed title, from the libraries of Ward E. Terry, R. B. Adam, A. Edward Newton, Bois Penrose and Wolfgang A. Herz with their respective bookplates and book labels. Joseph J. Felcone Inc. Fall Miscellany 2010 - 35 2011 $16,000

Joutel, Henri *A Journal of the Last Voyage Perform'd by Monsr. De La Sale to the Gulph of Mexico...* London: for A. Bell, B. Lintott, J. Baker, 1714. First edition in English; 8vo., (2), xxi, (9), 191, 194-205, (5) pages, engraved folding map, short closed tear, contemporary calf, extremities rubbed, top of spine bit worn, else lovely, untouched copy, text clean and fresh, entirely unfoxed, Peter Porter bookplate and Wolfgang Herz label. Joseph J. Felcone Inc. Fall Miscellany 2010 - 67 2011 $15,000

Ludolf, Hiob *A New History of Ethiopia.* London: for Samuel Smith, 1682. First edition in English; folio, (8), 88, 151-370, 375-398 pages, 8 engraved plates, engraved plate, folding genealogical table, contemporary or early 18th century calf, front hinge cracked but held by cords, corners worn, some light browning but very good, signatures of Edmund and Rufus Marsden, latter dated 1762, Herz booklabel.   Joseph J. Felcone Inc.   Fall Miscellany 2010 - 78   2011 $2200

Wafer, Lionel *A New Voyage and Description of the Isthmus of America, giving an Account of the Author's Abode there...* London: for James Knatpon, 1699. First edition; (8), 224, (16) pages, engraved folded map, 3 folding plates, 19th century morocco, hinges and extremities scuffed, very faint toning to edges of text, else excellent internally, Wolfgang Herz booklabel.   Joseph J. Felcone Inc.   Fall Miscellany 2010 - 123   2011 $2400

Association – Hesketh, Thomas

MacKenzie, Mary Jane *Geraldine; or Modes of Faith and Practice.* London: T. Cadell & W. Davies, 1820. First edition; 3 volumes, contemporary full calf, borders in gilt and blind, spines with raised and gilt bands, devices in gilt, leading hinges slightly worn, spine slightly darkened, small labels of Easton Neston Library and Sir Thomas Hesketh, Rufford Hall, good plus.   Jarndyce Antiquarian Booksellers   CLXC - 196   2011   £480

Association – Hess, Robert

Swift, Jonathan 1667-1745 *Miscellaneous Poems.* Waltham St. Lawrence: Golden Cockerel Press, 1928. One of 375 copies; 273 x 203mm., viii, 67, (2) pages, original quarter vellum over marbled paper boards, titling in gilt on spine, publisher's orange printed dust jacket, woodcut printer's device, 12 wood engravings by Robert Gibbings, titlepage printed in red and black; two prelim leaves, embossed ownership stamp of Robert Hess; edges of volume little faded, one leaf slightly torn at top as result of uncareful opening, otherwise fine in very good dust jacket, with clean covers, but with darkened, torn and chipped spine and with fraying along upper edge of cover panels.   Phillip J. Pirages   59 - 223   2011 $300

Association – Hiaasen, Carl

Naked Came the Manatee. New York: Putnam, 1996. First edition; fine in fine dust jacket, signed by all authors on single tipped in leaf, including Carl Hiaasen, Elmore Leonard, John Dufresne, Dave Barry, Vicki Hendricks, Edna Buchanan, Les Standiford and James W. Hall, etc.   Ken Lopez Bookseller   154 - 5   2011 $200

Association – Higginson, Alfred

Martineau, Harriet 1802-1876 *The History of England During the Thirty Years' Peace 1816-1846. (with) Introduction to the History of the Peace.* London: Charles Knight, 1849-1850. 1851. First edition; foldout maps, plates, half brown morocco, gilt spines, bit rubbed, good plus, this copy presentation copy signed by author for brother in law Alfred Higginson.   Jarndyce Antiquarian Booksellers   CLXC - 283   2011   £380

Martineau, Harriet 1802-1876 *Letters from Ireland.* London: John Chapman, 1852. First edition; 36 page catalog (Dec. 20th 1852), original green morocco grained cloth by Westleys, blocked in blind, spine lettered in gilt, spine slightly darkened and little rubbed, head and tail carefully repaired, good plus, signed "Higginson", almost certainly author's brother-in-law, Alfred Higginson.   Jarndyce Antiquarian Booksellers   CLXC - 318   2011   £220

Association – Higginson, Edward

Martineau, Harriet 1802-1876 *Poor Laws and Paupers Illustrated.* London: Charles Cox, 1833-1834. First edition; slightly spotted, 4 volumes in 2, contemporary olive green moire cloth, paper label, spine slightly dulled, signed by Edward Higginson, father-in-law of author's brother James.   Jarndyce Antiquarian Booksellers   CLXC - 335   2011   £200

Association – Higginson, Ellen Martineau

Martineau, Harriet 1802-1876 *Biographical Sketches.* London: Macmillan, 1869. First edition; half title, 2 pages ads, 48 page catalog (July 1868), original blue cloth by Burn & Co., spine lettered in gilt, slightly dulled, rubbed at tail of spine, presentation inscription from author for Ellen Higginson.   Jarndyce Antiquarian Booksellers   CLXC - 266   2011   £200

Martineau, Harriet 1802-1876 *The Crofton Boys.* London: Charles Knight & Co., 1841. First edition; contemporary half maroon calf, spine faded to brown, bit rubbed, inscribed by author to sister Ellen Higginson.   Jarndyce Antiquarian Booksellers   CLXC - 331   2011   £150

Martineau, Harriet 1802-1876 *Eastern Life, Present and Past.* London: Edward Moxon, 1848. First edition; 3 volumes, half title volume I, occasional light foxing, 19th century half maroon calf, little rubbed, inscription to Mrs. A. Higginson from author (this is married name of author's younger sister, Ellen).   Jarndyce Antiquarian Booksellers   CLXC - 276   2011   £450

Martineau, Harriet 1802-1876 *England and Her Soldiers.* London: Smith, Elder & Co., 1859. First edition; half title, foldout, color frontispiece, 2 foldout diagrams at end, 2 page ads + 24 page catalog (May 1859), some light browning, original red cloth by Westleys & Co., blocked in blind and gilt spine lettered in gilt, spine little darkened, hinges slightly rubbed, presentation inscription from author to sister Ellen Higginson.   Jarndyce Antiquarian Booksellers   CLXC - 278   2011   £380

Martineau, Harriet 1802-1876 *Feats on the Fiord.* London: Charles Knight Co., 1841. First edition; contemporary half maroon calf, spine faded to brown, bit rubbed, signed presentation from author for sister Ellen Higginson.   Jarndyce Antiquarian Booksellers   CLXC - 327   2011   £200

Martineau, Harriet 1802-1876 *Miscellanies.* Boston: Hilliard, Gray and Co., 1836. First edition; 19th century half maroon calf, spines faded to brown, rubbed, this the copy of author's sister, Ellen, signed by Ellen, loosely inserted small sheet of paper listing in contemporary hand 'pencil jottings in Aunt Harriet's copy of Miscellanies".   Jarndyce Antiquarian Booksellers   CLXC - 322   2011   £200

Martineau, Harriet 1802-1876 *The Peasant and The Prince. A Tale.* London: Charles Knight and Co., 1841. First edition; contemporary half maroon calf, spine faded to brown, slightly rubbed, presentation from author to sister Ellen Higginson.   Jarndyce Antiquarian Booksellers   CLXC - 325   2011   £150

Martineau, Harriet 1802-1876 *Retrospect of Western Travel.* London: Saunders & Otley, 1838. First edition; 3 volumes, occasional light spotting, 19th century half maroon calf, spines rubbed, uniformly faded to brown, slight wear to head of spine, volume II, attractive copy, signed presentation inscription by author for sister Ellen.   Jarndyce Antiquarian Booksellers   CLXC - 338   2011   £400

Martineau, Harriet 1802-1876 *Traditions of Palestine. (bound with) Devotional Exercises... Reflections and Prayers. (bound with) Addresses; with Prayers and Original Hymns.* London: Longman, Rees, Orme, Brown and Green, 1830. London: Rowland Hunter, 1832. London: C. Fox, 1838. First, third and second edition respectively; 3 volumes in 1 in 19th century half maroon calf, spine and edges little rubbed, with presentation by author for sister Ellen.   Jarndyce Antiquarian Booksellers   CLXC - 344   2011   £280

Association – Hind, Jesse

Stevenson, W. H. *Royal Charters Granted to the Burgesses of Nottingham A.D. 1155-1712.* London: Bernard Quaritch 15 Piccadilly Nottingham: Thomas Forman & Sons, 1890. First edition; half title, viiii, 155, (1) pages, original cloth, calf backed, spine slightly worn, title in gilt on spine, bookplate of Jesse Hind, nice clean copy.   Anthony W. Laywood   May 26 2011 - 21700   2011 $76

Association – Hippisley, Violet

Paget, Violet 1856-1935 *Pope Jacynth and Other Fantastic Tales.* London: Grant Richards, 1904. First edition, publisher's proof copy with stamps of T. & A. Constable throughout, several minor ms. alterations in text; half title, original pale purple binder's cloth, spine lettered in gilt, slightly dulled, top edge gilt, good plus, scarce, signed presentation inscription by author for Violet Hippisley.   Jarndyce Antiquarian Booksellers   CLXC - 110   2011   £500

Association – Hoare, H. P. R.

Hoare & Co. *Hoare' Bank. A Record 1673-1932.* privately published, 1932. Large 8vo., original cloth, gilt, dust jacket little rubbed and darkened, few short edge tears, pages xi, 88, 33 illustrations, genealogical table, TLS from H. P. R. Hoare to E. A. Jones, presentation copy presented by Bank to Jones.   R. F. G. Hollett & Son Antiquarian Booksellers   175 - 636   2011   £40

Association – Hodges, J.

Blackmore, Richard Doddridge 1825-1900 *Lorna Doone: a Romance of Exmoor.* London: Sampson Low, Son & Marston, 1869. First edition, apparently one of 500 copies printed; 3 volumes, octavo, vi, 332; lv, 340; iv, 342 pages, bound without prelim blank leaf in volume I and final blank leaf in volume III, but with 16 page publisher's catalog dated March 1869, at end volume III, bound circa 1960 by Bayntun-Riviere (stamp signed in gilt on front turn-in), full red morocco, covers with gilt double fillet border, spines panelled and lettered in gilt on front turn-in), in full red morocco, covers with gilt double fillet border, spines panelled and lettered in gilt compartments with five raised bands, board edges and turn-ins decoratively tooled in gilt, all edges gilt, marbled endpapers, spines very slightly sunned, few short, expertly repaired margin tears, some occasional minor foxing or soiling, bookplate of J. Hodges, overall, excellent copy, laid in is ALS from author to James Payn, Teddington, Dec. 34d 1877.   David Brass Rare Books, Inc.   May 26 2011 - 00726   2011 $6500

Association – Hodson, W. L.

Knight, Charles 1791-1873 *Shadows of the Old Booksellers.* London: Ball & Daldy, 1865. First edition; original brown cloth, slight rubbing, with signature of W. L. Hodson.   Jarndyce Antiquarian Booksellers   CXCI - 451   2011   £75

Association – Hoe, Robert

Guevara, Antonio De *Vita Di M. Avrelio Imperadore.* Venice: Bartolomeo Imperador and Francesco Veneziano, 1543. 160 x 103mm., 8 p.l., 132, (2) leaves, fine contemporary Roman red morocco Apollo and Pegasus medallion binding done for Giovanni Battista Grimaldi by Marc Antonio Guillery, (genuine Apollo and Pegasus binding) covers with gilt frame formed by two widely spaced fillets with lobes interlaced at ends and sides, space between fillets decorated with broad foliate curls, small floral tools, inner pane of each board with gilt titling above a horizontal oval Apollo and Pegasus plaquette centerpiece showing Pegasus atop black painted heights of Parnassus and Apollo racing his chariot (drawn by two straining steeds) across steep terrain with reins and whip held aloft and caps fluttering behind, plaquette with gilt motto in Greek in the collar above and below vignette, spine (very expertly rebacked) with four thin and three thick raised bands decorated with gilt rope pattern or plain rules (this being original backstrip?), newer (perhaps 19th century) endpapers, all edges gilt (apparently some remarkably skillful restoration at one or more corners and edges, perhaps some gold added, as well as to the chariot part of the plaquettes); woodcut printer's device on , morocco bookplate and separate gilt monogram of Robert Hoe as well as inscription and vellum bookplate of Swedish collector Thore Virgin, ownership inscription of J. T. Payne dated 1850; covers with half dozen insignificant tiny dark spots, titlepage faintly soiled, thin light brown stain just at top edge of leaves, small wormhole at upper inner margin (text not affected), occasional minor stains, other trivial imperfections, but no defects that are even remotely serious and in general really excellent specimen of a very special binding, text fresh and leather quite lustrous; also from the collection of bibliophile Johannes Gennadius, Liverpool oculist T. Shadford Walker and Swedish collector Rolfe Wistrand.   Phillip J. Pirages   59 - 2   2011 $35,000

Gresset, Jean Baptiste Louis *Poemes.* Paris: D. Jouaust, 1867. One of 2 copies Printed on vellum, there were also 118 on paper; 215 x 140mm., 6 p.l., (two vellum blanks, half title, title, two frontispieces (on paper), iv, 132 pages, (4) leaves (variants, contents/colophon, two vellum blanks), folio Cii unsigned and misnumbered but copy complete; very attractive contemporary midnight blue crushed morocco handsomely gilt by Thibaron (stamp signed), covers with French fillet border, raised bands, spines ornately gilt in compartments filled with delicately stippled swirling designs accented with small tools, gilt inner dentelles, marbled endpapers, all edges gilt, 9 engraved on (on paper), 2 frontispiece portraits, 7 plates, large paper copy, bookplates of Robert Hoe and Mortimer Schiff, engraved bookplate of Marcellus Schlimovich, library stamp of Sociedad Hebraica Argentina, just hint of wear top and bottom of joints, one side of first and last vellum flyleaf discolored (apparently from a reaction to the gilt on pastedowns(?), plates with variable freckled foxing (never serious), otherwise fine, elegant binding quite lustrous and leaves clean, fresh and bright.   Phillip J. Pirages   59 - 343   2011 $3250

La Fontaine, Jean De 1621-1695   *Fables Choisies, Mises en Vers.* Paris: Denys Thierry, 31 March, 1668. First edition; 4to., (58), 284 (2) pages, leaf o2 present as both cancellans and cancellandum, roman type, woodcut typographic head and tailpieces, floriated initials, 118 etchings by Francois Chauveau, crushed green morocco, gilt triple rule outer border, spine and wide turn-ins gilt, all edges gilt by Lortic, fils (spine and extremities faded to brown, front hinge worn), neat repair to five leaves (one touching two letters), very light overall toning, Robert Hoe's copy, inscribed in pencil on front flyleaf to his Granddaughter Thyrza Benson.   Joseph J. Felcone Inc.   Fall Miscellany 2010 - 72   2011 $30,000

Association – Hoensbroech, Paul Graf Von

Gerson, Johannes *De Pollutione Nocturna.* Cologne: Johann Guldenschaff, circa, 1480. Rare incunable edition; 8vo., pages (32), including initial blank, some light foxing, two old repairs to initial blank, generally crisp, fresh and wide margined, later paper covered boards, cloth spine and tips rubbed, title to initial blank in early manuscript, sporadic underlining in text, bookplate of Paul Graf von Hoensbroech, his crest stamped to first two leaves.   Simon Finch Rare Books   Zero - 101   2011   £3750

Association – Hogan, Frank

Day, Clarence *Life with Father.* New York: Alfred A Knopf, 1935. First edition; fine in attractive, very good or better, price clipped dust jacket with faint stain on front panel, little nicking at crown, small elegant bookplate of noted collector Frank Hogan, small pencil note on rear pastedown that a previous owner bought this at the Hogan sale in 1945.   Between the Covers   169 - BTC344723   2011 $250

Association – Hoggarth, M.

Potter, Beatrix 1866-1943 *The Tale of Tom Kitten.* London: F. Warne & Co. Ltd. n.d. early 1920's, 12mo., original brown boards lettered in white with pictorial onlay, two small marks to upper board, spine lettering rather rubbed, little defective and repaired at foot, pages 86, illustrations in color, early inscription (Miss M. Hoggarth of Windermere), signed in full by Potter.   R. F. G. Hollett & Son Antiquarian Booksellers   General Catalogue Summer 2010 - 553   2011   £650

Association – Holcomb, Irving

United States. War Department - 1855 *Reports of Explorations and Surveys, to Ascertain the Most Practicable and Economical Route Railroad from the Mississippi River to the Pacific Ocean, made in the Direction of the Secretary of War in 1853-4, According to Acts of Congress March 3 1953 May 31 1854 and August 5 1854.* Washington: A. O. P. Nicholson, Printer, 1855-1861.   Each volume has been rebound in black buckram, signatures resewn, titles stamped in gold on spine panel, while each volume is stamped with word "Senate" on spine, five of the volumes are actually for House of Representatives; flaws as noted - volume I with small stamp of Library of Washington and Jefferson College and word 'withdrawn', else very good, tight copy; volume IV with presentation inscription to Irving Holcomb from Hon. F. E. Sprimer (?) dated Nov. 1857, small waterstain to bottom edges of front flyleaf which continues lightly to page 3, else very good, tight copy; volume X - light foxing to first 8 pages in front of volume and last 8 pages in rear of volume, else very good, tight copy; volume XI - moderate foxing and two small waterstains that diminish over first 16 pages, else very good, tight copy, a majority of the color lithographic plates are in fine condition as are the majority of black and white plates; volume XI contains maps and plates, including desirable large folding map done by Lt. Warren, all maps and plates in this volume are tightly secured.   Buckingham Books   May 26 2011 - 26611   2011 $15,000

Association – Holiambe, Hercules

Chaucer, Geoffrey 1340-1400 *Workes of Geoffrey Chaucer.* London: Imprinted by Jhon Kyngston for Jhon Wight, 1561.   Rare first issue; folio, (14), ccclxxviii leaves (irregular foliation), title within woodcut border, woodcut border, 22 woodcuts, large and small historiated and decorative initials and other ornaments, black letter, fifty-six lines, double columns, early 20th century antique style dark brown calf, expertly and almost invisible rebacked with original spine laid down, covers with double blind fillet border, spine in six compartments with five raised bands, ruled in blind and dated in gilt at foot and with brown morocco gilt lettering label, title lightly soiled with upper blank margin renewed, lower corner of first two leaves strengthened, few tiny holes or paper flaws, occasional foxing or faint dampstaining on few leaves, short (2 inch) repaired tear to lower margin of Mmm6, not affecting text, bookplate with monogram of Dr. George Osborne Mitchell, early ink signature of Anne Abdy and Hercules Holiambe (?) and some additional early ink annotations on title.   David Brass Rare Books, Inc.   May 26 2011 - 00642   2011 $48,500

Association – Holland House

Barrow, Isaac *A Brief Exposition of the Lord's Prayer and the Decalogue.* London: M. Flesher for Brabazon Aylmer, 1681.   8vo., pages (vi), 269, (iii) + engraved portrait frontispiece; later dark blue polished turkey, spine decorative roll gilt in compartments with small corner and centre pieces, lettered in gilt direct, boards gilt rule bordered with small stylised floweret in corners, board edges and turn-ins 'zig-zag' decorative roll gilt, crimson turkey doublures with 'dentelle' gilt border, blue 'made' end flyleaves, all edges gilt, pale blue and white sewn endbands (suggestions here of James Brindley binding), faint dampmark to fore-edge, joints rubbed, splitting, endcaps and corners worn, "Shelburne" armorial bookplate, and "Holland House" heraldic bookplate on doublure, from the collection of Christopher Ernest Weston 1947-2010.   Unsworths Booksellers   24 - 4   2011   £175

Association – Holland, L. P.

Dangell, M. S. *The Cabinet or Philosopher's Masterpiece Containing a Fore-Knowledge of Future Events.* Philadelphia: reprinted from the Dublin edition, 1824.   First American edition?; 24mo., 139 pages, illustrated with cyphers, disbound, title loose, soiled & chipped, early ink inscription "Miss L. P. Holland's Book for Rev. F. W.", corners turned and hand soiling in text.   M & S Rare Books, Inc. 90 - 135   2011 $500

Association – Holman, Charles

McKenney, Thomas Lorraine *History of the Indian Tribes of North America, with Biographical Sketches and Anecdotes of the Principal Chiefs.* Philadelphia: D. Rice & A. N. Hart, 1858. Fourth edition; 3 volumes, 8vo., pages (2), iv, (3-) 333; xvii, (9-) 290; iv, (17-) 392, 120 hand colored lithographic plates by J. T. Bowen of Philadelphia, most are after Charles Bird King (marginal brown spot to 2 plates), contemporary morocco, elaborately blocked with stylistic foliage in corners and 5 raised bands to spine with 6 tooled panels, 2 of which are gilt lettered, some light scuffing, chipping to head of spine, text virtually clean, worming in gutter of few pages of volume 1, all edges gilt, Prexel copy with coat of arms; Charles Holman copy with coat of arms, very good. Raymond M. Sutton, Jr. May 26 2011 - 55944 2011 $25,000

Association – Holyoake, J. Percy

Rowcroft, Charles *Tales of the Colonies; or the Adventures of an Emigrant.* London: Smith Elder & Co., 1858. New edition; half title, final ad leaf, ads on endpapers, original printed orange glazed cloth, dulled and little marked, presentation "J. Percy Holyoake with his father's best love June 4th 1864". Jarndyce Antiquarian Booksellers CXCI - 476 2011 £35

Association – Honeyman, H. L.

Headlam, Cuthbert *The Three Northern Counties of England.* Gateshead: Northumberland Press, 1939. Limited to 500 copies; small 4to., original full dark blue levant morocco gilt, pages xii, 343, untrimmed, 23 plates and 8 maps and plans, few spots to half title and fore-edge, but most attractive copy, loosely inserted are several letters relating to the production of the book between H. L. Honeyman (one of the contributors), the publishers and others, with press cuttings etc. R. F. G. Hollett & Son Antiquarian Booksellers 173 - 536 2011 £120

Association – Hope-Nicholson, J. L. R.

Molesworth, Mary Louisa 1839-1921 *A Christmas Posy.* London: Macmillan, 1888. First edition; frontispiece and illustrations by Walter Crane, 32 page catalog (April 1888), original red cloth, blocked and lettered in black and gilt, little dulled and slightly rubbed, bookplate of J. L. R. Hope-Nicholson. Jarndyce Antiquarian Booksellers CLXC - 430 2011 £35

Association – Hopkey, J.

Braun, Ernst *Novissimum Fundamenturm & Praxis Artilleriae Oder Nachitziger Besten Mannier.* Danzig: J. F. Grafen for the author, 1682. First edition; folio, (4), 197 (7) pages, no dedication, additional engraved title, 24 plates on 22 (of 23) sheets, lacking final double page engraving, annotated in German hand by J. Hopkey with inscription on title and his initials on cover, from the library of the Earls of Macclesfield at Shirburn Castle. Maggs Bros. Ltd. 1440 - 42 2011 £2800

Association – Hoppin, Frederick

Randall-MacIver, David *Mediaeval Rhodesia.* London: Macmillan, 1906. First edition; quarto, pages xv, 106, 36 plates, original green decorative cloth with recent reback, small stain on lower cover, inscribed to Frederick Hoppin with author's compliments. J. & S. L. Bonham Antiquarian Booksellers Africa 4/20/2011 - 8901 2011 £40

Association – Hopton

Certain Sermons or Homilies Appointed to Be Read in Churches, in the Time of Queen Elizabeth of Famous Memory... London: printed by T. R. for Andrew Croke, Samuel Mearne and Robert Pawlet, 1673. Folio, contemporary blindstamped panelled calf, edges little chipped, top and tail of spine slightly defective, pages (vi), 388, printed in black letter with engraved headpieces and large historiated initials, front flyleaves worn at fore-edges, title little browned and worn at fore-edge, joints cracked, early signature of Hopton, Suffolk. R. F. G. Hollett & Son Antiquarian Booksellers 175 - 1207 2011 £175

Association – Horblit, Harrison

Lorimer, John *A Concise Essay on Magnetism with an Account Declination and Inclination of the Magnetic Needle and an Attempt to Ascertain the Cause of the Variation Thereof.* London: printed for the author and sold by W. Faden, 1795. First edition; inscribed by author to General Melville, from the collection of Harrison D. Horblit with his booklabel, very good, inscribed copy in later half leather, cloth binding with gilt lettering on spine and bottom 1.5" of spine cover chipped, covers edge wear, marbled endpapers with f.f.e.p. clipped, six foldout plates as issued, plates foxed, scattered foxing. By the Book, L. C. 26 - 105 2011 $900

Association – Hornby, Charles Harry St. John

Bacon, Francis, Viscount St. Albans 1561-1626 *Two Essays of Francis Lord Bacon; of Bvildings & Gardens.* Ashendene Press, 1897. One of 16 copies printed for private circulation (this copy #6); 225 x 170mm., viii, 36 pages, original gray printed paper wrappers, fore-edge and tail edge untrimmed, green linen clamshell case (slightly soiled) with gilt titling on spine, printer's device on final page, pencilled initials on front free endpaper, apparently those of printer Hornby, professional repairs to bottom edges and one fore edge of overlapping wrapper and to two places on covers, front cover with long faint diagonal crease, very fragile original wrapper entirely intact and mostly quite clean, very fine internally with clean, fresh, bright text. Phillip J. Pirages 59 - 73 2011 $14,000

Association – Hornby, E. G. S.

Keble, John *The Christian Year: thoughts in Verse for the Sundays and Holydays throughout the Year.* London: Bickers & Son, 1875. 24 illustrations, half title, frontispiece, illustrated title, original full dark brown crushed morocco, heavy boards in gilt decorated with diving bird, wings outstretched, in each corner, central gilt design of cross with brown morocco onlay with title, raised bands, compartments ruled and decorated in gilt, contemporary gift inscription facing half title "E.G.S. Hornby with his mother's love July 20 1880", booklabel of Robert J. Hayhurst, all edges gilt, very attractive. Jarndyce Antiquarian Booksellers CXCI - 440 2011 £125

Association – Houghton, F. B.

Oliver, J. A. *Directory of the City of Los Angeles, California for 1875.* Los Angeles: printed at the Mirror Book and Job Printing House, 1875. First edition of the first separate general directory of the city of LA alone; octavo, (2, blank), 1-80, (2, ad), 81-174, 175 (pastedown), titlepages (i), (3), ads on pastedowns and throughout text, with one leaf of ads inserted between pages 80 and 81, half title (?) inserted and trimmed at upper, lower and fore edge margin and reads "Directory of Los Angeles for 1875", publisher's quarter leather over printed paper boards bearing ads; very light general wear and rubbing, some professional restoration to spine, boards with some soiling, small stain on back cover, altogether a remarkably clean, sound copy, very rare, the copy of noted historian F. B. Houghton. Heritage Book Shop Holiday 2010 - 93 2011 $4000

Association – Houlgate, W. J.

Hebert, Septimus *Whispers of Truth from the Stars.* London: James Nisbet and Co., 1896. First edition; original cloth silvered, spine rather dulled and creased, several indented ring marks to lower board, pages xiv, 214, (iii), 5 diagrams and 2 tables, inserted is 4 page ALS from author to Rev. W. J. Houlgate concerning the book and folded leaflet of "Opinions of the Press", scarce. R. F. G. Hollett & Son Antiquarian Booksellers 175 - 614 2011 £45

Association – How, John

Williams, William *The Duty and Interest of a People Among Who Religion Has Been Planted, to Continue Steadfast and Sincere...* Boston: printed and sold by S. Kneeland and T. Green, 1736. First edition; 12mo., (2), 8, 120, (2), 38, 19 pages, contemporary blindstamped sheep over wooden boards, with lines, flowers and leaves, highly appealing contemporary binding, very slight cracking to outer hinges, top and bottom, lower outer corners lacking from front endleaves, slight break in lower edge of title, occasional staining of text, but remarkably good, tight and sound, ownership signature of John How 1770. M & S Rare Books, Inc. 90 - 123 2011 $3000

Association – Howard, John

Watts, Isaac *The Psalms of David. (bound with) Hymns and Spiritual Songs.* London: printed by and for J. W. Pasham, 1778. 123 x 70mm., 2 p.l., 240 pages, (10) leaves; 4 p.l., 216 pages, (12) leaves (index leaves for "Hymns an Spiritual Songs" bound out of order but all present), 2 parts in one volume, superb hand painted and gilt decorated vellum by Edwards of Halifax, both covers with very prominent oval paintings, front covers depicting a statue in grisaille of a female figure, probably representing Faith, casting her eyes upward to heaven, one arm aloft, other holding a cross, whole against a sky blue oval, back cover with very dynamic grisaille painting of the Resurrection, with Christ flying upward from the tomb amidst brilliant light, three soldiers beneath shielding themselves in protective wonderment and presiding angel supplying adoration at right, both covers bordered by gilt chain motif, flat spine divided by blue wash bands into compartments featuring gilt lyres and swirling gilt cornerpieces, blue wash label, all edges gilt in original soft green leather slipcase bordered by gilt chain matching that of binding, this in turn housed in modern morocco backed folding box with raised bands and gilt titling, bookplate of James Gordon, Esquire, Moor Place; inscription "Harriot Whitbread/The Gift of John Howard Esq(ui)re/ Cardington/ 1785", similar inscription to Harriot from M. Howard of Cardington dated 1787; blue spine label trifle faded, blue cover background on front board showing little soil, small ink blot on three pages, wonderful binding in very fine condition, text nearly pristine, original slipcase bit worn and faded but remarkable survival. Phillip J. Pirages 59 - 13 2011 $6900

Association – Howard, M.

Watts, Isaac *The Psalms of David. (bound with) Hymns and Spiritual Songs.* London: printed by and for J. W. Pasham, 1778. 123 x 70mm., 2 p.l., 240 pages, (10) leaves; 4 p.l., 216 pages, (12) leaves (index leaves for "Hymns and Spiritual Songs" bound out of order but all present), 2 parts in one volume, superb hand painted and gilt decorated vellum by Edwards of Halifax, both covers with very prominent oval paintings, front covers depicting a statue in grisaille of a female figure, probably representing Faith, casting her eyes upward to heaven, one arm aloft, other holding a cross, whole against a sky blue oval, back cover with very dynamic grisaille painting of the Resurrection, with Christ flying upward from the tomb amidst brilliant light, three soldiers beneath shielding themselves in protective wonderment and presiding angel supplying adoration at right, both covers bordered by gilt chain motif, flat spine divided by blue wash bands into compartments featuring gilt lyres and swirling gilt cornerpieces, blue wash label, all edges gilt in original soft green leather slipcase bordered by gilt chain matching that of binding, this in turn housed in modern morocco backed folding box with raised bands and gilt titling, bookplate of James Gordon, Esquire, Moor Place; inscription "Harriot Whitbread/The Gift of John Howard Esq(ui)re/ Cardington/ 1785", similar inscription to Harriot from M. Howard of Cardington dated 1787; blue spine label trifle faded, blue cover background on front board showing little soil, small ink blot on three pages, wonderful binding in very fine condition, text nearly pristine, original slipcase bit worn and faded but remarkable survival. Phillip J. Pirages 59 - 13 2011 $6900

Association – Howell, John

Watson, Douglas S. *California in the Fifties. Fifty Views of Cities and Mining Towns in California and the West.* San Francisco: John Howell, 1936. First edition, limited to 850 copies (of an edition of 1000); oblong folio, (113) pages, 50 full page reproductions with accompanying text on facing page, wine cloth, gilt lettered paper label on front cover, half inch dent to center of spine, else very fine, presentation inscription signed by publisher, John Howell, to bibliographer, Robert Cowan. Argonaut Book Shop Recent Acquisitions Summer 2010 - 232 2011 $400

Association – Howell, Warren

Hoe, Richard M. *The Literature of Printing. A Catalogue of the Library Illustrative of the History and Art of Topography, Chalcography and Lithography of Richard M. Hoe.* London: 1877. (4), 149, (2) pages, frontispiece, contemporary cloth, decorated endpapers, front inner hinge open, crown of spine (quarter inch) torn off, presentation copy inscribed by Hoe to his cousin, Samuel J. Barrows, on two front blanks are pasted (bit artlessly) pieces of blue paper containing Hoe family notes in hand of Richard Hoe's great-great granddaughter, who purchased this copy from Warren Howell in 1945. Joseph J. Felcone Inc. Fall Miscellany 2010 - 60 2011 $900

Association – Howes, Barbara

Compton-Burnett, Ivy 1892-1969 *Daughters and Sons.* London: Gollancz, 1937. First edition; 8vo., pages 320, blue cloth, owner's bookplate, name on flyleaf, cover slightly soiled, otherwise very good, author Barbara Howes' copy with her signature. Second Life Books Inc. 174 - 103 2011 $60

Holland, Rupert Sargent *Pirate of the Delaware.* Philadelphia: Lippincott, 1925. First edition; 8vo., pages 318, 4 illustrations, author's presentation on flyleaf to poet Barbara Howes, cream cloth with pictorial stamping in dark blue, edges slightly spotted, cover somewhat scuffed and soiled spine little worn at ends, otherwise very good, tight copy. Second Life Books Inc. 174 - 182 2011 $65

Smith, Pauline *The Little Karoo.* New York: Vanguard, 1952. 8vo., pages 188, black cloth stamped in red and gilt, poet Barbara Howes' bookplate, edges and endpapers little spotted, else very good, tight copy. Second Life Books Inc. 174 - 290 2011 $75

Thoby-Marcelin, Philippe *The Beast of the Haitian Hills.* New York: Rinehart & Co., 1946. First edition; fine in near fine, mildly spine dulled dust jacket, with slight edge wear, very nice, scarce signed, inscribed by author to Barbara Howes, with Howes/Smith bookplate. Ken Lopez Bookseller 154 - 73 2011 $450

Thoby-Marcelin, Philippe *Canape-Vent.* New York: Farrar & Rinehart, 1994. First edition; fine in good, price clipped dust jacket with small corner chips but splitting at flap folds, inscribed by author to poet Barbara Howes in 1971, nice association, scarce signed. Ken Lopez Bookseller 154 - 72 2011 $450

Woolf, Virginia 1882-1941 *A Room of One's Own.* London: Hogarth, 1931. Second edition; 8vo., 172 pages, green cloth, owner's bookplate, name on flyleaf, edges slightly spotted, few pencil notations in margins, cover slightly spotted, otherwise very good, poet Barbara Howes' copy with her bookplate and signature. Second Life Books Inc. 174 - 333 2011 $135

Association – Howes, Wright

Haley, James Evetts *The XIT Ranch of Texas and the Early Days of the Llano Estacado.* Chicago: Lakeside Press, 1929. First edition; 8vo., presentation inscription by author to R. G. Long, also laid in is penned note on Prince George Hotel (NYC) stationery, to Wright Howes advising that they would meet him for breakfast and afterwards, go to a sale together; decorated cloth, xvi, 261 pages, gilt top, frontispiece, fine bright copy in protective transparent dust jacket, exceptional copy. Buckingham Books May 26 2011 - 28028 2011 $1875

Association – Howson, James

Rousseau, Jean Jacques 1712-1778 *Emilius or a Treatise on Education.* Edinburgh: printed by A. Donaldson, 1768. 3 volumes, contemporary full speckled calf gilt, hinges just cracking in places but sound, pages 344, 274, (ii), 246, (xlii), titles with ornamental borders, contemporary inscription of James Howson dated 1769 on each flyleaf, very attractive early English edition.   R. F. G. Hollett & Son Antiquarian Booksellers   175 - 1156 2011   £450

Association – Hoyle, Mary

Thomson, James 1700-1748 *The Seasons.* London: printed for John Sharpe, 1821. 170 x 105mm., 215, (1) pages, extremely pleasing etruscan style calf in the style of and quite probably by Edwards of Halifax, covers with gilt Greek key border, wide inner frame of stencilled palmettes, central panel of tree calf framed by a gilt broken cable, flat spine gilt in compartments separated by Greek key roll and with a lyre centerpiece framed by foliate cornerpieces, with black morocco label, marbled endpapers, all edges gilt, very attractive fore-edge painting of an English stately home, perhaps Stourhead House, extra engraved titlepage with vignette and fine engraved plates, inscription "Mary Williams/The last gift of her affectionate Aunt/Mary Hoyle, July 31st 1826"; extremities and joints bit dry and rubbed, rear joint just starting at tail, gilt eroded from head and tail of spine, half a dozen small patches of lost patina in frame around outside of stencilled central panel, plates little foxed, one more noticeably but still quite pleasing copy, appealing unrestored original binding entirely sound, text clean and smooth and rich colors of painting beautifully preserved.   Phillip J. Pirages   59 - 196 2011 $1100

Association – Hubbard, Gardiner Green

Pedley, Charles *The History of Newfoundland from the Earliest Times to the Year 1860.* London: Longman, Green, Longman, Roberts & Green, Spottiswoods and Co. London, 1863. Pages xix, 531, (40 pages of ads and index) brown cloth with gilt to spine, half title, large map in pocket in front, 8vo., expertly rebacked in original cloth, bookplate of Gardiner Green Hubbard and "GBF" in ink front endpaper.   Schooner Books Ltd.   96 - 80 2011 $450

Association – Hudleston, Mary

Camp, John *Discovering Bells and Bellringing.* Tring: Shire Publications, 1968. First edition; small 8vo., original stiff wrappers, pages 48, illustrations, few annotations by Mary Hudleston (folk song collector), small cutting taped inside front panel.   R. F. G. Hollett & Son Antiquarian Booksellers   175 - 220 2011   £30

Association – Hudson, Herbert

Tasso, Torquato 1544-1595 *Jerusalem Delivered.* London: printed for J. Dodsley, 1787. Sixth edition; 214 x 130mm., 2 volumes, handsome contemporary flamed calf, backstrips with wide Greek key roll at head and tail and with six compartments formed by decorative rolls, two of these with a central urn and graceful dangling fronds, two with unusual oval ornament composed of a central floral lozenge encircled first by a garland of leaves and then by a string of beads, each spine with two red morocco labels, one of them a circular volume label, engraved frontispiece by Thomas Stothard in each volume; late 19th century(?) bookplate of Harvey Bonnell (and with evidences of removed bookplate); gift inscription in pencil to Christopher Carter from Herbert Hudson at Wickham Bishops in Essex, dated June 1946, recto of front free endpaper of volume II with two newspaper cuttings about this work dated in 1830's tipped in; vaguest hint of rubbing to joints and corners, occasional minor smudges and other trivial imperfections internally, fine contemporary copy, text remarkably fresh, clean and bright, most attractive bindings especially lustrous and scarcely worn.   Phillip J. Pirages   59 - 60 2011 $750

Association – Hughes, Fanny

Hughes, Thomas 1822-1896 *Early Memories for the Children by the Author of Tom Brown's Schooldays.* Thomas Burleigh for Private Circulation only, 1899. First edition; Presentation copy from author's widow, Fanny to Edward Clifford, pages (2), 78, 8vo., uncut, original grey blue card wrappers with title printed in blue on upper cover, olive green paper backstrip, backstrip sometime reinforced with clear tape, but now defective at centre, presentation inscription slightly touched by glue adhering to cover, sound.   Blackwell Rare Books   B166 - 52 2011   £275

Association – Hughes, Olwyn

Hughes, Ted 1930-1998 *Wolfwatching.* London: Faber & Faber, 1989. First edition; signed presentation to Audrey (Nicholson) the actress, from the author, loosely inserted card signed by Olwyn Hughes, author's sister for Audrey, fine in very good+ dust jacket slightly rubbed at edges.   Any Amount of Books   May 29 2011 - A68490 2011 $272

Association – Hughes, Robert Vaughan

Radclyffe, William *Graphic Illustrations of Warwickshire.* Birmingham: Beilby, Knott and Beilby, 1829. First edition, large paper copy; frontispiece (tissue guard), 31 engraved proof plates on India paper (each with tissue guard), 12 engraved vignettes in text, very mild foxing to prelim and final leaves, pages (viii) xii, 128, 4to., near contemporary half red morocco, smoth backstrip longitudinally gilt lettered within ornate floral border designs, red moire cloth sides, blindstamped rules on returns, minor shelfwear at board extremities, all edges gilt, yellow chalked endpapers, contemporary steel engraved bookplate of Robert Vaughan Hughes of Wyelands, publisher's ad tipped to front free endpaper, near fine, tipped at front is 4 page publisher's ad with list of subscribers. Blackwell Rare Books B166 - 87 2011 £700

Association – Hull, Josephine

Kelly, George *Craig's Wife a Drama.* Boston: Little Brown, 1926. First edition; 8vo., pages 174, very nice, tight copy, inscribed by author to Josephine Williams who played the part of Mrs. Harold in the NY production, also signed by rest of the cast - Annie Sutherland, Crystal Herne, Arthur Shaw, C. Stewart, Eleanor Marsh, Charles Trowbridge, Josephine Hull, J. A. Curtis, Nelan Jaap, Arline Alcine & Mary Gildea, also inscribed by the producer, Rosalie Stewart to whom the play was dedicated. Second Life Books Inc. 174 - 213 2011 $2000

Association – Hume, M.

London, Jack 1876-1916 *The Son of the Wolf. Tales of the Far North.* Boston and New York: Houghton, Mifflin and Co., 1900. First American edition, first issue; with "Houghton Mifflin & Co. at foot of spine and without the "dots" separating the "&", with comma (not a period) after the date on copyright page, frontispiece illustration tipped-in, not sewn; (6), 251 pages, frontispiece, slate gray cloth stamped in silver on cover and spine (silver belt and buckle design), very small spot to front cover, owner's name to flyleaf (M. Hume), slight rubbing, much less than usual, to silver corners on front, overall very fine. Argonaut Book Shop Recent Acquisitions Summer 2010 - 120 2011 $3000

Association – Hunnewell, James Frothingham

West, Thomas *The Antiquities of Furness; or an Account of the Royal Abbey of St. Mary...* printed for the author by T. Spilsbury, 1774. First edition; 4to., contemporary full polished calf gilt, edges rather rubbed, rebacked in matching calf gilt with raised bands, original spine label retained, pages (xx) lvi, 288, 3A-3R4 (appendices), folding engraved map, folding plan, 2 engraved plates, attractive copy, pictorial bookplate of James Frothingham Hunnewell. R. F. G. Hollett & Son Antiquarian Booksellers 173 - 1179 2011 £350

Association – Hunt, Edith

Jafir Barmukee; or Jafir the Barmecide. A Tragedy in Five Acts in Which are Combined and Faithfully Represented, the Real Incidents Which Attended the Fall and Death of that Able and Accomplished Minister of the Khalif Haroon Al Rusheed, in the Year of the Hejira 186 Corresponding with A.D. 802. London: printed by Emily Faithfull & Co., Victoria Press (for the employment of women), 1861. First edition; 8vo., pages 100, recently rebound in thick card boards preserving printed front wrapper which is effectively the titlepage, titlepage also reproduced and pasted on front, some ar and slight chipping to front wrapper and prelims not affecting text, else sound, complete about very good, loosely inserted are 3 good letters to Edith Hunt, second wife of William Holman Hunt. Any Amount of Books May 29 2011 - A40829 2011 $238

Association – Hunt, Sylvia Kingsley

MacDonald, George 1824-1905 *Gutta Percha Willie, The Working Genius.* Blackie & Son, 1887. New edition; half title, frontispiece and 7 plates by Arthur Hughes, 32 page catalog, slightly marked, original blue pictorial cloth, spine slightly rubbed, inscription "Sylvia Kingsley Hunt from Iss Jolly 1875". Jarndyce Antiquarian Booksellers CXCII - 166 2011 £65

Association – Hunt, W. F.

Park, Mungo *Travels in the Interior Districts of Africa, Performed in the Years 1795, 1796 and 1797.* London: John Murray, 1817. 1816. Second Murray enlarged edition; 2 volumes, 8vo., large folding map, text figures, original half calf over decorative boards, raised bands, gilt stamped spine titles, neatly restored, preserving original spines and endsheets, ink signatures of W. F. Hunt, very good. Jeff Weber Rare Books 163 - 202 2011 $400

Association – Hunter, James

Burns, Robert 1759-1796 *The Works.* London: James Cochrane and Co., 1834. First printing of this edition; 8 volumes, 165 x 102mm., very attractive contemporary or slightly later dark maroon calf, covers decorated in gilt and blind with border of multiple gilt fillets and blind scrolling roll, gilt thistle cornerpieces, very large lyre centerpiece in blind, raised bands, spines gilt in compartments featuring scrolling foliate cornerpieces an sidepieces an lyre centerpiece, dark green morocco label, all edges gilt, one folding manuscript facsimile and 17 engraved plates, 8 engraved titlepages and frontispieces, armorial bookplate of James Hunter of Hafton; trivial rubbing to bindings, perhaps a score of leaves with minor marginal soiling or isolated faint foxing, few creased corners (one frayed), otherwise, very fine and pretty set, bindings bright and scarcely worn, text quite fresh and smooth. Phillip J. Pirages 59 - 157 2011 $1100

Association – Hunter, Mary

Paget, Violet 1856-1935 *Genius Loci: Notes on Places.* London: Grant Richards, 1899. First edition; half title, title in red and black, final ad leaf, uncut in original pale brown buckram, lettered gilt, little dulled, dust jacket, bookplate of collector Mary Hunter. Jarndyce Antiquarian Booksellers CLXC - 101 2011 £110

Association – Hunter, Russell

Prokosch, Frederic *Storm and Echo.* Garden City: Doubleday & Company Inc., 1948. First edition; copy 379 of only 85 signed copies with leaf of original manuscript bound in, this is the dedication copy, inscribed and signed by author to dedicatee, Russell Hunter, publisher's slipcase with pictorial front reproducing dust jacket art, fine in very good slipcase with edges split but intact. Charles Agvent 2010 Summer Miscellany - 57 2011 $750

Association – Hurd, Nathaniel

An Interesting Appendix to Sir William Blackstone's Commentaries on the Laws of England. Philadelphia: Robert Bell, 1773. Second American edition; 8vo., contemporary calf, crudely rebacked, very good, browned, Institutional name stamped on free endpaper, name erased from title, with John C. Williams bookplate, engraved by Nathaniel Hurd. M & S Rare Books, Inc. 90 - 44 2011 $3500

Association – Huskison, William

Hooke, Robert 1635-1703 *Micrographia Restaurata; or the Copper-Plates of Dr. Hooke's Wonderful Discoveries by the Microscope...* London: for John Bowles, R. Dodsley and John Cuff, 1745. Folio, iv, 65 (5) pages, 33 engraved plates, contemporary calf, very skillfully rebacked to style retaining original spine label, both text and plates moderately and uniformly foxed, armorial bookplate of Wm. Huskison Esqr. Joseph J. Felcone Inc. Fall Miscellany 2010 - 61 2011 $7500

Association – Hutchinson, James

Clarkson, Christopher *The History of Richmond, in the County of York, Including a Description of the Castle Friary, Easeby Abbey and Other Remains of Antiquity in the Neighbourhood.* Richmond: printed by and for T. Bowman at the Albion Press, 1814. 8vo., pages 436 + aquatint frontispiece and 3 other engraved plates, late 19th century dark olive green hard grain half morocco (color fugitive on spine to uniform mid-brown), spine double rule gilt with decorative rolls to flat raised bands and extremities, lettered direct in gilt, 'place & date' gilt direct at foot, boards decorative roll gilt bordered with "Sanspareil" design marbled book cloth sides, "Sanspareil Peacock swirl 'made' endpapers, edges uncut, maroon & primrose mutilcore made applied endbands, browned and spotted in places, spine and edges faded, just touch rubbed, ink inscription, "Coll & perf. F.C.B. Decr. 1879" (Captain F. C. Brooks of Ufford, Suffolk), ink inscription "James Hutchinson/Brigg/1814", heavily annotated by way of ink marginalia and by sewn-in folding sheets with historical agricultural gleanings, from the collection of Christopher Ernest Weston 1947-2010. Unsworths Booksellers 24 - 79 2011 £600

Association – Hutt, F. H.

Jefferies, Richard 1848-1887 *Field and Hedgerow: Being the Last Essays of Richard Jefferies.* London: Longmans, 1889. First edition; half title, 16 page catalog (June 1888), original grey green decorated cloth, blocked in black and light green, booksellers stamp of F. H. Hutt, very good. Jarndyce Antiquarian Booksellers CXCI - 333 2011 £68

Association – Hyde, James Hazen

Pinckney, Mary Stead *Letter-Book of Mary Stead Pinckney November 14th 1796 to August 29th 1797.* New York: Grolier Club, 1946. Limited to 300 copies; octavo, vi, 116 pages, bookplate of James Hazen Hyde, fine. Jeff Weber Rare Books 163 - 205 2011 $60

Association – Hytych, Frederick J.

Jennings, Hargrave *One of the Thirty: a Strange History, Now for the First Time Told.* London: John Camden Hotten, 1873. First edition; 8vo, pages 359, frontispiece (tissue guarded), signed presentation from author to Frederick J. Hytych dated August 1873, also tipped in at front is good lettered dated Jan. 2nd 1873 where HJ asks the same person discussing the progress of the book, also loosely inserted is signed note of 100+ words possibly to same person, original royal blue cloth, lettered/ruled in gold with silver gilt decorations, covers show little general wear and slight marking, spine tanned, little scuffed with wear at spine ends, overall near very good. Any Amount of Books May 29 2011 - A46391 2011 $398

Association – Ilchester, Earl of

Commines, Philippe De, Sieur D'Argenton 1445-1511
The Historie of Philip de Commines, Knight Lord of Argenton. London: John Bill, 1614. Third edition; folio, (16), 366, blank (3) pages, ornate woodcut title, woodcut headpieces, woodcut initials, woodcut tailpieces, genealogical chart, title marginally trimmed with minor loss of image, G^1 I^6 L^4 Q^2 V^3 marginally scorched with faint waterstains (text bright and readable), early full Cambridge calf, gilt raised bands, red leather spine label, extremities rubbed, bookplate of Earl of Ilchester, very good. Jeff Weber Rare Books 163 - 9 2011 $500

Association – Ingram, H. V.

Terentius Afer, Publius *Comoediae Sex.* Lvgd. Batavorvm: Ex Officina Elzeviriana, 1635. 122 x 70mm, 1 p.l., 304, (8) pages, (lacking (23 prefatory leaves, apparently never bound in), excellent contemporary maroon morocco elaborately gilt covers with blind rule border, flat spine gilt in single compartment with densely repeated scrolling foliate tools at either end and titling in panel at center, marbled endpapers, turn-ins, all edges gilt; with woodcut initials, headpiece, portrait tondo and Medusa tailpiece, engraved titlepage by C. C. Duysend, morocco bookplate of H. V. Ingram; a sliver of leather worn away at bottom of backstrip, corners little rubbed, infrequent light foxing, one or two small stains, excellent copy in pretty binding, leather lustrous, text very fresh and pleasing. Phillip J. Pirages 59 - 31 2011 $375

Association – Ingram, Thomas

Bateman, William *The Colonist; a Work on the Past and Present Position of the Colony of New Zealand.* Christchurch: J. T. Smith and Co., 1881. First edition; half title, presentation inscription by author to Thomas Ingram, (12), tables in text, 9-486 pages, original cloth, appendix (pages 255-486). Anthony W. Laywood May 26 2011 - 19080 2011 $84

Association – Innes, Alexander

Jacson, Frances *Isabella.* London: Henry Colburn & Co., 1823. First edition; 3 volumes in 2, contemporary half calf by J. Philip of Aberdeen, spines gilt ruled, maroon labels, spines little rubbed at head and tails, good+, armorial bookplates of Alexander Innes. Jarndyce Antiquarian Booksellers CLXC - 1 2011 £225

Association – Ishimoto, Yasuhiro

Taken by Design: Photographs from The Institute of Design 1937-1971. Chicago: University of Chicago Press, 2002. First edition; very fine in photo illustrated boards, issued without dust jacket, signed by a large number of photographers and some of the editors, among the signatures are Yasuhiro Ishimoto, Marvin E. Newton (twice), Barbara Crane, Ray K. Metzker, Joseph Jachna, Joseph Sterling (twice), Kenneth Josephson, David Travis, Keith Davis and quite a few others, unique copy. Jeff Hirsch Books ny 2010 2011 $750

Association – Jaap, Nelan

Kelly, George *Craig's Wife a Drama.* Boston: Little Brown, 1926. First edition; 8vo., pages 174, very nice, tight copy, inscribed by author to Josephine Williams who played the part of Mrs. Harold in the NY production, also signed by rest of the cast - Annie Sutherland, Crystal Herne, Arthur Shaw, C. Stewart, Eleanor Marsh, Charles Trowbridge, Josephine Hull, J. A. Curtis, Nelan Jaap, Arline Alcine & Mary Gildea, also inscribed by the producer, Rosalie Stewart to whom the play was dedicated. Second Life Books Inc. 174 - 213 2011 $2000

Association – Jachna, Joseph

Taken by Design: Photographs from The Institute of Design 1937-1971. Chicago: University of Chicago Press, 2002. First edition; very fine in photo illustrated boards, issued without dust jacket, signed by a large number of photographers and some of the editors, among the signatures are Yasuhiro Ishimoto, Marvin E. Newton (twice), Barbara Crane, Ray K. Metzker, Joseph Jachna, Joseph Sterling (twice), Kenneth Josephson, David Travis, Keith Davis and quite a few others, unique copy. Jeff Hirsch Books ny 2010 2011 $750

Association – Jack, Ian

Blanchard, Laman *Life and Literary Remains of L.E.L.* London: Henry Colburn, 1841. First edition; 2 volumes, half titles, engraved frontispiece, uncut in original brown vertical grained cloth, spines lettered in gilt, lower margin of back board slightly affected by damp volume II, expert minor repairs to heads and tails of spines, small later booklabels of Ian Jack. Jarndyce Antiquarian Booksellers CLXC - 81 2011 £250

Landon, Letitia Elizabeth *Poetical Works.* London: Longman, Brown, Greens & Longman, 1844. 4 volumes, half titles, fronts little browned, ads on endpapers, untrimmed in original blue cloth, spines lettered in gilt, spines uniformly faded, slight rubbing, bookseller's ticket; Godwin, Bath, later booklabels of Ian Jack, very good. Jarndyce Antiquarian Booksellers CLXC - 75 2011 £125

Association – Jackson, Harry

Pointer, Larry *Harry Jackson.* New York: Harry N. Abrams, 1981. First edition; large quarto, 308 pages, 397 photo illustrations, light brown cloth lettered in dark brown, very fine, pictorial dust jacket, presentation inscription signed by co-author, Donald Goddard, additionally signed by artist, Harry Jackson. Argonaut Book Shop Recent Acquisitions Summer 2010 - 160 2011 $300

Association – Jackson, Henry

Sallustius Crispus, Caius *C. Crispi Sallustii Belli Catilinarii et Jugurthini Historiae.* Glasguae: in aedibus Roberti Urie, 1749. 8vo., pages iv, 250, (ii), contemporary polished calf, untooled spine, red lettering piece gilt, boards double rule bordered in blind with extra double rule and decorative roll in blind at joint side, board edges 'zip-zag' decorative roll gilt, all edges red speckled, pink and white sewn endbands, lightly age toned, few stains, rubbed and bit chipped, joints cracking, spine darkened, contemporary ink inscription John Pelch, first name covered by pasted slip and later ink inscription "Wm. Clark, also pencil inscription "From Prof. Henry Jackson's Sale...", from the collection of Christopher Ernest Weston 1947-2010. Unsworths Booksellers 24 - 139 2011 £50

Association – Jackson, Holbrook

Morris, William 1834-1896 *Signs of Change. Seven Lectures Delivered on Various Occasions.* Reeves and Turner, 1888. First edition; one leaf of undated ads at front and another at rear, few fox spots and marginal pencil ticks, portrait of Morris from newspaper pasted to verso of half title, another image tipped to verso of contents leaf, pages (ii), viii, (i), 202, (2), 8vo., original dark red cloth, backstrip lettered in gilt, boards with single blind fillet border, booklabel and ownership inscription of Holbrook Jackson to front endpapers, slightly bumped and scuffed at extremities, good. Blackwell Rare Books B166 - 195 2011 £100

Association – Jackson, J. E.

Smith, Alexander *City Poems.* Cambridge: Macmillan, 1857. First edition; half title, final ad leaf + 24 page catalog Feb. 1857, original blue cloth, slightly rubbed, embossed W. H. Smith stamp, contemporary signature of J. E. Jackson. Jarndyce Antiquarian Booksellers CXCI - 494 2011 £35

Association – Jackson, Thomas

Mill, John Stuart 1806-1873 *Principles of Political Economy with Some of Their Applications to Social Philosophy...* London: John W. Parker,, 1852. Third edition; 2 volumes, 8vo., xx, 604, xv, (1), 571, (1) pages, contemporary maroon morocco gilt, double gilt fillets on sides, spines fully gilt in compartments with raised bands and contrasting red and green lettering pieces, marbled edges, fine, late 19th century library of Sir George Bowen, armorial bookplate, ALS presenting this copy to Sir Thomas Jackson. John Drury Rare Books 153 - 96 2011 £600

Association – James, Alice

James, William *The Literary Remains of the Late Henry James.* Boston: James R. Osgood and Co., 1885. First edition; 8vo., original publisher's red cloth lettered gilt at spine, pages 469, uncut, frontispiece, pencilled ownership signature of historian F. R. Cowell author of 'Cicero and the Roman Republic", signed presentation by A(lice) J(ames) for friend Constance Maude, slight fading at spine, slight mottling and slight marking, otherwise very good. Any Amount of Books May 29 2011 - A47621 2011 $340

Association – James, Arthur Godfrey

Boswell, James 1740-1795 *The Life of Samuel Johnson.* London: George Routledge & Sons, circa, 1889. Text in double columns, pages xvi, 526, 8vo., contemporary vellum, double gilt ruled borders on sides, spine richly gilt, very good, inscribed to A. Godfrey James from A. C. Benson, Eton, Xmas 1889. Blackwell Rare Books B166 - 19 2011 £85

Holland, Elizabeth Vassall, Lady 1770-1845 *A Memoir of the Rev. Sidney Smith.* London: Longmans, Green and co., circa, 1885. Couple of fox spots, pages x, 628, 8vo. contemporary tree calf, spine gilt, second compartment gilt lettered direct by Riviere and Son, slightly sunned, near fine, inscribed by author to Arthur Godfrey James. Blackwell Rare Books B166 - 49 2011 £70

Association – James, Harry Arthur

Dixon, E. *Fairy Tales from the Arabian Nights. First and Second Series.* London: J. M. Dent, 1893-1895. 2 volumes, square 8vo., original decorated green cloth gilt, slight crease to one lower board, spines trifle dulled, pages (ii), 268; (ii), 256, with green floral endpapers, titles in red and black, 10 full page plates and 32 other illustrations, half titles and faintly page rather browned, presentation inscription, Welsh boxing bookplate of Harry Arthur James, very good. R. F. G. Hollett & Son Antiquarian Booksellers 175 - 87 2011 £250

Association – James, Henry

Hudson, William Henry   1841-1922   *Nature in Downland.*   London: Longmans, Green and Co., 1900. First edition; half title, frontispiece, engraved titlepage, plates and illustrations, uncut in original green buckram, slightly marked, presentation inscription to Paul Harvey, from friend Henry James.   Jarndyce Antiquarian Booksellers   CXCI - 221   2011   £850

Association – James, John

Barrow, Isaac   *The Works of the Learned Isaac Barrow...*   London: James Round, Jacob Tonson, and William Taylor, 1716. Third/fourth editions; 3 volumes bound in two, large 4to., (20), 783, (5); (4), 381, (7); (8), 390, (6) pages, frontispiece, full paneled Cambridge style speckled calf, raised bands, gilt stamped spine titles, expertly rebacked, retaining covers and spines, ownership signatures of David Jenks and John A. James, fine.   Jeff Weber Rare Books   163 - 31   2011 $1000

Association – Jarrett, John

Caesar, Gaius Julius   *C. Julii Caesaris quae Extant Accuratissime...*   London: Sumptibus & typis Jacobi Tonson, 1712. Large folio, pages (6), 560, 87 engraved plates and maps, 31 engraved head and tailpieces, vignettes and 17 engraved historiated initials, double page plate of bison, usually lacking, contemporary red straight grain morocco, rebacked, original spine laid down, boards ruled in gilt and borders roll tooled in blind, spine elaborately tooled in gilt and blind in compartments, spine lettered in gilt, board edges stamped in gilt, gilt dentelles, all edges gilt, marbled endpaper, corners with some wear, occasional light toning, four inch closed marginal tear on leaf L11, professionally repaired, not affecting text, 2 previous owner's bookplates of John Jarrett and C. Kalbfleisch, small old bookseller's label, overall excellent copy, very wide margined, clean and in attractive contemporary binding.   Heritage Book Shop   Holiday 2010 - 16   2011 $15,000

Association – Jeans, James

Shaw, George Bernard   1856-1950   *In Good King Charles's Golden Days: a History Lesson by a Fellow of The Royal Society of Literature.*   London: privately printed, 1939. First edition; 8vo., original publisher's printed wrappers designated "First Rehearsal Copy" on cover and "Strictly Private", signed presentation from author to scientist/astronomer James Jeans, few marginal linings in text, presumably in hand of Jeans, clean, very good example with slight creasing to one corner and short split at lower top hinge.   Any Amount of Books   May 26 2011 - A73446   2011 $1845

Association – Jeffreys, W.

Blackstone, William   1723-1780   *Commentaries on the Laws of England.*   Oxford: printed at the Clarendon Press, 1768-1769. Volumes I & II third edition, volumes III & IV first edition; 4to., full contemporary calf, raised bands, red and green gilt labels, joints cracked but firm, surface abrasion to boards, contemporary signature of W. Jeffreys Jr. dated 1769, later bookplate of Fort Augustus Abbey, very good, clean set.   Jarndyce Antiquarian Booksellers   CXCI - 70   2011   £2800

Association – Jeffreys, Walter Powell

Kingsley, Charles   1819-1875   *Westward Ho!*   Cambridge: Macmillan, 1855. First edition; 3 volumes, half titles, handsomely bound in tan calf by R. D. Steadman, Newcastle upon Tyne, gilt borders, raised bands, gilt compartments & dentelles, brown and dark green morocco labels, some slight marking or darkening to boards, armorial bookplates of Walter Powell Jeffreys, very good, handsome.   Jarndyce Antiquarian Booksellers   CXCI - 529   2011   £450

Association – Jenkins, Roy

Who Was Who.   London: Adam & Charles Black, 1966-1991. 9 volumes, 8vo., all very good or better in like dust jackets, first 6 volumes presentation from Roy Jenkins to Ian Gilmour.   Any Amount of Books   May 26 2011 - A70295   2011 $419

Association – Jenks, David

Barrow, Isaac   *The Works of the Learned Isaac Barrow...*   London: James Round, Jacob Tonson, and William Taylor, 1716. Third/fourth editions; 3 volumes bound in two, large 4to., (20), 783, (5); (4), 381, (7); (8), 390, (6) pages, frontispiece, full paneled Cambridge style speckled calf, raised bands, gilt stamped spine titles, expertly rebacked, retaining covers and spines, ownership signatures of David Jenks and John A. James, fine.   Jeff Weber Rare Books   163 - 31   2011 $1000

Association – Jennings, Annie Burr

Stevenson, Robert Louis Balfour 1850-1894 *Poems.* London: printed at the Florence Press for Chatto & Windus in association with Longmans Green & Co., 1913. One of 500 numbered copies on handmade paper (this being copy #472); 225 x 185mm., xvi, 399, (1) pages, stunning contemporary rose colored morocco, elaborately onlaid and inlaid as well as lavishly tooled in gilt by Riviere (stamp signed on front turn-in), covers with frame composed of two parallel borders, outer one featuring a curving gilt vine bearing green inlaid morocco blossom, the inner one with small inlaid black morocco circles connected by single gilt rule, two borders joined by interlacing strapwork cornerpieces inner border interrupted at center of each side with very intricate strapwork, each lobe containing three red onlaid morocco roses and connected on its inside tip, with prominent central mandorla featuring a beautiful onlaid composition of four lilies and four acanthus leaves in ivory, red and green morocco, the panel surrounding the centerpiece filled in with some 200 gilt leaves and flowers on twining stems, entire surface of boards covered with gilt stippling (sidepieces, cornerpieces and mandorla very densely stippled), raised bands, spine elaborately gilt in double ruled compartments of a complex design, each with four inlaid black morocco flowers, central inlaid circle and much stippling, extremely pretty white morocco doublures with very flamboyant floral gilt cornerpieces, doublure framed by very wide and unusually lovely turn-ins heavily gilt in repeating floral pattern, moss green watered silk endleaves, top edges gilt, other edges untrimmed, in binder's original (rather worn) folding morocco box with one defective metal closure, title printed in blue and black, front doublure with ivory morocco bookplate with monogram of "ABJ (apparently Annie Burr Jennings) above motto from Seneca "Otium sine litteris ors est", bookplate of Mrs. A. H. Ely, bookplate faintly discolored upper corner of front free endpaper just slightly crumpled, front flyleaf with two small stains, very short closed fore-edge tear, one leaf with rust spot, remarkably fine, unusually bright text pristine, dazzling binding with virtually no signs of wear. Phillip J. Pirages 59 - 127 2011 $15,000

Association – Jessopp, Augustus

Anderson, James S. M. *The History of the Church of England in the Colonies and Foreign Dependencies of the British Empire.* London: Rivingtons, 1856. Second edition; original brown cloth, blindstamp design to boards and gilt titles to spine, pages xl, 512, (8 pages ads); xix, 582, (2 ads); xx, 654, (2 ads), index, large folding table and folding color map to volume i and folding geological table to volume III, small 8vo., each volume has one outer hinge crack, otherwise very good, very good interiors with small signature "Augustus Jessopp Feburary 1858". Schooner Books Ltd. 96 - 274 2011 $175

Association – Jex-Blake, T. W.

Ruskin, John 1819-1900 *The Political Economy of Art: Being the Substance...* London: Smith, Elder & Co., 1857. First edition; small 8vo., original printed cloth, rather rubbed and neatly recased, pages vii, 248, blindstamp on title of Rev. T. W. Jex-Blake, Headmaster of Rugby School 1874-87, few spots to fore-edge. R. F. G. Hollett & Son Antiquarian Booksellers 175 - 1164 2011 £65

Association – Johnson, A.

Strype, John *The History of the Life and Acts of... Edmund Grindal...* London: printed for John Wyat and John Hartley, 1710. Folio, pages (i), xviii, 314, 108, (vi) + engraved frontispiece, contemporary calf, untooled spine, red lettering piece gilt, boards panelled in blind (Cambridge style) board edges decorative roll gilt, all edges red sprinkled, blue and white sewn endbands, lightly browned and spotted, rubbed and chipped, corners worn, joints cracking at ends, strong, contemporary inscription "Ant. Johnson, ink inscriptions crossed out on both pastedowns, from the collection of Christopher Ernest Weston 1947-2010. Unsworths Booksellers 24 - 51 2011 £250

Association – Johnson, Charles Plumptre

Dickens, Charles 1812-1870 *A Christmas Carol.* Philadelphia: Carey & Hart, 1844. Half title, color frontispiece, plates and illustrations, lager half green crushed morocco by Zaehnsdorf, spine blocked and lettered in gilt, original blue cloth bound in to precede half title, top edge gilt, very good, booklabel of Charles Plumptre Johnson, top edge gilt, very good. Jarndyce Antiquarian Booksellers CXCI - 154 2011 £1500

Association – Johnson, F. D.

Surtees, Robert Smith 1803-1864 *Mr. Sponge's Sporting Tour.* London: Bradbury & Evans, 1853. First edition; half title, frontispiece, hand colored steep engraved plates, illustrations, original brown cloth, borders in blind, pictorially blocked in gilt, neatly recased, little dulled, inscribed by author to F. D. Johnson, all edges gilt, tipped in 3 page ALS from author to Johnson. Jarndyce Antiquarian Booksellers CXCI - 501 2011 £280

Association – Johnson, Malcolm

Maugham, William Somerset 1874-1965 *Of Human Bondage.* New York: Doubleday, Doran, 1936. First illustrated edition, one of 751 numbered copies signed by author and artist, this is copy #4; additionally inscribed by author for Doubleday editor Malcolm Johnson, illustrations by Randolph Schwabe, small quarto, full dark blue morocco with raised bands and heavily stamped in gilt, just about fine, laid in is 1936 letter from artist, Schwabe in his calligraphic hand. Between the Covers 169 - BTC346497 2011 $4250

Association – Johnson, Mr.

Saunders, Louise *The Knave of Hearts.* New York: Charles Scribner's Sons, 1925. First edition; large quarto, (6), 46, (1) (3, blank) pages, color frontispiece and tissue guards, many full page color illustrations by Maxfield Parrish, laid into this copy is ANS by artist for Mr. Johnson, original black cloth with color pictorial label on front cover, color pictorial endpapers, some very light scuffing of back board, very clean internally, about fine in most of original glassine wrappers, however torn quite a bit, original issue cardboard box, box heavily worn, bottom of box intact but cracked at corners, top of box has its sides detached, however this box usually not present at all.   Heritage Book Shop   Holiday 2010 - 94   2011 $5500

Association – Johnson, Oliver

Garrison, William Lloyd *Sonnets and Other Poems.* Boston: Oliver Johnson, 1843. First edition; 16mo., 96 pages, original cloth, some browning, near fine, inscribed in ink by publisher O(liver) Johnson to his sister.   M & S Rare Books, Inc.   90 - 144   2011 $600

Association – Johnston, Ollie

Thomas, Frank *Disney Animation. The Illusion of Life.* New York: Abbeville, 1981. First edition; fine in fine dust jacket, inscribed by Thomas and Ollie Johnston.   Bella Luna Books   May 26 2011 - t6520   2011 $247

Association – Johnston, William

Bible. Greek - 1750 *(Greek). Novum Testamentum.* Glasguae: in Aedibus R. Urie, 1750. Large paper copy, 8vo., pages (iv), 572 i.e. formula (pi)2, A-Bbbb4, Cccc2 = 228 leaves, text in Greek, contemporary crimson morocco, spine panel gilt, black lettering piece gilt, boards broad decorative roll gilt bordered, board edges and turn-ins obliquely broken rule gilt, 'Antique Spot' 'made' endpapers, all edges gilt, pink and white sewn endpapers, little light spotting, joints touch rubbed, spine slightly darkened, armorial bookplate William Johnston Esq, from the collection of Christopher Ernest Weston 1947-2010.   Unsworths Booksellers   24 - 10   2011   £300

Association – Johnstone, H. H.

Martineau, Harriet 1802-1876 *A Complete Guide to the English Lakes.* Windermere: John Garnett, 1862. Third edition; engraved frontispiece, vignette title, additional printed title, foldout maps, plates, 15 pages commercial ads, original purple cloth, blocked in blind, lettered in gilt, bit worn, contemporary ownership inscription of H. H. Johnstone, Fairfield.   Jarndyce Antiquarian Booksellers CLXC - 269   2011   £68

Association – Jolliffe

Blackwell, Thomas *Memoirs of the Court of Augustus.* London: printed for A. Millar, 1764. third edition; 3 volumes, 4to., pages (vi) 384 + 9 engraved plates of roundel portraits, viii, 456 + 8 engraved plates of roundel portraits; (vi) 573 (xlix) + 8 engraved plates of roundel portraits, contemporary sprinkled and polished tan calf, spines panel gilt, red and black lettering and numbering pieces gilt, boards double rule gilt bordered, board edges 'zig-zag' decorative roll in blind, turn-ins obliquely striped with dark stain, all edges lightly red sprinkled, red and white sewn endbands, lightly toned and spotted, joints cracking but strong, spine ends bit worn with small repairs to headcaps, armorial bookplate of Jolliffe, from the collection of Christopher Ernest Weston 1947-2010.   Unsworths Booksellers   24 - 70   2011   £300

Association – Jolly, Iss

MacDonald, George 1824-1905 *Gutta Percha Willie, The Working Genius.* Blackie & Son, 1887. New edition; half title, frontispiece and 7 plates by Arthur Hughes, 32 page catalog, slightly marked, original blue pictorial cloth, spine slightly rubbed, inscription "Sylvia Kingsley Hunt from Iss Jolly 1875".   Jarndyce Antiquarian Booksellers   CXCII - 166   2011   £65

Association – Jones, E. Alfred

Hoare & Co. *Hoare' Bank. A Record 1673-1932.* privately published, 1932. Large 8vo., original cloth, gilt, dust jacket little rubbed and darkened, few short edge tears, pages xi, 88, 33 illustrations, genealogical table, TLS from H. P. R. Hoare to E. A. Jones, presentation copy presented by Bank to Jones.   R. F. G. Hollett & Son Antiquarian Booksellers 175 - 636   2011   £40

Association – Jones, Geraint

Burney, Charles *An Account of the Musical Performances in Westminster Abbey and the Pantheon May 26th, 27th, 29th and June the 3d and 5th 1748 in Commemoration of Handel.* London: printed for the Benefit of the Musical Fund and Sold by T. Payne and Son, 1785. First edition; 4to., pages vii (1), xvi, 8 *8, 9-20, *19-*24, 21-56, 21, (6), 46-90, (5), 94-139, (3), frontispiece and 7 other engraved plates, half dark green leather lettered gilt at spine with marbled boards and marbled endpapers, slight rubbing at spine hinges and corners, very slightly occasional foxing, slightly more pronounced at titlepage, else very good, from the library of classical musician Geraint Jones (1917-1998), 3 small drawings by Burney pasted to 2 supplied blanks inserted before title, pencilled beneath 2 drawings are notes, presumably in hand of former owner or past bookseller. Any Amount of Books   May 26 2011 - A46347   2011 $1256

Spender, Stephen *Three Versions from the German.* London: privately published, 1956. First edition, no. 50 of 100 copies; inscribed by author for Winnie and Geraint Jones, also signed by author's wife Natasha Spender, 8vo., original gold paper wrappers, titles to pink label on upper wrapper in black, gold wrappers in very good order, but creased at lower front and rear corner.   Any Amount of Books   May 29 2011 - A46011   2011 $272

Association – Jones, Gwilym Peredur

Fowler, J. T. *Adamnani Vita S. Columbae.* Oxford: Clarendon Press, 1894. Pages lxxxvii, 202, (ii), 8, original quarter roan gilt, spine rather frayed at head, some pencilled notes and underlinings, distinguished trio of earlier historian owners, Gwilym Peredur Jones, F. Lindstead Downham and Geoffrey Martin.   R. F. G. Hollett & Son Antiquarian Booksellers   175 - 464   2011   £35

Association – Jones, H. T.

Jones, Edward *A Peep Into the Palace; or a Voice from the House of Correction.* London: J. Pattie, 1841. Seventh edition; some faint damp marking, 64 pages, contemporary half green calf, lacking spine strip, signature of H. T. Jones on titlepage.   Jarndyce Antiquarian Booksellers   CXCI - 597   2011   £250

Association – Jones, Horace

Goblet, Y. M. *A Topographical Index of the Parishes and Towlands of Iceland in Petty's Barony Maps.* IMC, 1932. Only 500 copies printed; very good, ex-libris Horace Jones (Cork genealogist).   C. P. Hyland   May 26 2011 - 259/158   2011 $362

Association – Jones, Isaac

Pushkin, Aleksandr Sergeevich 1799-1837 *The Golden Cockerel.* New York: Heritage Press, 1950. 4to., original publisher's blue cloth with cockerel printed in gilt in repeat pattern on covers, spine lettered gilt, pages 42, copiously illustrated in color, signed by artist, Edmund Dulac with presentation from Dulac for Isaac Jones, slight marks, head of spine slightly rubbed, slight soiling otherwise very good+.   Any Amount of Books   May 29 2011 - A43024   2011 $340

Association – Jones, Margaret

Scott, George *The Memoires of Sir James Melhil of Hal-Hill...* London: printed by E. H. For Robert Boulter, 1683. First edition; 4to., (xvi), 204, (26) pages, heavily foxed and browned, title and first 5 leaves chipped at extremities, contemporary full calf, raised bands, leather scuffed, hinges neatly repaired, modern red title spine label, handsomely with gilt rolls, ownership signature of Margaret Jones, Philadelphia, very good.   Jeff Weber Rare Books   163 - 22   2011 $1000

Association – Jones, William

Dilich, Wilhelm *Peribologia.* Frankfurt: A. Humm etc., 1641. Folio, 5-202, 10) pages, engraved title and 7 section titles, 410 plus numbered engravings, contemporary English calf, gilt fillet on covers, spine with gilt ornaments, red edges, from the library of the Earls of Macclesfield at Shirburn Castle, this copy may well stem from the library of John Collins/William Jones, and has the old Macclesfield Library class mark.   Maggs Bros. Ltd.   1440 - 68   2011   £2000

Association – Jones, Winifred

Spender, Stephen *Three Versions from the German.* London: privately published, 1956. First edition, no. 50 of 100 copies; inscribed by author for Winnie and Geraint Jones, also signed by author's wife Natasha Spender, 8vo., original gold paper wrappers, titles to pink label on upper wrapper in black, gold wrappers in very good order, but creased at lower front and rear corner.   Any Amount of Books   May 29 2011 - A46011   2011 $272

Association – Joseph, E.

Milton, John 1608-1674 *Comus.* London: William Heinemann/New York: Doubleday Page, 1921. One of 550 copies; signed by artist, 300 x 233mm., 3 p.l., ix-xviii, 76 pages, (1) leaf, very attractive deep blue morocco by Zaehnsdorf for E. Joseph (stamp signed), upper board with very large gilt pictorial presentation and titling, raised bands, gilt spine titling, densely gilt turn-ins, marbled endpapers, top edge gilt, other edges untrimmed and partly unopened, illustrated titlepages, numerous black and white drawings, and 24 particularly pleasing color plates by Arthur Rackham, mounted on brown paper, original tissue guard, with descriptive letterpress; bookplate of Robert J. Wickenheiser, virtually faultless copy.   Phillip J. Pirages   59 - 292   2011 $3900

Association – Josephson, Kenneth

Taken by Design: Photographs from The Institute of Design 1937-1971. Chicago: University of Chicago Press, 2002. First edition; very fine in photo illustrated boards, issued without dust jacket, signed by a large number of photographers and some of the editors, among the signatures are Yasuhiro Ishimoto, Marvin E. Newton (twice), Barbara Crane, Ray K. Metzker, Joseph Jachna, Joseph Sterling (twice), Kenneth Josephson, David Travis, Keith Davis and quite a few others, unique copy. Jeff Hirsch Books ny 2010 2011 $750

Association – Josey, Clint

Garrard, Lewis H. *Wah-To-Yah and the Taos Trail; or Prairie and Scalp Dances, with a Look at Los Rancheros....* Cincinnati: H. W. Derby & Co., 1850. First edition, first state; from the library of Clint and Dorothy Josey with their bookplate affixed to front pastedown sheep, original black blindstamped cloth with original spine replaced, original title in gilt on spine, vi, (2), 349 pages, professionally rebacked with tiny portion of original spine remaining, front and rear endpapers replaced, some pages lightly foxed, else near fine, tight copy, housed in slipcase. Buckingham Books May 26 2011 - 28736 2011 $3000

Association – Josey, Dorothy

Garrard, Lewis H. *Wah-To-Yah and the Taos Trail; or Prairie and Scalp Dances, with a Look at Los Rancheros....* Cincinnati: H. W. Derby & Co., 1850. First edition, first state; from the library of Clint and Dorothy Josey with their bookplate affixed to front pastedown sheep, original black blindstamped cloth with original spine replaced, original title in gilt on spine, vi, (2), 349 pages, professionally rebacked with tiny portion of original spine remaining, front and rear endpapers replaced, some pages lightly foxed, else near fine, tight copy, housed in slipcase. Buckingham Books May 26 2011 - 28736 2011 $3000

Association – Juel-Jensen, Bent

Sparrow, John *A Day with Myself.* Burford - Cygnet Press, 1979. One of 100 copies; pages (8) 16mo., original black wrappers, printed front cover label, fine, inscribed by John Sparrow for Bent J(uel) J(ensen). Blackwell Rare Books B166 - 247 2011 £50

Association – Kael, Pauline

Shawn, Wallace *The Designated Mourner.* New York: Noonday Press, 1997. First Noonday Press edition; inscribed by author for Pauline Kael, together with Shawn's interview with Mark Strand in The Paris Review, Volume 40, No. 148 (NY: Paris Review 1998), laid in is APS from Shawn to Kael first book fine in wrappers, second book and card near fine. Ken Lopez Bookseller 154 - 201 2011 $350

Association – Kalbfleisch, Charles

Caesar, Gaius Julius *C. Julii Caesaris quae Extant Accuratissime...* London: Sumptibus & typis Jacobi Tonson, 1712. Large folio, pages (6), 560, 87 engraved plates and maps, 31 engraved head and tailpieces, vignettes and 17 engraved historiated initials, double page plate of bison, usually lacking, contemporary red straight grain morocco, rebacked, original spine laid down, boards ruled in gilt and borders roll tooled in blind, spine elaborately tooled in gilt and blind in compartments, spine lettered in gilt, board edges stamped in gilt, gilt dentelles, all edges gilt, marbled endpaper, corners with some wear, occasional light toning, four inch closed marginal tear on leaf L11, professionally repaired, not affecting text, 2 previous owner's bookplates of John Jarrett and C. Kalbfleisch, small old bookseller's label, overall excellent copy, very wide margined, clean and in attractive contemporary binding. Heritage Book Shop Holiday 2010 - 16 2011 $15,000

Lefevre, Raoul *Recuyell of the Historyes of Troye.* Hammersmith: Kelmscott Press, 1892. One of 300 copies; 3 books in 2 volumes, large quarto, xv, (1), 295, (1 blank); (297)-507, (1, blank), (509)-718 pages, printed in red and black in Troy and Chaucer type, decorative woodcut borders and initials, bound by Cedric Chivers in beautiful Art Nouveau "Vellucent" binding, binding elaborately decorated in vivid colors and detail and all boards and spine ruled in gilt, front covers framed by green vines with pink and orange flowers and gilt stamped detail, inside frame of vines stands Helen of Troy on volume I and Cassandra on volume II, title of book shown on a scroll beneath women's feet, spines of both volumes contain similar scroll decoration, also containing title of book on back cover of each volume is image of the towers of Troy in flames, and gauffered, others uncut, marbled endpapers, gilt ruled dentelles, bookplates of former owners Rudloph August Williams and "CKC" Charles C. Kalbfleisch and bookplate of other previous owner on back pastedown of each volume, each volume in its own chemise and quarter calf slipcase, dentelles slightly lifting, otherwise beautiful, near fine set in extraordinary binding. Heritage Book Shop Holiday 2010 - 67 2011 $22,500

Association – Kallir, Otto Nirenstein

Birnbaum, Uriel *Der Kaiser und Der Architekt: ein marchn in funzig Bildern. (The Emperor and the Architect: a Tale of Fifty Pictures).* Leipzig und Wien: Thyrsas Verlag, 1924. First edition; large 4to., blue cloth stamped in gold, 82 page, corner of cover faded, else near fine, 50 full page richly color illustrations, this copy inscribed by Birnbaum to Otto Nirenstein Kallir who founded Viennese modern art Neue Galerie in 1923, stunning book quite scarce with nice inscription. Aleph-Bet Books, Inc. 95 - 101 2011 $800

Association – Kapp, Yvonne

Brooke, Jocelyn *The Birth of a Legend.* London: Bertram Rota, 1964. One of 65 copies signed by author, this "out of series"; 4to., stiff plain card with printed green self wrappers, pages 7, signed presentation from publisher Anthony Rota to writer and activist Yvonne Kapp. Any Amount of Books   May 29 2011 - A49029 2011 $383

Association – Kaye, John

Cosin, John *Scholastical History of the Canon of the Holy Scripture.* London: E. Tyler and R. Holt for Robert Pawlett, 1672. 4to., pages (xxxvi), 224, (xlviii) + additional engraved titlepage, contemporary speckled calf, boards double ruled in blind, board edges broken ruled gilt, all edges blue 'swirl' marbled blue and white sewn endbands, early 1990's calf reback + corners by Chris Weston, touch of dust soiling, old leather bit flaked and rubbed, ink inscription "J. Lincoln", 20th century ink inscription "This volume belonged to/ John Kaye D.D./Bishop of Lincoln/1827-1853. It belonged to his son/William Frederick John Kaye/Archdeacon of Lincoln/1863-1919", ink inscription "Peter B.G. Binnall/ Barkwith Rectory/Wragby/Lincoln/ (rule) Bought in Lincoln/30 April 1951", 19th century bookseller's ticket "J. Leslie/52 Great Queen Street/Lincoln's Inn Fields/London; from the collection of Christopher Ernest Weston 1947-2010. Unsworths Booksellers   24 - 19 2011   £275

Association – Kaye, William Frederick John

Cosin, John *Scholastical History of the Canon of the Holy Scripture.* London: E. Tyler and R. Holt for Robert Pawlett, 1672. 4to., pages (xxxvi), 224, (xlviii) + additional engraved titlepage, contemporary speckled calf, boards double ruled in blind, board edges broken ruled gilt, all edges blue 'swirl' marbled blue and white sewn endbands, early 1990's calf reback + corners by Chris Weston, touch of dust soiling, old leather bit flaked and rubbed, ink inscription "J. Lincoln", 20th century ink inscription "This volume belonged to/ John Kaye D.D./Bishop of Lincoln/1827-1853. It belonged to his son/William Frederick John Kaye/Archdeacon of Lincoln/1863-1919", ink inscription "Peter B.G. Binnall/ Barkwith Rectory/Wragby/Lincoln/ (rule) Bought in Lincoln/30 April 1951", 19th century bookseller's ticket "J. Leslie/52 Great Queen Street/Lincoln's Inn Fields/London; from the collection of Christopher Ernest Weston 1947-2010. Unsworths Booksellers   24 - 19 2011   £275

Association – Keene, Charles

Layard, George Somes *The Life and Letters of Charles Samuel Keene.* London: Sampson Low, 1893. New edition; half title, frontispiece, illustrations, text slightly spotted, original dark blue cloth, gilt, slightly marked and rubbed, inner hinges slightly cracked, loosely inserted printed invitation completed by hand to Charles Keene for a "Punch" supper on 5th July 1871.   Jarndyce Antiquarian Booksellers   CXCI - 231 2011   £110

Association – Kelly, Thomas

Vergilius Maro, Publius *Bucolica, Georgica et Aeneis.* Birmingham: John Baskerville, 1757. First Baskerville edition; glorious copy, 4to., (10), 432 pages, contemporary English or Irish green morocco, gilt floral borders on covers, spine richly gilt with floral and ornamental tools, red morocco lettering piece, fine, beautifully, 18th century engraved bookplate of Thomas Kelly, contemporary signature of Hen. Gore.   Joseph J. Felcone Inc.   Fall Miscellany 2010 - 11 2011 $3800

Association – Kemp-Welch, John

Kynaston, David *Cazenove & Co. A History.* London: Batsford, 1991. First edition; pages 359, illustrations in color, inscribed "Duff (Hart-Davis) with best wishes John Kemp-Welch (partner, Cazenove & Co.) Oct. 1991".   R. F. G. Hollett & Son Antiquarian Booksellers   175 - 796 2011   £35

Association – Kendall, Percy

Conder, C. R. *The Tell Amarna Tablets.* Palestine Exploration Fund, 1892. First edition; original cloth, gilt, rather marked, hinges little rubbed, pages xi, 212, (iv), the copy of Percy F. Kendall (Yorkshire geologist) with his signature, later from the library of Dr. Arthur Raistrick with his bookplate.   R. F. G. Hollett & Son Antiquarian Booksellers   177 - 205 2011   £35

Association – Kennedy, Chessborough MacKenzie

Roustam, Bek *Aerial Russia. The Romance of the Giant Aeroplane.* London: Bodley Head, 1916. First edition; 8vo., original publisher's cloth lettered blue on cover and brown on spine, pages xvi, 154, uncut, frontispiece and 19 plates, signed presentation from Chessborough MacKenzie Kennedy, remains of dust jacket loosely inserted, slight browning to pages, else very good or better.   Any Amount of Books   May 29 2011 - A39876 2011 $221

Association – Kennedy, P.

Brooke, Henry *Memoirs of the Life of the Late Excellent and Pious Mr. Henry Brooke, Collected from Original Papers and Other Authentic Sources.* Dublin: printed by R. Napper and sold by M. Keane &c, 1816. 12mo., uncut in original blue boards, brown paper spine, worn paper label, leading hinge weakening, Dublin bookseller's ticket "P. Kennedy, Anglesea Street, Six Doors of College Green".   Jarndyce Antiquarian Booksellers   CXCI - 91 2011   £85

Association – Kennedy, T. F.

Thomson, Robert *Treatise on the Progress of Literature, and Its Effects on Society...* Edinburgh: Adam & Charles Black, 1834. Half title, odd spot, few repairs in inner margins with sellotape by previous owner, uncut in original drab boards, purple cloth, recased, paper label chipped and faded, inscribed presentation from author to T. F. Kennedy. Jarndyce Antiquarian Booksellers CXCI - 516 2011 £35

Association – Kenyon, Lloyd, Baron

Great Britain. Royal Commission on Historical Manuscripts - 1884 *Reports.* 1884-1917. 8vo., uniform red quarter morocco gilt, some little rubbed at head and foot of spines, handsome set, ex-libris Lloyd Lord Kenyon, Baron of Gredington with his armorial bookplate and family crest in gilt to centre of each upper cover. C. P. Hyland May 26 2011 - 257/249 2011 $5073

Great Britain. Royal Commission on Historical Manuscripts - 1895 *Report on the Manuscripts of the Marquis Of Ormonde.* Historical Manuscripts Commission, 1895. 1909. 1902.1912; together 10 volumes, red quarter morocco gilt, ex-libris, Lloyd, Lord Kenyon, with armorial bookplate and family rest in gilt on each upper cover, slight rubbing at head and foot of spines, 8vo. C. P. Hyland May 26 2011 - 255/338 2011 $1015

Association – Kermode, Frank

Kelly, Dollin *New Max Worthies.* Douglas: Manx Heritage Foundation, 2006. First edition; 4to., illustrations in black and white, 504 pages, fine in very good dust jacket with slight edgewear, Frank Kermode's copy with letter to him from Bureau Chief of NY Times and some xeroxes. Any Amount of Books May 29 2011 - A76394 2011 $204

Association – Kern, Jerome

Shaw, George Bernard 1856-1950 *The Perfect Wagnerite: a Commentary on the Niblung's Ring.* London: Grant Richards, 1898. First edition; quart cloth and silk or linen over boards, sizing under silk little toned, silk worn through a little on edges, very good, small leather bookplate of composer Jerome Kern. Between the Covers 169 - BTC342152 2011 $1000

Association – Kerr, Charles

Newte, Thomas *Prospects and Observations; on a Tour in England and Scotland: Natural, Economical and Literary.* London: printed for G. G. J. and J. Robinson, 1791. 4to., pages viii, 440 + a folding engraved map frontispiece and 23 other engraved plates, contemporary polished tan calf, board edges 'zig-zag' decorative roll in blind, red and white sewn endbands, late 1990's calf reback by Chris Weston, original red lettering piece gilt relaid, some foxing, old leather scratched and bit rubbed at edges, armorial bookplate of C. Kerr Esqr/Calder Bank, ink inscription "Charles Kerr/ Georges Square", from the collection of Christopher Ernest Weston 1947-2010. Unsworths Booksellers 24 - 126 2011 £350

Association – Kerr, Douglas

Combe, William 1742-1823 *The Three Tours of Dr. Syntax...* London: R. Ackermann's Repository of Arts, 1812. 1820. 1821. First editions in book form, first issue of the first work with plates in first state; 235 x 146mm., 3 volumes, remarkably pretty sky blue crushed morocco, handsomely gilt by Riviere (signed at foot of front turn-in), covers gilt with double rule border, French fillet center frame and floral cornerpieces, raised bands, spines elaborately gilt in compartments featuring elegant floral tools used for corner-pieces and centerpiece, broad and ornate gilt inner dentelles, all edges gilt, one woodcut illustration, one engraved tailpiece and 80 artfully hand colored aquatint plates by Thomas Rowlandson; engraved bookplate of Douglas Kerr; rear joint of one volume with thin crack along bottom inch or so, two covers with faint soiling, spines evenly faded to very pleasing, blue-grey, otherwise beautiful bindings in lovely condition with bright gilt, leaves opposite plates lightly offset, otherwise very fine internally text clean and with substantial margins, plates finely colored. Phillip J. Pirages 59 - 303 2011 $590

Association – Kertesz, Andre

Ducrot, Nicolas *Andre Kertesz: Sixty Years of Photography 1912-1972.* New York: Grossman Publishers, 1972. First edition; clean, very near fine with small owner name on front free endpaper in fine dust jacket with crease to front flap, signed and inscribed by Keretsz in 1975 on titlepage. Jeff Hirsch Books ny 2010 2011 $1000

Association – Kesselstan, Christopher, Count

Diogenes Laertius *Diogenis Laertii Clariss Historici De Vitis Ac Moribus Priscorum Philosophorum Librai Decem.* Cologne: ex offinia Eucharii Cervicorni, 1542. contemporary calf, panelled with triple rules and broad fillets with cornerpieces and central emblem, all in blind, extremities rather worn and spine dulled, silk ties worn away, pages 30, 671, (i, blank), title little stained, name scribbled out, label and few old stamps of Treves Cathedral Library, with ownership inscription of Christopher of Kesselstan, Dean of Paderborn, Count Kesselstan.   R. F. G. Hollett & Son Antiquarian Booksellers   General Catalogue Summer 2010 - 637   2011   £450

Association – Keyes, John Shepard

Thoreau, Henry David   1817-1862   *The Maine Woods.* Boston: Ticknor & Fields, 1864. First edition; original plum TR cloth, true first printing with list of Thoreau's books priced, no catalog bound into this copy, from the library of John Shepard Keyes with his ownership signature, contents clean, spine sunned, gilt little dull and frayed at tips and along edges, large vertical piece missing but not affecting lettering.   Charles Agvent   Transcendentalism 2010 - 36   2011 $2000

Association – Kidd, E. L.

James, Montague Rhodes   *Thin Ghost.*   London: Arnold, 1919. First edition; pages (viii), 152, foolscap 8vo., original grey cloth, backstrip and front cover lettered in blue with blue cobweb design to front cover, contemporary ownership signature of E. L. Kidd, very good.   Blackwell Rare Books   B166 - 168   2011   £200

Association – Kidd, John

MacDonald, George   1824-1905   *There and Back.* London: Kegan Paul, Trench, Trubner & Co., 1891. First edition; 3 volumes, half titles, final note volume III, original smooth red cloth, spines slightly faded with minor wear at heads and tail of spines and traces of labels at tails of front boards, good plus copy, black endpapers with booklabels of John Kidd and of George MacDonald Library, The Farm, Huntly.   Jarndyce Antiquarian Booksellers   CXCII - 283   2011 £2000

Ramon Y Cajal, Santiago   1852-1934   *Precepts and Counsels on Scientific Imagination: Stimulants of the Spirit.* New York: Oxford University Press, 1951. First edition in English, trade issue; 8vo., xii, 180 pages, frontispiece tipped in, maroon cloth, gilt stamped spine title, ownership signature of John G. Kidd, 1952, fine, from the Medical Library of Dr. Clare Gray Peterson.   Jeff Weber Rare Books   162 - 250   2011 $100

Association – King, A. W.

Laclos, Pierre Ambroise Francois Choderlos De   1741-1803   *Les Liasions Dangereuses.*   Brussels: J. Rosez, 1869. 2 volumes bound as one, pages 99; 291, internally clean and bright, minor chip to half title, contemporary blue black quarter morocco, gilt lettered on spine, original lime green printed wrappers bound in, top edge gilt, marbled boards and endpapers, spine and joints expertly repaired, edges of boards slightly rubbed, front endpapers chipped with some restoration also to front wrapper, Aubrey Beardsley's copy with his ink signature at head of titlepage and presentation inscription from his mother to A. W. King, later inscription from his mother, bookplate of Robert Booth.   Simon Finch Rare Books   Zero - 205   2011   £3500

Association – King, Florrie

MacDonald, George   1824-1905   *A Book of Strife.* London: printed for the author and to be had by Writing to Mr. Hughes 43 Beaufort Street, Chelsea, 1882. Tall 12mo., colophon leaf, original plain red cloth, slightly dulled, paper label browned with corner clip, ownership inscription of Florrie King, June 1883, good.   Jarndyce Antiquarian Booksellers   CXCII - 224   2011   £50

Association – Kingman, Catherine

Siringo, Charles Angelo   1855-1928   *Riata and Spurs. The Story of a Lifetime Spent in the Saddle as Cowboy and Detective.*   Boston and New York: Houghton Mifflin Co., 1927. First edition; 8vo., 14, (1), 276 pages, original cloth, dust jacket, complete and present, but one flap detached, fine, presentation by author to Miss Catherine Kingman, on half title is photo of Siringo taken in Pasadena by Spencer Kingman, with long pencil written explanation above.   M & S Rare Books, Inc.   90 - 387   2011 $850

Association – Kingsley, E. W.

Sumner, Charles   *The Crime Against Kansas. The Apologies for the Crime. The True Remedy. Speech...in the Senate of the United States 19th and 20th May 1856.* Washington: Buell & Blanchard printers, 1856. 8vo., 32 pages, as issued, uncut, inscribed in ink by author on titlepage to E. W. Kin(g)sley (sic).   M & S Rare Books, Inc.   90 - 408   2011 $3000

Association – Kingsley, Fanny

Kingsley, Charles   1819-1875   *Out of the Deep: Words for the Sorrowful.*   London: Macmillan, 1880. First edition; half title, final ad leaf, original grey cloth, dulled and rubbed, inner hinges cracking, photo of the Kings's laid down on leading pastedown, presentation from Fanny Kingsley.   Jarndyce Antiquarian Booksellers   CXCI - 234   2011   £65

Kingsley, Charles 1819-1875 *Prose Idylls New and Old.* London: Macmillan, 1884. Half title, frontispiece, added volume title, final ad leaf, unopened in original blue cloth, spine faded and slightly rubbed, inscribed by author's wife for Hugh and Margaret Egerton, with signature of M.A. Egerton.   Jarndyce Antiquarian Booksellers   CXCI - 233   2011   £35

Association – Kingsolver, Barbara

Gunther, Ken *Lilith: a Biography.* N.P.: 2005. First edition; 956 pages, fine in wrappers, this copy inscribed and signed by author to Barbara Kingsolver.   Bookworm & Silverfish   671 - 47   2011 $75

Association – Kinkead, A. S.

Gregory, Isbaella Augusta Perse 1859-1932 *Irish Folk-History Plays... First Series.... Second Series... (with) Our Irish Theatre/A Chapter of Autobiography.* New York and London: G. P. Putnams Sons, 1912-1913. First edition; First work in 2 volumes, 8vo., pages (ii), vi, 207, (i) blank, (3) ads; (ii), vi, 198, (5) ads, both volumes internally very fresh, short closed tear to one leaf of prelims in volume i, contemporary quarter cloth and blue paper covered boards, labels to spines with text in black, bumped and lightly rubbed, upper hinge volume i repaired, upper hinge volume ii cracked but firmly hold, John Quinn's autograph inscription volume ii, ownership inscription of A. S. Kinkead; second work 8vo., pages (ii), vi, 319, (i) blank, (5) ads, frontispiece and 3 plates, last leaves very slightly spotted otherwise extremely fresh, tight copy, contemporary quarter cloth and blue paper covered boards, label to spine with text in black, slightly bumped, some signs of wear to boards, endpapers lightly spotted, Quinn's presentation inscription to Joseph Conrad, ownership inscription of A. S. Kinkead.   Simon Finch Rare Books   Zero - 232   2011   £1250

Association – Kirby, Florence

Meynell, Alice *Poems.* London: Elkin Mathews & John Lane, 1893. Half title, final ad leaf, spotting in text, uncut in original brown buckram, bevelled boards, faded and slightly marked inscribed by author to Pucky (i.e. Florence Kirby).   Jarndyce Antiquarian Booksellers   CLXC - 390   2011   £45

Meynell, Alice *Poems.* London: Elkin Mathews & John Lane, 1893. Second edition; half title, 7 pages ads, some spots and pencil marginal marks, full contemporary plain green calf by Bumpus, gilt dentelles, slight rubbed, inscribed by author for Florence Kerry Kirby.   Jarndyce Antiquarian Booksellers   CLXC - 391   2011   £45

Meynell, Alice *The Rhythm of Life and Other Essays.* London: Elkin Mathews & John Lane, 1893. Second edition; half title, 4 pages ads + 7 page catalog, slight spotting, uncut in original light green cloth, spine faded to brown, inscribed by author for Florence Kirby.   Jarndyce Antiquarian Booksellers   CLXC - 393   2011   £45

Association – Kirley, John

O'Brien, Tim *The Things They Carried.* Boston: Houghton Mifflin, 1990. First edition; fine in like dust jacket, inscribed by author for John Kirley.   Bella Luna Books   May 29 2011 - t4918   2011 $137

Association – Kitchen, Herman

Peterson, Roger Tory *A Field Guide to the Birds, Giving Field marks of all Species Found in Eastern North America.* Boston and New York: Houghton Mifflin, 1934. First edition, third state; 36 plates, several drawings, 12mo., pages xxi, 167, original green silver printed cloth, near fine, signed inscription, signed in red ink from author to Herman Kitchen.   Raymond M. Sutton, Jr.   May 26 2011 - 43572   2011 $1200

Association – Knapp, Mr.

Spofford, Harriet Elizabeth Prescott 1835-1921 *In Titian's Garden and Other Poems.* Boston: Little Brown and Co., 1903. Reissue; (iv, 108) pages, 8vo., original green cloth, dark blue floral decorated front cover, gilt titled front and spine, very good, inscribed by author to Mr. Knapp (who wrote "Female Biography").   Paulette Rose Fine and Rare Books   32 - 163   2011 $100

Association – Knewstub, Christina

Ruskin, John 1819-1900 *Studies in Both Arts: Being Ten Subject Drawn and Described.* London: George Allen, 1895. First edition; folio, original decorated cream cloth with design by Edward Burne-Jones on upper board, trifle marked, pages 72, 10 tinted or colored photogravure plates, very nice, neat inscription "Christina Knewstub from J.W.P.L. May 19 1898".   R. F. G. Hollett & Son Antiquarian Booksellers   177 - 785   2011   £180

Association – Knight, Montagu George

Lactantius, Lucius Coelius Firmianus *Opera quae Exstant... et Commentariis Illustrata a Tho. spark.* Oxonii: E Theatro Sheldoniano, 1684. 8vo., pages (xviii), 912, (ii), 24, 17-38, contemporary speckled calf, boards double rule bordered in blind with stylized 'dahlia' tool in corners, board edges decorative 'zig-zag' roll in blind, turn-ins single ruled in blind, pink and white sewn endbands, early 21st century calf reback by Chris Weston with original decorative red lettering piece gilt relaid, little light spotting, small dampmark in upper corner of first few leaves, old leather scratched and marked, contemporary inscription "E Libris Gui. Brodnag", heraldic bookplate of Montagu George Knight of Chawton, from the collection of Christopher Ernest Weston 1947-2010. Unsworths Booksellers   24 - 28   2011   £250

Thoresby, Ralph *Ducatus Leodiensis; or the Topography of the Ancient and Populous Town and Parish of Leedes and Parts Adjacent in the West Riding of the County of York...* London: printed for Maurice Atkins, 1715. Folio, pages iv (ii) v-xii 628 (xii), frontispiece, folding engraved map, 4 extending engraved plates and 7 other engraved plates, mid 18th century sprinkled and polished tan calf spine panel gilt with made-up centre pieces, 'frond' corner-pieces, six raised bands and head and foot identically tooled using 'opposing multi rule triangles' pallet, orange lettering piece gilt, boards double rule gilt bordered, board edges 'exaggerated-wavy' roll in blind, all edges red sprinkled, pink and white sewn endbands, browned and spotted in places, little surface damage to boards, small loss from headcap, corners slightly worn, 19th century armorial bookplate of Montagu George Knight of Chawton, from the collection of Christopher Ernest Weston 1947-2010.   Unsworths Booksellers   24 - 147   2011   £1000

Association – Knight, R. P.

Caro, Annibale   1507-1566   *De Le Lettere Familiari del Commendatore Annibal Caro.* Venice: Bernardo Giunti e Fratelli, 1592.   1591. Later edition; 2 volumes bound together, 8vo., (8), 716; (8), 272 pages, 2 engraved title vignettes, engraved initials, engraved headpieces, early ink marginalia pages 272 (crossed out in early hand), neat marginal repair to page 213-214, early full vellum, early ms. title/author on spine, all edges gauffered in Pointille style with groups of fleur-de-lys in spaces, early ownership rubber-stamp of R. P. Knight.   Jeff Weber Rare Books   163 - 6   2011 $825

Association – Knipe, George

Bennett, Anna Maria *Viscissitudes Abroad.* London: printed at the Minerva Press for Lane, Newman and Co., 1806.   First (only) edition, complete as issued; 6 volumes, large 12mo., full contemporary mottled calf with crimson and black morocco spine labels, gilt rules to spine, minor tear at pages 191-192 of volume five with no loss, small chip to upper fore margin of volume five just touching page number, completely unsophisticated with small loss to spine head of volumes one and four, some occasional spotting, expected wear, armorial bookplate of George M. Knipe, overall, an excellent set, extremely rare, housed in two clamshell boxes.   David Brass Rare Books, Inc.   May 26 2011 - 01475   2011 $8500

Association – Knox, Mary

Shepard, Ernest H. *Drawn from Memory.* London: Methuen, 1957. First edition; 8vo., 190 pages, frontispiece, copious illustrations, loosely inserted by E. H. Shepard and his wife to their daughter Mary Knox, very good in slightly used and slightly rubbed, about very good dust jacket.   Any Amount of Books   May 26 2011 - A39617   2011 $503

Association – Kofoid, Charles Atwood

Sutherland, James *The Adventures of an Elephant Hunter.* London: Macmillan & Co., 1912.   First edition, first issue; 8vo., xviii, 324 (2 ads) pages, frontispiece, 52 illustrations, original blue cloth, gilt stamped cover ornament and spine title, top edge gilt, extremities rubbed, corners bumped, library card inside rear cover, bookplate of Charles Atwood Kofoid, very good, rare.   Jeff Weber Rare Books   163 - 218   2011 $600

Association – La Pierre, Julian

Thoreau, Henry David   1817-1862   *A Yankee in Canada, with Anti-Slavery and Reform Papers.* Boston: Ticknor and Fields, 1866.   First edition; original green C cloth, binding C, no priority given, bookplate of Julian La Pierre, M.D. dated 1904, scattered light foxing, cloth with no wear, but old staining to spine, especially rear cover, still very good.   Charles Agvent   Transcendentalism 2010 - 50   2011 $900

Association – Lachevre, F.

Pradon, Nicolas *Reponse a la Satire X du Sieur D****.* Paris: Chez Robert J. B. de la Caille, 1694.   (1), (11) pages, 12mo., recent blue cloth, gilt lettered spine, from the library of F. Lachevre with his ex-libris, very fine, scarce.   Paulette Rose Fine and Rare Books   32 - 135   2011 $700

Association – Laing, Dr.

Rivius, Gregorius *Puritani Monastica Historia...* Leipzig: Jo. Christiani Martini, 1737. Pages xxxvi, (ii), 510, (80, index), old half calf gilt with marbled boards, edges and corners worn and chipped, later spine label, upper hinge cracking, pages xxxvi, (ii) 510, (80, index), title in red and black (rather browned), engraved frontispiece and 6 engraved plates, small wormhole in lower margin of index leaves, from Dr. Laing's library. R. F. G. Hollett & Son Antiquarian Booksellers 175 - 1133 2011 £150

Association – Lakeland, Robert

Gale, Roger *Registrum Honoris De Richmond Exhibens Terrarum & Villarum.* Londini: Impensis R. Gosling, 1722. Large paper copy, folio, pages (ii), xxxv, (i), 106, (xxvi), 286, (xxx) + folding engraved map, one extending engraved plate, another 8 engraved plates and 6 extending plates of pedigrees, lacking the list of subscribers leaf, early 19th century calf, boards sided with 'French Shelf' marbled paper, 1970's renewal of leather with half reversed calf by John Henderson (spotted and lightly browned, old boards scuffed), armorial and masonic bookplate of "Robt. Lakeland" and inscription "from Major Sir Edw. Coates' Library", from the collection of Christopher Ernest Weston 1947-2010. Unsworths Booksellers 24 - 95 2011 £400

Association – Lambert, Thomas

Brooks, Shirley *Sooner or Later.* London: Bradbury, Evans & Co., 1868. First edition; 2 volumes, half titles, frontispiece, engraved titlepages, plates, slightly later half green calf, raised bands, decorated in gilt, contemporary signature of Thomas Lambert, handsome copy. Jarndyce Antiquarian Booksellers CXCI - 93 2011 £75

Association – Land, A. A.

Epictetus *Manuale et Sententiae Quibus Accedunt Tabula Cerebtis...* Utrecht: Ex officina Gulielmi Broedelet, 1711. Some browning and spotting in places, one index leaf with 2 small repairs in text area so that a few words are supplied in manuscript, pages (xx), 151, (1), 124, 152, (60), 4to., contemporary unlettered vellum, touch dusty, booklabel of A. A. Land, good. Blackwell Rare Books B166 - 37 2011 £250

Association – Lanesborough, J. E.

Long, Catherine *Sir Roland Ashton.* London: James Nisbet & Co., 1844. First edition; 2 volumes, half title, some light foxing, uncut in original blue vertical grained cloth, boards blocked in blind, spines lettered in gilt, spines faded and slightly rubbed, hinges chipped, each volume signed J. E. Lanesborough in contemporary hand, good plus. Jarndyce Antiquarian Booksellers CLXC - 161 2011 £150

Association – Lang, William

Grenfell, Wilfred *Forty Years for Labrador.* Boston & New York: Houghton Mifflin Co., 1932. Large 8vo., pages (xii), (3)-372, half title, frontispiece, map and 26 black and white photo illustrations, blue cloth with gilt title to spine, some light wear to binding, else very good, first flyleaf with drawing of large walrus with Eskimo in kayak and spear drawn in black ink, signed "With best wishes Wilfred T. Grenfell, Labrador 1934", also written by previous owner "Presented to me by Sir Wilfred Nov. 1935 William Lang", with TLS from Grenfell to Lang. Schooner Books Ltd. 96 - 42 2011 $150

Association – Langdell, Mrs.

Cole, John *Memoirs of the Life, Writings and Character of the Late Thomas Hinderwell, Esqr. Scarborough.* London: published by John Cole and Longman, Rees, Orme, Brown and Green, 1826. 8vo., pages (ii) 3 (i) 57, (iii) 55, (i) vii (i), engraved frontispiece, publisher's original green canvas, dark green morocco lettering piece gilt by Jenny Aste, late 1980's, some light spotting, especially to title, cloth little spotted and faded, slightly worn at endcaps, contemporary ink inscription to Mrs. Langdell, presented by author, also blue paper ex-libris of John William Clay, from the collection of Christopher Ernest Weston 1947-2010. Unsworths Booksellers 24 - 82 2011 £125

Association – Langley, Emily

Mitford, Mary Russell 1787-1855 *Lights and Shadows of American Life.* London: Henry Colburn and Richard Bentley, 1832. First edition; contemporary half calf, spines with raised bands and devices in gilt, black leather labels, owner's signature "Emily Langley 1847", very good, bright. Jarndyce Antiquarian Booksellers CLXC - 405 2011 £380

Association – Lanier, Charles

Jewett, Sophie *The Pilgrim and Other Poems.* New York: Macmillan, 1896. First edition; 12mo., 99 pages, 2 page publisher's ads, original pictorial grey boards, white cloth spine, top edge gilt, others uncut, light foxing, otherwise nice, inscribed presentation by author to Mary Day Lanier, bookplate indicating that the volume was presented to the Johns Hopkins University Library by Lanier's Son, Charles D. Lanier and subsequently released by that institution. Paulette Rose Fine and Rare Books 32 - 101 2011 $325

Association – Lanier, Mary Day

Jewett, Sophie *The Pilgrim and Other Poems.* New York: Macmillan, 1896. First edition; 12mo., 99 pages, 2 page publisher's ads, original pictorial grey boards, white cloth spine, top edge gilt, others uncut, light foxing, otherwise nice, inscribed presentation by author to Mary Day Lanier, bookplate indicating that the volume was presented to the Johns Hopkins University Library by Lanier's Son, Charles D. Lanier and subsequently released by that institution. Paulette Rose Fine and Rare Books   32 - 101   2011 $325

Association – Lansburg, Mrs.

Kelly, George *Craig's Wife, a Drama.* Boston: Little Brown, 1926. First edition; 8vo., pages 174, very nice tight copy, inscribed by author to Mrs. Lansburg, housed in calf backed cloth slipcase and chemise.   Second Life Books Inc.   174 - 214   2011 $1000

Association – Lansdowne, Lord

Eliot, George, Pseud. 1819-1880 *Adam Bede.* Edinburgh and London: William Blackwood and Sons, 1859. 2 volumes, from Lord Lansdowne's library, half titles, publisher's ads discarded, pages viii, 431; viii, 3-382, 8vo., original wave grain orange brown cloth, backstrips ruled and lettered in gilt, sides with blind decorated panels and paper labels of Lord Lansdowne with his cypher on front covers, slightly rubbed at extremities, joints of volume i skillfully repaired, good.   Blackwell Rare Books   B166 - 35   2011   £180

Association – Latham, Francis Law

Malory, Thomas *Le Morte D'Arthur.* London: published by David Nutt, 1889. One of 100 copies signed by publisher, there were 8 additional copies not for sale; 330 x 260mm. tipped in editor's note at back of first volume, 3 volumes, very appealing dark brown morocco, Jansenist, by Zaehnsdorf (signed), boards panelled with 11 thick and thin gilt and blind fillets, corners of central panel with outward extending gilt fleurons, raised bands, flanked by gilt and blind rules (and with gilt rule across the middle of each), two spine panels with gilt titling and four with arabesque centerpiece, very wide and very intricate gilt scrolling foliate and fleuron inner dentelles, marbled endpapers, top edge gilt, other edges untrimmed, one plate reproducing a page from Caxton, one folding facsimile, 3 folding tables; armorial bookplate of Francis Law Latham, tab at end of volume I with editor's note tipped on, explaining the various typographical alterations from Caxton; titlepages printed in red and black, first initial in red; handful of superficial marks to covers (one very small abrasion), trivial foxing or spotting in perhaps 10 leaves, one table creased, fine, lovely bindings lustrous and virtually unworn and text clean, fresh, bright and with vast margins.   Phillip J. Pirages   59 - 260 2011 $3500

Association – Laurencin, Marie

Mansfield, Katherine 1888-1923 *The Garden Party and Other Stories.* London: Verona Press, 1939, really, 1947. First illustrated edition, one of 1200 numbered copies (the first 30 were signed); color lithographs by Marie Laurencin, tall octavo, original green pastepaper over boards with printed red paper spine label gilt, slight foxing on front fly, still easily fine, this copy nicely inscribed by Laurencin with elaborate filigree decoration surrounding inscription.   Between the Covers   169 - BTC343218   2011 $3500

Association – Lawrence, George N.

Elliot, Daniel Giraud *A Monogram of the Pittidae; or Family of Ant Thrushes.* New York: D. Appleton & Co., 1863. First edition; 31 beautiful hand colored lithographed plates, and one unsigned plate after C. P. Tholey, of which 24 are after Elliot, folio, pages 23 and a lettepress for each bird illustrated, modern green three quarter morocco over contemporary marbled boards with matching marbled endpapers (light rubbing to marbled boards, fine copy, plates and text in immaculate, pristine condition, all edges gilt, signature of George N. Lawrence.   Raymond M. Sutton, Jr.   May 26 2011 - 51134   2011 $16,000

Association – Lawrence, Gertrude

The Art Journal for 1910. London: Virtue & Co., 1910. 4 etchings, many tipped in color and black and white plates, folio, gray cloth, good, bookplate of Gertrude M. Lawrence. Barnaby Rudge Booksellers   Art & Architecture & Photography - 017188   2011 $75

Association – Lawrence, Robert

Rogers, Samuel *Recollections of the Table Talk of Samuel Rogers to Which is added Porsoniana.* London: Edward Moxon, 1856. Apparently the first edition; 199 x 130 mm., viii, 355 pages, bound with half title with inserted plate as frontispiece, very pleasing later dark brown crushed morocco, attractively gilt, covers with French fillet border and elegant botanical cornerpieces, raised bands, heavily gilt spine in compartments featuring elaborate scrolling cornerpieces, an intricate fleuron centerpiece, and tiny circlets, turn-ins with plain and stippled rules and filigree with gilt decoration at corners and midpoints of two sides, textured (silk?) brown and cream millefleur-patterned endpapers, all edges gilt, extra illustrated with 55 portrait plates, five in color, all with tissue guards, engraved bookplate of Robert B. Lawrence, hint of browning to some of the inserted plates, fine, handsomely bound copy, text especially fresh, clean and smooth, binding bright and virtually unworn; hint of browning to some of the inserted plates, fine, handsomely bound copy, text especially fresh, clean and smooth, binding bright and virtually unworn.   Phillip J. Pirages   59 - 131   2011 $650

Association – Lawrence, Seymour

Hannah, Barry *Nightwatchmen.* New York: Viking, 1973. First edition; edge sunned cloth, near fine in very good dust jacket, spine and edge faded, inscribed by author to Seymour Lawrence. Ken Lopez Bookseller 154 - 74 2011 $475

Association – Lawrence, Thomas Edward

Shaw, George Bernard 1856-1950 *Adventures of the Black Girl in Her Search for God.* London: Constable, 1932. First edition; several wood engravings by John Farleigh, final leaves lightly foxed, pages 80, foolscap 8vo., original black boards, illustrated overall and with author and title printed on slightly sunned backstrip and front cover in white, joints trifle worn, good, T. E. Lawrence's copy with gift inscription to him from George Bernard Shaw's wife Charlotte. Blackwell Rare Books B166 - 173 2011 £2000

Association – Lawson, John

Pemble, William *A Briefe Introduction to Geography Containing a Description of the Grounds and Generall Part Thereof...* Oxford: Iohn Lichfield for Edward Forrest, 1630. First edition; Small 4to., (4), 64 (i.e. 46) pages, 1 folding table, 18 woodcut figures, printer's device on titlepage, 2 woodcut headpieces, very faint waterstain to few pages, modern full vellum, gilt stamped spine, booklabel of John Lawson, fine, rare. Jeff Weber Rare Books 163 - 11 2011 $2500

Association – Laxton-Hames, A.

Barrie, James Matthew 1860-1937 *Rosalind.* New York: Charles Scribner's Sons, 1914. 190 x 130mm., 1 p.l., 89-151 pages, very pleasing dark green pebble grain morocco, attractively gilt by J. S. H. Bates of Leicester (stamp signed on rear turn-in), covers with border of plain and broken gilt fillets around a central rectangular panel formed by the same broken rule (four flap-like panels surrounding the central rectangle in an arrangement resembling fold-over closures) large and very attractive cornerpieces of five grouped tulips on leaves stems, spine with two raised bands, large gilt tulips at either end, vertical titling in middle, gilt turn-ins, top edge gilt, gilt stamped presentation "To Lady Kathleen Curzon-Herrick/ A Memento of June 1918/ from Mr. and Mrs. A. Laxton-Hames", spine faded (as always with green morocco) to a pleasing olive green, hint of wear to extremities, still quite fine, especially attractive, very bright and clean inside and out. Phillip J. Pirages 59 - 87 2011 $850

Association – Le Boyer, Jean Francois

Bouguer, Pierre *Traite d'Optique sur la Gradation de la Lumiere: Ouvrage Posthume de M. Bouguer de l'Acaemie Royale des Sciences &c.* Paris: H. L. Guerin & L. F. Delatour, 1760. First edition; 4to., xviii, (2), 368 pages, engraved printer's device on titlepage, 7 engraved folding plates, contemporary full mottled calf, raised bands, gilt stamped spine panels and spine title, few minor covers scars, joints starting, bookplate of Jean Francois Le Boyer and Andras Gedeon, fine, from the Bern Dibner reference library, with Burndy bookplate. Jeff Weber Rare Books 161 - 51 2011 $2500

Association – Le Cain, Errol

De La Mare, Walter 1873-1956 *Molly Whuppie Retold by.* London: Faber and Faber, 1983. First edition thus; oblong 4to., full color pictorial boards, as new, full page color illustrations by Errol Le Cain, this copy signed in full. Jo Ann Reisler, Ltd. 86 - 154 2011 $200

Grimm, The Brothers *The Twelve Dancing Princesses.* New York: Viking Press, 1978. First American edition; oblong 4to., grey cloth backed lavender boards with elaborate blindstamped border design to boards, full color pictorial dust jacket, signed in full presentation from Le Cain, illustrations by Le Cain. Jo Ann Reisler, Ltd. 86 - 153 2011 $200

Longfellow, Henry Wadsworth 1807-1882 *Hiawatha's Childhood.* New York: Farrar Straus Giroux, 1984. Stated first American edition; red cloth with gold lettering on spine, full color pictorial dust jacket, as new, signed in full by artist, Errol Le Cain, illustrations by Le Cain. Jo Ann Reisler, Ltd. 86 - 155 2011 $275

Miles, Sally *Crisis at Crabtree.* Cambridge: Lutterworth Press, 1986. First edition; 8vo., full color pictorial boards, as new, front free endpaper signed in full and dated 1986 by artist, Errol Le Cain, illustrations by Le Cain. Jo Ann Reisler, Ltd. 86 - 156 2011 $200

Association – Le Clerc, Jean

Newton, Henry *Epistolae, Orationes, et Carmina. (bound with) Orationes quarum Altera Florentiae Anno MDCCV.* Lucca: D. Ciufetti, 1710. Amsterdam: 1710-(1712); 2 works in 1 volume, (6), 250, 115, (3) pages, engraved frontispiece, 58 pages (final quire signed * (pages 51-58) reprinted to include items dated 1711 and 1712, contemporary English panelled calf, spine gilt, rubbed, upper joint slightly cracked, one corner worn, number of small corrections, from the library of the Earls of Macclesfield at Shirburn Castle, bound at end are two manuscript letters from Newton at Florence, one to Jean Le Clerc at Amsterdam and the other to Gisbert Cuper at Deventer, both dated 1710. Maggs Bros. Ltd. 1440 - 155 2011 £800

Association – Le Mesurier, John

Dodwell, William *The Sick Man's Companion: or The Clergyman's Assistant in Visiting the Sick.* London: printed for B. White, 1768. Second edition; (8), xlvii, 48-260 pages, 8vo., little waterstaining to foot of final few leaves, contemporary calf, head and tail of spine and first 2 inches of upper joint worn, 19th century bookplate of Rev. John T. H. Le Mesurier, with his pencil notes to endpaper and in several margins; 18th century prayer written in earlier hand on final blank.   Jarndyce Antiquarian Booksellers   CXCI - 162   2011   £90

Association – Lee, Manfred

Doyle, Arthur Conan 1859-1930 *Adventures of Sherlock Holmes.* London: George Newnes, 1892. First edition, first issue with no street name on front cover; "Violent" for "Violet" on page 317, large octavo, (4), 317, (1, printer's imprint) (2, blank) pages, 104 illustrations by Sidney Paget in text, original light blue cloth over beveled boards, front cover and spine blocked and lettered in gilt and black, all edges gilt, gray flower and leaf endpapers, small ink initials to front free endpaper, front hinge professionally and invisibly repaired, back hinge starting but firm, slight bit of shelf wear to top and bottom of spine, some light foxing to few prelim and final pages, else near fine, exceptionally clean and bright, housed in tan cloth clamshell, the fine "Ellery Queen" (Manfred Lee) and "Barnaby Ross" (Frederic Dannay) names in ink on half title.   Heritage Book Shop Holiday 2010 - 30   2011 $17,500

Association – Leete, J.

Sala, George Augustus *Paris Herself Again in 1878-9.* London: Remington & Co., 1879. First edition; 2 volumes, half titles in volume I, frontispiece in volume I, plates and illustrations, original olive green pictorial cloth, blocked in black, largely inoffensive damp marking to back boards, little rubbed, presentation inscription, "Octobre 1879. A Monsieur L. Gillet. Souvenir de sincere amitie J. Leete", good copy.   Jarndyce Antiquarian Booksellers   CXCI - 577   2011   £150

Association – Legman, Gershon

Farny, Henry F. *"The Lady and the Flea."A Tale of a Tale".* Honolulu: Pretoria and Hammerfest (Cincinnati): published by the Society for the Dissemination of Useless Knowledge and the League for the Propagation of the Castanea Vulgaris, 1897. Only edition; Gershon Legman's copy, 8vo., pages (32), 14 illustrations on tracing paper pasted in, uncut, light offsetting to some pages, centre spread brown at inner margin, pages unattached from boards and bound in single gathering, original brown/green cloth with git lettering to upper panel and gilt decoration to upper and lower panel, some light shelfwear and rubbing, bump to upper hinge.   Simon Finch Rare Books   Zero - 230   2011   £750

Association – Leibovitz, Annie

Sontag, Susan *Women.* New York: Random House, 1999. First edition; photographs by Annie Leibovitz, fine in very near fine dust jacket with some minute wear, signed and inscribed by Leibovitz to another photographer and additionally signed by Sontag, genuinely uncommon signed by both.   Jeff Hirsch Books   ny 2010   2011 $450

Association – Leicester, Anne

Sharp, John *Fifteen Sermons Preached on Several Occasions by... John Lord Arch Bishop of York.* London: printed for Walter Kettilby, 1709. Third edition; 8vo., pages (vi) 472 + engraved frontispiece, contemporary crimson turkey, spine gilt panelled with salitred compartments, lettered direct in gilt, boards panelled in gilt, board edges decorative roll gilt, turn-ins decorative roll gilt, 'Dutch-comb' 'made' endpapers, all edges gilt, blue and white sewn endbands, light spotting, occasional dampmark in lower margin, tidy repairs to headcap with new matching endband, black leather gilt decorative roll bordered label "To Mrs./E.B." ink inscription "Eliz. Battell/Juner", in different hand "The Gift of my Good Aunt Mrs. Eliz Battell to me Anne Hallows junr. May ye 26 1728", in same hand "Anne Leicester", ink inscription "John Roberts No 2 May 14 1792", from the collection of Christopher Ernest Weston 1947-2010.   Unsworths Booksellers   24 - 40   2011   £200

Association – Leigh, Edward Chevenix Austen

Elliott, W. G. *Amateur Clubs and Actors.* London: Edward Arnold, 1898. First edition; original blind decorated green cloth gilt, few slight nicks and scratches, pages 320, uncut, 19 plates, joints cracked, scarce, armorial bookplate of Edward Chevenix Austen Leigh.   R. F. G. Hollett & Son Antiquarian Booksellers   175 - 413   2011   £65

Association – Leigh, Theodosia

Tacitus, Gaius Cornelius *The Works of...* London: printed for G. G. J. and J. Robinson, 1793. 4 volumes, 4to., engraved maps, contemporary densely speckled calf, spine fully gilt with triple rules, interweaving front and graded pebbles' roll and 'sun-burst brooche' centerpieces, red and black lettering and numbering pieces gilt, board edges decorative roll gilt, all edges blue sprinkled, red and white sewn endbands, plates somewhat foxed, rubbed at corners, endcaps worn, joints cracking, labels lost from volumes 1 and 2 and partly lost on volume 3, stipple engraved booklabel of Theo. Leigh/Toft", ink ownership Theodosia Leigh, from the collection of Christopher Ernest Weston 1947-2010.   Unsworths Booksellers   24 - 146   2011   £300

Association – Leighton, Baldwyn

MacDonald, George   1824-1905   *A Threefold Cord.*   not to be had of any bookseller, but by application to Mr. W. Hughes, 43 Beaufort Street, Chelsea, London, 1883.   First edition, first issue; original plain red sand grained cloth, printed paper label on spine, dulled and marked on front board, inscribed by author for Sir Baldwyn Leighton.   Jarndyce Antiquarian Booksellers   CXCII - 258   2011   £1250

Association – Leo, E. F.

Davenant, William   1606-1668   *The Works of Sr. William Davenant Kt. Consisting of those Which were Formerly printed and Those which He Design'd for the Press...*   London: by T. N. for Henry Herringman, 1673.   First collected edition; folio, (8), 402, (4), 486, 111 pages, portrait, turn-of-the-century red levant morocco, gilt arabesque centerpiece on covers, all edges gilt by Riviere, very skillfully rebacked, though new leather at joints and on cords has uniformly faded, unusually fine, fresh, wide margined copy, fine impression of portrait, leather tipped fleece lined slipcase, edges rubbed, Duke of Beaufort, E. F. Leo, A. E, Newton, with their bookplates.   Joseph J. Felcone Inc.   Fall Miscellany 2010 - 37   2011 $2200

Association – Leon, Herbert

Bronte, Anne   1820-1849   *The Tenant of Wildfell Hall.*   London: T. C. Newby, 1848.   First edition, first issue; 12mo., 3 volumes, (4), 358; (2), 366; (2), 342 pages, excessively rare half title in volume I, but without final leaf of ads in volume I, no half titles called for in volumes II and III, bound circa 1900 by Riviere & Son (stamp signed on verso of front free endpaper) in full tan polished calf, covers with gilt triple fillet border and gilt corner ornaments, spine decoratively tooled in gilt in compartments with two brown morocco gilt lettering pieces, board edges ruled in gilt, turn-ins decoratively tooled in gilt, top edge gilt, others uncut, armorial bookplate of Herbert S. Leon, housed in custom made half tan calf clamshell case with raised bands and two green morocco lettering labels and felt lined dividers, exceptionally copy, minimal foxing and mostly marginal soiling, volume I with tiny dampstain outer margin of P6, volume II with small very neat paper repairs to outer blank margin of D7 and F7, small faint stain in upper corner of G3-G7 and small paper flaw in upper blank margin of H5, volume III with faint stain in upper margin of D4 and D5, tiny tear in outer margin of G3, short tear neatly repaired in upper margin of G6, tiny tear in outer margin of P4.   David Brass Rare Books, Inc.   May 26 2011 - 00031   2011 $42,500

Association – Leonard, Elmore

Naked Came the Manatee.   New York: Putnam, 1996.   First edition; fine in fine dust jacket, signed by all authors on single tipped in leaf, including Carl Hiaasen, Elmore Leonard, John Dufresne, Dave Barry, Vicki Hendricks, Edna Buchanan, Les Standiford and James W. Hall, etc. Ken Lopez Bookseller   154 - 5   2011 $200

Association – Leopold, King of Belgium

Mitchell, John M.   *The Herring/Its Natural History and National Importance.*   Edinburgh: Edmonston and Douglas and London: Longman, Green, Roberts and Green, 1864.   First edition; 8vo., pages xii, 372, folding color lithographed frontispiece, 5 lithographed plates, some foxing, publisher's blue cloth, brown endpapers, bumped spines slightly faded, review pasted to rear endpapers, author's presentation inscription to half title dated 1865, very good; presentation copy to King Leopold I of Belgium dated 1865.   Simon Finch Rare Books   Zero - 131   2011   £400

Association – Leverhulme, Lord

Cuneo, Terence   *The Mouse and His Master. The Life and Work of Terence Cuneo.*   New Cavendish Books, 1977.   Limited, signed edition, no. 70 of 250 copies; oblong large 4to., original quarter faux morocco gilt with suede boards, matching slipcase, pages 244, illustrations, mostly in color, very special copy, with 3 ALS's from Cueno loosely inserted, a number of signatures laid in against relevant illustrations and portraits, including Lord Leverhulme and Sir Bernard Waley-Cohen, Lord Mayor of London, both with accompanying letters loosely inserted), Co. Sir Richard Glyn, Sir Lionel Denny and Robert Runcie, the letters are all addressed to Harold Ogden, managing Director of Broughton Moor, Slate Quarries, Coniston and signatures assembled by him.   R. F. G. Hollett & Son Antiquarian Booksellers   General Catalogue Summer 2010 - 96   2011   £1500

Association – Lewis, Alfred Hartley

Lewis, Arthur, Mrs.   *Salthurst.*   London: Samuel Tinsley, 1878.   First edition; 3 volumes, 6 page and 32 page catalog volume III, text slightly browned, facsimile title volume II, original crimson cloth by W. Bone & Son, rubbed and seriously affected by damp, small splits in spine volume III, inner hinges cracking, inscribed by author for her son, Alfred Hartley Lewis.   Jarndyce Antiquarian Booksellers   CLXC - 136   2011   £90

Association – Lewis, Jeremy

Lazzaro, Claudia *Italian Renaissance Garden from the Conventions of Planting, Design, and Ornament to the Grand Gardens of Sixteenth Century Central.* New Haven and London: Yale University Press, 1990. First edition; 4to., illustrations in color and black and white, 352, fine in fine dust jacket, in very good slipcase, bookplate of Jeremy Lewis.   Any Amount of Books   May 29 2011 - A70569   2011 $204

Association – Lewthwaite, George

Pope, Alexander 1688-1744 *A Supplement to the Works of Alexander Pope Esq. Containing Such Poems, Letters &c as are Omitted in the Edition Published by the Reverend Dr. Warburton...* London: privately Printed for M. Cooper, 1757. First edition; 8vo., full brown leather, pages viii 206, spine title label missing, some wear and rubbing to leather, otherwise sound, near very good, bookplate of George Lewthwaite and his neat name on endpaper.   Any Amount of Books   May 29 2011 - A32736   2011 $221

Association – Liddell Hart, Basil

Ruskin, John 1819-1900 *War.* Woolwich: printed for private circulation, 1866. Half title, partially erased pencil notes at end, original red cloth, dulled & rubbed, all edges gilt, good, sound copy, exceedingly scarce, bookplate of military historian Sir Basil Liddell Hart, with 4 page ALS to him from art historian Reginald Wilenski, July 23 1961.   Jarndyce Antiquarian Booksellers   CXCI - 478   2011   £380

Association – Lillie, William

Smith, Adam 1723-1790 *An Inquiry into the Nature and Causes of the Wealth of Nations...* Edinburgh: printed for Oliphant, Waugh, & Innes and John Murray, London, 1814. 4 volumes, 8vo., complete with all half titles, contemporary uniform diced russia, simply gilt and lettered, marbled edges, very minor wear to bindings but very good, near contemporary presentation inscription recording (in Latin) presentation prize of this copy on 9th April 1820 to William Lillie at King's College, Aberdeen by Andrew Alexander, the professor of moral philosophy.   John Drury Rare Books   153 - 138   2011   £850

Association – Lindbergh, Charles

Lindbergh, Anne Morrow *North to the Orient.* New York: Harcourt Brace and Co., 1935. First edition; octavo, (1)-255, (1, blank) pages, black and white photo frontispiece and numerous printed maps by Charles Lindbergh, publisher's original blue cloth, spine stamped and lettered in silver, top edge gilt, map printed endpapers, inscription on half title, publisher's dust jacket, jacket bit chipped at extremities and creased along top front edge, fine copy, inscribed by Charles and Anne Lindbergh for Albert H. Ebeling.   Heritage Book Shop   Holiday 2010 - 73   2011 $1500

Association – Linder, Samuel

Collins, W. Lucas *Ancient Classics for English Readers.* Edinburgh: William Blackwood & Sons, 1871-1874. Initial ad leaf in volume 1, half titles, publisher's ads, 20 volumes, original light brown cloth, decorated in black, slight rubbing to head and tail of spines, armorial bookplates of Samuel Linder, very good, bookseller's tickets of J. Gilbert, very good.   Jarndyce Antiquarian Booksellers   CXCI - 8   2011   £400

Association – Ling, Katharine

MacDonald, George 1824-1905 *Rampolli: Growths from a Long Planted Root: Being Translations, New and Old.* London: Longmans, Green & Co., 1897. First edition; half title, 32 page catalog (5/97), original crimson buckram, spine faded, uneven fading to boards, inscribed by author for cousin Katharine Ling, bookplate and guard of C. H. O. Scaife.   Jarndyce Antiquarian Booksellers   CXCII - 324   2011   £1200

Association – Linton, J.

Marryat, Frank *Mountains and Molehills, or Recollections of a Burnt Journal.* New York: Harper & Brothers, 1855. First American edition; x, (11)-393 pages, frontispiece, plus 25 wood engravings, publisher's blindstamped, royal blue cloth, gilt lettered spine, light and minimal scattered foxing, bit more so to first 10 leaves, early owner's name and date on endpaper (Jos. A. Linton/Aug. 25th 1870), slight darkening to spine, but fine, bright, tight copy.   Argonaut Book Shop   Recent Acquisitions Summer 2010 - 121   2011 $500

Association – Little, Denys

Ridley, Guy *The Wood of Treregor.* London: James Nisbet, 1914. First edition; 8vo., original publisher's blue cloth lettered gilt at spine and cover, pages 125, pages uncut, rare, fore-edge very slightly foxed, else about fine, exceptional condition, presentation copy to Denys C. Little from writer.   Any Amount of Books   May 29 2011 - A67184   2011 $255

Association – Littlecote

Cordiner, Charles *Remarkable Ruins and Romantic Prospects of North Britain.* London: published by I. and J. Taylor, 1795. 2 volumes, 4to., pages iv (cxxxvi) + engraved titlepage, engraved frontispiece and another 56 engraved plates (ccxii) + engraved titlepage, 40 engraved plates (of 41), lacking plate "personification of Events etc." in volume 2, contemporary mottled calf, 6 compartmented spine divided up by back to back double rules and polished pinhead decorative roll all gilt compartments, contain 'made'up' central device of gouges and small flowerets, all gilt, black lettering and numbering pieces gilt, place and date gilt direct at foot, boards double rule gilt border with decorative roll within, board edges decorative roll gilt turn-ins, hooded acanthus, roll gilt green 'sugarpaper' 'made' endpapers, all edges pale green "French Shell" marbled, red and pale blue sewn endbands, dark blue silk page markers, slightest bit of rubbing at extremities but very nice, armorial bookplate of "Littlecote" surmounting printed label of "E. W. Leyborne Popham", from the collection of Christopher Ernest Weston 1947-2010. Unsworths Booksellers 24 - 83 2011 £750

Association – Livingston, William

Monro, Thomas Kirkpatrick *Raynaud's Disease Local Syncope, Local Asphyxia, Symmetrical Gangrene): Its History, Causes, Symptoms, Morbid Relations, Pathology & Treatment.* Glasgow: James Maclehose & Sons, 1899. 8vo., xii, 251 pages, frontispiece, 3 tables, green cloth, gilt stamped spine title, very good, inscribed by John F. Fulton to William Livingston, from the Medical Library of Dr. Clare Gray Peterson. Jeff Weber Rare Books 162 - 218 2011 $150

Association – Llangattock

Wraxall, L. *Life in the Sea; or Nature and Habits of Marine Animals.* London: Houlston & Wright, 1860. First edition; frontispiece and illustrations, original purple wavy grained cloth by Leighton, Son & Hodge, spines slightly faded, armorial bookplate of Llangattock, very good. Jarndyce Antiquarian Booksellers CXCI - 344 2011 £68

Association – Lloyd-Jones, Hairlie

Milton, John 1608-1674 *The Poetical Works of John Milton.* London: T. Nelson & Sons, 1855. Frontispiece, additional engraved title, plates, original black morocco heavily blocked in blind, lettered in gilt on boards and spine, all edges gilt, booklabel of Hairlie Lloyd-Jones, fine. Jarndyce Antiquarian Booksellers CXCI - 442 2011 £75

Association – Lloyd-Jones, Hugh

Semonides *De Mulieribus.* Gottingen: Sumtibus viduae Vandenboek, 1781. Some spotting throughout, small wormtrail to margin of last five leaves, pages xxiv, 103, 8vo., contemporary half sprinkled calf with sprinkled paper boards, backstrip with five raised bands between darkened gilt fillets, dark label in second compartment, joints rubbed and cracking but strong, corners lightly worn, paper bit scuffed, ownership inscription of J. H. Lupton, sound, loosely inserted is letter addressed to (Sir Hugh) Lloyd-Jones dated 14 Feb. (no year). Blackwell Rare Books B166 - 95 2011 £350

Association – Lloyd-Russell, Vincent

Cervantes Saavedra, Miguel De 1547-1616 *The First (and Second) Part of the Histoty of the Various and Wittie Knight-Errant Don Quixote of the Mancha.* Ashendene Press, 1927-1928. One of 225 copies; 2 volumes, text in the 1620 English translation of Thomas Shelton, original luxurious white pigskin by W. H. Smith, thick raised bands, gilt titling on spine, sturdy cloth double slipcases (little marked), morocco labels, lovely woodcut initials and borders designed by Louise Powell, cut on wood by W. M. Quick and George H. Ford, bookplate of Vincent Lloyd-Russell in each volume, as well as shadow of another small bookplate now removed; pigskin of first volume, just shade different from second (a common defect as the volumes issued more than a year apart), in all other ways, extremely fine, magnificent binding unusually clean, text in perfect condition. Phillip J. Pirages 59 - 76 2011 $9500

Lilly, William *William Lilly's History of His Life and Times from the Year 1602 to 1681.* London: Reprinted for Charles Baldwyn, 1822. 252 x 154mm. 2 p.l., 260 pages, lovely dark brown crushed morocco, lavishly gilt by Zaehnsdorf (stamp signed on front turn-in, and with Zaehnsdorf's gilt oval stamp on rear turn-in), covers with wide lacy filigree border scalloped at inner edge and filled with densely gilt floral tools and sprigs on stippled ground, this border around an inner frame composed of double gilt rules with tiny shamrock at each corner and inside this frame, central panel with ornate cornerpieces filled with flowers, volutes and drawer handles on stippled ground, raised bands, spine densely and handsomely gilt in scallop edged compartments featuring a central quatrefoil containing a rose surrounded by floral sprays, open dots and much stippling, gilt turn-ins, top edge gilt, 12 engraved portraits printed on India paper and mounted, as called for; armorial bookplate of Vincent Lloyd-Russell; leaves faintly toned (no doubt as in all copies because of paper stock used), moderate offsetting from plates, other trivial imperfections, but excellent copy internally text generally clean and fresh, gleaming binding in especially fine condition with no perceptible wear. Phillip J. Pirages 59 - 149 2011 $1250

Association – Lloyd, Lt.

Campbell, Thomas 1777-1844 *Gertrude of Wyoming and Other Poems.* London: Longman Hurst, Rees, Orme & Brown, 1816. Sixth edition; half title, frontispiece, slightly foxed, uncut in original light brown paper boards, paper label, some very slight wear to lower following hinge, else exceptional copy in its original state; contemporary signature, modern booklabel of Vincent Walmsley and earlier ownership inscription of Lt. Lloyd. Jarndyce Antiquarian Booksellers CXCI - 347 2011 £75

Association – Loger, Vincent

Suetonius Tranquillus, Caius *(Opera).* Paris: Typographia Regia, 1645. 12mo., (12), 558, (30) pages, engraved title, engraved medallion portraits, engraved head and tailpiece, contemporary French calf, gilt fleurs de lys on covers within double gilt fillet, spine gilt in compartments, marbled edges, signature of Vincent Loger 1667, from the library of the Earls of Macclesfield at Shirburn Castle. Maggs Bros. Ltd. 1440 - 206 2011 £700

Association – Long, Harald

Heister, Lorenz 1683-1758 *Chirurgie, in Welcher Alles was Zur Wundarzney Gehoret... Deutlich Vorgestelelt Werden.* Nurnberg: Bey Gabriel Nicolaus Raspe, 1779. 216 x 183mm., 8 p.l. (including frontispiece), 378, (4) pages, 379-1078 (i.e. 1076) pages, 12 leaves, stunning contemporary painted calf, elaborately gilt decorated, covers each with four very large and graceful gilt floral tools within large compartments formed by interlacing strapwork that is painted black, an equally prominent central compartment with dense gilt foliage, flowers and fleurons and much supporting gilt decoration of a similar kind in 20 smaller compartments around the board edges and between the large compartments, raised bands, spine very handsomely gilt with lovely central flower and botanical side pieces, olive green spine label, gilt decorated turn-ins, marbled endpapers, all edges gilt; ornamental headpieces, initial and tailpieces, frontispiece and 38 sometimes startling folding plates, titlepage in red and black, inscribed "Dr. Harald Long 1895"; tiny cracks in label, text printed on inferior paper stock (so not particularly bright), but almost nothing else in the way of a significant defect; superb, even exceptional copy in wonderful binding, text absolutely fresh and leather with virtually no signs of wear. Phillip J. Pirages 59 - 52 2011 $17,500

Association – Long, R. G.

Haley, James Evetts *The XIT Ranch of Texas and the Early Days of the Llano Estacado.* Chicago: Lakeside Press, 1929. First edition; 8vo., presentation inscription by author to R. G. Long, also laid in is penned note on Prince George Hotel (NYC) stationery, to Wright Howes advising that they would meet him for breakfast and afterwards, go to a sale together; decorated cloth, xvi, 261 pages, gilt top, frontispiece, fine bright copy in protective transparent dust jacket, exceptional copy. Buckingham Books May 26 2011 - 28028 2011 $1875

Association – Longfellow, Henry Wadsworth

Agassiz, Louis 1807-1873 *Contributions to the Natural History of the United States of America.* Boston: Little Brown and Co., 1857-1862. 4 volumes, 77 plates, foxing, sometimes heavy to many, dampstaining, mostly marginal to plates in volumes 3 and 4, colored plates of turtles are virtually clean, large 4to., pages li, 452; (4), (451-) 643; xi, 306, 26; viii, 380, 12, original brown cloth (rebacked with later brown cloth, wear to corners and several edges to covers, head of spine perished, staining to front cover, some foxing to front and back pages, dampstaining to gutters and or margins of front and back pages, paper on some inner hinges cracked), from the library of Henry Wadsworth Longfellow, with his signature included twice, tipped into volume 1 is brief ALS, 1 page, from Agassiz to unknown recipient. Raymond M. Sutton, Jr. May 26 2011 - 55815 2011 $1200

Association – Lonsdale, Hugh Cecil, Earl of

Corner, Miss *Little Plays for Little People.* London: Dean & Son, n.d., First edition; original blue cloth gilt over bevelled boards, oval central chromolithograph on upper board, extremities little rubbed, pages 46, (ii), all edges gilt, woodcut illustrations by Alfred Crowquill, upper joint cracked, few spots, armorial bookplate of Hugh Cecil Earl of Lonsdale. R. F. G. Hollett & Sons Antiquarian Booksellers 170 - 172 2011 £95

Freke, John *The Princes of the Several Stocks, Anuities and Other Publick Securities &c with the Course of Exchange. From Saturday March 26th 1715 to Friday June 22d 1716.* London: sold by author at his office over against Jonathan's Coffee-House in Exchange Alley, 1716. 8vo., general titlepage (blank verso) + dedication leaf (blank verso), followed by 104 + 26 single sheet price lists, each 2 pages on facing leaves, some imprints cropped at foot, some printed on thick paper, contemporary panelled calf, skilfully rebacked and labelled to match, very good, from the 19th century library of Hugh Cecil 5th Earl of Lonsale, with his armorial bookplate, and from the early 20th century library of Harold Charles Drayton, the financier, exceptionally rare. John Drury Rare Books 153 - 49 2011 £3500

Reynard the Fox *The Most Delectable History of Reynard the Fox. (bound with) The Most Pleasant and Delightful History of Reynard the Fox. The Second Part (and) The Shifts of Reynardine the Son of Reynard the Fox...* London: printed by T. Ilive for Edward Brewster, 1701. London: Printed by A. M. and R. R. for Edward Brewster, 1681. London: Printed by T. J. for Edward Brewster and Thomas Passenger, 1684. Early English edition; 3 parts in one, small quarto, (156), (2 table of contents), (2, publisher's ads); (111), (1, publisher's ads); (8), 160 pages, mostly black letter with titles and side notes in roman letter, 62 woodcuts in first part, printed from 39 blocks and 15 woodcuts in second part, five repeated, all repeats from the first part, woodcut on C1 recto (Part I) printed upside down, contemporary sprinkled sheep, covers ruled and decoratively tooled in blind, spine decoratively tooled in gilt in compartments with two red morocco gilt lettering labels, minor restoration to covers, some browning, occasional light dampstaining and soiling, part I with tiny puncture marks in lower blank margin through gathering 1, just touching one letter in imprint of titlepage, 6 small holes in I3 and one tiny hole in I4, causing loss of a couple of letters, Part III with paper flaw in upper blank corner of A3 and A4, tiny tear (quarter inch) in lower blank margin of F4, and paper flaw in lower blank corner of I2, none affecting text, armorial bookplate of Gloucester on front free endpaper, bookplate of Hugh Cecil Lowther, 5th Earl of Lonsdale (1857-1944), (his sale 12 July 1937 lot 445), excellent copy, housed in quarter morocco clamshell box.   David Brass Rare Books, Inc.   May 26 2011 - 00654   2011 $17,500

Wordsworth, William   1770-1850   *Yarrow Revisited and Other Poems.* London: Longman, Rees, Orme, Brown, Green and Longman, Paternoster Row and Edward Moxon, Dover Street, 1835. First edition; small 8vo., full contemporary cranberry calf gilt, marbled edges, green morocco label on spine and with Earl of Lonsdale's coat of arms on front cover, extremities of calf trifle rubbed, otherwise superb copy in unusually fine contemporary binding, preserved in maroon half morocco slipcase, presentation copy to poet's patron, William Lowther, Earl of Lonsdale, with bookplate of recipients descendant, Hugh Cecil, Fifth Earl of Lonsdale. James S. Jaffe Rare Books   May 26 2011 - 13824   2011 $7500

Association – Lonsdale, William Lowther, Earl of

Wordsworth, William   1770-1850   *Yarrow Revisited and Other Poems.* London: Longman, Rees, Orme, Brown, Green and Longman, Paternoster Row and Edward Moxon, Dover Street, 1835. First edition; small 8vo., full contemporary cranberry calf gilt, marbled edges, green morocco label on spine and with Earl of Lonsdale's coat of arms on front cover, extremities of calf trifle rubbed, otherwise superb copy in unusually fine contemporary binding, preserved in maroon half morocco slipcase, presentation copy to poet's patron, William Lowther, Earl of Lonsdale, with bookplate of recipients descendant, Hugh Cecil, Fifth Earl of Lonsdale. James S. Jaffe Rare Books   May 26 2011 - 13824   2011 $7500

Association – Lorant, Stefan

Krull, Germaine   *100 x Paris.* Berlin-Westend: Verlag der Reihe, 1929. First edition; small quarto, 100 photo engraved plates, minor dampstains at extremities, else near fine in tattered, poor dust jacket, housed in cloth custom clamshell case, lengthy inscription by Krull to Stefan Lorant in German, rare in jacket.   Between the Covers   169 - STC346670   2011 $5000

Association – Lord, Winifred

Tennyson, Alfred Tennyson, 1st Baron   1809-1892 *Maud a Monodrama.* Kelmscott Press, 1893. One of 500 copies on paper (there were also five vellum copies not for sale; first state of text, without corrections later made on page 16, 19, 26 and 69; original limp vellum, vertical gilt titling on spine, silk ties, original (slightly soiled but generally well preserved) green cardboard slipcase with gilt tilting on front, initial opening with elaborate woodcut initials with decorative marginal extensions, device at end, printed in red and black, gift inscription "Winifred Lord/with her Uncle's love/and best wishes/may 20, 1895", half inch closed tear to fore edge of one leaf, otherwise virtually pristine, extraordinarily clean, fresh and bright inside and out.   Phillip J. Pirages   59 - 249   2011 $2750

Association – Louis Philippe, King of the French

Balzac, Honore De   *Les Cent Contes Drolatiques.* Paris: Charles Gosseli and Ed Werdet, 1832. First edition; 3 volumes, octavo, titlepages printed in red and black, later quarter tan calf over marbled boards, spines with four raised bands ruled in gilt and decoratively tooled in blind in compartments with two black morocco gilt lettering labels, marbled endpapers, edges sprinkled red, excellent copy, from the library of the Duc D'Orleans, Louis Philippe (King of the French), with armorial stamp on half title volume two, extremely scarce.   David Brass Rare Books, Inc.   May 26 2011 - 00914   2011 $5500

Association – Louis, Moira

MacDonald, George   1824-1905   *Within and Without: a Dramatic Poem.* London: Longman, Brown, Green, Longmans & Roberts, 1857. Second edition; 2 pages ads, original dark brown morocco coarse weave cloth, boards decorated in blind, spine lettered gilt, small splits at head of following hinge and tail of leading hinge, ownership inscriptions of Moira Louis, 61 Eaton Place, good plus.   Jarndyce Antiquarian Booksellers   CXCII - 4   2011   £350

Association – Lovett, Adele

Benchley, Robert *No Poems or Around the World Backwards and Sideways.* New York: Harper, 1932. First edition; illustrations by Gluyas Williams, modest age toning on spine and edge of rear board, tiny tears at crown, very good, without dust jacket, inscribed by author for Adele Lovett. Between the Covers 169 - BTC347389 2011 $950

Association – Lowdell, Stephen

Livius, Titus *Titi Livii Patavini Historiarum Libri Qui Extant.* Parisiis: apud Fredericum Leonard, 1679. 5 volumes bound as 6, 4to., pages (lxx) 544 (ix) + engraved half title and 2 engraved maps; (ii) 10 545-876, 3-191, (xix); (viii) 620 (lii) + 1 extending engraved plate and 1 other engraved plate; (viii) 757, (lxv) 678 (xxvi) 776, (xvi), contemporary calf, stain darkened spine panel gilt, brick red lettering piece gilt, numbered direct in gilt boards panelled in blind (Cambridge style), board edges decorative roll gilt, all edges red speckled, blue and white sewn endbands, light toning and some spotting, rubbed at joints and corners, joints cracked, endcaps worn, some labels lost, contemporary armorial bookplate of Sir Robert Clayton , early 19th century armorial bookplate of Stephen Lowdell, from the collection of Christopher Ernest Weston 1947-2010. Unsworths Booksellers 24 - 115 2011 £450

Association – Lowe, John

Tooke, John Horne 1736-1812 *Ptereonta or the Diversions of Purley.* London: 1798. 1805. Volume I is second edition, volume II is first edition; 2 volumes, large 4to., very free of foxing, text with wide margins, three quarter diced morocco and marbled boards, shelfwear, surface of leather at front edge of backstrip of volume I wearing but still tight, volume II has 3 inch split to right side of backstrip (marbling shelf rubbed), chip to backstrip extremities, bookplate of John Lowe. Bookworm & Silverfish 670 - 77 2011 $295

Association – Lowell, Anna Cabot

Emerson, Ralph Waldo 1803-1882 *May-Day and Other Pieces.* Boston: Ticknor and Fields, 1867. One of only 100 copies bound thus, from a total edition of 2000; original gilt decorated white linen, gift binding, few pages unopened, spine slightly darkened with minor wear to tips, near fine and scarce, signed and inscribed by author for Anna Cabot Lowell. Charles Agvent Transcendentalism 2010 - 15 2011 $8500

Association – Lowenstein, Eleanor

Moynier *De La Truffe, Traite Complet de ce Tubercule, Contenant sa Description et son Histoire Naturelle la Plus Detaillee, on Exploitation Commerciale et sa Position dans l'Art Culinaire...* Paris: Barba an Legrand et Bergougnious, 1836. 8vo., pages 204, uncut, internally excellent with only little light spotting, publisher's wrappers, blue, text in black, worn at spine with some loss, upper panel partially detached, light blue morocco backed clamshell box lined with fine chamois leather by Sangorski & Sutcliffe, bookplate of Eleanor Lowenstein, rare, entirely unsophisticated. Simon Finch Rare Books Zero - 128 2011 £2000

Association – Lucatelli, Austin

Austin, William *A Specimen of Sketching Landscapes in a Free and Masterly Manner with a Pen or Pencil; Exemplified in thirty Etchings done from original drawings of Lucatelli after the Life in and about Rome.* by the author in George Street, Hanover Square..., 1781. 4 pages, 30 etchings, some signed Austin F (or Fecit) Lucatelli, inscribed by Frederick Finden for Catherine Ward, very good, contemporary half calf with red morocco label, dark blue glazed paper boards which are rubbed and marked, marginal stain to one plate but clear of image and little old and faint waterstaining the inner lower corner, again not affecting images. Ken Spelman Rare Books 68 - 13 2011 £2200

Association – Luciani, Tomaso

Bude, Guillaume *De Asse et Partibvs Eivs Libri V.* Lvgdvni: Apvd Seb. Gryphivm, 1550. 185 x 120mm., 815, (79) pages, (1) leaf (with errors in pagination), fine contemporary ivory blindstamped pigskin over wooden boards, covers with frames formed by multiple blind rules and foliate roll featuring laurel-wreathed heads in medallions, upper cover with central panel stamp showing Justice with her sword and scales, the letters "C A N" stamped on panel above Justice and date "1566" on panel below, lower cover with central panel stamp depicting virtuous Roman matron Lucretia in act of suicide, raised bands, two fore-edge clasps and front free endpaper missing; printer's device on title, intermittent (presumably early) underlining in brown pencil, front pastedown with modern bookplate showing a ship above mott "Novus Orbis", titlepage with early ink ownership inscriptions and library stamp of Tomaso Luciani of Albona; tip of lower corner of front cover chipped off, adjacent half inch of pigskin missing along tail edge, covers bit smudged, other minor external defects binding very sturdy and still extremely attractive deeply impressed stamps retaining much of their detail and all of their charm, and front cover still rather clean, leaves bit toned with age, occasional minor stains, text quite smooth, few signs of use. Phillip J. Pirages 59 - 8 2011 $950

Association – Lunt, Alfred

Coward, Noel 1899-1973 *Qaudrille. A romantic Comedy in Three Acts.* London: Heienmann, 1952. First edition; 8vo., pages 116, signed by 17 members of the English cast and by producer Jack Wilson and by Lynn Fontanne and Alfred Lunt on dedication page (play is dedicated to them), inscribed by Coward to Dorothy Sands (Octavia in the NY production), two more signed cards by Lunt and Fontanne tipped in and 3 notes by Lunt to Sands laid in, with tipped in signed photo of Sands, nice copy in somewhat chipped dust jacket. Second Life Books Inc. 174 - 111 2011 $700

Association – Luntz, Florence

Caldwell, Erskine Preston 1903-1987 *Some American People.* New York: McBride, 1935. First edition; review copy, inscribed by author to Stuart Wright, owner signature of Florence Luntz, trace wear to spine ends, very near fine in near fine, slightly dusty dust jacket with tiny tear at upper front spine fold, publisher's review slip laid in, giving publication date Oct. 21 135, very nice association, rare as advance issue, particularly signed. Ken Lopez Bookseller 154 - 23 2011 $500

Association – Lupton, J. H.

Semonides *De Mulieribus.* Gottingen: Sumtibus viduae Vandenboek, 1781. Some spotting throughout, small wormtrail to margin of last five leaves, pages xxiv, 103, 8vo., contemporary half sprinkled calf with sprinkled paper boards, backstrip with five raised bands between darkened gilt fillets, dark label in second compartment, joints rubbed and cracking but strong, corners lightly worn, paper bit scuffed, ownership inscription of J. H. Lupton, sound, loosely inserted is letter addressed to (Sir Hugh) Lloyd-Jones dated 14 Feb. (no year). Blackwell Rare Books B166 - 95 2011 £350

Association – Luschier, Jennie

Odlum, Jerome *Each Dawn I Die.* Indianapolis and New York: Bobbs Merrill Co., 1938. First edition; spine heavily bleached, good only in internally lined, good dust jacket with small chip at crown, inscribed by author to Jennie and Lee Luschier, scarce in jacket, especially signed. Between the Covers 169 - BTC347393 2011 $2200

Association – Luschier, Lee

Odlum, Jerome *Each Dawn I Die.* Indianapolis and New York: Bobbs Merrill Co., 1938. First edition; spine heavily bleached, good only in internally lined, good dust jacket with small chip at crown, inscribed by author to Jennie and Lee Luschier, scarce in jacket, especially signed. Between the Covers 169 - BTC347393 2011 $2200

Association – Luveri, Michael

Fowles, John *The Enigma of Stonehenge.* London: Jonathan Cape, 1980. First edition; fine, dust jacket near fine, small rub on front fold, color plates, inscribed and dated by Fowles for Michael Luveri 8 Oct. 1982. Bella Luna Books May 29 2011 - t6805 2011 $82

Association – Lyon, Nelson

Elliott, Bob *Write If You Get Work: the Best of Bob & Ray.* New York: Random House, 1975. First edition; this copy inscribed by Elliott and Ray Goulding to Nelson Lyon, small stain to fore edge and shallow sunning to board edges, near fine in very good, spine sunned dust jacket, mild edgewear, very uncommon signed and nice association as well. Ken Lopez Bookseller 154 - 50 2011 $300

Ginsberg, Allen *Howl.* New York: Harper & Row, 1986. First edition thus, 30th anniversary original draft facsimile edition; remainder mark lower page edges foxing to top page edges, else fine in near fine dust jacket, inscribed by author to Nelson Lyon in 1992 with drawing. Ken Lopez Bookseller 154 - 62 2011 $750

Association – Macaulay, A.

Herbert, George *A Priest to the Temple.* London: printed by T. R. for Benj. Tooke, 1675. Third impression; small 8vo., old milled calf, rebacked in matching calf gilt with raised bands, pages (xxxvi), 166, (lxx), (viii, ads), imprimatur leaf (contemporary signature of A. Macaulay on recto). R. F. G. Hollett & Son Antiquarian Booksellers 175 - 620 2011 £395

Association – Macclesfield, Earl of

Abarbanel, Isaac *Don Vitzhaq Abravaniel & R. Mosis Alschechi Comment in Essiae Propbetian 30 (Actually Isaiah 52 v. 13 to 53 v. 12)...* Leiden: B. & A. Elzevier, 1631. 8vo., (16) 291, (13) pages, title printed in red and black, Square & Rabbinic letter, some Arabic type, contemporary English calf, from the library of the Earls of Macclesfield at Shirburn Castle. Maggs Bros. Ltd. 1440 - 1 2011 £550

Adronicus Rhodius *Ethicorum Nichomacheorum Paraphrasis.* Cambridge: Excudebat Johannes Hayes, 1679. Titlepage in red and black, one or two small spots, embossment of Earls of Macclesfield to first two printed leaves, pages (xviii), 530, (30), 8vo., contemporary plain biscuit calf, backstrip with five raised bands, old paper labels in top and bottom compartments, edges speckled red, merest touch of rubbing to edges, South Library bookplate, very good. Blackwell Rare Books B166 - 4 2011 £400

Agopian, Yovhannes *l'Argmanout 'iwn Italakansrbazani Xorhdatetern. La Laichiaratione Della Liturgia Armena.* Venice: M. A. Barboni, 1690. 4to., 51, (1) pages, title and text printed in red and black, some leaves cropped close at head, with loss of page numbers, modern half calf, from the library of the Earls of Macclesfield at Shirburn Castle. Maggs Bros. Ltd. 1440 - 2 2011 £2000

Ainsworth, Robert *Thesaurus... or a Compendius Dictionary of the Latin Tongue: Designed for the Use of the British Nations...* London: for various booksellers, 1746. Second edition; 4to., 2 volumes, contemporary Russia gilt, extremely handsome copy, from the library of the Earls of Macclesfield at Shirburn Castle. Maggs Bros. Ltd. 1440 - 3 2011 £450

Althuysen, Jan *Langaene oer dy Fortziesing fin zyn Trogloftigste Haegheyt byrymme Trog Jan Althuysen.* Harlingen: F. van der Plaats, 1747. 4to., 18 pages, imprint and catchwords trimmed, modern half calf over marbled boards, from the library of the Earls of Macclesfield at Shirburn Castle. Maggs Bros. Ltd. 1440 - 4 2011 £500

Ammianus Marcellinus *Rerum Gestarum Libri Decem et Octo.* Lyons: S. Gryphius, 1552. 12mo., 736 (8) pages, aa2 missing, aa3, last 2 leaves blank, contemporary French binding of smooth calf, gilt arabesque in centre of covers, spine in 5 compartments each with small gilt ornament, gilt edges, binding little rubbed, deleted contemporary inscription on titlepage Jacobus Rubeus, from the library of the Earls of Macclesfield at Shirburn Castle. Maggs Bros. Ltd. 1440 - 6 2011 £450

Anacreon *Opera.* London: W. Bowyer, 1725. 4to., (8), xlii, xlii, xliii-lxxiv, 75, (3) pages, list of subscribers, contemporary sprinkled calf gilt, rubbed, subscriber's copy, from the library of the Earls of Macclesfield at Shirburn Castle. Maggs Bros. Ltd. 1440 - 7 2011 £450

Angeli, Pietro *Syrias hoc est Expeditio illa Celeberrima Christianorum Principium Qua Hierosolyma Ductu Goffredi Blionis Lotharinguiae...* Florence: F. Giunto, 1591. First edition; 4to., (24), 406 pages, italic type, woodcut initials, 18th century English calf, triple gilt fillet on covers, little rubbed, 17th century French inscription of Vallognes on titlepage, from the library of the Earls of Macclesfield at Shirburn Castle. Maggs Bros. Ltd. 1440 - 8 2011 £950

Aretino, Pietro *Quatro Comedie...coe Il Marescoalco la Talanta. La Cortegiana L'Hipocrito.* London: J. Wolfe, 1588. 8vo., ff. (8), 485, (3 (errata), early 18th century English calf, spine gilt in compartments, very nice, from the library of the Earls of Macclesfield at Shirburn Castle. Maggs Bros. Ltd. 1440 - 5 2011 £900

Aristoteles *I tre Libri della Retorica...* Venice: Francesco de' Franceschi, 1571. First edition of this translation by Piccolomini; 4to., (12), 292 pages, device on titlepage, English calf c. 1720, gilt fillet on covers, spine gilt, colored silk marker, from the library of the Earls of Macclesfield at Shirburn Castle. Maggs Bros. Ltd. 1440 - 12 2011 £550

Artemidorus *Artemidori Daldiani & Achmetis Sereimi f. Oneirocritica. Astrampsychi & Nicephori Versus Etiam Oneirocritici.* Paris: M. Orry, 1603. 4to. (12), 269, L14 blank, (23) P2 blank, 20, 65; 275, (17) pages, title printed in red and black, 2 columns, later 17th century Cambridge binding of panelled calf, spine gilt, red edges, extremely handsome, inscription Stephanus Joann(is) Stephanius, from the library of the Earls of Macclesfield at Shirburn Castle. Maggs Bros. Ltd. 1440 - 14 2011 £900

Ascham, Roger *The English Works.* London: printed for R. and J. Dodsely, 1761. First edition, first issue with leaf of additional subscribers; 4to., (10), xvi, 395 pages, engraved armorial headpiece (Earl of Shaftesbury), contemporary calf, spine gilt, red morocco lettering piece (short split at head of upper joint), from the library of the Earls of Macclesfield at Shirburn Castle. Maggs Bros. Ltd. 1440 - 15 2011 £400

Asterius, Saint *Homiliae Graece & Latine Nunc Primum Editae Philppo Rubernio Interprete...* Antwerp: in off. Plantiniana, widoe & sons of J. Moretus, 1615. 4to., (12), 284, (4) pages, engraved device on titlepage, last leaf with woodcut device on recto, engraved portrait by Galle after Rubens, contemporary limp vellum, lower cover slightly damaged, very fine, from the library of the Earls of Macclesfield at Shirburn Castle. Maggs Bros. Ltd. 1440 - 10 2011 £1200

Bacon, Roger *Specula Mathematica in Qua de Specierum Muiltiplicatione Agitur. Liber... editus Opera.* Frankfurt: W. Richter for A. Hummius, 1614. 4to., (8), 83 pages, woodcut figures in text, rebound in half calf, old style, from the library of the Earls of Macclesfield at Shirburn Castle. Maggs Bros. Ltd. 1440 - 18 2011 £1200

Baif, Lazare De *De Re Vestiaria Libellus ex Bayfi Excerptus...* Paris: Ambroise Girault, 1535. 8vo., 68, (10) pages, later vellum, from the library of the Earls of Macclesfield at Shirburn Castle. Maggs Bros. Ltd. 1440 - 20 2011 £650

Bainbridge, John *An Astronomicall Description of the Late Comet from the 18 of Novemb. 1618 to 16 of December following.* London: by Edward Griffin for Iohn Parker, 1619. First edition (2nd state of imprint); 4to., (8), 24 "17" (i.e. 25) (26 (blank), 27-42 pages, folding engraved plate, lacking last blank leaf, errata leaf lightly stained, some light browning, few headlines slightly shaved, from the library of the Earls of Macclesfield at Shirburn Castle.   Maggs Bros. Ltd.   1440 - 21   2011   £2500

Barba, Alvaro Alonso *A Collection of Scarce and Valuable Treatises Upon Metals, Mines and Minerals.* London: C. Jephson for Olive Payne, 1738. 12mo., (12), 170 (10) 173-275 (5), 66, (2) pages, engraved plate, woodcut illustrations, contemporary morocco, gilt triple fillet and roll tooled border, gilt corner fleurons, spine gilt in compartments, gilt edges, spine chipped at head, joints rubbed and cracking, lacking lettering piece, fine, with publisher's ads (2 pages) at end, glossary (6 pages); from the library of the Earls of Macclesfield at Shirburn Castle.   Maggs Bros. Ltd.   1440 - 22   2011   £550

Bardet De Villeneuve, P. P. A. *Cours De La Science Militaire, A L'Usage De L'Infanterie, De La Cavalerie, De L'Artillerie, Du Genie & De La Marine.* The Hague: Jean Van Duren, 1740-1742. First edition; 202 x 118mm., 10 volumes bound in nine, first and fifth volumes bound without half titles, extremely pleasing late 18th century sprinkled calf, spines very elaborately gilt in diapered compartments (two of the compartments featuring unusual checkerboard and floral pattern), each (flat spine with red and green titling label; engraved vignette devices on all 10 volume titlepages, 8 engraved frontispieces (as called for) and a total of 142 folding plates, titlepages printed in red and black, front pastedown of each volume with armorial bookplate of Lt. Gen. G. L. Parker (4th Earl of Macclesfield), first endpaper with similar armorial bookplate of Macclesfield library, first two leaves of each volume with small embossed Macclesfield stamp, front joint of first volume (only) with just hint of wear, one cover with few small blemishes (superficial worm burrows?), light offsetting from frontispiece, about half the plates in three volumes with headlines and or/plate number partly cropped), no cropping elsewhere), two or three gatherings with minor foxing, but beautifully bound set in remarkably fine condition, bindings showing only most negligible wear, entire series clean and fresh internally.   Phillip J. Pirages   59 - 1   2011 $4800

Barlow, William *Magneticall Advertisements or Divers Pertinent Observations and Approved Experiments Concerning the Nature and Properties of the Load-stone...* London: Edward Griffin for Timothy Barlow, 1616. First edition; 4to., (16), 86, (2) pages, woodcut illustrations in text, without final leaf of "Faults escaped" but with penultimate leaf, short tear at head of A4, title and final page dust soiled, small dampstain in upper fore corner and fore margin at beginning and end, disbound, from the library of the Earls of Macclesfield at Shirburn Castle.   Maggs Bros. Ltd.   1440 - 25   2011   £4500

Basta, Giorgio *Counti d'Huszt.* Rouen: Jean Berthelin, 1627. Folio, (12), 76 pages, title within engraved border, woodcut initials and headpieces, 12 double page engraved plates, water damaged at foot throughout with some fraying, including foot of titlepage and on some plates, binding scraped; from the library of the Earls of Macclesfield at Shirburn Castle.   Maggs Bros. Ltd.   1440 - 26   2011   £450

Baxter, William *Glossarium Antiquitatum Britannicarum sive Syllabus Etymologicus Antiquitatum Vetris Britannae atque Iberniae Temporibus Romanorum etc.* London: W. Bowyer, 1719. Royal 8vo., (6), xiv, (4), 277, (19) pages, engraved portrait, contemporary russia binding, gilt border on covers, spine gilt, red edges, spine somewhat faded, without list of subscribers, from the library of the Earls of Macclesfield at Shirburn Castle.   Maggs Bros. Ltd.   1440 - 27   2011   £600

Benedetti, Giovanni Battista *Resolutio Omnium Euclidis Problematum Aliorumque ad hoc Necessaro Inventrum una Tantummodo...* Venice: Bartolommeo Cesano, 1553. 4to., ff. (12), 57, (1), woodcut diagrams, large device on titlepage, from the library of the Earls of Macclesfield at Shirburn Castle.   Maggs Bros. Ltd.   1440 - 28   2011   £5000

Berkenmeyer, Paul Ludolph *Le Curieux Antiquaire ou Recueil Geographique et Historique des Choses les Plus Remarquables qu'on Trouve dans les Quatre Parties de l'Univers...* Leiden: Pierre Vander Aa, 1729. First and only French edition; 3 volumes in one, 8vo., (22), 385, (2), 386-736, (10), 737-1062 pages, each volume has special titlepage, 2 engraved folding maps, 2 engraved folding plans, 46 engraved plates, title printed in red and black; from the library of the Earls of Macclesfield at Shirburn Castle.   Maggs Bros. Ltd.   1440 - 29   2011   £700

Bianchini, Francesco *De Kalendario et Cyclo Caesaris ac de Paschali Canone S. Hippolyti Martyris Dissertationes Duae...* Rome: A. & F. de Conte, 1703. First edition; handsome copy, 3 parts in 1 volume, folio, 10 engraved plates (of 11), engraved illustrations, contemporary Dutch calf, gilt spine; from the library of the Earls of Macclesfield at Shirburn Castle.   Maggs Bros. Ltd.   1440 - 30   2011   £550

Bible. Hebrew - 1656 *The Hebrew text of the Psalmes and Lamentations....* London: printed for the author and are to be sold by H. Robinson, A. Crook, L. Fawn, J. Kirton, S. Thomson and G. Sawbrige.., 1656. (8), 248, 22, (2), text in 2 columns printed in vocalised Hebrew and transliterated, last leaf with errata, contemporary English calf over pasteboard, contemporary English calf over pasteboard, upper joint cracking, from the library of the Earls of Macclesfield at Shirburn Castle.   Maggs Bros. Ltd.   1440 - 31   2011   £1800

Bible. Hebrew - 1656 *The Hebrew text of the Psalmes and Lamentations....* London: printed for the author and sold by H. Robinson, A Crook, L. Fawn, J. Kirton, S. Thomson..., 1656. 12mo., (12), 266, 149-191, 15, (2) pages, last leaf with errata, contemporary calf, from the library of John Christy 1717, from the library of the Earls of Macclesfield at Shirburn Castle. Maggs Bros. Ltd. 1440 - 32 2011 £450

Bible. Latvian - 1704 *Dahwida Dseesmu-Grahmata no Deewa, Sehta Wahrda Grabmatas pa Wahrdu Wahrdeem Insemta. (Pslams). (bound with) Salamana sakkami-wahrdi no deewa swehta Wahrda Grahmatas... (Proverbs).* Riga: G. N. Noller, 1704-1707. 2 works in 1 volume, 8vo., later 18th century English polished calf, gilt spine, red morocco lettering piece, red edges, few headlines slightly shaved, from the library of the Earls of Macclesfield at Shirburn Castle. Maggs Bros. Ltd. 1440 - 33 2011 £550

Bissel, Johann *Icaria.* Ingolstadt: C. Haemli, 1637. First edition; 12mo., (24), 343, (17) pages, engraved title, map in text, contemporary vellum, yapp edges, paper shelf labels on spine, from the library of the Earls of Macclesfield at Shirburn Castle, old Macclesfield classmark A IX 23 and number 35 written in ink (slightly dusty). Maggs Bros. Ltd. 1440 - 35 2011 £450

Blundeville, Thomas *M. Blundeville His Exercises Containing Eight Treatises...* London: William Stansby, 1613. Fourth edition; 4to., (16 first leaf blank), 799, (1 (blank) pages, folding table at page 80, folding table at page 695 (loosely inserted), folding woodcut "Mappe of Fraunce" at page 784, folding woodcut of empty globe divided into lines of longitude and latitude at page 798 (loosely inserted), the fifth folding woodcut is a woodcut of a set of compass points linked by thumb lines, it has become detached and is now loosely inserted at page 749, numerous woodcut illustrations, that at page 315 with piece of string as a pointer, that at page 315 a woodcut volvelle with pointer loosely inserted (this has attached to it the semi-circular "flie" missing from page 775 (cf. the 1638 edition on EEBO) in place of the circular? Globe found in 1597 and 1638 editions on EEBO; that at page 660 has pointer loosely inserted, a woodcut pointer tipped to margin (?incorrectly) at page 585, that at page 720 has woodcut vovelle and pointer, that at 744 lacks the volvelle, the space for the "Flie" at page 775 is blank as in the Huntington copy on EEBO; mid 17th century calf, gilt spine, marbled edges (joints and spine rubbed, foot of spine torn away exposing the tailband); from the library of the Earls of Macclesfield at Shirburn Castle. Maggs Bros. Ltd. 1440 - 36 2011 £1500

Bonaventura, Saint, Cardinal 1221-1274 *Meditationes to Yest Bogosliubna Razmiscglianya od Otaystva Odkupplienya Covicanskogo...* Rome: typis sacr. congreg. de progag fide, 1638. 12mo., (12), 226, (2 blank) pages, 19th century sprinkled calf, gilt fillet on covers, red morocco lettering pieces, red edges, from the library of the Earls of Macclesfield at Shirburn Castle. Maggs Bros. Ltd. 1440 - 38 2011 £700

Borel, Pierre *Tresor de Recherches et Antiquitez Gauloises et Francoises Reduites en Ordre Alphabetqiue et Renrichies de Beaucoup d'Origines...* Paris: August Courbe, 1655. First edition; 4to., (104), 61 (i.e. 609 pages 73-74 omitted), (23) pages, engraved printer's device, head-piece and initial, all by Jean Picart after F. C. Chauveau?, woodcut headpieces and initials, contemporary speckled calf, spine gilt in compartments, morocco lettering piece, severe worming in bottom right hand corners of 3 quires, affecting text, spine dry, from the library of the Earls of Macclesfield at Shirburn Castle. Maggs Bros. Ltd. 1440 - 39 2011 £500

Boschius, Jacobus *Symbolographia sive de Arte Symbolica Sermones Septem.* Augsburg & Eillingen: Johan Kaspar Bencard, 1702. First edition; 5 parts, folio, frontispiece, title vignette, 171 plates, contemporary English calf, spine gilt in compartments, from the library of the Earls of Macclesfield at Shirburn Castle. Maggs Bros. Ltd. 1440 - 40 2011 £5000

Boxhorn, Marcus Zuerius *Commentariolus de Statu Confoederatarum Provinciarum Belguii...* The Hague: A. Vlacq for J. Vlacq, 1668. 12mo., (12 (including engraved title dated 1659), 202, (2 blank) pages, contemporary English calf, gilt fillet on covers, gilt floral cornerpieces, spine gilt, edges gilt, first 2 leaves with slight dampstain, from the library of the Earls of Macclesfield at Shirburn Castle. Maggs Bros. Ltd. 1440 - 41 2011 £450

Branschweig-Luneburg, August, Duke of *Gustavi Seleni Cryptomenytices et Cryptographiae Libri IX etc.* Luneburg: J. & H. Stern, 1624. First edition; folio, (36), 493, (1) pages, half title, folding letterpress table, engraved border on titlepage, 3 engraved illustrations, woodcut diagrams, printer's device on final verso, contemporary Dutch vellum, yapp edges, title leaf trimmed at foot and mounted on stub, extremely fine, unspotted copy, from the library of the Earls of Macclesfield at Shirburn Castle. Maggs Bros. Ltd. 1440 - 17 2011 £7000

Braun, Ernst *Novissimum Fundamenturm & Praxis Artilleriae Oder Nachitziger Besten Mannier.* Danzig: J. F. Grafen for the author, 1682. First edition; folio, (4), 197 (7) pages, no dedication, additional engraved title, 24 plates on 22 (of 23) sheets, lacking final double page engraving, annotated in German hand by J. Hopkey with inscription on title and his initials on cover, from the library of the Earls of Macclesfield at Shirburn Castle. Maggs Bros. Ltd. 1440 - 42 2011 £2800

Bry, Gilles *Historie des Pays et Comte du Perche et Duche d'Alencon etc.* Paris: Pierre Le Mur, 1620. First edition; 4to., (16), 382, (14) pages, title printed in red and black, 18th century English calf, gilt fillets on covers, gilt spine, very handsome copy, from the library of the Earls of Maccleesfield at Shirburn Castle. Maggs Bros. Ltd. 1440 - 43 2011 £650

Callimachus *Hymni (cum Scholiis Graecis) & Epigrammatia Eiusdem Poemtaium de Coma Berenices...* Geneva: H. Estienne, 1578. 2 parts, 4to., (16), 72, 134, (2 blank) pages, device on titlepage, initials headpieces, Dutch early18th century mottled calf, gilt spine, handsome copy, from the library of the Earls of Macclesfield at Shirburn Castle. Maggs Bros. Ltd. 1440 - 44 2011 £600

Callimachus *Hymni, Epigrammata et Fragmenta...* Paris: S. Mabre-Cramoisy, 1675. 4to., (20), 262, (56) pages, engraved armorial headpiece to dedication, engraved initial, 19th century olive green morocco by Hatton of Manchester, gilt, from the library of the Earls of Macclesfield at Shirburn Castle, Macclesfield arms on upper cover, edges gilt, title leaf slightly browned, spine slightly faded, extremely handsome, printed on fine paper. Maggs Bros. Ltd. 1440 - 45 2011 £450

Cameli, Francesco *Nummi Antiqui Aurei Argentei & Acrei Primae, Secundae, Seu Mediae, Minimae & Maximae Formae.* Rome: G. G. de Buagni, 1690. 4to., 218, (2 blank) pages, French smooth calf c. 1700, spine gilt, engraved bookplate of Nicolas Joseph Foucault, from the library of the Earls of Macclesfield at Shirburn Castle. Maggs Bros. Ltd. 1440 - 232 2011 £1000

Camus, Francois Joseph De *Traite des Forces Mouvantes, avec la Description de 23 machines Nouvelles de son Invention.* Paris: C. Jombert and L. Le Cotne, 1722. 8vo., (16), 535, (7) pages, 8 folding engraved plates, woodcut device on title, woodcut initials, head and tailpieces, speckled calf, spine gilt in compartments, red morocco lettering piece, few quires lightly brown, extremities rubbed, red mottled edges, from the library of the Earls of Macclesfield at Shirburn Castle. Maggs Bros. Ltd. 1440 - 46 2011 £800

Chartier, Alain *Les Oeuvres.* Paris: S. Thiboust, Jan. 25th, 1617. 4to., (16), 868, (20) pages, title printed in red and black, woodcut device, woodcut head and tailpieces, woodcut initials, contemporary calf with triple fillet rule on boards and fleurons in corners, spine gilt in compartments, morocco lettering piece, colored silk page marker, manuscript ex-libris "Normand", manuscript annotations in margins (many trimmed), from the library of the Earls of Macclesfield at Shirburn Castle. Maggs Bros. Ltd. 1440 - 50 2011 £900

Chenu, Jean *Recueil d'Antiquitez et Privileges de la Ville de Bourges et de Plusieurs Autres Villes Capitales du Royaume Divise e Trois Parties.* Paris: Robert Fouet, 1621. First edition; 4to., (4), 503, (9) pages, (page 156 misnumbered 457), engraved portrait by L. Gauthier, mid 17th century French calf with triple fillets on boards and fleurons in corner, spine gilt in compartments, morocco lettering piece, from the library of the Earls of Macclesfield at Shirburn Castle. Maggs Bros. Ltd. 1440 - 51 2011 £500

Cicero, Marcus Tullius *Tusculanae Quaestiones.* Paris: Robert Estienne, 1537. 8vo., 223, (15) pages, woodcut printer's device on titlepage, late 17th century calf, spine gilt in compartments, manuscript annotations in margins, nice, from the library of the Earls of Macclesfield at Shirburn Castle. Maggs Bros. Ltd. 1440 - 53 2011 £450

Clairac, Louis Andre De La Mamie De *L'Ingenieur de Campagne, ou Traite de la Fortification Passagere.* Paris: Charles Antoine Jombert, 1749. First edition dedicated to the Comte d'Argenson; 4to., xxiii,(1), 24, (3) pages, 36 folding engraved plates, one engraved headpiece by Cochin contemporary speckled calf, spine gilt in compartments, some light spotting, foxing throughout pages 217-224, fine, Gen. G. L. Parker bookplate, manuscript ex-libris, from the library of the Earls of Macclesfield at Shirburn Castle. Maggs Bros. Ltd. 1440 - 56 2011 £400

Claudianus, Claudius *(Minor Works) Quotquot... extant Opuscula...* Paris: S. de Colines, 1530. 8vo., ff. 185 (=183, ff. 177-178 omitted), (1) (blank), printed in italic, late 17th century French binding of calf, double gilt fillet on covers, spine gilt, beautiful, clean copy, from the library of the Earls of Macclesfield at Shirburn Castle. Maggs Bros. Ltd. 1440 - 57 2011 £500

Clenardus, Nicolaus *Institutiones ac Meditationes in Graecum Linguam...* Paris: H. le Be, 1581. (1580); 4to., (108), 414, (2), 23, (1) pages, contemporary brown calf over pasteboards, gilt centerpiece within single gilt fillet, spine gilt in 6 compartments, covers scuffed, handsome copy, from the library of the Earls of Macclesfield at Shirburn Castle. Maggs Bros. Ltd. 1440 - 59 2011 £800

Clenardus, Nicolaus *Institutiones Grammaticae, Latinae.* Lyons: G. & M. Berringen, 1551. 8vo., 155 pages, 18th century mottled calf, spine gilt, second known copy, from the library of the Earls of Macclesfield at Shirburn Castle. Maggs Bros. Ltd. 1440 - 58 2011 £800

Columnis, Guido De *Historia Destructionis Troiae (with Epitaphium Hectoris and Epitaphium Achillis etc.).* Netherlands?: printer of Alexander Magnus, 1477-1479. First edition; fine large copy with "Historia Troiana" written possibly in the atelier of the printer, in red crayon on both first and final blank, chancery folio, ff. (132), first and least leaves blank, lines, type, rubricated, English binding of the first half of the 17th century of brown calf over pasteboard, slightly worn, from the library of the Earls of Macclesfield at Shirburn Castle. Maggs Bros. Ltd. 1440 - 61 2011 £40,000

contemporary calf, titlepage torn with loss of lower right corner (repaired, first page torn with loss (repaired), both not affecting text, from the library of the Earls of Macclesfield at Shirburn Castle. Maggs Bros. Ltd. 1440 - 159 2011 £500

Corradi, Sebastiano *Commentarius in Quo P. Virgilij Maronis Liber Primus Aeneidos Explicatur.* Florence: L. Torrentino, 1555. First edition; 8vo., 390 (2 (blank) pages, device on titlepage, English calf c. 1700, spine gilt, slightly rubbed, from the library of the Earls of Macclesfield at Shirburn Castle. Maggs Bros. Ltd. 1440 - 62 2011 £450

Crinesius, Christoph *Babel sive, Discursus de Confusione Linguarm tum Orientalium... tum Occidentalium... Statuens Hebraicam Omnium esse Priman & Ispissimam Matricem, etc.* Nurnberg: S. Halbmayer, 1629. 4to., (16), 144, (4), engraved text, small paper repair to recto of last leaf, ff. T1-2 (contents and errata) bound in prelims, 18th century English mottled calf, gilt, some leaves browned, binding slightly rubbed, from the library of the Earls of Macclesfield at Shirburn Castle. Maggs Bros. Ltd. 1440 - 63 2011 £900

Daniel, Gabriel *Histoire De La Milice Francoise.* Paris: Denis Mariette et al, 1721. First edition; 2 volumes, 280 x 204mm., very attractive late 18th century tree calf, handsomely gilt, raised bands, spine compartments with dense gilt field featuring undulant strapwork floral stamps, each spine with two red morocco labels, yellow edges, device on titlepage of both volumes, vignette headpieces, floral tailpieces, foliated initials and 70 full page engraved plates; front pastedown of each volume with armorial bookplate of Lt. Gen. G. L. Parker (4th Earl of Macclesfield), first endpaper with similar armorial bookplate of Macclesfield library, first two leaves of volume I and first three leaves of volume II with small embossed Macclesfield stamp; bit of rubbing where bands intersect with joints, rear joint of first volume with crack just alongside top compartment (and spine end slightly torn), minor wear at extremities, few trivial abrasions, extremely pretty bindings in generally excellent condition, entirely solid with lustrous leather and bright gilt, number of gatherings faintly mottled or with overall light browning, one plate with stain in margin, three marginal tears (one of them, three inches long, neatly mended), handful of other trivial faults, still quite appealing internally, leaves clean and especially fresh, despite flaws, very pleasing set. Phillip J. Pirages 59 - 27 2011 $2500

Desmarets De Saint Sorlin, Jean *L'Ariane.. Enrichie de Plusieurs Figures.* Paris: Matthieu Guillemat, 1639. 4to., (8), 775, (1) pages, 17 engraved full page illustrations by Abraham Bosse after Claude Vignon, woodcut head and tailpieces, woodcut initials, 17th century speckled calf, spine gilt in compartments, binding rubbed, fine, from the library of the Earls of Macclesfield at Shirburn Castle. Maggs Bros. Ltd. 1440 - 66 2011 £500

Dilich, Wilhelm *Peribologia.* Frankfurt: A. Humm etc., 1641. Folio, 5-202, 10) pages, engraved title and 7 section titles, 410 plus numbered engravings, contemporary English calf, gilt fillet on covers, spine with gilt ornaments, red edges, from the library of the Earls of Macclesfield at Shirburn Castle, this copy may well stem from the library of John Collins/William Jones, and has the old Macclesfield Library class mark. Maggs Bros. Ltd. 1440 - 68 2011 £2000

Dilich, Wilhelm *Peribologia.* Frankfurt: A. Humm for J. W. Dilich, 1641. Folio, 5-202 (10) pages, engraved title and 7 section titles, 410 plus numbered engravings on c. 240 plates, text and plates mounted on guards, 18th century English calf, gilt, red edges, very handsome, clean copy, from the library of the Earls of Macclesfield at Shirburn Castle. Maggs Bros. Ltd. 1440 - 67 2011 £2000

Dionysius, Periegetes *(Greek) Dionysij Orbis Descriptio Arati Astronomicon.* Basel: Thomas Wolf, 1534. Greek texts printed consecutively, and followed by Latin versions, 8vo., ff. (2) 68, (2); (64), last leaf with device etc. on verso, contemporary English brown calf over pasteboard, blind-stamped shield on covers with letters G F & H stamped in blind at sides, spine gilded later with red morocco label, contemporary ms. notes in margins of D3v and D4r, from the library of the Earls of Macclesfield at Shirburn Castle. Maggs Bros. Ltd. 1440 - 69 2011 £500

Drusius, Joannes *Animadversionum Libri Duo. (bound with) De Quaesitis per Epistolam.* Leiden: Jan Paets, 1585. Franeker: Gilles van den Rade, 1595; 2 volumes in 1, 8vo., 2 parts, 79, (1); 68 (i.e. 86) (2) pages, printer's device, woodcut head and tailpieces, initials; Oxford contemporary calf, strips of musical manuscript of vellum used as spine liner, extremities slightly rubbed, manuscript notes on prelim leaf and on pasteboard, from the library of the Earls of Macclesfield at Shirburn Castle. Maggs Bros. Ltd. 1440 - 71 2011 £500

Drusius, Joannes *Annotationum in Totum Iesu Christi Testamentum sive Praeteritorum Libri Decem. (bound with) Ad Voces Ebraicas Novi Testamenti Commentarius Duplex.* Amsterdam: J. Janssz, 1632. Franeker: F. Heyns for Jan. Jansz, 1616; 2 works in 1 volume, 4to., (8), 456, (12) pages; (8), 226, (10), 138, (8), 1-183, (8), 185-192, 9-52 pages, small clear tear in Ff2 of part I, contemporary English calf, red edges, head of spine slightly worn, from the library of the Earls of Macclesfield at Shirburn Castle. Maggs Bros. Ltd. 1440 - 70 2011 £400

Du Verdier, Claude *In Autores Pene Omnes Antiquos Potissimum Censio qua.. Grammaticorum, Potissimum, Censio; Wua.. Grammaticorum, Poetarum....* Lyons: B. Honore, 1586. First edition; 4to., 187, (5) pages, errata on page *188-189), (190-192) blank, device on titlepage, English binding of brown calf, gilt, fillets on covers, gilt spine lettering piece, red, green and white silk maker, from the library of the Earls of Macclesfield at Shirburn Castle. Maggs Bros. Ltd. 1440 - 74 2011 £950

Dumas, Louis *La Biblioteque des Enfans ou Les Premiers Elemens des Lettres, Contenant le Sisteme du Bureau Tipographique... a l'Usage de Monseigneur le Dauphin, et des Augustes Enfans de France.* Paris: Pierre Simon P. Witte, 1733. First edition; 4to., viii, 216, xix, (5), 96, xx, 97-306, 16, (2), vi, 124, 24, woodcut printer's device, etc., contemporary calf, spine gilt in compartments, morocco lettering piece, fine, large copy, uncommon, from the library of the Earls of Macclesfield at Shirburn Castle. Maggs Bros. Ltd. 1440 - 73 2011 £1500

Eber, Paulus *Vocabula rei Nummariae Ponderum et Mensurarum Graeca, Latina, Ebraica...* Leipzig: J. Rhamba, 1570. 8vo., ff. (112) smooth calf c. 1700, gilt fillet on covers, spine gilt, gilt edges, from the library of the Earls of Macclesfield at Shirburn Castle. Maggs Bros. Ltd. 1440 - 75 2011 £400,

Eenberg, Johann *Kort Berattelse af de Markwadigste Saker som for de Frammande are Besee Och Fornimma uti Upsala stad Och Nast om Gransande Orter.* Uppsala: Johann H. Werner, 1704. (1703); Agenda 12mo., (32) 185 pages, pages 185-191, 193-236; 53 (=54) (2(blank) pages, frontispiece (added) and 5 folding woodcut inserted illustrations in part 2, with extra folding titlepage to second part with woodcut of the fire, woodcut illustrations in text, contemporary half calf over marbled boards, most uncommon, from the library of the Earls of Macclesfield at Shirburn Castle. Maggs Bros. Ltd. 1440 - 76 2011 £1500

Equicola, Mario *Dell'istoria di Mantova Libri Cinque... Riformata Secondo l'Uso Moderne si Scrivere Istorie...* Mantua: F. Osanna, 1607. 4to., (26), 307, (5), Rrl with register and imprint Rr2 with list of errata, English calf, c. 1700, gilt fillet on covers, spine gilt in compartments, green, red silk marker, from the library of the Earls of Macclesfield at Shirburn Castle. Maggs Bros. Ltd. 1440 - 78 2011 £750

Erasmus, Desiderius *Paraphrasis seu Potius Epitome...in Elegantiarum Libros Laurentii Vallae...* Paris: R. Estienne, October, 1542. One of 3 editions of 1542; (Lyons and Cologne being the place of printing of the other two), 8vo., 192, (36) pages, last leaf blank, printer's device, 17th century calf, spine gilt in compartments, seems to be extremely uncommon, from the library of the Earls of Macclesfield at Shirburn Castle. Maggs Bros. Ltd. 1440 - 79 2011 £850

Erasmus, Desiderius *Paraphrasis seu Potius Epitome...in Elegantiarum Laurentij Vallae.. cum Gallica... Expositione.* Lyons: S. Gryphe, 1547. 8vo., 199, (17) pages, 17th century vellum over pasteboards, bottom edge lettered Erasmus in Vallam, from the library of the Earls of Macclesfield at Shirburn Castle. Maggs Bros. Ltd. 1440 - 80 2011 £400

Erizzo, Sebastiano *Discorso...Sopra le Medaglie de Gli Antichi con la Dichiaratione delle Monete Consulari & Delle Medaglie de Gli Imperadori Romani...* Venice: Giovanni Varisco & Paganino Paganini, not before, 1584. Splendid copy, 2 parts, 4to., (16), 282, (2 blank); 572 pages, title within woodcut border, woodcut initials and headpieces, woodcut illustrations, 17th century mottled calf, gilt arms of Foucault on covers, spine gilt in compartments, mottled red edges, Y1 torn at head with loss, extremities slightly rubbed, from the library of the Earls of Macclesfield at Shirburn Castle. Maggs Bros. Ltd. 1440 - 82 2011 £700

Erpenius, Thomas *Orationes tres, de Linguarum Ebraeae, Atque Arabicae Dignitate.* Leiden: ex typographia auctoris, 1621. 8vo., (12), 132 pages, contemporary English calf, printed pastedowns (Italian text), repaired, from the library of the Earls of Macclesfield at Shirburn Castle. Maggs Bros. Ltd. 1440 - 83 2011 £1000

Euclides *Elucidis Phaenomena Posta Zamberti & Maurolyci Editionem...* Rome: G. Martinelli, 1591. First edition of this Latin version; 4to., (22), 89 (=99) pages, woodcut diagrams, ownership inscription of William Charke, from the library of the Earls of Macclesfield at Shirburn Castle. Maggs Bros. Ltd. 1440 - 85 2011 £1200

Euclides *Geometricorum Elemntorum Libri XV.* Paris: H. Estienne after Jan., 1516-1517. First edition printed outside Italy; folio, ff. 261 (of 262 without final blank), woodcut diagrams in margins, woodcut initials, 19th century calf by Hatton of Manchester, marbled edges, title leaf cut down and remounted, from the library of the Earls of Macclesfield at Shirburn Castle. Maggs Bros. Ltd. 1440 - 84 2011 £4000

Ex Ctesia, Agatharchide, Memnone Excerptiae Historiae. Appiani Iberica. Item de Gestis Annibalis... Cum Henrici Stephani Castigationibus. Geneva: ex officina Henrici Stephani Parisiensis typographi, 1557. Editio princeps; 8vo., (16)m., 248, 17th century smooth calf, spine gilt, red edges, extremely handsome, from the library of the Earls of Macclesfield at Shirburn Castle. Maggs Bros. Ltd. 1440 - 65 2011 £1000

Fabre, Pierre Jean *Sapientia Universalis Quatuor Libris Comprehensa. Videlicet 1. quad sit Sapientia... 2. De Cognitione Hominis. 3. De Medendis Morbis Hominum. 4. De Meliorandis Metallis.* Frankfurt: J. Beyer, 1656. 4to., (2), 418 (=400) , (8) pages, contemporary English calf, ms. index notes at end, slightly browned, hinges weak, from the library of the Earls of Macclesfield at Shirburn Castle. Maggs Bros. Ltd. 1440 - 86 2011 £850

Falconieri, Ottavio *Inscriptiones Athleticae Nuper Repertae Editae & Notis Illustratae...* Rome: Fabio de Falco, 1668. 4to., (12), 230 pages, engraved illustrations, contemporary vellum with spine gilt in compartments and lettering piece, 2 leaves detached, pages browning within two quires, from the collection of Nicolas Joseph Foucault with his bookplate, from the library of the Earls of Macclesfield at Shirburn Castle. Maggs Bros. Ltd. 1440 - 87 2011 £650

Farinato, Paolo *Diverses Figures a l'Eau Forte de Petits Amours Anges Vollants et Enfans Propre a Mettre sur Frontons Portes...* Paris: A. Bosse, 1644. Oblong 4to., 30 numbered engraved plates, early 18th century vellum backed boards, acquisition date on fly leaf Jan. 7 1727/8, from the library of the Earls of Macclesfield at Shirburn Castle. Maggs Bros. Ltd. 1440 - 88 2011 £3500

Fertel, Martin Dominique *La Scencie Pratique de l'Imprimerie.* St. Omer: M.D. Fertel, 1723. 4to., (2), 230, (2), 231-292, (10) pages, 5 engraved plates, 2 folding letterpress tables, woodcut diagrams etc., contemporary speckled calf, spine gilt in compartments, slight dampstainin in outer margins an on covers, spine chipped and little rubbed, from the library of the Earls of Macclesfield at Shirburn Castle. Maggs Bros. Ltd. 1440 - 89 2011 £750

Finck, Kaspar *Poetica Latina Nova Methodo Perspicua Tradita Commentariis Luculentis Declarata Exemplis tum Veterum Tum Recentiorum Poetarum Illustrata...* Giessen: N. Hampel, 1607. 8vo., (8), 393, (7) pages, 18th century sprinkled calf, spine gilt, from the library of the Earls of Macclesfield at Shirburn Castle. Maggs Bros. Ltd. 1440 - 233 2011 £550

Florilegium Diversorum Epigrammatum Veterum, in Septem Libros Diversum... Geneva: E. Estienne, H. Fuggeri typographus, 1566. 4to., (4), 539 (=545, pages 283-288 bis), (35) pages, device on titlepage, later Dutch vellum over pasteboard, yapp edges, fine, clean, large copy, inscription "M. Bruningen 29 June 1657), from the library of the Earls of Macclesfield at Shirburn Castle. Maggs Bros. Ltd. 1440 - 234 2011 £2200

Foy-Vaillant, Jean *Numismata Imperatorum Romanorum Praestantiora a Julio Caesare ad Postumum et Tyrannos...* Paris: Jean Jombert, 1692. 2 volumes, 4to., (12), 256, (8); (8), 397, (35) pages, last leaf blank, numerous engravings, contemporary calf, spine gilt in compartments, binding rubbed, spine gilt erased, lacks lettering piece, from the library of the Earls of Macclesfield at Shirburn Castle. Maggs Bros. Ltd. 1440 - 92 2011 £450

Frick, Johann Georg *Commentatio de Druidis Occidentalium Populorum Philosophia...* Ulm: Daniel Bartholomaei & Son, 1744. 4to., (20) 226, (2 blank) pages, engraved frontispiece, contemporary vellum backed decorated paper boards, from the library of the Earls of Macclesfield at Shirburn Castle. Maggs Bros. Ltd. 1440 - 93 2011 £500

Fronsperger, Leonhard *Kriegsbuch... Jetzt von Neuem Gemehrt und Gebessert Usw.* Frankfurt: J. Feyerabend for the heirs of S. Feyerabend, 1596. 3 parts, folio, engraved plates, woodcuts, late 18th century tree calf, occasional spotting, very handsome, from the library of the Earls of Macclesfield at Shirburn Castle. Maggs Bros. Ltd. 1440 - 94 2011 £2000

Gaya, Louis De *A Treatise of the Arms and Engines of War of Fire-works, Ensigns, and Military Instruments, both Ancient and Modern...* London: printed for Robert Harford, 1678. 8vo., (16), 143, (1) pages, frontispiece (mounted) and 18 plates, 18th century smooth calf, gilt spine, lacking A the printed title, from the library of the Earls of Macclesfield at Shirburn Castle. Maggs Bros. Ltd. 1440 - 96 2011 £500

Gaya, Louis De *Traite des Armes des Machines de Guerre, Des Feux d'Artifice, des Ensignes & Des Instruments Militaires Anciens & Modernes.* Paris: Sebastien Cramoisy, 1678. 12mo., (6), 172 pages, additional engraved titlepage, 19 engraved plates, woodcut initials and tailpieces, contemporary calf, spine gilt in compartments, spine partly detached, sides rubbed, from the library of the Earls of Macclesfield at Shirburn Castle. Maggs Bros. Ltd. 1440 - 95 2011 £600

Gelasius, of Cyzicus *(Greek) ...commentarius Actorum Nicaeni Concilii, cum Corollario Theodori Presbyteri, de Incarnatione Domini...* Paris: F. Morel, 1599. 8vo., 15, (1), 287, (3), device on verso of title, last leaf with imprint, later sprinkled vellum, from the library of the Earls of Macclesfield at Shirburn Castle. Maggs Bros. Ltd. 1440 - 97 2011 £450

Geoffrey of Monmouth *Prophetia Anglicana, Merlini Ambrosii Britanni ex Incubo Olim (jut Hominum Fama est) Ante Annos Mille Ducentos Circiter in Anglia Nati...* Frankfurt: Ioachim Brathering, 1603. Small 8vo., (16),269 (3) pages, woodcut portrait on verso of title, mid 18th century English mottled calf, gilt spine, lightly browned, label missing, joints rubbed, from the library of the Earls of Macclesfield at Shirburn Castle. Maggs Bros. Ltd. 1440 - 98 2011 £800

Gesualdo, Filippo *Plutosofiae.... Nella Quale si Spiega l'Arte Della Memoria con Altre Crose Notabili Pertinenti Tanto alla Memoria Naturale...* Padua: P. Meietti, 1592. First edition; 4to., ff. (6), 64, device on titlepage, full page woodcut figure of a man on f. (27), very slightly cropped at foot, English binding c. 1700 of brown calf, gilt fillets on covers, gilt spine, morocco lettering piece, from the library of the Earls of Macclesfield at Shirburn Castle. Maggs Bros. Ltd. 1440 - 99 2011 £3000

Giger, Matthias *Artificium Muniendi Geometricum quo Delineatio Regularium Munimentorum non Solum Absque Omni Calcuo...* Stockholm: H, Kayser, 1650. 4to., ff. (4), woodcut on verso of title, disbound, from the library of the Earls of Macclesfield at Shirburn Castle. Maggs Bros. Ltd. 1440 - 100 2011 £400

Godfrey, Ambrose *A Curious Research in the Element of Water...* London: T. Gardner, 1747. First edition; 4to., (2), 18 pages, disbound, from the library of the Earls of Macclesfield at Shirburn Castle. Maggs Bros. Ltd. 1440 - 101 2011 £850

Guillard, Rene *Histoire du Conseil du Roy Depuis le Commencement de la Monarchie Jesqu a la fin du Regne de Louis Le Grand...* Paris: A-U Cousteiler, 1738. Uncommon, 4to., viii, (4), 855 pages, contemporary sprinkled calf, gilt border on covers, with floral cornerpieces, spine gilt, morocco lettering piece, silk bookmark, from the library of the Earls of Macclesfield at Shirburn Castle. Maggs Bros. Ltd. 1440 - 103 2011 £750

Halley, Edmond *Catalouge des Estoilles Australes ou Supplements du Catalgoue Thycho qui Montre les Longitudes & Latitudes...* Paris: J. B. Coignard, 1679. 12mo., (36), 118, (2 blank), contemporary calf, spine gilt, spine worn, lacking map, from the library of the Earls of Macclesfield at Shirburn Castle. Maggs Bros. Ltd. 1440 - 105 2011 £2000

Hartsoeker, Nicolaas *Suite des Conjectures Physiques.* Amsterdam: H. Desbordes, 1708. First edition; 4to., (8), 147, (1) pages, large paper copy, 5 medical engraved plates, 2 engraved armorial headpieces, woodcut figures, contemporary vellum backed boards, uncut, prelims slightly soiled, particularly titlepage, spine worn, from the library of the Earls of Macclesfield at Shirburn Castle. Maggs Bros. Ltd. 1440 - 106 2011 £700

Hase, Johann Matthias *Regni Davidici et Salomonaei Descripto Geographica et Historica...* Nurnberg: J. H. G. Bieling, prostat in off. Homanniana, 1739. 2 parts, flio, ff. (4), col. 320, ff. (2) ff. (2) (first blank), col. 132, f. (1), title printed in red and black, 6 folding engraved maps, contemporary sprinkled calf, gilt spine, red edges, very handsome, from the library of the Earls of Macclesfield at Shirburn Castle. Maggs Bros. Ltd. 1440 - 107 2011 £1500

Heliodorus *Aethiopicorum Libri X.* Paris: L. Feburier, 1619. 8vo., (16), 519, (1); 123, 5 (blank) pages, text in Greek and Latin in parallel columns, 17th century Dutch Prize binding of vellum over pasteboard arms of Amsterdam on covers within double gilt fillet with armorial cornerpieces, flat spine gilt, later 18th century red morocco label added at head, lacking green silk ties, from the library of the Earls of Macclesfield at Shirburn Castle. Maggs Bros. Ltd. 1440 - 109 2011 £400

Helmont, Franciscus Mercurius Van *Alphabeti vere Naturalis Hebraici Brevissima Delineatio Quae Simul Methodum Suppeditat...* Sulzbach: Abraham Lichtenthaler, 1657. (1667); 12mo., (36 including additional engraved title), 107, (1) pages, 36 engraved plates, 18th century smooth calf, gilt, handsome copy, from the library of the Earls of Macclesfield at Shirburn Castle. Maggs Bros. Ltd. 1440 - 110 2011 £1800

Hexham, Henry *The Principles of the Art Militarie etc. Parts I-III.* London: M. P(arsons) for M. Symons; Delft: Jan Peterson Waelpte, 1637. London: R Young, 1639. The Hague: F. vander Spruyt, 1640. First, second and First editions; 3 parts in 1 volume, folio, engraved illustrations, engraved volvelles, engraved plates, contemporary red morocco gilt, narrow roll borders, central cartouche formed of sprays of olive, spine gilt in compartments, gilt edges, small hole in text of dedication (paper flaw), tear in pages 15-16 of part I, lacks ties, tear from paper flaw across the top corner of page 19/20 in appendix to part 1, from the library of the Earls of Macclesfield at Shirburn Castle. Maggs Bros. Ltd. 1440 - 111 2011 £10,000

Howell, James *Lustra Ludovici or the late Victorius King of France, Lewis the XIII and his Cardinal de Richelieu.* London: by John Legate II for Humphrey Moseley, 1646. First edition; folio, (12), 188, (8) pages, engraved medallion portrait, woodcut initials and headpieces, rule borders, 17th century red morocco gilt, panelled sides with fleuron at corners, spine gilt in compartments, gilt edges, long tear in P3 with slight loss, occasional other short tears in margins, occasional manuscript notes in margins, small tear on upper cover, from the P. J. Wright collection with note on flyleaf dated September 1720, from the library of the Earls of Macclesfield at Shirburn Castle. Maggs Bros. Ltd. 1440 - 112 2011 £450

Hulsius, Levinus *Chronolgoia, hoc est Brevis Descriptio Rerum Memorabilium in Provinciis hac Adiuncta Tabula Topographica Comprehensis Gestarum...* Nurnberg: C. Lochner, 1597. 4to., (6), 89 (recte 90) pages large armorial engraving on title (arms of imperial provinces) and of Eberhard, Bishop of Spier on f A2v, contemporary vellum, foot of spine worn, from the library of the Earls of Macclesfield at Shirburn Castle. Maggs Bros. Ltd. 1440 - 113 2011 £500

Hyginus, Caius Julius *Fabularum Liber... Poeticon Astronomicon Libri Quatuor... Arati Phaenomena Graece...* Basel: ex officina Hervagiana, per E. Episcopium August, 1570. Folio, (8), 251, (29) pages, last leaf blank device on titlepage, woodcut illustrations, contemporary vellum over pasteboards, spine slightly cracked, from the library of the Earls of Macclesfield at Shirburn Castle, the Georgius Melchior copy, 1664 with inscription. Maggs Bros. Ltd. 1440 - 114 2011 £1500

Iamblichus (Greek)... *De Vita Phythagorica Liber... Notisque...* Amsterdam: widow of S. Petzold & C. Petzold, 1707. First separate edition; 2 parts, 4to., (16 (including engraved frontispiece), 219, (17), 93, (1) pages, 2 columns, title printed in red and black, contemporary English panelled calf, gilt spine, red morocco lettering piece, fine, large copy, armorial bookplate of Edward Wake, Christ Church, from the library of the Earls of Macclesfield at Shirburn Castle. Maggs Bros. Ltd. 1440 - 115 2011 £700

Isocrates *Orationes et Epistolae.* Geneva: H. Estienne, 1593. Folio, (14) ff., 427, 131, XXXIV pages, (1) f. (blank), (4) ff, 31 pages, (9) ff., early 18th century English mottled calf, covers panelled in blind, spine gilt in compartments, red morocco label, printed pastedowns, slight worming, upper joint split at head an foot, inscription on titlepage T. Osborne 17th century and Wm. Robinson (18th century), fine armorial bookplate of William Robinson & Coll. Jes. Soc. Com., from the library of the Earls of Macclesfield at Shirburn Castle. Maggs Bros. Ltd. 1440 - 116 2011 £900

Jones, William *Observations in a Journey to Paris by Way of Flanders in the Month of August 1776.* London: printed for G. Robinson, 1777. 2 volumes, 8vo., viii, 196, (4), 200 pages, engraved caricature of Voltaire in volume 1, original blue paper wrappers, volume 2 split, from the library of the Earls of Macclesfield at Shirburn Castle. Maggs Bros. Ltd. 1440 - 117 2011 £550

Junius, Hadrianus *Emblemata Eiusdem Aenigmata Libellus.* Leiden: F. Raphelengius ex off. Plantiniana, 1596. 58 woodcuts, mostly unsigned, 16mo., 167 pages, woodcuts, speckled calf, c. 1700, gilt spine, red morocco lettering piece, from the library of the Earls of Macclesfield at Shirburn Castle. Maggs Bros. Ltd. 1440 - 119 2011 £950

Kepler, Johann *Prodromus Dissertationum Cosmographicarum...* Frankfurt: Erasmus Kempfer for G. Tampach, 1621-1622. Second edition; folio, (8), 114, 119-163, (1); (50) pages, 4 'tabellae' with woodcut diagrams and with letterpress, (pages 18, IV at p. 54, V at pg. 56), woodcut diagrams, contemporary speckled calf, spine gilt in compartments, some browning, lacking engraved plate numbered III, from the library of the Earls of Macclesfield at Shirburn Castle. Maggs Bros. Ltd. 1440 - 120 2011 £15,000

Koran *L'Alcoran de Mahomet.* Antwerp: J. F. Lucas, 1719. 8vo., (8), 485, (3) pages, title printed in red and black, contemporary speckled calf, spine gilt in compartments, morocco lettering piece, from the library of the Earls of Macclesfield at Shirburn Castle. Maggs Bros. Ltd. 1440 - 174 2011 £300

Krag, Niels *De Republica Lacedaemoniorum Libri III... Opus Politicarum...* Geneva: P. Saintandre, 1593. First edition; 3 parts, 4to., (16), 269, (3 blank), 35, (1), 23 pages, contemporary ?Scandinavian vellum over thin wooden boards, yapp edges, from the library of the Earls of Macclesfield at Shirburn Castle.   Maggs Bros. Ltd.   1440 - 121   2011   £400

Krause, Johann *Neuer Bucher-Saal der Gelehrten Welt Oder Ausfuhrliche Nachtrichten von alelrehand Neuen Buchrern...* Leipzig: Gleditsch & Weidmanishe Buchhandlung, 1710-1711.   Issues 1-12 (with index), 8vo., (16), 969, (76) pages, frontispiece and portraits, contemporary vellum backed paper boards, from the library of the Earls of Macclesfield at Shirburn Castle.   Maggs Bros. Ltd.   1440 - 122   2011   £550

Lasena, Pietro *Dell'antico Ginnasio Napoletano. Opera Psothuma.* Naples: a spese di C. Porpora, 1688.   Second edition; 4to., (20), 229, (3) pages, plus engraved title, titlepage cropped, 17th century mottled calf, gilt fillet on covers, spine gilt in compartments, from the library of the Earls of Macclesfield at Shirburn Castle.   Maggs Bros. Ltd.   1440 - 123   2011   £850

Lauret, Christophe *La Doctrine des Temps et de l'Astronomie Universelle Contenant la Demonstration du Vray Nombre....* Paris: Cramoisy, 1610.   Folio, ff. (8) 133 (=135, several mispaginations etc.) 1), large woodcut printer's device on titlepage, woodcut headpieces, tailpieces, initials, mid 19th century calf by Hatton in Manchester, triple blind fillet on boards, blind fleuron in boards' corner and in spine compartments, morocco lettering piece, red edges, f. 58 stained, small hole with loss of text in f. 126, few manuscript annotations in margin, dedication (signed to Clement VIII by Cayet bound at end), from the library of the Earls of Macclesfield at Shirburn Castle.   Maggs Bros. Ltd.   1440 - 124   2011   £6000

Leopold, Johann Friedrich *Relatio Epistolica de Itinere Suo Sueccio Anno MDCCVII Facto ...* London: T. Childe, 1720.   First edition; 8vo., viii (vi) (2) 111 pages, fly title, 8 numbered folding engraved plates, and maps, woodcut head and tailpieces, contemporary calf, gilt border on covers, gilt spine, gilt edges, little rubbed, handsome copy, from the library of the Earls of Macclesfield at Shirburn Castle.   Maggs Bros. Ltd.   1440 - 129   2011   £525

Leto, Giulio Pomponio *Romanae Historiae Compendium etc.* Paris: Jean Dupre 7 May, 1501.   4to. in 6's, ff. (62), woodcut illustration on titlepage, large device at end, 18th century smooth calf, gilt spine, red edges, handsome copy, the copy of Nicolas Maillard of Rouen, from the library of the Earls of Macclesfield at Shirburn Castle.   Maggs Bros. Ltd.   1440 - 130   2011   £1500

Lewis, John *The Life of Mayster Wyllyam Caxton etc.* London: printed in the year, 1737.   Royal 8vo., xxii (engraved portrait on page (iii), 156, (6) pages, 2 full page woodcut illustrations of watermarks on pages (160-161), contemporary parchment backed blue paper boards, spine completely worn, deckle edges, with Proposals for Printing an Historical Account of that Most Universally Celebrated as well as useful art of typography (The Life of William Caxton) by John Bagford folded in; from the library of the Earls of Macclesfield at Shirburn Castle.   Maggs Bros. Ltd.   1440 - 19   2011   £8000

Livius, Titus *Historiarum ab Urbe Condita, Libri Qui Extant XXXV.* Venice: P. Manutius, 1555.   2 parts, folio, ff. (4), 1-429, 428-430, 433-478; 98, (40), calf, title leaf mounted, scholia bound first, from the library of the Earls of Macclesfield at Shirburn Castle.   Maggs Bros. Ltd.   1440 - 235   2011   £1000

Livius, Titus *Historiarum... Libri Qui Extant XXXV.* Niccolo Bevilaqua for P. Manutius, 1566.   2 parts, folio, (52), 399, (1); 107, (1), later calf, f. 70 with small stain, odd leaf slightly browned, light marginal dampstaining on ff. 140-141, some margins washed near beginning with traces of annotations, from the library of the Earls of Macclesfield at Shirburn Castle.   Maggs Bros. Ltd.   1440 - 236   2011   £1000

Llwyd, Humphrey *Commentarioli Britannicae Descriptionis Fragmentium.* Cologne: J. Birckmann, 1572.   First edition; 8vo., ff. (8), 79 (=78) (2(blank), 18th century smooth calf, gilt spine, without final blanks, from the library of the Earls of Macclesfield at Shirburn Castle.   Maggs Bros. Ltd.   1440 - 131   2011   £900

Loccenius, Johan *Antiquitatum Sueo-Gothicarum, cum Huius aevi Moribus, Institutis ac Ritibus Indigenis Pro re Nata Comparaatrum Libri Tres.* Stockholm: Johan Jansson, 1654.   8vo., (8), 168 pages, 17th century English sprinkled calf, very nice, from the library of the Earls of Macclesfield at Shirburn Castle.   Maggs Bros. Ltd.   1440 - 132   2011   £400

Loisel, Antoine *Memoires des Pays villes Comte et Comies...* Paris: S. Thiboust, 1617.   First (and only) edition; 4to., (4), 367, (19) pages, title printed in red and black, woodcut device on titlepage, woodcut head and tailpieces, initials, 1 engraved illustration, 17th century calf, triple fillet gilt with fleuron in each corner on boards, spine gilt in compartments, morocco lettering piece, spine used, slightly waterstained on titlepage, and in upper corner of first pages, manuscript ex-libris on titlepage, from the library of the Earls of Macclesfield at Shirburn Castle.   Maggs Bros. Ltd.   1440 - 133   2011   £700

Longinus, Dionysius *On the Sublime.* London: for W. Sandby, 1742. Second edition; 8vo., (16), xxxiv, 189, (1) pages, engraved frontispiece, woodcut head and tailpieces, woodcut initials, contemporary red morocco, wide gilt border on covers, spine gilt in compartments, gilt edges, slight wear to joints, the dedication copy, specially bound for George, second Earl of Macclesfield. Maggs Bros. Ltd. 1440 - 134 2011 £750

Lucanus, Marcus Annaeus *Lucan's Pharsalia.* London: for Jacob Tonson, 1718. Large paper copy; subscriber's copy, folio, (6), xxv, (5), 446, 55 pages, frontispiece, double page map, engraved head and tailpieces by Elisha Kirskhall after Cheron, contemporary calf, panelled in blind, gilt spine (upper joint cracked but firm), some light browning, from the library of the Earls of Macclesfield at Shirburn Castle. Maggs Bros. Ltd. 1440 - 136 2011 £600

Machiavelli, Niccolo 1469-1527 *Historie.* Piacenza: Gli heredi di Gabriel Giolito de Ferrari, i.e. London: John Wolfe, 1587. 12mo., (12), 559, (9) pages, Italic letter, woodcut printer' service on titlepage, woodcut headpiece and initials, 17th century speckled calf binding, spine gilt in compartments, lettering piece, lacking, binding rubbed, spine gilt detaching, small hole on last page, Lt. Gen. George Parker bookplate, from the library of the Earls of Macclesfield at Shirburn Castle. Maggs Bros. Ltd. 1440 - 137 2011 £700

Macrobius, Ambrosius Theodosius *In Somnium Scipionis Lib. II. Saturnaliorum Lib. VII.* Lyons: S. Gryphe, 1556. 8vo., 567, (73) pages, device on titlepage, contemporary limp vellum, yapp edges, lacking ties, very attractive copy, from the library of the Earls of Macclesfield at Shirburn Castle. Maggs Bros. Ltd. 1440 - 138 2011 £550

Manfredi, Eustachio *Elementi Della Cronologia con Diverse Scritture Appartenenti al Calendario Romano. Opera Postuma.* Bologna: Lelio dalla Volpe, 1744. First edition; 4to., (14), 362, (2 imprimatur) pages, engraved device on titlepage, woodcut initials, woodcut diagrams, engraved headpiece, 19th century half calf by Hatton of Manchester, red morocco lettering piece, red speckled edges, lacking frontispiece, from the library of the Earls of Macclesfield at Shirburn Castle. Maggs Bros. Ltd. 1440 - 139 2011 £450

Manutius, Aldus *De Quaesitis per Epistolam Libri III.* Venice: Aldus Manutius, 1576. First edition; 3 parts, 8vo., (8), 125, (3 blank); 106, (6 blank); 103 pages, 17th century German blindstamped pigskin over pasteboard, red edges, very nice, titlepage inscribed "Paulus Johanne?? Patavii MDLXXVII", from the library of the Earls of Macclesfield at Shirburn Castle. Maggs Bros. Ltd. 1440 - 140 2011 £450

Marolles, Michel De *Tableaux Du temple des Muses Representant les Vertus, et les Vices sur les Plus Illustres Fables De l'Antiquite.* Paris: Nicolas Langlois, 1655. First edition; folio, (20), 477, (9) pages, 58 engraved plates and portrait, engraved folding titlepage, woodcut head and tailpieces, initials woodcut, contemporary calf, rubbed, spine gilt in compartments, crackled, waterstained in corners throughout half of book, bookplate of Nicolas Joseph Foucault, from the library of the Earls of Macclesfield at Shirburn Castle. Maggs Bros. Ltd. 1440 - 141 2011 £900

Maupas Du Tour, Henri Couchon De *La Vie du Venerable Serviteur de Dieu, Francois de Sales, etc.* Paris: J. & E. Langlois, 1657. 2 parts, 4to., 411; 53, (3) pages, ruled in red, added engraved plates, 6 engraved plates, engraved headpieces and initials, contemporary French panelled, red morocco, gilt floral cornerpieces, spines gilt, turn-ins, edges gilt, slight damage to upper cover, paper flaw in plate at page 1 with consequent tear, handsome copy, ruled in red and from the Foucault library, De Cohon inscription, from the library of the Earls of Macclesfield at Shirburn Castle. Maggs Bros. Ltd. 1440 - 142 2011 £850

Mears, Abraham *The Book of Religion, Ceremonies and Prayers of the Jews as Practised in Their Synagogues and Families on all Occasions.* London: for J. Wilson, 1738. First English adaptation; 8vo., (xiv), 291, (7) pages, fine in contemporary mottled calf, covers ruled with gilt double fillet, gilt spine, slightly rubbed, from the library of the Earls of Macclesfield at Shirburn Castle. Maggs Bros. Ltd. 1440 - 143 2011 £1500

Melanchthon, Philipp 1497-1560 *Grammatica Latina.* Paris: R. Estienne, 1550. (1548); 8vo., 368 pages, contemporary French binding of calf, blindstamped panel on covers with central vase of flowers stamp, vellum ms. guards (15th century), binding slightly worn, with note on flyleaf (quotation from Melanchthon) in small neat English hand, from the library of the Earls of Macclesfield at Shirburn Castle. Maggs Bros. Ltd. 1440 - 144 2011 £550

Mennens, Frans *Miltitarium Ordinum Origines, Statuta, symbola et Insignia Iconibus, Additis Genuinis.* Macerata: P. Salvioni for F. Manolessi, 1623. 4to., 12, 120 pages, woodcut illustrations, late 18th century English tree calf, spine gilt, yellow edges, from the library of the Earls of Macclesfield at Shirburn Castle. Maggs Bros. Ltd. 1440 - 146 2011 £800

More, Henry *An Account of Virtue: or Dr. Henry More's Abridgement of Morals.* London: printed or B. Tooke, 1701. Second edition; 8vo., (16), 264 pages, panelled sheep, from the library of the Earls of Macclesfield at Shirburn Castle, inscription of Bibliothecae Gilberti Walmsley. Maggs Bros. Ltd. 1440 - 148 2011 £400

Muzo, Pio *Considerationi Sopra il Primo Libro di Cornelio Tacito.* Venice: Marco Ginammi, 1642. 4to., (56), 544, (4), (36), 360, (4) pages, 18th century English calf, spine gilt in compartments, red morocco lettering piece, errata and ad leaves for each part are all bound in part 2, from the library of the Earls of Macclesfield at Shirburn Castle.   Maggs Bros. Ltd.   1440 - 150 2011   £500

Nannini, Remigio *Orationi Militari... da Tutti Gli Historici Greci e Latini etc.* Venice: all insegna della concordio (G. A. Bertano), 1585. Second edition; 4to., (40), 1004 pages, italic letter, 18th century tree calf, gilt spine, red morocco lettering piece, red edges, from the library of the Earls of Macclesfield at Shirburn Castle.   Maggs Bros. Ltd.   1440 - 151 2011   £700

Neve, Richard *The City and Country Purchaser's and Builder's Dictionary...* London: printed for B. Sprint, D. Browne, J. Osborn, S. Birt, H. Lintot and A, Wilde, 1736. Third edition; 8vo., in 4's, xvi (including frontispiece), ff. (192), contemporary smooth calf, gilt fillet on covers, spine gilt, from the library of the Earls of Macclesfield at Shirburn Castle.   Maggs Bros. Ltd.   1440 - 154 2011   £650

Newton, Henry *Epistolae, Orationes, et Carmina. (bound with) Orationes quarum Altera Florentiae Anno MDCCV.* Lucca: D. Ciufetti, 1710. Amsterdam: 1710-(1712); 2 works in 1 volume, (6), 250, 115, (3) pages, engraved frontispiece, 58 pages (final quire signed * (pages 51-58) reprinted to include items dated 1711 and 1712, contemporary English panelled calf, spine gilt, rubbed, upper joint slightly cracked, one corner worn, number of small corrections throughout, from the library of the Earls of Macclesfield at Shirburn Castle, bound at end are two manuscript letters from Newton at Florence, one to Jean Le Clerc at Amsterdam and the other to Gisbert Cuper at Deventer, both dated 1710.   Maggs Bros. Ltd.   1440 - 155 2011   £800

Nicolai, Johann *Disquisitio de Mose Alpha Dicto.* Leiden: H. Teering, 1703. 12mo., 148, (4) pages, last leaf blank, contemporary vellum backed marbled paper boards, from the library of the Earls of Macclesfield at Shirburn Castle.   Maggs Bros. Ltd.   1440 - 156 2011   £500

Noceti, Caroli *De Iride et Aurora Boreali Carmina...* Rome: N. & M. Pagliarini ex typ. Palladis, 1747. First edition; 4to., (12), 127, (1) pages, printed on thick paper, 2 engraved plates, 18th century English sprinkled calf, gilt spine, morocco lettering piece, first plate slightly torn, from the library of the Earls of Macclesfield at Shirburn Castle.   Maggs Bros. Ltd.   1440 - 158 2011   £400

Nouvelle Grammaire Flamnade... Amsterdam: P. Mortier, 1688. 8vo., (4), 156 pages, contemporary calf, upper joint split, from the library of the Earls of Macclesfield at Shirburn Castle.   Maggs Bros. Ltd.   1440 - 90 2011   £400

Occo, Adolf *Impp. Romanorum Numismata a Pompeio Magno ad Heraclium... Summa Diligentia & Magno Labhore Collecta ab Adolpho Occone R. P. Aug. medico...* Antwerp: Christopher Plantin for the author, 1579. (1578). First edition; 4to., (16), 398, (10), (5 blank) pages, printer's device on titlepage, initials,

Ovidius Naso, Publius *Operum... Tomus Primus (Tertius)...* Frankfurt: C. Marny & Heirs of J. Aubry, typis Wechelianis, 1601. 3 volumes, folio, (4), 500, (16); (2), 388, 116, 244, (12), 340, 199 pages, later 17th century mottled calf, gilt fillet on covers, spines gilt, green silk ties lacking, slightly foxed but highly desirable, handsome copy, from the library of the Earls of Macclesfield at Shirburn Castle, bequeathed by Iosephi Scaliger to D. Heinsius.   Maggs Bros. Ltd.   1440 - 160 2011   £3000

Panchaud, Benjamin *Entretiens ou Lecons Mathematiques sur la Maniere d'Etudier Cette Science et su les Principles Utilites...* Lausanne & Geneva: Marc Michel Bousquet, 1743. 2 parts, 12mo., v i, (ii), 372, (2); 250, (2) pages, title printed in black and red, woodcut headpieces and initials, contemporary English blond calf with nice gilt border on boards, spine gilt in compartments, morocco lettering piece, elegant binding, from the library of the Earls of Macclesfield at Shirburn Castle.   Maggs Bros. Ltd.   1440 - 161 2011   £450

Papin, Denys *La Maniere d'Amolir les os, et de Faire Cuire Toutes Sortes de Viandes en Fort Peu de Temps & a Peu de Frais.* Paris: E. Michallet, 1682. First French edition; 12mo., (12), 164, (12), 2 folding engraved plates (first with 8 figures, second with X), contemporary calf, first few leaves slightly stained at head of leaf, spine slightly worn, from the library of the Earls of Macclesfield at Shirburn Castle.   Maggs Bros. Ltd.   1440 - 162 2011   £700

Parrhasio, Aulo Giano *Liber de Rebus per Epistola Quaesitis...* Geneva: H. Estienne, 1567. 8vo., (8), 272, (8) pages, English binding circa 1700 of black morocco, panelled in gilt on covers with floral cornerpieces, spine gilt, edges gilt, handsome collection, from the library of the Earls of Macclesfield at Shirburn Castle.   Maggs Bros. Ltd.   1440 - 164 2011   £700

Perez De Mendoza Y Quixada, Miguel *Resumen de la Vera Destreza de las Armas en Treinta y Ocho Asserciones.* Madrid: Francisco Sanz, 1675. 4to., ff. (21), 73, title printed in red and black, engraved portrait frontispiece and armorial title vignette, large folding plate (small tear), bound before f. 69, modern half calf, large engraved bookplate; from the library of the Earls of Macclesfield at Shirburn Castle.   Maggs Bros. Ltd.   1440 - 165 2011   £3000

Persons, Robert *An Answere to the Fifth Part of Reportes Lately Set Forth by Syr Edward Cooke Knight, the Kinges Attorney Generall.*   Saint Omer: imprinted with licence by F. Bellet, 1606.   First edition; small 4to., (72), 351, 353-386, (15) pages, contemporary limp vellum, loose in case, covers bit creased, short slit and few small holes in upper cover, ties missing, lightly browned in places, few corners creased, first few leaves cut close at foot, single wormhole through last few leaves, from the library of the Earls of Macclesfield at Shirburn Castle.   Maggs Bros. Ltd.   1440 - 166 2011   £950

Piganiol De la Force, Jean Aimar *Nouvelle Description De La France Dans Laquelle on Voit Le Gouvernement General De Ce Royaume, Celui De Chaque Province en Particulier...*   Paris: T. Legras fils, 1718.   First edition; 6 volumes, 12mo.,(32), 10, 462, (56) pages, engraved frontispiece, 4 engraved folding plates, (18), 304, (62) pages; 7 engraved folding plates, (8), 524, (54) pages, 1 engraved plate, (12), 527, (1 blank), (59) pages, 1 engraved plate, (10), 574, (62) pages; (12), 682, (38) pages, 1 engraved folding map, contemporary speckled calf with fillet gilt on boards and fleurons in corners, spine gilt in compartments, morocco lettering piece, silk page marker, label torn and detaching (2), label detached (6), light patch apparently due to leather treatment that was defective on this upper board (6); from the library of the Earls of Macclesfield at Shirburn Castle.   Maggs Bros. Ltd.   1440 - 167 2011   £550

Pitseus, Joannes *Relationum Historicarum de rebus Anglicis tomus Primus (ed. William Bishop).*   Paris: R. Thierry for Joseph Cottereau, 1623.   4to., (20), 990, (2) pages, last leaf blank, title printed in red and black, engraved device, contemporary vellum, lacking ties, motto on titlepage, from the library of the Earls of Macclesfield at Shirburn Castle.   Maggs Bros. Ltd.   1440 - 168 2011   £450

Poleni, Giovanni, Marchese *Miscellanea. Hoc est. 1. Dissertatio de Barometris & Thermmetris. II. Machinae Aritmeticae, ejusque Usus Descriptio. III. De Sectionibus Comicis Parallerum in Horologiis Solaribus Tractatus.*   Venice: Alvise Pavini, 1709.   4to., (8), 56, 9 folding engraved plates, contemporary Italian 'carta rustica', fine, large, clean copy in beautiful condition, from the library of the Earls of Macclesfield at Shirburn Castle.   Maggs Bros. Ltd.   1440 - 169 2011   £4500

Proclus Diadochus *Elementa Theologica et Physica...*   Ferrara: D. Mammarello, 1583.   4to., ff. (3), 69 device at end, modern half calf, with Roldolph Weckherlin manuscript ex-libris, from the library of the Earls of Macclesfield at Shirburn Castle.   Maggs Bros. Ltd.   1440 - 171 2011   £3000

Procopius, of Caesarea *Historiarum... Libri VIII...*   Augsburg: D. Franck, 1607.   Editio princeps of the Greek text; folio, (8), 376; 56, (84) pages, engraved title, dust jacket English (?Oxford) binding of brown calf, double gilt fillet on covers, spine with gilt ornament in compartments, chain mark on upper cover, from the library of the Earls of Macclesfield at Shirburn Castle, this the copy of Thomas Tonkys.   Maggs Bros. Ltd.   1440 - 239 2011   £800

Puente, Francisco De La *Tratado Breve De La Antiguedad del Linaie de Vera, y Memoria de Personas Senaladas de, que se Hallan en Histoias...*   Lima: G. de Contrerars, 1635.   4to., ff. *6), 180 (corrected to 182), 12, marginal notes printed in italic, armorial woodcut on page (ii), contemporary limp velum, lacking ties, minor marginal dampstains to few leaves, handsome, crisp copy, from the library of the Earls of Macclesfield at Shirburn Castle.   Maggs Bros. Ltd.   1440 - 172 2011   £6500

Puig, Andres *Arithemtca, Especulativa y Practica y Arte de Algebra en la Qual Se Contiene Todo lo Que Pertence al Art Mentor...*   Barcelona: A. Lacavalleria vendense e casa del mismo autor, 1672.   Second edition; 4to., (16), 576 (8) pages, 19th century English sprinkled calf, gilt spine, red morocco lettering piece, mottled edges, very handsome, from the library of the Earls of Macclesfield at Shirburn Castle.   Maggs Bros. Ltd.   1440 - 173 2011   £800

Richter, Edmond *Grammatica Obstetricia.*   Paris: P. L. Febvrier, 1607.   8vo., ff. (8), 162, (1 errata), folding table at page 126, device on titlepage, 17th century calf, gilt fillet on covers, gilt spine, top of upper hinge weak, marbled edges, uncommon, from the library of the Earls of Macclesfield at Shirburn Castle.   Maggs Bros. Ltd.   1440 - 177 2011   £550

Robert, Prior of Shrewsbury *The Admirable Life of Saint Wenefride...*   St. Omer: English College Press Superiorum Permissu, 1635.   8vo., (32), 275, (13) pages, plus added engraved titlepage by Martin Baes (loose), text printed within double line border, last leaf blank (here lacking), 18th century English vellum backed boards, signature of James Elcocks and note of his birth on 6 Jan. 1679, from the library of the Earls of Macclesfield at Shirburn Castle.   Maggs Bros. Ltd.   1440 - 178 2011   £500

Robortello, Francesco *De Artificio Dicendi... Eiusdem Tabulae Oratoriae.*   Bologna: Alessandro Benacci, 1567.   First edition; extremely handsome, 4to., ff. 52, 20; 32, (18), italic type, large device on titlepage, 9 line woodcut mythological initials, Dutch polished calf, c. 1700, spine gilt, red edges, from the library of the Earls of Macclesfield at Shirburn Castle.   Maggs Bros. Ltd.   1440 - 179 2011   £650

Roelands, David *T'magazi oft' pac-huys der loffelycker penn-const.* Vlissingen: letterpress printed at Middleburg by R. Schilders, 1616. (1617); Oblong folio, ff., (47) (44 engraved leaves including title and 3 leaves of letterpress comprising dedication to the Aldermen of Flushing (in French) and "To the reader" (in Dutch), engraved portrait of Roelands, later vellum backed blue paper boards, title leaf creased, few plates very slightly shaved at top edge, just touching swirls, from the library of the Earls of Macclesfield at Shirburn Castle.   Maggs Bros. Ltd.   1440 - 180 2011 £800

Romanus, Adrianus *Ventorum Secundum Recentiores Distinctorum Usus.* Wurzburg: G. Fleischman, 1596. Small 4to., ff. (9), rebound in half calf, old style, from the library of the Earls of Macclesfield at Shirburn Castle. Maggs Bros. Ltd.   1440 - 181 2011   £900

Rosselli, Cosmo *Thesaurus Artificiosae Memorae... Perutilis...* Venice: A. Paduano bibliopola Fiorentino, 1579. First edition; 4to., ff. (16), 145 (errata), printed in italic, 2 leaves with double page, woodcut at centre signed E4 and a similar 2 leaves at R3 with single woodcut on first recto and second verso, full page woodcut, with some repeats, contemporary limp vellum, lacking ties, from the library of the Earls of Macclesfield at Shirburn Castle.   Maggs Bros. Ltd. 1440 - 182 2011   £5000

Rousseau, Josue *Ensayo da Arte Grammatical Portugueza & Franceza, Para Aquelles que Sabendo a Lingua Franceza Querem Aprender a Portugueza Primeira Parte.* Lisbon: A. P. Galram, 1705. First edition; 4to., (8), 176 pages, hand colored woodcut device on titlepage, woodcut illustrations, woodcut initials and headpiece, contemporary vellum over boards, few small tears with slight loss, pages browned, spine cracking, from the library of the Earls of Macclesfield at Shirburn Castle.   Maggs Bros. Ltd. 1440 - 183 2011   £500

Rucellai, Bernardo *De Bello Italico Commentarius ex authentici Manuscripti Apographo nun Primum in Lucem Editus.* London: William Bowyer for John Rindley, 1724. Large 4to., (8), 102, (2) pages, last leaf blank, small errata slip pasted to pages (vii & viii), contemporary London Harleian style binding of sprinkled calf, by Brindley, from the library of the Earls of Macclesfield at Shirburn Castle. Maggs Bros. Ltd.   1440 - 185 2011   £750

Ruscelli, Girolamo *Kriegs und Archeley Kunst.* Frankfurt: Lukas Jennis (second part: Jakob de Zetter), 1620. First edition in German; 2 parts in one volume, 288 x 188 mm; 6 p.l., 145, (3) pages; 4 p.l., 71, (5) pages, very fine late 18th century tree calf, flat spine handsomely gilt in compartments filled with closely spaced horizontal gilt in compartments filled with closely spaced horizontal rows of alternating strapwork and flowing floral and foliate stamps, reddish orange morocco label, historiated headpieces and tailpieces, both titlepages attractively framed with design of military implements, with 24 double page engraved military plates, 15 accompanying the first section and 9 the second; front pastedown of each volume with armorial bookplate of Lt. Gen. G. L. Parker (4th Earl of Macclesfield), first endpaper with similar armorial bookplate of Macclesfield library, first three leaves with small embossed Macclesfield stamp; bottom of second titlepage just barely touched by binder's knife, three gatherings with inoffensive dampstain at lower inner margin, light offsetting on some of the plates, handful of leaves (including the first title) with light overall browning, additional trivial defects, otherwise really fine, lovely binding lustrous and scarcely worn, text very clean and execptionally fresh.   Phillip J. Pirages   59 - 58 2011 $5500

Sadler, John *Rights of the Kingdom or Customs of Our Ancestours: Touching the Duty, Power, Election or Succession of Our Kings and Parliaments, Our True Liberty Due Allegiance...* London: Richard Bishop, 1649. First edition; 4to, (2), (6), 93, 30-191 176-182 (i.e. 198) (4) pages, mid 19th century calf by Hatton of Manchester, panelled in blind, red edges, browned, spine slightly faded, signature of Sum Ashursti, a number of manuscript notes/corrections in text, from the library of the Earls of Macclesfield at Shirburn Castle.   Maggs Bros. Ltd.   1440 - 186 2011   £500

Samerius, Henricus *Sacra Chronologia (a) Mundo Condito ad Christum.* Antwerp: Hieronymum Verdussen, 1608. Folio, (4), 67, (i.e. 65) (1) pages, damage to title leaf with loss of word 'a', 19th century crimson hard grained morocco by Hatton of Manchester, from the library of the Earls of Macclesfield at Shirburn Castle, with Macclesfield arms gilt on upper cover, vertical gilt lettering, gilt edges, manuscript annotations (some extensive), white stains on boards, ex-libris William Godolphin, slightly trimmed, from the library of the Earls of Macclesfield at Shirburn Castle. Maggs Bros. Ltd.   1440 - 187 2011   £750

Sarpi, Paolo 1552-1623 *Histoire du Concile de Trente de Fra'Paolo Sarpi...* Amsterdam: G. P. & J. Blaeu, 1713. 4to., (48), 800, (46) pages, titlepage printed in red and black, woodcut printer's device, woodcut tailpieces and initials, contemporary calf, spine gilt in compartments, morocco lettering piece, binding rubbed, slight foxing, from the library of the Earls of Macclesfield at Shirburn Castle. Maggs Bros. Ltd.   1440 - 188 2011   £450

Savaron, Jean *Les Origines de la Ville de Clairmont... Augmentees de Remarques.* Paris: F. Muguet, 1662. Folio, (12), 593, (31) pages, title printed in red and black, engravings in text, 18th century English calf, gilt fillet on covers, spine gilt in compartments, red speckled edges, from the library of the Earls of Macclesfield at Shirburn Castle. Maggs Bros. Ltd. 1440 - 240 2011 £900

Savary, Jacques *Le Parfait Negociant ou Instruction Generale Pour ce Qui Regarde le Commerce des Marchandises de France...* Amsterdam: Etienne Roger, 1717. Eighth edition; 2 volumes in 1, 4to., xx, 651, (25); xxiv, 631 (1) pages, titlepages printed in red and black, 18th century panelled calf, spine gilt in compartments, title piece "parfait negociant", light dampstaining towards centre of volume, scarce, from the library of the Earls of Macclesfield at Shirburn Castle. Maggs Bros. Ltd. 1440 - 189 2011 £500

Savery, Thomas *The Miner's Friend or an Engine to Raise Water by Fire Described.* London: for S. Crouch, 1702. 8vo., (10), 84 pages, folding engraved plates, contemporary mottled calf gilt, spine gilt in compartments, red edges, without final leaf, plate slightly creased with small tear (repaired), from the library of the Earls of Macclesfield at Shirburn Castle. Maggs Bros. Ltd. 1440 - 190 2011 £10,000

Scala, Giovanni *Delle Fortificationi etc.* Rome: Giuseppe de Rossi, 1627. Enlarged edition; folio, ff. (64), 18th century half calf, spine gilt, red morocco lettering piece, lacking plan of Macerata, few illustrations shaved, from the library of the Earls of Macclesfield at Shirburn Castle. Maggs Bros. Ltd. 1440 - 1191 2011 £750

Scaliger, Josephus *(Greek) Proverbiales Graecorum versus Ios. Scaliger...* Paris: F. Morel, 1594. 2 parts, 8vo., 15, (1), 20 (4), 32 pages, device on royal Greek printer on titlepages, large 'decalogue' device with motto Pietas et Iustitia and Morel's initials on part 2 page (iv), contemporary limp vellum, fine, crisp copy, from the library of the Earls of Macclesfield at Shirburn Castle. Maggs Bros. Ltd. 1440 - 193 2011 £450

Scaliger, Josephus *Collectanea in M. Terentium Varronem de Lingua Latina.* Paris: R. Estienne 22 August, 1565. First edition; 8vo., (8), 221, (3) pages, device on gilt, last leaf blank, contemporary limp vellum, first few leaves, dampstained at head, title leaf little frayed at bottom, from the library of the Earls of Macclesfield at Shirburn Castle. Maggs Bros. Ltd. 1440 - 192 2011 £475

Schickard, Wilhelm *Tarich h.e. Series Regum Persiae... Cum Proemio Longiori...* Tubingen: T. Werlin, 1628. 4to., 231 pages, woodcut illustrations, 18th century calf, gilt spine, red edges, last 2 leaves cropped at outer margin with loss of letters, cropped signature at head of title "Nathan Wright of Englefield", from the library of the Earls of Macclesfield at Shirburn Castle. Maggs Bros. Ltd. 1440 - 194 2011 £1800

Schubler, Johann Jacob *Erste (Beylag zur Ersten Ausgab... Zweyte-Funffzehende). (bound with) Nutzliche Vorstellung, wie man... (bound with) Natzliche Vorstellung und Deutlicher Unterricht von Zierlichen....* Augsburg: Jeremias Wolff, circa, 1715-1730. Nuremberg: L. Bieling for J. C. Weigel, 1730, 1728.; Together 3 works in one volume, folio, woodcut headpieces and initials, contemporary speckled calf, spine gilt in compartments, binding slightly rubbed, tears on both covers, from the library of the Earls of Macclesfield at Shirburn Castle. Maggs Bros. Ltd. 1440 - 196 2011 £900

Schulze, Johann *De Suspecta Poli Declinatione et Eccentricitate Firmamenti vel ruina Cocli, Ultro Citroque Ventilata Materia, Potissimum Tamen hei Contra Domin.* Leipzig: C. Michaelis, 1675. 4to., 239, (1) pages, 18th century English calf, spine gilt uncommon, from the library of the Earls of Macclesfield at Shirburn Castle. Maggs Bros. Ltd. 1440 - 170 2011 £3000

Sems, Johan *Practijck des Kantmetens.* Leiden: Jan Bouwensz, 1600. First edition; 2 parts, 4to., (80, 303, (5); (8), 126, (2) pages, 7 engraved plates in part 2, engraving on both titlepages, woodcut diagrams, contemporary vellum, upper hinge split, ms. vellum guards and strengtheners, probably from the library of John Collins, from the library of the Earls of Macclesfield at Shirburn Castle. Maggs Bros. Ltd. 1440 - 197 2011 £3500

Siemienowicz Kazimierz *(Grand art d'Artillerie) Ausfuhrliche Beschreibung der Grossen Feuerwercks.* Frankfurt: J. D. Zunner, 1676. Reissue of 1651 French edition; folio, (2), 410, (6) pages, text in French, engraved title (in German) and 22 plates, contemporary English calf, lacking 4 leaves of printed prelims, the copy of R. Andersson, from the library of the Earls of Macclesfield at Shirburn Castle. Maggs Bros. Ltd. 1440 - 199 2011 £550

Snell, Willebrord *Tiphys Batavus sive Histriodromice de Navium Cursibus et re Navali.* Leiden: Officinana Elzeviriana, 1624. 4to., (56), 109, (3), 62, (2) pages, last leaf with errata, 2 engraved plates, woodcut diagrams, contemporary turkey morocco, gilt and blind fillet borders, spine gilt in compartments, blue edges, binding rubbed, spine crackling and chipped at head, on front endpapers are 3 pages of manuscript followed by page of tables, the copy of Christophorus Plass, Leiden 1671 who gave it to Benjamin de Munchausen, the Hague 1675, from the library of the Earls of Macclesfield at Shirburn Castle. Maggs Bros. Ltd. 1440 - 200 2011 £950

Somner, William *The Antiquities of Canterbury.* London: by I. L(egat) for Richard Thrale, 1640. First edition; 4to., (16), 516, (12) pages, full page woodcut cut of arms of William Laud, Archbishop of Canterbury on verso of title, folding engraved plan of Canterbury, folding engraved plan of the High altar and surrounding chapels in the cathedral, folding engraved plate, contemporary sprinkled calf, covers panelled in gilt and with gilt lozenge in centre, smooth spine divided into 11 panels by gilt rules (headcap broken, front flyleaf loose, occasional light browning/spotting, outer margin of page 411/2 and 425/8 spotted by damp, light purple, otherwise good, presentation copy inscribed in ink to unidentified recipient, from the library of the Earls of Macclesfield at Shirburn Castle. Maggs Bros. Ltd. 1440 - 201 2011 £950

Sophocles *(Greek) Sophoclis Tragoediae Septem.* Paris: Simon de Colines 16 December, 1528. 8vo., ff. (200), last leaf blank, device on titlepage, late 17th century sprinkled calf, gilt spine, few (cropped), marginal notes on first 2 leaves of Ajax, from the library of the Earls of Macclesfield at Shirburn Castle. Maggs Bros. Ltd. 1440 - 202 2011 £850

Spanheim, Ezechiel *Dissertationes de Praestantia et Usu Numismatum Antiquorum.* London: R. Smith, Amsterdam: Rodolph & Gerhard Wetstein, 1717. 2 volumes, folio, (36), 1 f. pl.), 656 (50) pages, (1 f. pl.); (6), xxviii, 726, (42), engraved frontispiece, engraved folding portrait of author, title printed in red and black, engraved illustrations in text, contemporary calf, spine gilt in compartments, binding extremely rubbed, from the library of the Earls of Macclesfield at Shirburn Castle. Maggs Bros. Ltd. 1440 - 203 2011 £450

Strada, Famiano *Histoire de la Guerre de Flandre.* Leiden: B. & A. Elzevier, 1652. 2 volumes, 8vo., (12), 768, (36); (12), 881, (65) pages, titles printed in red and black, engraved portraits in text, late 18th century English tree calf, spines gilt, joints little weak, bookplate of Hon. Lieut Gen. G. L. Parker, from the library of the Earls of Macclesfield at Shirburn Castle. Maggs Bros. Ltd. 1440 - 204 2011 £500

Sturm, Leonhard Christoph *Prodomus Architecturae Goldmannianae oder Betreue und Grundliche Anweisung.* Ausburg: Peter Detleff for Jermias Wolff, 1714. Oblong folio, bound as upright folio, ff. (10), engraved illustration in text, 22 (of 25) plates, bound as 29 engraved double page plates, contemporary calf backed, spine gilt in compartments, lacking plate VI, bookplate of Hon. Lieut. Gen. G. L. Parker, from the library of the Earls of Macclesfield at Shirburn Castle. Maggs Bros. Ltd. 1440 - 205 2011 £450

Suetonius Tranquillus, Caius *(Opera).* Paris: Typographia Regia, 1645. 12mo., (12), 558, (30) pages, engraved title, engraved medallion portraits, engraved head and tailpiece, contemporary French calf, gilt fleurs de lys on covers within double gilt fillet, spine gilt in compartments, marbled edges, signature of Vincent Loger 1667, from the library of the Earls of Macclesfield at Shirburn Castle. Maggs Bros. Ltd. 1440 - 206 2011 £700

The Bird-Fancier's Recreation. London: printed for T. Ward, 1735. Third edition; 12mo., 89, (5) pages, engraved frontispiece, very lightly browned, small closed tear to B4, overall good copy, contemporary sheep, front joint cracked, cords firm, from the library of the Earls of Macclesfield at Shirburn Castle. Maggs Bros. Ltd. 1440 - 34 2011 £450

Theodore Metochites *Annalium Liber III Theodori Metochitae Historiae Romanae a Iulio Caesare ad Constantinum Magnum Liber Singularius.* Leiden: J. Colster, 1618. 4to., ff. (22), 103, (5), Greek text printed in Plantin's large Greek font, last leaf with short list of errata, mid 17th century English binding of brown calf over pasteboard, blindstamped fillets, red edges, very nice, from the library of Thomas Smith (1638-1710), from the library of the Earls of Macclesfield at Shirburn Castle. Maggs Bros. Ltd. 1440 - 207 2011 £450

Thomas Magister *(Greek) Thomae Magistri Dictionum Atticarum Collectio.* Paris: M. Vascosan, 1532. 2 parts, 8vo., ff. (128); (148), Greek letter, French 17th century calf, gilt fillet on covers, gilt spine, red edges, binding slightly worn, from the library of the Earls of Macclesfield at Shirburn Castle. Maggs Bros. Ltd. 1440 - 209 2011 £450

Tomasini, Giacomo Filippo *Elogia Virorum Literis & Sapientia Illustrium ad Vivum Expressis Imaginibus Exornata.* Padua: S. Sardi, 1644. Handsome copy, 4to., (12), 411, (1) pages, device on titlepage, engraved portraits, contemporary vellum over pasteboard, from the library of the Earls of Macclesfield at Shirburn Castle. Maggs Bros. Ltd. 1440 - 210 2011 £550

Torre, Filippo Del, Bp. of Adria *Moumenti Veteris Antii hoc est Inscriptio M. Aquilii et Tabula Solis Mithrae...* Rome: Gaetano Zenobi & G. Placho, 1700. First edition; 4to., (16), 400, (32) pages, 4 engraved plates at page 6, 159, 161, 257, contemporary smooth French calf, gilt stamp of N. J. Foucault on covers, gilt spine, red edges, some occasional marginal dampstaining, from the library of the Earls of Macclesfield at Shirburn Castle.   Maggs Bros. Ltd.   1440 - 211   2011   £1100

Vlacq, Adriaan *Ephemerides of the Celestiall Motions for the Yeeres of the Vulgar Era 1633, 1634, 1635, 1636.* London: by William Iones, 1635. 4to., (2), 22, (104) (tables) pages closely shaved, cropping some signatures and catchwords and part of the one rule border, text itself untouched, in first part (A-C4) and in the tables touching a few signatures with some slight damage to extreme upper outer corners on few leaves, affecting a few dates, rebound in half calf, old style, from the library of the Earls of Macclesfield at Shirburn Castle.   Maggs Bros. Ltd.   1440 - 222   2011   £4000

Volcyre De Serouville, Nicolas *L'Histoire & Recueil de (la Triumphante et Glorieuse Victoire Obtenue Contre les Seduyctz et (Abusez) Lutheriens Mescreans du Pays Daulsays et Autres...* Paris: for Galliot du Pre, 1526. First edition; folio, ff., (10), xcviii, text in 2 columns, woodcut illustration on titlepage, woodcut of a scribe, 5 woodcut illustrations, 18th century calf with triple fillet gilt, spine gilt in compartments, red speckled edges, 3 colored silk markers, first 4 leaves torn with loss, H-3-H4 transposed, last leaf torn in margin, occasional slight staining, despite heavily damaged first leaves (woodcut on titlepage untouched), overall good copy, rare, from the library of the Earls of Macclesfield at Shirburn Castle.   Maggs Bros. Ltd.   1440 - 223   2011   £2500

Voltaire, Francois Marie Arouet De   1694-1778   *Letters Concerning the English Nation.* London: for C. Davis and A. Lyon, 1733. First edition; 8vo., (16), 253, (19) pages, fine, contemporary calf, gilt spine, small dampstain in upper inside corner of title, fading away over next few leaves, from the library of the Earls of Macclesfield at Shirburn Castle. Maggs Bros. Ltd.   1440 - 224   2011   £600

Watin, Jean Felix *L'Art de Faire et d'Employer le Vernis, ou l'Art de Vernisseur...* Paris: Chez Quillau & Chez L'Auteur, 1772. 8vo., xvi, 249 (1 errata), 6 (table/privilege), 8 (supplement), contemporary English half calf, marbled boards, red morocco label, from the library of the Earls of Macclesfield at Shirburn Castle.   Maggs Bros. Ltd.   1440 - 225   2011   £750

Werndly, Georg Henrik *Maleische Spraakkunst uit de Eige Schriften der Malaiers Opgemaakt...*   Amsterdam: R. & G. Wetstein op kosten va de E. A. Heren Bewindhebberen der oost indische maatschappye, 1736. First edition; 8vo., (120, lxviii, (23) pages, 18th century English polished calf, spine gilt in compartments, morocco lettering piece lacking, from the library of the Earls of Macclesfield at Shirburn Castle.   Maggs Bros. Ltd.   1440 - 226   2011   £1400

Worcester, Edward Somerset, Marquis of *A Century of the Names and Scantlings of Such Inventions as a Present I Can Call to Mind...* London: J. Grismond, 1663. First edition; 12mo., (24), 72, (12), (2), 34 pages (A1 blank (here lacking), A11v, E5v, E6r blank, woodcut royal arms on Flv, 18th century speckled calf, spine gilt in compartments, red morocco lettering piece, hinges cracked, binding rubbed, rare, from the library of the Earls of Macclesfield at Shirburn Castle.   Maggs Bros. Ltd.   1440 - 230   2011   £4500

Zosimus *(Greek) Historiarum Libri VIII.*   Geneva: H. Estienne, 1581. 2 parts in 1, (8), 182, (2); 79, (1 (blank) pages, small burn holes in margins on pages 35-40 (part I), affecting odd letter of printed marginal notes, late 17th century English panelled calf, somewhat rubbed, from the library of the Earls of Macclesfield at Shirburn Castle. Maggs Bros. Ltd.   1440 - 231   2011   £750

Association – MacColl, Alexander

MacDonald, George   1824-1905   *The Miracles of Our Lord.* London: Strahan & Co., 1870. First edition; half title, 16 page catalog (Nov. 1870), original mauve cloth, spine faded, monogram bookplate of M.E.J., signed presentation from author to Uncle, Alexander S. Maccoll.   Jarndyce Antiquarian Booksellers   CXCII - 129   2011   £2000

Association – MacDonald, Dwight

Dreiser, Theodore   1871-1945   *The Financier.* New York: Boni & Liveright, 1927. Revised edition; spine soiled and bit darkened, good plus without dust jacket, Dwight Macdonald's copy with his bookplate, Macdonald has made a number of slightly insouciant marginal critical notations in pencil in text.   Between the Covers   169 - BTC335183   2011 $450

Association – MacDonald, G.

Kennedy, Grace *Father Clement: a Roman Catholic Story.* Edinburgh: W. Oliphant & Son, 1838. Ninth edition; engraved frontispiece slightly spotted, contemporary half calf, gilt spine, maroon leather label, slightly rubbed, ownership signature G. MacDonald, nice.   Jarndyce Antiquarian Booksellers   CLXC - 52   2011   £40

Association – MacDonald, George

Bible. English - 1881 *The Gospel According to S. John.* Cambridge: Cambridge University Press, circa, 1881. Interleaves with plain rubricated pages, plain red calf, gilt dentelles & edges by Philip Tout, all edges gilt, inscribed "This gift to my father George MacDonald from Miss Violet Cavendish-Bentinck, now offered in much love & gratitude to the Rev. M. C. D'Arcy by Greville MacDonald". Jarndyce Antiquarian Booksellers CXCII - 335 2011 £250

Dickens, Charles 1812-1870 *Letters of Charles Dickens to Wilkie Collins 1851-1870.* London: James R. Osgood, McIlvaine & Co., 1892. Half title, original dark blue cloth, dulled, inner hinges cracking, inscribed by A. J. Watt for George MacDonald. Jarndyce Antiquarian Booksellers CXCII - 337 2011 £380

Dickens, Charles 1812-1870 *Little Dorrit.* London: Bradbury & Evans, 1857. First edition, Rigaud issue; frontispiece, added engraved title and plates, errata slip, slightly foxed and damp marked, contemporary half calf, marbled boards, well rebacked, black leather, with George Macdonald's bookplate. Jarndyce Antiquarian Booksellers CXCII - 336 2011 £500

O'Brien, Michael Fitz-James *The Diamond Lens and Other Stories.* London: Ward & Downey, 1887. Half title, blue cloth blocked in blind and squared pattern, spine faded and worn at head and tail, with George MacDonald's bookplate. Jarndyce Antiquarian Booksellers CXCII - 338 2011 £150

Shakespeare, William 1564-1616 *Shakespeare's Hamlet: the First Quarto 1603 a Facsimile...* London: W. Griggs, 1880. Final ad leaf, original quarter maroon roan, spine worn and slightly chipped, with George MacDonald's red ink signature and his larger bookplate, at end are extensive pencil notes by MacDonald. Jarndyce Antiquarian Booksellers CXCII - 339 2011 £850

Trollope, Anthony 1815-1882 *An Editor's Tales.* London: Strahan & Co., 1870. First edition; half title, original brown cloth, expertly recased with spine strip slightly trimmed at head and tail, binder's ticket of Burn & Co., inscribed by publisher, A. Strahan for George MacDonald, with MacDonalds bookplate. Jarndyce Antiquarian Booksellers CXCII - 340 2011 £450

Association – MacDonald, Greville

Bible. English - 1881 *The Gospel According to S. John.* Cambridge: Cambridge University Press, circa, 1881. Interleaves with plain rubricated pages, plain red calf, gilt dentelles & edges by Philip Tout, all edges gilt, inscribed "This gift to my father George MacDonald from Miss Violet Cavendish-Bentinck, now offered in much love & gratitude to the Rev. M. C. D'Arcy by Greville MacDonald". Jarndyce Antiquarian Booksellers CXCII - 335 2011 £250

Association – MacDonald, James

MacDonald, George 1824-1905 *A Book of Strife.* London: printed for the author and to be had by Writing to mr. Hughes 43 Beaufort Street, Chelsea, 1882. Second edition; tall 12mo., colophon leaf, original plain red cloth, marked, spine faded, inner hinges splitting, paper label browned and chipped, inscribed by author for cousin George MacDonald and with signature of Robt. G. Troup, husband of MacDonald's cousin, Margaret. Jarndyce Antiquarian Booksellers CXCII - 222 2011 £1200

Association – MacDonald, S.

MacDonald, George 1824-1905 *Paul Faber, Surgeon.* London: Kegan Paul, Trench, Trubner & Co., circa, 1890? New edition; 2 pages ads and colophon leaf, original red cloth blocked with black acanthus (style D), slightly marked, signature of S. MacDonald. Jarndyce Antiquarian Booksellers CXCII - 210 2011 £85

Association – MacDonald, Sara

MacDonald, George 1824-1905 *Donal Grant.* London: Kegan Paul, Trench & Co., 1892. New edition; half title, original red cloth (style D), slightly marked, inscribed S.M.D. (Sara MacDonald). Jarndyce Antiquarian Booksellers CXCII - 266 2011 £65

MacDonald, George 1824-1905 *The Elect Lady.* London: Kegan Paul, Trench & Co., 1888. First edition sheets but this issue does not have the frontispiece and ads; elaborate inscribed S. MacDonald 23.4.92 on half title and signed Sara MacDonald, half title, original red cloth, Style D, very good. Jarndyce Antiquarian Booksellers CXCII - 281 2011 £75

MacDonald, George 1824-1905 *Guild Court.* London: Sampson, Low, Marston, Searle & Rivington, 1887. New edition; 32 page Sampson Low catalog (Sept. 1888), original red cloth blocked and lettered in black (style B), very good, signature of young Sara MacDonald 1892. Jarndyce Antiquarian Booksellers CXCII - 78 2011 £85

MacDonald, George   1824-1905   *Heather and Snow.* London: Chatto & Windus, 1893. 2 volumes, half titles, 32 page catalog (March 1893), original dark blue morocco grained cloth, slightly dulled and rubbed, signed SMD (Sara MacDonald).   Jarndyce Antiquarian Booksellers   CXCII - 306   2011   £950

MacDonald, George   1824-1905   *The Seaboard Parish.* London: Kegan Paul, Trench & Co., 1888.   New edition; original red cloth with elaborate decoration black (style D), signature of Sara MacDonald 23.4.92.   Jarndyce Antiquarian Booksellers   CXCII - 99   2011   £65

MacDonald, George   1824-1905   *Stephen Archer and Other Tales.*   London: Sampson Low Marston, Searle & Rivington, 1888. New and cheaper edition; half title, original red cloth, style B, spine slightly faded, with signature of Sara MacDonald.   Jarndyce Antiquarian Booksellers CXCII - 252   2011   £50

MacDonald, George   1824-1905   *Wilfrid Cumbermede: an Autobiographical Story.*   London: Kegan Paul, Trench & Co., 1892?   New edition; half title, original red cloth, style D, very good, inscription from Sara MacDonald 23.4.92.   Jarndyce Antiquarian Booksellers   CXCII - 134   2011   £120

Association – MacEwen, Douglas

Shelley, Percy Bysshe   1792-1822   *The Poetical Works.* London: Reeves & Turner, 1886.   Second edition; 2 volumes, 191 x 135mm., very fine early 20th century olive crushed morocco handsomely gilt by C. and C. McLeish (stamp signed on rear turn-ins), covers bordered with single plain gilt rule, raised bands, spines densely and very attractively gilt in compartments featuring a large centerpiece in the form of a rose with four emanating springs of rose leaves, this quatrefoil design enclosed by a semis field punctuated with trefoil leaves, turn-ins with gilt French fillet border and trefoil cornerpieces, all edges gilt, each volume with frontispiece, engraved armorial bookplate of Douglas and Mary MacEwen; spines lightly sunned, offsetting from frontispieces, isolated minor foxing, otherwise especially fine set in lovely bindings, gilt bright, leather unworn, text with virtually no signs of use.   Phillip J. Pirages   59 - 119   2011 $1950

Association – MacEwen, Mary

Shelley, Percy Bysshe   1792-1822   *The Poetical Works.* London: Reeves & Turner, 1886.   Second edition; 2 volumes, 191 x 135mm., very fine early 20th century olive crushed morocco handsomely gilt by C. and C. McLeish (stamp signed on rear turn-ins), covers bordered with single plain gilt rule, raised bands, spines densely and very attractively gilt in compartments featuring a large centerpiece in the form of a rose with four emanating springs of rose leaves, this quatrefoil design enclosed by a semis field punctuated with trefoil leaves, turn-ins with gilt French fillet border and trefoil cornerpieces, all edges gilt, each volume with frontispiece, engraved armorial bookplate of Douglas and Mary MacEwen; spines lightly sunned, offsetting from frontispieces, isolated minor foxing, otherwise especially fine set in lovely bindings, gilt bright, leather unworn, text with virtually no signs of use.   Phillip J. Pirages   59 - 119   2011 $1950

Association – MacIver, Loren

Bishop, Elizabeth   *Poem.*   Phoenix Book Shop, 1973.   First edition, copy "L" (for Loren) of 26 lettered copies (Out of a total edition of 126) signed by Bishop on colophon; oblong small 8vo., original string tied unprinted stiff wrappers, marbled outer wrapper, printed paper label, housed in custom green cloth clamshell box with black morocco spine label, with author's presentation for Loren MacIver & Lloyd Frankenberg, laid in is exceptionally interesting TLS from Bishop for MacIver and Frankenberg.   James S. Jaffe Rare Books   May 26 2011 - 20762   2011 $8500

Association – Mackau, Baron De

Orleans, Pierre Joseph De   *Histoire des Revolutions D'Angleterre Depuis Le Commencement De La Monarchie.* Paris: Chez Claude Barbin, 1693-1694.   First edition; 250 x 193 mm., 3 volumes, splendid and unusual sumptuously gilt early 19th century marbled calf with red morocco spines in the style of Bozerian, covers with gilt borders of two decorative rules and elegant undulating floral vine, flat straight grain morocco spines very handsomely gilt in compartments with pointille ground and central circlet from which radiate four lillies and four leaves on twining stems, turn-ins gilt with plain and decorative rolls, marbled endpapers, all edges gilt, engraved head and tailpieces and 8 engraved portraits, verso of front free endpaper with bookplate of Baron de Mackau, titlepage with ink ownership inscription of Alexander Paul Ludwig Goupy? in contemporary hand; isolated gatherings with variable browning (small handfull rather browned), one leaf in first volume with expert early repair of four inch tear (letters of four words partly obscured or displaced, and text and facing page somewhat discolored), few additional trivial imperfections internally, but text generally quite fresh and clean, one joint with five small wormholes, few hardly noticeable, shallow scratches to covers hint of wear to extremities, lovely bindings in fine condition, lustrous leather and gilt with only minor wear, with their very considerable original visual appeal entirely intact.   Phillip J. Pirages   59 - 14   2011 $2250

Association – MacKenize, Compton

Turner, W. J. *Mozart. The Man and His Works.* London: Victor Gollancz, 1938. Uncorrected proof copy; original printed wrappers, edges little stained, pages 391, 16 plates, some edges little dampstained, TLS from Victor Gollancz to Compton MacKenzie loosely inserted. R. F. G. Hollett & Son Antiquarian Booksellers 175 - 1368 2011 £45

Association – MacKintosh, H. S.

One Hundred and One Ballades. London: Cobden-Sanderson, 1931. First edition; original cloth, gilt, dust jacket by John Nash, backstrip faded, lower half lacking, pages (vi), 108, illustrations by Nash throughout, presentation copy from H. S. MacKintosh. R. F. G. Hollett & Son Antiquarian Booksellers General Catalogue Summer 2010 - 854 2011 £60

Association – MacLagan, Mr.

Dixie, Florence *In the Land of Misfortune.* London: Richard Bentley and Son, 1882. First edition; octavo, xvi, 434 pages, frontispiece, plates, original lime green pictorial cloth stamped in black and white by Burn, corners showing, rubbed, author's presentation, inscribed to Mr. Maclagan, from author, very good. Jeff Weber Rare Books 163 - 154 2011 $300

Association – MacVeagh, Lincoln

Hinton, James *Life in Nature.* New York: Lincoln MacVeagh/The Dial Press, 1931. First edition; presumably later pencil ownership signature, boards little soiled, very good in good or better dust jacket with couple of small external tape repairs, some faint stains, neatly tipped ot half title is one page ALS from editor, Havelock Ellis to publisher Lincoln MacVeagh returning the proofs for this book (no present), questioning some of the author's premises and inquiring when the book will be released, letter near fine. Between the Covers 169 - BTC335143 2011 $500

Association – Magee, Florence

Dodgson, Charles Lutwidge 1832-1898 *Alice's Adventures in Wonderland. (and) Through the Looking Glass and What Alice Found There.* London: Macmillan and Co., 1866. Second, but first published edition; 183 x 125mm., 2 separately published works bound in 2 volumes, extremely pleasing crimson levant morocco by Root & son (stamp-signed on front turn-in of both volumes), each cover with panels formed by double gilt rules and central gilt medallion, the "Wonderland" medallion depicting Alice holding baby pig, the "Looking-Glass" medallion showing grumpy Red Queen, raised bands, spines gilt in compartments with double ruled frames and small central quatrefoil, gilt ruled turn-ins, marbled endpapers, all edges gilt, with 92 illustrations, letter laid in from bookseller John Newbegin elucidating issue points, bookplate of Florence Magee; spines slightly and evenly a darker red, handful of leaves with very minor foxing or smudges, one leaf with neat repair to tail edge (no text affected), but fine and attractive set, text clean, fresh, and smooth and bindings lustrous and virtually unworn. Phillip J. Pirages 59 - 176 2011 $11,500

Association – Maillard, Nicolas

Leto, Giulio Pomponio *Romanae Historiae Compendium etc.* Paris: Jean Dupre 7 May, 1501. 4to. in 6's, ff. (62), woodcut illustration on titlepage, large device at end, 18th century smooth calf, gilt spine, red edges, handsome copy, the copy of Nicolas Maillard of Rouen, from the library of the Earls of Macclesfield at Shirburn Castle. Maggs Bros. Ltd. 1440 - 130 2011 £1500

Association – Mainwaring, A. E.

Romer, C. F. *The Second Battalion Royal Dublin Fusiliers in the South African War.* London: A. L. Humphrys, 1908. First edition; 8vo., pages xiv, 271, numerous illustrations, original green cloth, very good, presentation copy from Major A. E. Mainwaring. J. & S. L. Bonham Antiquarian Booksellers Africa 4/20/2011 - 8300 2011 £175

Association – Mainwaring, Randolph

Martineau, Harriet 1802-1876 *Feats on the Fiord.* London: Charles Knight & Co., 1841. First edition; half title, original brown cloth, blocked in blind, spine lettered in gilt, bit rubbed, front inner hinge cracking, one or two gatherings slightly proud, inscription "Randolph Mainwaring from Mrs. Foley 1848". Jarndyce Antiquarian Booksellers CLXC - 328 2011 £45

Association – Mansfield, J.

Porter, Jane *Thaddeus of Warsaw.* London: printed by A. Strahan for T. N. Longman, 1804. Second edition; half titles, contemporary marbled boards, excellently rebacked, retaining original red labels, signature of J. Mansfield 1806, very good, clean copy,. Jarndyce Antiquarian Booksellers CLXC - 762 2011 £420

Association – Manso, Leo

Thomajan, P. K. *The White Lie.* Philadelphia: Ritten House, 1940. First edition; illustrations by Leo Manso, glazed illustrated boards, small nick on front gutter, else near fine, probably issued without dust jacket, this copy inscribed by Manso for the author. Between the Covers 169 - BTC340320 2011 $750

Association – Manville, Ira Albert

Peters, John P. *Body Water: The Exchange of Fluids in Man.* Springfield and Baltimore: Charles C. Thomas, 1935. 8vo., viii, 405 pages, figures, tables, green cloth, gilt stamped spine title, dust jacket, fine, scarce in jacket, bookplate and inkstamp of Ira Albert Manville, Portland, from the Medical Library of Dr. Clare Gray Peterson. Jeff Weber Rare Books 162 - 242 2011 $65

Association – Marceau, Robert

Doctor Comicus, or the Frolics of Fortune. London: B. Blake, 1825? 210 133mm., 269 pages without printed titlepage, very attractive light tan smooth calf by Sangorski & Sutcliffe/Zaehnsdorf (stamp signed verso of front endpaper), covers bordered with French fillet and fleuron cornerpieces, raised bands, spine gilt in compartments featuring decorative bands, scrolling cornerpieces, fleuron centerpiece and small tools, maroon morocco labels, gilt inner dentelles, marbled endpapers, all edges gilt, 12 plates, all color by hand, bookplate of Robert Marceau; engraved title and two plates, little foxed, three plates slightly trimmed at fore edge, without apparent loss, few leaves with light marginal foxing, or soiling, otherwise excellent, plates bright and well preserved, leaves clean and fresh, sympathetic binding in mint condition. Phillip J. Pirages 59 - 331 2011 $400

Association – Marcham, Genevieve

Cocteau, Jean *Le Sang D'un Poete.* Paris: Robert Marin, 1948. First edition, no. IV of 20 "Hors Commerce" copies on velin d'arches; 8vo., pages 106, photos by Sacha Masour, signed presentation from author for Genevieve Marcham, with superb ink drawing by Cocteau, about fine, very faint wear at head of spine. Any Amount of Books May 26 2011 - A68702 2011 $2013

Association – Marches, Monsieur

Fortolis, Ludovic *Hantises.* Paris: Bibliotheque De La Critique, 1901. First edition; 8vo., pages 94, (1) imprint (1) blank, 4 plates, numerous small illustrations, uncut, plates browned at edges, otherwise very clean copy, original illustrated wrappers, printed in black, discolored with some light foxing, inscription offset to inner front cover, worn, chipped, spine cracked, but holding, glassine cover chipped, inscribed presentation by author to Monsieur Marches. Simon Finch Rare Books Zero - 314 2011 £500

Association – Mardon, Edward

Inchbald, Elizabeth *A Simple Story.* London: Richard Bentley, 1833. Half title, bound at Seargeant's Abergavenny in contemporary half dark green calf, armorial bookplate of Edward K. E. Mardon, very good. Jarndyce Antiquarian Booksellers CXCI - 216 2011 £40

Association – Markham, Christopher Alexander

MacPherson, James 1736-1696 *The Poems of Ossian.* London: Lackington, Allen & Co., 1803. 2 volumes, contemporary quarter calf gilt with marbled boards, spines evenly darkened, one hinge tender, pages xvi, 320; (ii), 363 with 2 engraved frontispieces and 4 engraved plates, scattered foxing, engraved roundel bookplate of Christopher Alexander Markham in each volume. R. F. G. Hollett & Son Antiquarian Booksellers General Catalogue Summer 2010 - 664 2011 £120

Association – Markland, James Heywood

Murray, John *Genuine Memoirs of John Murray, Esq. Late Secretary to the Young Pretender.* London: printed for J. Wilford, 1747. First edition, variant issue; 8vo., (2), 64 pages, mid 19th century green half roan over marbled boards, spine lettered gilt, minor rubbing of extremities, excellent copy from mid 19th century library of the antiquary James Heywood Markland with his signature and armorial bookplate. John Drury Rare Books 153 - 98 2011 £275

Association – Marks, Harry

Boschere, Jean De 1878-1953 *Job le Pauvre.* Paris: Jacques Povolozky & Cie, 1922. First edition, no. 47 of 50 copies on Simili Japon Van Gelder from the tirage de tete,; with Bosschere's presentation inscription to Harry F. Marks, 8vo., pages (iv), 124, (i) contents, (1 blank, frontispiece, 2 sets of 14 plates, fore-edge and lower edge uncut, partly unopened, closed tear to frontispiece at gutter, otherwise exceptionally crisp and fresh, black morocco grain paper covered boards, paper label with black text to spine, bumped, chipped at head and foot of spine, some loss to label, author' presentation inscription. Simon Finch Rare Books Zero - 303 2011 £850

Association – Marryat, Frederick

Cruikshank, George 1792-1878 *Scraps and Sketches.* Published by the artist, 1828. Oblong folio, title and 6 leaves of plates, tear to lower margin of 3rd leaf not affecting image, contemporary half dark brown morocco, marbled paper boards, dark brown morocco label with elaborate gilt borders, extremities, little rubbed, leading inner hinge slightly cracking, presentation inscription on title to Capt. Marryat RN with best compliments, of George Cruikshank; armorial bookplate of Sir Robert Peel.   Jarndyce Antiquarian Booksellers   CXCI - 147   2011   £650

Association – Marsden, Edmund

Ludolf, Hiob *A New History of Ethiopia.* London: for Samuel Smith, 1682. First edition in English; folio, (8), 88, 151-370, 375-398 pages, 8 engraved plates, engraved plate, folding genealogical table, contemporary or early 18th century calf, front hinge cracked but held by cords, corners worn, some light browning but very good, signatures of Edmund and Rufus Marsden, latter dated 1762, Herz booklabel.   Joseph J. Felcone Inc.   Fall Miscellany 2010 - 78   2011 $2200

Association – Marsden, Rufus

Ludolf, Hiob *A New History of Ethiopia.* London: for Samuel Smith, 1682. First edition in English; folio, (8), 88, 151-370, 375-398 pages, 8 engraved plates, engraved plate, folding genealogical table, contemporary or early 18th century calf, front hinge cracked but held by cords, corners worn, some light browning but very good, signatures of Edmund and Rufus Marsden, latter dated 1762, Herz booklabel.   Joseph J. Felcone Inc.   Fall Miscellany 2010 - 78   2011 $2200

Association – Marsh-Caldwell, Elaine

Marsh, Anne *The Song of Roland as Chanted Before the Battle of Hastings by the Minstrel Taillefer.* London: Hurst and Blackett, 1854. First edition; frontispiece, rubricated text, original dark blue cloth, borders blocked in blind, lettered in gilt, at some time rebacked retaining most of original spine strip, leading inner hinge strengthened, following endpapers replaced, presentation inscription to Dean of Lichfield from daughters of the authoress, Elaine and Georgina Marsh-Caldwell - Linley Wood Sept 22nd 1879. Jarndyce Antiquarian Booksellers   CLXC - 241   2011   £110

Association – Marsh-Caldwell, Georgina

Marsh, Anne *The Song of Roland as Chanted Before the Battle of Hastings by the Minstrel Taillefer.* London: Hurst and Blackett, 1854. First edition; frontispiece, rubricated text, original dark blue cloth, borders blocked in blind, lettered in gilt, at some time rebacked retaining most of original spine strip, leading inner hinge strengthened, following endpapers replaced, presentation inscription to Dean of Lichfield from daughters of the authoress, Elaine and Georgina Marsh-Caldwell - Linley Wood Sept 22nd 1879. Jarndyce Antiquarian Booksellers   CLXC - 241   2011   £110

Association – Marsh, Eleanor

Kelly, George *Craig's Wife a Drama.* Boston: Little Brown, 1926. First edition; 8vo., pages 174, very nice, tight copy, inscribed by author to Josephine Williams who played the part of Mrs. Harold in the NY production, also signed by rest of the cast - Annie Sutherland, Crystal Herne, Arthur Shaw, C. Stewart, Eleanor Marsh, Charles Trowbridge, Josephine Hull, J. A. Curtis, Nelan Jaap, Arline Alcine & Mary Gildea, also inscribed by the producer, Rosalie Stewart to whom the play was dedicated.   Second Life Books Inc.   174 - 213   2011 $2000

Association – Marshall, Mervyn

Martineau, Harriet 1802-1876 *Eastern Life, Present and Past.* London: E. Moxon Sons & Co., 1850. New edition; contemporary full vellum, black leather labels, bit discolored, armorial bookplate of Mervyn Marshall.   Jarndyce Antiquarian Booksellers   CLXC - 277   2011   £70

Association – Martin, Geoffrey

Fowler, J. T. *Adamnani Vita S. Columbae.* Oxford: Clarendon Press, 1894. Pages lxxxvii, 202, (ii), 8, original quarter roan gilt, spine rather frayed at head, some pencilled notes and underlinings, distinguished trio of earlier historian owners, Gwilym Peredur Jones, F. Lindstead Downham and Geoffrey Martin.   R. F. G. Hollett & Son Antiquarian Booksellers   175 - 464   2011   £35

Association – Martin, H. Bradley

Blunt, Wilfred Scawen 1840-1922 *Sonnets and Songs.* London: John Murray, 1875. First edition; foolscap 8vo., pages viii, 112 page 53 misnumbered 5), internally bright and fresh, original yellow sand grain cloth over bevelled boards, upper side with gilt lettering and flaming sun design, dark green endpapers, spine and board edges dust soiled, front hinge cracked by holding, bookseller's ticket and bookplates of H. Bradley Martin and J. O. Edwards, author's presentation inscription, leaf from old bookseller's catalog loosely inserted.   Simon Finch Rare Books   Zero - 301   2011   £650

Clare, John *The Village Minstrel and Other Poems.* London: printed for Taylor and Hessey, Fleet Street and E. Drury, Stamford, 1821. First edition; 2 volumes, small 8vo., frontispieces, original cloth backed boards with paper spine labels, former owner's neat signature "Edw. Cragg 1843" in upper right hand corner of titlepages and on pastedowns, extremities of boards trifle rubbed, spines and covers bit soiled, but in general exceptionally fine set in original condition, preserved in folding cloth box, the Bradley Martin copy, Carter's variant binding "B".   James S. Jaffe Rare Books   May 26 2011 - 20616   2011 $8750

Radcliffe, Alexander *The Ramble an Anti-Heroick Poem. Together with Some Terrestrial Hymns and Carnal Ejaculations.* London: for the author and to be sold by Walter Davis, 1682. First edition; 8vo., pages (xvi), 128, including initial blank Ai, contemporary black morocco, sides panelled in gilt, spine richly gilt in compartments, marbled pastedowns, gilt edges, lightly rubbed, little marginal browning, fine, the Heber(?) Britwell-Hewyard-Bradley Martin, Edwards copy with modern bookplates of H. Bradley Martin and J. O. Edwards.   Simon Finch Rare Books   Zero - 348   2011   £2500

Stevenson, Robert Louis Balfour 1850-1894 *Treasure Island.* London: Cassell & Co., 1883. First edition, first issue; frontispiece printed in three colors, with tissue guard, original olive green diagonal fine ribbed cloth with covers ruled in blind and spine ruled and lettered in gilt, original black coated endpapers, absolute minimum of wear to corners and extremities, rear hinge expertly and almost invisibly repaired, some very occasional browning and soiling, previous owner's neat ink inscription, exceptionally fresh, bright and fine, chemised in quarter green morocco slipcase, the Bradley Martin copy, bookplate of Mildred Greenhill on front pastedown, in this copy the "7" in the pagination on page 127 has been hand stamped in larger font and darker ink, and, as with other copies of the first issue, the "8" is not present in the pagination on page 83 (copies are known with the "8" present on page 83 and with the "7" missing from pagination on page 127),.   David Brass Rare Books, Inc.   May 26 2011 - 00036   2011 $32,500

Wolfe, Thomas *The Crisis in Industry.* Chapel Hill: University of North Carolina, 1919. First edition, one of 300 copies; pamphlet, pages (iv), 5-14, (2) blank, original grey wrappers printed in black, green cloth chemise with bookplate of H. Bradley Martin, green cloth slipcase, spine with lettering and filleting in gilt and with morocco lettering piece in gilt, fine.   Simon Finch Rare Books   Zero - 142   2011   £4000

Association – Martin, James

Dickens, Charles 1812-1870 *A Tale of Two Cities.* London: Chapman & Hall, 1859. First edition, second state with titlepage still dated 1859 but with corrected pagination on page 213 and no signature 'b' on the list of plates; octavo, (i-vii) viii (ix-x), (1)2-254 pages, 16 inserted plate, including frontispiece and vignette title by Phiz, publisher's secondary binding of moderate olive green fine diaper cloth, covers stamped in blind, spine lettered in gilt, original pale yellow coated endpapers, boards remarkably fresh, text and plates very clean and bright with just minimal scattering of unobtrusive foxing, just tiny amount of wear to top and bottom of spine, inner hinges very expertly and almost invisibly strengthened, armorial bookplate of Sir James Martin, chemised in full green morocco slipcase case, superlative condition.   David Brass Rare Books, Inc.   May 26 2011 - 00734   2011 $18,500

Association – Martin, John

Beaumont, Cyril Winthrop *New Paths.* London: C. W, Beaumont, 1918. First edition, one of 6 copies on Japan specially printed for presentation in addition to the stated 30 copies, with Anne Estelle Rice's illustrations and Edgar Tytgat's frontispiece lithograph, all hand colored; 8vo., pages (xii), 164, complete with frontispiece, illustrations and 18 photogravures, uncut, spotting to endpapers and first and last leaves as often with this title, light offsetting from frontispiece colouring to titlepage, original tan paper boards, printed with illustrations in blue, white paper label printed in blue to spine, some light shelfwear, short crack to lower hinge but holding firm, glassine cover, from the library of John Martin, publisher of Black Sparrow Press. Simon Finch Rare Books   Zero - 331   2011   £300

Crosby, Harry *Transit of Venus.* Paris: Black Sun Press, 1929. Second edition, no. 130 of 200 copies on Holland Van Geler Zonen; small 8vo., pages (x, 62, (i) blank, (1) ads, (1) imprint, (1) blank, unopened and uncut, internally very fresh, publisher's ivory wrappers printed in red and black with illustration to lower wrapper, original glassine, silver and gold slipcase, lightly worn at edges, diminutive library ticket of John Martin (publisher of Black Sparrow Press).   Simon Finch Rare Books   Zero - 309   2011   £500

Dahlberg, Edward *Bottom Dogs.* London: G. P. Putnam's Sons, 1929. First edition, for subscriber's only, one of 520 copies, number 461 of 520; 8vo., pages xxi, (i) blank, (ii) half title, 285, (1) blank, (1) imprint, (1 blank, top edge gilt, others uncut, publisher's black cloth, gilt lettering to upper board and spine, original grey dust jacket, printed in black, spine lightly browned, small chips at head and foot of folds, unclipped, John Martin's (publisher of Black Sparrow Press) book ticket, 2 small bookseller's tickets, previous owner's pencil inscription, fine in about very good dust jacket.   Simon Finch Rare Books   Zero - 226   2011   £250

Lawrence, David Herbert 1885-1930 *Rawdon's Roof.* London: Elkin Mathews & Marrot, 1928. First edition, signed limited issue, number 304 of 500 copies signed by Lawrence; 8vo., pages 32, original grey paper boards, printed in blue, decorative endpapers, edges untrimmed, original grey dust jacket printed in blue, author's signature in black ink to limitation page, endpapers slightly browned, from the library of John Martin (publisher of Black Sparrow Press), with his small book ticket to rear pastedown, fine. Simon Finch Rare Books Zero - 248 2011 £500

Some Imagist Poets, 1916: An Annual Anthology. Boston and New York: Houghton Mifflin Co., Riverside Press, Cambridge, 1916. 8vo., pages (k), (i) ads, xvi, 96, (i) blank, (1), imprint, uncut, lower and fore-edge, crease to upper fore-edge, otherwise very crisp and clean, original leaf green paper wrappers, spine lettered in black, upper wrapper printed in black with decoration, shelfwear and discoloring, some small cracks and rubbing to spine, from the library of John Martin, publisher of Black Sparrow Press with his small book ticket. Simon Finch Rare Books Zero - 330 2011 £150

Association – Martineau, A. D.

Martineau, Philip Meadows *A Memoir of the Late Philip Meadows Martienau, Surgeon.* Norwich: Bacon & Kinnebrook, Mercury Office, 1831. First edition; 4to., frontispiece, tear in lower margin of leading f.e.p., with slight loss, original blue silk, spine little worn, with presentation inscription from A. D. Martineau for P. E. Elwin. Jarndyce Antiquarian Booksellers CLXC - 362 2011 £350

Association – Martineau, Charles

Martineau, Harriet 1802-1876 *Dawn Island.* Manchester: J. Gadsby, 1845. First edition; 12mo., engraved frontispiece, vignette title, additional printed title, odd spot, original blue vertical ribbed cloth, front board decorated with central gilt vignette within blind borders, spine blocked and lettered in gilt, spine very slightly rubbed, all edges gilt, very good, signed by C(harles) E. Martineau (author's great nephew). Jarndyce Antiquarian Booksellers CLXC - 270 2011 £180

Martineau, James *National Duties and Other Sermons and Addresses.* London: Longmans, Green & Co., 1903. First edition; uncut in original dark blue cloth, spine lettered in gilt, slightly marked, good plus, signed Charles Martin(eau), Harriet' great nephew. Jarndyce Antiquarian Booksellers CLXC - 359 2011 £35

Association – Martineau, E. K.

Martineau, Harriet 1802-1876 *A Complete Guide to te English Lakes.* Windermere: John Garnett, 1855. First edition; 4to., half title, color frontispiece and 3 color plates on plate paper, illustrations, color foldout map, original morocco grained blue cloth, blocked in blind, lettered in gilt, slightly rubbed, boards slightly affected by damp, all edges gilt, in Rivlin's alternative binding with centre of back board lettered in blind, signed E.K. Martineau on leading f.e.p., family copy. Jarndyce Antiquarian Booksellers CLXC - 268 2011 £250

Martineau, Harriet 1802-1876 *History of the Peace; Pictorial History of England During the Thirty Years' Peace 1816-1846.* London: W. & R. Chambers, 1858. New edition; large 8vo., color folding map preceding title, illustrations, index, uncut in original brown morocco grained cloth, blocked in blind, spine lettered in gilt, bit rubbed, expert repairs to head and tail of spine, with signature of E. K. Martineau. Jarndyce Antiquarian Booksellers CLXC - 285 2011 £180

Association – Martineau, Edward

Martineau, James *Endeavours After the Christian Life.* London: John Chapman, 1843-1847. First edition; 2 volumes, half titles, final ad leaves, contemporary half brown morocco, spines lettered and with devices in gilt, spines slightly darkened and bit rubbed, each volume with ownership inscription of Martineau family members, Robt. Martineau, Edwd. K. Martineau, author's representation inscription to R. R. Martineau. Jarndyce Antiquarian Booksellers CLXC - 354 2011 £125

Martineau, Harriet 1802-1876 *Traditions of Palestine: Times of the Saviour.* London: George Routledge & Sons, 1870. New edition; frontispiece, illustrations, 4 pages ads, original blue cloth, front board with central vignette in gilt, spine lettered in gilt, spine faded and little worn at head and tail, all edges gilt, presentation by author for her nephew, Edward Martineau. Jarndyce Antiquarian Booksellers CLXC - 345 2011 £180

Association – Martineau, Ellen

Martineau, Harriet 1802-1876 *Five Years of Youth; or Sense and Sentiment.* London: Harvey and Darton, 1831. First edition; 12mo., half title, engraved frontispiece, 3 plates, contemporary half tan calf, raised gilt bands, black leather label, spine darkened and little rubbed, hinges carefully repaired, pasted on half tile small piece of paper signed Ellen Martineau. Jarndyce Antiquarian Booksellers CLXC - 279 2011 £225

Martineau, Alice *The Herbaceous Garden.* London: Williams & Norgate, 1913. Second impression; half title, color frontispiece, plates, foldout diagram, 8 pages ads, edges slight spotted, original green cloth lettered in gilt, slightly faded, good plus, signed Ellen J. Martineau. Jarndyce Antiquarian Booksellers CLXC - 353 2011 £45

Martineau, James *A Study of Religion, Its Sources and Contents.* Oxford: Clarendon Press, 1889. Second edition; 2 volumes, half titles, 8 page catalog volume II, original blue cloth, spine lettered in gilt, spines slightly rubbed, good plus, presentation from Robert to Ellen Martineau, great niece of Harriet Martineau. Jarndyce Antiquarian Booksellers CLXC - 360 2011 £35

Association – Martineau, Frances Anne

Martineau, Harriet 1802-1876 *Society in America.* London: Saunders & Otley, 1837. First edition; 3 volumes, half titles, contemporary half maroon calf, spines slightly rubbed, faded to brown, this was the copy author's cousin, Frances Anne Martineau. Jarndyce Antiquarian Booksellers CLXC - 340 2011 £500

Association – Martineau, Harriet

Nightingale, Florence *Notes on Nursing; What It Is and What It Is Not.* London: Harrison, 1860. New edition; half title, original maroon wavy grained cloth by Burn & Co., borders blocked in blind, spine lettered in gilt, carefully rebacked, very good, inscribed by author for Harriet Martineau July 1860. Jarndyce Antiquarian Booksellers CLXC - 595 2011 £2500

Association – Martineau, James

Martineau, Harriet 1802-1876 *Illustrations of Political Economy.* London: Charles Fox, 1832-1834. First edition; 25 parts in 9 volumes in contemporary half dark brown calf, slight rubbing, very good, signed James Martineau, author's younger brother. Jarndyce Antiquarian Booksellers CLXC - 290 2011 £950

Association – Martineau, Jane

Martineau, Harriet 1802-1876 *Deerbrook.* London: Edward Moxon, 1839. First edition; 3 volumes, contemporary half calf, bevelled boards, spines with raised bands and devices in gilt, black leather labels, some minor careful repairs to hinges, top edge gilt, signed by author's niece, Jane Martineau. Jarndyce Antiquarian Booksellers CLXC - 272 2011 £580

Association – Martineau, Margaret

Martineau, Harriet 1802-1876 *Health, Husbandry and Handicraft.* London: Bradbury & Evan, 1861. First edition; half title, 12 page catalog (Jan. 1861), uncut in original red pebble grained cloth, blocked in blind, spine lettered in gilt, carefully recased, spine darkened cloth, slightly wormed on following board, signed presentation inscription Catherine Salt, from author, also signed in pencil Margaret Martineau. Jarndyce Antiquarian Booksellers CLXC - 282 2011 £420

Association – Martineau, Maria

Napier, William Francis Patrick *History of the War in the Peninsula and in the South of France from the Year 1807 to the Year 1814.* London: Thomas William Boone, 1862. New edition; 6 volumes, numerous engraved maps, later 18th century full tan calf, bevelled boards, at some time rebacked, spines gilt in compartments, maroon and black leather labels, hinges and hinges little worn, signed presentation inscription to Maria Martineau from friend, Richd. Napier, with additional signature of Anne Louise Napier, also tipped into prelims volume I is 19 line ALS from Richard Napier to Maria Martineau. Jarndyce Antiquarian Booksellers CLXC - 363 2011 £380

Martineau, Harriet 1802-1876 *Sketches from Life.* Whittaker & Co., 1856. First edition; original brown morocco grained cloth by Westleys, bevelled boards, lettered in gilt, head of spine slightly rubbed, half title, vignette title and plates by W. Banks, nice copy, signed presentation by author for her niece, Maria Martineau. Jarndyce Antiquarian Booksellers CLXC - 339 2011 £250

Martineau, Harriet 1802-1876 *Suggestions Towards the Future Government of India.* London: Smith, Elder & Co., 1858. First edition; half title, final ad leaf, 16 page catalog (Jan. 1858), original brown cloth, paper label, spine little chipped and slightly worn at head and tail, signed presentation from author to niece, Maria Martineau. Jarndyce Antiquarian Booksellers CLXC - 343 2011 £350

Association – Martineau, Robert

Martineau, James *Endeavours After the Christian Life.* London: John Chapman, 1843-1847. First edition; 2 volumes, half titles, final ad leaves, contemporary half brown morocco, spines lettered and with devices in gilt, spines slightly darkened and bit rubbed, each volume with ownership inscription of Martineau family members, Robt. Martineau, Edwd. K. Martineau, author's representation inscription to R. R. Martineau. Jarndyce Antiquarian Booksellers CLXC - 354 2011 £125

Martineau, James *A Study of Religion, Its Sources and Contents.* Oxford: Clarendon Press, 1889. Second edition; 2 volumes, half titles, 8 page catalog volume II, original blue cloth, spine lettered in gilt, spines slightly rubbed, good plus, presentation from Robert to Ellen Martineau, great niece of Harriet Martineau.   Jarndyce Antiquarian Booksellers   CLXC - 360   2011   £35

Association – Marton, George

Cumberland's British Theatre with Remarks, Biographical and Critical, Printed from the Acting Copies as Performed at the Theatres Royal London Volume I. London: John Cumberland, 1826. Volume I, small 8vo., old half calf gilt, hinges cracked but sound, frontispiece, armorial bookplate of George Marton.   R. F. G. Hollett & Son Antiquarian Booksellers   175 - 341   2011   £65

Association – Martyn, Ann

Allestree, Richard *The Whole Duty of Man, laid Down in a Plain and Familiar Way for the Use of All...* London: printed for N. Norton for George Pawles, 1689. Contemporary calf, rather worn, spine cracked and defective, pages xxii, 472, (vi), (ii ad), engraved frontispiece and title, (both little chipped), little loose, good, complete edition, inscription "Ann Martyn her book....1690".   R. F. G. Hollett & Son Antiquarian Booksellers   175 - 22   2011   £350

Association – Marx, Enid

Mawe, John   1764-1829 *The Voyager's Companion; or Shell Collector's Pilot...* by the author, 1821. Third edition; xiv, (2), 56 pages, 2 hand colored plates, original boards, backstrip and corners worn, but in good clean condition, apart from some browning to a tissue guard, Enid Marx's copy with inscription on front endpaper, very scarce.   Ken Spelman Rare Books   68 - 155   2011   £225

Association – Mason, George William

Jeffrey, Francis *Contributions to the Edinburgh Review.* London: printed for Longman, Brown, Green and Longmans, 1844. First collected edition; 222, x14mm., 4 volumes, very attractive contemporary purple morocco, boards framed in blind with multiple rules on either side of a decorative roll and featuring complex scrolling floral cornerpieces, raised bands, spines with gilt titling and compartments decorated in blind with scrolling cornerpieces, intricately gilt turn-ins, all edges gilt, armorial bookplate of George William Mason, trivial wear to leather, backstrips lightly and evenly faded, extremely fine set, joints and hinges entirely unworn and virtually as new internally.   Phillip J. Pirages   59 - 187   2011 $750

Association – Mason, William

Kames, Henry Home   1696-1782 *Sketches of the History of Man.* Edinburgh: for W. Creech, Edinburgh: and for W. Strahan and T. Cadell, 1774. First edition; 2 volumes, 4to., (iii)-xii, 519, (1); (2), 507, (1) pages, wanting half titles, titlepage of volume I little soiled and/or foxed, small blank strip cut away from foot (repaired and not near printed surface), intermittent minor soiling and foxing in volume I, two or three leaves with tears (but not with loss), small old ink stain in one leaf causing small hole with loss of few letters on each page, several early (and interesting) annotations in very good 19th century green half calf gilt with raised bands, minor blemishes apart, very good in sound and pleasing binding with mid 19th century ownership inscription in each volume "Wm. G. Mason 3 Bedford Circus, Exeter 1850".   John Drury Rare Books   153 - 62   2011   £1250

Association – Massingberd, Henry

Smith, Matthew *Memoirs of Secret Service.* Printed for A. Baldwin near the Oxford Arms, 1699. First edition; endpapers foxed, few spots, pages 160, 24, 8vo., early sprinkled calf, rebacked, backstrip with five raised bands, green morocco lettering piece, touch rubbed at extremities with slight wear to one corner, bookplate of Henry Massingberd of Gunby, good.   Blackwell Rare Books   B166 - 97   2011   £695

Association – Matheson, David, Mrs.

MacDonald, George   1824-1905 *A Book of Strife in the Form of the Diary of an Old Soul.* London: printed for the author and to be had by writing to Mr. Hughes 43 Beaufort St. Chelsea, 1880. First edition; tall 12mo., colophon leaf, original plain red cloth, slightly affected by damp, lacking leading f.e.p., slightly worn at head and tail of spine, paper label browned and slightly chipped, inscribed by author for Mrs. David Matheson.   Jarndyce Antiquarian Booksellers   CXCII - 220   2011   £1250

Association – Maude, Constance

James, William *The Literary Remains of the Late Henry James.* Boston: James R. Osgood and Co., 1885. First edition; 8vo., original publisher's red cloth lettered gilt at spine, pages 469, uncut, frontispiece, pencilled ownership signature of historian F. R. Cowell author of 'Cicero and the Roman Republic", signed presentation by A(lice) J(ames) for friend Constance Maude, slight fading at spine, slight mottling and slight marking, otherwise very good.   Any Amount of Books   May 29 2011 - A47621   2011 $340

Association – Maury, Richard

Bernard, George S. *War Talks of Confederate Veterans.* Petersburg: 1892. First edition; xxiii, 335 pages, 2 folding maps, patterned endpapers, CSA gray, both inner joints reglued, ownership inscription of Col. Richard L. Maury, very nice, small ripple to right of backstrip.   Bookworm & Silverfish   679 - 40   2011 $150

Fontaine, James   *A Tale of the Huguenots or Memoirs of a French Refugee Family.*   New York: 1838. First edition; 266 (8) pages, 12mo., Richard L. Maury's copy, endpapers foxed, some foxing to text, patterned cloth with drink ring, signature and bookplate of Col. Richard L. Maury, edges well rubbed, backstrip gilt legible but rubbed.   Bookworm & Silverfish   679 - 196   2011 $225

Hood, Thomas   *"When's & Oddities".*   Philadelphia: 1828. 146, (1) pages, 12mo., with 39 full page cartoon illustrations, half leather rubbed at backstrip edges, with enough label chipping to make it illegible, marbled endpapers, mouse chewed starting at back cover into text block affecting two bottom lines of print diminishing so that only last five leaves are affected through bottom edge of previous 100 pages, damage affects rear terminus cover as a diminishing scrape almost at top, bookplate of Col. Richard L. Maury, Plymouth NC.   Bookworm & Silverfish   662 - 33   2011 $75

Macaulay, Thomas Babington Macaulay, 1st Baron 1800-1859   *Essays, Critical and Miscellaneous.* Philadelphia: 1849.   New edition; 744 pages, half leather rubbed, all edges of backstrip and corners, modest foxing, bookplate of Col. Richard L. Maury with pencil presentation of C. Blackford.   Bookworm & Silverfish   679 - 67   2011 $60

Slaughter, Philip   *A Brief Sketch of the Life of William Green, LL.D.*   Richmond: 1883. First edition; 131 pages, pencil signature of Col. R. L. Maury, good, rear 1/8" of free edge has lost it's cloth and same amount on inner fear free edge, one other small scrape.   Bookworm & Silverfish 678 - 82   2011 $95

Association – Mavrogordato, J.

Boswell, James   1740-1795   *Boswell's Life of Johnson Including Boswell's Journal of a Tour to the Hebrides and Johnson's Diary of a Journey into North Wales.*   Oxford: at the Clarendon Press, 1887.   6 volumes, 229 x 152mm., especially pleasing contemporary prize bindings of polished calf, handsomely gilt for H. Sotheran & Co. (stamp signed on front pastedown), boards with gilt double rule border and with gilt scholastic arms on each of the six front covers, raised bands, spines elaborately gilt in compartments featuring scrolling foliate cornerpieces and intricate floral centerpiece, brown morocco labels, ornate gilt turn-ins, marbled endpapers, all edges gilt, with 14 plates as called for (8 of them folding), including facsimiles of Johnson's handwriting, map and chart of Johnson's contemporaries; Latin presentation bookplate to J. Mavrogordato indicating that this set was a prize given to him by the headmaster, William Rutherford of the College of Saint Peter, Westminster, one volume with very minor flaking to one join, odd trivial mark to covers but in exceptionally fine condition, bindings essentially unworn and text probably unread.   Phillip J. Pirages   59 - 155   2011 $1800

Association – Mawer, John

Gent, Thomas   *The Most Delectable, Scriptural and Pious History of the Famous and Magnificent Great Eastern Window .. in St. Peter's Cathedral, York...*   York: impress for the author in St. Peter's Gate, 1762. 8vo., pages (iv), xxiii, (i), 196, 12, (iv), 24, (vi) + large folding engraved plates (crudely hand colored) of E. Window and one other engraved plate headed "Pious Contemplations", contemporary sprinkled sheep boards, double rule bordered in blind, all edges red sprinkled, 1970's sheep reback + corners, browned, spotted, few page and plate edges just cropped, folding engraved plate splitting at folds and with handling tear, in places sometime repaired on rear, last leaf cut down, old leather darkened and chipped in places, bound in after titlepage is special presentation seal to Revd. John Mawer from author, from the collection of Christopher Ernest Weston 1947-2010.   Unsworths Booksellers   24 - 100 2011   £650

Association – Max Muller, Georgina

Aytoun, William Edmonstoun   *The Book of Ballads.* William Blackwood Sons, 1903.   New edition; illustrations, original blue cloth, gilt, bevelled boards, all edges gilt, fine, presentation inscription to W. G. (Wilhelm) Max Muller Xmas 1903, signed G.M.M. (Georgina Max Muller, 1853-1911, wife of Freidrich Max Muller 1832-1907, to her son).   Jarndyce Antiquarian Booksellers   CXCI - 318   2011   £50

Association – Max Muller, Wilhelm G.

Aytoun, William Edmonstoun *The Book of Ballads.* William Blackwood Sons, 1903. New edition; illustrations, original blue cloth, gilt, bevelled boards, all edges gilt, fine, presentation inscription to W. G. (Wilhelm) Max Muller Xmas 1903, signed G.M.M. (Georgina Max Muller, 1853-1911, wife of Freidrich Max Muller 1832-1907, to her son). Jarndyce Antiquarian Booksellers   CXCI - 318   2011   £50

Association – Maxwell, William Stirling

Collier, Jane *An Essay on the Art of Ingeniously Tormenting...* London: A. Millar, 1757. Second edition; 8vo., pages (2), iv, 234, little toned around fore edge of titlepage, clean copy with wide margins, bound in contemporary calf, bit worn, rebacked some time ago in brown morocco gilt, large armorial bookplate of Sir William Stirling Maxwell, engraved cat and mouse frontispiece.   Second Life Books Inc.   174 - 101   2011 $450

Association – Mayall, F. Murray

Montagu, Mary Pierrepone Wortley 1689-1762 *Letters of the Right Hon. Lady M--y W-----y M-----.* London: printed for T. Cadell, 1784. 2 volumes, small octavo ix, (), 220; (2), 272 pages, some penciling, original full calf, hinges broken, mended, extremities worn, bookplate of F. Murray H. Mayall, signature of F. Mayall.   Jeff Weber Rare Books   163 - 197   2011 $125

Association – Mayhew, Rosa

Scenes and Incidents of Foreign Travel. London: Robert Tyas, circa, 1844. Frontispiece and plates, slightly foxed, small internal tear to leading f.e.p., original dark blue cloth, blocked in blind, spine decorated in gilt, spine slightly faded, signature of Rosa Mayhew, Renier booklabel, all edges gilt, very good.   Jarndyce Antiquarian Booksellers   CXCI - 536   2011   £58

Association – McAllister, John

Benezet, Anthony *Observations on the Inslaving, Importing and Purchasing of Negores.* Germantown: Christopher Sower, 1760. Second edition; small 8vo. original full leather Saur binding, fine, splendid set (small partial chip on top of spine, contemporary bookplate and signature of John McAllister.   M & S Rare Books, Inc.   90 - 37   2011 $2000

Association – McAlpin, Charles Williston

Field, Michael, Pseud. *Stephania: a Trialogue.* London: Elkin Mathews & John Lane, 1892. One of 250 copies; 200 x 150mm., 6 p.l., 1, 100 pages, 4 leaves (colophon and ads), exceptionally attractive modeled goatskin by Mrs. Annie MacDonald of the Guild of Women Binders, front cover with large lobed frame, its upper corner enclosing the binder's initial and the date (1897), lower corners with daffodil blooms, large central panel showing an elaborately detailed scene featuring a woman with long, flowing hair entreating the god Mercury in his signature winged hat and sandals, the two figures, surmounted by an imperial crown through which twines a sprig of mistletoe (a design that appears in the woodcut frame on titlepage), lower cover showing the woman kneeling by a man reclining on a couch, this scene enclosed in an oval beaded frame, flat spine with modeled title flanked by pine cone device at head an tail, green watered silk pastedowns framed in unusual turn-ins, decorated with gilt vines and calf circles painted green and blue, leather hinges, top edge gilt, other edges untrimmed, titlepage with full woodcut border filled with intertwined pine branches and mistletoe, colophon with pine cone device, verso of front flyleaf with engraved bookplate of Charles Williston McAlpin, extra paper title labels tipped onto rear blank; two tiny red (ink?) marks to upper cover, inevitable offsetting from turn-ins to endpapers, one detached front flyleaf tipped onto front free endpaper, other trivial defects, still very attractive copy, binding lustrous and scarcely worn, leaves fresh and clean.   Phillip J. Pirages   59 - 107   2011 $4500

Association – McCauley, Michael

Thompson, Jim *Fireworks: the Lost Writings of Jim Thompson.* New York: Donald I. Fine, 1988. First edition; very good, light bumping to extremities, dust jacket near fine, corresponding creasing, signed note signed by Polito laid in, signed by editors Robert Polito and Michael McCauley.   Bella Luna Books   May 29 2011 - t6144   2011 $82

Association – McClure, Michael

Charters, Ann *The Portable Beat Reader.* New York: Viking, 1992. First edition; 600+ pages, fine in fine dust jacket, exceptional copy, this copy belonged to Nelson Lyon, inscribed to him or signed and dated by William Burroughs, Allen Ginsberg, Gregory Corso, Ed Sanders, Michael McClure and Anne Waldman.   Ken Lopez Bookseller   154 - 12   2011 $1250

Association – McConnors, Frank

Sterling, George *A Wine of Wizardry and Other Poems.* San Francisco: A. M. Robertson, 1909. First edition; 8vo., 137 pages, signed presentation from author for Frank McConnors, original publisher's burgundy red cloth lettered gilt on spine, gilt illustration on front cover, slight fading at spine, otherwise bright, very good+ copy. Any Amount of Books   May 26 2011 - A39601   2011 $503

Association – McCoy, Bill

Van De Water, Frederic *The Real McCoy.* Garden City: Doubleday, Doran and Co., 1931. First edition; fine in near fine dust jacket but for small chip on spine, inscribed by subject of the book "To Bob Davis, the man who suggested that this yarn be put in print. Bill McCoy", scarce either in jacket or signed. Between the Covers   169 - BTC342132   2011 $950

Association – McFarland, A. J. B.

Caprilli, Frederico *The Caprilli Papers: Principles of Outdoor Equitation.* London: J. A. Allen & Co. Ltd., 1967. First edition; frontispiece, pages 40 + 40 illustrations on 26 further pages, original red cloth, white lettering on spine, slightly bumped at lower spine, otherwise very good in very good dust jacket with some ink underlining on 8 pages by former owner, this was Lieut. Col. A. J. B. McFarland, scarce. Any Amount of Books   May 26 2011 - A722285   2011 $402

Association – McIntosh, George

Stanley, Henry Morton 1841-1904 *In Darkest Africa of the Quest, Rescue an Retreat of Emin Governor of Equatoria.* New York: Charles Scribner's Sons, 1891. 2 volumes, octavo, xiv, 547; xvi, 540 pages, 2 steel engravings, 150 illustrations and maps, 3 maps located in rear pockets, one map has repaired tear, two smaller maps have chips at corner folds, generally in very good condition, original full green cloth with black stamped image of Africa on upper cover, gilt titles and reproduction of author's signature, gilt spine titles, rubbed, bookplate of George W. McIntosh, Doylestown, PA. Jeff Weber Rare Books   163 - 214   2011 $75

Association – McKnight, J.

Scott, Joseph *The United States Gazetteer: Containing an Authentic Description of the Several States, Their Situation....* Philadelphia: F. and R. Bailey, 1795. First edition; 12mo., (iii)-vi, (294) pages, engraved title, large engraved folding map, 18 smaller engraved folding maps, contemporary sheep, very skillfully rebacked retaining original spine label, endpapers neatly replaced with period paper, usual light offsetting on maps and on facing text pages, few stray spots, else very good, very attractive, early signature of J. McKnight. Joseph J. Felcone Inc.   Fall Miscellany 2010 - 107   2011 $10,000

Association – McManaway, J. G.

Woodward, G. L. *English Play 1641-1700.* Chicago: The Newbury Library, 1945. Full leather with lovely gilt decorations to covers and spine, as well as matching inner gilt, decorations, very nearly fine, inscribed by co-compiler, J. G. McManaway for Mary Morley Crapo, Viscountess Eccles. Lupack Rare Books   May 26 2011 - ABE345163586   2011 $100

Association – McMaster, Gilbert

Symington, Andrew *The Duty of Stated and Select Private Christian Fellowship Briefly Inculcated and Directed.* Paisley: printed by Stephen Young, 1823. First edition; 8vo., 44 pages, couple of short closed marginal tears, near contemporary ink inscription on upper margin of titlepage, rebound recently in cloth, spine lettered gilt, original blue upper wrapper preserved on which is early 19th century ownership inscription of Rev. Gilbert McMaster (of) Duanesburgh (i.e Duanesbury in Schenactady County, NY). John Drury Rare Books   153 - 144   2011   £175

Association – McNeill, William

United States. War Department - 1825 *Military Laws of the United States to which is Prefixed the Constitution of the United States.* Washington: Edward De Krafft, 1825. First edition; xxxi, (1), 279 pages, contemporary sheep, foxed, binding scuffed but very tight and solid, William G. McNeill's copy, signed and dated 1827 on titlepage and with his name neatly lettered ink on front cover, portfolio and fine morocco backed slipcase. Joseph J. Felcone Inc.   Fall Miscellany 2010 - 121   2011 $2200

Association – McPherson, James Allan

Jones, Ann *Women Who Kill.* New York: Holt, Rinehart and Winston, 1980. First edition; near fine in near fine dust jacket with half inch tear on front panel, presentation copy, inscribed by James Allan McPherson for Peter Taylor. Between the Covers   169 - BTC336596   2011 $650

Association – McQueen, M.

Taylor, Jeremy 1613-1667 *The Rule and Exercise of Holy Living and Holy Dying...* London: Miles Flesher for Richard Royston, 1680. Twelfth edition; 2 volumes, 8vo., pages (xiv), 335, (i) + engraved titlepage and 1 double page engraved plates stub-mounted; (xiv), 259, (v) + engraved titlepage and 1 double page engraved plate stub mounted, contemporary black polished turkey, spines multi rule panelled in blind with contrasting stylised flower centerpieces, boards entirely blind tooled with triangular and rectangular densely ruled blocks, tulip & carnation heads, gouges and small 5 pointed stars, board edges and turn-ins decorative roll gilt, "Dutch-comb swirl" "made" endpapers, all edges gilt, 3 color pink, white and pale blue 2 core-sewn endbands, pink silk page markers, wholly unrestored "Sombre" bindings (age toned, few small stains, edges trimmed close, joints and edges rubbed, spines slightly faded, contemporary ink inscription M. McQueen", armorial bookplate of Shute Barrington, from the collection of Christopher Ernest Weston 1947-2010. Unsworths Booksellers 24 - 52 2011 £950

Association – McQuerry, Mary Noble

Bateman, James *A Second Century of Orchidaceous Plants.* London: L. Reeve & Co., 1867. 100 hand colored lithographed plates (light foxing to a few, mostly marginal), slight tanning to 3, 2 small marginal stains to a plate, most plates clean and fresh, each with one or two pages of descriptive letterpress, 4to., pages viii, plates and letterpress, original green gilt lettered cloth (flecking to lower margin & lower edge of covers, also slightly to head of spine, few small scuffs & minor stains to covers, corners worn, light rubbing to edges of spine, light foxing to 2 edges of pages, pages and plates restitched, half title and last page tanned, correction slip pasted over imprint on title, scattered light foxing to letterpress pages, heavy to 1, few inner joints open, the copy of Mary Noble McQuerry. Raymond M. Sutton, Jr. May 26 2011 - 13000 2011 $6000

Association – McSavaney, Ray

Misrach, Richard *Richard Misrach.* San Francisco: Grapestake Gallery, 1979. First edition, of a total edition of 100 cloth bound copies, this unnumbered; fine in fine glassine jacket, signed and warmly inscribed in year of publication by Misrach to his friend and fellow photographer Ray McSavaney. Jeff Hirsch Books ny 2010 2011 $3500

Association – Medcalfe, Violet

Potter, Beatrix 1866-1943 *The Tale of Peter Rabbit.* London and New York: Frederick Warne and Co., 1904. Second published edition; with double page colored endpapers (i.e. seventh or eighth printing), 12mo., 85, (1, printer's slug) pages, color illustrated endpapers, color frontispiece and 26 color illustrations, dark green boards, white lettered with pictorial label in color, original glazed paper glassine dust jacket printed in black with vertical lines at top and bottom of spine indicating where the fold should be for the front panel, with ad on rear panel for "The Peter Rabbit Books" listing five titles, top half inch and part of bottom half inch of jacket spine (including the " of the word net in the price) are missing as well as small piece 5/8 x 1/2 inch missing on top of back panel at spine, overall very bright, fine copy, in very good example of exceptionally are dust jacket, printed glassine jacket is of the utmost rarity, presentation copy inscribed by author for Violet Medcalfe. David Brass Rare Books, Inc. May 26 2011 - 01527 2011 $9500

Association – Melchior, Georgius

Hyginus, Caius Julius *Fabularum Liber... Poeticon Astronomicon Libri Quatuor... Arati Phaenomena Graece...* Basel: ex officina Hervagiana, per E. Episcopium August, 1570. Folio, (8), 251, (29) pages, last leaf blank device on titlepage, woodcut illustrations, contemporary vellum over pasteboards, spine slightly cracked, from the library of the Earls of Macclesfield at Shirburn Castle, the Georgius Melchior copy, 1664 with inscription. Maggs Bros. Ltd. 1440 - 114 2011 £1500

Association – Melville

Defoe, Daniel *A Tour thro' the Whole Island of Great Britain.* London: printed for S. Birt et al, 1753. Fifth edition; 4 volumes, 12mo., pages viii, 388, (xii); iv, 418, (xviii); iv, 312, (xviii); iv, 371 (xxi), contemporary sprinkled calf, spine double rule gilt, dark red lettering pieces gilt, volume number gilt direct, boards double rule gilt bordered, board edges decorative roll in blind, all edges slightly red sprinkled, red and white sewn endbands, browned and spotted, most so in volume I, dark offsetting from turn-ins, rubbed and worn, especially headcaps, joints cracking, front joint of volume 1 nearly split, labels lost from spines of volumes 1 and 4, armorial bookplate of 'Melville', from the collection of Christopher Ernest Weston 1947-2010. Unsworths Booksellers 24 - 85 2011 £260

Association – Melville, General

Lorimer, John *A Concise Essay on Magnetism with an Account Declination and Inclination of the Magnetic Needle and an Attempt to Ascertain the Cause of the Variation Thereof.* London: printed for the author and sold by W. Faden, 1795. First edition; inscribed by author to General Melville, from the collection of Harrison D. Horblit with his booklabel, very good, inscribed copy in later half leather, cloth binding with gilt lettering on spine and bottom 1.5" of spine cover chipped, covers edge wear, marbled endpapers with f.f.e.p. clipped, six foldout plates as issued, plates foxed, scattered foxing. By the Book, L. C. 26 - 105 2011 $900

Association – Merrill, Charles Edmund

Lawrence, David Herbert 1885-1930 *Amores.* New York: B. W. Huebsch, 1916. First American edition; 8vo., pages (xii), 116, internally fine, original brown cloth boards, spine and upper board lettered in gold, top edge gilt, original cream dust jacket printed in black, dust jacket expertly restored at spine and top edge, small tear not affecting text to upper panel, small bookplate of Charles Edmund Merrill Jr. to pastedown, bookplate of Constance M. and Karl Andrew Muir. Simon Finch Rare Books Zero - 329 2011 £500

Association – Metzker, Ray

Taken by Design: Photographs from The Institute of Design 1937-1971. Chicago: University of Chicago Press, 2002. First edition; very fine in photo illustrated boards, issued without dust jacket, signed by a large number of photographers and some of the editors, among the signatures are Yasuhiro Ishimoto, Marvin E. Newton (twice), Barbara Crane, Ray K. Metzker, Joseph Jachna, Joseph Sterling (twice), Kenneth Josephson, David Travis, Keith Davis and quite a few others, unique copy. Jeff Hirsch Books ny 2010 2011 $750

Association – Mexborough

Selby, Charles *Maximums and Specimens of William Muggins, Natural Philosopher and Citizen of the World.* London: Routledge, 1846. Plates, bound by Zaehnsdorf in half maroon calf, raised bands, decorated in gilt, black morocco labels, endpapers replaced, original cloth spine, one cloth cover bound in at end, Mexborough armorial bookplate, top edge gilt, handsome. Jarndyce Antiquarian Booksellers CXCI - 487 2011 £140

Association – Meynell, Wilfrid

Meynell, Alice *Poems.* London: Burns & Oates, 1914. Eleventh thousand; half title, frontispiece by Sargent slightly browned, 2 pages ads, original grey-brown cloth, rubbed, spine darkened, Wilfrid Meynell's presentation copy to Margot Ross, with holograph poem "The Modern Poet" numbered in corner '75' by Alice Meynell on slightly browned lined paper tipped in at end, with 2 cuttings inserted. Jarndyce Antiquarian Booksellers CLXC - 392 2011 £85

Association – Milburn, Geoff

Jones, Trevor *Cumbrian Rock. 100 Years fo Climbing in the Lake District.* Pic Publications, 1988. Limited signed edition, no. 164 of 250 copies; large 8vo., original glazed pictorial boards, pages 256, well illustrated, signed by Jones and co-author Geoff Milburn, with short inscription by Milburn. R. F. G. Hollett & Son Antiquarian Booksellers 173 - 632 2011 £95

Association – Milford Haven, George, 2nd Marquis of

Voltaire, Francois Marie Arouet De 1694-1778 *La Pucelle D'Orleans.* Londres: Paris, 1775. First enlarged edition; large 8vo., pages xv, (1), 447, (1), frontispiece and 21 engraved plates, all edges gilt, very crisp, fresh copy, contemporary full deep green morocco, red morocco spine lettering piece lettered in gilt, within gilt decorative compartments, triple gilt borders on each panel with fleur-de-lis devices at each corner, royal blue floral endpapers, slight signs of wear at head and foot of spine and outer corners, bookplate of George, Second Marquis of Milford Haven. Simon Finch Rare Books Zero - 407 2011 £3500

Association – Miller, Charles

Burroughs, Stephen *Memoirs of Stephen Burroughs.* Hanover: Benjamin True, 1798. Boston: Caleb Bingham 1804. First edition; 2 volumes, original calf, first volume 8vo., (2), vi-vii, (8), 296 pages, errata bottom of page 296, title in red leather on spine, bookplate of William L. Clements Library of American History, University of Michigan, top edge titlepage repaired with old paper, name in ink of Charles Miller, Feb. 14, 1848 on titlepage, small hole on pages 111 and 112 affecting few letters, minor foxing throughout, else very good, exceedingly rare; second volume 16mo., original calf with title in gilt on red leather label on spine, five gilt bands on spine, 202 pages, former owner's name on front pastedown sheet, waterstain to bottom third of front endpapers and titlepage, moderately rubbed to spine ends and extremities, else very good, exceedingly rare. Buckingham Books May 26 2011 - 25797 2011 $6750

Association – Miller, James

Johnson, Joseph *George MacDonald: a Biographical and Critical Appreciation.* London: Sir Isaac Pitman & Sons, 1906. Half title, engraved frontispiece, title in red and black uncut in secondary binding of slightly lighter maroon cloth without title and name on front board, spine faded with small splits at head and tail, bookplate of James L. Miller with inscription. Jarndyce Antiquarian Booksellers CXCII - 353 2011 £50

Association – Millers, W.

Garnett, Thomas *Popular Lectures on Zoonomia or the Laws of Animal Life in Health and Disease.* Printed by W. Savage Printer to the Royal Institution of Great Brtain for the benefit of the author's children by his executors, 1804. First edition; 4to., old half calf, gilt, elegantly tooled spine and Spanish marbled boards, extremities little rubbed and worn, pages xxii, 325, copper engraved portrait frontispiece, 3 text illustrations, few margins little creased, portrait little foxed in margins and slightly offset on to title, contemporary signature of W. Millers, St. John's on title. R. F. G. Hollett & Son Antiquarian Booksellers General Catalogue Summer 2010 - 974 2011 £225

Association – Million, J. M., Mrs.

Brown, Hallie Q. *Homespun Heroines and Other Women of Distinction...* Xenia: Aldine Publishing Co., 1926. First edition; 8vo., pages viii (252), green cloth (little soiled and faded), stamped in gilt, signed by author, previous owner's name "Mrs. J. M. Millon", some pencil underlining of the Harriet Tubman section, front hinge tender, very good. Second Life Books Inc. 174 - 74 2011 $950

Association – Mills, Edgar

Goldsmith, Oliver 1730-1774 *The Vicar of Wakefield: a Tale Supposed to be Written by Himself.* Salisbury: Printed for B. Collins for F. Newbery, 1766. First edition, variant B; 2 volumes, 172 x 108mm., terminal blank in volume I, beautiful scarlet crushed morocco, heavily gilt by Riviere & Son, covers with French fillet frame, spine with raised bands and handsomely gilt compartments, lovely gilt inner dentelles, all edges gilt, leather book labels of Roderick Terry, (Edgar) Mills and Doris Louise Benz, lower corner of terminal blank in first volume skillfully renewed, artful repair and faint glue stains at inner margin of B3 in second volume, other isolated trivial defects, very fine, text nearly pristine, especially bright and handsome binding. Phillip J. Pirages 59 - 50 2011 $6500

Association – Mills, Isaac

Edgeworth, Maria 1768-1849 *Practical Education.* New York: George F. Hopkins for Self and Brown and Stansbury, 1801. Providence: Lippitt, Boston, Wait, 1815. First American edition volume I, Second US edition volume II; 8vo., pages vi, 344; 312, contemporary leather, hinges loose, some foxing but good set, nice contemporary binder's ticket on front pastedown of volume I, contemporary ownership signature of Isaac Mills in volume I. Second Life Books Inc. 174 - 136 2011 $225

Association – Milne, Alexander

Bain, William *An Essay on the Variation of the Compass, Showing How far It Is Influence by a Change in the Direction of the Ship's Head, with an Exposition of the Dangers Arising to Navigators from Not Allowing for This Change of Variation.* (bound with) *Magnetism.* (and) *A Popular View of Mr. Barlow's Magnetical Experiments and Discoveries...* (article from Edinburgh Philosophical Journal Volume XI No. 21 July 1824, pages 65-86). Edinburgh: printed for William Blackwood and John Murray, 1817. 3 works in 1 volume, 8vo., pages (vi), 140, tables, throughout, folding chart; pages 96, numerous small illustrations; half calf and marbled boards, spine with lettering and decoration in gilt, slightly rubbed, bookplate of Sir Alexander Milne to front pastedown, his signature, occasional pencil annotations throughout, bookplate of Turner Collection, University of Keele. Simon Finch Rare Books Zero - 124 2011 £475

Association – Milner, J. A.

Barrow, Isaac *Several Sermons Against Evil Speaking.* London: printed for Barbazon Aylmer, 1678. 8vo., pages (viii), 243, (i), 140, (iv), contemporary speckled calf, boards blind ruled, board edges 'broken rule', gilt, text block edges densely red sprinkled, blue and white sewn endbands, late 20th century blind ruled and unlettered calf reback, touch of minor spotting, leather rubbed at extremities, corners just worn, contemporary ink inscription "Rd Scott", ink inscription "Jonathan Scott 1746 Betton", also "J. A. Milner/Shrewsbury/1889", from the collection of Christopher Ernest Weston 1947-2010. Unsworths Booksellers 24 - 2 2011 £275

Association – Minet, William

Paule, George *Life of the Most Reverend and Religious Prelate John Whitgift, Lord Archbishop of Canterbury.* London: printed by Thomas Snodham, 1612. small 4to., pages (viii), 94, (ii), woodcut portrait of Whitgift on titlepage verso, early 21st century retrospective ruled calf binding by CEW, title soiled text block trimmed to printed border and sometimes just inside at top and fore-edge, old f.e.p. corner repaired, early hand has annotated head of blank leaf A1 and final blank leaf N4 armorial bookplate of "James Comerford" on front pastedown, mid 19th century ownership in Philip Bliss's hand on 17th century flyleaf reading "Bodleian Catalogue 1843, p. 62" and at foot of page I signature "P.B.43": and flowery label, presented by William Minet at foot of front pastedown, from the collection of Christopher Ernest Weston 1947-2010. Unsworths Booksellers 24 - 34 2011 £450

Association – Minor, Berkeley

Edmonds, George *Facts and Falsehoods Concerning the War on the South 1861-1865.* Memphis: 1904. (2), (1) viii, (1)-271 pages, issued in wrappers, here in later half leather and marbled boards, new backstrip, f.f.e.p. is pulling, extensive inscription from Berkeley Minor family. Bookworm & Silverfish 678 - 31 2011 $325

Association – Minto, Earl of

Hamilton, Anthony 1646-1720 *Memoires Du Comte De Gramont.* Londres: Chez Edwards, 1793. 299 x 241mm., 5 p.l. (including portrait of Grammont, portrait of author and frontispiece), 313, 77 pages, (3) leaves, once very handsome and still quite pleasing period crimson straight grain morocco, covers with tooled and ruled border in gilt and blind (including very delicate gilt floral tools at corners), raised bands, spine ends with rows of stippled scales, spine panels with stippled gilt quatrefoil superimposed over elaborate blind tooled centerpiece incorporating various fleurons, all edges gilt, 78 engraved plates (some dated 1792 or 1793), 77 of them portraits, shelf label with motto "Credunt Quod Vient" (identified in pencil on front flyleaf as belonging to the Earl of Minto), large paper copy; joints bit flaked, spine uniformly dulled, but stately binding completely solid and certainly attractive, bright covers, 3 gatherings toward end with prominent (though faint) mottle foxing, intermittent minor foxing elsewhere, light offsetting opposite a number of plates, isolated marginal soiling and other minor imperfections but still quite pleasing, copy internally, leaves extremely fresh and margins vast. Phillip J. Pirages 59 - 51 2011 $1900

Association – Mirehouse

Plautus, Titus Maccius *Comedies of Plautus.* London: printed for T. Becket and P. A. De Hondt, 1769-1774. Volumes 1 and 2 are second edition, volumes 3-5 all First editions; 5 volumes, 8vo., full brown leather bindings, hinges bit used, sides dull, slight splitting otherwise reasonable complete near very good set with clean text, pages 1957, volumes 1 and 2 have 2 neat names and dates on front blanks, all have Mirehouse bookplate. Any Amount of Books May 29 2011 - A32674 2011 $306

Association – Mitchell, Arthur

Ford, Richard *A Hand-Book for Travellers in Spain and Readers at Home.* London: John Murray, 1845. First edition; half titles, engraved folding map, pages xii, 1-556; vi, 557-1064, 8vo., recent red buckram, gilt lettered backstrips (titles between gilt rules), gilt dated at foot, ads on laid down yellow chalked endpapers, ink ownership inscription of Arthur C. Mitchell dated Sept. 2nd 1871 at head of titlepages, red sprinkled edges, good. Blackwell Rare Books B166 - 39 2011 £675

Association – Mitchell, George Osborne

Chaucer, Geoffrey 1340-1400 *Workes of Geoffrey Chaucer.* London: Imprinted by John Kyngston for John Wight, 1561. Rare first issue; folio, (14), ccclxxviii leaves (irregular foliation), title within woodcut border, woodcut border, 22 woodcuts, large and small historiated and decorative initials and other ornaments, black letter, fifty-six lines, double columns, early 20th century antique style dark brown calf, expertly and almost invisible rebacked with original spine laid down, covers with double blind fillet border, spine in six compartments with five raised bands, ruled in blind and dated in gilt at foot and with brown morocco gilt lettering label, title lightly soiled with upper blank margin renewed, lower corner of first two leaves strengthened, few tiny holes or paper flaws, occasional foxing or faint dampstaining on few leaves, short (2 inch) repaired tear to lower margin of Mmm6, not affecting text, bookplate with monogram of Dr. George Osborne Mitchell, early ink signature of Anne Abdy and Hercules Holiambe (?) and some additional early ink annotations on title. David Brass Rare Books, Inc. May 26 2011 - 00642 2011 $48,500

Association – Modarressi, Mitra

Tyler, Anne 1941- *Tumble Tower.* New York: Orchard Books, 1993. First edition; illustrations by Mitra Modarressi, near fine, spine ends bumped, dust jacket fine, inscribed by author and signed by artist. Bella Luna Books May 29 2011 - t5321 2011 $82

Association – Moiroud, P. A.

Huygens, Christiaan *Opera Varia.* Lugduni Batavvorum: Janssonios Vander Aa, 1724. First collected edition; 4 books in one volume, 4to., (18), (1-4) 5-776, (18) pages, frontispiece, 56 folding plates, contemporary full calf, raised bands, gilt stamped spine panels, gilt stamped red morocco spine label, covers and joints rubbed, hinges beginning to split, very good, bookplate of Andras Gedeon and P. A. Moiroud, with J. B. de Bouvou signature on title dated 1758, very good.   Jeff Weber Rare Books   161 - 224   2011 $5500

Association – Monda, Joe

Floyd, Bryan Alec *The Long War Dead.* New York: Avon, 1976. First edition; intended dedication, this copy inscribed by author to Joe Monda, rubbing and crease to spine, very good in wrappers.   Ken Lopez Bookseller   154 - 230   2011 $300

Association – Monnais, Edoaurd

Waldor, Melanie *Poesies du Coeur.* Paris: Louis Janet, 1835. First edition; (315 pages, including errata), 8vo., contemporary quarter brown calf over matching marbled boards, gilt decorated spine with floral design, contrasting gilt lettered title label, half title, scarce wood engraved frontispiece and title vignette by Jean Gigoux, except for light waterstain on margin to some sheets and small chip to lower spine edge, near fine copy, with ALS to Edouard Monnais.   Paulette Rose Fine and Rare Books   32 - 1182   2011 $400

Association – Montagu, Frederick

Robertson, David *A Tour through the Isle of Man; to Which is Subjoined a Review of all the Manks History.* London: printed for the author by E. Hodson, 1794. Large paper copy, 8vo., pages (xii), 235, (i) + 8 sepia aquatint plates, contemporary straight grained mauve morocco, five flat raised bands spine triple rule and decorative pallet gilt, top and bottom compartment have symmetrical oblong centrepieces, gilt between decorative pallets in blind, 3 other compartments filled with massed French influence 'rolling breakers' decorative pallets gilt, lettered in gilt direct, boards triple rule gilt borders with 'acanthus' roll in blind within, board edges alternating double full and single broken hatch fillet roll in blind, turn-ins similarly tooled, 'French Shell' 'made' endpapers, all edges similarly marbled, blue and white sewn endbands, pink silk page marker, plates bit foxed and few spots to pages, touch scratched, spines little faded and upper joint slightly rubbed, unidentified bookplate, decorative bookplate of Frederick J. G. Montagu, booklabel of John Sparrow, pencil inscription Catherine of Fountayne, pencil annotations in same hand, from the collection of Christopher Ernest Weston 1947-2010.   Unsworths Booksellers   24 - 138   2011   £350

Association – Montague, Silke

Voltaire, Francois Marie Arouet De   1694-1778 *Oeuvres Completes.* Kehl: De L'Imprimerie de la Societe Litteraire Typographique, 1784. 230 x 145mm., 69 volumes, exceptionally attractive contemporary flamed calf, covers with gilt braided border, flat spines with six compartments, each compartment with bands above and below consisting of gilt Greek key roll flanked by triple gilt rules, 3 compartments with large sunburst centerpiece within a circular wreath, other compartments with morocco labels, two conventional titling labels of red and olive green and circular volume number label of dark blue within a beaded collar, turn-ins with leafy foliate gilt stamps, marbled endpapers, edges painted yellow, 2 engraved portraits and 14 plates, front pastedown of each volume with at least faint vestiges of removed bookplate (usually hardly noticeable), front flyleaf of each volume with modern two-line ownership stamp of Silke Montague; 2 volumes with hints of now erased pencil annotations on many leaves (3 other volumes with lesser numbers of such erased penciled notes), 3 consecutive leaves in one volume slightly discolored by minor spill, occasional gatherings with very slight overall browning (isolated signatures bit more noticeably affected, but never seriously so), final volume with light browning and foxing, other trivial imperfections, outstanding copy, bindings extraordinarily bright and virtually without wear, text remarkably fresh and clean.   Phillip J. Pirages   59 - 61   2011 $16,000

Association – Montefiore, Francis

Ashley, Evelyn *The Life of Henry John Temple, Viscount Palmerston 1846-1865.* London: Richard Bentley & Son, 1876. 2 volumes, original cloth gilt, spines faded, pages viii, 380; viii, 341, with 2 frontispiece portraits, some joints tender, armorial bookplate of Sir Francis Montefiore.   R. F. G. Hollett & Son Antiquarian Booksellers   175 - 52   2011   £75

Association – Montgomery, M. F.

Landon, Letitia Elizabeth *Ethel Churchill; or the Two Brides.* London: Henry Colburn, 1837. First edition; 3 volumes, half title volume I, uncut in contemporary drab boards, maroon cloth spines, paper labels, spines faded and slightly darkened, labels little darkened, small booklabels of Lady Mary Stewart and M. F. Montgomery, Convoy, good plus, internally very clean set.   Jarndyce Antiquarian Booksellers   CLXC - 72   2011   £750

Association – Montgomery, Robert

Johnston's Penny Fireside Journal a Magazine of Amusing and Instructive Literature. London: W. Johnston, 1843-1845. 4 volumes (of 5), few spots and stains here and there, 8vo., contemporary maroon half roan, not quite uniform, contemporary signature on each title of Robert Montgomery of ?Conway and his armorial stamp inside front covers, good, rare.   Blackwell Rare Books   B166 - 56   2011   £400

Manstein, Cristof Hermann *Memoirs of Russia, Historical, Political and Military from the Year MDCCXXVII to MDCCXLIV.* Dublin: printed for James Williams at No. 5 in Skinner Row, 1770. viii, 424, (8) pages, index, 8vo., few pages little mottled, some worming not affecting text to outer top corner from pages 371 to end, full contemporary calf, raised bands, gilt label, some insect damage to several areas of surface leather and foot of top joint, bookplate of Robert Montgomery of Convoy.   Jarndyce Antiquarian Booksellers   CXCI - 568   2011   £520

Association – Moodey, Henricus Riddell

Herodotus *Herodoti Halicarnassei Historiarum Libri IX.* Oxonii: Sumtibus J. Cooke et J. Parker et J. Payne et J. Mackinlay, Londini, 1808. 2 volumes, 8vo., pages xxx, 409, (i); (ii), 394, (lvi), contemporary russia, four double raised bands spine, broken rule gilt compartments with blind tooled elaborate centre stars composed of small tools and centered with small circles gilt, lettered, numbered, 'placed & dated' direct in gilt, boards dual single rule intersecting gilt bordered with 'facing drawer handle' roll in blind between rules and 'curtain freize' roll in blind innermost, board edges 'broken-hatch' roll gilt at corners, turn-ins "Grecian Key" roll gilt, "French Shell" 'made' endpapers, all edges marbled thus, pale blue and purple double core sewn endbands, pale blue silk page markers, little light foxing, joints rubbed and cracking, top compartment of volume 2 spine defective, contemporary ink inscription "Henricus Riddell Moody e coll. Oriel", from the collection of Christopher Ernest Weston 1947-2010.   Unsworths Booksellers   24 - 108   2011   £40

Association – Moon, Marjorie

Cock Robin. A Pretty Painted Toy for Either Girl or Boy. London: John Harris, circa, 1830's, 12mo., yellow printed paper wrappers with some light overall soiling and some foxing, mostly on blank endpapers, this copy was Marjorie Moon's and has her bookplate on verso of front cover, 17 numbered pages and page of ads at end of book, half page hand colored engravings.   Jo Ann Reisler, Ltd.   86 - 92   2011 $600

Elliott, Mary Belson *Precept and Example or Midsummer Holidays.* London: W. Darton Jun. (sic), 1812. 12mo., 188 + 2 pages, original marbled paper on boards, red roan spine, gilt title and fillets, full page copper engraved frontispiece, wood engraved vignette, wanting front free endpaper, covers lightly rubbed including edges and corners, else fine, from the collection of Marjorie Moon and handmade dust jacket with inked title on cover and along spine.   Hobbyhorse Books   56 - 45   2011 $300

History of Little Tom Tucker. London: printed for the Booksellers, n.d. circa, 1820. 12mo., * + 1 page list on lower wrapper, yellow pictorial paper wrappers, 8 wood engravings, some colored by juvenile hand, from the collection of Marjorie Moon, top edges of pages crudely opened and repaired, good copy.   Hobbyhorse Books   56 - 85   2011 $190

Saint Pierre, Jacques Henri Bernardin De   1737-1814 *Paul and Virginia.* Edinburgh: Oliver & Boyd, 1824. 12mo., 282 pages, three quarter tooled leather with corners, marbled paper on boards, gilt title label on spine, brown endpapers, very fine full page copper engraved frontispiece, ex-libris from the collection of Marjorie Moon, very fine.   Hobbyhorse Books   56 - 133   2011 $250

Association – Moon, Theo

Sallustius Crispus, Caius *The History of Catiline's Conspiracy and the Jugurthine War.* London: printed for D. Browne, A. Millar et al, 1757. 8vo., pages xvi, 253, (iii), contemporary sprinkled calf, spine panel with 'asymetric flowering plant' centrepieces and 'flower head' cornerpieces, red lettering piece gilt, board edges decorative roll gilt, all edges red sprinkled, red and white sewn endbands, little spotting, corners worn, joints cracking but strong, ink ownership stamp "Theo A Moon", from the collection of Christopher Ernest Weston 1947-2010.   Unsworths Booksellers   24 - 141   2011   £150

Association – Moore, Elizabeth Stauffer

Tennyson, Alfred Tennyson, 1st Baron   1809-1892
The Holy Grail. New Rochelle: George D. Sproul, 1902. One of 30 copies (18 for America)) of the Saint Dunstan edition; this copy #5 especially prepared for socialite and philanthropist Elizabeth Stauffer Moore and signed by publisher and illuminator, 267 x 207mm., 52 unnumbered leaves, printed on one side only, all printed on vellum, arresting neo-gothic crushed morocco by Trautz-Bauzonnet (stamp signed), covers with outer frame of dark red flanked by onlaid green morocco adorned with gilt dots, each of the four sides of this frame with centered green framed roundel containing either a stylized gilt cross or a Christogram, frame enclosing a central panel of scarlet morocco with large central cross inlaid in white vellum decorated in Celtic pattern, red morocco square at center featuring a gilt chalice and inlaid white vellum Host, four small roundels (where the arms of the cross meet) with onlaid gilt and green shamrocks raised bands, vertical gilt titling inside dotted gilt frame, very pleasing onlaid white morocco doublures, surrounded and embellished by red and green morocco as well as gilt, repeating the cover frame and host and shamrock designs, vellum endleaves, all edges gilt; in original white silk box (fraying) with brass clasp, gilt titling along fore edge and padded satin interior, handsomely illuminated by W. Formilli in colors and gold, inevitable offsetting form doublure frame to vellum endleaves, some slight variation in whiteness of vellum, most leaves with hint of rumpling, otherwise handsome production in fine, creamy vellum leaves, bright colors and gold, lustrous, unworn binding.   Phillip J. Pirages   59 - 341 2011 $5000

Association – Moore, George

Gosse, Edmund   1849-1928   *On Viol and Flute.* London: Heinemann, 1896. First Selected edition; small 8vo., pages xi, 212, original publisher's green cloth lettered gilt on spine and cover, frontispiece, signed presentation from author to George Moore, from the library of Henry "Chips" Channon with note at rear in his hand "Given me by Lady Cunard, Christmas 1938, slight tanning, slight fading, very small nick at head of spine, otherwise very good.   Any Amount of Books   May 29 2011 - A69860 2011 $255

Association – Moore, Joseph

Kendall, Edward Augustus   *Keeper's Travels in Search of His Master.* Philadelphia: Johnson & Warner, Lydia R. Bailey, 1808. Early American edition; 12mo., 87, (3) pages, wood engraved frontispiece, contemporary marbled paper covered boards, red roan spine, covers rubbed, usual light foxing but tight and lovely, 1809 ownership of Joseph Moore.   Joseph J. Felcone Inc.   Fall Miscellany 2010 - 69   2011 $400

Association – Morgan, Bill

Bradbury, Ray   *The Golden Apples of the Sun.* Garden City: Doubleday and Co. Inc., 1953. First edition; 8vo., pages 250, drawings by Joe Mugnaini, edges toned, original brown imitation cloth, spine lettered in yellow, head and foot of spine rubbed, original illustrated dust jacket printed in yellow, grey and black, lightly rubbed, spine sunned, price clipped, inscribed "Bill Morgan/(signed) Ray Bradbury/ Oct. 18 1980".   Simon Finch Rare Books   Zero - 210 2011   £500

Association – Morgan, J. Howard

Elliot, Frances Minto   *Diary of an Idle Woman in Constantinople.* London: John Murray, 1893. First edition; (12) (sic), 425 pages, including index, 8vo., contemporary half red calf over marbled boards, gilt decorated spines, contrasting gilt lettered spine, frontispiece, 3 plates, folding map printed in red and black, some rubbing to extremities, small chip to head of spine, upper hinge slightly cracking, unobtrusive light spotting to endpapers, repair to small tear on verso of map, nonetheless attractive copy, from the library of Welsh architect J. Howard Morgan.   Paulette Rose Fine and Rare Books   32 - 175 2011 $480

Association – Morgan, Johannes

Collins, Samuel   *A Systeme of Anatomy, Treating of the Body of Man, Beasts, Birds, Fish, Insects and Plants.* In the Savoy: printed by Thomas Newcomb, 1685. Folio, pages (16), lvi, (14), 52, 49-52, (53-) 678; (10), 679-) 740 739-740, (7451-) 1263, (42), engraved frontispiece, portrait (some light spotting), 74 engraved plates, one or two plates with shaved down fore-edge and just touching engraved border, due to bad setting, both titles printed in red and black (spotting to first), contemporary calf, professionally rebacked and repaired, some scattered marginal wormholes, light dampstaining to several pages in volume 1, with 6 additional dedications (of two leaves each) inserted and extra to collation given above, second volume inscribed "Johannes Morgan E. Coll. Jesus 1718" (possibly John Morgan), very good.   Raymond M. Sutton, Jr.   May 26 2011 - 55971 2011 $10,000

Association – Morgan, John

Vergilius Maro, Publius   *The Nyne Fyrst Bookes of the Eneidos of Virgil...* London: by Rouland Hall for Nicholas Englande, 1562. Rare early edition in English; 4to., (220) pages, woodcut on title, text in black letter, 19th century morocco, ruled in gilt, edges gilt, extremities lightly worn, minor scuffing, first quire washed and neatly extended at top edge, possibly supplied from another copy, few internal repairs, else very good, excellent full margins, Rubislaw House bookplate of John Morgan.   Joseph J. Felcone Inc. Fall Miscellany 2010 - 122 2011 $11,000

Association – Morison, Stanley

Dodgson, Campbell *Prints in the Dotte Manner and Other Metal-Cuts of the XV Century in the Department of Prints and Drawings British Museum.* London: British Museum, 1937. First edition; 34 pages, frontispiece, 43 plates, very good in slightly rubbed original dark green cloth, bookplate of Denis Tegetmeier and note 'gift of Stanley Morison', folio. Ken Spelman Rare Books   68 - 120   2011   £90

Association – Morrell, Ottoline

Vaughan, Henry *The Poems of Henry Vaughan, Silurist.* London: Lawrence & Bullen, 1896. 2 volumes, series and half titles, titles in red and black, uncut in original blue cloth, slightly sunned, top edge gilt, signed presentation from George MacDonald to Lady Ottoline Morrell.   Jarndyce Antiquarian Booksellers   CXCII - 341   2011   £650

Association – Morris, May

Morris, William   1834-1896   *Gothic Architecture: a Lecture for the Arts and Crafts Exhibition Society.* Kelmscott Press, 1893. One of 1500 copies on paper, there wer also on 45 on vellum; 145 x 108mm., 1 p.l., 68 pages, original holland backed paper boards, edges untrimmed, woodcut initials and small woodcut decorations in text, headlines and sidenotes printed in red, front flyleaf with pencilled ownership signature of May Morris; covers rather faded and bit soiled, one faint spot of foxing to two leaves, otherwise fine internally, text clean, fresh and bright. Phillip J. Pirages   59 - 242   2011 $500

Association – Morris, William

Gronow, Rees Howell   1794-1865   *The Reminiscences and Recollections of Captain Gronow, Being Anecdotes of the Camp Court, Clubs, and Society 1810-1860.* London: John C. Nimmo, 1889. One of 875 copies (this #10); 265 x 170 mm., 2 volumes extended to 4, especially lovely contemporary crimson crushed morocco, very lavishly gilt by Tout (stamp signed) covers with wide, elaborate gilt frames in the style of Derome, this intricate design rich with fleurons, volutes, curls, festoons an small floral tools, raised bands, spine gilt in double ruled compartments with central cruciform ornament sprouting curling leaves and flowers from its head and tail, these swirls accented with dotted rules and small tools filling the compartments, very wide turn-ins with complex curling botanical decoration, silk endleaves with tiny gold floral sprays, all edges gilt, frontispiece, 24 plates, all in two states as called for, one proof before letters on plate paper, other with captions on Whatman paper and colored by hand, extra illustrated with 227 plates, primarily portraits, 18 of these in color, armorial bookplate of William Ewert Baron Camrose pasted over bookplate of William Morris; hint of rubbing to corners, mild shelfwear, occasional minor foxing affecting inserted plates and adjacent leaves, handsome set, clean and fresh internally, sumptuous bindings in fine condition, lustrous and virtually unworn.   Phillip J. Pirages   59 - 144   2011 $4800

Association – Morris, Wright

Meatyard, Ralph Eugene *Ralph Eugene Meatyard.* New York: Aperture, 1974. First edition; fine in clean, very near fine dust jacket with none of the usual fading to spine, very clean copy, less common cloth copy, author Wright Morris' copy with his ownership signature.   Jeff Hirsch Books   ny 2010 2011 $350

Association – Morrison, Toni

Berman, Robert *A Kind of Rapture.* New York: Pantheon, 1998. First edition; color photos, signed by Toni Morrison, fine in fine dust jacket.   Ken Lopez Bookseller   154 - 124   2011 $425

Association – Morrow, William

Du Maurier, George Louis Palmella Busson   1834-1896 *Trilby.* Osgood, McIlvaine & Co.,, 1894. Serialised in Harper's Monthly Magazine, Volume LXXXVIII Dec. 1893 to May 1894; Titlepage of the European edition, illustrations, contemporary half maroon morocco, raised bands, gilt compartments, hinges neatly repaired, 6 page news paper article "Trilby" from Publishers' Weekly Aug. 1928 tipped in, 4 page ALS from author to Sir William Morrow, original brown cloth bound in at end of volume, armorial bookplate of Albert Henry Wiggin, very good.   Jarndyce Antiquarian Booksellers   CXCI - 166   2011   £150

Association – Mortimer, Raymond

Banting, John *The Blue Book of Conversation.* London: Editions Poetry/Nicholson and Watson, 1946. First edition; small quarto, pages 57 with 25 plates, one of which is double page, all of which are printed in blue, some slight foxing to endpapers, else near fine in about very good dust jacket that is slightly browned and slightly foxed at rear and has one inch chip at head of spine, loosely inserted is good longish 2 page letter to Raymond Mortimer from Banting. Any Amount of Books   May 26 2011 - A39855   2011 $629

Association – Moser, Barry

Melville, Herman 1819-1891 *Moby Dick; or, The Whale.* San Francisco: Arion Press, 1979. One of 265 copies of the book (of which 250 were for sale); along with one of 30 extra suites issued of the 100 engravings appearing in the book, the regular 100 in the volume and the extra 100, all signed by artist; with 10 original drawings used for the book's illustrations, each of these signed as well, colophon signed by artist, Barry Moser and with inscription for Becky and Gill Desmarais; 385 x 265mm., 576 pages, (2) leaves, "Moby Dick" volume plus companion portfolio of plates; publisher's fine cerulean crushed morocco, silver vertical titling on spine, in original cloth covered slipcase (hint of fading as usual), extra plates and original drawings in custom made morocco backed folding cloth box with gilt lettering, virtually pristine. Phillip J. Pirages 59 - 70 2011 $27,500

Association – Mostyn, Roger

Ussher, James *A Body of Divinity, or the Summe and Substance of Christian Religion...* London: M. F. for Tho. Downes and Geo. Badger, 1648. Third edition; folio, pages (xii) 3-451, (xv), 24 + engraved portrait frontispiece, signed "W. Marshall Sculpsit 1647", contemporary sprinkled calf, boards double ruled in blind, board edges single rule gilt, all edges rouge with black ink hand written "Ussher" at head of fore-edge, pink & white sewn endbands, evidence of chaining staple at head of fore-edge of upper board, also evidence of later ties, early 1990's calf reback by Chris Weston, spotting and staining (mostly light), small tear to titlepage border repaired with sellotape, old leather marked and bit chipped at edges, near contemporary ink inscription "Roger Mostyn Anno 1685" at head of titlepage and underneath later ink inscription, booklabel of Gloddaeth Library, also ex-libris of Rev. John F. Brencher, his MS mini biography of Ussher on f.e.p. and his signature on reverse, from the collection of Christopher Ernest Weston 1947-2010. Unsworths Booksellers 24 - 54 2011 £450

Association – Moulthrop, Daniel

Eggers, Dave *Teachers Have It Easy.* New York: New Press, 2005. First edition; signed by Eggers and co-authors Daniel Moulthrop and Ninive Clements Calegari, fine in fine dust jacket, uncommon. Ken Lopez Bookseller 154 - 48 2011 $200

Association – Mountbatten, Louis, Lady

Paul, James Balfour *The History of the Royal Company of Archers.* Edinburgh & London: William Blackwood and Sons, 1875. First edition; 250 x 200mm., ix, (i), 393 (1), 78 pages, 20 leaves, very fine contemporary dark green morocco, sumptuously gilt, covers with French fillet border, elaborate gilt picture like central frame around gilt emblem with motto "Dat Gloria Vires" above and "In Peace and War" below, showing figures associated with archery and love, peace, and war, raised bands between compartments with foliate cornerpieces and bow and quiver centerpiece, densely gilt inner dentelles, silk endleaves, gilt edges, in red and black felt lined buckram slipcase, with 6 full page color portraits, six black and white photo plates, and four line drawings, titlepage in red and black, inked note "This book formerly belonged to Lady Louis Mountbatten 4.8.34", bottom 4 inches of front joint just beginning to crack, covers slightly bumped, else beautiful copy, very handsome decorative binding, quite bright, text and plates in perfect state of preservation, luxuriously bound. Phillip J. Pirages 59 - 66 2011 $750

Association – Muir, Constance

Lawrence, David Herbert 1885-1930 *Amores.* New York: B. W. Huebsch, 1916. First American edition; 8vo., pages (xii), 116, internally fine, original brown cloth boards, spine and upper board lettered in gold, top edge gilt, original cream dust jacket printed in black, dust jacket expertly restored at spine and top edge, small tear not affecting text to upper panel, small bookplate of Charles Edmund Merrill Jr. to pastedown, bookplate of Constance M. and Karl Andrew Muir. Simon Finch Rare Books Zero - 329 2011 £500

Association – Muir, Karl Andrew

Lawrence, David Herbert 1885-1930 *Amores.* New York: B. W. Huebsch, 1916. First American edition; 8vo., pages (xii), 116, internally fine, original brown cloth boards, spine and upper board lettered in gold, top edge gilt, original cream dust jacket printed in black, dust jacket expertly restored at spine and top edge, small tear not affecting text to upper panel, small bookplate of Charles Edmund Merrill Jr. to pastedown, bookplate of Constance M. and Karl Andrew Muir. Simon Finch Rare Books Zero - 329 2011 £500

Association – Munby, A. N. L.

De La Ramee, Louise 1839-1908 *Two Offenders.* London: Chatto & Windus, 1894. First edition; 32 pages ads, half title, original dark green cloth, decorated in black and yellow, spine gilt lettered, George Ryland's booklabel, nice, fine full page inscription signed by author for Marie Corelli, pencil inscription "To Dalie with love on his 60th birthday from Tim", inserted typed note by Rylands, "Given me by A. N. L. Munby on my 60th birthday. Jarndyce Antiquarian Booksellers CLXC - 714 2011 £600

Association – Murao, Shigeyoshi

Brautigan, Richard *A Confederate General from Big Sur.* New York: Grove Press, 1964. First edition; inscribed by author for Shigeyoshi Murao, long-time manager of City Lights Bookstore, foxing to top edge of text block, else fine in near fine dust jacket with strip of foxing to upper rear flap and shallow creasing to upper rear panel.   Ken Lopez Bookseller   154 - 15 2011 $7500

Association – Murray, Jock

Hart, Davis *The Lyttelton Hart-Davis Letters: Correspondence of George Lyttelton and Rupert Hart-Davis.* London: John Murray, 1979-1987. Volume 1 reprint, others first editions, volumes 5 and 6 first edition paperback; 8vo, 6 volumes (5 and 6 bound in one book), volume II signed presentation copy from author to Dadie Rylands, 4 volumes have short letters laid in from publisher "Jock" Murray to Dadie Rylands, all very good, clean copies, dust jackets where called for.   Any Amount of Books   May 29 2011 - B9967 2011 $221

Association – Napier, Anne Louise

Napier, William Francis Patrick *History of the War in the Peninsula and in the South of France from the Year 1807 to the Year 1814.* London: Thomas William Boone, 1862. New edition; 6 volumes, numerous engraved maps, later 18th century full tan calf, bevelled boards, at some time rebacked, spines gilt in compartments, maroon and black leather labels, hinges and hinges little worn, signed presentation inscription to Maria Martineau from friend, Richd. Napier, with additional signature of Anne Louise Napier, also tipped into prelims volume I is 19 line ALS from Richard Napier to Maria Martineau.   Jarndyce Antiquarian Booksellers   CLXC - 363 2011   £380

Association – Napier, Richard

Napier, William Francis Patrick *History of the War in the Peninsula and in the South of France from the Year 1807 to the Year 1814.* London: Thomas William Boone, 1862. New edition; 6 volumes, numerous engraved maps, later 18th century full tan calf, bevelled boards, at some time rebacked, spines gilt in compartments, maroon and black leather labels, hinges and hinges little worn, signed presentation inscription to Maria Martineau from friend, Richd. Napier, with additional signature of Anne Louise Napier, also tipped into prelims volume I is 19 line ALS from Richard Napier to Maria Martineau.   Jarndyce Antiquarian Booksellers   CLXC - 363 2011   £380

Association – Nash, W. M.

The Modern Family Physician, or the Art of Healing Made Easy, Being a Plain Description of Diseases to Which Persons of Every Age are Most Liable...   London: printed for F. Newbery, 1775. First edition; 12mo., viii, 279, (1) pages, first few leaves somewhat creased, old tape mark to gutter of title, some paper browning and very occasional light spotting, well bound in recent quarter calf over plain boards, spine with raised bands, gilt lines and letters, good copy with early 19th century signature of W. M. Nash 1814, rare.   John Drury Rare Books   153 - 97 2011   £350

Association – Nederburgh

Doyle, Arthur Conan **1859-1930**   *Our African Winter.* London: John Murray, 1929. First edition; photographic frontispiece, Doyle's presentation inscription on titlepage for friend Nederburgh (possibly author H. G. Nederburgh), very good copy, some wear and rubbing at extremities, especially at top of spine, nice spine gilt, tight.   Lupack Rare Books   May 26 2011 - ABE4707850377 2011 $875

Association – Neeld, Joseph

Dodsley, Robert **1703-1764**   *Oeconomy of Human Life.* London: printed by T. Rickaby for S. and E. Harding, 1795. First edition with these illustrations; 272 x 85mm., 2 p.l., (5)-22 pages, (1) leaf, (119 pages (pages 117-119 ads as called for), large paper copy, apparently one of 25 in this format, quite attractive contemporary English crimson straight grain morocco, handsomely gilt, covers with borders of one plain and one decorative gilt rule and small fleuron in each corner, raised bands, spine elegantly gilt in compartments with foliate cornerpieces framing a large cruciform ornament with ribbon outlines enclosing a central starburst on stippled background, turn-ins with gilt Greek key roll, marbled endpapers, all edges gilt; 49 mostly large and always charming engraved emblematic headpieces and tailpieces by Sylvester Harding, typically showing human or angelic figures representing such abstract ideas as contentment, pity, or fortitude; armorial bookplate of Joseph Neeld, modern bookplate of John Porter, handwritten bookseller's? description signed "EB" and dated 1 Feb. 1804 tipped onto front flyleaves; covers slightly marked with minor spotting and soiling, trivial smudges internally, nearly fine and especially pretty copy, original luxury binding lustrous and with virtually no wear, text printed with vast margins extremely fresh and smooth, rare format.   Phillip J. Pirages   59 - 28 2011 $1250

Association – Nellen

Quincy, John *Lexicon Physico Medicum; or a New Medicinal Dictionary...* London: printed for J. Osborn and T. Longman at the Ship in Pater-Noster Row, 1730. xvi, 480 pages, diagrams in text, ownership inscription dated 1949, 8vo., full contemporary panelled calf, raised bands, early handwritten paper label, joints cracked but firm, head and tail of spine slightly chipped, tinted bookplate of Cholmondely Library, later bookplate ex-libris Nellen, fine, clean copy. Jarndyce Antiquarian Booksellers CXCI - 461 2011 £350

Association – Nelson, Mr.

Hull, William *Memoirs of the Campaign of the North Western Army of the United States A.D. 1812.* Boston: True & Greene, 1824. First edition; 8vo., 229, 10 pages, original printed wrappers, uncut, foxed, inscribed presentation by author to Honble. Mr. Nelson. M & S Rare Books, Inc. 90 - 434 2011 $950

Association – Nelson, Paul

MacDonald, Ross *The Chill.* Knopf, 1964. First edition; 8vo., inscribed by author for Paul Nelson, Rolling Stone writer who interviewed author extensively, fine in dust jacket with tiny chip at top edge of rear panel. Buckingham Books May 26 2011 - 20958 2011 $2500

Association – Newbegin, John

Dodgson, Charles Lutwidge 1832-1898 *Alice's Adventures in Wonderland. (and) Through the Looking Glass and What Alice Found There.* London: Macmillan and Co., 1866. Second, but first published edition; 183 x 125mm., 2 separately published works bound in 2 volumes, extremely pleasing crimson levant morocco by Root & son (stamp-signed on front turn-in of both volumes), each cover with panels formed by double gilt rules and central gilt medallion, the "Wonderland" medallion depicting Alice holding baby pig, the "Looking-Glass" medallion showing grumpy Red Queen, raised bands, spines gilt in compartments with double ruled frames and small central quatrefoil, gilt ruled turn-ins, marbled endpapers, all edges gilt, with 92 illustrations, letter laid in from bookseller John Newbegin elucidating issue points, bookplate of Florence Magee; spines slightly and evenly a darkened red, handful of leaves with very minor foxing or smudges, one leaf with neat repair to tail edge (no text affected), but fine and attractive set, text clean, fresh, and smooth and bindings lustrous and virtually unworn. Phillip J. Pirages 59 - 176 2011 $11,500

Association – Newbold, H. LeRoy

Lugar, Robert *Villa Architecture: a Collection of Views with Plans, of Buildings Executed in England, Scotland &c.* London: J. Taylor, 1828. First edition; folio, (2), x, 34 pages, 42 plates of which 26 are hand colored aquatints and 16 floor plans, modern half red morocco, margins of first two leaves bit soiled, few tiny chips, two leaves of preface moderately foxed, occasional spot of foxing, plates clean and bright, fine, signature of H. Le Roy Newbold, NY 1836. Joseph J. Felcone Inc. Fall Miscellany 2010 - 5 2011 $4500

Association – Newbury, Evy

Lancaster, Marie Jaqueline *Brian Howard. Portrait of a Failure.* London: Blond, 1968. First edition; portrait, pages xx, 639 16 pages of photos, loosely inserted are 10 signed cards from author to Mrs. Newbury, bookplate of Evy Newbury, she has pasted in flower card on verso of half title and few slight marks to prelims, else book is very good. Any Amount of Books May 29 2011 - A70276 2011 $213

Association – Newman, Arnold

Knowles, John *A Separate Peace.* New York: Macmillan Co., 1960. First edition; in the more commonly encountered second state dust jacket with reviews printed on front and rear panels and with corners of inside front flap clipped, not affecting price, this copy with signature of photographer, Arnold Newman, inscribed and signed to him by author, red ink mark at base of spine of both dust jacket and book, near fine. Charles Agvent 2010 Summer Miscellany - 40 2011 $6000

Association – Newman, William

Robinson, Robert *A Political Catechism.* London: J. Buckland, C. Dilly, J. Mathews, J. Debrett and W. Lepard, 1782. First edition; 8vo., iv, 140 pages, last page little soiled, contemporary ownership inscription (Wm. Newman 1782 No. 6), recently well bound in old style quarter mottled calf over marbled boards, spine with raised bands and label, very good. John Drury Rare Books 153 - 128 2011 £275

Association – Newton

Chaucer, Geoffrey 1340-1400 *Troilus and Criseyde.* Waltham St. Lawrence: Golden Cockerel Press, 1927. One of 225 numbered copies (first six of which were printed on vellum); 316 x 198mm., xi, (i), 309, (1) pages, (2) leaves (blank and colophon), original publisher's russet quarter morocco by Sangorski & Sutcliffe, patterned paper sides, top edge gilt, others untrimmed, publisher's (only just slightly rubbed and soiled) slipcase, fore margins of every text page with woodcut borders and five full page wood engravings, all by Eric Gill, section titlepages with red or blue lettering, occasional text initials in red or blue; bookplate of the Newton library (begun by Sir Alfred Newton, 1st Baronet and mostly assembled by Sir Harry Newton, 2nd Bart. 1871-1951); some minor spotting or soiling on part of the morocco on front board, otherwise faultless copy, spine unusually bright, corners (which are always rubbed) in virtually perfect condition, text as bright and fresh as new.   Phillip J. Pirages   59 - 219 2011 $19,500

Association – Newton, A. Edward

Coryate, Thomas *Coryats Crudities Hastily Gobbled Up in Five Moneths Travells in France, Savoy, Italy, Rhetia Comonly Called the Grisons Country, Helvetia Alias Switzerland, some Parts of High Germany and the Netherlands.* London: by William Stansby, 1611. First edition; printed title present, engraved allegorical title by William Hole (shaved very slightly at head), engraved plates, woodcut, text portrait, errata leaf present, many woodcut initials and headpieces, 19th century brown crushed levant morocco, gilt by Bedford, unusually tall, very handsome copy, rare printed title, from the libraries of Ward E. Terry, R. B. Adam, A. Edward Newton, Bois Penrose and Wolfgang A. Herz with their respective bookplates and book labels. Joseph J. Felcone Inc.   Fall Miscellany 2010 - 35 2011 $16,000

Davenant, William 1606-1668 *The Works of Sr. William Davenant Kt. Consisting of those Which were Formerly printed and Those which He Design'd for the Press...* London: by T. N. for Henry Herringman, 1673. First collected edition; folio, (8), 402, (4), 486, 111 pages, portrait, turn-of-the-century red levant morocco, gilt arabesque centerpiece on covers, all edges gilt by Riviere, very skillfully rebacked, though new leather at joints and on cords has uniformly faded, unusually fine, fresh, wide margined copy, fine impression of portrait, leather tipped fleece lined slipcase, edges rubbed, Duke of Beaufort, E. F. Leo, A, E, Newton, with their bookplates.   Joseph J. Felcone Inc. Fall Miscellany 2010 - 37 2011 $2200

Association – Newton, Marvin

Taken by Design: Photographs from The Institute of Design 1937-1971. Chicago: University of Chicago Press, 2002. First edition; very fine in photo illustrated boards, issued without dust jacket, signed by a large number of photographers and some of the editors, among the signatures are Yasuhiro Ishimoto, Marvin E. Newton (twice), Barbara Crane, Ray K. Metzker, Joseph Jachna, Joseph Sterling (twice), Kenneth Josephson, David Travis, Keith Davis and quite a few others, unique copy.   Jeff Hirsch Books   ny 2010 2011 $750

Association – Nichola, Pamela

Kithchin, C. H. B. *The Sensitive One.*   London: Hogarth Press, 1931. First edition; 8vo., original publisher's grey cloth lettered gilt on spine, pages 181, signed presentation copy with drawing, "C.P. from C.H.B.K. 18-2-31", also signed "Pamela Nichola from Clifford Kittchin", spine ends slightly rubbed, very slight shelf wear and bumping to covers, very good in somewhat worn good only, chipped, nicked and soiled dust jacket.   Any Amount of Books   May 29 2011 - A76003 2011 $340

Association – Nichols, Melvin J.

Roe, Charles Francis *Custer's Last Battle.*   New York: 1927. 40 pages, maps and illustrations, 12 x 9 inches, pamphlet, original printed wrappers, light soil and edgewear, top corner slightly bumped, else near fine presentation to noted Custer collector Melvin J. Nichols.   Dumont Maps & Books of the West   111 - 38 2011 $100

Association – Nicholson, Audrey

Hughes, Ted 1930-1998 *Wolfwatching.* London: Faber & Faber, 1989. First edition; signed presentation to Audrey (Nicholson) the actress, from the author, loosely inserted card signed by Olwyn Hughes, author's sister for Audrey, fine in very good+ dust jacket slightly rubbed at edges. Any Amount of Books   May 29 2011 - A68490 2011 $272

Association – Nicholson, Norman

Reilly, Paul *An Introduction to Regency Architecture.* London: Art and Technics, 1948. First edition; large 8vo., original cloth, gilt, dust jacket trifle torn and chipped, pages 96, 60 plates, 15 text illustrations, from the library of Lake District poet Norman Nicholson, with his bookplate.   R. F. G. Hollett & Son Antiquarian Booksellers   177 - 734 2011 £30

Williams, W. M. *The Sociology of an English Village - Gosforth.* London: Routledge & Kegan Paul, 1956. First edition; original cloth, gilt, dust jacket, few small chips and tears to extremities, pages 245, 16 with 12 maps, text figures, scarce, Norman Nicholson's copy with his bookplate, loosely inserted 2 postcards of Gosforth an 2 different 3 sided typescript reviews by Nicholson for the work, with alterations and corrections throughout both typescripts in his hand, much pencilled lining of text by Nicholson throughout. R. F. G. Hollett & Son Antiquarian Booksellers   173 - 1214   2011   £150

Association – Nolty, John

Cosway, Richard   *Catalogue of a Collection of Miniatures by Richard Cosway.*   For Private Ciculation Only, 1883. Limited edition, limitation not stated; folio, (32) ff., frontispiece, 26 full page mounted photo plates, original half brown morocco, marbled boards, morocco corners, raised bands, gilt spine title, all edges gilt, bound by J. Leighton, inscribed on titlepage by author, bookplate of John Nolty, fine, rare. Jeff Weber Rare Books   163 - 100   2011 $750

Association – Nomikos, Christopher

Cavafy, Constantine P.   *Poiemata (1908-1914).* Alexandria: Kasimath & Iona (Print Shop), circa, 1920. Tall 8vo., 29 numbered pages, printed on recto only with table of contents, in beige printed wrapper, very fine, half morocco folding box, presentation from poet to one of his closest friends, Christopher Nomikos.   James S. Jaffe Rare Books   May 26 2011 - 8185   2011 $25,000

Association – Nonnenmacker, E.

Leach, Bernard   *A Potter's Book.*   London: Faber & Faber, 1940. First edition; 8vo., pages xxvii, 293, 4 color plates, 77 half tone illustrations and numerous drawings in text, frontispiece tipped in, neat name on front pastedown (H. & E. Nonnenmacker), inner front hinge slightly cracked, edges of oatmeal boards very slightly stained but nice, bright very good+ in rather tatty worn, good only dust jacket.   Any Amount of Books   May 29 2011 - B22969   2011 $221

Association – Nonnenmacker, H.

Leach, Bernard   *A Potter's Book.*   London: Faber & Faber, 1940. First edition; 8vo., pages xxvii, 293, 4 color plates, 77 half tone illustrations and numerous drawings in text, frontispiece tipped in, neat name on front pastedown (H. & E. Nonnenmacker), inner front hinge slightly cracked, edges of oatmeal boards very slightly stained but nice, bright very good+ in rather tatty worn, good only dust jacket.   Any Amount of Books   May 29 2011 - B22969   2011 $221

Association – Nordmann, G.

Argens, Jean Baptiste De Boyer, Marquis De   1704-1771 *Therese Philosophe ou Memoires Pour servir a l'Histoire du P. Dirrag & De Mademoiselle Eradice...Premiere Partie. Therese Philosophe &c Seconde & Derniere Partie.*   A La Haye: circa, 1748.   2 'parties' bound in one, 8vo., pages viii (titlepage) 'explication' of the 17 plates, 'Table des Matieres de la Premiere Partie', page 72 misnumbered 24), 69, 70-72 (Table des matieres de la seconde partie' Page 72 misnumbered 70), (1) (Fautes a Coriger'), final leaf was probably printed as leaf I8 (pages 143-144) of the first partie and subsequently bound in at end of joint volume, frontispiece, 16 erotic plates, all edges gilt, slight scattered age darkening and soiling of paper, original 18th century maroon morocco (slight restoration), marbled endpapers, spine decorated and title label reading "T. PH" in gilt, all within raised bands, bookplate of G. Nordmann.   Simon Finch Rare Books   Zero - 403   2011   £25,000

Borde, Charles   *Parapilla, et Autres Oeuvres Libres...* Florence: 1784.   Small 12mo., pages (iv), 164, 1 plate by Marillier, numerous small wood engraved head and tailpieces, engraved portrait of Borde added as frontispiece, all edges gilt, full green long grain morocco fully gilt decorated in gilt with red dots, by Bozerain, pink silk lined endpieces, bookplate of Bibliotheque Mirault and G. Nordmann, few discrete pencil annotations.   Simon Finch Rare Books   Zero - 411   2011   £1750

Chorier, Nicolas   *L'Academie des Dames.*   A Venise: chez Pierre Arretin but Holland, circa, 1775.   8vo., pages 420, frontispiece, engraved titlepage, 35 engraved erotic plates, some light foxing and browning, contemporary full calf, red morocco lettering piece to spine, lettering in gilt, expertly rebacked, bookplate of Gerard Nordmann.   Simon Finch Rare Books   Zero - 408   2011   £5750

Cleland, John   *La Fille De Joie, ou Memoires de Miss Fanny, Ecrits par elle-meme.*   Paris: Madame Gourdan, 1786. (1787); Large 8vo., pages (iv), 235, plus frontispiece, 2 supplementary engraved titlepages, 34 engraved plates (numbered 1-33 and 5 bis) by Delcroche (unsigned), all edges gilt, small discrete old repair to titlepage, full mid brown gilt decorated and titled morocco by Hardy, c. 1860, Bookplate of G. Nordmann, fine, stunning copy.   Simon Finch Rare Books   Zero - 413   2011   £9500

Letters Galantes et Philosophiques De Deux Nones Publiees par un Apotre du Libertinage avec des Notes. Paris: pan ile de la republique francaise, 1794. First illustrated edition; 18mo., pages (iv), 172, 4 engravings, first in 2 states, one 'avant la lettre', all edges gilt, some very light spotting and soiling, mid 19th century mid brown full morocco, gilt decorated and titled on spine, bookplate of G. Nordmann, near fine.   Simon Finch Rare Books   Zero - 417   2011   £4000

Le Putanisme d'Amsterdam, Livre Contenant les Tours & Les Ruses Don Se Servent les Putains & Les Maquereles... Amsterdam: Elie Jogehemse de Rhin, 1681. First edition; rare, small 12mo., pages (vi), 277, (1) blank, engraved frontispiece and 4 plates, all edges gilt, discreet old repairs to frontispiece and final ad leaf, occasional light spotting early 20th century full black morocco, by Bernasconi, gilt lettering and raised bands to spine, gilt decoration to inside boards, marbled endpapers, bookplate of G. Nordmann. Simon Finch Rare Books   Zero - 401   2011   £3000

Mannoury D'Ectot, La Marquise   *Les Cousines de la Colonelle par Madame la Vicomtesse de Coeur-Brulant.* Lisbon: Antonio de Boa Vista, 1887. Fifth edition; 2 volumes in one, numbered continuously, 8vo., pages 440, plus 3 frontispieces and 6 engraved plates, 11 extra original watercolors in margins, top edge gilt, others roughly trimmed, internally fine, later red morocco, gilt lettering to spine, ex-libris G. Nordmann, his discreet bookplate to front free endpaper, unique copy with 11 extra watercolors added in margins, in superb condition.   Simon Finch Rare Books   Zero - 430   2011   £3300

Association – Norfolk, Charlotte, Duchess of

Twopenny, William   *Extracts from Various Authors...*   privately printed at the Chiswick Press, 1868. Half title, original brown cloth, borders blocked in blind, upper board blocked in gilt, few small marks, armorial bookplate of Charlotte, Duchess of Norfolk with inscription, presented by her to Thomas Henry Foley, 4th Baron Foley.   Jarndyce Antiquarian Booksellers   CXCI - 591   2011   £50

Association – Norman, Haskell

Darwin, Charles Robert   1809-1882   *The Foundations of the Origin of Species, A Sketch Written in 1842...* Cambridge: printed at the University Press, 1909. First printing; 8vo., pages xxii, 53, plus frontispiece and 1 plate, uncut, internally fine, original grey paper covered boards, vellum spine, upper board with text and coat of arms in black, bumped with light shelfwear, presentation copy to Prof. W. H. Bragg, label of H. F. Norman.   Simon Finch Rare Books   Zero - 141   2011   £450

Schoepf, Johann David   *Materia Medica Americana Potissimum Regni Vegetabilis.*   Erlangae: Sumtibus Io. Iac. Palmii, 1787. First edition; 8vo., pages (2), xviii, 170, (4), contemporary quarter sheep, some worming to edges of spine, dark stain to lower third of pages and pastedowns, marginal tear to a leaf, ex-libris Johann Thomas Bosch with signature, the Norman copy.   Raymond M. Sutton, Jr.   May 26 2011 - 51773   2011 $5500

Association – Normand

Chartier, Alain   *Les Oeuvres.*   Paris: S. Thiboust, Jan. 25th, 1617. 4to., (16), 868, (20) pages, title printed in red and black, woodcut device, woodcut head and tailpieces, woodcut initials, contemporary calf with triple fillet rule on boards and fleurons in corners, spine gilt in compartments, morocco lettering piece, colored silk page marker, manuscript ex-libris "Normand", manuscript annotations in margins (many trimmed), from the library of the Earls of Macclesfield at Shirburn Castle.   Maggs Bros. Ltd.   1440 - 50   2011   £900

Association – Norris, James

Barton, William P. C.   *Vegetable Materia Medica of the United States; or Medical Botany.*   Philadelphia: M. Carey & Son, 1817-1818. First edition; 50 hand colored engraved plates (1 folding, occasional foxing, offsetting from text to many plates in volume I, less so in volume II, 4to., pages vi, (17-) 76, (ad - 4 pages); 273; xvi, (9-) 243, list of subscribers at end volume II, contemporary full sheep (wear to extremities, some splitting to 2 outer hinges but solid, old abrasion to rear cover of volume II, foxing, mostly to volume I, small dark stain to a leaf, ex-libris Dr. James Norris with his signature on titles, a bookplate).   Raymond M. Sutton, Jr.   May 26 2011 - 55847   2011 $6000

Association – Norris, Thomas Wayne

London, Jack   1876-1916   *The Call of the Wild.*   New York: Macmillan, 1903. First American edition, only issue (vertically ribbed cloth); 231, (2) pages, frontispiece, 17 plates, vertically ribbed green pictorial cloth stamped in white, rust and black, lettering on front cover and spine in gilt, short presentation inscription in pencil by previous owner dated August 1903, bookplate, slightest of rubbing to spine ends, light foxing and stamped name to verso of color frontispiece, lower rear corner just slightly jammed, else very handsome, tipped in bookplate of famous collector Thomas Wayne Norris.   Argonaut Book Shop   Recent Acquisitions Summer 2010 - 118   2011 $1250

Association – Northumberland, Duke of

Shakespeare, William   1564-1616   *Mr. William Shakespare's Comedies, Histories and Tragedies.*   London: printed for H. Herringman, sold by Joseph Knight and Francis Saunders, 1685. Fourth folio; Folio in sixes, pages (xiv), 274, 328, 304, (2) blank, facsimile frontispiece, some light spotting throughout, few small paper flaws, minor repairs, overall generally a crisp and fresh copy, all edges gilt, dark green morocco gilt, rebacked marbled endpapers, light shelfwear, from the library of the Dukes of Northumberland.   Simon Finch Rare Books   Zero - 264   2011   £65,000

Association – Norton, Charles Eliot

Machiavelli, Niccolo 1469-1527 *Tvtte le Opere di Nicolo Machiavelli...* Geneva: Pierre Aubert, 1550, i.e. after, 1649. First "estina" edition; 4to., (4), 351, (1 blank, 4), 116, 14, (2 blank) 304, 16, 170 pages, woodcut portrait on titlepage, double page woodcut, occasional spotting ad toning, small wormhole in lower margin, later half brown levant over marbled boards, gilt stamped spine title, top edge gilt, minor repairs, early ink marginalia on endleaves and titlepage, bookplate, ink signature and notations by Charles Eliot Norton, ex-library ink stamps, monogram ownership mark, fine.   Jeff Weber Rare Books   163 - 15   2011 $2700

Association – Norton, Michael

Robbins, Tom *Another Roadside Attraction.* Garden City: Doubleday & Co., 1971. First edition; 8vo. pages 400, original green cloth backed black cloth boards, spine lettered in silver, green endpapers, original color pictorial dust jacket, author's photograph to rear panel, small stain to bottom edge of text block, light shelf wear to dust jacket extremities, light soiling to rear panel, author's inscription in blue felt tip pen to first blank, bookplate of Michael T. Norton, presentation from author.   Simon Finch Rare Books   Zero - 260   2011   £450

Association – Nottidge, Thomas

Madox, Thomas *History and Antiquities of the Exchequer of the Kings of England, in Two Periods; To Wit, from the Norman Conquest to the end of the Reign of K. John and from the End of the Reign of K. John to the End of the Reign of K. Edward II...* London: Robert Knaplock, 1711. First edition; folio, contemporary full panelled calf, rather worn, joints cracked, pages xviii, 752, xii, 75, (v), 2 divisional titles, copper engraved head pieces and initials and text illustrations, little light brown spotting to flyleaves and title, armorial bookplate of Thomas Nottidge, excellent copy.   R. F. G. Hollett & Son Antiquarian Booksellers   175 - 898   2011   £650

Association – Novello, Ivor

Shakespeare, William 1564-1616 *The Works of Shakespeare.* London: Virtue & Co., circa, 1873. Imperial edition; c, 810; (x), 778 pages, 2 volumes, folio, full page steel engravings, leather gilt with gilt lettering to spines and all page edges gilt, very good, slight external fading and handling wear, internally clean, from the library of British songwriter and thespian Ivor Novello with bookplate.   Any Amount of Books   May 26 2011 - A77056   2011 $503

Association – Nowell-Smith, Simon

Wordsworth, William 1770-1850 *Poems.* London: printed for Longman, Hurst, Orme, 1807. First edition, one of 500 copies Printed; with cancels D11-12 in volume I and B2 in volume II, volume I has half title and erratum leaf H8, volume II has half title, sectional half title leaf B1 and first state of sheet F9(i) in volume 2 with misprint "Thy fnuction" on page 98, last line; 2 volumes 8vo., original drab boards with pink paper covered spines as issued, contemporary ownership inscription to Anne Watson in volume I, with pencil ownership signature on titlepage, bookplates of Simon Nowell-Smith and his wife, light foxing, covers slightly chipped and worn but very good.   James S. Jaffe Rare Books   May 26 2011 - 21014   2011 $27,500

Association – O'Connell, Daniel

Dionysius of Halicarnassus *The Roman Antiquities of Dionysius Halicarnassensis.* London: printed and sold by booksellers of London and Westminster, 1758. 4 volumes bound as 2, 4to., pages lviii, 456, (ii); (ii), 439, (iii) + 1 double sided engraved sheet with "The Herodian Inscription" on recto, "The Athenian Inscription" on verso, (ii), 438, (ii); (ii), 516 (ii), contemporary diced Russia, boards "Grecian Key' gilt bordered, board edges 'milled' decorative roll gilt, turn-ins single rule gilt, 'Antique spot' 'made' endpapers, all edges lemon, early 21st century reback an corners by Chris Weston, age toned and foxed in places, bit of staining including large mark in gutter at end volume 1, old leather rubbed at edges, armorial bookplate of Daniel O'Connell, ink inscription, from the collection of Christopher Ernest Weston 1947-2010.   Unsworths Booksellers   24 - 87   2011   £600

Association – O'Donnell, Kim

Mitchell, John *The Bottom of the Harbor.* New York: Limited Editions Club, 1991. First edition with these illustrations, one of 250, signed on justification page by John Mitchell; 5 hors-texte photogravures hand pulled by Jon Goodman after Berenice Abbott, 12 x 10 inches, 250 pages, hand sewn and bound in black quarter Nigerian goatskin and black Irish linen, very slight binder's imperfection on cloth, otherwise excellent copy in publisher's slipcase, this copy additionally inscribed "binder's copy" signed by Kim O'Donnell of the Garthegaat Bindery.   Gemini Fine Books & Arts, Ltd.   Art Reference & Illustrated Books: First Editions 2011 $750

Mitchell, John *The Bottom of the Harbor.* New York: Limited Editions Club, 1991. First edition with these illustrations, one of 250 copies signed by Mitchell; 5 hors texte hand pulled photogravures by Berenice Abbot, 12 x 10 inches, 250 pages, hand sewn and bound in black Nigerian goatskin and black Irish linen, fit in publisher's cloth slipcase, excellent copy, binder Kim O'Donnell's copy, unnumbered, with extra engraving by Abbot bound in, colophon additionally signed by binder. Gemini Fine Books & Arts, Ltd. Art Reference & Illustrated Books: First Editions 2011 $950

Pound, Ezra Loomis 1885-1972 *Cathay.* New York: Limited Editions Club, 1992. First Clemente edition; one of 300 copies, signed and numbered by artist, 7 unsigned original color woodcuts by Francesco Clemente, printed on handmade Japanese Ogawashi paper, 12 x 8.5 inches, spine of book and edges of slipcase faded, otherwise as new, inscribed "binder's copy" and signed by Kim O'Donnell of the Garthegaat Bindery. Gemini Fine Books & Arts, Ltd. Art Reference & Illustrated Books: First Editions 2011 $1350

Association – O'Farrell, David

Loguen, J. W. *The Rev. J. W. Loguen as a Slave and as a Fireman.* New York: J. G. K. Truair, 1859. First edition; 12mo., x, (11)-444 pages, frontispiece original ful olive green blindstamped cloth, gilt spine title, extremities worn, few signatures sprung from binding, ownership labels of W. M. O'Farrell and David Mc. O'Farrell, good. Jeff Weber Rare Books 163 - 86 2011 $75

Association – O'Farrell, W. M.

Loguen, J. W. *The Rev. J. W. Loguen as a Slave and as a Fireman.* New York: J. G. K. Truair, 1859. First edition; 12mo., x, (11)-444 pages, frontispiece original ful olive green blindstamped cloth, gilt spine title, extremities worn, few signatures sprung from binding, ownership labels of W. M. O'Farrell and David Mc. O'Farrell, good. Jeff Weber Rare Books 163 - 86 2011 $75

Association – O'Kane, Helen Marguerite

Aucassin et Nicolete *The Son Story of Aucassin and Nicolete.* New Rochelle: Elston Press, 1902. One of 240 copies; 165 x 125mm., 2 p.l., 66, (3) pages, original publisher's quarter linen, gray paper boards, paper spine label with vertical titling, fore and tail edges untrimmed, introductory facing pages filled with decoration in white vine style by Helen Marguerite O'Kane, text in red and black, penned signature date 1934, 2 very small dark ink(?) spots on rear board, otherwise virtually pristine, text in mint condition. Phillip J. Pirages 59 - 188 2011 $250

Association – Oakeley, Walter

Bailey, Nathaniel *An Universal Etymological English Dictionary.* London: Printed for R. Ware, J. & P. Knapton &c., 1749. Thirteenth edition; rebound in half brown reverse calf, red morocco label, signature of Walter Oakeley on titlepage, very good. Jarndyce Antiquarian Booksellers CXCI - 155 2011 £280

Association – Oakley, Violet

Haywood, Carolyn *Here's a Penny.* New York: Harcourt Brace and Co., 1944. (I). First edition; 8vo., pictorial cloth, 158 pages, fine in very good+ dust jacket, full page and half page pen and ink drawings, this copy inscribed by Haywood for fellow artists Violet Oakley and Edith Emerson. Aleph-Bet Books, Inc. 95 - 284 2011 $350

Association – Oates, Robert Washington

Martineau, Harriet 1802-1876 *Life in the Sick Room.* London: Edward Moxon, 1844. Second edition; 8 page catalog (March 1844), preceding half title, spine bit chipped and worn, back hinge with some repairs, following board slightly marked, armorial bookplate of renowned book, collector Robert Washington Oates, good plus. Jarndyce Antiquarian Booksellers CLXC - 320 2011 £220

Association – Offutt, Chris

Beattie, Ann *Where You'll Find Me.* New York: Linden Press, 1986. First edition; near fine, spine lightly bumped, frontispiece near fine, light creasing, inscribed to Chris Offutt. Bella Luna Books May 29 2011 - t581 2011 $82

Association – Ofili, Chris

Choon, Angela *Chris Ofili: Devil's Pie.* New York and Gottingen: Steidl and David Swirner, 2008. First edition; 4to. original publisher's purple cloth lettered silver on spine and over, signed presentation from Ofili for Louise, illustrations in color, about fine. Any Amount of Books May 29 2011 - A7550 2011 $272

Association – Ogden, Charles

Bucke, Charles *On the Beauties, Harmonies and Sublimities of Nature.* London: Thomas Tegg & Son, 1837. New edition; 3 volumes, half titles, 8 page catalog (1846) in volume I, volume III lacking leading f.e.p., original red vertical grained cloth by Westley's & Clark, blocked in blind, spines faded, some slight wear to head and tail, booklabels of Charles Ogden, bookseller's ticket of H. Whitmore, Manchester. Jarndyce Antiquarian Booksellers CXCI - 329 2011 £110

Association – Ogilvie, T. W.

Rawnsley, H. D. *Ruskin and the English Lakes.* Glasgow: James MacLehose and Sons, 1901. First edition; contemporary cloth, gilt, extremities trifle rubbed, pages xii, 244, 10 plates, front joint trifle strained, scarce, signatures of T. W. Ogilvie, F. G.S. of Barrow and St. Bees, loosely inserted is autograph postcard initialled from Rawnsley to Ogilvie apologising for being too busy to help him.   R. F. G. Hollett & Son Antiquarian Booksellers   173 - 949 2011   £65

Association – Ogle, Mary

Linton, Eliza Lynn   *The Lake Country.* London: Smith, Elder & Co., 1864. First edition; original red cloth gilt extra, designed by John Leighton, over heavy bevelled boards, corners trifle frayed, pages xl, 351, all edges gilt, with 100 illustrations, double page map, frontispiece lightly spotted, signature of Mary Ogle (wife of Thomas Ogle, Lake District photographer) dated 1863, laid on top of title, handsome tight copy.   R. F. G. Hollett & Son Antiquarian Booksellers 173 - 690 2011   £225

Association – Olds, William

Ford, Worthington Chauncey   *George Washington.* New York: Goupil and Co. and Charles Scribner's Sons, 1900. One of 200 copies of Edition de Luxe; 2 volumes, 270 x 205mm., attractive green crushed morocco, covers with two line gilt frame, raised bands, gilt framed compartments and gilt titling, red morocco doublures surrounded by inch wide green morocco turn-ins, with four gilt fillets, watered silk endleaves, top edges gilt, other edges untrimmed, 8 full page plates in sepia, 42 in black and white and two frontispieces in color, as well as 32 tailpieces, chapter initials in black and red; bookplate of William P. Olds laid in at front of each volume; large paper copy; hint of wear to joints and extremities, spines mildly faded to olive green, spine of second volumned with just slightly irregular fading, still fine, binding solid and pleasing, text and plates virtually pristine. Phillip J. Pirages   59 - 345 2011 $1500

Association – Ollier, Edmund

Hotten, John Camden   *Charles Dickens, the Story of His Life.* London: John Camden Hotten, 1870.   First edition; 193 x 130mm., xvi, 367 pages, (10) leaves (ads), fine butterscotch colored straight grain morocco, handsomely gilt by Morrell (stamp signed verso front free endleaf), covers with French fillet border and rosette cornerpieces, raised bands, spine attractively gilt in double ruled compartments with ornate central lozenge surrounded by small tools and cornerpieces formed by arabesques and volutes, turn-ins heavily gilt in floral design, top edge gilt, other edges rough trimmed, front joint neatly repaired, extra illustrated with 73 portraits and engravings plus 2 folding facsimiles, titlepage with ink ownership inscription of Edmund Ollier, whose neat manuscript marginalia appears occasionally in text; just hint of wear to extremities, one leaf with one inch loosed tear to head margin (not affecting text), otherwise only trivial imperfections internally, nearly fine, lustrous and scarcely worn. Phillip J. Pirages   59 - 174 2011 $950

Association – Onslow, Florence

De La Ramee, Louise   1839-1908   *Princess Napraxine.* Leipzig: Bernhard Tauchnitz, 1884. Copyright edition; 3 volumes, half titles volumes II and III, original pink cloth, front boards lettered "Florence" and with small crown monograms in gilt, dark green leather labels, spines slightly dulled, very good, booklabels of Florence Onslow. Jarndyce Antiquarian Booksellers   CLXC - 699 2011   £45

Association – Ortiz, Alfonso

Bennett, Wendell C.   *Tarahumara, An Indian Tribe of Northern Mexico.* Chicago: 1935.   First edition; xix, 412 pages, illustrations, bookplate, name on titlepage and edges (of noted Pueblo ethnologist Alfonso Ortiz), spine faded, else very good.   Dumont Maps & Books of the West   111 - 56 2011 $125

Association – Osborne, T.

Isocrates   *Orationes et Epistolae.* Geneva: H. Estienne, 1593. Folio, (14) ff., 427, 131, XXXIV pages, (1) f. (blank), (4) ff, 31 pages, (9) ff., early 18th century English mottled calf, covers panelled in blind, spine gilt in compartments, red morocco label, printed pastedowns, slight worming, upper joint split at head an foot, inscription on titlepage T. Osborne 17th century and Wm. Robinson (18th century), fine armorial bookplate of William Robinson & Coll. Jes. Soc. Com., from the library of the Earls of Macclesfield at Shirburn Castle. Maggs Bros. Ltd.   1440 - 116 2011   £900

Association – Osgood, Rev.

Everett, Edward *Inauguration of Washington University at Saint Louis Missouri April 23 1857.* Boston: Little Brown and Co., 1857. First edition; 8vo., 104 pages, removed, presentation inscription from Everett to Rev. Osgood dated 14 Dec. 1857. M & S Rare Books, Inc. 90 - 437 2011 $150

Association – Osmond, T. S.

Maximus Tyrius *The Dissertations of Maximus Tyrius.* London: printed by C. Whittenham, Dean Street for the Translator and sold by R. H. Evans Pall Mall, 1804. First edition; small 8vo., 2 volumes in 1, pages xv, (1) 235, (1); 272 pages, later bottle green cloth (circa 1900), neat label of Pantiles (Tunbridge Wells) Library and Reading Room, no other library markings, booklabel of T. S. Osmond of St. John's College, Oxford (donor of the book), pencilled ownership signature of historian F. R. Cowell, very good, clean text free of foxing, couple of gatherings very slightly protruding but sound attractive copy. Any Amount of Books May 26 2011 - A46360 2011 $470

Association – Ouseley, Gore

Savioli, Lodovico Vittorio *Amri.* Crisopoli (Parma): Co'tipi Bodoniani, 1795. Fine stipple engraved medallion portrait on title just touch of faint dust soiling, pages (viii), 133, (3), 4to., contemporary mottled paper boards backed with mottled sheep, backstrip divided by triple gilt fillets, brown label in second compartment, rest with central gilt portrait tools, marbled pastedowns, stitching strained after title, bit scuffed in places, bookplate of Sir Gore Ouseley, Bt., good. Blackwell Rare Books B166 - 93 2011 £400

Association – Page, Hariette Story

Webster, Daniel 1782-1852 *An Address Delivered Before the New York Historical Society February 23, 1852.* New York: Press of the Historical Society, 1852. First edition; octavo, pamphlet bound in printed wrappers, 57 pages, moderate age toning, minor wear to wrappers, front wrapper neatly detached, vertical crease down center, very good, inscribed and signed by Webster for Mrs. (Harriette Story) Page. Charles Agvent 2010 Summer Miscellany - 64 2011 $950

Association – Paine, Robert Treat

Abbot, Abiel *Self Preservation. A Sermon Preached Before the Ancient and Honorable Artillery Company in Boston June 7 1802...* First edition; 8vo., 23, (1) pages, illustrated half title, sewn and uncut, original plain front wrapper, presented by militia commander General John Winslow to Judge (Robert Treate) Paine. M & S Rare Books, Inc. 90 - 1 2011 $125

Association – Pakington, John

Barruel, Augustin *Memoirs, Illustrating the History of Jacobinism....* London: printed for the translator by T. Burton, 1798. Second edition in English; 4 volumes, 8vo., (4), xvi, 401, (1), and (4), 479, (1); and xviii, 414; xviii, 601, (1), 50 pages, engraved plate of alphabets in volume III, large folding chart in volume IV (slightly cropped at foot affecting letters), one or two very minor marks here and there, contemporary uniform half calf gilt with contrasting red and black labels, vellum tips, little wear to joints but very good in first bindings, 19th century armorial bookplate in each volume of John S. Pakington. John Drury Rare Books 153 - 10 2011 £400

Association – Palmerston, Henry John Temple, 3rd Earl of

Macaulay, Zachary *Negro Slavery; or a View of Some of the More Prominent Features of that State of Society as it Exists in the United States of America and in the Colonies of the West Indies, Especially in Jamaica.* London: for Hatchard and Son... and J. and A. Arch, 1823. First edition; (4), 118 pages, attractive modern half calf by Bayntun, fine, fresh copy inside and out, Lord Palmerston's copy with his signature, (Henry John Temple, 3rd Viscount Palmerston). Joseph J. Felcone Inc. Fall Miscellany 2010 - 80 2011 $900

Association – Parker, James

Sullivan, J. *Cumberland & Westmorland, Ancient and Modern...* Whittaker & Co. and Kendal: John Hudson, 1837. First edition; original blindstamped cloth, gilt, pages iii, 171, scarce, James Parker's copy. R. F. G. Hollett & Son Antiquarian Booksellers 173 - 1082 2011 £95

Association – Parker, Thomas Towneley

Ronalds, Alfred *The Fly-Fisher's Entomology.* London: Longman, Green and Co., 1877. Eighth edition; original blindstamped green cloth, gilt, extremities little frayed and bumped, lower hinge repaired at foot, pages xiv, (ii), 132, 24, 20 finely hand colored plates, front joint strained and strengthened, armorial bookplates of Thomas Towneley Parker and Reginald Arthur Tatton. R. F. G. Hollett & Son Antiquarian Booksellers General Catalogue Summer 2010 - 1277 2011 £195

Association – Parks, Gordon

Carisella, P. J. *The Black Swallow of Death...* Boston: Marlbourough House Inc., 1972. 8vo., pages xiv, 271, 22 illustrations in text, one page slightly soiled, otherwise internally fine, publisher's cloth, blue, red lettering to upper board, white lettering and red motif to spine, fine, original color illustrated dust jacket, unclipped, lightly worn with short closed tears to head and foot of spine, presentation letter to Gordon Parks loosely inserted.   Simon Finch Rare Books   Zero - 213   2011   £375

Association – Parrish, Maxfield

Saunders, Louise *The Knave of Hearts.* New York: Charles Scribner's Sons, 1925. First edition; large quarto, (6), 46, (1) (3, blank) pages, color frontispiece and tissue guards, many full page color illustrations by Maxfield Parrish, laid into this copy is ANS by artist for Mr. Johnson, original black cloth with color pictorial label on front cover, color pictorial endpapers, some very light scuffing of back board, very clean internally, about fine in most of original glassine wrappers, however torn quite a bit, original issue cardboard box, box heavily worn, bottom of box intact but cracked at corners, top of box has its sides detached, however this box usually not present at all.   Heritage Book Shop   Holiday 2010 - 94   2011 $5500

Wharton, Edith   1862-1937   *Italian Villas and Their Gardens.* New York: Century, 1904. First and only edition; heavily illustrated with photos, drawings, 26 full color plates by Maxfield Parrish, with 3 page ALS from Wharton tipped in, written to Mrs. Sage, with two page ALS from Maxfield Parrish, written in his elegant calligraphic hand, owner's small tasteful bookplate adorns front pastedown.   Ken Lopez Bookseller   154 - 241   2011 $10,000

Association – Patavii, Paulus Johanne

Manutius, Aldus   *De Quaesitis per Epistolam Libri III.* Venice: Aldus Manutius, 1576. First edition; 3 parts, 8vo., (8), 125, (3 blank); 106, (6 blank); 103 pages, 17th century German blindstamped pigskin over pasteboard, red edges, very nice, titlepage inscribed "Paulus Johanne?? Patavii MDLXXVII", from the library of the Earls of Macclesfield at Shirburn Castle. Maggs Bros. Ltd.   1440 - 140   2011   £450

Association – Patterson, Virginia

Arnow, Harriette   *The Dollmaker.* London: Heinemann, 1955. First British edition; warmly inscribed by author for Virginia Patterson, laid into book are two autograph Christmas cards signed by Arnow 1968 and 1972 with lengthy notes, uncommon thus, book has tear at upper edge of front endpaper, and lower corner bump, otherwise near fine in fair dust jacket, corner chipped dust jacket fully split at front flap fold, pictorial dust jacket differs markedly from that of US edition, cards are fine.   Ken Lopez Bookseller   154 - 8   2011 $650

Association – Payn, James

Blackmore, Richard Doddridge   1825-1900   *Lorna Doone: a Romance of Exmoor.* London: Sampson Low, Son & Marston, 1869. First edition, apparently one of 500 copies printed; 3 volumes, octavo, vi, 332; lv, 340; iv, 342 pages, bound without prelim blank leaf in volume I and final blank leaf in volume III, but with 16 page publisher's catalog dated March 1869, at end volume III, bound circa 1960 by Bayntun-Riviere (stamp signed in gilt on front turn-in), full red morocco, covers with gilt double fillet border, spines panelled and lettered in gilt on front turn-in), in full red morocco, covers with gilt double fillet border, spines panelled and lettered in gilt compartments with five raised bands, board edges and turn-ins decoratively tooled in gilt, all edges gilt, marbled endpapers, spines very slightly sunned, few short, expertly repaired margin tears, some occasional minor foxing or soiling, bookplate of J. Hodges, overall, excellent copy, laid in is ALS from author to James Payn, Teddington, Dec. 34d 1877.   David Brass Rare Books, Inc.   May 26 2011 - 00726   2011 $6500

Association – Payne, John Thomas

Guevara, Antonio De *Vita Di M. Avrelio Imperadore.* Venice: Bartolomeo Imperador and Francesco Veneziano, 1543. 160 x 103mm., 8 p.l., 132, (2) leaves, fine contemporary Roman red morocco Apollo and Pegasus medallion binding done for Giovanni Battista Grimaldi by Marc Antonio Guillery, (genuine Apollo and Pegasus binding) covers with gilt frame formed by two widely spaced fillets with lobes interlaced at ends and sides, space between fillets decorated with broad foliate curls, small floral tools, inner pane of each board with gilt titling above a horizontal oval Apollo and Pegasus plaquette centerpiece showing Pegasus atop black painted heights of Parnassus and Apollo racing his chariot (drawn by two straining steeds) across steep terrain with reins and whip held aloft and caps fluttering behind, plaquette with gilt motto in Greek in the collar above and below vignette, spine (very expertly rebacked) with four thin and three thick raised bands decorated with gilt rope pattern or plain rules (this being original backstrip?), newer (perhaps 19th century) endpapers, all edges gilt (apparently some remarkably skillful restoration at one or more corners and edges, perhaps some gold added, as well as to the chariot part of the plaquettes); woodcut printer's device on , morocco bookplate and separate gilt monogram of Robert Hoe as well as inscription and vellum bookplate of Swedish collector Thore Virgin, ownership inscription of J. T. Payne dated 1850; covers with half dozen insignificant tiny dark spots, titlepage faintly soiled, thin light brown stain just at top edge of leaves, small wormhole at upper inner margin (text not affected), occasional minor stains, other trivial imperfections, but no defects that are even remotely serious and in general really excellent specimen of a very special binding, text fresh and leather quite lustrous; also from the collection of bibliophile Johannes Gennadius, Liverpool oculist T. Shadford Walker and Swedish collector Rolfe Wistrand. Phillip J. Pirages   59 - 2   2011 $35,000

Association – Pears, Betty

MacDonald, George   1824-1905   *Sir Gibbie.* London: Cassell & Co., 1927.   Half title, original grey blue cloth, slightly sunned, bookplate of Betty Pears.   Jarndyce Antiquarian Booksellers   CXCII - 219   2011   £30

Association – Pearson, L. B.

Elliott, Charles Boileau   *Two Letters Addressed to the Supreme Government of British India, Regarding the Abolition of Suttees, and the Best Means of Ameliorating the Moral and Intellectual Condition of the Natives of India.* Salisbury: Printed by Brodie and Dowding, n.d. but, 1827. First edition; 8vo., (2), 45, (1) pages, recent marbled boards, lettered on spine, very good, presentation copy inscribed by author L. B. Pearson Sept. 1828, very rare.   John Drury Rare Books   154 - 47   2011   £175

Association – Pease, Joseph Robinson

Cave, Henry   *Antquities of York.*   London: published by R. Ackermann, York: printed at the Office of G. Peacock, 1813. 1807; 2 works bound together as 1, 4to., pages iv, (ii), 31, (i) + engraved titlepage and 40 engraved plates (iv), iii, (i), 10, (ii) (xxiv) + engraved titlepage and 34 engraved plates, contemporary empanelled calf boards double bordered with decorative roll of consecutive polished pinheads gilt, central 'French Shell' 'made' endpapers, all edges marbled as per outer panels, green & vermillion sewn flat endbands, mid 20th century calf reback, some browning and foxing, few plates significantly but mostly light, old boards scuffed and little rubbed around edges, armorial bookplate of Joseph Robinson Pease, from the collection of Christopher Ernest Weston 1947-2010.   Unsworths Booksellers   24 - 75 2011 £1000

Association – Peel, Robert

Cruikshank, George   1792-1878   *Scraps and Sketches.* Published by the artist, 1828.   Oblong folio, title and 6 leaves of plates, tear to lower margin of 3rd leaf not affecting image, contemporary half dark brown morocco, marbled paper boards, dark brown morocco label with elaborate gilt borders, extremities, little rubbed, leading inner hinge slightly cracking, presentation inscription on title to Capt. Marryat RN with best compliments, of George Cruikshank; armorial bookplate of Sir Robert Peel.   Jarndyce Antiquarian Booksellers   CXCI - 147   2011   £650

Association – Peirce, Joseph

Walter, William   *A Discourse Delivered before the Humane Society of Massachusetts at the Semi-annual Meeting Twelfth of June 1798.* Boston: printed by John & Thomas Fleet, 1798.   First edition; small 4to., 48, (2) (blank leaf) pages, half title, sewn as issued, small blank piece missing from half title, edges slightly frayed, contemporary signature of Joseph Peirce at top of half title.   M & S Rare Books, Inc.   90 - 433   2011 $325

Association – Pelch, John

Sallustius Crispus, Caius   *C. Crispi Sallustii Belli Catilinarii et Jugurthini Historiae.*   Glasguae: in aedibus Roberti Urie, 1749. 8vo., pages iv, 250, (ii), contemporary polished calf, untooled spine, red lettering piece gilt, boards double rule bordered in blind with extra double rule and decorative roll in blind at joint side, board edges 'zip-zag' decorative roll gilt, all edges red speckled, pink and white sewn endbands, lightly age toned, few stains, rubbed and bit chipped, joints cracking, spine darkened, contemporary ink inscription John Pelch, first name covered by pasted slip and later ink inscription "Wm. Clark, also pencil inscription "From Prof. Henry Jackson's Sale…", from the collection of Christopher Ernest Weston 1947-2010.   Unsworths Booksellers   24 - 139   2011   £50

Association – Pembroke, Earl of

Rigge, Henry Fletcher *Cartmel Priory Church, North Lancashire.* Cartmel: E. Wilson, 1879. First edition; small 8vo., original blue cloth gilt with Earl of Pembroke's arms on upper board, pages 36, all edges gilt, frontispiece, scarce. R. F. G. Hollett & Son Antiquarian Booksellers 173 - 968 2011 £75

Association – Penrose, Bois

Coryate, Thomas *Coryats Crudities Hastily Gobbled Up in Five Moneths Travells in France, Savoy, Italy, Rhetia Comonly Called the Grisons Country, Helvetia Alias Switzerland, some Parts of High Germany and the Netherlands.* London: by William Stansby, 1611. First edition; printed title present, engraved allegorical title by William Hole (shaved very slightly at head), engraved plates, woodcut, text portrait, errata leaf present, many woodcut initials and headpieces, 19th century brown crushed levant morocco, gilt by Bedford, unusually tall, very handsome copy, rare printed title, from the libraries of Ward E. Terry, R. B. Adam, A. Edward Newton, Bois Penrose and Wolfgang A. Herz with their respective bookplates and book labels. Joseph J. Felcone Inc. Fall Miscellany 2010 - 35 2011 $16,000

Association – Pepler, Richard

The Lady's Law; or a Treatise of Feme Converts: containing al the Laws and Statutes Relating to Women Under Several Heads... London: in the Savoy: printed by E. and R. Nutt and R. gosling (assigns of E. Sayer, Esq.) for H. L. and sold by C. Corbett and E. Littleton, 1737. Second edition; 8vo., (iii)-viii 264 (16) pages, wanting initial leaf of ads, contemporary ruled calf, rebacked and labelled, very good, crisp copy, early ownership signature of James Crummer, 20th century bookplate of Richard Pepler. John Drury Rare Books 153 - 75 2011 £850

Association – Pepper, Lt. Col.

Stewarton *The Female Revolutionary Plutarch.* London: printed for John Murray, 1806. 1805. First editions; 196 x 11mm., 3 volumes, publisher's original blue paper boards, paper title labels on flat spines, edges untrimmed, frontispiece portraits, page one of each volume with lightly written signature of Lt. Col. Pepper(?), some (surprisingly minor) chafing and soiling to covers and spines, upper corner of one leaf torn off by rough opening (no loss of text), insignificant tiny round wormhole in gutter margin of first two gatherings of volume III, but exceptionally fine set, bindings all completely sound and showing no serious wear, text especially clean, bright and fresh. Phillip J. Pirages 59 - 351 2011 $1900

Association – Pepper, Michael

Dobson, Susanna *The Life of Petarch.* London: T. Bensely, 1797. Third edition; 2 volumes, engraved plates, manuscript poem on front endpaper, few fox marks to plates, half titles discarded, pages xviii, 388, (12); (ii), 410, (8), 8vo., 19th century vellum over boards, backstrips ruled in gilt with brown morocco labels, gilt lettering, boards bowing, marbled endpapers and edges, good, bookplates of Michael Pepper. Blackwell Rare Books B166 - 78 2011 £200

Association – Perlman, Alfred

Burns, Robert 1759-1796 *Poems, Chiefly in the Scottish Dialect.* Edinburgh: printed for author and sold by William Creech, 1787. First Edinburgh edition, first issue; first issue with "Roxburgh" misprinted "Boxburgh" on page xxxvii in list of subscribers with page 232 correctly printed and with 'skinking' on page 263, line 13, octavo, xlviii, (9)-368 pages, half title, frontispiece, bookplate of Alfred B. Perlman, original blue grey paper boards, uncut, few leaves carelessly opened, bookplate and name in ink on front pastedown, small ink presentation inscription on head of title, chemised within green cloth clamshell box, extraordinary copy, rarely found in original state, quite rare. David Brass Rare Books, Inc. May 26 2011 - 01388 2011 $5500

Association – Perry, Thomas

Latham, John *A General History of Birds.* Winchester: Jacob and Johnson, 1821-1828. New edition; 193 hand colored copper engraved plates after Latham (minor offsetting from text to some plates, only occasional foxing to plates, plates near fine), 4to., contemporary three quarter leather over marbled boards, spines beautifully replaced with gilt decorated polished calf, rubbing to marbled boards, several corners showing, black stain to inside margin of a page of text, occasional foxing to text, sometimes heavy, ex-libris Thomas Perry, marbled endpapers. Raymond M. Sutton, Jr. May 26 2011 - 50931 2011 $11,00

Association – Peterson, Clare Gray

Contributions to Medical and Biological Research, Dedicated to Sir William Osler in Honour of His Seventieth Birthday July 12 1919 by His Pupils and Co-Workers. New York: Paul B. Hoeber, 1919. Limited to 1600 copies; 2 volumes, 8vo., xix, (xx), 649; xi, (xii), 651-1268 pages, decorative orange title border, frontispiece of Osler with tissue guard (volume I), plates, navy cloth, gilt stamped cover and spine titles, top edge gilt, near fine, from the Medical Library of Dr. Clare Gray Peterson. Jeff Weber Rare Books 162 - 231 2011 $95

Cushing, Harvey Williams 1869-1939 *The Life of Sir William Osler.* Oxford: Clarendon Press, 1925. First edition; 2 volumes, xiii, (2), 685; x, (2), 728 pages, frontispiece (both volumes), 42 plates, index, original navy cloth, gilt stamped spine titles, little tears to spine ends, previous owner's inked signature and rubber stamp, good, from the Medical Library of Dr. Clare Gray Peterson. Jeff Weber Rare Books 162 - 232 2011 $75

Harsell, Olof *The Comparative Anatomy and Histology of the Cerebellum: The Human Cerebellum, Cerebellar Connections and Cerebellar Cortex.* Minneapolis: University of Minnesota Press, 1972. First edition; 4to., ix, (ii), 268 pages, 67 plates, figures, index, original green cloth, gilt stamped spine title, dust jacket, fine, from the Medical Library of Dr. Clare Gray Peterson. Jeff Weber Rare Books 162 - 185 2011 $125

Jackson, Chevalier *Bronchoscopy an Esophagoscopy.* Philadelphia & London: W. B. Saunders, 1922. First edition; 8vo., 346 pages, 5 plates, numbered figures, index, original black cloth, gilt stamped spine title, ex-library bookplate stamp, spine call number, very good, from the Medical Library of Dr. Clare Gray Peterson. Jeff Weber Rare Books 162 - 168 2011 $100

Jefferson, Geoffrey *Selected Papers.* Springfield: Charles C. Thomas, 1960. First US edition; 8vo., xi, (xii), 563 pages, frontispiece, 51 plates, 69 numbered figures, yellow cloth, gilt stamped orange spine label, dust jacket bit soiled, else fine, previous owner's signature, from the Medical Library of Dr. Clare Gray Peterson. Jeff Weber Rare Books 162 - 172 2011 $125

Jones, Frederic Wood *The Principles of Anatomy as Seen in the Hand.* London: J. & A. Churchill, 1920. 8vo., viii, 325 pages, 2 plates, including frontispiece, 123 numbered figures, original brown cloth, gilt stamped spine title, extremities speckled, very good, this copy belonged to C. Elmer Carlson, M.D. Orthopedic Surgery (Oregon) with his signature, from the Medical Library of Dr. Clare Gray Peterson. Jeff Weber Rare Books 162 - 173 2011 $120

Kocher, Emil Theodor *Text-Book of Operative Surgery.* London: Adam and Charles Black, 1903. Large 8vo., xxv, 440 pages, 255 numbered figures, dark blue cloth, gilt stamped spine title, ex-library bookplate with embossed stamp on title, spine call number painted over, ownership signature of Ernst A. Sommer, very good, from the Medical Library of Dr. Clare Gray Peterson. Jeff Weber Rare Books 162 - 177 2011 $200

Krogh, Schack August Steenberg *The Anatomy and Physiology of Capillaries.* New Haven & London: Yale University Press & Oxford University Press, 1922. First edition; 8vo., xvii, 276 pages, numbered figures, original navy cloth, gilt stamped spine title, previous owner's inked signature and rubber stamp, from the Medical Library of Dr. Clare Gray Peterson. Jeff Weber Rare Books 162 - 178 2011 $100

Larrey, Dominique Jean *Observations on Wounds, and Their Complications by Erysipelas, Gangrene and Tetanus and on the Principal Diseases and Injuries of the Head, Ear and Eye.* Philadelphia: Mielke & Biddle, 1832. Small 4to., viii, 332 pages, 2 plates, original speckled calf, neatly rebacked, gilt spine rules, black morocco spine label, original endleaves preserved, short period inscription on front pastedown and previous owner's inked signature, embossed stamp on title, very good, from the Medical Library of Dr. Clare Gray Peterson. Jeff Weber Rare Books 162 - 182 2011 $650

Larsell, Olof *The Comparative Anatomy and Histology of the Cerebellum from Myxinoids through Birds.* Minneapolis: University of Minnesota Press, 1967. First edition; 4to., viii, (ix-x), 291 pages, 242 numbered figures, index, original red cloth, gilt stamped spine title, dust jacket, fine, from the Medical Library of Dr. Clare Gray Peterson. Jeff Weber Rare Books 162 - 184 2011 $125

Larsell, Olof *The Comparative Anatomy and Histology of the Cerebellum from Monotremes through Apes.* Minneapolis: University of Minnesota Press, 1970. First edition; 4to., v, (ii), 269 pages, 233 numbered figures, original blue cloth, gilt stamped spine title, dust jacket, top jacket edge bit worn, near fine, from the Medical Library of Dr. Clare Gray Peterson. Jeff Weber Rare Books 162 - 184 2011 $125

Le Fanu, William *A Catalogue of the Portrait and Other Paintings, Drawings and Sculpture in the Royal College of Surgeons of England.* Edinburgh and London: E. & S. Livingstone, 1960. 8vo., xii, 119, plates, 52 pages, color frontispiece, numerous plates, blue cloth, gilt stamped cover emblem and spine title, dust jacket, very good, signed presentation inscription from author, from the Medical Library of Dr. Clare Gray Peterson. Jeff Weber Rare Books 162 - 188 2011 $60

Livingston, William Kenneth *The Clinical Aspects of Visceral Neurology: with Special Reference to the Surgery of the Sympathetic Nervous System.* Springfield and Baltimore: Charles C. Thomas, 1935. First edition; 8vo., xi, 254 pages, 3 color plates, figures, indexes, original blue cloth, gilt stamped spine title, dust jacket, near fine, author's signed presentation to Homer Rush, from the Medical Library of Dr. Clare Gray Peterson. Jeff Weber Rare Books 162 - 198 2011 $125

Longet, Francois Achille *Experiences Relatives avec Effets de l'Inhalation de l'ether Suffurique sur le Systeme Nerveux.* Paris: Victor Masson, 1847. First edition; 8vo., 54 pages, pages lightly foxed, original printed wrappers, uncut, housed in gray cloth clamshell box with gilt stamped black leather spine label, ownership inked signature on front cover, fine, from the Medical Library of Dr. Clare Gray Peterson.   Jeff Weber Rare Books   162 - 199 2011 $3500

Lorentz, Hendirk Antoon *Versuch Einer Theorie der Electrischen und Optischen Erscheinungen in Bewegten Korpern.* Leiden: E. J. Brill, 1895. First edition; 8vo. 138, (1) pages, modern quarter brown cloth and printed paper boards, gilt stamped black leather spine label, fine, library and release stamp of University of Groningen, from the Medical Library of Dr. Clare Gray Peterson.   Jeff Weber Rare Books   162 - 197 2011 $5000

McGill University *Neurological Biographies and Addresses. Foundation Volume.* London: Humphrey Milford, Oxford University Press, 1936. First edition; 8vo. viii 178 pages, frontispiece, plates, navy cloth, gilt stamped spine title, small ownership signature blacked over, fine, scarce, from the Medical Library of Dr. Clare Gray Peterson.   Jeff Weber Rare Books   162 - 203 2011 $100

McLean, Arthur J. *Intercranial Tumors.* Berlin: Julius Springer, 1936. 8vo., (iv), (131-285), errata (1) pages, 138 figures, green cloth, gilt stamped spine title, ownership signature of Lawrence Selling this copy with signed TLS from author to Selling, fine, rare, from the Medical Library of Dr. Clare Gray Peterson.   Jeff Weber Rare Books   162 - 206 2011 $250

Meigs, Jon Vincent *Tumors of the Female Pelvic Organs.* New York: Macmillan, 1934. First edition; 8vo., xxxiv, 533 pages, color frontispiece, numerous figures and tables, original navy cloth, gilt stamped spine title, previous owner's inked signature and rubber stamp, near fine, from the Medical Library of Dr. Clare Gray Peterson.   Jeff Weber Rare Books   162 - 215 2011 $100

Monro, Thomas Kirkpatrick *Raynaud's Disease Local Syncope, Local Asphyxia, Symmetrical Gangrene): Its History, Causes, Symptoms, Morbid Relations, Pathology & Treatment.* Glasgow: James Maclehose & Sons, 1899. 8vo., xii, 251 pages, frontispiece, 3 tables, green cloth, gilt stamped spine title, very good, inscribed by John F. Fulton to William Livingston, from the Medical Library of Dr. Clare Gray Peterson.   Jeff Weber Rare Books   162 - 218 2011 $150

Moore, Francis D. *The Metabolic Response in Surgery.* Springfield: Charles C. Thomas, 1952. Small 4to., xv, 156 pages, figures, tables, black pebbled cloth, gilt stamped cover and spine titles, blue ink underlining on page 136-7, previous owner's inked signature and rubber stamps, signed presentation inscription, from the Medical Library of Dr. Clare Gray Peterson.   Jeff Weber Rare Books   162 - 220 2011 $150

Morison, Alexander *The Physiognomy of Mental Diseases.* Weiler im Allgau: Editions Medicina Rara, n.d., Limited to 2500 copies, facsimile reproduction of 1843 second edition; 8vo., unpaginated, illustrations, quarter tan leather with black paper boards, blindstamped spine title, housed in paper slipcase, fine, from the Medical Library of Dr. Clare Gray Peterson.   Jeff Weber Rare Books   162 - 221 2011 $95

Osler, William 1849-1919 *Bibliotheca Osleriana. A Catalogue of Books Illustrating the History of Medicine and Science.* Mansfield Centre: Maurizio Martino, n.d., Facsimile reprint of 1929 Oxfored edition limited to 150 copies; thick 8vo. xxxv, 785 pages, index, light gray cloth, gilt stamped red spine label, fine, from the Medical Library of Dr. Clare Gray Peterson.   Jeff Weber Rare Books   162 - 230 2011 $90

Pare, Ambroise 1510-1590 *Oeuvres Completes d'Ambroise Pare...* Paris: J. B. Bailliere, 1840-1841. 3 volumes, 8vo., cccli, (1), 459; (4), 811; (4), xxxii, 878 pages, frontispiece in volume I and 217 line engravings by A. Chazal, original printed wrappers, uncut, unopened, fine, near mint set, from the Medical Library of Dr. Clare Gray Peterson.   Jeff Weber Rare Books   162 - 233 2011 $1900

Pare, Ambroise 1510-1590 *Ten Books of Surgery and the Magazine of the Instruments Necessary for It.* Athens: University of Georgia, 1969. First edition; 8vo., xvi, 264 pages, illustrations, brown cloth, gilt ruled cover borders and gilt stamped spine title, near fine, presentation inscription by translator Nathan Womack, from the Medical Library of Dr. Clare Gray Peterson.   Jeff Weber Rare Books   162 - 234 2011 $50

Pare, Ambroise 1510-1599 *The Collected Works of Ambroise Pare.* Pound Ridge: Milford House, 1968. Facsimile reprint of the 1634 first edition in English; (xii), 1173, table/index 22 pages, brown cloth, black stamped spine title, housed in black paper slipcase with printed cloth label, book in excellent condition, slipcase has bit of wear to extremities, hinges strong and intact, very good+, from the Medical Library of Dr. Clare Gray Peterson.   Jeff Weber Rare Books   162 - 235 2011 $250

Penfield, Wilder Graves *Epilepsy and Cerebral Localization: a Study of the Mechanism, Treatment and Prevention of Epileptic Seizures.* Springfield and Baltimore: Charles C. Thomas, 1941. 8vo., x, 623 pages, illustrations, original navy cloth, gilt stamped cover illustrations, spine title, previous owner's inked signature and rubber stamp, fine, from the Medical Library of Dr. Clare Gray Peterson. Jeff Weber Rare Books 162 - 241 2011 $250

Peters, John P. *Body Water: The Exchange of Fluids in Man.* Springfield and Baltimore: Charles C. Thomas, 1935. 8vo., viii, 405 pages, figures, tables, green cloth, gilt stamped spine title, dust jacket, fine, scarce in jacket, bookplate and inkstamp of Ira Albert Manville, Portland, from the Medical Library of Dr. Clare Gray Peterson. Jeff Weber Rare Books 162 - 242 2011 $65

Peterson, Clare Gray *Perspectives in Surgery.* Philadelphia: Lea and Febiger, 1972. First edition; 8vo., xvi, 339 pages, frontispiece, 83 numbered figures, blue cloth, gilt stamped cover and spine titles, all edges gilt, fine, author's personal copy and probably a deluxe edition, from the Medical Library of Dr. Clare Gray Peterson. Jeff Weber Rare Books 162 - 243 2011 $75

Pugh, John *A Treatise on the Science of Muscular Action.* London: Editions Medicina Rara, n.d., Facsimile reprint of original 1794 London edition, limited to 2500 copies (total edition of 2800) bound thus; 330 x 240mm., ix (mis-numbered xi), vi-xvi, 106 pages, 15 plates, each accompanied by duplicate outline plate, three quarter burgundy leather with maroon buckram sides, silver stamped spine title, housed in paper slipcase, fine, from the Medical Library of Dr. Clare Gray Peterson. Jeff Weber Rare Books 162 - 246 2011 $100

Purves-Stewart, James *Intracranial Tumours and Some Errors in Their Diagnosis.* London, et al: Humphrey Milford, Oxford University Press, 1927. First edition; 8vo., xiii, 206 pages, illustrations, index, maroon cloth, black stamped cover title and gilt stamped spine title, ex-library bookplate with embossed stamp on title, spine call numbered painted over, rubber stamp of Dr. Ernst A. Sommer, from the Medical Library of Dr. Clare Gray Peterson. Jeff Weber Rare Books 162 - 247 2011 $65

Quick, Armand James *The Physiology and Pathology of Hemostasis.* Philadelphia: Lea & Febiger, 1951. First edition; 8vo., 188 pages, figures, index, original blue cloth, gilt stamped spine title, previous owner's inked signature and stamp, fine, from the Medical Library of Dr. Clare Gray Peterson. Jeff Weber Rare Books 162 - 248 2011 $75

Ramon Y Cajal, Santiago 1852-1934 *Histology of the Nervous System of Man and Vertebrates.* New York: Oxford University Press, 1995. First printing of this edition; thick 8vo., xl, 805; x, 806 pages, 1025 figures, gilt and green stamped pictorial blue cloth, new, from the Medical Library of Dr. Clare Gray Peterson. Jeff Weber Rare Books 162 - 249 2011 $210

Ramon Y Cajal, Santiago 1852-1934 *Precepts and Counsels on Scientific Imagination: Stimulants of the Spirit.* New York: Oxford University Press, 1951. First edition in English, trade issue; 8vo., xii, 180 pages, frontispiece tipped in, maroon cloth, gilt stamped spine title, ownership signature of John G. Kidd, 1952, fine, from the Medical Library of Dr. Clare Gray Peterson. Jeff Weber Rare Books 162 - 250 2011 $100

Scarff, John E. *Fifty Years of Neurosurgery 1905-1955.* N.P. given: Franklin H. Martin Memorial Foundation, 1955. Reprint from Surgery Gynecology & Obstetrics, Nov. 1955, Volume 101; 8vo., 303-399 pages, 85 numbered figures, printed wrappers, previous owner's inked signature and rubberstamps, title info inked on spine, near fine, signed presentation inscription from author, from the Medical Library of Dr. Clare Gray Peterson. Jeff Weber Rare Books 162 - 270 2011 $75

Sharpey-Schafer, Edward Albert *The Endocrine Organ: a Introduction to the Study of Internal Secretion.* London, et al: Longmans, Green and Co., 1924-1926. Second edition; 2 volumes, 8vo., ix, 175; xxii, 177-418 pages, 204 numbered figures, indexes, original green cloth, blindstamped cover title and gilt stamped spine title, previous owner's inked signature and rubber stamp, near fine, from the Medical Library of Dr. Clare Gray Peterson. Jeff Weber Rare Books 162 - 274 2011 $100

Sherrington, Charles Scott *The Integrative Action of the Nervous System.* New York: Charles Scribner's Sons, 1906. First American edition; 8o., xvi, 411 pages, 85 text figures, original blue cloth, gilt stamped spine title, fine, from the Medical Library of Dr. Clare Gray Peterson. Jeff Weber Rare Books 162 - 276 2011 $2700

Sherrington, Charles Scott *The Integrative Action of the Nervous System.* New Haven: Yale University Press, 1947. Reprint; 8vo., xxiv, 433 pages, frontispiece, 85 numbered figures, beige cloth, black stamped spine title, previous owner's inked signature, very good, from the Medical Library of Dr. Clare Gray Peterson. Jeff Weber Rare Books 162 - 277 2011 $75

V. Muller & Co. *A Comprehensive Guide to Purchasing Hospital Professional Instruments-Equipment-Supplies.* Chicago: V. Mueller, 1956. 8vo., 611 pages, illustrations, stiff leatherette wrappers, top spine bit worn, previous owner's inked signature, very good, from the Medical Library of Dr. Clare Gray Peterson. Jeff Weber Rare Books 162 - 296 2011 $75

Waller, Erik *Bibliotheca Walleriana.* Stockholm: Almqvist & Wiksell, 1955. Limited to 100 copies; 2 volumes 8vo., xi, (xii), 471; 494 pages, frontispiece with facsimile signature, two color title printed in brown and black, 55 plates, original printed wrapper, like new in original shipping box, from the Medical Library of Dr. Clare Gray Peterson. Jeff Weber Rare Books 162 - 266 2011 $150

Watson-Jones, Reginald *Fractures and Joint Injuries.* Baltimore: Williams and Wilkins, 1944. Third edition; 2 volumes, 4to. xi, 407; vii, 409-960 pages, numerous figures, original navy cloth, gilt stamped spine titles, extremities lightly rubbed, ownership signature stamp of Clare Gray Peterson, near fine, signed and inscribed to Peterson by author. Jeff Weber Rare Books 162 - 307 2011 $500

Wood, Horatio Charles *A Treatise on Therapeutics, Comprising Materia Medica and Toxiology...* Philadelphia: J. B. Lippincott, 1876. Second edition; thick 8vo., 674 (ads), 12 pages, figures, pencil marginalia, original full sheepskin, black leather spine label, gilt spine, lightly rubbed, ownership signature and rubber stamp, very good, from the Medical Library of Dr. Clare Gray Peterson. Jeff Weber Rare Books 162 - 311 2011 $100

Association – Peyson, Emma

More, Hannah 1745-1833 *Sacred Dramas:... Sensibility: an Epistle.* London: T. Cadell and W. Davies, 1817. Twenty-first edition; frontispiece, title vignette, full contemporary calf, gilt spine and borders, green label, very good, attractive copy, inscription to Emma Peyson. Jarndyce Antiquarian Booksellers CLXC - 529 2011 £35

Association – Phillimore, A.

Trollope, Anthony 1815-1882 *How the "Mastiffs" Went to Iceland.* London: Virtue and Co., 1878. First edition; 4to., half title, frontispiece map and full page illustrations, 2 silver print photos, original blue cloth, bevelled boards, gilt, slight rubbing but nice, tight copy, all edges gilt, inscribed "R. Admiral A. Phillimore with Mr. John Burns' kind regards, from Castle Wemyss Jany 21 1874". Jarndyce Antiquarian Booksellers CXCI - 583 2011 £750

Association – Phillips, Frances Maria

Gray, Thomas 1716-1771 *The Poems.* London: printed by T. Bensley for F. J. Du Roveray, 1800. 190 x 120, xxx, 162, (1) pages, (ads), with half title, extremely pleasing etruscan style calf in the style of quite probably by Edwards of Halifax, very expertly rebacked to style and corners repaired by Courtland Benson, covers with gilt broad and narrow rules and Greek-key roll framing wide inner panel of stencilled palmettes, gilt foliate roll enclosing central flamed panel, raised bands flanked by double blind rules, spine panels with large oval sunburst ornament supported by a floral nest, original black spine label, turn-ins with linked gilt roll, marbled endpapers, all edges gilt, with fore-edge painting of Yarmouth Castle and Harbor, 6 engraved plates, inscription "Frances Maria Phillips June 1824. in remembrance of her grandmother", covers little marked and dried but expertly restored binding solid and pleasing, the painting with a number of very thin parallel uncolored striped where edges of leaves are not quite even or here the fore-edge was not carefully fanned out during painting, one flyleaf with upper corner clipped off, some offsetting from plates, otherwise fine internally with only trivial effects. Phillip J. Pirages 59 - 195 2011 $800

Association – Pierce, Israel

Baker, Samuel White 1821-1893 *Ismailia: a Narrative of the Expedition to Central Africa for the Suppression of the Slave Trade.* New York: Harper and Brothers, 1875. First American edition; 542 pages, octavo, steel plate portrait (tissue guard), frontispiece, map, numerous other plates, couple of signatures sprung a bit, original brick red cloth, gilt stamped upper cover and spine, rear cover blindstamped, signature of Israel Pierce, 1882, very good. Jeff Weber Rare Books 163 - 129 2011 $125

Association – Pim, J. N. R.

MacDonald, George 1824-1905 *David Elginbrod.* London: Hurst & Blackett, circa, 1890. Half title, frontispiece, 4 pages ads, 16 page catalog, original dark blue cloth, plain gilt borders, all edges gilt, with signature of J. N. R. Pim 1881. Jarndyce Antiquarian Booksellers CXCII - 22 2011 £40

Association – Pinker, James Brand

Conrad, Joseph 1857-1924 *The Works.* Garden City and New Yorj: Doubleday Page & Co., 1920-1926. Sun Dial edition, one of 735 copies signed by author; 22 volumes, 220 x 150mm., fine and especially flamboyant lilac morocco, elaborately gilt by Stikeman, covers panelled with single and double gilt fillets and intricate scrolling foliate cornerpieces, raised bands, spine attractively gilt in ruled compartments with margin ornaments (seashell or anchor) as centerpiece and with scrolling cornerpieces, crimson morocco doublures, front doublures with central panel to blue morocco, wide turn-ins with alternating floral tools, doublures decorated with very gilt lines and (at corners) floral bouquets, blue central panels with large gilt sailing vessel at middle, watered silk endleaves, morocco hinges, all edges gilt, frontispiece; with APS by author to James Brand Pinker (Conrad's agent) tipped in at front, also with signature of Richard Curle; spines uniformly faded to an even chestnut brown, hint of rubbing to handful of joints and corners (only), one opening in one volume with marginal spots, but quite fine set in very decorative bindings, text virtually pristine, volumes completely solid, covers bright and wear to leather entirely minor.   Phillip J. Pirages   59 - 168   2011 $15,000

Association – Pinkney, Robert

Tennyson Turner, Charles *Sonnets and Fugitive Pieces.* Cambridge: B. Bridges, 1830. Half title, green crushed morocco by Zaehnsdorf, gilt spine borders and dentelles, bookplate of Robert Pinkney, top edge gilt, inscribed with author's compliments, for T. H. Rawnsley.   Jarndyce Antiquarian Booksellers   CXCI - 509   2011   £500

Association – Pitt, George

Johnson, Samuel 1709-1784 *A Dictionary of the English Language.* Philadelphia: Moses Thomas, 1818. First unabridged American edition; 4to., 2 large volumes, unpaginated, full calf, elaborately stamped in gilt, worn at extremities of the spine, weak on hinges, frontispiece, all edges gilt, ownership signature of George Pitt from 1824 and note by his son John that the set was rebound in 1849, waterstain to inner margin of half title and titlepage of volume two, generally very good set.   Second Life Books Inc. 174 - 206   2011 $4000

Association – Pittner, Jean-Marc

Cocteau, Jean *Ceremonial Espagnol Du Phenix Suivi de La Partie D'Echecs.* Paris: Gallimard, 1961. First edition, service de presse copy; 4to., pages 32, (4), uncut, internally bright and clean, publisher's cream wrappers, text in black and red, lightly soiled in places, author's presentation inscription to Andre Marissel (i.e. Jean Marc Pittner) on first half title dated 1961, with 1 leaf, 8 lines autograph MS. signed by Cocteau, defining 'le poete" in envelope addressed to Pittner, 2 news clippings regarding Cocteau, flyer and card advertising Cocteau-Moretti exhibition in Librairie St. Germain des Pres 1967.   Simon Finch Rare Books   Zero - 307   2011   £375

Association – Plass, Christophorus

Snell, Willebrord *Tiphys Batavus sive Histriodromice de Navium Cursibus et re Navali.* Leiden: Officiana Elzeviriana, 1624. 4to., (56), 109, (3), 62, (2) pages, last leaf with errata, 2 engraved plates, woodcut diagrams, contemporary turkey morocco, gilt and blind fillet borders, spine gilt in compartments, blue edges, binding rubbed, spine crackling and chipped at head, on front endpapers are 3 pages of manuscript followed by page of tables, the copy of Christophorus Plass, Leiden 1671 who gave it to Benjamin de Munchausen, the Hague 1675, from the library of the Earls of Macclesfield at Shirburn Castle.   Maggs Bros. Ltd. 1440 - 200   2011   £950

Association – Plath, Aurelia

Hughes, Ted 1930-1998 *Roosting Hawk.* Grecourt Review, 1959. First edition; 8vo., printed wrappers, offsetting from newspaper insert on inside front cover, otherwise fine, presentation copy inscribed on inside front wrapper by poet to his mother-in-law, Aurelia Plath June 24 1959. James S. Jaffe Rare Books   May 26 2011 - 20984   2011 $7500

Association – Polito, Robert

Thompson, Jim *Fireworks: the Lost Writings of Jim Thompson.* New York: Donald I. Fine, 1988. First edition; very good, light bumping to extremities, dust jacket near fine, corresponding creasing, signed note signed by Polito laid in, signed by editors Robert Polito and Michael McCauley.   Bella Luna Books   May 29 2011 - t6144   2011 $82

Association – Pollack, Peter

Halsman, Philippe *Halsman" Sight and Insight. Words & Photographs.* Garden City: Doubleday & Co., 1972. First edition; photos, signed and inscribed by Halsman for Peter Pollack.   Jeff Hirsch Books   ny 2010   2011 $650

Association – Poole, Eric

Bede, the Venerable *Historiae Ecclesiasticae Gentis Anglorum...* Cantabrigiae: Typis Academicis, 1722. Folio, pages (xvi), 823 (xv) + 2 engraved plates and 1 folding map, early 19th century sprinkled an polished calf, spine fully gilt, red lettering piece gilt boards decorative roll gilt bordered, board edges decorative roll gilt, turn-ins decorative roll gilt, "French Shell" "made" endpapers, all edges 'Gloster' marbled, 3 colour (blue, red & white), sewn endbands, early 21st century conservation by Chris Weston, some browning to initial leaves and plates, little minor spotting elsewhere, few old scratched to old boards, signed binding with ticket of Nichols, Wakefield, unidentified armorial bookplate, and below, the later booklabel of Eric Poole, from the collection of Christopher Ernest Weston 1947-2010. Unsworths Booksellers 24 - 7 2011 £1500

Association – Popham, E. W. Leyborne

Cordiner, Charles *Remarkable Ruins and Romantic Prospects of North Britain.* London: published by I. and J. Taylor, 1795. 2 volumes, 4to., pages iv (cxxxvi) + engraved titlepage, engraved frontispiece and another 56 engraved plates (ccxii) + engraved titlepage, 40 engraved plates (of 41), lacking plate "personification of Events etc." in volume 2, contemporary mottled calf, 6 compartmented spine divided up by back to back double rules and polished pinhead decorative roll all gilt compartments, contain 'made'up' central device of gouges and small flowerets, all gilt, black lettering and numbering pieces gilt, place and date gilt direct at foot, boards double rule gilt border with decorative roll within, board edges decorative roll gilt turn-ins, hooded acanthus, roll gilt green 'sugarpaper' 'made' endpapers, all edges pale green "French Shell" marbled, red and pale blue sewn endbands, dark blue silk page markers, slightest bit of rubbing at extremities but very nice, armorial bookplate of "Littlecote" surmounting printed label of "E. W. Leyborne Popham", from the collection of Christopher Ernest Weston 1947-2010. Unsworths Booksellers 24 - 83 2011 £750

Association – Portal, W. S.

Wanley, Nathaniel *The Wonders of the Little World; or a General History of Man.* London: printed for W. J. and J. Richardson, Otridge & Son, &c, 1806. 2 volumes, frontispiece and plates, text in two columns, index, handsome plain contemporary calf, gilt borders, armorial bookplates of W. S. & Wyndham Portal, very good. Jarndyce Antiquarian Booksellers CXCI - 601 2011 £180

Association – Portal, Wyndham

Wanley, Nathaniel *The Wonders of the Little World; or a General History of Man.* London: printed for W. J. and J. Richardson, Otridge & Son, &c, 1806. 2 volumes, frontispiece and plates, text in two columns, index, handsome plain contemporary calf, gilt borders, armorial bookplates of W. S. & Wyndham Portal, very good. Jarndyce Antiquarian Booksellers CXCI - 601 2011 £180

Association – Porter, John

Dodsley, Robert 1703-1764 *Oeconomy of Human Life.* London: printed by T. Rickaby for S. and E. Harding, 1795. First edition with these illustrations; 272 x 85mm., 2 p.l., (5)-22 pages, (1) leaf, (119 pages (pages 117-119 ads as called for), large paper copy, apparently one of 25 in this format, quite attractive contemporary English crimson straight grain morocco, handsomely gilt, covers with borders of one plain and one decorative gilt rule and small fleuron in each corner, raised bands, spine elegantly gilt in compartments with foliate cornerpieces framing a large cruciform ornament with ribbon outlines enclosing a central starburst on stippled background, turn-ins with gilt Greek key roll, marbled endpapers, all edges gilt; 49 mostly large and always charming engraved emblematic headpieces and tailpieces by Sylvester Harding, typically showing human or angelic figures representing such abstract ideas as contentment, pity, or fortitude; armorial bookplate of Joseph Neeld, modern bookplate of John Porter, handwritten bookseller's? description signed "EB" and dated 1 Feb. 1804 tipped onto front flyleaves; covers slightly marked with minor spotting and soiling, trivial smudges internally, nearly fine and especially pretty copy, original luxury binding lustrous and with virtually no wear, text printed with vast margins extremely fresh and smooth, rare format. Phillip J. Pirages 59 - 28 2011 $1250

Association – Porter, Peter

Joutel, Henri *A Journal of the Last Voyage Perform'd by Monsr. De La Sale to the Gulph of Mexico...* London: for A. Bell, B. Lintott, J. Baker, 1714. First edition in English; 8vo., (2), xxi, (9), 191, 194-205, (5) pages, engraved folding map, short closed tear, contemporary calf, extremities rubbed, top of spine bit worn, else lovely, untouched copy, text clean and fresh, entirely unfoxed, Peter Porter bookplate and Wolfgang Herz label. Joseph J. Felcone Inc. Fall Miscellany 2010 - 67 2011 $15,000

Association – Portland, William Arthur, 6th Duke of

Eastlake, C. L. *Contributions to the Literature of the Fine Arts.* London: John Murray, 1848. First edition; xiii, (3), 396 pages + (4) + 16 pages ads, half title, fine in original blindstamped and gilt lettered cloth, armorial bookplate of William Arthur, 6th Duke of Portland. Ken Spelman Rare Books 68 - 42 2011 £180

Association – Portsmouth, Earl of

Phillips, Charles *The Speeches of Charles Phillips, Esq. Delivered at the Bar and on Various Public Occasions in Ireland and England.* London: printed for W. Simpkin and R. Marshall... and Millikin, Dublin, 1822. Second edition; 8vo., frontispiece (vi), ii, 304 pages, including half title, occasional light foxing, later 19th century full polished calf gilt with raised bands and crimson spine label, top edge gilt, others uncut, fine, late 19th century library of Earl of Portsmouth with his armorial bookplate and inscription. John Drury Rare Books   153 - 112   2011   £150

Swedenborg, Emanuel *De Coelo et Eius Mirabilibus et de Inferno.* London: by John Lewis of Hyde, 1758. First edition; 4to., pages 272, without final errata leaf sometimes present, woodcut title vignette, decorative woodcut head and tailpieces, contemporary sprinkled calf, gilt ruled raised bands, red sprinkled edges, from the Hurstbourne Park Library of Earl of Portsmouth, with gilt shelf mark '2303' in top compartment, inserted slip, inscribed in contemporary manuscript "from the author", upper joint repaired, chipping to head and foot of spine, some stripping to lower cover, wormhole at inner margin of last few leaves, internally very crisp and clean, extremely good, large copy.   Simon Finch Rare Books   Zero - 118   2011   £1600

Swedenborg, Emanuel *De Nova Hierosolyma et Ejus Doctrina Coelesti.* London: by John Lewis of Hyde, 1758. First edition; 4to., pages 156, (2) errata, verso blank, woodcut title vignette, decorative woodcut head and tailpieces, light dampstains on corners of few leaves, generally very crisp and clean, contemporary sprinkled calf, raised bands with later gilt shelfmark '2304' in top compartment, red sprinkled edges, hinges repaired, very good, from the library of the Earls of Portsmouth at Hurstbourne Park.   Simon Finch Rare Books   Zero - 117   2011   £1600

Association – Poske, Friedrich

Chamberlain, Houston Stewart *Richard Wagner.* London: J. M. Dent, 1900. Second edition; large 8vo., original publisher's green cloth lettered gilt on spine and cover, pages xvii, 402, copious plates and illustrations, loosely inserted signed card from Houston Stewart Chamberlain dated 1906 to fellow writer Friedrich Poske, clean, very good.   Any Amount of Books   May 29 2011 - A68665   2011 $255

Association – Potter, Stephen

Partridge, Eric *The Shaggy Dog Story.* London: Faber, 1953. First edition; inscription from author for Stephen Potter, pages 107, illustrations, original cloth, gilt, dust jacket price clipped.   R. F. G. Hollett & Son Antiquarian Booksellers   General Catalogue Summer 2010 - 863   2011   £120

Association – Poulter, J. Holmes

Dibdin, Thomas Frognall   1776-1847   *Reminiscenes of a Literary Life.* London: John Major, 1836. First edition; 2 volumes, frontispiece, plates and illustrations, subscriber's list pages xvii-xxxii, plates slightly foxed, some quite heavily, uncut in contemporary or slightly later half maroon calf, slight rubbing, crimson labels, contemporary signatures of J. Holmes Poulter.   Jarndyce Antiquarian Booksellers   CXCI - 153   2011   £200

Association – Poynder, Thomas

Polybius *The General History of Polybius.* London: printed for J. Dodsley, 1772. 2 volumes, 4to., pages xxiv, (viii) 559 (i) + extending engraved map frontispiece and one other extending engraved map, (xvi), 423, (xvii), contemporary sprinkled calf, spines panel gilt with 'Rococo' floral centrepieces, five raised bands and head and foot identically gilt using 'alternating full & broken hatch' pallet, red & black lettering & numbering pieces gilt, board edges decorative roll gilt, all edges lemon, red and white sewn endbands, lightly toned and bit spotted in places, rubbed, joints cracked, spine ends worn, some scrapes to boards, armorial bookplate of Thomas Poynder, from the collection of Christopher Ernest Weston 1947-2010.   Unsworths Booksellers   24 - 136   2011   £360

Association – Prabhavanda, Swami

Isherwood, Christopher *How to Know God, The Yoga Aphorisms of Patanjali.* New York: Harper & Brothers, 1953. First US edition; 16mo., 224 pages, faint rubbing, endpapers slightly browned, else fine in very good+ dust jacket with very small inked initials on cover (N,A.B. 1953) faintly rubbed at corners, signed by Isherwood and Swami Prabhavananda, very slight lean otherwise fine in slightly used price clipped, very good dust jacket, neat stamped on pastedown, hidden by dust jacket flap.   Any Amount of Books   May 29 2011 - A66357   2011 $306

Association – Pratt, Mildred

Thorndike, Russell *Jet and Ivory.* London: Rich and Cowan, 1934. First edition; pages viii, 9-443, 8vo., original publisher's black cloth lettered white on spine, with 36 page publisher's catalog at rear, signed presentation from author to Mildred Pratt, prelims very slightly foxed, white lettering at spine very slightly flaked, but title legible, slight rubbing, slight shelfwear, otherwise sound very good.   Any Amount of Books   May 29 2011 - A70325   2011 $230

Association – Preome, Dom

Merton, Thomas 1915-1968 *The Sign of Jonas.* New York: Harcourt Brace and Co., 1953. First edition; fine in near fine dust jacket with couple of old tape repairs on verso at spine ends, in specially made cloth slipcase, presentation copy inscribed in French by Thomas Merton (as Father Louis) on second endpaper to Dom Preome of the Oka-La Trappe in Quebec, further inscribed by Father James Fox, Merton's Abbot (superior) at Gethsemani at a time to dear Dom Preome with gratitude.   Between the Covers   169 - BTC342154   2011 $1650

Association – Preston

Lawless, Emily *With the Wild Geese.* London: Isbister & Co., 1902. First edition; half title, title in red and black, uncut in original olive green cloth, blocked and lettered in light green, lettered in gilt, Preston armorial bookplate, very good, bright.   Jarndyce Antiquarian Booksellers   CLXC - 85   2011   £65

Association – Preston, John

Gerarde, John 1545-1612   *The Herball or Generall Historie of Plantes.* London: Adam Islip, Joice Norton and Richard Whitakers, 1633. Second edition; approximately 2800 text woodcuts, woodcut initials, folio, engraved architectural title by John Payne, pages (38), 1-30, 29-30, 29-1630, (2), (1 page of additional illustrations, verso blank), (45), errata, contemporary full calf (professionally rebacked with sympathetic leather, old wear to edges and corners, lacking 1 leaf, H1, 89-90, endpapers renewed, engraved title somewhat soiled and with short marginal tears, some soiling to prelim pages, scattered pages with repairs with no loss to text, tear here and there, some dampstaining, mostly to back third of pages, an old ink annotation to a page, small brown stains to 2 leaves, several index pages soiled, chipped and frayed at fore edges, resulting in partial loss of text to 2 leaves, the copy of John Preston and of John Averill.   Raymond M. Sutton, Jr.   May 26 2011 - 55850   2011 $2400

Association – Prexel

McKenney, Thomas Lorraine *History of the Indian Tribes of North America, with Biographical Sketches and Anecdotes of the Principal Chiefs.* Philadelphia: D. Rice & A. N. Hart, 1858. Fourth edition; 3 volumes, 8vo., pages (2), iv, (3-) 333; xvii, (9-) 290; iv, (17-) 392, 120 hand colored lithographic plates by J. T. Bowen of Philadelphia, most are after Charles Bird King (marginal brown spot to 2 plates), contemporary morocco, elaborately blocked with stylistic foliage in corners and 5 raised bands to spine with 6 tooled panels, 2 of which are gilt lettered, some light scuffing, chipping to head of spine, text virtually clean, worming in gutter of few pages of volume 1, all edges gilt, Prexel copy with coat of arms; Charles Holman copy with coat of arms, very good.   Raymond M. Sutton, Jr.   May 26 2011 - 55944   2011 $25,000

Association – Priaulx, Edward

Fraunce, Abraham *The Lawiers Logike, Exemplifying the Praecept of Logike by the Practise of the Common Lawe.* London: by William How for Thomas Gubbin and T. Newman, 1588. First edition; 4to, (1), 151, (i.e. 152) leaves including blank leaf 2A2, folding table, title within type ornament border, woodcut initials, mixed black letter and roman, full red gilt panelled morocco, edges gilt by Bedford, first two leaves lightly washed, short closed tear on table, blank corner of 2K4 replaced, else fine, clean, armorial bookplate of Sir Edward Priaulx and book label of Abel Berland.   Joseph J. Felcone Inc.   Fall Miscellany 2010 - 52   2011 $8000

Association – Pulsford, Mrs.

MacDonald, George 1824-1905   *Dealings with the Fairies.* London: Alexander Strahan & Co., 1868. Second edition; half title, frontispiece and plates by Arthur Hughes, 4 pages ads (Dec. 1867), few marks, original green cloth blocked in black and gilt, slightly dulled with small split in leading hinge, all edges gilt, inserted at head of titlepage "Mrs. Pulsford for her ministering children with the author's love & thanks" in author's hand.   Jarndyce Antiquarian Booksellers   CXCII - 84   2011   £2500

Association – Purdy, James

Albee, Edward *Malcolm.* New York: Atheneum, 1966. First edition; Albee's play adaptation of James Purdy's first novel, fine in near fine dust jacket with light rubbing and edge wear, signed by Purdy and Albee, uncommon signed by both.   Ken Lopez Bookseller   154 - 3   2011 $250

Association – Puttnam, David

Brandt, Bill *Perspective of Nudes.* London: The Bodley Head, 1916. First edition, signed in year of publication; 4to., pages 120, 90 black and white photos printed in gravure, original decorated paper covered boards, spine and upper side lettered in red, original black and white photo illustrated dust jacket, text printed in red and black, crease to spine fold of upper panel, 2 chips at top and bottom edges of upper and lower panel, tape repairs to both sides, short closed tear to lower panel, tips lightly rubbed, bookseller's ticket to front pastedown, inscription from David Puttnam in black ink to front free endpaper for Julian, fine in very good dust jacket.   Simon Finch Rare Books   Zero - 511   2011   £2000

Association – Pym, Horace

Patmore, Coventry *How I Managed and Improved my Estate.* London: George Bell & Sons, 1886. First edition; half title, 24 page catalog (July 1883), original salmon pink cloth, boards ruled and lettered in black, spine lettered in gilt, bookplate and signature of Horace Pym, V, scarce. Jarndyce Antiquarian Booksellers CXCI - 383 2011 £150

Association – Quayle, Eric

Porter, Anna Maria *Roche-Blanche; or the Hunters of the Pyrenees.* London: Longman, 1822. First edition; 3 volumes, 12mo., half titles volumes II & III, inserted 4 pages at front volume I (June 1822), uncut in original blue boards, drab paper spines, paper labels, spines chipped at tails, good copy, 1926 bookplate of Eric Quayle, signatures of Mary Chandos August 1822, tipped in is folded holograph ms. signed by Porter. Jarndyce Antiquarian Booksellers CLXC - 758 2011 £650

Association – Queen, Ellery

Doyle, Arthur Conan 1859-1930 *Adventures of Sherlock Holmes.* London: George Newnes, 1892. First edition, first issue with no street name on front cover; "Violent" for "Violet" on page 317, large octavo, (4), 317, (1, printer's imprint) (2, blank) pages, 104 illustrations by Sidney Paget in text, original light blue cloth over beveled boards, front cover and spine blocked and lettered in gilt and black, all edges gilt, gray flower and leaf endpapers, small ink initials to front free endpaper, front hinge professionally and invisibly repaired, back hinge starting but firm, slight bit of shelf wear to top and bottom of spine, some light foxing to few prelim and final pages, else near fine, exceptionally clean and bright, housed in tan cloth clamshell, the fine "Ellery Queen" (Manfred Lee) and "Barnaby Ross" (Frederic Dannay) names in ink on half title. Heritage Book Shop Holiday 2010 - 30 2011 $17,500

Association – Quinn, John

Harris, Frank *Oscar Wilde/His Life and Confessions.* New York: privately published, 1916. First edition; 2 volumes, 4to., pages (x), vii, 320; (iv), 321-603, top edge gilt, others uncut, original quarter morocco with green paper boards, morocco worn, upper board of volume i detached, lacking spine but textblock firm, joints of volume ii starting, spine partially detached, bookplate of John Quinn, inscribed by author and Quinn, TLS from Quinn laid in. Simon Finch Rare Books Zero - 235 2011 £750

Gregory, Isabella Augusta Perse 1859-1932 *Irish Folk-History Plays... First Series.... Second Series... (with) Our Irish Theatre/A Chapter of Autobiography.* New York and London: G. P. Putnams Sons, 1912-1913. First edition; First work in 2 volumes, 8vo., pages (ii), vi, 207, (i) blank, (3) ads; (ii), vi, 198, (5) ads, both volumes internally very fresh, short closed tear to one leaf of prelims in volume i, contemporary quarter cloth and blue paper covered boards, labels to spines with text in black, bumped and lightly rubbed, upper hinge volume i repaired, upper hinge volume ii cracked but firmly hold, John Quinn's autograph inscription volume ii, ownership inscription of A. S. Kinkead; second work 8vo., pages (ii), vi, 319, (i) blank, (5) ads, frontispiece and 3 plates, last leaves very slightly spotted otherwise extremely fresh, tight copy, contemporary quarter cloth and blue paper covered boards, label to spine with text in black, slightly bumped, some signs of wear to boards, endpapers lightly spotted, Quinn's presentation inscription to Joseph Conrad, ownership inscription of A. S. Kinkead. Simon Finch Rare Books Zero - 232 2011 £1250

Association – Quinn, Marc

Incarnate. London: Booth-Clibborn Editions, 1998. First edition; 4to. pages 222 (unpaginated), illustrations in color and black and white, signed by contributor Marc Quinn, loosely inserted post card to Norman Rosenthal, fine in fine dust jacket. Any Amount of Books May 29 2011 - A45925 2011 $340

Association – Rackham, Arthur

Goldsmith, Oliver 1730-1774 *The Vicar of Wakefield.* London: Harrap, 1929. First Rackham edition, 4/775 copies signed by artist; 12 color printed plates and other illustrations in text, all by Arthur Rackham, title and Rackham design on titlepage printed in red, prelim leaves foxed, one leaf little creased, pages 232, 4to., original cream parchment, lettering and design on backstrip and lettering on front covers within double rule border, all blocked in gilt, endpapers with designs in green by Rackham, top edge gilt, others untrimmed, board slipcase from The Compleat Angler with printed label to that affect, very good, publisher George Harrap's copy with his bookplate, beneath statement of limitation is pen and ink drawing by Rackham, drawn for Harrap. Blackwell Rare Books B166 - 224 2011 £10,000

Shakespeare, William 1564-1616 *A Midsummer Night's Dream.* London: William Heinemann, 1908. First of this edition; 4to., top edge tinted, beige cloth with gold lettering and decoration on front cover and spine, lovely copy with bookplate on front pastedown, signed in full with drawing by the artist, Arthur Rackham, 40 mounted color plates plus black and white decorations within text. Jo Ann Reisler, Ltd. 86 - 202 2011 $3500

Association – Radford, C. H.

Honorius of Autun *Elucidarius Dvalogicus Theologie Tripertitus: Infinitarum questionum Resolutiuus.* colophon: Landshut: Johann Weyssenburger 20 June, 1514. Title printed in red and below it five vignettes, four within circles and altogether surrounded by a square frame, inner margin of first leaf strengthened, few minor spots and stains, ff., xxvii, (4 index), 4to. in sixes, early 20th century calf backed buckram, spine faded, blindstamped of C. H. Radford on first flyleaf, good, scarce.   Blackwell Rare Books   B166 - 50   2011   £1500

Association – Radford, Maitland

Farjeon, Eleanor *The Soul of Kol Nikon.* N.P.: (U.K.), n.p., n.d., 1914. First edition; 8vo., pages 107, original publisher's blue cloth lettered gilt on spine, signed presentation copy from author for Maitland Radford, some fading, front and rear covers dampstained, otherwise sound near very good, clean text.   Any Amount of Books   May 26 2011 - A62451   2011 $461

Lawrence, David Herbert   1885-1930 *Love Poems and Others.* London: Duckworth, 1913. First edition; 8vo. original publisher's blue cloth lettered gilt on spine and on front cover, pages lxiii, presentation from Margaret Radford to her brother Maitland Radford, endpapers very slightly browned, covers very faintly rubbed, near fine.   Any Amount of Books   May 26 2011 - A62565   2011 $419

Association – Radford, Margaret

Lawrence, David Herbert   1885-1930 *Love Poems and Others.* London: Duckworth, 1913. First edition; 8vo. original publisher's blue cloth lettered gilt on spine and on front cover, pages lxiii, presentation from Margaret Radford to her brother Maitland Radford, endpapers very slightly browned, covers very faintly rubbed, near fine.   Any Amount of Books   May 26 2011 - A62565   2011 $419

Association – Rae, Kenneth

Landon, Letitia Elizabeth *The Improvisatrice; and Other Poems.* London: Hurst, Robinson & Co., 1824. Second edition; frontispiece and engraved title and little spotted, additional printed title, contemporary half calf, spine ruled and with devices in gilt, tan leather label, following inner hinge cracking, bit rubbed and worn, good sound copy, signed presentation copy, pasted to leading pastedown, engraved presentation label completed in ink "to Rosina Lytton Bulwer from L.E.L. 1831", also with later booklabel of Kenneth Rae.   Jarndyce Antiquarian Booksellers   CLXC - 74   2011   £225

Association – Raistrick, Arthur

Barley, M. W. *The English Farmhouse and Cottage.* London: Routledge and Kegan Paul, 1961. First edition; original cloth, gilt, dust jacket (little worn), pages xxi, 297, with 24 pages on plates, 38 text figures and 8 tables, Dr. Arthur Raistrick's copy with his bookplate and stamps, inscribed on flyleaf by his wife.   R. F. G. Hollett & Son Antiquarian Booksellers   177 - 63   2011   £45

Conder, C. R. *The Tell Amarna Tablets.* Palestine Exploration Fund, 1892. First edition; original cloth, gilt, rather marked, hinges little rubbed, pages xi, 212, (iv), the copy of Percy F. Kendall (Yorkshire geologist) with his signature, later from the library of Dr. Arthur Raistrick with his bookplate.   R. F. G. Hollett & Son Antiquarian Booksellers   177 - 205   2011   £35

Hoskins, W. G. *Fieldwork in Local History.* London: Faber, 1967. First edition; original cloth, gilt, dust jacket, pages 192, with 5 illustrations, Dr. Arthur Raistrick's copy with his bookplate and signature and one or two marginal notes, printed compliments slip from author.   R. F. G. Hollett & Son Antiquarian Booksellers   177 - 474   2011   £30

Innocent, G. F. *The Development of English Building Construction.* David & Charles, 1971. Tall 8vo., original cloth, gilt, dust jacket, pages (xxii), 294, with 73 illustrations, Dr. Arthur Raistrick's copy with his signature.   R. F. G. Hollett & Son Antiquarian Booksellers   177 - 494   2011   £45

Lidbetter, Hubert *The Friends Meeting House.* York: Ebor Press, 1961. Limited edition, no. 8; original cloth, gilt, dust jacket, pages xvi, 84, with 72 plates and 47 plans, sections and elevations, Dr. Arthur Raistrick's copy with his stamp.   R. F. G. Hollett & Son Antiquarian Booksellers   177 - 548   2011   £35

O'Riordain, Sean P. *Antiquities of the Irish Countryside.* London: Methuen, 1953. Third edition; Original cloth, gilt, dust jacket (top and base of spine defective), pages xii 108, 88 plates and 5 text illustrations, from the library of Dr. Arthur Raistrick with his bookplate and signature.   R. F. G. Hollett & Son Antiquarian Booksellers   177 - 604   2011   £35

Sellman, R. R. *Devon Village Schools in the Nineteenth Century.* London: Davis & Charles, 1967. First edition; original cloth, gilt, dust jacket, pages 171 with 12 plates and 12 diagrams and maps, from the library of Dr. Arthur Raistrick, with his bookplate.   R. F. G. Hollett & Son Antiquarian Booksellers   175 - 1203   2011   £35

Association – Ramos, Manuel

A Dozen on Denver. Gulden: Fulcrum, 2009. First edition; fine, signed by Connie Willis, Nick Arvin, Robert Greer, Margaret Coel, Manuel Ramos and Arnold Grossman. Bella Luna Books   May 29 2011 - p3633   2011 $104

Association – Randall, Elizabeth

Kettilby, Mary *A Collection of Above Three Hundred Receipts in Cookery, Physick and Surgery for the Use of all Good Wives, Tender Mothers and Careful Nurses.* London: for Richard Wilkin, 1714. First edition; (16), 218, (13) pages, contemporary paneled calf, neatly rebacked, light overall toning, minor marginal foxing and dampstaining, upper margin of A3 clipped and neatly restored, just grazing running head on verso, 3 leaves of early owners' recipes bound in at end, early ownership signature of Tho. Tipping, dated at several locations in Hertfordshire 1714-1739, later signature of Elizabeth Randall 1771, modern cookery bookplate, very nice in portfolio and leather backed slipcase. Joseph J. Felcone Inc.   Fall Miscellany 2010 - 32   2011 $2800

Association – Randolph, Anna

Park, Mungo *Travels in the Interior Districts of Africa Performed Under the Direction an Patroange of the African Association in the Years 1795, 1796 and 1797...* Philadelphia: printed from the London quarto edition by James Humphreys, 1800. Octavo, xxi, (1), (23)-484 pages, large folding map, original full calf, gilt ruled spine, red spine label, hinges repaired, signature on title of Anna J. M. Randolph 1895, very good "Attleborough Library 6 weeks" on title, very good.   Jeff Weber Rare Books   163 - 203 2011 $300

Association – Ransome, Edwin

Fox, George *A Journal or Historical Account of the Life, Travels, Sufferings, Christian Experiences and Labour of Love in the Work of the Ministry...* London: printed by W. Richardson and S. Clark and sold by Luke Hinde, 1765. Third edition; folio, modern full blind ruled calf, gilt, pages lix, 679, (xxviii), excellent, clean, sound copy with signature of Robert Coleman, inscribed "given to Edwin R. Ransome in 1871...". R. F. G. Hollett & Son Antiquarian Booksellers 175 - 469 2011   £450

Association – Rattier, Leon

Lacroix, Paul *Ma Republique.* Paris: Librairie L. Conquet, 1902. One of 40 special copies with 2 extra states of the plates and inscribed by publisher to Monsieur L. Rattier (no doubt French bibliophile Leon Rattier; of the limited edition of 100 copies on Japan vellum (of a total edition of 400 copies) 205 x 140mm., 2 p.l., 150, (1) pages, very fine crimson morocco gilt and onlaid by Chambolle-Duru (stamp signed on front doublure), covers with broad border comprised of seven gilt fillets, raised bands, with broad border comprised of seven gilt fillets, raised bands, spine compartments outlined with five concentric gilt rules, doublures of brown crushed morocco featuring stylized flowers of onlaid olive brown morocco on elegant arching gilt stems, cloth and then marbled endleaves, all edges gilt, original printed wrappers bound in, 7 etchings, each in 3 states (for a total of 21 plates), virtually mint.   Phillip J. Pirages   59 - 91   2011 $3250

Association – Rawlett, John

Wemys, Thomas *Beth-Hak-Kodesh. Or the Separation and Consecration of Places in God's Publick Service and Worship.* London: printed for Thomas Dring, at the Harrow, over against the Inner Temple-gate in Fleet Street, 1674. First and only edition; 12mo., (24) 164 pages, complete with initial imprimatur leaf (A1), wormtracks affect lower margins throughout, occasionally with loss of single letter of text, small tear in margin of leaf F4 with loss of single letter on recto, contemporary sheep, unlettered, spine and corners rather worn but sound, from the 17th century library of John Rawlett with his signature and shelfmark on tag affixed to lower board, scarce.   John Drury Rare Books   153 - 170 2011   £650

Association – Rawnsley, Canon Hardwick

Cook, Theodore Andrea *The Water-Colour Drawings of J. M. W. Turner, R.A. in the National Gallery.* London: Cassell and Co., 1904. Limited edition, no. 217 of 1200 copies; folio, original cloth, gilt folder with linen ties, pages vi, 88, with 5 plates, plus 88 color plates set into mounts, top edges gilt, all loose in folder as issued, scarce, presentation copy from Canon Hardwick Rawnsley.   R. F. G. Hollett & Son Antiquarian Booksellers   173 - 256 2011   £450

Association – Rawnsley, T. H.

Tennyson Turner, Charles *Sonnets and Fugitive Pieces.* Cambridge: B. Bridges, 1830. Half title, green crushed morocco by Zaehnsdorf, gilt spine borders and dentelles, bookplate of Robert Pinkney, top edge gilt, inscribed with author's compliments, for T. H. Rawnsley.   Jarndyce Antiquarian Booksellers   CXCI - 509 2011   £500

Association – Ray, Reginald

Eccleston, Robert *Overland to California on the Southwestern Trail 1849. Diary of Robert Eccleston.* Berekely & Los Angeles: University of California Press, 1950. Limited to 750 copies, this number 95; inscribed by both authors to Reginald Ray and Grace Dell Stuart, with their bookplate, 8vo., xvii, 256 pages, brown cloth, gilt stamped spine title, dust jacket chipped.   Jeff Weber Rare Books   163 - 67   2011 $100

Association – Reclus, Elie

Arts & Crafts Exhibition Society *Art and Life and the Building and Decoration of Cities...* Rivington, Percival & Co., 1897. Half title, recent ownership inscription, uncut, original red brown publisher's gilt monogram on front board, worn paper label on spine, little sunned, presentation inscription for Elie Reclus, from T. J. and Annie Cobden-Sanderson, 5 volumes.   Jarndyce Antiquarian Booksellers   CXCI - 53   2011   £250

Association – Reddy, C. R.

Hussain, Iqbalunnisa *Purdah and Polygamy. Life in an Indian Muslim Household.* Bangalore: S. R. Zaman, 1944. First edition; original boards, spine and edges faded, spine rather cracked in places, dust jacket, pages 310 compliment slip of Sir C. R. Reddy and authoress tipped in, very scarce.   R. F. G. Hollett & Son Antiquarian Booksellers   175 - 690   2011   £75

Association – Redeke, H. C.

Schaeffer, Jacob Christian *Piscium Bavarico Ratisbonensium Pentas. (bound with) Epistola ad Regio-Borussicam Societatem Litterariam Du'isburgensem de Studii Ichthyologici Facililori...* Ratisbonae: Montagii et Typis Weissianis, 1761. Ratisbonae: Typis Weissianis et Impensis Montagii, 1760; 4to., 4 hand colored engraved plates (light foxing to 1), pages (12), 82; 4to., pages 24, scattered light foxing, contemporary calf backed boards, rubbed, bump to upper edges of covers, 1 inch split to upper edges of spine, old paper label to heel of spine, some worming to upper blank corner of all pages and plates, old ink number to front flyleaf, 3 handstamps on first title, scattered light foxing, from the Musee d'Histoire Naturelle de Geneve, also the copy of H. C. Redeke, P. F. Geiger, and R. Harry, Jr.   Raymond M. Sutton, Jr.   May 26 2011 - 41627   2011 $1500

Association – Redwell, John

Memoir of the Early Campaigns of the Duke of Wellington in Portugal and Spain. London: John Murray, 1820. First edition; 8vo., 234 pages, ex-British Foreign Office library with few library markings, else very good in modern red cloth lettered gilt at spine, presentation copy from author for John Redwell, 1821.   Any Amount of Books   May 26 2011 - A73970   2011 $503

Association – Regrave, Gilbert

Gesner, Konrad   1516-1565 *Historiae Animalium Liber III qui est de Avium Natura.* Francofurti: Henrici Laurentii, 1617. Later edition; over 230 woodcuts, folio, pages (12), 732, (21) contemporary full calf, 6 raised bands and gilt lettered red label on spine (front cover detached, corners showing, one being perished, dampstaining to corner and/or margins of many pages, lower corner of title partly disintegrated, marginal tear to 2 front leaves, ocasional foxing, slight worming to upper corner of few leaves, offsetting to text from woodcuts, many pages misnumbered, although sequence is correct, leaf 413/415 is printed twice, leaf 411/412 omitted), good, the copy of Gilbert R. Regrave, also Aquatic Research Institute.   Raymond M. Sutton, Jr. May 26 2011 - 45718   2011 $2500

Association – Reichenthal, Nathaniel

Graves, Robert   1895-1985   *Poems 1930-1933.* London: Arthur Barker, 1931. First edition; 8vo., 38 pages, presentation copy signed on piece of paper pasted to top f.e.p. "Nathaniel with love from Robert. 1933" (Nathaniel Reichenthal, father of Laura Riding), slight browning at edges, head of spine slight chafed, slight soiling, else very good, slight wear, otherwise very good.   Any Amount of Books   May 29 2011 - A36807   2011 $272

Association – Renier, Anne

Britton, John *A Brief Memoir of the Life and Writings of John Britton.* London: printed by J. Moyes, 1825. Half title, titlepage, dedication, 44 pages text, 2 page catalog, original boards, paper label on front board, marked and rubbed, hinges splitting, booklabel of Anne and F. G. Renier, inscribed presentation from author to J. Bull.   Jarndyce Antiquarian Booksellers   CXCI - 76   2011   £125

Chambers, William *Memoir of William and Robert Chambers.* Edinburgh: W. & R. Chambers, 1893. Frontispiece, illustrations, portraits, original brown cloth, very good, Renier booklabel.   Jarndyce Antiquarian Booksellers   CXCI - 448   2011   £35

De La Ramee, Louise 1839-1908 *Wisdom, Wit and Pathos, Selected from the Works of Ouida.* London: Chatto & Windus, 1889. Second edition; half title, final ad leaf, 32 page catalog (Oct. 1888), 'yellowback', original printed boards, spine slightly rubbed, Renier booklabel, good plus. Jarndyce Antiquarian Booksellers CLXC - 726 2011 £50

Gent, Thomas *The Life of Mr. Thomas Gent, Printer of York.* London: printed for Thomas Thorpe, 1832. Engraved frontispiece, uncut, original pink moire cloth, at some time rebacked, retaining original paper label, faded, cloth slightly creased on back board, Renier booklabel, according to pencil note work was edited by Joseph Hunter. Jarndyce Antiquarian Booksellers CXCI - 449 2011 £150

Kelty, Mary Anne *The Favourite of Nature.* London: G. & W. B. Whittaker, 1822. Third edition; 3 volumes, 12mo. contemporary half speckled calf, black leather labels, rubbed, leading hinges weak and repaired, volume I heads and tails of spines slightly worn, Renier booklabels, good, sound copy. Jarndyce Antiquarian Booksellers CLXC - 41 2011 £60

Kennedy, Grace *Dunallan; or Know What You Judge: a Story.* Edinburgh: W. Oliphant, 1825. Second edition; 3 volumes, 12mo., half titles, final ad leaf volume I, contemporary half dark blue calf, armorial bookplate, Cotton & Renier booklabel, very good. Jarndyce Antiquarian Booksellers CLXC - 48 2011 £120

Le Ros, Christian *Christmas Day and How It Was Spent by Four Persons in the House of Fograss, Fograss, Mowton and Snorton, Bankers.* London: George Routledge, circa, 1873. 2 pages ads, frontispiece and plates, illustrations by Phiz, yellowback, original printed boards, slightly rubbed and dulled, very good, Renier booklabel. Jarndyce Antiquarian Booksellers CXCI - 255 2011 £65

MacDonald, George 1824-1905 *Adela Cathcart.* London: Sampson Low, Marston, Searle & Rivington, 1889. New edition; yellowback with pale blue color pictorial boards, spine darkened, rubbed and cracked, blue endpapers, same ads as the 1887 edition, Renier booklabel. Jarndyce Antiquarian Booksellers CXCII - 29 2011 £45

MacDonald, George 1824-1905 *Guild Court.* London: Sampson Low, Marston, Searle & Rivington, 1890. New edition; booklabel of Anne and Fernand Renier, original white boards, printed in blue and red, rubbed with crack in spine, blue endpapers with ads. Jarndyce Antiquarian Booksellers CXCII - 80 2011 £50

MacDonald, George 1824-1905 *Paul Faber, Surgeon.* London: Chatto & Windus, 1883. New edition; initial ad leaf, yellowback in original cream pictorial boards, spine and hinges rubbed, corners knocked, Renier bookplate. Jarndyce Antiquarian Booksellers CXCII - 209 2011 £65

MacDonald, George 1824-1905 *Unspoken Sermons.* London: Strahan & Co., 1869. Third edition; half title removed, title in red and black, original royal blue cloth, dulled and slightly rubbed, Renier booklabel, ownership inscription, with Strahan & Co. in large & small caps at tail of spine. Jarndyce Antiquarian Booksellers CXCII - 70 2011 £85

Morley, Susan *Throstlethwaite.* London: Henry S. King & Co., 1875. First edition; 3 volumes in 1 in dulled red cloth remainder binding bit dulled and rubbed, inner hinges cracking, Renier booklabel. Jarndyce Antiquarian Booksellers CLXC - 545 2011 £60

Muhlbach, Luise, Pseud. *Joseph II and His Court.* New York: D. Appleton & Co., 1888. Frontispiece, 2 pages ads, 2 column text, original blue cloth, little rubbed, Renier booklabel. Jarndyce Antiquarian Booksellers CLXC - 552 2011 £40

Muhlbach, Luise, Pseud. *The Daughter of an Empress.* New York: D. Appleton & Co., 1867. Frontispiece, 3 full page plates, 1 page ads, original dark blue-green pebble grained cloth, slightly rubbed and dulled, Renier booklabel and "Victoria Library Rules". Jarndyce Antiquarian Booksellers CLXC - 551 2011 £50

Oliphant, Margaret Oliphant Wilson 1828-1897 *Salem Chapel and The Doctor's Family.* London: William Blackwood & Sons, 1902. New edition; half title, 32 page catalog (coded 6/02), original olive green cloth lettered in black and gilt, spine very slightly rubbed, very good, Renier booklabel. Jarndyce Antiquarian Booksellers CLXC - 608 2011 £35

Scenes and Incidents of Foreign Travel. London: Robert Tyas, circa, 1844. Frontispiece and plates, slightly foxed, small internal tear to leading f.e.p., original dark blue cloth, blocked in blind, spine decorated in gilt, spine slightly faded, signature of Rosa Mayhew, Renier booklabel, all edges gilt, very good. Jarndyce Antiquarian Booksellers CXCI - 536 2011 £58

Association – Renier, Fernand

Britton, John *A Brief Memoir of the Life and Writings of John Britton.* London: printed by J. Moyes, 1825. Half title, titlepage, dedication, 44 pages text, 2 page catalog, original boards, paper label on front board, marked and rubbed, hinges splitting, booklabel of Anne and F. G. Renier, inscribed presentation from author to J. Bull. Jarndyce Antiquarian Booksellers CXCI - 76 2011 £125

Chambers, William *Memoir of William and Robert Chambers.* Edinburgh: W. & R. Chambers, 1893. Frontispiece, illustrations, portraits, original brown cloth, very good, Renier booklabel. Jarndyce Antiquarian Booksellers CXCI - 448 2011 £35

De La Ramee, Louise 1839-1908 *Wisdom, Wit and Pathos, Selected from the Works of Ouida.* London: Chatto & Windus, 1889. Second edition; half title, final ad leaf, 32 page catalog (Oct. 1888), 'yellowback', original printed boards, spine slightly rubbed, Renier booklabel, good plus. Jarndyce Antiquarian Booksellers CLXC - 726 2011 £50

Gent, Thomas *The Life of Mr. Thomas Gent, Printer of York.* London: printed for Thomas Thorpe, 1832. Engraved frontispiece, uncut, original pink moire cloth, at some time rebacked, retaining original paper label, faded, cloth slightly creased on back board, Renier booklabel, according to pencil note work was edited by Joseph Hunter. Jarndyce Antiquarian Booksellers CXCI - 449 2011 £150

Kelty, Mary Anne *The Favourite of Nature.* London: G. & W. B. Whittaker, 1822. Third edition; 3 volumes, 12mo. contemporary half speckled calf, black leather labels, rubbed, leading hinges weak and repaired, volume I heads and tails of spines slightly worn, Renier booklabels, good, sound copy. Jarndyce Antiquarian Booksellers CLXC - 41 2011 £60

Kennedy, Grace *Dunallan; or Know What You Judge: a Story.* Edinburgh: W. Oliiphant, 1825. Second edition; 3 volumes, 12mo., half titles, final ad leaf volume I, contemporary half dark blue calf, armorial bookplate, Cotton & Renier booklabel, very good. Jarndyce Antiquarian Booksellers CLXC - 48 2011 £120

Le Ros, Christian *Christmas Day and How It Was Spent by Four Persons in the House of Fograss, Fograss, Mowton and Snorton, Bankers.* London: George Routledge, circa, 1873. 2 pages ads, frontispiece and plates, illustrations by Phiz, yellowback, original printed boards, slightly rubbed and dulled, very good, Renier booklabel. Jarndyce Antiquarian Booksellers CXCI - 255 2011 £65

MacDonald, George 1824-1905 *Adela Cathcart.* London: Sampson Low, Marston, Searle & Rivington, 1889. New edition; yellowback with pale blue color pictorial boards, spine darkened, rubbed and cracked, blue endpapers, same ads as the 1887 edition, Renier booklabel. Jarndyce Antiquarian Booksellers CXCII - 29 2011 £45

MacDonald, George 1824-1905 *Guild Court.* London: Sampson Low, Marston, Searle & Rivington, 1890. New edition; booklabel of Anne and Fernand Renier, original white boards, printed in blue and red, rubbed with crack in spine, blue endpapers with ads. Jarndyce Antiquarian Booksellers CXCII - 80 2011 £50

MacDonald, George 1824-1905 *Paul Faber, Surgeon.* London: Chatto & Windus, 1883. New edition; initial ad leaf, yellowback in original cream pictorial boards, spine and hinges rubbed, corners knocked, Renier bookplate. Jarndyce Antiquarian Booksellers CXCII - 209 2011 £65

MacDonald, George 1824-1905 *Unspoken Sermons.* London: Strahan & Co., 1869. Third edition; half title removed, title in red and black, original royal blue cloth, dulled and slightly rubbed, Renier booklabel, ownership inscription, with Strahan & Co. in large & small caps at tail of spine. Jarndyce Antiquarian Booksellers CXCII - 70 2011 £85

Morley, Susan *Throstlethwaite.* London: Henry S. King & Co., 1875. First edition; 3 volumes in 1 in dulled red cloth remainder binding bit dulled and rubbed, inner hinges cracking, Renier booklabel. Jarndyce Antiquarian Booksellers CLXC - 545 2011 £60

Muhlbach, Luise, Pseud. *Joseph II and His Court.* New York: D. Appleton & Co., 1888. Frontispiece, 2 pages ads, 2 column text, original blue cloth, little rubbed, Renier booklabel. Jarndyce Antiquarian Booksellers CLXC - 552 2011 £40

Muhlbach, Luise, Pseud. *The Daughter of an Empress.* New York: D. Appleton & Co., 1867. Frontispiece, 3 full page plates, 1 page ads, original dark blue-green pebble grained cloth, slightly rubbed and dulled, Renier booklabel and "Victoria Library Rules". Jarndyce Antiquarian Booksellers CLXC - 551 2011 £50

Oliphant, Margaret Oliphant Wilson 1828-1897 *Salem Chapel and The Doctor's Family.* London: William Blackwood & Sons, 1902. New edition; half title, 32 page catalog (coded 6/02), original olive green cloth lettered in black and gilt, spine very slightly rubbed, very good, Renier booklabel. Jarndyce Antiquarian Booksellers CLXC - 608 2011 £35

Scenes and Incidents of Foreign Travel. London: Robert Tyas, circa, 1844. Frontispiece and plates, slightly foxed, small internal tear to leading f.e.p., original dark blue cloth, blocked in blind, spine decorated in gilt, spine slightly faded, signature of Rosa Mayhew, Renier booklabel, all edges gilt, very good. Jarndyce Antiquarian Booksellers CXCI - 536 2011 £58

Association – Renny, William John

Cave, William *Antiquitate Apostolicae; or the History of the Lives, Acts and Martyrdoms of the Holy Apostles of Our Saviour...* London: printed by F. Flesher for R. Royston, 1684. Fifth edition; folio, old full calf gilt with spine label, rather scuffed and bumped, pages (vi), lxviii, (vi), xviii, 238, frontispiece dated 1683 (little soiled, some edge tears and old repair), first title in red and black, second title, double page plate of Church Catholic Tree dated 1679, rather stained, some edge tears partly laid down, 30 engraved plates in pairs within text, later endpapers, few small old repairs and marks, armorial bookplate of William John Renny. R. F. G. Hollett & Son Antiquarian Booksellers 175 - 234 2011 £275

Association – Renouad, A. A.

Valerius Flaccus *Argonautica.* Venice: Aldus and Andrea Asulani, May, 1523. First and only Aldine edition; small 8vo., 148 leaves, Aldine dolphin and anchor woodcut device on titlepage and colophon leaf, 19th century red pebble grain morocco, fully gilt (upper hinge splitting), very occasional marginal dampstaining, else fine, A. A. Renouard's copy. Joseph J. Felcone Inc. Fall Miscellany 2010 - 1 2011 $4500

Association – Reynolds, John Taylor

Thomson, James 1700-1748 *The Works.* London: printed by A. Strahan for J. Rivington and Sons, 1788. 227 x 145mm., 3 volumes, elegant and still pleasing contemporary scarlet straight grained morocco simply gilt, covers with single gilt fillet border, raised bands flanked by plain gilt rules, gilt titling, turn-ins with gilt chain roll, marbled endpapers, all edges gilt; fine fore-edge paintings of Folkestone, Dublin and Worcester; volumes in recent sturdy buckram slipcase with marbled paper sides; frontispiece portrait, 10 engraved plates; 19th century armorial bookplate of Richard Davies, morocco bookplate of Estelle Doheny and modern engraved bookplate of John Taylor Reynolds, titlepage with ink ownership inscription of Mihill Slaughter 1811 (Secretary of the Railways Department); hint of soil to covers, joints and extremities with little rubbing (but well refurbished), leaves with intermittent minor foxing, engravings bit more foxed (half of them rather browned), offset onto facing page, text with general light browning and occasional trivial soiling, four leaves with short marginal or paper flaw tears (no loss); although not without problems, set nevertheless appealing, internal flaws never really unsightly, bindings all solid and paintings where it really matters, entirely well preserved. Phillip J. Pirages 59 - 45 2011 $4500

Association – Richards, Roger

Purdy, James *63: Dream Palace.* New York: William Frederick Press, 1956. First edition; inscribed by author to legendary NY bookseller Roger Richards, one letter rubbed from Purdy's name on spine, else fine in wrappers. Ken Lopez Bookseller 154 - 165 2011 $150

Association – Ricketts, Betty

Hudson, William Henry 1841-1922 *153 Letters from W. H. Hudson.* London: Nonesuch Press, 1923. One of 1000 copies; 260 x 172mm., 1 p.l. 191, (1) pages, (1) leaf, original brown buckram over bevelled boards, flat spine with paper label, edges untrimmed, titlepage with photogravure portrait of Hudson, one full page illustration, spare paper label tipped onto rear endpaper, partly torn bookplate of Betty Ricket(ts), boards bit marked and with one small puncture, trivial creasing to few leaves, otherwise nearly fine. Phillip J. Pirages 59 - 272 2011 $150

Association – Ridler, Vivian

Delamotte, Freeman Gage *A Primer of the Art of Illumination for the Use of Beginners...* Lockwood, 1874. Printed in black and red, 20 chromolithographed plates of initial letters, pages 44, 20 plates, 1 (ad), (1) (blank), small 4to., original bevel edged maroon cloth, plain backstrip faded, sides with blindstamped double line border and fleur-de-lys corner pieces, upper side elaborately gilt blocked with title and passion flowers, yellow, chalked endpapers, gilt edges, Vivian Ridler's copy with his embossed address on front free endpaper. Blackwell Rare Books B166 - 29 2011 £200

Hullmandel, Charles *The Art of Drawing on Stone, Giving a Full Explanation of the Various Styles of the Different Methods to be Employed to Ensure Success...* London: C. V. Hullmandell and R. Ackermann, 1824. First edition; lithographed titlepage, 6 lithographed plates, including two in colors and one on India paper, occasional minor spotting or browning, uncut, pages xvi, vii, 92, (2, ads, browned and window mounted), royal 8vo., later drab boards, paper lettering piece on spine, but any lettering once thereupon now vanished, trifle worn, original front of printed paper wrapper tipped on to inside front cover, booklabel of Vivian Ridler, good. Blackwell Rare Books B166 - 53 2011 £1500

Mardersteig, Hans *The Officina Bodoni.* Editions Officinae Bodoni (at Verona) At the Sign of the Pegasus, Paris, New York, 1929. 191/500 copies printed on Lafuma Rag paper using Arrighi Bodoni and Pastonchi types, with several specimens tipped in of press' work printed on handmade paper and reproductions of number of facsimiles; also with series of 12 full page woodcuts by Frans Masereel, pages (iv) (blanks), 82, (2) (blanks), large 4to., original cream buckram, backstrip gilt lettered, gilt blocked press device on front cover, endpapers lightly foxed, untrimmed, dust jacket, very good, Vivian Ridler's copy with his booklabel. Blackwell Rare Books B166 - 268 2011 £750

Marrot, H. V. *William Bulmer: Thomas Bensley.* London: The Fleuron, 1930. First edition, one of 300 copies, this unnumbered, printed on handmade paper; prelims and final few leaves lightly foxed, pages (v) (blanks), xi, 84, 4to., original dark green cloth, printer Vivian Ridler's copy with his booklabel and signature. Blackwell Rare Books B166 - 246 2011 £115

Association – Rigden, Margaret

Pope, Alexander 1688-1744 *The Poetical Works of Alexander Pope with His Life by Samuel Johnson.* London: printed by Whittingham and Howard for Sharpe and Hailes, 1811. 222 x 142 mm., 2 volumes, once very striking and still quite handsome contemporary crimson straight grain morocco by Taylor & Hessey (stamp-signed on the narrow board edge of upper cover of each volume), covers with border of thick and thin gilt rules enclosing a fine lacy gilt frame incorporating palmettes and volutes, inner frame formed by single gilt rule terminating at corners in floral sprays, raised bands dividing spine into four large and three small panels, the three narrow panels featuring a gilt rosette flanked by fleurons, the large panels at head and tail with prominent ornate fleuron on a stippled background with scalloped edges, and two middle panels with gilt titling, all edges gilt, the two fore edges with especially attractive paintings of Windsor Castle and Twickenham, frontispiece portraits, 16 engraved plates; contemporary ink ownership inscription of "Miss M(argare)t Rigden", spines uniformly faded to soft rose (with consequent slight muting of gilt), joints and extremities bit rubbed (though well refurbished), considerable foxing to plates as well as foxing and offsetting to adjacent leaves, other trivial imperfections, nevertheless very appealing set in important ways, elegant original bindings entirely sound and with lustrous boards, text almost entirely very smooth and fresh, fore edge paintings in excellent state of preservation. Phillip J. Pirages 59 - 198 2011 $2900

Association – Riker, Richard

Colden, Cadwallader D. *Memoir... at the Celebration of the Completion of the Erie Canal... New York 1826. (an) Narrative of the Festivities Observed in Honor of the Completion of the Grand Erie Canal.* New York: W. A. Davis, 1825. 1826. 1825. First edition; 4to., (8), 408, (2) pages, maps, lithographic plates, portraits, many folding, some in color, old marbled boards, rebacked, presentation inscription from Recorder of New York, Richard Riker. M & S Rare Books, Inc. 90 - 287 2011 $2250

Association – Ritchie, Ward

Bentley, Wilder *The Poetry of Learning.* Berkeley: Archetype Press, 1973-1985. 20 of 26 letterpress scrolls only, includes scrolls A-S and U, handset in Lutetia type and printed on damp, BFK Rives paper, scrolls A-C are printed on a single sheet, A and B are 14 inches in height, scroll C is 20 1/2 inches in height, remaining scrolls consist of several sheets joined together, longest being nearly 15 feet in length, height 15 1/2 inches, each scroll housed in its own individual storage tube with printed paper labels, storage tube for Scroll C has a woodcut illustration, scroll F with light dust stains, otherwise only a few light fox marks, mostly marginal, overall fine set, very rare; Ward Ritchie's set. Jeff Weber Rare Books 163 - 107 2011 $1000

Association – Rittenhouse, Jack

Hertzog, Carl *The Composing Stick as Paint Brush.* Irving: Quoin Press, n.d., 1970. #15 of 150 copies; not paginated (16) pages, signed, original printed wrappers in paper slipcase which shows some soil and glued flaps have come loose, front wrapper has couple of spots probably form aforementioned flaps, otherwise bright and near fine, miniature book, just 3 1/2 x 3 inches, with ALS from Steve Schuster who was The Quoin Press transmitting the book to New Mexico printer, Jack Rittenhouse. Dumont Maps & Books of the West 112 - 24 2011 $65

Association – Roane, John

Virginia. Laws, Statutes, Etc. *A Collection of All Such Acts of the General Assembly of Virginia.* Richmond: 1803. First edition; 454, (2) blank, 72 (index) pages, early law calf, 2 inch surface crack top right and bottom left of backstrip, most presentable copy with signature of John Roane. Bookworm & Silverfish 671 - 194 2011 $195

Association – Robert, Ray

Pynchon, Thomas 1937- *Vineland.* Boston: Little Brown, 1990. Advance copy in the form of unbound signatures and with trail bindings; pages uncut, fine, laid into green binding, which has Ray Robert's bookplate and in fine dust jacket. Ken Lopez Bookseller 154 - 178 2011 $2500

Association – Roberts, John

Sharp, John *Fifteen Sermons Preached on Several Occasions by... John Lord Arch Bishop of York.* London: printed for Walter Kettilby, 1709. Third edition; 8vo., pages (vi) 472 + engraved frontispiece, contemporary crimson turkey, spine gilt panelled with saltired compartments, lettered direct in gilt, boards panelled in gilt, board edges decorative roll gilt, turn-ins decorative roll gilt, 'Dutch-comb' 'made' endpapers, all edges gilt, blue and white sewn endbands, light spotting, occasional dampmark in lower margin, tidy repairs to headcap with new matching endband, black leather gilt decorative roll bordered label "To Mrs./E.B." ink inscription "Eliz. Battell/Juner", in different hand "The Gift of my Good Aunt Mrs. Eliz Battell to me Anne Hallows junr. May ye 26 1728", in same hand "Anne Leicester", ink inscription "John Roberts No 2 May 14 1792", from the collection of Christopher Ernest Weston 1947-2010. Unsworths Booksellers 24 - 40 2011 £200

Association – Roberts, Ray

Farina, Richard *Been Down so Long It Looks Like Up to Me.* New York: Viking, 1983. Reissue of author's first and only novel; issued simultaneously in paperback and hardcover, this is hardcover copy and has bookplate of Pynchon's editor, Ray Roberts, printed on cheap paper which is darkening with age, otherwise fine, near fine dust jacket with couple of small spots of rubbing and closed tear to rear flap fold. Ken Lopez Bookseller 154 - 188 2011 $100

Pynchon, Thomas 1937- *Against the Day.* New York: Penguin, 2006. Review copy; bookplate of Pynchon's editor, Ray Roberts, fine in fine dust jacket with press release laid in, text which appears to be an early draft of front jacket flap, uncommon. Ken Lopez Bookseller 154 - 186 2011 $450

Pynchon, Thomas 1937- *The Crying of Lot 49.* Philadelphia: Lippinoctt, 1966. First edition; minimal tanning to board edges, else fine in very near fine dust jacket with trace rubbing, nice, small bookplate of Ray Roberts (Pynchon's editor). Ken Lopez Bookseller 154 - 166 2011 $1000

Pynchon, Thomas 1937- *The Crying of Lot 49.* London: Cape, 1967. First British edition; small bookplate of Ray Roberts, fine in near fine dust jacket with small tear and crease at crown. Ken Lopez Bookseller 154 - 167 2011 $1000

Pynchon, Thomas 1937- *Gravity's Rainbow.* N.P.: n.p., n.d., Taiwan piracy; bookplate of Ray Roberts, Tapei bookstore label on rear flyleaf, offsetting to endpages, near fine in good, spine sunned dust jacket with several edge chips and one long tear in upper rear spine fold. Ken Lopez Bookseller 154 - 171 2011 $300

Pynchon, Thomas 1937- *Gravity's Rainbow.* London: Cape, 1973. Uncorrected proof of the British edition; fine in wrappers, small bookplate of Pynchon's editor, Ray Roberts. Ken Lopez Bookseller 154 - 169 2011 $3500

Pynchon, Thomas 1937- *Gravity's Rainbow.* London: Cape, 1973. First British softcover edition; issued simultaneously with hardcover edition, very nice, none of the spine fading typical to this title, quite uncommon, bookplate of Ray Roberts inside front cover. Ken Lopez Bookseller 154 - 170 2011 $350

Pynchon, Thomas 1937- *Gravity's Rainbow.* New York: Viking Press, 1973. Uncorrected proof; tall blue wrappers, pencil number ("7" - all copies seen by us have been numbered), sunning to spine and little offsetting to wrappers, else near fine, on inside front wrapper is small bookplate of Ray Roberts, Pynchon's editor when he went to Little Brown, uncommon issue. Between the Covers 169 - BTC342428 2011 $3750

Pynchon, Thomas 1937- *Gravity's Rainbow.* New York: Viking, 1973. First edition; small hardcover first printing of 4000 copies, the balance of the first edition, 16,000 copies, issued as softcover, small bookplate of Pynchon's editor, Ray Roberts, fine in near fine dust jacket with small creased tear to crown. Ken Lopez Bookseller 154 - 168 2011 $2750

Pynchon, Thomas 1937- *Mason and Dixon.* New York: Henry Holt, 1997. Second issue, uncorrected proof; blue wrappers, tipped in titlepage that adds the ampersand missing in first issue, small bookplate of Ray Roberts, Pynchon's editor, fine, with two dust jackets (bit crimped at crown where they extend past the proof) and fine printed acetate wrapper. Ken Lopez Bookseller 154 - 183 2011 $4000

Pynchon, Thomas 1937- *Mason and Dixon.* New York: Henry Holt, 1997. Uncorrected proof copy; plain blue wrappers, first issue proof, which leaves out the ameprsand from "Mason & Dixon" on titlepage, small bookplate of Ray Roberts, Pynchon's editor, inside front cover. Ken Lopez Bookseller 154 - 182 2011 $4500

Pynchon, Thomas 1937- *Mason and Dixon.* New York: Henry Holt, 1997. Advance reading copy; beige wrappers, the number of the copies of each of the two variant issues of the advance reading copy was rumored to be 500, the issues vary only on rear wrapper, this is the one with rear panel featuring publication and promotional data, fine in wrappers, bookplate of Ray Roberts, Pynchon's editor. Ken Lopez Bookseller 154 - 185 2011 $250

Pynchon, Thomas 1937- *Mason and Dixon.* New York: Henry Holt, 1997. Of a total of 4 leather bound copies of this title, this one of two copies without topstain; this copy belonged to Pynchon's editor, Ray Roberts, with Roberts bookplate, fine. Ken Lopez Bookseller 154 - 181 2011 $3500

Pynchon, Thomas 1937- *Of a Fond Ghoul.* New York: Blown Litter Press, 1990. One of only 50 numbered copies; fine in stapled wrappers, bookplate of Ray Roberts, Pynchon's editor. Ken Lopez Bookseller 154 - 180 2011 $2000

Pynchon, Thomas 1937- *Slow Learner.* Boston: Little Brown, 1984. One of only two leatherbound copies prepared by publisher, one which went to Pynchon; this one belonged to Pynchon's editor, Ray Roberts, small bookplate of Roberts on pastedown, letterhead note card identifying the issue laid in, fine. Ken Lopez Bookseller 154 - 172 2011 $6500

Pynchon, Thomas 1937- *Slow Learner.* Boston: Little Brown, 1984. Review copy of the first paperback edition; issued simultaneously with hardcover edition, bit of edge sunning to rear cover, else fine in wrappers, with review slip laid in, bookplate of Ray Roberts, Pynchon's editor. Ken Lopez Bookseller 154 - 174 2011 $125

Pynchon, Thomas 1937- *Slow Learner.* Boston: Little Brown, 1984. Advance issue; very small number of folded and gathered signatures were prepared and laid into proof dust jackets and issued as advance copies, the usual number cited for such copies is 'about 10', this is one of those sets of "f&g's" laid into trial binding and dust jacket, the mock-up of the boards is black, bookplate of Pynchon's editor, Ray Roberts on first signature, fine in very good dust jacket, worn where it overlays sheets, probably unique item. Ken Lopez Bookseller 154 - 173 2011 $2500

Pynchon, Thomas 1937- *Slow Learner.* London: Cape, 1985. First British edition; bookplate of Ray Roberts, fine in fine dust jacket. Ken Lopez Bookseller 154 - 175 2011 $125

Pynchon, Thomas 1937- *Slow Learner.* London: Cape, 1985. Uncorrected proof copy of the British edition; bookplate of Ray Roberts, rear pages edge sunned, last blank has corner turn, near fine in wrappers. Ken Lopez Bookseller 154 - 176 2011 $200

Pynchon, Thomas 1937- *Vineland.* London: Secker & Warburg, 1990. First British edition; bookplate of Ray Roberts, Pynchon's editor, age toning to pages, else fine in fine dust jacket. Ken Lopez Bookseller 154 - 179 2011 $125

Pynchon, Thomas 1937- *Vineland.* Boston: Little Brown, 1990. First edition; inscribed by author to his editor, Ray Roberts, fine in fine dust jacket. Ken Lopez Bookseller 154 - 177 2011 $25,000

Siegel, Jules *Limeland. Mortality and Mercy on the Internet' Pynchon-L@Waste.Org Discussion List.* Philadelphia: Intangible Assets Manufacturing, 1997. First edition; fine in wrappers, bookplate of Ray Roberts, together with bound galleys of the book, 8 1/2 x 11 inches, velobound, lower inch of binding broken, else fine in acetate cover. Ken Lopez Bookseller 154 - 191 2011 $200

Thomas Pynchon. Modern Critical Views. New York: Chelsea House, 1986. First edition; fine in fine dust jacket, bookplate of Ray Roberts, Pynchon's editor. Ken Lopez Bookseller 154 - 189 2011 $75

Weiseenburger, Steven *A Gravity's Rainbow Companion.* Athens: University of Georgia Press, 1988. Review copy; simultaneous issue in wrappers, near fine, review slip and press release laid in, bookplate of Ray Roberts, Pynchon's editor. Ken Lopez Bookseller 154 - 190 2011 $75

Association – Robertson, C.

Pope, Alexander 1688-1744 *The Poetical Works.* London: published by Thomas M'Lean, 1821. One of 100 copies; 241 x 159mm, 2 volumes, contemporary dark green straight grain morocco, handsomely gilt, covers bordered with various gilt rules flanking a wide roll of linked drawer handle ornaments, blind floral roll forming a tangent inner frame, wide raised bands decorated in gilt, spines gilt with decorative rolls at head and foot with elaborate all over scrolling foliate design within panels, all edges gilt, designated large paper copy on titlepage and with margins that are quite wide but volume at least slightly trimmed down, engraved bookplate of Charles Costello (partially removed from first volume), first volume with pencilled ownership signature (perhaps of "Capt. C. Robertson"), hint of wear to leather and of fading to spines, intermittent light foxing, one opening little soiled, additional trivial defects, but quite appealing, decorative bindings bright, clean and very pretty, text quite fresh with nothing approaching a serious problem. Phillip J. Pirages 59 - 280 2011 $650

Association – Robertson, J. M.

Shakespeare, William 1564-1616 *The Sonnets of William Shakespeare.* London: Kegan Paul Trench & Co., 1881. First edition thus; 8vo., original publisher's dark brown cloth lettered gilt on spine and on front cover, pages x, 306, with 44 page publisher's catalog at rear, ownership signature of J. M. Robertson with some pencilled notes and marginal linings in his hand, very slight rubbing at spine which has been neatly rebacked, otherwise very good+ with slight lean,. Any Amount of Books May 29 2011 - A49454 2011 $296

Association – Robinson, Gladys

Papworth, John B. 1775-1847 *Select Views of London.* London: printed for R. Ackermann by J. Diggens, 1816. First edition, first issue; with Papworth's name on titlepage, large octavo, (8), 159 pages, 76 hand colored aquatint plates including five double page folding plates, plates watermarked 1815, contemporary Regency calf, neatly rebacked with original spine laid down, covers decoratively bordered gilt, spine decoratively tooled in gilt in compartments with black morocco gilt lettering label, little light offsetting form plates to text, armorial bookplate of Frank Brewer Bemis and bookplate of Gladys Robinson, excellent early copy, housed in tan cloth slipcase.   David Brass Rare Books, Inc.   May 26 2011 - 00640   2011 $8500

Association – Robinson, William

Isocrates *Orationes et Epistolae.* Geneva: H. Estienne, 1593. Folio, (14) ff., 427, 131, XXXIV pages, (1) f. (blank), (4) ff, 31 pages, (9) ff., early 18th century English mottled calf, covers panelled in blind, spine gilt in compartments, red morocco label, printed pastedowns, slight worming, upper joint split at head an foot, inscription on titlepage T. Osborne 17th century and Wm. Robinson (18th century), fine armorial bookplate of William Robinson & Coll. Jes. Soc. Com., from the library of the Earls of Macclesfield at Shirburn Castle. Maggs Bros. Ltd.   1440 - 116   2011   £900

Association – Rock, Joseph

Millais, John Guille 1865-1931 *Rhododendrons in Which is Set Forth an Account of all Species of the genus Rhododendron (including Azaleas) and the Various Hybrids. First and Second Series.* London: Longmans, Green and Co., 1917-1924. First editions, limited to 550 copies, of which these volumes are numbers 9 and 8; 34 colored plates, 28 collotype plates, 28 half tone plates, 24 photographic plates, folio, pages xi, 268; xii, 2265, original maroon gilt lettered cloth (some wear to ends of spines, light rubbing, scuff marks to rear cover of second volume, and 1 1/2 inch split to upper edge of spine near back cover of second volume, text pages tanned), from the collection of Joseph F. Rock with his attractive bookplates.   Raymond M. Sutton, Jr.   May 26 2011 - 55811   2011 $2000

Association – Rockey, A. A.

Ricketts, Benjamin Merrill *The Surgery of the Heart and Lungs: a History and Resume of Surgical Conditions Found Therein and Experimental and Clinical Research in Man and Lower Animals...* New York: Grafton Press, 1904. First edition; 8vo., xvi 510 pages, 87 photo plates (including frontispiece), navy cloth, gilt stamped spine title, ex-library bookplate and titlepage embossed stamp, spine call numbers, very good, signature of A. A. Rockey.   Jeff Weber Rare Books   162 - 257   2011 $200

Association – Roethke, Theodore

Plath, Sylvia 1932-1963 *The Colossus. Poems.* London: Heinemann, 1960. First edition; fine, 8vo., original green cloth, dust jacket, fine, preserved in half morocco slipcase, presentation copy inscribed by author to poet Theodore Roethke.   James S. Jaffe Rare Books   May 26 2011 - 18792   2011 $50,000

Association – Rofen, Robert

Aldrovandi, Ulyssis *De Piscibus Libri V et de Cetis Lib. Unus.* Bononiae: Apud Nicolaum Thebaldinum, Engraved allegorical title (some light foxing), about 389 woodcuts, engraved headpieces, folio, pages (6), 732, (26), contemporary full vellum, old soiling, vellum missing from a panel on spine, upper rear corner showing, endpapers and last leaf foxed, few tears to lower margin of title and 2 leaves professionally reinforced, some stains to lower margin of first 13 leaves, small dampspot to upper margin of few leaves, browning or tanning to several leaves, 6 raised bands with panel lettered in gilt, later edition, the copy of Robert Rofen. Raymond M. Sutton, Jr.   May 26 2011 - 42653   2011 $4500

Richter, Johann Gottfried Ohnefalsch *Ichthyotheolgie Oder; Vernnunft und Schriftmassiger...* Leipzig: Friedrich Lankischens, 1754. First edition; 8 copper engraved plates, folding table, 8vo., pages (32), 912, (32), contemporary goatskin (edges rubbed, dark discoloration to upper third of front cover, also going across upper panel of spine), small paper label to head of spine, 3 small wormholes to edges of spine, bookplate, faint ink inscription to front blank, small stain to upper corner of prelim pages, small dampstain to lower margin of several pages, not affecting text, lower corner of several pages, small dampstain to lower margin of several pages, not affecting text, lower corner of several pages bumped, minor worming to rear pastedown and flyleaf, ex-libris Robert Rofen, good copy.   Raymond M. Sutton, Jr.   May 26 2011 - 42317   2011 $1750

Association – Rogers, Clement

Dodgson, Charles Lutwidge 1832-1898 *The Hunting of the Snark an Agony in Eight Fits.... (with) An Easter greeting to every child who loves 'Alice'.* London: Macmillan, 1876. First edition; 4to., pages (14), 86, frontispiece and 9 illustrations, including blank map fine except for occasional spotting, red cloth, border of six lines broken by circles enclosing illustrations on front and back, all gilt, gilt lettering to spine, all edges gilt, dark grey endpapers, hinges cracked but holding, endpapers almost detached, author's presentation inscription to his godson, Clement Rogers, with leaflet 16mo., pages (4) in staining running along outer fold, otherwise fine, disbound with single leaf, presentation inscription from author to Rogers.   Simon Finch Rare Books   Zero - 214   2011   £2750

Association – Rollo, George

Forrester, Andrew *The Revelations of a Private Detective.* London: Ward & Lock, 1863. Trimmed cloth, original blue green binder's cloth, slightly faded, booklabel of George Rollo. Jarndyce Antiquarian Booksellers CXCI - 178 2011 £180

Association – Rolls, Etherington Welch

Whitling, Henry John *Pictures of Nuremberg; and Rambles in the Hills and Valleys of Franconia.* London: Richard Bentley, 1850. First edition; 2 volumes, half titles, frontispiece, illustrations, slight foxing to illustrations, original orange cloth, slightly dulled, small armorial booklabels of Etherington Welch Rolls, very good, crisp copy. Jarndyce Antiquarian Booksellers CXCI - 584 2011 £280

Association – Rolls, John

Montgomery, Fanny Charlotte *On the Wing: a Southern Flight.* London: Hurst & Blackett, 1875. First edition; half title, (2), 16 page catalog, original dark green cloth, slight rubbing, armorial bookplate of John Allan Rolls, very good. Jarndyce Antiquarian Booksellers CLXC - 505 2011 £85

Yeats, William Butler 1865-1939 *Essays 1931-1936.* Dublin: Cuala Press, 1937. One of 300 copies; Uncut and unopened, original blue boards, cream cloth spine, paper label, original glassine wrappers, slightly chipped, fine, from the library of the grandfather of John Rolls who was the Rolls of Rolls-Royce. Jarndyce Antiquarian Booksellers CXCI - 623 2011 £250

Association – Ronald, Nigel

MacDonald, George 1824-1905 *Alec Forbes of Howglen.* London: Hurst & Blackett, 1865. First edition; 3 volumes, half titles, initial a leaf volume I, 14 page catalog volume III (apparently lacking one leaf), original orange cloth, spines little darkened and little rubbed at tails, bookplates of Nigel Ronald, inscription "S. J. Selby in remembrance of Miss Manning Aug. 10th 1905". Jarndyce Antiquarian Booksellers CXCII - 33 2011 £3000

Association – Roosevelt, Elfrida

MacDonald, George 1824-1905 *At the Back of the North Wind.* New York: George Routledge & Sons, circa, 1890? 76 illustrations by Arthur Hughes, original green cloth "branch & basket" design blocked in brown and gilt, very good, ownership signature of Elfridia Roosevelt. Jarndyce Antiquarian Booksellers CXCII - 118 2011 £130

Association – Rosenbloom, Charles

Moore, Thomas 1779-1852 *Lalla Rookh, an Oriental Romance.* London: printed for Longman, Hurst, Rees, Orme and Brown, 1817. First edition; 292 x 222mm., 2 p.l., 405, (1) pages, nothing short of spectacular early 20th century dark blue levant morocco extravagantly gilt, richly inlaid and gloriously bejewelled by Sangorski & Sutcliffe (stamp-signed on front doublure), binding with overall Oriental design (befitting the poem) with upper cover featuring a sunken central panel, its unusual nine-sided shape resembling a clump of hanging grapes, within which two birds of paradise, inlaid in lilac, green and brown morocco with two rubies for eyes, perch in a grape arbor, its inlaid leaves with fruit clusters on densely stippled gilt around accented with 19 turquoises, the whole central tableau surrounded by a border of interweaving bands of inlaid brown morocco set with 9 bands of Mother-of-Pearl, the entire sunken panel surrounded by two ornate frames filled with flowering vines of Oriental design composed of hundreds of pieces of inlaid morocco in red, blue, violet and green on a background of brown morocco and heavily stippled gilt, outer frame accented with 20 blue chalcedonies and 20 garnets; lower cover with similar frame and central panel, this one featuring two lovebirds inlaid with multiple colors and with two amethyst eyes, birds in a similar grape arbor above, large Mother-of-Pearl heart, panel further adorned with 3 sapphires, four blue chalcedonies five turquoises, four Carnelians and 10 additional bands of Mother-of-Pearl, raised bands, spine gilt in compartments with large inlaid arabesque in green and brown morocco on a gilt background, gilt titling on inlaid compartments of chestnut brown morocco, glorious front doublure of ivory morocco covered in gilt vines with inlaid violet morocco flowers, the whole framed in green morocco decorated with gilt vines and red morocco posies and berries, at center, a hand painted Cosway-Style portrait of author on ivory surrounded by gilt frame, with 12 flowers composed of no fewer than 72 turquoises and 36 garnets, oval portrait in sunken panel enclosed by wreath of inlaid morocco flowers, rear doublure of similar design, but its medallion featuring 8 amethysts set among sinuously curving inlaid lilac strapwork twining around a large (approximately one carat) Mexican fire opal encircled by 12 pearls, the binding containing 226 jewels in all; free endleaves of cream colored watered silk, gilt edges, in original well made (somewhat scuffed), silk and plush lined blue morocco box with shuttered lid; extra illustrated with 12 hand colored engraved plates mounted on lettered Japan vellum bookplate of Charles J. Rosenbloom; two leaves with neatly renewed marginal tears, but magnificent copy of a masterpiece of bookbinding. Phillip J. Pirages 59 - 111 2011 $65,000

Association – Rosenthal, Norman

Incarnate. London: Booth-Clibborn Editions, 1998. First edition; 4to. pages 222 (unpaginated), illustrations in color and black and white, signed by contributor Marc Quinn, loosely inserted post card to Norman Rosenthal, fine in fine dust jacket. Any Amount of Books May 29 2011 - A45925 2011 $340

Renton, Andrew *Marc Quinn: Chemical Life Support.* London: White Cube, 2005. First edition; 4to., color illustrated wrappers, illustrations in color, signed presentation from author to Norman Rosenthal, 40 pages, fine. Any Amount of Books   May 29 2011 - A47541   2011 $204

Association – Ross, Margot

Meynell, Alice *Poems.* London: Burns & Oates, 1914. Eleventh thousand; half title, frontispiece by Sargent slightly browned, 2 pages ads, original grey-brown cloth, rubbed, spine darkened, Wilfrid Meynell's presentation copy to Margot Ross, with holograph poem "The Modern Poet" numbered in corner '75' by Alice Meynell on slightly browned lined paper tipped in at end, with 2 cuttings inserted. Jarndyce Antiquarian Booksellers   CLXC - 392 2011   £85

Association – Rossetti, Dante Gabriel

Swinburne, Algernon Charles 1837-1909 *Pomes and Ballads. (with) Poems and Ballads. Second Series.* London: Edward Moxon and Co., 1866. London: Chatto & Windus 1878. First editions; 2 volumes, 8vo., (first series 164 x 100mm, second series 180 xm), pages viii, 344; x, 240, internally very crisp and fresh, uniformly bound in contemporary green half morocco, marbled boards and endpapers, all edges marbled, some rubbing to extremities, ALS from D. G. Rossetti for John Skelton, presenting the book with envelope tipped into volume i, address panel of letter from Swinburne to Shelton tipped into volume ii, numerous pencil notes throughout volume i by Skelton, with presentation letter from Rossetti to Skelton.   Simon Finch Rare Books   Zero - 355 2011   £1800

Association – Rossetti, William Michael

Scott, William Bell *The Year of the World: a Philosophical Poem on "Redemption from the Fall".* Edinburgh: William Tait, 1846. First edition; original green cloth, lettered in gilt, blocked in blind, inscribed by author for Miss Lucy Madox Brown, further signed presentation inscription from W. M. Rossetti.   Jarndyce Antiquarian Booksellers   CXCI - 486   2011   £750

Tupper, John Lucas *Hiatus: the Void in Modern Education, Its Cause and Antidote.* London: Macmillan, 1869. First edition; 8vo., disbound, pages 251 with 51 page publisher's catalog at rear, presentation copy on verso of front endpaper to W. M. Rossetti from the author, last page has note about errata on 3 pages, possibly in hand of Rossetti, disbound, otherwise in decent, sound condition with clean text.   Any Amount of Books   May 26 2011 - A62731 2011 $419

Association – Rota, Anthony

Brooke, Jocelyn *The Birth of a Legend.* London: Bertram Rota, 1964. One of 65 copies signed by author, this "out of series"; 4to., stiff plain card with printed green self wrappers, pages 7, signed presentation from publisher Anthony Rota to writer and activist Yvonne Kapp.   Any Amount of Books   May 29 2011 - A49029   2011 $383

Association – Rothschild, Leopold De

Disraeli, Benjamin 1804-1881 *Novels and Tales by the Earl of Beaconsfield: with Portrait and Sketch of His Life.* London: Longmans, 1881. Hughenden edition; 11 volumes, half titles, frontispiece in volume I, engraved titles, largely unopened in original light brown cloth, oval blue morocco label on front boards, decorated in gilt, spines blocked in black, red and gilt, damp mark to back board of volume I, occasional slight rubbing, booklabels of L. R. Ascott, nice, bookplate of Leopold de Rothschild. Jarndyce Antiquarian Booksellers   CXCI - 11 2011   £280

Association – Roughton, Roger

Transition. Paris: Transition, 1930. First edition; large 8vo., original publisher's illustrated wrappers/paper back, pages 398, 21 plates, ownership signature of surrealist Roger Roughton, sound, near very good, decent copy with slight soiling, slight wear at spine hinge and slight browning. Any Amount of Books   May 29 2011 - A66993   2011 $306

Association – Roundell, Richard Henry

West, Thomas *The Antiquities of Furness; or, an Account of the Royal Abbey of St. Mary, in the Vale of Nightshade near Dalton in Furness...* 4to., old full speckled calf, gilt, elegantly gilt decorated spine, a little worn, corners bumped, pages (xvi), (ii), lvi, 288, 3A-3R4 (appendices), complete with folding engraved map (slightly torn in folds), folding plan, 2 engraved plates, armorial bookplate of Richard Henry Roundell, good, clean and sound.   R. F. G. Hollett & Son Antiquarian Booksellers   General Catalogue Summer 2010 - 1612 2011   £295

Association – Rowe, Richard

Saurat, Denis *Death and the Dreamer.* London: John Westhouse, 1946. First edition; original cloth, dust jacket, price clipped, pages 150 with full page illustrations, presentation copy, inscribed for Richard Rowe.   R. F. G. Hollett & Son Antiquarian Booksellers   General Catalogue Summer 2010 - 719   2011   £120

Association – Rowlandson, Richard

Tacitus, Gaius Cornelius *Annales of Cornelius Tacitus.* London: printed by John Bill, 1622. Fifth edition; small folio, pages (vi) 271, (vii), 12, 228, (ii), the second page 213 is a full page engraving, this copy lacks initial blank, contemporary speckled calf, spine double ruled in blind, unlettered, boards double rule bordered in blind with smaller double rule central panel fleurons outermost at corners and smaller stylised flower, innermost all in blind, board edges decorative roll in blind, all edges red speckled, pink and white sewn endbands, little spotting, dampmark in upper corner, excisions to title repaired, rubbed, corners and endcaps worn, joints cracked, upper just holding, original ownership inscription cut out, but may have been same as "Fran: Cornwallis" at head fore corner of first page 1 or may have been same as "Richard Rowlandson" verso front blank, 19th century unidentified circular armorial bookplate, from the collection of Christopher Ernest Weston 1947-2010. Unsworths Booksellers 24 - 145 2011 £300

Association – Rubeus, Jacobus

Ammianus Marcellinus *Rerum Gestarum Libri Decem et Octo.* Lyons: S. Gryphius, 1552. 12mo., 736 (8) pages, aa2 missing, aa3, last 2 leaves blank, contemporary French binding of smooth calf, gilt arabesque in centre of covers, spine in 5 compartments each with small gilt ornament, gilt edges, binding little rubbed, deleted contemporary inscription on titlepage Jacobus Rubeus, from the library of the Earls of Macclesfield at Shirburn Castle. Maggs Bros. Ltd. 1440 - 6 2011 £450

Association – Ruck, Berta

Louys, Pierre *Les Chansons de Bilitis.* Paris: Librairie Charpentier et Fasquelle, 1925. 8vo., pages (iv), xii, 356, plus 12 leaves of manuscript translations bound in, 300 engravings in text, top edge gilt, others uncut, pages lightly browned at edges, contemporary blue cloth, upper board and spine decorated in gilt, gilt lettering to spine, floral endpapers, light shelf wear, tips rubbed, spine darkened, manuscript list of bound in translations to front free endpaper, further manuscript translations to pages 17, 189, 228, 9, 244-5, 256, 330-1, unique Christmas gift from Berta Ruck to "Nony" who is possibly her husband Oliver Onions. Simon Finch Rare Books Zero - 339 2011 £350

Association – Ruetz, Michael

Becher, Bernhard *Anonyme Skulpturen. Eine Typologie Technischer Bauten.* Dusseldorf: Art Press Verlag, 1970. First edition of Becher's first book; 4to., pages (215) (i) blank, 196 black and white photos, text in German, English and French, original blue cloth, spine and upper side lettered in white, light marks to boards at fore-edge, original dust jacket illustrated with black and white photos, text printed in black, little light soiling, two short closed tears to lower panel and one to upper and light nicks to head of spine, ex-libris of German photographer Michael Ruetz, near fine. Simon Finch Rare Books Zero - 507 2011 £3000

Association – Rumney, Mark

Stackhouse, Thomas *A New and Practical Exposition of the Apostles Creed...* London: Thomas Longman, Thomas Shewell and Charles Hitch, 1747. First edition; folio, contemporary full polished calf with raised ands, few old surface scratches and small defects, pages (ii), xxviii (ii, analysis, verso blank), 208, 217-421, (i, ad), (xiv, index and table, final leaf blank), text and signature complete despite pagination, nice contemporary inscription on flyleaf in Latin from William Stratford, Commissary of the Archdeaconry of Richmond, presenting the book to the Curate of Dent, Mark Rumney and his successors. R. F. G. Hollett & Son Antiquarian Booksellers 175 - 1277 2011 £350

Association – Rush, Homer

Livingston, William Kenneth *The Clinical Aspects of Visceral Neurology: with Special Reference to the Surgery of the Sympathetic Nervous System.* Springfield and Baltimore: Charles C. Thomas, 1935. First edition; 8vo., xi, 254 pages, 3 color plates, figures, indexes, original blue cloth, gilt stamped spine title, dust jacket, near fine, author's signed presentation to Homer Rush, from the Medical Library of Dr. Clare Gray Peterson. Jeff Weber Rare Books 162 - 198 2011 $125

Association – Rushout, Anne

Hayley, William *Posthumous Writings of William Cowper, Esqr.* Chichester: Printed by J. Seagraves for J. Johnson, 1803-1804. First edition; 4to., 3 volumes, pages 413, 422, 436, contemporary calf, neatly rebacked with speckled calf spine and leather labels, some light foxing, generally very nice, wide margins, early bookseller's note on endper says this is "probably" a large paper copy, includes 2 portraits of Cowper, bookplate of Hon. Anne Rushout. Second Life Books Inc. 174 - 172 2011 $825

Association – Russell, A. F.

Walker, Eric A. *W. P. Schreiner: a South African.* Oxford: University Press, 1937. First edition; 8vo., pages xii, 386, 6 plates, original red cloth, spine slightly faded, presentation copy to A. F. Russell from author's son.   J. & S. L. Bonham Antiquarian Booksellers   Africa 4/20/2011 - 5166   2011   £45

Association – Russell, Edward

Jayne, Caroline Furness *String Figures.* New York: Charles Scribner's Sons, 1906. First edition; small 4to., original blue cloth, gilt, neatly recased, pages xxiii, 407, with 867 figures, inscribed by author's father to Sir Edward Russell dated 1906, few marginal pencil lines to introduction, otherwise excellent copy.   R. F. G. Hollett & Son Antiquarian Booksellers   175 - 726   2011   £250

Association – Russell, William

Rich, Henry *What Is to be Done? or Past, Present and Future.* London: James Ridgway, 1844. First edition; 8vo., (iv), 123 pages, recent blue boards, lettered on upper cover, paper label on spine, very good, from the contemporary library of Lord William Russell with his signature on titlepage, scarce.   John Drury Rare Books   153 - 125   2011   £100

Association – Rust, George Bernard

MacDonald, George 1824-1905 *The Lost Princess; or the Wise Woman.* Wells Gardner, Darton & Co., 1895. Half title, frontispiece and illustrations, 2 pages ads, original deep olive green cloth blocked in black and gilt, bookplates of Bibliotheca Churchilliana" and George Bernard Rust, very good.   Jarndyce Antiquarian Booksellers   CXCII - 184   2011   £120

MacDonald, George 1824-1905 *Phantastes: a Faerie Romance for Men and Women.* London: Arthur C. Fifield, 1905. New edition; half title, frontispiece, illustrations by Arthur Hughes, uncut in original dark blue cloth, spine slightly dulled, bookplate of George Bernard Rust, top edge gilt.   Jarndyce Antiquarian Booksellers   CXCII - 12   2011   £85

Association – Rutherford, William

Addison, Joseph 1672-1719 *The Works.* London: George Bell and Sons, 1893-1898. 7 volumes, 185 x 115 mm., attractive contemporary prize binding of light polished calf done for H. Sotheran & Co. (stamp signed on front turn-in of each volume), covers with double gilt fillet border, upper board of each volume with central gilt crest of St. Peter's College, Westminster, raised bands, spines ornately gilt in compartments with elegant central floral spray, surrounded by a lozenge of small tools and elaborate side and cornerpieces composed of fleurons, curls, volutes and circulets, two pale green morocco labels, filigree gilt turn-ins, marbled endpapers, all edges gilt, volume I with portrait frontispiece and 8 plates of medal and coin designs, pastedown with affixed presentation certificate to B. H. Willet, signed by William ("Gulielmus") Rutherford and dated 1899, leather with bit of dryness, extremities little rubbed, labels slightly faded, one minor neatly repaired tear (into text, but no loss), otherwise fine, elaborately gilt bindings lustrous and with other minor wear and text virtually pristine, pretty set.   Phillip J. Pirages   59 - 62   2011 $275

Boswell, James 1740-1795 *Boswell's Life of Johnson Including Boswell's Journal of a Tour to the Hebrides and Johnson's Diary of a Journey into North Wales.* Oxford: at the Clarendon Press, 1887. 6 volumes, 229 x 152mm., especially pleasing contemporary prize bindings of polished calf, handsomely gilt for H. Sotheran & Co. (stamp signed on front pastedown), boards with gilt double rule border and with gilt scholastic arms on each of the six front covers, raised bands, spines elaborately gilt in compartments featuring scrolling foliate cornerpieces and intricate floral centerpiece, brown morocco labels, ornate gilt turn-ins, marbled endpapers, all edges gilt, with 14 plates as called for (8 of them folding), including facsimiles of Johnson's handwriting, map and chart of Johnson's contemporaries; Latin presentation bookplate to J. Mavrogordato indicating that this set was a prize given to him by the headmaster, William Rutherford of the College of Saint Peter, Westminster, one volume with very minor flaking to one join, odd trivial mark to covers but in exceptionally fine condition, bindings essentially unworn and text probably unread.   Phillip J. Pirages   59 - 155   2011 $1800

Association – Rylands, George

De La Ramee, Louise 1839-1908 *Two Offenders.* London: Chatto & Windus, 1894. First edition; 32 pages ads (Nov. 1893), half title, original dark green cloth, decorated in black and yellow, spine gilt lettered, George Ryland's small booklabel, nice, fine full page inscription signed by author for Marie Corelli, also pencil inscription "To Dalie with love on his 60th birthday from Tim", loosely inserted typed note by Rylands, "Given me by A. N. L. Munby on my 60th birthday.   Jarndyce Antiquarian Booksellers   CLXC - 714   2011   £600

Hart, Davis *The Lyttelton Hart-Davis Letters: Correspondence of George Lyttelton and Rupert Hart-Davis.* London: John Murray, 1979-1987. Volume 1 reprint, others first editions, volumes 5 and 6 first edition paperback; 8vo, 6 volumes (5 and 6 bound in one book), volume II signed presentation copy from author to Dadie Rylands, 4 volumes have short letters laid in from publisher "Jock" Murray to Dadie Rylands, all very good, clean copies, dust jackets where called for.   Any Amount of Books   May 29 2011 - B9967   2011 $221

Association – Sachs

Bacon, Francis, Viscount St. Albans 1561-1626 *The Twoo Bookes of Francis Bacon. Of the Proficience and Advancement of learning, Divine and Humane.* London: for Henrie Tomes, 1605. First edition; 4to., (1), 45, 118 (i.e. 121), leaves, lacks final blank 3H2 an, as always, the rare two leaves of errata at end, late 18th century half calf and marbled boards, extremities of boards worn, very skillfully and imperceptively rebacked retaining entire original spine, small worm trail in bottom margin of quires 2D-2F, occasional minor marginalia in an early hand, else lovely, early signature of Row'd Wetherald on title, signature of Horatio Carlyon 1861, Sachs bookplate and modern leather booklabel, calf backed clamshell box.   Joseph J. Felcone Inc.   Fall Miscellany 2010 - 8   2011 $7500

Association – Sackett, T.

Cooper, James Fenimore 1789-1851 *Leatherstocking Tales.* Philadelphia: Lea & Blanchard, 1848. 1848. 1849. 1848. 1849 (but maybe all 1848?). Early reprint of first collected edition; 5 volumes, publisher's uniform brown cloth stamped in blind and titled in gilt, each title is two volumes in one, 3 volumes have ownership signature of Thos. Sackett dated in 1848, corners bumped and worn, some erosion to cloth on spine with minor loss at spine ends considerable foxing, but handsome, about very good set and very uncommon.   Between the Covers   169 - BTC3408333   2011 $2200

Association – Sadleir, Michael

Whitman, Walt 1819-1892 *Leaves of Grass.* Brooklyn: published by the author, 1856. Second edition; 12mo., original grey-green cloth, decoratively blindstamped, gilt decorations and lettering, engraved frontispiece by Samuel Hollyer, bookplates of E. M. Cox and Michael Sadleir, cloth slightly rubbed, some light to moderate foxing, fine, from the collection of Samuel Charters.   The Brick Row Book Shop   Bulletin 8 - 6   2011 $22,500

Association – Sage, Mrs.

Wharton, Edith 1862-1937 *Italian Villas and Their Gardens.* New York: Century, 1904. First and only edition; heavily illustrated with photos, drawings, 26 full color plates by Maxfield Parrish, with 3 page ALS from Wharton tipped in, written to Mrs. Sage, with two page ALS from Maxfield Parrish, written in his elegant calligraphic hand, owner's small tasteful bookplate adorns front pastedown.   Ken Lopez Bookseller   154 - 241   2011 $10,000

Association – Salin, Edgar

Nietzsche, Friedrich *Gotzen-Dammerung, Oder Wie man Mit Dem Hammer Philosophiert.* Leipzig: C. G. Naumann, 1889. First edition; 8vo., pages (vii), 144, later cloth, spine lettered in gilt, original drab wrappers printed in red and black bound in, pencilled note to front pastedown "Ex Biblioth. E. Salin" (Edgar Salin 1892-1974 prominent German sociologist), light wear to wrappers, but excellent, fresh copy.   Simon Finch Rare Books   Zero - 134   2011   £2250

Association – Salmon William

Churchill, Charles *Poems.* London: printed for John Churchill and W. Flexney, 1769. Fourth edition; (4), 369, (1), (2) pages ads, half title; (4), 330 pages, half title, 8vo., full contemporary calf, gilt decorated spines, red and olive green gilt labels, some rubbing to gilt, slight crack to upper joint volume I, signature of J. Churchill at foot of final leaf of text, volume II with armorial bookplates of William Salmon and J. P. Turbervill, very good, attractive.   Jarndyce Antiquarian Booksellers   CXCI - 119   2011   £200

Association – Salt, Catherine

Martineau, Harriet 1802-1876 *Health, Husbandry and Handicraft.* London: Bradbury & Evan, 1861. First edition; half title, 12 page catalog (Jan. 1861), uncut in original red pebble grained cloth, blocked in blind, spine lettered in gilt, carefully recased, spine darkened cloth, slightly wormed on following board, signed presentation inscription Catherine Salt, from author, also signed in pencil Margaret Martineau.   Jarndyce Antiquarian Booksellers   CLXC - 282   2011   £420

Association – Saltoun, Alexander William Fraser, 19th Lord

Morgan, Sydney Owenson 1776-1859 *Lady Morgan's Memoirs: Autobiography, Diaries and Correspondence.* London: Wm. H. Allen & Co., 1863. Second edition; engraved frontispiece, contemporary full maroon calf, double ruled borders in gilt, spines gilt in compartments, black title labels, lacking volume no. labels, spines faded to brown and slightly rubbed, Eton leaving inscription E. W. Danby to Alexander William Fraser, 19th Lord Saltoun, Saltoun bookplates, good plus. Jarndyce Antiquarian Booksellers CLXC - 542 2011 £125

Association – Sandell, Richard

Great Britain. Royal Commission on Historical Monuments - 1970 *An Inventory of the Historical Monuments in Dorset. Volume two - South East.* London: HMSO, 1970. First edition; 3 volumes, 4to., original cloth, gilt, dust jackets, pages lxiv, 188; xviii, 189-417; ix, 418-701, numerous plans, plates and maps, including color frontispiece, bookplate of Richard Sandell, god-son of Sir Emery Walker. R. F. G. Hollett & Son Antiquarian Booksellers 177 - 765 2011 £140

Association – Sanders, Ed

Charters, Ann *The Portable Beat Reader.* New York: Viking, 1992. First edition; 600+ pages, fine in fine dust jacket, exceptional copy, this copy belonged to Nelson Lyon, inscribed to him or signed and dated by William Burroughs, Allen Ginsberg, Gregory Corso, Ed Sanders, Michael McClure and Anne Waldman. Ken Lopez Bookseller 154 - 12 2011 $1250

Association – Sands, Dorothy

Coward, Noel 1899-1973 *Qaudrille. A romantic Comedy in Three Acts.* London: Heienmann, 1952. First edition; 8vo., pages 116, signed by 17 members of the English cast and by producer Jack Wilson and by Lynn Fontanne and Alfred Lunt on dedication page (play is dedicated to them), inscribed by Coward to Dorothy Sands (Octavia in the NY production), two more signed cards by Lunt and Fontanne tipped in and 3 notes by Lunt to Sands laid in, with tipped in signed photo of Sands, nice copy in somewhat chipped dust jacket. Second Life Books Inc. 174 - 111 2011 $700

Association – Saumarez, Rear Admiral

Sheridan, Thomas *Sheridan's and Henderson's Practical Method of Reading and Reciting English Poetry...* London: Printed for E. Newbery, 1796. xii, 264 pages, 12mo., small stain to outer edge of final leaves, paper flaw to page 261-2 with slight loss, missing words being supplied in margin in neat contemporary hand, excellently rebacked in half calf, gilt ruled spine, original marbled boards, ownership label of Rear Admiral Saumarez with note presenting the book to his granddaughter May Snowden. Jarndyce Antiquarian Booksellers CXCI - 491 2011 £125

Association – Saunders, William

Jefferies, Richard 1848-1887 *The Scarlet Shawl.* London: Tinsley Bros., 1874. First edition; text slightly spotted, contemporary half blue morocco by Bumpus, raised bands, decorated and lettered gilt on spine, slightly rubbed, armorial bookplate of William Henry Radcliffe Saunders, very good. Jarndyce Antiquarian Booksellers CXCI - 223 2011 £420

Ponsonby, Arthur *The Priory and Manor of Lynchmere and Shulbrede.* Taunton: Barnicott & Pearce, 1920. First edition; original holland backed boards, edges little stained, pages xiv, 207, uncut with 57 illustrations by author, few spots in places, attractive bookplate of William Saunders, 10 line autograph note by author on his headed notepaper tipped on to flyleaf. R. F. G. Hollett & Son Antiquarian Booksellers 175 - 1069 2011 £120

Association – Savitsch, Eugene Constantin

Pound, Ezra Loomis 1885-1972 *The Cantos of Ezra Pound.* New York: New Directions, 1948. First edition, 2nd printing; presentation copy from author to Russian emigre surgeon Eugene Constantin de Savitsch, 8vo., pages (iv), 150, 56, 46, (2), 168, 118, plus frontispiece with reproduction of photo of author by Arnold Genthe, internally clean and bright, original black cloth with white lettering to spine, faded, very light wear to extremities, original sea gray dust jacket, unclipped, maroon text, Gaudier Breska drawing of Pound to upper panel, chipped, spine sunned. Simon Finch Rare Books Zero - 346 2011 £1250

Association – Scaife, C. H. O.

MacDonald, George 1824-1905 *Rampolli: Growths from a Long Planted Root: Being Translations, New and Old.* London: Longmans, Green & Co., 1897. First edition; half title, 32 page catalog (5/97), original crimson buckram, spine faded, uneven fading to boards, inscribed by author for cousin Katharine Ling, bookplate and guard of C. H. O. Scaife. Jarndyce Antiquarian Booksellers CXCII - 324 2011 £1200

Association – Scaliger, Joseph

Ovidius Naso, Publius *Operum... Tomus Primus (Tertius)...* Frankfurt: C. Marny & Heirs of J. Aubry, typis Wechelianis, 1601. 3 volumes, folio, (4), 500, (16); (2), 388, 116, 244, (12), 340, 199 pages, later 17th century mottled calf, gilt fillet on covers, spines gilt, green silk ties lacking, slightly foxed but highly desirable, handsome copy, from the library of the Earls of Macclesfield at Shirburn Castle, bequeathed by Iosephi Scaliger to D. Heinsius.   Maggs Bros. Ltd.   1440 - 160 2011   £3000

Association – Schiff, Mortimer

Gresset, Jean Baptiste Louis *Poemes.* Paris: D. Jouaust, 1867. One of 2 copies Printed on vellum, there were also 118 on paper; 215 x 140mm., 6 p.l., (two vellum blanks, half title, title, two frontispieces (on paper), iv, 132 pages, (4) leaves (variants, contents/colophon, two vellum blanks), folio Cii unsigned and misnumbered but copy complete; very attractive contemporary midnight blue crushed morocco handsomely gilt by Thibaron (stamp signed), covers with French fillet border, raised bands, spines ornately gilt in compartments filled with delicately stipped swirling designs accented with small tools, gilt inner dentelles, marbled endpapers, all edges gilt, 9 engraved on (on paper), 2 frontispiece portraits, 7 plates, large paper copy, bookplates of Robert Hoe and Mortimer Schiff, engraved bookplate of Marcellus Schlimovich, library stamp of Sociedad Hebraica Argentina, just hint of wear top and bottom of joints, one side of first and last vellum flyleaf discolored (apparently from a reaction to the gilt on pastedowns(?), plates with variable freckled foxing (never serious), otherwise fine, elegant binding quite lustrous and leaves clean, fresh and bright. Phillip J. Pirages   59 - 343   2011 $3250

Association – Schmidt, Frederikke

Ibsen, Henrik *Et Dukkehjem. (Doll's House).* Copenhagen: Gyldendalske Boghandels Forlag, 1879. First edition; 8vo., pages 180, original paper wrappers, printed in black, pages slightly and evenly toned, Frederikke Schmidt's neat ownership signature and Doris Arentz's to half title, chips to spine head and wrappers, front wrappers sometime strengthened, very good.   Simon Finch Rare Books   Zero - 242   2011   £900

Association – Schneider, H. W.

Graham, Henry *The New Coinage.* privately published Civil Service Printing and Publishing Co., 1878. Pages 152, original black cloth, gilt, rather bubbled and stained by damp, pages 152, endpapers rather cockled ad stained, presentation copy inscribed by H. W. Schneider with author's compliments.   R. F. G. Hollett & Son Antiquarian Booksellers   173 - 486   2011   £75

Association – Scholes, Ellen

Burke, William *The Greek-English Derivative Dictionary showing in English Characters, the Greek Originals of Such Words in the English Language as are Derived from the Greek...* London: J. Johnson, 1806. 8vo., pages 248, 2 neat inscriptions on front endpaper in 19th century handwriting of the Fanny Desborough of Russell Square, also Mary Desborough, Ellen Scholes and Mrs. Geldart, soundly bound in full plain unlettered (but with 7 gold bands at spine), tree calf which is lightly scuffed and slightly marked), very good.   Any Amount of Books   May 29 2011 - A72178 2011 $238

Association – Schuster, Stephen Mathew

Fay, Bernard *Notes on the American Press at the End of the Eighteenth Century.* New York: Grolier Club, 1927. Limited to 325 copies; tall 4to., (10), 29 pages, 25 folding double page facsimiles of early American newspapers, original blue cloth boards, printed paper cover and spine labels, second cover and spine labels pasted inside rear cover, housed in blue paper slipcase, extremities worn, small piece of box missing, with officer's commission certificate: USN Reserve commission for Stephen Mathew Schuster to the rank of Ensign, signed by secretary of Navy, Frank Knox 6 March 1944, fine.   Jeff Weber Rare Books   163 - 113 2011 $85

Association – Schuster, Steve

Hertzog, Carl *The Composing Stick a a Paint Brush.* Irving: Quoin Press, n.d., 1970. #15 of 150 copies; not paginated (16) pages, signed, original printed wrappers in paper slipcase which shows some soil and glued flaps have come loose, front wrapper has couple of spots probably form aforementioned flaps, otherwise bright and near fine, miniature book, just 3 1/2 x 3 inches, with ALS from Steve Schuster who was The Quoin Press transmitting the book to New Mexico printer, Jack Rittenhouse.   Dumont Maps & Books of the West   112 - 24   2011 $65

Association – Schuyler, James

O'Hara, Frank *Meditations in an Emergency.* New York: Grove Press, 1957. First edition, one of an unknown number of unnumbered (out of series) hardbound copies, perhaps author's copies, out of a total of 90 cloth bound copies; small 8vo., original green cloth, glassine dust jacket, very fine, lacking slipcase, presentation copy inscribed by author to James Schuyler for Jimmy and Alfred and Guinevere. James S. Jaffe Rare Books   May 26 2011 - 13191 2011 $7500

Association – Schwabe, Randolph

Maugham, William Somerset 1874-1965 *Of Human Bondage.* New York: Doubleday, Doran, 1936. First illustrated edition, one of 751 numbered copies signed by author and artist, this is copy #4; additionally inscribed by author for Doubleday editor Malcolm Johnson, illustrations by Randolph Schwabe, small quarto, full dark blue morocco with raised bands and heavily stamped in gilt, just about fine, laid in is 1936 letter from artist, Schwabe in his calligraphic hand.   Between the Covers   169 - BTC346497   2011 $4250

Association – Scott, A. J., Mrs.

Ruskin, John 1819-1900 *The Queen of the Air: Being a Study of the Greek Myths of Cloud and Storm.* London: Smith, Elder and Co., 1869. Second edition; 8vo., pages 199, presentation from author for Mrs. A. J. Scott, decent, clean copy in original publisher's green cloth lettered gilt at spine, top of titlepage has been cut out to reveal the presentation at top of next page (not affecting text), slight rubbing at spine ends, else very good.   Any Amount of Books May 29 2011 - A63060   2011 $374

Association – Scott, Jonathan

Barrow, Isaac *Several Sermons Against Evil Speaking.* London: printed for Brabazon Aylmer, 1678. 8vo., pages (viii), 243, (i), 140, (iv), contemporary speckled calf, boards blind ruled, board edges 'broken rule', gilt, text block edges densely red sprinkled, blue and white sewn endbands, alte 20th century blind ruled and unlettered calf reback, touch of minor spotting, leather rubbed at extremities, corners just worn, contemporary ink inscription "Rd Scott", ink inscription "Jonathan Scott 1746 Betton", also "J. A. Milner/Shrewsbury/1889", from the collection of Christopher Ernest Weston 1947-2010.   Unsworths Booksellers   24 - 2   2011   £275

Association – Scott, R.

Barrow, Isaac *Several Sermons Against Evil Speaking.* London: printed for Brabazon Aylmer, 1678. 8vo., pages (viii), 243, (i), 140, (iv), contemporary speckled calf, boards blind ruled, board edges 'broken rule', gilt, text block edges densely red sprinkled, blue and white sewn endbands, late 20th century blind ruled and unlettered calf reback, touch of minor spotting, leather rubbed at extremities, corners just worn, contemporary ink inscription "Rd Scott", ink inscription "Jonathan Scott 1746 Betton", also "J. A. Milner/Shrewsbury/1889", from the collection of Christopher Ernest Weston 1947-2010.   Unsworths Booksellers   24 - 2   2011   £275

Association – Scott, Thomas

Catlin, George 1796-1872 *O'Kee-Pa: a Religious Ceremony and Other Customs of the Mandans.* London: Trubner and Co., 1867. First edition; small 4to., vi, (2), 52 pages plus iii page "Folium Reservatum, 13 chromolithographed plates after Catlin by Simonau & Toovey, publisher's purple cloth, gilt, all edges gilt, binding lightly soiled and faded, extremities lightly worn (spine ends more so), occasional minor foxing, very good, fragile to find in fine condition, presentation copy inscribed by publisher Nicholas Trubner to Thomas Scott.   Joseph J. Felcone Inc.   Fall Miscellany 2010 - 22   2011 $20,000

Association – Searle, George

Martin, Theodore *The Life of His Royal Highness the Prince Consort.* London: Smith, Elder, 1879. First volume is sixth edition from 1879 and the second a fourth edition from 1877; stout 8vo., 2 volumes, original publisher's brown cloth lettered gilt at spine, about 1100 pages in all, both very good condition, with one small gathering slightly sprung in first volume, signed presentation from Queen Victoria to George Searle.   Any Amount of Books   May 26 2011 - A39542   2011 $604

Association – Seed, Harris

MacDonald, Ross *The Galton Case.* New York: Knopf, 1959. First edition; inscribed by author to his lawyer and friend Harris and Nancy (Seed), fine in dust jacket with light wear to spine ends and with one small closed tear to top edge of rear panel.   Buckingham Books   May 26 2011 - 20956   2011 $3750

Association – Seed, Nancy

MacDonald, Ross *The Galton Case.* New York: Knopf, 1959. First edition; inscribed by author to his lawyer and friend Harris and Nancy (Seed), fine in dust jacket with light wear to spine ends and with one small closed tear to top edge of rear panel.   Buckingham Books   May 26 2011 - 20956   2011 $3750

Association – Selby, S. J.

MacDonald, George 1824-1905 *Alec Forbes of Howglen.* London: Hurst & Blackett, 1865. First edition; 3 volumes, half titles, initial a leaf volume I, 14 page catalog volume III (apparently lacking one leaf), original orange cloth, spines little darkened and little rubbed at tails, bookplates of Nigel Ronald, inscription "S. J. Selby in remembrance of Miss Manning Aug. 10th 1905".   Jarndyce Antiquarian Booksellers   CXCII - 33   2011   £3000

Association – Self, William

Dickens, Charles 1812-1870 *Dombey and Son.* London: Bradbury & Evans, 1848. First edition in book form, first state following all points in Smith; octavo, xvi, (1, errata), (1, blank), 624 pages, frontispiece, titlepage and 38 plates after Phiz, publisher's variant binding of moderate green fine diaper grain cloth, front and back covers entirely stamped in blind with thin double line border which enclosed a rectangular frame, frame contains a loop-scroll design in each corner and string of 16 beads runs along its inner edge, lineal globe shaped design stamped in center of both covers, spine stamped in blind with thick and thin band at top and thin and thick one at bottom, between which are three decorative rectangular panels, each containing heart shaped flower design in its center, spine lettered in gilt original pale yellow coated endpapers, spine very slightly faded, corners very slightly bumped with just tiny amount of board show through, otherwise binding is as fresh as one could possibly wish for, chemised in half green morocco slipcase with bookplate of William Self on chemise, bookplates of Gilfrid William Hartley and William Self, and Dickens Centenary Testimonial label on front pastedown, signature of original owners Eleanor Trotter September 11th 1859", signature of Kenyon Starling.   David Brass Rare Books, Inc.   May 26 2011 - 01693   2011 $13,500

Dickens, Charles 1812-1870 *The Personal History of David Copperfield.* London: Bradbury & Evans, 1850. First edition in book form, first state (following all but one of the twenty points listed in Smith), in the primary binding; octavo, xiv, (1, errata), (1, blank), 624 pages, frontispiece, titlepage and 38 engraved plates after Phiz, the single point not in its first state is page 132, line 20 "screamed" for "screwed", publisher's primary binding of moderate green fine diaper grain cloth, front and back covers entirely stamped in blind with thin double line border which encloses a rectangular frame, frame contains a loop-scroll design in each corner and string of 16 beads runs along its inner edge, lineal globe shaped design is stamped in center of both covers, spine stamped in blind with thick and thin band at top and a thin ad thick one at bottom, between which there are three decorative rectangular panels, each containing heart shaped flower design in its center, spine lettered in gilt, original pale yellow coated endpapers, The Kenyon Starling - William Self copy, original owner's signature "Eleanor Trotter/September 1812-1912) to front pastedown endpaper, spine very slightly darkened, few very minor and pale stains on cloth sides, corners very slightly bumped with little show through of boards, chemised in half green morocco slipcase with bookplates of Starling and Self on chemise,.   David Brass Rare Books, Inc.   May 26 2011 - 01692   2011 $14,500

Association – Selling, Lawrence

McLean, Arthur J. *Intercranial Tumors.* Berlin: Julius Springer, 1936. 8vo., (iv), (131-285), errata (1) pages, 138 figures, green cloth, gilt stamped spine title, ownership signature of Lawrence Selling this copy with signed TLS from author to Selling, fine, rare, from the Medical Library of Dr. Clare Gray Peterson.   Jeff Weber Rare Books   162 - 206   2011 $250

Association – Selwin, Gertrude

More, Hannah 1745-1833 *Poems.* London: T. Cadell & W. Davies, 1816. First edition; engraved title, handsomely bound in contemporary full dark blue calf, spine gilt in compartments, gilt borders and dentelles, red leather label, slight rubbing, small owner's label, Gertrude Selwin, good plus.   Jarndyce Antiquarian Booksellers   CLXC - 526   2011   £150

Association – Sendak, Maurice

Brentano Clemens *Schoolmaster Whackwell's Wonderful Sons.* New York: Random House, 1962. First edition; 8vo., (88) pages, fine in dust jacket with price intact (few edge chips and some rubbing), illustrations in color by Maurice Sendak, this copy has wonderful 8 line inscription from Sendak to fellow children's book illustrator, very scarce.   Aleph-Bet Books, Inc.   95 - 512   2011 $1250

Wilder, Alex *Lullabies and Night Songs.* New York: Harper & Row, 1965. First edition; large 4to., black cloth with gold lettering on spine and within decorated box on front cover, full color pictorial dust jacket with some wear and tear on front wrappers, charming drawing with presentation signed in full and dated by the artist, Maurice Sendak.   Jo Ann Reisler, Ltd.   86 - 228   2011 $975

Association – Senhouse, Robert

Taylor, Tom *Life of Benjamin Robert Haydon, Historical Painter...* London: Longman, Brown and Longmans, 1853. First edition; 3 volumes, original blindstamped brown cloth, gilt, little soiled and faded, spines little worn and frayed at head and foot, pages vi, 386, (vi); 368; 358, 32, endpapers little spotted, very good set, Roger Senhouse's set with his label and pencilled notes on first pastedown and neat signature in each volume.   R. F. G. Hollett & Son Antiquarian Booksellers   General Catalogue Summer 2010 - 471   2011   £140

Association – Sergeant, Edward

Tyson, John *Dalton-in-Furness District Local Board Abstract of Account for the Year Ending 2th March 1887.* Dalton-in-Furness: 1887. Pages 224, folding tables, compiler's printed presentation slip tipped in, redated Feb. 1892, scarce, bookplate of Edward Sergeant. R. F. G. Hollett & Son Antiquarian Booksellers 173 - 1140 2011 £120

Association – Sessions, Juliette

Hughes, Langston *The Weary Blues.* New York: Alfred A. Knopf, 1926. First edition, one of 1500 copies; Advance copy with publisher's review slip giving publication date laid in, small 8vo., original blue cloth backed decorated boards, pictorial dust jacket by Covarrubias, extremities of boards slightly rubbed, former owner's signature "Juliette Sessions" on front endpaper, else fine in lightly chipped dust jacket which is faintly darkened along spine, extremely rare in dust jacket. James S. Jaffe Rare Books May 26 2011 - 21624 2011 $25,000

Association – Sewell, Rufus

Stoppard, Tom *Rock 'n' Roll.* London: Faber & Faber, 2006. First edition thus; 8vo., wrappers, signed by Stoppard, Rufus Sewell, Brian Cox and Sinead Cusak, pages 128, fine. Any Amount of Books May 29 2011 - A68668 2011 $340

Association – Shackleton, Ernest Henry

Churchyard, Albert *The Arcana of Freemasonry.* London: George Allen, 1915. First edition; very good, inscribed presentation from author with masonic bookplate and typed name slip of E. H. Shackleton, original cloth, rubbed along rear edge of spine with occasional light fading, else very good, uncommon. I. D. Edrich May 26 2011 - 98666 2011 $478

Association – Shaftesbury, Earl of

Ascham, Roger *The English Works.* London: printed for R. and J. Dodsely, 1761. First edition, first issue with leaf of additional subscribers; 4to., (10), xvi, 395 pages, engraved armorial headpiece (Earl of Shaftesbury), contemporary calf, spine gilt, red morocco lettering piece (short split at head of upper joint), from the library of the Earls of Macclesfield at Shirburn Castle. Maggs Bros. Ltd. 1440 - 15 2011 £400

Association – Sharpe, Arthur Hartley

MacDonald, George 1824-1905 *Castle Warlock.* Hamburg: Karl Gardener & J. F. Richter, 1882. Copyright edition; 3 volumes, half titles, slight spotting and browning, tear in last leaf repaired, contemporary half red calf, green label, very good, armorial bookplate of Arthur Hartley Sharpe. Jarndyce Antiquarian Booksellers CXCII - 237 2011 £125

Association – Shaw, Arthur

Kelly, George *Craig's Wife a Drama.* Boston: Little Brown, 1926. First edition; 8vo., pages 174, very nice, tight copy, inscribed by author to Josephine Williams who played the part of Mrs. Harold in the NY production, also signed by rest of the cast - Annie Sutherland, Crystal Herne, Arthur Shaw, C. Stewart, Eleanor Marsh, Charles Trowbridge, Josephine Hull, J. A. Curtis, Nelan Jaap, Arline Alcine & Mary Gildea, also inscribed by the producer, Rosalie Stewart to whom the play was dedicated. Second Life Books Inc. 174 - 213 2011 $2000

Association – Shaw, Charlotte

Shaw, George Bernard 1856-1950 *Adventures of the Black Girl in Her Search for God.* London: Constable, 1932. First edition; several wood engravings by John Farleigh, final leaves lightly foxed, pages 80, foolscap 8vo., original black boards, illustrated overall and with author and title printed on slightly sunned backstrip and front cover in white, joints trifle worn, good, T. E. Lawrence's copy with gift inscription to him from George Bernard Shaw's wife Charlotte. Blackwell Rare Books B166 - 173 2011 £2000

Association – Shearman, Montague

Fielding, Henry 1707-1754 *The Journal of a Voyage to Lisbon.* London: Millar, 1755. First published edition, first issue; 12mo., pages (iv), iv, (xviii), (19)-240, 193-228, leather backed contemporary marbled boards, fine, contemporary bookplate of Montague Shearman, bound with half title,. Second Life Books Inc. 174 - 146 2011 $1125

Association – Shedden, George

Dobie, James *Memoir of William Wilson of Crummock.* Edinburgh: privately printed, 1896. First edition, number 12 of 60 copies; 8vo., original publisher's quarter leather lettered gilt on spine and on front cover, pages xliii, 238, uncut, slight wear at rear corner, slight splitting at head of spine, otherwise about very good+, with "George Shedden Esq./ with the editor's kind regards". Any Amount of Books May 29 2011 - A47872 2011 $340

Association – Sheffield

Kant, Immanuel *The Principles of Critical Philosophy...* London: sold by J. Johnson, W. Richardson; Edinburgh: P. Hill, Manners and Miller; Hamburg: B. G. Hoffmann, 1797. First English edition; 8vo., lxxx, 454, (ads 2) pages, occasional light foxing, original full mottled calf, spine with gilt rules, black leather spine label, early ownership signature of Jacob Barker, Glasgow, 14 April crossed out from blank, Sheffield library bookplate, very good, scarce.   Jeff Weber Rare Books   161 - 246   2011 $4000

Association – Shelburne

Barrow, Isaac *A Brief Exposition of the Lord's Prayer and the Decalogue.* London: M. Flesher for Barbazon Aylmer, 1681. 8vo., pages (vi), 269, (iii) + engraved portrait frontispiece; later dark blue polished turkey, spine decorative roll gilt in compartments with small corner and centre pieces, lettered in gilt direct, boards gilt rule bordered with small stylised floweret in corners, board edges and turn-ins 'zigzag' decorative roll gilt, crimson turkey doublures with 'dentelle' gilt border, blue 'made' end flyleaves, all edges gilt, pale blue and white sewn endbands (suggestions here of James Brindley binding), faint dampmark to fore-edge, joints rubbed, splitting, endcaps and corners worn, "Shelburne" armorial bookplate, and "Holland House" heraldic bookplate on doublure, from the collection of Christopher Ernest Weston 1947-2010.   Unsworths Booksellers   24 - 4   2011   £175

Association – Sheldon, Benjamin

Burr, Aaron *The Watchman's Answer to the Question, What of the Night &c. A Sermon Preached Before the Synod of New York, Convened at Newark in New Jersey.* Boston: S. Kneeland, 1757. 46 pages, stitched in contemporary blue paper wrappers, then sewn into early (18th century?) homemade covers, stain on both wrappers and first few leaves of text, upper corner of titlepage worn away costing one letter, outer cover chipped at edges, else very good, 18th century ownership signatures of Benjamin Sheldon and Josepha (?) Ely, latter dated 1777.   Joseph J. Felcone Inc.   Fall Miscellany 2010 - 21   2011 $900

Association – Sherrington, Charles Scott

Beevor, Charles *The Croonian Lectures on Muscular Movements and Their Representation in the Central Nervous System.* London: Adlard and Son, 1904. First edition; 8vo., original publisher's red cloth lettered gilt at spine, pages xii, 100 with 6 figures, ownership signature of C. S. Sherrington (i.e. Charles Scott Sherrington 1857-1952), tipped in "With the Author's compliments", slight fading at top edge, very slight fading at spine, else very good+.   Any Amount of Books   May 29 2011 - A48318   2011 $213

Association – Sherwin, Henry

Lowe, Richard Thomas *History of the Fishes of Madeira.* London: Bernard Quaritch, 1843-1860. Large paper copy; L28 lithographed plates of which 18 are hand colored (minor marginal spotting to 4 plain plates), 4to., pages xvi, 4, (4*-) 196, contemporary half calf (edges rubbed, tips of corners worn, a corner slightly bumped, ink number to a margin of a page, very good), raised bands and gilt decorations on spine, top edge gilt, rare, the copy of Henry A. Sherwin (founder of Sherwin-Williams Co.) and bookplate of R. Harry Jr.   Raymond M. Sutton, Jr.   May 26 2011 - 41582   2011 $2350

Association – Shettle, Harriet MacKenzie

Landon, Letitia Elizabeth *The Golden Violet with Its Tales of Romance and Chivalry and Other Poems.* London: Longman &c, 1827. First edition; engraved frontispiece, contemporary full calf, boards decorated with elaborate borders in blind within triple ruled gilt borders, spine gilt in compartments, spine worn but sound, label missing, signed Harriet Mackenzie Shettle(?) on leading blank.   Jarndyce Antiquarian Booksellers   CLXC - 73   2011   £110

Association – Shilleto, William

Gent, Thomas *The Antient and Modern History of the Loyal Town of Rippon...* York: printed and sold at the Printing Office, 1733. 8vo., pages xvi, (ii) 165, (i), 73, (vii) + folding engraved plan frontispiece, 2 full page woodcuts and 2 extra illustrated engraved plates, modern (March 1982) calf binding by Jenny Aste, some browning and spotting, folding plates rehinged, one extra plate (unflattering portrait of author, bound as frontispiece), substantially smaller and frayed at edge, other copy of folding plate from Gent's "Annales Regioduni Hullini", 2 flyleaves from earlier binding tipped in at end, ink inscription "William Shilleto 1841" and pencil inscription, from the collection of Christopher Ernest Weston 1947-2010.   Unsworths Booksellers   24 - 97   2011   £450

Association – Shorrock, Joseph

Chambers, Robert *The Book of Days.* London: W. & R. Chambers, 1864. 2 volumes, large 8vo., original half crimson morocco, gilt, little scraped, pages (iv), 832; (ii), 840, all edges and endpapers marbled, printed in double columns, red and black pictorial titles, woodcut illustrations, scattered foxing, mainly to flyleaves, but handsome sound set, green morocco presentation label "Mr. & Mrs. Joseph Shorrock from Egerton W. Wood 1865".   R. F. G. Hollett & Son Antiquarian Booksellers   175 - 243   2011   £150

Association – Sibon, Marcelle

Barker, George *The Dead Seagull.* London: John Lehman, 1950. First edition; 8vo., pages 142, (2) blank, original bright orange cloth, blocked in black and lettered in gilt to spine, original pictorial dust jacket designed by Humphrey Spender, extremities lightly rubbed, lower panel lightly soiled, couple of nicks to lower edge, inscribed in blue by Stephen And Natasha Spender for Marcelle (Sibon). Simon Finch Rare Books   Zero - 204   2011   £75

Association – Silliman, Benjamin

Burney, James *A Chronological History of the Discoveries in the South Seas or Pacific Ocean.* London: printed by Luke Hansard and sold by G. and W. Nicol, 1803-. 1806-1813. First edition; 12 engraved plates, some foxing, including some charts, 21 engraved maps (missing 1 map from volume 3), separation to lower fold of a map, creases to another map reinforced, offsetting and/or light foxing to some maps, few engravings in text, 4to., pages (10), xii, 391; v, (11), 482; (10) 437, contemporary quarter calf over marbled boards, light rubbing, few small abrasions, heel of spine chipped, one inch split to front edge of spine, near head of volume 2, splitting to calf still solid, on rear edge of spine to volume 1, endpapers foxed, ex-libris Benjamin Silliman, browning to upper margin of 4 pages, offsetting from plates, marginal tear to a page, dampstain to lower corner of 3 leaves, occasional foxing.   Raymond M. Sutton, Jr.   May 26 2011 - 44145   2011 $3500

Association – Simpkins, E. B.

Thoreau, Henry David 1817-1862 *A Week on the Concord and Merrimack Rivers.* Boston: Ticknor and Fields, 1862. First edition; original brown z cloth, binding D, no priority, owner name of Elizabeth dated 1865 on front along with ink name "E. B. Simpkins on dark brown front endpaper, possibly a relation to Emerson's publisher Samuel G. Simpkins, contents clean, couple of signatures slightly pulled, spine tips frayed with about a quarter inch piece lacking at head not affecting any lettering, gilt quite dull but readable, light wear to corners, good to very good.   Charles Agvent   Transcendentalism 2010 - 46   2011 $2000

Association – Simpson, Eli

Andrews, William *The Book of Oddities.* London: Simpkin, Marshall and Co., 1882. First edition; pages (ii), 86, title lightly browned in red and black, bound for Eli Simpson of Autwick by Edmondson & Wilson of Settle, with note to that effect by Simpson with his faint stamp on title, very scarce.   R. F. G. Hollett & Son Antiquarian Booksellers   General Catalogue Summer 2010 - 623 2011   £120

Association – Simpson, John

Graham, Rigby *Rigby Graham's Leicestershire.* Leicester: Sycamore Press for the Gadsby Galleries, 1980. Limited signed edition, out of series copy, number of 150 copies; oblong folio, original morocco backed green buckram, gilt, slipcase, pages 160, with 160 illustrations, including original lithographs and full color lino blocks, fine, inscribed "Publisher's copy" and signed by John Simpson.   R. F. G. Hollett & Son Antiquarian Booksellers   General Catalogue Summer 2010 - 1420   2011   £650

Association – Singer, Charles

Bell, A. E. *Christian Huygens and the Development of Science in the Seventeenth Century.* London: Edward Arnold, 1947. First edition; 8vo., 220 pages, frontispiece, plates, figures, brown cloth, silver stamped spine title, dust jacket, jacket chipped, very good, Charles Singer's copy with his small booklabel, from the Bern Dibner reference library, with Burndy bookplate.   Jeff Weber Rare Books   161 - 226   2011 $95

Hewson, J. B. *A History of the Practice of Navigation.* Glasgow: Brown, Son & Ferguson, 1951. First edition; 8vo., vii, 270 pages, illustrations, dark blue cloth, gilt stamped cover and spine titles, dust jacket worn with pieces missing and tape repair, else very good, rare in jacket, Charles Singer's copy with his bookplate, from the Bern Dibner reference library, with Burndy bookplate.   Jeff Weber Rare Books   161 - 204   2011 $125

Association – Singleton, Anketell

Watson, Robert *The History of the Reign of Philip the Second, King of Spain.* London: printed for W. Strahan, 1777. 2 volumes, 4to., pages (iv) 443, (i); (iv) 437 (xix), contemporary 'Antique Spot' sided boards, original ultra worn quarter sheep renewed in 1990s by Chris Weston, all text uncut, bit of light spotting, boards scuffed and corners worn, ink ownership inscription "Anketell Singleton", from the collection of Christopher Ernest Weston 1947-2010.   Unsworths Booksellers   24 - 149   2011   £200

Association – Skelton, John

Swinburne, Algernon Charles 1837-1909 *Pomes and Ballads. (with) Poems and Ballads. Second Series.* London: Edward Moxon and Co., 1866. London: Chatto & Windus 1878. First editions; 2 volumes, 8vo., (first series 164 x 100mm, second series 180 xm), pages viii, 344; x, 240, internally very crisp and fresh, uniformly bound in contemporary green half morocco, marbled boards and endpapers, all edges marbled, some rubbing to extremities, ALS from D. G. Rossetti for John Skelton, presenting the book with envelope tipped into volume i, address panel of letter from Swinburne to Shelton tipped into volume ii, numerous pencil notes throughout volume i by Skelton, with presentation letter from Rossetti to Skelton. Simon Finch Rare Books   Zero - 355   2011   £1800

Association – Skinner, Jacob

Leslie, Charles Robert *A Short and Easy Method with the Deists... (bound with) The Truth of Christianity Demonstrated...* London: F. and C. Rivington, 1799. New edition; bound together in contemporary full polished tree calf gilt, edges little bumped and cracked, spine rather dulled, engraved roundel bookplate of Jacob Skinner.   R. F. G. Hollett & Son Antiquarian Booksellers   175 - 821   2011   £85

Association – Skipton, J. Sunderland

Grainge, William *Yorkshire Longevity: or Records and Biographical Anecdotes of Persons Who Have Attained to extreme Old Age Within that County.* Pateley Bridge: printed and published by Thomas Thorpe, London: T. T. Lemare, 1864. First edition; 2 pages ads, original purple brow cloth, little rubbed and faded, small circular ownership label of J. Sunderland Skipton, good sound copy.   Jarndyce Antiquarian Booksellers   CXCI - 191   2011   £35

Association – Slater, James

MacDonald, George 1824-1905 *The Flight of the Shadow.* London: Kegan Paul, Trench, Trubner & Co. circa, 1900? New edition; half title, rougher text paper slightly browned, slightly shorter copy in original orange cloth blocked in brown and gilt (style H), spine slightly faded, slightly torn booklabel of James Slater.   Jarndyce Antiquarian Booksellers   CXCII - 301 2011   £50

MacDonald, George 1824-1905 *St. George and St. Michael.* London: Kegan Paul, Trench, Trubner & Co. circa, 1900. Half title, paper slightly browning, original orange cloth (style H), spine slightly faded, booklabel of James Slater.   Jarndyce Antiquarian Booksellers   CXCII - 179 2011   £40

Association – Slaughter, Mihill

Thomson, James 1700-1748 *The Works.* London: printed by A. Strahan for J. Rivington and Sons, 1788. 227 x 145mm., 3 volumes, once elegant and still pleasing contemporary scarlet straight grained morocco simply gilt, covers with single gilt fillet border, raised bands flanked by plain gilt rules, gilt titling, turn-ins with gilt chain roll, marbled endpapers, all edges gilt; with fine fore-edge paintings of Folkestone, Dublin and Worcester; volumes in recent sturdy buckram slipcase with marbled paper sides; frontispiece portrait, 10 engraved plates; 19th century armorial bookplate of Richard Davies, morocco bookplate of Estelle Doheny and modern engraved bookplate of John Taylor Reynolds, titlepage with ink ownership inscription of Mihill Slaughter 1811 (Secretary of the Railways Department); hint of soil to covers, joints and extremities with little rubbing (but well refurbished), leaves with intermittent minor foxing, engravings bit more foxed (half of them rather browned), offset onto facing page, text with general light browning and occasional trivial soiling, four leaves with short marginal or paper flaw tears (no loss); although not without problems, set nevertheless appealing, internal flaws never really unsightly, bindings all solid and paintings where it really matters, entirely well preserved.   Phillip J. Pirages   59 - 45 2011 $4500

Association – Sly, R.

Burney, Charles *General History of Music.* London: printed for the author and sold by T. Beckett, J. Robson and G. Robinson, 1776. First edition; 4 volumes, large quarto, xx, (12), 522, (1, blank), (4), 597, (1, blank), (1 errata); xi, (1, blank), 622, (11, index) (1, errata); (4), 685, (1, blank), (2 publisher's ads), (12 index), (1, errata), (1 blank) pages, 12 engraved plates, including 4 frontispieces, engraved frontispieces in volumes I-III, 9 additional plates, engraved musical illustrations, contemporary full calf, rebacked to style, green morocco spine labels, spines and labels stamped and lettered in gilt, board edges gilt, gilt dentelles, marbled endpapers, boards rubbed and corners bumped, inner hinges reinforced, some foxing and dampstaining throughout, mainly to prelim pages, previous owner's ink stamp, previous owner R. Sly's old ink signature, he has made ink corrections in accordance with errata throughout each volume, overall very nice.   Heritage Book Shop   Holiday 2010 - 14   2011 $2500

Association – Smith, Cyril Stanley

Brock, Alan St. H. *A History of Fireworks.* London. et al: George J. Harrap, 1949. First edition; 8vo., 280 pages, 40 plates, text illustrations, dark blue cloth, gilt stamped spine title, dust jacket worn, very good, from the Bern Dibner reference library, with Burndy bookplate, signed by Cyril Stanley Smith.   Jeff Weber Rare Books   161 - 66 2011 $125

Ffoulkes, Charles *Armour & Weapons.* Oxford: Clarendon Press, 1909. First edition; 8vo., 112 pages, frontispiece, plates, illustrations, paper boards, black stamped cover title and illustration, very good, signed by former owner, Cyril Stanley Smith, from the Bern Dibner reference library, with Burndy bookplate.   Jeff Weber Rare Books   161 - 145   2011 $60

Association – Smith, E.

De La Ramee, Louise 1839-1908 *Pipistrello.* London: Chatto & Windus, 1882. New edition; half title, initial ad leaf, 32 page catalog (Mary 1882), few pencil note in text, 'yellowback', original printed boards, small booklabel of E. Smith, Stratton Strawless, near fine.   Jarndyce Antiquarian Booksellers   CLXC - 697   2011   £85

Association – Smith, Eric Carrington

Porter, Anna Maria *The Recluse of Norway.* London: Longman, 1814. First edition; 4 volumes, slight spotting, handsome contemporary half calf, gilt spines, black labels, armorial bookplates of Eric Carrington Smith, very good, attractive.   Jarndyce Antiquarian Booksellers   CLXC - 756   2011   £380

Association – Smith, Fred Sumner

Bigelow, Jacob 1787-1879 *American Medical Botany, Being a Collection of the Native Medicinal Plants of the United States.* Boston: Cummings and Hilliard, 1817-1820. First edition, mixed state; 60 colored plates (few hand colored, most color printed, foxing to several, occasional light offsetting to plates), tall 8vo., pages xi, (17-) 197, (5); xiv, (15-) 199, (1);x, (11-) 193, contemporary calf, upper corner of back cover bumped, corner to head of spine bumped and with piece missing, scattered foxing, offsetting to some pages, opposite plates, pages 195 through 198 from volume III misbound following page 198 of volume I, inner hinges reinforced, from the Yale College Library, presented by the estate of Benjamin Barrett, M.D., bought from Yale for Dr. Fred. Sumner Smith by his Father.   Raymond M. Sutton, Jr. May 26 2011 - 39722   2011 $3700

Association – Smith, H. A.

Prosser, Sophie Amelia *Original Fables.* London: R.T.S., 1870? Ad leaf preceding frontispiece, illustrations, original brown cloth, bevelled boards, pictorially blocked and lettered in blue and gilt, blocked in black, little rubbed, back board slightly marked, signed H.A. Smith in contemporary hand, all edges gilt, good plus.   Jarndyce Antiquarian Booksellers   CLXC - 785   2011   £40

Association – Smith, Marion

Tudor, Tasha *Amanda and the Bear.* New York: Oxford University Press, 1951. First edition; 12mo., light blue textured cloth with color paste label and red orange lettering on spine, quite nice, full color pictorial dust jacket, clean, fresh copy, front free endpaper signed in full with presentation for Marion Smith.   Jo Ann Reisler, Ltd.   86 - 251   2011 $1000

Tudor, Tasha *Dorcas Porkus.* New York: Oxford University Press, 1942. First printing; 16mo., yellow cloth with white dots, lovely clean copy color pictorial dust jacket with dusting to point of being darkened, this copy signed and dated on front free endpaper by Tudor, along with presentation to Marion Smith.   Jo Ann Reisler, Ltd.   86 - 249   2011 $1000

Tudor, Tasha *Edgar Allan Crow.* New York: Oxford University Press, 1953. First edition; 12mo., dark blue textured boards (with gold lettering on spine), color decorated paste label, full color pictorial dust jacket, quite fresh, clean copy, signed in full by Tudor with presentation for Marion Smith, full page color illustrations.   Jo Ann Reisler, Ltd.   86 - 252   2011 $1000

Tudor, Tasha *Snow Before Christmas.* New York: Oxford University Press, 1941. First edition; square 8vo., grey cloth with color paste label with decorated title on front cover, bright fresh copy, color pictorial dust jacket with little spot to rear cover, otherwise nice, presentation by Tudor signed in full on front free endpaper for Marion Smith.   Jo Ann Reisler, Ltd.   86 - 248   2011 $950

Association – Smith, Thomas

Theodore Metochites *Annalium Liber III Theodori Metochitae Historiae Romanae a Iulio Caesare ad Constantinum Magnum Liber Singularius.* Leiden: J. Colster, 1618. 4to., ff. (22), 103, (5), Greek text printed in Plantin's large Greek font, last leaf with short list of errata, mid 17th century English binding of brown calf over pasteboard, blindstamped fillets, red edges, very nice, from the library of Thomas Smith (1638-1710), from the library of the Earls of Macclesfield at Shirburn Castle.   Maggs Bros. Ltd.   1440 - 207   2011   £450

Ward, Robert Plummer *Illustrations of Human Life.* London: Henry Colburn, 1837. First edition; pages viii, 359; viii, 324; (iv), 301, 8vo., contemporary dark green half morocco, backstrips panelled with gilt fillets and repeated leafy and drawer handle tools, marbled boards, slightly rubbed, all edges gilt, bookplates of Thomas Smith, good.   Blackwell Rare Books   B166 - 116   2011   £300

Association – Smith, William

Mitford, Mary Russell 1787-1855 *Belford Regis; or Sketches of a Country Town.* London: Richard Bentley, 1835. First edition; 3 volumes, contemporary half calf, maroon labels, bit rubbed, good plus, armorial bookplates of William Smith. Jarndyce Antiquarian Booksellers CLXC - 400 2011 £280

Oliver, George *Signs and Symbols Illustrated and Explained in a Course of Twelve Lectures on Free Masonry.* Grimsby: printed for the author by Br. Skelton, 1826. First edition; contemporary half calf gilt by Anthony Birdsall of Northampton (with his label), masonic emblem to spine compartments, double spine labels and Spanish marbled boards, extremities little rubbed, pages lx, 248, text illustrations, slight spotting to few leaves, but excellent copy, with ownership inscriptions of Richard Griffiths, architect and William Smith, both of Northampton, 2 small press cuttings relating to death of latter's unmarried daughter in Northampton are tipped to pastedown, S. S. Birdsall of Pomfret Lodge Northampton was a subscriber, rare. R. F. G. Hollett & Son Antiquarian Booksellers 175 - 1020 2011 £350

Association – Smith, William Henry

Bible. Greek - 1812 *Psalterium Graecum E Codice Ms. Alexandrino.* Londini: Ex Prelo Ricardi Taylor et Socii, 1812. One of 17 copies printed on vellum; 356 x 299mm., (1) leaf (blank), xii, (32) leaves, 18 pages, (1) leaf (blank), very handsome contemporary deep blue morocco lavishly gilt, apparently by Charles Lewis, covers with broad elaborately gilt border and simple inner frame, wide gilt decorated raised bands, spine compartments with complex gilt decoration featuring scrolling floral stamps and unusual trapezoidal ornaments on either side of a central stem, very wide and sumptuously gilt inner dentelles, yellow watered silk pastedowns, front and rear free endleaves, made of matching watered silk pasted to vellum sheets, all edges gilt; monogram booklabel and armorial bookplate of William Henry Smith and oval morocco bookplate of Estelle Doheny, subscriber list, slight variation in color of binding and of vellum leaves, but very fine, stunning. Phillip J. Pirages 59 - 340 2011 $15,000

Association – Snape, M.

Allen, John *The Humiliation and Exaltation of Our Redeemer.* London: George Routledge & Co., 1856. First edition; 32 prints, square 8vo. original printed pictorial cloth, faded, pages 64, complete with 22 plates, etched bookplate of M. Snape. R. F. G. Hollett & Son Antiquarian Booksellers 175 - 20 2011 £85

Association – Snow, Edith

Werfel, Franz *Hearken Unto the Voice.* New York: Viking, 1938. First American edition; warmly inscribed by author for Edith Snow, minor fore edge foxing and offsetting to hinges, very good in very good dust jacket with mild edge-wear, books signed by author scarce. Ken Lopez Bookseller 154 - 239 2011 $500

Association – Snowden, May

Sheridan, Thomas *Sheridan's and Henderson's Practical Method of Reading and Reciting English Poetry...* London: Printed for E. Newbery, 1796. xii, 264 pages, 12mo., small stain to outer edge of final leaves, paper flaw to page 261-2 with slight loss, missing words being supplied in margin in neat contemporary hand, excellently rebacked in half calf, gilt ruled spine, original marbled boards, ownership label of Rear Admiral Saumarez with note presenting the book to his granddaugther May Snowden. Jarndyce Antiquarian Booksellers CXCI - 491 2011 £125

Association – Snyder, Gary

Hepworth, J. *Resist Much, Obey Little - Some Notes on Edward Abbey.* Salt Lake City: Dream Garden Press, 1985. First edition; fine, signed by J. Hepworth and Gary Snyder. Bella Luna Books May 26 2011 - 6500 2011 $165

Association – Somers, John

Cicero, Marcus Tullius *The Letters of Marcus Tullius Cicero to Several of His Friends...* London: printed for R. Dodsley, 1753. Octavo, (iv), 477, (2); (ii), 468, (iii); (ii), 384, (iv) pages, original full calf, hinges cracked, spine ends worn, corners showing, bookplate of John Somers, Lord, good. Jeff Weber Rare Books 163 - 144 2011 $125

Association – Sommer, Ernst

Kocher, Emil Theodor *Text-Book of Operative Surgery.* London: Adam and Charles Black, 1903. Large 8vo., xxv, 440 pages, 255 numbered figures, dark blue cloth, gilt stamped spine title, ex-library bookplate with embossed stamp on title, spine call number painted over, ownership signature of Ernst A. Sommer, very good, from the Medical Library of Dr. Clare Gray Peterson. Jeff Weber Rare Books 162 - 177 2011 $200

Purves-Stewart, James *Intracranial Tumours and Some Errors in Their Diagnosis.* London, et al: Humphrey Milford, Oxford University Press, 1927. First edition; 8vo., xiii, 206 pages, illustrations, index, maroon cloth, black stamped cover title and gilt stamped spine title, ex-library bookplate with embossed stamp on title, spine call numbered painted over, rubber stamp of Dr. Ernst A. Sommer, from the Medical Library of Dr. Clare Gray Peterson.   Jeff Weber Rare Books   162 - 247 2011 $65

Association – Soper, George

Munnings, Alfred J. *Pictures of Horses and English Life.* London: Eyre & Spottiswoode, 1927. First edition; small folio, original cloth over bevelled boards, lettered in black, pages x, 215, all edges gilt, with 29 color plates, with captioned tissues and 109 monochrome illustrations, scattered spots and slight marks, tissues lightly foxed in places, excellent sound copy, from the collection of George Soper RI (1870-1942), signed by him in pencil on title.   R. F. G. Hollett & Son Antiquarian Booksellers   General Catalogue Summer 2010 - 278 2011   £350

Association – Sorley, M. S.

Miller, Anna Riggs *Letters from Italy, Describing the Manners, Customs, Antiquities, Paintings &c of that Country in the Years MDCCLXX and MDCCLXXI...* London: Edward & Charles Dilly, 1777. Second edition; 2 volumes, half titles, contemporary full tree calf, spines gilt in compartments, maroon and dark green leather labels, rebacked retaining original spine strips, little rubbed and worn, later bookplates and signatures of M. S. Sorley, good plus, internally very clean.   Jarndyce Antiquarian Booksellers   CLXC - 398 2011   £285

Association – Southern, Terry

Kerouac, Jack 1922-1969 *The Dharma Bums.* New York: Viking Press, 1958. First edition; worn, fair only copy, heavily rubbed and frayed at extremities, in very good dust jacket, rubbed, almost certainly married to book (but which came to us thus) in fine custom made quarter morocco clamshell case, inscribed by author to Terry Southern. Between the Covers   169 - BTC346433 2011 $35,000

Association – Spalding, John Tricks

Belloc, Hilaire 1870-1953 *The Historic Thames.* London: J. M. Dent, 1907. First edition; 4to., original green decorated cloth, gilt, pages vii, 224, top edges gilt, 60 color plates, bookplate of John Tricks Spalding.   R. F. G. Hollett & Son Antiquarian Booksellers   General Catalogue Summer 2010 - 1558 2011   £150

Association – Sparrow, John

Hassell, John *Tour of the Isle of Wight.* London: printed by John Jarvis for Thomas Hookham, 1790. 2 volumes, 8vo., pages xxiv, 224 + engraved titlepage and 17 tinted aquatint plates; viii, 248 + engraved titlepage and 13 tinted aquatint plates, contemporary 'Etruscan' calf almost certainly by Edwards of Halifax, spine gilt compartmented with gilt 'coil' cornerpieces and 'classical urn' centre-pieces in blind, black lettering piece gilt, numbered direct in gilt within an open central blind tooled oval, boards 'metope and pentaglyph' roll gilt bordered and concentric borders within (one of palmettes & trident in blind) surrounding a central gilt 'Grecian key' roll edges marbled panel, board edges & turn-ins single rule gilt, vivid pink 'made' endpapers, all edges gilt, brown and white double core sewn endbands, bit foxed in places, neat restoration to endcaps and joints, spines slightly cracked, printed booklabel of John Sparrow at top left of verso of 'made' front endpaper, from the collection of Christopher Ernest Weston 1947-2010.   Unsworths Booksellers   24 - 107 2011   £750

Robertson, David *A Tour through the Isle of Man; to Which is Subjoined a Review of all the Manks History.* London: printed for the author by E. Hodson, 1794. Large paper copy, 8vo., pages (xii), 235, (i) + 8 sepia aquatint plates, contemporary straight grained mauve morocco, five flat raised bands spine triple rule and decorative pallet gilt, top and bottom compartment have symmetrical oblong centrepieces, gilt between decorative pallets in blind, 3 other compartments filled with massed French influence 'rolling breakers' decorative pallets gilt, lettered in gilt direct, boards triple rule gilt borders with 'acanthus' roll in blind within, board edges alternating double full and single broken hatch fillet roll in blind, turn-ins similarly tooled, 'French Shell' 'made' endpapers, all edges similarly marbled, blue and white sewn endbands, pink silk page marker, plates bit foxed and few spots to pages, touch scratched, spines little faded and upper joint slightly rubbed, unidentified bookplate, decorative bookplate of Frederick J. G. Montagu, booklabel of John Sparrow, pencil inscription Catherine of Fountayne, pencil annotations in same hand, from the collection of Christopher Ernest Weston 1947-2010.   Unsworths Booksellers   24 - 138 2011   £350

Sparrow, John *A Day with Myself.* Burford - Cygnet Press, 1979. One of 100 copies; pages (8) 16mo., original black wrappers, printed front cover label, fine, inscribed by John Sparrow for Bent J(uel) J(ensen).   Blackwell Rare Books   B166 - 247 2011   £50

Association – Spencer, Eliza

Herodotus *The History of Herodotus.* London: printed for D. Midwinter et al, 1737. Third edition; 2 volumes, 8vo., pages xvi, 447 (xvii) + 3 extending engraved maps, (ii), 430, (xviii), contemporary orangey tan calf boards triple rule gilt bordered with broad dentelle inner border of individual small tools, board edges decorative roll gilt, late 19th century 'swirl' 'made' endpapers with pale green block cloth, inner joint strengtheners, all edges original blue swirl/marbled pale blue and white sewn endbands, early 21st century retrospective reback + corners by Chris Weston, little toning and marginal dust soiling, some marginal pencil notes, old leather chipped at edges, contemporary ink inscription "Eliza Spencer" at head of titlepages, verso of volume I marbled endpaper has ms. note by Rev. John Bourton/Banningham Rectory/Norfolk referring to early provenance of Sunderland Library and subsequent purchase at Puttick & Simpson's auction in 1882, from the collection of Christopher Ernest Weston 1947-2010.   Unsworths Booksellers   24 - 109   2011   £400

Association – Spender, Natasha

Barker, George   *The Dead Seagull.*   London: John Lehman, 1950.   First edition; 8vo., pages 142, (2) blank, original bright orange cloth, blocked in black and lettered in gilt to spine, original pictorial dust jacket designed by Humphrey Spender, extremities lightly rubbed, lower panel lightly soiled, couple of nicks to lower edge, inscribed in blue by Stephen And Natasha Spender for Marcelle (Sibon).   Simon Finch Rare Books   Zero - 204   2011   £75

Association – Spender, Stephen

Barker, George   *The Dead Seagull.*   London: John Lehman, 1950.   First edition; 8vo., pages 142, (2) blank, original bright orange cloth, blocked in black and lettered in gilt to spine, original pictorial dust jacket designed by Humphrey Spender, extremities lightly rubbed, lower panel lightly soiled, couple of nicks to lower edge, inscribed in blue by Stephen And Natasha Spender for Marcelle (Sibon).   Simon Finch Rare Books   Zero - 204   2011   £75

Spender, Stephen   *Three Versions from the German.* London: privately published, 1956. First edition, no. 50 of 100 copies; inscribed by author for Winnie and Geraint Jones, also signed by author's wife Natasha Spender, 8vo., original gold paper wrappers, titles to pink label on upper wrapper in black, gold wrappers in very good order, but creased at lower front and rear corner.   Any Amount of Books   May 29 2011 - A46011   2011 $272

Association – Spingarn, Arthur

Whitman, Walt 1819-1892   *Leaves of Grass.*   Brooklyn: published by author, 1855.   First edition, 2nd issue binding, second state of page iv; the 795 copies were bound in different stages, and this one of the 262 bound between Dec. 1855 and Jan. 1856, 4to., original decoratively blindstamped green cloth, gilt lettering, engraved frontispiece, 8 pages of extracts of reviews and notices tipped in before frontispiece, bookplate of Arthur B. Spingarn (1878-1971), from the collection of Samuel Charters.   The Brick Row Book Shop Bulletin 8 - 5   2011 $125,000

Association – Spottiswoode, John

Barry, George   *The History of the Orkney Islands...* Edinburgh: printed for the author by D. Willison, 1805. 4to., pages (ii) viii, 509 + engraved frontispiece, 1 folding map, 19 other engraved plates, later tan calf, spine panelled in gilt with 'crowned dolphin" center pieces, dark brown lettering piece gilt, boards double rule gilt bordered with decorative roll gilt within, board edges and turn-ins decorative roll gilt, 'Dutch-curl' 'made' endpapers and all edges matching, brown and white sewn flat endbands, some minor spotting, little foxing to plates, spine bit rubbed, front joint cracking at foot, subscriber's copy of John Spottiswoode of Spottiswoode with his armorial gilt stamped on both boards, from the collection of Christopher Ernest Weston 1947-2010. Unsworths Booksellers   24 - 67   2011   £400

Association – Sprimer. F. E.

United States. War Department - 1855   *Reports of Explorations and Surveys, to Ascertain the Most Practicable and Economical Route Railroad from the Mississippi River to the Pacific Ocean, made in the Direction of the Secretary of War in 1853-4, According to Acts of Congress March 3 1953 May 31 1854 and August 5 1854.*   Washington: A. O. P. Nicholson, Printer, 1855-1861.   Each volume has been rebound in black buckram, signatures resewn, titles stamped in gold on spine panel, while each volume is stamped with word "Senate" on spine, five of the volumes are actually for House of Representatives; flaws as noted - volume I with small stamp of Library of Washington and Jefferson College and word 'withdrawn', else very good, tight copy; volume IV with presentation inscription to Irving Holcomb from Hon. F. E. Sprimer (?) dated Nov. 1857, small waterstain to bottom edges of front flyleaf which continues lightly to page 3, else very good, tight copy; volume X - light foxing to first 8 pages in front of volume and last 8 pages in rear of volume, else very good, tight copy; volume XI - moderate foxing and two small waterstains that diminish over first 16 pages, else very good, tight copy, a majority of the color lithographic plates are in fine condition as are the majority of black and white plates; volume XI contains maps and plates, including desirable large folding map done by Lt. Warren, all maps and plates in this volume are tightly secured.   Buckingham Books   May 26 2011 - 26611   2011 $15,000

Association – St. George, Sylvia Marguerite Agnes

Craik, Dinah Maria Mulock 1826-1887 *Alice Learmont: a Fairytale.* London: Macmillan and Co., 1884. New edition; half title, frontispiece + illustrations, 2 pages ads, original pale blue cloth, pictorially blocked in gilt, lettered in gilt and maroon, spine slightly darkened, ownership inscription of Sylvia Marguerite Agnes St. George dated August 1892. Jarndyce Antiquarian Booksellers CLXC - 557 2011   £35

Association – Standiford, Les

Naked Came the Manatee. New York: Putnam, 1996. First edition; fine in fine dust jacket, signed by all authors on single tipped in leaf, including Carl Hiaasen, Elmore Leonard, John Dufresne, Dave Barry, Vicki Hendricks, Edna Buchanan, Les Standiford and James W. Hall, etc. Ken Lopez Bookseller 154 - 5 2011 $200

Association – Standing, George

Noel, E. B. *First Steps to Rackets.* London: Mills & Boon, 1926. First edition; octavo, 136, 16 ads pages, plates, green cloth, slight bump on front board, very good or better, without dust jacket, inscribed by one of the co-authors, Clarence Bruce for George Standing. Between the Covers 169 - BTC342222 2011 $650

Association – Standish, Hannah

Muir, John 1838-1914 *The Writings.* Boston and New York: Houghton Mifflin Co., 1916-1924. Manuscript edition, one of 750 copies; 226 x 160mm., 10 volumes, very fine contemporary dark brown morocco , handsomely gilt with front flyleaf in first volume stamped "Bound at the Riverside Press", cover border of triple gilt fillets, large center panel with triangular cornerpieces composed of massed floral and foliate tools, including a Tudor rose, raised bands, spines intricately gilt in compartments, with leaves, flowers and interlacing stems, wide turn-ins, similar gilt decoration framing doublures of white pigskin, doublures with center panel formed by two gilt rules an featuring circled monogram HMS (Hannah M. Standish), watered silk flyleaves, top edge gilt, other edges untrimmed and unopened, few illustrations in text, 127 plates, mostly on Japanese vellum, 8 of them hand colored, five of them maps; virtually mint, bindings essentially unworn, unopened, text (not surprisingly) without sign of use. Phillip J. Pirages 59 - 268 2011 $10,000

Association – Standish, Thomas

Glover, Richard *Leonidas, a Poem.* London: T. Bensley for F. J. Du Voveray, 1798. Sixth edition according to titlepage; fine contemporary highly polished marbled calf, covers with gilt border of thick and thin rules and central panel formed by gilt fillet with scalloped corners, flat spines divided into panels by multiple gilt rules, two panels with black morocco labels, other four with central gilt patera, turn-ins with beaded gilt rule, marbled endpapers, frontispiece, 6 more engraved plates, large modern bookplate of Thomas S. Standish from Wigan; very short portions of joints of first volume cracked, just at top, covers slightly marked, margins and versos of plates foxed, otherwise very fine, bindings extremely lustrous and with no significant wear and text fresh, clean and bright, very ample margins. Phillip J. Pirages 59 - 49 2011 $475

Association – Stanger, Joshua, Mrs.

Bush, James *The Choice or Line of the Beatitudes.* London: R. Sayweel; Cockermouth: Baily & Sons and Carlisle: C.. Thurnam, 1841. square 8vo., full polished calf gilt, edges rubbed, pages 102, engraved frontispiece (foxed), scattered foxing in places, scarce presentation copy , inscribed by author to Mrs. Joshua Stanger. R. F. G. Hollett & Son Antiquarian Booksellers 173 - 204 2011   £75

Association – Stannard, Christopher

Woodhouselee, Alexander Fraser Tytler, Lord 1747-1813 *Plan and Outlines of a Course of Lectures on University History, Ancient and Modern, Delivered in the University of Edinburgh.* Edinburgh: William Creech, 1782. First edition; small 4to., (iv) 216 (2) (217)-250 pages, full contemporary black calf, gilt ruled covers and spine, gilt stamped spine title, contemporary ink inscription by John Gordon to Christopher Stannard, 1795, fine. Jeff Weber Rare Books 163 - 50 2011 $850

Association – Starling, Kenyon

Dickens, Charles 1812-1870 *Dombey and Son.* London: Bradbury & Evans, 1848. First edition in book form, first state following all points in Smith; octavo, xvi, (1, errata), (1, blank), 624 pages, frontispiece, titlepage and 38 plates after Phiz, publisher's variant binding of moderate green fine diaper grain cloth, front and back covers entirely stamped in blind with thin double line border which enclosed a rectangular frame, frame contains a loop-scroll design in each corner and string of 16 beads runs along its inner edge, lineal globe shaped design stamped in center of both covers, spine stamped in blind with thick and thin band at top and thin and thick one at bottom, between which are three decorative rectangular panels, each containing heart shaped flower design in its center, spine lettered in gilt original pale yellow coated endpapers, spine very slightly faded, corners very slightly bumped with just tiny amount of board show through, otherwise binding is as fresh as one could possibly wish for, chemised in half green morocco slipcase with bookplate of William Self on chemise, bookplates of Gilfrid William Hartley and William Self, and Dickens Centenary Testimonial label on front pastedown, signature of original owners Eleanor Trotter September 11th 1859", signature of Kenyon Starling.   David Brass Rare Books, Inc.   May 26 2011 - 01693   2011 $13,500

Dickens, Charles 1812-1870 *The Personal History of David Copperfield.* London: Bradbury & Evans, 1850. First edition in book form, first state (following all but one of the twenty points listed in Smith), in the primary binding; octavo, xiv, (1, errata), (1, blank), 624 pages, frontispiece, titlepage and 38 engraved plates after Phiz, the single point not in its first state is page 132, line 20 "screamed" for "screwed", publisher's primary binding of moderate green fine diaper grain cloth, front and back covers entirely stamped in blind with thin double line border which encloses a rectangular frame, frame contains a loop-scroll design in each corner and string of 16 beads runs along its inner edge, lineal globe shaped design is stamped in center of both covers, spine stamped in blind with thick and thin band at top and a thin ad thick one at bottom, between which there are three decorative rectangular panels, each containing heart shaped flower design in its center, spine lettered in gilt, original pale yellow coated endpapers, The Kenyon Starling - William Self copy, original owner's signature "Eleanor Trotter/September 1812-1912) to front pastedown endpaper, spine very slightly darkened, few very minor and pale stains on cloth sides, corners very slightly bumped with little show through of boards, chemised in half green morocco slipcase with bookplates of Starling and Self on chemise,.   David Brass Rare Books, Inc.   May 26 2011 - 01692   2011 $14,500

Association – Staunton, Isabella

Crabbe, George *Tales.* J. Hatchard, 1812. First edition; presentation copy, inscribed on half title "The very Reverend The Dean of Lincoln with respects of the Author" (almost certainly George Gordon who held that position between 1810 and his death in 1845), also signed "Isabella Staunton 1848", pages (xxiv), 398, (2) (publisher's catalog), 8vo., contemporary mottled calf, binder's ticket of Johnston, Lincoln, neatly rebacked, backstrip with five flat bands with gilt Greek key-style rolls, black morocco label in second compartment, rest with central blind tools, corners neatly restored, marbled endpapers, hinges neatly relined, very good.   Blackwell Rare Books   B166 - 25   2011   £350

Association – Stephanius, Joannis

Artemidorus *Artemidori Daldiani & Achmetis Sereimi f. Oneirocritica. Astrampsychi & Nicephori Versus Etiam Oneirocritici.* Paris: M. Orry, 1603. 4to. (12), 269, L14 blank, (23) P2 blank, 20, 65; 275, (17) pages, title printed in red and black, 2 columns, later 17th century Cambridge binding of panelled calf, spine gilt, red edges, extremely handsome, inscription Stephanus Joann(is) Stephanius, from the library of the Earls of Macclesfield at Shirburn Castle.   Maggs Bros. Ltd.   1440 - 14   2011   £900

Association – Sterling, Joseph

Taken by Design: Photographs from The Institute of Design 1937-1971. Chicago: University of Chicago Press, 2002. First edition; very fine in photo illustrated boards, issued without dust jacket, signed by a large number of photographers and some of the editors, among the signatures are Yasuhiro Ishimoto, Marvin E. Newton (twice), Barbara Crane, Ray K. Metzker, Joseph Jachna, Joseph Sterling (twice), Kenneth Josephson, David Travis, Keith Davis and quite a few others, unique copy.   Jeff Hirsch Books   ny   2010 2011 $750

Association – Stevens, Anne

Pellew, Claughton *Five Wood Engravings Printed from Original Wood Blocks with Biographical Note by Anne Stevens.* Wakefield: Fleece Press, 1987.   One of 150 sets printed on Zerkal mouldmade paper; pages (15), folio, original plain white sewn wrappers, untrimmed, dust jacket with wood engraving by Pellew reproduced in line block on label on front cover; (with) Five Wood Engravings by Claughton Pellew, each printed on separate sheet and loosely enclosed in pale or mid blue card folder with printed title, book and prints enclosed in grey buckram, card lined, fold down back box, same design of label as that used for book on its front, fine, Anne Stevens' copy, but without mark of ownership.   Blackwell Rare Books   B166 - 252 2011   £250

Association – Stewart, Angus

Williams, Tennessee 1911-1983 *Five Plays: Cat on a Hot Tin Roof. The Rose Tattoo. Something Unspoken. Suddenly Last Summer. Orpheus Descending.* London: Secker & Warburg, 1962. First English collected edition; pages xvi, 376, 8vo., original pale blue cloth, backstrip gilt lettered, dust jacket, fine, authorial gift inscription to Angus Stewart, novelist. Blackwell Rare Books B166 - 242 2011 £600

Association – Stewart, C.

Kelly, George *Craig's Wife a Drama.* Boston: Little Brown, 1926. First edition; 8vo., pages 174, very nice, tight copy, inscribed by author to Josephine Williams who played the part of Mrs. Harold in the NY production, also signed by rest of the cast - Annie Sutherland, Crystal Herne, Arthur Shaw, C. Stewart, Eleanor Marsh, Charles Trowbridge, Josephine Hull, J. A. Curtis, Nelan Jaap, Arline Alcine & Mary Gildea, also inscribed by the producer, Rosalie Stewart to whom the play was dedicated. Second Life Books Inc. 174 - 213 2011 $2000

Association – Stewart, H.

Fox, R. Hingston *Dr. John Fothergill and His Friends: Chapters in Eighteenth Century Life.* London: Macmillan, 1919. 8vo., xxiv, 434 pages, frontispiece, 13 illustrations, original blue cloth, gilt stamped spine title, spine ends rubbed, ownership signature of H. Stewart, very good, from the Bern Dibner reference library, with Burndy bookplate. Jeff Weber Rare Books 161 - 153 2011 $85

Association – Stewart, Mary

Landon, Letitia Elizabeth *Ethel Churchill; or the Two Brides.* London: Henry Colburn, 1837. First edition; 3 volumes, half title volume I, uncut in contemporary drab boards, maroon cloth spines, paper labels, spines faded and slightly darkened, labels little darkened, small booklabels of Lady Mary Stewart and M. F. Montgomery, Convoy, good plus, internally very clean set. Jarndyce Antiquarian Booksellers CLXC - 72 2011 £750

Association – Stewart, Robert

Waller, J. F. *Inauguration Ode Performed at the Opening of the National Exhibition Cork 1852.* Cork: Bradford, 1852. Titlepage, 4 pages text, 32 pages music, quarter cloth, signed by Robert Stewart. C. P. Hyland May 26 2011 - 259/84 2011 $507

Association – Stewart, Rosalie

Kelly, George *Craig's Wife a Drama.* Boston: Little Brown, 1926. First edition; 8vo., pages 174, very nice, tight copy, inscribed by author to Josephine Williams who played the part of Mrs. Harold in the NY production, also signed by rest of the cast - Annie Sutherland, Crystal Herne, Arthur Shaw, C. Stewart, Eleanor Marsh, Charles Trowbridge, Josephine Hull, J. A. Curtis, Nelan Jaap, Arline Alcine & Mary Gildea, also inscribed by the producer, Rosalie Stewart to whom the play was dedicated. Second Life Books Inc. 174 - 213 2011 $2000

Association – Stickland

Disraeli, Benjamin 1804-1881 *Sybil; or the Two Nations.* London: Henry Colburn, 1845. First edition; 3 volumes, bound without half titles, slight spotting to prelims of volume III, slightly later half red pebble grained morocco, raised bands in gilt, "Stickland" ownership stamp on titlepages, very good. Jarndyce Antiquarian Booksellers CXCI - 519 2011 £480

Association – Stokes, Anson Phelps

Morse, Jedidiah 1761-1826 *The American Geography; or a View of the Present Situation of the United States of America.* Elizabeth Town: Shepard Kollock, 1789. xii, 534, (3) pages, 2 folding maps, contemporary sheep, very skillfully rebacked in correct period style, rear endpaper sympathetically replaced, light foxing and occasional browning throughout as usual with early American paper, few short splits and one map tear skillfully mended, 20th century owner's stamp at foot of dedication page and on verso of one map, Rev. Anson Phelps Stokes bookplate. Joseph J. Felcone Inc. Fall Miscellany 2010 - 91 2011 $5500

Association – Stone, Richard

Champernowne, D. G. *Uncertainty & Estimation in Economics.* Edinburgh & San Francisco: Oliver & Boyd/Holden Day, 1969. First edition; 3 volumes, 8vo., pages viii, 280; vi, 426; v, 108, tables, figures, signed presentation from author to Richard Stone, very good+ in like dust jacket (spines slightly tanned). Any Amount of Books May 29 2011 - A75931 2011 $204

Friedman, Milton *Income from Independent Professional Practice.* New York: National Bureau of Economic Research, 1945. First edition; 8vo. original publisher's blue cloth lettered gilt at spine, pages xxxiii, 599, tables, charts, from the library of Cambridge economist Sir Richard Stone (1913-1991), slight scuffing to rear boards, else very good+, overall ownership stamp of Stone. Any Amount of Books May 29 2011 - A67478 2011 $255

Association – Stone, Robert

Carver, Raymond *Fires.* London: Collins Harvill, 1985. First British edition; inscribed by author to novelist, Robert Stone, uncommon thus, foxing to page edges and endpapers, not affecting inscription, very good in very good dust jacket, lightly edgeworn with foxing, mostly on verso and slight fading to spine title,. Ken Lopez Bookseller 154 - 26 2011 $2500

Association – Stout, M. E.

Fairy Poster Book. Racine: Whitman, 1929. Oblong 4to., stiff pictorial wrappers, some cover wear, else near fine, fine and unused, illustrations M. E. Stout who has inscribed the book. Aleph-Bet Books, Inc. 95 - 397 2011 $250

Association – Strahan, A.

Trollope, Anthony 1815-1882 *An Editor's Tales.* London: Strahan & Co., 1870. First edition; half title, original brown cloth, expertly recased with spine strip slightly trimmed at head and tail, binder's ticket of Burn & Co., inscribed by publisher, A. Strahan for George MacDonald, with MacDonald's bookplate. Jarndyce Antiquarian Booksellers CXCII - 340 2011 £450

Association – Strahan, Alexander

MacDonald, George 1824-1905 *The Poetical Works of George MacDonald.* London: Chatto & Windus, 1893. 2 volumes, half titles, some spotting, original plain crimson buckram, spines faded, volume I slightly marked, with 2 page ALS from author to Alexander Strahan dated only Friday without address. Jarndyce Antiquarian Booksellers CXCII - 313 2011 £750

Association – Stratford, William

Stackhouse, Thomas *A New and Practical Exposition of the Apostles Creed...* London: Thomas Longman, Thomas Shewell and Charles Hitch, 1747. First edition; folio, contemporary full polished calf with raised ands, few old surface scratches and small defects, pages (ii), xxviii (ii, analysis, verso blank), 208, 217-421, (i, ad), (xiv, index and table, final leaf blank), text and signature complete despite pagination, nice contemporary inscription on flyleaf in Latin from William Stratford, Commissary of the Archdeaconry of Richmond, presenting the book to the Curate of Dent, Mark Rumney and his successors. R. F. G. Hollett & Son Antiquarian Booksellers 175 - 1277 2011 £350

Nelson, Robert *A Companion for the Festivals and Fasts of the Church of England...* London: J. & J. Bonwicke S. Brit etc., 1752. Twentieth edition; contemporary full speckled sheep gilt, few slight old tape marks and surface defects, pages (iv), 636, (xvi), engraved frontispiece, prelim leaves slightly creased, sound, clean copy, nice contemporary (1754) inscription in Latin from William Stratford. R. F. G. Hollett & Son Antiquarian Booksellers 175 - 988 2011 £175

Association – Strathallan

Spence, Joseph 1699-1768 *Polymetis or an Enquiry Concerning the Agreement Between the Works of the Roman Poets and the Remains of the Ancient Artists.* London: printed for R. and J. Dodsley, 1755. Second edition; folio, pages vi, 361, (i) + engraved frontispiece and 41 other engraved plates, contemporary calf, spine fully gilt with 'sun-spot filled lattice' compartments, boards single rule gilt bordered with elaborate stencil design of interlocking 'eared' ovoids and quatrefoil corners, board edges decorative roll gilt, 'Dutch swirl' 'made' endpapers, all edges lemon, some minor spotting, frontispiece offset onto title, joints and corners skillfully repaired, old leather bit rubbed and scratched, contemporary engraved armorial bookplate lettered "southouse" pasted to verso of first plain flyleaf signed "Timbrell & Harding" later armorial bookplate of Strathallan, from the collection of Christopher Ernest Weston 1947-2010. Unsworths Booksellers 24 - 142 2011 £675

Association – Streeter, Frank S.

Beechey, Frederick William 1796-1856 *Narrative of a Voyage to the Pacific and Beering's Strait...Performed in His Majesty's Ship Blossom... in the Years 1825, 1826, 1827, 1828...* London: Henry Colburn and Richard Bentley, 1831. First edition; 2 volumes, quarto, (iii)-xxi, (1, errata), (1, directions to the binder), (1, blank), 392; (iii)-vii, (1, directions to binder), (393)-742 pages, bound without publisher's ads (2) pages at end volume II and bound without half titles, 3 engraved maps, two of which are folding and 23 engraved plates, contemporary diced calf, rebacked in style, boards ruled in gilt, each volume with red and black, spine labels, spines stamped and lettered in gilt, board edges stamped in gilt, all edges marbled, bit of spotting and offsetting, three quarter inch closed tear to outer margin of b4 in volume I, not affecting text, boards with few light scrapes and spots, overall very good, handsome, the Frank S. Streeter copy with his bookplate. Heritage Book Shop Holiday 2010 - 8 2011 $8500

Association – Stuart, Grace Dell

Eccleston, Robert *Overland to California on the Southwestern Trail 1849. Diary of Robert Eccleston.* Berkeley & Los Angeles: University of California Press, 1950. Limited to 750 copies, this number 95; inscribed by both authors to Reginald Ray and Grace Dell Stuart, with their bookplate, 8vo., xvii, 256 pages, brown cloth, gilt stamped spine title, dust jacket chipped.   Jeff Weber Rare Books   163 - 67   2011 $100

Association – Sturcke, Arthur

Patchen, Kenneth *The Memoirs of a Shy Pornographer.* New York: New Directions, 1945. First edition, first impression; clippings on rear endpapers, else near fine, tattered remnants of dust jacket (lacking front panel and front flap), booklabel of Greenwich Village artist Arthur Sturcke on titlepage, inscribed to same by author.   Between the Covers   169 - BTC34088   2011 $1500

Association – Suave, Francesco

Homerus *Odyssea (and other works).* Venice: Melchiorre Sessa, 1540? 165 x 108mm., 238, (2) leaves, contemporary olive brown calf over pasteboard, ends of spine repaired (probably late in 19th century), gilt covers framed with two sets of double rules, outer panel with broad foliate curl cornerpieces and sidepieces with trefoil of three rings between each, inner panel with blindstamped horizontal oval centerpiece of Apollo and Pegasus, the gilt collar with Greek motto touching rules at sides, large foliate sprays at head and foot curling to left and right and rising to a fleuron tool at ends, raised bands, spine panelled in gilt featuring broad rules and fleuron centerpiece, brown morocco label; woodcut historiated initials and charming cat and mouse printer's device, leaves at front and back with various marks of ownership, including signature of Francesco Suave at head of titlepage and "proprieta di Carlo Balzi 1884", contemporary marginal annotations in Latin and Greek; joints partly cracked (wormed in two places), corners somewhat worn, some scuffing to leather, binding completely solid, gilt still distinct, plaquettes (not surprisingly) bright and volume altogether pleasing even with its defects, final leaf cropped at fore edge (with loss of first [verso] or last [recto] on two thirds of the lines), upper corner of two gatherings with small, faint dampstain, one minor paper flaw costing half dozen letters, otherwise unusually well preserved internally, text exceptionally bright, fresh and clean, according to Hobson a fraudulent Apollo and Pegasus binding, volume looks absolutely convincing, with usual signs of age and restoration (wheels of Apollo's chariot have four spokes, in the genuine article, they have six.   Phillip J. Pirages   59 - 4   2011 $7500

Association – Sunderland

Herodotus *The History of Herodotus.* London: printed for D. Midwinter et al, 1737. Third edition; 2 volumes, 8vo., pages xvi, 447 (xvii) + 3 extending engraved maps, (ii), 430, (xviii), contemporary orangey tan calf boards triple rule gilt bordered with broad dentelle inner border of individual small tools, board edges decorative roll gilt, late 19th century 'swirl' 'made' endpapers with pale green block cloth, inner joint strengtheners, all edges original blue swirl/marbled pale blue and white sewn endbands, early 21st century retrospective reback + corners by Chris Weston, little toning and marginal dust soiling, some marginal pencil notes, old leather chipped at edges, contemporary ink inscription "Eliza Spencer" at head of titlepages, verso of volume I marbled endpaper has ms. note by Rev. John Bourton/Banningham Rectory/Norfolk referring to early provenance of Sunderland Library and subsequent purchase at Puttick & Simpson's auction in 1882, from the collection of Christopher Ernest Weston 1947-2010.   Unsworths Booksellers   24 - 109   2011   £400

Association – Surtees, Anthony Conyers

Hardy, Thomas 1840-1928 *A Pair of Blue Eyes.* London: Tinsley Brothers, 1873. First edition in book form, one of presumably 500 copies; 3 volumes, small octavo, (6), 303, (1, blank); (6), 311, (1, blank); (6), 262 pages, complete with half titles, bound circa 1910 by Zaehnsdorf in three quarter green crushed morocco gilt over green cloth boards ruled in gilt, spines lettered and decoratively tooled in gilt, marbled endpapers, top edges gilt, bookplate of Anthony Conyers Surtees on front pastedown, superb copy, very rare.   David Brass Rare Books, Inc.   May 26 2011 - 01306   2011 $9500

Association – Sutherland, A.

Hawthorne, Nathaniel 1804-1864 *Transformation or the Romance of Monte Beni.* London: Smith, Elder & Co., 1860. Third edition; 3 volumes, slight spotting to prelims, contemporary grained tan calf, gilt borders, raised bands, gilt spine, brown and green morocco labels, booklabels of W. M. Graham, signature of A. Sutherland in volume I, very good.   Jarndyce Antiquarian Booksellers   CXCI - 526   2011   £175

Association – Sutherland, Annie

Kelly, George *Craig's Wife a Drama.* Boston: Little Brown, 1926. First edition; 8vo., pages 174, very nice, tight copy, inscribed by author to Josephine Williams who played the part of Mrs. Harold in the NY production, also signed by rest of the cast - Annie Sutherland, Crystal Herne, Arthur Shaw, C. Stewart, Eleanor Marsh, Charles Trowbridge, Josephine Hull, J. A. Curtis, Nelan Jaap, Arline Alcine & Mary Gildea, also inscribed by the producer, Rosalie Stewart to whom the play was dedicated.   Second Life Books Inc.   174 - 213   2011 $2000

Association – Sutherland, Duke of

Anacreon *Anacreontis Odaria. (The Odes).* Londini: Ex Officina B. R. Howlett, Veneunt apud J. Murray, 1813. 188 x 112mm., 2 p.l., 130 pages, very pleasing contemporary crimson straight grain morocco, covers bordered by single gilt fillet upper cover with gilt arms of the Duke of Sutherland, raised bands flanked by gilt rules, spine panels with central gilt wheel ornament, gilt turn-ins, marbled endpaper, all edges gilt, 20 charming hand colored engraved head and tailpieces vignettes, text in Greek, spine slightly and uniformly faded, text with occasional minor foxing and slight yellowing, one opening with offsetting from a pressed flower, otherwise quite excellent contemporary copy, high quality binding with only most minor wear, beautifully set text quite fresh and hand coloring subtly done and very pleasing. Phillip J. Pirages   59 - 63   2011 $600

Association – Sutherland, Rod

Bonwick, James *Port Phillip Settlement.* London: Sampson Low, Marston, Sarle & Rivington, 1883. First edition; octavo, original blue cloth, gilt decoration on front cover, x, 537, (1), (- ads) pages, 4 folding facsimiles of letters, one folding facsimile of handwritten newspaper, folding map, double page plate with numerous facsimile, signatures of Men of the Period, 4 full page lithographed views, 42 half page illustrations on 21 lithographed plates, 4 lithographed portraits, color lithograph frontispiece, pencil signature of H. Britton dated 1884 on front endpaper and below of Rod M. Sutherland dated Nv. 1949, occsional light spotting to text, half inch tear to top of spine, mild rubbing to edges, near fine, uncommon.   Charles Agvent   2010 Summer Miscellany - 13   2011 $350

Association – Swetenham, Roger

Bentley, Richard *Designs by Mr. Bentley for Six Poems by Mr. Gray.* London: printed for R. Dodsley, 1753. First edition; folio, modern half calf gilt, page (iv), 35, half title, title with vignette, 6 full page copper engraved plates, 12 engraved decorations and 6 engraved initials, half title rather soiled and abraded in places, short tears repaired, little creasing in places, armorial bookplate of Roger Swetenham. R. F. G. Hollett & Son Antiquarian Booksellers   General Catalogue Summer 2010 - 627   2011   £750

Association – Swetman, George

Beston, Henry *The Outermost House: a Year of Life of the Great Beach of Cape Cod.* New York: Rinehart & Co., 1949. Twelfth printing; photos by William A. Bradford and others, corners bit bumped, near fine in about fine dust jacket with very short tear, warmly inscribed by author to George Swetman, ALS signed twice by Beston to Mrs. Swetman.   Between the Covers   169 - BTC347882   2011 $5000

Association – Swinglehurst, Henry

Nicholson, Cornelius *The Annals of Kendall.* Kendal: Hudson and Nicholson, 1832. First edition; near contemporary full polished calf gilt, boards panelled with broad rolls in gilt, spine faded, pages ix, 260, engraved frontispiece and folding plan of Kendal (defective and partly replaced with modern photocopy taped on), single sheet ALS laid in from author to Henry Swinglehurst, Nicholson's 19 page pamphlet "History and Incidents connected with the grant of the three Royal Charters of Incorporation of the Borough of Kendal (privately published 1876) bound in at end, frontispiece and titlepage laid down, small engraving of Kendal Castle laid down on dedication leaf.   R. F. G. Hollett & Son Antiquarian Booksellers   173 - 825   2011   £175

Association – Symonds, Frederick

Hunter, John *The Natural History of Human Teeth: Explaining their Structure, Use, Formation, Growth and Diseases.* London: for J. Johnson, 1771. First edition; 4to., (8), 128 pages, 16 engraved plates, with facing letterpress, 19th century half roan, headcap neatly replaced, lightly scuffed, corners worn), just hint of foxing in top margin, else clean, wide margined copy, armorial bookplate of Frederick Symonds.   Joseph J. Felcone Inc.   Fall Miscellany 2010 - 38   2011 $4500

Association – Symons, A. J. A.

Lancaster, Osbert *Progress at Pelvis Bay.* London: John Murray, 1936. First edition; original cloth backed pictorial boards, matching dust jacket little rubbed and dusty, pages vi, 70, line drawings by author, pictorial endpapers, from the library of A. J. A. Symons with his small label, part of original wraparound band loosely inserted.   R. F. G. Hollett & Son Antiquarian Booksellers   General Catalogue Summer 2010 - 828   2011   £85

Whitman, Walt   1819-1892 *Good-Bye My Fancy: 2nd Annex to Leaves of Grass.* Philadelphia: David McKay, 1891. First edition; 8vo. original maroon cloth, beveled edges, gilt lettered, top edge gilt, frontispiece, from the library of A. J. A. Symons, with his Brick House bookplate, small nick in spine, edges little rubbed and faded, good, from the collection of Samuel Charters.   The Brick Row Book Shop   Bulletin 8 - 36   2011 $400

Association – Symons, William Hales

Opie, Amelia *Adeline Mowbray, or the Mother and Daughter: a Tale.* London: Longman, 1805. Second edition; 3 volumes, half title and final ad leaf volume I, some occasional light foxing, contemporary full tree calf, spines with gilt devices and black leather labels, little rubbing, hinges slightly cracked, armorial bookplates of William Hales Symons, good plus.   Jarndyce Antiquarian Booksellers   CLXC - 656   2011   £450

Association – Syston Park

Dalrymple, John *Memoirs of Great Britain and Ireland from the Dissolution of the Last Parliament of Charles II Until the Sea Battle of La Hogue.* London and Edinburgh: for W. Strahan and T. Cadell and A. Kincaid, J. Bell and J. Balfour, 1771. Second edition; 285 x 215mm., viii, (4) leaves, 509, (1) pages, originally illustrated with separate appendix not present here; handsome contemporary oxblood morocco, gilt, in style of Robert Payne, expertly and sympathetically rebacked, covers with wide and intricate gilt tooled frame composed of closely spaced alternating palm fronds and lancets, cornerpieces composed of 10 different botanical and geometric tools, flat spine divided into compartments by decorative gilt rolls, each compartment with central floral sprig inside a lozenge of stars, circles and other small tools and corners with curling palm fronds, gilt turn-ins, marbled endpapers, all edges gilt; with fine foreedge painting of Limerick and the River Shannon, as seen from the tower of Limerick Cathedral; early 19th century engraved bookplate of Syston Park and with smaller 20th century bookplate of "A.A.H.", with notation in what appears to be late 18th century hand of John Thorold; half dozen small abrasions to covers with minimal loss of gilt, extremities bit rubbed, occasional minor foxing or smudging, other trivial imperfections, excellent copy, binding solidly restored and certainly appealing, text very fresh, quite clean, generous margins, expert fore-edge painting in fine condition, colors soft but clear, composition especially pleasing. Phillip J. Pirages 59 - 41 2011 $2400

Association – Sze, Mai Mai

Watts, Alan W. *The Way of Zen.* New York: Pantheon, 1957. First edition; fine in near fine dust jacket with mild sunning to spine and edges, inscribed by author to Mai-Mai Sze. Ken Lopez Bookseller 154 - 237 2011 $1500

Association – Taft, A. C.

Copeia. New York/Ann Arbor: American Society of Ichthyologists and Herpetologists, 1913-2006. Most first editions, approximately 20 of the earlier issues are reprints; Complete except for 1998 (nos. 1-4), 8vo. (Nos. 1-173 smaller 8vo), numerous photos, text illustrations, folded tables, charts, etc., wrappers beginning with no. 162 (some tears to No. 1), all repaired with cello tape, rest with very modest wear including occasional smudges, tanning, creases, etc, handstamp to front pages or front wrapper, very nice set, issues 1930-1948 with A. C. Taft's name in pencil. Raymond M. Sutton, Jr. May 26 2011 - 55023 2011 $1750

Association – Talbot, R. A.

Bible. English - 1836 *New Testament of Our Lord and Saviour Jesus Christ: Published in 1526.* London: Samuel Bagster, 1836. 8vo., pages iv, 98 ff., ii-ccxvii + engraved titlepage and frontispiece, later calf, spine panelled in blind, lettered in 'Old English' type and dated at foot both in gilt, boards elaborately panelled in blind with rules and decorative rolls, central panel double rule diced board edges decorative roll n blind, turn-ins elaborately decorated with rolls tooled in blind, 'Peacock swirl' 'made' endpapers, all edges gilt & gauffered, 3 color (blue white & pink), sewn flat endbands, maroon silk page marker, frontispiece foxed, spine quite rubbed, joints split and boards loose, armorial bookplate of York Minster /Library / Bequeathed by the Rev. R. A. Talbot 1993", from the collection of Christopher Ernest Weston 1947-2010. Unsworths Booksellers 24 - 12 2011 £95

Association – Tanner, Heather

Tanner, Robin *Double Harness.* Impact Books, 1987. First edition; large 8vo., original cloth, gilt, dust jacket (red spine lettering faded), pages (iv), 215, 7 etchings and 10 pen drawings, fine, label signed by Robin and Heather Tanner and dated July 1987 laid on flyleaf. R. F. G. Hollett & Son Antiquarian Booksellers General Catalogue Summer 2010 - 912 2011 £45

Association – Tanner, Wesley

McClure, Michael *Solstice Blossom.* N.P.: Arif Press, 1973. Of a total edition of 130 copies, this is an out-of-series copy labeled as an "Artist's Copy" and signed by author; inscribed by Welsey Tanner who provided an original water color as frontispiece, one small edge tear, else fine in saddle stitched wrappers, attractive, uncommon. Ken Lopez Bookseller 154 - 111 2011 $250

Association – Tatton, Reginald Arthur

Ronalds, Alfred *The Fly-Fisher's Entomology.* London: Longman, Green and Co., 1877. Eighth edition; original blindstamped green cloth, gilt, extremities little frayed and bumped, lower hinge repaired at foot, pages xiv, (ii), 132, 24, 20 finely hand colored plates, front joint strained and strengthened, armorial bookplates of Thomas Towneley Parker and Reginald Arthur Tatton. R. F. G. Hollett & Son Antiquarian Booksellers General Catalogue Summer 2010 - 1277 2011 £195

Association – Taubman-Goldie, George

White, Arthur Silva *The Expansion of Egypt: under Anglo-Egyptian Condominium.* London: Methuen, 1899. First edition; 8vo., pages xv, 438, ads, 4 maps, original red decorative cloth, presentation copy to Sir George Tabuman-Goldie in 1899. J. & S. L. Bonham Antiquarian Booksellers Africa 4/20/2011 - 8260 2011 £100

Association – Taylor, Arthur

Tapping, Thomas *A Treatise on the Derbyshire Mining Customs and Mineral Court Act 1852 (15 & 16 Vict. CCLXIII) Analytically and Practically Arranged...* Shaw and Sons, 1854. First edition; pages xi, 166, original printed boards, rather rubbed, spine and corners worn, scarce, signature of Arthur G. Taylor and W. B. Brooke-Taylor, successive stewards and barmasters of the Marmote Court.   R. F. G. Hollett & Son Antiquarian Booksellers   175 - 1313 2011   £220

Association – Taylor, Nathaniel Pendleton

Godwin, William 1756-1836 *Memoirs of the author of a Vindication of the Rights of Woman.* Philadelphia: James Carey, 1799. First American edition; 8vo., pages 158, front blank tissued and remounted, bound in new boards with calf spine, some little marginal staining, very good, this copy was owned and annotated by a contemporary American reader, Nathaniel Pendleton Taylor, who signed and dated titlepage.   Second Life Books Inc. 174 - 331 2011 $1500

Association – Taylor, Peter

Jones, Ann *Women Who Kill.* New York: Holt, Rinehart and Winston, 1980. First edition; near fine in near fine dust jacket with half inch tear on front panel, presentation copy, inscribed by James Allan McPherson for Peter Taylor.   Between the Covers 169 - BTC336596 2011 $650

Association – Taylor, R. G.

Oliphant, Margaret Oliphant Wilson 1828-1897 *A House in Bloomsbury.* New York: Dodd, Mead & Co., 1894. First American edition; original grey cloth, blocked with floral design in dark green lettered in gilt, spine slightly dulled, R. G. Taylor booklabel, very good.   Jarndyce Antiquarian Booksellers   CLXC - 624 2011   £120

Association – Tegetmeier, Denis

Dodgson, Campbell *Prints in the Dotte Manner and Other Metal-Cuts of the XV Century in the Department of Prints and Drawings British Museum.* London: British Museum, 1937. First edition; 34 pages, frontispiece, 43 plates, very good in slightly rubbed original dark green cloth, bookplate of Denis Tegetmeier and note 'gift of Stanley Morison', folio.   Ken Spelman Rare Books   68 - 120 2011   £90

Association – Tempest, J. P.

Vernon, W. V. *A Second Letter to Viscount Milton on the Restoration of York Minster and the Proposed Removal of the Choir Screen.* W. Hargrove for John and George Todd, 1830. 8vo., 62 pages, engraved plate, large uncut copy in later gilt lettered blue cloth, outer leaves rather dusty, contemporary signature of J. P. Tempest.   Ken Spelman Rare Books   68 - 24 2011   £75

Association – Temple, Edward

Thoreau, Henry David 1817-1862 *Excursions.* Boston: Ticknor & Fields, 1863. First edition; original blue green z cloth, portrait frontispiece, one signature pulled, scattered foxing and staining, covers lightly soiled, minor wear to spine, gilt bright, very good, early owner name of Edward L. Temple, early bookplate of Rutland High School.   Charles Agvent   Transcendentalism 2010 - 31 2011 $850

Association – Terry, Roderick

Goldsmith, Oliver 1730-1774 *The Vicar of Wakefield: a Tale Supposed to be Written by Himself.* Salisbury: Printed for B. Collins for F. Newbery, 1766. First edition, variant B; 2 volumes, 172 x 108mm., terminal blank in volume I, beautiful scarlet crushed morocco, heavily gilt by Riviere & Son, covers with French fillet frame, spine with raised bands and handsomely gilt compartments, lovely gilt inner dentelles, all edges gilt, leather book labels of Roderick Terry, (Edgar) Mills and Doris Louise Benz, lower corner of terminal blank in first volume skillfully renewed, artful repair and faint glue stains at inner margin of B3 in second volume, other isolated trivial defects, very fine, text nearly pristine, especially bright and handsome binding.   Phillip J. Pirages 59 - 50 2011 $6500

Association – Terry, Ward

Coryate, Thomas *Coryate's Crudities Hastily Gobbled Up in Five Moneths Travells in France, Savoy, Italy, Rhetia Comonly Called the Grisons Country, Helvetia Alias Switzerland, some Parts of High Germany and the Netherlands.* London: by William Stansby, 1611. First edition; printed title present, engraved allegorical title by William Hole (shaved very slightly at head), engraved plates, woodcut, text portrait, errata leaf present, many woodcut initials and headpieces, 19th century brown crushed levant morocco, gilt by Bedford, unusually tall, very handsome copy, rare printed title, from the libraries of Ward E. Terry, R. B. Adam, A. Edward Newton, Bois Penrose and Wolfgang A. Herz with their respective bookplates and book labels.   Joseph J. Felcone Inc.   Fall Miscellany 2010 - 35 2011 $16,000

Association – Thiersch, Ludwig

Goethe, Johann Wolfgang Von 1749-1832 *Zur Farbenlehre and Erklarung der Zu Goethe's Fabrenlehre Gehorigen Tafeln and Anzeige und Uebersicht des Goethischen Werkes zur Fabenlehre (the latter two in the plate volume).* Tubingen: J. G. Cotta, 1810. First editions of both text volumes and plate volume; text volumes 200 x 125mm., plate volume 240 x 202mm., 3 volumes, two text volumes and quarto atlas volume as issued), unusual period binding of contemporary paper treated to look like tree calf, paper put on over original half calf, flat spines with plain and decorative gilt rules, orange paper labels, with 17 plates, 12 of them hand colored, bookplate OS?, ink ownership inscription of German painter Ludwig Thiersch; variable foxing because of inferior paper stock, perhaps a dozen gatherings in first volume rather foxed, but problem never severe, the foxing quite minor or absent in many places and plates, done on better paper, almost entirely unaffected, paper covering the binding little worn and chipped at places along joints (revealing gilt decorated leather underneath), corners slightly bumped, atlas volume with two minor scratches to upper cover, still quite an appealing set, original insubstantial board bindings entirely sturdy, remarkably clean and surprisingly bright, text quite fresh and with almost no signs of use. Phillip J. Pirages 59 - 218 2011 $24,000

Association – Thomajan, P. K.

Perelman, S. J. *Dawn Ginsbergh's Revenge.* New York: Horace Liveright, 1929. Third printing (same month as first printing, curiously in the same green plush binding as the first issue); bookplate of Madison Ave. advertising marvel and bibliophile P. K. Thomajan, little wear at bottom of boards, near fine in very good or better third printing dust jacket with shallow chips at top of front panel, inscribed by author at a later date to P. K. Thomajan, rare, some modest wear, still very nice, abrasive plush material of binding tended to rub jacket away to nothing. Between the Covers 169 - BTC347866 2011 $1600

Association – Thomas, Anthony

Craig, Edward Gordon 1872-1966 *The Page. Volume Two. Number Four.* Hackbridge: At the Sign of the Rose and printed by Arthur Chilver, 1899. Limited edition, number 2 of 410 copies); large square 8vo., original brown printed wrappers, overlapping edges trifle chipped, backstrip defective, pages (116), 4 woodcuts with hand coloring, other woodcuts, text printed on rectos only, presentation copy, inscribed by Craig for Anthony Thomas. R. F. G. Hollett & Son Antiquarian Booksellers 175 - 330 2011 £1200

Williams, Emlyn *Emlyn. An Early Autobiography.* London: The Bodley Head, 1973. First edition; original cloth, gilt, dust jacket, little worn, pages 424, presentation copy, inscribed to Anthony Thomas with author's affection Jan. 1974. R. F. G. Hollett & Son Antiquarian Booksellers 175 - 1447 2011 £30

Association – Thomas, Caron

Willans, John *Marc Bolan: Wilderness of the Mind.* London: Xanadu, 1992. First edition; 8vo., pages 176, illustrations in black and white, signed by Willans and Caron Thomas, fine in very good dust jacket with slight edgewear, stamp with note "This edition signed by authors is limited to one thousand copies, of which this is number 179". Any Amount of Books May 29 2011 - A66474 2011 $238

Association – Thomas, Molly

Manvell, Roger *Ellen Terry.* London: Heinemann, 1968. First edition; original cloth, gilt, dust jacket little worn, pages x, 390, with 41 illustrations, presentation copy from Manvell for Molly Thomas (curator of Ellen Terry Museum in Smallhythe, Kent). R. F. G. Hollett & Son Antiquarian Booksellers 175 - 911 2011 £30

Association – Thomason, Dustin

Caldwell, Ian *The Rule of Four.* New York: Dial Press, 2004. First edition; near fine, very light bump to heel of spine, fine dust jacket, signed by Ian and co-author Dustin Thomason. Bella Luna Books May 29 2011 - t6860 2011 $82

Association – Thomlinson, William

Baker, Samuel White 1821-1893 *The Nile Tributaries.* London: Macmillan, 1867. First edition; 8vo., xxii, 596 pages, engraved frontispiece, 23 plates, 2 colored maps, modern quarter calf, marbled boards, gilt spine, bookplate of William Thomlinson, fine. Jeff Weber Rare Books 163 - 130 2011 $225

Association – Thompson, W. B.

Kipling, Rudyard 1865-1936 *Actions and Reactions.* London: Macmillan, 1909. First edition; half title, 12 page catalog, original red cloth gilt, contemporary owner inscription of W. B. Thompson on leading f.e.p. verso, top edge gilt, very good. Jarndyce Antiquarian Booksellers CXCI - 238 2011 £50

Association – Thomson, G. S.

Alexander, Patrick Proctor *Spiritualism: a Narrative with a Discussion.* Edinburgh: William P. Nimmo, 1871. First edition; 2 pages ads, original yellow printed boards, neatly rebacked, dulled, slightly rubbed, slight creasing to boards, contemporary signature of G. S. Thomson on leading pastedown, good, sound copy. Jarndyce Antiquarian Booksellers CXCI - 34 2011 £65

Association – Thomson, Samuel

Dugdale, William 1605-1686 *Monasticon Anglicanum; or the History of the Ancient Abbies, Monasteries, Hospitals...in England and Wales. (with) ... Two Additional volumes to Sir William Dugdale's Monasticon Anglicanum.* London: R. Harbin for D. Browne and J. Smith (et al) for Tho. Taylor..., 1718. 1722-1723; 3 volumes, folio, plates (lacking plates 42-44 in volume 1, contemporary mottled calf, stain darkened, spine panel gilt, red lettering piece gilt, numbered direct in panel gilt compartment, board edges 'zig-zag' roll gilt, all edges 'French Shell' marbled, blue and red sewn endleaves, some damp and mould marking, a few plates loose but present, rather rubbed, joints worn but strong, some loss from endcaps, contemporary ink inscription "Samuel Thomson Esq. of Bradfield Berks", ink stamped armorial of "Samuel Thomson of Bradfield Esqr", armorial bookplates of Honble James Bertie Esqr. of Stanwell in Com. Middx. Second Son to James late/Earle of Abingdon 1702", from the collection of Christopher Ernest Weston 1947-2010. Unsworths Booksellers 24 - 21 2011 £600

Association – Thore, Virgin

Guevara, Antonio De *Vita Di M. Avrelio Imperadore.* Venice: Bartolomeo Imperador and Francesco Veneziano, 1543. 160 x 103mm., 8 p.l., 132, (2) leaves, fine contemporary Roman red morocco Apollo and Pegasus medallion binding done for Giovanni Battista Grimaldi by Marc Antonio Guillery, (genuine Apollo and Pegasus binding) covers with gilt frame formed by two widely spaced fillets with lobes interlaced at ends and sides, space between fillets decorated with broad foliate curls, small floral tools, inner pane of each board with gilt titling above a horizontal oval Apollo and Pegasus plaquette centerpiece showing Pegasus atop black painted heights of Parnassus and Apollo racing his chariot (drawn by two straining steeds) across steep terrain with reins and whip held aloft and caps fluttering behind, plaquette with gilt motto in Greek in the collar above and below vignette, spine (very expertly rebacked) with four thin and three thick raised bands decorated with gilt rope pattern or plain rules (this being original backstrip?), newer (perhaps 19th century) endpapers, all edges gilt (apparently some remarkably skillful restoration at one or more corners and edges, perhaps some gold added, as well as to the chariot part of the plaquettes); woodcut printer's device on , morocco bookplate and separate gilt monogram of Robert Hoe as well as inscription and vellum bookplate of Swedish collector Thore Virgin, ownership inscription of J. T. Payne dated 1850; covers with half dozen insignificant tiny dark spots, titlepage faintly soiled, thin light brown stain just at top edge of leaves, small wormhole at upper inner margin (text not affected), occasional minor stains, other trivial imperfections, but no defects that are even remotely serious and in general really excellent specimen of a very special binding, text fresh and leather quite lustrous; also from the collection of bibliophile Johannes Gennadius, Liverpool oculist T. Shadford Walker and Swedish collector Rolfe Wistrand. Phillip J. Pirages 59 - 2 2011 $35,000

Association – Thorold, John

Dalrymple, John *Memoirs of Great Britain and Ireland from the Dissolution of the Last Parliament of Charles II Until the Sea Battle of La Hogue.* London and Edinburgh: for W. Strahan and T. Cadell and A. Kincaid, J. Bell and J. Balfour, 1771. Second edition; 285 x 215mm., viii, (4) leaves, 509, (1) pages, originally illustrated with separate appendix not present here; handsome contemporary oxblood morocco, gilt, in style of Robert Payne, expertly and sympathetically rebacked, covers with wide and intricate gilt tooled frame composed of closely spaced alternating palm fronds and lancets, cornerpieces composed of 10 different botanical and geometric tools, flat spine divided into compartments by decorative gilt rolls, each compartment with central floral sprig inside a lozenge of stars, circles and other small tools and corners with curling palm fronds, gilt turn-ins, marbled endpapers, all edges gilt; with fine foreedge painting of Limerick and the River Shannon, as seen from the tower of Limerick Cathedral; early 19th century engraved bookplate of Syston Park and with smaller 20th century bookplate of "A.A.H.", with notation in what appears to be late 18th century hand of John Thorold; half dozen small abrasions to covers with minimal loss of gilt, extremities bit rubbed, occasional minor foxing or smudging, other trivial imperfections, excellent copy, binding solidly restored and certainly appealing, text very fresh, quite clean, generous margins, expert fore-edge painting in fine condition, colors soft but clear, composition especially pleasing.   Phillip J. Pirages 59 - 41 2011 $2400

Association – Thorold, R. F.

Carey-Hobson, Mary *At Home in the Transvaal.* London: W. Swan Sonnenschein, 1884. 2 volumes, small octavo (iv), 268; (iv), (260)-524 pages, original green cloth, blind rules, gilt spines, speckled edges, titlepage embossed with library stamps, bookplate of R. F. Thorold, very good plus, rare.   Jeff Weber Rare Books 163 - 140 2011 $85

Association – Thorp, Willard

Fitzgerald, Francis Scott Key 1896-1940 *Tender is the Night.* New York: Scribner's, 1934. First edition, 2nd printing; (8), 408 pages, cloth, spine lettering very faint, general cover wear, good to very good, Willard Thorp's copy.   Joseph J. Felcone Inc. Fall Miscellany 2010 - 48 2011 $400

Association – Thorshead, O.

Jones, E. Alfred *Catalogue of the Plate of Clare College Cambridge.* Cambridge: University Press, 1938. First edition; large 4to., original plum cloth, gilt, pages xxxvii, 88, with 27 plates, loosely inserted is single sheet TLS from O. Thorshead (Librarian at Windsor Castle) to author. R. F. G. Hollett & Son Antiquarian Booksellers 175 - 744 2011 £250

Association – Throckmorton, Lilian

Shaw, George Bernard 1856-1950 *Saint Joan.* London: Constable, 1924. First edition; 12mo., pages 114, inscribed by author to Lilian Throckmorton, original silverprint of GBS and recipient posing in a garden, Throckmorton's bookplate, fine. Second Life Books Inc. 174 - 283 2011 $900

Association – Tiby, Anais Duret

Bible. French - 1843 *Les Saints Evangiles.* Paris: L. Curmer, 1843. First edition thus; the handsomely designed presentation page at the front tells us that this beautiful object was assembled at the order of C. J. T. Tiby and given to his dear wife Anais Duret Tiby on 2 June 1855 as a "Souvenir of 25 years of Happiness", 260 x 184mm., 4 p.l. 552 pages; 2 p.l, 372 pages, 2 volumes bound in one, extremely elegant mid 19th century Neo-gothic presentation binding by Gruel-Engelmann in dark green silk velvet, covers mounted with delicately amd elaborately carved boxwood frames after designs by Martin Riester, upper cover with wooden grapevine cornerpieces forming a large ogival central velvet panel featuring carved wooden vines forming the prominent monogram "A T" (for Anais Tiby) at middle, lower cover with central carved cross twined with grape vines arising from a cluster of leaves, flat spine with carved head and tailpieces, repeating grapevine motif and a carved boxwood banderolle at center on which the title appears in red, blue and gold; two pierced metal clasps at fore edge, saffron yellow moire silk endleaves, morocco hinges, edges very elaborately gauffered with gilt neo-gothic floral pattern on a red background, housed in handsome and very sturdy morocco backed wooden box lined with gold velvet, ornamental borders around text, numerous ornamental headpieces, initials and tailpieces (37 of these illuminated by hand), two chromolithographed titlepages, four woodcut titles for each Gosepl, two engraved maps, two steel engraved frontispieces by Lecomte after Decaisne and by Cousin after Meissonier and 17 steel engraved plates after Tony Johannot by Cousin, Fontaine, Revel and others; extra illustrated with 11 steel engraved topographical plates printed on chine, one leaf inscribed in gothic hand with the Prophecies of Isaiah in red, blue and gold inks, a presentation page with calligraphy and a full border with flowers and acanthus leaves of a burnished gold ground, both done by Langlume, in the style of a 15th century Book of Hours, with accompanying original watercolor of the Tiby wedding by Fauquet within an illuminated border by Langlume, with 22 (blank) genealogical pages, printed in colors with ruled centers surrounded by ornamental borders bound in below beginning of text; one barely perceptible chip to one of the grapevine cornerpieces on upper cover, 9 of the Johannot plates rather browned and offset to text, one border slightly soiled, otherwise extraordinarily fine copy of a unique work, text clean, fresh and bright, interior and exterior colors and gold shimmering and quite lovely delicate binding astonishingly well preserved. Phillip J. Pirages 59 - 105 2011 $15,000

Association – Tiby, C. J. T.

Bible. French - 1843 *Les Saints Evangiles.* Paris: L. Curmer, 1843. First edition thus; the handsomely designed presentation page at the front tells us that this beautiful object was assembled at the order of C. J. T. Tiby and given to his dear wife Anais Duret Tiby on 2 June 1855 as a "Souvenir of 25 years of Happiness", 260 x 184mm., 4 p.l. 552 pages; 2 p.l, 372 pages, 2 volumes bound in one, extremely elegant mid 19th century Neo-gothic presentation binding by Gruel-Engelmann in dark green silk velvet, covers mounted with delicately and elaborately carved boxwood frames after designs by Martin Riester, upper cover with wooden grapevine cornerpieces forming a large ogival central velvet panel featuring carved wooden vines forming the prominent monogram "A T" (for Anais Tiby) at middle, lower cover with central carved cross twined with grape vines arising from a cluster of leaves, flat spine with carved head and tailpieces, repeating grapevine motif and a carved boxwood banderolle at center on which the title appears in red, blue and gold; two pierced metal clasps at fore edge, saffron yellow moire silk endleaves, morocco hinges, edges very elaborately gauffered with gilt neo-gothic floral pattern on a red background, housed in handsome and very sturdy morocco backed wooden box lined with gold velvet, ornamental borders around text, numerous ornamental headpieces, initials and tailpieces (37 of these illuminated by hand), two chromolithographed titlepages, four woodcut titles for each Gospel, two engraved maps, two steel engraved frontispieces by Lecomte after Decaisne and by Cousin after Meissonier and 17 steel engraved plates after Tony Johannot by Cousin, Fontaine, Revel and others; extra illustrated with 11 steel engraved topographical plates printed on chine, one leaf inscribed in gothic hand with the Prophecies of Isaiah in red, blue and gold inks, a presentation page with calligraphy and a full border with flowers and acanthus leaves of a burnished gold ground, both done by Langlume, in the style of a 15th century Book of Hours, with accompanying original watercolor of the Tiby wedding by Fauquet within an illuminated border by Langlume, with 22 (blank) genealogical pages, printed in colors with ruled centers surrounded by ornamental borders bound in below beginning of text; one barely perceptible chip to one of the grapevine cornerpieces on upper cover, 9 of the Johannot plates rather browned and offset to text, one border slightly soiled, otherwise extraordinarily fine copy of a unique work, text clean, fresh and bright, interior and exterior colors and gold shimmering and quite lovely delicate binding astonishingly well preserved. Phillip J. Pirages 59 - 105 2011 $15,000

Association – Tinkler, S. H.

Gray, John 1866-1934 *Silverpoints.* London: Elkin Mathews and John Lane, 1893. First edition, no. 192 of 250 copies on Van Gelder; pages xxviii, (1) imprint, (1) blank, uncut lower and fore-edge, few black ink spots to fore-edge not affecting text, some foxing to endpapers, original green cloth with gilt design by Charles Ricketts, boards worn at top edge, gilt slightly faded, spine bumped, spots of black ink to upper and lower panels, but still very attractive copy, scarce, ownership inscription of S. H. Tinkler. Simon Finch Rare Books Zero - 321 2011 £2000

Association – Tipping, Thomas

Kettilby, Mary *A Collection of Above Three Hundred Receipts in Cookery, Physick and Surgery for the Use of all Good Wives, Tender Mothers and Careful Nurses.* London: for Richard Wilkin, 1714. First edition; (16), 218, (13) pages, contemporary paneled calf, neatly rebacked, light overall toning, minor marginal foxing and dampstaining, upper margin of A3 clipped and neatly restored, just grazing running head on verso, 3 leaves of early owners' recipes bound in at end, early ownership signature of Tho. Tipping, dated at several locations in Hertfordshire 1714-1739, later signature of Elizabeth Randall 1771, modern cookery bookplate, very nice in portfolio and leather backed slipcase. Joseph J. Felcone Inc. Fall Miscellany 2010 - 32 2011 $2800

Association – Todd, Albert May

Jacobus De Varagine 1230-1298 *The Golden Legend.* Kelmscott Press, 1892. One of 500 copies; 300 x 215mm., 3 volumes, handsome contemporary burgundy morocco by Fazakerley of Liverpool (stamp signed on front turn-ins), covers with three concentric frames each formed by single gilt rule and one thick and one thin black rule, outer frame with elaborate cascading cornerpieces formed by flowers, leafy volutes and small round tools, middle frame with gilt anular dot at each corner, corners of innermost panel with two entwined gilt leaves, raised bands decorated with gilt fillet and flanked by blood and gilt rule, spine panels with elegant gilt floral centerpiece, gilt turn-in, marbled endpapers, top edges gilt, other edges untrimmed, elaborate woodcut title (first designed by Morris) and first page with full white vine borders, 2 woodcut illustrations and 2 full borders designed by Edward Burne-Jones, large and small decorative woodcut initials, printer's device; decorative bookplate of Samuel Cross, with Tiffany engraved bookplate of Albert May Todd; endpapers (which are ot a part of the collation) with sparse and light mottling, five gatherings with perhaps half of their leaves faintly yellowed (a single leaf only that is more than slightly affected), otherwise only most trivial imperfections, extremely attractive, handsome bindings lustrous and with just negligible signs of use and text virtually immaculate. Phillip J. Pirages 59 - 240 2011 $9500

Association – Todd, Alexander

MacDonald, George 1824-1905 *Unspoken Sermons.* London: Strahan and Co., 1870. Fourth edition; half title, title in red and black, original royal blue cloth, dulled and rubbed, initial printed ad slip for Dora Greenwell's Colloquia Crucis, signature of Alexander Todd 1880. Jarndyce Antiquarian Booksellers CXCII - 71 2011 £85

Association – Tonkys, Thomas

Procopius, of Caesarea *Historiarum... Libri VIII...* Augsburg: D. Franck, 1607. Editio princeps of the Greek text; folio, (8), 376; 56, (84) pages, engraved title, dust jacket English (?Oxford) binding of brown calf, double gilt fillet on covers, spine with gilt ornament in compartments, chain mark on upper cover, from the library of the Earls of Macclesfield at Shirburn Castle, this the copy of Thomas Tonkys. Maggs Bros. Ltd. 1440 - 239 2011 £800

Association – Torphichen, Lord

Drexelius, Jeremias *The Considerations of Drexelius Upon Eternitie.* London: printed by John Redmayne, 1663. 18mo., old splashed calf, nicely rebacked in matching calf gilt with raised bands and lettering piece, pages (xxii), 358, engraved title printed at Cambridge by Roger Daniel and 8 woodcut plates, signature of Matthew Wren on engraved title and some marginal annotations, probably in his hand, some later annotations in another hand (probably that of Lord Torphichen, whose armorial bookplate is on pastedown), few pencilled marginal crosses, originally the copy of Matthew Wren (1585-1667), Christopher Wren's uncle. R. F. G. Hollett & Son Antiquarian Booksellers 175 - 389 2011 £650

Association – Tout, Mary

Block, Maurice *The Huntington Art Collections.* San Marino: Huntington Library, 1942. Large 8vo. original pictorial wrappers, pages 96 with numerous illustrations, loosely inserted 4 page ALS from Block to Mary Tout, historian recounting the history of the Huntington collection and its staff during the second world war. R. F. G. Hollett & Son Antiquarian Booksellers General Catalogue Summer 2010 - 55 2011 £35

Association – Towneley, John

Carr, John 1772-1832 *The Stranger in Ireland; or a Tour in the Southern and Western Parts of that Country in the Year 1805.* London: Richard Phillips, 1806. First edition; 4to., xiv, (2), 530, (2) pages, 16 sepia tinted aquatint plates (several folding), engraved map, uncut, modern morocco backed paper covered boards, endpapers bit foxed, internally clean and fresh, large unpressed copy, retaining most of original tissue guards, armorial bookplate of John Towneley, modern booklabel. Joseph J. Felcone Inc. Fall Miscellany 2010 - 64 2011 $2000

Clarke, James *A Survey of the Lakes of Cumberland, Westmorland and Lancashire...* printed for the author, 1789. Second edition; tall folio, full diced calf gilt with gilt rule borders, edges rather worn, rebacked in polished calf, gilt, one small scrape, pages xlii, 194, complete with 11 large folding plans and maps, few small creases or repairs to back of the maps as usual, excellent uncut, clean and sound with maps tipped on to guards for easier opening, several printed on heavy paper, armorial bookplate of John Towneley (re-laid). R. F. G. Hollett & Son Antiquarian Booksellers 173 - 239 2011 £1500

Association – Toynbee, A. J.

Stoddard, Lathrop *Scientific Humanism.* New York: Charles Scribner's Sons, 1926. First edition; original blue cloth, pages 177, fore-edges spotted, presentation copy, inscribed to Dr. A. J. Toynbee (historian) by the author and dated 1926, with compliments slip of publisher loosely inserted. R. F. G. Hollett & Son Antiquarian Booksellers 175 - 1298 2011 £35

Association – Trafton, A. G.

Bronte, The Sisters *Poems by Currer, Ellis and Acton Bell.* Philadelphia: Lea and Blanchard, 1848. First American edition; iv, (1), 13-176, (24) pages, original brown paper covered boards, printed paper spine label, outer brown paper worn along hinges and at tips of spine revealing lighter paper underneath, scattered foxing, else very nice, very tight in fragile original boards, 1848 ownership signature of A. G. Trafton. Joseph J. Felcone Inc. Fall Miscellany 2010 - 20 2011 $2800

Association – Traherne, Louisa

Mitford, Mary Russell 1787-1855 *Our Village: Sketches of Rural Character and Scenery.* London: Whittaker, Treacher, 1830. Fifth edition of volume I, new edition volume II; 2 volumes, uniformly bound in half calf, blocked in blind, gilt band, red labels, slightly rubbed, splits in hinges, 1 label chipped, booklabel of Louisa Traherne. Jarndyce Antiquarian Booksellers CLXC - 408 2011 £40

Association – Traubel, Horace

Whitman, Walt 1819-1892 *Leaves of Grass.* Philadelphia: McKay, 1891-1892. Deathbed edition; 8vo., portrait inserted, original heavy grey wrappers, printed yellow spine label The Garden copy, front lower wrapper split approximately 2 1/2 inches at joint, otherwise fine, unopened in half morocco slipcase, inscribed in Horace Traubel's hand "To Warren Fitzinger Jan. 7 1892 given by direction of Walt Whitman from his sick bed. H.L.T.". James S. Jaffe Rare Books May 26 2011 - 21628 2011 $35,000

Association – Travis, David

Taken by Design: Photographs from The Institute of Design 1937-1971. Chicago: University of Chicago Press, 2002. First edition; very fine in photo illustrated boards, issued without dust jacket, signed by a large number of photographers and some of the editors, among the signatures are Yasuhiro Ishimoto, Marvin E. Newton (twice), Barbara Crane, Ray K. Metzker, Joseph Jachna, Joseph Sterling (twice), Kenneth Josephson, David Travis, Keith Davis and quite a few others, unique copy. Jeff Hirsch Books ny 2010 2011 $750

Association – Tredegar, Evan Morgan, Lord

Sidney, Philip 1554-1586 *Astrophel and Stella. The Sonnets of Sir Philip Sidney.* London: Hacon and Ricketts (Vale Press), 1898. First edition, 10 copies only; 8vo., green and white patterned paper covered boards, olive green matt spine with printed paper label, pages 67, corners rubbed, spine very slightly stained, spine label slight chipped, endpapers slightly browned red inkstain to corner of rear cover, bookplate of Evan Morgan (Lord Tredegar) overall sound, near very good with bright clean text and illustrations. Any Amount of Books May 29 2011 - B27468 2011 $238

Association – Trotter

Lamy, Bernard *Traitez de Mechanique, de l'Equilibre des Solides et des Liqueurs...* Paris: Andre Pralard, 1679. First edition; 12mo., pages (ii) title and permission leaf, 263 (misprinted 163), (1), title with woodcut vignette, numerous woodcut diagrams to text, ornamental head and tailpieces, folding engraved plate, contemporary sprinkled calf, gilt panelled spine, sprinkled edges, minor repair to joints, otherwise excellent copy in contemporary condition, engraved Trotter bookplate, inscription noting purchase at auction in Jan. 1712. Simon Finch Rare Books Zero - 108 2011 £800

Association – Trotter, Eleanor

Dickens, Charles 1812-1870 *Dombey and Son.* London: Bradbury & Evans, 1848. First edition in book form, first state following all points in Smith; octavo, xvi, (1, errata), (1, blank), 624 pages, frontispiece, titlepage and 38 plates after Phiz, publisher's variant binding of moderate green fine diaper grain cloth, front and back covers entirely stamped in blind with thin double line border which enclosed a rectangular frame, frame contains a loop-scroll design in each corner and string of 16 beads runs along its inner edge, lineal globe shaped design stamped in center of both covers, spine stamped in blind with thick and thin band at top and thin and thick one at bottom, between which are three decorative rectangular panels, each containing heart shaped flower design in its center, spine lettered in gilt original pale yellow coated endpapers, spine very slightly faded, corners very slightly bumped with just tiny amount of board show through, otherwise binding is as fresh as one could possibly wish for, chemised in half green morocco slipcase with bookplate of William Self on chemise, bookplates of Gilfrid William Hartley and William Self, and Dickens Centenary Testimonial label on front pastedown, signature of original owners Eleanor Trotter September 11th 1859", signature of Kenyon Starling.   David Brass Rare Books, Inc.   May 26 2011 - 01693   2011 $13,500

Dickens, Charles 1812-1870 *The Personal History of David Copperfield.* London: Bradbury & Evans, 1850. First edition in book form, first state (following all but one of the twenty points listed in Smith), in the primary binding; octavo, xiv, (1, errata), (1, blank), 624 pages, frontispiece, titlepage and 38 engraved plates after Phiz, the single point not in its first state is page 132, line 20 "screamed" for "screwed", publisher's primary binding of moderate green fine diaper grain cloth, front and back covers entirely stamped in blind with thin double line border which encloses a rectangular frame, frame contains a loop-scroll design in each corner and string of 16 beads runs along its inner edge, lineal globe shaped design is stamped in center of both covers, spine stamped in blind with thick and thin band at top and a thin ad thick one at bottom, between which there are three decorative rectangular panels, each containing heart shaped flower design in its center, spine lettered in gilt, original pale yellow coated endpapers, The Kenyon Starling - William Self copy, original owner's signature "Eleanor Trotter/September 1812-1912) to front pastedown endpaper, spine very slightly darkened, few very minor and pale stains on cloth sides, corners very slightly bumped with little show through of boards, chemised in half green morocco slipcase with bookplates of Starling and Self on chemise,.   David Brass Rare Books, Inc.   May 26 2011 - 01692   2011 $14,500

Association – Troup, Francis William

MacDonald, George 1824-1905 *Cross Purposes and Other Stories.* London: Alexander Strahan, 1884. Reissue with additional title and half title; original grey green cloth blocked with Grolier pattern, spine slightly dulled, with signature of F. W. Troup Mar/1901.   Jarndyce Antiquarian Booksellers   CXCII - 148   2011   £30

MacDonald, George 1824-1905 *St. George and St. Michael.* London: Kegan Paul Trench & Co., 1883. Fourth edition; half title, frontispiece, 39 page catalog (10.83), original red cloth, bevelled boards (style F), dulled and slightly rubbed, but good, inscribed by author for Francis William Troup, signed twice by Troup.   Jarndyce Antiquarian Booksellers   CXCII - 173   2011   £850

Association – Troup, Margaret

MacDonald, George 1824-1905 *England's Antiphon.* London: Macmillan & Co., 1868. First edition; frontispiece, color engraved title and plates after Arthur Hughes, original royal blue cloth, borders in blind "The Sunday Library for Household Reading" devices blocked on front board and spine dulled, slightly chipped, binder's ticket of Burn & Co., inscribed by author for cousin Margaret MacDonald Troup.   Jarndyce Antiquarian Booksellers   CXCII - 109   2011 £1250

MacDonald, George 1824-1905 *Unspoken Sermons.* London: Alexander Strahan, 1867. (1866). First edition; half title, title in red and black, original royal blue cloth, little dulled, presentation copy from author for cousin "Robert & Margaret Troup...Dec. 7 1866", with Strahan alone in caps at tail of spine with two heavy rules & publisher's device in gilt on front boards.   Jarndyce Antiquarian Booksellers CXCII - 68   2011   £850

Association – Troup, Robert

MacDonald, George 1824-1905 *A Book of Strife.* London: printed for the author and to be had by Writing to Mr. Hughes 43 Beaufort Street, Chelsea, 1882. Second edition; tall 12mo., colophon leaf, original plain red cloth, marked, spine faded, inner hinges splitting, paper label browned and chipped, inscribed by author for cousin George MacDonald and with signature of Robt. G. Troup, husband of MacDonald's cousin, Margaret.   Jarndyce Antiquarian Booksellers CXCII - 222 2011   £1200

MacDonald, George 1824-1905 *Unspoken Sermons.* London: Alexander Strahan, 1867. (1866). First edition; half title, title in red and black, original royal blue cloth, little dulled, presentation copy from author for cousin "Robert & Margaret Troup...Dec. 7 1866", with Strahan alone in caps at tail of spine with two heavy rules & publisher's device in gilt on front boards.   Jarndyce Antiquarian Booksellers CXCII - 68   2011   £850

MacDonald, George 1824-1905 *Lilith: a Romance.* London: Chatto & Windus, 1895. First edition; half title, title in red and black, 32 page catalog (Oct. 1895), original plain black buckram, rather rubbed, signature on titlepage of Robert G. Troup, MacDonald's cousin by marriage. Jarndyce Antiquarian Booksellers   CXCII - 319   2011   £200

MacDonald, George 1824-1905 *Phantastes: a Faerie Romance for Men and Women.* London: Arthur C. Fifield, 1905. New edition; half title, frontispiece, illustrations by Arthur Hughes, piece torn from margin pages 221-22 by careless opening, original dark blue cloth, spine dulled, inner hinge cracking, inscribed for Robert Troup from Uncle Edward & Aunt Winifred.   Jarndyce Antiquarian Booksellers   CXCII - 13   2011   £160

Association – Trowbridge, Charles

Kelly, George *Craig's Wife a Drama.* Boston: Little Brown, 1926. First edition; 8vo., pages 174, very nice, tight copy, inscribed by author to Josephine Williams who played the part of Mrs. Harold in the NY production, also signed by rest of the cast - Annie Sutherland, Crystal Herne, Arthur Shaw, C. Stewart, Eleanor Marsh, Charles Trowbridge, Josephine Hull, J. A. Curtis, Nelan Jaap, Arline Alcine & Mary Gildea, also inscribed by the producer, Rosalie Stewart to whom the play was dedicated.   Second Life Books Inc.   174 - 213   2011 $2000

Association – Troyle, Elizabeth

Waterland, Daniel *A Criticial History of the Athanasian Creed.* Cambridge: University Press for Corn. Crownfield, 1724. 8vo., pages xxiv, 533, (xi), Francis Hoffman head-piece on page 1, contemporary calf untooled spine, boards panelled in blind (Cambridge style), board edges decorative roll gilt, all edges red speckled, pale blue and white sewn endbands, replacement lettering piece, dampstain to lower corner at beginning and end, touch of wear to corners, repairs to spine ends, later ink inscription "Richard Troyle his book 1774" and below "Elizabeth Troyle" on final f.e.p. (inverted), from the collection of Christopher Ernest Weston 1947-2010.   Unsworths Booksellers   24 - 56   2011   £250

Association – Troyle, Richard

Waterland, Daniel *A Criticial History of the Athanasian Creed.* Cambridge: University Press for Corn. Crownfield, 1724. 8vo., pages xxiv, 533, (xi), Francis Hoffman head-piece on page 1, contemporary calf untooled spine, boards panelled in blind (Cambridge style), board edges decorative roll gilt, all edges red speckled, pale blue and white sewn endbands, replacement lettering piece, dampstain to lower corner at beginning and end, touch of wear to corners, repairs to spine ends, later ink inscription "Richard Troyle his book 1774" and below "Elizabeth Troyle" on final f.e.p. (inverted), from the collection of Christopher Ernest Weston 1947-2010.   Unsworths Booksellers   24 - 56   2011   £250

Association – Trubner, Nicholas

Catlin, George 1796-1872 *O'Kee-Pa: a Religious Ceremony and Other Customs of the Mandans.* London: Trubner and Co., 1867. First edition; small 4to., vi, (2), 52 pages plus iii page "Folium Reservatum, 13 chromolitho-graphed plates after Catlin by Simonau & Toovey, publisher's purple cloth, gilt, all edges gilt, binding lightly soiled and faded, extremities lightly worn (spine ends more so), occasional minor foxing, very good, fragile to find in fine condition, presentation copy inscribed by publisher Nicholas Trubner to Thomas Scott.   Joseph J. Felcone Inc.   Fall Miscellany 2010 - 22   2011 $20,000

Association – Trumpp, Marilyn

Berry, Wendell *Findings (Poems).* Iowa City: Prairie Press, 1969. First edition; 8vo., pages 63, fine in dust jacket, scarce, with ownership signature of Marilyn Trumpp, August. 1969, noting it was a gift from book designer Carroll Coleman.   Second Life Books Inc.   174 - 44   2011 $300

Association – Tudor, Tasha

First Poems of Childhood. New York: Platt & Munk Publishers, 1967. First edition; 8vo., dark grey cloth spine with grey cloth, gold vignette on front cover and gold lettering on spine, full color pictorial dust jacket with some surface rubbing to rear cover of wrapper, signed in full by Tasha Tudor on titlepage, 46 numbered pages with every page illustrated to enhance verses, illustrations both in black and white in full color for an overall pictorial presentation.   Jo Ann Reisler, Ltd.   86 - 254   2011 $275

Association – Turbervill, J. P.

Churchill, Charles *Poems.* London: printed for John Churchill and W. Flexney, 1769. Fourth edition; (4), 369, (1), (2) pages ads, half title; (4), 330 pages, half title, 8vo., full contemporary calf, gilt decorated spines, red and olive green gilt labels, some rubbing to gilt, slight crack to upper joint volume I, signature of J. Churchill at foot of final leaf of text, volume II with armorial bookplates of William Salmon and J. P. Turbervill, very good, attractive. Jarndyce Antiquarian Booksellers CXCI - 119 2011 £200

Association – Turner, B. B.

Poole, Sophia *The Englishwoman in Egypt: Letters from Cairo, Written During a Residence There in 1842, 3 and 4. (with) Second Series... Letters written 1845-46.* London: Charles Knight & Co., 1844-1846. 3 volumes, half title volume II, frontispiece volume I, plates volumes I & II, original dark green cloth, elaborate borders in blind, spines lettered in gilt, name erased from leading pastedown volume I, otherwise near fine set, bookplates of B. B. Turner. Jarndyce Antiquarian Booksellers CXCI - 574 2011 £1100

Association – Turner, E. A.

Maitland, Julia Charlotte *Cat and Dog or Memoirs of Puss and the Captain.* London: Grant & Griffith, 1856. Third edition; frontispiece + 3 plates, 8 pages ads, original olive green morocco cloth, borders in blind, pictorially blocked and lettered in gilt, leading hinges with small neat repairs, bit dulled and slightly affected by damp, signed E. A. Turner in contemporary hand, good. Jarndyce Antiquarian Booksellers CLXC - 198 2011 £85

Association – Turner, Henry Whitelock

Foster, Joseph *The Royal Lineage of Our Noble and Gentle Families Together with their Paternal Ancestry (Volume 3).* Aylesbury: privately published by Hazell, Watson and Viney, n.d., 4to., original blue cloth over bevelled boards, neatly recased with new endpapers, pages (iv, family register), xvi, 367-462, interleaved, register and first 3 blank leaves filled with genealogy of Whitelock and Turner in mss., armorial bookplate of Revd. Henry Whitelock Turner relaid. R. F. G. Hollett & Son Antiquarian Booksellers 175 - 462 2011 £225

Association – Turner, Joseph

Shelley, Percy Bysshe 1792-1822 *The Cenci.* Italy: for C. and J. Ollier, London, 1819. First edition one of 250 copies; 8vo., pages xiv, 104, occasional light spotting, bound without initial blank in later morocco by Ramage, upper and lower boards filleted in gilt, spine with raised bands and compartments delineated in gilt, gilt lettering, inner dentelles, marbled endpapers, top edge gilt, others uncut, bookplate of Joseph Turner. Simon Finch Rare Books Zero - 353 2011 £3500

Association – Turner, Robert Samuel

Thackeray, William Makepeace 1811-1863 *Ballads.* London: Smith, Elder & Co., 1879. Illustrated edition; this edition was given to C. R. Ashbee by family friend and bibliophile, Robert Samuel Turner, 8vo., pages 323, illustrations, pasted on reverse of frontispiece is 5 x 5 inch square of light blue paper upon which are written just over 12 lines of prose in blue ink and underneath which, in Ashbee's hand, are pencilled the words "Autograph of Thackeray", original publisher's cloth little used, snagged at head of spine, slightly shaken and scuffed, very good. Any Amount of Books May 26 2011 - A49450 2011 $587

Association – Tyringham, William Backwell

Luard, John *Views in India, Saint Helena and Car Nicobar. Drawn from Nature and on Stone.* London: J. Graf, printer to her Majesty, 1838. unpaged, lithographic title, 60 lithographic plates mounted on india paper, folio, contemporary crimson morocco over boards, spine tooled and lettered gilt, 5 raised bands, bound by Harrison Bookbinder (Pall Mall, small stamp to front blank), moderate foxing to text leaves and plate mounts, boards rubbed, some discoloration and scuff marks to front board, spine with few minor chips, edgewear, still very good; bookplate of William Backwell Tyringham, neat stamp of A. J. Combridge, Bombay and Madras. Kaaterskill Books 12 - 124 2011 $5250

Association – Tyson, Michael

Bolingbroke, Henry St. John, 1st Viscount 1678-1751 *Letters on the Study and Use of History.* London: printed for A. Millar, 1752. New edition; 8vo., pages 481, (iii), errata slip pasted at foot of page 481 covering up signature "Hh", contemporary sprinkled calf, boards double rule gilt bordered, board edges zig zag decorative roll in blind, all edges red speckled, red and white sewn endbands, light spotting, small marginal stain to few leaves, corners touch worn, but of scuffing elsewhere, armorial bookplate of Michael Tyson, from the collection of Christopher Ernest Weston 1947-2010. Unsworths Booksellers 24 - 143 2011 £75

Association – Tytler, Alex Fraser

Addison, Joseph 1672-1719 *Dialogues Upon the Usefulness of Ancient Medals Especially in Relation to the Latin and Greek Poets.* Glasgow: printed by R. Urie, 1751. 8vo., pages 267 (i) 4, contemporary polished tan calf, spine single rule gilt, red lettering piece gilt, board edges decorative roll in blind, all edges lightly red sprinkled, red and white sewn endbands, marginal browning to first few leaves, joints cracking, extremities bit rubbed, few small marks, ink inscription "Alex Fraser Tytler", from the collection of Christopher Ernest Weston 1947-2010. Unsworths Booksellers 24 - 65 2011 £250

Association – Upward, Allen

Pound, Ezra Loomis 1885-1972 *Ripostes of Ezra Pound.* London: Stephen Swift & Co., 1912. First edition, first issue; 8vo., original gray cloth, covers lightly soiled, spine darkened, some offsetting as usual to endpapers, otherwise very good, presentation copy inscribed to Allen Upward from author Sept. 1913, publisher's ads at end are present in this copy,.   James S. Jaffe Rare Books   May 26 2011 - 16359 2011 $6500

Association – Urie, D. M. L.

MacDonald, George 1824-1905 *Robert Falconer.* London: Hurst & Blackett, circa, 1895. New edition; frontispiece, contemporary half red morocco, spine slightly faded, bookplate of D. M. L. Urie, very good.   Jarndyce Antiquarian Booksellers   CXCII - 62 2011   £160

Association – Vail, Laurence

Miller, Henry 1891-1980 *Tropic of Cancer.* Paris: Obelisk Press, 1934. First edition; 8vo., pages 323, (1) imprint, internally fresh, pale blue grey pictorial wrappers, printed in blue and black from a design by Maurice Kahane, extremities rubbed, spine cracked in places, old repair to upper panel, black morocco backed clamshell box, lettered gilt, amusing pencil inscription, initialled L. (Laurence Vail?), increasingly difficult to find in acceptable original condition.   Simon Finch Rare Books   Zero - 255 2011   £9500

Association – Vaillant, Leon

Forskal, Petrus *Descriptiones Animalium, Avium, Amphibiorum, Piscium Insectorum Vermium... (bound with) Icones Rerum Naturalium quad In Itinere Orientali.* Hauniae: Molleri, 1775-1776. Folding engraved map, 4to., pages 19, (1), xxxlv, 164, contemporary quarter calf (some rubbing, wear to edges, small abrasions to spine, front cover detached, text is quite clean), 43 engraved plates (8 are folding, light marginal foxing to last few plates) of which 20 are of plants, 1 of a bird, the remaining plates are of marine animals, from the collection of J. Van der Hoeven, Leon Vaillant the George Vanderbilt Foundation.   Raymond M. Sutton, Jr.   May 26 2011 - 42066 2011 $7000

Association – Vallis, V.

Australian Poetry. Australia: 1942-1970. First edition; 1942-1948, 1951-1952, 1954, 1955, 1956, 1958, 1961-1963, 1965-1968, 1970, 20 volumes, all save one with dust jackets, all very good, 1955 presentation copy inscribed by V. Vallis, one of the contributors.   I. D. Edrich   May 26 2011 - 84608 2011 $419

Association – Vallognes

Angeli, Pietro *Syrias hoc est Expeditio illa Celeberrima Christianorum Principium Qua Hierosolyma Ductu Goffredi Blionis Lotharinguiae...* Florence: F. Giunto, 1591. First edition; 4to., (24), 406 pages, italic type, woodcut initials, 18th century English calf, triple gilt fillet on covers, little rubbed, 17th century French inscription of Vallognes on titlepage, from the library of the Earls of Macclesfield at Shirburn Castle.   Maggs Bros. Ltd.   1440 - 8 2011   £950

Association – Van Court, John H.

Bible. Polyglot - 1809 *Liber Psalmorum Hebraice.* London: Cambridge, 1809. First Printing of any part of the Bible in Hebrew in America; 12mo, (8), (1)-495, (1, blank) pages, with translation and notes in Latin, full contemporary calf, front board attached but loose, lacking part of the backstrip, back cover with some leather lacking, corners and edges chipped, leaves bit toned, some foxing, as usual for American books of this era, old pencil inscription on front free endpaper, very good, extremely scarce, housed in custom calf clamshell, undated gift inscription from Rev. John H. Van Court (1793-1867) to the Rev. John Dorrance (1800-1861).   Heritage Book Shop   Holiday 2010 - 65 2011 $20,000

Association – Van Der Hoeven, J.

Forskal, Petrus *Descriptiones Animalium, Avium, Amphibiorum, Piscium Insectorum Vermium... (bound with) Icones Rerum Naturalium quad In Itinere Orientali.* Hauniae: Molleri, 1775-1776. Folding engraved map, 4to., pages 19, (1), xxxlv, 164, contemporary quarter calf (some rubbing, wear to edges, small abrasions to spine, front cover detached, text is quite clean), 43 engraved plates (8 are folding, light marginal foxing to last few plates) of which 20 are of plants, 1 of a bird, the remaining plates are of marine animals, from the collection of J. Van der Hoeven, Leon Vaillant the George Vanderbilt Foundation.   Raymond M. Sutton, Jr.   May 26 2011 - 42066 2011 $7000

Association – Van Pelt, D. N.

Darwin, Charles Robert 1809-1882 *A Naturalist's Voyage. Journal of Researches into the Natural History and Geology of the Countries visited During the Voyages of H.M.S. "Beagle" Round the World...* London: John Murray, 1890. Later edition; small 8vo., xi, 500 pages, frontispiece, additional engraved portrait loosely inserted, original green cloth, gilt stamped cover ornament and spine title, ANS by Darwin glued to verso of titlepage and dedication page, ink stamp of D. N. Van Pelt, very good, with Darwin's signature written on slip of paper 200 x 72mm, mounted inside volume, additional engraved portrait of Darwin loosely inserted, from the Bern Dibner reference library, with Burndy bookplate, inscription " to my dear grandson Nevill Forbes, from E.F.".   Jeff Weber Rare Books   161 - 106 2011 $5000

Association – Vandale, Earl

Thompson, Albert W. *The Story of Early Clayton, New Mexico.* Clayton: Clayton News, 1933. First edition; 8vo., brief inscription by Earl Vandale, a book collector, fine, housed in cloth four point clamshell case with leather label on spine with titles stamped in gold. Buckingham Books May 26 2011 - 26281 2011 $2500

Association – Vane, Harry

Tryon, Thomas *The New Art of Brewing, Ale and Other Sorts of Liquors.* London: printed for Tho. Salusbury, 1691. 12mo., (6), 138 pages with ad leaf and contents leaf immediately following titlepage, general paper browning throughout, gutter of titlepage frayed (not touching printed surface), numeral entered in red ink in early hand on title, ms. inscription in ink on flyleaf, signed by Henry Cope recording the gift of the book to him by Sir Harry Fane (Vane) on January 4th 1699 with 4 pages of ms. notes" in ink apparently by Henry Cope on prelim blanks and 19th century armorial bookplate of Alfred Chadwick, contemporary ruled sheep, neatly appropriately rebacked and labeled, good copy. John Drury Rare Books 153 - 161 2011 £1250

Association – Vansittart, Ann May

Dodd, William 1729-1777 *The Visitor, by Several Hands, Published by William Dodd...* London: Printed for Edward and Charles Dilly, 1764. First edition; 12mo., 2 volumes, 6.5 x 4 inches, pages (10), 310; (2), 307, index (5), frontispiece in volume 1, contemporary full brown calf, gilt lined with 5 raised bands, spine unlettered, or most probably lacking spine labels, faint gilt volume numbers, hinges slightly tender, neat name at head of titlepages "Ann May Vansittart 1825", overall very good examples of scarce work. Any Amount of Books May 29 2011 - A34287 2011 $255

Association – Vaz-Ferreira, Raul

Azara, Felix De *Essais sur l'Histoire Naturelle des Quadrupedes de la Province du Paraguay...* Paris: Charles Pougens, 1801. First French edition; 8vo., pages lxxx, 366; 2 (5-) 499, contemporary calf backed boards (missing half titles, corners worn, 1 bumped, spines scuffed, a 1 1/2 inch split to front edge of spine, calf on ends of spine perished, small, old sticker on heel of spines, ink number on front flyleaf and blank, small handstamp on titles, scattered tanning and light foxing to text, sometimes heavier in volume 2, short marginal tear to 2 leaves, with gilt lettering and gilt decorations on spines, marbled page edge, rare, the copy of Raul Vaz-Ferreira with his handstamp. Raymond M. Sutton, Jr. May 26 2011 - 45608 2011 $2000

Association – Velis, George

Steinbeck, John Ernst 1902-1968 *Sweet Thursday.* New York: Viking, 1954. Intermediate edition, with red and black titlepage, unstained top edge red dot at lower corner rear cover and testimonials under the Halsman photo on dust jackets rear panel; x, 273 pages, cloth, spine canted, dust jacket price clipped, light chipping at spine ends and corner, few dampstains, inscribed George "Sonny Boy" Velis, Velis operated the restaurant and bar in Montgomery that is the subject of the entire chapter 23 in Sweet Thursday as well as a paragraph in Travels with Charley. Joseph J. Felcone Inc. Fall Miscellany 2010 - 112 2011 $450

Association – Veydt, L.

Commines, Philippe De, Sieur D'Argenton 1445-1511 *Les Memoires.* A Leide: Chez les Elzeviers, 1648. Derniere edition; 140 x 80 mm., 12 p.l., 765, (19) pages, very pretty early 19th century dark green morocco by Thouvenin (stamp-signed at tail of spine), covers with large frame formed by decorative rules and dense, complex cornerpieces in blind, this frame punctuated with a dozen thick gilt dots and enclosing an intricate lozenge in blind and gilt featuring elegant flowers, fronds and seashells, as well as many small tools and curls, raised bands, spine compartments with small, simple gilt lozenge at center of very elaborate quatrefoil fleuron in blind, gilt turn-ins, salmon pink watered silk endpapers, all edges gilt; with four tondo portraits; engraved bookplate of Bibliotheque L. Veydt; spine uniformly sunned to pleasing olive brown, first gathering with quarter inch dampstain to tail edge margin, occasional minor foxing or other trivial imperfections, especially appealing copy in fine condition, clean, fresh leaves, very lustrous binding showing only most superficial wear. Phillip J. Pirages 59 - 30 2011 $1250

Association – Vickery, Willis

Cervantes Saavedra, Miguel De 1547-1616 *History of the Valorous and Witty Knight Errant, Don Quixote of the Mancha.* London: printed for R. Scot, T. Basset, J. Wright, R. Chiswell, 1675. Early edition of The Thomas Shelton translation in two parts; small folio, (8), 137; (5), 138-214, 216-244, 244-273 leaves, full red morocco, boards and spine tooled and lettered in gilt boards with and attractive art nouveau style tooling with center lozenge containing the gilt initials "FB" (for Fletcher Battershall), gilt dentelles, lower front dentelle with small gilt bat device with initial "B", all edges gilt and rough cut, edges and outer hinges bit rubbed, small bit of splitting to front joint at top and bottom of spine, some minor paper repairs to fore edge margin of titlepage and following leaf as well as final leaf, 2 bookplates belonging to Willis Vickery and binders Fletcher and Maude Battershall, old catalog clippings tipped to front flyleaf by previous owner, overall very good. Heritage Book Shop Holiday 2010 - 18 2011 $5000

Association – Victoria, Queen of Great Britain

Martin, Theodore *The Life of His Royal Highness the Prince Consort.* London: Smith, Elder, 1879. First volume is sixth edition from 1879 and the second a fourth edition from 1877; stout 8vo., 2 volumes, original publisher's brown cloth lettered gilt at spine, about 1100 pages in all, both very good condition, with one small gathering slightly sprung in first volume, signed presentation from Queen Victoria to George Searle.   Any Amount of Books   May 26 2011 - A39542   2011 $604

Association – Vines, Sidney

Whitman, Walt   1819-1892   *Leaves of Grass.*   Camden: Author's Edition, 1876. Fifth edition, third printing, second issue, one of 600 copies signed by author; 8vo., original cream quarter calf and corners, marbled boards, gilt lettering, 2 portraits, this copy inscribed to English botanist Sidney H. Vines, from the author, binding little soiled and rubbed, some slight foxing, very good, much nicer than usual for this fragile binding, from the collection of Samuel Charters.   The Brick Row Book Shop   Bulletin 8 - 18   2011 $9000

Association – Waddington, T.

Moseley, Henry Nottidge *Notes by a Naturalist.* London: John Murray, 1892. New edition; map, portrait, woodcuts, half title, index, 4 pages ads, tear in half title, pencil notes on endpaper and half title by previous owner, T. Waddington, original dark blue half cloth, lighter blue cloth sides, boards dulled.   Jarndyce Antiquarian Booksellers   CXCI - 340   2011   £45

Association – Wake, Edward

Iamblichus   (Greek)... *De Vita Phythagorica Liber... Notisque...*   Amsterdam: widow of S. Petzold & C. Petzold, 1707. First separate edition; 2 parts, 4to., (16 (including engraved frontispiece), 219, (17), 93, (1) pages, 2 columns, title printed in red and black, contemporary English panelled calf, gilt spine, red morocco lettering piece, fine, large copy, armorial bookplate of Edward Wake, Christ Church, from the library of the Earls of Macclesfield at Shirburn Castle.   Maggs Bros. Ltd.   1440 - 115   2011   £700

Association – Wakeman, Stephen

Emerson, Ralph Waldo   1803-1882   *Miscellanies: Embracing Nature, Addresses and Lectures.*   Boston: Phillips, Sampson, 1856. First edition; original brown cloth, the Stephen H. Wakeman copy with his bookplate, moderate wear to spine tips and corners, few scrapes to spine, numerous pencil markings, very good.   Charles Agvent   Transcendentalism 2010 - 16   2011 $250

Association – Waldie, John

Dalyell, John Graham   *Musical Memoirs of Scotland with Historical Annotations and Numerous Illustrative Plates.*   London: William Pickering and Edinburgh: Thomas G. Stevenson, 1849. First edition; 4to., plates, original half morocco gilt with marbled boards, hinges and edges rubbed, pages xii, 300, top edge gilt, engraved title and 40 engraved plates, few tinted, engraved armorial bookplate of John Waldie of Hendersyde, fine, clean copy.   R. F. G. Hollett & Son Antiquarian Booksellers   175 - 348   2011   £450

Association – Waldman, Anne

Charters, Ann   *The Portable Beat Reader.*   New York: Viking, 1992. First edition; 600+ pages, fine in fine dust jacket, exceptional copy, this copy belonged to Nelson Lyon, inscribed to him or signed and dated by William Burroughs, Allen Ginsberg, Gregory Corso, Ed Sanders, Michael McClure and Anne Waldman.   Ken Lopez Bookseller   154 - 12   2011 $1250

Association – Waldron, Laurence Ambrose

Rutter, John   *Delineations of Fonthill and its Abbey.*   London: (Shaftesbury) Charles Knight for the author, 1893. First edition; xvi, 127 pages; 4to., 13 full page engraved plates, 3 exquisitely hand colored and 20 x 26 inch foldout plan with hand colored walks and further 15 woodcut vignettes in text, additional engraved plate of the abbey from the south west, original endpapers, rear endpaper torn, bookplate of Laurence Ambrose (Larky) Waldron (1858-1823), excellent, clean text, foldout plan, one 3 inch closed tear at fold.   Any Amount of Books   May 26 2011 - A76292   2011 $1426

Association – Waley-Cohen, Bernard

Cuneo, Terence   *The Mouse and His Master. The Life and Work of Terence Cuneo.*   New Cavendish Books, 1977. Limited, signed edition, no. 70 of 250 copies; oblong large 4to., original quarter faux morocco gilt with suede boards, matching slipcase, pages 244, illustrations, mostly in color, very special copy, with 3 ALS's from Cueno loosely inserted, a number of signatures laid in against relevant illustrations and portraits, including Lord Leverhulme and Sir Bernard Waley-Cohen, Lord Mayor of London, both with accompanying letters loosely inserted), Co. Sir Richard Glyn, Sir Lionel Denny and Robert Runcie, the letters are all addressed to Harold Ogden, managing Director of Broughton Moor, Slate Quarries, Coniston and signatures assembled by him.   R. F. G. Hollett & Son Antiquarian Booksellers   General Catalogue Summer 2010 - 96   2011   £1500

Association – Walker, Emery

Morris, William 1834-1896 *The Hollow Land and Other Contributions to the Oxford and Cambridge Magazine.* London: Chiswick Press, 1903. First edition; printed on handmade paper using Morris' Golden typeface, in black with the titles and shoulder titles printed in red, pages (viii) (blanks), iv, 334, (7) (blanks), crown 8vo., original quarter blue grey cloth, printed label (spare label tipped in), pale blue boards lightly soiled and edges rubbed, cloth faded and little worn at backstrip head, free endpapers lightly browned, rough trimmed, front flyleaf inscribed by Emery Walker to Margaret Dickinson.   Blackwell Rare Books   B166 - 194   2011   £500

Association – Walker, T. Shadford

Guevara, Antonio De *Vita Di M. Avrelio Imperadore.* Venice: Bartolomeo Imperador and Francesco Veneziano, 1543. 160 x 103mm., 8 p.l., 132, (2) leaves, fine contemporary Roman red morocco Apollo and Pegasus medallion binding done for Giovanni Battista Grimaldi by Marc Antonio Guillery, (genuine Apollo and Pegasus binding) covers with gilt frame formed by two widely spaced fillets with lobes interlaced at ends and sides, space between fillets decorated with broad foliate curls, small floral tools, inner pane of each board with gilt titling above a horizontal oval Apollo and Pegasus plaquette centerpiece showing Pegasus atop black painted heights of Parnassus and Apollo racing his chariot (drawn by two straining steeds) across steep terrain with reins and whip held aloft and caps fluttering behind, plaquette with gilt motto in Greek in the collar above and below vignette, spine (very expertly rebacked) with four thin and three thick raised bands decorated with gilt rope pattern or plain rules (this being original backstrip?), newer (perhaps 19th century) endpapers, all edges gilt (apparently some remarkably skillful restoration at one or more corners and edges, perhaps some gold added, as well as to the chariot part of the plaquettes); woodcut printer's device on , morocco bookplate and separate gilt monogram of Robert Hoe as well as inscription and vellum bookplate of Swedish collector Thore Virgin, ownership inscription of J. T. Payne dated 1850; covers with half dozen insignificant tiny dark spots, titlepage faintly soiled, thin light brown stain just at top edge of leaves, small wormhole at upper inner margin (text not affected), occasional minor stains, other trivial imperfections, but no defects that are even remotely serious and in general really excellent specimen of a very special binding, text fresh and leather quite lustrous; also from the collection of bibliophile Johannes Gennadius, Liverpool oculist T. Shadford Walker and Swedish collector Rolfe Wistrand.   Phillip J. Pirages   59 - 2   2011 $35,000

Association – Walker, William

Specimens of the Early English Poets. London: printed for Edwards, 1790. First edition; 190 x 127mm., 5 p.l., 323 pages, extremely pleasing etruscan style calf in the style of and quite probably by, Edwards of Halifax, covers with gilt metope and pentaglyph border, wide inner frame of stencilled palmettes, sprinkled central panel featuring at middle a stained obelisk tool draped with four slender fronds on either side, this centerpiece painted over in red, recently and beautifully rebacked by Courtland Benson to replicate original (flat) spine with all over gilt lattice design, black titling label, marbled endpapers, turn-ins and all edges gilt; with attractive fore-edge painting, very probably by Edwards, apparently showing Walton Hall near Wakefield; large paper copy, armorial bookplate of Thomas Walker, that bookplate as well as verso of endpaper inscribed in ink "Wm. Walker", former dated August 1848 and later "Wilsick, July 1848", titlepage with painted armorial laid down beneath imprint; minor pitting (as inevitable with acid treated calf), few leaves with small faint stains, otherwise fine, expertly restored binding with lustrous covers and bright gilt, text especially clean, fresh and bright with very spacious margins.   Phillip J. Pirages   59 - 39   2011 $1400

Association – Waller, Captain

Victoria, Queen of Great Britain 1819-1901 *Leaves from the Journal of Our Life in the Highlands from 1848 to 1861.* London: Smith, Elder and Co., 1868. First edition thus; 4to., pages xvii, 198, frontispiece, 6 engraved plates and 2 color chromolithographs and numerous vignettes, original publisher's red cloth highly decorated and illustrated on covers and spine in gilt with some black patterning, illustrations, inscribed by Queen Victoria for Captain Waller, R.E, sound, clean attractive about very good copy with slight wear at lower hinge of spine and spine ends with corners rubbed.   Any Amount of Books   May 26 2011 - A66337   2011 $604

Association – Walmsley, Gilbert

More, Henry *An Account of Virtue: or Dr. Henry More's Abridgement of Morals.* London: printed or B. Tooke, 1701. Second edition; 8vo., (16), 264 pages, panelled sheep, from the library of the Earls of Macclesfield at Shirburn Castle, inscription of Bibliothecae Gilberti Walmsley.   Maggs Bros. Ltd.   1440 - 148   2011   £400

Association – Walmsley, Vincent

Campbell, Thomas 1777-1844 *Gertrude of Wyoming and Other Poems.* London: Longman Hurst, Rees, Orme & Brown, 1816. Sixth edition; half title, frontispiece, slightly foxed, uncut in original light brown paper boards, paper label, some very slight wear to lower following hinge, else exceptional copy in its original state; contemporary signature, modern booklabel of Vincent Walmsley and earlier ownership inscription of Lt. Lloyd.   Jarndyce Antiquarian Booksellers   CXCI - 347   2011   £75

Association – Walters, Maurice

Lange, Jakob E. *Flora Agaricina Danica.* Copenhagen: 1935-1940. 200 chromolithographed plates, 4to., pages (3), xxiv, 90; 105; 96; 119; 105 (12), binder's buckram, fine, plates are superb, the copy of Maurice Walters, inserted A.S. postcard from author to Walters, proof for volume 4 titlepage, order form for subscription and two letters from publication office to Mr. Walters.   Raymond M. Sutton, Jr. May 26 2011 - 25548   2011 $1500

Association – Walton, E. Russell

Backhouse, James *Upper Teesdale, Past and Present.* London: Simpkin, Marshall etc. and Barnard Castle; w. R. Atkinson, 1896.   First edition; original pictorial boards, little soiled and worn, hinges cracked, pages (iv), 87, (ii), 8 plates and map, flyleaves browned or spotted, upper joint cracked, signature of E. Russell Walton of Cotherstone on half title. R. F. G. Hollett & Son Antiquarian Booksellers   General Catalogue Summer 2010 - 1320   2011   £35

Association – Wanamaker, Rodman

Ryley, Samuel William *The Itinerant; or Memoirs of an Actor. (with) The Itinerant in Scotland.* London: Sherwood Neely & Jones, 1817. 1816. 1827. Second edition of volumes 1-3 and First edition of volumes 4-6 and 7-9; 12mo., in all 9 volumes, three quarter calf, spine gilt, some rubbed along extremities, untrimmed (rear cover separate on volume 1), armorial bookplate of Rodman Wanamaker on each front pastedown.   Second Life Books Inc.   174 - 271 2011 $900

Association – Warburton, N.

De La Ramee, Louise 1839-1908   *Pascarel.* Leipzig: Bernhard Tauchnitz, 1873. 2 volumes in 1, contemporary half vellum, gilt spine and trim, spine dulled, slightly rubbed, good, sound copy, bound without half titles, booklabel of N. Warburton.   Jarndyce Antiquarian Booksellers   CLXC - 695 2011   £35

Association – Ward, Catherine

Austin, William *A Specimen of Sketching Landscapes in a Free and Masterly Manner with a Pen or Pencil; Exemplified in thirty Etchings done from original drawings of Lucatelli after the Life in and about Rome.* by the author in George Street, Hanover Square..., 1781.   4 pages, 30 etchings, some signed Austin F (or Fecit) Lucatelli, inscribed by Frederick Finden for Catherine Ward, very good, contemporary half calf with red morocco label, dark blue glazed paper boards which are rubbed and marked, marginal stain to one plate but clear of image and little old and faint waterstaining the inner lower corner, again not affecting images. Ken Spelman Rare Books   68 - 13 2011   £2200

Association – Wardington, Lord

Bible. English - 1901 *The Boke off the Revelacion off Sanct Jhon the Devine Done into Englysshe by WilliamTyndale.* Ashendene Press, 1901. One of 54 copies; 218 x 165 mm., 1 p.l., xxx, (i) pages, plus 6 blank leaves at front and three at back, original limp velum dyed dark green, gilt titled flat spine, custom made folding cloth box with gilt titling, initials and chapter headings printed in red, booklabel "From the Books of Crosby Gaige", bookplate of Lord Wardington, little loss of dark green present along fore edges of binding, in all other ways a faultless copy. Phillip J. Pirages   59 - 74   2011 $4250

Association – Wardour, Arundell

Drake, Francis *The History and Antiquities of the City of York, from its Origin to the Present Times.*   York: printed by A. Ward, 1785.   3 volumes, 12mo., pages (iv), 400 + folding engraved plan frontispiece and 17 other engraved plates; (ii), 402 + 2 other extending engraved plates; (iv), 292 + folding engraved map and one other folding engraved plate, contemporary polished tan calf, spine single rule gilt, red and green lettering and numbering pieces gilt, board edges obliquely broken fillet roll in blind, a lemon, fawn and white sewn endbands, some toning and spotting edges of few folding plates little darkened and frayed, touch of wear to endcaps, front joint of volume I cracked, armorial bookplate of Lord Arundell Wardour, from the collection of Christopher Ernest Weston 1947-2010.   Unsworths Booksellers   24 - 90 2011   £300

Association – Waring, James

Hutchinson, William *An Excursion to the Lakes in Westmoreland and Cumberland, with a Tour through Part of the Northern Counties in the Years 1773 and 1774.*   J. Wilkie and W. Charnley, 1776. First edition; near contemporary half calf with marbled boards, neatly rebacked to match, original spine label re-laid, pages 382, (iv), 2 engraved text vignettes, contemporary inscription of James Waring on title, few pencilled marginalia by later owner William Ball of Glen Rothay.   R. F. G. Hollett & Son Antiquarian Booksellers   173 - 603 2011   £295

Association – Warner, Henry Lee

Dods, Mary Diana *Tales of the Wild and the Wonderful.* London: Hurst, Robinson and Co., Edinburgh: A. Constable and Co., 1825. First edition; scarce, 8vo., pages xii, 356, extremely bright and fresh, all edges marbled, contemporary calf, upper and lower boards ruled in gilt, spine blind-stamped with gilt spots and decorative pattern at head and foot, green morocco lettering piece with gilt lettering, marbled endpapers, very light shelfwear only, engraved bookplate of Henry Lee Warner and small bookseller's sticker to front pastedown, ownership inscriptions dated 1827 and 1853 to front free endpaper, fine.   Simon Finch Rare Books Zero - 228   2011   £1200

Association – Warner, Sylvia Townsend

Powys, Theodore Francis *The Left Leg.* London: Chatto & Windus, 1923. First edition; 8vo., pages 311, inscribed presentation from dedicatee, Sylvia Townsend Warner to Angus (Davidson), with a quatrain also inscribed to same, three quarter red morocco, spine gilt in compartments, little browned on fore edge, else fine. Second Life Books Inc. 174 - 262 2011 $713

Association – Warren, C. Henry

Smith, Dodie *I Capture the Castle.* Boston: Little Brown, 1948. First edition; 8vo., 343 pages, illustrations by Ruth Steed, signed presentation from author to friend C. Henry Warren, full dark blue morocco titles and decoration to spine gilt, rule to boards gilt, marbled endpapers, 5 raised bands at spine, excellent condition.   Any Amount of Books   May 26 2011 - A71762 2011 $1761

Association – Warren, John

Stanhope, Philip Henry Stanhope, Earl of *Life of William Pitt...* London: John Murray, 1879. New edition; 3 volumes, half titles, frontispieces in volumes I and II, finely bound by Riviere & Son in full tree calf, gilt borders and dentelles, raised bands, gilt compartments, maroon and brown morocco labels, spines slightly sunned, armorial bookplates of John Warren, very handsome set.   Jarndyce Antiquarian Booksellers   CXCI - 25 2011 £165

Association – Warren, S.

Collins, Wilkie 1824-1889 *The Dead Secret.* London: Chatto & Windus, 1902. New edition; final ad leaf, original light pink original pictorial paper wrappers, odd mark and crease, stationer's stamp of S. Warren, Ipswich.   Jarndyce Antiquarian Booksellers   CXCI - 127 2011 £40

Association – Waterhouse, W. T.

Prescott, William Hickling 1796-1859 *History of the Conquest of Mexico.* London: Swan Sonnenschein & Co., 1906. 2 maps, one handwriting facsimile plate, pages xxiv, 713, 8vo., contemporary tree calf, boards with gilt roll border, spine in five compartments with raised bands, green morocco lettering piece, compartments with gilt floral centre pieces and corner vine sprays, marbled edges and endpapers, gilt prize stamp (Cambridge Local Examinations, Southport Centre) to front board, prize bookplate inside, binder's ticket of Edward Howell, Liverpool, spine gently sunned, near fine, award to W. T. Waterhouse of First Class Honours in History and Geography, 1908.   Blackwell Rare Books   B166 - 83 2011 £95

Prescott, William Hickling 1796-1859 *History of the Conquest of Peru.* London: Swan Sonnenschein & Co., 1907. New edition; pages xxiv, 510, (2), 8vo., contemporary tree calf, boards with gilt roll border, spine in five compartments with raised bands, green morocco lettering piece, compartments with gilt floral center-pieces and corner vine sprays, marbled edges and endpapers, gilt prize stamp (Cambridge Local Examinations, Southport Centre) to front board and prize bookplate inside, binder's ticket of Edward Howell, Liverpool, spine gently sunned, near fine, awarded to W. T. Waterhouse for First Class Honours in English, 1908.   Blackwell Rare Books   B166 - 84 2011 £95

Southey, Robert 1774-1843 *The Life of Nelson.* Bickers and Son, 1902. 12 woodburytype plates and one folding map, one illustration, pages xiv, (ii), 351, 8vo., contemporary green polished calf, prize binding of Southport Centre Cambridge Local Examinations (awarded to W. T. Waterhouse in 1907), spine gilt just slightly faded, red morocco lettering piece by B. Howell, Liverpool, near fine.   Blackwell Rare Books   B166 - 101 2011 £125

Association – Watson, Anne

Wordsworth, William 1770-1850 *Poems.* London: printed for Longman, Hurst, Orme, 1807. First edition, one of 500 copies Printed; with cancels D11-12 in volume I and B2 in volume II, volume I has half title and erratum leaf H8, volume II has half title, sectional half title leaf B1 and first state of sheet F9(i) in volume 2 with misprint "Thy function" on page 98, last line; 2 volumes 8vo., original drab boards with pink paper covered spines as issued, contemporary ownership inscription to Anne Watson in volume I, with pencil ownership signature on titlepage, bookplates of Simon Nowell-Smith and his wife, light foxing, covers slightly chipped and worn but very good.   James S. Jaffe Rare Books   May 26 2011 - 21014 2011 $27,500

Association – Watson, James

Watson, Elizabeth L. *Houses for Science.* (with) *Landmarks in Twentieth Century Genetics.* Plainview: Cold Spring Harbor Laboratory Press, 1991. First edition; 4to., xiii, 351 pages, fine in near fine dust jacket, signed and inscribed and dated by Elizabeth Watson and James Watson.   By the Book, L. C.   26 - 90 2011 $275

Association – Watson-Taylor, Simon

Mesens, E. L. T. *Troisieme Front/Poemes de Guerre...* London: London Gallery editions, 1944. First edition, no. 31 of 500 copies; 8vo., pages 47, (1) limitation, 6 full page illustrations in text, uncut, crisp, fresh copy, publisher's wrappers, green, text in black to upper side and spine, slightly faded and discolored at edges, dust jacket with light shelfwear, chipped at head and foot of spine, dated presentation inscription for Simon Watson-Taylor to half title and signature to limitation page.   Simon Finch Rare Books   Zero - 340 2011 £350

Association – Watt, A. P.

Dickens, Charles 1812-1870 *Letters of Charles Dickens to Wilkie Collins 1851-1870.* London: James R. Osgood, McIlvaine & Co., 1892. Half title, original dark blue cloth, dulled, inner hinges cracking, inscribed by A. J. Watt for George MacDonald.   Jarndyce Antiquarian Booksellers   CXCII - 337 2011   £380

MacDonald, George 1824-1905 *David Elginbrod.* London: Hurst & Blackett, 1863. First edition; 3 volumes, half titles, original red coarse morocco grained cloth, plain blind borders on boards, gilt lettered spines, dulled with slight wear to spines, inner hinges weakening, endpapers replaced volume I, A. P. Watt's bookplate in each volume.   Jarndyce Antiquarian Booksellers   CXCII - 19 2011   £1650

MacDonald, George 1824-1905 *The Flight of the Shadow.* London: Kegan Paul, Trench, Trubner & Co., 1891. First edition; half title, frontispiece by Gordon Browne, 32 page catalog, original red cloth, bevelled boards (style E), spine faded with slight wear at head and tail, inscribed by author for A. P. Watt with Watt's bookplate.   Jarndyce Antiquarian Booksellers   CXCII - 295 2011   £2000

MacDonald, George 1824-1905 *Heather and Snow.* London: Chatto & Windus, 1893. First edition; 2 volumes, half titles, 32 page catalog (March 1893), original dark blue morocco grained cloth, very good, bright copy, inscribed by author for A. P. Watt, with Watt's bookplate.   Jarndyce Antiquarian Booksellers   CXCII - 305 2011   £2500

MacDonald, George 1824-1905 *There and Back.* London: Kegan Paul, Trench, Trubner & Co., 1891. Second edition; half title, frontispiece, original red cloth bevelled boards (Style F), spine faded, otherwise very good, signed presentation from author to A. P. Watt, with Watt's bookplate.   Jarndyce Antiquarian Booksellers   CXCII - 284 2011   £1500

MacDonald, George 1824-1905 *What's Mine's Mine.* London: Kegan Paul, Trench & Co., 1886. First edition; half titles, 44 page catalog (3.86) volume III, some spotting caused by endpapers, original red fine bead grained cloth, black borders and device on back board, gilt spine lettering, slightly dulled, rubbing on leading hinge volume I, but very good, inscribed by author for A. P. Watt", with Watt's bookplate.   Jarndyce Antiquarian Booksellers   CXCII - 271 2011   £2500

Association – Watting, Maurice

Crane, Walter 1845-1915 *Renascence. A Book of Verse.* London: Elkin Mathews, 1891. First edition, no. 6 of 25 copies (plus 3 for author and 15 for America) o Japanese vellum; 4to., pages (xiv) 164 (1) imprint, (19) blank, with errata slip, numerous illustrations, unopened, some light rubbing to margin of titlepage, otherwise internally fine, loosely inserted into original parchment backed folder of drab boards with ties, gold lettering to spine, upper and lower ties worn, folder extremities rubbed, folds cracked in places, old paper tape mend to lower fold, booklabel of Maurice Watting on inner front cover of folder.   Simon Finch Rare Books   Zero - 308 2011   £750

Association – Weaver, William

Calvino, Italo *Le Cosmicomiche.* Torino: Einaudi, 1965. First edition; 8vo., original pale green cloth, dust jacket, fine, jacket with few short tears, presentation copy inscribed by Calvino to William Weaver, the English translator of Cosmicomics, with a number of discreet pencil annotations by Weaver.   James S. Jaffe Rare Books   May 26 2011 - 20757 2011 $5000

Association – Webster, Erwin

Hornaday, William T. *Two Years in the Jungle.* New York: Charles Scribner's, 1885. Octavo, xxii, 512 pages, frontispiece, 2 folding maps, plates, index, original tan-mustard pictorial cloth, stamped in black and gilt, spine bottom showing wear, rubbed, ownership signature of E(rwin) W. Webster, Ansonia, Conn. 1886, initials of SJW, very good, scarce.   Jeff Weber Rare Books   163 - 177 2011 $400

Association – Weckherlin, Rodolph

Proclus Diadochus *Elementa Theologica et Physica...* Ferrara: D. Mammarello, 1583. 4to., ff. (3), 69 device at end, modern half calf, with Roldolph Weckherlin manuscript ex-libris, from the library of the Earls of Macclesfield at Shirburn Castle.   Maggs Bros. Ltd.   1440 - 171 2011   £3000

Association – Wedgwood, Frances Emma

Carlyle, Thomas 1795-1881 *Sartor Resartus.* Boston: James Munroe; Philadelphia: James Kay: Pittsburg: John I. Kay, 1837. Excellent rebound in half red brown calf, spine gilt, ownership signature of F. E. (Frances Emma) Wedgwood 11 July 1837".   Jarndyce Antiquarian Booksellers   CXCI - 109 2011   £480

Association – Wells, H. G.

Dollard, John *Criteria for the Life History with Analyses of Six Notable Documents.* New Haven: Yale University Press for the Institute of Human Relations, 1935. First edition; 8vo., original publisher's grey cloth with printed spine label, pages v, 288, loosely inserted is good 1935 TLS from author to H. G. Wells, spine label very slightly soiled, otherwise very good+.   Any Amount of Books   May 29 2011 - A45555   2011 $230

Association – Werner, Arno

Baskin, Leonard *Birds and Animals.* Gehenna Press, 1972-1974. First edition; square 4to., 65 original wood engravings, full red pigskin with gilt cat profile on front cover by Arno Werner, very fine copy in beautiful Werner binding, half morocco folding box, unique copy, specially bound by Werner, with his pencil annotation on prelim leaf, binder's own copy with his bookplate.   James S. Jaffe Rare Books   May 26 2011 - 20923   2011 $9500

Tate, Allen *The Hovering Fly and Other Essays.* Cummington: Cummington Press, 1949. One of only 12 copies on Van Gelder paper with original drawing and woodcuts hand colored, specially bound and signed by author and artist, out of a total edition of 245; 8vo., woodcuts by Wightman Williams, full russet morocco with inlaid hand colored panel on front cover by Arno Werner, very fine, in half morocco folding box, binder's copy, signed by Arno Werner.   James S. Jaffe Rare Books   May 26 2011 - 11551   2011 $15,000

Association – West, Eli

Skidmore, Thomas *The Rights of Man to Property! Being a Proposition to make It Equal Among the Adults of the Present Generation.* New York: printed for the author by Alexander Ming Jr., 1829. First edition; 12mo., 405, (1) pages, original calf, sides stamped "Rights of Man to Property!", binding rubbed and slightly worn, some foxing, very good, early bookplate of Eli West of Carthage, Jefferson County NY.   M & S Rare Books, Inc.   90 - 388   2011 $7500

Association – West, Herbert

Hughes, Richard *A High Wind in Jamaica.* London: Chatto & Windus, 1929. First edition; one of 150 deluxe copies, signed by author, 8vo., 284 pages, fine, buckram backed printed boards, contemporary bookplate of bookseller Herbert F. West, spine trifle faded, some light foxing, very nice, clean copy.   Second Life Books Inc.   174 - 185   2011 $525

Association – Westminster, Duke of

MacDonald, George 1824-1905 *Alec Forbes of Howglen.* London: Hurst & Blackett, circa, 1875. Half title, frontispiece, bound without ads in half light brown morocco with coronet on spine, armorial bookplate of Duke of Westminster, 1884, very good, handsome copy.   Jarndyce Antiquarian Booksellers   CXCII - 37   2011   £85

MacDonald, George 1824-1905 *Robert Falconer.* London: Hurst & Blackett, 1869. Half title, frontispiece, handsome half brown morocco with coronet, marbled endpapers and edges, bookplate of Hugh, Duke of Westminster 1884 with corner marked.   Jarndyce Antiquarian Booksellers   CXCII - 59   2011   £150

Association – Weston, Brett

Armitage, Merle *Brett Weston: Photographs.* New York: E. Weyhe, Publisher, 1956. First edition; clean, very near fine copy, very small stain to bottom of first two pages in bright near fine dust jacket with small chip and couple of tears to top of spine, as well as some other very minor wear, signed and inscribed by Weston, additionally, a vintage silver gelatin self portrait of Weston is affixed to front endpaper, image signed by Weston in negative, unique copy.   Jeff Hirsch Books   ny 2010 2011 $5000

Association – Weston, Christopher Ernest

Addison, Joseph 1672-1719 *Dialogues Upon the Usefulness of Ancient Medals Especially in Relation to the Latin and Greek Poets.* Glasgow: printed by R. Urie, 1751. 8vo., pages 267 (i) 4, contemporary polished tan calf, spine single rule gilt, red lettering piece gilt, board edges decorative roll in blind, all edges lightly red sprinkled, red and white sewn endbands, marginal browning to first few leaves, joints cracking, extremities bit rubbed, few small marks, ink inscription "Alex Fraser Tytler", from the collection of Christopher Ernest Weston 1947-2010.   Unsworths Booksellers   24 - 65   2011   £250

Allen, Thomas *A New and Complete History of The County of York.* London: published by I. T. Hinton, 1828. 6 volumes, 8vo., pages (iii)-viii, ii, 359 + engraved title and frontispiece, ii, 431 + engraved title, frontispiece and 12 other plates; ii, 443 + engraved title frontispiece and 7 other plates; ii, 532 + engraved title, frontispiece and 22 other plates; ii, 488 + engraved title, frontispiece and 28 other plates; ii, 404 + engraved title, frontispiece and 67 other plates, contemporary tan half calf, four flat banded spines gilt with blind double rule open centred compartments, green lettering and numbering pieces gilt boards double ruled in blind with green 'swirl' marbled paper sides, matching 'made' endpapers, all edges gilt "French Shell marbled, pink and white sewn flat endbands, light age toning, little offsetting from plates, extremities little rubbed, volume 6 joints just cracking at ends, boards scuffed, bindings blindstamped "I.L" within a 3/8 inch diameter circle at head of front board of all volumes, from the collection of Christopher Ernest Weston 1947-2010.   Unsworths Booksellers   24 - 66   2011   £360

Athanasius, Alexandrini Archiepiscopi *Omnia Quae Extant Opera.* Parisiis: Apud Michaelem Sonnium, 1581. Folio, pages (xii), 699 (lxxxvii), contemporary blind tooled pigskin, spine simply ruled, boards panelled with a stylised wheatsheaf roll and two sizes of medallion rolls, paper title label in MS ink at head of spine, inner chamber of boards blind ruled, pink and white sewn endbands, original brass staples but modern clasps, toned bit of spotting, boards marked and bit rubbed at edges, spine darkened, ink inscription "Collegii Caroli iv Paerum No. 17" and lower down "Collegii Soctii Jesu Pragae and S. Clementen Bibliothecae Minoris", from the collection of Christopher Ernest Weston 1947-2010.   Unsworths Booksellers   24 - 1   2011   £750

Barrow, Isaac *A Brief Exposition of the Lord's Prayer and the Decalogue.* London: M. Flesher for Brabazon Aylmer, 1681. 8vo., pages (vi), 269, (iii) + engraved portrait frontispiece; later dark blue polished turkey, spine decorative roll gilt in compartments with small corner and centre pieces, lettered in gilt direct, boards gilt rule bordered with small stylised floweret in corners, board edges and turn-ins 'zig-zag' decorative roll gilt, crimson turkey doublures with 'dentelle' gilt border, blue 'made' end flyleaves, all edges gilt, pale blue and white sewn endbands (suggestions here of James Brindley binding), faint dampmark to fore-edge, joints rubbed, splitting, endcaps and corners worn, "Shelburne" armorial bookplate, and "Holland House" heraldic bookplate on doublure, from the collection of Christopher Ernest Weston 1947-2010.   Unsworths Booksellers   24 - 4   2011   £175

Barrow, Isaac *A Treatise of the Pope's Supremacy.* London: Miles Flesher for Barbazon Aylmer, 1680. Small 4to., pages (viii), 428, (ii), 49, (i), engraved portrait frontispiece, contemporary mottled calf, boards blind double rule bordered, board edges "morse code" rule gilt, early 21st century rebacked and restoration by CEW, little faint spotting, old leather crackled, from the collection of Christopher Ernest Weston 1947-2010.   Unsworths Booksellers   24 - 3   2011   £275

Barrow, Isaac *Several Sermons Against Evil Speaking.* London: printed for Brabazon Aylmer, 1678. 8vo., pages (viii), 243, (i), 140, (iv), contemporary speckled calf, boards blind ruled, board edges 'broken rule', gilt, text block edges densely red sprinkled, blue and white sewn endbands, late 20th century blind ruled and unlettered calf reback, touch of minor spotting, leather rubbed at extremities, corners just worn, contemporary ink inscription "Rd Scott", ink inscription "Jonathan Scott 1746 Betton", also "J. A. Milner/Shrewsbury/1889", from the collection of Christopher Ernest Weston 1947-2010.   Unsworths Booksellers   24 - 2   2011   £275

Barry, George *The History of the Orkney Islands...* Edinburgh: printed for the author by D. Willison, 1805. 4to., pages (ii) viii, 509 + engraved frontispiece, 1 folding map, 19 other engraved plates, later tan calf, spine panelled in gilt with 'crowned dolphin" center pieces, dark brown lettering piece gilt, boards double rule gilt bordered with decorative roll gilt within, board edges and turn-ins decorative roll gilt, 'Dutch-curl' 'made' endpapers and all edges matching, brown and white sewn flat endbands, some minor spotting, little foxing to plates, spine bit rubbed, front joint cracking at foot, subscriber's copy of John Spottiswoode of Spottiswoode with his armorial gilt stamped on both boards, from the collection of Christopher Ernest Weston 1947-2010. Unsworths Booksellers   24 - 67   2011   £400

Barwick, Peter *The Life of the Reverend Dr. John Barwick, D.D.* London: printed by J. Bettenham, 1724. Large paper copy, 8vo., pages (xxiv), 552, (xl) + 2 engraved portrait frontispieces, contemporary calf, gilt panelled spine, orange lettering piece gilt, boards panelled in blind (Cambridge style), board edges decorative roll gilt, 'Dutch-comb' 'made' endpapers, all edges red and grey sprinkled green and white sewn endbands, rubbed at extremities, spine darkened, joints cracked but strong, endcaps worn "James Affleck" book label, contemporary ink inscription "Eliz. Dolben" and above "James Affleck", mid 20th century provenance note by Peter B. G. Binnall, from the collection of Christopher Ernest Weston 1947-2010.   Unsworths Booksellers   24 - 6   2011   £200

Barwick, Peter *Vita Johannis Barwick.* London: Typis Gulielmi Bowyer, 1721. Large paper copy; from the collection of Christopher Ernest Weston 1947-2010, 8vo., pages (lxvi), 464 (44) + 2 engraved portrait plates, contemporary sprinkled calf, gilt panelled spine, boards "Harleian style" gilt bordered board edges, decorative roll gilt, 'Dutch-comb' 'made' endpapers, all edges gilt, mid 1990's conservation/restoration by Weston, little surface wear to leather. Unsworths Booksellers   24 - 5   2011   £250

Bawden, William *Dom Bloc. A Translation of the Record Called Domesday, so Far as Relates to the County of York... and to the Counties of Middlesex (et al) and Gloucester.* Doncaster: printed by W. Sheardown, 1809-1812. 2 volumes, 4to., pages (iv) iv, 31, (i), 628, 61, (iii); (iv), 26, 76, (3)-82, 62, 72, 2, 4, 3, i), 4, 6, contemporary tan half calf, spines double rule and single broken rule gilt orange and red lettering and numbering pieces gilt, place and date gilt direct at foot, boards single rule gilt bordered with "nonpareil" marbled sides, matching 'made' endpapers, dark olive green sewn flat endbands, volume I in mid 198's calf reback, little light spotting titlepage toned, some marginal pencil marks, boards bit scuffed, corners and volume 2 spine rubbed, armorial bookplate of Edward Balme Wheatley-Balme, from the collection of Christopher Ernest Weston 1947-2010.   Unsworths Booksellers   24 - 68 2011   £300

Bede, the Venerable *Historiae Ecclesiasticae Gentis Anglorum...* Cantabrigiae: Typis Academicis, 1722. Folio, pages (xvi), 823 (xv) + 2 engraved plates and 1 folding map, early 19th century sprinkled an polished calf, spine fully gilt, red lettering piece gilt boards decorative roll gilt bordered, board edges decorative roll gilt, turn-ins decorative roll gilt, "French Shell" "made" endpapers, all edges 'Gloster' marbled, 3 colour (blue, red & white), sewn endbands, early 21st century conservation by Chris Weston, some browning to initial leaves and plates, little minor spotting elsewhere, few old scratched to old boards, signed binding with ticket of Nichols, Wakefield, unidentified armorial bookplate, and below, the later bookabel of Eric Poole, from the collection of Christopher Ernest Weston 1947-2010.   Unsworths Booksellers   24 - 7   2011   £1500

Bible. English - 1653 *The Holy Bible containing ye Old and New Testaments.... (with, bound at end of volume 2: The Psalms of David in Meeter).* London: printed by Iohn Field, 1653. Edinburgh: i.e. Amsterdam: printed by Evan Tyler, 1653; The first work divided after Dd2, 12mo., ff. (314); (282), 89, (i), contemporary red morocco, unlettered spine panel gilt, boards fully gilt in Scottish 'Herringbone' style, board edges decorative roll gilt, turn-ins decorative roll gilt, 'Dutch floral gilt' endpapers to volume 1, 'dutch-comb' endpapers to volume 2, all edges gilt, pale blue and white sewn endbands, text rubricated throughout, browned, some soiling and staining, one leaf in second work with corner torn away affecting a dozen lines of text, 20th century MS poem to last text leaf in volume 2 signed "Phineas Fletcher", binding rubbed, joints splitting, endpapers worn, spines darkened, old repair to head volume i, ink ownership inscription "MARY ADAMS/1769", from the collection of Christopher Ernest Weston 1947-2010.   Unsworths Booksellers   24 - 9 2011   £700

Bible. English - 1836 *New Testament of Our Lord and Saviour Jesus Christ: Published in 1526.* London: Samuel Bagster, 1836. 8vo., pages iv, 98 ff., ii-ccxvii + engraved titlepage and frontispiece, later calf, spine panelled in blind, lettered in 'Old English' type and dated at foot both in gilt, boards elaborately panelled in blind with rules and decorative rolls, central panel double rule diced board edges decorative roll n blind, turn-ins elaborately decorated with rolls tooled in blind, 'Peacock swirl' 'made' endpapers, all edges gilt & gauffered, 3 color (blue white & pink), sewn flat endbands, maroon silk page marker, frontispiece foxed, spine quite rubbed, joints split and boards loose, armorial bookplate of York Minster /Library / Bequeathed by the Rev. R. A. Talbot 1993" , from the collection of Christopher Ernest Weston 1947-2010.   Unsworths Booksellers   24 - 12 2011   £95

Bible. Greek - 1750 (Greek). *Novum Testamentum.* Glasguae: in Aedibus R. Urie, 1750.   Large paper copy, 8vo., pages (iv), 572 i.e. formula (pi)2, A-Bbbb4, Cccc2 = 228 leaves, text in Greek, contemporary crimson morocco, spine panel gilt, black lettering piece gilt, boards broad decorative roll gilt bordered, board edges and turn-ins obliquely broken rule gilt, 'Antique Spot' 'made' endpapers, all edges gilt, pink and white sewn endpapers, little light spotting, joints touch rubbed, spine slightly darkened, armorial bookplate William Johnston Esq, from the collection of Christopher Ernest Weston 1947-2010.   Unsworths Booksellers   24 - 10 2011   £300

ASSOCIATION COPIES

Blackwell, Thomas *Memoirs of the Court of Augustus.* London: printed for A. Millar, 1764. third edition; 3 volumes, 4to., pages (vi) 384 + 9 engraved plates of roundel portraits, viii, 456 + 8 engraved plates of roundel portraits; (vi) 573 (xlix) + 8 engraved plates of roundel portraits, contemporary sprinkled and polished tan calf, spines panel gilt, red and black lettering and numbering pieces gilt, boards double rule gilt bordered, board edges 'zig-zag' decorative roll in blind, turn-ins obliquely striped with dark stain, all edges lightly red sprinkled, red and white sewn endbands, lightly toned and spotted, joints cracking but strong, spine ends bit worn with small repairs to headcaps, armorial bookplate of Jolliffe, from the collection of Christopher Ernest Weston 1947-2010. Unsworths Booksellers 24 - 70 2011 £300

Bolingbroke, Henry St. John, 1st Viscount 1678-1751 *Letters on the Study and Use of History.* London: printed for A. Millar, 1752. New edition; 8vo., pages 481, (iii), errata slip pasted at foot of page 481 covering up signature "Hh", contemporary sprinkled calf, boards double rule gilt bordered, board edges zig zag decorative roll in blind, all edges red speckled, red and white sewn endbands, light spotting, small marginal stain to few leaves, corners touch worn, but of scuffing elsewhere, armorial bookplate of Michael Tyson, from the collection of Christopher Ernest Weston 1947-2010. Unsworths Booksellers 24 - 143 2011 £75

Bowen, Emanuel *Britannia Depicta; or Ogilby Improv'd: Being a Correct Coppy of Mr. Ogilby's actual Survey of all ye Direct & Principal Cross Roads in England and Wales.* London: printed and sold by Tho. Bowles, 1736. Fourth edition; 4to., pages 5, (iii) 273 + engraved titlepage, contemporary reversed calf, boards double rule bordered in blind with decorative roll adjacent joint border board edges 'zig-zag' roll in blind, all edges lightly red sprinkled, red and white sewn endpapers, green silk page markers, 2009 reversed calf reback with original red lettering piece relaid by Chis Weston, bit of toning and spotting, corners little worn, from the collection of Christopher Ernest Weston 1947-2010. Unsworths Booksellers 24 - 71 2011 £1000

Bryant, Jacob *A New System, or an Analysis of Ancient Mythology: Wherein an Attempt is Made to Divest Tradition of Fable.* London: printed for P. Elmsly, 1774. 1774. 1776; 3 volumes, 4to., pages (iii)-xx (ii) 516 + 8 engraved plates, vii, (i), 537, (i) + 18 engraved plates; (iii)-viii, 601, (i) + 3 engraved maps, 4 engravings included within letterpress, contemporary sprinkled tan calf, spines panel gilt with lozenge and wheel centered compartments alternating, red lettering and numbering pieces, gilt board edges 'milled' decorative roll gilt, pink sewn endbands, spotted and bit toned, plates offset, rubbed, joints worn and splitting, front board of volume 1 lost, armorial bookplate "Eardley" from the collection of Christopher Ernest Weston 1947-2010. Unsworths Booksellers 24 - 73 2011 £360

Bryant, Jacob *Observations and Inquiries Relating to Various Parts of Ancient History...* Cambridge: printed by J. Atchdeacon, printer to the University, 1767. Mixed issue, page 7 has the press figure '2' but page 62 has no press figure and page 63 has '3', errata leaf comes at beginning; 4to., pages (ii) iiii, (v), 324, 7 engraved extending plates, contemporary tan calf, spine panel gilt, red lettering piece gilt, boards double rule gilt bordered, board edges 'zig zag' decorative roll in blind, all edges densely red sprinkled, pink and white sewn endbands, (gathering *1 - 4 leaves of prelims) not bound in this copy (apparently not infrequent error), light toning and spotting, closed tear to one leaf, through but not affecting text, small wormtrack in lower corner at beginning, rubbed at extremities, joints cracked, little loss from headcap, armorial bookplate of "Dacre", from the collection of Christopher Ernest Weston 1947-2010. Unsworths Booksellers 24 - 72 2011 £300

Burnet, Gilbert, Bp. of Salisbury 1643-1715 *An Exhortation to Peace and Union. A Sermon at St. Lawrence - Jury at the Election of Lord Mayor of London on the 29th of September 1681.* London: printed for Richard Chiswell, 1681. Small 4to., pages (iv) 35 (i), disbound, first and last leaves bit soiled, faint dampmark to upper corner, now bound in quarter calf, red morocco lettering piece lettered vertically down, boards sided out with marbled paper by Chris Weston, contemporary (not Burnet's) ink inscription, from the collection of Christopher Ernest Weston 1947-2010. Unsworths Booksellers 24 - 15 2011 £95

Burnet, Gilbert, Bp. of Salisbury 1643-1715 *An Exposition of the Thirty-nine Articles of the Church of England.* London: printed for Ri. Chiswell, 1705. Third edition; contemporary vellum, spine blind ruled, 19th century dark red lettering piece gilt, boards panelled in blind with large open central lozenge centre piece, pink and white sewn endbands, little spotting in places, vellum soiled, slight cracking at joint ends, ink inscription "C. J. Hardey/May 18th 1838", is lightly scored out in ink in favour of "Robt. Hardey Hull 1840", from the collection of Christopher Ernest Weston 1947-2010. Unsworths Booksellers 24 - 16 2011 £150

Burnet, Gilbert, Bp. of Salisbury 1643-1715 *Bishop Burnet's History of His Own Time.* London: printed for Thomas Ward, Printed for the editor, by Joseph Downing... and Henry Woodfall, 1724. 1734; Large paper copy, 2 volumes, folio, pages (xvi), 836, (xx); (xxii), 765, (i), Frances Hoffman headpieces in volume 2 on pages i, 1. 139, 309 & 729, later mottled calf, boards gilt double rule bordered, board edges obliquely-broken fillet gilt, 'Dutch-comb' 'made' endpapers, all edges densely red sprinkled, mid 20th century calf reback with original red and green lettering and numbering pieces relaid, bit of light browning, slightly rubbed, old boards little scratched and flaked, all boards have unidentified ducal armorial blindstamped impression (motto" Finem Respice) volume 2 top edge gilt verso has contemporary ink inscription, "The Original Manuscript of both volumes of this/ History will be deposited in the Cotton Library by/ T. Burnett" within red ink double rule border, from the collection of Christopher Ernest Weston 1947-2010. Unsworths Booksellers 24 - 17 2011 £400

Burnet, Gilbert, Bp. of Salisbury 1643-1715 *Memoires of the Lives and Actions of James and William Dukes of Hamilton and William Dukes of Hamilton and Castleherald... (half title) The History of the Church and State of Scotland, the II Part.* London: J. Grover for R. Royston, 1677. Large paper copy, folio, pages (xxii), 436 (xvi) + 1 engraved plates, 3 engraved portraits within text, contemporary calf boards panelled in blind, central having marbled effect, board edges decorative roll gilt, all edges blue 'swirl' marbled, 'Dutch-comb' 'made' endpapers, early 1990's calf reback and corners by Chris Weston, little dust soiling and browning, old leather scraped and scratched, unidentified armorial bookplate, from the collection of Christopher Ernest Weston 1947-2010. Unsworths Booksellers 24 - 14 2011 £300

Cave, Henry *Antquities of York.* London: published by R. Ackermann, York: printed at the Office of G. Peacock, 1813. 1807; 2 works bound together as 1, 4to., pages iv, (ii), 31, (i) + engraved titlepage and 40 engraved plates (iv), iii, (i), 10, (ii) (xxiv) + engraved titlepage and 34 engraved plates, contemporary empanelled calf boards double bordered with decorative roll of consecutive polished pinheads gilt, central 'French Shell' 'made' endpapers, all edges marbled as per outer panels, green & vermillion sewn flat endbands, mid 20th century calf reback, some browning and foxing, few plates significantly but mostly light, old boards scuffed and little rubbed around edges, armorial bookplate of Joseph Robinson Pease, from the collection of Christopher Ernest Weston 1947-2010. Unsworths Booksellers 24 - 75 2011 £1000

Charlton, Lionel *The History of Whitby and of Whitby Abbey... (with) History and Antiquities of Scarborough and the Vicinity.* York: printed by A. Ward; William Blanchard for E. Bayley, successor to J. Schofield, 1779. 1798; 4to., pages xvii, (i), 379, (i) + engraved extending plan of Whitby as frontispiece and 3 other engraved plates, xi (i), 352, (viii) + engraved frontispiece, 2 engraved plans and 2 other engraved plates, early 19th century marbled half calf, 6 compartmented spine divided by back to back 'acanthus' roll gilt, two black lettering pieces gilt, boards sided with 'French Shell' marbled paper, red and white sewn endbands, early 1970's calf rebacked with old backstrip relaid by John Henderson, intermittent foxing, titlepage creased and spotted, corners touch worn, boards scuffed, from the collection of Christopher Ernest Weston 1947-2010. Unsworths Booksellers 24 - 76 2011 £600

Clarkson, Christopher *The History of Richmond, in the County of York.* Richmond: printed for the author by Thomas Bowman, 1821. Large paper copy, 4to., pages iv, 446, cxxxii, + engraved titlepage and extending engraved plan, frontispiece and 16 other engraved plates, contemporary marbled half calf, spine double rule gilt, red lettering piece gilt, date gilt direct at foot, boards double rule bordered in blind with 'French Shell" marbled paper sides, uncut, pink & white sewn flat endbands, calf reback, backstrip relaid & corners by Jenny Aste, decorative 1979, plates foxed, some spotting elsewhere, edges untrimmed, few scratches to boards, contemporary ink inscription from the author, from the collection of Christopher Ernest Weston 1947-2010. Unsworths Booksellers 24 - 80 2011 £475

Clarkson, Christopher *The History of Richmond, in the County of York, Including a Description of the Castle Friary, Easeby Abbey and Other Remains of Antiquity in the Neighbourhood.* Richmond: printed by and for T. Bowman at the Albion Press, 1814. 8vo., pages 436 + aquatint frontispiece and 3 other engraved plates, late 19th century dark olive green hard grain half morocco (color fugitive on spine to uniform mid-brown), spine double rule gilt with decorative rolls to flat raised bands and extremities, lettered direct in gilt, 'place & date' gilt direct at foot, boards decorative roll gilt bordered with "Sanspareil" design marbled book cloth sides, "Sanspareil Peacock swirl 'made' endpapers, edges uncut, maroon & primrose multicore made applied endbands, browned and spotted in places, spine and edges faded, just touch rubbed, ink inscription, "Coll & perf. F.C.B. Decr. 1879" (Captain F. C. Brooks of Ufford, Suffolk), ink inscription "James Hutchinson/Brigg/1814", heavily annotated by way of ink marginalia and by sewn-in folding sheets with historical agricultural gleanings, from the collection of Christopher Ernest Weston 1947-2010. Unsworths Booksellers 24 - 79 2011 £600

Cole, John *Memoirs of the Life, Writings and Character of the Late Thomas Hinderwell, Esqr. Scarborough.* London: published by John Cole and Longman, Rees, Orme, Brown and Green, 1826. 8vo., pages (ii) 3 (i) 57, (iii) 55, (i) vii (i), engraved frontispiece, publisher's original green canvas, dark green morocco lettering piece gilt by Jenny Aste, late 1980's, some light spotting, especially to title, cloth little spotted and faded, slightly worn at endcaps, contemporary ink inscription to Mrs. Langdell, presented by author, also blue paper ex-libris of John William Clay, from the collection of Christopher Ernest Weston 1947-2010.   Unsworths Booksellers   24 - 82   2011   £125

Comber, Thomas *Roman Forgeries in the Councils During the First Four Centuries...* London: Samuel Roycroft for Rover Clavell, 1689. Small 4to., pages (xvi), 175, (i), contemporary sprinkled sheep, spine blind ruled and gilt lettered direct, boards blind double rule bordered with blind decorative roll toward hinges and blind 'tulip' tool in corners, additional gilt and blind tooling indicative of early 19th century decorative update to spine and boards, board edges decorative roll gilt, blue and white sewn endbands, 20th century calf rebacked with old backstrip relaid, little faint spotting, old leather crackled and rubbed, relaid spine heavily worn, from the collection of Christopher Ernest Weston 1947-2010.   Unsworths Booksellers   24 - 18   2011   £450

Cordiner, Charles *Remarkable Ruins and Romantic Prospects of North Britain.* London: published by I. and J. Taylor, 1795. 2 volumes, 4to., pages iv (cxxxvi) + engraved titlepage, engraved frontispiece and another 56 engraved plates (ccxii) + engraved titlepage, 40 engraved plates (of 41), lacking plate "personification of Events etc." in volume 2, contemporary mottled calf, 6 compartmented spine divided up by back to back double rules and polished pinhead decorative roll all gilt compartments, contain 'made'up' central device of gouges and small flowerets, all gilt, black lettering and numbering pieces gilt, place and date gilt direct at foot, boards double rule gilt border with decorative roll within, board edges decorative roll gilt turn-ins, hooded acanthus, roll gilt green 'sugarpaper' 'made' endpapers, all edges pale green "French Shell" marbled, red and pale blue sewn endbands, dark blue silk page markers, slightest bit of rubbing at extremities but very nice, armorial bookplate of "Littlecote" surmounting printed label of "E. W. Leyborne Popham", from the collection of Christopher Ernest Weston 1947-2010.   Unsworths Booksellers   24 - 83 2011   £750

Cosin, John *Scholastical History of the Canon of the Holy Scripture.* London: E. Tyler and R. Holt for Robert Pawlett, 1672. 4to., pages (xxxvi), 224, (xlviii) + additional engraved titlepage, contemporary speckled calf, boards double ruled in blind, board edges broken ruled gilt, all edges blue 'swirl' marbled blue and white sewn endbands, early 1990's calf reback + corners by Chris Weston, touch of dust soiling, old leather bit flaked and rubbed, ink inscription "J. Lincoln", 20th century ink inscription "This volume belonged to/ John Kaye D.D./Bishop of Lincoln/1827-1853. It belonged to his son/William Frederick John Kaye/Archdeacon of Lincoln/1863-1919", ink inscription "Peter B.G. Binnall/ Barkwith Rectory/Wragby/Lincoln/ (rule) Bought in Lincoln/30 April 1951", 19th century bookseller's ticket "J. Leslie/52 Great Queen Street/Lincoln's Inn Fields/London; from the collection of Christopher Ernest Weston 1947-2010.   Unsworths Booksellers   24 - 19   2011   £275

D'Oyly, George *The Life of William Sancroft, Archbishop of Canterbury.* London: John Murray, 1821. 2 volumes, 8vo., pages (iii-xvi, 470; (iv) 446 + engraved portrait frontispiece in volume 1, contemporary russia, spines tooled in gilt and in blind with 3 sets of triple raised bands, lettered/numbered/dated in gilt direct, boards alternatively gilt and blind decorative rooled and ruled with central diced panel, board edges 'broken-hatch' gilt at corners, turn-ins 'Grecian Key' roll gilt, 'French Shell' 'made' endpapers and all edges marbled, 3 color (green white & red) patterned 'flat' endbands, some light foxing, frontispiece offset, joints tiny bit rubbed and front joint volume 1 cracking but strong, signed binding, pink ticket "Warren/Bookseller/ & Stationer/ 19 Old Bond St" at top left of front pastedown of both volumes, ink stamp "Bound by Warren Old Bond St.", from the collection of Christopher Ernest Weston 1947-2010.   Unsworths Booksellers   24 - 20   2011   £200

Darell, William *The History of Dover Castle.* London: printed for S. Hooper, 1786. 4to., pages (ii), vi, 68 + engraved title, engraved frontispiece, double page engraved plan mounted on stub and another 7 engraved plates, contemporary diced Russia, boards decorative roll gilt (interweaving frond and graded pebbles) bordered, board edges decorative roll gilt, turn-ins decorative roll (alternating metope between quadraglyphs and pearl necklace) gilt, 'Gloster' 'made' endpapers, green silk page marker, early 21st century reback + corners by Chris Weston, some foxing and offsetting, little sunning to spine, from the collection of Christopher Ernest Weston 1947-2010.   Unsworths Booksellers   24 - 84   2011   £200

Defoe, Daniel *A Tour thro' the Whole Island of Great Britain.* London: printed for S. Birt et al, 1753. Fifth edition; 4 volumes, 12mo., pages viii, 388, (xii); iv, 418, (xviii); iv, 312, (xviii); iv, 371 (xxi), contemporary sprinkled calf, spine double rule gilt, dark red lettering pieces gilt, volume number gilt direct, boards double rule gilt bordered, board edges decorative roll in blind, all edges slightly red sprinkled, red and white sewn endbands, browned and spotted, most so in volume I, dark offsetting from turn-ins, rubbed and worn, especially headcaps, joints cracking, front joint of volume 1 nearly split, labels lost from spines of volumes 1 and 4, armorial bookplate of 'Melville", from the collection of Christopher Ernest Weston 1947-2010.   Unsworths Booksellers   24 - 85   2011   £260

Dibdin, Charles   1745-1814 *Observations on a Tour through Almost the Whole of England and a Considerable Part of Scotland, in a Series of Letters.* London: published by G. Goulding etc. circa, 1803. 2 volumes bound as 1, 4to., pages 404 + 26 engraved plates; 407 (i) + 34 engraved plates, extending table of distances in Scotland, contemporary straight grained crimson morocco, spine fully gilt in religious sense with cross, chalice and stylised lily tools, lettered direct in gilt and 'dated' at foot, boards double rule gilt bordered with decorative roll (linked looped-leaf), within, board edges decorative roll gilt, turn-ins decorative roll gilt, mauvish brown sugar paper 'made' endpapers, all edges gilt, dark green double core sewn endbands, dark blue silk page marker, offsetting from plates, bit of foxing, spine bit darkened, slightly rubbed at extremities and some scratches to boards, evidence of removal of two early bookplates, armorial bookplate of "Brown", from the collection of Christopher Ernest Weston 1947-2010.   Unsworths Booksellers   24 - 86   2011   £550

Dionysius of Halicarnassus *The Roman Antiquities of Dionysius Halicarnassensis.* London: printed and sold by booksellers of London and Westminster, 1758. 4 volumes bound as 2, 4to., pages lviii, 456, (ii); (ii), 439, (iii) + 1 double sided engraved sheet with "The Herodian Inscription" on recto, "The Athenian Inscription" on verso, (ii), 438, (ii); (ii), 516 (ii), contemporary diced Russia, boards "Grecian Key' gilt bordered, board edges 'milled' decorative roll gilt, turn-ins single rule gilt, 'Antique spot' 'made' endpapers, all edges lemon, early 21st century reback an corners by Chris Weston, age toned and foxed in places, bit of staining including large mark in gutter at end volume 1, old leather rubbed at edges, armorial bookplate of Daniel O'Connell, ink inscription, from the collection of Christopher Ernest Weston 1947-2010.   Unsworths Booksellers   24 - 87   2011   £600

Douglas, Robert *The Peerage of Scotland: containing an Historical and Genealogical Account of the Nobility of that Kingdom.* Edinburgh: printed by George Ramsay and Co. for Archibald Constable and Co., 1813. Second edition; 2 volumes, folio, pages xiii, (i), ,759, (i), xiv, 9 engraved plates; iv, 748, xiii, (i), 8 engraved plates, contemporary diced Russia, five flat raised banded spine decorative roll gilt and blind tooled, elaborate symmetrical centerpieces gilt in compartments, lettered and numbered direct in gilt, boards triple rule gilt bordered with decorative roll lozenge in blind, board edges single rule gilt, turn-ins decorative roll gilt, 'French Shell' 'made' endpapers, all edges 'Stormont' marbled, 3 color (fawn, white and blue) symmetrical patterned sewn endbands (toned and foxed in places, rubbed and scratches, spine ends and joints worn and defective in places, board edges sometime renewed in lighter leather, hinges cracked but sound, armorial bookplate of William Gordon Esqr. of Fyvie, signed binding by or produced for A. Brown & Co., with his ticket, from the collection of Christopher Ernest Weston 1947-2010.   Unsworths Booksellers   24 - 88   2011   £400

Drake, Francis *Eboracum; or the History and Antiquities of the City of York... together with the History of the Cathedral Church...* London: printed by William Bowyer for the author, 1736. Folio, pages (xxviii) 398 (ii) 399-627 (i) cx (xxv) + 59 engraved plates, there are a further 55 engravings among the letterpress, some full page, second half of 18th century diced Russia consummately rebacked & recornered . 1830, seven compartment spine gilt extra with multi rule bands and massed decorative roll infills, original brown lettering piece gilt relaid, boards decorative roll gilt bordered with cornerpieces, board edges decorative roll gilt, all edges gilt & gauffered, blue and mauve sewn endbands, little light toning, slight dust soiling at beginning, boards touch sunned in places, extra illustrated copy, principally by inclusive of i - mezzotint portrait engraving of Francs. Drake, ii - mezzotint portrait engraving of Mr. Thos. Gent, also 8 minor embellishments at pages 27, 224, 258, 286, 301, 398, additional titlepage and 483, from the collection of Christopher Ernest Weston 1947-2010.   Unsworths Booksellers   24 - 89   2011   £1750

Drake, Francis *The History and Antiquities of the City of York, from its Origin to the Present Times.* York: printed by A. Ward, 1785. 3 volumes, 12mo., pages (iv), 400 + folding engraved plan frontispiece and 17 other engraved plates; (ii), 402 + 2 other extending engraved plates; (iv), 292 + folding engraved map and one other folding engraved plate, contemporary polished tan calf, spine single rule gilt, red and green lettering and numbering pieces gilt, board edges obliquely broken fillet roll in blind, a lemon, fawn and white sewn endbands, some toning and spotting edges of few folding plates little darkened and frayed, touch of wear to endcaps, front joint of volume I cracked, armorial bookplate of Lord Arundell Wardour, from the collection of Christopher Ernest Weston 1947-2010.   Unsworths Booksellers   24 - 90   2011   £300

Dugdale, William 1605-1686 *Monasticon Anglicanum; or the History of the Ancient Abbies, Monasteries, Hosptials...in England and Wales. (with) ... Two Additional volumes to Sir William Dugdale's Monasticon Anglicanum.* London: R. Harbin for D. Browne and J. Smith (et al) for Tho. Taylor..., 1718. 1722-1723; 3 volumes, folio, plates (lacking plates 42-44 in volume 1, contemporary mottled calf, stain darkened, spine panel gilt, red lettering piece gilt, numbered direct in panel gilt compartment, board edges 'zig-zag' roll gilt, all edges 'French Shell' marbled, blue and red sewn endleaves, some damp and mould marking, a few plates loose but present, rather rubbed, joints worn but strong, some loss from endcaps, contemporary ink inscription "Samuel Thomson Esq. of Bradfield Berks", ink stamped armorial of "Samuel Thomson of Bradfield Esqr", armorial bookplates of Honble James Bertie Esqr. of Stanwell in Com. Middx. Second Son to James late/Earle of Abingdon 1702", from the collection of Christopher Ernest Weston 1947-2010.   Unsworths Booksellers   24 - 21 2011   £600

Englefield, Henry C.   *A Description of the Principal Picturesque Beauties, Antiquities and Geological Pheonmena of the Isle of Wight.* London: printed by William Bulmer and Co. for Payne and Foss, 1816.   Large paper copy, 4to., pages (viii) vi 238 (iv) (vi)-xxvii, (i) + oval engraved frontispiece, 50 other engraved plates, contemporary russia leather, boards intricately gilt bordered with double triple rules and back to back decorative roll between, within blind tooled acanthus roll and innermost a single rule gilt panel with elaborate made up corner pieces gilt, board edges, 'broken hatch fillet' roll at corners, turn-ins 'composite double rule' gilt, all edges gilt, 3 color double core patterned sewn endbands, orange silk page markers, early 20th century in brown goatskin, spine divided into five compartments by triple raised bands, one flat between two ordinary and tooled in gilt and in blind, lettering gilt direct in two compartments, toned, some foxing to plates, touch of rubbing to extremities, crowned and belted heraldic crest, gilt stamp of Earl of Derby in centre of front board, this copy is extra illustrated by the inclusion of Ordnance Survey sheet 10 of Isle of Wight dated 1810, large folding map bound in, from the collection of Christopher Ernest Weston 1947-2010. Unsworths Booksellers   24 - 92 2011   £1400

Eutropius   *Eutropii Historiae Romanae Breviarium...* Parisiis: Apud Viduam Antonii Cellier via Citaraea, 1683. 4to., pages (xiv) 183, (i), this copy lacks engraved half title, found with some copies of the Delphin editions, contemporary vellum, spine fully gilt in compartments, green lettering piece gilt, all edges gilt red and grey sprinkled, green and white sewn endbands, small faint dampmark to upper edge, fore edges of first c. 20 leaves little creased, vellum touch soiled, from the collection of Christopher Ernest Weston 1947-2010.   Unsworths Booksellers   24 - 93 2011   £125

Florus, Lucius Annaeus   *A Compendious History of Rome...* York: printed by Thomas Gent for Arthur Bettesworth, 1727. 8vo., pages (vi), 217, (i), contemporary calf, boards panelled in blind, Cambridge style, board edges 'zig-zag' decorative roll in blind, all edges red sprinkled, pink and white sewn endbands, late 20th century calf reback by CEW (some thumbing and soiling, title rehinged, hinge cracked at title), old leather scratched and chipped, substantial portion on front renewed with rebacking, from the collection of Christopher Ernest Weston 1947-2010.   Unsworths Booksellers   24 - 94 2011   £175

Gale, Roger   *Registrum Honoris De Richmond Exhibens Terrarum & Villarum.* Londini: Impensis R. Gosling, 1722. Large paper copy, folio, pages (ii), xxxv, (i), 106, (xxvi), 286, (xxx) + folding engraved map, one extending engraved plate, another 8 engraved plates and 6 extending plates of pedigrees, lacking the list of subscribers leaf, early 19th century calf, boards sided with 'French Shelf' marbled paper, 1970's renewal of leather with half reversed calf by John Henderson (spotted and lightly browned, old boards scuffed), armorial and masonic bookplate of "Robt. Lakeland" and inscription "from Major Sir Edw. Coates' Library", from the collection of Christopher Ernest Weston 1947-2010.   Unsworths Booksellers   24 - 95 2011   £400

Gent, Thomas   *Historia Compendiosa Anglicana; or a Compendious History of England.*   York: printed and sold by the author, 1741. 2 volumes, 8vo., pages (iv), xvi, (ii), 268, (iv); (iv), 269-376, (ii), 70, xxxviii, later 18th century marbled calf, boards decorative roll gilt bordered, board edges obliquely broken fillet, roll gilt, all edges red speckled, early 20th century calf reback, fully gilt spines, red and black lettering and numbering piece gilt, dark green & purple sewn endbands, some browning, few fore edges cut close and few frayed but no loss of text, little rubbed at extremities, corners sometime, at different times renewed, from the collection of Christopher Ernest Weston 1947-2010. Unsworths Booksellers   24 - 99 2011   £300

Gent, Thomas   *The Antient and Modern History of the Famous City of Yrok and i a Particular Manner of its Magnificent Cathedral...*   York: at the Printing Office in Coffe Yard, 1730. 8vo., pages viii, 256, (viii) + extending engraved frontispiece and one other engraving, contemporary hand colored extending plan, this copy is the first issue with woodcut of framed celestial crown with Latin quotation from Rev. II 10 as a headpiece to page 84, also tall copy, modern (1982) calf by Jenny Aste, browned and spotted, frontispiece and plan rehinged, from the collection of Christopher Ernest Weston 1947-2010.   Unsworths Booksellers   24 - 96 2011   £400

Gent, Thomas *The Antient and Modern History of the Loyal Town of Rippon...* York: printed and sold at the Printing Office, 1733. 8vo., pages xvi, (ii) 165, (i), 73, (vii) + folding engraved plan frontispiece, 2 full page woodcuts and 2 extra illustrated engraved plates, modern (March 1982) calf binding by Jenny Aste, some browning and spotting, folding plates rehinged, one extra plate (unflattering portrait of author, bound as frontispiece), substantially smaller and frayed at edge, other copy of folding plate from Gent's "Annales Regioduni Hullini", 2 flyleaves from earlier binding tipped in at end, ink inscription "William Shilleto 1841" and pencil inscription, from the collection of Christopher Ernest Weston 1947-2010. Unsworths Booksellers 24 - 97 2011 £450

Gent, Thomas *The Most Delectable, Scriptural and Pious History of the Famous and Magnificent Great Eastern Window .. in St. Peter's Cathedral, York...* York: impress for the author in St. Peter's Gate, 1762. 8vo., pages (iv), xxiii, (i), 196, 12, (iv), 24, (vi) + large folding engraved plates (crudely hand colored) of E. Window and one other engraved plate headed "Pious Contemplations", contemporary sprinkled sheep boards, double rule bordered in blind, all edges red sprinkled, 1970's sheep reback + corners, browned, spotted, few page and plate edges just cropped, folding engraved plate splitting at folds and with handling tear, in places sometime repaired on rear, last leaf cut down, old leather darkened and chipped in places, bound in after titlepage is special presentation leaf to Revd. John Mawer from author, from the collection of Christopher Ernest Weston 1947-2010. Unsworths Booksellers 24 - 100 2011 £650

Gibbon, Edward *The History of the Decline and Fall of the Roman Empire.* London: printed for W. Strahan and T. Cadell, 1777-1781. Third edition volume 1, First editions volumes 2-3; 3 volumes only (of 6), 4to., pages vi, (vi), 704, engraved frontispiece; (xii) 640, (ii) + 1 folding engraved map and 1 extending engraved map (xii), 640, (ii), 1 folding engraved map, contemporary sprinkled tan calf, six compartmented spine fully gilt with 'paterae row' decorative roll bands and 'frond' cornered panels with 'doves and urn' center pieces red & green lettering & numbering pieces gilt, board edges 'obliquely-broken fillet' roll gilt, 'Dutch swirl' 'made' endpapers, all edges lemon, russet and white sewn endbands, green silk page markers, little light spotting, merest touch rubbed at edges, corners gently worn, joints of volumes 1 and 3 cracking a bit at foot, from the collection of Christopher Ernest Weston 1947-2010. Unsworths Booksellers 24 - 101 2011 £450

Godden, Thomas *Catholicks no Idolaters. Or a Full Refutation of Doctor Stillingfleet's Unjust Charge.* London: printed in the year, 1672. 8vo., pages (xxxii), 48, 448, contemporary sprinkled calf, spine double rule panelled in blind, paper label lettered in ink, boards double rule bordered in blind, board edges decorative roll gilt, all edges gilt, densely red sprinkled, white and pink sewn endleaves, just touch marked but very well preserved binding, free endpaper ink stamped angus dei within two leafy springs and underneath "SHEPPARD" (suggestive of heraldic crest), from the collection of Christopher Ernest Weston 1947-2010. Unsworths Booksellers 24 - 22 2011 £275

Gordon, C. A. *A Concise History of the Antient and Illustrious House of Gordon from the Origin of the Name to the Present Time.* Aberdeen: printed for the author, 1754. 8vo., pages ix (iii) 309, (xi) contemporary crimson sheep, boards double rule gilt bordered with flowerets at corners and in centre black morocco lozenge onlay double rule gilt bordered with flowerets outermost at extremities and 'Scottish Herringbone" design within all gilt, 'Dutch gilt' endpapers, all edges gilt, pale blue and white sewn endbands, early 21st retrospective reback in sheep by Chris Weston, toned and little spotted, old leather bit scratched, ink inscription "Honble Colonel Cosmo Gordon to his friend and relation David Gordon Esre. Abergeldie, further inscriptions signed "Emilia Lucy Gordon/Ivy Lodge August 1873", reverse of loose paper has information about Cosmo Gordon who shot dead a fellow officer, fled abroad for a year then faced a trial at which the jury pronounced him not guilty, from the collection of Christopher Ernest Weston 1947-2010. Unsworths Booksellers 24 - 103 2011 £500

Great Britain. Laws, Statutes, etc. - 1683 *Acts Made in the First Parliament...of Charles the First. (& First and Third Parliament of Charles the Second. With an index or abridgement of the Acts of Parliament.* Edinburgh: printed by David Lindsay, John Reid, 1683-1685. 12mo., pages 130 (iv) 133-371 (xiii) 373-640, (ii), 292, browned, bit of soiling, titlepage foxed, from the collection of Christopher Ernest Weston 1947-2010. Unsworths Booksellers 24 - 64 2011 £150

Gregorius Nazianazenus *Opera nunc Primum Graece Latine Coniunctin Edita.* Lutetiae Parisiorum: Typis Regiis apud Claudium Morellum, 1609. 2 volumes, folio pages (lxviii), 916 (cxvi) (viii), 308, (viii) cols. 1544 (xliv), contemporary calf - an Oxford; spine ruled in blind, boards triple rule panelled in blind with double outer and single inner foliage panelled roll, board edges single ruled in blind, endleaves taken from a 16th century edition of Mesue, all edges rouge, blue and white sewn endbands small paper labels lettered and numbered in ink, lightly browned, titlepage slightly dust soiled, little rubbed and scratched, labels worn, ties removed, headcap of 2 defective, both volumes have inscription "Brentley/Library...", from the collection of Christopher Ernest Weston 1947-2010. Unsworths Booksellers 24 - 23 2011 £1200

Hargrove, William *History and Description of the Ancient City of York...* York: published and sold by Wm. Alexander, 1818. 2 volumes, 8vo., pages (iii)-xvi, (17)-396 397*-412*, (397)-407 (iii) + engraved frontispiece and 3 other engraved plates; iv, (5)-688, (ii) + engraved frontispiece, an extending hand colored plan and 6 other engraved plates, this copy extra illustrated by the inclusion of Volume I - 16 pages of text and 8 engraved plates between pages xvi and (17) and volume 2 - engraved plate facing page 522 and tipped-in slip with view of gatehouse to Archbishop's palace at Bishopthorpe facing page 518, all additions except the last slip have been taken from James Storer's History and Antiquities of the Cathedral Churches of Great Britain" volume 4 (London 1818), contemporary polished maroon calf, four flat raised band spine ruled in gilt with massed 'intersecting circles' pallet in compartments, lettered and numbered direct in gilt, boards double rule gilt bordered and 'intersecting broken waves' roll within, centrally a large panel 'straight grain' tooled, board edges decorative roll gilt, turn-ins 'intersecting broken waves' roll gilt, 'Spanish' 'made' endpapers, dark blue and white sewn endbands, dark blue silk page markers, some light spotting, split at fold of one extending plate, volume I repaired at head of spine, front joint of volume 2 cracking a bit, little rubbing at extremities, spines lightly sunned, signed binding by Douglas, bookbinder, Blackburn with his paper ticket, printed label of Thomas Butler, from the collection of Christopher Ernest Weston 1947-2010.   Unsworths Booksellers   24 - 106   2011   £450

Hassell, John *Tour of the Isle of Wight.* London: printed by John Jarvis for Thomas Hookham, 1790. 2 volumes, 8vo., pages xxiv, 224 + engraved titlepage and 17 tinted aquatint plates; viii, 248 + engraved titlepage and 13 tinted aquatint plates, contemporary 'Etruscan' calf almost certainly by Edwards of Halifax, spine gilt compartmented with gilt 'coil' cornerpieces and 'classical urn' centre-pieces in blind, black lettering piece gilt, numbered direct in gilt within an open central blind tooled oval, boards 'metope and pentaglyph' roll gilt bordered and concentric borders within (one of palmettes & trident in blind) surrounding a central gilt 'Grecian key' roll edges marbled panel, board edges & turn-ins single rule gilt, vivid pink 'made' endpapers, all edges gilt, brown and white double core sewn endbands, bit foxed in places, neat restoration to endcaps and joints, spines slightly cracked, printed booklabel of John Sparrow at top left of verso of 'made' front endpaper, from the collection of Christopher Ernest Weston 1947-2010.   Unsworths Booksellers   24 - 107   2011   £750

Herodotus *Herodoti Halicarnassei Historiarum Libri IX.* Oxonii: Sumtibus J. Cooke et J. Parker et J. Payne et J. Mackinlay, Londini, 1808. 2 volumes, 8vo., pages xxx, 409, (i); (ii), 394, (lvi), contemporary russia, four double raised bands spine, broken rule gilt compartments with blind tooled elaborate centre stars composed of small tools and centered with small circles gilt, lettered, numbered, 'placed & dated' direct in gilt, boards dual single rule intersecting gilt bordered with 'facing drawer handle' roll in blind between rules and 'curtain freize' roll in blind innermost, board edges 'broken-hatch' roll gilt at corners, turn-ins "Grecian Key" roll gilt, "French Shell" 'made' endpapers, all edges marbled thus, pale blue and purple double core sewn endbands, pale blue silk page markers, little light foxing, joints rubbed and cracking, top compartment of volume 2 spine defective, contemporary ink inscription "Henricus Riddell Moody e coll. Oriel", from the collection of Christopher Ernest Weston 1947-2010.   Unsworths Booksellers   24 - 108   2011   £40

Herodotus *The History of Herodotus.* London: printed for D. Midwinter et al, 1737. Third edition; 2 volumes, 8vo., pages xvi, 447 (xvii) + 3 extending engraved maps, (ii), 430, (xviii), contemporary orangey tan calf boards triple rule gilt bordered with broad dentelle inner border of individual small tools, board edges decorative roll gilt, late 19th century 'swirl' 'made' endpapers with pale green block cloth, inner joint strengtheners, all edges original blue swirl/marbled pale blue and white sewn endbands, early 21st century retrospective reback + corners by Chris Weston, little toning and marginal dust soiling, some marginal pencil notes, old leather chipped at edges, contemporary ink inscription "Eliza Spencer" at head of titlepages, verso of volume I marbled endpaper has ms. note by Rev. John Bourton/Banningham Rectory/Norfolk referring to early provenance of Sunderland Library and subsequent purchase at Puttick & Simpson's auction in 1882, from the collection of Christopher Ernest Weston 1947-2010.   Unsworths Booksellers   24 - 109   2011   £400

Hooker, Richard   1554-1600 *The Works of... Mr. Richard Hooker...* London: printed for R.C.S.S. B.W. M.W. G.C., 1705. Folio, pages (x), 553, (I) + engraved portrait frontispiece, contemporary calf (laid on top of original panelled calf), boards panelled in blind Cambridge style (compared with the single panel of binding underneath), board edges decorative roll in blind (previous binding a decorative roll gilt), all edges gilt, all edges red speckled, calf reback, boards restoration and relaying contemporary red lettering piece gilt by Jenny Aste, invoice 4 v 1983 £46, touch of minor staining, boards scratched and marked, from the collection of Christopher Ernest Weston 1947-2010.   Unsworths Booksellers   24 - 24   2011   £500

Horsley, John *Britannia Romana; or the Roman Antiquities of Britain...* London: printed for John Osborn and Thomas Longman, 1732. Folio, pages (viii), xxxii, 520, (xl) + 5 extending engraved maps and 100 other engraved plates, early 19th century polished russia, five flat raised banded spine double rule gilt with 'quatrefoil-title' roll gilt bands, compartment with blind tooled elaborate centre pieces composed of stylised plant tools, lettered direct in gilt, boards triple rule gilt bordered with decorative rule in blind within, board edges 'zig-zag' roll gilt, turn-ins decorative roll gilt, 'French Shell' 'made' endpapers, all edges gilt, 3 color (pink, white and green) double core sewn and patterned endbands, dark blue silk page markers, calf reback and relay by John Henderson, some light spotting, unidentified Knight of the Garter armorial gilt stamped on both boards, from the collection of Christopher Ernest Weston 1947-2010. Unsworths Booksellers 24 - 110 2011 £900

Hunter, Joseph *Hallamshire. The History and Topography of the Parish of Sheffield in the County of York.* London: printed for the author by Richard and Arthur Taylor, published by Lackington, Hughes, Harding, Mavor and Jones, 1819. Large paper copy, folio, pages x, (ii) 299 (I) + engraved frontispiece and 8 other engraved plates, later hard grain purple morocco, spine single ruled in blind, lettered direct in gilt, 'place & date' direct in gilt at foot, turn-ins decorative roll gilt, 'French Shell' 'made' endpapers, all edges gilt, dark blue and pink sewn flat endbands, some foxing to plates and facing leaves, little rubbed at extremities, unidentified Knight of the Gater armorial gilt stamped on both boards, signed binding stamp "Tuckett Binder to the Queen", from the collection of Christopher Ernest Weston 1947-2010. Unsworths Booksellers 24 - 111 2011 £400

Jackson, Thomas *The Life of the Rev. Charles Wesley...* London: John Mason, 1841. from the collection of Christopher Ernest Weston 1947-2010, 2 volumes, 8vo., pages xvi, 592 + engraved frontispiece, viii, 578, (ii) + signed agreement facsimile plate facing page 577, late 1990's retrospective half calf by Chris Weston, frontispiece foxed, otherwise just faint age toning and few tiny spots. Unsworths Booksellers 24 - 25 2011 £180

Jacob, Alexander *A Complete English Peerage.* London: printed for the author, 1766. 2 volumes, bound as 3, folio, pages (vi), 354 + engraved frontispiece, 25 other engraved plates and 39 plates of pedigrees (ii), 355)-614 (ii) + engraved frontispiece, 36 other engraved plates and 52 plates of pedigrees, 707, (i) + engraved frontispiece, 143 other engraved plates and 1 plate of pedigree, contemporary reversed calf, remains of black morocco spinal onlay panel gilt with compartments 'saltired', red lettering piece gilt, numbering gilt direct, boards panelled in blind, board edges decorative roll in blind, all edges lightly red sprinkled, red and white sewn endbands, green silk page markers, small marginal dampstain to first few leaves of volume 1, little minor spotting elsewhere, joints cracked and spines quite rubbed and cracked, bit of wear to endcaps, boards showing few scratches but relatively well preserved, heraldic stencilled bookplate bearing monograph the letters of which appear to be E.T.H. & C., from the collection of Christopher Ernest Weston 1947-2010. Unsworths Booksellers 24 - 112 2011 £750

Junius, Pseud. *Junius Stat Nominius Umbra.* London: printed by T. Bensley for Vernor and Hood et al, 1801. 2 volumes, 8vo., pages (ii) xxxiii-xxxii 274 + engraved titlepage (dated 1797), engraved portrait frontispiece and 10 other engraved portrait plates, v, (iii), 318, (ii) + engraved titlepage, engraved portrait frontispiece and 7 other engraved portrait plates, contemporary straight grained dark blue morocco, fully gilt six compartmented spine with 'liberty cap atop oak leaved staff' centerpieces, lettered & numbered direct in gilt, boards full and brown rule gilt bordered with decorative roll (interweaving front and graded pebbles) within, board edges single rule gilt, turn-ins decorative roll gilt, pink 'made' endpapers, all edges gilt, dark green double core sewn endbands, pale blue silk page markers, foxed, bit rubbed at extremities and touched up with blue dye, small printed booklabel of "Gwendolen Brandt", from the collection of Christopher Ernest Weston 1947-2010. Unsworths Booksellers 24 - 113 2011 £160

King, Daniel *The Vale Royall of England.* London: printed by John Streater, 1656. folio, pages (x), 99, (v), 239 (x), 55, (vii) 34 + 2 (***) double page engraved maps mounted on stubs, 1 double page plan of Chester and 1 other double page engraving of cathedral, both mounted on their own stubs, 11 plates of armorials and 3 other engraved plates, full page of Beaumont armorials on page (12) in the isle of man section, contemporary sprinkled calf, spine originally double ruled in blind but updated in early 18th century by superimposition of panel gilding, dark orange lettering piece gilt, boards double ruled in blind, board edges originally single rule gilt by superimposed with decorative roll gilt, all edges, dark brown sprinkled pink and white sewn endbands, some spotting in places, boards scratched and marked, joint ends and endcaps sometime restored in a different shade of leather, from the collection of Christopher Ernest Weston 1947-2010. Unsworths Booksellers 24 - 114 2011 £1600

Kinge, John *Lectures Upon Jonas, Delivered at Yorke in the yeare of Our Lorde 1594.* Oxford: Joseph Barnes, 1599. Small 4to., pages (x), 660, (ii), 661-706, N.B. leaves *1 and 2Y4 are blanks (first except for a fleuron) missing in this copy, early 19th century tan calf, spine gilt, red lettering piece gilt, place and date gilt direct, boards gilt double rule bordered, board edges decorative roll gilt turn-ins decorative roll gilt, "Gloster' 'made' endpapers, all edges red mottled, pink sewn endbands, light age toning and few tiny spots, couple of small marks to leather, headcap slightly worn, early ink inscription of titlepage largely cut off (and undecipherable) and repaired and matching paper, early initials "WPL" on titlepage, heraldic bookplate of Marquis of Devonshire, from the collection of Christopher Ernest Weston 1947-2010.   Unsworths Booksellers   24 - 26 2011   £500

Knowles, John *A Separate Peace.* New York: Macmillan, 1960. First American edition; signed by author, from the collection of Christopher Ernest Weston 1947-2010 owner name stamp and gift inscription noting this is an Autographed copy from a Fairmont Man, minor spine tanning and offsetting to joints from binder's glue, near fine in very good, price clipped, second issue dust jacket,.   Ken Lopez Bookseller   154 - 91 2011 $1500

Knox, John *The Historie of the Reformation of the Church of Scotland.* London: John Raworth for George Thomason and Octavian Pullen, 1644. Folio, pages (lxxxiv), 276, 279-397, (i) 401-460, 91, (ii), 92-122, contemporary sprinkled calf, boards blind triple ruled, board edges single rule gilt, turn-ns single ruled in blind, all edges rouge, pink and white sewn endbands, calf reback & corners by John Henderson, little light spotting, couple of old scrapes to leather, modern booklabel of Robert J. Hayhurst, from the collection of Christopher Ernest Weston 1947-2010. Unsworths Booksellers   24 - 27 2011   £950

Lactantius, Lucius Coelius Firmianus *Opera quae Exstant... et Commentariis Illustrata a Tho. spark.* Oxonii: E Theatro Sheldoniano, 1684. 8vo., pages (xviii), 912, (ii), 24, 17-38, contemporary speckled calf, boards double rule bordered in blind with stylized 'dahlia' tool in corners, board edges decorative 'zig-zag' roll in blind, turn-ins single ruled in blind, pink and white sewn endbands, early 21st century calf reback by Chris Weston with original decorative red lettering piece gilt relaid, little light spotting, small dampmark in upper corner of first few leaves, old leather scratched and marked, contemporary inscription "E Libris Gui. Brodnag", heraldic bookplate of Montagu George Knight of Chawton, from the collection of Christopher Ernest Weston 1947-2010. Unsworths Booksellers   24 - 28 2011   £250

Laud, William *A Relation of the Conference Between William Lawd...and Mr. Fisher the Jesuite.* London: printed by Richard Badger, 1639. Folio, pages (xxiv), 388, later dark brown turkey, spine panel gilt extra (7 compartments tooled in four designs arranged symmetrically about the centre), boards gilt panelled with double corner pieces out with the elaborately gilt rolled outer frame of centre panel, board edges elaborately decorative roll gilt 'Dutch-comb-swirl' endpapers, all edges gilt, fawn and white sewn endbands, joints and corners conserved, early 21st century by Chris Weston, lightly browned, dust soiled in places, corner of f.e.p. excised, old leather little bit rubbed and chipped, 19th century armorial bookplate of "James Bank M.A./Linc. Coll. Oxon" on front pastedown, from the collection of Christopher Ernest Weston 1947-2010.   Unsworths Booksellers   24 - 29 2011   £325

Livius, Titus *Titi Livii Patavini Historiarum Libri Qui Extant.* Parisiis: apud Fredericum Leonard, 1679. 5 volumes bound as 6, 4to., pages (lxx) 544 (ix) + engraved half title and 2 engraved maps; (ii) 10 545-876, 3-191, (xix); (viii) 620 (lii) + 1 extending engraved plate and 1 other engraved plate; (viii) 757, (lxv) 678 (xxvi) 776, (xvi), contemporary calf, stain darkened spine panel gilt, brick red lettering piece gilt, numbered direct in gilt boards panelled in blind (Cambridge style), board edges decorative roll gilt, all edges red speckled, blue and white sewn endbands, light toning and some spotting, rubbed at joints and corners, joints cracked, endcaps worn, some labels lost, contemporary armorial bookplate of Sir Robert Clayton , early 19th century armorial bookplate of Stephen Lowdell, from the collection of Christopher Ernest Weston 1947-2010.   Unsworths Booksellers   24 - 115 2011   £450

MacKenzie, Eneas *A Descriptive and Historical Account of the Town and County of Newcastle upon Tyne...* Newcastle upon Tyne: printed & published by Mackenzie & Dent, 1827. 2 volumes bound as 1, 4to., pages x, 414, frontispiece and 10 other engraved plates; (ii), (415)-770, (ii) + engraved frontispiece and 3 other engraved plates, modern half calf by John Henderson, foxed in places, armorial bookplate of Archibald Dawnay, from the collection of Christopher Ernest Weston 1947-2010.   Unsworths Booksellers   24 - 116 2011   £300

MacKenzie, Eneas *An Historical, Topographical and Descriptive View of the County Palatine of Durham...* Newcastle upon Tyne: printed and published by MacKenzie and Dent, 1834. 2 volumes, 4to., pages cxxii, 518 + extending engraved map frontispiece and 9 other engraved plates (ii) 450 + engraved frontispiece and 9 other engraved plates, contemporary tan half calf, four flat raised bands, spines double ruled gilt, compartments textured by massed decorative pallets in blind brown lettering pieces, gilt, numbered direct in gilt, 'author' gilt direct at foot, boards decorative roll bordered in blind with 'French Shell' marbled sides, all edges brown sprinkled, pink cloth over core applied endbands, plates foxed, frontispiece onset onto title, from the collection of Christopher Ernest Weston 1947-2010. Unsworths Booksellers   24 - 117 2011   £350

Martin, Martin *A Description of the Western Islands of Scotland...* London: printed for Andrew Bell, 1703. 8vo., pages (xxxii) 392 + folding engraved map and one other folding engraved plate, early 21st century retrospective panelled calf by ChrisWeston, touch of faint spotting, small handling tear to folded map, from the collection of Christopher Ernest Weston 1947-2010. Unsworths Booksellers 24 - 121 2011 £800

Montagu, Edward Wortley 1713-1776 *Reflections on the Rise and Fall of the Ancient Republicks.* London: printed for A. Millar and T. Cadell, 1769. 8vo., pages (vi) 392, contemporary sprinkled tan calf, spine fully gilt with massed flowers, board edges 'alternating full and brown hatch fillet' roll gilt, turn-ins as above but in blind, all edges densely red speckled, pink and white sewn endbands, little faint spotting, rubbed at extremities, joints cracking but strong, little wear to endcaps, lettering piece lost, from the collection of Christopher Ernest Weston 1947-2010. Unsworths Booksellers 24 - 123 2011 £95

Morritt, J. B. S. *A Vindication of Homer and of the Ancient Poets and Historians who Have Recorded the Siege and Fall of Troy.* York: printed by W. Blanchard for T. Cadell, Jun. and W. Davies, 1798. 4to., pages 124 + 1 double page engraved map and 5 other double page engraved plates all mounted on stubs, contemporary diced Russia, spine double gilt with 'perched peacock' centre-piece gilt in compartments, lettered direct in gilt, boards decorative roll gilt bordered with central gilt ruled panel and quadrant arc corners gilt, board edges decorative roll gilt, turn-ins 'rope-twist' roll gilt, 'French shell' 'made' endpapers, all edges brown speckled, pale blue silk page marker, mid 20th century calf reback, backstrip relaid (partly inserted) + corners, faint dust soiling and toning, little offsetting from plates, old leather darkened around repairs, parts of old spines lost, Devonshire monogrammed heraldic booklabel on front pastedown, from the collection of Christopher Ernest Weston 1947-2010. Unsworths Booksellers 24 - 124 2011 £600

Nepos, Cornelius *De Vita Excellentium Imperatorum. Interpretatione et Notis Illustravit Nicolaus Courtin...* Parisiis: Apud Fredericum Leonard, 1675. 4to., pages (xlii) 163 (lxxvi) + engraved half title, contemporary polished tan calf, spine panel gilt with 'crowned dolphin' centre pieces, green 'Delph' lettering piece gilt, boards single rule gilt bordered, board edges 'exaggerated -wavy' roll gilt, 'Dutch-swirl' endpapers, all edges rouge, early 21st century restoration by Chris Reston, light toning, few spots and faint dampmark in early leaves, old leather little chipped at edges, rebacked preserving spine panel but new red lettering piece, unidentified gilt stamped armorial motto within circular frame, from the collection of Christopher Ernest Weston 1947-2010. Unsworths Booksellers 24 - 125 2011 £225

Newte, Thomas *Prospects and Observations; on a Tour in England and Scotland: Natural, Economical and Literary.* London: printed for G. G. J. and J. Robinson, 1791. 4to., pages viii, 440 + a folding engraved map frontispiece and 23 other engraved plates, contemporary polished tan calf, board edges 'zig-zag' decorative roll in blind, red and white sewn endbands, late 1990's calf reback by Chris Weston, original red lettering piece gilt relaid, some foxing, old leather scratched and bit rubbed at edges, armorial bookplate of C. Kerr Esqr/Calder Bank, ink inscription "Charles Kerr/ Georges Square", from the collection of Christopher Ernest Weston 1947-2010. Unsworths Booksellers 24 - 126 2011 £350

Newton, Isaac 1642-1727 *Observations upon the Prophecies of Daniel and the Apocalypse of St. John.* London: printed by J. Darby and T. Browne, 1733. 4to., pages vi, (ii), 323, (i), early 21st century retrospective blind tooled calf by Chris Weston, title slightly dusty, otherwise very clean, from the collection of Christopher Ernest Weston 1947-2010. Unsworths Booksellers 24 - 32 2011 £2250

Newton, Isaac 1642-1727 *The Chronology of Ancient Kingdoms Amended.* London: printed for J. Tonson &c, 1728. 4to., pages xiv, (ii), 376, 3 extending plates, early 21st century retrospective panelled calf binding by Chris Weston, title washed and repaired at edge, minor spotting elsewhere, from the collection of Christopher Ernest Weston 1947-2010. Unsworths Booksellers 24 - 31 2011 £950

Oldmixon, John *The History and Life of Admiral Blake; General and Admiral of the Fleets and Naval Forces of England...* London: printed for R. Davis and J. Millan, 1746. Second edition; 12mo., pages (xvi) 128, engraved portrait frontispiece, early 21st century retrospective sheep binding by Chris Weston, some spotting and dust soiling, from the collection of Christopher Ernest Weston 1947-2010. Unsworths Booksellers 24 - 127 2011 £300

Oliver, George *The History and Antiquities of the Town and Minister of Beverley in the County of York.* Beverley: printed and sold by M. Turner, 1829. Large paper copy, 4to., pages xxiii (i) 576 + engraved frontispiece, 5 other engraved plates, folding pedigree, contemporary tan calf, boards double rule gilt bordered with triple rule in blind within, board edges single rule gilt, turn-ins single rule gilt, all edges gilt 'peacock swirl' marbled, calf reback by John Henderson (1976) with original red lettering piece gilt relaid, plates foxed and some spotting elsewhere, old leather chipped and scratched, corners worn, from the collection of Christopher Ernest Weston 1947-2010. Unsworths Booksellers 24 - 128 2011 £250

Osburn, William *Ancient Egypt, her Testimony to the Truth of the Bible...* London: Samuel Bagster and Sons, 1846. 8vo., pages x, 242, (ii) + color printed frontispiece, additional titlepage and 4 other color printed plates, publisher's original interlinked concentric circle design brown book cloth, spine lettered red on gilt background at head, lemon 'coated' endpapers, early 21st century cloth reback, old backstrip relaid by Chris Weston, corners bit rubbed, from the collection of Christopher Ernest Weston 1947-2010.   Unsworths Booksellers   24 - 129   2011   £50

Pagan, James *Sketch of the History of Glasgow.* Glasgow: Robert Stuart & co., 1847. 8vo., pages (vi) 198 + engraved titlepage, extending lithographic plan and 22 other lithograph plates, later polished calf by Ramage, signed in gilt above bottom front turn-in, spine panel-gilt, dark orange lettering & 'place & date' pieces gilt, boards panelled in gilt and in blind reinterpreting the 'Cambridge' style, board edges 'broken hatch' roll gilt at corners, turn-ins 'dentelle' roll gilt, 'French Shell' 'made' endpapers, all edges lemon, 3 color double core sewn endbands, replacement lettering piece for author's name, little spotting to plates, pages lightly large toned, from the collection of Christopher Ernest Weston 1947-2010.   Unsworths Booksellers   24 - 130   2011   £200

Parker, Samuel *The Ecclesiastical Histories of Eusebius, Socrates, Sozomen and Theodorit.* London: printed for C. Rivington, 1729. Third edition; 4to., pages 16 (viii), 17-368, (i), ccclxii-ccclxviii, 369-651, (xxv) + engraved frontispiece and 4 other plates, contemporary calf, boards panelled in blind Cambridge style, board edges, decorative roll in blind, all edges red sprinkled, contrasting calf reback + corners by W. R. Wiltshire, little light spotting, few early notes in margins and one on tipped in sheet, old leather rubbed and chipped at edges, from the collection of Christopher Ernest Weston 1947-2010.   Unsworths Booksellers   24 - 33   2011   £200

Patercullus, Velleius *C. Velleii Paterculi Historiae Romanae and M. Vinicium Cos Libri Duo.* Parisiis: Apud Fredericum Leonard, 1675. 4to., pages (xxviii) 151, (lxxx-ix) + engraved half title, bound facing title contemporary mottled calf, spine panel gilt, dark red lettering piece gilt, boards double rule bordered in blind with central triple rule panel having fleurons at corners all in blind, board edges decorative roll gilt, all edges red speckled, blue and white sewn endbands, few minor spots, title bit dusty, old leather somewhat scratched, contemporary ink inscription, armorial bookplates of John Peyto Verney/Lord Willoughby de Broke, and of Robert John Verney/Lord Willoughby de Broke, from the collection of Christopher Ernest Weston 1947-2010.   Unsworths Booksellers   24 - 131   2011   £250

Patercullus, Velleius *The Roman History of C. Velleius Paterculus.* Edinburgh: printed for the author by John Mosman and Co., 1722. 8vo., pages (vi) x, 258, contemporary tan calf, untooled spine, red lettering piece gilt, boards panelled in blind 'Cambridge style' board edges decorative roll in blind, all edges gilt lightly red speckled, pink and white sewn endbands, some browning, few marks, touch rubbed at extremities, from the collection of Christopher Ernest Weston 1947-2010.   Unsworths Booksellers   24 - 132   2011   £150

Paule, George *Life of the Most Reverend and Religious Prelate John Whitgift, Lord Archbishop of Canterbury.* London: printed by Thomas Snodham, 1612. small 4to., pages (viii), 94, (ii), woodcut portrait of Whitgift on titlepage verso, early 21st century retrospective ruled calf binding by CEW, title soiled text block trimmed to printed border and sometimes just inside at top and fore-edge, old f.e.p. corner repaired, early hand has annotated head of blank leaf A1 and final blank leaf N4 armorial bookplate of "James Comerford" on front pastedown, mid 19th century ownership in Philip Bliss's hand on 17th century flyleaf reading "Bodleian Catalogue 1843, p. 62" and at foot of page I signature "P.B.43": and flowery label, presented by William Minet at foot of front pastedown, from the collection of Christopher Ernest Weston 1947-2010.   Unsworths Booksellers   24 - 34   2011   £450

Peck, Francis *Desiderata Curiosa; or a Collection of Divers Scarce and Curious Peices.* London: printed, 1732-1735. 2 volumes bound as 1, folio, pages (viii) viii (xii) 66, 26, 52, 50, 44, 56 (xii) + engraved portrait frontispiece and 6 other engraved plates, (xxii), 68, 58, 52, 32, 50, 36, 32, 56, 25 (xix) + engraved portrait frontispiece and 3 other engraved plates, contemporary tan calf over re-used late 16th century, 17th century pasteboards, spine panel gilt, lettered and dated together in gilt direct, boards single rule gilt bordered, board edges decorative roll in blind, all edges red speckled, brown and white sewn endbands, little marginal dust soiling but quite clean, rear joint cracked, front joint sometime restored but now split again with board loose, spine ends and corners worn, old scrapes and scratches to boards, armorial bookplate of Wm. Constable, Esqr, from the collection of Christopher Ernest Weston 1947-2010.   Unsworths Booksellers   24 - 133   2011   £450

Pennant, Thomas   1726-1798 *Of London.* London: printed for Robt. Faulder, 1790. 4to., pages iii-vi, (ii) 439 (ix) + engraved frontispiece, engraved and 11 other engraved plates, contemporary speckled and polished calf, spine emblematically panel gilt with 'classical urn' centerpieces, cornerpieces, black lettering piece gilt, boards decorative roll gilt bordered, board edges 'alternating full & broken hatch fillet' roll gilt, turn-ins alternating bands of light and dark stain, all edges red and grey sprinkled, green and white sewn endbands, green silk page marker, early 21st century conservation by Chris Weston, few spots, plates lightly foxed, titlepage dusty, from the collection of Christopher Ernest Weston 1947-2010.   Unsworths Booksellers   24 - 134   2011   £300

Polybius *The General History of Polybius.* London: printed for J. Dodsley, 1772. 2 volumes, 4to., pages xxiv, (viii) 559 (i) + extending engraved map frontispiece and one other extending engraved map, (xvi), 423, (xvii), contemporary sprinkled calf, spines panel gilt with 'Rococo' floral centrepieces, five raised bands and head and foot identically gilt using 'alternating full & broken hatch' pallet, red & black lettering & numbering pieces gilt, board edges decorative roll gilt, all edges lemon, red and white sewn endbands, lightly toned and bit spotted in places, rubbed, joints cracked, spine ends worn, some scrapes to boards, armorial bookplate of Thomas Poynder, from the collection of Christopher Ernest Weston 1947-2010. Unsworths Booksellers 24 - 136 2011 £360

Poulson, George *Beverlac; or the Antiquities and History of the Town of Beverley...* London: printed for George Scaum, 1829. 2 volumes bound as 1, large paper copy 4to., pages xx, 510 + engraved frontispiece, 1 extending engraved plate of facsimiles and 3 other plates (ii) (512)-816, 84, tipped in errata slip + 1 engraved plates, vignette "Beverley Foundry" pasted to page 816, folding plan of the "Boundary of the New Borough of Beverley" with hand colored outlines, contemporary purple morocco, four flat raised banded spine, bands and extremities 'paired tool' gilt with connecting gilt rules, compartments blind tooled in concentric panel, green lettering piece gilt, boards panelled in blind, decorative roll between rules all gilt within, quintuple rule with rose head corners innermost panel in blind, board edges single rule gilt, turn-ins 'quintuple zig-zag rules' in blind, 'Spanish' 'made' endpapers (green pasted), all edges 'Spanish' marbled (fawn based), fawn sewn flat endbands, purple silk page marker, plates bit foxed, few offset, spine faded, extremities rubbed, bit of wear to endcaps and top of joints, (?) lettering piece replaced armorial bookplate of Christopher Harrison, from the collection of Christopher Ernest Weston 1947-2010. Unsworths Booksellers 24 - 137 2011 £250

Robertson, David *A Tour through the Isle of Man; to Which is Subjoined a Review of all the Manks History.* London: printed for the author by E. Hodson, 1794. Large paper copy, 8vo., pages (xii), 235, (i) + 8 sepia aquatint plates, contemporary straight grained mauve morocco, five flat raised bands spine triple rule and decorative pallet gilt, top and bottom compartment have symmetrical oblong centrepieces, gilt between decorative pallets in blind, 3 other compartments filled with massed French influence 'rolling breakers' decorative pallets gilt, lettered in gilt direct, boards triple rule gilt borders with 'acanthus' roll in blind within, board edges alternating double full and single broken hatch fillet roll in blind, turn-ins similarly tooled, 'French Shell' 'made' endpapers, all edges similarly marbled, blue and white sewn endbands, pink silk page marker, plates bit foxed and few spots to pages, touch scratched, spines little faded and upper joint slightly rubbed, unidentified bookplate, decorative bookplate of Frederick J. G. Montagu, booklabel of John Sparrow, pencil inscription Catherine of Fountayne, pencil annotations in same hand, from the collection of Christopher Ernest Weston 1947-2010. Unsworths Booksellers 24 - 138 2011 £350

Rutland, John Henry Manners, 5th Duke of *Journal of a Tour to the Northern Parts of Great Britain.* London: printed for J. Triphook, 1813. 8vo., pages (iv) 300 + 10 sepia aquatint plates, 2 floor plans for Haddon Hall and 2 plates of room dimensions, contemporary mottled calf with early 20th century reback, spine double rule gilt with 'milled' roll gilt raised bands, compartments with 'covered urn' centre pieces gilt, red lettering piece gilt, number erased from 'open centred' centre piece gilt, boards single rule gilt bordered, board edges 'obliquely-broken fillet' roll gilt turn-ins 'double-rule' gilt, 'French Shell' 'made' endpapers, all edges mottled as per boards, pale blue and white sewn flat endbands, occasional minor spot, bit of chipping to head of spine, small area of surface insect damage at corner of lower board, armorial bookplate of James Comerford, from the collection of Christopher Ernest Weston 1947-2010. Unsworths Booksellers 24 - 120 2011 £150

Rutland, John Henry Manners, 5th Duke of *Travels in Great Britain. Journal of a Tour Round the Southern Coasts of England...* London: printed for J. Triphood, 1805. 1813. 1805; 3 volumes, 8vo., pages (viii) 229, (iii) + 2 sepia aquatint plates; (iv), 300 + 10 sepia aquatints, 2 floor plans, 2 plates of room dimensions, (viii), 389, (iii), + 7 sepia aquatint plates, contemporary sprinkled and polished calf, spines triple rule gilt, red lettering and numbering pieces gilt, boards single rule gilt bordered, board edges 'obliquely-broken fillet' roll gilt, turn-ins as above but in blind, all edges blue sprinkled, red and white sewn endbands, touch of faint spotting in places, quite rubbed, little wear to spine ends, some joints cracking, lettering piece of volume I and numbering piece of volume 3 lost, numbering piece of volume 1 upside down, from the collection of Christopher Ernest Weston 1947-2010. Unsworths Booksellers 24 - 119 2011 £750

Sallustius Crispus, Caius *C. Crispi Sallustii Belli Catilinarii et Jugurthini Historiae.* Glasguae: in aedibus Robert Urie, 1749. 8vo., pages iv, 250 (ii), rear board only of contemporary polished calf binding remains, board edges being decorative roll gilt, text block edges roughed, late 1980's attempts at rebacking with new front board by Chris Weston, lightly age toned, old leather bit scratched and rubbed, from the collection of Christopher Ernest Weston 1947-2010. Unsworths Booksellers 24 - 140 2011 £125

Sallustius Crispus, Caius *C. Crispi Sallustii Belli Catilinarii et Jugurthini Historiae.* Glasguae: in aedibus Roberti Urie, 1749. 8vo., pages iv, 250, (ii), contemporary polished calf, untooled spine, red lettering piece gilt, boards double rule bordered in blind with extra double rule and decorative roll in blind at joint side, board edges 'zig-zag' decorative roll gilt, all edges red speckled, pink and white sewn endbands, lightly age toned, few stains, rubbed and bit chipped, joints cracking, spine darkened, contemporary ink inscription John Pelch, first name covered by pasted slip and later ink inscription "Wm. Clark, also pencil inscription "From Prof. Henry Jackson's Sale...", from the collection of Christopher Ernest Weston 1947-2010. Unsworths Booksellers   24 - 139   2011   £50

Sallustius Crispus, Caius *The History of Catiline's Conspiracy and the Jugurthine War.* London: printed for D. Browne, A. Millar et al, 1757. 8vo., pages xvi, 253, (iii), contemporary sprinkled calf, spine panel with 'asymetric flowering plant' centrepieces and 'flower head' cornerpieces, red lettering piece gilt, board edges decorative roll gilt, all edges red sprinkled, red and white sewn endbands, little spotting, corners worn, joints cracking but strong, ink ownership stamp "Theo A Moon", from the collection of Christopher Ernest Weston 1947-2010.   Unsworths Booksellers   24 - 141   2011   £150

Sharp, John *Fifteen Sermons Preached on Several Occasions by... John Lord Arch Bishop of York.* London: printed for Walter Kettilby, 1709. Third edition; 8vo., pages (vi) 472 + engraved frontispiece, contemporary crimson turkey, spine gilt panelled with saltired compartments, lettered direct in gilt, boards panelled in gilt, board edges decorative roll gilt, turn-ins decorative roll gilt, 'Dutch-comb' 'made' endpapers, all edges gilt, blue and white sewn endbands, light spotting, occasional dampmark in lower margin, tidy repairs to headcap with new matching endband, black leather gilt decorative roll bordered label "To Mrs./E.B." ink inscription "Eliz. Battell/Juner", in different hand "The Gift of my Good Aunt Mrs. Eliz Battell to me Anne Hallows junr. May ye 26 1728", in same hand "Anne Leicester", ink inscription "John Roberts No 2 May 14 1792", from the collection of Christopher Ernest Weston 1947-2010.   Unsworths Booksellers   24 - 40   2011   £200

Sparrow, Anthony *A Rationale Upon the Book of Common Prayer of the Church of England...* London: printed for Robert Pawlet, 1672. 12mo., pages (viii), 353 (xxvii) 52 + engraved frontispiece, two engraved titles and 3 engraved portrait plates, contemporary speckled calf, boards double rule bordered in blind, board edges 'zig-zag' decorative roll gilt, all edges blue 'swirl' marbled, early 21st century re-sew and calf reback by Chris Weston, edges of frontispiece and first engraved title repaired, little spotting elsewhere, old leather a touch rubbed and chipped, contemporary ink inscription, from the collection of Christopher Ernest Weston 1947-2010.   Unsworths Booksellers   24 - 41   2011   £250

Spence, Joseph   1699-1768 *Polymetis or an Enquiry Concerning the Agreement Between the Works of the Roman Poets and the Remains of the Ancient Artists.* London: printed for R. and J. Dodsley, 1755.   Second edition; folio, pages vi, 361, (i) + engraved frontispiece and 41 other engraved plates, contemporary calf, spine fully gilt with 'sun-spot filled lattice' compartments, boards single rule gilt bordered with elaborate stencil design of interlocking 'eared' ovoids and quatrefoil corners, board edges decorative roll gilt, 'Dutch swirl' 'made' endpapers, all edges lemon, some minor spotting, frontispiece offset onto title, joints and corners skillfully repaired, old leather bit rubbed and scratched, contemporary engraved armorial bookplate lettered "southouse" pasted to verso of first plain flyleaf signed "Timbrell & Harding" later armorial bookplate of Strathallan, from the collection of Christopher Ernest Weston 1947-2010.   Unsworths Booksellers   24 - 142   2011   £675

Spottiswood, John *The History of the Church of Scotland, Beginning the Year of Our Lord 203 and Continued to the End of the Regn of King James the VI.* London: J. Flesher for R. Royston, 1655. Folio, pages (xx), 546, (xiv), engraved frontispiece and engraved portrait dedication leaf, contemporary calf, spine double ruled in blind, boards double rule double bordered connected by stylised mitre pieces at corners, board edges, single rule gilt, all edges red sprinkled and with black ink handwritten "Spotiswood" on fore edge, bit of spotting and dust soiling, rubbed and marked, some surface damage at extremities, recent amateur red lettering piece gilt, touch of wear to corners and front joint, booklabel "Abrahamus Francke, now detached and loosely inserted, ink inscription "Affrancke/ A.M. / T.C.C. of Soc./ Ecc. de W. D,. Paul/1716", later ink inscription "Little Horksley Library" at inner head, from the collection of Christopher Ernest Weston 1947-2010.   Unsworths Booksellers   24 - 42   2011   £400

Stillingfleet, Edward *A Defence of the Discourse Concerning the Idolatry Practised in the Church of Rome.* London: Robert White for Henry Nortlock, 1676. 8vo., pages (xxxii), 877, (i), contemporary calf, spine panel gilt, boards double ruled in blind, board edges 'zig-zag' decorative roll gilt, all edges red and grey sprinkled, pink and white sewn endbands, small inkmark to half title and titlepage, endcaps worn, old leather scratched and conserved, recent replacement red lettering piece gilt, dust jacket ink inscription "JJ.20", from the collection of Christopher Ernest Weston 1947-2010.   Unsworths Booksellers   24 - 46   2011   £250

Stillingfleet, Edward *A Discourse Concerning the Doctrine of Christ's Satisfaction...* London: J. Heptinstall for Henry Mortlock, 1696. 8vo., pages xlvi, (ii) 35, (i), contemporary sprinkled calf, spine double ruled in blind, red lettering piece, boards double rule bordered in blind with stylized plant at corners, board edges decorative roll gilt, all edges gilt, lightly red speckled, blue and white sewn endbands, little thumbsoiling, front joint just cracking at foot, slight rubbing to extremities, contemporary ink printing, ink inscription, from the collection of Christopher Ernest Weston 1947-2010. Unsworths Booksellers   24 - 50   2011   £200

Stillingfleet, Edward *An Answer to Some Papers... Concerning the Authority of the Catholick Church in Matters of Faith and the Reformation of the Church of England.* London: printed for Ric. Chiswel, 1686. 4to., (iv), 72, (ii) late 1990's half calf by Chris Weston, few minor spots, some early ink annotations, from the collection of Christopher Ernest Weston 1947-2010.   Unsworths Booksellers   24 - 48   2011   £95

Stillingfleet, Edward *Origines Sacrae, or a Rational Account of the Grounds of Christian Faith.* London: R. W. for Henry Mortlock, 1663. Small 4to., pages (xxxvi), 619, (i), contemporary calf, unlettered spine double ruled in blind, boards double ruled in blind, board edges single rule gilt, inner face of boards exposed all edges rouge, browned and spotted, some dust soiling, rubbed and scratched, front board detached, rear joint splitting, endcaps worn, early ink inscription "Robert Whitaker" on front endpaper, also "George Stead/Book May 16 1833" reading downwards at fore-edge of same leaf, from the collection of Christopher Ernest Weston 1947-2010.   Unsworths Booksellers   24 - 43   2011   £150

Stillingfleet, Edward *The Unreasonableness of Separation; or an Impartial Account of the... Present.* London: T. N. for Henry Mortlock, 1681. 4to., pages (ii), xciv, (xvi), 450, contemporary calf, boards double rule bordered in blind, board edges 'zig-zag' decorative roll gilt, all edges blue 'swirl' marbled, mid 1980's calf rebacked and corners by Chris Weston, some spotting and toning, first few leaves soiled, titlepage touch worn at fore-edge, old leather scratched and crackled, early ink inscriptions "Christopher Metcalfe" (reading across) and in a different hand "Christopher Metcalfe book" reading upwards, contemporary ink inscription "C.M.", also printed booklabel of Revd. Richard Gibbons Binnall, from the collection of Christopher Ernest Weston 1947-2010.   Unsworths Booksellers   24 - 47   2011   £275

Strype, John *The History of the Life and Acts of... Edmund Grindal...* London: printed for John Wyat and John Hartley, 1710. Folio, pages (i), xviii, 314, 108, (vi) + engraved frontispiece, contemporary calf, untooled spine, red lettering piece gilt, boards panelled in blind (Cambridge style) board edges decorative roll gilt, all edges red sprinkled, blue and white sewn endbands, lightly browned and spotted, rubbed and chipped, corners worn, joints cracking at ends, strong, contemporary inscription "Ant. Johnson, ink inscriptions crossed out on both pastedowns, from the collection of Christopher Ernest Weston 1947-2010. Unsworths Booksellers   24 - 51   2011   £250

Tacitus, Gaius Cornelius *Annales of Cornelius Tacitus.* London: printed by John Bill, 1622. Fifth edition; small folio, pages (vi) 271, (vii), 12, 228, (ii), the second page 213 is a full page engraving, this copy lacks initial blank, contemporary speckled calf, spine double ruled in blind, unlettered, boards double rule bordered in blind with smaller double rule central panel fleurons outermost at corners and smaller stylised flower, innermost all in blind, board edges decorative roll in blind, all edges red speckled, pink and white sewn endbands, little spotting, dampmark in upper corner, excisions to title repaired, rubbed, corners and endcaps worn, joints cracked, upper just holding, original ownership inscription cut out, but may have been same as "Fran: Cornwallis" at head fore corner of first page 1 or may have been same as "Richard Rowlandson" verso front blank, 19th century unidentified circular armorial bookplate, from the collection of Christopher Ernest Weston 1947-2010.   Unsworths Booksellers   24 - 145   2011   £300

Tacitus, Gaius Cornelius *C. Cornelii Taciti Opera quae exstant...* Antwerpiae: Ex Officina Plantiniana Balthasaris Moreti, 1648. Folio, pages (xvi) 547 (xxxiii) 36 84 (xvi), contemporary Dutch blind panelled vellum, spine lettered in MS. ink, all edges red sprinkled, green sewn endbands, green ties, early 21st century conservation by Chris Weston, lightly soiled, vellum dusty, little bit ruckled, from the collection of Christopher Ernest Weston 1947-2010.   Unsworths Booksellers   24 - 144   2011   £600

Tacitus, Gaius Cornelius *The Works of...* London: printed for G. G. J. and J. Robinson, 1793. 4 volumes, 4to., engraved maps, contemporary densely speckled calf, spine fully gilt with triple rules, interweaving front and graded pebbles' roll and 'sun-burst brooche' centerpieces, red and black lettering and numbering pieces gilt, board edges decorative roll gilt, all edges blue sprinkled, red and white sewn endbands, plates somewhat foxed, rubbed at corners, endcaps worn, joints cracking, labels lost from volumes 1 and 2 and partly lost on volume 3, stipple engraved booklabel of Theo. Leigh/Toft", ink ownership Theodosia Leigh, from the collection of Christopher Ernest Weston 1947-2010. Unsworths Booksellers   24 - 146   2011   £300

Taylor, Jeremy 1613-1667 *The Rule and Exercise of Holy Living and Holy Dying...*   London: Miles Flesher for Richard Royston, 1680. Twelfth edition; 2 volumes, 8vo., pages (xiv), 335, (i) + engraved titlepage and 1 double page engraved plates stub-mounted; (xiv), 259, (v) + engraved titlepage and 1 double page engraved plate stub mounted, contemporary black polished turkey, spines multi rule panelled in blind with contrasting stylised flower centerpieces, boards entirely blind tooled with triangular and rectangular densely ruled blocks, tulip & carnation heads, gouges and small 5 pointed stars, board edges and turn-ins decorative roll gilt, "Dutch-comb swirl" "made" endpapers, all edges gilt, 3 color pink, white and pale blue 2 core-sewn endbands, pink silk page markers, wholly unrestored "Sombre" bindings (age toned, few small stains, edges trimmed close, joints and edges rubbed, spines slightly faded, contemporary ink inscription M. Mcqueen", armorial bookplate of Shute Barrington, from the collection of Christopher Ernest Weston 1947-2010.   Unsworths Booksellers   24 - 52   2011   £950

Thoresby, Ralph *Ducatus Leodiensis; or the Topography of the Ancient and Populous Town and Parish of Leedes and Parts Adjacent in the West Riding of the County of York...*   London: printed for Maurice Atkins, 1715. Folio, pages iv (ii) v-xii 628 (xii), frontispiece, folding engraved map, 4 extending engraved plates and 7 other engraved plates, mid 18th century sprinkled and polished tan calf spine panel gilt with made-up centre pieces, 'frond' cornerpieces, six raised bands and head and foot identically tooled using 'opposing multi rule triangles' pallet, orange lettering piece gilt, boards double rule gilt bordered, board edges 'exaggerated-wavy' roll in blind, all edges red sprinkled, pink and white sewn endbands, browned and spotted in places, little surface damage to boards, small loss from headcap, corners slightly worn, 19th century armorial bookplate of Montagu George Knight of Chawton, from the collection of Christopher Ernest Weston 1947-2010.   Unsworths Booksellers   24 - 147 2011   £1000

Torr, James *The Antiquities of York City and the Civil Government Thereof...*   York: printed by G. White for F. Hildyard, 1719. 8vo., pages (viii), 148, (v), late 19th/early 20th century half sheep, cloth sides, text block uncut, height 210mm., some browning and soiling to page edges, spine and corners sunned, from the collection of Christopher Ernest Weston 1947-2010.   Unsworths Booksellers   24 - 148 2011   £200

Ussher, James *A Body of Divinity, or the Summe and Substance of Christian Religion...*   London: M. F. for Tho. Downes and Geo. Badger, 1648. Third edition; folio, pages (xii) 3-451, (xv), 24 + engraved portrait frontispiece, signed "W. Marshall Sculpsit 1647", contemporary sprinkled calf, boards double ruled in blind, board edges single rule gilt, all edges rouge with black ink hand written "Ussher" at head of fore-edge, pink & white sewn endbands, evidence of chaining staple at head of fore-edge of upper board, also evidence of later ties, early 1990's calf reback by Chris Weston, spotting and staining (mostly light), small tear to titlepage border repaired with sellotape, old leather marked and bit chipped at edges, near contemporary ink inscription "Roger Mostyn Anno 1685" at head of titlepage and underneath later ink inscription, booklabel of Gloddaeth Library, also ex-libris of Rev. John F. Brencher, his MS mini biography of Ussher on f.e.p. and his signature on reverse, from the collection of Christopher Ernest Weston 1947-2010.   Unsworths Booksellers   24 - 54 2011   £450

Ussher, James *A Speech Delivered in the Castle-Chamber at Dublin the XXII of November Anno 1622 at the Censuring of Certain Officers Who Refused to Take the Oath of Supremacie.*   London: printed by R. Y. for the Partners of the Irish Stocke, 1631. Small 4to., pages (ii), 12, (ii) disbound, age toned, soiled an spotted, now bound in quarter calf, red lettering piece lettered vertically down, boards sided out with marbled paper by Chris Weston, from the collection of Christopher Ernest Weston 1947-2010.   Unsworths Booksellers   24 - 53 2011   £75

Waterland, Daniel *A Critical History of the Athanasian Creed.*   Cambridge: University Press for Corn. Crownfield, 1724. 8vo., pages xxiv, 533, (xi), Francis Hoffman headpiece on page 1, contemporary calf untooled spine, boards panelled in blind (Cambridge style), board edges decorative roll gilt, all edges red speckled, pale blue and white sewn endbands, replacement lettering piece, dampstain to lower corner at beginning and end, touch of wear to corners, repairs to spine ends, later ink inscription "Richard Troyle his book 1774" and below "Elizabeth Troyle" on final f.e.p. (inverted), from the collection of Christopher Ernest Weston 1947-2010.   Unsworths Booksellers   24 - 56 2011   £250

Waterland, Daniel *A Second Vindication of Christ's Divinity or a Second Defense of Some Queries Relating to Dr. Clarke's Scheme of the Holy Trinity...*   London: for W. and J. Innys and Corn. Crownfield, 1723. 8vo., pages xxiv, 533, (xi), headpiece on p. 1, contemporary calf, boards panelled in blind (Cambridge style), board edges decorative roll gilt, all edges sprinkled red, early 21st calf reback and corners by Chris Weston, touch of marginal dust soiling, old leather slightly rubbed at edges.   Unsworths Booksellers   24 - 55 2011   £150

Waterland, Daniel *Scripture Vindicated: in Answer to Book Intituled, Christianity as Old as the Creation.* London: printed for W. Innys, Cambridge printed for Cornelius Crownfield and John Crownfield, 1730-1731. 2 parts bound as 1, with collective half title, 8vo., pages (iv), 96, (iv), 160, disbound and subsequently (late 1980's) calf bound by Chris Weston, few minor spots, lower corner of first leaf worn, from the collection of Christopher Ernest Weston 1947-2010. Unsworths Booksellers   24 - 57   2011   £150

Watson, Richard *Anecdotes of the Life of Richard Watson, Bishop of Landaff.* London: printed for T. Cadell and W. Davies, 1818. 2 volumes, 8vo., pages (ii), 476, contemporary polished dark blue half calf, spines decoratively gilt in six compartments, lettered direct in gilt numbered direct within a geometrical frame gilt, boards, single rule with 'tight French shell' marbled sides, all edges densely red sprinkled, pink and white patterned sewn endbands, titlepages foxed, light foxing elsewhere, boards little scuffed touch of rubbing at spine ends, from the collection of Christopher Ernest Weston 1947-2010.   Unsworths Booksellers   24 - 58   2011   £120

Watson, Robert *The History of the Reign of Philip the Second, King of Spain.* London: printed for W. Strahan, 1777. 2 volumes, 4to., pages (iv) 443, (i); (iv) 437 (xix), contemporary 'Antique Spot' sided boards, original ultra worn quarter sheep renewed in 1990s by Chris Weston, all text uncut, bit of light spotting, boards scuffed and corners worn, ink ownership inscription "Anketell Singleton", from the collection of Christopher Ernest Weston 1947-2010. Unsworths Booksellers   24 - 149   2011   £200

Weever, John *Antient Funeral Monuments of Great Britain, Ireland and the Islands Adjacent.* London: printed by W. Tooke for the editor, 1767. 4to., pages (x) clxxvii (i) 608 + engraved portrait frontispiece and 5 other engraved plates, extending table, contemporary calf much worn, board edges 'milled' decorative roll gilt, pink & white, sewn endbands, removal of amateur reback, revealed fragment of a once fully gilt spine with massed decorative pallets, awaiting restoration, now with early 21st century reback to corners by Chris Weston, light toning and some spotting, frontispiece offset, old leather somewhat scratched and bit rubbed at extremities, ink ownership inscription "Robt. Entwisle", from the collection of Christopher Ernest Weston 1947-2010. Unsworths Booksellers   24 - 150   2011   £400

Wellbeloved, Charles *Some Account of the Ancient and Present State of the Abbey of St. Mary, York and the Discoveries Recently Made in Excavating the Ground... (bound with) Some Remarks on the Pillar, or Obelisk at Forres...* London: published by the Society of Antiquaries, 1829. Large folio, pages 17 (i) 10 lithographic engraved plates numbered LI-LX (plus) extra illustration "Details of St. Mary's Abbey York" a tinted lithograph plate by F. Bedford, 2 + 2 lithographic engraved plates, contemporary half calf, boards triple rule bordered in blind, 'French Shell' sides, awaiting restoration, plates foxed, some dust soiling, rubbed, worn at edges, spine perished, boards detached, from the collection of Christopher Ernest Weston 1947-2010. Unsworths Booksellers   24 - 151   2011   £250

Wharton, Henry *The History of the Troubles and Tryal of.... William Laud...to which is prefixed the Diary of His Own Life.* London: printed for Ri. Chiswell, 1695. Folio, pages (xx) 616, (ii), engraved frontispiece, contemporary speckled calf, spine double ruled in blind decorative red lettering piece gilt, boards blind double ruled with decorative rollout with the supplementary ruling, board edges decorative roll gilt, all edges lightly red sprinkled, pink and white sewn endbands, title bit dusty, few minor spots elsewhere, touch rubbed joints cracking but strong, front joint bit defective at head, some scratches to boards, ink inscription "W. Danby", armorial 18th century bookplate "William Danby Esqr.", from the collection of Christopher Ernest Weston 1947-2010. Unsworths Booksellers   24 - 59   2011   £400

Whitaker, Thomas Dunham *Ducatus Leodiensis or the Topography of the Ancient and Populous Town and Parish of Leedes.* Leeds: printed by B. Dewhirst for Robinson, Son and Holdsworth etc. Printed by T. Davison for Robinson Son and Holdsworth etc., 1816. 2 works together as issued in 2 volumes, large paper copy, folio, pages (iv), xvii, (i), xvii, (i), 268, (ii) 123, (i), 159, 11, (i), engraved frontispiece and 10 other engraved plates, (vi), 404, 2, 88 + engraved portrait frontispiece and 52 other engraved plates, original grey sugar paper covered boards, white paper printed title labels with "Vol. 1" for the Ducatus volume and "vol. II" for the Loidis vol., all edges uncut, toned and spotted, rubbed and soiled, spine ends worn and rumpled, label edges and joints chipped, unidentified armorial bookplates, contemporary ink inscription Hallen Edge 1844, from the collection of Christopher Ernest Weston 1947-2010. Unsworths Booksellers   24 - 153   2011   £900

Whitaker, Thomas Dunham *History and Antiquities of the Deanery of Craven in the County of York.* London: printed by Nichols and sold, 1805. Folio, pages xii, 437, (i) 16 + engraved frontispiece and 36 other engraved plates, early 20th century marbled half leather, maroon bookcloth (watered design) sides, all edges uncut, toned and bit spotted, some foxing in plates, spine rubbed and faded, front joint bit worn, from the collection of Christopher Ernest Weston 1947-2010.   Unsworths Booksellers   24 - 152   2011   £250

Wright, G. N. *China, in a Series of Views Displaying the Scenery, Architecture and Social Habits of that Ancient Empire, Drawn from Original and Authentic Sketches...* London: and Paris: Fisher, Son and Co., 1843. 4 volumes bound as 2, 4to., pages 96, 72; 68, 56 72 + engraved vignette title and 31 steel engraved plates in each volume, contemporary tan half calf, spines panel gilt extra, green and black lettering and numbering pieces gilt, green 'publisher & date' piece gilt at foot, boards double rule gilt bordered with broken rule in blind within, 'pin head' design blue bookcloth sides, orange 'coated' endpapers, all edges gilt, multi core made red and yellow applied endbands, plates little foxed at edges, spine chipped at ends, numbering pieces mostly lost, joints cracking, ink inscription, from the collection of Christopher Ernest Weston 1947-2010.   Unsworths Booksellers   24 - 154   2011   £1000

Association – Wetherald, R.

Bacon, Francis, Viscount St. Albans 1561-1626 *The Twoo Bookes of Francis Bacon. Of the Proficience and Advancement of learning, Divine and Humane.* London: for Henrie Tomes, 1605.   First edition; 4to., (1), 45, 118 (i.e. 121), leaves, lacks final blank 3H2 an, as always, the rare two leaves of errata at end, late 18th century half calf and marbled boards, extremities of boards worn, very skillfully and imperceptively rebacked retaining entire original spine, small worm trail in bottom margin of quires 2D-2F, occasional minor marginalia in an early hand, else lovely, early signature of Row'd Wetherald on title, signature of Horatio Carlyon 1861, Sachs bookplate and modern leather booklabel, calf backed clamshell box.   Joseph J. Felcone Inc. Fall Miscellany 2010 - 8   2011 $7500

Association – Wharton, Elizabeth Kenneys-Tynte, Baroness

Paget, Violet 1856-1935 *Althea; a Second Book of Dialogues on Aspirations and Duty.* London: Osgood, McIlvaine & Co., 1894.   First edition; half title, original dark green cloth, spine lettered in gilt, spine darkened and rubbed at head and tail, inner hinges slightly cracked, armorial bookplate of Elizabeth Kenneys-Tynte (Baroness Wharton).   Jarndyce Antiquarian Booksellers   CLXC - 98   2011   £40

Association – Wheatley-Balme, Edward Balme

Bawden, William *Dom Bloc. A Translation of the Record Called Domesday, so Far as Relates to the County of York... and to the Counties of Middlesex (et al) and Gloucester.* Doncaster: printed by W. Sheardown, 1809-1812.   2 volumes, 4to., pages (iv) iv, 31, (i), 628, 61, (iii); (iv), 26, 76, (3)-82, 62, 72, 2, 4, 3, i), 4, 6, contemporary tan half calf, spines double rule and single broken rule gilt orange and red lettering and numbering pieces gilt, place and date gilt direct at foot, boards single rule gilt bordered with "nonpareil" marbled sides, matching 'made' endpapers, dark olive green sewn flat endbands, volume I in mid 198's calf reback, little light spotting titlepage toned, some marginal pencil marks, boards bit scuffed, corners and volume 2 spine rubbed, armorial bookplate of Edward Balme Wheatley-Balme, from the collection of Christopher Ernest Weston 1947-2010.   Unsworths Booksellers   24 - 68   2011   £300

Association – Whinfield, W. H.

Bentham, Jeremy 1748-1832 *Official Aptitude Maximized, Expense Minimized as Shown on the Several Papers Comprised in this Volume.* London: printed for the author and published by Robert Heward, 1830.   First edition of this collection; 8vo., 11 parts with paginations and signatures by Chuo, original boards, neatly rebacked and labelled, partially unopened, very good, old booklabel of W. H. Whinfield.   John Drury Rare Books   154 - 22   2011   £500

Association – Whistler, Laurence

Jones, Barbara *Follies & Grottoes.* London: Constable, 1953.   First edition; original cloth, gilt, dust jacket, slight wear and few short tears to edges, pages xii, 246, colored lithograph title, 28 drawings by author and 17 plates, the copy of engraver poet Laurence Whistler, with his pencilled signature, label removed from flyleaf.   R. F. G. Hollett & Son Antiquarian Booksellers   177 - 508   2011   £65

Association – Whitaker, Robert

Stillingfleet, Edward *Origines Sacrae, or a Rational Account of the Grounds of Christian Faith.* London: R. W. for Henry Mortlock, 1663.   Small 4to., pages (xxxvi), 619, (i), contemporary calf, unlettered spine double ruled in blind, boards double ruled in blind, board edges single rule gilt, inner face of boards exposed all edges rouge, browned and spotted, some dust soiling, rubbed and scratched, front board detached, rear joint splitting, endcaps worn, early ink inscription "Robert Whitaker" on front endpaper, also "George Stead/Book May 16 1833" reading downwards at fore-edge of same leaf, from the collection of Christopher Ernest Weston 1947-2010.   Unsworths Booksellers   24 - 43   2011   £150

Association – Whitbread, Harriot

Watts, Isaac *The Psalms of David. (bound with) Hymns and Spiritual Songs.* London: printed by and for J. W. Pasham, 1778. 123 x 70mm., 2 p.l., 240 pages, (10) leaves; 4 p.l., 216 pages, (12) leaves (index leaves for "Hymns an Spiritual Songs" bound out of order but all present), 2 parts in one volume, superb hand painted and gilt decorated vellum by Edwards of Halifax, both covers with very prominent oval paintings, front covers depicting a statue in grisaille of a female figure, probably representing Faith, casting her eyes upward to heaven, one arm aloft, other holding a cross, whole against a sky blue oval, back cover with very dynamic grisaille painting of the Resurrection, with Christ flying upward from the tomb amidst brilliant light, three soldiers beneath shielding themselves in protective wonderment and presiding angel supplying adoration at right, both covers bordered by gilt chain motif, flat spine divided by blue wash bands into compartments featuring gilt lyres and swirling gilt cornerpieces, blue wash label, all edges gilt in original soft green leather slipcase bordered by gilt chain matching that of binding, this in turn housed in modern morocco backed folding box with raised bands and gilt titling, bookplate of James Gordon, Esquire, Moor Place; inscription "Harriot Whitbread/The Gift of John Howard Esq(ui)re/ Cardington/ 1785", similar inscription to Harriot from M. Howard of Cardington dated 1787; blue spine label trifle faded, blue cover background on front board showing little soil, small ink blot on three pages, wonderful binding in very fine condition, text nearly pristine, original slipcase bit worn and faded but remarkable survival.   Phillip J. Pirages   59 - 13   2011 $6900

Association – White, Della Quinn

Plutarchus *The Live of the Nobel Grecians and Romanes...* Shakespeare Head Press, 1928. One of 500 copies; printed for sale in Great Britain, this copy # 309, another 500 sets were printed for the U.S. and an additional 100 were printed on handmade paper and signed by artist, 233 x 160mm., 8 volumes, quite attractive mid 20th century burgundy half morocco over matching linen, gilt decorated raised bands, spines with large central compartment featuring an intricate gilt filigree lozenge and cornerpieces, marbled endpapers, top edge gilt, other edges untrimmed and largely unopened, engraved headpieces, front flyleaf with tipped on typed note from Harry E. Davis, ABAA describing the book and noting the binding was done by hand for Della Quinn White of Houston Texas in 1952; very small gouge to front cover of volume I (but deep enough to cause a small crack in pastedown), otherwise very fine set, largely unopened, text nearly pristine and handsome bindings lustrous and virtually unworn.   Phillip J. Pirages   59 - 318   2011 $1500

Association – White, John Chambers

James, William *The Naval History of Great Britain.* London: Richard Bentley, 1837. 8vo., 6 volumes, xiv, xxxii, 404; vii, 396; viii, 376; viii, 376; viii, 404; viii, 568 pages, contemporary tan half calf on marbled boards, black spine labels, gilt decoration to spines including ship motifs, from the library of John Chambers White with armorial bookplates, half titles present but without loose charts and abstracts seen accompanying some copies, 24 engraved plates numerous battle plans in text, very little foxing, some occasional light offsetting from plates, slight overall rubbing, withal a still robust, clean handsome set.   Any Amount of Books   May 26 2011 - A63567   2011 $629

Association – Whitehead, Robert Bovill

Morris, Francis Orpen   1810-1893   *A History of the British Birds.* London: George Bell and Sons, 1870. Second edition; 365 hand colored plates, some foxing to few, tall 8vo., over 1600 pages, original green cloth, some wear, mostly to lower corners, partial splitting to cloth on rear edge of 2 volumes, several corners bumped, soiling to some endpapers, few inner joints open, occasional light foxing, Robert Bovil Whitehead armorial bookplates.   Raymond M. Sutton, Jr.   May 26 2011 - 30708   2011 $1250

Association – Wickenheiser, Robert

Milton, John   1608-1674   *Comus.* London: William Heinemann/New York: Doubleday Page, 1921. One of 550 copies; signed by artist, 300 x 233mm., 3 p.l., ix-xviii, 76 pages, (1) leaf, very attractive deep blue morocco by Zaehnsdorf for E. Joseph (stamp signed), upper board with very large gilt pictorial presentation and titling, raised bands, gilt spine titling, densely gilt turn-ins, marbled endpapers, top edge gilt, other edges untrimmed and partly unopened, illustrated titlepages, numerous black and white drawings, and 24 particularly pleasing color plates by Arthur Rackham, mounted on brown paper, original tissue guard, with descriptive letterpress; bookplate of Robert J. Wickenheiser, virtually faultless copy.   Phillip J. Pirages   59 - 292   2011 $3900

Association – Wiggin, Albert Henry

Du Maurier, George Louis Palmella Busson   1834-1896 *Trilby.* Osgood, McIlvaine & Co.,, 1894. Serialised in Harper's Monthly Magazine, Volume LXXXVIII Dec. 1893 to May 1894; Titlepage of the European edition, illustrations, contemporary half maroon morocco, raised bands, gilt compartments, hinges neatly repaired, 6 page news paper article "Trilby" from Publishers' Weekly Aug. 1928 tipped in, 4 page ALS from author to Sir William Morrow, original brown cloth bound in at end of volume, armorial bookplate of Albert Henry Wiggin, very good.   Jarndyce Antiquarian Booksellers   CXCI - 166   2011   £150

Association – Wightman, Arthur

Hirschfelder, J. O. *The Effects of Atomic Weapons.* Washington: Combat Forces Press, 1950. First edition; slight wear at spine ends, else near fine in fair dust jacket, lacking top inch or so to spine and split at spine fold, Arthur S. Wightman's copy with his ownership signature. Between the Covers 169 - BTC340930 2011 $475

MOVE Association – Wingfield, E. A.

Marsh, Anne *Father Darcy.* London: Chapman and Hall, 1846. First edition; 2 volumes, half titles, contemporary half dark green calf, spines gilt in compartments, maroon leather labels, slight rubbing, each volume signed by E. A. Wingfield, Digby with associated inscriptions, John Fowles booklabel, good plus. Jarndyce Antiquarian Booksellers CLXC - 238 2011 £180

Association – Wilbur, Marguerite Eyer

Venegas, Miguel *Juan Maria de Salvatierra of the Company of Jesus: Missionary in the Province of New Spain and Apostolic Conqueror of the Californias.* Cleveland: Arthur H. Clark Co., 1929. First edition, one of 755 copies; 350 pages, illustrations, maps, facsimiles, portraits, red cloth, gillt, slight rubbing to spine ends, fine, presentation copy signed by editor, Marguerite Eyer Wilbur to author Lindley Bynum. Argonaut Book Shop Recent Acquisitions Summer 2010 - 218 2011 $275

Association – Wilenski, Reginald

Ruskin, John 1819-1900 *War.* Woolwich: printed for private circulation, 1866. Half title, partially erased pencil notes at end, original red cloth, dulled & rubbed, all edges gilt, good, sound copy, exceedingly scarce, bookplate of military historian Sir Basil Liddell Hart, with 4 page ALS to him from art historian Reginald Wilenski, July 23 1961. Jarndyce Antiquarian Booksellers CXCI - 478 2011 £380

Association – Wilkie, Gary

Ginsberg, Allen *Sad Dust Glories/ Poems During Work Summer in Woods.* Berkeley: The Workingham Press, 1975. First edition; 8vo., pages (iv), 27, (i) imprint, original stapled green pictorial wrappers, some slight discoloration to wrappers, still near fine, inscribed by author for Gregory Corso, with TLS from Gary Wilkie to Corso loosely inserted. Simon Finch Rare Books Zero - 318 2011 £675

Association – Wilkind, Sam

Phillippo, James Mursell *Jamaica: its Past and Present State.* London: John Snow, 1843. First edition; 8vo., pages xvi, 487, 16 full page woodcut illustrations and woodcut vignettes, inscribed by Rev. Th. H. Clarke/Dry Harbor Jamaica Novb. 1843 for Sam. J. Wilkind. Any Amount of Books May 29 2011 - A45552 2011 $255

Association – Wille, Franz

Collins, Wilkie 1824-1889 *The Moonstone.* Leipzig: Bernhard Tauchnitz, 1868. (1894). Copyright edition; 2 volumes in 1, half titles, contemporary half dark brown sheep, publisher's binding, rubbed and little worn, good, sound copy, booklabel of Franz Wille, Jerusalem library stamp on half title volume 1. Jarndyce Antiquarian Booksellers CXCI - 131 2011 £85

Association – Willet, B. H.

Addison, Joseph 1672-1719 *The Works.* London: George Bell and Sons, 1893-1898. 7 volumes, 185 x 115 mm., attractive contemporary prize binding of light polished calf done for H. Sotheran & Co. (stamp signed on front turn-in of each volume), covers with double gilt fillet border, upper board of each volume with central gilt crest of St. Peter's College, Westminster, raised bands, spines ornately gilt in compartments with elegant central floral spray, surrounded by a lozenge of small tools and elaborate side and cornerpieces composed of fleurons, curls, volutes and circulets, two pale green morocco labels, filigree gilt turn-ins, marbled endpapers, all edges gilt, volume I with portrait frontispiece and 8 plates of medal and coin designs, pastedown with affixed presentation certificate to B. H. Willet, signed by William ("Gulielmus") Rutherford and dated 1899, leather with bit of dryness, extremities little rubbed, labels slightly faded, one minor neatly repaired tear (into text, but no loss), otherwise fine, elaborately gilt bindings lustrous and with other minor wear and text virtually pristine, pretty set. Phillip J. Pirages 59 - 62 2011 $275

Association – Williams, Joe

Oliver, Paul *Conversation with the Blues.* London: Cassell, 1965. First edition; original cloth, gilt, dust jacket, pages xix, 217, with 80 illustrations and 2 maps, part of a menu signed by Count Basie and his vocalist Joe Williams (twice) (April 1960), another (indecipherable) loosely inserted. R. F. G. Hollett & Son Antiquarian Booksellers 175 - 1021 2011 £120

Association – Williams, John

Caussin, Nicholas *The Holy Court in Five Times....* London: printed by William Bentley, 1650. Folio, near contemporary speckled calf with raised bands and spine label, sometime nicely re-cased, rather rubbed, corners restored, pages (xx), 522, (viii) (viii) 319 (i, blank), 13, (vii), half title, printed title in red and black, 6 further titles, engraved head and tailpieces, historiated initials in each section and numerous engraved portraits within text, some 10 leaves in first section have several closed cuts to text, without loss, one leaf fine with lower corner torn off affecting 3 lines of table, otherwise excellent, clean and sound copy, early ownership signatures of John and Jane Comberbach of Barker Street, Nantwich, Cheshire, later armorial bookplate of Sir John Williams of Bodelwyddan Castle in North Wales.   R. F. G. Hollett & Son Antiquarian Booksellers   175 - 233 2011   £350

An Interesting Appendix to Sir William Blackstone's Commentaries on the Laws of England. Philadelphia: Robert Bell, 1773. Second American edition; 8vo., contemporary calf, crudely rebacked, very good, browned, Institutional name stamped on free endpaper, name erased from title, with John C. Williams bookplate, engraved by Nathaniel Hurd.   M & S Rare Books, Inc.   90 - 44 2011 $3500

Association – Williams, Jonathan

Niedecker, Lorine *My Friend Tree. Poems.* Edinburgh: Wild Hawthorn Press, 1961. First edition; oblong 8vo., original wrappers, dust jacket, fine association copy, inscribed by author for her later publisher, Jonathan Williams.   James S. Jaffe Rare Books   May 26 2011 - 7948 2011 $7500

Spicer, Jack *After Lorca.* San Francisco: White Rabbit Press, 1957. One of 26 lettered copies signed by Spicer with drawing by poet out of a total edition of 500 copies typed on an Olivetti Lexikon 80 by Robert Duncan; 8vo., original pictorial wrappers with cover drawing by Jess, covers somewhat foxed, some portion rubbed, otherwise very good, rare, although not noted, this copy belonged to poet and Jargon Press publisher, Jonathan Williams.   James S. Jaffe Rare Books   May 26 2011 - 21279 2011 $6500

Association – Williams, Josephine

Kelly, George *Craig's Wife a Drama.* Boston: Little Brown, 1926. First edition; 8vo., pages 174, very nice, tight copy, inscribed by author to Josephine Williams who played the part of Mrs. Harold in the NY production, also signed by rest of the cast - Annie Sutherland, Crystal Herne, Arthur Shaw, C. Stewart, Eleanor Marsh, Charles Trowbridge, Josephine Hull, J. A. Curtis, Nelan Jaap, Arline Alcine & Mary Gildea, also inscribed by the producer, Rosalie Stewart to whom the play was dedicated.   Second Life Books Inc.   174 - 213 2011 $2000

Association – Williams, Mary

Thomson, James   1700-1748   *The Seasons.* London: printed for John Sharpe, 1821. 170 x 105mm., 215, (1) pages, extremely pleasing etruscan style calf in the style of and quite probably by Edwards of Halifax, covers with gilt Greek key border, wide inner frame of stencilled palmettes, central panel of tree calf framed by a gilt broken cable, flat spine gilt in compartments separated by Greek key roll and with a lyre centerpiece framed by foliate cornerpieces, with black morocco label, marbled endpapers, all edges gilt, very attractive fore-edge painting of an English stately home, perhaps Stourhead House, extra engraved titlepage with vignette and fine engraved plates, inscription "Mary Williams/The last gift of her affectionate Aunt/Mary Hoyle, July 31st 1826"; extremities and joints bit dry and rubbed, rear joint just starting at tail, gilt eroded from head and tail of spine, half a dozen small patches of lost patina in frame around outside of stencilled central panel, plates little foxed, one more noticeably but still quite pleasing copy, appealing unrestored original binding entirely sound, text clean and smooth and rich colors of painting beautifully preserved.   Phillip J. Pirages   59 - 196 2011 $1100

Association – Williams, Rudolph August

Lefevre, Raoul *Recuyell of the Historyes of Troye.* Hammersmith: Kelmscott Press, 1892. One of 300 copies; 3 books in 2 volumes, large quarto, xv, (1), 295, (1 blank); (297)-507, (1, blank), (509)-718 pages, printed in red and black in Troy and Chaucer type, decorative woodcut borders and initials, bound by Cedric Chivers in beautiful Art Nouveau "Vellucent" binding, binding elaborately decorated in vivid colors and detail and all boards and spine ruled in gilt, front covers framed by green vines with pink and orange flowers and gilt stamped detail, inside frame of vines stands Helen of Troy on volume I and Cassandra on volume II, title of book shown on a scroll beneath women's feet, spines of both volumes contain similar scroll decoration, also containing title of book on back cover of each volume is image of the towers of Troy in flames, and gauffered, others uncut, marbled endpapers, gilt ruled dentelles, bookplates of former owners Rudolph August Williams and "CKC" Charles C. Kalbfleisch and bookplate of other previous owner on back pastedown of each volume, each volume in its own chemise and quarter calf slipcase, dentelles slightly lifting, otherwise beautiful, near fine set in extraordinary binding.   Heritage Book Shop   Holiday 2010 - 67 2011 $22,500

Association – Williamson, George Charles

Somervell, John *Some Westmorland Wills 1686-1738.* Kendal: Titus Wilson, 1928. First edition; pages 119, uncut, 9 plates, slight stain to gutter of flyleaf, bookplates of George Charles Williamson and Helen Mary Garnett.   R. F. G. Hollett & Son Antiquarian Booksellers   173 - 1068 2011   £60

Association – Willink, William Williamson

Lytton, Edward George Earle Bulwer-Lytton, 1st Baron 1803-1873 *The Last Days of Pompeii.* London: Richard Bentley, 1834. First edition; 210 x 130mm., volume 1 lacking half title, 3 volumes, publisher's drab paper boards backed with maroon muslin, flat spines with original printed paper labels, edges untrimmed, housed in red buckram chemise, inside very handsome red morocco backed case, its spine designed to appear as three attractively found volumes with raised bands and gilt compartments filled with interlacing floral vines, ALS by apparently written by author's elder brother, the diplomat, Sir Henry Lytton Earle Bulwer to his banker, 19th century armorial bookplate of William Williamson Willink, each volume with morocco bookplate of Estelle Doheny; paper boards bit soiled (one cover with slight dampstain), minor wear at joints and extremities, isolated trivial smudges internally, otherwise excellent unsophisticated set, especially clean and fresh, extremely handsome. Phillip J. Pirages 59 - 259 2011 $950

Association – Willis, Connie

A Dozen on Denver. Gulden: Fulcrum, 2009. First edition; fine, signed by Connie Willis, Nick Arvin, Robert Greer, Margaret Coel, Manuel Ramos and Arnold Grossman. Bella Luna Books May 29 2011 - p3633 2011 $104

Association – Willis, John Ralph

Armistead, Wilson *Tribute for the Negro: Being a Vindication of the Moral, Intellectual and Religious Capabilities of the Coloured Portion of Mankind.* Manchester: William Irwin, 1848. First edition; octavo, (i)-xxxv, (1, blank), (1)- 564, (4, publisher's ads), (2, blank) pages, frontispiece and 11 additional engraved plates, half title and engraved titlepage, text within decorative border, publisher's deluxe gilt binding, full plum morocco, boards ruled in blind, front board and spine decoratively stamped gilt with vignettes of shackled slaves, all edges gilt, yellow endpapers, bookplate of John Ralph Willis, prominent collector of Rare Africana, previous owner's ink inscription dated '48, inner front hinge cracked but firm, hardly noticeable, some light foxing, overall better condition than usually found in publisher's rare deluxe binding. Heritage Book Shop Holiday 2010 - 3 2011 $2750

Burton, Richard Francis 1821-1890 *To the Gold Coast for Gold. A Personal Narrative.* London: Chatto & Windus, 1883. First edition; 2 volumes, octavo, xii (1, contents) (1, blank), (1)-354, (2), (32, publisher's ads); (2, blank), (i)-vi,(1)-381, (3) pages, 2 colored folding maps in volume I and colored frontispiece in volume II, publisher's original red cloth, stamped in black and gilt on boards, spines lettered in gilt and stamped in black, black coated endpapers, spines slightly rubbed and sunned, top edges bit foxed, minimal and invisible restoration to inner hinges, bookplate of previous owner John Ralph Willis, very good, handsome. Heritage Book Shop Holiday 2010 - 15 2011 $5500

Association – Willoughby De Broke, John Peyto Verney

Patercullus, Velleius *C. Velleii Paterculi Historiae Romanae and M. Vinicium Cos Libri Duo.* Parisiis: Apud Fredericum Leonard, 1675. 4to., pages (xxviii) 151, (lxxxix) + engraved half title, bound facing title contemporary mottled calf, spine panel gilt, dark red lettering piece gilt, boards double rule bordered in blind with central triple rule panel having fleurons at corners all in blind, board edges decorative roll gilt, all edges red speckled, blue and white sewn endbands, few minor spots, title bit dusty, old leather somewhat scratched, contemporary ink inscription, armorial bookplates of John Peyto Verney/Lord Willoughby de Broke, and of Robert John Verney/Lord Willoughby de Broke, from the collection of Christopher Ernest Weston 1947-2010. Unsworths Booksellers 24 - 131 2011 £250

Association – Willoughby De Broke, Robert John Verney

Patercullus, Velleius *C. Velleii Paterculi Historiae Romanae and M. Vinicium Cos Libri Duo.* Parisiis: Apud Fredericum Leonard, 1675. 4to., pages (xxviii) 151, (lxxxix) + engraved half title, bound facing title contemporary mottled calf, spine panel gilt, dark red lettering piece gilt, boards double rule bordered in blind with central triple rule panel having fleurons at corners all in blind, board edges decorative roll gilt, all edges red speckled, blue and white sewn endbands, few minor spots, title bit dusty, old leather somewhat scratched, contemporary ink inscription, armorial bookplates of John Peyto Verney/Lord Willoughby de Broke, and of Robert John Verney/Lord Willoughby de Broke, from the collection of Christopher Ernest Weston 1947-2010. Unsworths Booksellers 24 - 131 2011 £250

Association – Willoughby, Francis

Grew, Nehemiah 1641-1712 *Musaeum Regalis Societatis or a Catalogue & Description of the Natural and Artificial Rarities Belonging to the Royal Society...* London: printed by W. Rawlins for the author, 1681. First edition; folio, pages (12), 386, (4), (2), 43, contemporary tooled full calf professionally rebacked with sympathetic leather, restored tears to corners near spine, bump to fore-edge of front cover, stains to front endpaper, bookplate removal, edges to front blanks chipped, occasional foxing, ink correction to a page, restored tear to rear endpaper, the copy of Francis Willoughby. Raymond M. Sutton, Jr. May 26 2011 - 55886 2011 $2000

Association – Willoughby, Mrs.

Crawford, W. S. *Synesius the Hellene.* London: Rivingtons, 1901. First edition; 8vo., pages xiv, 585, signed presentation from author to Mrs. Willoughby Dominique, original publisher's maroon cloth lettered gilt at spine, faint shelfwear, else very good+ with loosely inserted flyer with quotes from library reviews. Any Amount of Books May 29 2011 - A45131 2011 $221

Association – Willyams, W. B.

Taylor, Jane 1783-1824 *Hymns for Infant Minds.* London: Jackson and Walford, 1840. Thirty-second edition; 12mo., original roan backed marbld boards, gilt, edges and corners little rubbed or worn, pages (iv), 98, (ii), woodcut vignette frontispiece, some early leaves little fingered, some contemporary annotations, this copy inscribed "Master W. B. Willyams Oct. 1841".   R. F. G. Hollett & Sons Antiquarian Booksellers   170 - 676   2011   £45

Association – Wilson, Dr.

Robertson, Eric *Wordsworthshire.*   Kirkby Stephen: Hayloft Pub., 2000.   First edition; thick 8vo., original cloth, gilt, spine little faded and hinges trifle rubbed, pages xii, 352, 47 illustrations by Arthur Tucker and maps, endpapers little spotted, presentation copy inscribed by author to Dr. Wilson, Dalston.   R. F. G. Hollett & Son Antiquarian Booksellers   173 - 979 2011   £45

Association – Wilson, Jack

Coward, Noel 1899-1973   *Qaudrille. A romantic Comedy in Three Acts.*   London: Heinemann, 1952.   First edition; 8vo., pages 116, signed by 17 members of the English cast and by producer Jack Wilson and by Lynn Fontanne and Alfred Lunt on dedication page (play is dedicated to them), inscribed by Coward to Dorothy Sands (Octavia in the NY production), two more signed cards by Lunt and Fontanne tipped in and 3 notes by Lunt to Sands laid in, with tipped in signed photo of Sands, nice copy in somewhat chipped dust jacket.   Second Life Books Inc.   174 - 111   2011 $700

Association – Wilson, James

Longus *Daphnis & Chloe.*   London: Geoffrey Bles, 1925.   First edition thus; large 4to., pages 200, with 12 tipped in colored and 4 black and white full plate illustrations by John Austen, original vellum backed blue cloth, from the Daphnis and Chloe collection of bookplate expert James Wilson with his D&C bookplate (by Mark Severin), hand numbered limitation signed by Austen (number 91), very faint soiling of vellum spine, corners very slightly rubbed, very good or better.   Any Amount of Books   May 26 2011 - A65762   2011 $604

Association – Wilson, James Lee

Craig, Edward Gordon 1872-1966   *Nothing or the Bookplate.*   London: Chatto & Windus, 1924.   First edition; crown 8vo., original russet buckram lettered gilt on spine and cover, pages vii, 27 and 50 pages of figures, loosely inserted 2 original bookplates by E. C. Craig, limited edition, no. 33 of 280 copies, this with a further bookplate signed by Gordon Craig, bookplates hand colored, from the library of James Lee Wilson with his small neat bookplate by Leo Wyatt, loosely inserted is a compliments slip from London Mercury 1925 with review of book extracted, spine slightly sunned, very good+.   Any Amount of Books   May 26 2011 - A66401   2011 $419

Association – Wilton, Ann

Smith, Dodie   *Call It a Day.*   London: Victor Gollancz, 1936.   First edition; 8vo., 151 pages, very good in slightly tanned and slightly marked decent and very good dust jacket, signed presentation form author to Ann Wilton.   Any Amount of Books   May 29 2011 - A71753   2011 $408

Association – Wimbush, Evelyn

Paget, Violet 1856-1935   *A Phantom Lover: a Fantastic Story.*   London: William Blackwood & Sons, 1886.   First edition; contemporary maroon binder's cloth, spine faded and slightly worn at head and tail, signs of label removed from front board, signed "Evelyn Wimbush, 1887" (friend of author).   Jarndyce Antiquarian Booksellers   CLXC - 109   2011   £650

Association – Windele, John

O'Brien, Henry   *The Round Towers of Ireland or The Mysteries of Freemasonry of Sabaism and of Budhism for the First Time Unveiled.*   1834.   First edition; half calf, (2), 524 pages, 4 plates, many text illustrations, quarter leather library binding, not a pretty copy, but it has owner inscription of doyen of Cork antiquaries John Windele.   C. P. Hyland   May 26 2011 - 259/350   2011 $362

Association – Winningham, Geoff

Martin, William C.   *Going Texas: the Days of the Houston Livestock Show and Rodeo.*   Houston: Mavis P. Kelsey Jr., 1972.   First edition; limited to 500 numbered copies, very near fine, some minor rubbing to photo mounted on front panel in very near fine cloth slipcase, signed by photographer, Geoff Winningham, laid in is original silver gelatin photo that is also signed by Winningham, very uncommon.   Jeff Hirsch Books   ny 2010 2011 $1250

Association – Winslow, John

Abbot, Abiel *Self Preservation. A Sermon Preached Before the Ancient and Honorable Artillery Company in Boston June 7 1802...* First edition; 8vo., 23, (1) pages, illustrated half title, sewn and uncut, original plain front wrapper, presented by militia commander General John Winslow to Judge (Robert Treate) Paine. M & S Rare Books, Inc. 90 - 1 2011 $125

Association – Wise, Mary

Morgan, Sydney Owenson 1776-1859 *Woman; or Ida of Athens.* London: Longman, Hurst, Rees and Orme, 1809. First edition; 4 volumes, contemporary full calf, borders in blind and gilt, gilt spines, black leather labels, spines little dulled and slightly rubbed, good plus, with gift inscription in prelims of each volume, "Mary Wise, the gift of her beloved and affect. husband, 1809". Jarndyce Antiquarian Booksellers CLXC - 541 2011 £650

Association – Wistrand, Rolfe

Guevara, Antonio De *Vita Di M. Avrelio Imperadore.* Venice: Bartolomeo Imperador and Francesco Veneziano, 1543. 160 x 103mm., 8 p.l., 132, (2) leaves, fine contemporary Roman red morocco Apollo and Pegasus medallion binding done for Giovanni Battista Grimaldi by Marc Antonio Guillery, (genuine Apollo and Pegasus binding) covers with gilt frame formed by two widely spaced fillets with lobes interlaced at ends and sides, space between fillets decorated with broad foliate curls, small floral tools, inner pane of each board with gilt titling above a horizontal oval Apollo and Pegasus plaquette centerpiece showing Pegasus atop black painted heights of Parnassus and Apollo racing his chariot (drawn by two straining steeds) across steep terrain with reins and whip held aloft and caps fluttering behind, plaquette with gilt motto in Greek in the collar above and below vignette, spine (very expertly rebacked) with four thin and three thick raised bands decorated with gilt rope pattern or plain rules (this being original backstrip?), newer (perhaps 19th century) endpapers, all edges gilt (apparently some remarkably skillful restoration at one or more corners and edges, perhaps some gold added, as well as to the chariot part of the plaquettes); woodcut printer's device on , morocco bookplate and separate gilt monogram of Robert Hoe as well as inscription and vellum bookplate of Swedish collector Thore Virgin, ownership inscription of J. T. Payne dated 1850; covers with half dozen insignificant tiny dark spots, titlepage faintly soiled, thin light brown stain just at top edge of leaves, small wormhole at upper inner margin (text not affected), occasional minor stains, other trivial imperfections, but no defects that are even remotely serious and in general really excellent specimen of a very special binding, text fresh and leather quite lustrous; also from the collection of bibliophile Johannes Gennadius, Liverpool oculist T. Shadford Walker and Swedish collector Rolfe Wistrand. Phillip J. Pirages 59 - 2 2011 $35,000

Association – Wittock, Michel

Appianus, Alexandrinus *Romanorum Historiarum Libri.* Basel: Hieronymus Froben and Nicolaus Episcopius, 1554. 318 x 216mm., 8 p.l., 506 pages (duplicate leaves pages 437-440), 22 leaves, early 20th century dark brown morocco over pasteboard, covers panelled in gilt and blind with three sets of blind rules, gilt double ruled frame interlaced at lobes on ends and sides, decorated with broad foliate curls, cornerpieces and small bird tools, inner panel with titling in lobed compartment at head, small foliate curl endpiece and sidepieces, flanking upright oval Apollo and Pegasus centerpiece embossed and with traces of gilt and silvering on black background, showing Pegasus with raised foreleg on cliff before a charging Apollo, who races his chariot across steep terrain with reins and whip held aloft and cape fluttering behind, gilt collar with motto in Greek in upper half and chain roll in lower, raised single and double bands, spine panelled gilt and blind with double rules, gilt cinquefoil centerpiece, all edges gilt, fleece lined brown buckram clamshell case, brown morocco labels on spine; woodcut historiated initials, printer's device on titlepage and verso of last leaf; morocco bookplate of Michel Wittock; slightly soiled and with several tiny wormholes, much of text with light overall browning, sprinkled foxing and very occasional faint spotting, little soiling (done on purpose?) to covers, still an obviously appealing volume, wonderful (according to Hobson fraudulent) binding virtually unworn and text perfectly satisfactory with no serious problems, superb example of a replica binding with remarkably persuasive tooling and just enough purposefully applied "wear" and discoloration to be deceiving, according to Hobson this example would not be genuine because Apollo does not lean far enough forward in his chariot and his steeds' front hooves incorrectly touch the cliff. Phillip J. Pirages 59 - 3 2011 $8500

Oribasius *Synopseos ad Evstathivm Filivm Lib. Novem.* Paris: Maurice Meunier for Oudin Petit, 1554. First edition; splendid 16th century Parisian citron morocco, very lavishly gilt for Pietro Duodo, boards with elegant frame of leafy fronds enclosing a large central panel occupied by five horizontal rows of three ovals, each of these ovals enclosing lovely flower tool, covers also with large number of gilt thistles, passion flowers and other small tools, slightly larger central oval on upper cover with armorial crest of Duodo, lower cover with three lilies on hillock as well as a collar containing Duodo's motto "Expectata non eludet", flat spine similarly gilt with two flower medallions above and below a central oval containing author's name, spine ends raised above top and bottom board edges in a la grecque style, all edges gilt, felt lined folding cloth box, woodcut initials and woodcut device on titlepage, ruled in red throughout, green morocco bookplate of Michel Wittock, ink inscription "Cuthell Martin 23 May (18)04" (presumably recording purchase from London Booksellers Cuthell & Martin); hint of uniform darkening to backstrip, two tiny wormholes near tail of spine, corners and joints slightly rubbed, isolated insignificant stains internally, still very fine, text remarkably fresh and clean, exquisite little binding lustrous and generally in especially pleasing state of preservation, minor wear far outweighed by bright, sumptuous gilt. Phillip J. Pirages 59 - 11 2011 $17,500

Association – Woburn Abbey

Darrah, H. Z. *Sport in the Highlands of Kashmir.* London: Rowland Ward, 1898. First edition; large 8vo., pages xviii, 506 2 folding maps (in envelope at rear), 52 illustrations, original publisher's maroon cloth lettered gilt at spine, 'Zebra skin' endpapers with ducal Woburn Abbey bookplate, very good, clean. Any Amount of Books May 26 2011 - A74330 2011 $671

Association – Wolfe, Humbert

Pound, Ezra Loomis 1885-1972 *Umbra: the Early Poems of Ezra Pound.* London: Elkin Mathews, 1920. First edition; 8vo., pages 128, original publisher's printed grey boards with cloth spine, slight soiling slight marks but decent, very good, ownership signature of Humbert Wolfe Jan. 18 1926. Any Amount of Books May 29 2011 - A64843 2011 $255

Association – Womack, Nathan

Pare, Ambroise 1510-1590 *Ten Books of Surgery and the Magazine of the Instruments Necessary for It.* Athens: University of Georgia, 1969. First edition; 8vo., xvi, 264 pages, illustrations, brown cloth, gilt ruled cover borders and gilt stamped spine title, near fine, presentation inscription by translator Nathan Womack, from the Medical Library of Dr. Clare Gray Peterson. Jeff Weber Rare Books 162 - 234 2011 $50

Association – Wood, Egerton

Chambers, Robert *The Book of Days.* London: W. & R. Chambers, 1864. 2 volumes, large 8vo., original half crimson morocco, gilt, little scraped, pages (iv), 832; (ii), 840, all edges and endpapers marbled, printed in double columns, red and black pictorial titles, woodcut illustrations, scattered foxing, mainly to flyleaves, but handsome sound set, green morocco presentation label "Mr. & Mrs. Joseph Shorrock from Egerton W. Wood 1865". R. F. G. Hollett & Son Antiquarian Booksellers 175 - 243 2011 £150

Association – Wood, L. Duncan

Emerson, Ralph Waldo 1803-1882 *Representative Men: Seven Lectures.* Boston: Ticknor and Fields, 1863. Contemporary half calf, marbled boards, with calf corners, marbled endpapers and edges, neatly rebacked retaining original spine, signed by author, armorial bookplate of L. Duncan Wood, near fine, scarce. Charles Agvent Transcendentalism 2010 - 21 2011 $4500

Association – Woods, Lucius

Douglas, William O. *Go East, Young Man, the Early Years.* New York: Random House, 1974. First edition; fine, dust jacket near fine, very light use, laid in is gift letter to Walter Gerash from Lucius Woods dated Feb. 25, 1991. Bella Luna Books May 29 2011 - t9174 2011 $82

Association – Wordsworth, Jonathan

Wordsworth, William 1770-1850 *My Dearest Love. Letters of William and Mary Wordsworth 1810.* Grasmere: Dove Cottage, 1981. Limited edition (no. 196 of 300 copies; large 4to., original quarter morocco gilt with marbled boards, oval leather label, gilt monogram, cloth slipcase with matching marbled boards, pages 81, untrimmed, 25 facsimile plates, loosely inserted prospectus with 1 page (folded as issued), original invoice with 4 line autograph postcard from Jonathan Wordsworth (St. Catherine's College, Oxford '81), fine. R. F. G. Hollett & Son Antiquarian Booksellers 173 - 1241 2011 £400

Association – Wren, Matthew

Drexelius, Jeremias *The Considerations of Drexelius Upon Eternitie.* London: printed by John Redmayne, 1663. 18mo., old splashed calf, nicely rebacked in matching calf gilt with raised bands and lettering piece, pages (xxii), 358, engraved title printed at Cambridge by Roger Daniel and 8 woodcut plates, signature of Matthew Wren on engraved title and some marginal annotations, probably in his hand, some later annotations in another hand (probably that of Lord Torphichen, whose armorial bookplate is on pastedown), few pencilled marginal crosses, originally the copy of Matthew Wren (1585-1667), Christopher Wren's uncle. R. F. G. Hollett & Son Antiquarian Booksellers 175 - 389 2011 £650

Association – Wright, A. E. G.

Bell, Edward Allen *A History of Giggleswick School from its Foundation 1499 to 1912.* Leeds: Richard Jackson, 1912. Limited large paper edition, no. 40 of 100 copies; original full vellum gilt over bevelled boards, spine trifle rubbed, pages xii, 294 (v), top edge gilt, untrimmed with 44 plates, excellent copy, very scarce deluxe edition, bookplate of A. E. G. Wright, this copy was purchased new by his grandfather T. W. Wright. R. F. G. Hollett & Son Antiquarian Booksellers General Catalogue Summer 2010 - 1331 2011 £180

Association – Wright, Abner

Smith, Samuel *The History of the Colony of Nova Caesaria or New Jersey...* Burlington: James Parker, 1765. First edition; x, 573, (1) pages, modern calf backed marbled paper covered boards, very skillfully executed in period style, noticeably foxed as usual, few blank corners torn away without loss, contemporary ownership signatures of Burlington County residents Saml. Black and Abner Wright.   Joseph J. Felcone Inc.   Fall Miscellany 2010 - 108   2011 $2000

Association – Wright, Frank Lloyd

Wendingen The Life Work of the American Architect Frank Lloyd Wright. Santpoort: 1925-1926. First English language edition; numbers I-VII of the magazine Wendingen, inscribed by the artist on titlepage, oblong folio, publisher's full beige cloth, inscribed by Frank Lloyd Wright.   Heritage Book Shop   Booth A12 51st NY International Antiquarian Book Fair April 8-10 2011 - 142   2011 $4000

Association – Wright, Nathan

Schickard, Wilhelm *Tarich h.e. Series Regum Persiae... Cum Proemio Longiori...* Tubingen: T. Werlin, 1628. 4to., 231 pages, woodcut illustrations, 18th century calf, gilt spine, red edges, last 2 leaves cropped at outer margin with loss of letters, cropped signature at head of title "Nathan Wright of Englefield", from the library of the Earls of Macclesfield at Shirburn Castle.   Maggs Bros. Ltd.   1440 - 194   2011   £1800

Association – Wright, P. J.

Howell, James *Lustra Ludovici or the late Victorius King of France, Lewis the XIII and his Cardinal de Richelieu.* London: by John Legate II for Humphrey Moseley, 1646. First edition; folio, (12), 188, (8) pages, engraved medallion portrait, woodcut initials and headpieces, rule borders, 17th century red morocco gilt, panelled sides with fleuron at corners, spine gilt in compartments, gilt edges, long tear in P3 with slight loss, occasional other short tears in margins, occasional manuscript notes in margins, small tear on upper cover, from the P. J. Wright collection with note on flyleaf dated September 1720, from the library of the Earls of Macclesfield at Shirburn Castle.   Maggs Bros. Ltd.   1440 - 112   2011   £450

Association – Wright, Stuart

Caldwell, Erskine Preston   1903-1987 *Some American People.* New York: McBride, 1935. First edition; review copy, inscribed by author to Stuart Wright, owner signature of Florence Luntz, trace wear to spine ends, very near fine in near fine, slightly dusty dust jacket with tiny tear at upper front spine fold, publisher's review slip laid in, giving publication date Oct. 21 135, very nice association, rare as advance issue, particularly signed.   Ken Lopez Bookseller   154 - 23   2011 $500

Association – Wright, T. W.

Bell, Edward Allen *A History of Giggleswick School from its Foundation 1499 to 1912.* Leeds: Richard Jackson, 1912. Limited large paper edition, no. 40 of 100 copies; original full vellum gilt over bevelled boards, spine trifle rubbed, pages xii, 294 (v), top edge gilt, untrimmed with 44 plates, excellent copy, very scarce deluxe edition, bookplate of A. E. G. Wright, this copy was purchased new by his grandfather T. W. Wright.   R. F. G. Hollett & Son Antiquarian Booksellers   General Catalogue Summer 2010 - 1331   2011   £180

Association – Wright, W. A.

Babington, Churchill *An Introductory Lecture on Archaeology Delivered Before the University of Cambridge.* Cambridge: Deighton Bell and Co., 1865. First edition; original cloth, gilt, spine chipped at head and tail, pages (iv), 80, 8, presentation copy inscribed to W. A. Wright.   R. F. G. Hollett & Son Antiquarian Booksellers   177 - 60   2011   £65

Association – Wright-Smith, Lesley

Marine Biological Association of the United Kingdom *Journal of...* Plymouth/Cambridge: Marine Biological Association of the United Kingdom/Cambridge University Press, 1887-2006. First editions and reprint; Old Series Volumes 1 and 2 (of 2) and New Series Volumes 1-84 (complete), volume 85 (Nos. 1, 2, 3, 6) and Volume 86 (nos.1-3) in 112; very good, numerous plates, text figures and some photos, occasional minor soiling, few short tears along folds and tear along fold of a panel in 1, few tears repaired with tape, tall 8vo., some 4to., volumes 1/2, 1-3, 5 an 12-21 contemporary hardbound, volumes, 4, 6-11 and 22-48 recent hardbound, original wrappers bound into volumes 6-11 & 22-48, volumes 49-68 in original printed wrappers, volumes 69-86 paperbound (modest wear to extremities in 6 oldest volumes, spine faded to brown in 3 older volumes and with splitting to cover along edges of spine in 2, some endpapers browned, handstamp to front wrappers and or front endpapers contents and index pages are photocopies in volumes 6 and 10, plates are photocopies in volume 7, occasional tear to soiling to original wrappers or text pages, some pencil notations to text pages, in early issues, occasional bump, short tear or wrinkling to paper on spine, light soiling or pages tanned, recent issues mostly fine; with W(alter) Garstang's signature and handstamp to 3 volumes, A(lister) C(lavering) Hardy's signature to 24 volumes, Lesley D. Wright-Smith's copy with his name on title, numerous dates and some notes on page margins.   Raymond M. Sutton, Jr.   May 26 2011 - 48790   2011 $2400

Association – Wyatt, Stephen

Kneale, Nigel *The Year of the Sex Olympics and Other TV plays.* London: Ferret Fantasy, 1976. First edition; 8vo., pages 143, original publisher's ochre cloth lettered gilt on spine, ownership signature of S. J. Wyatt (i.e. Stephen Wyatt, author of Doctor Who books), about fine in very good, slightly tanned dust jacket (complete, with no nick or tears), excellent condition.   Any Amount of Books   May 29 2011 - A68822   2011 $255

Powell, Michael *A Life in the Movies: an Autobiography.* London: Heinemann, 1986. First edition; 8vo., pages 705, original green boards lettered gilt on spine, signed by author on titlepage, ownership signature of Stephen Wyatt, playwright, slight lean bumping, otherwise near fine, in like dust jacket (very slight creasing).   Any Amount of Books   May 26 2011 - A68824   2011 $461

Association – Wyndham, J.

Martineau, Harriet   1802-1876   *Retrospect of Western Travel.* London: Saunders and Otley, 1838. First edition; 3 volumes, half titles, 2 pages ads volume III (unopened), uncut and partially unopened in original drab boards, labels on spines little browned, very good, signature J. Wyndham 1948.   Jarndyce Antiquarian Booksellers   CLXC - 337   2011   £380

Association – Yasinski, Rene

Bonnefoy, Yves   *Pierre Ecrite.*   Paris: Mercure de France, 1965. 8vo., pages 88, (1) imprint, partly unopened, very bright, clean copy, original printed ivory wrappers as issued, with original protective tissue, blue and black text to upper and lower wrapper and spine, upper hinge detached but text block firm, glassine wrapper, chipped in places, author's presentation inscription for Monsieur et Madame Rene Yasinksi.   Simon Finch Rare Books   Zero - 302   2011   £350

Association – Yates, Edmund

Fenn, William Wilthew   *Half Hours of Blind Man's Holiday; or Summer and Winter Sketches in Black and White.* London: Sampson Low, 1878. First edition; 2 volumes, half titles, largely unopened in original dark olive green cloth, armorial bookplate of novelist Edmund Yates, very good.   Jarndyce Antiquarian Booksellers   CXCI - 174   2011   £180

Association – Yeager, Mr.

Anaya, Rudolfo   *Bless Me. Ultima.*   Berkeley: Quinto Sol, 1972. First edition; near fine, light bumping to corners, dust jacket very good-, moderate rubbing, several repaired closed tears, but complete, inscribed by author for Mr. & Mrs. Yeager.   Bella Luna Books   May 26 2011 - t9349   2011 $1650

Association – Yorke, Henry Francis Redhead

Kerner Von Marilaun, Anton   *The Natural History of Plants Their Forms, Growth, Reproduction and Distribution.* Blackie & Son, 1894-1895. 2 volumes, thick small 4to., contemporary three quarter green levant morocco gilt with marbled boards by Riviere, spines mellowed, top edge gilt, 16 color plates and some 2000 woodcut text illustrations, handsome, bookplate of Sir Henry Francis Redhead Yorke. R. F. G. Hollett & Son Antiquarian Booksellers   General Catalogue Summer 2010 - 1008   2011   £220

Association – Yoshi

Wells, Ruth   *A to Zen. A Book About Japanese Culture.* Saxonville: Picture Book Studio, 1992. First edition; 4to., pictorial boards, as new in dust jacket, illustrations by Yoshi, this copy inscribed by Yoshi.   Aleph-Bet Books, Inc.   95 - 23   2011 $100

Association – Young, Noel

Metz, Jerred *The Temperate Voluptuary. Rendered From Platina's Cookbook on Its 500th Anniversary.* Santa Barbara: Capra Press, 1975. First edition, a total of 50 numbered, signed copies; pictorial boards, handbound by Emily Paine, this copy not numbered but rather designated as "Noel Young's copy" in red ink, woodcuts by Thomas Lang, fine in glassine dust jacket.   Charles Agvent   2010 Summer Miscellany - 47   2011 $100

Association – Yudkin, John

Godwin, William   1756-1836   *Of Population. An Enquiry Concerning the Power of Increase in the Numbers of Mankind...*   London: printed for Longman, Hurst, Rees, Orme and Brown, 1820.   First edition; 235 x 152, xvi, (17)-22, 626 page, publisher's original temporary brown paper boards, paper label, edges untrimmed, text unopened (except for the introduction), folding cloth box with morocco spine label, old armorial bookplate of Jonathan Hargreaves and modern bookplate of John Yudkin; backstrip chipped at head (costing perhaps a square inch of paper), vertical crack at top reaching two-thirds of the way down the spine, loss of paper along half the length of joints (and with short cracks in joints), slight rubbing to corners (as usual), but binding still solid and otherwise well preserved, covers unusually clean, one opening of preface with noticeable ink staining in upper margin, minor foxing and marginal tears, but exceptionally clean and well preserved internally, unopened text obviously unread.   Phillip J. Pirages   59 - 217   2011 $3900

Association – Zimbalist, Efrem

Cather, Willa Sibert   1873-1947   *One of Ours.* New York: Knopf, 1922.   First edition; of the limited edition of 345 large paper copies, signed by author, this one of 35 on Imperial Japon vellum, signed twice, once on endpaper and again on limitation page, fine, untrimmed copy in custom slipcase, bookplate of collector Efrem Zimbalist.   Second Life Books Inc.   174 - 90   2011 $3750

Association – Zimmerman, Fred

Wildlife Society   *The Journal of Wildlife Management. (with) Wildlife Monographs.*   Bethesda: Washington. Menasha: The Wildlife Society, 1937.   First edition; very good plus, 8vo., volumes 1-66 (missing 3 issues, volume 35 (No. 4) 36 (1) and 49 (1), includes indies for volumes 40 and with Wildlife Monographs Nos. 1-2, 8-51 and 142-150; volumes 1-29 bound in red cloth by year, remaining volumes as published by number in original wrappers, occasional minor scuff, short tear smudge, light bump, Fred R. Zimmerman's handstamp and or signature to early volumes, very nice.   Raymond M. Sutton, Jr.   May 26 2011 - 55375 2011 $1200

Association – Zyw, Aleksander

Muir, Edwin   *Poles in Uniform.* London: Thomas Nelson, 1943.   Oblong 4to., original cloth, gilt, few slight marks, pages 128, illustrations, presentation copy inscribed by artist, Aleksander Zyw.   R. F. G. Hollett & Son Antiquarian Booksellers   175 - 1484   2011   £45

Fine Bindings

Binding – 16th Century

Baif, Lazare De *Annotationes in L. II. De Captivis, et Postiliminio Reversis in Qvibvs Tractatvr de Re Navali (and three other works).* Paris: Robert Estienne, 1536. First edition of "De re Navali", first printing of this collection; 215 x 150mm., 4 p.l., (1)-168, (8), (1)-203, (13) pages (with pagination anomalies), striking 16th century calf, heavily and beautifully gilt, covers gilt with border formed by two plain rules flanking a floral roll, this frame enclosing a central file of very many tiny star tools, intricate strapwork, cornerpieces and large central arabesque composed of strapwork interspersed with lilies and volutes; flat spine divided into latticed gilt panels by double plain rules and floral bands, newer (17th or 18th century?) black morocco label, binding almost certainly with some restoration (joints probably worked on, though repairs executed with such skill as to make difficult identifying exactly what has been done), old stock used for replacement endpapers, 32 fine woodcuts in text, 11 of them full page or nearly so, woodcut printer's device on title, decorative initials 4 woodcut diagrams, text in Latin and Greek, covers with minor discoloration, little crackling and minor scratching, gilt bit dulled and eroded, one corner somewhat bumped, half dozen leaves with faint dampstains to lower outer corner, hint of soil in isolated places, extremely pleasing copy, binding solid, serious wear, still very attractive, text clean, fresh and bright, margins generous. Phillip J. Pirages 59 - 5 2011 $7500

Bude, Guillaume *De Asse et Partibvs Eivs Libri V.* Lvgdvni: Apvd Seb. Gryphivm, 1550. 185 x 120mm., 815, (79) pages, (1) leaf (with errors in pagination), fine contemporary ivory blindstamped pigskin over wooden boards, covers with frames formed by multiple blind rules and foliate roll featuring laurel-wreathed heads in medallions, upper cover with central panel stamp showing Justice with her sword and scales, the letters "C A N" stamped on panel above Justice and date "1566" on panel below, lower cover with central panel stamp depicting virtuous Roman matron Lucretia in act of suicide, raised bands, two fore-edge clasps and front free endpaper missing; printer's device on title, intermittent (presumably early) underlining in brown pencil, front pastedown with modern bookplate showing a ship above mott "Novus Orbis", titlepage with early ink ownership inscriptions and library stamp of Tomaso Luciani of Albona; tip of lower corner of front cover chipped off, adjacent half inch of pigskin missing along tail edge, covers bit smudged, other minor external defects binding very sturdy and still extremely attractive deeply impressed stamps retaining much of their detail and all of their charm, and front cover still rather clean, leaves bit toned with age, occasional minor stains, text quite smooth, few signs of use. Phillip J. Pirages 59 - 8 2011 $950

Oribasius *Synopseos ad Evstathivm Filivm Lib. Novem.* Paris: Maurice Meunier for Oudin Petit, 1554. First edition; splendid 16th century Parisian citron morocco, very lavishly gilt for Pietro Duodo, boards with elegant frame of leafy fronds enclosing a large central panel occupied by five horizontal rows of three ovals, each of these ovals enclosing lovely flower tool, covers also with large number of gilt thistles, passion flowers and other small tools, slightly larger central oval on upper cover with armorial crest of Duodo, lower cover with three lilies on hillock as well as a collar containing Duodo's motto "Expectata non eludet", flat spine similarly gilt with two flower medallions above and below a central oval containing author's name, spine ends raised above top and bottom board edges in a la grecque style, all edges gilt, felt lined folding cloth box, woodcut initials and woodcut device on titlepage, ruled in red throughout, green morocco bookplate of Michel Wittock, ink inscription "Cuthell Martin 23 May (18)04" (presumably recording purchase from London Booksellers Cuthell & Martin); hint of uniform darkening to backstrip, two tiny wormholes near tail of spine, corners and joints slightly rubbed, isolated insignificant stains internally, still very fine, text remarkably fresh and clean, exquisite little binding lustrous and generally in especially pleasing state of preservation, minor wear far outweighed by bright, sumptuous gilt. Phillip J. Pirages 59 - 11 2011 $17,500

Binding – 17th Century

Aristoteles *Commentarii Colelgii Conimbricensis Societatis Iesu in Tres Libros de Anima Aristotelis Stagiritae.* Cologne: Impensis Lazari Zetzneri, 1609. Some light browning and spotting, few marginal paper flaws and touch of marginal worming near end (never affecting text) pages (viii), columns 694, pages (19), 4to., contemporary Oxford blind tooled dark calf boards, outer border of triple blind fillet, frame of triple blind fillet with cornerpieces and central decorative blind lozenge, spine with four raised bands between blind fillets, hatched at top and bottom, little rubbed in places, bit of wear to corners and head of spine, pastedowns lifted and early printed binder's waste exposed to front, ownership inscription of "Chesterton", good. Blackwell Rare Books B166 - 17 2011 £950

Binding – 18th Century

Catholic Church. Liturgy & Ritual. Breviary *Breviarium Romanum.* Venetiis: Ex Typographia Balleoniana, 1744. 187 x 112 mm., 4 volumes, very attractive contemporary dark brown crushed morocco, handsomely gilt, covers with simple border of plain and stippled gilt rules and fleuron cornerpieces, raised bands, spines intricately and elegantly gilt in compartments formed by plain and decorative gilt rules and featuring cornerpieces of leaves and volutes framing a central curling lozenge incorporating palmettes with fleur-de-lys, marbled endpapers, all edges gilt with gauffering on top and bottom edges next to endbands, apparently original elaborate ribbon markers comprised of four silk strands held together at top by large tassel, 14 engravings by M. Beylbrouck, engraved printer's device on titlepages, woodcut tailpieces and floriated initials, printed in red and black, one opening with small wax (?) stain, other very trivial imperfections, nearly flawless copy, binding with only faintest signs of age, clean, fresh and bright text with virtually no signs of use.   Phillip J. Pirages   59 - 7   2011 $1500

Dodsley, Robert   1703-1764   *A Collection of Poems... by Several Hands.* London: For J. Dodsley, 1782. 6 volumes, 173 x 116mm., half titles, superb contemporary sprinkled calf, flat spines, wide gilt bands forming elegantly gilt compartments with scrolling cornerpieces and large sunburst centerpiece, red and green morocco labels, engraved vignette titlepage, engraved and woodcut headpieces and tailpieces, 2 engraved plates; perhaps 20 leaves with moderate foxing, small dent and puncture in fore edge of four gatherings of first volume (text unaffected), frequent offsetting in text, otherwise only insignificant defects internally, leaves quite fresh and clean, covers with only trivial imperfections, especially attractive bindings remarkably well preserved.   Phillip J. Pirages   59 - 10   2011 $1900

Heister, Lorenz   1683-1758   *Chirurgie, in Welcher Alles was Zur Wundarzney Gehoret... Deutlich Vorgestelelt Werden.* Nurnberg: Bey Gabriel Nicolaus Raspe, 1779. 216 x 183mm., 8 p.l. (including frontispiece), 378, (4) pages, 379-1078 (i.e. 1076) pages, 12 leaves, stunning contemporary painted calf, elaborately gilt decorated, covers each with four very large and graceful gilt floral tools within large compartments formed by interlacing strapwork that is painted black, an equally prominent central compartment with dense gilt foliage, flowers and fleurons and much supporting gilt decoration of a similar kind in 20 smaller compartments around the board edges and between the large compartments, raised bands, spine very handsomely gilt with lovely central flower and botanical side pieces, olive green spine label, gilt decorated turn-ins, marbled endpapers, all edges gilt; ornamental headpieces, initial and tailpieces, frontispiece and 38 sometimes startling folding plates, titlepage in red and black, inscribed "Dr. Harald Long 1895"; tiny cracks in label, text printed on inferior paper stock (so not particularly bright), but almost nothing else in the way of a significant defect; superb, even exceptional copy in wonderful binding, text absolutely fresh and leather with virtually no signs of wear.   Phillip J. Pirages   59 - 52   2011 $17,500

Binding – 19th Century

Crowe, J. A.   *History of Painting in Italy. (and) History of Painting in North Italy. (and) Early Flemish Painters.* London: John Murray, 1864-1872. First edition of first two works, second edition of the third; 222 x 144mm., 3 separately published works bound in 6 volumes, uniformly bound in handsome contemporary dark green pebble grain morocco, lavishly gilt, covers with gilt frame formed by multiple plain and decorative rules flanking a central Greek key roll, raised bands, spines heavily gilt in double ruled compartment with Greek key roll at top and bottom, inner dotted frame with scrolling cornerpieces and elongated central fleuron, turn-ins gilt with multiple decorative rules and floral cornerpieces, marbled endpapers, all edges gilt, 148 black and white plates, two of them folding, pencilled ownership inscriptions of C. M. Brewster, fore edge of one upper board just slightly bumped, trivial imperfections internally, but very fine set, sumptuously gilt bindings, especially lustrous and virtually unworn, text and plates showing almost no signs of use.   Phillip J. Pirages   59 - 81   2011 $1500

Filhol, Antoine Michel   *Galerie Du Musee de France.* Paris: Chez Filhol, 1814-1815. First edition in book form; (with Poussin's "Paysage" in volume VIII misidentified in the contents as plate 557, rather than 577), 305 x 229mm., with half titles, 10 volumes, marvelous contemporary dark green morocco sumptuously gilt in romantic style, covers with complex scrolling and undulant cornerpieces connected by triple gilt rules, raised bands, spine compartments densely and very handsomely gilt with massed scrolling and foliate stamps, very wide turn-ins gilt with thick and thin rules framing a border composed of the same kind of decoration as on spine, all edges gilt, 718 very pleasing engraved plates of famous works of art (numbered 1-720 but with plates #552 and 553 omitted as always), original tissue guards, 4 plates supplied from another copy; large paper copy, more area occupied by margins than by either text or plates; some boards with slightest variation in color, few trivial marks to covers, lovely bindings beautifully preserved, with rich coloring, leather and gilt extraordinarily lustrous, tissue guards and versos of plates normally foxed, variable foxing to plates with only marginal or light foxing, perhaps 30 plates with more noticeable foxing, about as many entirely clean, rest moderately foxed, otherwise in fine condition internally, few signs of use and with fine impressions of engravings.   Phillip J. Pirages   59 - 71   2011 $4800

Paul, James Balfour *The History of the Royal Company of Archers.* Edinburgh & London: William Blackwood and Sons, 1875. First edition; 250 x 200mm., ix, (i), 393 (1), 78 pages, 20 leaves, very fine contemporary dark green morocco, sumptuously gilt, covers with French fillet border, elaborate gilt picture like central frame around gilt emblem with motto "Dat Gloria Vires" above and "In Peace and War" below, showing figures associated with archery and love, peace, and war, raised bands between compartments with foliate cornerpieces and bow and quiver centerpiece, densely gilt inner dentelles, silk endleaves, gilt edges, in red and black felt lined buckram slipcase, with 6 full page color portraits, six black and white photo plates, and four line drawings, titlepage in red and black, inked note "This book formerly belonged to Lady Louis Mountbatten 4.8.34", bottom 4 inches of front joint just beginning to crack, covers slightly bumped, else beautiful copy, very handsome decorative binding, quite bright, text and plates in perfect state of preservation, luxuriously bound.   Phillip J. Pirages   59 - 66   2011 $750

Rogers, Samuel *Recollections of the Table Talk of Samuel Rogers to Which is added Porsoniana.* London: Edward Moxon, 1856. Apparently the first edition; 199 x 130 mm., viii, 355 pages, bound with half title with inserted plate as frontispiece, very pleasing later dark brown crushed morocco, attractively gilt, covers with French fillet border and elegant botanical cornerpieces, raised bands, heavily gilt spine in compartments featuring elaborate scrolling cornerpieces, an intricate fleuron centerpiece, and tiny circlets, turn-ins with plain and stippled rules and filigree with gilt decoration at corners and midpoints of two sides, textured (silk?) brown and cream millefleur-patterned endpapers, all edges gilt, extra illustrated with 55 portrait plates, five in color, all with tissue guards, engraved bookplate of Robert B. Lawrence, hint of browning to some of the inserted plates, fine, handsomely bound copy, text especially fresh, clean and smooth, binding bright and virtually unworn; hint of browning to some of the inserted plates, fine, handsomely bound copy, text especially fresh, clean and smooth, binding bright and virtually unworn.   Phillip J. Pirages   59 - 131   2011 $650

Binding – 20th Century

Goldsmith, Oliver   1730-1774 *The Vicar of Wakefield.* London: George G. Harrap & Co., 1929. First edition; 4to., top edge gilt, publisher's leather with elaborate and lovely inlay on front cover, very nice with no notable faults, 12 full page color plates and line drawings by Arthur Rackham, 232 numbered pages, housed in original publisher's box with title label on one end, box has some wear and side missing, magnificent publisher's inlaid leather binding.   Jo Ann Reisler, Ltd.   86 - 203   2011 $1500

Pollok, Robert *The Course of Time: a Poem in Ten Books.* Edinburgh: William Blackwood and London: T. Cadell, 1833. 169 x 105mm., 2 p.l. 394 page, charming early 20th century sky-blue crushed morocco, onlaid and gilt, front cover with onlaid red morocco flanked and decorated with gilt, this border expanding into wedge shaped cornerpieces featuring a stylized gilt rosebud with curling gilt stems and onlaid green morocco leaves (veins delicately traced with gilt), border enclosing large center panel featuring prominent round centerpiece of onlaid red morocco containing the same gilt rosebuds and green morocco leaves found in corners (but here seen in graceful interlacing form), back cover repeating same design but entirely in gilt raised bands, heavily gilt spine with rose and leaf patterns repeated wide turn-ins with three gilt fillets, all edges gilt, top of spine with very shallow piece of leather loss approximately half its width, hint of soiling to covers, spine uniformly sunned to pleasing blue green, otherwise fine, quite pretty binding with virtually no wear to joints or hinges and with only trivial problems internally.   Phillip J. Pirages   59 - 122   2011 $575

Binding – Allix, Susan

Allix, Susan *Rosas: Roses Real and Imaginary with Poems.* London: Susan Allix, 2009. One of 10 copies, signed by artist (this copy #8); 369 x 277mm., 14 unnumbered leaves, in an exuberant binding of multi-colored morocco and embroidery by Susan Allix, covers inlaid with irregular morocco pieces in various shades of yellow, pink, blue, green, orange and burgundy to achieve a quilt like effects; upper cover with large octagonal centerpiece of hand embroidered roses in reds, yellows and pinks on dark green background, flat spine with vertical titling in blind, handmade endpapers in bright pink and black with pink polka dots, edges untrimmed, original red felt lined folding cloth box with morocco labels and accents in two colors, 9 illustrations, one an original watercolor unique to this volume, as new.   Phillip J. Pirages   59 - 83   2011 $4800

Binding – Andrews

Architectural and Archeological Society of Durham and Northumberland *Transactions. Volume II 1869-1870.* Durham: Andrews and Co., 1883. Old half morocco gilt with raised bands by Andrews of Durham, pages xciii, 272, iv, with 15 photo plates and 4 folding plans and plates, some little stained.   R. F. G. Hollett & Son Antiquarian Booksellers   177 - 19   2011   £75

Binding – Apollo and Pegasus

Guevara, Antonio De *Vita Di M. Avrelio Imperadore.* Venice: Bartolomeo Imperador and Francesco Veneziano, 1543. 160 x 103mm., 8 p.l., 132, (2) leaves, fine contemporary Roman red morocco Apollo and Pegasus medallion binding done for Giovanni Battista Grimaldi by Marc Antonio Guillery, (genuine Apollo and Pegasus binding) covers with gilt frame formed by two widely spaced fillets with lobes interlaced at ends and sides, space between fillets decorated with broad foliate curls, small floral tools, inner pane of each board with gilt titling above a horizontal oval Apollo and Pegasus plaquette centerpiece showing Pegasus atop black painted heights of Parnassus and Apollo racing his chariot (drawn by two straining steeds) across steep terrain with reins and whip held aloft and caps fluttering behind, plaquette with gilt motto in Greek in the collar above and below vignette, spine (very expertly rebacked) with four thin and three thick raised bands decorated with gilt rope pattern or plain rules (this being original backstrip?), newer (perhaps 19th century) endpapers, all edges gilt (apparently some remarkably skillful restoration at one or more corners and edges, perhaps some gold added, as well as to the chariot part of the plaquettes); woodcut printer's device on , morocco bookplate and separate gilt monogram of Robert Hoe as well as inscription and vellum bookplate of Swedish collector Thore Virgin, ownership inscription of J. T. Payne dated 1850; covers with half dozen insignificant tiny dark spots, titlepage faintly soiled, thin light brown stain just at top edge of leaves, small wormhole at upper inner margin (text not affected), occasional minor stains, other trivial imperfections, but no defects that are even remotely serious and in general really excellent specimen of a very special binding, text fresh and leather quite lustrous; also from the collection of bibliophile Johannes Gennadius, Liverpool oculist T. Shadford Walker and Swedish collector Rolfe Wistrand.
Phillip J. Pirages   59 - 2 2011 $35,000

Binding – Apollo and Pegasus, Forgery

Appianus, Alexandrinus *Romanorum Historiarum Libri.* Basel: Hieronymus Froben and Nicolaus Episcopius, 1554. 318 x 216mm., 8 p.l., 506 pages (duplicate leaves pages 437-440), 22 leaves, early 20th century dark brown morocco over pasteboard, covers panelled in gilt and blind with three sets of blind rules, gilt double ruled frame interlaced at lobes on ends and sides, decorated with broad foliate curls, cornerpieces and small bird tools, inner panel with titling in lobed compartment at head, small foliate curl endpiece and sidepieces, flanking upright oval Apollo and Pegasus centerpiece embossed and with traces of gilt and silvering on black background, showing Pegasus with raised foreleg on cliff before a charging Apollo, who races his chariot across steep terrain with reins and whip held aloft and cape fluttering behind, gilt collar with motto in Greek in upper half and chain roll in lower, raised single and double bands, spine panelled gilt and blind with double rules, gilt cinquefoil centerpiece, all edges gilt, fleece lined brown buckram clamshell case, brown morocco labels on spine; woodcut historiated initials, printer's device on titlepage and verso of last leaf; morocco bookplate of Michel Wittock; slightly soiled and with several tiny wormholes, much of text with light overall browning, sprinkled foxing and very occasional faint spotting, little soiling (done on purpose?) to covers, still an obviously appealing volume, wonderful (according to Hobson fraudulent) binding virtually unworn and text perfectly satisfactory with no serious problems, superb example of a replica binding with remarkably persuasive tooling and just enough purposefully applied "wear" and discoloration to be deceiving, according to Hobson this example would not be genuine because Apollo does not lean far enough forward in his chariot and his steeds' front hooves incorrectly touch the cliff.   Phillip J. Pirages   59 - 3 2011 $8500

Homerus *Odyssea (and other works).* Venice: Melchiorre Sessa, 1540? 165 x 108mm., 238, (2) leaves, contemporary olive brown calf over pasteboard, ends of spine repaired (probably late in 19th century), gilt covers framed with two sets of double rules, outer panel with broad foliate curl cornerpieces and sidepieces with trefoil of three rings between each, inner panel with blindstamped horizontal oval centerpiece of Apollo and Pegasus, the gilt collar with Greek motto touching rules at sides, large foliate sprays at head and foot curling to left and right and rising to a fleuron tool at ends, raised bands, spine panelled in gilt featuring broad rules and fleuron centerpiece, brown morocco label; woodcut historiated initials and charming cat and mouse printer's device, leaves at front and back with various marks of ownership, including signature of Francesco Suave at head of titlepage and "proprieta di Carlo Balzi 1884", contemporary marginal annotations in Latin and Greek; joints partly cracked (wormed in two places), corners somewhat worn, some scuffing to leather, binding completely solid, gilt still distinct, plaquettes (not surprisingly) bright and volume altogether pleasing even with its defects, final leaf cropped at fore edge (with loss of first [verso] or last [recto] on two thirds of the lines), upper corner of two gatherings with small, faint dampstain, one minor paper flaw costing half dozen letters, otherwise unusually well preserved internally, text exceptionally bright, fresh and clean, according to Hobson a fraudulent Apollo and Pegasus binding, volume looks absolutely convincing, with usual signs of age and restoration (wheels of Apollo's chariot have four spokes, in the genuine article, they have six. Phillip J. Pirages 59 - 4 2011 $7500

Binding – Arts & Crafts

Barham, Richard Harris 1788-1845 *Ingoldsby Legends or Mirth & Marvels.* London: J. M. Dent & Co., 1898. First Rackham edition; 200 x 135mm., 2 p.l., including frontispiece, xxiii, (i), 638, (1) pages, very attractive contemporary Arts and Crafts style binding of russet Niger Goatskin lavishly gilt, covers with central panel of gilt ruled squares within wide frame of flowers and foliage, raised bands, spine compartments densely gilt with tooling repeating cover frame design, gilt turn-ins, top edge gilt, other edges gilded on the rough, titlepage with green ornamental border, numerous black and white illustrations and 13 color plates, including frontispiece by Arthur Rackham; slight and even darkening to spine, covers with minor soiling, title and frontispiece rather foxed, text with hint of browning at edges, but very attractive copy, nevertheless animated gilt of binding still bright, leather with only insignificant wear and text almost entirely bright, clean and fresh. Phillip J. Pirages 59 - 84 2011 $1500

Binding – Aste, Jenny

Cole, John *Memoirs of the Life, Writings and Character of the Late Thomas Hinderwell, Esqr. Scarborough.* London: published by John Cole and Longman, Rees, Orme, Brown and Green, 1826. 8vo., pages (ii) 3 (i) 57, (iii) 55, (i) vii (i), engraved frontispiece, publisher's original green canvas, dark green morocco lettering piece gilt by Jenny Aste, late 1980's, some light spotting, especially to title, cloth little spotted and faded, slightly worn at endcaps, contemporary ink inscription to Mrs. Langdell, presented by author, also blue paper ex-libris of John William Clay, from the collection of Christopher Ernest Weston 1947-2010. Unsworths Booksellers 24 - 82 2011 £125

Gent, Thomas *The Antient and Modern History of the Famous City of York and in a Particular Manner of its Magnificent Cathedral...* York: at the Printing Office in Coffe Yard, 1730. 8vo., pages viii, 256, (viii) + extending engraved frontispiece and one other engraving, contemporary hand colored extending plan, this copy is the first issue with woodcut of framed celestial crown with Latin quotation from Rev. II 10 as a headpiece to page 84, also tall copy, modern (1982) calf by Jenny Aste, browned and spotted, frontispiece and plan rehinged, from the collection of Christopher Ernest Weston 1947-2010. Unsworths Booksellers 24 - 96 2011 £400

Binding – Bagguley

Irving, Washington 1783-1859 *The Alhambra.* London and New York: Macmillan and Co., 1896. One of 500 extra illustrated copies; 263 x 189mm. xx, 436 pages, magnificent contemporary dark green crushed morocco, extravagantly gilt by Bagguley (signed with the firm's ink "Sutherland" patent stamp on verso of front endleaf), covers with borders of multiple plain and decorative gilt rules, lobed inner frame with fleuron cornerpieces, whole enclosing a large and extremely intricate gilt lozenge, raised ands, spine lavishly gilt in double ruled compartments, gilt titling and turn-ins, beautiful vellum doublures elaborately tooled in diapered gilt red, and green moorish pattern, green weathered silk endleaves, top edge gilt, other edges rough trimmed, numerous illustrations in text and 12 inserted lithographs by Joseph Pennell, bookplate of Harold Douthit; in beautiful condition inside and out, lovely bind with lustrous morocco, vellum and gilt, text virtually pristine. Phillip J. Pirages 59 - 86 2011 $5500

Binding – Batten, D.

Allom, Thomas 1804-1872 *Picturesque Rambles in Westmorland, Cumberland, Durham and Northumberland From Drawings Taken on the Spot.* Peter Jackson late Fisher Son & Co., The Caxton Press, n.d. circa, 1832. 3 volumes, 4to., original half calf gilt by D. Batten of Clapham Common, spines with broad raised bands, and lettering pieces, evenly mellowed, pages (ii), 96; (ii), 80; (i), 72, complete with 3 engraved titles and 215 fine full page steel engraved plates, glazed endpapers, occasional spot or mark but clean handsome set of best form of this work, engraved plates, printed on superior paper. R. F. G. Hollett & Son Antiquarian Booksellers 173 - 18 2011 £850

Binding – Bayntun

Ainsworth, William Harrison 1805-1882 *The Works of Cheviot Tichburn.* Manchester: with the type of John Leigh, 1825. Half title, small tear to upper margin of half title and contents leaf, 20th century half calf by Bayntun, very good. Jarndyce Antiquarian Booksellers   CXCI - 33 2011 £1850

Bronte, The Sisters *The Novels of...* Edinburgh: John Grant, 1907. Thornton edition; 12 volume, 8vo., titlepages printed in red and black, frontispiece portraits and numerous photo plates, bound in dark green three quarter calf and green cloth, spine gilt in compartments, top edge gilt, by Bayntun of Bath, hinge of one volume little tender, fine. Second Life Books Inc. 174 - 73 2011 $2625

Bunyan, John 1628-1688 *The Pilgrim's Progress.* London: Henry G. Bohn, 1856. Eleventh edition; 205 x 145mm., xxxvi, 476 pages, pleasing early 20th century marbled calf by Bayntun, covers framed by an elegant scrolling roll featuring artichokes and strawberry leaves, raised bands, compartments at head and tail of spine filled by three different and pleasing gilt rolls, two compartments with scrolling floral cornerpieces, one dark blue and one green morocco label, turn-ins densely gilt in botanical pattern, marbled endpapers, all edges gilt, in slightly soiled tan linen slipcase; historiated initials, 6 illustrations in text, 17 charming plates by Thomas Stothard, as called for, ours most pleasing colored by a contemporary hand; bit of wear to joints, minor crackling and dulling to spine, isolated foxing, excellent copy, very clean and fresh internally with pretty colored plates, attractive decorative binding that is solid and without any significant defect. Phillip J. Pirages 59 - 88 2011 $850

Cervantes Saavedra, Miguel De 1547-1616 *Life and Adventures of Don Quixote de la Mancha.* London: printed for Hurst, Robinson and Co., 1820. New edition; 4 small octavo volumes, (2), xx, (1)-371, (1 colophon); (6), (1)-388; (8), (1)-367, (1, colophon); (8), (1)-436 pages, numerous engravings by Richard Westall inserted throughout, full red morocco bound by Bayntun, boards panelled and ruled in gilt with geometric diamond over rectangle design, spines decoratively tooled and lettered in gilt in six compartments with five raised bands, gilt board edges and dentelles, all edges gilt marbled endpapers, previous owner's bookplate on front pastedown of each volume, some very minor occasional foxing to prelim and final leaves, overall about fine. Heritage Book Shop   Holiday 2010 - 19 2011 $1000

Clemens, Samuel Langhorne 1835-1910 *The Adventures of Huckleberry Finn.* London: Chatto & Windus, 1884. First edition; 191 x 133mm., xvi, 438 pages, very pleasing red morocco by Bayntun (stamp signed on verso of front free endpaper), covers with two frames formed by simple gilt rules, inner frame with cornerpieces of stylized fleurs-de-lys, raised bands, spine gilt in double ruled compartments with central lily and open dot corners, very pretty intricate floral gilt turn-ins, marbled endpapers, top edge gilt, original red cloth covers bound in at rear, frontispiece and many illustrations in text, spine slightly and evenly a darker red just a breath of rubbing to joints, two small closed tears, other trivial imperfections internally, still fine, difficult to find this good, text clean, fresh and smooth and appealing binding lustrous with only insignificant wear. Phillip J. Pirages 59 - 167 2011 $2750

Clemens, Samuel Langhorne 1835-1910 *Adventures of Huckleberry Finn.* New York: Charles L. Webster, 1885. First edition, first issue; with titlepage and page 283/4 as cancel sheets, and with the three required points - "Huck Decided" on page 9, with illustration for page 87 ("Him and Another Man") listed as page 88; and with misprint "with the was" (for "with the saw") on page 57, the book has been bound and signed by Bayntun in full dark green morocco with raised bands, gilt spine decorations, gilt lines to boards, lovely gilt inner dentelles, feathered endpapers and all edges gilt, original cloth covers and spine bound in at end, book housed in green cloth slipcase, book is near fine (light foxing to endpapers, one minor closed tear to one page), binding books fine and attractive. Lupack Rare Books May 26 2011 - ABE4707853086 2011 $2100

Craik, Dinah Maria Mulock 1826-1887 *John Halifax, Gentleman.* London: Hurst and Blackett, 1856. First edition; 3 volumes, 3 pages of ads at end of the first volume and two pages at end of the third; extremely pleasing medium green straight grain morocco, attractively gilt by Bayntun stamp signed on front flyleaf), gilt double fillet border on covers, raised bands, gilt spine compartments with filigree lozenge centerpiece and cornerpiece volutes, blue and red morocco labels, heavily gilt turn-ins, marbled endpapers, all edges gilt; joints of first volume bit flaked (with tiny cracks just beginning), two leaves with neatly repaired tear (one in lower fore margin, other into text but without loss), text faintly browned at edges because of inexpensive paper, but still quite appealing set, decorative bindings bright and almost entirely unworn, text very clean and smooth.   Phillip J. Pirages   59 - 269   2011 $950

Eliot, George, Pseud. 1819-1880 *Scenes of Clerical Life.* Edinburgh & London: William Blackwood & Sons, 1858. First edition; 2 volumes, half titles, slight foxing in prelims volume II, contemporary half brown crushed morocco by Bayntun, spines with raised gilt bands, and ruled and lettered in gilt, all edges gilt, very good, attractive.   Jarndyce Antiquarian Booksellers CXCI - 171   2011   £850

Hardy, Thomas 1840-1928 *The Mayor of Casterbridge: The Life and Death of a Man of Character.* London: Smith, Elder & Co., 1886. First edition in book form; 2 volumes, octavo, (4), 313, (1, blank), (2, ads); (4), 312, (4, ads) pages, with all ads and half titles called for, beautifully bound by Bayntun in green polished calf, boards and spines printed in gilt, each volume with red and blue spine labels, lettered gilt, gilt dentelles, all edges gilt, marbled endpapers, few pages with minor professionally repaired closed tears and reinforced corners, including title and half title volume I.   Heritage Book Shop   Holiday 2010 - 52   2011 $2500

Hawthorne, Nathaniel 1804-1864 *A Wonder Book.* London: J. M. Dent & Sons, 1957. Full powder blue calf gilt by Bayntun, contrasting spine labels, spine and top edges of boards little faded, pages x, 195, all edges gilt, 8 colored plates, 4 black and white illustrations.   R. F. G. Hollett & Sons Antiquarian Booksellers   170 - 704   2011   £75

Kirby, Mary *The Discontented Children and How They Were Cured.* London: Grant & Griffith, 1855. First edition; color frontispiece and 2 black and white plates, odd spot, half dark green crushed morocco by Bayntun of Bath, green cloth boards, gilt spine, spine faded to brown, booklabel of J. Brocklebank, slightly torn, top edge gilt, very good.   Jarndyce Antiquarian Booksellers   CLXC - 58   2011   £65

Leslie, Charles Robert *Life and Times of Sir Joshua Reynolds.* London: John Murray, 1865. First edition; 222 x 143 mm., 4 volumes, very handsome chestnut brown crushed morocco by Bayntun (signed on turn-in), covers gilt with interlocking strapwork frame and large central lozenge, lancet corner ornaments, spines gilt in compartments of similar design, turn-ins with gilt French fillets ad palmette cornerpieces, marbled endpapers, all edges gilt, housed in brown buckram covered slipcase, upper seams of slipcase neatly reinforced with library tape; extra illustrated with 194 plates, 40 of them in color in addition to the 11 called for; spines lightly but uniformly sunned to pleasing honey brown, one leaf with small neat repair to fore-edge, other trivial imperfections but lovely set in very fine condition, leaves and plates fresh, clean and bright, binding nearly pristine.   Phillip J. Pirages   59 - 298   2011 $2400

Macaulay, Zachary *Negro Slavery; or a View of Some of the More Prominent Features of that State of Society as it Exists in the United States of America and in the Colonies of the West Indies, Especially in Jamaica.* London: for Hatchard and Son... and J. and A. Arch, 1823. First edition; (4), 118 pages, attractive modern half calf by Bayntun, fine, fresh copy inside and out, Lord Palmerston's copy with his signature, (Henry John Temple, 3rd Viscount Palmerston).   Joseph J. Felcone Inc.   Fall Miscellany 2010 - 80   2011 $900

Shelley, Percy Bysshe 1792-1822 *Queen Mab.* London: W. Clark, 1821. First published edition; 8vo., 182 page, three quarter blue morocco with raised bands and spine gilt by Bayntun, top edge gilt, little worn along hinges, leaves little darkened, very good, bound with the rare dedicatory poem to author's first wife, Harriet, but without ad leaf.   Second Life Books Inc.   174 - 288   2011 $1800

Binding – Bayntun-Riviere

Blackmore, Richard Doddridge 1825-1900 *Lorna Doone: a Romance of Exmoor.* London: Sampson Low, Son & Marston, 1869. First edition, apparently one of 500 copies printed; 3 volumes, octavo, vi, 332; lv, 340; iv, 342 pages, bound without prelim blank leaf in volume I and final blank leaf in volume III, but with 16 page publisher's catalog dated March 1869, at end volume III, bound circa 1960 by Bayntun-Riviere (stamp signed in gilt on front turn-in), full red morocco, covers with gilt double fillet border, spines panelled and lettered in gilt on front turn-in), in full red morocco, covers with gilt double fillet border, spines panelled and lettered in gilt compartments with five raised bands, board edges and turn-ins decoratively tooled in gilt, all edges gilt, marbled endpapers, spines very slightly sunned, few short, expertly repaired margin tears, some occasional minor foxing or soiling, bookplate of J. Hodges, overall, excellent copy, laid in is ALS from author to James Payn, Teddington, Dec. 34d 1877.   David Brass Rare Books, Inc.   May 26 2011 - 00726   2011 $6500

Dodgson, Charles Lutwidge 1832-1898 *Alice's Adventures in Wonderland. (with Through the Looking Glass. (with) Through the Looking Glass and What Alice Found There.* London: MacMillan and Co., 1866-1872. First published edition with inverted 's' on last line of contents page; first edition of Though the Looking Glass and What Alice Found There; octavo, (xii) (1)-192 pages, 42 illustrations by John Tenniel, including frontispiece, original cloth bound in at end; octavo, (xii), (1)-224, (4) pages, with misprint 'wade' instead of 'wabe' on page 21, 50 illustrations by Tenniel including frontispiece, one page publisher's ads, original cloth binding bound in at end; the 2 volumes uniformly bound by Bayntun-Riviere in red calf, boards ruled in gilt, gilt dentelles, all edges gilt, stamped and lettered in gilt, spines stamped and lettered in gilt with blue and green spine label on each volume, marbled endpapers, three quarter inch closed tear professionally repaired to outer margin of K3 of volume I, bit of very light spotting on few pages, otherwise extremely nice housed together in red cloth slipcase. Heritage Book Shop Holiday 2010 - 17 2011 $12,500

Haggard, Henry Rider 1856-1925 *King Solomon's Mines.* London: Cassell & Co., 1885. First edition; first issue with "Bamamgwato" for "Bamangwato" on page 10, line 14; "to let twins to live" for "to let Twins live" on page 122, line 27 and "wrod" instead of "word" on page 307, line 29, with publisher's catalog dated "5G.8.85" and "5B.8.85", small octavo, (4), vi, (7)-320, (16, publisher's catalog) pages, folding color facsimile map inserted as frontispiece, black and white map on page 27, original front cover cloth bound in at back, beautifully bound by Bayntun-Riviere in full red morocco, boards ruled gilt, spine printed and lettered gilt, gilt dentelles, all edges gilt, marbled endpapers, few professional repaired closed tears to folding map, about fine. Heritage Book Shop Holiday 2010 - 50 2011 $5000

Walton, Izaak 1593-1683 *The Compleat Angler or the Contemplative Man's Recreation.* London: Hodder & Stoughton, 1911. Hodder's first trade edition; quarto, xvi, 166, (1) pages, 25 plates tipped in on green paper, each plate with descriptive tissue guards, original green cloth from front cover bound in at back, beautifully bound by Bayntun Riviere for Asprey in full black morocco, boards ruled in gilt, inner rule with floral corners, front board with mutiple colors of morocco inlays to create shape of a fisherman, rear board with central gilt device, spine elaborately stamped and lettered gilt, all edges gilt, gilt dentelles, marbled endpapers, Bayntun Riviere stamped in blind on dentelles, Asprey stamped in gilt on lower edge of back pastedown, some very light foxing to text, plates very clean, previous owner's small leather bookplate, near fine, green cloth slipcase. Heritage Book Shop Holiday 2010 - 124 2011 $2000

Binding – Bedford

Coryate, Thomas *Coryats Crudities Hastily Gobbled Up in Five Moneths Travells in France, Savoy, Italy, Rhetia Comonly Called the Grisons Country, Helvetia Alias Switzerland, some Parts of High Germany and the Netherlands.* London: by William Stansby, 1611. First edition; printed title present, engraved allegorical title by William Hole (shaved very slightly at head), engraved plates, woodcut, text portrait, errata leaf present, many woodcut initials and headpieces, 19th century brown crushed levant morocco, gilt by Bedford, unusually tall, very handsome copy, rare printed title, from the libraries of Ward E. Terry, R. B. Adam, A. Edward Newton, Bois Penrose and Wolfgang A. Herz with their respective bookplates and book labels. Joseph J. Felcone Inc. Fall Miscellany 2010 - 35 2011 $16,000

Fraunce, Abraham *The Lawiers Logike, Exemplifying the Praecept of Logike by the Practise of the Common Lawe.* London: by William How for Thomas Gubbin and T. Newman, 1588. First edition; 4to, (1), 151, (i.e. 152) leaves including blank leaf 2A2, folding table, title within type ornament border, woodcut initials, mixed black letter and roman, full red gilt panelled morocco, edges gilt by Bedford, first two leaves lightly washed, short closed tear on table, blank corner of 2K4 replaced, else fine, clean, armorial bookplate of Sir Edward Priaulx and book label of Abel Berland. Joseph J. Felcone Inc. Fall Miscellany 2010 - 52 2011 $8000

MacDonald, George 1824-1905 *Lilith: a Romance.* London: George Allen & Unwin, 1924. Centenary edition; half title with reproduction of MacDonald's bookplate, front plate after F. D. Bedford, few spots, original crimson cloth, spine slightly faded, very good, cutting of the TLS review of the 1962 Gollancz edition laid down on leading f.e.p. Jarndyce Antiquarian Booksellers CXCII - 321 2011 £45

Ruskin, John 1819-1900 *The Ethics of the Dust: Ten Lectures to Little Housewives on the Elements of Crystallisation.* London: Smith, Elder & Co., 1866. First edition; 191 x 127mm., x, (iv), (3)-244 pages, very fine dark green crushed morocco by Bedford (stamp signed on front turn-in), covers bordered in gilt with French fillet, raised bands, spine handsomely gilt in compartments featuring decorative bands at head and foot, scrolled cornerpieces and thistle centerpiece with surrounding small tools, densely gilt inner dentelles, marbled endpapers, all edges gilt, titlepage with ownership inscription "Walter Macfarlane, Saracen Foundry", boards with hint of soiling, very fine in lovely binding, gilt very bright, text virtually pristine. Phillip J. Pirages 59 - 90 2011 $500

Tennyson, The Brothers *Poems by Two Brothers.* London: printed for W. Simpkin and J. and J. Jackson, Louth, 1827. First edition; 197 x 127mm., xii, 228 pages, especially attractive apple green crushed morocco by Bedford (signed on inside front dentelle), covers bordered with gilt French fillet, raised bands, compartments handsomely gilt with double bands and decorative rolls, scrolled floral cornerpieces and floral centerpiece surround by small tools, elaborately gilt inner dentelles, top edge gilt, spine uniformly faded to a pleasing sea green, cover with uneven fading (browned at top and fore edge), just hint of rubbing to joints, isolated faint foxing, otherwise fine, pretty binding still pleasing because still bright and without any significant wear, text clean and fresh, no real signs of use. Phillip J. Pirages 59 - 333 2011 $3500

Binding – Bernasconi

Le Putanisme d'Amsterdam, Livre Contenant les Tours & Les Ruses Don Se Servent les Putains & Les Maquereles... Amsterdam: Elie Jogehemse de Rhin, 1681. First edition; rare, small 12mo., pages (vi), 277, (1) blank, engraved frontispiece and 4 plates, all edges gilt, discreet old repairs to frontispiece and final ad leaf, occasional light spotting early 20th century full black morocco, by Bernasconi, gilt lettering and raised bands to spine, gilt decoration to inside boards, marbled endpapers, bookplate of G. Nordmann. Simon Finch Rare Books Zero - 401 2011 £3000

Binding – Bianchi

Apollinaire, Guillaume *Les Onze Mille Verges ou les Amours d'un Hospodar.* Monte Carlo: Les Ygrees; Paris: Rene Bonnet and Pascal Pia, 1930. First bibliophile edition, no. 3 of 3 copies on Imperial Japan; large square 8vo., pages (vi), xii, 168 + limitation leaf, bound in are 14 highly erotic original watercolor drawings , attributed by a penciled note on the flyleaf to Jean Auscher, contemporary full crimson, marbled endpapers, top edge gilt others rough trimmed, in matching (lined) slipcase, original grey printed wrappers bound in, by Bianchi of Nice, fine in immaculate binding. Simon Finch Rare Books Zero - 441 2011 £6000

Binding – Bickers

Donaldson, John William *The Theatre of the Greeks, a Treatise on the History and Exhibition of the Greek Drama...* London: Longman and Co., 1860. Seventh edition; pages xii, 414, all edges and endpapers marbled, 5 engraved plates, full tan calf gilt prize binding over bevelled boards by Bickers, upper hinge cracked, spine rubbed and defective at head. R. F. G. Hollett & Son Antiquarian Booksellers 175 - 384 2011 £50

Binding – Birdsall

Blount, Thomas 1618-1679 *Boscobel.* London: reprinted for Houslton and Son, 1832. Small 8vo., finely bound in three quarter morocco gilt with raised bands by Birdsall, pages xix, 91, (i), all edges gilt, engraved frontispiece, folding bird eye view of Boscobel and text woodcut vignette of Boscobel House. R. F. G. Hollett & Son Antiquarian Booksellers 175 - 142 2011 £120

Dodgson, Charles Lutwidge 1832-1898 *Alice's Adventures in Wonderland.* London: Philip Lee Warner, Publisher to the Medici Society Ltd., 1914. Limited, numbered edition of 1000 copies on handmade Riccardi paper; 8vo., top edge gilt, full leather signed "Birdsall London & Northampton) with color inlay on front cover of the White Rabbit and raised bands and gold lines on spine, slight rubbing to raised bands of otherwise clean, fresh copy, cloth slipcase, at most a touch of rubbing at corners, lovely copy, 131 numbered pages, illustrations by Tenniel. Jo Ann Reisler, Ltd. 86 - 32 2011 $1500

Hardy, Thomas 1840-1928 *The Patriot.* Edinburgh: Printed for and sold by J. Dickson, London, sold by G. Nicol, 1793. 8vo., (2), 78 pages, contents leaf misbound after A1, late 19th century maroon morocco fully gilt by Birdsall, fine in handsome binding. John Drury Rare Books 153 - 57 2011 £200

Hardy, Thomas 1840-1928 *The Trumpet Major.* London: Smith Elder & Co., 1880. Half titles, luxuriously bound in full brown crushed morocco by Birdsall of Northampton, gilt spines, borders and dentelles, top edge gilt, very good, handsome. Jarndyce Antiquarian Booksellers CXCI - 525 2011 £1250

Hawker, Peter *Instructions to Young Sportsmen in All that Relates to Guns and Shooting.* London: printed for Longman, Hurst, Rees, Orme Brown and Green, 1824. Third edition; 240 x 155mm., xxii, 470 pages; with 10 plates; evidence of bookplate removal; handsome scarlet crushed morocco by Birdsall (stamp signed on front turn-in), covers with double gilt fillet border, raised bands, spine very attractively gilt in compartments with central figure of shooter and his dog framed by tree branch cornerpieces, gilt turn-ins, marbled endpapers, all edges gilt, in felt lined red straight grain morocco slipcase (very slightly marked); spine just shade darker than boards, little faded, with tail compartment bit rubbed, faint soiling to rear cover, trivial imperfections to few plates, isolated minor thumbing, corner creases, marginal stains, still nearly fine and quite attractive, leaves fresh and bright and decorative binding lustrous and virtually unworn. Phillip J. Pirages 59 - 234 2011 $1250

Lemon, Mark *Mr. Punch: His Origin and Career, with Facsimile of His Original prospectus...* London: printed by Jas. Wade Covent Garden, 1870. First edition; folding facsimile frontispiece on blue paper, 4 pages ads at front, 16 pages ads at back, 1 page with small tear slightly affecting text, original printed wrappers, bound into half tan morocco by Birdsall & Son, Northampton, top edge gilt, very good. Jarndyce Antiquarian Booksellers   CXCI - 254   2011   £100

Oliver, George *Signs and Symbols Illustrated and Explained in a Course of Twelve Lectures on Free Masonry.* Grimsby: printed for the author by Br. Skelton, 1826. First edition; contemporary half calf gilt by Anthony Birdsall of Northampton (with his label), masonic emblem to spine compartments, double spine labels and Spanish marbled boards, extremities little rubbed, pages lx, 248, text illustrations, slight spotting to few leaves, but excellent copy, with ownership inscriptions of Richard Griffiths, architect and William Smith, both of Northampton, 2 small press cuttings relating to death of latter's unmarried daughter in Northampton are tipped to pastedown, S. S. Birdsall of Pomfret Lodge Northampton was a subscriber, rare.   R. F. G. Hollett & Son Antiquarian Booksellers   175 - 1020   2011   £350

Binding – Blunson & Co.

Dickens, Charles   1812-1870   *Charles Dicken's Works.* London: Chapman and Hall, 1881. Edition deluxe, first issue, no. 361 of 1000 numbered copies; 30 volumes, half titles, frontispieces, illustrations with India proofs after original plates, reprint of front wrapper from original part publication, some occasional light foxing, contemporary half maroon morocco by Blunson & Co., spines lettered in gilt, top edge gilt.   Jarndyce Antiquarian Booksellers   CXCI - 10   2011   £4800

Binding – Bone

Collins, Wilkie   1824-1889   *Basil: a Story of Modern Life.* London: Sampson, Low, Son & Co., 1862. Revised edition; frontispiece, 16 page catalog (May 1863), pencil ownership inscription of George Jones, original mauve cloth by Bone & Son, front board slightly dulled, spine faded to brown.   Jarndyce Antiquarian Booksellers   CXCI - 126   2011   £180

Gilbert, William Schwenck   1836-1911   *The "Bab" Ballads.* London: John Camden Hotten, 1869. First edition; preface dated October 1868, illustrations by author, 4 pages ads, original green cloth, bevelled boards by W. Bone & Son, decorated and lettered gilt, slightly dulled, all edges gilt.   Jarndyce Antiquarian Booksellers   CXCI - 186   2011   £250

Lewis, Arthur, Mrs.   *Salthurst.* London: Samuel Tinsley, 1878. First edition; 3 volumes, 6 page and 32 page catalog volume III, text slightly browned, facsimile title volume II, original crimson cloth by W. Bone & Son, rubbed and seriously affected by damp, small splits in spine volume III, inner hinges cracking, inscribed by author for her son, Alfred Hartley Lewis.   Jarndyce Antiquarian Booksellers   CLXC - 136   2011   £90

MacDonald, George   1824-1905   *Mary Marston.* London: Sampson Low Marston, Searle & Rivington, 1881. Fifth edition; half title, 32 page catalog (Jan. 1881), original red cloth, bevelled boards (Style A) by W. Bone & Son, spine dulled.   Jarndyce Antiquarian Booksellers   CXCII - 230   2011   £65

MacDonald, George   1824-1905   *Orts.* London: Sampson Low, Marston, Searle & Rivington, 1882. First edition; half title, 2 page catalog (April 1888), original brown cloth, bevelled boards blocked in black and gilt, blind ornament on back board by W. Bone & Sone, brown endpapers, following hinge splitting.   Jarndyce Antiquarian Booksellers   CXCII - 256   2011   £350

MacDonald, George   1824-1905   *Orts.* London: Sampson Low, Marston, Searle & Rivington, 1882. half title, 2 pages ads + 32 page catalog (Nov. 1882), original brown cloth, bevelled boards blocked in black and gilt with blind ornament on back board, by W. Bone & Son, brown endpapers, inner hinges cracking, good, inscribed by author for Sophia Corey, also signed by MacDonald in pencil with considerable ink alterations.   Jarndyce Antiquarian Booksellers   CXCII - 255   2011   £3800

MacDonald, George   1824-1905   *Stephen Archer and Other Tales.* London: Sampson Low, Marston, Searle & Rivington, 1883. half title, 2 pages ads, 32 page catalog (Nov. 1882), original red cloth, bevelled boards by W. Bone & Son (style A), spine slightly faded and bukled.   Jarndyce Antiquarian Booksellers   CXCII - 251   2011   £65

Mayhew, The Brothers   *Acting Charades or Deeds Not Words.* London: D. Bogue, 1850. First edition; small square 8vo., original red cloth gilt by Bone and Son, stamped in blind and gilt, extremities trifle rubbed, pages x (ii), 158, (ii), all edges gilt, hand colored frontispiece and title and silhouette illustrations in text.   R. F. G. Hollett & Sons Antiquarian Booksellers   170 - 431   2011   £120

Binding – Bourbeau, David

Robinson, Alan James *Cetacea, The Great Whales.* Easthampton: Cheloniidae Press, 1981.   Artist's own copy, artist's proof #1, signed by artist, binders and printer, Harold Patrick McGrath; all on Arches Cover Buff, page size 22 x 15 inches, bound loose as issued with sheets laid in a full black Niger oasis goat folder sculpted in low relief with head of a Right Whale by David Bourbeau at The Thistle Bindery, beautiful folder housed in quarter leather moroccan goat drop back box by Gray Parrot, short split at lower joint of box, else fine; the 7 bleed etchings by Robinson depict the major species of whales, numerous blindstamped line-cut and two wood engravings, text contains biological information, 12 two-color maps showing migration routes and breeding areas printed by Harold McGrath at Hampshire Typothetae; artist printed at Cheloniidae Press.   Priscilla Juvelis - Rare Books   48 - 5   2011 $3000

Binding – Bozerian

Borde, Charles *Parapilla, et Autres Oeuvres Libres...* Florence: 1784.   Small 12mo., pages (iv), 164, 1 plate by Marillier, numerous small wood engraved head and tailpieces, engraved portrait of Borde added as frontispiece, all edges gilt, full green long grain morocco fully gilt decorated in gilt with red dots, by Bozerain, pink silk lined endpieces, bookplate of Bibliotheque Mirault and G. Nordmann, few discrete pencil annotations.   Simon Finch Rare Books   Zero - 411   2011   £1750

Orleans, Pierre Joseph De *Histoire des Revolutions D'Angleterre Depuis Le Commencement De La Monarchie.* Paris: Chez Claude Barbin, 1693-1694.   First edition; 250 x 193 mm., 3 volumes, splendid and unusual sumptuously gilt early 19th century marbled calf with red morocco spines in the style of Bozerian, covers with gilt borders of two decorative rules and elegant undulating floral vine, flat straight grain morocco spines very handsomely gilt in compartments with pointille ground and central circlet from which radiate four lillies and four leaves on twining stems, turn-ins gilt with plain and decorative rolls, marbled endpapers, all edges gilt, engraved head and tailpieces and 8 engraved portraits, verso of front free endpaper with bookplate of Baron de Mackau, titlepage with ink ownership inscription of Alexander Paul Ludwig Goupy? in contemporary hand; isolated gatherings with variable browning (small handful rather browned), one leaf in first volume with expert early repair of four inch tear (letters of four words partly obscured or displaced, and text and facing page somewhat discolored), few additional trivial imperfections internally, but text generally quite fresh and clean, one joint with five small wormholes, few hardly noticeable, shallow scratches to covers hint of wear to extremities, lovely bindings in fine condition, lustrous leather and gilt with only minor wear, with their very considerable original visual appeal entirely intact.   Phillip J. Pirages   59 - 14   2011 $2250

Binding – Bradley

Crane, Stephen 1871-1900   *War is Kind.* New York: Frederick A. Stokes, 1899.   First edition; 8vo., 96 pages, 22 illustrations, uncut paper, original gray pictorial boards by Bradley, original printed paper, spine and portion of book cover moderately sunstruck, unrubbed, fine, early owner's inscription dated Christmas 1900.   M & S Rare Books, Inc.   90 - 101   2011 $1500

Binding – Bradstreet

Thoreau, Henry David 1817-1862   *A Week on the Concord and Merrimack Rivers.* Boston and Cambridge: James Munroe and Co., 1849.   First edition, first printing, first issue; 12mo., 413, (1, blank), [1, publisher's ads ("Will Soon be Published, "Walden, or Life in the Woods. By Henry D. Thoreau")], (1, blank) pages, original brown cloth, BAL binding variant A, Trade binding) with five rule border stamped in blind on covers, spine lettered in gilt with rules and decorative leaf design stamped in blind, original buff endpapers, some wear to spine extremities, contemporary ink signatures on first prelim blank, armorial bookplate of Jacob Chester Chamberlain, with his acquisition slip tipped in between rear endpapers: From "Che Col." (filled in in pencil) Through "Dodd Mead & Co." (filled in in pencil) and date "Dec. 27/00" (filled in in pencil) "J.CC." Sold at the Chamberlain Sale First Editions of Ten American Authors, The Anderson Auction Company, February 16 and 17, 1909, with note by late owner inserted discussing its purchase from Seven Gables Bookshop in NY 1951, some neat marginal pencil notes and underlining, 3 lines of type dropped by printer on page 396 are provided in pencil, with Chamberlain's note concerning this textual point, spectacular copy, totally untouched, gilt on spine bright and fresh, chemised in full dark green straight grain morocco pull-off case by Bradstreet.   David Brass Rare Books, Inc.   May 26 2011 - 00541   2011 $19,500

Binding – Brentanos

Bacon, Francis, Viscount St. Albans 1561-1626 *Works of Francis Bacon.* London: William Pickering, 1825. New edition; 16 volumes, bound in 17, octavo, several volumes with inserted frontispieces and plates, uniformly bound by Brentanos in half brown morocco over brown cloth, spines lettered and stamped in gilt, some scattered foxing, headcaps of few volumes slightly chipped, previous owner's bookplate on front pastedown of each volume, previous owner's old ink inscription on prelim blank of each volume dated 1928, overall very good, handsome copy.   Heritage Book Shop   Holiday 2010 - 7   2011 $1500

Surtees, Robert Smith 1803-1864 *Handley Cross.* London: Edward Arnold, 1912. First edition with these illustrations; one of 250 copies signed by artist, this is copy #34, 2 volumes, 249 x 190mm., especially pleasing modern scarlet highly polished calf, handsomely gilt "stamp signed" "Bound by Brentanos" on verso of front free endpaper, covers with gilt double fillet, raised bands, spine attractively gilt in a hunting theme, double ruled compartments featuring a fox head, hunter's horn or riding hat and crop as centerpieces, each framed by ornate scrolling cornerpieces, each spine with one tan and one dark brown morocco label, turn-ins with intricate gilt floral vine, marbled endpapers, all edges gilt, titlepage vignettes, 97 illustrations in text, 24 tipped-on color plates, all by Cecil Aldin, one tiny scratch to one title label, one leaf with upper corner and narrow portion of top half of fore-edge margin expertly renewed (perhaps after rough opening?), but very fine and quite pretty set with only trivial imperfections in text, especially fresh, clean and bright, plates in pristine condition, very attractive decorative bindings unusually lustrous and virtually unworn. Phillip J. Pirages   59 - 143   2011 $950

Binding – Brindley

Rucellai, Bernardo *De Bello Italico Commentarius ex authentici Manuscripti Apographo nun Primum in Lucem Editus.* London: William Bowyer for John Rindley, 1724. Large 4to., (8), 102, (2) pages, last leaf blank, small errata slip pasted to pages (vii & viii), contemporary London Harleian style binding of sprinkled calf, by Brindley, from the library of the Earls of Macclesfield at Shirburn Castle. Maggs Bros. Ltd.   1440 - 185   2011   £750

Binding – Bufford

MacDonald, George 1824-1905 *Princess Rosamond.* Boston: D. Lothrop & Co., 1879. Second American edition of The Wise woman; 4to., frontispiece, plates, illustrations, text in two columns, original green cloth, color printed pictorial boards by Bufford, Boston, slight rubbing at corners. Jarndyce Antiquarian Booksellers   CXCII - 182   2011   £300

Binding – Bumpus

Jefferies, Richard 1848-1887 *The Scarlet Shawl.* London: Tinsley Bros., 1874. First edition; text slightly spotted, contemporary half blue morocco by Bumpus, raised bands, decorated and lettered gilt on spine, slightly rubbed, armorial bookplate of William Henry Radcliffe Saunders, very good.   Jarndyce Antiquarian Booksellers   CXCI - 223   2011   £420

Meynell, Alice *Poems.* London: Elkin Mathews & John Lane, 1893. Second edition; half title, 7 pages ads, some spots and pencil marginal marks, full contemporary plain green calf by Bumpus, gilt dentelles, slight rubbed, inscribed by author for Florence Kerry Kirby.   Jarndyce Antiquarian Booksellers   CLXC - 391   2011   £45

Ritchie, Anne Isabella Thackeray 1837-1919 *Bluebeard's Keys and Other Stories.* London: Smith, Elder & Co., 1874. (x, 512 pages), 8vo., three quarter green morocco over marbled boards, top edge gilt, half title, attractive copy bound by John Bumpus, scarce.   Paulette Rose Fine and Rare Books   32 - 172   2011 $150

Swinburne, Algernon Charles 1837-1909 *The Tragedies.* London: Chatto & Windus, 1905. First collected edition; one of 110 large paper copies, this #6, 230 x 150mm., especially fine contemporary burgundy crushed morocco by Bumpus (signed on front turn-in), covers and board edges with double gilt rule, spines with attractively and densely gilt in compartments, filled with massed stippled volutes, enclosing a quatrefoil at center, elegant inner gilt dentelles, top edge gilt, other edges rough trimmed, entirely unopened, photograuvre frontispiece in final volume, titles printed in red and black; one spine just barely darker than the others, couple of mild corner bumps, otherwise beautifully bound set in splendid condition.   Phillip J. Pirages   59 - 330   2011 $1250

Binding – Burn

Arnold, Matthew 1822-1888 *New Poems.* London: Macmillan & Co., 1867. First edition; half title, original green cloth by Burn, booksellers ticket of G. G. Walmsley. Jarndyce Antiquarian Booksellers   CXCI - 51   2011   £150

Beatrice Mary, Princess of England *A Birthday Book.* London: Smith Elder & Co., 1881. 4to., color litho plates, half title, light brown decorated cloth by Burn & Co., little marked, all edges gilt, very good.   Jarndyce Antiquarian Booksellers   CXCI - 73   2011   £125

Bible. English - 1874 *The Gospel According to St. Matthew.* London: Sampson Low, etc., 1874. Folio, original brown cloth gilt by Burn & Co., over bevelled boards, corners trifle worn, unpaginated, all edges gilt, engraved title with lettering in red title in red and black and 40 magnificent full page etched plates after Alexandre Bida, handsome, clean copy.   R. F. G. Hollett & Son Antiquarian Booksellers   175 - 128   2011   £295

Bible. English - 1877 *The Gosepl According to St. Mark.* London: Sampson Low etc., 1877. Folio, original brown cloth gilt by Burn & Co., over bevelled boards, unpaginated, all edges gilt, engraved title with lettering to red, title in red and black and 38 magnificent full page etched plates after French artist and engraver Alexandre Bida, handsome, clean copy.   R. F. G. Hollett & Son Antiquarian Booksellers   175 - 126   2011   £295

Dixie, Florence *In the Land of Misfortune.* London: Richard Bentley and Son, 1882. First edition; octavo, xvi, 434 pages, frontispiece, plates, original lime green pictorial cloth stamped in black and white by Burn, corners showing, rubbed, author's presentation, inscribed to Mr. Maclagan, from author, very good.   Jeff Weber Rare Books   163 - 154 2011 $300

L'Estrange, A. G.   *The Life of Mary Russell Mitford....* London: Richard Bentley, 1870. First edition; 3 volumes, half titles, original brown cloth by Burn & Co., bevelled boards, spines lettered in gilt, inner hinges slightly cracking, very good.   Jarndyce Antiquarian Booksellers   CLXC - 415 2011   £65

Lubke, Wilhelm *History of Art.* London: Smith, Elder, 1868. Tall 8vo., 2 volumes, half titles, vignette illustrations in text, 2 pages ads in each volume, original brown cloth, bevelled boards by Burn & Co., decorated in black and gilt, lettered in gilt, very good bright copy.   Jarndyce Antiquarian Booksellers   CXCI - 299 2011   £75

MacDonald, George 1824-1905   *At the Back of the North Wind. in Good Words for the Young 1869 & 1870.* London: Strahan & Co., 1869-1870. Color frontispiece and title, 1869, frontispiece & engraved title 1870, plates, illustrations, some browning, 2 volumes in original blue decorated cloth by Burn & Co., 1869 more faded and rubbed, inner hinges cracking, all edges gilt.   Jarndyce Antiquarian Booksellers   CXCII - 112 2011   £850

MacDonald, George 1824-1905   *England's Antiphon.* London: Macmillan & Co., 1868? First edition, later issue?; frontispiece, color engraved title and plates by Arthur Hughes, original royal blue, bevelled boards with borders of gilt rules and crosses to front board, inner hinge cracking, slightly dulled, binder's ticket of Burn & Co, all edges gilt, very good.   Jarndyce Antiquarian Booksellers   CXCII - 111 2011   £200

MacDonald, George 1824-1905   *England's Antiphon.* London: Macmillan & Co., 1868. First edition; frontispiece, color engraved title and plates after Arthur Hughes, original royal blue cloth, borders in blind "The Sunday Library for Household Reading" devices blocked on front board and spine dulled, slightly chipped, binder's ticket of Burn & Co., inscribed by author for cousin Margaret MacDonald Troup.   Jarndyce Antiquarian Booksellers   CXCII - 109 2011 £1250

MacDonald, George 1824-1905   *The Princess and the Goblin. in Good Words for the Young: Annual for 1871.* London: A. Strahan & Co., 1871. Frontispiece and engraved title, plates, illustrations, some spotting, few pages torn at fore edge, original blue decorated cloth by Burn & Co., spine faded and slightly rubbed, inner hinges cracking, all edges gilt.   Jarndyce Antiquarian Booksellers   CXCII - 137 2011   £300

Manning, Anne *The Spanish Barber: a Tale.* London: James Nisbet & Co., 1869. First edition; half title, with two color transfers, frontispiece, original green cloth by Burn & Co., front board and spine blocked and lettered in black and gilt, slightly dulled, Morningside school prize label, good plus.   Jarndyce Antiquarian Booksellers   CLXC - 229 2011   £40

Martineau, Harriet 1802-1876   *Biographical Sketches.* London: Macmillan, 1869. First edition; half title, 2 pages ads, 48 page catalog (July 1868), original blue cloth by Burn & Co., spine lettered in gilt, slightly dulled, rubbed at tail of spine, presentation inscription from author for Ellen Higginson.   Jarndyce Antiquarian Booksellers   CLXC - 266 2011   £200

Myers, Frederic William Henry *Saint Paul.* London: Macmillan & Co., 1867. First edition; half title, occasional pencil and ink notes, original red cloth by Burn, blocked in black and gilt, slightly rubbed, cloth little lifted in places, label removed from f.e.p., ownership signature of E. W. Gosse, Jan. 1868.   Jarndyce Antiquarian Booksellers   CXCI - 327 2011   £125

Nightingale, Florence *Notes on Nursing; What It Is and What It Is Not.* London: Harrison, 1860. New edition; half title, original maroon wavy grained cloth by Burn & Co., borders blocked in blind, spine lettered in gilt, carefully rebacked, very good, inscribed by author for Harriet Martineau July 1860.   Jarndyce Antiquarian Booksellers   CLXC - 595 2011   £2500

Trollope, Anthony 1815-1882   *An Editor's Tales.* London: Strahan & Co., 1870. First edition; half title, original brown cloth, expertly recased with spine strip slightly trimmed at head and tail, binder's ticket of Burn & Co., inscribed by publisher, A. Strahan for George MacDonald, with MacDonalds bookplate.   Jarndyce Antiquarian Booksellers   CXCII - 340 2011   £450

Binding – Carswell

Oliphant, Margaret Oliphant Wilson 1828-1897   *The Victorian Age of English Literature.* Leipzig: Heinemann and Balestier, 1893. 2 volumes in 1, contemporary dark blue patterned cloth by R. Carswell of Belfast, spine lettered in gilt, very good.   Jarndyce Antiquarian Booksellers   CLXC - 654 2011   £35

FINE BINDINGS

Binding – Chambolle-Duru

Gontaut-Biron, Marie Josephine Louise, Duchesse De *Memoirs of the Duchesse De Gontaut...* New York: Dodd Mead and Co., 1894. Of this edition on deckle edge paper, 175 copies were printed; 235 x 155mm., 2 volumes, elegant dark green crushed morocco, sumptuously gilt by Chambolle-Duru (stamp signed on front turn-ins), covers ornately gilt with triple ruled borders surrounding a wide internal frame of fleurons, scallops, curls and floral bouquets in urns, raised bands, spine compartments with floral urn centerpiece within a frame of scrolling foliate stamps, elaborate inner gilt dentelles, marbled endpapers, top edge gilt, other edges uncut, each volume with mezzotint color frontispiece and window mount, 12 additional engraved plates with captioned tissue guards, titlepages printed in red and black, joints partly rubbed, front joint of first volume beginning to crack at top and bottom, slight browning at edges of leaves because of acidic paper, still very appealing, especially lovely bindings, solid and bright, text without significant signs of use. Phillip J. Pirages 59 - 226 2011 $650

Lacroix, Paul *Ma Republique.* Paris: Librairie L. Conquet, 1902. One of 40 special copies with 2 extra states of the plates and inscribed by publisher to Monsieur L. Rattier (no doubt French bibliophile Leon Rattier; of the limited edition of 100 copies on Japan vellum (of a total edition of 400 copies) 205 x 140mm., 2 p.l., 150, (1) pages, very fine crimson morocco gilt and onlaid by Chambolle-Duru (stamp signed on front doublure), covers with broad border comprised of seven gilt fillets, raised bands, with broad border comprised of seven gilt fillets, raised bands, spine compartments outlined with five concentric gilt rules, doublures of brown crushed morocco featuring stylized flowers of onlaid olive brown morocco on elegant arching gilt stems, cloth and then marbled endleaves, all edges gilt, original printed wrappers bound in, 7 etchings, each in 3 states (for a total of 21 plates), virtually mint. Phillip J. Pirages 59 - 91 2011 $3250

Binding – Chivers, Cedric

Lefevre, Raoul *Recuyell of the Historyes of Troye.* Hammersmith: Kelmscott Press, 1892. One of 300 copies; 3 books in 2 volumes, large quarto, xv, (1), 295, (1 blank); (297)-507, (1, blank), (509)-718 pages, printed in red and black in Troy and Chaucer type, decorative woodcut borders and initials, bound by Cedric Chivers in beautiful Art Nouveau "Vellucent" binding, binding elaborately decorated in vivid colors and detail and all boards and spine ruled in gilt, front covers framed by green vines with pink and orange flowers and gilt stamped detail, inside frame of vines stands Helen of Troy on volume I and Cassandra on volume II, title of book shown on a scroll beneath women's feet, spines of both volumes contain similar scroll decoration, also containing title of book on back cover of each volume is image of the towers of Troy in flames, and gauffered, others uncut, marbled endpapers, gilt ruled dentelles, bookplates of former owners Rudloph August Williams and "CKC" Charles C. Kalbfleisch and bookplate of other previous owner on back pastedown of each volume, each volume in its own chemise and quarter calf slipcase, dentelles slightly lifting, otherwise beautiful, near fine set in extraordinary binding. Heritage Book Shop Holiday 2010 - 67 2011 $22,500

Binding – Cockerell, Douglas

Malory, Thomas *The Noble and Joys Book Entitled Le Morte D'Arthur...* Chelsea: The Ashendene Press, 1913. Limited to 145 copies and the most deluxe format; folio, (6 blank, 4) xxii, 500, (2, 8 blank) pages, 29 woodcut illustrations, 2 full page, initials in red and blue by and after Graily Hewitt, original full dark brown calf designed by Douglas Cockerell and executed by W. H. Smith, binder, raised bands, gilt stamped spine title, neatly rebacked preserving original covers, fine. Jeff Weber Rare Books 163 - 106 2011 $8000

Malory, Thomas *The Noble and Joys Book Entitled Le Morte D'Arthur...* Chelsea: The Ashendene Press, 1913. Limited to 145 copies and the most deluxe format; folio, (6 blank, 4) xxii, 500, (2, 8 blank) pages, 29 woodcut illustrations, 2 full page, initials in red and blue by and after Graily Hewitt, original full dark brown calf designed by Douglas Cockerell and executed by W. H. Smith, binder, raised bands, gilt stamped spine title, neatly rebacked preserving original covers, fine. Jeff Weber Rare Books 163 - 106 2011 $8000

Binding – Cohen, Claudia

Morrow, Bradford *A Bestiary.* New York: Grenfell Press, 1990. Limited to 100 copies (entire edition) of which only 50 were for sale; original full multi-colored morocco by Claudia Cohen, in morocco and linen slipcase, each copy signed by author and each of the artists, the present copy is accompanied by one of only 3 complete sets of 36 original prints assembled at time of publication, each print is one of an edition of only 10 copies signed by artist, only 10 separate prints of each of the illustrations in book were produced, with the contributing artists receiving 7 copies of each of their prints, remaining 3 copies of the prints were gathered into 3 sets containing the full complement of 36 prints, 2 of these sets were retained by publisher and one by author, folio, 36 original prints by 18 different artists.   James S. Jaffe Rare Books   May 26 2011 - 5770 2011 $50,000

Plimpton, Sarah *Keeping Time.* New York: 2009. Artist's book one of 15 copies all on Tosa Washi paper, each signed and numbered by the artist/author, Sarah Plimpton; page size 15 5/8 x 11 7/8 inches, plus letterpress printed text of poem on small sheet 6 3/8 x 5 3/8 inches, 10 pages, bound loose in grey paper wrappers and housed in custom made cloth over boards clamshell box by Claudia Cohen, label printed in gold gilt on paper on spine with title and author's name, book was set in Filosophia type and printed letterpress by Brad Ewing at the Grenfell Press, 10 reduction woodcuts printed in several shades of grey, black, magenta, blue, brown and chartreuse.   Priscilla Juvelis - Rare Books   48 - 21 2011 $1200

Poe, Edgar Allan 1809-1849 *The Raven.* Easthampton: Cheloniidae Press, 1986. Artist's Proof copy; one of a handful of such bound as the state proof edition in full red morocco, with additional two suites of working proofs (21 prints total, 17 wood engravings and 3 states of frontispiece etching), from a total issue of 225 copies, 150 regular edition, 50 deluxe with extra suite of prints, bound in quarter morocco by Claudia Cohen, 25 state proof copies with two extra suites and an original drawing, full morocco binding, all copies on Magnani Letterpress paper and all signed and numbered by Alan James Robinson; page size 6 7/16 x 9 3/8 inches, this is an all new original edition in which the artist revisits the text of the first book of the press, text is letterpress by Dan Keliher at Wild Carrot Letterpress, the 9 original wood engravings and one original etching, frontispiece portrait of Poe, the full red morocco binding is by Daniel Kelm and Sarah Pringle at the Wide Awake Garage, the front panel blindstamped with one of Robinson's wood engravings of a raven, the two additional suites are housed in grey cloth over boards folder with white label printed in black on front "The Raven/Prints" and both housed in grey cloth-over boards clamshell box, red morocco label on spine, blindstamped with title, author and title logo of Cheloniidae Press, both bit worn, book and prints fine.   Priscilla Juvelis - Rare Books   48 - 4 2011 $2000

Binding – Cosway

Forester, Cecil Scott 1899-1966 *Josephine, Napoleon's Empress.* London: Methuen & Co., 1925. First edition; 218 x 145mm., vii (i), 246 pages, superb contemporary deep blue morocco by Sangorski & Sutcliffe for Asprey with more than 60 onlays, front cover with center medallion featuring onlaid teal blue crossed "J's", surrounded by gilt wreath and crown as well as onlaid pink flowers, lovely gilt floral sprays with more onlaid pink flowers in corners of both covers, raised bands, spine beautifully gilt and onlaid in same floral vine pattern, doublures of crimson morocco with onlaid blue flowers in corners as well as intricate series of patterned rules against deep blue morocco border, front doublure with fine inset hand painted ivory miniature of Josephine, watered silk free endpapers, gilt edges, in slightly scuffed but sturdy and attractive morocco backed plush-lined folding cloth box, gilt titling on spine; with 12 illustrations, all photos of portraits, as called for, choice binding in immaculate condition.   Phillip J. Pirages 59 - 96 2011 $5500

Kingsley, Charles 1819-1875 *The Water-Babies.* London: Macmillan and Co., 1885. First edition illustrated by Linley Sambourne; small quarto, viii, 371, (1, printers imprint) pages, wood engravings, text illustrations, fine Cosway binding by Riviere & Son (stamp signed in gilt on front turn-in), full red crushed levant morocco, covers with gilt triple fillet border, front cover set a fine rectangular miniature portrait on ivory under bevelled glass 89 x 66mm. of Charles Kinglsey by Miss C. B. Currie, within inner gilt double fillet border and wide outer gilt floral and leaf border (in the style of Charles MacLeish), spine in 6 compartments, five raised bands, lettered gilt in two compartments and decoratively tooled in gilt in a similar floral and leaf design in remaining four compartments, with date in gilt at foot, board edges with gilt double fillet, turn-ins ruled in gilt with similar gilt floral corner ornaments, dark green watered silk doublures and liners, all edges gilt, stamped in gilt on rear doublure "Miniatures by C. B. Currie", additionally stamped in gilt on fore-edges of front and rear boards "Cosway Binding" and "Invented by J. H. Stonehouse", inserted certificate leaf signed by Stonehouse and Currie and numbered in ink identifies the present copy as being "No 951 of the Cosway Bindings invented by J. H. Stonehouse with Miniatures on Ivory by Miss Currie", original front and rear blue cloth covers bound in at end, superb example, housed in velvet lined red cloth clamshell case.   David Brass Rare Books, Inc.   May 26 2011 - 00892 2011 $11,500

Manson, James A. *Sir Edwin Landseer, R.A.* London: Walter Scott Publishing Co. Ltd., 1902. First edition; octavo, (i-vi), vii-xvi, 219, (220) pages, titlepage printed in blue and black, 21 engraved plates and photogravure frontispiece, full dark green levant Cosway-stye binding by Riviere & Sons for Sotheran & Co., stamp signed to front turn-in, spine decoratively tooled and lettered in gilt, after floral and leaf design, compartments ruled in gilt, front and back covers ruled and decoratively tooled in a gilt floral and leaf design, surrounding 10 oval-round miniature paintings under glass, 9 miniatures on front cover depict 8 hunting dogs around a stag, miniature on back cover is portrait of Landseer, extremities double ruled in gilt, with turn-ins ruled and decoratively tooled in gilt, green marbled endpapers, joints expertly and totally invisibly repaired, fine, housed in original burgundy roan slipcase,. David Brass Rare Books, Inc. May 26 2011 - 01191 2011 $23,500

Moore, Thomas 1779-1852 *Lalla Rookh, an Oriental Romance.* London: printed for Longman, Hurst, Rees, Orme and Brown, 1817. First edition; 292 x 222mm., 2 p.l., 405, (1) pages, nothing short of spectacular early 20th century dark blue levant morocco extravagantly gilt, richly inlaid and gloriously bejewelled by Sangorski & Sutcliffe (stamp-signed on front doublure), binding with overall Oriental design (befitting the poem) with upper cover featuring a sunken central panel, its unusual nine-sided shape resembling a clump of hanging grapes, within which two birds of paradise, inlaid in lilac, green and brown morocco with two rubies for eyes, perch in a grape arbor, its inlaid leaves with fruit clusters on densely stippled gilt around accented with 19 turquoises, the whole central tableau surrounded by a border of interweaving bands of inlaid brown morocco set with 9 bands of Mother-of-Pearl, the entire sunken panel surrounded by two ornate frames filled with flowering vines of Oriental design composed of hundreds of pieces of inlaid morocco in red, blue, violet and green on a background of brown morocco and heavily stippled gilt, outer frame accented with 20 blue chalcedonies and 20 garnets; lower cover with similar frame and central panel, this one featuring two lovebirds inlaid with multiple colors and with two amethyst eyes, birds in a similar grape arbor above, large Mother-of-Pearl heart, panel further adorned with 3 sapphires, four blue chalcedonies five turquoises, four Carnelians and 10 additional bands of Mother-of-Pearl, raised bands, spine gilt in compartments with large inlaid arabesque in green and brown morocco on a gilt background, gilt titling on inlaid compartments of chestnut brown morocco, glorious front doublure of ivory morocco covered in gilt vines with inlaid violet morocco flowers, the whole framed in green morocco decorated with gilt vines and red morocco posies and berries, at center, a hand painted Cosway-Style portrait of author on ivory surrounded by gilt frame, with 12 flowers composed of no fewer than 72 turquoises and 36 garnets, oval portrait in sunken panel enclosed by wreath of inlaid morocco flowers, rear doublure of similar design, but its medallion featuring 8 amethysts set among sinuously curving inlaid lilac strapwork twining around a large (approximately one carat) Mexican fire opal encircled by 12 pearls, the binding containing 226 jewels in all; free endleaves of cream colored watered silk, gilt edges, in original well made (somewhat scuffed), silk and plush lined blue morocco box with shuttered lid; extra illustrated with 12 hand colored engraved plates mounted on lettered Japan vellum bookplate of Charles J. Rosenbloom; two leaves with neatly renewed marginal tears, but magnificent copy of a masterpiece of bookbinding. Phillip J. Pirages 59 - 111 2011 $65,000

Napoleon, Emperor of the French *Maxims of Napoleon.* London: Arthur L. Humphreys, 1903. Small quarto, bound by Riviere & son in full light brown paneled morocco, with two miniature paintings on Ivory by Miss C. B. Currie, almost invisible rebacked with original spine laid down. Heritage Book Shop Booth A12 51st NY International Antiquarian Book Fair April 8-10 2011 - 33 2011 $15,000

Binding – Courteval

Labillardiere, Jacques Julien Houton De *Relation du Voyage a la Recherche de La Perouse.* Paris: Chez H. J. Jansen, 1799-1800. First edition; 2 quarto text volumes and one folio atlas, atlas with engraved title, double page route map and 43 plates, contemporary French mottled calf by Courteval.   Heritage Book Shop   Booth A12 51st NY International Antiquarian Book Fair April 8-10 2011 - 82   2011 $20,000

Binding – Crombie & Lamothe

Thoreau, Henry David   1817-1862   *Walden; or Life in the Woods.* Boston: Ticknor & Fields, 1854. First edition; rebound around the turn of the twentieth century by Crombie & Lamothe in three quarter brown morocco and marbled paper boards, five raised bands, gilt ruling and lettering, matching marbled paper used as pastedowns and endpapers, original cloth covers and spine in very nice condition, gilt still bright, bound at rear, 8 page publisher's catalog not bound in, engraved titlepage and map inserted, marginal dampstain in outer top and bottom corners throughout, except on map, rarely just touching text, but mostly not affecting any text, small neat bookplate of Abram Joseph Abeloff, very minor rubbing to joints, very good or better.   Charles Agvent   Transcendentalism 2010 - 41   2011 $6500

Binding – David, S.

Croze-Magnan, Simon Celestin   *L'Aretin d'Aguustin Carrache, ou Recueil de Postures Erotiques, d'Apres les Gravures a l'eau-forte par cet Artiste Celebre avec le texte Explicatif des sujets.* Paris: A La Nouvelle Cythere, Didot, 1798. First edition; 4to., pages (iv), 12, 80, with 20 dry points and burin engraved plates by J. J. Coiny after Carnach, top edge trimmed, others uncut, very occasional light spotting, otherwise fine, fresh, wide margined copy, red morocco, elaborately gilt, inner gilt decorations and dentelles, silk and marbled endpaper by S. David (mid 20th century), fine, red morocco and marbled paper chemise, red silk lining, matching slipcase, light shelf wear only.   Simon Finch Rare Books   Zero - 419   2011   £9500

Binding – Davies & Hands

Oliphant, Margaret Oliphant Wilson   1828-1897   *Margaret Maitland of Sunnyside.* New York: G. P. Putnam & Vo., 1856. First American edition; 12 page catalog, original dark green cloth by Davies & Hands, boards blocked in blind, spine lettered gilt, very slight rubbing to tail of spine, very good, bright.   Jarndyce Antiquarian Booksellers   CLXC - 634   2011   £120

Binding – Davison

Prosser, Sophie Amelia   *The Cheery Chime of Garth and Other Stories.* London: R.T.S., 1874. First edition; frontispiece, illustrations, original green cloth by Davison, blocked and lettered in black and gilt, slight rubbing, owner's inscription Christmas 1875, good plus.   Jarndyce Antiquarian Booksellers   CLXC - 776   2011   £35

Binding – De Coverley, Roger

Malory, Thomas   *Morte D'Arthur.* London: David Nutt, 1889. Limited edition; 3 volumes, quarto, uniformly bound by Roger De Coverley in half brown morocco over marbled boards, gilt lettering on spine, titlepage, others uncut, marbled endpapers, previous owner's armorial bookplate to front pastedown of each volume, corners lightly bumped and edges slightly rubbed, folding chart in volume 3 with closed tear, expertly repaired, very good.   Heritage Book Shop Holiday 2010 - 77   2011 $1350

Binding – De La Rue & Co.

Sheridan, Louisa Henrietta   *The Comic Offering; or Ladies' Melange of Literary Mirth for MDCCCXXXII.* London: Smith, Elder and Co., 1832. Frontispiece, additional engraved title, illustrations, 6 pages ads, original black calf, heavily and pictorially embossed, spine lettered in gilt, slightly rubbed, endpapers replaced, all edges gilt, very good, binding signed "De La Rue & Co. London", superb example.   Jarndyce Antiquarian Booksellers   CXCI - 443   2011   £85

Binding – Delaney, Roberta

Delaney, Roberta   *Plants and Insects from Spring Snow.* Sherborn: 1989. Artist's book, one of 10 copies only; all on French fold Rives heavyweight cream paper, each signed and numbered by artist, page size 9 1/2 x 11 1/2 inches, 2 volumes identically bound by artist in handmade Japanese nacreous paper with various leaves and grasses in paper itself ivory colored background with leaves, etc. in grey/green and buff, handsewn and housed in folding case of handmade green Japanese paper over boards lined with handmade Mexican Bark paper, ivory colored plastic clasps, artist has taken text for Yukio Mishima's "Spring Snow" and illuminated it with hand colored woodcuts, 6 in the volume of "Plants" and 8 in the volume of "Insects", recto page contains the print, verso a graphite rubbing from part of same block, woodcuts printed and hand colored by artist, some printed in color with mica reflecting Edo period techniques, woodcuts were cut from Japanese 5 layered plywood with boxwood exterior surface, enabling artist to print on an etching press (mantle), graphite rubbings on verso wear from a graphite stick, paper laid over block and rubbed in random manner, each print titled by artist in pencil blow print, as each print is hand colored, no two copies the same, delicately beautiful book.   Priscilla Juvelis - Rare Books   48 - 7   2011 $5000

Binding – Derome

Achilles, Tatius *De Clitophontis et Leucippes Amoribus Libri VIII.* Leipzig: Sumtibus Io. Friderici Iunii, 1776. Facing pages of Greek and Latin text, pages xvi, 731, (13), 8vo., contemporary red morocco, boards bordered with triple gilt fillet, spine divided by gilt square chain rolls between gilt fillets, second compartment gilt lettered direct, rest with central gilt tools, marbled endpapers, all edges gilt, small ink spot to lower board, note on endpaper above binding, near fine, binding unsigned, but 20th century pencil note on verso of front flyleaf attributes it to Derome le Jeune. Blackwell Rare Books B166 - 16 2011 £800

Anacreon *(Title in Greek, then) Anacreontis Teii Odaria (i.e. The Odes).* Parmae: ex Regio Typographeio, 1785. One of 250 copies on "Blue" paper (of a total of 310 copies); 305 x 223mm., 2 p.l., xciv, 100 (1) pages, splendid contemporary crimson morocco, handsomely gilt by Derome Le Jeune (with his ticket), covers framed with double gilt rules, inner rule with scalloped corners, raised bands, compartments with very appealing all over diaper pattern, chain pattern (asterisk and four petal flower) on board edges, endleaves of lavender watered silk, very wide and intricate inner dentelles extending in unusual way from turn-ins onto silk pastedowns, all edges gilt, small author portrait in style of ancient coin to titlepage, large and elaborate armorial vignette on dedication page; tiny bit of wear to spine ends, few leaves with very minor wear or paper flaw at fore edge, especially fine, beautiful book with elegant original binding scarcely worn, text very clean, bright and fresh, margins nothing short of immense. Phillip J. Pirages 59 - 9 2011 $8500

Henault, Charles Jean Francois *Nouvel Abrege Chronologique de l'Histoire de France.* Paris: Chez Prault et al, 1756. Fifth edition; 165 x 105mm., 2 volumes with continuous pagination, 5 p.l., (1), 545, (1), 1 blank leaf; (549)-928 pages, (48) leaves, including final blank, second volume with half title but no titlepage, apparently as issued, lovely contemporary olive green morocco, elegantly gilt in style of Derome, covers with plain and stippled fillet border around a frame containing large and graceful gilt floral and botanical stamps as well as dots and circlets, raised bands, spines gilt in compartments featuring charming flower centerpiece and small scrolling foliate cornerpieces, turn-ins with gilt zig-zag decoration, stenciled gilt endpapers, all edges gilt, publisher's device on titlepage, historiated headpieces, foliated initials, ornamental tailpieces; small bookplate of Jean Furstenberg and Henri Beraldi; spines slightly and uniformly faded to an attractive amber, just hint of wear to joints and corners, isolated minor foxing, few trivial stains, but fine, pretty binding sound, lustrous and with only insignificant wear and text, very clean and fresh. Phillip J. Pirages 59 - 53 2011 $2900

Binding – Dillon, L. J.

Swisher, Mary *The Stones of Mani. Views of the Southern Peloponnese.* Sacramento: Stalwart Press, 2008. Limited edition, one of 50 copies, signed; text on Rives Heavyweight paper and each of the 12 platinum-palladium photograph on Crane's 90-lb. business card stock with preceding legend for each photo on Wyndstone vellum, each copy signed and numbered by author/photographer, who has also signed and numbered each of her photos, pages size 11 3/4 x 10 inches, text volume 72 pages, print volume 24 leaves, bound by L. J. Dillon, text volume in tan linen over boards with stitched binding in natural linen thread using Greek key design, plate volume is loose as issued housed in tan linen portfolio identical in trim size to text volume, both housed in publisher's slipcase of same tan linen with blue Hahnemuhle Bugra papers on front and back, title and author in black with cross and lion motifs used also as decorations in text, same blue Hahnemuhle paper used as endsheets in text volume and to line plate portfolio case. Priscilla Juvelis - Rare Books 48 - 22 2011 $3000

Binding – Douglas

Hargrove, William *History and Description of the Ancient City of York...* York: published and sold by Wm. Alexander, 1818. 2 volumes, 8vo., pages (iii)-xvi, (17)-396 397*-412*, (397)-407 (iii) + engraved frontispiece and 3 other engraved plates; iv, (5)-688, (ii) + engraved frontispiece, an extending hand colored plan and 6 other engraved plates, this copy extra illustrated by the inclusion of Volume I - 16 pages of text and 8 engraved plates between pages xvi and (17) and volume 2 - engraved plate facing page 522 and tipped-in slip with view of gatehouse to Archbishop's palace at Bishopthorpe facing page 518, all additions except the last slip have been taken from James Storer's History and Antiquities of the Cathedral Churches of Great Britain" volume 4 (London 1818), contemporary polished maroon calf, four flat raised band spine ruled in gilt with massed 'intersecting circles' pallet in compartments, lettered and numbered direct in gilt, boards double rule gilt bordered and 'intersecting broken waves' roll within, centrally a large panel 'straight grain' tooled, board edges decorative roll gilt, turn-ins 'intersecting broken waves' roll gilt, 'Spanish' 'made' endpapers, dark blue and white sewn endbands, dark blue silk page markers, some light spotting, split at fold of one extending plate, volume I repaired at head of spine, front joint of volume 2 cracking a bit, little rubbing at extremities, spines lightly sunned, signed binding by Douglas, bookbinder, Blackburn with his paper ticket, printed label of Thomas Butler, from the collection of Christopher Ernest Weston 1947-2010. Unsworths Booksellers 24 - 106 2011 £450

Binding – Doves Bindery

Irving, Washington   1783-1859   *Bracebridge Hall.* London: Macmillan, 1877. First edition with these illustrations; extremely fine dark green crushed morocco handsomely gilt by the Doves Bindery (stamp signed and dated 1905 on rear turn-in), covers with double gilt fillet border and Tudor rose cornerpieces set among leafy sprays and circlets, raised bands, spine compartments heavily gilt with central Tudor rose framed by trefoil cornerpieces and accented with small tools, gilt turn-ins, all edges gilt, stippled gauffering, illustrations by Randolph Caldecott, including frontispiece, titlepage and five full page plates; engraved bookplate of William F. Gable; edges of free endpaper at front and back with usual (but here rather pronounced) offsetting from turn-ins, otherwise magnificent copy, text with virtually no signs of use, beautiful binding absolutely flawless.   Phillip J. Pirages   59 - 99   2011 $4500

Swinburne, Algernon Charles   1837-1909   *Astrophel and Other Poems.* London: Chatto & Windus, 1894. First edition; 190 x 130mm., 4 p.l., 228 pages, exquisite garnet red crushed morocco beautifully gilt by Doves Bindery, signed on rear turn-in and dated 1894), covers with gilt border accented with small tools enclosing a center panel framed by a single gilt rule, roseleaf cornerpieces, raised bands, spine lavishly gilt in compartments with large central Tudor rose (Doves tool 1h) surrounded by leaves and stippling, gilt titling, turn-ins adorned with gilt rules and roseleaf cornerpieces, all edges gilt, housed in suede lined black straight grain morocco pull-off case (slightly scuffed), front pastedown with faint evidence of bookplate removal, minor offsetting to endpapers from turn-ins (as usual), old bookseller's description taped to front free endpaper causing two small adhesive stains, otherwise really beautiful book, text clean and fresh, splendid binding in superb condition. Phillip J. Pirages   59 - 102   2011 $6500

Binding – Easton, Malcolm

Hubbard, Hesketh   *Architectural Painting in Oils.* Sir Isaac Pitman, 1938. First edition; pages 28, 2 color plates and black and white illustrations, large 8vo., original pictorial boards by Malcolm Easton, scattered spotting, uncommon. R. F. G. Hollett & Son Antiquarian Booksellers   177 - 479   2011   £35

Binding – Edmond & Spark

Murray, Charles Augustus   *The Prairie Bird.* London: Richard Bentley, 1844. First edition; 3 volumes, 12mo., slightly later half green morocco grained sheep by J. and J. P. Edmond & Spark, Aberdeen, gilt bands, very slightly rubbed, Fasque booklabels, very good, loosely inserted is opened stamped envelope address to H. Magnac (?), Fasque, Lawrencekirk.   Jarndyce Antiquarian Booksellers   CXCI - 531   2011   £330

Binding – Edmonds & Remnants

Knight, Charles   1791-1873   *The Old Printer and the Modern Press.* London: John Murray, 1854. First edition; illustrations, lacking leading f.e.p., original brown cloth by Edmonds & Remnants, decorated in blind, slightly rubbed. Jarndyce Antiquarian Booksellers   CXCI - 450   2011   £75

MacDonald, George   1824-1905   *Poems.* London: Longman, Brown, Green, Longmans & Roberts, 1857. March 1856 24 page catalog, original dark brown morocco grained cloth by Edmonds & Remnants, spine marked and worn, following inner hinge cracking, poor copy, but sound. Jarndyce Antiquarian Booksellers   CXCII - 8   2011   £250

MacDonald, George   1824-1905   *Within and Without: a Dramatic Poem.* London: Longman, Brown, Green & Longmans, 1855. First edition; 4 pages ads, 24 page catalog (March 1856), few spots, original brown morocco grained cloth by Edmonds & Remnants, small hole in spine, almost imperceptibly repaired, frontispiece, in this copy grain of cloth is vertical.   Jarndyce Antiquarian Booksellers   CXCII - 1   2011   £950

Manning, Anne   *The Old Chelsea Bun-House.* London: Arthur Hall, Virtue and Co., 1855. First edition; engraved frontispiece, 5 pages ads, red brown endpapers, labels removed from pastedowns, original dark brown cloth by Edmonds & Remnants, bevelled boards, blocked in blind, spine lettered in gilt, very good.   Jarndyce Antiquarian Booksellers   CLXC - 217   2011   £75

Binding – Edwards

Gray, Thomas   1716-1771   *The Poems.* London: printed by T. Bensley for F. J. Du Roveray, 1800. 190 x 120, xxx, 162, (1) pages, (ads), with half title, extremely pleasing etruscan style calf in the style of quite probably by Edwards of Halifax, very expertly rebacked to style and corners repaired by Courtland Benson, covers with gilt broad and narrow rules and Greek-key roll framing wide inner panel of stencilled palmettes, gilt foliate roll enclosing central flamed panel, raised bands flanked by double blind rules, spine panels with large oval sunburst ornament supported by a floral nest, original black spine label, turn-ins with linked gilt roll, marbled endpapers, all edges gilt, with fore-edge painting of Yarmouth Castle and Harbor, 6 engraved plates, inscription "Frances Maria Phillips June 1824. in remembrance of her grandmother", covers little marked and dried but expertly restored binding solid and pleasing, the painting with a number of very thin parallel uncolored striped where edges of leaves are not quite even or here the fore-edge was not carefully fanned out during painting, one flyleaf with upper corner clipped off, some offsetting from plates, otherwise fine internally with only trivial effects.   Phillip J. Pirages   59 - 195   2011 $800

Hassell, John *Tour of the Isle of Wight.* London: printed by John Jarvis for Thomas Hookham, 1790. 2 volumes, 8vo., pages xxiv, 224 + engraved titlepage and 17 tinted aquatint plates; viii, 248 + engraved titlepage and 13 tinted aquatint plates, contemporary 'Etruscan' calf almost certainly by Edwards of Halifax, spine gilt compartmented with gilt 'coil' cornerpieces and 'classical urn' centre-pieces in blind, black lettering piece gilt, numbered direct in gilt within an open central blind tooled oval, boards 'metope and pentaglyph' roll gilt bordered and concentric borders within (one of palmettes & trident in blind) surrounding a central gilt 'Grecian key' roll edges marbled panel, board edges & turn-ins single rule gilt, vivid pink 'made' endpapers, all edges gilt, brown and white double core sewn endbands, bit foxed in places, neat restoration to endcaps and joints, spines slightly cracked, printed booklabel of John Sparrow at top left of veros of 'made' front endpaper, from the collection of Christopher Ernest Weston 1947-2010. Unsworths Booksellers 24 - 107 2011 £750

Johnson, Samuel 1709-1784 *Prince of Abissinia. a Tale.* London: printed for J. F. and C. Rivington et al, 1790. Eighth edition; 182 x 108mm., viii, 304 pages; extremely pleasing etruscan style calf in style of and quite probably by Edwards of Halifax, covers with gilt metope and pentaglyph border as well as a wide frame of stenciled palmettes enclosing a sprinkled central panel with lightened slats radiating from an oval sunburst and laurel garland at middle, raised bands flanked by plain gilt rules, spine panels with central black urn or ewer framed by gilt floral spray cornerpieces, black morocco label, turn-ins and all edges gilt; with attractive fore-edge painting, quite possibly by Edwards, apparently showing a landscape with Rievaulx Abbey Yorkshire in background; contemporaneous armorial bookplate of "Rycroft", covers with very minor marks and stains, joints and extremities with hint of rubbing (top of spine with very small losses of leather), with no significant wear, only trivial defects internally and with the fore-edge scene very well preserved. Phillip J. Pirages 59 - 37 2011 $1950

La Serre, Jean Puget De *The Mirrour Which Flatters Not Concerning the Contempt of the World, or the Meditation of Death, of Philip King of Macedon, Saladine, Adrian and Alexander the Great.* London: E. T. and R. H. for R. Thrale, 1673. 146 x 89mm., 12 p.l., 216 pages, quite pleasing early 19th century vellum in the style of Edwards of Halifax, covers bordered with narrow decorative gilt roll flanked by blue rules and with gilt floral cornerpieces, flat spine with decorative gilt bands forming panels, five of these with charming floral centerpiece, titling and date panels colored blue, unusual additional gilt titling between four pairs of decorative bands, marbled endpapers, woodcut headpieces and five engraved folding plates, including frontispiece, vellum very slightly soiled, front board just barely splayed but binding in excellent condition, completely sound and rather pretty, one plate accidentally cut into at crease (with minor loss of background detail), each plate with small tear in crease near gutter (with no loss), small portion of lower blank fore margin of one leaf cut away, front pastedown very roughened (from lifted bookplate?), leaves slightly browned at edges, bit foxed, text still rather fresh, surprisingly clean, generally well preserved. Phillip J. Pirages 59 - 12 2011 $650

Rogers, Samuel *The Pleasures of Memory with Other Poems.* London: printed for T. Cadell Jun. and W. Davies, 1799. 165 x 102mm., 8 p.l., (9)-188 pages, extremely pleasing etruscan style calf in the style of, and quite probably by, Edwards of Halifax, covers with Greek-key roll border, wide inner frame of stencilled palmettes, and central flamed calf panel formed here by foliate roll, raised bands, spine compartments with gilt wheat and horn centerpiece and foliate corner ornaments, black morocco label, chained gilt turn-ins, marbled endpapers, all edges gilt; with pleasing pastel fore-edge painting of a scene from the (Italian?) countryside, featuring long arched ridge and title roofed villa, 4 engraved plates; joints and extremities just little dried and worn, trivial foxing and offsetting in text, still excellent, unrestored copy, binding entirely sound, with no cracks in joints, text very clean an fresh, bright copy. Phillip J. Pirages 59 - 38 2011 $1750

Specimens of the Early English Poets. London: printed for Edwards, 1790. First edition; 190 x 127mm., 5 p.l., 323 pages, extremely pleasing etruscan style calf in the style of and quite probably by, Edwards of Halifax, covers with gilt metope and pentaglyph border, wide inner frame of stencilled palmettes, sprinkled central panel featuring at middle a stained obelisk tool draped with four slender fronds on either side, this centerpiece painted over in red, recently and beautifully rebacked by Courtland Benson to replicate original (flat) spine with all over gilt lattice design, black titling label, marbled endpapers, turn-ins and all edges gilt; with attractive fore-edge painting, very probably by Edwards, apparently showing Walton Hall near Wakefield; large paper copy, armorial bookplate of Thomas Walker, that bookplate as well as verso of endpaper inscribed in ink "Wm. Walker", former dated August 1848 and later "Wilsick, July 1848", titlepage with painted armorial laid down beneath imprint; minor pitting (as inevitable with acid treated calf), few leaves with small faint stains, otherwise fine, expertly restored binding with lustrous covers and bright gilt, text especially clean, fresh and bright with very spacious margins. Phillip J. Pirages   59 - 39   2011 $1400

Thomson, James   1700-1748   *The Seasons.* London: printed for John Sharpe, 1821. 170 x 105mm., 215, (1) pages, extremely pleasing etruscan style calf in the style of and quite probably by Edwards of Halifax, covers with gilt Greek key border, wide inner frame of stencilled palmettes, central panel of tree calf framed by a gilt broken cable, flat spine gilt in compartments separated by Greek key roll and with a lyre centerpiece framed by foliate cornerpieces, with black morocco label, marbled endpapers, all edges gilt, very attractive fore-edge painting of an English stately home, perhaps Stourhead House, extra engraved titlepage with vignette and fine engraved plates, inscription "Mary Williams/The last gift of her affectionate Aunt/Mary Hoyle, July 31st 1826"; extremities and joints bit dry and rubbed, rear joint just starting at tail, gilt eroded from head and tail of spine, half a dozen small patches of lost patina in frame around outside of stencilled central panel, plates little foxed, one more noticeably but still quite pleasing copy, appealing unrestored original binding entirely sound, text clean and smooth and rich colors of painting beautifully preserved. Phillip J. Pirages   59 - 196   2011 $1100

Watts, Isaac   *The Psalms of David.* (bound with) *Hymns and Spiritual Songs.* London: printed by and for J. W. Pasham, 1778. 123 x 70mm., 2 p.l., 240 pages, (10) leaves; 4 p.l., 216 pages, (12) leaves (index leaves for "Hymns and Spiritual Songs" bound out of order but all present), 2 parts in one volume, superb hand painted and gilt decorated vellum by Edwards of Halifax, both covers with very prominent oval paintings, front covers depicting a statue in grisaille of a female figure, probably representing Faith, casting her eyes upward to heaven, one arm aloft, other holding a cross, whole against a sky blue oval, back cover with very dynamic grisaille painting of the Resurrection, with Christ flying upward from the tomb amidst brilliant light, three soldiers beneath shielding themselves in protective wonderment and presiding angel supplying adoration at right, both covers bordered by gilt chain motif, flat spine divided by blue wash bands into compartments featuring gilt lyres and swirling gilt cornerpieces, blue wash label, all edges gilt in original soft green leather slipcase bordered by gilt chain matching that of binding, this in turn housed in modern morocco backed folding box with raised bands and gilt titling, bookplate of James Gordon, Esquire, Moor Place; inscription "Harriot Whitbread/The Gift of John Howard Esq(ui)re/ Cardington/ 1785", similar inscription to Harriot from M. Howard of Cardington dated 1787; blue spine label trifle faded, blue cover background on front board showing little soil, small ink blot on three pages, wonderful binding in very fine condition, text nearly pristine, original slipcase bit worn and faded but remarkable survival.   Phillip J. Pirages 59 - 13   2011 $6900

Binding – Edwards, George Wharton

Irving, Washington   1783-1859   *Tales of a Traveller.* New York: Putnam, 1895. First edition, Buckthorne edition; 2 volumes, large 8vo., white cloth with extensive gilt pictorial bindings, signed GWE (George Wharton Edwards), top edge gilt, fine in original printed cloth dust jackets, 5 illustrations in half tone by Arthur Rackham, also illustrated by others.   Aleph-Bet Books, Inc.   95 - 478   2011 $450

Binding – Fazakerley

Jacobus De Varagine   1230-1298   *The Golden Legend.* Kelmscott Press, 1892.   One of 500 copies; 300 x 215mm., 3 volumes, handsome contemporary burgundy morocco by Fazakerley of Liverpool (stamp signed on front turn-ins), covers with three concentric frames each formed by single gilt rule and one thick and one thin black rule, outer frame with elaborate cascading cornerpieces formed by flowers, leafy volutes and small round tools, middle frame with gilt anular dot at each corner, corners of innermost panel with two entwined gilt leaves, raised bands decorated with gilt fillet and flanked by blood and gilt rule, spine panels with elegant gilt floral centerpiece, gilt turn-in, marbled endpapers, top edges gilt, other edges untrimmed, elaborate woodcut title (first designed by Morris) and first page with full white vine borders, 2 woodcut illustrations and 2 full borders designed by Edward Burne-Jones, large and small decorative woodcut initials, printer's device; decorative bookplate of Samuel Cross, with Tiffany engraved bookplate of Albert May Todd; endpapers (which are ot a part of the collation) with sparse and light mottling, five gatherings with perhaps half of their leaves faintly yellowed (a single leaf only that is more than slightly affected), otherwise only most trivial imperfections, extremely attractive, handsome bindings lustrous and with just negligible signs of use and text virtually immaculate.   Phillip J. Pirages   59 - 240   2011 $9500

Binding – Fisher, George

Rossetti, Christina   1830-1894   *Poems Chosen by Walter De La Mare.* Gregynog Press, 1930.   One of 25 copies specially bound, of a total edition of 300; 235 x 159mm., 3 p.l., vii-xliii, (1), 107, (1) pages, very fine animated scarlet morocco by Gregynog (signed in gilt by R. Ashwin Maynard and George Fisher on rear turn-in), gilt tooled covers dominated by two large cruciform foliate ornaments elaborated with diagonal blind and gilt decoration (something like evergreen leaves), ornaments on a field of gold dots, covers bordered by gilt and blind rules from which emanate a series of similar gilt and blind evergreen decorations, spine with raised bands, panels outlined in blind, gilt titling, turn-ins with double gilt rule, top edge gilt, other edges untrimmed, original publisher's board slipcase (slightly soiled but sturdy), initial openings and frontispiece after drawings by Dante Gabriel Rossetti, printed in red and black throughout, one page with trivial stain, otherwise virtually pristine.   Phillip J. Pirages   59 - 228   2011 $7500

Binding – Four Hands Bindery

Brassai   *The Artists of My Life.*   New York: Witken Berley Ltd., 1982.   First edition, deluxe edition comprising 'specially selected sheets", this number 11 of 150 copies, signed and numbered by Brassai, issued with hand pulled dust grained photogravure also signed by Brassai of Henri Matisse drawing a nude woman, 19193; large 4to., full page reproductions of photos, pictorial patterned paper covered boards over cloth lettered silver at spine, special presentation folder housing photogravure, in special binding designed by Sage Reynolds and executed at Four Hands Bindery NY, fine in very good plain buff slipcase.   Any Amount of Books   May 26 2011 - A68250   2011 $1845

Binding – Frost

Arabian Nights   *The Book of the Thousand Nights and a Night. (and) Supplemental Nights.*   Benares: printed by the Kamashastra Society for private subscribers only, 1885-1888.   First printing of this edition; 250 x 1600, 16 volumes, very pleasing rose colored crushed half morocco over buckram boards by Brian Frost & Co. (signed on verso of front endpaper of each volume), raised bands, spine panels with gilt floral centerpiece or titling, marbled endpapers, top edge gilt, titlepages printed in red and black, first and last leaves of each volume generally with light foxing (few of these leaves bit more foxed), text a shade less than bright because of paper stock chose, still very fine, especially lustrous binding without fault, no signs of use internally.   Phillip J. Pirages   59 - 64   2011 $12,500

Hamilton, Edith   *The Greek Way. (and) The Roman Way.* New York: W. W. Norton & Co. Inc., 1942.   1932. First edition of the second work; 211 x 143mm., 2 volumes, excellent dark blue crushed morocco by Frost and Co. (signed on front turn-ins), covers with gilt double fillet border, raised bands, spines gilt in double ruled compartments with central lozenge formed by small leaf tools, turn-ins with gilt rules and volute cornerpieces, marbled endpapers, all edges gilt, slight offsetting as usual from turn-ins onto free endleaves (from binder's glue), but very fine with virtually no signs of use.   Phillip J. Pirages   59 - 232   2011 $475

Binding – Garthegaat Bindery

Mitchell, John   *The Bottom of the Harbor.*   New York: Limited Editions Club, 1991.   First edition with these illustrations, one of 250, signed on justification page by John Mitchell; 5 hors-texte photogravures hand pulled by Jon Goodman after Berenice Abbott, 12 x 10 inches, 250 pages, hand sewn and bound in black quarter Nigerian goatskin and black Irish linen, very slight binder's imperfection on cloth, otherwise excellent copy in publisher's slipcase, this copy additionally inscribed "binder's copy" signed by Kim O'Donnell of the Garthegaat Bindery.   Gemini Fine Books & Arts, Ltd.   Art Reference & Illustrated Books: First Editions 2011 $750

Mitchell, John *The Bottom of the Harbor.* New York: Limited Editions Club, 1991. First edition with these illustrations, one of 250 copies signed by Mitchell; 5 hors texte hand pulled photogravures by Berenice Abbot, 12 x 10 inches, 250 pages, hand sewn and bound in black Nigerian goatskin and black Irish linen, fit in publisher's cloth slipcase, excellent copy, binder Kim O'Donnell's copy, unnumbered, with extra engraving by Abbot bound in, colophon additionally signed by binder.   Gemini Fine Books & Arts, Ltd.   Art Reference & Illustrated Books: First Editions 2011 $950

Pound, Ezra Loomis 1885-1972 *Cathay.* New York: Limited Editions Club, 1992.   First Clemente edition; one of 300 copies, signed and numbered by artist, 7 unsigned original color woodcuts by Francesco Clemente, printed on handmade Japanese Ogawashi paper, 12 x 8.5 inches, spine of book and edges of slipcase faded, otherwise as new, inscribed "binder's copy" and signed by Kim O'Donnell of the Garthegaat Bindery.   Gemini Fine Books & Arts, Ltd.   Art Reference & Illustrated Books: First Editions 2011 $1350

Binding – Gazel, Jeanne

Louys, Pierre *Pybrac Illustre de Trente Pointes Seches d'un Artiste Inconnu.* Paris: Aux depens d'un amateur (Marcel Vertes), 1928.   Second (first illustrated) edition; 4to., pages (iv), 78, etched frontispiece and 30 erotic dry point etchings (10 hors texte), 2 original aquarelles, 5 original sketches (one foxed), two duplicate suites of 31 engraving (one hand colored, one on Japan nacre), 5 refused plates, 1 original copper plate, red crushed half morocco, spine gilt titled and decorated within raised bands, gilt initialled "A.P."" (i.e. Arpad Pletsch) at base of spine, top edge gilt, others untrimmed, short closed tear to upper hinge at head of spine, bottom edge lightly rubbed, printed wrappers bound in, signed "Jeanne Gazel (c. 1930), presentation inscription and original drawing, choice copy, with original erotic drawing and autograph presentation from Vertes to Pletch, sumptuously bound for collector Pletch.   Simon Finch Rare Books   Zero - 439   2011   £10,000

Binding – Gray, Earle

Durrell, Lawrence George 1912-1990 *The Plant-Magic Man.* Santa Barbara: Capra Press, 1973.   First edition, #54 of 200 numbered and signed copies; handbound by Earle Gray, pictorial boards, fine in glassine dust jacket, illustrated with color blocks by Margaret Wilson and 2 photos.   Charles Agvent 2010 Summer Miscellany - 27 2011 $75

Binding – Gregynog Binder

Rossetti, Christina 1830-1894 *Poems Chosen by Walter De La Mare.* Gregynog Press, 1930.   One of 25 copies specially bound, of a total edition of 300; 235 x 159mm., 3 p.l., vii-xliii, (1), 107, (1) pages, very fine animated scarlet morocco by Gregynog (signed in gilt by R. Ashwin Maynard and George Fisher on rear turn-in), gilt tooled covers dominated by two large cruciform foliate ornaments elaborated with diagonal blind and gilt decoration (something like evergreen leaves), ornaments on a field of gold dots, covers bordered by gilt and blind rules from which emanate a series of similar gilt and blind evergreen decorations, spine with raised bands, panels outlined in blind, gilt titling, turn-ins with double gilt rule, top edge gilt, other edges untrimmed, original publisher's board slipcase (slightly soiled but sturdy), initial openings and frontispiece after drawings by Dante Gabriel Rossetti, printed in red and black throughout, one page with trivial stain, otherwise virtually pristine.   Phillip J. Pirages   59 - 228   2011 $7500

Binding – Grieve, Andrew

Shakespeare, William 1564-1616 *The Works.* London: Edward Moxon, 1857.   6 volumes, 220 x 143mm., one gathering in third volume with leaves bound out of order, but complete; 6 volumes, beautiful contemporary tree calf by Andrew Grieve of Edinburgh for William Paterson, Edinburgh bookseller (stamp-signed), covers with gilt double fillets and twining leaf border, raised bands, spines very attractively gilt in compartments with graceful floral corner-pieces and elaborate fleuron centerpiece, red and dark green morocco title labels, gilt ruled turn-ins, marbled endpapers and edges, engraved frontispiece, frontispiece and one title leaf bit foxed, isolated very minor foxing elsewhere, couple of very faint scratches to covers, but exceptionally fine, lovely bindings lustrous and virtually unworn, text showing no signs of use.   Phillip J. Pirages   59 - 317   2011 $4800

Binding – Gruel-Engelmann

Bible. French - 1843 *Les Saints Evangiles.* Paris: L. Curmer, 1843. First edition thus; the handsomely designed presentation page at the front tells us that this beautiful object was assembled at the order of C. J. T. Tiby and given to his dear wife Anais Duret Tiby on 2 June 1855 as a "Souvenir of 25 years of Happiness", 260 x 184mm., 4 p.l. 552 pages; 2 p.l, 372 pages, 2 volumes bound in one, extremely elegant mid 19th century Neo-gothic presentation binding by Gruel-Engelmann in dark green silk velvet, covers mounted with delicately amd elaborately carved boxwood frames after designs by Martin Riester, upper cover with wooden grapevine cornerpieces forming a large ogival central velvet panel featuring carved wooden vines forming the prominent monogram "A T" (for Anais Tiby) at middle, lower cover with central carved cross twined with grape vines arising from a cluster of leaves, flat spine with carved head and tailpieces, repeating grapevine motif and a carved boxwood banderolle at center on which the title appears in red, blue and gold; two pierced metal clasps at fore edge, saffron yellow moire silk endleaves, morocco hinges, edges very elaborately gauffered with gilt neo-gothic floral pattern on a red background, housed in handsome and very sturdy morocco backed wooden box lined with gold velvet, ornamental borders around text, numerous ornamental headpieces, initials and tailpieces (37 of these illuminated by hand), two chromolithographed titlepages, four woodcut titles for each Gospel, two engraved maps, two steel engraved frontispieces by Lecomte after Decaisne and by Cousin after Meissonier and 17 steel engraved plates after Tony Johannot by Cousin, Fontaine, Revel and others; extra illustrated with 11 steel engraved topographical plates printed on chine, one leaf inscribed in gothic hand with the Prophecies of Isaiah in red, blue and gold inks, a presentation page with calligraphy and a full border with flowers and acanthus leaves of a burnished gold ground, both done by Langlume, in the style of a 15th century Book of Hours, with accompanying original watercolor of the Tiby wedding by Fauquet within an illuminated border by Langlume, with 22 (blank) genealogical pages, printed in colors with ruled centers surrounded by ornamental borders bound in below beginning of text; one barely perceptible chip to one of the grapevine cornerpieces on upper cover, 9 of the Johannot plates rather browned and offset to text, one border slightly soiled, otherwise extraordinarily fine copy of a unique work, text clean, fresh and bright, interior and exterior colors and gold shimmering and quite lovely delicate binding astonishingly well preserved.   Phillip J. Pirages   59 - 105 2011 $15,000

Binding – Guild of Women Binders

Field, Michael, Pseud. *Stephania: a Trialogue.* London: Elkin Mathews & John Lane, 1892. One of 250 copies; 200 x 150mm., 6 p.l., 1, 100 pages, 4 leaves (colophon and ads), exceptionally attractive modelled goatskin by Mrs. Annie MacDonald of the Guild of Women Binders, front cover with large lobed frame, its upper corner enclosing the binder's initial and the date (1897), lower corners with daffodil blooms, large central panel showing an elaborately detailed scene featuring a woman with long, flowing hair entreating the god Mercury in his signature winged hat and sandals, the two figures, surmounted by an imperial crown through which twines a sprig of mistletoe (a design that appears in the woodcut frame on titlepage), lower cover showing the woman kneeling by a man reclining on a couch, this scene enclosed in an oval beaded frame, flat spine with modelled title flanked by pine cone device at head and tail, green watered silk pastedowns framed in unusual turn-ins, decorated with gilt vines and calf circles painted green and blue, leather hinges, top edge gilt, other edges untrimmed, titlepage with full woodcut border filled with intertwined pine branches and mistletoe, colophon with pine cone device, verso of front flyleaf with engraved bookplate of Charles Williston McAlpin, extra paper title labels tipped onto rear blank; two tiny red (ink?) marks to upper cover, inevitable offsetting from turn-ins to endpapers, one detached front flyleaf tipped onto front free endpaper, other trivial defects, still very attractive copy, binding lustrous and scarcely worn, leaves fresh and clean.   Phillip J. Pirages   59 - 107 2011 $4500

Binding – Guillery, Marc Antonio

Guevara, Antonio De *Vita Di M. Avrelio Imperadore.* Venice: Bartolomeo Imperador and Francesco Veneziano, 1543. 160 x 103mm., 8 p.l., 132, (2) leaves, fine contemporary Roman red morocco Apollo and Pegasus medallion binding done for Giovanni Battista Grimaldi by Marc Antonio Guillery, (genuine Apollo and Pegasus binding) covers with gilt frame formed by two widely spaced fillets with lobes interlaced at ends and sides, space between fillets decorated with broad foliate curls, small floral tools, inner pane of each board with gilt titling above a horizontal oval Apollo and Pegasus plaquette centerpiece showing Pegasus atop black painted heights of Parnassus and Apollo racing his chariot (drawn by two straining steeds) across steep terrain with reins and whip held aloft and caps fluttering behind, plaquette with gilt motto in Greek in the collar above and below vignette, spine (very expertly rebacked) with four thin and three thick raised bands decorated with gilt rope pattern or plain rules (this being original backstrip?), newer (perhaps 19th century) endpapers, all edges gilt (apparently some remarkably skillful restoration at one or more corners and edges, perhaps some gold added, as well as to the chariot part of the plaquettes); woodcut printer's device on , morocco bookplate and separate gilt monogram of Robert Hoe as well as inscription and vellum bookplate of Swedish collector Thore Virgin, ownership inscription of J. T. Payne dated 1850; covers with half dozen insignificant tiny dark spots, titlepage faintly soiled, thin light brown stain just at top edge of leaves, small wormhole at upper inner margin (text not affected), occasional minor stains, other trivial imperfections, but no defects that are even remotely serious and in general really excellent specimen of a very special binding, text fresh and leather quite lustrous; also from the collection of bibliophile Johannes Gennadius, Liverpool oculist T. Shadford Walker and Swedish collector Rolfe Wistrand.   Phillip J. Pirages   59 - 2   2011 $35,000

Binding – Hamady, Walter

Lindbergh, Reeve *John's Apples. thirteen Paintings by John Wilde. Twelve Poems by Reeve Lindberg.* Mt. Horeb: Perishable Press, 1995. One of 125 numbered copies; on 10 different papers, this one of the printer's own copies with his pencil notations, page size 9 7/8 x 6 1/4 inches, 102 pages, 78 of which printed, bound by printer in drab paper over boards with rondel cut-out on upper panel showing color image of two Golden Delicious apples (one bitten on), linen spine, printed on Heidelberg CPC and an old Vandercook, 14 pt. Stempel Syntax was set by hand, the unfinished looking front cover is not glued down and two of the 7 signatures are left uncut and untrimmed, replete with colorbars, etc, lovely, intriguing book.   Priscilla Juvelis - Rare Books   48 - 18   2011 $1500

Binding – Hanbury & Simpson

Inman, Thomas *Ancient Faiths Embodied in Ancient Names...* printed for the author, 1868-1869. 2 volumes, presentation copy inscribed by author for Liverpool Philomathic Society, lithograph frontispiece (touch foxed), 4 further plates in volume I, 8 in volume II, numerous figures in letterpress, little dust soiling in places, purple stamp of Philomathic Society to titles, tissue guards, some leaves, their bylaws pasted to front endpapers and slip recording purchase from Society in March 1925, signed by secretary pasted to flyleaf, pages (viii, 789; 1, 1028, 8vo., original brown cloth by Hanbury & Simpson, boards with frames blocked in blind containing gilt figures blocked in gilt on front, backstrips with gilt figures and titles, just slightly rubbed and darkened at extremities, backstrip ends bumped, hinges almost invisibly reinforced, good.   Blackwell Rare Books   B166 - 54   2011   £375

Binding – Harcourt Bindery

Cellini, Benvenuto *The Life of Benvenuto Cellini.* London: printed for the Navarre Society by Riverside Press, 1927. One of 1500 copies; 209 x 140mm., 2 volumes, fine burgundy morocco, handsomely gilt and onlaid by the Harcourt Bindery of Boston (stamp signed on front flyleaf of each volume), boards with triple fillet border each cover with elaborate heraldic frame of gilt and onlaid green morocco around an empty oval, raised bands, very pretty gilt spine compartments featuring looping tendril frame enclosing charming flower centerpiece, densely gilt turn-ins, marbled endpapers, titlepage, double page genealogical table and 62 plates, as called for; one cover with short, vague scratch, but in especially fine condition, fresh, bright and internally, with lustrous bindings with virtually no wear.   Phillip J. Pirages   59 - 108   2011 $800

Krause, Dorothy Simpson *Losing Ground.* Marshfield Hills: Viewpoint Editions, 2008. Artist's book; one of 6 deluxe copies from a total issue of 106 (100 regular and 6 deluxe), all on Mohawk Options 65 cover made from 100 per cent post consumer content with renewable wind power, each signed and numbered on colophon by artist/author, page size 12 x 12 inches, 40 pages, bound by Harcourt Bindery in aubergine Nigerian goatskin with onlay of copper inset 7 7/8 x 7 7/8 inches that has been manipulated by artist (acid washed with "wrinkles") title blindstamped in center of copper, gold endpapers, housed in matching gold cloth over boards, custom made clamshell box, printed on HP Indigo 5500 Press by Acme Bookbinding that have been manipulated by Ms. Krause with graphite, metallic pigments, gold and silver leaf, text is mainly taken from Intergovernmental Panel on Climate Change, although a notable page spread in text taken from the Holy Bible, Malachi, Chapter 4, Verses 16, beautiful book.   Priscilla Juvelis - Rare Books   48 - 13   2011 $2500

Smollett, Tobias George 1721-1771 *The Adventures of Covent Fathom.* London: Navarre Society Ltd. circa, 1902. One of only 2000 copies; 180 x 113mm., 2 volumes, very fine burgundy morocco, handsomely gilt and onlaid by the Harcourt Bindery of Boston (stamp-signed), boards with triple fillet border, each cover with elaborate heraldic frame of gilt and onlaid green morocco, around an empty oval, raised bands, very pretty gilt spine compartments featuring looping tendril frame enclosing a charming flower centerpiece, densely gilt turn-ins marbled endpapers, top edge gilt, two frontispieces by George Cruikshank; very fine, bindings especially bright and text with virtually no signs of use. Phillip J. Pirages   59 - 322   2011 $400

Smollett, Tobias George 1721-1771 *The Aventures of Roderick Random.* London: Navarre Society Ltd. circa, 1902. One of 2000 copies; 3 volumes, 180 x 113mm., very fine burgundy morocco, handsomely gilt and onlaid by Harcourt Bindery of Boston (stamp signed), boards with triple fillet border, each cover with elaborate heraldic frame of gilt and onlaid green morocco around an empty oval, raised bands, very pretty gilt spine compartments featuring looping tendril fame enclosing charming flower centerpiece, densely gilt turn-ins, marbled endpapers, top edge gilt, 3 frontispiece drawings by George Cruikshank, very fine, bindings especially bright and text with virtually no signs of use. Phillip J. Pirages   59 - 324   2011 $550

Sterne, Laurence 1713-1768 *A Sentimental Journey through France and Italy.* London: Navarre Society, circa, 1926. One of 200 copies; 180 x 113mm., 2 p.l. (including frontispiece), 147 pages, very fine burgundy morocco, handsomely gilt and onlaid by the Harcourt Bindery of Boston (stamp-signed), boards with triple fillet border, each cover with elaborate heraldic frame of gilt and onlaid green morocco, around an empty oval, raised abands, very pretty gilt spine compartments featuring looping tendril frame enclosing a charming flower centerpiece, densely gilt turn-ins marbled endpapers, top edge gilt, frontispiece by George Cruikshank; very fine.   Phillip J. Pirages   59 - 327   2011 $375

Binding – Hardy

Andrea De Nerciat, Andre Robert *Felicia ou Mes Fredaines, Orne de Figures en taille Douce.* Londres: Paris: Cazin, 1782. First edition; 4 parts bound in 2, 18mo., pages (iv), 160, (iv), 161-352; (iv), 204, (iv), 205-396, with 24 plates by Elluin after Borel, one supplied from another, slightly later copy, apres la lettre, the others all avant la lettre, initial blanks to parts 1 and 3, short tear to margin of volume II A1, otherwise internally fine, all edges gilt, mid 19th century full morocco, gilt filleting to boards, gilt decoration and lettering to spines, marbled endpapers by Hardy, firm, bright with very light negligible shelfwear, bookplates of Leigh D. Brownlee to each volume.   Simon Finch Rare Books   Zero - 409   2011   £5000

Cleland, John *La Fille De Joie, ou Memoires de Miss Fanny, Ecrits par elle-meme.* Paris: Madame Gourdan, 1786. (1787); Large 8vo., pages (iv), 235, plus frontispiece, 2 supplementary engraved titlepages, 34 engraved plates (numbered 1-33 and 5 bis) by Delcroche (unsigned), all edges gilt, small discrete old repair to titlepage, full mid brown gilt decorated and titled morocco by Hardy, c. 1860, Bookplate of G. Nordmann, fine, stunning copy.   Simon Finch Rare Books   Zero - 413   2011   £9500

Binding – Harrison Bookbinder

Luard, John *Views in India, Saint Helena and Car Nicobar. Drawn from Nature and on Stone.* London: J. Graf, printer to her Majesty, 1838. unpaged, lithographic title, 60 lithographic plates mounted on india paper, folio, contemporary crimson morocco over boards, spine tooled and lettered gilt, 5 raised bands, bound by Harrison Bookbinder (Pall Mall, small stamp to front blank), moderate foxing to text leaves and plate mounts, boards rubbed, some discoloration and scuff marks to front board, spine with few minor chips, edgewear, still very good; bookplate of William Backwell Tyringham, neat stamp of A. J. Combridge, Bombay and Madras.   Kaaterskill Books   12 - 124 2011 $5250

Binding – Hatchards

Emerson, Ralph Waldo 1803-1882 *Complete Works.* Cambridge: Riverside Press, 1883. Riverside edition, one of 500 copies; 235 x 150m., 11 volumes, very attractive green straight grain morocco (stamp signed "Hatchards of Piccadilly" on front turn-in), covers with border of two gilt fillets, wide raised bands decorated with floral ornaments and three gilt rules, ruled gilt compartments with large fleuron centerpiece, marbled endpapers, top edge gilt, other edges rough trimmed, 2 frontispiece portraits, large paper copy, armorial bookplates of Henry Martin Gibbs of Barrow Court, Flax Bourton, Somerset, backstrips uniformly faded to pleasing caramel color, top of one spine slightly rubbed, three or four joints with trivial wear, three corners bit bumped, endpapers (of a different stock from text), somewhat foxed, otherwise quite appealing set, leather lustrous, wear insignificant and text especially bright, fresh and clean.   Phillip J. Pirages   59 - 189   2011 $2500

Surtees, Robert Smith 1803-1864 *Handley Cross; or Jorrock's Hunt.* Bradbury Agnew, circa, 1880. Hand colored frontispiece, title vignette and 16 hand colored plates, one or two foxmarks, pages viii, 550, 8vo., full polished calf, spine panelled in gilt, central haunting emblems and morocco labels, with gilt lettering, upper cover with running fox in gilt and triple gilt fillet borders, top edge gilt, by Hatchards, with their stamp on endpaper, very good.   Blackwell Rare Books   B166 - 104   2011   £250

Wentz, W. Y. Evans *The Fairy Faith in Celtic Countries.* Rennes: 1909. First (and only) edition; 22, 314 pages, original wrappers under fine full crushed morocco by Hatchards (rubbing on pressure points), very good.   C. P. Hyland   May 26 2011 - 258/1083   2011 $1305

Wilkinson, J. Gardiner *The Manners and Customs of the Ancient Egyptians.* London: John Murray, 1878. 3 volumes, early 29th century three quarter scarlet levant morocco gilt by Hatchards with broad flattened raised bands, hinges rather rubbed and cracked in places but sound, pages xxx, 510; xii,5 16; xi, 528, top edge gilt, complete with 74 plates, 643 text figures and woodcut vignettes, handsome clean set.   R. F. G. Hollett & Son Antiquarian Booksellers   177 - 906   2011   £650

Binding – Hatton

Callimachus *Hymni, Epigrammata et Fragmenta...* Paris: S. Mabre-Cramoisy, 1675. 4to., (20), 262, (56) pages, engraved armorial headpiece to dedication, engraved initial, 19th century olive green morocco by Hatton of Manchester, gilt, from the library of the Earls of Macclesfield at Shirburn Castle, Macclesfield arms on upper cover, edges gilt, title leaf slightly browned, spine slightly faded, extremely handsome, printed on fine paper.   Maggs Bros. Ltd.   1440 - 45   2011   £450

Euclides *Geometricorum Elemntorum Libri XV.* Paris: H. Estienne after Jan., 1516-1517. First edition printed outside Italy; folio, ff. 261 (of 262 without final blank), woodcut diagrams in margins, woodcut initials, 19th century calf by Hatton of Manchester, marbled edges, title leaf cut down and remounted, from the library of the Earls of Macclesfield at Shirburn Castle.   Maggs Bros. Ltd.   1440 - 84   2011   £4000

Lauret, Christophe *La Doctrine des Temps et de l'Astronomie Universelle Contenant la Demonstration du Vray Nombre....* Paris: Cramoisy, 1610. Folio, ff. (8) 133 (=135, several mispaginations etc.) 1), large woodcut printer's device on titlepage, woodcut headpieces, tailpieces, initials, mid 19th century calf by Hatton in Manchester, triple blind fillet on boards, blind fleuron in boards' corner and in spine compartments, morocco lettering piece, red edges, f. 58 stained, small hole with loss of text in f. 126, few manuscript annotations in margin, dedication (signed to Clement VIII by Cayet bound at end), from the library of the Earls of Macclesfield at Shirburn Castle.   Maggs Bros. Ltd.   1440 - 124   2011   £6000

Manfredi, Eustachio *Elementi Della Cronologia con Diverse Scritture Appartenenti al Calendario Romano. Opera Postuma.* Bologna: Lelio dalla Volpe, 1744. First edition; 4to., (14), 362, (2 imprimatur) pages, engraved device on titlepage, woodcut initials, woodcut diagrams, engraved headpiece, 19th century half calf by Hatton of Manchester, red morocco lettering piece, red speckled edges, lacking frontispiece, from the library of the Earls of Macclesfield at Shirburn Castle.   Maggs Bros. Ltd.   1440 - 139   2011   £450

Binding – Hayday

MacDonald, George 1824-1905 *Within and Without: a Dramatic Poem.* London: Longman, Brown, Green, Longmans & Roberts, 1857. Second edition; contemporary black morocco by Hayday, at some time very neatly recased, all edges gilt.   Jarndyce Antiquarian Booksellers   CXCII - 5   2011   £200

Roby, J. *Traditions of Lancashire.* London: Longman, Rees &c., 1829-1831. First edition; 4 volumes, finely bound in half maroon morocco gilt by Hayday, spines with 5 raised bands, marbled boards, top edge gilt, 2 engraved titles, 22 engraved plates, text woodcut vignettes, occasional patch of foxing or finger marking, few inked emendations, handsome, sound set.   R. F. G. Hollett & Son Antiquarian Booksellers   175 - 1142   2011   £450

Binding – Hayday & Mansell

Church of England. Book of Common Prayer *Book of Common Prayer and Administration of the Sacraments.* Oxford: University Press, 1861. Small 8vo., original full morocco gilt by Hayday & Mansell over heavy bevelled boards, panelled and tooled in gilt, upper board with ornate central brass cross, boards brass bound with broad clasps (one pin missing), heavily gilt turn-ins with marbled endpapers, unpaginated, all edges gilt, very handsome.   R. F. G. Hollett & Son Antiquarian Booksellers   175 - 1084   2011   £180

Binding – Henderson, John

Gale, Roger *Registrum Honoris De Richmond Exhibens Terrarum & Villarum.* Londini: Impensis R. Gosling, 1722. Large paper copy, folio, pages (ii), xxxv, (i), 106, (xxvi), 286, (xxx) + folding engraved map, one extending engraved plate, another 8 engraved plates and 6 extending plates of pedigrees, lacking the list of subscribers leaf, early 19th century calf, boards sided with 'French Shelf' marbled paper, 1970's renewal of leather with half reversed calf by John Henderson (spotted and lightly browned, old boards scuffed), armorial and masonic bookplate of "Robt. Lakeland" and inscription "from Major Sir Edw. Coates' Library", from the collection of Christopher Ernest Weston 1947-2010.   Unsworths Booksellers   24 - 95   2011   £400

MacKenzie, Eneas *A Descriptive and Historical Account of the Town and County of Newcastle upon Tyne...* Newcastle upon Tyne: printed & published by Mackenzie & Dent, 1827. 2 volumes bound as 1, 4to., pages x, 414, frontispiece and 10 other engraved plates; (ii), (415)-770, (ii) + engraved frontispiece and 3 other engraved plates, modern half calf by John Henderson, foxed in places, armorial bookplate of Archibald Dawnay, from the collection of Christopher Ernest Weston 1947-2010. Unsworths Booksellers 24 - 116 2011 £300

Binding – Himebauch & Browne

Wollaston, A. F. R. *From Ruwenzori to the Congo: a Naturalist's Journey Across Africa.* New York: E. P. Dutton, 1908. Octavo, xxv, 315 pages, frontispiece, numerous plates, 2 maps, half brown morocco, cloth, raised bands, gilt spine top edge gilt by Himebauch & Browne, front hinge repaired, very. Jeff Weber Rare Books 163 - 230 2011 $400

Binding – Hodgson

Knight, Charles 1791-1873 *Passages of a Working Life during Half a Century; with a Prelude of Early Reminiscences.* London: Bradbury & Evans, 1864-1865. First edition; 3 volumes, 8vo., 346 (4) 336 (4) 344 pages, contemporary uniform polished calf gilt with raised bands, fully gilt in compartments with contrasting labels, all edges marbled by Hodgson of Liverpool, fine set in most attractive binding, contemporary unidentified armorial bookplate. John Drury Rare Books 153 - 73 2011 £150

Binding – Hoffmann, Christoph

Schultz, Christoph *Kurze Fragen Ueber die Christliche Glaubens Lehre... Den Christlichen Glaubens Schulern...* Philadelphia: Carl Cist, 1784. (1), 104 pages, contemporary sprinkled calf, blind roll and fillets on boards and spine, red sprinkled edges, by Christoph Hoffmann, nice, tight copy. Joseph J. Felcone Inc. Fall Miscellany 2010 - 41 2011 $900

Binding – Howell, B.

Southey, Robert 1774-1843 *The Life of Nelson.* Bickers and Son, 1902. 12 woodburytype plates and one folding map, one illustration, pages xiv, (ii), 351, 8vo., contemporary green polished calf, prize binding of Southport Centre Cambridge Local Examinations (awarded to W. T. Waterhouse in 1907), spine gilt just slightly faded, red morocco lettering piece by B. Howell, Liverpool, near fine. Blackwell Rare Books B166 - 101 2011 £125

Binding – Howell, Edward

Prescott, William Hickling 1796-1859 *History of the Conquest of Mexico.* London: Swan Sonnenschein & Co., 1906. 2 maps, one handwriting facsimile plate, pages xxiv, 713, 8vo., contemporary tree calf, boards with gilt roll border, spine in five compartments with raised bands, green morocco lettering piece, compartments with gilt floral centre pieces and corner vine sprays, marbled edges and endpapers, gilt prize stamp (Cambridge Local Examinations, Southport Centre) to front board, prize bookplate inside, binder's ticket of Edward Howell, Liverpool, spine gently sunned, near fine, award to W. T. Waterhouse of First Class Honours in History and Geography, 1908. Blackwell Rare Books B166 - 83 2011 £95

Prescott, William Hickling 1796-1859 *History of the Conquest of Peru.* London: Swan Sonnenschein & Co., 1907. New edition; pages xxiv, 510, (2), 8vo., contemporary tree calf, boards with gilt roll border, spine in five compartments with raised bands, green morocco lettering piece, compartments with gilt floral center-pieces and corner vine sprays, marbled edges and endpapers, gilt prize stamp (Cambridge Local Examinations, Southport Centre) to front board and prize bookplate inside, binder's ticket of Edward Howell, Liverpool, spine gently sunned, near fine, awarded to W. T. Waterhouse for First Class Honours in English, 1908. Blackwell Rare Books B166 - 84 2011 £95

Binding – Hyman, N. A.

Bursill, Henry *Hand Shadows to be Thrown Upon the Wall.* London: Griffith and Farran, 1860. Fourth edition; 4to., modern three quarter levant morocco gilt by N. A. Hyman, pages 4, with 18 hand colored plates, attractive, coloring probably later, but well done. R. F. G. Hollett & Sons Antiquarian Booksellers 170 - 122 2011 £120

Binding – Ipsley Bindery

Bartlett, Benjamin *Manduessedum Romanorum; Being the History and Antiquities of the Parish of Manceter...* printed by and for J. Nichols, Printer to the Society of Antiquaries, 1791. First edition; 24 engraved plates (as called for), chronological charts (some folding, pages viii, 136, 137*-167- (1), 137-142, 143*-146*, 143-168, 4to., modern half tan calf by Ipsley bindery (their ink stamp at foot of rear pastedown), backstrip divided into six compartments by raised bands between blindstamped rules, gilt lettered direct in second compartment, remainder empty, gilt dated at foot, marbled sides, buff endpapers, marbled edges, very good. Blackwell Rare Books B166 - 9 2011 £150

Binding – Jenkins & Cecil

Pepys, Samuel 1633-1703 *Memoirs of Samuel Pepys... Comprising His Diary... and a Selection from His Private Correspondence.* London: Henry Colburn, 1828. Second edition; 229 x 146mm., 5 volumes, especially attractive polished tree calf (stamp signed by Jenkins and Cecil), covers bordered with gilt chain roll, raised band, spine compartments handsomely gilt with knotwork centerpiece surrounded by small tools and with scrolling foliate cornerpieces, decorative rolls on bands and at head and foot of spine, red and blue morocco labels, turn-ins with fine foliate roll marbled edges and endpapers, engraved frontispiece, 6 additional portraits, tailpiece, folding map, two double page views and two page facsimile of Pepys' handwriting, hint of wear to extremities, plates little foxed, very good handsome set in quite fine and bright condition, text especially fresh and clean.   Phillip J. Pirages   59 - 277   2011 $1900

Binding – Jevne, Jill

Bart, Harriet *The Poetry of Chance Encounters.* Minneapolis: Mnemonic Press, 2003. One of 35 numbered copies, all on Rives BFK, from a total edition of 40 (35 + 5 artist proof copies); page size 9 x 6 1/8 inches, 42 pages, bound by Jill Jevne, full brown box calf, matching calf edged and gold paste paper by Claire Maziarcyzk, matching calf over boards slipcase, book contains 16 visual poems on multi-color fields, each imprinted with an icon in 22 karat gold, each printed page has total of five press runs, including a varnish over icon and field with the impression of the gold leaf imparting an embossed effect to the icon, basic typeface is Lydian, a stressed sans serif chose to complement the treatment of image and type throughout the page.   Priscilla Juvelis - Rare Books   48 - 1   2011 $2400

Binding – Jewelled

Moore, Thomas 1779-1852 *Lalla Rookh, an Oriental Romance.* London: printed for Longman, Hurst, Rees, Orme and Brown, 1817. First edition; 292 x 222mm., 2 p.l., 405, (1) pages, nothing short of spectacular early 20th century dark blue levant morocco extravagantly gilt, richly inlaid and gloriously bejewelled by Sangorski & Sutcliffe (stamp-signed on front doublure), binding with overall Oriental design (befitting the poem) with upper cover featuring a sunken central panel, its unusual nine-sided shape resembling a clump of hanging grapes, within which two birds of paradise, inlaid in lilac, green and brown morocco with two rubies for eyes, perch in a grape arbor, its inlaid leaves with fruit clusters on densely stippled gilt around accented with 19 turquoises, the whole central tableau surrounded by a border of interweaving bands of inlaid brown morocco set with 9 bands of Mother-of-Pearl, the entire sunken panel surrounded by two ornate frames filled with flowering vines of Oriental design composed of hundreds of pieces of inlaid morocco in red, blue, violet and green on a background of brown morocco and heavily stippled gilt, outer frame accented with 20 blue chalcedonies and 20 garnets; lower cover with similar frame and central panel, this one featuring two lovebirds inlaid with multiple colors and with two amethyst eyes, birds in a similar grape arbor above, large Mother-of-Pearl heart, panel further adorned with 3 sapphires, four blue chalcedonies five turquoises, four Carnelians and 10 additional bands of Mother-of-Pearl, raised bands, spine gilt in compartments with large inlaid arabesque in green and brown morocco on a gilt background, gilt titling on inlaid compartments of chestnut brown morocco, glorious front doublure of ivory morocco covered in gilt vines with inlaid violet morocco flowers, the whole framed in green morocco decorated with gilt vines and red morocco posies and berries, at center, a hand painted Cosway-Style portrait of author on ivory surrounded by gilt frame, with 12 flowers composed of no fewer than 72 turquoises and 36 garnets, oval portrait in sunken panel enclosed by wreath of inlaid morocco flowers, rear doublure of similar design, but its medallion featuring 8 amethysts set among sinuously curving inlaid lilac strapwork twining around a large (approximately one carat) Mexican fire opal encircled by 12 pearls, the binding containing 226 jewels in all; free endleaves of cream colored watered silk, gilt edges, in original well made (somewhat scuffed), silk and plush lined blue morocco box with shuttered lid; extra illustrated with 12 hand colored engraved plates mounted on lettered Japan vellum bookplate of Charles J. Rosenbloom; two leaves with neatly renewed marginal tears, but magnificent copy of a masterpiece of bookbinding.   Phillip J. Pirages   59 - 111   2011 $65,000

Binding – Jones, John

Landon, Letitia Elizabeth *The Troubadour; Catalogue of Pictures and Historical Sketches.* London: Hurst, Robinson & Co., 1825. First edition; engraved title, additional printed title, slight damp staining in prelims, contemporary half vellum by John Jones of Liverpool, spine finely tooled in gilt, maroon leather label, blue paper covered boards, very slight rubbing, good plus, handsome copy. Jarndyce Antiquarian Booksellers   CLXC - 78 2011   £125

Binding – Joyce, Carol

Snodgrass, W. D. *These Trees Stand.* New York: Carol Joyce, 1981. One of two artist's proofs signed by poet ad photographer (of a total of 12 copies, 10 of them for sale); 238 x 285mm., 15 French-fold leaves, memorable original pictorial maroon morocco with molded onlays and gilt highlights by Carol Joyce binding featuring a molded cream colored onlaid calf tree its trunk occupying almost all of the flat spine, its bare limbs spread across both covers with wrinkling gilt stars visible between its branches, trunk dividing in two at head of spine with author's name in gilt appearing in fork, original matching burgundy cloth clamshell box with morocco spine label, with 12 black and white photos of poet by Robert Mahon, virtually mint.   Phillip J. Pirages   59 - 140 2011 $6000

Binding – Kelly & Sons

Blackmore, Richard Doddridge 1825-1900 *Erema; or My Father's Sin.* London: Smith, Elder and Co., 1877. First edition; 3 volumes, half titles, later 19th century half dark maroon calf by Kelly & Sons, top edge gilt, very good. Jarndyce Antiquarian Booksellers   CXCI - 518 2011   £220

Binding – Kelm, Daniel

Clemens, Samuel Langhorne 1835-1910 *The Jumping Frog.* Easthampton: Cheloniidae Press, 1985. One of 15 State Proof copies; one extra suite of the wood engravings and portrait etching of author, a state-proof suite of prints and copy of regular edition of the book, all signed and numbered by artist and signed on colophon by artist, regular edition as limited to 250 and is bound in green paper wrappers, all editions printed on Saunders paper in Centaur and Arrighi types at Wild Carrot Letterpress with assistance of Arthur Larson - the 15 wood engravings printed by Harold Patrick McGrath, page size 6 x 8.5 inches; bound by Daniel Kelm, full undyed Oasis with onlays of the frog in repose - before the jump on the front panel and after jump on back panel, doublures showing frog in mid-jump, onlays in green oasis of frog jumping are on front and back pastedowns, housed in linen clamshell box with pull-out portfolio for extra suites and book, lovely copy.   Priscilla Juvelis - Rare Books   48 - 6 2011 $3500

Poe, Edgar Allan 1809-1849 *The Raven.* Easthampton: Cheloniidae Press, 1986. Artist's Proof copy; one of a handful of such bound as the state proof edition in full red morocco, with additional two suites of working proofs (21 prints total, 17 wood engravings and 3 states of frontispiece etching), from a total issue of 225 copies, 150 regular edition, 50 deluxe with extra suite of prints, bound in quarter morocco by Claudia Cohen, 25 state proof copies with two extra suites and an original drawing, full morocco binding, all copies on Magnani Letterpress paper and all signed and numbered by Alan James Robinson; page size 6 7/16 x 9 3/8 inches, this is an all new original edition in which the artist revisits the text of the first book of the press, text is letterpress by Dan Keliher at Wild Carrot Letterpress, the 9 original wood engravings and one original etching, frontispiece portrait of Poe, the full red morocco binding is by Daniel Kelm and Sarah Pringle at the Wide Awake Garage, the front panel blindstamped with one of Robinson's wood engravings of a raven, the two additional suites are housed in grey cloth over boards folder with white label printed in black on front "The Raven/Prints" and both housed in grey cloth-over boards clamshell box, red morocco label on spine, blindstamped with title, author and title logo of Cheloniidae Press, both bit worn, book and prints fine.   Priscilla Juvelis - Rare Books   48 - 4 2011 $2000

Binding – Kimbrough, F. R.

Magruder, Julia *Miss Ayr of Virginia & Other Stories.* Chicago: Herbert S. Stone and Co., 1896. First edition; (395, 1 pages, 8 page publisher's Ads dated October 1896), small 8vo., pale green cloth covered pictorial boards, very fine, in most attractive binding designed by F. R. Kimbrough. Paulette Rose Fine and Rare Books   32 - 119 2011 $200

Binding – Larkins

Lennox, Sarah *The Life and Letters of Lady Sarah Lennox...Also a Short Political Sketch of the Years 1760 to 1763 by Henry Fox, 1st Lord Holland.* London: John Murray, 1901. First edition; 223 x 143mm., 2 volumes, lovely contemporary loden green crushed morocco, handsomely gilt by J. Larkins (stamp signed on verso of front free endpaper), covers framed with one decorative and two plain gilt rules, raised bands, spines in especially attractive gilt compartments, featuring central pomegranate lozenges and scrolling corner decoration, densely gilt inner dentelles, marbled endpapers, all edges gilt, with 30 photogravures of portraits; spines uniformly sunned to a soft hazel, three very small and hardly noticeable dents in one cover, trivial defects internally but quite handsome set in fine condition, bindings lustrous and virtually unworn, text clean and fresh. Phillip J. Pirages   59 - 114 2011 $400

Binding – Launder, W.

Perceval of Galles *Syr Perecyvelle of Gales.* Kelmscott Press, 1895. One of 350 copies on paper, 8 additional copies were on vellum; 212 x 150mm., 98 pages, without final blank, quite attractive contemporary olive-brown half morocco by W. Launder (stamp signed), flat spine gilt in one long compartment with leafy vines at head and tail, vertical titling in ornate Gothic majuscules, marbled sides and endpapers, top edge gilt, elaborate woodcut frontispiece by Edward Burne-Jones, wide white vine borders on first opening, one page with half border, decorative woodcut initials, device in colophon; spine sunned to a pleasing hazel brown, some irregular fading to leather elsewhere, extremely fine, binding very lustrous and virtually unworn, text immaculate. Phillip J. Pirages   59 - 247   2011 $1900

Binding – Laurenchet

Le Maingre De Bouciqualt, Don Luis *Les Amazones Revoltees.* Rotterdam: n.p., 1730. First edition; (1) blank, (4) 274 pages & errata (2) blank), 12mo., modern dark gray cloth a la Bradel, gilt lettered spine with floral ornament in gilt centered, all edges gilt, nice copy, bound by Laurenchet. Paulette Rose Fine and Rare Books   32 - 113   2011 $1200

Binding – Leighton

Cosway, Richard *Catalogue of a Collection of Miniatures by Richard Cosway.* For Private Ciculation Only, 1883. Limited edition, limitation not stated; folio, (32) ff., frontispiece, 26 full page mounted photo plates, original half brown morocco, marbled boards, morocco corners, raised bands, gilt spine title, all edges gilt, bound by J. Leighton, inscribed on titlepage by author, bookplate of John Nolty, fine, rare. Jeff Weber Rare Books   163 - 100   2011 $750

Binding – Leighton, Son & Hodge

MacDonald, George   1824-1905   *Alec Forbes of Howglen.* London: Hurst & Blackett, circa, 1875? Later one volume edition; this copy with 1879 inscription, half title, frontispiece, 4 pages ads, ink note on title, original dark green cloth by Leighton, Son & Hodge, slightly damp marked, labels partially removed from pastedowns. Jarndyce Antiquarian Booksellers   CXCII - 38   2011   £45

MacDonald, George   1824-1905   *Paul Faber, Surgeon.* London: Hurst & Blackett, 1879. First edition; 3 volumes, half titles, 16 pages catalog volume III, some spotting caused by endpaper, original brown cloth blocked in black and gilt by Leighton Son & Hodge, slightly marked with title wear to heads ad tails of spines, W. H. Smith Library labels marked "sold" on pastedowns.   Jarndyce Antiquarian Booksellers   CXCII - 208   2011   £2000

MacDonald, George   1824-1905   *Sir Gibbie.* London: Hurst & Blackett, 1879. First edition; 3 volumes, half titles, 16 page catalog volume III, internal mends volume III with occasional torn corners, original brown cloth by Leighton Son & Hodge, neatly recased, little rubbed with traces of label removal on front boards and slight damp marking on brown endpapers.   Jarndyce Antiquarian Booksellers   CXCII - 212   2011   £1600

Wraxall, L.   *Life in the Sea; or Nature and Habits of Marine Animals.* London: Houlston & Wright, 1860. First edition; frontispiece and illustrations, original purple wavy grained cloth by Leighton, Son & Hodge, spines slightly faded, armorial bookplate of Llangattock, very good.   Jarndyce Antiquarian Booksellers   CXCI - 344   2011   £68

Binding – Lewis, Charles

Bible. Greek - 1812   *Psalterium Graecum E Codice Ms. Alexandrino.* Londini: Ex Prelo Ricardi Taylor et Socii, 1812. One of 17 copies printed on vellum; 356 x 299mm., (1) leaf (blank), xii, (32) leaves, 18 pages, (1) leaf (blank), very handsome contemporary deep blue morocco lavishly gilt, apparently by Charles Lewis, covers with broad elaborately gilt border and simple inner frame, wide gilt decorated raised bands, spine compartments with complex gilt decoration featuring scrolling floral stamps and unusual trapezoidal ornaments on either side of a central stem, very wide and sumptuously gilt inner dentelles, yellow watered silk pastedowns, front and rear free endleaves, made of matching watered silk pasted to vellum sheets, all edges gilt; monogram booklabel and armorial bookplate of William Henry Smith and oval morocco bookplate of Estelle Doheny, subscriber list, slight variation in color of binding and of vellum leaves, but very fine, stunning.   Phillip J. Pirages   59 - 340   2011 $15,000

Clarendon, Edward Hyde, 1st Earl of 1609-1674 *The History of the Rebellion and Civil Wars in England. (and) The Life of Edward Earl of Clarendon.* Oxford: At the Claredon Press, 1826-1827. 11 volumes, 254 x 160mm., contemporary deep purple hard grain morocco, very lavishly gilt, apparently by Charles Lewis, covers with gilt double fillet border and with central panel formed by a thick band of volutes, large outward facing fleurons as panel cornerpieces, the center of each board with armorial cresh, including mottoe "Vincit qui Patitur", gilt decorated raised bands, extremely handsome gilt spine compartments, formed by triple rules and featuring dense masses of fleurons, volutes and dots, attractively gilt turn-ins, marbled endpapers, all edges gilt (over marbling), extra illustrated with 8 frontispiece portraits, from other editions with manuscript letter signed by Charles I tipped in at front volume II, letter lacking its seal, otherwise in excellent condition, apart from some minor foxing (folded over covering sheet with address and notes in contemporaneous hand recording letter's reception torn along folds), sometimes noticeable foxing to endpapers and especially to inserted engraved portraits, along with consequent darkening to titlepages, opposite engraved material, in all other ways, superb set, margins very ample, text smooth, clean and fresh, wonderful binding with only most trivial wear.   Phillip J. Pirages   59 - 166 2011 $9500

Binding – Liddell, Sandra

Gibb, Robert *Whalesongs.* Berkeley: Turkey Press, 1979. Second edition, #91 of 100 numbered and signed copies of the first hardcover edition; cloth backed boards, printed letterpress on Rives heavy weight paper and bound by Sandra Liddell using Harry Reese's handmade paper on cover inset, illustrations, near fine.   Charles Agvent   2010 Summer Miscellany - 32 2011 $100

Binding – Lintott, Mark

Hugo, Victor 1802-1865 *Aux Etats Unis d'Amerique.* Octon: Verdigris Press, 2007. One of 4 deluxe copies, each with original pencil and Chinese ink wash painting, double page spread which is preparatory study for the book's mezzotint, from a total edition of 45, all on Rives BFK for text and Hahnemuhle for double page foldout mezzotint, each signed and numbered by artist, Judith Rothchild; page size 7 7/8 x 4 5/8 inches, 14 pages, bound by printer, Mark Lintott, leporello style with brown marbled paper over boards and black cloth showing at spine and edges, title and author in black on spine and front panel, interior guards with tan marbled paper over boards, opening with French text on left and English translation on right, double page mezzotint unfolds across middle, book and special portfolio housing the original painting are both in publisher's custom made black cloth clamshell box with tan and brown marbled papers on spine and front panel with title on front and title, author, artist and press on spine.   Priscilla Juvelis - Rare Books   48 - 25 2011 $1250

Verlaine, Paul 1844-1896 *Clair de Lune.* Octon: Verdigris Press, 2009. Artist's book, one of 4 deluxe copies, from a total issue of 24 copies; (4 deluxe with original copperplate and 20 regular), all on Hahnemuhle paper, each signed and numbered by artist, Judith Rothchild, page size 7 3/4 x 4 inches, 14 pages, bound by Mark Lintott, leporello style laid into bordeaux paper over boards folder, title in black on front panel, laid into matching paper over boards clamshell box with original copperplate laid into back of box, protected by paper over boards folder with ribbon pull, paper are original serigraph prints made by Ms Rothchild with darker bordeaux printing in pattern of sunflowers and tendril border, matching label on spine with title, author, artist and press printed in black; Mr. Lintott has handset and printed Verlaine's poem in Vendome romain, taken from his Fetes Galantes.   Priscilla Juvelis - Rare Books   48 - 26 2011 $1250

Binding – Lloyd, Trevor

Smith, Adam 1723-1790 *An Inquiry into the Nature and Causes of the Wealth of Nations.* London: for A. Strahan and T. Cadell, 1789. Fifth edition; 3 volumes, 8vo., x, 499, (1) (1) and vi 518 (6) and v (1), 465 (51) pages, contemporary uniform calf gilt, sides with gilt borders, almost imperceptibly rebacked, spines fully gilt tooled in compartments with contrasting crimson and black lettering pieces by Trevor Lloyd, superb set of presentation quality.   John Drury Rare Books   153 - 137 2011   £3500

Binding – Lortic

La Fontaine, Jean De 1621-1695 *Fables Choisies, Mises en Vers.* Paris: Denys Thierry, 31 March, 1668. First edition; 4to., (58), 284 (2) pages, leaf o2 present as both cancellans and cancellandum, roman type, woodcut typographic head and tailpieces, floriated initials, 118 etchings by Francois Chauveau, crushed green morocco, gilt triple rule outer border, spine and wide turn-ins gilt, all edges gilt by Lortic, fils (spine and extremities faded to brown, front hinge worn), neat repair to five leaves (one touching two letters), very light overall toning, Robert Hoe's copy, inscribed in pencil on front flyleaf to his Granddaughter Thyrza Benson.   Joseph J. Felcone Inc.   Fall Miscellany 2010 - 72 2011 $30,000

Binding – Loutrel, Patrick

Thomas, Dylan Marlais 1914-1953 *Twenty-Six Poems.* N.P. London: Jams Laughlin & J. M. Dent & Sons Ltd., 1949. One of only 10 copies printed on Japan vellum, out of a total edition of 150 Printed by Hans Mardersteig at the Officina Bodoni in Verona and signed by author, this copy #2 of the vellum issue; 4to, full black French morocco gilt with inner dentelles, matching chemise and slipcase by Patrick Loutrel of Rouen, very fine, extremely rare issue.   James S. Jaffe Rare Books   May 26 2011 - 17107 2011 $25,000

Binding – Lubbett, Denise

Besterman, Theodore *The Pilgrim Fathers.* Waltham St. Lawrence: Golden Cockerel Press, 1939. One of 300 copies (this copy #65); 255 x 160mm., 3 p.l. (including frontispiece), 7-87, (1) pages, (1) leaf (blank), very inventive gray-green onlaid pictorial crushed morocco by Denise Lubbett, covers and (flat unlettered) spine with large areas of onlaid tan morocco in the shape of a portion of the New England coastline, in felt lined morocco backed folding cloth box with gilt spine titling, box slightly rubbed and faded; with 9 woodcuts by Geoffrey Wales; spine just bit sunned, otherwise in especially fine condition inside and out. Phillip J. Pirages 59 - 115 2011 $2250

Binding – MacDonald

Lowell, James Russell 1819-1891 *Poems.* Cambridge: John Owen, 1844. First edition; royal 8vo., 12, 279 pages, contemporary full black tooled morocco, gilt gone from outside covers, all edges gilt, marbled endpapers with binder's ticket of MacDonald of Cambridge, inner front hinge trifle weak, despite loss of gilding, very fine in handsome binding, this copy 9 3/8 inches tall. M & S Rare Books, Inc. 90 - 220 2011 $750

Binding – MacDonald, Annie

Field, Michael, Pseud. *Stephania: a Trialogue.* London: Elkin Mathews & John Lane, 1892. One of 250 copies; 200 x 150mm., 6 p.l., 1, 100 pages, 4 leaves (colophon and ads), exceptionally attractive modelled goatskin by Mrs. Annie MacDonald of the Guild of Women Binders, front cover with large lobed frame, its upper corner enclosing the binder's initial and the date (1897), lower corners with daffodil blooms, large central panel showing an elaborately detailed scene featuring a woman with long, flowing hair entreating the god Mercury in his signature winged hat and sandals, the two figures, surmounted by an imperial crown through which twines a sprig of mistletoe (a design that appears in the woodcut frame on titlepage), lower cover showing the woman kneeling by a man reclining on a couch, this scene enclosed in an oval beaded frame, flat spine with modelled title flanked by pine cone device at head an tail, green watered silk pastedowns framed in unusual turn-ins, decorated with gilt vines and calf circles painted green and blue, leather hinges, top edge gilt, other edges untrimmed, titlepage with full woodcut border filled with intertwined pine branches and mistletoe, colophon with pine cone device, verso of front flyleaf with engraved bookplate of Charles Williston McAlpin, extra paper title labels tipped onto rear blank; two tiny red (ink?) marks to upper cover, inevitable offsetting from turn-ins to endpapers, one detached front flyleaf tipped onto front free endpaper, other trivial defects, still very attractive copy, binding lustrous and scarcely worn, leaves fresh and clean. Phillip J. Pirages 59 - 107 2011 $4500

Binding – Mansell

Haggard, Henry Rider 1856-1925 *Cetwayo and His White Neighbours; or Remarks on Recent Events in Zululand, Natal & the Transvaal.* London: Trubner & Co., 1882. First edition; half title, followed by leaf printed verso, half red morocco, marbled boards by Mansell, very slight rubbed at head of spine, booklabel of Geo. Evelyn Cower, top edge gilt, fine. Jarndyce Antiquarian Booksellers CXCI - 197 2011 £450

Haggard, Henry Rider 1856-1925 *A Winter Pilgrimage.* London: Longmans, Green and Co., 1901. First edition; half title, frontispiece, illustrations, half red morocco, marbled boards by W. J. Mansell, top edge gilt, fine. Jarndyce Antiquarian Booksellers CXCI - 553 2011 £160

Binding – Marius, Michel

L'Art Revue Hebdomadaire Illustre. Cinquieme Annee Tome III. Paris: Librairie de l'Art, 1879. 440 x 310mm., 2 p.l., 322, (1) pages, in very elaborately inlaid morocco binding by Marius Michel (stamp signed on front turn-in), covers with all over design of entwined floral and foliate sprays incorporating many morocco inlays in 8 different colors (predominately browns, but with some red and two shades of green), front cover with journal title (L'Art) inlaid on a scroll that straps around a foliated branch and budding stem, rear cover similarly decorated but without titling, raised bands, spine compartments with onlaid frame and foliate centerpiece in two shades of brown morocco, wide turn-ins with six gilt rules, especially pleasing brocaded endleaves in very animated floral pattern, marbled flyleaves, all edges gilt, elaborate historiated and decorative initials, headpieces and tailpieces, nearly 200 illustrations in text, 24 full page illustrations, four illustrated borders and 67 engraved plates, including 14 plates, each appearing four times, 28 of these plates done on special paper and mounted, little cockling to some of the mounted plates, otherwise only trivial imperfections, in very fine condition, binding bright and virtually unworn. Phillip J. Pirages 59 - 117 2011 $5500

Binding – Martin

Burnand, Francis Cowley *Strapmore!* London: Bradbury, Agnew & Co., 1878. Half title, original brown sand grained cloth by Martin of Marylebone, spine lettered in gilt, very good. Jarndyce Antiquarian Booksellers CLXC - 707 2011 £75

Binding – Maynard, R. Ashwin

Rossetti, Christina 1830-1894 *Poems Chosen by Walter De La Mare.* Gregynog Press, 1930. One of 25 copies specially bound, of a total edition of 300; 235 x 159mm., 3 p.l., vii-xliii, (1), 107, (1) pages, very fine animated scarlet morocco by Gregynog (signed in gilt by R. Ashwin Maynard and George Fisher on rear turn-in), gilt tooled covers dominated by two large cruciform foliate ornaments elaborated with diagonal blind and gilt decoration (something like evergreen leaves), ornaments on a field of gold dots, covers bordered by gilt and blind rules from which emanate a series of similar gilt and blind evergreen decorations, spine with raised bands, panels outlined in blind, gilt titling, turn-ins with double gilt rule, top edge gilt, other edges untrimmed, original publisher's board slipcase (slightly soiled but sturdy), initial openings and frontispiece after drawings by Dante Gabriel Rossetti, printed in red and black throughout, one page with trivial stain, otherwise virtually pristine. Phillip J. Pirages 59 - 228 2011 $7500

Binding – McKim, Alicia

McKim, Alicia *Greetings from California.* Denver: 2009. Artist's book, one of 50 copies; each containing five dioramas of three separate layers each of vintage postcards, printed on an inkjet printer with pigmented ink on neutral ph paper, each copy numbered by author, page size 5 1/2 x 6 1/2 inches, carousel book, bound by artist, paper over boards with blue cloth spine and blue ribbon ties, housed in publisher's stiff white board folding box. Priscilla Juvelis - Rare Books 48 - 16 2011 $500

Binding – McLeish

Shelley, Percy Bysshe 1792-1822 *The Poetical Works.* London: Reeves & Turner, 1886. Second edition; 2 volumes, 191 x 135mm., very fine early 20th century olive crushed morocco handsomely gilt by C. and C. McLeish (stamp signed on rear turn-ins), covers bordered with single plain gilt rule, raised bands, spines densely and very attractively gilt in compartments featuring a large centerpiece in the form of a rose with four emanating springs of rose leaves, this quatrefoil design enclosed by a semis field punctuated with trefoil leaves, turn-ins with gilt French fillet border and trefoil cornerpieces, all edges gilt, each volume with frontispiece, engraved armorial bookplate of Douglas and Mary MacEwen; spines lightly sunned, offsetting from frontispieces, isolated minor foxing, otherwise especially fine set in lovely bindings, gilt bright, leather unworn, text with virtually no signs of use. Phillip J. Pirages 59 - 119 2011 $1950

Binding – Morrell

Booth, William *The Trial at Large of William Booth and His Associates, George Scot the Three Yates's, John Barrows and Elizabeth Childow for Forgery Coining &c. at the Stafford Summer Assizes 1812 before Mr. Justice Le Blanc.* Wolverhampton: printed and sold by Gower and Smart, 1812. First edition; 8vo., 46 pages, well bound by Morrell, ca. 1900 in half calf over marbled boards, spine lettered in gilt, upper joint and head of spine worn, very good, early 20th century bookplate of numismatist, Samuel Hamer and ms. note in his hand. John Drury Rare Books 153 - 150 2011 £475

Church of England. Book of Common Prayer *Book of Common Prayer and Administration of the Sacraments....* Oxford: University Press, circa, 1960. 12mo., chestnut crushed morocco gilt by Morrell for Mowbray with Cockerell paper marbled boards, all edges gilt, crimson silk markers, printed in red and black throughout. R. F. G. Hollett & Son Antiquarian Booksellers 175 - 1087 2011 £75

Gueulette, Thomas Simon *The Thousand and One Quarters of an Hour (Tartarian Tales).* London: H. S. Nichols and Co., 1893. One of 5 copies on Japanese vellum (of an edition of 680 copies); 254 x 159mm, viii, 308 pages, quite pleasing dark green crushed morocco by Morrell (signed), covers bordered in gilt with French fillet elaborate oblique gilt scrolling cornerpieces with blank oval center with raised bands, spine in handsome gilt compartment similarly decorated, wide green morocco turn-ins with simple gilt ornaments and rules, crimson crushed morocco doublures and free endpapers, other edges untrimmed, middle raised band of spine with small expert repair, front endpaper with morocco bookplate of W. A. Foyle, Beeleigh Abbey, titlepage printed in red and black; spine now sunned to uniform warm brown, top and top edge of cover also slightly sunned, few leaves of one gathering with small stain just at fore edge, additional trifling imperfections, otherwise fine, binding lustrous with very little wear, beautifully luxurious paper of text especially fresh and clean. Phillip J. Pirages 59 - 321 2011 $650

Hotten, John Camden *Charles Dickens, the Story of His Life.* London: John Camden Hotten, 1870.   First edition; 193 x 130mm., xvi, 367 pages, (10) leaves (ads), fine butterscotch colored straight grain morocco, handsomely gilt by Morrell (stamp signed verso front free endleaf), covers with French fillet border and rosette cornerpieces, raised bands, spine attractively gilt in double ruled compartments with ornate central lozenge surrounded by small tools and cornerpieces formed by arabesques and volutes, turn-ins heavily gilt in floral design, top edge gilt, other edges rough trimmed, front joint neatly repaired, extra illustrated with 73 portraits and engravings plus 2 folding facsimiles, titlepage with ink ownership inscription of Edmund Ollier, whose neat manuscript marginalia appears occasionally in text; just hint of wear to extremities, one leaf with one inch loosed tear to head margin (not affecting text), otherwise only trivial imperfections internally, nearly fine, lustrous and scarcely worn.   Phillip J. Pirages   59 - 174   2011 $950

Macaulay, Thomas Babington Macaulay, 1st Baron 1800-1859 *Critical and Historical Essays Contributed to the Edinburgh Review.* London: Longman, Brown, Green, Longmans & Roberts, 1858.   Ninth edition; 3 volumes, 230 x 150mm., lovely contemporary honey brown full crushed morocco, elegantly gilt by Morrell (signed on front turn-in), covers with double gilt rule frame, raised bands, spine gilt in charming Arts and Crafts design of interlacing flowers and leaves, gilt titling, turn-ins, extra illustrated with 122 engraved plates; upper cover of a third volume with one inch and two three-inch scratches (all shallow and well masked with dye), thin band of offsetting to free endpapers from gilt turn-ins (as usual), some of the plates with minor foxing and bit offset onto facing pages, otherwise quite handsome set in fine condition, text fresh and clean, bindings very lustrous and with virtually no wear to joints or extremities.   Phillip J. Pirages   59 - 121   2011 $850

Binding – Mudie

Collins, Wilkie 1824-1889 *Antonina, or The Fall of Rome.* London: Chatto & Windus, circa, 1890. New edition; original half tan calf by Mudie, gilt spine, maroon morocco labels, signature of M.D. Baron, very good.   Jarndyce Antiquarian Booksellers   CXCI - 122   2011   £110

Collins, Wilkie 1824-1889 *The New Magdalen: a Novel.* London: Chatto & Windus, 1893.   New edition; contemporary half tan calf by Mudie, gilt spine, maroon morocco labels, booklabel of M. D. Baron, very good.   Jarndyce Antiquarian Booksellers   CXCI - 132   2011   £120

MacDonald, George 1824-1905 *At the Back of the North Wind.* London: Strahan & Co., 1872? 76 illustrations by Arthur Hughes, few spots, rebound in half dark green morocco by Mudie, spine faded and slightly rubbed.   Jarndyce Antiquarian Booksellers   CXCII - 115   2011   £200

Binding – Muir, Ann

Barrie, James Matthew 1860-1937 *Peter Pan or the Boy Who Would Not Grow Up.* London: Folio Society, 1992.   First edition thus, 1 of 100 numbered copies; large tall 8vo., pages xx, 106, (2), 27.5 x 18 cm., frontispiece and 14 color illustrations by Paula Rego, specially bound in quarter Nigerian goatskin with hand marbled sides by Ann Muir, signed by artist, lettered gilt at spine with, fine in fine slipcase, this copy no. "staff 2", superb example of sumptuous special edition.   Any Amount of Books   May 26 2011 - A48124   2011 $805

Binding – Mullen

Scott, Walter 1771-1832 *The Works of.* Edinburgh: 1806. 5 volumes, large paper set presented to the Countess of Granard, Mullen's binding is morocco, a gilt tooled red spine, somewhat dull, boards black and red corners, plain but for three line panelling, three edges gilded with typical Mullen tooled panel top, bottom and fore-edge.   C. P. Hyland   May 26 2011 - 258   2011 $644

Binding – Nash, John Henry

Emerson, Ralph Waldo 1803-1882 *The Essays of Ralph Waldo Emerson.* San Francisco: Limited Editions Club, 1934.   #196 of 1500 beautifully designed copies, singed by John Henry Nash; folio, cloth backed blue paper boards, bound by John Henry Nash, spine little darkened, slight chipping to spine label, near fine in very good, intact slipcase.   Charles Agvent   Transcendentalism 2010 - 11   2011 $175

Binding – Nichols

Bede, the Venerable *Historiae Ecclesiasticae Gentis Anglorum...* Cantabrigiae: Typis Academicis, 1722. Folio, pages (xvi), 823 (xv) + 2 engraved plates and 1 folding map, early 19th century sprinkled an polished calf, spine fully gilt, red lettering piece gilt boards decorative roll gilt bordered, board edges decorative roll gilt, turn-ins decorative roll gilt, "French Shell" "made" endpapers, all edges 'Gloster' marbled, 3 colour (blue, red & white), sewn endbands, early 21st century conservation by Chris Weston, some browning to initial leaves and plates, little minor spotting elsewhere, few old scratched to old boards, signed binding with ticket of Nichols, Wakefield, unidentified armorial bookplate, and below, the later bookabel of Eric Poole, from the collection of Christopher Ernest Weston 1947-2010.   Unsworths Booksellers   24 - 7   2011   £1500

Binding – Noulhac

La Fontaine, Jean De 1621-1695 *Contes et Nouvelles en Vers.* Paris: De l'Imprimerie de P. Didot l'aine, 1795. First printing of the Fragonard edition; 322 x 250mm., 2 volumes, very fine honey brown crushed morocco handsomely gilt by Noulhac (stamp signed and dated 1902 on front turn-ins), covers with French fillet border and sawtooth edging and very elegant large floral ornaments in corners, raised bands, spines very attractively gilt in compartments formed by triple rules and featuring a poppy centerpiece framed by leafy sprays and ribbons, marbled endpapers, all edges gilt, 3 full page portraits of Fragonard, one smaller portrait tondo of La Fontaine, one vignette of Venus, vignette of Cupid on each titlepage and 20 very fine plates "Before Letters" from original edition, 16 of them after Fragonard and, in addition, the 57 etchings "Before Letters? published in 1880 by Roquette based on Fragonard's 57 planned illustrations of the 1795 edition, along with 36 original sepia wash drawings done in 1869 and based on a selection of Fragonard originals (these drawings done in reverse), like images bound next to each other (meaning that sometimes there are three versions of the same illustration bound together); slightest hint of foxing internally (perhaps a half dozen leaves more foxed, but worst being just about negligible), perhaps 10 leaves with expertly repaired short marginal tears (typically less than an inch and never anywhere near text), very special copy in beautiful condition, finely executed lovely bindings lustrous and virtually without wear, margins nothing short of vast, text, plates and inserted material all extraordinarily fresh and clean.   Phillip J. Pirages   59 - 48   2011 $17,500

Binding – Nutt, W.

Lodge, Edmund *Portraits of Illustrious Personages of Great Britain...* printed for Harding & Leopard, 1834. 12 volumes, tall 8vo., contemporary full bottle green morocco gilt by W. Nutt, little rubbing to hinges and feet of backstrips, few slight scrapes to one or two boards, all edges gilt, 240 steel engraved portraits, one or two plates little foxed, most handsome set.   R. F. G. Hollett & Son Antiquarian Booksellers   General Catalogue Summer 2010 - 436   2011   £1250

Binding – O'Donnell, Kim

Mitchell, John *The Bottom of the Harbor.* New York: Limited Editions Club, 1991. First edition with these illustrations, one of 250, signed on justification page by John Mitchell; 5 hors-texte photogravures hand pulled by Jon Goodman after Berenice Abbott, 12 x 10 inches, 250 pages, hand sewn and bound in black quarter Nigerian goatskin and black Irish linen, very slight binder's imperfection on cloth, otherwise excellent copy in publisher's slipcase, this copy additionally inscribed "binder's copy" signed by Kim O'Donnell of the Garthegaat Bindery.   Gemini Fine Books & Arts, Ltd.   Art Reference & Illustrated Books: First Editions 2011 $750

Mitchell, John *The Bottom of the Harbor.* New York: Limited Editions Club, 1991. First edition with these illustrations, one of 250 copies signed by Mitchell; 5 hors texte hand pulled photogravures by Berenice Abbot, 12 x 10 inches, 250 pages, hand sewn and bound in black Nigerian goatskin and black Irish linen, fit in publisher's cloth slipcase, excellent copy, binder Kim O'Donnell's copy, unnumbered, with extra engraving by Abbot bound in, colophon additionally signed by binder.   Gemini Fine Books & Arts, Ltd.   Art Reference & Illustrated Books: First Editions 2011 $950

Pound, Ezra Loomis 1885-1972 *Cathay.* New York: Limited Editions Club, 1992. First Clemente edition; one of 300 copies, signed and numbered by artist, 7 unsigned original color woodcuts by Francesco Clemente, printed on handmade Japanese Ogawashi paper, 12 x 8.5 inches, spine of book and edges of slipcase faded, otherwise as new, inscribed "binder's copy" and signed by Kim O'Donnell of the Garthegaat Bindery.   Gemini Fine Books & Arts, Ltd.   Art Reference & Illustrated Books: First Editions 2011 $1350

Binding – Okamoto Bindery

Michener, James A. *Modern Japanese Print.* Rutland: & Tokyo: Charles E. Tuttle Co., 1962. First edition, one of 510 numbered copies, this being #46, signed by author and 10 contributing artists; large folio, (1)-55, (1, colophon) pages, 10 original full page prints, each signed by artist, text handset in Perpetua type, printed on handmade kyokushi or Japanese vellum, bound at Okamoto Bindery in original tri-tone line, stamped in gilt on front boards and spine, uncut, housed in original slipcase of unvarnished spruce or Japanese cedar, Japanese title burned into wood on front panel of slipcase, book fine, slipcase with few minor bumps and scuffs, altogether, lovely, fine copy.   Heritage Book Shop   Holiday 2010 - 84   2011 $4500

Binding – Oldbach, Albert, & Son

Hepplewhite, Alice *The Cabinet Maker and Upholsterer's Guide.* London: published I. and J. Taylor, 1789. Second edition; folio, 127 engraved plates on 126 sheets, bound by Albert Oldach & Son in modern full brown morocco.   Heritage Book Shop   Booth A12 51st NY International Antiquarian Book Fair April 8-10 2011 - 66   2011 $7500

Binding – Paine, Emily

Metz, Jerred *The Temperate Voluptuary. Rendered From Platina's Cookbook on Its 500th Anniversary.* Santa Barbara: Capra Press, 1975. First edition, a total of 50 numbered, signed copies; pictorial boards, handbound by Emily Paine, this copy not numbered but rather designated as "Noel Young's copy" in red ink, woodcuts by Thomas Lang, fine in glassine dust jacket.   Charles Agvent   2010 Summer Miscellany - 47   2011 $100

Binding – Painted

Monkhouse, William Cosmo *Corn and Poppies.* London: Elkin Mathews, 1890. First edition; half title, uncut in original painted vellum binding. bevelled boards, very slightly dulled, bookplate of Alban Dobson, very good, tipped on to leading f.e.p. a 13 line poem on single sheet of paper signed by author with note by Alban Dobson "found among Austin Dobson's papers".   Jarndyce Antiquarian Booksellers   CXCI - 325 2011   £150

Binding – Parrot, Gray

Browne, Thomas 1605-1682 *Pseudodoxia Epidemica; of Unicornes Hornes.* N.P. but Williamsburg: Cheloniidae Press, 1984. First edition, Artist proof issue, one of 5 copies only; all on obsolete Whatman paper (blue-white laid ca. 1962) from a total issue of 225, all signed by artist, as follows, 5 AP copies (this copy), in elegant full limp vellum non-adhesive binding, title in gilt on spine, frontispiece etching in 2 states, extra suite (14), each signed and numbered, and two extra suites of working proofs (28), each signed and labeled "wp", original drawing, unicorn within an oval border signed in full by Alan J. Robinson, housed in quarter vellum folder with Narwhal 'horn' tooled in gold, gilt on spine, housed in tan cloth over boards with vellum spine stamped with title in gold gilt, with 15 state proof copies, bound in full vellum non-adhesive limp binding with original drawing and an extra suite of prints plus a suite of working proofs of the prints and state proofs of the etching, 60 deluxe copies in vellum binding and extra suite: 150 regular copies on TH Saunders laid, page size 9 1/2 x 7 inches, bound by Gray Parrot with his binder's ticket at lower rear turn-in, full limp vellum, matching quarter vellum sleeve for extra suites all housed in vellum and linen clamshell box, box slightly worn with 2 or 3 minor bumps, book fine; 15 wood engravings and one etching by Robinson, text set and cast in Van Dyck monotype by Winifred and Michael Bixler and printed by Harold Patrick McGrath in black and blue at Hampshire Typothetae, lovely book.   Priscilla Juvelis - Rare Books 48 - 2 2011 $2500

A Fowl Alphabet. Easthampton: Cheloniidae Press, 1986. Issued in a regular edition of 150 copies in vellum backed marbled boards, a deluxe edition of 50 signed and numbered copies and a full vellum edition of 50 signed and numbered copies and full vellum edition of 26 copies, this number III of only 5 artist proof copies of the full vellum edition that has each plate signed by artist and numbered "AP III", there is no drawing mentioned in prospectus, printed on Rives paper french fold; 8vo., bound in full vellum by Gray Parrot, includes the alphabet bound in full vellum, separate suite of proof plates and a blind alphabet housed in vellum backed chemise folder, all housed in vellum backed cloth case, as new with prospectus laid in, 26 wood engravings by Alan James Robinson, magnificent alphabet.   Aleph-Bet Books, Inc. 95 - 7 2011 $2500

McPhee, John *Roadkills. A Collection of Prose and Poetry.* Easthampton: Cheloniidae Press, 1981. First edition; one of 5 AP copies, inscribed by artist on first wood engraving in extra suite which is laid in, "for ****", from a total issue of 305. 5 AP copies with original drawing, extra suite of 11 wood engravings, each signed by artist who has signed the colophon as have all the authors, titlepage etching, as well an additional copy of the book, all on white Sakamto paper (text and wood engravings) including all 10 text pages, colophon again signed by all authors and Robinson and 11 wood engravings loose in folder, the 50 deluxe copies were issued (as this copy of the book) with text printed on Sakomoto and Mulberry paper and the prints on Cha-u-ke plus an extra suite of the prints, colophon of text signed by artist and all authors: 250 regular copies with text on Mulberry paper signed by artist on colophon; page size 12 x 8 3/4 inches, 58 pages, bound by Gray Parrot, quarter grey morocco with tire tracks blind tooled across spine and title in blind, matching black chemise, all housed in grey morocco and black cloth clamshell box, tiny bit of sunning to clamshell box morocco spine, else fine, illustrated with 11 wood engravings and one etching, text printed in red and black by Harold Patrick McGrath at Hampshire Typothetae in Bruce Rogers' Centaur and Frederick Warde's Arrighi which was hand set in 18 point by P. Chase Twichell, very rare, Artist's Proof with extra suite each plate signed by artist, colophon with signatures of authors, drawing and extra copy of book on different paper.   Priscilla Juvelis - Rare Books 48 - 3 2011 $3500

Robinson, Alan James *Cetacea, The Great Whales.* Easthampton: Cheloniidae Press, 1981. Artist's own copy, artist's proof #1, signed by artist, binders and printer, Harold Patrick McGrath; all on Arches Cover Buff, page size 22 x 15 inches, bound loose as issued with sheets laid in a full black Niger oasis goat folder sculpted in low relief with head of a Right Whale by David Bourbeau at The Thistle Bindery, beautiful folder housed in quarter leather moroccan goat drop back box by Gray Parrot, short split at lower joint of box, else fine; the 7 bleed etchings by Robinson depict the major species of whales, numerous blindstamped line-cut and two wood engravings, text contains biological information, 12 two-color maps showing migration routes and breeding areas printed by Harold McGrath at Hampshire Typothetae; artist printed at Cheloniidae Press.   Priscilla Juvelis - Rare Books   48 - 5 2011 $3000

Thoreau, Henry David 1817-1862 *The Maine Woods.* Portland: Ascensius Press, 1998. Copy #44 of only 45 total copies; folio, bound by Gray Parrot in full dark green morocco, gilt lettered and ruled brown morocco spine label inlay, author's signature stamped in black on front cover, frontispiece and several illustrations by Jon Luoma, printed on paper handmade in Maine, laid into the book is sheet of paper presenting the book from the nature Conservancy to a Maine Environmentalist fine in about fine slipcase made of solid Maine white pine.   Charles Agvent Transcendentalism 2010 - 37 2011 $2000

Wakefield, D. R. *Alphabet of Extinct Mammals.* Poole, East Yorkshire: Chevington Press, 2009. One of 55 copies; all on Somerset satin white mould made paper, each copy signed and numbered by Wakefield, page size 11 x 15 inches, 70 pages, 4 of which are double page foldouts etching of extinct mammal, bound by Gray Parrot, gold morocco spine with fabulous green and gold pastepaper over boards, title in gilt on spine, binder's ticket on lower rear turn-in, Wakefield has printed in color 26 etchings plus frontispiece etching with accompanying text, hand set in 12 pt. Plantin, on an early Ullmer and Watts Ablion Press. Priscilla Juvelis - Rare Books 48 - 27 2011 $3000

Binding – Paterson, M.

Arabian Nights *The Thousand and One Nights Commonly Called in England the Arabian Nights' Entertainments.* London: John Murray, 1849. 222 x 150mm., 3 volumes, 222 x 150mm., elegant contemporary green pebble grain morocco, elaborately gilt by M. Paterson of Edinburgh (his ticket on front pastedown), cover with alcove design, frames with ornate floral decoration, top and bottom panels with semi-circular central portion formed by multiple gilt rules, whole enclosing large central urn filled with flowers, spines gilt in double ruled compartments, with intricate fan style cornerpieces and large complex central fleuron, densely gilt turn-ins, marbled endpapers, all edges gilt, extra engraved titlepage and about 700 wood engravings from designs by William Harvey; spines just slightly and uniformly sunned toward a pleasing olive green, inner half inch of front free endpaper of volume on glued to pastedown and slightly torn, small additional defect, otherwise fine, extremely pretty set, decorative original binding with bright gilt and only trivial wear, text with virtually no signs of use. Phillip J. Pirages 59 - 65 2011 $1250

Binding – Payne, Robert

Dalrymple, John *Memoirs of Great Britain and Ireland from the Dissolution of the Last Parliament of Charles II Until the Sea Battle of La Hogue.* London and Edinburgh: for W. Strahan and T. Cadell and A. Kincaid, J. Bell and J. Balfour, 1771. Second edition; 285 x 215mm., viii, (4) leaves, 509, (1) pages, originally illustrated with separate appendix not present here; handsome contemporary oxblood morocco, gilt, in style of Robert Payne, expertly and sympathetically rebacked, covers with wide and intricate gilt tooled frame composed of closely spaced alternating palm fronds and lancets, cornerpieces composed of 10 different botanical and geometric tools, flat spine divided into compartments by decorative gilt rolls, each compartment with central floral sprig inside a lozenge of stars, circles and other small tools and corners with curling palm fronds, gilt turn-ins, marbled endpapers, all edges gilt; with fine fore-edge painting of Limerick and the River Shannon, as seen from the tower of Limerick Cathedral; early 19th century engraved bookplate of Syston Park and with smaller 20th century bookplate of "A.A.H.", with notation in what appears to be late 18th century hand of John Thorold; half dozen small abrasions to covers with minimal loss of gilt, extremities bit rubbed, occasional minor foxing or smudging, other trivial imperfections, excellent copy, binding solidly restored and certainly appealing, text very fresh, quite clean, generous margins, expert fore-edge painting in fine condition, colors soft but clear, composition especially pleasing. Phillip J. Pirages 59 - 41 2011 $2400

Binding – Period Binders

Farington, Joseph 1747-1821 *Thirty-One Views in Derbyshire. Part VI of Britannia Depicta...* London: Cadell & Davies, 1818. First edition; oblong folio, modern half calf gilt with marbled boards by Period Binders of Bath, original elegant lettering piece relaid on upper band, complete with title, list of plates and 31 tissue guarded steel engraved plates with accompanying leaf of leaves of text, light spotting to few plate margins, but excellent copy, plates in strong impressions. R. F. G. Hollett & Son Antiquarian Booksellers General Catalogue Summer 2010 - 1391 2011 £1200

Binding – Philip, J.

Jacson, Frances *Isabella.* London: Henry Colburn & Co., 1823. First edition; 3 volumes in 2, contemporary half calf by J. Philip of Aberdeen, spines gilt ruled, maroon labels, spines little rubbed at head and tails, good+, armorial bookplates of Alexander Innes. Jarndyce Antiquarian Booksellers CLXC - 1 2011 £225

Binding – Pisano, Maria

Pisano, Maria G. *Patterned to the Fabric.* Plainsboro: Memory Press, 2008. Artist's book; one of 10 copies, all on Sekishu and BFK paper, each signed and numbered by artist, page size 5 x 6 inches, 26 pages, bound by artist, accordion fold with intaglio prints in red over boards as covers and endpapers, opening to blue intaglio prints, some with red of blue ground text, printed cyanotype on white Sekishu paper with blue border, Sekishu text pages hand-sewn with blue thread to Rives pages, housed in red paper publisher's slipcase with label printed in red within black rule on front panel showing title, artist and press.   Priscilla Juvelis - Rare Books   48 - 19   2011 $500

Binding – Potter

Brown, J. *Tourist Rambles in the Northern and Midland Counties. Second Series.*   London: Simpkin Marshall Co. and York: J. Sampson and E. H. Pickering, 1885. Deluxe edition; pages (iv), 308, all edges gilt, 7 photo plates, scattered spots to prelims, original green cloth gilt extra by Potter and Son of York, little rubbed and marked in places.   R. F. G. Hollett & Son Antiquarian Booksellers   173 - 158   2011   £150

Roberts, Mary *Ruins and Old Trees, Associated with Memorable Events in English History.*   London: Harey and Darton, n.d., 1843. First edition; half green calf gilt by Potter and Sons of York, rather rubbed and little scraped.   R. F. G. Hollett & Son Antiquarian Booksellers   177 - 749   2011   £120

Binding – Pratt

Lamb, Charles 1775-1834 *Tales from Shakespeare.* London: printed for Thomas Hodgkins, 1807. First edition, first issue, with printer's imprint on verso of page 235 of volume I and with ad at end of volume II giving the earlier Hanway Street address for the Juvenile Library; 172 x 108mm., 2 volumes, very fine citron morocco handsomely gilt by W. Pratt, stamp signed, covers framed in gilt with French fillet border, inner panel with double fillets and outwear extending fleuron cornerpieces, raised bands, spines ornately gilt in compartments featuring scrolling foliate cornerpieces and lozenge centerpiece with black inlaid (?) circle and fleuron elements at ends and sides, blue morocco title and volume labels with scrolling foliate cornerpieces, elaborate gilt inner dentelles, all edges gilt, in suede lined morocco edged marbled paper slipcase, with 20 plates printed on special thick paper after designs by William Mulready and said to have been engraved by William Blake; spines slightly and evenly faded to a pleasant caramel color, front board of first volume with few small spots, breath of foxing in isolated places but a wonderful copy, text and plates clean, fresh and bright, lovely decorative binding unworn.   Phillip J. Pirages   59 - 250   2011 $2500

Binding – Price

Reynolds, Herbert Edward *Wells Cathedral its Foundation, Constitutional History and Statutes.*   Wells: privately printed for the editor, 1881. Small folio, contemporary half calf gilt by Price of Wells with double contrasting spine labels, spine and edges little rubbed, pages (xvi, subscribers and errata), cxcviii (preface, 280, engraved frontispiece, numerous woodcuts, photographic and facsimile plates, folding table little creased, bookplate of Wells Cathedral library.   R. F. G. Hollett & Son Antiquarian Booksellers   General Catalogue Summer 2010 - 1565   2011   £120

Binding – Prideaux, Sarah

Villon, Francois *Les Ballades.* Eragny Press, 1900. One of 226 copies (of which 200 were for sale); 198 x 128mm., 2 p.l., 88, (4) pages, lovely contemporary olive green crushed morocco by Sarah Prideaux (stamp signed "STP" and dated 1901 on rear turn-in), covers with wide double ruled gilt frame filled with curling tendrils, 12 of these terminating in leaves, six more connected to large pomegranates located at each corner and at midpoint of the left and right side, frame with interspersed large and small dots, raised bands, spine panels with single leaf on a curling vine, gilt turn-ins, edges gilt on the rough, with woodcut printer's device on opening page, titlepage with woodcut vignette surrounded by full border of leaves and berries, 37 woodcut foliate initials all by Lucien Pissarro, printed in red and black, isolated spots of foxing, spine perhaps just a shade darker than covers, but very fine, text especially clean, fresh and smooth, lustrous binding without perceptible wear.   Phillip J. Pirages   59 - 123   2011 $7500

Binding – Pringle, Sarah

Poe, Edgar Allan 1809-1849 *The Raven.*
Easthampton: Cheloniidae Press, 1986. Artist's Proof copy; one of a handful of such bound as the state proof edition in full red morocco, with additional two suites of working proofs (21 prints total, 17 wood engravings and 3 states of frontispiece etching), from a total issue of 225 copies, 150 regular edition, 50 deluxe with extra suite of prints, bound in quarter morocco by Claudia Cohen, 25 state proof copies with two extra suites and an original drawing, full morocco binding, all copies on Magnani Letterpress paper and all signed and numbered by Alan James Robinson; page size 6 7/16 x 9 3/8 inches, this is an all new original edition in which the artist revisits the text of the first book of the press, text is letterpress by Dan Keliher at Wild Carrot Letterpress, the 9 original wood engravings and one original etching, frontispiece portrait of Poe, the full red morocco binding is by Daniel Kelm and Sarah Pringle at the Wide Awake Garage, the front panel blindstamped with one of Robinson's wood engravings of a raven, the two additional suites are housed in grey cloth over boards folder with white label printed in black on front "The Raven/Prints" and both housed in grey cloth-over boards clamshell box, red morocco label on spine, blindstamped with title, author and title logo of Cheloniidae Press, both bit worn, book and prints fine.   Priscilla Juvelis - Rare Books   48 - 4   2011 $2000

Binding – Prize

Bible. Greek - 1625 *(Greek text) Noveum Testamentum.*
Leiden: Elzevier, 1625. First Elzevier Greek New Testament; woodcut printer's device on title, pages (xii), 863, 12mo., contemporary vellum, elaborate gilt arms of Rotterdam supported by lions rampant and surmounted by a crown on both covers, spine with gilt fleuron in each of four compartments, lettered late in English in ink, yapp edges, gilt edges, gauffered frames, traces of green silk ties, vellum somewhat rubbed with loss of some gilt, slightly discolored, very good, prize binding from Rotterdam with inscription dated 1625 on flyleaf presenting it to a young scholar (his name unfortunately crossed out, possibly Franciscus van den Brouck).   Blackwell Rare Books   B166 - 14   2011   £600

Binding – Ramage

Pagan, James *Sketch of the History of Glasgow.*
Glasgow: Robert Stuart & co., 1847. 8vo., pages (vi) 198 + engraved titlepage, extending lithographic plan and 22 other lithograph plates, later polished calf by Ramage, signed in gilt above bottom front turn-in, spine panel-gilt, dark orange lettering & 'place & date' pieces gilt, boards panelled in gilt and in blind reinterpreting the 'Cambridge' style, board edges 'broken hatch' roll gilt at corners, turn-ins 'dentelle' roll gilt, 'French Shell' 'made' endpapers, all edges lemon, 3 color double core sewn endbands, replacement lettering piece for author's name, little spotting to plates, pages lightly large toned, from the collection of Christopher Ernest Weston 1947-2010.   Unsworths Booksellers   24 - 130   2011   £200

Ruskin, John 1819-1900 *The King of the Golden River or the Black Brothers.* London: Smith Elder & Co., 1863. Fifth edition; 64 pages, half title, frontispiece, decorative titlepages and text engravings, fine in three quarter dark green crushed morocco by Ramage, top edge gilt, marbled boards, original gilt cloth covers bound in at end.   Ken Spelman Rare Books   68 - 50   2011   £125

Shakespeare, William 1564-1616 *Julius Caesar.*
London: printed by H. H. Jun. for Hen. Herringman and R. Bentley in Russel-Street in Covent Garden and sold by Joseph Knight and Francis Saunders at the Blew Anchor in the Lower Walk of the Nuw-Exchange in the Strand, n.d. circa, 1684. Early quarto edition; later full brown and tan panelled calf by Ramage.   Heritage Book Shop   Booth A12 51st NY International Antiquarian Book Fair April 8-10 2011 - 116   2011 $15,000

Shelley, Percy Bysshe 1792-1822 *The Cenci.* Italy: for C. and J. Ollier, London, 1819. First edition one of 250 copies; 8vo., pages xiv, 104, occasional light spotting, bound without initial blank in later morocco by Ramage, upper and lower boards filleted in gilt, spine with raised bands and compartments delineated in gilt, gilt lettering, inner dentelles, marbled endpapers, top edge gilt, others uncut, bookplate of Joseph Turner.   Simon Finch Rare Books   Zero - 353   2011   £3500

Shelley, Percy Bysshe 1792-1822 *Poems.* London: Macmillan, 1913. Small 8vo., full crushed scarlet morocco gilt by Ramage, raised bands, pages lxvi, 340, all edges gilt, engraved title vignette, light crayon scribble on flyleaf, otherwise fine.   R. F. G. Hollett & Son Antiquarian Booksellers General Catalogue Summer 2010 - 904   2011   £60

Wordsworth, William 1770-1850 *Poems.* London: Macmillan, 1911. Small 8vo., full crushed scarlet morocco gilt by Ramage (although unsigned), with raised bands, pages xxxi, 331, all edges gilt, engraved title vignette portrait, fine in lovely little gift binding.   R. F. G. Hollett & Son Antiquarian Booksellers   General Catalogue Summer 2010 - 930   2011   £75

Binding – Relfe Brothers

Jameson, Anna Brownell 1794-1860 *Shakespeare's Heroines.* London: Ernest Nister, n.d. circa, 1895. Large 8vo., full calf, gilt prize binding by Relfe Brothers, pages 308, all edges gilt, 6 color plates, 70 half tone illustrations by W. Paget.   R. F. G. Hollett & Son Antiquarian Booksellers 175 - 722   2011   £75

Kingsley, Charles 1819-1875 *The Water Babies.* London: Macmillan, 1891. Pages 330, 100 woodcut illustrations by Linley Sambourne, full scarlet calf gilt prize binding by Relfe Brothers, few slight scratches, pages 330, 100 woodcut illustrations. R. F. G. Hollett & Sons Antiquarian Booksellers 170 - 365 2011 £50

Binding – Reynolds, Sage

Brassai *The Artists of My Life.* New York: Witken Berley Ltd., 1982. First edition, deluxe edition comprising 'specially selected sheets", this number 11 of 150 copies, signed and numbered by Brassai, issued with hand pulled dust grained photogravure also signed by Brassai of Henri Matisse drawing a nude woman, 19193; large 4to., full page reproductions of photos, pictorial patterned paper covered boards over cloth lettered silver at spine, special presentation folder housing photogravure, in special binding designed by Sage Reynolds and executed at Four Hands Bindery NY, fine in very good plain buff slipcase. Any Amount of Books May 26 2011 - A68250 2011 $1845

Binding – Riviere

Ainsworth, William Harrison 1805-1882 *Saint James's or the Court of Queen Anne. an Historical Romance.* London: John Mortimer, 1844. First (Magazine) issue; 8vo., full red levant, elaborate gilt dentelles, all edges gilt, gilt lettered by Riviere, frontispiece after Maclise and 14 engraved plates by Cruikshank, first appearance in print as extracted from "Ainsworth's Magazine" volume 4 and bound with titlepage apparently issued by Mortimer who was publisher of both Magazine and three volume first book edition of this, nice, clean, unfoxed, scarce. Second Life Books Inc. 174 - 8 2011 $638

Bacon, Francis, Viscount St. Albans 1561-1626 *Essayes or Counsels, Civill and Morall.* London: printed by John Haviland for Hanna Barret and Richard Whitaker, 1625. First complete edition, first issue with titlepage bearing imprint of Barret and Whitaker and the qualifier "Newly enlarged"; small quarto, (xii), 340, (2, blank) pages, complete with both first and final blank, text within printed borders, woodcut initials, full light brown morocco by Riviere, covers with triple gilt fillet borders, densely gilt spine compartments, gilt spine lettering, gilt board edges and dentelles, all edges gilt, leaves O-O3 with light dampstain on lower outer corner, very small wormhole through outer upper corners of leaves Nn-Tt, in slipcase, overall, excellent copy, very clean and complete. Heritage Book Shop Holiday 2010 - 6 2011 $5500

Beaumont, Francis *Comedies and Tragedies Written by Francis Beaumont and John Fletcher, Gentlemen.* London: printed for Humphrey Robinson and for Humphrey Moseley, 1647. First collected edition; folio, 20th century crimson morocco by Riviere & Sons. Heritage Book Shop Booth A12 51st NY International Antiquarian Book Fair April 8-10 2011 - 11 2011 $7500

Boswell, James 1740-1795 *Boswell's Life of Johnson...* Oxford: Clarendon Press, 1887. 6 volumes in 11, half titles, frontispiece, extra illustrated, additional titlepages, plates as called for + 1293 additional plates, some occasional foxing and offsetting, heavy in places but largely internally, very good, handsomely bound in full crushed red morocco by Riviere & Son, double ruled gilt borders, raised gilt bands, compartments ruled in gilt, bookplates of Edith Bessie Cooke, top edge gilt. Jarndyce Antiquarian Booksellers CXCI - 20 2011 £5800

Bouchot, Henri *La Miniature Francaise 1750-1825.* Paris: Goupil, 1907. One of 200 copies; 330 x 260 mm., 2 p.l., 245, (1) pages, magnificent sky blue crushed levant, lavishly gilt by Riviere, covers with gilt double fillet border and grand central panel formed by use of 11 plain and decorative rules (as well as small seashell centerpieces), raised bands between richly gilt compartments of rinceaux like decoration around central lozenge elegantly gilt inner dentelles, watered silk endleaves, marbled flyleaves, all edges gilt, with 72 fine plates (containing a total of 154 images, 45 of the plates tinted and 20 fully colored) and 108 illustrations in text, all but two of them tinted, printed tissue guards, even in the case of text illustrations, titlepage in red and black; hint of wear to corners and edges, spine just slightly sun faded, offsetting from two engraved pages, minor dots of foxing in isolated places, otherwise fine, beautifully bound volume, gilt and covers still very bright and text and plates quite clean, bright and fresh. Phillip J. Pirages 59 - 72 2011 $1600

Bronte, Anne 1820-1849 *The Tenant of Wildfell Hall.* London: T. C. Newby, 1848. First edition, first issue; 12mo., 3 volumes, (4), 358; (2), 366; (2), 342 pages, excessively rare half title in volume I, but without final leaf of ads in volume I, no half titles called for in volumes II and III, bound circa 1900 by Riviere & Son (stamp signed on verso of front free endpaper) in full tan polished calf, covers with gilt triple fillet border and gilt corner ornaments, spine decoratively tooled in gilt in compartments with two brown morocco gilt lettering pieces, board edges ruled in gilt, turn-ins decoratively tooled in gilt, top edge gilt, others uncut, armorial bookplate of Herbert S. Leon, housed in custom made half tan calf clamshell case with raised bands and two green morocco lettering labels and felt lined dividers, exceptionally copy, minimal foxing and mostly marginal soiling, volume I with tiny dampstain outer margin of P6, volume II with small very neat paper repairs to outer blank margin of D7 and F7, small faint stain in upper corner of G3-G7 and small paper flaw in upper blank margin of H5, volume III with faint stain in upper margin of D4 and D5, tiny tear in outer margin of G3, short tear neatly repaired in upper margin of G6, tiny tear in outer margin of P4. David Brass Rare Books, Inc. May 26 2011 - 00031 2011 $42,500

Browning, Elizabeth Barrett 1806-1861   *Two Poems by Elizabeth Barrett and Robert Browning.*   London: Chapman & Hall, 1854.   First edition; full dark green crushed morocco by Riviere & Son, gilt dentelles, slightly sunned, booklabel and another removed from following pastedown, top edge gilt, very good.   Jarndyce Antiquarian Booksellers CXCI - 95 2011   £200

Combe, William 1742-1823   *The Three Tours of Dr. Syntax...*   London: R. Ackermann's Repository of Arts, 1812. 1820. 1821. First editions in book form, first issue of the first work with plates in first state; 235 x 146mm., 3 volumes, remarkably pretty sky blue crushed morocco, handsomely gilt by Riviere (signed at foot of front turn-in), covers gilt with double rule border, French fillet center frame and floral cornerpieces, raised bands, spines elaborately gilt in compartments featuring elegant floral tools used for cornerpieces and centerpiece, broad and ornate gilt inner dentelies, all edges gilt, one woodcut illustration, one engraved tailpiece and 80 artfully hand colored aquatint plates by Thomas Rowlandson; engraved bookplate of Douglas Kerr; rear joint of one volume with thin crack along bottom inch or so, two covers with faint soiling, spines evenly faded to very pleasing, blue-grey, otherwise beautiful bindings in lovely condition with bright gilt, leaves opposite plates lightly offset, otherwise very fine internally text clean and with substantial margins, plates finely colored.   Phillip J. Pirages 59 - 303 2011 $590

Davenant, William 1606-1668   *The Works of Sr. William Davenant Kt. Consisting of those Which were Formerly printed and Those which He Design'd for the Press...*   London: by T. N. for Henry Herringman, 1673.   First collected edition; folio, (8), 402, (4), 486, 111 pages, portrait, turn-of-the-century red levant morocco, gilt arabesque centerpiece on covers, all edges gilt by Riviere, very skillfully rebacked, though new leather at joints and on cords has uniformly faded, unusually fine, fresh, wide margined copy, fine impression of portrait, leather tipped fleece lined slipcase, edges rubbed, Duke of Beaufort, E. F. Leo, A. E, Newton, with their bookplates.   Joseph J. Felcone Inc. Fall Miscellany 2010 - 37 2011 $2200

Dickens, Charles 1812-1870   *The Works.*   London: Chapman and Hall, 1873-1876.   30 volumes, 220 x 140mm. very pleasing dark blue straight grain morocco, handsomely gilt, by Riviere & Son (stamp signed verso front free endpaper), covers bordered with gilt double rule and wide ornate floral roll incorporating fleuron cornerpieces, raised bands, spines heavily gilt in double ruled compartments with ornate central lozenge, surrounded by small tools and intricate scrolling volute cornerpieces, inner gilt dentelles, marbled endpapers, titlepage (one volume very expertly rebacked using original backstrip), copiously illustrated with 461 plates, plus numerous illustrations in text, half the volumes with shallow chips at head (only noticeable upon close inspection) just hint of wear to joints and extremities, occasional minor foxing, other trivial imperfections internally, but excellent, even with wear at spine ends, text clean and fresh and very decorative bindings quite pleasing, unusually lustrous covers, sumptuously bound.   Phillip J. Pirages 59 - 173 2011 $6500

Goldsmith, Oliver 1730-1774   *The Vicar of Wakefield: a Tale Supposed to be Written by Himself.*   Salisbury: Printed for B. Collins for F. Newbery, 1766.   First edition, variant B; 2 volumes, 172 x 108mm., terminal blank in volume I, beautiful scarlet crushed morocco, heavily gilt by Riviere & Son, covers with French fillet frame, spine with raised bands and handsomely gilt compartments, lovely gilt inner dentelles, all edges gilt, leather book labels of Roderick Terry, (Edgar) Mills and Doris Louise Benz, lower corner of terminal blank in first volume skillfully renewed, artful repair and faint glue stains at inner margin of B3 in second volume, other isolated trivial defects, very fine, text nearly pristine, especially bright and handsome binding.   Phillip J. Pirages 59 - 50 2011 $6500

Goldsmith, Oliver 1730-1774   *The Vicar of Wakefield.*   London and New York: Macmillan, 1927.   185 x 125mm., xxxvi, 306 pages, charming contemporary fawn colored pictorial crushed morocco by Riviere and Son, covers with frame formed by multiple gilt rules with onlaid green dot cornerpieces and gilt festoons at head and tail of frame, central pictorial inlay in four colors depicting a vicar pontificating (and in front of him as an indication of shadow, thin penwork lines inscribed into the morocco), raised bands, spine gilt in French fillet compartments with central gilt patera, wide gilt framed turn-ins with ribbon cornerpieces, leather hinges, marbled endpapers, all edges gilt, linen covered slipcase; frontispiece and 181 illustrations in text by Hugh Thomson, spine very slightly and uniformly sunned toward a butterscotch color, but very fine, text clean, fresh and bright and lustrous, appealing binding with only the most insignificant wear.   Phillip J. Pirages 59 - 128 2011 $950

Hamilton, Charles Gillingham, Mrs. *The Exiles of Italy.* Edinburgh: Thomas Constable and Co., 1857. First edition with bound-in limitation page signed by artist on fore-edge painting proclaiming, "This is No. 122 of the Books with Fore-edge Paintings by Miss Currie/ The Painting Under the gold is a view of The Temples of Paestrum"; 185 x 125mm., xxxii, (1) leaf (half title), 502 pages, beautiful early 20th century dark blue straight grain morocco sumptuously gilt by Riviere and Son (stamp signed), covers richly decorated in gilt and blind with outer gilt frame featuring pairs of triple fillets flanking a chain roll composed of leaf fronds and then daisy cornerpieces, next to outer frame, blind rolled border in cresting pattern and further in a central panel composed of plain gilt rules and gilt botanical cornerpieces accented with blindstamped daisy tools around outer edge and with tangent dogtooth roll in blind closer to middle of board, raised bands, spine gilt in triple filleted compartments, intricate central lozenge and blind tooled leaf cornerpieces, densely gilt turn-ins, all edges gilt, with fine fore-edge paintings by Miss Currie of the Temple of Hera and the Second Temple of Hera at Paestum; top corners little bumped, mild offsetting to endpapers from gilt turn-ins (as almost always) isolated minor foxing and other trivial imperfections internally, otherwise fine in lovely binding, text clean and fresh binding exceptionally lustrous and virtually unworn and fore-edge painting well preserved. Phillip J. Pirages 59 - 204 2011 $5500

Holland, Elizabeth Vassall, Lady 1770-1845 *A Memoir of the Rev. Sidney Smith.* London: Longmans, Green and co., circa, 1885. Couple of fox spots, pages x, 628, 8vo. contemporary tree calf, spine gilt, second compartment gilt lettered direct by Riviere and Son, slightly sunned, near fine, inscribed by author to Arthur Godfrey James. Blackwell Rare Books B166 - 49 2011 £70

Kerner Von Marilaun, Anton *The Natural History of Plants Their Forms, Growth, Reproduction and Distribution.* Blackie & Son, 1894-1895. 2 volumes, thick small 4to., contemporary three quarter green levant morocco gilt with marbled boards by Riviere, spines mellowed, top edge gilt, 16 color plates and some 2000 woodcut text illustrations, handsome, bookplate of Sir Henry Francis Redhead Yorke. R. F. G. Hollett & Son Antiquarian Booksellers General Catalogue Summer 2010 - 1008 2011 £220

Kingsley, Charles 1819-1875 *The Water-Babies.* London: Macmillan and Co., 1885. First edition illustrated by Linley Sambourne; small quarto, viii, 371, (1, printers imprint) pages, wood engravings, text illustrations, fine Cosway binding by Riviere & Son (stamp signed in gilt on front turn-in), full red crushed levant morocco, covers with gilt triple fillet border, front cover set a fine rectangular miniature portrait on ivory under bevelled glass 89 x 66mm. of Charles Kingsley by Miss C. B. Currie, within inner gilt double fillet border and wide outer gilt floral and leaf border (in the style of Charles MacLeish), spine in 6 compartments, five raised bands, lettered gilt in two compartments and decoratively tooled in gilt in a similar floral and leaf design in remaining four compartments, with date in gilt at foot, board edges with gilt double fillet, turn-ins ruled in gilt with similar gilt floral corner ornaments, dark green watered silk doublures and liners, all edges gilt, stamped in gilt on rear doublure "Miniatures by C. B. Currie", additionally stamped in gilt on fore-edges of front and rear boards "Cosway Binding" and "Invented by J. H. Stonehouse", inserted certificate leaf signed by Stonehouse and Currie and numbered in ink identifies the present copy as being "No 951 of the Cosway Bindings invented by J. H. Stonehouse with Miniatures on Ivory by Miss Currie", original front and rear blue cloth covers bound in at end, superb example, housed in velvet lined red cloth clamshell case. David Brass Rare Books, Inc. May 26 2011 - 00892 2011 $11,500

Kitton, Frederic G. *Charles Dickens by Pen and Pencil, Including Anecdotes and Reminiscences Collected from his Friends and Contemporaries.* London: Frank T. Sabin, and John F. Dexter, 1890-1892. Large paper edition; 390 x 300 mm., 3 volumes, elegant crimson morocco attractively gilt by Riviere (signed at foot of front turn-in), boards gilt with lozenge centerpiece of scrolled floral tooling around a blind oval center, raised bands, gilt spines with fleuron centerpiece, marbled endpapers, inner gilt dentelles incorporating lovely floral tools, top edge gilt, other edges untrimmed, complete set of the 15 wrappers bound in at back of third volume, text illustrations throughout, 195 fine plates (containing 236 images), all of these added (either as part of the usual Large Paper version, or, in the case of some 70 plates, as inserted, extra illustrations), engraved bookplate of Johannis Neville Cross, titlepage printed in red and black; slight dulling to covers (from leather preservative), trivial soiling, but impressive bindings scarcely worn and very pleasing, dozen of the extra engraved plates and adjacent leaves somewhat foxed, one plate creased in lower corner (not affecting image), few instances of minor marginal soiling, slight offset browning opposite few plates, other trivial defects, generally quite clean and bright. Phillip J. Pirages 59 - 175 2011 $3500

Manson, James A. *Sir Edwin Landseer, R.A.* London: Walter Scott Publishing Co. Ltd., 1902. First edition; octavo, (i-vi), vii-xvi, 219, (220) pages, titlepage printed in blue and black, 21 engraved plates and photogravure frontispiece, full dark green levant Cosway-stye binding by Riviere & Sons for Sotheran & Co., stamp signed to front turn-in, spine decoratively tooled and lettered in gilt, after floral and leaf design, compartments ruled in gilt, front and back covers ruled and decoratively tooled in a gilt floral and leaf design, surrounding 10 oval-round miniature paintings under glass, 9 miniatures on front cover depict 8 hunting dogs around a stag, miniature on back cover is portrait of Landseer, extremities double ruled in gilt, with turn-ins ruled and decoratively tooled in gilt, green marbled endpapers, joints expertly and totally invisibly repaired, fine, housed in original burgundy roan slipcase,. David Brass Rare Books, Inc. May 26 2011 - 01191 2011 $23,500

Mill, John Stuart 1806-1873 *The Subjection of Women.* London: Longmans, Green Reader and Dyer, 1869. First edition; presentation copy "from the author", octavo, full contemporary tan polished calf by Riviere and Son. Heritage Book Shop Booth A12 51st NY International Antiquarian Book Fair April 8-10 2011 - 90 2011 $3500

Mill, John Stuart 1806-1873 *Subjection of Women.* London: Longmans Green, Reader and Dyer, 1869. First edition; presentation "From the author", octavo, (4), (1)-188 pages, full contemporary tan polished calf gilt stamp decoration on boards and spine, spine with two brown morocco spine labels, lettered in gilt, all edges gilt, blue endpapers, bound by Riviere and Son, some light foxing to endpapers, minor cracking to joints and light wear to tips of spine, very good. Heritage Book Shop Holiday 2010 - 86 2011 $4500

Napoleon, Emperor of the French *Maxims of Napoleon.* London: Arthur L. Humphreys, 1903. Small quarto, bound by Riviere & son in full light brown paneled morocco, with two miniature paintings on Ivory by Miss C. B. Currie, almost invisible rebacked with original spine laid down. Heritage Book Shop Booth A12 51st NY International Antiquarian Book Fair April 8-10 2011 - 33 2011 $15,000

Pratt, Anne *The Flowering Plants, Grasses, Sedges & Ferns of Great Britain...* London: Frederick Warne & Co., 1889. 4 volumes, three quarter morocco gilt by Riveire with floral emblems to spine panels and marbled boards, few slight scuffs here and there, top edge gilt, 318 color plates, handsome tall set. R. F. G. Hollett & Son Antiquarian Booksellers General Catalogue Summer 2010 - 1036 2011 £750

Shelley, Percy Bysshe 1792-1822 *Alastor; or the Spirit of Solitude and Other Poems.* London: printed for Baldwin, Cradock and Joy by S. Hamilton, 1816. First edition; 8vo., pages (viii without half title as issued), 101, (7) blank, gilt edges, some minor spotting to margins of endpapers, otherwise internally very clean, late 19th century navy blue morocco with ornate red, green and gilt decoration, brown fabric to inside of boards and endpapers, gilt lettering to spine, raised bands by Riviere, blue morocco and marbled paper covered slipcase, binding fine with light wear to edges of slipcase, bookplate of John Whipple Frothingham. Simon Finch Rare Books Zero - 352 2011 £4500

Stanhope, Philip Henry Stanhope, Earl of *Life of William Pitt...* London: John Murray, 1879. New edition; 3 volumes, half titles, frontispieces in volumes I and II, finely bound by Riviere & Son in full tree calf, gilt borders and dentelles, raised bands, gilt compartments, maroon and brown morocco labels, spines slightly sunned, armorial bookplates of John Warren, very handsome set. Jarndyce Antiquarian Booksellers CXCI - 25 2011 £165

Stevenson, Robert Louis Balfour 1850-1894 *Poems.* London: printed at the Florence Press for Chatto & Windus in association with Longmans Green & Co., 1913. One of 500 numbered copies on handmade paper (this being copy #472); 225 x 185mm., xvi, 399, (1) pages, stunning contemporary rose colored morocco, elaborately onlaid and inlaid as well as lavishly tooled in gilt by Riviere (stamp signed on front turn-in), covers with frame composed of two parallel borders, outer one featuring a curving gilt vine bearing green inlaid morocco blossom, the inner one with small inlaid black morocco circles connected by single gilt rule, two borders joined by interlacing strapwork cornerpieces inner border interrupted at center of each side with very intricate strapwork, each lobe containing three red onlaid morocco roses and connected on its inside tip, with prominent central mandorla featuring a beautiful onlaid composition of four lilies and four acanthus leaves in ivory, red and green morocco, the panel surrounding the centerpiece filled in with some 200 gilt leaves and flowers on twining stems, entire surface of boards covered with gilt stippling (sidepieces, cornerpieces and mandorla very densely stippled), raised bands, spine elaborately gilt in double ruled compartments of a complex design, each with four inlaid black morocco flowers, central inlaid circle and much stippling, extremely pretty white morocco doublures with very flamboyant floral gilt cornerpieces, doublure framed by very wide and unusually lovely turn-ins heavily gilt in repeating floral pattern, moss green watered silk endleaves, top edges gilt, other edges untrimmed, in binder's original (rather worn) folding morocco box with one defective metal closure, title printed in blue and black, front doublure with ivory morocco bookplate with monogram of "ABJ (apparently Annie Burr Jennings) above motto from Seneca "Otium sine litteris ors est", bookplate of Mrs. A. H. Ely, bookplate faintly discolored upper corner of front free endpaper just slightly crumpled, front flyleaf with two small stains, very short closed fore-edge tear, one leaf with rust spot, remarkably fine, unusually bright text pristine, dazzling binding with virtually no signs of wear. Phillip J. Pirages 59 - 127 2011 $15,000

Tristram, William Outram *Coaching Days and Coaching Ways.* London: Macmillan and Co., 1924. 185 x 125mm., green pictorial crushed morocco by Riviere & Son, covers with frames formed by multiple gilt rules with onlaid red dot cornerpieces and gilt festoons at head and tail of frame, front cover with central pictorial inlay in five colors depicting a mounted groom holding another horse by its reins, raised bands, spine gilt in French fillet compartments with central gilt ornament of horseshoe, bridle, or riding hat, gilt ruled turn-ins with horseshoe with bridle cornerpieces, leather hinges, marbled endpapers, all edges gilt, 214 illustrations in text by Hugh Thomson and Herbert Railton, joints little worn (though rubbing well masked with dye), spine slightly darkened and with four tiny abrasions at bottom, still excellent copy, attractive inlaid binding solid and lustrous and text virtually pristine. Phillip J. Pirages 59 - 130 2011 $750

Voltaire, Francois Marie Arouet De 1694-1778 *Romances, Tales and Smaller Pieces.* London: printed for P. Dodsley, 1794. First edition; 2 volumes, pages (4) vii, (1) 9-340; (iv), 341, frontispiece, 23 engraved plates, all edges gilt, extremely bright, crisp copy, brown morocco, gilt ruled, gilt decoration and lettering to spine, red endpapers by Riviere, light spotting to boards. Simon Finch Rare Books Zero - 265 2011 £600

Wagstaffe, William *The Character of Richard St-le Esq. with Some Remarks.* London: printed for J. Morphew near Stationers Hall, 1713. First edition; (4), 32, 1 f. blank, with half title, engraved frontispiece, 8vo. in fours, fine, clean, crisp, frontispiece very slightly shaved, full polished calf by Riviere, gilt fillet borders, gilt panelled spine, red gilt morocco labels, all edges gilt. Jarndyce Antiquarian Booksellers CXCI - 498 2011 £280

White, Gilbert 1720-1793 *Natural History and Antiquities of Selborne, in the County of Southampton.* London: printed by T. Bensley for B. Shite and Son, 1789. First edition; quarto, v, (1, blank), 468 (i.e. 466), (12, index) (1, errata), (1 blank) pages, folding engraved frontispiece, 2 engraved title vignettes, 6 engraved plates, engravings by Peter Mazell and Daniel Lerpinire after drawing by Samuel Grimm, bound by Riviere & Son in full olive morocco, boards ruled in gilt, spine decoratively stamped and lettered in gilt, marbled endpapers, all edges gilt, very good. Heritage Book Shop Holiday 2010 - 129 2011 $2750

Binding – Root

Contes et Legendes Des Nations Aliees. Paris: H. Piazza, 1917. One of 1000 copies signed by Edmund Dulac; 305 x 241mm., (2 p.l., 149. (3) pages, lovely burgundy morocco by Root and son (signed on rear turn-in), covers framed in gilt with triple fillet border, multiple fillet inner panel with foliate cornerpieces facing outwards, raised bands, spine gilt in compartments formed by concentric plain and stippled rules and featuring ivy leaf cornerpieces, titling compartments with single rule frame and foliate curl cornerpieces, wide gilt ruled turn-ins with ivy leaf cornerpieces, marbled endpapers, top edges gilt, other edges rough trimmed, original paper covers bound in at back, decorative initials, decorative head and tailpieces for all text leaves, decorative and illustrated title and 15 color plates by Dulac (each laid down within ornamental printed frame with captioned tissue guard), bookplate of Joseph H. Haines; printed in green and black throughout (original wrappers printed in blue and black), very small stain in one fore margin, otherwise mint in unworn, very bright and appealing decorative binding. Phillip J. Pirages 59 - 185 2011 $1750

Dodgson, Charles Lutwidge 1832-1898 *Alice's Adventures in Wonderland. (and) Through the Looking Glass and What Alice Found There.* London: Macmillan and Co., 1866. Second, but first published edition; 183 x 125mm., 2 separately published works bound in 2 volumes, extremely pleasing crimson levant morocco by Root & son (stamp-signed on front turn-in of both volumes), each cover with panels formed by double gilt rules and central gilt medallion, the "Wonderland" medallion depicting Alice holding baby pig, the "Looking-Glass" medallion showing grumpy Red Queen, raised bands, spines gilt in compartments with double ruled frames and small central quatrefoil, gilt ruled turn-ins, marbled endpapers, all edges gilt, with 92 illustrations, letter laid in from bookseller John Newbegin elucidating issue points, bookplate of Florence Magee; spines slightly and evenly a darkened red, handful of leaves with very minor foxing or smudges, one leaf with neat repair to tail edge (no text affected), but fine and attractive set, text clean, fresh, and smooth and bindings lustrous and virtually unworn. Phillip J. Pirages 59 - 176 2011 $11,500

Hardy, Thomas 1840-1928 *Works.* London: Macmillan and Co. Ltd., 1912. Wessex edition; 21 volumes, octavo, photogravure frontispiece, maps, bound by Root & Son in contemporary three quarter blue morocco gilt over blue cloth boards, spines panelled gilt, top edge gilt, blue gray endpapers. David Brass Rare Books, Inc. May 26 2011 - 01081 2011 $9500

La Princesse Badourah; Conte Des Mille et Une Nuits. Paris: H. Piazza, 1914. One of 500 copies, signed by Edmund Dulac; 305 x 241mm., 2 p.l. (5)-114 (3) pages, very fine brown crushed morocco by Root and Son (signed on rear turn-in), covers bordered in gilt with French fillet, central panel formed by single rule with foliate branch on stippled ground in each corner of panel raised bands, spine gilt in compartments formed by double rules foliate cornerpieces on stippled ground forming a lobed frame for a floral tool centerpiece, very wide inner gilt dentelles featuring two decorative rolls, each between rules, marbled endpapers, top edge gilt, other edges rough trimmed, original tan front wrapper printed in gilt, blue and white bound in before half title, decorative initials, leaves and decorative border, decorated titlepage and 10 color plates by Edmund Dulac (each laid down with an ornamental frame and with captioned tissue guard), front pastedown with bookplate of Joseph H. Haines, titlepage printed in gilt, muted yellow and blue and leaves throughout in yellow and black, virtually mint, especially bright inside and out. Phillip J. Pirages 59 - 186 2011 $1600

Shelley, Mary Wollstonecraft 1797-1851 *Monsieur Nongtongpaw.* London: Alfred Miller, 1830. First illustrated edition; 12mo., pages 19 (11) (4), 6 engraved plates with contemporary hand coloring, bound in later three quarter morocco and marbled boards by Root and Son (front cover very loose), very clean copy. Second Life Books Inc. 174 - 286 2011 $600

Binding – Sangorski & Sutcliffe

Blanchard, Jean Pierre *Exact and Authentic Narrative of M. Blanchard's Third Aerial Voyage.* London: C. Heydigner, 1784. First English edition; small folio, viii, 17, (1, blank) pages, frontispiece, early dark brown paper wrappers, housed in dark blue cloth folder by Sangorski & Sutcliffe for E. P. Dutton, gilt lettering on outside of folder, balloon themed bookplate of previous owner William G. Gerhard on inside front of folder, lacking half title as called for in ESTC, slight offsetting to titlepage from frontispiece and some light foxing to final leaf, very good. Heritage Book Shop Holiday 2010 - 11 2011 $2750

Borrow, George 1803-1881 *Lavengro; The Scholar- The Gypsy - The Priest.* London: John Murray, 1851. First edition; 8vo., pages xx, 360, 32; xii, 366, 32, xii, 426, bound in three quarter red morocco, gilt on spines in compartments, top edge gilt by Sangorski and Sutcliffe, hinges tender, lovely set. Second Life Books Inc. 174 - 70 2011 $563

Chaucer, Geoffrey 1340-1400 *Troilus and Criseyde.* Waltham St. Lawrence: Golden Cockerel Press, 1927. One of 225 numbered copies (first six of which were printed on vellum); 316 x 198mm., xi, (i), 309, (1) pages, (2) leaves (blank and colophon), original publisher's russet quarter morocco by Sangorski & Sutcliffe, patterned paper sides, top edge gilt, others untrimmed, publisher's (only just slightly rubbed and soiled) slipcase, fore margins of every text page with woodcut borders and five full page wood engravings, all by Eric Gill, section titlepages with red or blue lettering, occasional text initials in red or blue; bookplate of the Newton library (begun by Sir Alfred Newton, 1st Baronet and mostly assembled by Sir Harry Newton, 2nd Bart. 1871-1951); some minor spotting or soiling on part of the morocco on front board, otherwise faultless copy, spine unusually bright, corners (which are always rubbed) in virtually perfect condition, text as bright and fresh as new. Phillip J. Pirages 59 - 219 2011 $19,500

Doctor Comicus, or the Frolics of Fortune. London: B. Blake, 1825? 210 133mm., 269 pages without printed titlepage, very attractive light tan smooth calf by Sangorski & Sutcliffe/Zaehnsdorf (stamp signed verso of front endpaper), covers bordered with French fillet and fleuron cornerpieces, raised bands, spine gilt in compartments featuring decorative bands, scrolling cornerpieces, fleuron centerpiece and small tools, maroon morocco labels, gilt inner dentelles, marbled endpapers, all edges gilt, 12 plates, all color by hand, bookplate of Robert Marceau; engraved title and two plates, little foxed, three plates slightly trimmed at fore edge, without apparent loss, few leaves with light marginal foxing, or soiling, otherwise excellent, plates bright and well preserved, leaves clean and fresh, sympathetic binding in mint condition. Phillip J. Pirages 59 - 331 2011 $400

Forester, Cecil Scott 1899-1966 *Josephine, Napoleon's Empress.* London: Methuen & Co., 1925. First edition; 218 x 145mm., vii (i), 246 pages, superb contemporary deep blue morocco by Sangorski & Sutcliffe for Asprey with more than 60 onlays, front cover with center medallion featuring onlaid teal blue crossed "J's", surrounded by gilt wreath and crown as well as onlaid pink flowers, lovely gilt floral sprays with more onlaid pink flowers in corners of both covers, raised bands, spine beautifully gilt and onlaid in same floral vine pattern, doublures of crimson morocco with onlaid blue flowers in corners as well as intricate series of patterned rules against deep blue morocco border, front doublure with fine inset hand painted ivory miniature of Josephine, watered silk free endpapers, gilt edges, in slightly scuffed but sturdy and attractive morocco backed plush-lined folding cloth box, gilt titling on spine; with 12 illustrations, all photos of portraits, as called for, choice binding in immaculate condition. Phillip J. Pirages 59 - 96 2011 $5500

Hyde, H. Montgomery *John Law. the History of an Honest Adventurer.* London: W. H. Allen, 1969. Revised edition; pages 228, top edge gilt, 9 plates, three quarter crimson levant morocco gilt by Sangorski & Sutcliffe, spine trifle mellowed, original dust jacket bound in at end, author's own copy with his Lamb House bookplate initialled NR 1964. R. F. G. Hollett & Son Antiquarian Booksellers   175 - 698 2011   £85

Hyde, H. Montgomery *Room 3603.* Mayflower-Dell, 1964. Small 8vo., three quarter crimson levant morocco gilt by Sangorski & Sutcliffe, spine rather mellowed, pages 286, (ii), top edge gilt with 9 plates, original paperback wrappers bound in, author's own copy his Lamb House bookplate initialled NR.   R. F. G. Hollett & Son Antiquarian Booksellers 175 - 700 2011   £65

Hyde, H. Montgomery *The Trials of Oscar Wilde.* William Hodge and Co., 1948. First edition; pages (x), 384, top edge gilt, 16 plates, three quarter green levant morocco gilt by Sangorski & Sutcliffe, spine little mellowed, author's own copy with his Lamb House bookplate initialled NR 1964. R. F. G. Hollett & Son Antiquarian Booksellers   175 - 701 2011   £140

Lowell, James Russell   1819-1891   *The Writings.* London: Macmillan and Co., 1890. Riverside edition; 193 x 130mm., 10 volumes beautiful early 20th century olive green textured calf, handsomely gilt by Sangorski & Sutcliffe (stamp signed on verso of front free endpaper), covers with double ruled gilt border and blindstamped in basket weave pattern, raised bands, spines lavishly gilt in compartments with central cruciform ornament framed by wide densely gilt cornerpieces, filled with leaves, flowers and small tools, each with two maroon morocco labels, turn-ins gilt in lacy filigree, marbled endpapers, top edge gilt, other edges rough trimmed, 3 volumes with portrait frontispiece, light rubbing and flaking to one joint (only), spines uniformly sunned to a mellow olive brown, one leaf with triangular tear at upper right just into text (no loss), isolated very minor stains or foxing, otherwise beautiful set in fine condition, handsome bindings very lustrous with no significant wear, text fresh, clean and bright.   Phillip J. Pirages   59 - 135 2011 $1750

Moore, Thomas   1779-1852   *Lalla Rookh, an Oriental Romance.* London: printed for Longman, Hurst, Rees, Orme and Brown, 1817. First edition; 292 x 222mm., 2 p.l., 405, (1) pages, nothing short of spectacular early 20th century dark blue levant morocco extravagantly gilt, richly inlaid and gloriously bejewelled by Sangorski & Sutcliffe (stamp-signed on front doublure), binding with overall Oriental design (befitting the poem) with upper cover featuring a sunken central panel, its unusual nine-sided shape resembling a clump of hanging grapes, within which two birds of paradise, inlaid in lilac, green and brown morocco with two rubies for eyes, perch in a grape arbor, its inlaid leaves with fruit clusters on densely stippled gilt around accented with 19 turquoises, the whole central tableau surrounded by a border of interweaving bands of inlaid brown morocco set with 9 bands of Mother-of-Pearl, the entire sunken panel surrounded by two ornate frames filled with flowering vines of Oriental design composed of hundreds of pieces of inlaid morocco in red, blue, violet and green on a background of brown morocco and heavily stippled gilt, outer frame accented with 20 blue chalcedonies and 20 garnets; lower cover with similar frame and central panel, this one featuring two lovebirds inlaid with multiple colors and with two amethyst eyes, birds in a similar grape arbor above, large Mother-of-Pearl heart, panel further adorned with 3 sapphires, four blue chalcedonies five turquoises, four Carnelians and 10 additional bands of Mother-of-Pearl, raised bands, spine gilt in compartments with large inlaid arabesque in green and brown morocco on a gilt background, gilt titling on inlaid compartments of chestnut brown morocco, glorious front doublure of ivory morocco covered in gilt vines with inlaid violet morocco flowers, the whole framed in green morocco decorated with gilt vines and red morocco posies and berries, at center, a hand painted Cosway-Style portrait of author on ivory surrounded by gilt frame, with 12 flowers composed of no fewer than 72 turquoises and 36 garnets, oval portrait in sunken panel enclosed by wreath of inlaid morocco flowers, rear doublure of similar design, but its medallion featuring 8 amethysts set among sinuously curving inlaid lilac strapwork twining around a large (approximately one carat) Mexican fire opal encircled by 12 pearls, the binding containing 226 jewels in all; free endleaves of cream colored watered silk, gilt edges, in original well made (somewhat scuffed), silk and plush lined blue morocco box with shuttered lid; extra illustrated with 12 hand colored engraved plates mounted on lettered Japan vellum bookplate of Charles J. Rosenbloom; two leaves with neatly renewed marginal tears, but magnificent copy of a masterpiece of bookbinding.   Phillip J. Pirages 59 - 111 2011 $65,000

Moore, Thomas   1779-1852   *Paradise and the Peri.* London: 1909. Quarto, beautiful frontispiece with elaborate burnished gold, additional 8 miniatures, beautifully bound by Sangorski & Sutcliffe in full royal blue levant morocco jeweled binding.   Heritage Book Shop   Booth A12 51st NY International Antiquarian Book Fair April 8-10 2011 - 111 2011 $30,000

Moynier *De La Truffe, Traite Complet de ce Tubercule, Contenant sa Description et son Histoire Naturelle la Plus Detaillee, on Exploitation Commerciale et sa Position dans l'Art Culinaire...* Paris: Barba an Legrand et Bergougnious, 1836. 8vo., pages 204, uncut, internally excellent with only little light spotting, publisher's wrappers, blue, text in black, worn at spine with some loss, upper panel partially detached, light blue morocco backed clamshell box lined with fine chamois leather by Sangorski & Sutcliffe, bookplate of Eleanor Lowenstein, rare, entirely unsophisticated. Simon Finch Rare Books   Zero - 128   2011   £2000

Pepys, Samuel   1633-1703   *The Diary.*   London: G. Bell and Sons Lts., 1924.   188 x 120mm., 8 volumes bound in 3, fine contemporary terra cotta rushed morocco by Sanorski & Sutcliffe (singe don front turn-ins), double gilt fillet border on covers, upper covers with gilt insignia incorporating the initials "S P", crossed anchors and looping ropes with Pepys' (misspelled) motto in Latin on a ribbon above it, raised bands, spines gilt in double ruled compartments with central ornament of either a crown, a sailor's knot, an anchor or crossed quills, turn-ins ruled in gilt, marbled endpapers, all edges gilt, frontispiece, spines slightly and uniformly sunned toward pink, otherwise extremely pleasing set in beautiful condition inside and out.   Phillip J. Pirages   59 - 137   2011 $1250

Poe, Edgar Allan   1809-1849   *Tales of Mystery and Imagination.*   London: George G. Harrap & Co., 1935. Limited to 460 numbered copies (of which 450 were for sale), One of 10 special copies with original watercolor drawing, signed by artist; containing original watercolor drawing on inserted leaf, signed and dated "Arthur Rackham/1935", large quarto, (2, blank), 317, (1), (2, blank) pages, 12 mounted color plates with descriptive tissue guards, 17 black and white plates, 11 small black and white drawings in text by Arthur Rackham, specially bound by Sangorski Sutcliffe (stamp-signed in gilt) in full green morocco, covers stamped in gilt, top edge gilt, others uncut, "Cockerell" marbled endpapers, original black and white pictorial endpapers bound in at front and back, spine slightly faded, otherwise fine, in original cardboard slipcase with printed spine label, matching limitation number, lower edge of slipcase expertly and almost invisibly replaced, housed in quarter morocco clamshell box.   David Brass Rare Books, Inc.   May 26 2011 - 00267   2011 $37,500

Swinburne, Algernon Charles   1837-1909   *Pasiphae.* Waltham St. Lawrence: Golden Cockerel Press, 1950. One of 100 specially bound volumes with an extra engraving; (of a total of 500 printed), 229 x 152mm., 2 p.l., 5-40 pages, beet colored vellum, stamp signed on front pastedown by Sangorski & Sutcliffe, gilt titling on spine, head of a bull in gilt on cover, top edge gilt, other edges untrimmed, buckram slipcase (just slightly worn), 7 charming copper engravings by John Buckland Wright (including titlepage), spine slightly and uniformly sunned, cover slightly faded, with color lost on corners and right at fore edges, otherwise fine.   Phillip J. Pirages   59 - 224   2011 $375

Binding – Schulze, Otto, & Co.

Burns, Robert   1759-1796   *Songs.*   Edinburgh: printed by George Robb and Co. for Otto Schulze and Co., 1901. One of 500 copies; 220 x 180mm., 3 p.l. including half title, 99 pages, (3) leaves (index and colophon), lovely contemporary olive brown crushed morocco by Otto Schulze & Co. of Edinburgh (signed on front turn-in), covers with single gilt rule border, upper cover with 11 horizontal bows of gilt and inlaid red morocco thistles, the thistles (numbering 72 in all), separated by small round tools, two raised bands flanked by gilt rules, gilt vertical titling, turn-ins with single gilt rule top edge gilt, woodcut title and frontispiece surrounded by wide, elaborate border of twining thistles and bluebells, large woodcut initials foliated with similar thistles and bluebells at beginning of each poem; spine a definite (pleasing) brown rather than an olive brown, minor offsetting from turn-ins to endleaves, slender trailing two inch marginal (glue?), stain to last two pages of index, occasional thumbing and other trivial imperfections, otherwise fine, text and decorations clean, fresh and bright, handsome binding lustrous and unworn.   Phillip J. Pirages   59 - 138   2011 $750

Binding – Seargeant's Abergavenny

Inchbald, Elizabeth   *A Simple Story.*   London: Richard Bentley, 1833.   Half title, bound at Seargeant's Abergavenny in contemporary half dark green calf, armorial bookplate of Edward K. E. Mardon, very good.   Jarndyce Antiquarian Booksellers   CXCI - 216   2011   £40

Binding – Seton

MacDonald, George   1824-1905   *Exotics.*   London: Strahan & Co., 1876.   First edition; half title, original brown cloth, bevelled boards blocked in gilt, slightly dulled, binder's ticket of Seton, Edinburgh, very good.   Jarndyce Antiquarian Booksellers   CXCII - 203   2011   £850

Binding – Settle, Smith

Chaucer, Geoffrey   1340-1400   *The Works of...* London: Folio Society, 2002. First edition thus, number 44 of 1010 copies; full Nigerian white goatskin designed by David Eccles after T. J. Cobden Sanderson; the paper, specially made at James Cropper Mill at Burneside in Cumbria and supplied by John Purcell Paper, binding design redrawn by Eccles from a copy of the Kelmscott Chaucer bound by Coben-Sanderson, elaborate gilt decorated binding by Smith Settle at Otley, Yorkshire, excellent slipcase (bumped at one corner), with gilt goatskin spine label, tipped in at front of slipcase is 15 page booklet with essay by William Peterson on Kelmscott Chaucer.   Any Amount of Books   May 26 2011 - A68251   2011 $1761

Gill, Eric 1882-1940 *The Engravings.* Wellingborough: Christopher Skelton, 1983. First edition, 1350 copies; folio, original two-tone cloth gilt by Smith Settle, upper board blindstampd with design by Gill, slipcase, pages xxiv, 545, with over 1000 illustrations, fine.   R. F. G. Hollett & Son Antiquarian Booksellers   General Catalogue Summer 2010 - 172   2011   £450

Binding – Sickles

Turgenieff, Ivan 1818-1883 *The Jew and Other Stories.* New York: Charles Scribner's Sons, 1904. 213 x 145mm., viii, (2), 357 pages; lovely contemporary dark rose colored morocco, ornately gilt by Sickles (stamp signed), covers with border of double gilt rules enclosing an Art Nouveau style frame of wavy rules connecting large cornerpieces, these with small oval medallion of onlaid black morocco, enclosed by gilt drawer handle tools and leafy sprays, upper cover with circular stylized monogram of "CEB" at center, raised bands, spines gilt in double ruled compartments decorated with drawer handles and circlets, wide turn-ins with gilt frame featuring pretty fleuron cornerpieces, ivory watered silk pastedowns and free endleaves, top edge gilt, frontispiece; spine evenly faded to soft rose, 3 leaves with uneven fore edges from rough opening, half a dozen leaves with corner creased, other trival imperfections but fine, text clean, fresh and bright, handsome binding lustrous and virtually unworn.   Phillip J. Pirages   59 - 335 2011 $375

Turgenieff, Ivan 1818-1883 *Phantoms and Other Stories.* New York: Charles Scribner's Sons, 1904. 213 x 145mm., ix, (3), 321 pages, lovely contemporary dark rose colored morocco, ornately gilt by Sickles (stamp signed), covers with border of double gilt rules enclosing an Art Nouveau style frame of wavy rules connecting large cornerpieces, these with small oval medallion of onlaid black morocco enclosed by gilt drawer handle tools and leafy sprays, upper cover with circular stylized monogram of "CEB" at center, raised bands, spines gilt in double ruled compartments, decorated with drawer handles and circlets, wide turn-ins with gilt frame featuring pretty fleuron cornerpieces, ivory watered silk pastedowns and free endleaves, top edge gilt, frontispiece, except for even fading of spine, very fine, pretty copy.   Phillip J. Pirages   59 - 336 2011 $350

Binding – Smith, J. P. J.

Stockdale, James *Annales Caermoelenses; or Annals of Cartmel.* Ulverston: William Kitchin, 1872. First edition; thick 8vo., modern full maroon morocco gilt over bevelled boards with raised bands and double spine labels by J. P. J. Smith of Cartmel, with matching slipcase, pages (ii), 595, (iii), 2, vii, top edge gilt, complete with engraved frontispiece, 4 photos plates, genealogical table printed in red and black, gilt ruled dentelles and patterned endpapers, few neat repairs, scattered foxing, very scarce.   R. F. G. Hollett & Son Antiquarian Booksellers   173 - 1080 2011   £350

Binding – Smith, W. H.

Cervantes Saavedra, Miguel De 1547-1616 *The First (and Second) Part of the Histoty of the Various and Wittie Knight-Errant Don Quixote of the Mancha.* Ashendene Press, 1927-1928. One of 225 copies; 2 volumes, text in the 1620 English translation of Thomas Shelton, original luxurious white pigskin by W. H. Smith, thick raised bands, gilt titling on spine, sturdy cloth double slipcases (little marked), morocco labels, lovely woodcut initials and borders designed by Louise Powell, cut on wood by W. M. Quick and George H. Ford, bookplate of Vincent Lloyd-Russell in each volume, as well as shadow of another small bookplate now removed; pigskin of first volume, just shade different from second (a common defect as the volumes issued more than a year apart), in all other ways, extremely fine, magnificent binding unusually clean, text in perfect condition.   Phillip J. Pirages 59 - 76 2011 $9500

Malory, Thomas *The Noble and Joys Book Entitled Le Morte D'Arthur...* Chelsea: The Ashendene Press, 1913. Limited to 145 copies and the most deluxe format; folio, (6 blank, 4) xxii, 500, (2, 8 blank) pages, 29 woodcut illustrations, 2 full page, initials in red and blue by and after Graily Hewitt, original full dark brown calf designed by Douglas Cockerell and executed by W. H. Smith, binder, raised bands, gilt stamped spine title, neatly rebacked preserving original covers, fine.   Jeff Weber Rare Books   163 - 106 2011 $8000

Binding – Sotheran

Addison, Joseph 1672-1719 *The Works.* London: George Bell and Sons, 1893-1898. 7 volumes, 185 x 115 mm., attractive contemporary prize binding of light polished calf done for H. Sotheran & Co. (stamp signed on front turn-in of each volume), covers with double gilt fillet border, upper board of each volume with central gilt crest of St. Peter's College, Westminster, raised bands, spines ornately gilt in compartments with elegant central floral spray, surrounded by a lozenge of small tools and elaborate side and cornerpieces composed of fleurons, curls, volutes and circulets, two pale green morocco labels, filigree gilt turn-ins, marbled endpapers, all edges gilt, volume I with portrait frontispiece and 8 plates of medal and coin designs, pastedown with affixed presentation certificate to B. H. Willet, signed by William ("Gulielmus") Rutherford and dated 1899, leather with bit of dryness, extremities little rubbed, labels slightly faded, one minor neatly repaired tear (into text, but no loss), otherwise fine, elaborately gilt bindings lustrous and with other minor wear and text virtually pristine, pretty set.   Phillip J. Pirages   59 - 62 2011 $275

Boswell, James 1740-1795 *Boswell's Life of Johnson Including Boswell's Journal of a Tour to the Hebrides and Johnson's Diary of a Journey into North Wales.* Oxford: at the Clarendon Press, 1887. 6 volumes, 229 x 152mm., especially pleasing contemporary prize bindings of polished calf, handsomely gilt for H. Sotheran & Co. (stamp signed on front pastedown), boards with gilt double rule border and with gilt scholastic arms on each of the six front covers, raised bands, spines elaborately gilt in compartments featuring scrolling foliate cornerpieces and intricate floral centerpiece, brown morocco labels, ornate gilt turn-ins, marbled endpapers, all edges gilt, with 14 plates as called for (8 of them folding), including facsimiles of Johnson's handwriting, map and chart of Johnson's contemporaries; Latin presentation bookplate to J. Mavrogordato indicating that this set was a prize given to him by the headmaster, William Rutherford of the College of Saint Peter, Westminster, one volume with very minor flaking to one join, odd trivial mark to covers but in exceptionally fine condition, bindings essentially unworn and text probably unread. Phillip J. Pirages 59 - 155 2011 $1800

Galsworthy, John 1867-1933 *The Forsythe Saga.* London: Heinemann, 1936. Pages 1104, contemporary three quarter calf gilt by Sotheran, corners and edges little rubbed and darkened, extending genealogy, top edge gilt. R. F. G. Hollett & Son Antiquarian Booksellers General Catalogue Summer 2010 - 784 2011 £45

Galsworthy, John 1867-1933 *A Modern Comedy.* London: Heinemann, 1936. Pages 1088, contemporary three quarter calf gilt by Sotheran, corners and edges little rubbed and darkened, top edge gilt, extending genealogy. R. F. G. Hollett & Son Antiquarian Booksellers General Catalogue Summer 2010 - 785 2011 £45

Manson, James A. *Sir Edwin Landseer, R.A.* London: Walter Scott Publishing Co. Ltd., 1902. First edition; octavo, (i-vi), vii-xvi, 219, (220) pages, titlepage printed in blue and black, 21 engraved plates and photogravure frontispiece, full dark green levant Cosway-stye binding by Riviere & Sons for Sotheran & Co., stamp signed to front turn-in, spine decoratively tooled and lettered in gilt, after floral and leaf design, compartments ruled in gilt, front and back covers ruled and decoratively tooled in a gilt floral and leaf design, surrounding 10 oval-round miniature paintings under glass, 9 miniatures on front cover depict 8 hunting dogs around a stag, miniature on back cover is portrait of Landseer, extremities double ruled in gilt, with turn-ins ruled and decoratively tooled in gilt, green marbled endpapers, joints expertly and totally invisibly repaired, fine, housed in original burgundy roan slipcase,. David Brass Rare Books, Inc. May 26 2011 - 01191 2011 $23,500

Thackeray, William Makepeace 1811-1863 *The Works.* London: Smith, Elder & Co., 1898. 26 volumes, near contemporary three quarter calf gilt by Sotheran with raised bands and double spine labels, top edge gilt, endpapers marbled, illustrations by author, handsome, sound set. R. F. G. Hollett & Son Antiquarian Booksellers General Catalogue Summer 2010 - 679 2011 £750

Binding – Sparre, Eva

Morris, William 1834-1896 *Gothic Architecture: a Lecture for the Arts and Crafts Exhibition Society.* Kelmscott Press, 1893. One of 1500 copies on paper (there were also 45 on vellum); 145 x 110mm., 1 p.., 68 pages, remarkably graceful contemporary calf modelled to an Art Nouveau design by Eva Sparre (signed with her initials at bottom of front cover), upper board dominated by graceful anthhemion of leaves emerging from an intricately tooled base (which resembled stylized feathers, perhaps from a peacock), titling inscribed in blind on either side of this large central object, back covers with floral medallion in middle, flat spine edges untrimmed, woodcut initials and small woodcut decorations in text, headlines and sidenotes printed in red, dozen little spots (perhaps from water droplets) on front cover and two dozen on back, small chip at head of spine, endpapers with offsetting from leather turn-ins, three or four pages with tiny dots of foxing, otherwise excellent, binding with very little wear to joints or extremities, text quite clean and fresh. Phillip J. Pirages 59 - 141 2011 $2500

Binding – Squires

Marsh, Anne *Two Old Men's Tales. the Deformed and The Admiral's Daughter.* London: Richard Bentley, 1844. Contemporary half olive green morocco by Squires of Woolwich, gilt spine, spine faded to brown, little rubbed at head, bookplate of Colonel William Kemmis of Ballincor, nice copy. Jarndyce Antiquarian Booksellers CLXC - 245 2011 £58

Binding – Staggemeier & Welcher

Fenelon, Francois Salignac De La Mothe, Abp. 1651-1715 *Les Aventures de Telemaque.* Paris: Imprimerie de Monsieur (i.e. Pierre Francois Didot, 1785. 340 x 264mm., 4 p.l., 305, (1) pages; 2 p.l., 297, (3) pages, 2 volumes bound in 1; elegant red contemporary straight grain morocco by Staggemeier & Welcher, the covers with wide gilt border, composed of onlaid strips of blue goatskin onlay at corners tooled with a medallion, and with an inner frame composed of onlaid citron goatskin band and large, graceful gilt impressions of flowers, foliage, and ears of wheat; smooth spine divided into four unequal compartments by a strip of onlaid green goatskin tooled with gilt pentaglyph and metope roll, lettered in second compartment on green goatskin label and directly on spine at foot, the first compartment tooled with a face-in-the-sun, third (elongated) compartment featuring a strange figure with winged helmet holding festoons of flowers balancing on top of a flower issuing from a large neo-classical vase, vase in turn perched on a candelabrum, edges of boards and turn-ins tooled with gilt rolls, marbled endpapers, all edges gilt; with fore-edge painting, very probably contemporary, of two boats sailing on a lake with a stately home in background; engraved printer's device on titlepages and two frontispiece portraits of author engraved by Dequevauviller, one in early state before letters, and one printed on India paper and mounted; hint of wear to corners, spine little darkened, slight variation in color of leather covers, other minor defects, but extremely handsome binding entirely solid, nothing approaching a significant fault, covers especially lustrous with bright gilt, intermittent pale foxing in text (few gatherings with faint overall browning or more noticeably foxed), leaves remarkably fresh (they crackle as you turn them), very clean and printed within vast margins. Phillip J. Pirages   59 - 40   2011 $9500

Binding – Steadman, R. D.

Kingsley, Charles 1819-1875 *Westward Ho!* Cambridge: Macmillan, 1855. First edition; 3 volumes, half titles, handsomely bound in tan calf by R. D. Steadman, Newcastle upon Tyne, gilt borders, raised bands, gilt compartments & dentelles, brown and dark green morocco labels, some slight marking or darkening to boards, armorial bookplates of Walter Powell Jeffreys, very good, handsome. Jarndyce Antiquarian Booksellers   CXCI - 529   2011   £450

Binding – Stikeman

Conrad, Joseph 1857-1924 *The Works.* Garden City and New Yorj: Doubleday Page & Co., 1920-1926. Sun Dial edition, one of 735 copies signed by author; 22 volumes, 220 x 150mm., fine and especially flamboyant lilac morocco, elaborately gilt by Stikeman, covers panelled with single and double gilt fillets and intricate scrolling foliate cornerpieces, raised bands, spine attractively gilt in ruled compartments with margin ornaments (seashell or anchor) as centerpiece and with scrolling cornerpieces, crimson morocco doublures, front doublures with central panel to blue morocco, wide turn-ins with alternating floral tools, doublures decorated with very gilt lines and (at corners) floral bouquets, blue central panels with large gilt sailing vessel at middle, watered silk endleaves, morocco hinges, all edges gilt, frontispiece; with APS by author to James Brand Pinker (Conrad's agent) tipped in at front, also with signature of Richard Curle; spines uniformly faded to an even chestnut brown, hint of rubbing to handful of joints and corners (only), one opening in one volume with marginal spots, but quite fine set in very decorative bindings, text virtually pristine, volumes completely solid, covers bright and wear to leather entirely minor.   Phillip J. Pirages   59 - 168   2011 $15,000

Hearn, Lafcadio 1850-1904 *Writings.* Boston: Houghton Mifflin Co., 1922. Limited to 750 numbered copies; 16 volumes, octavo, mounted color frontispiece and photograuvre plates, mostly from photos by Charles S. Olcott, several in color and mounted, all on Japanese vellum, with descriptive tissue guards, text illustrations, handsomely bound by Stikeman in contemporary three quarter maroon morocco ruled in gilt over lilac cloth boards, spines with two raised bands decoratively tooled and lettered in gilt, marbled endpapers, top edge gilt, others uncut, fine set. David Brass Rare Books, Inc.   May 26 2011 - 01581   2011 $5750

Irving, Washington 1783-1859 *History of New York, from the Beginning of the World to the End of the Dutch Dynasty.* New York: published by Inskeep & Bradford, 1809. First edition; 2 volumes, 12mo, xxiii, (1, blank), 268, (2, blank); (2 blank) (2) 258, (2, blank) pages, rare folding frontispiece bound in by bottom edge, full red morocco, ruled in gilt on boards and spine, lettered in gilt on spine, bound by Stikeman & Co. NY, all edges gilt, marbled endpapers, small repair to plate at fold, repair to small portion of top edge of titlepage (probably to remove former owner's name), tops of spines very lightly rubbed, pages 140 and 246 volume II, with few ink underlines, very good. Heritage Book Shop   Holiday 2010 - 59   2011 $2750

Porter, William Sydney 1862-1910 *The Complete Writings of O. Henry.* Garden City: Doubleday Page and co., 1917. One of 1075 copies, Memorial edition and edition deluxe; 230 x 150mm., 14 volumes, lavishly gilt by Stikeman, covers with very broad and animated gilt borders of swirling foliage flowers and butterflies in style of Derome, raised bands, spine compartments attractively gilt with antique tools, red morocco doublures with multiple rules and other gilt elaboration, watered silk free endleaves, top edge gilt, other edges untrimmed, entirely unopened; with 90 plates, including colored frontispiece in each volume, the one in volume 1 signed by artist and engraved half title with vignette, signed by publisher; original tissue guards, prelim page of first volume with folding leaf of manuscript, apparently in Porter's hand, tipped in; titlepages and half titles in blue and black; spines evenly sunned, one leaf with minor marginal tear at fore edge, otherwise extraordinarily beautiful set in virtually faultless condition. Phillip J. Pirages   59 - 281   2011 $11,500

Binding – Stoakley

Bunyan, John 1628-1688 *A Book for Boys and Girls.* London: Elliot Stock, 1889. Large paper copy; large square 8vo., later quarter levant morocco gilt by Stoakley of Cambridge (but unsigned), pages xxvi, 79, top edge gilt, untrimmed, handsome.   R. F. G. Hollett & Sons Antiquarian Booksellers   170 - 117   2011   £120

Binding – Taylor & Hessey

Montgomery, James *The World Before the Flood.* London: printed for Longman, Hurst, Rees, Orme and Brown, 1814. Third edition; 168 x 103mm., xvi, (2), 328 pages, attractive and intriguing contemporary calf, heavily gilt by Taylor and Hessey (board edges along fore edge stamp signed in gilt), covers with wide filigree gilt frame, large central panel dominated by an elongated octagon painted in black with gold dot at each of its eight corners, these corners radiating stippled gilt lines that intersect to form 12 triangles of various sizes plus a large central lozenge (lozenge also with gilt dots at its four angles), wide raised bands decorated in blind dividing the spine into four panels, gilt titling, turn-ins with gilt broken cables, all edges gilt, expertly rebacked using original spine, with very pretty fore-edge painting of Pope's Villa at Twickenham, small abrasions to lower spine, bit discolored and with gilt difficult to read, partly because it is so small, tiny nicks here and there in painting, still excellent copy, text unusually clean and fresh, binding solidly restored and with only minor wear, painting generally quite well preserved.   Phillip J. Pirages   59 - 197   2011 $950

Pope, Alexander 1688-1744 *The Poetical Works of Alexander Pope with His Life by Samuel Johnson.* London: printed by Whittingham and Howard for Sharpe and Hailes, 1811. 222 x 142 mm., 2 volumes, once very striking and still quite handsome contemporary crimson straight grain morocco by Taylor & Hessey (stamp-signed on the narrow board edge of upper cover of each volume), covers with border of thick and thin gilt rules enclosing a fine lacy gilt frame incorporating palmettes and volutes, inner frame formed by single gilt rule terminating at corners in floral sprays, raised bands dividing spine into four large and three small panels, the three narrow panels featuring a gilt rosette flanked by fleurons, the large panels at head and tail with prominent ornate fleuron on a stippled background with scalloped edges, and two middle panels with gilt titling, all edges gilt, the two fore edges with especially attractive paintings of Windsor Castle and Twickenham, frontispiece portraits, 16 engraved plates; contemporary ink ownership inscription of "Miss M(argare)t Rigden", spines uniformly faded to soft rose (with consequent slight muting of gilt), joints and extremities bit rubbed (though well refurbished), considerable foxing to plates as well as foxing and offsetting to adjacent leaves, other trivial imperfections, nevertheless very appealing set in important ways, elegant original bindings entirely sound and with lustrous boards, text almost entirely very smooth and fresh, fore edge paintings in excellent state of preservation.   Phillip J. Pirages   59 - 198   2011 $2900

Young, Edward *Night Thoughts and a Paraphrase on Part of the Book of Job.* London: printed at the Chiswick Press by C. Whittingham for Taylor and Hessey, 1812. 240 x 145mm., lxvi, (2), 353, (1) pages, striking contemporary black morocco elaborately tooled in blind and gilt by Taylor & Hessey (board edges at middle on either side of painting stamped in gilt "Taylor and Hessey/Booksellers London"), covers with frame outlined by gilt rules and with cornerpieces in form of a stylized gilt satire, frame also featuring a chain of blindstamped oval medallions connected by palm fronds of an unusual ground of blind stippling, the whole enclosing a large central panel ornately tooled in blind, with cornerpieces composed of shells, leaves and volutes and with intricate sunburst medallion centerpiece, central panel further decorated in blind with complex of elaborate strapwork between the centerpiece and cornerpieces, highlighted by botanical and other tools, raised bands, spine with rows of gilt tools at head and tail, three spine panels tooled in blind and highlighted with gilt lancets with flowers, gilt turn-ins in Greek key style, all edges gilt, with exceptionally fine fore-edge painting depicting Westminster Bridge and Westminster Hall; with engraved frontispiece, armorial bookplate of David Gill, ink presentation inscription "Eliza Gill/the gift of her attached and affectionate Husband/Decem(ber) 3rd 1812", joints and extremities with touch of rubbing (though well marked with dye), offsetting to titlepage from frontispiece, occasional trivial imperfections internally, exceptionally pleasing copy, binding especially lustrous, text unusually clean, fresh and bright, painting beautifully preserved.   Phillip J. Pirages   59 - 199   2011 $2500

Binding – Thibaron

Gresset, Jean Baptiste Louis *Poemes.* Paris: D. Jouaust, 1867. One of 2 copies Printed on vellum, there were also 118 on paper; 215 x 140mm., 6 p.l., (two vellum blanks, half title, title, two frontispieces (on paper), iv, 132 pages, (4) leaves (variants, contents/colophon, two vellum blanks), folio Cii unsigned and misnumbered but copy complete; very attractive contemporary midnight blue crushed morocco handsomely gilt by Thibaron (stamp signed), covers with French fillet border, raised bands, spines ornately gilt in compartments filled with delicately stipped swirling designs accented with small tools, gilt inner dentelles, marbled endpapers, all edges gilt, 9 engraved on (on paper), 2 frontispiece portraits, 7 plates, large paper copy, bookplates of Robert Hoe and Mortimer Schiff, engraved bookplate of Marcellus Schlimovich, library stamp of Sociedad Hebraica Argentina, just hint of wear top and bottom of joints, one side of first and last vellum flyleaf discolored (apparently from a reaction to the gilt on pastedowns(?), plates with variable freckled foxing (never serious), otherwise fine, elegant binding quite lustrous and leaves clean, fresh and bright. Phillip J. Pirages 59 - 343 2011 $3250

Binding – Thistle Bindery

Robinson, Alan James *Cetacea, The Great Whales.* Easthampton: Cheloniidae Press, 1981. Artist's own copy, artist's proof #1, signed by artist, binders and printer, Harold Patrick McGrath; all on Arches Cover Buff, page size 22 x 15 inches, bound loose as issued with sheets laid in a full black Niger oasis goat folder sculpted in low relief with head of a Right Whale by David Bourbeau at The Thistle Bindery, beautiful folder housed in quarter leather moroccan goat drop back box by Gray Parrot, short split at lower joint of box, else fine; the 7 bleed etchings by Robinson depict the major species of whales, numerous blindstamped line-cut and two wood engravings, text contains biological information, 12 two-color maps showing migration routes and breeding areas printed by Harold McGrath at Hampshire Typothetae; artist printed at Cheloniidae Press. Priscilla Juvelis - Rare Books 48 - 5 2011 $3000

Binding – Thompson Bros.

Hoggarth, James *Echoes from Years Gone By.* Kendal: Thompson Brothers, 1892. Pages x, 168, very scarce, affixed to pastedown is ALS from author soliciting purchase of his book, original brown cloth gilt by Thompson Bros. of Kendal. R. F. G. Hollett & Son Antiquarian Booksellers 173 - 562 2011 £140

Binding – Thouvenin

Commines, Philippe De, Sieur D'Argenton 1445-1511 *Les Memoires.* A Leide: Chez les Elzeviers, 1648. Derniere edition; 140 x 80 mm., 12 p.l., 765, (19) pages, very pretty early 19th century dark green morocco by Thouvenin (stamp-signed at tail of spine), covers with large frame formed by decorative rules and dense, complex cornerpieces in blind, this frame punctuated with a dozen thick gilt dots and enclosing an intricate lozenge in blind and gilt featuring elegant flowers, fronds and seashells, as well as many small tools and curls, raised bands, spine compartments with small, simplie gilt lozenge at center of very elaborate quatrefoil fleuron in blind, gilt turn-ins, salmon pink watered silk endpapers, all edges gilt; with four tondo portraits; engraved bookplate of Bibliotheque L. Veydt; spine uniformly sunned to pleasing olive brown, first gathering with quarter inch dampstain to tail edge margin, occasional minor foxing or other trivial imperfections, especially appealing copy in fine condition, clean, fresh leaves, very lustrous binding showing only most superficial wear. Phillip J. Pirages 59 - 30 2011 $1250

Binding – Toovey, James

Bray, Anna Eliza *Life of Thomas Sothard.* London: John Murray, 1851. First edition; 217 x 172mm., xxiv, 246 pages, excellent contemporary dark green morocco, handsomely gilt by James Toovey (stamp signed), covers with French fillet border, raised bands, heavily gilt spine compartments featuring scrolling cornerpieces and large and intricate floral centerpiece, turn-ins densely gilt with botanical tools, marbled endpapers, all edges gilt, frontispiece, engraved titlepage frame and more than 50 illustrations in text; spine evenly faded to a pleasing olive brown, covers with just touch of fading and soiling, handful of pages with extensive freckled foxing, trivial to minor foxing in much of the rest of the text, still extremely fresh, in scarcely worn, very attractive decorative binding. Phillip J. Pirages 59 - 328 2011 $550

Binding – Tout

Bible. English - 1881 *The Gospel According to S. John.* Cambridge: Cambridge University Press, circa, 1881. Interleaves with plain rubricated pages, plain red calf, gilt dentelles & edges by Philip Tout, all edges gilt, inscribed "This gift to my father George MacDonald from Miss Violet Cavendish-Bentinck, now offered in much love & gratitude to the Rev. M. C. D'Arcy by Greville MacDonald". Jarndyce Antiquarian Booksellers CXCII - 335 2011 £250

Dickens, Charles   1812-1870   *Sketches by Boz.* London: John Macrone, 1836.   First edition; first printing (Whiting), 2 volumes, 12mo., (i-iii) iv-v (vi-vii) viii, (1) 2-348; (i-iv), (1) 2-342, 16 engraved plates by George Cruikshank; bound by Tout in full green morocco, covers decoratively ruled in gilt, spines lettered and decoratively tooled in gilt in compartments, gilt dentelles, all edges gilt, rust color coated endpapers, bit of light browning to plates as usual, still excellent copy,.   Heritage Book Shop   Holiday 2010 - 29   2011 $2500

Dickens, Charles   1812-1870   *Works.* London: Chapman & Hall, n.d., 1874-1891.   Reprint of illustrated library edition; octavo, 30 volumes, plates, late 19th century full tan polished calf by Tout (stamp signed on verso of front free endpaper), covers with gilt triple fillet border with gilt corner ornaments, spines elaborately tooled in gilt in compartments with five gilt dotted raised bands and red and green morocco gilt, others uncut, marbled endpapers, minor rubbing to extremities, headcaps on volumes IX, X, and XXI expertly repaired, small bookseller's ticket on rear pastedown of each volume, near fine, partially unopened.   David Brass Rare Books, Inc.   May 26 2011 - 00785   2011 $20,000

Gronow, Rees Howell   1794-1865   *The Reminiscences and Recollections of Captain Gronow, Being Anecdotes of the Camp Court, Clubs, and Society 1810-1860.*   London: John C. Nimmo, 1889.   One of 875 copies (this #10); 265 x 170 mm., 2 volumes extended to 4, especially lovely contemporary crimson crushed morocco, very lavishly gilt by Tout (stamp signed) covers with wide, elaborate gilt frames in the style of Derome, this intricate design rich with fleurons, volutes, curls, festoons an small floral tools, raised bands, spine gilt in double ruled compartments with central cruciform ornament sprouting curling leaves and flowers from its head and tail, these swirls accented with dotted rules and small tools filling the compartments, very wide turn-ins with complex curling botanical decoration, silk endleaves with tiny gold floral sprays, all edges gilt, frontispiece, 24 plates, all in two states as called for, one proof before letters on plate paper, other with captions on Whatman paper and colored by hand, extra illustrated with 227 plates, primarily portraits, 18 of these in color, armorial bookplate of William Ewert Baron Camrose pasted over bookplate of William Morris; hint of rubbing to corners, mild shelfwear, occasional minor foxing affecting inserted plates and adjacent leaves (as well as a small handful of other pages), quite handsome set, clean and fresh internally, sumptous bindings in fine condition, lustrous and virtually unworn.   Phillip J. Pirages   59 - 144   2011 $4800

Rowley, Hugh   *Gamosagammon or Hints on Hymen.* London: John Camden Hotten, n.d., 1871.   First edition; square 8vo., full tan calf gilt by Tout, boards elegantly panelled with triple fillets and cornerpieces, spine with raised bands and contrasting triple lettering pieces, pages xvi, 327, (xviii), all edges gilt, profusely illustrated by author, original cloth laid in at end, handsome copy.   R. F. G. Hollett & Son Antiquarian Booksellers   175 - 1157   2011   £180

Binding – Trautz-Bauzonnet

Tennyson, Alfred Tennyson, 1st Baron   1809-1892 *The Holy Grail.* New Rochelle: George D. Sproul, 1902. One of 30 copies (18 for America)) of the Saint Dunstan edition; this copy #5 especially prepared for socialite and philanthropist Elizabeth Stauffer Moore and signed by publisher and illuminator, 267 x 207mm., 52 unnumbered leaves, printed on one side only, all printed on vellum, arresting neo-gothic crushed morocco by Trautz-Bauzonnet (stamp signed), covers with outer frame of dark red flanked by onlaid green morocco adorned with gilt dots, each of the four sides of this frame with centered green framed roundel containing either a stylized gilt cross or a Christogram, frame enclosing a central panel of scarlet morocco with large central cross inlaid in white vellum decorated in Celtic pattern, red morocco square at center featuring a gilt chalice and inlaid white vellum Host, four small roundels (where the arms of the cross meet) with onlaid gilt and green shamrocks raised bands, vertical gilt titling inside dotted gilt frame, very pleasing onlaid white morocco doublures, surrounded and embellished by red and green morocco as well as gilt, repeating the cover frame and host and shamrock designs, vellum endleaves, all edges gilt; in original white silk box (fraying) with brass clasp, gilt titling along fore edge and padded satin interior, handsomely illuminated by W. Formilli in colors and gold, inevitable offsetting form doublure frame to vellum endleaves, some slight variation in whiteness of vellum, most leaves with hint of rumpling, otherwise handsome production in fine, creamy vellum leaves, bright colors and gold, lustrous, unworn binding.   Phillip J. Pirages   59 - 341   2011 $5000

Binding – Turnam

Cumberland and Westmorland Antiquarian & Archaeological Society   *Transactions - Old Series. Volumes 1-16.*   Kendal: T. Wilson, 1874-1899.   16 volumes matching half morocco gilt by Turnam of Carlisle, with raised bands and marbled boards, stamped in blind "Westminster Public Libraries" in roundel on upper boards, few old scrapes here and there, top edge gilt, uncut, numerous illustrations, diagrams, text drawings, folding pedigrees etc., all wrappers bound in, handsome complete run of this very scarce, each volume with armorial bookplate of Spencer Charles Ferguson and later label (small stamps to back of titles and few other places).   R. F. G. Hollett & Son Antiquarian Booksellers   173 - 287   2011   £2500

Binding – Warren

D'Oyly, George *The Life of William Sancroft, Archbishop of Canterbury.* London: John Murray, 1821. 2 volumes, 8vo., pages (iii-xvi, 470; (iv) 446 + engraved portrait frontispiece in volume 1, contemporary russia, spines tooled in gilt and in blind with 3 sets of triple raised bands, lettered/numbered/dated in gilt direct, boards alternatively gilt and blind decorative rolled and ruled with central diced panel, board edges 'broken-hatch' gilt at corners, turn-ins 'Grecian Key' roll gilt, 'French Shell' 'made' endpapers and all edges marbled, 3 color (green white & red) patterned 'flat' endbands, some light foxing, frontispiece offset, joints tiny bit rubbed and front joint volume 1 cracking but strong, signed binding, pink ticket "Warren/Bookseller/ & Stationer/ 19 Old Bond St" at top left of front pastedown of both volumes, ink stamp "Bound by Warren Old Bond St.", from the collection of Christopher Ernest Weston 1947-2010.   Unsworths Booksellers   24 - 20   2011   £200

Binding – Wascher-James, Sande

Wascher-James, Sande *In Your Hands.* Whidbey Island: 2010. Artist's book, one of 18 copies; all hand painted and digitally printed on Lutradur, designed and bound by Sande Wascher-James, signed and numbered by her on colophon, page size in shape of a hand 8 x 5.5 inches, hand shaped pages cut with Graphtec Robo cutter, 32 pages including covers, handsewn by artist in blue thread matching the Liberty of London floral fabric on which text and stamp images of women, especially Eleanor Roosevelt were collaged, scanned and then printed, housed in custom made box of pale blue handmade paper over boards with collage of stamp of Eleanor Roosevelt on lid.   Priscilla Juvelis - Rare Books   48 - 28   2011 $850

Binding – Webb, Wareing

Taylor, Joseph *Mirabilia; or the Wonders of Nature and Art.* London: F. J. Mason, 1829. First edition; 12mo., frontispiece and plates, untrimmed in original pink glazed cloth by Wareing Webb, Manchester, slightly chipped paper label (7s 6d), cloth faded mostly to brown, little rubbed, inscriptions and embossed stamp of James Smith, Darley Dale Nurseries, nice.   Jarndyce Antiquarian Booksellers   CXCI - 507   2011   £125

Binding – Welcher, Samuel

Le Sage, Alain Rene   1668-1747   *The Adventures of Gil Blas of Santillana.* London: printed for Richard Phillips, 1807. 4 volumes, 203 x 121mm., extremely pleasing contemporary deep blue straight grain morocco handsomely gilt by Samuel Welcher (with his ticket), covers bordered gilt with triple rules and framed with wide palmette roll, inside of which is a rule with small ring and floral tools at corners, raised bands, spines ornately gilt in lobed compartments featuring stippled ground, quatrefoil centerpiece with delicate foliate sprays at sides and fleurons at ends, turn-ins gilt with single rule an fleuron and ring tools at corners, all edges gilt, 100 copperplates by Warner, Tomlinson and others, extra illustrated with 60 plates by Conrad Martin Metz for a total of 160 engravings; armorial bookplate of H. Holland Edwards, Pennant Ereithlyn, North Wales; front joints just little flaked, backstrips slightly sunned, covers with minor variation in color, several plates little foxed, generally only in margins and more frequently on added plates), one leaf with light ink stain in lower margin, light dampstain in margin at head of one plate, isolated very minor marginal soiling, very pleasing set, decorative bindings very well preserved and internally clean, fresh and bright.   Phillip J. Pirages   59 - 254   2011 $1800

Binding – Wells

Arnold, Matthew   1822-1888   *Poems.* London: Macmillan, 1888-1890. Volume 1 Popular edition, volumes II & III New edition; 3 volumes, half titles, full dark brown morocco by Wells of Winchester, gilt, gilt dentelles, decorated endpapers, slightly rubbed, contemporary inscription, all edges gilt, very good, handsome set.   Jarndyce Antiquarian Booksellers   CXCI - 52   2011   £150

Binding – Werner, Arno

Baskin, Leonard *Birds and Animals.* Gehenna Press, 1972-1974. First edition; square 4to., 65 original wood engravings, full red pigskin with gilt cat profile on front cover by Arno Werner, very fine copy in beautiful Werner binding, half morocco folding box, unique copy, specially bound by Werner, with his pencil annotation on prelim leaf, binder's own copy with his bookplate.   James S. Jaffe Rare Books   May 26 2011 - 20923   2011 $9500

Tate, Allen *The Hovering Fly and Other Essays.* Cummington: Cummington Press, 1949. One of only 12 copies on Van Gelder paper with original drawing and woodcuts hand colored, specially bound and signed by author and artist, out of a total edition of 245; 8vo., woodcuts by Wightman Williams, full russet morocco with inlaid hand colored panel on front cover by Arno Werner, very fine, in half morocco folding box, binder's copy, signed by Arno Werner.   James S. Jaffe Rare Books   May 26 2011 - 11551   2011 $15,000

Binding – Westleys

Howitt, William *Visits to Remarkable Places: Old Halls, Battle-Fields and Scenes Illustrative of Striking Passages in English History and Poetry.* London: Longman Brown, Green, Longmans & Roberts, 1856. Third edition; engraved titles, illustrations, original green cloth by Westleys & Co., decorated in gilt, spines slightly faded, hinges slightly cracked, nice. Jarndyce Antiquarian Booksellers   CXCI - 557   2011   £75

MacDonald, Diana Louisa *Villa Verocchio; or the Youth of Leonardo Da Vinci: a Tale.* London: Longmans, 1850. First editions, half title, few spots, 32 page catalog (June 10, 1850); original dark blue cloth by Westleys, small splits at heads of hinges, ads on endpapers. Jarndyce Antiquarian Booksellers   CLXC - 186   2011   £45

Manning, Anne *Deborah's Diary.* London: A. Hall, Virtue and Co., 1858. First edition; half title, initial 4 page catalog, 24 page catalog (Oct. 1858), original maroon embossed cloth, bevelled boards by Westleys, spine faded, slightly worn at head and tail, presentation inscription. Jarndyce Antiquarian Booksellers   CLXC - 208   2011   £45

Manning, Anne *Family Pictures.* London: Arthur Hall, Virtue & Co., 1861. First edition; half title, 24 page catalog (May 1860), original mauve cloth by Westleys, slightly rubbed and discolored, inner hinges cracking, working copy, c. 1900, belonging to publisher Arthur Hall with his notes and revisions. Jarndyce Antiquarian Booksellers   CLXC - 210   2011   £250

Martineau, Harriet   1802-1876   *England and Her Soldiers.* London: Smith, Elder & Co., 1859. First edition; half title, foldout, color frontispiece, 2 foldout diagrams at end, 2 page ads + 24 page catalog (May 1859), some light browning, original red cloth by Westleys & Co., blocked in blind and gilt spine lettered in gilt, spine little darkened, hinges slightly rubbed, presentation inscription from author to sister Ellen Higginson. Jarndyce Antiquarian Booksellers   CLXC - 278   2011   £380

Martineau, Harriet   1802-1876   *Letters from Ireland.* London: John Chapman, 1852. First edition; 36 page catalog (Dec. 20th 1852), original green morocco grained cloth by Westleys, blocked in blind, spine lettered in gilt, spine slightly darkened and little rubbed, head and tail carefully repaired, good plus, signed "Higginson", almost certainly author's brother-in-law, Alfred Higginson. Jarndyce Antiquarian Booksellers   CLXC - 318   2011   £220

Martineau, Harriet   1802-1876   *Sketches from Life.* Whittaker & Co., 1856. First edition; original brown morocco grained cloth by Westleys, bevelled boards, lettered in gilt, head of spine slightly rubbed, half title, vignette title and plates by W. Banks, nice copy, signed presentation by author for her niece, Maria Martineau. Jarndyce Antiquarian Booksellers   CLXC - 339   2011   £250

Binding – Westleys & Clark

Bucke, Charles *On the Beauties, Harmonies and Sublimities of Nature.* London: Thomas Tegg & Son, 1837. New edition; 3 volumes, half titles, 8 page catalog (1846) in volume I, volume III lacking leading f.e.p., original red vertical grained cloth by Westley's & Clark, blocked in blind, spines faded, some slight wear to head and tail, bookabels of Charles Ogden, bookseller's ticket of H. Whitmore, Manchester. Jarndyce Antiquarian Booksellers   CXCI - 329   2011   £110

Trollope, Thomas Adolphus   1810-1892   *A Summer in Brittany.* London: Henry Colburn, 1840. 2 volumes, hand colored engraved frontispiece, engraved titles, 10 plates drawn and etched by A. Hervieu, 2 pages ads, volume I and II, uncut in original olive green cloth by Westleys and Clark, blocked in blind, sympathetically rebacked in plain cloth. Jarndyce Antiquarian Booksellers   CXCI - 583   2011   £150

Binding – Weston, Chris

Jackson, Thomas *The Life of the Rev. Charles Wesley...* London: John Mason, 1841. from the collection of Christopher Ernest Weston 1947-2010, 2 volumes, 8vo., pages xvi, 592 + engraved frontispiece, viii, 578, (ii) + signed agreement facsimile plate facing page 577, late 1990's retrospective half calf by Chris Weston, frontispiece foxed, otherwise just faint age toning and few tiny spots. Unsworths Booksellers   24 - 25   2011   £180

Martin, Martin *A Description of the Western Islands of Scotland...* London: printed for Andrew Bell, 1703. 8vo., pages (xxxii) 392 + folding engraved map and one other folding engraved plate, early 21st century retrospective panelled calf by Chris Weston, touch of faint spotting, small handling tear to folded map, from the collection of Christopher Ernest Weston 1947-2010. Unsworths Booksellers   24 - 121   2011   £800

Newton, Isaac   1642-1727   *Observations upon the Prophecies of Daniel and the Apocalypse of St. John.* London: printed by J. Darby and T. Browne, 1733. 4to., pages vi, (ii), 323, (i), early 21st century retrospective blind tooled calf by Chris Weston, title slightly dusty, otherwise very clean, from the collection of Christopher Ernest Weston 1947-2010. Unsworths Booksellers   24 - 32   2011   £2250

Oldmixon, John *The History and Life of Admiral Blake; General and Admiral of the Fleets and Naval Forces of England...* London: printed for R. Davis and J. Millan, 1746. Second edition; 12mo., pages (xvi) 128, engraved portrait frontispiece, early 21st century retrospective sheep binding by Chris Weston, some spotting and dust soiling, from the collection of Christopher Ernest Weston 1947-2010. Unsworths Booksellers   24 - 127   2011   £300

Paule, George *Life of the Most Reverend and Religious Prelate John Whitgift, Lord Archbishop of Canterbury.* London: printed by Thomas Snodham, 1612. small 4to., pages (viii), 94, (ii), woodcut portrait of Whitgift on titlepage verso, early 21st century retrospective ruled calf binding by CEW, title soiled text block trimmed to printed border and sometimes just inside at top and fore-edge, old f.e.p. corner repaired, early hand has annotated head of blank leaf A1 and final blank leaf N4 armorial bookplate of "James Comerford" on front pastedown, mid 19th century ownership in Philip Bliss's hand on 17th century flyleaf reading "Bodleian Catalogue 1843, p. 62" and at foot of page I signature "P.B.43": and flowery label, presented by William Minet at foot of front pastedown, from the collection of Christopher Ernest Weston 1947-2010.   Unsworths Booksellers   24 - 34 2011   £450

Stillingfleet, Edward *An Answer to Some Papers... Concerning the Authority of the Catholick Church in Matters of Faith and the Reformation of the Church of England.* London: printed for Ric. Chiswel, 1686. 4to., (iv), 72, (ii) late 1990's half calf by Chris Weston, few minor spots, some early ink annotations, from the collection of Christopher Ernest Weston 1947-2010.   Unsworths Booksellers   24 - 48 2011   £95

Waterland, Daniel *Scripture Vindicated: in Answer to Book Intituled, Christianity as Old as the Creation.* London: printed for W. Innys, Cambridge printed for Cornelius Crownfield and John Crownfield, 1730-1731. 2 parts bound as 1, with collective half title, 8vo., pages (iv), 96, (iv), 160, disbound and subsequently (late 1980's) calf bound by Chris Weston, few minor spots, lower corner of first leaf worn, from the collection of Christopher Ernest Weston 1947-2010. Unsworths Booksellers   24 - 57   2011   £150

Binding – Wood

Hassell, John *Picturesque Rides and Walks, with Excursions by Water Thirty Miles Round the British Metropolis.* London: printed for J. Hassell, 1817-1818. First edition; 163 x 102mm., 2 volumes, quite attractive late 19th century jade green crushed morocco in Arts and Crafts design by Wood of London (stamp signed on front turn-ins), covers with gilt rule border and stippled cornerpieces incorporating drawer handles and three graceful tulips, raised bands, spines gilt in compartments with wide frame formed by drawer handles, heart ornaments and much stippling, turn-ins decorated with charming gilt tulips, marbled endpapers, top edge gilt, other edges rough trimmed; with 120 hand colored aquatint engravings; front joint of one volume with just hint of rubbing at head, faint minor spotting to covers, spines just slightly sunned to richer green trivial imperfections internally, but particularly fine and pretty set, text and plates very clean and fresh, ornate bindings lustrous and with no significant wear.   Phillip J. Pirages   59 - 233 2011 $2900

Ireland, William Henry   1777-1835   *The Life of Napoleon Bonaparte.* London: G. Berger (for the first volume) and John Cumberland (for the others), 1828. (this date in Volume II the other volumes undated); 216 x 142mm., bound without half titles in first 3 volumes, 4 volumes, extremely fine 19th century crimson morocco, handsomely gilt by Wood, stamp signed on front turn-ins, coves with single gilt rule border and with gilt springs and Napoleonic bee in each corner, raised bands, spines gilt in compartment repeating the same stamps (but with top compartment featuring the same stamps (but with top compartment featuring instead an "N" surmounted by a crown), marbled endpapers, top edge gilt, other edges rough trimmed, sturdy linen covered slipcase; with one facsimile plate, three black and white plates, 24 hand colored plates, all but two of the folding, plates expertly backed with silk, front pastedown of each volume with modern bookplate; margins of some of the folding plates, little soiled and with few expert repairs without loss (a handful of text also expertly repaired in text), titlepages of second and third volumes as well as a portion of one black and white plate bit soiled, two contents leaves in volume IV gracelessly remargined, other trivial problems with leaves, still very good internally without any fatal flaw, with text still rather fresh and with virtually no foxing, just hint of superficial chafing on covers, lovely decorative bindings in very fine condition especially bright and virtually unworn.   Phillip J. Pirages   59 - 237 2011 $4250

Binding – Worsfold

Piozzi, Hester Lynch Salusbury Thrale   1741-1821 *Autobiography Letters and Literary Remains of Mrs. Piozzi (Thrale).* London: Longman, Green, Longman & Roberts, 1861. 2 volumes, small octavo, xiii, 375; vi 479 pages, 2 frontispieces, index, later half navy blue morocco, marbled boards, raised bands, gilt spines, top edge gilt by W. Worsford, London, fine. Jeff Weber Rare Books   163 - 50 2011 $250

Binding – Zaehnsdorf

The Aldine Poets. The Complete Series. London: printed by Charles Whittingham for William Pickering, 1830-1845. 160 x 103mm., 53 volumes, especially pretty polished light brown calf, attractively gilt by Zaehnsdorf (stamp signed), covers with gilt double fillet border and gilt Aldine/Pickering anchor centerpiece, raised bands, spines in gilt compartments with scrolling foliate cornerpieces and looping stem centerpiece surrounded by a diamond frame of circlets and tiny stars, each spine with red and green titling label and at bottom, a red date label elaborately gilt turn-ins, marbled endpapers, all edges gilt, 24 frontispiece portraits, spines uniformly faded to a darker brown, a number of small nicks or tiny scuffs to backstrips, slight offsetting from engraved frontispieces, but fine and in many ways an amazing set, joints and remarkably bright covers almost entirely without wear and text pristine. Phillip J. Pirages 59 - 279 2011 $7800

Banks, Joseph *Captain Cook's Florilegium.* London: Lion and Unicorn Press, Royal College of Art, 1973. One of 100 copies on handmade paper; folio, black half Nigerian goatskin and Japanese silk by Zaehnsdorf (fine), matching buckram solander case (very good plus), text printed in various colors, list of subscribers, 30 engraved plates. Raymond M. Sutton, Jr. May 26 2011 - 55737 2011 $15,000

Dickens, Charles 1812-1870 *A Christmas Carol.* Philadelphia: Carey & Hart, 1844. Half title, color frontispiece, plates and illustrations, lager half green crushed morocco by Zaehnsdorf, spine blocked and lettered in gilt, original blue cloth bound in to precede half title, top edge gilt, very good, booklabel of Charles Plumptre Johnson, top edge gilt, very good. Jarndyce Antiquarian Booksellers CXCI - 154 2011 £1500

Dickens, Charles 1812-1870 *Christmas Books. A Christmas Carol. The Chimes. The Cricket on the Hearth. The Battle of Life. The Haunted Man and the Ghost's Bargain. (with) The Chimes. (with) The Cricket on the Hearth. (with) The Battle of Life. (with) The Haunted Man and The Ghost's Bargain.* London: Chapman and Hall, 1843. London: Chapman and Hall 1845 (i.e. Dec. 1844). London: printed and published for the author by Bradbury and Evans 1846, i.e. Dec. 1845. London: Bradbury & Evans, 1846. London: Bradbury & Evans 1848. First edition, first issue, i.e. "Stave I"; remainder first editions; blue half title, red and blue title, small octavo, (viii), (1) 2-166, (2, publisher's ads) pages, 4 inserted hand colored plates, including frontispiece, in text black and white illustrations, 2 pages of publisher's ads, original green coated endpapers bound in at front, original complete cloth, including front, back and spine, bound in at back; small octavo, (viii), (1) 2-175, (1, colophon), first state additional engraved title and frontispiece, 11 in text black and white illustrations, publisher's prelim ad leaf for tenth edition Christmas Carol, original complete cloth, including front back and spine, bound in at back; small octavo, (viii), (1) 2-174 (2 publisher's ads) pages, engraved title and frontispiece, 12 in text black and white illustrations, with second state of final leaf of publisher's ads for new edition of Oliver Twist, original complete cloth, including front, back and spine bound in at back; small octavo, (viii), (1-3) 4-175, (1, colophon), (2, publisher's ads) pages, second state engraved title and frontispiece, 11 in text black and white illustrations, original complete cloth, including front back and spine, bound in at back; small octavo, (viii), (1) 2-188 pages, prelim leaf of publisher's ads, additional pictorial frontispiece, 15 in text black and white illustrations, original complete cloth, including front back and spine, bound in at back, all books beautifully uniformly bound by Zaehnsdorf in full red morocco, covers ruled in gilt, spines ruled and lettered in gilt in compartments with five raised bands, all edges gilt, gilt board edges and dentelles, marbled endpapers, each volume with original complete cloth (including front back and spine), bound in at back of volume, a Christmas Carol with original coated endpapers bound in at front, slightest rubbing to extremities, superb set, housed in red cloth slipcase. Heritage Book Shop Holiday 2010 - 27 2011 $12,500

Doctor Comicus, or the Frolics of Fortune. London: B. Blake, 1825? 210 133mm., 269 pages without printed titlepage, very attractive light tan smooth calf by Sangorski & Sutcliffe/Zaehnsdorf (stamp signed verso of front endpaper), covers bordered with French fillet and fleuron cornerpieces, raised bands, spine gilt in compartments featuring decorative bands, scrolling cornerpieces, fleuron centerpiece and small tools, maroon morocco labels, gilt inner dentelles, marbled endpapers, all edges gilt, 12 plates, all color by hand, bookplate of Robert Marceau; engraved title and two plates, little foxed, three plates slightly trimmed at fore edge, without apparent loss, few leaves with light marginal foxing, or soiling, otherwise excellent, plates bright and well preserved, leaves clean and fresh, sympathetic binding in mint condition. Phillip J. Pirages 59 - 331 2011 $400

Gray, Thomas 1716-1771 *An Elegy Wrote in a Country Church Yard.* London: for R. Dodsley and sold by M. Cooper, 1751. First edition; 4to., 11 pages, full black crushed levant morocco by Zaehnsdorf (very lightly rubbed at extremities), fine, with no loss of punched-through type, bookplates. Joseph J. Felcone Inc. Fall Miscellany 2010 - 57 2011 $15,000

Hamilton, Anthony 1646-1720 *Memoirs of Count Grammont.* London and Edinburgh: printed by Jas. Ballantyne & Co. for William Miller and James Carpenter, 1811. 2 volumes, splendid crimson straight grain morocco, elegantly and attractively gilt by Zaehnsdorf (stamp signed and dated 1900 on front turn-ins), covers gilt with double ruled border enclosing a lacy frame formed by drawer handles, fleurons and floral sprays, large fleuron cornerpieces accented with circlets and dots, broad raised bands adorned with six gilt rules, spine compartments with filigree frames echoing cover decoration, densely gilt filigree turn-ins, marbled endpapers, top edge gilt, other edges untrimmed, with a total of 143 engraved portraits, including 64 called for, and extra illustrated with 79 additional portraits apparently take from 1793 edition of the work printed by S. & E. Harding and inserts specially in this copy, large paper copy; noticeable offsetting from portraits whenever there is a facing text page (as opposed to verso of another plate) and rather conspicuous in about a half dozen cases, otherwise extremely fine set, text very fresh and clean, beautiful bindings unworn and extraordinarily bright. Phillip J. Pirages 59 - 147 2011 $1600

Hardy, Thomas 1840-1928 *A Pair of Blue Eyes.* London: Tinsley Brothers, 1873. First edition in book form, one of presumably 500 copies; 3 volumes, small octavo, (6), 303, (1, blank); (6), 311, (1, blank); (6), 262 pages, complete with half titles, bound circa 1910 by Zaehnsdorf in three quarter green crushed morocco gilt over green cloth boards ruled in gilt, spines lettered and decoratively tooled in gilt, marbled endpapers, top edges gilt, bookplate of Anthony Conyers Surtees on front pastedown, superb copy, very rare. David Brass Rare Books, Inc. May 26 2011 - 01306 2011 $9500

Lamb, Charles 1775-1834 *A Tale of Rosamund Gray and Old Blind Margaret.* London: Printed for Lee & Hurst, 1798. First edition, 2nd issue; full brown morocco by Zaehnsdorf, gilt dentelles, all edges gilt, very good, handsome, scarce. Jarndyce Antiquarian Booksellers CXCI - 248 2011 £1500

Lilly, William *William Lilly's History of His Life and Times from the Year 1602 to 1681.* London: Reprinted for Charles Baldwyn, 1822. 252 x 154mm. 2 p.l., 260 pages, lovely dark brown crushed morocco, lavishly gilt by Zaehnsdorf (stamp signed on front turn-in, and with Zaehnsdorf's gilt oval stamp on rear turn-in), covers with wide lacy filigree border scalloped at inner edge and filled with densely gilt floral tools and sprigs on stippled ground, this border around an inner frame composed of double gilt rules with tiny shamrock at each corner and inside this frame, central panel with ornate cornerpieces filled with flowers, volutes and drawer handles on stippled ground, raised bands, spine densely and handsomely gilt in scallop edged compartments featuring a central quatrefoil containing a rose surrounded by floral sprays, open dots and much stippling, gilt turn-ins, top edge gilt, 12 engraved portraits printed on India paper and mounted, as called for; armorial bookplate of Vincent Lloyd-Russell; leaves faintly toned (no doubt as in all copies because of paper stock used), moderate offsetting from plates, other trivial imperfections, but excellent copy internally text generally clean and fresh, gleaming binding in especially fine condition with no perceptible wear. Phillip J. Pirages 59 - 149 2011 $1250

Malory, Thomas *Le Morte D'Arthur.* London: published by David Nutt, 1889. One of 100 copies signed by publisher, there were 8 additional copies not for sale; 330 x 260mm. tipped in editor's note at back of first volume, 3 volumes, very appealing dark brown morocco, Jansenist, by Zaehnsdorf (signed), boards panelled with 11 thick and thin gilt and blind fillets, corners of central panel with outward extending gilt fleurons, raised bands, flanked by gilt and blind rules (and with gilt rule across the middle of each), two spine panels with gilt titling and four with arabesque centerpiece, very wide and very intricate gilt scrolling foliate and fleuron inner dentelles, marbled endpapers, top edge gilt, other edges untrimmed, one plate reproducing a page from Caxton, one folding facsimile, 3 folding tables; armorial bookplate of Francis Law Latham, tab at end of volume I with editor's note tipped on, explaining the various typographical alterations from Caxton; titlepages printed in red and black, first initial in red; handful of superficial marks to covers (one very small abrasion), trivial foxing or spotting in perhaps 10 leaves, one table creased, fine, lovely bindings lustrous and virtually unworn and text clean, fresh, bright and with vast margins. Phillip J. Pirages 59 - 260 2011 $3500

Poe, Edgar Allan 1809-1849 *Tales of Mystery and Imagination.* London: George G. Harrap & Co., 1935. Half title, color frontispiece, plates by Arthur Rackham, full red crushed morocco by Zaehnsdorf, borders in gilt, raised bands, spine decorated in gilt, gilt dentelles, top edge gilt, fine. Jarndyce Antiquarian Booksellers CXCI - 396 2011 £1200

Rivers, John *Greuze and His Models.* London: Hutchinson & Co., 1912. First edition; 225 x 170mm., 9 p.l. including frontispiece, 282 pages, fine contemporary emerald green crushed morocco for Hatchards (done according to a pencilled note at front, by Zaehnsdorf), covers gilt in Arts and Crafts design of interlocking plain rule frames with floral stamps at corners and gilt titling flanked by leaves and berries, raised bands, spine gilt in double ruled compartments, with central floral sprig and three circles to each corner, gilt ruled turn-ins, gray endpapers, all edges gilt, with extra engraved titlepage and 44 plates, 40 with tissue guards (four reproductions of sketches bound in without guards); spine faintly sunned to pleasing slightly darker green, front free endpaper with two small very faint vestiges of tape, but quite fine, handsomely bound, binding unworn and clean, fresh and bright inside and out. Phillip J. Pirages 59 - 151 2011 $500

Ruskin, John 1819-1900 *Time and Tide by Weare and Tyne.* London: George Allen, 1891. Fourth edition; 185 x 125mm., 6 p.l., 235 pages (bound with half title), splendid later maroon morocco lavishly gilt by Zaehnsdorf (with their oval stamped in gilt on rear pastedown), covers with wide gilt border featuring a twining vine with charming little leaves and flowerheads, vine on stippled ground, center panel outlined by single gilt rule with intricate cornerpieces, small flowering vine sprouting from each corner, raised bands, spine sumptuously gilt in pointille, compartments within which four gilt pomegranates spring from the central circle toward the four corners and flowers grow from top and sides of circle, turn-ins with lovely floral garlands extending around corners as well as approaching the hinge at top and bottom, gold dog-tooth roll where pastedowns and turn-ins meet, marbled endpapers, all edges gilt, beautiful volume in very fine condition, binding lustrous and virtually unworn, text immaculate. Phillip J. Pirages 59 - 152 2011 $850

Selby, Charles *Maximums and Specimens of William Muggins, Natural Philosopher and Citizen of the World.* London: Routledge, 1846. Plates, bound by Zaehnsdorf in half maroon calf, raised bands, decorated in gilt, black morocco labels, endpapers replaced, original cloth spine, one cloth cover bound in at end, Mexborough armorial bookplate, top edge gilt, handsome. Jarndyce Antiquarian Booksellers CXCI - 487 2011 £140

Tennyson Turner, Charles *Sonnets and Fugitive Pieces.* Cambridge: B. Bridges, 1830. Half title, green crushed morocco by Zaehnsdorf, gilt spine borders and dentelles, bookplate of Robert Pinkney, top edge gilt, inscribed with author's compliments, for T. H. Rawnsley. Jarndyce Antiquarian Booksellers CXCI - 509 2011 £500

Trollope, Frances Milton 1780-1863 *Jessie Phillips.* London: Henry Colburn, 1844. First one volume edition; (352) pages, 8vo., later three quarter dark red morocco over marbled boards, gilt lettered and gilt decorated spines, raised bands, 6 compartments, , frontispiece, 11 additional full page engraved illustrations by John Leach, very fine and handsome copy bound by Zaehnsdorf. Paulette Rose Fine and Rare Books 32 - 178 2011 $625

Zaehnsdorf, Joseph W. *The Art of Bookbinding.* Gregg International Publishers, 1969. Facsimile of second edition; original green cloth gilt by Zaehnsdorf, pages ii, new introductory note), xix, 190, (i), illustrations. R. F. G. Hollett & Son Antiquarian Booksellers General Catalogue Summer 2010 - 353 2011 £45

Fore-edge Paintings

Fore-edge – 1617

Spenser, Edmund   1552-1599   *The Faerie Queen. The Shepheardes Calendar.*   London: printed for H. L. Lownes, 1617.   Early reprint of 1611 first collected edition; here with magnificent fore-edge painting by John Beer "Shepheard's Pastoral", tall quarto in sixes, (iv), 363, (1); (x), 56, (2, blank); 16, (14), (2, blank; (136) pages, decorative woodcut title, woodcut head - tailpieces, initials, colophon misprinted "16012", with an additional four pages in manuscript at rear as index, contemporary full oxblood morocco, gilt tooled panels, corner tulips, gilt ruled border, neatly rebacked with original spine laid down, new spine label to style, all edges gilt, later endleaves, small mid leaf burr chip to colophon, occasional small stain, beautiful copy,.   David Brass Rare Books, Inc.   May 26 2011 - 01595   2011 $6500

Fore-edge – 1771

Dalrymple, John   *Memoirs of Great Britain and Ireland from the Dissolution of the Last Parliament of Charles II Until the Sea Battle of La Hogue.*   London and Edinburgh: for W. Strahan and T. Cadell and A. Kincaid, J. Bell and J. Balfour, 1771.   Second edition; 285 x 215mm., viii, (4) leaves, 509, (1) pages, originally illustrated with separate appendix not present here; handsome contemporary oxblood morocco, gilt, in style of Robert Payne, expertly and sympathetically rebacked, covers with wide and intricate gilt tooled frame composed of closely spaced alternating palm fronds and lancets, cornerpieces composed of 10 different botanical and geometric tools, flat spine divided into compartments by decorative gilt rolls, each compartment with central floral sprig inside a lozenge of stars, circles and other small tools and corners with curling palm fronds, gilt turn-ins, marbled endpapers, all edges gilt; with fine fore-edge painting of Limerick and the River Shannon, as seen from the tower of Limerick Cathedral; early 19th century engraved bookplate of Syston Park and with smaller 20th century bookplate of "A.A.H.", with notation in what appears to be late 18th century hand of John Thorold; half dozen small abrasions to covers with minimal loss of gilt, extremities bit rubbed, occasional minor foxing or smudging, other trivial imperfections, excellent copy, binding solidly restored and certainly appealing, text very fresh, quite clean, generous margins, expert fore-edge painting in fine condition, colors soft but clear, composition especially pleasing.   Phillip J. Pirages   59 - 41   2011 $2400

Fore-edge – 1785

Fenelon, Francois Salignac De La Mothe, Abp.   1651-1715   *Les Aventures de Telemaque.*   Paris: Imprimerie de Monsieur (i.e. Pierre Francois Didot, 1785.   340 x 264mm., 4 p.l., 305, (1) pages; 2 p.l., 297, (3) pages, 2 volumes bound in 1; elegant red contemporary straight grain morocco by Staggemeier & Welcher, the covers with wide gilt border, composed of onlaid strips of blue goatskin onlay at corners tooled with a medallion, and with an inner frame composed of onlaid citron goatskin band and large, graceful gilt impressions of flowers, foliage, and ears of wheat; smooth spine divided into four unequal compartments by a strip of onlaid green goatskin tooled with gilt pentaglyph and metope roll, lettered in second compartment on green goatskin label and directly on spine at foot, the first compartment tooled with a face-in-the-sun, third (elongated) compartment featuring a strange figure with winged helmet holding festoons of flowers balancing on top of a flower issuing from a large neo-classical vase, vase in turn perched on a candelabrum, edges of boards and turn-ins tooled with gilt rolls, marbled endpapers, all edges gilt; with fore-edge painting, very probably contemporary, of two boats sailing on a lake with a stately home in background; engraved printer's device on titlepages and two frontispiece portraits of author engraved by Dequevauviller, one in early state before letters, and one printed on India paper and mounted; hint of wear to corners, spine little darkened, slight variation in color of leather covers, other minor defects, but extremely handsome binding entirely solid, nothing approaching a significant fault, covers especially lustrous with bright gilt, intermittent pale foxing in text (few gatherings with faint overall browning or more noticeably foxed), leaves remarkably fresh (they crackle as you turn them), very clean and printed within vast margins.   Phillip J. Pirages   59 - 40   2011 $9500

Fore-edge – 1788

Thomson, James   1700-1748   *The Works.*   London: printed by A. Strahan for J. Rivington and Sons, 1788.   227 x 145mm., 3 volumes, once elegant and still pleasing contemporary scarlet straight grained morocco simply gilt, covers with single gilt fillet border, raised bands flanked by plain gilt rules, gilt titling, turn-ins with gilt chain roll, marbled endpapers, all edges gilt; with fine fore-edge paintings of Folkestone, Dublin and Worcester; volumes in recent sturdy buckram slipcase with marbled paper sides; frontispiece portrait, 10 engraved plates; 19th century armorial bookplate of Richard Davies, morocco bookplate of Estelle Doheny and modern engraved bookplate of John Taylor Reynolds, titlepage with ink ownership inscription of Mihill Slaughter 1811 (Secretary of the Railways Department); hint of soil to covers, joints and extremities with little rubbing (but well refurbished), leaves with intermittent minor foxing, engravings bit more foxed (half of them rather browned), offset onto facing page, text with general light browning and occasional trivial soiling, four leaves with short marginal or paper flaw tears (no loss); although not without problems, set nevertheless appealing, internal flaws never really unsightly, bindings all solid and paintings where it really matters, entirely well preserved.   Phillip J. Pirages   59 - 45   2011 $4500

Fore-edge – 1790

Specimens of the Early English Poets. London: printed for Edwards, 1790. First edition; 190 x 127mm., 5 p.l., 323 pages, extremely pleasing etruscan style calf in the style of and quite probably by, Edwards of Halifax, covers with gilt metope and pentaglyph border, wide inner frame of stencilled palmettes, sprinkled central panel featuring at middle a stained obelisk tool draped with four slender fronds on either side, this centerpiece painted over in red, recently and beautifully rebacked by Courtland Benson to replicate original (flat) spine with all over gilt lattice design, black titling label, marbled endpapers, turn-ins and all edges gilt; with attractive fore-edge painting, very probably by Edwards, apparently showing Walton Hall near Wakefield; large paper copy, armorial bookplate of Thomas Walker, that bookplate as well as verso of endpaper inscribed in ink "Wm. Walker", former dated August 1848 and later "Wilsick, July 1848", titlepage with painted armorial laid down beneath imprint; minor pitting (as inevitable with acid treated calf), few leaves with small faint stains, otherwise fine, expertly restored binding with lustrous covers and bright gilt, text especially clean, fresh and bright with very spacious margins.   Phillip J. Pirages   59 - 39   2011 $1400

Fore-edge – 1790

Johnson, Samuel   1709-1784   *Prince of Abissinia. a Tale.* London: printed for J. F. and C. Rivington et al, 1790. Eighth edition; 182 x 108mm., viii, 304 pages; extremely pleasing etruscan style calf in style of and quite probably by Edwards of Halifax, covers with gilt metope and pentaglyph border as well as a wide frame of stenciled palmettes enclosing a sprinkled central panel with lightened slats radiating from an oval sunburst and laurel garland at middle, raised bands flanked by plain gilt rules, spine panels with central black urn or ewer framed by gilt floral spray cornerpieces, black morocco label, turn-ins and all edges gilt; with attractive fore-edge painting, quite possibly by Edwards, apparently showing a landscape with Rievaulx Abbey Yorkshire in background; contemporaneous armorial bookplate of "Rycroft", covers with very minor marks and stains, joints and extremities with hint of rubbing (top of spine with very small losses of leather), with no significant wear, only trivial defects internally and with the fore-edge scene very well preserved.   Phillip J. Pirages   59 - 37   2011 $1950

Fore-edge – 1791

Church of England. Book of Common Prayer   *The Book of Common Prayer.* Paris: printed by P. Didot, Sen. and sold by W. Edwards & Sons, Halifax, 1791. 160 x 100mm., (348) leaves, appealing contemporary vellum, handsomely gilt and painted in style of Edwards of Halifax, covers framed with border featuring a Greek key roll superimposed on blue wash and on inner side of border, each an elegant gilt roll of undulant foliage and flowers, rounded spine (without raised bands) decorated with all over honeycomb pattern in gilt and with blue wash label for title near top and publisher near bottom, marbled endpapers, gilt edges; fore edge with very fine painting depicting the ruins of a medieval English castle; blue wash somewhat faded to places (as almost always), vellum little soiled, otherwise fine example, fresh and clean, internally with painting remarkably well preserved.   Phillip J. Pirages   59 - 36   2011 $2400

Fore-edge – 1795

Thomson, James   1700-1748   *The Seasons.* London: printed by and for T. Chapman, 1795. 224 x 140mm., 1 p.l. (frontispiece), xiv, 233, (1) pages, (1) leaf (ads), pleasing contemporary mottled calf expertly rebacked using original spine leather, covers with wide border of stippled, knotted and Greek key rolls, flat spine in panels formed by bands of massed plain and decorative rules, simple gilt floral ornament used as panel centerpiece, marbled endpapers, all edges gilt, immensely pleasing fore-edge painting showing a snowy skating scene on a wooded canal; engraved frontispiece, engraved vignette titlepage, large and attractive engraved head and tailpieces and with four full page engravings, early ink ownership inscription of Cathe Cassin; leather little dry and pitted (as always with early mottled calf), small losses of gilt on spine, minor foxing to initial leaves and to plates and adjacent leaves, otherwise fine, carefully restored binding quite solid and still attractive, text generally clean, fresh and bright with especially pleasing fore-edge painting exceptionally bright and fresh.   Phillip J. Pirages   59 - 43   2011 $1800

Fore-edge – 1797

The Spectator. London: printed by H. Baldwin for Longman, Dodsley, et al, 1797. 264 x 165mm., 8 volumes, excellent contemporary light green straight grain morocco sides with gilt double fillet, raised bands decorated with stippled rule an flanked by plain rules, second and third panels of each spine gilt lettered, marbled endpapers, all edges gilt, in two modern fleece lined matching cloth slipcases; each of the 8 volumes with beautiful fore-edge painting; engraved vignette on each titlepage, large paper copy, ownership signature of Mary Erskine dated 1803 with inscription "This book was given her when she married by her cousin Lord Wodehouse"; spines somewhat darkened and gilt titling consequently dulled, leather slightly varied in color (due partly to refurbishing), soiled and marked, bindings nevertheless in remarkably good condition, entirely sound and with little wear to joints, each volume with isolated openings just bit foxed in (typically upper) margins (one volume with slightly more foxing), three or four leaves with frayed corner or minor tear in margin at foot, other trivial imperfections, still fine internally, almost entirely very clean, bright and fresh. Phillip J. Pirages   59 - 42   2011 $11,000

Fore-edge – 1799

Rogers, Samuel   *The Pleasures of Memory with Other Poems.* London: printed for T. Cadell Jun. and W. Davies, 1799. 165 x 102mm., 8 p.l., (9)-188 pages, extremely pleasing etruscan style calf in the style of, and quite probably by, Edwards of Halifax, covers with Greek-key roll border, wide inner frame of stencilled palmettes, and central flamed calf panel formed here by foliate roll, raised bands, spine compartments with gilt wheat and horn centerpiece and foliate corner ornaments, black morocco label, chained gilt turn-ins, marbled endpapers, all edges gilt; with pleasing pastel fore-edge painting of a scene from the (Italian?) countryside, featuring long arched ridge and title roofed villa, 4 engraved plates; joints and extremities just little dried and worn, trivial foxing and offsetting in text, still excellent, unrestored copy, binding entirely sound, with no cracks in joints, text very clean an fresh, bright copy.   Phillip J. Pirages   59 - 38 2011 $1750

Fore-edge – 1800

Gray, Thomas   1716-1771   *The Poems.* London: printed by T. Bensley for F. J. Du Roveray, 1800. 190 x 120, xxx, 162, (1) pages, (ads), with half title, extremely pleasing etruscan style calf in the style of quite probably by Edwards of Halifax, very expertly rebacked to style and corners repaired by Courtland Benson, covers with gilt broad and narrow rules and Greek-key roll framing wide inner panel of stencilled palmettes, gilt foliate roll enclosing central flamed panel, raised bands flanked by double blind rules, spine panels with large oval sunburst ornament supported by a floral nest, original black spine label, turn-ins with linked gilt roll, marbled endpapers, all edges gilt, with fore-edge painting of Yarmouth Castle and Harbor, 6 engraved plates, inscription "Frances Maria Phillips June 1824. in remembrance of her grandmother", covers little marked and dried but expertly restored binding solid and pleasing, the painting with a number of very thin parallel uncolored striped where edges of leaves are not quite even or here the fore-edge was not carefully fanned out during painting, one flyleaf with upper corner clipped off, some offsetting from plates, otherwise fine internally with only trivial effects.   Phillip J. Pirages   59 - 195   2011 $800

Fore-edge – 1809

Addison, Joseph   1672-1719   *The Evidences of the Christian Religion.* Oxford: Clarendon Press, 1809. 165 x 100 mm., 354 pages, very attractive dark green straight grain morocco, handsomely gilt, covers with border of multiple blind rules as well as intricate scrolling gilt cornerpieces, wide raised bands, spine compartments densely gilt cornerpieces, wide raised bands, spine compartments densely gilt with many floral and foliate tools emanating from central flower, all edges gilt, excellent fore-edge painting showing Eton College, front flyleaf with signature of Jefry Goddard dated 1819; joints just slightly rubbed, covers bit marked, isolated very minor foxing, generally in quite attractive condition, binding bright and scarcely worn, text fresh and clean.   Phillip J. Pirages   59 - 194   2011 $1100

Fore-edge – 1810

Cowper, William 1731-1800 *Poems.* London: Published by John Sharpe, 1810. New edition; 202 122mm., 432 pages, volume I only, of 2 volumes, once splendid and still pleasing contemporary dark green straight grain morocco, extravagantly gilt, covers with wide gilt frames featuring interlocking circles and arcs accented with leaves and flowers on densely stippled backgrounds, central panel formed by gilt fillet and multiple blindstamped rolls and with foliate spray cornerpieces on stippled ground, board raised bands dividing spine into five panels, three with large animated central gilt fleuron, two with gilt titling, gilt turn-ins and edges, with excellent fore-edge painting of a bustling Regent Street scene in London; with extra engraved titlepage, 21 engraved head and tailpieces designed by Thurston with five engraved plates designed by Richard Westall, R.A., with engraved bookplate of George Ramsay Feilden, with Feilden's ink ownership signature, spine sunned to light olive, joints and extremities somewhat rubbed tiny chip to head of spine, isolated minor foxing, otherwise excellent copy, binding sturdy and retaining its charm, leaves clean and fresh and fore-edge painting generally well preserved. Phillip J. Pirages 59 - 202 2011 $650

Fore-edge – 1811

Hesiod *Works of Hesiod.* London: printed at the Stanhope Press by Whittingham and Rowland, 1811. 2 volumes, small octavo, (4), 136; (4), 138, (2 blank) pages, frontispiece in each volume, full red straight grain morocco, boards ruled in gilt floral pattern, spine stamped and lettered in gilt, drab grey endpapers, edges lightly rubbed, boards slightly soiled, with double fore-edge painting depicting of St. John's College in Cambridge on one side and King's College Chapel in Cambridge on the other, very good, red cloth slipcase. Heritage Book Shop Holiday 2010 - 42 2011 $1500

Fore-edge – 1811

Pope, Alexander 1688-1744 *The Poetical Works of Alexander Pope with His Life by Samuel Johnson.* London: printed by Whittingham and Howard for Sharpe and Hailes, 1811. 222 x 142 mm., 2 volumes, once very striking and still quite handsome contemporary crimson straight grain morocco by Taylor & Hessey (stamp-signed on the narrow board edge of upper cover of each volume), covers with border of thick and thin gilt rules enclosing a fine lacy gilt frame incorporating palmettes and volutes, inner frame formed by single gilt rule terminating at corners in floral sprays, raised bands dividing spine into four large and three small panels, the three narrow panels featuring a gilt rosette flanked by fleurons, the large panels at head and tail with prominent ornate fleuron on a stippled background with scalloped edges, and two middle panels with gilt titling, all edges gilt, the two fore edges with especially attractive paintings of Windsor Castle and Twickenham, frontispiece portraits, 16 engraved plates; contemporary ink ownership inscription of "Miss M(argare)t Rigden", spines uniformly faded to soft rose (with consequent slight muting of gilt), joints and extremities bit rubbed (though well refurbished), considerable foxing to plates as well as foxing and offsetting to adjacent leaves, other trivial imperfections, nevertheless very appealing set in important ways, elegant original bindings entirely sound and with lustrous boards, text almost entirely very smooth and fresh, fore edge paintings in excellent state of preservation. Phillip J. Pirages 59 - 198 2011 $2900

Fore-edge – 1812

Cowper, William 1731-1800 *Poems.* London: printed for J. Johnson and Co., 1812. New edition; 2 volumes, 168 x 107mm., handsome contemporary crimson straight grain morocco elaborately gilt, covers with border of interlacing circles in blind enclosing a broader frame comprised of two parallel rules, flanking a string of floral fleurons emanating in both directions from square cornerpieces featuring a heavily stippled ground, raised bands, spine panels with gilt tilting or else intricately gilt in an all over pattern with floral centerpiece with dense stippling, gilt tooled turn-ins, all edges gilt, 2 volumes with very attractive fore-edge paintings of Ludlow Castle and of Malmsbury, Wiltshire; minor wear, (as expected) to joints, corners with hint of rubbing, cover very slightly soiled, still lovely set, bindings extremely lustrous and text consistently clean, bright and fresh. Phillip J. Pirages 59 - 203 2011 $2500

Fore-edge – 1812

Young, Edward *Night Thoughts and a Paraphrase on Part of the Book of Job.* London: printed at the Chiswick Press by C. Whittingham for Taylor and Hessey, 1812. 240 x 145mm., lxvi, (2), 353, (1) pages, striking contemporary black morocco elaborately tooled in blind and gilt by Taylor & Hessey (board edges at middle on either side of painting stamped in gilt "Taylor and Hessey/Booksellers London"), covers with frame outlined by gilt rules and with cornerpieces in form of a stylized gilt satire, frame also featuring a chain of blindstamped oval medallions connected by palm fronds of an unusual ground of blind stippling, the whole enclosing a large central panel ornately tooled in blind, with cornerpieces composed of shells, leaves and volutes and with intricate sunburst medallion centerpiece, central panel further decorated in blind with complex of elaborate strapwork between the centerpiece and cornerpieces, highlighted by botanical and other tools, raised bands, spine with rows of gilt tools at head and tail, three spine panels tooled in blind and highlighted with gilt lancets with flowers, gilt turn-ins in Greek key style, all edges gilt, with exceptionally fine fore-edge painting depicting Westminster Bridge and Westminster Hall; with engraved frontispiece, armorial bookplate of David Gill, ink presentation inscription "Eliza Gill/the gift of her attached and affectionate Husband/Decem(ber) 3rd 1812", joints and extremities with touch of rubbing (though well marked with dye), offsetting to titlepage from frontispiece, occasional trivial imperfections internally, exceptionally pleasing copy, binding especially lustrous, text unusually clean, fresh and bright, painting beautifully preserved.   Phillip J. Pirages   59 - 199   2011 $2500

Fore-edge – 1814

Montgomery, James *The World Before the Flood.* London: printed for Longman, Hurst, Rees, Orme and Brown, 1814. Third edition; 168 x 103mm., xvi, (2), 328 pages, attractive and intriguing contemporary calf, heavily gilt by Taylor and Hessey (board edges along fore edge stamp signed in gilt), covers with wide filigree gilt frame, large central panel dominated by an elongated octagon painted in black with gold dot at each of its eight corners, these corners radiating stippled gilt lines that intersect to form 12 triangles of various sizes plus a large central lozenge (lozenge also with gilt dots at its four angles), wide raised bands decorated in blind dividing the spine into four panels, gilt titling, turn-ins with gilt broken cables, all edges gilt, expertly rebacked using original spine, with very pretty fore-edge painting of Pope's Villa at Twickenham, small abrasions to lower spine, bit discolored and with gilt difficult to read, partly because it is so small, tiny nicks here and there in painting, still excellent copy, text unusually clean and fresh, binding solidly restored and with only minor wear, painting generally quite well preserved.   Phillip J. Pirages   59 - 197   2011 $950

Fore-edge – 1821

Burns, Robert 1759-1796   *The Poetical Works.* Chiswick: from the Press of C. Whittingham, 1821. 130 x 85mm., 2 volumes, very attractive contemporary red straight grain morocco, covers with wide gilt leaf border and central panel formed in multipled blind rules, raised bands, spine panels intricately gilt with leaves, acorns, foliage and small tools, gilt turn-ins, all edges gilt, each volume with pleasing fore-edge painting, one of Burns' Birthplace, the Other of His Cenotaph and Brig O'Doon, in (slightly scuffed) rose colored cloth lined linen folding box with gilt titling, extra engraved titlepage with vignette in each volume; covers with touch of soiling, vague scratch across central panel of one board, joints and extremities very slightly rubbed, small spill-over of fore-edge paint onto a couple of leaves at front of each volume, engraved titles bit foxed, other trivial imperfections internally, very pretty set in excellent condition, bindings solid and shining, text fresh and bright, fore-edge paintings quite well preserved.   Phillip J. Pirages   59 - 200   2011 $1500

Fore-edge – 1821

Thomson, James 1700-1748   *The Seasons.* London: printed for John Sharpe, 1821. 170 x 105mm., 215, (1) pages, extremely pleasing etruscan style calf in the style of and quite probably by Edwards of Halifax, covers with gilt Greek key border, wide inner frame of stencilled palmettes, central panel of tree calf framed by a gilt broken cable, flat spine gilt in compartments separated by Greek key roll and with a lyre centerpiece framed by foliate cornerpieces, with black morocco label, marbled endpapers, all edges gilt, very attractive fore-edge painting of an English stately home, perhaps Stourhead House, extra engraved titlepage with vignette and fine engraved plates, inscription "Mary Williams/The last gift of her affectionate Aunt/Mary Hoyle, July 31st 1826"; extremities and joints bit dry and rubbed, rear joint just starting at tail, gilt eroded from head and tail of spine, half a dozen small patches of lost patina in frame around outside of stencilled central panel, plates little foxed, one more noticeably but still quite pleasing copy, appealing unrestored original binding entirely sound, text clean and smooth and rich colors of painting beautifully preserved.   Phillip J. Pirages   59 - 196   2011 $1100

Fore-edge – 1857

Hamilton, Charles Gillingham, Mrs. *The Exiles of Italy.* Edinburgh: Thomas Constable and Co., 1857. First edition with bound-in limitation page signed by artist on fore-edge painting proclaiming, "This is No. 122 of the Books with Fore-edge Paintings by Miss Currie/ The Painting Under the gold is a view of The Temples of Paestrum"; 185 x 125mm., xxxii, (1) leaf (half title), 502 pages, beautiful early 20th century dark blue straight grain morocco sumptuously gilt by Riviere and Son (stamp signed), covers richly decorated in gilt and blind with outer gilt frame featuring pairs of triple fillets flanking a chain roll composed of leaf fronds and then daisy cornerpieces, next to outer frame, blind rolled border in cresting pattern and further in a central panel composed of plain gilt rules and gilt botanical cornerpieces accented with blindstamped daisy tools around outer edge and with tangent dogtooth roll in blind closer to middle of board, raised bands, spine gilt in triple filleted compartments, intricate central lozenge and blind tooled leaf cornerpieces, densely gilt turn-ins, all edges gilt, with fine fore-edge paintings by Miss Currie of the Temple of Hera and the Second Temple of Hera at Paestum; top corners little bumped, mild offsetting to endpapers from gilt turn-ins (as almost always) isolated minor foxing and other trivial imperfections internally, otherwise fine in lovely binding, text clean and fresh binding exceptionally lustrous and virtually unworn and fore-edge painting well preserved.   Phillip J. Pirages   59 - 204   2011 $5500

ISBN-13: 978-1-4144-0661-9
ISBN-10: 1-4144-0661-4